Hornbook Series and Basic Legal Texts
Nutshell Series

and

Black Letter Series

of

WEST PUBLISHING COMPANY
P.O. Box 64526
St. Paul, Minnesota 55164-0526

Accounting

FARIS' ACCOUNTING AND LAW IN A NUTSHELL, 377 pages, 1984. Softcover. (Text)

Administrative Law

AMAN AND MAYTON'S HORNBOOK ON ADMINISTRATIVE LAW, Approximately 750 pages, 1993. (Text)

GELLHORN AND LEVIN'S ADMINISTRATIVE LAW AND PROCESS IN A NUTSHELL, Third Edition, 479 pages, 1990. Softcover. (Text)

Admiralty

MARAIST'S ADMIRALTY IN A NUTSHELL, Second Edition, 379 pages, 1988. Softcover. (Text)

SCHOENBAUM'S HORNBOOK ON ADMIRALTY AND MARITIME LAW, Student Edition, 692 pages, 1987 with 1992 pocket part. (Text)

Agency—Partnership

REUSCHLEIN AND GREGORY'S HORNBOOK ON THE LAW OF AGENCY AND PARTNERSHIP, Second Edition, 683 pages, 1990. (Text)

STEFFEN'S AGENCY-PARTNERSHIP IN A NUTSHELL, 364 pages, 1977. Softcover. (Text)

NOLAN-HALEY'S ALTERNATIVE DISPUTE RESOLUTION IN A NUTSHELL, 298 pages, 1992. Softcover. (Text)

RISKIN'S DISPUTE RESOLUTION FOR LAWYERS VIDEO TAPES, 1992. (Available for purchase by schools and libraries.)

American Indian Law

CANBY'S AMERICAN INDIAN LAW IN A NUTSHELL, Second Edition, 336 pages, 1988. Softcover. (Text)

Antitrust—see also Regulated Industries, Trade Regulation

GELLHORN'S ANTITRUST LAW AND ECONOMICS IN A NUTSHELL, Third Edition, 472 pages, 1986. Softcover. (Text)

HOVENKAMP'S BLACK LETTER ON ANTITRUST, Second Edition approximately 325 pages, April 1993 Pub. Softcover. (Review)

HOVENKAMP'S HORNBOOK ON ECONOMICS AND FEDERAL ANTITRUST LAW, Student Edition, 414 pages, 1985. (Text)

SULLIVAN'S HORNBOOK OF THE LAW OF ANTITRUST, 886 pages, 1977. (Text)

Appellate Advocacy—see Trial and Appellate Advocacy

Art Law

DUBOFF'S ART LAW IN A NUTSHELL, Second Edition, approximately 325 pages, 1993. Softcover. (Text)

Banking Law

LOVETT'S BANKING AND FINANCIAL INSTI-

Banking Law—Cont'd

TUTIONS LAW IN A NUTSHELL, Third Edition, 470 pages, 1992. Softcover. (Text)

Civil Procedure—see also Federal Jurisdiction and Procedure

CLERMONT'S BLACK LETTER ON CIVIL PROCEDURE, Third Edition, approximately 350 pages, May, 1993 Pub. Softcover. (Review)

FRIEDENTHAL, KANE AND MILLER'S HORNBOOK ON CIVIL PROCEDURE, Second Edition, approximately 1000 pages, May 1993 Pub. (Text)

KANE'S CIVIL PROCEDURE IN A NUTSHELL, Third Edition, 303 pages, 1991. Softcover. (Text)

KOFFLER AND REPPY'S HORNBOOK ON COMMON LAW PLEADING, 663 pages, 1969. (Text)

SIEGEL'S HORNBOOK ON NEW YORK PRACTICE, Second Edition, Student Edition, 1068 pages, 1991. Softcover. (Text) 1992 Supplemental Pamphlet.

SLOMANSON AND WINGATE'S CALIFORNIA CIVIL PROCEDURE IN A NUTSHELL, 230 pages, 1992. Softcover. (Text)

Commercial Law

BAILEY AND HAGEDORN'S SECURED TRANSACTIONS IN A NUTSHELL, Third Edition, 390 pages, 1988. Softcover. (Text)

HENSON'S HORNBOOK ON SECURED TRANSACTIONS UNDER THE U.C.C., Second Edition, 504 pages, 1979, with 1979 pocket part. (Text)

MEYER AND SPEIDEL'S BLACK LETTER ON SALES AND LEASES OF GOODS, Approximately 300 pages, 1993. Softcover. (Review)

NICKLES' BLACK LETTER ON COMMERCIAL PAPER, 450 pages, 1988. Softcover. (Review)

STOCKTON AND MILLER'S SALES AND LEASES OF GOODS IN A NUTSHELL, Third Edition, 441 pages, 1992. Softcover. (Text)

STONE'S UNIFORM COMMERCIAL CODE IN A NUTSHELL, Third Edition, 580 pages, 1989. Softcover. (Text)

WEBER AND SPEIDEL'S COMMERCIAL PAPER IN A NUTSHELL, Third Edition, 404 pages, 1982. Softcover. (Text)

WHITE AND SUMMERS' HORNBOOK ON THE UNIFORM COMMERCIAL CODE, Third Edition, Student Edition, 1386 pages, 1988. (Text)

Community Property

MENNELL AND BOYKOFF'S COMMUNITY PROPERTY IN A NUTSHELL, Second Edition, 432 pages, 1988. Softcover. (Text)

Comparative Law

FOLSOM, MINAN AND OTTO'S LAW AND POLITICS IN THE PEOPLE'S REPUBLIC OF CHINA IN A NUTSHELL, 451 pages, 1992. Softcover. (Text)

GLENDON, GORDON AND OSAKWE'S COMPARATIVE LEGAL TRADITIONS IN A NUTSHELL. 402 pages, 1982. Softcover. (Text)

Conflict of Laws

HAY'S BLACK LETTER ON CONFLICT OF LAWS, 330 pages, 1989. Softcover. (Review)

SCOLES AND HAY'S HORNBOOK ON CONFLICT OF LAWS, Student Edition, 1160 pages, 1992. (Text)

SIEGEL'S CONFLICTS IN A NUTSHELL, 470 pages, 1982. Softcover. (Text)

Constitutional Law—Civil Rights

BARRON AND DIENES' BLACK LETTER ON CONSTITUTIONAL LAW, Third Edition, 440 pages, 1991. Softcover. (Review)

BARRON AND DIENES' CONSTITUTIONAL LAW IN A NUTSHELL, Second Edition, 483 pages, 1991. Softcover. (Text)

ENGDAHL'S CONSTITUTIONAL FEDERALISM IN A NUTSHELL, Second Edition, 411 pages, 1987. Softcover. (Text)

MARKS AND COOPER'S STATE CONSTITUTIONAL LAW IN A NUTSHELL, 329 pages, 1988. Softcover. (Text)

Constitutional Law—Civil Rights—
Cont'd

NOWAK AND ROTUNDA'S HORNBOOK ON CONSTITUTIONAL LAW, Fourth Edition, 1357 pages, 1991. (Text)

VIEIRA'S CONSTITUTIONAL CIVIL RIGHTS IN A NUTSHELL, Second Edition, 322 pages, 1990. Softcover. (Text)

WILLIAMS' CONSTITUTIONAL ANALYSIS IN A NUTSHELL, 388 pages, 1979. Softcover. (Text)

Consumer Law—see also Commercial Law

EPSTEIN AND NICKLES' CONSUMER LAW IN A NUTSHELL, Second Edition, 418 pages, 1981. Softcover. (Text)

Contracts

CALAMARI AND PERILLO'S BLACK LETTER ON CONTRACTS, Second Edition, 462 pages, 1990. Softcover. (Review)

CALAMARI AND PERILLO'S HORNBOOK ON CONTRACTS, Third Edition, 1049 pages, 1987. (Text)

CORBIN'S TEXT ON CONTRACTS, One Volume Student Edition, 1224 pages, 1952. (Text)

FRIEDMAN'S CONTRACT REMEDIES IN A NUTSHELL, 323 pages, 1981. Softcover. (Text)

KEYES' GOVERNMENT CONTRACTS IN A NUTSHELL, Second Edition, 557 pages, 1990. Softcover. (Text)

SCHABER AND ROHWER'S CONTRACTS IN A NUTSHELL, Third Edition, 457 pages, 1990. Softcover. (Text)

Copyright—see Patent and Copyright Law

Corporations

HAMILTON'S BLACK LETTER ON CORPORATIONS, Third Edition, 732 pages, 1992. Softcover. (Review)

HAMILTON'S THE LAW OF CORPORATIONS IN A NUTSHELL, Third Edition, 518 pages, 1991. Softcover. (Text)

HENN AND ALEXANDER'S HORNBOOK ON LAWS OF CORPORATIONS, Third Edition, Student Edition, 1371 pages, 1983, with 1986 pocket part. (Text)

Corrections

KRANTZ' THE LAW OF CORRECTIONS AND PRISONERS' RIGHTS IN A NUTSHELL, Third Edition, 407 pages, 1988. Softcover. (Text)

Creditors' Rights

EPSTEIN'S DEBTOR-CREDITOR LAW IN A NUTSHELL, Fourth Edition, 401 pages, 1991. Softcover. (Text)

EPSTEIN, NICKLES AND WHITE'S HORNBOOK ON BANKRUPTCY, Approximately 1000 pages, January, 1992 Pub. (Text)

NICKLES AND EPSTEIN'S BLACK LETTER ON CREDITORS' RIGHTS AND BANKRUPTCY, 576 pages, 1989. (Review)

Criminal Law and Criminal Procedure—see also Corrections, Juvenile Justice

ISRAEL AND LaFAVE'S CRIMINAL PROCEDURE—CONSTITUTIONAL LIMITATIONS IN A NUTSHELL, Fourth Edition, 461 pages, 1988. Softcover. (Text)

LaFAVE AND ISRAEL'S HORNBOOK ON CRIMINAL PROCEDURE, Second Edition, 1309 pages, 1992 with 1992 pocket part. (Text)

LaFAVE AND SCOTT'S HORNBOOK ON CRIMINAL LAW, Second Edition, 918 pages, 1986. (Text)

LOEWY'S CRIMINAL LAW IN A NUTSHELL, Second Edition, 321 pages, 1987. Softcover. (Text)

LOW'S BLACK LETTER ON CRIMINAL LAW, Revised First Edition, 443 pages, 1990. Softcover. (Review)

SUBIN, MIRSKY AND WEINSTEIN'S THE CRIMINAL PROCESS: PROSECUTION AND DEFENSE FUNCTIONS, Approximately 450 pages, February, 1993 Pub. Softcover. Teacher's Manual available. (Text)

Domestic Relations

CLARK'S HORNBOOK ON DOMESTIC RELA-

Domestic Relations—Cont'd

TIONS, Second Edition, Student Edition, 1050 pages, 1988. (Text)

KRAUSE'S BLACK LETTER ON FAMILY LAW, 314 pages, 1988. Softcover. (Review)

KRAUSE'S FAMILY LAW IN A NUTSHELL, Second Edition, 444 pages, 1986. Softcover. (Text)

MALLOY'S LAW AND ECONOMICS: A COMPARATIVE APPROACH TO THEORY AND PRACTICE, 166 pages, 1990. Softcover. (Text)

Education Law

ALEXANDER AND ALEXANDER'S THE LAW OF SCHOOLS, STUDENTS AND TEACHERS IN A NUTSHELL, 409 pages, 1984. Softcover. (Text)

Employment Discrimination—see also Gender Discrimination

PLAYER'S FEDERAL LAW OF EMPLOYMENT DISCRIMINATION IN A NUTSHELL, Third Edition, 338 pages, 1992. Softcover. (Text)

PLAYER'S HORNBOOK ON EMPLOYMENT DISCRIMINATION LAW, Student Edition, 708 pages, 1988. (Text)

Energy and Natural Resources Law— see also Oil and Gas

LAITOS AND TOMAIN'S ENERGY AND NATURAL RESOURCES LAW IN A NUTSHELL, 554 pages, 1992. Softcover. (Text)

Environmental Law—see also Energy and Natural Resources Law; Sea, Law of

FINDLEY AND FARBER'S ENVIRONMENTAL LAW IN A NUTSHELL, Third Edition, 355 pages, 1992. Softcover. (Text)

RODGERS' HORNBOOK ON ENVIRONMENTAL LAW, 956 pages, 1977, with 1984 pocket part. (Text)

Equity—see Remedies

Estate Planning—see also Trusts and Estates; Taxation—Estate and Gift

LYNN'S INTRODUCTION TO ESTATE PLANNING IN A NUTSHELL, Fourth Edition, 352 pages, 1992. Softcover. (Text)

Evidence

BROUN AND BLAKEY'S BLACK LETTER ON EVIDENCE, 269 pages, 1984. Softcover. (Review)

GRAHAM'S FEDERAL RULES OF EVIDENCE IN A NUTSHELL, Third Edition, 486 pages, 1992. Softcover. (Text)

LILLY'S AN INTRODUCTION TO THE LAW OF EVIDENCE, Second Edition, 585 pages, 1987. (Text)

McCORMICK'S HORNBOOK ON EVIDENCE, Fourth Edition, Student Edition, 672 pages, 1992. (Text)

ROTHSTEIN'S EVIDENCE IN A NUTSHELL: STATE AND FEDERAL RULES, Second Edition, 514 pages, 1981. Softcover. (Text)

Federal Jurisdiction and Procedure

CURRIE'S FEDERAL JURISDICTION IN A NUTSHELL, Third Edition, 242 pages, 1990. Softcover. (Text)

REDISH'S BLACK LETTER ON FEDERAL JURISDICTION, Second Edition, 234 pages, 1991. Softcover. (Review)

WRIGHT'S HORNBOOK ON FEDERAL COURTS, Fourth Edition, Student Edition, 870 pages, 1983. (Text)

First Amendment

GARVEY AND SCHAUER'S THE FIRST AMENDMENT: A READER, 527 pages, 1992. Softcover. (Reader)

Future Interests—see Trusts and Estates

Gender Discrimination—see also Employment Discrimination

THOMAS' SEX DISCRIMINATION IN A NUTSHELL, Second Edition, 395 pages, 1991. Softcover. (Text)

Health Law—see Medicine, Law and

Human Rights—see International Law

Immigration Law

WEISSBRODT'S IMMIGRATION LAW AND

Immigration Law—Cont'd

Procedure in a Nutshell, Third Edition, 497 pages, 1992. Softcover. (Text)

Indian Law—see American Indian Law

Insurance Law

Dobbyn's Insurance Law in a Nutshell, Second Edition, 316 pages, 1989. Softcover. (Text)

Keeton and Widiss' Insurance Law, Student Edition, 1359 pages, 1988. (Text)

International Law—see also Sea, Law of

Buergenthal's International Human Rights in a Nutshell, 283 pages, 1988. Softcover. (Text)

Buergenthal and Maier's Public International Law in a Nutshell, Second Edition, 275 pages, 1990. Softcover. (Text)

Folsom's European Community Law in a Nutshell, 423 pages, 1992. Softcover. (Text)

Folsom, Gordon and Spanogle's International Business Transactions in a Nutshell, Fourth Edition, 548 pages, 1992. Softcover. (Text)

Interviewing and Counseling

Shaffer and Elkins' Legal Interviewing and Counseling in a Nutshell, Second Edition, 487 pages, 1987. Softcover. (Text)

Introduction to Law—see Legal Method and Legal System

Introduction to Law Study

Hegland's Introduction to the Study and Practice of Law in a Nutshell, 418 pages, 1983. Softcover. (Text)

Kinyon's Introduction to Law Study and Law Examinations in a Nutshell, 389 pages, 1971. Softcover. (Text)

Judicial Process—see Legal Method and Legal System

Sinha's Jurisprudence (Legal Philosophy) in a Nutshell. Approximately 350 pages, 1993. Softcover. (Text)

Juvenile Justice

Fox's Juvenile Courts in a Nutshell, Third Edition, 291 pages, 1984. Softcover. (Text)

Labor and Employment Law—see also Employment Discrimination, Workers' Compensation

Leslie's Labor Law in a Nutshell, Third Edition, 388 pages, 1992. Softcover. (Text)

Nolan's Labor Arbitration Law and Practice in a Nutshell, 358 pages, 1979. Softcover. (Text)

Land Finance—Property Security—see Real Estate Transactions

Land Use

Hagman and Juergensmeyer's Hornbook on Urban Planning and Land Development Control Law, Second Edition, Student Edition, 680 pages, 1986. (Text)

Wright and Wright's Land Use in a Nutshell, Second Edition, 356 pages, 1985. Softcover. (Text)

Legal Method and Legal System—see also Legal Research, Legal Writing

Kempin's Historical Introduction to Anglo-American Law in a Nutshell, Third Edition, 323 pages, 1990. Softcover. (Text)

Reynolds' Judicial Process in a Nutshell, Second Edition, 308 pages, 1991. Softcover. (Text)

Legal Research

Cohen and Olson's Legal Research in a Nutshell, Fifth Edition, 370 pages, 1992. Softcover. (Text)

Cohen, Berring and Olson's How to Find the Law, Ninth Edition, 716 pages, 1989. (Text)

Legal Writing and Drafting

Mellinkoff's Dictionary of American

Legal Writing and Drafting—Cont'd

Legal Usage, 703 pages, 1992. Softcover. (Text)

Squires and Rombauer's Legal Writing in a Nutshell, 294 pages, 1982. Softcover. (Text)

Legislation—see also Legal Writing and Drafting

Davies' Legislative Law and Process in a Nutshell, Second Edition, 346 pages, 1986. Softcover. (Text)

Local Government

McCarthy's Local Government Law in a Nutshell, Third Edition, 435 pages, 1990. Softcover. (Text)

Reynolds' Hornbook on Local Government Law, 860 pages, 1982 with 1990 pocket part. (Text)

Mass Communication Law

Zuckman, Gaynes, Carter and Dee's Mass Communications Law in a Nutshell, Third Edition, 538 pages, 1988. Softcover. (Text)

Medicine, Law and

Hall and Ellman's Health Care Law and Ethics in a Nutshell, 401 pages, 1990. Softcover (Text)

Jarvis, Closen, Hermann and Leonard's AIDS Law in a Nutshell, 349 pages, 1991. Softcover. (Text)

King's The Law of Medical Malpractice in a Nutshell, Second Edition, 342 pages, 1986. Softcover. (Text)

Military Law

Shanor and Terrell's Military Law in a Nutshell, 378 pages, 1980. Softcover. (Text)

Mining Law—see Energy and Natural Resources Law

Mortgages—see Real Estate Transactions

Natural Resources Law—see Energy and Natural Resources Law, Environmental Law

Teply's Legal Negotiation in a Nutshell, 282 pages, 1992. Softcover. (Text)

Office Practice—see also Computers and Law, Interviewing and Counseling, Negotiation

Hegland's Trial and Practice Skills in a Nutshell, 346 pages, 1978. Softcover (Text)

Oil and Gas—see also Energy and Natural Resources Law

Hemingway's Hornbook on the Law of Oil and Gas, Third Edition, Student Edition, 711 pages, 1992. (Text)

Lowe's Oil and Gas Law in a Nutshell, Second Edition, 465 pages, 1988. Softcover. (Text)

Partnership—see Agency—Partnership

Patent and Copyright Law

Miller and Davis' Intellectual Property—Patents, Trademarks and Copyright in a Nutshell, Second Edition, 437 pages, 1990. Softcover. (Text)

Products Liability

Phillips' Products Liability in a Nutshell, Third Edition, 307 pages, 1988. Softcover. (Text)

Professional Responsibility

Aronson and Weckstein's Professional Responsibility in a Nutshell, Second Edition, 514 pages, 1991. Softcover. (Text)

Lesnick's Being a Lawyer: Individual Choice and Responsibility in the Practice of Law, 422 pages, 1992. Softcover. Teacher's Manual available. (Coursebook)

Rotunda's Black Letter on Professional Responsibility, Third Edition, 492 pages, 1992. Softcover. (Review)

Wolfram's Hornbook on Modern Legal Ethics, Student Edition, 1120

Professional Responsibility—Cont'd
pages, 1986. (Text)

Wydick and Perschbacher's California Legal Ethics, 439 pages, 1992. Softcover. (Coursebook)

Property—see also Real Estate Transactions, Land Use, Trusts and Estates

Bernhardt's Black Letter on Property, Second Edition, 388 pages, 1991. Softcover. (Review)

Bernhardt's Real Property in a Nutshell, Second Edition, 448 pages, 1981. Softcover. (Text)

Boyer, Hovenkamp and Kurtz' The Law of Property, An Introductory Survey, Fourth Edition, 696 pages, 1991. (Text)

Burke's Personal Property in a Nutshell, Second Edition, approximately 400 pages, May, 1993 Pub. Softcover. (Text)

Cunningham, Stoebuck and Whitman's Hornbook on the Law of Property, Second Edition, approximately 900 pages, May, 1993 Pub. (Text)

Hill's Landlord and Tenant Law in a Nutshell, Second Edition, 311 pages, 1986. Softcover. (Text)

Real Estate Transactions

Bruce's Real Estate Finance in a Nutshell, Third Edition, 287 pages, 1991. Softcover. (Text)

Nelson and Whitman's Black Letter on Land Transactions and Finance, Second Edition, 466 pages, 1988. Softcover. (Review)

Nelson and Whitman's Hornbook on Real Estate Finance Law, Second Edition, 941 pages, 1985 with 1989 pocket part. (Text)

Regulated Industries—see also Mass Communication Law, Banking Law

Gellhorn and Pierce's Regulated Industries in a Nutshell, Second Edition, 389 pages, 1987. Softcover. (Text)

Remedies

Dobbs' Hornbook on Remedies, Second Edition, approximately 1000 pages, April, 1993 Pub. (Text)

Dobbyn's Injunctions in a Nutshell, 264 pages, 1974. Softcover. (Text)

Friedman's Contract Remedies in a Nutshell, 323 pages, 1981. Softcover. (Text)

O'Connell's Remedies in a Nutshell, Second Edition, 320 pages, 1985. Softcover. (Text)

Sea, Law of

Sohn and Gustafson's The Law of the Sea in a Nutshell, 264 pages, 1984. Softcover. (Text)

Securities Regulation

Hazen's Hornbook on the Law of Securities Regulation, Second Edition, Student Edition, 1082 pages, 1990. (Text)

Ratner's Securities Regulation in a Nutshell, Fourth Edition, 320 pages, 1992. Softcover. (Text)

Sports Law

Champion's Sports Law in a Nutshell,. Approximately 300 pages, January, 1993 Pub. Softcover. (Text)

Schubert, Smith and Trentadue's Sports Law, 395 pages, 1986. (Text)

Tax Practice and Procedure

Morgan's Tax Procedure and Tax Fraud in a Nutshell, 400 pages, 1990. Softcover. (Text)

Taxation—Corporate

Schwarz and Lathrope's Black Letter on Corporate and Partnership Taxation, 537 pages, 1991. Softcover. (Review)

Weidenbruch and Burke's Federal Income Taxation of Corporations and Stockholders in a Nutshell, Third Edition, 309 pages, 1989. Softcover. (Text)

Taxation—Estate & Gift—see also Estate Planning, Trusts and Estates

McNulty's Federal Estate and Gift Taxation in a Nutshell, Fourth Edition, 496 pages, 1989. Softcover. (Text)

Peat and Willbanks' Federal Estate and Gift Taxation: An Analysis and Critique, 265 pages, 1991. Softcover. (Text)

Taxation—Individual

Dodge's The Logic of Tax, 343 pages, 1989. Softcover. (Text)

Hudson and Lind's Black Letter on Federal Income Taxation, Fourth Edition, 410 pages, 1992. Softcover. (Review)

McNulty's Federal Income Taxation of Individuals in a Nutshell, Fourth Edition, 503 pages, 1988. Softcover. (Text)

Posin's Federal Income Taxation, Second Edition, approximately 650 pages, May, 1993 Pub. Softcover. (Text)

Rose and Chommie's Hornbook on Federal Income Taxation, Third Edition, 923 pages, 1988, with 1991 pocket part. (Text)

Taxation—International

Doernberg's International Taxation in a Nutshell, 325 pages, 1989. Softcover. (Text)

Bishop and Brooks' Federal Partnership Taxation: A Guide to the Leading Cases, Statutes, and Regulations, 545 pages, 1990. Softcover. (Text)

Burke's Federal Income Taxation of Partnerships in a Nutshell, 356 pages, 1992. Softcover. (Text)

Schwarz and Lathrope's Black Letter on Corporate and Partnership Taxation, 537 pages, 1991. Softcover. (Review)

Taxation—State & Local

Gelfand and Salsich's State and Local Taxation and Finance in a Nutshell, 309 pages, 1986. Softcover. (Text)

Torts—see also Products Liability

Kionka's Black Letter on Torts, 339 pages, 1988. Softcover. (Review)

Kionka's Torts in a Nutshell, Second Edition, 449 pages, 1992. Softcover. (Text)

Prosser and Keeton's Hornbook on Torts, Fifth Edition, Student Edition, 1286 pages, 1984 with 1988 pocket part. (Text)

Trade Regulation—see also Antitrust, Regulated Industries

McManis' Unfair Trade Practices in a Nutshell, Third Edition, approximately 450 pages, 1993. Softcover. (Text)

Schechter's Black Letter on Unfair Trade Practices, 272 pages, 1986. Softcover. (Review)

Trial and Appellate Advocacy—see also Civil Procedure

Bergman's Trial Advocacy in a Nutshell, Second Edition, 354 pages, 1989. Softcover. (Text)

Clary's Primer on the Analysis and Presentation of Legal Argument, 106 pages, 1992. Softcover. (Text)

Dessem's Pretrial Litigation in a Nutshell, 382 pages, 1992. Softcover. (Text)

Goldberg's The First Trial (Where Do I Sit? What Do I Say?) in a Nutshell, 396 pages, 1982. Softcover. (Text)

Hegland's Trial and Practice Skills in a Nutshell, 346 pages, 1978. Softcover. (Text)

Hornstein's Appellate Advocacy in a Nutshell, 325 pages, 1984. Softcover. (Text)

Jeans' Handbook on Trial Advocacy, Student Edition, 473 pages, 1975. Softcover. (Text)

Trusts and Estates

ATKINSON'S HORNBOOK ON WILLS, Second Edition, 975 pages, 1953. (Text)

AVERILL'S UNIFORM PROBATE CODE IN A NUTSHELL, Second Edition, 454 pages, 1987. Softcover. (Text)

BOGERT'S HORNBOOK ON TRUSTS, Sixth Edition, Student Edition, 794 pages, 1987. (Text)

MCGOVERN, KURTZ AND REIN'S HORNBOOK ON WILLS, TRUSTS AND ESTATES– INCLUDING TAXATION AND FUTURE INTERESTS, 996 pages, 1988. (Text)

MENNELL'S WILLS AND TRUSTS IN A NUTSHELL, 392 pages, 1979. Softcover. (Text)

SIMES' HORNBOOK ON FUTURE INTERESTS, Second Edition, 355 pages, 1966. (Text)

TURANO AND RADIGAN'S HORNBOOK ON NEW YORK ESTATE ADMINISTRATION, 676 pages, 1986 with 1991 pocket part. (Text)

WAGGONER'S FUTURE INTERESTS IN A NUTSHELL, 361 pages, 1981. Softcover. (Text)

Water Law—see also Environmental Law

GETCHES' WATER LAW IN A NUTSHELL, Second Edition, 459 pages, 1990. Softcover. (Text)

Wills—see Trusts and Estates

Workers' Compensation

HOOD, HARDY AND LEWIS' WORKERS' COMPENSATION AND EMPLOYEE PROTECTION LAWS IN A NUTSHELL, Second Edition, 361 pages, 1990. Softcover. (Text)

*

WEST'S LAW SCHOOL ADVISORY BOARD

CURTIS J. BERGER
Professor of Law, Columbia University

JESSE H. CHOPER
Dean and Professor of Law,
University of California, Berkeley

DAVID P. CURRIE
Professor of Law, University of Chicago

YALE KAMISAR
Professor of Law, University of Michigan

MARY KAY KANE
Professor of Law, University of California,
Hastings College of the Law

WAYNE R. LaFAVE
Professor of Law, University of Illinois

RICHARD C. MAXWELL
Professor of Law, Duke University

ARTHUR R. MILLER
Professor of Law, Harvard University

GRANT S. NELSON
Professor of Law, University of California, Los Angeles

ROBERT A. STEIN
Dean and Professor of Law, University of Minnesota

JAMES J. WHITE
Professor of Law, University of Michigan

CHARLES ALAN WRIGHT
Professor of Law, University of Texas

The Hornbook

Dr. Johnson described the hornbook as "the first book of children, covered with horn to keep it unsoiled." Pardon's *New General English Dictionary* (1758) defined it as "A leaf of written or printed paper pasted on a board, and covered with horn, for children to learn their letters by, and to prevent their being torn and daubed."

It was used throughout Europe and America between the late 1400s and the middle 1700s.

Shaped like an old-fashioned butter paddle, the first hornbooks were made of wood. The paper lesson the child was to learn was fastened to the wooden paddle and covered with a piece of horn. The transparent strip of horn was made by soaking a cow's horn in hot water and peeling it away at the thickness of a piece of celluloid. The horn was necessary to protect the lesson from the damp and perhaps grubby hands of the child. Hornbooks commonly contained the alphabet, the vowels, and the Lord's Prayer. Later hornbooks were made of various materials: brass, copper, silver, ivory, bronze, leather, and stone.

As the art of printing advanced, the hornbook was supplanted by the primer in the book form we know today. Subsequently, West Publishing Company developed its "Hornbook Series", a series of scholarly and well-respected one volume treatises on particular areas of law. Today they are widely used by law students, lawyers and judges.

BANKRUPTCY

By

David G. Epstein
King & Spalding
Atlanta, Georgia

Steve H. Nickles
Roger F. Noreen Professor of Law
University of Minnesota

James J. White
Robert A. Sullivan Professor of Law
University of Michigan

Reprinted from Epstein, Nickles & White,
Bankruptcy, Practitioner Treatise Series,
Vols. 1–3 (West, 1992)

HORNBOOK SERIES®

WEST PUBLISHING CO.
ST. PAUL, MINN., 1993

Reprinted from Epstein, Nickles & White, Bankruptcy, Practitioner Treatise Series, Volumes 1–3 (West, 1992).
COPYRIGHT © 1993 By WEST PUBLISHING CO.
610 Opperman Drive
P.O. Box 64526
St. Paul, MN 55164–0526

All rights reserved
Printed in the United States of America

Library of Congress Cataloging-in-Publication Data

Epstein, David G., 1943–
    Bankruptcy / by David G. Epstein, Steve H. Nickles, and James J. White.
        p.   cm. — (Hornbook series)
    Includes Index.
    ISBN 0–314–01124–2
    1. Bankruptcy—United States. I. Nickles, Steve H., 1949–   . II. White, James J., 1934–
III. Title. IV. Series.
KF1524.E67 1993
346.73'078—dc20
[347.30678]
                                                                                                              92–44067
                                                                                                               CIP

ISBN 0–314–01124–2

(E., N.& W.) Bankr. HB

The authors disagree on many matters of style and substance but not about the dedication of this book. We are cheerfully united in dedicating it, with much affection and respect, to our mutual good friends,

Roger and Violet Noreen

Editorial Note to Student Edition

This book is the student edition of a three-volume treatise for practitioners. The two versions are the same, except that the student edition leaves out many footnotes and some whole sections that are much more important to practicing lawyers than to student lawyers.

The student edition concentrates on the essentials that a law teacher is likely to cover in class or on an examination. Nevertheless, the student edition marks every place where materials are deleted that appear in the practitioner edition. This alerts readers that more is available in the full, three-volume treatise. Cross-reference is easy because the section and footnote numbers are identical between the two versions of the book.

The purpose of having a downsized student edition is to focus attention on central, important issues and, equally, to produce a book for students that is more portable and more affordable than the complete treatise.

*

Preface to Three Volume Treatise

In 1956, West published a hornbook on bankruptcy by James A. MacLachlan. The preface to the book began, "A one volume text on Bankruptcy cannot be comprehensive." Today, in 1992, a year in which about one million bankruptcy cases will be filed and West will report thousands of opinions in more than a dozen volumes of the Bankruptcy Reporter, three volumes on bankruptcy cannot be comprehensive.

Professor MacLachlan described his 1956 bankruptcy hornbook as "what one man thinks is appropriate to say about bankruptcy within the limitations of space imposed by the general nature of this undertaking." Similarly, this book is what each of us thinks is appropriate to say about bankruptcy in three volumes. And, Dave Epstein or Steve Nickles or Jim White's thoughts about what is appropriate to say about bankruptcy are not only different from Professor MacLachlan's, but in many respects are also different from his coauthors.

This book uses a variety of pronouns and expresses a variety of views that sometimes conflict. At times, "it" is used to represent "he," "she," or "it"; at times, "he" is used to represent "he," "she," or "it"; at times, "she" is used to represent "he," "she," or "it." More important, at times, "we" is used to represent Epstein, Nickles, and White; at times, "we" is used to represent some combination of two of us; at times, "we" is used to represent only one of us.

Readers (especially lawyers who are negotiating or litigating against Dave Epstein) need to understand how this book was written. Dave Epstein wrote the manuscript for Chapters 1, 2, and 5; Steve Nickles wrote the manuscript for Chapters 3, 6, and 8; and Jim White wrote the manuscript for Chapters 4, 7, and 9 through 12. Each chapter was reviewed and criticized by the other two "coauthors". All such comments were carefully considered; many, if not most, were disregarded. Accordingly, notwithstanding the use of the editorial "we," the pronouns used and the opinions expressed in any chapter of this book should be attributed, at most, only to the "author" of that chapter.

Even then, readers should understand that no chapter completely represents its author. Every chapter contains some compromises and accommodations. Each of us made a few of them, usually to leave room for very strongly-held beliefs of his coauthors.

We are agreed that the issues of bankruptcy law are compounded in number and complexity by the wide disagreement everywhere on the purpose and role of bankruptcy itself, as well as the objectives of its constituent laws.

This disagreement comforts us. It means that the reader's own perspective on these matters is likely different from our own; and he or she will see, more easily even than we, the discussions that are askew because of our different view.

DAVID G. EPSTEIN
Atlanta

STEVE H. NICKLES
Minneapolis

JAMES J. WHITE
Ann Arbor

September, 1992

Acknowledgments

David Epstein thanks Lynda Walton who with good cheer and uncommon care added manuscript preparation to the burdens of serving as secretary to a lawyer and two paralegals. He also publicly acknowledges his debt to his partners at King & Spalding who truly supported his work on this book.

For their work and laughter while helping to build this book, Steve Nickles thanks his research assistants: Todd Pearson '92, Peter Carter '91, Terri Georgen '93, Anne Marrs '92, and Kevin Saville '92.

Jim White acknowledges the work of Cynthia Baker '88, Richard Ziegler '88, Patrick Potter '89, John Castenada '90, Ronald G. DeWaard '90, John Klein '90, Clara Rubinstein '90, Karl Weber '90, Julia Goatley '91, Maureen McAndrew '91, David Gaskey '92, Patrick Romain '92, Julie Smith '92, David Kravitz '93, and Robert Fogler '94. Particularly deserving is Kathryn West, who not only typed, spell checked, and cite checked much of the manuscript, but who read the entire manuscript and often scolded not only White, but also Nickles and Epstein for their excesses. Nickles and Epstein nevertheless join White in thanking Ms. West, and Nickles and White join Epstein in thanking Ms. Walton. These two women helped all three authors and helped the book even more.

*

Bankruptcy Law Research on Westlaw®

Analysis

Sec.
1. Introduction.
2. Bankruptcy Databases.
3. Menu–Driven WESTLAW: EZ ACCESS.™
4. Retrieving a Document with a Citation: Find and Jump.
5. Query Formulation.
    - 5.1 Terms.
    - 5.2 Alternative Terms.
    - 5.3 Connectors.
    - 5.4 Restricting Your Search by Field.
    - 5.5 Restricting Your Search by Date.
6. Verifying Your Research with Citators.
    - 6.1 Insta–Cite.®
    - 6.2 Shepard's® Citations.
    - 6.3 Shepard's PreView.™
    - 6.4 QuickCite.™
    - 6.5 Using WESTLAW as a Citator.
    - 6.6 Citator Commands.
7. Research Examples.
    - 7.1 Retrieving Law Review Articles.
    - 7.2 Retrieving Statutes.
    - 7.3 Retrieving Federal Regulations.
    - 7.4 Using Citator Services.
    - 7.5 Retrieving Bankruptcy Cases.
    - 7.6 Following Recent Developments.
    - 7.7 Accessing the Online Bankruptcy Treatises.

Section 1. Introduction

Epstein, Nickles & White's *Bankruptcy* provides a strong base for analyzing bankruptcy law problems. Whether your research requires examination of case law, statutes, administrative materials, commentary or technical information, West books and WESTLAW are excellent sources of research materials.

In the area of bankruptcy law, WESTLAW expands your library by giving you access to documents issued by state and federal courts and legislatures. To assist you in keeping up-to-date with changes to bankruptcy law, WESTLAW provides a topical highlights database for bankruptcy issues, as well as text from the publications in *Clark Boardman's Bankruptcy Law Library,* and the treatise *Bankruptcy Evidence Manual.*

Additional Resources

If you have not used WESTLAW or have questions not addressed in this appendix, see the *WESTLAW Reference Manual* or contact the West Reference Attorneys at 1–800–688–6363. The West Reference Attorneys are trained, licensed attorneys, available throughout the workday and on weekends to answer your WESTLAW or West book research questions.

Section 2. Bankruptcy Databases

Each database on WESTLAW is assigned an abbreviation called an identifier, which you use to access the database. You can find identifiers for all databases in the WESTLAW Directory and in the *WESTLAW Database List.* When you need to know more detailed information about a database, use the Scope command. Scope displays coverage, unique commands and related databases for each database and service.

The chart below lists WESTLAW databases that contain information on bankruptcy law. Because new information is continually being added to WESTLAW, you should check the WESTLAW Directory for any new database information.

Description	Database Identifier	Coverage (see Scope for more specific information)
FEDERAL DATABASES		
Federal materials combines: FBKR–CS, FBKR–USCA, FBKR–FR, and FBKR–CFR	FBKR–ALL	Varies by database
Case Law		
Federal Bankruptcy	FBKR–CS, FBKR–CS–OLD	1789–present
U.S. Supreme Court Cases	FBKR–SCT, FBKR–SCT–OLD	1790–present
U.S. Courts of Appeals Cases	FBKR–CTA, FBKR–CTA–OLD	1891–present

Description	Database Identifier	Coverage
U.S. District Courts	FBKR–DCT, FBKR–DCT–OLD	1789–present
U.S. Bankruptcy Courts	FBKR–BCT	1979–present
U.S. Claims Court	CLCT, CLCT–OLD	1929–present

Statutes and Regulations

U.S. Code Annotated	FBKR–USCA	Current
Federal Rules	FBKR–RULES	Current
Federal Register	FBKR–FR	1980–present
Code of Federal Regulations	FBKR–CFR	Current
Combines: FBKR–USCA, FBKR–FR and FBKR–CFR	FBKR–CODREG	Varies by individual database
Combines: FBKR–FR and FBKR–CFR	FBKR–REG	Varies by individual database
United States Public Laws	US–PL	Current
Legislative History—U.S. Code	LH	From 1986
Congressional Record	CR	From 1985

STATE DATABASES

Statutes and Regulations

State Statutes—Annotated	ST-ANN-ALL	Varies by state
Statutes and annotations from all fifty states, the District of Columbia, Puerto Rico and the Virgin Islands		
State Statutes—Unannotated	STAT-ALL	Current
Statutes from all fifty states, the District of Columbia, Puerto Rico and the Virgin Islands		
Individual State Statutes Annotated *	XX-ST-ANN	Current
Individual State Statutes Unannotated *	XX-ST	Current
Multistate Legislative Service	LEGIS-ALL	Varies by state
Documents passed by the legislative bodies from all fifty states, the		

* XX is a state's two-letter postal abbreviation.

Description	Database Identifier	Coverage
District of Columbia, Puerto Rico and the Virgin Islands		
Individual State Legislative Service *	XX–LEGIS	Varies by state
Individual State Statute Indexes *	XX–ST–IDX	Varies by state
General index references for the statutes and constitutions of all fifty states and the District of Columbia		
Individual State Attorney General Opinions *	XX–AG	Varies by state

SPECIALIZED MATERIALS

Description	Database Identifier	Coverage
BNA Bankruptcy Law Daily	BNA–BLD	From 9/89
Current Index to Legal Periodicals	CILP	Current
Directory of Bankruptcy Attorneys	BKR–DIR	Current
Dow Jones Highlights	DJH	Current
Federated Department Stores Bankruptcy	FBKR–FDS	Current
Index to Legal Periodicals	ILP	From 8/81
Legal Resource Index ™	LRI	From 1/80
Practising Law Institute	PLI	From 9/84
United States Law Week	BNA–USLW	From 1/86
United States Law Week–Daily Edition	BNA–USLWD	From 3/87
West's® Legal Directory	WLD	Current
West's Legal Directory—Individual States *	WLD–XX	Current
WESTLAW Topical Highlights–Bankruptcy	WTH–BKR	Current

GATEWAY DATABASES

Description	Database Identifier	Coverage
Dialog Information Services, Inc.	DIALOG	
Dow Jones News/Retrieval®	DJNS	
Dun & Bradstreet Information Services' Online Service for WESTLAW	DUNS	

TEXTS & TREATISES

Description	Database Identifier	Coverage
Bankruptcy Evidence Manual, 1991 Edition	BKRMANUAL	Current
Bankruptcy Law Reviews, Texts & Bar Journals	BKR–TP	Varies by publication

Description	Database Identifier	Coverage
Clark Boardman–Bankruptcy Law Fundamentals	CB–BKRFUND	Through last supplement
Clark Boardman–Federal Rules of Bankruptcy	CB–BKRULES	Through last supplement
Clark Boardman–Guidebook to Security Interests in Personal Property	CB–GSI	Through last supplement
Clark Boardman–Herzog's Bankruptcy Forms and Practice	CB–BKRFP	Through last supplement
Clark Boardman–Law of Distressed Real Estate	CB–DRE	Through last supplement

Section 3. Menu–Driven WESTLAW: EZ ACCESS™

EZ ACCESS is West Publishing Company's menu-driven research system. It is ideal for new or infrequent WESTLAW users because it requires no experience or training on WESTLAW.

To access EZ ACCESS, type **ez**. Whenever you are unsure of the next step, or if the choice you want is not listed, simply type **ez**; additional choices will be displayed. Once you retrieve documents with EZ ACCESS, use standard WESTLAW commands to browse your documents. For more information on browsing documents, see the *WESTLAW Reference Manual.*

Section 4. Retrieving a Document with a Citation: Find and Jump

Find is a WESTLAW service that allows you to retrieve a document by entering its citation. Find allows you to retrieve documents from anywhere in WESTLAW without accessing or changing databases or losing your search result. Find is available for many documents including case law (federal and state), state statutes, the *United States Code Annotated*®, the *Code of Federal Regulations,* the *Federal Register,* and state and federal public laws.

To use Find, type **fi** followed by the document citation. Below is a list of examples.

To Find This Document:	Type:
In re Roberson, 1992 WL 78014 (N.D.Ill.)	**fi 1992 wl 78014**
Toibb v. Radloff, 111 S.Ct. 2197	**fi 111 sct 2197**
11 U.S.C.A. § 726	**fi 11 usca 726**
55 FR 38649	**fi 55 fr 38649**
34 CFR § 673.59	**fi 34 cfr 673.59**

To Find This Document:	Type:
In re Hancock, 22 Bankr.Ct.Dec. 1157	**fi 22 bankr ct dec 1157**
Bankruptcy Evidence Manual Section 22. *Exclusion of Parol Evidence*	**fi bkrmanual s 22**
BNA Bankruptcy Law Daily May 6, 1992	**fi 5/6/92 bld**
In re SLC Limited V, Bankruptcy Law Reports (CCH) § 74,509 (Bankr.D.Utah, 1992)	**fi bankr l rep 74,509**
Bankruptcy Official Form # 7 Statement of Financial Affairs	**fi bankr official 7**
In re Capital Center Equities, 137 B.R. 600 (Bankr.E.D.Pa.1992)	**fi 137 br 600**
Rules of Bankruptcy Procedure, Rule 1018: *Contested Involuntary Petitions*	**fi bankr rule 1018**
In re Federated Department Stores, Motion of debtors and debtors in possession for authorization to renew insurance policies, court filing number 358 (S.D.Ohio W.D. 1990)	**fi camp 358**
Whitson v. Middleton, 22 C.B.C. 258 (4th Cir.1990)	**fi 22 cbc 258**
In re Sun Valley Ranches, Inc., 17 Collier Bankr.Cas.2d 449 (9th Cir.1987)	**fi 17 collier bankr cas 2d 449**

Use Jump to retrieve a case or U.S.C.A. section cited in a case you are viewing. Click your mouse on the > or ► symbol displayed before the citation, or press the **Tab** key until the cursor reaches the desired location, then press **Enter**. The cited document will be displayed automatically.

Section 5. Query Formulation

Overview: A query is a request you make to WESTLAW specifying the information you wish to retrieve. The terms in a query are words or numbers that you include in your request so that WESTLAW will retrieve documents containing those words or numbers. These terms are linked together by connectors, which specify the relationship in which the terms must appear.

5.1 Terms

Plurals and Possessives: Plurals are automatically retrieved when you enter the singular form of a term. This is true for both regular and irregular plurals (e.g., **child** retrieves *children*). If you enter the plural form of a term, you will not retrieve the singular form.

If you enter the non-possessive form of a term, WESTLAW automatically retrieves the possessive form as well. However, if you enter the possessive form, only the possessive form is retrieved.

Automatic Equivalencies: Some terms have alternative forms or equivalencies; for example, *5* and *five* are equivalent terms. WESTLAW automatically retrieves equivalent terms. The *WESTLAW Reference Manual* contains a list of equivalent terms.

Compound Words and Acronyms: When a compound word is one of your search terms, use a hyphen to retrieve all forms of the word. For example, the term **long-term** retrieves *long-term, long term* and *longterm*.

When using an acronym as a search term, place a period after each of the letters in the acronym to retrieve any of its forms. For example, the term **c.e.r.c.l.a.** retrieves *cercla, c.e.r.c.l.a., c e r c l a* and *c. e. r. c. l. a.*

Root Expander and Universal Character: Placing a root expander (!) at the end of a root term generates ALL other terms with that root. For example, adding the ! symbol to the root *develop* in the query

develop! /s covenant

instructs WESTLAW to retrieve such words as *develop, develops, developed, developer* and *development*.

The universal character (*) stands for one character and can be inserted in the middle or at the end of a term. For example, the term

s****holder

will retrieve *shareholder* and *stockholder*. But adding only two asterisks to the root *jur* in the query

jur**

instructs WESTLAW to retrieve all forms of the root with up to two additional characters. Terms like *jury* or *juror* are retrieved by this query. However, terms with more than two letters following the root, such as *jurisdiction,* are not retrieved. Plurals are always retrieved, even if more than two letters follow the root.

Phrase Searching: To search for a phrase on WESTLAW, place it within quotation marks. For example, to search for references to the Rule Against Perpetuities, type **"rule against perpetuities"**. You should use phrase searching only when you are certain that the phrase will not appear in any other form.

5.2 Alternative Terms

After selecting the terms for your query, consider which alternative terms are necessary. For example, if you are searching for the term *contract,* you might also want to search for the term *agreement.* You should consider both synonyms and antonyms as alternative terms.

5.3 Connectors

After selecting terms and alternative terms for your query, use connectors to specify the relationship that should exist between search terms in your retrieved documents. The connectors you can use are described below:

Use:	To retrieve documents with:	Example:
& (and)	search terms in the same document	**discharge & judgment**
or (space)	one search term or the other	**loan debt indebtedness**
/p	search terms in the same paragraph	**fraud! /p transfer!**
/s	search terms in the same sentence	**homestead /s exempt!**
+s	one search term preceding the other within the same sentence	**preferen! +s transfer**
/n	search terms within "n" words of each other (where "n" is a number)	**discharge /3 debtor**
+n	one search term preceding the other by "n" words (where "n" is a number)	**secured +1 transaction**
Use:	To exclude documents with:	Example:
% (but not)	search terms following the % symbol	**nondischarge!/3fraud& da(1992) % to(110)**

5.4 Restricting Your Search by Field

Overview: Documents in each WESTLAW database consist of several segments, or fields. One field may contain the citation, another the title, another the synopsis, and so forth. A query can be formulated to retrieve only those documents that contain search terms in a specified field. Not all databases contain the same fields. Also, depending on the database, fields of the same name may contain different types of information.

To view the fields and field content for a specific database, type **f** while in the database. Note that in some databases, not every field is available for every document. To restrict your search to a specific field, type the field name or two-letter abbreviation followed by search terms enclosed in parentheses. For example, to retrieve a case entitled *Hancock Bank v. Jefferson*, restrict your search to the title field:

ti(hancock & jefferson)

The fields discussed below are available in WESTLAW databases you might use for bankruptcy research.

Digest and Synopsis Fields: The digest and synopsis fields, provided in case law databases by West Publishing Company's editors, summarize the main points of a case. A search in these fields is useful because it retrieves only cases in which a search term was significant enough to be included in a summary.

Consider restricting your search to one or both of these fields if

- [ ] you are searching for common terms or terms with more than one meaning, and you need to narrow your search; or

- [ ] you cannot narrow your search by moving to a smaller database.

For example, to retrieve cases that discuss whether condominium fees are dischargeable in bankruptcy, access the Federal Bankruptcy Cases database (FBKR–CS) and type:

> sy,di(condominium condo association   /p   fee   /p   discharge!)

Headnote Field: The headnote field is a part of the digest field, but does not contain the topic number, the key number, the case citation or the title. The headnote field contains only the one-sentence summary of the point of law and any supporting statutory citations given by the author of the opinion. A headnote field search is useful when you are searching for references to specific code sections or rule numbers. For example, to retrieve headnotes that cite 11 U.S.C.A. § 722, type the following query:

> he(11 +5 722)

Topic Field: The topic field is also a part of the digest field. It contains the West digest topic name and number, the key number, and the key line text. You should restrict search terms to the topic field in a case law database if

- [ ] a digest field search retrieves too many documents; or

- [ ] you want to retrieve cases with digest paragraphs classified under more than one topic.

An example of the first type of topic field search is the following: The topic *Bankruptcy* has the topic number 51. To retrieve cases that discuss the dischargeability of environmental cleanup liability under the Comprehensive Environmental Response, Compensation, and Liability Act (CERCLA), access the Federal Bankruptcy Cases database (FBKR–CS) and type:

> to(51) /p c.e.r.c.l.a. (comprehensive /3 response /3 compensation) /p discharge!

The second type of topic field search allows you to retrieve West headnotes classified under more than one topic and key number. Search for the topic name in the topic field; for example, to search for cases that discuss the effects of bankruptcy on child support or maintenance awards, access the Federal Bankruptcy—Bankruptcy Court Cases database (FBKR–BCT) and type a query like the following:

> to(divorce) /p support maintenance alimony

The TOPIC database contains a complete list of West Digest topics and their corresponding topic numbers.

Be aware that slip opinions and cases from looseleaf services do not contain the digest, synopsis, headnote or topic fields.

Prelim and Caption Fields: When searching in a database containing statutes or regulations, restrict your search to the prelim and caption fields to retrieve documents in which your terms are important enough to appear in a section name or heading. For example, to retrieve code sections discussing involuntary bankruptcy under Chapter 7, access the Federal Bankruptcy—U.S. Code Annotated database (FBKR–USCA) and type the following:

> pr,ca(involuntary) & "chapter 7"

5.5 Restricting Your Search by Date

You can instruct WESTLAW to retrieve documents *decided or issued* before, after, or on a specified date, as well as within a range of dates. The following are examples of queries that contain date restrictions:

> da(bef 1992 & aft 1990) & revoke revocation /3 discharge!
> da(1992) & revoke revocation /3 discharge!
> da(10/20/89) & revoke revocation /3 discharge!

You can also instruct WESTLAW to retrieve documents *added to a database* on or after a specified date, as well as within a range of dates. The following are examples of queries that contain added date restrictions:

> ad(aft 1/1/90) & revoke revocation /3 discharge!
> ad(aft 6/1/92 & bef 3/1/92) & revoke revocation /3 discharge!

Section 6. Verifying Your Research with Citators

Overview: WESTLAW contains four citator services that assist you in checking the validity of cases you are relying on. These four citator services—Insta–Cite®, Shepard's® Citations, Shepard's PreView™ and Quick-Cite™—help you perform many valuable research tasks, saving you hours of manual research. Sections 6.1 through 6.4 provide further information on these services.

For citations that are not covered by one of these services, a fifth technique, called *using WESTLAW as a citator*, can assist you. Section 6.5 explains how to use this technique.

6.1 Insta–Cite®

Insta–Cite is West Publishing Company's case history and citation verification service. It is the most current case history service available, providing direct history within hours of when a case is received at West. Use Insta–Cite to see if your case is still good law. Insta–Cite provides the following types of information about a citation:

> **Direct History.** In addition to reversals and affirmances, Insta–Cite gives you the complete reported history of a litigated matter including any related cases. Insta–Cite provides the federal direct history of a case from 1754 and the state direct history from 1879. Related references (cases related to the litigation) are provided from 1983 to date.
>
> **Negative Indirect History.** Insta–Cite lists subsequent cases that have a substantial negative impact on your case, including cases overruling your case or calling it into question. Cases affected by decisions from 1972 to date will be displayed on Insta–Cite. To retrieve negative

indirect history prior to 1972, use Shepard's Citations (discussed in Section 6.2).

Secondary Source References. Insta–Cite also provides references to secondary sources that cite your case. These secondary sources currently include legal encyclopedias such as *Corpus Juris Secundum*®.

Parallel Citations. Insta–Cite provides parallel citations for cases including citations to *American Law Times Bankruptcy Reports, National Bankruptcy Register Reports* and many other looseleaf reporters.

Citation Verification. Insta–Cite confirms that you have the correct volume and page number for a case. Citation verification information is available from 1754 for federal cases and from 1879 for state cases.

6.2 Shepard's® Citations

Shepard's provides a comprehensive list of cases and publications that have cited a particular case or United States Code Annotated® section. Shepard's also includes explanatory analysis to indicate how the citing cases have treated the case, e.g., "followed," "explained."

In addition to citations from federal, state, and regional citators, Shepard's on WESTLAW includes citations from specialized citators, such as *Bankruptcy Citations*. *Bankruptcy Citations* contains cross-references to the same cases in various other citators, including *Opinions of the U.S. Attorney General, Bankruptcy Law Reporter* and *Collier Bankruptcy Cases*.

6.3 Shepard's PreView™

Shepard's PreView gives you a preview of citing references from West's® National Reporter System® that will appear in Shepard's Citations. Depending on the citation, Shepard's PreView provides citing information days, weeks or even months before the same information appears in Shepard's online. Use Shepard's PreView to update your Shepard's results.

6.4 Quick*Cite*™

Quick*Cite* is a citator service that enables you to retrieve the most recent citing cases on WESTLAW, including slip opinions, automatically.

There is a four- to six-week gap between a citing case's availability on WESTLAW and its listing in Shepard's PreView. This gap occurs because cases go through an editorial process at West before they are added to Shepard's PreView. To retrieve the most recent citing cases, therefore, you need to search case law databases on WESTLAW for references to your case. Quick*Cite* does this for you automatically by retrieving and displaying the complete text of recent citing cases.

Quick*Cite* formulates a query using the title, the case citation(s), and an added date restriction. Quick*Cite* then accesses the appropriate database, either ALLSTATES or ALLFEDS, and runs the query for you. Quick*Cite* also allows you to choose a different date range and database for your query so you can tailor it to your specific research needs.

Quick*Cite* is designed to retrieve documents that cite cases. To retrieve citing references to other documents, such as state statutes and law review articles, use WESTLAW as a citator (discussed below).

6.5 Using WESTLAW as a Citator

Using WESTLAW as a citator, you can search for documents citing a specific statute, regulation, rule, agency decision or other authority. To retrieve documents citing Rhode Island General Laws § 3–5–19, for example, access the Federal Bankruptcy—District Courts Cases database (FBKR–DCT) and search for the citation alone:

> **3-5-19**

If the citation is not a unique term, add descriptive terms. For example, to retrieve cases citing Oklahoma Statute Title 31 § 1 discussing the exemption of a debtor's interest in a personal injury award, access the Oklahoma Cases database (OK–CS) and type a query like the following:

> **31 + 5 1 & "personal injury"**

6.6 Citator Commands

The following are some of the commands that can be used in the citator services. For a complete list, see the *WESTLAW User Guide* or the *WESTLAW Reference Manual.*

Type:	To retrieve:
ic xxx or **ic**	An Insta–Cite result when followed by a case citation (where xxx is the citation), or when entered from a displayed case, Shepard's result or Shepard's PreView result.
sh xxx or **sh**	A Shepard's result when followed by a case citation (where xxx is the citation), or when entered from a displayed case, Insta–Cite result or Shepard's PreView result.
sp xxx or **sp**	A Shepard's PreView result when followed by a case citation (where xxx is the citation), or when entered from a displayed case, Insta–Cite result or Shepard's result.
qc xxx or **qc**	A Quick*Cite* result when followed by a case citation (where xxx is the citation), or when entered from a displayed case, Insta–Cite result, Shepard's result or Shepard's PreView result.
xx sc	The scope of coverage (where xx is the citator).
sh sc xxx	The scope of coverage for a specific publication in Shepard's, where xxx is the publication abbreviation (e.g., **sh sc b.r.**).

Type:	To retrieve:
xx pubs	A list of publication abbreviations available with the citator (where xx is the citator).
xx cmds	A list of commands (where xx is the citator).

Section 7. Research Examples

7.1 Retrieving Law Review Articles

A colleague refers you to a law review article by Daniel Keating, *Offensive Uses of the Bankruptcy Stay,* 45 Vand.L.Rev. 71 (1992). How can you retrieve the article on WESTLAW?

Solution

☐ If you know the citation, access the Vanderbilt Law Review database (VNLR). Search for terms from the citation in the citation field:

ci(45 +5 71)

☐ If you know the title of the article, but not which journal it appears in, access the Bankruptcy—Law Reviews, Texts & Bar Journals database (BKR–TP). Search for key terms in the title field:

ti(offensive /s stay)

7.2 Retrieving Statutes

You need to retrieve any Kentucky statutes that discuss property that is exempt in a bankruptcy proceeding.

Solution

☐ Access the Kentucky Statutes—Annotated database (KY–ST–ANN). Search for your terms in the prelim and caption fields:

pr,ca(property /s exempt! /s debtor)

☐ When you know the citation for a specific section of a state statute, use Find to retrieve the statute. (Note: For more information on Find, see Section 4 of this appendix.) For example, to retrieve Kentucky Revised Statute § 427.170, discussing the application of federal bankruptcy exemptions, type

fi ky st s 427.170

☐ To look at surrounding statutory sections, use the Documents in Sequence command. To retrieve the section preceding § 427.170, type **d-**. To retrieve the section immediately following § 427.170, type **d**.

☐ To see if a statute has been amended or repealed, use the Update service. Simply type **update** while viewing the statute to display any session law on WESTLAW that amends or repeals the statute.

Because slip copy versions of laws are added to WESTLAW before they contain full editorial enhancements, they are not retrieved with Update. To retrieve slip copy documents, access a legislative service database and type **ci(slip)** and descriptive terms. Update also does not retrieve legislation that enacts a new statute or covers a topic that will not be incorporated in the statutes. To retrieve this legislation, run a descriptive word search in the appropriate legislative service database.

7.3 Retrieving Federal Regulations

While browsing a case, you note that 40 CFR § 264.117 provides for continued liability for thirty years after the closure of a hazardous waste site. You want to look at the other post-closure requirements for your client.

Solution

☐ Because you have the citation, use Find; type **fi 40 cfr s 264.-117**.

☐ After retrieving this regulation, use Update to display any document from the *Federal Register* on WESTLAW that amends or repeals this regulation; type **update**.

7.4 Using Citator Services

One of the cases retrieved in your research is *Matter of Bundles*, 856 F.2d 815 (7th Cir.1988). You wish to see if this case is still good law and if other cases have cited this case.

Solution

☐ Use Insta–Cite to retrieve the direct and negative indirect case history of *Bundles*. While viewing the case, type **ic**.

☐ You want to Shepardize *Bundles*. Type **sh**.

☐ Limit your Shepard's result to decisions containing a reference to a specific headnote, such as headnote two. Type **Loc 2**.

☐ Check Shepard's PreView for more current cases citing *Bundles*. Type **sp**.

☐ Check Quick*Cite* for the most current cases citing *Bundles*. Type **qc** and follow the online instructions.

7.5 Retrieving Bankruptcy Cases

Your client obtained a malpractice judgment against her former doctor. Unfortunately, her doctor has filed for bankruptcy under Chapter 7. She is concerned that any judgment or settlement that she is awarded will be discharged. You need to locate cases that discuss dischargeability of judgment debts in malpractice cases.

Solution

☐ Access the Federal Bankruptcy Cases database (FBKR–CS). Type a query containing descriptive terms, restricting your search to the synopsis and digest fields:

    sy,di(malpractice /p discharge! nondischarge!)

7.6 Following Recent Developments

As the new associate in the firm, you are expected to keep up with and summarize recent legal developments in the area of bankruptcy law. How can you do this efficiently?

Solution

☐ One of the easiest ways to stay abreast of recent developments in bankruptcy law is by accessing the WESTLAW Topical Highlights—Bankruptcy database (WTH–BKR). The WTH–BKR database summarizes recent legal developments, including court decisions, legislation and materials released by administrative agencies.

☐ To access the database, type **db wth-bkr**. You automatically retrieve a list of documents added to the database in the last two weeks.

☐ To read a summary of a document listed, type its corresponding number.

☐ You can also search this database by typing **s** to display the Enter Query screen. At the Enter Query screen, type your query. For example, to retrieve documents discussing avoiding liens on household goods, type a query like the following:

household & lien /s avoid!

7.7 Accessing the Online Bankruptcy Treatises

Your first client as a bankruptcy attorney asks you about the feasibility of transferring property to his daughter for her birthday before he files for bankruptcy next month. A colleague remembers seeing something on this topic in Hon. Barry Russell's *Bankruptcy Evidence Manual,* and suggests you use this as a starting point.

Solution

☐ Because you don't know the citation, access the *Bankruptcy Evidence Manual* database (BKRMANUAL) by typing **db bkrmanual**. Retrieve the Table of Contents for the treatise by typing

ci(content)

☐ Browse through the document by entering page mode by typing **p** and pressing **Enter**. You see a pertinent heading under § 301.6, *Dischargeability of Transfers to Relatives*. To display your query for editing, type **q**. Edit your query to search for the number 301.6 in the citation field:

ci(301.6)

*

Summary of Contents

	Page
EDITORIAL NOTE TO STUDENT EDITION	v
PREFACE TO THREE VOLUME TREATISE	vii
ACKNOWLEDGMENTS	ix
BANKRUPTCY LAW RESEARCH ON WESTLAW	xi

Chapter

1. Overview of Bankruptcy 1
2. Commencement, Dismissal, and Conversion 15
   - A. Commencement 16
   - B. Dismissal 42
   - C. Conversion 55
3. Automatic Stay 57
   - A. Scope of the Stay 64
   - B. Duration of the Stay 127
   - C. Consequences of Violating the Stay 155
4. Use/Sale/Lease of Estate Property 171
5. Leases and Executory Contracts 223
   - A. Scope of Section 365 226
   - B. Consequences of Section 365 234
   - C. Assumption or Rejection 243
   - D. Executory Contracts and Unexpired Leases That Cannot Be Assumed 251
   - E. Contracts That Cannot Be Assigned 259
   - F. Requirements for Assumption and Assignment 261
   - G. Gap Period 266
   - H. "Special" Leases and Contracts 271
6. Avoidance Powers 272
   - A. Preference, Section 547 278
   - B. Setoff, Section 553 359
   - C. Fraudulent Transfers 365
   - D. "Strong-Arm" Powers, Section 544(a) 390
   - E. Statutory Liens, Section 545 401
   - F. Sellers' Right of Reclamation, Section 546(c) 406
   - G. Postpetition Transfers, Sections 549, 542 and 552 ... 406
   - H. Consequences of Avoidance 419
   - I. Pseudo Avoidance Powers 435
7. Liquidation 447
   - A. Claims, Expenses, and Distributions in Chapter 7 ... 454
   - B. Discharge 472
   - C. Reaffirmation, Section 524(c) 552

Chapter			Page
7.	Liquidation—Continued		
	D.	Protection Against Discriminatory Treatment, Section 525	564
	E.	Dismissal	575
	F.	Redemption, Section 722	584
8.	Exempt Property		592
	A.	Property That Is Exempt in Bankruptcy	598
	B.	Debtor's Avoidance of Transfers of Exempt Property	621
	C.	Exemption "Planning" in Anticipation of Bankruptcy	646
	D.	Pseudo–Exemptions	650
9.	Individual Reorganization: Chapters 13 and 12		651
	A.	Individuals With Regular Income	652
	B.	Chapter 12—Family Farmers With Regular Income	729
10.	Business Reorganization: Chapter 11		731
	A.	Operating the Business After the Chapter 11 Filing	737
	B.	The Trustee, Examiners, Committees	745
	C.	The Plan of Reorganization	756
	D.	Claims	769
	E.	Post-Confirmation Issues	780
	F.	Retrospective	780
11.	Selected Topics in Chapter 11 Proceedings		781
	A.	Claims	782
	B.	Mega–Claims	799
	C.	Waiting for the Debtor's Plan: The "Exclusivity Period," Section 1121(d)	812
	D.	Disclosure and Plan Approval	819
	E.	Absolute Priority and New Value	838
	F.	Bankruptcies Involving Partnerships	854
	G.	Substantive Consolidation	855
12.	Jurisdiction and Procedure		856
	A.	Jurisdiction and Allocation of Judicial Power	856
	B.	Venue	872
	C.	Appeals	882
	D.	Jury Trial	886

TABLE OF CASES — 901
TABLE OF STATUTES — 1001
INDEX — 1055

Table of Contents

	Page
EDITORIAL NOTE TO STUDENT EDITION	v
PREFACE TO THREE VOLUME TREATISE	vii
ACKNOWLEDGMENTS	ix
BANKRUPTCY LAW RESEARCH ON WESTLAW	xi

CHAPTER 1. OVERVIEW OF BANKRUPTCY

Sec.		
1–1	Origins of American Bankruptcy Law	1
1–2	What Is (Are) the Purpose(s) or Goal(s) of Bankruptcy Laws?	2
1–3	What Is Bankruptcy Law?	3
	a. Legislative History	5
	b. State Law	5
1–4	Who Is Involved in a Bankruptcy Case: A Vocabulary List	6
1–5	What Is Bankruptcy?	8
1–6	What Happens in a Bankruptcy Case?	9
1–7	What Happens in a Chapter 7 Bankruptcy Case?	9
	a. Commencement	9
	b. Collection	10
	c. Liquidation	10
	d. Distribution	11
	e. Discharge	11
1–8	Chapter 13 and How It Differs From Chapter 7	11
1–9	Chapter 11 and How It Differs From Chapters 7 and 13	12
	a. Comparison of 7 and 11	13
	b. Comparison of 11 and 13	13
1–10	Chapter 12 and How It Differs From the Other Chapters	13

CHAPTER 2. COMMENCEMENT, DISMISSAL, AND CONVERSION

A. COMMENCEMENT

2–1	Overview of Commencement	16
2–2	Voluntary Cases, Section 301	16
	a. Eligibility	18
	Chapter 7	18
	Chapter 11	18
	Chapter 13	18
	Chapter 12	19
	b. Partnerships	20
	c. Code Limitations on Frequent Filing	20
	d. Filing Fees	21
2–3	Joint Cases	21
2–4	Substantive Consolidation	22

Sec.			Page
2–5	Involuntary Cases, Section 303		23
	a.	Debtors Subject to Involuntary Petitions	24
	b.	Partnerships	24
	c.	Petitioning Creditors	25
	d.	Commencement of the Case/Order for Relief	27
	e.	Grounds for Involuntary Relief	28
	f.	Rights of Debtor and Creditors in the "Involuntary Gap"	28
	g.	Dismissal and Conversion	31
2–6	Case Ancillary to a Foreign Proceeding *		31
2–7	Legal Consequences of Commencing a Case		31
2–8	Legal Consequences of Commencing a Case—Property of the Estate		32
	a.	Importance of the Concept	32
	b.	Scope of Property of the Estate	33
	c.	Postpetition Property as Property of the Estate	36
	d.	Individual Debtor's Postpetition Earnings in Chapter 7 or 11 Cases	37
	e.	Other Statutory Exclusions From Property of the Estate	40
	f.	Effect of Transfer Restrictions on Property of the Estate	41

B. DISMISSAL

Sec.			Page
2–9	Who Can Cause Dismissal		43
2–10	Abstention, Section 305		43
2–11	Consequences of Dismissal		43
	a.	Past Actions	43
	b.	Future Actions	44
2–12	Grounds for Dismissal		45
2–13	Voluntary Dismissal *		45
	a.	Chapter 7 and Chapter 11 *	45
	b.	Chapters 12 and 13 *	45
2–14	Dismissal of Certain Consumer Chapter 7 Cases for "Substantial Abuse"		45
2–15	Creditors' Motions to Dismiss a Chapter 11 Petition for Lack of Good Faith		46
	a.	Filing by a Financially Strong Business Such as Johns-Manville	48
	b.	Filing by the Single Asset Debtor on the Eve of Foreclosure	48
	c.	Filing After a "Last Minute" Transfer of Assets to a Newly Created Entity	49
2–16	Good Faith Problems in Serial Filings		50
	a.	Successive Chapter 13 Filings	50
	b.	Chapter 19 or 20 (or More) Cases	51

* For the full text of this section, see Epstein, Nickles and White, Bankruptcy, Practitioner Treatise Series, Vol. 1.

Sec.			Page
2–16	Good Faith Problems in Serial Filings—Continued		
	c.	Filing a New Chapter 11 Petition After Default Under a Confirmed Chapter 11 Plan	52
	d.	Simultaneous Petitions	55

C. CONVERSION

2–17	Consequences of Conversion *		55
	a.	Property of the Estate *	55
	b.	Exempt Property *	55
	c.	Avoidance of Postpetition/Preconversion Transfers	55
2–18	Debtor's Right to Convert *		55
2–19	Creditor's Right to Convert *		56

CHAPTER 3. AUTOMATIC STAY

3–1	Introduction and Overview		59

A. SCOPE OF THE STAY

3–2	When the Stay Arises		64
3–3	Whom the Stay Affects		65
3–4	What the Stay Generally Covers: Its Three Dimensional Scope		66
3–5	Actions Against the Debtor		67
3–6	Actions Against the Debtor—Actions and Proceedings		69
	a.	Common Coverage and Even Wider Scope	70
	b.	Purpose Requirement	70
	c.	Who Is Protected	71
	d.	Process/Procedure Affected	72
	e.	"Against the Debtor"	75
	f.	The Prepetition Limitation	76
3–7	Actions Against the Debtors—"Exception" for Collective Bargaining *		80
3–8	Actions Against the Debtor—Collection Efforts		80
3–9	Actions Against the Debtor—Special Treatment of Utility Service *		87
3–10	Actions Against the Debtor—Exceptionally Protecting Nondebtors by Extending Section 362 *		87
	a.	Purposive Application (Mainly, the Piccinin "Identity-of-Interest" "Rule") *	87
	b.	Incidental Protection of Nondebtors When Covered Property Is Involved *	87
	c.	"Codebtors" in Chapter 12 and 13 Cases (Sections 1201 and 1301) *	87
3–11	Actions Against the Debtor's Property		87
3–12	Actions Against the Debtor's Property—Exception for Certain Domestic Obligations (Section 362(b)(2)) *		91
3–13	Actions Against Estate Property		91

* For the full text of this section, see Epstein, Nickles and White, Bankruptcy, Practitioner Treatise Series, Vol. 1.

Sec.			Page
3–14	Actions Against Estate Property—Obtaining Possession and Exercising Control Over Estate Property, Section 362(a)(3)		92
	a.	Fundamentals	92
	b.	Causes of Action	96
	c.	Rights to Payment and Other Contract Rights	98
	d.	Letters of Credit	102
	e.	Leases	103
	f.	Rights From Government	106
3–15	Actions Against Estate Property—Setoff		106
3–16	Actions Against Estate Property—Effecting Liens Against Property of the Estate		109
3–17	Actions Against Estate Property—Excepting Purchase–Money Security Interests In Aircraft (Section 1110) *		112
	a.	Substantive Requirements *	112
	b.	Cure *	112
	c.	Expiration of the Stay *	112
3–18	Respecting Certain Grace Periods for Perfection (Section 362(b)(3))		112
	a.	Bankruptcy Preference Law	112
	b.	State Priority Law	114
3–19	Excepting Certain Actions by Government		117
3–20	Excepting Certain Actions by Government—Criminal Actions (Section 362(b)(1)) *		118
3–21	Excepting Certain Actions by Government—Regulatory Actions (Section 362(b)(4–5)) *		118
	a.	Legislative Design of the Exceptions	121
	b.	Meaning of "Governmental Unit" *	122
	c.	Action or Proceeding Enforcing Police or Regulatory Power Under (b)(4) *	122
		i. Enforcement *	122
		ii. Action or Proceeding *	122
		iii. Police or Regulatory Power *	122
	d.	Enforcement of a Judgment Under (b)(5) and the Internal Limit Excluding Money Judgments *	122
	e.	External Limits on the Exceptions *	122
		i. Unexcepted, Unaffected Parts of Section 362(a) *	122
		ii. Discretionary Injunctions Under Section 105(a) *	122
3–22	Supplemental Injunctions		123

B. DURATION OF THE STAY

3–23	How Long the Stay Continues *		127
	a.	Case Is Ended *	128
	b.	Discharge Is Granted or Denied *	128
	c.	Property Leaves the Estate *	128
	d.	Relief Is Granted *	128

* For the full text of this section, see Epstein, Nickles and White, Bankruptcy, Practitioner Treatise Series, Vol. 1.

Sec.		Page
3-24	Judicial Relief That Lifts the Stay—Overview	128
3-25	Judicial Relief That Lifts the Stay—Debtor Lacks Equity in Property That Is Not Needed for Reorganization (Section 362(d)(2))	130
	a. Does the Debtor Have an Equity in the Property?	131
	b. Is the Property Necessary to an Effective Reorganization?	133
3-26	Judicial Relief That Lifts the Stay—Cause (Section 362(d)(1))	138
3-27	Judicial Relief That Lifts the Stay—Cause (Section 362(d)(1))—Lack of Adequate Protection	140
	a. Identifying and Valuing the Secured Interest That Deserves Adequate Protection	141
	b. Defining the Risks (When Adequate Protection Is Needed)	143
	c. Determining and Providing Protection That Is Adequate	144
	d. Making Adjustments	148
3-28	Judicial Relief That Lifts the Stay—Cause (Section 362(d)(1))—True Leases *	149
3-29	Judicial Relief That Lifts the Stay—Cause (Section 362(d)(1))—Bad Faith Filing	149
3-30	Judicial Relief That Lifts the Stay—Cause (Section 362(d)(1))—More Appropriate Forum Elsewhere *	154
3-31	Some (Mostly) Procedural Concerns *	154
	a. Who Can Request Relief ("Party in Interest") *	154
	b. When and How Relief Is Requested and Decided *	154
	i. Relief by Judicial Default (Section 362(e)) *	155
	ii. Nature of the Hearing *	155
	iii. Burdens of Proof *	155
	iv. Ex Parte Relief (Section 362(f)) *	155
	c. Effect of Lifting the Stay *	155
	d. Appeal *	155

C. CONSEQUENCES OF VIOLATING THE STAY

Sec.		Page
3-32	Voidance	155
	a. General Rule	155
	b. Judicial Annulment	156
	c. Statutory Exceptions	158
	d. Competing Rule of "Voidable" Only	159
3-33	Damages (Section 362(h))	161
	a. Who Is the Plaintiff?	162
	b. Who Is the Defendant?	162
	c. What Is the Wrong?	163
	d. What Are the Damages?	164
	e. Overlapping Wrongs and Remedies	165

* For the full text of this section, see Epstein, Nickles and White, Bankruptcy, Practitioner Treatise Series, Vol. 1.

Sec.		Page
3-34	Damages (Section 362(h))—Sovereign Immunity	166
	a. The States	166
	b. The United States	168
	c. Waiving Immunity to Section 362(h) Damages by Section 106(a-b)	168
3-35	Damages (Section 362(h))—Contempt	170

CHAPTER 4. USE/SALE/LEASE OF ESTATE PROPERTY

Sec.		Page
4-1	Introduction: Sections 363 and 364	171
4-2	Introduction to Section 363—Use, Sale or Lease of Property	173
4-3	Ordinary Course of Business, Use, Sale or Lease, Section 363(c)(1)	173
4-4	Use, Sale or Lease Not in the Ordinary Course, Section 363(b)(1)	177
	a. Routine Sales	177
	b. Sale of All or Substantially All Assets Under Section 363(b)	179
4-5	Cash Collateral, Section 363(c)(2)	186
4-6	Cash Collateral, Section 363(c)(2)—Sanctions for Unauthorized Use of Cash Collateral	188
4-7	Sales Free of Others' Interests—Secured Parties, Section 363(f)	191
4-8	Sales Free of Others' Interests—Bidding in: Section 363(k)	196
4-9	Sales Free of Others' Interests—Co-owners, Section 363(h)	197
4-10	Application of Section 363(f) and (h) in Unconventional Cases *	200
4-11	Section 364: Introduction	200
4-12	Ordinary Course and Non-ordinary Course Unsecured Loans, Section 364(a) and (b)	202
4-13	Loans With Priority Over Other Administrative Expenses, With Security or With Senior Security, Section 364(c) and (d)	203
4-14	Loans With Priority Over Other Administrative Expenses, With Security or With Senior Security, Section 364(c) and (d)—Section 364(d)	206
4-15	Payment of and Granting Security for Prepetition Debt: Herein of Cross-Collateralization and *Texlon*	208
4-16	Notice and Hearing Under Sections 363 and 364	215
4-17	Appeals, Sections 363(m) and 364(e)	218

CHAPTER 5. LEASES AND EXECUTORY CONTRACTS

Sec.		Page
5-1	Introduction to Leases and Executory Contracts	224

A. SCOPE OF SECTION 365

5-2	What Is a Lease?	226
5-3	What Is an Unexpired Lease?	228
5-4	What Is an Executory Contract?	229
	a. Absence of a Statutory Definition	229
	b. "Countryman Definition": Performance Due on Both Sides	229
	c. Legislative History	230

* For the full text of this section, see Epstein, Nickles and White, Bankruptcy, Practitioner Treatise Series, Vol. 1.

Sec.			Page
5-4	What Is an Executory Contract?—Continued		
	d.	"Booth" Test: Consequences of Applying Section 365	231
	e.	Two or More Executory Contracts in a Single Document	232

B. CONSEQUENCES OF SECTION 365

Sec.			Page
5-5	Consequences of Assumption		234
	a.	Property of the Estate	234
	b.	Administrative Expense Priority	235
5-6	Consequences of Assignment		235
	a.	Comparison of Section 365 Assignment With Common Law Assignment	235
	b.	Comparison of Assigning a Lease With Subleasing	236
5-7	Consequences of Rejection		237
	a.	Rejection as a Breach	237
	b.	Rejection by Real Property Lessor	237
	c.	Rejection by Licensors of "Intellectual Property": Cases Commenced on or After November 3, 1988	238
	d.	Rejection by Licensors of Intellectual Property: Cases Commenced Before November 3, 1988	239
	e.	Rejection as an Avoiding Power	240
	f.	Rejection and Contract Provisions Such as Liquidated Damages Clauses	241
	g.	Rejection and Covenants Not to Compete	242

C. ASSUMPTION OR REJECTION

Sec.		Page
5-8	Role of the Court	243
5-9	Time for Rejection or Assumption	245
5-10	Time for Rejection or Assumption—Section 365(d)(4)	246
5-11	Time for Rejection or Assumption—Contract Provisions and Section 108(b)	250

D. EXECUTORY CONTRACTS AND UNEXPIRED LEASES THAT CANNOT BE ASSUMED

Sec.		Page
5-12	Contract and Lease Clauses	251
5-13	"Loans" or "Financial Accommodations"	253
5-14	"Loans" or "Financial Accommodations"—Consent to Assumption of Financial Accommodation Contracts	255
5-15	Nonassignability Under Applicable Law	256

E. CONTRACTS THAT CANNOT BE ASSIGNED

Sec.		Page
5-16	Statutory Restrictions on Assignments	259
5-17	Contractual Restrictions on Assignment	260

F. REQUIREMENTS FOR ASSUMPTION AND ASSIGNMENT

Sec.		Page
5-18	Overview of Requirements of Section 365(b)	261
5-19	Default Cure and Compensation	263

Sec.		Page
5-20	Adequate Assurance of Future Performance	263
	a. Adequate Assurance and Shopping Center Leases	263
	b. Adequate Assurance of Future Payment	264
	c. Adequate Assurance of Performance of Lease or Contract Provisions Not Requiring the Payment of Money	264
5-21	Adequate Assurance of Assignee Performance Requirements of Section 365(f)(2)	265

G. GAP PERIOD

5-22	Performance Obligations of the Nondebtor Party	266
5-23	Performance Obligations of the Debtor	268
	a. Nonresidential Real Property Leases	268
	b. Other Leases and Contracts	270
5-24	Right of Nondebtor Lessor to Adequate Protection *	271
5-25	Recoupment by Other Party During the Gap Period *	271

H. "SPECIAL" LEASES AND CONTRACTS

5-26	"Special" Leases and Contracts *	271

CHAPTER 6. AVOIDANCE POWERS

6-1	Introduction to Avoidance Powers	274
6-2	Who Can Avoid Transfers	275

A. PREFERENCE, SECTION 547

6-3	Introduction to Preferences	278

1. Elements of a Preference

6-4	Transfer of an Interest of the Debtor in Property	281
	a. The Critical Terms (Especially "Transfer")	281
	b. Most Common Transfers	284
6-5	Transfer of an Interest of the Debtor in Property—Increase in Value	284
6-6	Transfer of an Interest of the Debtor in Property—Transfers of Exempt Property	284
6-7	Transfer of an Interest of the Debtor in Property—Property of Third Party and Earmarked Funds	284
6-8	To or for the Benefit of a Creditor	287
6-9	To or for the Benefit of a Creditor—Preferences That Indirectly Benefit (a/k/a Indirect Preferences)	288
6-10	To or for the Benefit of a Creditor—Remedying an Indirect Preference (and the Levit Case)	290
6-11	Within the Preference Period	295
6-12	Within the Preference Period—General Rule: Time of Transfer Is Time of Perfection	299

* For the full text of this section, see Epstein, Nickles and White, Bankruptcy, Practitioner Treatise Series, Vol. 1.

Sec.		Page
6–13	Within the Preference Period—Exception: Perfection Within Ten Days	299
6–14	Within the Preference Period—Caveat: No Transfer Until Debtor Acquires Rights	299
6–15	Within the Preference Period—The Caveat Applied to Garnishment During Preference Period	299
6–16	Within the Preference Period—Payment by Check	299
6–17	Within the Preference Period—Insiders	301
6–18	When the Debtor Is Insolvent	306
6–19	For or on Account of an Antecedent Debt	308
6–20	Preferential Effect	310
6–21	Preferential Effect—Foreclosure Sales	314

2. Exceptions, Section 547(c)

6–22	Introduction to Exceptions	314
6–23	Contemporaneous New Value, Section 547(c)(1)	315
6–24	Contemporaneous New Value, Section 547(c)(1)—Scope of the Exception	316
6–25	Contemporaneous New Value, Section 547(c)(1)—New Value	317
6–26	Contemporaneous New Value, Section 547(c)(1)—Exchange	323
6–27	Contemporaneous New Value, Section 547(c)(1)—Contemporaneous in Fact	325
6–28	Contemporaneous New Value, Section 547(c)(1)—Contemporaneous by Design	328
6–29	Ordinary Payment of Ordinary Debts, Section 547(c)(2)	329
6–30	Ordinary Payment of Ordinary Debts, Section 547(c)(2)—Debt Incurred in the Ordinary Course	331
6–31	Ordinary Payment of Ordinary Debts, Section 547(c)(2)—Payment Made in the Ordinary Course and on Ordinary Business Terms	332
6–32	Ordinary Payment of Ordinary Debts, Section 547(c)(2)—Payments on Long-Term Debt	335
6–33	Enabling Security Interests, Section 547(c)(3)	337
6–34	Subsequent New Value, Section 547(c)(4)	341
6–35	Floating Liens on Inventory or Receivables, Section 547(c)(5)	345
6–36	Statutory Liens, Section 547(c)(6)	355
6–37	Small Transfers in Consumer Cases, Section 547(c)(7)	358

B. SETOFF, SECTION 553

6–38	Overview: The Meaning of Setoff and Its Significance in Bankruptcy, Section 553	359

1. Bankruptcy's Substantive Effect on Right of Setoff

6–39	General Rule of Section 553	362
6–40	Requirements of the General Rule	364
	a. Existence of Substantive Right	365
	b. Both Debts Prepetition	365
	c. Mutuality	365

2. Substantive Exceptions to the General Rule

Sec.		Page
6–41	Statutory	365
6–42	Equitable	365

3. Bankruptcy's Procedural Effect on Exercise of Section 553 Setoff

6–43	Automatic Stay	365
6–44	Waiver	365

4. Recoupment

6–45	Recoupment	365

C. FRAUDULENT TRANSFERS

6–46	Introduction to Fraudulent Transfers	365

1. Transfers Fraudulent Under Bankruptcy Law, Section 548

6–47	Introduction to Section 548	366
6–48	Actual Fraud	368
6–49	Constructive Fraud	371
6–50	Remedies and Defenses	380

2. Special Problems

6–51	Guaranties *	385
6–52	LBOs *	385
6–53	Foreclosure Sales *	385
6–54	Foreclosure Sales—Forced Sale as "Transfer" of Debtor's Interest in Property *	386
6–55	Foreclosure Sales—Timing of the Transfer *	386
6–56	Foreclosure Sales—Determining "Reasonably Equivalent Value" *	386
6–57	Transfers of Exempt Property *	386
6–58	Converting Nonexempt Property to Exempt Property *	386
6–59	Preferential Transfers *	386

3. Transfers Fraudulent Under State Law, Section 544(b)

6–60	Transfers Fraudulent Under State Law (Trustee as Successor to Actual Creditor, Section 554(b))	386

D. "STRONG–ARM" POWERS, SECTION 544(a)

6–61	Trustee as Hypothetical Lien Creditor or Purchaser ("Strong–Arm" Powers, Section 544(a))	390

E. STATUTORY LIENS, SECTION 545

6–62	Statutory Liens, Section 545	401

F. SELLERS' RIGHT OF RECLAMATION, SECTION 546(c)

6–63	Reclamation Under State Law *	406

* For the full text of this section, see Epstein, Nickles and White, Bankruptcy, Practitioner Treatise Series, Vol. 2.

Sec.		Page
6–64	Importance of Preserving State–Created Reclamation in Buyer's Bankruptcy—Role of Section 546(c) *	406
6–65	Effect of Section 546(c) *	406
6–66	State Law Requirements for Reclamation and Federal Requirements of Section 546(c) *	406
6–67	The Possession and Priority Requirement *	406

G. POSTPETITION TRANSFERS, SECTIONS 549, 542 AND 552

6–68	Introduction to Postpetition Transfers and Their Avoidance	406

1. Postpetition Transfers in General, Section 549

6–69	General Rule Regarding Avoidance of Postpetition Transfers	408
6–70	Exception: Authorized Transfers *	409
6–71	Exception: Involuntary Cases *	409
6–72	Exception: Transfers of Real Estate *	409
6–73	Time Limitation on Avoidance Under Section 549 *	409

2. Postpetition Transfers by Third Parties

6–74	Special Protection for Innocent Transferors, Section 542(c)	409

3. Postpetition Effect of Prepetition Security Agreements, Section 552

6–75	Introduction	411
6–76	General Rule, Section 552(a)	412
6–77	Exception, Section 552(b)	413
6–78	Exceptions to the Exception—The "Except" Clauses of Section 552(b)	417

H. CONSEQUENCES OF AVOIDANCE

6–79	Overview of Consequences	419

1. Nullification of the Transfer

6–80	The Nullifying Effect of Avoidance Per Se and the Difference From Recovery	421
6–81	Time Limitations on Avoidance, Section 546(a) *	424
6–82	Time Limitations on Avoidance, Section 546(a)—Applicability *	425
6–83	Time Limitations on Avoidance, Section 546(a)—Mechanics *	425
6–84	Time Limitations on Avoidance, Section 546(a)—Qualifications *	425
6–85	"Stockbroker" Defense (and Other Protections of Financial Markets) *	425

2. Preservation of the Avoided Transfer, Section 551

6–86	Preservation of the Avoided Transfer, Section 551	425

* For the full text of this section, see Epstein, Nickles and White, Bankruptcy, Practitioner Treatise Series, Vol. 2.

3. Recovery From Transferees, Section 550

Sec.		Page
6–87	Basic Remedial Rule: Recovery of the Property or Its Value	427
6–88	Persons Liable	429
6–89	Improvement Lien for All Good Faith Transferees *	435
6–90	Time Limitations on Recovery *	435

I. PSEUDO AVOIDANCE POWERS

6–91	Subordinating Claims, Section 510	435
6–92	Consensual Subordination, Section 510(a)	435
6–93	Equitable Subordination, Section 510(c)	436
6–94	Asserting Debtor's Defenses, Section 558	445

CHAPTER 7. LIQUIDATION

7–1	Introduction	448
7–2	Procedural Overview	450

A. CLAIMS, EXPENSES, AND DISTRIBUTIONS IN CHAPTER 7

7–3	Introduction	454
7–4	Definition of Claim	457
7–5	When Does the Claim Arise?	457
7–6	When Does the Claim Arise?—Pension Obligations *	459
7–7	When Does the Claim Arise?—Condominium Fees *	459
7–8	Does a Right to an Equitable Remedy Constitute a "Claim"?	459
7–9	Hierarchy of Claims	461
7–10	Hierarchy of Claims—Secured Claims	461
7–11	Hierarchy of Claims—Administrative Expenses	463
7–12	Hierarchy of Claims—Other Priority Claims	465
7–13	Hierarchy of Claims—Superpriority Claims, Section 507(b)	466
7–14	Distribution Under Section 726	467
7–15	Distribution Under Section 726—Interpretive Difficulties With Section 726(a)	469
	a. What Is a Penalty?	469
	b. Tardy Claims	469

B. DISCHARGE

7–16	Discharge: Overview	472
7–17	Denial of Discharge: Introduction	473
7–18	Denial of Discharge: Introduction—Individuals, Section 727(a)(1)	475
7–19	Denial of Discharge: Introduction—Fraudulent Conveyances, Section 727(a)(2)	476
7–20	Denial of Discharge: Introduction—Financial Disclosure: Section 727(a)(3) *	480

* For the full text of this section, see Epstein, Nickles and White, Bankruptcy, Practitioner Treatise Series, Vol. 2.

Sec.		Page
7–21	Denial of Discharge: Introduction—"Bankruptcy Crimes," Section 727(a)(4) *	480
7–22	Denial of Discharge: Introduction—Delivery of Assets, Section 727(a)(5) *	480
7–23	Denial of Discharge: Introduction—Refusal to Testify or Obey Court Order, Section 727(a)(6)	480
7–24	Exceptions to Discharge, Section 523, Introduction	480
7–25	Exceptions to Discharge, Section 523, Introduction—Taxes, Section 523(a)(1)	488
7–26	Exceptions to Discharge, Section 523, Introduction—False Pretense, Fraud and False Financial Statements, Section 523(a)(2)	494
	a. Section 523(a)(2)(A): False Pretenses, False Representation and Actual Fraud	498
	b. Section 523(a)(2)(B): False Financial Statement Materiality, Reasonable Reliance and Intent	505
	c. Section 523(a)(2)(C)	509
	d. Fraud—Causal Connection	511
7–27	Exceptions to Discharge, Section 523, Introduction—Unscheduled Debts, Section 523(a)(3)	515
7–28	Exceptions to Discharge, Section 523, Introduction—Fraud, Defalcation and Embezzlement, Section 523(a)(4)	517
7–29	Exceptions to Discharge, Section 523, Introduction—Alimony, Maintenance and Support, Section 523(a)(5)	521
	a. Substantive Rule	523
	b. Drafting Note for Divorce Lawyers	528
7–30	Exceptions to Discharge, Section 523, Introduction—Willful and Malicious Injury, Section 523(a)(6)	529
	a. Overview	529
	b. Willful and Malicious	531
	c. Malicious	532
	d. Summary	536
7–31	Exceptions to Discharge, Section 523, Introduction—Fines and Penalties, Section 523(a)(7)	537
7–32	Exceptions to Discharge, Section 523, Introduction—Fines and Penalties, Section 523(a)(7)—Tax Penalties	540
7–33	Exceptions to Discharge, Section 523, Introduction—Student Loans, Section 523(a)(8)	542
	a. Overview	542
	b. Substantive Rules	544
	c. The Exceptions to Nondischargeability	545
	d. Summary	548
7–34	Exceptions to Discharge, Section 523, Introduction—Driving While Intoxicated, Section 523(a)(9)	548

* For the full text of this section, see Epstein, Nickles and White, Bankruptcy, Practitioner Treatise Series, Vol. 2.

C. REAFFIRMATION, SECTION 524(c)

Sec.		Page
7-35	Introduction and Overview of Reaffirmation	552
7-36	Procedure	556
7-37	Best Interest and Undue Hardship	559
7-38	Timing and Omission of the Admonition Hearing	560
7-39	Reaffirmation, Redemption, Negotiation and the Secured Creditor	561

D. PROTECTION AGAINST DISCRIMINATORY TREATMENT, SECTION 525

7-40	Introduction to Protection Against Discrimination	564
7-41	Protection Against Discrimination by Governmental Units, Section 525(a)	567
	a. Governmental Unit	568
	b. "Solely"	568
	c. Acts Prohibited	572
	d. Remedies	573
7-42	Protection Against Discrimination by Private Employees, Section 525(b)	573

E. DISMISSAL

7-43	Section 707(a)	575
7-44	Section 707(b)	576
7-45	Section 707(b)—Substantive Requirements	578
	a. "Primarily"	578
	b. "Consumer" Debts	579
	c. Substantial Abuse	581
7-46	Section 707(b)—Retrospective	583

F. REDEMPTION, SECTION 722

7-47	Introduction and Overview of Redemption	584
7-48	Substantive Requirements	586
7-49	Valuation	588

CHAPTER 8. EXEMPT PROPERTY

8-1	Introduction: Meaning and Importance of Exemptions Under Nonbankruptcy Law and in Bankruptcy	593
8-2	Persons Entitled to Exemptions in Bankruptcy	598

A. PROPERTY THAT IS EXEMPT IN BANKRUPTCY

8-3	Source of Law for Exemptions in Bankruptcy	598

1. Exemptions of Nonbankruptcy Law

8-4	Introduction	602
8-5	State Exemptions	602
8-6	State Exemptions—Personal Property Exemptions	603
8-7	State Exemptions—Exempt Real Property (Homestead)	604
8-8	State Exemptions—Applying Value Limitations on Exemptions (Centrality of the Debtor's Interest)	607

Sec.		Page
8–9	State Exemptions—How Far State Law Controls in Determining State Law Exemptions Under the Code	608
8–10	Property Held by the Entirety *	610
	a. Immune Under State Law *	610
	b. Exempt in Bankruptcy *	610
8–11	Federal Exemptions (Nonbankruptcy Law) *	610

2. Exemptions of Bankruptcy Law, Section 522(d)

Sec.		Page
8–12	Introduction	610
8–13	Debtor's Residence	613
8–14	Personal Property Exemptions	615
8–15	Personal Property Exemptions—Goods *	616
8–16	Personal Property Exemptions—Income: Generally *	616
8–17	Personal Property Exemptions—Income: Support *	616
8–18	Personal Property Exemptions—Income: Losses *	616
8–19	Personal Property Exemptions—Life Insurance *	616
8–20	"Wild Card" Exemption	616

3. Joint Cases, Section 522(m)

Sec.		Page
8–21	Joint Cases, Section 522(m) *	617

4. Claiming Exemptions in Property the Trustee Recovers, Section 522(g)

Sec.		Page
8–22	Claiming Exemptions in Property the Trustee Recovers, Section 522(g)	617

B. DEBTOR'S AVOIDANCE OF TRANSFERS OF EXEMPT PROPERTY

1. Asserting Trustee's Avoidance Powers, Section 522(h)

Sec.		Page
8–23	Asserting Trustee's Avoidance Powers, Section 522(h)	621

2. Debtor's Personal Powers of Avoidance, Section 522(f)

Sec.		Page
8–24	Introduction	624
8–25	Determining if the Lien Is Within the Scope of Section 522(f)	625
8–26	Determining if the Property Is Exempt	632
8–27	Determining if the Lien Affixed to Debtor's Interest	636
8–28	Determining Impairment	639
8–29	Procedural Concerns	644

3. Claiming Property as Exempt Upon Debtor's Avoidance (§ 522(i))

Sec.		Page
8–30	Claiming Property as Exempt Upon Debtor's Avoidance (522(i))	645

C. EXEMPTION "PLANNING" IN ANTICIPATION OF BANKRUPTCY

Sec.		Page
8–31	Planning by Creditors: Getting Debtors to Waive Exemptions and Related Rights	646

* For the full text of this section, see Epstein, Nickles and White, Bankruptcy, Practitioner Treatise Series, Vol. 2.

Sec.		Page
8-32	Planning by Debtors: Converting Their Nonexempt Property to Exempt Property	647

D. PSEUDO-EXEMPTIONS

8-33	Property Excluded From the Estate (Herein, ERISA—Qualified Plans and Other Pension Funds *	650
	a. Excluding a Pension Plan From the Estate *	650
	b. Exempting a Pension Plan From the Estate *	650
	c. Enforcing Against the Estate a Pension Plan's Restrictions on Access *	650

CHAPTER 9. INDIVIDUAL REORGANIZATION: CHAPTERS 13 AND 12

A. INDIVIDUALS WITH REGULAR INCOME

9-1	History	652
9-2	Chapter 13 and Chapter 7 Compared	654
	a. The Number of Chapter 13s	657
	b. Reasons for the Chapter 13 Increase	658
9-3	Eligibility	659
9-4	Chapter 13 Procedure	664
	a. The Opening Events: Petition, Statement, Notice, and Plan	664
	b. Filing Proof of Claims	664
	c. Significance of Filing Proof of Claim for Payment Under the Plan and for Discharge of the Debt	665
	d. Filing and Allowance of Postpetition Claims	667
	e. Secured Claims	668
	f. Meeting of the Creditors	668
	g. Confirmation Hearing: Form of Creditor Objections	670
	h. The Chapter 13 Trustee: Appointment, Duties, and Payment	671
	i. Payment to Trustee	672
	j. Codebtor Stay	675
9-5	The Plan: Priorities and Payment—Introduction	676
9-6	Priorities and Payment—Secured Creditors and Priority Claims	677
	a. Secured Creditors	677
	b. Priority Claims	678
9-7	General Creditor, Discrimination and the Floor	679
9-8	Determining the Amount of Payments to Be Made Under the Plan: Introduction	685
9-9	The Best Interest Test—In General	687
9-10	The Best Interest Test—Computing Present Value—The Best Interest Test Applied	688
9-11	Duration of the Plan and the Disposable Income Test	694
9-12	Duration of the Plan and the Disposable Income Test—Section 1322(c): The Duration of the Plan	695

* For the full text of this section, see Epstein, Nickles and White, Bankruptcy, Practitioner Treatise Series, Vol. 2.

Sec.		Page
9–13	Duration of the Plan and the Disposable Income Test—Projected Disposable Income	698
9–14	Good Faith	701
9–15	Modification of the Rights of Creditors—Introduction	707
9–16	Modification of the Rights of Creditors—Modification of Secured and Unsecured Claims and the Long Term Limitation	709
9–17	Modification of the Rights of Creditors—Deacceleration and Cure, Section 1322(b)(5)	711
9–18	Modification of the Rights of Creditors—Restrictions on the Modification of Home Mortgages	714
9–19	Feasibility, Section 1325(a)(6)	719
9–20	Confirmation and Discharge	721
9–21	Confirmation and Discharge—Hardship Discharge	726
9–22	Modification and Revocation of Confirmed Plan	727

B. CHAPTER 12—FAMILY FARMERS WITH REGULAR INCOME

9–23	History of Chapter 12 *	729
	a. Comparison of Chapters 11 and 12 *	729
	b. Comparison of Chapters 13 and 12 *	729
9–24	Eligibility for Chapter 12 *	729
	a. Farming Operation *	729
	b. Strategic Considerations *	729
	c. Retrospective *	729
9–25	Procedure and the Timing of Events in Chapter 12 *	730
9–26	Procedure and the Timing of Events in Chapter 12—Lessons for Chapter 11 *	730
9–27	Conversion and Dismissal From Chapter 12 *	730
	a. Conversion or Dismissal at Debtor's Request *	730
	b. Conversion or Dismissal at Creditor's Request *	730
	c. Retrospective *	730
9–28	Substantive Rules in Chapter 12 *	730
9–29	Substantive Rules in Chapter 12—Feasibility *	730
9–30	Chapters 19 and 20: The Filing of a Chapter 7 Shortly Followed by a Chapter 12 or 13 *	730

CHAPTER 10. BUSINESS REORGANIZATION: CHAPTER 11

10–1	History and Introduction	732
10–2	History and Introduction—Nature of the Chapter 11 Process	733
10–3	History and Introduction—Roadmap	735

A. OPERATING THE BUSINESS AFTER THE CHAPTER 11 FILING

10–4	Debtor in Possession Usually Operates	737
10–5	Limits on Conducting Business	738

* For the full text of this section, see Epstein, Nickles and White, Bankruptcy, Practitioner Treatise Series, Vol. 2.

Sec.		Page
10–6	Discretion in Operating Business	740
10–7	Effect on Corporate Governance	741

B. THE TRUSTEE, EXAMINERS, COMMITTEES

Sec.		Page
10–8	Grounds for Appointment of Trustee	745
10–9	Grounds for Appointment of Trustee—Powers of the Trustee	748
10–10	Examiners	748
10–11	Committees and Their Operation	750
10–12	Committees and Their Operation—Composition of the Committee	750
10–13	Committees and Their Operations—Powers and Duties of a Committee	753
10–14	Committees and Their Operations—Who Pays and How	755

C. THE PLAN OF REORGANIZATION

Sec.		Page
10–15	A Practical Overview	756
10–16	The Basic Contents of the Plan of Reorganization: Best Interest, Cramdown, and Absolute Priority	759
10–17	The Basic Contents of the Plan of Reorganization: Best Interest, Cramdown, and Absolute Priority—Acceptance Requirements	760
10–18	The Basic Contents of the Plan of Reorganization: Best Interest, Cramdown, and Absolute Priority—Best Interest Test	761
10–19	The Basic Contents of the Plan of Reorganization: Best Interest, Cramdown, and Absolute Priority—Requirements for Cramdown Under Section 1129(b)	762
10–20	The Basic Contents of the Plan of Reorganization: Best Interest, Cramdown, and Absolute Priority—Requirements for Cramdown Under Section 1129(b)—Fair and Equitable Treatment—Secured Claims	762
10–21	The Basic Contents of the Plan of Reorganization: Best Interest, Cramdown, and Absolute Priority—Requirements for Cramdown Under Section 1129(b)—The Absolute Priority Rule—Unsecured Claims	764
10–22	The Basic Contents of the Plan of Reorganization: Best Interest, Cramdown, and Absolute Priority—Requirements for Cramdown Under Section 1129(b)—Unfair Discrimination	767

D. CLAIMS

Sec.		Page
10–23	Impairment of Claims	769
10–24	Manipulation of Classes	771
10–25	Special Rules for Secured Claims in Chapter 11	774
10–26	Special Rules for Secured Claims in Chapter 11—Section 1111(b)(1): Right of Recourse	775
10–27	Special Rules for Secured Claims in Chapter 11—Section 1111(b)(2)	775

Sec.		Page
10–28	Special Rules for Secured Claims in Chapter 11—Exceptions to 1111(b)(2)	779

E. POST-CONFIRMATION ISSUES

10–29	Return of Property to the Debtor *	780
10–30	Discharge of the Debtor *	780
10–31	Binding Effect of the Plan of Reorganization *	780
10–32	Implementation, Adjustment, and Modification *	780
10–33	Revocation and Modification *	780

F. RETROSPECTIVE

10–34	Retrospective: The Unpractical View *	780

CHAPTER 11. SELECTED TOPICS IN CHAPTER 11 PROCEEDINGS

A. CLAIMS

11–1	Significance and Overview of Problems	782
11–2	What Is a Claim (Section 101(5))?	784
11–3	When Does a Claim Arise?	787
11–4	Filing Claims in Bankruptcy	791
11–5	Estimating Claims (Section 502(c))	794
11–6	Estimating Claims (Section 502(c))—Estimation for Voting Purposes	795
11–7	Estimating Claims (Section 502(c))—Estimation for Distribution Purposes	797

B. MEGA–CLAIMS

11–8	Bankruptcy and Mass Torts	799
11–9	Claims for Environmental Cleanup in Chapters 11 and 7	803
11–10	Claims for Environmental Cleanup in Chapters 11 and 7—Relative Priority Under the Code	805
11–11	Claims for Environmental Cleanup in Chapters 11 and 7—Cleanup Expenses as Secured Claims	809
11–12	Claims for Environmental Cleanup in Chapters 11 and 7—Retrospective: The Better Judicial and Legislative Answers	811

C. WAITING FOR THE DEBTOR'S PLAN: THE "EXCLUSIVITY PERIOD," SECTION 1121(d)

11–13	Introduction: Exclusivity and Delay	812
11–14	Procedure for Extending the Period	814
11–15	Cause for Extension	816

D. DISCLOSURE AND PLAN APPROVAL

11–16	Overview	819

* For the full text of this section, see Epstein, Nickles and White, Bankruptcy, Practitioner Treatise Series, Vol. 3.

Sec.		Page
11-17	Standards for Adequate Information	824
11-18	Solicitation of Rejection or Acceptance of Competing Plans	828
11-19	Voting Agreements	832
11-20	Voting in Multiple Plan Cases, Rule 3016	833
11-21	Pre-packaged Plans	834
11-22	Pre-packaged Plans—Prepetition Disclosure	835
11-23	Pre-packaged Plans—Prepetition Solicitation	836
11-24	Pre-packaged Plans—Why Use Prepackaged Plans	837
	a. Advantages of Prepackaged Plan Over Nonbankruptcy Workout	837
	Binds All Creditors	837
	Tax Benefits	837
	Original Issue Discount	837
	b. Advantages of Prepackaged Chapter 11 Over Ordinary Chapter 11	838
	c. Disadvantage of Prepackaged Chapter 11	838

E. ABSOLUTE PRIORITY AND NEW VALUE

Sec.		Page
11-25	Overview of "Absolute Priority" Rule	839
11-26	Origin and Development of the "New Value" Exception	840
11-27	The "New Value" Exception Under the Code	843
11-28	Applying the Exception	846
11-29	Applying the Exception—The Cases	849
	In re Greystone III Joint Venture	851
	In re Marston Enterprises, Inc.	852
	Potter Material Service, Inc.	853
	Jartran	853
11-30	Applying the Exception—Arguing Against the Exception *	854

F. BANKRUPTCIES INVOLVING PARTNERSHIPS

Sec.		Page
11-31	Introduction *	854
11-32	Liability of Partnerships and General Partners to the Creditors of Each *	855
11-33	Priority *	855
11-34	Staying Creditors *	855
11-35	Staying Creditors—Automatic Stay, Section 362 *	855
11-36	Staying Creditors—Injunctions, Section 105 *	855
11-37	Partner Bankruptcy Effects on the Enforcement of the Partnership Agreement *	855
11-38	Partner Bankruptcy Effects on the Enforcement of the Partnership Agreement—Assumption, Assignment and Rejection: Sections 365(c) and 365(e) *	855
11-39	Partner Bankruptcy Effects on the Enforcement of the Partnership Agreement—Partner's Settlement and Contribution *	855

* For the full text of this section, see Epstein, Nickles and White, Bankruptcy, Practitioner Treatise Series, Vol. 3.

G. SUBSTANTIVE CONSOLIDATION

Sec.		Page
11–40	Meaning and Reasons *	855
11–41	Cases and Rules *	855

CHAPTER 12. JURISDICTION AND PROCEDURE

A. JURISDICTION AND ALLOCATION OF JUDICIAL POWER

12–1	Introduction and Overview	856
12–2	Marathon and the Core Proceeding	860
12–3	Marathon and the Core Proceeding—Related Proceedings	865
12–4	Personal Injury Cases	867
12–5	Abstention	870

B. VENUE

12–6	Venue of Cases, Section 1408(1)	872
12–7	Venue of Cases, Section 1408(1)—Affiliates, Section 1408(2)	875
12–8	Venue of Proceeding, Section 1409	876
12–9	Change of Venue, Section 1412	878
12–10	Change of Venue, Section 1412—Proper Venue	878
12–11	Change of Venue, Section 1412—Improper Venue	880

C. APPEALS

12–12	Appeals	882

D. JURY TRIAL

12–13	The Right to Jury Trial	886
12–14	The Right to Jury Trial—Granfinanciera	889
12–15	The Right to Jury Trial—Jury Cases After Granfinanciera	895
12–16	Which Judge Presides	898

TABLE OF CASES	901
TABLE OF STATUTES	1001
INDEX	1055

*

---

* For the full text of this section, see Epstein, Nickles and White, Bankruptcy, Practitioner Treatise Series, Vol. 3.

BANKRUPTCY

*

Chapter 1

OVERVIEW OF BANKRUPTCY

Table of Sections

Sec.
1–1 Origins of American Bankruptcy Law.
1–2 What Is (Are) the Purpose(s) or Goal(s) of Bankruptcy Laws?
1–3 What Is Bankruptcy Law?
    a. Legislative History.
    b. State Law.
1–4 Who Is Involved in a Bankruptcy Case: A Vocabulary List.
1–5 What Is Bankruptcy?
1–6 What Happens in a Bankruptcy Case?
1–7 What Happens in a Chapter 7 Bankruptcy Case?
    a. Commencement.
    b. Collection.
    c. Liquidation.
    d. Distribution.
    e. Discharge.
1–8 Chapter 13 and How It Differs From Chapter 7.
1–9 Chapter 11 and How It Differs From Chapters 7 and 13.
    a. Comparison of 7 and 11.
    b. Comparison of 11 and 13.
1–10 Chapter 12 and How It Differs From the Other Chapters

---

§ 1–1 Origins of American Bankruptcy Law

Historians have traced the origins of bankruptcy law to Roman law in 118 B.C.[1] By the 18th century, bankruptcy laws were well-established in England. When our Constitution was framed in 1787, Article I, section 8, clause 4 gave Congress the right to establish "uniform laws of bankruptcy." The first American bankruptcy law, adopted in 1800, copied the English bankruptcy laws of that time: it was limited to creditor-initiated petitions against merchants. Through the 19th century, other bankruptcy acts were adopted by Congress and repealed.[2]

---

§ 1–1

1. See Countryman, A History of American Bankruptcy Law, 81 Com. L.J. 226 (1976); see generally F. Noel, A History of the Bankruptcy Law (1919); C. Warren, Bankruptcy in United States History ch. 1 (1935); McCord, The Origins of Voluntary Bankruptcy, 5 Bankr. Dev. J. 361 (1988); Riesenfeld, The Evolution of Modern Bankruptcy Law, 31 Minn.L.Rev. 401 (1947); Tabb, The Historical Evolution of the Bankruptcy Discharge, 65 Am. Bankr. L.J. 325 (1991).

2. The Bankruptcy Act of 1898 remained in effect until 1979. More precisely, the Bankruptcy Reform Act of 1978 (hereafter referred to as the Bankruptcy Code) governs cases filed since October 1, 1979. The Bankruptcy Act of 1898 governed cases filed prior to October 1, 1979. Accordingly, the Bankruptcy Act of 1898 would apply in 1983 litiga-

According to Professor Max Radin, the common characteristic of these various English and American bankruptcy statutes is that

> whatever else was present or absent, there was always some method by which all the creditors were compelled to accept some arrangement or some disposition of their claims against the bankrupt's property, whether they all agreed to it or not. Everything else is clearly incidental. The bankrupt might be stripped of all his property and thrown into prison. He might be allowed certain exemptions. He might be relieved of his debts or have them scaled down or postponed. All these are stages of increasing humanity toward an unsuccessful member of the commercial community. He might even be helped to reconstruct and carry on his business, and this, with a view to maintaining an economic unit that involved a great many persons who are not properly creditors. But whatever happens to the debtor, in every case the creditors have been assembled in some formal way, their claims examined and classified, and assigned for satisfaction in definite proportions to an existing or prospective fund.[3]

§ 1–2 What Is (Are) the Purpose(s) or Goal(s) of Bankruptcy Laws?

The provisions of the bankruptcy laws of the United States reflect a variety of separate and discrete policies. For example, courts and commentators agree that section 547 of the Bankruptcy Code, which empowers a bankruptcy trustee to recover certain prebankruptcy transfers from creditors, is based on a bankruptcy policy of equality. It is helpful to identify and understand the policy basis for a Bankruptcy Code provision in interpreting and applying that provision to a particular bankruptcy problem.

Many bankruptcy problems involve either more than one Bankruptcy Code provision or no Bankruptcy Code provision at all. In dealing with such problems, it is helpful to identify and understand the more general purposes or goals of bankruptcy law.

As Professor Radin indicates, a purpose of all bankruptcy laws is to provide a collective forum for sorting out the rights of the various claimants against the assets of a debtor where there are not enough assets to go around. Professor Warren has much more recently written:

> In bankruptcy, with an inadequate pie to divide and the looming discharge of unpaid debts, the disputes center on who is entitled to shares of the debtor's assets and how these shares are to be divided. Distribution among creditors is not incidental to other concerns; it is the center of the bankruptcy scheme.[1]

Both Radin and Warren suggest that at its core, bankruptcy law historically was, and presently is, a debt collection system. Bankruptcy is not, however, the only debt collection system. State law and, to a lesser extent, federal laws other than the bankruptcy law provide for collection of debts.

---

tion arising in a bankruptcy case filed in September, 1979.

3. Radin, The Nature of Bankruptcy, 89 U.Pa.L.Rev. 1, 3–4 (1940).

§ 1–2

1. Warren, Bankruptcy Policy, 54 U.Chi. L.Rev. 775, 785 (1987).

Both Radin and Warren suggest differences between the bankruptcy and state and federal nonbankruptcy debt collection laws: (1) State and federal nonbankruptcy debt collection laws provide a means for collection of a single debt, but bankruptcy is a collective debt collection device; (2) bankruptcy provides for some sort of financial fresh start for certain debtors.

Consider the possible, practical significance of bankruptcy's role as a collective creditor collection system. A collective creditor collection system should consider whether individual creditors in pursuing their individual remedies decrease the aggregate value of assets available to creditors generally. Assume that C has a lien on D's equipment and that C could sell that equipment to a third party for $200,000, leaving other assets that could be sold for $300,000. What if selling all of D's assets in a single transaction would produce more than $500,000? What if D's continued operations can produce more than $500,000 to pay its creditors?

Under such facts, bankruptcy law perhaps should help D stay in business. What if it is unclear that D's continued operations will result in creditors' being paid more than $500,000? Or it is highly unlikely that continuing the operations of D will yield as much for D's creditors as liquidating D's assets now? Should bankruptcy's goal still be to keep D in operation? Should the bankruptcy court consider the interests and needs of D's employees? Of the community where D is located? To what extent can and should a bankruptcy court put a specific creditor at risk by deferring its collection in order to increase possible collections by creditors generally later in the case. To what extent can and should a bankruptcy court put creditors generally at risk in order to continue the debtor's business operations?

There are no "right" or "wrong" answers to these questions. There are no right or wrong answers to the question "What is the purpose or goal of bankruptcy law"?[2] While a bankruptcy judge is never called on to answer expressly "What is the purpose or goal of bankruptcy law," the bankruptcy judge's view with respect to this general question obviously affects her answers to the specific disputes that she is called on to resolve.

§ 1-3 What Is Bankruptcy Law?

Bankruptcy law is federal law.[1] It is primarily statutory law. It is Title

---

2. But cf. T. Jackson, The Logic and Limits of Bankruptcy Law (1989); Bowers, Groping and Coping in the Shadow of Murphy's Law: Bankruptcy Theory and the Elementary Economics of Failure, 68 Mich.L.Rev. 2098 (1990); Eisenberg, Bankruptcy Law in Perspective, 28 UCLA L. Rev. 953 (1981); Korobkin, Rehabilitating Values: A Jurisprudence of Bankruptcy, 91 Colum.L.Rev. 718 (1991); LoPucki, A General Theory of the Dynamics of the State Remedies/Bankruptcy System, 1982 Wis. L.Rev. 311; Shanker, The Abuse and Use of Federal Bankruptcy Power, 26 Case Western L. Rev. 3 (1976), for various "right" answers.

§ 1-3

1. States may regulate the debtor-creditor relationship, but this regulation may not be a bankruptcy law. In determining whether a state statute is invalid as a bankruptcy law, the courts have seemed to place primary importance on the presence or absence of discharge provisions. See, e.g., International Shoe Co. v. Pinkus, 278 U.S. 261, 49 S.Ct. 108, 73 L.Ed. 318 (1929); Carlson's for Music., Inc. v. Gould, 176 Colo. 172, 489 P.2d 1038 (1971), appeal after remand, 524 P.2d 651 (Colo.App. 1974); but cf. Johnson v. Star, 287 U.S. 527, 53 S.Ct. 265, 77 L.Ed. 473 (1933).

The late Professor Glenn criticized this focus on discharge:

[T]he discharge of the debtor is not an inherent trait of bankruptcy laws; on the contrary it is an innovation—of considerable age, no doubt, but still an innovation,— * * * The real test of a bankruptcy law * * * should relate to the distinction be-

11 of the United States Code.² A lawyer or law student encounters two different federal bankruptcy statutes:

Bankruptcy Act of 1898 (commonly referred to as the "Act"). Bankruptcy cases filed prior to October 1, 1979, were governed by the Act. A significant number of cases reported in the 1980's still involved the Act. A significant number of cases decided in the 1990's still cite to and rely on Act cases.

Bankruptcy Reform Act of 1978 (commonly referred to as the "Bankruptcy Code"). Bankruptcy cases filed since October 1, 1979, are governed by the Bankruptcy Reform Act of 1978. Many of the Code's sections are derived from the Act. The Bankruptcy Code was amended significantly in 1984, 1986, 1988 and 1990.

The Bankruptcy Code divides the substantive law of bankruptcy into the following chapters:

> Chapter 1. General Provisions, Definitions and Rules of Construction
>
> Chapter 3. Case Administration
>
> Chapter 5. Creditors, the Debtor, and the Estate
>
> Chapter 7. Liquidation
>
> Chapter 9. Adjustment of the Debts of a Municipality
>
> Chapter 11. Reorganization
>
> Chapter 12. Adjustment of Debts of a Family Farmer with Regular Annual Income
>
> Chapter 13. Adjustment of the Debts of an Individual With Regular Income

The provisions in Chapters 1, 3, and 5 apply in every bankruptcy case, unless otherwise specified.³

Bankruptcy law is also the Bankruptcy Rules.⁴ Pursuant to the authority of 28 U.S.C.A. section 2075, the United States Supreme Court promulgated Bankruptcy Rules. These rules, not the Federal Rules of Civil Procedure, "govern procedure in United States Bankruptcy Courts." ⁵ The Bankruptcy Rules are divided into ten parts. Each part governs a different stage of the bankruptcy process. In theory, these rules deal only with the process, only with procedural and not substantive matters.⁶

---

tween proceedings by way of agreement and proceedings wholly in invitum through the direct aid of the courts. The general assignment, no matter how minutely regulated by state it may be, still retains its original character of a trust created by the debtor's own conveyance. The assignee is the debtor's selection, not the choice of the court, nor yet of the creditors.

G. Glenn, Liquidation § 125 at 210–12 (1935); see also D. Baird and T. Jackson, Cases, Materials, and Problems in Bankruptcy 1013 (1985).

2. In this book, we often cite or refer to provisions in the Bankruptcy Code by simply stating "section" and then the number.

3. 11 U.S.C.A. § 103.

4. In 1991, Rule 1001 was amended to change the name of the Bankruptcy Rules to "Federal Rules of Bankruptcy Procedure."

5. Fed. R. Bankr. P. 1001. Bankruptcy Rules hereafter are cited as "Bankr. R."

6. From 1973–1976, the Supreme Court promulgated Rules of Bankruptcy Procedure pursuant to 28 U.S.C.A. section 2075, as enacted by Congress in 1964. These rules rendered

a. Legislative History

Courts and commentators have looked to the legislative history of the Bankruptcy Code for help in ascertaining the meaning of Code provisions and for help in determining the significance of Code omissions. The legislative history of the Bankruptcy Code is voluminous.[7] It begins in 1968 with hearings conducted by the Subcommittee on Bankruptcy of the Senate Judiciary Committee and ends with the Code enactment in 1978.[8]

The Supreme Court's decision in *United States v. Ron Pair Enterprises, Inc.*[9] has reduced significantly bankruptcy courts' use of legislative history in interpreting the provisions of the Bankruptcy Code. The Court there held that section 506(b) changed pre-Code case law so that a nonconsensual lien creditor is entitled to postpetition interest on its claim. Justice Blackmun based this holding on "the plain meaning" of section 506(b). Justice Blackmun's majority opinion[10] contained a number of statements about construing the Bankruptcy Code that are now regularly quoted by bankruptcy courts in rejecting arguments based on legislative history and pre-Code case law.[11]

b. State Law

Bankruptcy law also includes state law. While principles of federal supremacy and the inability of states to impair the obligations of contracts preclude state legislatures from enacting bankruptcy laws, the Bankruptcy

---

a part of the Bankruptcy Act of 1898 obsolete because according to the last sentence of 28 U.S.C.A. section 2075, "All laws in conflict with such rules shall be of no further force or effect after such rules have taken effect." In enacting the Bankruptcy Reform Act of 1978, Congress amended 28 U.S.C.A. section 2075 by omitting this last sentence. See § 405(d) of Title IV of Pub. L. No. 95–598, 92 Stat. 2685. As the Advisory Committee Note to Rule 1001 states, "The effect of the amendment is to require that procedural rules promulgated pursuant to 28 U.S.C. § 2075 to be consistent with the bankruptcy statute[s]."

7. See Practitioner Treatise, Vol. 1.

8. Courts have even looked to the post-enactment statements by members of a subsequent Congress regarding the meaning of an earlier enacted statute. See Bundles v. Baker, 61 B.R. 929, 934–35 (Bankr. S.D. Ind.1986), aff'd, 78 B.R. 203 (S.D.Ind.1987) (quoting 130 Cong. Rec. 512771–72 (Oct. 5, 1985) on intent of Congress in enacting 1984 amendments).

9. 489 U.S. 235, 109 S.Ct. 1026, 103 L.Ed.2d 290 (1989), on remand, 872 F.2d 778 (6th Cir. 1989); see generally Falk, Ron Pair Enterprises: Supreme Court Finds Oversecured Creditors Entitled to Postpetition Interest, 1 Faulkner & Gray's Bankruptcy Law Review 9 (Summer 1989).

10. This meaning was "plain" only to some. Ron Pair is a 5–4 decision.

11. In the Court's words:

Initially, it is worth recalling that Congress worked on the formulation of the Code for nearly a decade. It was intended to modernize the bankruptcy laws * * *. In such a substantial overhaul of the system, it is not appropriate or realistic to expect Congress to have explained with particularity each step it took. Rather, as long as the statutory scheme is coherent and consistent, there generally is no need for a court to inquire beyond the plain language of the statute.

The task of resolving the dispute over the meaning of § 506(b) begins where all such inquiries must begin: with the language of the statute itself * * *. In this case it is also where the inquiry should end, for where, as here, the statute's language is plain, "the sole function of the courts is to enforce it according to its terms." Caminetti v. United States, 242 U.S. 470, 485, 37 S.Ct. 192, 194, 61 L.Ed. 442 (1917). The language before us expresses Congress' intent—that postpetition interest be available—with sufficient precision so that reference to legislative history and to pre-Code practice is hardly necessary.

489 U.S. at 241–42, 109 S.Ct. at 1030, 103 L.Ed.2d at 297–98.

Code often expressly incorporates state law.[12] Additionally, in applying the Bankruptcy Code, reference is commonly made to state common-law concepts.

There are a few basic differences between bankruptcy law and state debtor-creditor law. State law puts a premium on prompt action by creditors: the first creditor to attach the debtor's property, the first creditor to execute on the property, etc. is the one most likely to be paid. Bankruptcy law, on the other hand, emphasizes equality of treatment, rather than a race of diligence. After the commencement of a bankruptcy case, a creditor generally cannot improve its position vis-a-vis other creditors by obtaining a lien on the assets of the debtor.[13] Similarly, a creditor's ability to improve its position before bankruptcy is limited considerably by bankruptcy law.[14]

Second, the prospects for debtor relief are much greater in bankruptcy. The concept of "discharge" is unique to bankruptcy. A discharge relieves the debtor from any further liability on her debts. While no debtor is guaranteed a bankruptcy discharge, most debtors who file for bankruptcy do receive a discharge. As the Supreme Court pointed out in *Local Loan Co. v. Hunt*,[15] "[O]ne of the primary purposes of the bankruptcy act is to 'relieve the honest debtor from the weight of oppressive indebtedness and permit him to start afresh * * *.'"[16]

Third, the vocabulary of bankruptcy law is different from the vocabulary in state law. Both ordinary terms such as "debtor" and "insolvent" and more technical terms such as "inventory" and "notice and hearing" are given special and unique meanings by the Bankruptcy Code. As you work with the provisions of the Bankruptcy Code, it is very important that you always check for definitions of the statutory terms. Section 101 of the Code is the primary, but not exclusive, source of such definitions.

§ 1–1 Who Is Involved in a Bankruptcy Case: A Vocabulary List

1. Nobody is a *bankrupt*. There is no such person under the Bankruptcy Code.

2. The *debtor* is the person who files a voluntary petition or person against whom an involuntary petition is filed. In other words, the debtor is the "bankrupt."

3. A *holder of a claim* is a creditor. If D owes C $300,000 and D files a bankruptcy petition, D will be a debtor and C will be the holder of a claim.

4. A *holder of a secured claim* is a creditor with a lien on property of the debtor or a right of setoff against property of the debtor. The amount of a secured claim is limited by both the debt and the value of the collateral. If D owed C $300,000 and the debt is secured by Blackacre, the amount of C's secured claim will depend on the value of Blackacre. The Code leaves unanswered the question of how the collateral is to be valued. If Blackacre is valued at $200,000, then C's secured claim will only be $200,000. Under

---

12. See, e.g., 11 U.S.C.A. §§ 522, 544.
13. See id. § 362.
14. See id. § 547.
15. 292 U.S. 234, 54 S.Ct. 695, 78 L.Ed. 1230 (1934).
16. Id. at 244, 54 S.Ct. at 699, 78 L.Ed. at 1235.

these facts, C will also have an unsecured claim for $100,000. A single credit transaction can thus be the basis for two claims: a secured claim and an unsecured claim.

5. A *holder of an unsecured claim* is a creditor that does not have a lien or right of setoff against the debtor's property or a creditor that has a lien on or right of setoff against property of the debtor that has a value less than the amount of the debt.

6. The *bankruptcy judge* is a judicial officer of the district court. [Prior to the Bankruptcy Rules of 1973, they were known as "referees."]

7. The *trustee* is representative of the creditors. She is generally a private citizen, not an employee of the federal government. There will be a trustee in every Chapter 7, 12, and 13 case and some Chapter 11 cases.[1] Her powers and duties vary from chapter to chapter. The trustee is generally appointed by the United States trustee. Creditors can elect a trustee to replace an appointed trustee.[2]

8. A *United States trustee*[3] is a federal government official that performs appointing and other administrative tasks[4] that a bankruptcy judge would otherwise have to perform. In Chapter 7 cases, the United States trustee appoints an interim trustee for each case. When no trustee from the private sector is willing to so serve, the United States trustee, i.e., a member of the U.S. trustee staff, is permitted to act as trustee in that Chapter 7 case. The United States trustee also appoints a private trustee in a Chapter 11 case, if the court so orders. Neither the United States trustee nor a staff member may serve as trustee in a Chapter 11 case.

9. A *creditors' committee* is composed of representatives of creditors in Chapter 11 cases.[5]

10. The *debtor in possession,* also known as the *DIP,* is the debtor in a Chapter 11 or Chapter 12 case. To illustrate, in a Chapter 11 case either the debtor will remain in control of its business and assets as debtor in possession or a trustee will be appointed to take control of the property.[6]

§ 1–4

1. See generally Given, When and Why Courts Appoint a Trustee in Bankruptcy, 34 Prac. Law 29 (Sept. 1988).

2. Trustees are rarely elected in Chapter 7 cases primarily because of the substantial creditor effort involved. Creditors holding at least 20% of the outstanding shares must call for the election. 11 U.S.C.A. § 702(c).

3. The United States is divided into 21 regions for purposes of the United States trustee program. The Attorney General appoints a United States trustee for each region for a five-year term.

4. The United States trustee is not a judicial officer. Accordingly, the United States trustee does not resolve disputes as to the propriety of its actions. Rule 2020 provides a procedure for judicial review of the United States trustee's actions or inaction.

5. See generally Forman, The Role of Creditor Committee in Reorganizations Under Chapter 11, 11 ALI–ABA Course Materials Journal 47 (1986); Cuevas, Due Process and Adequate Representation in a Chapter 11 Case: The Appointment and Removal of Members of a Creditors' Committee in a Corporate Reorganization, 24 New Eng. L. Rev. 333 (1989).

6. The Bankruptcy Code equates the "debtor in possession" with both the "debtor" and the trustee. Section 1101(1) provides that " 'debtor in possession' means debtor except when a person that has qualified under section 322 of this title is serving as trustee in the case." Section 1107 provides that a debtor in possession shall have the rights, powers, functions, and duties of a trustee. Sections 1103(c), 1106(b), 1110, 1112(a) and 1168 are the only other Chapter 11 provisions that use the term "debtor in possession." Elsewhere, Chapter 11 uses the term "debtor."

It can perhaps be argued from section 1101(1) and section 1107 that any Code section

11. An *examiner* is appointed in some Chapter 11 cases to investigate and perform such other duties as the court might order.[7] In theory the role of an examiner is different from the role of a trustee in a Chapter 11 case: the trustee runs the debtor's business; the trustee runs the debtor's Chapter 11 case. In practice, the lines between the roles of an examiner and the roles of a trustee are being blurred. An examiner can not be appointed in a case in which a trustee has already been appointed. The court can, however, appoint a trustee in a case in which an examiner has been appointed. Examiners are appointed in relatively few cases. The grounds for appointment of an examiner are (i) appointment is "in the interests of creditors, any equity security holders and other interests of the estate" or (ii) nontrade, nontax unsecured debts exceed $5,000,000.[8]

§ 1–5 What Is Bankruptcy?

There are two general forms of bankruptcy: (1) liquidation and (2) rehabilitation.

Chapter 7 of the Code is entitled "Liquidation." The terms "straight bankruptcy" or "bankruptcy" often are used to describe liquidation cases under the bankruptcy laws because the vast majority of bankruptcy cases are liquidation cases. In a typical Chapter 7 liquidation case, the trustee collects the nonexempt property of the debtor, converts that property to cash, and distributes the cash to the creditors.[1] The debtor gives up all of the nonexempt property she owns at the time of the filing of the bankruptcy petition and hopes to obtain a discharge.

Chapters 11, 12, and 13 of the Bankruptcy Code contemplate debtor rehabilitation. In a rehabilitation case, creditors look to future earnings of the debtor, not to the property of the debtor at the time of the initiation of the bankruptcy proceeding, to satisfy their claims. The debtor generally

that uses both the term "debtor" and the term "trustee" means "debtor" and "debtor in possession." For example, both the "debtor" and the "trustee" are a "party in interest" under section 1109(b). In light of section 1107, does that mean that both the "debtor" and the "debtor in possession" are a "party in interest"?

The obvious and more important question is whether the "debtor" and the "debtor in possession" are separate legal entities. Most of the cases that have discussed this issue involve the effect of a bankruptcy filing on an employer's obligations under a collective bargaining contract. In National Labor Relations Board v. Bildisco and Bildisco, 465 U.S. 513, 104 S.Ct. 1188, 79 L.Ed.2d 482 (1984), the Supreme Court rejected the Third Circuit's holding that a debtor in possession was a separate entity, stating: "For our purposes, it is sensible to view the debtor in possession as the same 'entity' which existed before the bankruptcy petition, but empowered by the Bankruptcy Code to deal with its contracts and property in a manner it could not have employed absent the bankruptcy filing." Id. at 528, 104 S.Ct. at 1197, 79 L.Ed.2d at 497. Similar statements can be found in cases such as In re Triangle Chemicals, Inc., 697 F.2d 1280, 1290 (5th Cir.1983) and In re Chapel Gate Apts., Ltd., 64 B.R. 569, 576 (Bankr. N.D.Tex.1986), and also in this book.

7. See generally Kaplan, The Role of the Examiner: Some Observations, 4 Bankr. Dev. J. 439 (1987); Snider, The Examiner in the Reorganization Process: A Need to Modify, 45 Bus. Law. 35 (1989).

8. 11 U.S.C.A. § 1104.

§ 1–5

1. In a Chapter 7 case, the court may authorize the trustee to operate a business until that business can be sold. 11 U.S.C.A. § 721. Assume, for example, that D Ski Resort, Inc., files a Chapter 7 petition. The trustee may request authorization to operate D Ski Resort, Inc. because she can sell an operating ski resort for significantly more than could be realized by selling the various assets of D Ski Resort, Inc. separately.

retains its assets [2] and makes payments to creditors, usually from postpetition earnings, pursuant to a court-approved plan.

Chapter 9 (Adjustment of Debts of a Municipality), Subchapters III and IV of Chapter 7 (Stockbroker and Commodity Broker Liquidation), and Subchapter 14 of Chapter 11 (Railroad Reorganization) are beyond the scope of this book.

§ 1–6 What Happens in a Bankruptcy Case?

The answer to the question, "what happens in a bankruptcy case?" is "it depends." It depends in part on the nature of the debtor (business or non-business), and it depends in part on the nature of the form of bankruptcy relief (Chapter 7, Chapter 11, Chapter 12 or Chapter 13). Typically, 80 or 90 percent of the debtors involved in bankruptcy cases are non-business debtors. Typically, 70 to 80 percent of the bankruptcy filings are under Chapter 7. Typically a Chapter 11 case or a Chapter 12 case generates more legal issues and involves more lawyers than a Chapter 7 case or a Chapter 13 case.

§ 1–7 What Happens in a Chapter 7 Bankruptcy Case?

A Chapter 7 case has five stages:

(1) getting the debtor into bankruptcy court;

(2) collecting the debtor's property;

(3) selling this property;

(4) distributing the proceeds of the sale to creditors, and

(5) determining whether the debtor is discharged from further liability to these creditors.

a. Commencement

A Chapter 7 case is commenced with the filing of a petition with the Bankruptcy Court.[1] The petition shall conform substantially to the petitions set out in the Official Forms.[2]

Generally, the debtor files the bankruptcy petition. While creditors have a limited statutory right to initiate bankruptcy under Chapter 7 against a debtor, very few Chapter 7 petitions are filed by creditors.[3] Debtor-initiated proceedings are often referred to as "voluntary;" creditor-initiated proceedings are often labelled "involuntary."

---

2. In a Chapter 11 case, the debtor or trustee can sell assets to finance operations pending confirmation of a plan or under the plan to fund payments under the plan. See 11 U.S.C.A. §§ 363, 1123(b)(4); see generally Hurley, Chapter 11 Alternative: Section 363 Sales of All of the Debtor's Assets Outside a Plan of Reorganization, 58 Am. Bankr. L.J. 233 (1984); Lander, Key Issues Regarding Liquidating Plans in Small and Medium Size Chapter 11 Cases, Norton Bankruptcy Law Adviser at 8 (November 1989).

§ 1–7

1. 11 U.S.C.A. §§ 301, 303(b).
2. Bankr. R. 9009.

3. The number of Chapter 7 filings by creditors probably does not accurately represent the practical significance of the involuntary bankruptcy provisions. It does not reflect the number of debtors who enter into workout agreements or file voluntary petitions because of the possibility of creditors' filing an involuntary petition.

b. Collection

Section 704 charges the bankruptcy trustee with the duty of collecting the property of the estate in a Chapter 7 bankruptcy case. Who is the bankruptcy trustee and what is property of the estate?

Recall that the bankruptcy trustee is different from the United States trustee. The bankruptcy trustee is not a government employee; rather she is a private citizen who will be paid for her work in the Chapter 7 case in accordance with a statutory formula that looks to the moneys disbursed to creditors in the case.[4] A trustee is typically appointed by the United States trustee. Under section 702, creditors can replace this appointed trustee with a trustee of their choice.

Whether appointed by the United States trustee or elected by the creditors, the bankruptcy trustee is not a neutral observer. She is not neutral in that she is trying to recover as much property as possible from the debtor for creditors. She is not an observer in that a Chapter 7 trustee is an active trustee.

One of the most important activities of the Chapter 7 trustee is the collection of the property of the estate from the debtor. The filing of a bankruptcy petition creates "property of the estate." Property of the estate includes all of the debtor's interests in property as of the time of the filing of the petition. The Chapter 7 trustee must collect the property of the estate from the debtor. Additionally, the trustee is statutorily empowered to recover some property that the debtor transferred prior to bankruptcy.

How does the bankruptcy trustee learn what property the debtor owns and what property the debtor transferred prior to the petition? The schedules that the debtor is required to file by section 521 are one important source of such information; the meeting of creditors is another. Section 343 requires that the debtor appear at a meeting of creditors and submit to questioning under oath. Through such questioning the trustee and creditors try to locate and evaluate assets of the debtor and determine if any previous transfer of property by the debtor can be avoided.

Section 522 allows an individual debtor to claim as "exempt" from property of the estate "certain assets." In the typical Chapter 7 case of a consumer debtor, all or almost all property is exempt. In such a "no asset" case, there are no assets for the trustee to collect and liquidate.

c. Liquidation

In a Chapter 7 case, any distribution to creditors is in cash, not in kind. Accordingly, it is necessary for the trustee to sell the property that he collects. Some of the "property of the estate" will have little if any resale value. Property owned by a business debtor may require extensive repairs to be made saleable. The trustee has the power to "abandon" such "burdensome" property under section 554.

---

4. 11 U.S.C.A. § 326.

d. Distribution

A creditor with a valid lien on property will receive either its collateral or the proceeds from its sale.

Section 726 governs the proceeds from the sale of unencumbered property of the estate. Section 726 reflects the bankruptcy policy of treating similar creditors similarly. It provides for a pro rata distribution to the holders of allowed unsecured claims. If, for example, the sale of the unencumbered property of the estate nets $3,000 and there is $30,000 of allowed unsecured, non-priority claims, each general creditor will receive 10% of its claim. The preceding sentence suggests the three principal exceptions to the general policy of pro rata distribution. First, creditors whose claims are secured are treated more favorably. Second, certain unsecured claims enjoy a priority in distribution and are paid before other unsecured claims. Section 507 lists the claims with a priority status in bankruptcy. Third, section 726 does not call for dividends to be paid on all claims—only on allowed claims. Section 502 answers the question which claims are allowed.

e. Discharge

A discharge is a release of the debtor from any further personal liability for his or her pre-bankruptcy debts. If the debtor receives a discharge, all a creditor will receive will be its pro rata distribution even though the amount of the debt far exceeds the amount of this bankruptcy dividend.

To illustrate, assume that Mr. Bill files a Chapter 7 petition. At the time of the petition, he owes Sluggo $1,000. The amount of Mr. Bill's debts far exceeds the value of his non-exempt property. The liquidation of Mr. Bill's non-exempt property only yields $800 for $16,000 of unsecured debts. On these facts, Sluggo and Mr. Bill's other creditors with unsecured claims would receive only "five cents on the dollar." And, if Mr. Bill receives a discharge, Sluggo would be barred from attempting to collect the remaining $950 of his debt from Mr. Bill.

As the preceding paragraph implies, a discharge is not granted to each and every debtor. Section 727(a) lists ten grounds for barring the debtor from receiving a discharge. Even if he is able to receive a discharge, a debtor will not necessarily be freed from all creditors' claims. Section 523 excepts a number of debts from the operation of any discharge.

§ 1–8 Chapter 13 and How It Differs From Chapter 7

The typical Chapter 13 case is not a liquidation case. Generally, in Chapter 13, the debtor retains his or her property and prepares a plan proposing payments to creditors.

A Chapter 13 case has five stages. First, an individual debtor files a petition. Only the debtor can file a Chapter 13 petition. Only certain individuals are eligible for Chapter 13 relief. Second, the debtor files a plan providing for payments to creditors. The Code specifies what the plan must provide and what the plan may provide. The Code does not require that the plan provide for full payment of creditors; the plan may alter the rights of creditors. Third, the court reviews and determines whether the plan meets the requirements for confirmation of the plan. Fourth, after confirmation, the debtor makes the payments called for by the plan. Fifth, the debtor receives a discharge.

In Chapter 13 cases, as in Chapter 7 cases, the provisions in Chapters 1, 3, and 5 are applicable.

There are important differences between Chapter 7 cases and Chapter 13 cases. Some of these differences are:

(1) Only debtors can file a Chapter 13 case; debtors and creditors can file Chapter 7 cases.

(2) Chapter 7 relief is more generally available. Use of Chapter 13 is restricted to individual debtors "with a regular income" who meet the debt limits of section 109(e). Chapter 7 can be used by corporations, partnerships and individuals, with no debt limits.

(3) In a Chapter 7 case, the bankruptcy trustee takes control of the property of the estate. In a Chapter 13 case, the debtor retains the property of the estate.

(4) In a Chapter 7 case, creditors are paid from the liquidation of the property of the estate, and the amount a particular creditor receives is governed by statute. The Chapter 7 distribution to creditors generally occurs within months of the bankruptcy filing. In a Chapter 13 case, creditors are generally paid from the debtor's postpetition earnings, and the amount a particular creditor receives is governed by a court-approved plan. A Chapter 13 plan usually provides for payments over a three to five year period.

(5) In a Chapter 7 case, the availability of a discharge depends on whether a creditor can establish one of the statutory grounds for withholding a discharge. In a Chapter 13 case, the availability of a discharge depends primarily on whether the debtor makes his payments called for by the plan.

(6) A Chapter 13 discharge typically covers more kinds of debts than a Chapter 7 discharge, i.e., the exceptions to discharge are fewer.

§ 1–9 Chapter 11 and How It Differs From Chapters 7 and 13

Chapter 11, like Chapter 13, usually involves rehabilitation rather than liquidation. Although the Bankruptcy Code does not expressly restrict the use of Chapter 11 to business cases, the typical Chapter 11 case is a business case.[1] A Chapter 11 case involving a business will typically have the following stages: (1) getting the debtor into bankruptcy, (2) operating the business, (3) formulating a plan of rehabilitation, (4) creditor acceptance of

---

§ 1–9

1. Even though section 109(d) does not restrict use of Chapter 11 to business debtors, some courts (including circuit courts) barred individual nonbusiness debtors from filing under Chapter 11 until the Supreme Court ruled that individual nonbusiness debtors may file for relief under Chapter 11. Toibb v. Radloff, ___ U.S. ___, 111 S.Ct. 2197, 115 L.Ed.2d 145 (1991).

the plan, (5) court confirmation of the plan, (6) discharge as a result of confirmation, and (7) payments under the plan.

a. Comparison of 7 and 11

There are important differences between Chapter 11 and Chapter 7. Some of the differences are:

(1) There is a trustee in every Chapter 7 case. In most Chapter 11 cases, there is not a trustee.

(2) In a Chapter 7 case, the trustee takes possession of the property of the estate and liquidates it. Creditors are paid from the liquidation of the property, and the amount a particular creditor receives is governed by statute. In a Chapter 11 case, the debtor as "debtor in possession" retains the property of the estate. Creditors are generally paid from the postpetition earnings of the debtor, and the amount a particular creditor receives is governed by a plan approved by both creditors and the court.

(3) In a Chapter 7 case, the availability of a discharge depends on whether a creditor can establish one of the statutory grounds for withholding a discharge. Typically in Chapter 11, the debtor receives a discharge when its plan is confirmed.

b. Comparison of 11 and 13

There are also important differences between Chapter 11 cases and Chapter 13 cases. Some of these differences are:

(1) Debtors and creditors can file a Chapter 11 petition; only certain debtors can file Chapter 13 petitions.

(2) Chapter 11 is more generally available. Chapter 11 can be used by corporations, partnerships and individuals with no debt limits. Chapter 13 is restricted to individuals with a regular income who meet the debt limits of section 109(e).

(3) Chapter 11 contemplates creditors' plans as well as a debtor's plan, and plans are generally filed months, if not years, after the petition. In Chapter 13, the plan can only be filed by the debtor and generally is filed at the same time as the bankruptcy petition.

(4) In Chapter 11, creditors vote on the plan. Creditors do not vote on a Chapter 13 plan.

(5) In Chapter 13 cases, discharge is delayed until the debtor performs under the plan. In Chapter 11, the discharge occurs at the confirmation of the plan.

§ 1–10 Chapter 12 and How It Differs From the Other Chapters

Chapter 12 was added to the Bankruptcy Code. It became effective on November 9, 1986. It provides an additional bankruptcy alternative for the "family farmer with a regular income" as defined in section 101. Chapter 12 is intended as a temporary measure; it expires on October 1, 1993.

Chapter 12 is modeled on Chapter 13. In Chapter 12, as in Chapter 13,

(1) Only the debtor can file the petition.

(2) The debtor retains the property of the estate.

(3) Payments to creditors are determined by the plan, and only the debtor can file the plan.

(4) Creditors do not vote on the plan; only the bankruptcy judge approves the plan.

(5) Chapter 12 debtors do not receive a discharge until they perform under the plan.

While Chapter 12 was based on Chapter 13, it differs from Chapter 13 in a number of important respects. Eligibility is only the most obvious difference. Chapter 13 can be used by individuals with a regular income, regardless of the source of that income. Chapter 12 can only be used by debtors with a regular income from farming operation, regardless of whether the debtor is an individual or a corporation or partnership. Moreover, the debt limits for Chapter 12 are significantly higher than the debt limits for Chapter 13.

Because of its specialized nature, its similarity to Chapter 13, and its 1993 expiration, Chapter 12 is not covered in this book as completely as Chapters 7, 11 and 13. They are the main focus.

Chapter 2

COMMENCEMENT, DISMISSAL, AND CONVERSION

Table of Sections

A. Commencement.

Sec.
2–1 Overview of Commencement.
2–2 Voluntary Cases, Section 301.
    a. Eligibility.
        Chapter 7.
        Chapter 11.
        Chapter 13.
        Chapter 12.
    b. Partnerships.
    c. Code Limitations on Frequent Filing.
    d. Filing Fees.
2–3 Joint Cases.
2–4 Substantive Consolidation.
2–5 Involuntary Cases, Section 303.
    a. Debtors Subject to Involuntary Petitions.
    b. Partnerships.
    c. Petitioning Creditors.
    d. Commencement of the Case/Order for Relief.
    e. Grounds for Involuntary Relief.
    f. Rights of Debtor and Creditors in the "Involuntary Gap".
    g. Dismissal and Conversion.
2–6 Case Ancillary to a Foreign Proceeding.
2–7 Legal Consequences of Commencing a Case.
2–8 __ Property of the Estate.
    a. Importance of the Concept.
    b. Scope of Property of the Estate.
    c. Postpetition Property as Property of the Estate.
    d. Individual Debtor's Postpetition Earnings in Chapter 7 or 11 Cases.
    e. Other Statutory Exclusions From Property of the Estate.
    f. Effect of Transfer Restrictions on Property of the Estate.

B. Dismissal.

2–9 Who Can Cause Dismissal.
2–10 Abstention, Section 305.
2–11 Consequences of Dismissal.
    a. Past Actions.
    b. Future Actions.
2–12 Grounds for Dismissal.
2–13 Voluntary Dismissal.
    a. Chapters 7 and 11.
    b. Chapters 12 and 13.

Sec.
2–14 Dismissal of Certain Consumer Chapter 7 Cases for "Substantial Abuse".
2–15 Creditors' Motions to Dismiss a Chapter 11 Petition for Lack of Good Faith.
   a. Filing by a Financially Strong Business Such as Johns–Manville.
   b. Filing by the Single Asset Debtor on the Eve of Foreclosure.
   c. Filing After a "Last Minute" Transfer of Assets to a Newly Created Entity.
2–16 Good Faith Problems in Serial Filings.
   a. Successive Chapter 13 Filings.
   b. Chapter 19 or 20 (or More) Cases.
   c. Filing a New Chapter 11 Petition After Default Under a Confirmed Chapter 11 Plan.
   d. Simultaneous Petitions.

C. Conversion

2–17 Consequences of Conversion.
   a. Property of the Estate.
   b. Exempt Property.
   c. Avoidance of Postpetition/Preconversion Transfers.
2–18 Debtor's Right to Convert.
2–19 Creditor's Right to Convert.

A. COMMENCEMENT

§ 2–1 Overview of Commencement

Sections 101, 109, 301, 302, and 303 deal with the commencement of a bankruptcy case.[1] These provisions answer the questions: (1) how is a bankruptcy case commenced and (2) who can commence a bankruptcy case.

The filing of a bankruptcy petition with the bankruptcy court commences the bankruptcy case. The Bankruptcy Rules govern the form of the petition.[2] Generally, the debtor files the petition. Such debtor-initiated cases are often referred to as "voluntary." Creditors have a limited right to initiate "involuntary" cases under Chapters 7 and 11 by filing a bankruptcy petition "against" the debtor.

§ 2–2 Voluntary Cases, Section 301

Section 301 deals with the commencement of a voluntary case under Chapter 7, or Chapter 11, or Chapter 12, or Chapter 13. Note that section 301 does not require that the debtor be insolvent.[1] It does not condition a debtor's use of bankruptcy on her owing any minimum amount of debt.

§ 2–1

1. "Case" is a term of art. It needs to be distinguished from "proceeding." The "case" is the entire Chapter 7, 11, 12, or 13 matter pending in the bankruptcy court. A "proceeding" is a particular dispute or matter arising within a pending case. A single case can involve many proceedings.

2. Rule 9009 provides that official forms should be used "with alterations as may be appropriate." Official Form 1 is a voluntary petition.

§ 2–2

1. In re Johns–Manville Corp., 36 B.R. 727 (Bankr. S.D.N.Y. 1984), appeal denied, 39 B.R. 234 (S.D.N.Y.1984), reargument denied, 39 B.R. 998 (S.D.N.Y.1984).

Section 301 simply provides that a bankruptcy petition may be filed by any "entity that may be a debtor under such chapter."

Merely filing the voluntary petition results automatically in "an order for relief." The Bankruptcy Code phrase "order for relief" is equivalent to the Bankruptcy Act term "adjudication"; it is "tantamount to an order approving the court's exercise of jurisdiction to grant relief pursuant to the provisions of the law." [2] While neither the Bankruptcy Code nor the Bankruptcy Rules provide for answering or contesting voluntary petitions, creditors can and have challenged a voluntary petition filed by an ineligible debtor by filing a motion to dismiss.[3]

Section 109 defines who may be a debtor. Paragraph (a) makes it clear that only a person who resides in the United States or has a domicile, place of business, or property in the United States may be a debtor under Chapter 7, 11, 12, or 13. The remaining paragraphs of section 109 set out limits on who may be a debtor under a particular chapter of the Code.

Several cases have considered whether the eligibility requirements in paragraphs (b) through (f) of section 109 are jurisdictional in nature. For example, *In re Koehler*[4] granted a creditor's motion to dismiss filed after the Chapter 13 plan had been confirmed because the debtor exceeded section 109(e)'s debt limits. In so ruling, the court held that section 109's eligibility standards, were like jurisdiction questions. Similarly, *In re Wulf*[5] reasoned that a bankruptcy court lacked jurisdiction to convert a Chapter 13 case filed by a debtor not eligible for Chapter 13.

The better view is that section 109 is not jurisdictional.[6] An order confirming a plan should be a binding determination of the debtor's eligibility. A court should have the power to convert a case filed by a debtor who does not meet section 109's eligibility standards for the chapter she has selected.[7]

Support for the position that section 109 eligibility is not jurisdictional can be found in the language of the Code—in both what the Bankruptcy Code says and does not say. Note that the definition of debtor uses the phrase "under this title [i.e., Title 11 of the U.S. Code]", rather than "under Chapter ___." Note also that section 109 states nothing about bankruptcy court jurisdiction.

---

2. Kennedy, The Commencement of a Case Under the New Bankruptcy Law, 36 Wash. & Lee. L. Rev. 977, 983 (1979); contra Ayers, Commencing a Case Under the Bankruptcy Reform Act of 1978: A Primer, 51 Miss. L.J. 639, 651 (1981).

3. See, e.g., In re Bankwest Boulder Industrial Bank, 82 B.R. 559 (Bankr. Colo.1988): In re Koehler, 62 B.R. 70 (Bankr. Neb. 1986).

4. 62 B.R. 70 (Bankr. Neb.1986); see also Kennedy, supra note 2, at 983, n.34 ("The bankruptcy court would have no jurisdiction of a petition filed by an ineligible debtor.").

5. 62 B.R. 155 (Bankr. Neb.1986).

6. See, e.g., Rudd v. Laughlin, 866 F.2d 1040, 1042 (8th Cir.1989); Promenade Nat'l Bank v. Phillips, 844 F.2d 230, 235-36 (5th Cir.1988).

7. See, e.g., In re Wenberg, 94 B.R. 631 (Bankr. 9th Cir.1988), decision aff'd, 902 F.2d 768 (9th Cir.1990); In re Tatsis, 72 B.R. 908 (Bankr. W.D.N.C.1987). Assume, for example, that D makes payments on her antecedent debts and then files a Chapter 13 petition. Ninety-one days after the payments, she files a motion to dismiss her Chapter 13 petition. If the bankruptcy case is dismissed, D will have effectively precluded any trustee challenge to her preferential payments. Under these facts, should the bankruptcy court have power (jurisdiction) to convert D's Chapter 13 to Chapter 7?

a. Eligibility

Chapter 7

Section 109(b) contains two limitations on the availability of Chapter 7 relief to a debtor:

1. The debtor must be a "person." "Person" is defined in section 101 as including individuals, corporations, and partnerships. A sole proprietorship is not a "person." [8]

2. The debtor may not be a railroad, insurance or financial institution.[9] Holding companies of an entity ineligible for bankruptcy relief—e.g., a savings and loan holding company—are eligible.

Chapter 11

Section 109(d) governs eligibility for Chapter 11 relief. With two exceptions, any person who is eligible to file a petition under Chapter 7 is also eligible to file a petition under Chapter 11. The first exception is railroads. Railroads are eligible for Chapter 11, but not Chapter 7. The second exception is for stockbrokers and commodity brokers. They are eligible for Chapter 7, but not Chapter 11.

While most Chapter 11 debtors are business debtors, there is no statutory language that restricts the use of Chapter 11 to businesses. The Supreme Court resolved a conflict among the circuits by holding that nonbusiness debtors can file for Chapter 11 relief: "In our view, the plain language of the Bankruptcy Code disposes of the question before us * * *. The Code contains no 'ongoing business' requirement for reorganization under Chapter 11." [10]

Chapter 13

Chapter 13 is generally regarded as more favorable to debtors than Chapter 7 or Chapter 11. Accordingly, debtors often endeavor to qualify for Chapter 13 relief; creditors often endeavor to "disqualify" the debtor from using Chapter 13. In order to qualify for Chapter 13 relief, the debtor must meet the requirements of section 109(e). There are three significant limitations in section 109(e) on the availability of Chapter 13:

1. The debtor must be an "individual." Compare the term "individual" in section 109(e) with the word "person" that appears in section 109(b)

---

8. See 11 U.S.C.A. § 101(41); In re T.W. Koeger Trucking Co., 105 B.R. 512 (Bankr. E.D.Mo.1989). In Koeger, the court was concerned that if it allowed a filing in the company's name, the individual's assets may be shielded from creditors. Id. at 515.

9. A foreign insurance company or bank may be a Chapter 7 debtor if it has property in the United States but is not engaged in the insurance or banking business in this country. See generally Kennedy, supra note 2, at 990. The cases are divided as to whether a health maintenance organization is an insurance company and so ineligible for bankruptcy relief. Compare In re Family Health Services, Inc., 104 B.R. 279 (Bankr. C.D. Calif. 1989) (eligible) with In re Beacon Health, Inc., 105 B.R. 178 (Bankr. N.H. 1989) (ineligible). See generally Comment, Maxicare as a Guide for Health Maintenance Organizations (HMOs) in Bankruptcy, 8 Bankr. Dev. J. 271 (1991).

10. Toibb v. Radloff, __ U.S. __, 111 S.Ct. 2197, 2199, 115 L.Ed.2d 145 (1991). See generally Herbert, Consumer Chapter 11 Proceedings: Abuse or Alternative? 91 Com. L.J. 234 (1986).

and (d). An "individual" is always a "person"; a "person" is not always an "individual." A corporation or a partnership is a "person" but not an "individual" so a Chapter 13 petition cannot be filed by a corporation or a partnership.

2. The individual must have "income sufficiently stable and regular to enable such individual to make payments under a Chapter 13 plan." [11] Thus, Chapter 13 includes not only wage earners but also self-employed individuals, individuals on welfare, pensions, and retirement income.[12]

3. The debtor must have noncontingent, liquidated, unsecured debts of less than $100,000 and noncontingent, liquidated, secured debts of less than $350,000. Most of the reported cases have involved the debt limit. This litigation raises issues such as whether a disputed debt is noncontingent and liquidated, how section 109(e) treats a debt secured by collateral that has a value less than the amount of a debt, and when a contention that the debtor exceeds the debt limits can be raised. We consider these Chapter 13 eligibility issues later in the book.[13]

Chapter 12

Chapter 12, like Chapter 13, is generally viewed as more advantageous to debtors than Chapter 7 or Chapter 11. Thus, in Chapter 12, as in Chapter 13, there has been considerable litigation over debtor eligibility.

Section 109(f) uses the qualifying phrase "family farmer" which is defined in section 101(18). In summary, all of the following requirements must be met for an *individual* to qualify for relief under Chapter 12:

(1) the debtor must be "engaged in farming";

(2) aggregate debts may not exceed $1,500,000; [14]

(3) 80% of all noncontingent, liquidated debts must arise from farming;

(4) 50% of the debtor's gross income must come from a "farming operation." [15]

In addition, if the debtor is a partnership or a corporation, the farming operation must be conducted by the family and relatives, more than 80% of

---

11. Section 101 defines the phrase "individual with regular income." The definition is not absolute but relative, "sufficiently stable and regular to enable such individual to make payments under a plan." Accordingly, it would seem that if the Chapter 13 plan provided for nominal or no payments, a debtor would be eligible for Chapter 13 even though she did not have a job or other income source. Courts and commentators have rejected this argument. See In re Gavia, 24 B.R. 573 (Bankr. 9th Cir.1982).

12. See, e.g., In re Hammonds, 729 F.2d 1391 (11th Cir.1984) (AFDC benefits as regular income); In re Ballard, 4 B.R. 271 (Bankr. E.D.Va.1980) (attorney); see generally Drake & Morris, Eligibility for Relief Under Chapter 13, 57 Am. Bankr. L.J. 195 (1983); Moller, It Isn't Only for Wage Earners Anymore: The Individual in Business and Chapter 13 of the Bankruptcy Code, 17 Houston L. Rev. 331 (1980). Chapter 13 replaces Chapter XIII of the Bankruptcy Act of 1898 which was expressly limited to wage earners.

13. See infra §§ 2–2 & 9–3.

14. Note that this includes all debts, secured and unsecured, contingent and noncontingent, etc.

15. In deciding whether 50% or the debtor's gross income was derived from a farming operation, courts have relied on the debtor's income tax returns. See In re Nelson, 73 B.R. 363 (Bankr. Kan.1987); In re Shepherd, 75 B.R. 501 (Bankr. N.D.Ohio 1987). Renting farmland or renting farm equipment is not a "farming operation". See, e.g., In re Seabloom, 78 B.R. 543 (Bankr. C.D.Ill. 1987); In re Cobb, 76 B.R. 557 (Bankr. N.D.Miss.1987); contra In re Rott, 73 B.R. 366 (Bankr. N.D. 1987).

the value of the debtor's assets must relate to the farming operation, and, if the debtor is a corporation, the stock may not be publicly traded. In our Chapter 9 we say more about Bankruptcy Chapter 12.

b. Partnerships

The Bankruptcy Code's definition of "person" includes a partnership.[16] Thus, in bankruptcy, a partnership is a legal entity, distinct from the general partners. The partnership itself may file for relief under Chapter 7, Chapter 11 or Chapter 12 if it meets the definition of a "family farmer." Partnerships are not eligible for Chapter 13 relief.

All of the general partners must consent to the filing.[17] A partner's consent to the filing can be based on the partnership agreement.[18] A bankruptcy petition on behalf of the partnership to which all of the general partners do not consent must be filed as an involuntary petition.[19] The consent of limited partners is not required.[20]

c. Code Limitations on Frequent Filing

Section 109(g) adds what could be roughly called a "frequent filing" limitation on filings by individuals. Under section 109(g), an individual is not eligible to be a debtor under Chapter 7, 11, 12, or 13 if she was a debtor in a bankruptcy case that in the past 180 days was:

(1) dismissed by the court for "willful" failure of the debtor to abide by court orders or appear before the court,[21] or

(2) dismissed on motion of the debtor "following" the filing of a motion requesting relief from the automatic stay.

There is a division in the case law interpreting the word "following" in section 109(g)(2). Obviously, section 109(g)(2) bars another bankruptcy filing by a debtor who dismisses her bankruptcy petition *because* a creditor files a motion requesting relief from the automatic stay or obtains relief from the stay. Does "following" in this context mean "because of" or "in response to"? What if the debtor dismisses her bankruptcy petition for other rea-

---

16. 11 U.S.C.A. § 101(41). The Bankruptcy Code does not define "partnership." Generally, the court looks to the state law of the domicile of the association to determine whether it is a partnership. See generally Hanley, Partnership Bankruptcy Under the New Act, 31 Hastings L.J. 149, 151 (1979).

17. Cf. 11 U.S.C.A. § 303(b)(3); see Bankr. R. 1004(a). While all general partners must consent to the filing of a partnership petition, it is not necessary that all partners sign the petition. The Code and Rules leave to state law and the partnership agreement who may authorize a voluntary case on behalf of a partnership. See Kennedy, Partnerships and Partners Under the Bankruptcy Reform Act and the New (Proposed) Bankruptcy Rules, 27 St. Louis U. L.J. 507, 521–32 (1983).

18. In re Channel 64 Joint Venture, 61 B.R. 255 (Bankr. S.D.Ohio 1986) (partnership agreement provided that a majority vote of the management committee of the partnership could authorize the filing of a bankruptcy petition).

19. 11 U.S.C.A. § 303(b)(3).

20. See, e.g., In re Westover Hills, Ltd., 46 B.R. 300 (Bankr. Wy. 1985); In re Bel Air Assoc., Ltd., 4 B.R. 168 (Bankr. W.D. Okla. 1980).

21. Section 109(g)(1) deals with two types of conduct: (i) failure to abide by court orders and (ii) failure to appear before the court in prosecution of the case. The court in In re Arena, 81 B.R. 851, 855 (Bankr. E.D.Pa. 1988), rejected the argument that a showing of willfulness is required only in connection with failure to abide by court orders.

sons? Assume, for example, that the debtor dismisses his Chapter 13 case because he loses his job. If he later obtains employment and wants to file another Chapter 13 petition, will he be barred by section 109(g)(2) from filing another bankruptcy petition because a creditor had filed a motion for relief from stay in the first case? The cases disagree.[22]

Section 109(g)(2) deals only with a filing by an individual or family farmer whose earlier case was dismissed. Section 109(g)(2) does not expressly bar an individual or other person who has completed a Chapter 7, 11, 12 or 13 case within the past 180 days from filing for bankruptcy again. Some cases have dismissed a person's bankruptcy filing for lack of good faith because of her prior bankruptcy filings. However, in *Johnson v. Home State Bank*,[23] the Supreme Court relied on section 109(g) to hold that a debtor who had recently obtained Chapter 7 relief was still eligible for later Chapter 13 relief. While *Johnson* precludes any per se bar to bankruptcy based on the debtor's recent bankruptcy relief, we believe that courts can and will consider any such relief in ruling on a motion to dismiss based on bad faith.

d. Filing Fees

A debtor who files a bankruptcy petition must pay a filing fee. No provision is made for in forma pauperis bankruptcy. Failure to pay filing fees is a statutory basis for dismissal.[24]

§ 2–3 Joint Cases

A husband and wife may file for bankruptcy together. Section 302 authorizes the initiation of a joint case by filing a joint petition. Two petitioners. Two debtors. Only one petition. Only one filing fee. A joint petition may be filed by a husband and a wife under Chapter 7, Chapter 11, Chapter 12 or Chapter 13.[1]

How is a husband and wife's filing a section 302 joint petition different from a husband and wife each filing a voluntary petition under section 301? As noted above, filing a joint petition saves the couple one filing fee.

Section 109 sets out another difference between a joint petition and

---

22. Compare In re Patton, 49 B.R. 587 (Bankr. M.D.Ga.1985) (debtor barred only if earlier dismissal was in response to creditor's stay motion) with In re Keziah, 46 B.R. 551 (Bankr. W.D.N.C.1985) (debtor's reasons irrelevant). See generally Morris, Substantive Consumer Bankruptcy Reform in the Bankruptcy Amendments Act of 1984, 27 William & Mary L. Rev. 91, 100–103 (1985). There is also a division on the question of whether eligibility under section 109(g) raises an issue of subject matter jurisdiction; the case authority is collected in In re Phillips, 844 F.2d 230, 235, n. 2 (5th Cir.1988), which properly holds that it is not a subject matter jurisdiction issue.

23. __ U.S. __, 111 S.Ct. 2150, 115 L.Ed.2d 66 (1991), on remand, 940 F.2d 609 (10th Cir.1991). Johnson and other serial filing cases are considered infra at § 2–16.

24. See, e.g., 11 U.S.C.A. § 707(a)(2). In a 5–4 decision, the Supreme Court ruled in United States v. Kras, 409 U.S. 434, 93 S.Ct. 631, 34 L.Ed.2d 626 (1973), that it was constitutional for Congress to limit relief to petitioners who can pay filing fees.

§ 2–3

1. Section 302 is the only Bankruptcy Code provision permitting joint filing. Courts have not been willing to extend section 302 to unmarried, cohabiting couples. See In re Malone, 50 B.R. 2 (Bankr. E.D.Mich.1985). Parents and children have not been permitted to file a joint petition. See In re Lam, 98 B.R. 965 (Bankr. W.D.Mo.1988).

separate filings.² When a husband and wife file a joint Chapter 12 or Chapter 13 petition, they are held to a single debt limit. If, on the other hand, the husband and wife file separately, the debt limit would be separately applied to the husband and wife.³

While a joint petition results in a single debt limit, a husband and wife joint petition under section 302 still leaves two separate bankruptcy estates for administration absent a consolidation order.

In re Birch,⁴ for example, the husband owned a lumber business that he operated in his own name alone; the wife owned real property that she had inherited. Most of the debts related to the husband's business. Mr. and Mrs. Birch filed a joint Chapter 7 petition under section 302. Even though they filed only one bankruptcy petition, their filing created two separate bankruptcy estates. The claims of the husband's lumber business creditors could be satisfied only from the husband's bankruptcy estate assets even though the wife's estate had some $50,000 in assets and few liabilities.

Section 302(b) empowers the court to determine the "extent if any to which the debtors' estates shall be consolidated." The Bankruptcy Code does not provide any standards for determining when husband and wife cases should be consolidated. Legislative history suggests that relevant factors include "the extent of jointly held property and the amount of jointly owned debts."⁵

§ 2–4 Substantive Consolidation

Although section 302(b) is the only Bankruptcy Code reference to consolidation of estates, i.e., "*substantive consolidation*," bankruptcy courts have relied on section 105, which authorizes the court to "issue any order * * * necessary or appropriate to carry out the provisions of this title," to order substantive consolidation in business situations.¹ Substantive consolidation is a process by which the assets and liabilities of different entities are consolidated in bankruptcy and treated as a single entity for purposes of a bankruptcy case. These consolidated assets then create a single fund from which all of the claims against the consolidated debtors are satisfied. To illustrate, if A files a bankruptcy petition and B files a bankruptcy petition,² and A and B are consolidated substantively, the creditors of A and the creditors of B become joint creditors of the consolidated A and B debtors. These joint creditors share equally in the assets of A and B. Substantive consolidation also eliminates claims among the consolidated debtors. In other words, the claims of A against B, and the claims of B against A will be eliminated by substantive consolidation.

2. See 11 U.S.C.A. § 109(e), (f); cf. id. § 101(18).

3. If a husband and wife each file a Chapter 13 petition, their joint obligations are counted in full in each bankruptcy in applying the debt limits.

4. 72 B.R. 103 (Bankr. N.H.1987).

5. H.R. Rep. No. 595, 95th Cong., 1st Sess. 321 (1977).

§ 2–4

1. See generally P. Blumberg, The Law of Corporate Groups: Bankruptcy Law ch. 10 (1985); Note, Substantive Consolidation in Bankruptcy: A Primer, 43 Vand.L.Rev. 207 (1990).

2. See Practitioner Treatise, Vol. 1.

Substantive consolidation can prejudice the rights of creditors because different debtors ordinarily have different ratios of assets to liabilities. If the asset to liability ratio of A is higher than that of B, the creditors of A will receive a proportionally smaller return on its claim after substantive consolidation because the asset to liability ratio of the merged estates will be lower.

As noted above, section 105 is the only statutory authority for substantive consolidation. Because of the absence of any statutory prerequisites for substantive consolidation, courts examine the facts and circumstances of each case to determine whether consolidation is warranted. Courts frequently cite seven factors from *In re Vecco Construction Industries, Inc.*[3] when considering a motion for substantive consolidation: (1) the presence or absence of consolidated financial statements; (2) the unity of interests and ownership between various corporate entities; (3) the existence of parent and intercorporate guarantees on loans; (4) the difficulty in segregating and ascertaining individual assets and liabilities; (5) the existence of transfers of assets without formal observance of corporate formalities; (6) the commingling of assets in business functions; and (7) the profitability of consolidation at a single physical location.[4]

Substantive consolidation should not be confused with either the corporate law concept of piercing the corporate veil or the bankruptcy law concept of joint administration. Unlike piercing the corporate veil, substantive consolidation does not seek to hold shareholders liable for acts of their incorporated entity. A corporate law concept closer to substantive consolidation is merger of two corporations under state law.[5]

Later, in our Chapter 11, we say more about consolidation in the context of business reorganizations.[6]

Joint administration is a procedure under which courts hear cases involving two or more entities that have filed different bankruptcy petitions as a single case.[7] Joint administration does not affect the substantive rights of creditors and other interested parties. In joint administration, unlike substantive consolidation, the estate of each debtor is kept separate and distinct and inter-entity claims survive. The creditors of each jointly administered entity may look only to the assets of their debtor.

§ 2–5 Involuntary Cases, Section 303

Section 303 empowers creditors to start a Chapter 7 or a Chapter 11 bankruptcy case (but not a Chapter 12 or Chapter 13 case) by filing a bankruptcy petition. Such creditor-initiated cases are generally referred to as "involuntary cases." While the first American bankruptcy laws permitted only creditor petitions, today very few bankruptcy cases are involuntary

---

3. 4 B.R. 407 (Bankr. E.D.Va.1980).
4. See Eastgroup Properties v. Southern Motel Assoc., 935 F.2d 245 (11th Cir.1991). For a more extensive discussion of substantive consolidation cases, see § 11–41 infra.
5. In re Parkway Calabasas Ltd., 89 B.R. 832, 836 (Bankr. C.D.Cal.1988).
6. See §§ 11–40 & 11–41 infra.
7. See Bankr. R. 1015.

cases. *Generally,* creditors are better off using state collection proceedings.[1] Involuntary bankruptcy is threatened far more than it is actually used.

a. *Debtors Subject to Involuntary Petitions*

Section 303(a) explains which debtors are subject to creditor-initiated bankruptcy. With two exceptions, an involuntary case can be commenced against any debtor who is eligible for voluntary bankruptcy under the chapter chosen. The exceptions are farmers and corporations that are not "moneyed, business, or commercial."[2] There has been considerable controversy as to whether farmers and non-profit corporations should be protected from involuntary petitions and which non-profit corporations are protected by the language "not moneyed, business or commercial." The Bankruptcy Act of 1898 contained the same language, and Code cases look to and rely on Act cases in determining whether or not the debtor is subject to an involuntary petition.[3] The cases are not clear if the issue of whether or not a debtor is protected by section 303(a) from creditor-initiated bankruptcy is a jurisdictional issue that the creditors must establish or an affirmative defense that the debtor must prove and plead.[4]

Most involuntary Chapter 7 petitions are filed against corporate or partnership debtors. Creditors are less likely to file an involuntary Chapter 7 petition against an individual for fear that the unpaid portions of their claims will be discharged. In Chapter 7 cases involving individual debtors, creditors will usually find the unpaid portions of their claims discharged. Discharge is unique to bankruptcy, and, in Chapter 7 cases, is limited to individual debtors.

b. *Partnerships*

Recall that an involuntary petition must be used whenever less than all

§ 2–5

1. For a discussion of the reasons that creditors file involuntary bankruptcy petitions, see T. Eisenberg, Bankruptcy and Debtor–Creditor Law 458–59 (2d ed. 1988); Weintraub & Resnick, Involuntary Petitions Under the New Bankruptcy Code, 97 Banking L.J. 292, 294–96 (1980).

2. Arguably, there is a third category of debtors able to file voluntary petitions but protected from involuntary petitions—husbands and wives. Recall that section 302 permits a husband and wife to file a joint petition. Section 302 is read as permitting only a voluntary joint petition. Creditors cannot file a joint involuntary petition. If creditors want to force a husband and wife into bankruptcy, they need to file an involuntary petition against each and establish a section 303(h) ground as to each. See In re Benny, 842 F.2d 1147 (9th Cir.1988), cert. denied, 488 U.S. 1014, 109 S.Ct. 806, 102 L.Ed.2d 796 (1989); In re Jones, 112 B.R. 770 (Bankr. E.D.Va.1990).

There is also a category of debtors ineligible for voluntary bankruptcy, but vulnerable to involuntary bankruptcy. Generally, financial institutions are not eligible for voluntary bankruptcy, section 109(b)(2). Section 109 creates an exception for foreign banks not engaged in the business of banking in the United States but possessing assets here. Section 303(k) permits an involuntary petition to be filed against such a foreign bank only if a foreign bankruptcy proceeding relating to the bank is already pending. See generally Kennedy, The Commencement of a Case Under the New Bankruptcy Code, 36 Wash. & Lee L. Rev. 977, 1002–3 (1979).

3. See, e.g., In re Caucus Distributors, Inc., 83 B.R. 921, 930 (Bankr. E.D.Va.1988); In re United Kitchen Associates, Inc., 33 B.R. 214, 216 (Bankr. W.D.La.1983); see generally Sovern, Section 4 of the Bankruptcy Act: The Excluded Corporation, 42 Minn.L.Rev. 171, 231–43 (1957).

4. See Practitioner Treatise, Vol. 1.

of the general partners want the partnership in bankruptcy.[5] A voluntary petition cannot be filed for the partnership over the objection of even one of the general partners. Objections by limited partners, however, do not prevent the filing of a voluntary petition.

In re Sunset Developers[6] held that a general partner who had filed a Chapter 11 petition in his individual capacity did not have the authority to file an involuntary bankruptcy petition for the partnership. The court looked to the Uniform Partnership Act which provides in section 31 that the "bankruptcy" of an individual partner causes a dissolution of the partnership, and in section 33 that dissolution terminates all authority of a partner to act for the partnership.

We disagree with the *Sunset Developers* holding. We believe that the court should have focused on the Bankruptcy Code, rather than the Uniform Partnership Act.[7] Under section 303(b) of the Bankruptcy Code, a general partner can file an involuntary petition against the partnership. Section 303(b) makes no reference to the filing partner's bankruptcy status or bankruptcy history: if she is a partner, she can file. While, under state law, bankruptcy is a cause for dissolution of the partnership, it does not result in termination of the partnership. The partnership continues to exist, and the partner who filed an individual bankruptcy petition continues to be a partner.[8] The Uniform Partnership Act or other state law can limit such a partner's power to act for the partnership in matters not controlled by federal law. The Bankruptcy Code controls that partner's power to file a bankruptcy petition for the partnership.[9]

c. *Petitioning Creditors*

There are two questions regarding petitioning creditors: (i) who may be a petitioning creditor and (ii) how many petitioning creditors are required. Section 303(b) deals with both questions.

In order to have standing to file an involuntary petition, a creditor must hold a claim that is "not contingent as to liability or subject to a bona fide dispute." The Bankruptcy Code does not define the term "contingent." A "contingent" claim for this purpose, as distinguished from a claim that is

---

5. 11 U.S.C.A. § 303(b)(3).
6. 69 B.R. 710 (Bankr. Idaho 1987).
7. The Sunset Developers interpretation of the UPA is open to question on two grounds. First, is a Chapter 11 filing a cause of dissolution? Section 31 of the UPA lists "bankruptcy" as a cause of dissolution. It has been argued that the UPA was not using the term "bankruptcy" in its "technical sense—that the UPA only intended to make a liquidation bankruptcy a cause of dissolution. E.g., In re Safren, 65 B.R. 566 (Bankr. C.D. Calif. 1986); Eibl, Strategies for Partners Under the Bankruptcy Code When the Partnership is Insolvent, 61 Am. Bankr. L.J. 37, 52 (1987). Second, even if a Chapter 11 filing by a general partner results in dissolution of the partnership, the Sunset Developers interpretation of the powers of a partner on dissolution can be challenged. Section 35 of the UPA speaks of a partner not acting "for" the partnership after dissolution. Arguably, a section 303 filing is an act against the partnership, not for the partnership.

8. Note that the Revised Uniform Limited Partnership Act provides that a general partner ceases to be a general partner if she files for bankruptcy. R.U.L.P.A. § 402.

9. See In re B C & K Cattle Co., 84 B.R. 69 (Bankr. N.D.Tex.1988). The effect of a partner's bankruptcy filing is considered more generally in Kennedy, Partnerships and Partners Under the Bankruptcy Reform Act and the New Proposed Bankruptcy Rules, 27 St. Louis L.J. 507 (1983).

unliquidated or unmatured, is one as to which there is some remaining condition precedent to liability. The leading reported case on "not contingent as to liability" under section 303 is *In re All Media Properties, Inc.*,[10] in which the court described the claim against a guarantor on a note and a tort claim not yet reduced to judgment as "contingent" and a debt arising from the sale of merchandise as not contingent. A guarantor is only contingently liable until there is a dishonor or default by the primary obligor. Outside of the tort area, a claim does not have to be reduced to judgment to be "not contingent as to liability."

The requirement that the petitioning creditor's claim cannot be the subject of a "bona fide dispute" was added in 1984. How is a court to determine whether the debtor's dispute of her liability is "bona fide"? Although the court will not have to determine the outcome of the dispute, it will have to look into the merits of the dispute the debtor has raised. A number of cases use the test from *In re Lough*,[11] which asks "if there is a genuine issue of material fact that bears upon the debtor's liability or a meritorious contention as to the application of law to undisputed facts."[12]

Generally, three or more creditors with unsecured [13] claims totalling at least $5,000 must join the petition.[14] If, however, the debtor has less than 12 unsecured creditors, a single creditor with an unsecured claim of at least $5,000 is sufficient. While a single petitioning creditor is sufficient to commence an involuntary case against a debtor that has less than 12 eligible creditors, courts have been reluctant to grant a petition where there is only a single creditor.[15] These cases suggest that nonpayment of a single creditor is not the "generally not paying" debts contemplated by section 303(h)(1) and that bankruptcy contemplates more than a two party dispute.

We do not read section 303(h)(1) as prohibiting single-creditor involuntary cases. The word "generally" in section 303(h)(1) is comparative, not absolute. Nor do we apply bankruptcy policy to prohibit all single-creditor involuntary cases. In *In re Concrete Pumping Service, Inc.*,[16] the Sixth Circuit properly permitted a single creditor petition. There the petitioning creditor, PC, alleged that the debtor, D, had transferred all of its assets to an insider creditor, IC. IC then used her own funds to pay all of D's creditors,

---

10. 5 B.R. 126, 133 (Bankr. S.D.Tex.1980), aff'd, 646 F.2d 193 (5th Cir.1981).

11. 57 B.R. 993 (Bankr. E.D.Va.1986).

12. Id. at 997; see In re Busick, 831 F.2d 745, 749–50 (7th Cir.1987); In re Leach, 92 B.R. 483 (Bankr. Kan.1988), opinion amended, 102 B.R. 805 (Bankr. Kan.1989); In re B.B.S.I., Ltd., 81 B.R. 227, 230 (Bankr. E.D.N.Y.1988); In re Garland Coal & Mining Co., 67 B.R. 514, 521 (Bankr. W.D.Ark.1986); cf. In re Ramm Industries, Inc., 83 B.R. 815, 822 (Bankr. M.D.Fla.1988); but cf. In re Johnston Hawks, Ltd., 49 B.R. 823, 830 (Bankr. Haw. 1985); In re Stroop, 51 B.R. 210 (Bankr. Colo. 1985). See generally Ponoroff, Involuntary Bankruptcy and the Bona Fides of a Bona Fide Dispute, 65 Ind. L.J. 315 (1990).

13. It is not necessary that each of the petitioning creditors holds an unsecured claim. A fully secured creditor is a qualified petitioner. See Paradise Hotel Corp. v. Bank of Nova Scotia, 842 F.2d 47 (3d Cir.1988). Note, however, that only the holder of an unsecured claim can join as a petitioning creditor on a previously filed involuntary petition. 11 U.S.C.A. § 303(c).

14. Section 303(b)(3) contains additional options for the commencement of an involuntary case against a partnership; section 303(b)(4) provides another alternative for the commencement of an involuntary case against a debtor that is involved in a foreign bankruptcy case.

15. See, e.g., In re Nordbrock, 772 F.2d 397 (8th Cir.1985); Paroline v. Doling, 116 B.R. 583 (Bankr. S.D.Ohio 1990); but cf. In re 7H Land & Cattle Co., 6 B.R. 29 (Bankr. Nev. 1980).

16. 943 F.2d 627 (6th Cir.1991).

other than PC, leaving D with no assets and one creditor and leaving that creditor, PC, with no real remedy other than section 303 and section 547.[17]

In computing the number of creditors, section 303(b) expressly excludes employees, insiders, and transferees of voidable transfers. The statute does not specifically exclude creditors with small recurring claims, and most cases include creditors with small, recurring claims in determining whether there are at least 12 unsecured creditors.[18] Another question about petitioning creditors that is not answered by either section 303 or the reported cases is how limited partners are to be treated. Professor Kennedy has argued that a limited partner's right of return of its capital contribution qualifies it as a petitioning creditor.[19] Professor Kennedy acknowledges that such a right is subordinated to other claims against the partnership but argues that "[t]he [limited partner's] claim is not rendered contingent, however, because it is subordinated to other claims against the estate * * *. Merely because a postponed claim is less likely to be paid than one given a higher priority does not make the postponed claim contingent." [20]

Similarly, it would seem that limited partners should be included in a count of creditors for the purpose of determining whether three petitioners are required. Section 303(b)(2) excludes "insider" creditors from the count, but section 101 does not include limited partners in the definition of "insider."

Creditors may join in the petition after filing with the same effect as if the joining creditor had been one of the original petitioners.[21] So, if after the filing of an involuntary petition, the claim of one of the three petitioning creditors is found to be contingent as to liability, the petition will not be dismissed for want of three qualified petitioning creditors if another qualified creditor joins in the petition. If, however, the original petition was filed by one creditor with knowledge that the debtor had 12 or more creditors, the petition may not be cured by the later joinder of two more creditors.[22]

d. Commencement of the Case/Order for Relief

The filing of an involuntary petition is treated as commencing the bankruptcy case. The date of the filing is thus the critical date in applying other Bankruptcy Code provisions such as section 362 (automatic stay), section 541 (property of the estate), section 547 (preferences), and section 548 (fraudulent conveyances) which refer to date of filing or commencement of the case.

---

17. PC alleges that D's payment to IC was an avoidable preference under section 547, which is considered infra in our Chapter 6 at §§ 6–3 through 6–37.

18. See, e.g., In re Rassi, 701 F.2d 627 (7th Cir.1983); In re Hoover, 32 B.R. 842 (Bankr. W.D. Okla. 1983). Contra In re Atwood, 124 B.R. 402 (S.D.Ga.1991); In re Blaine Richards & Co., 10 B.R. 424, 429–31 (Bankr. E.D.N.Y. 1981).

19. Kennedy, supra note 9, at 526.

20. Id.

21. 11 U.S.C.A. § 303(c); In re Braten, 74 B.R. 1021 (Bankr. S.D.N.Y.1987).

22. See, e.g., Basin Electric Power Co-op. v. Midwest Processing Co., 769 F.2d 483, 486 (8th Cir.1985), cert. denied 474 U.S. 1083, 106 S.Ct. 854, 88 L.Ed.2d 894 (1986); In re Alta Title Co., 55 B.R. 133, 143 (Bankr. Utah 1985). Debtor has no obligation to provide a creditor with the names and addresses of other creditors. See In re McDonald Trucking Co., Inc., 74 B.R. 474 (Bankr. W.D.Pa.1987).

While the filing of a voluntary petition both commences the case and effects the order for relief, the filing of an involuntary petition does not operate as an order for relief, as an adjudication of bankruptcy. The debtor has the right to file an answer to the involuntary petition.[23] If the debtor does not timely answer the petition, the court "shall order relief."[24] If the debtor does timely answer the petition, the court shall order relief against the debtor only if one of the two grounds set out in section 303(h) is established.

e. Grounds for Involuntary Relief

Under the Bankruptcy Act of 1898, creditors seeking to force a debtor into bankruptcy had to allege and prove that the debtor had committed one of six "acts of bankruptcy" within four months of the time of the filing of the petition.[25] These acts were difficult to understand and difficult to establish.

The Bankruptcy Code eliminated the concept of acts of bankruptcy. Under Section 303(h), the first basis for involuntary relief is that the debtor is "generally" not paying debts as they come due. Note how this differs from the Bankruptcy Code's definition of insolvency in section 101, the Uniform Commercial Code's definition of insolvency in section 1–201(23) and the traditional equity insolvency test. Here the focus is on whether the debtor is actually paying her debts rather than on the debtor's ability to pay as shown on her balance sheet.[26]

Neither the Bankruptcy Code nor the case law provides specific standards as to the number or the size of the claims that the debtor is not paying. Since 1984, the Code has provided that nonpayment of debts that are the subject of a "bona fide dispute" is not to be considered in applying this first ground for involuntary relief.

The alternative basis for involuntary relief is that within 120 days before the petition was filed, a general receiver, assignee, or custodian took possession of substantially all of the debtor's property or was appointed to take charge of substantially all of the debtor's property. The appointment of a receiver in a state court real estate foreclosure action satisfies section 303(h)(2) only if the real estate involved is substantially all of the debtor's property.

f. Rights of Debtor and Creditors in the "Involuntary Gap"

Usually there will be an interval of at least several weeks between the filing of an involuntary petition and the order of relief against the debtor. This period of time is often referred to as the involuntary gap. During the

---

23. 11 U.S.C.A. § 303(d); Bankr. R. 1011. The general partner of a partnership that did not join in the petition may also answer an involuntary petition. Neither creditors nor shareholders may answer the petition.

24. 11 U.S.C.A. § 303(h).

25. See generally Treiman, Acts of Bankruptcy: A Medieval Concept in Modern Bankruptcy Law, 52 Harv.L.Rev. 189 (1938).

26. See Kennedy, supra note 2, at 1009; In re All Media Properties, Inc., 5 B.R. 126, 142 n. 5 (Bankr. S.D.Tex.1980), order aff'd, 646 F.2d 193 (5th Cir.1981); see generally McCoid, The Decision for Involuntary Bankruptcy, 61 Am. Bankr. L.J. 195 (1987).

involuntary gap in a Chapter 7 case,[27] the bankruptcy court may appoint an interim trustee to take possession of the debtor's property or operate the debtor's business "if necessary to preserve the property of the estate or to prevent loss to the estate." [28]

During this involuntary gap period, some, but not all, of the provisions of the Bankruptcy Code apply. Some Code provisions are triggered by the filing of a petition; others do not become effective until the order for relief. The automatic stay of section 362 applies as soon as the involuntary petition is filed;[29] creditors' actions to collect prepetition debts will be barred. Similarly, the filing of an involuntary petition creates the bankruptcy estate, and the interests of the debtor in property become property of the estate under section 541.[30] The restrictions on use and disposition of property of the estate of section 363, however, do not apply.[31]

The debtor is able to dispose of property. The court may, under section 303(f), restrict transfers but such restrictions are rarely imposed where there is no fraudulent conduct. The debtor is able to make voluntary payments to its creditors. After an order for relief, however, the trustee will be able to recover any such payments on prepetition debts. Under section 549, creditors who receive payments during this gap period are protected only to the extent of value given after the filing of the petition. The creditors' knowledge or lack of knowledge of the involuntary filing is irrelevant.[32]

The principal problems confronting a business debtor against whom an involuntary petition has been filed will be (i) extensions of credit to it and (ii) collection by it on the credit it has extended.[33] A person who extends credit to such a debtor "in the ordinary course of the debtor's business or financial affairs" during the involuntary gap is given what seems to be a second priority, unsecured claim, that comes behind secured claims and administrative expenses.[34] Because so many claims will have priority over this second priority,[35] most trade creditors refuse to extend credit to a business against

27. An interim trustee cannot be appointed to take possession of the property in a Chapter 11 case. Cf. In re Beaucrest Realty Assoc., 4 B.R. 164 (Bankr. E.D.N.Y.1980).

28. 11 U.S.C.A. § 303(g). If an interim trustee is appointed, the debtor may regain possession of its property from the interim trustee by posting a bond.

29. Section 362 is considered infra in our Chapter 3.

30. Section 541 is considered infra at § 2–8.

31. Section 363 is considered infra in Chapter 4.

32. 11 U.S.C.A. § 549. We consider section 549 at §§ 6–68 through 6–73 infra. The trustee will not have to prove the various elements of a preference set out in section 547(b). The law of preferences is limited to prepetition transfers.

33. While a bankruptcy filing of any kind often inhibits customers from buying from a business, there is no Bankruptcy Code basis for these inhibitions. A customer who buys personal or real property from a business against whom an involuntary petition has been filed will be protected by section 549(b) from a later suit by a bankruptcy trustee to recover the property it bought. Of course, if no order for relief is entered, all who dealt with the debtor during the involuntary gap are unaffected by the bankruptcy filing. It is as if no bankruptcy petition was ever filed. The protection and lack of protection described above are important only if the order for relief is entered.

34. See 11 U.S.C.A. §§ 507(a)(2), 502(f).

35. Most of the unsecured debt incurred after an order for relief will qualify for the higher, administrative expense priority. And, all of the priority claims from a Chapter 11 case that fails and is converted to Chapter 7 will come behind the priority claims of the later Chapter 7 case. See 11 U.S.C.A. § 726(b).

whom an involuntary petition has been filed.[36]

For both business and legal reasons, a person against whom an involuntary petition has been filed will find it even more difficult to obtain loans or other non-ordinary course trade credit. The Bankruptcy Code does not expressly deal with the needs of a person against whom an involuntary petition has been filed for loans or other nonordinary course credit. Subsections 364(b), (c), and (d) govern nonordinary course extensions of credit to a debtor. It is not clear, however, whether section 364(b), (c) and (d) apply to the gap period between the filing of an involuntary petition and the order for relief. Recall that the filing of an involuntary petition triggers some, but not all, of the provisions of the Bankruptcy Code.

In re Roxy Roller Rink Joint Venture[37] involved an effort to obtain a $120,000 secured loan after the commencement of an involuntary case but before any order for relief. In holding that an involuntary gap debtor can not take advantage of section 364(b), (c) and (d), Judge Abram looked to section 303(f) which allows the debtor to operate as if no petition has been filed. She found this freedom under section 303(f) to be inconsistent with the fiduciary duties imposed upon a trustee or a debtor in possession under section 1107 and so concluded that an involuntary gap debtor could not qualify as "trustee" to invoke section 364.[38] We find Judge Abram's analysis persuasive.

And, for both business and legal reasons, customers are reluctant to pay a business that is subject to an involuntary petition. Customers who know of the pending involuntary bankruptcy petition and still pay the debtor are at risk of being required to make a second payment to the trustee unless there has been a court order authorizing payments to the debtor.[39]

Section 303(e) empowers the court to order petitioning creditors to post a bond to cover possible liability under section 303(i). Debtors against whom an involuntary petition has been filed commonly move for such a bond to "encourage" petitioning creditors to dismiss their petition. The bankruptcy court will decide in its discretion whether to require a bond and the amount of the bond. Even if this strategy is successful, the debtor will still operate under the shadow and stigma of bankruptcy for at least twenty-one more days. The Code requires notice to all creditors of dismissal of an involuntary petition,[40] and the Rules provide a twenty-one day prior notice period.[41]

---

36. See generally 1 R. Ginsberg, Bankruptcy § 2.05(c) (2d ed. 1989).

37. 73 B.R. 521 (Bankr. S.D.N.Y. 1987).

38. "It is a sensible statutory scheme to preclude the debtor from taking advantage of the powers of the Bankruptcy Code, such as the right to incur debt under section 364 on a priming lien, superpriority basis or the right to recover fraudulent conveyances or set aside preferences under sections 547 and 548, while the debtor opposes the entry for an order for relief and when no order for relief may ever be entered." Id. at 527; contra 2 Collier on Bankruptcy ¶ 364.03 at 364-9. Judge Abram acknowledged in a footnote that any interim trustee appointed under section 303(g) might be able to borrow under section 364(b), (c) or (d). 73 B.R. at 527 n.5.

39. See 11 U.S.C.A. § 542(c).

40. 11 U.S.C.A. § 303(j).

41. Bankr. R. 2002(a).

g. Dismissal and Conversion [42]

Because the filing of an involuntary petition adversely affects the debtor's financial reputation and business operations, section 303(i) attempts to protect debtors from ill-founded petitions by setting out the following remedies in cases in which an involuntary petition is dismissed "other than on consent of all petitioners and the debtor." [43]

　　1. The court may grant judgment for the debtor against the petitioning creditors for costs and a reasonable attorney's fee.

　　2. If an interim trustee took possession of the debtor's property, the court may grant judgment for "any damages proximately caused by the taking."

　　3. If the petition was filed in "bad faith," the court may award "any damages proximately caused by such filing," such as loss of business, and also punitive damages.[44]

Section 303(i) contemplates dismissal of an involuntary petition for want of prosecution or inability to satisfy the requirements of section 303. Additionally, an involuntary petition that satisfies all of the requirements of section 303 can be dismissed under section 305 [45] if the court decides that the "interests of creditors and the debtor would be better served." If a case is dismissed under section 305, there is no recovery under section 303(i).[46]

An involuntary Chapter 7 case can be converted to a case under Chapter 11, 12, or 13. Section 706 allows conversion from Chapter 7 to Chapter 11, 12, or 13 as a matter of right. While the Code expressly provides for conversion of a case from one chapter to another, there is nothing in the Code or Rules that explains the procedure to convert an involuntary petition to a voluntary petition. It would seem that a debtor's motion to convert will not alone automatically transform an involuntary case into a voluntary one. Additionally, the debtor should file a voluntary petition—particularly if she is converting to Chapter 12 or 13 which do not permit involuntary cases.[47]

§ 2–6 Case Ancillary to a Foreign Proceeding

For full text of this section, see Epstein, Nickles & White, Bankruptcy, Practitioner Treatise Series, Vol. 1.

§ 2–7 Legal Consequences of Commencing a Case

The mere filing of a bankruptcy petition, voluntary or involuntary, has important legal consequences on both the debtor and creditors. The filing of

---

42. Dismissal and conversion of bankruptcy cases are more generally considered at §§ 2–9 through 2–19 infra.

43. Even with "consent of all petitioners and the debtor," dismissal of an involuntary petition requires notice and hearing. 11 U.S.C.A. § 303(j). This requirement protects other creditors from a collusive settlement.

44. See generally D. Pollard & J. Burton, Guide to Effective Bankruptcy Litigation § 5.08 (1988).

45. Section 305 is considered infra at § 2–10.

46. See In re Sun World Broadcasters, Inc., 5 B.R. 719 (Bankr. M.D.Fla.1980); In re Luftek, 6 B.R. 539 (Bankr. E.D.N.Y.1980).

47. See In re Longhorn 1979–II Drilling Program, 32 B.R. 923, 929 (W.D. Okla. 1983); but cf. In re Technical Fabricators, Inc., 65 B.R. 197, 199 (S.D. Ala.1986).

a *voluntary* bankruptcy petition effects the commencement of the case. The filing of a voluntary or involuntary bankruptcy petition triggers the automatic stay that bars creditors' collection efforts.[1] Claims against the debtor that arose before the filing of a bankruptcy petition are treated differently in bankruptcy than claims that arose after the bankruptcy petition.[2] Different Bankruptcy Code provisions govern the avoidance of prepetition and postpetition transactions.[3] And the commencement of the case creates an estate. The bankruptcy estate is considered below.

§ 2–8 Legal Consequences of Commencing a Case—Property of the Estate

a. *Importance of the Concept*

Section 541(a) provides that the filing of a bankruptcy petition automatically creates an estate. In a Chapter 7 case, "property of the estate" is collected by the bankruptcy trustee and sold; the proceeds from the sale of the property of the estate is then distributed to creditors. In other words, the loss of possession and ownership of property of the estate is the primary cost of a Chapter 7 bankruptcy case to the debtor, and the receipt of the proceeds from the sale of property of the estate is the primary benefit creditors receive from a Chapter 7 bankruptcy.

Generally, a Chapter 11 or 12 or 13 case does not result in the debtor's loss of possession or ownership of property of the estate. In most Chapter 11 and 12 cases, the debtor will retain and remain in possession of "property of the estate" as "debtor in possession." However, the Chapter 11 or Chapter 12 debtor in possession's use of the property of the estate will be subject to bankruptcy court supervision. While Chapter 13 contemplates that there will be a trustee in every case, a Chapter 13 trustee does not take possession of "property of the estate." A debtor who files for Chapter 13 relief retains possession of his property interests. Again, the use and sale of "property of the estate" is subject to the supervision of the bankruptcy court. Additionally, in Chapters 11, 12, and 13 cases, the value of the "property of the estate" determines the minimum amount that must be offered to holders of unsecured claims in the debtor's plan of repayment.

Finally, a number of general provisions in Chapters 3 and 5 of the Bankruptcy Code that are applicable in all bankruptcy cases use the phrase "property of the estate." For example, the automatic stay bars a creditor from collecting a claim from "property of the estate" in provisions such as section 362(a)(3).

In short, in all bankruptcy cases, it is necessary to know what property of the estate includes.

§ 2–7

1. We devote all of our Chapter 3 to the automatic stay.

2. Claims are discussed infra in Chapters 7, 10, and 11.

3. Our Chapter 6 covers the avoidance of transactions in bankruptcy.

b. Scope of Property of the Estate

With only minor exceptions, property of the estate includes all property interests of the debtor as of the time of the commencement of the bankruptcy case.

Section 541(a) in seven numbered subparagraphs identifies the property interests that become "property of the estate." Subparagraph 1 is by far the most comprehensive and significant. According to the legislative history, section 541(a)(1) "will bring everything of value that the debtor has into the estate." [1]

Section 541(a)(1) provides that "property of the estate" includes "all legal or equitable interests of the debtor in property as of the commencement of the case." Property of the estate thus includes both real property interests and personal property interests, both tangible and intangible property interests, both property in the debtor's possession and property that is held by others [2] in which the debtor has retained an interest.

The application in section 541(a)(1) involves three questions:

(1) Is the item in question "property" for purposes of section 541(a)(1)?

(2) If so, what is the debtor's interest in that property? (Note that section 541(a)(1) reaches merely the debtor's interest in property, rather than the debtor's property.)

(3) If so, did the debtor have this interest in the property as of the time of commencement of the bankruptcy case?

---

§ 2-8

1. H.R. Rep. 95-595, 95th Cong., 1st Sess. 176 (1977).

2. Generally, a third party who is in possession of property in which the debtor has an interest will be required to turn the property over to the debtor or the trustee when a bankruptcy petition is filed. Sections 542 and 543 govern such "turnovers." Section 543 covers a "custodian"; section 542 covers anyone other than a "custodian." Assume, for example, that S extended credit to D and obtained a security interest in D's inventory. D defaulted. S repossessed the inventory pursuant to section 9-503 of the Uniform Commercial Code. D filed for Chapter 11 relief. Under section 542, S will be compelled to return the inventory to D although S can demand adequate protection of its interest in the inventory. See In re Ayscue, 123 B.R. 28 (Bankr. E.D.Va.1990) (pledged collateral); In re Aegean Fare, Inc., 34 B.R. 965 (Bankr. Mass. 1983); see also 11 U.S.C.A. § 362(d)(1) (lift stay for lack of adequate protection). Section 542(a) compels the turnover of "property that the trustee may use, sell, or lease under section 363" "unless such property is of inconsequential value or benefit to the estate." What is the antecedent of the pronoun "such"? If it is "property that the trustee may use, sell, or lease under section 363," then it is necessary to look at section 363. Section 363 provides for the use, sale, or lease of "property of the estate." It is thus necessary to look at section 541 which describes property of the estate in terms of the "interests of the debtor in property." What is the interest of the debtor in inventory that has been pledged or repossessed? A right of redemption under section 9-506? A right to any surplus produced by a forced sale under 9-504? Are these rights of "inconsequential value" for purposes of section 542? The Supreme Court worked through these questions in United States v. Whiting Pools, Inc., 462 U.S. 198, 103 S.Ct. 2309, 76 L.Ed.2d 515 (1983), and concluded that section 542 requires that a creditor that seized its collateral prior to bankruptcy turn over the property to a Chapter 11 debtor. Whiting Pools involved a seizure by the IRS of property subject to a tax lien. It seems clear from dicta in Whiting Pools that the Court would reach a similar result if a private creditor seized property subject to its security interest. And, it seems clear from dicta in Whiting Pools and the language of section 542 that the Court would and should reach a different result in a Chapter 7 case. In the typical Chapter 7 case, the trustee is liquidating and so the property in the possession of a third party is not "property that the trustee may use, sell, or lease under section 363." See generally 1 R. Ginsberg, Bankruptcy § 5.04 (2d ed. 1989).

The question of what is property for purposes of section 541(a)(1) is a question of federal law. The Supreme Court considered the question of "property" under the Bankruptcy Act's counterpart to section 541, section 70a,[3] in the *Board of Trade of Chicago v. Johnson*.[4] There the "bankrupt" owned a membership on the Chicago Board of Trade. The issue before the Court was whether this CBT membership was property of the estate. The Illinois Supreme Court had earlier held that CBT memberships were not "property" for purposes of Illinois state law. In this case, the Supreme Court held that the CBT membership was "property of the estate" for purposes of bankruptcy law. In declining to limit the definition of property of the estate by state law property concepts, the Court stated:

> Congress derived its power to enact a bankruptcy law from the Federal Constitution, and the construction of it is a federal question. Of course, where the bankruptcy law deals with property rights which are regulated by the State law, the Federal courts in bankruptcy will follow the State Court; but when the language of Congress indicates a policy referring to broader construction of the statute than the state decisions were giving, federal courts cannot be concluded by them.[4.5]

While state law does not control the question of what is "property," bankruptcy courts look to state law in determining what is the debtor's interest in that property.[5] If, for example, a question arises in a bankruptcy case whether Blackacre belongs to the debtor who has been occupying it or to X who holds record title to Blackacre, the state law of adverse possession would and should answer the question. It is neither practical nor desirable for bankruptcy courts to formulate an entirely new law of property. Or new law of torts. Or new law of corporations. Courts are currently divided as to whether property of the estate of a debtor corporation includes that corporation's alter ego claims against its principals.[6] In determining whether the alter ego action is property of the estate, courts have looked to state corporate law to determine if a corporation has standing (i.e., an "interest in") to bring an alter ego cause or action or whether only creditors [7] of the corporation can assert the cause of action.

---

3. For a review of cases under section 70a, see Countryman, The Use of State Law in Bankruptcy Cases, 47 N.Y.U.L.Rev. 407, 431–473 (1972). Property of the estate under section 541 is significantly broader than under section 70a. For a comparison of the two provisions, see generally Aaron, The Bankruptcy Reform Act of 1978: The Full Employment for Lawyers Bill, 1979 Utah L. Rev. 405, 416–29.

4. 264 U.S. 1, 44 S.Ct. 232, 68 L.Ed. 533 (1924). For a case under section 541(a)(1) holding that a CBT seat is property of the estate, see In re Drexel Burnham Lambert Group Inc., 120 B.R. 724 (Bankr. S.D.N.Y. 1990).

4.5 Board of Trade of Chicago v. Johnson, 264 U.S. at 10, 44 S.Ct. at 234, 68 L.Ed at 536.

5. See Butner v. United States, 440 U.S. 48, 99 S.Ct. 914, 59 L.Ed.2d 136 (1979).

6. Compare In re Ozark Restaurant Equipment Co., 816 F.2d 1222 (8th Cir.1987), cert. denied, 484 U.S. 848, 108 S.Ct. 147, 98 L.Ed.2d 102 (1987) (Arkansas law would not permit a corporation to assert an alter ego action on its own behalf) with Koch Refining v. Farmer's Union Central Exchange, Inc., 831 F.2d 1339 (7th Cir. 1987), cert. denied, 485 U.S. 906, 108 S.Ct. 1077, 99 L.Ed.2d 237 (1988) (corporation could assert alter ego cause of action under Illinois and Indiana corporate law); see generally Epling, Trustee's Standing to Sue in Alter Ego or Other Damage Remedy Actions, 6 Bankr. Dev. J. 191 (1989).

7. The phrase "all legal or equitable interests of the debtor in property" in section 541 empowers the trustee to assert all of the debtor's causes of action. Section 544(b) permits the trustee to assert certain causes of action of certain creditors. The application of section 544(b) to alter ego causes of action is noted infra at § 6–61 n. 8.

Because property of the estate under section 541(a)(1) is limited to the interest of the debtor in property,[8] if the debtor is leasing the building at 191 Peachtree from its owner at the time of its bankruptcy filing, it is that leasehold interest and not the building that becomes property of the estate. Similarly, if the debtor is the sole stockholder of Acme Corporation at the time she files for bankruptcy, the property of the estate includes her Acme stock but not the assets of Acme Corporation. If the debtor owns Blackacre at bankruptcy but has executed a mortgage on Blackacre, then property of the estate includes Blackacre subject to the mortgage.[9] If the debtor and Gilligan own an island as tenants in common,[10] or tenants in the entirety,[11] only the debtor's limited interest in the island would be property of the estate.[12]

Note that in these hypotheticals, the debtor's property interest in 191 Peachtree, in Acme, in Blackacre, and in the island, existed as of the time of the filing of the petition. And recall that section 541(a)(1) contains the limiting phrase, "as of the time of the commencement of the case." Subject to significant exceptions discussed below, property of the estate is limited to the debtor's prepetition interests in property.

---

8. Property of the estate under section 541(a)(2), however, is not so limited. Section 541(a)(2) deals with community property. Even if only one spouse files, the interests of both spouses in community property becomes property of the estate if the debtor has any management or control over the property of if the property is subject to claims of the debtor's creditors or if the property is subject to the claims of the joint creditors of the husband and the wife. See In re Bartlett, 24 B.R. 605 (Bankr. 9th Cir.1982). Section 541(a)(2) should be read together with sections 101(7), 524(a)(3), and 726(c). Professor Hart summarizes these provisions as follows:

> Even if only one spouse is in bankruptcy, the general pattern of the Code is to bring all community property into the bankruptcy estate, to allow all community debts, including those incurred by the other spouse as claims, and to protect after-acquired community property from debts acquired prior to the bankruptcy * * *. The Code provides for marshalling of debts and claims so that separate debts are paid first out of separate property and community claims are paid first out of community property.

Hart, Commercial Law, 11 New Mexico L. Rev. 69, 70 (1981). Professor Hart's article provides a very helpful eight-page survey of the Bankruptcy Code's treatment of community property. For a much more extensive treatment of the topic, see Pedlar, Community Property and the Bankruptcy Reform Act of 1978, 11 St. Mary's L.J. 349 (1979).

9. In bankruptcy, some prepetition transactions that comply completely with nonbankruptcy law can be avoided. The avoiding powers are considered infra in our Chapter 6. If a bankruptcy trustee is able to avoid the mortgage on Blackacre, then an unencumbered Blackacre is the property of the estate. Property recovered by the trustee pursuant to the exercise of the avoidance powers becomes property of the estate, section 541(a)(3).

10. See In re Panholzer, 36 B.R. 647 (Bankr. Md.1984) (joint tenancy interest).

11. Napotnik v. Equibank & Parkvale Sav. Ass'n, 679 F.2d 316 (3d Cir.1982) (tenancy by the entirety). Napotnik and most of the reported cases involving tenancy by the entirety property deal primarily with the issue of whether the property is exempt. See 11 U.S.C.A. § 522(b)(2)(B); see generally Kalevitch, Some Thoughts on Entireties in Bankruptcy, 60 Am. Bankr. L.J. 141 (1986); Note, Estates By The Entirety in Bankruptcy, 15 J.L. Ref. 399 (1982). Under section 522(b)(2)(B), a debtor may exempt any interest in entirety property to the extent that creditors can not reach that property under state law.

12. Under certain circumstances, a bankruptcy trustee can sell encumbered property free and clear of encumbrances. See 11 U.S.C.A. § 363(f); see generally Note, Selling Out Undersecured Creditors: "Value" Under Section 363(f) of the Bankruptcy Code, 8 Cardozo L. Rev. 1251 (1987). Similarly, under certain circumstances, a bankruptcy trustee can sell property only partially owned by the debtor. See 11 U.S.C.A. § 363(h). If the four numbered conditions in section 363(h) are satisfied, the trustee can sell not only the interest of the debtor but also the interest of the nondebtor.

Sometimes it is not obvious whether an interest in property is prepetition or postpetition. The time of payment to or realization by the debtor should not be and is not controlling. Tax benefits that result from a debtor's prepetition losses but realizable, if at all, only in postpetition tax years have been held to be property of the estate.[13] Similarly, fees that a debtor receives postpetition for services performed prepetition are property of the estate.[14]

c. Postpetition Property as Property of the Estate

While generally property of the estate is limited to the interests of the debtor as of the time of the filing of the bankruptcy petition, certain postpetition property is property of the estate. There are five significant statutory exceptions to the general proposition that property of the estate is limited to prepetition property.

The first exception applies only in Chapter 12 and Chapter 13 cases. Under section 1207(a) and section 1306, a Chapter 12 or 13 debtor's postpetition income earned or property acquired before the case is closed, dismissed, or converted is property of the estate. If D files for Chapter 13 relief on January 15 and wins $20,000 in a lottery on April 5, her postpetition earnings and her lottery prize will be property of the estate.[15] If D's Chapter 13 case is converted to Chapter 7 on June 6, her post-June 6 earnings will *not* be property of the estate. Courts are divided as to whether her January 15 to June 6 earnings and property will continue to be property of the estate in the Chapter 7 case.[16]

Second, under section 541(a)(3) and (4), property recovered or preserved pursuant to the avoiding or recovery powers is property of the estate.[17] Assume, for example, that D, while insolvent, gave $100,000 to her son. D later filed for bankruptcy. If, after bankruptcy, the gift of $100,000 is avoided as a fraudulent conveyance, the $100,000 would become property of the estate.

Third, section 541(a)(5) includes property that the debtor acquires or "becomes entitled to acquire" within 180 days after the petition by (i) bequest, devise or inheritance;[18] (ii) property settlement or divorce decree, or

---

13. See, e.g., Kokoszka v. Belford, 417 U.S. 642, 94 S.Ct. 2431, 41 L.Ed.2d 374 (1974), reh'g denied 419 U.S. 886, 95 S.Ct. 160, 42 L.Ed.2d 131 (1974) (tax refund); Segal v. Rochelle, 382 U.S. 375, 86 S.Ct. 511, 15 L.Ed.2d 428 (1966) (NOL carryback); In re Prudential Lines Inc., 928 F.2d 565 (2d Cir.1991), cert. denied, ___ U.S. ___, 112 S.Ct. 82, 116 L.Ed.2d 55 (1991) (NOL carryforward); cf. 11 U.S.C.A. § 346(i).

14. In re Calder, 94 B.R. 200 (Bankr. Utah 1988), appeal decided, 912 F.2d 454 (10th Cir. 1990) (fees an attorney received postpetition for prepetition work). Fees that a debtor receives postpetition for services that are performed in part prepetition and in part postpetition present much harder problems—require interpretation of section 541(a)(6) and balancing Congress' intention "to bring anything of value into the estate" with the fundamental bankruptcy policy of a fresh start for an individual debtor who receives a bankruptcy discharge. See infra § 2–8(d).

15. Cf. In re Koonce, 54 B.R. 643 (Bankr. S.C.1985).

16. See infra § 2–17(a).

17. Recovery from and preservation of avoided transfers are dealt with in sections 550 and 551. Sections 550 and 551 are dealt with infra at §§ 6–86—6–90.

18. Postpetition rejection of an inheritance can be challenged under section 549. See In re Watson, 65 B.R. 9 (Bankr. C.D.Ill. 1986).

(iii) as beneficiary of a life insurance policy.[19]

Fourth under section 541(a)(6), property of the estate includes property received from a conversion of property of the estate. To illustrate, D owns Blackacre at the time he files for bankruptcy. After filing for bankruptcy, D sells Blackacre to X for $100,000. The $100,000 is property of the estate.[20] Similarly, D owns the Blackacre Bar and Grill at the time of her Chapter 11 filing. Postpetition, Blackacre Bar and Grill is destroyed in a fire, and D receives $100,000 pursuant to a fire insurance policy that she had obtained prepetition. The $100,000 is property of the estate.[21]

Fifth, under section 541(a)(6) and (7) property of the estate includes rents, profits, and earnings of or from property of the estate. If D's book is published by West before he files for bankruptcy, his postpetition royalties from the book are property of the estate. The postpetition rents that D receives from buildings that D owned when he filed for bankruptcy are property of the estate. The postpetition earnings of D Corp. from its business operations would be property of the estate.

d. *Individual Debtor's Postpetition Earnings in Chapter 7 or 11 Cases* [22]

One of the fundamental purposes of bankruptcy law is to provide a "fresh start" for individual debtors. Section 541(a)(6) reflects this fundamental policy. Under section 541(a)(6) "earnings from services performed by an individual debtor after the commencement of the case" are *excepted* from property of the estate.

The application of this section 541(a)(6) exception of postpetition "earnings from services performed by an individual debtor" is difficult in situations involving either (1) *post* petition earnings that are attributable in part to *pre* petition services and in part to *post* petition services or (2) *post* petition earnings that are attributable in part to *pre* petition property and in part to *post* petition services.

Assume, for example, that D is an insurance agent. She sells term life insurance policies. D receives a commission when she sells such a policy and an additional commission each time the term life insurance policy is renewed. D files for bankruptcy. Are her postpetition renewal commissions property of the estate? If the sale of the policy took place before D's bankruptcy but the renewal occurred after D's filing, is the renewal commission property of the estate? Arguably, D's right to the renewal commission was, at least in part, earned by D's prepetition efforts in selling the policy. Arguably, only a part of the postpetition renewal commissions qualifies for the section 541(a)(6) exception from property of the estate for "earnings from services performed by an individual debtor after the commencement of the

---

19. Section 541(a)(5) should be read together with Rule 1007(h) which requires the debtor to notify the court of the new property interest.

20. Blackacre also might be property of the estate. If the trustee is able to avoid the postpetition transfer under section 549, considered infra at § ___, Blackacre will be property of the estate. 11 U.S.C.A. § 541(a)(3).

21. See Practitioner Treatise, Vol. 1.

22. Recall that in a Chapter 12 case or a Chapter 13 case, postpetition earnings are expressly included in property of the estate by section 1207 or section 1306.

case." Arguably, only a part of the renewal commission should be allocated to property of the estate.

Courts, however, have generally rejected the argument that a part of postpetition earnings attributable to both prepetition and postpetition services performed by an individual debtor should be allocated to property of the estate. In cases involving an insurance agent's renewal commissions, courts have generally excepted from property of the estate all postpetition commissions if the debtor's receipt of the renewal commission requires her to continue to service the policy or even to continue to work as an insurance agent.[23]

Similarly, the Seventh Circuit held in *In re Haynes*,[24] that all of the postpetition retirement pay of a retired naval officer was excluded from property of the estate by section 541(a)(6). In concluding that the retirement benefits were not part of the bankruptcy estate, the court in *Haynes* focused on the continuing obligations imposed on a military retiree as conditions of receipt of retirement benefits.[25] In *Haynes,* as is in the insurance renewal commissions cases, the courts relied on the "services performed by an individual debtor after the commencement of the case" and disregarded the services performed by an individual debtor before the commencement of the case.

Decisions such as *Haynes* are consistent with the approach taken by the Supreme Court in property of the estate cases under section 70a of the Bankruptcy Act of 1898. For example, in *Lines v. Frederick*,[26] the Court held that the debtor's vacation pay that (i) was earned before his bankruptcy filing but (ii) collectible only after the bankruptcy filing was not property of the estate.[27] In determining whether the debtor's rights to earned but unpaid vacation pay was property of the estate, the Court did not look to the language of the Bankruptcy Act in section 70a or elsewhere; instead the Court looked to the purposes of the Bankruptcy Act, particularly the purpose of a fresh start for individual debtors. The Court stated "the function of the accrued vacation pay is to support the basic requirements of life for them and their families during brief vacation period or in the event of layoff * * *. The wage earning bankrupt who must take a vacation without pay or forego a vacation altogether cannot be said to have achieved the 'new opportunity in life and the clear field for future effort, unhampered by the pressure and discouragement of preexisting debt' which it was the purpose of the statute to provide." [28]

While *Haynes* and the renewal commission cases are consistent with cases under section 70a of the Bankruptcy Act, they seem inconsistent with

---

23. See In re Rankin, 102 B.R. 439 (Bankr. W.D.Pa.1989); In re Hodgson, 54 B.R. 688 (Bankr. W.D. Wisc.1985); In re Kervin, 19 B.R. 190 (Bankr. S.D. Ala.1982); In re Selner, 18 B.R. 420 (Bankr. S.D.Fla.1982); contra, In re Froid, 109 B.R. 481 (Bankr. M.D.Fla.1989).

24. 679 F.2d 718 (7th Cir.1982), cert. denied, 459 U.S. 970, 103 S.Ct. 299, 74 L.Ed.2d 281 (1982).

25. The court noted that a military retiree remains subject to the Uniform Military Code of Justice and can be called to active duty in time of war or national emergency.

26. 400 U.S. 18, 91 S.Ct. 113, 27 L.Ed.2d 124 (1970).

27. In Lines, the vacation pay was collectible after the bankruptcy filing either during the employer's annual shut down for vacation or on the final termination of the debtor's employment.

28. 400 U.S. at 20, 91 S.Ct. at 114, 27 L.Ed. at 127.

section 541.[29] We read the Bankruptcy Code as requiring an allocation of at least a part of an individual debtor's postpetition earnings to property of the estate where the earnings are at least in part attributable to the debtor's prepetition services. In applying the Bankruptcy Code to such earnings, we look at the word "any" in section 541(a)(1) which suggests that the concept of property of the estate is comprehensive and all inclusive and the word "from" in section 541(a)(6) which indicates that the postpetition earnings exception from property of the estate involves attribution or allocation.[30]

We also look to the word "any" in section 541(a)(1) and the word "from" in section 541(a)(6) in concluding that the Bankruptcy Code requires allocating a part of an individual debtor's postpetition earnings to property of the estate where the earnings are in part attributable to that individual debtor's postpetition services and in part attributable to that individual debtor's prepetition property. The Ninth Circuit required such an allocation in *In re Fitzsimmons*.[31]

Fitzsimmons was the Chapter 11 case of an individual lawyer who practiced law as a sole proprietorship, employing other lawyers, paralegals, and secretaries. A trustee was appointed. The trustee and Fitzsimmons then litigated the question of whether Fitzsimmons individually or the bankruptcy estate was entitled to the earnings from the law practice. The Seventh Circuit held that the earnings had to be allocated:

> "His contention that all the earnings of a sole proprietorship constitute 'earnings from services performed by an individual debtor' and are excluded from the estate means that the estate—and the creditors who look to the estate for satisfaction of their claims—would not enjoy the benefit of any profits earned by a sole proprietorship operated under Chapter 11. This contrasts with the situation that prevails when the debtor business is a partnership or a corporation. In those cases, there is no 'individual debtor' so the earnings exception is not applicable and the earnings of the business all accrue to the estate under § 541(a)(6). At the same time, although Fitzsimmons maintains that the estate should not enjoy the profits earned by a sole proprietorship operated under § 1108, any losses suffered by such a sole proprietorship would be borne by the estate, since such losses would reduce the value of the estate's assets.
>
> We do not believe that Congress intended such an anomalous result. To avoid it, we hold that § 541(a)(6) excepts from the proceeds of the estate only those earnings generated by services personally performed by the individual debtor. Fitzsimmons is thus entitled to monies generated by his law practice only to the extent that they are attributable to personal services that he himself performs. To the extent that the law

---

29. While the Haynes result is inconsistent with the language Congress used in section 541, it is probably consistent with Congressional intent. Congress intended that Commander Haynes would be able to retain his retirement benefits as exempt property under section 522(d)(10). As a result of a last minute compromise, states were allowed to "opt out" of section 522(d).

30. We also look at the legislative history that expressly states that section 541 is intended to overrule Lines v. Frederick. See S. Rep. 95–989, 95th Cong., 2d Sess. 82 (1978); H. R. Rep. No. 95–595, 1st Sess. 367–68 (1977); but cf. Eisenberg, Bankruptcy Law in Perspective, 28 UCLA L. Rev. 953, 972, n. 60 (1981).

31. 725 F.2d 1208 (9th Cir.1984).

practice's earnings are attributable not to Fitzsimmons' personal services but to the business' invested capital, accounts receivable, good will, employment contracts with the firm's staff, client relationships, fee agreements, or the like, the earnings of the law practice accrue to the estate.[32]

Several later bankruptcy court decisions expressly reject *Fitzsimmons*.[33] The Seventh Circuit's decision in *Fitzsimmons* can and has been criticized as unworkable [34] and inconsistent with the language of section 541(a)(6).[35] While there is merit in this criticism of *Fitzsimmons,* we believe that a part of an individual debtor's earnings that are attributable to both her postpetition services and to prepetition property must be allocated to property of the estate in a Chapter 11 case [36]. Creditors of a corporate or a partnership debtor share in the earnings and losses of the debtor. Creditors of a sole proprietorship debtor share in the losses of the debtor. Creditors of a sole proprietorship debtor should also share in the earnings of the debtor. As Judge Leif Clark stated in *In re Herberman*,[37]

> Were the debtor a corporation wholly owned by an individual who also served as the corporation's principal employee, we would not question a creditor's challenging the wages which that person was drawing out of the debtor corporation. That the enterprise which files bankruptcy happens to be a sole proprietorship rather than a corporation should not make a difference.[38]

e. *Other Statutory Exclusions From Property of the Estate*

The statement in section 541(a)(1) that all legal and equitable interests of the debtor in property as of the commencement of the case are property of

---

32. Id. at 1211.

33. See In re Altchek, 124 B.R. 944 (Bankr. S.D.N.Y. 1991); In re Cooley, 87 B.R. 432 (Bankr. S.D. Texas 1988); In re Herberman, 122 B.R. 273 (Bankr. W.D. Texas 1990); see generally Pitts, Rights to Future Payment as Property of the Estate in Bankruptcy, 64 Am. Bankr. L.J. 61 (1990).

34. Pitts, Rights to Future Payment as Property of the Estate in Bankruptcy, 64 Am. Bankr. L.J. 61, 71–73 (1990).

35. "The role of Subsection (a)(6) is restricted to a discussion of proceeds, etc. 'of or from property of the estate.' The exception clause is contained within this provision and commences 'except such as are earnings from services performed * * * .' The word 'such' can only refer to the 'proceeds (etc.) of or from property of the estate' referenced in the first part of the subsection. Earnings from services which are not proceeds, etc. of or from property of the estate in the first place are not governed by the exception clause in subsection (a)(6)." In re Herberman, 122 B.R. 273, 278 (Bankr. W.D. Texas 1990).

36. Problems of postpetition earnings that are attributable to both prepetition property and postpetition services performed by an individual debtor arise primarily in Chapter 11 cases. As originally proposed, the exception for earnings from postpetition service was limited to Chapter 7 cases. See Report of the Commission on Bankruptcy Laws of the United States, H.R. No. 93–197, 93rd Cong., 1st Sess. 195 (1973).

37. 122 B.R. 273 (Bankr. W.D. Texas 1990). The bankruptcy concept of discharge and the bankruptcy policy of fresh start are not reasons for distinguishing between corporations and sole proprietorships on this question. Remember, the question is whether the debtor is able to retain all postpetition earnings that are attributable both to prepetition property of the estate and to services performed by the individual debtor in the gap between the filing of a Chapter 11 petition and the confirmation of a Chapter 11 plan. (Confirmation vests the property back in the debtor, section 1141). In Chapter 11, both debtors that are corporations and debtors that are individuals operating sole proprietorship can receive a discharge. And, in Chapter 11, a debtor can not receive a discharge until the plan has been confirmed.

38. Id. at 282.

the estate is prefaced by an exception for exclusions from property of the estate contained in section 541(b) and (c)(2).[39] Section 541(b)(1) excludes any power that the debtor can exercise only for someone else's benefit. For example, if the debtor has a power of appointment under a will that prohibits appointment to the debtor or her estate, that power of appointment is not property of the estate. Section 541(b)(3), added in 1990, is of even more limited significance, excluding accreditation status as an educational institution and rights to participate under certain Higher Education Act programs from property of the estate. And, section 541(b)(2), added in 1984, is of *no* significance. It excludes nonresidential real property leases that terminated prior to the bankruptcy filing from property of the estate. If a lease terminated prior to the bankruptcy filing—whether it is residential, nonresidential, or equipment—there is no interest of the debtor in property to become property of the estate under section 541(a)(1).

The property of the estate exclusion in section 541(c)(2) is arguably significant. Section 541(c)(2) excludes the debtor's beneficial interest in a trust from property of the estate if that interest is subject to restrictions on transfer that are enforceable under nonbankruptcy law. The language of section 541(c)(2) is arguably broad enough to exclude the debtor's interest in an ERISA pension plan from property of the estate. Such arguments, however, have generally been rejected by courts which instead limit section 541(c)(2) to traditional spendthrift trusts; such arguments are considered in our chapter on exemptions later in this book.[40]

f. *Effect of Transfer Restrictions on Property of the Estate*

As the facts of *Chicago Board of Trade* illustrate, private parties sometimes contract to prevent transfers of property interests. Additionally, governmental entities sometimes legislate or regulate against the transfer of property interests. Such transfer restrictions raise two separate and distinct questions:

1. Does the transfer restriction prevent the debtor's interest in the property from becoming property of the estate?

2. Does the transfer restriction prevent the trustee or debtor in possession from later transferring the property to some third party?

Section 541(c)(1)(A) deals only with the first of these two questions.

Section 541(c)(1) generally provides that the interest of the debtor in property becomes property of the state notwithstanding a transfer restriction in an agreement or in applicable non-bankruptcy law. The rule of section 541(c)(1) is consistent with one of the conclusions of the Supreme Court in the *Chicago Board of Trade v. Johnson*[41] case. Recall, the debtor there had a seat on the Chicago Board of Trade. The bankruptcy trustee wanted to sell the seat for cash. A rule of the Chicago Board of Trade provided that members could transfer their seats only after they paid

---

39. See Practitioner Treatise, Vol. 1.
40. See Practitioner Treatise, Vol. 1.
41. 264 U.S. 1, 44 S.Ct. 232, 68 L.Ed. 533 (1924). The rule of section 541(c) for interests in property is generally consistent with the rules for executory contracts in section 365(e), (f).

everything they owed to other board members as well as all they owed to the Board itself. Notwithstanding these transfer restrictions, the Supreme Court, applying Section 70a of the Bankruptcy Act of 1898, held that the seat was property of the estate. A court, applying section 541(c)(1), should similarly hold.

Courts have applied section 541(c)(1) to liquor licenses more often than to Board of Exchange seats.[42] In the liquor license cases, the transfer restrictions are imposed by state legislation or regulation,[43] rather than by private party contracts.

Generally, a liquor store's right to transfer its license is restricted by state law that prohibits the transfer of the license if the store owes any taxes to the state based on transactions involving the sale of liquor. Courts have applied Section 541(c)(1) to hold that a liquor license is property of the estate notwithstanding outstanding taxes and such a state law requirement.

Again, that section 541(c)(1) simply answers one of the two questions presented by transfer restrictions: section 541(c)(1) simply determines that contractual and statutory restrictions on transfer do not prevent property from becoming property of the estate. Section 541(c)(1) does not deal with the related, yet separate, question of whether the transfer restrictions will apply to the trustee in bankruptcy when she sells the property.

In *Chicago Board of Trade*, the Court answered this second question by concluding that the transfer restriction applied to a transfer of the board seat by the trustee to a third party. Such a result is consistent with the general concept that the trustee takes only the debtor's interest in property and the general rule that while bankruptcy law determines what is "an interest in property" nonbankruptcy law determines the attributes of that property interest.

Liquor license cases under section 541(c)(1) have reached similar results. For example, in *In re Farmers Markets, Inc.*,[44] the Ninth Circuit held that a debtor's liquor license became property of the estate notwithstanding state regulatory transfer restrictions, but it was property of the estate "subject to the restrictions imposed on the debtor by its transferor." The court concluded that the State of California had a first claim to the proceeds received when the estate transferred the license to a third party.[45]

B. DISMISSAL

The bankruptcy court can dismiss a voluntary bankruptcy case even though it was filed by an eligible debtor. And, the bankruptcy court can dismiss an involuntary case even though all of the requirements of section 303 are satisfied.

---

42. See In re Terwilliger's Catering Plus, Inc., 911 F.2d 1168 (6th Cir.1990), cert. denied, ___ U.S. ___, 111 S.Ct. 2815, 115 L.Ed.2d 987 (1991); In re Farmers Markets, Inc., 792 F.2d 1400 (9th Cir.1986); In re Hoffman, 65 B.R. 985 (D.R.I.1986); In re Miller, 68 B.R. 385 (Bankr. W.D.Pa.1986).

43. State statutes that condition transfers on payments of taxes and fees raise issues under section 545 and 507. Does the state statute create a statutory lien that meets the requirements of section 545 or does the state statute create a mere priority that is preempted by the Bankruptcy Code's priorities in section 507?

44. 792 F.2d 1400 (9th Cir.1986).

45. Id. at 1403.

A lawyer or law student needs to be able to answer the following questions about dismissal of a bankruptcy case:

(1) Who can cause the dismissal of a bankruptcy case?

(2) What are the effects of dismissal?

(3) What are the grounds for dismissal?

§ 2–9 Who Can Cause Dismissal

Dismissal is generally "caused" by a motion filed by the debtor, creditor or trustee. Although the Code and the Bankruptcy Rules seem to require a hearing on a motion to dismiss, most bankruptcy judges hold a formal hearing on a motion to dismiss only if a party so requests.[1] The bankruptcy court can act *sua sponte* in dismissing a bankruptcy petition.[2]

§ 2–10 Abstention, Section 305

Section 305 empowers the court, after notice and hearing, to dismiss a case filed under section 301, section 302, section 303, or section 304 or to suspend proceedings in such a case. Dismissal or suspension under section 305 is not reviewable in any manner. The ground for dismissing or suspending a case filed under section 301, section 302, or section 303 is "the interests of creditors and the debtor would be better served by such dismissal or suspension."[1]

When will dismissal be beneficial to both the creditors and the debtor? The legislative history offers the example of an involuntary petition filed by creditors seeking to obstruct a workout,[2] and there are cases that seek to limit section 305 dismissal to that fact pattern,[3] or, at least, to involuntary cases. As the court in *In re Pine Lake Village Apartment Co.*[4] reasoned, dismissal under section 305 must benefit the debtor as well as creditors and the interests of a debtor will not be "better served" by denying that debtor the relief it just requested.[5]

§ 2–11 Consequences of Dismissal

a. Past Actions

Section 349 deals with the consequences of dismissal. Unless the court orders otherwise, dismissal vacates orders issued during the bankruptcy case

§ 2–9

1. Cf. 11 U.S.C.A. § 102.

2. See, e.g., In re Chandler, 89 B.R. 1002 (Bankr. N.D.Ga.1988); In re Brown, 88 B.R. 280 (Bankr. Haw. 1988); cf. 11 U.S.C.A. § 105(a). The holding of In re Gusam Restaurant Corp., 737 F.2d 274 (2d Cir. 1984), is that a bankruptcy court has no power to dismiss a case sua sponte. After the Gusam decision, the 1986 Amendments added the second sentence to section 105(a).

§ 2–10

1. Abstention in a section 304 case ancillary to a foreign proceeding turns on the six factors in section 304(c). 11 U.S.C.A. § 305(2)(B); In re Axona International Credit & Commerce Ltd., 88 B.R. 597 (Bankr. S.D.N.Y. 1988), decision aff'd, 115 B.R. 442 (S.D.N.Y.1990), appeal dism'd, 924 F.2d 31 (2d Cir.1991).

2. H.R. Rep. 95–595, 1st Sess. 325 (1978); S. Rep. 989, 95th Cong., 2d Sess., 36 (1978).

3. See In re RAI Marketing Services, Inc., 20 B.R. 943 (Bankr. Kan.1982).

4. 16 B.R. 750 (Bankr. S.D.N.Y. 1982).

5. See also In re G–N Partners, 48 B.R. 459 (Bankr. Minn.1985); R. Ginsberg, Bankruptcy, 2034 (1985); G. Treister, J.R. Trost, L. Forman, K. Klee, R. Levin, Fundamentals of Bankruptcy Law, 117 (2d ed. 1988); Rowin, Abstention Under Section 305: When Is It Appropriate?, 59 Am. Bankr. L.J. 89 (1983); contra In re The Fax Station, Inc., 118 B.R. 176 (Bankr. R.I.1990); In re Colonial Ford, Inc., 24 B.R. 1014 (Bankr. Utah 1982).

and restores the debtor and creditors to their prepetition positions.[1] If another bankruptcy petition is later filed, the date of the later petition becomes the relevant date in applying various Code provisions such as section 547's 90–day preference rule.[2]

Assume, for example, that D pays one of its creditors, X, $50,000 on 1/15/91; D then files for bankruptcy on 2/2/91. The bankruptcy trustee recovers the $50,000 payment from creditor X on 3/3 as a preferential transfer. Dismissal of D's bankruptcy case will "reinstate" the $50,000 payment to X unless the court orders otherwise. If D later files a bankruptcy petition on 3/3/91, D will *not* be able to recover the 1/15/91 payment as a preference.[3]

b. *Future Actions*

A dismissal is usually without prejudice: the debtor or petitioning creditors can refile.[4] In *In re Frieouf*,[5] the Tenth Circuit reversed a bankruptcy court order that dismissed a case with prejudice to the filing of any bankruptcy petition by the debtor for three years. In so ruling, Judge Seth read section 349(a) as instructed by the Supreme Court in *Ron Pair Enterprises*,[6] and concluded that

> section 349(a) must be read as allowing a bankruptcy court, "for cause" to permanently disqualify a class of debts from discharge but a bankruptcy court may not deny future access to bankruptcy court, except under the circumstances of section 109(g). Any other reading of section 349(a) is contrary to the language and punctuation used by Congress.[7]

The *Frieouf* opinion does not expressly consider whether section 105 empowers a bankruptcy court to dismiss a case with prejudice to future bankruptcy filings.[8]

---

§ 2–11

1. 11 U.S.C.A. § 349(b); see generally D. Pollard & J. Burton, Guide to Effective Bankruptcy Litigation § 19.03 (1988).

2. Note this important difference between dismissal and conversion. A case converted from one chapter to another generally retains the original filing date. See 11 U.S.C.A. § 348(a).

3. Cf. In re Sadler, 935 F.2d 918 (7th Cir. 1991).

4. While a dismissal is generally without prejudice, there are both statutory and judicial exceptions. Section 109(f) describes two situations in which dismissal is with prejudice in the sense that the debtor is barred from any kind of bankruptcy petition for 180 days. And, there are cases where the debtor's conduct (or lack of conduct) caused the court to condition the dismissal so as to prevent immediate refiling or to preclude later discharge of the debts scheduled in the dismissed case.

See, e.g., In re Dilley, 125 B.R. 189, 197 (Bankr. N.D.Ohio 1991) (one year); In re Hundley, 103 B.R. 768 (Bankr. E.D.Va.1989) (one year).

5. 938 F.2d 1099 (10th Cir.1991).

6. United States v. Ron Pair Enterprises, Inc., 489 U.S. 235, 109 S.Ct. 1026, 103 L.Ed.2d 290 (1989), on remand, 872 F.2d 778 (6th Cir. 1989), summarized supra in § 1–3(a).

7. In re Frieouf, 938 F.2d 1099, 1103 (10th Cir.1991). Section 349(a) consists of two clauses connected with a semicolon. The first clause deals with discharge in a later case of the debts from the dismissed case; the second clause deals with the filing of a later bankruptcy petition. The phrase "Unless the court for cause orders otherwise" appears only at the beginning of the first clause.

8. Cf. Lerch v. Federal Land Bank, 94 B.R. 998, 1000 (N.D.Ill. 1989). Frieouf expressly considered and rejected Lerch because it "dis-

§ 2-12 Grounds for Dismissal

Each bankruptcy relief chapter has its own dismissal provision: sections 707, 1112, 1208, and 1307. Under all of the provisions, involuntary dismissal requires a showing of "cause." Each of the sections lists circumstances constituting cause for dismissal; each of these lists is non-exclusive.

The ability of a debtor to effect a dismissal of her bankruptcy case varies from chapter to chapter. Chapters 7 and 11 treat voluntary dismissal the same as involuntary: a debtor who has filed for relief under Chapter 7 or Chapter 11 must establish "cause" in order to dismiss. A debtor who has filed for relief under Chapter 12 or Chapter 13 has a right to dismiss without first establishing cause.

§ 2-13 Voluntary Dismissal

For full text of this section, see Epstein, Nickles & White, Bankruptcy, Practitioner Treatise Series, Vol. 1.

a. Chapter 7 and Chapter 11

b. Chapters 12 and 13

§ 2-14 Dismissal of Certain Consumer Chapter 7 Cases for "Substantial Abuse"

The 1984 Amendments to the Bankruptcy Code added a ground for dismissal of Chapter 7 cases involving individual debtors owing primarily consumer debts. Acting *sua sponte* or on motion of the United States trustee,[1] the court can dismiss such a consumer Chapter 7 case if it finds that the granting of relief would be a "substantial abuse" of the provisions of Chapter 7.

Congress's purpose in enacting section 707(b) was to preclude individuals from using Chapter 7 who have the ability to make meaningful payments to their creditors. The language used by Congress in section 707(b) limits its usefulness. Section 707(b)'s "substantial abuse" standard can only be applied if the debts in the bankruptcy case are "primarily consumer debts." "Consumer debt" is defined in section 101(8) as a "debt incurred by an individual primarily for a personal, family, or household purpose." Under the language of this definition and the reported cases applying it, section 707(b) can not be used to dismiss a Chapter 7 bankruptcy filed by a wealthy individual such as a doctor or general manager of WSIX in Nashville whose debts arise primarily from bad investments even though such an individual is earning more than $200,000 a year.

While the Bankruptcy Code defines "consumer debt,"[2] the other critical section 707(b) term "substantial abuse" is not statutorily defined. "Substan-

---

regarded the binary structure of section 349(a) as reflected by both its punctuation and substantive content." Frieouf did not expressly consider Lerch's consideration of section 105.

§ 2-14

1. See Practitioner Treatise, Vol. 1.

2. 11 U.S.C.A. § 101(8). In re Booth, 858 F.2d 1051 (5th Cir.1988), held that the district court had erred in classifying all loans secured by the debtor's residence as consumer "debt." Looking to decisions under the Truth in Lending Law and earlier bankruptcy court decisions, the Fifth Circuit held that the test for

tial abuse" has been widely and variously interpreted by the courts. It is clear from the case law and from the legislative history that the debtor's ability to pay her debts is the most important factor in determining whether her Chapter 7 filing constitutes "substantial abuse"; it is not clear whether the debtor's ability to pay is the only relevant factor.[3] There is a line of cases holding that a showing of the debtor's ability to pay a significant part of her debts without undue hardship establishes substantial abuse.[4] Such an interpretation compels debtors with discretionary income to choose Chapter 13 or be denied bankruptcy relief. Congress has consistently rejected proposals for "mandatory" Chapter 13.[5] Another view is that ability to pay creditors is not in and of itself sufficient to establish substantial abuse.[6] As Judge Sam Erwin, Jr. stated in *In re Green*,

> [A] totality of the circumstances analysis is much to be preferred to the application of a per se rule not only because it better accords with what we know of Congressional thinking surrounding the adoption of section 707(b) but also because it is consistent with the statutory presumption in favor of granting the relief requested by the debtor.[7]

§ 2–15 Creditors' Motions to Dismiss a Chapter 11 Petition for Lack of Good Faith

The Bankruptcy Act of 1898 expressly required that a petition for reorganization under Chapter X be filed in "good faith."[1] The Bankruptcy Code expressly requires "good faith" from debtors filing for relief under Chapter 9.[2] And, "good faith" is a confirmation requirement in Chapters 11, 12, and 13.[3] Congress did not, however, retain the statutory requirement that petitions for reorganization be filed in good faith or list "good faith" as one of the examples of "cause" for dismissal in the Chapter 11 dismissal provision. Indeed, the examples of cause in section 1112 are based on the

classifying a debt as a consumer debt for purposes of section 707(b) is "whether it was incurred with an eye toward profit." In In re Manning, 126 B.R. 984 (M.D.Tenn.1991), the district court reversed a bankruptcy court's use of section 707(b) to dismiss a Chapter 7 case filed by a radio station manager whose debts were attributable primarily to his investments in his sister's business. The bankruptcy judge had relied on Truth in Lending law and the debtor's purpose of helping his sister. In reversing, Judge Wiseman stated, "To hold that an investment debt may be classified as a consumer debt would stand the English language on its ear." Contra In re Berndt, 127 B.R. 222 (Bankr. N.D.1991).

3. See generally Breitowitz, New Developments in Consumer Bankruptcy Chapter 7 Dismissal on the Basis of "Substantial Abuse", 59 Am. Bankr L. 327 (1985); Wells, Kurtz, and Calhoun, The Implementation of Bankruptcy Code Section 707(b): The Law and the Reality, 39 Cleve. St. L. Rev. 15 (1991); Young, The Increasing Impact of Bankruptcy Code Section 707(b), 49 Bus. Law 2043 (1990).

4. See, e.g., In re Walton, 866 F.2d 981 (8th Cir.1989); In re Kelly, 841 F.2d 908 (9th Cir. 1988); In In re Strong, 84 B.R. 541 (Bankr. N.D.Ind. 1988), the court looked to the earnings of both the debtor and the nondebtor spouse.

5. In re Walton, 866 F.2d 981, 986–87 (8th Cir.1989).

6. In re Green, 934 F.2d 568 (4th Cir.1991); accord Gross, Preserving a Fresh Start for the Individual Debtor, 135 U.Pa.L.Rev. 59, 101 (1986).

7. 934 F.2d at 572–73.

§ 2–15

1. Chapter X of the Bankruptcy Act required good faith in filing in section 141.

2. Section 921 provides for dismissal of a Chapter 9 case "if the debtor did not file the petition in good faith."

3. See 11 U.S.C.A. §§ 1129(a)(3), 1225(a)(3), 1325(a)(3).

debtor's postpetition actions and in actions.[4] Nevertheless, in ruling on motions to dismiss, bankruptcy courts continue to consider the motives of debtors who file voluntary petitions for reorganization under Chapter 11.[5] The justification most often relied on was offered initially in *In re Northwest Recreational Activities, Inc.*[6]:

> Good faith * * * is merged into the power of the court to protect its jurisdictional integrity from schemes of improper petitioners seeking to circumvent jurisdictional restrictions and from petitioners with demonstrable frivolous purposes absent any economic reality.[7]

While it is clear that bankruptcy courts can and will dismiss a Chapter 11 petition because of the debtor's lack of "good faith" in filing, it is not clear what standards a bankruptcy court will apply. Two recent circuit court decisions, *In re Phoenix Piccadilly, Ltd.*,[8] and *Carolin Corp. v. Miller*[9] represent two very different tests. *Phoenix Piccadilly* looked solely to the debtor's intentions in filing—to "subjective good faith." The Eleventh Circuit identified six "circumstantial factors" which evidence bad faith filing.[10] *Carolin Corp.*, on the other hand, required not only subjective bad faith but also "objective futility"—whether there is reasonable prospect of reorganization. We find the reasoning of Judge Dickson Phillips in *Carolin Corp.* persuasive:

> Such a test obviously contemplates that it is better to risk proceeding with a wrongly motivated invocation of Chapter 11 protections whose futility is not immediately manifest than to risk cutting off even a remote chance that a reorganization effort so motivated might nonetheless yield a successful rehabilitation.[11]

Similarly, it is not clear what facts establish that the debtor lacked good faith in filing. No one fact controls the resolution of a good faith challenge. Three fact patterns, however, merit consideration: (1) filing by the financially strong business; (2) filing by the single asset debtor on the eve of foreclosure and (3) filing after a last minute transfer to a newly created entity.[12]

---

4. In urging greater use of section 1112 by bankruptcy courts, Judge Carolyn Randall King discusses only the debtor's postpetition actions and inactions in In re Timbers of Inwood Forest Associates, Ltd., 808 F.2d 363, 371–72 (5th Cir.1987), cert. granted, 481 U.S. 1068, 107 S.Ct. 2459, 95 L.Ed.2d 868 (1987).

5. See generally, Ordin, The Good Faith Principle in the Bankruptcy Code: A Case Study, 38 Bus. Law, 1795 (1983); Ponoroff & Knippenberg, The Implied Good Faith Filing Requirement: Sentinel of an Evolving Bankruptcy Policy, 85 Nw. U.L. Rev. 919 (1991).

6. 4 B.R. 36 (Bankr. N.D.Ga.1980).

7. Id. at 39.

8. 849 F.2d 1393 (11th Cir.1988).

9. 886 F.2d 693 (4th Cir.1989).

10. 849 F.2d at 1394. The court also suggested that filing a Chapter 11 case in Florida for a Kentucky apartment complex "may itself be evidence of bad faith." Id. at 1395.

11. 886 F.2d at 701.

12. It is important to be mindful of Judge Phillips' warning:

> The dangers of overemphasis on particular indicia or patterns, of engaging in mere indicia-counting, and of forcing particular facts into previously identified patterns is obvious, and must be guarded against. We simply note, as have other courts, that a totality of circumstance inquiry is required; that "any conceivable list of factors is not exhaustive"; and that there is no "single factor that will necessarily lead to a finding of bad faith."

Carolin Corp. v. Miller, 886 F.2d 693, 701 (4th Cir.1989).

a. Filing by a Financially Strong Business Such as Johns-Manville

When Johns-Manville, a Fortune 500 corporation with a net worth (exclusive of tort liability) of approximately 1.1 billion dollars filed its Chapter 11 petition, the popular press and law journals questioned the propriety of its filing.[13] Later, various creditor committees raised the question by filing motions to dismiss, alleging Johns-Manville "lack of good faith" in filing its petition. The newspaper and magazine articles and the motions to dismiss focused on Johns-Manville's resources and its motives.

The *Johns-Manville* decision properly denied the motions to dismiss.[14] The financial strength of the debtor should not be a basis for dismissal of a Chapter 11 case. Insolvency is not a Chapter 11 eligibility requirement.[15] In omitting any such requirement, Congress recognized that reorganization was more efficient than liquidation and that "belated commencement of a case may kill an opportunity for reorganization."[16] In denying the motions to dismiss, Judge Lifland recognized that

> Manville must not be required to wait until its economic picture has deteriorated beyond salvation to file for reorganization. Manville's purported motivation in filing to obtain a breathing spell from asbestos litigation should not conclusively establish its lack of intent to rehabilitate and justify the dismissal of its petition.[17]

The *Johns-Manville* decision noted that the good faith requirement in the old Bankruptcy Act had been deleted from the Code and stated that good faith is not a "strict and absolute * * * predicate to filing" but rather an "elastic" concept that can be "read into the statute on a limited ad hoc basis."[18] "Manville's good faith filing is measured by the existence of massive unmanageable real debt owed to real claimants."[19]

b. Filing by the Single Asset Debtor on the Eve of Foreclosure

When a debtor that owns a single asset files for bankruptcy to fend off foreclosure, the existence of "real debt" and "real claimants" is often an important issue. In motions to dismiss such filings on the eve of foreclosure,

---

13. See, e.g., Cifelli, Management by Bankruptcy, Fortune at 72 (October 31, 1983); Kennedy, Use and Abuse of the Bankruptcy Law—Reflection on Some Recent Cases, 71 Iowa L. Rev. 199 (1985).

14. 36 B.R. 727 (Bankr. S.D.N.Y. 1984), appeal denied, 39 B.R. 234 (S.D.N.Y.1984), reargument denied 39 B.R. 998 (S.D.N.Y.1984).

15. But cf. T. Jackson, The Logic and Limits of Bankruptcy Law 194–203 (1986) (arguments for an insolvency type test). If Johns-Manville had been required to allege and prove insolvency, it would have been necessary to consider the various studies of its liability exposure and evaluate potential liabilities. Cf. 11 U.S.C.A. § 502(c)(1). Experts indicated that liability costs could exceed five billion dollars. Recall the bankruptcy definition of insolvency in section 101. Johns-Manville may have been insolvent in the "bankruptcy sense."

16. The commission Congress established to propose new bankruptcy legislation recommended removing this good faith requirement. See Report of the Commission on the Bankruptcy Laws of the United States, H.R. Doc. 137, 93d Cong., 1st Sess. 183, 222 (1973). The elimination of the good faith requirement is not discussed in the House and Senate Reports accompanying the bills that became the Bankruptcy Code.

17. 36 B.R. at 737.

18. Id.

19. Id.

creditors have argued that a debtor lacks good faith who has only one encumbered asset and owes only creditors holding liens on that asset lacks "real debts" and "real claimants." Courts have dealt with this argument on a case by case basis, listing factors rather than establishing rules.[20] *In re Phoenix Piccadilly, Ltd.*,[21] is representative.

In *Phoenix Piccadilly,* a limited partnership which owned an apartment complex filed a Chapter 11 petition the day before a hearing in state court to appoint a receiver for the debtor's property. The three secured creditors filed motions for relief from stay and motions to dismiss. The bankruptcy court dismissed, finding that the debtor had filed the petition in bad faith. In affirming, the Eleventh Circuit listed the following factors:

(i) The Debtor has only one asset, the Property, in which it does not hold legal title;

(ii) The Debtor has few unsecured creditors whose claims are small in relation to the claims of the Secured Creditors;[22]

(iii) The Debtor has few employees;

(iv) The Property is the subject of a foreclosure action as a result of arrearages on the debt;

(v) The Debtor's financial problems involve essentially a dispute between the Debtor and the Secured Creditors which can be resolved in the pending State Court Action; and

(vi) The timing of the Debtor's filing evidences an intent to delay or frustrate the legitimate efforts of the Debtor's secured creditors to enforce their rights.[23]

c. *Filing After a "Last Minute" Transfer of Assets to a Newly Created Entity*

A number of the eve-of-foreclosure cases involve a newly created entity to whom a nonproductive asset has been transferred from an otherwise

---

20. See generally Cohn, Good Faith and the Single Asset Debtor, 62 Am. Bankr. L.J. 131 (1988). Courts have also read a "good faith in filing test" into the word "cause" in section 362(d)(1) and have granted relief from the automatic stay in these single asset cases. It would seem more appropriate to deal with these cases under section 362(d)(2). If the debtor lacks equity in the encumbered property and has no realistic plans for using the collateral in a manner that would lead to an effective reorganization, the secured creditors should be granted relief from the stay to foreclose on the single asset.

21. 849 F.2d 1393 (11th Cir.1988).

22. Of the various factors listed in Phoenix Piccadilly and other reported cases involving motions to dismiss for lack of good faith, we consider the absence of significant, unsecured creditors as providing the strongest ground for dismissing the Chapter 11 petition. Courts have consistently and properly questioned the use of bankruptcy to resolve what is essentially a two party dispute. See, e.g., In re Panache Development Co., Inc., 123 B.R. 929 (Bankr.M.D. Fla.1991); In re Nancant, Inc., 8 B.R. 1005 (Bankr. Mass.1981).

23. 849 F.2d at 1394. The court also considered a Florida bankruptcy filing on a Kentucky apartment complex to be "evidence of bad faith," "although perhaps technically proper." When the debtor is a partnership, the only meaningful venue test is the principal place of business or the principal location of the assets. Cf. 28 U.S.C.A. § 1408. A partnership does not have a "domicile" or a "residence." See In re Garden Manor Associates, L.P., 99 B.R. 551, 553 (Bankr. S.D.N.Y. 1988). A partnership debtor's principal place of business is not necessarily the location of its principal assets. In re Bell Tower Associates, Ltd., 86 B.R. 795, 799 (Bankr. S.D.N.Y. 1988). The location of the general partners may fix the "principal place of business" because the general partners are making the decision for the business. Id.

solvent entity. Assume, for example, that X owns several apartment projects and faces foreclosure proceedings on one of them. Instead of filing a bankruptcy petition that would cover all of its property, X creates a new corporation, D Inc., transfers the asset subject to foreclosure to D Inc., and immediately causes D Inc. to file a bankruptcy petition. This prevents the foreclosure without subjecting all of X's other assets to bankruptcy court supervision.[24]

In re Yukon Enterprises, Inc.,[25] involved such a fact pattern. In granting the motion to dismiss, the court held that the transfer of distressed property to a newly created debtor shortly before the bankruptcy filing was prima facie evidence of bad faith. While most of the reported decisions simply include transfers to a newly created entity in a list of factors, it is clearly an important factor.[26] Eve of foreclosure transfers to a new entity could be proper where the new owners offer either new capital or new management expertise. There are reported cases holding that the newly created debtor was organized for legitimate business purposes and so last-minute transfers are not evidence of bad faith filing.[27]

§ 2–16 Good Faith Problems in Serial Filings

Recall that section 109(g) details circumstances under which repetitive filings is a basis for dismissal.[1] Reported cases suggest three other situations in which a debtor's prior bankruptcy filings have been a basis for a motion to dismiss for lack of good faith in filing.

a. Successive Chapter 13[2] Filings

Courts have generally dismissed for lack of good faith where a debtor files a petition after an earlier petition was dismissed unless the debtor can establish a change in circumstances. *In re McElveen*[3] is representative. In this case the debtors had filed three previous Chapter 13 petitions, all of which had been dismissed. The court dismissed a fourth petition, filed three years later, for bad faith because the debtors failed to demonstrate a change in circumstances.

---

24. Carolin Corp. v. Miller, 886 F.2d 693 (4th Cir.1989) illustrates a different type of last minute transfer to a newly created entity. There a single asset real estate company was facing foreclosure of its building. Investors formed a new holding company to acquire the stock of the real estate company and then filed a Chapter 11 petition for the real estate company. Judge Phillips characterized the transaction as "a speculative venture which had as its sole purpose the riskless achievement of a one short profit, rather than ongoing involvement by the investment of venture capital in a rehabilitative effort." Id. at 705.

25. 39 B.R. 919 (Bankr. C.D.Cal.1984).

26. See, e.g., In re Adkinson, 94 B.R. 730 (Bankr. N.D.Fla.1988); In re Nelson, 66 B.R. 231 (Bankr. N.J.1986), appeal decided, 838 F.2d 1207 (3d Cir.1988).

27. See In re Spenard Ventures, Inc., 18 B.R. 164 (Bankr. Alaska 1982); In re Conquest Offshore International, Inc., 73 B.R. 171 (Bankr. S.D.Miss.1986); In re Levinsky, 23 B.R. 210 (Bankr. S.D.N.Y. 1982).

§ 2–16

1. Section 109(g) is considered supra at § 2–2(c).

2. A filing by a debtor whose previous Chapter 7 case or Chapter 11 case was dismissed can occur and is also generally dismissed absent a change of circumstances. See In re Mandalay Shores Cooperative Housing Association, 112 B.R. 440 (Bankr. M.D.Fla. 1990). Dismissal and refiling of a Chapter 13 is much more common. Recall that in Chapter 13, but not in Chapter 7 or 11, the debtor has a right to dismiss its voluntary petition.

3. 78 B.R. 1005 (Bankr. S.C.1987).

b. *Chapter 19 or 20 (or More) Cases*

In cases like *McElveen* and decisions under section 109(g), courts are dismissing bankruptcy petitions because prior petitions were dismissed. Can a court dismiss a bankruptcy petition because the debtor's prior bankruptcy petition resulted in bankruptcy relief? While section 727 bars a Chapter 7 discharge because of prior bankruptcy relief, the Code nowhere expressly bars bankruptcy filing because of earlier bankruptcy relief. So many debtors who have obtained a Chapter 7 discharge immediately file a Chapter 12 or 13 petition that courts use the phrases "chapter 19" and "chapter 20."[4] Should a court dismiss a Chapter 12 or Chapter 13 petition for lack of good faith in filing if the debtor recently received a Chapter 7 discharge?

There are many situations in which a debtor would find it advantageous to obtain a Chapter 7 discharge and then file for Chapter 12 or Chapter 13 relief. Assume, for example, that D has a relatively high-paying job but little, if any, exempt property. D owes over $100,000 to various unsecured creditors. One of the creditors, C, has a claim that would be excepted from a Chapter 7 discharge under section 523. Because of the amount of unsecured debt she owes, D is not now eligible for Chapter 13 relief. If D files a Chapter 7 petition and receives a discharge, she is free from any further legal obligation to her prepetition creditors other than C and is still free to spend her postpetition salary as she pleases. The Chapter 7 discharge does not, however, affect D's liability to C who holds a claim excepted from the discharge. Can D now file a Chapter 13 petition to deal with C's claim? What if D also was delinquent on her home mortgage payments to M? The Chapter 7 case does not help D with her home mortgage problems. M can obtain relief from the stay and foreclose then or foreclose at the close of D's Chapter 7 case. There is no provision in Chapter 7 for curing defaults on home mortgages or other secured debts. Chapter 12 and Chapter 13 do so provide.[5] Can D who has recently received a Chapter 7 discharge now file for Chapter 12 or Chapter 13 relief to cure her home mortgage default?

Creditors have raised the good faith issue by motions to dismiss, motions for relief from stay under section 362(d), and/or objections to confirmation under section 1225(a)(3) or 1325(a)(3). Most of the courts that have considered this question have focused on the debtor's good faith, usually citing to section 1225(a)(3) or section 1325(a)(3), rather than section 1208 or section 1307. The cases have generally rejected any *per se* bad faith rule in Chapter 19 or Chapter 20 cases.[6] Instead, most cases have decided whether the later Chapter 12 or Chapter 13 filing was made in bad faith based on the "totality of the circumstances."[7]

In some of the cases where a debtor who has received a Chapter 7 discharge and is now looking to Chapter 13 to cure mortgage defaults, courts

---

4. See In re Hagberg, 92 B.R. 809, 815 (Bankr. W.D.Wis.1988); see generally, Morris, Serial Bankruptcies and Good Faith in Chapter 20, 1 Faulkner & Gray's Bankruptcy L. Rev. 48 (Winter 1990).

5. See 11 U.S.C.A. §§ 1222(b)(3) & 1322(b)(3).

6. See, e.g., In re Chaffin, 836 F.2d 215 (5th Cir.1988); In re Chisum, 847 F.2d 597 (9th Cir.1988), cert. denied, 488 U.S. 892, 109 S.Ct. 228, 102 L.Ed.2d 218 (1988). Chisum was actually a "Chapter 46" case—three successive 13s and then a 7.

7. See Practitioner Treatise, Vol. 1.

focused on whether the mortgagor is a creditor rather than whether the debtor is acting in good faith. It has been argued that

> (1) A Chapter 13 plan can only deal with creditors;
>
> (2) The Chapter 7 discharge eliminated the mortgagor's contractual right to payment;
>
> (3) Accordingly, the mortgagor did not hold a claim and was not a creditor under the section 101 definitions;
>
> (4) Accordingly, the debtor who has received a Chapter 7 discharge cannot later file a Chapter 13 plan to deal with the mortgagor's lien.

The Supreme Court rejected this argument in *Johnson v. Home State Bank*,[8] holding that the mortgage lien remains a "claim."[9] The Court also directly rejected an argument against "Chapter 20", stating:

> Congress has expressly prohibited various forms of serial filings* * *. The absence of a like prohibition on serial filings of Chapter 7 and Chapter 13 petitions, * * * convinces us that Congress did not intend categorically to foreclose the benefits of a Chapter 13 reorganization to a debtor who has previously filed for Chapter 7 relief.[10]

It is important to note that the Court added dictum acknowledging that previous Chapter 7 relief could be the basis for denying confirmation under section 1325(a)(3) for lack of good faith.[11] We believe that a bankruptcy judge who would prevent the use of "Chapter 20" by granting a motion to dismiss for lack of good faith will still prevent the use of "Chapter 20" by refusing to confirm the Chapter 13 plan for lack of good faith.

c. Filing a New Chapter 11 Petition After Default Under a Confirmed Chapter 11 Plan

Confirmation of a Chapter 11 plan requires a court finding of feasibility.[12] Notwithstanding this finding, real life debtors often find themselves in default on their plan obligations. Section 1127 bars a debtor from modifying its confirmed Chapter 11 plan after "substantial consummation."[13] Can the Chapter 11 debtor who has defaulted under its plan avoid this prohibition on modification by simply filing a new Chapter 11 case?[14]

In re Northampton Corp.[15] was the first reported Code case to answer this question. The bankruptcy court there concluded that a second filing aimed at curing defaults in a previously confirmed plan was tantamount to a modification after substantial consummation and was thus inconsistent with section 1127.

---

8. __ U.S. __, 111 S.Ct. 2150, 115 L.Ed.2d 66 (1991), on remand, 940 F.2d 609 (10th Cir. 1991).

9. "Claims" are dealt with infra in Chapters 7, 10, and 11.

10. __ U.S. at __, 111 S.Ct. at 2151. 115 L.Ed.2d at 77.

11. Id.

12. See 11 U.S.C.A. § 1129(a)(11).

13. See 11 U.S.C.A. § 1127(b). Chapter X of the Bankruptcy Act, in section 229c, allowed modification even after substantial consummation unless the proposed alteration or modification materially and adversely affects the participation provided for any class of creditors or stockholders by the plan.

14. See generally Comment, The Advent of the Serial Chapter 11 Filing and Its Implications, 8 Bankr. Dev. J. 245 (1991).

15. 39 B.R. 955 (Bankr. E.D.Pa.1984), aff'd, 59 B.R. 963 (E.D.Pa. 1984).

In re AT of Maine, Inc.,[16] relied on this reasoning in granting a motion to dismiss a Chapter 11 case initiated after a default under a confirmed Chapter 11 plan. The *AT of Maine* decision also looked to section 1112(b) and concluded that the second petition had been filed in bad faith. In so concluding, the court carefully limited its ruling to "the facts of this case." The confirmed *AT of Maine* plan had provided for the transfer of all of the debtor's assets in trust to a new entity for the benefit of the sole owner of both the transferor and the transferee. This new entity, the debtor in the second Chapter 11 case, had no assets other than those held in trust and no creditors other than those affected by the earlier case. The bad faith finding in *AT of Maine* seemed to focus more on the lack of a business to reorganize in the second case than on the fact of the first filing.[17]

In *In re Jartran, Inc.*,[18] a second Chapter 11 filing was permitted by a debtor still operating under the terms of a confirmed Chapter 11 plan. There, Jartran filed its first Chapter 11 petition in December, 1981, and obtained confirmation of its Chapter 11 plan in September, 1984. That plan contemplated continued operation of Jartran's truck and trailer leasing business, using equipment leased from Fruehauf. The Jartran–Fruehauf leases were assumed under the plan.

In March, 1986, more than four years after the initial Jartran filing, Jartran filed a second Chapter 11 petition. In the second Chapter 11 case, Jartran acknowledged that it was unable to continue operating its business and stated its intention to file a liquidating plan, as permitted by section 1123. Seven months later, Fruehauf initiated litigation seeking either dismissal of the second case or an administrative expense priority in the second case for obligations owing under the leases assumed in the first case. Fruehauf's argument for the administrative expense priority was based on the premise that the second Chapter 11 case was merely a continuation of the first case. The bankruptcy court rejected this argument and stated that it considered the two bankruptcy filings as "separate cases characterized by different objectives, assets, and claims."[19] Fruehauf appealed and the United States Court for the Northern District of Illinois and the United States Court of Appeals for the Seventh Circuit affirmed.

In its unsuccessful litigation and appeals, Fruehauf relied heavily on section 1129, *A.T. of Maine* and *Northampton*. Fruehauf also used section 1112(b) to argue that the second case should be dismissed or converted to Chapter 7. Recall that section 1112(b) provides that "the court *may* convert a case under this chapter to a case under chapter 7 of this title or may dismiss a case under this chapter, whichever is in the best interest of creditors and the estate, for cause." The Seventh Circuit held "conversion or dismissal under section 1112(b) is in the bankruptcy court's discretion and we cannot discern that the court abused that discretion in refusing to convert or dismiss this case."[20]

16. 56 B.R. 55 (Bankr. Me.1985).

17. Id. at 58.

18. 886 F.2d 859 (7th Cir.1989).

19. In re Jartran, Inc., 71 B.R. 938, 941 (Bankr. N.D.Ill.1987).

20. 886 F.2d at 868. Regrettably, the Seventh Circuit opinion does not speculate as to the consequences of conversion of the first Jartran Chapter 11 to Chapter 7. The Bankruptcy Code deals with consequences of conversion in section 348(d). It is clear from section 348(d) that claims against Jartran aris-

In *Jartran*, the second Chapter 11 petition was filed to liquidate rather than to rehabilitate. Is the precedential effect of *Jartran* restricted to these facts?

In the bankruptcy court opinion in *Jartran*, Judge Schwartz distinguished *Jartran* from *A.T. of Maine* and *Northampton* in that in *Jartran* six years had elapsed since the original Chapter 11 filing and the debtor had conducted business during that time. Accordingly, Judge Schwartz concluded that the second *Jartran* case represented "a new case with assets, liabilities, and objectives different than those in the first case."[21] Second, Judge Schwartz emphasized that the second filing in *Jartran* involved a liquidating plan, and thus the debtor was not seeking a second reorganization.

The Seventh Circuit first describes *Jartran* as a case in which "the central issue is whether a debtor whose original plan of reorganization has failed may file a new liquidating Chapter 11 rather than converting to Chapter 7 for liquidation."[22] Later language in the opinion, however, is much more general, suggesting the possibility of successive Chapter 11 restructurings:

> There is no prohibition of serial good faith Chapter 11 filings in the Code—indeed there is not even a time limit on successive filings parallel to those imposed on individuals or family farmers. As the District Court noted, Congress could easily have included repeat corporate debtors in that section; its failure to do so indicates that corporate debtors are exempt from even the minimal constraints on the serial filings imposed on other kinds of debtors. Once a bankruptcy plan is effectuated, all indications from the Code would incline us to treat the reorganized entity as we would any other company.[23]

In re Casa Loma Associates,[24] relied on this language in denying a motion to dismiss a second Chapter 11 reorganization case.

ing in the gap between the time of confirmation of the first Jartran plan and the filing of the second Jartran petition would be treated as prepetition claims in the event that Jartran had been converted to Chapter 7. It is, however, not clear from sections 348 or 541, or any other section of the Bankruptcy Code, whether the earnings of Jartran after the confirmation of its first Chapter 11 plan would be treated as property of the estate if the first Jartran Chapter 11 case had been converted to Chapter 7.

The confirmation of a Chapter 11 plan generally revests property of the estate in the debtor. See section 1141(b). Does this mean that there is no longer property of the estate? Does this mean that Jartran's postconfirmation earnings would not be property of the estate in the event that the case was later converted to Chapter 7?

In a recent decision dealing with the dismissal of a Chapter 11 case in which a plan had been confirmed, Judge Grant concluded: "Once a plan of reorganization is confirmed, the bankruptcy estate ceases to exist unless the plan specifically provides otherwise and all estate property revests in the debtor subject to the terms and conditions imposed by the plan * * *. Since the bankruptcy estate ceased to exist upon confirmation, there was no longer any property of the estate as to which section 349(b) could operate. Consequently, there was no property of the estate upon which FMAHA's lien could be restored." In re Depew, 115 B.R. 965 (Bankr. N.D.Ind. 1989).

21. 71 B.R. at 942.
22. 886 F.2d at 866.
23. 866 F.2d at 870.
24. 122 B.R. 814 (Bankr. N.D.Ga.1991).

d. Simultaneous Petitions

There is nothing in the Bankruptcy Code that expressly prohibits a person from filing a second bankruptcy petition while his or her first bankruptcy case is still pending. Some cases have read the Supreme Court Decision in *Freshman v. Atkins*[25] as prohibiting simultaneous petitions.[26] Other cases, however, read *Freshman* as merely standing for the proposition that two applications for discharge for the same debts cannot be pending at the same time.[27] In still other cases, this issue is never expressly considered. For example, In re Saylors,[28] the debtor received a discharge in his Chapter 7 case in August, 1987. On December 30, 1987, he filed a second bankruptcy petition, this time a Chapter 13 petition. A week later, the Chapter 7 trustee filed his final report.

C. CONVERSION

Remember that there are five forms of bankruptcy relief: Chapter 7, Chapter 9, Chapter 11, Chapter 12, and Chapter 13. The party filing a petition elects one of these chapters: she files a petition for relief under Chapter 7 or ___ (You fill in the blank.). The petitioner's choice of a chapter is reversible: Chapter 7, Chapter 11, Chapter 12, and Chapter 13 have provisions governing conversion of a case under that chapter to another chapter.[29]

While the grounds for conversion vary from chapter to chapter, there are three common conversion concerns: (1) what are the consequences of conversion, (2) does the debtor have a right to convert, and (3) when can a party other than the debtor cause the conversion of a case.

§ 2–17 Consequences of Conversion

For full text of this section, see Epstein, Nickles & White, Bankruptcy, Practitioner Treatise Series, Vol. 1.

   a. Property of the Estate

   b. Exempt Property

   c. Avoidance of Postpetition/Preconversion Transfers

§ 2–18 Debtor's Right to Convert

For full text of this section, see Epstein, Nickles & White, Bankruptcy, Practitioner Treatise Series, Vol. 1.

---

25. 269 U.S. 121, 46 S.Ct. 41, 70 L.Ed. 193 (1925).

26. See e.g. In re Keen, 121 B.R. 513 (Bankr. W.D.Ky.1990); In re Bodine, 113 B.R. 134, 135 (Bankr. W.D.N.Y.1990); Prudential Insurance Company of America v. Colony Square Company, 29 B.R. 432, 436 (W.D.Pa. 1983), appeal dism'd, 725 F.2d 666 (3d Cir. 1983).

27. See, e.g., In re Grimes, 117 B.R. 531 (Bankr. 9th Cir.1990); In re Kosenka, 104 B.R. 40 (Bankr. N.D.Ind. 1989).

28. 869 F.2d 1434 (11th Cir.1989).

29. See 11 U.S.C.A. §§ 706, 1112, 1208, and 1307.

§ 2–19 Creditor's Right to Convert

For full text of this section, see Epstein, Nickles & White, Bankruptcy, Practitioner Treatise Series, Vol. 1.

Chapter 3

AUTOMATIC STAY

Table of Sections

Sec.
3–1 Introduction and Overview.

A. Scope of the Stay.

3–2 When the Stay Arises.
3–3 Whom the Stay Affects.
3–4 What the Stay Generally Covers: Its Three Dimensional Scope.
3–5 Actions Against the Debtor.
3–6 ___ Actions and Proceedings.
    a. Common Coverage and Even Wider Scope.
    b. Purpose Requirement.
    c. Who Is Protected.
    d. Process/Procedure Affected.
    e. ""Against the Debtor".
    f. "The Prepetition Limitation.
3–7 ___ "Exception" for Collective Bargaining.
3–8 ___ Collection Efforts.
3–9 ___ Special Treatment of Utility Service.
3–10 ___ Exceptionally Protecting Nondebtors by Extending Section 362.
    a. Purposive Application (Mainly, the Piccinin "Identity-of–Interest" "Rule").
    b. Incidental Protection of Nondebtors When Covered Property Is Involved.
    c. "Codebtors" in Chapter 12 and 13 Cases (Sections 1201 and 1301).
3–11 Actions Against the Debtor's Property.
3–12 ___ Exception for Certain Domestic Obligations (Section 362(b)(2)).
3–13 Actions Against Estate Property.
3–14 ___ Obtaining Possession and Exercising Control Over Estate Property, Section 362(a)(3).
    a. Fundamentals.
    b. Causes of Action.
    c. Rights to Payment and Other Contract Rights.
    d. Letters of Credit.
    e. Leases.
    f. Rights From Government.
3–15 ___ Setoff.
3–16 ___ Effecting Liens Against Property of the Estate.
3–17 ___ Excepting Purchase–Money Security Interests in Aircraft (Section 1110).
    a. Substantive Requirements.
    b. Cure.
    c. Expiration of the Stay.

Sec.
3-18 Respecting Certain Grace Periods for Perfection (Section 362(b)(3)).
    a. Bankruptcy Preference Law.
    b. State Priority Law.
3-19 Excepting Certain Actions by Government.
3-20 ___ Criminal Actions (Section 362(b)(1)).
3-21 ___ Regulatory Actions (Section 362(b)(4–5)).
    a. Legislative Design of the Exceptions.
    b. Meaning of "Governmental Unit".
    c. Action or Proceeding Enforcing Police or Regulatory Power Under (b)(4).
        i. Enforcement.
        ii. Action or Proceeding.
        iii. Police or Regulatory Power.
    d. Enforcement of a Judgment Under (b)(5) and the Internal Limit Excluding Money Judgments.
    e. External Limits on the Exceptions.
        i. Unexcepted, Unaffected Parts of Section 362(a).
        ii. Discretionary Injunctions Under Section 105(a).
3-22 Supplemental Injunctions.

                B. Duration of the Stay.

3-23 How Long the Stay Continues.
    a. Case Is Ended.
    b. Discharge Is Granted or Denied.
    c. Property Leaves the Estate.
    d. Relief Is Granted.
3-24 Judicial Relief That Lifts the Stay—Overview.
3-25 ___ Debtor Lacks Equity in Property That Is Not Needed for Reorganization (Section 362(d)(2)).
    a. Does the Debtor Have an Equity in the Property?
    b. Is the Property Necessary to an Effective Reorganization?
3-26 ___ Cause (Section 362(d)(1)).
3-27 ___ ___ Lack of Adequate Protection.
    a. Identifying and Valuing the Secured Interest That Deserves Adequate Protection.
    b. Defining the Risks (When Adequate Protection Is Needed).
    c. Determining and Providing Protection That Is Adequate.
    d. Making Adjustments.
3-28 ___ ___ True Leases.
3-29 ___ ___ Bad Faith Filing.
3-30 ___ ___ More Appropriate Forum Elsewhere.
        Balancing Test.
        Contextually Unimportant Actions.
        Domestic Relations.
        Specialized Forums.
        Ordinary Claims.
        Bottom Line.
3-31 Some (Mostly) Procedural Concerns.
    a. Who Can Request Relief ("Party in Interest").
    b. When and How Relief Is Requested and Decided.
        i. Relief by Judicial Default (Section 362(e)).
            The First 30 Days.
            The Second 30 Days.
            The Final 30 Days.
            Getting Around Section 362(e).
        ii. Nature of the Hearing.
        iii. Burdens of Proof.
        iv. Ex Parte Relief (Section 362(f)).

Sec.
    c. Effect of Lifting the Stay.
    d. Appeal.
       C. Consequences of Violating the Stay.
3–32 Voidance.
    a. General Rule.
    b. Judicial Annulment.
    c. Statutory Exceptions.
    d. Competing Rule of "Voidable" Only.
3–33 Damages (Section 362(h)).
    a. Who Is the Plaintiff?
    b. Who Is the Defendant?
    c. What Is the Wrong?
    d. What Are the Damages?
    e. Overlapping Wrongs and Remedies.
3–34 __ Sovereign Immunity.
    a. The States.
    b. The United States.
    c. Waiving Immunity to Section 362(h) Damages by Section 106(a-b).
3–35 __ Contempt.

§ 3–1 Introduction and Overview

After filing bankruptcy a debtor needs immediate protection from the collection efforts of creditors. In a voluntary Chapter 7 case the trustee needs time to identify and collect the property of the estate which will be distributed pro rata to general creditors. In a voluntary reorganization case the debtor needs time to prepare a plan. In an involuntary case the debtor needs time to controvert the petition. In every case creditors' collection efforts must be stopped quickly in order to accomplish the orderly and even administration of the debtor's property and financial affairs that is a chief goal of bankruptcy.

For these reasons section 362 essentially commands that all collection efforts should cease upon the filing of a voluntary or involuntary petition.[1] It does so by providing that the filing of a bankruptcy petition "operates as a stay"[2] of the activities described in eight numbered subparts of section 362(a).[3] These activities are:

    (1) the commencement or continuation, including the issuance or employment of process, of a judicial, administrative, or other action or proceeding against the debtor that was or could have been commenced before the commencement of the case under this title, or to recover a claim against the debtor that arose before the commencement of the case under this title;

    (2) the enforcement, against the debtor or against property of the estate, of a judgment obtained before the commencement of the case under this title;

---

§ 3–1
1. 11 U.S.C.A. § 362(a).
2. Id.
3. Id.

(3) any act to obtain possession of property of the estate or of property from the estate or to exercise control over property of the estate;

(4) any act to create, perfect, or enforce any lien against property of the estate;

(5) any act to create, perfect, or enforce against property of the debtor any lien to the extent that such lien secures a claim that arose before the commencement of the case under this title;

(6) any act to collect, assess, or recover a claim against the debtor that arose before the commencement of the case under this title;

(7) the setoff of any debt owing to the debtor that arose before the commencement of the case under this title against any claim against the debtor; and

(8) the commencement or continuation of a proceeding before the United States Tax Court concerning the debtor.[4]

This is the automatic stay of bankruptcy. The stay is "applicable to all entities";[5] it applies in every case; and it does so automatically: the stay arises and is effective, without any request or order, when a bankruptcy petition is filed simply and solely as a result of the filing. Nothing more is necessary to the existence or force of the stay.

Because of the automatic stay, bankruptcy provides an immediate and fundamental benefit to the debtor:

> It gives the debtor a breathing spell from his creditors. It stops all collection efforts, harassment, and all foreclosure actions. It permits the debtor to attempt a repayment or reorganization plan, or simply to be relieved of the financial pressures that drove him into bankruptcy.[6]

There are other, equally important goals and effects of the stay. It freezes and maintains the status quo among creditors.[7] None of them can advance her claim over the other creditors. The stay locks in, fixes the creditors' state-law relationships and the priorities among them.[8] Also, because creditor action is suppressed during the bankruptcy case, claims and property can be handled in an orderly manner consistent with bankruptcy principles and policies, including bankruptcy priorities that can reflect, supplement, or override state law.

For unsecured creditors the stay thus provides protection from each other. Without the stay these creditors

---

4. Id.

5. Id.

6. H.R. Rep. No. 595, 95th Cong., 1st Sess. 340, *reprinted in* 1978 U.S. Code Cong. & Admin. News 5963, 6296–97; S. Rep. No. 989, 95th Cong., 2d Sess. 54, *reprinted in* 1978 U.S. Code Cong. & Admin. News 5787, 5840.

7. Interstate Commerce Commission v. Holmes Transportation, Inc., 931 F.2d 984, 987 (1st Cir.1991) ("The automatic stay is designed to effect an immediate freeze of the status quo at the outset of the chapter 11 proceedings, by precluding and nullifying most postpetition actions and proceedings against the debtor in nonbankruptcy fora, judicial or nonjudicial, as well as most extrajudicial acts against the debtor, or affecting property in which the debtor, or the debtor's estate, has a legal, equitable or possessory interest.").

8. "The stay is intended * * * to fix the rights and priorities of the creditors as of the time of the filing of the petition and to prohibit any further acts to advance those rights and priorities." In re Richardson Builders, Inc., 123 B.R. 736, 738 (Bankr. W.D. Va. 1990).

would be able to pursue their own remedies against the debtor's property. Those who acted first would obtain payment of the claims in preference to and to the detriment of other creditors. Bankruptcy is designed to provide an orderly liquidation procedure under which all [general, unsecured] creditors are treated equally. A race of diligence by creditors for the debtor's assets prevents that.[9]

By preventing this race the stay promotes the stated policy of equal treatment.

The stay intends to stop virtually every creditor from all collection activities. The scope of the stay, which is set by section 362(a), is thus very wide and comprehensive. Not only is the creditor stayed from pursuing legal and administrative actions against the debtor personally,[10] the creditor is also stayed from undertaking any act to get payment[11] or to create or enforce a lien.[12] Even polite requests to the debtor for voluntary payment are stayed. Broadly, "*any* action to collect"[13] is prohibited. It therefore strains the imagination to think of something a creditor might wish to do *with* or *to* a creditor that is not prohibited by some subsection of section 362(a). In short, after the petition is filed the debtor's creditors may continue to breathe, eat and sleep and are free to dream about the debtor, but they may do little else having anything to do with the debtor.

Section 362(b) creates exceptions to the stay by describing certain activities that are beyond it, that is, not stayed by the filing of a petition.[14] They are very narrow activities such as the continuation of a criminal action against the debtor,[15] the exercise by government of its police or regulatory powers,[16] and the collection of alimony and child support.[17] Moreover, the exceptions are narrowly read and applied to secure the broad relief that Congress intended the stay to provide.[18] In the ordinary case none of the section 362(b) exceptions applies to the typical creditor. In the extraordinary case in which an exception applies, the covered conduct is automatically allowed without the need for court-ordered relief from the stay.[19]

The stay itself does not extinguish a creditor's claim, lien or other rights.[20] Rather, it only delays realizing or enforcing them. Yet, during this delay the creditor's rights will be filtered through other Code provisions that may kill, reduce or change them. A lien may be avoided. An unsecured claim may be discharged. Eventually, however, the stay ends in one way or another, and the rights that have survived bankruptcy are enforceable in the shape and form that bankruptcy law has left them.

Generally, because of the debtor's discharge, unsecured creditors have no rights that survive bankruptcy.[21] The stay thus marks the end of their

9. H.R. Rep. No. 595, 95th Cong., 1st Sess. 340, *reprinted in* 1978 U.S. Code Cong. & Admin. News 5963, 6297.

10. 11 U.S.C.A. § 362(a)(1).

11. Id. § 362(a)(6).

12. Id. § 362(a)(4) & (5).

13. Id. § 352(a)(6) (emphasis added).

14. See Practitioner Treatise, Vol. 1.

15. Id. § 362(b)(1).

16. Id. § 362(b)(4).

17. Id. § 362(b)(2).

18. In re Stringer, 847 F.2d 549, 552 (9th Cir.1988).

19. See Practitioner Treatise, Vol. 1.

20. See Practitioner Treatise, Vol. 1.

21. The discharges operates as a permanent injunction "against the commencement

collection efforts. The unpaid balance of their claims is a loss they must suffer. It is a cost of doing business as an unsecured creditor.

In contrast, because liens are generally unaffected by bankruptcy, secured creditors retain their rights to their collateral during and after the case. They can collect their secured claims from the property even after the debtor's bankruptcy. The stay itself is nevertheless costly to secured creditors if only because time is money. Most significantly, a secured creditor loses her collateral's reinvestment value during the stay unless her claim is sufficiently oversecured to cover the loss. The stay can thereby reduce the creditor's net recovery or increase her overall loss. The size of this cost grows as the stay lengthens. Secured creditors are thus interested in having the stay end as soon as possible.

The automatic stay automatically ends upon certain occurrences,[22] most notably the closing or dismissal of the case or the discharge of the debtor.[23] None of these events always and reliably happens quickly, especially not when the aim of the bankruptcy is reorganization rather than liquidation. While the typical Chapter 7 case is completed in a matter of months, a Chapter 11 or 12 case may continue for several years.

A stay as to particular property (such as a secured creditor's collateral) can sooner end for either of the reasons described in section 362(d): (1) "for cause, including the lack of adequate protection"[24] or, specifically, (2) the debtor lacks equity in the property which is not necessary for reorganization.[25] The end of the stay is not automatic under this section. The court orders it, i.e., grants relief from the stay, upon the creditor's motion to lift the stay (i.e., a lift-stay motion).

The typical lift-stay motion is aimed at property that is the movant-creditor's collateral. Her motion triggers an adversary proceeding in which objections can be made by people who could be harmed by lifting the stay. The person most likely to object is the trustee or debtor in possession. The usual basis for the objection is the belief that the property holds value that belongs to the estate or that the estate can profitably use. In the event someone objects to the lift-stay motion, the dispute is decided by the court on stipulated facts and briefs or in a plenary hearing.

Cause and lack of equity are alternative reasons for lifting the stay under section 362(d), and the secured creditor seeking relief from the stay will probably argue both of them. Because lack of equity is more specific and is essentially an instance of cause, the creditor is likely to begin with the no-equity argument of subsection (d)(2). If this argument fails, the creditor will fall back on the more general argument of (d)(1): there is some other "cause" for relief from the stay, "including lack of adequate protection." Lack of adequate protection is sufficient but not necessary for relief under (d)(1); undoubtedly, however, lack of adequate protection is the cause for relief that secured creditors most often argue.

or continuation of an action, the employment of process, or an act, to collect, recover or offset any * * * [discharged] debt as a personal liability of the debtor * * *." 11 U.S.C.A. § 524(a)(2). "Once the debtor receives a discharge § 362 no longer is applicable but is replaced by the permanent injunction of § 524." In re Peterson, 118 B.R. 801, 804 (Bankr. D.N.M.1990).

22. See 11 U.S.C.A. § 362(c) & (e).
23. Id. § 362(c)(2).
24. Id. § 362(d)(1).
25. Id. § 362(d)(2).

Adequate protection is a critically important concept of bankruptcy law which appears in other provisions of the Code and in other settings of a bankruptcy case. It refers generally to safeguarding the value of a third-party's interest in property affected by the bankruptcy. In the setting of section 362(d)(1), the issue of adequate protection usually concerns preserving the value of a secured creditor's lien during the period of the stay.

A lien is a property interest in the collateral. The value of the lien is the amount of the secured debt, but the value of the property as a whole is a natural limit on the value of the lien. The Code intends that the stay will not shrink lien value. The largest, most common threat to this value is a decline in the collateral's worth during the stay that consumes any equity and reduces the property's realizable value below the amount of the secured debt.

If the lien value is at risk during the stay, the creditor is entitled either to adequate protection against the risk or to relief from the stay so that she can dispose of the property before her lien is eroded. She enjoys this right even with respect to collateral that is needed for an effective reorganization.

Section 361 suggests several ways of providing adequate protection. It amounts to giving insurance. The object is not so much to protect against a decline in the worth of the collateral itself as to insure that if a decline occurs and results in a loss of lien value, the creditor will be compensated for this loss from other property or sources. It is the value of the creditor's interest that must be protected rather than the interest itself. If sufficient insurance is given for this purpose, relief from the stay is rightly denied even if the collateral's worth is then falling and causing a present decline of the creditor's lien in the property.

A creditor gains nothing by knowingly or even innocently violating the stay by engaging in conduct that section 362 proscribes. Any action that violates the stay is void or voidable so that any nonbankruptcy consequences diluting the rights of the debtor or the estate are deemed ineffective, including the transfer of rights in property that the stay protects. Additionally, a willful violator of the stay may be held in contempt and is liable in any event for compensatory and punitive damages.[26]

Every year there are hundreds of reported proceedings that implicate section 362. More often the difficulty is deciding the facts required to apply section 362 rather than construing the law that it states. Nevertheless, because critical terms are open and fluid, the proper application of section 362 even in common situations is not entirely settled. Also, because the stay applies in every bankruptcy case, it is stretched and pulled by many unusual circumstances and by very many clever lawyers. The tension regularly produces novel issues of interpretation and application.

Lying just beneath the surface in much of our discussion that follows, and in the hundreds of cases we cite in the body and in the footnotes, is the general policy question: How broad a stay? It is possible that the stay has spread and been interpreted more broadly than its advocates could have imagined when the stay was put in the Code in 1978. Although the pre-Code rules and every knowledgeable lawyer would have barred traditional collec-

---

26. Id. § 362(h).

tion activities after the petition was filed, we suspect that at least some of them would not have anticipated that the section 362 stay would reach to the debtor's divorce proceedings, to communications between debtors and creditors and to a host of other things that are well removed from traditional debt collection. There are now bitter lawsuits not only over the foregoing matters, but also over the power of the court to extend the stay (or something like it under section 105), to suits against guarantors and quasi-guarantor partners. Clever lawyers have greatly stretched and pulled the stay.

The policy question is whether it has been pulled too far. One can easily acknowledge that traditional collection procedure should be stopped upon filing of a petition without also conceding that the stay should bar a creditor's claim against a third party or should intrude upon behavior that is not directly associated with the active collection of a debt. Disagreement among lawyers on this point is wide.

Some lawyers would identify the extensive and expansive application of the stay as unfortunate and troublesome. They would argue that the expansive stay is one of the factors that may make Chapter 11 so expensive and damaging to legitimate creditor's interests as to call its future into doubt.

Other lawyers take the opposite position. They see more virtue in an expansive stay and equal danger from both direct and indirect attempts by creditors to enhance their positions.

Everyone must agree, however, as we do, that continuous expansion of the stay is not a costless good.

A. SCOPE OF THE STAY

§ 3–2 When the Stay Arises

The stay arises or becomes effective as soon as the bankruptcy petition is filed,[1] which is when the petition is placed in the clerk's possession.[2] The petition itself "operates as" the stay.[3] It is "automatic and self-operating."[4] The irreparable harm that is usually necessary for an injunction is not required: "The automatic stay comes into play upon the filing of a bankruptcy petition whether or not the debtor would suffer irreparable harm in the absence of the stay."[5] Moreover, notice is not required to anyone,[6] although a violator's lack of notice may affect the consequences of her violation of the stay.[7] Indeed, no further procedure or process of any kind is necessary. Filing the petition accomplishes the stay.

The conversion of a case from one chapter to another under the Code effects a large change in the proceedings, but does not create a new case. No

---

§ 3–2

1. 11 U.S.C.A. § 362(a).

2. In re Godfrey, 102 B.R. 769, 771 (Bankr. 9th Cir.1989) (Bankruptcy petition is filed so as to create the stay as soon as the petition is placed in clerk's possession, not when the petition is time stamped.).

3. 11 U.S.C.A. § 362(a).

4. NLT Computer Services Corp. v. Capital Computer Systems, Inc., 755 F.2d 1253, 1258 (6th Cir.1985).

5. In re Minoco Group of Companies, Ltd., 799 F.2d 517, 520 (9th Cir.1986).

6. See Practitioner Treatise, Vol. 1.

7. See § 3–33 infra, which is part of our discussion of the consequences of violating the stay.

new petition of commencement is required, and the conversion does not even affect a change in the date of the filing.[8] Thus, a conversion does not trigger a different or fresh stay because "[t]he filing of a petition * * * operates as a stay. A conversion * * * does not." [9]

§ 3–3 Whom the Stay Affects

The stay protects against "the pursuit of actions by *any* party of *any* character * * *"[1] because the stay operates against "*all* entities."[2] Basically, entity means anyone, including natural people, business forms and organizations, and governments and governmental units.[3] Thus, even the United States, the states, and their subdivisions are bound by the stay.[4] Their sovereign immunity sometimes protects them, but only against damages for having violated the stay.[5] Government generally is not otherwise immune from the stay, and government action that violates the stay is as legally ineffective as any private person's violation.[6] The reason is simple:

> The automatic stay ensures that no creditor receives more than an equitable share of the bankrupt's estate. This equitable treatment requires that all creditors, both public and private, be subject to the automatic stay. [Thus] Congress used broad language to prohibit 'all entities', including a 'governmental unit,' from taking action against a debtor's property during bankruptcy.[7]

The term "entities" is broad not only because it covers everybody, whether natural or fictional, private or public. It is also broad because the term covers the persons described without regard to their purpose. The stay thus applies to an entity whether or not the entity is a creditor of the debtor.[8]

Generally, therefore, everyone (regardless of motive or reason) is prohibited during the life of the stay from doing anything that section 362(a)

---

8. 11 U.S.C.A. § 348(a).

9. In re State Airlines, Inc., 873 F.2d 264, 267–69 (11th Cir.1989). As a consequence, a creditor who gets relief from the stay in the debtor's Chapter 11 case is not required to seek relief again when the case is converted to Chapter 13. In re Greetis, 98 B.R. 509 (Bankr. S.D.Cal.1989).

§ 3–3

1. Williford v. Armstrong World Industries, Inc., 715 F.2d 124, 126 (4th Cir.1983) (emphasis added) (dicta).

2. 11 U.S.C.A. § 362(a) (emphasis added). This includes the debtor herself. In re Shapiro, 124 B.R. 974, 981 (Bankr. E.D.Pa. 1991) (The stay of § 362(a)(3) is violated by the debtor effecting a postpetition transfer of estate property.).

3. The word "entity" includes "person, estate, trust, governmental unit, and United States trustee." 11 U.S.C.A. § 101(15). " '[P]erson' includes individual, partnership, and corporation * * *." Id. § 101(41). " '[G]overnmental unit' means United States; State; Commonwealth; District; Territory; municipality; foreign state; department, agency, or instrumentality of the United States * * *, a State, a Commonwealth, a District, a Territory, a municipality, or a foreign state; or other foreign or domestic government." Id. § 101(27).

4. See Practitioner Treatise, Vol. 1.

5. See Practitioner Treatise, Vol. 1.

6. See § 3–32 infra.

7. Matter of Guterl Special Steel Corp., 111 B.R. 107, 110 (W.D.Pa.1990), judgm't aff'd, 916 F.2d 890 (3d Cir.1990), cert. denied, ___ U.S. ___, 111 S.Ct. 1640, 113 L.Ed.2d 735 (1991).

8. In re Claussen, 118 B.R. 1009, 1015 (Bankr. D.S.D.1990) ("Congress could not have been more inclusive in expressing which entities are stayed, since 'all' means whole or a totality. This includes those who are not creditors of the estate."); In re Firstcorp, Inc., 122 B.R. 484, 490 n.8 (Bankr. E.D.N.C.1990) (The stay applies to all entities, not just creditors.).

describes, unless the activity is excepted from the stay by subsection (b) or the court orders relief from it through subsection (d). In short, the stay is not limited by whom it affects because it affects everyone. The limits of the stay concern the events and actions that the stay bars: what the stay covers, not who.

§ 3–4 What the Stay Generally Covers: Its Three Dimensional Scope

The scope of what the stay covers is very broad because its purpose is very large: to stop "*all* collection efforts, *all* harassment, and *all* foreclosure actions"[1] and even more. Generally speaking, the stay intends to stop occurrences (mostly conduct and other activities) from beginning or continuing that would financially pressure the debtor, that would complicate sorting out her financial affairs during the liquidation or reorganization process, or that would advantage any person or class of people claiming her property or property of the estate. Naturally, the principal target of the stay is creditor action. The aim is three dimensional: certain actions against the debtor personally, her property, and property of the estate.

In simple terms, here is the reason the stay is multi-dimensional in the archetypical bankruptcy, a Chapter 7 case: Bankruptcy gives the debtor a discharge from prepetition claims. Creditors are permanently enjoined from collecting the claims. Any payment must ordinarily come from the estate. Because prepetition claims cannot be prosecuted against the debtor, they cannot ripen into liens, which means that property the debtor acquires after bankruptcy (including any property she gets from the estate) is effectively immune from these claims. Because the debtor and her own separate property are immune from prepetition claims, section 362(a) stays any act against the debtor to collect, assess or recover a prepetition claim, and also stays any act to create, perfect or enforce against the debtor's property any lien for a prepetition debt.

The bankruptcy discharge gives no immunity as to debts arising after bankruptcy. The stay thus provides no protection for the debtor or her property from post-petition claims.[2]

Postpetition claims against the debtor cannot be collected from the estate which is a separate legal entity. The estate assumes only its own obligations and the debtor's prepetition obligations. These debts are paid or otherwise dealt with, however, pursuant to the priority rules and overall scheme of the Code that the bankruptcy courts administer in an orderly, disciplined fashion to maximize value and protect third-party interests. Therefore, neither creditors nor anyone else can help themselves to estate property. The stay stops everyone from any act to get possession of or

---

§ 3–4

1. H.R. Rep. No. 595, 95th Cong., 1st Sess. 340, reprinted in 1978 U.S. Code Cong. & Admin. News 5963, 6297; S. Rep. No. 989, 95th Cong., 2d Sess. 54, reprinted in 1978 U.S. Code Cong. & Admin. News 5787, 5840 (emphasis added).

2. In a reorganization case the discharge can cover postpetition claims which participate, along with prepetition claims, in the bankruptcy distribution. Correspondingly, the estate is enlarged to include property that the debtor acquires postpetition. This property, as estate property, is protected by the stay. The debtor's own property is unprotected but insignificantly because the debtor acquires little or no property for itself during the bankruptcy.

exercise control estate property. This injunction includes creditors with postpetition claims for the more basic reason that the estate is not liable for them.

An important part of bankruptcy is determining the existence and amount of claims chargeable to the estate. For the sake of efficiency the Code centralizes the process in the bankruptcy court. Therefore, no other court or other body can properly decide a prepetition claim against the debtor after bankruptcy has been filed. The stay prevents or stops any action or proceeding against the debtor that could have been brought before bankruptcy, specifically including any action or proceeding to recover a prepetition claim. Litigation is effectively shifted to the bankruptcy court for coordination and appropriate decision.

The three dimensional aim of the stay is focused by the subparts of section 362(a). Its eight subsections define the specific acts, events and happenings against which the debtor, her property and the property are protected. Each subsection is limited by what and who is covered, but the subsections themselves describe multiple events and use language that is universally very general, wide and open. Commonly, therefore, the same event is covered by more than one subsection or covered more than once within the same subsection. Overlap can occur in two ways: several parts of the section can apply to a single event that affects only the debtor, her property, or property of the estate. Additionally or alternatively, the same single event can be doubly covered because the event affects, by one or more prohibited means, two or all three of the entities which the stay protects (the debtor, her property or property of the estate).

On the other hand, redundant coverage is unnecessary to trigger the stay, and an event is stopped that matches any of the parts of section 362(a). They apply alternatively, and an event that escapes one part can be caught and stopped (equally dead) by another part.

An event or happening that section 362(a) covers, even redundantly, is not stayed if the happening is also covered by an exception described in subsection (b). These exceptions also apply alternatively, but they are narrow as written and applied. In the typical case none of them applies. Still, no decision that the stay applies is completely sound unless the decision has considered and ruled out the exceptions of subsection (b). They are therefore merged and mingled throughout our discussion of the scope of the stay.

§ 3–5 Actions Against the Debtor

In general, section 362 stays actions or proceedings and collection efforts aimed at the debtor herself,[1] and also stays acts to create, perfect or enforce liens on the debtor's own property.[2] Specifically, with respect to the debtor and her property, section 362(a) stays:

> (1) the commencement or continuation, including the issuance or employment of process, of a judicial, administrative, or other action or proceeding against *the debtor* that was or could have been commenced

---

§ 3–5
1. 11 U.S.C.A. § 362(a)(1–2), (6) & (8).

2. Id. § 362(a)(5).

before the commencement of the case under this title, or to recover a claim against *the debtor* that arose before the commencement of the case under this title;

(2) the enforcement, against *the debtor* or against property of the estate, of a judgment obtained before the commencement of the case under this title;

* * *

(5) any act to create, perfect, or enforce against property of *the debtor* any lien to the extent that such lien secures a claim that arose before the commencement of the case under this title;

(6) any act to collect, assess, or recover a claim against *the debtor* that arose before the commencement of the case under this title;

(7) the setoff of any debt owing to *the debtor* that arose before the commencement of the case under this title against any claim against the debtor; and

(8) the commencement or continuation of a proceeding before the United States Tax Court concerning *the debtor*.[3]

The "debtor" for these purposes is the person concerning whom the case was commenced,[4] a/k/a the bankrupt; the object of the bankruptcy case; the person who filed bankruptcy or, in an involuntary case, the person against whom bankruptcy was filed. With very few exceptions the stay generally protects only this debtor and no one else. Thus, the stay of actions against the debtor does not affect actions against people (or their property) who are related to the debtor or who are participants in the harm or liability underlying the claims against the debtor.

For example, the section 362 stay, by its terms, does not generally protect the following people simply because of their relationship to the debtor:

- The debtor's spouse;[5]
- A surety for the debtor's obligations;[6]
- The debtor's insurer;[7]
- The owner of property that is subjected to a construction lien because of the contractor-debtor's default;[8]
- The debtor-assignor's obligor who is sued on the account by the debtor's assignee;[9]
- A transferee of the debtor's property;[10]
- The prime tenant of a subtenant in bankruptcy;[11]
- Officers, directors, and other principals of a corporate debtor;[12]

3. Id. § 362(a) (emphasis added).
4. Id. § 101(13).
5. See Practitioner Treatise, Vol. 1.
6. See Practitioner Treatise, Vol. 1.
7. See Practitioner Treatise, Vol. 1.
8. See Practitioner Treatise, Vol. 1.
9. See Practitioner Treatise, Vol. 1.
10. See Practitioner Treatise, Vol. 1.
11. See Practitioner Treatise, Vol. 1.
12. See Practitioner Treatise, Vol. 1.

- Subsidiaries of a corporate debtor; [13]
- The parent of a subsidiary in bankruptcy; [14]
- Partners of a partnership debtor; [15]
- A partnership in which the debtor is an individual partner; [16] or,
- A company when its principals are debtors. [17]

The debtor's protection from actions and proceedings against her does not even extend to the debtor's own bankruptcy estate as an obligor.[18]

Other people are not usually protected by the debtor's stay even when they are sued or otherwise pursued for liability shared with the debtor. The stay does not usually reach actions or proceedings against joint tortfeasors, contract co-obligors, or other codefendants of the debtor who are liable with her on other legal theories.[19]

In sum, the general rule is that the stay is personal to the debtor: the protection that section 362 provides the debtor and her property stops with the debtor herself and provides no shelter, directly or indirectly, for anyone else. Nondebtors are generally entirely beyond it regardless of their relational or transactional connections to the debtor. Therefore, actions or proceedings against them or their property are unaffected by the stay of the debtor's bankruptcy, save in a few extraordinary cases in which very narrow exceptions to the rule, or end runs around it, apply.

In contrast to this narrowness of the stay in protecting only the debtor, the stay is very wide in terms of the range of protection the debtor gets.

§ 3–6 Actions Against the Debtor—Actions and Proceedings

In its first clause subsection 362(a)(1) declares a very wide prohibition against

> the commencement or continuation, including the issuance or employment of process, of a judicial, administrative, or other action or proceeding against the debtor that was or could have been commenced before the commencement of the case under this title.

As if to emphasize and illustrate rather than to limit, the second clause of (a)(1) stays any action "to recover a [prepetition] claim against the debtor." Specifically prohibited by subsection (a)(8) is a proceeding "before the United States Tax Court concerning the debtor."

The intent is to channel all actions and proceedings against the debtor into the bankruptcy court and there coordinate and consolidate them with each other and with everything else going on in the case that affects the debtor's financial fate. The results of this channeling are more consistent decisions and more efficient decision making that reduce the time, trouble, and costs of bankruptcy administration and thereby increase the benefits of bankruptcy for the debtor and her creditors.

---

13. See Practitioner Treatise, Vol. 1.
14. See Practitioner Treatise, Vol. 1.
15. See Practitioner Treatise, Vol. 1.
16. See Practitioner Treatise, Vol. 1.
17. See Practitioner Treatise, Vol. 1.
18. See Practitioner Treatise, Vol. 1.
19. See Practitioner Treatise, Vol. 1.

a. Common Coverage and Even Wider Scope

Section 362(a)(1) most obviously and commonly covers ordinary civil litigation against the debtor that seeks damages or other relief for a prepetition claim. Lawsuits for this purpose—whether in law or equity, in tort or contract, or for violation of a statute—cannot be brought anywhere against the debtor in state or federal courts.[1] It makes no difference that the claim is based on a nondischargeable debt.[2] Suits on any prepetition claim pending anywhere against the debtor when bankruptcy is filed must immediately stop as to the debtor[3] regardless of the stage of the proceedings, even if the case is on appeal. Anything done thereafter in the case with respect to the debtor is void or voidable, especially including any verdict, judgment or other ultimate decision against her.[4] Jurisdiction is not lost;[5] rather, the right to exercise jurisdiction is suspended by force of overriding federal law, i.e., section 362.

In theory and practice the scope of (a)(1) is very much wider in two dimensions. First, the ordinary civil lawsuit is not the only kind of action or proceeding that (a)(1) targets. It equally reaches any other form and forum of an action or proceeding against the debtor whether in court, before some other governmental body (legislative, administrative, regulatory or quasi-judicial body)[6], or in arbitration[7] or some other private forum.[8] In sum:

> The scope of this paragraph [§ 362(a)(1)] is broad. All proceedings are stayed, including arbitration, license revocation, administrative, and judicial proceedings. Proceeding in this sense encompasses civil actions and all proceedings even if they are not before governmental tribunals.[9]

Second, it is sufficient but not necessary that the purpose of the action or proceeding is to recover a claim. Section 362(a)(1) routinely stops proceedings as varied as divorce,[10] eviction,[11] civil forfeiture, and license revocation.[12] Indeed, the broadest language of (a)(1) requires only that the proceeding is "against the debtor." The object of the proceeding is seemingly unimportant, but the underlying purposes of the law are naturally limiting.

b. Purpose Requirement

Section 362(a)(1) probably requires, when the purpose is not to recover a claim, that the action or proceeding offends the policies of the stay or undermines the goals of the bankruptcy case. This alternative requirement is most obviously satisfied whenever the aim or effect of the action or proceeding is to create liability, reduce property or limit rights that financially affect the debtor or her estate. The effect can be slight and indirect,

---

§ 3–6

1. See Practitioner Treatise, Vol. 1.
2. See Practitioner Treatise, Vol. 1.
3. See Practitioner Treatise, Vol. 1.
4. See Practitioner Treatise, Vol. 1.
5. See Practitioner Treatise, Vol. 1.
6. See Practitioner Treatise, Vol. 1.
7. See Practitioner Treatise, Vol. 1.
8. See Practitioner Treatise, Vol. 1.
9. H.R. Rep. No. 595, 95th Cong., 1st Sess. 340, reprinted in 1978 U.S. Code Cong. & Admin. News 5963, 6297; S. Rep. No. 989, 95th Cong., 2d Sess. 50, reprinted in 1978 U.S. Code Cong. & Admin. News 5787, 5836.
10. See Practitioner Treatise, Vol. 1.
11. See Practitioner Treatise, Vol. 1.
12. See Practitioner Treatise, Vol. 1.

but the connection (however slim) between the action and the purposes of (a)(1) is necessary.

The connection is missing with respect to actions against the debtor in which she is a nominal defendant only,[13] or actions that seek relief unrelated to her property and business or financial affairs. Therefore, the stay will not save a debtor's marriage[14] or guarantee her position as personal representative of a decedent's estate.[15] Arguably, even an interpleader action against the debtor is beyond (a)(1) when the purpose is to determine if the debtor owns property rather than to take property she already owns.[16]

In practice, the required connection between the action and purposes of (a)(1) does not substantially limit (a)(1)'s reach. Any action or proceeding worth bringing against the debtor will ordinarily affect her pecuniarily. Also, the proceeding most commonly pursued against a debtor is an action to recover a claim, which is expressly within the scope of (a)(1). Moreover, the law should (and usually does) err in favor of reading and applying (a)(1) broadly, almost without end, because relief to an interested third party is always possible, relatively cheaply, through section 362(d). In addition, the damages should be little or nothing for a proceeding that unoffensively violates the stay. The cost to bankruptcy would be higher from a narrow construction that errs the other way and fails to stops actions or proceedings which prejudice the case.

The bottom line, therefore, is that in applying (a)(1), the forum is unimportant and the purpose requirement is very general, loose and routinely met by any proceeding anywhere that affects the debtor's financial affairs. Also, because the concern is the effect of the action or proceeding, the nature of the relief sought should not decide, in itself, the applicability of (a)(1). It is the end rather than the means that counts in applying (a)(1).

c. Who Is Protected

Significantly, an action or proceeding against the debtor is no less affected by (a)(1) when other people are sued along with her. On the other hand, the stay of (a)(1) protects only the debtor.[17] Therefore, when an action or proceeding against the debtor is stayed, it is stopped only as to her and can begin or continue as to everyone else.

The whole action stops in the rare case in which the debtor is an indispensable party.[18] In this event, the reason for protecting the nondebtor is nonbankruptcy procedure law rather than section 362 itself. It is very uncommon, however, that any party is indispensable within the strict meaning of procedure law.[19] Significantly, a debtor is typically not an indispensable party if she has been sued with someone else as a joint tortfeasor[20] or as a co-obligor on a contract debt.[21] Therefore, staying the suit against her does not prevent, for lack of joinder, continuing the suit against the other defendant.

---

13. See Practitioner Treatise, Vol. 1.
14. See Practitioner Treatise, Vol. 1.
15. See Practitioner Treatise, Vol. 1.
16. See Practitioner Treatise, Vol. 1.
17. See Practitioner Treatise, Vol. 1.
18. See Practitioner Treatise, Vol. 1.
19. See Practitioner Treatise, Vol. 1.
20. See Practitioner Treatise, Vol. 1.
21. See Practitioner Treatise, Vol. 1.

d. Process/Procedure Affected

Section 362(a)(1) reaches process and procedure within an action or proceeding that (a)(1) covers. The explanation is not that procedure itself is an "action or proceeding." These terms refer to the main matter or case in chief. The component processes and procedures are stayed because they continue the action or proceeding, and (a)(1) stops the continuation of an action against the debtor just as clearly as it stops the action itself. An even more basic explanation is that, in a real sense, an action or proceeding is the collection of process and procedure which comprise it: collectively, the process and procedure are the action or proceeding. Section 362(a)(1) therefore stays, for example: an award or other decision of the matter,[22] even a decision favoring the debtor;[23] hearings or other proceedings that are associated with the action;[24] and motions or other process that powers, rouses or otherwise affects or moves the proceeding in any direction or fashion.[25]

The courts disagree whether dismissal of an action against the debtor is stayed. The obvious analysis is that dismissal is the opposite of continuation and is therefore not covered by section 362(a)(1).[26] Some courts decide the other way, holding that the stay applies to dismissal of an action against the debtor.[27] Effectively, they define "continuation" in (a)(1) more broadly to include any change or happening in the action.[28] The argument for this view is that preserving an action against the debtor may somehow advantage the estate. Matters affecting the estate are usually best decided by the bankruptcy court rather than by the court where the action is pending. Dismissal, therefore, should usually be stayed and decided through and by the bankruptcy court taking the broadest and best view of the issue.

Appeals in actions or proceedings against the debtor are stayed, too. If the debtor won a suit filed against her, the plaintiff cannot appeal the judgment, and any pending appeal by the plaintiff is stopped.[29] Similarly, any planned or pending appeal by the debtor in the action is also stayed.[30] The key issue is not who is appealing, that is, whether *the appeal* is by or against the debtor. Rather, the key issue is whether *the original action* was

---

22. See Practitioner Treatise, Vol. 1.
23. See Practitioner Treatise, Vol. 1.
24. See Practitioner Treatise, Vol. 1.
25. See Practitioner Treatise, Vol. 1.
26. See Practitioner Treatise, Vol. 1.
27. See Practitioner Treatise, Vol. 1.
28. As explained by the Fifth Circuit:

   We recognize that the stay, by its statutory words, operates against "the commencement or continuation" of judicial proceedings. No specific reference is made to "dismissal" of judicial proceedings. Nevertheless, it seems to us that ordinarily the stay must be construed to apply to dismissal as well. First, if either of the parties takes any step to obtain dismissal, such as motion to dismiss or motion for summary judgment, there is clearly a continuation of the judicial proceeding. Second, in the more technical sense, just the entry of an order of dismissal, even if entered sua sponte, constitutes a judicial act toward the disposition of the case and hence may be construed as a "continuation" of a judicial proceeding. Third, dismissal of a case places the party dismissed in the position of being stayed "to continue the judicial proceeding," thus effectively blocking his right of appeal. Thus, absent the bankruptcy court's lift of the stay, or perhaps a stipulation of dismissal, a case such as the one before us must, as a general rule, simply languish on the court's docket until final disposition of the bankruptcy proceeding.

   Pope v. Manville Forest Products Corp., 778 F.2d 238, 239 (5th Cir.1985).

29. See Practitioner Treatise, Vol. 1.
30. See Practitioner Treatise, Vol. 1.

against the debtor. Any appeal by anybody in a case that was filed against the debtor is stayed by section 362(a)(1) because anybody's appeal is a continuation of the original action against the debtor. This continuation, even if by the debtor, is stopped by (a)(1). In short: "section 362 should be read to stay all appeals in proceedings that were originally brought against the debtor, regardless of whether the debtor is the appellant or appellee."[31]

The analysis is properly different if the original action was brought by the debtor rather than against her. In this event (a)(1) does not apply to the original action and thus has no application to anybody's appeal as a "continuation" of an action against the debtor.

It might be argued that an appeal by the non-debtor side is stayed on the different basis that the appeal is a distinct "proceeding" against the debtor which (a)(1) views separately and independently without regard to the underlying action. We believe that the terms "action" and "proceeding" refer to the whole of an original cause against the debtor and not separately to its component processes and procedures. The terms must refer to a cause against the debtor because of the requirement in (a)(1) respecting when the action or proceeding was or could have been commenced or when it arose. Also, "proceeding" is distinct from "action" and equal to it. It would be redundant to define "proceeding," in this context, to mean stage or component of an "action" because the latter term, which itself appears in (a)(1), naturally embraces its own parts. "Proceeding" is probably used here as an alternative to "action," rather than as a part of it, to cover cases and causes pursued before non-judicial bodies, which more commonly describe matters they hear as proceedings rather than actions.

Thus, an appeal by the other side in an action brought by the debtor is not itself a proceeding against the debtor and does not continue an action against her, so that nothing in section 362(a)(1) stays the non-debtor's appeal in the debtor's action.[32] More certainly, nothing there stays an appeal by the debtor in an action she brought.[33]

We quickly add that other law can possibly limit appeals in actions brought by the debtor. In the typical case the debtor's cause of action and any judgment on it (or its other proceeds) are property that passed to the estate when bankruptcy was filed. An appeal by the other side would presumably aim to dilute this property and is therefore very likely an act against property of the estate that is stayed by section 362(a)(3).[34] The same (a)(3) may also stay an appeal by the debtor who, by appealing, is violating (a)(3) by exercising control over estate property. In any event, the debtor is not a proper person to prosecute an appeal because the action now belongs to the estate.

Remember that even when the stay of (a)(1) applies, it protects only the debtor and not third persons. This rule carries over to the process or procedure within the action that is stayed. The goings on involving other parties to the action are unaffected by the (a)(1) stay. The action and

---

31. Association of St. Croix Condominium Owners v. St. Croix Hotel Corp., 682 F.2d 446, 449 (3d Cir.1982).

32. See Practitioner Treatise, Vol. 1.

33. See Practitioner Treatise, Vol. 1.

34. See Practitioner Treatise, Vol. 1.

processes and procedures, including appeals, stop only as to the debtor and continue as to everyone else.[35]

Essentially everything freezes as to the debtor. Nobody can do anything to her in the nonbankruptcy forum. A party who wishes to press the action or proceeding against the debtor must turn to the bankruptcy court. There she can file a claim or otherwise appropriately pursue the matter. The stay does not apply to actions, proceedings or other matters in bankruptcy court.[36] An alternative strategy is to ask the bankruptcy court for relief from the stay to commence or continue the action or proceeding in the other forum. Technically, therefore,

> the stay does not prevent a * * * creditor from seeking [a claim] * * * from the debtor. Rather, it forces the creditor to look to the estate for the amount or to get permission from the court to pursue it outside the bankruptcy proceeding.[37]

Only the bankruptcy court can grant this relief. The nonbankruptcy forum cannot give it, not even a higher federal court.[38] In the event relief is granted, the other body can only act within the license granted—to the extent permitted—by the bankruptcy court's order in lifting the stay.[39] The stay continues in force beyond the bounds of this license.

Some process and procedure affecting the debtor is permitted in an action or proceeding against her that is otherwise stayed. Common practice allows the debtor or another party in a lawsuit to file a suggestion of bankruptcy that gently, actually warns everybody that a bankruptcy case has been filed. In this event, or however the news is heard, the forum court can freely determine if the stay affects the action or proceeding before it.[40]

Also, section 362(a)(1) does not block reporting, after bankruptcy, a decision in an action or proceeding that was made before bankruptcy. The stay bars any step in making the decision so that, if any deliberations are necessary after bankruptcy, the decision cannot be made.[41] The stay probably also bars any procedural step necessary to make the decision effective under non-bankruptcy law.[42] The tiny exception for post-petition reporting of a decision in an action or proceeding permits "only rote post-petition activity."[43] The test is whether the matter was decided "in word and deed" before bankruptcy "leaving only the clerical act of recording * * *."

It is not clear that section 362(a)(1) stays a prepetition decision, resulting from a covered action or proceeding that first becomes effective, automatically, after bankruptcy. On the one hand, the maturing of the decision involves no action. On the other hand, (a)(1) covers the continuation of an action or proceeding without requiring, expressly, that the continuation itself involve action. So read, (a)(1) could stay the decision as a continuation of the proceeding that produced it. Probably, however, the term "continuation" is limited by the meaning of "action" and "proceeding." These parent

---

35. See Practitioner Treatise, Vol. 1.
36. See Practitioner Treatise, Vol. 1.
37. Delta Sav. & Loan Ass'n, Inc. v. I.R.S., 847 F.2d 248, 250 (5th Cir. 1988.)
38. See Practitioner Treatise, Vol. 1.
39. See Practitioner Treatise, Vol. 1.
40. See Practitioner Treatise, Vol. 1.
41. See Practitioner Treatise, Vol. 1.
42. See Practitioner Treatise, Vol. 1.
43. In re Knightsbridge Development Co. Inc., 884 F.2d 145, 148 (4th Cir.1989).

terms naturally imply affirmative actions [44]—process and procedures—in reaching a decision; and they naturally exclude the inert decision itself. The decision results from the proceeding and is the ending rather than a continuation of it.

e. "Against the Debtor"

Section 362(a)(1) very clearly limits itself to actions or proceedings that are "against the debtor." Most obviously, this language excludes from (a)(1) suits that the debtor brings against other people.[45] Some courts believe the language also excludes the debtor's counterclaims when she is sued, so that the debtor can continue her claims against the plaintiff who is stayed from continuing against her.[46]

The plaintiff will likely argue that although the debtor's counterclaim, alone, is an action by the debtor rather than against her, the counterclaim nevertheless continues the lawsuit that was filed against the debtor. For this reason, (a)(1) stays the counterclaim equally with the plaintiff's action itself. The problem with this argument is that the plaintiff's action that started the lawsuit is stayed. The lawsuit continues but only to determine the debtor's counterclaim against the plaintiff. No action against the debtor is continued by pursuing the counterclaim.

A different argument for stopping both the debtor's actions as plaintiff and her counterclaims as defendant is that the underlying causes are property of the estate. The trustee is therefore the proper party to pursue them, and the debtor herself continuing either an action or counterclaim is stayed by (a)(3) which stops anyone's exercise of control over property of the estate. This argument has divided the courts.[47] Nobody much doubts that the debtor's causes of action pass to the estate, but not everybody agrees that the debtor is thereby completely robbed of the right or power to prosecute them.

On the other side of the coin are counterclaims against the debtor in actions by her. Whether they are stayed by (a)(1) depends on whether the coverage of the provision is determined by the nature of the original action and limited by it, so that (a)(1) applies to everything in a lawsuit filed against the debtor but applies to nothing in a suit she filed. We believe that the meaning of "action or proceeding" in (a)(1) is limited but not so narrowly. A counterclaim against the debtor is a cause of action that was or could have been commenced, or arose, and thus seems plainly covered by (a)(1).[48] The stay surely would have stopped the action if the defendant had pursued it in the form of a lawsuit commenced against the debtor. Stopping the action as a counterclaim is no more unfair. Only the form has changed.

In any event the defendant remains free to fight the debtor's action against her,[49] even if doing so requires countering for declaratory relief in the same [50] or a different forum.[51] Also, her claim against the debtor is not

---

44. See Practitioner Treatise, Vol. 1.
45. See Practitioner Treatise, Vol. 1.
46. See Practitioner Treatise, Vol. 1.
47. See Practitioner Treatise, Vol. 1.
48. See Practitioner Treatise, Vol. 1.
49. See Practitioner Treatise, Vol. 1.
50. See Practitioner Treatise, Vol. 1.
51. See Practitioner Treatise, Vol. 1.

lost. She can pursue the claim in bankruptcy court. Only the forum has changed.

Not everybody will be quite so sanguine about the rights of a defendant who is sued by the debtor. These are people who are concerned that staying a creditor's hand who has been sued would expose the defendant-creditor to inconsistent findings of fact, would unduly complicate the suit and might add considerable expense to the litigation. They would either interpret section 362 to prohibit the debtor's suit or be quite generous in allowing a defendant to bring counterclaims and affirmative defenses, even though these matters could not be brought against the debtor as an original matter.

f. The Prepetition Limitation

Section 362(a)(1) is also limited by its requirement on the timing of the cause that is asserted against the debtor. No action to recover a claim is stayed by (a)(1), not even a classic lawsuit on a contract debt, unless the claim "*arose*" before bankruptcy, i.e., "before the commencement of the case."[52] Any other kind of action or proceeding is stayed by (a)(1) only if it "was or could have been commenced" before bankruptcy.[53] "Since claims arising postpetition are not dischargeable, there is no compelling reason to stay judicial proceedings predicated on such claims."[54] When an action could have been commenced is usually determined by reference to nonbankruptcy law; but when a claim "arose" is decided according to a federal standard in light of bankruptcy policy that is not dictated by state law.[55] The standard can surely incorporate and reflect state law but need not mirror it.

Bankruptcy law does not define when a claim "arose" in terms of when an action based on it could have been commenced. The two events are thus different. Coincidentally, they can occur simultaneously and sometimes do; but a claim can arise much earlier and often does. The common explanation is that "claim" is itself defined very broadly to include:

> [any] right to payment, whether or not such right is reduced to judgment, liquidated, unliquidated, fixed, contingent, matured, unmatured, disputed, undisputed, legal, equitable, secured or unsecured.[56]

---

52. 11 U.S.C.A. § 362(a)(1) (emphasis added); see, e.g., In re Gull Air, Inc., 890 F.2d 1255, 1263 (1st Cir.1989) (Proceeding to withdraw airport landing slots was not stayed by (a)(1) because the proceeding could not have been commenced before the debtor's bankruptcy.); Holland America Ins. Co. v. Succession of Roy, 777 F.2d 992 (5th Cir.1985) (After bankruptcy a fire destroyed the debtor's building. The insurer filed an interpleader action. The action was not stayed by (a)(1). The true explanation is that the action was impossible prior to bankruptcy because the loss was postpetition.); Broadcast Music, Inc. v. Game Operators Corp., 107 B.R. 326, 327 (D.Kan.1989) (Section 362(a) does not bar actions for infringements occurring postpetition.); In re Shuman, 122 B.R. 317 (Bankr. S.D.Ohio 1990) (The action against the debtor was not stayed because the alleged negligent entrustment, which was the basis of the action, occurred postpetition. The stay does not stop any action on a postpetition claim, although relief may be necessary to enforce any judgment resulting from the action.).

53. 11 U.S.C.A. § 362(a)(1).

54. Matter of M. Frenville Co., Inc., 744 F.2d 332, 338 (3d Cir.1984), cert. denied, 469 U.S. 1160, 105 S.Ct. 911, 83 L.Ed.2d 925 (1985).

55. This view is dominant. See, e.g., Grady v. A.H. Robins Co., Inc., 839 F.2d 198, 200–03 (4th Cir.1988), cert. dism'd, 487 U.S. 1260, 109 S.Ct. 201, 101 L.Ed.2d 972 (1988).

56. 11 U.S.C.A. § 101(5).

Thus, a claim exists even though it is contingent, provisional or otherwise indefinite. On the other hand, there is no claim without a right to payment. Substituting the latter for the former only begs the question.

The explanation is slightly more complicated. A claim or right to payment exists because the debtor becomes obligated to pay. This obligation tracks ultimately to certain defining conduct identified by law. The actions that create obligations, and the conditions and circumstances that limit or further define the obligations, are properly determined by nonbankruptcy law; but bankruptcy law properly determines, for purposes of section 362(a)(1) and its other inventions, the point from which to date the obligation and corresponding right to pay it, i.e., the point at which the claim arose.

> So, the bankruptcy Code is superimposed upon the law of the State which has created the obligation. * * * Congress intended that all legal obligations of the debtor, no matter how remote or contingent, will be able to be dealt with in bankruptcy. The Code contemplates the broadest possible relief in the bankruptcy court. Also, * * * the automatic stay is one of the fundamental debtor protections provided by the bankruptcy laws.[57]

These bankruptcy policies argue for determining that a claim arises at an early point. With this thought in mind most courts date a claim, for purposes of (a)(1), from the time of the debtor's actions that are the root of the obligation.

In sum, a claim arises under bankruptcy law when the debtor acts to obligate herself (whether by law or agreement) to pay money (either now or later) even though the obligation is contingent. Therefore, in the case of an obligation that was contingent by state law by postponing the right to immediate payment and suit, the claim nevertheless dates from the time of the debtor's conduct that underlies the obligation.[58]

By this definition a tort claim arises when the tortious conduct itself occurs.[59] It is because of this conduct that the tortfeasor becomes obligated to pay even for injuries and damages that may occur later. An action on a tort claim is therefore stayed if the conduct occurred prepetition even though the harm did not occur or was not discovered until after bankruptcy.

A contract claim can arise as soon as the contract is made. Making the contract immediately gives each party a right to performance by the other party. The seller of the property or services gets a right to the price conditioned upon her performance and the terms of payment. This right, though conditioned, is a right to payment or claim that arose, for purposes of section 362(a)(1), when the contract was made. Suppose, for example, that a lender or seller makes a loan or sells goods on credit and awaits payment due later from the buyer. The buyer files bankruptcy and defaults. An action by the lender or seller to recover the claim is stayed by section 362(a)(1).

57. Grady v. A.H. Robins Co., Inc., 839 F.2d 198, 202 (4th Cir.1988), cert. dism'd, 487 U.S. 1260, 109 S.Ct. 201, 101 L.Ed.2d 972 (1988).

58. See Practitioner Treatise, Vol. 1.

59. See Practitioner Treatise, Vol. 1.

Similarly, when a suretyship contract is made before the principal debtor's bankruptcy and the surety pays thereafter, the surety's action against the debtor for reimbursement is stayed by (a)(1). The surety's right to reimbursement did not mature, under state law, until the surety paid the debt; but the right to reimbursement arose, under bankruptcy law, when the suretyship contract was made because the law immediately obligated the debtor to reimburse the surety upon the surety's payment of the debt.[60] This right of the surety to reimbursement was initially contingent, but a contingent right to payment is nevertheless a claim.

The problem in reverse is harder: the debtor is the supplier of promised property or services. The buyer has paid for them and expects delivery as promised at a date that is preceded by the debtor's bankruptcy. The debtor's default gives the buyer a right to damages. Whether (a)(1) stays an action to recover these damages depends, as always, on whether the claim arose pre- or post-petition.

On the one hand, the buyer had no right to damages, under state law, until the seller's breach, which was postpetition. Before then the buyer had a right to performance but not money. Moreover, the conduct that created the right to damages, per se, was the breach.

On the other hand, the right to damages substitutes for the right to performance which tracks, in turn, to the prepetition conduct of the parties in creating the contract. Upon making the contract the buyer got a right to performance or, alternatively, a right to damages if the seller defaulted. A contingent right to payment is nevertheless a claim.

We could accept that the buyer's claim is prepetition because she would be treated the same as the lender or financing seller whose debtor defaults in payment after filing bankruptcy. The pre-paying buyer is basically, like them, a financer. Also, the drag on the debtor's fresh start is the same whether the obligation is to pay the price of property or services supplied to her or to pay damages for not supplying them to someone else.

The problem is made easier if the buyer has not paid the price when the supplier-debtor files bankruptcy. In this event the contract is executory. Section 365 forces the trustee to assume or reject the contract. No claim matures if the contract is assumed and performed. A breach occurs if the contract is rejected, and the buyer's right to damages is treated, by express provision, as a prepetition claim.[61] Section 362(a)(1) naturally stays any action to recover the claim. This treatment may imply or endorse a larger policy that the debtor's postpetition breach of any prepetition contract amounts to a prepetition claim.

Tort and other non-contract claims that are related to a contract do not necessarily date from the same time as claims based on the contract itself. Rather, the non-contract claims arise when the different or further conduct occurred on which they, as distinct claims, are based.[62] This conduct can occur earlier or later than the conduct producing the contract claims.

---

60. See Practitioner Treatise, Vol. 1.

61. 11 U.S.C.A. § 365(g)(1). A claim based on a breach before the contract is assumed or rejected "would be considered a pre-petition claim, even if the activities which allegedly constitute the breach occurred post-petition, and would be stayed under 11 U.S.C. § 362." In re Ionosphere Clubs Inc., 124 B.R. 635, 639 (S.D.N.Y. 1991).

62. See Practitioner Treatise, Vol. 1.

Determining if a claim arose prepetition based on root conduct is not limited to the usual, straight tort or contract action. The approach applies generally, as in *In re Transportation Systems International, Inc.*[63] Before bankruptcy the debtor, TSI, carried goods for Honeywell and, a later audit revealed, undercharged for the services. Honeywell responded to a bill for the undercharges by contesting them before the ICC. Honeywell contended that the ICC proceeding escaped (a)(1) because the audit revealing the undercharges did not occur until after bankruptcy, which is when Honeywell first learned of them. The court rejected the argument because

> a claim is considered to arise, for bankruptcy purposes, at "the time when acts giving rise to the alleged liability were performed." This is true even though at the time the acts giving rise to liability were performed the claimant had not discovered his or her injury and did not have access to the courts. Thus, in this case, TSI's claim arose at the time Honeywell paid TSI less than the applicable tariff rate and must be considered pre-petition.[64]

Like reasoning marks *In re Chateaugay Corp.*[65] The debtor, LTV, created and maintained an employee pension plan that was eventually terminated, postpetition, because of insufficient funding. The termination resulted from action by the PBGC, a government-owned entity that insured the plan. Upon termination LTV became accountable to the PBGC for certain claims, including "termination liability" equalling the amount by which the pension plan assets were insufficient to satisfy insured benefits that PBGC paid pensioners. This liability was part of the law that governed LTV's creation and maintenance of the pension plan. LTV argued that the termination liability was a prepetition claim and that any nonbankruptcy proceeding to recover it was stayed. The court agreed:

> Consistent with the goals of uniform treatment for creditors and a fresh start for debtors, courts have determined when a claim arises for Code purposes by focusing upon "the time when the acts giving rise to the alleged liability were performed" * * *. Where the debtors' obligations stem from contractual liability, even a post-petition breach will be treated as giving rise to a prepetition liability where the contract was executed prepetition.
>
>   * * *
>
> Therefore, in order to determine the status of PBGC's claims, this court must consider what acts gave rise to LTV's pension liabilities, when they occurred * * *.
>
> Here, the events that gave rise to the PBGC's claims and that mark them as prepetition were LTV Steel's creation and maintenance of a pension plan that was subject to [federal law's] termination liability

---

63. 110 B.R. 888 (D.Minn.1990), aff'd on somewhat diff. grounds sub nom., Lovett v. Honeywell, Inc., 930 F.2d 625 (8th Cir. 1991).

64. 110 B.R. at 894 (The proceeding nonetheless escaped (a)(1) because it was not "against the debtor."); compare Taylor v. First Fed. Sav. & Loan Ass'n, 843 F.2d 153, 154 (3d Cir.1988) (Section 362(a)(1) does not prevent the state from filing a judgment to secure repayment of welfare payments paid postpetition.).

65. 87 B.R. 779 (S.D.N.Y. 1988), aff'd, 875 F.2d 1008 (2d Cir. 1989), rev'd and remanded, 496 U.S. 633, 110 S.Ct. 2668, 110 L.Ed.2d 579 (1990).

provisions * * *. The PBGC's right to payment upon termination was, on the petition date, a classic example of a contingent claim—"one which the debtor will be called upon to pay only upon the occurrence or happening of an extrinsic event." If the extrinsic event occurs post-petition, the contingent claim simply becomes a liquidated one; it, however, is not thereby elevated to the status of a post-petition claim. Here, the extrinsic event was plan termination, which simply fixed LTV's liability to PBGC.[66]

We agree with these cases but warn against their shorthand. The courts here and elsewhere describe their approach, for determining when a claim arose, as focusing upon "the time when the acts giving rise to the alleged liability were performed."[67] This common description is accurate but misleading unless you remember that the "alleged liability" is the debtor's underlying obligation to pay rather than the later tortious harm or the contractual breach that triggers or matures the obligation. The courts focus on the acts that created this obligation and corresponding right to payment rather than on the events that triggered the right to collect it. If these acts of creation occurred prepetition, the claim arose then and section 362(a)(1) stays any action to recover it even though the action, by state law, could not have been commenced prepetition. Defining when a claim arose in these terms weakens this limitation on the scope of (a)(1) and thereby strengthens the force of the stay, which is exactly the result the definition intends.

As a final matter we also warn that an action that escapes (a)(1) is nevertheless affected by the stay at the enforcement stage. The action can freely continue even so far as entry of judgment against the debtor. The judgment, however, cannot be enforced against property of the estate. The main reasons are (a)(3-4), which guard estate property from liens and any act to get possession of it. The judgment is enforceable, but only against the debtor's individual property. The stay protects this property only from prepetition claims, not postpetition claims that can be pursued to judgment despite (a)(1).

§ 3–7 Actions Against the Debtors—"Exception" for Collective Bargaining

For full text of this section, see Epstein, Nickles & White, Bankruptcy, Practitioner Treatise Series, Vol. 1.

§ 3–8 Actions Against the Debtor—Collection Efforts

Section 362(a)(1) stays, specifically, any action or proceeding to recover a prepetition claim against the debtor. Section (a)(6) covers the same ground and goes beyond it by staying "any act to collect, assess, or recover a

---

66. 87 B.R. at 796–97 (S.D.N.Y. 1988).

67. The source is In re Johns–Manville Corp., 57 B.R. 680, 690 (Bankr. S.D.N.Y. 1986). In this case the buyers of goods had claims for indemnification and contribution against the debtor-seller resulting from harm suffered by the buyers' customers in using the goods. The court determined that these claims tracked all the way back to the seller-debtor providing the defective goods to the buyers.

[prepetition] claim against the debtor * * *."[1] This broad language principally adds to (a)(1) by reaching collection efforts that occur without or apart from litigation or other action or proceeding: (a)(6) "prevents creditors attempting *in any way* to collect a prepetition debt."[2]

Relatedly (even redundantly), section 362(a)(2) prevents enforcing a prepetition judgment against the debtor. Any effort to do so, whether formal or informal, would also fall within the broad language of (a)(6) as an act to collect a prepetition claim. Formal enforcement, as by execution process, is further stayed by (a)(1) and, because a lien is typically involved, (a)(4) or (5). Section 362(a) is repeatedly redundant.

A major unique contribution of (a)(6) is in staying a creditor's informal collection efforts, even telephone calls because:

> [c]reditors in consumer cases occasionally telephone debtors to encourage repayment in spite of bankruptcy. Inexperienced, frightened, or ill-counseled debtors may succumb to suggestions to repay notwithstanding their bankruptcy. This provision prevents evasion of the purpose of the bankruptcy laws by sophisticated creditors.[3]

Collection letters and the like are covered,[4] too, as well as more coercive tactics.

In the case *In re Sechuan City, Inc.*,[5] the debtor, which operated a restaurant, had not paid the rent. The landlord ran the hotel in which the restaurant was located. Upon learning of the debtor's bankruptcy, the hotel manager posted signs near the restaurant that reported the debtor's bankruptcy and the nonpayment of rent and asked the public not to patronize the restaurant because "IT DOES NOT PAY IT'S [sic] BILLS."[6] The admitted purpose was "to 'shame' and 'embarrass' the debtor into paying its bills."[7] Posting the signs violated (a)(6):

> [the lessor] undertook a studied effort to coerce payment of the lessor's prepetition claim. * * * While the lessor did not bring a suit against the debtor, its actions were designed to place the debtor in a position of either paying the lessor's prepetition claim or losing business due to defendants' actions. Such a choice runs counter to the purpose of § 362(a).[8]

§ 3–8

1. 11 U.S.C.A. § 362(a)(6).

2. H.R. Rep. No. 595, 95th Cong., 1st Sess. 342, reprinted in 1978 U.S. Code Cong. & Admin. News 5963, 6298; S. Rep. No. 989, 95th Cong., 2d Sess. 50, reprinted in 1978 U.S. Code Cong. & Admin. News 5787, 5836 (emphasis added).

3. H.R. Rep. No. 595, 95th Cong., 1st Sess. 342, reprinted in 1978 U.S. Code Cong. & Admin. News 5963, 6298; S. Rep. No. 989, 95th Cong., 2d Sess. 50–51, reprinted in 1978 U.S. Code Cong. & Admin. News 5787, 5836–37.

4. In re Bulson, 117 B.R. 537, 539 (Bankr. 9th Cir.1990) (IRS collection notice); In re Nelson, 123 B.R. 993, 1000 (Bankr. D.S.D.1991) ("A letter apprising a debtor's attorney of the existence of legal rights does not violate the automatic stay. A letter demanding the debtor contact a creditor within a certain period of days or lose legal rights violates 11 U.S.C. § 362(a)."); In re Newell, 117 B.R. 323, 324 (Bankr. S.D.Ohio 1990) (The stay of (a)(6) is violated by inadvertently sending invoices to debtor.); In re Still, 117 B.R. 251, 254 (Bankr. E.D.Tex.1990) (notice of condemnation hearing to take easement across debtor's land).

5. 96 B.R. 37 (Bankr. E.D.Pa. 1989).

6. Id. at 39.

7. Id.

8. Id. at 41–42.

The landlord's free-speech defense failed. The first amendment only weakly protects speech falling at this point on the constitutional spectrum, that is, speech on matters of purely private concern; and this protection fades when, as here, the competing governmental interest is very strong.[9]

Subsection (a)(6) is not limitless. It does not ban every report of a debtor's bankruptcy, and does not prevent all communications by a creditor. No act is stayed by (a)(6) unless the purpose is "to collect, assess or recover" a prepetition claim. Benign reports of information to the debtor or third persons are therefore beyond (a)(6),[10] and so too are creditors' acts toward the debtor that are threatening for reasons not covered by (a)(6). For example, (a)(6) does not stop the federal government from investigating or even revoking the debtor's preferred tax status.[11]

The purpose threshold of (a)(6) is even higher. The courts interpret (a)(6) or add to it by requiring, ordinarily, some element or coercion or harassment in the act to collect. As explained by the Ninth Circuit in *Morgan Guaranty Trust Co. v. American Savings and Loan Ass'n*[12]:

> The case law supports a distinction between communications between the creditor and debtor that contain threats or harassment and those that merely set forth the fact that money is owing. Thus, courts have held the automatic stay violated by letters giving notice of intent to terminate a lease, by a letter informing the debtor that a creditor medical clinic would provide no future medical services due to his refusal to pay, by a letter from an attorney informing the debtor he had been retained by a creditor to collect a delinquent account, by a college that refused to give transcripts to the debtor to force payment, and by a creditor who made repeated visits and telephone calls to the debtor. On the other hand, a court has said that a letter from a credit union announcing it would do no further business with the debtor unless the debt was reaffirmed would not have violated the automatic stay if it had been sent to the debtor's attorney, and we have treated other communications that merely set forth the fact of the debt as amendable proofs of claim not voided by the automatic stay.[13]

Honoring this distinction the court held that "mere requests for payment" are not barred absent coercion or harassment by the creditor. Specifically, (a)(6) does not stay presentment of a negotiable instrument for payment, which is an act that Congress in 1984 expressly excepted from the stay through section 362(b)(11).[14]

Despite this purpose requirement which somewhat limits the reach of

---

9. See Practitioner Treatise, Vol. 1.
10. See Practitioner Treatise, Vol. 1.
11. See Practitioner Treatise, Vol. 1.
12. 804 F.2d 1487 (9th Cir.1986), cert. denied, 482 U.S. 929, 107 S.Ct. 3214, 96 L.Ed.2d 701 (1987).
13. Id. at 1491 n.4.
14. "The filing of a petition * * * does not operate as a stay * * * under subsection (a) of this section, of the presentment of a negotiable instrument and the giving of notice of and protesting dishonor of such an instrument." 11 U.S.C.A. § 362(b)(11); In re Roete, 936 F.2d 963, 965–66 (7th Cir.1991) (Creditor did not violate stay in attempting, postpetition, to cash check that debtor wrote prepetition.). "Presentment is a demand for acceptance or payment made upon the maker, acceptor, drawee or other payor [of a negotiable instrument] by or on behalf of the holder." U.C.C. § 3–504(1).

(a)(6), there are reports, as in *In re Sechuan City, Inc.*,[15] that "the band of permitted activities is narrow, given the broad language utilized by Congress in the catch-all provision of § 362(a)(6) and the purposes behind the stay."[16] Indeed, by reading (a)(6) in light of the general, broad purposes of section 362 in whole, the courts are wrong to limit (a)(6) to acts designed only to harass. This reading shrinks (a)(6) short of its terms and reason.

On the other hand, a person who doubts the stay's efficacy would also doubt the merit of the report in *Sechuan City* and wonder if the court correctly articulates the rules in (a)(6). Debtors, after all, are not potted plants; they can say no. By this view, the stay should be applied only to communications that are themselves harassing.

Assessing a claim is expressly covered by the terms of (a)(6), as if acting to assess is distinct and different from an action to collect or recover. The clearest example is the process whereby government formally determines or imposes tax liability as a preliminary step in creating a tax lien.[17] On the other hand, the act of notifying the debtor of a tax deficiency, which can be a component of or closely related to assessment, is expressly excepted from the stay by section 362(b)(9).[18] The purpose of the notice exception, which is rooted in the federal tax system, is "'to permit the debtor to take his personal tax case to the Tax Court, if the bankruptcy judge authorizes him to do so * * *.'"[19]

In the federal system this deficiency notice is required when the debtor has understated her tax liability. It essentially warns the debtor that the IRS believes more taxes are owed than the debtor admits. The notice then triggers the taxpayer's right to a redetermination in the Tax Court, and is a necessary condition for assessment and a tax lien. Therefore, in a case of understated tax liability, the combination of (a)(6) and (b)(9) has this effect on the United States:

> It can calculate the amount of unpaid taxes, and it can notify the taxpayer of the total deficiency, but it cannot formally assess tax liability and create a lien.[20]

Neither the (a)(6) stay of assessment nor the (b)(9) notice exception is limited to the collection of federal taxes. Both apply equally and comparably to the collection of state and local taxes.[21] Possibly, the (a)(6) stay of

---

15. 96 B.R. 37 (Bankr. E.D.Pa. 1989).

16. Id. at 14.

17. In re Schwartz, 119 B.R. 207, 208 (Bankr. 9th Cir.1990), decision rev'd on other grounds, 954 F.2d 569 (9th Cir.1992) (Postpetition assessment of prepetition taxes violates § 362(a)(4–6)); Anglemyer v. United States, 115 B.R. 510, 512 (D.Md.1990) (IRS making tax assessments against debtor violates the stay.).

18. 11 U.S.C.A. § 362(b)(9).

19. H & H Beverage Distributors v. Department of Revenue of the Commonwealth of Pennsylvania, 850 F.2d 165, 167 (3d Cir.1988), cert. denied, 488 U.S. 994, 109 S.Ct. 560, 102 L.Ed.2d 586 (1988).

20. H & H Beverage Distributors v. Department of Revenue of the Commonwealth of Pennsylvania, 850 F.2d 165, 169 (3d Cir.1988), cert. denied, 488 U.S. 994, 109 S.Ct. 560, 102 L.Ed.2d 586 (1988) (dicta); see also In re Apex Oil Co., 122 B.R. 559, 566 (Bankr. E.D.Mo. 1990) (Customs' assessment of import duties and postpetition claim liquidation were not excepted from the stay of § 362(b)(9).).

21. H & H Beverage Distributors v. Department of Revenue of the Commonwealth of Pennsylvania, 850 F.2d 165, 167–70 (3d Cir. 1988), cert. denied, 488 U.S. 994, 109 S.Ct. 560, 102 L.Ed.2d 586 (1988) (The stay was not violated by the state's audit of the debtor to determine extent of any tax claim, or by sending the debtor notice of audit assessment. The notice was excepted under § 362(b)(9) as the functional equivalent of a notice of federal tax deficiency. On the other hand, the state

assessment has even broader application because, unlike (b)(9), the terms of (a)(6) are not tied to tax debts.

We have saved for last the most interesting question about the scope of (a)(6): Does "*act* to collect" include refusing to deal or otherwise to act with the debtor? Suppose, for example, that the creditor is a long-time supplier of goods on open account that are critically important to the debtor's business. The debtor can most efficiently deal with this creditor because of their experience together and well-established course of conduct. Continuing this relationship is thus financially important to the debtor. After the debtor's bankruptcy, however, the creditor refuses to sell to the debtor even for cash. Finding another supplier will cost time and money that the debtor's bankruptcy probably cannot afford.

If the creditor were contractually obligated to continue supplying the debtor, the debtor could of course assume the contract.[22] By complying with section 365 the debtor could force the creditor to continue to perform. Even apart from section 365, the contract would become property of the estate; and it is arguable that the creditor would be barred from cancelling or breaching the contract by section 362(a)(3), which prohibits interference with property of the estate.[23] By this argument, section 362(a)(3) alone would shield the contract from cancellation or breach.

Put aside for now the issue whether or not (a)(3) condemns cancelling a contract and failing to perform under it. We say more on this issue later.[24]

There are other refusals to act with respect to property of the estate that, more certainly, amount to interference with the property in violation of (a)(3). In this event, whenever such a refusal occurs whereby (a)(3) is violated, (a)(3) is a sufficient basis for finding a violation of the stay without resorting to (a)(6). For example, *In re Farmers Markets, Inc.*,[25] which was decided on (a)(6), could be based on (a)(3). In this case, the debtor had sold its liquor license, but the state refused to transfer the license to the buyer until the debtor's taxes were paid. The court held that this refusal violated (a)(6).[26]

The more substantial holding in *Farmers Markets* was that the license had become property of the estate subject to the state's right to payment under a local statute that disallows transfer until taxes are paid.[27] In light of this holding, one could explain the stay violation in terms of (a)(3):

could not actually create a lien without making a demand and filing, and these acts are stayed.).

22. 11 U.S.C.A. § 365.

23. Subsection (a)(3) stays "any act to obtain possession of property of the estate or of property from the estate or to exercise control over property of the estate." 11 U.S.C.A. § 362(a)(3).

24. See § 3–14 infra.

25. 792 F.2d 1400 (9th Cir.1986).

26. Id. at 1404 ("The State refused to transfer the licenses in an effort to obtain payment of its claims without first seeking relief from the automatic stay from the bankruptcy court."); but compare In re Feature Homes, Inc., 116 B.R. 731 (Bankr. E.D.Cal. 1990) (Before bankruptcy the state had suspended the debtor's corporate privileges for failure to pay taxes, and refused to revive them when bankruptcy occurred. The court held that the state had not thereby violated (a)(6), which is not offended absent affirmative action. A refusal to act is not covered.); In re Nu–Process Brake Engineers, Inc., 119 B.R. 700, 702–03 (Bankr. E.D.Mo.1990) (The stay was not violated by the state failing to reinstate the debtor's business sales tax license because of the debtor's failure to pay prepetition taxes.).

27. In re Farmers Markets, Inc., 792 F.2d 1400, 1402–04 (9th Cir.1986).

refusing to transfer the license, which was estate property, was an exercise of control over property of the estate.

Section (a)(6) is also unnecessary to the result in *In re Figgers*.[28] It is explainable in terms of section 362(a)(5), which stays any act to enforce against the debtor's property any lien that secures a prepetition claim.[29] In *Figgers* the creditor froze the debtor's share account that was filled with postpetition earnings. This money belonged to the debtor, not the bankruptcy estate. The creditor's acted pursuant to a pledge of the account to secure a prepetition debt. The court decided that this act violated (a)(6), but the conduct better fits (a)(5). The same is true of *Matter of Hellums*,[30] in which the Seventh Circuit stuck within (a)(6) the automatic garnishment of a debtor's postpetition wages. Whether or not an "act" occurred postpetition as (a)(6) requires, the language of (a)(5) is a better fit because, despite the automation, the garnishment enforced a lien against the debtor's property for a prepetition debt.

In our example, however, neither (a)(3) or (5) is implicated. By refusing to deal with the debtor the supplier has not breached a contractual commitment as to future performance; is not otherwise exercising control over any estate property or property of the debtor; and is not otherwise keeping, withholding or interfering with something to which the debtor or the estate is legally entitled.

Whether or not (a)(6) covers this situation was almost decided in *In re Sportfame of Ohio, Inc.*[31] Here are the facts as the court reported them:

> Plaintiff, Sportfame of Ohio, Inc. (Sportfame), runs four retail sporting goods stores in Ohio, three of which are located in Toledo, one in Findlay. Plaintiff carries a wide variety of goods and, in addition to supplying customers at its stores, employs salespeople to call on schools and institutions with sports programs directly.
>
> Defendant, Wilson Sporting Goods Company (Wilson), has sold its line of sporting goods to plaintiff at wholesale for almost 10 years until recently when it refused to ship any further goods to plaintiff. Defendant had supplied plaintiff with a wide variety of its name brand products which are widely advertised and promoted.
>
> On February 14, 1983 plaintiff filed a voluntary petition under Chapter 11 of the Bankruptcy Code. In the twelve month period prior to the filing of the petition, plaintiff had purchased some $45,000 worth of goods from defendant at wholesale and sold them at retail to its customers for approximately $70,000. Sometime prior to the filing of the petition, plaintiff became in arrears with defendant for shipments of goods in the amount of approximately $18,000. Due to the arrearage, defendant ceased shipping goods to plaintiff prior to the filing of the petition.
>
> In March and April of 1983 Sam R. Shible, president of Sportfame, contacted defendant's credit manager by telephone in an attempt to have shipments of inventory resumed. On these occasions, Mr. Shible

---

28. 121 B.R. 772 (Bankr. S.D.Ohio 1990).

29. 11 U.S.C.A. § 362(a)(5).

30. 772 F.2d 379 (7th Cir.1985).

31. 40 B.R. 47 (Bankr. N.D.Ohio 1984).

attempted to buy goods from defendant for cash. Defendant, while aware of the Chapter 11 proceeding, refused to resume shipments of goods unless plaintiff brought its account current or made arrangements to pay 100% of the arrearage.

As a result of defendant's refusal to fill plaintiff's orders, plaintiff can no longer supply its customers with the Wilson line of sporting goods. According to the evidence adduced at trial, many of plaintiff's individual and institutional customers have asked for certain Wilson goods by name. These same customers many times either refuse or are reluctant to accept as replacements other lines of goods carried by plaintiff. Plaintiff's president testified that its inability to fill orders for Wilson goods will result in customer dissatisfaction and loss of profits.[32]

The court decided that Wilson violated (a)(6) but circumscribed its holding: the violation occurred "by refusing to enter into *cash* transactions with debtor *absent payment of its prepetition debt* where its *sole* motivation was to collect its prepetition debt."[33] The key to this decision is not Wilson's refusal to deal but Wilson's repeated coercive demands for payment. It is irrelevant to the court that the coercion was by carrot rather than stick. In this case, because of the debtor's extraordinary dependency on Wilson, the effect was the same.

The *Sportfame* case does not decide our example in which the supplier has simply refused to deal with the debtor. We do not believe that our supplier has violated (a)(6), not even if her reason for refusing to deal is the debtor's default and bankruptcy. This conduct may well constitute an act, but not an act to collect or recover a claim which (a)(6) requires and which was at the bottom of *Sportfame*. The court in *Sportfame* itself recognized:

> Wilson could have simply refused, for any reason, to sell goods to debtor or offered no explanation for its refusal. Instead, its sole reason for refusing to sell goods to debtor was its desire to collect its prepetition claim.

If any violation of (a)(6) occurred in *Sportfame,* and we are not certain that is so, it was Wilson's act of attempting to collect by insisting on payment. Refusing to deal, for any reason or no reason, is not itself prohibited by (a)(6) or even by section 362(a) in whole absent a contractual or other legal commitment of future performance. As the Third Circuit has so clearly said,

> Nothing in the bankruptcy code requires [a] creditor to do business with [a] debtor. * * * [A] mere refusal to do business does not amount to improper coercion. The refusal can be "designed to protect the ... coffers against repeated defaults, a permissible purpose."[34]

Reading (a)(6) otherwise would seriously undermine freedom of and from contract without the very clear and very strong justification that should be required to do so.[35]

---

32. Id. at 48–49.
33. Id. at 51 (emphasis added).
34. Brown v. Pennsylvania State Employees Credit Union, 851 F.2d 81, 85–86 (3d Cir. 1988), quoting In re Goldrich, 771 F.2d 28, 31–32 (2d Cir.1985).
35. See Practitioner Treatise, Vol. 1.

This analysis does not justify, rather it argues against, a school holding hostage a debtor's transcript. First, the debtor may enjoy some "right" to the transcript which, technically, passed to the estate. By withholding the transcript the school arguably exercises control over estate property in violation of (a)(3). It is possible, however, that the right to the transcript is unenforceable even by the estate, perhaps because the right expired before bankruptcy; property was suspended, before or after bankruptcy, against the world; or passed to the estate and, by some means, left the estate. In any event, even if neither the debtor nor the estate is entitled to the transcript, the school runs a risk of offending the stay by using the transcript as leverage to collect a prepetition debt. Doing so is likely an act to collect that violates (a)(6) a la *Sportfame*.[36]

§ 3–9 Actions Against the Debtor—Special Treatment of Utility Service

For full text of this section, see Epstein, Nickles & White, Bankruptcy, Practitioner Treatise Series, Vol. 1.

§ 3–10 Actions Against the Debtor—Exceptionally Protecting Nondebtors by Extending Section 362

For full text of this section, see Epstein, Nickles & White, Bankruptcy, Practitioner Treatise Series, Vol. 1.

a. Purposive Application (Mainly, the Piccinin "Identity-of-Interest" "Rule")

b. Incidental Protection of Nondebtors When Covered Property Is Involved

c. "Codebtors" in Chapter 12 and 13 Cases (Sections 1201 and 1301)

§ 3–11 Actions Against the Debtor's Property

Commencing a bankruptcy case creates an estate that is immediately filled with all of the debtor's property.[1] Typically, nothing is excepted, and thus the debtor is usually left with nothing. This emptiness of the debtor's personal estate is brief. The debtor gets property that the estate abandons. Additionally, an individual debtor can reclaim estate property that is exempt. Also, in a Chapter 7 case the debtor keeps most of the property she acquires postpetition.

In these and other ways the debtor begins soon after bankruptcy to rebuild her personal estate. This process is the debtor's new start that is a fresh start because the debtor's own property is immune to liens for prepetition claims that had not already attached when the case commenced. The immunity first arises, principally and most directly, through the automatic stay of section 362(a)(5). It stays:

---

36. See Practitioner Treatise, Vol. 1.

§ 3–11

1. 11 U.S.C.A. § 541(a).

any act to create, perfect, or enforce against property of the debtor any lien to the extent that such lien secures a claim that arose before the commencement of the case under this title.[2]

As a result, for example, the court in *In re Schroff*[3] declared void several judgment liens that creditors secured postpetition[4] in violation of (a)(5).

The immunity of the debtor's property survives after the stay dies. It is continued by the debtor's discharge.[5] The discharge itself prevents the creation of liens for prepetition claims by permanently enjoining any action, proceedings or act to collect these claims.[6]

Preexisting liens on property that the debtor owns at the time of bankruptcy are not extinguished by the bankruptcy itself. These liens survive the filing and continue with the property into the bankruptcy estate, which honors the principle of derivative title. To the extent of the avoiding powers, the trustee can repeal the liens for the purpose of enriching the estate.

In a reorganization case, any of the preexisting liens that still survive will eventually die upon confirmation of the plan when the property is returned to the debtor.[7] They are often reborn as new liens that are created by the plan of reorganization. The purpose in a Chapter 11 case is to meet the requirement that the plan treat secured creditors fairly and equitably by allowing them to retain their liens.[8] The law is similar in a Chapter 13 case.[9]

Although confirmation passes the property of the estate to the debtor,[10] section 362(a)(5) does not then protect the property from the liens that the plan created, not even in a Chapter 13 case in which the stay generally survives throughout the plan's implementation. The explanation is that section 362(a)(5) protects the debtor's property against liens for prepetition debts. A lien that a plan creates does not secure such a debt. Rather, as explained by the court in *In re Nicholson:*[11]

> [O]nce a plan is confirmed, and the property of the estate has vested in the debtor, the secured creditor's rights and interests are then defined by the provisions of the plan. * * * In other words, the plan itself has the effect of making a new agreement between the debtor and the creditor with a new obligation to be paid in the manner provided for by the terms of the plan.

---

2. Id. § 362(a)(5).

3. 94 B.R. 279 (Bankr. E.D.N.Y.1988).

4. Id. at 283. Liens that attached prepetition cannot be foreclosed. The (a)(5) stay prevents even the IRS from levying on the debtor's exempt property to perfect and enforce statutory tax liens even though the liens are nondischargeable and the government's right to tax payments is a priority claim. In re Miller, 98 B.R. 110, 113 (Bankr. N.D.Ga.1989).

5. See 11 U.S.C.A. § 727(b) (The debtor is discharged from prepetition debts.); § 1141(d)(1)(A) (Confirmation of a plan discharges the debtor from pre-confirmation debts.); § 1228(c) (When the debtor completes making payments under the plan, the court grants a discharge which discharges the debtor from all unsecured debts provided by the plan or disallowed.); § 1328(c) (essentially the same).

6. Id. § 524(a)(2).

7. Id. § 1141(c).

8. Id. § 1129(b)(2).

9. See id. §§ 1325(a)(5) & 1327(c).

10. The property remains in the estate, however, if the plan so provides. In re Denn, 37 B.R. 33, 35–36 (Bankr. D.Minn.1983) (The court honored provision of Chapter 13 plan that kept property of the estate in the estate until one of the enumerated events occurred.).

11. 70 B.R. 398 (Bankr. D.Colo.1987).

If the debtor defaults post-confirmation in the performance of his obligations under the plan, the secured creditor's remedy is to foreclose the lien which the creditor was granted by the terms of the plan as security for the payments to be made as agreed under the plan. The foreclosure of the lien, under these circumstances, does not constitute an act by the creditor to enforce against property of the debtor a lien securing a claim that arose before the commencement of the Chapter 13 case, nor does it constitute an act to collect a pre-petition claim from the debtor within the meaning of 11 U.S.C.A. § 362(a)(5) and (6). It is, instead, enforcement of the new agreement evidenced by the plan.[12]

Estate property is not generally returned to the debtor in a liquidation case, with some important exceptions. For example, any property with preexisting liens that are not avoided is surrendered to the secured creditor, save any equity which is distributed to unsecured creditors. Technically, if the surrender is accomplished by the trustee abandoning the property, the abandonment actually puts title in the debtor and only possession in the creditor for purposes of foreclosure.[13] Technically, therefore, the property is returned to the debtor. An even larger exception is an individual debtor's exempt property: it passes to the estate but is returned to the debtor when she properly asserts her exemptions in bankruptcy.

Preexisting liens, which survived into the estate, continue in property that the debtor exempts or otherwise reclaims from the estate (as by abandonment). Nevertheless, (a)(5) stops any act to perfect or enforce these liens even though the property now belongs to the debtor rather than to the estate.[14]

Unperfected liens are typically avoided in bankruptcy. The trustee commonly erases them using, principally, sections 544(a), 547 or 545 of her avoiding powers.[15] The trustee focuses, however, on building the estate. There is little incentive for her to avoid liens on property that the debtor exempts and thereby removes from the estate. The Code therefore empowers the debtor to use the trustee's avoiding powers against certain liens on exempt property, including the powers that are easily and commonly used to avoid unperfected liens.[16] It is significant, therefore, that (a)(5) stays not only the creation and enforcement of a lien against the debtor's property, but also perfection of the lien.[17] Unless the stay is lifted, a lien that enters bankruptcy unperfected cannot be perfected while the property remains in the estate; and, because of (a)(5), the lien cannot be perfected if the property returns to the debtor by reason of exemption or otherwise. In any event the

---

12. Id. at 400; cf. In re Erie Hilton Joint Venture, 125 B.R. 140, 147–48 (Bankr. W.D.Pa.1991) (Upon confirmation of Chapter 11 plan, the property of the estate vested in the debtor and the property was thereupon subject to liens for postpetition real estate taxes.); but see In re Harrell, 57 B.R. 88, 89–90 (Bankr.D.S.C.1985) (The (a)(5) stay protects the property of the Chapter 11 debtor even against liens for liabilities accruing after confirmation.) (dicta).

13. In re D'Annies Restaurant, Inc., 15 B.R. 828, 830 (Bankr. D.Minn.1981); In re Tyler, 15 B.R. 258, 260 (Bankr. E.D.Pa. 1981).

14. See Practitioner Treatise, Vol. 1.

15. 11 U.S.C.A. §§ 544(a), 547(b) & 545. We discuss these and other avoiding powers in Chapter 7, infra.

16. Id. § 522(h). The debtor is also given unique, special avoiding powers of her own to avoid certain liens on exempt property. See id. § 522(f). The whole subject of the debtor avoiding liens on exempt property is discussed at §§ 8–23—8–29 infra.

17. See, e.g., In re Brooks, 871 F.2d 89, 90 (9th Cir.1989) (Rerecording a deed to perfect a prepetition lien violates § 362(a)(5).).

lien is therefore easy prey for the avoiding powers; and, if the lien is avoided, the creditor violates the stay by trying to revive it.[18]

A different concern is a lien that floats by law or agreement and, by force of nonbankruptcy law, would attach to property the debtor newly acquires after bankruptcy. Clearly, consensual liens sink in bankruptcy because of section 552(a), which provides:

> Except as provided in subsection (b) of this section, property acquired by the estate or *by the debtor* after the commencement of the case is not subject to any lien resulting from any security agreement entered into by the debtor before the commencement of the case.[19]

This provision thus neuters the effect of an after-acquired property clause in a mortgage or an Article 9 security agreement, or any other provision of a consensual lien that extends the lien, otherwise than allowed by section 552(b), to property the debtor acquired postpetition.[20]

Section 552(a) itself is limited, by its terms, to liens resulting from security agreements. A "security agreement" is an agreement providing for a "security interest"[21] which, in turn, is a "lien created by agreement."[22] Thus, 552(a) is limited to consensual liens.

Some nonconsensual liens float. A good example is a judgment or tax lien. Section 552(a) does not stop these liens from attaching to property acquired after bankruptcy. In no event could they attach to estate property. By their own terms the liens only reach property of the debtor.[23] Also, estate property is protected by section 549 [24] which allows the trustee to avoid postpetition transfers of property of the estate.

The issue we finally reach is whether the stay of (a)(5) stops a nonconsensual lien from floating to property the debtor acquires postpetition. The precise question is whether the creation of a lien in this fashion, automatically by operation of law, is an "*act*" that (a)(5) stays. On the one hand, the usual meaning of "act" does not naturally cover a lien that arises automatically and by operation of law. We think so. On the other hand, it makes no great sense to distinguish between liens on the basis of how they arise, or to to dilute the debtor's fresh start by allowing a lien to cross bankruptcy simply because of the operation of the lien. Also, the word "act" is used throughout section 362 and in these other places is interpreted to include automatic occurrences.[25]

---

18. In re Esser, 20 B.R. 178, 179 (Bankr. E.D.Pa. 1982) (State held in contempt for trying to revive a lien on exempt property that was voided under § 522(f).).

19. 11 U.S.C.A. § 552(a)(emphasis added). Subsection (b) makes exception for proceeds and the like. We discuss section 552 at §§ 6–75—6–78 infra.

20. See, e.g., In re Figgers, 121 B.R. 772, 776–77 (Bankr. S.D.Ohio 1990) (In a Chapter 7 case that had been converted from a Chapter 13, the prepetition pledge of the debtor's share or deposit account did not capture funds deposited after bankruptcy that were postpetition wages.).

21. 11 U.S.C.A. § 101(50).

22. Id. § 101(51).

23. See Practitioner Treatise, Vol. 1.

24. 11 U.S.C.A. § 549(a), which we discuss in § 6–69 infra.

25. See, e.g., Matter of Hellums, 772 F.2d 379, 381 (7th Cir.1985) (automatic wage assignment) ("We hold that Congress intended the stay of section 362(a)(6) to apply to the automatic * * * transfer and application of post-petition funds to the pre-petition debts of Chapter 7 debtors.").

It is therefore possible to read (a)(5) to cover and stop, during the bankruptcy, floating liens for prepetition debts.[26] Coordinately, the discharge may permanently suppress floating liens for dischargeable debts.[27] It is also possible that a lien that would float can altogether die during the bankruptcy, if only upon proper request, because of section 506 which voids liens to the extent they are undersecured.[28]

§ 3–12 Actions Against the Debtor's Property—Exception for Certain Domestic Obligations (Section 362(b)(2))

For full text of this section, see Epstein, Nickles & White, Bankruptcy, Practitioner Treatise Series, Vol. 1.

§ 3–13 Actions Against Estate Property

Every bankruptcy case runs on property of the estate. This property is the corpus of the bankruptcy and funds it. Not surprisingly, therefore, the automatic stay widely protects estate property. Generally, nobody can touch it because section 362(a)(3) stays everybody from

> any act to obtain possession of property of the estate or of property from the estate or to exercise control over property of the estate.[1]

The protection is made more specific and widened with respect to liens on estate property: (a)(4) stays "any act to create, perfect, or enforce any lien against property of the estate."[2] As if this language was not entirely inclusive, section 362 gets even more specific and stays, through (a)(2), the enforcement of any prepetition judgment against estate property[3] and, through (a)(7), the setoff of any prepetition debt.[4]

These prohibitions are broad because a wide range of conduct is covered, but equally because the subject, "property of the estate," is so inclusive. Section 541 defines the term, very generally, to include everything the debtor owns when she files bankruptcy and certain property she or the estate thereafter acquires. Even exemptible property is property of the estate before the debtor exempts it and, until then, is protected by these provisions of section 362.[5]

---

26. See Practitioner Treatise, Vol. 1.

27. The discharge enjoins any "action, the employment of process, or an act, to collect, recover or offset" a discharged debt "as a personal liability of the debtor * * *." 11 U.S.C.A. § 524(a)(2). The same reasoning argues for interpreting the language "act, to collect, recover" to cover and enjoin a prepetition lien that would float to the debtor's postpetition property.

It is possible that the spread of a prepetition judgment lien is also stopped by the language of (a)(1) that "voids any judgment." Id. § 524(a)(1). The judgment is a debt which the lien of judgment secures. Without the debt there is nothing to secure and no basis for the lien. The lien is most probably preserved to the extent of property to which it has already attached. To any further extent, however, the judgment lien is seemingly undermined, quite literally, by voiding the judgment debt.

28. Id. § 506(a) & (d).

§ 3–13

1. 11 U.S.C.A. § 362(a)(3).

2. Id. § 362(a)(4).

3. Id. § 362(a)(2) ("the enforcement, against the debtor or against property of the estate, of a judgment obtained before the commencement of the case under this title").

4. Id. § 362(a)(7) ("the setoff of any debt owing to the debtor that arose before the commencement of the case under this title against any claim against the debtor").

5. Sovran Bank v. Anderson, 743 F.2d 223, 224 (4th Cir.1984). After the debtor exempts the property, it will be protected to some

Moreover, section 541 generally applies without regard to where the property is or who holds or controls it and without any qualitative or quantitative threshold. Concomitantly, the same is true of the stay in protecting estate property. Also, sections 541 and 362 equally guard interests and rights in real estate and in tangible and intangible personal property. Even very minor property interests that belong to the estate, whether legal or equitable, trigger this protection,[6] including bare legal title.[7]

§ 3–14 Actions Against Estate Property—Obtaining Possession and Exercising Control Over Estate Property, Section 362(a)(3)

a. Fundamentals

Section 362(a)(3) is, perhaps, the stay's broadest prohibition: "any act to obtain possession of property of the estate or of property from the estate or to exercise control over property of the estate."[1] The purpose is clear:

> to prevent dismemberment of the estate. Liquidation must proceed in an orderly fashion. Any distribution of property must be by the trustee after he has had an opportunity to familiarize himself with the various rights and interests involved and with the property available for distribution.[2]

To achieve this purpose the stay of (a)(3) is very wide in terms of the conduct that is covered. As Bankruptcy Judge Nancy Dreher has observed, its language "stays three distinct, although not mutually exclusive, types of actions:"[3] (1) obtaining possession of property (a) of the estate or (b) from the estate or (2) exercising control over estate property.

Actually, even attempting any of these actions is, itself, an "act to" obtain possession or exercise control that violates (a)(3). This prohibition can therefore reach legal or self-help proceedings that target estate property without ever hitting it.[4]

Taking property of and from the estate is not entirely redundant. The latter covers property that the estate possesses or controls without any interest, including property that the debtor held without interest when she filed bankruptcy.[5] It is not property of the estate because the estate consists

extent by section 362 as property of the debtor. See discussion at § 3–11 supra.

6. See, e.g., In re Bialac, 712 F.2d 426, 432 (9th Cir.1983) (Property of the estate that consists of an option or a contingent or fractional interest is protected by § 362, as in this case where a sale of a note would affect the debtor's one-sixth undivided interest and would also cut off the debtor's right to redeem.); In re CS Associates, 121 B.R. 942, 960 (Bankr. E.D.Pa. 1990) ("slight" interest of settlor of trust that was a bond fund).

7. In re Jones, 121 B.R. 122, 124 (Bankr. M.D.Fla.1990).

§ 3–14

1. 11 U.S.C.A. § 362(a)(3).

2. H.R. Rep. No. 595, 95th Cong., 1st Sess. 341, reprinted in 1978 U.S. Code Cong. & Admin. News 5963, 6298; S. Rep. No. 989, 95th Cong., 2d Sess. 50, reprinted in 1978 U.S. Code Cong. & Admin. News 5787, 5836.

3. In re Crawley, 117 B.R. 457, 459 (Bankr. D.Minn.1990).

4. See Practitioner Treatise, Vol. 1.

5. "Property from the estate" means "property over which the estate has control or possession." H.R. Rep. No. 595, 95th Cong., 1st Sess. 341, reprinted in 1978 U.S. Code

only of property interests, but is nevertheless considered within the estate because of the estate's power over it.

In truth, however, property of the estate is so broadly defined that the overlap here is virtually complete. Arguably, even mere possession is a property interest. In sum, obtaining possession of property "from the estate" applies, independently, only at the tiny margins of the estate to protect bare dominion where there is no ownership. It does not extend (a)(3) to property that once belonged to the estate but was excluded by way of exemption, abandonment, or other cause.

Expressly extending the stay to this marginal, grey area is only a small enlargement but is important and makes sense. It means that from the beginning, the only legitimate arbiter of control and ownership is the bankruptcy court rather than other courts or, at least, claimants themselves. If they were free to grab property from the debtor that she did not own, they would naturally err in their own favor in deciding ownership and, as often as not, grab property that actually belongs the estate. As often as not, therefore, this free-for-all would dilute and disrupt the bankruptcy process.

The stay of (a)(3) reaches farthest in prohibiting, beyond obtaining possession of estate property, *exercising control* over any of it. The latter is longer, if not as wide as, the former. Getting possession of property without control is unlikely because possession itself enables control. Also, some property is impossible to possess. Controlling property without possession is thus easier done and, practically, more likely and common.

A common example is exercising control of intangible property rights that belong to the estate, such as contract rights or causes of action. These rights are incapable of real possession unless they are reified. Yet, (a)(3) preserves and guards against interference with them by staying any act to exercise control over estate property.

With respect to property capable of possession, "to exercise control" extends the stay of (a)(3) by picking up where "to obtain possession" leaves off. For example, in the case *In re Knaus*,[6] the creditor had lawfully seized collateral before the debtor's bankruptcy. Despite the creditor having a security interest in the property, the debtor retained rights in it (i.e., title) which passed to the estate when bankruptcy was filed. The creditor was therefore in possession of estate property but had not *obtained* possession in violation of (a)(3). The stay applies only to postpetition acts.[7] Therefore, while (a)(3) is violated when property of the estate is repossessed or otherwise seized after the debtor files bankruptcy,[8] nothing in section 362(a) is violated when the repossession occurs, as in *Knaus*, before the bankruptcy.

Yet, remaining in possession is itself, arguably, a kind or degree of control. It more certainly amounts to exercising control if the estate is

---

Cong. & Admin. News 5963, 6298; S. Rep. No. 989, 95th Cong., 2d Sess. 50, reprinted in 1978 U.S. Code Cong. & Admin. News 5787, 5836; Proyectos Electronics, S.A. v. Alper, 37 B.R. 931, 932–33 (E.D.Pa. 1983); In re Turbowind, Inc., 42 B.R. 579, 585–86 (Bankr. S.D.Cal. 1984).

6. 889 F.2d 773 (8th Cir.1989).

7. United States v. Inslaw, Inc., 932 F.2d 1467, 1474 (D.C. Cir. 1991), cert. denied, ___ U.S. ___, 112 S.Ct. 913, 116 L.Ed.2d 813 (1992).

8. See, e.g., In re R. & L. Cartage & Sons, Inc., 118 B.R. 646, 650–51 (Bankr. N.D.Ind. 1990) (Bank with no security interest violated stay by repossessing and disposing of property after debtor's bankruptcy.).

entitled to possession of the property over the possessor. The secured party in *Knaus* could not enforce its security interest by sale or otherwise. Any unauthorized disposition of estate property is the clearest example of an exercise of control in violation of (a)(3);[9] and the crime is doubled if the purpose is to foreclose because (a)(4) specifically forbids any to enforce a lien against property of the estate.[10]

Moreover, section 542 obligates any entity in possession of estate property to turn it over if the trustee can make use of it.[11] "[P]roperty of the debtor repossessed by a secured creditor falls within this rule * * *."[12] The turn-over duty "is not contingent upon any predicate violation of the stay, any order of the bankruptcy court, or any demand * * *."[13] The duty arises automatically as soon as bankruptcy is filed. The court thus held in *Knaus* that

> [t]he failure to fulfill this duty, regardless of whether the original seizure was lawful, constitutes a prohibited attempt to "exercise control over the property of the estate" in violation of the automatic stay.[14]

The bottom line is that simply retaining possession of estate property can violate (a)(3) because doing so—most certainly in the face of an obligation to return the property—can amount to an exercise of control that (a)(3) prohibits.[15]

Knaus justified giving (a)(3) such a long reach because the creditor's continued possession "prevented the debtor [in Chapter 11] from continuing his business with all his available assets." This explanation suggests a loose, very general definition of exercising control, or implies a far limit on its meaning, that is echoed in other cases: it is conduct affecting specific property of the estate that directly, adversely affects the bankruptcy.

For instance, the Fourth Circuit held in *In re Knightsbridge Development Co., Inc.*,[16] that filing a lis pendens did not violate (a)(3) because:

> The lis pendens noticed a distinct proceeding, without operating to satisfy or secure the claim that inspired it. The notice did not interfere with [the debtor's] possession of or control over the [property described in the notice] and, though intended to inform prospective purchasers of a potential encumbrance, was not an "exercise of control" over the property.[17]

In sum, the lis pendens was not stayed because it "had no effect on the bankruptcy estate, and was hence innocuous * * *."[18]

---

9. See, e.g., In re BNT Terminals, Inc., 125 B.R. 963, 972 (Bankr. N.D.Ill. 1990) (The sale of estate property and payment of proceeds to someone else violate § 362(a)(3).).

10. 11 U.S.C.A. § 362(a)(4).

11. Id. § 542(a).

12. United States v. Whiting Pools, Inc., 462 U.S. 198, 206, 103 S.Ct. 2309, 2314, 76 L. Ed.2d 515, 522 (1983).

13. In re Knaus, 889 F.2d 773, 775 (8th Cir.1989).

14. Id.

15. See Practitioner Treatise, Vol. 1.

16. 884 F.2d 145 (4th Cir.1989).

17. Id. at 148.

18. Id. We should note that filing a lis pendens does not violate section 362(a)(4) or (5), as an act to create or perfect a lien, because a lis pendens is not a lien.

Requiring a direct effect is supported and defined by cases such as *In re Chateaugay*.[19] In this case a federal regulatory agency (Pension Benefit Guaranty Corporation (PBGC)) ordered the debtor, LTV, to restore a pension plan that earlier, upon proper authority, the debtor had discontinued. The order of restoration was issued postpetition and obligated the debtor to make contributions to the plan which would dilute the estate. Nevertheless, the order did not violate (a)(3). The district court explained:

> LTV equates the compulsory accrual of liabilities under the Plans with the exercise of control over property of the debtor which is barred by section 362(a)(3). However, the scope of section 362(a)(3) does not by its terms encompass such indirect effects of restoration.
>
> The purpose of section 362(a)(3) "is to protect the estate from direct action taken by creditors against a debtor's personal or real property, and to prevent an uncontrolled scramble to liquidate the estate." Cases interpreting section 362(a)(3), therefore, "have generally involved direct action taken by creditors against a debtor's personal or real property." Courts, moreover, "have clearly distinguished between the entry of judgment, and attempts to enforce a judgment against property of the estate in determining whether a violation of subsection 362(a)(3) has occurred."

Restoration does not constitute direct action against LTV's property or assets. Restoration simply reimposes on LTV Steel the obligation to provide pension benefits for employees. This obligation is an ordinary cost of doing business and one that LTV Steel has readily accepted under the 1987 CBA Plans, albeit outside the regulatory framework of ERISA. However, contrary to LTV Steel's assumption, termination did not remove the company and its Plans from ERISA's regulatory framework. The PBGC's authority to restore terminated pension plans to their pretermination status necessarily implies that termination does not erase a plan sponsor's obligations under ERISA but rather suspends certain obligations and transforms others into liability claims. For example, although termination relieves the plan sponsor of its obligation to make minimum funding contributions directly to the Plans, section 4062 of ERISA recasts the sponsor's minimum funding obligations as liabilities directly to the PBGC. The district court explained:

> "[T]he Code does not change the business and regulatory environment in which a debtor operates." Although LTV Steel seeks to minimize the application of ERISA to its post-petition pension activities, ERISA's restoration provision compels the conclusion that an employer who funds a qualified ongoing pension plan may under appropriate circumstances be required to resume its statutory obligations for a plan that has been terminated. Therefore, the continued accrual of employee pension benefits results from maintaining a qualified pension plan under ERISA. The liability that LTV Steel incurs as such benefits accrue does not transfer or exercise control over LTV Steel's property.[20]

---

19. 87 B.R. 779 (S.D.N.Y. 1988), aff'd, 875 F.2d 1008 (2d Cir. 1989), rev'd & remanded, 496 U.S. 633, 110 S.Ct. 2668, 110 L.Ed.2d 579 (1990).

20. 87 B.R. at 801. We would also cite, in very general support, In re Golden Distributors, Ltd., 122 B.R. 15 (Bankr. S.D.N.Y. 1990), which held that the stay of section 362(a)(3) was not violated when former employees, in

Similar reasoning explains why the stay of (a)(3) does not cover acts against property of a separate legal entity that the debtor owns or in which she has an interest.[21] The debtor's property is the other entity itself rather than the entity's property. The former gives the debtor no interest in the latter. Therefore, the acts only indirectly affect the debtor's property and, for this reason, are beyond (a)(3).

While we agree with *Chateaugay* and *Knightsbridge,* we also recognize that the requirement they impose on (a)(3) of a direct and adverse affect on the estate and the bankruptcy is not a rigid rule. It is rather a principle that is wide and general and only loosely defines (a)(3); and whether or not this principle is satisfied always depends on the peculiar facts of the particular case. Even the specific conduct that the courts let pass in *Chateaugay* and *Knightsbridge* could trigger (a)(3) under different circumstances that push harder against its underlying concerns.

In any event, the principle sets very far boundaries for (a)(3). There is a surprisingly wide range of conduct that easily fits there. Indeed, the usual reason for excluding conduct is not because of the nature of the act itself but because the property acted upon is not property of the estate. On the other hand, property of the estate is itself so widely defined that this concept extends (a)(3) in ways that are more surprising and significant than the limits it imposes on (a)(3), especially in regard to conduct that affects intangible property. We focus now on a few very important examples.

b. *Causes of Action*

Causes of action against third parties are added to the estate, like any other property, under section 541. Thus, for example, any cause of action the debtor carries with her into bankruptcy becomes property of the estate.

breach of contracts with the debtor not to compete, solicited business for themselves from the debtor's customers. We agree with the result and the court's reasoning as far as it goes, and we would add that the effect on the estate was too remote to implicate (a)(3).

It is not required, additionally, that the conduct is aimed specifically at the debtor, so long as the effect on the estate and the bankruptcy is direct. See In re Prudential Lines Inc., 928 F.2d 565 (2d Cir.1991), cert. denied, ___ U.S. ___, 112 S.Ct. 82, 116 L.Ed.2d 55 (1991), in which the court opined:

> [Elsewhere] we held that a landlord's attempt to terminate its lease with a non-debtor was subject to the automatic stay since it would have had the legal effect of terminating the debtor's sublease. Despite the fact that the landlord's action was not directed specifically at the debtor, we held that
>
> "where a non-debtor's interest is intertwined ... with that of a bankrupt debtor ... [and an] action taken against the non-bankrupt party would inevitably have an adverse impact on property of the bankrupt estate, then such action should be barred by the automatic stay."
>
> Similarly, where a non-debtor's action with respect to an interest that is intertwined with that of a bankrupt debtor would have the legal effect of diminishing or eliminating property of the bankrupt estate, such action is barred by the automatic stay.

Id. at 574, quoting In re 48th St. Steakhouse, Inc., 835 F.2d 427, 431 (2d Cir.1987), cert. denied, 485 U.S. 1035, 108 S.Ct. 1596, 99 L.Ed.2d 910 (1988) (The debtor's corporate parent was stayed from taking a worthless stock deduction on its tax return that would effectively eliminate the value of the debtor's NOL carryforward.); see also Matter of Colonial Realty Co., 122 B.R. 1 (Bankr. D. Conn. 1990) (The debtor was the manager of property subject to a mortgage that was foreclosed. The mortgagee got a receiver appointed who took possession of the property and displaced the debtor. The debtor's contract to manage the place was property of the estate, so that the mortgagee's acts in removing the debtor as manager violated (a)(3).).

21. See Practitioner Treatise, Vol. 1.

It is therefore protected by section 362(a)(3). Any act to exercise control over the cause of action violates the stay. Nobody can buy it. More commonly important, no third person can sue on it.

A person likely to try is a creditor of a corporate debtor seeking to vindicate some wrong to the debtor that diminished the debtor's worth and contributed (if only indirectly) to the debtor's nonpayment of the creditor. The rule is that "[t]he automatic stay prevents individual creditors from suing to enforce a right of action belonging to a corporation when that corporation is in bankruptcy," [22] including an action to recover the debtor's property that someone else controls.[23] The reason is not that the proceeding itself is stayed by section 362. Actions and proceedings in themselves are stayed only when they are against the debtor. The reason is that the cause of action belongs to the estate, and prosecuting the action is thereby an exercise of control over property of the estate in violation of (a)(3).

Thus, (a)(3) stays a suit against a third party based on a tort claim that is exclusively owned by the estate.[24] It also stays a creditor's suit against the debtor's officers and directors on an alter ego or similar theory because this action belongs to the debtor and thus the estate.[25]

The creditor is generally free to pursue her own claim against the defendant,[26] with a couple exceptions. First, she cannot sue if doing so would involve seeking recovery on behalf of the debtor as well as for herself.[27] The reason is not wholly the stay. It is also the rule that only the trustee can represent the estate.[28]

Another, more important exception is that the creditor cannot sue to recover property the debtor fraudulently transferred.[29] The law of fraudulent conveyances usually gives this action exclusively to the creditor. In bankruptcy, however, this action by the creditor is barred because the debtor retained an equitable interest in the property. This interest belongs to the estate. Therefore, the action seeks possession or control of estate property, or property in which the estate holds an interest, which (a)(3) prohibits.[30] The prohibition equally applies if the creditor asks for substitutional damages from the transferee-defendants instead of their return of the property itself.[31]

The stay of (a)(3) does not bar a suit on a cause of action the trustee abandons. " '[A]bandonment constitutes a divestiture of all interests in

---

22. In re Crysen/Montenay Energy Co., 902 F.2d 1098, 1101 (2d Cir.1990).

23. See Practitioner Treatise, Vol. 1.

24. In re Crysen/Montenay Energy Co., 902 F.2d 1098 (2d Cir.1990).

25. Matter of S.I. Acquisition, Inc., 817 F.2d 1142, 1148–54 (5th Cir.1987) (suit based on alter ego theory); In re MortgageAmerica Corp., 714 F.2d 1266, 1276–77 (5th Cir.1983) (corporate trust fund or denuding theory).

26. "If, however, the right of action belongs to the creditor, the action is not part of the debtor's estate and the stay does not apply." In re Crysen/Montenay Energy Co., 902 F.2d 1098, 1104 (2d Cir.1990).

27. Id. (dictum).

28. Id.

29. Matter of Sherk, 918 F.2d 1170, 1177 (5th Cir.1990); In re MortgageAmerica Corp., 714 F.2d 1266, 1275–76 (5th Cir.1983); Kommanditselskab Supertrans v. O.C.C. Shipping, Inc., 79 B.R. 534 (S.D.N.Y. 1987); In re AP Industries, Inc., 117 B.R. 789, 798–801 (Bankr. S.D.N.Y. 1990).

30. In re MortgageAmerica Corp., 714 F.2d 1266, 1275–76 (5th Cir.1983).

31. In re AP Industries, Inc., 117 B.R. 789, 798–801 (Bankr. S.D.N.Y. 1990).

property that were property of the estate.'"[32] Therefore, "the right of action, * * * once abandonment by the trustee took place, reposed in [the creditor] free of any stay."[33]

c. *Rights to Payment and Other Contract Rights*

Rights to the payment of money and other contract rights owed the debtor become property of the estate like everything else she owns. The estate also includes rights under contracts that the trustee makes.[34] These contract rights that belong to the estate are protected by section 362(a)(3), as is any other property of the estate, even when the rights are entirely abstract and incapable of possession by anyone. They are guarded against acts to exercise control over them. Also, the stay's protection of contract rights is two dimensional, guarding against interference by third persons and cancellation by the obligor.

The easiest example is the obligor on a contract who has purchased property or services from the debtor and owes her the price. This obligation runs to the debtor and thus the estate: the right to the money is property of the estate. A creditor of the debtor who tries to collect from the obligor violates (a)(3) because this conduct is an act to exercise control over estate property. Actually collecting the money or other consideration from an obligor is a further wrong. The money itself, as proceeds of estate property, also belongs to the estate.[35] Taking it thus amounts to obtaining possession of property of the estate, which is a separate violation of (a)(3).

Similarly, the debtor's rights under her liability or casualty insurance are property of the estate. The stay of (a)(3) bars other people from trying to collect the insurance.[36]

Beyond these examples, section 362(a)(3) is sometimes read to bar, much more generally, any conduct by third parties that would dilute the value of the debtor's rights under any of her contracts. An example is *Matter of Colonial Realty Co.*[37] The debtor was the manager of a real estate complex subject to a mortgage that was foreclosed. The mortgagee got a receiver appointed who took possession of the complex and displaced the debtor. The debtor's contract to manage the place was property of the estate, so that the mortgagee's acts in removing the debtor as manager violated (a)(3). It made no difference in applying section 362 that the debtor lacked any interest in

---

32. Unisys Corp. v. Dataware Products, Inc., 848 F.2d 311, 314 (1st Cir.1988).

33. Id. (The suit was based on allegations that the debtor and its officers had conspired to defraud creditors by liquidating the debtor's assets and transferring them to customers or a successor entity.).

34. 11 U.S.C.A. § 541(a)(7) (The estate includes "[a]ny interest in property that the estate acquires after the commencement of the case."); In re Carroll, 903 F.2d 1266, 1270–71 (9th Cir.1990) (A contract that the trustee makes is property of the estate that § 362(a)(3) protects, and it cannot be terminated without prior court approval.); Matter of Gulf Tampa Drydock Co., 49 B.R. 154 (Bankr. M.D.Fla.1985) (Insurance policies issued to the debtors after bankruptcy are property of the estate.).

35. 11 U.S.C.A. § 541(a)(6) (The estate includes "[p]roceeds, product, offspring, rents, or profits of or from property of the estate * * *.").

36. See, e.g., Tringali v. Hathaway Machinery Co., Inc., 796 F.2d 553, 560–61 (1st Cir. 1986) (suit against insurer for proceeds of liability policy stayed); In re Circle K Corp., 121 B.R. 257, 258–61 (Bankr. D.Ariz.1990) (same).

37. 122 B.R. 1 (Bankr. D.Conn.1990).

the complex itself, or that the debtor's contract rights under the management contract were unassignable and of little benefit to the estate.[38]

We are certain that there are critics of cases such as *Colonial Realty* who would not read (a)(3) so broadly. They doubt the wisdom of staying conduct on this basis when the link between the conduct and the debtor's property is thin, especially when the property that is affected is also quite thin.

Even more often, but no less controversially, the stay of (a)(3) is read to protect contract rights against acts of the obligor herself. Specifically, it preserves them against cancellation of the contract by the obligor that would permit her to escape performance, if not liability. For example, the debtor's insurer cannot cancel the insurance policy because doing so is an exercise of control over the property that (a)(3) prohibits.[39]

Similarly, a person who has contracted to buy or sell property or services to the debtor cannot unilaterally terminate the deal.[40] This contract is executory and will be assumed or rejected by the trustee under section 365.[41] Even before assumption, however, the contract cannot be terminated without relief from the stay, not even if reason exists for terminating it by the terms of the contract itself [42] or by the provision of section 365 that permits terminating personal contracts and contracts for financial accommodations.[43]

---

38. Id. at 4–5. On the other hand, (a)(3) is not offended every time a third party butts into the debtor's contracts. Informing the obligors of their contractual rights against the debtor, or their duties to another person, is not obtaining possession or exercising control of the contracts that is sufficient to violate (a)(3), least if the estate is unaffected by the conduct. See Matter of Hughes–Bechtol, Inc., 117 B.R. 890, 905–07 (Bankr.S.D. Ohio 1990) (Debtor-contractor's surety wrote letters to debtor's obligor warning of the surety's claim against them if they prejudiced the surety's rights to retainages. The court thought the question was close but decided that (a)(3) was not violated. "[A]bsent coercion or harassment, mildly worded correspondence which does not adversely impact on the estate, does not constitute an actionable violation of the automatic stay."); In re U.S. Electric, Inc., 123 B.R. 262 (Bankr. S.D.Ohio 1990) (Materialman did not violate stay by contacting debtor-contractor's customers and informing them of their right to setoff to satisfy directly the material suppliers who might file liens against them.).

39. See Practitioner Treatise, Vol. 1.

40. See Practitioner Treatise, Vol. 1.

41. 11 U.S.C.A. § 365(a) ("the trustee, subject to the court's approval, may assume or reject any executory contract or unexpired lease of the debtor").

42. In re Computer Communications, Inc., 824 F.2d 725, 728 (9th Cir.1987) (The defendant, Codex, unilaterally terminated contract to purchase computer equipment from the debtor. This conduct violated (a)(3): "Even if Codex had a valid reason for terminating the Agreement, it was still required to petition the court for relief from the automatic stay * * *.").

43. See 11 U.S.C.A. § 365(e)(2) (It permits the termination of an executory contract or unexpired lease of the debtor if applicable law excuses the other party from accepting performance from or rendering performance to anyone other than the debtor, or if the contract is a contract to make a loan or other financial accommodation.); In re Computer Communications, Inc., 824 F.2d 725, 730 (9th Cir.1987). (The defendant, Codex, unilaterally terminated a contract to purchase computer equipment from the debtor. "[E]ven if § 365(e)(2) allowed Codex to terminate the contract, § 362 automatically stayed termination."); Matter of Edwards Mobile Home Sales, Inc., 119 B.R. 857, 860 (Bankr. M.D.Fla.1990) (Although an obligor of a financial accommodation can terminate under § 365, must get relief from the stay or be in violation. "The Court does not find that Section 365(e)(2) exempts non-assumable executory contracts from the scope of the automatic stay."); cf. Matter of West Electronics Inc., 852 F.2d 79, 82 (3d Cir.1988) (The government had a defense contract with the debtor that could not be assumed in bankruptcy because overriding federal law prohibited any assumption without the government's consent. The court assumes, without deciding, that the government was nevertheless barred by § 362 from terminating the contract without obtaining an order for relief

The stay's preservation of contract rights against the other party's cancellation is important. The estate honors the principle of derivative title, even as to contracts that are property of the estate. Therefore, a right under a contract to cancel upon the debtor's default or for other reason would be enforceable against the estate if the stay did not prevent exercising the right. Because of the stay, the trustee has time to decide whether to assume or reject the contract. Upon assumption, any default that triggered the other party's right to cancel must be cured.

Some contracts would circumvent this scheme by providing that cancellation occurs automatically when, or immediately before, the debtor files bankruptcy. This kind of provision is called an *ipso facto clause*. It is ineffective in bankruptcy.[44]

On the other hand, cancellation before bankruptcy, for reasons other than an ipso facto clause, is effective. The stay applies only to postpetition acts, and thus (a)(3) cannot prevent prepetition cancellation. Bankruptcy cannot revive dead contracts.[45] Also, although the stay stops a postpetition act to cancel a contract and the Code neuters ipso facto clauses, nothing in the bankruptcy law generally prevents a contract from expiring automatically, by its own terms, even after the bankruptcy filing.[46]

Further, even when bankruptcy intervenes during the term of a contract so as to prevent cancellation, a mere breach of the contract is generally not stayed. This point is very well made in *In re Golden Distributors, Ltd.*[47] The debtor's former employees had made covenants not to compete with the debtor, but they nevertheless solicited the debtor's customers for their own business. This conduct as a breach of the employees' contract with the debtor did not, per se, violate (a)(3).

> Manifestly, the employment contracts with the defendants might qualify as property of the debtor's estate. However * * * the fact that the defendants may have breached the restrictive covenants in their employment contracts or that they may have improperly solicited the debtor's customers, for which the defendants might ultimately be liable to the debtor for damages or enjoined from engaging in such improper conduct, does not mean that the defendants attempted to obtain possession or control of property of the estate in violation of 11 U.S.C.A. § 362(a)(3).[48]

under § 362(d).); but see Watts v. Pennsylvania Housing Finance Co., 876 F.2d 1090, 1094–96 (3d Cir.1989) (Stay did not prevent agency from terminating mortgage assistance benefits upon debtor filing bankruptcy because same is implicitly excepted from stay through § 365(c)(2) & 365(e)(2)(B) as contract to make financial accommodation for debtor's benefit. This is exception from rule prohibiting termination of contracts because of bankruptcy. Debtor cannot force lender to keep lending.).

44. 11 U.S.C.A. § 541(c)(1)(B), which provides:

> [A]n interest of the debtor in property becomes property of the estate * * * notwithstanding any provision in an agreement, transfer instrument, or applicable nonbankruptcy law * * * that is conditioned on the insolvency or financial condition of the debtor, on the commencement of a case under this title, or on the appointment of or taking possession by a trustee in a case under this title or a custodian before such commencement and that effects or gives an option to effect a forfeiture, modification, or termination of the debtor's interest in property.

Id.

45. See Practitioner Treatise, Vol. 1.

46. See Practitioner Treatise, Vol. 1.

47. 122 B.R. 15 (Bankr. S.D.N.Y. 1990).

48. Id. at 19–20.

Also, the conduct did not violate (a)(3) by its affect on the affairs between the debtor and the customers whom the employees solicited for business. It did not amount to contractual interference because the debtor had no contracts with these customers.

> Absent any evidence as to exclusivity agreements between the debtor and its customers or that such customers are required to purchase from the debtor specific quantities of products, the debtor can point to no property interest with respect to its potential customers which can be interfered with by the defendants, or which is capable of being lost to the possession or control of the defendants in violation of 11 U.S.C. § 362(a)(3). Although the debtor argues that the good will of its customers is an intangible property right which the defendants have misappropriated, this argument loses sight of the fact that the restriction which the debtor seeks to enforce against the defendants arises out of a contract executed by the defendants and not by virtue of any other property right which the debtor may have with respect to its potential customers.
>
> Under certain circumstances where a debtor has contractual arrangements with its customers which can be translated into assured sales or income, such intangible property rights or good will can be protected from interference by others within the context of 11 U.S.C.A. § 362(a)(3).[49]

Nor did the employees' conduct amount to interference with property in the form of "good will."

> The debtor reasons that its relation with its customers is a valuable asset and property right in the nature of good will * * *.
>
> * * *
>
> Manifestly, good will may exist in some cases as an asset * * *. Thus, good will of a business, to the extent it exists, may be included as property of an estate in bankruptcy. There was no evidence that the defendants sought to continue the debtor's business or hold themselves out as related in any way to the debtor's business so as to acquire the good will that was associated with such business.[50]

In essence, competing against the debtor is not same as taking debtor's good will.

The debtor in *Golden Distributors* could have argued further that (a)(3) was violated by the net effect, overall, of the employees' conduct: soliciting the debtor's customers and taking their business from the debtor reduced the size of the debtor's bankruptcy estate. The causal link is too speculative and tenuous. The stay of (a)(3) requires a more direct affect on the estate.[51]

Nothing is lost by failing to stay breach of contract. The cause of action for the breach belongs to the estate. It can remedy the wrong by any appropriate means as in any other action for breach of contract, including the recovery of compensatory, consequential and other damages or an order of specific performance.

---

49. Id. at 20.
50. Id.

51. See § 3-14 supra.

Damages for nonpayment of a debt typically do not include consequential loss and therefore fail to cover the full range of harm that the obligee can suffer. Appropriately, a person who owes money to a bankruptcy debtor under an executed contract, i.e., owes for property or services already received, cannot withhold payment that is due or set it off against an obligation the debtor owes her. This prohibition, which is founded on (a)(3), is confirmed and reiterated by section 542, which provides that "an entity that owes a debt that is property of the estate and that is matured, payable on demand, or payable on order, shall pay such debt to, or on the order of, the trustee * * *."[52] Also, setoff is specifically stayed by section 362(a)(7).[53] While the substantive right of setoff is recognized and honored in bankruptcy,[54] the procedural right to accomplish the setoff unilaterally is barred by both section 362(a)(3) and (a)(7). A creditor/obligor with a basis for setoff must get relief from the stay to effect the right.

Setoff is so important in bankruptcy, as a form of security, that we devote an entire section of another chapter to the topic.[55] Look there for a complete analysis.

d. Letters of Credit

We have said that a debtor's right to payment is property of the estate. Third parties cannot act to obtain possession or exercise control over it in violation of section 362(a)(3). The same is true of the obligor herself. She must pay the debt to the estate.

In general, these principles should ordinarily apply to a right to payment under a letter of credit issued to the debtor as the beneficiary. The issuer is simply an account debtor who owes payment of the credit upon compliance with its terms.[56] This right to payment, so limited, passes to the estate when the debtor files bankruptcy.[57] Therefore, notwithstanding cases such as *Swift Aire Lines*[58], we believe that a debtor in possession should normally be authorized to draw on a letter of credit as to which the debtor is beneficiary. Whether the American commercial law ultimately will sustain such a right is unclear at this point; we, at least, think it should.

These principles do *not* apply to letters of credit that are issued for the account of the debtor who is the account party or customer. Neither the credit nor its proceeds are property of the estate. They are property of the beneficiary to whom the issuer-bank owes payment by the terms of U.C.C. Article 5 and the credit itself. This obligation runs directly from the issuer to the beneficiary and is independent of the debtor-customer's relations with the issuer and beneficiary. Moreover, the bank uses its own funds in paying the credit. Therefore, section 362(a)(3) does not stay the issuer from pay-

---

52. 11 U.S.C.A. § 542(b).

53. Id. § 362(a)(7) ("the setoff of any debt owing to the debtor that arose before the commencement of the case under this title against any claim against the debtor").

54. See id. § 553(a).

55. See § 3–15 infra.

56. The assignment of proceeds under a letter of credit is treated as the assignment of an account. U.C.C. § 5–116(2). The obligor on an account is the "account debtor." U.C.C. § 9–105(1)(a).

57. See Practitioner Treatise, Vol. 1.

58. 30 B.R. 490 (9th Cir. BAP 1983).

ing.[59]

It might be argued that by making demand for payment, the beneficiary arguably violates section 362(a)(6), which stays "any act to collect, assess, or recover" a prepetition claim against the debtor. The weakness in this argument is that the credit itself represents a claim against the bank, not the debtor. By paying the credit the bank is satisfying its own debt to the beneficiary, not paying a claim against the debtor.

In any event, whether or not the stay is violated, the net result of the whole transaction is possibly an indirect preference to the beneficiary that is avoidable under section 547(b).[60] The issuer who pays is entitled to reimbursement from the debtor who will satisfy this obligation by transferring property in payment or as security. This transfer is not to the beneficiary, but is sufficient to establish a preference to her because the transfer is for her benefit.[61] The remedy for such a preference includes recovery from the beneficiary herself [62] or, arguably, the bank as the "initial transferee" of the transfer.[63]

e. Leases

Some of the important principles we have discussed about contract rights apply most often to leases, especially leases of real estate. A debtor's leasehold interest in property, and any other rights to property under a lease contract, are property that passes to the estate, including subleases. The stay of (a)(3) therefore protects them,[64] and the lessor violates this stay by any act that would terminate the lease or that would end the debtor's occupancy of the property under it. Also, the stay of (a)(3) covers a debtor's tenancy at sufferance or a mere possessory interest without any accompanying legal interest.[65] If the debtor has any legal or equitable interest or right to possession when bankruptcy begins, any act to terminate the right or dispossess her is stayed by (a)(3).

On the other hand, (a)(3) does not apply if the debtor lost every right to possession before bankruptcy and acquired nothing new after bankruptcy.[66] Mere possession alone, without any right to it, is not covered. Also, the protection of (a)(3) lapses if her rights and thus her complete interest end by their own terms during bankruptcy.

In practice, however, a person who occupies property can often find some continuing interest or right that accompanies her possession, even if this right is very small and less than her original interest.[67] The stay of (a)(3) will protect it, and so can section 362(a)(1) which stays any action or proceeding against the debtor that could have been commenced before

---

59. See, e.g., Lower Brule Const. Co. v. Sheesley's Plumbing & Heating Co., Inc., 84 B.R. 638 (D.S.D.1988); In re Skylark Travel, Inc., 120 B.R. 352, 354 (Bankr. S.D.N.Y. 1990).

60. 11 U.S.C.A. § 547(b).

61. Id. § 547(b)(1).

62. Id. § 550(a)(1) ("entity for whose benefit such transfer was made").

63. Id.

64. See Practitioner Treatise, Vol. 1.

65. See Practitioner Treatise, Vol. 1.

66. See Practitioner Treatise, Vol. 1.

67. See Practitioner Treatise, Vol. 1.

bankruptcy.[68] Indeed, (a)(1) arguably protects mere possession alone against any action or proceedings that (a)(1) covers.

The safe course is always to proceed in bankruptcy court to get possession of property that a debtor holds. No other course is even possible if the debtor holds by virtue of possession or rights that, by terms of the lease, she continues to enjoy in the absence of the lessor acting to terminate the rights. In this event, the terminating acts themselves are stayed. For the lessor to do the acts that would terminate the debtor's rights, and for her to take possession of the property, will both require relief from the stay by the bankruptcy court.

The trustee can assume an unexpired lease,[69] and in doing so she must cure any default and provide adequate assurance of future performance. If a default later occurs,

> the Bankruptcy Code provides two basic forms of relief. First, the landlord may seek payment as a first priority creditor [§§ 507, 503(b)(1)(A)]. There is no question, of course, that the payment of rent for the use and occupancy of real estate ordinarily counts as an "actual, necessary" cost to which a landlord, as a creditor, is entitled. * * *

> When a debtor is unable to meet the obligation to pay rent, a second form of relief is available to the landlord. As a general matter, landlords are barred by section 362(a)(3) of the Code from seeking to evict debtors in forums other than the bankruptcy court. * * *

> This presumption against collateral proceedings is rebuttable, however, under section 362(d), which empowers the bankruptcy court to lift the stay "for cause, including the lack of adequate protection of an interest in property of [a] party in interest." In the case of a tenant who neglects to pay rent, the upshot of § 362(d) is to permits the landlord to challenge the stay against state court remedies upon a showing of "extraordinary or compelling equitable circumstances." In this way, the failure of a debtor to pay rent affords the landlord the opportunity to convince the bankruptcy court to lift the stay and permit the landlord to seek an ejectment order from state court.[70]

In the absence of timely assumption, the lease is deemed rejected by operation of law.[71] Rejection is not a signal, however, that the lessor can freely re-enter and oust the debtor from possession. It is, technically, only a breach of the lease,[72] not necessarily an abandonment of any residual property interest that (a)(3) protects. Yet, if the trustee constructively rejects a lease of nonresidential real estate, she must "immediately surrender such nonresidential real property to the lessor."[73] Here, minimally, is grounds for relief, if not abandonment.[74]

---

68. 11 U.S.C.A. § 362(a)(1); In re Onio's Italian Restaurant Corp., 42 B.R. 319, 320–21 (Bankr. S.D.N.Y. 1984) (The stay of § 362(a)(2) stays eviction of debtor from property in which she had an equitable interest, even though she lost her legal interest prior to bankruptcy by way of proceedings begun then.).

69. 11 U.S.C.A. § 365(a).

70. Zagata Fabricators, Inc. v. Superior Air Products, 893 F.2d 624, 627 (3d Cir.1990).

71. See 11 U.S.C.A. § 365(d).

72. Id. § 365(g).

73. Id. § 365(d)(4).

74. See Practitioner Treatise, Vol. 1.

Leases of nonresidential real estate are also the subject of a limited exception to the whole of section 362(a) that in every case, from the beginning, immunizes them from the stay. It is section 362(b)(10), which provides that the stay does not apply to:

> any act by a lessor to the debtor under a lease of nonresidential real property that has terminated by the expiration of the stated term of the lease before the commencement of or during a case under this title to obtain possession of such property.[75]

This exception is obviously helpful if the debtor entered bankruptcy without any rights in the property due to the lease having already expired before she filed. In this case (a)(3) would not have barred the lessor from taking action against the debtor, outside of bankruptcy, for possession of the property; but (a)(1) could have stopped the lessor in the absence of (b)(10), even if the debtor lacked any interest in the property, because (a)(1) stops actions solely on the basis that they are against the debtor.

The (b)(10) exception, by itself, is not helpful if, despite expiration of the lease before or during bankruptcy, the debtor retains some interest, even a mere equitable possessory interest, in the property. Under the usual rules, this interest belongs to the estate and is guarded by (a)(3). While (b)(10) is an exception to everything in section 362(a), including (a)(3), the only conduct that (b)(10) excepts is an act "to [against?] the debtor" and not acts with respect to property of the estate. Therefore, the (b)(10) exception would not push aside the stay of (a)(3).

Enter section 541(b)(2), which is an exception to the usual rules about property of the estate. It excludes from the estate:

> any interest of the debtor as a lessee under a lease of nonresidential real property that has terminated at the expiration of the stated term of such lease before the commencement of the case under this title, and ceases to include any interest of the debtor as a lessee under a lease of nonresidential real property that has terminated at the expiration of the stated term of such lease during the case.[76]

This exclusion means that when a nonresidential lease expires before or after bankruptcy, any residual property interest escapes the estate and thus the protection of section 362(a)(3). Only the stay of section 362(a)(1) prevents action against the debtor for possession of the property, and the (b)(10) exception neuters it. Thus, the lessor of nonresidential real estate is free to take possession of the property as soon as the lease term expires.[77] Relief from the stay is not necessary because the stay does not apply.

The (b)(10) exception was slightly stretched in *In re Urbanco, Inc.*[78] The court assumed that (b)(10) was triggered and the stay was terminated by constructive or deemed rejection of the lease under section 365,[79] requiring surrender of the property to the lessor. Effectively, the court defined the phrase "expiration of the stated term" in (b)(10) to include such rejection.

---

75. 11 U.S.C.A. § 362(b)(10).
76. Id. § 541(b)(2).
77. Erickson v. Polk, 921 F.2d 200, 201–02 (8th Cir.1990) (unimproved farmland); In re Neville, 118 B.R. 14, 18 (Bankr. E.D.N.Y.1990).
78. 122 B.R. 513, 520 (Bankr. W.D.Mich. 1991).
79. 11 U.S.C.A. § 365(d)(4).

Even when triggered, however, (b)(10) terminates the stay only with respect to the lessor's acts "to the debtor," not with respect to acts against estate property that (a)(3) stays. Yet, by so defining the same phrase in section 541(b)(2), the effect of the rejection is to exclude from the estate any residual property interests of the nonresidential lease. The stay of (a)(3) is thereby rendered useless against the lessor's action to obtain possession of the property. With (b)(10) allowing the action against the debtor herself, section 362 stays nothing else that can stop the lessor.

So bolstered by section 541(b)(2), the (b)(10) exception rips a large tear in section 362(a) for nonresidential real estate leases. By itself, however, the exception is a pinhole that reliably allows very little to escape the stay.

f. Rights From Government

Debtors get all kinds of rights from government that are not ordinary contract rights. Good examples are business licenses and income entitlements. The stay of section 362(a)(3) generally protects these government rights that are property.[80] Specifically, the government is stayed from cancelling them.

Controlling certain of these rights is sometimes within the government's police or regulatory power. Action to enforce such power is excepted from the stay of section 362(a)(1) by section 362(b)(4–5).[81] These exceptions do not, by their terms, trump the stay of (a)(3)[82] and should override (a)(3), if at all, only to the extent that (a)(3) overlaps (a)(1).

§ 3–15 Actions Against Estate Property—Setoff

A right to the payment of money is property. If it belongs to the estate, the stay of section 362(a)(3) applies and bars the obligor from exercising control over the property. This general prohibition, by itself, should prevent the obligor from setting off the obligation, that is, subtracting the amount of the obligation from the total of an unrelated debt that the debtor owes her. The stay of section 362(a)(7) removes any doubt that set off of prepetition debts is covered. It stays:

> the setoff of any debt owing to the debtor that arose before the commencement of the case under this title against any claim against the debtor.[1]

Section 542(b) directs the obligor, instead, to pay the trustee any debt owed to the debtor that is property of the estate.[2]

---

80. See Practitioner Treatise, Vol. 1.

81. 11 U.S.C.A. § 362(b)(4–5). These exceptions provide that bankruptcy is not a stay:

(4) under subsection (a)(1) of this section, of the commencement or continuation of an action or proceeding by a governmental unit to enforce such governmental unit's police or regulatory power;

(5) under subsection (a)(2) of this section, of the enforcement of a judgment, other than a money judgment, obtained in an action or proceeding by a governmental unit to enforce such governmental unit's police or regulatory power.

Id. We discuss them at § 3–21 infra.

82. See Practitioner Treatise, Vol. 1.

§ 3–15

1. 11 U.S.C.A. § 362(a)(7).
2. Id. § 542(b).

Setoff is allowed and common under state law. It is a favorite remedy of banks. They use it to satisfy loans by setting off the customers' deposit accounts. Setoff is not limited to banks, but they are peculiarly well-situated to use it. The effect of setoff is to give a creditor security to the extent of the amount owed the debtor.

Bankruptcy does not extinguish this security. Rather, the Code expressly provides in section 553 for preserving and honoring setoff of prepetition debts in bankruptcy.[3] Every other provision, save two, are subject to section 553, including the turnover order of section 542(b). The exceptions are section 362 and section 363.[4] The latter governs the use of collateral, especially including cash collateral which includes funds held subject to setoff.[5] The 362 exception means that despite the creditor having a right of setoff that is good in bankruptcy, unilateral enforcement of the right is stayed.[6] The right is properly exercised only by getting relief from the stay to do so.

This topic is so important that we devote an entire section to it in our chapter on the trustee's avoiding powers.[7] We put our main discussion of setoff there because of its important effect as an exception to preference law. The coverage nevertheless includes much about the stay as a procedural limit on setoff and also as a limit on the close relatives of recoupment and the "administrative freeze" of a debtor's funds.

Three very narrow instances of setoff are explicitly excepted from the stay. All three exceptions concern sophisticated arrangements involving financial markets and are designed to minimize volatility. Section 362(b)(6) excepts the setoff of any mutual debt and claim for certain commodity and stock transactions, that is,

> under subsection (a) of this section, of the setoff by a commodity broker, forward contract merchant, stockbroker, financial institutions, or securities clearing agency of any mutual debt and claim under or in connection with commodity contracts, as defined in section 761(4) of this title, forward contracts, or securities contracts, as defined in section 741(7) of this title, that constitutes the setoff of a claim against the debtor for a margin payment, as defined in section 101(34), 741(5), or 761(15) of this title, or settlement payment, as defined in section 101(35) or 741(8) of this title, arising out of commodity contracts, forward contracts, or securities contracts against cash, securities, or other property held by or due from such commodity broker, forward contract merchant, stockbroker, financial institutions, or securities clearing agency to margin, guarantee, secure, or settle commodity contracts, forward contracts, or securities contracts [8]

---

3. Id. § 553(a) ("Except as otherwise provided in this section and in sections 362 and 363 of this title, this title does not affect any right of a creditor to offset a mutual debt owing by such creditor to the debtor that arose before the commencement of the case under this title against a claim of such creditor against the debtor that arose before the commencement of the case * * *.").

4. Id. §§ 362 & 363.
5. See Practitioner Treatise, Vol. 1.
6. See Practitioner Treatise, Vol. 1.
7. See §§ 6–38—6–44 infra.
8. 11 U.S.C.A. § 362(b)(6).

The purpose is "to ensure that brokers and clearinghouses [can] immediately protect themselves and the market by rapidly closing out open positions upon the happening of a customer insolvency."[9] Protecting the securities market, especially against a possible chain reaction of insolvencies, overrides the importance of preserving the single customer's estate against the narrow disruption that (b)(6) allows.

Similar reasoning is behind the other exception, section 362(b)(7). It concerns repurchase (a/k/a "repo") agreements, which consist of:

> a sale of government-guaranteed securities for cash and a simultaneous agreement by the seller to repurchase the same securities, or ones of equivalent value, at a later date for a premium above the original price. Typically, the securities are sold for an amount of cash less than their face value. The seller may agree to repurchase the securities the next day, or after some longer period. The premium for repurchase is determined by market forces and is unrelated to the interest rates of the underlying securities.[10]

Repo agreements are important in financing the national debt and in providing liquidity of mortgage-backed securities. Their essential attribute "is liquidity—the assurance that the repo will be completed without delay."[11] Also, the participants must have quick protection against open-ended market loss in the event of the bankruptcy of a dealer or other counter-party in the repo market. To these ends of liquidity and stability (b)(7) excepts from the stay:

> the setoff by a repo participant, of any mutual debt and claim under or in connection with repurchase agreements that constitutes the setoff of a claim against the debtor for a margin payment, as defined in section 741(5) or section 761(15) of this title, or settlement payment, as defined in section 741(8) of this title, arising out of repurchase agreements against cash, securities, or other property held by or due from such repo participant to margin, guarantee, secure or settle repurchase agreements.[12]

The third narrow exception is section 362(a)(14). It concerns swap agreements and exceptions from the stay

> the setoff by a swap participant, of any mutual debt and claim under or in connection with any swap agreement that constitutes the setoff of a claim against the debtor for any payment due from the debtor under or in connection with any swap agreement against any payment due to the debtor from the swap participant under or in connection with any swap agreement or against cash, securities, or other property of the debtor held by or due from such swap participant to guarantee, secure or settle any swap agreement.[13]

The explanation is this:

---

9. In re Amcor Funding Corp., 117 B.R. 549, 551 (D.Ariz.1990).

10. Matter of Bevill, Bresler & Schulman Asset Mgmt., 896 F.2d 54, 55 (3d Cir.1990).

11. Bevill, Bresler & Schulman v. Spencer Sav. & Loan, 878 F.2d 742, 753 (3d Cir.1989).

12. 11 U.S.C.A. § 362(b)(7).

13. 11 U.S.C.A. § 362(b)(14).

Interest rate and foreign currency rate swap agreements are entered into by corporations, financial institutions, and governmental entities to minimize borrowing costs and to hedge against fluctuations in interest rates and foreign exchange rates. A corporation typically enters into swap agreements in order to obtain more advantageous interest and foreign exchange rates that are not available to it through conventional means. For example, because of low credit ratings, a company may not be able to obtain long-term, fixed-rate financing at acceptable rates. Instead, it may have to settle for more volatile, short-term floating rates that can expose it to uncertain interest rate costs over the life of the loan. To counter this risk, the company may, by paying a high premium, enter into agreements with a financial institution to "swap" the short-term floating rates for favorable long-term rates. The financial institution may, in turn, enter into other swap arrangements to minimize its own overall exposure to risk. The two parties to a swap agreement typically enter into a number of such agreements, occurring over a period of 1 to 12 years. Fluctuations in the rate of return can be expected to occur in both directions in the course of an agreement, or over the course of multiple agreements which are incorporated into a single master agreement. At the end of the swap agreement term, or upon default, the total of the periodic fluctuations, measured at specified periods during the term, are calculated, the amounts the first party owes to the second are set off against the amounts the second party owes the first, and the net sum owing from one party to the other is "netted out." The setoff process, which is at the center of the swap agreement, may be skewed if one of the parties has filed for bankruptcy.[14]

Because of this exception, which Congress added in 1990, the stay does not get in the way of a swap participant using setoff, postpetition, to make "a final accounting of the net amount due from or owed to the debtor * * *."[15] A related provision makes clear that the bankruptcy does not prevent the swap participant from terminating a swap agreement after the debtor's bankruptcy.[16]

§ 3–16 Actions Against Estate Property—Effecting Liens Against Property of the Estate

Section 362(a)(4) stays "any act to create, perfect, or enforce any lien against property of the estate."[1] This provision is the easiest part of section 362 to understand. There are no significant traps or unexpected turns. It

---

14. H.R. Rep. No. 484, 101st Cong., 2d Sess. (1990).

15. Id.

16. 11 U.S.C.A. § 560 (preserves a swap participant's contractual right to terminate a swap agreement and offset any amounts under it). This provision was added, along with section 362(b)(14), because of concerns

that under current bankruptcy law, termination and setoff of a swap agreement would be automatically stayed when one of the parties files a bankruptcy petition, whereupon the trustee, after indefinitely postponing termination of the swap agreement, could refuse setoff and unfairly "cherry pick" only the portions of the agreement advantageous to the debtor, while rejecting the portions unfavorable to the debtor.

H.R. Rep. No. 484, 101st Cong., 2d Sess. (1990).

§ 3–16

1. 11 U.S.C.A. § 362(a)(4).

applies as written to all liens, whether consensual or nonconsensual,[2] and to all creditors, including governments,[3] and applies without regard to the nature of the underlying claim or collateral and without regard to when the claim arose.[4] It stays every step in the creation, perfection, or enforcement of a lien,[5] including automatic steps[6] and also the very last step when everything else was done before bankruptcy. Thus, (a)(4) stays a sale of collateral that was repossessed prior to bankruptcy so long as the debtor retains an interest at the time of bankruptcy.[7] The stay of (a)(4) is triggered solely by the estate having an interest in the property,[8] not by where the property is physically located or the stage of the lien process.

Significantly, it is a hair trigger. Any interest sets it off. This aspect of (b)(4) causes the courts to consider, recurringly, whether and how (b)(4) applies in a very common case. The case involves foreclosing a lien on real estate. Everything was done before bankruptcy, including the sale of the property. In bankruptcy, the debtor claims that after filing the petition, she retained some interest or right in or to the property; that the stay preserved this right; and that she can now use it to undo or upset the sale.

The first and last issues are generally decided by state law. It defines property rights, including any rights that a mortgagee retains after foreclosure that can subordinate the buyer's title.[9]

The middle issue is really pretty easy. Any interest or right of the debtor at the time of bankruptcy passed to the estate, and (b)(4) stayed any act of lien enforcement against this right.[10] Any such act, even though actually taken, was legally ineffective. The stay thus preserved the right.

---

2. The term "lien" means any "charge against or interest in property to secure payment of a debt or performance of an obligation." Id. § 101(37). The various forms include a security interest, which is a lien created by agreement, id. § 101(51), a statutory lien, id. § 101(53), and a judicial lien. Id. § 101(36).

An exception is a maritime lien for a crew member's wages. The stay of (b)(4) does not affect such a lien which will arise, automatically, for postpetition labor. United States v. ZP Chandon, 889 F.2d 233 (9th Cir.1989) ("Maritime liens for seamen wages have priority over a preferred ship mortgage, and are 'sacred liens' entitled to protection 'as long as a plank of the ship remains.' * * * [I]t is unlikely that the drafters of the Bankruptcy Act would have casually neglected to express its intention to rewrite a 'sacred' principle of maritime law. We construe Congress' omission of any reference to maritime law in section 362(a)(4) as evidence of its intention to limit the reach of that statute to land-based transactions where (1) a recording of a lien interest is required and (2) the creditor first in time is entitled to priority. The district court erred in holding that the automatic stay provisions of the Bankruptcy Act apply to seamen's wages.").

3. See Practitioner Treatise, Vol. 1.

4. Matter of Reserves Development Corp., 78 B.R. 951, 958 (W.D.Mo.1986) (In applying (a)(4), the time the claim arose, whether pre- or postpetition, is irrelevant.).

5. It does not reach mere preparation to take any such step. In re de Jesus Saez, 721 F.2d 848, 853 (1st Cir.1983) (Sale of collateral upon dismissal of Chapter 13 petition was not stay violation because dismissal immediately ended stay. Preparing for auction sale before dismissal was not itself a violation, not even rescheduling date or advertising.).

The stay itself, however, does not extinguish a prepetition lien, but only prevents perfecting or enforcing such a lien or creating a lien after bankruptcy. See, e.g., Equibank v. Wheeling–Pittsburgh Steel Corp., 884 F.2d 80, 84–85 (3d Cir.1989) (The stay does not affect the secured status of a debt.); New York Life Ins. Co. v. Bremer Towers, 714 F.Supp. 414, 418 (D.Minn.1989) ("The fact that a creditor did not enforce [its] perfected interest prior to bankruptcy does not invalidate the interest, it merely stays the enforcement of that interest pending the bankruptcy court's determination of the party's entitlement.").

6. See Practitioner Treatise, Vol. 1.

7. See Practitioner Treatise, Vol. 1.

8. See Practitioner Treatise, Vol. 1.

9. See Practitioner Treatise, Vol. 1.

10. See Practitioner Treatise, Vol. 1.

A common, related issue is whether, in this fashion, the stay preserves a state-law right of redemption that expired, by the running of time, after the debtor filed bankruptcy. The precise question is whether the stay tolls or otherwise suspends the redemption period. The common answer is no.[11] The essential explanation is that (b)(4) works only against an "act" with respect to a lien. A right of redemption expiring by its own terms is not an "act." It is rather "self-destruction" that (b)(4) does not prevent.[12] The same reason explains why the right is not saved by (a)(3), which more broadly stays acts to possess or control property of the estate, or by (a)(1) which even more generally stays actions and proceedings against the debtor.[13]

The same analysis applies, with the same result, to any other right or interest of contract or property that would expire by its own terms after bankruptcy.[14] Neither (a)(3) nor (a)(4) stays the self-destructive expiration even though the estate owns the right that is thereby lost.

A debtor's redemption right can be suspended, apart from the stay, by section 108(b).[15] It extends the time that is set by law or agreement for a debtor to act to preserve her rights, including any act to cure a default or perform any similar act, *if* the time would expire before 60 days after the order for relief. In this event, section 108(b) stretches the time for acting to the end of those 60 days.[16] The time is not extended if the time set for expiration is later than the 60 days.[17]

A creditor's lien rights, too, can expire, as by the lapse of a judgment lien or the expiration of a recorded notice that perfects a lien.[18] By section 108(c) the Code saves a judgment lien from death caused by the running of the statute of limitations for enforcing the judgment: the debtor's bankruptcy suspends the statute throughout the case.[19]

It is not clear that section 108 covers revivor of a judgment lien in a state where the lien can lapse before the period of enforcement expires. It is even less likely that section 108 covers acts of recordation and the like that are necessary under state law to preserve liens or their perfection. It would seem, however, that a creditor can take freely these steps during the debtor's bankruptcy and, by these usual means of state law, perpetuate her lien rights. Acts to continue or preserve liens are not acts to create, perfect or

---

11. See Practitioner Treatise, Vol. 1.

12. Oulman v. Rolling Green, Inc., 851 F.2d 1032, 1034 (8th Cir.1988) ("Under the law of this Circuit, a notice of forfeiture in advance of bankruptcy automatically divests the purchaser's estate (and hence likewise the derivative bankruptcy estate) if default is not cured by the date specified in the notice of forfeiture. Hence no 'act' or 'enforcement' precluded by the automatic stay is required to perfect the foreclosure. The [debtors'] estate 'self-destructed' when they failed to pay up their arrears in timely fashion.").

13. See Practitioner Treatise, Vol. 1.

14. See Practitioner Treatise, Vol. 1.

15. 11 U.S.C.A. § 108(b); In re Maanum, 828 F.2d 459, 460 (8th Cir.1987), reh'g denied, 838 F.2d 991 (8th Cir.1988). ("We have no doubt that [a statutory period for curing the cancellation of a contract for deed] constitutes such a law" that § 108(b) tolls.); Matter of Tynan, 773 F.2d 177, 179 (7th Cir.1985) ("We * * * hold that when a petition in bankruptcy is filed before the expiration of the applicable state redemption period, § 108(b) extends the redemption period for 60 days from the commencement of bankruptcy proceedings.").

16. 11 U.S.C.A. § 108(b)(2).

17. Id. § 108(b)(1).

18. The debtor's stay does not save the creditor's rights. In re Morton, 866 F.2d 561, 563–65 (2d Cir.1989).

19. 11 U.S.C.A. § 108(c) (extends statute of limitations for creditors); In re Morton, 866 F.2d 561, 565–67 (2d Cir.1989) (§ 108(c) tolls New York's ten-year period governing judgment liens).

enforce them that (a)(4) stays.[20] We worry, however, that a judicial proceeding to revive a judgment or a similar action is stayed by section 362(a)(1), especially if the action could have been brought before bankruptcy.[21]

An Article 9 secured party is not bothered by this issue. Ordinarily, a filed financing statement that perfects her security interest [22] is effective for only five years from the date of filing.[23] She must file a continuation statement during the last six months to continue the filing's effectiveness.[24] An exception applies if bankruptcy or other insolvency proceedings are commenced by or against the debtor. In this event, state law suspends the five-year term of a financing statement.[25] Its effectiveness automatically continues throughout the bankruptcy case without any need to file a continuation statement, not even if the five-year period expires during the case. By operation of law, "the security interest remains perfected until termination of the insolvency proceedings and thereafter for a period of sixty days or until expiration of the five year period, whichever occurs later." [26]

§ 3–17 Actions Against Estate Property—Excepting Purchase-Money Security Interests In Aircraft (Section 1110)

For full text of this section, see Epstein, Nickles & White, Bankruptcy, Practitioner Treatise Series, Vol. 1.

a. Substantive Requirements

b. Cure

c. Expiration of the Stay

§ 3–18 Respecting Certain Grace Periods for Perfection (Section 362(b)(3))

a. Bankruptcy Preference Law

Property is not washed of liens simply by passing to the bankruptcy estate. Rather, the estate honors the principle of derivative title and takes property subject to all liens, including liens that are unperfected. Typically, however, the trustee can avoid unperfected liens using the avoiding powers of sections 544(a), 545(2), or 547(b).[1]

Section 547 is preference law.[2] Even a lien perfected before bankruptcy can be avoided as a preference under section 547(b), which enforces bank-

---

20. See Practitioner Treatise, Vol. 1.

21. This provision stays "the commencement or continuation, including the issuance or employment of process, of a judicial, administrative, or other action or proceeding against the debtor that was or could have been commenced before the commencement of the case under this title, or to recover a claim against the debtor that arose before the commencement of the case under this title." 11 U.S.C.A. § 362(a)(1).

22. See U.C.C. §§ 9–302(1); 9–401; 9–402.

23. Id. § 9–403(2).

24. Id. § 9–403(2–3).

25. Id. § 9–403(2).

26. Id.

§ 3–18

1. 11 U.S.C.A. §§ 544(a), 545(2) & 547(b).

2. The trustee can avoid a preference by force of section 547(b), id. § 547(b), which describes a preference as:

Any transfer of an interest of the debtor in property;

ruptcy policy against the debtor playing favorites in paying or securing antecedent debts. An unperfected lien at bankruptcy is especially vulnerable.

For purposes of preference law, a lien is deemed to occur at the time of perfection unless the lien is perfected within 10 days after actually taking effect between the parties.[3] By force of section 547(e)(2)(A), perfection within this 10-day grace period dates the transfer as of the time of its actual effectiveness,[4] so that a kind of relation back occurs. This time is usually closer to when the debt was incurred, so that the relation back works against finding the key requirement of a preference that the transfer was for an antecedent debt.[5]

A lien that is unperfected at the time of bankruptcy is deemed to have occurred immediately before bankruptcy.[6] This time is usually much later than when the secured debt was incurred, and the gap establishes that the transfer was for an antecedent debt. The relation-back effect of section 547(e)(2)(A) would reduce or eliminate the gap if any of the 10-day grace period remains and the creditor can and does perfect within it.[7] The circumstances control expiration of the 10-day period, but section 362 controls whether or not the creditor can perfect after the debtor's bankruptcy.

Ordinarily, section 362(a)(4) or (5) stays any act to perfect a lien against property of the estate or the debtor,[8] but section 362 creates an exception for the 10-day grace period of section 547(e)(2)(A). The exception is part of section 362(b)(3) which covers:

> *any act to perfect an interest in property* to the extent that the trustee's rights and powers are subject to such perfection under section 546(b) of this title or *to the extent that such act is accomplished within the period provided under section 547(e)(2)(A) of this title.*[9]

Thus, the stay does not prevent perfecting a lien after bankruptcy so long as the perfection occurs within the 10-day period that section 547(e)(2)(A) describes, i.e., within 10 days after the lien took effect between the parties.

This exception of (b)(3) does not extend beyond section 547(e)(2)(A), and section 547(e)(2)(A) does not extend beyond these 10 days. Thus, the exception does not apply if the 10-day period has expired before bankruptcy. Even if the period continues after bankruptcy, the creditor must actually

---

To or for the benefit of a creditor;

For or on account of an antecedent debt owed by the debtor before such transfer was made;

Made while the debtor was insolvent;

Made on or within 90 days before the date of the filing of the petition, or within one year of the filing if the creditor is an insider; and,

That enables the creditor to receive more than she would receive in a Chapter 7 distribution of the bankruptcy estate had the transfer not been made.

We thoroughly discuss preference law elsewhere. See §§ 6-3—6-37 infra.

3. Id. § 547(e)(2)(A-B).

4. Id. § 547(e)(2)(A).

5. See id. § 547(b)(2) (transfer "for or on account of an antecedent debt owed by the debtor before such transfer was made").

6. Id. § 547(e)(2)(C).

7. Id. § 547(e)(2)(C)(ii).

8. Id. § 362(a)(4) ("any act to create, perfect, or enforce any lien against property of the estate"); § 362(a)(5) ("any act to create, perfect, or enforce against property of the debtor any lien to the extent that such lien secures a claim that arose before the commencement of the case under this title").

9. Id. § 362(b)(3) (emphasis added).

perfect her lien during the 10 days in order to trigger section 547(e)(2)(A). The only effect of doing so, however, is that the lien is thereby deemed to have occurred, for section 547 purposes, when the lien actually took effect between the parties. The lien was nevertheless a transfer made for an antecedent debt if the debt was incurred before the lien became so effective, and is avoidable under section 547(b) if the other elements of preference are satisfied. Further, even if the lien is not a preference or otherwise escapes section 547, the trustee will probably, almost surely, avoid it under section 544 or 545.

b. *State Priority Law*

Because of sections 544(a) and 545(2), the trustee can ordinarily avoid liens that are unperfected at the time of bankruptcy.[10] In general, these avoiding powers give the trustee the same priority in relation to liens on the debtor's property as a person who became a lien creditor or good faith purchaser of the collateral at the time of bankruptcy. Because such a third person would normally prime unperfected liens under the nonbankruptcy law that governs them, the trustee asserting the same priority can entirely avoid the liens under bankruptcy law.

The creditor cannot save her lien by perfecting it before the trustee sues to avoid the lien. Section 362(a)(4-5) stays any act to perfect a lien against property of the estate or the debtor. Also, perfection after bankruptcy could possibly be attacked as a postpetition transfer that the trustee can avoid under section 549(a).[11] Moreover, avoidance under section 544(a) or 545(2) turns on the trustee's priority, under state law, as a lien creditor or purchaser. The trustee assumed this status at the moment of bankruptcy.

---

10. Section 544(a) provides:

(a) The trustee shall have, as of the commencement of the case, and without regard to any knowledge of the trustee or of any creditor, the rights and powers of, or may avoid any transfer of property of the debtor or any obligation incurred by a debtor that is voidable by—

(1) a creditor that extends credit to the debtor at the time of the commencement of the case, and that obtains, at such time and with respect to such credit, a judicial lien on all property on which a creditor on a simple contract could have obtained such a judicial lien, whether or not such a creditor exists;

(2) a creditor that extends credit to the debtor at the time of the commencement of the case, and obtains, at such time and with respect to such credit, an execution against the debtor that is returned unsatisfied at such time, whether or not such a creditor exists; or

(3) a bona fide purchaser of real property, other than fixtures, from the debtor, against whom applicable law permits such transfer to be perfected, that obtains the status of a bona fide purchaser and has perfected such transfer at the time of the commencement of the case, whether or not such a purchaser exists.

11 U.S.C.A. § 544(a). Section 545(2) allows the trustee to avoid a statutory lien that

is not perfected or enforceable at the time of the commencement of the case against a bona fide purchaser that purchases such property at the time of the commencement of the case, whether or not such a purchaser exists.

Id. § 545(2).

11. This section provides:

(a) Except as provided in subsection (b) or (c) of this section, the trustee may avoid a transfer of property of the estate—

(1) that occurs after the commencement of the case; and

(2)(A) that is authorized only under section 303(f) or 542(c) of this title; or

(B) that is not authorized under this title or by the court.

Id. § 549(a). This argument would analogize to preference law which deems that a transfer occurs at the time of perfection.

Her priority is set then and would not be undermined by subsequent perfection of the lien. The reason is that under state law, which defines the trustee's priority, this happening would not affect the priority of a real lien creditor or purchaser. Neither section 544(a) nor 545(2) provides a grace period for perfection such as section 547(e)(2)(A).[12]

Occasionally, however, state law makes an exception to the usual priority rules that allows subsequent perfection of a lien to relate back to the time of the lien's creation. The lien thereby trumps an intervening lien creditor or purchaser whose claim was otherwise entitled to priority because it attached when the first creditor's lien was unperfected.

A common example is a construction lien. Typically, this lien favors, by law, a supplier of goods or services that are used for the improvement of real estate. The lien attaches to the real estate at the time of use or sooner and is perfected by filing a notice or suing. A buyer, mortgagee, or other creditor who takes an interest in the collateral during the interim, between attachment and perfection of the construction lien, takes subject to it even though the lien was secret when they intervened.[13] Another common example is a mortgagee's claim to rents and profits that, in some states, is perfected after the mortgagor's default.[14]

For certain purposes, bankruptcy law honors such a state-law rule of related-back perfection and priority. The trustee's avoiding powers of sections 544, 545 and 549 are subject to it, by force of section 546(b):

> The rights and powers of a trustee under sections 544, 545, and 549 of this title are subject to any generally applicable law that permits perfection of an interest in property to be effective against an entity that acquires rights in such property before the date of such perfection. If such law requires seizure of such property or commencement of an action to accomplish such perfection, and such property has not been seized or such action has not been commenced before the date of the filing of the petition, such interest in such property shall be perfected by notice within the time fixed by such law for such seizure or commencement.[15]

The stay is also subject to a relation-back rule, by force of section 362(b)(3) which excepts:

---

12. Preference law deems that a transfer is made when it is perfected unless perfection occurs within 10 days after it takes effect between the parties, in which event the transfer is made when it took effect between them. Id. § 547(e)(2)(A).

13. For further discussion and examples, see our discussion of the trustee's power to avoid construction and other statutory liens by force of section 545, id. § 545, at 6–62 infra.

14. We thoroughly cover this claim of a mortgagee, and its priority against the trustee, in our discussion of the postpetition transfers and the trustee's power to avoid them under section 549 and related provisions. Id. § 546. See especially § 6–77 infra.

15. Id. § 546(b). We imagine that this rule covers section 549 not only because of the possibility that the postpetition perfection is itself a postpetition transfer. Another reason is that the postpetition perfection gives some immunity to transfers that the trustee could otherwise have avoided. In a sense, therefore, the perfection indirectly and remotely takes (or keeps) property from the estate even if the perfection is not itself, technically and directly, a transfer. For this reason the perfection could be attacked as a postpetition transfer. We doubt any argument that perfection is a transfer within section 549, but we can understand the wisdom of section 546(b) covering section 549 just to make clear and certain that the latter is not used to undermine the former.

any act to perfect an interest in property *to the extent that the trustee's rights and powers are subject to such perfection under section 546(b) of this title* or to the extent that such act is accomplished with the period provided under section 547(e)(2)(A) of this title.[16]

This exception removes the stay as a procedural bar to a creditor perfecting after bankruptcy in order to take advantage of a relation-back rule and thereby prevent the trustee's avoidance of the lien. Because (b)(3) applies against the whole of section 362(a), it allows postpetition related-back perfection whether the collateral is property of the estate or the debtor's own property. Nothing in section 362(a) prevents the perfection.[17]

We discuss later, in some detail, the avoiding powers of sections 544, 545 and 549. The discussions cover specific applications of section 362(b)(3) and section 546(b) in relation to these three avoiding powers.[18]

In every instance, however, these general, common principles govern:

1. The section 362(b)(3) exception applies, to shield from the stay an act intended to take advantage of section 546(b), only if section 546(b) itself applies and is satisfied.[19]

2. Section 546(b) applies only if the lien itself actually exists prepetition. It does not permit the creation or attachment of a lien after bankruptcy even though, by state law, the lien would relate back to a time before bankruptcy.[20] The scope of section 546(b) is strictly limited to the relation back of postpetition perfection of a prepetition lien.

3. Section 546(b) is not itself a provision that provides for relation back. It recognizes state law that does so, and only such state law that results in subordinating intervening claims, i.e., "generally applicable law that permits perfection of an interest in property to be effective against an entity that acquires rights in such property before the date of such perfection."[21] It does not apply when the state law merely provides for subsequently perfecting a lien, after an intervening claim, and dating the lien's priority forward from the time of perfection.

---

16. Id. § 362(b)(3) (emphasis added).
17. See Practitioner Treatise, Vol. 1.
18. See §§ 6–61 (section 544(a)), 6–62 (section 545(2)) and 6–69 (section 549) infra.
19. See Practitioner Treatise, Vol. 1.
20. See Practitioner Treatise, Vol. 1.
21. 11 U.S.C.A. § 546(b); see, e.g., In re Alberto, 823 F.2d 712, 722–23 (3d Cir.1987) (Postpetition recording of ship mortgage to perfect security interest and also subsequent endorsement of mortgage upon vessel's documents are violations of stay so that they are null and ineffective. Recording not protected by §§ 362(b)(3) and 546(b) because law (Ship Mortgage Act) did not provide that recordation would relate back to a time before bankruptcy.); In re Ian Homes, Inc., 126 B.R. 933 (Bankr. D.Md.1991) (Stay barred state court litigation to perfect mechanic's lien that did not relate back to the time of the underlying debt's creation.); In re Westchase I Associates, L.P., 119 B.R. 521, 525–26 (Bankr. W.D.N.C. 1990), remanded, 126 B.R. 692 (W.D.N.C.1991) (Stay stops appointment of a receiver to sequester rents and profits for that is an attempt to perfect or create lien postpetition, and §§ 362(b) & 546(b) are inapplicable because there is no relation back.); In re Westport–Sandpiper Associates, 116 B.R. 355, 358 (Bankr. D. Conn. 1990) (Rents are cash collateral only to extent there is a perfected security interest in them. Postpetition perfection is generally void by section 362(a)(4), and § 546(b) applies only if state law provides that perfection relates back.); In re Wynnewood House Associates, 121 B.R. 716, 726–27 (Bankr. E.D.Pa. 1990) (Cannot perfect interest in postpetition rents by actual or constructive possession; and § 362(b)(3) does not apply, because § 546 does not apply, because no relation back.).

4. Even when section 546(b) applies, the creditor must actually take the steps for perfection that state law requires within the time for doing so fixed by the state relation-back law, except that substituted action is required if the steps involve seizure of the collateral or filing a lawsuit. In this event, instead of seizing or suing, the secured creditor perfects, by overriding authority of section 546(b) itself, "by notice within the time fixed by * * * [the state law] for such seizure or commencement." [22] Nothing else satisfies section 546(b) and thus anything else violates the stay.[23]

5. Even when section 546(b) applies and the creditor's postpetition perfection is shielded by section 362(b)(3), this exception to the stay shields only the acts to perfect and nothing else in furtherance of the lien, least acts to enforce it.[24]

6. The related-back perfection that section 546(b) respects, while protecting against sections 544 and 545, does not itself protect against section 547(b), by which the trustee can avoid certain preferential transfers for antecedent debt.[25] If the perfection is not within the 10-day period of section 547(e)(2)(A),[26] the lien is deemed perfected, and the transfer made, immediately before bankruptcy.[27] This grace period of bankruptcy preference law, which section 362(b)(3) also respects,[28] is not extended by the grace period of state perfection and priority law. Also, section 546(b) subjects sections 544, 545 and 549 to this state law, *but not section 547*. The largest possible significance, however, is only that the lien is deemed a transfer for an antecedent debt by dating the transfer from a point immediately before bankruptcy. Other elements of preference must be satisfied in order to avoid the lien under section 547. Also, any defense to preference that applies can save the lien from section 547 avoidance even if the lien is a preference.[29]

§ 3–19 Excepting Certain Actions by Government

Federal, state and local governments are generally subject to the automatic stay.[1] Government is enjoined, as is everyone else, from engaging in any of the acts that section 362(a) describes; and government's acts in violation of the stay are always void or voidable, as is true for everyone else.[2]

---

22. 11 U.S.C.A. § 546(b).

23. In re Coated Sales, Inc., 124 B.R. 17 (Bankr. S.D.N.Y. 1991).

24. Matter of Chief Charley's, Inc., 122 B.R. 785, 787–88 (Bankr. M.D.Fla.1990) (The (b)(3) exception does not cover issuance of tax warrants that are acts of collection rather than perfection.); In re Richardson Builders, Inc., 123 B.R. 736 (Bankr. W.D. Va. 1990) (Action to enforce mechanic's lien is not excepted by (b)(3).); Northwest Wholesale Lumber, Inc. v. Citadel Co., 457 N.W.2d 244 (Minn. App.1990) (An action to enforce a mechanic's lien does not fit into the § 362(b)(3) stay exception.).

25. 11 U.S.C.A. § 547(b).

26. Id. § 547(e)(2)(A).

27. Id. § 547(e)(2)(C).

28. Id. § 362(b)(3). We have earlier discussed this aspect of the exception, at § 3–18 supra.

29. A perfect example is a construction or other statutory lien that is unavoidable under section 545. Such a lien cannot be avoided under § 547(b) even though the lien satisfies fully the elements of preference. See id. § 547(c)(6). A statutory lien can be saved from avoidance under 545 by state related-back perfection, § 546(b) and 362(b)(3), and can thereby be saved from avoidance as a preference.

§ 3–19

1. For authorities, see § 3–3, where we discuss people and entities whom the stay affects.

2. See § 3–32 infra.

The only effect of sovereign immunity is, sometimes, to prevent liability for damages for having violated the stay.[3]

Government is favored, however, by several of the section 362(b) exceptions. The exceptions that concern the government as an ordinary creditor are small, even tiny, and relatively insignificant.[4] Two of the exceptions are large and important. They concern the government as cop and except criminal actions against the debtor, section 362(b)(1),[5] and actions to enforce police or regulatory power against her, section 362(b)(4–5).[6]

§ 3–20 Excepting Certain Actions by Government—Criminal Actions (Section 362(b)(1))

For full text of this section, see Epstein, Nickles & White, Bankruptcy, Practitioner Treatise Series, Vol. 1.

§ 3–21 Excepting Certain Actions by Government—Regulatory Actions (Section 362(b)(4–5))

For full text of this section, see Epstein, Nickles & White, Bankruptcy, Practitioner Treatise Series, Vol. 1.

---

3. See § 3–34 infra.

4. Bankruptcy does not operate as a stay—

(8) under subsection (a) of this section, of the commencement of any action by the Secretary of Housing and Urban Development to foreclose a mortgage or deed of trust in any case in which the mortgage or deed of trust held by the Secretary is insured or was formerly insured under the National Housing Act and covers property, or combinations of property, consisting of five more living units;

(9) under subsection (a) of this section, of the issuance to the debtor by a governmental unit of a notice of tax deficiency;

* * *

(12) under subsection (a) of this section, after the date which is 90 days after the filing of such petition, of the commencement or continuation, and conclusion to the entry of final judgment, of an action which involves a debtor subject to reorganization pursuant to chapter 11 of this title and which was brought by the Secretary of Transportation under the Ship Mortgage Act, 1920 (46 U.S.C.A. App. § 911 et seq.) (including distribution of any proceeds of sale) to foreclose a preferred ship or fleet mortgage, or a security interest in or relating to a vessel or vessel under construction, held by the Secretary of Transportation under section 207 or title XI of the Merchant Marine Act, 1936 (46 U.S.C.A. App. §§ 1117 and 1271 et seq., respectively), or under applicable State law; or

(13) under subsection (a) of this section, after the date which is 90 days after the filing of such petition, of the commencement or continuation, and conclusion to the entry of final judgment, of an action which involves a debtor subject to reorganization pursuant to chapter 11 of this title and which was brought by the Secretary of Commerce under the Ship Mortgage Act, 1920 (46 U.S.C.A. App. § 911 et seq.) (including distribution of any proceeds of sale) to foreclose a preferred ship or fleet mortgage in a vessel or a mortgage, deed of trust, or other security interest in a fishing facility held by the Secretary of Commerce under section 207 or title XI of the Merchant Marine Act, 1936 (46 U.S.C.A. App. §§ 1117 and 1271 et seq., respectively).

The provisions of paragraphs (12) and (13) of this subsection shall apply with respect to any such petition filed on or before December 31, 1989.

11 U.S.C.A. § 362(b)(8–9, 12–13).

5. It excepts "the commencement or continuation of a criminal action or proceeding against the debtor." Id. § 362(b)(1).

6. These except "the commencement or continuation of an action or proceeding by a governmental unit to enforce such governmental unit's police or regulatory power," id. § 362(b)(4), and the enforcement of a judgment in such a proceeding. Id. § 362(b)(5).

Section 362(a)(1) stays actions and proceedings against the debtor.[1] An important exception is section 362(b)(4). It permits actions and proceedings by a "governmental unit to enforce * * * [the] unit's police or regulatory power."[2] Section 362(b)(5) widens the exception by taking the next step and allowing the enforcement of a judgment, "other than a money judgment,"[3] that the governmental unit obtains in such an action.

The exceptions provide, in full, that the filing of a petition does not operate as a stay:

[(b)](4) under subsection (a)(1) of this section, of the commencement or continuation of an action or proceeding by a government unit to enforce such government unit's police or regulatory power;

(5) under subsection (a)(2) of this section, of the enforcement of a judgment, other than a money judgment, obtained in an action or proceeding by a governmental unit to enforce such governmental unit's police or regulatory power.[4]

The effect of these exceptions is to allow a governmental unit to pursue actions against a debtor, that are within (b)(4–5), despite the debtor having filed bankruptcy.[5] Relief from the stay is not necessary.[6] Thus, for example, the federal government or a state can initiate or continue a suit against the debtor, even though she is in bankruptcy, to determine and correct violations of environmental protection laws,[7] or to fix liability for unlawful labor and employment practices.[8] Other examples of excepted actions are:

- state licensing activities that enforce regulatory and police laws;[9]
- civil forfeiture action;[10]
- enforcing state statute prohibiting odometer tampering;[11]
- forcing a debtor to comply with zoning laws by requiring him to clear

§ 3–21

1. It provides:

(a) Except as provided in subsection (b) of this section * * * a petition filed * * * operates as a stay, applicable to all entities, of * * * the commencement or continuation, including the issuance or employment of process, of a judicial, administrative, or other action or proceeding against the debtor that was or could have been commenced before the commencement of the case under this title, or to recover a claim against the debtor that arose before the commencement of the case under this title * * *.

11 U.S.C.A. § 362(a)(1). For our discussion of (a)(1), see § ____ supra.

2. Id. § 362(b)(4).

3. Id. § 362(b)(5).

4. Id. § 362(b)(4), (5).

5. There is authority that limits the § 362(b)(4-5) exceptions to government action that itself complies with the police or regulatory laws that the government acts to enforce. Matter of Nat'l Hospital and Institutional Builders Co., 658 F.2d 39 (2d Cir.1981), cert. denied, 454 U.S. 1149, 102 S.Ct. 1014, 71 L.Ed.2d 303 (1982) (§ 362(b)(4) does not prevent court from enjoining bad faith enforcement of local regulation). A bankruptcy court is not licensed, however, to dispute a state court's judgment about these laws and compliance with them. In re James, 940 F.2d 46 (3d Cir.1991) (Federal court lacked power to examine merits of state forfeiture proceeding that had been decided against the debtor.).

6. Because the filing of a petition in bankruptcy "does not operate as a stay" against actions described in the exceptions of section 362(b), there is no reason to seek relief from the stay to pursue them. See e.g., N.L.R.B. v. Edward Cooper Painting, Inc., 804 F.2d 934, 939 (6th Cir.1986); In re Chateaugay Corp., 87 B.R. 779, 806 (S.D.N.Y. 1988).

7. See Practitioner Treatise, Vol. 1.

8. See Practitioner Treatise, Vol. 1.

9. See Practitioner Treatise, Vol. 1.

10. See Practitioner Treatise, Vol. 1.

11. See Practitioner Treatise, Vol. 1.

his land of truck parts and junk;[12]

- government's review of the financial fitness of a common carrier in order to protect shippers against financially irresponsible carriers;[13]
- administrative proceedings by Office of Thrift Supervision to fix and ascertain the debtor's liability for violating federal banking laws;[14]
- action by the CFTC to stop violations of the commodities trading laws,[15] or by the SEC seeking injunctive and other forms of relief to protect investors under the anti-fraud provisions of the federal securities laws;[16]
- state's adjudication of workers' compensation claims;[17]
- Pension Benefit Guaranty Corporation moving to require debtor to restore employees' pension plan and to fund and administer it and other plans;[18]
- Secretary of Labor's suit to enjoin interstate sale of "hot" goods manufactured in violation of federal minimum wage laws,[19] to require compliance with OSHA safety requirements;[20] or to rescind debtor's purchase of securities for employees' profit sharing plan and to require debtor to restore any losses to the plan;[21]
- state's suit for an injunction, civil penalties and attorney fees and costs against debtor for violations of local consumer protection laws;[22]
- INS citing debtor for violating immigration laws;[23]
- New York's action to recover excess rent that debtor-landlord had already collected and to enjoin him from collecting excess rent in the future;[24] and,
- state proceeding to establish debtor's liability for overpayment of unemployment benefits because the purpose was to stop fraud.[25]

If the government wins the action, enforcement of any judgment or other decision in its favor, other than a money judgment, is also excepted.[26]

If the debtor, trustee, or another interested party believes the action is outside of (b)(4–5), she can seek to stop the government by arguing that the exceptions are inapplicable and that the stay thus applies.[27] Moreover, neither (b)(4) nor (5) provides a complete escape from the stay even when the exception applies. Each of them overrides only a single subsection of section 362(a). In allowing government actions, (b)(4) only trumps (a)(1), which generally bans actions and proceedings against the debtor. The accompanying (b)(5), permitting the government to enforce its judgment, overrides only the general prohibition of (a)(2) against enforcing prepetition judgments

---

12. Cournoyer v. Town of Lincoln, 790 F.2d 971, 976 (1st Cir.1986).
13. See Practitioner Treatise, Vol. 1.
14. See Practitioner Treatise, Vol. 1.
15. See Practitioner Treatise, Vol. 1.
16. See Practitioner Treatise, Vol. 1.
17. See Practitioner Treatise, Vol. 1.
18. See Practitioner Treatise, Vol. 1.
19. See Practitioner Treatise, Vol. 1.
20. See Practitioner Treatise, Vol. 1.
21. See Practitioner Treatise, Vol. 1.
22. See Practitioner Treatise, Vol. 1.
23. See Practitioner Treatise, Vol. 1.
24. See Practitioner Treatise, Vol. 1.
25. See Practitioner Treatise, Vol. 1.
26. 11 U.S.C.A. § 362(b)(5).
27. See Practitioner Treatise, Vol. 1.

against the debtor or property of the estate.[28] By the express terms of section 362, everything else in subsection (a) applies against governmental police and regulatory power despite (b)(4–5).

If the exceptions apply and the action is not otherwise stayed by section 362, the only way to stop it is to ask the bankruptcy court to enjoin the government, on other grounds, from pursuing the action. Even when governmental action is excepted from the automatic stay by (b)(4–5), the bankruptcy court can act beyond section 362 and stay the action by a discretionary injunction based on section 105(a).[29]

In practice, however, the exceptions of (b)(4–5) cut a very noticeable, increasingly-travelled and ever-widening path through section 362(a) that is seldom blocked by section 105 injunctions. In combination (which is how we usually treat them), their boundaries are almost certain to move even more in order to accommodate any growth in the social problems that government fights with police or regulatory laws.

a. Legislative Design of the Exceptions

The legislative history of section 362(b)(4) reports a noble purpose and wide scope. The exception is intended to remove the stay of the debtor's bankruptcy as a procedural bar

> where a governmental unit is suing [the] debtor to prevent or stop violation of fraud, environmental protection, consumer protection, safety, or similar police or regulatory laws, or attempting to fix damages for violation of such a law.[30]

On the other hand, there is evidence that (b)(4) was not intended to allow government "to protect a pecuniary interest in property of the debtor or property of the estate."[31] Thus, (b)(4) was built, in some part, on a distinction between actions enforcing police or regulatory laws and actions protecting pecuniary interests. The line between them helps to define, by exclusion, the reach of the (b)(4) exception, but does not fully decide its scope.

---

28. Section 362(a)(2) provides:

(a) Except as provided in subsection (b) of this section * * * a petition filed * * * operates as a stay, applicable to all entities, of * * * (2) the enforcement, against the debtor or against property of the estate, of a judgment obtained before the commencement of the case under this title * * *.

11 U.S.C.A. § 362(a)(2).

29. This provision allows the bankruptcy court to "issue any order, process, or judgment that is necessary or appropriate to carry out the provisions of this title." 11 U.S.C.A. § 105(a). We discuss later how section 105(a) overrides section 362. See ___ infra.

30. H.R. Rep. No. 595, 95th Cong., 1st Sess. 340, 343, reprinted in 1978 U.S. Code Cong. & Admin. News 5963, 6299; S. Rep. No. 989, 95th Cong., 2d Sess. 54–55, reprinted in 1978 U.S. Code Cong. & Admin. News 5787, 5838.

31. 124 Cong. Rec. H 11089, Sept. 28, 1978 (statement by Cong. Edwards) reprinted in 1978 U.S. Code Cong. & Admin. News 6444–45; 124 Cong. Rec. S 17406, Oct. 6, 1978 (statement by Sen. DeConcini) reprinted in 1978 U.S. Code Cong. & Admin. News 6513. The statement in full states:

Section 362(b)(4) indicates that the stay under section 362(a)(1) does not apply to affect the commencement or continuation of an action or proceeding by a governmental unit to enforce the governmental unit's police or regulatory power. This section is intended to be given a narrow construction in order to permit governmental units to pursue actions to protect the public health and safety and not to apply to actions by a governmental unit to protect a pecuniary interest in property of the debtor or property of the estate.

Id.

The accompanying exception, section 362(b)(5), "extends" (b)(4) "to permit an injunction and enforcement of an injunction, and to permit the *entry* of a money judgment."[32] After all, a judgment or its equivalent is the immediate aim of an action of proceeding. There is little reason to permit the latter without the former. On the other hand, Congress denied the ultimate aim by explicitly excluding from (b)(5) the *enforcement* of a money judgment. Congress reasoned:

> Since the assets of the debtor are in the possession and control of the bankruptcy court, and since they constitute a fund out of which all creditors are entitled to share, enforcement by a government unit of a money judgment would give it preferential treatment to the detriment of all other creditors.[33]

The usual balancing is everywhere. Congress created these exceptions so that in providing financial relief for a debtor, the bankruptcy process would not compromise enforcing the laws that promote the health and welfare of the debtor's community. On the other hand, permitting government enforcement stops short of preferring government with respect to the bankruptcy estate. Government is not to get a priority over other creditors and, thus, enforcing its money judgments is excluded from the exception and is thereby subjected to the stay.

There is a middle case which does not neatly fit this design. It is the case of police or regulatory enforcement that is not a money judgment but nevertheless costs the debtor's estate money, such as a mandated environmental clean-up. Allowing this enforcement would appear, effectively, to give the government a "super priority." This kind of case eventually leads to a very basic, tough conflict between, on the one hand, serving the bankruptcy goal of preserving the estate for an equal distribution among the debtor's creditors, and, on the other hand, paying off the top to repair the debtor's damage to public health and safety. This issue is always in the background of decisions interpreting (b)(4–5). We now turn to these decisions and toward the ultimate issue, which we believe is finally resolved in favor of the bankruptcy estate more than the government.

b. Meaning of "Governmental Unit"
c. Action or Proceeding Enforcing Police or Regulatory Power Under (b)(4)
  i. Enforcement
  ii. Action or Proceeding
  iii. Police or Regulatory Power
d. Enforcement of a Judgment Under (b)(5) and the Internal Limit Excluding Money Judgments
e. External Limits on the Exceptions
  i. Unexcepted, Unaffected Parts of Section 362(a)
  ii. Discretionary Injunctions Under Section 105(a)

---

32. H.R. Rep. No. 595, 95th Cong., 1st Sess. 340, 343, reprinted in 1978 U.S. Code Cong. & Admin. News 5963, 6299; S. Rep. No. 989, 95th Cong., 2d Sess. 54–55, reprinted in 1978 U.S. Code Cong. & Admin. News 5787, 5838.

33. Id.

§ 3–22 Supplemental Injunctions

The stay of section 362(a) is the only injunction that results automatically from the debtor's bankruptcy, but section 362(a) is not the only law for enjoining conduct that affects the bankruptcy. Principally important is section 105(a), which very broadly empowers the bankruptcy court to "issue any order, process, or judgment that is necessary or appropriate to carry out the provisions of this title." [1] Using this power the court can issue injunctions, in appropriate cases, that supplement the stay in several dimensions. The court can enjoin acts that are beyond the stay because:

- Section 362(a) does not cover them; [2]

- they are excepted by section 362(b); [3] or

- their initial coverage by section 362 has lapsed by the stay's expiration or the court's grant of relief from it. [4]

Most significant in practice, section 105(a) enables the court in proper circumstances to enjoin acts and actions against third parties and their property who are not themselves in bankruptcy. [5]

Section 105(a) gives general equitable powers to bankruptcy courts and district courts sitting in bankruptcy, but the authority to issue section 105(a) injunctions is not unlimited and is not limited only by equity. Rather, the authority of section 105(a) is to issue injunctions and exercise other equitable powers only when necessary to further the Code's substantive provisions. The powers of section 105(a) cannot be used "to create substantive rights that would otherwise be unavailable under the Code," [6] nor "in a manner that is inconsistent with the other, more specific provisions of the Code." [7]

---

§ 3–22

1. 11 U.S.C.A. § 105(a). There are other sources of injunctive relief. For example, in Equal Employment Opportunity Comm. v. Rath Packing Co., 787 F.2d 318, 325 (8th Cir. 1986), cert. denied, 479 U.S. 910, 107 S.Ct. 307, 93 L.Ed.2d 282 (1986), the court noted that the All Writs Act, 28 U.S.C.A. § 1651(a), authorizes bankruptcy courts to issue stays, ("The Supreme Court and all courts established by Act of Congress may issue all writs necessary or appropriate in aid of their respective jurisdictions and agreeable to the usages and principles of law."). It is also said that bankruptcy courts are inherently empowered to grant stays. Matter of S.I. Acquisition, Inc., 817 F.2d 1142, 1146 n.3 (5th Cir.1987); A.H. Robins Co., Inc. v. Piccinin, 788 F.2d 994, 1003 (4th Cir.1986), cert. denied, 479 U.S. 876, 107 S.Ct. 251, 93 L.Ed.2d 177 (1986).

2. See Practitioner Treatise, Vol. 1.

3. See Practitioner Treatise, Vol. 1.

4. See Practitioner Treatise, Vol. 1.

5. See Practitioner Treatise, Vol. 1.

6. In re Morristown & Erie Railroad Co., 885 F.2d 98, 100 (3d Cir.1989) (Bankruptcy court could not require the debtor-railroad to initiate accelerated procedures with state environmental agency, including posting bond that debtor claimed it could not afford. No provision of the Code gives the trustee the right to require the debtor to assume the liability that the court imposed.).

7. In re Western Real Estate Fund, Inc., 922 F.2d 592, 601 (10th Cir.1990); see also In re American Hardwoods, 885 F.2d 621 (9th Cir.1989) (The bankruptcy court could not permanently enjoin, beyond the confirmation of the plan, a creditor's enforcement of a state court judgment against the debtor's guarantors.); United States v. Carolina Parachute Corp., 907 F.2d 1469 (4th Cir.1990) (In issuing a § 105(a) injunction a bankruptcy court cannot disregard the bankruptcy statute and rules and cannot enjoin the government's right to terminate a contract, as its terms allowed, that the debtor in possession had assumed. To allow the injunction would disregard the rule that a contract is assumed with all its burdens, including the right to terminate.); In re Compton Corp., 90 B.R. 798, 806–07 (N.D.Tex.1988), appeal dism'd, 889 F.2d 1104 (Em.App.1989) (A injunction issues under § 105(a) to carry out the provisions of the Code, not to contravene them.); but compare In re Ionosphere Clubs, Inc., 922 F.2d 984

Rather, the authority of section 105(a) is to use the powers of equity, consistent with the law's purpose and policy, to fill gaps and to trim or mold statutes that apply imperfectly in the particular case because of peculiar circumstances.

As a supplement to the stay, section 105(a) injunctions are most often sought and issued in Chapter 11 cases. Indeed, " '[t]his provision [§ 105] has been construed liberally to enjoin [actions] that might impede the reorganization process.' "[8] Injunctions in reorganization cases are most popular to stop actions and proceedings against third parties who are linked to the debtor.[9] The stay itself generally protects only the debtor and nobody else. It will not stop suits against other people, not even people who are intimately connected to the debtor generally or in terms of the plaintiff's specific claims.[10] For injunctive relief, third parties must depend on other law; and their favorite source, when the relief is based on a connection to the debtor, is section 105(a). It helps them in certain cases but is never certain and remains always exceptional.

The Fourth Circuit has had the most to say on the issue of enjoining actions against third-party nondebtors. Its first significant opinion on the issue was *A.H. Robins Co. v. Piccinin,*[11] in which the corporate debtor sought to enjoin products liability actions in state court against the debtor's insiders and insurer. The court recognized, in dicta, that section 105(a), backed by a broad grant of jurisdiction, empowers the bankruptcy court to enjoin nondebtors from commencing or continuing litigation against other nondebtors.[12] As to the "circumstances under which the power or jurisdiction may be exercised," the Fourth Circuit adopted the views of lower courts: generally, section 105(a) is properly used " 'to enjoin actions excepted from the automatic stay which might interfere in the rehabilitative process whether in a liquidation or in a reorganization case.' "[13] More specifically, a bankruptcy court can enjoin a creditor's action against a third party that would "have an adverse impact on the Debtor's ability to formulate a Chapter 11 plan"[14] or, in particular, " 'would adversely or detrimentally influence and pressure the debtor through the third party.' "[15]

The plaintiffs' actions in *Piccinin* threatened the debtor's reorganization if only because the litigation would seriously distract Robins' officers, directors, and employees. The actions were stayed, however, on grounds more narrow than 105(a). The court's holding, most tightly stated, is that 362(a)(3) stopped them because the actions could reduce the pool of the debtor's insurance that was property of the estate.[16]

(2d Cir.1990) (Although section 1113(f) excepts enforcement of collective bargaining agreements from the stay, the section does not prohibit the bankruptcy court from enjoining such enforcement.)

8. In re Prudential Lines Inc., 928 F.2d 565, 574 (2d Cir.1991), cert. denied, ___ U.S. ___, 112 S.Ct. 82, 116 L.Ed.2d 55 (1991) quoting In re Johns–Manville Corp., 837 F.2d 89, 93 (2d Cir. 1988), cert. denied, 488 U.S. 868, 109 S.Ct. 176, 102 L.Ed.2d 145 (1988).

9. See authorities cited note 5 supra.

10. See our discussion at § 3–5 supra.

11. 788 F.2d 994 (4th Cir. 1986), cert. denied, 479 U.S. 876, 107 S.Ct. 251, 93 L.Ed.2d 177 (1986).

12. Id. at 1001–03.

13. Id. at 1002.

14. Id. at 1003.

15. Id.

16. See id. at 1001–02, 1007–08. The (a)(3) stay covers any act to obtain possession of estate property or exercise control over it. 11 U.S.C.A. § 362(a)(3). For more on this reason for enjoining actions against nondebtors, see our discussion at § 3–10 supra.

In a later *Robins* proceeding the Fourth Circuit practiced what it had only preached in *Piccinin* and relied on section 105(a) to enjoin products liability suits against the debtor's insurer.[17] The plaintiffs' suits aimed at Aetna for its own actions and sought recovery from Aetna's own assets. Every attempt was made to leave the debtor alone. The plaintiffs even agreed to minimize their discovery of Robins' officers, directors, and employees. These tactics failed.

The court enjoined the actions because of the "harm" of the "burden" the actions would cause these people, "which would exhaust their energies and thus interfere with the debtor's reorganization."[18] Although the plaintiffs' themselves could promise to go easy on the debtor and its insiders, the plaintiffs could not force Aetna to do the same.

> Inevitably, Aetna must involve Robins in this litigation. Aetna's primary defense logically will be that Robins—not Aetna—is responsible for the injuries suffered by these plaintiffs, and that any detrimental actions taken by Aetna were on behalf of or at the direction of Robins. Under a system of comparative negligence, the trier of fact must determine Robins' relative fault in order to determine Aetna's relative fault. Despite the plaintiffs' good intentions, Robins will inexorably be drawn into this litigation. Because this involvement will put a substantial burden on Robins, it will detract from the reorganization process. We therefore hold that under section 105, the [bankruptcy] court had authority to stay these actions.[19]

This basis is the slimmest support of any section 105(a) injunction to stop an action against a nondebtor. As another court describes it, "simply the debtor's inevitable, burdensome involvement in the ancillary litigation can justify preemptive injunctive relief."[20] We would note, however, that this *Robins* precedent is actually very limited: it was a Chapter 11 case, and the burden of the litigation was so very great due to the complexity of the legal issues and the hugeness of the claims. *Robins* does not justify using section 105(a) to enjoin actions that are significantly less bothersome to the debtor with a correspondingly smaller affect on its reorganization; nor does *Robins* justify enjoining even large actions if the bankruptcy is a liquidation

---

17. In re A.H. Robins Co., Inc., 828 F.2d 1023 (4th Cir.1987), cert. denied, 485 U.S. 969, 108 S.Ct. 1246, 99 L.Ed.2d 444 (1988).

18. Id. at 1025.

19. Id. at 1026; see also In re Chateaugay, 109 B.R. 613, 621 (S.D.N.Y. 1990), appeal dism'd and remanded, 924 F.2d 480 (2d Cir. 1991) (District court affirmed the bankruptcy court's decision to enjoin actions against the debtor's subsidiaries which was partly based on the fear that the actions would divert the energies of the debtor's legal and managerial talents away from the reorganization effort.); In re Zenith Laboratories, Inc., 104 B.R. 659 (D.N.J.1989) (Court stayed actions brought against debtor's directors and officers and other defendants for securities violations and tort claims. The injunction was based on § 105 and extended even to codefendants not connected to debtor. Any suit would necessarily involve the debtor, though not a party, in depositions and document production that would distract employees at critical time of reorganization.); cf. United States v. Seitles, 106 B.R. 36, 40–42 (S.D.N.Y. 1989), order vac'd on parties' settlement, 742 F.Supp. 1275 (S.D.N.Y. 1990) (The court properly issued a § 105(a) injunction to stop action against the corporate-debtor's principal and sole remaining executive because the claims against him were so closely interwoven with the claims against the debtor that defending himself would necessarily detract from his ability to continue the debtor's business.).

20. In re Western Real Estate Fund, Inc., 922 F.2d 592, 599 (10th Cir.1990).

or other case in which the goals are not seriously frustrated by ancillary litigation.

The point is that a section 105(a) injunction is never justified simply because some interference is possible with the debtor's reorganization or other bankruptcy effort,[21] not even when the debtor itself is threatened directly by an action that is excepted from the stay. The interference must be so significant that injunctive relief is more than merely convenient, but is important or even "essential"[22] for the success of the bankruptcy.

The cases identify a few factors or circumstances that reliably increase the odds, even in more routine cases, of a court enjoining a creditor's action against a nondebtor, either because the circumstances amplify the interference that the action causes or because they argue in themselves for injunctive relief. These circumstances include:

- the nondebtor is an important director, officer, employee, or partner of the corporate-debtor, which is trying to reorganize, who will be distracted from her duties (if not loyalty) to the debtor by the threat of personal liability;[23]
- the nondebtor-defendant can seek indemnity, contribution, or other recovery over from the estate;[24]
- the claims against the nondebtor are so interwoven with the creditor's claims against the debtor that everything is more efficiently resolved in a single proceeding, which is especially compelling if the action against the nondebtor "would likely prejudice the debtor's future defense" of the claims against her;[25]
- the ancillary litigation could affect matters or property that is critical to the reorganization.[26]

It is not entirely clear that equity's usual requirements for an injunction are also necessary for injunctive relief under section 105(a). Some courts believe that "'[s]ince injunctions in bankruptcy cases are authorized by statute [§ 105(a)], the usual equitable grounds for relief, such as irreparable damage, need not be shown.'"[27] Most courts, however, routinely include irreparable harm among the elements necessary for a section 105(a) injunction, as did the court in *In re Stadium Management Corp.*[28] It listed four elements the debtor must prove by a preponderance of the evidence:

(1) there is a danger of imminent, irreparable harm to the estate or [the debtor's] ability to reorganize;

(2) there is a reasonable likelihood of a successful reorganization;

---

21. See Practitioner Treatise, Vol. 1.

22. In re Ionosphere Clubs, Inc., 114 B.R. 379, 402–05 (S.D.N.Y. 1990), decision aff'd in part, rev'd in part. 922 F.2d 984 (2d Cir.1990).

23. See Practitioner Treatise, Vol. 1.

24. See Practitioner Treatise, Vol. 1.

25. See Practitioner Treatise, Vol. 1.

26. See Practitioner Treatise, Vol. 1.

27. In re AP Industries, Inc., 117 B.R. 789, 802 (Bankr. S.D.N.Y. 1990), quoting In re Neuman, 71 B.R. 567, 571 (S.D.N.Y. 1987), opinion after remand, 75 B.R. 966 (Bankr.S.D.N.Y. 1987); see also In re Chateaugay Corp., Reomar, Inc., 93 B.R. 26, 29 (S.D.N.Y. 1988) ("The usual grounds for injunctive relief such as irreparable injury need not be shown in a proceeding for an injunction under section 105(a). Rather, a bankruptcy court may enjoin proceedings in other courts when it is satisfied that such a proceeding would defeat or impair its jurisdiction with respect to a case before it.").

28. 95 B.R. 264 (D.Mass.1988).

(3) the harm [to the debtor] outweighs the damage which the injunction causes [to the person enjoined];

(4) the public interest in a successful bankruptcy reorganization outweighs other competing social interests.[29]

Actually, whether or not the debtor must prove irreparable harm is often a false issue. Showing proper purpose for resorting to section 105(a) in the first place argues very strongly, even establishes, that irreparable harm is likely in the absence of an injunction. In any event, whether considered at the level of triggering section 105(a) or justifying an injunction, the money that a debtor spends in litigating actions that escape the stay is typically not sufficient harm, in itself, to justify enjoining them.[30] This drain on the estate is also too indirect to stay the actions under section 362(a)(3).

Significantly, the focus here is on avoiding harm to the bankruptcy rather than to the third parties against whom action is enjoined. The harm they will suffer if the action continues, without injunction, is not totally unimportant but is typically not decisive or even very significant under 105(a),[31] least in determining proper purpose or substantive cause for resorting to its equitable powers in the first place. The courts are not moved even by the hardships of multiple litigation against the third parties,[32] or their having to defend actions that, because of the stay, cannot involve the debtor as a party or a witness.[33] On the other hand, culpable conduct by the third parties counts against injunctive relief that would stop actions against them.[34]

The harm that the injunction would cause to the person whom it would stay is typically weightier.[35] Her very right to proceed in the first instance is, by itself, fairly heavy and counts much against issuing any injunction which, minimally, would delay and thereby dilute the right.

B. DURATION OF THE STAY

§ 3–23 How Long the Stay Continues

For full text of this section, see Epstein, Nickles & White, Bankruptcy, Practitioner Treatise Series, Vol. 1.

The stay lasts until its purposes are served or its reasons for continuing are overcome by competing concerns. This very general rule is the sum of section 362(c) which is the basic law that governs the length of the stay. It provides:

(c) Except as provided in subsections (d), (e), and (f) of this section—

(1) the stay of an act against property of the estate under subsection (a) of this section continues until such property is no longer property of the estate; and

(2) the stay of any other act under subsection (a) of this section continues until the earliest of—

(A) the time the case is closed;

---

29. Id. at 268.
30. See Practitioner Treatise, Vol. 1.
31. See Practitioner Treatise, Vol. 1.
32. See Practitioner Treatise, Vol. 1.
33. See Practitioner Treatise, Vol. 1.
34. See Practitioner Treatise, Vol. 1.
35. See Practitioner Treatise, Vol. 1.

(B) the time the case is dismissed; or

(C) if the case is a case under chapter 7 of this title concerning an individual or a case under chapter 9, 11, 12, or 13 of this title, the time a discharge is granted or denied.[1]

The stay continues until any of the events described in section 362(c) occurs. Chronologically last is "the time the case is closed,"[2] which is therefore the outside limit on the length of the stay. Every case that is not dismissed is closed; but in most cases another event of section 362(c) happens first. Usually, therefore, the stay ends, in whole or part, before the case closes.

a. Case Is Ended

b. Discharge Is Granted or Denied

c. Property Leaves the Estate

d. Relief Is Granted

§ 3–24 Judicial Relief That Lifts the Stay—Overview

It is possible that in a particular case, the purpose for generally staying a certain act is overcome by a circumstantially more compelling reason for permitting the act to be done. The Code recognizes this possibility by empowering the bankruptcy court, in section 362(d)(1), to lift the stay "for cause." Specifically, section 362(d)(1) provides:

> On request of a party in interest and after notice and a hearing, the court shall grant relief from the stay provided under subsection (a) of this section, such as by terminating, annulling, modifying, or conditioning such stay—
>
> (1) for cause, including the lack of adequate protection of an interest in property of such party in interest * * *.[1]

Basically, (d)(1) works very simply. A person affected by the stay asks the court, by motion, for permission to do whatever the stay prevents her from doing. If her reason is sufficient, i.e., she establishes "cause," the court will grant her request by formally ordering that she can proceed to the extent and in the manner provided in this order. This order is the grant of relief that (d)(1) mentions. Everybody refers to this process as *lifting the stay,* and the motion requesting the relief is called a *lift-stay motion.*

We say more later about the procedure.[2] It is fairly straightforward. The hard part is establishing cause for lifting the stay. In truth, very few reasons are sufficient. Relief is usually limited to people who have property interests that the stay threatens to erode. Unsecured creditors seldom get relief from the stay.

§ 3–23
1. 11 U.S.C.A. § 362(c).
2. Id. § 362(c)(2)(A).

§ 3–24
1. 11 U.S.C.A. § 362(d)(1). The "court" that grants the relief is the bankruptcy court, not the district court or a multidistrict litigation transferee court. In re Pan Am Corp., 128 B.R. 59, 63 (S.D.N.Y. 1991), aff'd in part, rev'd in part, 950 F.2d 839 (2d Cir. 1991).

2. See § 3–31 infra.

The general explanation is that bankruptcy honors the interests of third parties in the debtor's property. The bankruptcy itself does not affect their interests. Even the property that comprises the estate is limited to the debtor's interests. Third-party interests generally survive the bankruptcy whether they are legal or equitable, recorded or secret, large or small. These interests are sometimes avoided by the trustee but only exceptionally. Avoidance is based on relatively narrow concerns that do not significantly undermine the Code's respect for the huge general policy of derivative title.

The stay itself does not offend this policy. It does not cut off or reduce any third-party interest in property that is affected by the bankruptcy.

Yet, the stay can stop third parties, temporarily, from taking action with respect to their interests in the property that could affect the debtor's interest, the debtor herself or her bankruptcy case. This delay by itself can reduce a third party's interest, most commonly when it is a security interest or lien. The costs of time and the depreciation of the collateral consume the security; and, when the declining value falls below increasing debt, the size of the secured creditor's interest begins to shrink.

In theory, bankruptcy law protects against this erosion by providing the secured creditor with two shots at relief from the stay. "Cause" under (d)(1) is actually the creditor's second shot or fall-back position. Her first shot is usually section 362(d)(2), which is essentially a standardized cause or reason for giving relief with respect to an act against property. Under (d)(2) the stay is lifted if:

(A) the debtor does not have an equity in such property; and

(B) such property is not necessary to an effective reorganization.[3]

Property that lacks equity is useless in bankruptcy unless the debtor is reorganizing and needs the property itself in order to make it. There is no reason to continue the stay with respect to property that the bankruptcy cannot use.

Even if equity exists or the property is needed for reorganization or both, the secured creditor's interest will shrink if the bankruptcy's use of her collateral or other circumstances will consume any equity and further devalue the collateral so as to cut into her interest. Proving that this risk to her interest is likely to occur is "cause" for relief under section 362(d)(1). The court must lift the stay to permit the secured creditor to realize on her collateral unless the debtor provides the creditor with "adequate protection" against the loss of value that would result from the erosion of the creditor's interest.

Unsecured creditors have no property interests to protect so that relief from the stay under (d)(2) is never possible. Their other concerns are usually unimportant against the stay because the bankruptcy will discharge the debts owed them. Essentially, these creditors' reasons for wanting relief from the stay contradict the fundamental purposes of the bankruptcy. Typically, therefore, they lack "cause" for relief under (d)(1). About the only halfway common reason to lift the stay for an unsecured creditor is to permit liquidation of the claim in a forum that is substantially more appropriate

---

3. 11 U.S.C.A. § 362(d)(2).

than the bankruptcy court, or because the debtor filed bankruptcy in bad faith. Even these reasons are seldom established, and the bottom line is that relief from the stay is rare for the unsecured creditor.

Now we take a wider and deeper look at the law and issues of judicial relief under 362(d), considering them in the same basic order as here.

§ 3–25 Judicial Relief That Lifts the Stay—Debtor Lacks Equity in Property That Is Not Needed for Reorganization (Section 362(d)(2))

The debtor's bankruptcy should not continue to hold a secured creditor's collateral that cannot serve the aims of the bankruptcy, which are to liquidate, reorganize or do some of both. The property lacks any liquidation value if the debtor owns no equity in it; and the property lacks any other value for bankruptcy purposes if the property is not needed for a reorganization. Therefore, section 362(d)(2) provides for lifting the stay:

> with respect to an act against property under subsection (a) of this section, if—
>
> (A) the debtor does not have an equity in such property; and
>
> (B) such property is not necessary to an effective reorganization.[1]

Both elements must be established to lift the stay under (d)(2),[2] but the secured creditor or other person seeking the relief is burdened to prove only the debtor's lack of equity.[3] The burden of proof is on the party opposing the relief from stay, who wants to keep the property in the bankruptcy, to prove that the property is needed for a reorganization.[4]

Some courts have suggested that by keying relief on the need for the property in a reorganization, (d)(2) limits itself to reorganization cases.[5] Other courts and the three of us disagree. Relief is generally available under (d)(2) even in liquidation cases; and, because none of the property in such a case is needed to reorganize, (d)(2) relief in such a case usually turns on the single issue whether or not the debtor lacks equity in the property.[6]

On the other hand, the reference to reorganization in (d)(2)(B) contemplates more than a Chapter 11 case. The whole of (d)(2), specifically including (d)(2)(B), fully applies to "any form of [bankruptcy] rehabilitation of a debtor's debt structure," including a Chapter 13.[7] Therefore, a Chapter 13 debtor can prevent losing her home, car or other property under (d)(2), even though she lacks equity in it, by showing that she needs the property for financial rehabilitation.[8]

Significantly, subsections (d)(2) and (1) are disjunctive: they provide entirely alternate grounds for relief. Thus, the stay should be lifted if (d)(2) is met even if the secured creditor's interest is adequately protected within

---

§ 3–25
1. 11 U.S.C.A. § 362(d)(2).
2. See Practitioner Treatise, Vol. 1.
3. 11 U.S.C.A. § 362(g)(1).
4. Id. § 362(g)(2).
5. See Practitioner Treatise, Vol. 1.

6. See Practitioner Treatise, Vol. 1.
7. In re Scott, 121 B.R. 605, 607 (Bankr. E.D. Okla. 1990).
8. See Practitioner Treatise, Vol. 1.

the meaning of (d)(1).[9] Remember that (d)(2) is really a specific expression of (d)(1). The circumstances of (d)(2) are themselves, by operation of law, sufficient cause for relief from the stay. The absence of any other cause, such as lack of adequate protection, can (practically) influence the decision whether or not (d)(2) is met, but cannot trump relief under (d)(2) when its requirements are proved.

a. Does the Debtor Have an Equity in the Property?

Deciding section 362(d)(2)(A) is mechanical and easy once certain values are determined. Equity basically "is the value, above all secured claims against the property [including both security interests and liens], that can be realized from the sale of the property for the benefit of the unsecured creditors."[10] Thus, section 362(d)(2)(A) is decided by determining the market value of the property and subtracting the amount of debts that it secures. The debtor has no equity in the property if the difference is zero or less.

In applying (d)(2)(A), the fact questions regarding value are usually tough, but not the legal issues about how the test is supposed to work. Only a few details of decisional law are added to the basic formula to fully equip (d)(2)(A) for application in the typical case.

1. No "particular appraisal method" is used in valuing the property.[11] "Rather, valuation is determined case-by-case, taking into account the nature of the debtor's business, market conditions, the debtor's prospects for rehabilitation, and the type of collateral."[12] This flexibility does not diminish the requirement that the creditor prove the property's value. Relief under (d)(2) is not possible without this proof,[13] which requires "more than bare-bones, paper allegations."[14]

2. The property's value is properly "reduced by an amount sufficient to cover the usual costs of foreclosure and sale" in order "to assure that the usual costs incurred in foreclosure and sale will not compromise the allowed secured claim."[15] In essence, therefore, equity means net equity. Another way of seeing this point is that equity is measured not as of the time of the lift-stay hearing, but as of the time immediately after the property's disposition when the creditor would apply the proceeds. This broader view also explains why, in deciding equity under (d)(2)(A), some courts account presently for future increases in the secured debt that accrue through the time of sale, including principal, interest, and other charges to the collateral.[16]

---

9. See Practitioner Treatise, Vol. 1.

10. In re Mellor, 734 F.2d 1396, 1400 n. 2 (9th Cir.1984).

11. Matter of Sutton, 904 F.2d 327, 330 (5th Cir.1990).

12. Id.

13. In re Camellia Court Apartments, Ltd., 117 B.R. 316 (Bankr. S.D.Ohio 1990).

14. In re Ward, 837 F.2d 124, 128 (3d Cir. 1988).

15. In re Figueroa Ruiz, 121 B.R. 419, 422 (D.P.R.1990); see also In re Stratford Hotel Co., 119 B.R. 695, 696 (Bankr. E.D.Mo.1990) (Court takes into account "additional expenses such as sales commissions, other costs of sale, [and] real estate taxes, which would substantially reduce the amount of [the] apparent equity.").

16. In re Figueroa Ruiz, 121 B.R. 419, 422 (D.P.R.1990) (Court takes into account interest that would accrue until the time of sale, and also attorneys' fees in the event of foreclosure.).

3. The secured debt that is subtracted is the sum of all valid liens and security interests against the property, not just the encumbrance of the person who filed the lift-stay motion. Even junior claims are included. As explained by the court in *Stewart v. Gurley:* [17]

> The bankruptcy courts that have confronted this issue have differed over the proper definition of "equity" for purposes of section 362(d)(2)(A). The majority has adopted the definition relied upon by the bankruptcy court below: that "equity" refers to the difference between the value of the property and all encumbrances upon it.
>
> The minority view subtracts from the value of the property only the amounts owed to the lienholder challenging the stay and to more senior lienholders. * * * [The reasoning is] that dissolving the stay when some value remains after that subtraction would not be in the best interest of junior lienholders because foreclosure by the senior lienholder might force the junior lienholders to choose between purchasing the interest of the senior lienholder or losing their own security interests.
>
> We choose not to follow the minority view. The language of the statute simply refers to the debtor's "equity," which has been defined as "the amount or value of a property above the total liens or charges." The statute does not refer to the debtor's equity as against the only plaintiff-lienholder seeking to lift the stay or persons holding liens senior to that of the plaintiff-lienholder. The minority view improperly focuses upon the interests of junior lienholders as opposed to the interests of the debtor or senior lienholder. * * * Chapter 11 reorganization should benefit the debtor's interests and not exclusively those of junior lienholders. Unless the debtor can demonstrate that the property is necessary to an effective reorganization, the property is of no value to him. Refusing to grant relief from the automatic stay under those circumstances would only promote the junior lienholders' interests over those of the senior lienholder. Should the junior lienholders want to protect their interests, they may bid at the foreclosure sale just as if the bankruptcy proceedings had not intervened. The junior lienholders might also find it advantageous in certain instances to have a senior lienholder shoulder the burden of commencing foreclosure proceedings.[18]

At bottom, accounting for all secured claims is the only way to determine if the property holds value that the bankruptcy can use.

4. Only valid encumbrances are counted. The formula should exclude liens or security interests that the trustee is likely to avoid even though she has not yet done so.[19]

5. Finally, it is not important to (d)(2) that other property also supports the creditor's secured debt, not even if the total collateral exceeds the debt so that, on the whole, the creditor is adequately protected. According to the court in *In re New Era Company*,[20] it is wrong to consider the entire collateral package in applying (d)(2) because doing so

---

17. 745 F.2d 1194 (9th Cir.1984).
18. Id. at 1195–96.
19. See Practitioner Treatise, Vol. 1.
20. 125 B.R. 725 (S.D.N.Y. 1991).

mixes section 362(d)(2) with 362(d)(1), notwithstanding the fact that they are independent bases for granting a creditor relief from the automatic stay. Section 362(d)(1) * * * refers to a creditor's ability to seek relief from the automatic stay "for cause, including the lack of adequate protection of an interest in property of such party in interest." * * * [I]t is clear that one way to assure such protection is to have an "equity cushion." * * * However, while the concepts of equity cushions and adequate protection are relevant for section 362(d)(1), where one looks to the adequate protection of the creditor, there is no mention of these concepts in section 362(d)(2). Instead, section 362(d)(2) only demands an analysis of the debtor's equity in the property * * *. In this case, notwithstanding the possible availability of [other collateral] to help satisfy its debt to the Bank, New Era has no equity in the property since it owes more than the property is worth. This is the only inquiry that is necessary.[21]

On the other hand, though the existence of adequate protection cannot bar relief under section 362(d)(2), the lack of such protection will justify relief "for cause" under section 362(d)(1) if relief under (d)(2) is denied. We discuss (d)(1) shortly.[22]

b. Is the Property Necessary to an Effective Reorganization?

The debtor's lack of an equity in the property is not sufficient for relief under section 362(d)(2). A second, equal requirement, imposed by (d)(2)(B), is that "such property is not necessary to an effective reorganization."[23] In other words, (d)(2) allows the bankruptcy to hold onto property that is needed to reorganize even though the debtor lacks any equity in it.

The trustee or debtor bears the burden of proving two points. First, the property must be important to the reorganization. Merely helpful or convenient is not enough.[24] On the other hand, Judge Leif Clark of Texas is right in *In re Fields*,[25] that a "literal reading of the term must be eschewed"[26] because it would encourage postpetition dismemberment of the estate—"a post-petition race to the courthouse in direct conflict with clear bankruptcy policy which discourages such *pre*-petition races. It would also discourage consensual workouts" and, "in short, leads to absurd results."[27] Most important, the need for property "must be measured against the kind of

21. Id. at 728–29.
22. See § 3–26 et seq. infra.
23. 11 U.S.C.A. § 362(d)(2)(B).
24. In re Endrex Exploration Co., 101 B.R. 474, 476 (N.D.Tex.1988).
25. 127 B.R. 150 (Bankr. W.D.Tex.1991) (The court decided that a complex of 447 self-storage units was necessary to the debtor's Chapter 11 reorganization even though the debtor owned other income-producing properties and other assets that could form the basis of the reorganization.).
26. Id. at 154.
27. Id. at 152 (emphasis in original); see also In re Ledgemere Land Corp., 125 B.R. 58, 64 (Bankr. D.Mass.1991) ("The Bank contends that the Debtors' reorganization, visionary and unrealistic though it may be, does not depend upon any of these three properties. Surely the necessity test means more than this. Otherwise, in a large and complex real estate case such as this, each property could be viewed to be as dispensable as individual items in a manufacturer's inventory; under that reasoning, the Debtors' entire inventory of real estate could be foreclosed upon.").

reorganization contemplated in a given case."[28] As Judge Clark explains:

> [O]ne enterprise might well need to shed all nonincome producing property in order to develop a reorganization plan, while another might, as part of its plan, legitimately contemplate maintaining an inventory of such property for future development.[29]

The question is always whether or not "in *this* case, *this* property is necessary to *this* Debtor's reorganization."[30]

We would only emphasize that part of the consideration is, most fundamentally, the kind of case and the kind of debtor. The reason the property is necessary can differ, for example, between a Chapter 13 and a Chapter 11 corporate business reorganization. Courts in some Chapter 13 cases have defined need in broader, softer terms that consider not only if the property can directly produce income, but also if the property is important to the debtor's well-being.[31] In effect, (d)(2)(B) becomes a quasi-exemption law. This approach makes some sense if only because, in a Chapter 13, the debtor herself is the most important asset for producing income.

It is not sufficient, however, even that the property is essential or indispensable to the reorganization.[32] The debtor or trustee must prove a second point, that the planned reorganization is feasible. In truth, (d)(2) relief in Chapter 11 business cases usually turns solely on this issue, which the Supreme Court more fully described in *United Savings Association of Texas v. Timbers of Inwood Forest Associates, Ltd.*[33]:

> Once the movant under § 362(d)(2) establishes that he is an undersecured creditor, it is the burden of the debtor to establish that the collateral at issue is "necessary to an effective reorganization." What this requires is not merely a showing that if there is conceivably to be an effective reorganization, this property will be needed for it; but that the property is essential for an effective reorganization that is in prospect. This means, as many lower courts, including the en banc court in this case, have properly said, that there must be a "reasonable possibility of a successful reorganization within a reasonable time."[34]

This rule or test of feasibility—whether or not a successful reorganization is reasonably possible within a reasonable time—was merely dicta in *Timbers,* but was the law that most courts followed before *Timbers* and that everybody follows now.

The reason is very simple for requiring proof that reorganization is feasible in addition to proof that the property is important or necessary to the effort:

> The plain language of the statute refers to an "effective" reorganization. * * * [I]t seems pointless and wasteful to deny a stay because of the relationship of certain property to a reorganization that will never occur * * *. Even if the word effective was not in the statute, a similar

---

28. In re Fields, 127 B.R. 150, 154 (Bankr. W.D.Tex.1991).
29. Id. at 154 n.5.
30. Id. at 155–56 (emphasis in original).
31. See Practitioner Treatise, Vol. 1.
32. See Practitioner Treatise, Vol. 1.
33. 484 U.S. 365, 108 S.Ct. 626, 98 L.Ed.2d 740 (1988).
34. Id. at 375–76 108 S.Ct. at 632–33, 98 L.Ed.2d at 751.

construction would result. A condition is not *necessary* to a result if that result will not occur even if the condition is satisfied—i.e., a piece of property is not necessary to a reorganization if a reorganization will not occur even if the property remains in the estate.[35]

This feasibility test is really the heart of (d)(2) and is also the hardest part to apply, even to write about helpfully, because it is so entirely indeterminate and completely fact-bound. General legal rules about feasibility become pitifully empty in specific cases. In truth, whether or not a plan of reorganization is feasible is a business decision that considers factors such as cash flow, market conditions, past experience, future trends, and the like. Probably no other decision in a bankruptcy case involves more discretionary judgment and educated guessing. The law here is really secondary and not very helpful, and is limited to some basic notions that frame the issue and guide the inquiry but that never actually decide it.

1. To prove feasibility the debtor must "do more than manifest unsubstantiated hopes for a successful reorganization,"[36] but the debtor is not required to show that its plan for reorganization is confirmable.[37] Confirmation in Chapter 11 is the process whereby the court signs off on an accepted plan under section 1129(a)[38] or approves—"crams down"—a plan under section 1129(b)[39] despite the dissent of certain creditors.

A hearing on a motion to lift-stay under section 362(d)(2) is not a confirmation hearing on the debtor's or anybody else's plan. As explained in *In re Ledgemere Land Corp.*,[40]

> That plan may be amended several times before it is formally proposed or confirmed. What is subject to scrutiny here is the Debtors' general ability to reorganize, not whether any particular plan will be confirmed. Moreover, even if we focus upon the * * * plan on file, the Debtors need not demonstrate that the plan meets the requirements of § 1129 [confirmation], only that there is a reasonable possibility of it doing so.[41]

2. On the other hand, "[a] court may," even must, "analyze the debtor's plan 'using the feasibility test as a guidepost * * * because [the plan] provides the basis for determining whether the debtor can successfully reorganize.' "[42] The purpose is not to decide, full-blown, confirmation. The analysis is "mini"[43] to determine only "whether the components of the plan

---

35. In re 8th Street Village Ltd. Partnership, 94 B.R. 993, 996 (N.D.Ill. 1988).

36. Matter of Canal Place Limited Partnership, 921 F.2d 569, 577 (5th Cir.1991); see also In re Endrex Exploration Co., 101 B.R. 474 (N.D.Tex.1988) ("To prevail against the secured creditor who has moved to lift the stay under § 362(d)(2), the debtor must do more than evince high hopes * * *.").

37. See Practitioner Treatise, Vol. 1.

38. 11 U.S.C.A. § 1129(a).

39. Id. § 1129(b).

40. 125 B.R. 58 (Bankr. D.Mass.1991).

41. Id. at 64–65.

42. In re Ritz–Carlton of D.C., Inc., 98 B.R. 170, 172 (S.D.N.Y. 1989), quoting In re National Real Estate Limited Partnership II, 87 B.R. 986, 991 (Bankr. E.D.Wis.1988); see also Matter of East–West Associates, 106 B.R. 767, 775 (S.D.N.Y. 1989), on remand, 110 B.R. 675 (S.D.N.Y.1990).

43. In re Oklahoma P.A.C. First Limited Partnership, 122 B.R. 394, 400 (Bankr. D.Ariz. 1990) ("This Court must review this Debtor's Plan of Reorganization, determine how the Debtor intends to treat this particular parcel of real property—the Surprise Property—in its Plan, and going one step further, determine that this Property is essential for an effective reorganization of the Debtor that is in prospect. In essence, a mini-feasibility analysis of the Debtor's Plan is required.").

which are to be done after confirmation can be accomplished as a practical matter."[44] In practice, however, the analysis deepens as firm dissent to the plan widens. In the extreme case of creditors opposing the plan who can block acceptance of it, the court in a Chapter 11 bankruptcy is often forced to test, directly and rather fully, the plan's confirmability under the cramdown provisions and to decide, as part of the process, very complex legal issues.[45]

3. Timing is very important in a couple of respects. Substantively, feasibility requires success within a reasonable time. Procedurally, Bankruptcy Judge Barbara Sellers, in Ohio, believes that the showing itself must come within a reasonable time, and she formalizes and separates this requirement from everything else: "Once a showing of a reasonable possibility of a successful reorganization has been made, [the Court must examine] whether that showing has come within a 'reasonable time' * * *."[46] She is really asking if, in the bankruptcy case, the debtor has progressed "meaningfully" toward reorganization.[47]

Most courts more subtly blend these two issues. The detail and soundness that are required to show feasibility are affected by when in the bankruptcy, early or late, relief is sought and the debtor's showing is responsively made. The principle is:

> The debtor's burden of demonstrating a reasonable possibility of a successful reorganization increases with time. "During the early stages of a proceeding, a less detailed showing may succeed. The same showing at a later time, however, may be insufficient."[48]

Judge Sellers also recognizes this linkage, having written that the showing of feasibility "necessarily must be stronger as the case ages or if the financial information shows a marginal operation."[49] She very helpfully explained why in *In re Ashgrove Apts. of Dekalb County, Ltd.,*[50]

> [The cases] acknowledge the need for a balancing test in this area. Requiring the debtor to establish a "reasonable possibility of a successful

---

44. In re Ritz–Carlton of D.C., Inc., 98 B.R. 170, 173 (S.D. N.Y.1989); see also Matter of East–West Associates, 106 B.R. 767, 775 (S.D.N.Y. 1989), on remand, 110 B.R. 675 (Bankr.S.D.N.Y.1990).

45. See Practitioner Treatise, Vol. 1.

46. In re Northgate Terrace Apartments, Ltd., 126 B.R. 520, 523 (Bankr.S.D.Ohio 1991), related proceeding, 126 B.R. 762 (Bankr. S.D.Ohio 1991). Judge Sellers follows this non-exclusive list of factors as guides in determining the issue:

  1. the length of time the case has been pending;

  2. the presence or absence of pre-petition or post-petition negotiations among the parties;

  3. the length of time the debtor has been in possession and operating its business;

  4. the presence or absence of good faith efforts by the parties to negotiate a consensual solution to the case;

  5. the level of cooperation from any recent state court appointed receiver in making available to the debtor records of the receiver's operations;

  6. the length of time since the expiration of the exclusivity period; and

  7. any other relevant legal factors.

126 B.R. at 523–24.

47. Id. at 523, 525.

48. In re Ritz–Carlton of D.C., Inc., 98 B.R. 170, 172 (S.D.N.Y. 1989), quoting In re Grand Sports, Inc., 86 B.R. 971, 974 (Bankr. N.D.Ind. 1988).

49. In re Northgate Terrace Apartments, Ltd., 126 B.R. 520, 523 (Bankr. S.D.Ohio 1991), related proceeding, 126 B.R. 762 (Bankr. S.D.Ohio 1991).

50. 121 B.R. 752 (Bankr. S.D.Ohio 1990).

reorganization within a reasonable time," has different meanings depending on the stage of the proceeding. Debtors should be given a full opportunity to work under the Bankruptcy Code toward a successful reorganization. However, at the same time, debtors must be realistic. Debtors must make some showing that successful reorganization is possible. As stated by one court: "The court should not, at the conclusion of the debtor's case, be left to speculate about important elements and issues relating to the likelihood of an effective reorganization."

[I]n the initial stages of a Chapter 11 proceeding, the debtor should be granted significant leeway in attempting to establish that successful reorganization is a reasonable possibility. However, as the case progresses, so too does the debtor's burden of proving that successful reorganization may be reasonably expected. Even at the later stages, a motion for relief from stay should not be turned into a confirmation hearing; that is not the debtor's burden of proof. Rather, the test should be viewed as a continuum with the scales tipping in favor of the debtor in the early stages and the burden of proof becoming greater in the later stages.[51]

Very often, therefore, part of the reason for granting relief under section 362(d)(2) is that the debtor's plan falls short compared to the length of the case, or simply that the case has continued so long that the absence of success so far argues against any possibility of success in the future.[52] By contrast, as in *In re Swansea Consolidated Resources, Inc.*,[53] a court may well deny relief at a "relatively early stage" in the case based on the debtor showing feasibility "not by a very comfortable margin."[54]

No absolute grace period is recognized, however. At the earliest stage, even during the first four months when only the debtor can propose a plan,[55] the court is free to grant relief under (d)(2) in the absence of any realistic chance of an effective reorganization.[56] In a borderline case, the court can hedge and deny relief on the condition that a plan is confirmed in the near future.[57]

We perceive that many courts, even before *Timbers of Inwood* and a larger number thereafter, are losing patience with optimistic debtors. Creditors have been the first to realize the injury that can be done to all creditors by the continued operation of a losing business in Chapter 11. They in turn have pressed their case with the courts and the courts have responded by making earlier decisions and by a more restricted willingness to continue the stay. We endorse this activity, for we believe that almost no one is benefitted by a long residence in Chapter 11.

4. Peripheral matters can affect the debtor's burden. Most significant, the burden is made heavier by the debtor's own delay and negligence as debtor in possession of the estate. Indeed, dilatory conduct that prejudices

---

51. Id. at 756, quoting In re Anderson Oaks (Phase I) Limited Partnership, 77 B.R. 108, 110 (Bankr. W.D. Texas 1987).

52. See Practitioner Treatise, Vol. 1.

53. 127 B.R. 1 (Bankr. D.R.I.1991).

54. Id. at 3.

55. See 11 U.S.C.A. § 1121(b) & (c)(2).

56. See Practitioner Treatise, Vol. 1.

57. See Practitioner Treatise, Vol. 1.

the creditor can be reason in itself for lifting the stay.[58] Relatedly, an impure motive for filing bankruptcy can increase the load and even break the debtor's back, as when the purpose was to delay creditors.[59]

The debtor's burden can be lightened if the creditor's interest is adequately protected. Adequate protection is not a defense to relief under (d)(2), but "the adequate protection status of a moving creditor might, along with other considerations, influence the sufficiency of the [feasibility] showing that need be made in a particular case * * *."[60] Specifically, it can buy the debtor more time, as in *In re Royal Palm Square Associates*.[61] In this case the possibility of an effective reorganization was "quite slim, if not nil."[62] Nevertheless, because the creditor was adequately protected, its motion for relief from stay was denied "in order to give the Debtor one last chance to obtain confirmation, with the proviso, however, that this Court will not enter any further extensions or continuances."[63]

On the other hand, the absence of adequate protection works against the debtor. Relief that is denied for any reason under (d)(2) can be sought, alternatively, under (d)(1). Relief there is "for cause, including the lack of adequate protection * * *."[64]

§ 3–26 Judicial Relief That Lifts the Stay—Cause (Section 362(d)(1))

Section 362(d)(2) provides no relief from the stay with respect to property that is necessary for an effective reorganization, not even if the debtor lacks an equity in the property. This news is good for the debtor but possibly very bad for the third-party claimant of the property, such as a secured creditor. Using the property in the bankruptcy, or merely keeping it from the secured creditor, can imperil her lien or other interest. Harming the interest would violate bankruptcy's usual policy of honoring third-parties' claims to property that is affected by the case.

Section 362(d)(1) therefore trumps (d)(2) and orders relief for the secured creditor or other third-party claimant if she can show a threat to her interest that is not adequately protected. This exposure, called "lack of adequate protection," is actually only a specific example of reason for relief under section 362(d)(1). Its few words are much wider and appear very generous in ordering relief

> *for cause,* including the lack of adequate protection of an interest in property of such party in interest [who requests the relief].[1]

For purposes of (d)(1), "'[c]ause' has no clear definition and is determined on a case-by-case basis,"[2] in light of "all the facts and circumstances of the case,

---

58. In re Belmont Realty, 124 B.R. 422 (Bankr. D.R.I.1991).

59. See Practitioner Treatise, Vol. 1.

60. In re Embassy Enterprises of St. Cloud, 125 B.R. 552, 555 (Bankr. D.Minn.1991) (The existence of adequate protection, however, "cannot obviate the need for any [feasibility] showing at all.").

61. 124 B.R. 129 (Bankr. M.D.Fla.1991).

62. Id. at 132.

63. Id.

64. 11 U.S.C.A. § 362(d)(1).

§ 3–26

1. 11 U.S.C.A. § 362(d)(1) (emphasis added).

2. In re Universal Life Church, Inc., 127 B.R. 453, 455 (E.D.Cal.1991); see also In re Revco D.S., Inc., 99 B.R. 768, 777 (N.D.Ohio 1989) (same).

taking into account the purposes of the automatic stay, the behavior of the parties, considerations of judicial efficiency, and the balance of hardships involved."[3]

In theory, cause is endless: "*any* reason cognizable to the equity power and conscience of the court as constituting an abuse of bankruptcy process."[4] Even in practice (d)(1) has justified relief in a wide range of circumstances and for many reasons. For example, relief "for cause" has allowed:

- the government to terminate a contract that the debtor in possession could not assume because of overriding federal law;[5]
- the equitable owner of property to gain legal title held by the debtor "where [only] naked legal title to property has passed into the estate," as "when a purchaser receives equitable title at a sheriff's sale but legal title remains in a debtor * * *;"[6]
- a landlord to reenter premises the debtor held under an unassumable lease;[7]
- foreclosing a mortgage because the debtor's "unfulfilled representations, its dilatory conduct as debtor in possession during the pendency of this case, and its administration of the assets have been negligent at best, and said behavior has caused unreasonable delay that is prejudicial to the movant;"[8]
- enforcing the right to specific performance decreed by a state court;[9]
- enforcing a lien held by debtor's former spouse who had exhausted her financial reserves and was suffering hardship,[10] and
- lifting the stay because the debtor failed to comply with an adequate protection agreement made with the creditor.[11]

In truth, however, for creditors in typical cases, few causes regularly trigger relief under (d)(1) other than lack of adequate protection, which only secured creditors can claim. Only two other causes are important and common (if only in the sense that they are commonly argued): (1) the debtor

---

3. In re Sonnax Industries, Inc., 99 B.R. 591, 595 (D.Vt.1989), aff'd, 907 F.2d 1280 (2d Cir.1990).

4. Little Creek Dev. Co. v. Commonwealth Mortgage Corp., 779 F.2d 1068, 1072 (5th Cir. 1986) (emphasis added); Victory Constr. Co., Inc., 9 B.R. 549, 560 (Bankr.C.D.Cal. 1981), modified on other grounds, 9 B.R. 570 (Bankr. C.D.Cal. 1981), vacated as moot, 37 B.R. 222 (B.A.P. 9th Cir.1984), on remand, 42 B.R. 145 (Bankr. C.D.Cal.1984).

5. Matter of West Electronics Inc., 852 F.2d 79, 82–84 (3d Cir.1988).

6. Matter of Spencer, 115 B.R. 471, 476, 485 (D.Del.1990).

7. See § 3–28 infra.

8. In re Belmont Realty, 124 B.R. 422, 425–26 (Bankr. D.R.I.1991); see also Matter of Canal Place Limited Partnership, 921 F.2d 569, 579 (5th Cir. 1991) (The debtor was not forthcoming, refusing to disclose the names of its individual principal investors. The court did not know with whom it was really dealing.).

9. In re Roxse Homes, Inc., 74 B.R. 810 (D.C. Mass.1987), order aff'd, 83 B.R. 185 (D.Mass.1988), judgment aff'd, 860 F.2d 1072 (1st Cir.1988) (The right does not involve a money judgment, and thus the holder has no means of enforcing its right in post-confirmation bankruptcy proceedings.).

10. In re Kelly, 125 B.R. 301, 303 (Bankr. D.Kan.1991); compare In re Apex Oil, 85 B.R. 538 (Bankr. E.D.Mo.1988) (The bankruptcy court held that it may not take into account the financial needs of the creditor in determining if cause exists.).

11. See, e.g., In re Cambridge Properties, Inc., 82 B.R. 35 (E.D.La.1988); In re Blanton, 78 B.R. 442 (D.S.C.1987); Matter of Lafayette Dial, Inc. 92 B.R. 798 (Bankr. N.D.Ind. 1988); In re Polries Bros., 49 B.R. 669 (Bankr. D.N.D. 1985).

filed bankruptcy in bad faith and (2) a more appropriate forum exists than the bankruptcy court for determining a claim against the debtor. These reasons for relief are about the only tickets out of the stay that are commonly available to unsecured creditors. Even these tickets are seldom valid.

A movant can prove sufficient cause for relief under section 362(d)(1) without proving either of the elements of (d)(2), and the debtor disproving even both of the elements of (d)(2) is no defense to relief established under (d)(1). Relief for (d)(1) cause is an entirely alternative, independent basis for relief from the stay.[12] This book often treats (d)(1) as residual relief, that is, a fall-back argument in the event (d)(2) relief is not possible; but we do so only as a means of conceptually organizing the materials to reflect ordinary practice patterns. Nothing about the law requires a movant to exhaust (d)(2) before arguing for relief under (d)(1).

§ 3–27 Judicial Relief That Lifts the Stay—Cause (Section 362(d)(1))—Lack of Adequate Protection

A person with an interest in property that is affected by the stay is entitled to relief "for cause" under section 362(d)(1) if her interest is not adequately protected.[1] The precise reason is "lack of adequate protection of [her] interest in [the] property * * *."[2] It applies most often (almost exclusively) to creditors with liens and security interests in property seized by the stay. It never applies to unsecured creditors who have no property interests to protect.[3]

Bankruptcy intends to safeguard secured creditors' encumbrances, but the stay threatens them by preventing the secured creditors from foreclosing or taking other actions to apply the property's value against the secured debt. Bankruptcy aims to guard against this threat by ordering relief under (d)(1) for lack of adequate protection of the secured interest.

In very general terms, adequate protection means that the value of an interest is reasonably well insured. If the circumstances do not naturally provide this insurance and the debtor cannot buy or otherwise supply it, the interest is not adequately protected and this lack of protection itself justifies relief "for cause" under section 362(d)(1). The secured creditor can then grab her collateral and apply its value to the secured debt.

Determining if an interest is adequately protected involves these three basic steps, reported by the Eighth Circuit in *In re Martin:*[4]

(1) establish the value of the secured creditor's interest,

(2) identify the risks to the secured creditor's value * * *, and

---

12. In re Wieseler, 934 F.2d 965, 968 (8th Cir.1991) ("§ 362(d)(1) and § 362(d)(2) are phrased as alternative means of obtaining relief, and a creditor is therefore not bound to pursue relief to recover property under § 362(d)(2), but is instead presented that remedy as an alternative."); Matter of Mueller, 123 B.R. 613, 615–16 (Bankr. D.Neb.1990) (Secured party granted relief as to its collateral because of lack of adequate protection even though the property was necessary to an effective reorganization.).

§ 3–27

1. 11 U.S.C.A. § 362(d)(1).
2. Id.
3. See Practitioner Treatise, Vol. 1.
4. 761 F.2d 472 (8th Cir.1985).

(3) determine whether the debtor's adequate protection proposal protects value as nearly as possible against risks to that value * * *.[5]

The burden of non-persuasion is on the trustee or debtor: to defeat relief under (d)(1) she is burdened to prove that the creditor's interest is adequately protected.[6]

a. Identifying and Valuing the Secured Interest That Deserves Adequate Protection

The Supreme Court explained in *United Savings Association of Texas v. Timbers of Inwood Forest Associates, Ltd.*,[7] that "the 'interest in property' referred to by § 362(d)(1) includes the right of a secured creditor to have the security applied in payment of the debt * * *."[8] The value of this interest is measured by the secured debt but is naturally limited by the value of the collateral.[9]

The value of the interest is also reduced by the amount of senior encumbrances. If they exceed the collateral's value, the creditor's junior interest lacks any value that (d)(1) is designed to protect. She is essentially unsecured. Therefore, relief is impossible under (d)(1) for lack of adequate protection,[10] as is true for any unsecured creditor.[11]

The *Timbers* case involved a creditor who was undersecured. It had a first secured claim to value in collateral that was less than the secured debt. Specifically, the creditor held a first mortgage for $4.7 million on an apartment complex worth as little as $2.6 million. The mortgage was an interest that (d)(1) protected to the extent of the collateral's value, but it was not threatened. The creditor nevertheless argued for (d)(1) relief because of another right with respect to the collateral that was not adequately protected: it is the right to immediate foreclosure that the stay suspended. Adequately protecting this right would require paying the secured creditor interest for the term of the stay on the proceeds that the immediate foreclosure, at the beginning of the case, would have produced.

At bottom, the base issue in *Timbers* was whether or not an undersecured creditor is entitled to postpetition interest on its secured claim. The Court answered no. The short reason is that the Code clearly provides for paying interest that accrues postpetition to oversecured creditors and is silent, at best, on paying the same to undersecured creditors.[12]

---

5. Id. at 477.
6. See Practitioner Treatise, Vol. 1.
7. 484 U.S. 365, 108 S.Ct. 626, 98 L.Ed.2d 740 (1988).
8. Id. at 370, 108 S.Ct. at 629, 98 L.Ed.2d at 748.
9. The collateral is valued in terms of net liquidation value, not fair market value. In re Robbins, 119 B.R. 1, 4–5 (Bankr. D.Mass. 1990).
10. See Practitioner Treatise, Vol. 1.
11. See Practitioner Treatise, Vol. 1.
12. 484 U.S. 365, 370–73, 108 S.Ct. 626, 630–31, 98 L.Ed.2d 740, 748–50 (1988). Because undersecured creditors are not entitled to postpetition interest, any postpetition payments that the debtor makes to such a creditor reduce the creditor's claim if the collateral is not depreciating in value. In re Reddington/Sunarrow Ltd. Partnership, 119 B.R. 809 (Bankr. D.N.M.1990).

To some critics of Timbers, the Code is not silent on this matter. They read section 361(3) to direct the payment of interest by promising "the indubitable equivalent" of such entity's interest. Part of the indubitable equivalent of a party's interest in property is the income (i.e., interest on reinvestment or opportunity cost) that would be produced by reinvestment after liquidation of collateral.

The source of law for paying this interest to an oversecured creditor, which means her claim "is for an amount less than the value of the property securing it,"[13] is section 506(b), which provides:

> To the extent that an allowed secured claim is secured by property the value of which * * * is greater than the amount of such claim, there shall be allowed to the holder of such claim, interest on such claim, and any reasonable fees, costs, or charges provided for under the agreement under which such claim arose.[14]

The source of payment is the equity cushion, which is the value of the collateral that exceeds the secured debt. In essence, the creditor's lien or other secured claim grows, postpetition, to cover accruing interest and the other charges that section 506(b) describes.[15] The lien feeds on the equity cushion and reaches maximum size when it equals the collateral's value.

This postpetition increase in the secured claim is an "interest" within the meaning of section 362(d)(1). It must be adequately protected together with the part of the lien that accrued prepetition.

We are not saying, however, that a right to payment of postpetition interest must itself be protected. On this issue we agree with *In re Westchase I Associates, L.P.*[16] In the *Westchase* case the interest of the oversecured creditor was adequately protected because the value of the collateral was stable. The bankruptcy court nevertheless ordered the debtor to make a monthly interest payment. The purpose was to maintain the equity cushion. Paying postpetition interest would stop the growth of the creditor's lien and thereby prevent it from eating any of the cushion.

The effect of the bankruptcy order was to protect the right to the payment of postpetition interest as opposed to the increase in the value of the secured claim resulting from accruing interest. The latter was already protected because the collateral was not declining in value. The district court correctly overruled the order, opining that "if the value of the property itself is not declining, as is the case here, the creditor would not be entitled to protection of the accruing interest value of the claim."[17]

Rather, the accruing interest is properly charged against the equity cushion until the cushion is fully consumed. At this point the right to postpetition interest is exhausted and the secured claim is full grown. No payment to the secured creditor or other form of adequate protection is required unless, at full growth of the claim or before, the value of the collateral threatens to decline.

---

13. United States v. Ron Pair Enterprises, Inc., 489 U.S. 235, 239, 109 S.Ct. 1026, 239, 103 L.Ed.2d 290 (1989), on remand, 872 F.2d 778 (6th Cir.1989).

14. 11 U.S.C.A. § 506(b). This provision covers not only consensually secured claims, but also involuntary secured claims such as judicial and statutory liens. United States v. Ron Pair Enterprises, Inc., 489 U.S. 235, 109 S.Ct. 1026, 103 L.Ed.2d 290 (1989), on remand, 872 F.2d 778 (6th Cir.1989) (United States was entitled to receive postpetition interest on its oversecured, prepetition tax lien.); In re Rozel Industries, Inc., 120 B.R. 944, 948 (Bankr. N.D.Ill. 1990) ("Ron Pair establishes that the right to post-petition interest applies in the context of a claim which is oversecured as defined in § 506(a) by virtue of the creditor's right of setoff.").

15. See Practitioner Treatise, Vol. 1.

16. 126 B.R. 692 (W.D.N.C.1991).

17. Id. at 694.

This threat was missing in *Westchase*. Therefore, the bankruptcy order effectively recognized the payment of postpetition interest as an independent right that is itself entitled to adequate protection, which is wrong. Postpetition interest that has accrued and become part of the secured claim gets protection. We could even imagine protecting the right to receive unaccrued interest to the extent of the equity cushion: a decline in the cushion would trigger adequate protection to preserve the value for future interest. Doing so would stretch the meaning of the "interest" that (d)(1) protects to include a prospective secured claim. Not everyone would stretch so far, not even all of us. We all agree, however, that there is nothing to protect and thus no need for or lack of adequate protection if, as in *Westchase*, neither an accrued secured claim nor even the equity cushion is threatened.

b. *Defining the Risks (When Adequate Protection Is Needed)*

The basic risk that adequate protection covers is a decline, during the stay, in the value of the creditor's encumbrance or, synonymously, secured claim. It is frequently said that this value or claim is determined at the time of bankruptcy,[18] which is generally true. We would only note the important exception for oversecured creditors whose secured claim can grow after bankruptcy to cover postpetition interest.[19]

The usual cause of a decline in the value of an encumbrance is a drop in the value of the collateral which, in turn, usually results from a falling market for the property or depreciation by someone using it. The most common reason for adequate protection is a predicted drop in the collateral's value, from one or both of these causes, that will cut into or reduce the secured creditor's lien or security interest.[20]

Another common reason is the lack of property casualty insurance. It guarantees the property's value against a precipitous drop or complete loss by fire, robbery, or other unnatural calamity. The insurance is paid to encumbrancers of the property if a covered risk occurs. Without this insurance an encumbrancer risks losing every bit of the value of her lien. It is often an unacceptable risk for which adequate protection must be provided,[21] which usually means that the stay is lifted unless the debtor buys or pays for a casualty policy.

Adequate protection is never needed or lacking absent a threat to the value of the encumbrance. It is not sufficient either that the debtor lacks an equity in the property [22] or the creditor's claim is undersecured.[23] Even a decline in the collateral's value is not always sufficient, in itself, to trigger

---

18. In re Westchase I Associates, L.P., 126 B.R. 692, 694 (W.D.N.C.1991) ("[A] secured creditor is entitled to adequate protection of the value of its collateral on the petition date."); In re Reddington/Sunarrow Ltd. Partnership, 119 B.R. 809, 812–13 (Bankr. D.N.M. 1990) (The date for valuing an undersecured claim for purposes of adequate protection and § 362 is the date of filing, not the date the Chapter 11 is confirmed. Undersecured creditor thus does not receive the benefit of appreciation between the two dates.); In re Dahlquist, 34 B.R. 476, 480 (Bankr. D.S.D.1983) ("The value of an allowed secured claim for purposes of adequate protection is determined as of the time the bankruptcy petition is filed.").

19. See 11 U.S.C.A. § 506(b).
20. See Practitioner Treatise, Vol. 1.
21. See Practitioner Treatise, Vol. 1.
22. See Practitioner Treatise, Vol. 1.
23. See Practitioner Treatise, Vol. 1.

adequate protection. The decline must threaten to reduce the value of the creditor's encumbrance.

For this reason an oversecured creditor is usually denied relief for lack of adequate protection so long as the equity cushion is reasonably thick. Also, a creditor in the opposite position, whose secured claim is zeroed out because of senior encumbrances, gets no relief even if the collateral's value begins to fall sharply. The drop could not further reduce the value of her encumbrance.

The value of an encumbrance can decline so as to justify adequate protection without any drop in the collateral's value. The best example is an encumbrance that is junior to an oversecured senior lien. The senior lienor is entitled to postpetition interest which will swell her encumbrance so long as there is value in the collateral beyond the amount of her lien. At some point the growing lien will displace the junior encumbrance. This displacement is a decline in the value of the collateral that entitles the junior encumbrancer to adequate protection.[24]

In sum, a drop in the collateral's value is sometimes not sufficient and sometimes not necessary for adequate protection. The trigger is always a decline in the value of the encumbrance, which is determined and affected by factors in addition to the collateral's value.

c. *Determining and Providing Protection That Is Adequate*

Finding an interest that deserves protection and is threatened leads to the ultimate issue of how adequately to protect it. The debtor and creditor very often negotiate and settle the issue through an adequate protection agreement that is filed as an agreed order of adequate protection and approved by the court upon proper notice.[25] The debtor's breach of the agreement and order is itself reason to lift the stay.[26]

Often enough, the creditor rejects the debtor's offer of adequate protection and takes the issue to court by requesting relief from the stay. On the creditor's lift-stay motion, the court will decide if the debtor's proposal is sufficient; can order additional protection; and will grant relief from the stay if adequate protection is not forthcoming. If the creditor's interest is adequately protected, her motion is denied unless she establishes other "cause" for relief under (d)(1) or that the grounds for relief under (d)(2) are satisfied.

An important key to understanding and deciding adequate protection is that the actual purpose is not to protect the creditor's interest itself, but to insure the value of the interest. Therefore, many different kinds of protection are possible. The Code gives examples in section 361:

> When adequate protection is required under sections 362, 363, or 364 of this title of an interest of an entity in property, such adequate protection may be provided by—
>
> > (1) requiring the trustee to make a cash payment or periodic cash payments to such entity, to the extent that the stay under

---

24. See Practitioner Treatise, Vol. 1.
25. See Practitioner Treatise, Vol. 1.
26. See Practitioner Treatise, Vol. 1.

section 362 of this title, use, sale, or lease under section 363 of this title, or any grant of a lien under section 364 of this title results in a decrease in the value of such entity's interest in such property;

(2) providing to such entity an additional or replacement lien to the extent that such stay, use, sale, lease, or grant results in a decrease in the value of such entity's interest in such property; or

(3) granting such other relief, other than entitling such entity to compensation allowable under section 503(b)(1) of this title as an administrative expense, as will result in the realization by such entity of the indubitable equivalent of such entity's interest in such property.[27]

Behind this veneer of a list in section 361 are the thick, heavy reason and purpose of adequate protection. They confirm that providing equivalent value to insure an interest is sufficient rather than preserving the interest in specie. This substitution is even necessary to allow the flexibility that is often essential to the bankruptcy process. As the court explained in *In re Bobroff,*[28] reciting legislative history and concluding in stock terms which everybody accepts as gospel:

"The concept is derived from the fifth amendment protection of property interests. It is not intended to be confined strictly to the constitutional protection required, however. The section, and the concept of adequate protection, is based as much on policy grounds as on constitutional grounds. Secured creditors should not be deprived of the benefit of their bargain. There may be situations in bankruptcy where giving a secured creditor an absolute right to his bargain may be impossible or seriously detrimental to the bankruptcy laws. Thus, this section recognizes the availability of alternate means of protecting a secured creditor's interest. Though the creditor might not receive his bargain in kind, the purpose of the section is to insure that the secured creditor receives in value essentially what he bargained for." The legislative history indicates that adequate protection for a secured creditor means that the creditor must receive the same measure of protection in bankruptcy that he would have had outside of bankruptcy although *the type of protection may differ from the bargain initially struck* between the parties.[29]

Moreover, adequate protection can and should differ among cases and between proceedings. It "must * * * be determined on a case-by-case basis, permitting the debtors 'maximum flexibility in structuring a proposal for adequate protection.' * * * [i]n order to encourage reorganization * * *."[30]

Still, the protection that is provided, though it can be different from the creditor's interest, must be equivalent—the "indubitable equivalent"—in terms of the power to guarantee and realize the value of the interest.[31] This

27. 11 U.S.C.A. § 361.

28. 32 B.R. 930 (Bankr. E.D.Pa. 1983).

29. Id. at 931–32 (emphasis added), referring to H.R. Rep. No. 95–595, 95th Cong., 1st Sess. 339, reprinted in 1978 U.S. Code Cong. & Admin. News 5787, 6295.

30. In re Martin, 761 F.2d 472, 474, 476 (8th Cir.1985), quoting In re American Mariner Industries, Inc., 734 F.2d 426, 435 (9th Cir.1984).

31. "Indubitable equivalence requires 'such relief as will result in the realization of value.'" In re Martin, 761 F.2d 472, 477 (8th Cir.1985), citing In re Sheehan, 38 B.R. 859, 864 (D.S.D.1984).

requirement of equivalency can affect the nature of the protection that is appropriate. Its larger role is to test the protection for safety and reliability in preserving an amount of value that equals the creditor's interest.

The sum and bottom line of theory is that "adequate protection" is a "flexible concept to be tailored to the individual facts and circumstances of each case." [32] It can work to safeguard the interest itself, or can provide a substitute for the interest that equally insures the value of the secured claim. "This flexibility, however, must not operate to the detriment of the secured creditor's interest." [33] In every case, adequate protection " 'should as nearly as possible under the circumstances of the case provide the creditor with the value of his bargained for rights.' * * * [I]ts requirement of indubitable equivalence remains constant." [34]

In the typical case, the threat to the creditor's encumbrance is a decline in the value of the collateral. The threat is compounded because interest is accruing on the secured debt. Adequate protection to counter this threat is most commonly provided in any one of these forms or by a combination of them:

- identifying an equity cushion, which is the value of the collateral in excess of the secured debt;
- making cash payments (commonly called a "stream of payments") to satisfy interest and, more certainly, to reduce the principal in sufficient amount to keep it below declining value;
- transferring the encumbrance to other collateral or creating a security interest in additional collateral; or,
- proposing to use the original collateral, or otherwise affect it, in such a way that its value is enhanced.

Acting to enhance the collateral's value is the most uncommon form of adequate protection, especially in a common bankruptcy case. The opportunities and possibilities for it are small, and the risk is large. It usually involves repairing, improving, or developing the collateral [35] and sometimes uses money that the creditor also claims as proceeds. The expected return should be sufficient to recover the proceeds as well as to protect the value of the interest in the collateral.

Occasionally, the adequate protection is indirect, and the link is quite tenuous between it and the immediate use of the money. For example, in *In re Mid–Atlantic Fuels, Inc.*,[36] Quaker State had sold the debtor a refinery and retained a purchase-money interest. Quaker State initially received quarterly adequate-protection payments of $50,000. After environmental testing reports revealed some soil and groundwater contamination at the refinery, the trustee asked the court to change the adequate-protection order to permit using the rent to assess and monitor pollution in the vicinity of the plant. The court agreed:

32. In re Tellier, 125 B.R. 348, 349 (Bankr. D.R.I.1991).

33. In re Martin, 761 F.2d 472, 476 (8th Cir.1985).

34. Id.

35. See Practitioner Treatise, Vol. 1.

36. 121 B.R. 207 (Bankr. S.D. W.Va.1990).

> Because Quaker State is potentially liable under state and federal law for any trespass or injury resulting from out-migration of hazardous substances from the refinery site, and because conditions found at the plant indicate the existence of a substantial threat to ground water quality, the Court finds that reasonable study of the site to further assess any migration of hazardous substances in the ground water in the area of the refinery is adequate protection in the form of an indubitable equivalent of Quaker's interest in the equipment, vehicles and other collateral under the control of the Trustee of the estate.[37]

The reasoning could be that fixing the pollution helps maintain the value of the collateral and the mortgage interest, or reduces the creditor's risk of liability for environmental clean-up costs that counters the risk of decline in the value of the mortgage's interest. We have no trouble accepting this reasoning, which impliedly approves proving adequate protection indirectly and even circuitously, so long as the proof adequately supports it and the court adequately accounts for an important risk. Anytime one party is empowered to spend another's money, and moreover, to claim that he is doing so "in the interest of the other party," there is real risk that expenditures will not be properly monitored and that money will not be spent in the interest of the supposed beneficiary.

An equity cushion is undoubtedly the single most common form of adequate protection. An existing cushion works even more fundamentally in determining when the creditor's interest is threatened. Measuring a cushion for any purpose under section 362(d)(1) is very different from determining if the debtor has equity for purposes of (d)(2). The debtor's equity is calculated by totaling all of the encumbrances on the property and subtracting the sum from the property's value. A creditor's equity cushion in the collateral is found by subtracting from the property's value only the creditor's lien or interest and any senior encumbrances.[38]

Whenever an equity cushion is proposed as adequate protection, the question is seldom asked if a cushion is an appropriate means of protection. Always asked, and often hotly debated, is the question how much cushion is enough. Obviously, the necessary size of the cushion depends on several factors, including mainly the certainty of a drop in the collateral's value, how quickly it will drop and how far. Equally important are the effect and strength of other protections that are proposed in combination with an equity cushion. Every situation is different, posing an entirely fresh guessing game every time the necessary size of an equity cushion is calculated. Nevertheless, there are general rules of thumb, as reported in *In re Kost:*[39]

> Whether an equity cushion provides adequate protection to a creditor is determined on a case-by-case basis rather than by mechanical application of a formula. Over time, however, various bankruptcy decisions have provided this court with guidance. "Case law has almost uniformly held that an equity cushion of 20% or more constitutes adequate

---

37. Id. at 210.

38. In re Mellor, 734 F.2d 1396, 1400–01 (9th Cir.1984) (Junior liens are not considered in determining if a senior lien is adequately protected by an equity cushion.); In re Royal Palm Square Associates, 124 B.R. 129, 132 (Bankr. M.D. Fla.1991) (All liens are considered in determining equity under (d)(2) but not equity cushion under (d)(1).).

39. 102 B.R. 829 (D.Wyo.1989).

protection. Case law has almost as uniformly held that an equity cushion under 11% is insufficient to constitute adequate protection. Case law is divided on whether a cushion of 12% to 20% constitutes adequate protection." [40]

In sum, it is a "general law of bankruptcy" that "the likelihood of lift of stay is inversely proportional to the amount of equity that the debtor possesses in the collateral." [41]

On the other hand, it is not a general law of bankruptcy that a cushy equity cushion is always adequate protection in itself that bars relief under section 362(d)(1). Uncertainty can falsely inflate the cushion. Time will usually deflate it. Moreover, an equity cushion does not always respond to or answer fully the whole range of risks to the value of the creditor's encumbrance, such as the threat of calamitous loss because of the lack of casualty insurance. Finally, an equity cushion solves only the problem of the lack of adequate protection which is " 'but one "cause" for which relief can be granted under § 362(d)(1).' " [42] In sum, "[t]he mere fact that the debtor enjoys a so-called equity cushion above the secured claim of [the creditor] Citibank does not mean that the debtor may float on this cushion out of the troubled waters stirred up by Citibank's request for relief from the stay." [43]

d. Making Adjustments

Adequate protection is an estimate that is always, to some extent, uncertain and unreliable. Fortunately, it is adjustable. The rule is:

> While an order of adequate protection is final, in the sense that it is capable of being appealed, it is not final in the sense that it is immutable. Consequently, even after it is entered, the order is subject to change, if the circumstances upon which it was premised also change.[44]

This rule works both sides of the street: it allows either the creditor or the debtor to request and get adjustments in adequate protection because of changed circumstances.

---

40. Id. at 832–33.

41. In re Novak, 121 B.R. 18, 19 (Bankr. W.D.Mo.1990).

42. In re Wieseler, 934 F.2d 965, 968 (8th Cir.1991), quoting In re Family Investments, Inc., 8 B.R. 572, 576 (Bankr. W.D. Kan.1981) (An equity cushion does not automatically bar relief from the stay. A creditor need not prove both "cause" under § 362(d)(1) and the absence of an equity cushion.).

43. In re Westchester Ave. Marina Realty, Inc., 124 B.R. 161, 166 (Bankr. S.D.N.Y. 1991). The court added:

> This is especially true if the debtor has offered no additional payments, there exists a declining value of the secured claim in the face of declining real estate values, there is unpaid interest required to be paid under 11 U.S.C. § 506(b), there are unpaid real estate taxes and there is no plan of reorganization proposed by the debtor after more than four months following the filing of the Chapter 11 petition. In these circumstances, Citibank is entitled to some relief while the debtor is given an opportunity to demonstrate that it is in a position to achieve an effective reorganization.
>
> Accordingly, Citibank's motion for relief from the stay is denied, provided that the debtor pays * * * all real estate taxes which became payable after it filed * * *. Additionally, the debtor must promptly proceed to establish [the voidable preference it claims which will reduce secured debt] and must file by * * * a Chapter 11 plan which reflects realistic prospects for achieving an effective reorganization.

Id.

44. Matter of Lafayette Dial, Inc., 92 B.R. 798, 799 (Bankr. N.D.Ind. 1988), citing United States v. Swift & Co., 286 U.S. 106, 114, 52 S.Ct. 460, 462, 76 L.Ed. 999 (1932).

With or without adjustments, adequate protection sometimes proves inadequate, and the creditor's interest actually loses value. The Code's apology for the miscalculation—this gap of adequate protection insurance—is section 507(b). It often grants an administrative expense superpriority for loss that results when adequate protection fails.[45] This priority is guaranteed compensation only to the extent that there is free value in the estate to pay it.

§ 3–28 Judicial Relief That Lifts the Stay—Cause (Section 362(d)(1))—True Leases

For full text of this section, see Epstein, Nickles & White, Bankruptcy, Practitioner Treatise Series, Vol. 1.

§ 3–29 Judicial Relief That Lifts the Stay—Cause (Section 362(d)(1))—Bad Faith Filing

Filing bankruptcy in bad faith is independent "cause" for relief under section 362(d)(1).[1] It triggers lifting the stay even if adequate protection exists and no other reason for relief is proved.[2] It means that the debtor abused the bankruptcy process by filing the case under circumstances or for reasons that are beyond the legitimate purposes and aims of the bankruptcy. The concern is broader than a threat to a secured creditor's collateral. It is rather that the debtor should not use bankruptcy law to dilute any person's rights in a situation for which the law was not designed and the dilution was not intended. As the Fifth Circuit explained more fully in *Matter of Little Creek Development Co.*:[3]

> Every bankruptcy statute since 1898 has incorporated literally, or by judicial interpretation, a standard of good faith for the commencement, prosecution, and confirmation of bankruptcy proceedings. Such a standard furthers the balancing process between the interests of debtors and creditors which characterizes so many provisions of the bankruptcy laws and is necessary to legitimize the delay and costs imposed upon parties to a bankruptcy. Requirement of good faith prevents abuse of the bankruptcy process by debtors whose overriding motive is to delay creditors without benefitting them in any way or to achieve reprehensible purposes. Moreover, a good faith standard protects the jurisdictional integrity of the bankruptcy courts by rendering their powerful equitable weapons (i.e., avoidance of liens, discharge of debts, marshalling and turnover of assets) available only to those debtors and creditors with "clean hands."[4]

---

45. 11 U.S.C.A. § 507(b). It provides:

If the trustee, under sections 362, 363, or 364 of this title, provides adequate protection of the interest of a holder of a claim secured by a lien on property of the debtor and if, notwithstanding such protection, such creditor has a claim allowable under subsection (a)(1) of this section arising from the stay of action against such property under section 362 of this title, from the use, sale, or lease of such property under section 363 of this title, or from the granting of a lien under section 364(d) of this title, then such creditor's claim under such subsection shall have priority over every other claim allowable under such subsection.

§ 3–29

1. See Practitioner Treatise, Vol. 1.
2. See Practitioner Treatise, Vol. 1.
3. 779 F.2d 1068 (5th Cir.1986).
4. Id. at 1072.

With relief based on bad-faith filing so broadly explained, anybody affected by the stay can request lifting it on this basis, including an unsecured creditor.

Relief from the stay for bad-faith filing is more commonly sought and won in reorganization cases, especially Chapter 11. The explanation is that reorganization sets a goal that is more specific than liquidation and imposes a greater risk on creditors. The meaning of abuse is thus wider, and, for this reason and also the greater risk, creditors are more likely to complain about abuse.

This relief in Chapter 11 is not displaced or even duplicated by section 1112(b) which permits dismissing a case for cause, including bad faith.[5] The two remedies address the same concerns but at different times and for different reasons and with different effects, including the parties affected.[6] Lift stay protects the creditor. Dismissal goes further and denies the debtor the benefits of bankruptcy, however few, that survive the lift stay.

Always, however, even in Chapter 11 and perhaps especially there, lifting the stay for bad faith requires that the debtor's abuse of the bankruptcy process is clear.[7] Erring in the debtor's favor on this issue is necessary to insure that bankruptcy law applies in every situation for which it was intended.

No particular test determines bad faith. It is a fact-bound inquiry that asks if the reasons and circumstances of the bankruptcy case are in line with the purposes and aims of the bankruptcy law. Lots of factors are always considered, and no single factor is ever conclusive. Nevertheless, the cases that are the easiest to understand are the Chapter 11 filings by debtors who are not financially distressed or only mildly so, or who are so greatly

---

5. 11 U.S.C.A. § 1112(b) ("[O]n request of a party in interest or the United States trustee, and after notice and a hearing, the court may convert a case [to chapter 7] * * * or may dismiss a case * * * whichever is in the best interest of the creditors and the estate, for cause * * *.").

6. Here is a very good explanation of the relationship between stay relief and case dismissal for bad faith:

> We disagree that bad faith constituting "cause" for relief from a stay automatically equates to bad faith warranting dismissal of the petition. If that were true, there would not be a need to ever lift a stay for bad faith, because the petition would necessarily have to be dismissed. That seems at odds with the intent of the Bankruptcy Code. It is at least inconsistent with the practice in many courts which have lifted a stay on a finding of bad faith but which nonetheless permit the petition to be maintained.
>
> That the bankruptcy court has seen fit to grant relief from the stay is not equivalent to a decision by that court that Dixie may not maintain its petition. Rather, the decision on whether to grant or deny relief from an automatic stay may be analogized to a decision whether or not to grant preliminary injunctive relief. The fact that preliminary relief is obtained does not mean that permanent relief also must be forthcoming. Likewise here, the purposes and considerations that weigh in the determination of relief from a stay are distinct from the inquiry into whether the proceeding may be maintained at all.
>
> A panel of this Court stated in dicta in In re Phoenix Piccadilly, Ltd. that "what amounts to bad faith is the same for both proceedings." We interpret that statement to mean that the factors used to demonstrate bad faith are the same in both contexts, but that a bankruptcy judge may nonetheless take into consideration the number of factors and their certainty in determining whether they constitute bad faith for dismissal purposes.

In re Dixie Broadcasting, Inc., 871 F.2d 1023, 1029 (11th Cir.1989), cert. denied, 493 U.S. 853, 110 S.Ct. 154, 107 L.Ed.2d 112 (1989).

7. In re Arnold, 806 F.2d 937, 939 (9th Cir.1986).

distressed that reorganization within a reasonable time is clearly, utterly impossible without a large miracle.

Chapter 11 is an expensive, wholesale way of dealing with crowds of creditors that, by peculiar process, stops and subordinates their self-interested attacks on the debtor for the greater good of preserving or creating value that would otherwise be lost. Only cases that realistically fit this mold are ripe for Chapter 11. This test most certainly closes Chapter 11 to debtors who lack either real financial problems or a real chance of solving them through reorganization. If these debtors file anyway, they do so in bad faith, at least for purposes of granting stay relief "for cause" under section 362(d)(1).

Typically, however, when a court decides for this purpose that a case does not fit Chapter 11, the judge relies on facts in addition to the debtor's financial condition. A good reason for doing so is that a reliable judgment on the debtor's finances is not always possible in a lift-stay proceeding. The motion often comes early in the case and the hearing is usually rather quick and summary. The available financial information can suggest that the case is not right for Chapter 11 but not so convincingly that, at this stage, the judge is willing to decide the lift-stay motion on it alone. A wrong decision will deny a principal bankruptcy right to a debtor who, actually, is rightfully entitled to full bankruptcy protection. A possible further effect is to undermine the whole case.

The court looks for additional facts confirming that the case ill fits Chapter 11 or, in base terms, that the debtor's filing was an abuse of the bankruptcy process. A very good example is *In re Dixie Broadcasting, Inc.*[8] The corporate debtor, Dixie, owned a radio station that it agreed to sell to WBHP Radio, owned by Pollard. The debtor later got a better price from someone else and reneged on the contract, claiming that a secured creditor, Barclays, would not approve the sale to WBHP. Barclays had a security interest in the debtor's assets to secure a loan that benefitted related entities, not the debtor or its radio station. This deal was arranged by Donald Martin who was a principal behind Dixie and all of its relatives.

WBHP sued the debtor, mainly for specific performance. This suit and related proceedings rocked along for years. At a hearing at the end of December, 1986, the state court explained that it was leaning in WBHP's favor but ordered the parties to try to settle the matter. They met immediately and again on January 30, 1987. During a lunch break at this later meeting, Dixie filed for Chapter 11 bankruptcy.

WBHP asked the bankruptcy court to dismiss Dixie's petition, or in the alternative, to lift the stay so the pending action in state court could continue. The court granted WBHP's lift-stay motion because Dixie filed bankruptcy in bad faith. The district court affirmed, and the case went to the Eleventh Circuit. It, too, affirmed in an opinion that is helpful in showing how courts decide the bad-faith filing question. We therefore quote a large chunk of it:

---

8. 871 F.2d 1023 (11th Cir.1989), cert. denied, 493 U.S. 853, 110 S.Ct. 154, 107 L.Ed.2d 112 (1989).

We hold that the bankruptcy court did not err in its determination that there was bad faith to justify lifting the stay. The evidence of bad faith in this case includes: (1) the filing of the petition during a lunch recess in eleventh-hour court ordered settlement negotiations in the state court litigation; (2) use of bankruptcy proceedings despite the apparent good financial health of the debtor; (3) use of bankruptcy to avoid a contract that had become less profitable in light of a better purchase offer; (4) execution of a security agreement giving Barclays the right of consent to a sale of Dixie's assets on May 10, 1984, after Dixie and WBHP had entered into a Memorandum of Agreement to sell the station, and just one week prior to execution of the Purchase and Sale Agreement; (5) use of Dixie's assets to secure a loan which benefited some of Donald Martin's other enterprises and the sale of one of these enterprises on which Barclays had a collateral assignment and lien at the same time Dixie entered into the security agreement; and (6) Mr. Bramlett's statements to creditors that the petition was filed as a "diversionary tactic" and that Dixie was not in financial distress.

Although there is no precise test for determining bad faith, courts have recognized factors which show an "intent to abuse the judicial process and the purposes of the reorganization provisions." These factors include the timing of the filing of the petition; whether the debtor is "financially distressed;" whether the petition was filed strictly to circumvent pending litigation; and whether the petition was filed solely to reject an unprofitable contract.

In light of these factors, we find no error with the bankruptcy court's determination that Dixie and Martin filed their petition in bad faith to justify lifting the stay. Contrary to the arguments of Dixie and Barclays, neither the bankruptcy court nor the district court improperly seized upon any single factor in determining the existence of bad faith. Rather, the cumulative effect of all the evidence was appropriately considered. As both the bankruptcy court and the district court noted, the petition was filed when it appeared that a ruling adverse to Dixie was imminent in state court litigation that had been underway for more than two years. Moreover, the state court litigation arose because Dixie had received a better offer for its radio station and refused to perform an executed sales agreement for the station. It does not appear that Dixie was in financial distress and needed the protection of the bankruptcy court. It was substantially current on its debts and remained only secondarily liable on the Barclays loan which the debtors make much of. Its sales were increasing as the result of the relocation of a transmitter tower to a better site. Further, one year prior to the filing, Dixie began paying Martin a $5,000 per month consulting fee, and continued to pay more than $500 a month for a Lincoln Continental automobile which Martin used in Vermont. Dixie also paid $36,000 per year to Bramlett to manage the station and, about six months before the filing, increased Bramlett's wife's salary from $12,000 to $36,000 per year to keep the station's books. As the district court stated, "[t]hese facts are not indicative of a business in financial distress."

It seems clear that Dixie entered bankruptcy to get out of its bad deal. There was testimony that Mr. Bramlett told creditors that the petition was filed to prevent WBHP's purchase, that Dixie did not have financial problems, and that the petition was filed as a "diversionary tactic." This Court has found similar comments as one factor leading to a finding of bad faith.

The Bankruptcy Code is not intended to insulate financially secure sellers or buyers from the bargains they strike. Thus, we hold that the bankruptcy court's * * * conclusion as to bad faith for this purpose was correct as a matter of law.[9]

The pattern of bad faith that *Dixie* identifies is the *financially secure debtor* who files bankruptcy to beat a bad bargain. It is a classic case, but lift stay for bad-faith filing is not limited to it. Rather, the *Dixie* pattern is matched by the *financially distressed debtor* who files bankruptcy to delay the inevitable end of its business. The paradigm case, involving a single-asset debtor, is described by the Fifth Circuit in *Matter of Little Creek Development Co.:*[10]

> The debtor has one asset, such as a tract of undeveloped or developed real property. The secured creditors' liens encumber this tract. There are generally no employees except for the principals, little or no cash flow, and no available sources of income to sustain a plan of reorganization or to make adequate protection payments * * *. Typically, there are only a few, if any, unsecured creditors whose claims are relatively small. The property has usually been posted for foreclosure because of arrearages on the debt and the debtor has been unsuccessful in defending actions against the foreclosure in state court. Alternatively, the debtor and one creditor may have proceeded to a stand-still in state court litigation, and the debtor has lost or has been required to post a bond which it cannot afford. Bankruptcy offers the only possibility of forestalling loss of the property. There are sometimes allegations of wrongdoing by the debtor or its principals. * * *
>
> Resort to the protection of the bankruptcy laws is not proper under these circumstances because there is no going concern to preserve, there are no employees to protect, and there is no hope of rehabilitation, except according to the debtor's "terminal euphoria." The * * * "purpose of Chapter 11 reorganization is to assist financially distressed business enterprises by providing them with breathing space in which to return to a viable state." '[I]f there is not a potentially viable business in place worthy of protection and rehabilitation, the Chapter 11 effort has lost its raison d'etre * * *." Neither the bankruptcy courts nor the creditors should be subjected to the costs and delays of a bankruptcy proceeding under such conditions.[11]

The courts have found bad-faith filings in other kinds of cases. Some of these cases are variants of *Dixie* and *Little Creek* and differ only in degree,[12] but other cases represent somewhat different patterns.[13] They all stress the same fundamental themes even if they emphasize different facts and pat-

---

9. Id. at 1026–28. There are two main factors here, and each is very strong by itself and decisive in combination. The more narrow factor is using bankruptcy as a means of undoing an unfavorable deal.

10. 779 F.2d 1068 (5th Cir.1986).

11. Id. at 1073.

12. See Practitioner Treatise, Vol. 1.

13. See Practitioner Treatise, Vol. 1.

terns. The point is that finding the same circumstances of these or any other case is neither required nor sufficient to decide in a new case that the debtor filed bankruptcy in bad faith. This decision does not turn on any particular combination of facts, and no single fact is ever decisive. Filing bankruptcy immediately before foreclosure does not itself establish bad faith;[14] and it is not established by the lone fact that the debtor is a single-asset entity,[15] not even if the debtor files principally to avoid an unfavorable contract.[16]

The presence of facts that were suspicious or supportive of bad faith in other cases is, in itself, meaningless: a "slavish recitation of facts reminiscent of the illustrative factors will not suffice to establish bad faith."[17] The issue is their sum: do they add to the conclusion that the case misses the point of Chapter 11 to "provide the debtor with a means of avoiding premature or unnecessary liquidations in order to maximize payments to creditors and save jobs."[18]

For some, the calculation is hardest when the debtor's financial condition seems to fit Chapter 11, but her motive for filing the case was out of line with the aim of reorganization. She lacked any real intent to reorganize. She filed the case for the benefits of bankruptcy, which would hinder her creditors, without intending to assume any burdens that could compensate them. The case is hard because of the argument that motive is irrelevant so long as a need and chance to reorganize exist.

We believe that improper motive is terribly important, even usually decisive,[19] because a debtor who lacks the will to reorganize also lacks, almost surely, any real chance to reorganize. For us, the only hard issue in this case is whether or not the evidence really establishes improper motive. The debtor's motive for filing bankruptcy is usually mixed. Moreover, in deciding the true or main reason the debtor filed, the court must consider her financial condition. The circle is complete.

§ 3–30 Judicial Relief That Lifts the Stay—Cause (Section 362(d)(1))—More Appropriate Forum Elsewhere

For full text of this section, see Epstein, Nickles & White, Bankruptcy, Practitioner Treatise Series, Vol. 1.

§ 3–31 Some (Mostly) Procedural Concerns

For full text of this section, see Epstein, Nickles & White, Bankruptcy, Practitioner Treatise Series, Vol. 1.

a. Who Can Request Relief ("Party in Interest")
b. When and How Relief Is Requested and Decided

---

14. See Practitioner Treatise, Vol. 1.
15. See Practitioner Treatise, Vol. 1.
16. See Practitioner Treatise, Vol. 1.
17. In re Sentry Park, Ltd., 87 B.R. 427, 430 (Bankr. W.D.Tex.1988).
18. In re HBA East, Inc., 87 B.R. 248, 258–259 (Bankr. E.D.N.Y.1988).
19. See Practitioner Treatise, Vol. 1.

  i. *Relief by Judicial Default (Section 362(e))*
  ii. *Nature of the Hearing*
  iii. *Burdens of Proof*
  iv. *Ex Parte Relief (Section 362(f))*
 c. **Effect of Lifting the Stay**
 d. **Appeal**

C. CONSEQUENCES OF VIOLATING THE STAY

Compared to the issues of the scope and duration of the stay, there is little to say about the consequences of violating it. The reason is not that the consequences are small. They are few but very big. The reason is that the two major consequences are clear and simple. First, and mainly, any conduct that violates the stay is legally ineffective (void or voidable): normally, the conduct accomplishes nothing in the law. Second, damages are recoverable for any willful violation. The former is routinely true against anybody who violates the stay; the latter is not always possible against governments because of their immunity. Occasionally, the courts use their contempt powers to supplement the usual consequences of violating the stay.

It is, however, the first consequence—voidance—that gives teeth to the stay, and life to the bankruptcy, by actually preserving the debtor's property and affairs until they can be handled, in an organized fashion, pursuant to bankruptcy law and process. The provision for damages discourages creditors from disturbing the debtor's peace. The effect of voidance makes it impossible for them to disturb her property. Conduct that would ordinarily change the debtor's rights and interest in the absence of the stay changes nothing if done in the face of the stay.

§ 3–32 Voidance

a. *General Rule*

The dominant, general rule is that any act or occurrence that violates the stay is *void ab initio*.[1] The rule means that to the extent that the stay is violated by anyone, including government, the act or occurrence itself lacks any legal effect against the debtor and other people whom the rule protects, as if the act or occurrence never happened.[2] As against them, anyone who claims through the act or occurrence takes nothing because it "is null and void ab initio and has no validity for any purpose."[3]

Although this rule works against anyone who violates the stay, the voidness that results does not work in favor of everyone who could possibly benefit from it. The only entities who can take advantage of the rule are the congressionally intended beneficiaries of section 362: most certainly, the bankruptcy estate and the debtor in the case in which the violation oc-

---

§ 3–32
1. See Practitioner Treatise, Vol. 1.
2. See Practitioner Treatise, Vol. 1.

3. Anglemyer v. United States, 115 B.R. 510, 514 (D.Md.1990) (referring to a tax assessment violating the stay).

curred.[4] Arguably, their creditors are also entitled to benefit,[5] but "[w]hatever argument may be made for extending the protection of section 362 to creditors, it clearly does not confer any rights to outside parties." [6]

The ineffectiveness of acts or occurrences violating the stay is not a temporary condition but is permanent. They are legally empty—not just suppressed or dormant—and thus remain void and ineffective even after the stay and the bankruptcy end.[7]

This rule is self-effective and carries no conditions, least of all knowledge of the stay or lack of innocence.[8] It applies by its own force in every instance against anyone who violates the stay, including people acting completely in good faith and in complete ignorance of the bankruptcy. The rule itself is decisional and admits no excuses or defenses, but the Code trumps it in two important respects by allowing judicial annulment and creating statutory exceptions.

b. Judicial Annulment

Section 362(d) permits the bankruptcy court not only to lift the stay but also to annul it.[9] An order annulling the stay retroactively validates, nunc pro tunc, the act or occurrence that violated the stay: it means that the act or occurrence accomplished the legal effects provided by any applicable law, as if the stay never applied to it.[10]

The courts actually recognize two bases for annulment: legal and equitable. The legal track is section 362(d) itself, which authorizes annulment. Annulment is technically just a form of relief from the stay that is justified, in the court's discretion, when any of the section 362(d) grounds for relief is met. The most apt ground is general "cause."

The courts in a few cases have ordered annulment on this legal basis. The typical reason is that for independent cause under 362(d), the creditor is entitled to have the stay lifted to take the very same action that she earlier took in violation of the stay, and requiring her to redo this conduct would be useless. Therefore, for the purpose of saving time and money for everyone, including the debtor, the court annuls the stay as to the action already taken instead of lifting the stay that would only allow taking the action again.[11] In every case, the creditor's violation was innocent and without knowledge of the bankruptcy.

The equitable basis for annulment tracks to *In re Smith Corset Shops, Inc.*[12] In this case Smith, the debtor, closed his shop after having failed to pay the rent. On March 25, the Brodeurs, the landlords, sued to eject him and eventually won a default judgment. The constable thereafter entered the shop and removed the inventory. Unbeknownst to the Brodeurs, the

---

4. See Practitioner Treatise, Vol. 1.
5. See Practitioner Treatise, Vol. 1.
6. In re Globe Inv. and Loan Co., Inc., 867 F.2d 556, 560 (9th Cir.1989) (Mortgagee foreclosed in violation of the stay and, by state law, extinguished interests of debtor and third parties).
7. See Practitioner Treatise, Vol. 1.
8. See Practitioner Treatise, Vol. 1.
9. 11 U.S.C.A. § 362(d).
10. See Practitioner Treatise, Vol. 1.
11. See Practitioner Treatise, Vol. 1.
12. 696 F.2d 971 (1st Cir.1982).

state court, and the constable, Smith had filed Chapter 11 bankruptcy on March 21. Several weeks later he sued the Brodeurs in bankruptcy court alleging that they had converted his inventory by having it removed in violation of the automatic stay. The bankruptcy court decided the proceeding against him, and the First Circuit agreed on this reasoning:

> The *Brodeurs not only acted without knowledge of the bankruptcy filing but did so after having notified Smith and securing a court order.* They personally did not dispossess Smith; the constable did so acting under the execution. Smith, for its part, not only had advance notice of the proposed action, it apparently had an agent on hand while the property was moved. Yet Smith made no effort to advise either the Brodeurs, the court, or the constable of the pending bankruptcy action until the property had been moved and stored. If successful in its conversion action, Smith would extract from the innocent Brodeurs the full original cost of an inventory which may have become unmarketable. Given these facts, we hold that Smith may not recover in conversion for the removal of the inventory.
>
> Our holding does not undermine the automatic stay. The stay is one of the "fundamental debtor protections" provided by the bankruptcy act, designed to "stop[ ] all collection efforts, all harassment, and all foreclosure actions" against debtors. It must be given full effect. We only hold that *Smith could not remain stealthily silent* when it knew that the goods were being moved pursuant to court order and then turn around and successfully sue the Brodeurs for the alleged conversion of the goods. We do not think Congress envisioned any such misuse of the automatic stay.[13]

Technically, the bankruptcy court in *Smith Corset* did not annul the stay but simply ignored it in judging the legality of the landlords' conduct. The First Circuit's reasoning for affirmance has nevertheless become a prime test for annulment and a principal justification for ordering it. As the court explained in *In re Williams*,[14] the cases that have followed *Smith Corset* "apply traditional equitable principles of laches and estoppel to prevent deceptive or incredibly ignorant debtors from unfairly benefitting by an eleventh-hour ambush of their unsuspecting opponents."

Technically, the courts could explain *Smith Corset* in terms of the legal basis for annulment, as "cause" under section 362(d). Usually, however, the case and its progeny are treated separately, as authority to annul the stay for equitable reasons apart from section 362(d).

The basic reasons for ignoring the stay in *Smith Corset* were the defendant-creditor's innocence and, equally, the plaintiff-debtor's guilt. This test is very decidedly two-pronged. The creditor's innocence to some degree is always necessary [15] but, as with legal annulment, is never sufficient in itself.[16] The debtor must be guilty of deliberate conduct [17] that, as in *Smith*

---

13. Id. at 977 (emphasis added).

14. 124 B.R. 311, 316 (Bankr. C.D.Cal. 1991).

15. See, e.g., In re Shamblin, 890 F.2d 123, 126 (9th Cir.1989) (Annulment not justified because creditors' conduct with respect to tax sale proceeding bordered on bad faith.).

16. In re Smith, 876 F.2d 524, 526–27 (6th Cir.1989).

17. See Practitioner Treatise, Vol. 1.

Corset, would estop her to complain of the creditor's action or that, more generally, "contributed to the creditor's plight." [18] In other words, the debtor "bears some responsibility for creating the problems." [19]

The debtor's conduct is really the linchpin of equitable annulment, so much so that the innocence required of the creditor lessens or changes as the debtor's culpability grows. Specifically, the creditor's ignorance of the bankruptcy, which is a hallmark of *Smith Corset,* is not necessary where the debtor's contribution to the "creditor's plight" is large and causes serious prejudice.[20]

In the final analysis, however, for both equitable and legal annulment, the decisive balance compares the gain and loss of annulment. The loss surely includes the violence done to the goals of the stay, especially the harm that the estate will suffer and the injury to other creditors who by their inaction implicitly rely on the stay. Any appreciable harm to them should weigh so heavily against annulment as almost always to prevent it. The very possibility of annulment undermines the deterrent force of the stay. These reasons justify the view of many courts that annulment is a "radical form of relief" [21] and "should be narrow and applied only in extreme circumstances," [22] very "sparingly." [23]

There is another view. It is held by critics who believe that much injury is done to creditors by the stay in general, particularly by long applications of the stay. In their opinion some restraint in application of the stay is a good idea. They are more willing to see annulment and would encourage courts to use it.

c. *Statutory Exceptions*

Postpetition transfers of estate property are doubly doomed. They violate the stay and are void for this reason. Also, section 549 allows the trustee to avoid the transfers and recover the property for the estate.[24]

Section 549 creates exceptions but only to itself. The provision identifies two classes of transfers that the trustee cannot avoid under section 549: transfers during the "gap" in an involuntary case that are made for new value,[25] and transfers of real estate to good faith purchasers who buy the property without knowledge of the bankruptcy.[26]

Section 362 does not expressly repeat or incorporate these exceptions. Therefore, if literally applied, section 362 would void the excepted transfers and undermine the section 549 exceptions themselves. The courts handle this misfit between sections 362 and 549 by treating the section 549 excep-

---

18. In re Calder, 907 F.2d 953, 956 (10th Cir.1990).

19. Matthews v. Rosene, 739 F.2d 249, 251 (7th Cir.1984).

20. See Practitioner Treatise, Vol. 1.

21. Scrima v. John Devries Agency, Inc., 103 B.R. 128, 135 (W.D.Mich. 1989), on remand, 116 B.R. 951 (Bankr. W.D.Mich. 1990).

22. In re Shamblin, 890 F.2d 123, 126 (9th Cir.1989).

23. In re Williams, 124 B.R. 311, 316 (Bankr. C.D. Cal.1991).

24. The general rule of section 549 is that "the trustee may avoid a transfer of property of the estate * * * that occurs after the commencement of the case * * *." 11 U.S.C.A. § 549(a)(1). We thoroughly discuss section 549 in Chapter 6. See §§ ___ infra.

25. Id. § 549(c).

26. Id.

tions as implied limits on the voiding effect of section 362.[27] Therefore, a transfer that section 549 excepts is not void even though the act of transferring the property violates the stay. The result is that the transferee can keep whatever property interests were conveyed to her, as permitted and limited by any applicable law.[28]

The courts sometimes report that section 362 is similarly limited by section 542, especially section 542(c). It authorizes people holding property of the debtor at the time of bankruptcy, who are ignorant of the filing, to transfer or pay the property to someone other than the estate.[29] We believe the effect of section 542 is greater. It works as an exception to the whole of section 362 by approving, more fundamentally, the very making of the transfer. Therefore, not only is the transfer effective to the extent of applicable law, the transferor has not violated the stay in making it. While section 549 protects transferees from the stay's effects, section 542 excepts transfers from the stay and thereby protects both transferors and transferees.

d. Competing Rule of "Voidable" Only

Occasionally, a bankruptcy court declares that an act or occurrence violating the stay is *voidable* rather than void. Sometimes, the court means only that the act is not irretrievably void because the court can annul the stay.[30] This meaning does not contradict the general rule that acts violating the stay are void ab initio.

Other times, a court fully intends to reject the general rule and means, by "voidable," that acts violating the stay are not automatically void. Rather, as explained by the Ninth Circuit Bankruptcy Appellate Panel in *In re Schwartz*,[31] "these actions can be declared invalid in an appropriate proceeding but are capable of being cured by confirmation or ratification or if no proceeding is brought to avoid the voidable act."[32] This "appropriate proceeding" is "an action by the debtor or trustee during the bankruptcy case in which the stay violation occurred."[33]

Undoubtedly, a proceeding under this rule will almost always void any act in violation of the stay that materially harms the estate or the bankruptcy. Similarly, an annulment proceeding under the general rule will usually deny relief for such an act. In the end, the act is void under both the void and voidable rules. The conflict between them appears insignificant, even false.

In truth, the difference between the two rules can be very real and important. The best example is the bankruptcy case that is complete, and someone asserts a right or claim against the debtor based on an action that violates the stay. The claim fails if the act was void unless the bankruptcy court annuls the stay.[34] The claim prevails if the act was only voidable and

---

27. See Practitioner Treatise, Vol. 1.
28. See Practitioner Treatise, Vol. 1.
29. 11 U.S.C.A. § 542(c-d).
30. See Practitioner Treatise, Vol. 1.
31. 119 B.R. 207 (Bankr. 9th Cir.1990), rev'd, 954 F.2d 569 (9th Cir. 1992).
32. Id. at 209.
33. Id. at 211.
34. See Practitioner Treatise, Vol. 1.

is not voided by the bankruptcy court.[35] The default outcome is entirely different depending on which rule controls, as is who bears the burden and risk of trying to change the outcome. Changing it can become procedurally difficult or even impossible if the case is formally closed or dismissed, or for some other reason the court in bankruptcy lacks original basis for acting on the issue.

The main technical argument for the voidable rule is that section 549, which empowers the trustee to avoid postpetition transfers of estate property, is unnecessary if acts violating the stay are void ad initio.[36] This argument hangs everything on an inference of congressional intent for which there is no further proof, and it ignores that the overlap between sections 549 and 362 is not complete so that any superfluity that supposedly proves the voidable rule is incomplete. Moreover, the two sections can be reconciled so that section 549 compliments the dominant rule that acts violating section 362 are void.[37] Most important, the voidable rule lacks any substantial reason or policy to support it very long or far, much less enough force to overcome the threat it poses to the deterrence of the stay and the stability of the bankruptcy process.

The thin argument for the voidable rule explains why only a few bankruptcy courts in a handful of courts have followed it. Even among state courts, acceptance, although probably wider, is not complete.[38] They should naturally prefer the rule because it is softer on local law.

Most bankruptcy courts are committed to the opposing general rule that acts violating the stay are void ab initio. Strong practical arguments and policy reasons support this rule. The court in *In re Williams*[39] gets to the heart of the matter in disagreeing with the opinion of the Bankruptcy Appellate Panel in *In re Schwartz*, which adopted the voidable rule and was subsequently reversed:

> The *Schwartz* opinion does not fully examine the consequences of its holding. The BAP grudgingly acknowledges that declaring actions in violation of the stay to be merely voidable, not void, " * * * may have the effect of impairing the fresh start purposes of the automatic stay by requiring the debtor to enforce the stay through actions to avoid certain transfers, [but] any impairment can be offset by rigorous application of section 362(h). By thus casually brushing aside the implications of its decision, the Panel has failed to give due weight to the fundamental issue at stake here. In effect, the BAP approach to the problem of the unauthorized post-petition transfer chooses to protect the "good faith" creditor who proceeded in violation of the stay, at the expense of the "good faith" debtors who rely on the stay to prevent creditors from seizing or selling their property. The "voidable" rule implicitly imposes on the debtor (or trustee) the burden of persuading the court that the transfer should be set aside.
>
> This court declines to follow the BAP approach, choosing instead to follow the * * * [majority rule] that actions violating the stay are void,

---

35. See Practitioner Treatise, Vol. 1.
36. 11 U.S.C.A. § 549(a).
37. See Practitioner Treatise, Vol. 1.
38. See Practitioner Treatise, Vol. 1.
39. 124 B.R. 311 (Bankr. C.D. Cal.1991).

thereby imposing on the creditor/transferee the burden of proving that the transfer falls within the narrow exceptions to the rule of voidness.

The BAP's optimistic assumption that "more rigorous" enforcement of Section 362(h) can and will deter potential violations of the stay is unsupported, and probably unwarranted. Section 362(h) only provides sanctions for willful, not inadvertent violations of the stay. Moreover, remedies under that subsection are available only to [certain] debtors * * * [and there are problems of proof] * * *.

More importantly, deterrence of violations is not the only—nor even the major—issue here. The question is whether the debtor has the right to undo the violative action. Under the * * * [majority] rule [that the action is void], the answer is yes, unless the narrow statutory exceptions apply or bad faith on the debtor's part is proven by the creditor. Under the minority view, the answer is maybe, if the debtor avoids procedural pitfalls, and can establish an equitable right to have the transfer set aside. This shifting in the burden of proof is fundamentally inconsistent with the basic premise of the automatic stay.[40]

This analysis convinced the Ninth Circuit. On further appeal of the *Schwartz* case, the Ninth Circuit favorably cited *Williams* and flatly reversed the BAP, "making clear that violations of the automatic stay are void, not voidable."[41] In policy terms, the Ninth Circuit reasoned:

If violations of the stay are merely voidable, debtors must spend a considerable amount of time and money policing and litigating creditor actions. If violations are void, however, debtors are afforded better protection and can focus their attention on reorganization. Given the important and fundamental purpose of the automatic stay, we find that Congress intended violations of the automatic stay to be void rather than voidable. Nothing in the Code or legislative history suggests that Congress intended to burden a bankruptcy debtor with the obligation to fight off unlawful claims. [A rule of voidable only] would impose severe hardships on debtors trying to regain their financial footing.[42]

§ 3–33 Damages (Section 362(h))

Conduct that violates the stay is void against the stay's beneficiaries. This effect always occurs and is the primary consequence of violating the stay. A secondary consequence which sometimes occurs is damages prescribed by section 362(h). It provides:

An individual injured by any willful violation of a stay provided by this section shall recover actual damages, including costs and attorneys' fees and, in appropriate circumstances, may recover punitive damages.[1]

The relationship between the two consequences is this:

[T]here is a difference between the effect of actions taken in violation of the stay, and the culpability of the actors who take such acts. The

---

40. Id. at 318.

41. In re Schwartz, 954 F.2d 569, 571 (9th Cir.1992), rev'g, 119 B.R. 207 (Bankr. 9th Cir. 1990).

42. Id.

§ 3–33

1. 11 U.S.C.A. § 362(h).

actions may be void ab initio, but the actor's culpability is a question to be settled by reference to some extrinsic legal standard, whether it is * * * § 362(h), or [alternatively applicable] * * * common-law and statutory theories under which * * * [the debtor] [chooses] to bring suit.[2]

a. Who Is the Plaintiff?

The meaning of "individual," who can recover damages under section 362(h), includes the debtor and, probably, creditors.[3] The stay intends limited protection for creditors, and section 362(h) should logically permit them to repair harm resulting from a breach in the protection intended for them.

The larger debate about the meaning of "individual" is whether the term is limited to natural persons or also includes corporations and other legal entities. The Code elsewhere uses the term "individual" exclusive of corporations, partnerships, government.[4] Some courts therefore limit its meaning in section 362(h) to natural persons.[5] By this view a corporate debtor can never recover damages under section 362(h). Other courts believe that the role of section 362(h) in deterring and repairing violations of the stay is overridingly important. These courts, a probable majority, define "individual" more broadly, for purposes of section 362(h), to include a debtor corporation and thereby allow the corporation to recover section 362(h) damages.[6]

In any event, this "individual" gets a "private cause of action."[7] In the usual case, in which the injured individual is the debtor, she will pursue her action in bankruptcy as a disputed matter.[8]

b. Who Is the Defendant?

Damages are recoverable under section 362(h) from any entity responsible for the violation, except governmental units protected by sovereign immunity.[9] Significantly, the people accountable include not only the person whose actions violated the stay, but also people who counselled or aided

---

2. Vahlsing v. Commercial Union Ins. Co., 928 F.2d 486, 489 (1st Cir.1991).

3. Homer Nat'l Bank v. Namie, 96 B.R. 652, 654–55 (W.D.La.1989).

4. The definition of "'person' includes individual, partnership, and corporation, but does not include governmental unit * * *." 11 U.S.C.A. § 101(41).

5. In re Chateaugay Corp., 920 F.2d 183, 184 (2d Cir.1990); In re Ionosphere Clubs, Inc., 124 B.R. 635 (S.D.N.Y. 1991); In re Prairie Trunk Railway, 125 B.R. 217, 220–22 (Bankr. N.D.Ill. 1991); In re Williams, 124 B.R. 311 (Bankr. C.D.Cal.1991) (dicta).

6. See, e.g., In re Atlantic Business and Community Corp., 901 F.2d 325, 329 (3d Cir. 1990); Budget Service Co. v. Better Homes of Virginia, Inc., 804 F.2d 289, 292 (4th Cir.1986); In re Academy Answering Service, Inc., 100 B.R. 327, 329 (N.D.Ohio 1989); United States v. INSLAW, Inc., 113 B.R. 802, 820 (D. D.C. 1989), rev'd on other grounds, 932 F.2d 1467 (D.C. Cir. 1991); In re Jim Nolker Chevrolet–Buick–Oldsmobile, Inc., 121 B.R. 20, 22 (Bankr. W.D.Mo.1990).

7. Pettitt v. Baker, 876 F.2d 456, 457 (5th Cir.1989); see also Martin–Trigona v. Champion Federal Sav. and Loan Ass'n, 892 F.2d 575 (7th Cir.1989).

8. It is handled as a contested matter, In re Zumbrun, 88 B.R. 250 (Bankr. 9th Cir. 1988), upon motion and without a finding of contempt or the like. In re Karsh Travel, Inc., 102 B.R. 778, 780–81 (N.D.Cal.1989), appeal dism'd, vac'd in part as moot, 942 F.2d 792 (9th Cir. 1991).

9. See § 3–34 infra.

the actions, including the actor's lawyer.[10] This group includes representatives acting for the debtor.[11]

c. *What Is the Wrong?*

The wrong that triggers section 362(h) is a "willful violation" of the stay. No damages of any kind are recoverable under section 362(h) without it. Virtually everybody agrees that a violation is willful when a creditor acts intentionally with knowledge of the stay [12] or, more generally, the bankruptcy.[13] Actually, the courts do not disagree on the event about which the creditor must be aware because "knowledge of the bankruptcy filing is the legal equivalent of knowledge of the stay." [14]

A specific intent to violate the stay is not required, or even an awareness by the creditor that her conduct violates the stay.[15] It is sufficient that the creditor knows of the bankruptcy and engages in deliberate conduct that, it so happens, is a violation of the stay. Moreover, "[w]here there is actual notice of the bankruptcy it must be presumed that the violation was deliberate or intentional." [16]

Satisfying these requirements itself creates strict liability. There is nothing more to prove except damages. Specifically, liability is not conditioned on proving a request and refusal to quit the violation.[17] Also, establishing civil contempt is not necessary.[18] Imposing sanctions for contempt was the principal answer to willful violations of the stay before section 362(h) was enacted. It remains an alternative or additional remedy in some circumstances, but section 362(h) is entirely independent and triggered solely by its own terms.

The reason the section 362(h) trigger is so quick and easy is simple:

> This standard encourages would-be violators to obtain declaratory judgments before seeking to vindicate their interests in violation of an automatic stay, and thereby protects debtors' estates from incurring potentially unnecessary legal expenses in prosecuting stay violations.[19]

The same policy explains why good faith is not a defense and is irrelevant to liability.[20] Specifically, " '[w]hether the party believes in good faith that it had a right to the property is not relevant to whether the act was "willful." ' "[21] " 'Not even a "good faith" mistake of law or a "ligitimate dispute" as to legal rights relieve a willful violator of the consequences of the act,' "[22] or even good faith reliance on an attorney's advice.[23] Inadvertence

---

10. See Practitioner Treatise, Vol. 1.

11. See Practitioner Treatise, Vol. 1.

12. See Practitioner Treatise, Vol. 1.

13. See Practitioner Treatise, Vol. 1.

14. In re Wagner, 74 B.R. 898, 904 (Bankr. E.D.Pa. 1987).

15. See Practitioner Treatise, Vol. 1.

16. Homer Nat'l Bank v. Namie, 96 B.R. 652, 654 (W.D.La.1989).

17. See Practitioner Treatise, Vol. 1.

18. See Practitioner Treatise, Vol. 1.

19. In re Crysen/Montenay Energy Co., 902 F.2d 1098, 1105 (2d Cir.1990).

20. See Practitioner Treatise, Vol. 1.

21. In re Atlantic Business and Community Corp., 901 F.2d 325, 329 (3d Cir.1990), quoting In re Bloom, 875 F.2d 224, 227 (9th Cir. 1989); see also In re Karsh Travel, Inc., 102 B.R. 778, 780 (N.D.Cal.1989), appeal dism'd, vac'd in part as moot, 942 F.2d 792 (9th Cir. 1991).

22. In re Chateaugay Corp., 112 B.R. 526, 530 (S.D.N.Y.1990), rev'd on other grounds, 920 F.2d 183 (2d Cir.1990), quoting In re San-

23. See note 23 on page 164.

can be a defense[24] because it negates intention, not because of innocence and not when there is a pattern of inattentiveness.[25]

d. What Are the Damages?

The damages recoverable under section 362(h) are actual damages, including costs and attorneys' fees, and punitive damages in appropriate circumstances. Actual damages "must be based on losses actually suffered" as a result of the violation[26] and are not awarded without sufficient proof to support them.[27]

Sometimes, the only damages proved are the costs and attorneys' fees in addressing the violation. The courts disagree on whether or not these expenses are recoverable without actual damages.[28] We would allow the recovery because the costs and fees are themselves a form of actual damages. Otherwise, the practical effect is to narrow the stay by limiting enforcement to violations that cause damages that can be proved with certainty.

Punitive damages are a different form, and the requirements for recovering them are greater. Reportedly, actual damages are a predicate for punitive damages,[29] but very minimal actual damages will support them.[30] More substantially, "appropriate circumstances" are required,[31] which means heightened culpability of the defendant.

A bare willful violation that justifies actual damages is not sufficient for punitive damages. "An additional finding of maliciousness or bad faith on the part of the offending creditor warrants the further imposition of punitive damages * * *."[32] They require "a higher state of mind standard" than simple willfulness[33] producing "egregious, intentional misconduct"[34] that is oppressive,[35] outrageous,[36] fraudulent,[37] reckless[38] or in bad faith.[39]

---

sone, 99 B.R. 981 (C.D.Cal.1989). Most courts would likely agree, but a couple of cases go the other way and have decided that a violation is not willful if legitimate doubt and uncertainty existed on whether or not the stay covered the conduct. University Medical Center v. Sullivan, 125 B.R. 121, 126–28 (E.D.Pa. 1991) (rejecting the rule that willful is a violation with knowledge of the bankruptcy); In re Reiter, 126 B.R. 961, 966 n.4 (Bankr. W.D.Tex. 1991).

23. In re Taylor, 884 F.2d 478, 482–83 (9th Cir.1989); Homer Nat'l Bank v. Namie, 96 B.R. 652, 654 (W.D.La.1989).

24. See Practitioner Treatise, Vol. 1.

25. See Practitioner Treatise, Vol. 1.

26. Archer v. Macomb County Bank, 853 F.2d 497, 500 (6th Cir.1988) (Damages against creditor for violating the stay were reversed because evidence of lost contracts too speculative and the evidence of causal relation was conjecture.).

27. See Practitioner Treatise, Vol. 1.

28. See Practitioner Treatise, Vol. 1.

29. See Practitioner Treatise, Vol. 1.

30. See Practitioner Treatise, Vol. 1.

31. 11 U.S.C.A. § 362(h).

32. In re Crysen/Montenay Energy Co., 902 F.2d 1098, 1105 (2d Cir.1990); accord, In re DaShiell, 124 B.R. 242, 251–52 (Bankr. N.D.Ohio 1990) (Punitive damages awarded because creditor refused to remove lien after the court ordered it done.).

33. United States v. Ketelsen, 104 B.R. 242, 254 (D.S.D.1988), aff'd, 880 F.2d 990 (8th Cir. 1989); see also In re Bloom, 875 F.2d 224, 228 (9th Cir. 1989) (higher state of mind required).

34. In re Ketelsen, 880 F.2d 990, 993 (8th Cir.1989); see also In re Knaus, 889 F.2d 773, 776 (8th Cir.1989) (Punitive damages appropriate because creditor attempted to have debtor excommunicated from church after debtor sought turnover from creditor.); In re Omni Graphics, Inc., 119 B.R. 641, 644–45 (Bankr. E.D.Wis.1990).

35. See Practitioner Treatise, Vol. 1.

36. See Practitioner Treatise, Vol. 1.

37. See Practitioner Treatise, Vol. 1.

38. See Practitioner Treatise, Vol. 1.

39. See note 39 on page 165.

Here, good faith is important. It is irrelevant in determining liability for actual damages but works, effectively, as a defense to punitive damages. Specifically, they are inappropriate if the creditor acted in good faith on legal advice that her conduct would be lawful.[40]

e. *Overlapping Wrongs and Remedies*

Sometimes, conduct that violates the stay also violates another rule of the Code, or breaches other law, which can carry its own remedies. For example, section 542 requires third persons holding property of the estate to surrender it to the trustee.[41] Refusing to do so is a violates both the stay[42] and section 542. Disposing of property of the estate violates the stay and, in effect, section 549 which empowers the trustee to avoid unauthorized, postpetition transfers of such property.[43] In turn, the avoidance entitles the trustee, acting under section 550, to recover the property or damages from various people.[44] Similarly, conduct toward property that violates the stay can also violate non-bankruptcy law, such as the law of conversion which would create liability for the value of the property wrongfully taken or detained.

Nothing in or about section 362 displaces these other wrongs and remedies. Rather, section 362 and the other law can operate alternatively or work cumulatively in the absence of inconsistency between them. An even tighter fit between sections 542 and 362 is possible, with section 542 providing "the *right* to the return of estate property, while section 362(h) provides the *remedy* for the failure to do so,"[45] including the recovery of punitive damages if the failure amounts to egregious, intentional misconduct.[46]

Sometimes, however, the relationship is strained, as when recovery under the other law is prohibited by procedural restrictions that section 362 does not share. The issue then is whether the other law displaces recovery under section 362(h). The best example is the trustee attempting to use section 362(h) to recover estate property, or its value, that was wrongly transferred and that cannot be recovered under section 549 because the limitations period of section 549(d) has expired.[47] We believe that section 549 displaces section 362(h) in this case,[48] but this example is a very tiny precedent. It argues for displacement only when the other law is also bankruptcy law, and the match in substance between it and section 362 is so close that they serve essentially the same ends with only different means. Meeting this test would fairly establish the other law, as far as it goes, as an exception to section 362(h), and allowing recovery under section 362 would accomplish nothing of purpose.

39. See Practitioner Treatise, Vol. 1.
40. See Practitioner Treatise, Vol. 1.
41. 11 U.S.C.A. § 542(a-b).
42. See Practitioner Treatise, Vol. 1.
43. 11 U.S.C.A. § 549(a).
44. Id. § 550(a).

45. In re Abrams, 127 B.R. 239, 242 (Bankr. 9th Cir.1991) (suggesting that this proposition is the basis for certain decisions by other courts) (emphasis in original).
46. See Practitioner Treatise, Vol. 1.
47. 11 U.S.C.A. § 549(d).
48. See § 6–73 infra.

§ 3-34 Damages (Section 362(h))—Sovereign Immunity

a. The States

Government is traditionally shielded from liability by the decisional doctrine of sovereign immunity. The states are further protected by the Eleventh Amendment immunity from suit in federal court. The Congress can waive this immunity in bankruptcy, including the states' constitutional protection, and—to some extent—did so in section 106, which provides:

> (a) A governmental unit is deemed to have waived sovereign immunity with respect to any claim against such governmental unit that is property of the estate and that arose out of the same transaction or occurrence out of which such governmental unit's claim arose.
>
> (b) There shall be offset against an allowed claim or interest of a governmental unit any claim against such governmental unit that is property of the estate.
>
> (c) Except as provided in subsections (a) and (b) of this section and notwithstanding any assertion of sovereign immunity—
>
>> (1) a provision of this title that contains "creditor," "entity," or "governmental unit" applies to governmental units; and
>>
>> (2) a determination by the court of an issue arising under such a provision binds governmental units.[1]

The meaning of this provision determines the extent to which the states, and probably the federal government, can be held liable for violating the stay and other provisions of the Code.

The key to interpreting 106 is *Hoffman v. Connecticut Dept. of Income Maintenance*.[2] In this case a bankruptcy trustee sought damages from Connecticut on two different bases in two unrelated cases: the turnover of certain payments the state owed one of the debtors for prepetition services, and the recovery of preferential tax payments the other debtor had paid the state shortly before bankruptcy. The former was based on section 542 and the latter on section 547. The state resisted the trustee's actions because of the Eleventh Amendment. The bankruptcy court decided that section 106 waived this immunity, specifically section 106(c). Neither (a) nor (b) was applicable because the state had not filed a proof of claim.

The bankruptcy court reasoned that the trigger words of section 106(c)(1) are used in both section 542 ("entity") and section 547 ("creditor") and that these provisions therefore bind the state by force of section 106(c)(2), "notwithstanding any assertion of sovereign immunity." Moreover, because the turnover and preference sections use the section 106(c)(1) trigger words, the effect of section 106(c)(2) is to waive entirely the state's sovereign immunity with respect to turnover and preference actions. Therefore, Connecticut could be required to pay the trustee a debt that is property of the estate, and the trustee could avoid and recover a preference to the state.

---

§ 3-34

1. 11 U.S.C.A. § 106.

2. 492 U.S. 96, 109 S.Ct. 2818, 106 L.Ed.2d 76 (1989).

The Second Circuit agreed with everything except how far section 106(c)(2) waives immunity. This court concluded that when section 106(c) applies, immunity is waived "only to the extent necessary for the bankruptcy court to determine a state's rights in the debtor's estate,"[3] not to the extent of allowing any recovery of damages against the state. The Second Circuit affirmed the District Court which had reversed for Connecticut.

The Supreme Court affirmed the decision for the state but only four of the justices (Kennedy, O'Connor, Rehnquist, and White) agreed with the Second Circuit that the section 106(c) waiver is limited. This plurality believes

> that § 106(c)(2) operates as a further limitation on the applicability of § 106(c), narrowing the type of relief to which the section applies. * * * The language of § 106(c)(2) is more indicative of declaratory and injunctive relief than of monetary recovery. * * * We therefore construe § 106(c) as not authorizing monetary recovery from the States. Under this construction of § 106(c), a State that files no proof of claim would be bound, like other creditors, by discharge of debts in bankruptcy, including unpaid taxes, but would not be subjected to monetary recovery.[4]

Four others (Brennan, Blackmun, and Stevens, and Marshall) dissented and would have reversed for the trustee, agreeing with the bankruptcy court that waiver of immunity by section 106(c) is complete. Justice Scalia broke the tie by voting to affirm for Connecticut on the further basis that Congress cannot waive the states' Eleventh Amendment immunity. In any event, the *Hoffman* plurality controls because the sum of opinions is that a majority of the Court will not approve awarding damages in bankruptcy against a state when the only waiver of immunity is section 106(c).

The courts basically agree on what *Hoffman* means to the states' liability under section 362. The states are always and fully subject to the avoiding effect of section 362(a).[5] Even if their immunity would shield them from the effect, section 106(c) waives the immunity in this respect because section 362(a) uses the trigger word "entities," and the avoiding effect is declaratory or injunctive relief that section 106(c)(2) covers.

The story is different for damages under section 362(h). It uses none of the trigger words, and they would make no difference if all of them were there. The section 106(c) waiver does not cover liability for damages of any kind. Therefore a state which has not filed a proof of claim cannot be liable for damages under section 362(h),[6] not even if the state knowingly acts in deliberate disregard of the stay.

The story under section 362(h) changes some, but not entirely, if the state files a proof of claim. By doing so the state is deemed to have waived sovereign immunity completely, even for damages, but only with respect to the claims against the state that are described in section 106(a) and (b).

---

3. In re Willington Convalescent Home, Inc., 850 F.2d 50, 55 (2d Cir.1988), aff'd, Hoffman v. Connecticut Dept. of Income Maintenance, 492 U.S. 96, 109 S.Ct. 2818, 106 L.Ed.2d 76 (1989).

4. Hoffman v. Connecticut Dept. of Income Maintenance, 492 U.S. 96, 102, 109 S.Ct. 2818, 2822-23, 106 L.Ed.2d 76, 84-85 (1989).

5. See Practitioner Treatise, Vol. 1.

6. See Practitioner Treatise, Vol. 1.

b. The United States

The federal government is not protected by the Eleventh Amendment, but the decisional law is settled that "the United States may not be sued absent a waiver of its sovereign immunity."[7] For bankruptcy, the federal waiver is determined, as is a state's, under section 106; and the majority of courts have interpreted and applied section 106 to the United States in the same way that *Hoffman* applies it to the states. They were proved right in *United States v. Nordic Village Inc.*[7.5] In this case an officer of the corporate debtor made a postpetition transfer to the Internal Revenue Service. The debtor's trustee sued to avoid the transfer and won judgment against the IRS, including a monetary judgment under section 550(a). *Hoffman* did not control this case but the Court followed the plurality's reasoning in *Hoffman* which led to the decision in *Nordic Village* that "[n]either § 106(c) nor any other provision of law established * * * waiver of the [federal] Government's immunity from a bankruptcy trustee's claims for monetary relief."[7.10] Therefore, the United States is always, fully subject to the avoiding effect of section 362(a),[8] but is never liable for damages under section 362(h) unless it files a proof of claim.[9] Even then, the federal immunity to damages is waived only to the limits of section 106(a) and (b).

c. Waiving Immunity to Section 362(h) Damages by Section 106(a-b)

Government's immunity from damages under section 362(h) is waived by subsections 106(a) and (b). They provide:

> (a) A governmental unit is deemed to have waived sovereign immunity with respect to any claim against such governmental unit that is property of the estate and that arose out of the same transaction or occurrence out of which such governmental unit's claim arose.
>
> (b) There shall be offset against an allowed claim or interest of a governmental unit any claim against such governmental unit that is property of the estate.[10]

These two provisions look confusingly alike but are different and complimentary. As the Eighth Circuit has explained:

> Subsection (b) does not require [as does (a)] that the two claims "arise from the same transaction or occurrence." Unlike subsection (a), how-

---

7. In re Professional Sales Corp., 56 B.R. 753, 760 (N.D.Ill. 1985), citing, Lehman v. Nakshian, 453 U.S. 156, 160, 101 S.Ct. 2698, 2701, 69 L.Ed.2d 548 (1981); see also In re Bulson, 117 B.R. 537, 539 (Bankr. 9th Cir. 1990), relying on Edwards v. United States, 163 F.2d 268, 269 (9th Cir.1947) and citing Alyeska Pipeline Serv. Co. v. Wilderness Soc'y, 421 U.S. 240, 267–69, 95 S.Ct. 1612, 1626–27, 44 L.Ed.2d 141 (1975); NAACP v. Civiletti, 609 F.2d 514, 518–21 (D.C.Cir.1979), cert. denied, 447 U.S. 922, 100 S.Ct. 3012, 65 L.Ed.2d 1114 (1980) ("We begin our analysis with the basic notion that governmental bodies enjoy immunity from suit, and that the doctrine of sovereign immunity protects the federal government from suits brought by the debtor in a bankruptcy case. However, the government's sovereign immunity maybe waived, provided that the waiver is clear and explicit and not merely inferred.").

7.5 ___ U.S. ___, 112 S.Ct. 1011, 117 L.Ed.2d 181 (1992).

7.10 Id. at ___, 112 S.Ct. at 1017, 117 L.Ed.2d at ___.

8. See Practitioner Treatise, Vol. 1.

9. See Practitioner Treatise, Vol. 1.

10. 11 U.S.C.A. § 106(a-b).

ever, subsection (b) limits the waiver of sovereign immunity to an offset of the governmental unit's claim against the estate. * * * [R]ead together * * * [s]ection 106(a) is applicable only where the debtor's claim exceeds the claim of the governmental unit, and then, affirmative recovery is allowed only to the extent of such excess.[11]

Yet, a waiver of immunity under section 106(a) for affirmative recovery requires that the two claims arise out of the same transaction. Moreover, and very significantly, the Supreme Court has described both section 106(a) and (b) as "narrow * * * waivers of sovereign immunity."[12] The first, section 106(a), "carefully limits the waiver" by "requiring that the claim against the governmental unit arise out of the same transaction or occurrence as the governmental unit's claim."[13] The second, section 106(b), is likewise "a narrow waiver, with the amount of the offset limited to the value of the governmental unit's allowed claim."[14]

The claims that section 106(a-b) describe—for which the government's immunity to damages is dropped—do not naturally include violations of the stay, even less so if the Supreme Court's dicta is followed that the exceptions are only "narrow waivers" of sovereign immunity. The lower courts, however, have stretched section 106(a-b), in several directions, in order to impose section 362(h) damages on governmental units.

For example, the district court decided in *United States v. INSLAW, Inc.*,[15] that section 106(a) applies even without the government filing a proof of claim. Other conduct is sufficient that casts the government as a creditor in the bankruptcy.[16] Even more significantly, the court concluded that "because § 106(a) forms the basis of the waiver, it is complete; the entire bankruptcy code applies including those provisions such as § 362(h) which provide for monetary damages."[17] The language is ignored in 106(a) that limits the government's exposure to the debtor's claims "that arose out of the same transaction or occurrence" that produced the government's claim.

In another case, *United States v. McPeck*,[18] the government violated the stay by continuing its tax collection efforts after the debtor filed her Chapter 13 case. The Eighth Circuit decided that the debtor's 362(h) claim for damages (including attorney's fees) against the government belonged to the estate and, to the extent allowed by 106(b), were properly set off against the government's claim for taxes.[19]

The section 106(b) waiver allows setting off the debtor's claim against the government's claim, but allows no affirmative recovery for any excess of

---

11. United States v. McPeck, 910 F.2d 509, 512–13 (8th Cir.1990).

12. Hoffman v. Connecticut Dept. of Income Maintenance, 492 U.S. 96, 101, 109 S.Ct. 2818, 2822, 106 L.Ed.2d 76, 84 (1989).

13. Id. at 101–02, 109 S.Ct. at 2822, 106 L.Ed.2d at 84.

14. Id. at 102, 109 S.Ct. at 2822, 106 L.Ed.2d at 84.

15. 113 B.R. 802 (D. D.C. 1989), rev'd on other grounds, 932 F.2d 1467 (D.C. Cir. 1991).

16. Id. at 810–12 (United States waived its immunity, though it asserted no formal claim against debtor, where Government behaved like creditor, involved itself directly in deliberations of debtor's efforts to reorganize, expressly represented to bankruptcy court that it was creditor, and asserted monetary claims against debtor in another forum.).

17. Id. at 813.

18. 910 F.2d 509 (8th Cir.1990).

19. Id. at 512–13; see also Matter of Fernandez, 125 B.R. 317, 319–21 (Bankr. M.D.Fla. 1991), aff'd in part and rem'd, 132 B.R. 775 (M.D.Fla.1991).

the debtor's claim, i.e., the amount by which it exceeds the government's claim. The section 106(a) waiver exposes government to this affirmative recovery, but (a) requires that the two claims arise out of the same transaction. Here, too, the courts have stretched the waiver of immunity. In *In re Bulson*,[20] the Bankruptcy Appellate Panel concluded that a claim for damages like that in *McPeck* was related to the government's claim for taxes and, therefore, the wider waiver of section 106(a) applied.[21]

§ 3–35 Damages (Section 362(h))—Contempt

The damages remedy of section 362(h) is new. It was added to the Code in 1984. Before then, any award of damages for violating the stay was usually based on the court's civil contempt power.[1] Many courts, probably the majority of them, believe that this use of contempt survives section 362(h).[2] The survival of contempt for this purpose is meaningful, however, only if contempt is more generous (is a wider basis) than section 362(h) in providing damages for violations of the stay. Some courts believe so but, typically, their view of section 362(h) is stingy. For example, they would use contempt to award damages to corporations[3] and against creditors' lawyers[4] and in the absence of an intent to violate the stay,[5] but the same awards are possible under section 362(h) depending on how it is read and applied. Contempt is typically an equal remedy in the courts that interpret and apply section 362(h) as fully as possible; and, when used against government as an alternative to section 362(h), it is probably (even most certainly) equally limited by sovereign immunity.[6] Contempt is even smaller if, as some authorities suggest, it requires for this purpose the breach of an actual court order.[7]

The bottom line is that no description is very reliable about the relationship between section 362(h) and contempt as sources of damages for stay violations. How the two remedies fit together depends on how the courts size both of them, and the courts are not agreed on the exact shape of even one of them.

---

20. 117 B.R. 537 (Bankr. 9th Cir.1990).

21. Id. at 541 ("In this case, the IRS's claim against the debtor arises from the debtor's failure to pay taxes owed. The debtor's claim arises pursuant to the attempt by the IRS to collect these taxes owed by the debtor. The basis of both cases revolve around the aggregate core of facts regarding the debtor's unpaid taxes. Therefore, we find that under these circumstances the essential facts relating to the tax claim itself are logically related to the government's collection activities. As a result, the United States sovereign immunity is waived under § 106(a)."); see also United States v. Ketelsen, 104 B.R. 242 (D.S.D.1988), aff'd, 880 F.2d 990 (8th Cir. 1989) (By force of both 106(a) and (b), FmHA was subject to debtor's claim for tax refund that FmHA setoff in violation of the stay.).

§ 3–35

1. See Practitioner Treatise, Vol. 1.
2. See Practitioner Treatise, Vol. 1.
3. See Practitioner Treatise, Vol. 1.
4. See Practitioner Treatise, Vol. 1.
5. See Practitioner Treatise, Vol. 1.
6. See Practitioner Treatise, Vol. 1.
7. See Practitioner Treatise, Vol. 1.

Chapter 4

USE/SALE/LEASE OF ESTATE PROPERTY

Table of Sections

Sec.
4–1 Introduction: Sections 363 and 364.
4–2 Introduction to Section 363—Use, Sale or Lease of Property.
4–3 Ordinary Course of Business, Use, Sale or Lease, Section 363(c)(1).
4–4 Use, Sale or Lease Not in the Ordinary Course, Section 363(b)(1).
    a. Routine Sales.
    b. Sale of All or Substantially All Assets Under Section 363(b).
4–5 Cash Collateral, Section 363(c)(2).
4–6 __ Sanctions for Unauthorized Use of Cash Collateral.
4–7 Sales Free of Others' Interests—Secured Parties, Section 363(f).
4–8 __ Bidding In: Section 363(k).
4–9 Sale Free of Others' Interests—Co–Owners, Section 363(h).
4–10 Application of Section 363(f) and (h) in Unconventional Cases.
4–11 Section 364: Introduction.
4–12 Ordinary Course and Non-ordinary Course Unsecured Loans, Section 364(a) and (b).
4–13 Loans With Priority over Other Administrative Expenses, With Security or With Senior Security, Section 364(c) and (d).
4–14 __ Section 364(d).
4–15 Payment of and Granting Security for Prepetition Debt: Herein of Cross–Collateralization and *Texlon*.
4–16 Notice and Hearing Under Sections 363 and 364.
4–17 Appeals, Sections 363(m) and 364(e).

§ 4–1 Introduction: Sections 363 and 364

Because most Chapter 11 filings never produce a confirmed plan even though they may chug and jerk along for months and even years, the rules that govern the operation of the business after the petition is filed and before a plan is confirmed may be even more important than the rules that determine the nature of the plan. Under sections 1107 and 1108, the debtor in possession or a trustee is given the right to operate a business after it files its Chapter 11 petition.[1] Sections 363 and 364 are chief among the rules

---

§ 4–1
1. Similar rights exist in the other chapters. 11 U.S.C.A. §§ 1203, 1307, and 721.

that govern the operation of the business after the petition and before confirmation.

Consider the kinds of things that must be done on a routine and non-routine basis in the operation of an industrial company in Chapter 11. Such a company will have hundreds of suppliers, thousands of employees; it will need to continue selling assets and to buy raw materials to feed manufacturing or resale operations. To do all of this it will need to draw checks, sign contracts, and to pay obligations such as the claims of trade creditors, of employees, and even of postpetition financial lenders. Moreover, if the business depends upon the goodwill of customers or of employees, and if that goodwill will be destroyed by even a temporary cessation of operations (as for example, when an airline strands its clientele all around the country by ceasing to operate for even a few days), the loss may be irretrievable.

To meet these short-term concerns, section 363 and 364 authorize a variety of activities, some without court approval (if they are in the ordinary course), and others only with court approval. The former section authorizes sale, lease and other "uses" of the debtor's assets. These uses would include acts such as flying the aircraft of a bankrupt airline on a revenue producing route on the day after the petition is filed, operating the machinery subject to a security interest and selling goods out of inventory and free of the security interest of the floor-planner. Ultimately they will also include making payments on debt incurred after the petition was filed and perhaps more extensive transactions such as the sale of all the assets of the company or signing of long-term leases that will have a dramatic impact on the debtor's future activities.

Section 364 authorizes various forms of borrowing. The most simple is trade credit—unsecured, open-term credit routinely granted by sellers of supplies. Typically this can be incurred without court intervention. It also contemplates the possibility, now with court approval, for large-scale borrowing to facilitate extraordinary transactions undertaken to preserve assets and to make the reorganization possible.

Few would argue with the proposition that any successful Chapter 11 program requires provisions that authorize ordinary course transactions without court approval. The first difficulty arises when a debtor, and possibly some of the creditors, claim that a transaction is in the ordinary course, but others classify it as out of the ordinary course and so in need of court blessing. The Code gives no guidance to distinguish "ordinary" from "non-ordinary" course, and courts have had to grope for a definition.

If one concludes that a particular transaction is not in the ordinary course, a second question arises: what standards should courts apply in approving some non-ordinary course transactions while denying others? Presumably a hearing before the judge is not merely a formality; it is implicit in the idea of a hearing that the judge is sometimes to approve the sale and sometimes to disapprove, but what are the standards?

Both section 363 and section 364 have a number of intricate rules designed to protect the interests of creditors and others. Some of these are substantive; many are procedural. Because sections 363 and 364 will have an application in nearly every Chapter 11 case, and indeed in every business that is continued after a petition is filed in whatever chapter, every lawyer should have a good grasp of both sections. In some cases, as when a sale of all the debtor's assets is proposed in lieu of a reorganization, the fight under section 363 or section 364 will not be merely the preliminary bout; it will be the main event.

§ 4–2 Introduction to Section 363—Use, Sale or Lease of Property

The basic substantive subsections of section 363 are 363(c)(1) (use without court approval in ordinary course transactions) and section 363(b)(1) (use, sale or lease after notice and hearing *not* in the ordinary course). Below we devote considerable discussion both to the distinction between these two subsections and to their operation.

One particularly important subset of ordinary course transactions are subjected to the *non*-ordinary course rules in (b), i.e., to the requirement of a court hearing and approval for use. These transactions are those dealing with "cash collateral." In a typical case, cash collateral includes bank accounts on deposit with a bank that is a creditor of the estate and cash proceeds of collateral such as accounts receivable or inventory.

Two important and specialized subsections ((f) and (h)) authorize the sale of property that is subject to the interests of third parties. Subsection (f) deals mostly with cases in which the debtor wishes to sell property free and clear of an existing and valid security interest. Subsection (h) deals particularly with co-owned property; most frequently it comes into play when a debtor seeks to sell property owned jointly by the debtor and a spouse who is not in bankruptcy.

In addition to the substantive sections discussed above, there are a series of procedural subsections. Among these considered below are (k) (allowing a secured creditor to bid in his debt at a sale) and (m) (having to do with the limitation on reversal or modification on appeal).

Section 363 is beguiling in its simplicity. A casual reading does not alert one to the multitude of transactions that a debtor may propose and that a court must consider under its aegis.

§ 4–3 Ordinary Course of Business, Use, Sale or Lease, Section 363(c)(1)

Section 363(c)(1) authorizes the debtor to "enter into transactions, including the sale or lease of property of the estate, in the ordinary course of business, without notice or a hearing" and to "use property of the estate" on a similar basis.[1] Even though the concept of ordinary course is not new to the law [2] and even though a wide array of transactions could be identified as

---

§ 4–3
1. 11 U.S.C.A. § 363(c)(1).
2. Under Article 6 of the Uniform Commercial Code there is a well developed body of case law on the question what is and what is not ordinary course. The terms usually used to describe a "bulk transfer" are "rare, irregular events, occurring but few times in the life of a merchant". Martin Marietta Corp. v. New Jersey Nat'l Bank, 505 F.Supp. 946, 950 (D.N.J.1981), judgment aff'd and rem'd, 653 F.2d 779 (3d Cir.1981), was found not to fit

clearly within the ordinary course, the margin between what is ordinary course and what is not is quite ragged and hard to distinguish.

For example, would the sale to one buyer of one hundred pairs of shoes by a retailer constitute a non-ordinary course sale where the sale of one pair would clearly be ordinary course? Would transactions that are routine in any significant business such as the settlement of a dispute or lawsuit be non-ordinary course transactions because they are not associated with the principal purpose of the business? Is it in the ordinary course for a company in Chapter 11 to hire lobbyists to argue its cause in Congress?[3]

The richness and the variety of different factual circumstances—each raising issues never before considered, and most calling for a subtle judgment based upon the particular business involved—make it unlikely that even the most sophisticated test can make the boundary between ordinary course and non-ordinary course smooth and clear. Nevertheless, we turn to some of the cases and to the tests there proposed. At minimum they give one a taste for the questions presented and an understanding of the formulae stated by the courts.

As an initial matter one might ask how these questions are presented. Presumably the debtor in possession makes a judgment that a particular use or sale of an asset would be in the ordinary course. If the debtor so decides, presumably the transaction proceeds without court intervention. How then does the court get involved?

When the transaction is a loan, the creditor will ultimately have a claim against the estate if it is not routinely paid. This claim will be classified as an administrative expense under section 364(a) and can be challenged by other creditors as a part of a liquidation or plan. If the transaction is a lease or some other executory contract under section 363, it can be challenged in exactly the same way. More difficult is the outright sale under section 363 where the challenger will have to trace the asset into the hands of the buyer and then ask the court to require the buyer to disgorge. As we will see below, the problem becomes particularly acute when the debtor has spent cash collateral and the cash has disappeared into the pocket of a

---

this description. Martin Marietta's purpose in contracting to buy 50,000 tons of sand per month for three months to keep Hollander afloat pending a decision whether to acquire the plant was rare. Buyers interested in purchasing the whole business do not appear every day. But Martin Marietta's method of "testing the waters" was to make ordinary purchases. Thus, while the underlying purpose was unusual, the sale of the sand itself was not. Indeed, Martin Marietta's very purpose makes the sale a far cry from the danger that the bulk transfer act is intended to prevent. The primary danger is that the transferor will more easily go out of business leaving creditors remediless.

Although it was a large contract for the normally slow winter season, the selling price was market price, not cut-rate. Also, the sale constituted less than one-third of the overall six-month inventory (as opposed to the inventory at "time of transfer").

See U.C.C. § 6–102(1); Sternberg v. Rubenstein, 305 N.Y. 235, 112 N.E.2d 210 (1953). See also Aab v. Loehmann's, Inc., 8 B.R. 777 (S.D.N.Y. 1981); Matter of Curtina Intern., Inc., 23 B.R. 969 (Bankr. S.D.N.Y. 1982); Davis v. Lawrence–Cedarhurst Bank, 206 F.2d 388 (2d Cir.1953) (mortgaging "currently salable" goods without such an existing customary practice held to be out of the ordinary course); see also note 3 infra.

3. See Park Terrace Townhouses v. Wilds, 852 F.2d 1019 (7th Cir.1988) (hiring a new property manager and maintenance supervisor held in ordinary course); In re Johns–Manville Corp., 60 B.R. 612 (Bankr. S.D.N.Y. 1986) (court approves of hiring of non attorney lobbyist as in the ordinary course).

routine seller. For these reasons we suspect only a small share of all questionable transactions are in fact challenged by unhappy creditors.

The most widely followed articulation of the ordinary-course standard in a bankruptcy case was given by Judge Sofaer in *In re James A. Phillips Inc.*[4] Phillips, a ceiling and wall contractor, applied for authority to make payment to certain prepetition creditors who would otherwise have asserted mechanic's liens on projects already completed. Such filing would in turn have caused the general contractor to hold back money already earned by Phillips. The bankruptcy judge approved the payments but there was no notice of the request to any of Phillips' other creditors. The district court concluded that payments made on an accelerated basis to creditors who are threatening to assert mechanics' liens are not ordinary course payments.

Since *Phillips* is one of the few cases that blesses full postpetition payment of a prepetition debt, it is a considerable understatement to say that the payments were not in the ordinary course. Nevertheless Judge Sofaer put some flesh on the section 363(c)(1) bones. He suggests transactions *not* in the ordinary course are those where there is the need to

> assure interested persons of an opportunity to be heard concerning transactions different from those that might be expected to take place so long as the debtor in possession is allowed to continue normal business operations. The touchstone of "ordinariness" is thus the interested parties' reasonable expectations of what transactions the debtor in possession is likely to enter in the course of its business.[5]

The judge instructs one to examine the reasonable expectations of a creditor of this particular business. If outside of bankruptcy, such use, sale or lease of the debtor's assets (here payment of a debt) would be expected, they can be undertaken without court approval and without notice to the creditors. If, on the other hand, the use would go beyond the normal expectations of creditors outside of bankruptcy, the debtor must give notice and receive court approval.

The court correctly points out that when creditors object to transactions that are in fact ordinary course, they are really making strategic objections based upon the "bankrupt's Chapter 11 status, not the particular transactions themselves."[6] In effect the congressional adoption of Chapter 11 has withdrawn that argument from the creditors' arsenal. Many creditors would be happier if there were no Chapter 11 or if it did not authorize the debtor to operate its business with only modest control by the creditor. With the adoption of Chapter 11 that battle has been lost. Like it or not, ordinary course transactions are permitted without court approval.

Returning to the *Phillips* formula, how does one test creditors' reasonable expectations about what is and is not ordinary? The court in *Waterfront Companies, Inc. v. Johnston*[7] suggests the use of a "horizontal" and a "vertical" test. The horizontal dimension encompasses the general activities of that business. For example, an automobile manufacturer could not sell groceries at retail, for to do so would violate Judge Kressel's "horizontal"

---

4. 29 B.R. 391 (S.D.N.Y. 1983).
5. Id.
6. Id. at 394.

7. 56 B.R. 31 (Bankr. D.Minn.1985); see also In re Dant & Russell, Inc., 853 F.2d 700 (9th Cir. 1988).

standard. The vertical requirement says that there may be transactions within the "horizontal" scope of the debtor's normal business operations but which are so large they bump the ceiling. Waterfront's business was to develop a railroad station that had formerly been used by the Milwaukee Road in Minneapolis. In the process of that development a dispute arose among the various parties; the dispute was resolved with an indemnity agreement. The agreement indemnified certain beneficiaries against "any and all liabilities, loss, damage, cost or expenses" which they "may sustain or incur as a result of any liabilities or any indebtedness of the partnership * * *." Several parties asserted claims against the debtor amounting to $1,650,846.90 and arising out of the indemnity agreement that had been entered into after the petition had been filed. The claimants argued that their claim was in the ordinary course because it arose out of a deal (indemnity agreement) that was entirely conventional and normal for a real estate developer.

Finding that the magnitude of the transaction (the potential liability arising out of an unlimited indemnity) was so great it could not have been in the ordinary course, the court rejected the claim. Surely the court was correct to consider the size of the transaction as an element to determine ordinary course. In fact, the experience with Article 6 [8] of the Uniform Commercial Code shows that size of the transaction is one of the principal events that may cause an otherwise ordinary transaction to become not ordinary. For example, the sale of one pair of shoes by a shoe store would clearly be an ordinary transaction. However, the sale of 80 percent of the inventory of that same store to one buyer would be a non-ordinary course transaction that might run afoul of Article 6. It is entirely appropriate to transplant the U.C.C. learning to sections 363 and 364. The foregoing case gives some idea how the courts might look at a transaction.

A final test that may be useful in section 363 appears in *In re Selgar Realty Corp.*[9] Finding that the sale of real estate by a company whose principal business was renting real estate is not an ordinary course sale, the judge offered an interesting test: will the court have to think about this more than a minute? One way for a lawyer to test his or her intuition about ordinary course is to ask whether there would be automatic and nearly certain approval of the sale or loan if it were presented to the judge and known to the creditors. If the answer to that question is no (assuming such disapproval by the creditors does not arise merely out of intransigence), then lawyers should be doubtful that the transaction is in the ordinary course.

Before we pass from the question of what is and what is not ordinary course, we note one application of the rule with which we do not agree. In

---

8. See also In re Wicaco Machine Co., Inc., 55 B.R. 588 (Bankr. E.D.Pa. 1985), appeal denied, 60 B.R. 415 (E.D.Pa.1986) (citing 1942 case, court decided test of whether transfer outside of ordinary course of business is whether sale is substantially different in *amount* or character from those regularly made by seller); compare Sternberg v. Rubenstein, 305 N.Y. 235, 240, 112 N.E.2d 210, 212 (1953) (where court held that a sale of a large batch of off-season shoes was still in the ordinary course partly because "in the business of shoe retailing the sale of off-season wares is no rare and irregular occurrence").

9. 85 B.R. 235 (Bankr. E.D.N.Y.1988); see also United States v. Goodstein, 883 F.2d 1362 (7th Cir.1989) (it is not a routine or ordinary event to transfer control of one manufacturing company to another, effectively merging the two companies, or to relocate substantial portions of a company's equipment and inventory to the premises of another).

In re Hilyard Drilling Co., Inc.,[10] the court found that the debtor in possession's sale of $60,000 of used equipment was not in the ordinary course. Despite the fact that business was moribund, the principal shareholder had been paying himself $22,000 a month out of the bank account in which the $60,000 was deposited. Given those facts, it is easy to see how the court concluded this was not an ordinary course sale.

However, the court's articulation of the rule in this case seems incorrect to us. Because the business of the debtor was drilling oil wells, the court stated that no sale of any of the used equipment could be in the ordinary course "of that business." It made that statement despite the fact that Hilyard routinely sold excess and obsolete equipment before its Chapter 11 filing. Following the court's statement to its logical conclusion, one would decide that only sales of inventory could be in the ordinary course, for by hypothesis every other sale would not be in the ordinary course of *the* business in which the debtor was engaged. That is too narrow a reading of the ordinary course rule. Following *Phillips* (what would the creditors reasonably expect?), we would say that routine sales of non-inventory assets in the style and amount that were characteristic of the business before it filed Chapter 11 should be regarded as ordinary course sales and permitted without court approval.

§ 4–4 Use, Sale or Lease Not in the Ordinary Course, Section 363(b)(1)

Cases under section 363(b) present two significant legal issues. First, what standard is a court to apply in approving or denying a challenged request? The Code is silent on this issue. Second, when may a court approve a sale of all or substantially all the assets of a debtor under section 363(b) where such sale would foreclose the possibility of reorganization under section 1129?

a. Routine Sales

Turning to the first question, what are the standards? Courts commonly say there must be a "business justification" for a non-ordinary course sale[1] and that the sale be "in good faith"[2] or that it be in the "best

---

10. 74 B.R. 5 (W.D.Ark.1986).

§ 4–4

1. In re Lionel, 722 F.2d 1063 (2d Cir.1983); Continental Air Lines, 780 F.2d 1223 (5th Cir. 1986); In re Industrial Valley Refrigeration and Air Conditioning Supplies, 77 B.R. 15 (Bankr. E.D.Pa. 1987); In re Rebeor, 93 B.R. 16 (Bankr. N.D.N.Y.1988); In re Ionosphere Clubs, Inc., 98 B.R. 174 (Bankr. S.D.N.Y. 1989) (debtor must articulate some business justification other than appeasement of major creditors); In re Naron & Wagner, Chartered, 88 B.R. 85 (Bankr. D.Md.1988); In re Schipper, 109 B.R. 832 (Bankr. N.D.Ill. 1989), aff'd, 112 B.R. 917 (N.D.Ill.1990); Matter of Plaza Family Partnership, 95 B.R. 166 (E.D.Cal.1989). Consider the court's justification in Matter of Met–L–Wood Corp., 861 F.2d 1012 (7th Cir. 1988), cert. denied, 490 U.S. 1006, 109 S.Ct. 1642, 104 L.Ed.2d 157 (1989):

> Often, filing a petition for bankruptcy makes it difficult to keep the bankrupt in operation. Suppliers and customers, fearing interruption of service, may shy away and creditors be reluctant to advance fresh credit, even though such credit carries a high priority in bankruptcy. The bankrupt may be shunned like a leper. Because of these possible consequences, it may make sense—not least from the creditor's standpoint—to shift the bankrupt's assets to another owner as quickly as possible, so that the business can continue in other hands, free of the stigma and uncertainty of bankruptcy.

2. See note 2 on page 178.

interests"[3] of the creditors. If one puts aside sales that might somehow foreclose a possible reorganization, all of these tests come to only one question: IS THIS THE BEST PRICE? If the present value of the stream of payments to be earned by the asset in the Chapter 11 business is higher than the proposed sale price or, alternatively, if other buyers can be found who will pay a higher price, the sale should not normally be approved. If the contrary is true, it should be approved. In our view the "business justification" or "best interest" rule at bottom come to this and to no more.

The courts instinctively realize this, and the hearings under section 363(b)(1) are hearings mostly about the value of the asset to be sold and about the fairness of the price. Characteristic of these cases is *In re Karpe*.[4] After some negotiation the price of the real estate to be sold in that case was set at $105,000 and notice was given to creditors of the proposed sale price and of the opportunity to submit a higher offer three days prior to the proposed sale. It appears that the last day for objection was August 3. Because of failure to serve certain parties, the motion was not heard until some time late in October. Well after the objection date but before the hearing date, a third party, A.R.K. Hess Association, offered $125,000 for the property. Finding Hess not a party in interest, the court approved the negotiated sale for $105,000.

Often the courts are plagued by competing offers that appear to be more favorable than the one offered for the court's approval, but are in fact ill-financed or conditional. In cases like *Karpe* there may be a conflict between getting the best price in *this* case and the best price *generally*. If the court routinely allows third parties to overturn negotiated deals by bidding small increments above an agreed price, negotiations will soon become sham transactions in which the negotiating buyer will not give its best price.

Where there are two or more serious bidders, the courts have been ingenious in ordering or conducting auctions. In one case the trustee actually conducted an auction in the courtroom.[5]

Questions about the "good faith" of the proposed sale are often coded challenges to disguised payments to insiders. For example, in *Industrial Valley Refrigerating and Air Conditioning Supply*[6] a buyer originally offered to purchase the assets of the debtor for $640,000. Only a few weeks later, the debtor in possession sought approval of a sale to the same buyer for $482,000. The latter transaction included a promise by the buyer to employ

Id. at 1017.

2. In re Industrial Valley Refrigeration and Air Conditioning Supplies, 77 B.R. 15 (Bankr. E.D.Pa. 1987); Matter of Specialty Products, Inc., 94 B.R. 781 (Bankr. N.D.Ga. 1989) (duty to disclose the existence of a deal between an insider and a purchaser: the court might well imply wrongdoing on the part of either or both parties and hold either or both liable to the estate for the turnover of the amounts involved in the undisclosed arrangement).

3. In re Apex Oil Co., 92 B.R. 847 (Bankr. E.D.Mo.1988); In re Coastal Industries, Inc., 63 B.R. 361 (Bankr. N.D.Ohio 1986).

4. 84 B.R. 926 (Bankr. M.D.Pa.1988); see also In re Joshua Slocum, Ltd., 99 B.R. 261 (Bankr. E.D.Pa. 1989).

5. In re Alves, 52 B.R. 353, 355 (Bankr. D.R.I.1985) (Trustee "acted prudently and in the best interests of the estate" by conducting an auction in the courtroom when prospective buyer indicated an intention to improve upon another's offer. The court noted that all parties objecting to the trustee's Notice of Intended Sale were in attendance, that property was given adequate marketing exposure, and that original offer was fair and reasonable.); see also In re Planned Systems, Inc., 82 B.R. 919 (Bankr. S.D.Ohio 1988).

6. 77 B.R. 15 (Bankr. E.D.Pa. 1987).

an insider for five years at $60,000 annually. The insider had previously been paid $50,000 annually. Suspecting that the buyer had deducted the value of these payments from the original purchase price, the court refused to approve the sale. Here, lack of good faith means favoritism to insiders.[7]

For the most part the courts seem to be applying section 363(b) in a sensible and straightforward way. Instinctively the courts are searching for the process that will produce the best price in a particular case. They are appropriately skeptical of those who ask rejection of a true or negotiated offer in favor of an undisclosed, conditional or ill-defined offer at a higher price. They are inquisitive about side payments that go into the pockets of insiders when such payments are not part of the purchase price in theory but are part of that price in fact. Moreover, the courts have been quite innovative and sophisticated in their use of appraisals and combination of negotiated deals and open auctions to get the best prices.[8]

b. *Sale of All or Substantially All Assets Under Section 363(b)*

Under the Bankruptcy Act of 1898, the Courts of Appeals disagreed over the right of the bankruptcy court to approve the sale of all or substantially all of the assets of a Chapter XI debtor under the predecessor of section 363(b). In *In re Solar Manufacturing Corp.*,[9] a 1949 Third Circuit opinion, the court found that a sale of substantially all of the assets of the debtor in reorganization could be approved without a reorganization plan only if there was an "actual emergency."[10] In *In re Dania Corp.*[11] the Court of Appeals for the Fifth Circuit found that such sales could be approved without any finding of emergency. The Bankruptcy Commission bill originally submitted to Congress in 1973 explicitly rejected the requirement of an actual emergency. Section 7–205 provided that "a sale or lease of all or substantially all of the property of the estate may be authorized by a court if in the best interest of the estate." The note to that section recognizes the "split of authority in the case law" but states that the "section makes it clear that a showing of emergency is not necessary."[12]

When section 363 was enacted as part of the Code in 1978, the explicit authorization for the sale of all of the assets was gone. Apparently the Department of Justice argued against authorizing sales of all the assets of a

---

7. In re Onouli–Kona Land Co., 846 F.2d 1170 (9th Cir.1988) (good faith does not depend on "value" and does not require the Bankruptcy Court to make an explicit finding of good faith); In re Levine, 100 B.R. 537 (Bankr. D.Colo.1989) (no fraudulent or "sweetheart" deals allowed); In re Sovereign Estates, Ltd., 104 B.R. 702 (Bankr. E.D.Pa. 1989) (insider perks indicated lack of good faith, settlement not approved). See also In re Abbotts Dairies of Pennsylvania, Inc., 788 F.2d 143 (3d Cir. 1986).

8. See In re Vanguard Oil and Service Co., Inc., 88 B.R. 576 (E.D.N.Y.1988); In re Selgar Realty Corp., 85 B.R. 235 (Bankr. E.D.N.Y. 1988); In re Alpha Industries, Inc., 84 B.R. 703 (Bankr. D. Mont. 1988) (sale pursuant to liquidating plan); In re NEPSCO, Inc., 36 B.R. 25 (Bankr. D.Me.1983) (sale approved as part of a deal for immediate payment to security creditor in return for large reduction of secured creditor's claim); In re Alves, 52 B.R. 353 (Bankr. D.R.I.1985) (auction in the courtroom).

9. 176 F.2d 493 (3d Cir.1949).

10. Id. at 494.

11. 400 F.2d 833, 837 (5th Cir.1968), cert. denied, 393 U.S. 1118, 89 S.Ct. 994, 22 L.Ed.2d 122 (1969), rehearing denied, 394 U.S. 994, 89 S.Ct. 1455, 22 L.Ed.2d 711 (1969).

12. Report of the Commission on the Bankruptcy Laws of the U.S., H.R. Doc. 137, Part II, 93rd Cong., 1st Sess. 239 (1973).

reorganized company without a plan.[13] Because there is no explicit reference in the Judiciary Committee Report about the removal of this language, it is impossible to say with certainty whether Congress removed the language with the intention of retaining the rule of *In re Solar* or for some other reason.[14] For reasons set out below, we agree with the majority of courts that have held that 363(b) authorizes the sale of all or substantially all of the assets of a company in Chapter 11, even though there is no finding of actual emergency.

Since 1981, four federal Courts of Appeal, the Second, Third, Fifth and Sixth, have addressed this general question as have many bankruptcy and district courts.[15] All of the circuit courts and most of the lower courts have concluded that an emergency need not be found in order to authorize a section 363 sale of all the assets of a Chapter 11 debtor. Beyond that there has been only limited agreement among the courts about proper standards for a sale of all assets under section 363. To some extent the apparent disagreement among the courts rises not from different views of the law but from the substantial differences in the proposals by the particular debtors that have been faced by various courts.

At one end of the spectrum is a clean cash sale of all of the assets of the debtor. In many ways this is the simplest case, for it presents only one question: Is the price right? It is like the routine sale of a single asset. If the price is right, the relative claims of the creditors and other claimants can be determined after the fact and can attach to the proceeds of the sale in the same ratio as they attached to the other assets.

More difficult is a second class of cases where the debtor proposes the sale of less than all, but of certain critical assets. In those cases a synergistic relationship between the assets may be ruined and the sale of some assets at a fair price may dramatically lower the value of other assets. Sale in such circumstances may constitute a silent judgment about or alteration of the relative priority of various claims. If, for example, one creditor had a claim on a chemical plant that was dependent upon an adjacent plant, the sale of the latter, even for a very high price, would impair the value of the former. That would be particularly true if none of the proceeds of the sale were to go to the creditor whose remaining asset was reduced in value. Such a judgment should be made only in a conscious way, most commonly during the bargaining of a plan.

A third and troublesome proposal is one for the sale of all or part of the assets not in exchange for cash, but as part of a complex deal that governs

---

13. Hearings on H.R. 31 and H.R. 32, Before the Subcommittee on Civil and Constitutional Rights of the House Comm. on the Judiciary, 94th Cong. 1st and 2nd Sess., ser. 27, pt. 4 at 2123 (1975–76).

14. Cases finding emergency to be necessary under section 363(b) include: In re D. M. Christian Company, 7 B.R. 561 (Bankr. N.D.W.Va.1980); In re White Motor Credit Corp., 14 B.R. 584 (Bankr. N.D.Ohio 1981).

15. See, In re Cedar Tide Corp., 859 F.2d 1127 (2d Cir.1988), cert. denied, 490 U.S. 1035, 109 S.Ct. 1933, 104 L.Ed.2d 405 (1989); In re Naron & Wagner, Chartered, 88 B.R. 85 (Bankr. D.Md.1988); In re Abbotts Dairies of Pennsylvania, Inc., 788 F.2d 143 (3d Cir. 1986), on remand, 61 B.R. 156 (Bankr. E.D.Pa.1986); In re Continental Air Lines Inc., 780 F.2d 1223 (5th Cir. 1986); Stephens Industries, Inc. v. McClung, 789 F.2d 386 (6th Cir. 1986); In re Lionel, 722 F.2d 1063 (2d Cir. 1983); In re Rausch Mfg. Co., Inc., 59 B.R. 501 (Bankr. D.Minn.1985); In the Matter of Baldwin United Corporation, 43 B.R. 888 (Bankr. S.D.Ohio 1984); In re WHET, Inc., 12 B.R. 743 (Bankr. D. Mass. 1981).

the use of those assets or for non-cash payments. If the sale contract provides that some of the assets are to go to particular creditors and not to others, or if the non-cash assets "paid" by the buyer are of value in one reorganization scenario but not another or if some but not all of the debts are assumed, it means that the sale is not merely an exchange of value but may be a redistribution of wealth among the creditors.

A fourth class of cases is one involving multiple debtors such as a parent and a subsidiary, each with shared and individual creditors. Here the sale of the assets of one subsidiary will have a disproportionate impact on the creditors of that subsidiary compared with other creditors. For example, the sale of the stock or assets in a subsidiary that would give the subsidiary's creditors a claim against a parent but allow the sale of the subsidiary's assets free and clear would obviously change the status of those creditors. It might enhance or detract from their position.

Before we turn to the cases, consider the players in this theater and understand what consideration each deserves. First are fully secured creditors, who often wish for an early sale in the fear that continued operation of a losing business will erode their security. Second are creditors who have only slight hope of any payoff and shareholders who have even less hope. The latter desperate actors may oppose a sale, not because they truly believe that continued operation will produce a plan that will give them more money, but because they hope to win concessions from the secured and other powerful senior creditors by raising the threat of a long and expensive court battle.

We find significant cases under the Code illustrating each of the categories. The first of these is *In re WHET*.[16] In that case Judge Lavien authorized the sale of all of the operating assets and licenses of a radio station for the price of $1,250,001.50 It appears to have been a cash sale without strings or contingency; essentially it turned the Chapter 11 estate into a pot of cash that could be divided at the court's leisure in accordance with appropriate findings about the relative priorities of the claimants. The court devoted most of its effort to assure that the trustee had achieved the highest possible price on the sale of the station. It examined various appraisals, the mode of advertising, and heard testimony from a variety of persons about the station's value. Because the principal shareholder of the debtor was serving a prison term for a felony at the time, it would have been easy to believe that the station was not operating at its most efficient level.

With this case in mind, consider the arguments that are commonly put forward by those who object to a section 363(b) sale. First they argue that section 1125 has not been met, for there has been no detailed disclosure statement about a plan or a specific solicitation of votes. Second, they argue there has been no opportunity under section 1126 to vote for or against the plan, and that the various creditors may have been deprived of protections under section 1129, such as the assurance under section 1129(a)(7) that each creditor will receive under the plan at least as much as the creditor would have received on liquidation. Finally, of course, one can argue that the good faith provisions of section 1129 have not been met where those provisions would require a different distribution among creditors similarly situated.

---

16. 12 B.R. 743 (Bankr. D.Mass.1981).

To see how those arguments can easily be met in a situation where all of the assets are to be turned into cash, consider the *WHET* bankruptcy.[17] First, questions about the best interest test can be solved by assuring that the assets are sold for a fair price, and by later determining the exact share that each is to receive. While there is no possibility to vote against the plan, the principal reason to vote against a plan is that one will receive too little because the sale is at too low a price. That issue can be raised by any creditor and examined by the court at the hearing to approve the sale under section 363(b). Disclosure under section 1125 is a more difficult issue; but if the principal function of disclosure is to assure the creditors that the maximum amount is being realized on the sale, that can be done by the court and the parties in the approval hearing.

The sale of all of the assets for cash is very much like a conventional section 363(b) sale of a single asset. The beginning and the end of the responsibility of the debtor in possession, of the trustee, and of the court is to insure the best possible price is received. If they do that, no creditor can have a legitimate complaint. Particularly in a case such as *WHET* where the assets were probably being operated in a marginally competent way, there is a possibility that a passage of time will see the assets decline in value and that a sale sooner rather than later will enlarge the creditors' recovery. Even if that is not true, there is no *a priori* reason why the sale of any set of assets will bring more or less than its true value later rather than sooner. Put another way, creditors who assert that the assets could be used in the Chapter 11 business to produce a greater return than would be realized on an early sale, should have the burden of explaining why the current market price for those assets is not the proper value for the potential stream of earnings.

The final reason for the courts to be receptive to such sales under section 363(b) arises from the expense of operating in Chapter 11. Although there are certain virtues about operating in Chapter 11 (e.g., interest-free loans by the continued use of prepetition debt), we expect those are far outweighed in most cases by the expense inherent in running a business by committee under court supervision. If the strength of the leveraged buyout is to stimulate the managers by giving them an ownership interest, Chapter 11 must be the converse. While the executives of competing businesses are free to make decisions that maximize their income, businesses in Chapter 11 must bear the burden of court supervision, lawyer interference, creditor consultation, and committee decisionmaking. In addition to making payments to lawyers, accountants, and others for expenses that would not be suffered outside of Chapter 11, they pay all the costs of working under a slow, ponderous, and conservative management.

17. In re WHET, Inc., 12 B.R. 743 (Bankr. D. Mass.1981) (In this Chapter 11 bankruptcy case, confirmation of the sale of the debtor's assets was sought. The bankruptcy court held that cash sale of substantially all assets of debtor was appropriate, where independent trustee had widely advertised the assets, debtor had no connection with proposed buyer, radio station was operating on "temporary authority," so that it was vulnerable to proposals to FCC for takeover of license, causing debtor's principal assets to be at risk which increased with passage of time, station's existence to date had only been made possible by loan from lessor of debtor's facilities and, if sale did not go forward, lessor would be free to convey its fee interest in land to others, and cash bid was probably equivalent to, if not superior to, highest appraisal figure.).

An example of the second case described above—sale of critical assets in a complex non-cash transaction—is *In re Braniff Airways, Inc.*[18] In reversing the decision of the district and bankruptcy courts, the Fifth Circuit disapproved the proposed sale. Although the court protested that it "need not express an opinion" on the merits of the sale under section 363(b) (because the transaction was "much more" than a use, sale or lease), we believe it did so. The conditions to which the court objected are terms of sale and are part and parcel of a section 363(b) decision. Despite the court's protestation to the contrary, we interpret this case to be a decision under section 363(b).

The court identified three aspects of the sale that could not be authorized under section 363(b). First, PSA (the buyer) proposed that Braniff pay $2.5 million to PSA in exchange for $7.5 million of scrip that entitled the holders of the scrip to travel on PSA. The court correctly noted that taking scrip had the practical effect of dictating some of the terms of any future reorganization, for any reorganized company would have to use the scrip on PSA flights or forfeit a valuable asset. Second, Braniff and its creditors were required to vote a portion of their deficiency claims in favor of any reorganization plan approved by a majority of the unsecured creditors' committee. Finally, the PSA transaction "provided for release of claims by all parties against Braniff, its secured creditors, its officers and directors."

The court states that it cannot approve a sale agreement containing any of the three items, for they are not authorized by section 363(b). We believe the court may have been correct in declining to approve, but we would not agree that these terms are beyond the scope of "use, sale or lease." Any lease, most uses, and many sales have elaborate terms that are related in one way or another with the ultimate price but do not go directly to the transfer of title or to the payment for it. In our view the terms of the PSA agreement fall well within that sphere.

Nevertheless, the court may have been correct in concluding that terms of the kind specified necessarily allocated resources among creditors and determined the rights of various parties in a way that should be done only as a part of a reorganization plan. Even so, we have some doubt about the court's judgment. First, it is unclear to us why a creditor cannot agree to vote in a particular way or why doing so would be a violation of the policy under section 1126. Nor do we understand why a release of claims by parties to the sale transaction should be regarded as beyond the bounds of a section 363(b) sale. We would think it routine for any sale that is in settlement of a dispute to include such hold-harmless agreements. For all of that, we are sympathetic to the court's dilemma. As any transaction becomes more complex, as it includes not merely payment of cash for assets but also transfers of non-cash assets of peculiar value and other executory promises, the possibility grows that the transaction will predetermine the reorganization in ways that favor the informed and aggressive over others.

Representative of the last genus described above—those involving sales of assets of related corporations—is *In re Crutcher Resources Corp.*[19] A

---

18. 700 F.2d 935 (5th Cir.1983), reh'g denied 705 F.2d 450 (1983); see also In re Pioneer Ford Sales, Inc., 729 F.2d 27 (1st Cir. 1984) (ability to assign a franchise denied).

19. 72 B.R. 628 (Bankr. N.D.Tex.1987).

trustee representing debenture holders issued by one subsidiary of Crutcher objected to the proposed sale of two other profitable subsidiaries. Noting that a petition had been filed in October, that the parties sought a sale in December, that there was no proof of a business reason for the sale, and the suspicion that the principals of the debtor were motivated to sell in hopes of escaping their personal guarantees, the court declined to approve a section 363(b) sale. This decision seems correct. It was possible not only that insiders were self dealing but also that assets available to the creditors of one of the subsidiaries in reorganization might have been taken beyond the creditors' reach by sale. Since the profitable subsidiaries were not in danger of liquidation and since there were plausible allegations that certain creditors would be favored over others by a sale, it seems to us that the court made the right choice.

On the other hand, we agree with the contrary decision of Judge Newsome in a similar case. In *In the Matter of Baldwin United*,[20] the judge approved the sale of the debtor's Colorado banking subsidiary. The sale settled an otherwise interminable and expensive litigation involving the banks. The court intimated that the cost in time and money of that litigation endangered the prospect of a successful reorganization. It seems to us that those are exactly the kind of factors that properly influence the judge in determining whether to permit a sale under section 363(b) of a large share of a debtor's assets.

Finally, consider the two most widely-cited, major use or sale cases, *Lionel*[21] and *Continental*.[22] In *Lionel*, the debtor in possession wished to sell its 82 percent interest in a profitable subsidiary. The interest in the subsidiary constituted approximately 34 percent of the debtor's assets. Overturning the decision of the district court, the court of appeals held the sale should not have been authorized under section 363(b). Although it rejected the argument that an emergency was necessary for a large-scale sale, the court found that other conditions had not been met. Stating that some "articulated business justification" must be put forward other than the "appeasement of major creditors," the opinion is full of rhetoric requiring that the judge "expressly find the evidence presented before him at the hearing a good business reason to grant such an application." The court is less clear on particulars, but it does list a set of factors that reappear in later lower court decisions. The court suggests that the bankruptcy judge look to

> relevant factors [such] as the proportionate value of the asset to the estate as a whole, the amount of elapsed time since the filing, the likelihood that the plan of reorganization will be proposed and confirmed in the near future, the effect of the proposed disposition on future plans of reorganization, the proceeds to be obtained from the disposition vis à vis any appraisals of property, which of the alternatives of use, sale or lease the proposal envisions and, most importantly perhaps, whether the asset is increasing or decreasing in value.[23]

20. 43 B.R. 888 (Bankr. S.D.Ohio 1984); see also In re Apex Oil Co., 92 B.R. 847 (Bankr. E.D.Mo.1988) (approved partly on the ground that expensive litigation would be avoided).

21. In re Lionel Corp., 722 F.2d 1063 (2d Cir.1983).

22. In re Continental Air Lines Inc., 780 F.2d 1223 (5th Cir.1986).

23. In re Lionel Corp., 722 F.2d at 1071.

Some of these factors are common-sense rules that the bankruptcy judge should follow to determine whether the price being paid is the best that can be obtained. Others sensibly suggest that the judge should not authorize a section 363(b) sale if a plan of reorganization is about to be proposed and can shortly be confirmed.

We are less certain about the intent or wisdom behind the remaining factors. For example, why should it matter that the proposed transaction is a sale as opposed to a lease? Why is it important the assets be increasing or decreasing in value? Rapid and certain decline in value (the peaches are rotting) calls for a prompt sale, but absent such an obvious change in value, it is unclear why one's guess about climbing or declining values should have any impact on the decision to sell. Presumably if the business is getting marginally better one should get a better price for it than if that were not true, and vice versa. Already this list is appearing in other cases, but we doubt it is much more than window dressing. To the extent it hides the principal question—namely, is this the best price?—we fear it may be an impediment to the correct analysis.

Finally, there is *In re Continental Air Lines, Inc.*[24] As in *Lionel*, the court in *Continental* reversed the decision of the bankruptcy and district courts and sent the case back with instructions. It found that the proposed transaction could not be authorized under section 363(b) at least on the record as it stood. Continental proposed to lease two DC-10s for ten years for a total lease commitment in excess of $70 million. It proposed to use the aircraft to serve its Pacific routes. Continental argued that its Pacific routes had considerable value which could be realized only if it had the proper aircraft to fly them. The court concluded that a lease was a "use" of property under section 363(b) and that the bankruptcy court did not err in finding that there was an adequate business justification.

It nevertheless sent the case back with instructions that the lower court should hear the objectors' claims and deny the lease only if those objecting "could have defeated a plan of reorganization containing the Leases." Recognizing that a section 363 lease would deprive creditors of certain rights (section 1125 disclosure, section 1126 voting, section 1129(a)(7) best interest, section 1129(b)(2)(B) absolute priority rule), the court states that first the debtor should show a business purpose, and then any creditor who wished to object "must specify exactly what protection is being denied."[25] In effect, the burden on rehearing below should be on the objectors. The lower court must require them to show exactly how they would have been better treated had there been a reorganization and not a section 363(b) lease of the aircraft.

This seems a clever model. It is easy for a creditor (who simply wishes to increase its take by being mean and obstreperous) to object to almost any business transaction. Here the court demands that such creditor show how the proposed transactions will injure. Presumably, the lease will be approved if the creditor is tongue tied in response to the opportunity to show how it will be injured by the section 363(b) transaction. This procedure makes more sense than one demanding that the debtor anticipate and

---

24. 780 F.2d 1223 (5th Cir.1986).   25. Id. at 1228.

answer every possible complaint of the creditors. We embrace the *Continental* scheme.

In concluding we reiterate: notwithstanding *In re White Motor Credit Corp.*,[26] the requirement of an emergency as a condition to the sale of all or substantially all the assets is moribund, perhaps dead. Most courts find that sale is permitted without any finding of emergency.[27] Second, any sale of all or substantially all of the assets under section 363(b) must first meet the same tests that one would apply to the sale of any asset under section 363(b); the court should take care to find that the seller has achieved the best price. This means, for example, that a court should be skeptical of side payments to insiders and that it should listen with care to appraisals and encourage all imaginative attempts to produce the best price.

Ultimately we suspect that the division in the case law should not be between sale of a particular asset and sale of all assets, but between sales, whether large or small, that critically affect any reorganization and cause potential reordering of priorities, and sales that do not do so. For example, the sale of all the debtor's assets for cash, as was done in *WHET*, presents few issues. On the other hand, the sale of even a small part of an airline's assets, such as gates or landing rights, might have a dramatic impact on the value of other assets.

Because courts cannot depend on creditors to express their honest views in these settings, finding the truth will require clever procedural devices like those suggested in *Continental*. Creditors who hope to gain by threatening others with delay will oppose sales even in circumstances where they have no legitimate hope of receiving a larger payment out of a fairly bargained reorganization. To distinguish legitimate from illegitimate claims, we endorse the suggestion of the Court of Appeals for the Fifth Circuit in *Continental*. It is not enough for complaining creditors to fill the air with buckshot in the form of claims about injuries under sections 1125, 1126, and 1129; the courts should demand that the objectors take aim at particular sections and show how those sections will give them tangible benefits which they are being denied by the proposed sale under section 363(b).

§ 4–5 Cash Collateral, Section 363(c)(2)

To limit the temptation to which the debtor might otherwise succumb, Congress has restricted certain ordinary course transactions. Specifically, section 363(c)(2) prohibits even the ordinary course use of "cash collateral" unless the creditor claiming the collateral consents or unless the court authorizes the use. Presumably Congress enacted this subsection in full appreciation of the temptation before a desperate debtor and of the precarious nature of a security interest in a deposit account or the like. Absent

---

26. 14 B.R. 584 (Bankr. N.D.Ohio 1981) (Sale for cash was approved. There the remaining assets of White Motor were sold to Volvo. Even though the court approved that sale, ironically it did so by finding that there was an emergency and that the Solar standard had been met.).

27. Even the landmark emergency case In re Solar Manufacturing, 176 F.2d 493 (3d Cir. 1949) may no longer reign in its home circuit.

See In re Cedar Tide Corp., 859 F.2d 1127 (2d Cir.1988), cert. denied, 490 U.S. 1035, 109 S.Ct. 1933, 104 L.Ed.2d 405 (1989); In re Abbotts Dairies of Pennsylvania, Inc., 788 F.2d 143 (3d Cir.1986); see also, In re Lionel, 722 F.2d 1063 (2d Cir.1983); In re Continental Air Lines, Inc., 780 F.2d 1223 (5th Cir.1986); In re Braniff Airways, Inc., 700 F.2d 935 (5th Cir.1983), reh'g denied, 705 F.2d 450 (1983).

such a restriction, one would suppose that a security interest in such collateral in the hands of a desperate debtor would be worthless. Even in the face of such limitation, we suspect that debtors often use cash collateral to meet pressing needs without complying with (c)(2).

Section 363(a) defines cash collateral to mean "cash, negotiable instruments, documents of title, securities, deposit accounts, or other cash equivalents * * *" provided the estate and an "entity other than the estate have an interest" in the assets. In a conventional Chapter 11 case a debtor's bank account, held at the bank where the debtor borrows (and so subject to setoff against that borrowing) would be cash collateral. The same would be true of deposit accounts, cash or other assets that are proceeds of perfected security interests, as well as checks received in payment for collateral and the occasional document of title or security. There is no evidence from the decisions that courts have had any difficulty in applying the definition.

Note that the definition does not include inventory or accounts receivable themselves, items nearly as liquid as negotiable instruments and cash equivalents. One of the bills before Congress in 1978 would have subjected all "soft collateral" to the cash collateral rules,[1] but the Code does not contain that provision. Because "proceeds, products, offspring, rents or profits" that are subject to a security interest perfected at the time of filing continue to be subject to the security interest under section 552(b), the creditor enjoys the cash collateral protection when the inventory, accounts and such turn into cash equivalents. Put another way, the payments on the sale of inventory and the collection of accounts are proceeds subject to the security interest, thus become cash collateral and so subject to the protection of section 363(c)(2).

The presence of (c)(2) means that in a typical Chapter 11, the debtor must either enter into an agreement with its principal secured creditor or must bring the creditor to court in the process of seeking an order that permits it to use its bank account and other liquid assets. Commonly these negotiations produce what is known as a *"cash collateral order."* Out of such an order, the debtor typically gets a limited right to use the collateral in its business. The quid pro quo for the creditor may be several things. First, the creditor may insist upon additional accounting and reporting by the debtor. It may require a *"drop dead clause"* (a clause giving it the right to seize the collateral upon default of the debtor without further court hearing). It may also procure rights in certain additional collateral, or even an agreement for the debtor to make certain payments.

When the debtor has filed in Chapter 11 and is in dire need of the liquid funds, the secured creditor's position is at its height. This power is diminished if the creditor refuses to negotiate and is ultimately forced to give up the collateral by court order. So it is typically in the interest of both parties to negotiate some form of cash collateral order. One suspects too that this most powerful secured creditor and the debtor sometimes conspire in such orders to maximize their interests at the expense of creditors who are not privy to the negotiations.

§ 4–5
1. 124 Cong. Rec. H. 11,093 (Daily ed. Sept. 28, 1978) ¶ 363.01 n.17.

If the parties cannot reach agreement, the hearing on the debtor's right to use the cash collateral is likely to turn into a hearing on the grant of adequate protection under section 363(e). The debtor will ask for authority under section 363(c) to use the cash collateral, and the creditor will respond that such use cannot be permitted because the creditor is not adequately protected. Because of section 363(e), there can be no order without adequate protection. So it is that this cash collateral dispute descends into another boring discussion of adequate protection, the equity cushion and all of that under sections 362 and 361. Therefore, the real issues that come up in a cash collateral hearing are likely to be issues that we discuss elsewhere.[2]

§ 4–6 Cash Collateral, Section 363(c)(2)—Sanctions for Unauthorized Use of Cash Collateral

One of the few distinct questions associated with the debtor's use of cash collateral is the question what penalty the debtor will suffer for its unauthorized use. Based on highly anecdotal evidence, we believe that debtors often use cash collateral without authority. In some cases, debtors have atoned by giving replacement collateral.[1] But, of course, giving additional collateral is really no punishment at all, for that is what the debtor would have had to have done if it had asked permission to use cash collateral. Is it possible to hold the debtor in contempt for such act or somehow to give the debtor additional incentive to come to the court for permission?

Where a debtor in possession sells collateral under section 363 without the proper authority or where a lender makes a postpetition loan without court approval under section 364, the court can often punish the lender (by reducing its priority) or the buyer (requiring the buyer to return the asset or its value). When cash collateral is spent by the debtor in possession, there is no such easy or obvious sanction. Unless the cash is given in a lump sum to a particular creditor who took it in bad faith, one would not expect to be able to recover the cash from the payee. Presumably the most common improper use of cash collateral is to pay it out in satisfaction of various liabilities over a period of time. In such circumstances no recipient of the cash collateral would have reason to believe that it had received anything improper, and it would be inappropriate in such cases to force the innocent recipient to disgorge the proceeds.

If there is no creditor whose loan can be subordinated and no buyer to disgorge, how is the court to enforce section 363(c)(2)? The most obvious answer is to grant the creditor, whose cash collateral was spent, a security interest on other assets or to require the debtor to repay the cash collateral. Neither of these solutions is entirely satisfactory. If the debtor is insolvent, either solution is likely to punish unsecured creditors not the debtor; that is, if the claimant to the cash collateral is given a substitute lien on other assets that in liquidation would go to unsecured creditors, those unsecured creditors, not the debtor, have been made to pay for the debtor's transgression.

---

2. See §§ 3–24–3–31 supra, on relief from the stay.

§ 4–6
1. In re Casbeer, 793 F.2d 1436 (5th Cir. 1986).

For yet another reason, such a "sanction" may be no sanction at all. Presumably if the debtor in possession had done what it should have, namely, come to court and asked authority to use the cash collateral, the quid pro quo for that use would have been adequate protection, possibly a form of a lien on other assets to the secured creditor. If, having failed to ask permission, the debtor suffers only what it would have suffered had it asked permission, the debtor in possession will have no incentive to comply with the law in the first place. For both of these reasons, the granting of a lien or similar adequate protection is not a satisfactory solution to the problem of policing debtors' use of cash collateral.[2]

Particularly where the debtor's behavior has been egregious, courts have imposed various sanctions with considerable bite. Among these are finding the debtor in contempt, disallowing the confirmation of a Chapter 11 plan, denying the discharge of an individual debtor, and holding of the principals liable in conversion. Even a few lawyers who have advised debtors in possession have felt the sting of the bankruptcy court's lash.[3]

Although debtors are not frequently found in contempt, creditors have asked for contempt findings in several reported cases and the bankruptcy judges have sometimes granted those requests. Representative of these cases is *In re Krisle*.[4] While he was in Chapter 11, debtor Krisle withdrew $94,000 of cash collateral from the debtor in possession deposit account and purchased a certificate of deposit from another bank. When, on the witness stand, he refused either to return the cash or to tell the court where the certificate was located, the court held him (and ultimately his lawyer) in contempt and put him (and ultimately his lawyer) in jail. The propriety of the judge's order was considered in the district court when the debtor filed a writ of habeas corpus; the court's order was upheld.

Notwithstanding *Krisle,* a creditor should not expect a contempt finding for every violation of section 363. In *In re Continental Marine Corp.,*[5] the judge expressed considerable doubt about his power to issue a contempt decree. Moreover, the court found the mere failure to follow section 363, a statutory obligation, was not contemptuous behavior. The court distinguished section 362 on the ground that the latter provision specifically provides for contempt (which is not actually true). Thus, except in unusual cases, there will be no finding of contempt unless there has been an explicit court order that the debtor has violated.

Even the violation of an order may not be enough. In *In re Etch–Art Inc.,*[6] there was an order prohibiting the debtor from disposing its interest in "gold, inventory [and] proceeds of accounts receivable." When the sole owner disposed of some of the cash collateral, the creditor sought contempt against both the corporation and the sole owner. The court declined the request on the ground that mere use of cash collateral was not enough and that the creditor would have to establish "willful contempt." The court,

---

2. For a case in which the court ordered substitute liens and little else, see In re Placid Oil Co., 80 B.R. 824 (Bankr. N.D.Tex.1987).

3. See e.g., In re Krisle, 54 B.R. 330 (Bankr. D.S.D.1985); Midwest Properties No. Two v. Big Hill Investment Co., 93 B.R. 357 (N.D. Tex.1988).

4. 54 B.R. 330 (Bankr. D.S.D.1985).

5. 35 B.R. 990 (Bankr. E.D.Mo.1984).

6. 48 B.R. 143 (Bankr. D.R.I.1985).

however, invited the creditor to return with more extensive proof that such willfulness existed.

Finally, consider *Midwest Properties II v. Big Hill Investment Co.*[7] In this case the bankruptcy judge ordered the president of the debtor to repay the estate $141,660, and ordered two lawyers to pay respectively, $18,888 and $28,332. When the parties did not make payment in accordance with the order, the court held them in contempt. On appeal the district judge reversed. The district judge concluded the court had authority to order the parties to make payment where they had spent $550,000 of cash collateral in a one and one-half month period without authority. However, the district court concluded that the bankruptcy judge had not followed the proper procedures to find them in contempt, and sent the case back for compliance with Rule 9020, and for various findings to support the contempt conclusions. The debtor in *Midwest Properties* had filed ten separate Chapter 11 petitions in the prior two years. In each he had transferred an asset to a new debtor immediately prior to foreclosure and immediately filed a Chapter 11 for the new debtor with the sole intention of forestalling the foreclosure. The improper expenditure of $550,000 on top of this behavior obviously angered the creditors and, ultimately, the judge. One suspects that the debtor did not fare well on remand.

The boundaries of the contempt power are necessarily unclear, subject to change with each decision. However, a few things can be learned from the cases decided thus far. First, the court will not find someone in contempt simply for violating a statutory provision that does not itself invite a contempt sanction; ordinarily, therefore, one must violate a court order as a condition to any finding of contempt. Second, some bankruptcy judges are still uncertain about their power to find parties in contempt, and this uncertainty doubtless restricts their willingness to make such findings. Finally, courts are not likely to make contempt findings except in egregious cases, such as the ones discussed above.

Depending upon the circumstances, other more hospitable routes may be open to creditors who seek to punish debtors that have improperly spent cash collateral. In one case a debtor in possession who had received more than $6,000 cash collateral and not reported it to the court, was denied a discharge when the case was converted to Chapter 7.[8] The court concluded that the debtor's use of such property constituted a "fraud or defalcation while acting in a fiduciary capacity" under section 523(a)(4). It concluded that a debtor in possession is a fiduciary and that the burden of proof for a plaintiff under (a)(4) was easier to meet than that needed to show fraud under (a)(2).

In another case the court dismissed a Chapter 11 and denied a confirmation to a farmer's Chapter 11 plan partly on the ground that the debtors had appropriated cash collateral. The court held that a failure to comply with section 363(c)(2) was a violation of section 1129(a)(2) (failure to comply with the "applicable provisions of this title"). The court also found that unautho-

---

7. 93 B.R. 357 (N.D.Tex.1988).

8. In re Alvey, 56 B.R. 170 (Bankr. W.D.Ky.1985).

rized use of the cash collateral violated section 1107(a) (the duties of the debtor in possession) and it dismissed under section 1112.[9]

There are also cases where the courts find individual officers or agents of debtors to be liable for conversion or orders them, without a finding of conversion, to make up the amount of the payments. *Matter of Koran Enterprises, Inc.*[10] is an example of the former. There the court held the CEO liable for conversion on the ground that he had used $19,675 of cash collateral improperly. This outcome is similar to the one in *Midwest Properties*,[11] where, without a conversion rationale, the court held the debtor individually liable for $141,660 because of the debtor's violation of section 363. Whether this finding is made after a trial on conversion liability or simply as a sanction arising directly out of sections 105 and 363 is probably unimportant. However, the former theory is more sympathetic to a lawyer's ears. The latter, directing repayment by one who is himself not in bankruptcy, seems more radical.

Note that these liabilities imposed on individuals who are merely the agents of the corporate debtor avoid the dilemma that we discussed above. If the individuals have assets outside the debtor corporation, the court's order does not take assets out of the hands of unsecured creditors to give them to secured creditors. By forcing the converters to put their own money into the bankruptcy estate, the courts are increasing the net worth of the estate at no cost to any creditor of the estate.

The cases recited above are a testament to the strength of our case-law system. One thinking of the dilemma posed above and reading section 363, might ask how the court is to manipulate the statute in order to achieve its purposes where there is no apparent sanction for violation of section 363(c). The cases show that the courts and the creditors' imagination are adequate to the task. Although we have not yet had enough case law clearly to delineate when contempt will be granted when conversion is charged and when no sanctions will apply, the courts have traveled a considerable distance down a road toward a sensible sanction for debtor misbehavior here.

Finally, lawyers should not overlook the fact that sanctions were imposed on lawyers in both *Midwest Properties*[12] and *Krisle*[13]. Part of the claim in *Midwest* was based on Rule 9011 which states that an attorney's signature on a paper "constitutes a certificate" that the attorney has read the document and that the attorney's knowledge and belief is that "it is well grounded in fact and is warranted by existing law or a good faith argument for the extension, modification, or reversal of existing law."

§ 4–7 Sales Free of Others' Interests—Secured Parties, Section 363(f)

To prove that a proposed sale is proper under section 363(b) is only to cross the threshold in cases where others have interests in the asset. In

---

9. Cothran v. United States, 45 B.R. 836 (S.D.Ga.1984).

10. 61 B.R. 321 (Bankr. W.D.Mo.1986).

11. Midwest Properties II v. Big Hill Investment Co., 93 B.R. 357 (N.D.Tex.1988).

12. Midwest Properties II v. Big Hill Investment Co., 93 B.R. 357 (N.D.Tex.1988).

13. In re Krisle, 54 B.R. 330 (Bankr. D.S.D. 1985).

many cases, assets of the estate will be subject to security interests or other liens. Occasionally others such as spouses or children have undivided interests in such assets. Section 363(h) deals with the latter question, treatment of co-owners. Section 363(f) deals with the former, mostly cases involving secured creditors. It reads in full as follows:

> (f) The trustee may sell property under subsection (b) or (c) of this section free and clear of any interest in such property of an entity other than the estate, only if—
>
> (1) applicable nonbankruptcy law permits sale of such property free and clear of such interest;
>
> (2) such entity consents;
>
> (3) such interest is a lien and the price at which such property is to be sold is greater than the aggregate value of all liens on such property;
>
> (4) such interest is in bona fide dispute; *or*
>
> (5) such entity could be compelled, in a legal or equitable proceeding, to accept a money satisfaction of such interest.[1]

First, one should understand that section 363(b) or 363(c) must be satisfied before section 363(f) becomes relevant; it is proper to look at (f) as a further condition on the right to sell under (b) and (c).

Note that the five conditions of (f) are disjunctive; they are connected with an "or." Thus, a sale can be authorized if the debtor in possession can prove any one of the five conditions; the debtor need not prove all.

Nothing like section 363(f) existed in the bankruptcy commission's statute.[2] Nor was there anything as detailed in the Act of 1898.[3] To the extent that the subsection has an identifiable ancestry, those ancestors are cases under the Act. We fear that the message of those cases was muddled in translation into (f) and that the message has become yet more confused by some of the cases we discuss below.

Turning to the explicit terms of section 363(f), subsections (2), (3), and (4) seem relatively straightforward. If the person, other than the debtor in possession, who has an interest in the property consents, it should be obvious there could be a sale and so says (2). Subsection (3) contemplates the case in which the debtor has an equity so that no secured creditor could be injured because the property will be sold for more than the value of all the liens, so that all can be satisfied out of the proceeds. The rule is not quite that simple, but almost. Subsection (4) arises out of pre-Code law which recognized the importance of selling property that had a declining value even in circumstances in which there was a dispute over the rights to it, but where long litigation might be required to clarify those rights. As we will see, there are minor interpretive difficulties with (2), (3), and (4).

§ 4–7
1. 11 U.S.C.A. § 363(f).
2. Compare Bankruptcy Commission Report §§ 7–203, 7–205, H.R. Doc. 137, Part II, 93rd Cong., 1st Sess. 236, 239 (1973).
3. For the closest analogue, see, Bankruptcy Act §§ 70(f), 70(g), 11 U.S.C.A. § 110 (superseded 1978); see also Bankr. R. 606 (superseded 1978).

Then what is the meaning of (1), sale is permitted where "applicable nonbankruptcy law permits sale"? Perhaps it is to bar the converse, namely, to show deference to state law interests and to bar sale if applicable state law would bar sale free and clear of the competing interest. This result, however, does not seem likely since the subsection appears within a disjunctive list of reasons authorizing sales, not prohibiting them. Any one of the subsections is sufficient to justify a sale.

An obvious case for the application of section 363(f) arises under U.C.C. section 9-307(1). That section of the Uniform Commercial Code permits the debtor to sell collateral free of a security interest as long as it sells to a buyer in the ordinary course of business. Perhaps that is the case the drafters had in mind when they put (f)(1) in.

We have found no case in which a debtor successfully justified a sale under (f)(1). In *In re Fandrich* [4] a debtor argued that he had a right to sell his homestead under North Dakota law because under that law the homestead was exempt from the claims of creditors. The court denied the request on the ground that the homestead exemption did not belong to the debtor, but to his wife who was occupying the homestead at the time of the request.

The debtor in *In re 523 East Fifth St. Housing Preservation Development Fund Corp.* [5] was likewise unsuccessful in invoking (f)(1). That debtor argued that the property could be sold free of a covenant that required the property to be used solely for low income housing. The debtor argued that sale was permitted under either of two state statutes or under the common law of New York. As in *Fandrich* the court seemed to accept the potential application of (f)(1), but concluded that the debtor's substantive intentions were unfounded. Other cases have treated (f)(1) in a similar way. [6]

In section 363(f)(2) one would expect the consent rule to be applied frequently and without any significant contention. One should note, however, that "consent" under (f)(2) may be found from the creditor's inaction in certain circumstances. [7] In *In re Gabel* [8] the creditor claimed never to have received notice of the hearing that would have authorized the sale under section 363(b). Under Rules 6004 and 2002, a creditor who receives notice, but fails to oppose the proposed sale, is deemed to have consented. Despite the testimony of the creditor, the court in *Gabel* found that the creditor had received actual notice from a representative of the court. The creditor's silence was enough to fulfill (f)(2).

Presumably the theory that supports (f)(3) is that no creditor can complain about a sale if the proceeds of the sale will fully liquidate the creditor's claim. Put another way, a creditor has a right to no more than 100 percent of its claim, and having received that, has no right to say that a particular sale should or should not be made. It is implicit in (f)(3) either

---

4. 63 B.R. 250 (Bankr. D.N.D.1986).
5. 79 B.R. 568 (Bankr. S.D.N.Y. 1987).
6. See In re Manning, 37 B.R. 755 (Bankr. D.Colo.1984), vac'd on other grounds, 831 F.2d 205 (10th Cir. 1987) (debtor unsuccessfully attempted to use Colorado partnership law to sell assets free of partnership interests). For conclusory use of (f)(1), see Matter of Spain, 83 B.R. 61 (Bankr. N.D.Ala.1988); In re Hunt Energy Co., Inc., 48 B.R. 472 (Bankr. N.D.Ohio 1985); In re Red Oak Farms, 36 B.R. 856 (Bankr. W.D.Mo.1984).

7. Equibank, N.A. v. Wheeling-Pittsburgh Steel Corp., 884 F.2d 80 (3d Cir.1989).

8. 61 B.R. 661 (Bankr. W.D.La.1985).

that the proceeds of the sale will be paid to the creditors with claims or that the money will be held subject to the creditors' security interests.

Prior to the 1984 amendments, (f)(3) required that the price be greater "than the aggregate value of such interest." In 1984 the language was changed to require that the price be greater than "the aggregate value *of all liens on such property.*" [9] At minimum the new language requires the court to consider all security interests, not just the first lien or the one before the court. We believe that the amendments were designed also to make it clear that the debtor must have an equity in the property as a condition to the use of (f)(3). Put another way, we believe the debtor in possession may not use (f)(3) unless the *face amount* of the secured claims against a piece of property are less than the price for which that property will be sold.

Consider, for example, the *Matter of Stroud Wholesale, Inc.*,[10] where the district court reversed the bankruptcy court's sale authorization. There the combination of claims secured by tax liens and other security interests far exceeded the value of the asset. The debtor argued that the sale could be permitted under (f)(3) on the ground that the "value" of the liens could not exceed the value of the property and thus that (f)(3) was satisfied. Of course, that reading makes (f)(3) tautological. If the debtor's only interest in a particular asset is economic, by hypothesis a lien on that asset can have no greater value than the asset itself. Thus, if one were to conclude that (f)(3) were satisfied in such circumstances, it would never fail to be satisfied and it would authorize the sale free of security interests in all cases.

In a contrary decision, *In re Beker Industries Corp.*,[11] Judge Buschman construed (f)(3) to permit a sale even though the debtor had no equity on the ground the "value" of the lien was less than the price at which the property was to be sold. We find the *Beker* analysis unpersuasive. The policy that supports (f)(3) is a policy that says the creditors have no interest in controlling the sale where the debtor has an equity and thus the creditors will be paid 100 cents on the dollar. To read the section otherwise would be to violate that policy and to render most of the rest of (f) insignificant. For example, as long as the property were to be sold at its fair market value, there would never be any requirement for consent under (f)(2) because (f)(3) would always be satisfied. Thus, we agree with the court in *Stroud Wholesale* and read the word "value" in (f)(3) to mean the face amount of the secured debts, not to mean value in the sense in which that term is used in section 506 (where it is limited to the value of the underlying collateral).

To reiterate, consider an example. Assume an asset worth $1,000,000 subject to two mortgages with total claims of $800,000. In such case, (f)(3) would be met because the value (face amount) of all liens would be $800,000. If, however, the two mortgages totalled $1,200,000, (f)(3) would not be

---

9. 11 U.S.C.A. § 363(f)(3) (emphasis added). Section 442(d) of the 1984 Act states that "Section 363(f)(3) of title 11 of the United States Code is amended by striking out 'such interest' the second place it appears and inserting in lieu thereof 'all liens on such property.'" Federal Judgeship Act of 1984, Pub. L. No 98–353 (1984). Weintraub & Resnick believe that the section was amended "to require that the sale price be greater than the aggregate value of all liens on the property. B. Weintraub & A. Resnick, Bankruptcy Law Manual ¶ 4.11 at 4–53 n.8 (rev. ed. 1986). For a similar interpretation, see 2 Collier on Bankruptcy, para. 363.07, pp. 363–30, 31 (15th ed., 1988).

10. 47 B.R. 999 (E.D.N.C.1985).

11. 63 B.R. 474 (Bankr. S.D. N.Y 1986).

satisfied because the value of the mortgages (face amount) would then exceed the price at which the property could be sold. The majority of the courts are in agreement with the *Stroud* case.[12]

Subsection (f)(4) is the statutory descendant of a judge-made rule that permitted certain expedient sales of third party interests.[13] Particularly with an asset that is declining in value or for which there is a current buyer but a doubtful future market, it makes sense for the court to sell the property even though it has not yet established precisely the interests of the various claimants in the property. It is clear that the debtor in possession cannot invoke subsection (4) merely by arguing that the amount of the third party's claim is in doubt;[14] it is properly invoked only when there is a bona fide argument by the DIP that the third party's interest is voidable as a preference under section 547,[15] or under one of the other trustee powers, or where there is some substantive challenge to the interest.

Finally, there is subsection (5), authorization to sell where the third party could be compelled to accept a money satisfaction. Like (f)(4), subsection (f)(5) is a bit of an enigma. On the face of it, every security interest seems to fit under (f)(5) and (f)(5) seems to authorize sale free of every such security interest. The court in *Stroud Wholesale*[16] pointed out that such a holding would render subsections (1) through (4) superfluous in their most common applications. For example, it would never be necessary to get the consent of a secured creditor or to make a finding under subsection (3) that the total amount of the security interest and other liens were less than the value of the property; these sales could be approved automatically under (f)(5). Rejecting that broad interpretation of (f)(5) the court in *Stroud Wholesale* held that (f)(5) could not normally be satisfied unless there was a full satisfaction, namely, full payment of the competing security interests. Of course this reading of (f)(5) still leaves it covering most of the same ground now covered by (f)(3).

What else could it mean? Several courts have held that (f)(5) is satisfied if the court finds the sale and payment of the proceeds to the secured creditor is the kind that could be crammed down under a plan under section 1129(b)(2). Indeed section 1129(b)(2)(A)(ii) refers to sales "subject to section 363(k)" and for security interests to attach to the proceeds of such sales. In dictum the court in *In re Red Oak Farms*[17] found that a sale could be approved under (f)(5) if the secured creditor were given substitute collateral that would be the "indubitable equivalent" under section 1129(b)(2)(A).[18]

12. In re Red Oak Farms, 36 B.R. 856 (Bankr. W.D.Mo.1984); In re Bobroff, 40 B.R. 526 (Bankr. E.D.Pa. 1984); In re Murphy, 34 B.R. 78 (Bankr. D.MD.1983). Cf. Matter of Rouse, 54 B.R. 31 (Bankr. W.D.Mo.1985); In re Hatfield Homes, Inc., 30 B.R. 353 (Bankr. E.D.Pa. 1983) (decided prior to 1984 amendments); but see, In re Terrace Gardens Park Partnership, 96 B.R. 707 (Bankr. W.D.Tex. 1989).

13. See Coulter v. Blieden, 104 F.2d 29, 32 (8th Cir.1939), cert. denied, 308 U.S. 583, 60 S.Ct. 106, 84 L.Ed. 488 (1939).

14. Matter of Stroud Wholesale, 47 B.R. 999 (E.D.N.C.1985).

15. In re Millerburg, 61 B.R. 125 (Bankr. E.D.N.C.1986).

16. Matter of Stroud Wholesale, 47 B.R. 999 (E.D.N.C.1985).

17. 36 B.R. 856 (Bankr. W.D.Mo.1984).

18. For other cases reading § 363(f)(5) to be satisfied where there could have been a sale under § 1129(b)(2), see In re Hunt Energy Co. Inc., 48 B.R. 472 (Bankr. N.D.Ohio 1985); In re Hatfield Homes, Inc., 30 B.R. 353 (Bankr. E.D.Pa. 1983); contra In re Beker Industries Corp., 63 B.R. 474 (Bankr. S.D.N.Y. 1986); cf. In re Wing, 63 B.R. 83 (Bankr. M.D.Fla.1986).

Except for the reference to section 363(k) in section 1129, there is no suggestion in the statutory history or in the statute itself that (f)(5) was intended to be mated with the indubitable equivalent rules in section 1129 and to permit sale in any circumstance in which similar sale could be done under section 1129 as part of a plan. Thus, we are doubtful that Congress intended to authorize sales under (f)(5) every time a sale could have been approved under section 1129(b). On the other hand, if those are not the cases covered by (f)(5), what cases are covered? Rejecting the section 1129 analogy, the court in *Beker* [19] simply says that (f)(5) is to apply to those "few interests" that can be reduced to dollars by operation of law. The court, however, fails to tell what those few interests are and we are uncertain about them. The courts seem equally uncertain about (f)(5)'s application; mostly they have explained why (f)(5) does not apply to the case before them.[20]

In summary, it seems fair to regard section 363(f) mainly as a device designed to protect secured creditors' interests, but also to facilitate sales of assets where the interests of both the secured creditor and the debtor might be served. We believe (f)(2) and (f)(3) should be the work horses. In cases where there is no consent and where the debtor has no equity, we see little value in twisting (f)(1) or (f)(5) to permit sales where the secured creditors are opposed. After all, if the secured creditors' claims exceed the value of the collateral and if those claims are not avoidable, presumably the secured creditors, not the debtor in possession, have the greatest interest in procuring a sale and in such cases it should be their opinion, not that of the debtor in possession to which we should listen.

§ 4–8 Sales Free of Others' Interests—Bidding in: Section 303(k)

When the secured creditor believes its position will be undermined by an unfair sale and section 363(f), or that the court may allow the debtor to use the proceeds in inappropriate ways, the creditor may sometimes be able to protect itself under section 363(k). Unless the court "for cause orders otherwise," the creditor may bid and offset its claim against the purchase price on the sale of the property. Thus, if property is to be put up for auction, the secured creditor can appear and bid its debt if it believes the price is not right, or if it believes that the proceeds will be used inappropriately by the debtor in possession. Then at least it can take away the collateral and resell at its leisure.

---

19. In re Beker Industries Corp., 63 B.R. 474 (Bankr. S.D.N.Y. 1986).

20. For more (f)(5) cases, see In re Wing, 63 B.R. 83 (Bankr. M.D.Fla.1986) ((f)(5) not available where no compelling equitable considerations existed to force creditors to accept less than full money satisfaction for their liens); In re Manning, 37 B.R. 755 (Bankr. D. Colo. 1984), vac'd on other grounds, 831 F.2d 205 (10th Cir. 1987) ((f)(5) would not apply where other members of partnership could not be forced to accept money interest); In re Gerdes, 33 B.R. 860 (Bankr. S.D.Ohio 1983) (would not apply where offering expectancy instead of money); In re Cox Cotton Co., 24 B.R. 930 (E.D.Ark.1982), vac'd, 732 F.2d 619 (8th Cir. 1984), cert. denied 469 U.S. 881, 105 S.Ct. 247, 83 L.Ed.2d 185 (1984), ((f)(5) appropriate where creditor would have to accept money interest in judgment); In re 18th Avenue Development Corp., 14 B.R. 862 (Bankr. S.D.Fla.1981) (reasonable marketing strategy would insure that all lienholders would be protected).

In certain circumstances, of course, the court may choose to forestall such bidding, particularly where a privately negotiated sale seems to be the best mode of disposing of the property and the court fears the secured creditor will merely chill the negotiations by a later bid. Here a court faces the same problem discussed above under section 363(b), namely, the fear that the secured creditor may show up as an eleventh hour bidder after there have been hard negotiations between the debtor in possession and a third party. In *In re Miami General Hospital, Inc.*,[1] the court allowed the bank to bid in its secured debt of $15 million over such an argument. In that case others argued that the bid should not be accepted because the bank's lien was in dispute. Apparently to solve this problem the bank proposed to bid its debt and agreed that if its lien were set aside, it would substitute cash for the debt.

Because the bank had entered into some negotiations with third parties prior to the auction, at least one party argued that the bank had violated section 363(n) by entering into a collusive arrangement. The court properly rejected that argument. When one secured party holds an interest that far exceeds the value of the property, it is only rational to expect some negotiation by potential bidders with that secured creditor.

Any arrangements made by the parties prior to the bidding should be revealed to the court. Absent such revelation, there is potential for collusive arrangement, as, for example, where the secured creditor bids less than the proper value with the understanding that the third party will buy the asset for a higher price from the secured creditor later on. Such an agreement goes well beyond the kind of negotiations in *Miami General Hospital.*

§ 4–9 Sales Free of Others' Interests—Co-owners, Section 363(h)

Section 363(h) deals with the vexing problem that arises when one of two co-owners is in bankruptcy. The section finds its principal use where property is owned as tenants in common or by the entireties or as joint tenants between husband and wife (or between a man and woman who formerly were married), one of whom is in bankruptcy. If all of the conditions are met in (h),[1] the property of both the debtor and of the co-owner can be sold. The sale can occur in the words of (h) only if:

(1) partition in kind of such property among the estate and such co-owners is impracticable;

(2) sale of the estate's undivided interest in such property would realize significantly less for the estate than sale of such property free of the interests of such co-owners;

(3) the benefit to the estate of a sale of such property free of the interests of co-owners outweighs the detriment, if any, to such co-owners; and

§ 4–8
1. 81 B.R. 682 (S.D.Fla.1988).

§ 4–9
1. Unlike (f), subsection (h) is not disjunctive.

(4) such property is not used in the production, transmission, or distribution, for sale, of electric energy or of natural or synthetic gas for heat, light, or power.[2]

An initial question is the constitutionality of this provision. Some co-owners have argued that section 363(h) is unconstitutional as a taking without compensation and without due process under the Fifth Amendment.[3] In some states 363(h) effectively amends the pre-existing state law property rights of an entireties property owner as they existed prior to 1978. It is normally not possible for a creditor of one spouse to force the partition of or to seize the present possessory interest of either spouse when the property is held by the entirety. Section 363(h) purports to grant that power to the trustee in bankruptcy, not merely in the tenancy in common or joint tenancy cases, but also in the entirety cases. Arguably, therefore, the passage of 363(h) was itself a taking in the sense that it diminished the property rights of the non-consenting and non-debtor spouse.

Although the section has been applied in many cases, only one court has squarely faced the constitutional question. *Matter of Tsunis*[4] presented a paradigm entirety scenario where 363(h) allowed the non-debtor's interest, which was inseparable under state law, to be sold along with the debtor's property. In response to the non-debtor's due process argument, the court ruled that such "taking" was constitutional.[5] The court relied on *United States v. Rodgers*,[6] a tax case involving an analogous property situation, where the Supreme Court ruled that the taking was constitutional because compensation was paid to the spouse, and the taking was not a "gratuitous confiscation." The court in *Tsunis* did not address, however, one important basis for *Rodgers* not present in bankruptcy, namely the long-held axiom of tax collection that federal law attaches tax consequences to the property interests defined by state law. In *Rodgers* the Supreme Court also noted that such a result would facilitate the prompt and certain enforcement of the tax laws.[7]

Presumably one can construct exactly the same kind of argument on a bankruptcy law basis that one sees constructed on a tax law basis in *Rodgers*. Surely section 363(h) facilitates prompt and certain enforcement of the bankruptcy law, a bankruptcy law that contains a variety of provisions that alter state law property rights. Of course one can maintain that the owner never had the rights he thought he had under state law, because even those state law rights contain a germ of federal law that could grow into a limitation upon or deprivation of a state law right. Carried to its conclusion this becomes an argument that justifies every federal taking. Although this argument is not entirely satisfactory, it may ultimately carry the day. As it exists, section 363(h) certainly has the utilitarian virtue of providing for

2. 11 U.S.C.A. § 363(h).

3. See In re Levenhar, 24 B.R. 331 (Bankr. E.D.N.Y.1982); Matter of Tsunis, 39 B.R. 977 (E.D.N.Y.1983), aff'd, 733 F.2d 27 (2d Cir. 1984).

4. 39 B.R. 977, 980 (E.D.N.Y.1983), aff'd, 733 F.2d 27 (2d Cir. 1984).

5. Cf. Matter of Spain, 85 B.R. 874 (Bankr. N.D.Ala.1988), rev'd, 103 B.R. 286 (N.D.Ark. 1988) (constitutionality of § 363(h) questioned on jurisdictional grounds).

6. 461 U.S. 677, 103 S.Ct. 2132, 76 L.Ed.2d 236 (1983), on remand, 712 F.2d 990 (5th Cir. 1983).

7. Id. at 683, 103 S.Ct. at 2137, 76 L.Ed.2d at 246.

sensible liquidation and distribution of property, even at the risk of trampling upon state-law property rights and on the state's own power to set those property rights. In general we are not sympathetic to the claims that section 363(h) violates the Constitution, but then we are not confident that we have seen and understood all of the arguments.[8]

Reading the first three conditions under (h), it will come as no surprise that most courts are sympathetic to the usual co-owner's claim and, more often than not, reject the creditor's argument for sale of the homestead over the non-debtor spouse's objection. Representative of the discussions that are hostile to the creditor's claim here is *Matter of Spain*.[9] In that case the court refused the sale on the ground that the benefit did not outweigh the "detriment" to the co-owners. The property at issue was the homestead of the parties. It was subject to an $80,000 mortgage; there was a $15,000 joint exemption and it would have cost approximately $2,500 to sell the property. The court started with $100,000 as the value of the property (that had been the value at the time the petition was filed, although there was evidence nine years later, at the time of the hearing, that the value had risen to $117,000). The court concluded that the payoff to the unsecured creditors would amount to only $2,500 and that the $2,500 benefit did not outweigh the dislocation sufficiently to justify the sale.

Several courts have now openly held that the "detriment" spoken of in (h)(3) can be composed in substantial part of the psychological and emotional injury to the person who is forced to give up his or her home.[10] In the usual case subsection (1) and (2) are met and subsection (4) is not relevant. Ultimately these cases come to an equitable judgment by the court about the economic value to the creditor compared with the emotional and economic loss to the debtor and the co-owner. Because there are many factors at work here, one should not expect fixed rules soon to appear from the cases. The injury to the other party who must move out of the homestead, even though that spouse is not in bankruptcy, is obvious and the courts are appropriately sensitive to it. Less obvious is the factor that seems to exist in some cases, namely, the vindictiveness of a divorced debtor who might derive obscene delight in seeing a former spouse dispossessed of a homestead.[11] Fortunately, where the co-owned property is not the homestead of one of the parties or where the parties are not husband and wife, and where there is a large amount to be gained by the creditors, the courts have allowed sales under (h).[12]

8. For a case where the constitutional argument was raised but not reached, see, In re Levenhar, 24 B.R. 331 (Bankr. E.D.N.Y.1982).

9. 85 B.R. 874 (Bankr. N.D.Ala.1988), rev'd, 103 B.R. 286 (N.D.Ala.1988); see also Matter of Glass, 92 B.R. 880 (Bankr. W.D.Mo. 1988).

10. For a long discussion of this question, see In re Persky, 78 B.R. 657 (Bankr. E.D.N.Y. 1987), aff'd, 108 B.R. 418 (E.D.N.Y.1989); see also In re Coombs, 86 B.R. 314 (Bankr. D. Mass. 1988); In re Addario, 53 B.R. 335 (Bankr. D.Mass.1985); In re Oswald, 90 B.R. 218 (Bankr. N.D.W.Va.1988); In re McCoy, 92 B.R. 750 (Bankr. N.D.Ohio 1988).

11. For cases where these matters may be at work between estranged spouses, see In re Wilson, 85 B.R. 722 (Bankr. E.D.Pa. 1988); In re Coombs, 86 B.R. 314 (Bankr. D.Mass.1988); In re Vassilowitch, 72 B.R. 803 (Bankr. D.Mass.1987); Matter of Ray, 73 B.R. 544 (Bankr. M.D.Ga.1987).

12. In re Vassilowitch, 72 B.R. 803 (Bankr. D.Mass.1987) (permitted sale of former marital home where wife owned two-thirds of a house worth approximately $200,000); Kepler v. Atkinson, 63 B.R. 266 (Bankr. W.D.Wis. 1986) (vacant farm land owned by debtor and her son); In re Bell, 80 B.R. 104 (M.D.Tenn. 1987) (property co-owned by debtor and nine

Doubtless the courts are correct in considering not merely the economic detriment to the co-owner from a sale, but also the emotional and psychological; there remain a few loose ends, however. For example, some courts seem to believe that there is no benefit to the estate unless there would be a payment as a result of the sale to the general creditors of the estate.[13] Others find payment of administrative claims and even payments to secured creditors to be a "benefit to the estate."[14] We agree with the latter conclusion and see no reason to limit the estate's interest to the interest of one set of creditors.

§ 4–10 Application of Section 363(f) and (h) in Unconventional Cases

For full text of this section, see Epstein, Nickles & White, Bankruptcy, Practitioner Treatise Series, Vol. 1.

§ 4–11 Section 364: Introduction

A common reason why debtors file for reorganization under Chapters 11 and 12 is that they are too illiquid to meet their current obligations. Necessarily this condition means that such debtors must be able to borrow while in Chapter 11 if the reorganization provisions of Chapters 11 and 12 are to offer any real hope of avoiding liquidation. Therefore, section 364, titled "Obtaining Credit" is properly regarded as a central provision of the Code; it is one of a handful of critical provisions that affect every successful Chapter 11 reorganization.

Section 364 establishes a hierarchy of postpetition credit. Together with the case law, it makes possible at least six different levels of credit.

The most junior form of postpetition credit is one that no creditor seeks, but some creditors receive. This is postpetition credit sharing parity with the prepetition general creditors. Only a fool or a good friend would willingly extend credit to someone in bankruptcy with the understanding that he would share equally with the pre-existing general creditors.

Those who wind up in that position are mostly those who have extended credit believing it to be covered by section 364(a) (and so entitled to administrative expense treatment) only to find that that is not so. Or they may have loaned under section 364(b) (non-ordinary course) without giving the required notice. As we will see, these creditors are sometimes rudely sent to the purgatory of general credit to punish them for their failure to comply with section 364.

The first level of credit explicitly contemplated by section 364 is that entitled to "priority" under section 503(b)(1) as an administrative expense. That is to say, the typical ordinary course credit in section 364(a) and the typical non-ordinary course credit authorized after notice and a hearing

---

year old son, the smell of a fraudulent conveyance); In re Probasco, 839 F.2d 1352 (9th Cir.1988) (allowed sale of co-owner's interest in a sewer easement); In re Satterfield, 90 B.R. 484 (N.D. Ala. 1988).

13. Matter of Spain, 85 B.R. 874 (Bankr. N.D. Ala.1988), rev'd on other grounds, 103 B.R. 286 (N.D.Ala.1988); see also In re Oberlies, 94 B.R. 916 (Bankr. E.D.Mich.1988).

14. In re Bell, 80 B.R. 104 (M.D.Tenn. 1987); see also In re Haley, 100 B.R. 13 (Bankr. N.D. Cal.1989).

under section 364(b) enjoys administrative expense priority; in any liquidation or in a plan it will be paid before the general creditors are paid.

If the debtor is unable to obtained unsecured credit under (b), it can apply for credit under (c). Credit under (c)(1) may be entitled to administrative expense "super" priority (i.e., administrative expense with a status higher than that of other administrative expenses). Alternatively, the creditor may receive a security interest in property that is unencumbered, or a junior security interest on property that is encumbered. Thus (c) offers us two new levels of credit.

Subsection (d) is the most senior level of credit contemplated by section 364. It may be granted only if there are no lenders willing to lend under (a), (b) or (c), and if there is adequate protection given to other creditors whose interests will be subordinated by the new security. Under (d) the new credit can have a lien "senior or equal" to the existing liens. It truly enjoys "superpriority." As one might expect, the battles in (d) tend to be fought over the question whether there is adequate protection for the existing secured creditor whose interest will be subordinated to the new loan.

The final level of credit, the apotheosis of postpetition credit, is not specifically contemplated by section 364. This is the credit that carries with it "cross-collateralization." In it the creditor bargains not only to have security for its new loan that the creditor will make postpetition, but also to have its prepetition unsecured debt secured by the new collateral. This credit is different from all others under section 364 because it grants security not merely for new dollars put into the estate after the petition, but also for dollars put in before the petition was filed. Cross-collateralization is not covered by section 364 and its status in the law is still uncertain.

Before we go through the various sections of 364 in order, consider the general problems that face the courts in deciding section 364 issues. Commonly a postpetition creditor with the debtor in possession in tow will argue for the most senior form of credit for which any case can be made under section 364. It will be up to the other creditors to show that the debtor could have got credit elsewhere at lesser cost, and it will be up to the judge to determine who speaks the truth. For example, secured credit may be granted under (c) only if the trustee is "unable to obtain unsecured credit allowable under (b)." But how does one determine that the particular creditor who is now willing to lend under (c) or (d) would not have lent under (b)? How does one determine that there are others who will lend under (b) who are not in court? Mostly, these questions are answered by testimony in the first place from the creditor itself and by testimony from the debtor about the many places it has applied for credit and has been rejected.

The trouble with the testimony of the creditor is that it is self-serving. If one were a creditor and were told by his lawyer that he could get security if he refused to lend without security and were then asked what he would wish to do, he could truthfully say that he would not lend without security? Indeed, he would be a fool to lend without security if merely by refusing to do so he could get it. Thus, one should be suspicious of the creditor who is quite willing to lend under (d), but who is offended at the suggestion that it might become a lender unsecured under (b) or with only a junior lien under (c).

One might also be suspicious of the debtor's testimony that it had sought credit in many places and had been rejected. This brings to mind the motorist who dutifully procures three bids for accident repair from body shops, but manipulates them in such a way to insure that the body shop he wishes to use will be the one that is authorized by his insurance company. It will not be difficult for a debtor in possession to procure a handful of loan rejections, for by hypothesis, as a debtor in Chapter 11 he is a pariah already and a whispered aside to the loan officer ("just turn me down, this is only pro forma anyway") may be quite enough to procure a denial.

One fears that the only way a judge is likely to get to the bottom of the question is by playing chicken. Only by denying the motion for superpriority and observing the creditor will one test the truth of the parties' assertions. These are tough decisions for the courts to make, but given the structure of section 364, we think they are unavoidable.

§ 4–12 Ordinary Course and Non-ordinary Course Unsecured Loans, Section 364(a) and (b)

Most cases on the meaning of the phrase ordinary course have arisen under 363, not under section 364. We believe the tests are essentially the same in both sections and that the articulation given by Judge Sofaer in the *Phillips*[1] case works as well in section 364 as in 363. Routine credit purchases of goods and routine draws on lines of credit of the kind experienced in the business prior to the filing of the petition should be recognized as in the ordinary course. Moreover the *Waterfront*[2] elaboration on the *Phillips* test (Is the transaction abnormal because it is too large, even though it falls within the general scope?) is as useful in section 364 as in 363.

Because a loan under section 364(a) or (b) produces a claim against the bankruptcy estate that will receive treatment as an administrative expense and thus enjoy priority under section 503(b)(1), it is possible to find an additional and perhaps different test for "ordinary course" in section 364 than in section 363. For example, in *In re Club Development and Management Corp.*,[3] the court held that the standard for approving a loan under section 364(b) was that the loan standing alone would have met the tests under section 503(b)(1)(A) as an "actual, necessary" cost and expense "of preserving the estate." The court in that case was discussing section 364(b); presumably it would have applied the same rule to section 364(a), for loans under both subsections are treated as administrative expenses. The loans were to pay members of the controlling family $12,700 per month even though debtor in possession had been liquidated and its assets consisted of $2.6 million in cash and a $500,000 promissory note. The court could have

---

§ 4–12

1. In re James A. Phillips, Inc., 29 B.R. 391 (S.D.N.Y. 1983).

2. In re Waterfront Companies, Inc. v. Johnston, 56 B.R. 31 (Bankr. D.Minn.1985); see also, In re C.E.N., Inc., 86 B.R. 303 (Bankr. D.Me.1988).

3. 27 B.R. 610 (Bankr. 9th Cir.1982). For cases denying § 364 motion because loan was not necessary for preserving the estate, see In re Crouse Group, Inc., 71 B.R. 544 (Bankr. E.D.Pa. 1987); Matter of Patch Graphics, 58 B.R. 743 (Bankr. W.D.Wis.1986). For cases where bankruptcy court approved § 364 motion because loan was necessary for preserving the estate, see In re Gloria Mfg. Corp., 47 B.R. 370 (E.D.Va.1984); In re AAA Produce Co., Inc., 58 B.R. 430 (Bankr. E.D.Mo.1986).

easily found such a payment not in the ordinary course and not in the best interest of the estate under section 364(b), but that is not what it said.

In denying the section 364 approval the court relied upon the definition from section 503(b). It found that the loan was not in the ordinary course because it was not necessary for "preserving the estate." We fear that one might read this definition from section 503(b) as substantially more restrictive than a general "ordinary course" rule. For example, a debtor in possession might incur debt to purchase inventory as it had prior to the Chapter 11. Such trade debt would clearly be ordinary course under *Phillips*, yet it might not be regarded as a "necessary cost and expense of preserving the estate." This is particularly true of credit for a line of business that was destined to be abandoned in the reorganization.

We doubt the wisdom of using section 503(b) to impose a higher standard than the *Phillips* "creditors' expectation" test. Use of a more stringent test might force trade creditors who have little knowledge of the specific workings or plans of a Chapter 11 debtor to stop advancing trade credit or risk subordination because, by hindsight, their credit did not constitute an "actual necessary cost or expense of preserving the estate." We think it enough to ask the trade creditors to determine that their extension of credit is generally consistent with their behavior prior to Chapter 11. The imposition of a higher standard might strangle a Chapter 11 debtor by cutting off the flow of trade credit from sellers who could not be assured that they would receive priority.

§ 4–13 Loans With Priority Over Other Administrative Expenses, With Security or With Senior Security, Section 364(c) and (d)

It is not uncommon for existing secured creditors to continue to lend to a debtor in Chapter 11 on terms similar to those that governed their loans prior to the petition. We suspect there are many such loans and they are often authorized without court opinion and without complaint by junior creditors. If that is true, the cases we discuss below under 364(c) and (d) are sports, cases in which the existing secured creditors have thrown in the towel or in which there has been a falling out between the debtor and the existing secured creditor so that the debtor is forced to look elsewhere.

At least in theory the basic tests are relatively straightforward for procuring a loan under section 364(c) or under (d). Turning first to section 364(c), the trustee must show an inability to "obtain unsecured credit allowable under section 503(b)(1) * * * as an administrative expense." As we have indicated, this is done by procuring the testimony of the creditor, and of the debtor about its search for credit and possibly from the testimony of those creditors who have declined to lend. There are no hard and fast rules. Sometimes the cases will be easy, as where a prepetition secured creditor simply wishes to continue lending more or less as it has been lending. Others will be difficult, as where a prepetition unsecured now wishes to be secured.

Under both (c) and (d) the debtor in possession is required to show inability to obtain credit with more generous terms. Most courts require that the debtor show an unsuccessful attempt to procure such credit from more than one creditor. Apart from conclusory statements, the opinions do not disclose how diligent this search must be or how far the mating dance has to go with each of the potential creditors in order for it to count as a turn-down. As we have indicated above, we suspect in some cases this is a minuet, manipulated by the debtor in possession to procure a number of rejections so that it can take the loan it wants with the creditor it wants. Perhaps we are afflicted with an excess of cynicism, but we doubt it.

In other cases the debtor will be so near death's door that no one will seriously challenge the proposition that unsecured credit is unavailable.[1] Thus, the inability to obtain more generous credit is a rather loose standard dependent upon the judge's judgment, and on the circumstances of the particular case. In a case that has been long before a court and struggling in reorganization, it may take little to convince a court to make the proper finding. In others, where other creditors are claiming no attempt to look elsewhere and where the plight of the debtor is not so obvious, the debtor may have to show diligent and dedicated attempts to procure credit on a more generous basis at many other lenders. As the Fourth Circuit put it: the debtor need not look at every possible lender[2] but at least the debtor must do some hunting.[3]

The second condition for procuring credit under section 364(c) and (d) is the same as section 364(b)'s condition, that it be necessary for "preserving the estate." Because credit under section 364(b) receives administrative expense treatment, arguably it must meet the test of administrative expense under section 503(b)(1)(A), which includes only "actual, necessary costs and expenses of preserving the estate." *A fortiori*, if that is a condition to getting credit under section 364(b), it is a condition under (c) and (d).

Often the courts are quite general about these conditions, but some have spelled them out in some detail. For example, *In re Crouse Group Inc.*[4] concluded that a debtor in possession could borrow under section 364(c) only if three conditions were met. First, the debtor in possession had to show that it could not obtain credit unencumbered by super-priority status. Second, it had to show that the credit was necessary to preserve the assets of the estate. Finally, the DIP had to prove that the credit was "fair, reasonable, and adequate."

In *Crouse* the court denied the application on the ground that the debtor had not proved even one of the three conditions. The Crouse group was a collection of contracting companies. It had stopped work on a series of construction projects; the lender who sought superpriority was its bonding company, Federal. The court found that Crouse had failed on the first

§ 4-13

1. See In re Au Natural Restaurant, Inc., 63 B.R. 575 (Bankr. S.D.N.Y. 1986); In re Phoenix Steel Corp., 39 B.R. 218, 222 (D.Del. 1984) (debtor "leveraged out"); Matter of St. Petersburg Hotel Associates, Ltd., 44 B.R. 944 (Bankr. M.D.Fla.1984) ("absolutely no doubt").

2. In re Snowshoe Co., Inc., 789 F.2d 1085 (4th Cir.1986); see also In re Sky Valley, Inc., 100 B.R. 107 (Bankr. N.D.Ga.1988), aff'd, 99 B.R. 117 (N.D.Ga.1989) (debtor satisfied burden of showing that it could not obtain credit other than by granting superpriority lien, though debtor approached a total of only four lenders).

3. In re Reading Tube Industries, 72 B.R. 329 (Bankr. E.D.Pa. 1987)(approached not even one additional potential lender); see also In re Executive Air Services, 62 B.R. 474 (D. Utah 1986); Matter of London, Inc., 70 B.R. 63 (Bankr. E.D.Wis.1987).

4. 71 B.R. 544 (Bankr. E.D.Pa. 1987).

ground because the parent company (which was apparently not in bankruptcy) had assets that it had refused to lend, but might lend in other circumstances, and because it had not even approached either of the two banks who were its largest creditors. Second, the court found it was unclear that the loan would benefit the estate because it suspected that Federal, the bonding company, would replace Crouse as soon as it was able to find a solvent contractor. Thus the credit was "not necessary to preserve the assets of the estate." Finally, it found that the terms of the credit were not fair, reasonable or adequate, mostly because they did not meet the first two tests.

It is unclear where Judge Scholl found his third test. Nothing of that kind appears in the statute and at least in this case that condition seems to add nothing to the first two. We have some doubt therefore whether such a finding should be necessary in order to approve credit under section 364(c) and (d). Reading between the lines of the *Crouse* case, one can imagine tension between the debtor in possession and the creditor and can guess at some of the court's concerns. The court was obviously bothered by the fact that the parent had assets that it would not use for the subsidiaries. It specifically directed that there be no more payments to the vacationing president of the bankrupt company who had been drawing a substantial income. The fact that the debtor had not negotiated with either of its principal secured creditors also bothered the court and suggests there was something unusual in this case. Ultimately the court may have sensed that the bonding company would lend the money because it had no better alternative and thus that the first condition was almost certainly not met. It appears from Judge Scholl's opinion in a later case that is in fact what happened, namely, Federal did extend the money without superpriority.[5]

Matter of Ellingsen MacLean Oil Co. Inc.[6] is probably a more representative case. The debtors in that case were retail sellers of home heating oil in Marquette, Michigan. Late in December they ran out of credit and cash and the debtor in possession petitioned the court to grant super-priority to the banks who would lend money to enable the debtor to purchase heating oil and thus serve its customers (who were about to run out of oil in the bitter northern Michigan winter). Notice was given on an expedited basis to the principal creditors and the hearing was actually held by phone conference call. Subsequently the district court upheld the loan despite the fact that it included a cross-collateralization clause. It concluded that there was no evidence the crisis was "manufactured" and recognized the need for expedited notice and unconventional hearing in the circumstances.

These cases demonstrate the unenviable position of the judge. The judge must often make a judgment on the basis of limited and self-interested testimony about what various actors will do and about the consequences that will befall the debtor if the judge does not grant the requested order. In *Crouse* the judge appears correctly to have read the tea leaves. Whether the judge did so in *Ellingsen* we will never know.

---

5. See In re St. Mary Hospital, 86 B.R. 393, 402 (Bankr. E.D.Pa. 1988).

6. 65 B.R. 358 (W.D.Mich.1986), aff'd, 834 F.2d 599 (6th Cir.1987), cert. denied, 488 U.S. 817, 109 S.Ct. 55, 102 L.Ed.2d 33 (1988); see also In re FCX, Inc., 54 B.R. 833 (Bankr. E.D.N.C.1985); In re AAA Produce Co., Inc., 58 B.R. 430 (Bankr.E.D. Mo.1986); In re Gloria Mfg. Corp., 65 B.R. 341 (E.D.Va.1985).

§ 4–14 Loans With Priority Over Other Administrative Expenses, With Security or With Senior Security, Section 364(c) and (d)—Section 364(d)

Even though section 364(d) is different only in kind from section 364(c), to the creditor it may seem to be a long step beyond (c). The reason is that subsection (d) involves an actual reduction of the status of an existing secured creditor's rights in a particular asset. By authorizing the new creditor to have a senior or equal lien on property that is already subject to a security interest, (d) authorizes an explicit reduction in the rights of the existing creditors. At least in tone, if not in practical effect, this seems a much more serious event, one with dramatic and symbolic qualities that may not be associated with loans under (b) or (c). Because the existing secured creditors' position is going to be usurped by the loan, section 364(d)(1)(B) explicitly requires that there be adequate protection of the existing creditors' rights.

We discuss adequate protection in Chapter 3,[1] but it deserves an additional word here. By hypothesis no loan is permitted under (d) unless the same or similar credit is unavailable under (b) or (c). But if no creditor will lend under (c) against the existing unencumbered asset, or as a junior lienor, or for administrative expense, arguably that in and of itself is good evidence that there will be no adequate protection for the displaced existing creditors! In effect, we would say anytime a debtor makes a case for a loan under section 364(d), it is, by that fact alone, raising a presumption that there will be no adequate protection and thus that the loan should not be permitted.

Because of the explicit reference to adequate protection in section 364(d)(1)(B), the cases under (d) tend to be cases about the valuation of existing assets, about the existence of equity cushion and potential payment to various parties. In section 364(d) cases the courts have not been generous to debtors. They have been appropriately solicitous of the existing secured creditors and have properly concluded, even in some hard cases, that the new loan with superpriority should not be permitted under section 364(d).

To understand how the transaction develops, consider two cases, one in which the loan was granted and one in which it was denied. In *In re Snowshoe*[2] the Court of Appeals affirmed a lower court's granting of a section 364(d) motion for a new loan. The debtor operated a large ski resort in West Virginia that had a value variously estimated at $12 to $35 million. Shenandoah Savings and Loan, the objecting creditor, had an existing first mortgage securing a debt of approximately $13 million. It would have granted a new loan without superpriority, but only on condition that the trustee drop his challenges to the validity of its existing security. Over the objection of Shenandoah, the court approved a loan of up to $2 million by another bank. This bank was granted priority over Shenandoah, who was found to be adequately protected because the court concluded that the value of the ski resort was $19 million.

Here, as in cases under section 364(c), there are a variety of intangible matters at work that probably and properly influenced the court's judgment.

---

§ 4–14
1. See § 3–27 supra.

2. 789 F.2d 1085 (4th Cir.1986).

Among other things, the court pointed out that the application for the loan was by a "respected trustee." In other words, this was not merely a case of a failed debtor putting forward yet another unrealistic estimation. Moreover, the court noted that at the time of the hearing at the Court of Appeals, the loan had been made and a substantial part had already been repaid and there were realistic prospects for repayment of the rest.

Compare *Snowshoe* with *In re Phoenix Steel Corp.*[3] There the debtor owed $26 million to a consortium of French banks and sought to subordinate that loan to a new loan from a subsidiary of the Bank of America. The court engaged in a long and careful analysis of the value of the available collateral and ultimately denied the section 364(d) motion on the ground the French banks could not be offered adequate protection.

The court pointed out that the debtor had lost $6.2 million after the filing of the petition, but before the hearing. It had a severe shortage of cash and was "leveraged out," i.e., almost all of its assets were already subject to security interests. In that case the court denied the loan even though a substantial number of jobs would be lost if the debtor liquidated. Apparently the debtor did liquidate.[4]

Although the (d) cases are first cousins to the cases under (c) and (b), they look quite different. In fact the cases look much more like those one might see under section 362, where a secured creditor is seeking the lifting of the stay so it can foreclose. Like the section 362 cases, those under section 364(d) tend to revolve around the existing value, about the prospects of the debtor and about the impact those prospects will have on those values. Where the equity cushion is large and the prospects are relatively certain and put forward in a business-like and persuasive way, the courts grant section 364(d) loans.[5] Where, on the other hand, the existing values are uncertain, and those values are likely to be undermined by continuing losses, the court will deny section 364(d) coverage.[6]

How, ultimately, does one look at section 364(d)? When does one find its conditions satisfied and when not? Judge Mund, in *In re Chevy Devco,*[7] gives an interesting insight that may be useful both for the parties and for the

---

3. 39 B.R. 218 (D.Del.1984).

4. See In the Matter of Phoenix Steel Corp., 82 B.R. 334 (Bankr. D.Del.1987) (sale of debtor's equipment for cash plus cost of removal was to be accepted where extensive media coverage and advertising could not generate a sale of business as a going concern).

5. For cases where section 364(d) motion was granted, see In re Chicago, Missouri and Western Railway Co., 90 B.R. 344 (Bankr. N.D.Ill. 1988), decision rev'd, 109 B.R. 308 (Bankr.N.D.Ill.1989), dism'd, 899 F.2d 17 (7th Cir.1990); In re Beker Industries Corp., 58 B.R. 725 (Bankr. S.D.N.Y. 1986); In re Dunes Casino Hotel, 69 B.R. 784 (Bankr. D.N.J.1986); In re Snowshoe, 789 F.2d 1085 (4th Cir. 1986); In re Center Wholesale, Inc., 759 F.2d 1440 (9th Cir. 1985), appeal after remand, 788 F.2d 541 (9th Cir.1986); In the Matter of Stanley Hotel, Inc., 15 B.R. 660 (D. Colo. 1981); In re Universal Profile, Inc. 5 B.R. 572 (Bankr. N.D.Ga.1980); In the Matter of Stratbucker, 4 B.R. 251 (Bankr. D.Neb.1980); see also In re Olsen, 87 B.R. 148 (Bankr. D. Colo., 1988); In re Chicago, Missouri & Western Ry. Co., 90 B.R. 344 (Bankr. N.D.Ill. 1988), decision rev'd, 109 B.R. 308 (N.D.Ill.1989), dism'd, 899 F.2d 17 (7th Cir.1990).

6. For cases where section 364(d) motion was denied, see In re Reading Tube Industries, 72 B.R. 329 (Bankr. E.D.Pa. 1987); In re Stacy Farms, 78 B.R. 494 (Bankr. S.D.Ohio 1987); In re Chevy Devco, 78 B.R. 585 (Bankr. C.D.Cal. 1987); In the Matter of St. Petersburg Hotel Assoc., Ltd., 44 B.R. 944 (Bankr. M.D.Fla. 1984); In re Phoenix Steel Corp., 39 B.R. 218 (D.Del.1984); In re Roamer Linen Supply, Inc., 30 B.R. 932 (Bankr. S.D.N.Y. 1983); In re Dunckle Associates, Inc., 19 B.R. 481 (Bankr. E.D.Pa. 1982).

7. 78 B.R. 585 (Bankr. C.D.Cal.1987).

courts as a way to look at such cases. In that case the single asset of the debtor was a small shopping center in Los Angeles. The debtor in possession proposed a new $1.2 million loan and a subordination of the existing tax liens and mortgage loans to the new loan. The loan was to allow for the conversion of a building that had been used as a health club into retail sales and office space. According to the debtor, the conversion would have increased the value of the shopping center by well more than the $1.2 million cost and would have enabled it to produce revenue that would have paid off not only the new loan but also the existing debts.

In denying the debtor's request, the judge makes several points. First, she points out that authorizing a loan of this magnitude on the sole asset of the estate is tantamount to approving a plan of reorganization. She says that the loan should not be approved unless the subordination of the first mortgage could be done under section 1129.[8] The Judge also points out that the debtor is really seeking to make the existing secured creditors into "investors," albeit investors with diminished prospects. As she points out, the typical investor is the first to suffer a loss, but also the one who monopolizes the gains. Where the unwilling investor is a secured creditor with a mortgage, that investor's enjoyment of the additional gains is zero, for its claim rises no higher than its total debt and the interest on it. On the other hand, a substantial increase in debt means that the probability of loss is increased. Thus, in every case in which the debtor is additionally leveraged by new loans the risks of loss are increased, but there are no offsetting increases in the potential benefits to fully secured creditors.

Of course, the judge's point could be made with respect to Chapter 11 as a whole. The very operation of Chapter 11 tends to increase the existing risks of secured (and in some cases of unsecured) creditors, without giving any significant new benefits to them. Nevertheless, Judge Mund's approach seems an appropriate one for testing for the existence of adequate protection under section 364(d)(1)(B). Conceivably, one way to sweeten the adequate protection pot for the secured creditors would be to allow them to share in the gains in return for their giving up a portion of the collateral that would otherwise be theirs. As we indicate above, if that is not done, almost by hypothesis the existing secured creditors' rights are diminished by a new loan under section 364(d). Since by hypothesis the "free assets" or equity cushion are not adequate to induce a third party to loan under section 364(c), only smoke and mirrors will make those assets appear to be sufficient for adequate protection.

In conclusion we share Judge Mund's skepticism about section 364(d) loans. We believe they should be granted only in the extraordinary cases and that the courts and debtors should listen with a sympathetic mind to the arguments of the existing secured creditors.

§ 4–15 Payment of and Granting Security for Prepetition Debt: Herein of Cross–Collateralization and *Texlon*

All of the cases that we discuss above under section 364 deal with new credit—credit granted the debtor *after* the debtor has filed a petition in

---

8. In this case she finds it could not have been done, but, of course, that would not always be true. There could have been an "indubitable equivalent" under section 1129(b).

Chapter 11. The section is entitled "Obtaining Credit" and contemplates only postpetition debt and the granting of security under (c) and (d) for that debt.

Section 363's relation to prepetition debt is less clear. The cases under section 363 also deal almost exclusively with the transfer of property after the petition and with the "use" of cash to pay not prepetition, but postpetition debt that arose under section 364. It is fair, therefore, to characterize the many terms of sections 363 and 364 as dealing largely, if not exclusively, with the incurring of postpetition debt, with the payment of that debt under section 363 and with other postpetition transfers under section 363.

What then of the postpetition liability to the various prepetition creditors? To what extent may these be paid under section 363 or be granted security under section 364 or under the common law of bankruptcy?

It is tempting to read the Bankruptcy Code to say that no prepetition debt may ever be paid under section 363 or secured under section 364 and that all such debt must await ultimate disposition in a liquidation or in a plan approved under section 1129. Indeed, the very idea of bankruptcy is that creditors similarly situated at the time of filing be treated the same, namely, to wait. A central purpose of the avoidance powers, such as section 547, is to reign in the swift and to control the meanest and most powerful creditors in the exercise of their particular state law rights that might otherwise allow them to enjoy payment when others, less aggressive or less powerful would not be paid.[1]

Moreover, one can cite a number of sections that collectively seem to say that no prepetition creditor should be paid or should receive security except as part of a liquidation or a plan. Most explicit is section 549 that prohibits postpetition transfers of the property of the estate unless it is authorized "under this title or by the court." Section 1123(a)(4) states that members of the same class must be treated the same; that implies that neither of two general creditors should be treated better than the other. There are also implications from section 547 (which does not apply directly here because it deals only with prepetition payments) and from section 1129(a)(3) requiring good faith, that similarly situated creditors be treated the same. Thus, the grand idea, bringing all creditors before a single court and there disabling their state-law and self-help weapons, is supported by individual specific sections such as sections 549, 1123(a)(4), and by the implications from other sections.

Yet it is clear that this theoretical barrier to special treatment for the mean and powerful in fact gives way, more than occasionally. The most

§ 4–15

1. The reported objectives of section 547, in regard to preferences, are as follows:

The purpose of the preference section is two-fold. First, by permitting the trustee to avoid prebankruptcy, creditors are discouraged from racing to the courthouse to dismember the debtor during his slide into bankruptcy. The protection thus afforded the debtor often enables him to work his way out of a difficult financial situation through cooperation with all his creditors.

Second, and more important, the preference provisions facilitate the prime bankruptcy policy of equality of distribution among creditors of the debtor ... The operation of the preference section to deter the "race of diligence" of creditors to dismember the debtor before bankruptcy furthers the second goal of the preference section—that of equality of distribution.

H.R. Rep. No. 595, 95th Cong., 1st Sess. 177–179, reprinted in 1978 U.S. Code Cong. & Admin. News 5963, 6138.

prominent recurring question involves "cross-collateralization" proposals under which prepetition, unsecured debt is secured by postpetition assets and so is lifted higher than its siblings in the unsecured prepetition class. But there are also cases in which courts authorize the outright payment of prepetition debt.

Consider again *In re James A. Phillips, Inc.*[2] Phillips, a subcontractor, had nearly completed two jobs in which it was owed $27,294 and $104,306 respectively. It owed two suppliers $10,065 and $36,665 respectively on the two jobs. Under New York law the suppliers had the right to perfect a mechanic's lien and those liens would have been valid in bankruptcy under section 546(b). In addition, Phillips was owed $42,261 on a third job and it owed its supplier on that job $69,421. The third supplier also had the power to exercise a mechanic's lien against the job.

The bankruptcy judge authorized Phillips' payment of all the suppliers without notice to the other creditors or the opportunity for a hearing. On appeal Judge Sofaer affirmed that finding. Although the court never says so, it appears to have relied on section 363 to authorize the debtor's payment. The contesting creditor argued the payment was not an ordinary course payment under section 363, and therefore that notice was required. By implication that argument concedes that section 363 would have covered the transaction and that it might have been within the power of the court to have authorized a payment after hearing. Presumably one "use" of money is to pay debt and it is clear that section 363 authorizes the payment of postpetition debt. Because subsections 363(b) and (c) make no reference to the time when such a debt arose, they can be read, as Judge Sofaer apparently read them, to authorize payment of prepetition debt.

Although such payments are in conflict with the general principles discussed above, one could fit them technically within section 549(a)(2)(B) as authorized "under this title" by section 363—if that is what 363 means.

Of course section 363 cannot possibly contemplate payment of some debts and a refusal to pay others willy nilly, and—if it contemplates payment of some—which are those? It is easy to see why the debtor wished to make payment to the general contractors in the first two cases in *Phillips*. By paying approximately $46,000, it stood to recover more than $131,000 from the general contractors. Faced with the threat of mechanics' liens to be asserted against their jobs by the suppliers, the general contractors threatened not to pay and undoubtedly would have had a right at minimum to set off sufficient funds to pay the mechanics' liens. At least in those two cases it makes sense to allow Phillips to pay and thus to recover a net benefit of nearly $90,000.

If there had been a hearing and the suppliers and general contractors were called before the court, the court could have ordered the payments and then have either granted the payments directly to the suppliers or given them adequate protection in the form of a lien on the money so paid or on other assets of the debtor. In any event, as Judge Sofaer points out, it is hard to see how any creditors were injured by payments in those two cases.

2. 29 B.R. 391 (S.D.N.Y. 1983).

The same is not true of the third case. There the debtor paid $69,000 in order to recover $42,000 at the most. Even if that payment were thought necessary to maintain Phillips' position on the job, it is hard to see how it should be approved from the facts that are recited in the court's opinion. Particularly because of this third part of the transaction, we have difficulty justifying the *Phillips* outcome.

We suspect, however, that payments are routinely made to certain creditors who are particularly powerful and obstreperous. For example, we would wager a small amount of money on the proposition that employees are routinely paid wages earned prior to the filing of the petition out of postpetition funds. Of course these employees would enjoy priority status under section 507(a)(3), but that does not entitle them to payment in advance of other priority claimants, particularly in circumstances where there are few assets in the estate and the administrative expenses might eat up all of the available funds. Without justifying such payments under any particular section of the Act or Code, former Judge Ordin has candidly admitted authorizing such payments to key creditors.[3]

Presumably most of these payments were done under the pre-Code law where the "necessity of payment" rule (from railroad reorganization law) arguably authorized them. It is unclear that the necessity of payment doctrine survived the enactment of the Code; we doubt that it did. In *Matter of B & W Enterprises Inc.*,[4] Judge Young ordered a series of suppliers to disgorge postpetition payments of prepetition debt. These were payments for prepetition diesel fuel obligations and other expenses in connection with a trucking business. There Judge Young concluded section 1171(b) along with section 103(g) had restricted the necessity doctrine to railroad reorganizations. Without specific reference to the necessity doctrine, Judge Lundin, in *McCormick Enterprises*,[5] ruled that the postpetition payment for prepetition debt was a direct violation of section 549 and had to be disgorged.

Because of the large temptation for the debtor to favor one creditor who is particularly important for its survival, we favor the courts' conclusions in *McCormick Enterprises* and *B & W*. We are sympathetic to Judge Sofaer's decision in *Phillips,* but only as to the first two situations, and even there we would think that the transaction could be better handled by an order and a grant of adequate protection to the parties asserting the lien. We believe vigilance is important here because the debtor is essentially spending other people's money. Where the debtor has individually guaranteed the debt to be paid, the incentive to pay that debt with other's money is redoubled by the debtor's desire to avoid personal liability. For those reasons we would read section 549 broadly and read the authorization to pay under section 363 narrowly.

---

3. R.L. Ordin, Case Comment 54 Am. Bankr. L.J. 173, 177 (1980) ("I can recall authorizations to pay: (i) prepetition wages to key employees; (ii) hospital malpractice premiums incurred prior to filing; (iii) debts to suppliers of unique and irreplaceable 'widgets'; and (iv) peripheral benefits under labor contracts. These orders typify the twilight zone: struggles for survival, played against a background of economic chaos and disintegration.").

4. 19 B.R. 421 (Bankr. D.Idaho 1982), aff'd, 713 F.2d 534 (9th Cir. 1983).

5. In re Tom McCormick Enterprises, Inc., 26 B.R. 437 (Bankr. M.D.Tenn.1983); see also In re 222 Liberty Associates, 94 B.R. 381 (Bankr. E.D.Pa. 1988), order rev'd, 110 B.R. 686 (E.D.Pa.1989).

The foregoing cases are only egregious examples of the more widely known and commonly recognized cross-collateralization case in which the creditor does not seek payment, but asks instead for security for a prepetition debt. Typically this security is an inducement for the creditor to make a postpetition loan.

By way of definition first consider two cases that are sometimes described as "cross-collateralization" cases, but which do not in fact present the issues with which we are concerned. Assume, for example, that the creditor proposes making a new loan to the debtor after the petition and provides that the loan will be secured by pre- and postpetition assets. Although this is "cross-collateralization" in the sense that the postpetition loan will be secured by prepetition assets, it is explicitly provided for in the Code and does not violate the Code policies. This is the very case considered above under section 364(c) and (d). Those sections explicitly authorize the court to grant security under the conditions that we have discussed in the foregoing sections. There is no limitation on the kind of security that can be given; in the usual case, much of the collateral offered (real estate would be an example) must have been owned by the debtor prior to the petition. This, then, is a case that Congress explicitly considered and authorized. It is bounded by the protections that we have discussed and that Congress explicitly provided and it is clearly within the authority of the court to grant it.[6]

Also identified as cross-collateralization cases, but distinguishable in our minds, are the cases of creditors who were fully secured prepetition and who ask that their postpetition lending and prepetition lending be secured by postpetition assets. If the creditor is fully secured at the time the petition is filed, it is entitled to adequate protection under section 362, and leaving it fully secured by either pre- or postpetition assets causes no injury to other creditors. Unlike *Phillips* and unlike the cross-collateralization cases discussed below, there is no potential for improving the position of a fully secured creditor by allowing that debt to be secured by postpetition collateral. By hypothesis, had there been liquidation on the date the petition was filed, the creditor would have been paid in full. Merely to permit that loan to be secured by postpetition collateral is to do no more than would have been required under section 362. Of course, there is a possibility that a creditor might exaggerate the value of its collateral at the date the petition was filed and thus enjoy more protection than it is entitled to. Short of that, we see no reason why the creditor's request ought not be granted in a case like this and why this ought not be treated as quite different from the classic cross-collateralization case discussed below. Indeed, there may well be other reasons why it should be done, for the creditor might find efficiencies in administering both pre- and postpetition loans as a single loan with claims on a single set of collateral. There surely are some costs involved in segregating such loans. If the court concludes that there should be no postpetition payment of interest on the prepetition loan, that item will have to be factored into the formula for the combined loan, but there is no reason why that could not be done.

---

6. See In re Antico Manufacturing Co., Inc., 31 B.R. 103 (Bankr. E.D.N.Y.1983).

Finally, we come to the true and difficult cross-collateralization cases. These sometimes pass under the rubric of the "*Texlon*" cases, named for the opinion *In re Texlon Corp.*[7] by Judge Friendly, who discussed the matter at great length. *Texlon* was decided under the Bankruptcy Act of 1898. When the petition was filed, the creditor was owed $1,000,000, partially secured. The creditor proposed to lend more money to the debtor in return for security for the pre- and postpetition debt. Without notice to other creditors the bankruptcy judge approved the arrangement *ex parte* and the creditor ultimately lent $667,000 postpetition. Upon liquidation and after payment of the postpetition loans, there remained $267,000 which the lender claimed as security to satisfy its prepetition loan.

Reversing the bankruptcy judge's ruling, Judge Friendly held against the creditor. The holding is based upon the fact that the bankruptcy judge gave no notice to the other creditors. In dictum, Judge Friendly casts doubt upon the wisdom of cross-collateralization:

> a financing scheme so contrary to the spirit of the Bankruptcy Act should not have been granted by an ex parte order, where the bankruptcy court relies solely on the representations by a debtor in possession that credit essential to the maintenance of operations is not otherwise obtainable. The debtor in possession is hardly neutral.[8]

The court went on to say that it need not find that all cross-collateral arrangements were invalid in order to reach the decision.

Thus, Judge Friendly has given a little to both sides in the cross-collateralization debate. Declining to rule such a proposal to be impermissible under the pre-Code law, he nevertheless held against the creditor in the case before him and cast doubt on the wisdom of cross-collateralization arrangements.

The issue has come up in a handful of cases since *Texlon*. Cross-collateralization has been permitted in many of them, but grudgingly so. For example, in *In re Tennessee Wheel & Rubber Co.*,[9] the court allowed a cross-collateralization clause because no other creditor challenged it. Judge Lundin cautiously stated that he need express "no opinion of the general propriety" of cross-collateralization.[10] In *In re Adams Apple, Inc.*,[11] Judge Fletcher happily avoided a ruling on the merits of cross-collateralization by ruling that section 364(e) precluded a challenge to the cross-collateralization provision.

The closest thing to an indorsement of the idea is found in *In re Vanguard Diversified, Inc.*[12] There the court adopts the four-part test proposed by Professor Weintraub and Mr. Resnick.[13] It concludes that cross-collateralization should be permitted only if the four following conditions are met: (1) the creditor will not survive without the loan; (2) the debtor is

---

7. 596 F.2d 1092 (2d Cir.1979).

8. Id. at 1098.

9. 64 B.R. 721 (Bankr. M.D.Tenn.1986), order aff'd, 75 B.R. 1 (Bankr.M.D.Tenn.1987).

10. Id. at 723 n.1.

11. 829 F.2d 1484 (9th Cir.1987).

12. 31 B.R. 364 (Bankr. E.D.N.Y.1983); see also In re Tenney Village Co., Inc., 104 B.R. 562, 569–70 (Bankr. D.N.H.1989).

13. See Weintraub & Resnick, Cross-Collateralization of Prepetition Indebtedness as an Inducement for Postpetition Financing: A Euphemism Comes of Age, 14 UCC L.J. 86, 90 (1981).

unable to gets loans from alternative sources on acceptable terms; (3) the proposed lender, who proposes to make the cross-collateralized loan, will not agree to lend without a cross-collateralization; and (4) the loan is in the best interest of the creditors.

It is not surprising that the tests look quite familiar to one who has studied the cases under sections 364(b), (c) and (d). On the other hand, the four tests suffer from exactly the same problem here that they do in section 364(d), namely, the questions posed answer themselves; they are likely to be answered in a highly predictable and self-interested way by the lender's agents. For example, in *Vanguard,* Ms. Cohen, the agent of Bank Leumi, the creditor, testified that her bank would not make the loan on any other terms. She and others, of course, testified that the debtor would have to be liquidated if the loan were not made. Here, as in section 364(d), the court cannot test such assertions except by playing chicken with the debtor, namely, by denying the order and observing the lender to see if the lender makes the additional loans notwithstanding the lender's testimony. It is not an enviable position for the court to be in, but we see no way out of it. Ultimately if the court is to allow cross-collateralization, the courts will have to make the kind of ad hoc judgments based on faulty information that will be made under section 364(c) and section 364(d). Neither the four *Vanguard* tests nor any other will substitute for a court's good sense, based on many factors about the probability of a loan without a cross-collateralization and about the need for the loan.

On the other side of the fence, one court has held flatly that cross-collateralization is not permitted under the Bankruptcy Code. In *In re Monach Circuit Industries,*[14] Judge Goldhaber refused a creditor's request for security for a prepetition loan of approximately $500,000. The judge held that such a provision would violate the policy of section 547 and concluded that section 364 permitted only postpetition loans and, by implication, denied the power to grant security for prepetition loans.[15]

Clearly the courts are nervous here, and well they should be. Allowing a postpetition security for a prepetition unsecured loan conflicts with all the same principles and sections that were discussed above in connection with the payment of a prepetition loan. Indeed, cross-collateralization may be even more corrosive than an outright payment of the loan because it often will be unclear to all but the creditor itself (and possibly to the debtor in possession) about the magnitude of the diversion of assets that is likely to occur. Other creditors may believe the proponent of such a plan is already

---

14. 41 B.R. 859 (Bankr. E.D.Pa. 1984); see also In re J.L. Graphics, Inc., 62 B.R. 750 (Bankr. D.N.H.1986), aff'd, In re Cross Baking Co., 818 F.2d 1027 (1st Cir. 1987).

15. For cases allowing cross-collateralizations, see In re Adams Apple, Inc., 829 F.2d 1484 (9th Cir.1987) (section 364(e) forecloses challenge); In re Tennessee Wheel & Rubber Co., 64 B.R. 721 (Bankr. M.D.Tenn.1986), order aff'd, 75 B.R. 1 (Bankr.M.D.Tenn.1987) (no challenge); In re Beker Industries Corp., 58 B.R. 725 (Bankr. S.D.N.Y. 1986) (unsecured creditors consented); In re FCX, Inc., 54 B.R. 833 (Bankr. E.D.N.C.1985) (postpetition security okay for prepetition loan that was fully perfected and covered by existing collateral); see also Matter of Borne Chemical, Inc., 9 B.R. 263 (Bankr. D.N.J.1981); In re Roblin Industries, Inc., 52 B.R. 241 (Bankr. W.D.N.Y.1985) (applies Vanguard test); cf. Matter of Texas Research, Inc., 862 F.2d 1161 (5th Cir.1989); In re Ellingsen MacLean Oil Co., 834 F.2d 599 (6th Cir.1987), cert. denied, 488 U.S. 817, 109 S.Ct. 55, 102 L.Ed.2d 33 (1988); In re B & W Tractor Co., Inc., 38 B.R. 613 (Bankr. E.D.N.C. 1984); In re General Oil Distributors, Inc., 20 B.R. 873 (Bankr. E.D.N.Y.1982).

fully secured, or nearly so, when the proponent may know that is not true. Others may believe there are few postpetition assets when a proponent knows that there are or there can be generated a substantial number of postpetition assets that will be subject to the proposed security interest. Thus, there is the possibility where security is granted that the debtor will really make a large and secret payment that appears small and insignificant and thus does not arouse the interest of competing creditors.

This quality of uncertainty, moreover, is what distinguishes the cross-collateralization from other forms of outright payment for a postpetition loan. For example, one might argue that cross-collateralization should be permitted as a mode of paying for a postpetition loan since the interest and other payments to be made under that loan are themselves merely a transfer of wealth of the debtor to the creditor in return for making the postpetition loan. What then, the argument goes, distinguishes this relatively high interest rate charged on the postpetition loan from a cross-collateralization, which is merely another form of payment? One answer is the point made in the immediately preceding paragraph, namely, the form and amount of the payment in a cross-collateralization case may be large and well known to the creditor, but unknown to and carefully hidden from competing creditors.

If cross-collateralization were routinely denied, would the bankruptcy world change? Arguably any cross-collateralization arrangement has a monetary value and that monetary value could be replaced by a direct payment for the postpetition loan. This payment could come in the form of added interest over the life of the loan or of an outright fee. So we are unsure.

Because cross-collateralization is in fundamental conflict with the basic policies of the Bankruptcy Code and with various sections such as 549 and 1123, and because it offers substantial potential for undisclosed overpayment, we believe that courts should be hesitant in approving cross-collateralization. We are not prepared to say that it should never be done; but, for the reason suggested, we think it should be infrequent. We are inherently doubtful of the protestations of creditors who say they will lend if they get cross-collateralization, but will not do so under any circumstances if they fail to get it. A flat rule to deny cross-collateralization would at least have the virtue of minimizing duplicitous testimony by loan officers in front of bankruptcy judges.

In any event, the secured creditor should be regarded as not more than a particularly powerful creditor, like those identified by Judge Ordin, who is seeking to overturn the theoretical balance that the filing in bankruptcy strikes among the various creditors. We believe that such credit should never be approved without notice and that if there are objections when notice has been given, courts should rarely approve it. If it is denied, in some cases the creditors will nevertheless lend and in others, liquidation may occur; but even then there may be no loss if there was no going concern value.

§ 4–16 Notice and Hearing Under Sections 363 and 364

Sections 363(b)(1) and 364(b), (c), and (d) all provide that action may be taken only "after notice and a hearing." An innocent reader of these provisions might conclude that no sale or use under 363(c) and no loan under 364(b), (c), or (d) thus could occur without an actual hearing before a bankruptcy judge. That would be wrong. Section 102(1) defines "after notice and a hearing" as follows:

(1) "after notice and a hearing", or a similar phrase—

(A) means after such notice as is appropriate in the particular circumstances, and such opportunity for a hearing as is appropriate in the particular circumstances; but

(B) authorizes an act without an actual hearing if such notice is given properly and if—

(i) such a hearing is not requested timely by a party in interest; or

(ii) there is insufficient time for a hearing to be commenced before such act must be done, and the court authorizes such act[.] [1]

Note particularly section 102(1)(B) which tells us there can be a hearing without there being a hearing provided there is insufficient time or, in the more common case, no party in interest requests one. Thus, there must be many cases in which the debtor in possession proposes to sell an asset or to borrow money, sends notice to that effect to various creditors and, receiving no timely objection, proceeds with the sale or loan without a court hearing.

Note that the language of section 364 is slightly different from the language of section 363. Section 363(b) simply permits the sale if there is notice and no objection. Section 364(b), (c), and (d), on the other hand, does not permit the loan, rather it permits "the court" to authorize the loan. Thus, presumably, if one were careful, he would always procure a court order under 364; this would not be necessary under section 363(b), but it might be the sensible thing to do even there.

Although detailed consideration of the form, timing, and procedure on notice is beyond the scope of this book, we spend a moment to identify the relevant bankruptcy rules. The basic notice requirement is Rule 2002. Rule 2002(a) requires 20 days notice to the parties in interest in the usual case. Rule 2002(c) requires that the notice state "the time and place of any public sale, the terms and conditions of any private sale and the time fixed for filing objections." Rule 6004 is an elaboration of 2002. It distinguishes among conventional sales under section 363(b)(2), sales free and clear of liens and other interests, and sales of property under $2,500. It makes it clear that there need be no hearing in the ordinary section 363(b) case if there is no objection and under Rule 6004(d) it permits a general notice without specifically identifying property where all the non-exempt property of the estate has a gross value of less than $2,500.

On the other hand, Rule 6004(c) appears to contemplate an actual hearing and a more formal motion where the sale will be free of liens or other interests. Rule 6004(c) contains a specific cross reference to Rule 9014 "Contested Matters." Presumably one should look at his or her own local rules and customs to see how local bankruptcy judges handle those. At minimum they contemplate "a court order" in cases under section 363(f) and

§ 4–16

1. 11 U.S.C.A. § 102(1).

(g); apparently they also contemplate an actual appearance in open court even in the absence of an objection to the motion. In Rule 9013, such a motion must state "with particularity the grounds therefor." One would expect, therefore, that a motion to sell under section 363(f) would state the facts and make appropriate references to the subsection so that the recipient of the motion could understand what the claim was to be.[2]

To summarize the conventional cases, one should understand that despite the requirement for "notice and a hearing," there need not be any hearing in many of the cases unless there is a request for one by an objecting party. Second, one should see that the requirements are somewhat more stringent when one wishes to sell property out from under a creditor's security interest or a co-owner's interest than when there is no such specific claim in the property. Finally, one should note that the bankruptcy court has broad powers both to shorten the 20-day notice period provided in Rule 2002(a) and to direct that notice be given by a method other than mail. Such authority is granted in 2002(a) and also in Rule 9006(c). A court's power to alter the notice and shorten the time is subject to a variety of limitations that we do not consider.

The need for a shorter time and quicker notice commonly arises where the debtor will not be able to continue its operation without a loan and the prospective creditor will not lend unless it is given the protection under sections 364(b), (c), or (d). *In re Ellingsen MacLean Oil Co.*[3] is a nice illustration of the problem. Recall in *Ellingsen* the debtor was a retail home heating oil seller in Marquette, Michigan. Its lender was willing to give additional credit, but only if it received security. Ellingsen needed the credit in order to procure oil to meet its sales obligations to consumers in the middle of winter in Marquette, Michigan. In response to that crisis the court authorized telex and telephone notice and, in fact, conducted the hearing by conference call.

Such emergency circumstances are much more likely to arise under section 364 than under section 363. As *Ellingsen* and other cases demonstrate the bankruptcy courts have considerable discretion when they are faced with such circumstances and are not likely to be reversed on appeal.[4]

---

2. Failure to give proper notice may invalidate the section 363 or section 364 transaction. See In re Fernwood Markets, 73 B.R. 616 (Bankr. E.D.Pa. 1987); MRR Traders, Inc. v. Cave Atlantique, Inc., 788 F.2d 816 (1st Cir. 1986); In re First Baptist Church, Inc., 564 F.2d 677 (5th Cir. 1977); In re Stanley Engineering Corp., 164 F.2d 316 (3d Cir. 1947), cert denied, 332 U.S. 847, 68 S.Ct. 351, 92 L.Ed. 417 (1948); In re First Internat'l Services Inc., 25 B.R. 66 (Bankr. D.Conn.1982); In re Foster, 19 B.R. 28 (Bankr. E.D.Pa. 1982).

3. 65 B.R. 358 (W.D.Mich.1986), aff'd, 834 F.2d 599 (6th Cir.1987), cert. denied, 488 U.S. 817, 109 S.Ct. 55, 102 L.Ed.2d 33 (1988).

4. For section 364(b) and section 364(c) cases, see In re Ellingsen MacLean Oil Co., 65 B.R. 358 (W.D.Mich.1986), decision aff'd, 834 F.2d 599 (6th Cir.1987), cert. denied, 488 U.S. 817, 109 S.Ct. 55, 102 L.Ed.2d 33 (1988) (telex, letters, telephone notice and immediate authorization of section 364(c) held proper where heating oil needed to be purchased); In re AAA Produce Co., 58 B.R. 430 (Bankr. E.D.Mo.1986) (limited notice, expedited hearing proper where great need on part of debtor); In re FCX, Inc., 54 B.R. 833 (Bankr. E.D.N.C.1985) (four day notice by telephone and mailgram sufficient where business would deteriorate); In re Adamson Co., 29 B.R. 937 (Bankr. E.D.Va.1983); Matter of Sullivan Motor Sales, 2 B.R. 350 (Bankr. D.Me.1980) (business needed to be threatened with "irreparable injury"); In re Monach Circuit Industries, Inc., 41 B.R. 859 (Bankr. E.D.Pa. 1984) (very high showing needed to forego at least telephone notice).

For a section 364(d) case, see In re Center Wholesale, Inc., 759 F.2d 1440 (9th Cir.1985), appeal after remand, 788 F.2d 541 (9th Cir.

§ 4–17 Appeals, Sections 363(m) and 364(e)

Sections 363(m) and 364(e) are nearly identical. The first provides:

> The reversal or modification on appeal of an authorization under subsection (b) or (c) of this section of a sale or lease of property does not affect the validity of a sale or lease under such authorization to an entity that purchased or leased such property in good faith, whether or not such entity knew of the pendency of the appeal, unless such authorization and such sale or lease were stayed pending appeal.

The other, section 364(e), provides:

> The reversal or modification on appeal of an authorization under this section to obtain credit or incur debt, or of a grant under this section of a priority or lien, does not affect the validity of any debt so incurred, or any priority or lien so granted, to an entity that extended such credit in good faith, whether or not such entity knew of the pendency of the appeal, unless such authorization and the incurring of such debt, or the granting of such priority or lien, were stayed pending appeal.

The former protects any purchaser who buys or leases property in good faith from the bankruptcy estate, and the latter protects a lender who extends credit in good faith from reversal on appeal. The subsections explicitly protect the buyer in the one case and the lender in the other, even though they knew of the pendency of the appeal.

The fear the drafters are seeking to assuage is obvious. Necessarily bankruptcy is a contentious setting; almost always some party will believe that a proposed sale under section 363 or a loan under section 364 is contrary to its interest and can argue that it is a violation of the provisions of the Code. Since such sales under section 363 and loans under section 364 are usually made in the presence of such inchoate threats or challenges, the drafters feared the buyers would not buy from sellers in bankruptcy and the lenders would not lend to them. By foreclosing appeal—except where there has been something tantamount to bad faith—the Congress has taken extraordinary measures to encourage purchases and loans.

The general message of these sections is that one must protest before the bankruptcy judge, and if a person is not successful there, must get a stay pending the appeal, or forsake his case. Even where the bankruptcy judge has misread the law or granted an impermissible right to a lender or buyer, the decision cannot be overturned on appeal if the buyer purchased in good faith or the lender made its loan in good faith.

In general the courts have been true to these sections: the district and circuit courts have been appropriately hesitant to overturn bankruptcy judges' decisions. We suspect the Congress and the courts were right in trading the challengers' due process rights of appeal for the speed and certainty that may have been necessary, particularly under section 364, to allow transactions needed to keep the debtor in business. In many cases a sale or a loan will provide capital that is critical to the continued operation of the debtor. In at least some and perhaps many of those cases, the losses that will result from even a temporary cessation of business will foreclose

1986) (one day notice violated Due Process Clause).

the possibility of a successful reorganization. If one balances that fact against the possibility that a bankruptcy judge is likely to be at least as wise and well informed as a district judge or a judge on a court of appeals, the trade is relatively easy to make.

Because the transactions contemplated by the two sections are a bit different, the consequences of undoing one transaction as opposed to the other also differ. Presumably the consequence of overturning a section 363 transfer on appeal would be to require the buyer to disgorge the property or its value. On the other hand, disallowing a loan under section 364 is not likely to cause the transaction to be undone. In that case the debtors will have spent the money and thus will be unable to return the loan and put the lender back in the status quo. The consequence of reversal on appeal under section 364 is a reduction in priority of the lender's claim. Thus, for example, if a loan made with security under section 364(c) were deemed to have been improperly made and reversed on appeal, the security would be withdrawn and the lender would be treated as a creditor with an administrative claim or possibly even as a general creditor. For those reasons more is at stake on appeal under section 364 than under section 363. The one who disgorges in section 363 merely loses its expectancy. The lender who is subordinated under section 364 may lose not only its expectancy (the interest payment), but also its capital.

For the most part, section 364(e) has worked fairly effectively. In *In re Ellingsen*[1] the debtor's customers needed fuel oil at once. The court held a telephone hearing and authorized the loan. The court of appeals affirmed the lower court's order despite the fact there was a cross-collateralization clause and in the face of an argument that section 363(e) did not protect cross-collateralization. *Ellingsen* is representative of the cases where the section seems to have worked in a conventional and effective way.[2]

But there are some holes in the safety net of 364(e). For example, in *In re St. Mary Hospital*[3] the court granted an emergency order to allow a parent to lend $700,000 to a failing subsidiary hospital with security in certain previously unencumbered assets and with priority over administrative expenses. The original emergency order contained a waiver of the lender's 364(e) rights. A later hearing produced angry testimony by the operators of the hospital that the parent-lender was actually "manufacturing" the crisis and manipulating the hospital to produce its closure without complying with various rules and regulations. The court then withdrew its authorization for priority as an administrative expense and left the lender (who in the meantime had extended the $700,000) as a general creditor. The lessons of the case are fairly clear. A lender's bargaining leverage in Chapter 11 is greatest before it has extended the money and only reluctantly should it make the loan if it will not receive the protection of section 364(e).[4]

§ 4–17

1. Matter of Ellingsen MacLean Oil Co. Inc., 65 B.R. 358 (W.D.Mich.1986), aff'd, 834 F.2d 599 (6th Cir.1987), cert. denied, 488 U.S. 817, 109 S.Ct. 55, 102 L.Ed.2d 33 (1988).

2. For other cases, see e.g., Matter of Stanley Hotel, Inc., 15 B.R. 660 (D.Colo.1981); In re Snowshoe Co., Inc., 789 F.2d 1085 (4th Cir. 1986); In re Texaco Inc., 92 B.R. 38 (S.D.N.Y. 1988).

3. 86 B.R. 393 (Bankr. E.D.Pa. 1988).

4. Cf. In re FCX, Inc., 54 B.R. 833, 837 (Bankr. E.D.N.C.1985) (creditor agreed to allow terms of its loan agreement to be considered at a subsequent hearing if any objections

Although the cases are not in direct conflict, one might argue that the decision of Judge Fletcher in *In re Adams Apple, Inc.*[5] is inconsistent with Judge Posner's Seventh Circuit decision in *Matter of EDC Holding Co.*[6] In the latter case the court found that the priority of a $77,000 loan which was earmarked for the payment of attorney's fees of a creditor was not protected by section 364(e). Judge Posner held that payment to an individual creditor's attorney is not permissible under the Bankruptcy Code and is, *a fortiori*, not in good faith, even though the bankruptcy judge had approved it.

In affirming a cross-collateralization clause—also a suspect transaction under the Bankruptcy Code—Judge Fletcher of the Ninth Circuit read section 364(e) to grant greater protection in *In re Adams Apple, Inc.*[7] In that case the bankruptcy court had approved a new loan by a bank to a debtor who was operating apple orchards. Under the agreement Central Washington Bank would advance $450,000 to the debtor and might, in addition, loan an additional $325,000. It was to retain a first lien not only for the postpetition loan, but also for its prepetition loan. Over the objection of other creditors, the bankruptcy court tentatively approved the agreement in an oral ruling on June 15. The court issued a final authorization on July 14. The bank lent debtor $48,000 before June 15 and an additional $200,000 before July 14. Later it lent the remaining $202,000. On July 14 the competing creditor filed a motion for a stay pending the appeal. The bankruptcy court denied that motion, but on August 19 reversed itself and ordered a stay.

On appeal the competing creditors argued, first, that section 364(e) did not preclude a reexamination because there had been a stay pending the appeal. The court rejects that argument on the ground that some of the loans had been made prior to the stay, but after the oral order, and secondly on the ground that the stay was entered after the appeal had already lodged jurisdiction in the district court.[8]

On appeal the court concluded not only that there was no stay but also that the cross-collateralization clause itself should be protected by section 364(e) and that the making of such a cross-collateralization arrangement was not in and of itself bad faith. Although the case is not in direct conflict with *Matter of EDC Holding Co.*,[9] its tone and the breadth with which the court reads section 364(e) are in conflict with *EDC*.

In general we favor Judge Fletcher's approach in *Adams Apple*. The need for speed and the virtue of finality of decisions under section 364 are apparent to us. We doubt the law would be improved much by allowing first the district court and then courts of appeal to second guess the bankruptcy judge. In most of these circumstances we suspect the bankruptcy court has a better general understanding of the implications of postpetition lending

---

ensued after all creditors had been given notice).

5. 829 F.2d 1484 (9th Cir.1987).
6. 676 F.2d 945 (7th Cir.1982).
7. 829 F.2d 1484 (9th Cir.1987).
8. The case presents but does not answer an interesting question about section 364(e)'s application when loans are first authorized by a bankruptcy court, but a motion for stay is taken under advisement. In most cases the court should make these judgments simultaneously (loan and stay).

9. 676 F.2d 945 (7th Cir.1982).

and of the merits of the proposal before it in a particular case than would be true of the district or appellate court.

Turning to section 363(m), note first the acts to be examined by the court in section 363 are slightly different from those in section 364. In section 364 the creditor must lend in "good faith"; in section 363 the buyer must buy in "good faith." Section 363(m) introduces a familiar person, namely, the bona fide purchaser, one well known to any student of the law. Analogous rules for bona fide purchase or holder in due course under the Uniform Commercial Code would normally require purchase without knowledge of a defense, for value, and in good faith.

Since section 363(m) specifically provides that knowledge of the appeal is not knowledge of a defense and, *a fortiori,* that knowledge of the competitor's claim is not normally a defense, what are the questions one would expect to see under section 363(m)? *Willemain v. Kivitz*[10] is representative. There the debtor Willemain's sole asset was his interest in a real estate partnership that owned 94 acres of land in Baltimore County, Maryland. The interest was encumbered by the limitation that no member of the partnership was free to sell to one not associated to the partnership. After searching for five months, Kivitz, the trustee, agreed to sell the property for $100,000 to somebody associated with the partnership. Willemain argued that his interest was worth more than $1,400,000. In support of his claim he brought forth an appraisal that estimated its value to be $907,500 and he procured an "eleventh hour" conditional offer for $200,000. Despite the appraisal and the high conditional offer, the bankruptcy judge approved the sale for $100,000. The district court held that the sale was protected from challenge on appeal by 363(m).

First, the court concluded that Willemain lacked standing to prosecute the appeal. This surprising conclusion arises from the fact that Willemain was so hopelessly insolvent that even if the higher offer of $200,000 had been granted, the proceeds of that offer would not have gone to Willemain, but to his other creditors. Thus, the initial question under section 363 whether the debtor is in such dismal shape that he has no interest even if the better offers were accepted. If that is so, it is the other creditors who would enjoy the excess, not he, and it is they, not he, who are the parties in interest.

Most courts find that value has been given if the amount paid exceeds 70 or 75 percent of the appraised value of the asset. Rejecting the $907,500 appraisal as not persuasive, the court concluded that this test had been met.

If the drafters intended to adopt the model of the bona fide purchaser by their reference to good faith purchaser in section 363(m), we believe this and the courts' requirement that 70 or 75 percent be paid is technically inaccurate. All that is required for "value" to be given is that *some* value be given. The comparison between the worth of the asset and the amount paid may determine the buyer's "good faith," but it does not affect the giving of value. Thus, one who buys property worth $100,000 for $5,000 has given "value" as that term is commonly used in the Uniform Commercial Code and the common law, yet it is unlikely that he has purchased in "good faith."

10. 764 F.2d 1019 (4th Cir.1985).

Perhaps the 75 percent rule has been imported from fraudulent conveyance cases where the question is different. There one must determine whether the buyer gave "reasonably equivalent value." In such cases, use of a percentile number of the kind discussed in the *Willemain* case would be appropriate. In any event, our complaint is a professors' quibble; we might engage in the same kind of inquiry the court in *Willemain* used, but we would do so under the rubric of determining the buyer's "good faith."

In general, creditors and, even more, debtors who seek to challenge sales on appeal have not fared well in the courts. As we have indicated above, the appellate courts, like the bankruptcy courts have been skeptical of claims that unidentified buyers are prepared to pay exponentially greater sums than the amount paid by the particular buyer who did purchase. We think the skepticism by the appellate courts is appropriate and that their confidence in the bankruptcy judges is generally well placed.[11]

In summary, section 363(m) and section 364(e) are sensible trade-offs between the need for quick action to save a failing debtor and the due process right of competing creditors. For the most part the appellate courts have been respectful of the Congressional wishes expressed in these subsections and have been appropriately vigorous in turning aside appeals.

---

11. See In re Karpe, 84 B.R. 926 (Bankr. M.D.Pa.1988); In re Vanguard Oil & Service Co., Inc., 88 B.R. 576 (E.D.N.Y.1988); In re Gabel, 61 B.R. 661 (Bankr. W.D.La.1985); In re Wieboldt Stores, Inc., 92 B.R. 309 (N.D.Ill. 1988); In re Abbotts Dairies of Pennsylvania, Inc., 788 F.2d 143 (3d Cir.1986), on remand, 61 B.R. 156 (Bankr.E.D.Pa.1986); In re Onouli–Kona Land Co., 846 F.2d 1170 (9th Cir.1988).

Chapter 5

LEASES AND EXECUTORY CONTRACTS

Table of Sections

Sec.
5–1 Introduction to Leases and Executory Contracts.

    A. Scope of Section 365.

5–2 What Is a Lease?
5–3 What Is an Unexpired Lease?
5–4 What Is an Executory Contract?
    a. Absence of a Statutory Definition.
    b. "Countryman Definition": Performance Due on Both Sides.
    c. Legislative History.
    d. "Booth" Test: Consequences of Applying Section 365.
    e. Two or More Executory Contracts in a Single Document.

    B. Consequences of Section 365.

5–5 Consequences of Assumption.
    a. Property of the Estate.
    b. Administrative Expense Priority.
5–6 Consequences of Assignment.
    a. Comparison of Section 365 Assignment With Common Law Assignment.
    b. Comparison of Assigning a Lease With Subleasing.
5–7 Consequences of Rejection.
    a. Rejection as a Breach.
    b. Rejection by Real Property Lessor.
    c. Rejection by Licensors of "Intellectual Property": Cases Commenced on or After November 3, 1988.
    d. Rejection by Licensors of "Intellectual Property": Cases Commenced Before November 3, 1988.
    e. Rejection as an Avoiding Power.
    f. Rejection and Contract Provisions Such as Liquidated Damages Clauses.
    g. Rejection and Covenants Not to Compete.

    C. Assumption or Rejection.

5–8 Role of the Court.
5–9 Time for Rejection or Assumption.
5–10 ___ Section 365(d)(4).
5–11 ___ Contract Provisions and Section 108(b).

    D. Executory Contracts and Unexpired Leases That Cannot Be Assumed.

5–12 Contract and Lease Clauses.
5–13 "Loans" or "Financial Accommodations".
5–14 ___ Consent to Assumption of Financial Accommodation Contracts.
5–15 Nonassignability Under Applicable Law.

    E. Contracts That Cannot Be Assigned.

Sec.
5–16 Statutory Restrictions on Assignments.
5–17 Contractual Restrictions on Assignment.

    F. Requirements for Assumption and Assignment.

5–18 Overview of Requirements of Section 365(b).
5–19 Default Cure and Compensation.
5–20 Adequate Assurance of Future Performance.
    a. Adequate Assurance and Shopping Center Leases.
    b. Adequate Assurance of Future Payment.
    c. Adequate Assurance of Performance of Lease or Contract Provisions Not Requiring the Payment of Money.
5–21 Adequate Assurance of Assignee Performance Requirements of Section 365(f)(2).

    G. Gap Period.

5–22 Performance Obligations of the Nondebtor Party.
5–23 Performance Obligations of the Debtor.
    a. Nonresidential Real Property Leases.
    b. Other Leases and Contracts.
5–24 Right of Nondebtor Lessor to Adequate Protection.
5–25 Recoupment by Other Party During the Gap Period.

    H. "Special" Leases and Contracts.

5–26 "Special" Leases and Contracts.

---

§ 5–1 Introduction to Leases and Executory Contracts

Bankruptcy involves both the assets and the obligations of the debtor. Bankruptcy deals with these assets and obligations through the creation of a fictional estate. The assets of the debtor become property of the estate. The estate is administered by a trustee or debtor in possession to satisfy the secured and unsecured obligations of the debtor. In the course of administration, the estate will incur its own obligations; these administrative expenses are given priority over the debtor's unsecured obligations.

Generally, the Bankruptcy Code's provisions dealing with the debtor's assets are separate from the Bankruptcy Code's provisions dealing with the debtor's obligations and the estate's obligations: property of the estate in section 541 and allowable claims and administrative expenses in sections 502 and 503. Similarly, this book generally separately deals with the debtor's assets and obligations.

A lease or executory contract involves potentially both property of the estate and a claim against the debtor or the estate. This hybrid nature of a lease or executory contract is most apparent in lease situations in which the debtor is the lessee. Assume, for example, that D Store, Inc. (D) leases its store in the mall from O. D later files for bankruptcy. D's rights to the use of the space in the mall is an asset of the estate. D's lease, however, involves burdens as well as benefits. D has performance obligations under the lease such as paying rent. If these obligations are not performed, O will have a claim.

For over fifty years, the American bankruptcy statutes have had special sections for leases and executory contracts. In 1938, the Chandler Act Amendments added sections 70b and 63c. In 1978, the Bankruptcy Code replaced these provisions with sections 365 and 1110. And, later, section

1113. And, still later, section 1114 and then section 559 and section 560. While there are now a few pages of bankruptcy statutes on leases and executory contracts instead of a couple of paragraphs, the core concepts from the Chandler Act have been retained.

The bankruptcy treatment of a lease or executory contract can take one of three possible forms:

1. Rejection,
2. Assumption and retention, or
3. Assumption and assignment.

In this chapter we review the consequences of, procedures for, and limitations on these three alternatives for leases and executory contracts in bankruptcy.

In comparing rejection, assumption, and assignment, it is important to keep in mind that the lease or contract involves potentially both property of the estate and a claim against the estate. The following chart provides a general view of the effect of rejection, assumption, and assignment on property of the estate and claims against the estate.

	Rejection	Assumption	Assignment
Property of the estate	No property of the estate	Debtor's rights under contract or lease	Proceeds, if any, from assignment of debtor's rights under contract or lease
Claims	Unsecured claim for (1) pre-petition defaults and (ii) breach resulting from rejection; administrative expense priority claim for post-petition obligations, if any.	Administrative expense priority claim for all obligations under contract or lease, post-petition or pre-petition	No claim against the estate. Nondebtor party to an assigned contract or lease looks solely to the assignee

An understanding of the bankruptcy law of leases and executory contracts requires an understanding not only of rejection, assumption, and assignment, which are the three different elections available to the debtor under the Bankruptcy Code. It also requires an understanding of the election that is not available to the debtor under the Bankruptcy Code.[1] A

---

§ 5–1

1. Arguably, there is a fourth alternative in Chapter 11 cases. Under the Bankruptcy Act, the term "ride through" was used to describe a situation in which the debtor neither assumed, nor rejected a contract or lease. Under this ride through case law, the conse-

quences of a debtor's failure to assume or reject were (1) the non-debtor had no claim in the case because there was no breach and (2) discharge did not affect the enforceability of the contract against the debtor. See, e.g., Federal's Inc. v. Edmonton Investment Company, 555 F.2d 577 (6th Cir.1977); In re Alfar

debtor does not have a legal right to modify or change the terms of an unexpired lease or an executory contract.[2]

To illustrate, assume that D Stores, Inc., (D) leases space in a mall from O for $20,000 a year. D owes $600,000 in to unsecured trade creditors and $3,000,000 to secured lenders. D files a Chapter 11 petition. D wants to continue operating in the mall and wants to retain the leasehold. D will have to assume the lease and also the lease payment as is: $20,000 a year, no change. In its Chapter 11 plan, D will be able to alter its payment obligations to lenders and trade creditors, secured and unsecured. D cannot, however, use bankruptcy to effect a modification in its obligations under its leases or executory contracts. Rejection, assumption, or assignment. Not modification.

A. SCOPE OF SECTION 365

Section 365 applies to "unexpired leases" and to "executory contracts." There is no Bankruptcy Code definition of either phrase.

§ 5–2 What Is a Lease?

The Bankruptcy Code does not define the term "lease." For accounting and tax reasons, a transaction that is in substance a secured installment sale of equipment is sometimes documented as a lease. In determining whether a deal characterized as a lease of personal property was a "true lease" or a secured credit transaction, the bankruptcy courts look to state law.[1] More specifically, the courts in bankruptcy look to section 1–201(37) of the Uniform Commercial Code to distinguish a true lease which is subject to section 365 from a "security lease" of personal property which is not subject to section 365.[2]

Dairy, Inc., 458 F.2d 1258 (5th Cir.1972), cert. denied, 409 U.S. 1048, 93 S.Ct. 517, 34 L.Ed.2d 501 (1972), see generally Countryman, Executory Contracts in Bankruptcy, Part II, 58 Minn.L.Rev. 479, 561–63 (1974).

There are statements by way of dicta in Bankruptcy Code cases suggesting that the "ride through" concept continues. In his concurring and dissenting opinion in Bildisco, Justice Brennan wrote: "In the unlikely event that the contract is neither assumed nor rejected, it will 'ride through' the bankruptcy proceeding and be binding on the debtor even after a discharge is granted. The non-debtor party's claim will therefore survive the bankruptcy proceeding," National Labor Relations Board v. Bildisco and Bildisco, 465 U.S. 513, 546 n.12, 104 S.Ct. 1188, 1198 n. 12, 79 L.Ed. 482 (1984); see also In re Greystone III Joint Venture, 948 F.2d 134 (5th Cir.1991); International Union v. Miles Machinery, 34 B.R. 683, 687 (E.D.Mich.1982).

2. The statement in the text is both correct and misleading. There are only the three elections under the Bankruptcy Code. A debtor does not have a right under the Bankruptcy Code to change the terms of an unexpired lease or executory contract. Nonetheless, a debtor is often able to use its bargaining power and other legal rights under the Bankruptcy Code to "persuade" the other party to the lease or contract to "agree" to modifications in the lease or contract. For example, D is leasing a building from L. D files for bankruptcy. D wants L to reduce her rent. D presents L with the choice that either D will reject the lease which will leave L with an empty building and a general claim in D's bankruptcy case or L will agree to modifications in the lease. L will often choose to modify the lease.

§ 5–2

1. "Whether a consignment of a lease constitutes a security interest under the Bankruptcy Code will depend on whether it constitutes a security interest under applicable State or local law." H.R. Rep. No. 595, 95th Cong., 1st Sess. 313–14 (1977), reprinted in 1978 U.S. Code Cong. & Admin. News 5963, 6271.

2. See, e.g., In re Royal Food Markets, Inc., 121 B.R. 913 (Bankr. S.D.Fla.1990); In re Torgerson Co., 114 B.R. 899 (Bankr. S.D. Texas 1990).

Similarly, section 365 does not apply to real property transactions that are leases in form but secured installment sales in substance. There is legislative history accompanying section 502(b)[3] stating that economic realities rather than labels should control so that where the purported "'lease' involves a sale of the real estate and the rental payments are, in substance, the payments of principal and interest on * * * sale * * * the 'lessors' are essentially sellers or lenders and should be treated as such for purposes of the bankruptcy law."[4] There have been comparatively few reported cases under section 365 on whether real estate transactions structured as leases are in fact and substance leases.[5]

In re PCH Associates[6] held that a transaction documented by a "Sale-Leaseback Agreement" and a "Ground Lease" was not an unexpired nonresidential real property lease for purposes of section 365. There the debtor PCH owned and operated a hotel. Through the "Sale-Leaseback Agreement" and the "Ground Lease" the land owned by PCH, but not the hotel, was sold to Purchase Estates, Ltd. (and later assigned to Liona) and immediately leased back to PCH. Liona therefore held title to the land and leased it to PCH, which owned and operated the hotel. The Ground Lease explicitly provided that the relationship between Liona and PCH was that of landlord and tenant.

PCH filed for Chapter 11 relief. One month later, pursuant to section 365(d)(3) and (4), Liona filed an application seeking an order directing PCH to continue paying rent under the terms of the Ground Lease. PCH sought a declaration that the Ground Lease was not an unexpired lease within the scope of section 365 of the Code, but rather constituted a joint venture or subordinate financing scheme. The bankruptcy court found that although the transaction was labeled a sale and a lease, its true nature was that of a joint venture and therefore no landlord/tenant relationship existed. The district court and the Second Circuit affirmed. The Second Circuit held that the Ground Lease was not a true or bona fide lease as contemplated by section 365(d)(4). It found it therefore unnecessary "to identify the transaction as a joint venture, security agreement, subordinated financing, or other investment scheme. Suffice it to say that it is not a bona fide lease for

---

3. Section 502(b)(6) limits the amount of damages that a landlord can recover in bankruptcy as a result of rejection of a real property lease.

4. S. Rep. 989, 95th Cong., 2d Sess. 64, reprinted in 1978 U.S. Code Cong. & Admin. News 5787, 5850.

5. See, e.g., In re Harris Pine Mills, 862 F.2d 217, 220 (9th Cir.1988); In re MCorp Financial, Inc., 122 B.R. 49, 52 (Bankr. S.D. Tex. 1990); cf. 11 U.S.C.A. § 502(b). "The term 'lease of real property' appears in section 502(b)(6), a provision which limits the amount of damages for unpaid rent a landlord can recover as a result of the termination of a lease of real property." In re Moreggia & Sons, Inc., 852 F.2d 1179, 1182 (9th Cir.1988). The Senate Report to section 502(b)(6) observes that as used in that section, "the phrase 'lease of real property' applies only to a 'true' or 'bona fide' lease and does not apply to financing leases of real property or interest therein, or to leases of such property which are intended as security. * * * Whether a 'lease' is [a] true or bona fide lease or, in the alternative, a financing 'lease' or a lease intended as security depends upon the circumstances of each case. The distinction between a true lease and a financing transaction is based upon the economic substance of the transaction and not, for example, upon the locus of title, the form of the transaction or the fact that the transaction is denominated as a 'lease'." S. Rep. No. 989, 95th Cong. 2d Sess. 64, reprinted in 1978 U.S. Code Cong. & Admin. News 5787, 5850.

6. 804 F.2d 193 (2d Cir.1986).

§ 5–3 What Is an Unexpired Lease?

Assuming that the transaction is a lease in substance as well as form, section 365 only applies if the lease was "unexpired."[1] The term "unexpired leases" is not defined in the Bankruptcy Code. According to the Report of the Commission on Bankruptcy Laws of the United States, the phrase "unexpired leases" excludes a lease "terminated pursuant to a contractual provision or nonbankruptcy law prior to the date of the petition because of a default of the debtor."[2]

The reported cases under the Code are consistent with this legislative history: a lease is treated as not "unexpired" and so not subject to section 365 not only if the term of the lease has been completed but also if one of the parties to the lease has taken the action required by state law to terminate the lease.[3] What actions are required to terminate a lease vary from state to state.[4] A lease that has been terminated prior to the bankruptcy filing not only is not an "unexpired lease," it is not a lease at all. It no longer exists.

---

7. Id. at 198–199; see also International Trade Administration v. Rensselaer Polytechnic Institute, 936 F.2d 744 (2d Cir.1991); In re Moreggia & Sons, Inc., 852 F.2d 1179 (9th Cir.1988); but cf. In re Martin Bros. Toolmakers, Inc., 796 F.2d 1435 (11th Cir.1986). Martin Bros. declined to look beyond the form of the transaction. The Huntsville Industrial Development Board (IDB) issued $500,000 in industrial development bonds to build a manufacturing facility to debtor's specifications so that debtor would relocate in Huntsville. Debtor then entered into a lease with IDB that provided for rental payments measured by the principal and interest due on the bonds; the lease term ran through the bond payment period. On expiration of the lease, debtor had the option to purchase the building for $5,000. Before expiration of the lease, the debtor filed a Chapter 11 petition. A representative of IDB filed a complaint seeking an order under section 365 to compel debtor to affirm or reject the lease; the debtor argued that the lease agreement must be construed as a mortgage. Concerned about the adverse impact on Huntsville's industrial development bond program, the court refused to characterize the lease as a mortgage for bankruptcy purposes. The Martin Bros. opinion includes dictum that "a real estate lease * * * may be the functional equivalent of a secured financing transaction." Id. at 1439.

§ 5–3

1. Section 70b of the Bankruptcy Act used the phrase "executory contract including an unexpired lease of real property." Cases under the Bankruptcy Act consistently held Section 70b inapplicable to leases terminated prior to bankruptcy for reasons other than the operation of a lease clause that terminated the lease because of the bankruptcy filing.

2. Report of the Commission on the Bankruptcy Laws of the United States, pt. II, H.R. Doc. 137, 93d Cong. 1st Sess. p. 156 (1973). "A lease that is validly terminated pursuant to state law may not be resurrected by the filing of a bankruptcy petition." In re Hickory Point Industries, Inc., 83 B.R. 805, 806 (Bankr. M.D.Fla.1988); see also In re Seven Stars Restaurant, Inc., 122 B.R. 213 (Bankr. S.D.N.Y. 1990); but cf. In re Mimi's of Atlanta, Inc., 5 B.R. 623, 628–629 (Bankr. N.D.Ga.1980), aff'd and remanded, 11 B.R. 710 (N.D.Ga.1981) (where a lease has been validly terminated by the landlord prior to bankruptcy, there is no lease available to the debtor under § 365 "absent equitable consideration sufficient to justify the extraordinary remedy of resurrecting the lease"); see also 11 U.S.C.A. §§ 541(b)(2) & 362(b)(10).

3. Termination of a lease is a "transfer" for purposes of fraudulent conveyance law. A bankruptcy trustee can avoid a prepetition termination of a lease if she can establish the other elements of a fraudulent conveyance. See In re Indri, 126 B.R. 443 (Bankr. N.J. 1991); see generally Goodman, Avoidance of Lease Terminations as Fraudulent Transfers, 43 Bus. Law. 807 (1988).

4. Compare In re Waterkist, 775 F.2d 1089 (9th Cir.1985) (debtor could still assume lease since state anti-forfeiture law allowed reinstatement) with In re Escondido West Travelodge, 52 B.R. 376 (Bankr. S.D.Cal.1985) (lease terminated when lessor filed unlawful detainer action); In re Darwin, 22 B.R. 259 (Bankr. E.D. N.Y 1982) (lease terminated when warrant of possession issued).

§ 5–4 What Is an Executory Contract?[1]

a. Absence of a Statutory Definition

The term "executory contract" is, of course, not unique to bankruptcy. Nor is it a term that is in any way "new" to bankruptcy law. Prior to the Chandler Act amendments in 1938, the term "executory agreement" and "executory contract" appeared in bankruptcy cases, including Supreme Court cases.[2]

In proposing what became the Chandler Act's section 70b, Professor MacLachlan used the term "executory contract" in his suggested amendment to section 70a without discussing what he meant by the term.[3] There was no definition of "executory contract" in section 70b.

In proposing what became the Bankruptcy Code, the Commission on the Bankruptcy Laws of the United States used the term "executory contract" without defining it. Part I of the Commission's Report stated, "[T]he term 'executory contract' should not be defined. In general, its meaning is well understood, and any succinct statutory language risks an unintended omission or inclusion."[4]

The Commission proposed to replace section 70b with section 4–602. Like section 70b, section 4–602(a) used the term "executory contract;" like section 70b, section 4–602(a) did not define the term "executory contract." Section 365 is in many respects very different from the Commission's proposed section 4–602(a) and from section 70b. Again, however, section 365, like section 4–602(a) and section 70b, uses the term "executory contract" but does not define it.

b. "Countryman Definition": Performance Due on Both Sides

In what is undoubtedly the most widely cited law review article on a bankruptcy topic, Professor Vern Countryman reviewed the 1898 Act case law on executory contract and synthesized the cases in the following definition of "executory contracts" for purposes of section 70b:

---

§ 5–4

1. Similarly, a contract that has been terminated prior to the bankruptcy filing not only is not an "executory contract," it is not a contract at all. It does not exist at the time of the bankruptcy. Moreover, if all of the acts necessary to terminate the contract have occurred prior to the bankruptcy filing except for the running of a period of time, the process of termination is irreversible and section 365 does not apply. Cf. In re Windmill Farms, Inc., 841 F.2d 1467, 1471 (9th Cir.1988), on remand, 116 B.R. 755 (Bankr.S.D.Cal.1990); 11 U.S.C.A. § 541(b)(2).

2. See, e.g., Central Trust Co. v. Chicago Auditorium Ass'n, 240 U.S. 581, 36 S.Ct. 412, 60 L.Ed. 811 (1916).

3. McLaughlin, Amendment of the Bankruptcy Act, 40 Harv.L.Rev. 583, 605 (1927).

Just as a debtor in possession is physically (if not "metaphysically") the same person as the debtor, Professor MacLachlan is the same person as Professor McLaughlin. In 1948, Professor McLaughlin of the Harvard Law School faculty became Professor MacLachlan of the Harvard Law School faculty "correcting an ancestral error made in Scotland in about 1835." J. Hanna & J. MacLachlan, Case and Materials on Creditors Rights viii, n. 1 (4th ed. 1951). Professors Nickles and White are too busy making and correcting their own errors to consider correcting any ancestral error by becoming Professors Nichols and Whyte.

4. Report of the Commission on the Bankruptcy Laws of the United States, (Part I) H.R. Doc. No. 137, 93d Cong., 1st Sess., 198–9 (1973).

a contract under which the obligation of both the bankrupt and the other party to the contract are so far unperformed that the failure of either to complete performance would constitute a material breach excusing performance by the other.[5]

In approaching the question of what is an executory contract, Countryman begins by stating:

> The concept of "executory contract" in bankruptcy should be defined in light of the purpose for which the trustee is given the option to assume or reject.[6]

He then excludes contracts fully performed by the nondebtor party (or so nearly fully performed that failure to complete performance would not be sufficiently material to excuse performance by the debtor) from his definition of "executory contracts":

> The estate has whatever benefit it can obtain from the other party's performance and the trustee's rejection would neither add to nor detract from the creditor's claim or the estate's liability. His assumption, on the other hand, would in no way benefit the estate and would only have the effect of converting the claim into a first priority expense of administration.[7]

The article then considers contracts performed by the bankrupt. Countryman concludes that it makes no sense to say that the debtor has "breached" a contract that she has fully performed because she does not assume the contract. And, even without assumption under section 70b, the right to performance under the contract from the nondebtor was property of the estate under section 70a. Accordingly, contracts performed by the bankrupt are not "executory contracts" under the Countryman definition.

c. Legislative History

The Commission described the Countryman definition as reflecting the generally accepted understanding of "executory contract." The legislative reports accompanying early drafts of what became the Bankruptcy Code use language similar to the Countryman definition: "it [executory contracts] generally includes contracts on which performance remains due to some extent on both sides."[8] The Fourth Circuit quoted this language and commented that it "ratified the pre-Code practice, also uniformly followed by courts construing section 365, of relying on Professor Countryman's definition of executory contract.[9]

Congress probably was relying on Professor Countryman and Professor Countryman's definition. The language in the Congressional reports is,

---

5. Countryman, Executory Contracts in Bankruptcy Part I, 57 Minn.L.Rev. 439, 460 (1973) (hereafter, Countryman I).
6. Id. at 450.
7. Id. at 451–52.
8. S. Rep. No. 989, 95th Cong., 2d Sess. 58 (1978), reprinted in 1978 U.S. Code Cong. & Admin. News 5787, 5844; H.R. Rep. No. 595, 95th Cong. 1st Sess. 347 (1977), reprinted in 1978 U.S. Code Cong. & Admin. News 5963, 6303.
9. Gloria Mfg. Corp. v. International Ladies' Garment Workers Union, 734 F.2d 1020, 1021–22 (4th Cir.1984); see also In re Maralak, Ltd., 104 B.R. 446 (Bankr. M.D.Fla.1989) ("Application of the definition of executory contracts in section 365 is supported by the legislative history of the Code.").

however, different from the language in Professor Countryman's *Minnesota Law Review* article. The Report's requirement of "performance remains due to some extent" is different from Countryman's "material breach" test.[10] While it is possible to question the Fourth Circuit's statement that Congress followed the Countryman definition, no one questions its statement that courts are looking to the Countryman definition.[11]

d. *"Booth" Test: Consequences of Applying Section 365*

Although most reported cases rely on the Countryman definition, there are cases employing a different, result oriented-test. Under this approach, the decision whether to apply section 365 turns on the consequences of applying section 365. If treatment of the contract as an executory contract produces a result that is considered consistent with the purposes of section 365, then the contract is "executory." If, on the other hand, treatment of the contract as an executory contract yields a result deemed contrary to section 365's purposes, then the contract is called non-executory and section 365 does not apply.

In a case under Chapter XIII of the Bankruptcy Act, the Sixth Circuit dismissed the Countryman definition with the statement:

> Such definitions are helpful but do not resolve the problem. The key, it seems, to deciphering the meaning of the executory contract rejection provisions is to work backward, preceding from an examination of the purposes that rejection is expected to accomplish. If those objectives have already been accomplished or if they can not be accomplished through rejection, then the contract is not executory within the meaning of the Bankruptcy Act.[12]

---

10. In re Harms, 10 B.R. 817 (Bankr. Colo. 1981) is the most commonly used example of a reported case in which the result under the Countryman language differs from the result under the language in the legislative history to section 365. The contract there in question was a limited partnership agreement. In finding that the limited partnership agreement was an executory contract for purposes of section 365, the bankruptcy court applied the Tenth Circuit's definition of executory contract—"neither party completely performed and the obligations of each remained complex." This Tenth Circuit test is compatible with the Congressional test; it is less compatible with the Countryman test. If the court had applied the Countryman test, it would have concluded that the limited partnership agreement was not an executory contract because failure of a limited partner to perform does not excuse a general partner from performing. See generally M. Bienenstock, Bankruptcy Reorganization 441–42 (1987).

11. An important recent law review article dismisses the question of what is an executory contract for purposes of section 365 as "generally meaningless." Andrew, Executory Contracts in Bankruptcy: Understanding Rejection, 59 U.Colo.L.Rev. 845, 849 (1988). Under the analysis in the Andrew article, the definition of "executory contract" matters only when the assumption of the contract is at issue: rejection simply places the non-debtor party in the same position as other holders of claims. Id. at 890. Andrew criticizes the Countryman definition for "using conceptual intermediaries to express what surely could be expressed more understandably in direct fashion" and suggests the following definition for "executory contract": "simply a contract under which (a) debtor and non-debtor each have unperformed obligations and (b) the debtor, if it ceases further performance, would have no right to the other party's continued performance." Id. at 892–93; but cf. Westbrook, A Functional Analysis of Executory Contracts, 74 Minn.L.Rev. 227 (1989) (supporting the Countryman articles).

12. In re Jolly, 574 F.2d 349, 351 (6th Cir. 1978), cert. denied, 439 U.S. 929, 99 S.Ct. 316, 58 L.Ed.2d 322 (1978). This statement was quoted with approval by the Eleventh Circuit in In re Martin Bros. Toolmakers Inc., 796 F.2d 1435, 1439 (11th Cir.1986).

Most of the recent cases using this result-oriented approach have involved land sales contracts in which the debtor is the vendee. *In re Booth* [13] is the leading such case.

The debtor in *Booth* was a broker and dealer in land who engaged in the purchase and sale of land on "contracts for deed." After the bankruptcy filing, the non-debtor vendor on one of the contracts moved for an order requiring the debtor to assume or reject the contract under section 365. Judge Mabey denied the motion and allowed the debtor to treat the agreement as a sale secured with a lien.

Judge Mabey engaged in a lengthy review and analysis of the law of executory contracts. He acknowledged that the result was inconsistent not only with the language of the Countryman definition but also with the language of section 365(i) which treats a contract for the sale of land as an executory contract where the debtor is the vendor.

> The court is reluctant to depart from a rule as workable as the Countryman test. Our application of the rule in this case contradicts the reason for its existence. Classifying the contract for deed, where debtor is vendee, as a lien rather than an executory contract benefits the estate by enlarging the value of the estate and furthering the rehabilitation of the debtor. Seller, as lienors, enjoys adequate protection. This is in harmony with sections 365(i) and 365(j). The blessings and burdens of reorganization are fairly distributed between creditors and the estate.[14]

Under the laws of some states, contracts for deeds are treated no differently from mortgage or deed of trust transactions. Utah was not such a state. *Booth* in essence treated Utah as such a state for bankruptcy purposes.

e. Two or More Executory Contracts in a Single Document

An executory contract must be assumed or rejected in its entirety. If the debtor assumes an executory contract, it must assume both the burdens and the benefits: the debtor cannot pick and choose from the desirable and undesirable portions of the contract. Can a single "document" contain two or more distinct executory contracts, so that the debtor can elect to assume one of the executory contracts without assuming the other? *In re Gardinier, Inc.*[15] is the leading, recent case that deals with this question at length.

Prior to its Chapter 11 filing, Gardinier, Inc., entered into a contract for sale of real estate in which it agreed to sell a tract of land to X for $5,117,000

---

13. 19 B.R. 53 (Bankr. D. Utah 1982); see generally Westbrook, A Functional Analysis of Executory Contracts, 74 Minn.L.Rev. 227, 320–21 (1989).

14. 19 B.R. at 53. There are reported cases that follow the Booth result and reasoning. In re Fox, 83 B.R. 290 (Bankr. E.D.Pa. 1988); In re Adolphsen, 38 B.R. 780 (Bankr. D.Minn.1983); cf. In re Streets & Beard Farm Partnership, 882 F.2d 233 (7th Cir. 1989). A larger number reject the Booth test. See, e.g., In re Terrell, 892 F.2d 469 (6th Cir. 1989);

Brown v. First National Bank in Lenox, 844 F.2d 580 (8th Cir. 1988), cert. dism'd, 487 U.S. 1260, 109 S.Ct. 20, 101 L.Ed.2d 971 (1988); see generally Weintraub and Resnick, What Is An Executory Contract: A Challenge to the Countryman Test, 15 U.C.C. L.J. 273 (1983); T. Jackson, The Logic and Limits of Bankruptcy Law 120 (1986).

15. 831 F.2d 974 (11th Cir.1987), reh'g denied, 849 F.2d 1480 (11th Cir.1988); see also In re Cutters, Inc., 104 B.R. 886 (Bankr. M.D.Tenn.1989).

and to pay Y a 10% commission for its services. Debtor filed a motion to assume the contract. The creditors committee objected to payment of Y's brokerage commission on the ground that the brokerage agreement was a separate and fully executed agreement that could not be assumed postpetition. The bankruptcy court sustained the committee's objection. The district court reversed the bankruptcy court, finding that the brokerage provision was a part of the entire contract between the buyer, seller, and broker and so was not severable.

Judge Kravitch, writing for the Eleventh Circuit, concluded that the agreement to pay the brokerage commission was a separate and distinct contract from the purchase and sale agreement, even though it was in the same document as the purchase and sale agreement. In so ruling, she stated:

> Although there is only one document memorializing this transaction, there is otherwise no clear indication from the face of the instrument that the parties intended to make only one contract. Instead, the terms of the instrument demonstrate that the parties intended to make two separate contracts. In its order, the bankruptcy court noted three aspects of the transaction that we agree are persuasive evidence of this intent. First, the nature and purpose of the agreements are different. One agreement addresses the sale of property and the other contemplates an employment contract related to the sale of the property. Second, the consideration for each agreement is separate and distinct. Kilgore agreed to pay Gardinier in excess of $5 million in consideration for the Goldstein tract. Gardinier separately agreed to pay Kilgore a commission as consideration for services rendered in making the sale of the property. There was no consideration flowing between the broker and the buyer. Finally, the obligations of each party to the instrument are not interrelated. Gardinier obligated itself to deliver the deed to Burley upon payment of the purchase price, and it obligated itself to pay a commission to Kilgore upon completion of the broker's responsibilities. There are no promises running between the broker and the purchaser; their only relation is that each has separate contractual rights with the seller.[16]

Not only can a single document be multiple section 365 transactions but also multiple documents can be a single section 365 transaction. In *In re Harrison*,[17] the debtor filed a voluntary petition for reorganization under Chapter 11 of the Bankruptcy Code. Shell Oil filed an application for an order to compel the debtor to surrender two nonresidential real properties known as Don's Shell No. 1 and Don's Shell No. 2 because the debtor did not assume or reject the Motor Fuel Station Leases within 60 days of filing the

---

16. 831 F.2d at 976. In a concluding footnote, Judge Kravitch discusses In re SteelShip Corp., 576 F.2d 128 (8th Cir.1978), which held that where a trustee assumed a contract for the sale of assets of a business, it also assumed an agreement to pay the broker a commission for procuring the buyer. The court found that SteelShip was "not persuasive in this case because the precise issue we face—whether the brokerage agreement was separate and distinct from the purchase and sale agreement—was not presented to the court in SteelShip." Nor was this "precise issue" presented (or at least expressly addressed) in In re Clavis Smith Building, Inc., 112 B.R. 768 (Bankr. E.D.Va.1990). Judge Bonney there held that the debtor seller was obligated to pay the broker's fee; Gardinier was not discussed in the opinion.

17. 117 B.R. 570 (Bankr. C.D. Calif. 1990).

Chapter 11 case herein. In response, the debtor contended that the leases were part of a single agreement between the debtor and Shell Oil that included the Auto Care Agreement, the Auto Care Limited Warranty, and the Motor Fuel Station Leases. The debtor successfully argued that all of these writings must be read as one agreement for purposes of section 365.

B. CONSEQUENCES OF SECTION 365
§ 5–5 Consequences of Assumption

The Bankruptcy Code does not expressly deal with the consequences of assumption of a lease or executory contract. It is clear from the cases and commentary that the consequences of assumption are those we discuss here.

a. Property of the Estate

If the trustee or debtor in possession assumes a lease or executory contract, the debtor's rights under the lease or contract continue as property of the estate. There is some question as to whether leases and executory contracts become property of the estate only if assumed by the trustee.

Under English law a lease did not become a part of a general bankruptcy assignment until the assignee accepted the lease. In *Copeland v. Stevens*,[1] the bankrupt attempted to avoid liability on his lease by arguing that the leasehold had passed to his bankruptcy assignee under the general assignment of property affected by his bankruptcy, and so, there was no longer the necessary privity of estate to make him liable for rent. In holding the bankrupt liable on the lease, the court concluded that the bankruptcy assignment did not vest the assignee with the lease until the assignee accepted the lease.

Early American case law followed *Copeland*. The rule in the United States prior to the Chandler Act Amendments was that a lease or executory contract became part of the estate and the estate became bound to the debtor's lease or contract liabilities only after the bankruptcy trustee acted affirmatively to accept the lease or contract.[2]

This was also the understanding and intent of Professor MacLaughlin, principal draftsman of section 70b. He viewed the assumption of executory contracts as a property of the estate issue. Professor MacLaughlin proposed the executory contracts be added to section 70, which was entitled "Title to Property" because "the question of what contracts pass to the trustee is properly treated in section 70."[3]

The Bankruptcy Code separates the executory contract provisions from the property of the estate provisions. The former is in Chapter 3; the latter in Chapter 5. Cases under the Bankruptcy Code are divided as to whether executory contracts and leases are property of the estate prior to assumption. The Ninth Circuit's division on this question is all too typical.

---

§ 5–5

1. 106 Eng. R. 218 (King Bench 1818).
2. United States Trust Company v. Wabash Western Railway, 150 U.S. 287, 299–300, 14 S.Ct. 86, 89–90, 37 L.Ed. 1085 (1893); see generally Andrew, Executory Contracts in Bankruptcy: Understanding "Rejection", 59 U.Colo.L.Rev. 845, 857–860 (1988).

3. McLaughlin, Amendment of the Bankruptcy Act, 40 Harv.L.Rev. 583, 606–07 (1927).

In 1985, the Ninth Circuit stated in *In re Lovitt:*[4]

[B]ecause executory contracts in leases involve future liabilities as well as rights, * * * an affirmative act of assumption by the trustee is required to bring the property into the estate in order to ensure that the estate is not charged with the liabilities, except upon deliberation. Thus, executory contracts and leases—unlike all other assets—do not vest in the trustee as of the date of the filing of the bankruptcy petition. They vest only upon the trustee's timely and affirmative act of assumption. Because assumption of an executory contract is retroactive to the date of the filing of the petition, such a contract never becomes property of the bankruptcy estate.[5]

Two years later the Ninth Circuit, in *In re Computer Communications, Inc.,*[6] treated an unassumed executory contract as property of the estate, without discussing or even acknowledging the *Lovitt* case. Relying on the language of and the legislative history for section 541(a)(1), *Computer Communications* held that the automatic stay barred the nondebtor party from terminating an executory contract that was not assumable.

While there are aspects of the *Computer Communications* decision with which we strongly disagree, the *Computer Communications'* treatment of an unassumed executory contract as property of the estate seems appropriate. Such an interpretation is consistent with the sweeping language of section 541(a) and the apparent Congressional purpose to include all property interests as property of the estate.

b. *Administrative Expense Priority*

The debtor's obligations under the lease or executory contract become obligations of the estate. A later breach of an assumed lease or executory contract creates an administrative expense priority.[7] The nondebtor party is entitled to an administrative expense priority for prepetition obligations as well as postpetition obligations.[8]

§ 5–6 Consequences of Assignment

a. *Comparison of Section 365 Assignment With Common Law Assignment*

The consequences of assignment under section 365 differ from the consequences of an assignment under nonbankruptcy contract law. Generally, an assignment or delegation does not relieve the assignor from liability for later breach of the contract by the assignee. Section 365(k) does relieve the estate from any further liability on assigned executory contracts and leases.

---

4. 757 F.2d 1035 (9th Cir.1985), cert. denied, 474 U.S. 849, 106 S.Ct. 145, 88 L.Ed.2d 120 (1985).

5. Id. at 1041.

6. 824 F.2d 725 (9th Cir.1987).

7. See generally Ehrlich, The Assumption and Rejection of Unexpired Real Property Leases Under the Bankruptcy Code—A New Look, 12 Buffalo L. Rev. 1, 66–67 (1983).

8. See In re Norwegian Health Spa, 79 B.R. 507 (Bankr. N.D.Ga.1987); In re Mushroom Transportation Co., 78 B.R. 754 (Bankr. E.D.Pa. 1987); cf. 11 U.S.C.A. § 365(b).

While section 365(k) relieves the trustee and the estate from any further liability on an assigned executory contract or unexpired lease after the assignment, there is no language in section 365(k) or elsewhere in the Bankruptcy Code that expressly obligates the assignee. It is anticipated that the assignee's assumption of the obligations under the contract or lease will be part of the adequate assurance of future performance required by section 365(f)(2).

The consequences of assignment under section 365 are different from the consequences of an assignment under nonbankruptcy law because the requirements for a section 365 assignment differ from the requirements for a common law assignment. Section 365(k) must be read together with section 365(f)(2)(B).[1] Section 365(f)(2)(B) conditions assignment on adequate assurance of future performance by the assignee. There is no comparable condition to a common-law assignment.

b. Comparison of Assigning a Lease With Subleasing

In determining how to dispose of favorable leases, a trustee or debtor in possession may consider subleasing instead of assigning the leases. Section 365 nowhere expressly deals with subleasing. While section 365 expressly provides for the consequences of assignment and the requirements for assignments, there are no corresponding provisions for the consequences of subleasing or the requirements for subleasing. We do not believe that the section 365 provisions on assignments should be applied to subleases.[2]

Outside of bankruptcy, a sublease does not extinguish the lessee's liability on a lease. In bankruptcy, a sublease should not extinguish a debtor/lessee's liability on a lease. Section 365(k) is silent as to subletting so that an assumption and subletting, unlike an assumption and assignment, results in the continued liability of the debtor under the lease. Similarly, section 365(f) which invalidates prohibitions on assignments does not speak to the question of subletting so that restrictions on subletting will be recognized in bankruptcy.[3]

Section 365(f)(2) conditions assignments on adequate assurance of future performance regardless of whether there has been a default. Section 365(f)(2) does not mention subleases. Under section 365(b), which governs assumption, adequate assurance of future performance is required only if there has been a default. Accordingly, a debtor should be able to assume[4] and sublet a lease in good standing without providing adequate assurance of future performance.

§ 5–6

1. Section 365(f)(2)(B) is considered infra at § 5–21.

2. See In re LaFayette Radio Electronics, 8 B.R. 528 (Bankr. E.D.N.Y.1981).

3. See In re Pin Oaks Apartments, 7 B.R. 364 (Bankr. S.D. Texas 1980).

4. In theory, a debtor could seek to sublease without first assuming the lease. Such a sublease should be governed by section 363, rather than section 365. Generally, the sublessee will require the debtor to assume the lease first.

§ 5-7 Consequences of Rejection

While the consequences of assumption and assignment of a lease or executory contract are well-settled, there is considerable confusion and controversy over the consequences of rejection.

a. Rejection as a Breach

Section 365 deals briefly with the consequences of rejection of a lease or executory contract in paragraph (g). Section 365(g) sets out two important rules about rejection:

(1) rejection "constitutes a breach" and

(2) this breach is deemed to have occurred prior to the filing of the petition.[1]

The following hypothetical illustrates the operation of a rejection as a breach in a general, simple situation. Suppose that on January 15, D enters into a contract with O. April 5, D files for bankruptcy while his contract with O is still executory. July 13, D rejects the contract. O incurs additional costs of $5,000 in having X perform D's contract.

O will have a $5,000 unsecured claim. Although this claim resulted from D's postpetition breach of contract, it will be treated the same as general claims that arose before the filing of the bankruptcy petition for purposes of bankruptcy distribution and for purposes of discharge. D's obligations on the contract with O will be within the scope of the bankruptcy discharge since O's claim is treated as a debt that arose before the bankruptcy filing.[2]

b. Rejection by Real Property Lessor

Section 365(h) limits the effect of rejection of a lease of real property when the debtor is the landlord. While a debtor landlord has the power to reject leases, the effect of any such rejection is quite limited. The significant limitation on such rejection is that the landlord will not regain the premises unless the tenant voluntarily vacates.

Section 365(h), in effect, gives the lessee a choice when the lessor files for bankruptcy and elects to reject the lease. Under 365(h)(1), the lessee can, at its option, treat the lease as terminated by the rejection. The lessee vacates the premises and asserts a claim against the estate for any damages it has incurred from the rejection of the lease. This will be a general unsecured claim.[3]

§ 5-7

1. Section 365(g) should be read together with section 502(g) which states the claim of the other party to a lease or executory contract is allowable as if it had arisen as the time of the filing of the bankruptcy petition.

2. See 11 U.S.C.A. §§ 727, 1141, 1228 & 1338.

3. Consider the effect of a lessee's election to treat the lease as terminated on third parties. What if there are sublessees? The sublease and nonbankruptcy state law will determine the rights of any of the sublessees under section 365(h). See In re Stalter & Co., Ltd., 99 B.R. 327, 330–31 (E.D.La.1989); In re Elmhurst Transmission Corp., 60 B.R. 9 (Bankr. E.D.N.Y.1986). What if the lessee borrowed money and used the long term lease as collat-

Alternatively, under section 362(h)(2), the lessee can elect to remain in the leased premises even though the lessor has filed for bankruptcy and rejected a lease. The lessee may so remain in the premises for the balance of the term of the lease plus any renewals or extension rights it would have a right to assert under the lease. If the lessee remains in possession of the leasehold, it must continue to pay rent to the trustee.[4]

While a debtor lessor cannot use rejection to force the lessee to leave the premises, the debtor lessor can use rejection as a means for avoiding some of its contractual obligations under a lease such as repairs and maintenance. The lessee may then offset the amount of rent it pays by the damages caused by the debtor lessor's nonperformance. This right of offset is the sole remedy against the estate for damages arising after the rejection. The lessee may not file a claim in the bankruptcy case for damages resulting from the debtor lessor's failure to render services called for by the lease.

There are very few reported cases involving rejection of leases by lessors. Because of section 365(h), it would seem that the trustee's power to reject real property leases is almost illusory.[5]

c. Rejection by Licensors of "Intellectual Property": Cases Commenced on or After November 3, 1988

Section 365(n) was added in 1988. It deals with the rejection of "intellectual property" licenses by a bankrupt licensor.[6] Section 365(n) applies in cases commenced on or after November 3, 1988.

Just as section 365(h) provides two options for the lessee when its lessor files for bankruptcy and rejects its real property lease, section 365(n) provides two options for a technology licensee in the event that its licensor files for bankruptcy and rejects its license in its bankruptcy case. The first alternative is to treat the license as terminated and file a claim against the bankruptcy estate for breach of contract damages. The claim will be a general, unsecured claim. If the licensee elects this option, it forfeits any or all rights to continued use of the intellectual property that is the subject matter of the license.

The second alternative provided by section 365(n) allows the licensee to retain its rights under the license to the technology, including rights of exclusivity. The licensee may retain these rights for the initial term of the

---

eral? A clause requiring the lessee mortgagor to obtain the mortgagee's consent before electing to treat the lease as terminated should be effective. See generally Winfield, Rejection of Nonresidential Leases and Real Property in Bankruptcy: What Happens to the Mortgagee's Security Interest?, 17 Pepperdine L. Rev. 429 (1990).

4. The phrase "rent reserved under such lease" has been read as supporting the rule that a debtor/lessor cannot use rejection to raise the rent. See In re Upland/Euclid, Ltd., 56 B.R. 250, 252 (Bankr. 9th Cir.1985); In re TM Carlton House Partners, Ltd., 97 B.R. 819 (Bankr. E.D.Va.1989).

5. See generally Ehrlich, The Assumption and Rejection of Unexpired Real Property Leases Under the Bankruptcy Code—A New Look, 32 Buffalo L. Rev. 1, 82 (1983).

6. "Intellectual property" is a term defined in section 101(56) of the Bankruptcy Code. Intellectual property includes patents and patent applications, works of authorship protected under copyright law, mask works, and trade secrets. The definition does not include trademark or tradename rights. See generally Lieb, The Interrelationship of Trademark Law and Bankruptcy Law, 62 Am. Bank. L.J. 1 (1989).

contract as well as for any optional extension periods available at the licensee's discretion.

If the licensee elects to continue to use the licensed technology notwithstanding the rejection of the license by the debtor licensor, the licensee must continue to pay all royalties due the licensor. Additionally the licensee waives any rights of setoff it might have against the licensor and also waives any administrative claims against the estate that it might have.

Rejection relieves the debtor licensor of any burdens to take on any additional affirmative action pursuant to the license such as training or updating the intellectual property. Accordingly, it would seem that the licensee would not have a right to use technology developed after the rejection, even if covered by the license.[7]

d. Rejection by Licensors of Intellectual Property: Cases Commenced Before November 3, 1988

While earlier cases on the effect of rejection of license agreements are now of limited direct precedential value, these cases—particularly the *Lubrizol* case—remain important in understanding the effect of rejection.

Lubrizol Enterprises v. Richmond Metal Finishers, Inc.[8] involved a non-exclusive license to a technical process. The license allowed *Lubrizol* to utilize a metal coating process technology owned by Richmond Metal Finishers. Richmond Metal Finishers filed for bankruptcy relief and rejected its contract with Lubrizol. While the Fourth Circuit's opinion in *Lubrizol* focuses primarily on the question of whether the contract was "executory" for purposes of section 365, it also held that the debtor in possession's rejection of the licensing agreement terminated Lubrizol's right to use the metal coating process.[9]

In explaining why the nondebtor party, Lubrizol, could not rely on the provisions in the licensing agreement for continued use of the technology upon rejection by Richmond Metal Finishers, the court stated:

> [W]e can only conclude that the District Court was under a misapprehension of controlling law in thinking that by rejecting the agreement the debtor could not deprive Lubrizol of all rights to the process. Under section 365(g), Lubrizol would be entitled to treat rejection as a breach and seek a money damages remedy; however, it could not seek to retain

---

7. Accordingly, a licensee should consider negotiating for a security interest in the intellectual property with a broadly drafted "dragnet" clause securing performance of all obligations of the licensor under the intellectual property license. See generally Duvall, Defensive Drafting to Protect Intellectual Property Agreements, 2 Faulkner & Gray's Bankruptcy Law Review 21 (Fall 1990). Rejection of the license should not affect the executed security agreement. See In re Leasing Serv. Corp., 826 F.2d 434 (6th Cir.1987).

8. 756 F.2d 1043 (4th Cir.1985), cert. denied sub nom., Lubrizol Enterprises v. Canfield, 475 U.S. 1057, 106 S.Ct. 1285, 89 L.Ed.2d 592 (1986). The Bankruptcy Court citation is 34 B.R. 521 (Bankr. E.D.Va.1983), stay denied, 36 B.R. 270 (Bank. E.D.Va.1984), and the District Court citation is 38 B.R. 341 (E.D.Va. 1984), judgment rev'd, 756 F.2d 1043 (4th Cir. 1985), cert. denied, 475 U.S. 1057, 106 S.Ct. 1285, 89 L.Ed.2d 592 (1986).

9. The District Court in Lubrizol had ruled that the rejection of a non-exclusive technology does not deprive the licensee of the right to use the technology, analogizing the license to a completed sale of property. The Fourth Circuit rejected this analogy, stating that "licensing agreements are more similar to leases than to sales of property because of the limited nature of the property involved." 56 F.2d at 1048.

its contract rights in the technology by specific performance even if that remedy would ordinarily be available upon breach of this type of contract. Even though section 365(g) treats rejection as a breach, the legislative history of section 365(g) makes clear that the purpose of the provision is to provide only a damages remedy for the non-bankrupt party. For the same reason, Lubrizol cannot rely on provisions within its agreement with RMF for continued use of the technology by Lubrizol upon breach by RMF. Here again, the statutory breach contemplated by section 365(g) controls, and provides only a money damages remedy for the non-bankruptcy party. Allowing specific performance would obviously undercut the core purpose of rejection under 365(a) and that consequence cannot therefore be read into congressional intent.[10]

The *Lubrizol* decision is significant because it viewed rejection as both (i) relieving the estate of postbankruptcy performance obligations and also as (ii) avoiding a prebankruptcy transfer. In *Lubrizol,* rejection not only permitted the debtor RMF to avoid a future performance of its postbankruptcy obligations under the licensing contract but also to recover technology previously transferred.[11]

e. *Rejection as an Avoiding Power*

The question of whether section 365 rejection operates as a kind of avoiding power to bring back into the estate assets transferred by the debtor prior to its bankruptcy filing is now moot in license cases like *Lubrizol:* section 365(n) now protects licensees of intellectual property. The question remains important, however, in other section 365 situations, such as leases of personal property and franchise contracts.[12]

In *real property* leases, the bankruptcy laws have long expressly recognized that rejection is not an avoiding power. Section 70b provided that rejection by a debtor/lessor "does not deprive the lessee of his estate."

---

10. 756 F.2d at 1048.

11. See generally Andrew, Executory Contracts in Bankruptcy: Understanding "Rejection", 59 U.Colo.L.Rev. 846, 901–931 (1988).

12. Other situations in which the question of whether section 365 rejection works as avoidance of a transfer of a property right or interest include contracts for the sale or real property and franchise licenses. See generally Andrew id. at 901; Westbrook, A Functional Analysis of Executory Contracts, 74 Minn. L.Rev. 227 (1989); Andrew, Executory Contracts Revisited: A Reply to Professor Westbrook, 62 U.Colo.L.Rev. 1 (1991). We believe that the most difficult problem is presented by a rejection of a contract that includes a license of the debtor's trade name or trademark. Assume for example, Jim & Steve Inc. makes ice cream. People in Minnesota, Michigan, and throughout the Midwest believe that Jim & Steve Inc.'s ice cream is unique—different from and better than its competitors. X Corp. becomes Jim & Steve Inc.'s Georgia franchisee. The franchise agreement provides that X Corp. can use the Jim & Steve Inc. name but can sell only ice cream produced by Jim & Steve Inc. While X Corp. prospers as a Jim & Steve Inc. franchisee, Jim & Steve Inc. finds that the costs of shipping ice cream to Georgia are far greater than it had contemplated. Jim & Steve Inc. files for Chapter 11 relief and rejects the franchise agreement with X Corp. What are the consequences of that rejection? Does rejection "avoid" the transfer of the franchise to X Corp.? Andrew and Westbrook and now Judge Conrad in In re Drexel Burnham Lambert Group, Inc., 1992 WL 36294 (Bankr.S.D.N.Y.1992), say that rejection does not terminate nonbankruptcy rights in specific property such as X Corp.'s rights in the trade name. Unless, however, rejection terminates or "avoids" X Corp.'s rights to the trade name, then either Jim & Steve Inc. will have to continue supplying ice cream to X Corp. or suffer the possible damage to its trade name and reputation from a Jim & Steve Inc. store not selling Jim & Steve Inc. ice cream.

There is similar language in section 365(h). Accordingly, rejection of a real property lease by a debtor/lessor does not terminate the lessee's rights under the lease to the leasehold. Courts, however, have looked to this language dealing with the effect of rejection in *real* property lease situations to conclude that rejection does work as an avoiding power in other situations.[13] We do not believe that rejection should work as a kind of avoiding power to bring back into the estate assets transferred by the debtor under the contract.

Assume for example that D leases equipment. D files for bankruptcy while the lease is still in effect and is in possession of the equipment pursuant to the lease. At the time of the bankruptcy filing, D's property of the estate includes D's nonpossessory, reversionary "interest" in the equipment, not the equipment.[14] Unless rejection under section 365 somehow operates as an avoiding power, the trustee takes the debtor's limited interest in the equipment. X should be able to continue to retain and use the leased equipment for the remainder of the lease term.

Section 365 rejection is not an avoiding power that somehow clears title to the underlying property covered by the lease or contract. Section 365 rejection does not make the other party's interest in the property disappear. Section 365 rejection does not even make the rejected lease or contract disappear.

f. Rejection and Contract Provisions Such as Liquidated Damages Clauses

Under non-bankruptcy contracts law, a liquidated damages clause in a contract will generally be upheld if (i) damages are not readily ascertainable at the time the contract was formed and (ii) the measure of damages in the liquidated damages clause is a reasonable estimation of potential damages. What is the effect of rejection in bankruptcy on such a provision for liquidated damages?

Assume, for example, that D enters into a contract with O. The contract contains a liquidated damages clause. The clause meets the relevant state law criteria. D files for bankruptcy at a time when the contract is still executory. The trustee rejects the contract. Obviously, O has a general claim. What is the amount of O's claim? More specifically, does the liquidated damages clause in the contract between D and O still apply despite the rejection?

In *In re TransAmerican Natural Gas Corp.*,[15] a bankruptcy court in Texas faced this question. The issue arose in the context of judicially estimating a claim for the purpose of voting on a plan of reorganization. The creditor sought to value the claim pursuant to the contract's liquidated damages clause. The court refused to apply a liquidated damages clause in a

---

13. Lubrizol Enterprises v. Richmond Metal Finishers, Inc., 756 F.2d 1043, 1048 (4th Cir.1985), cert. denied, 475 U.S. 1057, 106 S.Ct. 1285, 89 L.Ed.2d 592 (1986); In re O.P.M. Leasing Services, Inc., 23 B.R. 104 (Bankr. S.D.N.Y. 1982); In re New York Investors Mutual Group, Inc., 143 F.Supp. 51 (S.D.N.Y. 1956).

14. See 11 U.S.C.A. § 541(a)(1) ("interests of the debtor in property as of the commencement of the case").

15. 79 B.R. 663 (Bankr. S.D.Tex.1987).

rejected executory contract. The court estimated the claim for voting purposes at $10.5 million and not $38 million sought under the liquidated damages clause. In so ruling, the court stated: "If an executory contract is rejected, the damages clause is also rejected * * *. To enforce the liquidated clause of a duly rejected executory contract would in effect enforce the executed contract." [16]

We disagree with the *TransAmerican* result and reasoning. Enforcing the liquidated damages clause of a duly rejected executory contract is not enforcing the contract. As a result of the rejection, contract performance is not an obligation of the estate. The nondebtor party does not have a postpetition claim against the estate, does not have an administrative expense priority.

Enforcing the liquidated damages clause of a duly rejected executory contract is recognizing that rejection of an executory contract does not rescind or cancel the contract. Section 365(g) describes rejection as a "breach," not as a cancellation or rescission or a termination. Sections 365(g) and 502(g) further provide that the breach resulting from rejection creates an allowable, unsecured claim. The damages for the breach and the amount of the allowed claim are to be determined by state law.[17] We believe that a liquidated damages clause that is valid and enforceable under state law should be recognized in bankruptcy, notwithstanding rejection of the executory contract.

g. Rejection and Covenants Not to Compete

The effect of rejection on a debtor's obligations under a covenant not to compete has been an issue in franchise contracts and other kinds of contracts. *In re Rovine*,[18] a Chapter 11 case, is probably the leading case. There, the debtor was a franchisee of Burger King. The franchise agreement contained a clause providing that upon termination of the franchise agreement the debtor would not engage in any similar business within a

---

16. Id. at 667. The TransAmerican court had found In re Davies, 27 B.R. 898 (Bankr. E.D.N.Y.1983), "authoritative on its holding on the matter of the liquidated damages clause in the context of rejection of contracts in bankruptcy." 79 B.R. at 668 n.3. In the Davies case, a layaway contract which contained a liquidated damages clause was rejected. In Davies, however, unlike TransAmerican, the court found the liquidated damages clause to be unenforceable under applicable state law. Similarly, In re OPM Leasing Services, Inc., 23 B.R. 104 (Bankr. S.D.N.Y. 1982), involved a liquidated damages clause that was unenforceable under state law as a penalty. The bankruptcy court in In re El International, 123 B.R. 64 (Bankr. D.Idaho 1991) relied on TransAmerican in holding a liquidated damages clause inapplicable after rejection. The El International opinion only cited and relied on the TransAmerican decision.

17. See Butner v. United States, 440 U.S. 48, 99 S.Ct. 914, 59 L.Ed.2d 136 (1979); In re Custom Millwork, Inc., 35 B.R. 171 (Bankr. D. Haw. 1983). Congress has expressly provided for a different measure of damages for real estate leases and for employment contracts in sections 502(b)(6), (7). Absent such an express Congressional provision limiting or changing the nonbankruptcy damages rules, the amount of the breach claim from rejection should be governed by nonbankruptcy damages rules. The language of sections 502(b)(6) and (7) can also be used to argue a contrary rule and result. Sections 502(b)(6) and (7) used the word "termination"—"if such claim is the claim * * * resulting from termination." It can be argued that the limits of sections 502(b)(6) and (7) do not apply to section 365 rejection if rejection only breaches the contract or leases but does not terminate it. Cf. In re Emple Knitting Mills, Inc., 123 B.R. 688 (Bankr. D. Maine 1991).

18. 6 B.R. 661 (Bankr. W.D.Tenn.1980).

specified radius of the franchised premises for a limited time. The debtor filed for Chapter 11 relief and rejected the franchise agreement under section 365. Burger King asked the bankruptcy court to issue a temporary injunction enforcing the covenant not to compete. In denying the request, the court stated:

> An executory contract must be rejected in its entirety or not at all. The effect of rejection is to relieve a debtor and its estate of the obligation imposed under an executory contract. In the instant case, the covenant not to compete was a part of the franchise agreement. Since the franchise agreement has been rejected by the defendant as an executory contract, the covenant not to compete must also be deemed rejected.[19]

There is dicta to the contrary in later decisions involving covenants not to compete in executory contracts other than franchise agreements.[20]

We question the reasoning of the court in *Rovine*. Note the statement that "the effect of rejection is to relieve a *debtor* and its estate of the obligation imposed under an executory contract." Section 365 does not have anything to do with relief for the debtor. Rather, section 365 provides relief for the estate. It is not the debtor who rejects an executory contract; it is the representative of the estate (although that representative may, in some circumstances, be the debtor acting as debtor in possession). The issue of whether the covenant not to compete can be enforced against the debtor should be treated as a discharge issue, rather than an executory contract issue.[21]

C. ASSUMPTION OR REJECTION

§ 5–8 Role of the Court

Section 365(a) contemplates court approval of rejection or assumption. Rule 6006 provides that assumption or rejection is a contested matter governed by Rule 9014. Neither the Code nor the Rules explain the standard the court should apply in determining whether to grant or withhold its approval of rejection or assumption.

Section 70b of the 1898 Act did not expressly provide for court approval of assumption or rejection. There were, however, provisions in Chapters X, XI, XII and XIII that required court approval of *rejection*.[1] The cases under these various rehabilitation chapters of the Bankruptcy Act of 1898 suggest

---

19. Id. at 666. In Silk Plants, Etc. Franchise Systems, Inc. v. Register, 100 B.R. 360 (M.D.Tenn.1989), the court looked to Rovine in affirming the bankruptcy court's holdings that (1) a covenant not to compete in a franchise agreement was rejected at the same time that the franchise agreement was rejected and (2) the franchisor was entitled to file a general claim for breach of the covenant not to compete. See also In re JRT, Inc., 121 B.R. 314 (Bankr. W.D.Mich.1990).

20. See In re Don and Lin Trucking Company, Inc., 110 B.R. 562 (Bankr. N.D. Ala. 1990); In re Noco, Inc., 76 B.R. 839 (Bankr. N.D.Fla.1987).

21. The discharge issue is whether the nonbankruptcy rights of the franchisor to enforce a covenant not to compete constitutes a "claim" as defined in section 101, since a bankruptcy discharge only frees the debtor from personal liability on "claims." See generally Julis, Classifying Rights and Interest Under the Bankruptcy Code, 55 Amer. L. J. 223, 261 (1981).

§ 5–8
1. Bankruptcy Act §§ 116(1), 313(1), 413(1)

various standards for reviewing rejection of leases and executory contracts.[2] There are 1898 Act cases limiting the trustee's rejection of contracts to those that were burdensome to the estate.[3] Prior to the effective date of the Bankruptcy Code, however, the "business judgment" test was a test adopted by most Bankruptcy Act cases.[4]

The following example illustrates the possible difference in application of the "burdensome" and "business judgment" tests. D is leasing property to O at $10,000 a month at the time of the D's bankruptcy filing. O's $10,000 rental rate exceeds D's costs: D is making a profit. The lease with O is not burdensome to D's estate. T is willing to rent the property from D for $15,000 a month. Under these facts, the trustee may exercise her "business judgment" to reject the lease with O even though it is not "burdensome."

The Commission on the Bankruptcy Laws of the United States recommended against a statutorily imposed "burdensome" requirement, stating: "Such a requirement is unnecessary in light of the Trustee's general duty to maximize return to creditors and might stimulate after the fact reappraisals demanding from the trustee the quality of prescience."[5]

From over thirteen years of case law under the Bankruptcy Code, it is clear that the "business judgment" standard is the majority view. For example, the Supreme Court in *National Labor Relations Board v. Bildisco and Bildisco*[6] referred to the "*traditional* 'business judgment' standard." And, it is clear that the "business judgment" standard is less demanding than a "burdensome" standard. What is unclear is what the business judgment standard means. While there are numerous cases that invoke the business judgment standard, very few discuss the application of that standard.

There are cases suggesting that the business judgment standard effectively means no review. For example, the United States District Court in *Johnson v. Fairco Corp.*,[7] described the business judgment standard as a "lax standard" so that "only where the debtor's actions are in bad faith or in gross abuse of its managerial discretion should the decision be disturbed."[8]

In *In re W & L Associates, Inc.*[9], a Chapter 11 case, the debtor had contracted to sell a parcel of real estate for $252,000. The court found that the land was worth at least $300,000. In holding the "business judgment"

and 613(1).

2. See generally Cook, Judicial Standards for Rejection of Executory Contracts in Bankruptcy Code Reorganization Cases, 1980 Annual Survey of American Law 689.

3. See, e.g., In re Chicago Rapid Transit Company, 129 F.2d 1 (7th Cir.1942), cert. denied, 317 U.S. 683, 63 S.Ct. 205, 87 L.Ed. 547 (1942); In re New York Investors Mutual Group, 143 F.Supp. 51, 54 (S.D.N.Y. 1956); see Creedon and Zinman, Landlord's Bankruptcy: Laissez Les Lessees, 26 Bus. Law. 1391, 1395 (1971) ("[T]he fact that the right of rejection is a part of the right to abandon results in the obvious conclusion that a trustee may not reject or disaffirm a contract or lease unless the contract is burdensome to the estate of the bankrupt.").

4. See, e.g., In re Jackson Brewing Company, 567 F.2d 618 (5th Cir.1978); In re Tilco, 558 F.2d 1369 (10th Cir.1977).

5. Report of the Commission on the Bankruptcy Laws of the United States H.R. Doc. No. 137, 93d Cong. 1st Sess. (pt. 1) 200 (1973).

6. 465 U.S. 513, 523, 104 S.Ct. 1188, 1194, 79 L.Ed.2d 482, 493 (1984) (emphasis added).

7. 61 B.R. 317 (N.D.Ill. 1986).

8. Id. at 320; see also In re Central Florida Fuels, Inc., 89 B.R. 242, 245 (Bankr. M.D.Fla. 1988); In re Summit Land, 13 B.R. 310, 315 (Bankr. Utah 1981).

9. 71 B.R. 962 (Bankr. E.D.Pa. 1987).

test satisfied, the Bankruptcy Court stated, "clearly the lack of 'fairness' to the Buyer in allowing the rejection of the contract is irrelevant."[10] Is it clear that the impact of the rejection on the other party to a lease or executory contract is always "irrelevant" to court approval of the rejection of a contract or a lease?

As early as 1979, Professor Morris Shanker urged courts to look at the impact of rejection on the other party in applying the business judgment standard.[11] There have been a few cases in which such a balancing approach has been applied.[12]

We do not believe that there should be a "balancing" or other special consideration of the interest of the other party to the executory contract. The other party to an executory contract or lease is the holder of a unsecured claim, contingent on the debtor's rejecting the contract or lease. The other party will have an unsecured claim for its provable damages caused by the rejection. Applying such a balancing test gives this other party more favorable treatment than that afforded to other unsecured creditors.

General discussion of the business judgment standard in reported cases and commentary does not distinguish between court approval of a motion to reject and court approval of a motion to assume. It is at least arguable that the court's review of assumption should be different from and more rigorous than its review of rejection. The administrative priority claim that arises from assumption has a greater effect on other creditors than the general claim that arises from rejection.[13]

Arguably, the language of the Bankruptcy Code supports court deference to a trustee's decision to reject and greater scrutiny of a decision to assume.[14] The deemed-rejected rule in section 365(d)(1) and (4) supports such a view. Under section 365(d)(1), a lease or executory contract in a Chapter 7 case is deemed rejected—without court approval—if the trustee takes no action within 60 days.

§ 5–9 Time for Rejection or Assumption

Paragraph (d) of section 365 imposes time deadlines for assumption or rejection. Prior to the 1984 Amendments, section 365(d) imposed a single set

---

10. Id. at 968; accord, Borman's Inc. v. Allied Supermarkets, Inc., 706 F.2d 187, 189 (6th Cir.1983); In re Mammoth Mart, 536 F.2d 950, 954 (1st Cir.1976); In re Prime Motor Inns, 124 B.R. 378 (Bankr. S.D.Fla.1991).

11. See Shanker, The Treatment of Executory Contracts and Leases in the 1978 Bankruptcy Code, 25 Prac. Law. 11, 21 (1979).

12. See In re Petur U.S.A. Instrument Company, Inc., 35 B.R. 561 (Bankr. W.D. Wash.1983); Infosystems Technology, Inc. v. Logical Software, Inc., 1987 WL 13805 (D. Mass. 1987); In re Monarch Tool & Mfg. Co., 114 B.R. 134 (Bankr. S.D.Ohio 1990).

13. Cf. In re Food City, Inc., 94 B.R. 91, 92 (Bankr. W.D.Tex.1988) ("[W]hen the issue is assumption, the focus usually turns on the estate's ability to cure outstanding defaults and assure future performance so that the business judgment test is seldom referenced."). The Bankruptcy Act of 1898 distinguished between approval of assumption and approval of rejection. Under the first sentence of section 70b, the trustee was deemed to have rejected any lease or executory contract that she has not assumed within the prescribed time. The fourth sentence of Section 70b required that the trustee file a list with the court indicating any contracts rejected within the statutory time period. The Collier treatise relied on this statutory language to conclude that in straight bankruptcy cases, court approval was required for assumption but not rejection. See 4A Collier on Bankruptcy ¶ 70.43(5) at 529–31 (14th Ed. 1972).

14. Cf. In re Summit Land Co., 13 B.R. 310, 315 (Bankr. Utah 1981).

of rules for all leases and executory contracts. In a Chapter 7 case, there was a 60-day rule. All leases and executory contracts that were not assumed within 60 days after the Chapter 7 order for relief were deemed rejected.[1] Before 1984, there was no similar time limit for Chapters 11 and 13 cases. In a case under Chapter 11 or Chapter 13, a lease or executory contract could be assumed or rejected as a part of the plan or prior to the formulation of the plan. The court could, upon request of the other party to the lease or contract, set a time by which the trustee or debtor in possession must act.[2]

§ 5–10 Time for Rejection or Assumption—Section 365(d)(4)

In 1984, Congress passed section 365(d)(4) to expedite the assumption of "nonresidential real property" leases in Chapter 11 cases.[1] Section 365(d)(4) applies only if (1) the transaction is a lease of real property[2] and (2) the subject matter is nonresidential real property,[3] and (3) the debtor is the

§ 5–9

1. 11 U.S.C.A. § 365(d)(1).
2. 11 U.S.C.A. § 365(d)(2).

§ 5–10

1. Senator Hatch, one of the major proponents of this legislation, stated:

The first problem which this bill would remedy is the long-term vacancy or partial operation of space by a bankrupt tenant. Although in a Chapter 7 case, the Bankruptcy Code presently requires that the trustee decide whether to assume or reject an unexpired lease within 60 days after the bankruptcy petition is filed, there is no deadline for this decision in a Chapter 11 case. Because of the unprecedented number of bankruptcy cases, the consequent delay in the bankruptcy courts, tenant space has been vacated for extended periods of time before the Bankruptcy Court forced the trustee to decide whether to assume or reject the lease. During this time, the other tenants of the shopping center are hurt because of the reduced customer traffic in the shopping center. Tenants and landlords in other nonresidential structures have encountered similar problems.

130 Cong. Rec. S8894 (daily edition June 29, 1984).

2. See 11 U.S.C.A. § 365(m). There has been considerable litigation over whether an oil and gas lease is a lease of real property for purposes of section 365(m). Many of the decisions seem to focus on whether the transaction would be characterized as a lease under state law. See generally Byers & Tuggery, Oil and Gas Leases and Section 365 of the Bankruptcy Code: A Uniform Approach, 63 Am. Bankr. L. J. 337 (1989). We question whether the definition of a phrase in a federal statute and the applicability of that statute should turn on state law. In re Moreggia & Sons, Inc., 852 F.2d 1179 (9th Cir. 1988), held that something that was a "lease" under state law was not within Section 365(d)(4). There the document was labelled a "lease." It gave the debtor the right to use space in the San Francisco Produce Terminal, a bond-financed project to house produce sellers displaced by another city project. The court in Moreggia acknowledged that the agreement was a lease under California law but stated, "not every interest that might qualify as a lease under state law is subject to (§ 365(d)(4))." 852 F.2d at 1182. In finding that section 365(d)(4) did not apply, the court added, "the appropriate focus is on the federal law purposes of Section 365(d)(4) and the economic realities of the particular arrangement." Id.; but see In re Harris Pine Mills, 862 F.2d 217 (9th Cir. 1988) ("whether an agreement is a lease or rental agreement for purposes Section 365(m) and 365(d)(4) * * * generally depends on state law").

3. The phrase "nonresidential real property lease" is not statutorily defined. What makes it "nonresidential"? Is it the nature of the property or the nature of the lease? Assume, for example, that D operates a nursing home that it leases from X. D files for bankruptcy. Is the D–X lease "nonresidential"? If the court focuses on the nature of the lease, it is "nonresidential." If, however, the court focuses on the nature of the property, it is residential. The cases are divided. Compare In re Care Givers, Inc., 113 B.R. 263 (Bankr. N.D. Texas 1989) (nature of property controls—nursing home residential) with In re Sonora Convalescent Hosp. Inc., 69 B.R. 134 (Bankr. E.D. Calif. 1986) (nature of lease controls—convalescent home "nonresidential" even though people live there). We believe that Care Givers' focus on the property is more consistent with the legislative history and with the language of the statute. Note

lessee.[4]

Section 365(d)(4) extends the deadline for leases and executory contracts in Chapter 7 cases to leases of nonresidential real property in all of the chapters. More specifically, section 365(d)(4) mandates that the trustee must act within 60 days after the order for relief to assume or obtain an extension of time to assume or reject a nonresidential real property lease under which the debtor is the lessee.

The changes effected by section 365(d)(4) are largely procedural. In essence, section 365(d)(4) shifts the burden of making time requests from the lessor to the debtor/lessee. Prior to the 1984 Amendments, the burden was on the lessor to request the court to reduce the time of the debtor/lessee to assume or reject. Section 365(d)(4) shifts to the debtor/lessee the burden of requesting the court to extend the time to assume or reject.

The application of section 365(d)(4) has presented several interpretative questions. One such question is what part of the process of assumption must be completed prior to the expiration of the 60-day period. Assume, for example, that the debtor files a motion to extend the time to assume or reject a nonresidential real property lease. The motion is filed 48 days after the bankruptcy filing. The bankruptcy court does not rule on the motion until after the 60-day period has elapsed. Does the Code require court action within the 60-day period or is debtor's submitting a motion to assume or extend the time period sufficient? On its face, the statute would seem to require court action. Note the language of section 365(d)(4): "assume or reject * * * within 60 days after the date of the order for relief, or within such additional time as the court, for cause, within such 60-day period, fixes." Recall that assumption or rejection of a lease must be approved by the court. Thus, read literally, section 365(d)(4) requires a court order within the 60-day period. There are reported cases that so read section

---

that the word "nonresidential" comes before the word "property," not before the word "lease." See generally In re Lippman, 122 B.R. 206 (Bankr. S.D.N.Y. 1990).

4. Compare section 365(d)(2) with section 365(d)(4). Section 365(d)(2) establishes the time period for assuming or rejecting (1) executory contracts and (2) leases of residential real estate and (3) leases of personal property. Section 365(d)(4) establishes the time period for assuming or rejecting nonresidential real property leases in which the debtor is the lessee. Neither section 365(d)(2) nor section 365(d)(4) nor any other part of section 365 establishes a time period for assuming or rejecting nonresidential real property leases in which the debtor is the lessor. What is the practical significance, if any, of this apparently inadvertent gap in the Code? Does it mean there is no time period in which assumption or rejection of a nonresidential real property lease by a debtor/lessor must occur? Does it mean that a debtor/lessor is not required to assume or reject nonresidential real property leases? Is it significant that section 365(a) uses the phrase "may assume or reject" instead of "must assume or reject"?

A review of the reported cases suggests that courts have not considered these questions. In In re Oklahoma Plaza Investors, Ltd., 124 B.R. 108 (Bankr. N.D. Okla. 1991), the debtor/lessor failed to assume or reject its Wal-Mart shopping center lease. Wal-Mart contended that this failure constitutes rejection. Judge Covey looked to the gap in section 365(d) and the word "may" in section 365(a) and the 1108 authorization of a debtor to continuing operating its business without court order to conclude that a debtor/lessor is not required to assume or reject. Subsequently, the Fifth Circuit stated, by way of dicta, in In re Greystone III Joint Venture, 948 F.2d 134 (5th Cir. 1991), that "[a] debtor in Chapter 11 must either assume or reject its leases with third parties. If the debtor does neither, the lease continues in effect and the lessees have no provable claim against the bankruptcy estate." Id. at 141.

A review of Chapter 11 plans suggests that the reason that more courts have not considered the question of whether a debtor/lessor is required to assume or reject nonresidential real property leases is because Chapter 11 plans generally contain a blanket assumption or rejection of executory contracts and leases.

365(d)(4).⁵ Most courts, however, merely require that the debtor act prior to the expiration of the 60-day period and permit court approval of the debtor's motion to assume or the debtor's motion to extend the time period to be granted after the expiration of the initial 60-day time period.[6]

Notwithstanding the statutory language, this would seem to be the preferable position. A debtor has no control over a court docket. Even if a debtor performed in a timely fashion, a court might not be able to act on the debtor's assumption or extension request prior to the expiration of the 60-day period. As the Ninth Circuit Court of Appeals stated in *In re Southwest Aircraft Services, Inc.*,[7]

> it is frequently the case that if an act must be undertaken within a particular time, a request for an extension must be made before that time period has expired. Such a rule can hardly be said to be unusual or worthy of special discussion in the legislative history. On the other hand, a rule that forfeits a party's rights, benefits, privileges or opportunities simply because a court fails to act within a particular time period would be quite extraordinary. We think that Congress would not adopt any such rule without clearly indicating in the legislative history its intention to do so and explaining its reasons.[8]

A related time issue is whether a court can grant more than one extension of time, that is, whether an extension of time can be granted after the initial 60-day time period. Again, the language of section 365(d)(4) would seem to answer the question. Note the phrase "court, for cause, within such 60-day period, fixes." A strict reading of the statute would preclude multiple extensions. Again, most of the reported cases take a different position.

In re American Healthcare Management, Inc.[9] is representative of the majority rule. There, the debtor filed a Chapter 11 petition on August 7. On September 9, the debtor filed a motion to extend the time to assume or reject nonresidential real property leases and the motion was granted on October 5. The court at that time extended the time period until December 7. On November 24, the debtor again requested an extension and the court granted the motion. When the court finally heard the debtor's motion to assume the leases, the lessor argued that the lease had been automatically rejected because the only time the court could extend the time to assume or reject a nonresidential real property lease was within the initial 60-day period.

In rejecting the lessor's argument, the Fifth Circuit reasoned that since section 365(d)(4) places no limit on the length of any extension granted by a bankruptcy court, a holding that limited bankruptcy courts to the granting of only one extension would cause bankruptcy judges to extend the time for much longer periods. Indeed, a court could and probably would extend the

---

5. See, e.g., In re House of Deals of Broward, Inc., 67 B.R. 23 (E.D.N.Y.1986); In re Coastal Industries, Inc., 58 B.R. 48 (Bankr. N.J.1986).

6. See, e.g., In re Victoria Station, Inc., 840 F.2d 682 (9th Cir.1988); In re Mushroom Transp. Co., Inc., 78 B.R. 754 (Bankr. E.D.Pa. 1987).

7. 831 F.2d 848 (9th Cir.1987), cert. denied sub nom., Long Beach v. Southwest Aircraft Services, Inc., 487 U.S. 1206, 108 S.Ct. 2848, 101 L.Ed.2d 885 (1988).

8. 831 F.2d at 851.

9. 900 F.2d 827 (5th Cir.1990).

time until confirmation of a reorganization plan. *American Healthcare Management* viewed the purpose of section 365(d)(4) as enabling a bankruptcy court to monitor the treatment of nonresidential real property leases. Accordingly, the court concluded that it was preferable to permit the debtor to justify multiple extensions rather than granting the debtor a virtually unlimited extension at the outset.

The Bankruptcy Code does not set out the factors that a court should consider in determining whether to extend the time provided in section 365(d)(4). Section 365(d)(4) should be read together with section 365(d)(3) which requires a debtor/lessee under a nonresidential real property lease to continue paying rent after bankruptcy. It is hard to envision a situation in which a debtor/tenant, current in its postpetition lease obligations, will not be granted an extension. There is, however, no reported case that establishes a per se rule that an extension is to be granted if the debtor/lessee is paying rent.

Also, there is no per se rule that nonpayment of rent as required by section 365(d)(3) precludes an extension of the section 365(d)(4) 60-day period. The Ninth Circuit rejected such a per se rule in *In re Southwest Aircraft Services, Inc.*[10] There a landlord argued that a debtor's failure to pay rent required by section 365(d)(3) should, without more, result in denying the debtor's right to extend the 60-day period under section 365(d)(4). The Ninth Circuit stated:

> We hold that the failure to make payments under Subsection (d)(3) constitutes simply one element to be considered along with all of the other relevant factors in determining whether cause exists under Subsection (d)(4) to extend the 60-day period for assumption or rejection.[11]

It should be noted that in *Southwest Aircraft Services, Inc.*, the debtor tendered its past due rent at the bankruptcy court hearing on its extension motion.

In determining whether to extend the 60-day period, section 365(d)(4) should also be read together with section 365(d)(1) and section 1121(b). Recall that section 365(d)(1) imposes a 60-day deemed rejected rule. Section 1121(b) provides for a 120-day exclusivity period. In adding section 365(d)(4), Congress used the 60-day period from 365(d)(1), rather than the 120-day period from 1121(b). The court in *In re Perfectlite Co.*[12] properly dealt with the debtor's argument to extend so that it would have the exclusivity period to decide what to do about its nonresidential real property lease. The court stated, "[T]here is nothing in the Code or legislative history to warrant extending the 60-day period in section 365(d)(4) to coincide with the Debtor's exclusivity period."[13]

Section 365(d)(4) also deals with the consequences of the debtor's failure to assume in a timely manner. It states that if the lease is deemed rejected,

---

10. 831 F.2d 848 (9th Cir.1987), cert. denied, 487 U.S. 1206, 108 S.Ct. 2848, 101 L.Ed.2d 885 (1988).

11. 831 F.2d at 854.

12. 116 B.R. 84 (Bankr. N.D.Ohio 1990).

13. Id.; contra In re Taber Farm Associates, 115 B.R. 455 (Bankr. S.D.N.Y. 1990).

"the trustee shall immediately surrender such nonresidential real property to the lessor."[14] The reported cases are divided as to whether section 365(d)(4) contemplates the lessor moving for relief from the stay. The majority of the bankruptcy courts which have addressed the issue have held that upon rejection of the lease under section 365(d)(4), the court is authorized to order the debtor to surrender the premises immediately.[15] There are, however, cases that have held that a lessor may only regain possession of the premises through first obtaining relief from the stay and then bringing a state court eviction action.[16] According to the legislative history, the purpose of section 365(d)(4) is to assist lessors in obtaining a speedy resolution of the status of their property. The majority view seems more consistent with that purpose and with the language of section 365(d)(4).[17]

§ 5–11 Time for Rejection or Assumption—Contract Provisions and Section 108(b)

Can a party to a contract or lease avoid the possibility of extensions under section 365(d)(4), or the problems of persuading a court to order a Chapter 11 debtor or trustee to decide whether to assume or reject other leases and executory contracts, by adding a provision to the contract or lease that requires assumption or rejection within a certain number of days after the filing of a bankruptcy petition? We do not believe that such a contract provision would be enforceable in bankruptcy. Section 365(d) would supersede the contract language.

There are no reported cases under the Bankruptcy Code involving such a contract provision. There are reported cases that deal with a contract provision that requires a debtor to cure a default within X days, and those cases are instructive. Assume, for example, that the contract between O and D lists events of default, requires notice of termination, and provides that the defaulting party can avoid termination by curing the triggering default within 30 days. D defaults. O sends a notice of termination. Ten days later, D files a Chapter 11 petition. Can D wait until confirmation to act on the contract?

Section 108(b) provides in pertinent part:

> if * * * an agreement fixes a period within which the debtor * * * may * * * cure a default, * * * the trustee may only * * * cure * * * before the later of—(1) the end of such period * * * or (2) 60 days after the order for relief.

While section 108(b) would seem to control, there are cases that hold section

---

14. Note that both section 365(d)(1), which applies in Chapter 7 cases, and section 365(d)(4), which applies to nonresidential real property leases, "deem" leases rejected. Only, however, section 365(d)(4) provides for immediate "surrender." Accordingly, it is important to recall that section 365(d)(4) applies to nonresidential real property leases in all cases under all chapters, including Chapter 7.

15. See, e.g. In re Elm Inn, Inc., 942 F.2d 630 (9th Cir.1991); In re Urbanco, 122 B.R. 513 (Bankr. W.D.Mich.1991); In re U.S. Fax, Inc., 114 B.R. 70 (Bankr. E.D.Pa. 1990); In re Hurst Lincoln–Mercury, Inc., 70 B.R. 815 (Bankr. S.D.Ohio 1987).

16. See In re Adams, 65 B.R. 646 (Bankr. E.D.Pa. 1986); In re Re–Trac Corp., 59 B.R. 251 (Bankr. D.Minn.1986).

17. We also discuss this issue in our chap-

365 overrides section 108. For example, in *Moody v. Amoco Oil Co.*,[1] the Court of Appeals reversed the District Court holding that the debtor could not assume a jobbership contract. There the debtor was given notice of termination on February 3 that provided for 15 days within which it could cure the default. The debtor filed a Chapter 11 petition on February 4. The debtor did not cure the default within the 15 days as required by the contract. On April 14, the debtor commenced an action to assume the contract. In holding that the debtor could still elect to assume the contract, the court stated:

> [T]he purpose behind section 108(b) is to permit the debtor an extension of time for doing certain acts necessary to preserve his rights. It would be anomalous to apply section 108 to restrict debtor's rights as Amoco would have us do here. Applying section 108(b) here would force debtors to decide to cure long before they must decide whether to assume or reject the contract and long before they know any reorganization plan will be confirmed * * *. Debtors must be permitted a certain amount of flexibility in determining whether to assume or reject the contract. Specific provisions of the Code should be interpreted with this goal in mind. To interpret the Code so as to minimize flexibility and rush the debtor into what may be an improvident decision does not further the purposes of reorganization provisions.[2]

D. EXECUTORY CONTRACTS AND UNEXPIRED LEASES That Cannot Be Assumed

There is and should be a substantial amount of litigation involving the question of whether an executory contract can be assumed in bankruptcy. The trustee is not obligated to assume an executory contract. In the exercise of her business judgment, the trustee will be assuming only those executory contracts that are favorable to the estate. Thus, the issue of assumption often arises in situations in which the other party to the contract would prefer for the contract to end. Moreover, the trustee's assumption of an executory contract is not tantamount to the trustee's performance of that contract. While assumption renews the promise to perform and creates an administrative expense priority for any loss resulting from nonperformance, circumstances may still render performance and payment in full of administrative expenses impossible.

§ 5–12 Contract and Lease Clauses

Under the Bankruptcy Act of 1898, clauses in contracts and leases could preclude a trustee from assuming and/or assigning a contract or lease. Section 70b provided that "an express covenant that an assignment by operation of law or the bankruptcy of a specified party thereto or either

---

ter on the stay. See § 3–14(e) supra.

§ 5–11

1. 734 F.2d 1200 (7th Cir.1984), cert. denied, 469 U.S. 982, 105 S.Ct. 386, 83 L.Ed.2d 321 (1984).

2. 734 F.2d at 1216; see also In re Round Hill Travel, Inc., 52 B.R. 807 (Bankr. Nev. 1985) (debtor allowed to cure default before confirmation notwithstanding lapse of 30–day cure period prescribed in contract and 60–day period allowed by section 108(b)).

party shall terminate the lease or give the other party an election to terminate the same is enforceable."

While section 70b dealt expressly only with *lease* provisions prohibiting *assignment,* courts in applying the 1898 Act also generally recognized *termination* clauses in leases and contracts.[1] The contents of these termination clauses varied greatly. Generally, however, they permitted one party to terminate the contract or lease if the other party became insolvent or was involved in a bankruptcy case. The term *"ipso facto"* was used to refer to those clauses that provided that the contract or lease terminated instantly, or "ipso facto" upon the filing of a bankruptcy petition by one of the parties.

The Supreme Court refused to permit termination of a lease notwithstanding an unequivocal insolvency termination provision in *Smith v. Hoboken Railroad, Warehouse and Steamship Connecting Co.*[2] In *Smith,* a debtor attempted to reorganize under section 77 of the Bankruptcy Act. In section 77 proceedings, special authority was granted to the Interstate Commerce Commission to prepare a plan compatible with the public interest. The debtor in *Smith* had leased substantially all of its assets. A forfeiture of the leasehold to the lessor would have made reorganization impossible. Relying on the special role of the Interstate Commerce Commission and the public interest, the Court refused to enforce the termination clause.

Later 1898 Act cases expanded considerably the equitable powers of a bankruptcy court under the Bankruptcy Act to refuse to enforce termination clauses. *Queens Boulevard Wine and Liquor Company v. Blum*[3] is perhaps the leading such case. The facts of the case are that a liquor store filed for Chapter XI relief. The lease in question was a simple retail space used by the debtor for the purpose of operating its liquor store. The lessor wanted to exercise its right to terminate the lease because of its ability to re-rent the property to another tenant at a higher rate. Holding the termination clause unenforceable, the Second Circuit noted that enforcement of the clause would injure creditors, provide a windfall to the lessor in the form of increased rent, and deprive the debtor "of its most valuable asset—its location."[4]

Queens Boulevard recognized the unfairness of bankruptcy termination clauses. By exercising its option to terminate the lease, the lessor could deprive the estate of an asset essential to a successful rehabilitation, even though continuation of the lease would provide no real harm to the lessor. Termination and anti-assignment provisions were harmful to the estate even in liquidation cases. Any value in the leasehold resulting from the difference between the rent under the lease and current market rates would go to the lessor—one, unsecured creditor—rather than be distributed proportionally to all of the unsecured creditors of the estate.

The drafters of the Bankruptcy Code were persuaded by the reasoning of *Queens Boulevard.* Under the Bankruptcy Code, a bankruptcy trustee or

§ 5–12

1. See Finn v. Meighan, 325 U.S. 300, 65 S.Ct. 1147, 89 L.Ed. 1624 (1945); In re D.H. Overmeyer, 510 F.2d 329 (2d Cir.1975).

2. 328 U.S. 123, 66 S.Ct. 947, 90 L.Ed. 1123 (1946).

3. 503 F.2d 202 (2d Cir.1974).

4. Id. at 206, 207; see generally Simpson, Leases and the Bankruptcy Code: The Protean Concept of Adequate Assurance of Future Performance, 56 Am. Bankr. L. J. 233, 234 (1982).

debtor in possession is free to disregard bankruptcy termination provisions in executory contracts and unexpired leases. Section 365(e)(1) bars insolvency-related terminations after the filing of the petition.[5] For example, in *In re Taylor*,[6] the court properly held that the debtor lessee could assume a lease notwithstanding a lease provision authorizing the nondebtor lessor to terminate the lease if a bankruptcy case commenced by or against the lessee was not dismissed within 30 days.

Notice that the Bankruptcy Code provision denying enforceability of a bankruptcy termination clause in an executory contract or unexpired lease was included in a Chapter 3 section, rather than in a section in Chapter 11. Accordingly, section 365 nullifies bankruptcy termination clauses in liquidation cases under Chapter 7 as well as reorganization cases under Chapter 11. In essence, Congress has not only codified *Queens Boulevard*, but also extended it to liquidation cases. The Commission on Bankruptcy Laws of the United States had recommended that bankruptcy termination clauses remain effective in Chapter 7 cases.[7] In a Chapter 11 case, permitting the trustee or debtor to assume the executory contract or unexpired lease arguably fosters rehabilitation. In a Chapter 7 case, permitting the trustee to assume and then assign a favorable lease, notwithstanding a lease provision that terminated the lease on the bankruptcy filing, simply transfers value from the nondebtor lease party to the other parties of the estate.[8]

The application of section 365(e) is not limited to contracts with express bankruptcy or insolvency termination provisions. In *In re Siegel*,[9] the bankruptcy court looked to section 365(e) to permit assumption of an insurance contract with a three year term but terminable at will where the termination by the nondebtor insurer was triggered by the bankruptcy filing.

The application of section 365(e) is, however, limited to the time of the bankruptcy case. Section 365(e) should be viewed as tolling the enforcement of insolvency termination provisions, not prohibiting or voiding their use. If the contract is terminated because of insolvency prior to a bankruptcy filing, section 365(e) is ineffective.[10] Similarly, section 365(e) does not prevent insolvency termination after the close of the bankruptcy case.

§ 5-13 "Loans" or "Financial Accommodations"

Section 365(c)(2) provides that the trustee cannot assume a "contract to make a loan, or extend other debt financing or *financial accommodations*." What is a "financial accommodation"? The term is not defined in the Bankruptcy Code. Generally, an executory contract or unexpired lease involves some extension of credit by the other party to the contract—that is why the other party wants to prevent the debtor's assumption of the

---

5. Similarly and perhaps redundantly, section 365(b)(2) exempts the trustee from satisfying the cure requirements of section 365(b) if the only default has been an insolvency related default.

6. 6 B.R. 370 (Bankr. N.D.Ga.1980).

7. Report of the Commission on the Bankruptcy Laws of the United States, H.R. Doc. No. 137, pt. 1, 93d Cong., 1st Sess. 198 (1977).

8. See generally T. Jackson, The Logic and Limits of Bankruptcy Law 113-119 (1986).

9. 51 B.R. 159 (Bankr. E.D.Mich.1985).

10. See In re LJP, Inc., 22 B.R. 556 (Bankr. S.D. Fla.1982); Krasnowiecki, Terminating Lease if the Tenant Is Insolvent, 3 Bankr. Strategist No. 8, p. 1 (June, 1986).

contract. Do all such contracts extend "financial accommodations"? Congress's use of the ambiguous phrase "financial accommodations" has left to the courts the question of how much of a credit component in the contract precludes the debtor's assumption.

The first reported case interpreting section 365(c)(2) was *In re Adana Mortgage Bankers, Inc.*,[1] in which the court held that a surety bond from a bank backing mortgage based-securities issued by the debtor was a "financial accommodation." In so holding, the court relied on the legislative history to state that section 365(c)(2) should be read narrowly.[2] Later cases have consistently looked to this same legislative history and applied it *in*consistently.

The contract most frequently litigated under section 365(c)(2) has been the contract between Airlines Reporting Company (ARC) and a travel agency. ARC contracts with travel agencies to provide blank, standard form airline tickets. This blank ticket stock has value. The ARC/travel agency contract provides for periodic payments by the travel agency to ARC to cover the agency's cash ticket sales during that period. ARC is obligated to the carrier for the travel agency's cash ticket sales. While ARC is extending credit to the travel agency, most courts have permitted travel agency debtors to assume ARC contracts.[3] The courts permitting assumption of the ARC contracts look to the legislative history and "insightful" statements, such as "this would allow the exception to swallow the rule,"[4] to conclude that section 365(c)(2) was not intended to cover contracts for sale of services or goods merely because the seller is extending credit.

In re Thomas B. Hamilton Co.[5] relied on these travel agency clearinghouse cases to find that an agreement between a debtor and a bank pursuant to which the bank agreed to serve as the clearing bank for the debtor's credit card charges did not constitute a financial accommodation under section 365(c)(2) and (c)(2)(B) of the Code. The bank had claimed that the agreement constituted a financial accommodation because the debtor was permitted to withdraw funds based on credit card receipts from a depository account before the bank actually received funds from the customer's banks. The court held, however, that " 'such an interpretation would turn every contract into a financial accommodation contract where a debtor owes any money to a claimant from whom it obtained either goods or services' * * * thereby

§ 5–13

1. 12 B.R. 977 (Bankr. N.D.Ga.1980).

2. 124 Cong. Rec. H 11,093 (Sept. 28, 1978) [H.R. 95–595, 95th Cong., 1st Sess. 348 (1977)]; see also Hearings on S. 2266 & H.R. 8200 Before the Senate Subcommittee on Improvements in Judicial Machinery of the Senate Committee on the Judiciary, 95th Cong., 1st Sess., p. 576 (1977).

3. See, e.g., In re Charrington Worldwide Enterprise, Inc., 110 B.R. 973 (M.D.Fla.1990), remanded, 922 F.2d 847 (11th Cir.1990); In re Travel Shoppe, Inc., 88 B.R. 466 (Bankr. N.D.Ga.1988); contra In re Lockspur, Inc., 82 B.R. 37 (Bankr. E.D.La.1987). Courts are also divided as to whether unexpired leases with construction allowances are assumable by a debtor tenant. Compare In re United Press International, Inc., 55 B.R. 63 (Bankr. D. D.C. 1983) (assumable) with In re Postle Enterprises, Inc., 48 B.R. 721 (Bankr. D.Ariz.1985) (nonassumable) United Press International and Postle are arguably distinguishable on their facts. In Postle, the landlord was obligated to provide $150,000 to the debtor to pay for improvements. In United Press, the lease required the landlord to build the improvements at its own expense.

4. In re Charrington Worldwide Enterprises, Inc., 98 B.R. 65, 69 (Bankr. M.D.Fla.1989), order aff'd, 110 B.R. 973 (M.D.Fla.1990), remanded, 922 F.2d 847 (11th Cir.1990).

5. 115 B.R. 384 (Bankr. N.D.Ga.1990).

allowing the exception to swallow the rule."[6] In its holding, the court focused on the central purpose of the contract, which was to provide services to the debtor, not to loan money or provide credit. Arguably the bankruptcy court in *Thomas B. Hamilton* allowed the rule to swallow the exception.

The only circuit court decision that applies section 365(c)(2)'s "financial accommodations" standard seems to read the legislative history and the case law differently than the bankruptcy court in *Thomas B. Hamilton*. In *In re Easebe Enterprises, Inc.*,[7] the Ninth Circuit held that a lease with an option to purchase involving seller-financing was a nonassumable financial accommodation contract. In so holding, the court relied on the statement in the House Report that the purpose of section 365(c)(2) was to prevent the trustee from "requiring new advances of money or other property."[8] *Easebe* summarized case law as establishing the test that "contracts requiring money or property to be delivered in exchange for a promise to pay are nonassumable while those that require money or property to be delivered in exchange for goods or services are assumable."[9]

Neither this test from *Easebe* nor the "central purpose" test of *Thomas B. Hamilton* is workable or defensible. As *Easebe* and *Thomas B. Hamilton* illustrate, the section 365(c)(2) phrase "financial accommodations" is ambiguous, and the legislative history is confusing. Moreover, there is no policy basis for determining which contracts should be excepted from assumption because of the credit component.[10] If seller S can be compelled to continue to honor its prebankruptcy contract to sell goods on credit to buyer D notwithstanding S's bankruptcy-driven reservations about D's ability to pay, why should creditor C be able to avoid its prepetition obligation to make a loan to D? Similarly, why should seller S or creditor C be treated more favorably than landlord L who is being compelled to continue making the leasehold available to its debtor tenant notwithstanding its reservations about the debtor's ability to pay rent? In all executory contract or unexpired lease situations, the other party to the contract is confronted with a significant change in the debtor's situation that fundamentally affects its deal with the debtor. If "adequate assurance of future performance" under section 365(b) and an administrative expense priority under section 503 are sufficient to protect L from risk and compensate L for risk, why should S or C be treated more favorably?

§ 5–14 "Loans" or "Financial Accommodations"—Consent to Assumption of Financial Accommodation Contracts

There is dicta in *Easebe* that financial accommodation contracts are assumable with the consent of the nondebtor party to the contract.[1] There are other cases that so hold.[2] It can be argued that the Bankruptcy Code

---

6. Id. at 387.

7. 900 F.2d 1417 (9th Cir.1990).

8. H.R. Rep. No. 595, 95th Cong., 2d Sess. 348, reprinted in 1978 U.S. Code Cong. & Admin. News 5963, 6304.

9. 900 F.2d at 1419.

10. See Nimmer, Executory Contracts in Bankruptcy: Protecting the Fundamental Terms of the Bargain, 54 U.Colo.L.Rev. 507, 534–36 (1983).

§ 5–14

1. In re Easebe Enterprises, Inc., 900 F.2d 1417, 1420 (9th Cir.1990).

2. See In re Prime, Inc., 15 B.R. 216 (Bankr. M.D. Mo.1981); In re Charrington Worldwide Enterprises, Inc., 98 B.R. 65, 67–8

does not permit assumption of financial accommodation contracts even if the other party consents. Section 365(c)(1), which sets out another prohibition on assumption, provides that its prohibition applies only when the other party does not consent. There is no comparable limitation in section 365(c)(2).[3]

§ 5–15 Nonassignability Under Applicable Law

The other major statutory limitation on assumption of an executory contract or unexpired lease is in section 365(c)(1), which provide that an executory contract or unexpired lease cannot be *assumed* or assigned if it cannot be *assigned* under applicable law. The phrase "applicable law" encompasses both common law restrictions on assignments and statutory prohibitions on assignments. For example, certain "personal services" contracts are not assignable (or delegable) under the common law of contracts.[1] Under contract law, for example, Andrew Dice Clay could not assign or delegate his contract to perform at the Omni during the Olympics to J.J. A bankruptcy filing by the Dice Man (Mr. Clay) should not change that result.

It is easy to understand the need for limitations on *assignment* of executory contracts. Assignment changes the parties to the contract. Assignment in bankruptcy, like assignment under contract law, introduces and substitutes a new party to the contract; and, under bankruptcy law, the substitution is even more complete than under contract law. Assignment in bankruptcy frees the debtor/assignor from any contractual obligation. If Andrew Dice Clay assigns the Omni contract to J.J., then section 365(k) would relieve Clay completely from any liability or legal responsibility under the Omni contract and leave the Omni with recourse only against J.J., a stranger to it.

It is not as easy to understand a need for such a limitation on *assumption* of executory contracts. Assumption provides different and seemingly easier issues than assignment. Assumption does not change the parties to the contract. Andrew Dice Clay after bankruptcy is the same actual and legal person as Andrew Dice Clay before bankruptcy. As the Supreme Court made clear in *National Labor Relations Board v. Bildisco and Bildisco*,[2] a person is not a different legal entity because it files for bankruptcy. If the Omni chooses to contract with Andrew Dice Clay, it is hard to understand the need for precluding Clay's continued performance under the contract because of his bankruptcy. Read literally, section 365(c)(1) means that if

(Bankr. M.D.Fla.1989), aff'd, 110 B.R. 973 (M.D.Fla.1990), remanded, 922 F.2d 847 (11th Cir.1990). In re TS Industries, Inc., 117 B.R. 682 (Bankr. Utah 1990), relied in part on these cases in holding that section 365(c)(2) did not preclude a debtor's assumption of a credit agreement it entered into in contemplation of bankruptcy. There the parties had negotiated a workout that was contingent on the confirmation of a plan of reorganization. After filing for Chapter 11, the debtor changed its mind and moved to reject the workout agreement, relying in part on section 365(c)(2).

3. See generally Slome, Assuming Pre-Petition Workout Agreements Under Section 365: The "Workout" Decade Begins With Innovation, 3 BNA Bankr. L. Rep. 104 (1991). Mr. Slome also argues that section 364 limits the debtor and other party's ability to continue prepetition financing arrangements by their agreement. See also In re Sun Runner Marine, Inc., 945 F.2d 1089 (9th Cir. 1991). Section 364 is considered at §§ ___-___ supra.

§ 5–15

1. See J. Calamari and J. Perillo, Contracts § 18–28 (3d Ed. 1987).

2. 465 U.S. 513, 528, 104 S.Ct. 1188, 1197, 79 L.Ed.2d 482, 497 (1984).

Andrew Dice Clay files for bankruptcy he cannot hold the Omni to the contract, but rather, the Omni can escape its contractual obligations by invoking section 365(c)(1).

There are cases that read section 365(c)(1) literally: there are cases that prohibit *assumption* by a debtor in possession because of an applicable law that precludes *assignment*. The leading such case is the Third Circuit decision in *In re West Electronics, Inc.*[3]

In *West Electronics*, the court held that a Chapter 11 debtor could not assume its prepetition contract with the United States. Under the contract, the debtor defense contractor was to supply missile launcher power supply units to the Air Force. After its Chapter 11 filing, the debtor continued to supply this equipment. Irregularities in accounting procedures and delinquencies in delivery prompted the Air Force to file a motion to lift the automatic stay so that the Air Force could terminate the contract.[4] The government relied on 41 U.S.C.A. section 15 which requires the government's consent to the *assignment* of government contracts and provides, in relevant part:

> no [government] contract * * * or any interest therein shall be transferred by the party to whom such contract * * * is given to any other party, and any such transfer shall cause the annulment of the contract transfer, so far as the United States are concerned.

The court accepted the government's argument that because this statute precluded *assignment* of the contract, section 365(c)(1) precluded assumption of the contract. The court stated:

> 365(c)(1) creates a hypothetical test, i.e. under the applicable law, could the government refuse performance from an entity other than the debtor or the debtor-in-possession. Thus the relevant inquiry is not whether 41 U.S.C. § 15 would preclude an assignment from West as a debtor to West as a debtor in possession, but whether it would foreclose an assignment by West to another defense contractor.[5]

---

3. 852 F.2d 79 (3d Cir.1988).

4. West Electronics did not involve a personal services contract. "[A]pplicable law" under section 365(c)(1) is not limited to the common law prohibition on assignment of certain personal services contract. There is dictum in In re Taylor, 913 F.2d 102, 107 (3d Cir.1990), indicating that the Third Circuit would apply West Electronics and reach the same result in the Andrew Dice Clay example. Taylor involved (1) Kool and the Gang, not Andrew Dice Clay; (2) rejection, not assumption; and (3) a discussion of law of property of the estate, more than a discussion of the law of executory contracts. In In re Fastrax, Inc., 129 B.R. 274 (Bankr. M.D.Fla.1991), Judge Paskay, rejected West Electronics in concluding that a debtor in possession could assume personal services contracts notwithstanding section 365(c)(1). See also Texaco, Inc. v. Louisiana Land & Exploration Co., 136 B.R. 658 (M.D.La.1992).

5. 852 F.2d at 83. Similarly, the district court, in In re Carolina Parachute Corp., 108 B.R. 100 (N.D.N.C.1989), aff'd in part, vac'd in part on other grounds sub nom., Department of Air Force v. Carolina Parachute Corp., 907 F.2d 1469 (4th Cir.1990) prohibited a defense contractor from assuming its contracts with the United States. There, the defense contracts at issue were the debtor's only source of revenue. Again, because of the debtor's delinquency in performing its contractual obligations, the government sought to have the automatic stay lifted to enable it to terminate the contract. Again, the government argued that it would not consent to the assumption of the contract by the debtor and invoked section 365(c)(1). Again, the court held for the government indicating that a contract that could not be assigned outside of bankruptcy cannot be assumed in bankruptcy.

West Electronics is consistent with the language of section 365(c)(1). The Code does link nonassignability under "applicable law" together with a prohibition on assumption in bankruptcy. Such a result, however, not only ignores the very real practical differences between assignment and assumption, but also other provisions of the Bankruptcy Code.

As noted earlier in this chapter, the interest of a debtor in a executory contract is property of the estate; under section 541 property of the estate includes the debtor's interest in intangible property. Section 541(c)(1) provides in pertinent part: "an interest of the debtor in property becomes property of the estate under subsection (a)(1), (a)(2), or (a)(5) of this section, notwithstanding any provision in * * * applicable nonbankruptcy law—(A) that restricts * * * transfer of such interest by the debtor." As the legislative history indicates, "[s]ubsection (c) invalidates restrictions on the transfers of property of the debtor, in order that all interests of the debtor in property will become property of the estate."[6] Under section 541(c), no statute can directly provide for the termination of a debtor's property interest. Section 365(c)(1) read literally, indirectly provides for the termination of the debtor's property interest because of a bankruptcy filing.

West Electronic's literal reading of section 365(c)(1) also seems to ignore the protection provided to the nondebtor party in section 365(b). A debtor who is in default under its executory contract cannot assume that contract unless and until it provides adequate assurance of future performance to the other party to the contract.

Accordingly, we believe that Congress should amend section 365(c)(1) to make clear that "applicable law" prohibitions on assignment do not preclude assumption in bankruptcy. It is generally believed that Congress attempted such an amendment in 1984. At that time, section 365(c)(1)(A) was changed as indicated below:

> The trustee may not assume or assign *any* executory contract or unexpired lease of the debtor, whether or not such contract or lease prohibits or restricts assignment of rights or delegation of duties, if—(1)(A) applicable law excuses such a party, other than the debtor, to such contract or lease from accepting performance from or rendering performance to [the trustee or] *an entity other than the debtor or the debtor in possession* whether or not such contract, or lease, prohibits or restricts assignment of rights or delegation of duties.[7]

The bracketed language was deleted by the 1984 amendment and the italicized language was added.

There is a relatively obscure committee report for a technical corrections bill, which was a predecessor to the 1984 amendments to section 365(c)(1). It states:

> [T]his amendment makes it clear that a prohibition against a trustee's power to assume an executory contract does not apply when it is the debtor that is in possession and the performance to be given or received

---

6. H.R. 595, 95th Cong., 1st Sess. 368 (1977)), reprinted in 1978 U.S. Code Cong. & Admin. News 5963, 6325; see generally 2 W. Norton, Bankruptcy Law and Practice § 29.15 (1988).

7. 11 U.S.C.A. § 365(c)(1)(A).

under a personal service contract will be the same as if no petition had been filed because of the personal service nature of the contract.[8]

Even assuming that this report is relevant to the 1984 amendments, Congress's change in section 365(c) did not accomplish the change presumably intended. Insertion of the phrase "or debtor in possession" did not change the linkage between prohibition of assignment under "applicable law" and prohibition of assumption in bankruptcy.[9]

Until Congress amends section 365(c)(1), courts should read section 365(c)(1) "harmonious with other sections of the Code and with the Code's purposes"[10] and permit a debtor or trustee[11] to assume a contract notwithstanding an "applicable law" prohibition on the assignment of the contracts.

E. CONTRACTS THAT CANNOT BE ASSIGNED
§ 5–16 Statutory Restrictions On Assignments

The Bankruptcy Code's provisions governing which executory contracts and unexpired leases are assignable are set out in paragraphs (c) and (f) of section 365. As noted above, the Bankruptcy Code's restrictions on *assignments* of executory contracts and unexpired leases are the same as the Bankruptcy Code's restrictions on *assumptions* of executory contracts and unexpired leases.

Section 365(f)(2)(A) requires the trustee to assume an executory contract or unexpired lease in accordance with the other provisions of section 365 before she assigns it. Accordingly, the trustee cannot assign any executory contract or unexpired lease that she can not assume. Accordingly, by reason of section 365(f)(2)(A) and section 365(c), a trustee cannot assign an executory

---

8. See H.R. Rep. No. 1195, 96th Cong., 2nd Sess., section 27(b) (1980) (explaining section 27(b) of the proposed Bankruptcy Technical Correction Act of 1980).

9. See G. Munitz, Executory Contracts and Unexpired Leases Under The Bankruptcy Code, in M. Cook, Bankruptcy Litigation Manual 305, 344–346 (1988); see also T. Jackson, The Logic and Limits of Bankruptcy Law 117 (1986).

10. In re Fastrax, Inc., 129 B.R. 274 (Bankr. M.D.Fla.1991); see also In re Hartec Enterprises, Inc., 117 B.R. 865 (Bankr. W.D.Tex.1990), judgment vac'd and set aside, 130 B.R. 929 (W.D.Tex.1991), on remand, 130 B.R. 930 (Bankr. W.D.Tex.1991); In re Ontario Locomotive and Industrial Railway Supplies Inc., 126 B.R. 146 (Bankr. W.D.N.Y. 1991); In re Terrace Apartments, Limited, 107 B.R. 382 (Bankr. N.D.Ga.1989); cf. In re Cardinal Industries Inc., 116 B.R. 964, 979 (Bankr. S.D.Ohio 1990). Judge Aug recently refused to read section 365(c)(1) literally in an assignment case, In re Federated Department Stores, Inc., 122 B.R. 313 (Bankr. S.D.Ohio 1990). There a state statute prohibited assignments without the lessor's consent. The statute provided: "During the term of a lease, the tenant may not rent the leasehold to any other person without the prior consent of the Landlord." In refusing to prohibit assignment, the court adopted the debtor's argument that section 365(c)(1) is limited to cases "where the 'applicable law' involves overriding public policy concerns." Id. at 315.

11. In In re Hartec Enterprises, Inc., 117 B.R. 865 (Bankr. W.D. 1990), judgment vac'd and set aside, 130 B.R. 929 (W.D.Tex.1991), on remand, 130 B.R. 930 (Bankr. W.D.Tex.1991). Judge Clark distinguishes between assumption by a debtor in possession and assumption by a trustee. Id. at 870; see also In re Ontario Locomotive and Industrial Railway Supplies, Inc., 126 B.R. 146, 148 (Bankr. W.D.N.Y. 1991). Such a distinction is not consistent with the Code's basic approach of providing equal rights and powers for trustees and debtors in possession. Nor is such a distinction required to protect the other party to the contract. The appointment of a trustee in a Chapter 11 case should be analogized to a change in management. If a contract would survive a change in management outside of bankruptcy, it should survive the appointment of a trustee in bankruptcy. Cf. T. Jackson, The Logic and Limits of Bankruptcy Law 116–17 (1986) (Dean Jackson compares the appointment of a trustee with a change in ownership.).

contract that would not be assignable under nonbankruptcy law and cannot assign rights under a loan or "financial accommodations" contract.

For example, *In re Pioneer Ford Sales, Inc.*[1] reversed a district court decision that had permitted a debtor Ford dealer to assign its rights under its executory franchise contract with Ford to a Toyota dealer, notwithstanding Ford's objections to the assignment. Relevant state law provided that "[n]o dealer * * * shall have the right to * * * assign the franchise * * * without the consent of the manufacturer." Please understand that *Pioneer Ford* does not stand for the proposition that the other party to an executory contract can prevent its assignment by withholding consent. Rather, the *Pioneer Ford* case simply applied section 365(c)(1) to hold that an executory contract can not be assigned without the consent of the other party where "applicable law" so provides.[2]

It can be argued from section 365(f)(1)'s use of the phrase that "or in applicable law," that a contract can be assigned in bankruptcy even though it could not be assigned under common law.[3] Such an argument is contrary to section 365(c), section 365(f)(2), and common sense. There is *dictum* in *Pioneer Ford* that suggests that section 365(c)(1)(A) and section 365(f)(1) be reconciled as follows:

> [Section] (c)(1)(A) refers to state laws that prohibit assignment 'whether or not' the contract is silent while (f)(1) contains no such limitation. Apparently, (f)(1) includes state laws that prohibit assignment only when the contract is not silent about assignment, that is to say state laws that enforce contract provisions prohibiting assignments * * *. These state laws are to be ignored.[4]

Nice try.

§ 5–17 Contractual Restrictions on Assignment

Section 365(f)(1) and (f)(3)[1] deal with contractual restrictions on assignment. It is clear from the language of section 365(f), and the cases applying the language, that contractual clause prohibitions or restrictions on assignment are not enforceable in bankruptcy. A provision in a lease granting the landlord a right of first refusal in connection with any assignment was held unenforceable.[2] A provision in a lease requiring payment of proceeds from the assignment to the landlord was held unenforceable.[3] A lease provision

---

§ 5–16

1. 729 F.2d 27 (1st Cir.1984).

2. See also In re Van Ness Auto Plaza, Inc., 120 B.R. 545 (Bankr. N.D. Calif. 1990); contra In re Federated Department Stores, Inc., 122 B.R. 313 (Bankr. S.D.Ohio 1990).

3. Cf. 1 R. Ginsberg, Bankruptcy 530 n.72 (2d ed. 1989); see generally Fogel, Executory Contracts and Unexpired Leases in the Bankruptcy Code, 64 Minn.L.Rev. 341, 360–61 n.79 (1980).

4. 729 F.2d at 29.

§ 5–17

1. See 11 U.S.C.A. § 365(f)(1) & (3). It is not clear what if anything section 365(f)(3) adds to section 365(f)(1). See Fogel, Executory Contracts and Unexpired Leases In the Bankruptcy Code, 64 Minn.L.Rev. 341, 360–61 n.79 (1980).

2. In re Mr. Grocer, Inc., 77 B.R. 349 (Bankr. D.N.H.1978).

3. In re Standor Jewelers West, Inc., 129 B.R. 200 (Bankr. 9th Cir.1991); see also In re Howe, 78 B.R. 226 (Bankr. S.D.1987) (invalidated assignment fee); but cf. L. Cherkin, Real Estate Transactions Under the Bankruptcy Code 206(2) (1990) ("It may be argued that nothing prevents the parties from contracting with respect to the ownership of the proceeds of an assignment so long as the right

increasing the rent on assignment would not be enforceable.[4]

It is less clear from the language of section 365(f) whether a lease provision that restricts the tenant's use of the leasehold is unenforceable in bankruptcy as a disguised restriction on assignment. Under section 365(f)(2)(B), assignment of a lease requires "adequate assurance of future performance by the assignee." Congress's use of the term "performance" indicates that the assignee must comply not only with the payment obligations, but with all of the contract terms including terms governing the use of the leasehold. Accordingly, it would seem that a lease that requires the premises be used as an electronics store could not be assigned to a bistro. *In re U.L. Radio*[5] held otherwise.

U.L. Radio was a Chapter 7 case involving a lease to an electronics store on the ground floor of a New York department store. The lease was substantially below market. The trustee wanted to sell the lease to a bistro named Just Heaven. The lease expressly required that the premises be used as an electronics store. In permitting the assignment, Judge Galgay, stated:

> Section 365(f) in broad language empowers the Court to authorize assignment of an unexpired lease and invalidate any lease provision which would terminate or modify the lease because of the assignment of the lease. Any lease provision, not merely one entitled 'anti-assignment clause' would be subject to the Court's scrutiny regarding its anti-assignment effect. The Court could render unenforceable any provision whose sole effect is to restrict assignment as contrary to the policy of [section 365(f)(3)].[6]

While there have been other reported cases that have permitted assignments of leases that contravene use restrictions, there have been very few such cases.[7] In assessing the precedential significance of *U.L. Radio,* it is important that Judge Galgay there made an express finding that "the landlord has shown no actual harm or substantial detriment to him from the proposed assignment."[8]

It is also important *U.L. Radio* involved an apartment building lease, not a shopping center lease.[9] Section 365(b)(3) provides special protection for shopping center lessors,[10] and the legislative history to the 1984 Amendments to section 365(b)(3) indicates an important part of that special protection is "strict compliance with the provisions of use clauses in shopping center leases."[11]

F. REQUIREMENTS FOR ASSUMPTION AND ASSIGNMENT

§ 5–18 Overview of Requirements of Section 365(b)

Paragraph (b) section 365 sets out the requirements for assumption of an executory contract or unexpired lease. Section 365(b), however, only applies

---

of assignment is not prohibited, restricted or conditioned.").

4. In re J.F. Hink & Son, 815 F.2d 1314, 1317–18 (9th Cir.1987) (dictum).

5. 19 B.R. 537 (Bankr. S.D.N.Y. 1982).

6. Id. at 543.

7. In re Grudoski, 33 B.R. 154 (Bankr. D.Hawaii 1983) is the only such reported case outside the Southern District of New York.

8. 19 B.R. at 545.

9. Cf. M. Bienenstock, Bankruptcy Reorganization 494–98 (1987).

10. These special shopping center provisions are considered infra at § 5–20(a).

11. Remarks of Senator Robert Dole, 130 Cong. Rec. at S8895 (June 29, 1984).

to assumptions of executory contracts or unexpired leases if there has been a default, other than a breach of a provision relating to bankruptcy filing or insolvency. While most Bankruptcy Code provisions focus on the date of the petition, section 365(b) does not. The default that triggers section 365(b) can occur either prepetition or postpetition, but there must be a default.

Assume, for example, that D rents a building from L. D files a bankruptcy petition. D is current on all of its obligations under the Lease at the time of the petition and remains current during the bankruptcy. If D decides to assume the Lease, then the requirements of section 365(b) will not apply because of the absence of any default.

If there has been a default, section 365(b) imposes requirements relating to past failures to perform and requirements with respect to the future performance obligations under the executory contract or unexpired lease. The critical phrase under section 365(b) is "adequate assurance." As to past defaults, section 365(b)(1) requires, first, cure of past defaults or "adequate assurance" of prompt cure of the past defaults and, second, compensation for actual pecuniary loss resulting from past defaults or "adequate assurance" of prompt compensation. As to future performance, section 365(b)(1)(C) requires "adequate assurance" of future performance.

Do not confuse "adequate assurance" with "adequate protection." "Adequate assurance" is limited to section 365. A secured creditor's property interest in its collateral can be adequately protected; the debtor's performance of its contract or lease can be adequately assured. Section 361 sets out examples of adequate protection; the Code does not give examples of adequate assurance.[1] A comparison of the two phrases suggests that adequate *protection* is a more demanding standard than adequate *assurance*.

The phrase "adequate assurance" is not defined in the Bankruptcy Code. The Commission on the Bankruptcy Laws of the United States adopted this phrase "adequate assurance" from section 2–609 of the Uniform Commercial Code.[2] Section 2–609 of the Uniform Commercial Code not only contains language similar to section 365(b) of the Bankruptcy Code, but also serves a similar purpose. In section 2–609, a party to an unperformed contract for the sale of goods is demanding adequate assurance of performance because it does not want to perform until it is reasonably certain of the other party's ability to perform.

Most reported cases on "adequate assurance" under section 365 are not helpful precedents. The courts quite properly tend to tie the holding of "adequate assurance" to the facts of the case. As was stated in *In re Grayhall Resources, Inc.*,[3] "each case must rest on a pragmatic analysis taking into account the lessor's rights and expectations as they existed prior to the filing of the bankruptcy proceeding."[4]

§ 5–18

1. Section 365(b)(3), considered infra, sets out examples of adequate assurance of future performance of leases of real property in a shopping center.

2. See Report of Commission on Bankruptcy Laws of the United States, H.R. Doc. No. 137, 93d Cong. 1st Sess. 156 (1973).

3. 63 B.R. 382 (Bankr. Colo.1986).

4. Id. at 388–89.

§ 5–19 Default Cure and Compensation

The Code does not condition assumption of an executory contract that is in default on a cash cure payment at the time of assumption. Instead, the Code requires that the trustee act "promptly" with respect to the cure and compensation for pecuniary loss.

In applying this vague, statutory standard of "promptly," courts have looked to the specific facts and circumstances. The amount of time varies from weeks to years. For example, *In re Coors of North Mississippi, Inc.*[1] permitted a three-year cure of defaults,[2] while *In re Grayhall Resources, Inc.*[3] limited the cure period to twenty-one days.[4]

What if the contract that the debtor moves to assume requires that all defaults must be cured within 30 days? Does such a contract provision control, i.e., is "promptly" then 30 days? No reported case has considered the precise question of whether the parties can, prebankruptcy, define what "promptly" under section 365(b) means.[5] We believe the bankruptcy court should still be free to approve a cure on other terms. While the general common-law concept is that a debtor assumes the contract in full, without change, section 365(b)'s standard ("provide adequate assurance that the trustee will promptly cure") should displace any contract provision regarding time for cure of defaults or terms for curing defaults under section 365(b).[6]

§ 5–20 Adequate Assurance of Future Performance

Recall that section 365(b)(2) requires adequate assurance of future performance only if the debtor is in default and does not define "adequate assurance." The statute does, however, give examples of adequate assurance of future performance of leases of real property in a shopping center in section 365(b)(3).

a. Adequate Assurance and Shopping Center Leases

It is clear from the legislative history that section 365(b)(3) is intended to provide shopping center landlords with greater assurance that their debtor/tenants will pay their rent and perform their other lease obligations.[1] More specifically, section 365(b)(3) was enacted for three reasons: (1) alleviate the hardship to landlord and other tenants resulting from vacancy or partial use of the debtor's space in the shopping center; (2) insure continuation of payments under the lease; and (3) guarantee to the landlord and the other shopping center tenants that the tenant mix will not be disrupted.[2]

§ 5–19
1. 27 B.R. 918 (Bankr. N.D.Miss.1983).
2. Id. at 922.
3. 63 B.R. 382 (Bankr. D.Colo.1986).
4. Id. at 384, 386–92.
5. There are reported cases that deal with contract time limitations on curing default. These cases involve the very different question of how quickly the debtor must cure a prepetition default to avoid termination of the contract. See supra at §§ 5–9 through 5–11.
6. Cf. Moody v. Amoco Oil Co., 734 F.2d 1200, 1215 n.15 (7th Cir.1984), cert. denied, 469 U.S. 982, 105 S.Ct. 386, 83 L.Ed.2d 321 (1984).

§ 5–20
1. See H.R. Rep. No. 595, 95th Cong., 1st Sess. 348–49 (1977), reprinted in 1978 U.S. Code Cong. & Admin. News 5963, 6305.
2. Id.

It is not clear, however, who qualifies as a shopping center landlord. The phrase "shopping center" is not defined in the Bankruptcy Code, but there is helpful language in the legislative history:

> A shopping center is often a carefully planned enterprise, and though it consists of numerous individual tenants, the center is planned as a single unit, often subject to a master lease or financing agreement. Under these agreements the tenant mix in a shopping center may be as important to the lessor as the actual promised rental payments, because certain mixes will attract higher percentages of the stores in the center and thus a higher rental for the landlord from those stores that are subject to a percentage of gross receipts rental agreements.[3]

In determining whether a group of stores is a "shopping center" for purposes of section 365(b)(3), physical characteristics such as contiguity of stores and common parking are important, but less important than contractual considerations such as common landlord, master lease with use restrictions, and joint advertising. *In re Joshua Slocum, Inc.*[4] reversed the bankruptcy judge's determination that the Denney Block in the downtown shopping district of Freeport, Maine was not a "shopping center."[5] The Third Circuit acknowledged that Denney Block does not look at all like a shopping mall. (It is three semi-adjacent buildings with a courtyard between two of the buildings and a common parking lot for the three buildings.) The Joshua Slocum decision listed fourteen characteristics of a shopping center, eleven of which existed at Denney Block.[6]

b. Adequate Assurance of Future Payment

Although the first two examples in section 365(b)(3) of adequate assurance of future performance of shopping center leases deal with future rent payments, the reported cases on adequate assurance of future payment do not seem to distinguish between shopping center leases and other leases or executory contracts. The requirement of adequate assurance of future performance is generally satisfied by the debtor's financial position and prospects[7] or some sort of deposit or guarantee.[8]

c. Adequate Assurance of Performance of Lease or Contract Provisions Not Requiring the Payment of Money

Section 365(b)(3) conditions assumption of an executory contract or

---

3. Id.

4. 922 F.2d 1081 (3d Cir.1990); see generally Bloom & Jannetta, Limits on the Assumption and Assignment of Shopping Center Leases, 3 Faulkner & Gray's Bankruptcy Law Review 5 (Summer 1991).

5. In so holding, the Third Circuit acknowledged that the definition of "shopping center" is left to case by case interpretation. 922 F.2d at 1086. Other cases interpreting "shopping center" include In re Goldblatt Brothers, Inc., 766 F.2d 1136 (7th Cir.1985); In re 905 International Stores, Inc., 57 B.R. 786 (E.D.Mo.1985); In re Ames Department Stores, 121 B.R. 160 (Bankr. S.D.N.Y. 1990).

6. 922 F.2d at 1087–88.

7. See, e.g., Richmond Leasing v. Capital Bank, 762 F.2d 1303, 1310–11 (5th Cir.1985); Seacoast Products, Inc. v. Spring Valley Farms, Inc., 34 B.R. 379, 380–81 (N.D.N.C. 1983).

8. See, e.g., In re Belize Airways, Ltd., 5 B.R. 152, 156 (Bankr. S.D.Fla.1980) (three months rent); In re Westview 74th Street Drug Corp., 59 B.R. 747 (Bankr. S.D.N.Y. 1986) (two months rent).

unexpired leases that is in default on adequate assurance of future *performance,* not adequate assurance of future *payment.* A contract or lease often creates performance obligations in addition to an obligation to pay. Surprisingly few reported cases have dealt with adequate assurance of future performance of nonmonetary obligations; most of these few cases deal with use clauses in nonshopping center leases.[9]

The language from the cases, the Bankruptcy Code and the legislative history support the following general observations about use clauses:

    1. Courts will not require strict compliance with all contract or lease provisions;

    2. Courts will be more strict in shopping center cases, than in nonshopping center cases;

    3. Shopping center cases decided after the 1984 amendments should reflect a stricter compliance standard than shopping cases decided before the 1984 amendments;[10] and,

    4. Courts will and should determine whether use restrictions and other contract or lease clauses have a valid business purpose or are disguised bankruptcy termination or anti-assignment clauses.[11]

§ 5-21 Adequate Assurance of Assignee Performance Requirements of Section 365(f)(2)

Subparagraph (f)(2) of section 365 sets out the two requirements for an

---

9. In re Joshua Slocum, Ltd., 922 F.2d 1081 (3d Cir.1990); In re Haute Cuisine, Inc., 58 B.R. 390 (Bankr. M.D.Fla.1986); In re Grudoski, 33 B.R. 154 (Bankr. D. Haw. 1983); In re Peterson's Ltd., 31 B.R. 524 (Bankr. S.D.N.Y. 1983); In re Fifth Avenue Originals, 32 B.R. 648 (Bankr. S.D.N.Y. 1983); In re TSW Stores of Nanuet, Inc., 34 B.R. 299 (Bankr. S.D.N.Y. 1983); In re U.L. Radio Corp., 19 B.R. 537 (Bankr. S.D.N.Y. 1982); In re Consolidated Southeastern Group, Inc., 75 B.R. 102 (Bankr. N.D.Ga.1987); In re Vista VI, Inc., 35 B.R. 564 (Bankr. N.D.Ohio 1983).

10. The 1984 Amendments deleted the word "substantially" from section 365(b)(3) and (4). It would thus seem that a court is no longer free to sanction noncompliance with a provision of a shopping center lease by finding that it is not a substantial breach. Cf. M. Bienenstock, Bankruptcy Reorganization 498 (1987); 1 R. Ginsberg, Bankruptcy 527 (2d ed. 1989). In re Joshua Slocum Ltd., 922 F.2d 1081 (3d Cir.1990), seems to ignore, if not overlook, the 1984 amendments. See id. at 1090 ("Congress did not envision literal compliance with all lease provisions; insubstantial disruptions in, inter alia, tenant mix, and insubstantial breaches in other leases or agreements were contemplated and allowed"); id. at 1086 n.3 (1978 text of § 365(b)(3) without the 1984 Amendments).

11. Most shopping center leases contain clauses restricting use or otherwise protecting the tenant mix of the center. What if the shopping center lease does not contain any such express language? Read literally, section 365(b)(2)(D) protects the tenant mix from a bankruptcy assignment even where there is no such express protection in the lease. Compare the language of section 365(b)(2)(D) with that of section 365(b)(2)(C):

(C) that assumption or assignment of such lease is subject to all the provisions thereof, including (but not limited to) provisions such as a radius, location, use, or exclusivity provision, and will not breach any such provision contained in any other lease, financing agreement, or master agreement relating to such shopping center; and

(D) that assumption or assignment of such lease will not disrupt any tenant mix or balance in such shopping center."

Note that (D), unlike (C), does not make any reference to lease provisions. Indeed, it can be argued that requiring any such reference to a lease provision in (D) makes (D) surplus since (C) already requires compliance with all lease provision. In re Ames Department Stores, Inc., 127 B.R. 744 (Bankr. S.D.N.Y. 1991), rejected such an argument, relying on (i) the language of section 365(f)(2) ("adequate assurance of future performance * * * of such contract or lease"), (ii) legislative history, and (iii) a policy against landlord's realizing a windfall because of a tenant's bankruptcy.

assignment of an executory contract or an unexpired lease.[1] First, the assumption requirements discussed above must be satisfied. Second, the trustee or debtor in possession must provide adequate assurance of performance by the assignor.

Compare the requirement of adequate assurance of future performance in section 365(f)(2) with the similar requirement of adequate assurance of future performance in section 365(b). Notice that section 365(f)(2) conditions assignment of an executory contract or unexpired lease on adequate assurance of future performance regardless of whether there has been a default in the contract or lease while section 365(b) requires adequate assurance of future performance to assume only if there has been a default. Note also that section 365(f) focuses on the assignee—adequate assurance of future performance by the assignee. Section 365(f)(2), like section 365(b), does not define "adequate assurance of future performance." The examples of adequate assurance of future performance of a lease of real property in a shopping center in section 365(b)(3) are expressly applicable to assignments of shopping center leases.

Section 365(f) should be read together not only with section 365(b), but also with section 365(l). Section 365(l) authorizes a lessor[2] to require a deposit or other security for performance under as assigned lease to the same extent that it would require it from a similar lessee on initial leasing. Although section 365(l) does not refer to section 365(f)(2), a court may treat this deposit or other security as the adequate assurance of future performance.

Also, section 365(f)(2) must be read together with section 365(k). Adequate assurance of the assignor's future performance is important because after an assignment of an executory contract or unexpired lease, the estate is not liable for default.

G. GAP PERIOD

A gap occurs between the filing of a bankruptcy petition and any action to assume, assign, or reject an executory contract or unexpired lease. This interim period is rarely significantly shorter than 90 days and often significantly longer.[3] Accordingly, it is necessary to consider the question of what are the rights and responsibilities of the debtor and the other party to an executory contract or unexpired lease during the gap period between the filing of the bankruptcy petition and the assumption/rejection decision. This question is important primarily in Chapter 11 cases.

§ 5–22 Performance Obligations of the Nondebtor Party

Section 365 does not deal directly with the performance obligations of the nondebtor party to an executory contract or unexpired lease during the

---

§ 5–21

1. A proceeding to assign an executory contract is a contested matter, governed by Rule 9014, and so is initiated by the filing of a motion. See Bankr. R. 6004(a).

2. It is unclear whether section 365(l) is limited to real property leases. Paragraph (l) was added to the Bankruptcy Code in 1984 as a part of a package of amendments to section 365 which enhanced the rights of a lessor of commercial real estate. Section 365(l) first uses the general word "lessor" but later uses the more limited term "landlord."

3. Cf. 11 U.S.C.A. § 365(d), considered supra at §§ 5–9 through 5–11.

gap period. Both section 365(b)(4) and section 362 indirectly indicate that the nondebtor party to an *unexpired lease* is obligated to continue its performance, i.e., to make the leasehold or leased goods available to the debtor.

Section 365(b)(4) excuses a nondebtor lessor from providing "services or supplies incidental to such lease" on credit prior to assumption where the debtor lessee is in default; this "suggests" that a nondebtor lessor is *not* excused from continuing to provide the leased premises or goods to the debtor. To illustrate, N leases machinery to D. The lease requires N to service the machinery. D files a bankruptcy petition. D is in default under the lease. Section 365(b)(4) states that N is not obligated to service the machine on credit during the gap but suggests that N remains obligated to provide the leased machine during the gap.

Section 362(a)(3) reinforces that suggestion. Any action by N to recover the leased equipment during the gap would violate the automatic stay which reaches "any act to obtain possession of property of the estate or of property from the estate."[1] Stated differently, the automatic stay in essence compels the nondebtor lessor to perpetuate unexpired leases during the gap period.[2]

If the nondebtor party to an unexpired lease is required to continue its performance during the gap period, is there any reason to treat the nondebtor party to executory contracts differently?[3] In Chapter 11 cases, the debtor in possession's ability to compel performance with respect to executory contracts can be essential to the business operations and to the reorganization effort. If that ability is eliminated, a debtor in possession may be compelled to make its assumption/rejection decision as soon as it files.

Most courts seem simply to assume that the nondebtor party to an executory contract or lease is obligated to continue performance or, at minimum, is prevented from cancelling the contract so that a failure to perform is a contract breach. The very few cases that have expressly dealt with the question of gap period performance obligations of the nondebtor party to an executory contract have so stated.

In re Feyline Presents, Inc.[4] rejected the argument by a nondebtor party, Coke, that its executory contract with the debtor was not enforceable prior to assumption. There Coke repudiated the contract prior to the trustee's rejection. Coke argued that since the contract was deemed breached as of a date immediately prior to the filing of the petition, there was no contract on which it was obligated to perform and so its repudiation cannot give rise to a claim for breach. The court held that, prior to assumption or rejection, an executory contract is enforceable against the nondebtor party but not against the debtor. In so holding, the court stated:

§ 5–22
1. 11 U.S.C.A. § 362(a)(3).
2. Elsewhere we discuss the extent to which the stay protects a debtor's contract rights as property of the estate. See § 3–14 supra.
3. Professor Westbrook has argued that leases and executory contracts that transfer an interest in property, i.e., an ITI, "interest in the thing itself" should be treated different from other executory contracts. See generally Westbrook, A Functional Analysis of Executory Contracts, 74 Minn.L.Rev. 227 (1989). And, surely some law professor has or will incorrectly argue somewhere that section 365(d)(3), considered infra, justifies requiring gap period performance from nondebtor lessors but not from nondebtor parties to executory contracts.
4. 81 B.R. 623 (Bankr. Colo.1988).

The suggestion by Coke that, until assumption, there is no contract would effectively deprive a debtor-in-possession or a trustee of the benefits of the breathing spell provided by § 365 of the Code. The debtor is given the option of assuming or rejecting. In order to make that option effective, the contract must remain in effect and the other party must be bound to perform under the terms of the contract. If a nondebtor could unilaterally cease performance on an executory contract, the powers provided to a debtor under § 365(d) would have no meaning. Coke could have availed itself of the provisions of § 365(d)(2) to force Feyline [the debtor] to an early decision to assume.[5]

The facts make the holding of *Feyline* fairly outrageous. Coke was obligated to make advance payments of money for future services of the debtor prior to the debtor's assumption of the contract. We doubt that a nondebtor party should be required to make an advance payment to a debtor who has not even assumed the executory contract.

It would be an even more outrageous case that would require performance by the nondebtor party to a contract the debtor cannot assume. As noted in the statement from *Feyline,* the purpose of the gap period is to afford the debtor in possession or trustee an opportunity to decide whether to assume or reject an executory or unexpired lease. If the contract in question is a kind that cannot be assumed, then there really is no gap period for that contract. The argument is thus much weaker that the nondebtor party is obligated to continue such a contract postpetition.[6] We do not believe that a nondebtor is obligated to perform during the gap on a *nonassumable* contract.

§ 5–23 Performance Obligations of the Debtor

a. *Nonresidential Real Property Leases*

Section 365(d)(3) expressly deals with the performance obligations of the debtor under a nonresidential real property lease.[1] Until a nonresidential real property lease is assumed or rejected, the debtor tenant must perform all obligations under the lease accruing after commencement of the case. Rent accrues as per the lease. For cause, however, the court may give the debtor until 60 days after the filing of the bankruptcy petition to perform any lease obligations that arose during those first 60 days in bankruptcy.

---

5. Id. at 627; see also In re Public Service Co. of New Hampshire, 884 F.2d 11, 15 (1st Cir.1989); In re Whitcomb & Keller Mortgage Co., 715 F.2d 375, 378 (7th Cir.1983); In re McLean Industries, Inc., 96 B.R. 440 (Bankr. S.D.N.Y. 1989); Bordewieck, The Post-Petition, Pre-Rejection, Pre-Assumption Status of an Executory Contract, 59 Am. Bankr. L.J. 197 (1983); Buschman, Benefits and Burdens: Post-Petition Performance of Unassumed Executory Contracts, 5 Bankr. Dev. J. 341 (1988); but cf. NLRB v. Bildisco & Bildisco, 465 U.S. 513, 532, 104 S.Ct. 1188, 1199, 79 L.Ed.2d 482 (1984) ("the filing of a petition in bankruptcy under Chapter 11 makes the contract unenforceable"); G. Treister, J. Trost, L. Forman, K. Klee, R. Levin, Fundamentals of Bankruptcy Law 251 (2d ed. 1988).

6. See Buschman, Benefits and Burdens: Post-Petition Performance of Unassumed Executory Contracts, 5 Bankr. Dev. J. 341, 348–49 (1988); but cf. In re Computer Communications, Inc., 824 F.2d 725 (9th Cir. 1987) (The court held that the nondebtor party's termination of a unassumable contract was a violation of the automatic stay, regardless of whether the contract was assumable.).

§ 5–23

1. The automatic stay also deals specially with nonresidential leases. For a discussion of the stay issues, see § 3–14 supra.

While section 365(d)(3) requires a debtor/tenant to make timely payments of rent on nonresidential real property, it does not set out the landlord's remedies if the debtor-tenant defaults. Section 365(d)(3) has created confusion over the consequences of noncompliance with its requirements both because of what it does say—"notwithstanding section 503(b)(1)"—and what it does not say—anything about the lease being "deemed rejected."

Assume, for example, that D Inc. rents a building from L. The lease provides for bimonthly rental payments of $10,000. D Inc. files for Chapter 11 relief. Section 365(d)(3) contemplates that D Inc. will make the initial postpetition rental payment within 60 days after the bankruptcy filing and remain current thereafter. 61 days after the bankruptcy filing, what are L's rights if D Inc. has not paid any postpetition rent? Can L recover the $10,000? Can L terminate lease?

In dealing with L's demand for payment under section 365(d)(3) of the $10,000 postpetition rent, the court will have to deal with the language "notwithstanding section 503(b)(1) of this title." Under section 503(b)(1), administrative expenses include the actual, necessary costs of preserving the estate. Courts and commentators have variously read section 365(d)(3)'s reference to section 503(b)(1) to mean that the landlord's section 365(d)(3) claims have (i) a superpriority above administrative expenses and are to be paid immediately,[2] or (ii) the same priority as other administrative expenses and so can be paid immediately only where there is a reasonable likelihood that all administrative expenses will be paid in full in the case,[3] or (iii) no priority by reason of section 365(d)(3) and so qualify for an administrative

---

2. In re Rare Coin Galleries of America, Inc., 72 B.R. 415, 416–18 (D.Mass.1987); In re Longua, 58 B.R. 503, 505 (Bankr. W.D.Wis. 1986).

3. See, e.g. In re Wingspread Corp., 116 B.R. 915 (Bankr. S.D.N.Y. 1990); In re Virginia Packaging Supply Co., Inc., 122 B.R. 491 (Bankr. E.D.Va.1990). There is limited case authority for an additional award of interest. In re Far West Corporation of Shasta County, 120 B.R. 551 (Bankr. E.D.Cal.1990) stands for the proposition that administrative rent and similar charges due and owing pursuant to section 365(d)(3) should accrue interest from the date the lease in question is rejected. See also United States v. Friendship College, Inc., 737 F.2d 430, 433 (4th Cir.1984) (postpetition interest on unpaid taxes is an administrative expense); In re Mesa Refining, Inc., 66 B.R. 36 (Bankr. D. Colo. 1986) (interest on a reclamation claim as an administrative expense); In re Pharmadyne Laboratories, Inc., 53 B.R. 517, 523 (Bankr. D.N.J.1985) (interest on FICA taxes as an administrative expense). The Far West Corporation court only permitted interest after it had made a determination that the debtor's estate had at all relevant times sufficient funds to satisfy all potential administrative expense claims in full. 120 B.R. at 556.

We believe that Far West Corporation is wrongly decided. The Far West Corporation court acknowledges that all reported decisions addressing the issue of interest on allowed administrative expense claims run counter to its decision. Id. at 554. See e.g., In re Brooks & Woodington, Inc., 505 F.2d 794, 799 (7th Cir.1974); In re Fred Swain, Inc., 97 B.R. 660, 661 (Bankr. S.D.Fla.1989); In re Goldblatt Bros., Inc., 61 B.R. 459 (Bankr. N.D.Ill. 1986).

As noted by the court in In re Fred Swain, Inc.:

Because the presumption in bankruptcy cases is that the debtor's limited resources will be equally distributed among his creditors, statutory priorities are narrowly construed ... [I]f one claimant is to be preferred over others, the purpose should be clear from the statute.

* * *

The explicit provision in § 506(b) for recovery [of interest] by a limited class of creditors under limited circumstances is an unmistakable indication that such charges are not recoverable by any other claimant in the absence of an equally explicit provision. Any other reading of § 503(b) would be the antithesis of the strict and narrow construction that has always been placed on priority treatment of claims in bankruptcy.

97 B.R. at 661.

expense priority only if the requirements of section 503(b)(1) can be satisfied.[4] We do not believe that the language or legislative history of section 365(d)(3) compels any of these readings. The "majority" rule is (ii), i.e. a claim under section 365(d)(3) should have administrative expense priority but not a superpriority.[5]

In dealing with L's demand to terminate the lease because of D's noncompliance with section 365(d)(3), the court will have to deal with section 365(d)(3)'s lack of the "deemed rejected" language that appears in both section 365(d)(1) and (4). Courts have been reluctant to evict a debtor tenant for noncompliance with section 365(d)(3). The following statement from *In re Westview 74th Street Drug Corp.*[6] is representative:

> [I]t would be inappropriate for the judiciary to fashion a harsh rule of forfeiture where Congress did not provide one. Thus, we hold that the failure to meet lease obligations required by section 365(d)(3) within the first sixty days after the date of the order for relief does not effect an automatic termination of the lease. Rather, the appropriate remedy for such a failure is one which should be formulated by the court after a review of the facts of the particular case."[7]

b. *Other Leases and Contracts*

It is generally stated that the debtor party to an executory contract or lease is not obligated to perform during the gap period.[8] Such a statement is somewhat misleading. The Code does require gap period performance from certain debtors under certain kinds of executory contract and leases.[9] More important, when the debtor finally assumes the contract or lease or rejects it, she will be liable for the goods or services she received under executory contracts or leases during the gap period.

Assume, for example, that D Inc. is leasing an airplane from L. The monthly lease payments are $5,000. D Inc. files a Chapter 11 petition on February 1. D Inc. does not assume or reject the airplane lease until December 1. During the ten month gap period, D Inc. does not make lease payments to L. If D Inc. assumes the lease, it will be obligated to pay the $50,000 in gap-period rent as a part of the section 365(b) cure of defaults. If D Inc. rejects the lease, the gap period rent will be a part of L's claim.

---

4. See, e.g., In re Orvco, Inc., 95 B.R. 724 (Bankr. 9th Cir.1989); In re Tammey Jewels, Inc., 116 B.R. 292 (Bankr. M.D.Fla.1990).

5. See generally Battershall, Commercial Leases and Section 365 of the Bankruptcy Code, 64 Am. Bankr. L.J. 329 (1990); Zaretsky, Nonresidential Leases. New York Law Journal, September 20, 1990, page 3.

6. 59 B.R. 747 (Bankr. S.D.N.Y. 1986). The failure to pay rent required by section 365(d)(3) does not even effect an automatic denial of extensions of the section 365(d)(4) time requirements. See In re Southwest Aircraft Services, Inc., 831 F.2d 848, 854 (9th Cir.1987), cert. denied, 487 U.S. 1206, 108 S.Ct. 2848, 101 L.Ed.2d 885 (1988), considered supra at § 5–10.

7. 59 B.R. at 754. For more, see our discussion in Chapter 3 on a lessor's right for relief from the stay during the gap period before rejection or assumption, at § 3–28 supra.

8. See, e.g., In re Gunter Hotel Associates, 96 B.R. 696, 700 (Bankr. N.D. Texas 1988); Bordewieck, The Prepetition, Pre-Rejection, Pre-Assumption, Status of an Executory Contract, 59 Am. Bankr. L.J. 197, 213–15 (1985).

9. For example, section 365(h) compels a debtor landlord to perform during the gap by making the leasehold available to the debtor. Similarly, section 365(n) requires a debtor licensor of intellectual property to make the licensed intellectual property available during the gap.

There are two lines of cases dealing with whether a claim for gap period rent qualifies as an administrative expense under section 503(b)(1). Some cases hold that the lessor is entitled to an administrative expense priority for gap period rent regardless of whether the debtor uses the leased property.[10] The majority and better view is that the lessor is entitled to an administrative expense only if the debtor actually uses the leased property and a benefit to the estate can be established.[11] The existence of an administrative expense priority should turn on whether the estate has realized a benefit, not on whether a particular creditor has sustained a loss.

§ 5–24 Right of Nondebtor Lessor to Adequate Protection

For full text of this section, see Epstein, Nickles & White, Bankruptcy, Practitioner Treatise Series, Vol. 1.

§ 5–25 Recoupment by Other Party During the Gap Period

For full text of this section, see Epstein, Nickles & White, Bankruptcy, Practitioner Treatise Series, Vol. 1.

H. "SPECIAL" LEASES AND CONTRACTS

§ 5–26 "Special" Leases and Contracts

For full text of this section, see Epstein, Nickles & White, Bankruptcy, Practitioner Treatise Series, Vol. 1.

---

10. See, e.g., In re Fred Sanders Co., 22 B.R. 902 (Bankr. E.D.Mich.1982); In re Schulz, 63 B.R. 163 (Bankr. Neb.1986).

11. See, e.g., In re Subscription Television of Greater Atlanta, Inc., 789 F.2d 1530 (11th Cir.1986); Kinnan & Kinnan Partnership v. Agristor Leasing, 116 B.R. 162 (D.Neb.1990) (rejecting Schulz).

Chapter 6

AVOIDANCE POWERS

Table of Sections

Sec.
6–1 Introduction to Avoidance Powers.
6–2 Who Can Avoid Transfers.

A. Preference, Section 547
6–3 Introduction to Preferences.

1. Elements of a Preference
6–4 Transfer of an Interest of the Debtor in Property.
    a. The Critical Terms (Especially "Transfer").
    b. Most Common Transfers.
6–5 ____ Increase in Value.
6–6 ____ Transfers of Exempt Property.
6–7 ____ Property of Third Party and Earmarked Funds.
6–8 To or for the Benefit of a Creditor.
6–9 ____ Preferences That Indirectly Benefit (a/k/a Indirect Preferences).
6–10 ____ Remedying an Indirect Preference (and the *Levit* Case).
6–11 Within the Preference Period.
6–12 ____ General Rule: Time of Transfer Is Time of Perfection.
6–13 ____ Exception: Perfection Within Ten Days.
6–14 ____ Caveat: No Transfer Until Debtor Acquires Rights.
6–15 ____ The Caveat Applied to Garnishment During Preference Period.
6–16 ____ Payment by Check.
6–17 ____ Insiders.
6–18 When the Debtor Is Insolvent.
6–19 For or on Account of an Antecedent Debt.
6–20 Preferential Effect.
6–21 ____ Foreclosure Sales.

2. Exceptions, Section 547(c)
6–22 Introduction to Exceptions.
6–23 Contemporaneous New Value, Section 547(c)(1).
6–24 ____ Scope of the Exception.
6–25 ____ New Value.
6–26 ____ Exchange.
6–27 ____ Contemporaneous in Fact.
6–28 ____ Contemporaneous by Design.
6–29 Ordinary Payment of Ordinary Debts, Section 547(c)(2).
6–30 ____ Debt Incurred in the Ordinary Course.
6–31 ____ Payment Made in the Ordinary Course and on Ordinary Business Terms.
6–32 ____ Payments on Long–Term Debt.
6–33 Enabling Security Interests, Section 547(c)(3).
6–34 Subsequent New Value, Section 547(c)(4).
6–35 Floating Liens on Inventory or Receivables, Section 546(c)(5).
6–36 Statutory Liens, Section 547(c)(6).

Sec.
6–37 Small Transfers in Consumer Cases, Section 547(c)(7).
                B. Setoff, Section 553
6–38 Overview: The Meaning of Setoff and Its Significance in Bankruptcy, Section 553.
        1. Bankruptcy's Substantive Effect on Right of Setoff
6–39 General Rule of Section 553.
6–40 Requirements of the General Rule.
    a. Existence of Substantive Right.
    b. Both Debts Prepetition.
    c. Mutuality.
        2. Substantive Exceptions to the General Rule
6–41 Statutory.
6–42 Equitable.
        3. Bankruptcy's Procedural Effect on Exercise of Section 553 Setoff
6–43 Automatic Stay.
6–44 Waiver.
                4. Recoupment
6–45 Recoupment.
            [Contained in Volume 2]
            C. Fraudulent Transfers
6–46 Introduction to Fraudulent Transfers.
        1. Transfers Fraudulent Under Bankruptcy Law, Section 548
6–47 Introduction to Section 548.
6–48 Actual Fraud.
6–49 Constructive Fraud.
6–50 Remedies and Defenses.
        2. Special Problems
6–51 Guaranties.
6–52 LBOs.
6–53 Foreclosure Sales.
6–54 ____ Forced Sale as "Transfer" of Debtor's Interest in Property.
6–55 ____ Timing of the Transfer.
6–56 ____ Determining "Reasonably Equivalent Value".
6–57 Transfers of Exempt Property.
6–58 Converting Nonexempt Property to Exempt Property.
6–59 Preferential Transfers.
        3. Transfers Fraudulent Under State Law, Section 544(b)
6–60 Transfers Fraudulent Under State Law (Trustee as Successor to Actual Creditors, Section 544(b)).
        D. "Strong–Arm" Powers, Section 544(a)
6–61 Trustee as Hypothetical Lien Creditor or Purchaser ("Strong–Arm" Powers, Section 544(a)).
        E. Statutory Liens, Section 545
6–62 Statutory Liens, Section 545.
        F. Sellers' Right of Reclamation, Section 546(c)
6–63 Reclamation Under State Law.
6–64 Importance of Preserving State–Created Reclamation in Buyer's Bankruptcy—Role of Section 546(c).
6–65 Effect of Section 546(c).
6–66 State Law Requirements for Reclamation and Federal Requirements of Section 546(c).
6–67 The Possession and Priority Requirement.
        G. Postpetition Transfers, Sections 549, 542 and 552
6–68 Introduction to Postpetition Transfers and Their Avoidance.
        1. Postpetition Transfers in General, Section 549
6–69 General Rule Regarding Avoidance of Postpetition Transfers.

Sec.
6–70 Exception: Authorized Transfers.
6–71 Exception: Involuntary Cases.
6–72 Exception: Transfers of Real Estate.
6–73 Time Limitation on Avoidance Under Section 549.
    2. Postpetition Transfers by Third Parties
6–74 Special Protection for Innocent Transferors, Section 542(c).
    3. Postpetition Effect of Prepetition Security Agreements, Section 552
6–75 Introduction.
6–76 General Rule, Section 552(a).
6–77 Exception, Section 552(b).
6–78 Exceptions to the Exception—The "Except" Clauses of Section 552(b).
    H. Consequences of Avoidance
6–79 Overview of Consequences.
    1. Nullification of the Transfer
6–80 The Nullifying Effect of Avoidance Per Se and the Difference From Recovery.
6–81 Time Limitations on Avoidance, Section 546(a).
6–82 —— Applicability.
6–83 —— Mechanics.
6–84 —— Qualifications.
6–85 "Stockbroker" Defenses (and Other Protections of Financial Markets).
    2. Preservation of the Avoided Transfer, Section 551
6–86 Preservation of the Avoided Transfer, Section 551.
    3. Recovery From Transferees, Section 550
6–87 Basic Remedial Rule: Recovery of the Property or Its Value.
6–88 Persons Liable.
6–89 Improvement Lien for All Good Faith Transferees.
6–90 Time Limitations on Recovery.
    I. Pseudo Avoidance Powers
6–91 Subordinating Claims, Section 510.
6–92 Consensual Subordination, Section 510(a).
6–93 Equitable Subordination, Section 510(c).
6–94 Asserting Debtor's Defenses, Section 558.

§ 6–1 Introduction to Avoidance Powers

Bankruptcy principally aims to give the debtor a fresh financial start while allowing creditors to share equally, to a fair and equitable extent, in the debtor's accumulated assets that form the bankruptcy estate. This broad objective and its constituent goals are undermined by pre- and postbankruptcy transfers of property that unfairly or discriminatorily withhold or rob property from the estate to the prejudice of the debtor or her creditors.

To remedy this theft the Bankruptcy Code condemns and provides for the *avoidance,* i.e., the undoing and recovery, of some prebankruptcy transfers of the debtor's property and most postbankruptcy transfers of estate property. The person primarily responsible for avoiding these transfers and recapturing the property for the estate's benefit is usually the bankruptcy trustee or, in her stead in reorganization cases, the debtor in possession. The major statutes providing for avoidance are referred to collectively as the trustee's *avoiding* or *avoidance powers.*

These avoidance powers are sections:

- 544 Trustee as hypothetical lien creditor [1] and bona fide purchaser [2] and as successor to actual creditors [3]
- 545 Statutory liens [4]
- 546 Reclamation [5]
- 547 Preferences [6]
- 548 Fraudulent transfers and obligations [7]
- 549 Postpetition transfers [8]
- 553 Setoff [9]

We devote this entire chapter primarily to explaining and illustrating these powers separately because each of them largely works independently of the others; but we also frequently note their interrelationships and often intersperse coverage of various statutes that are closely and importantly connected to the avoiding powers and their aims.

There are other Code sections that allow avoiding transfers of property. Some of them explicitly authorize avoidance; [10] and others effectively operate as avoidance powers. We concentrate, however, on the major, explicit avoidance provisions of the Code's Chapter 5. They are most important theoretically, and in practice they fuel most adversary efforts to avoid transfers.

§ 6–2 Who Can Avoid Transfers

Transfers condemned through the avoiding powers are not automatically avoided in a bankruptcy case. Avoidance does not occur by operation of law.[1] Rather, a person whom the Code empowers to avoid transfers must bring an action or proceeding to do so, and the bankruptcy court then determines the matter. As a broad, general rule, the bankruptcy trustee wields the avoiding powers; but in some cases or instances the powers are asserted by the debtor, the debtor's surrogate, or the debtor's creditors.

The statutes that describe the Code's principal avoiding powers explicitly give them only to the trustee. They repeatedly declare that the "trustee" is the person who "may avoid," [2] which actually means that only she is authorized to bring an action or proceeding asking the court to order

§ 6–1

1. 11 U.S.C.A. § 544(a)(1) & (2).
2. 11 U.S.C.A. § 544(a)(3).
3. 11 U.S.C.A. § 544(b); see also 11 U.S.C.A. § 551.
4. 11 U.S.C.A. § 545.
5. 11 U.S.C.A. § 546(c).
6. 11 U.S.C.A. § 547(b).
7. 11 U.S.C.A. § 548(a) & (b).
8. 11 U.S.C.A. § 549(a).
9. 11 U.S.C.A. § 553(a) & (b).
10. See, e.g., 11 U.S.C.A. § 724(a) (trustee may avoid lien that secures a fine, penalty, forfeiture or penal damages). Another example is section 522, which empowers individual debtors to avoid certain transfers that impair their exemptions. See 11 U.S.C.A. § 522(f) & (h). We devote a large part of another chapter to discussing section 522 and its avoidance powers. See §§ 8–23—8–29 infra.

§ 6–2

1. See Practitioner Treatise, Vol. 1.
2. 11 U.S.C.A. §§ 544(a) & (b); 545; 547(b); 548(a) & (b); 553(b)(1) ("trustee may recover"); 549(b).

avoidance.[3] The basic reason is that avoidance is designed to enlarge the estate for the benefit of creditors; and, for conceptual and practical reasons, representation of the estate, and authority to act for creditors collectively, are centered in the single person of the trustee.[4] The trustee is not required, however, to request avoidance of a transfer; rather, she is the person empowered to do so if, in her discretion, avoidance is appropriate.[5] The trustee cannot even assign her right to exercise the avoidance powers.[6] This general rule, that only the trustee avoids, applies broadly in every kind of bankruptcy except a Chapter 9 case.[7]

Usually, however, a trustee is not appointed in a Chapter 11 case. In place of a trustee is the debtor in possession who, by express statutory authorization, exercises all of the functions and duties of a trustee.[8] Thus, in a typical Chapter 11 case, the avoiding powers are enforced by the debtor in possession.[9] We would assume that in the unusual Chapter 11 case in which a trustee is appointed,[10] especially when the appointment results from the debtor's fraud or incompetence, the trustee displaces the debtor in possession and acquires the exclusive power to avoid transfers.

A trustee is always appointed in a Chapter 12 case,[11] but the debtor may also serve simultaneously as debtor in possession. A Chapter 12 debtor in possession, like her Chapter 11 counterpart, is expressly authorized to assert the trustee's powers.[12] Presumably, therefore, she can assert the avoiding powers concurrently with the trustee or even exclusively.[13]

A trustee is always appointed, too, in a Chapter 13 case.[14] There is no debtor in possession, but the debtor herself is expressly given some of the trustee's powers through section 1303.[15] The powers expressly given to her, however, do not include the trustee's avoiding powers. For this reason some courts have held that a Chapter 13 debtor lacks authority to exercise the avoiding powers.[16] Yet, the legislative history makes clear that the purpose of section 1303 was to specify "rights and powers that the debtor has exclusive of the trustee" [17] without implying "that the debtor does not also possess other powers concurrently with the trustee." [18] Moreover, the Code explicitly makes the provisions of Chapter 5, which includes the avoiding powers, generally applicable in Chapter 13 cases.[19] For these reasons a majority of courts have concluded that a Chapter 13 debtor is free, concurrently with the Chapter 13 trustee, to exercise the trustee's avoiding powers for the benefit of the estate.[20]

In cases under other chapters of the Code, especially Chapter 7 cases, debtors themselves (i.e., personally) generally cannot exercise the trustee's

3. See Practitioner Treatise, Vol. 1.
4. See Practitioner Treatise, Vol. 1.
5. See Practitioner Treatise, Vol. 1.
6. See Practitioner Treatise, Vol. 1.
7. See Practitioner Treatise, Vol. 1.
8. 11 U.S.C.A. § 1107(a).
9. See Practitioner Treatise, Vol. 1.
10. See 11 U.S.C.A. §§ 1104 & 1106.
11. See 11 U.S.C.A. § 1202.
12. 11 U.S.C.A. § 1203.
13. See Practitioner Treatise, Vol. 1.
14. See Practitioner Treatise, Vol. 1.
15. 11 U.S.C.A. § 1303.
16. See Practitioner Treatise, Vol. 1.
17. 124 Cong.Rec. 32,409 (1978) (remarks of Rep. Edwards).
18. Id.
19. 11 U.S.C.A. § 103(a).
20. See Practitioner Treatise, Vol. 1.

avoiding powers for anyone's benefit.[21] In Chapter 7 and other kinds of bankruptcy cases, however, individual debtors are expressly empowered to avoid, for their own benefit, certain transfers that impair exemptions.[22] We discuss these limited avoiding powers of debtors in our separate discussion of exempt property.[23]

Individual creditors generally are not empowered to use the trustee's avoiding powers in any kind of case [24] either for their own benefit or for the benefit of the estate, not even to attack transfers the creditors could have avoided under state law because of harm to them personally.[25] Creditors most often try to pursue avoidance actions in Chapter 11 cases that are managed by a debtor in possession, complaining that avoiding transfers for the benefit of creditors is often against the interests of the debtor who thus refuses to act. The courts are sensitive to this conflict-of-interest argument, but not to the extent of conferring the avoiding powers on creditors carte blanche.

Instead, the courts have outlined and endorsed more limited "powers" that frustrated creditors can assert to overcome and remedy indirectly the inaction of self-interested debtors-in-possession. For instance, in the case *Nebraska State Bank v. Jones*,[26] the Eighth Circuit suggested that an unsatisfied individual creditor can alternatively:

- move to dismiss the Chapter 11 case;
- seek to convert the case to Chapter 7;
- move to replace the debtor in possession with a Chapter 11 trustee;
- petition the court to compel the debtor in possession to act; or,
- petition the court to allow the creditor herself to institute an avoidance action.[27]

The last option, getting the bankruptcy court's permission for the creditor to act herself, really involves the creditor bringing an avoidance action in the form of a derivative suit for the estate's benefit. Other courts have endorsed this option as a means for creditors to overcome inaction by debtors and even by trustees in Chapter 11 and other cases;[28] but authority to so proceed, though presumably available to any appropriately interested creditor in any case, is most often actually given to *creditors' committees* in Chapter 11 cases.[29] Moreover, most courts have held that the authority generally exists only on a case-by-case basis, when specifically approved beforehand by the court, and only upon a showing of good cause.[30]

Apparently, however, after confirmation of a reorganization plan in a Chapter 11 case, someone other than the trustee or the debtor in possession can freely exercise the avoiding powers carte blanche. According to section 1123, the plan may provide for "the retention and enforcement by the

---

21. See Practitioner Treatise, Vol. 1.
22. See 11 U.S.C.A. § 522(f) & (h).
23. See §§ 8–24—8–29.
24. See Practitioner Treatise, Vol. 1.
25. See Practitioner Treatise, Vol. 1.
26. 846 F.2d 477 (8th Cir.1988).
27. Id. at 478, quoting Saline State Bank v. Mahloch, 834 F.2d 690, 695 (8th Cir.1987); see also In re Curry & Sorensen, Inc., 57 B.R. 824, 828 (Bankr. 9th Cir.1986) (same listing of options).
28. See Practitioner Treatise, Vol. 1.
29. See Practitioner Treatise, Vol. 1.
30. See Practitioner Treatise, Vol. 1.

debtor, by the trustee, *or by a representative of the estate* appointed for such purpose, of any * * * claim or interest [belonging to the debtor or to the estate]."[31] The courts construe this provision as giving the avoiding powers to the person named in the plan as the debtor's or estate's representative, even though this person is a third party whom the court has not specifically or formally authorized to bring avoidance actions.[32]

This authority is specific and limited, flowing from the statute (section 1123(b)(3)(B)) and the plan. Neither the trustee nor debtor in possession enjoys the general power to assign the right to pursue avoidance actions. Thus, a third person who acquires assets from the estate, as through an asset purchase agreement in Chapter 11, is not thereby empowered to avoid, and the debtor in possession is precluded from asserting her avoiding powers for the benefit of the third person.[33]

A. PREFERENCE, SECTION 547
§ 6–3 Introduction to Preferences

Bankruptcy law aims to distribute the bankruptcy estate to the debtor's creditors in an order that corresponds to a prescribed hierarchy of classes of creditors.[1] The primary goal is to treat creditors within each class equally by giving every class member a pro rata share of the property available for distribution to the class. Of course, the real importance of establishing and ranking classes of creditors, and treating members of the same class equally, is tied to the size of the estate. An equal share of nothing is still nothing.

Generally speaking, the bankruptcy estate consists only of property the debtor owns at the time the bankruptcy petition is filed.[2] Prepetition transfers of the debtor's property are usually respected and left undisturbed. Any other rule would undermine the credibility and reliability of property transactions.

Yet, respecting transfers of the debtor's property that occur prior to bankruptcy, while seeking to order and equalize distribution of the balance of the estate after bankruptcy ensues, encourages creditors to rush to collect their claims under discriminatory state law before a financially troubled debtor ends up in bankruptcy. The effects are to increase the likelihood of the debtor's bankruptcy; to reduce the assets available for distribution to creditors if bankruptcy occurs; and, ultimately, to make less meaningful the order and equality of distribution that are the goals of bankruptcy law.

Section 547 softens these effects by allowing a trustee to avoid a prepetition transfer that is a *preference*. In unofficial and general terms, a preference is "a transfer of the debtor's property on the eve of bankruptcy to satisfy an old debt."[3] The official, technical definition appears in section 547(b) which describes a preference as:

- Any transfer of an interest of the debtor in property;

---

31. 11 U.S.C.A. § 1123(b)(3)(B) (emphasis added).
32. See Practitioner Treatise, Vol. 1.
33. See Practitioner Treatise, Vol. 1.

§ 6–3
1. See 11 U.S.C.A. § 726.

2. See 11 U.S.C.A. § 541.
3. Orelup, Avoidance of Preferential Transfers Under the Bankruptcy Reform Act of 1978, 65 Iowa L. Rev. 209 (1979).

- To or for the benefit of a creditor;
- For or on account of an antecedent debt owed by the debtor before such transfer was made;
- Made while the debtor was insolvent;
- Made on or within 90 days before the date of the filing of the petition, or within one year of the filing if the creditor is an insider; and,
- That enables the creditor to receive more than she would receive in a Chapter 7 distribution of the bankruptcy estate had the transfer not been made.

The principal purposes of avoiding preferences are to discourage creditors "from racing to the courthouse to dismember the debtor during his slide into bankruptcy" in order to "facilitate the prime bankruptcy policy of equality of distribution among creditors of the debtor. Any creditor that received a greater payment than others of his class is required to disgorge so that all may share equally."[4]

The creditor's subjective innocence is no defense. "Congress considered equality of distribution so important that it specifically eliminated consideration of creditors' good faith or knowledge from preference actions * * *."[5] Similarly, the debtor's motive and intent is irrelevant:

All that is required for an avoidable preference is the actual transfer being made within the preferential period, in addition to establishing the other elements of § 547(b).[6]

Moreover, "[a]ny wrongdoing on the part of the debtor is not imputed to the Trustee so as to avoid his avoidance powers [with respect to preferences]."[7]

Suppose, for example, that the amount of D's debts vastly exceeded the value of her property. She paid her last $1,000 in cash to C in satisfaction of a one-year-old, unsecured trade debt in the same amount. D filed for bankruptcy the next week. The bankruptcy estate is poor: if D's assets are liquidated, as would happen in a Chapter 7 case, her general creditors will be paid, from the bankruptcy estate, no more than ten percent of the amounts owed them.

D's prepetition payment to C is unassailable under state law. In bankruptcy, however, the payment is a voidable section 547(b) preference.

All the elements of a preference are satisfied. D is the debtor.[8] Her $1,000 payment was a transfer of the debtor's property, and the money was transferred to a creditor, C.[9] The transfer was made within 90 days before D's bankruptcy petition and when D was insolvent, inasmuch as her liabili-

---

4. H.R. Rep. No. 595, 95th Cong., 1st Sess. 177–78, reprinted in 1978 U.S. Code Cong. & Admin. News 5963, 6138.

5. In re Southern Indus. Banking Corp., 92 B.R. 297, 301 (Bankr. E.D.Tenn.1988).

6. In re Service Bolt & Nut Co., Inc., 98 B.R. 759, 761 (Bankr. N.D.Ohio 1989).

7. In re Lendvest Mortg., Inc., 123 B.R. 623, 624 (Bankr. N.D.Cal.1991).

8. The term "debtor" essentially means any person concerning whom a bankruptcy case has been commenced. 11 U.S.C.A. § 101(13).

9. The term "creditor" includes any "entity that has a claim against the debtor that arose at the time of or before the order for relief concerning the debtor." 11 U.S.C.A. § 101(10)(A). "Claim" includes any "right to payment." 11 U.S.C.A. § 101(5)(A).

ties exceeded her assets at the time of the transfer.[10] Finally, the transfer had a preferential effect, that is, the $1,000 payment enabled C to receive more than she would get in a Chapter 7 case had the transfer not been made. The $1,000 cash would have been included in the bankruptcy estate if the payment had not occurred, and the distribution to each general creditor would therefore have been slightly larger. Yet, none of the general creditors, including C, would have been paid in full. Thus, the $1,000 payment to C, which fully satisfied her claim, enabled her to get more than she otherwise would have received in a Chapter 7 distribution of the bankruptcy estate.

Preferential effect is the harm of a preference. There is no preference without it. Preferential effect, however, is not sufficient in itself to establish that a transfer was a section 547 preference. Every element of section 547(b) must be satisfied, and preferential effect is only one of the elements.

For another example, suppose that instead of paying her debt to C, D gave C a perfected security interest in personal property, or a recorded mortgage on real property, as collateral for the $1,000 debt. D had sufficient equity in the collateral to support the encumbrance. As a general rule, the transfer cannot be attacked under state law or in bankruptcy. On these facts, however, the transfer is a section 547(b) preference that is avoidable in D's bankruptcy. Similarly, "the substitution of a secured loan for an unsecured loan during the preference period * * * results in a preference to the extent of the value of the collateral transferred." [11]

All of the elements of a preference are again satisfied. The only difference is that D made a security transfer rather than an absolute conveyance, of her property. Nevertheless, the creation of this security interest or mortgage, which gave C a lien on the collateral, is a transfer of an interest in D's property. The creation of the lien also had a preferential effect. As a general rule, a lien perfected before a debtor's bankruptcy is enforceable against the bankruptcy estate, which means that C could enforce her lien despite the bankruptcy and therefore fully satisfy her claim. Had the transfer not occurred so that C was a general, unsecured creditor, her claim would not have been fully satisfied. Thus, the security transfer enabled C to receive more than a Chapter 7 distribution would have given her.

Transfers will occur that are technically preferences under section 547(b) but that do offend the purposes of the law or that involve competing policies that override those purposes. Congress did not give the courts an open-ended power to save all inoffensive preferences. Congress did identify, however, seven limited, discrete exceptions to section 547(b) which are collected in section 547(c). A transfer that matches any of these section 547(c) exceptions cannot be avoided by the trustee even though the transfer is a preference as defined by section 547(b). None of these exceptions applies to the preceding examples.

---

10. The Bankruptcy Code uses this legal test of insolvency. See 11 U.S.C.A. § 101(32)(A) (sum of debts is greater than fair valuation of all property).

11. In re Continental Country Club, Inc., 108 B.R. 327, 330 (Bankr. M.D.Fla.1989).

The trustee or other person attacking a transfer as preferential has the burden of establishing that the transfer involved all six elements of a section 547(b) preference.[12] The transferee, if she defends by invoking a section 547(c) exception, has the burden of establishing that the transfer satisfied every requirement of the exception.[13] The courts tend to read section 547(b) broadly, but construe section 547(c) narrowly. The effect is to err in favor of the bankruptcy estate.

1. Elements Of A Preference
§ 6–4 Transfer of an Interest of the Debtor in Property

a. The Critical Terms (Especially "Transfer")

Preference law attacks a "*transfer* of an *interest* of the debtor in *property*."[1] All of these terms are very broadly defined. "Property" means any kind of property,[2] including tangible and intangible, regardless of exemption under state or federal law.[3] "Interest" includes all or part of a legal or equitable claim to or right in property.[4] Equally broad is the meaning of "transfer," which is

> every mode, direct or indirect, absolute or conditional, voluntary or involuntary, of disposing of or parting with property or with an interest in property, including retention of title as a security interest and foreclosure of the debtor's equity of redemption.[5]

Put simply, "transfer" includes, for purposes of section 547(b), any event that results in eliminating or diluting the debtor's interest in property. The form and circumstances of the event are irrelevant, as are the nature and size of the interest that is transferred. A transfer occurs whenever the debtor's interest in property is diminished by deliberate or intentional action or by default as the result of the debtor's own choosing, by someone else's choice, or by operation of law.

A few cases imply, for purposes of section 547, a limit on this very broad definition of transfer. We have in mind, principally, cases such as *Matter of Newcomb*.[6] The debtor, Arthur Newcomb, suffered a judgment in favor of

---

12. 11 U.S.C.A. § 547(g). This burden of proof is met by a preponderance of the evidence. In re Harvard Mfg. Corp., 97 B.R. 879, 882 (Bankr. N.D.Ohio 1989).

13. Id. The defense's burden is preponderance, too. In re Cook United, Inc., 117 B.R. 884, 887 (Bankr. N.D.Ohio 1990).

§ 6–4

1. 11 U.S.C.A. § 547(b) (emphasis added).

2. Bankruptcy law does not actually define "property." The meaning is determined by reference to state law. WJM, Inc. v. Massachusetts Dept. of Public Welfare, 840 F.2d 996, 1007 (1st Cir.1988); In re Hulm, 738 F.2d 323, 326 (8th Cir.1984), cert. denied, 469 U.S. 990, 105 S.Ct. 398, 83 L.Ed.2d 331 (1984) (state law determines whether the debtor had an interest in property); In re Sierra Steel, Inc., 96 B.R. 271, 273 (Bankr. 9th Cir.1989) ("Generally, the existence and nature of the debtor's interest in property are determined by state law," but "[s]tate law * * * must be applied in a manner consistent with federal bankruptcy law."); In re Kleckner, 93 B.R. 143, 149 (N.D.Ill. 1988) (state law determines "interest of the debtor in property").

3. In re Richards, 92 B.R. 369, 371 (Bankr. N.D.Ind. 1988) ("makes no difference whether the property involved is exempt or not").

4. Naturally, if the debtor owns property jointly with another person, the preference attack is limited to the debtor's interest, i.e., the part of the property the debtor owns. Matter of Van Kylen, 98 B.R. 455, 470–72 (Bankr. W.D.Wis.1989).

5. 11 U.S.C.A. § 101(54).

6. 744 F.2d 621 (8th Cir.1984).

the FHA, the United States. The judgment was appealed, and the debtor placed in escrow a sum of money sufficient to satisfy the judgment. The escrow agreement provided that if the judgment was affirmed, the money would be turned over to the United States; if the judgment was reversed, the money would be returned to the debtor. The escrow was established prior to the preference period. On July 15, the appeal was decided in favor of the United States. Within 90 days the debtor filed bankruptcy. The trustee sought the escrow funds.

The trustee argued that a transfer of the funds occurred when the condition of the escrow was met upon affirmance of the judgment. The United States argued that the transfer occurred when the escrow was created.

The court agreed with both of the parties, concluding that the definition of "transfer" is "broad enough to include both the transfer that occurs when an escrow is created and the transfer that occurs when the condition of an escrow is met."[7] Thus, the real issue is "which of these two 'transfers' is controlling in this case."[8] The court decided that the latter transfer controlled because:

> the transfer that occurred when the condition of the escrow was met is not the type of transfer that can be avoided. *To be avoidable a transfer must deprive the debtor's estate of something of value which could otherwise be used to satisfy creditors.* Once the escrow was created, the only interest in the escrowed funds remaining in the debtor was a contingent right to the funds if * * * the judgment for the United States [was reversed]. This interest is worthless in light of * * * [the] affirmance of the judgment for the United States. Therefore, the 'transfer' of this interest did not deprive the estate of anything of value. It follows that this 'transfer' cannot be avoided.[9]

A technical explanation of *Newcomb* is that it limits the meaning of transfer for purposes of section 547 by adding an additional requirement: a transfer is not a transfer for avoidance purposes unless the transfer sought to be avoided is valuable to the debtor's estate.

This caveat could explain the decision in *Matter of Wey*.[10] The debtor in *Wey* had contracted to buy real estate and made a substantial downpayment. When the debtor failed to pay the balance of the price, the contract terminated and, according to its terms, the debtor lost the downpayment.

---

7. Id. at 626.

8. Id.

9. Id. at 626–27 (emphasis added); accord, In re Shapiro, 124 B.R. 974, 983 (Bankr. E.D.Pa. 1991) ("The most significant transfer of the [escrow] fund appears to have occurred when the Debtor made the deposit which created it," which was outside the 90-day period.); In re Cedar Rapid Meats, Inc., 121 B.R. 562, 569–70 (Bankr. N.D.Iowa 1990) ("[T]he relevant transfer of property in an escrow arrangement is the deposit of funds into the escrow, not any transfers later made out of the funds."); In re Coco, 67 B.R. 365, 369–70 (Bankr. S.D.N.Y. 1986) ("[T]he escrow cases are uniform in holding that it is the debtor's deposit of funds into escrow and not the * * * release of the funds that is the controlling transfer for preference purposes."); Matter of O.P.M. Leasing Services, Inc., 46 B.R. 661, 666–69 (Bankr. S.D.N.Y. 1985); cf. In re Berman, 95 B.R. 833 (S.D.Fla.1989), appeal dism'd, 885 F.2d 879 (11th Cir.1989) (in deciding when enabling loan made for purposes of § 547(c)(3), loan occurred when proceeds placed in escrow rather than when proceeds actually delivered); but compare In re M.B.K., Inc., 92 B.R. 429, 434 (Bankr. C.D.Cal.1987) (involving local law regulating transfer of liquor licenses).

10. 854 F.2d 196 (7th Cir.1988).

The formation of the contract and payment of the downpayment occurred beyond the preference period; the forfeiture occurred within it.

The trustee sought the downpayment, arguing that the forfeiture of the downpayment was a preferential transfer. The court decided that after making the downpayment, the debtor had no rights remaining in the money. What really happened upon the forfeiture was that the debtor lost an equitable interest in the real estate. The court concluded, however, that loss of this interest was not a transfer. Thus, there was no preference.[11]

The broad conclusion in *Wey* that no transfer occurred seems clearly wrong, but the result is consistent with *Newcomb* and is better explained in terms of *Newcomb*. The loss of the equitable interest was a transfer, but the interest was worthless to the estate because the debtor had forfeited it pursuant to the parties' contract. Thus, in terms of *Newcomb* the transfer was not of a kind subject to avoidance. Moreover, in *Wey,* as in *Newcomb,* the trustee was chasing the money; and the only transfer with respect to the money itself was when the downpayment was made, which occurred before the preference period.

We would certainly discourage trustees from chasing worthless property, but not by redefining "transfer" in section 547 to mean something valuable. So long as there is a transfer, as Congress defined it, there is a preference if the other elements of section 547(b) are met. A single transaction can involve several transfers and, as we read the law, the trustee is free to avoid any of them that meets the tests for avoidance without having to prove worth.

The law discourages the trustee from avoiding worthless transfers but only indirectly. It surgically limits the effect of avoidance and recovery to the very transfer that is avoided. The trustee will not attack a transfer that is truly worthless, and avoiding such a transfer should not cause loss to anyone else. Moreover, worth and value and loss are affected by context and circumstances that are better considered in the wider administration of the estate, perhaps in an abandonment proceeding, rather than during an avoidance hearing. In sum, we agree with Congress that, for purposes of section 547, "transfer" is not limited by any adjective of worth or value.

We should warn, however, that the scope of section 547 is not coextensive with the very broad meaning of "transfer." For example, the meaning of "transfer" is probably sufficiently broad to encompass setoff, which involves the cancellation of a debt a person owes in satisfaction of a debt owed her. Section 547, however, does not apply to setoffs. The only provision that limits prepetition setoffs is section 553.[12]

This exclusion from section 547 is triggered, however, only when the transfer is a true, proper setoff, as when a bank offsets a customer's general deposit account in satisfaction of an overdue note or in other circumstances where setoff is permitted and is appropriately effected.[13] Section 547 is fully applicable, rather than section 553, when a transfer that looks like a setoff is

---

11. Id. at 199–200.

12. 11 U.S.C.A. § 553, which we fully discuss at §§ 6–38 through 6–44 infra.

13. See, e.g., In re Hinson, 65 B.R. 675 (W.D.Tenn.1986) (bank offsetting depositor's account); In re Morgan, 77 B.R. 81 (Bankr. S.D.Miss.1987) (utility offset refund due customer against bill owed for electricity).

actually a seizure or other application of funds or monetary credit that is, in substance, not a true setoff or is a setoff that is beyond the scope of (or not permitted by) the local law of setoff.[14]

Certain statutory liens are also beyond the scope of section 547 and are dealt with in section 545, but this exclusion is expressly referenced in section 547 itself.[15]

b. Most Common Transfers

Three kinds of frequently recurring transfers are the most common foundations for preferences: (1) The debtor makes an absolute conveyance of her money, personalty or realty in satisfaction of a debt; (2) she creates a consensual, legal or equitable encumbrance on her rights in property as security for a debt;[16] or (3) her property is subjected to an involuntary encumbrance such as a judgment, execution or garnishment lien at law,[17] or a constructive trust or lien in equity. These situations are only typical instances of preferential transfers, however, and set no limits on the meaning of transfer for purposes of section 547(b).

§ 6–5 Transfer of an Interest of the Debtor in Property—Increase in Value

For full text of this section, see Epstein, Nickles & White, Bankruptcy, Practitioner Treatise Series, Vol. 1.

§ 6–6 Transfer of an Interest of the Debtor in Property—Transfers of Exempt Property

For full text of this section, see Epstein, Nickles & White, Bankruptcy, Practitioner Treatise Series, Vol. 1.

§ 6–7 Transfer of an Interest of the Debtor in Property—Property of Third Party and Earmarked Funds

No matter how a transfer occurs, section 547(b) is satisfied only if a property interest of the debtor is transferred. The Bankruptcy Code does not explain when property is "*of the debtor,*" but the courts have done so: "Generally, property belongs to the debtor for purposes of § 547 if its transfer will deprive the bankruptcy estate of something which could otherwise be used to satisfy the claims of creditors."[1]

---

14. See, e.g., In re WJM, Inc., 84 B.R. 268 (D.Mass.1986); In re Savig, 50 B.R. 1003 (D.Minn.1985); In re Kroh Bros. Development Co., 86 B.R. 186 (Bankr. W.D.Mo.1988); In re 4–S Corp., 69 B.R. 499 (Bankr. W.D.Mo.1987).

15. See 11 U.S.C.A. § 547(c)(6), which is discussed at § 6–36.

16. See Practitioner Treatise, Vol. 1.

17. See Practitioner Treatise, Vol. 1.

§ 6–7

1. In re Bullion Reserve of North America, 836 F.2d 1214, 1217 (9th Cir.1988), cert. denied, 486 U.S. 1056, 108 S.Ct. 2824, 100 L.Ed.2d 925 (1988); see also In re Lill, 116 B.R. 543, 548 (Bankr. N.D.Ohio 1990) (payment of monies by third person was transfer of debtor's property because debtor had control over the funds and directed the payment); In re Adams, 102 B.R. 271, 274–75 (Bankr. M.D.Ga.1989) (third party's transfer of funds held in trust for debtor was preferential because the funds would have been property of the estate and third party simply acted as debtor's agent in effecting the transfer); compare In re Glassley, 124 B.R. 579, 581 (Bankr.

A transfer of someone else's property cannot be a preference in the debtor's case even if all of the other elements of section 547(b) are satisfied and the deliberately intended effect was to prefer a creditor of the debtor on the very eve of bankruptcy. The explanation is that preference law protects only the bankruptcy estate, that is, the law is designed to avoid transfers that will deprive the estate of something which could otherwise be used to satisfy creditors' claims. The bankruptcy estate is composed only of property of the debtor.[2] Protecting transfers of other people's property is thus beyond the purpose of preference law.

There is an exception of sorts:

> If the debtor determines the disposition of funds from the third party and designates the creditor to be paid, the funds are available for payment to creditors in general and the funds are assets of the estate.[3]

In this event, because the debtor controlled the funds and could have paid them to anyone, the money is treated as having belonged to her for purposes of preference law whether or not she actually owns it.

The section 547(b) requirement that the transfer involves the debtor's property explains why a debtor's transfer of property held in trust by her is never a preference.[4] Property so held belongs to the beneficiary of the trust rather than to the debtor.

The requirement also explains the much more common case in which D's debt to C is paid by E who pays C, on D's behalf, gratuitously; as a surety for the debt or a principal comaker of it; or as a lender who refinances the debt. D files bankruptcy the next day. The trustee seeks to recover the payment to C, arguing that it was a preference. The trustee loses.[5] Section 547(b) is not satisfied, and thus the payment is not a preference, because the money paid to C was not D's property.

This reasoning supports the "earmarking doctrine," which holds that:

> [I]f a third party advances funds or property to the Debtor with instructions to use them to pay off another creditor, there is no avoidable preference since there has been no transfer of an interest of the Debtor in property. Such funds or property, said to be "earmarked" for payment to a specific creditor or creditors of the Debtor, never really become property of the Debtor's estate. Thus, other creditors are not harmed by the payment.[6]

For example, suppose that E loaned money to D for the purpose of paying D's debt to C. E did not, however, remit the proceeds directly to C. Instead, E gave the money to D with instructions to use it to pay C, which D did. There is no preference. The technical explanation is that for purposes of section 547(b), D made no transfer of her own property; rather, she simply passed along property of E. A broader justification is that the transaction did not

---

D.Kan.1991) (There was no preference because the transfer consisted of property that belonged to the joint venture in which the debtor was involved. It was not property of the debtor herself.).

2. See 11 U.S.C.A. § 541.

3. In re Knapp, 119 B.R. 285, 287 (Bankr. M.D.Fla.1990).

4. See Practitioner Treatise, Vol. 1.

5. See Practitioner Treatise, Vol. 1.

6. Matter of Van Huffel Tube Corp., 74 B.R. 579, 585 (Bankr. N.D.Ohio 1987).

violate the policies behind preference law because the debtor simply substituted one creditor, E, for another creditor, C. The estate was not diminished.

The earmarking doctrine applies only if the debtor's use of the property is restricted, i.e., earmarked, for the purpose of paying a specific creditor or creditors so that the debtor rightfully and actually lacks dispositive control over the funds.[7] In the absence of such a restriction, the property that is passed to the debtor is deemed to have become her own property even though she pays it to other creditors. Thus, the earmarking doctrine would not apply to protect D's payment of a debt to C if E loaned the money to D without any restrictions on its use, or for the general purpose of paying a subset of D's creditors determined by D alone. Nor would the doctrine apply if D borrowed the money from E to pay a particular debt to C but actually used the money to pay C a different debt,[8] or if D enjoyed such control of the funds that she could in fact do with them as she wished despite an agreement dedicating them to a particular purpose.[9] The reason is that D necessarily had control over the money, which precludes applying the earmarking doctrine, inasmuch as D did or could apply the loan proceeds in a manner different from the agreement with E.

The earmarking doctrine can be applied, however, in proportion to the satisfaction of its elements. Assume, for example, that E loaned D $1,000. They had agreed that $500 of the loan would be used to pay a debt that D owed C. The use of the balance of the loan was unrestricted. D paid C $500 and used the balance to pay another creditor, F. The earmarking doctrine would protect the payment to C but not the payment to F.[10]

Notwithstanding the earmarking doctrine, and even if a third person transfers her property directly to the debtor's creditor, the property-of-the-debtor requirement of a preference is satisfied if the transfer to the creditor, though involving the third person's property, is secured by the debtor's own property. For example, suppose that D owes C an unsecured debt. The debt matures, but D cannot pay it. During the preference period before D's bankruptcy, E refinances the obligation by paying C and taking a note from D that is secured by a lien on D's property.

E's payment to C was a transfer of E's property. This conclusion is correct, due to the earmarking doctrine, even if the payment was channeled through D. The creation of the lien, however, was a transfer of D's property. The lien is a preference if the other elements of section 547(b) are satisfied.[11] This conclusion stands, despite the earmarking doctrine, if E's money passed to C through D.

The earmarking doctrine is no defense to a preference to the extent that credit extended by a third person but secured by the debtor's property is used to pay the debtor's unsecured debts.[12] The net result of such a

---

7. See Practitioner Treatise, Vol. 1.

8. In re Bohlen Enterprises, 859 F.2d 561 (8th Cir.1988).

9. In re New York City Shoes, Inc., 98 B.R. 725, 729–30 (Bankr. E.D.Pa. 1989), aff'd, 106 B.R. 58 (E.D.Pa. 1989); see also Beck v. General Accident Ins., 114 B.R. 168, 173 n.8 (S.D.Ind.1990).

10. In re Bohlen Enterprises, Ltd., 78 B.R. 556 (Bankr. N.D.Iowa), aff'd, 91 B.R. 486 (N.D.Iowa 1987), rev'd on related but other grounds, 859 F.2d 561 (8th Cir.1988); see also Beck v. General Accident Ins., 114 B.R. 168, 173 (S.D.Ind.1990).

11. See Practitioner Treatise, Vol. 1.

12. See Practitioner Treatise, Vol. 1.

transaction is to convert unsecured credit to secured credit and thereby to diminish the debtor's estate. Thus, the earmarking doctrine would protect the transfer to C, if C was an unsecured creditor, only to the extent that E's loan to D was unsecured by real or personal property belonging to D.[13]

The difficult issue in this example, whether E paid the money directly to C or indirectly through D, is to whom the transfer is chargeable. Resolution of this issue begins by considering the separate requirement of a preference: "to or for the benefit of a creditor."

§ 6–8 To or for the Benefit of a Creditor

A transfer of the debtor's property is a preference only if the transfer is made "to or for the benefit of a creditor."[1] The "creditor" component of this requirement causes few problems because the term is very widely defined. It basically means any "entity that has a claim against the debtor,"[2] and claim has the "broadest possible definition"[3] which is any

(A) right to payment, whether or not such right is reduced to judgment, liquidated, unliquidated, fixed, contingent, matured, unmatured, disputed, undisputed, legal, equitable, secured or unsecured; or

(B) right to an equitable remedy for breach of performance if such breach gives rise to a right to payment, whether or not such right to an equitable remedy is reduced to judgment, fixed, contingent, matured, unmatured, disputed, undisputed, secured, or unsecured.[4]

In short and general terms, "creditor" includes anyone to whom the debtor owes any kind of legal obligation no matter how remote or contingent.[5]

On the other hand, the meaning of the term "creditor" is not unbounded, and the limits of the term restrict, by themselves, the scope of section 547(b). For example, when the debtor makes a gratuitous transfer of her property, i.e., a transfer to a person without a claim against her, the transfer is not a preference.[6]

The separate component—"to or for the benefit"—is not restrictive or limiting; rather, it actually widens the circumstances in which preferences are possible because "to" and "for the benefit" are alternative conditions. A transfer that is for the benefit of a creditor can be a preference even though it was not made to her. In such a case the transfer is often referred to as an indirect preference, which typically is preference that indirectly benefits a creditor.

---

13. See Practitioner Treatise, Vol. 1.

§ 6–8

1. 11 U.S.C.A. § 547(b)(1).
2. 11 U.S.C.A. § 101(10).
3. H.R.Rep. No. 95–595, 95th Cong. 1st Sess. 309, reprinted in 1978 U.S. Code Cong. & Admin. News 5963, 6266; S.Rep. No. 95–989, 95th Cong., 2d Sess. 21 (1978), reprinted in 1978 U.S. Code Cong. & Admin. News 5787, 5808.
4. 11 U.S.C.A. § 101(5).

5. Directly related to this "creditor" requirement is the additional requirement that the transfer be "for or on account of an antecedent debt," 11 U.S.C.A. § 547(b)(2), which we discuss later. See § 6–19 infra. The relationship between these requirements is close because "creditor" requires a claim; and if there is a claim there is a debt; and if there is a debtor there is both a debtor and a creditor. Thus the later discussion on antecedent debt is entirely relevant here.

6. See Practitioner Treatise, Vol. 1.

§ 6–9 To or for the Benefit of a Creditor—Preferences That Indirectly Benefit (a/k/a Indirect Preferences)

A transfer of the debtor's property can be a preference to a creditor who is not a transferee of the property if the transfer nevertheless reduces her claim. This odd preference is possible because section 547(b)(1) is alternatively satisfied by a transfer of the debtor's property either "to" a creditor *or* "for the benefit of a creditor." Here is an example:

- D is obligated to C.
- C is obligated to B.
- D satisfies her obligation to C by paying C's debt to B.

D's payment to B is not a preference to B because B is not D's creditor.[1] C is the creditor, but the payment was not made to her. It was made, however, for C's benefit. The payment is therefore a preference to C if the other requirements of section 547(b) are met.[2]

The "for the benefit" language of section 547(b) reflects or even codifies a long-standing decisional principle of bankruptcy law known as the *indirect transfer* (or *indirect preference*) *doctrine*. According to this doctrine,

> "[t]o constitute a preference, it is not necessary that the transfer be made directly to the creditor. If the bankrupt has made a transfer of his property, the effect of which is to enable one of his creditors to obtain a greater percentage of his debt than another creditor of the same class, circuity of arrangement will not avail to save it." To combat such circuity, the courts have broken down certain transfers into two transfers, one direct and one indirect. The direct transfer to the third party may be valid and not subject to preference attack. The indirect transfer, arising from the same action by the debtor, however, may constitute a voidable preference as to the creditor who indirectly benefitted from the direct transfer to the third party.[3]

Actually, only one transfer of the debtor's property occurs. The "indirect transfer" is a technical fiction. The doctrine uses it to establish a preference that the trustee can avoid for the purpose of claiming the preferential value that the creditor indirectly received from the "direct" or actual transfer.

Section 547 does not need this doctrine for the purpose of finding a preference in these circumstances. Because of (a)(1), preference is expressly defined to include a transfer that only benefits a creditor without conveying the property to her.

The most common indirect preference is a payment to a creditor that benefits a surety. Here is the common case:

- D is obligated to C on a unsecured debt.

§ 6–9

1. See Practitioner Treatise, Vol. 1.
2. See Practitioner Treatise, Vol. 1.
3. Matter of Compton Corp., 831 F.2d 586, 591 (5th Cir.1987), on reh'g, 835 F.2d 584 (5th Cir.1988) (emphasis in original), quoting National Bank of Newport v. National Herkimer County Bank, 225 U.S. 178, 184, 32 S.Ct. 633, 635, 56 L. Ed. 1042, 1046 (1912).

- E is surety for this debt. Significantly, E is entitled to reimbursement from D if E pays the debt.[4] E thus has a contingent claim against D and therefore E, like C, is a creditor of D.
- As it happens, however, D dutifully pays the debt.

D's payment to C is obviously a transfer of the debtor's property to a creditor, C. The payment is also for the benefit of E because the payment reduces E's contingent claim against D. If the other elements of 547(b) are satisfied, the payment is thus a preference to E even though the debtor's property was actually transferred to C.[5]

Conversely, the indirect preference doctrine can be turned against C when she is paid by E using E's own money.[6] In this event, the payment itself is never a preference because property of the debtor is not transferred. Suppose, however, that D secured her obligation to reimburse E by giving E a lien on her property. The lien was given to E, but it was a transfer for the benefit of C. The lien is thus an indirect preference to C if the balance of section 547(b) is satisfied.[7]

The result is the same—C is indirectly preferred—if E paid the debt not because she was a surety, but because she was a creditor who refinanced the debt by paying the debt owed C and taking a secured note from D. E's payment to C is not itself a preference because the property transferred to C was E's money, not D's property. On the other hand, D transferred her property to E by securing the note to E. The courts agree that although this security transfer is made to E, it is for the benefit of C and is an indirect preference to C if the other elements of section 547(b) are satisfied.[8]

A more complex example involves the issuance of a letter of credit. Suppose, for example, that D owes C an unsecured debt of $10,000. A transfer to C would obviously occur if D paid C the debt, or secured the debt by providing collateral for it. This kind of transfer does not occur, however. Instead, D's bank, E, issues a letter of credit to C, and D secures her obligation to reimburse E[9] by securing the credit with a lien on D's property. C makes a demand under the credit; E honors the demand; and D files for bankruptcy. The trustee sues C, arguing that C received a preference. Is there a transfer of D's property "to or for the benefit of a creditor?"

The money paid to C was not D's property. D's property was transferred as collateral for the credit, but that property was transferred to E. Yet, the transfer of the collateral to E was a necessary condition to the issuance of the credit. Because the credit and its proceeds benefitted C, the

---

4. Restatement of Security § 104 (1941) (principal debtor must reimburse surety if surety makes a payment or otherwise performs on default by principal debtor, or if surety's property is used to satisfy principal debtor's duty); U.C.C. § 3–415(5) (an accommodation party who pays the instrument has right of recourse on the instrument against the party accommodated); L. Simpson, Handbook on the Law of Suretyship § 48 (1950).

5. See Practitioner Treatise, Vol. 1.

6. Do not confuse earmarked-funds cases with indirect-preference cases. In the former property of a third party moves through the debtor and directly from the debtor to the creditor. In the latter the debtor's property moves from the debtor to a third party, and property of the third party moves directly from the third party to the creditor.

7. See Practitioner Treatise, Vol. 1.

8. See Practitioner Treatise, Vol. 1.

9. The customer who procures a letter of credit is obligated by law to reimburse the issuer upon the issuer duly honoring the credit. U.C.C. § 5–114(3).

transfer of the collateral for the credit was for C's benefit even though the transfer was made directly to E. If the other conditions of section 547 are satisfied, there is a preference (albeit indirect) to C that the trustee can rectify by recovering the value of the transferred property, that is, the value of the collateral given E.[10]

Carefully note that in each of these examples of indirect preferences, the indirect benefit satisfied an unsecured claim. No preference would occur to the extent that the claim which was indirectly paid was secured by an unavoidable lien the creditor could have enforced in the debtor's bankruptcy. The technical reason is that to this extent, the transfer would lack the preferential effect that (b)(5) requires. The practical explanation is that to this extent, the transfer would indirectly release equity and therefore not diminish the debtor's estate. No harm, no foul.

This caveat fully applies in the case of the surety whose contingent claim is reduced by the debtor paying the principal creditor even if only the principal creditor takes collateral.[11] The surety's contingent claim is secured by this same property because the surety inherits the collateral if she pays the principal creditor. Therefore, if the debtor pays the principal creditor who is fully secured, the payment is not a preference to the principal creditor or the surety because preferential effect is missing as to each of them. The surety is independently saved from preference for the same reason the principal creditor is saved, not derivatively because the principal creditor is saved.

§ 6–10 To or for the Benefit of a Creditor—Remedying an Indirect Preference (and the Levit Case)

The standard means of remedying a preference is to avoid the transfer under section 547 and, pursuant to section 550, recover the property transferred or its value from "the initial transferee of such transfer or the entity for whose benefit such transfer was made * * *."[1] A creditor who gets an indirect preference is not a transferee of the property. Therefore, the apparently proper remedy for an indirect transfer is to recover its value from this creditor as the entity whom the transfer benefitted.

The issue, however, is thoroughly muddled, principally because of the Seventh Circuit's decision in *Levit v. Ingersoll Rand Financial Corp.*[2] Essentially, the case involved a series of indirect preferences to a surety or guarantor, Richard Deprizio, because the debtor, which was his company, made payments to a lender and other creditors. An important twist is that these payments occurred more than 90 days but within a year before bankruptcy. For this reason, the payments were not preferences to the principal creditors. Richard, however, was an insider for whom the preference period was one year. No one doubted that he received indirect preferences, but the issue in this case was not about recovering from him.

---

10. See Practitioner Treatise, Vol. 1.
11. See Practitioner Treatise, Vol. 1.

§ 6–10

1. 11 U.S.C.A. § 550(a)(1). People who fit these descriptions, and the descriptions in (a)(2), are jointly and severally liable, but "[t]he trustee is entitled to only a single satisfaction * * *." Id. § 550(c). In another place we thoroughly discuss liability under section 550. See §§ 6–87 through 6–90 infra.

2. 874 F.2d 1186 (7th Cir.1989).

The trustee sought to remedy the indirect preferences to Richard by recovering from the principal creditors. The trustee based the claim against the lender on the language of section 550 that imposes liability on the entity who benefitted from an avoided transfer or, alternatively, the "initial transferee." On this theory, a principal creditor who is an outsider may be required, by section 550, to repay transfers it received during the one-year preference period that applies, by section 547, only to insiders.

The principal creditors did not defend by arguing they were not "initial transferees." Their defense was rather that

> § 550 allows the trustee to recover only "to the extent that a transfer is avoided under" § 547. Viewing each payment as two "transfers"—one to Lender, another to Guarantor—they insist that the only transfer avoidable under § 547 is the one to Guarantor.[3]

In other words, the direct transfers to the principal creditors were not avoidable under section 547 because the transfers were before the 90-day preference period that applied to outsiders, and thus the remedies of section 550 could not be used against them.

The short answer would have been that recovery under section 550 is not limited to persons who receive transfers that are avoided under section 547 as preferences to them. If section 547 avoids a preference to anyone, section 550 imposes joint and several liability on everyone it describes. In cases before and after *Levit*, the courts have given this answer and imposed liability on principal creditors in situations like *Levit* involving indirect preferences to a surety.

The Seventh Circuit decided on a longer answer. It rejected the two-transfer theory, rather straightforwardly deciding that "[a] single payment * * * is one 'transfer' no matter how many persons gain thereby."[4] Yet, in deciding that the trustee could recover from the principal creditors under section 550, the court's reasoning, especially on the issue of preference, is more extensive than the short answer to the case, arguably confused and muddled.

As to the exact nature of the preference that occurred, the court reasoned that the one-year preference period applied to the transfers to the principal creditors because an insider benefitted from them; that these transfers were therefore preferences the trustee avoided; and these avoided transfers triggered section 550. In justifying the decision, the court used language such as extending and "[a]pplying the longer preference-recovery period to outside creditors"[5] and even declared, in the very end, "[w]e hold * * * that the preference-recovery period for outside creditors is one year when the payment produces a benefit for an insider creditor * * *."[6]

This approach ignores that even though only one transfer actually occurs, it can affect multiple creditors and differently, so that the transfer can satisfy the avoidance requirements of section 547(b) as to a subset of creditors whom it affects. Significantly, section 547(b) is creditor-specific in describing these requirements, and there is no preference to a particular

---

3. Id. at 1191.
4. Id. at 1196.
5. Id. at 1197.
6. Id. at 1200–01.

creditor unless all of the requirements are satisfied as to the creditor. Mixing and matching is not allowed.[7] Specifically, the one-year preference period applies to "*such* creditor" who is an insider.[8] It does cover a transfer to a creditor just because the transfer was an indirect preference for the benefit of an insider creditor.

On the other hand, because of the single-transfer truth, if all of the section 547(b) requirements are met as to any creditor, the transfer is avoided as to all creditors even though none of the others received a preference. If they are to be saved from preference law, it is not by denying that a preference occurred under section 547 simply because no preference occurred as to them. They are saved to the extent the terms of section 550 protect them from accountability.

The court's mix-and-match approach persists in the *Levit* dicta. There the court argues, in effect, that no preference occurs—not even indirectly to the surety—if any of the section 547(c) defenses fits the transfer to the principal creditor.[9] These defenses, however, are also creditor-specific. They must be satisfied by the creditor with respect to whom the transfer is avoidable under (b). The legislative history is clear that the defenses are tied to the creditor, not the transfer: "[i]f a creditor can qualify under any one of the exceptions, then *he* is protected to that extent."[10] Yet, protecting the transfer from avoidance as a preference to him does not mean completely immunizing the transfer so that it cannot be avoided as a preference to someone else. If an indirect preference were saved whenever a section 547(c) defense applies to the direct transferee, the most classic indirect preferences are protected, including the cases in which an unsecured debt is refinanced by a fresh lender who takes collateral or an unsecured debt is paid by a draw against a secured letter of credit.

Therefore, if the section 547(b) requirements of preference are met with respect to the surety as a creditor who indirectly benefitted from the transfer, the defenses of section 547(c) are irrelevant unless they are satisfied with respect to this creditor. The creditor to which section 547(c) applies is the creditor with respect to whom the transfer is avoidable under section 547(b).

As it happens, none of these defenses applied in *Levit* itself. Therefore, despite our disagreements with *Levit* about how to apply both section 547(b) and (c), we reach the same conclusion under section 547 that the transfers were avoidable preferences. The court apparently concluded that the transfers were avoidable because the section 547(b) requirements were satisfied by the principal creditors. We would base avoidance on the surety satisfying them.

The case, however, is not done. Indeed, we only now get to the question of how to remedy the preference and arrive at the critical issue, which is the

---

7. See Practitioner Treatise, Vol. 1.

8. 11 U.S.C.A. § 547(b)(4)(B) (emphasis added).

9. 874 F.2d at 1200; see also In re H & S Transportation Co., Inc., 939 F.2d 355, 358 (6th Cir.1991).

10. H.R. Rep. No. 595, 95th Cong., 2d Sess. 373, reprinted in 1978 U.S. Code Cong. & Admin. News 5963, 6329; S. Rep. No. 989, 95th Cong., 2d Sess. 87, reprinted in 1978 U.S. Cong. & Admin. News 5787, 5873.

meaning of section 550(a). It assigns personal liability with respect to transfers that the trustee avoids using her bankruptcy avoiding powers:

> Except as otherwise provided in this section, to the extent that a transfer is avoided under sections 544, 545, 547, 548, 549, 553(b), or 724(a) of this title, the trustee may recover, for the benefit of the estate, the property transferred, or, if the court so orders, the value of such property, from
>
> (1) the *initial transferee* of such transfer or the entity for whose benefit such transfer was made; or
>
> (2) any immediate or mediate transferee of such initial transferee.[11]

The trustee in *Levit* contended that the principal creditors were "initial transferees." This contention is the big issue in Levit.

Significantly, section 550 is triggered in any case, including *Levit,* by any avoidance under section 547 on any basis. Section 550 only cares that a "transfer is avoided under" section 547, not which or how or why. Even the *Levit* opinion notes that "it is the novel text of § 550(a)(1), allowing recovery from either transferee or beneficiary, that underlies the Trustee's claim."[12] This claim did not really depend on how many transfers are involved in an indirect preference or even on which creditor satisfies the preference requirement. The trustee could make a section 550 claim in *Levit* so long as section 547 avoided a preference, and nobody in Levit doubted that a section 547 avoidable preference had occurred. Therefore, *Levit* is largely dicta with respect to how section 547 applies to indirect preferences.

The true holding in *Levit* is limited to the meaning of section 550, specifically whether or not the principal creditors were "initial transferees." On this precise issue *Levit* is very clear: yes. Other courts agree.[13] The favorite reason is plain meaning.

It is not plain, however, that a direct transferee is necessarily an "initial" transferee. Reasons of policy and purpose argue against treating them synonymously. First, holding a person liable for a transfer that was not preferential as to her effectively negates the limits of section 547(b), as applied to her, and thereby indirectly extends the reach of preference law. Second, this effect is not within the likely purpose of section 550(a):

> Section 550(a) was an attempt by Congress to stop the situation present under the old Bankruptcy Act in which fraudulent transfers were run through third parties before being accepted by their intended recipient, thereby frustrating the trustee's recovery of the transfer. When Congress passed section 550(a) of the Bankruptcy Code it corrected the problem present under the Act by giving the trustee the flexibility to recover from any transferee in the chain.[14]

Some cases resembling *Levit* have gone the other way and denied recovery from a principal creditor who received a transfer that was preferential only to the surety.[15] These cases sometimes reason very basically that

---

11. 11 U.S.C.A. § 550(a) (emphasis added).
12. 874 F.2d at 1196 n.9.
13. See Practitioner Treatise, Vol. 1.
14. In re Anchorage Marina, Inc., 93 B.R. 686, 694 (Bankr. D.N.D.1988).
15. See Practitioner Treatise, Vol. 1.

sense and equity argue against holding the principal creditor liable when, as to her, the transfer was unoffensive.

We would add that this argument, that shields the direct transferee from accountability based solely on indirect preference, is even stronger in the letter of credit and refinancing situations, which *Levit* also threatens,[16] than in the surety cases. In the surety cases the creditor-direct transferee, who forfeits a debtor's payment that was an indirect preference, is legally entitled to recover over from the surety; and the creditor expected from the beginning to rely ultimately on the surety's willingness and ability to pay the debt. In contrast, letter of credit law does not generally allow an issuer-bank to look to the beneficiary in the event that reimbursement by the debtor fails;[17] so the bank never anticipated (much less expected) recoupment from the beneficiary. Similarly, in a refinancing case, the original creditor is not a surety for the refinanced debt. The new lender cannot turn to the original creditor for payment upon losing the debtor's payment and never planned on doing so. So, whether or not the direct transferee in a surety case is accountable for the indirect preference, there are stronger reasons for immunizing the direct transferees in these other indirect preference cases.[18] They never expected having to recover over against a third party, and the law does not clearly and certainly provide for doing so.

The *Levit* case would argue that in these cases, the lenders are safe because a section 547(c) exception applies, probably (c)(1).[19] We have already noted, a few paragraphs back, our disagreement with this answer because its effect in each case is to shield not only the lender but also the other creditor who indirectly benefitted. The *Levit* answer is technically wrong and works too broadly. The correct answer is that the indirect preference to the other creditor is not saved from section 547(b) by a section 547(c) defense that fits only the lender, but that recovery under section 550(a) is limited to the other creditor for whose benefit the transfer was made because the lender is not an "initial transferee."

A few people defend *Levit*. Professor Jay Westbrook finds the court's policy analysis "compelling" and agrees with the result.[20] He likes the case because, in his view, it mitigates against the "undesirable effects" of the "enormous leverage" that pure-leverage guarantees give lenders.

Many more people want to "fix" *Levit* by legislatively overruling it. Basically, they would tie recovery from any person under 550(a)(1) to the trustee's ability to avoid the transfer against same person. In other words, the trustee could recover only from a person against whom the transfer was avoided. On the facts of *Levit,* the trustee could not recover from the lender because the transfer was avoidable only against the insider and not against the lender. This change would also "fix" the other letter-of-credit, refinanc-

---

16. See Practitioner Treatise, Vol. 1.
17. See Practitioner Treatise, Vol. 1.
18. See Practitioner Treatise, Vol. 1.
19. "The trustee may not avoid under this section a transfer * * * to the extent that such transfer was (A) intended by the debtor and the creditor to or for whose benefit such transfer was made to be a contemporaneous exchange for new value given to the debtor; and (B) in fact a substantially contemporaneous exchange." 11 U.S.C.A. § 547(c)(1).
20. Westbrook, Two Thoughts About Insider Preferences, 76 Minn.L.Rev. 73 (1991).

ing, and other cases in which, because of Levit's wooden reading of 550(a), indirect preferences are recoverable from the direct transferee.

§ 6–11 Within the Preference Period

The purpose of avoiding preferences is to discourage dismemberment of the debtor's estate by creditors acting out of fear that the debtor is approaching bankruptcy.[1] Thus, bankruptcy law's concern with transfers that have a preferential effect is limited to transfers that occur during the debtor's financial "slide into bankruptcy."[2] For purposes of section 547(b), this slide is deemed to begin 90 days before the date of the filing of the petition.[3] It begins earlier with respect to transfers by insiders—one year before the filing[4]—because insiders know sooner that a debtor is in financial trouble and can thereby get a head start in dismembering the estate for the protection of their own interests.[5] This 90-day or one-year period, prescribed by section 547(b)(4), is known as the *preference period.* No transfer is a preference under section 547(b) unless the transfer occurs, or is deemed to occur, within this period.[6]

Most courts compute the preference period by counting backward from the date the bankruptcy petition was filed.[7]

> The filing date itself is excluded, but "[t]he last day of the period so computed shall be included, unless it is a Saturday, a Sunday, or a legal holiday * * *."[8]

The most difficult problem in deciding whether a transfer falls within the preference period is determining precisely when the transfer occurred for purposes of section 547(b). This timing issue is resolved by applying state law in tandem with federal law of section 547, particularly the following subsection 547(e):

(1) For purposes of this section:

(A) a transfer of real property other than fixtures, but including the interest of a seller or purchaser under a contract for the sale of real property, is perfected when a bona fide purchaser of such property from the debtor against whom applicable law permits such transfer to be

---

§ 6–11

1. H.R. Rep. No. 595, 95th Cong., 1st Sess. 177–78, reprinted in 1978 U.S. Code Cong. & Admin. News 5963, 6138.

2. Id.

3. 11 U.S.C.A. § 547(b)(4)(A).

4. 11 U.S.C.A. § 547(b)(4)(B).

5. A fuller explanation of the policy behind the extended preference period for insider transfers is:

> Transactions involving parties with a close relationship to the debtor have traditionally been subjected to closer scrutiny by the courts. Persons on the inside naturally have access to more information and can exert greater influence on the debtor. Thus, transactions between insiders are less vulnerable to the market pressures that govern and shape arm's-length transactions. In addition, the close relationship of insider creditor and debtor can veil a potentially preferential transfer or may even be used to deliberately conceal the preference. The [extended one-year rule] * * * seeks to give the trustee an enhanced avoiding power to combat the greater ability of the insider creditor to procure a preference.

Orelup, Avoidance of Preferential Transfers Under the Bankruptcy Reform Act of 1978, 65 Iowa L. Rev. 209, 219 (1979).

6. See Practitioner Treatise, Vol. 1.

7. See Practitioner Treatise, Vol. 1.

8. Bankr. R. 9006(a).

perfected cannot acquire an interest that is superior to the interest of the transferee; and

(B) a transfer of a fixture or property other than real property is perfected when a creditor on a simple contract cannot acquire a judicial lien that is superior to the interest of the transferee.

(2) For the purposes of this section, except as provided in paragraph (3) of this subsection, a transfer is made—

(A) at the time such transfer takes effect between the transferor and the transferee, if such transfer is perfected at, or within 10 days after, such time;

(B) at the time such transfer is perfected, if such transfer is perfected after such 10 days; or

(C) immediately before the date of the filing of the petition, if such transfer is not perfected at the later of—

(i) the commencement of the case; or

(ii) 10 days after such transfer takes effect between the transferor and the transferee.

(3) For the purposes of this section, a transfer is not made until the debtor has acquired rights in the property transferred.[9]

Two pieces of background information are useful in understanding section 547(e). First, under nonbankruptcy law, a transfer of property that is valid and enforceable between the transferor and the transferee is not necessarily effective against third parties. Very often, third parties are not affected by the transfer, even though the transfer is complete between the immediate parties to it, until additional steps are taken. Thus, the time when a transfer actually occurs, i.e., when it is effective between the transferor and transferee, may be different from, typically earlier than, the time when the transfer is effective against third parties. For example, an Article 9 security interest is valid between the debtor and secured party-creditor when there is a security agreement, value has been given and the debtor has rights in the collateral.[10] Although the creditor's security interest so created is fully enforceable against the debtor, the interest is typically not effective against a lien creditor of the debtor who acquires her lien on the collateral before an Article 9 financing statement has been properly filed.[11] This filing makes the security interest effective against a subsequent lien creditor.

The added step that nonbankruptcy law requires to make a transfer effective against third parties is commonly referred to as perfection. Perfection usually involves public filing, such as the filing of an Article 9 financing statement or the recording of a real estate mortgage, that is designed to notify the world of the transferee's interest. The purpose of this notice, and thus the purpose of perfection, is to broadcast transfers of the property so

---

9. 11 U.S.C.A. § 547(e).
10. U.C.C. § 9–203(1).
11. Article 9 provides that ordinarily, a secured party interest in collateral is subordinate to the claim of a person who becomes a lien creditor before the security interest is perfected. U.C.C. § 9–301(1)(b). The usual means of perfecting a security interest is filing a financing statement. U.C.C. § 9–302(1).

that third parties dealing with it will not be mislead as to the true state of the property's title.

The second piece of useful background information is that section 547 is designed to serve a subsidiary purpose beyond its main goal of discouraging discriminatory dismemberment of the debtor's estate on the eve of bankruptcy. The secondary purpose is to discourage secret transfers that could mislead the debtor's creditors as to the true size of the debtor's estate. This purpose is achieved by the somewhat cumbersome language of section 547(e).

The core of subsection 547(e) is that a transfer is deemed made, for preference purposes, when the transfer is effective between the transferor and transferee only if the transfer is perfected at or within ten days after that time.[12] If perfection is delayed beyond the ten-day period, the transfer is deemed to have occurred at the time the transfer is perfected.[13] If the transfer is not perfected before the debtor's bankruptcy, the transfer is deemed to have been made immediately before the filing of the bankruptcy petition,[14] except where the transfer is perfected after the filing but within ten days of the time the transfer took effect between the immediate parties. A transfer of real property is perfected when it is effective against a bona fide purchaser;[15] a transfer of personal property or fixtures is perfected when it is effective against a lien creditor.[16] In no event is a transfer made, however, until the debtor acquires rights in the property.[17] Nonbankruptcy law determines when a transfer is effective between the parties and against third persons, and also when the debtor acquires rights in the property transferred.

The consequence of section 547(e) is that a delay in perfecting a transfer of the debtor's property, pursuant to nonbankruptcy law, can postpone the timing of the transfer for purposes of section 547. This postponement increases the risk that the transfer will have occurred during the preference period, and thereby increases the risk that the transfer is an avoidable preference. Creditors manage this risk by quickly perfecting transfers of a debtor's property to them. Section 547 thereby achieves the goal of discouraging secret, i.e., unperfected, transfers that can mislead creditors as to the true size of the debtor's estate.

The easiest way to work with section 547(e) is to restate and apply the provision in three parts: a general rule, a broad exception, and an overriding caveat. The general rule is that the time of transfer, for purposes of section 547, is the time the transfer is perfected. The exception to this rule is that the time of perfection relates to the time of actual transfer, i.e., the time the transfer is valid between the immediate parties, if perfection occurs at or within ten days of the actual transfer. The caveat is that a transfer never occurs until the debtor acquires rights in the property even if all of the other steps had earlier been taken to make the transfer valid between the immediate parties and effective against third parties.

Suppose, for example, that D borrows money from C and the parties agree to secure the loan by a non-possessory, Article 9 security interest in

---

12. 11 U.S.C.A. § 547(e)(2)(A).
13. 11 U.S.C.A. § 547(e)(2)(B).
14. 11 U.S.C.A. § 547(e)(2)(C)(i).
15. 11 U.S.C.A. § 547(e)(1)(A).
16. 11 U.S.C.A. § 547(e)(1)(B).
17. 11 U.S.C.A. § 547(e)(3).

equipment that D purchased a year earlier. D has rights in the collateral from the very beginning of the deal between her and C because D already owned the property then;[18] but a transfer has not yet occurred. The security interest is not effective even between the immediate parties themselves, much less against third parties, until the requirements for creating a security interest under state law, U.C.C. Article 9, are satisfied.

Creating a non-possessory, Article 9 security interest requires not only that the debtor has agreed to the secured transaction and have rights in the collateral, but also that value has been given and that the debtor has signed a written security agreement.[19] In the example, the loan from C to D is value,[20] and D already has the necessary rights. So, when D signs a security agreement, a security interest is created, that is, the security arrangement is effective and fully enforceable between D and C.

Still, however, the transfer has not occurred for purposes of section 547 because state law requires a further step in order to make the security interest effective against a lien creditor. The security interest must be perfected in a manner required or permitted by Article 9.[21] Therefore, the transfer of the security interest is not made, for purposes of section 547, until the interest is perfected under state law Article 9, which in this case requires properly filing a financing statement.

In the end, therefore, the timing of the transfer of the security interest, for purposes of Bankruptcy Code section 547, depends on when the filing is made under local Article 9 law. If the filing is made within ten days after the security interest is created, section 547(e) will relate the time of perfection back to the time the interest became effective between C and D, so that the transfer will be deemed to have been made when the interest was actually created.[22] In this event, no preference will have occurred if the time of creation was outside the preference period even if the filing was within it. If the filing is delayed beyond the ten-day period, there is no relation back: the transfer is deemed to have occurred when the filing was made, without regard to when the security interest was actually created and became effective between the parties.[23]

Article 9 allows a financing statement to be filed before the security interest is actually created[24] so that, for purposes of local law, the security interest will be perfected as soon as the interest attaches to the collateral. When filing precedes creation, the time of transfer is the time of creation for preference purposes. The explanation is that a security interest is not perfected under Article 9 until the interest itself has been created;[25] and thus there is no section 547 transfer until then because the time of transfer is the time of perfection as determined by applicable nonbankruptcy law.

If the secured transaction between C and D involved equipment that D was later to purchase, the transfer of a security interest in that property would not occur until the time D actually purchased the equipment and

---

18. D's seller's title to the equipment passed to D no later than delivery of the property to D. See U.C.C. §§ 2–401(2) & 2–403(1).
19. U.C.C. § 9–203(1).
20. See U.C.C. § 1–201(44).
21. See U.C.C. § 9–301(1)(b).
22. 11 U.S.C.A. § 547(e)(2)(A).
23. 11 U.S.C.A. § 547(e)(2)(B).
24. U.C.C. § 9–402(1).
25. U.C.C. § 9–303(1).

through that transaction acquired rights in the property. The transfer would be so delayed even if D had signed a security agreement and C had filed a financing statement before the purchase occurred.

This example is relatively easy. Deciding when the transfer occurred in many other common situations can be much harder. Indeed, resolving the issue even in the simplest cases such as the preceding example may trigger complicated questions of state law and complex problems and exceptions hiding in the details of section 547, especially in the corners of subsection 547(e). Questions of state law are mostly beyond the scope of this book. We focus here primarily on the details of section 547(e), and on a selection of common problems that arise in deciphering them.

§ 6–12 Within the Preference Period—General Rule: Time of Transfer Is Time of Perfection

For full text of this section, see Epstein, Nickles & White, Bankruptcy, Practitioner Treatise Series, Vol. 1.

§ 6–13 Within the Preference Period—Exception: Perfection Within Ten Days

For full text of this section, see Epstein, Nickles & White, Bankruptcy, Practitioner Treatise Series, Vol. 1.

§ 6–14 Within the Preference Period—Caveat: No Transfer Until Debtor Acquires Rights

For full text of this section, see Epstein, Nickles & White, Bankruptcy, Practitioner Treatise Series, Vol. 1.

§ 6–15 Within the Preference Period—The Caveat Applied to Garnishment During Preference Period

For full text of this section, see Epstein, Nickles & White, Bankruptcy, Practitioner Treatise Series, Vol. 1.

§ 6–16 Within the Preference Period—Payment by Check

A recurring issue under section 547 is the precise time of the transfer of the debtor's property when the transfer is a payment of money by check. Does the transfer occur as soon as the debtor delivers the check to the creditor, or as late as when the drawee-bank pays the instrument? The answer to this question can be critically important. Suppose that D gives C a check on Monday in satisfaction of an antecedent debt that D owes C. The check is presented to the drawee-bank for payment on Wednesday, and is actually paid by the bank on Thursday. D files bankruptcy 90 days following the intervening Tuesday. The payment cannot be a preference if the transfer is deemed to have occurred upon delivery of the check to C because, in that event, the transfer occurred outside the preference period. The payment is subject to attack, however, if the transfer is deemed to have occurred when the check was paid.

To further illustrate the importance of the issue, suppose that D actually files bankruptcy on the intervening Tuesday. If the transfer occurs on Thursday when drawee-bank pays the check, rather than on the date D delivers the check to C, section 547 does not apply because it only governs prepetition transfers. Section 549, which governs postpetition transfers, would determine the validity of the transfer to C.

The issue, when the transfer occurs upon payment by check, arises not only under section 547(b)(4) in determining whether the transfer was preferential, but also under section 547(c) in determining whether an exception to subsection (b) applies. For purposes of section 547(b)(4) only, the majority view has long been that the transfer occurs when the check is paid by the drawee-bank.[1] The Supreme Court eventually embraced this view in *Barnhill v. Johnson*[2] and ended the debate on this issue under section 547(b). The issue may be answered differently for all or certain parts of section 547(c).

The majority view of the issue under section 547(b)(4) rests mainly on the law of U.C.C. Articles 3 and 4, which govern negotiable instruments and check collection, respectively. A check does not, in itself, effect an assignment of funds in a bank account,[3] and the drawee of a check has no liability on the instrument.[4] Thus, a check gives the payee no rights against the drawee-bank until the check is paid. Upon payment of a check, the drawee-bank is accountable for the instrument to the payee.[5] Moreover, taking a check for an underlying debt does not ordinarily discharge the debt for which the check is taken; rather, the debt is only suspended.[6] Discharge of the drawer awaits payment of the check.[7] Also, a drawer's right to stop payment of a check is absolute, in the ordinary case, until the drawee-bank pays the instrument or demonstrates its intention to do so.[8] Moreover, a judicial lien attaching to the account before that time has priority over the check.[9] In sum, until the check is paid, the instrument itself is little more than a different form of the debt for which it was given by the debtor and taken by the creditor.

In sum, it is payment of the check that actually gives the payee or other transferee a claim against the drawee-bank for the amount of the instrument. This claim moving from the drawer-debtor to the payee-creditor is the property that is transferred, and this movement or transfer occurs upon payment of the check rather than upon its delivery.

The argument has been made that the ten-day rule of section 547(e)(2)(A) applies to payment by check, so that the transfer occurs upon delivery of the check if it is paid within ten days. The argument has been rejected on the basis that the rule only applies to transfers of security transactions, not payment by check.[10] A better, more fundamental reason for rejecting the argument is that actual transfer and perfection are one and

§ 6–16
1. See Practitioner Treatise, Vol. 1.
2. ___ U.S. ___, 112 S.Ct. 1386, 118 L.Ed.2d 39 (1992).
3. U.C.C. § 3–409(1).
4. See U.C.C. §§ 3–401(1) & 3–409(1).
5. U.C.C. § 4–213(1).
6. U.C.C. § 3–802(1)(b).
7. U.C.C. §§ 3–603(1) & 3–802(1)(b).
8. U.C.C. §§ 4–303(1) & 4–403(1).
9. U.C.C. § 4–303(1).
10. In re Newman Companies, Inc., 83 B.R. 571, 572–73 (Bankr. E.D.Wis.1988).

the same with respect to payment by check. Delivery of the instrument does not operate, in any sense, as a transfer of the debtor's property. As is made clear above, the actual and only transfer occurs upon payment of the check, and that is also the point when the transfer is perfected in the sense that no judicial lienor can thereafter acquire superior rights to the funds in the checking account. Thus, though payment is perfection, this perfection does not relate back to the delivery of the check because the payment itself, rather than the delivery, effects both the actual and perfected transfer.

§ 6–17 Within the Preference Period—Insiders

The preference period is one year, rather than 90 days, if the transferee is an "insider." The purpose of the longer preference period is to balance the greater ability of insider creditors, compared to non-insiders, to procure a preference.[1] Because of insiders' close relationships with the debtor, they have greater access to more information about the debtor's financial position;[2] they "can exert greater influence on the debtor, which causes insider transactions to be less vulnerable to the market pressures that help control arm's-length transactions;"[3] and, because of their greater knowledge and influence, insiders may more easily than other creditors "veil a potentially preferential transfer, or may even deliberately conceal the preference."[4]

The Code does not actually define "insider." It rather describes a wide sampling of relationships with a debtor that make a creditor an insider. According to section 101(31), "insider" includes:

(A) if the debtor is an individual—

    (i) relative of the debtor or of a general partner of the debtor;

    (ii) partnership in which the debtor is a general partner;

    (iii) general partner of the debtor; or

    (iv) corporation of which the debtor is a director, officer, or person in control;

(B) if the debtor is a corporation—

    (i) director of the debtor;

    (ii) officer of the debtor;

    (iii) person in control of the debtor;

    (iv) partnership in which the debtor is a general partner;

    (v) general partner of the debtor;

    (vi) relative of a general partner, director, officer, or person in control of the debtor;

(C) if the debtor is a partnership—

    (i) general partner in the debtor;

---

§ 6–17

1. Orelup, Avoidance of Preferential Transfers Under the Bankruptcy Reform Act of 1978, 65 Iowa L. Rev. 209, 219 (1979).

2. Note, The Term Insider Within Section 547(b)(4)(B) of the Bankruptcy Code, 57 Notre Dame Law. 726, 729 (1982).

3. Id. at 729–30.

4. Id. at 730.

(ii) relative of a general partner in, general partner of, or person in control of the debtor;

(iii) partnership in which the debtor is a general partner;

(iv) general partner of the debtor; or

(v) person in control of the debtor;

(D) if the debtor is a municipality, elected official of the debtor or relative of an elected official of the debtor;

(E) affiliate, or insider of an affiliate if such affiliate were the debtor; and

(F) managing agent of the debtor.[5]

If the creditor's relationship with the debtor is listed here, the transferee is an insider.[6] It is not necessary to prove that the creditor actually used her position to gain the preference that she is alleged to have received. Thus, a creditor of a corporation is an insider of the company if she is a sister or other relative (within the third degree [7]) of a company official.[8] It is irrelevant that the creditor-relative herself played no role in running the company; had no special leverage there; was not directly or indirectly responsible for the transfer to her; and, since childhood, has not spoken to her relative who sits on the debtor's board.[9] For the most part, a creditor's actual conduct in dealing with the debtor is pertinent only when the claim of insider is based on the creditor having been a "person in control of the debtor," or when the claim is based on a relationship between the creditor and debtor that does not appear in the section 101(31) non-exclusive list [10] of insiders.

Because "person in control of the debtor" is so relatively general, the courts have often been asked to explore the meaning and boundaries of this basis for insider status. The only firm conclusion the cases yield is that a creditor is not a "person in control of the debtor" simply because she enjoys the leverage, influence and financial power that naturally and ordinarily accompany a debtor-creditor relationship.[11] Because the allegations of control have typically been based only on that kind of power, the courts have

---

5. 11 U.S.C.A. § 101(31). This listing is exemplary, not exclusive. The meaning of "insider" is not limited to the examples listed. In re Hydraulic Industrial Products Co., 101 B.R. 107, 109 (Bankr. E.D.Mo.1989); see also In re Polk, 125 B.R. 293, 296–97 (Bankr. D.Colo.1991) ("Insider" is a term of inclusion rather than exclusion, and the list the Code provides to illustrate the term is not exhaustive.); Matter of Hollar, 100 B.R. 892, 893 (Bankr. N.D.Ohio 1989) (the definition of "insider" is not exclusively limiting).

Notice that the list does not include a limited partner when a corporate debtor is the general partner, and the courts will not necessarily add this relationship to the list. See In re Pittsburgh Cut Flower Co., Inc., 124 B.R. 451, 459–60 (Bankr. W.D.Pa.1991).

6. See Practitioner Treatise, Vol. 1.

7. A "relative" is an "individual related by affinity or consanguinity within the third degree as determined by the common law, or individual in a step or adoptive relationship within such third degree." 11 U.S.C.A. § 101(45) (emphasis added). " '[C]ommon law' refers to the body of applicable state law in effect at the time of the action which is the subject of the proceeding." In re Hydraulic Industrial Products, Co., 101 B.R. 107, 108 (Bankr. E.D.Mo.1989) (instead of applying common-law method of determining the degree of relationship by counting generations from the common ancestor, court applies local statute governing descent and distribution and finds thereunder that first cousins are not related within third degree).

8. See Practitioner Treatise, Vol. 1.

9. See Practitioner Treatise, Vol. 1.

10. See Practitioner Treatise, Vol. 1.

11. See Practitioner Treatise, Vol. 1.

seldom had the occasion to consider what additional power a creditor must wield in order to be "in control of the debtor" for insider purposes. The very few opinions that go beyond the standard fare suggest that the creditor must have meaningfully involved itself in actually managing or otherwise running the debtor's affairs so as to prevent the debtor from acting independently.

Thus, in *In re Babcock Dairy Co. of Ohio, Inc.*,[12] the court concluded that, in the absence of this kind of substantial meaningful involvement, a man who sold his company and stayed on as an advisor to the new owner was not sufficiently in control of the company to qualify, on the basis of control, as an insider of it. The former owner, though he was a vocal advisor to, a creditor of and also a stockholder in the company, was not in control of it because he did not "make any dispositive corporate decisions," "had no authority to dispose of corporate assets," did not "prevail in any decisions regarding the operations of the * * * business," could not "command authority over any corporate affair," and, in sum, "had no meaningful control over any corporate affair."[13]

The issue of a creditor's insider status, based on control of the debtor, was decided differently in *In re Bellanca Aircraft Corp.*[14] The court pinned the label "insider" on two creditors, AGCO and Aviation, because the officers and directors of the creditors sat on the debtor's board and also assumed certain executive positions in the debtor's management. Additionally, the creditors were controlling shareholders, inasmuch as Aviation had the right to vote 68% of the common shares of the debtor and AGCO owned 100% of Aviation.[15]

Voting control is not necessary, however, for insider status based on control of the debtor. In the case, *In re Rubin Bros. Footwear, Inc.*[16], the court determined that insider status through control of the debtor can be established by other means of substantial involvement by a creditor in the operation of a debtor's business. In this case the debtor, Rubin Bros., owed Chemical Bank approximately $700,000 at a time when the debtor was having financial problems. The problems were so severe that the debtor told Chemical of its intention to file bankruptcy. The Bank recommended a different plan: Rubin should hire Solomon, a business consultant, to help turn around the debtor's business. Rubin took this advice and hired Solomon who, the debtor alleged, covertly worked on the Bank's behalf, from within the debtor's operation, to secure and reduce the debt to the Bank. The court decided in *Rubin* that if this allegation were proved, Chemical was an insider, based on control, because the bank had not dealt at "arms length" with the debtor, but had " 'a special relationship with the debtor through which it [could] * * * compel payment of its debt * * *.' "[17]

12. 70 B.R. 668 (Bankr. N.D.Ohio 1986).

13. Id. at 673; see also In re UVAS Farming Corp., 89 B.R. 889, 893 (Bankr. D.N.M. 1988) (creditor had no day-to-day control, and debtor was free to act independently); cf. In re Belco, Inc., 38 B.R. 525, 530 (Bankr. W.D. Okla. 1984) (control requires evidence that creditor enjoyed means of restraint and authority over debtor beyond that enjoyed in usual debtor-creditor relationship).

14. 56 B.R. 339 (Bankr. D.Minn.1985), appeal decided, 850 F.2d 1275 (8th Cir.1988), on remand, 96 B.R. 913 (Bankr.D.Minn.1989).

15. Id. at 389.

16. 73 B.R. 346 (S.D.N.Y. 1987).

17. Id. at 354.

The claim of insider status in *Rubin* was not based solely on creditor involvement in the management of the debtor's business. The claim was also based on creditor self-dealing. Self-dealing is not essential, however, to insider status based on control of the debtor. The courts have used the equitable power of subordination to handle the creditor who manipulates the debtor for the purpose of enhancing the creditor's own position to the detriment of other creditors.[18] Moreover, Congress intended the term insider to include a person with "a sufficiently close relationship with the debtor that his conduct is made subject to closer scrutiny than those dealing at arm's length with the debtor."[19] It is therefore the person's relationship with the debtor that is critical to insider status, not the person's motive, purpose or behavior in the relationship. A creditor that controls a debtor managerially or operationally is thus an insider for that reason alone, notwithstanding the absence of creditor self-dealing in exercising the control.

On the other hand, the courts' hesitance to make creditors insiders merely because they exercise some influence over the debtor is sensible. A secured creditor's influence over a debtor is invariably self-interested, and at least to that limited extent, constitutes "self dealing." Yet such influence by an aggressive creditor that has a large enough stake to justify some intrusion into the debtor's affairs may benefit not only that creditor, but other creditors as well. Where the managers of the debtor are incompetent, misguided, or dishonest, not only the strong, but also the weak may profit by early intervention of a strong and self-interested creditor.

Whether or not the creditor's relationship with the debtor is close enough to justify closer scrutiny is an important issue not only in deciding if a creditor was a "person in control of the debtor." The issue is determinative by itself in deciding if a creditor is an "insider" on the basis of a relationship that, unlike control of the debtor, is not included in the insider relationships listed in section 101(31). In theory, a creditor can be an insider even though she did not control the debtor and does not fit within any of the other relationships described in section 101(31), inasmuch as that list is illustrative only and is not exclusive.[20] For example, the court held in *In re Polk*[21] "that a trust, including a profit sharing trust of a debtor's employer, can qualify as an insider of an individual debtor * * *,"[22] depending on the facts of the particular case and whether there was a "sufficiently close relationship" between the debtor and the trust. In practice, however, the courts have not generally agreed on any relationship, beyond the examples in section 101(31), that in itself usually and generally establishes insider status.

A likely candidate is the relationship between a debtor and creditor who are close friends. After all, a relative is an insider; and friends are often closer than relatives. More often than not, however, courts have refused to conclude that a creditor is an insider solely because of her close friendship with the debtor or with persons in charge of a corporate debtor.[23]

---

18. See 11 U.S.C.A. § 510(c).

19. S. Rep. No. 989, 95th Cong., 2d Sess. 25, reprinted in 1978 U.S. Code Cong. & Admin. News 5787, 5810.

20. See authorities cited note 5 supra.

21. 125 B.R. 293 (Bankr. D.Colo.1991).

22. Id. at 297.

23. See Practitioner Treatise, Vol. 1.

Instead of adding to the section 101(31) list of insiders, the courts are more apt expansively to interpret and apply the examples provided there. For example, in *Matter of Montanino*,[24] the court appears to have decided that the debtor's fiancee (who had lived with the debtor for more than five years) and the fiancee's parents, were insiders because they were "relatives" of the debtor. The court reasoned that

> Congress did not intend to limit the classification of insiders to relatives by marriage or consanguinity. The true test of an "insider" is one who has such a relationship with the debtor that their dealing with one another cannot be characterized as an arm's-length transaction.[25]

In this case, the debtor's fiancee was his relative because of their close affinity, and the relationship between the debtor and his fiancee's parents "was more than sufficiently close to eliminate any finding of an arms-length transaction" so that they, too, were insiders.[26]

Separate and apart from the definitional issue, i.e., who is an insider, is the issue of timing, i.e., when must the person have been an insider in order to trigger the one-year preference period. The Code declares that the one-year period applies if the "creditor *at the time of such transfer* was an insider."[27] In other words, "[t]he insider relationship must exist on the date of the transfer."[28] Thus, as a general rule, the 90-day preference period applies, rather than the one-year period, if the creditor had been an insider prior to the transfer but had terminated the relationship before the transfer occurred;[29] but the one-year period applies if the creditor was an insider when the transfer was made but thereafter shed the status prior to the debtor's bankruptcy.

The rule is somewhat flexible, however, as demonstrated in *In re F & S Central Manufacturing Corp.*[30] In this case the creditor sold the debtor company to a corporate buyer pursuant to an agreement that required the debtor, after the sale, to reduce an antecedent debt owed the creditor-seller. Shortly after the sale, the debtor got a loan and paid the antecedent debt. The trustee argued that this transfer was a preference to an insider, basing the claim of insider status on the creditor's ownership of the debtor company. The creditor argued, however, that it was not an insider at the time of the debtor's reduction of the antecedent debt because, three days earlier, the creditor had sold and delivered all of its stock in the debtor to the buyer of the company.

The court rejected the creditor's argument, disagreeing with the assumption "that only those who are insiders on the very day the debtor transfers its property are insiders at the time of transfer."[31] In the court's view, "[a] creditor who is an insider *at the time the transfer of the debtor's property is*

---

24. 15 B.R. 307 (D.N.J.1981).
25. Id. at 310.
26. Id. at 310–11. Another example of an expansive reading of the examples listed in section 101(31) is In re Landbank Equity Corp., 83 B.R. 362 (E.D.Va.1987), in which the court held that a company was an insider because it was the corporate alter ego of a relative of an owner-officer of the debtor. Id. at 391.
27. 11 U.S.C.A. § 547(b)(4)(B) (emphasis added).
28. In re Tennessee Wheel and Rubber Co., 62 B.R. 1002, 1005 (Bankr. M.D.Tenn.1986).
29. See Practitioner Treatise, Vol. 1.
30. 53 B.R. 842 (Bankr. E.D.N.Y.1985).
31. Id. at 848.

arranged is an insider at the time of the transfer."[32] If the law were otherwise, insiders could "escape the insider provisions by delaying * * * the date the debtor transfers its property."[33] There is authority contrary to *F & S*. The court in *Dent v. Martin*[34] rejected *F & S* because the "plain meaning" of section 547(b)(4)(B) requires determining insider status on the exact date of the transfer.[35]

A statute's "plain meaning," however, should not be applied to thwart the statute's obvious purpose. We agree with *F & S*.

§ 6–18 When the Debtor Is Insolvent

A transfer is a not a preference under section 547 unless the transfer was "made while the debtor was insolvent."[1] "Insolvent" means that the debtor's financial condition is such that the sum of her debts is greater than all of her property at a fair valuation.[2] A "balance sheet" test determines insolvency.[3] "The debtor is insolvent when its liabilities exceed its assets at a fair valuation."[4]

Property that was transferred with the intention of defrauding creditors is excluded from the assets side of the balance sheet.[5] Exempt property is also excluded.[6] On the other hand, property that was the subject of an alleged preference is included in the calculation.[7]

The worth of all property that is included must be determined "at a fair valuation."[8] According to the court in *In re Joe Flynn Rare Coins, Inc.*,[9]

fair value does not mean the amount the property would bring in the worst circumstances or the best, but the amount it would bring if the debtor took a reasonable time to collect its debts and sell its property. For example, a forced sale price is not fair value though it may be used as evidence on the question of fair value. Likewise, the fair value of saleable assets is not what they would sell for in the slow process of the debtor's trade as if the debtor were continuing business unhampered. The general idea of fair value is the amount of money the debtor could

---

32. Id. at 849 (emphasis added).

33. Id.

34. 86 B.R. 290 (S.D.Fla.1988), on remand, 103 B.R. 322 (Bankr. S.D.Fla.1988), opinion aff'd, 104 B.R. 477 (Bankr. S.D.Fla.1989).

35. Id. at 292.

§ 6–18

1. 11 U.S.C.A. § 547(b)(3).

2. 11 U.S.C.A. § 101(32).

3. See Practitioner Treatise, Vol. 1.

4. In re Joe Flynn Rare Coins, Inc., 81 B.R. 1009, 1017 (Bankr. D.Kan.1988); accord, Briden v. Foley, 776 F.2d 379 (1st Cir. 1985); In re Excello Press, Inc., 96 B.R. 840, 842 (Bankr. N.D.Ill. 1989); Matter of Plihal, 97 B.R. 554, 557–58 (Bankr. D.Neb.1989); Matter of Writing Sales Ltd. Partnership, 96 B.R. 175, 177 (Bankr. E.D.Wis.1989); In re F.H.L., Inc., 91 B.R. 288, 293 (Bankr. D.N.J.1988); In re Rose, 86 B.R. 193, 194 (Bankr. W.D.Mo.1988). There is no set, rigid approach to determining this "fair valuation;" and it is not accomplished in only one way. Porter v. Yukon Nat'l Bank, 866 F.2d 355, 356–57 (10th Cir. 1989).

"[T]he fact that the debtor cannot pay its debts as they mature is not the correct test, but this does not mean that this fact cannot be relied upon as evidence of insolvency." Dent v. Martin, 104 B.R. 477, 479 (S.D.Fla. 1989) (emphasis in original).

5. 11 U.S.C.A. § 101(32)(A)(i).

6. 11 U.S.C.A. § 101(32)(A)(ii); In re Lewis, 94 B.R. 789, 793 (Bankr. D.Mass.1988); In re Wommack, 74 B.R. 638 (Bankr. N.D.Fla.1987) (but debt owed on exempt property not excluded in calculating liabilities); In re Espinoza, 51 B.R. 170 (Bankr. D.N.M.1985).

7. Matter of K & R Mining, Inc., 103 B.R. 136, 140 (Bankr. N.D.Ohio 1988).

8. 11 U.S.C.A. § 101(32)(A) & (B).

9. 81 B.R. 1009 (D.Kan.1988).

raise from its property in a short period of time, but not so short as to approximate a forced sale, if the debtor operated as a reasonably prudent and diligent businessman with his interests in mind, especially a proper concern for the payment of his debts.[10]

In a particular case the proper standard for valuing assets can depend to some extent on the peculiar circumstances affecting value at the time of the transfer, including the debtor's financial situation. If the debtor was still operating in a somewhat regular fashion when the transfer occurred, the proper standard is the going-concern value of the assets at the time, not the property's liquidation value.[11] On the other hand, "going-concern value is not the proper standard if the business is 'on its deathbed.' "[12]

The critical time for insolvency is "when the alleged preferential transfer occurred and not when the petition was filed."[13] Correspondingly, the debtor's "assets must be valued at what they are reasonably worth at the time of the allegedly preferential transfers and not what they turned out to be worth at some time after the bankruptcy intervened."[14]

Debts owed for the price of exempt assets are included on the liabilities side of the balance sheet even though the assets themselves are excluded in determining the worth of the debtor's property at the time of the transfer.[15] The debt that an alleged preference satisfied is also included in liabilities.[16] Contingent or doubtful liabilities, such as tort claims against the debtor and debts on which the debtor is a surety only, are properly included,[17] but not necessarily at face value. Rather, the size of these liabilities should be discounted to account for the uncertainty that they would be collected from the debtor.[18]

Although the trustee is burdened with proving every element of a preference,[19] she is greatly aided in establishing the insolvency element by a legal presumption: For the purposes of section 547, "the debtor is presumed to have been insolvent on and during the 90 days immediately preceding the date of the filing of the petition."[20] This presumption works in the trustee's favor in every case except insider transfers that occurred between 90 days and one year before bankruptcy was filed.[21]

The presumption of insolvency is not conclusive. The defendant-creditor can rebut it by going forward with " '*some evidence* tending to prove solvency * * * ' "[22] that is sufficient " 'to cast into doubt the statutory presumption of insolvency, i.e., that the debtor's assets exceeded its liabilities.' "[23] This standard of rebuttal is not satisfied, however, by the mere assertion that the

10. Id. at 1017.

11. See Practitioner Treatise, Vol. 1.

12. Matter of Taxman Clothing Co., Inc., 905 F.2d 166, 170 (7th Cir.1990).

13. In re Davis, 120 B.R. 823, 825 (Bankr. W.D.Pa.1990).

14. Id.

15. In re Wommack, 74 B.R. 638, 640 (Bankr. N.D.Fla.1987); In re Pereau, 37 B.R. 902, 903 (Bankr. M.D.Fla.1984).

16. Matter of K & R Mining, Inc., 103 B.R. 136, 140 (Bankr. N.D.Ohio 1988).

17. See 11 U.S.C.A. § 101(5), defining "claim," which gives rise to debt of the debtor, to include contingent and unliquidated rights to payment.

18. See Practitioner Treatise, Vol. 1.

19. 11 U.S.C.A. § 547(g).

20. 11 U.S.C.A. § 547(f).

21. See Practitioner Treatise, Vol. 1.

22. In re Wommack, 74 B.R. 638, 640 (Bankr. N.D.Fla.1987) (emphasis added).

23. In re World Financial Services Center, Inc., 78 B.R. 239, 241 (Bankr. 9th Cir.1987).

debtor was solvent;[24] by evidence of equitable solvency, that is, the debtor was paying her debts as they became due;[25] by testimony of the conclusions of the debtor's officers, or the creditor's representatives, that the debtor was legally solvent at the time of the transfer;[26] or by unaudited financial statements of the debtor that cover a period long before the challenged transfer.[27] Moreover, "[t]he shorter the time between the transfer and bankruptcy, the greater the proof required to rebut the presumption."[28]

If the presumption applies and is not rebutted, the court is bound to rule in the trustee's favor on the insolvency issue even though the trustee has offered no proof whatsoever on the issue.[29] The presumption alone carries the day. If, on the other hand, the creditor rebuts the presumption, the trustee is saddled with the ultimate burden of proof, that is, the trustee bears the burden of persuasion to prove actual insolvency.[30]

§ 6–19 For or on Account of an Antecedent Debt

A transfer is a preference only if the transfer is made "for or on account of an antecedent debt owed by the debtor before such transfer was made."[1] This element of a preference actually embodies two principal requirements: (1) The transfer must have been for or on account of a *debt* that was *owed by the debtor;* and (2) the debt must have been on *antecedent* debt, that is, the debtor must have owed the debt *before the transfer was made.*

The first requirement essentially reiterates an element of a preference considered earlier, i.e., that the transfer be "to or for the benefit of a creditor."[2] A creditor is a person with a claim against the debtor.[3] The terms "claim" and "debt" are coextensive.[4] Thus, whenever there is a transfer to a creditor for or on account of the creditor's claim against the debtor, there is likewise a transfer for or on account of a debt that the debtor owed.[5] The nondischargeability of the debt makes no difference.[6] There is

---

24. See Practitioner Treatise, Vol. 1.

25. See Practitioner Treatise, Vol. 1.

26. See Practitioner Treatise, Vol. 1.

27. See Practitioner Treatise, Vol. 1.

28. In re Rose, 86 B.R. 193, 194 (Bankr. W.D.Mo.1988).

29. See Practitioner Treatise, Vol. 1.

30. See Practitioner Treatise, Vol. 1.

§ 6–19

1. 11 U.S.C.A. § 547(b)(2).

2. 11 U.S.C.A. § 547(b)(1), which we discuss at § 6–8.

3. 11 U.S.C.A. § 101(10)(A).

4. "'[D]ebt' means liability on a claim." 11 U.S.C.A. § 101(12); Matter of Barge, 875 F.2d 508, 510 (5th Cir.1989) ("The terms creditor and debt are * * * statutorily congruent."); In re Bullion Reserve of North America, 836 F.2d 1214, 1219 (9th Cir.1988), cert. denied, 486 U.S. 1056, 108 S.Ct. 2824, 100 L.Ed.2d 925 (1988) ("debt" and "claim" are coextensive); In re Energy Co-op, Inc., 832 F.2d 997, 1001 (7th Cir.1987) (same); Matter of Cavalier Homes of Georgia, Inc., 102 B.R. 878, 886 (Bankr. M.D.Ga.1989) (same); In re Financial Partners Ltd., 116 B.R. 629, 635 (Bankr. N.D.Ill. 1989) (same).

The definition of "debt" is very broad because the meaning of "claim" is so expansive, providing that "claim" includes "any right to payment." 11 U.S.C.A. § 101(5)(A). Thus, any obligation to pay money is a debt, at least "so long as any person or entity has a right to enforce that obligation." In re Johnson–Allen, 871 F.2d 421, 426 (3d Cir.1989), aff'd sub nom., Pennsylvania Dept. of Welfare v. Davenport, 495 U.S. 552, 110 S.Ct. 2126, 109 L.Ed.2d 588 (1990) (obligation to make criminal restitution is a debt that is discharged in Chapter 13). Even "[u]nauthorized loans created through the fraud of a check kiting scheme constitute 'debts' * * *;" moreover, "[t]hat the extension of credit effected by the check kite was not authorized is of little consequence in preference analysis." In re Montgomery, 123 B.R. 801, 808, 809 (Bankr. M.D.Tenn.1991), aff'd, 136 B.R. 727 (M.D.Tenn.1992).

5. See Practitioner Treatise, Vol. 1.

no preference, however, if the transfer is made to someone who is not a creditor of the debtor [7] or to a creditor of the debtor for or on account of someone else's debt [8] or for some purpose other than satisfying the debt.[9]

The requirement of antecedent debt is satisfied if the debt was owed or incurred before the transfer was made.[10] There are three issues here. The first issue, the timing of the transfer, has already been considered.[11] Remember that, as a general rule, a transfer is not deemed to have been made until the transfer is perfected.[12]

Second, when is a debt "owed?" Generally speaking, a debt is owed as of the time the debt is incurred,[13] and "'a debt is "incurred" on the date upon which the debtor first becomes legally bound to pay.'"[14] A debtor does not become legally bound to pay for services or property when the contract is made; rather, for purposes of section 547(b), a debtor becomes legally obligated to pay for services when they are rendered;[15] for a loan when the proceeds are advanced;[16] and for goods or other property when the debtor obtains an interest in the property.[17] It makes no difference that the debt is then unmatured, contingent, unliquidated or disputed,[18] or that an invoice or other demand for payment is not sent or made until a later time.[19] Indeed, it makes no difference that the creditor was ignorant of the debt when it was incurred.[20]

The third issue with respect to antecedence is whether the requirement is satisfied by any gap, however small, between the time the debt was incurred and the time the transfer was made, or whether some gap between these times is properly tolerated, in appropriate circumstances, to prevent stretching preference law beyond its purposes. If the language of section 547(b)(2) is literally read and applied, a transfer is for an antecedent debt if the transfer was made even one second after the time the debtor incurred the debt.

This literal approach does not deny that preference law is aimed at transfers that deplete the debtor's estate during the preference period; that transfers for "new value" (somehow defined) do not deplete the estate; and that Congress intended to protect such transfers (as Congress would define them) from avoidance under section 547. Rather, the approach simply recognizes that the exclusive source of this protection is section 547(c), which creates a series of exceptions to subsection (b) and thereby immunizes certain transfers, including certain new-value transfers, from avoidance as preferences.

The argument for this approach is simple and strong. Though everyone might agree (as we do) on immunizing new-value transfers, everyone (including each of us) has his or her own definition of new value that is wide or

6. See Practitioner Treatise, Vol. 1.
7. See Practitioner Treatise, Vol. 1.
8. See Practitioner Treatise, Vol. 1.
9. See Practitioner Treatise, Vol. 1.
10. See Practitioner Treatise, Vol. 1.
11. See §§ 6–11 through 6–17.
12. 11 U.S.C.A. § 547(e).
13. See Practitioner Treatise, Vol. 1.
14. In re Wathen's Elevators, Inc., 37 B.R. 870, 871 (Bankr. W.D.Ky.1984).
15. See Practitioner Treatise, Vol. 1.
16. See Practitioner Treatise, Vol. 1.
17. See Practitioner Treatise, Vol. 1.
18. See Practitioner Treatise, Vol. 1.
19. See Practitioner Treatise, Vol. 1.
20. See Practitioner Treatise, Vol. 1.

narrow depending on the person's own notion of the purposes of preference law. It is Congress' meaning that counts, however; and the requirement of "antecedent debt" is not a good means of deciding the range of "new value" transfers that Congress decided was beyond the purpose of preference law. The language is too loose and uncertain and has too much play to insure that the actual reach of section 547, as judicially applied, is consistent with the statute's intended range, as congressionally decided.

The subsection (c) exceptions, though not without ambiguity, are comparatively fuller, tighter and more specific in their language and legislative history. They therefore serve as better, more reliable guides in defining the new-value transfers that are beyond the aims and reach of preference law. (Similar reasoning leads us to apply section 547 in any case by reading subsection (b) broadly and literally, while construing the subsection (c) exceptions narrowly and purposively.) We discuss the exceptions separately below.[21]

On the other hand, we are not 100 percent certain about how literal the courts should be in applying section 547(b)(2). It may be safer to allow some leeway there, even if only a tiny bit, to insure an escape for "slightly antecedent" transfers that, properly, should be freed from the grasp of section 547.

§ 6–20 Preferential Effect

The final element of a preference, as listed in section 547(b)(5), is that the transfer must have enabled the creditor to receive more than such creditor would receive if

(A) the case were a case under chapter 7 of this title;

(B) the transfer had not been made; and

(C) such creditor received payment of such debt to the extent provided by the provisions of this title.[1]

Put more simply, the transfer must have enabled the creditor to receive more, when added to the potential recovery on the balance of her claim,[2] than the creditor would have received if (1) the transfer had not been made, (2) the debtor's estate were liquidated under Chapter 7 of the Bankruptcy Code, and (3) the creditor got only the distribution to which the creditor would be entitled in the liquidation case.[3] A creditor's receiving more from the transfer than she would have received in a Chapter 7 liquidation is often referred to as "preferential effect."

To determine if a transfer resulted in a preferential effect, a purely "hypothetical [Chapter 7] liquidation case must be created to determine if the creditor's position was improved by the transfer."[4] The date of the imaginary case, and also the date of the imaginary liquidation and distribution, is the day on which the debtor filed her petition in the actual

21. See §§ 6–22 through 6–37.

§ 6–20
1. 11 U.S.C.A. § 547(b)(5).
2. See Practitioner Treatise, Vol. 1.

3. See Practitioner Treatise, Vol. 1.

4. Young, Preference Under the Bankruptcy Reform Act of 1978, 54 Am. Bankr. L. J. 221, 224 (1980).

bankruptcy case. Actual postpetition developments are ignored.[5] This Chapter 7 liquidation must be imagined even if the debtor has actually filed for Chapter 11 reorganization or for relief under another chapter of the Bankruptcy Code.[6] The trustee must prove that upon the hypothesized Chapter 7 distribution of the debtor's liquidated assets, the creditor would have received less than the amount the creditor would actually have received in such a case from the actual transfer plus the amount she would have recovered on the balance of her claim. Proof is sufficient that establishes preferential effect to any extent.[7] "[I]t is not necessary to quantify the amount of preferential effect * * * with actuarial certainty."[8]

If the creditor's claim would not have been allowable in a Chapter 7 case, the trustee need go no further. The preferential effect requirement is satisfied because the creditor would have received nothing from the distribution of the estate.[9]

If the claim would be allowable, these major steps are required to determine preferential effect:

Step 1. Value the amount of the debtor's assets that would be distributed in a liquidation case. This property should be valued as of time of the actual petition.[10] The property actually transferred to the creditor should be included if that property would have been liquidated and distributed in a Chapter 7 case.[11]

Step 2. Determine the size of the distribution the creditor would have received in the Chapter 7 case if the transfer had not been made and the creditor had made a claim for the full amount of the debt owed her. In making this determination, fully respect the Code's priority scheme for making payments to creditors in a Chapter 7 case.[12]

Step 3. Measure the value of the property actually transferred to the creditor;[13] and add to this amount the distribution that the creditor would receive on the balance of her claim,[14] taking into account that the pool of assets available for distribution should not, for this step, include the value of the actual transfer.[15]

Step 4. Finally, compare the results in steps 2 and 3. If the latter is larger than the former, the transfer had a preferential effect and section 547(b)(5) is satisfied. If step 2 is larger than step 3, the transfer is not avoidable as a preference,[16] even if all of the other elements of a preference are satisfied.

For example, assume that D makes a $1,000 payment to C, a general creditor with a $10,000 unsecured claim, on January 10. On February 20, D files a bankruptcy petition. The property of the estate, including hypothetically the $1,000 paid to C, would be sufficient to pay each general, unsecured creditor only 50% of her claim. Thus, had the transfer not been made to C,

5. See Practitioner Treatise, Vol. 1.
6. See Practitioner Treatise, Vol. 1.
7. See Practitioner Treatise, Vol. 1.
8. Matter of Craig, 92 B.R. 394, 398 (Bankr. D.Neb.1988).
9. See Practitioner Treatise, Vol. 1.
10. See Practitioner Treatise, Vol. 1.
11. See Practitioner Treatise, Vol. 1.
12. See Practitioner Treatise, Vol. 1.
13. See Practitioner Treatise, Vol. 1.
14. See Practitioner Treatise, Vol. 1.
15. See Practitioner Treatise, Vol. 1.
16. See Practitioner Treatise, Vol. 1.

she would have received $5,000. C, however, would actually receive a total of about $5,500: this amount includes the $1,000 transfer of January 10, and slightly less than 50% of C's remaining claim (about $4,500). The percentage payment is a bit smaller here because the value of the January 10 transfer is excluded from the pool of assets available for distribution in deciding the dividend that C would get on the balance of her claim.

Fortunately, the courts have recognized certain shorthand tests for deciding if a transfer had a preferential effect. The most commonly used test is as follows: In the case of a payment to an unsecured, nonpriority (general) creditor, the preferential effect requirement is satisfied unless general, unsecured creditors would have received 100% of their claims in the hypothesized Chapter 7 distribution.[17] The same is true in such a case if the transfer that is attacked as a preference is a lien created voluntarily or involuntarily on the debtor's property.[18] In either case the trustee need only show, in order to establish preferential effect, that the debtor's liabilities exceeded her assets at the time of the bankruptcy petition. To make this showing the trustee can rely on the debtor's schedules of property and debts that accompanied the bankruptcy petition.[19]

On the other hand, a payment to a *fully secured creditor,* with a valid in-bankruptcy lien or other invulnerable secured claim, has no preferential effect.[20] The reason is that a secured claim would have been satisfied from

---

17. See Practitioner Treatise, Vol. 1.
18. See Practitioner Treatise, Vol. 1.
19. See Practitioner Treatise, Vol. 1.
20. Matter of EDC, Inc., 930 F.2d 1275, 1283 (7th Cir.1991) (There would be no preference if goods ended up with secured creditor which held senior lien on them.); In re Hagen, 922 F.2d 742, 745–46 (11th Cir.1991) ("A transfer to a secured creditor in the amount of its lien during the preference period does not constitute an avoidable preference."); Lewis v. Diethorn, 893 F.2d 648, 650–51 (3d Cir.1990), cert. denied, ___ U.S. ___, 111 S.Ct. 369, 112 L.Ed.2d 332 (1990) (payment to holder of equitable lien, which lien was immune to trustee's attack, was not a preference because no preferential effect); Braniff Airways, Inc. v. Exxon Co., U.S.A., 814 F.2d 1030, 1033–40 (5th Cir.1987) (payments to fully secured creditor, including one secured by right of setoff, are not preferential); Matter of Missionary Baptist Foundation, 796 F.2d 752, 759 (5th Cir. 1986), on remand, 69 B.R. 540 (Bankr. N.D.Tex.1987) ("It is commonplace that preference law exempts fully secured creditors from its grasp."); In re Presidents Mortg. Indus. Bank, 110 B.R. 508, 510–13 (D.Colo.1989) (repayment of loan with proceeds held subject to constructive trust is not preferential); In re Julien Co., 127 B.R. 604, 619 (Bankr. W.D.Tenn.1991) (Wire transfers were not preference because they satisfied secured debt in full and the secured creditor received no more than it would have received had its lien been satisfied in a Chapter 7 liquidation.); In re Cedar Rapids Meats, Inc., 121 B.R. 562, 572–73 (Bankr. N.D.Iowa 1990) (Payment to an over-secured creditor with a perfected lien is not a preference because there is no preferential effect to the extent of the secured debt.); In re Lill, 116 B.R. 543, 549–50 (Bankr. N..Ohio 1990) ("Section 547 is not applicable to fully secured creditors."); In re Holland, 102 B.R. 208, 210 (Bankr. S.D. Cal.1989) (IRS prepetition collection had no preferential effect because the tax liabilities were fully secured by federal tax lien); In re Sunnyside Beverage, Inc., 104 B.R. 51, 54 (Bankr. N.D.Ind. 1989) (payment to creditor fully secured by real estate and inventory); In re Parkway Calabasas Ltd., 89 B.R. 832, 840 (Bankr. C.D.Cal. 1988) (payment of secured debt not subject to preference attack); Matter of Phoenix Steel Corp., 76 B.R. 373, 376 (Bankr. D.Del.1987) (payment to a fully secured Article 9 secured party); In re Rimmer Corp., 80 B.R. 337, 339 (Bankr. E.D.Pa. 1987); In re U.S. Lines, Inc., 79 B.R. 542, 545–46 (Bankr. S.D.N.Y. 1987) (payment of property held under a duty of restitution is not preferential as property would have been subject to constructive trust and remedy that would be enforceable against trustee); In re Zuni, 6 B.R. 449, 451 (Bankr. D.N.M.1980) (Code excepts from preference attack payments to fully secured creditor with a perfected lien); Duncan, Loan Payments to Secured Creditors as Preferences Under the 1984 Bankruptcy Amendments, 64 Neb. L. Rev. 83, 86 (1985) (loan payments to fully secured creditors are not preferences); cf. First Fed. Sav. & Loan Ass'n v. Standard Bldg. Ass'n, 87 B.R. 221 (N.D.Ga.1988) (§ 547 does not apply to valid nonjudicial foreclosure by a fully secured mortgage holder).

the collateral in a Chapter 7 case ahead of all other claims to and payments from the estate. Thus, a payment to a fully secured creditor does not enable her to get more than she would have received had the estate been liquidated. Moreover, the payment does not harm the estate because the payment caused a compensating reduction in the size of the creditor's lien and a corresponding increase in the amount of equity available to the estate.[21] If, however, the creditor's putative lien is voidable in bankruptcy, or is otherwise worthless, the creditor's claim is unsecured; so any transfer to the creditor in satisfaction of the claim is preferential in the absence of a 100 percent Chapter 7 distribution to the creditor.[22]

Under secured creditors have claims that are not completely collateralized, that is, the value of their collateral is less than the debts owed them. A transfer to a general undersecured creditor is deemed preferential, at least to the extent that the transfer is equal to or less than the size of the unsecured part of the creditor's claim, if general, unsecured creditors would receive less than a 100 percent distribution on their claims in the hypothesized Chapter 7 case.[23] Arguably, the undersecured creditor could avoid this

---

The general rule that payment of a fully secured claim lacks preferential effect does not apply if the collateral is someone else's property because, in this event, the payment reduces the estate. See generally, e.g., In re C–L Cartage Co., Inc., 899 F.2d 1490, 1493 (6th Cir.1990). The payment releases equity to the third person and compensates this person rather than the estate.

The general rule does not fully apply to tax liens because of section 724(b). It subordinates unavoidable tax liens to unsecured claims having a higher priority than unsecured tax claims. In re Healthcare Services, Inc., 80 B.R. 563, 565 (Bankr. N.D.Ga.1987).

The general rule has no application if the creditor's claim of fully secured status is built on a security interest or lien in collateral that is avoided or could have been avoided. In such a case the payments are deemed made to an unsecured creditor and, of course, have a preferential effect. See, e.g., In re Melon Produce, Inc., 122 B.R. 641, 644–45 (D.Mass.1991) (Payment to secured party not immune from preference attack because the security interest was perfected within the preference period and was voidable.); Venn v. Roberts Supply, Inc., 124 B.R. 858 (N.D.Fla.1991) (Return of collateral to secured party was a preference because the security interest was unperfected and avoidable under § 544(a).); In re Chambers, 125 B.R. 788, 792 (Bankr. W.D.Mo.1991) (Car buyer's return of vehicle to dealer was a preference despite the dealer's security interest because the security interest was unperfected.); In re Kittrell, 115 B.R. 873, 882–83 (Bankr. N.D.N.C.1990) (payments to creditor were avoidable because the creditor's setoff and statutory lien was invalid); In re Adams, 102 B.R. 271, 74 (Bankr. M.D.Ga.1989) (payment on debt secured by unperfected security interest had preferential effect because unperfected interest was avoidable, leaving debt unsecured); In re King Arthur Clock Co., Inc., 105 B.R. 669 (Bankr. S.D.Ala.1989) (same); In re L & T Steel Fabricators, Inc., 102 B.R. 511, 518–19 (Bankr. M.D.La.1989) (same); In re Singer Products Co., Inc., 102 B.R. 912, 923–33 (Bankr. E.D.N.Y.1989) (payments made toward debt secured by a security interest that was itself an avoidable preference); In re Hoffman, 96 B.R. 46, 48 (Bankr. W.D.Pa.1988) (payment was preferential that satisfied judicial lien debtor could have avoided under § 522(f)); Matter of Washkowiak, 62 B.R. 884 (Bankr. N.D.Ill. 1986) (payment of money to satisfy lien that could have been avoided is preferential).

21. This reasoning, logically extended, should protect a fully secured creditor in the case of collateral substitution. The commentators disagree on whether the technical basis of the protection is the absence of a preferential effect so that section 547(b)(5) is not satisfied, or the applicability of the exceptions in section 547(c). Compare Countryman, The Concept of a Voidable Preference in Bankruptcy, 38 Vand.L.Rev. 713, 745 (1985) (arguably no preferential effect); cf. In re Nelson Co., 117 B.R. 813, 818–19 (Bankr. E.D.Pa. 1990), order aff'd, 128 B.R. 930 (Bankr. E.D.Pa.1991) (substitution of liens); In re Cosper, 106 B.R. 377, 381 (Bankr. M.D.Pa.1989) (continuation of lien by revival of judgment continued existing interest and had no preferential effect) with Nimmer, Security Interests in Bankruptcy: An Overview of section 547 of the Code, 17 Houston L. Rev. 289, 309–16 (1980) (protection of substituted collateral should come only through § 547(c)).

22. See Practitioner Treatise, Vol. 1.

23. See Practitioner Treatise, Vol. 1.

result by releasing her lien to the extent of the transfer.[24] The release would negate the implicit assumption of the courts that a transfer to an undersecured creditor is always first credited against the unsecured part of her claim.

In no event is the payment preferential beyond the amount of undersecurity.[25] The reason is that while preferential effect is necessary to a preference, a transfer is a preference only to the extent that the transfer causes this effect. Preference is pro tanto. Any payment to an undersecured creditor that reduces the secured part of the creditor's claim lacks preferential effect and to this extent, therefore, is not a preference.

Actually, the more accurate statement of the law is that payment on an undersecured *claim*, rather than to an undersecured *creditor*, is preferential to the extent of the undersecurity. This statement accounts for the case in which a creditor has multiple claims against the debtor that, in total, are undersecured, but one or more of the claims are fully secured. A payment on a fully secured claim in this case is not preferential even though, on the whole, the creditor is undersecured, not even if the payment decreases the undersecurity on another claim of the creditor.[26]

§ 6–21 Preferential Effect—Foreclosure Sales

For full text of this section, see Epstein, Nickles & White, Bankruptcy, Practitioner Treatise Series, Vol. 1.

2. Exceptions, Section 547(c)

§ 6–22 Introduction to Exceptions

A transfer that is a preference under section 547(b) is nevertheless safe from avoidance by the trustee to the extent the transfer fits within one or more of the exceptions described in section 547(c). The section 547(c) exceptions

> are designed to rescue from attack in bankruptcy those kinds of transactions, otherwise fitting the definition of a preference, that are essential to commercial reality and do not offend the purposes of preference law, or that benefit the ongoing business by helping to keep the potential bankrupt afloat.[1]

There are seven exceptions. They are "cumulative in nature"[2] and can be used "separately or jointly,"[3] which means that "[i]f a creditor can qualify under any one of the exceptions then he is protected to that extent. If he can qualify under several, he is protected by each to the extent that he can

---

24. See Practitioner Treatise, Vol. 1.
25. See Practitioner Treatise, Vol. 1.
26. See Practitioner Treatise, Vol. 1.

§ 6–22

1. Orelup, Avoidance of Preferential Transfers Under the Bankruptcy Reform Act of 1978, 65 Iowa L. Rev. 209, 233 (1979).

2. Nimmer, Security Interests in Bankruptcy: An Overview of Section 547 of the Code, 17 Hous. L. Rev. 289, 315 (1980). They are also exclusive: "The only affirmative defenses available to preference suits are those set out in Section 547(c)." In re Stanley-Southwest Investments, Inc., 96 B.R. 701, 705 (Bankr. W.D.Tex.1988) (theories such as waiver, estoppel, and detrimental reliance are not good defenses against a preference action).

3. Young, Preferences Under the Bankruptcy Reform Act of 1978, 54 Am. Bankr. L. J. 221, 225 (1980).

qualify under each."[4] The creditor bears the burden of proving that an exception applies.[5]

§ 6–23 Contemporaneous New Value, Section 547(c)(1)

Remember that if section 547(b)(2) is literally read and applied, a transfer is deemed to have been made "for or on account of an antecedent debt" if the transfer was made at any time, even immediately, after the the debtor incurred the debt.[1] By this approach, even a transfer in exchange for new value is preferential if the value precedes, by any time, the transfer because the value creates a debt for an instant that precedes the transfer. Technically, for example, a cash sale of goods over the seller's counter usually involves a transfer for an antecedent debt because the buyer's actual payment lags slightly behind the buyer's obligation to pay for the goods.

Yet, a transfer made in exchange for new value, such as a cash sale of goods, does not offend the purposes behind preference law because the transaction does not diminish the debtor's estate to the detriment of creditors. One form of property is substituted for another, e.g., the goods take the place of the payment. Indeed, avoiding such a transfer contradicts a main purpose of preference law, which is to forestall a debtor's slide into bankruptcy, because even "cash sellers would be discouraged from doing business with an unstable debtor because of the risk that an unintentional, minimal delay would turn an essentially cash transaction into an extension of credit accompanied by a voidable preference."[2] This result would speed, rather than prevent, the bankruptcy of a financially troubled debtor.

For these reasons, section 547(c)(1) saves a preferential transfer that is contemporaneously made in exchange for new value. In the words of the exception, a transfer that is a preference under section 547(b) is nevertheless not avoidable to the extent that the transfer was

> (A) intended by the debtor and the creditor to or for whose benefit such transfer was made to be a contemporaneous exchange for new value given to the debtor; and

> (B) in fact a substantially contemporaneous exchange.[3]

This exception purposely adds slack to the technically rigid meaning of "antecedent debt" in order to protect a transfer that, by design, actually and contemporaneously offsets a debt created by the giving of new value to the debtor.

Four separate requirements lurk here, however, and each of them must be satisfied in order to save a transfer under section 547(c)(1): First, the

---

4. H.R. Rep. No. 595, 95th Cong., 1st Sess. 88, reprinted in 1978 U.S. Code Cong. & Admin. News 5963, 6329; S. Rep. No. 989, 95th Cong., 2d Sess. 88, reprinted in 1978 U.S. Code Cong. & Admin. News 5787, 5874.

5. 11 U.S.C.A. § 547(g); In re Websco, 92 B.R. 1, 2 (Bankr. D.Me.1988); Matter of Wellington Constr. Corp., 82 B.R. 424, 430 (Bankr. N.D.Miss.1987). Moreover, in relying on a section 547(c) exception the creditor is technically asserting an affirmative defense that is waived if not pleaded. In re Fisher, 100 B.R. 351, 355–56 (Bankr. S.D.Ohio 1989), order amended, 101 B.R. 507 (Bankr. S.D.Ohio 1989).

§ 6–23

1. See 11 U.S.C.A. § 547(b)(2), which we discuss at § 6–19 supra.

2. Orelup, Avoidance of Preferential Transfers Under the Bankruptcy Reform Act of 1978, 65 Iowa L. Rev. 209, 234 (1979).

3. 11 U.S.C.A. § 547(c)(1).

debtor must get "new value." Second, the new value must be "in exchange" for the transfer. Third, the exchange of the new value for the transfer must be "substantially contemporaneous." Fourth, the parties must have "intended" a contemporaneous exchange. Before discussing these four requirements, however, we briefly explore a problem concerning the scope of section 547(c)(1) that tests the meaning of "transfer" as that term is used there.

§ 6–24 Contemporaneous New Value, Section 547(c)(1)—Scope of the Exception

Any kind of transfer of the debtor's property can be a preference that is avoidable under section 547(b). The Code defines "transfer" very broadly to mean every mode of disposing of an interest in property.[1] This definition easily and clearly includes the creation of a security interest or other lien, as well as payments of money.

On its face, the section 547(c)(1) exception also applies to any "transfer." The Code does not define the word "transfer" differently for purposes of section 547(c)(1). It would appear, therefore, that any transfer of a debtor's property, including the creation of a security interest, made in exchange for new value could potentially qualify for the protection of section 547(c)(1).

The majority of courts have concluded, however, that section 547(c)(1) does not apply to consensual, enabling, i.e., purchase-money liens.[2] The principal reason is that section 547*(c)(3)*[3] is expressly dedicated entirely to such liens, and Congress must therefore have intended (c)(3) as the exclusive source of protection for them. As a result, a purchase-money lien that does not satisfy the requirements of (c)(3) cannot be saved, alternatively, by (c)(1).

The courts sometimes give a broader reason for concluding that (c)(1) is inapplicable to consensual, purchase-money liens: the legislative history of the exception suggests that Congress intended (c)(1) to cover only transfers in the form of cash payments.[4] If this limitation is read into (c)(1), the exception is not a protector of any consensual lien, not even a nonpurchase-money one.

We do not agree that (c)(1) is generally limited to cash payments. The best and controlling evidence of the intention of Congress is the language used in the statute itself. Section (c)(1) plainly uses the unmodified, unlimited word "transfer" which is plainly and broadly defined to include any mode

---

§ 6–24

1. 11 U.S.C.A. § 101(54), discussed at § ___ supra.

2. See Practitioner Treatise, Vol. 1.

3. The exception is:
   The trustee may not avoid under this section [§ 547] a transfer * * * that creates a security interest in property acquired by the debtor
   (A) to the extent such security interest secures new value that was—
      (i) given at or after the signing of a security agreement that contains a description of such property as collateral;
      (ii) given by or on behalf of the secured party under such agreement;
      (iii) given to enable the debtor to acquire such property; and
      (iv) in fact used by the debtor to acquire such property; and
   (B) that is perfected on or before 10 days after the debtor receives possession of such property.

11 U.S.C.A. § 547(c)(3). This exception is discussed at § 6–33 infra.

4. See Practitioner Treatise, Vol. 1.

of disposing of property[5] and which therefore includes the creation of liens on property.[6]

We are unconcerned by the narrower holding that (c)(3) displaces (c)(1) in the case of consensual, purchase-money liens. The issue is moot when (c)(3) is satisfied. When (c)(3) is not satisfied, the usual reason is that the lien was not perfected within the ten-day period as (c)(3) requires.[7] In this event, resort to (c)(1) would be futile anyway because, in such a case, (c)(1) does not apply for a wholly different reason: section (c)(1) is limited by section 547(e)[8] so that a transfer qualifies for protection under (c)(1) only when the transfer is perfected, in accordance with (e), within ten days of the time the transfer takes effect between the parties.[9]

§ 6–25 Contemporaneous New Value, Section 547(c)(1)—New Value

Section 547(c)(1) does not shield a transfer from avoidance as a preference simply because the transfer was made in exchange, contemporaneously in fact and by design, for something of value to the debtor. The section is a shield only when such an exchange is made for something that is "new value" as defined by the Code[1] as follows:

> money or money's worth in goods, services, or new credit, or release by a transferee of property previously transferred to such transferee in a transaction that is neither void nor voidable by the debtor or the trustee under any applicable law, including proceeds of such property, but does not include an obligation substituted for an existing obligation.[2]

Naturally, paying an antecedent unsecured debt is not included. The reason is:

> That a payment be "for or on account of an antecedent debt" is one of the necessary elements for *voidability* of a transfer under section 547. If "new value" included credit toward such debts, thus rendering such transfers categorically *nonavoidable,* section 547 would be rendered a tautological nullity.[3]

---

5. 11 U.S.C.A. § 101(54).

6. See Practitioner Treatise, Vol. 1.

7. A purchase-money security interest qualifies for (c)(3) protection only if the interest "is perfected on or before 10 days after the debtor receives possession of such property [i.e., the collateral]." 11 U.S.C.A. § 547(c)(3)(B).

8. 11 U.S.C.A. § 547(e). This provision is quoted and discussed in §§ 6–11 through 6–17.

9. See 11 U.S.C.A. § 547(e)(2)(A). Section 547(e) as a limitation on (c)(1) is discussed in § —— infra.

§ 6–25

1. For the proposition that "new value" is an independent component of (c)(1) which must be satisfied to trigger the section's application, see In re George Rodman, Inc., 39 B.R. 855, 858 (Bankr. W.D. Okla. 1984).

2. 11 U.S.C.A. § 547(a)(2). The definition is exclusive rather than suggestive. In re Energy Co-op, Inc., 832 F.2d 997, 1003 (7th Cir.1987); In re Hatfield Electric, 91 B.R. 782, 785 (Bankr. N.D.Ohio 1988).

The definition is, however, somewhat pliable in combination with (c)(1) to the extent that "section 547(c)(1) does not require that a contemporaneous exchange for new value involve the same type of consideration as that originally envisioned by the parties." In re Lewellyn & Co., Inc., 929 F.2d 424, 429 (8th Cir.1991) (Transfer of stock to securities broker-dealer in lieu of cash was new value for securities purchased within preceding seven days.).

3. In re Chase & Sanborn Corp., 904 F.2d 588, 595 (11th Cir.1990) (emphasis in original).

The definition expressly repeats the word "new" only in connection with credit. There is no doubt, however, that "new" implicitly modifies every kind of value encompassed within the definition.

Congress intended "new value" to have its ordinary meaning,[4] but defined the term "to avoid any confusion or uncertainty."[5] It has not helped. Indeed, the stated intention of Congress, to use "new value" in the ordinary sense of the term, has been misread to mean that the definition codifies the usual rules of common-law consideration.[6]

The vast majority of courts actually define the term "new value" more narrowly than consideration. They insist that consideration or other value is "new value," for purposes of section 547, only if it is something of tangible economic value [7] that prevents the transfer, for which the value is given, from diminishing the debtor's assets. The reasoning for this judicial requirement, at least as applied in connection with 547(c)(1), is tied to the primary justification for (c)(1): a transfer of the debtor's property is harmless that does not deplete the debtor's estate to the detriment of other creditors. Thus, for (c)(1) to apply, the value given for the transfer must actually and in real terms enhance the worth of the debtor's estate so as to offset the reduction in the estate that the transfer caused.[8]

The strength of the "tangible value" requirement is made clear by the analysis and outcome in the case, *In re Vunovich*.[9] The debtor made a payment that reduced an unsecured line of credit. This payment was a preference. The creditor's defense was based in part on section 547(c)(1). The creditor argued that the availability of the credit line was renewed to the extent of the payment; that, in renewing the availability of the credit line, the creditor gave the debtor "new credit;" and that, therefore, new value was given because "new credit" is expressly included within the meaning of "new value."[10] The court rejected this argument because "[n]ew credit is extended only when [and if] the debtor actually used the line of credit by obtaining cash advances." [11] In this sense, consideration is new value only to the extent the consideration is actually performed or given and not merely promised.[12]

The requirement of tangible value explains the many cases holding that, although forbearance to assert a legal right is common-law consideration, such forbearance—including forbearance from establishing a lien, foreclosing on collateral, and pursuing other creditors' remedies—never constitutes new value for purposes of section 547(c)(1).[13] The same is true of an agreement releasing a debtor from contractual obligations.[14]

---

4. The three terms that are defined in section 547(a) "are defined in their ordinary senses, but are defined to avoid any confusion or uncertainty surrounding the terms." H.R. Rep. No. 595, 95th Cong., 1st Sess. 372, reprinted in 1978 U.S. Code Cong. & Admin. News 5963, 6328; S. Rep. No. 989, 95th Cong., 2d Sess. 87, reprinted in 1978 U.S. Code Cong. & Admin. News 5787, 5873.

5. Id.

6. In re Spada, 91 B.R. 668, 672 (Bankr. M.D.Pa.1988), aff'd, 115 B.R. 796 (M.D.Pa. 1989), aff'd in part, rev'd in part, 903 F.2d 971 (3d Cir. 1990).

7. See Practitioner Treatise, Vol. 1.

8. See Practitioner Treatise, Vol. 1.

9. 74 B.R. 629 (Bankr. D.Kan.1987).

10. 11 U.S.C.A. § 547(a)(2).

11. Id. at 632, relying on In re Rustia, 20 B.R. 131 (Bankr. S.D.N.Y. 1982).

12. See Practitioner Treatise, Vol. 1.

13. See Practitioner Treatise, Vol. 1.

14. See Practitioner Treatise, Vol. 1.

New value is given, however, when a creditor actually releases a valid lien that already exists on property of the debtor.[15] This situation is covered by the explicit language in the definition of "new value" that includes a transfer in release of other property of the debtor.[16] The same language can also cover the situation in which the release is accomplished by a third person rather than by the creditor to whom the transfer is actually made. For example, suppose that a debt to a creditor is secured by a letter of credit issued by a bank. The bank's right to seek reimbursement from the debtor,[17] should the bank have to pay the credit, is in turn secured by property of the debtor. The debtor satisfies her obligation to the creditor; the creditor releases the letter of credit; and the bank then releases its security interest in the debtor's property. A release of a lien is generally considered "new value." The problem in applying section 547(c)(1) here is that this release of collateral is actually effected by the bank, and the creditor's action in releasing the letter of credit is not expressly covered by the exclusive definition of new value.

On these facts, however, the court in *Matter of Fuel Oil Supply & Terminaling, Inc.*[18] reasoned that the "exchange did not result in a depletion of [the debtor's] estate, and therefore [the debtor's] unsecured creditors were not impaired by this transaction."[19] Therefore, the court held "that under these circumstances, new value received by a debtor need not be provided by the creditor to whom the transfer was made but may be provided by the fully secured third party."[20] This holding is only fair: inasmuch as a transfer can be indirectly preferential with respect to a creditor under section 547(b),[21] an indirect exchange of new value to the debtor should be safe under section 547(c)(1).[22]

A release of a lien, no matter by whom, is not new value, however, if the lien itself is "void" or "voidable by the debtor or the trustee under any applicable law."[23] A logical extension of this rule is that releasing a lien is not new value if, despite the lien's technical validity, the collateral is worthless. This corollary was announced in the case *In re Nucorp Energy, Inc.*[24] In *Nucorp*, the debtor in possession attacked as preferential certain payments that the debtor had made to Milchem. These payments satisfied Milchem's claim for materials and services he had rendered with respect to an oil well operated by the debtor. Milchem could have asserted a lien on

---

15. See Practitioner Treatise, Vol. 1.

16. 11 U.S.C.A. § 547(a)(2) ("release by a transferee of property previously transferred to such transferee in a transaction that is neither void nor voidable by the debtor or the trustee under any applicable law"). This language is probably broad enough to cover the case in which there is a substitution of collateral for a debt. See In re Quade, 108 B.R. 674, 679–80, further opin., 108 B.R. 681, 683 (Bankr. N.D.Iowa 1989); Countryman, The Concept of a Voidable Preference in Bankruptcy, 38 Vand.L.Rev. 713, 766 (1985); see also Kaye, Preferences Under the New Bankruptcy Code, 54 Am. Bankr. L. J. 197, 199–201 (1980); Nimmer, Security Interests in Bankruptcy: An Overview of Section 547 of the Code, 17 Hous. L. Rev. 289, 310–13 (1980).

17. U.C.C. § 5–114(3).

18. 837 F.2d 224 (5th Cir.1988).

19. Id. at 230.

20. Id. at 231.

21. See § 6–27 supra.

22. See Practitioner Treatise, Vol. 1.

23. 11 U.S.C.A. § 547(a)(2); In re Joseph M. Eaton Builders, Inc., 84 B.R. 56 (Bankr. W.D.Pa.1988) (payment to satisfy a mechanic's lien that had expired under state law is not new value).

24. 80 B.R. 517 (Bankr. S.D.Cal.1987), aff'd, 902 F.2d 729 (9th Cir.1990).

the well if he had not been paid, and thus he argued that forbearance from asserting the lien was "new value." The court rejected the argument not only because forbearance to assert a legal right is not new value,[25] but also because "the well against which Milchem's lien would have attached had been plugged and abandoned as worthless"[26] in an economic sense. For this reason alone section 547(c)(1) was inapplicable because an economically " 'valueless transfer falls outside the definition of "new value." ' "[27]

The *Nucorp* decision that "new value" implicitly contains a valuation requirement begs the next issue: is the requirement fully met by any value or is it satisfied pro tanto to the extent of the value. An important precedent is *In re George Rodman, Inc.*[28] Its facts are very similar to the facts of *Nucorp*. In *Rodman*, the defendant released a lien on an oil and gas well in exchange for a preferential payment from the debtor. At the time the well had "some value" but an unknown amount. The bankruptcy court decided that the lien's release was not new value because the collateral (the oil well) had no value at the time of the adversary proceeding to avoid the preference: "A valid but valueless transfer falls outside the definition of 'new value.' "[29]

The Tenth Circuit reversed in *Rodman*. It concluded that (c)(1) does not impose a valuation requirement at the time of the avoidance proceeding. We agree on this narrow point. The time for judging the exchange under (c)(1) is when it occurred.

The court went further. It strongly implied that (c)(1) is fully met if the debtor gets any value for the exchange when the exchange takes place. First, the court reasoned that the release of the lien satisfied the "literal requirements of the definition of 'new value,' "[30] which expressly includes "the release by a transferee of property previously transferred to such transferee in a transaction that is neither void nor voidable by the debtor or the trustee under any applicable law."[31] The court then concluded that "new value" does not contain a valuation requirement because the "plain language" does not impose it."[32] Finally, the court reversed the bankruptcy judge and remanded without instruction to measure the value of the property transferred at the time of the exchange. The Tenth Circuit apparently concluded that the preference was fully protected by (c)(1) because the debtor got "some value" for it when the exchange occurred. Thus, according to *Rodman*, the release of a technically valid lien is "new value" that shields a preference given in exchange, even if the property transferred to the debtor is worthless at the time of bankruptcy, so long as the collateral had "some

25. 80 B.R. at 518–19. For additional support, see authorities cited note 13 supra.

26. 80 B.R. at 519.

27. Id. at 518; accord, In re Grassmueck, 127 B.R. 869, 873–74 (Bankr. D.Or.1991); In re George Rodman, Inc., 39 B.R. 855, 858–59 (Bankr. W.D. Okla. 1984), rev'd, 792 F.2d 125 (10th Cir. 1986); see also In re Finelli Jewelry Co., 79 B.R. 521, 522 (Bankr. D.R.I.1987) ("The value given in a contemporaneous exchange must approximate the worth of the asset transferred to qualify as an exception to the preference provisions."); accord, In re Robinson Bros. Drilling, Inc., 877 F.2d 32, 34 (10th Cir. 1989).

28. 792 F.2d 125 (10th Cir.1986).

29. In re George Rodman, Inc., 39 B.R. 855, 857 (Bankr. W.D. Okla. 1984), rev'd, 792 F.2d 125 (10th Cir. 1986).

30. 792 F.2d at 128.

31. 11 U.S.C.A. § 547(a)(2).

32. 792 F.2d at 128, which view was confirmed and reasserted by the court in In re Allen, 888 F.2d 1299, 1302–03 (10th Cir.1989).

value" when the exchange took place. In sum, the protection of (c)(1) is all-or-nothing depending on whether any new value was given in exchange rather than pro tanto to the extent of the worth of the new value given.

We are doubtful about this aspect of the Tenth Circuit's analysis in *Rodman*. We would extend and project the bankruptcy court's reasoning in *Nucorp* so that (c)(1) applies pro tanto.[33] First, as the court in *Nucorp* points out, the literal language of the definition of new value does not certainly include any "release" of an unavoidable transfer. Arguably, the definition is limited to "money's worth" in such a release,[34] and worth implies valuation.[35] Second, the language of section 547(c)(1) also implies valuation, inasmuch as it protects a transfer "to the extent" that the transfer satisfies the requirements of the section. Also, the courts agree that, in general, "new value" requires something of "tangible" or "economic value."[36] Finally, section 547(c)(1) is primarily justified on the basis that a transaction fitting the exception does not diminish the debtor's estate. This justification is satisfied only to the extent the debtor's estate receives value in exchange for the payment of money or the transfer of something else by the debtor that, in real terms, diminishes the estate.

It is true that section 548 on fraudulent transfers guards the fairness of the debtor's prepetition exchanges.[37] Section 548, however, measures a different kind of fairness and does so differently. It does not condemn the preference in *Rodman* because the transfer was made to satisfy a preexisting debt owed the defendant for supplies. Fairness under section 547 is determined by its terms and policy which are offended by a transfer for a stale debt within the preference period and are satisfied only to the extent of compensating, offsetting new value at the time of the exchange.

The statutory definition of "new value" expressly excludes "an obligation substituted for an existing obligation."[38] Thus, the "new value" requirement cannot be satisfied by recasting an existing debt as a fresh obligation. In *Matter of Wellington Constr. Corp.*,[39] a stale debt was renewed by the debtor's execution of a new note. The proceeds of this note were applied to the old debt. When the transaction was attacked as a preferential transfer, the creditor argued that the note was new value given contemporaneously with the transfer of the proceeds. The creditor lost because the court concluded that there was no new value. The parties simply substituted a new obligation for an existing one.[40]

This exclusion codifies the common-law doctrine that a promise to pay a pre-existing debt or to perform any other pre-existing duty is not consideration.[41] A seemingly difficult issue is whether the definition of "new value" also incorporates the exception to the common-law pre-existing duty rule

---

33. This is the holding of In re Spada, 903 F.2d 971, 975–77 (3d Cir.1990).

34. "'[N]ew value' means money or money's worth in goods, services, or new credit, or release by a transferee of property previously transferred to such transferee * * *." 11 U.S.C.A. § 547(a)(2).

35. In re Nucorp Energy, Inc., 80 B.R. 517, 520 (Bankr. S.D.Cal.1987).

36. See authorities cited note 7 supra.

37. See 11 U.S.C.A. § 548(a). We thoroughly discuss section 548 beginning at § ___ infra.

38. 11 U.S.C.A. § 547(a)(2).

39. 82 B.R. 424 (Bankr. N.D.Miss.1987).

40. See Practitioner Treatise, Vol. 1.

41. Restatement (Second) of Contracts § 73 (1981) (first clause).

that consideration exists if the duty is modified [42] even slightly. In the case *In re Spada*,[43] the debtor consolidated and refinanced three unsecured debts owed a bank and, as part of the refinancing during the preference period, granted the bank a mortgage on certain real property. The mortgage was a preference, but the bank contended that the transfer was protected by section (c)(1). The bank argued that it gave "new value" for the mortgage by the changes made in the debtor's loan obligations: the interest rate was reduced from 21% to 15%; the debtor was not required to make a principal payment during the first year of the restructured debt; and the bank agreed that if the debtor could obtain financing to develop a shopping center on the mortgaged property, the bank would subordinate its encumbrance to the new lender.

The court decided in *Spada* that the refinancing involved more than simply substituting a new obligation for an existing one because the debtor's obligations were changed. Rather, relying on the common-law rule that modification in the terms of an existing duty may constitute consideration, the court concluded that the bank gave "new credit" and thus "new value" because the terms of the refinanced loan were different.[44]

In contrast is *In re White River Corp.*[45] The debtor's obligations under a lease of personal property were modified to increase the security deposit. In compliance with this change the debtor made an additional payment of $7,000 toward the security deposit. The lessor tried to shield the $7,000 payment under section 547(c)(1), arguing that it

> gave value to the debtor contemporaneously to receiving the $7000 * * * [by its] "forbearance from pursuing its remedies which became available upon the debtor's default (failure to pay * * * [two months'] rent in a timely manner pursuant to the lease) and the consideration provided in exchange for executing the amended lease agreement." [46]

The court in *White River* first embraced the widely-accepted rule that forbearance of contractual rights is not "new value." [47] The reasoning is familiar: Such forbearance is "of no economic solace to the creditors of the estate," that is, "it could not reasonably offset the diminution of the estate caused by the preferential transfer." [48]

The court then turned to the lessor's argument that consideration had been exchanged. Conceding the accuracy of the argument under common-law contract principles, the court nevertheless concluded that "it [the exchanged consideration] does not fall within the ambit of new value." The reason given was:

> It constitutes a substitution of the Amended Lease Agreement for the original Lease Agreement. An obligation substituted for an existing

---

42. Id. § 73 (second clause).

43. 91 B.R. 668 (Bankr. M.D.Pa.1988), aff'd, 115 B.R. 796 (M.D.Pa.1989), aff'd in part, rev'd in part, 903 F.2d 971 (3d Cir. 1990).

44. 91 B.R. at 671–72.

45. 50 B.R. 403 (Bankr. D.Colo.1985), appeal decided, 799 F.2d 631 (10th Cir.1986).

46. Id. at 408–09.

47. Id. at 409; see also authorities cited note 13 supra.

48. Id. at 409.

obligation is expressly excluded from the definition of "new value" * * *.[49]

The results in *White River* are correct, but the reasoning is wrong on the issue whether the lease modification was new value. *Spada* correctly determined that the exclusion of substituted obligations from the definition of new value does not apply when the new obligation is different. *Spada* erred, however, in concluding that when the terms of credit are changed, there is necessarily "new credit" and thus "new value."

The issue whether modification of a duty constitutes "new value" is governed by the overarching limitation that the courts have imposed on the general equation of consideration with new value: the debtor must in any event receive tangible, economic value offsetting the diminution of the estate that the transfer caused.[50] If the modification of the debtor's duty meets this test, there is new value *to the extent of the offset*.[51] Otherwise, there is none, notwithstanding the existence of common-law consideration.[52]

The court's analysis of this issue in *White River*, as well as its decision on the issue, would have been correct if the court had simply reiterated the reason for holding that forbearance is not new value, i.e., no tangible, economic value. There was no need to decide that new value cannot be found in a contact modification. It can be found but is not always there. The problem with *Spada* is that the court assumed that a contract modification produces new value without finding the peculiar value that "new value" requires. It cannot always be found in a contract modification.

In sum, we agree with the outcome in *White River* and seriously doubt *Spada*. Minimally, the courts should be slow to endorse modifications of existing loan documents as new value under this definition. Wide recognition of such modification as "new value" could lead to all sorts of shenanigans by creditors seeking to protect transfers within the 90 day period. We would not deny that some modifications might constitute new value, but we would look at all of them with a skeptical eye.

§ 6–26 Contemporaneous New Value, Section 547(c)(1)—Exchange

Section 547(c)(1) applies only when there is a contemporaneous *ex-*

---

49. Id.

50. See text accompanying notes 7–14 supra.

51. In re Spada, 903 F.2d 971, 975–77 (3d Cir.1990), qualifying the bankruptcy court's opinion which is discussed at text accompanying notes 43–44 supra.

52. In this sense, "new value" is narrower than common-law consideration. It is also narrower in another respect. A fundamental requirement of consideration is an exchange between the parties. ("To constitute consideration, a performance or a return promise must be bargained for." Restatement (Second) of Contracts § 71(1) (1981). "A performance or return promise is bargained for if it is sought by the promisor in exchange for his promise and is given by the promisee in exchange for that promise." Id. § 71(2).) The requirement of an exchange is not, however, an implicit component of "new value." Exchange is rather an explicit requirement of section 547(c)(1): the section applies only when there is a "contemporaneous exchange for new value." 11 U.S.C.A. § 547(c)(1)(A) (emphasis added). To read "exchange" into "new value" would render the exchange requirement of (c)(1) redundant, and would therefore violate the elementary rule of statutory construction that every word of a statute should be given effect. 2A N. Singer, Sutherland Statutory Construction § 46.06 (1984 rev.). Moreover, reading an exchange requirement into the meaning of "new value" would effectively add such a requirement into the other exceptions of section 547(c) that require new value but that may not have been intended, as was (c)(1), to require an exchange.

change, in fact and by design, for new value.[1] For purposes of (c)(1), "exchange" implies more than simply a coincidental swap of property between the parties. It also means more than the reciprocal inducement associated with bargained-for exchange in contract doctrine. That a transfer is induced by new value is not sufficient to find an exchange. Rather, to satisfy the (c)(1) requirement of "exchange," the transfer must be intended as, and must actually be, an offsetting reciprocal for the debt created by the giving of the new value.

For example, suppose D offers to buy goods on credit from C, to whom D owes a stale, pre-existing debt. C proposes supplying the desired goods if D will pay or reduce the old debt. D accepts the proposal. C performs, and D soon thereafter pays the old debt. Upon D's bankruptcy, the trustee attacks the payment as a preference, and D tries to hide behind section 547(c)(1). The courts properly conclude that C's payment to D is not protected by (c)(1).[2]

In a similar case, *In re Wadsworth Bldg. Components, Inc.,*[3] a seller sold the debtor goods and materials worth $21,691.45 in October, 1979. The debtor paid by check in December. The check was dishonored. When the debtor-buyer ordered additional goods, the seller refused to supply them until the December check was paid. The debtor promised payment, and the seller shipped supplies worth $21,484 to the debtor in late January, 1980. The December check was paid on February 14.

The seller argued that the February payment of the December check was protected by (c)(1) because new credit was extended on the basis of the debtor's promise to pay the dishonored check. The Ninth Circuit disagreed:

> The bankruptcy court held that the check was * * * only the payment of an [pre-]existing obligation. It therefore held that no new value was given for the check. The critical inquiry in determining whether there has been a contemporaneous exchange for new value is whether the parties intended such an exchange. Here, * * * the debtor was required to pay past debts before it would receive further credit. Value was given only for a future promise to pay. The check therefore is not exempted from treatment as a preference by § (c)(1).[4]

The reasoning in *Wadsworth* is fuzzy, but a panel of Ninth Circuit bankruptcy judges restated the *Wadsworth* holding in the later case, *In re World Financial Services, Center, Inc.*[5]:

> *In re Wadsworth* held that when a payment, made within the preference period, * * * [is] applied to an existing obligation it is not a 'contemporaneous exchange' pursuant to § 547(c)(1). This is so regardless of whether the creditor extended value when the payment was tendered by the debtor.[6]

§ 6-26

1. 11 U.S.C.A. § 547(c)(1)(A).

2. See, e.g., In re Wadsworth Bldg. Components, Inc., 711 F.2d 122, 124 (9th Cir.1983); In re World Financial Services Center, Inc., 78 B.R. 239, 241 (Bankr. 9th Cir.1987); In re Circleville Distributing Co., 84 B.R. 502, 505 (Bankr. S.D.Ohio 1988); In re Olympic Foundry Co., 51 B.R. 428, 430 (Bankr. W.D. Wash. 1985).

3. 711 F.2d 122 (9th Cir.1983).

4. Id. at 124.

5. 78 B.R. 239 (Bankr. 9th Cir.1987).

6. Id. at 241.

Clearly, however, supplying fresh goods on credit is new value; the giving of new value is obviously contemporaneous with a payment on an old debt when the latter is tendered when the former is given; and the parties certainly intend contemporaneity of the new value and the payment when the former is conditioned on the later.

We think *Wadsworth* and like cases are best explained on the basis that the exchange requirement of section (c)(1) has not been satisfied. The new value and the payment on the old debt are reciprocal inducements, but the payment, i.e., the transfer, was not exchanged for the new value. The debtor must still pay for the new value. Rather, for purposes of section 547(c)(1), the transfer was exchanged for reducing the old debt. The reduction, however, is not new value, and thus (c)(1) is inapplicable to protect the transfer.[7]

A critic of these decisions would argue that the courts read the law too narrowly in holding that the payment was on account of pre-existing debt and not for the new value contemporaneously exchanged. If the true motivation of payment was the simultaneous conveyance of new value, should the creditor lose the payment as a preference because it is not as careful as others to specify in the documents that the payment is for new value and not on the pre-existing debt? Functionally, the two transactions are the same. The same injury or lack of it will have occurred in both cases. Quaere whether the creditor should lose its claim as a preference because it has not hired the most clever accountant.

§ 6–27 Contemporaneous New Value, Section 547(c)(1)—Contemporaneous in Fact

A transfer of the debtor's property in exchange for new value is protected by section 547(c)(1) only if the parties intended the exchange to be contemporaneous and the exchange was *actually,* i.e., "*in fact,*" "substantially contemporaneous."[1] "Intent alone is not sufficient—the exchange must 'in fact' be contemporaneous in that there must be 'temporal proximity between the [new value] and the [debtor's] transfer * * *.' "[2] Suppose, for example, that D purchased goods from C. The parties intended a cash sale and even contracted for it, but for some reason D delayed making payment

---

7. Another possible explanation for cases such as Wadsworth and World Financial is that the new value was exchanged for the transfer, but not exclusively for it. The explanation assumes, however, that section 547(c)(1) requires the transfer to be made solely for the new value and not in any part for antecedent debt. There is reason to doubt this assumption. See In re Pitman, 843 F.2d 235, 240–42 (6th Cir.1988) (suggesting that a transfer is given for new value, within the meaning of subsection (c)(1), so long as the transfer was not made solely for an antecedent debt, and implying that the transfer is protected even though made only partly for new value).

§ 6–27

1. 11 U.S.C.A. § 547(c)(1)(B) (emphasis added).

2. In re Montgomery, 123 B.R. 801, 812 (Bankr. M.D.Tenn.1991), aff'd, 136 B.R. 727 (M.D.Tenn.1992) (This proximity was lacking in a case in which debtor made deposits so that a bank could escape a check-kiting scheme. The bank argued that the transfer was protected by (c)(1) because the bank gave value in not dishonoring checks that the debtor drew against the bank. This argument failed because the bank failed to prove the value of surrendering its right to dishonor and also because there was no contemporaneous exchange. Checks drawn against the bank were paid—not dishonored—without regard to the balance of deposits made by the debtor in the debtor's account.).

until three months after receiving the goods. Section 547(c)(1) does not protect the payment if the court decides that the three-month gap between the exchange of the goods and payment is so long that the exchange is not contemporaneous.[3] The same is true if C made a loan to D that the parties intended to secure immediately with a nonpurchase-money mortgage on real estate or a security interest in personal property, but that was not actually secured by a recorded mortgage or perfected security interest until three months later.

The Code does not define "contemporaneous," and the courts have established no set lengths of time for the gap between the giving of value and the transfer of the debtor's property that clearly mark an exchange as contemporaneous or not contemporaneous. The issue of contemporaneity is a fact-bound inquiry that turns on the peculiar facts and circumstances of each case. There are, however, some general bench marks. As noted in *In re Brown Family Farms, Inc.*,[4] the courts very rarely find that a transfer of property involving a time period of greater than one month is substantially contemporaneous.[5] On the other hand, a week hiatus is almost presumptively acceptable. Section 547(c)(1) codifies the result on the preference issue involved in *Dean v. Davis*.[6] In *Dean*, the Supreme Court held, under the old Bankruptcy Act, that a nonpurchase-money mortgage executed to secure a loan made a week earlier, and not recorded until eight days after the loan, was not a preference because the exchange was substantially contemporaneous and thus the mortgage was not given for an antecedent debt.[7]

Another suggested bench mark is that "[o]rdinarily, a [non-purchase money] security interest must be perfected within ten days * * * for the transfer of the security interest to be substantially contemporaneous."[8] Otherwise, non-purchase money interests would be handled more favorably than purchase money interests under section 547(c)(3), which would create an anomaly because the latter are generally favored over the former.[9]

A very important point to remember is that in measuring the gap, the time of the transfer is determined according to the usual rule of section 547(e) which deems that a transfer is made when the transfer is perfected.[10] Suppose, for example, that on May 1 bank makes a loan to a farmer, D, to cover crop expenses. At the very same time D grants bank a security

---

3. See Practitioner Treatise, Vol. 1.

4. 80 B.R. 404 (Bankr. N.D.Ohio 1987).

5. Id. at 412.

6. 242 U.S. 438, 37 S.Ct. 130, 61 L.Ed. 419 (1917).

7. Id. at 443, 37 S.Ct. at 131; see In re Quade, 108 B.R. 681, 683–84 (Bankr. N.D.Iowa 1989) (substitution of collateral was substantially contemporaneous despite a time lag of six days).

8. In re Minnesota Utility Contracting, Inc., 101 B.R. 72, 82 (Bankr. D.Minn.1989), judgment aff'd in part, rev'd in part, 110 B.R. 414 (D.Minn.1990); but see In re Carson, 119 B.R. 264, 267 (Bankr. E.D. Okla. 1990) ("The adoption by Congress of the ten (10) day rule for perfection of 'enabling loans' under § 547(c)(3) was an obvious attempt to create uniformity among the state laws governing perfection pursuant to the Uniform Commercial Code. If this same degree of uniformity was intended for establishing a security interest in non-purchase money transactions, we must presume that Congress would have clearly set forth an objective standard."); In re Telecash Industries, Inc., 104 B.R. 401, 403–04 (Bankr. D. Utah 1989) ("a ten-day limitation in the contemporaneous exchange exception [as applied to nonpurchase-money security interests] * * * is simply not there").

9. In re Minnesota Utility Contracting, Inc., 101 B.R. 72, 82 n.9 (Bankr. D.Minn.1989), judgment aff'd in part, rev'd in part, 110 B.R. 414 (Bankr. D.Minn.1990).

10. 11 U.S.C.A. § 547(e)(2)(B). This general rule is discussed at § 6–12 supra.

interest in the crops because the parties intended a secured transaction and also intended that making the loan and providing collateral would be contemporaneous. The security interest actually attaches on the same day the loan is made. Bank delays, however, until October 1 to perfect its security interest. Thus, for the purposes of both section 547(b) and the section 547(c)(1) exception, the gap between the loan (which is the value the bank gave and the debt D incurred) and the transfer is five months. The debt for which the transfer was made is clearly antecedent, and the exchange is clearly not substantially contemporaneous.[11]

On the other hand, the transfer would have been protected if the bank had perfected within ten days after the security interest attached. In this event, because of the exceptional rule of section 547(e), the transfer would be deemed to have been made when the security interest attached,[12] which was on the same day the loan was made. The creation of the security interest would have been for an antecedent debt if the interest attached after the loan was made; but the exchange, having occurred on the very same day, would certainly have been substantially contemporaneous as the parties intended and thereby would have been saved by section 547(c)(1).

Consider now a case that falls between the preceding two problems. Suppose that the bank perfected only 11 days after the time the loan was made and the security interest was created. The transfer in exchange for the loan would be deemed to have occurred on the date of perfection; yet, the gap is only 11 days. Nevertheless, the authorities generally hold that, on these facts, even an 11-day delay is too long to conclude that the exchange was substantially contemporaneous. Indeed, they conclude that in any case in which the transfer is not perfected in compliance with the exceptional, ten-day rule of section 547(e), the section 547(c)(1) exception is altogether inapplicable and cannot save the transfer under any circumstances.[13] The essential reasoning is that applying the exception in such a case (where perfection occurred more than ten days after the transfer was effective between the parties) would offend the secondary purpose of section 547 to punish and discourage secret conveyances, as expressed in the rules of section 547(e).

Be careful! Simply because section 547(c)(1) is inapplicable when the delay in perfecting a transfer exceeds the ten-day rule of section 547(e) does not mean that any transfer for new value perfected within ten days, in accordance with section 547(e), is a substantially contemporaneous exchange. Perfecting such a transfer within ten days of the time it was effective between the parties only means that the transfer is deemed to have occurred at the point that the transfer actually took effect between the parties. This point in time must then be compared to the time when the new value was given. It is the size of this gap—the period between the giving of value that created the debt and the making of the transfer in satisfaction of the debt— that determines whether the exchange was substantially contemporaneous.

The problem of determining the time of transfer for purposes of section 547(c)(1) also arises when the transfer involves payment of money by check.

---

11. See Practitioner Treatise, Vol. 1.

12. 11 U.S.C.A. § 547(e)(2)(A). This exceptional rule is discussed in § 6–13 supra.

13. See Practitioner Treatise, Vol. 1.

We have already discussed this same problem in the context of deciding whether a transfer is a preference under section 547(b).[14] We pointed out that a transfer of the debtor's property by check is deemed to occur, for purposes of section 547(b), when the check is paid by the drawee-payor bank. Typically, however, the problem is solved differently for purposes of section 547(c), including (c)(1). The majority view is that when a debt is paid by check, the transfer is considered to have been made, for purposes of section 547(c)(1), when the check is delivered to the creditor if the drawee-payor bank eventually pays the check in due course.[15] The legislative history of (c)(1) supports this view.[16] Congress clearly intended that the issue regarding the timing of payment by check would be resolved differently under sections 547(b) and (c).[17] The different treatment can be explained on the basis that the effect is to widen the applicability of both provisions.

§ 6–28 Contemporaneous New Value, Section 547(c)(1)—Contemporaneous by Design

Section 547(c)(1) does not protect a transfer simply because the transfer was contemporaneously made in exchange for new value. Another requirement must have been satisfied: the contemporaneity must have resulted from the parties' design, that is, they must have *intended* the exchange to be contemporaneous.[1]

Suppose, for example, that on Monday the bank made an unsecured loan to D that is due in six months. On Tuesday morning, because of unexpected market changes that affected D's business, the bank became concerned about D's ability to repay the loan at maturity. Bank therefore asked D to provide collateral. D agreed, and on Wednesday afternoon gave Bank a security interest in all of D's business property. Bank immediately perfected.

---

14. See § 6–16 supra.

15. See Practitioner Treatise, Vol. 1.

16. This history shows that Congress viewed payment by check as

> normally * * * a credit transaction. However, for the purposes of this paragraph [(c)(1)], a transfer involving a check is considered to be "intended to be contemporaneous," and if the check is presented for payment in the normal course of affairs, which the Uniform Commercial Code specifies as 30 days, that will amount to a transfer that is "in fact substantially contemporaneous."

H.R. Rep. No. 595, 95th Cong., 1st Sess. 373, reprinted in 1978 U.S.Code Cong. & Admin. News 5787, 6329. There is even more direct evidence that Congress intended payment by check to occur, for purposes of (c)(1), at the time the check was delivered:

> Payment of a debt by means of a check is equivalent to a cash payment, unless the check is dishonored. Payment is considered to be made when the check is delivered for purposes of Section 547(c)(1) and (2).

124 Cong. Rec. H11,097 (daily ed. Sept. 28, 1978); S17,414 (daily ed. Oct. 6, 1978).

17. Congress reported that normally, and thus for purposes of section 547(b), payment by check is considered a credit transaction with payment occurring upon the drawee's honor of the instrument. For purposes of section 547(c), the normal view did not apply, that is, payment by check occurred upon delivery rather than upon honor. See authorities cited note 15 supra, and discussion of payment by check under section 547(b) in § 6–16 supra.

§ 6–28

1. 11 U.S.C.A. § 547(c)(1)(A). A contemporaneous exchange must have been intended by both the parties, that is, both the creditor and the debtor. In re Fasano/Harriss Pie Co., 71 B.R. 287, 289 (W.D.Mich.1987); see also In re Jolly N, Inc., 122 B.R. 897, 904–05 (Bankr. D.N.J.1991) ("To fall within the * * * exception, both parties must intend, at the outset, that the exchange be contemporaneous." This requirement is not met when services are supplied, billed and paid on a monthly billing cycle, not even if this practice is the industry norm and the unique nature of the services (here, utility services) dictates the payment pattern.)

The security transfer was a preference under section 547(b); but the loan and the transfer were substantially contemporaneous; yet, section 547(c)(1) will not shield the transfer. The parties did not intend such a contemporaneous exchange when the value was given. Section 547(c)(1) cannot be applied unless the section's "intent" requirement is satisfied, along with the other requirements of new value and contemporaneity in fact.[2] Indeed, "without the requisite intent even a seven-hour gap between receipt of funds [or other value] and transfer of a security interest [or other property] [is] preferential [and beyond the protection of (c)(1)]."[3]

Of course, it is a literal reading of section 547(b)(2), the antecedency element of preference, that brings us here. If this section is not so strictly applied and tolerates some gap between debt and transfer, such as seven hours, there is no preference under (b) and no reason to find a defense in section 547(c). The creditor wins without even getting to (c).

§ 6–29 Ordinary Payment of Ordinary Debts, Section 547(c)(2)

A consumer debtor's payment of a utility bill is a preference even though the payment is in due course. A preference also results when a business debtor makes a timely payment for inventory that the seller regularly supplies upon 45–day credit. Neither of these preferences is protected by section 547(c)(1):[1] because the services or goods were supplied on credit, the parties did not intend a contemporaneous exchange of new value for the payment the debtor made.[2] Yet, in the view of Congress, these kinds of transfers, that is, payments that are part of "normal financial [or business] relations,"[3] do not offend the objectives of section 547(b). They do "not detract from the general policy of the preference section to discourage unusual action by either the debtor or his creditors during the debtor's slide into bankruptcy."[4] Moreover, avoiding payments that are part of normal business and financial relations would effectively discourage a financially troubled debtor's regular creditors from continuing to extend even short-term credit that is usual and essential to almost everyone. Avoiding such payments would thereby enhance, rather than reduce, the likelihood of the debtor's bankruptcy.[5]

To protect these payments Congress enacted section 547(c)(2). It provides that the trustee may not avoid a transfer to the extent that the transfer was:

---

2. See Practitioner Treatise, Vol. 1.

3. Kaye, Preferences Under the New Bankruptcy Code, 54 Am. Bankr. L. J. 197, 199 (1980). This warning is based on National City Bank v. Hotchkiss, 231 U.S. 50, 34 S.Ct. 20, 58 L.Ed. 115 (1913), which is the ultimate antecedent of the section 547(c)(1) "intent" requirement. In Hotchkiss a bank demanded collateral for an unsecured loan made earlier the same day. The debtor complied by pledging securities. The Court held that the pledge was a preference.

§ 6–29

1. For discussion of the (c)(1) exception to section 547(b), see §§ 6–23 through 6–28 supra.

2. See § 6–28.

3. H.R. Rep. No. 595, 95th Cong., 1st Sess. 373, reprinted in 1978 U.S. Code Cong. & Admin. News 5963, 6329; S. Rep. No. 989, 95th Cong., 2d Sess. 87, reprinted in U.S. Code Cong. & Admin. News 5787, 5874.

4. Id.

5. Countryman, The Concept of a Voidable Preference in Bankruptcy, 38 Vand.L.Rev. 713, 775 (1985); Orelup, Avoidance of Preferential Transfers Under the Bankruptcy Reform Act of 1978, 65 Iowa L. Rev. 209, 236 (1979).

(A) in payment of a debt incurred by the debtor in the ordinary course of business or financial affairs of the debtor and the transferee;

(B) made in the ordinary course of business or financial affairs of the debtor and the transferee; and

(C) made according to ordinary business terms.[6]

As originally enacted, (c)(2) carried an additional requirement: the transfer must have been made not later than 45 days after the debt was incurred. Congress eliminated the 45-day requirement in 1984.[7] This change in the section did not entirely eliminate, as a factor to consider in applying (c)(2), the length of time that elapsed between the debtor incurring the debt and paying it.[8] The period, however long or short, may be extraordinary and therefore disqualify the payment for (c)(2) immunity on the ground that the payment was not made in the ordinary course as (c)(2)(B) requires.[9]

Before considering further the several requirements of the current (c)(2) with respect to the ordinariness of payment, we briefly note two important aspects of the general scope of (c)(2). First, it does not protect every kind of ordinary-course transfer. Rather, the protection of (c)(2) is limited to a transfer that is a "*payment,*" which means that the purpose of the transfer is to reduce or satisfy a debt. A transfer for that purpose is a payment within the scope of (c)(2) whether the payment is in cash or other property;[10] but section 547(c)(2) never immunizes any kind of transfer, whether in cash or other property, that is for security,[11] such as an Article 9 security interest or a real estate mortgage, or that is for any other purpose that is not payment.[12]

Second, the ordinary-course payments protected by (c)(2) include payments that debtors make as consumers, as well as payments made by debtors

---

6. 11 U.S.C.A. § 547(c)(2). "This exception codifies the 'current expense' rule under the old Act which protected wages and rent, and general operational expenses including advertising expenses, general business expenses, warehousing expenses, and payment of rent/tax arrearages to realize value of leasehold." Kaye, Preferences Under the New Bankruptcy Code, 54 Am. Bankr. L. J. 197, 201–02 (1980).

7. The controlling date for applying the 1984 amendments and the new (c)(2) without the 45-day limit is the date the debtor filed her bankruptcy petition, not when the trustee commences the adversary proceeding. In re Republic Trust & Savings Co., 897 F.2d 1041, 1044–45 (10th Cir.1990), cert. denied, ___ U.S. ___, 111 S.Ct. 245, 112 L.Ed.2d 204 (1990).

8. "Most authorities indicate that a debt is incurred for purposes of section 547(c)(2)(B) upon the shipment or delivery of the goods, depending upon the contract terms." In re Powerine Oil Co., 126 B.R. 790, 793 (Bankr. 9th Cir.1991).

9. 11 U.S.C.A. § 547(c)(2)(B). Indeed, the usual reason that a payment fails to qualify for protection under (c)(2) is that the payment was untimely. See § 6–31 infra.

10. Countryman, The Concept of a Voidable Preference in Bankruptcy, 38 Vand.L.Rev. 713, 775 (1985). This view is not unquestioned. See In re Gentile, 114 B.R. 192 (Bankr. W.D.Mo.1990), in which the court cites authority to the contrary and makes clear the court's own uncertainty on the issue and its willingness to consider the competing arguments. Id. at 193.

11. See, e.g., In re Four Winds Enterprises, Inc., 100 B.R. 24, 25 (Bankr. S.D.Cal.1989) (§ 547(c)(2) inapplicable to re-perfection of an Article 9 security interest); In re Silve, 86 B.R. 230 (Bankr. D. Mont. 1988) ((c)(2) does not apply to a security interest in crops); Matter of Blackburn, 90 B.R. 569, 572 (Bankr. M.D.Ga.1987) ((c)(2) inapplicable to enabling security interest); Countryman, The Concept of a Voidable Preference in Bankruptcy, 38 Vand.L.Rev. 713, 775 (1985).

12. See, e.g., In re Gentile, 114 B.R. 192, 194 (Bankr. W.D.Mo.1990) ((c)(2) does not protect a transfer of property whereby the property was held by the transferee for the debtor's later use and was not a "done deal" in the sense of the transfer being payment).

in business. Congress intended to make this clear by referring throughout (c)(2) not only to "business," but also to "financial affairs." This term, "financial affairs," was designed "for the case of a consumer * * * to include such nonbusiness activities as payment of monthly utility bills." [13]

No payment by any debtor is protected, however, whether in business or as a consumer, unless the circumstances surrounding the payment were *"ordinary"* in three different senses: First, the debt toward which the payment was made must have been incurred in the ordinary course.[14] Second, the payment itself must have been made in the ordinary course.[15] Finally, the payment must also have been made according to ordinary business terms.[16] A payment is protected pro tanto to the extent these requirements are met.[17]

§ 6–30 Ordinary Payment of Ordinary Debts, Section 547(c)(2)—Debt Incurred in the Ordinary Course

The first requirement of the (c)(2) exception is that the debt, toward which the payment was made, must have been "a *debt incurred* by the debtor *in the ordinary course of business* or financial affairs of the debtor *and* the transferee."[1] Thus, (c)(2) does not protect payments, however regular and routine, made toward a debt arising from a need or purpose, or out of a transaction, that is extraordinary for either the debtor or the transferee.

The proper context for applying (c)(2)(A) is the experience of the particular parties. The court must determine what is ordinary for them.[2]

The issue is whether the debt is ordinary. It is not sufficient that the debtor had routinely made payments on the debt for a substantial period of time so that, as between the parties, the payments themselves were ordinary. The debt itself must have been ordinary in both directions. Incurring the obligation must have been ordinary in the overall business or financial affairs of the debtor.[3] Also, the right to payment, that the debt creates in the transferee, must have been ordinary as to transferee.

Suppose, for example, that T is a retailer or an individual. T is not in the business of making loans and never made a loan until D asked to borrow $25,000. D's repayment of the loan is unprotected by (c)(2) if for no other reason than that the loan transaction was not in the ordinary course of T's business or financial affairs.[4] An independent requirement of (c)(2) is that

---

13. H.R. Rep. No. 595, 95th Cong., 1st Sess. 373, reprinted in 1978 U.S. Code Cong. & Admin. News 5963, 6329; S. Rep. No. 989, 95th Cong., 2d Sess. 87, reprinted in 1978 U.S. Code Cong. & Admin. News 5787, 5874.

14. 11 U.S.C.A. § 547(c)(2)(A).

15. 11 U.S.C.A. § 547(c)(2)(B).

16. 11 U.S.C.A. § 547(c)(2)(C).

17. In re Miner Industries, Inc., 119 B.R. 6, 9 (Bankr. D.R.I.1990) (relying on pre-Code authorities to conclude that a payment may be split into preferential and nonpreferential portions).

§ 6–30

1. 11 U.S.C.A. § 547(c)(2)(A) (emphasis added).

2. In re Fulghum Const. Corp., 872 F.2d 739, 743 (6th Cir.1989) (the court must analyze "the business practices which were unique to the particular parties under consideration and not to the practices which generally prevailed in the industry of the parties").

3. See Practitioner Treatise, Vol. 1.

4. See Practitioner Treatise, Vol. 1.

the debt must have been ordinary for the transferee: having the particular right to payment, and having it arise as it did, must not have been unusual in the transferee's experience.

Cases such as *In re Southern Indus. Banking Corp.*[5] are therefore very easily resolved. In this case a savings and loan association deposited money with the debtor, Southern Industrial Banking Corp., which was not a bank. The association withdrew the funds. Its withdrawals were preferences, and (c)(2) did not save them from avoidance. The conduct of the association in having deposited the funds and, in effect, having made investments through the debtor was illegal; and an illegal transaction is not ordinary for either the debtor or the transferee.[6]

It is only slightly more difficult to resolve the case in which a perfectly legal and ordinary transaction not unusual for either the debtor and the transferee produces a debt the parties somehow settle, with or without court action. The debtor pays the settlement according to its terms. Although the settlement is based on an ordinary trade debt, the debtor's payment of the settlement is not spared from avoidance as a preference by section 547(c)(2).[7] A perfectly legitimate explanation is that the payment was not for a debt incurred in the ordinary course of the debtor's and transferee's affairs.[8] The debt paid was the debt created by the settlement, and debts arising from settlements are typically extraordinary as to the debtor and the creditor-transferee.

The courts are just as likely, however, to explain the settlement cases on the different basis that the payment itself was not made in the ordinary course because the payment was prompted by the extraordinary forces and circumstances that produced the settlement.[9] Payment of even the most ordinary debt is not protected by (c)(2) if the payment itself was unusual in any respect. Failure in this respect, that is, some oddity in payment itself rather than with respect to the debt, is the usual reason that (c)(2) protection is denied.

§ 6–31 Ordinary Payment of Ordinary Debts, Section 547(c)(2)—Payment Made in the Ordinary Course and on Ordinary Business Terms

Section (c)(2) requires, beyond ordinariness of the debt,[1] that the payment itself be "made in the ordinary course of business or financial affairs of the debtor and the transferee."[2] This requirement is satisfied only if every aspect of the payment is consistent with the usual routine of payments the debtor makes and the transferee receives. The language probably dictates that a payment is not made in the ordinary course if the payment or the receipt is unusual when compared with the overall financial routine of the debtor or the transferee in all their dealings, including transactions with third parties.

5. 72 B.R. 512 (Bankr. E.D.Tenn.1987).
6. See Practitioner Treatise, Vol. 1.
7. See Practitioner Treatise, Vol. 1.
8. See Practitioner Treatise, Vol. 1.
9. See Practitioner Treatise, Vol. 1.

§ 6–31

1. 11 U.S.C.A. § 547(c)(2)(A), discussed at § 6–30 supra.
2. 11 U.S.C.A. § 547(c)(2)(B).

§ 6–31   AVOIDANCE POWERS   333

The courts, however, generally compare the payment only against the pattern of payments between the immediate parties themselves.[3] Thus, the requirement that payment be made in the ordinary course is not met if, for example:

- the payment was made by wire transfer rather than by check as was customary between the parties;[4]
- the payment was drawn from a special account not customarily used to cover such expenses;[5]
- the payment was made by check that was not honored until re-presentment;[6]
- the payment was made involuntarily, such as
  - by way of levy, garnishment or the like,[7]
  - through setoff,[8] or
  - because of the creditor's own personal "amplified pressure" on the debtor;[9]
- the payment was made pursuant to a fresh arrangement between the parties that imposed new terms and constraints on the parties' dealings;[10]
- the payment on a credit line was extraordinarily large compared to the amount the debtor had ordinarily paid each month;[11]
- the payment was made after the debtor discontinued business operations in an attempt to wind up its affairs,[12] or
- (Surprise! Surprise!) the transfer was made in furtherance of an unlawful scheme.[13]

In sum, a payment is extraordinary and beyond the protection of (c)(2) if the payment was associated with any "variation from what theretofore had been the usual course of dealing" between the parties.[14]

The most common reason a payment fails the made-in-the-ordinary-course requirement is that the payment was untimely. Suppose, for example, that D regularly purchases goods on open account from S. The price of

---

3. See Practitioner Treatise, Vol. 1.
4. See Practitioner Treatise, Vol. 1.
5. See Practitioner Treatise, Vol. 1.
6. See Practitioner Treatise, Vol. 1.
7. See Practitioner Treatise, Vol. 1.
8. See Practitioner Treatise, Vol. 1.
9. See Practitioner Treatise, Vol. 1.
10. See Practitioner Treatise, Vol. 1.
11. See Practitioner Treatise, Vol. 1.
12. See Practitioner Treatise, Vol. 1.
13. See Practitioner Treatise, Vol. 1.
14. In re Singer Products Co., Inc., 102 B.R. 912, 935 (Bankr. E.D.N.Y.1989) (creditor began applying payments to unsecured debt, instead of crediting them to secured debt as had been the routine practice, upon learning of the debtor's precarious financial condition).

A payment can be ordinary, however, though it is not a kind of payment that is commonly made. " '[A]n extensive showing that such transactions occurred often, or even regularly, is not necessary * * *. [A] transaction can be ordinary and still occur only occasionally.' " In re Energy Cooperative, Inc., 103 B.R. 171 (N.D.Ill. 1986); see also First Software Corp. v. Micro Educ. Corp. of America, 103 B.R. 359, 360–61 (D. Mass. 1988) (payments on invoices were ordinary where they were made after due dates of invoices but pursuant to oral agreement for weekly payments, as parties had done on one other occasion in the past).

Also, erratic payments are ordinary if the parties had established no regular pattern of payment so that paying erratically was normal. In re National Office Products, Inc., 119 B.R. 896, 897 (Bankr. D.R.I.1990).

each shipment is due 30 days after delivery. This relationship extends over a period of several years, and D regularly makes timely payments. During the preference period, however, D makes several untimely payments, that is, D pays for shipments that D received more than 30 days before the payment. Section 547(c)(2) does not protect the untimely payments.[15]

Typically, of course, payments are made by check. In such a case the payment is deemed to have been made, for purposes of (c)(2), when the check was delivered to the transferee, as long as the check is eventually paid in due course by the drawee.[16]

An important exception significantly limits the general rule that untimely payments are beyond the scope of (c)(2). It is that *section 547(c)(2) protects untimely payments if they are customary in the relationship between the debtor and the transferee.*[17] This exceptions is the product of a broader principle that "the parties may adopt a payment practice at variance with their contract terms, which practice then becomes the ordinary course of business between them * * *.[18]

On the other hand, the exception itself is limited by an important qualification: *untimely payments are unprotected, even though they are common between the immediate parties, if late payments are uncommon within the industry, trade, or market in which the parties deal.* This qualification would be applied by the courts which hold that the ordinary-course requirement, with respect to the making of payment, contains an *objective* component, as well as a *subjective* component.[19] The latter concerns the pattern between the debtor and the transferee, while the former addresses practices in the relevant, wider community.

These courts are convinced that both components must be satisfied—subjective *and* objective—not only with respect to the timeliness of payment, but also with respect to every other aspect of the payment. Otherwise, (c)(2) is inapplicable.

There is an obvious argument that (c)(2) contains no objective component. The language of (c)(2)(B) itself, in black and white, requires only that the payment be "made in the ordinary course of business or financial affairs *of the debtor and the transferee.*"[20]

The courts which find an objective component in (c)(2) would agree that (c)(2)(B) imposes a subjective test. They focus rather on (c)(2)(C), which adds the apparently separate requirement that the payment must be "made according to ordinary business terms."[21] These courts reason that the two subsections (B) and (C) are redundant unless (c)(2)(C) imposes an objective test.

The subsections are easily interpreted, however, to share a purely subjective test without creating a redundancy. Read section (c)(2)(B) as governing the mechanics of the payment, i.e., the way in which the payment is "made," and read (c)(2)(C) as governing exactly what the language de-

15. See Practitioner Treatise, Vol. 1.
16. See Practitioner Treatise, Vol. 1.
17. See Practitioner Treatise, Vol. 1.
18. In re Richardson, 94 B.R. 56, 61 (Bankr. E.D.Pa. 1988) (dicta).
19. See Practitioner Treatise, Vol. 1.
20. 11 U.S.C.A. § 547(c)(2)(B) (emphasis added).
21. 11 U.S.C.A. § 547(c)(2)(C).

scribes, i.e., the "terms" of the payment, including the amount, the time the payment is made, and the like. Thus, if the payment is larger than the debtor normally makes to the transferee, (c)(2) is inapplicable and the precise reason is the failure to satisfy (c)(2)(C): the payment was not made according to ordinary business terms.[22] The same reason explains the inapplicability of (c)(2) if the payment is made after the contract between the parties has been terminated.[23]

In any event, we do not read into (c)(2) an objective component requiring that payment be made in accordance with general industry or trade customs or practices. To read it otherwise requires that creditors conform, at least when the debtor appears in financial trouble, to a vague community standard that cannot readily (if ever) be determined in advance. Yet, that is the worst time to change the comfortable and, perhaps, more flexible pattern the parties have established for themselves. Even if the community standard is not, in fact, more rigid, making any change requires the creditor accurately to define and properly to comply with an ambiguous and distant standard. The odds are against the creditor whose natural reaction may well be to abandon the debtor when the debtor most needs continuing credit.

In sum, we believe that (c)(2)(C) picks up where (c)(2)(B) leaves off. The latter requires that the mechanics of payment be in the ordinary course and the former continues the theme and applies it to the actual terms of payment. The two requirements are different but complimentary, and they are fully satisfied if the mechanics and terms of payment are ordinary for the debtor and transferee as between themselves. In other words, the test for each requirement is purely subjective, focusing exclusively on the experiences of the parties involved in the transfer. There is no objective test that determines ordinariness by comparing the way in which the payment was made, or its terms, to industry custom or practices.

§ 6–32 Ordinary Payment of Ordinary Debts, Section 547(c)(2)—Payments on Long-Term Debt

Here is a special problem in the application of section (c)(2): Suppose that D is obligated on an unsecured debt that she is repaying in monthly installments over a term of five years. D incurs and makes the payments in the ordinary course of her affairs and on ordinary terms in every sense and from every perspective. The regular monthly payments D makes during the preference period preceding her bankruptcy are preferences under section 547(b). The issue is whether the payments are eligible for protection by (c)(2).

Resolving the issue was easy before the 1984 change in (c)(2) eliminated the requirement that the payment be made within 45 days after the debt was incurred. Each monthly payment, at least of principal, is not made to satisfy a presently incurred debt for the installment then due. Rather, each payment is toward the whole debt that accrued when the principal balance

---

22. In re Vunovich, 74 B.R. 629, 631 (Bankr. D.Kan.1987). For other authority that (c)(2) does not protect a payment in an unusual amount, see Matter of Ullman, 80 B.R. 101, 103 (Bankr. S.D.Ohio 1987). (payments included late fee and interest).

23. In re Seawinds Ltd., 91 B.R. 88 (N.D.Cal.1988), aff'd sub nom., Matter of Seawinds Ltd., 888 F.2d 640 (9th Cir.1989).

was loaned. Thus, D's payments during the preference period, no matter how ordinary, fail the 45-day requirement, and (c)(2) is inapplicable.[1]

With the elimination of this requirement, the creditor-transferee could easily argue that payments on long-term debt are eligible for (c)(2) protection. The plain language no longer limits the exception to short-term obligations. There are only the several requirements of ordinariness which payments on long-term debt can satisfy. Thus, (c)(2) shields the payments if neither the debt itself nor any aspect of the payment is extraordinary. Some authorities so held as soon as the 45-day requirement of (c)(2) was eliminated.[2]

Not everyone accepted the plain-language argument. An opposing argument relied on purposive analysis. It assumed that that the aim of Congress in enacting (c)(2) was to protect "recurring, customary credit transactions that are incurred and paid in the ordinary course,"[3] or, put more succinctly, Congress intended to shield short-term credit for current expenses.[4] Therefore, payments on long-term credit obligations are beyond the section's scope. Some authorities so held.[5]

The reply was that by eliminating the 45-day requirement, Congress removed such a purposive limitation on the scope of the section. The rejoinder was that the 45-day requirement was not the only support for limiting (c)(2) to short-term credit deals, that the original congressional intent and purpose to so limit (c)(2) was pervasive and endogenous to the exception as a whole and thus survived the 1984 change; and that the elimination of the 45-day rule simply removed an artificial, arbitrary time limit and accomplished nothing else.

The Supreme Court ended this debate in *Union Bank v. Wolas*.[6] The Court endorsed the plain-language argument. Because of the "clarity of the statutory text," the arguments of history and policy behind 547 were not enough to convince the Court "that Congress intended to create or to preserve a special rule for long-term debt * * *." The holding of *Union Bank* is "that payments on long-term debt, as well as payments on short-term debt, may qualify for the ordinary course of business exception to the trustee's power to avoid preferential transfers."

Union Bank does not mean, however, that (c)(2) protects payments ordinarily made on all long-term debts. The elimination of the 45-day requirement did not remove the separate requirement that the debt must have been incurred in the ordinary course of the debtor's and transferee's affairs. Thus, in no event should (c)(2) protect payments on a long-term debt that is extraordinary in the experience of either the debtor or the transferee.

On this point some people have argued that incurring long-term debt is always extraordinary. We do not agree, not even with respect to consumers. It may be that, notwithstanding the elimination of the 45-day rule, (c)(2)

§ 6-32
1. See Practitioner Treatise, Vol. 1.
2. See Practitioner Treatise, Vol. 1.
3. WJM, Inc. v. Massachusetts Dept. of Public Welfare, 840 F.2d 996, 1011 (1st Cir. 1988); Hickey v. Nightingale Roofing, Inc., 83 B.R. 180, 183–84 (D.Mass.1988); Matter of Van Huffel Tube Corp., 74 B.R. 579, 588 (Bankr. N.D.Ohio 1987).
4. See Practitioner Treatise, Vol. 1.
5. See Practitioner Treatise, Vol. 1.
6. ___ U.S. ___, 112 S.Ct. 527, 116 L.Ed.2d 514 (1991).

should have been limited to payments on short-term credit for reasons of policy or enduring congressional purpose; but to so limit the section on the stated basis that long-term debt is always extraordinary simply ignores reality. Ask almost anyone who uses a credit card to buy Christmas or Hanukkah presents. Similarly, with respect to businesses, "[a]lthough incurring a long-term loan to provide working capital is not 'ordinary' in the sense that it occurs frequently, it is 'ordinary' in the sense that incurring such debt occasionally during its lifetime is not unusual for most businesses."[7]

Interest payments on long-term debt were probably eligible for (c)(2) protection from the beginning, even when the 45–day requirement was part of the exception. While the debt for the principal is incurred at the very inception of the credit transaction, the debt for interest is incurred as the interest periodically becomes due.[8] Regular payments of interest are therefore for short-term credit and within the original purpose, as well as the plain language, of (c)(2).[9] The peculiar facts of each case will determine if interest is ordinary in every sense that (c)(2) requires to trigger its protection.

§ 6–33 Enabling Security Interests, Section 547(c)(3)

The third exception to section 547(b), section 547(c)(3), protects enabling security interests, better known as purchase-money[1] security interests, and is a particular expression of section 547(c)(1), which protects contemporaneous exchanges for new value.[2] An enabling or purchase-money security interest is a consensual lien[3] on collateral given by the debtor to the person who gave new value,[4] usually in the form of the purchase money or credit, that enabled the debtor to buy or otherwise acquire rights in the property.

For example, suppose that D borrows money from Bank for the purpose of buying a new piece of equipment for D's factory. As collateral for the loan D signs a security agreement that will give Bank an Article 9 security interest in the equipment as soon as D buys and thereby acquires rights in the property. D also signs an Article 9 financing statement which the Bank immediately files in order to perfect its expectant interest. A week later, D acquires rights in the equipment under the sales contract with the seller, and a security interest in the property then attaches in Bank's favor, pursuant to the earlier security agreement. Moreover, because Bank has already filed, the interest is perfected as soon as it attaches.

---

7. In re Control Electric, 91 B.R. 1010, 1011–12 (Bankr. N.D.Ga.1988); see also In re Finn, 909 F.2d 903, 905–08 (6th Cir. 1990) (long-term consumer loans are not unusual for every person). Similarly, the frequent use of long-term debt is ordinary for some businesses and individuals. Fidelity Sav. & Inv. Co. v. New Hope Baptist, 880 F.2d 1172, 1177 (10th Cir.1989) (writing with respect to consumer loan company which raised capital by selling savings certificates).

8. See Practitioner Treatise, Vol. 1.

9. See Practitioner Treatise, Vol. 1.

§ 6–33

1. "Purchase-money" is a term the Uniform Commercial Code defines in U.C.C. § 9–107.

2. 11 U.S.C.A. § 547(c)(1).

3. Section 547(c)(3) protects a transfer that is a "security interest," which means a "lien created by an agreement." 11 U.S.C.A. § 101(51).

4. The meaning of "new value" for purposes is discussed earlier. See § 6–25 supra.

This secured transaction between D and Bank is technically a preference. The transfer, i.e., the creation of the security interest, followed the creation of the debt for the loan, which D owes Bank. Thus, the transfer was for an antecedent debt.

On the other hand, the parties intended the transfer, i.e., the security interest, to be exchanged contemporaneously for new value, i.e., the purchase money, given the debtor. Section (c)(1) protects such exchanges in general but does *not* apply to this particular exchange. Section (c)(3), with its peculiar procedural requirements, was designed especially for purchase-money security interests, and therefore (c)(1) is inapplicable to them.[5] Thus, if Bank's interest is to be protected as a contemporaneous exchange for new value, (c)(3) must be satisfied.

Section (c)(3) protects from avoidance as a preference any transfer:

that creates a security interest in property acquired by the debtor

(A) to the extent such security interest secures new value that was

(i) given at or after the signing of a security agreement that contains a description of such property as collateral;

(ii) given by or on behalf of the secured party under such agreement;

(iii) given to enable the debtor to acquire such property; and

(iv) in fact used by the debtor to acquire such property; and

(B) that is perfected on or before 10 days after the debtor receives possession of such property.[6]

The many small requirements of (c)(3), especially those in subsection (A), give the appearance that this exception will be difficult to satisfy, and that its protection is much more narrow than (c)(1)'s. In fact, the requirements of (c)(3) essentially mirror the steps that are normally followed in the typical purchase-money secured transaction. Thus, the usual transaction that gives a lender an Article 9, purchase-money security interest will usually satisfy (c)(3), including the hypothetical deal above between Bank and D.[7]

Moreover, in one respect, (c)(3) is more protective that (c)(1). The reason is (c)(3)(B). Suppose that in the deal between Bank and D, Bank fails to file a financing statement at the inception of the transaction. D buys the new piece of equipment on February 1, which is five days after getting the loan from Bank. On the same day, February 1, D acquires rights in the equipment because it is identified to the contract of sale between D and the seller. D, however, delays taking possession of the equipment until March 15, and Bank finally files on March 20.

The Bank actually acquired its security interest, under state law, when D acquired rights in the collateral, that is, on February 1. For purposes of preference law, the transfer would have been deemed to have been made on the same date, February 1, which is when the transfer was actually effective between Bank and D, if the Bank had perfected at, or within ten days after, such time. The Bank, however, did not perfect within the ten-day period.

---

5. See § 6–24.
6. 11 U.S.C.A. § 547(c)(3).
7. See Practitioner Treatise, Vol. 1.

Therefore, the transfer to the Bank is deemed to have occurred when the Bank perfected,[8] which was on March 20. As a result, more than 50 days elapsed between the time the Bank gave value and the time the transfer was made. Even if enabling security interests were generally within the scope of (c)(1), the requirements of (c)(1) would not be satisfied in this case. Because of the 50-day lapse of time, the exchange was not contemporaneous.

Section 547(c)(3) would be satisfied, however. Subsection (B) establishes a ten-day grace period for perfection that is measured not from the time the security interest was actually effective between the parties, but rather from the time the debtor *takes possession* of the collateral.[9] In the hypothetical problem, Bank perfected within ten days of D taking possession of the collateral, and Bank's security interest is therefore shielded from preference attack by (c)(3), assuming (as is true in the usual case) that the particulars of (c)(3)(A) are met. If the Bank had perfected more than ten days after the debtor got possession, the interest would not have been saved by (c)(3) from avoidance under section 547(b).[10]

The ten-day period naturally overrides and controls over a longer grace period allowed by state law.[11] The Eleventh Circuit carves an exception, however, if the state law relates the perfection back to a point within the ten-day period. In the case *In re Busenlehner*,[12] the secured party, GMAC, perfected its security interest under Georgia law by applying for a certificate of title that would reflect the security interest. The application occurred beyond the ten-day limit of section 547(c)(3), but it was timely under a local law that deems perfection to have occurred when the interest was created if application for title is made within 20 days. The court reasoned that by complying with the 20-day rule of local law, perfection related back to the time the interest was created which was within the ten-day period of (c)(3). Thus, perfection, too, occurred within the period.

We question *Busenlehner*. Subsection (c)(3) requires perfection within the ten-day period. GMAC did not satisfy this requirement. Even under local law GMAC did not perfect until it applied for the certificate of title. Relating back the perfection affects priority but does not change when perfection occurred. The very concept of relation back admits of itself that perfection occurred later than the time to which it is related back.

---

8. 11 U.S.C.A. § 547(e)(2).

9. 11 U.S.C.A. § 547(c)(3)(B). The term "possession" in (c)(3)(B) is defined according to its usual and ordinary meaning, that is, physical or manual control. The term is not necessarily synonymous with ownership. In re Trott, 91 B.R. 808, 811–12 (Bankr. S.D.Ohio 1988) (debtor's possession of automobile was not dependent upon delivery of certificate of title to him); In re Winnett, 102 B.R. 635, 637–38 (Bankr. S.D.Ohio 1989) (possession is not to be equated with ownership or limited to functional use, but is determined as of time debtor enjoys simple physical control). As originally enacted, the (c)(3)(B) grace period was measured from the time the security interest attached. In 1984 the language was changed, so that the grace period is measured from the time the debtor takes possession of the collateral, in order to match the language of U.C.C. provisions such as sections 9–301(2) and 9–312(4).

Also, Bankruptcy Rule 9006(a) applies to the ten-day period of section 547(c)(3), In re Lamons, 121 B.R. 748, 752 (Bankr. S.D.Ohio 1990), so that the date of possession is excluded and the last day of the period is included unless it is a Saturday, Sunday, or legal holiday.

10. See, e.g., Gibson v. General Motors Acceptance Corp., 104 B.R. 432, 434 (Bankr. N.D.Fla.1989); In re Phillips, 103 B.R. 893, 896 (Bankr. S.D.Ohio 1989).

11. Matter of Hamilton, 892 F.2d 1230, 1234–35 (5th Cir.1990).

12. 918 F.2d 928 (11th Cir.1990), reh'g denied, 924 F.2d 1067 (11th Cir.1991).

Our doubt is not dispelled by subsection 547(e), which explains that a transfer of personal property "is perfected when a creditor on a simple contract cannot acquire a judicial lien that is superior too the interest of the transferee." The court relied on (e) in *Busenlehner*. It reasoned that no creditor could beat GMAC after the security interest was created because GMAC's perfection would relate back and trump any intervening lien creditor. Thus, by complying with the local 20-day, relation-back law, GMAC was perfected within the meaning of (e) when the interest was created. This reasoning ignores, however, the essential truth of local law: GMAC could not have achieved this priority unless and until it properly applied for the certificate of title. Only then was priority assured and thus only then did perfection occur even in terms of section 547(e). We suspect that under (e) as under state law, perfection cannot occur before the steps for achieving it are taken, notwithstanding any relation back of the priority that results once the steps have been taken.

Few other problems arise in applying (c)(3), and there are very few cases construing it probably because, as already mentioned, the section's requirements reflect normal practice. There are, however, two questions about the scope of (c)(3) that deserve mention for the very reason that the questions are largely ignored in the cases and by other authorities. Scope questions under (c)(3) are especially important because of the relationship between (c)(1) and (c)(3). As we have already noted, the latter can be more protective than the former. On the other hand, if (c)(3) is applicable because the transfer involves an enabling security interest, (c)(1) is not alternatively available should the requirements of (c)(3) not be met.

The first scope question is whether (c)(3) applies if the secured party is a seller of the collateral rather than a lender supplying the purchase money. There is an argument that "Congress did not intend section 547(c)(3) to apply to a seller who retains a purchase money security interest in the goods sold * * * " because the earliest antecedent of (c)(3) is a proposal by the National Bankruptcy Conference to protect the security interests of an enabling *lender*.[13] Yet, the language of (c)(3) implies no such intention. By its own terms the section extends to any case in which the new value enables the debtor to acquire rights in the collateral. Nothing in the definition of "new value" confines the meaning of the term to a loan of money by a bank or other lender. Indeed, the definition explicitly includes "new credit." Moreover, the related law of commercial transactions defines "purchase-money security interest," which is the U.C.C.'s term for enabling interest, to include the interest of either a lender or seller who takes or retains an interest in "the collateral to secure all or part of its price."[14] Finally, there is no apparently good reason for discriminating between enabling secured parties, for purposes of (c)(3), on the basis of whether they enabled the debtor to acquire the collateral by loaning the purchase money or extended credit for the purchase price. We would thus conclude that (c)(3) is sufficiently broad to cover the enabling interest of a seller of the collateral.[15]

13. Countryman, The Concept of a Voidable Preference in Bankruptcy, 38 Vand.L.Rev. 713, 778 (1985).

14. U.C.C. § 9–107(a).

15. See Practitioner Treatise, Vol. 1.

The other scope question is whether (c)(3) applies when the collateral is real property. Again, the literal language answers, "Yes." The section applies to a "transfer" that creates an enabling "security interest" in "property." Although the U.C.C. limits the creation of a "security interest" to personal property, the Bankruptcy Code defines the term to mean "lien created by an agreement."[16] "Lien" means "charge against or interest in *property* to secure payment of a debt or performance of an obligation."[17] "Property" is not defined but is in the definition of "transfer,"[18] which is "as broad as possible,"[19] and universally includes realty as well as personalty. We would therefore conclude that (c)(3) applies to purchase-money mortgages and other consensual encumbrances on real property. No court has specifically so held, but no court has decided the question the other way.[20]

§ 6–34 Subsequent New Value, Section 547(c)(4)

Suppose that a creditor refuses to provide additional goods or services to the debtor until the debtor pays a previous balance that is overdue. The debtor thus makes a payment toward her account with the seller, and the seller immediately thereafter provides fresh goods or services on credit. Within 90 days thereafter the debtor files bankruptcy. The trustee argues that the payment was a preference and seeks to recover it from the seller.

The payment is not protected by section 547(c)(1). The seller gave new value but not in exchange for the payment. Rather, the payment was given to satisfy a preexisting debt for consideration previously supplied on credit. The payment is not protected by (c)(2) because the payment was not made in the ordinary course according to ordinary business terms. Rather, the payment was untimely and coerced. Section (c)(3) is inapplicable because it applies only to enabling security interests, not to payments of money.

Yet, though the payment depleted the estate, the estate was enriched by the fresh goods or services, i.e., the new value, that the seller supplied on credit. The payment, viewed in isolation as section 547(b) requires, was preferential; but the sum of the payment and the new value caused no preferential effect to the extent of the new value, and to this extent the payment is protected by section (c)(4). It covers any transfer:

> to or for the benefit of a creditor, to the extent that, after such transfer, such creditor gave new value to or for the benefit of the debtor—
>
> (A) not secured by an otherwise unavoidable security interest; and
>
> (B) on account of which new value the debtor did not make an otherwise unavoidable transfer to or for the benefit of such creditor.[1]

---

16. 11 U.S.C.A. § 101(51).

17. 11 U.S.C.A. § 101(37).

18. Transfer essentially means "every mode * * * of disposing of or parting with property * * *." 11 U.S.C.A. § 101(54).

19. H.R. Rep. No. 595, 95th Cong., 1st Sess. 314, reprinted in 1978 U.S. Code Cong. & Admin. News 5963, 6271; S. Rep. No. 989, 95th Cong., 2d Sess. 27, reprinted in 1978 U.S. Code Cong. & Admin. News 5787, 5813.

20. See Practitioner Treatise, Vol. 1.

§ 6–34

1. 11 U.S.C.A. § 547(c)(4).

In effect, (c)(4) treats subsequent new value "as a form of restitution, restoring the previously received preference."[2]

"Section 547(c) most obviously applies to revolving credit relationships,"[3] that is, "running accounts between sellers and buyers, where they make periodic payments and deliveries not coordinated to occur concurrently."[4] The exception is not so limited, however. "For instance, it also may include the value of insurance coverage provided after the payment of delinquent premiums, the value of leased equipment when the lessor permitted the debtor-lessee to continue using the equipment to produce inventory after default in rental payments, and may include the value of electricity supplied by a utility to the debtor after preferential payments."[5]

There are two keys to the application of (c)(4). The creditor must have given (1) "new value" and must have done so (2) *after* the preferential transfer. We have already explored the meaning of "new value" as part of our discussion of section 547(c)(1). What we say there about the meaning of "new value" applies equally here.

Even though the definition of "new value" is the same for sections (c)(1) and (c)(4), the two provisions differ substantially in two respects regarding the necessary relationship between the "new value" and the parties' transaction. First, for purposes of (c)(1), the new value must have been given in exchange for the preferential transfer. In contrast, (c)(4) contains no exchange requirement of any kind, that is, "there is no requirement that the [new value] * * * be extended as a result of the previously received preference."[6]

A second difference between (c)(1) and (c)(4) is that the former rigidly demands that the new value must have been "given to the debtor." Section (c)(4) is more flexible: it is sufficient that the new value was given "to *or for the benefit of* the debtor." Thus, (c)(4) applies when, after receiving a preference, the creditor pays an obligation of the debtor to a third person.[7]

The other key to the application of (c)(4) is that the new value must have been given *after* the preferential transfer that the creditor seeks to protect under (c)(4). Because of this requirement the (c)(4) exception is slimmer than the "net result rule" under pre-Code bankruptcy law. The old "net result rule" aggregated "all transfers during the preference period. A

---

2. Nimmer, Security Interests in Bankruptcy: An Overview of Section 547 of the Code, 17 Houston L. Rev. 289, 299 (1980).

3. Id.

4. Young, Preferences Under the Bankruptcy Reform Act of 1978, 54 Am. Bankr. L. J. 221, 229 (1980). See, e.g., Best Corp. v. Gibson Chemical & Oil Corp., 73 B.R. 69 (Bankr. D. Conn. 1987) (payment on prior invoice protected by value of subsequently required goods on credit); see also Matter of Global Int'l Airways Corp., 80 B.R. 983 (Bankr. W.D.Mo.1987) (payment for services protected by subsequent sales of goods on credit).

5. Countryman, The Concept of a Voidable Preference in Bankruptcy, 38 Vand.L.Rev. 713, 786 (1985); see also, e.g., In re Sounds Distrib., Inc., 80 B.R. 749 (Bankr. W.D.Pa. 1987) (payments for legal services that were preferential are protected by the value of services later provided).

6. Nimmer, supra note 2, at 299; but see In re Antinarelli Enterprises, Inc., 76 B.R. 247, 251 (Bankr. D.Mass.1987) ($100,000 preferential payment not protected by (c)(4) because the new value was not given in exchange for the payment).

7. In re Bellanca Aircraft Corp., 850 F.2d 1275, 1280 (8th Cir.1988), on remand, 96 B.R. 913 (Bankr. D.Minn.1989); Drabkin v. A.I. Credit Corp., 800 F.2d 1153, 1158 (D.C. Cir. 1986) (dicta); In re Amarex, 88 B.R. 362, 365 (W.D. Okla. 1988).

preference resulted only to the extent that payments by the debtor exceeded value given by the creditor."[8] In other words, the old rule "totals all payments and all advances and offsets one against the other."[9] Under (c)(4), however, the only advances or other new value that is offset is new value given after the preference sought to be protected by (c)(4), so that (c)(4) " 'has transformed the judicially created net result rule into * * * a subsequent advance rule."[10]

This requirement, that the new value must have been given *after* the transfer, is rigidly enforced by the courts even to the extent of refusing to apply (c)(4) when the transfer and the giving of new value occur simultaneously.[11] The timing of a transfer for purposes of section 547 has already been discussed.[12] We will not repeat ourselves on that issue, except to emphasize two points.

First, the timing of a transfer for any purpose under section 547, including the exceptions in (c), is highly regulated by section 547(e).[13] Thus, a transfer may be deemed to have occurred when it was perfected against third parties or at the time of the filing of bankruptcy rather than an earlier time when it was effective between the parties.[14] Consequently, for example, (c)(4) will not protect an unperfected mortgage or deed of property even though new value was given after the deed was executed.[15] The transfer of the property will be deemed to have occurred on the date of the bankruptcy filing,[16] and therefore the new value was given before the transfer rather than after it as (c)(4) requires.

Second, for purposes of (c)(4), as well as elsewhere in section 547(c), a transfer of money by check is usually deemed to have occurred when the check was actually delivered to the creditor if the check was paid in due course.[17]

The timing of the new value that the creditor gives is not ordinarily a problem. The only recurring issue is the timing of new value that consists of services. The courts agree that, in such a case, the new value is given when the services are actually rendered rather than when the creditor chooses to calculate the price of the services or to bill for them.[18] On the other hand, when the creditor gives new value by paying the debtor's obligation to a third person, such as a person who supplied the debtor with goods or services on credit, the new value is deemed given when the creditor actually pays the third person, not when the third person supplied the goods or services.[19]

The new value comes too late, however, if it is given after the debtor files her bankruptcy petition. Section 547(c)(4) only applies to unsecured

---

8. Orelup, Avoidance of Preferential Transfers Under the Bankruptcy Reform Act of 1978, 65 Iowa L. Rev. 209, 239–41 (1979).

9. Countryman, The Concept of a Voidable Preference in Bankruptcy, 38 Vand.L.Rev. 713, 784 (1985).

10. Id.

11. In re H & S Transp. Co., Inc., 80 B.R. 441, 448 (M.D.Tenn.1987).

12. See §§ 6–11 through 6–17 supra.

13. 11 U.S.C.A. § 547(e).

14. 11 U.S.C.A. § 547(e)(2).

15. In re Brown Family Farms, Inc., 80 B.R. 404 (Bankr. N.D.Ohio 1987).

16. 11 U.S.C.A. § 547(e)(2)(C).

17. See Practitioner Treatise, Vol. 1.

18. See Practitioner Treatise, Vol. 1.

19. See Practitioner Treatise, Vol. 1.

credit advanced *during the [prepetition] preference period.*" [20]

Section 547(c)(4) contains two other requirements beyond giving new value after the transfer. The new value must be *unsecured,* that is, it must not be secured "by an otherwise unavoidable security interest." [21] Two caveats are needed here. First, the authorities generally agree that having any security for the new value does not altogether preclude reliance on (c)(4). The exception applies, even if there is security, to the extent that the new value is undersecured.[22] In determining whether the new value was fully or only partially secured for (c)(4) purposes, the critical time is when the new value was given.[23]

It might be helpful to note that in a conventional revolving loan there may be monthly, weekly, or even daily loans in the form of new draws by the debtor against a continuing line of credit. When these periodic draws are made by a debtor against an undersecured credit line, they constitute unsecured credit to the extent they raise the debt above the value of the security.

The second caveat is that security for the new value is disregarded if the security is itself avoided in bankruptcy. Professor Nimmer explains:

> The purpose of * * * [requiring that the new value be unsecured] is obvious. To the extent that the subsequent new value is secured by a valid security interest, the transfer has not effectively replenished the estate. It should be emphasized at this point that the section requires a prior determination of whether any involved security interest is valid in bankruptcy. If the security interest is not valid, the creditor will lose the benefit of the security interest, but will be able to use the subsequent advance to exempt a prior preference.[24]

The final requirement of (c)(4) is that the debtor must not, "on account of" the new value, have made "an unavoidable transfer to or for the benefit of * * * [the] creditor." [25] This element of (c)(4) is often summarized as requiring that the new value "go unpaid." [26] Three caveats are in order here, too. First, the debtor's payment of the new value does not affect the application of (c)(4) if the payment itself is avoidable. The requirement that the new value "go unpaid" is offended, so that (c)(4) does not apply, only if the debtor's payment toward the new value is itself unavoidable.

In this situation, the creditor may keep his payment but has no section 547(c)(4) defense * * *. [T]he creditor gets credit only once for goods and services later supplied.[27]

---

20. In re Vunovich, 74 B.R. 629, 632 (Bankr. D.Kan.1987) (emphasis in original); accord, In re Jolly N, Inc., 122 B.R. 897, 909–10 (Bankr. D.N.J.1991) ("Post-petition advances of new value may not be applied to offset preferential transfers."); In re Ford, 98 B.R. 669, 683 (Bankr. D.Vt.1989) (postpetition advances are not new value for purposes of §§ 547(a)(2) and (c)(4)).

21. 11 U.S.C.A. § 547(c)(4)(A); see, e.g., In re Mid–South Cabinet & Millwork, Inc., 125 B.R. 16, 17 (Bankr. E.D. Ark.1990) ("Section 547(c)(4) is a variation of the 'net result rule' * * * and permits a creditor to offset * * * the amount of any subsequent unsecured credit * * *.").

22. See Practitioner Treatise, Vol. 1.

23. See Practitioner Treatise, Vol. 1.

24. Nimmer, supra note 2, at 300.

25. 11 U.S.C.A. § 547(c)(4)(B).

26. See Practitioner Treatise, Vol. 1.

27. Countryman, supra note 5, at 787–88; see also In re Kroh Bros. Dev. Co., 104 B.R. 182, 195 (Bankr. W.D.Mo.1989), decision aff'd,

Second, (c)(4) should not be woodenly construed to preclude entirely its application whenever the debtor makes any unavoidable payment toward the new value. The exception should be interpreted so that its inapplicability is limited to the extent of the amount of such a payment.[28]

Finally, the creditor does not lose the defense of (c)(4) if the new value was repaid by a third party whose repayment did not reduce or otherwise harm the debtor's estate to the detriment of other creditors.[29] In this event the net effect on the estate is a wash. No harm, no foul.

§ 6–35 Floating Liens on Inventory or Receivables, Section 547(c)(5)

A classic case of a preference is a transfer of security to an unsecured or undersecured creditor. Suppose, for example, that 90 days before D's bankruptcy she owes C an unsecured debt of $1,000. During the preference period D for the first time gives C a perfected security interest in collateral worth $1,000. D thereafter files bankruptcy. If D's estate is liquidated and distributed as a Chapter 7 case, general, unsecured creditors will receive ten percent of their claims. Thus, in the absence of the transfer, C would have received only $100. Because of the transfer C could fully satisfy her claim. Therefore, the transfer has a preferential effect and is avoidable under prior and present preference law.[1]

Change the facts slightly: Suppose that C acquires the security interest as a result of an after-acquired property clause in a security agreement executed and perfected long before the preference period preceding D's bankruptcy.[2] The after-acquired property clause causes C's interest to spread automatically to additional property of the kind described in the parties' security agreement. Because of this effect, C's security interest is commonly described as a "floating lien" that hovers above D's estate and attaches to fresh collateral as soon as D acquires it.

At the beginning of the preference period the secured debt is $10,000, but the collateral then existing is worth only $9,000. In this event C is undersecured $1,000. In other words, at the beginning of the preference period C has a $9,000 secured claim and a $1,000 unsecured claim. During the preference period D acquires rights in fresh collateral worth $1,000 to which C's perfected security interest automatically attaches. Once again, there is a preferential effect.

In the second problem, however, C's security interest in the collateral acquired during the 90-day period would not have been a preference under prior law. The courts effectively related back the transfer of this interest, which was effected by a floating lien, to the point in time when the original security interest was perfected. In our problem, as in the typical case, this

---

114 B.R. 658 (Bankr. W.D.Mo.1990), judgment aff'd in part, rev'd in part on somewhat different reasoning, 930 F.2d 648 (8th Cir.1991), on remand, 131 B.R. 717 (Bankr. W.D.Mo.1991) (there is no "unpaid new value requirement" in applying (c)(4) if the payment of the new value is itself avoidable).

28. See Practitioner Treatise, Vol. 1.

29. See Practitioner Treatise, Vol. 1.

§ 6–35

1. Regarding preferential effect as a requirement of a preference, see 11 U.S.C.A. § 547(b)(5) and our discussion of it at § 6–20 supra.

2. The law expressly authorizes after-acquired property clauses in security agreements covering personal property or fixtures. U.C.C. § 9–204(2).

point is well beyond the preference period. Thus, no preference occurred under pre-Code law even though the security interest in the after-acquired collateral did not actually attach until the debtor acquired rights in the collateral during the preference period.[3]

Section 547 expressly prohibits the pre-Code habit of relating back transfers in this fashion. Subsection (e) provides that a transfer cannot occur in any event until the debtor acquires rights in the collateral.[4] Thus, C's after-acquired interest is deemed to have been acquired, i.e., the transfer of that interest occurs, when the debtor actually acquired rights in the new collateral,[5] which was during the preference period. Therefore, C's floating lien or after-acquired interest in the new collateral (or security interest in the after-acquired collateral) is a preference under section 547(b).

The result under modern law is that any floating lien that attaches to collateral during the preference period is ordinarily a preference under section 547(b) if, at the time the interest attaches, the creditor is undersecured. This is true regardless of the kind of collateral involved.

The most common use of floating liens is in the financing of inventory and accounts or other rights to the payment of money. Technically, the secured party gets an interest in all of the specific pieces of goods and rights to payment that comprise the debtor's inventory and receivables. In reality, the secured party's interest is in the mass of such property existing at any one time. The individual components of the collateral mass are always changing: inventory is sold, and receivables are produced; the proceeds are used to buy new inventory; this inventory is sold producing new receivables; and so forth. (The water changes, and the flow varies; but the Mississippi River is the Mississippi River from Itasca, Minnesota, to New Orleans, Louisiana.) Throughout this process the debtor is paying part of the proceeds to the secured party; and the secured party is making fresh advances which are secured by the mass of collateral.

Theoretically, any security snared during the preference period by the secured party's floating lien is a preference. In the usual case the secured party cannot rely on section 547(c)(1)[6] or (c)(3)[7] as a defense to the preference attack. New value might have been extended but not in contemporaneous exchange for, or to enable D to buy, specific collateral. The (c)(4) exception that gives credit for subsequent new value might apply,[8] but the secured party will have a difficult burden of proof in establishing the extent of its applicability. C must match specific collateral with subsequent extensions of new value and must account for payments that D made. What an evidentiary mess! Practically speaking, C will seldom succeed in establishing a (c)(4) or other subsection (c) defense without incurring large costs.

---

3. See Practitioner Treatise, Vol. 1.

4. 11 U.S.C.A. § 547(e)(3).

5. See Practitioner Treatise, Vol. 1.

6. 11 U.S.C.A. § 547(c)(1), which protects transfers contemporaneously exchanged for new value. We discuss this exception at §§ 6–23 through 6–28 supra.

7. 11 U.S.C.A. § 547(c)(3), which protects enabling security interests. Our discussion is at § 6–33 supra.

8. See 11 U.S.C.A. § 547(c)(4), which we discuss at § 6–34 supra; but compare In re J.A.S. Markets, Inc., 113 B.R. 193, 199 (Bankr. W.D.Pa.1990) (creditor is not entitled to a further reduction of the preference amount on account of new value if the value is considered in computing the creditor's change in position under (c)(5)).

Also, C will usually have no solid assurance in the beginning that the end net result will significantly favor her. On the other hand, the trustee will have a similarly difficult job of establishing a preference in the first instance because she must identify the particular items of property that became collateral during the preference period.

Section 547(c)(5) was designed to strike a fair compromise of the competing interests to collateral in the form of inventory and receivables acquired during the preference period. It protects a floating lien on inventory, receivables, and the proceeds of either kind of collateral to a limited extent that is relatively easy to determine mathematically. Keep in mind that floating liens do not in themselves offend the policies behind preference law. Those policies are offended only when the lien enables the secured party to improve her secured position, i.e., the size of her secured claim, during the preference period. Thus, the goal of (c)(5) is to avoid only improvement "measured in terms of the extent to which any deficiency between the debt and the security existing at the outset of the preference time period is reduced at the time of bankruptcy." [9]

The goal is accomplished in a backhanded manner: First, (c)(5) creates a very broad, general exception to (b) that fully shields a perfected security interest in inventory, receivables, or the proceeds of either kinds of property. Second, (c)(5) immediately cuts back on the exception by denying protection to the extent the secured creditor's secured position is increased during the preference period. The denial is not expressed in these simple terms, however. Rather, in very complicated language (c)(5) creates

> a two-point test, and requires determination of the secured creditor's [security] position 90 days before the petition [or one year in the case of an insider] and on the date of the petition. If new value was first given after 90 days before the case, the date on which it was first given substitutes for the 90-day period.[10]

We reiterate that, if the secured creditor is an insider, the period is one-year before the petition rather than 90 days. In any event, there is an avoidable preference to the extent of the positive difference between the unsecured debt on the former date (one year, 90 days or less, as the case may be) minus the unsecured debt on the latter date (the date of filing). In other words, "[t]he amount by which * * * the excess [of] (debt minus security) is reduced during the ninety-day [or other appropriate] period will be deemed a preference." [11]

The language of (c)(5) itself provides that a transfer is not an avoidable preference

> that creates a perfected security interest in inventory or a receivable or the proceeds of either, except to the extent that the aggregate of all such transfers to the transferee caused a reduction, as of the date of the filing of the petition and to the prejudice of other creditors holding unsecured

---

9. Nimmer, Security Interests in Bankruptcy: An Overview of Section 547 of the Code, 17 Houston L. Rev. 289, 301 (1980).

10. H.R. Rep. No. 595, 95th Cong., 1st Sess. 374, reprinted in 1978 U.S. Code Cong. & Admin. News 5963, 6330; S. Rep. No. 989, 95th Cong., 2d Sess. 88, reprinted in 1978 U.S. Code Cong. & Admin. News 5787, 5874.

11. Orelup, Avoidance of Preferential Transfers Under the Bankruptcy Reform Act of 1978, 65 Iowa L. Rev. 209, 249–50 (1979).

claims, of any amount by which the debt secured by such security interest exceeded the value of all security interests for such debt on the later of—

(A)(i) with respect to a transfer to which subsection (b)(4)(A) of this section applies, 90 days before the date of the filing of the petition; or

(ii) with respect to a transfer to which subsection (b)(4)(B) of this section applies, one year before the date of the filing of the petition; or

(B) the date on which new value was first given under the security agreement creating such security interest.

Everything clear? To help clarify the process, here is a step-by-step approach suggested by the Seventh Circuit in the case, *In re Ebbler Furniture and Appliances, Inc.*[12] This approach can be used in the typical case in which the transferee is not an insider and new value was first given under the security agreement beyond the 90–day preference period.

Step 1. "The first step in applying section 547(c)(5) is to determine the amount of the loan outstanding 90 days prior to filing and the 'value' of the collateral on that day." [13]

Step 2. "The difference between these figures [obtained in Step I] is then computed [by subtracting the value of the collateral from the amount of the loan]." [14]

Step 3. "Next, the same determinations are made as of the date of filing the petition." [Determine the value of the collateral on the date of the petition, determine the amount of the loan then, and subtract the former from the latter.][15]

Step 4. "A comparison is made [of the computations made in Steps II and III] * * *." [16]

Step 5. "[I]f there is a reduction during the 90 day period of the amount by which the initially existing debt exceeded the security [i.e., if the net figure in Step II is more than the net figure in Step III], then a preference for section 547(c)(5) purposes exists [to the extent that a net net positive sum results from subtracting the Step III figure from the Step II figure]." [17]

Step 6. "Of course, if the creditor is fully secured 90 days before the filing of the petition [i.e., the resulting figure in Step II is zero or less], then that creditor will never be subject to a preference attack [because the outcome in Step V could not net a positive sum, which would mean

---

12. 804 F.2d 87 (7th Cir.1986).

13. Id. at 89. Although 90 days before the petition is correct in the typical case, the proper beginning point is one year if the transferee is an insider and less than 90 days if new value was first given under the security agreement sometime after the beginning of the 90–day period.

14. In re Ebbler Furniture and Appliances, Inc., 804 F.2d 87, 89–90 (7th Cir.1986).

15. Id. at 90. Be careful here! Any payments that reduced the loan are themselves potential preferences that are not protected by (c)(5). We discuss the point a little later in this section.

16. Id.

17. Id.

there has been no improvement in the secured position during the preference period]."[18]

Here are a few problems that illustrate the main principles of when and how (c)(5) applies (more or less) in the main: First, suppose that at the time of its bankruptcy petition, D owes C $100,000 and has inventory $60,000. C has a perfected security interest in all of D's inventory. Exactly 90 days before bankruptcy, D owed C $90,000 and had inventory of $70,000. All of D's inventory was acquired within the last 90 days and therefore C's security interest in the inventory is preferential. This security interest is, however, protected by the opening language in section 547(c)(5) which provides that the trustee cannot avoid a preferential transfer of a perfected security interest in inventory or receivables, except to the extent that the creditor's secured position improved during the 90-day period before bankruptcy.

C was undersecured by $20,000 [$90,000 debt minus $70,000 inventory] at the beginning point, i.e., 90 days before D filed for bankruptcy; at the point of bankruptcy C was undersecured by $40,000 [$100,000 in debt minus $60,000 in inventory]. C's secured position worsened rather than improved during the preference period. Thus the "except" part of (c)(5) is not satisfied, and C's perfected security interest in the inventory is fully protected.

Change the facts slightly. Suppose that 90 days prior to D's bankruptcy the debt was $90,000 and the inventory was worth $30,000. At the time of bankruptcy the debt was $100,000 and the inventory was worth $75,000. C's secured position improved by $35,000. Thus, the "except" clause of (c)(5) limits C's security interest in the collateral to $40,000. In the end, therefore, C loses $35,000 in collateral.[19]

Suppose, however, that shortly before bankruptcy the inventory (worth $75,000) had been seized and sold for that amount. This change does not affect the analysis. The application of the $75,000 in proceeds to the secured debt is a preference that, unprotected by an exception in (c), can be recovered from C. Yet, because the proceeds are proceeds of inventory, C's claim to them is protected by (c)(5), except to the extent of the improvement in C's secured position during the preference period.[20] As before, C was undersecured by $60,000 at the beginning of the 90-day period. At the time of D's bankruptcy, C was undersecured by $25,000. Thus, the trustee can recover $35,000 from C if none of the other exceptions in (c) protect the transfer to her. Once again, therefore, C loses $35,000 in collateral.

---

18. Id. See, e.g., Matter of Lackow Bros., Inc., 19 B.R. 601, 604–05 (Bankr. S.D.Fla. 1982), aff'd, 752 F.2d 1529 (11th Cir.1985) (no improvement in position occurs and thus no preference occurs if the creditor was fully secured on both pivotal dates); In re Ken Gardner Ford Sales, Inc., 10 B.R. 632, 644–45 (Bankr. E.D.Tenn.1981), decision aff'd, 23 B.R. 743 (Bankr. D.C.Tenn. 1982) (an improvement in position can occur only if there is an unsecured deficiency 90 days before bankruptcy, and cannot occur if on that date the collateral was worth more than the secured debt); Kaye, Preferences Under the New Bankruptcy Code, 54 Am. Bankr. L. J. 197, 207 (1980) ("A creditor fully secured 90 days prior to bankruptcy will never be subject to preference attack no matter how much he subsequently loans and how much his inventory or receivables collateral increases."); Ross, The Impact of Section 547 of the Bankruptcy Code Upon Secured and Unsecured Creditors. 69 Minn.L.Rev. 39, 59 (1984) (essentially the same).

19. See generally, e.g., In re J.A.S. Markets, Inc., 113 B.R. 193, 199–200 (Bankr. W.D.Pa.1990).

20. See generally, e.g., id. at 200.

Change the facts again so that the collateral was equipment rather than inventory. In this case C's security interest is not protected to any extent by (c)(5). It applies only when the collateral is inventory, receivables, or the proceeds of either kinds of property.

The (c)(5) exception would apply if the collateral were a farmer's crops or livestock because the Bankruptcy Code's definition of "inventory" includes farm products.[21] Indeed, a security interest in farm products that increase in value by natural processes may get unusually good treatment under (c)(5).

Suppose that bank makes a $100,000 loan to a debtor, who is a farmer, for the purpose of producing a crop of corn. The bank acquires a perfected security interest in the crop that attaches as soon as the crop begins to grow. Unfortunately, the debtor is eventually forced to file bankruptcy. At that point the crop has been harvested and is worth $65,000. As late as 90 days earlier, however, the crop was still in the field and had not matured; so its value at the 90-day point was little or nothing. The bank's security interest is protected by the opening part of (c)(5), but the trustee will argue that the "except" clause applies so as to avoid the entire security interest because the bank's secured position has improved $65,000.

Enter now a qualification, albeit small, on the general principle of (c)(5) that an improvement in position is avoidable: An improvement in position is unavoidable that causes no "prejudice of other creditors holding unsecured claims."[22] The meaning and scope of this qualification are not entirely clear. The evidence strongly suggests, however, that its main purpose is

> to reduce from the avoidable excess increases due to appreciated values and not to the debtor's acquisition of fresh inventory or receivables, usually the result of cannibalization of other assets of the debtor to the preference of the secured creditor. [The "prejudice" qualification] was intended to except from the trustee's avoidance powers increases due to such things as *harvesting crops,* transforming work in progress to more valuable completed goods, conversion of inventory into more valuable accounts, and seasonal fluctuations in value.[23]

In short, general creditors are not prejudiced and therefore there is no avoidable improvement in secured position if the collateral grows in value without consuming other assets of the estate.

Thus, because of the requirement that the improvement in position prejudice general creditors, the "except" clause of (c)(5) may not apply to the improvement in C's secured position to the extent it is attributable to the natural appreciation in the value of the collateral as it grew in the field.[24] Thus, to that extent C's security interest in the crops will be protected by the opening part of (c)(5). The same reasoning arguably protects the growth of a security interest in livestock when the herd expands by propagation.[25] The

---

21. 11 U.S.C.A. § 547(a)(1). For further discussion, see text accompanying notes 30–34 infra.

22. 11 U.S.C.A. § 547(c)(5).

23. Young, Preferences Under the Bankruptcy Reform Act of 1978, 54 Am. Bankr. L. J. 221, 234 (1980) (emphasis added).

24. See Practitioner Treatise, Vol. 1.

25. Section 547(c)(5) and this reasoning better explains the result in Fairchild v. Lebanon Prod. Cred. Ass'n, 31 B.R. 789, 794 (Bankr. S.D.Ohio 1983). In the Fairchild case the court held that such an enlarged security interest in cattle was not subject to avoidance

same reasoning also shields improvement in secured position if the value of collateral that is inventory grows as a result of market forces.[26]

The "prejudice" requirement is really a small point, and will not be a factor in the typical case in which (c)(5) may apply. Indeed, the (c)(5) exception raises an almost infinite number of narrow issues that can, in varying circumstances, significantly affect its application. We do not have an infinite amount of space; moreover, very few reported cases deal with (c)(5), suggesting that the exception is practically unimportant[27] or is smoothly applied in practice despite its many theoretical potholes. Therefore, in further discussing (c)(5) we limit ourselves to coloring in only a few of the more universally important details.

First, remember that (c)(5) does not apply to all kinds of transfers. It only protects a transfer that is a "perfected *security interest.*"[28] The term "security interest" generally includes any consensual lien but typically means a perfected Article 9 security interest.[29]

Second, the (c)(5) exception only applies to security interests in *inventory, receivables,* and the *proceeds* of inventory and receivables, and only these kinds of property are the "collateral" that is valued in Step I above. Section 547 itself defines "inventory"[30] and "receivable."[31] Do not use the U.C.C. definitions of these terms, or the definitions of them learned in business law classes. It is especially important to note that, for purposes of section 547, "inventory" includes "farm products such as crops or livestock,"[32] and that "receivables"—though the term certainly includes accounts—is not limited to accounts but includes any earned or unearned right to payment.[33] The

---

under section 547 because no "transfer" occurred and thus there was no preference in the first instance. We disagree with this reasoning, but not the result in the case. We would get to the same place but use the different route of (c)(5).

26. In re Nivens, 22 B.R. 287, 293 (Bankr. N.D.Tex.1982) ("if there is only an increase in value of inventory due to market fluctuations, without an accompanying increase in volume of inventory, there is no avoidable preference") (dicta) (emphasis in original).

27. For the view that section 547(c)(5) is unimportant in light of the actual practices of financers, see Ross, The Impact of Section 547 of the Bankruptcy Code Upon Secured and Unsecured Creditors. 69 Minn.L.Rev. 39 (1984).

28. 11 U.S.C.A. § 547(c)(5) (emphasis added).

29. Each of the kinds of collateral that (c)(5) covers is personal property. The Code defines security interest as "lien created by an agreement." 11 U.S.C.A. § 101(51). All consensual liens on personal property are governed by U.C.C. Article 9, U.C.C. § 9–102(1), except those liens expressly excluded. U.C.C. § 9–104.

Section 547(c)(5) has no application to liens created by law, such as a lien of garnishment on a debtor's wages. In re Larson, 21 B.R. 264, 266 (Bankr. D. Utah 1982).

30. " '[I]nventory' means personal property leased or furnished, held for sale or lease, or to be furnished under a contract for service, raw materials, work in process, or materials used or consumed in a business, including farm products such as crops or livestock, held for sale or lease." 11 U.S.C.A. § 547(a)(1).

31. " '[R]eceivable' means right to payment, whether or not such right has been earned by performance * * *." 11 U.S.C.A. § 547(a)(3).

32. 11 U.S.C.A. § 547(a)(1).

33. 11 U.S.C.A. § 547(a)(3). Thus a right to payment that is not an account under the U.C.C., such as a general intangible, chattel paper or an instrument, see U.C.C. §§ 9–105(1)(i) & 9–106, would nevertheless be a receivable for purposes of section 547. But see Matter of Fitterer Engineering Associates, Inc., 27 B.R. 878, 881 (Bankr. E.D.Mich.1983) (Congress intended the definition of receivable to conform to the U.C.C.'s definition of account) (dicta); Matter of Jefferson Mortg. Co., Inc., 25 B.R. 963, 967 (Bankr. D.N.J.1982) (equates receivables with accounts so that (c)(5) is inapplicable to a right to payment (tax refund) in the form of a general intangible) (dicta).

definition of "proceeds" is presumably the same as the U.C.C. definition.[34]

Third, even if the transfer involves a security interest in inventory, receivables, or the proceeds of either, (c)(5) does not apply if the security interest is unperfected.[35] The exception is triggered only if the transfer is effected by a "*perfected* security interest"[36] in such collateral.

Fourth, in no event does (c)(5) protect a payment simply because the debt was secured by a perfected security interest in accounts or other receivables. The exception itself only applies to perfected security interests, i.e., consensual liens, in that kind of collateral. It applies to payments only when the payments consist of proceeds of inventory or receivables that is collateral subject to an unavoidable, perfected security interest. Of course, payments may be protected otherwise, and will not even constitute a preference if the transferee is fully secured.[37]

Assume a case in which the debt is $100,000 and the collateral is worth $70,000 90 days prior to bankruptcy. Within 90 days the debtor first acquires $10,000 of new collateral, procures additional loans of $10,000 and subsequently makes a $10,000 payment. At the end of the period, therefore, debtor will owe $100,000 and the collateral will be worth $80,000. If one simply compares the gap at 90 days ($30,000) with the gap at the date of the petition ($20,000), there would be a preference of only $10,000 by a combination of 547(b) and (c)(5); yet that understates the case for there has really been a total of $20,000 in preferences here. The payment, $10,000 (here not saved by (c)(4)), may well constitute a preference and is not saved by (c)(5) which applies only to after-acquired property. This amount of preference, added to the $10,000 of after-acquired property which is also a preference by (b) and (c)(5), yields $20,000. Sometimes courts are not as careful as they should be in distinguishing between preferences that arise because of after-acquired property (that may be protected under (c)(5)) and preferences that arise because of payments within the 90 days (that are never saved by (c)(5)).

Fifth, (c)(5) may not cover every transfer that involves a perfected security interest in inventory, receivables or their proceeds. Consider, for example, this problem: D is indebted to C on an unsecured note that was executed years ago. Within 90 days of D filing bankruptcy, she gives C a security interest in her inventory and receivables. The purpose of this transfer is to secure D's note to C. C perfects the security interest 30 days after the parties created it. D files bankruptcy.

The transfer of the security interest to C is undoubtedly a preference under section 547(b). C argues, however, that the transfer is protected by section 547(c)(5): her security interest is perfected and the collateral is accounts and receivables; thus, the interest is avoidable only to the extent of the improvement in her secured position during the 90 days before D's filing.

C's argument is supported by the literal language of (c)(5) but nevertheless fails if the scope of the exception is purposively limited to floating liens.

---

34. The U.C.C. defines "proceeds" as "whatever is received upon the sale, exchange, collection or other disposition of collateral or proceeds." U.C.C. § 9–306(1).

35. In re Slater, 54 B.R. 186, 188–89 (Bankr. D.S.D.1985); In re Furniture Discount Stores, Inc., 11 B.R. 5, 7 (Bankr. N.D.Tex. 1980).

36. 11 U.S.C.A. § 547(c)(5) (emphasis added).

37. There is no preferential effect as required by section 547(b)(5). See § 6–20 supra.

In the case *In re Auto–Train Corp.*[38] the court opined that the purpose of (c)(5) is "to protect creditors with a security interest in 'a floating mass' whose composition and value inevitably fluctuates during the 90–day period." The court held that satisfying this underlying purpose of (c)(5) is a prerequisite to the application of the exception. It does not apply if the collateral is an unchanging collection of rights to payment even though the value of the collateral varies during the preference period. The district court in *Auto–Train* further limited the exception's scope by agreeing with the bankruptcy judge that (c)(5) only applies "to a creditor who receives additional collateral [during the preference period] by virtue of a perfected security interest in inventory or accounts receivable [that is perfected beyond the preference period]."[39] Other cases similarly suggest that (c)(5) is so limited to floating liens.[40]

Not everyone agrees with this limitation on the scope of (c)(5). The court in *In re American Ambulance Service, Inc.*[41] flatly rejected the view that (c)(5) is confined to floating liens perfected outside the preference period. In *American Ambulance*, the bank advanced $35,000 to the debtor on October 1, 1982. On the same day the debtor granted the bank a security interest in all of the debtor's inventory and receivables, but the interest was not perfected until 40 days later on November 10. Thus, the transfer of the security interest did not occur, for section 547 purposes, until then.[42] The debtor filed bankruptcy a month later on December 9, 1982.

The transfer was obviously a preference under section 547(b), and the bank relied on (c)(5) as a defense. The main question was whether (c)(5) was even applicable to these facts, inasmuch as the bank's interest was unlike a floating lien. The collateral was not additional collateral that the bank had acquired pursuant to an after-acquired property clause in a security agreement that was originally perfected outside the preference period. The court expressly disagreed with the notion that (c)(5) was limited to floating liens. The court specifically held that (c)(5) applies, if the collateral is inventory or accounts, provided the security interest is perfected before bankruptcy is filed. In such a case (c)(5) applies without regard to when the security interest is perfected and despite a long delay, even exceeding 10 days, in perfecting the interest.[43]

The literal language of (c)(5) supports the holding in *American Ambulance*. Moreover, the language that Congress actually used speaks most loudly and persuasively about congressional intent.

38. 49 B.R. 605 (D. D.C. 1985).

39. Id. at 612.

40. Matter of Val Decker Packing Co., 61 B.R. 831, 839 (Bankr. S.D.Ohio 1986) (finds (c)(5) inapplicable "[s]ince the creditor did not have a floating lien"); In re Phillips, 24 B.R. 712, 715 (Bankr. E.D.Cal.1982) ("This section is directed to floating liens that have been perfected outside the ninety day to one year avoiding period of 547(b) so as to limit the amount of security that they can encumber and not the instant situation of a transfer that occurs when a security interest is perfected within the voidable preference period.").

The opinion in In re Bourgeois, 58 B.R. 657 (Bankr. W.D.La.1986), reports that (c)(5) does not apply to long-term trade debt, id. at 660, but the report is probably a typographical error or a misprint. The sense of the opinion is that the court was actually referring to the scope of section 547(c)(2), which is also the section dealt with in the cases cited in Bourgeois.

41. 46 B.R. 658 (Bankr. S.D.Cal.1985).

42. See 11 U.S.C.A. § 547(e)(2)(B).

43. 46 B.R. at 660–61.

Sixth, whenever (c)(5) applies, the trustee bears the burden of proving an improvement of the secured party's position.[44] Presumably, if the trustee fails in this regard, the opening portion of (c)(5) shields the transfer from avoidance as a preference to the extent that the secured party has established that the transfer involves a perfected security interest in accounts, receivables, or the proceeds of such collateral.

Seventh, the test used in valuing the collateral is critically important in determining the occurrence and size of any improvement of the creditor's secured position. For instance, in determining the debt-to-collateral ratio at the point 90 days before the petition (or other applicable beginning point), the trustee will argue for using a measure that puts the smallest value on the collateral at the beginning of the 90–day period (such as liquidation value). The creditor wants the opposite: a measure that put the highest value on the property (such as face value of receivables or retail value of inventory). As the value increases the size of the unsecured portion of the debt decreases until the creditor is fully secured. If the creditor was fully secured at the beginning point, no improvement of position could have occurred as of the time of the bankruptcy petition irrespective of the ratio of debt to collateral at that latter point. The creditor and trustee will swap approaches in measuring the collateral's value as of the date when bankruptcy was filed.

The developing general rule is that, in valuing collateral for (c)(5) purposes, there is no standard measure. Rather, though always from the creditor's perspective,[45] "value should be defined on a case by case basis"[46] so that the assessment is "particularized, individualized."[47] Consistent with this rule, different measures of value have been approved in different cases, including the cost of inventory,[48] the wholesale value of inventory,[49] the liquidation value of inventory,[50] and the ongoing concern value of inventory.[51] This flexible test of value also accommodates different measures of the value of receivables. They need not be measured at face value.[52] Professor Neil Cohen has argued that whenever receivables have actually been disposed of or collected, the test used to value the collateral should match the

---

44. In re 4–S Corp., 69 B.R. 499, 502 (Bankr. W.D.Mo.1987); In re American Ambulance Service, Inc., 46 B.R. 658, 660 (Bankr. S.D.Cal.1985); In re Beattie, 31 B.R. 703, 714 (Bankr. W.D.N.C.1983); Fairchild v. Lebanon Prod. Cred. Ass'n, 31 B.R. 789, 794 (Bankr. S.D.Ohio 1983) (debtor in possession) (dicta); Matter of Fitterer Engineering Associates, Inc., 27 B.R. 878, 882 (Bankr. E.D.Mich.1983) (debtor in possession); In re Music House, Inc., 11 B.R. 139, 140 (Bankr. D.Vt.1980); but see In re Auto–Train Corp., 49 B.R. 605, 612 (D. D.C. 1985) (creditor has the burden of establishing no improvement) (dicta).

45. Matter of Clark Pipe and Supply Co., Inc., 893 F.2d 693, 698 (5th Cir.1990), reh'g denied, 899 F.2d 11 (5th Cir.1990).

46. In re Ebbler Furniture and Appliances, Inc., 804 F.2d 87, 91 (7th Cir.1986).

47. Matter of Missionary Baptist Found. of America, Inc., 796 F.2d 752, 761 (5th Cir.1986), on remand, 69 B.R. 540 (Bankr. N.D.Tex.1987); accord, In re Ebbler Furniture and Appliances, Inc., 804 F.2d 87, 91 (7th Cir.1986); In re Joe Flynn Rare Coins, Inc., 81 B.R. 1009, 1018–21 (Bankr. D.Kan.1988).

48. In re Ebbler Furniture and Appliances, Inc., 804 F.2d 87, 91 (7th Cir.1986).

49. In re Joe Flynn Rare Coins, Inc., 81 B.R. 1009, 1018–21 (Bankr. D.Kan.1988).

50. Matter of Clark Pipe & Supply Co., Inc., 893 F.2d 693, 697–98 (5th Cir.1989), reh'g denied, 899 F.2d 11 (5th Cir.1990).

51. Matter of Lackow Bros., Inc., 752 F.2d 1529, 1531–33 (11th Cir.1985).

52. Matter of Missionary Baptist Found. of America, Inc., 796 F.2d 752, 761 (5th Cir.1986), on remand, 69 B.R. 540 (Bankr. N.D.Tex.1987).

manner of actual disposition.[53]

Eighth, regardless of how value is measured when determining improvement in secured position, compare only the net secured positions at the two pivotal points: the time the petition was filed and, usually, 90 days before then. Unlike section 547(c)(4) (the subsequent value rule), section (c)(5) is effectively a true net result rule. For (c)(5) purposes, give no attention to payments made during the preference period. The "proper approach" disregards "fluctuations in the [size of the] account throughout the preference period. The difference between the balances on those two dates is the amount of the transfer to be avoided." [54]

§ 6–36 Statutory Liens, Section 547(c)(6)

Special policy and technical problems are posed by a kind of nonconsensual lien known as a "statutory lien," which essentially means a "lien arising solely by force of a statute on specified circumstances or conditions" [1] apart from an agreement or judicial action. Because of these special problems with statutory liens, Congress decided to deal separately with them in a provision dedicated exclusively to describing the circumstances under which the trustee can avoid such liens. It is section 545.[2] Because of this special, comprehensive treatment of statutory liens, preference law need not concern itself with them. Thus, section 547(c)(6) exempts from preference attack any preference "that is the fixing of a statutory lien that is not avoidable under section 545 of this title." In other words, a statutory lien that is safe from avoidance by the trustee under section 545 is safe from avoidance as a preference.[3]

Suppose, for example, that D underpaid her federal income taxes. A deficiency was assessed against her but D refuses to pay it. The result is that, solely by force of federal statutory law, a lien in favor of the United

---

53. Cohen, "Value" Judgments: Accounts Receivable Financing and Voidable Preferences Under the New Bankruptcy Code, 66 Minn.L.Rev. 639, 664 (1982).

54. In re Savig, 50 B.R. 1003, 1009 (D.Minn.1985); see also Nimmer, Security Interests in Bankruptcy: An Overview of Section 547 of the Code, 17 Hous. L. Rev. 289, 301 (1980) (the timing of any transfers and any advances within the relevant period is immaterial).

§ 6–36

1. 11 U.S.C.A. § 101(53).

2. It provides:

The trustee may avoid the fixing of a statutory lien on property of the debtor to the extent that such lien—

(1) first becomes effective against the debtor—

(A) when a case under this title concerning the debtor is commenced;

(B) when an insolvency proceeding other than under this title concerning the debtor is commenced;

(C) when a custodian is appointed or authorized to take possession;

(D) when the debtor becomes insolvent;

(E) when the debtor's financial condition fails to meet a specified standard; or

(F) at the time of an execution against property of the debtor levied at the instance of an entity other than the holder of such statutory lien;

(2) is not perfected or enforceable at the time of the commencement of the case against a bona fide purchaser that purchases such property at the time of the commencement of the case, whether or not such a purchaser exists;

(3) is for rent; or

(4) is a lien of distress for rent.

11 U.S.C.A. § 545. We discuss the scope and application of this provision at § 6–62 infra.

3. See Practitioner Treatise, Vol. 1.

States arises and attaches to all of D's property.[4] Some months later the United States filed locally for the purpose of establishing priority of its lien over the claims of certain third persons.[5] Within 90 days after the federal tax lien was filed, D filed bankruptcy. She has been insolvent for months.

The federal tax lien will follow D's property into bankruptcy. It is, however, a transfer that is deemed to have occurred, for preference purposes, upon filing the lien.[6] Thus, the lien is a classic section 547(b) preference, but it is not avoidable thereunder because the federal tax lien is also a classic statutory lien that is not avoidable under section 545. Because section 545 does not avoid the lien, section 547(c)(6) immunizes the lien from preference attack.[7]

Like any other exception to section 547(b), (c)(6) applies only if its requirements are met, and the courts have strictly construed them. To win (c)(6) protection the transfer must be (1) the "fixing" of (2) a "statutory lien" that (3) is "not avoidable under section 545."

A lien is a statutory lien only if it arises automatically and solely by force of law without judicial action of any kind.[8] Examples are mechanics' and materialmen's liens, warehousemen's liens, and tax liens.[9] A lien that is obtained by judgment, levy or the like involving some legal or equitable process or judicial action is a judicial lien [10] rather than a statutory lien. The two categories of liens are mutually exclusive. A judicial lien, such as a judgment or garnishment lien, is therefore not protected by (c)(6) and is subject to preference attack if no other exception applies.[11]

Moreover, only statutory liens that are unavoidable under section 545 qualify for (c)(6) immunity. A transfer that matches a section 545 description of an avoidable statutory lien is doubly vulnerable. The lien can, of course, be avoided under 545; and, for the very reason that the lien is not unavoidable under section 545, it is not saved from preference attack by section 547(c)(6).[12]

Finally, the section 547(c)(6) exception immunizes only the "*fixing*" of a statutory lien that is unavoidable under section 545. It is not clear that the voluntary payment or involuntary satisfaction of such a lien is "fixing" within the scope and protection of (c)(6). Suppose, for example, that D hires a general contractor, GC, to construct a building on land owned by D. GC is regularly paid as the improvement progresses, but GC failed to pay SC, the plumbing subcontractor. Under local statutory law SC acquires, solely by force of law, a lien on the building and the land where it rests. Typically, the lien's effectiveness, at least as against third persons, is conditioned on public filing within a certain time period after the lienor supplies the materials or services that are the basis of her claim; but the lien usually

---

4. 26 U.S.C.A. § 6321.

5. See id. § 6323(a) (purchasers, holders of security interests, mechanic's lienors, and judgment lien creditors).

6. See 11 U.S.C.A. § 547(e)(2).

7. See Practitioner Treatise, Vol. 1.

8. See 11 U.S.C.A. § 101(53).

9. H.R. Rep. No. 595, 95th Cong., 1st Sess. 314, reprinted in 1978 U.S. Code Cong. & Admin. News 5963, 6271; S. Rep. No. 989, 95th Cong., 2d Sess. 27, reprinted in 1978 U.S. Code Cong. & Admin. News 5787, 5813.

10. 11 U.S.C.A. § 101(36).

11. See Practitioner Treatise, Vol. 1.

12. See Practitioner Treatise, Vol. 1.

arises in the first instance without filing and never requires, for its existence, court approval or other judicial action.

This lien is typically referred to as a mechanics', materialmen's or construction lien. A supplier in whose favor the lien arises can enforce it by having D's property sold if the supplier's claim is not timely paid. In many states D cannot defend on the basis that GC breached the construction contract with D by not paying suppliers. In effect, therefore, D can be required to pay twice for SC's plumbing work in the building.

Suppose that D cannot raise the money to pay SC. GC is liable to D for the misused contract proceeds, but GC has filed bankruptcy. D decides to file bankruptcy herself because she is completely broke. SC's construction lien against D's property is a transfer that is deemed to have occurred when the lien was filed.[13] As it happens, SC filed her lien within 90 days before D filed bankruptcy. The lien survives D's filing, is unavoidable under section 545 because it is a statutory lien not avoidable thereunder, and is safe from preference attack due to section 546(c)(6). SC will therefore be paid, notwithstanding D's bankruptcy, to the extent that the collateral has value exceeding the worth of prior claims.

Change the facts slightly. Suppose that D managed to find sufficient funds to pay SC just before she collapsed into bankruptcy. Is this payment recoverable as a preference? Some courts would decide that, because the payment satisfied a lien protected by (c)(6), the payment itself is also protected by (c)(6).[14] Other courts would decide that (c)(6) does not protect the payment because the exception protects only the fixing, not the satisfaction, of a statutory lien.[15]

Yet, if SC's claim was fully secured by the collateral, the payment to her is not avoidable under section 547 because the payment was not a preference. The reason is the lack of a preferential effect: payment of a claim that is fully secured by an unavoidable lien is not preferential because the payment did not enable the creditor to receive more than she would receive in a Chapter 7 liquidation of D's estate.[16] This rule generally applies to payment of statutory liens.[17]

Be careful here! This rule cannot properly be applied willy nilly to the payment of a federal tax lien because the rule assumes that the lienor's claim could be completely satisfied from the collateral had the debtor filed a Chapter 7 case. Complete satisfaction would occur in the typical case in which the lienor's claim is fully secured by a state statutory lien because no one else would share in the proceeds ahead of the lienor. The United States, however, though fully secured by an unavoidable federal tax lien, must share the proceeds of its collateral in a Chapter 7 case. Several classes of claims, including administrative expenses, must be satisfied before the tax lien is paid.[18] Thus, when a federal tax lien is paid voluntarily or involuntarily during the preference period, the transfer is vulnerable under section 547(b) if the payment results in the government having received more than

---

13. 11 U.S.C.A. § 547(e)(2).
14. See Practitioner Treatise, Vol. 1.
15. See Practitioner Treatise, Vol. 1.
16. See 11 U.S.C.A. § 547(b)(5), and discussion at § 6–20 supra.
17. See Practitioner Treatise, Vol. 1.
18. 11 U.S.C.A. §§ 507 & 724(b).

it would have received in a Chapter 7 liquidation from the proceeds of the tax lien collateral after satisfaction of priority claims.[19]

Also be careful to note that here we have focused only on the relationship between section 545 and section 547. We discuss the substance of 545 itself elsewhere.[20]

§ 6–37 Small Transfers in Consumer Cases, Section 547(c)(7)

In 1984 Congress added a seventh exception to section 547(b). The exception, section 547(c)(7), is narrow in scope but wide in application. It applies only to "a case filed by an individual debtor whose debts are primarily consumer debts,"[1] but it exempts from preference attack *any transfer* that is less than $600.[2] Thus, as long as the dollar limitation is not exceeded, (c)(7) shields the entire range of transfers that a consumer debtor can make, including payments of money; consensual security interests[3] affecting any kind of property; and involuntary transfers of every kind such as a transfer pursuant to a garnishment lien.[4]

Perhaps the most important question about the application of (c)(7) is whether the exception applies to any extent when the challenged transfer exceeded $600. This question was answered by the court in *In re Vickery*.[5] In this case the debtor made a payment of $957.45 in satisfaction of a past-due account at a clothing store. The creditor argued that (c)(7) protected the payment up to $599.99 and that the trustee could recover only the excess of $357.46. The court disagreed, concluding that any transfer of $600 or more is completely and entirely beyond the protection of (c)(7). The exception does not protect the first $599.99 of any consumer transfer; rather, it only protects a consumer transfer that is $599.99 or less. "[T]he court believes this kind of cut-off point is exactly what Congress had in mind"[6] because the purpose of (c)(7) is "to stop recoveries by bankruptcy trustees of small installment payments made in the ninety days before bankruptcy."[7]

Because this purpose is behind (c)(7), the court in *Vickery* projected that the exception would not only protect payments of $500 each to three different creditors; (c)(7) will also protect "several payments, each less than $600, to the same creditor during the preference period."[8] This projection is probably accurate and is supported by the literal terms of the exception. Plainly read, (c)(7) applies anew to every discrete payment or other transfer and, as to each of them, is reached only when "the aggregate value of all property that constitutes or is affected by such *transfer*" is $600 or more.

---

19. See Practitioner Treatise, Vol. 1.
20. See § 6–62 infra.

§ 6–37
1. 11 U.S.C.A. § 547(c)(7).
2. The actual language is that a transfer is protected "if * * * the aggregate value of all property that constitutes or is affected by such transfer is less than $600." 11 U.S.C.A. § 547(c)(7).
3. See Practitioner Treatise, Vol. 1.
4. See Practitioner Treatise, Vol. 1.
5. 63 B.R. 222 (Bankr. E.D.Tenn.1986).

6. Id. at 223; accord, In re Via, 107 B.R. 91, 95 (Bankr. W.D.Va.1989).
7. Id.
8. Id. at 224; see also In re Irvine, 95 B.R. 464, 465 (Bankr. W.D.Ky.1988) (debtor's wages garnished six times within the preference period by three different creditors, and the transfer to each creditor was less than $600); compare In re Lewis, 116 B.R. 54 (Bankr. D.Md.1990) (exception did not apply where total of creditor's continuing garnishment against the same employer exceeded $600).

Clearly, the limit is not triggered by aggregating the value of all transfers to a creditor. In sum, therefore, the (c)(7) exception is "unlimited as to the total amount of preferential payments that are protected so long as each is less than $600."[9]

Remember, however, that (c)(7) is limited to consumer cases. The exception is available only "in a case filed by an individual debtor whose debts are primarily consumer debts."[10] "Consumer debt" means "debt incurred by an individual primarily for a personal, family or household purpose."[11] It is not clear whether "primarily" is judged in terms of the total number or dollar amount of consumer debts in relation to all of the debtor's obligations. In the case *McDaniel v. Nationwide*,[12] the court assumed that the proper test was dollar amount,[13] and also concluded that, in applying the test, consumer debt secured by property, including real estate, is counted [14] because the term "consumer debt" generally means liability on any right to payment whether the liability is secured or unsecured.[15]

Interestingly, although (c)(7) is available only in consumer cases, the exception is apparently not limited to transfers for or on account of consumer debts. In a case in which (c)(7) applies, i.e., the case of an individual owing primarily consumer debts, the exception shields any transfer of less than $600 without regard to purpose of the transfer. Thus, small transfers, or a series of them, for business purposes would be protected.

B. SETOFF, SECTION 553

§ 6–38 Overview: The Meaning of Setoff and Its Significance in Bankruptcy, Section 553

Section 553 [1] is entitled "Setoff" and its purpose is, generally, "to preserve the [nonbankruptcy] right of setoff in bankruptcy cases * * *."[2] Under nonbankruptcy law, setoff is essentially the extinguishment of *unrelated* cross-demands between parties indebted to each other.[3] It occurs in litigation when the plaintiff and defendant both successfully complain and counterclaim for damages. Each litigant does not recover money from the other. Rather, the party with the larger award recovers an amount reduced by the sum she owes the other party. This form of setoff derives from the

---

9. In re Vickery, 63 B.R. 222, 224 (Bankr. E.D.Tenn.1986). The court added, and correctly so, that it is irrelevant whether or not the debt was incurred or paid in the ordinary course of the debtor's financial affairs. Id.

10. 11 U.S.C.A. § 547(c)(7).

11. 11 U.S.C.A. § 101(8).

12. 85 B.R. 69 (Bankr. N.D.Ill. 1988).

13. Id. at 70.

14. Id. at 70–71.

15. See 11 U.S.C.A. § 101(8), (12) & (5)(A); In re Kelly, 841 F.2d 908, 912 (9th Cir.1988) (a debt secured by real property is not excluded from the meaning of "consumer debt").

§ 6–38

1. 11 U.S.C.A. § 553.

2. H.R. Rep. No. 595, 95th Cong., 1st Sess. 377, reprinted in 1978 U.S. Code Cong. & Admin. News 5963, 6333; S. Rep. No. 989, 95th Cong., 2d Sess. 91, reprinted in 1978 U.S. Cong. & Admin. News 5787, 5877.

3. By "unrelated" we mean that the opposing demands arose from different transactions. The extinguishment of related cross-demands, i.e., mutual obligations arising from the same transaction, is governed by the separate doctrine of recoupment. This distinction is especially significant in bankruptcy. Section 553 applies only to setoff and limits it. Generally speaking, recoupment is not affected by bankruptcy, and the limitations of section 553 limitations do not apply to it. See discussion at § 6–45 infra.

Roman law of *compensatio*[4] and is sometimes a statutory procedure.

Another form of setoff is equitable setoff which works as a creditor's remedy. It occurs extra-judicially between two parties who are mutually indebted, i.e., each of them is both a creditor and debtor of the other party. It works very simply: one of the parties determines that her obligation to the other person is offset. This debt is thereby reduced by the amount the other person owes her.

The remedy of equitable setoff is most commonly used by banks to satisfy loans made to people who are depositors as well as borrowers. As a depositor the borrower is a creditor of the bank to the extent of the balance in the deposit account.[5] The bank is therefore both creditor and debtor of the borrower, and the borrower also wears both hats as to the bank. The two parties are mutually indebted. Setoff thus allows the bank to apply the borrower's deposit account to reduce the borrower's obligation to the bank.[6]

Equitable setoff exists as decisional law and its availability, incidents, and limitations are mostly prescribed by the same law. Only a very few states significantly regulate equitable setoff by statute. Generally, the remedy is available only with respect to mature debts, which mainly means debts that are due.[7] Thus, a bank can set off its borrower's account only upon the borrower's default on the debt she owes the bank. In some states, however, setoff is available to a bank upon a borrower-depositor's insolvency, even though the borrower's debt to the bank has not yet matured.[8]

There are not many restrictions on equitable setoff, even as a bank's remedy. The major restrictions, as applied to banks, are three: First, a bank can set off only a borrower's general deposits. Special deposits are immune to setoff.[9] Second, a bank cannot knowingly set off the funds of a third party even though the funds are mingled in a debtor's general deposit account.[10] Finally, setoff traditionally requires mutuality of obligation between the bank and the borrower-depositor, that is, both of them must be indebted to each other in the same capacity or right. The borrower must stand in exactly the same relation to the bank as depositor and as debtor.[11]

Significantly, setoff by a bank does not require the borrower's consent,[12] and the bank is not required to notify the borrower before effecting the setoff.[13] There are no constitutional problems because setoff does not involve state action and thus does not trigger due process protection.[14]

The use of setoff as a remedy by creditors other than banks is occasionally confirmed or established by statute, mainly when the creditor is government. A familiar example is the federal law that allows the United States to set off tax refunds against taxpayers' federally guaranteed student loans.[15]

4. Dunn, Banker's Lien and Equitable Setoff: Constitutional and Policy Considerations for Protecting Bank Customers, 27 Stan. L.Rev. 1149, 1152 (1975).
5. See Practitioner Treatise, Vol. 1.
6. See Practitioner Treatise, Vol. 1.
7. See Practitioner Treatise, Vol. 1.
8. See Practitioner Treatise, Vol. 1.
9. See Practitioner Treatise, Vol. 1.
10. See Practitioner Treatise, Vol. 1.
11. See Practitioner Treatise, Vol. 1.
12. See Practitioner Treatise, Vol. 1.
13. See Practitioner Treatise, Vol. 1.
14. See Practitioner Treatise, Vol. 1.
15. See Practitioner Treatise, Vol. 1.

There are other federal setoffs,[16] and many states have similar laws allowing various state obligations to be offset against debts owed the state.[17]

So much for setoff as a judicial procedure and a creditor's remedy. Now consider the intersection of setoff and bankruptcy law, and the significance of section 553 preserving the right of setoff in bankruptcy.

Suppose that bank is owed $50,000 on a unsecured loan made to borrower who maintains a checking account with bank. Borrower defaults on the loan, and the bank sets off borrower's account, which contains $50,000, in compliance with the state created right of setoff. The borrower files bankruptcy the next day.

If the setoff is avoided in bankruptcy, the bank will be required to pay $50,000 to the estate and will have a $50,000 unsecured claim. Very little of this claim will be paid if the borrower's bankruptcy is typical. The bank is thus a big loser. The bank is a big winner, however, if the setoff is unaffected by the bankruptcy. In this event, the bank will keep the $50,000 in full satisfaction of its claim.

The bank's setoff satisfies all of the requirements of a preference under section 547(b), but the setoff cannot be avoided as a preference *if* it is within the scope of section 553. The validity or avoidability of a setoff is determined exclusively by section 553 and is immune from all of the trustee's other avoiding powers, including section 547. The relationship between sections 547 on preferences and 553 on setoffs is clear: " 'When Section 553 is determined to be applicable, Section 547 cannot hereafter be utilized to undo its effect.' " [18]

The issue of the bank's right to set off the debtor's account might arise in another way that also implicates section 553. Suppose that the bank did not have time to effect the setoff before the debtor filed bankruptcy. The automatic stay now prevents the bank from acting unilaterally to offset the debtor's account.[19] Thus, the bank seeks relief from the stay to effect the setoff, and the trustee responds by resisting the relief and seeking a turnover of the funds in the debtor's account pursuant to section 542(b), which requires an entity owing a debt that is property of the estate to pay such debt to the trustee.[20]

The bank will prevail against the trustee. It will be permitted to make the setoff postpetition if its right of setoff is protected by section 553.[21] The obligation under section 542 to pay the account to the estate does not apply to the bank to the extent that the account may be offset under section 553.[22] Moreover, the trustee's strong-arm powers under section 544(a), which arise upon bankruptcy, are powerless against a setoff protected by section 553.[23] Once again, the bank is a big winner *if* it enjoys a right of setoff that is within the protection of section 553.

1. Bankruptcy's Substantive Effect on Right of Setoff

16. See Practitioner Treatise, Vol. 1.
17. See Practitioner Treatise, Vol. 1.
18. In re Lott, 79 B.R. 869, 870 (Bankr. W.D.Mo.1987), quoting In re Brooks Farms, 70 B.R. 368, 372 (Bankr. E.D.Wis.1987).
19. 11 U.S.C.A. § 362(a)(7).
20. 11 U.S.C.A. § 542(b).
21. See Practitioner Treatise, Vol. 1.
22. See Practitioner Treatise, Vol. 1.
23. See Practitioner Treatise, Vol. 1.

§ 6–39 General Rule of Section 553

Section 553 exclusively determines the validity or avoidability of setoff in bankruptcy. The core rule of the section is that nothing in the Bankruptcy Code affects:

> any right of a creditor to offset a mutual debt owing by such creditor to the debtor that arose before the commencement of the case * * * against a claim of such creditor against the debtor that arose before the commencement of the case, except to the extent [provided herein] * * *.[1]

In other words, as a general rule, bankruptcy does *not* affect a creditor's right of setoff so long as the setoff satisfies the criteria described in section 553(a).

This rule of section 553 applies to setoffs exercised by banks against deposit accounts,[2] but is not so limited. It applies to any creditor who enjoys a right, under nonbankruptcy law, to offset a mutual debt she owes the debtor. For example, section 553 allows:

- a person who traded goods with the debtor to set off sums she owes debtor against amounts the debtor owes her;[3]
- a financial institution which traded securities with the debtor to set off the value of securities it owes the debtor against the value of securities debtor owes the financial institution under repurchase agreements;[4]
- a seller who owes sales commissions to debtor to set them off against price of purchases debtor had made from seller;[5]
- a trucking company to offset funds collected upon deliveries for the debtor against the cost of services rendered by the company for the debtor;[6]
- a lawyer to offset her fee against funds of the client-debtor representing the debtor's recovery of attorney's fees awarded in litigation successfully prosecuted by the lawyer;[7]
- creditor to set off her liability to the debtor (for costs, damages, and attorney's fees) for having filed in bad faith an involuntary bankruptcy petition against the debtor;[8]
- a debtor's claim against creditor for freight damage to be offset against creditor's claim for freight charges;[9]
- a state agency to offset any amount due to the agency against any amount owing by the agency to same person or entity;[10]
- the state to set off income tax refund against debtor's child support obligation which had been assigned to the state;[11]

§ 6–39

1. 11 U.S.C.A. § 553(a).
2. See Practitioner Treatise, Vol. 1.
3. See Practitioner Treatise, Vol. 1.
4. See Practitioner Treatise, Vol. 1.
5. See Practitioner Treatise, Vol. 1.
6. See Practitioner Treatise, Vol. 1.
7. See Practitioner Treatise, Vol. 1.
8. See Practitioner Treatise, Vol. 1.
9. See Practitioner Treatise, Vol. 1.
10. See Practitioner Treatise, Vol. 1.
11. See Practitioner Treatise, Vol. 1.

- a real property tenant to set off prepetition claims against prepetition rentals;[12]
- a landlord to set off a tenant's security deposit against the landlord's claim for prepetition rent;[13]
- a contractor to offset contract retainage funds in satisfaction of claim for debtor's breach and rejection of subcontract;[14]
- the United States to set off federal farm benefits and entitlements against debtor-farmer's debt to United States;[15]
- the government to set off a federal income tax refund against a defaulted student loan obligation;[16]
- the United States to setoff account owed debtor against taxes the debtor owed;[17]
- a state to do the same for local taxes even though the mutual debts involve different state agencies;[18]
- the IRS to setoff a tax refund against taxes owed;[19]
- the IRS to offset prepetition tax overpayments against unpaid prepetition tax obligations;[20]
- a bank to offset its liability to debtor for wrongful foreclosure against debtor's obligation to bank;[21]
- a bank to set off its obligation to fund loan balance against debtor's obligation to repay funds already advanced;[22]
- a probate estate to offset bequests made to the debtor against debts owed by the debtor to the decedent;[23]
- a surety to offset the amount it paid on debtor's obligation against surety's liability on note to debtor;[24]
- account obligor of debtor to offset account that debtor owed to person who assigned account to obligor five months before debtor's bankruptcy;[25]
- obligor on note to debtor to offset obligor's claim against debtor arising out of avoidance of bulk sale to obligor;[26]
- maker of note on which debtor was payee to set off against maker's liability on note the debtor's obligation for the price of goods the debtor had purchased on credit from the maker;[27]
- public utility to set off refund for electric service against debtor's electric service bills;[28]

12. See Practitioner Treatise, Vol. 1.
13. See Practitioner Treatise, Vol. 1.
14. See Practitioner Treatise, Vol. 1.
15. See Practitioner Treatise, Vol. 1.
16. See Practitioner Treatise, Vol. 1.
17. See Practitioner Treatise, Vol. 1.
18. See Practitioner Treatise, Vol. 1.
19. See Practitioner Treatise, Vol. 1.
20. See Practitioner Treatise, Vol. 1.
21. See Practitioner Treatise, Vol. 1.
22. See Practitioner Treatise, Vol. 1.
23. See Practitioner Treatise, Vol. 1.
24. See Practitioner Treatise, Vol. 1.
25. See Practitioner Treatise, Vol. 1.
26. See Practitioner Treatise, Vol. 1.
27. See Practitioner Treatise, Vol. 1.
28. See Practitioner Treatise, Vol. 1.

- partner of the debtor to set off the partner's claim for indemnification upon satisfying the partnership's indebtedness against the debtor's claim against the partner on a note for money loaned to him by the debtor;[29]
- an officer of the corporate debtor to offset her claims for wages, expense reimbursements, etc. against the debtor's cross-demands for breach of contract, money had and received, and money lent;[30]
- debtor's former employer, a stockbroker, to set off debtor's deferred compensation account against debtor's obligations to employer based on deficit in debtor's own margin account;[31]
- wife to offset alimony due her and proceeds of one-half interest in note and mortgage she owned with debtor-husband against her obligation to husband for certain expenses for which she was liable to him as co-owner of real property;[32]
- judgment debtor to offset the bankruptcy debtor's obligation to her.[33]

The general rule of section 553 means that a setoff exercised before bankruptcy cannot ordinarily be avoided. As a consequence the obligation owed the debtor, which was satisfied through setoff before bankruptcy, cannot be collected for the benefit of the estate.[34] Additionally, if the debtor paid her obligation to the creditor instead of the creditor setting it off against the creditor's obligation to the debtor, the payment cannot be avoided as a preference or otherwise recovered.[35] In effect, "setoff constitutes an affirmative defense to the trustee's preference action * * *."[36]

The rule also means that if a right to setoff has not been exercised before bankruptcy, the right to make the setoff survives and can be enforced despite the bankruptcy, subject to certain procedural limitations imposed by the automatic stay.[37] The creditor can do so by asserting the right affirmatively (usually by seeking relief from the stay) or raising it defensively (usually as a response to a turnover action).[38]

In effect, the Code treats a creditor's right of setoff as a form of collateral or security so that the creditor's claim against the debtor is treated like a secured claim.[39] Just as a perfected Article 9 security interest in property or a recorded mortgage is generally enforceable against the debtor and her bankruptcy estate, so too is a right of setoff to the extent of the debt that the creditor owes the debtor. This is true notwithstanding that the effect of the setoff is to give the creditor preferential treatment.

§ 6–40 Requirements of the General Rule

For full text of this section, see Epstein, Nickles & White, Bankruptcy, Practitioner Treatise Series, Vol. 1.

29. See Practitioner Treatise, Vol. 1.
30. See Practitioner Treatise, Vol. 1.
31. See Practitioner Treatise, Vol. 1.
32. See Practitioner Treatise, Vol. 1.
33. See Practitioner Treatise, Vol. 1.
34. See Practitioner Treatise, Vol. 1.
35. See Practitioner Treatise, Vol. 1.

36. In re Woker, 120 B.R. 454, 458 (Bankr. S.D.Ill.1990).

37. See 11 U.S.C.A. § 362(a)(7) (stay blocks unilateral setoff), and § 6–43 infra.

38. See Practitioner Treatise, Vol. 1.

39. See Practitioner Treatise, Vol. 1.

a. Existence of Substantive Right

b. Both Debts Prepetition

c. Mutuality

2. Substantive Exceptions to the General Rule

§ 6–41 Statutory

For full text of this section, see Epstein, Nickles & White, Bankruptcy, Practitioner Treatise Series, Vol. 1.

§ 6–42 Equitable

For full text of this section, see Epstein, Nickles & White, Bankruptcy, Practitioner Treatise Series, Vol. 1.

3. Bankruptcy's Procedural Effect on Exercise of Section 553 Setoff

§ 6–43 Automatic Stay

For full text of this section, see Epstein, Nickles & White, Bankruptcy, Practitioner Treatise Series, Vol. 1.

§ 6–44 Waiver

For full text of this section, see Epstein, Nickles & White, Bankruptcy, Practitioner Treatise Series, Vol. 1.

4. Recoupment

§ 6–45 Recoupment

For full text of this section, see Epstein, Nickles & White, Bankruptcy, Practitioner Treatise Series, Vol. 1.

C. FRAUDULENT TRANSFERS

§ 6–46 Introduction to Fraudulent Transfers

Rather than see their property seized by creditors, debtors sometimes transfer their property to friends or relatives for little or no consideration or with the understanding that the debtor shall continue to have the use and benefit of the property. Since Roman law, such attempts to defraud creditors have been ineffective. The source of modern fraudulent transfer law is the Statute of 13 Elizabeth, chapter 5, enacted by Parliament in 1570. This law condemned any conveyance of property made with the intent "to delay, hinder or defraud" creditors. As interpreted and applied, the Statute of 13 Elizabeth, and its more modern counterparts, render fraudulent transfers voidable by creditors of the debtor.

American jurisdictions either recognized the Statute of 13 Elizabeth as part of inherited common law or enacted identical or very similar versions of it. More recently, about one-half of the states adopted the Uniform Fraudulent Conveyance Act.[1] Very recently, a successor to the UFCA was promulgated by the National Conference of Commissioners on Uniform State Laws. The new model statute is entitled the Uniform Fraudulent Transfer Act.[2] For the most part, the two uniform laws are very similar.

Like the Statute of 13 Elizabeth, both the UFCA and the UFTA condemn transfers of property that are *actually fraudulent,* meaning that the debtor makes the transfer with the actual, subjective intention of defrauding, hindering or delaying her creditors.[3] The two uniform statutes go much further, however, and render certain transfers of a debtor's property ineffective against creditors without regard to the debtor's actual subjective intention.[4] This latter class of conveyances, which are *constructively fraudulent,* describes circumstances under which the law deems that a transfer of the debtor's property is unfair to her creditors and is ineffective as to them, irrespective of the debtor's intention in making the transfer, solely because certain circumstances existed at the time of the transfer.

A version of the UFCA has long been part of the federal bankruptcy laws and presently appears as section 548 of the Bankruptcy Code.[5] Like similar state laws, section 548 condemns, as a matter of federal law, transfers that the debtor made with actual intent to defraud creditors[6] and certain other transfers that are deemed to be constructively fraudulent.[7] A closely-related avoiding power is section 544(b),[8] which allows a trustee to invoke state fraudulent conveyance law to avoid a transfer. Section 544(b) is useful when the letter of the state law, or judicial interpretations of it, condemn a wider range of transfers than section 548.

The purpose of fraudulent conveyance law, whatever its form, is simple: it protects a debtor's unsecured creditors from unfair reductions in the debtor's estate to which they look, generally, for their security. Presumably, as a result of this protection, the creditors "need not monitor debtors so closely, and the savings in monitoring costs make businesses more productive."[9]

§ 6–46

1. Uniform Fraudulent Conveyances Act (withdrawn 1984). This model law, hereinafter referred to as the UFCA, was promulgated in 1918. It was withdrawn in 1984 by the National Conference of Commissioners on Uniform State Laws in favor of a new successor law of fraudulent transfers.

2. Uniform Fraudulent Transfer Act (1984). This law, which was promulgated in 1984, is hereinafter referred to as the UFTA.

3. See UFCA § 7; UFTA § 4(a)(1).

4. See UFCA §§ 4, 5, 6 & 8; UFTA §§ 4(a)(2) & 5.

5. 11 U.S.C.A. § 548.

6. Id. § 548(a)(1).

7. Id. § 548(a)(2) & (b).

8. 11 U.S.C.A. § 544(b).

9. Bonded Financial Services v. European American Bank, 838 F.2d 890, 892 (7th Cir. 1988). In this case the Seventh Circuit also helpfully noted the difference between fraudulent and preferential transfers:

The fraudulent conveyance must be distinguished from a preferential transfer to a creditor, which does not diminish the total payoff for the group, but which may be undone to reduce the incentive individual creditors have to rush to dismember the debtor before rival creditors can do so. The collective bankruptcy proceeding solves the common pool problem, which otherwise may produce a reduction in the value of the productive assets taken jointly.

Id.

1. Transfers Fraudulent Under Bankruptcy Law, Section 548

§ 6–47 Introduction to Section 548

Section 548 of the Bankruptcy Code [1] empowers the trustee to avoid a transfer of the debtor's property, or any obligation incurred by her, that was fraudulently made or incurred on or within one year before the filing of the bankruptcy petition. Section 548 itself, as a matter of federal law, defines in its subsections (a) and (b) when a transfer or obligation is fraudulently made or incurred. The first and most obvious is when the debtor made the transfer or incurred the obligation with actual fraudulent intent, that is, she acted

> with actual intent to hinder, delay, or defraud any entity to which the debtor was or became, on or after the date such transfer was made or such obligation incurred, indebted * * *.[2]

Section 548 also describes four instances of constructive fraud, that is, four situations in which a transfer or obligation is deemed to have been fraudulently made or incurred irrespective of the debtor's intention. The first three such situations are when a transfer was made for less than reasonably equivalent value and the debtor (1) was or thereby became insolvent;[3] (2) was engaged in business with an unreasonably small capital;[4] or (3) intended to incur debts that would be beyond her ability to pay.[5] The fourth constructively fraudulently situation is any transfer of partnership property to a partner in the debtor if the debtor was or thereby became insolvent.[6]

Certain requirements are common to both kinds of fraudulent transfers under section 548. First, a transfer must have occurred [7] involving property of the debtor.[8] Second, the transfer must have been made, directly or indirectly, by the debtor herself.[9] Finally, the transfer must have occurred within the one-year period preceding bankruptcy.[10]

Significantly, for purposes of section 548, a transfer that must be perfected under local law in order to be valid against a bona fide purchaser is deemed not to have been made until the necessary steps for perfection have been taken.[11] If those steps are not taken before the debtor's bankruptcy the transfer is deemed to have occurred immediately before the date of the bankruptcy petition.[12] Suppose, for example, that the debtor transfers part of her real property under circumstances that render the transfer fraudulent under section 548. Local law provides that no conveyance of real estate is effective against a bona fide purchaser unless and until the conveyance is recorded. Therefore, for purposes of section 548, the timing of the transfer is not determined on the basis of when it was effective between the debtor and transferee. Rather, the timing is determined according to when the transfer was recorded.[13] So, if the transfer was actually made 18

---

§ 6–47
1. 11 U.S.C.A. § 548.
2. Id. § 548(a)(1).
3. Id. § 548(a)(2)(A) & (B)(i).
4. Id. § 548(a)(2)(A) & (B)(ii).
5. Id. § 548(a)(2)(A) & (B)(iii).
6. See Practitioner Treatise, Vol. 2.
7. See Practitioner Treatise, Vol. 2.
8. See Practitioner Treatise, Vol. 2.
9. See Practitioner Treatise, Vol. 2.
10. See Practitioner Treatise, Vol. 2.
11. 11 U.S.C.A. § 548(d)(1).
12. Id.
13. See Practitioner Treatise, Vol. 2.

months before the debtor's bankruptcy, but was not recorded until 11 months before then, the transfer is deemed to have occurred within the one-year period preceding bankruptcy and is therefore avoidable under section 548.

Each kind of fraud—actual and constructive—involves other peculiar requirements. We thus segregate the two kinds of fraudulent transfers and separately discuss their unique components. Thereafter we describe certain transfers that raise unusual problems when the law of fraudulent transfers is applied to them. Finally, we briefly cover the trustee's remedies upon avoiding a transfer under section 548 and the major defenses that are available to a transferee of a fraudulent transfer.

§ 6–48 Actual Fraud

Section 548(a)(1) empowers the trustee to avoid a transfer that the debtor made "with actual intent to hinder, delay or defraud" any creditor to whom the debtor was or became obligated at the time the transfer was made or thereafter.[1] Direct evidence of the requisite intent is rarely available. People seldom admit their fraudulent intent. It would therefore seem that the trustee could almost never avoid a transfer under section 548(a)(1) because she bears the burden of proving actually fraudulent intention[2] which is established by direct proof, i.e., an admission, only in the most extraordinary case.[3] Moreover, the standard of proof that the trustee must satisfy under section 548(a)(1) is "clear and convincing."[4]

The trustee's burden in proving actual fraud is significantly lightened, however, by two evidentiary twists in her favor. First, direct evidence of actual fraudulent intent is unnecessary. Rather, circumstantial evidence will suffice. As is repeatedly explained by the courts:

> "The finding of the requisite intent may be predicated upon the occurrence of facts which, while not direct evidence of actual intent, lead to the irresistible conclusion that the transferor's conduct was motivated by such intent."[5]

Indeed, the courts have recognized that certain facts commonly circumstantially imply actual fraud and have labeled these facts "badges of fraud." The badges of fraud that are universally recognized by the courts, including courts deciding section 548(a)(1) cases, have been collected in the new Uniform Fraudulent Transfer Act which would codify the tell-tale facts and make them part of state statutory law:

(1) the transfer * * * was to an insider;

(2) the debtor retained possession or control of the property transferred after the transfer;

(3) the transfer * * * was disclosed or concealed;

(4) before the transfer was made * * *, the debtor had been sued or threatened with suit;

§ 6–48

1. 11 U.S.C.A. § 548(a)(1). Having this intention even as a secondary purpose is sufficient for purposes of section 548(a)(1). Matter of Davenport, 64 B.R. 411, 415 (Bankr. M.D.Fla.1986).

2. See Practitioner Treatise, Vol. 2.

3. See Practitioner Treatise, Vol. 2.

4. See Practitioner Treatise, Vol. 2.

5. In re Bridge, 90 B.R. 839, 845 (Bankr. E.D.Mich.1988), on reh'g, 106 B.R. 474 (Bankr. E.D.Mich. 1989).

(5) the transfer was of substantially all of the debtor's assets;

(6) the debtor absconded;

(7) the debtor removed or concealed assets;

(8) the value of the consideration received by the debtor was [not] reasonably equivalent to the value of the asset transferred * * *;

(9) the debtor was insolvent or became insolvent shortly after the transfer was made * * *;

(10) the transfer occurred shortly before or shortly after a substantial debt was incurred; and

(11) the debtor transferred the essential assets of the business to a lienor who transferred the assets to an insider of the debtor.[6]

The courts have identified other badges of actual fraud under section 548(a)(1) and state fraudulent transfer law.[7] Even under the UFTA this list is exemplary only, not exclusive. The point is that actual fraud is usually and often proved indirectly by the trustee using proof of circumstances accompanying and surrounding the transfer, like the badges of fraud listed above, that collectively imply the required intent.[8]

No single badge of fraud, not even a badge included in the UFTA's authoritative list, conclusively establishes, in and by itself, actual intent to defraud. Rather, it is the combined force of multiple badges of fraud that tilts the balance of the evidence so that it preponderates in the trustee's favor. As the courts in Florida often state:

> Each of the * * * badges of fraud has evidentiary force in establishing the fraudulent character of a transfer. Although the badges of fraud may not be conclusive to establish fraud when considered separately, if they exist in combination, they "may by their number and joint consideration be sufficient to constitute conclusive proof" of fraud.[9]

A second evidentiary twist that helps the trustee establish actual fraud is that the occurrence of certain combinations of badges of fraud creates a presumption of fraudulent intent. The burden of proof (the burden of going forward with the evidence if not the burden of persuasion) then shifts to the transferee to establish the lack of such intent;[10] and, if the transferee fails to rebut the presumption, the trustee prevails on the intent issue.

The courts most often recognize such a presumption when an individual debtor transfers property to a natural relative for little, inadequate or no consideration.[11] Similarly, a presumption of actual fraud can arise when an

---

6. UFTA § 4(b). Trustees have already used this very list as authority for the badges of fraud that should indicate actual intent to defraud under section 548(a)(1). See In re Brantz, 106 B.R. 62, 67 (Bankr. E.D.Pa. 1989); In re Pinto Trucking Services, Inc., 93 B.R. 379, 386 (Bankr. E.D.Pa. 1988); In re BGNX, Inc., 75 B.R. 44 (Bankr. S.D.Fla.1987).

7. See Practitioner Treatise, Vol. 2.

8. See Practitioner Treatise, Vol. 2.

9. In re Kranich, 53 B.R. 821, 823 (Bankr. M.D.Fla.1985), quoting Florida Nat'l Bank v. Sherouse, 80 Fla. 405, 405, 86 So. 279, 279 (1920); see also Max Sugarman Funeral Home, Inc. v. A.D.B. Investors, 926 F.2d 1248, 1254–55 (1st Cir. 1991) ("The presence of a single badge of fraud may spur mere suspicion; the confluence of several can constitute conclusive evidence of an actual intent to defraud, absent 'significantly clear' evidence of a legitimate supervening purpose.").

10. See Practitioner Treatise, Vol. 2.

11. See Practitioner Treatise, Vol. 2.

inequivalent transfer occurs between related companies that are controlled by the same person.[12] Indeed, the obvious policy behind the presumption would seem to trigger it whenever any debtor receives less than equivalent value from a transfer to any insider. In any event, the courts always give closer than usual scrutiny to transfers between related persons, especially where the relationship is personally, organizationally, or financially close.

Section 548(a)(1) literally gives the trustee three bites at the apple, that is, she succeeds if she proves any of three intentions: to hinder, to delay, or to defraud. "An intent to hinder or delay is condemned equally with an intent to defraud, i.e., an intent not to pay creditors at all." [13] It is arguable, however, "that in order to constitute a fraudulent conveyance as contemplated by § 548(a)(1) the 'intent to hinder or delay' must also be [or involve] 'fraudulent intent.'" [14] In no event, however, is a debtor guilty of hindering or delaying a creditor, within the meaning of section 548(a)(2), when the creditor claimed to have been harmed is the very creditor to whom the transfer was made, and the theory is that the transfer (for security or in payment) caused the creditor to forbear making collection efforts.[15]

Showing that the debtor acted with malice is not necessary.[16] It is also unnecessary to prove that the debtor's motive was wrongful, inasmuch as a debtor can be guilty of effecting an actually fraudulent transfer even though she acted in good faith and in the firm belief that her conduct would ultimately benefit her creditors.[17] The real issue would therefore appear to be whether, irrespective of design and motivation, the actual effect of the conduct was to hinder, delay or defraud the debtor's creditors.

Proof of culpability on the transferee's part is also unnecessary to the avoidance of a transfer under section 548(a)(1). The intention to hinder, delay or defraud creditors is only required of the debtor-transferor, not of the transferee.[18] This fraudulent intention at the time of the transfer on the part of the debtor, or on the part of someone whose intention is attributable to the debtor,[19] is sufficient *in itself* to satisfy section 548(a)(1). There is no requirement of proof that the debtor was insolvent when the transfer was made.[20] It is no defense that the debtor received equivalent value for the transfer [21] or that she was solvent when the transfer was made,[22] although these facts would argue against a finding of wrongful intent in the first instance.

In contrast, the debtor's receipt of equivalent value for the transfer or her solvency at the time of the transfer is a defense to the avoidance in the usual case where the trustee relies on section 548(a)(2).[23] The reason is that, under section 548(a)(2), the combination of inequivalency of value and insolvency is typically the sole reason in itself for avoiding a transfer.

---

12. See Practitioner Treatise, Vol. 2.

13. Matter of Life Science Church of River Park, 34 B.R. 529, 534 (Bankr. N.D.Ind. 1983). See also In re Checkmate Stereo & Electronics, Ltd., 9 B.R. 585, 613–14 (Bankr. E.D.N.Y. 1981), aff'd, 21 B.R. 402 (E.D.N.Y. 1982) (intent to delay is separately sufficient).

14. In re Missionary Baptist Foundation of America, 24 B.R. 973, 977 (Bankr. W.D.Tex. 1982).

15. See Practitioner Treatise, Vol. 2.

16. See Practitioner Treatise, Vol. 2.

17. See Practitioner Treatise, Vol. 2.

18. See Practitioner Treatise, Vol. 2.

19. See Practitioner Treatise, Vol. 2.

20. See Practitioner Treatise, Vol. 2.

21. See Practitioner Treatise, Vol. 2.

22. See Practitioner Treatise, Vol. 2.

23. 11 U.S.C.A. § 548(a)(2)(A)-(B).

Actual fraudulent intent is not required. The fraud is implied by law rather than inferred from facts, that is, the fraud is *constructive* only.

§ 6–49 Constructive Fraud

Section 548 empowers a trustee to avoid certain transfers as fraudulent without requiring her to prove that the transfers were made with actual intent to defraud creditors.[1] A transfer that is avoidable as fraudulent without proof of actual fraud is labelled *constructively fraudulent*. Section 548 describes in subsections (a)(2) and (b) transfers that are avoidable due to constructive fraud:

(a) The trustee may avoid any transfer of an interest of the debtor in property, or any obligation incurred by the debtor, that was made or incurred on or within one year before the date of the filing of the petition, if the debtor voluntarily or involuntarily—

* * *

(2)(A) received less than a reasonably equivalent value in exchange for such transfer or obligation; and

(B)(i) was insolvent on the date that such transfer was made or such obligation was incurred, or became insolvent as a result of such transfer or obligation;

(ii) was engaged in business or a transaction, or was about to engage in a business or a transaction, for which any property remaining with the debtor was an unreasonably small capital; or

(iii) intended to incur, or believed that the debtor would incur, debts that would be beyond the debtor's ability to pay as such debts matured.

(b) The trustee of a partnership debtor may avoid any transfer of an interest of the debtor in property, or any obligation incurred by the debtor, that was made or incurred on or within one year before the date of the filing of the petition, to a general partner in the debtor, if the debtor was insolvent on the date such transfer was made or such obligation was incurred, or became insolvent as a result of such transfer or obligation.[2]

These subsections detailing constructive fraud share two requirements with subsection 548(a)(1) on actual fraud: (1) a transfer of property of the debtor (2) within the one-year period before bankruptcy.[3] Here the similarity ends.

Constructive fraud under section 548(a)(2) or (b) requires no actual intend to hinder, delay or defraud creditors. Instead, there is a requirement concerning the debtor's financial condition at the time, or as a result of, the

---

§ 6–49

1. See 11 U.S.C.A. § 548(a)(2) & (b); Stratton v. Equitable Bank, 104 B.R. 713, 727 (D.Md.1989), aff'd, 912 F.2d 464 (4th Cir. 1990) ("Even if actual intent to defraud creditors is absent pursuant to § 548(a)(1), a transfer may be deemed constructively fraudulent pursuant to § 548(a)(2).").

2. Id.

3. See Practitioner Treatise, Vol. 2.

transfer. Subsection (b) requires actual legal insolvency;[4] subsection (a)(2) alternatively requires actual legal insolvency,[5] subjective equitable insolvency,[6] or undercapitalization.[7] In practice, when a transfer is avoided on the basis of subsection (a)(2), the financial condition requirement is almost always satisfied by proof of actual insolvency. Only rarely is subjective insolvency or undercapitalization relied on.[8]

There is an additional requirement for constructive fraud under (a)(2): the debtor must have "received less than a reasonably equivalent value in exchange for such transfer or obligation."[9] This requirement must be satisfied to establish that any transfer is constructively fraudulent, except a transfer by a partnership debtor to a general partner. In this exceptional case, which is governed by subsection (b), constructive fraud can occur notwithstanding that equivalent value was exchanged.[10]

In practice, however, trustees almost never rely on section 548(b) in arguing constructive fraud. They routinely rely on section 548(a)(2), which has been described as allowing the recovery of "the assets of a bankruptcy estate from recent transferees who took more than their due;"[11] and trustees usually attempt to satisfy the requirements of (a)(2) by establishing that (1) the debtor was insolvent when the transfer was made or became insolvent as a result of it, and (2) she received less than reasonably equivalent value in exchange for the transfer. If both of these requirements are established, a transfer of the debtor's property within one year of bankruptcy is avoidable under section 548 without proof of actual intent to defraud [12] or anything else. Thus, virtually every reported case decided under section 548(a)(2) focuses in large part on the two critical issues of the debtor's solvency or insolvency about the time of the transfer and the value she received for the transfer. We adopt the same focus here.

We note preliminarily that in seeking to avoid a transfer under section 548(a)(2) due to constructive fraud, the trustee or other person challenging the transfer bears the burden of proof on all of the necessary elements, including the debtor's insolvency and the inequivalency of value.[13] The standard of proof, however, is not "clear and convincing" as when the basis of avoidance is actual fraud;[14] rather, in a constructive fraud case, the standard is preponderance of the evidence.[15] Moreover, the burden of going forward with the evidence may shift to the defendant upon the trustee establishing a prima facie case.[16] Also, in a few constructive fraud cases the

---

4. 11 U.S.C.A. § 548(b) ("if the debtor was insolvent on the date such transfer was made or such obligation was incurred, or became insolvent as a result of such transfer or obligation").

5. 11 U.S.C.A. § 548(2)(B)(i) ("insolvent on the date that such transfer was made or such obligation was incurred, or became insolvent as a result of such transfer or obligation").

6. Id. § 548(a)(2)(B)(iii) ("intended to incur, or believed that the debtor would incur, debts that would be beyond the debtor's ability to pay as such debts matured").

7. Id. § 548(a)(2)(B)(ii) ("was engaged in business or a transaction, or was about to engage in business or a transaction, for which any property remaining with the debtor was an unreasonably small capital").

8. See Practitioner Treatise, Vol. 2.

9. 11 U.S.C.A. § 548(a)(2)(A).

10. Id. § 548(b).

11. In re Rosenberg, 69 B.R. 3 (Bankr. E.D.N.Y.1986).

12. See Practitioner Treatise, Vol. 2.

13. See Practitioner Treatise, Vol. 2.

14. See Practitioner Treatise, Vol. 2.

15. See Practitioner Treatise, Vol. 2.

16. See Practitioner Treatise, Vol. 2.

courts have recognized presumptions (as is common in litigation involving actual fraud [17]) whereby certain facts, while failing in themselves to establish insolvency or inequivalency, nevertheless establish a prima facie case and shift the burden of proof to the defendant to establish the opposite.[18]

A standard definition of "insolvent" runs throughout the Code,[19] so that the meaning of the term "insolvency" for purposes of section 548(a)(2) is generally the same as its meaning in section 547 on preferences.[20] A person or other entity, except a partnership, is insolvent when

> the sum of such entity's debts is greater than all of such entity's property, at a fair evaluation, exclusive of
>
>> (i) property transferred, concealed, or removed with intent to hinder, delay, or defraud such entity's creditors; and
>>
>> (ii) property that may be exempted from property of the estate under section 522 * * *.[21]

This definition creates a standard balance sheet test for determining solvency [22] which, the courts are fond of saying, focuses on "the fair market value of the debtor's assets and liabilities within a reasonable time of the [challenged] transfer." [23]

The suggestion is somewhat misleading that proof of insolvency around the time of the transfer—within a reasonable time of it—is sufficient for purposes of section 548(a)(2). The section requires, and the trustee must prove as a fact, that the debtor was insolvent at the precise time of the transfer [24] or as a result of it.[25] Moreover, the presumption of insolvency during the 90-day period before filing that applies in preference actions under section 547 [26] does not apply under section 548.[27]

On the other hand, the trustee is not required to produce direct proof that the debtor was insolvent on the very day, hour and minute of the transfer. She can satisfy her burden of proof as to insolvency through the process of *retrojection*, i.e., showing that the debtor was insolvent a reasonable time before or after the transfer and that the debtor's financial condition did not materially change during the intervening period.[28] This evidence will create an inference of the debtor's insolvency at the time of the

---

17. See Practitioner Treatise, Vol. 2.
18. See Practitioner Treatise, Vol. 2.
19. 11 U.S.C.A. § 101(32).
20. See § 6–18 supra. Incorporate here what is written there about insolvency. Note, however, that while the trustee benefits from a presumption under section 547 that the debtor was insolvent during the 90-day period before the petition, 11 U.S.C.A. § 547(f), the trustee gets no such break under section 548. This latter provision creates no presumption of insolvency during any period of time. The trustee thus always bears the burden of proof on insolvency no matter when the challenged transfer took place.
21. Id. § 101(32)(A). For the definition of insolvency with respect to a partnership, see id. § 101(32)(B).
22. See Practitioner Treatise, Vol. 2.
23. In re Ohio Corrugating Co., 91 B.R. 430, 436 (Bankr. N.D.Ohio 1988); In re Ipswich Bituminous Concrete Products, Inc., 79 B.R. 511, 516 (Bankr. D. Mass. 1987); see also, e.g., In re Dugue Rodriguez, 75 B.R. 829, 831 (Bankr. S.D.Fla.1987) (for purposes of section 548, "fair valuation" is indistinguishable from "fair market value"). It is typically fair value on a going-concern basis rather than a liquidation basis. Moody v. Security Pacific Business Credit, Inc.,127 B.R. 958, 995 (W.D.Pa. 1991).
24. See Practitioner Treatise, Vol. 2.
25. See Practitioner Treatise, Vol. 2.
26. See Practitioner Treatise, Vol. 2.
27. See Practitioner Treatise, Vol. 2.
28. See Practitioner Treatise, Vol. 2.

transfer that will support a factual finding for the trustee on the insolvency requirement of section 548(a)(2).

In practice, however, proving insolvency is not nearly so difficult for the trustee as establishing that the debtor received "less than reasonably equivalent value."[29] This latter requirement not only causes hard problems of proof, but it also involves tough legal issues that essentially test the purposes and policies behind the law of fraudulent transfers. No other issue that arises under section 548 is more often litigated in the courts and discussed by the commentators than the meaning and application of the concept "reasonably equivalent value."

In deciding whether something that the debtor received in exchange for a transfer is "reasonably equivalent value," the first step is to determine whether the debtor got "value" and, if so, then to compare the worth of the value the debtor received to the property that she transferred or the obligation she incurred in exchange therefor. Section 548 defines "value" to mean

> property, or satisfaction or securing of a present or antecedent debt of the debtor, but does not include an unperformed promise to furnish support to the debtor or to a relative of the debtor.[30]

A debtor most obviously receives value when she transfers her property, absolutely or as security, in contemporaneous exchange for goods, real estate, a loan of money, or other property.[31] The meaning of value is not so limited, however.

Value also includes paying or securing a preexisting debt,[32] and in this regard value is broader than common-law consideration.[33] Thus, a debtor receives value in satisfying an antecedent claim [34] (as by paying an overdue account or an outstanding loan or by transferring property to vindicate a preexisting interest in it) or in providing collateral for a previously unsecured creditor.[35] It makes no difference that the debtor got nothing new, in terms of property added to her estate, at the time of the transfer.

The further meaning of value is surprisingly uncertain and confused, even on the seemingly basic issue whether the term includes an executory promise. Courts in several cases have opined that the Code's definition of value leaves "no room for a mere executory promise from the transferee as constituting that value."[36] Yet, the only executory promise that the defini-

---

29. 11 U.S.C.A. § 548(a)(2)(A).

30. See Practitioner Treatise, Vol. 2.

31. See Practitioner Treatise, Vol. 2.

32. 11 U.S.C.A. § 548(d)(2)(A); In re United Energy Corp., 102 B.R. 757, 761–63 (Bankr. 9th Cir.1989), decision aff'd, 944 F.2d 589 (9th Cir.1991) (damages claim against debtor operating Ponzi scheme was antecedent debt that was reduced or satisfied by debtor's payments to investors so that payments were made for value); Matter of Cavalier Homes of Georgia, Inc., 102 B.R. 878, 885–86 (Bankr. M.D.Ga. 1989) (satisfying preexisting contingent liability as guarantor). For cases in which the value consisted of securing an antecedent debt, see, e.g., In re Countdown of Connecticut, Inc., 115 B.R. 18, 21–22 (Bankr. D.Conn. 1990); In re 550 Les Mouches Fashions, Ltd., 24 B.R. 509 (Bankr. S.D.N.Y. 1982); Butz v. Pingel, 17 B.R. 236 (Bankr. S.D.Ohio 1982).

33. See Restatement (Second) of Contracts § 73 (1981) (performance of legal duty not consideration).

34. See Practitioner Treatise, Vol. 2.

35. See Practitioner Treatise, Vol. 2.

36. In re Wallace, 66 B.R. 834, 844 (Bankr. E.D.Mo.1986); see also Matter of Kaczorowski, 87 B.R. 1, 3 (Bankr. D.Conn.1988), citing Gray v. Snyder, 704 F.2d 709, 711 (4th Cir. 1983) (" '[R]easonably equivalent value under § 548 excludes future consideration, at least to the

tion explicitly excludes from the meaning of value is such a promise "to furnish support to the debtor or to a relative of the debtor."[37] The strong negative implication of this exclusion is that any other kind of enforceable executory promise is value for purposes of section 548.[38] Moreover, the "property" component of the definition of value is surely wide enough to reach executory promises.

Yet, neither an executory promise nor anything else is value unless it is economically beneficial to the debtor.[39] The explanation for this implicit requirement of "economic benefit," which is not a component of common-law contract consideration, is that the purpose of fraudulent conveyance law is to protect the debtor's unsecured creditors by preserving the value of the debtor's estate to which they must look for satisfaction of their claims. Thus, for purposes of section 548, there is no value in the making of a gift[40] or in the receipt of love and affection or the promise of same.[41]

On the other hand, the requirement of economic benefit to the debtor does not demand consideration that replaces the transferred property with money or something else tangible or leviable that can be sold to satisfy the debtor's creditors' claims. That the meaning of value is not so limited is made clear by the definition's explicit coverage of transfers that satisfy or secure an antecedent debt.[42] The courts have made clear that value also includes other kinds of intangible consideration that economically benefits the debtor without returning a leviable asset to her estate. Common examples are services that the debtor buys[43] and the consideration she gets in exchange for a transfer that settles a disputed claim or releases her from future obligations.[44]

The debtor nevertheless benefits economically by satisfying antecedent debts, paying for services (viewed as paying an antecedent debt for services), obtaining waivers of claims against her and the like: *her liability is reduced.* If the meaning of economic benefit is to account for such intangible consideration, it must therefore include either adding property to the debtor's estate *or* reducing the debtor's liability. This definition of economic benefit suggests that the purpose of fraudulent conveyance law is, precisely, to preserve the net worth of the debtor's estate rather than to preserve the value of the estate, i.e., the value of the collection of property that comprises it (or the value of the assets side of the balance sheet).

This wider definition of economic benefit, and corresponding reduction in the purpose of fraudulent conveyance law, makes sense in bankruptcy where creditors are dealt with collectively. Unpaid creditors generally, as a group, are not harmed by the debtor having paid antecedent debts and having otherwise reduced claims against her because, although she gets no

extent not actually performed.'"); In re Butcher, 72 B.R. 447, 450 (Bankr. E.D.Tenn. 1987) (promise to perform legal services is outside the scope of value which excludes future consideration); In re Total Acquisition Corp., 29 B.R. 836, 840 (Bankr. S.D. Fla.1983) (implies that promissory note and other executory promises not themselves value, but are value only to the extent that the promises they represent are performed).

37. 11 U.S.C.A. § 548(d)(2)(A).

38. See Practitioner Treatise, Vol. 2.

39. See Practitioner Treatise, Vol. 2.

40. See Practitioner Treatise, Vol. 2.

41. See Practitioner Treatise, Vol. 2.

42. 11 U.S.C.A. § 548(d)(2)(A).

43. See Practitioner Treatise, Vol. 2.

44. See Practitioner Treatise, Vol. 2.

leviable asset in return, the number of claimants sharing in the estate is reduced. The net effect on them is zero in terms of the percentage of their claims that will be satisfied.[45]

You can readily see that expanding the definition of value is a means of narrowing the reach of fraudulent conveyance law, and whether the law enjoys a narrow or wide scope depends ultimately upon the purposes and policies behind it. These underlying purposes and policies have been the subject of great debate recently as the courts and commentators have struggled to decide whether fraudulent conveyance law, with its ancient origins, properly applies to modern financing devices such as leveraged buyouts and intra-corporate guaranties. Later in these materials we deal separately with these devices and concentrate on the special problems involved in applying fraudulent conveyance law to them.

The essential problem, however, is not especially new or peculiar to modern, sophisticated financing methods. It arises whenever there is a *triangular transaction* in which the debtor makes a transfer or incurs an obligation to someone else that directly benefits a third person. While this typically happens in a LBO or as part of an intra-corporate up-, down- or cross-stream guaranty, it is also commonplace in simple, vintage kinds of transactions in which one person pays or provides collateral for another person's debt. There are well-established rules of fraudulent conveyance law that apply in these transactions to decide the value issue.

The first rule is entirely consistent with the traditional notion that value requires economic benefit to the debtor: *Value is completely lacking if the debtor makes a transfer or incurs an obligation for or on account of someone else and the debtor herself receives nothing of economic benefit in exchange.*[46] This would be the case, for example, if an individual paid or secured the debt of her penniless, jobless child for which only the child had theretofore been liable; or if a company gratuitously paid or secured the personal debts of its officers or employees.[47] Common-law contract consideration would be present in either case,[48] but not value within the meaning of section 548. In this respect, as in requiring economic benefit for the transfer, value is more demanding that consideration.

The second rule is a rather large qualification on the first rule: *Even though the debtor makes a transfer, or incurs an obligation, for consideration that moves (in form or substance) directly to a third person, the debtor nevertheless receives value if she receives an economic benefit* **indirectly**[49] *(in form or substance).* The consideration need not flow directly to her to satisfy the value component of reasonably equivalent value. Value requires only that the transfer result, whether directly or indirectly, in economic benefit to her. For example, the debtor gets value (though not necessarily reasonably equivalent value) as an indirect beneficiary of economic benefit running directly to someone else where:

    a. The other person was merely a conduit for the consideration so that

---

45. See Practitioner Treatise, Vol. 2.
46. See Practitioner Treatise, Vol. 2.
47. See Practitioner Treatise, Vol. 2.
48. See Practitioner Treatise, Vol. 2.
49. See Practitioner Treatise, Vol. 2.

the direct benefit really passed, albeit circuitously, to the debtor;[50]

b. The debtor and the other person share an identity of economic interest so that the debtor got some or all of the direct benefit straightforwardly even though, in form, it passed only to the other person because what benefits one will benefit the other;[51] or

c. Apart from sharing an identity of interest, and even though the direct benefit itself did not somehow pass to the debtor, the parties are nevertheless so connected or the deal was so structured that the debtor otherwise benefitted economically, though indirectly, from the other person getting the direct benefit of the consideration.[52]

The maxim that value includes indirect economic benefit to the debtor is recognized in many Code cases,[53] but the authority for the maxim that most of them cite is a decision under the Bankruptcy Act in the case *Rubin v. Manufacturers Hanover Trust Co.*[54] In *Rubin* the trustees sought to avoid, as fraudulent conveyances, the corporate debtors' promises to repay and provision of security for loans made to the debtors' affiliates. A principal issue was whether the debtors had received "fair consideration," which is the Act's counterpart to the Code's reasonably equivalent value. The two terms share essentially the same meaning.

The trustees argued very simply that the debtors did not receive value because the loan proceeds were channeled directly to the affiliates. The court disagreed. The trustees took "too narrow a view" of value because:

> The cases recognize * * * that a debtor may sometimes receive "fair" consideration even though the consideration given for his property or obligation goes initially to a third person. As we have recently stated, although "transfers *solely* for the benefit of third parties do not furnish fair consideration," * * * the transaction's benefit to the debtor "need not be direct; it may come indirectly through benefit to a third person." If the consideration given to the third person has ultimately landed in the debtor's hands, or if the giving of the consideration to the third person otherwise confers a benefit upon the debtor, then the debtor's net worth has been preserved, and [the requirement of fair consideration] * * * has been satisfied.
>
> * * *
>
> [In sum] the fact that a third party initially receives the consideration given for the debtor's property or obligation does not automatically mean [as the trustees contend] that fair consideration was lacking. Thus the simple fact that [the corporate debtors' affiliates] rather than [the debtor itself] received the loan line advances need not compel a ruling in favor of the trustees on this point. The relationships * * * were such that the advances to [the affiliates] very likely did facilitate transfers of funds from those firms to the bank accounts shared by [the debtors], benefitting each of those firms to some degree.[55]

50. See Practitioner Treatise, Vol. 2.
51. See Practitioner Treatise, Vol. 2.
52. See Practitioner Treatise, Vol. 2.
53. See Practitioner Treatise, Vol. 2.
54. 661 F.2d 979 (2d Cir.1981).
55. Id. at 991–93.

On this reasoning, the court therefore agreed with the trial judge's decision in rejecting the trustees' simple argument "that the corporate separateness of the loan recipients [the affiliates] from * * * [the debtors which guaranteed the loans] necessarily precluded a finding of fair consideration."[56]

The matter was not thereby ended, however. In an equally important part of the *Rubin* case the court rejected the trial judge's further decision that any indirect benefit satisfied the requirement of fair consideration.[57] As the term implies, the consideration must be fair, meaning that it must be a "fair equivalent" of the property transferred; or, in the case of a security transfer, the secured debt must not be disproportionately small as compared to value of the collateral. In modern terms, the benefit the debtor receives, directly or indirectly, must be *reasonably equivalent* to the value of the property transferred or the size of the obligation incurred.[58] The trial court in *Rubin* had not determined equivalency; so the case was remanded to decide that issue.

Thus revealed is the real problem in relying on the indirect benefit maxim to save a triangular transaction from attack as a fraudulent conveyance. Most people accept, intellectually and theoretically, that indirect benefits can flow to a person who makes a transfer for the direct benefit of someone else to whom the transferor is related in business. In court, however, a person wishing to uphold the transaction needs more than theories. She needs facts. She must have evidence that the debtor-transferor actually received an indirect benefit and, if the traditional standard of value applies, that the benefit had economic value. (Of course, this job would be easier if the court were convinced that the purpose of fraudulent conveyance law was narrower than preserving the value or net worth of the debtor's estate and accordingly adopted an accommodatingly wider definition of value.) Further, the benefit must have been in *exchange* for the transfer, i.e., the one must have been the *quid pro quo* for the other.[59] Tougher still, the evidence must also show that the worth of the benefit was reasonably equivalent to the value of the transfer made or the size of the obligation incurred.[60] More later on specialized triangular deals.

The immediate point is that value in itself is never sufficient to avoid constructive fraud. Reasonable equivalence of the value is always neces-

---

56. Id. at 993.

57. Id. at 993–94.

58. 11 U.S.C.A. § 548(a)(2). For triangular cases under the Code in which the court signalled the need to establish the reasonable equivalence of an indirect benefit, see, e.g., In re Metro Communications, Inc., 95 B.R. 921, 933 (Bankr. W.D.Pa.1989), order amended, 135 B.R. 17 (Bankr. W.D.Pa.1989) ("[I]ndirect benefits may furnish fair consideration, provided, however, that the value received by the Debtor is reasonably equal to the value of the obligation given."); In re Lawrence Paperboard Corp., 76 B.R. 866, 875–76 (Bankr. D.Mass.1987) (challenge to a corporate downstream guaranty by parent company to affiliate); Matter of Ohio Corrugating Co., 70 B.R. 920, 927 (Bankr. N.D.Ohio 1987) (LBO); In re Ear, Nose and Throat Surgeons of Worchester, Inc., 49 B.R. 316, 320 (Bankr. D. Mass. 1985) (trustee succeeded in proving that corporate debtor's guaranty of its presidents personal loans was for less than reasonably equivalent value); In re Royal Crown Bottlers of North America, Inc., 23 B.R. 28, 30 (Bankr. N.D.Ala. 1982) (although debtor gets value in the form of vicarious benefit derived from consideration following to third person with whom debtor shares "identity of interest," the ultimate question is whether the worth of the value is a reasonable equivalent of the property transferred).

59. See Practitioner Treatise, Vol. 2.

60. See Practitioner Treatise, Vol. 2.

sary, too. In this respect, as in others, value in fraudulent transfer law is more demanding than consideration under the common law.[61]

"Reasonably equivalent" is undefined in the Code.[62] Most courts would likely agree, however, that it generally implies a "fair economic bargain"[63] without requiring a penny-for-penny exchange.[64]

The courts are fond of saying that reasonable equivalence is always a fact question for which there is no set, precise formula,[65] and that all of the facts and circumstances surrounding the transfer are considered in answering the question.[66] In truth, however, the same general approach to the question is routinely followed in most cases: the value of the property transferred is compared to the value of that which the debtor got in return for it. The focus is not on whether the transfer was in the ordinary course of the debtor's affairs. The issue rather "is limited solely to the value of the property or services given to the debtor in exchange for the transfer * * *,"[67] measured when the transfer was made rather than sometime later when the value may have dropped.[68]

What counts in measuring the debtor's return on the transfer is the value of what the debtor obtained, not the value of what the transferee gave up;[69] but all of the direct and indirect benefits received by the debtor are taken into account.[70] There is also authority that in valuing the property the debtor transferred, the same perspective (the debtor's) is used: the value of the property the debtor transferred is determined by its value *to the debtor*.[71] Thus, the value of what the debtor gave up is used rather than the value of what the transferee received.

This process is easiest when the debtor paid money to satisfy a debt, and got a dollar-for-dollar reduction in the debt. Reasonably equivalent value has obviously been received.[72]

The process is considerably more complicated when, as in the typical case, the challenged transfer involves property of the debtor that has no established or absolute intrinsic value. In this event, the comparative value of the transferred property is typically based on market value.[73] The relevant market may depend, however, on the peculiar circumstances of the case.[74] Also, extraordinary circumstances affecting the market can be considered in establishing the market value,[75] but the debtor's peculiar circumstances that affect what price is satisfactory to her are not properly considered.[76]

61. See Practitioner Treatise, Vol. 2.
62. See Practitioner Treatise, Vol. 2.
63. In re Morris Communications NC Inc., 75 B.R. 619, 628 (Bankr. W.D.N.C.1987), order rev'd after district court affirmance, 914 F.2d 458 (4th Cir.1990); see also In re Ozark Restaurant Equipment Co., Inc., 850 F.2d 342, 344–45 (8th Cir.1988), on subsequent remand, 96 B.R. 187 (Bankr. W.D.Ark.1988) ("The concept of reasonably equivalent value is a means of determining if the debtor received a fair exchange in the market place for the goods transferred * * *.").
64. See Practitioner Treatise, Vol. 2.
65. See Practitioner Treatise, Vol. 2.
66. See Practitioner Treatise, Vol. 2.
67. See Practitioner Treatise, Vol. 2.
68. See Practitioner Treatise, Vol. 2.
69. See Practitioner Treatise, Vol. 2.
70. See Practitioner Treatise, Vol. 2.
71. See Practitioner Treatise, Vol. 2.
72. See Practitioner Treatise, Vol. 2.
73. See Practitioner Treatise, Vol. 2.
74. See Practitioner Treatise, Vol. 2.
75. See Practitioner Treatise, Vol. 2.
76. See Practitioner Treatise, Vol. 2.

The courts have not set an exact, absolute percentage of the value of the transferred property that the debtor must have received in order to support a finding of reasonable equivalency. Often, however, they use 70 percent as a bench mark. This bench mark is most commonly used in cases in which foreclosure sales of property are attacked as constructively fraudulent,[77] but its use has spread to other kinds of cases.[78]

Yet, the 70 percentage figure is not mechanically controlling in any kind of case. Reasonable equivalence may be lacking when more than 70% is paid,[79] and may be present when the debtor gets less than 70% of the transferred property's value. Moreover, the percentage paid, though very important, is not itself always controlling. Rather, it is properly considered in combination with all of the other facts surrounding the transfer in determining the ultimate issue which is whether, in light of the particular circumstances of the case, the debtor got a fair economic exchange.

Later we review a variety of fraudulent transfer cases that repeatedly arise and present special problems.[80] Collectively, these cases illustrate the importance of the reasonable equivalence issue and demonstrate that its resolution is often affected by the peculiar circumstances of the transfer.

§ 6–50 Remedies and Defenses

When a transfer is avoidable under section 548(a), either because of actual or constructive fraud by the debtor, the trustee's remedies are spelled out in section 550(a). The trustee may recover the property or its value from:

>   (1) the initial transferee of such transfer or the entity for whose benefit such transfer was made; or

>   (2) any immediate or mediate transferee of such initial transferee.[1]

This section means that, in the typical case, the debtor's immediate transferee and any subsequent transferee are accountable to the trustee.[2] The transferee's lack of involvement in the fraud, her ignorance that the transfer was fraudulent, or her complete innocence is not, in itself, a bar to the trustee's recovery.

The transferee is not defenseless, however. She enjoys two basic defenses: sections 550(b) and 548(c).[3] The former bars the trustee from recovering from any subsequent transferee who takes for value, in good faith, and without knowledge of the voidability of the transfer. *This defense does not*

---

77. See § 6–53 infra.
78. See Practitioner Treatise, Vol. 2.
79. See Practitioner Treatise, Vol. 2.
80. See §§ 6–51 through 6–59 infra.

§ 6–50

1. 11 U.S.C.A. § 550(a).

2. The trustee, of course, is limited to a single satisfaction, 11 U.S.C.A. § 550(c); but the whole "value of the transferred property should be restored to the estate, even if composite elements of that value must come from more than one transferee." Matter of Laughlin, 18 B.R. 778, 781 (Bankr. W.D.Mo.1982).

Section 550 is fully discussed in §§ 6–87 through 6–90 infra. We deal with it briefly here only to set the context for considering section 548(c).

3. See 11 U.S.C.A. §§ 548(c) & 550(b). A minor defense which we discuss elsewhere is section 550(d). It secures a good value transferee pro tanto for certain improvements to the property. See 11 U.S.C.A. § 550(d), discussed at § 6–89 infra.

protect the initial transferee. It only benefits people who take the property after the initial transferee.

The second basic defense, section 548(c), is available to any transferee, including the initial transferee from the debtor.[4] It provides:

> Except to the extent that a transfer or obligation voidable under this section is voidable under section 544, 545, or 547 of this title, a transferee or obligee of such a transfer or obligation that takes for value and in good faith has a lien on or may retain any interest transferred or may enforce any obligation incurred, as the case may be, to the extent that such transferee or obligee gave value to the debtor in exchange for such transfer or obligation.[5]

This defense, which must be proved by the person relying on it,[6] looks much like section 550(b). The two defenses are very similar, but not identical.

Both defenses are alike in general effect. Satisfying either of them does not negate the finding of actual or constructive fraud based upon section 548(a). Rather, each of them operates only to limit, completely or partly (as the case may be), the trustee's recovery because of the fraud.

Both defenses require "good faith." Here we focus on good faith for purposes of section 548(c). It "is an 'indispensable element' of this saving provision,"[7] but "is not susceptible of precise definition."[8] Good faith is a fact question that depends on the peculiar circumstances of each case.[9] Generally speaking, however, good faith requires an arm's length transaction[10] in which the transferee herself acts honestly and without malice or fraudulent design.[11] She must also act innocently. A transferee lacks good faith, even though her own conduct and motives are pure, if she knows or should have known something that signals the debtor's actual or constructive fraud.

For example, good faith is lacking in a case of actual fraud when the transferee shares or is aware of the debtor's intent to hinder, delay or defraud creditors,[12] as well as in any case in which the transferee independently acts with actual fraud.[13] If the transferee is innocent, however, the debtor's actual fraudulent intent does not, in itself, ordinarily bar the transferee's reliance on section 548(c).[14]

Good faith is also lacking under section 548(c) if the transferee knows, at the time of the transfer, that the debtor is insolvent[15] or, more generally, that the debtor is in financial trouble.[16] This knowledge is damning presum-

---

4. See, e.g., In re Richardson, 23 B.R. 434, 449 (Bankr. D. Utah 1982) (buyer of property at public sale forced by mortgagee got a § 548(c) lien even though buyer, as initial transferee, was unprotected by § 550(b)); In re Carr, 34 B.R. 653, 657–58 (Bankr. D.Conn. 1983), order aff'd, 40 B.R. 1007 (D.Conn.1984).

5. 11 U.S.C.A. § 548(c).

6. See Practitioner Treatise, Vol. 2.

7. In re Roco Corp., 701 F.2d 978, 984 (1st Cir.1983); see also In re Candor Diamond Corp., 76 B.R. 342, 351 (Bankr. S.D.N.Y. 1987).

8. In re Roco Corp., 701 F.2d 978, 984 (1st Cir.1983).

9. See Practitioner Treatise, Vol. 2.
10. See Practitioner Treatise, Vol. 2.
11. See Practitioner Treatise, Vol. 2.
12. See Practitioner Treatise, Vol. 2.
13. See Practitioner Treatise, Vol. 2.
14. See Practitioner Treatise, Vol. 2.
15. See Practitioner Treatise, Vol. 2.
16. See Practitioner Treatise, Vol. 2.

ably because it suggests an awareness that the transfer would be detrimental to the debtor's creditors.[17]

Significantly, the transferee is not charged only with information she actually knows. She is also charged with knowledge that a reasonable person in her position should have known.[18] In effect, therefore, the transferee is obligated to investigate the circumstances of the debtor's transfer to the extent that an ordinarily prudent person in her position would have done so. A subsequent transferee, however, is not usually required to investigate the original transfer involving the debtor.

Sections 550(b) and 548(c) are also alike in requiring that the transferee gave "value" for the transfer or obligation. "Even if the [transferee] was acting in good faith, * * * it still must have given value to qualify for the section 548(c) exception."[19] Section 548 provides an internal definition of value that applies throughout the entire provision: "property or satisfaction of a present or antecedent debt of the debtor."[20] We have already discussed this meaning of value in considering the lack of reasonably equivalent value as a requirement for constructive fraud under section 548(a)(2). The discussion of value there applies equally as well here.[21] Remember, however, that section 548(c) applies to the extent that any value was given. The transferee need not have given reasonably equivalent value to qualify for protection thereunder.

There are two important differences between sections 548(c) and 550(b). First, section 550(b) provides a complete defense so long as some value was innocently given. In contrast, section 548(c) is a pro tanto defense only, that is, the transferee can avoid the trustee's recovery only to the extent that the transferee gave value. The transferee forfeits any value in the property exceeding what she paid for it. Technically, when a fraudulent transfer of property is avoided and the property is returned to the trustee, the transferee's original claim therein is extinguished by force of section 548(a);[22] and, on the basis of subsection (c), she is awarded a lien on the property to the extent of the value she gave the debtor.[23] This lien must be satisfied or otherwise respected as is any other secured claim.[24] The trustee may sell the property free and clear of the lien, but the lien attaches to and must be paid from the sale proceeds.[25] If the trustee recovers the value of the property instead of the property itself, the recovery is reduced by the value paid by the transferee.

A very common case involves the avoidance, under section 548(a)(2), of a forced sale of property to enforce a lien. The sale terminates the lien and passes some proprietary interest to the buyer. Upon avoidance of the sale as a constructively fraudulent transfer, the buyer loses her interest resulting from the sale and, through section 548(c), gets a lien for the price she paid.[26]

17. See Practitioner Treatise, Vol. 2.
18. See Practitioner Treatise, Vol. 2.
19. In re Anchorage Marina, Inc., 93 B.R. 686, 693 (Bankr. D.N.D.1988).
20. 11 U.S.C.A. § 548(d)(2)(A).
21. See Practitioner Treatise, Vol. 2.
22. See Practitioner Treatise, Vol. 2.
23. See Practitioner Treatise, Vol. 2.
24. See Practitioner Treatise, Vol. 2.
25. See Practitioner Treatise, Vol. 2.
26. See Practitioner Treatise, Vol. 2.

Often, the buyer at a sale to enforce a lien is the secured creditor herself who forced the sale and who bids in the amount of her lien. In this case, too, if the sale is avoided, the lienor qua purchaser gets a lien. The cases do not agree whether this lien is a fresh encumbrance arising under section 548(c),[27] or is the original encumbrance that is reinstated by virtue of a decisional rule restoring the status quo ante upon avoidance of the sale.[28] This difference is important because, if the lien is based on section 548(c), the secured creditor must satisfy the section's conditions to qualify for the lien: value and good faith.[29]

There is no problem with the requirement of value. Value would be given to the extent the antecedent secured debt was satisfied and any additional amount was paid for the property. The problem is in the good faith requirement. A secured creditor who forces a sale of her collateral may well be aware of the debtor's insolvency. Having this knowledge qua purchaser means that the secured party lacked good faith, within the meaning of section 548(c), in buying the property at the forced sale.[30] Thus, she would not qualify for a section 548(c) lien.[31]

Yet, this disqualification for a lien under section 548(c), based on the secured creditor's status at the time of the forced sale, has no bearing on the validity of her original encumbrance. If the sale (which extinguished that encumbrance) is set aside, the natural and fair result would seem to be that the original encumbrance is resurrected, notwithstanding and apart from section 548(c). On the other hand, if the secured party's recovery upon avoidance of her forced sale is really her original encumbrance, she will be shorted if she bids more than the amount of her lien in buying the property at the sale.

A middle position is outlined by the court in *In re Cole*.[32] In this case a mortgagee won a judgment of foreclosure against the debtor and enforced the judgment by a sheriff's sale of the collateral. The mortgagee-judgment creditor itself purchased the property at the sale. In the mortgagor-debtor's bankruptcy, the sale was set aside under section 548(a). With respect to the issue whether the mortgagee had to satisfy the good faith requirement of section 548(c) in order to retain a lien on the property, the court opined:

> [I]t is clear that the Mortgagee is entitled to have its lien satisfied in the sale reinstated against the premises under 11 U.S.C. § 548(c) when the sale is set aside. We read § 548(c) as addressing solely the issue of whether the transferee or obligee, i.e., the purchaser at the sale, has a right to a lien against the Debtor's premises in light of the frustration of his bargain. It is the good faith of the purchaser which is the measure of whether a lien is warranted. There is no suggestion in § 548(c) that a judgment creditor whose lien was satisfied in the avoided sale should not have this lien reinstated. When a judgment creditor purchases at his own sale, he has rights in two capacities, i.e., as judgment creditor and as purchaser. We believe that, pertinent to its capacity as judgment creditor, nothing in § 548(c) suggests that it should lose its judgment

---

27. See Practitioner Treatise, Vol. 2.
28. See Practitioner Treatise, Vol. 2.
29. See Practitioner Treatise, Vol. 2.
30. See Practitioner Treatise, Vol. 2.
31. See Practitioner Treatise, Vol. 2.
32. 81 B.R. 326, further opinion, 89 B.R. 433 (Bankr. E.D.Pa. 1988).

lien, no matter what the circumstances of the sale were. The question of the judgment creditor's good faith is only relevant in determining whether it is entitled to an additional lien for any outlay of value to the Debtor pertinent to its capacity as purchaser.[33]

Thus, on the authority of *Cole,* when a secured creditor buys at her own forced sale which is thereafter avoided under section 548, she recovers in any event her original encumbrance, notwithstanding and apart from section 548(c). The original encumbrance is not, however, the limit of her recovery. If she paid more value for the property than the amount of the secured debt, she gets a section 548(c) lien for the excess, assuming she acted in good faith in buying the property at the sale.

Sections 550(b) and 548(c) also differ in a second respect. The former does not care to whom the transferee gave value so long as she gave value in good faith to someone.[34] Section 548(c), on the other hand, requires value given "to the debtor"[35] by the transferee.[36] In this respect, that is, requiring that the debtor receive the value,[37] section 548(c) simply mirrors the identical requirement of "reasonably equivalent value" in section 548(a)(2).

This restriction in section 548(c) causes no problems in the typical case in which the transferee and the debtor are the only players. They deal directly, and the transferee pays the debtor the consideration for the property that is transferred. The debtor herself gets the value.

The "to the debtor" language is also not a problem for a subsequent transferee of the debtor's initial transferee even though the subsequent transferee pays her transferor rather than the debtor. Although the subsequent transferee is disqualified for protection under section 548(c),[38] she gets the protection of section 550(b) which contains no "to the debtor" limitation.

The "to the debtor" language in section 548(c) becomes meaningful in three-sided (or triangular) transactions in which the debtor makes a transfer of her property (or incurs an obligation) to a second person so that this second person will give value of her own to a third person. Suppose, for example, that a closely-held, insolvent corporation gratuitously pays a debt

---

33. 81 B.R. at 331. The court that decided Cole reconsidered this reasoning and affirmed it in In re Orsa Associates, 106 B.R. 418, 421–23 (Bankr. E.D.Pa. 1989).

34. See Practitioner Treatise, Vol. 2.

35. 11 U.S.C.A. § 548(c) (emphasis added); Bonded Financial Services v. European American Bank, 838 F.2d 890, 897 (7th Cir.1988) (dicta); In re Energy Sav. Center, Inc., 61 B.R. 732, 736 (E.D.Pa. 1986) (for purposes of § 548(c), value can include satisfying antecedent debt but not when debt owed by someone other than the debtor); In re Candor Diamond Corp., 76 B.R. 342, 352 n.12 (Bankr. S.D.N.Y. 1987) (value was not given to the debtor when money transferred by corporate debtor was returned by transferee to principal of debtor); Matter of Frank, 39 B.R. 166, 177 (Bankr. E.D.N.Y.1984) (upon avoidance of forced sale of property that debtor owned jointly with spouse, § 548(c) protected transferee only to extent of price attributable to debtor's one-half interest).

36. For a literal interpretation of section 548(c), that the transferee herself must be the source of the value given the debtor, see In re Alexander Dispos–Haul Systems, 36 B.R. 612, 616 (Bankr. D.Or.1983).

37. Moreover, the lien of section 548(c), by its terms, only covers the amount of value the debtor received; thus the lien would not seem to accommodate the buyer's expenses associated with the sale such as costs and attorney's fees because these expenses conferred no benefit on the debtor. The courts disagree on this issue, however. Compare, e.g., In re Richardson, 23 B.R. 434, 449 (Bankr. D. Utah 1982) (§ 548(c) lien does not cover such expenses) with In re Jones, 20 B.R. 988, 995 (Bankr. E.D.Pa. 1982) (lien does cover costs).

38. But see Matter of Laughlin, 18 B.R. 778, 781 (W.D.Mo.1982).

that its principal owes someone else. Shortly thereafter, the corporation files bankruptcy. The payment is avoidable as constructively fraudulent under section 548(a)(2),[39] and section 548(c) is no defense for the third person because she gave no value "to the debtor." Section 550(b) is also useless to the third person because she is the initial transferee. This result is good. The transaction was detrimental to the corporation's creditors because the debtor's assets were reduced with no corresponding benefit, of any kind, to the debtor. That a debtor must account to its creditors before making gifts to its friends is a main lesson of, and a principal reason for, the prohibition against constructive fraud in section 548(a)(2). In the absence of the "to the debtor" limitation in section 548(c), the third person would have a defense and section 548(a)(2) would effectively be neutered with respect to the very kind of classic case it was designed to avoid.

The "to the debtor" limitation of section 548(c) is indiscriminate, however, when literally applied. It leaves transferees unprotected in certain kinds of triangular transactions that are commercially significant, that are (perhaps) useful in broad economic terms, and that can benefit (at least indirectly and in the longer run) the debtor and her creditors. Prime examples are intra-corporate guaranties and leveraged buyouts (LBOs), which are discussed separately below as special problems in the law of fraudulent transfers.[40] As a technical means of clearing the way for these financing devices, the courts have widened the meaning of "value" to include indirect benefits that the debtor receives,[41] and some authorities have argued for ignoring the "to the debtor" restriction in section 548(c).[42]

Yet, these kinds of deals—guaranties, LBOs and the like—are threatened by section 548 in the first instance because the law in section 548(a)(2) describes constructive fraud in terms of *the debtor* receiving less than reasonably equivalent value. Any complaint about section 548 is thus more properly aimed at section 548(a) and should rightly center on the result of applying old fraudulent conveyance law applied to modern financing devices. The "to the debtor" language in section 548(c) thus cannot honestly be avoided without first redefining, judicially or legislatively, the scope and reach of that law.

2. Special Problems

§ 6–51 Guaranties

For full text of this section, see Epstein, Nickles & White, Bankruptcy, Practitioner Treatise Series, Vol. 2.

§ 6–52 LBOs

For full text of this section, see Epstein, Nickles & White, Bankruptcy, Practitioner Treatise Series, Vol. 2.

§ 6–53 Foreclosure Sales

For full text of this section, see Epstein, Nickles & White, Bankruptcy, Practitioner Treatise Series, Vol. 2.

---

39. See § 6–49 supra.
40. See § 6–52 infra.
41. See § 6–49 supra.

42. See Carlson, Leveraged Buyouts in Bankruptcy, 20 Ga. L. Rev. 73, 86–87 (1985); Guaranties and Section 548(a)(2) of the Bankruptcy Code, 52 U.Chi.L.Rev. 194, 204 (1985).

§ 6–54 Foreclosure Sales—Forced Sale as "Transfer" of Debtor's Interest in Property

For full text of this section, see Epstein, Nickles & White, Bankruptcy, Practitioner Treatise Series, Vol. 2.

§ 6–55 Foreclosure Sales—Timing of the Transfer

For full text of this section, see Epstein, Nickles & White, Bankruptcy, Practitioner Treatise Series, Vol. 2.

§ 6–56 Foreclosure Sales—Determining "Reasonably Equivalent Value"

For full text of this section, see Epstein, Nickles & White, Bankruptcy, Practitioner Treatise Series, Vol. 2.

§ 6–57 Transfers of Exempt Property

For full text of this section, see Epstein, Nickles & White, Bankruptcy, Practitioner Treatise Series, Vol. 2.

§ 6–58 Converting Nonexempt Property to Exempt Property

For full text of this section, see Epstein, Nickles & White, Bankruptcy, Practitioner Treatise Series, Vol. 2.

§ 6–59 Preferential Transfers

For full text of this section, see Epstein, Nickles & White, Bankruptcy, Practitioner Treatise Series, Vol. 2.

3. Transfers Fraudulent Under State Law, Section 544(b)

§ 6–60 Transfers Fraudulent Under State Law (Trustee as Successor to Actual Creditor, Section 554(b))

Transfers that are fraudulent under state law, as opposed to the federal law of section 548,[1] are avoidable through section 544(b). It empowers the trustee to

> avoid any transfer of an interest of the debtor in property or any obligation incurred by the debtor that is voidable under applicable law by a creditor holding an unsecured claim that is allowable under section 502 of this title or that is not allowable only under section 502(e) of this title.[2]

This provision subrogates the trustee to the right of any unsecured creditor of the estate to void, under any "applicable law," a prepetition transfer of the debtor's property.[3] This "applicable law," which essentially means any

---

§ 6–60

1. 11 U.S.C.A. § 548, which is discussed at §§ 6–47 through 6–59 infra.

2. Id. § 544(b).

3. Id. "Section 554(b) * * * applies only to the prepetition transfer of an interest in property of a debtor. It does not apply to the postpetition transfer of an interest in property

nonbankruptcy law, includes state fraudulent transfer law.[4] Indeed, state fraudulent transfer law is, by far, the "applicable law" most often relied on by trustees under section 544(b).

For the most part, however, the content of the typical state fraudulent transfer law is very similar to the substance of section 548. Local law, like section 548, condemns any transfer that is made with actual intent to defraud, hinder or delay creditors;[5] and local law essentially mirrors section 548 with respect to transfers that are deemed constructively fraudulent.[6] Therefore, "cases construing [section 548] counterparts are persuasive authority due to the similarity of the laws in this area."[7] Nevertheless, state laws are somewhat unique in ways that permit the trustee under section 544(b) to avoid transactions that are beyond the reach of section 548.

First, although the main tenets of section 548 and state fraudulent transfer laws are generally the same, the laws of some states go beyond the substance of section 548 and define as fraudulent a slightly wider range of transfers. For example, the laws of several states include certain preferences on their lists of constructively fraudulent transfers, including preferences to insiders. Thus, in reliance on such a law, the trustee can avoid such a preference through section 544(b) even though the transfer cannot be attacked under section 548 or section 547.[8] On the other hand, some states' fraudulent transfer law are substantially more narrow than section 548, that is, they condemn a substantially smaller number of transfers than would be condemned by section 548 or even by the uniform state laws—the UFCA and UFTA.

Moreover, the trustee's avoidance power under section 544(b) is not defined solely in terms of state fraudulent transfer laws. Section 544(b) allows the trustee to avoid a transfer that is voidable by an unsecured creditor under any nonbankruptcy law, which includes nonbankruptcy federal law and state law other than local fraudulent conveyance law. For example, separate state law governs bulk sales. The governing law in most states is U.C.C. Article 6. A transfer subject to Article 6 but not made in compliance with the statute is ineffective against creditors.[9] The courts agree that a bulk sale that is ineffective under Article 6 is voidable under local law within the meaning of 544(b) and, on that basis, can be avoided.[10] Section 544(b) also permits the trustee to use a local preference statute rather than section 547 to avoid a preferential transfer.[11]

Also, even when a trustee relies on state fraudulent transfer laws that share the substance of section 548, the local law may condemn a wider range of transfers by defining differently from section 548 the critical terms and particulars. For example, state law agrees with section 548 in condemning, as constructively fraudulent, any transfer made by an insolvent debtor who

of an estate." In re Metropolitan Cosmetic Reconstructive Surgery P.A., 125 B.R. 556, 557 (Bankr. D.Minn.1991).

4. See Practitioner Treatise, Vol. 2.
5. See Practitioner Treatise, Vol. 2.
6. See Practitioner Treatise, Vol. 2.
7. In re Agricultural Research and Technology Group, 916 F.2d 528, 534 (9th Cir.1990).
8. See Practitioner Treatise, Vol. 2.
9. U.C.C. §§ 6–104(1) & 6–105.
10. See Practitioner Treatise, Vol. 2.
11. See, e.g., In re Wilson, 106 B.R. 125 (Bankr. W.D.Ky.1989).

does not receive equivalent value in exchange.[12] Commonly, however, local law defines equivalency in terms more demanding than the meaning of "reasonably equivalent value" in section 548. The most common local analog to "reasonably equivalent value" is "fair consideration."[13] It includes the requirement of section 548's "reasonably equivalent value" that the debtor received an economic equivalent in value, and then goes beyond this requirement to demand also that the transferee acted in good faith.[14] Thus, if a challenged transfer had been made by an insolvent debtor for a reasonably equivalent value but to a transferee who acted without good faith, the transfer would not be constructively fraudulent under section 548 or otherwise avoidable under the Code but could be avoided under state law through section 544(b).[15]

Finally, and most important, the reach-back period of local fraudulent transfer laws is typically much longer than the one-year period of section 548. Using section 548 the trustee can only avoid transfers that occurred within one year before the bankruptcy petition was filed.[16] When the trustee relies on local fraudulent transfer law through section 544(b), she is not restrained by section 548's one-year rule. Rather, the trustee gets the benefit of the local statute of limitations on voiding fraudulent conveyances which may be six or ten years or even longer.[17] The trustee also gets the benefit of any gloss on these local statutes that starts the limitations period running only from the time that the fraud is discovered or should have been discovered.[18]

A disadvantage of section 544(b) is that the trustee's rights thereunder are entirely derivative of an actual unsecured creditor. Section 544(b) permits the trustee to attack a transfer only on the basis of laws that would allow a transfer to be voided by a present creditor of the estate holding an allowable, unsecured claim.[19] Thus, when relying on section 544(b) to avoid a transfer under local law, the trustee must establish not only that the conditions of the local law have been satisfied; the trustee must also establish that at least one of the actual, unsecured creditors of the estate could have invoked the local law herself and voided the transfer for her own

---

12. Compare 11 U.S.C.A. § 548(a)(2) with Uniform Fraudulent Conveyance Act § 4 and Uniform Fraudulent Transfer Act § 5.

13. The Uniform Fraudulent Conveyance Act, or a statute very much like it, is the law in the majority of states. The Act generally requires the absence of "fair consideration" to find that a transfer was constructively fraudulent. Uniform Fraudulent Conveyance Act §§ 4, 5, 6 & 8(b).

14. The model definition of "fair consideration" is as follows:

Fair consideration is given for property, or obligation,

(a) When in exchange for such property, or obligation, as a fair equivalent therefor, and in good faith, property is conveyed or an antecedent debt is satisfied, or

(b) When such property, or obligation, is received in good faith to secure a present advance or antecedent debt in amount not disproportionately small as compared with the value of the property, or obligation obtained.

Uniform Fraudulent Conveyance Act § 3.

15. This possibly will lessen, however, as the states adopt the newly proposed Uniform Fraudulent Transfer Act. This law substitutes for "fair consideration" the Bankruptcy Code's concept of "reasonably equivalent value," and, consistent with the Code, defines "value" so as to exclude the element of "good faith." See Uniform Fraudulent Transfer Act § 3.

16. 11 U.S.C.A. § 548(a) ("on or within one year before the date of the filing of the petition").

17. See Practitioner Treatise, Vol. 2.

18. See Practitioner Treatise, Vol. 2.

19. "The trustee may avoid any transfer * * * voidable * * * by a creditor holding an unsecured claim * * *." 11 U.S.C.A. § 544(b).

benefit as of the time of the bankruptcy petition.[20] Thus, unlike section 544(a) which independently gives the trustee the power of a hypothetical creditor,[21] section 544(b) requires that an actual creditor have the power to void a transfer;[22] and, where such power exists, section 544(b) then allows the trustee to step into the actual creditor's shoes and use the power derivatively for the benefit of the estate and all unsecured creditors. This subrogation does not depend on the creditor, before bankruptcy, having already sued or otherwise acted herself to void the transfer.[23] All that is necessary is that the creditor have had a right, at the time of the debtor's bankruptcy, to void the transfer.

Because the trustee's power under section 544(b) is derivative, she must satisfy the same conditions, and is subject to the same defenses, that the local law would impose on the actual creditor whose shoes the trustee wears.[24] Thus, the trustee cannot avoid a transfer through section 544(b) on the basis of a local law that no actual creditor could have used at the time of bankruptcy due to the expiration by then of the applicable, local statute of limitations.[25] On the other hand, if the local statute had not expired prior to bankruptcy, the filing of the petition automatically tolls the running of the statute for a two-year period.[26] In any event, the trustee's power to avoid transfers through section 544(b) is restricted by the general statute of limitations that the Code imposes on all avoidance actions.[27]

In contrast, the consequences in bankruptcy of the voidability of a transfer under state law through section 544(b) are not defined, or at least not limited, by the applicable state law. Rather, the consequences are generally determined by the federal law of bankruptcy. This means that even if the local law on which the trustee relies declares the transfer voidable only to the extent of the actual creditor's claim, the transfer is nevertheless completely avoided by the trustee for the benefit of the estate generally.[28] Moreover, the trustee who avoids a transfer through section 544(b) is entitled to the remedies provided by the Code and is not restricted to the remedies described by the local "applicable law" on which the trustee relied to avoid the transfer.[29]

20. See Practitioner Treatise, Vol. 2.

21. 11 U.S.C.A. § 544(a), which is discussed at § 6-61 infra.

22. See Practitioner Treatise, Vol. 2.

23. See Practitioner Treatise, Vol. 2.

24. See Practitioner Treatise, Vol. 2.

25. In re McDowell, 87 B.R. 554, 558 (Bankr. S.D.Ill.1988); In re Express Liquors, Inc., 65 B.R. 952, 955 n.2 (Bankr. D.Md.1986).

26. 11 U.S.C.A. §§ 108(a) & 546(a); In re Dry Wall Supply, Inc., 111 B.R. 933, 935-37 (D.Colo.1990); Matter of Curtina Int'l, Inc., 23 B.R. 969, 975 (Bankr. S.D.N.Y. 1982).

27. 11 U.S.C.A. § 546(a).

28. Moore v. Bay, 284 U.S. 4, 52 S.Ct. 3, 76 L.Ed. 133 (1931); H.R. Rep. No. 595, 95th Cong., 1st Sess. 370, reprinted in 1978 U.S. Code Cong. & Admin. News 5963, 6326; S.R. No. 989, 95th Cong., 2d Sess. 85, reprinted in 1978 U.S. Code Cong. & Admin. News 5787, 5871 (§ 544(b) follows Moore v. Bay); In re Theisen, 45 B.R. 122, 126-27 (Bankr. D.Minn. 1984) ("[U]nder the rule in Moore v. Bay, a case decided under predecessor of § 544(b), once availability is determined under state law, the transfer is entirely avoidable by a trustee in bankruptcy regardless of the amount of the creditor's claim relied on by the trustee.").

29. See 11 U.S.C.A. § 550(a) (trustee entitled to remedies listed here when a transfer is avoided under any one of several Code provisions, including section 544); In re Leinheiser, 51 B.R. 164 (Bankr. E.D.Pa. 1985) (trustee entitled to § 550 remedies upon successfully attacking a transfer as constructively fraudulent under state law); In re O.P.M. Leasing Services, Inc., 32 B.R. 199 (Bankr. S.D.N.Y. 1983) (trustee may use § 550 to recover property from any subsequent transferee to the extent that the initial transfer has been avoided under § 544).

D. "STRONG-ARM" POWERS, SECTION 544(a)
§ 6–61 Trustee as Hypothetical Lien Creditor or Purchaser ("Strong–Arm" Powers, Section 544(a))

It is commonplace under state law that certain interests in property, especially unperfected encumbrances, are subordinate to the claims of subsequent lien creditors or bona fide purchasers. This universal theme of state law underlies the avoiding powers of section 544(a), commonly known as the trustee's "strong arm" powers. Section 544(a) provides:

(a) The trustee shall have, as of the commencement of the case, and without regard to any knowledge of the trustee or of any creditor, the rights and powers of, or may avoid any transfer of property of the debtor or any obligation incurred by a debtor that is voidable by

(1) a creditor that extends credit to the debtor at the time of the commencement of the case, and that obtains, at such time and with respect to such credit, a judicial lien on all property on which a creditor on a simple contract could have obtained such a judicial lien, whether or not such a creditor exists;

(2) a creditor that extends credit to the debtor at the time of the commencement of the case, and obtains, at such time and with respect to such credit, an execution against the debtor that is returned unsatisfied at such time, whether or not such a creditor exists; or

(3) a bona fide purchaser of real property, other than fixtures, from the debtor, against whom applicable law permits such transfer to be perfected, that obtains the status of a bona fide purchaser and has perfected such transfer at the time of the commencement of the case, whether or not such a purchaser exists.[1]

Most important, this federal law effectively gives the trustee, in her own right for the benefit of the estate, the status (technically, "rights and powers") of two classes of claimants of property who claim through the debtor as of the time of bankruptcy: (1) a lien creditor with a *judicial lien* [2] on *all* property that a contract creditor could subject to such a lien under

§ 6–61

1. 11 U.S.C.A. § 544(a).

2. A lien is any "charge against or interest in property to secure payment of a debt or performance of an obligation." 11 U.S.C.A. § 101(37). The Bankruptcy Code recognizes two primary classes of liens: liens that arises by contract and nonconsensual liens. Liens arising by contract, i.e., liens based on the parties' agreement, are referred to as "security interests," whether the collateral is real or personal property. 11 U.S.C.A. § 101(51).

The class of liens that are nonconsensual divides into two subsets of liens: judicial liens and statutory liens. A "statutory lien" is a lien "arising solely by force of a statute on specified circumstances or conditions, or lien of distress for rent, whether or not statutory, but does not include security interest or judicial lien." 11 U.S.C.A. § 101(53). A "judicial lien" is any "lien obtained by judgment, levy, sequestration, or other legal or equitable process or proceeding." 11 U.S.C.A. § 101(36). Typically, judicial liens are created by statute. They are distinguished from statutory liens on the basis that a judicial lien does not arise, attach or otherwise become effective against property without or apart from some kind of judicial process. In contrast, a statutory lien is not only created by statute, but attaches to property automatically without and apart from judicial process.

These three categories of liens—security interests, statutory liens, and judicial liens—are mutually exclusive, and the only kind of lien the trustee acquires under section 544(a) is a judicial lien. She does not acquire a statutory lien or security interest in any property.

state law,[3] and (2) a bona fide *purchaser*[4] of *real property* from the debtor to whom the transfer is made and perfected as of the time of bankruptcy.[5] (WARNING! Be especially careful to note the wider reach of the lien claim: It can stretch to both personal and real property, but the trustee's claim as purchaser reaches only real property and not personalty.[6]) Less important, section 544(a) also deems that the trustee is an unsecured creditor as of the filing of bankruptcy who on the same day caused execution to issue and suffered a nulla bona return.[7]

So what? Most important, third parties' prepetition liens and interests in property that could be claimed (under state law) by a judicial lien creditor of the debtor, or by a purchaser of real estate from her, are avoidable by the trustee (under section 544(a)) if at the time of bankruptcy the interests are subordinate (under state law) to the claim of such a lien creditor or purchaser,[8] even if the property involved is exempt as to the debtor.[9] Less important, section 544(a) also allows the trustee to avoid any *obligation* of the debtor that is voidable under state law by a lien creditor or purchaser.[10]

Federal and state law thus work in tandem: First, section 544(a) confers on the trustee the status of both a judicial lienor and bona fide purchaser who claim property through the debtor, and provides that the trustee enjoys their rights and powers with respect to the property. Second, the substance of these rights and powers, primarily the priority of these claims in relation to other interests in the property, is then determined by reference to state law.[11] Third, if state law provides that the trustee's claim (as a judicial lienor or bona fide purchaser) is entitled to priority over a third party's interest in the property, the consequence is prescribed by federal law, section 544(a), which is that the trustee can entirely avoid the inferior, third-party interest. Any claim of the third-party survives, but only as an unsecured claim. The third party's interest is completely eliminated as to the third party even though the result under state law would be less severe.[12]

On the other hand, the third person's interest is unaffected by section 544(a) if, under state law, her interest primes the trustee's claim as lien

---

3. 11 U.S.C.A. § 544(a)(1).

4. The Code defines "purchaser" broadly. The term is not limited to a buyer of property. It embraces any "transferee of a voluntary transfer, and includes immediate or mediate transferee of such a transfer." 11 U.S.C.A. § 101(43). Thus, for example, a mortgagee of property, as well as a buyer of it, is a purchaser.

5. 11 U.S.C.A. § 544(a)(3).

6. See Practitioner Treatise, Vol. 2.

7. 11 U.S.C.A. § 544(a)(2). This status insures that the trustee "will have all of the equitable remedies and procedural rights available under applicable state law only to such a creditor. In addition, this status may afford the trustee a presumption that the judgment debtor is insolvent and thereby materially assist him in avoiding transfers under applicable state law." Teofan & Creel, The Trustee's Avoiding Powers Under the Bankruptcy Act and the New Code: A Comparative Analysis, 11 St. Mary's L. J. 311, 313 (1979). Mainly, however, section 544(a)(2)

was intended to merely protect the trustee against 'quirks of local procedural law,' where certain remedial rights flowed to a creditor who had an execution returned unsatisfied. Thus, whenever a procedure was necessary under local law, such as exhausting the legal remedies of obtaining a writ before asserting equitable relief, the trustee would be deemed to have reached that stage in the proceedings.

In re Ozark Restaurant Equipment Co., Inc., 816 F.2d 1222, 1229–30 n.12 (8th Cir.1987), cert. denied, 484 U.S. 848, 108 S.Ct. 147, 98 L.Ed.2d 102 (1987).

8. See Practitioner Treatise, Vol. 2.

9. See Practitioner Treatise, Vol. 2.

10. See Practitioner Treatise, Vol. 2.

11. See Practitioner Treatise, Vol. 2.

12. See Practitioner Treatise, Vol. 2.

creditor or purchaser. This is true even if state law subordinates the third person's interest to other kinds of claims that the trustee cannot assert under section 544(a).[13]

To illustrate how section 544(a) works to avoid transfers, suppose that a bank acquires an Article 9 security interest in the debtor's existing inventory and equipment, but fails properly to perfect the interest. The debtor files bankruptcy. Because of section 544(a)(1), the trustee is deemed to have a judicial lien on the debtor's inventory and equipment from the very moment the case commenced.[14] Because of state law (usually, the Uniform Commercial Code Article 9), the trustee's claim of a judicial lien on the property enjoys priority over the bank's unperfected security interest.[15] Because of federal law, section 544(a), the bank's interest is avoided.[16] The debtor's obligation to the bank remains, but the bank's claim in bankruptcy is entirely unsecured.

As another example suppose that the bank's collateral is real estate of the debtor. The bank's mortgage is not properly recorded when the debtor files bankruptcy. State law provides that an unrecorded conveyance of real property is void against a good faith purchaser. The trustee's status as a judicial lienor will not entitle her to avoid the mortgage because the local law does not protect such a claimant from unrecorded mortgages. It only protects purchasers. The trustee will nevertheless prevail. Section 544(a)(3) deems that the trustee is also a purchaser of the debtor's real estate.[17] Thus, asserting this purchaser's status conferred by section 544(a) and a purchaser's priority under state law over the unrecorded interest of a mortgagee, the trustee can avoid the bank's unrecorded mortgage[18] with the result that the bank's claim against the debtor becomes completely unsecured.

In either case the trustee could probably avoid the encumbrance as a preference under section 547(b).[19] Because the encumbrance was unperfected under state law, the security interest or mortgage would be deemed to have occurred immediately before bankruptcy[20] and thus within the preference period. The trustee would nevertheless be required to prove the other elements of section 547(b). In the typical case of an unperfected encumbrance these elements can usually be proved, and ordinarily none of section 547(c) applies. Yet, attacking the encumbrance under section 544(a) is conceptually easier, cleaner and less risky. Moreover, section 544(a) operates entirely independently of section 547, so that an unperfected lien is avoidable under the former in the unlikely event the trustee cannot avoid it under the latter.

Consensual liens, such as the security interest and mortgage in the two examples, are the most common targets of the trustee's section 544(a) avoiding powers. These powers, however, can be aimed at non-consensual liens and also against any other kind of interest whether voluntary or involuntary, legal or equitable. In sum, section 544(a) can be used to avoid any right, claim, or interest in property that is inferior under state law for

13. See Practitioner Treatise, Vol. 2.
14. 11 U.S.C.A. § 544(a)(1).
15. U.C.C. § 9–301(1)(b).
16. See Practitioner Treatise, Vol. 2.
17. See Practitioner Treatise, Vol. 2.
18. See Practitioner Treatise, Vol. 2.
19. 11 U.S.C.A. § 547. Preference law is discussed at §§ 6–3–6–37 supra.
20. 11 U.S.C.A. § 547(e)(2)(C).

whatever reason to the claim of a judicial lienor or bona fide purchaser of real property who claims through the debtor as of the time of bankruptcy.

For example, through section 554(a) a trustee can avoid not only unperfected Article 9 security interests and real estate mortgages, but also:

- an unrecorded deed to real property;[21]
- the rights of a beneficiary of a restrictive covenant in a deed for real property;[22]
- the conveyance of property by an unrecorded divorce decree;[23]
- unrecorded or improperly perfected statutory liens;[24]
- the claims of a partnership to real property conveyed by a partner,[25] or to partnership property held in the name of a partner;[26]
- an unrecorded lease of farmland giving the lessor an interest in part of the crops grown upon the land;[27]
- the secret equitable title, interest or claim (including constructive trust or the like) to property, even if the debtor holds only bare legal title;[28]
- the right to reform a mortgage so as to include property mistakenly omitted from it;[29]
- an unperfected judicial lien;[30]
- a restraining notice covering funds of the debtor which enjoined the third person holding the funds from disposing of them;[31]
- an unperfected pledge or assignment of rents;[32]
- the unnoticed interest of the true owner of goods consigned to the debtor.[33]

We very deliberately describe the trustee's claim under section 544(a) as that of a lienor or purchaser who claims *through* the debtor upon bankruptcy, rather than such a person who then claims property *of* the debtor. Section 544(a) does not limit the trustee to avoiding interests in property that the debtor actually owns when the case commences.

The trustee can use section 544(a) even against interests in property in which the debtor actually has *no rights* when the petition is filed. The section expressly permits avoiding prepetition transfers of the debtor's property, and avoidance of such a transfer is possible through section 544(a) even if the transfer left the debtor without any rights to the property at the time of bankruptcy.[34] The key is whether, notwithstanding the transfer, a subsequent lien creditor or purchaser claiming through the debtor would, under local law, acquire rights to the property superior to the interest of the prior transferee.

21. See Practitioner Treatise, Vol. 2.
22. See Practitioner Treatise, Vol. 2.
23. See Practitioner Treatise, Vol. 2.
24. See Practitioner Treatise, Vol. 2.
25. See Practitioner Treatise, Vol. 2.
26. See Practitioner Treatise, Vol. 2.
27. See Practitioner Treatise, Vol. 2.
28. See Practitioner Treatise, Vol. 2.
29. See Practitioner Treatise, Vol. 2.
30. See Practitioner Treatise, Vol. 2.
31. See Practitioner Treatise, Vol. 2.
32. See Practitioner Treatise, Vol. 2.
33. See Practitioner Treatise, Vol. 2.
34. See Practitioner Treatise, Vol. 2.

Section 544(a) is also used against interests in property that are transferred to the debtor before bankruptcy, but are transferred in such a manner or form that the transferor retains true, equitable ownership and the debtor enjoys only *mere ostensible, legal rights*. A case in point is *Belisle v. Plunkett*.[35] Plunkett formed a set of partnerships to buy an expensive leasehold from W.O.F. Associates. Plunkett bought the leasehold using partnership funds, but he closed the deal and recorded the transfer in his own name. In Plunkett's bankruptcy the trustee and the partnerships fought over the leasehold. Local law gave the partnerships an equitable claim to the property—a constructive trust on it—because of Plunkett's fraud. The trustee argued that the partnerships' claim was avoided under section 544(a) because local law gave priority to a bona fide purchaser of the leasehold over an unrecorded claim such as that of the partnerships.

The court agreed with the trustee, and in so doing rejected the partners' argument that the strong arm powers allow the recovery of property transferred out of the estate before the filing but not property transferred to the debtor subject to a constructive trust:

> Nothing in the text or function of § 544(a)(3) makes the force of this turn on whether Plunkett once owned the leasehold and then sold it to the partnerships (but failed to record their interest) or whether, instead, Plunkett acquired the leasehold through the partnerships. The sequence of W.O.F. to Plunkett * * * to [the] partnerships to Plunkett, with Plunkett obtaining ostensible ownership, is identical in every respect to the sequence W.O.F. to [the] partnerships to Plunkett, with Plunkett obtaining ostensible ownership. Identical from the perspective of Plunkett, of the partners, and of Plunkett's (other) creditors—and identical from the perspective of § 544(a)(3). Section 544(a)(3) allows the trustee to have bona fide purchaser's rights or avoid a transfer, so a "transfer" by the debtor cannot be a necessary condition of the exercise of the strong-arm power. The statute mentions "transfer" only in the sense of the hypothetical transfer that measures the trustee's rights: if a hypothetical bona fide transferee from the debtor would come ahead of the "true" owner's rights, then the trustee takes ahead of the true owner.[36]

The court further reasoned in *Belisle* that section 541(d) did not limit the trustee's strong arm powers. This section excludes from the estate the equitable interests in property to which the debtor holds only legal title,[37] but the court concluded that this exclusion in section 541(d) does not conflict with avoidance of such an equitable interest through section 544(a).[38]

---

35. 877 F.2d 512 (7th Cir.1989), cert. denied, 493 U.S. 893, 110 S.Ct. 241, 107 L.Ed.2d 191 (1989).

36. Id. at 515.

37. The section provides in full:

Property in which the debtor holds, as of the commencement of the case, only legal title and not an equitable interest, such as a mortgage secured by real property, or an interest in such a mortgage, sold by the debtor but as to which the debtor retains legal title to service or supervise the servicing of such mortgage or interest, becomes property of the estate under subsection [541](a)(1) or (2) of this section only to the extent of the debtor's legal title to such property, but not to the extent of any equitable interest in such property that the debtor does not hold.

11 U.S.C.A. § 541(d).

38. See Practitioner Treatise, Vol. 2.

Section 541(d) does not have anything to say about the effects of § 544(a)(3). It forbids including property in the debtor's estate "under subsection (a) of this section [541]" and does not address whether property may be included under some other part of the Code.[39]

Moreover,

> allowing the estate to "benefit from property that the debtor did not own" is exactly what the strong arm powers are about: they give the trustee the status of a bona fide purchaser for value, so that the estate contains interests to which the debtor lacked good title. The estate gets what the debtor could convey under local law rather than what the debtor owned under local law * * *.[40]

We should emphasize that the outcome in *Belisle* was not determined only by the court's analysis of the Code. The outcome for the trustee was equally dependent on local law. Different local law could produce a different result despite faithful adherence to the *Belisle* Code analysis. In this case local law apparently characterized the leasehold as real property so that the trustee could attack as a bona fide purchaser. Where the trustee's target is personal property (and some states classify leases of real estate as personalty), the trustee can attack only as the holder of a judicial lien. State law often gives lien creditors less protection against third-parties' claims than is given to bona fide purchasers.

Also, the local law applied in *Belisle* protected innocent bona fide purchasers from the partners' unrecorded claim.[41] Where secret constructive trusts and the like or other claims of the third person are fully effective against the kind of claim the trustee asserts (whether lien creditor or purchaser), the trustee will lose notwithstanding the validity of the Code analysis in *Belisle*. Unlike the local law applied in *Belisle*, the law of some states sometimes protects entirely secret equitable interests, including constructive trusts, from the kinds of claims that a trustee can assert under section 544(a);[42] and in a case even exactly like *Belisle* but governed by such different local law that protects unnoticed equitable interests, the trustee would lose, even before the very same court that decided *Belisle*.

In sum, the particulars of local law are often decisive in section 544(a) cases without regard to how the courts interpret the Code.

The reference and deference to state law by section 544(a) are critical to achieving its underlying purpose, as is well explained by the court in *In re Wind Power Systems, Inc.*[43] In this case the debtor filed bankruptcy with an attachment lien clinging to her property as a result of a pending lawsuit in state court. The trustee sought to avoid the lien under section 544(a) because of the uncertainty that the lien would ever be reduced to judgment. (Such a lien is unenforceable unless and until the attaching creditor wins her case against the debtor.) The Ninth Circuit held in *Wind Power* that the trustee could not avoid the attachment lien on the basis of the trustee's claim as a judicial lienor under section 544(a)(1).

---

39. 877 F.2d at 515.
40. Id. at 516.
41. See Practitioner Treatise, Vol. 2.
42. See Practitioner Treatise, Vol. 2.
43. 841 F.2d 288 (9th Cir.1988).

Under state law the attachment lien survived and outranked the trustee's judicial lien as of the time the trustee's claim arose despite the possibility that the attachment lien would ultimately fail for lack of a judgment against the debtor. The court concluded that this possibility was no reason for the trustee to defeat the lien under section 544(a).[44] First, allowing the trustee to prevail would run "counter to a long line of cases upholding liens in the face of the trustee's section 544 powers and allowing lienholders to proceed to judgment after bankruptcy."[45] Second, and more importantly, defeating the attachment lien would contradict the purpose behind the trustee's strong arm powers:

> Section 544 preserves within the bankruptcy proceeding the equities among creditors that existed outside bankruptcy. It freezes the relative positions of secured and unsecured creditors at the time of the filing, reducing the incentive to file a strategic bankruptcy petition, and awarding [sic][rewarding] the diligent creditor.[46]

Avoiding attachment liens through section 544(a), when they could not be avoided under state law, would contrarily encourage "strategic bankruptcy filings which distort rights among creditors from what they would be outside bankruptcy proceedings."[47]

The trustee's section 544(a) claims are not dependent on the existence of an actual, third-party lienor or purchaser because, unlike section 544(b) which is discussed earlier,[48] section 544(a) is *not* based on the trustee succeeding to the rights and powers of real claimants.[49] Section 544(a) confers the rights and powers of a judicial lienor and bona fide purchaser on the trustee as if she herself acquired such claims, new and fresh, at the time the bankruptcy petition was filed. The trustee's status is constructive or hypothetical, that is, she is deemed by federal law to have the claims even though she actually did nothing in dealing with the debtor or under state law to acquire them. Nevertheless, this status, though hypothetical, allows the trustee to assert the full range of rights and powers that a real lienor or purchaser would acquire under state law.

Compared to the rights of the trustee as a successor to actual claims under section 544(b), there is good news and bad news for the trustee in her status as a hypothetical claimant under section 544(a). We begin with the bad news.

In asserting the rights of actual creditors under section 544(b), the trustee steps beyond the veil of bankruptcy and assumes the rights of creditors as of the time, prepetition, when the creditors acquired their claims.[50] The comparative bad news regarding section 544(a) is that the trustee's claims, as a hypothetical judicial lienor and bona fide purchaser, date only from the time the bankruptcy petition is filed.[51] The claims and their effects cannot be projected to any time before the petition or after it.[52] As a result, section 544(a) is impotent against a lien or interest that, as of

44. See Practitioner Treatise, Vol. 2.
45. 841 F.2d at 293.
46. Id.
47. Id. at 292–93.
48. 11 U.S.C.A. § 544(b), discussed at § 6–60 supra.
49. See Practitioner Treatise, Vol. 2.
50. See Practitioner Treatise, Vol. 2.
51. See Practitioner Treatise, Vol. 2.
52. See Practitioner Treatise, Vol. 2.

the time of bankruptcy, was fully effective or superior, through filing or otherwise, to a judicial lien and the claim of a bona fide purchaser of real estate.[53] This is true even if the steps necessary to achieve this superiority were taken only days or hours or minutes before the petition was filed, and is true too if no steps are taken if local law requires none for superiority.[54]

On the other hand, a third party whose interest is inferior to the trustee's claim prior to bankruptcy cannot ordinarily take steps after the filing that will improve her priority against the trustee's hypothetical section 544(a) claims.[55] There are two reasons. First, priority of the trustee's section 544(a) claims is determined by reference to state law; and state law usually preserves the priority of a lien creditor or bona fide purchaser despite a junior claimant's subsequent perfection of her interest. Second, the automatic stay enjoins the physical actions that typically are involved in enhancing the priority of an interest in property.[56] In sum, the state and stature of third-parties' interests at the moment of bankruptcy is usually decisive in determining whether the trustee can avoid them under section 544(a). Effectively, therefore, the filing of the bankruptcy petition *frame freezes* third-parties' interests for the purpose of deciding their priority in relation to the trustee's section 544(a) claims.

In rare instances, however, state law subordinates the claim of a lien creditor or bona fide purchaser to a competing interest in the property that is perfected after the lien or purchase occurred. U.C.C. Article 9 provides the best example of such a law. Generally, a security interest is subordinate to a judicial lien that attaches before the security interest is perfected by filing or otherwise.[57] If, however, the interest is a purchase-money security interest that is perfected by filing before or within ten days after the debtor receives possession of the collateral, section 9–301(2) gives the secured party "priority over the rights of * * * a lien creditor which arise between the time the security interest attaches and the time of filing." This exceptional rule, section 9–301(2), effectively permits the secured party's subsequent perfection to relate back to the time when the security interest attached and in so doing subordinates the intervening claim of the lien creditor.

Through section 546(b) the Bankruptcy Code subjects the trustee's section 544(a) claims to U.C.C. section 9–301(2) and other relation-back priority rules of state law. Section 546(b) provides that

> the rights and powers of the trustee under sections 544, 545, and 549 * * * are subject to any generally applicable law that permits perfection of an interest in property to be effective against an entity that acquires rights in such property before the date of perfection.[58]

This exception allows a third party to perfect and gain priority over the trustee after the filing of bankruptcy whenever state law would so favor the third party outside of bankruptcy against a person having the intervening rights asserted by the trustee.

---

53. See Practitioner Treatise, Vol. 2.
54. See Practitioner Treatise, Vol. 2.
55. See Practitioner Treatise, Vol. 2.
56. 11 U.S.C.A. § 362(a), especially § 362(a)(4) which expressly stays any act to "perfect" any lien in the debtor's property. See, e.g., In re Terkeltaub, 117 B.R. 47, 50 (Bankr. D.Conn.1990) (§ 362(a)(4) is violated by the postpetition creation and recording of a mortgage).
57. U.C.C. § 9–301(1)(b).
58. 11 U.S.C.A. § 546(b).

WARNING! Section 546(b) does not apply in a section 544(a) case simply because state law allows a third party to perfect after the intervention of a lien creditor or bona fide purchaser and the third party has done so. State law must also give priority to the third party based on her subsequent perfection. In the words of the legislative history behind section 546(b), it applies only if "perfection relates back to a date that is before the commencement of the case [i.e., that is prior to the filing of the bankruptcy petition]."[59] In addition, section 546(b) "does not come into play" unless the creditor actually exercises her bankruptcy right to perfect postpetition so as to trigger her state law right of relation-back priority.[60]

The automatic stay of bankruptcy does not bar taking advantage of section 546(b). Expressly excluded from the operation of the stay is "any act to perfect an interest in property to the extent that the trustee's rights and powers are subject to such perfection under section 546(b) * * *."[61] Yet, because relation-back priority rules are rare under state law, section 546(b) and this exclusion from the stay are rarely applicable.

Bankruptcy's usual freeze framing of third-parties' interests for purposes of section 544(a) is, however, two sided and nondiscriminatory. Although it works against third parties whose interests are unperfected prior to bankruptcy, the freeze can work in favor of third parties whose interests are perfected at the time of bankruptcy. Specifically, the lapse of perfection of an interest after the case has commenced does not necessarily destroy its priority over the trustee's section 544(a) claim as determined at the decisive moment of the bankruptcy filing.

For example, an Article 9 security interest is immune from attack under section 544(a) if the interest is properly perfected upon the debtor's bankruptcy.[62] Perfection is ordinarily accomplished by filing a financing statement.[63] Perfection by filing, however, is effective for only five years unless a continuation statement is filed.[64] At the end of the five-year period the effectiveness of the filing ends, i.e., lapses. The usual effect under state law is that the security interest becomes unperfected and is deemed to have been unperfected and subordinate "as against a person who became a purchaser or lien creditor before lapse."[65] The trustee, qua section 544(a) lien creditor, cannot take advantage of this state law when the perfection of a security interest lapses after bankruptcy because the priority of third-parties' interests in relation to the trustee's section 544(a) claims is set and determined as of the time the petition is filed; so the priority of an Article 9 security interest that is perfected by filing when bankruptcy begins is not lost by lapse of the filing during the bankruptcy case.[66]

The good news about the trustee's status as a hypothetical claimant under section 544(a), compared to her position as successor of real creditors under section 544(b), is that the trustee's 544(a) rights, powers and priority are not affected by the insider information of actual creditors that can

---

59. H.R. Rep. No. 595, 95th Cong., 1st Sess. 371, reprinted in 1978 U.S. Code Cong. & Ad. News 5963, 6327; S. Rep. No. 989, 95th Cong., 2d Sess. 86, reprinted in 1978 U.S. Code Cong. & Ad. News 5787, 5872.

60. See Practitioner Treatise, Vol. 2.

61. 11 U.S.C.A. § 362(b)(3).

62. See U.C.C. § 9–301(1)(b).

63. U.C.C. § 9–302(1).

64. U.C.C. § 9–403(2).

65. U.C.C. § 9–403(2).

66. See Practitioner Treatise, Vol. 2.

sometimes dilute the value of their claims. In asserting the rights of an actual creditor under section 544(b), the trustee's rights are derivative and coextensive with the rights of the creditor herself; therefore, the trustee's avoiding power under section 544(b) is diluted by any defects in the creditor's standing (such as preclusive knowledge) that would prevent the creditor herself from avoiding claims to the debtor's property.

In contrast, the trustee's claims under section 544(a) are original and independent, and in asserting them the trustee is a "well nigh 'ideal' "[67] lien creditor or bona fide purchaser. Section 544(a) thus puts the trustee, as lien creditor, "wherever he may need to be, replete with any incidentals, process, papers, proof, or whatever is required to make him the 'ideal creditor.' "[68] The trustee, as bona fide purchaser, is a person who:

(1) at the instance the petition is filed, purchases from the debtor;

(2) for value;

(3) in good faith;

(4) without actual knowledge of any defect or limitation in title;

(5) every interest in real property the debtor could have purported to convey without the terms of the conveyancing instrument itself evidencing irregularity;

(6) by an instrument that adheres to all formal requisites usually and regularly followed in the relevant jurisdiction * * *; and

(7) who as of the moment of purchase, takes all unilateral steps possible under relevant nonbankruptcy law to perfect the conveyance * * *.[69]

Most significant, like Sergeant Schultz of Hogan's Heros, the trustee as lien creditor and bona fide purchaser officially "knows nothing" notwithstanding her own personal knowledge and the knowledge of the debtor's real creditors. Section 544(a) is explicit: The avoidance powers it creates are unaffected by "any knowledge of the trustee or of any creditor."[70] Moreover, none of the debtor's knowledge is imputed to the trustee.[71]

Be careful to avoid reading this indulgence of innocence too broadly. The phrase in section 544(a), "without regard to the knowledge of the trustee," negates only "any *personal knowledge* the trustee may have."[72] It "does not give the trustee any greater rights than he, or any other person would have as a bona fide purchaser or creditor under applicable state law."[73] Consequently, if state law would charge a real judicial lienor or bona fide purchaser with constructive or inquiry notice (even beyond record, constructive notice) that denies her priority despite her actual, subjective

---

67. Matter of Quality Holstein Leasing, 752 F.2d 1009, 1013 (5th Cir.1985).

68. In re First City Mortg. Co., 69 B.R. 765, 770 (Bankr. N.D.Tex.1986) (on motion for rehearing).

69. In re Gurs, 27 B.R. 163, 165 (Bankr. 9th Cir.1983), reh'g denied, 34 B.R. 755 (Bankr. 9th Cir. 1983).

70. 11 U.S.C.A. § 544(a).

71. See Practitioner Treatise, Vol. 2.

72. In re Morse, 30 B.R. 52, 54 (Bankr. 1st Cir.1983) (emphasis in original).

73. Id.

innocence, the trustee as hypothetical, ideal lien creditor or bona fide purchaser is similarly charged and likewise denied priority.[74]

The debtor can sometimes assert the trustee's avoiding powers. Most significantly, a debtor operating as a Chapter 11 debtor-in-possession enjoys "all the rights * * * and powers * * * of a trustee serving in a [Chapter 11] case * * *,"[75] including the trustee's avoidance powers. Thus, a debtor in possession can use section 544(a) to avoid an interest that is subordinate to the claim of a third party even though, outside of bankruptcy, the interest is fully enforceable against the debtor herself. The explanation is that "[a] debtor in possession is a fiduciary holding the estate's assets and operating its business for the benefit of the creditors [rather than the debtor] and under the supervision of the court."[76]

A recurring issue in section 544(a) cases is whether and how far the debtor, in asserting the trustee's strong arm powers as debtor in possession or otherwise, is entitled to the trustee's ideal, subjectively innocent status when the debtor herself has personal knowledge that would deny priority to a lien creditor or purchaser charged with same. The simplest analysis is that whenever the debtor derivatively asserts the trustee's powers under section 544(a), the debtor stands fully in the trustee's shoes and takes the trustee's place; thus, if the trustee's personal knowledge is irrelevant, so is the debtor's own personal knowledge. This result is bolstered when the powers are not asserted by the debtor personally and for herself, but are asserted by her in the capacity of a legally separate entity, such as a Chapter 11 debtor-in-possession.

Most courts follow this simple analysis to a point. They deem that when a postpetition debtor asserts section 544(a) claims, she is innocent of personal knowledge about a third-party's interest that would subordinate the claim of a lien creditor or purchaser under state law.[77] This result is easy to swallow in most cases because typically, the third-party is herself responsible for the vulnerability of her claim under section 544(a): She failed properly to perfect or take other action that would have insured her claim against a lien creditor or bona fide purchaser. The third party's own fault in failing to perfect is not a compelling reason to dilute the strong arm powers of a postpetition debtor, especially when the debtor's success in asserting those powers will benefit other creditors of the estate whom perfection was designed to protect.

The fictional distinction between the prepetition debtor and the debtor asserting avoiding powers in bankruptcy is harder to accept when the debtor's personal fault is greater, as when the debtor engaged in unfair, prepetition conduct which caused the vulnerability of the third-party claim that is the object of the section 544(a) attack. The technical or conceptual basis for the distinction is the same, however, and is not eliminated by the increased culpability of the debtor; so there is a legal basis for honoring the distinction fully and thereby allowing the postpetition debtor the full,

---

74. See Practitioner Treatise, Vol. 2.

75. 11 U.S.C.A. § 1107(a).

76. In re Waldvogel, 125 B.R. 13, 15 (Bankr. E.D.Wis.1991).

77. See Practitioner Treatise, Vol. 2.

unrestrained use and benefit of the strong-arm powers regardless of her prepetition misconduct.[78]

On the other hand, honoring the distinction is understandably less palatable in cases of debtor misconduct because the debtor effectively escapes accountability for her own deliberate sins. One way to avoid this result is to ignore the distinction, straightforwardly, on the obvious policy basis that to honor it in such cases could encourage prepetition misbehavior designed to give debtors postpetition advantage in bankruptcy. An indirect way to avoid the result is to rely on equity for an end run: Recognize and honor the distinction; but supplement the third party's crippled legal interest (which is vulnerable under section 544(a)) with an invincible equitable interest of some kind which is justified by the debtor's misconduct.[79] The first approach is preferable because it is more intellectually honest and also because state law may not provide an equitable interest that outranks the strong arm powers of section 544(a).[80]

E. STATUTORY LIENS, SECTION 545

§ 6–62 Statutory Liens, Section 545

Section 545 gives the trustee a separate, specific power to avoid four kinds of statutory liens on any kind of property of the debtor. This avoidance power works against any statutory lien that:

(1) first becomes effective against the debtor—

   (A) when a case under this title concerning the debtor is commenced;

   (B) when an insolvency proceeding other than under this title concerning the debtor is commenced;

   (C) when a custodian is appointed or authorized to take or takes possession;

   (D) when the debtor become insolvent;

   (E) when the debtor's financial condition fails to meet a specified standard; or

   (F) at the time of an execution against property of the debtor levied at the instance of an entity other than the holder of such statutory lien;

(2) is not perfected or enforceable at the time of the commencement of the case against a bona fide purchaser that purchases such property at the time of the commencement of the case, whether or not such a purchaser exists;

(3) is for rent; or

(4) is a lien of distress for rent.[1]

The "fixing" of a statutory lien that fits into any of these four alternative categories can be avoided by the trustee on the basis of section 545 even

---

78. See Practitioner Treatise, Vol. 2.
79. See Practitioner Treatise, Vol. 2.
80. See Practitioner Treatise, Vol. 2.

§ 6–62
1. 11 U.S.C.A. § 545.

though the lien is beyond all of the trustee's other avoiding powers. Significantly, a lien that is avoidable under section 545 can be avoided notwithstanding that the lien has been enforced prior to bankruptcy by selling the property to which the lien attached.[2]

Any other statutory lien (i.e., a statutory lien not described in section 545) cannot be avoided under section 545[3] but is nevertheless subject to the trustee's other avoiding powers,[4] with one notable exception. A statutory lien that is not described in section 545, and that thereby escapes avoidance thereunder, cannot be avoided as a preference under section 547(b).[5] The basis for this preference immunity is that section 547(c) expressly excepts, from avoidance under section 547(b), "the fixing of a statutory lien that is not avoidable under section 545 * * *."[6]

Applying section 545 is basically a two-step procedure: First, decide whether the claim that the trustee seeks to avoid is a *statutory lien*. If not, neither section 545 nor the section 547(c) immunity from preference law applies. If the claim is a statutory lien, decide if the lien is a kind described in section 545. If so, the lien can be avoided on the basis of section 545 alone. If the lien is statutory but section 545 does not describe it, then section 545 is inapplicable and cannot be used to avoid the lien. The lien can be challenged, however, under other avoidance provisions, except section 547 on preferences.

The Code defines "statutory lien" to mean

> lien arising solely by force of a statute on specified circumstances or conditions, or lien of distress for rent, whether or not statutory, but does not include security interest or judicial lien, whether or not such interest or lien is provided by or is dependent on a statute and whether or not such interest or lien is made fully effective by statute.[7]

WARNING! This definition defines largely by exclusion, and it contains several important terms that are themselves explicitly defined. After following the instruction to exclude the most common kinds of liens, security interests[8] and judicial liens[9], the meaning of statutory lien is reduced to this: any nonconsensual lien (i.e., any charge on property to secure the payment or performance of an obligation[10]) that arises upon specified circumstances solely by statute without legal or equitable process or proceeding, and any lien of distress for rent.

An encumbrance that arises, i.e., is created and made effective, solely by statute does not avoid classification as a statutory lien because the lien is enforced through judicial process.[11] Also, a statutory lien does not lose the

---

2. See Practitioner Treatise, Vol. 2.
3. See Practitioner Treatise, Vol. 2.
4. See Practitioner Treatise, Vol. 2.
5. See Practitioner Treatise, Vol. 2.
6. 11 U.S.C.A. § 547(c)(6), which is fully discussed in our discussion of preference law, at § 6–36 supra.
7. 11 U.S.C.A. § 101(53).
8. " '[S]ecurity interest' means lien created by agreement." 11 U.S.C.A. § 101(51).
9. " '[J]udicial lien' means lien obtained by judgment, levy, sequestration, or other legal or equitable process or proceeding." 11 U.S.C.A. § 101(36).
10. 11 U.S.C.A. § 101(37).
11. See Practitioner Treatise, Vol. 2.

classification simply because the debtor somehow accepts or acquiesces to the lien.[12]

The list of liens that ARE NOT statutory liens includes most commercially and practically significant encumbrances, such as:

- Article 9 security interests in personal property or fixtures;
- Pledges and assignments of, and liens on, personalty beyond the scope of Article 9 that are created by contract;[13]
- Real estate deeds of trust, mortgages, land sale contracts and other real estate encumbrances created by agreement;[14]
- Liens of judgment, execution and sequestration;[15]
- Garnishment liens;[16] and,
- Uncodified, common-law liens (except distress for rent).

The list of practically significant encumbrances that ARE statutory liens is typically very small, including primarily:

- Construction liens for materials and services furnished for the improvement of real estate;[17]
- Liens for personal services[18] and for services or supplies furnished with respect to personalty;[19]
- Warehousemen's liens;[20]
- Lien on warehoused grain that arises, solely by force of statute, upon depositing grain there;[21]
- Tax liens and liens of government for services;[22]
- Statutory landlord liens for rent;[23] and,
- Common-law liens of distress for rent.[24]

In the final analysis, therefore, "statutory lien" is defined so narrowly that it covers very few important liens. Moreover, because section 545 only applies to a subset of four classes of statutory liens, its coverage is even less.

The largest class of statutory liens potentially within the scope of section 545 is the class defined by subsection (2): any and all statutory liens that are unperfected or otherwise unenforceable under state law against a bona fide purchaser who purchases at the time of bankruptcy.[25] If such a person hypothetically acquiring the property at that time would defeat the statutory lien under local law, the lien is avoidable under section 545 whether or not such a person actually exists.[26]

---

12. See Practitioner Treatise, Vol. 2.
13. See Practitioner Treatise, Vol. 2.
14. See Practitioner Treatise, Vol. 2.
15. See Practitioner Treatise, Vol. 2.
16. See Practitioner Treatise, Vol. 2.
17. See Practitioner Treatise, Vol. 2.
18. See Practitioner Treatise, Vol. 2.
19. See Practitioner Treatise, Vol. 2.
20. See Practitioner Treatise, Vol. 2.
21. See Practitioner Treatise, Vol. 2.
22. See Practitioner Treatise, Vol. 2.
23. See Practitioner Treatise, Vol. 2.
24. See Practitioner Treatise, Vol. 2.
25. 11 U.S.C.A. § 545(2). The Code defines "purchaser" very broadly to mean "transferee of a voluntary transfer, and includes immediate or mediate transferee of such a transferee." 11 U.S.C.A. § 101(43).
26. See Practitioner Treatise, Vol. 2.

In effect, the trustee is deemed to have the status of a bona fide purchaser as of the time of filing. The status results from federal law, section 545. By asserting this federal "purchaser" status the trustee can avoid any statutory lien that would then be subordinate to such a purchaser under local law. It is the local law that creates the lien that decides the lien's priority against the trustee's status as purchaser.[27] For this purpose the trustee is deemed to be an innocent purchaser: her personal knowledge of the lien, and the lien's validity between the debtor and statutory lienor, is irrelevant and is not imputed to the trustee in her role as hypothetical purchaser under section 545.[28]

On the other hand, this innocence will not enable the trustee to defeat a lien under section 545(2) that is enforceable against an innocent purchaser under applicable state law. In this case the trustee is powerless even against a secret, unrecorded lien that is locally enforceable against such a purchaser.[29]

To a large extent this power to avoid statutory liens under section 545 looks very much like and duplicates the strong-arm powers of section 544(a). The overlap is not total, however. Section 545 retains a bit of independent significance. The trustee's status as a hypothetical purchaser under section 544(a) is limited to real property; as to personal property she is only a lien creditor. In contrast, the trustee has no lien creditor status under section 545, but her purchaser status thereunder extends to all property. Thus, an unperfected statutory lien on personal property that is subordinate to a bona fide purchaser under local law can be defeated by the trustee under section 545, but not by her acting as purchaser under section 544(a). Even this sliver of independent significance is lost if local law would also subordinate the unperfected statutory lien to the holder of a judicial lien. In this case the statutory lien could fall to the trustee qua lien creditor under section 544(a).

Here is an example of a case in which only section 545 could make the trustee's day. Suppose that the federal government has tax liens on an automobile of the debtor and her stock in AT&T.[30] Both liens were perfected before bankruptcy.[31] The liens in this case are invulnerable to the strong arm powers of section 544(a): the trustee as section 544(a) lien creditor takes subject to a perfected tax lien, and as purchaser under section 544(a) she has no claim whatsoever to personal property.

Under section 545, however, the trustee's claim as purchaser extends to personal property. As a general rule, perfected federal tax liens are enforceable against bona fide purchasers;[32] but purchasers of securities and motor vehicles take free of filed liens on the property.[33] Thus, the trustee can

---

27. See Practitioner Treatise, Vol. 2.

28. See Practitioner Treatise, Vol. 2.

29. See Practitioner Treatise, Vol. 2.

30. "If any person liable to pay any tax neglects or refuses to pay the same after demand, the amount * * * shall be a lien in favor of the United States upon all property and rights to property, whether real or personal, belonging to such person." 26 U.S.C.A. § 6321. The lien dates from the time of tax assessment. Id. § 6322.

31. The federal tax lien is perfected by filing public notice as prescribed by federal law. See 26 U.S.C.A. § 6323(f).

32. 26 U.S.C.A. § 6323(a).

33. 26 U.S.C.A. § 6323(b)(1) & (2).

avoid the government's tax liens on the debtor's automobile and stock even though the liens are perfected at the time of the debtor's bankruptcy.[34]

We should note here that perfected federal tax liens on certain other kinds of personal property are subordinate to the claims of special bona fide purchasers. Most notably, a perfected tax lien on inventory is invalid against a "purchaser in the ordinary course of the seller's trade or business." [35] The legislative history of section 545 is unclear on whether or not a trustee can claim to be such a specialized purchaser under section 545.[36] The argument that the trustee acquires this status is based on the literal language of section 545(2): a statutory lien can be avoided if the lien "is not perfected or enforceable * * * against a bona fide purchaser * * *." [37] It is not required for avoidance that the lien be unenforceable against all bona fide purchasers. The requirement is only that it be unenforceable against "a," i.e., any, bona fide purchaser. Although a purchaser in the ordinary course is special, she is nevertheless a bona fide purchaser. Thus, because a perfected federal tax lien in inventory is not enforceable against a bona fide purchaser, i.e., a purchaser in the ordinary course, such a lien can be avoided on the basis of section 545(2). This argument fails if the congressional identification of "a bona fide purchaser" was aimed at a generic bona fide purchaser and not at a specialized bona fide purchaser such as a purchaser of a particular commodity or a buyer in the ordinary course.

The absolutely smallest class of statutory liens within the scope of section 545 is the class described in subsection (1): "springing" liens that do not arise unless and until the debtor suffers a kind financial stress described there, including bankruptcy, insolvency, or execution on her assets at the hands of another creditor. Significantly, section 545(1) is not satisfied simply because a statutory lien attaches to the debtor's property when she is insolvent or after the occurrence of other events described in subsection (1). The requirement is met only if the lien arises (i.e., is made effective) because of (i.e., due to) the debtor's insolvency or the happening of any of the other described events.[38] State statutes providing for this class of liens have almost entirely vanished because federal law has for so long condemned them as impermissible local efforts to circumvent federal priorities for paying creditors' claims in bankruptcy.

The real, separate importance of section 545 is in avoiding liens for rent that are perfected so as to be beyond the reach of section 544(a) and that are beyond the preference period of section 547(b). Statutory liens for rent are avoidable under section 545(3).[39] These liens are avoidable even if they are perfected upon the debtor's bankruptcy and are then fully enforceable against bona fide purchasers of the liened property. Avoidable, too, under subsection (4) is an uncodified, common-law lien of distress for rent.[40] Such a lien, though not actually statutory, is included within the definition of statutory lien; [41] is thus deemed to be a statutory lien; and is explicitly listed as a kind of lien that the trustee can avoid under section 545.[42]

34. See Practitioner Treatise, Vol. 2.
35. 26 U.S.C.A. § 6323(b)(3).
36. See Practitioner Treatise, Vol. 2.
37. 11 U.S.C.A. § 545(2) (emphasis added).
38. See Practitioner Treatise, Vol. 2.
39. 11 U.S.C.A. § 545(3).
40. 11 U.S.C.A. § 545(4).
41. See Practitioner Treatise, Vol. 2.
42. See Practitioner Treatise, Vol. 2.

F. SELLERS' RIGHT OF RECLAMATION, SECTION 546(c)

§ 6–63 Reclamation Under State Law

For full text of this section, see Epstein, Nickles & White, Bankruptcy, Practitioner Treatise Series, Vol. 2.

§ 6–64 Importance of Preserving State–Created Reclamation in Buyer's Bankruptcy—Role of Section 546(c)

For full text of this section, see Epstein, Nickles & White, Bankruptcy, Practitioner Treatise Series, Vol. 2.

§ 6–65 Effect of Section 546(c)

For full text of this section, see Epstein, Nickles & White, Bankruptcy, Practitioner Treatise Series, Vol. 2.

§ 6–66 State Law Requirements for Reclamation and Federal Requirements of Section 546(c)

For full text of this section, see Epstein, Nickles & White, Bankruptcy, Practitioner Treatise Series, Vol. 2.

§ 6–67 The Possession and Priority Requirement

For full text of this section, see Epstein, Nickles & White, Bankruptcy, Practitioner Treatise Series, Vol. 2.

G. POSTPETITION TRANSFERS, SECTIONS 549, 542 AND 552

§ 6–68 Introduction to Postpetition Transfers and Their Avoidance

Our discussion of the trustee's avoiding powers has focused thus far on her powers to avoid *pre* petition transfers of the debtor's property. Here we cross the great divide that results from the filing of a bankruptcy petition and emphasize the trustee's power to avoid *post* petition transfers of estate property and, in the case of section 552, property of the debtor.

The date of the filing of the bankruptcy petition is critically important in bankruptcy law. Subject to limited exceptions, only the property that the debtor owns on the date of the filing of the petition becomes property of the estate.[1] The trustee takes control of the use and disposition of all such property, and the debtor herself loses the right to transfer any interest in the property or otherwise affect it without Code or court authority.[2] Generally, however, property acquired by the debtor after the filing remains her own separate property. The date of the filing of the petition is significant

---

§ 6–68

1. 11 U.S.C.A. § 541(a).
2. See, e.g., Jones v. Harrell, 858 F.2d 667 (11th Cir.1988) (debtor could not settle tort claim that became property of the estate); In re Crevier, 820 F.2d 1553, 1556–57 (9th Cir. 1987) (debtors could not create postpetition security interest in their residence).

not only in determining what property becomes property of the estate but also in determining when the property becomes property of the estate. The filing of a bankruptcy petition, whether voluntary or involuntary, creates the estate,[3] and it is property the debtor then owns that then becomes property of the estate.

The date of the filing of the bankruptcy petition is not, however, the date when the debtor loses possession of her property that passes to the bankruptcy estate, not even in Chapter 7 cases. While the Code provides for the appointment of an interim trustee in Chapter 7 cases "promptly after the order for relief,"[4] there will always be some delay before the trustee can actually take charge of the estate property as she is obligated to do.

During the hiatus between the filing of the bankruptcy petition and the bankruptcy trustee's taking charge of the property of the estate, the debtor will usually have possession and control of it. Therefore, even after the petition is filed the debtor is in a position to transfer property of the estate to herself or a third party. Assume, for example, that B files a Chapter 7 petition on January 10. On January 12, B sells her summer home to X. On January 13, B sells her boat to Y.

Obviously, B should not have made these postbankruptcy transfers. Obviously, the trustee has a cause of action against B for conversion. Obviously, the trustee can claim any proceeds from the postbankruptcy transfers as property of the estate. Obviously, too, the claim against the debtor and the right to remaining proceeds will usually be of limited practical value.

The significant inquiry is whether or not the trustee can recover the summer house from X and the boat from Y. Does bankruptcy law protect X and Y. The same question arises with respect to transfers of estate property by third parties. The answer in each case depends on the extent to which the trustee is empowered to avoid postpetition transfers.

This power does not come from provisions of the Code we have already discussed in this chapter, such as sections 544, 545, 547 and 548. These sections apply only to prebankruptcy transfers. The trustee's power to avoid postbankruptcy transfers comes mainly from section 549, which we discuss here.

Another provision, section 552, governs a special kind of postpetition transfer: the transfer that results when property is subjected to a security interest created by a prepetition security agreement. Especially in business bankruptcies, the typical debtor's property is encumbered by U.C.C. Article 9 security interests that float over the debtor's estate and attach automatically to property of the kinds described in the parties' security agreement whenever the debtor acquires such property.[5] When this happens to property acquired after the debtor's bankruptcy as a result of a security agreement made before bankruptcy, the effect is determined by section 552 rather than section 549. The two sections partly overlap theoretically, but the former works differently and its scope is larger, covering property of both the estate and the debtor. We discuss section 552 here, too.

3. 11 U.S.C.A. § 541(a).
4. Id. § 701(a)(1).
5. See U.C.C. §§ 9–203(1) & 9–204(1).

1. Postpetition Transfers in General, Section 549

§ 6–69 General Rule Regarding Avoidance of Postpetition Transfers

The starting place when considering the effectiveness of postpetition transfers is the relatively easy, straightforward general rule of section 549(a): the trustee can avoid a postpetition transfer of estate property that is not authorized by the Bankruptcy Code or the bankruptcy court.[1] This means that transferees such as X and Y in the preceding hypothetical problem are unprotected, and they are accountable for the property unless an exception to section 549(a) applies.

BE CAREFUL! The general rule of section 549(a) is limited to transfers involving property *of the estate*. It does not extend to transfers involving anyone else's property,[2] not even property of the debtor.[3] Section 541 thoroughly describes "property of the estate,"[4] and we discuss section 541 elsewhere.[5] Thus, we will not get into it here. Keep section 541 in mind, however, as you work with section 549 because only property of the estate is affected by section 549.

Apart from deciding that property of the estate was involved in a transfer[6] that occurred postpetition,[7] there is nothing difficult in applying the general rule of section 549(a). It is plain and clear that the transfer is avoidable absent authorization by the court or the Code. Whether the debtor herself (acting personally or as debtor in possession[8]) or someone else made the transfer is unimportant under section 549(a).[9] It is also unimportant thereunder that the transferee lacked knowledge of the bankruptcy,[10] that the transfer satisfied obligations of the debtor,[11] that the property was the transferee's collateral or the fruits of collateral,[12] that she gave or the debtor received contemporaneous value for the transfer,[13] or that the value the transferee gave was so important as to entitle her to an administrative claim for reimbursement.[14] Section 549(a) is simple and very broad. It

---

§ 6–69

1. 11 U.S.C.A. § 549(a), which provides in whole:

    (a) Except as provided in subsection (b) or (c) of this section, the trustee may avoid a transfer of property of the estate—

    (1) that occurs after the commencement of the case; and

    (2)(A) that is authorized only under section 303(f) or 542(c) of this title; or

    (B) that is not authorized under this title or by the court.

2. See Practitioner Treatise, Vol. 2.
3. See Practitioner Treatise, Vol. 2.
4. 11 U.S.C.A. § 541(a).
5. See § 2–8 supra.
6. 11 U.S.C.A. § 549(a). " '[T]ransfer' means every mode, direct or indirect, absolute or conditional, voluntary or involuntary, of disposing of or parting with property or with an interest in property, including retention of title as a security interest and foreclosure of the debtor's equity of redemption." 11 U.S.C.A. § 101(54). In several other places we discuss the meaning and timing of "transfer," including §§ 6-4-6-7 supra. It most certainly includes the attachment of a lien, so that liens cannot generally attach postpetition without court approval. In re Chateaugay Corp., 115 B.R. 760, 780 (Bankr. S.D.N.Y. 1990) (not even lien that arises by operation of law); Matter of Timberline Property Development, Inc., 115 B.R. 787, 791 (Bankr. D.N.J.1990).

7. 11 U.S.C.A. § 549(a)(1).
8. See Practitioner Treatise, Vol. 2.
9. See Practitioner Treatise, Vol. 2.
10. See Practitioner Treatise, Vol. 2.
11. See Practitioner Treatise, Vol. 2.
12. See Practitioner Treatise, Vol. 2.
13. See Practitioner Treatise, Vol. 2.
14. See Practitioner Treatise, Vol. 2.

"allows the trustee to recover *all* postpetition transfers, except those that fit within the statute's narrow exceptions."[15]

§ 6–70 Exception: Authorized Transfers

For full text of this section, see Epstein, Nickles & White, Bankruptcy, Practitioner Treatise Series, Vol. 2.

§ 6–71 Exception: Involuntary Cases

For full text of this section, see Epstein, Nickles & White, Bankruptcy, Practitioner Treatise Series, Vol. 2.

§ 6–72 Exception: Transfers of Real Estate

For full text of this section, see Epstein, Nickles & White, Bankruptcy, Practitioner Treatise Series, Vol. 2.

§ 6–73 Time Limitation on Avoidance Under Section 549

For full text of this section, see Epstein, Nickles & White, Bankruptcy, Practitioner Treatise Series, Vol. 2.

2. Postpetition Transfers by Third Parties

§ 6–74 Special Protection for Innocent Transferors, Section 542(c)

Property of the estate is sometimes held or controlled by third parties in a position to effect transfers of it. They usually cannot freely transfer the property, however, not even on instructions from the debtor herself, without risking personal accountability to the estate for the value of the property. The most basic reason is that the property belongs to the estate and is properly transferred only as authorized in the Code. Moreover, persons holding certain property are expressly required to deliver it to the trustee,[1] and obligors of the debtor are required to pay their obligations to the trustee.[2] Also, a third person's transfer of estate property can violate the automatic stay of bankruptcy which is punishable by liability for actual and penal damages.[3]

The most common situation of someone else controlling estate property is the highly typical case in which the debtor owns a bank account. The bank is obligated to the debtor to the extent of the balance in the account. When the bankruptcy petition is filed, this obligation, i.e., the balance then in the debtor's account, becomes property of the estate. Moreover, under the general rule of section 542(b),[4] the bank would be obligated to pay the trustee the account balance as of the moment of the customer's bankruptcy.

---

15. See Practitioner Treatise, Vol. 2.

§ 6–74

1. See 11 U.S.C.A. § 542(a). Custodians are elsewhere provided for. 11 U.S.C.A. § 543.
2. Id. § 542(b).
3. See id. § 362(a) & (h).

4. This section provides:

Except as provided in subsection (c) or (d) of this section, an entity that owes a debt that is property of the estate and that is matured, payable on demand, or payable on order, shall pay such debt to, or on the order of, the trustee, except to the extent that such debt may be offset under section

This puts the debtor's bank between a rock and a hard place when, unbeknownst to the bank, the debtor enters bankruptcy. In the case of a checking account, for instance, local law obligates the bank to pay checks properly drawn against the account by making the bank liable to the customer for wrongful dishonor,[5] i.e., failing to pay properly drawn checks. To avoid this liability the bank will always routinely pay checks that are presented against the account. In the process of doing so the bank can easily violate the federal bankruptcy law of section 542(b) because the bank will usually not learn of the customer's bankruptcy until some time after the petition has been filed.

Bankruptcy law recognizes this problem of banks and other third parties holding or controlling estate property and has long protected them. Under the old Act this protection took the form of a decisional rule announced in *Bank of Marin v. England*,[6] which held under the Bankruptcy Act that a bank is not liable for paying a debtor's checks postpetition unless the bank knew of the bankruptcy. Under the Code the protection is a codification and expansion of the holding of *Bank of Marin*, which appears as section 542(c):

> Except as provided in section 362(a)(7) of this title, an entity that has neither actual notice nor actual knowledge of the commencement of the case concerning the debtor may transfer property of the estate, or pay a debt owing to the debtor, in good faith and other than in the manner specified in subsection (d) of this section, to an entity other than the trustee, with the same effect as to the entity making such transfer or payment as if the case under this title concerning the debtor had not been commenced.[7]

Because of section 542(c), a third person[8] who in "good faith"[9] transfers property of the estate, or pays to someone other than the trustee an obligation owed the debtor, in violation of the Code is nevertheless immune from liability if the third person was unaware of the bankruptcy when she acted.[10] Accordingly, a debtor's bank is protected from liability to the trustee when the bank innocently and in good faith pays the debtor's checks with estate property after the debtor's bankruptcy case has commenced.[11]

The protection of section 542(c) is not limited, however, to banks paying checks. Its protection extends to other entities misapplying money owed the

---

553 of this title against a claim against the debtor.

Id. § 542(b).

5. U.C.C. § 4–402.

6. 385 U.S. 99, 87 S.Ct. 274, 17 L.Ed.2d 197 (1966).

7. 11 U.S.C.A. § 542(c).

8. We say "third person" because "it would seem that the debtor himself could not qualify under section 542(c) as 'an entity that has neither actual notice nor actual knowledge of the commencement of the case.'" Matter of Newman, 59 B.R. 670, 672 n.1 (Bankr. W.D.Mo.1986).

9. "Good faith" is lacking where the transfer amounts to a breach of trust between the transferor and the debtor. In re NWFX, Inc., 864 F.2d 593, 596 (8th Cir.1989).

10. The section only applies if the transferor lacks both "actual notice" and "actual knowledge." 11 U.S.C.A. § 542(c). Such notice or knowledge in itself will disqualify the transferor for the protection of section 542(c), even in the absence of a demand for turnover of the property by the trustee. In re Lucas, 100 B.R. 969, 972–73 (Bankr. M.D.Tenn.1989), opinion aff'd and adopted, 110 B.R. 335 (M.D.Tenn.1989), judgment rev'd on other grounds, 924 F.2d 597 (6th Cir.1991), cert. denied, ___ U.S. ___, 111 S.Ct. 2275, 114 L.Ed.2d 726 (1991).

11. See Practitioner Treatise, Vol. 2.

debtor,[12] and to persons mishandling other kinds of property.[13]

WARNING! Note that section 542(c) protects only the party who transfers the property of the estate; it does not protect the transferee.[14] The transferee is fully subject to the trustee's section 549(a) power to avoid postpetition transfers of estate property. While it is true that the transfer was authorized (in a sense) by section 542(c), section 549(a) explicitly permits the trustee to avoid postpetition transfers of estate property *that are authorized* by section 542(c). Thus, the trustee can avoid the transfer as against the transferee unless the transfer is protected by section 549(b) or (c) or otherwise by the Code.

3. Postpetition Effect of Prepetition Security Agreements, Section 552

§ 6–75 Introduction

Section 552 deals with postpetition transfers effected by consensual, floating liens which are especially common in business bankruptcies. For example, suppose that debtor, a retailer, secures its financing bank with a perfected, U.C.C. Article 9 security interest in all of the debtor's inventory and equipment. The parties' security agreement describes these kinds of property as collateral, and also provides, by way of a so-called *after-acquired property clause*, that collateral will include such property the debtor later acquires.

Because of this clause the bank's security interest will float over the debtor's estate and automatically attach to any equipment and inventory the debtor at any time acquires. So inventory and equipment the debtor acquires after the security agreement is made will also become collateral for the bank. No new or amended security agreement is required. The bank need not provide the debtor with additional, new value. Any antecedent debt that the security agreement covers is sufficient value in itself to support a security interest in after-acquired collateral.

Also, because of state law the bank's security interest will automatically attach to any identifiable proceeds that the debtor receives upon disposing of any property that is the bank's collateral. A security interest in proceeds is not dependent upon the parties agreement. It arises by operation of law.

Suppose that the debtor files Chapter 11 bankruptcy and continues to operate her business as a debtor in possession. She sells inventory that was on hand when her petition was filed and acquires fresh inventory and equipment. Because of state law and the parties's security agreement, the bank's security interest attaches to the sale proceeds (whatever they are, including money and receivables) and also to the freshly acquired inventory and equipment. In other words, state law generally continues the force and effect of prepetition, floating security interests despite the debtor's bankruptcy. They are nevertheless highly vulnerable in bankruptcy due to section 552 which, as a general rule, defeats them.

---

12. See Practitioner Treatise, Vol. 2.
13. See Practitioner Treatise, Vol. 2.
14. See Practitioner Treatise, Vol. 2.

§ 6–76 General Rule, Section 552(a)

The general rule of section 552 is that "a prepetition security interest does not reach property acquired by the estate or debtor postpetition."[1] Thus floating security interests created before bankruptcy are sunk by bankruptcy. This general rule is embodied in section 552(a) which provides in full:

> Except as provided in subsection (b) of this section, property acquired by the estate or by the debtor after the commencement of the case is not subject to any lien resulting from any security agreement entered into by the debtor before the commencement of the case.[2]

The rule applies equally to security interests that float because of the parties' agreement (e.g., after-acquired property clauses) or as a result of law (e.g., proceeds).[3] Security interests, whatever their source, simply do not attach to property acquired after the petition is filed. The bankruptcy filing is a barrier they cannot cross.[4]

Note that section 552(a) is limited to liens resulting from *security agreements*. For purposes of bankruptcy, a "security agreement" is "an agreement that creates or provides for a security interest." A "security interest" is a "lien created by agreement." So section 552(a) applies only to consensual liens, not judicial or statutory liens.[5] On the other hand, the meaning of security interest includes a consensual lien on any kind of property. Thus, the application of section 552(a) is not affected by the nature of the collateral, and it applies equally to both real and personal property. Consensual, floating liens on real property are relatively uncommon, however, compared to the everyday routine and widespread use of floating Article 9 security interests on personal property.

If a prepetition, floating security interest could attach to postpetition property, it would cause a postpetition transfer. Section 549 deals with postpetition transfers. What does section 552 add to section 549? The answer is in the effect and coverage of 552. Section 549 empowers the trustee in her discretion to avoid postpetition transfers. In contrast, section 552 declares outright, as a matter of preemptive federal law, that postpetition property is immune from floating security interests created prepetition. There is nothing to avoid when section 552 applies because, as a result of its application, no transfer occurred.[6] More important, while section 549 applies only to estate property, section 552 equally immunizes both property of the estate and property of the debtor.

---

§ 6–76

1. United Sav. Ass'n v. Timbers of Inwood Forest, 484 U.S. 365, 374, 108 S.Ct. 626, 631, 98 L.Ed.2d 740, 750 (1988).

2. 11 U.S.C.A. § 552(a).

3. A proceeds security interest that itself arises by law and not specific agreement is nevertheless subject to section 552 if it "results" from a security agreement. 11 U.S.C.A. § 552(a) ("any lien resulting from any security agreement"). This is true, for example, of an Article 9 security interest in proceeds. In the absence of a security agreement there is no security interest, U.C.C. § 9–105(1)(*l*); without a security interest there is no collateral, U.C.C. § 9–105(1)(c); and, without collateral, there are no proceeds. U.C.C. § 9–306(1). An Article 9 proceeds interest thus results, albeit indirectly, from a security agreement.

This is not of great importance because section 552(b) largely excepts proceeds from the general rule of section 552(a).

4. See Practitioner Treatise, Vol. 2.

5. See Practitioner Treatise, Vol. 2.

6. See Practitioner Treatise, Vol. 2.

§ 6–77 Exception, Section 552(b)

Section 552(a) aims to kill the postpetition effectiveness of a prepetition floating security interest. Subsection (b) creates an exception. It saves and makes enforceable in bankruptcy such an interest that extends to proceeds, product, offspring, rents and profits of prepetition collateral. This exceptional rule of section 552(b) provides:

> [I]f the debtor and an entity entered into a security agreement before the commencement of the case and if the security interest created by such security agreement extends to property of the debtor acquired before the commencement of the case and to proceeds, product, offspring, rents, or profits of such property, then such security interest extends to such proceeds, product, offspring, rents, or profits acquired by the estate after the commencement of the case to the extent provided by such security agreement and by applicable non-bankruptcy law * * *.[1]

More simply stated, "Section 552(b) provides that if a pre-petition security interest encumbers proceeds of pre-petition collateral, the post-petition proceeds of prepetition collateral will be subject to the creditor's pre-petition security interest."[2]

Suppose, for example, that the debtor's bank enjoys a security interest in the debtor's inventory and receivables, present and after-acquired. After the debtor files bankruptcy, she sells inventory that was the bank's collateral before bankruptcy, and receivables result from the sale. The bank's security interest does not extend to the receivables on the basis of the after-acquired property clause in the security agreement. The postpetition effectiveness of that clause was killed by section 552(a). Yet, because the receivables were acquired upon the disposition of the bank's collateral, they are proceeds under state law,[3] and the bank's security interest would continue to some extent in these proceeds by operation of state law even in the absence of an after-acquired property clause.[4] To this same extent the security interest in the proceeds is valid and enforceable in the debtor's bankruptcy because of section 552(b), notwithstanding subsection (a).

Like the general rule of subsection (a), section 552(b) is most often applied in practice to secured transactions involving personal property that are governed by U.C.C. Article 9, but is not theoretically or practically so limited. It can also apply to proceeds or the like resulting from non-Article 9 security interests in personal property[5] and from consensual liens on real estate that is collateral so long as the conditions of section 552(b) are met.[6]

There are two important conditions on the applicability of section 552(b). First, it does not create, as an original matter, a security interest in proceeds or the like. It simply validates in bankruptcy a security interest in such property that attaches postpetition by virtue of nonbankruptcy law. So the first step in applying section 552(b) is to determine if local law gives the

---

§ 6–77
1. 11 U.S.C.A. § 552(b).
2. In re Ludford Fruit Products, Inc., 99 B.R. 18, 25 (Bankr. C.D.Cal.1989).
3. U.C.C. § 9–306(1).
4. U.C.C. §§ 9–306(2) & (4).
5. "Section 552 applies to all security interests, not just to security interests created under the Uniform Commercial Code." In re Oliver, 66 B.R. 426, 428 (Bankr. N.D.Tex. 1986).
6. See Practitioner Treatise, Vol. 2.

secured party an interest in the proceeds she claims.[7] If not, section 552(b) does not apply to protect the security interest for the simple reason that there is no security interest to protect.[8]

The express terms of section 552(b) seem clearly to limit its protection to interests in proceeds and the like that are provided by applicable nonbankruptcy law *and* by the parties' security agreement.[9] The language is actually not so restrictive. We believe section 552(b) is triggered when local law provides for an automatic interest in the proceeds without the parties' agreement confirming the interest.[10] Providing for the proceeds interest in the security agreement is necessary only when doing so is necessary for enforcement of the interest under local law.

In referring to local law for purposes of applying section 552(b), a particularly troublesome issue is whether a mortgagee of real estate is entitled to postpetition rents and profits assigned to the mortgagee as additional security with the land. A mortgage usually enjoys no inviolate right to rents and profits under state law simply because the security agreement covers such property and is recorded. Rather, the right is not effective against third parties, or even against the debtor in some instances, until some further "perfecting" steps are taken after the debtor's default such as taking possession of the land, impounding the rents, appointing a receiver to collect them, judicially sequestering the rents, or some similar action.[11] If the necessary steps to perfect have been taken prior to bankruptcy, the mortgagee enjoys a right to postpetition rents and profits pursuant to section 552(b).[12]

The trouble arises when the steps to perfect have not been taken before bankruptcy. When the petition is filed the trustee acquires the status of hypothetical lien creditor and bona fide purchaser.[13] She thus primes the mortgagee's so-far unperfected right to rents and profits. Under state law the mortgagee may be free to perfect despite the intervention of a third party claimant and thereby establish for the mortgagee a priority to future rents accruing subsequent to her perfection. In bankruptcy, however, the automatic stay prevents the mortgagee from perfecting postpetition;[14] and, if the mortgagee does nothing to perfect in compliance with state law, she establishes no superior rights to any rents and profits under bankruptcy law.[15]

Enter section 546(b). It allows a creditor to perfect her interest after bankruptcy if the local law that governs her interest permits perfection "against an entity that acquires rights in such property before the date of such perfection."[16] Specifically and significantly,

> [i]f such [local] law requires seizure of such property or commencement of an action to accomplish such perfection, and such property has not been seized or such action has not been commenced before the date of

---

7. See Practitioner Treatise, Vol. 2.
8. See Practitioner Treatise, Vol. 2.
9. 11 U.S.C.A. § 552(b).
10. See Practitioner Treatise, Vol. 2.
11. See Practitioner Treatise, Vol. 2.
12. See Practitioner Treatise, Vol. 2.
13. 11 U.S.C.A. § 544(a), which we thoroughly discuss in § 6–61 supra.
14. See 11 U.S.C.A. § 362(a).
15. See Practitioner Treatise, Vol. 2.
16. 11 U.S.C.A. § 546(b).

the filing of the petition, such interest in such property shall be perfected by notice within the time fixed by such law for such seizure or commencement.[17]

Moreover, when section 546(b) applies, the automatic stay does not prevent the creditor from perfecting in compliance with it.[18]

Mortgagees have argued that section 546(b) permits them to perfect postpetition by seeking possession or a receiver in a bankruptcy proceeding, or by providing the notice described in section 546(b), and that doing so thereby establishes a right to rents and profits accruing postpetition after the time of this perfection in bankruptcy. Many courts have accepted this argument,[19] but the growing trend is to reject it.[20]

The usual reasoning behind the widening minority view is that section 546(b) only applies when the local law not only allows an interest to be perfected after an intervening claim, but also relates the perfection back so as to antedate the creditor's priority over the intervening claimant. Because the typical local law governing collateral assignment of rents and profits does not have this relation back feature, section 546(b) is inapplicable. The mortgagee thus cannot perfect her claim to rents and profits after the case has commenced, and therefore lacks a valid claim to any pre- and postpetition rents and profits.

In sum, despite the absence of local law that explicitly allows relation back, real estate lenders frequently engage in bouts with trustees for postpetition rent, and even more often, try by various means to achieve priority as to those rents. As indicated above, these fights are always heavily dependent upon the local law. They are also dependent upon the acts that the lender undertook prior to the filing of the petition. In most jurisdictions there is no fool-proof way to protect one's rights to postpetition rent except by taking possession of the premises or having a receiver take possession prior to the filing of the petition.

The second important condition on the applicability of section 552(b) is that it only applies to postpetition proceeds of collateral that the debtor acquired *before* the case commenced.[21] For example, suppose the debtor acquires new inventory after filing her bankruptcy petition. This inventory is sold, and proceeds are produced. Under state law the bank's security interest would spread to the new inventory due to the security agreement's coverage of after-acquired property and would also continue in the proceeds of the new inventory by operation of law. Under section 552(a), however, the interest in the new collateral (both the inventory and its proceeds) is ineffective, most certainly if the new is not derivative of prepetition collateral; and the interest in the proceeds of the new inventory is not protected by section 552(b) because they are not proceeds of collateral that the debtor acquired before the commencement of the case. The assumption here is that the new collateral is not itself proceeds of prepetition collateral.

Similarly unprotected are proceeds of an account or other contract that was covered by the security agreement but that arose or was made postpeti-

---

17. Id.
18. See 11 U.S.C.A. § 362(b)(3).
19. See Practitioner Treatise, Vol. 2.
20. See Practitioner Treatise, Vol. 2.
21. See Practitioner Treatise, Vol. 2.

tion, or proceeds of crops that the security agreement covered but that were planted after bankruptcy. In these cases, too, as in the inventory hypothetical, the proceeds did not result from property that was itself collateral (i.e., subject to a security interest) before the case commenced, and thus section 552(b) is inapplicable. Section 552(a) applies and immunizes the postpetition property from the security interest.

The security interest in the proceeds of the new, postpetition inventory (or account or crops) is arguably protected by section 552(b) if the secured party can prove that the property is proceeds of proceeds (i.e., second generation proceeds) of property that was collateral before the case commenced.[22] The necessary proof would be difficult to muster. The secured party would be required to show that the new inventory was purchased with money traceable to prepetition collateral, and would also need to show that the new inventory produced the very pot of funds she now claims. Proof of direct lineage is required, and the proof fails if there is any gap in the chain linking the original collateral and the remote proceeds.

So long as the proceeds, product, or whatever results immediately or (arguably) mediately from prepetition collateral, we are satisfied that this condition to section 552(b) is met even if the product itself had no prepetition existence in some other form and arose wholly anew postpetition. For instance, if a secured party has an interest in a debtor's dairy cows that produced postpetition milk, the milk is a product protected by section 552(b) if under state law the secured party would have an interest in the milk as a product of the cows. It does not matter that the milk itself and its immediate components came into existence only after the case commenced.[23]

In other words, section 552(b) is *not* limited to protecting proceeds, products and the like that existed in a different form before bankruptcy and were only transformed thereafter by manufacturing or other processing.

Farm bankruptcies provide the best examples for illustrating the two conditions on section 552(b). Suppose that a bank has a perfected security interest in the debtor's crops and all receivables and intangibles of the debtor, present and after acquired. The debtor files bankruptcy in 1990 after having planting that year's crop. Under local law and section 552(b), the bank's security interest will extend to any and all proceeds of the 1990 crop, including government entitlements with respect to the 1990 crop that are considered proceeds of the crop under local law.[24] It does not matter that the proceeds are paid postpetition or even that the contracts or other arrangements for acquiring the proceeds were made postpetition. It is sufficient that the proceeds result from collateral in existence (e.g., crops that were planted) before the case commenced.

The bank's security interest will not extend to the debtor's 1991 crop or any of its proceeds [25] unless section 552(b) protects mediate proceeds and the

---

22. Proceeds of proceeds are themselves "proceeds" under state law, U.C.C. § 9–306(1), that are subject to the security interest in the original collateral if the secured party can link or trace the original interest through the various transformations of the property to the very proceeds that she claims. U.C.C. § 9–306(2) ("identifiable"). So mediate proceeds that are traceable to prepetition collateral are themselves "proceeds" of that collateral.

23. See Practitioner Treatise, Vol. 2.

24. See Practitioner Treatise, Vol. 2.

25. See Practitioner Treatise, Vol. 2.

bank can make the necessary, difficult proof.[26]

Suppose, however, that the debtor has decided against planting crops in 1991 and elected to participate in a government set aside program that pays her for not planting crops. If this deal was made with the government before bankruptcy so that the debtor acquired contract rights to the benefits prepetition, and if these rights are receivables or intangibles that are covered by the parties' security agreement, the payments that the debtor later receives under the set aside program (even postpetition) are subject to the bank's security interest and protected by section 552(b).[27] The contract that produced the payments was in existence before bankruptcy and was prepetition collateral. Thus, any proceeds of this contract are proceeds of such property and within the scope section 552.

If the set aside deal was made with the government after the debtor filed bankruptcy, the bank has no right to the set aside payments that the debtor receives.[28] Even if the set aside contract and the debtor's rights under it are within the scope of receivables and intangibles covered by the parties security agreement, any security interest in the property is cut off by section 552(a) because the set aside contract and rights arose postpetition; and the proceeds of the contract and rights are therefore not protected by section 552(b) because they are not proceeds of prepetition collateral. The debtor did not acquire the rights until postpetition.

The bank's only chance of prevailing as to set aside payments resulting from a postpetition deal with the government is to convince the court that the debtor's contract and rights under the set aside program are proceeds of prepetition crops or other collateral that existed before bankruptcy. This argument depends on local law and requires a very broad definition of proceeds that some courts have been unwilling to accept.

§ 6–78 Exceptions to the Exception—The "Except" Clauses of Section 552(b)

The exceptional rule of Section 552(b) is itself subject to two exceptions. The first exception, which is announced in the first words of the subsection, is that subsection (b) is subject to other provisions of the Code, specifically: sections 363, 506(c), 522, 544, 545, 547, and 548.[1] Thus, for example, despite the applicability of section 552(b) and the enforceability of a security interest in proceeds, the trustee may use, sell, or lease the property pursuant to section 363.[2] Also, the avoiding powers of sections 544, 545, 547, and 548 override section 552(b) to the extent they apply. This displacement of section 552(b) does not depend on avoiding the proceeds interest directly. The interest will fail upon the avoidance for any reason of the security interest in the collateral that produced the proceeds.[3]

26. See Practitioner Treatise, Vol. 2.
27. See Practitioner Treatise, Vol. 2.
28. See Practitioner Treatise, Vol. 2.

§ 6–78
1. The provision is: "Except as provided in sections 363, 506(c), 522, 544, 545, 547, and 548 of this title." 11 U.S.C.A. § 552(b).
2. See Practitioner Treatise, Vol. 2.
3. See Practitioner Treatise, Vol. 2.

The second exception is in the last words of section 552(b). A proceeds interest that would be enforceable is not valid "to any extent that the court, after notice and a hearing and based on the equities of the case, orders otherwise."[4] This exception cuts back on the protection that section 552(b) otherwise gives a proceeds security interest.[5] It does not allow a court for reasons of equity to enforce an interest that fails the conditions for applying section 552(b).[6]

The purpose is to reduce a postpetition, proceeds security interest to the extent that the estate acquired "the proceeds at the expense of other creditors holding unsecured claims,"[7] which thereby "increases the value of the collateral,"[8] and "which, if not adjusted, would lead to an unjust enrichment of the secured party's position."[9] For example, the proviso

> covers the situation where raw materials * * * are converted into inventory, or inventory into accounts, at some expense to the estate, thus depleting the fund available for general unsecured creditors, but is limited to the benefit inuring to the secured party thereby.[10]

Specifically,

> Suppose that a creditor had a security interest in raw materials worth $1 million, and the debtor invested $100,000 to turn those raw materials into a finished product which he then sold for $1.5 million. The proceeds of this sale (after deducting wages and other administrative expenses) would be added to the secured creditor's collateral unless the court decided that it would be inequitable to do so—as well it might be, since the general creditors were in effect responsible for much or all of the increase in the value of the proceeds over the original collateral.[11]

It is not limited to this exact situation, however, and applies in theory to any case "of the debtor's putting his own money (more precisely, the money of his other creditors) to work to increase the value of the secured creditor's collateral."[12] It applies, for example, in cases where:

- unsecured creditors furnished feed or other supplies essential to postpetition production of milk claimed as collateral by a secured

---

4. 11 U.S.C.A. § 552(b).

5. See Practitioner Treatise, Vol. 2.

6. See Practitioner Treatise, Vol. 2.

7. S. Rep. No. 989, 95th Cong., 2d Sess. 91, reprinted in 1978 U.S. Cong. Code & Admin. News, 5787, 5877. Compare In re George, 78 B.R. 886, 891 (C.D.Ill. 1987) (exception does not apply where debtor did not use assets of the estate to acquire the proceeds).

The exception has also been applied, however, to the extent that the proceeds were produced at the expense of the debtor's own personal funds or effort. In re Hofstee, 88 B.R. 308, 313–14 (Bankr. E.D.Wash.1988), decision aff'd in part, 116 B.R. 872 (Bankr. 9th Cir. 1990).

8. Matter of Village Properties, Ltd., 723 F.2d 441, 444 (5th Cir.1984), cert. denied, 466 U.S. 974, 104 S.Ct. 2350, 80 L.Ed.2d 823 (1984).

9. In re Cross Baking Co., Inc., 818 F.2d 1027, 1033 (1st Cir.1987).

The "equities" exception does not apply to the original, prepetition collateral. In re North County Place, Ltd., 92 B.R. 437, 443–44 (Bankr. C.D. Cal.1988). Compare section 506(c) which applies to all collateral but is limited to imposing a surcharge for the reasonable and necessary costs of the estate preserving or disposing of the property.

10. H.R. Rep. No. 595, 95th Cong., 1st Sess. 377, reprinted in 1978 U.S. Code Cong. & Admin. News 5963, 6333; S. Rep. No. 989, 95th Cong., 2d Sess. 91, reprinted in 1978 U.S. Code Cong. & Admin. News, 5787, 5877.

11. J. Catton Farms v. First Nat'l Bank, 779 F.2d 1242, 1246 (7th Cir.1985) (dicta).

12. Id. at 1247.

party;[13]

- the debtor or trustee expends funds of the estate toward the care and harvesting of a crop that is collateral of a secured party who is entitled to proceeds of the crop under section 552(b);[14]

- the debtor expends labor and funds to produce products from prepetition livestock that was the secured party's collateral;[15] or,

- the secured party claims proceeds of accounts that existed prepetition, but the trustee expends estate funds to create the goods or provide the services covered by the accounts.[16]

Moreover, a proceeds security interest that is valid under section 552(b) is also subject to reduction under section 506(c) which imposes a surcharge on a secured claim for expenses of the estate in preserving or disposing of the collateral.[17]

On the other hand, the "equities" exception of section 552(b) is inapplicable in the absence of sufficient evidence by the trustee justifying its application.[18] It has seldom been applied in practice, probably because of the difficulties in marshaling the necessary evidence.

H. CONSEQUENCES OF AVOIDANCE
§ 6–79 Overview of Consequences

The preceding umpteen pages mainly explain the trustee's avoiding powers, that is, the legal bases on which the trustee can avoid a transfer of property. A trustee is motivated to exercise those powers because of the three major consequences of avoidance: *nullification* of the transfer as against the trustee; *preservation* of the transfer for the benefit of the estate; and, in an appropriate case, *recovery* from transferees of the property or from other people who benefitted from the avoided transfer.

Nullification is the principal consequence of avoidance. It always occurs upon avoidance and predicates the other two consequences, but is also significant in its own right. Nullification essentially means that the transfer is retroactively ineffective and the transferee legally acquired nothing through it.

Preservation of the avoided transfer also occurs upon avoidance[1] but is rarely practically important. In effect, it is an avoiding power which is used to defeat transfers that were subordinate to the avoided transfer under nonbankruptcy law.

Recovery goes beyond avoidance. Recovery is a bankruptcy remedy for avoidance which makes transferees of the affected property, and also people for whose benefit the transfer was made, personally accountable to the estate for the return of the property or for its value.[2] Avoidance is always necessary for recovery, but recovery is not always necessary or even useful after avoidance.

---

13. See Practitioner Treatise, Vol. 2.
14. See Practitioner Treatise, Vol. 2.
15. See Practitioner Treatise, Vol. 2.
16. See Practitioner Treatise, Vol. 2.
17. See Practitioner Treatise, Vol. 2.

18. See Practitioner Treatise, Vol. 2.

§ 6–79

1. 11 U.S.C.A. § 551.
2. Id. § 550.

Before focusing on each of the three consequences separately, consider this hypothetical problem which illustrates and contrasts their different functions. Suppose that, six months before filing bankruptcy, the debtor, D, gave an insider creditor, IC, a perfected Article 9 security interest in goods to secure an antecedent debt of $13,000. The same property was subject to a competing security interest for $9,000 in favor of a bank, B, a non-insider creditor. B acquired its interest a year before IC, but perfected a few days after IC. Thus, IC enjoyed priority.[3]

In the six-month period preceding bankruptcy, D paid IC $3,000 on the secured debt. B was paid nothing.

When D files bankruptcy, the goods (which are now worth only $10,000 because of market forces) become property of the bankruptcy estate because, despite the security interests that D created, D retained title to and thus an interest in the goods.[4] On the other hand, the property remains subject to the security interests of IC and B. If their liens are valid in bankruptcy, they can eventually recover the property and satisfy their secured claims from its value without sharing it with anyone.

Soon after D's bankruptcy case commences, both IC and B ask for relief from the automatic stay for the purpose of enforcing their security interests in the goods. Simultaneously, the trustee seeks to avoid their interests. The trustee convinces the bankruptcy court that the security interest to IC was an avoidable preference under section 547(b).[5] The preference period as to IC is one year because she was an insider.[6] No section 547(c) exception applies. The bankruptcy court will order that the security interest to IC is avoided. This judgment effectively deems, as a matter of law, that the secured transaction between IC and D never occurred. It is nullified. Thus, IC's claim for the balance of the debt owed her, $4,000, is unsecured. IC becomes a general unsecured creditor of the estate.

The trustee cannot avoid B's security interest as a preference. The preference period as to B (a non-insider) is 90 days,[7] and B's security interest was created and perfected beyond the 90-day period preceding bankruptcy. The trustee is not defeated, however. Another consequence of avoiding the transfer to IC is that the transfer (i.e., the security interest that D gave IC) is automatically preserved for the benefit of the estate.[8] This preservation means that the trustee can use the avoided interest to reduce or eliminate secured claims that were subordinate to it under nonbankruptcy law. Outside of bankruptcy IC enjoyed priority over B.[9] In bankruptcy the trustee can assert the priority of IC's avoided, though preserved, interest and thereby avoid and thus nullify B's interest to the same extent that IC had priority over B under state law. B, too, thus becomes a general unsecured creditor because IC's avoided lien equaled the property's value and would therefore have entirely squeezed out B's interest under state law.

The goods were fully encumbered at the beginning of D's bankruptcy. Now the goods are completely unencumbered. The trustee has freed their

3. U.C.C. § 9–312(5)(a).
4. 11 U.S.C.A. § 541(a)(1).
5. Id. § 547(b).
6. Id. § 547(b)(4)(B).
7. Id. § 547(b)(4)(A).
8. Id. § 551.
9. See U.C.C. § 9–312(5)(a).

value, $10,000, for the benefit of the estate and its general creditors. A trustee's principal goal in exercising her avoidance powers is increasing the size of the estate.

The trustee is not finished. She wants the $3,000 that D paid IC during the six months before the bankruptcy case commenced. It is not property of the estate. The debtor had no interest in it when the case commenced. The payment, however, was preferential and avoidable under section 547(b).[10] No preference exception applies. The transfer, i.e., the payment of the money, was nullified when the bankruptcy court ordered that the transfer be avoided. In this instance, however, the nullification is a hollow victory. The property is not in the trustee's control. IC has it, and avoidance in itself does not constitute a judicial command for the return of the affected property or for other accountability with respect to it.

When the trustee wishes not only to nullify a transfer but also to impose accountability on third parties with respect to it, she must go beyond avoidance of the transfer and recover the affected property from the transferee. A person from whom the trustee can recover is liable for the property itself or its value.[11] It is through the recovery process that the trustee holds third parties personally accountable for the property involved in an avoided transfer. Whatever is recovered from them thereupon becomes property of the estate.[12]

Therefore, after avoiding the $3,000 payment from D to IC, the trustee will ask the bankruptcy court, in the same or a different proceeding, to order recovery of the money. In so ordering, the court will enter a judgment against IC directing her to return the money to the trustee for the benefit of the estate. It is even possible that B could be liable for the money. When the requirements of recovery are met, the class of persons liable to the trustee is not limited to people who received the transferred property from the debtor. The class can include subsequent transferees who never dealt with the debtor [13] and people who benefitted from the transfer even though they never received the property from anyone.[14]

Avoidance is a requirement for recovering from IC or B, but is not sufficient cause in itself to support recovery from anyone. The requirements of recovery go beyond avoidance, primarily because recovery carries defenses which are different from defenses to the trustee's avoiding powers.[15] Thus, it is possible for the trustee to succeed in avoiding a transfer but fail to recover the affected property from anyone. Whether this happenstance is a total loss for the trustee in practical terms depends on whether nullification and preservation are themselves practically meaningful in the case. They always occur as consequences of avoidance regardless of the trustee's ability or inability to recover the affected property or its value.

1. Nullification of the Transfer
§ 6–80 The Nullifying Effect of Avoidance Per Se and the Difference From Recovery

The Code provisions that describe the trustee's principal avoiding pow-

---

10. 11 U.S.C.A. § 547(b).
11. Id. § 550(a).
12. Id. § 541(a)(3).
13. Id. § 550(a)(2).
14. Id. § 550(a)(1).
15. See id. § 550(b) & (e).

ers do so by declaring that the trustee "may avoid."[1] These powers have been successfully exercised in many thousands of proceedings in which the courts have ordered transfers "avoided." Oddly, the Code does not explain if avoidance in itself has any effect, and the courts have explored the effect of avoidance per se in only a handful of reported cases.

It is tempting to conclude that the significance of avoidance is defined mainly (if not exclusively) by section 550, which governs recovery from transferees of avoided transfers.[2] Indeed, no less an authority than Professor Stefan Riesenfeld has written that "[t]he effects of avoidability are spelled out in §§ 550 and 551 [which governs preservation of an avoided transfer]."[3] Recovery under section 550, and preservation under section 551,[4] are undoubtedly consequences of avoidance, but they do not completely define avoidance.[5]

Avoidance of a transfer is significant in itself apart from sections 550 and 551. Here is the evidence: First, the Code provisions that describe the trustee's principal avoiding powers do not define them in terms used by other sections. Instead of providing that the trustee may recover under section 550, or preserve under section 551, the provisions declare flatly that the trustee "may avoid." The language itself suggests that avoidance differs from recovery and preservation and is meaningful in itself. Second, the word "avoid" is a forceful verb which is commonly understood to mean "to make legally void: annul."[6] To deny it this effect is to exclude the word from the Code. Third, the Code provides separate statutes of limitations for avoidance and recovery.[7] Two different limitation periods would have been unnecessary if avoidance were properly defined only in terms of recovery. Fourth, Congress deliberately intended to separate and distinguish "between the concepts of avoiding a transfer and recovering from the transferee."[8] This separation is meaningful only if avoidance is separately meaningful.

Finally, the few courts that have explored this issue have generally concluded that avoidance is separately meaningful from recovery. The issue seldom arises because, in practice, a trustee will seek recovery from transferees in the same proceeding in which she seeks to avoid the transfer. Thus, recovery and avoidance are procedurally combined within the applicable

---

§ 6–80

1. See, e.g., 11 U.S.C.A. §§ 544(a) & (b); 545; 547(b); 548(a) & (b); 549(a); but see § 553(b) ("may recover").

2. Id. § 550(a).

3. S. Riesenfeld, Cases and Materials on Creditors' Remedies and Debtors' Protection 681 (4th ed. 1987).

4. 11 U.S.C.A. § 551.

5. "Thus, § 550(a) is a secondary cause of action after a properly appointed representative has prevailed pursuant to the avoidance sections of the Code. Section 550(a) stands as a recovery statute only and not as a primary avoidance basis for an action, as it will only survive when coupled with the transfer avoidance sections of the Code." In re Mako, Inc., 127 B.R. 471, 473 (Bankr. E.D. Okla. 1991).

6. Webster's Ninth New Collegiate Dictionary 120 (1988).

7. 11 U.S.C.A. §§ 546(a) (avoidance) & 550(e) (recovery).

8. It is through section 550, which "prescribes the liability of a transferee of an avoided transfer," that the Code "enunciates the separation between the concepts of avoiding a transfer and recovering from the transferee." H.R. Rep. No. 595, 95th Cong., 1st Sess. 375, reprinted in 1978 U.S. Code Cong. & Admin. News 5963, 6331; S. Rep. No. 989, 95th Cong., 2d Sess. 90, reprinted in 1978 U.S. Code Cong. & Admin. News, 5787, 5876. This separation is made clear in the provision of different statutes of limitations for avoidance, 11 U.S.C.A. § 546(a), and recovery. 11 U.S.C.A. § 550(e). We discuss these statutes later. See §§ 6–81 & 6–90 infra.

periods of limitation, and there is no reason to determine their separate effects.

The issue of the difference between avoidance and recovery has most clearly surfaced when a debtor relied on section 522(f) to avoid a lien on exempt property [9] when recovery from a transferee was barred by the section 550 statute of limitation on recovery.[10] In these proceedings the majority of courts has decided that section 550 does not in any way limit a debtor's avoidance power under section 522(f).[11] In so doing the courts have enunciated separate, independent effects of avoidance and recovery. By allowing debtors to rid their property of liens apart from recovery under section 550, the courts implicitly define avoidance as nullifying the lien or other interest created in the affected property (i.e., the res in which the lien or other interest was created). Some of these courts explicitly define recovery (and limit it) to retrieving the affected property in the hands of third-party transferees.[12] Recovery is unnecessary if the affected property has not itself been transferred.

We readily accept giving avoidance such a separate nullifying effect, but we reject limiting recovery to situations in which the affected property has been transferred. Section 550 permits a trustee, upon avoiding a transfer, to recover from transferees and other third parties "the property transferred" or its value.[13] This phrase is sufficiently broad to include the property interest involved in the avoided transfer.[14] Thus, a transferee of the avoided interest is liable for recovery under section 550 even though the affected res was not itself conveyed to her or anyone else. Taking this broad view of recovery does not diminish the separate, nullifying consequence of avoidance per se which occurs even in the absence of recovery from transferees under section 550.

Nevertheless, it might be argued that the whole purpose of avoidance is to bring property within the bankruptcy estate for the benefit of the debtor and creditors, and that accomplishing this purpose requires recovery because section 541(a)(3) includes within the estate "[a]ny interest in property that the trustee *recovers* under section * * * 550."[15] Thus, even if avoidance has a separate effect theoretically, it achieves its intended purpose only through recovery. A trustee must therefore always recover under section 550 to give purposive meaning to avoidance. This argument ignores the fact that an automatic consequence of avoidance, beyond its nullifying effect, is preserva-

---

9. Section 522(f) empowers the debtor to avoid nonpossessory, nonpurchase-money security in certain goods and judicial liens that impair an exemption to which the debtor would otherwise be entitled. 11 U.S.C.A. § 522(f).

10. 11 U.S.C.A. § 550(e).

11. See, e.g., Beneficial Fin. Co. of Virginia v. Lazrovitch, 47 B.R. 358, 360–62 (E.D.Va. 1983); In re Goydoscik, 94 B.R. 72 (Bankr. W.D.Pa.1988); Matter of Barnett, 30 B.R. 119 (Bankr. N.D.Ala.1983).

12. See, e.g., Matter of Barnett, 30 B.R. 119, 122 (Bankr. N.D.Ala.1983) ("The only effect that 11 U.S.C. Section 550 has on the avoidance powers * * * is to limit those powers as to recovery of tangible property and property in the hands of third party transferees."); Matter of Conley, 17 B.R. 387, 390 (Bankr. S.D.Ohio 1982) ("§ 550 deals only with the right to recover property transferred to third parties prior to the time when the lien is avoided * * *."); Matter of Swanson, 13 B.R. 851, 854 (Bankr. D.Idaho 1981) (same).

13. 11 U.S.C.A. § 550(a).

14. Beneficial Finance Co. v. Franklin, 26 B.R. 636, 641–42 (W.D.Va.1983), vac'd and remanded without opinion, 714 F.2d 127 (4th Cir.1983).

15. 11 U.S.C.A. § 541(a)(3) (emphasis added).

tion of the lien or other interest that is avoided,[16] and that the preserved interest automatically becomes part of the estate without recovery.[17] Thus, when a transfer is avoided, the interest which the transfer created becomes part of the estate without further ado. It merges with any residual interest in the debtor which passed to the estate when the bankruptcy case commenced.[18]

In some cases, however, nullifying a transfer and automatically including the avoided interest within the estate is not a complete remedy. The transferee may have disposed of the transferred interest or the affected property by consuming it or by reconveying to a third person whose claim should be honored for overriding policy reasons; or, a transferee may effectively control the property despite the avoidance and consequent negation of her legal claim to it. In these and other circumstances in which the estate cannot easily or fully realize the value of the avoided interest, the trustee's further remedy is recovery, under section 550, from transferees and people who benefitted from the avoided transfer.

In sum, our view of the relationship between avoidance and recovery is that avoidance, per se, legally annuls the transfer, and the transferred interest automatically becomes part of the estate.[19] Recovery is a further step which makes transferees and beneficiaries of the transfer personally accountable to the estate with respect to the transferred property. Recovery does not define avoidance by providing the exclusive remedy for it; rather, recovery provides an additional remedy whenever avoidance alone provides incomplete relief. Recovery is necessary only when annulment of the transfer does not completely satisfy the estate.[20]

Avoidance, however, is always foundational. Nullification, preservation and recovery are conditioned on the trustee avoiding a transfer. Avoidance itself is limited not only by the peculiar requirements of the separate avoiding powers, but also by a statute of limitations that equally applies to all of the trustee's avoiding powers: section 546(a).[21] Because of its universal importance, we discuss this time limitation on avoidance before considering the consequences of preservation and recovery that derivatively flow from avoidance.

§ 6–81 Time Limitations on Avoidance, Section 546(a)

For full text of this section, see Epstein, Nickles & White, Bankruptcy, Practitioner Treatise Series, Vol. 2.

---

16. 11 U.S.C.A. § 551.

17. 11 U.S.C.A. § 541(a)(4); Beneficial Fin. Co. of Virginia v. Franklin, 26 B.R. 636, 641 n.16 (W.D.Va.1983), vac'd and remanded without opinion, 714 F.2d 127 (4th Cir.1983) (one can argue, reading § 541(a)(3) & (4) together, that avoided transfers automatically become property of the estate).

18. Section 541(a)(3) is not unnecessary, however, because recovery can affect property that is unaffected by avoidance and preservation alone, principally when a transferee is liable with respect to property in which the debtor never had an interest. Suppose, for instance, that a debtor makes a prepetition transfer of property to a transferee who consumes or disposes of it. The trustee avoids the transfer as preferential or fraudulent. The transferee is liable under section 550 for the value of the property, 11 U.S.C.A. § 550(a), despite having disposed of the property itself. This liability is satisfied in money damages that becomes property of the estate through section 541(a)(3) because it was recovered pursuant to section 550.

19. 11 U.S.C.A. §§ 551 and 541(a)(4).

20. See Practitioner Treatise, Vol. 2.

21. 11 U.S.C.A. § 546(a).

§ 6–82 Time Limitations on Avoidance, Section 546(a)—Applicability

For full text of this section, see Epstein, Nickles & White, Bankruptcy, Practitioner Treatise Series, Vol. 2.

§ 6–83 Time Limitations on Avoidance, Section 546(a)—Mechanics

For full text of this section, see Epstein, Nickles & White, Bankruptcy, Practitioner Treatise Series, Vol. 2.

§ 6–84 Time Limitations on Avoidance, Section 546(a)—Qualifications

For full text of this section, see Epstein, Nickles & White, Bankruptcy, Practitioner Treatise Series, Vol. 2.

§ 6–85 "Stockbroker" Defense (and Other Protections of Financial Markets)

For full text of this section, see Epstein, Nickles & White, Bankruptcy, Practitioner Treatise Series, Vol. 2.

2. Preservation of the Avoided Transfer, Section 551

§ 6–86 Preservation of the Avoided Transfer, Section 551

Section 551 provides that an avoided transfer is "preserved for the benefit of the estate."[1] The preservation is not discretionary and is effected without action. It occurs automatically.[2]

Preservation under section 551 has two effects. First, the property interest that was involved in the avoided transfer automatically becomes property of the estate.[3] Second, the trustee is subrogated to the rights and priority of the transferee of the avoided transfer as against other claimants of the property, and can therefore derivatively reduce or entirely eliminate their claims.[4] The intended effect is to prevent "junior lienors from improving their position at the expense of the estate when a senior lien is avoided."[5]

Suppose, for example, that a farmer files bankruptcy. Her crops are subject to two liens: a long perfected Article 9 security interest in favor of a bank for a production money loan, and a nonconsensual, statutory lien for rent in favor of her landlord. The trustee avoids the landlord's lien under

---

§ 6–86

1. 11 U.S.C.A. § 551. This occurs when a transfer is avoided "under section 522, 544, 545, 547, 548, 549, or 724(a)," and also occurs with respect to a lien that is "void under section 506(d)." Id.

2. See Practitioner Treatise, Vol. 2.

3. 11 U.S.C.A. § 541(a)(4); In re Brown, 33 B.R. 219, 221 (Bankr. N.D.Ohio 1983) (preserved transfer becomes property of the estate, and is not postpetition, after-acquired property of the debtor).

4. See Practitioner Treatise, Vol. 2.

5. H.R. Rep. No. 595, 95th Cong., 1st Sess. 376, reprinted in 1978 U.S. Code Cong. & Admin. News 5963, 6332; S. Rep. No. 989, 95th Cong., 2d Sess. 91, reprinted in 1978 U.S. Code Cong. & Admin. News, 5787, 5877.

section 545, which condemns any statutory lien "for rent."[6] The lien is preserved under section 551, and the trustee steps into the landlord's shoes. Applicable state law gives the landlord's lien priority over the bank's security interest. To the same extent the trustee can defeat the bank's security interest even though the interest cannot be voided directly by the trustee using any of her bankruptcy avoiding powers.[7]

The trustee's power to assert the derivative priority of avoided transfers is subject to three important limitations. First, the trustee's rights against other claimants are exactly coextensive with, and not greater than, the rights that the transferee of the avoided transfer enjoyed under nonbankruptcy law, that is:

> a * * * lien that is preserved under 11 U.S.C. § 551 cannot be greater than that which is avoided by the trustee * * *. By avoiding and preserving the lien, the trustee simply steps into the [lienor's] shoes and succeeds to the [lienor's] rights with regard to the lien. Clearly, the trustee cannot and does not obtain more than what the [lienor] could and should be able to claim * * *.[8]

Two corollaries combine to support this rule. First, a trustee cannot *entirely* defeat another claim simply because the trustee avoided a senior lien or other interest. The other claim is avoided under section 551 only to the extent that the avoided transfer extinguished the other claim under applicable nonbankruptcy law.[9] Thus, if the avoided transfer is a lien for $5,000 and the other claim is a junior lien in the same amount, the junior lien will be affected by the trustee's rights under section 551 only if the property is worth less than $10,000. Otherwise, the avoided senior lien does not impinge on the junior claim which is likewise unaffected by the trustee's subrogation to the rights of the senior lienor.

The other corollary is that section 551 does not cure defects in an avoided transfer to the detriment of other claimants who, as a result of the defects, would have priority under applicable nonbankruptcy law.[10] Suppose, for example, that C1 takes an Article 9 security interest in debtor's goods and immediately files a financing statement. C2 subsequently acquires a security interest in the same property and perfects. Six months later the debtor files bankruptcy. The trustee attacks C1's interest because C1 filed the financing statement in the wrong place; C1's interest was thus unperfected under local law; and it was therefore voidable under sections 544(a) and 547(b).

Avoiding C1's interest avails the trustee nothing with respect to C2's interest.[11] Because C1's interest was unperfected, C2's interest had priority under local law.[12] A trustee's succession to the rights of a lienor under section 551 has no affect on the validity of senior claims to the property.[13]

The second limitation on the trustee's derivative rights under section 551 is that the trustee can assert only the avoided lien or other interest

---

6. 11 U.S.C.A. § 545(3).
7. See Practitioner Treatise, Vol. 2.
8. In re Coal–X Ltd., "76", 103 B.R. 276, 280 (D. Utah 1986), decision aff'd in part, rev'd in part, 881 F.2d 865 (10th Cir.1989).
9. See Practitioner Treatise, Vol. 2.
10. See Practitioner Treatise, Vol. 2.
11. See Practitioner Treatise, Vol. 2.
12. U.C.C. § 9–312(5)(a).
13. See Practitioner Treatise, Vol. 2.

because section 551 preserves only that and nothing more. In the case, *In re Kors, Inc.,*[14] the trustee avoided a bank's unperfected security interest in goods. Stepping into the shoes of the bank as an unperfected secured party did not help the trustee avoid two subsequent security interests in the collateral that were perfected because, under local law, they ranked ahead of the bank's interest. The other secured parties, however, had agreed to subordinate their interests to the bank's claim. The trustee argued that section 551 allowed him to step into the bank's shoes as beneficiary of the subordination agreement and thereby take the proceeds of the collateral ahead of the other creditors. The court disagreed, holding that the trustee's subrogation powers under section 551 extend only to the rights against the debtor derived from the very interest that is avoided.[15]

The third limitation on the trustee's derivative rights under section 551 is that they can be asserted to defeat a junior lien *"only with respect to property of the estate."* [16] The purpose of this limitation, which is an explicit part of section 551, is to prevent the trustee from asserting an avoided lien that floats, such as a tax lien, against after-acquired property of the debtor.[17] Otherwise, if a trustee avoids a tax lien or lien of judgment that automatically reaches after-acquired property, she could arguably assert the lien against property that the debtor acquires postpetition and thereby enlarge the estate at the expense of the debtor's fresh start.

The phrase, "only with respect to property of the estate," has been construed to mean that an avoided transfer becomes property of the estate only if the avoided transfer involves estate property.[18] This construction is wrong. The clear purpose of the phrase is to limit only the subrogation powers of section 551, not to restrict the reach of sections 551 and 541 in bringing avoided transfers within the bankruptcy estate.[19]

3. Recovery From Transferees, Section 550
§ 6–87 Basic Remedial Rule: Recovery of the Property or Its Value

Congress deliberately distinguished between avoiding a transfer and recovering from the transferee.[1] They are conceptually different, and each of them is remedially significant. Recovery depends upon avoidance but does not exclusively define it. Rather, recovery is a remedy that supplements the remedial effect of avoidance per se. Elsewhere we discuss the relationship between avoidance and recovery.[2] Here we explain how recovery works.

---

14. 819 F.2d 19 (2d Cir.1987).

15. Id. at 23–24. These rights might nevertheless include more power than just priority over junior claimants, such as the power to force a senior creditor to marshall assets. In re John I. Paulding, Inc., 76 B.R. 7, 8–9 (Bankr. D.Mass.1987).

16. 11 U.S.C.A. § 551 (emphasis added).

17. In re Losieniecki, 17 B.R. 136, 140 (Bankr. W.D.Pa.1981), citing 124 Cong.Rec. H 11,097 (Sept. 28, 1978); 517, 414 (Oct. 6, 1978).

18. In re Ward, 42 B.R. 946, 950–53 (Bankr. M.D.Tenn.1984).

19. See Practitioner Treatise, Vol. 2.

§ 6–87

1. It is through section 550, which "prescribes the liability of a transferee of an avoided transfer," that the Code "enunciates the separation between the concepts of avoiding a transfer and recovering from the transferee." H.R. Rep. No. 595, 95th Cong., 1st Sess. 375, reprinted in 1978 U.S. Code Cong. & Admin. News 5963, 6331; S. Rep. No. 989, 95th Cong., 2d Sess. 90, reprinted in 1978 U.S. Code Cong. & Admin. News, 5787, 5876.

2. See § 6–80 supra.

Section 550 governs recovery. It provides in subsection (a) this basic remedial rule:

> "[T]o the extent that a transfer is avoided under section 544, 545, 547, 548, 549, 553(b), or 724(a) * * *, *the trustee may recover,* for the benefit of the estate, *the property transferred, or,* if the court so orders, *the value of such property* * * *."[3]

Property or its value that is recovered pursuant to section 550(a) thereupon becomes property of the estate.[4] The transferee has a claim for the amount she must disgorge which is treated as a pre-petition claim against the estate.[5]

Notice that the trustee can recover the value of the transferred property only "if the court so orders." The clear implication is that recovering the property itself is the usual remedy and that recovering its value is extraordinary relief.[6]

In practice, however, trustees recover damages about as often, maybe even more often, than they recover the transferred property itself. The main reason is that trustees commonly pursue defendants who are not in control of the property that was the subject of the avoided transfer.[7] These defendants reconveyed, lost, expended or commingled the property (as, for example, if the property transferred was money) or never had it, and thus they are unable to return the property in species. The only appropriate remedy against such a defendant, and the remedy that is therefore routinely ordered, is recovery of the property's value.[8] The substitutional remedy of damages is available even against a transferee that is a government if sovereign immunity is waived.[9]

Whenever the trustee's recovery is, or is tied to, the value of the property, the amount of the recovery is often based on the property's value when the avoided transfer occurred.[10] Interestingly, depreciation in the property's value during the interim (between the property transfer and the avoidance action) may be sufficient reason in itself to allow the trustee to recover value damages rather than the property itself.[11] On the other hand, if the property has appreciated in value during the interim, the trustee cannot necessarily be forced to accept value damages in lieu of recovering the property,[12] but the transferee gets a lien for appreciation that results from the transferee's improvements to the property.[13] In sum, the defendant bears the burden of any decline in value after the avoided transfer, and the trustee gains the benefit of any subsequent, fortuitous increase in value.

Recovery in a successful avoidance action is not always limited to the recovery described in section 550(a). For instance, trustees are often awarded prejudgment interest when preferences are avoided,[14] which theoretically

---

3. 11 U.S.C.A. § 550(a)(1) (emphasis added).
4. 11 U.S.C.A. § 541(a)(3).
5. 11 U.S.C.A. § 502(h); In re Coated Sales, Inc., 119 B.R. 452, 458 n.14 (Bankr. S.D.N.Y. 1990).
6. See Practitioner Treatise, Vol. 2.
7. See Practitioner Treatise, Vol. 2.
8. See Practitioner Treatise, Vol. 2.
9. See Practitioner Treatise, Vol. 2.
10. See Practitioner Treatise, Vol. 2.
11. See Practitioner Treatise, Vol. 2.
12. See Practitioner Treatise, Vol. 2.
13. See Practitioner Treatise, Vol. 2.
14. See Practitioner Treatise, Vol. 2.

compensates for loss in use of the property.[15] Also, in a rare but appropriate case, which usually involves a fraudulent conveyance, punitive damages are allowed if applicable state law so provides.[16] Trustees sometimes also recover attorney's fees on the basis of state law.[17] Finally, although section 550(a) does not explicitly provide for recovering the proceeds of property involved in a voided transfer, courts have subjected such proceeds to constructive trusts or equitable liens in favor of the trustee.[18] There is even authority that reads section 550 to allow the trustee to recover the fruits of the transferred property *in addition to* the property itself.[19]

§ 6–88 Persons Liable

Two parts of section 550 are critical in determining who is liable thereunder to the trustee. Subsection (a) states the general rule on liability. It provides that to the extent the trustee avoids a transfer, she can recover the property or its value from:

> (a)(1) the initial transferee of such transfer or the entity for whose benefit such transfer was made; or

> (2) any immediate or mediate transferee of such initial transferee.[1]

Note that the trustee "is not restricted to bringing a recovery action pursuant to § 550(a) against the same party" who was the target of the "primary avoidance action."[2] A person is liable under 550(a) simply because the terms of the section fit. It is irrelevant that no transfer to her was avoided.

Government often fits 550(a) and is not excepted from liability by the terms of the section itself. Indeed, 550(a) uses the word "entity," which includes governmental units.[3] Special protection for government is possible, however, because of its sovereign immunity, which is a topic we discuss elsewhere.[4]

Subsection (b) creates an exception to liability but only to a piece of (a). This (b) exception is:

> The trustee may not recover under *section (a)(2)* of this section from

> > (1) a transferee that takes for value, including satisfaction or securing of a present or antecedent debt, in good faith, and without knowledge of the voidability of the transfer avoided; or

---

15. See Practitioner Treatise, Vol. 2.
16. See Practitioner Treatise, Vol. 2.
17. See Practitioner Treatise, Vol. 2.
18. See Practitioner Treatise, Vol. 2.
19. See Practitioner Treatise, Vol. 2.

§ 6–88

1. 11 U.S.C.A. § 550(a).
2. In re Mako, Inc., 127 B.R. 471, 473 (Bankr. E.D.Okla.1991).
3. 11 U.S.C.A. § 101(15).
4. See § 3–34 supra, where we discuss government's immunity to liability for damages tied to violations of the automatic stay. The waiver of governmental immunity is mainly controlled by section 106. 11 U.S.C.A. § 106. Neither it nor any other law establishes a general waiver of the government's immunity from a trustee's claims for monetary relief. United States v. Nordic Village, Inc., ___ U.S. ___, 112 S.Ct. 1011, 117 L.Ed.2d 181 (1992), on remand, ___ F.2d ___ (6th Cir.1992) (immunity of federal government); Hoffman v. Connecticut Dept. of Income Maintenance, 492 U.S. 96, 109 S.Ct. 2818, 106 L.Ed.2d 76 (1989) (immunity of state government).

(2) any immediate or mediate good faith transferee of such transferee.[5]

In short, subsection (a) establishes who is liable. Subsection (b) creates a defense.

These rules are sometimes tricky to apply. Three points about them are most important. First, the *initial transferee* (of the property involved in the avoided transfer) is always liable under section 550(a)(1).[6] The good faith taker defense of section 550(b) is never available to the initial transferee,[7] and any such defense that state law would afford her is preempted and impotent.[8]

Second, any transferee of the property after the initial transferee is also liable,[9] except a subsequent transferee who took for value and in good faith [10] or who took in good faith through such a transferee for value.[11] This class of accountable people is very broad. It includes the person who took from the initial transferee, i.e., the secondary or immediate transferee,[12] and also later takers, i.e., mediate transferees.[13] Because there is a good faith taker defense for a subsequent transferee but not for the initial transferee, many battles fought within section 550 involve the issue whether the defendant was the "initial" or a subsequent transferee.[14] This issue is a matter for the court to decide as a matter of law even if a jury hears the avoidance action.[15]

Third, while liability is generally limited to transferees of the property involved in the avoided transfer, "an entity for whose benefit such transfer was made" is also liable [16] even though she is not a transferee of the property. Moreover, a person who is liable on this basis does not enjoy the good faith taker defense of subsection (b). This class of accountable persons is very small, however. It properly includes only an entity that was the direct beneficiary of the initial transfer.

To explain further these three points, and to add some detail and gloss to the black-letter law of section 550, we will walk you through a ten-step demonstration of how the liability rules of subsection (a) and (b) are applied:

Step 1. We begin with the simplest and easiest case. D makes a transfer of property to A that is avoided by the trustee for D's estate under section 544, 545, 547, 548, 549, 553(b), or 724(a). A, who in this instance retains the property, is liable under section 550(a)(1) as the initial transferee of the property.[17] She is defenseless, and she is accountable for the property or its value despite having paid full value, innocently, and in good faith. The section 550(b) defense is unavailable to A. It applies

---

5. 11 U.S.C.A. § 550(b).

6. 11 U.S.C.A. § 550(a)(1).

7. It is available only to a person whose liability is based on subsection (a)(2) dealing with subsequent transferees. 11 U.S.C.A. § 550(b).

8. In re Rice, 83 B.R. 8, 12 (Bankr. 9th Cir.1987); cf. In re Still, 113 B.R. 311 (N.D.Tex.1990), judgment aff'd, 124 B.R. 24 (N.D.Tex.1991) (D'Oench doctrine and federal holder in due course doctrine cannot bar trustee's action against FDIC); In re Kanterman, 97 B.R. 768, 773–77 (Bankr. S.D.N.Y. 1989), appeal granted, 99 B.R. 208 (S.D.N.Y.1989) (same).

9. 11 U.S.C.A. § 550(a)(2).

10. Id. § 550(b)(1).

11. Id. § 550(b)(2).

12. Id. § 550(a)(2).

13. Id. § 550(a)(2).

14. See Practitioner Treatise, Vol. 2.

15. See Practitioner Treatise, Vol. 2.

16. 11 U.S.C.A. § 550(a)(1).

17. See Practitioner Treatise, Vol. 2.

only to an immediate or mediate transferee of the initial transferee, not to the initial transferee herself.[18] A must account for the property or its value, and under section 550 she gets no credit in reduction of the recovery against her for any value she paid for the property.[19]

Step 2. Suppose now that A sold the property to B soon after acquiring it, and that B reconveyed the property to C. Nothing has changed to affect A's liability. Although she has disposed of the property and cannot return it, she is still the initial transferee who is liable to the trustee for the property's value under section 550(a)(1). "The fact that the property is no longer in the custody of the initial transferee does not prohibit recovery from that transferee."[20]

B is also liable to the trustee under section 550(a)(2) as the immediate transferee, and C is liable thereunder as the mediate transferee; but the section 550(b) defense is available to both B and C. B is protected by (b)(1) if she gave value in good faith and without knowledge of the voidability of the transfer that the trustee avoided.[21] The transferee who relies on this defense is burdened with proving its elements.[22]

Value that counts for purposes of the section 550(b) defense includes value given to the transferee's transferor, and is not limited to value given to the debtor.[23] The knowledge that counts is actual knowledge rather than mere constructive notice[24] or reason to know.[25] On the other hand, a transferee is charged with inferences that a reasonable person would draw from facts actually known to the transferee;[26] and, because of the requirement of good faith, the transferee is charged with facts that would have been learned from further investigation if the facts actually known to the transferee would have caused a reasonable person to investigate.[27]

If (b)(1) protects B, then C is protected by (b)(2) which requires only that C took in good faith.[28] Subsection (b)(2) has no value requirement. If B fails to qualify for the (b)(1) defense, C can defend herself directly on the basis of (b)(1);[29] but in this event C must establish both good faith and value.

Subsequent transferees who cannot establish the section 550(b) defense are liable to the trustee[30]—along with the initial transferee—for the transferred property or its value. The trustee can recover fully from all of them collectively,[31] or from any of them individually, because they are jointly and severally liable.[32] The trustee, however, cannot recover, in total, more than the property or its value even if a group of people are liable. The trustee "is entitled to only a single satisfaction."[33] In effect, therefore, "[s]ection 550 allows * * * [the trustee] to reach a 'deep pocket'—someone who is able to

18. See Practitioner Treatise, Vol. 2.
19. See Practitioner Treatise, Vol. 2.
20. See Practitioner Treatise, Vol. 2.
21. See Practitioner Treatise, Vol. 2.
22. See Practitioner Treatise, Vol. 2.
23. See Practitioner Treatise, Vol. 2.
24. See Practitioner Treatise, Vol. 2.
25. See Practitioner Treatise, Vol. 2.
26. See Practitioner Treatise, Vol. 2.
27. See Practitioner Treatise, Vol. 2.
28. See Practitioner Treatise, Vol. 2.
29. See Practitioner Treatise, Vol. 2.
30. See Practitioner Treatise, Vol. 2.
31. See Practitioner Treatise, Vol. 2.
32. See Practitioner Treatise, Vol. 2.
33. 11 U.S.C.A. § 550(c).

pay the amount of the transfer. It is left to the trustee's discretion to determine from whom he will be most likely to recover."[34]

Step 3. Change the problem. Assume that D pays money to A through A's lawyer, L. After D files for bankruptcy the trustee avoids the transfer, which was a preference, under section 547(b). The trustee seeks to recover from L who was joined in the avoidance proceeding, arguing that L is—technically or literally—the initial transferee. L may nevertheless avoid liability on the basis of the "conduit" exception to the liability of an initial transferee. Under this court-made exception, a person is not liable under section 550(a) as the initial transferee if she acquired no beneficial interest of her own and was merely a person who in the ordinary course facilitated passing the property to someone else for whom it was originally intended.[35] If L is characterized as a conduit then: L acted for A; L is ignored in the chain; and A is recognized as the true initial transferee.

Step 4. Because A is recognized as the initial transferee of the property in Step 3, A is liable under section 550(a).[36] Alternatively, she is liable under the same provision as the person for whose benefit the transfer was made.[37] In either case the section 550(b) defense is unavailable to her.

Step 5. L's immunity in Step 3 is not entirely certain. There are two significant limitations on the exceptional protection afforded a conduit:

> Side Step 5A. The conduit exception is not available to a person who acted without good faith in playing her role in the transaction.[38]
>
> Side Step 5B. The conduit exception is not available to a person who, despite having ultimately passed on the property, was free to do as she wished with it or enjoyed an interest of her own therein before passing it to the intended beneficiary.[39]

L is liable as the initial transferee if the conduit exception is unavailable to her.[40]

Step 6. L's liability as initial transferee does not automatically free A of accountability. A is still a transferee, and every transferee of the property involved in an avoided transfer is liable under section 550(a). At best, A is an immediate transferee who is liable under section 550(a)(2)[41] unless she can establish the section 550(b)(1) defense.[42] Arguably, however, A's role and liability are not so limited. We would argue that, if L acted for A, then L's status as initial transferee is imputed to A. Therefore, A, like L, is an initial transferee and is liable under subsection (a)(1). Alternatively, A is the person for whose benefit the transfer was made and on that basis she is liable under section 550(a)(1) even though she is also an initial or subsequent

---

34. In re Acadiana Elec. Service, Inc., 66 B.R. 164, 166, 168 (Bankr. W.D.La.1986).
35. See Practitioner Treatise, Vol. 2.
36. See Practitioner Treatise, Vol. 2.
37. See Practitioner Treatise, Vol. 2.
38. See Practitioner Treatise, Vol. 2.
39. See Practitioner Treatise, Vol. 2.
40. See Practitioner Treatise, Vol. 2.
41. See Practitioner Treatise, Vol. 2.
42. See Practitioner Treatise, Vol. 2.

transferee.[43] If A's liability is based on either role described in (a)(1), she does not qualify for the section 550(b) defense. This defense would be available to A only if her role were limited to that of immediate transferee under section 550(a)(2).

Step 7. Although every transferee of the property is potentially liable under section 550(a)(1) and (2), a non-transferee is also liable under section 550(a)(1) if she is "the entity for whose benefit such transfer was made."[44] By this language the Code makes clear that recovery is "not restrict[ed] to those persons or entities receiving the property."[45] Suppose, for example, that D transfers property to A to satisfy a debt that B owes to A. The trustee for D's estate avoids the transfer. B is not a transferee but is nevertheless liable.[46] The transfer was made for her benefit. Because her liability on this basis is described in subsection (a)(1), B is not entitled to the section 550(b) defense.[47]

Step 8. Liability imposed on "the entity for whose benefit such transfer was made" is limited in two respects. First, the words "for whose benefit" arguably imply the requirement that the transfer was made for the purpose, i.e., with the intention, of benefitting the person. Apparently, however, such a deliberate intention or designated purpose, while probably sufficient, is unnecessary to satisfy the "for whose benefit" portion of section 550(a)(1). Rather, the courts have usually considered only whether the person benefitted from the transfer without investigating whether benefitting her was the purpose of the transfer.[48] Yet, in all the cases the benefit conferred was a direct and primary benefit, i.e., reduction of the person's primary or secondary liability to a third party.

We thus conclude that the "for whose benefit" test is met without evidence of intention or purpose to benefit so long as the benefit is direct and primary. Conversely, the test is not satisfied if a person benefits only remotely and incidentally from a transfer, especially in the absence of evidence showing that the purpose or intention behind the transfer was to benefit her.

The second limitation is implied by the words, "such transfer." They refer to the transfer that the trustee avoided, which is the first or initial transfer of the property. In sum, therefore, "entity for whose benefit such transfer was made" means an entity who (1) directly benefitted from (2) the first or initial transfer of the property.[49]

These limitations are important. Suppose, for example, that D makes a transfer to A that satisfies B's debt to A. In an unrelated transaction A thereafter transfers the property to C.

43. See Practitioner Treatise, Vol. 2.
44. 11 U.S.C.A. § 550(a)(1). We do not mean to suggest, however, that not being a transferee is a condition to liability on this basis. Here we simply make the point that a non-transferee is potentially liable under section 550(a)(1) despite never getting the transferred property.
45. Matter of Ohio Corrugating Co., 70 B.R. 920, 924 (Bankr. N.D.Ohio 1987).
46. See Practitioner Treatise, Vol. 2.
47. See Practitioner Treatise, Vol. 2.
48. See Practitioner Treatise, Vol. 2.
49. See Practitioner Treatise, Vol. 2.

Side Step 8A. A and B are both liable under section 550(a)(1)—A as the initial transferee and B as the person for whose benefit the transfer was made. Neither of them is protected by the section 550(b) defense because the liability of each is based on subsection (a).

Side Step 8B. C is clearly liable under section 550(a)(2) as the immediate transferee, but in that role she enjoys the section 550(b) defense.

Side Step 8C. C cannot be denied the section 550(b) defense by classifying her under section 550(a)(1) as the person for whose benefit the transfer was made. Although C may have benefitted directly from the transfer to her (and thus remotely by the transfer to A), C was not the person who directly benefitted from the initial transfer to A.[50]

Side Step 8D. Similarly, because the transfer to A satisfied B's debt to A, B's other creditors benefitted in a broad sense if B's net worth was thereby increased. Yet, these other creditors of B are not liable under section 550(a)(1) as people for whose benefit the transfer was made because they were not the direct or primary beneficiaries of the transfer.[51] B was the only such beneficiary of the initial transfer.

Interestingly, liability is not limited to intended beneficiaries who actually benefitted from the transfer: "recovery * * * may be ordered * * * even though the entity [for whose benefit the transfer was made] did not actually receive a benefit as a result of the transfer."[52] We would think, however, that an intended beneficiary who got no benefit should get no liability unless she is chargeable, in whole or part, with responsibility for the transfer itself. Absolute liability without a foundation in either restitution (getting a benefit) or compensation (having caused the transfer) is unjustified and unfair.

Step 9. In Steps 7 and 8 (where D transfers property to A and thereby satisfies a debt that B owes to A), B's liability under section 550(a)(1) as the intended beneficiary of the transfer does not immunize A. Rather, A is also ordinarily liable under the same section as the initial transferee.[53]

Step 10. A difficult issue arises when the benefit to B is the only avoidable aspect of the deal and the initial transfer to A is unobjectionable under the trustee's avoiding powers. Is the initial transferee incidentally liable under section 550(a) even though the transfer to her is directly unavoidable? For example, suppose that six months before D Corporation's bankruptcy it repays an unsecured debt to A which was guaranteed by D's president, P. The payment to A cannot be avoided as a preference under section 547(b) because the transfer was beyond the 90-day period. Yet, the payment resulted in a preference to P who is an insider and with respect to whom the preferential period is one year. P is clearly liable under section 550(a)(1). The issue is whether A is

---

50. See Practitioner Treatise, Vol. 2.
51. See Practitioner Treatise, Vol. 2.
52. In re Richmond Produce Co., Inc., 118 B.R. 753, 758–59 (Bankr. N.D.Cal.1990).
53. See Practitioner Treatise, Vol. 2.

also liable thereunder as the initial transferee. The courts are split.[54] We discuss this issue more fully elsewhere.[55]

§ 6–89 Improvement Lien for All Good Faith Transferees

For full text of this section, see Epstein, Nickles & White, Bankruptcy, Practitioner Treatise Series, Vol. 2.

§ 6–90 Time Limitations on Recovery

For full text of this section, see Epstein, Nickles & White, Bankruptcy, Practitioner Treatise Series, Vol. 2.

I. PSEUDO AVOIDANCE POWERS

§ 6–91 Subordinating Claims, Section 510

The Bankruptcy Code describes in section 726 the priority of claims against the estate,[1] that is, the order in which property of the estate is distributed to creditors. The very first priority, however, which is not described there, consists of allowed secured claims that survive the trustee's avoiding powers. An allowed secured claim is generally satisfied by or from the collateral that secures it, and no one else can share in the collateral without fully honoring the secured claim. Priority between secured claims to the same collateral is determined by applicable nonbankruptcy law.

This ranking of claims, which puts secured claims at the top, is subject to an important exception: section 510. It provides for subordinating claims, including secured claims, on the basis of either consensual or equitable subordination.[2]

§ 6–92 Consensual Subordination, Section 510(a)

Consensual subordination is governed by section 510(a) which directs that a subordination agreement "is enforceable [in bankruptcy] * * * to the same extent [the agreement] * * * is enforceable under applicable nonbankruptcy law."[1]

A subordination agreement is a contract whereby a creditor agrees that her claim against the debtor or the debtor's property will be satisfied only after another person's claim, which by law is equal or junior in rank, is fully or partly paid.[2] In other words, the creditor agrees that notwithstanding the priority of her claim under local law, subordinate claims will be satisfied before her otherwise senior claim. The local law of priority is thereby displaced; and the subordination agreement, so far as it applies, controls the ranking and satisfaction of the parties' claims.

Subordination agreements are common among creditors' with competing liens on the debtor's property, especially among Article 9 secured parties

---

54. See Practitioner Treatise, Vol. 2.
55. See § 6–10 supra.

§ 6–91
1. 11 U.S.C.A. § 726(a).
2. Id. § 510(a) & (c).

§ 6–92
1. 11 U.S.C.A. § 510(a).
2. See Practitioner Treatise, Vol. 2.

with security interests in the debtor's personal property.[3] They are also sometimes made by secured creditors in favor of unsecured creditors, and between unsecured creditors *inter se* whose claims are otherwise ranked equally.

The principal source of law for enforcing a subordination agreement is ordinary contract law. It generally controls even when the agreement involves the subordination of an Article 9 security interest. A subordination agreement is therefore enforceable only when it satisfies the usual requirements of a contract, that is, the parties must have mutually assented to the terms of the agreement,[4] and the agreement must be supported by consideration.[5] Contract law, however, does not require a writing. Ordinarily, therefore, the enforceability of a subordination agreement is not conditioned on the agreement being written.[6] A subordination agreement can be established "by document, oral communication, or even a course of conduct," and no "written formal agreement" is required.[7] Moreover, neither contract law nor U.C.C. Article 9 requires public filing of a subordination agreement as a condition of enforcement or for any other reason.[8]

Another consequence of contract law ruling subordination agreements is that the effect and reach of the agreement is determined by its terms. In other words, a subordination agreement does not confer any priority beyond that defined by the terms of the agreement itself. If a subordinator agrees to defer only partly to another creditor, the other creditor's resulting priority based on the subordination agreement is accordingly so limited.[9]

The purpose served by section 510(a) is to confirm that a subordination agreement affecting the debtor's creditors, if it is effective under local law, is equally effective in the bankruptcy case. Thus, when the creditors of a debtor in bankruptcy have made a subordination agreement that is valid under local law, the junior creditors whom it benefits cannot be denied their contractual priority because of the debtor's bankruptcy.[10] In ranking for any purpose the claims of the parties, *inter se,* that the subordination agreement covers, the agreement itself controls and overrides state priority law and even section 726 in determining the priority of the claims among themselves upon distribution of the estate.

§ 6–93 Equitable Subordination, Section 510(c)

Section 510(c) empowers a bankruptcy court to employ "principles of *equitable subordination*" to subordinate claims and interests and, when a secured claim is involved, to transfer the creditor's lien to the estate.[1]

3. See Practitioner Treatise, Vol. 2.
4. See Practitioner Treatise, Vol. 2.
5. See Practitioner Treatise, Vol. 2.
6. See Practitioner Treatise, Vol. 2.
7. In re Mihalko, 87 B.R. 357, 365 (Bankr. E.D.Pa. 1988).
8. See Practitioner Treatise, Vol. 2.
9. See Practitioner Treatise, Vol. 2.
10. See Practitioner Treatise, Vol. 2.

§ 6–93
1. The whole rule is:

Notwithstanding subsections (a) and (b) of this section, after notice and hearing, the court may

(1) under principles of equitable subordination, subordinate for purposes of distribution all or part of an allowed claim to all or part of another allowed claim or all or part of an allowed interest to all or part of another allowed interest; or

(2) order that any lien securing such a subordinated claim be transferred to the estate.

11 U.S.C. § 510(c).

Subordination under section 510(c) results not from the creditor's agreement. Rather, it results from the force of law for reasons of equity and fairness. The purpose is to "'undo or offset any inequity in the claim position of a creditor that will produce injustice or unfairness to other creditors in terms of the bankruptcy results.'"[2]

This purpose is achieved in theory not by *disallowance* of the creditor's claim; rather, paying the claim is *delayed* until the claims of injured creditors are satisfied.[3] In practice, however, the delay has the same result as disallowance if the assets are consumed in first satisfying others creditors.

Equitable subordination is usually employed to rearrange priorities established by law. It can be used, however, to reorder priorities established consensually by subordination agreement.[4]

When a secured claim is subordinated, the ultimate possible effect is "a court order invalidating the security interest * * *, requiring the secured creditor to return [any] * * * proceeds of [the] collateral to the debtor, and reclassifying the claim as an unsecured claim subordinate to all other unsecured claims."[5] A lien that secures a claim subordinated under section 510(c) can be transferred to the estate[6] just as happens when a lien is voided through the exercise of the trustee's avoiding power.[7]

The complete outcome, however, is potentially even worse under section 510(c) than having the lien undone by the trustee's avoiding powers. When the avoiding powers are successfully exercised the creditor usually retains a claim that minimally ranks *equally* with other unsecured claims. Subordinating a secured claim can put it *behind* them in order of priority.[8] Thus, equitable subordination is used not only as a kind of avoidance tool instead of the trustee's avoiding powers; it is sometimes used as a further remedy in addition to them.[9]

Significantly, the power to compel equitable subordination is not limited to the trustee or debtor in possession.[10] Individual creditors, who usually cannot assert the trustee's avoiding powers, can nevertheless seek equitable subordination of other creditors' claims.[11] Indeed, it is normally a creditor rather than the trustee who asks for subordination under section 510(c).

2. In re EMB Associates, Inc., 92 B.R. 9, 15 (Bankr.R.I.1988), further proceeding, 100 B.R. 629 (Bankr. D.R.I.1989), aff'd in part, rev'd in part sub nom., Max Sugarman Funeral Home, Inc. v. A.D.B. Investors, 127 B.R. 508 (D.R.I. 1989), vacated & remanded, 926 F.2d 1248 (1st Cir.1991), citing Bostian v. Schapiro (In re Kansas City Journal–Post Co.), 144 F.2d 791, 800 (8th Cir. 1944).

3. In re UNR Industries, Inc., 46 B.R. 25, 28–29 (Bankr. N.D.Ill. 1984).

4. See In re W.T. Grant Co., 699 F.2d 599, 609 (2d Cir.1983), cert. denied, 464 U.S. 822, 104 S.Ct. 89, 78 L.Ed.2d 97 (1983) (dicta); In re Sepco, Inc., 36 B.R. 279, 287–88 (Bankr. D.S.D. 1984), aff'd, 750 F.2d 51 (8th Cir. 1984).

5. Chaitman, The Equitable Subordination of Bank Claims, 39 Bus. Law. 1561 (1984).

6. 11 U.S.C.A. § 510(c)(2) ("the court may * * * order that any lien securing such a subordinated claim be transferred to the estate"); see, e.g., In re Answerfone, Inc., 48 B.R. 24, 29, 31 (Bankr. E.D.Ark.1985); In re Loop Hosp. Partnership, 50 B.R. 565, 569–71 (Bankr. N.D.Ill. 1985); Matter of Pat Freeman, Inc., 42 B.R. 224, 232 (Bankr. S.D.Ohio 1984).

7. 11 U.S.C.A. § 551, which we discuss earlier in § 6–86 supra.

8. See Practitioner Treatise, Vol. 2.

9. See Practitioner Treatise, Vol. 2.

10. See Practitioner Treatise, Vol. 2.

11. See Practitioner Treatise, Vol. 2.

Also, "[t]he bankruptcy court itself may raise a claim on grounds of equitable subordination sua sponte if a party in interest fails to do so."[12]

Obviously, inasmuch as the target of equitable subordination is a relatively higher ranked claim, there is no basis for pursuing the remedy against someone who has not filed a proof of claim in the bankruptcy case.[13]

The Code does not describe the principles that justify equitable subordination under section 510(c). Rather, they "are defined by case law" which long predates the Code and which normally subordinates a claim "only if its holder is guilty of misconduct."[14]

In precise terms; the main key to equitable subordination is usually *inequitable conduct.*[15] It is the first and principal component of a three-pronged test for equitable subordination that is recited in almost every modern case in which a court considers section 510(c):

> (1) The claimant must have engaged in some type of inequitable conduct;
>
> (2) the misconduct must have resulted in injury to the creditors of the bankruptcy or conferred an unfair advantage on the claimant; and
>
> (3) equitable subordination of the claim must not be inconsistent with the provisions of the Bankruptcy Act.[16]

Inequitable conduct toward the debtor or her other creditors "can warrant subordination of a claim *irrespective of whether it was related to the acquisition or assertion of that claim,*"[17] and irrespective of "reliance or prudence" of the other creditors.[18]

"Inequitable conduct" is, of course, a very slippery concept with little predictive value. In very general terms, inequitable conduct is "conduct of the claimant in relation to other creditors [that] is or was * * * unjust or unfair * * *."[19] Somewhat more specifically,

> [i]nequitable conduct is that conduct which may be lawful, yet shocks one's good conscience. It means, *inter alia,* a secret or open fraud; lack of good faith or guardianship by a fiduciary; an unjust enrichment, not

---

12. In re Fargo Financial, Inc., 80 B.R. 247, 251 n.1 (Bankr. N.D.Ga.1987), citing M.H. Gordon & Son, Inc. v. Debtor and Committee of Unsecured Creditors, 62 B.R. 552, 554 (D.Mass.1986).

13. In re Pernie Bailey Drilling Co., Inc., 111 B.R. 565, 571 (Bankr. W.D.La.1990).

14. S. Rep. No. 989, 95th Cong., 2d Sess. 74, reprinted in 1978 U.S. Code Cong. & Admin. News, 5787, 5860.

15. See Practitioner Treatise, Vol. 2.

16. Cases reciting this exact test include Matter of Clark Pipe & Supply Co., Inc., 893 F.2d 693, 699 (5th Cir.1990), reh'g denied, 899 F.2d 11 (5th Cir. 1990); In re Universal Farming Industries, 873 F.2d 1334, 1337 (9th Cir. 1989); In re Bellanca Aircraft Corp., 850 F.2d 1275, 1282 (8th Cir.1988), on remand, 96 B.R. 913 (Bankr.D.Minn.1989); In re Giorgio, 862 F.2d 933, 938–39 (1st Cir.1988); In re N & D Properties, Inc., 799 F.2d 726, 731 (11th Cir. 1986); In re F.A. Potts & Co., Inc., 115 B.R. 66, 71 (E.D.Pa. 1990), judgment aff'd, 922 F.2d 830 (3d Cir.1990); In re Otis & Edwards, P.C., 115 B.R. 900, 914 (Bankr. E.D.Mich.1990).

17. Benjamin v. Diamond (Matter of Mobile Steel), 563 F.2d 692, 700 (5th Cir.1977) (emphasis added); see also, e.g., In re Western World Funding, Inc., 52 B.R. 743, 789 (Bankr. D.Nev.1985) ("The inequitable conduct need not be related to the acquisition or assertion of the claim, nor must actual fraud be shown."); In re Beverages Int'l Ltd., 50 B.R. 273, 281 (Bankr. D.Mass.1985) (same).

18. In re T. E. Mercer Trucking Co., 16 B.R. 176, 189 (Bankr. N.D.Tex.1981).

19. DeNatale & Abram, The Doctrine of Equitable Subordination as Applied to Non-management Creditors, 40 Bus. Law. 417, 419 (1985).

enrichment by bon chance, astuteness or business acumen, but enrichment through another's loss brought about by one's own unconscionable, unjust, unfair, close, or double dealing or foul conduct."[20]

Unfortunately, these definitions simply substitute equally vague terms for the root concept.

Many courts have categorized the kinds of conduct that have justified equitable subordination in past cases. A listing that is a favorite of the courts is:

    (1) fraud, illegality, breach of fiduciary duties;

    (2) undercapitalization; and

    (3) claimant's use of the debtor as a mere instrumentality or alter ego.[21]

A slightly different list is part of the opinion in the case, *Matter of CTS Truss, Inc.*,[22] in which the court wrote:

> The courts have actually confined equitable subordination of claims to three general categories of cases: those in which a fiduciary of the debtor misuses his position to the disadvantage of other creditors; those in which a third party, in effect, controls the debtor to the disadvantage of others; and those in which a third-party defrauds other creditors.[23]

These and similar lists do not completely agree; the categories are broad and non-exclusive; and they are often explained in terms that themselves need further definition and explanation to prove reliably helpful.

The search for a firmer grip on section 510(c), and the usually necessary "inequitable conduct," properly begins at the beginning: the two Supreme Court cases that are the bedrock of equitable subordination in bankruptcy. They are *Taylor v. Standard Gas & Electric Co.*[24] and *Pepper v. Litton.*[25] The Court in *Taylor* approved subordinating a parent corporation's claim against its subsidiary, the debtor, because the former had undercapitalized and mismanaged the latter to the detriment of preferred stockholders. In *Pepper* the Court approved subordinating or altogether denying the claim of the corporate debtor's dominant and controlling stockholder, Litton, who used his "strategic position," i.e., his dominant influence" over the debtor, "for his own preferment to the damage" of the debtor's creditors. Specifically,

---

20. In re Harvest Milling Co., 221 F.Supp. 836, 838 (D.Or.1963), quoted in In re Sleepy Valley, Inc., 93 B.R. 925, 933 n.13 (Bankr. W.D.Tex.1988).

21. For cases reciting this list of "bad acts" constituting "inequitable conduct," see, e.g., In re Otis & Edwards, P.C., 115 B.R. 900, 914 (Bankr. E.D.Mich.1990); In re Shelter Enterprises, Inc., 98 B.R. 224, 231, further opin., 99 B.R. 668 (Bankr. W.D.Pa.1989); In re EMB Associates, Inc., 92 B.R. 9, 15 (Bankr.R.I.1988), further proceeding, 100 B.R. 629, 634 n.6 (Bankr. D.R.I.1989), aff'd in part, rev'd in part sub nom., Max Sugarman Funeral Home, Inc. v. A.D.B. Investors, 127 B.R. 508 (D.R.I.1989), vacated & remanded, 926 F.2d 1248 (1st Cir. 1991); In re Sleepy Valley, Inc., 93 B.R. 925, 933 (Bankr. W.D.Tex.1988). In the Sleepy Valley case the court added: "At least one court has suggested that under certain circumstances, something less than actual fraud may suffice." Id., citing In re Beverages Int'l Ltd, 50 B.R. 273, 281–82 (Bankr. D. Mass. 1985).

22. 868 F.2d 146 (5th Cir.1989).

23. Id. at 148–49.

24. 306 U.S. 307, 59 S.Ct. 543, 83 L.Ed. 669 (1938).

25. 308 U.S. 295, 60 S.Ct. 238, 84 L. Ed. 281 (1939).

> [Litton] used his power not to deal fairly with the creditors of [the debtor] * * * but to manipulate its affairs in such a manner that when one of its creditors came to collect her just debt the bulk of the [debtor's] assets had disappeared into another Litton company. [He] * * * was enabled * * * to acquire most of the assets of the bankrupt not for cash or other consideration of value to creditors but for bookkeeping entries representing at best merely Litton's appraisal of the worth of Litton's services over the years.[26]

Moreover, Litton so acted in deliberate and calculated reaction to the creditor's efforts to collect from the debtor.

Because section 510(c) is rooted in *Taylor* and *Pepper,* they teach much about "inequitable conduct" that still applies in most modern cases. Their most important lesson is that inequitable conduct is broader than unlawful conduct. The claimant in neither *Taylor* nor *Pepper* violated a statute, breached a contract, or committed a tort. While any of these wrongs is almost surely within the meaning of "inequitable conduct" and can justify subordination under section 510(c), none of them is required to subordinate a creditor's claim. Self-serving inattention, manipulation or maneuvering, that is legal but harmful to other creditors, is sometimes sufficient.

Such lawful conduct is not always inequitable, however, despite being harmful. It was inequitable in *Taylor* and *Pepper* primarily because in each case the claimant was an insider who also controlled the debtor. A person who controls someone else must usually respect the other person's interests even if the other person is a corporation; and the person in control is expected to abide by the rules of fair play and good conscience in dealing with the corporation's stockholders and creditors.

> He cannot manipulate the affairs of his corporation to their detriment and in disregard of the standards of common decency and honesty. He cannot by the intervention of a corporate entity violate the ancient precept against serving two masters. He cannot by the use of the corporate device avail himself of privileges normally permitted outsiders in a race of creditors. He cannot utilize his insider information and his strategic position for his own preferment. He cannot violate rules of fair play by doing indirectly through the corporation what he could not do indirectly. He cannot use his power for his own personal advantage and to the detriment of the stockholders and creditors no matter how absolute in terms that power may be and no matter how meticulous he is to satisfy technical requirements. For that power is at all times subject to the equitable limitation that it may not be exercised for [his] * * * aggrandizement, preference, or advantage * * *. Where there is a violation of those principles, equity will undo the wrong or intervene to prevent its consummation.[27]

Because section 510(c) is rooted in *Taylor* and *Pepper,* the statute is most comfortably and often applied to subordinate the claims of insiders.[28] *Insider status is not, however, a sufficient basis in itself for equitable subordina-*

---

26. Id. at 311–12, 308 S.Ct. at 247–48, 84 L. Ed. at 292.

27. Pepper v. Litton, 308 U.S. 295, 311, 60 S.Ct. 238, 247 84 L. Ed. 281, 291–92 (1939).

28. See Practitioner Treatise, Vol. 2.

tion under section 510(c).[29] The courts insist that, as in *Taylor* and *Pepper,* the insider must be guilty of "inequitable conduct." This requirement is satisfied if the insider acted unlawfully,[30] or committed the inequities condemned in *Taylor* and *Pepper.*

Thus, in line with *Pepper,* an insider's claim will be subordinated under section 510(c) if she uses insider information and her strategic position for self-aggrandizement, preference, or advantage, or otherwise violates the rules of fair play by doing indirectly through the corporation what she could not do directly.[31]

Also, on the authority of *Taylor,* the debtor's undercapitalization will justify subordinating an insider's claim, especially when accompanied by mismanagement, a conscious plan to substitute debt funding for equity investment, or other insider improprieties not amounting in themselves to inequitable misconduct. An insider's "loan" to a debtor in such a case will likely be treated, in effect, as a capital contribution that is subordinate to all creditor's claims if the debtor was undercapitalized from the beginning, or if the "loan" was made when the debtor's condition was so poor that no commercial lender would loan to it.[32] In bankruptcy, equity holders stand in line behind debt claimants.[33]

Although insiders are the usual targets of equitable subordination, it is not restricted to them. It can also affect the claims of non-insiders who are guilty of inequitable conduct; but subordinating their claims under section 510(c) is much tougher both procedurally and substantively.

With respect to procedure, the burden of proof is divided when an insider's claim is attacked but is borne entirely by the challenger when the claim belongs to a non-insider. As explained by the bankruptcy court in the case, *In re Sleepy Valley, Inc.:*[34]

> A verified proof of claim establishes the claimant's prima facie case both for the validity of the claim and for the purpose of meeting an equitable subordination challenge, as the latter is considered a "defense," of sorts, to a creditor's claim. Thus, the party seeking to subordinate the claim must come forward with sufficient proof to justify modifying the claim's priority. If the claimant is a non-insider, the burden remains on the objectant throughout. However, if the claimant is an insider, fiduciary or alter ego, the burden begins with the objectant, but shifts to the claimant to prove the integrity of the claim once there is a substantial factual showing of inequitable conduct.[35]

With respect to the substance of the proof, the meaning of "inequitable conduct" is much broader for an insider. Generally speaking, because of *Taylor* and *Pepper* an insider's conduct is subject to exacting judicial scrutiny;[36] and the conduct is inequitable if it lacks the earmarkings of an arms-length transaction and, in terms of those cases, is merely unfair or lacking in good faith or conscience.[37] A non-insider's conduct is inequitable only if she

29. See Practitioner Treatise, Vol. 2.
30. See Practitioner Treatise, Vol. 2.
31. See Practitioner Treatise, Vol. 2.
32. See Practitioner Treatise, Vol. 2.
33. See Practitioner Treatise, Vol. 2.
34. 93 B.R. 925 (Bankr. W.D.Tex.1988).
35. Id. at 932 n.11.
36. See Practitioner Treatise, Vol. 2.
37. See Practitioner Treatise, Vol. 2.

is guilty of much "more egregious conduct," [38] that is, intentional, gross misconduct proved with particularity.[39]

More specifically, unlawfulness by a non-insider is inequitable and can result in subordination under section 510(c). On this point, however, there is no real difference in the treatment between insiders and non-insiders. Generally speaking, a person in either class acts inequitably for purposes of section 510(c) when her conduct is: explicitly proscribed by statutory law (most certainly, if the conduct forms the basis of her claim);[40] unlawful under much less specific, common-law proscriptions, including fraudulent misrepresentation and other torts;[41] or a breach of traditional or modern contract law, including estoppel.[42]

The substantial difference in the treatment of insiders and non-insiders under section 510(c) is in the range of lawful conduct that is considered inequitable. It is generally narrower for a non-insider because she is ordinarily free of the legal and equitable duties that an insider owes the debtor and the debtor's creditors.

Most obviously, for example, a non-insider's claim usually cannot be subordinated because of the debtor's undercapitalization,[43] or otherwise easily recharacterized as an equity investment subject to subordination.[44] Also, a non-insider is usually free to use every available legal device and technical maneuver for collecting or protecting her claim.[45] She is also free to maximize fully the protection of her claim. In doing so the non-insider can use any position of strength that comes from being a source of credit or having the power to foreclose or otherwise enforce her claim against the debtor.[46] Moreover, the non-insider creditor is not obligated to safeguard other creditors from the effects of her own legitimate efforts to protect or collect her claim, and she is not required to police the debtor's treatment of them.[47] In sum:

> "A creditor is under no fiduciary obligation to its debtor or to other creditors of the debtor in the collection of its claim * * * ." The permissible parameters of a creditor's efforts to seek collection from a debtor are generally those with respect to voidable preferences and fraudulent conveyances proscribed by the Bankruptcy Act; apart from these there is generally no objection to a creditor's using his bargaining position, including his ability to refuse to make further loans needed by the debtor, to improve the status of his existing claims.[48]

Finally, if a creditor is so positioned as to have a prior secured claim to the debtor's property that leaves other creditors with little or nothing, her enviable priority status in relation to their pitifully poor position is not sufficient cause to readjust the claims under section 510(c).[49]

---

38. In re N & D Properties, Inc., 799 F.2d 726, 731 (11th Cir.1986).
39. See Practitioner Treatise, Vol. 2.
40. See Practitioner Treatise, Vol. 2.
41. See Practitioner Treatise, Vol. 2.
42. See Practitioner Treatise, Vol. 2.
43. See Practitioner Treatise, Vol. 2.
44. See Practitioner Treatise, Vol. 2.
45. See Practitioner Treatise, Vol. 2.
46. See Practitioner Treatise, Vol. 2.
47. See Practitioner Treatise, Vol. 2.
48. In re W.T. Grant Co., 699 F.2d 599, 609–10 (2d Cir.1983), cert. denied, 464 U.S. 822, 104 S.Ct. 89, 78 L.Ed.2d 97 (1983).
49. See Practitioner Treatise, Vol. 2.

The range of acceptable lawful conduct for a non-insider narrows, however, when she strong-arms her way into actual control of the debtor, or by agreement with the debtor or otherwise positions herself so that she controls the debtor. In this event, which is actually very rare, the creditor becomes a real or de facto insider. She must therefore honor the principles of *Taylor* and *Pepper* and respect the debtor's interests, sometimes ahead of her own. Failing to do so is inequitable conduct justifying subordination of the creditor's claim even though the conduct is technically lawful.[50]

The scope of acceptable conduct for a creditor who controls the debtor depends on the degree of the creditor's control.[51] The least latitude is permitted in the rare case when the creditor effectively becomes the alter ego of the debtor who exists as a mere instrumentality. A close identity of interest, however, that fully satisfies the legally technical requirements of an alter ego relationship, is not essential to imposing on a controlling creditor the equitable duties and accountability of an insider under section 510(c).[52]

Usually, the degree of control that is necessary to trigger insider-like treatment is rather large control. Some courts would say "*virtually* complete control."[53] The probable explanation is that the creditor's accountability based on her control is ultimately based on the creditor having dictated the conduct as a real insider is able to do. Having this much power, so that the debtor is robbed of free and independent choice, ordinarily requires substantial control.

Remember, however, that it is not the existence of the creditor's contractual right or transactional power to influence the debtor's conduct which triggers insider-like equitable duties.[54] They are triggered by the creditor's actual control in unilaterally directing the debtor's conduct that affects creditors. Yet, it is not this control that is inequitable. Indeed, "[e]ven total control of a debtor's affairs [by a real insider] does not necessarily lead to equitable subordination of claims * * * ."[55] It is rather exercising the control inequitably, as by the creditor violating the lessons of *Pepper* and using its position for its own selfish advantage.[56]

The classic case is *In re American Lumber Co.*[57] In this case the debtor's major financer took over the management of the debtor and very deliberately kept the debtor in business solely for the purpose of advantaging the financer. It caused the debtor to generate receivables, in which the financer had a first priority, that were paid to the financer. Other creditors were paid little or nothing. The financer, using its position of power and its insider information, effectively shifted the debt from itself to the backs of unpaid inventory suppliers and trade creditors and in so doing acted inequitably within the meaning of *Pepper*.[58]

American Lumber is remarkable and stands out not because of the holding, but because the case is a rare finding of insider-like status by a

50. See Practitioner Treatise, Vol. 2.
51. See Practitioner Treatise, Vol. 2.
52. See Practitioner Treatise, Vol. 2.
53. See Practitioner Treatise, Vol. 2.
54. See Practitioner Treatise, Vol. 2.
55. In re Featherworks Corp., 25 B.R. 634, 648 (Bankr. E.D.N.Y.1982), order aff'd, 36 B.R. 460 (E.D.N.Y.1984).
56. See Practitioner Treatise, Vol. 2.
57. 5 B.R. 470 (D.Minn.1980).
58. See Practitioner Treatise, Vol. 2.

secured creditor. It is especially remarkable that the finding is rare considering that secured creditors are daily involved very deeply in the affairs of many thousands of debtors. This rarity, however, is right in terms of existing doctrine. By this law, the cases will be few in which an outsider creditor is deemed to have become as an insider and to have engaged in conduct that entitles the trustee to subordinate the creditor's claim. Specifically, when creditors intervene in the debtor's affairs to protect their own interests, it does not matter that they act aggressively and selfishly. Doing so, consistent with contract and law, is their right and is only natural. It matters only when they are unnaturally or unusually exploitative. Only then is there harm to other creditors that warrants subordination.

This harm in a case such as *American Lumber* is in continuing to extend credit to a debtor pursuant to a secret plan that provides no repayment to other creditors. These creditors are thus misled and essentially robbed of their property and services for the benefit of the controlling creditor who has exploited its unfair advantage.

BE CAREFUL! Finding injury or unfair advantage is always important to subordination. Inequitable conduct of an insider or non-insider does not automatically result in subordination under section 510(c). It is only the first requirement (albeit the major requirement) of a three-pronged test that usually must be satisfied to justify subordination.[59] The second requirement is resulting harm to the debtor's creditors or unfair advantage to the claimant.[60] Section 510(c) is not a penal statute designed to punish inequitable conduct. Its purpose is to remedy the injury that other creditors suffer as a result of the misconduct "and is applied only to the extent necessary to offset specific harm caused by inequitable conduct."[61] Inequitable conduct of a creditor that causes no continuing harm or unfair advantage does not justify subordination under section 510(c).[62] Relatedly, even where there is resulting harm, the "claim or claims should be subordinated only to the extent necessary to offset the harm which the bankrupt and its creditors suffered on account of the inequitable conduct."[63]

The third and final requirement of the usual test is that equitable subordination must be consistent with the provisions of the Code. In other words, there must be nothing in the language or policy of the statute as a whole that expressly or tacitly approves the claimant's conduct. This requirement has never prevented subordinating the claim of a creditor whose conduct passed the other prongs of the test. We are not surprised. It is very unlikely that a court would ever construe the Code to sanction conduct that, in the court's view, is harmfully inequitable.

The courts are occasionally asked to depart from the usual three-pronged test for subordination which is keyed to inequitable conduct, and are urged to use section 510(c) as authority for rearranging the usual priority of claims solely because of the nature of the claims. They almost always refuse, reasoning that section 510(c) is *not* a "license to weigh the moral quality of each debt or to compare creditors in terms of moral worth

---

59. See Practitioner Treatise, Vol. 2.
60. See Practitioner Treatise, Vol. 2.
61. In re Allegheny Internat'l, Inc., 118 B.R. 282, 312 (Bankr. W.D.Pa.1990).
62. See Practitioner Treatise, Vol. 2.
63. Matter of Mobile Steel Co., 563 F.2d 692, 700–01 (5th Cir.1977).

* * *."⁶⁴ Section 510(c) authorizes only subordination, "not evaluation of a creditor's claim based on the court's own rules of priority."⁶⁵ In short, the courts usually, regularly, and routinely stick to the long tradition of requiring harmful, inequitable conduct as if the requirement was an explicit part of section 510(c); and they will almost never subordinate in the absence of such conduct.⁶⁶

§ 6–94 Asserting Debtor's Defenses, Section 558

Section 558 gives "[t]he estate * * * the benefit of any defense available to the debtor as against any entity other than the estate."¹ Thus, when a person makes a claim against the estate, the claim can be reduced or even eliminated to the extent that the debtor has a defense to it under local or other law that governs the claim. Because the trustee represents the estate, she usually asserts the defense on its behalf.²

The trustee can use section 558 as a means for indirectly attacking transfers of property, especially secured transactions. A transfer of property for security is always prompted by a debt, and the size of debt determines the size of the lien or security interest. By asserting the debtor's defenses to the debt the trustee can attack the actuality, legality or amount of the debt. If these defenses reduce the debt or establish that it is unenforceable, the lien which the debt supports is concomitantly reduced or eliminated.³

The debtor's defenses that the trustee can assert by way of section 558 include "statutes of limitation, statutes of frauds, usury, and other personal defenses."⁴ This listing, which is part of section 558 itself, is representative only and not exclusive. The statute covers any defense of state or federal law the debtor could assert with respect to the transaction that produced the creditor's claim.⁵ It also permits the trustee to assert the debtor's right of setoff against claims.⁶

Any defense that benefits the estate under section 558 is unaffected by the debtor's waiver of the defense after the commencement of the case. It "does not bind the estate." If, however, the debtor validly waives a defense

---

64. In re Giorgio, 862 F.2d 933, 939 (1st Cir.1988). Neither is such a license given by section 105(a), 11 U.S.C.A. § 105(a), which confers equity powers upon bankruptcy courts. In re FCX, Inc., 60 B.R. 405, 410–11 (E.D.N.C. 1986).

65. Matter of B & W Enterprises, Inc., 713 F.2d 534, 537 (9th Cir.1983); see also Matter of David A. Rosow, Inc., 13 B.R. 203, 204 (Bankr. D.Conn.1981) (court will not elevate a claim above other claims on the basis that the equities attending the former are greater than those of the latter).

66. See Practitioner Treatise, Vol. 2.

§ 6–94

1. 11 U.S.C.A. § 558. Before this provision was isolated as section 558, it was buried elsewhere in the Code and appeared as section 541(e).

2. 11 U.S.C.A. § 323(a); In re Dominelli, 820 F.2d 313, 316–17 (9th Cir.1987) (trustee is proper person to assert § 558 defenses, but suggests that junior lien claimant can assert them to attack senior lien if trustee does not seek to do so); In re DiBona, 7 B.R. 798, 800 (Bankr. E.D.Pa. 1980). "The trustee's right under § 558 to assert debtor's defenses" is not, however, an "exclusive right" and in an appropriate case the defenses "may be asserted by the debtor," as when she defends against creditor's action to determine dischargeability. In re Nasr, 120 B.R. 855, 858 (Bankr. S.D.Tex. 1990).

3. See Practitioner Treatise, Vol. 2.

4. 11 U.S.C.A. § 558.

5. See Practitioner Treatise, Vol. 2.

6. See Practitioner Treatise, Vol. 2.

before her case commences, the prepetition waiver is effective and binding on the estate.[7] The trustee thus cannot assert it.

Section 558 does not cover the debtor's affirmative claims or causes of action against creditors of the estate and other persons. The debtor's estate nevertheless gets the benefit of these claims or actions. They pass to the estate and become part of it through section 541, and are enforceable by the trustee as the estate's representative.[8]

---

7. Matter of Wey, 827 F.2d 140, 142 (7th Cir.1987).

8. See 11 U.S.C.A. § 541(a)(1).

Chapter 7

LIQUIDATION

Table of Sections

Sec.
7-1 Introduction.
7-2 Procedural Overview.

A. Claims, Expenses, and Distributions in Chapter 7

7-3 Introduction.
    (a) Necessity for Filing.
    (c) Time for Filing.
7-4 Definition of Claim.
7-5 When Does the Claim Arise?
7-6 ____ Pension Obligations.
7-7 ____ Condominium Fees.
7-8 Does a Right to an Equitable Remedy Constitute a "Claim"?
7-9 Hierarchy of Claims.
7-10 ____ Secured Claims.
7-11 ____ Administrative Expenses.
7-12 ____ Other Priority Claims.
7-13 ____ Superpriority Claims, Section 507(b).
7-14 Distribution Under Section 726.
7-15 ____ Interpretive Difficulties With Section 726(a).
    a. What Is a Penalty?
    b. Tardy Claims.

B. Discharge

7-16 Discharge: Overview.
7-17 Denial of Discharge: Introduction.
7-18 ____ Individuals, Section 727(a)(1).
7-19 ____ Fraudulent Conveyances, Section 727(a)(2).
7-20 ____ Financial Disclosure, Section 727(a)(3).
7-21 ____ "Bankruptcy Crimes," Section 727(a)(4).
7-22 ____ Delivery of Assets, Section 727(a)(5).
7-23 ____ Refusal to Testify or Obey Court Order, Section 727(a)(6).
7-24 Exceptions to Discharge, Section 523, Introduction.
7-25 ____ Taxes, Section 523(a)(1).
7-26 ____ False Pretense, Fraud and False Financial Statements, Section 523(a)(2).
    a. Section 523(a)(2)(A): False Pretenses, False Representation and Actual Fraud.
    b. Section 523(a)(2)(B): False Financial Statement Materiality, Reasonable Reliance and Intent.
    c. Section 523(a)(2)(C).
    d. Fraud—Causal Connection.
7-27 ____ Unscheduled Debts, Section 523(a)(3).
7-28 ____ Fraud, Defalcation and Embezzlement, Section 523(a)(4).
7-29 ____ Alimony, Maintenance and Support, Section 523(a)(5).
    a. Substantive Rule.

Sec.
          b. Drafting Note for Divorce Lawyers.
7–30 ____ Willful and Malicious Injury, Section 523(a)(6).
          a. Overview.
          b. Willful and Malicious.
          c. Malicious.
          d. Summary.
7–31 ____ Fines and Penalties, Section 523(a)(7).
7–32 ____ ____Tax Penalties.
7–33 ____ Student Loans, Section 523(a)(8).
          a. Overview.
          b. Substantive Rules.
          c. The Exceptions to Nondischargeability.
          d. Summary.
7–34 ____ Driving While Intoxicated, Section 523(a)(9).

C. Reaffirmation, Section 524(c)

7–35 Introduction and Overview of Reaffirmation.
7–36 Procedure.
7–37 Best Interest and Undue Hardship.
7–38 Timing and Omission of the Admonition Hearing.
7–39 Reaffirmation, Redemption, Negotiation and the Secured Creditor.

D. Protection Against Discriminatory Treatment, Section 525

7–40 Introduction to Protection Against Discrimination.
7–41 Protection Against Discrimination by Governmental Units, Section 525(a).
          a. Governmental Unit.
          b. "Solely".
          c. Acts Prohibited.
          d. Remedies.
7–42 Protection Against Discrimination by Private Employees, Section 525(b).

E. Dismissal

7–43 Section 707(a).
7–44 Section 707(b).
7–45 ____ Substantive Requirements.
          a. "Primarily."
          b. "Consumer" Debts.
          c. Substantial Abuse.
7–46 ____ Retrospective.

F. Redemption, Section 722

7–47 Introduction and Overview of Redemption.
7–48 Substantive Requirements.
7–49 Valuation.

---

§ 7–1 Introduction

One who reads a generalized description of bankruptcy is quite likely to get a grossly distorted view of Chapter 7. Chapter 7 provides for liquidation. It is used mostly by individuals, and more than by any other class, by individuals who have little or nothing to give to their creditors. The generalized description of bankruptcy features the debtor, hounded by his creditors seeking to take his assets from him piecemeal, who invokes the federal bankruptcy law as a means of providing an equitable distribution of his assets to those creditors. In return the debtor is discharged from all liabilities and is granted the "fresh start." The latter part of the description is correct, but it understates the significance of the discharge. In fact, the norm in Chapter 7 is not for the collection and distribution of the debtor's assets, but rather for the discharge of the debtor without any distribution whatsoever to unsecured creditors. In a representative case, all the debtor's assets will be taken by secured creditors or be kept by the debtor under the various exemption laws discussed in our Chapter 8. Whatever remains is likely to be taken by the debtor's lawyer and the trustee as "administrative expenses." Thus, it is incorrect to think of Chapter 7 primarily as a mode of collecting and distributing assets of the debtor. For the most part Chapter 7 is a formal minuet danced by the debtor, to entitle the debtor to the fresh start that arises through the discharge under section 727, the effect of which is described in detail by section 524(a).

The avoidance powers discussed in Chapter 6 of this book, the automatic stay in Chapter 3, and most of the jurisdictional questions discussed in Chapter 12 have little to do with the routine bankruptcy Chapter 7 case. Most of those issues become relevant in a bankruptcy Chapter 11 case where there are sufficient assets to stimulate the parties to fight over them. On the contrary, the interesting intellectual and legal issues in a Chapter 7 case deal mostly with exemptions, the effect of the discharge, with exceptions of various debts from discharge under section 523 and with the peripheral effects of the discharge concerning things such as reaffirmations under section 524(c), discrimination against bankrupts under section 525, and with redemption of assets from secured creditors under section 722.

Congress has made a judgment expressed in section 523 that a debtor should not be freed from certain debts. For example, a debtor should not be permitted to rid himself of his child support obligations by going through Chapter 7; and for particularly heinous activity, the debtor may be denied a discharge not merely as to a particular debt (such as a support obligation), but to a discharge entirely under section 727. The law must also look to questions about the debtor's power to reaffirm debts that would otherwise be discharged and to the ways (under section 525) in which governmental units would be prohibited from discriminating against someone because he is in bankruptcy.

Occasionally a creditor will seek to deprive the debtor of the discharge by causing a dismissal of a Chapter 7 case or by requiring its conversion under section 706 or 707. Of course, there are some cases where the debtor has enough property to make the rights to that property a lively issue, but these are a minority. These cases give us a look at section 541 on "property of the estate" where the courts are called upon to decide whether future and contingent payments, for example, constitute property of the estate, and whether equitable interests in trusts are property of the estate.

Occasionally a debtor will assert a right in Chapter 7 to keep an asset that is subject to, but worth less than the face amount of a secured debt. Section 722 clearly gives the debtor the right to pay off such liabilities at less than the face amount (e.g., a $12,000 debt on a car worth $7,000 can normally be satisfied by a payment of $7,000 to the creditor). More recently debtors have attempted to keep their homes by continued payment of only that portion of the mortgage liability that is equal to the current value of the home. In effect, these debtors claim that section 506 gives them authority over real estate mortgages that section 722 gives over certain personal property.

So it would not be correct to conclude that all Chapter 7 cases are "no asset" cases. An occasional case presents a lively question about the property of the estate under section 541 or about the right of the debtor to redeem under section 722 or section 506 for less than the full obligation.

In this chapter we will deal with all those questions. Mostly we concentrate on the discharge, denial of the discharge, exceptions to the discharge, and matters peripheral to the discharge such as reaffirmation. Viewing Chapter 7 in proper perspective, one should regard these sections as the heart of Chapter 7. To them we devote our principal effort here.

§ 7–2 Procedural Overview

Involuntary Chapter 7 bankruptcies are possible [1]; but they are quite rare. The normal case is "voluntary" and is commenced by the filing of a Chapter 7 petition with the clerk of the bankruptcy court. Concurrently with the petition or shortly thereafter, the debtor in the voluntary case must file a list containing the name and address of each creditor and a schedule of assets and liabilities, of income and expenditures and, in some cases, a statement of financial affairs. All of these are specified in Bankruptcy Rule 1007.[2] Most of these filings are to be made on "Official Forms" that are

---

§ 7–2

1. 11 U.S.C.A. § 303.

2. This rule concerns lists, schedules and statements, and time limits, and provides:

(a)(1) Voluntary case. In a voluntary case, the debtor shall file with the petition a list containing the name and address of each creditor unless the petition is accompanied by a schedule of liabilities or a Chapter 13 Statement.

* * *

(b)(1) The debtor in a chapter 7 liquidation case or chapter 11 reorganization case, unless the court orders otherwise, shall file with the court schedules of assets and liabilities, prepared as prescribed by Official Form No. 6, a schedule of current income and expenditures, prepared as prescribed by Official Form No. 6A, if appropriate, a statement of financial affairs, prepared as prescribed by Official Form No. 7 or No. 8, whichever is appropriate, and a statement of executory contracts.

* * *

(b)(3) An individual debtor in a chapter 7 case shall file a statement of intention as required by § 521(2) of the Code, prepared as prescribed by Official Form No. 8A. A copy of the statement of intention shall be served on the trustee and the creditors named in the statement on or before the filing of the statement.

(c) Time limits. The schedules and statements, other than the statement of intention, shall be filed with the petition in a voluntary case, or if the petition is accompanied by a list of all the debtor's creditors and their addresses, within 15 days thereafter, except as otherwise provided in subdivisions (d), (e), and (h) of this rule. In an involuntary case the schedules and statements, other than the statement of intention, shall be filed by the debtor within 15 days after entry of the order for relief. Schedules and statements previously filed in a pending chapter 7 case shall be deemed filed in a superseding case unless the court directs otherwise. Any extension of time for the filing of the schedules and statements may be granted only on motion for cause shown and on notice to any committee, trustee, examiner, or other party as the court may direct. Notice of an extension shall be given to any committee, trustee, or other party as the court may direct.

* * *

(h) Interests acquired or arising after petition. If, as provided by § 541(a)(5) of the

published as part of the Rules. To make a public disclosure, open to all, not only of all of one's creditors, but also of one's assets and liabilities, current income and expenditures, and in some cases of "other financial affairs" is the first cost of a bankruptcy. Consider whether you would be comfortable in making such public disclosures about your own affairs and your own creditors. Many of us would be quite uncomfortable about such disclosure, and that, together with the lawyer's fee and the filing fee are the first and some of the most significant costs associated with bankruptcy.

The next significant event in the typical Chapter 7 case is likely to be the meeting of creditors under section 341. Rule 2002 requires the clerk to give 20 days notice by mail of the 341 meeting to all of the creditors that have been listed on the debtor's schedule. Under Rule 2003 this meeting must occur not earlier than 20 days nor later than 40 days after the petition is filed. Under section 341 the United States Trustee "shall convene and preside at a meeting." [3] Under section 343 the debtor must also appear and "submit to examination under oath" at the 341 meeting. The trustee appointed for that case, the U.S. trustee, or any of the creditors who appear at the 341 meeting "may examine the debtor."

Perhaps it is time to stop and consider some of the terms that are used in the Rules and in the sections quoted above. We have said that the time for appearing under 341 runs from the date the petition is filed, yet the rules and the statute speak not of the time of filing, but the time of the "order for relief." In a voluntary case the date of the "order for relief" is the date of the filing of the petition. In an involuntary case, the debtor may dispute the merits of the involuntary petition that has been filed against him and, if he succeeds in causing that petition to be dismissed, there will never be an order for relief. If, on the other hand, he ultimately consents to the involuntary petition or his challenge is unsuccessful, the court will then "order relief." In almost all cases, therefore, the date of the order for relief is the date of the petition.

We have spoken above of the "United States Trustee" and also of trustees in lower case. The United States Trustee is a federal official who is appointed by the Attorney General [4] and who serves as a full time adminis-

---

Code, the debtor acquires or becomes entitled to acquire any interest in property, the debtor shall within 10 days after the information comes to the debtor's knowledge or within such further time the court may allow, file a supplemental schedule in the chapter 7 liquidation case, chapter 11 reorganization case, or chapter 13 individual debt adjustment case. If any of the property required to be reported under this subdivision is claimed by the debtor as exempt, the debtor shall claim the exemptions in the supplemental schedule. The duty to file a supplemental schedule in accordance with this subdivision continues notwithstanding the closing of the case, except that the schedule need not be filed in a chapter 11 or chapter 13 case with respect to property acquired after entry of the order confirming a chapter 11 plan or discharging the debtor in a chapter 13 case.

* * *

(k) Preparation of list, schedules, or statements on default of debtor. If a list, schedule, or statement, other than a statement of intention, is not prepared and filed as required by this rule, the court may order the trustee, a petitioning creditor, committee, or other party to prepare and file any of these papers within a time fixed by the court. The court may approve reimbursement of the cost incurred in complying with such an order as an administrative expense.

Bankr. R. 1007.

3. 11 U.S.C.A. § 341(a). Within a reasonable time after the order for relief in a case under this title, the United States trustee shall convene and preside at a meeting of creditors.

4. 28 U.S.C. § 581.

trator of part of the bankruptcy process. This Trustee grew out of the Congressional attempt in 1978 to divide the judicial functions from the purely administrative functions in the bankruptcy court. It granted the former to the bankruptcy judge and the latter to the U.S. Trustee. In a few federal districts [5] there is no U.S. Trustee and accordingly the functions that are performed by the U.S. Trustee elsewhere must be performed by different people in those jurisdictions. One should understand, however, that the United States Trustee is a full time official who has overall authority for calling and conducting meetings and for a variety of other administrative details but who does not normally individually supervise particular Chapter 7 bankruptcies. That task falls to a person who is appointed as *the* trustee for a particular Chapter 7 case. A trustee is always appointed in a Chapter 7 case; that trustee normally comes from a panel authorized by section 701. Under the terms of 701(a)(1) the United States Trustee shall promptly appoint "one disinterested person that is a member of the panel of private trustees * * * to serve as interim trustee in the case." The person so appointed for our particular case may or may not be a lawyer and may or may not spend all or almost all of his or her time as a trustee. The identity of the person appointed by the United States Trustee as the trustee from the panel may depend upon the job to be undertaken. Moreover, section 701 provides only for an "interim trustee". That trustee serves only until the creditors elect a trustee of their own choosing under section 702.

If the Chapter 7 involves an individual or legal entity with substantial property, it is often in the creditors' interest to appoint a person who has the particular business skill, legal talent, or reputation to carry out the particular responsibilities of that case. In the typical case, where the creditors expect to receive nothing from the bankruptcy and doubtless put the notices of the 341 meeting in the waste basket, the interim trustee is the only trustee and no replacement is ever appointed. We suspect, therefore, that the trustee appointed shortly after the petition by the United States Trustee remains the trustee for the entire life of most cases.

In theory the section 341 hearing is a time when all of the creditors come to the bankruptcy court and, by examination of the debtor, attempt to determine the accuracy of the schedules he has filed, whether he has squirreled away assets, and what prospect there is for payment. Usually no creditors come to the meeting of creditors. In practice the meeting consists of a brief discussion among the debtor, the debtor's lawyer, and the person appointed as the trustee in the corner of a dingy federal courtroom. How searching the examination and how careful the questioning will be is entirely a function of the skill and interest of the trustee and of the prospect that there will be anything in the debtor's estate to pay any of the creditors.

---

5. Under the Bankruptcy Judges, United States Trustees, and Family Farmer Bankruptcy Act of 1986, P.L. No. 99–554, § 302(d)(3), districts within the states of Alabama and North Carolina were exempted from the U.S. Trustee system until those districts "opt-in" to the system or October 1, 1992, whichever occurs first. As a consequence, the amendments to the Bankruptcy Act made by subtitle A of title II of the Bankruptcy Judges, United States Trustees,

Since the trustee essentially works on a contingent fee, albeit a small one,[6] the trustee has an interest in enlarging the value of the estate.

The duties of the trustee are set out in section 704. In most cases one suspects that the obligation to "investigate the financial affairs of the debtor" constitutes an examination of the schedules and the posing of a few questions to the debtor at the section 341 meeting. Most cases merit no further investigation. In some cases there will be property of the estate to be collected under section 704(1). Occasionally the trustee may even seek to recover a preference or to avoid a transfer that the debtor made to a spouse or to a third party. We suspect these are the exceptions. Even more rarely the trustee may choose to "oppose the discharge of the debtor" because of information disclosed at the section 341 hearing or in the schedules.[7] Note that the court may order the trustee to investigate the acts and conduct of the debtor "to determine whether a ground exists for denial of discharge."[8] The section 341 hearing may be the only time that the debtor comes to the bankruptcy court. If the court chooses to hold a hearing under section 524(d) after it has decided whether to grant a discharge, the debtor must attend that hearing. However, one suspects that such hearings on discharge are few and far between and thus, that the debtor's one and only trip to the bankruptcy court is for the 341 hearing.

and Family Farmer Bankruptcy Act of 1986 are not effective until those districts "opt-in."

6. Under section 326, the court may award the trustee in a Chapter 7 or 11 case "reasonable compensation" as described in section 330. However, the amount of this reasonable compensation may not exceed fifteen percent on the first $1,000 or less, six percent on the next $2,000, and three percent on any amount in excess of $3,000, upon all moneys disbursed or turned over in the case by the trustee to parties in interest, excluding the debtor. In many cases, the trustee receives indirect compensation by employing members of his firm to perform legal services under § 327, which compensation is allowed by § 330 to the extent it is "reasonable compensation for actual, necessary services" rendered by the attorneys.

7. The duties of the trustee are these:

The trustee shall—

(1) collect and reduce to money the property of the estate for which such trustee serves, and close up such estate as expeditiously as is compatible with the best interests of parties in interest;

(2) be accountable for all property received;

(3) ensure that the debtor shall perform his intention as specified in section 521(2)(B) of this title;

(4) investigate the financial affairs of the debtor;

(5) if a purpose would be served, examine proofs of claims and object to the allowance of any claim that is improper;

(6) if advisable, oppose the discharge of the debtor;

(7) unless the court orders otherwise, furnish such information concerning the estate and the estate's administration as is requested by a party in interest;

(8) if the business of the debtor is authorized to be operated, file with the court, with the United States trustee, and with any governmental unit charged with responsibility for collection or determination of any tax arising out of such operation, periodic reports and summaries of the operation of such business, including a statement of receipts and disbursements, and such other information as the United States trustee or the court requires; and

(9) make a final report and file a final account of the administration of the estate with the court and with the United States trustee.

11 U.S.C.A. § 704.

8. 11 U.S.C.A. § 727(c), which provides:

(1) The trustee, a creditor, or the United States trustee may object to the granting of a discharge under subsection (a) of this section.

(2) On request of a party in interest, the court may order the trustee to examine the acts and conduct of the debtor to determine whether a ground exists for denial of discharge.

Section 705 indicates that the creditors at the 341 hearing may elect a creditors' committee. Such a committee could represent the creditors' interests in a variety of ways in cooperation with the trustee and the United States Trustee. In fact, such committees in individual Chapter 7 cases are rarer than hen's teeth. To form a committee and spend time at committee meetings is to throw good money after bad. The individual debtor's very presence at the gates of the bankruptcy court tells most creditors that the case is hopeless. Only in the unusual case of a wealthy individual who has gotten into a cash bind or the liquidation of a corporation with substantial assets would it make sense for a creditor to serve on a creditors' committee or to spend more than a few cents and a few moments on postpetition searches for assets or attempts to collect.

Two other procedural matters deserve passing reference here. First, under section 706 the debtor may convert the case to Chapters 11, 12 or 13. Although at some point it may be in the interest of the debtor to do that, such cases would be quite unusual. Note that the court has the power "on request of a party in interest" to convert the case to Chapter 11 despite the debtor's objection. There is no similar power to convert to Chapters 12 or 13.

Finally there is the possibility that the court will throw the debtor out of bankruptcy entirely. We will discuss this possibility at some length below, but one should understand that it is an unlikely event. Section 707(a) and (b) provide for such dismissal on relatively narrow grounds. Section 707(b) is almost all that remains from the 1984 attempt by consumer creditors to restrict debtors' power to use Chapter 7. Note that it applies only if there is "substantial abuse of the provisions" of Chapter 7 and that it can be invoked only at the request of the United States Trustee, but "not at the request or suggestion of any party in interest."

In summary, it is probably fair to describe the procedural aspects of Chapter 7 as much *less* than meets the eye. The rather elaborate provisions in Chapter 7 concerning creditors' committees, duties of the trustee, election of trustees, and meetings of creditors give the image of a much more elaborate and formal process than is likely to be practiced in the typical Chapter 7. Most Chapter 7's are perfunctory, informal, and uncontroversial. Yet, the number of Chapter 7s is so huge that even a very small percentage of difficult cases produces a ton of difficult issues and justifies a thorough study of Chapter 7 bankruptcy.

A. CLAIMS, EXPENSES, AND DISTRIBUTIONS IN CHAPTER 7

§ 7–3 Introduction

Claims, how they are made and what they do, is a considerable mystery to the law student, to the novice lawyer (who has never seen the inside of a bankruptcy court) and to most law professors. For a lawyer even slightly experienced in bankruptcy, his practice gives a framework to understand claims, how they are filed and proved, and what they do. This section is addressed to the novice and to the student; it is an attempt to remove some of the mystery associated with these important but non-substantive provisions.

Whether a person who identifies himself as a "creditor" has something that the Code recognizes as a "claim" or something else (a grudge? a 1979 Pontiac?) will affect the rights of the creditor and of the debtor in several ways. First, in a Chapter 11, only claimants can vote. We are not concerned with this rule here, but it can be important in a reorganization proceeding. Second, only claims are discharged. If the creditor's right against the debtor does not rise to the level of a claim, it is not discharged, therefore it survives the bankruptcy; and, if the debtor lives on (as an individual will, but a corporation will not), the right can be asserted against the postbankruptcy income and assets of the debtor. Finally, the status of the claim determines whether the creditor will receive a distribution and how much that distribution will be. Without a claim there can be no distribution. Some claims entitle the holder to priority in distribution over others.

To understand the nature of claims, how they are put before the court and how they interact, one needs to read sections 501, 502, 503, 506, and 507. Those sections and the bankruptcy rules applying them contain the procedure for the filing and proof of claim and contain rules about priority among various claims and expenses.

Consider first the procedure in a Chapter 7. A potential claim is revealed to the court by the papers that the debtor files together with his petition. The debtor is obliged to list his creditors and the amount and nature of their claims. Typically, he will do that. Of course, the debtor's recollection of the amount and type of claim may be different from the creditor's; but the debtor's papers, filed in connection with the petition and under Rule 1007, stimulate the bankruptcy clerk to send notice of the case. This notice in turn alerts the creditor to the debtor's bankruptcy and to the creditor's need to protect its rights.

Unlike a Chapter 11 case where the creditor need not file a proof of claim [1], a Chapter 7 creditor must file a proof of claim under Rule 3002. If he does not do so, the debtor or the trustee may do so in his behalf, but normally it will be up to the creditor to file this "proof of claim" to satisfy section 501 and to procure "allowance" under 502. Typically the proof of claim is filed on a official bankruptcy form, and it sets out the creditor's notion of the amount due and identifies the proper name and address of the creditor. This "proof" may also include documents, such as a promissory note signed by the debtor or some other form of contract. The purpose of all of this is obvious. If the bankruptcy court is to consolidate the debtor's liabilities and pay them off in some pro rata form, it must know the nature and amount of each liability in order to classify them and to determine the pro rata distribution.

Under section 502(a), a claim that is filed under 501 is "deemed allowed" unless somebody objects. Rather than requiring a formal procedure of the kind that was contemplated prior to 1978, the current Code assumes that the claims made by creditors are generally accurate and leaves it to the debtor,

---

§ 7–3

1. Congress apparently assumed that a Chapter 11 debtor's records will allow it to get the creditor's claim right.

other creditors or the trustee to challenge those claims. In most cases, allowance is pro forma, an event that occurs with the passage of time.

The procedural aspects of filing a proof of claim in connection with a Chapter 7 liquidation are governed by Rule 3002. This rule provides in part:

(a) Necessity for Filing. An unsecured creditor or an equity security holder must file a proof of claim or interest in accordance with this rule for the claim or interest to be allowed, except as provided in Rules 1019(4), 3003, 3004 and 3005. * * *

(c) Time for Filing. In a chapter 7 liquidation or chapter 13 individual's debt adjustment case, a proof of claim shall be filed within 90 days after the first date set for the meeting of creditors called pursuant to § 341(a) of the Code, except as follows:

> (1) on motion of the United States, a state, or subdivision thereof before the expiration of such period and for cause shown, the court may extend the time for filing of a claim by the United States, a state, or subdivision thereof.

> (2) In the interest of justice and if it will not unduly delay the administration of the case, the court may extend the time for filing a proof of claim by an infant or incompetent person or the representative of either. * * *

> (4) A claim arising from the rejection of an executory contract of the debtor may be filed within such time as the court may direct. * * *

> (6) In a chapter 7 liquidation case, if a surplus remains after all claims allowed have been paid in full, the court may grant an extension of time for the filing of claims against the surplus not filed within the time hereinabove prescribed.

A fairly common objection concerns the allowance of claims that are tardily filed. The time for filing a Chapter 7 claim is governed by Bankruptcy Rule 3002(c) quoted above. If a Chapter 7 creditor fails to file a claim within the time required in Rule 3002(c) and an objection is made to his late filing, he may lose the claim entirely. At least two Circuit Courts of Appeals have held that Rule 9006(b)(3)[2] prevents bankruptcy courts from extending the filing deadline unless one of the six situations described in Rule 3002(c) exists.[3] However, the Sixth Circuit has taken a different position. In *United States v. Cardinal Mine Supply, Inc.*,[4] the court held that bankruptcy courts as courts of equity can provide a remedy even when the specific provisions of the rule do not.[5]

What if the creditor did not receive notice? The *Cardinal Mine* court held that due process and equitable concerns mandate that when a creditor does not have notice or knowledge of a bankruptcy, it must be allowed to file

---

2. It provides that:
    The court may enlarge the time for taking action under * * * [Rule] 3002(c) * * *, only to the extent and under the conditions stated in [that] rule.
Bankr. R. 9006(b)(3).

3. In re Davis, 936 F.2d 771 (4th Cir.1991); In re Coastal Alaska Lines, Inc., 920 F.2d 1428, 1432–33 (9th Cir.1990).

4. 916 F.2d 1087 (6th Cir.1990).

5. Id. at 1091.

if it does so promptly after learning of the bankruptcy.[6] However, even a successful due process argument will not always save a claim. One court used the equitable doctrine of laches to bar a tardy claim.[7]

Note that section 502(b) and the remaining subsections of 502 contain a number of exceptions to allowance and specify that certain things that look like claims are not to be treated as such. Interest to be accrued but not yet matured when the petition is filed is a good example, see 502(b)(2). For the time being we ignore the rest of the exceptions in 502(b), but one should know of their existence.

§ 7–4 Definition of Claim

If the creditor's right is not a claim, *a fortiori* one need ask whether the right is secured or unsecured or is entitled to priority. There is no need for filing, allowance, or any of the other procedures that are applicable to "claims." Section 101(5) defines a claim as follows:

> (A) right to payment, whether or not such right is reduced to judgment, liquidated, unliquidated, fixed, contingent, matured, unmatured, disputed, undisputed, legal, equitable, secured, or unsecured; or

> (B) right to an equitable remedy for breach of performance if such breach gives rise to a right to payment, whether or not such right to an equitable remedy is reduced to judgment, fixed, contingent, matured, unmatured, disputed, undisputed, secured, or unsecured.

The Senate Judiciary Committee's report makes clear that "[b]y this broadest possible definition * * * the [Code] contemplates that all legal obligations of the debtor, no matter how remote or contingent, will be able to be dealt with in the bankruptcy case."[1] Despite this seemingly limitless expanse of "claim," the definition has presented two interpretive difficulties. First, and most significant, is the question when a creditor's right becomes sufficiently mature that it amounts to a "claim." Second is the problem associated with paragraph (B) concerning rights to injunctive relief that appear not to "give rise to a right to payment."

§ 7–5 When Does the Claim Arise?

"Claims" are discharged in Chapter 7, but rights that have not yet risen to the level of "claims" at the time the petition is filed survive or receive priority status as administrative expenses. It is always in the creditor's interest, therefore, to argue that its particular liability arose after the petition in any case where general unsecured creditors will receive no distribution.

---

6. Id. at 1089–90; see also In re Dodd, 82 B.R. 924, 928 (N.D.Ill. 1987) (debtor must show that notice has been provided before the Rules' time limits may be enforced); In re Kennedy, 40 B.R. 558, 560 (Bankr. N.D.Ala. 1984) (dictum) (where barring tardy filing of claim amounts to deprivation of property without due process, a court must prohibit the application of the Rules to the performance of the act which would otherwise be barred).

7. In re Barsky, 85 B.R. 550 (C.D.Cal.1988), aff'd, 933 F.2d 1013 (9th Cir.1991) (affirmed on doctrine of laches, thus due process question not reached).

§ 7–4

1. S. Rep. No. 989, 95th Cong., 2d Sess. 22, reprinted in 1978 U.S. Code Cong. & Admin. News 5787, 5808.

This timing issue is also relevant in determining when the stay applies and in certain other circumstances. It has been litigated most frequently and extensively in cases involving the stay. Technically the cases under section 362 deal with the question whether a "claim" arose before the commencement of the case and not with the question whether a "debt" arose then. However, because the definition of debt in section 101(12) means "liability on a claim", we believe that the length and breadth of "claim" and "debt" are coextensive. We see no other reason why the cases under section 362 cannot be used to define the time when the debt arises under sections 727 and 524 as well.

There are at least two ways to determine the birth of a claim or debt. The view of the Court of Appeals for the Third Circuit in *Matter of M. Frenville Co.*[1] is that a claim arises only when the party asserting the claim would have a cause of action against the debtor *under state law*. The Bankruptcy Code does not define either debt or claim. The courts must look to state law for definitions and, thought the Court of Appeals for the Third Circuit, must also look to that law to determine when the state-defined claim arises.

Yet if one wishes to include all possible claimants in the bankruptcy, provide for all under a plan in Chapter 11, and discharge the debtor to the largest possible extent, bankruptcy policy arguably calls for a broader definition than the kind contemplated in *Frenville*. Out of concern for these bankruptcy policies, most courts have disagreed with *Frenville* and have applied a broader definition of claim and debt.[2] These courts hold, and the majority rule is, that a claim (debt) arises at the time when the acts giving rise to the alleged liability were performed without regard to when the cause of action arises under state law. This rule is justified by section 101(5), formerly section 101(4)[3], which defines "claim" to include contingent, unliquidated and unmatured rights to payment.[4] Further, the legislative history of section 101(5) states Congress' intention to include in the definition "all legal obligations of the debtor, no matter how remote or contingent."[5] This meaning effectively expands the discharge, extends its scope and includes, most significantly, tort victims whose claims are both contingent and unknown at the time of the petition. Mass tort claims have become so important in bankruptcy that we discuss this problem separately in our Chapter 11.

§ 7–5

1. 744 F.2d 332 (3rd Cir.1984), cert. denied, 469 U.S. 1160, 105 S.Ct. 911, 83 L.Ed.2d 925 (1985).

2. Bush v. Taylor, 912 F.2d 989 (8th Cir. 1990) (en banc); Grady v. A.H. Robins Co., 839 F.2d 198 (4th Cir.1988), cert. dismissed 487 U.S. 1260, 109 S.Ct. 201, 101 L.Ed.2d 972 (1988); In re Chateaugay, 112 B.R. 513 (S.D.N.Y. 1990), judgment aff'd, 944 F.2d 997 (2d Cir.1991) (postpetition injury must attach to something prepetition); L.F. Rothschild & Co. v. Angier, 84 B.R. 274 (D. Mass. 1988); In re Poule, 91 B.R. 83 (BAP 9th Cir. 1988); In re Allied Mechanical Services, Inc., 38 B.R. 959 (Bankr. N.D.Ga.1984) (OSHA penalties levied postpetition but based on prepetition violation are treated as prepetition obligations.)

3. Many of the definitions in § 101 were renumbered in 1990. Crime Control Act of 1990, Pub. L. No. 101–647, § 2522(e), 104 Stat. 4789, 4867–68.

4. Matter of Rosteck, 899 F.2d 694 (7th Cir.1990).

5. S.Rep. No. 989, 95th Cong., 2d Sess. 22, reprinted in 1978 U.S.Code Cong. & Ad. News 5787; H.R. Rep. No. 595, 95th Cong. 2d Sess. 309, reprinted in 1978 U.S.Code Cong. & Ad. News, 5963.

In recent cases three other factual circumstances have presented issues about the date of birth of a claim. First are cases in which a spouse promises to pay a portion of a pension to another spouse as part of a divorce decree or a divorce settlement. After the divorce the promisor spouse takes bankruptcy and argues that the liability was a prepetition property settlement which is discharged in the bankruptcy. On a variety of theories, the promisee spouse argues—usually victoriously—that the duty to pay the pension arises after the petition and is not discharged. A second scenario involves a condominium owner who has a continuing obligation to pay periodic condominium fees. In that case there will be a similar dispute between the creditor condominium association who asserts that these periodic obligations are postpetition and therefore not discharged and the condominium owner who argues that his obligation arose prior to the petition and is thus discharged. Third are obligations analogous to tort claims, to the federal government under CERCLA for toxic waste discharges.

If one rejects *Frenville* and concludes that the time of birth of a debt is to be found in the Bankruptcy Code and is also to be pushed back to the earliest possible time, then one should regard all four of these cases as easy. All of them should be regarded as prepetition claims and all discharged. "On the law" they are the same or very close. In truth, the outcome on all four is not the same. A possible explanation is that extra-legal factors influence this issue. Regardless of the explanation, we would warn the lawyer from blindly carrying the rule expressed in one of these cases to another setting.

§ 7–6 When Does the Claim Arise?—Pension Obligations

For full text of this section, see Epstein, Nickles & White, Bankruptcy, Practitioner Treatise Series, Vol. 2.

§ 7–7 When Does the Claim Arise?—Condominium Fees

For full text of this section, see Epstein, Nickles & White, Bankruptcy, Practitioner Treatise Series, Vol. 2.

§ 7–8 Does a Right to an Equitable Remedy Constitute a "Claim"?

Under section 101(5)(B), a "claim" includes:

right to an equitable remedy for breach of performance if such breach gives rise to a right to payment, whether or not such right to an equitable remedy is reduced to judgment, fixed, contingent, matured, unmatured, disputed, undisputed, secured, or unsecured.

While any party holding an injunction should be wary of the implications of this definition, the issues surrounding section 101(5)(B) have most often arisen in the area of environmental clean-up obligations. In 1985, the Supreme Court faced the issue of environmental clean-up obligation injunctions when it decided the case of *Ohio v. Kovacs*.[1] In *Kovacs*, the chief

---

§ 7–8
1. 469 U.S. 274, 105 S.Ct. 705, 83 L.Ed.2d 649 (1985).

executive officer and stockholder of a corporation, Chem–Dyne, Inc., entered into a stipulation and judgment order to clean up the site of its industrial waste. Kovacs and Chem–Dyne later filed bankruptcy and the state of Ohio sought to have the clean-up stipulation declared nondischargeable because it was not a "debt" within the meaning of the Bankruptcy Code. Relying on the meaning of "claim" as found in section 101(5)(B), the Supreme Court found that Ohio's right did constitute a claim, and further, that the claim was dischargeable in bankruptcy.[2]

In its analysis, the Supreme Court first found that the State had the right to an equitable remedy under state law which had been reduced to a judgment in the form of an injunction ordering the clean-up. The Court then decided that the State was really looking for a payment in compensation for its costs to clean up the facility. Of critical importance to the Court's decision was the fact that when Kovacs failed to abide by the injunction, the State secured the appointment of a receiver to take charge of Kovac's assets rather than prosecute him under the environmental laws or bring civil or criminal contempt proceedings.

A second development in the area of environmental obligations arose in *United States v. Whizco, Inc.*[3] Concluding that the defendant would have to pay someone else to carry out the court order (to reclaim a mine), the court held that the plaintiff was really looking for "payment." To the extent that the obligation was really for an expenditure of money by the defendant, it was discharged.[4] However, if a debtor could personally act without spending money to hire an agent, the obligation would not be discharged.

The *Whizco* result has been properly criticized as an ill advised expansion of the definition of "right to payment" and section 101(5)(B).[5] Two recent district courts explicitly reject the *Whizco* rationale. In one of those cases, the court found that the fact the debtor must spend money to comply with an injunction does not make the obligation a dischargeable claim. According to that court only where the creditor has an option of converting an injunction into a right to monetary compensation should the debtor fail to comply with the injunction, the obligation should be regarded as a dischargeable claim.[6] This reasoning is sound. The real issue is not an expenditure

---

2. The Court quoted from the legislative history:

> Section 101(4)(B) [now (5)(B)] * * * is intended to cause the liquidation or estimation of contingent rights of payment for which there may be an alternative equitable remedy with the result that the equitable remedy will be susceptible to being discharged in bankruptcy. For example, in some States, a judgment for specific performance may be satisfied by an alternative right to payment in the event performance is refused; in that event, the creditor entitled to specific performance would have a "claim" for purposes of a proceeding under title 11.

Ohio v. Kovacs, 469 U.S. 274, 105 S.Ct. 705, 83 L.Ed.2d 649 (1985) (quoting 124 Cong. Rec. 32393 (1978) (remarks of Rep. Edwards); see also 124 Cong. Rec. at 33992 (1978) (remarks of Sen. DeConcini)).

3. 841 F.2d 147 (6th Cir.1988).

4. See also In re Robinson, 46 B.R. 136 (Bankr. M.D. Fla.1985) rev'd on other grounds, 55 B.R. 355 (M.D.Fla.1985) (while duty to restore marshland was facially nonmonetary, the debtor would be required to spend money in order to accomplish that result, therefore giving the plaintiff a right to payment).

5. In re Chateaugay Corp., 112 B.R. 513 (S.D.N.Y.1990), aff'd, 944 F.2d 997 (2d Cir. 1991); United States v. Hubler, 117 B.R. 160 (W.D.Pa.1990), judgment aff'd, 928 F.2d 1131 (3d Cir.1991).

6. In re Chateaugay Corp., 112 B.R. 513, 522 (S.D.N.Y.1990), aff'd, 944 F.2d 997 (2d Cir. 1991). The court stated: "Even an optional right to payment is nonetheless a right to payment and the fact that EPA may not choose to exercise that option in no way ne-

of money to comply with an injunction, but rather the existence of an obligation by the creditor allowing *it* to collect money from the debtor. The language of section 101(5)(B) makes clear that should the breach of performance give rise to a right to payment, then the equitable remedy is a "claim." Like it or not, the environmental authorities are, and should normally be treated as, creditors.

§ 7-9 Hierarchy of Claims

A consideration of sections 503 (administrative expenses), 506 (determination of secured status), 507 (priority), and 510 (subordination) shows that not all claims are created equal. Once one has determined that there is a claim, that claim ultimately receives different treatment under section 726 (distribution of the bankrupt's assets) if it is a secured claim or a claim arising out of an administrative expense, or some other form of priority claim with a right to be paid ahead of general unsecured claims.

In one sense there is less here than meets the eye. It would be inaccurate to suggest that the typical Chapter 7 case includes sufficient assets so that there will be payment down the line to various priority claimants and then to the general unsecured claimants. Those will be quite unusual cases. In the usual case, secured creditors will take their assets, there will be some payment to the administrative expense claimants, and that may be all that is available. Nevertheless, one must understand what the distribution would be in a Chapter 7 liquidation because that standard places a floor on what a creditor can receive in a Chapter 11, 12, or 13 plan, and thus has a direct impact on the kind of plan that can be approved in those chapters. For that reason, more than any other, one must be familiar with sections 503, 507, and 726.

§ 7-10 Hierarchy of Claims—Secured Claims

Secured claims are not listed in section 507 which establishes the hierarchy of claims or in 726 that describes distribution from the estate. Nevertheless, secured claims are always given top priority as to the assets subject to the security. Perhaps this was thought so obvious that it need not be stated in the Code, but a security interest that cannot be set aside (whether a mortgage, an Article 9 security interest, or some other form of lien) continues after the discharge as a claim on the assets subject to the security. The bankruptcy has no effect because bankruptcy honors the property principle of derivative title, and the lienor's interest in the debtor's property is excluded from the bankruptcy estate.

---

gates the existence of that right." Id. In affirming the district court's decision the Second Circuit distinguished between injunctions in which the enforcing agency has an alternative right to payment and injunctions in which no such alternative exists. The Second Circuit found that an injunction that does no more than impose an obligation entirely as an alternative to a right to payment is dischargeable. Recognizing that the EPA had no authority to accept payment as an alternative to continued pollution, the court held, however, that an injunctive order which accomplishes the dual objectives of removing accumulated wastes and "stopping or ameliorating ongoing pollution emanating from such wastes is not a dischargeable claim." In re Chateaugay Corp., 944 F.2d 997, 1008 (2d Cir. 1991), aff'g, 112 B.R. 513, 522 (S.D.N.Y.1990).

In effect, the secured claim that remains after the bankruptcy constitutes an *in rem* claim against the particular asset and—assuming the total value of the creditor's claim exceeds the value of the asset—constitutes a claim to that entire value.

By hypothesis a secured claim represents an interest in property. In the words of section 506(a), it is

> an allowed claim of a creditor secured by a lien on property in which the estate has an interest, or that is subject to setoff under section 553 * * * to the extent of the value of such creditor's interest in the estate's interest in such property, or to the extent of the amount subject to setoff.

Section 101(37) describes "lien" to mean a "charge against or interest in property" and "judicial lien" is defined by section 101(36) to be a lien "obtained by judgment, levy, sequestration, or other legal or equitable process or proceeding * * *." The Senate Committee confirms that the definition was intended to be "very broad"; it is intended to encompass judicial liens, statutory liens, security interests, and mortgages.[1]

Of course, to the extent that the lien or security interest is avoided—as a preference, because it is unperfected, or for any other reason—the claimant is left with an unsecured claim.

Because the conventional vernacular describing "secured" loans in mortgage law or under U.C.C. Article 9 would identify any claim as secured if the creditor had taken security in any collateral, no matter how small its value, the definition of secured claims in section 506 will be unfamiliar to and at odds with that conventional way of thinking. Under section 506 a mortgage securing a million dollar obligation on a piece of property worth $500,000 would be treated as and regarded as a "secured claim" only to the extent of the value "of such creditor's interest in the estate's interest in such property * * *." In the case posed, the secured creditor would have a claim on 100 percent of the estate's interest, but the estate's interest in the property is only $500,000. Therefore the creditor has a $500,000 secured claim and a $500,000 unsecured claim. Contrary to the common parlance, this creditor is a secured creditor and also an unsecured creditor. The upshot is that it will have one claim treated as a secured claim in bankruptcy, and one claim treated as an unsecured claim. All of that will be important for any plan under Chapter 11, 12, or 13. One of the fighting issues currently before the Supreme Court deals with the question of how one values property and, to a lesser extent, what rights section 506 grants to the debtor to divide property into secured and unsecured claims and to do what is known in the trade as "*lien stripping.*"[2]

§ 7–10

1. S. Rep. No. 989, 95th Cong., 2d Sess. 25, reprinted in 1978 U.S. Code Cong. & Admin. News 5787, 5811.

2. In a series of cases arising between 1985 and 1990, debtors who had granted mortgages on their homes sought to keep those homes in Chapter 7 proceedings by "lien stripping." Debtors argued that the creditors' claim should be divided into a secured and an unsecured claim against the home (assume a home worth $120,000 with a $170,000 mortgage). In that circumstance the debtor would argue that the $50,000 liability was to be discharged and that a claim equal only to $120,000 would remain in rem against the property under 506. The debtor would then borrow the $120,000 from someone else and assert the right to pay off the in rem liability, so keeping the house. The creditors, of course, argued that

§ 7-11 Hierarchy of Claims—Administrative Expenses

The claims with the highest priority in section 507—ranking right below secured claims—are technically not "claims," but only "expenses." These are so-called administrative expenses defined in section 503(b). They consist of "the actual, necessary costs and expenses of preserving the estate, including wages, salaries, or commissions for services rendered after the commencement of the case."[1] Because the conventional expenses of operating the business would be administrative expenses, as well as attorneys, accountants, and investment bankers' fees, these costs can be enormous in a Chapter 11. Since there is no business to operate in most Chapter 7s and since any business would be operated only for a brief time if there were one, the expenses will be significantly less in a Chapter 7. Nevertheless, even in a Chapter 7 case these expenses can eat up the lion's share of the available assets.

Although it may not be obvious at first, a little reflection reveals the rationale behind the administrative expense priority. In *Trustees of Amalgamated Insurance Fund v. McFarlin's*,[2] the court pointed out that

> Congress granted priority to administrative expenses in order to facilitate the efforts of the trustee or debtor in possession to rehabilitate the business for the benefit of all the estate's creditors* * *. Congress reasoned that unless the debts incurred by the debtor in possession could be given priority over the debts which forced the estate into bankruptcy in the first place, persons would not do business with the debtor in possession, which would inhibit rehabilitation of the business and thus harm the creditors.[3]

The court in *McFarlin's* went on to deny administrative expense priority to a claim of a multiemployer pension fund, since the contribution to the fund was consideration for services performed by employees prior to filing the bankruptcy petition, and hence the contribution would not benefit the estate's creditors.[4] However, because of the general concern of keeping the business afloat (in Chapter 11), "doing business" expenses such as insurance payments, utility bills, tort claims litigation expenses, and contract-related expenses are typically given administrative expense priority if they arise postpetition.[5] In addition, section 503(b)(4) specifically grants attorney's and accountant's fees administrative expense priority, presumably to insure that those professionals will be willing to provide their services to a bankrupt client.

---

their entire $170,000 claim remained as an in rem liability against the property and that the property could be taken from them against their will only by a payment of the full $170,000. Debtors pointed to 506 which seemed to permit such division; creditors pointed to § 722 that permits such redemption of personal property, but conspicuously excludes real property. The Third and Eleventh Circuits agreed with the debtor's position here, the Tenth Circuit agreed with the creditor's position. In re Dewsnup, 908 F.2d 588 (10th Cir. 1990), cert. granted, ___ U.S. ___, 111 S.Ct. 949, 112 L.Ed.2d 1038 (1991); In re Gaglia, 889 F.2d 1304 (3rd Cir.1989); Matter of Folendore, 862 F.2d 1537 (11th Cir.1989). The Supreme Court has granted certiorari in the Dewsnup case.

§ 7-11

1. 11 U.S.C.A. § 503(b)(1)(A).
2. 789 F.2d 98 (2d Cir.1986).
3. Id. at 101.
4. Id. at 104.
5. See Norton Bankr. L. and Prac. §§ 12.17–12.34 (1981).

The concern in a Chapter 7 case, where there is no ongoing business operation, is likely to be more with "maximizing the size of the estate to be distributed than with the Chapter 11 goal of inducing third parties to contribute towards the continued operations of the business,"[6] so the court may be more stingy in awarding administrative expenses in a Chapter 7 case, since there are likely to be fewer expenses required to preserve the estate. For example, in *Matter of Hayes*,[7] the court denied administrative expense priority to a farmer who had incurred expenses in caring for some of the debtor's cattle, on the grounds that the farmer had undertaken the expense for his own benefit, rather than for the sole benefit of the estate. Of course, the necessity for services of attorneys and accountants remains in a liquidation case, and section 503(b)(4) (allowance of administrative expense priority for attorney's and accountant's fees) applies to Chapter 7 just as to Chapter 11.

For an expense to qualify as an administrative expense, two things must happen. First, the claim must arise after the petition has been filed. Prior to the filing of the petition there is no estate to be preserved[8] and *a fortiori* prepetition expenses are not administrative expenses, but rather are likely to be conventional, pedestrian unsecured claims. The postpetition requirement has been strictly construed in *In re Gitex*,[9] where a creditor who delivered goods to the debtor just hours before the debtor filed for bankruptcy was denied administrative priority.

This requirement is merely one part of the question discussed above, when does a claim arise. Depending upon the circumstances, sometimes the claimant will wish to argue that no claim arose at any time until after the case was closed—so that the claim is not discharged. In other cases, the argument will be that the claim arose postpetition so that it is an expense, and in yet other cases there may be an argument by the creditor that the claim arose prior to the petition so that it can be a claim asserted in the bankruptcy estate and entitled to a vote.

Second, and less important, postpetition expenses must be "actual, necessary" costs of preserving the estate. The absence of cases on this issue suggests that there is relatively little difficulty with the latter requirement, but certainly it is possible to have expenses that are only tangentially related to the business of preserving the estate or to maintaining its property.[10] In such circumstances, even postpetition expenses would not be administrative expenses entitled to priority. Consider, for example, *Matter of Chicago, Rock Island & Pacific Railroad Co.*[11] In that case, a railroad was reorganizing into a real estate concern and abandoning its railroad operations. The state of Iowa wished to restore all of the Rock Island's railroad crossings in Iowa to their pre-railroad condition (which would entail removal

---

6. In re Dant & Russell, 853 F.2d 700, 706–707 (9th Cir.1988) (quoting Broadcast Corp. of Georgia v. Broadfoot, 54 B.R. 606, 611 (N.D.Ga.1985)).

7. 20 B.R. 469 (Bankr. W.D.Wis.1982).

8. Section 541(a) provides that "[t]he commencement of a case * * * creates an estate."

9. 4 B.C.D. (CRR) 1066 (Bankr. S.D.N.Y. 1978).

10. "A debt is not entitled to [administrative] priority simply because the right to payment arises after the debtor in possession has begun managing the estate." Trustees of Amalgamated Ins. Fund v. McFarlin's, Inc., 789 F.2d 98, 101 (2d Cir.1986) (citations omitted).

11. 756 F.2d 517 (7th Cir.1985).

of tracks from highways, removal of bridges, and filling in underpasses), and to receive an administrative expense priority against Rock Island for the cost of the operations. Iowa's theory was that the crossing would eventually become hazards, exposing the Rock Island to potential tort liability in the future. The court agreed that removal of a crossing that posed an *imminent* threat to the public would benefit the railroad's other creditors by avoiding tort liability during the reorganization period. However, the court denied Iowa's request, on the grounds that

> removals that will benefit the citizens of Iowa years after the reorganization is complete and the Rock Island ceases to be a railroad are unlikely to benefit the Rock Island's creditors * * *. [T]he benefit, if any, is too slight, indirect, conjectural, and remote to justify classifying the expense of restoration as an administrative expense.[12]

Hence, Iowa's claim, which clearly arose postpetition, was nonetheless denied as not an "actual, necessary" expense of preserving the estate.

§ 7–12 Hierarchy of Claims—Other Priority Claims

In the current version of section 507(a) there are eight numbered levels of priority claims. We devote no time to four of them: 507(a)(2), early expenses in involuntary cases; (5), grain producers and fishermen; (6) deposits; and (8), payments to the FDIC and the like.

The third and fourth priorities deal respectively with wages and claims for contributions to an employee benefit plan. These give a modest advantage to the employees of the debtor. Generally these rights are limited to $2,000 for wages earned but unpaid within 90 days before the filing, and for certain claims for contributions to an employee benefit plan arising from services rendered within 180 days before the filing of the petition. Both of these modest priorities recognize claims of employees as more deserving— but only slightly so—than claims of other unsecured creditors. Each is capped at $2,000 and the net effect of the other limitations is that most employees will not get even $2,000.

Recently the Congress has done a piecemeal improvement of the employees' priority in certain respects not directly related to section 507. For example, it enacted section 1113 on rejection of collective bargaining agreements. The effect of this provision will be somewhat to improve the lot of employees of companies that are in Chapter 11. More recently the Congress enacted section 1114 on payment of insurance benefits to retired employees. The effect of this provision is to give retired employees of Chapter 11 companies significantly increased priority for insurance benefits compared with what they would enjoy under section 507. While these provisions are technically not modifications to the priority system found in 507, they have that consequence and should properly be regarded as evidence of a spasmodic rethinking by Congress of the appropriate priority of employees as claimants.

The seventh priority deals primarily with taxes of many sorts. We deal at length with that provision in connection with the discussion of the exception of taxes from the discharge under section 523. A crude but

---

12. Id. at 520.

generally accurate statement is that most taxes are included in and enjoy priority under 507(a)(7).[1] It is not entirely true but is a good working presumption.

§ 7–13 Hierarchy of Claims—Superpriority Claims, Section 507(b)

One final situation deserves mention: the "superpriority" claim described in section 507(b). The automatic stay granted a debtor upon filing a petition for bankruptcy under section 362 prevents a secured creditor from taking possession of or enforcing a lien on any property of the debtor. However, section 362(d) provides that the court may grant the creditor relief from the stay "for cause, including the lack of adequate protection of an interest in property." If the court determines that adequate protection has been provided to the creditor, relief from the stay will not be granted to the creditor.[1]

Section 507(b) covers the case when despite the "adequate protection" given to the secured creditor, the creditor nonetheless has a claim allowable under section 507(a)(1) (i.e., an administrative expense claim). In that case, the creditor's claim is given priority over every other administrative expense claim.

When a creditor goes to court, asks for adequate protection and receives "adequate" protection that later proves "inadequate," that creditor clearly qualifies for superpriority under 507(b). But what if there is never a court finding of the need for and the requirement of adequate protection? Assume, for example, that creditor insists upon adequate protection and then receives it without a court hearing in an agreement between the creditor and the debtor in possession or between the creditor and the trustee in a Chapter 7 case. Assume further that the protection that is given proves to be inadequate. Is such a creditor entitled to the superpriority under 507(b)?

Although some courts require court approval of the agreement once the 507(b) request has been made, most courts seem to agree that private adequate protection agreements entitle the creditor to 507(b) relief. For example, in *In re Cheatham*,[2] the court allowed a 507(b) claim for failure of a private adequate protection agreement without any review of the agreement. The court held that "a creditor is entitled to superpriority status for unforeseeable, unexpected losses; however, it is not entitled to losses arising from foreseeable circumstances such as normal depreciation or wear and tear"[3] when a consensual adequate protection agreement has been worked

---

§ 7–12

1. Two of the enumerated priority classes of section 507(a), farmers and fishermen (paragraph (5)) and taxes (paragraph (7)) contain subparagraphs that create what could be interpreted as a priority ranking within the particular priority class. For example, section 507(a)(7) lists property taxes in subparagraph (B), but lists excise taxes in subparagraph (E), possibly suggesting that property tax claims should be paid in full before excise taxes receive any distribution. However, we have found no cases on this point, and authorities appear to assume that distribution within each priority class is equal (e.g., excise taxes and property taxes should receive equal pro rata shares). See, e.g., 2 Collier Bankr. Man. ¶ 507.08 (3d ed. 1991).

§ 7–13

1. For our discussion of relief from the stay for lack of adequate protection, see §§ —-— supra.

2. 91 B.R. 382 (E.D.N.C.1988).

3. Id. at 804.

out.[4] The court distinguished the situation where the court has determined what protection is adequate, in which case it would be "inequitable to tax the creditor with the burden of the court's error if the judicially determined adequate protection later turns out to be 'inadequate.'"[5]

In contrast, in *In re Blehm Land & Cattle Co.*,[6] the court held that private adequate protection agreements should be scrutinized before allowing 507(b) expenses. In that case, after a debtor defaulted on the private agreement, the court rejected the trustee's argument that a creditor could not assert a 507(b) claim since the court had never approved the agreement. It held that "neither the Code nor its legislative history supports the interpretation that court approval of an ex parte adequate protection agreement is a prerequisite to a 507(b) expense."[7] However, the court went on to hold that when a 507(b) claim is made, the court should first scrutinize the private adequate protection agreement to see if it passed a test set forth in an earlier case.[8] That test required that (1) the agreement be consistent with the Bankruptcy Code; (2) the conduct of the creditor be equitable; and (3) allowing the agreement would not produce an inequitable result.[9] So both *Cheatham* and *Blehm* allow creditors who have worked out private adequate protection agreements to assert 507(b) claims, but the *Blehm* court reserves the right to invalidate the agreement: "[w]hen an ex parte adequate protection agreement is determined to be 'too adequate,' it should be modified or set aside."[10]

A third approach, taken by *In re Becker*[11] and rejected by *Cheatham*, allowed the creditor to claim its entire proved loss (foreseeable as well as unforeseeable) as a 507(b) expense after failure of an ex parte agreement. Clearly, the law is unsettled, both as to the circumstances under which failed private adequate protection agreements will give rise to valid 507(b) superpriority claims, and the extent to which such claims will be allowed.[12]

§ 7-14 Distribution Under Section 726

As we have said before, most conventional Chapter 7s produce minimum distribution to the creditors. Nevertheless, there are some cases in which there will be substantial assets and there are larger numbers of cases in Chapters 11, 12 and 13, where certain of the rights of the creditors are established by reference to section 726. For example, under Chapter 11 a plan cannot be approved under 1129(a)(7)(A)(ii) unless "each holder of a claim" has accepted or "will receive or retain * * * property of a value * * * that is not less than the amount such holder would so receive * * * if the debtor were liquidated under Chapter 7 * * *." Thus, the *floor* for a Chapter

---

4. The court limited the creditor's right to recovery to unforeseeable damage on the grounds that "the creditor is generally at a distinct advantage over the debtor in working out consensual adequate protection agreements." Id. at 803.

5. Id.

6. 859 F.2d 137 (10th Cir.1988).

7. Id. at 140.

8. In re B & W Tractor Co., 38 B.R. 613 (Bankr. E.D.N.C.1984).

9. Id. at 617.

10. 859 F.2d at 140.

11. 51 B.R. 975 (Bankr. D.Minn.1985).

12. For a more extensive discussion of these matters, and a proposal to solve some of the inequities that can arise out of private adequate protection agreements, see Note, Adequate Protection and Administrative Expense: Toward a Uniform System for Awarding Superpriorities, 88 Mich.L.Rev. 2168 (1990).

11 creditor is what the Chapter 11 creditor would receive in a distribution under section 726. For that purpose, if for no other, it is important to understand how section 726 would distribute the assets of an estate were there substantial assets.

Section 726(a) has six classifications. It reads in full as follows:

(a) Except as provided in section 510 of this title, property of the estate shall be distributed—

(1) first, in payment of claims of the kind specified in and in the order specified in, section 507 of this title;

(2) second, in payment of any allowed unsecured claim, other than a claim of a kind specified in paragraph (1), (3), or (4) of this subsection, proof of which is—

(A) timely filed under section 501(a) of this title:

(B) timely filed under section 501(b) or 501(c) of this title; or

(C) tardily filed under section 501(a) of this title, if—

(i) the creditor that holds such claim did not have notice or actual knowledge of the case in time for timely filing of a proof of such claim under section 501(a) of this title; and

(ii) proof of such claim is filed in time to permit payment of such claim;

(3) third, in payment of any allowed unsecured claim proof of which is tardily filed under section 501(a) of this title, other than a claim of the kind specified in paragraph (2)(C) of this subsection;

(4) fourth, in payment of any allowed claim, whether secured or unsecured, for any fine, penalty, or forfeiture, or for multiple, exemplary, or punitive damages, arising before the earlier of the order for relief or the appointment of a trustee, to the extent that such fine, penalty, forfeiture, or damages are not compensation for actual pecuniary loss suffered by the holder of such claim;

(5) fifth, in payment of interest at the legal rate from the date of the filing of the petition, on any claim paid under paragraph (1), (2), (3), or (4) of this subsection; and

(6) sixth, to the debtor.

Above we have already discussed the provisions of section 507. Those 507 issues are in effect transmitted to 726 and played out in the distribution scheme. Here, as in section 507, a secured creditor has priority to the extent of its security even though the section is silent on that question.

Although the stream will almost certainly run dry before it reaches even subsection (2) under 726(a), one should understand some of the rules lurking in the subsequent provisions of 726(a). Note, for example, that although unaccrued interest is not an allowable claim because of section 502, interest is to be paid if there is money to do so under 726(a)(5) at the "legal rate." Thus in determining what goes to the creditors under 1129(a)(7) and what might be left to a debtor in Chapter 11, a creditor should not overlook his right to interest under 726(a)(5). That right might increase his share even in circumstances in which he is included in a class that as a whole accepts the plan where he does not accept.

§ 7-15 Distribution Under Section 726—Interpretive Difficulties With Section 726(a)

For the most part, the application of section 726(a) is mechanical. Once one has worked out the priority problems under section 507, that learning can easily be transferred to section 726. On the other hand, occasional problems are caused by the rules with respect to tardy claims under 726(a)(2) and (a)(3), and the distinction between a priority claim for taxes, for example, and a claim that is subordinated as a "fine, penalty or forfeiture" under subsection (4).

a. What Is a Penalty?

Most of these cases are easy. In one decision, the court had little trouble determining that the payment of a highway use tax without a proration for discontinued use was not a penalty, but a normal tax.[1] It was even easier to decide that RICO treble damages were in fact multiple damages under section 726(a)(4). Because the damages were not compensation for actual loss, the claim was subordinated.[2]

A more interesting question is raised when a company violates Department of Energy (DOE) regulations by overcharging private entities in resales of crude oil. How is the DOE's claim to recover the overcharges to be classified? Appellate courts addressing this issue have consistently held that the DOE claim is not a penalty; rather, it is a claim for restitution made on behalf of each overcharged entity. Thus, the DOE claim is to be treated as a general unsecured claim under section 726(a)(2).[3]

b. Tardy Claims

When a creditor's claim is not timely filed, a question arises as to what distribution the creditor ought to receive. Rule 3002(c) sets forth a filing deadline covering all claims in a Chapter 7 liquidation. The strict language of this rule has led many courts to find that it is preemptory in nature.[4] However, strict adherence to that view conflicts with the clear language of section 726, which provides for distribution of assets to tardily filed claims.[5] How is this conflict to be resolved?

Let us start from the beginning. A claim that has been timely filed according to Rule 3002(c) and is not objectionable in any other regard will be

---

§ 7-15

1. In re Graf Bros., 38 B.R. 237, 238 (Bankr. D. Maine 1984).

2. In re Comstock Financial Services, 111 B.R. 849, 860 (Bankr. C.D.Cal.1990).

3. United States Dep't of Energy v. West Texas Marketing, 763 F.2d 1411, 1426 (Temp. Emer. Ct.App.1985), on remand, 82 B.R. 829 (Bankr.N.D.Tex.1988); In re Seneca Oil, 906 F.2d 1445, 1455 (10th Cir. 1990).

4. See e.g., In re Davis, 936 F.2d 771 (4th Cir.1991); In re Coastal Alaska Lines, Inc., 920 F.2d 1428 (9th Cir.1990).

5. 11 U.S.C.A. § 726(a)(2)(C) and (a)(3).

allowed. Once this claim is allowed, assignment to the proper distribution level under section 726 is a routine matter.

A tardily filed claim to which no one objects should also be deemed allowed pursuant to section 502(a). If the creditor holds a general unsecured claim (one that does not otherwise qualify as a priority claim under section 507(a)), placement in a distribution group is still a relatively simple matter. The creditor's main worry is to avoid having its claim subordinated to the third level enumerated in section 726(a)(3). To avoid subordination the creditor must satisfy the requirements of section 726(a)(2)(C). (If the tardily filed claim would be a priority claim but for the tardy filing, the question of subordination is a bit more tricky. We will save that question until the end of this subsection.)

As we discussed earlier, creditors who tardily file and who face objections must address the possibility of disallowance of their claims.[6] If the creditor does not qualify for an extension under Rule 3002(c) and is not saved by a due process argument, what options remain for distribution?

We can think of at least three. First, the creditor might possess a nondischargeable claim under section 523. In this instance, the creditor would not worry about filing at all. However, the debtor is greatly interested in seeing as much of this nondischargeable claim satisfied out of the assets of the estate as possible. Thus, courts will often look for ways to involve nondischargeable claims as much as possible in the distribution process. As one court put it:

> In an asset case, when a nondischargeable creditor such as a priority tax creditor fails to file a timely proof of claim, the result is that debtors find themselves saddled with a liability that might have been satisfied out of the estate. By the enactment of 11 U.S.C.A. § 501(c) as implemented by Rule 3004, Congress provided a safety net for debtors prejudiced by the failure of a creditor to file a timely proof of claim.[7]

Second, many courts say that they may not extend the filing period for these creditors. Nonetheless, some of these same courts will still allow the tardy creditors to maintain their claims.[8] Last, and least likely to share in a distribution, are claims under Rule 3002(c)(6). Under this provision, any claims that were not filed according to Rule 3002(c)(1)-(5) may receive an extension to share in any surplus remaining after all other allowed claims are satisfied.

We now turn to the treatment of tardily filed priority claims. Once allowed, what distribution level should these claims occupy? The answer is hard to find in section 726. Section 726(a)(1) does not distinguish between

---

6. See § 7–3 supra.

7. In re Davis, 108 B.R. 95, 97 (Bankr. D.Md.1989), aff'd, 936 F.2d 771 (4th Cir. 1991); see also In re MacLochlan, 134 B.R. 2 (Bankr. N.D.Ohio 1991) (because debtor would suffer consequences of subordinating nondischargeable claim, court allowed creditor to maintain priority claim status under section 726(a)(1)).

8. See e.g., In re Kragness, 82 B.R. 553, 556 (Bankr. D. Ore. 1988) (although court unable to extend time for filing, claim allowed as tardily filed); In re Coastal Alaska Lines, Inc., 920 F.2d 1428 (9th Cir. 1990) (although finding that the legislative history clearly indicated that a creditor with knowledge of the bankruptcy did not qualify for relief under section 726, affirmed district court decision allowing claim as subordinated to third level); but see In re Davis, 936 F.2d 771 (4th Cir. 1991) (creditors not filing in accordance with Rule 3002(c) are barred from filing whether or not there was good reason).

timely and tardy claims, so some believe that all priority claims should receive distribution under that subsection. However, at least one court has found that these claims should be dealt with under sections 726(a)(2)(C) and (a)(3) along with all other tardy claims.

In *In re Kragness* an untimely priority claim was subordinated to the level provided in section 726(a)(3).[9] While recognizing that Rule 3002(c) would not allow an extension of the filing deadline, the *Kragness* court allowed the claim as tardily filed. That court found two policy reasons for subordination. Initially, the *Kragness* court decided that section 726 was designed to give preferential treatment to timely filed claims. That court also declared that subordination was a practical necessity. Otherwise, requiring a pro rata return of previously distributed funds in order to satisfy a tardy claim would cause administrative havoc. In light of these considerations, the court decided that Congress must have intended implicitly to require timely filing of section 726(a)(1) claims.[10]

In *United States v. Cardinal Mine Supply*[11] the Sixth Circuit ignored this case. Where the reason for the priority creditor's late filing was the lack of notice, the court found the claim was entitled to distribution under section 726(a)(1) just as if it had been timely filed, based on equitable and due process considerations.[12] However, the court went on to suggest in dicta that all tardily filed priority claims should maintain their preferred status, no matter what reason was given for the delay. The court said that the types of claims included in section 726(a)(1) all deserved special consideration regardless of when they were filed. They also found that it was reasonable to consider the priority more important than the time of filing because section 726(a)(1) explicitly sets out priorities, yet is silent as to filing deadlines.[13]

The decision in *In re MacLochlan*[14] supports the *Cardinal Mine Supply* dicta. Although the debtors did not file their motion to allow the IRS's claim in a timely fashion pursuant to Rule 3004, the court still allowed the claim and permitted the priority to remain intact based on equitable considerations. Because the IRS held a claim that was nondischargeable under section 523(a)(1)(A), the court found that the debtor—not the creditor—would suffer the consequences of subordination. This would have the effect of depriving the debtor of a fresh start as well as depriving the IRS of its congressionally recognized preferred position.

In re Mayville Feed & Grain[15] made it clear that filing deadlines are important for priority claims. In that case Judge Spector worried that the dicta in *Cardinal Mine* had gone too far and was advocating *allowing* all priority claims, no matter when they were filed. He cautioned that section 507(a), which defines priority claims to be distributed under section 726(a)(1), refers only to *allowed* claims. He also warned that the failure to file a proof of claim before the applicable bar date was sufficient basis for disallowing a

9. 82 B.R. 553, 557 (Bankr. D. Ore. 1988).
10. Id. at 556–57.
11. 916 F.2d 1087 (6th Cir.1990).
12. Id. at 1091–92.
13. Id. at 1091.
14. 134 B.R. 2 (Bankr. N.D.Ohio 1991).
15. 123 B.R. 245 (Bankr. E.D.Mich.1991).

creditor's claim entirely, and so renders the issue of distribution levels moot.[16]

We agree with Judge Spector. Like all tardily filed claims, a priority creditor's tardily filed claim may clearly be disallowed.[17] Such a claim might also be allowed because of due process concerns.[18] We further believe that the dicta in *Cardinal Mine Supply,* which argues against subordinating priority claims, is accurate but that the rule should apply only to allowed claims. Congress distinguished timely and tardy claims in section 726(a)(2). Such a distinction was clearly possible in section 726(a)(1), but one was not made. Apparently Congress intended that subsections (a)(2)(C) and (a)(3) apply only to tardily filed general unsecured claims, not to priority claims.[19]

B. DISCHARGE

§ 7–16 Discharge: Overview

For the debtor the end all and be all of a Chapter 7 is the *discharge,* together with exemptions. Discharge is the legal embodiment of the idea of the fresh start; it is the barrier that keeps the creditors of old from reaching the wages and other income of the new. Since there are some common elements in the discharges in all of the Chapters, but also different rules for the different Chapters, one must consider not only Chapter 5, section 524(a), but also Chapter 7, section 727(b). The basic discharge in Chapter 7 is stated as follows in section 727(b):

> Except as provided in section 523 of this title, a discharge under subsection (a) of this section discharges the debtor from all debts that arose before the date of the order for relief under this chapter, and any liability on a claim that is determined under section 502 of this title as if such claim had arisen before the commencement of the case, whether or not a proof of claim based on any such debt or liability is filed under section 501 of this title, and whether or not a claim based on any such debt or liability is allowed under section 502 of this title.

The effect of this discharge is spelled out in greater detail in 524(a).

> (a) A discharge in a case under this title—
>
> (1) voids any judgment at any time obtained, to the extent that such judgment is a determination of the personal liability of the debtor with respect to any debt discharged under section 727, 944, 1141, 1228, or 1328 of this title, whether or not discharge of such debt is waived;
>
> (2) operates as an injunction against the commencement or continuation of an action, the employment of process, or an act, to collect,

---

16. Id. at 246–47 (citing 3 Collier on Bankruptcy ¶ 502.01[1] (15th ed. 1990)).

17. See e.g., In re Davis, 936 F.2d 771 (4th Cir.1991).

18. See e.g., United States v. Cardinal Mine Supply, 916 F.2d 1087, 1092 (6th Cir. 1990).

19. "First, property is distributed among priority claimants, as determined by section 507 * * * Second, distribution is to general unsecured creditors. This class excludes priority creditors * * * The Provision [section 726(a)(2)] is written to permit distribution to creditors that tardily file claims if their tardiness was due to a lack of notice or knowledge of the case* * * Third distribution is to general unsecured creditors who tardily file." S. Rep. No. 989, 95th Cong., 2d Sess. 97, reprinted in 1978 U.S. Code Cong. & Admin. News 5787, 5883.

recover or offset any such debt as a personal liability of the debtor, whether or not discharge of such debt is waived; * * *.

To begin, consider what the discharge does not do. Because 727(b) discharges only debts that "arose before the date of the order for relief", it does not discharge debts that arose after the petition was filed. As one might expect, when a debt "arises" has become an item of hot contention.

Note, second, that section 524(a) bars and enjoins collection of only debts "as a personal liability of the debtor." As originally enacted 524(a)(2) enjoined the collection not only of debts "as a personal liability" but "from the property of the debtor." The latter language was removed to make it clear that 524 discharged the debtor only of his personal liability and did not free the debtor's property from valid security interests that attached to that property.

To understand this, assume a case in which GMAC has a perfected security interest in the debtor's non-exempt automobile. Assume that the automobile is worth $5,000 and that the debt is $10,000. By taking Chapter 7 the debtor frees himself from personal liability on the entire $10,000 debt. However, he does not free his automobile from the security interest of GMAC. Even though bankruptcy has occurred, GMAC has a right to the automobile and may repossess it after the case is closed, or while the case is going on if the stay is lifted.

One should also note that section 727(a)(1) denies the discharge to any debtor who is "not an individual." Neither corporations nor partnerships who go through Chapter 7 are discharged from their debts. Presumably, a liquidated partnership or corporation needs no discharge because it will have no continuing existence after its liquidation. What is everything for the individual, namely the discharge, is nothing in Chapter 7 for the corporate or partnership debtor.

The basic rules set out above in sections 727(b) and 524(a) raise only two significant problems. The first is the question when does the debt arise, before or after the petition. The second is the question whether a particular claim which the debtor seeks to discharge is a "debt" or something else. The latter question arises with respect to injunctions that order the debtor to perform certain acts, but require no payment of money. In those cases a reasonable argument can be made that there is no "debt" and thus that section 727(b) does not discharge the liability to perform.

Note, finally, that the price of the discharge is all of the debtor's nonexempt property, which is liquidated and distributed to creditors. The more property the debtor can exempt, the cheaper the discharge. In this conceptual sense, discharge and exemptions are closely related and equally important in a Chapter 7 case. We cover exemptions next, in our Chapter 8.

§ 7–17 Denial of Discharge: Introduction

One should first distinguish two events, denial of the discharge under 727(a) and "exceptions to discharge" under section 523. The consequences of the application of section 523 or of 727 are substantially the same from the point of view of the creditor whose debt is not discharged, but they are radically different from the point of view of the debtor. Under section 727(a) the debtor's discharge is denied entirely and his assets and future income remain subject to the claims of *all* of his creditors. Under section 523 only the particular debt "excepted" from the discharge survives and is a claim against those assets and that income. We will discuss the major issues under section 727(a) and then we will consider the exceptions for particular kinds of debts under section 523.

As one might guess, the denial of a discharge under section 727(a) is a much less frequent event than exceptions of a particular debt under section 523. To apply section 727(a) broadly and recklessly would conflict with the very idea of the fresh start. Thus it is not surprising that the debtor must engage in quite outrageous conduct if he is to suffer excommunication under section 727(a). Section 523, on the other hand, may be regarded as mere penance by the debtor for incurring an obligation to a particularly exalted creditor (such as an ex-spouse or child) or for more limited fraudulent or quasi-fraudulent behavior (as against a credit card issuer where the debtor runs up a large bill immediately prior to bankruptcy).

Return now to section 727(a). It has ten subsections and the debtor is denied a discharge if he fits under any one of them. Several are relatively mechanical and we can dismiss those without much discussion.

First, under 727(a)(1) there is no discharge if the debtor is a not an "individual." Thus, a corporation or partnership in Chapter 7 does not receive a discharge.

Second, section 727(a)(8) and (a)(9) deny a discharge to one who has been granted a discharge in an earlier case under Chapters 7 or 11 or, in more limited cases, under Chapters 12 or 13. Under the terms of section 727(a)(8) a debtor who has received a discharge in Chapters 7 or 11 cannot receive one in a now case that is *filed* within six years after the commencement of the earlier case.

Note what subsection (8) does not prohibit. First, it does not prohibit a discharge if the earlier case failed to result in one. Assume, for example, that the debtor commenced an earlier bankruptcy case, but the case was dismissed without a discharge. In that circumstance 727(a)(8) would not prohibit a discharge in a new case. Assume, secondly, that there was a discharge granted in the earlier case within six years of the new petition. That fact alone will not keep the discharge from being granted in the new case because the six years commences to run at the commencement of the earlier case, not at its closing or from the grant of the discharge in it. The discharge in a Chapter 7 speaks as of the date of the petition and at least in that sense there could be six years between discharges even though the end of the first case is within six years of the beginning of the second.

Section 727(a)(9) dealing with Chapters 12 and 13 is more complicated. If the plan in the earlier 12 or 13 provided for payments that were in fact made and totalled 100 percent of the allowed unsecured claims, then a new discharge can be granted in Chapter 7 without limitation as to time.

If a debtor failed to propose or to make a 100 percent payout in the earlier case, he may still have a Chapter 7 discharge within six years if the earlier plan was "proposed in good faith", constitutes the debtor's "best effort" and if the debtor paid at least 70 percent of the allowed unsecured claims. Since many Chapter 12 and Chapter 13 plans do not provide for anything approaching 70 percent of the unsecured claims, the granting of discharges in such cases will in fact bar a new discharge in a case commenced within six years of the commencement of the filing in Chapter 12 or 13.

Note that section 1328, on discharge in Chapter 13, does not include limitations of the kind found in section 727. Thus one may have a discharge under 727 and shortly thereafter file for and ultimately receive a discharge in Chapter 13. Like section 1328, section 1228 (the discharge provision in Chapter 12) is also free of such limitations. We elsewhere discuss "Chapter 20" cases (Chapter 7 followed by Chapter 13) and "Chapter 19" cases (Chapter 7 followed by Chapter 12).[1]

§ 7–18 Denial of Discharge: Introduction—Individuals, Section 727(a)(1)

Although one would suppose that there are no legal issues associated with the question whether someone other than an "individual" can be discharged, that is not quite true. In three recent cases before three separate Courts of Appeals, individuals, corporations, and labor unions have sought to avoid liability under the National Labor Relations Act because of a Chapter 7 bankruptcy. In all these cases those seeking protection of the discharge have been unsuccessful.

Representative of these cases is *In re Goodman*[1]. In this case the National Labor Relations Board and the Road Sprinkler Fitters Union, Local 669, filed unfair labor practices against Mr. Goodman and his company, Goodman Automatic Sprinkler Corp. Previously, Goodman had been the sole shareholder of E.G. Sprinkler Corp. (E.G.) and had been a principal in a company owned by his wife known as Goodman Piping Products (G.P.P.). Goodman had apparently used the latter company to avoid the contract that the union had negotiated with E.G. Sprinkler Corp. When the National Labor Relations Board ordered G.P.P. to bargain with Local 669 and to reimburse it for certain benefits, that company ceased operation, and Goodman filed a petition in Chapter 7. After he was discharged in Chapter 7 and after E.G. and G.P.P. also filed under Chapter 7, Goodman commenced operation as Goodman Automatic Sprinkler Corp. (G.A.S.C.). When the union and the National Labor Relations Board asserted that Goodman individually and G.A.S.C. were the alter egos of the former corporations and thus liable for their judgments, Goodman claimed that he and his corporation were free of liability because of his Chapter 7 discharge.

Noting 727(a)(1), the court found there could be no discharge of the corporations' liability. Moreover, the court found that while Goodman himself was discharged from his personal liability, if his subsequent acts made him an alter ego, he had liability because of those subsequent acts and despite the discharge of his prior liability. The court sent the case back for hearing on that and other issues.

§ 7–17

1. See § 9–30 infra.

§ 7–18

1. 873 F.2d 598 (2nd Cir.1989).

Only incidentally does the case deal with section 727, but it makes clear first that there is no discharge of the corporate liability and second, that an individual's own discharge will not free him from liabilities that arise after the original petition. The upshot of this is that Goodman may have personal liability that he may not be able to avoid because of the six year prohibition on a subsequent discharge in Chapter 7.

In a similar case the Court of Appeals for the Fifth Circuit has found that a labor union that went through Chapter 7 was not discharged from its unfair labor practice liability and that a successor union representing the identical members constituted an alter ego which also undertook those liabilities.[2]

Strictly speaking these cases present no significant legal issues under 727(a)(1). To the extent they show that a discharge will not free one from subsequent acts, they are more directly relevant to 727(b)'s definition of the kind of debt that is discharged. But they demonstrate that 727(a)(1) has some significant bite where the alter ego theory is to be applied and where, therefore, dissolution of a labor union or of a corporation does not amount to corporate death.

§ 7–19 Denial of Discharge: Introduction—Fraudulent Conveyances, Section 727(a)(2)

Under section 727(a)(2) the debtor is denied discharge if he is guilty of a major-league fraudulent conveyance within one year prior to the filing of the petition. The subsection reads in full as follows:

(a) The Court shall grant the debtor a discharge, unless—

(2) the debtor, with intent to hinder, delay, or defraud a creditor or an officer of the estate charged with custody of property under this title, has transferred, removed, destroyed, mutilated, or concealed or has permitted to be transferred, removed, destroyed, mutilated, or concealed—

(A) property of the debtor, within one year before the date of the filing of the petition; or

(B) property of the estate, after the date of the filing of the petition[.]

Essentially, the section requires the challenging creditor to show that the debtor made a fraudulent conveyance with actual (as opposed to presumed) intent within the year prior to the filing of the petition. Nominally the creditor must show four things: (1) the transfer; (2) within a year; (3) of property of the debtor; (4) with intent to hinder, delay, or defraud.[1] In practice only the fourth factor is likely to be difficult. In that sense these

---

2. N.L.R.B. v. Laborers' Intern. Union of North America, AFL–CIO, 882 F.2d 949 (5th Cir.1989); see also N.L.R.B. v. Better Building Supply Corp., 837 F.2d 377 (9th Cir.1988).

§ 7–19

1. Matter of Chastant, 873 F.2d 89 (5th Cir.1989); Matter of Agnew, 818 F.2d 1284 (7th Cir.1987); First Texas Savings Assoc., Inc. v. Reed, 700 F.2d 986 (5th Cir.1983); In re Aubrey, 111 B.R. 268 (Bankr. 9th Cir.1990); In re Martin, 88 B.R. 319 (D.Colo.1988); In re Ford, 53 B.R. 444 (W.D.Va.1984) aff'd, 773 F.2d 52 (4th Cir.1985).

cases are likely to be indistinguishable from certain fraudulent conveyances cases.

To put some flesh on these theoretical bones, consider a recent case before the Bankruptcy Appellate Panel in the Ninth Circuit, *In re Aubrey.*[2] In that case the debtor, Aubrey, produced a television movie concerning the experiences of William Thomas in a mental institution where he had been confined for eleven years. After the movie had been produced, Thomas sued Aubrey on the ground that Aubrey had converted money that should have gone to Thomas. Thomas alleged that the agreement between them for the movie was a joint venture. Ultimately, Thomas recovered a judgment against Aubrey for $123,201.50 in unpaid profits, $2,750 in unpaid fees, $39,000 in compensatory and $400,000 in punitive damages for conversion, and $9,059.09 in costs. Shortly after the state jury verdict, Aubrey executed two deeds of trust (mortgages) on property in which he had an equity of approximately $1,100,000 in favor of "Noble Lenale and Kenbashe Ltd." (Noble). Allegedly this mortgage was to secure a debt of $950,000 that, Aubrey claimed, had been incurred several years prior to the state court suit in connection with a gold purchase financed either by Noble, or by an affiliate doing business in Switzerland. Aubrey also filed a UCC–1 in favor of Noble on all of his personal property including numerous business and investment interests.

When Aubrey filed bankruptcy, Thomas claimed that his debt was not discharged because of section 523 and also that the discharge should be denied entirely under sections 727(a)(2) and (a)(4). The crucial issue was who had the burden of proof on Aubrey's intent and how that burden was to be satisfied.

Since one cannot expect a person engaged in fraudulent conveyances to admit as much on or off the witness stand, actual intent must be inferred from the behavior of the transferor. In this case Thomas proved the judgment and the conveyance shortly after the judgment. The trial court awarded summary judgment in Thomas's favor, and the Bankruptcy Appellate Panel affirmed. It appears that Thomas's case for fraudulent intent was based on several circumstances. First was the fact that the transfer occurred shortly after the state court judgment had been entered for Thomas. Second was the fact that Thomas had great difficulty through court process, depositions and otherwise in locating or finding out information about Aubrey's assets. The court characterizes Aubrey's behavior as disclosed in these depositions as "playing hide and seek" with his assets or "stonewalling" the creditor's discovery efforts. The court was willing to draw inferences about Aubrey's unsavory intent in considerable degree because of that behavior in the bankruptcy court.

Concluding that such evidence was enough to show a prima facie case, the court found that the burden then shifted to Aubrey to show that the transfer was not for a fraudulent intent. Aubrey was unable to produce any written evidence of the alleged $950,000 loan to Noble. The court concluded that it was so improbable that there would be a $950,000 loan without any written documentation that it was fair to conclude that no such loan existed and that *a fortiori* the transfer was with a fraudulent intent. Of course, one

---

2. 111 B.R. 268 (Bankr. 9th Cir.1990).

should not overlook the possibility the court was aided in this case by the fact that Aubrey, the film producer, was apparently taking advantage of a person who had spent eleven years in a mental institution and who could be expected to have a diminished capacity to look out for himself.[3]

Note too that a discharge can be denied under 727(a)(2) when a debtor decides to conduct business as usual even though he is already in bankruptcy. In *In re Devers*,[4] Cloyd Devers, a Montana farmer, filed in Chapter 11. Called into bankruptcy court by the creditor who accused him of selling secured livestock without remitting the proceeds and without the court's approval, Devers admitted that he was selling livestock and that he had not informed the creditor or paid the money over to the creditor. The court told the debtor to notify the creditor within five days of selling any secured property and to cease commingling the funds. When the reorganization failed and the case was converted to Chapter 7 for liquidation, the creditor discovered that most of the livestock had been sold and that some of the ranch equipment was missing. Cloyd was less than persuasive when he claimed that the disposition of 97 sows and 350 pigs was "culling" and that his garden tractor had "disappeared" in his absence. The Court of Appeals affirmed the bankruptcy court's finding that the discharge should be denied.

Note that Devers' behavior probably would not have constituted fraudulent conveyance had he done it prior to the filing of his Chapter 11 petition. It is commonplace for debtors to sell collateral without remitting the proceeds and use the proceeds in the conduct of their business or on the payment of other creditors. Although these acts may constitute conversion under state law, they seldom support a successful claim by the secured creditor of a fraudulent conveyance.

Devers is different because the sales were made after the Chapter 11 had been filed and after there had been a hearing at which the court had admonished Devers about his behavior. It is yet another illustration of a point that should not go unnoticed for debtors' counsel: the same acts that the debtor might get away with *vis á vis* a creditor will produce a more severe and immediate consequence if done *vis á vis* the court and the court's directions.

Although the circumstances from which one might infer actual intent are bounded only by the hyperactive imaginations of those committing fraud, perhaps it is worthwhile to identify some of the badges of fraud that the courts might recognize. First, of course, is a significant transfer to one to whom no debt is owed and who has some other relation to the debtor. An obvious example would be the transfer of an asset from one spouse to another or from a parent to a child. Second is the concealment of the fact of the transfer, or, if the transfer is in return for a payment, the debtor's absconding with or hiding the proceeds. The creation of a closely held corporation to receive the transfer may have the smell of fraud as will any transfer of property for far less than its fair market value.[5] Moreover, the

---

3. For cases analogous to Aubrey, see In re Roberts, 81 B.R. 354 (Bankr. W.D.Pa.1987); Camacho v. Martin, 88 B.R. 319 (D.Colo.1988).

4. In re Devers, 759 F.2d 751 (9th Cir. 1985).

5. See In re Kaiser, 32 B.R. 701 (S.D.N.Y. 1983), aff'd, 722 F.2d 1574 (2d Cir.1983); In re Marcus, 45 B.R. 338 (S.D.N.Y.1984); In re Bateman, 646 F.2d 1220 (8th Cir. 1981) (fact that valuable property is gratuitously trans-

inquiry is not limited to evidence presenting itself before or at the time of the transfer; subsequent conduct is probative of the debtor's intent on a prior occasion.[6]

Believing that lawyers are endowed with some power to purge a transfer of its fraud, debtors sometimes defend their transfers on the ground they were done on advice of counsel and therefore cannot be fraudulent. While advice of counsel in certain circumstances would be useful, courts are appropriately skeptical of such claims.[7]

Occasionally there is an argument about whether or not a "transfer" occurred. Because the definition of transfer in section 101(54) is very broad, this is seldom a serious issue.[8] A debtor may escape on the ground there has been no transfer or if the debtor recovers the asset prior to the filing of the petition.[9] Once the asset is back in the debtor's hands and subject to the jurisdiction and disposition of the bankruptcy court, presumably any fraud is remedied.

Finally, section 727(a)(3)(A) attacks only transfers made within one year before the filing of the bankruptcy. However, there is at least one important exception to that statute of limitations. Where the debtor transfers property earlier than one year before the petition, but retains a significant interest, such as the right to use the property, the courts have applied the doctrine of "continuing concealment" to deny the debtor a discharge.[10] In one case, where a transfer of ownership in real property was made seven years before the filing of the petition but the transferor retained possession, the court denied a discharge under 727(a)(2)(A).[11] With the exception of its timing, the transfer satisfied all other elements required for a denial of discharge.

ferred raises the presumption that there is actual fraudulent intent); Matter of Chastant, 873 F.2d 89 (5th Cir. 1989) (while the retention of the use of transferred property very strongly indicates a fraudulent motive, a presumption of actual fraudulent intent arises when the property is transferred gratuitously or is transferred to relatives).

6. Farmer's Co-Operative Ass'n of Talmage, Kan. v. Strunk, 671 F.2d 391 (10th Cir.1982); Future Time, Inc. v. Yates, 26 B.R. 1006 (M.D.Ga.1983), aff'd, 712 F.2d 1417 (11th Cir. 1983).

7. See In re Rice, 109 B.R. 405 (Bankr. E.D.Cal.1989), decision aff'd, 126 B.R. 822 (Bankr. 9th Cir.1991).

8. 11 U.S.C.A. § 101(54) provides:

"transfer" means every mode, direct or indirect, absolute or conditional, voluntary or involuntary, of disposing of or parting with property or with an interest in property, including retention of title as a security interest and foreclosure of the debtor's equity of redemption * * *.

See also S.Rep. No. 95-989, 95th Cong., 2d Sess. 26-27 (1978), reprinted in 1978 U.S. Code Cong. & Admin. News 5787, 5813 stating:

[a] transfer is a disposition of an interest in property. The definition of transfer is as broad as possible. Many of the potentially limiting words in current law are deleted, and the language is simplified. Under this definition, any transfer of an interest in property is a transfer, including a transfer of possession, custody, or control, even if there is not a transfer of title, because possession, custody, and control are interests in property. A deposit in a bank account or similar account is a transfer.

See Matter of Smiley, 864 F.2d 562 (7th Cir. 1989); In re Ford, 53 B.R. 444 (W.D.Va.1984), aff'd, 773 F.2d 52 (4th Cir.1985) (a debtor transferred property when he relinquished a fee simple interest in real estate to a tenancy by the entirety with a right of survivorship).

9. In re Adeeb, 787 F.2d 1339 (9th Cir. 1986); Matter of Smiley, 864 F.2d 562 (7th Cir.1989); In re Barney, 86 B.R. 105 (Bankr. N.D.Ohio 1987).

10. In re Olivier, 819 F.2d 550 (5th Cir. 1987); In re Espino, 48 B.R. 232 (Bankr. S.D.Fla.1985), aff'd, 806 F.2d 1001 (11th Cir. 1986) (finding no "continuing concealment" on the basis of the facts presented).

11. In re Olivier, 819 F.2d 550 (5th Cir. 1987).

§ 7–20 Denial of Discharge: Introduction—Financial Disclosure: Section 727(a)(3)

For full text of this section, see Epstein, Nickles & White, Bankruptcy, Practitioner Treatise Series, Vol. 2.

§ 7–21 Denial of Discharge: Introduction—"Bankruptcy Crimes," Section 727(a)(4)

For full text of this section, see Epstein, Nickles & White, Bankruptcy, Practitioner Treatise Series, Vol. 2.

§ 7–22 Denial of Discharge: Introduction—Delivery of Assets, Section 727(a)(5)

For full text of this section, see Epstein, Nickles & White, Bankruptcy, Practitioner Treatise Series, Vol. 2.

§ 7–23 Denial of Discharge: Introduction—Refusal to Testify or Obey Court Order, Section 727(a)(6)

A denial of the discharge under section 727(a)(6) is a punishment for a debtor who has "refused in the case" to obey the court's order or to respond to a material question approved by the court. The section specifically protects the debtor's privilege to refuse to testify on the grounds of self-incrimination, but also authorizes the granting of immunity and the attendant removal of that privilege. To go into the many questions that lurk behind the privilege is beyond the scope of this book.

Suffice it to say that section 727(a)(6) is likely to be reserved for people who hold bizarre or deviant views about their legal rights and others' duties. A nice illustration of such a case is *Kershaw v. Behm*[1]. In that case, Mr. Kershaw consistently refused to follow the orders of Judge Lundin, but nevertheless proposed his own plan under which he would keep his property outside the plan and beyond the jurisdiction of the court, yet do a "cramdown" on the bank. On appeal the district court described Mr. Kershaw's views as "the grossest misunderstanding of section 1129 by an attorney that this court has heard," quite a compliment. It appears that Mr. Kershaw was not only at odds with the court, but also with the trustee and ultimately both he and his wife received what one would have expected, namely, no discharge.

§ 7–24 Exceptions to Discharge, Section 523, Introduction

Section 523 is applied most frequently in Chapter 7, but it also applies in cases brought in the other chapters. Yet, as we discuss in our Chapter 9, many of the exceptions to discharge in section 523 are not applicable in Chapter 13 cases where the debtor is entitled to the "superdischarge."[1]

§ 7–23

1. 81 B.R. 897 (M.D.Tenn.1988).

§ 7–24

1. Note that § 523(a) lists the various sections that provide for discharge, but that it excludes § 1328(a), the principal discharge provision in Chapter 13. That is to allow for

§ 7-24   LIQUIDATION   481

Even there, however, the debtor must pay his tax liabilities that would not be discharged, and he is not discharged from liability for alimony and child support, student loans and judgments in drunk driving cases.

Clearly, section 523 is an important provision. It may well account for more litigation in Chapter 7 than any other single section. Consumers file bankruptcy today at the drop of the hat. Reaffirmations are few and far between. Many of the creditors will find themselves unsecured. For these reasons, a creditor's only hope against a debtor in bankruptcy may be to argue that his particular debt is excepted from the discharge under section 523.

The subsections of 523 deal, in this order, with:

- taxes;
- money procured by false pretenses;
- debts that are not scheduled;
- liability for fraud, embezzlement or larceny;
- liability for child support or alimony;
- intentional torts;
- liability for fines, penalties or forfeitures payable to a governmental unit;
- student loans;
- liability arising out of a debtor's operation of a motor vehicle while he is intoxicated;
- liabilities that could have been discharged in prior cases, but were excluded for one of several reasons;
- debts arising from an act of fraud or defalcation while acting in a fiduciary capacity committed with respect to any depositary institution or insured credit union; and
- liabilities for the malicious or reckless failure to maintain the capital of an insured depository institution.

The last two were added by the 1990 amendments.[2]

For one reason or another, Congress made the judgment that none of these liabilities should be discharged. To say there are policies that support each of the twelve provisions is not to say that everyone would agree to those policies. For example, (a)(1)—the exception for certain taxes—is best explained merely as an exercise of brute power by the King who excepts his claims (taxes) from discharge because he makes the law. On the other hand, the exceptions in subsection (a)(2) (money procured by fraud), (a)(4) (embezzlement and larceny), and (a)(6) (intentional tort) are all morally distinguishable from usual debt. Each carries with it a moral opprobrium. In some

---

the "superdischarge" in Chapter 13. As we see in Chapter 9 (of this book), one filing in Chapter 13 receives a much broader discharge than in the other chapters. For the most part the Chapter 13 discharge applies to all of the debts in § 523 except for most taxes (these must be paid as part of the plan under 1322(a)(2)) and except for alimony and child support under § 523(a)(5), student loans under § 523(a)(8), and liabilities incurred by driving while intoxicated § 523(a)(9).

2. Crime Control Act of 1990, Pub.L.No. 101-647, § 2522(a)(1), 104 Stat. 4789, 4865-66.

cases (larceny and embezzlement) the debtor's act will have been a concurrent violation of the criminal law.

Other exceptions such as that in subsection (a)(3) for debts not listed or scheduled, and for debts that were or could have been discharged in earlier bankruptcies, are protections for the integrity of the system. Subsection (3) is an incentive to the debtor to be truthful in revealing the names of his creditors and the amount owed them.

Some exceptions from the discharge arise out of more narrowly focused indignation at particular classes of debtors. Here we would list the drunk driving liability cases. Here, too, student loans probably fit. In 1990, Congress extended the five-year waiting period to seven (see 523(a)(8)(A)), and excluded student loans from a Chapter 13 discharge.

In summary, it would not be correct to look upon section 523(a) as arising from a careful and dispassionate analysis by a single body about the kind of debts that ought to be excluded from the discharge. For the most part the list comes from the Bankruptcy Act of 1898, but its shape has changed. In time, a huge judicial gloss will be applied to many of the subsections. Others will get small attention from the courts. We will consider the subsections in order.

Before one sets out on the long trip through section 523, a look back is in order. Consider the original (1973) proposal of the Bankruptcy Commission to Congress. Note particularly how much more generous it was to debtors than is the present law:[3]

> *Section 4–506. Exceptions from Discharge; Determination of Dischargeability and Liability on Nondischargeable Debt.*
>
> *(a) Exceptions from Discharge.* A discharge extinguishes all debts of an individual debtor, whether or not allowable, except the following:
>
> (1) any liability for taxes with respect to which (A) a priority is granted under section 4–405(a)(5), (B) a return, if required to be filed, was not filed more than one year prior to the date of the petition, or (C) the debtor made a false or fraudulent return or willfully attempted in any manner to evade or defeat;
>
> (2) any debt, other than a consumer debt, for obtaining money, property, or services, or an extension or renewal of credit by (A) fraud or false pretenses or false representations or (B) use of a materially false statement in writing respecting his financial condition relied on by the creditor and made or published in any manner whatsoever with intent to deceive;
>
> (3) any debt for obtaining money, property, or services within 90 days before the date of the petition without the intention, at the time it was incurred, to pay the debt and in contemplation of the filing of a petition under this Act by or against him;

---

3. Report of the Commission on the Bankruptcy Laws of the United States, H.R. Doc. No. 137, 93rd Cong., 1st Sess., pt. II, at 136–42 (1973).

(4) any debt not scheduled in time for allowance, with the name of the creditor, if known to the debtor, unless the creditor had notice or actual knowledge of the case under the Act permitting timely filing for allowance;

(5) any liability for embezzlement or larceny;

(6) any liability to a spouse or child for maintenance or support, for alimony due or to become due, or under a property settlement in connection with a separation agreement or divorce decree;

(7) any liability for willful and malicious injury to the person or property of another;

(8) any educational debt if the first payment of any installment thereof was due on a date less than five years prior to the date of the petition and if its payment from future income or other wealth will not impose an undue hardship on the debtor and his dependents;

(9) any liability to the extent it is for a fine for the benefit of a federal, state, or local government; and

(10) any debt which was scheduled, or could have been scheduled, in a prior case in which the debtor waived discharge or was denied discharge under any clause of section 4–505(a) of this Act except clause (7) or under section 14c of the former Act except clause (5) or (8). A debt not dischargeable under clause (4) or (8) of this subdivision may nevertheless be discharged in a subsequent case.

(b) Determination of Dischargeability. The debtor or any creditor may file a complaint with the court for determination of the dischargeability of any debt. A debt shall not be denied dischargeability under any clause of subdivision (a) other than (1), (4), or (6) unless a complaint to obtain a determination of dischargeability is filed within the time prescribed by Rules of Bankruptcy Procedure. An agreement entered in good faith and approved by the court settling litigation to determine the dischargeability of a debt may be enforced against the debtor.

(c) Jurisdiction of the Court to Determine Dischargeability. The court shall determine the dischargeability of a debt on the filing of a complaint for such determination. However, if an action on a debt is pending in another court at the filing of a complaint for determination of its dischargeability, the bankruptcy court may in the interest of justice suspend or decline the exercise of jurisdiction under this section.

(d) Determination of Issues of Liability on a Nondischargeable Debt. If the court determines a debt to be nondischargeable in a proceeding commenced under this section, it shall determine any remaining issues concerning liability on the debt unless, for cause shown and in the interest of justice, the court suspends or declines the exercise of its jurisdiction.

(e) Injunctive Relief. Prior to or during the pendency of a proceeding under this section a creditor may be enjoined on the complaint of a discharged debtor from instituting any action on a debt in another court, or from employing any process to collect the debt as a personal liability of the debtor. An injunction may nevertheless not be issued hereunder against enforcement of any debt, except one allowable under this Act that arises exclusively out of transactions or events occurring after the commencement of the case in which the debtor was discharged.

Note

1. Subdivision (a) is the successor to § 17a of the present Act.

2. The reference to "provable debts" in § 17a is dropped, in harmony with the elimination of the concept of provability in the proposed Act. See Note to § 4-403.

3. The only substantive change in the opening clause establishes that a discharge "extinguishes" a debt and does not, as in § 17a, merely "release a bankrupt" from a debt. Cf. § 4-507(a) of the proposed Act, which prohibits the reaffirmation of debts extinguished by discharge.

4. The judicial rules concerning postpetition interest and penalties are not disturbed. Although the rules have been developed in the context of tax claims, their applicability extends to all claims similarly treated under the Act. Postpetition interest is not allowable on any claim, whether or not dischargeable or fully secured by an indefeasible lien. New York v. Saper, 336 U.S. 328, 69 S.Ct. 554, 93 L.Ed. 710 (1949); Sword Line v. Industrial Comm'r, 212 F.2d 865 (2d Cir.1954), cert. denied, 348 U.S. 830, 75 S.Ct. 53, 99 L.Ed. 654 (1954); 1A Collier ¶ 17.14[9], at 1626-27 (1971). If the estate is solvent, postpetition interest (but not penalties) is payable. See § 4-405(a)(8) and accompanying Note. If however, the claim is nondischargeable, the debtor and his after acquired property are liable for postpetition interest and penalties as if a case under this Act had not occurred. Bruning v. United States, 376 U.S. 358, 84 S.Ct. 906, 11 L.Ed.2d 772 (1964). The dischargeability status of penalties is explained below.

5. Clause (1) of subdivision (a) excepts certain tax debts from discharge. The arrangement and style of § 17a(1) of the present Act, which this clause supplants, is entirely changed. Whereas § 17a(1) sets forth rules applicable also to determination of priority in the distribution of estate proceeds under § 64a(4), this clause relies on rules set forth in the corresponding priorities section of the proposed Act, § 4-405. The reversal of cross-reference conforms with the revised chronology of the discharges and priority sections in the proposed Act.

6. The substantive changes in § 4-405(a)(5) are explained in the Note to that section. The principal revisions are, first, the reduction from three years to one year of the time period for the nondischargeability and priority of tax debts, and, second, the shift from reference to "due and owing" and "assessed" to special rules tailored to the major categories of the debts. Compare § 17a(1) ("taxes * * * legally due and owing") and clauses (a) through (c) of the first proviso thereto with § 4-405(a)(5)(A) ("income taxes"), (6) ("ad valorem taxes"), (E) ("employment taxes"), and (F) ("excise taxes"). In addition, clause (d) of the first

proviso to § 17a(1) is continued as clause (c) of this clause, and clause (e) of the former proviso is replaced by § 4–405(a)(5)(D). Clause (B) of this clause is added to provide nondischargeability but not priority for a tax claim, for whatever tax period or wherever first payable, for which a return is not filed before a date one year preceding the date of the petition.

7. Clause (2) of subdivision (a) replaces § 17a(2) of the present Act. The word "services" is added to avoid an arbitrary limitation of the scope of the clause. Nondischargeability under this clause does not attach to consumer debts, in recognition of the spurious use of § 17a(2) by creditors to avoid the discharge of consumer debts owed them. Clause (A) is identical to the corresponding portion of § 17a(2), except for the addition of the word "fraud," removed from § 17a(4) of the present Act, as explained below in the discussion of clause (5) of this subdivision. Clause (B) also makes no substantive change. The last phrase of § 17a(2), concerning willful and malicious conversion of property has been removed to clause (7). See infra.

8. Clause (3) of subdivision (a) is new. It applies to both consumer and business debts. It is intended specially to deny the discharge of debts which a debtor never intended to pay and the liability for which he planned to avoid by obtaining a discharge.

9. Clause (4) of subdivision (a) continues § 17a(3) of the present Act without substantive change. The last five words of the clause, not found in § 17a(3), are a clarification.

10. Clause (5) of subdivision (a) replaces § 17a(4) of the present Act. The limiting words, "while acting as an officer or in any fiduciary capacity," the scope of which is controverted under the present Act, are eliminated. Thus, for example, the uncertainty whether this ground for nondischargeability applies only to a corporate or public officer or extends also to a corporate employee, partner, or other agent, compare 1A Collier ¶ 17.24, at 1707–1714.1 (1971), with Countryman, The New Dischargeability Law, 45 Am. Bankr. L.J. 1, 17 nn. 70–76 (1971), is abolished.

11. The terms "misappropriation" and "defalcation" are discarded as overbroad and uncertain in meaning. See Central Hanover Bank & Trust Co. v. Herbst, 93 F.2d 510 (2d Cir.1937). The standard of "fraud" is moved to a more appropriate location in clause (2), and the precisely definable term "larceny" is added to the remaining term "embezzlement" to cover conduct clearly within the intended scope of this ground for nondischargeability.

12. Clause (6) of subdivision (a) overhauls § 17a(7) of the present Act. Under the proposed Act debts denied dischargeability under the clause are limited to family support obligations; debts "for seduction of an unmarried female, or for breach of promise of marriage accompanied by seduction, or for criminal conversation" are eliminated as no longer responsive to prevailing social policy. The clause is broadened, however, to include any liability to a "spouse or child * * * under a property settlement in connection with a separation agreement or divorce decree." Under the present Act such property settlements are dischargeable. The change recognizes that obligations to support family dependents in the future may take the form of either a duty to make periodic

payments based on need or an obligation to pay a settlement based on the debtor's present or anticipated wealth. The choice of form frequently turns on tax considerations or other factors not directly related to the duty to provide support.

13. Clause (7) of subdivision (a) continues without substantive change § 17a(8) of the Act. The phrase "willful and malicious conversion of the property of another," now appearing as the last phrase of § 17a(2) of the Act, is reincorporated into this clause, undoing a technical change made by the 1970 Amendments to § 17a.

14. Clause (8) of subdivision (a) is new. It responds to the rising incidence of consumer bankruptcies of former students motivated primarily to avoid payment of educational loan debts. It can be anticipated that the incidence will continue to increase as greater numbers of higher educational loans become payable.

15. A separate clause to provide for a limited nondischargeability of educational loan debts is desirable for two kinds of reasons. First, a loan or other credit extended to finance higher education that enables a person to earn substantially greater income over his working life should not as a matter of policy be dischargeable before he has demonstrated that for any reason he is unable to earn sufficient income to maintain himself and his dependents and to repay the educational debt. Second, such a policy cannot be appropriately carried out under any other nondischargeability provision. Clauses (2) and (3) except from dischargeability, respectively, business debts incurred under fraud or other false representations and any debt incurred without the intention to pay it and in contemplation of a case in which the debt is dischargeable. These clauses neither provide for nondischargeability of debts incurred honestly which the debtor subsequently decides not to pay nor distinguish between persons scheduling educational debts who, under the general "fresh start" policy of the proposed Act, should and those who should not be enabled to discharge them.

16. This clause excepts from dischargeability any "educational debt," defined in § 1–102(23), that meets two requirements:

> First, at least one installment payment of the debt must have been payable for five years or longer. In usual circumstances, suspending dischargeability of the debt for five years is fair to both the debtor and creditor. The time period gives the debtor an opportunity to try to meet his payment obligation and affords the creditor a reasonable opportunity to seek enforcement of the obligation if the debtor does not pay.
>
> Second, the claimant must establish that the debtor can pay the educational debt from future earnings or other wealth, such as trust fund income or an inheritance. This requirement recognizes that in some circumstances the debtor, because of factors beyond his reasonable control, may be unable to earn an income adequate both to meet the living costs of himself and his dependents and to make the educational debt payments.

17. In order to determine whether nondischargeability of the debt will impose an "undue hardship" on the debtor, the rate and amount of his future resources should be estimated reasonably in terms of ability

to obtain, retain, and continue employment and the rate of pay that can be expected. Any unearned income or other wealth which the debtor can be expected to receive should also be taken into account. The total amount of income, its reliability, and the periodicity of its receipt should be adequate to maintain the debtor and his dependents, at a minimal standard of living within their management capacity, as well as to pay the educational debt.

18. Clause (9) of subdivision (a) is new. It is intended to clarify and rationalize the dischargeability status of debts for nonpecuniary loss, i.e., debts for fines, penalties, or forfeitures or for multiple, punitive, or exemplary damages. Under the present Act it has become "well settled" that "fines and penalties are not affected by a discharge." 1A Collier ¶ 17.05, at 1586 (1967). Such debts have been regarded as not dischargeable because they are not provable. However, debts owed to governments for fines, penalties, and forfeitures are expressly not allowable under § 57 of the present Act, notwithstanding the general rule that nonprovable debts are not subject to allowance. The status of judgment debts for punitive and exemplary damages has not been as well classified by judicial interpretations of the present Act. The general rule seems to be that the dischargeability of punitive damages follows the dischargeability of the debt for compensatory damages that arises from the same course of conduct. Coen v. Zick, 458 F.2d 326 (9th Cir.1972); Wilcox v. Rohr, 81 Cal.App. 2d 312, 183 P.2d 916 (1947).

19. The proposed Act abandons the concept of "provability," see Note to section 4-403, and permits all debts which can be liquidated as of the date of the petition (and certain other debts) to be allowed and discharged unless expressly excepted. The proposed Act does not disallow debts for nonpecuniary losses but subordinates their payment. See §§ 4-403(b), 4-406(a)(3). This clause denies dischargeability only to a fine for the benefit of a governmental unit. All other nonpecuniary debts, including a fine payable to a governmental unit but for the benefit of a private individual, are to be discharged unless they are expressly nondischargeable under another clause of this subdivision, or as considered in the preceding paragraph, arise from the same course of conduct as compensatory damages that are nondischargeable.

20. Thus it is intended that, for example, a prepetition tax penalty shall be discharged if and to the extent that the tax debt, the nonpayment of which has given rise to the penalty, is dischargeable. If, however, the tax debt itself is nondischargeable, e.g., because no return was ever filed, section 4-506(a)(1)(B), or the return was fraudulent, section 4-506(a)(1)(C), and penalty arising therefrom is also nondischargeable. A postpetition penalty is a nondischargeable liability of the debtor only if the tax liability from which it arises is nondischargeable. Cf., Bruning v. United States, 376 U.S. 358, 84 S.Ct. 906, 11 L.Ed.2d 772 (1964), concerning the debtor's liability for post petition interest.

21. Clause (10) of subdivision (a) and the sentence following it replace section 17b of the present Act. Section 17b was added in 1970 to settle divisions of judicial authority on issues arising from a successive discharge granted to the same debtor. The relocation is not intended to effect any substantive change except to reflect the elimination in § 4-505(a) of failure to pay filing fees as a ground denying discharge and the

addition in clause (8) of educational debts as nondischargeable debts under certain circumstances.

22. Clause (10) continues without substantive change the second sentence of § 17b, which overrules Bluthenthal v. Jones, 208 U.S. 64, 28 S.Ct. 192, 52 L.Ed. 390 (1908), and has the effect of recognizing the res judicata status of an earlier case without requiring a "split discharge" that distinguishes between debts scheduled, or capable of being scheduled, in the earlier case and debts arising thereafter.

23. The first sentence of present § 17b is not repeated in clause (10) because the sentence is a necessary corollary of the exceptions from clause (10)'s rule of nondischargeability; i,e., any debt that was scheduled or could have been scheduled in a prior case in which discharge was denied because of the operation of a time bar or because of the nonpayment of filing fees is nonetheless dischargeable in a subsequent case. The sentence adopts the rule followed in Turner v. Boston, 393 F.2d 683 (9th Cir.1968), and overrules such cases as Chopnick v. Tokatyan, 128 F.2d 521 (2d Cir.1942), cert. denied, 312 U.S. 667, 63 S.Ct. 72, 87 L.Ed. 536 (1942). The sentence following clause (10) codifies the rule in In re Berkowitz, 51 F.Supp. 80 (S.D.N.Y. 1942), and covers debts under clause (8), new in the proposed Act, as well as under clause (4), continued from the present Act.

24. Subdivision (b) carries forward § 17c(1) and (2), added to the present Act in 1970. The reference in § 17c(2) to "clause (2), (4), or (8)" of § 17a is changed substantively in only one respect. Clause (2) has been dropped because under the proposed Act it does not apply to consumer debts, old clause (4) appears as clause (5) of subdivision (a), former clause (8) appears as new clause (7), and clause (3) of subdivision (a), new in the proposed Act, is added for the same reasons that § 17a(2) was included in former section 17c(2).

25. Subdivisions (c) through (e) are derived from the remainder of § 17c of the present Act. The second sentence of subdivision (c) recognizes, however, the appropriateness of suspension or declination of jurisdiction to determine dischargeability in particular circumstances, e.g., when litigation in another court has proceeded to a point where it would be wasteful of judicial resources and inequitable to one or more of the parties to require reintroduction of evidence and reargument of issues in the bankruptcy court.

§ 7–25 Exceptions to Discharge, Section 523, Introduction—Taxes, Section 523(a)(1)

Section 523(a)(1) is a wretched piece of draftsmanship; it leads one on a wild goose chase, first, from section 523(a)(1), then to section 507(a)(2) and (a)(7), and in turn into the intricacies of federal and state income tax laws to find the definitions of verbs such as "assess" and adjectives such as "excise" and the distinctions between taxes measured by "income or gross receipts" compared with those "required to be collected or withheld" as opposed to "excise taxes." In a search for answers, one only starts with 523 and 507; ultimately he reaches deeply into the state or federal tax law for the meaning of "assessment," timing, etc.

To begin, let us summarize in a somewhat inaccurate way the kinds of taxes that are incorporated into section 523(a)(1) by its reference to section 507(a)(7), taxes that are thus exempt from discharge. Consider first section 523(a)(1)(B) and (C). Subsection (1)(B) excludes from discharge any tax or duty with respect to which returns should have been filed where there was no return filed. Thus, if one had an income tax liability that had not been cut off by the statute of limitations in the Internal Revenue Code and if the taxpayer had not filed a return at the time the petition was filed, the liability would not be discharged. For this we do not need to look at section 507, for section 523(a)(1)(B) tells that there is no discharge. The same is true if the return was filed late and within two years of the filing of the petition. Thus, if one owed a tax liability from several years past and wished to avoid subsection (B)(i) he could not file a tax return on day 1 and then file a petition in bankruptcy on day 2. Although subsection (B)(i) would no longer catch him because the tax return would have been "filed," it would have been filed within two years before the petition and late; therefore, the tax liability so disclosed would not be discharged because of subsection (B)(ii).

Subsection (C) picks up tax liability with respect to which the debtor made a fraudulent return or which involved the "willful" attempt to evade the tax. In these latter cases, the least of the debtor's problems may be his discharge in bankruptcy; he will likely be more concerned with his discharge from jail.

The real action occurs mostly under subsection (a)(1)(A) and specifically under the section there referenced, 507(a)(7); let us commence the goose chase.[1] If the tax would have priority under section 507(a)(7), it is excepted from the discharge under section 523(a)(1)(A). What cases therefore fit into section 507(a)(7) and are excepted from the discharge? Let us summarize.

First are income taxes for the three—or more frequently four—years prior to the date of filing of the petition. Subsection 507(a)(7)(A)(i) catches these. If a debtor filed a petition in bankruptcy on July 1, 1990, one could reach back until June 30, 1987, and then pick up the tax liability for all tax years for which a return was "last due" after June 30, 1987. Thus it would certainly include the tax (for a calendar year taxpayer) for the years 1987, 1988, and 1989. If for some reason the taxpayer had a filing extension for 1986 and it was not due on June 30, 1987, the year 1986 could be included as well. Crudely, therefore, it is fair to regard the basic section to exclude from discharge income tax liability for at least three, often four, and occasionally more years immediately preceding the bankruptcy.

With some exceptions, section 507(a)(7)(A)(ii) bars discharge of income tax assessed within 240 days of the filing of the petition. As we will see, "assessment" is a term of art, and it can occur long after a close of the relevant tax year. Thus, it is possible for section 507(a)(7)(A)(ii) to cause taxes for years well back in the past to be exempt from the discharge.

§ 7–25

1. Section 507(a)(2), which references § 502(f), refers to unsecured "gap" claims in involuntary cases. These "gap" claims are claims which accrue between the filing of an involuntary petition for bankruptcy relief and the granting of such relief, commonly referred to as the "gap." See In re Advanced Electronics, Inc., 107 B.R. 503 (Bankr. M.D. Pa. 1989) (discussing the operation of §§ 507(a)(2) and 502(f) to "gap" wages.)

Section 507(a)(7)(B) picks up taxes payable within the year prior to the petition and thus will render nondischargeable one and possibly two years of property taxes. Of course, those taxes will often be a lien on the property and thus the taxing authorities levying the property taxes may not need to concern themselves with exceptions from discharge.

Section 507(a)(7)(C) on taxes "required to be collected or withheld" are so-called trust fund taxes. On these there is no time limitation. The debtor remains eternally liable (at least as far as the Bankruptcy Code is concerned). These include amounts that were or should have been withheld from employee's wages for social security taxes and state and federal income taxes.

Although there is still some dispute in the courts, it appears now quite well settled that section 507(a)(7)(C) also includes sales taxes in most jurisdictions. There are also a few more obscure federal taxes that are doubtless included here, and certainly there are a variety of state taxes that also fit. The big ones, however, are sales taxes, social security taxes, and income taxes all withheld from the sale price of goods or services or from the wages of employees.[2]

Finally, under section 507(a)(7)(E) are excise taxes on transactions within three years prior to the filing of the petition or, if the return is required, on transactions which would be covered by a return filed within or after three years before the petition.

The legal issues posed by section 523(a)(1) arise almost exclusively out of section 507(a)(7). These issues in turn derive from two questions. First, under which of the subheadings does a particular tax fit (one with a three year limit or one with none)? Second, to the extent that there is a limitation period, what events start and what events conclude that period?

We do not have the space to deal with every possible permutation, but let us summarize the problems. First is the question whether certain state taxes, such as sales taxes, use tax, and other business taxes such as "occupation taxes" constitute excise taxes governed only by section 507(a)(7)(E) (subject to a three year statute of limitation), or whether they constitute trust fund taxes, under (C) (subject to no such limitation). Second are problems associated with the definition of "assessment" to determine whether the proper event has occurred so as to bring an income tax within

---

2. Section 507(a)(7)(D), formerly known as section 507(a)(6)(D), is a cryptic inclusion of priority and nondischargeable taxes. The few courts that have dealt with this section have been unable to determine precisely what taxes the section is intended to cover. Most courts have agreed that the section covers unemployment compensation taxes owed by the debtor based on the wages, salaries and commissions of the debtor's employees. See In re Ndosi, 116 B.R. 687 (Bankr. D.Minn.1990); In re Skjonsby Truck Line, Inc., 39 B.R. 971 (Bankr. D.N.D. 1984). One bankruptcy court has further held that § 507(a)(7)(D) covers Federal Insurance Contributions Act (FICA) taxes as well as Federal Unemployment Tax Act (FUTA) and state unemployment compensation taxes. Matter of Lackawanna Detective Agency, Inc., 82 B.R. 336 (Bankr. D.Del.1988). However, this result seems in dispute as most other courts have grouped FICA and other withholding taxes under section 507(a)(7)(C). See In re Ross, 122 B.R. 462 (Bankr. M.D. Fla.1990); In re Ridgley, 81 B.R. 65 (Bankr. D. Ore. 1987); In re Gould & Eberhardt Gear Machinery Corp., 69 B.R. 944 (Bankr. D. Mass. 1987), decision rev'd, 80 B.R. 614 (D.Mass. 1987), appeal dism'd, 852 F.2d 26 (1st Cir. 1988). Given that the language of § 507(a)(7)(D) includes only those taxes for which the debtor/employer is liable and based upon the wages of its employees, and not so called "trust fund" taxes included under section 507(a)(7)(C), the inclusion of FICA taxes into 507(a)(7)(D) is suspect.

the 240 day limitation found in subsection (a)(7)(A)(ii). Presumably there are similar problems lurking in the laws of all 50 states under subsection (a)(7)(E) on the definition of "assessment" concerning property taxes. Because "assessment" is a term of art in the Internal Revenue Code, but is not necessarily a defined term in the property tax law of each of the 50 states, those cases when they arise are likely to be yet more difficult and metaphysical than the ones we have now seen under the Internal Revenue Code.

The cases that have come to the Court of Appeals for the Seventh Circuit from the State of Illinois are nicely representative of the issues that are likely to arise in many jurisdictions. The most recent is *In re Groetken*[3]. The debtor in this case operated a restaurant, Pizza John's, in Alton, Illinois. In this role he was responsible for the Illinois Retailer's Occupation Tax and was ultimately held liable in the state court in Illinois in January of 1982. After he paid less than one-third of his tax liability, Groetken filed in Chapter 7 in May of 1984. In September of the same year he received a discharge in Chapter 7. Claiming that its debt was excepted from discharge, the State of Illinois sued him in July of 1985 in state court to collect the 1982 judgment. Groetken maintained that the occupation tax liability had been discharged and that the exception to discharge under section 523(a)(1) incorporating section 507(a)(7) did not except his liability, because it was either a tax on gross receipts, under section 507(a)(7)(A) or an excise tax under subsection (E).

The State of Illinois took the position that the occupation tax was a liability under (C), a trust fund liability without the three year cutoff.

The court concluded that the occupation tax was imposed directly upon retailers as a percentage of sales. The statute provided that the retailer had to pay; the tax was imposed "upon persons engaged in the business of selling tangible personal property at retail, at the rate of five percent of gross receipts from such sales of tangible personal property made in the course of such business."[4] The Illinois authorities argued that the tax should fit under (C), because the occupation tax was really in lieu of the use tax retailers are supposed to collect from their customers and remit to the state. The court refused to accept the state's argument and concluded that whether the tax in this case was a tax on gross income or an excise tax, it was applied directly to Groetken, was not a trust fund tax covered by (C), and thus was discharged.

The *Groetken* case followed closely on the heels of another Seventh Circuit case, *Rosenow v. State of Illinois, Department of Revenue*[5]. *Rosenow* held that the Illinois sales tax, unlike the occupation tax, was a trust fund tax and that the debtor's liability was not discharged, notwithstanding the fact that the liability had arisen more than three years prior to the petition. Consider how delicate and finespun the analysis must be and how careful the court must be to examine the particular state statutes.

Because the idea of true "collection" or actual "withholding" from a particular retail purchase, or indeed from an employee, is fictional, it is quite difficult to distinguish between trust fund taxes on the one hand and

---

3. 843 F.2d 1007 (7th Cir.1988).
4. Ill. Rev. Stat. Chap. 120 ¶ 441 (1955).
5. 715 F.2d 277 (7th Cir.1983); accord In re Shank, 792 F.2d 829 (9th Cir.1986).

other taxes, such as the occupation tax, which are merely levied on a percentage of the gross sales. The business person is likely to treat both of them as the same, and not to regard a part of each purchase price as a separate and identifiable tax payment to be put in a separate pocket and held for the state. For this reason, the two taxes cannot be distinguished on the basis of the behavior of the retailer or the customer, and they must be distinguished on the basis of the language of the statute, a fairly unsatisfactory state of affairs.

Quaere whether the trust fund rules make any sense at all. If, of course, there is continuing liability on the part of the employee to pay his taxes (that have not been withheld by his employer) or on the retail purchaser (who thinks he has paid his sales tax, but has not), this is a basis for distinction between trust fund taxes and non-trust fund taxes. If, on the other hand, the taxing authorities do not have or will not assert any claim against the employee or the retail purchaser, it makes little sense to distinguish between these kinds of taxes.

Groetken makes three other points that merit consideration. First, it concludes that the case is to be analyzed under section 507(a)(7), even though it appears what was being collected from Groetken was technically not a tax, but a "penalty" because of the failure of his business to pay the tax. The court finds that Congress intended to treat such penalties exactly the same as the underlying tax liability.[6] Second, concluding that interpretation of the Bankruptcy Code was a matter for the federal courts, the Court of Appeals applying both Illinois state law and the federal law comes to a different conclusion about the nature of the tax than the state courts of Illinois had previously reached.

Finally, *Groetken* illustrates a fact that is true about most but not all of the exceptions from discharge: the creditor who claims his debt was excepted from discharge may sue the debtor in state court without having a previous finding in the bankruptcy court about the exception from discharge. In this case the Illinois state taxing authority simply proceeded against Groetken, notwithstanding his discharge and notwithstanding the fact there had been no finding about the exception from discharge as to the tax. Note that the rule is different with respect to exceptions from discharge under section 523(a)(2), (4) and (6).[7]

To understand how income tax liability from years well beyond three can haunt the debtor, consider *In re Hartman*[8]. In that case the debtor filed a tax return for the calendar year 1983 in March of 1984. Ultimately the return was audited and the Internal Revenue Service claimed a deficiency by

---

6. See 843 F.2d at 1010 n.3.

7. The history of those subsections has led the Congress to require creditors claiming them make their arguments in bankruptcy court.

There can be some confusion in a debtor's mind who has been told by his lawyer and perhaps by the judge that he now has a fresh start free of his prior liability. Such a person may disregard a state-court suit based on liability that arose prior to his earlier bankruptcy and that he thought had been discharged in that bankruptcy. Where that threat is thought to be particularly threatening, as in subsection (2) (money obtained by false pretenses or use of a false financial statement), (4) (fraud or defalcation), or (6) (willful or malicious injury), the creditor must state his case in the bankruptcy court; he may not lie in the grass and later bring suit in the state court.

8. 110 B.R. 951 (D.Kan.1990).

a September, 1986 letter. In November of 1986 the IRS issued Form 3552 to the debtor and his wife stating that he was indebted to the United States for $32,865.60 in increased tax, $4,929.84 in additional penalties, and $11,768.52 in interest. In June of 1987 the debtor filed a petition in bankruptcy. Predictably the Internal Revenue Service argued that no part of the liability, the tax, the penalties or the interest were discharged. Although the liabilities were for a taxable year whose return was filed more than three years prior to the petition, the Internal Revenue Service argued the debtor was caught by section 507(a)(7)(A)(ii) because the assessment occurred within 240 days of the date of the petition.

Noting that assessment is a formal act undertaken by the Internal Revenue Service after there has been a notice of deficiency and after there has been a demand for payment [9], the court adopted the definition from the Internal Revenue Code and concluded that the assessment occurred under the Internal Revenue Code in November of 1986. Even where the debtor has filed a return and there are no allegations of fraud, tax liability from a year more remote than three before the filing of the petition can fail to be dischargeable.

A final question, answered in part by *Hartman* but more directly by other cases, involves the status of interest. *Matter of Larson* [10] concludes that prepetition interest on the underlying, nondischargeable liability is also nondischargeable. In that case the court correctly points out that section 502 excludes from claims only "unmatured interest" and presumably therefore intends that interest due at the time the petition is filed to be part of the "claim". It then reasons that the claim is either entirely dischargeable or entirely nondischargeable and that no distinction is to be made between the prepetition interest and the underlying claim for taxes. *In re Hanna* [11] applies the same rule to postpetition interest and penalties. Concluding that no inference as to postpetition interest should be drawn from 502(b)(2) (excluding unmatured interest), that court found that Congress intended to continue the ruling in *Bruning v. United States* [12] that postpetition interest on unpaid tax debt survives bankruptcy. The court noted that oversecured creditors continue to collect interest notwithstanding the filing of a petition and interpreted the somewhat confusing statutory history to support the proposition that postpetition interest and penalties survive and are not discharged.[13]

---

9. See 26 U.S.C.A. §§ 6303, 6201 et.seq., 6322, 6331(a).

10. 862 F.2d 112 (7th Cir.1988).

11. 872 F.2d 829 (8th Cir.1989).

12. 376 U.S. 358, 84 S.Ct. 906, 11 L.Ed.2d 772 (1964).

13. In Hanna v. United States, 872 F.2d 829, 831 (8th Cir.1989), the court concludes:

Sections 502(b)(2) and 523(a)(1) of the Code, read together, are not entirely clear. The House Report accompanying the Bankruptcy Reform Act of 1978, explaining section 523, states: "If the taxing authority's claim has been disallowed, then it would be barred by the more modern rules of collateral estoppel from reasserting that claim against the debtor after the case was closed." H.R.Rep. No. 595, 95th Cong., 2d Sess. at 363–64 (1978) reprinted in 1978 U.S.Code Cong. and Admin. News 5963, 6319.

On an initial reading, the language of the House Report appears to support the view that Congress intended that this claim be barred. See H.R. Rep. No. 595, 95th Cong., 2d Sess. at 363–64 (1978) reprinted in 1978 U.S. Code Cong. and Admin. News 5963, 6319. On further investigation, one discovers, however, that the language in the Report was not intended to cover all disallowed claims. The House Report cites to Plumb, The Tax Ramifications of the Com-

To summarize the status of tax claims, it is perhaps wise to start with the presumption that tax claims will not be discharged. Only after one has carefully examined the character and the timing of the various claims can one be certain that they will be discharged. Even if a person finds that the claims appear to fit within one of the sections of 507, that contain a one or a three year cutoff, a lawyer cannot be certain that they will be discharged because the taxing authority may still be able to persuade the court that failure to pay was made through a "fraudulent return" or was a "willful" attempt to evade such a tax. Thus, one who goes into bankruptcy in the hope of discharging a significant tax liability is undertaking a precarious trip.

§ 7–26 Exceptions to Discharge, Section 523, Introduction— False Pretense, Fraud and False Financial Statements, Section 523(a)(2)

Subsection 523(a)(2) is based on section 17(a)(2) of the Bankruptcy Act of 1898. Although it is somewhat changed from section 17(a)(2) by the addition, for example, of "fraud" from another portion of section 17, subsection 523(a)(2) excludes from discharge substantially the same kinds of debts that the prior act covered. There are now three subsections, each designed to cover a particular set of cases.

Subsection (A), excluding from discharge debts obtained by false pretenses and fraud, is as broad as the debtor's and creditor's imaginations. Under this section are debtors who lie about their accounts receivable, about the value of collateral, about a variety of other things that might somehow relate to the creditor's decision.

Subsection (B) on the other hand covers a specific and well-recognized kind of fraud, namely, the procuring of a loan by the use of a false financial statement. Subsection (B) has been the scene of bitter and continuing dispute between consumer creditors and consumer debtors. The former have maintained that consumer debtors often misrepresent their financial status knowingly and with the intention of misleading the creditor. The latter argue that creditors are likely to use financial statements and forms as traps and falsely to claim reliance upon such statements even when they had much other information and placed no reliance upon the financial statements. An example put forward by the debtor spokesmen might be a case in which a creditor dealt with a particular consumer debtor over ten years time and has renewed a loan tens or even dozens of times, based not on any financial disclosure, but on the continuing payment performance of the debtor.

mission on Bankruptcy Laws: Tax Procedure, 88 Harv.L.Rev. 1360, 1388 (1975), which states:

> Therefore, unless the disallowance of a claim is based upon nonprovability of the debt or other grounds not going to the merits, the creditor (including a tax creditor) cannot recover in a subsequent proceeding against the debtor personally if his claim was disallowed by the bankruptcy court. Id. at 1388 (citations omitted).

Unmatured interest is not disallowed on its merits. Rather, the bases for disallowing unmatured interest are the concerns pertaining to administrative convenience and fairness to other creditors, and collateral estoppel should not apply to prevent actions attempting to enforce such claims.

Taken together, sections 502 and 523 simply demonstrate Congress' intent to codify the general principle that applied under Bruning.

Subsection (C) was added in 1984. It is a watered down version of the consumer creditors' request that debts run up shortly before bankruptcy should be nondischargeable.[1] Liability for "luxury goods or services" and cash advances aggregating more than $1,000 within 20 days before the

§ 7-26

1. Section 523(a)(2)(C) addresses the problem of debtors who make purchases or obtain cash advances on credit immediately before declaring bankruptcy. These practices are known as "loading up." While subsection(a)(2)(C) is limited in scope, initial legislative attempts at dealing with the problem cast a much wider net. Consider the amendment as originally proposed:

> For purposes of subsection (a)(2) of [§ 523], any debt which is incurred on or within ninety days before the date of the filing of a petition under this title, is presumed to be nondischargeable under such subsection.

H.R. 4786, 97th Cong., 1st Sess., § 9(c) (1981). This bill was drafted by the National Coalition for Bankruptcy Reform, whose members represented many segments of the consumer credit industry. Making Their Mark on Bankruptcy Law, 14 Nat'l J. 632, April 10, 1982.

Creditors supported this amendment for many reasons. Their primary concern was with the proper allocation of the burden of proof. In most loading-up cases, creditors had to show fraudulent intent based on circumstantial evidence surrounding the use of credit cards. Many lenders maintained that this was an almost insurmountable burden of proof. They supported shifting the burden to debtors who were more familiar with their own circumstances. Promoters of this provision also pointed out that the presumption would not arise unless a creditor challenged a discharge under § 523(c). Personal Bankruptcy: Oversight Hearings Before the Subcomm. on Monopolies and Commercial Law of the House Comm. on the Judiciary, 97th Cong., 1st and 2nd Sess., at 813–14 (1981–1982) (prepared statement of A. Thomas Small on behalf of the Am. Bankers Ass'n and the Consumer Bankers Ass'n).

Lenders also defended the ninety day period for raising the presumption of nondischargeability. They contended that although a debtor may not have decided to file for bankruptcy during that period, the debtor would surely be aware of its financial situation. Creditors also argued that this presumption was based on another presumption, that of insolvency. Because § 547(b)(4) created a ninety day presumption of insolvency, they believed that a similar duration was appropriate for the proposed nondischargeability presumption. Finally, creditors claimed that the ninety day period would not be over inclusive. This argument was founded on the contention that most loading-up occurred within ninety days of filing while previous debts were likely to have been incurred without anticipating any discharge. Id. at 814–15.

This viewpoint was not shared by everyone. The primary opposition to this amendment was based on its overbreadth. For example, the presumption would reach ongoing credit obligations such as rent and utilities. In those cases, debtors could not wait ninety days to file for bankruptcy. Any delay would mean the risk of eviction or of being cut off from essential services. Consumer advocates were also worried about another type of liability that was indicative of overreaching on the creditors' part. This situation would arise when a creditor, who knew that a debtor was insolvent, encouraged that debtor to refinance an old loan or to take out a debt consolidation loan. Under the amendment these new liabilities would extinguish the old debts and presumptively escape discharge. Id. at 799 (prepared statement of Francis B. Stevens, Attorney and Professor of Law, and Ellen L. Sundlow, Attorney and Adjunct Professor of Law, The Urban Law Institute of the Antioch School of Law).

Perhaps in light of these objections, Senator Metzenbaum offered a different approach:

> For purposes of paragraph (2) of subsection (a) of [§ 523], any debt or debts aggregating more than $500 for items of a kind specified in section 622(d)(2), 522(d)(3), or 522(d)(4) of this title held primarily for personal, family, or household use, incurred on or within forty-five days before the date of the filing of a petition under this title, is presumed to be nondischargeable under such subsection.

S.333, 98th Cong., 1st Sess., § 6 (1983). Senator Dole answered with a bill containing a load-up provision similar to that in H.R. 4786. S.445, 98th Cong., 1st Sess., § 209(d) (1983) called for a forty day presumption, explicitly stated that the presumption was rebuttable, and excepted debts for the presumption that "were incurred for expenses which were reasonably necessary for the support of the debtor or the debtor's dependents[.]"

It appears that § 523(a)(2)(C) is a hybrid of these two bills. The actual presumption attaches to combined debts greater than $500 as in S.333, but includes all "luxury goods or services." There is also a threshold of $1,000 for cash advances. These provisions seem to be a compromise between the broad scope of Dole's bill and the narrow references to 522(d) contained in the Metzenbaum bill. Section 523(a)(2)(C) also contains distinct elements of S.445, such as the forty day period and the "support or maintenance" exception to the presumption.

petition is filed may be regarded as subsets of the cases under subsection (2)(A). Most of the cases under (C) and a substantial part of those under (A) presumably will arise out of the robust use of a credit card shortly before bankruptcy.

Section 523(a)(2) has been one of the important battlegrounds between consumer creditors and consumer debtors. Particularly in the consumers' heyday in the late 1960s and early 1970s, consumer debtors frequently argued that consumer creditors were using false financial statements as a snare. They argued that creditors would give them a form which had only a small space for all of their other debts or that the loan officer would tell the debtor not to concern himself with a complete disclosure—all in the hope that upon bankruptcy the consumer creditor would have in its file what later would be used as evidence of fraud. Creditors, of course, never admitted doing such things.

Partly as a consequence of this dispute, the predecessor to section 523(a)(2)(B) [2] was enacted. That provision requires that a consumer creditor who wishes to challenge the dischargeability of its debt under 523(a)(2) come to the bankruptcy court to make that challenge and present it in open court in front of a forum that is comparatively more inclined to the debtor than a state court might be.

The highwater mark of this sensitivity to the consumer debtors' interest came with the proposal in 1973 of section 4–506 of the National Bankruptcy Commission's proposed statute. Section 4–506(a)(2) was the predecessor of our 523(a)(2). It provided that consumer debts were always dischargeable, no matter that a consumer debtor had committed fraud or given a materially false financial statement on which the creditor relied. The debt would still have been dischargeable. As originally proposed, what became subsection (a)(2) would have dealt only with business debts, not at all with consumer debts. As we can see, the Commission proposal did not survive Congress; the enacted provision makes no distinction between consumer debt and business debt. In fact, most of the debtors who are challenged under section 523(a)(2) are consumer debtors.

The recent cases lead one to conclude that the consumer's stock has fallen yet further since 1978. All of the cases are full of assertions that the exceptions to discharge should be read "narrowly." True to these assertions the early cases under subsection (a)(2) (and decided almost exclusively by bankruptcy judges), followed the pre-Code cases and did interpret the section quite narrowly. For example, creditors routinely lost because they could not convince a court under section 523(a)(2)(B) that the creditor had "reasonably relied" on a false financial statement. They lost even in circumstances where it was clear the statement was false and despite the testimony of the creditor that he would not have made the loan had the statement been truthful.

As these cases have worked their way through the system and have come seriatum to the various courts of appeals, initial debtor successes have been reversed. One court, has described the creditor-reliance requirement as formerly a "debtor's" club that has now turned into a "feather". The

---

2. Act of July 12, 1960, Pub. L. No. 86–621, 74 Stat. 408 (1960).

implication, we take it, is that the appellate (and, a fortiori the lower courts governed by those appellate decisions) will now find reasonable reliance by a creditor where they would not have done so formerly. In general, the courts of appeals are more likely to find debts not dischargeable and are more likely to decide against the debtor and for the creditor than are the bankruptcy courts. The decisions under (a)(2) are consistent with that trend.[3]

Yet a further blow to the debtor's stock occurred recently in the case of *Grogan v. Garner.*[4] In that case, the Supreme Court resolved the dispute between the circuits regarding the standard of proof for a creditor to show fraud under section 523(a)(2). The majority of the Circuit Courts of Appeals had held that the creditor must meet a "clear and convincing" standard.[5] However, the Third and Fourth Circuits had held the standard to be merely a "preponderance of the evidence."[6] The Supreme Court sided with the Third and Fourth Circuits in accepting the lesser standard.

In *Grogan,* the petitioners brought an action against the respondent, Garner, alleging that he had defrauded them in connection with the sale of corporate securities. Grogan and his co-petitioners won before the jury, which had been instructed on a "preponderance of the evidence" standard by the trial court. While his appeal of this judgment was pending, defendant Garner filed a petition for relief under Chapter 11 and listed the fraud judgment as a dischargeable debt. The Eighth Circuit affirmed the fraud judgment after reducing the damage award. Grogan then filed a motion in the Bankruptcy Court seeking to except the fraud judgment from discharge under section 523(a)(2). After finding that all of the elements required to establish actual fraud under section 523(a)(2) had been proved in the original jury trial, the Bankruptcy Court applied collateral estoppel and held the debt not discharged.

Arguing before the Supreme Court, Garner asserted that doctrine of collateral estoppel should not apply since the trial court instructed the jury on a "preponderance of the evidence" standard instead of a "clear and convincing" standard applicable to section 523(a)(2) dischargeability determinations. In rejecting this argument and reversing the Eighth Circuit Court of Appeals, the Supreme Court held that the correct standard under section 523(a)(2) was a "preponderance of the evidence." The Court noted that both the language of section 523 and the legislative history are silent as to the correct standard of proof a creditor must meet. However, the court found that "because the preponderance-of-the-evidence standard results in a roughly equal allocation of the risk of error between litigants, [the Court] presume[s] that this standard is applicable in civil actions between private litigants unless 'particularly important individual interests or rights are at

---

3. See, e.g., In re Phillips, 804 F.2d 930 (6th Cir.1986); In re Ophaug, 827 F.2d 340 (8th Cir.1987); In re Dallam, 850 F.2d 446 (8th Cir.1988) (all reversing a lower court decisions on behalf of the debtor).

4. ___ U.S. ___, 111 S.Ct. 654, 112 L.Ed.2d 755 (1991).

5. See In re Phillips, 804 F.2d 930 (6th Cir.1986); In re Kimzey, 761 F.2d 421 (7th Cir.1985); In re Black, 787 F.2d 503 (10th Cir.1986); Chrysler Credit Corp. v. Rebhan, 842 F.2d 1257 (11th Cir.1988); In re Hunter, 780 F.2d 1577 (11th Cir.1986); In re Dougherty, 84 B.R. 653 (Bankr. 9th Cir.1988), on remand, 89 B.R. 840 (Bankr.E.D.Cal.1988).

6. In re Braen, 900 F.2d 621 (3d Cir.1990), cert. denied, ___ U.S. ___, 111 S.Ct. 782, 112 L.Ed.2d 845 (1991); Combs v. Richardson, 838 F.2d 112 (4th Cir.1988).

stake.' " [7] The Court having previously held that bankruptcy is not a "fundamental" or constitutional right, the result was clear.

In so holding, the Court rejected outright the argument that Congress, by its silence, intended the "clear and convincing" standard to apply because most States required the higher standard for civil fraud judgments at the time the Bankruptcy Code was enacted.[8] Instead, greater reliance was placed on the fact that Congress has consistently chosen the lesser standard when creating federal actions for fraud such as the False Claims Act, Medicare and Medicaid fraud, section 17(a) of the Securities Act of 1933, and most importantly, section 727(a)(4) of the Bankruptcy Code which denies a debtor a discharge altogether if the debtor has committed a fraud on the bankruptcy court.

The result of the Court's holding is that application of the "preponderance of the evidence" standard will permit exception from discharge of all fraud claims creditors have successfully reduced to judgment, whether those judgments had to pass the "clear and convincing" or the "preponderance of the evidence" standard at trial. This reduction in trial work for the bankruptcy courts also clearly represents a change in the "narrow" reading of section 523(a)(2) in favor of the debtor.

a. Section 523(a)(2)(A): False Pretenses, False Representation and Actual Fraud

As we have indicated above, an almost limitless number of cases could fall within the description in section 523(a)(2)(A): a John Deere dealer procuring loans from John Deere by making paper sales that never occurred;[9] fraudulently inducing a contract to sell a house for far less than its true value,[10] the certification by a contractor that he has paid materialmen and that no claims are outstanding;[11] a lie about the debtor's intention for loan proceeds (operating expenses in a failing business rather than purchase of land).[12] Almost all of these misrepresentations are fraudulent. They somehow exaggerate the security of the loan. Debtors either lie about having collateral or exaggerate its value. Sometimes the representations increase the apparent creditworthiness of the debtor.

Probably the most common case under (2)(A) arises when the loan is received by a debtor who has no intention of repaying it. The debtor thus has committed fraud or procured the loan under false pretenses merely by receiving the loan at a time when any rational person would have known that he could not repay it.

The most common of these cases are those involving credit cards. A common scenario might run as follows: Debtor uses a credit card over a

---

7. __ U.S. at __, 111 S.Ct. at 658, 112 L.Ed.2d at 764.

8. In rejecting the conclusion reached by a majority of the circuits, the Court stated that "it would not be reasonable to conclude that in enacting § 523 Congress silently endorsed a background rule that clear-and-convincing evidence is required to establish exemption from discharge." Id.

9. In re Gerlach, 897 F.2d 1048 (10th Cir. 1990).

10. In re Rubin, 875 F.2d 755 (9th Cir. 1989).

11. In re Dallam, 850 F.2d 446 (8th Cir. 1988).

12. In re Ophaug, 827 F.2d 340 (8th Cir. 1987).

period of time with a balance that fluctuates around $2,000. Late one year his financial circumstances become more difficult, and he consults a bankruptcy lawyer about the possibility of going into bankruptcy. Learning from a lawyer that his credit card debt will be among those discharged, he runs up his debt from $2,000 to the $8,000 credit limit (or perhaps beyond by clever manipulation) and declares bankruptcy a month later. Based on the dollar amount and the timing, this case might fit under 523(a)(2)(C), but many cases not covered by (C) fit under (A). In the case posed, the creditor will point to the financial status of the debtor and ask the court to draw the inference both from the visit to the lawyer and from the radical change in the amount outstanding on the credit card—combined with the timing of the bankruptcy—that the debtor had no intention of paying the debt and was thus guilty of fraud under 523(a)(2)(A).

What elements then must be proved under (2)(A)? What is the nature of the proof? Prior to the Supreme Court decision in *Grogan v. Garner*,[13] the courts routinely said that the level of evidence must be "clear and convincing"; now the rule is "preponderance of the evidence."[14] Of course, the creditor must prove the false pretense, the false misrepresentation or actual fraud. Where the debtor is actually fabricating[15] or making specific certifications known to be inaccurate[16] (e.g., that materialmen have been paid), or other explicit representations known to be false, these elements can be easily proven by showing the inaccuracy of the assertion and by proving that the assertions were made.

When the creditor asks the court to find fraud or false pretenses by inference from the debtor's use of a credit card or other line of credit at a time when the debtor has no hope of repayment, the proof of false pretenses is not as easy. To understand how such an inference might be drawn, consider *In re Karelin*.[17] Ms. Karelin had been a heavy casino gambler in Las Vegas and Reno for years. Routinely she had gone to one of those cities 15 to 20 times a year. Sometimes she was even picked up by one of the casino's private jets and taken there! She had gambled from $25,000 to $50,000 on each trip. In the year prior to her bankruptcy she lost her job and started a new and struggling business on her own.

Her modus operandi was to draw the entire credit limit on her card before she left San Jose for each of the gambling trips. At the time of her bankruptcy, her card had a $55,000 limit. Shortly before her bankruptcy and after she had lost her high paying job, she had refinanced the mortgage on her house, borrowed from various casinos (who made claims of $260,000 in her bankruptcy). On the ultimate trip to Nevada she received an $87,000 cash advance. The advance exceeded her credit limit because of a clerical error at the bank which had given her credit for a deposit but had not made an appropriate debit.

13. __ U.S. __, 111 S.Ct. 654, 112 L.Ed.2d 755 (1991).

14. See e.g., In re Phillips, 804 F.2d 930 (6th Cir.1986); Knoxville Teachers Credit Union v. Parkey, 790 F.2d 490 (6th Cir.1986); cf. In re Rubin, 875 F.2d 755 (9th Cir.1989) (in footnote 2 at 759 the court states that it expresses "no opinion" on this issue).

15. In re Gerlach, 897 F.2d 1048 (10th Cir. 1990).

16. In re Dallam, 850 F.2d 446 (8th Cir. 1988).

17. 109 B.R. 943 (Bankr. 9th Cir.1990).

The Bankruptcy Appellate Panel held that her debt to the bank was not dischargeable and concluded, in effect, that the very act of borrowing $87,000 by someone in her desperate circumstances constituted false pretenses or actual fraud. The court [18] and many others [19] conclude that it is actual fraud when she "makes charges with no intention of repaying them." Whether one concludes the making of a charge carries with it an implied representation (here false) that the debtor has the capacity and will to repay or whether one concludes the absence of such will and capacity is actual fraud is probably a matter of no consequence. Because both false pretentions and fraud are covered, either conclusion satisfies one of the terms of 523(a)(2)(A).

To understand what evidence might be sufficient to reach the conclusion of no intention to repay at the time the debt was incurred, consider the court's discussion in *Karelin:*

> The record is replete with evidence of Ms. Karelin's hopeless financial condition at the time of the cash advances. There was ample evidence before the bankruptcy court to support its finding that Ms. Karelin must have been aware of the extent of the debt she was incurring by taking the cash advances, and that she could not possibly have failed to perceive the hopelessness of repaying the resulting obligation. Although Ms. Karelin testified to the contrary, her testimony in various details was impeached repeatedly and the record supports the court's decision to give her testimony little weight.
>
> Under *Dougherty,* actual fraud is present when the cardholder made the charges with no intention of paying for them. Ms. Karelin asserts that despite the hopelessness of her financial condition, she manifested the clear intention, or at least hope, of repaying the debt by applying her meager $32,000 of gambling "winnings" (out of the $66,100 that she took to the casinos) to her credit card account after she had drawn the first cash advance.
>
> Care must be taken to stop short of a rule that would make every desperate, financially strapped debtor a guarantor of his ability to repay, on pain of nondischargeability. Such a rule would unduly expand the "actual fraud" discharge exception by attenuating the intent requirement. A substantial number of bankruptcy debtors incur debts with hopes of repaying them that could be considered unrealistic in hindsight. This by itself does not constitute fraudulent conduct warranting nondischarge.[20]

The quoted statement recognizes the risk of too readily drawing the inference of fraud from nonpayment even by desperate persons. Presumably the world is full of Mr. McCawbers who eternally believe that their ship is about to come in even when objective analysis would show that to be

---

18. In re Karelin, 109 B.R. 943 (Bankr. 9th Cir.1990).

19. See, e.g., In re Dougherty, 84 B.R. 653 (Bankr. 9th Cir.1988), on remand, 89 B.R. 840 (Bankr.E.D.Cal.1988); Matter of LaBuda, 37 B.R. 47 (Bankr. M.D.Fla.1984); In re Hable, 107 B.R. 356 (Bankr. M.D.Fla.1989); In re Rodgers, 115 B.R. 678 (Bankr. C.D.Cal.1990); In re Scarlata, 112 B.R. 279 (Bankr. N.D.Ill. 1990), aff'd in part, rev'd in part, 127 B.R. 1004 (N.D.Ill.1991); In re Beverly, 95 B.R. 500 (Bankr. N.D.Ohio).

20. 109 B.R. at 947–8.

highly unlikely.[21] In our view, it is sensible and appropriate to draw the inference of actual fraud from behavior of the kind described in the *Karelin* case and from behavior of the kind that apparently exists in thousands of other cases involving credit cards. Every credit card holder who uses his credit card at a particular level for a long period of time, who radically runs up the balance within a relatively short period prior to filing a petition in bankruptcy, should be examined with a skeptical eye.[22] Particularly when

21. For cases dealing with the credit card problem in general, see In re Ward, 857 F.2d 1082 (6th Cir.1988) (reliance on misrepresentation in application unreasonable absent even a minimal credit check); In re Touchard, 121 B.R. 397 (Bankr. D. Utah 1990) (debt nondischargeable to extent credit limit exceeded); In re Dorsey, 120 B.R. 592 (Bankr. M.D.Fla.1990) (debt nondischargeable); In re Hinman, 120 B.R. 1018 (Bankr. D.N.D. 1990) (debt nondischargeable); In re Graham, 122 B.R. 447 (Bankr. M.D.Fla.1990) (debt nondischargeable); In re Borste, 117 B.R. 995 (Bankr. W.D. Wash.1990) (obsessive-compulsive disorder not a defense to nondischargeability); In re Nogami, 118 B.R. 846 (Bankr. M.D. Fla.1990) (debt not dischargeable merely because it was incurred before revocation of the card); In re Sutliff, 112 B.R. 680 (Bankr. M.D.Pa.1990) (debt nondischargeable); In re Cirineo, 110 B.R. 754 (Bankr. E.D.Pa. 1990) (debt under credit limit dischargeable absent subjective intent not to pay charges); In re Hall, 101 B.R. 781 (Bankr. M.D.Fla.1989) (debt nondischargeable); In re Tondreau, 117 B.R. 397 (Bankr. N.D.Ind. 1989) (debt nondischargeable); In re Leaird, 106 B.R. 177 (Bankr. W.D.Wis.1989) (debt dischargeable); In re Conroy, 99 B.R. 113 (Bankr. S.D.Fla.1989); In re Landen, 95 B.R. 826 (Bankr. M.D.Fla.1989) (court must make finding of intent to deceive); In re Wellen, 95 B.R. 497 (Bankr. N.D.Ohio 1989) (cash advances nondischargeable); In re Chech, 96 B.R. 781 (Bankr. N.D.Ohio 1988); In re Solano, 85 B.R. 642 (Bankr. S.D.Fla.1988) (post-revocation charges); In re Dougherty, 84 B.R. 653 (Bankr. 9th Cir.1988), on remand, 89 B.R. 840 (Bankr. E.D.Cal.1988).

22. As a good example of legal skepticism, consider Judge Paskay's handling of the case of In re Dorsey, 120 B.R. 592 (Bankr. M.D.Fla. 1990). The debtor, Dixie Lee Dorsey, was a widow with two children; she had no income other than $480 per month from Social Security; she had not been gainfully employed for over ten years; and she resided in a mobile home in Winter Haven, Florida. Despite this stellar credit record, she possessed seven American Express credit cards, including a green card, a gold card, and an Optima card. However, as the court stated, "not being satisfied that the credit extended to her through these cards would be sufficient to meet her need for credit, she also collected various other credit cards, which resulted in * * * unsecured debt totaling $106,922.39." 120 B.R. at 594. Part of the debt was incurred at the suggestion of Dixie Lee's boyfriend, a mysterious "Jimmy Jones," who purportedly owned and operated dog kennels and a horse farm in Florida and supplemented her Social Security by paying her bills and giving her a modest $2,500 to $6,000 per month.

Much of the American Express debt of $24,000 was incurred on an extensive trip to West Central Europe with a side trip to the Greek Islands and a later trip to the Northern United States. She charged her travel costs to her "Sign and Travel" account with American Express and placed her incidental expenses, including French perfume purchased for $784.21, on her card. As the court found:

> In an attempt to explain this purchase [Dixie Lee] explained that she always liked to smell good. The purchase of this item, no doubt, triggered a not-to-well [sic] smelling sour note in the not very sensitive nostrils of American Express credit department when it received notice of the filing of the Chapter 7 petition by this debtor.

120 B.R. at 594.

While the court seemed nauseous at the idea of protecting a company such as American Express which had extended so much credit to someone in this financial position, the elements of fraud were nonetheless established. As Judge Paskay concluded:

> If the Guineas [sic] Book of World Records would include the misuse of credit as a category of records in its publication, this Debtor certainly would have a fighting chance to get the first prize considering what happened in this instance * * *. There is hardly any doubt that this Debtor was fully aware that she could never meet these obligations on her income even if she lived to be 100 years old, and her reliance on her mysterious boyfriend was unrealistic and unjustified to say the least. Although this relationship lasted four years, she claims they never lived together during those four years and she was not able to find out his real identity, she has no idea where he lives, and she certainly had no basis to believe that his generosity would continue forever.
>
> Thus, it should be evident that this is not merely a claim of nondischargeability

the borrowing constituted cash advances that are spent on the debtor's personal living or for the purchase of items that the debtor sold to others, the inference of fraud becomes irresistible.

Section 523(a)(2)(A) requires five elements for a successful cause of action based upon credit card fraud. The creditor must show (a) that the debtor made representations; (b) that at the time the debtor knew the representations were false; (c) that the debtor made them with the intention and purpose of deceiving the creditor; (d) that the creditor relied on such representations; and (e) that the creditor sustained the alleged loss and damage as the proximate result of the representations.[23] In reality, only the second, third, and fourth elements are usually in dispute. Because there are essentially two types of contracts at issue in the credit card cases, some interesting problems arise. First, there is the credit card agreement that the debtor fills out and presents to the card issuer. Second is the charge slip signed by the debtor at the time that he uses the card in which he agrees to repay the full amount borrowed to fund the purchase.

This distinction between the two contracts is central to many of the problems involved in showing credit card fraud. In looking at debtor misrepresentation, should the focus be on the credit agreement or on the charge slip? If the debtor made no misrepresentations on the former but knew he would be unable to repay the charges when he signed the charge slip, is there misrepresentation sufficient to deny a discharge of the debt? Further, when did the intent to deceive exist, in the earlier or the later contract? Finally, there must be reasonable reliance by the creditor upon the debtor's misrepresentations. Does the reliance occur by merely accepting the signature on the charge slip or by running an extensive credit check based upon the credit agreement? All of these questions have presented issues which the courts have attempted to resolve, not always consistently.

Three lines of authority have arisen to determine the nondischargeability of credit card debt under section 523(a)(2)(A). Prior to 1988, a number of courts concluded that when a credit card was used, the cardholder impliedly represented to the creditor that the user had the ability and the intention to pay for the goods or services charged. This theory, known as the "implied representation" theory, finds by implication the representation and reliance elements necessary for the section 523(a)(2)(A) test.[24] Another position, known as the "assumption of risk" theory, held that the cardholder makes a false representation to the issuer only when revocation of the card is communicated to the cardholder and the cardholder continues to use the card. Here, the credit card issuer assumes the risk that the cardholder will incur debts she cannot pay.[25]

---

based on misuse of a credit card by exceeding the credit limit * * *, but involves obtaining money by actual fraud when she had no intention to pay these charges. The fact of the matter is, when questioned about her European trip, she stated, with some pride, that she had a grand time on her trip and enjoyed every minute of it.
120 B.R. at 596.

23. See Comerica Bank–Midwest v. Kouloumbris, 69 B.R. 229 (N.D.Ill. 1986); In re Dougherty, 84 B.R. 653 (Bankr. 9th Cir.1988), on remand, 89 B.R. 840 (Bankr. E.D.Cal.1988).

24. See In re Hinman, 120 B.R. 1018 (Bankr. D.N.D.1990) (representation and reliance implied from mere use of the bank card); In re Faulk, 69 B.R. 743 (Bankr. N.D.Ind. 1986).

25. See First National Bank of Mobile v. Roddenberry, 701 F.2d 927 (11th Cir.1983); In re Ward, 857 F.2d 1082 (6th Cir.1988) (it is unreasonable for bank to rely upon mere sig-

In *In re Dougherty*,²⁶ a simple dischargeability action involving a credit card amount of $2,675, the Ninth Circuit Bankruptcy Appellate Panel declined to adopt either the assumption of risk or the implied representation theory. The court rejected the implied representation theory because it ran counter to the principle that the creditor must meet the standard of proof in showing each of the elements of a dischargeability action. Thus, the credit card issuer was placed in a preferred position as compared to other creditors in dischargeability actions. The court rejected the assumption of risk theory because it placed the credit card issuer in a virtually impossible position with respect to pre-revocation charges. As the court stated, "because representation and reliance are not meaningful in the credit card context, these elements are virtually impossible to prove." ²⁷ Further, the focus of the inquiry under this theory was not the dishonest debtor, but the "improvident creditor."

Instead, the court adopted what it considered to be a modified assumption of risk theory. Under its analysis, based upon the inclusion of "actual fraud" in section 523(a)(2)(A), post-revocation charges are nondischargeable where the debtor continues to use the card after the revocation is communicated to the debtor. With respect to pre-revocation charges, the creditor must prove that the debts were incurred with no intention of paying for them. In determining intention, the court provided a list of factors. ²⁸

A second element of the creditor's proof under (2)(A) is that the creditor rely upon the misrepresentation or on fraud in making the loan. Unlike subsection (B) there is no explicit statement that the creditor must have relied in order to state a cause of action, but without exception the courts have read a reliance requirement into the creditor's proof under (2)(A). Despite the fact one might draw the opposite inference from the presence of such an explicit reliance condition in (B) and the absence of one in (A), this is a sensible reading. If there is no reliance and therefore no causal connection between the false representation or fraud and the creditor's loss, the creditor should not recover. It is unimportant whether one reaches the conclusion by imposing an implicit reliance requirement or by finding no damage absent a causal connection between the fraud and the loan.²⁹

---

nature without credit check); In re Carpenter, 53 B.R. 724 (Bankr. N.D.Ga.1985).

26. 84 B.R. 653 (Bankr. 9th Cir.1988), on remand, 89 B.R. 840 (Bankr. E.D.Cal.1988).

27. Id. at 656.

28. As the court stated:

[T]rial courts should consider:

1. The length of time between the charges made and the filing of bankruptcy;

2. Whether or not an attorney has been consulted concerning the filing of bankruptcy before the charges were made;

3. The number of charges made;

4. The amount of the charges;

5. The financial condition of the debtor at the time the charges were made;

6. Whether the charges were above the credit limit of the account;

7. Whether the debtor made multiple charges on the same day;

8. Whether or not the debtor was employed;

9. The debtor's prospects for employment;

10. Financial sophistication of the debtor;

11. Whether there was a sudden change in the debtor's buying habits; and

12. Whether the purchases were made for luxuries or necessities.

In re Dougherty, 84 B.R. at 657 (citing In re Faulk, 69 B.R. at 757); see In re Borste, 117 B.R. 995 (Bankr. W.D. Wash.1990) (application of the Dougherty test).

29. In re Ward, 857 F.2d 1082 (6th Cir. 1988); In re Mullet, 817 F.2d 677 (10th Cir.

In *In re Ophaug*[30] the Court of Appeals for the Eighth Circuit held that the creditor need prove only actual reliance and need not meet the higher standard of "reasonable" reliance. In that case a farm debtor procured a loan of $90,000 from another farmer claiming that he was going to use the money for the purchase of neighboring land. In fact, the debtor was already in financial difficulty and used the loan for operating expenses. The lower court found that the creditor did rely upon the false statements of the debtor, but that such reliance was not reasonable and that the real cause of the creditor's loss was "his own carelessness."[31] Pointing out that 523(a)(2)(A) and (a)(2)(B) are mutually exclusive and finding no indication that Congress intended to "give additional support to debtors by imposing a reasonableness requirement in section 523(a)(2)(A)" the court concluded that subsection (A) required only actual reliance.[32] Accordingly the court reversed the lower court's finding on behalf of the debtor. We endorse the result and find support for its conclusion both in the careful statement of the reasonable reliance requirement in (B)(iii) and in the history of (B) on false financial statements in consumer credit transactions that we have discussed above.

In summary, one reading the cases under section 523(a)(2)(A) would do well to stick to the facts and to pay much less attention to the articulation of the rules of law. Although the cases routinely say that there must be explicit representation or "actual fraud", that there must be "scienter", that the reliance of the creditor must be reasonable, the courts are often quite willing to infer the presence of those legal requirements from facts that show nothing more than that the debtor lied about some significant element in order to get his loan. Representative of these cases is *In re Kimzey*[33] where the Court of Appeals for the Seventh Circuit held that a debt was nondischargeable that the debtor had procured by showing "invoices." Contrary to the inference from the existence of the "invoices", the goods had not been shipped and no account receivable created. The debtor argued that there was no fraud because he intended to ship the goods. The court found there was fraud because an invoice represented goods already shipped and an account receivable already created. The court addressed the law and the facts in that case as follows:

> The bank argues that Kimzey's representation to the bank that the thirteen purchase orders were invoices of goods already shipped satisfied the requirements of 11 U.S.C. § 523(a)(2)(A). That section provides that a Chapter 7 discharge does not relieve the debtor from any debt "for obtaining money * * * [by] false pretenses, a false representation, or actual fraud." 11 U.S.C. § 523(a)(2)(A)(1982). To succeed on a claim that a debt is nondischargeable under section 523(a)(2)(A), a creditor must prove three elements. First, the creditor must prove that the debtor obtained the money through representations which the debtor either knew to be false or made with such reckless disregard for the truth as to constitute willful misrepresentation. *Carini v. Matera*, 592 F.2d 378, 380 (7th Cir.1979). The creditor also must prove that the

1987); In re Kimzey, 761 F.2d 421 (7th Cir. 1985).

30. 827 F.2d 340 (8th Cir.1987).

31. Id. at 342.

32. The court relied substantially on the reasoning in In re Fosco, 14 B.R. 918 (Bankr. D.Conn.1981).

33. 761 F.2d 421 (7th Cir.1985).

debtor possessed scienter, *i.e.,* an intent to deceive. *Gabellini v. Rega,* 724 F.2d 579, 581 (7th Cir.1984). Finally, the creditor must show that it actually relied on the false representation, and that its reliance was reasonable. *Carini,* 592 F.2d at 381. The party objecting to discharge must prove the facts establishing each element by clear and convincing evidence. * * *

Appellant Kimzey contends that the bank failed to prove any of the elements for nondischargeability under section 523(a)(2)(A); we disagree. The bank officers testified that their agreement with Kimzey was to loan him the sale price of merchandise already shipped. Furthermore, the bankruptcy trustee testified that Kimzey told him that the normal course of business was for Kimzey to present the bank with orders for merchandise already shipped. Although Kimzey claims the agreement was for sales orders rather than for goods already shipped, we defer to the credibility determination of the bankruptcy court, especially since the agreement in dispute was oral. *See In re Martin,* 698 F.2d 883, 885–86 (7th Cir.1983). We therefore hold that it was not clearly erroneous for the bankruptcy court to find that, when Kimzey received loans with the thirteen purchase orders for which he had not shipped the goods, Kimzey obtained money through a false representation.

As for the scienter element of a section 523(a)(2)(A) claim, an intent to deceive may logically be inferred from a false representation which the debtor knows or should know will induce another to make a loan. *Carini,* 592 F.2d at 380. Since, as the bankruptcy court found, the agreement was to loan money for orders Kimzey had already shipped, Kimzey knew or should have known that he could not obtain loans with the thirteen unshipped orders unless he represented to the bank that he had shipped the goods. It was therefore not clearly erroneous for the bankruptcy court to find that the bank had proved scienter.

Finally, Kimzey argues that since the bank officers knew of his financial difficulties, they could not reasonably rely on a representation that the loans were on accounts receivable for goods already shipped. But the evidence supports the bankruptcy court's finding that the bank reasonably relied on Kimzey's representations. Although the bank officers knew that Kimzey was short of capital, it was not unreasonable for them to believe—as they testified they did—that Kimzey needed loans on orders already shipped in order to finance supplies for future orders. In addition, each order was presented to the bank on a form labeled "INVOICE," further suggesting that the goods had already been shipped. Thus the bankruptcy court's finding that the bank reasonably relied on Kimzey's false representations is not clearly erroneous and the court's holding that the $4,447.47 debt was nondischargeable under section 523(a)(2)(A) is affirmed.[34]

b. *Section 523(a)(2)(B): False Financial Statement Materiality, Reasonable Reliance and Intent*

Subsection (B) has a long and contentious history. Advocates of consumer debtors maintain that creditors entrap naive consumer debtors by discour-

---

34. 761 F.2d at 423–24.

aging them from completing financial statement forms that the creditors have provided. Creditors, on the other hand, have maintained that debtors, consumer and otherwise, are often quite sophisticated and routinely omit large debts or exaggerate assets because they know they will procure the loan only by that means. Subsection (B) contains four requirements. They are as follows:

> (B) use of a statement in writing—
>
> (i) that is materially false;
>
> (ii) respecting the debtor's or an insider's financial condition;
>
> (iii) on which the creditor to whom the debtor is liable for such money, property, services, or credit reasonably relied; and
>
> (iv) that the debtor caused to be made or published with intent to deceive; * * *

Unlike subsection (A), this subsection cannot be satisfied by an oral statement or by just any writing. It must be a statement in writing respecting the debtor's financial condition.[35] A distillation of the four conditions brings out three interrelated fighting issues.

How does one determine whether a misrepresentation is "material"? Debtors commonly argue that omissions on their financial statements are so small as to have no impact. For example, if one had liabilities of $500,000 and assets of $700,000, the omission of $10,000 of liabilities or the exaggeration by $10,000 of assets would not be "material." Therefore, the most obvious test of materiality is to see where it stands in the universe of the particular disclosures and financial statements of that debtor. Obviously, the larger the value misrepresented (as a percentage of the whole), the more likely it is to be material and vice versa.[36]

The second factor that might bear on materiality would be the nature of the debt that is not disclosed. For example, a creditor might view routine phone bills and other utility debts as inherently immaterial. The same creditor might draw negative inferences about outstanding debts—even at similar amounts—to small loan companies or to judgment creditors. Where one borrows tells something about that person's creditworthiness.

---

35. In re Engler, 744 F.2d 1060 (4th Cir. 1984) (oral assurance of first priority is not enough even if false); In re Phillips, 804 F.2d 930 (6th Cir.1986)(footnote 1 finds a deed insufficient to satisfy the writing requirement). For other cases testing the writing requirement, see In re Howard, 73 B.R. 694 (Bankr. N.D.Ind. 1987); In re Shelton, 42 B.R. 547 (Bankr. E.D.Mo.1984)(agreeing with Howard, no signature required); In re Allen, 65 B.R. 752 (E.D.Va.1986), appeal dism'd, 823 F.2d 548 (4th Cir.1987); In re Lansford, 822 F.2d 902 (9th Cir. 1987) (both dealing with the liability of a non-signing spouse). In our view there is no signature requirement. What should be required is that the debtor hold the writing out as something on which the creditor should rely.

36. See e.g., In re Harasymiw, 895 F.2d 1170 (7th Cir.1990) (omission of $128,000 mortgage on $267,000 property was material); In re Greene, 96 B.R. 279 (Bankr. 9th Cir.1989) (omission of prior secured loans totalling $100,000 for loan of $10,000 was material); In re Figge, 94 B.R. 654 (Bankr. C.D. Cal.1988) ($220,000 difference between actual value ($560,000) and represented value ($780,000) was material for loan of $200,000); In re Meyer, 89 B.R. 25 (Bankr. E.D.Wis.1988) (overstatement of net worth by at least seven percent was material); In re Roland, 65 B.R. 1003 (Bankr. D. Conn. 1986) ($72,000 difference between actual net worth of $206,500 rather than represented $278,500 was not material for $62,500 loan); In re Lambert, 64 B.R. 170 (Bankr. E.D. Tenn.1986) (overvaluation of equity held in a farm by 25% of the loan amount, household and personality by 51% of loan amount, and stock by 1.65 times the loan amount was material).

The debtor's second argument and the creditor's response to it on the materiality question invariably laps over into the reasonable reliance issue. The debtor is likely to argue that an omission is not material because the creditor did not rely and would not have relied upon such information. When that argument is made it becomes inextricably confused with the reasonable reliance issue. For example, a debtor might argue that a creditor routinely makes renewals of loans based exclusively on the past payment history of the debtor and without consideration of anything put down on a financial statement at the time of the renewal. This argument could go to the materiality of the representation but also to the reasonableness of the reliance, whether there was reliance at all. In short, materiality can be found in the size of the variation from the truth, in the message that would have been transmitted to the creditor by the omitted material, whatever its size, and to some extent, in the actual practices of particular creditors with the use of such information.[37]

A second condition related to the materiality condition has to do with the debtor's *mens rea*. Under subsection (iv) the use of the statement must be "published with intent to deceive." As we indicate above, intent is normally drawn in section 523(a)(2)(A) from the mere use of a materially false statement. One cannot omit his largest creditor from his financial statement and say that he did not intend to mislead when any reasonable person looking at the financial statement would find it misleading. Thus, the intention is almost always found or not found by reasonable inference from the facts that are used to prove other elements such as the inaccuracy and materiality.[38] Seldom, if ever, is the creditor able to prove that the debtor had truly malicious feelings against a particular creditor.

Note that it is sufficient that the debtor is deemed to have been "grossly reckless as to the truth" even in circumstances where the debtor is convincing in his testimony that he did not truly "intend" to mislead.[39]

The crux of most cases under (B) has to do with creditor's reasonable reliance. This argument seems to be declining in importance and strength for the debtor. Routinely debtors argue the creditor has a responsibility to check items other than financial statements and that any reasonable creditor can check their credit rating or who checked any other information would have known that the financial statement was false and therefore could not be relied upon. As some of the Courts of Appeals have recently pointed out, this argument tends to stink in the mouth of the debtor. In its

---

37. See e.g., Matter of Bogstad, 779 F.2d 370 (7th Cir.1985); In re Sanders, 110 B.R. 328 (M.D.Tenn.1989); In re Greene, 96 B.R. 279 (Bankr. 9th Cir.1989); In re Pretner, 110 B.R. 942 (Bankr. D. Colo. 1990); In re Calvo, 111 B.R. 1003 (Bankr. M.D.Fla.1990); In re Spilotros, 105 B.R. 708 (Bankr. M.D.Fla.1989), judgment aff'd, 115 B.R. 368 (M.D.Fla.1990); In re DiMarco, 105 B.R. 128 (Bankr. S.D.Fla.1989); In re Galizia, 108 B.R. 63 (Bankr. W.D.Pa. 1989); In re Anzman, 73 B.R. 156 (Bankr. D.Colo.1986); In re Roland, 65 B.R. 1003 (Bankr. D.Conn.1986); In re Levine, 6 B.R. 54 (Bankr. D. Fla. 1980), aff'd, Deel Rent–A–Car, Inc. v. Levine, 16 B.R. 873 (S.D.Fla.1982), aff'd, 721 F.2d 750 (11th Cir. 1983); In re Rosel, 63 B.R. 603 (Bankr. W.D.Ky.1986); In re Delano, 50 B.R. 613 (Bankr. D.Mass.1985); In re Lambert, 64 B.R. 170 (Bankr. E.D.Tenn.1986); In re Iverson, 66 B.R. 219 (Bankr. D. Utah 1986).

38. In re Martin, 761 F.2d 1163 (6th Cir.1985)(ratio of assets to liabilities shown to be two to one when in fact ratio of liabilities to assets was actually three to one).

39. In re Matera, 592 F.2d 378 (7th Cir. 1979); In re Houtman, 568 F.2d 651 (9th Cir. 1978); In re Martin, 761 F.2d 1163 (6th Cir. 1985); Knoxville Teachers Credit Union v. Parkey, 790 F.2d 490 (6th Cir.1986).

baldest form, the debtor is saying: "Granted that I misled you, and granted that I intended to mislead you, but I still should not have liability to you because you were more gullible than most." So posed, the argument is a hard one to win, yet it is one frequently made, albeit dressed in slightly better attire than we have used.

In re Martin[40] demonstrates the growing difficulty that debtors are having on this issue. While the court stated that the reasonableness requirement was intended to incorporate prior case law,[41] the requirement cannot be said to be "a rigorous requirement, but rather is directed at creditors acting in bad faith."[42] Recognizing that Congress intended that creditors use "other sources of information such as credit bureau reports to verify the accuracy of the list of debts",[43] the courts nevertheless show a growing skepticism about this claim of confession and avoidance:

> But in this case, the statement was intentionally false from the very beginning. Mr. Martin intentionally communicated the false statement to the bank with expectation that the bank would rely on it and he cannot now be heard to say that he did not intend the bank to continue this reliance.[44]

While it is too soon to be absolutely certain, it seems likely that we will look back upon the later 1980s and the early 1990s as a time when the appellate courts reigned in the bankruptcy courts' predisposition to allow debtors routinely to be discharged, even from debts that were procured by materially false financial statements. The courts now seem less willing to accept the argument—over the contrary testimony of the creditor—that the creditor did not really rely, or should not have relied. In some cases, the courts have found the reliance not reasonable on the ground the creditor should have done his homework in the form of studying the documents more carefully or procuring additional credit reports or other material.[45] More commonly now, we see cases in which the courts are unsympathetic to the debtor, who has by hypothesis presented a materially false financial statement.[46]

In summary, section 523(a)(2)(B) remains an important battleground between debtors and creditors. Although there are doubtless creditors who did not rely, yet who assert that they did, and attempt to avoid dischargeability under this section, we see a growing skepticism of the debtor's claim

---

40. 761 F.2d 1163 (6th Cir.1985), accord Knoxville Teachers Credit Union v. Parkey, 790 F.2d 490 (6th Cir 1986); In re Lansford, 822 F.2d 902 (9th Cir.1987) (the argument that the creditor failed to check the information was "unseemly" because the creditor had believed his lie); In re Liming, 797 F.2d 895 (10th Cir.1986).

41. S.Rep. 989, 95th Cong. 2nd Sess. 78, reprinted in 1978 U.S. Code Cong. & Admin. News, 5787, 5864; H.R. Rep. No. 595, 95th Cong. 1st Sess. 364, reprinted in 1978 U.S. Code Cong. & Admin. News, 5963, 6320.

42. 761 F.2d at 1166, citing also In re Garman, 643 F.2d 1252 (7th Cir.1980), cert. denied, 450 U.S. 910, 101 S.Ct. 1347, 67 L.Ed.2d 333 (1981).

43. H.R. Rep. 595, 95th Cong. 1st Sess. 130, reprinted in 1978 U.S. Cong. Code & Ad. News 1691.

44. In re Martin, 761 F.2d at 1167; see also In re Sanders, 110 B.R. 328 (M.D.Tenn. 1989) (suggesting the appellate decisions have substantially watered down the reliance requirement).

45. See e.g, In re Ward, 857 F.2d 1082 (6th Cir.1988).

46. In re Bonnett, 895 F.2d 1155 (7th Cir. 1989); In re Martin, 761 F.2d 1163 (6th Cir. 1985), Knoxville Teachers Credit Union v. Parkey, 790 F.2d 490 (6th Cir.1986); In re Liming, 797 F.2d 895 (10th Cir.1986).

here, at least where the creditor is able to establish there was a materially false statement. Courts seem increasingly and properly unreceptive to the argument that creditors have a duty to check out every statement made by a debtor whose own culpability tends to overshadow any fault of the creditor.

c. Section 523(a)(2)(C)

Immediately before going into bankruptcy, debtors sometimes charge items to their credit cards or secure a cash advance in anticipation that the debt will be discharged. While these problems can be dealt with under the actual fraud provisions of section 523(a)(2)(A), proving the elements of actual fraud can be difficult. To counter this problem, known as "loading up," Congress amended section 523(a)(2) in 1984 to make presumptively nondischargeable certain purchases of "luxury goods and services" on credit and cash advances incurred immediately before bankruptcy.[47] The intent of Congress was to place the burden for certain credit purchases upon the debtor rather than the creditor where the purchases seemed unnecessary or imprudent for a debtor in difficult financial straits.[48] Thus, once the requirements of the section are met, the burden shifts to the debtor to rebut the presumption that the purchases were made with a fraudulent intent.

As enacted, section 523(a)(2)(C) was made applicable to two types of credit transactions: consumer debts owed to a single creditor aggregating more than $500 incurred on or within 40 days before the order for relief, and cash advances aggregating more than $1,000 incurred under an open end credit agreement (credit card) and obtained by the debtor on or within 20 days before the order for relief. Under the language of the statute, either type of debt must be owed to a single creditor, but aggregating amounts to the creditor is permissible.

---

47. Section 523(a)(2)(C) reads:
[F]or purposes of subparagraph (A) of this paragraph, consumer debts owed to a single creditor and aggregating more than $500 for "luxury goods or services" incurred by an individual debtor on or within forty days before the order for relief under this title, or cash advances aggregating more than $1,000 that are extensions of consumer credit under an open end credit plan obtained by an individual debtor on or within twenty days before the order for relief under this title, are presumed to be nondischargeable; "luxury goods or services" do not include goods or services reasonably acquired for the support or maintenance of the debtor or a dependent of the debtor; an extension of consumer credit under an open end credit plan is to be defined for purposes of this subparagraph as it is defined in the Consumer Credit Protection Act (15 U.S.C. 1601 et seq.);
11 U.S.C.A. § 523(a)(2)(C).

48. As the legislative history to § 523(a)(2)(C) reveals:
Section 523 is amended and expanded to address a type of unconscionable or fraudulent debtor conduct not heretofore considered by the code—that of loading up. In many instances, a debtor will go on a credit buying spree in contemplation of bankruptcy. The new subsection [C] creates a rebuttable presumption that any debt incurred by the debtor within forty days before the filing of the petition has been incurred under the circumstances that would make the debt nondischargeable. Only that portion of a debt which was incurred within the 40-day time period is subject to this presumption. The burden is upon the debtor to demonstrate that the debt was not incurred in contemplation of a discharge in bankruptcy and thus a fraudulent debt. As the language makes clear, debts incurred for expenses reasonably necessary for support of the debtor and the debtor's dependents are not covered by the presumption.

S. Rep. No. 65, 98th Cong., 1st Sess. 58 (1983). This language describes S.445, 98th Cong.,1st Sess. § 209(b), which was an earlier attempt to legislate on the loading-up problem. However, we believe it adequately describes the basic meaning of section 523(a)(2)(C). See id. at 82 n.1.

The most obvious question under section 523(a)(2)(C) is what is a "luxury good or service"? The statute and the legislative history give very little guidance. Section 523(a)(2)(C) says that "luxury goods or services" does not include goods or services reasonably acquired for the support or maintenance of the debtor or a dependent of the debtor. The legislative history supports this same exclusion. However, this definition begs the real question: what *is* included in the term?

The boundaries of "luxury goods" and "necessities" do not necessarily abut.[49] Some goods that are not necessities are also not luxury goods. Most courts have proceeded on an ad hoc basis merely to identify the items presented in each case as either a luxury or not.[50] One court has suggested that the appropriate inquiry should be into the price and the function of the purchased goods or services, and whether the goods are exempt from the property of the estate.[51] Finding "luxury" to imply extravagance, superfluousness, self-indulgence or a going beyond or overflowing an implicit, indeterminate level of comfort, one court noted that "luxury" is inherently relative. The bare necessities for Marie Antoinette might seem quite luxurious to the rest of us.[52] Even a car may be a necessity to one because of the need for that vehicle and a luxury to one without such need. The conclusion that should be drawn is that while many goods or services such as Gucci handbags, diamond rings, or pedicures are easy to classify, many other goods and services will not demonstrate inherent attributes to show them to be necessities nor luxuries.

There is a final issue. What if a debtor uses the money from a bank loan to purchase luxury goods or services? If the advance is under an open-end credit agreement but outside of the twenty day period or not under an open-end credit agreement at all, the transaction does not technically fit within section 523(a)(2)(C). Under the analysis of the Bankruptcy Appellate Panel for the Ninth Circuit, the phrase "debts * * * for luxury goods or services" refers to a vendor's right to payment for luxury goods or services sold to the debtor, rather than to the creditor's right to repayment of a cash loan used to purchase luxury goods or services from another vendor.[53] As was noted, cash advances were intended to be dealt with under the second part of section 523(a)(2)(C) rather than under the luxury part.

---

49. In re Blackburn, 68 B.R. 870 (Bankr. N.D.Ind. 1987).

50. In re Orecchio, 109 B.R. 285 (Bankr. S.D.Ohio 1989) (audio tapes providing investment advice were luxury); In re Williams, 106 B.R. 87 (Bankr. E.D.N.C. 1989) ("Giorgio" colognes and "Gucci" handbags were luxury); In re Barger, 85 B.R. 756 (Bankr. S.D.Ohio 1988) (moderately priced clothing not a luxury); In re Barthol, 75 B.R. 305 (Bankr. S.D.Ohio 1987) (floral arrangement was luxury); Matter of Claar, 72 B.R. 319 (Bankr. M.D.Fla.1987) (purchase of additional days on lifetime membership at Heritage Campground, Heritage, U.S.A. was a luxury service); In re Faulk, 69 B.R. 743 (Bankr. N.D.Ind. 1986) (clothes, shoes, boots were not luxuries; gift sets, cologne, fashion accessories, auto blanket, and coffee maker were luxuries); In re Hussey, 59 B.R. 573 (Bankr. M.D.Ala.1986) (three-wheel off-road vehicle was a luxury); In re Davis, 56 B.R. 120 (Bankr. D. Mont. 1985) (used Plymouth Voyager Van used by the debtors and their family and acquired in exchange for their previous vehicle was not luxury); In re Ashton, 51 B.R. 712 (Bankr. W.D.Pa.1985) (computer and auto parts were luxury); In re Smith, 50 B.R. 573 (Bankr. M.D.N.C.1985) (clothing not luxury).

51. In re Davis, 56 B.R. 120 (Bankr. D.Mont.1985).

52. In re Blackburn, 68 B.R. 870 (Bankr. N.D.Ind. 1987).

53. In re Neal, 113 B.R. 607 (Bankr. 9th Cir.1990); see also In re Woods, 66 B.R. 984 (Bankr. E.D.Pa. 1986); but see Matter of Claar, 72 B.R. 319 (Bankr. M.D.Fla.1987); In re Hussey, 59 B.R. 573 (Bankr. M.D.Ala.1986).

d. Fraud—Causal Connection

Technically, there is no "damage" issue in a case under section 523(a)(2). For most of these cases the question whether the creditor suffered damage is only another way of asking whether there was a sufficient causal connection between the fraud and the creditor's loss to attribute that loss to this debtor's behavior. Causation of damages on the one hand and damages suffered on the other are merely the opposite sides of the same coin.

Consider *Birmingham Trust National Bank v. Case*.[54] Because the debtor's "collateral" was not owned by the debtor, the bank's security was worthless. The bankruptcy court and the Court of Appeals held that no part of the debt was dischargeable. The debtor argued that the debt should be held nondischargeable only to the extent of the value of the purported collateral. Only to that extent was the creditor's loss *caused* by the debtor's fraud. There is confusion among the bankruptcy courts on this issue.[55] In *Birmingham Trust*, the Court of Appeals for the Eleventh Circuit sides with the cases that hold that the entire debt is denied discharge.

However, the *Birmingham Trust* case relies upon particular language of section 523 and it may no longer be good law. In 1984 Congress added the words "to the extent obtained by" in 523(a)(2). This language makes it clear that dischargeability in (a)(2) is not an all or nothing proposition. Yet even under the new language, the *Birmingham* case should have come out the same way. The court pointed out [56] "there was evidence indicating that [the bank] never would have made the loan absent the Debtor's misrepresentations." If the small value of the collateral would have stopped the loan entirely, the bank would never have had to look to the collateral at all. Its loss, therefore, should not be limited merely to the underestimation in the collateral's value.

If the debtor in *Birmingham Trust* could have shown that the creditor would have made the loan even if the truth were known about the exaggerated value of collateral, then presumably the debt is dischargeable. This is so either because there was no reasonable reliance on the representation or because the loan was not obtained by false representations.

Considering this case in yet a third way, there is a possibility that a creditor would have lent a smaller amount had it known the truthful value of the collateral. If that were true, the new 1984 language "to the extent obtained by" would come into play and would cause only the added increment of the loan to be nondischargeable.

We suspect that the incremental addition (the last case) is the exception and that the more common case is one like *Birmingham Trust* as it played out, namely one in which the bank states persuasively that had it known the truth it would have made no loan at all, not a loan for a smaller amount. If

---

54. 755 F.2d 1474 (11th Cir.1985).

55. Compare In re Brewood, 15 B.R. 211 (Bankr. D. Kans. 1981); In re Easterly, 11 B.R. 206 (Bankr. E.D.Tenn.1981) (both holding limited dischargeability) with In re Benedict, 15 B.R. 671 (Bankr. W.D.Mo.1981); In re Swanson, 12 B.R. 688 (Bankr. S.D.Fla.1981) (entire debt nondischargeable).

56. Id. at 1477.

that is so, the causal connection is to the entire loan and the entire loan should be rendered not dischargeable.

The complexity increases when the fraud with respect to certain loans arguably causes the creditor to extend several loans. This is illustrated by the case *In re Gerlach*.[57] In this case a John Deere dealer and his father were running a quasi kite on John Deere. Under the scheme, they would produce a document showing sales of John Deere implements. The sales never occurred. On reporting such sham sales to John Deere, they would get immediate credit from John Deere even though the loan transactions were constructed so that when the loan documents were later presented for approval at John Deere, they would be rejected and the credit previously given would be withdrawn. The Gerlachs used the credit in the meantime.

Father Gerlach had been involved in certain of these sham transactions. Deere argued that its existing and outstanding unsecured credit to the dealership (for which the father was liable as a guarantor) should be nondischargeable on the ground that they would not have made *those* loans had they known about the *previous* sham transactions in which he engaged.

The lower courts found the causal connection to be too tenuous, but the Court of Appeals reversed. Noting that it was standard to hold not only a debt procured through fraud, but extensions and renewals to be nondischargeable,[58] the court found that one need prove only that the fraud was a "substantial factor" in the creditor's decision. Rejecting the debtor's proximate cause argument, the court relied on the Restatement.[59]

In our view, the court properly rejected a series of cases that have required a higher standard of causal proof from the creditor.[60] Contrary to the conclusion of some lower courts, this court finds that the 1984 "to the extent" language does not change the outcome of most of these cases. As indicated above, we would agree that the new language will have quite limited impact.

Renewals and extensions of loans have provided a yeasty medium for conflicts about damages suffered by creditors as a result of debtor's fraud. First is the question whether the entire debt is nondischargeable if it was originally procured without fraud, but it is renewed or extended by the fraudulent act of the debtor. Second is the question whether the debtor's original fraud in procuring the loan is cured by a non-fraudulent renewal.

The statutory history addresses these questions as follows:[61]

"The amount of the debt made nondischargeable * * * is not limited to 'new value' when a loan is rolled over. If an initial loan is made subject to a false financial statement and new money is advanced under a subsequent loan that is not made under conditions of fraud or false pretenses, then only the initial amount of the loan made on the original

---

57. 897 F.2d 1048 (10th Cir.1990).

58. Matter of Van Horne, 823 F.2d 1285 (8th Cir.1987).

59. See also Takeuchi Manufacturing v. Fields (In re Fields), 44 B.R. 322 (Bankr. S.D.Fla.1984); Zarate v. Baldwin (In re Baldwin), 578 F.2d 293 (10th Cir.1978) (found debt to be nondischargeable).

60. See, e.g, Muleshoe State Bank v. Black, 77 B.R. 91 (N.D.Tex.1987); In re Adelman, 90 B.R. 1012 (Bankr. D.S.D.1988); In re Eaton, 41 B.R. 800 (Bankr. E.D.Wis.1984).

61. In re Gerlach, 897 F.2d 1048, 1051 n.2 (10th Cir.1990).

financial statement is invalidated and excepted from discharge. On the other hand, where the original financial statement is made under nonfraudulent conditions and the entire loan in addition to new money is advanced under a subsequent false financial statement, the entire loan is made under fraudulent conditions."[62]

The quoted material makes it clear that where new money is added on an honest renewal of an originally fraudulent loan, only the outstanding amount of the original loan is to be held nondischargeable. Conversely, a fraudulent rewriting of an existing loan renders the entire loan—the original amount plus any new money added—nondischargeable. The assumption behind this view is that the renewal is an alternative to collection of the debt—proceeding at once against the debtor—and thus that there is a causal connection between the fraud committed on the renewal and the later inability of the creditor to collect the original debt.

One can imagine cases where the outcome would be different. Assume creditor makes a $100,000 loan in an honest transaction with a debtor. Debtor falls on hard times after the debt has been paid down to $80,000 and by fraud procures a renewal of the $80,000 debt with the addition of $20,000 new dollars. Clearly the new $20,000 should be nondischargeable, but what about the $80,000? If the creditor can show that it was unable to collect the $80,000 on bankruptcy and that the money could have been collected if it had tried at the time of the fraudulent renewal, the $80,000 should be nondischargeable as well.

On the other hand, what if the debt was uncollectible at the time of the renewal; and even if the creditor had been spurred to action at that time, he would have received no additional recovery. Then, it would seem to us, "to that extent" there was no loan or renewal procured by fraud and the $80,000 should be a dischargeable debt.

The *Gerlach* case stands for the proposition that "the use of fraud to obtain an extension of a debt originally procured non-fraudulently also renders the debt nondischargeable."[63] On its facts the case seems correct, for it seems plausible that the past fraud in the quasi-kiting scheme kept the current loans in existence and thus led John Deere deeper into the morass than would otherwise have been true. The language both in *Birmingham Trust* and in *Gerlach* goes beyond that necessary for the holding in those cases. We endorse both holdings as well as the analysis of the particular facts in those opinions, but we do not embrace the broad language in *Birmingham Trust* and we have some doubt about the *Gerlach* court's endorsement of the all or nothing language from *Birmingham Trust*.

In re Liming[64] is a similar case. There Liming procured his first loan with a financial statement showing him to be worth $183,000 with debts of only $88,000. Three months later in the course of procuring a renewal, he made the mistake of disclosing his debts as $264,000.

Liming asserts that, even if Central National relied on the financial statement when it issued the loan, it did not rely on the statement when

---

62. H.R. Rep. No. 595, 95th Cong., 1st Sess. 129–30 (1977) reprinted in 1978 U.S. Code Cong. & Admin. News 5787, 6090–91; see also 3 Collier on Bankruptcy ¶ 523.10, at 523–67.

63. Id. at 1051 n.2.

64. 797 F.2d 895 (10th Cir.1986).

it issued the renewal note—when it knew Liming's correct finances. He also argues that, because Central National passed up its opportunity to call the loan, it is now either estopped or has waived its right to object to the false statement.[65]

The court found that the renewal only maintained Liming's initial debt and that "[i]t did not represent a new debt incurred without regard to the initial false statement."[66] Thus Liming's entire debt was denied discharge.

Matter of Van Horne[67] is the converse of *Gerlach* and *Liming*. Van Horne attempted to stiff his mother-in-law, Mrs. Caspers, and so give the proverbial mother-in-law her due. He was unsuccessful. Initially, he borrowed $30,000 from the mother-in-law in exchange for a four-year note. Six months later when he had difficulty paying it, he gave her a new note. According to the bankruptcy court, he had already formed an intention to divorce Caspers' daughter when he gave the new note. The fraud consisted in procuring the extension without disclosing his intention to divorce the daughter of his creditor. The court found that Mrs. Caspers would not have renewed the note had she known of his intention to divorce the daughter.

Van Horne unsuccessfully argued that he was already into Mrs. Caspers for $30,000 at the time of the renewal and that in fact the renewal had nothing to do with her loss. He correctly pointed out that had he not renewed the note, but instead divorced the wife and gone into bankruptcy, the debt to the mother-in-law would clearly have been discharged. In a footnote, the court points out Van Horne "did not present any evidence to either of the courts below or to this court indicating he was insolvent at the time he renewed his loan obligation."[68] Ungrateful son-in-laws must prove their cases with precision.

In summary, we draw several conclusions from the statute and the cases concerning the causation questions. First, the addition of the "to the extent" language to section 523(a)(2) in 1984 must mean that Congress intends something different than an all or nothing approach—at least in some circumstances. Second, the number of cases seem quite limited where it is appropriate for partial nondischargeability because of the "to the extent" language. In most of the cases the creditor can argue plausibly that even if the misrepresentation was only about a certain percentage of the collateral or about part of the loan, he would not have made the loan at all had he known the truth. Where the creditor can make that argument persuasively, the limiting language "to the extent that" does not save the debtor.

Also, it seems clear that the courts here are willing to accept fairly limited evidence of proximate causation. That is to say, appellate courts, at least, seem to resolve causation questions against the debtor and to accept the creditor's claim that the fraud caused the loss, even in circumstances where one reasonably sympathetic to the debtor could come to the opposite conclusion.

---

65. Id. at 898.
66. Id.
67. 823 F.2d 1285 (8th Cir.1987).
68. Id. at 1289 n.1.

The upshot of this is that honest renewals of fraudulently procured debt do not render the original debts dischargeable. Fraudulent renewals of honest debt may render the entire debt nondischargeable. Finally, we suspect the level of outrage at the debtor's behavior has an impact on the court's judgment about proximate causation. For example, *In re Rubin*[69] involved a man who by fraud caused a husband and wife to lose their home. To call the debtor a thief would be charitable. In view of that behavior, the court brushes aside the argument that the husband and wife creditors would almost certainly have lost their house even if Rubin had not defrauded them. We believe that the same things are at work in the court's treatment of the sneaky son-in-law in *Van Horne* and possibly in other cases. In cases under 523(a)(2) as elsewhere, one sees much less sympathy for the debtor in the appellate courts and a more stern and calvinistic approach to the debtor's cries than one ever hears from bankruptcy judges.

§ 7–27 Exceptions to Discharge, Section 523, Introduction—Unscheduled Debts, Section 523(a)(3)

Section 523(a)(3) denies discharge for certain debts that are neither listed nor scheduled by the debtor in time to permit the creditor to file a timely proof of claim or a timely request for a determination of dischargeability. However, if the creditor had "notice or actual knowledge" of the case in time to permit such timely filings, even an unscheduled debt is discharged.[1] On its face, section 523(a)(3) protects the creditor's right to notice of the bankruptcy and of the potential discharge. The creditor need not show bad faith by the debtor; a completely innocent omission by the debtor is enough.[2]

Three issues recur in section 523(a)(3) cases. The first concerns the sufficiency of the debtor's schedule of creditors. The general requirements for creditor schedules are stated in Bankruptcy Rule 1007. Under this rule, the debtor must state the name and address of his creditors and has a burden of reasonable diligence to seek out the names and addresses of those not readily at hand.[3]

---

69. 875 F2d 755 (9th Cir.1989).

§ 7–27

1. Section 523(a)(3) states:

A discharge under section 727, 1141, 1228(a), 1228(b), or 1328(b) of this title does not discharge an individual debtor from any debt—

* * *

(3) neither listed nor scheduled under section 521(1) of this title, with the name, if known to the debtor, of the creditor to whom such debt is owed, in time to permit—

(A) if such debt is not of a kind specified in paragraph (2), (4), or (6) of this subsection, timely filing of a proof of claim, unless such creditor had notice or actual knowledge of the case in time for such timely filing; or

(B) if such debt is of a kind specified in paragraph (2), (4), or (6) of this subsection, timely filing of a proof of claim and timely request for a determination of dischargeability of such debt under one of such paragraphs, unless such creditor had notice or actual knowledge of the case in time for such timely filing and request; * * *.

2. In re Fauchier, 71 B.R. 212 (Bankr. 9th Cir.1987) (The correct test is whether or not the debt was scheduled in time to permit a timely request for dischargeability determination or a timely proof of claim determination.).

3. In re Fauchier, 71 B.R. 212 (Bankr. 9th Cir.1987) (The debtor must use reasonable diligence in scheduling the names and addresses of its creditors.).

The second interpretive issue involves the meaning of the adverb "timely" in section 523(a)(3)(A) and (B). One reason the creditor needs notice is to make a timely filing of its claim so to insure that it is eligible for a distribution in the Chapter 7 liquidation. More significant is the requirement of section 523(a)(3)(B) that the creditor get notice in time to challenge the dischargeability of a debt covered by 523(a)(2), (4), or (6). Recall that the debts classified in (2), (4) and (6) are automatically discharged even though they fall within the nondischargeability rules of 523 unless the creditor challenges this discharge in the bankruptcy court. To challenge the discharge, the creditor must have notice of the bankruptcy. Thus the real cases on timeliness arise in the uncommon situations where the creditor wishes to argue that its debt is not dischargeable because it was procured by fraud under (a)(2), or fraud or embezzlement under (a)(4), or arose out of willful or malicious injury under (a)(6).

According to Bankruptcy Rule 4007(c), a section 523(c) complaint is timely if it is brought within 60 days following the first meeting of the creditors. Under the same rule, creditors are to receive notice from the court's clerk of the bar date at least 30 days in advance. Often the creditor will neither be listed nor receive notice of the bankruptcy until immediately before the bar date. *Matter of Sam*[4] illustrates how courts respond to this issue. In *Sam* the creditor was not scheduled by the debtor, but he had knowledge of the bankruptcy 18 days before the bar date. The court held that technical compliance with the 30 day notice rule was not necessary. Instead, the court found that 523(c) and Rule 4007(c) require the creditor to protect his rights. Where there is enough time to object to discharge, or at least make a motion to extend the bar date,[5] the debt will be discharged even if the debtor failed to schedule the debt.[6]

The third issue in section 523(a)(3) is the meaning of "notice or actual knowledge." Under the Uniform Commercial Code knowledge means actually knowing something; notice means having received information from which one could infer the existence of the relevant fact. What the adjective "actual" adds to the idea of "knowledge" is unclear. Buried in the idea of notice and knowledge are several questions. First, notice or knowledge of what? The statute makes this relatively clear for it provides that one must have notice or actual knowledge "of the case." Presumably the assumption is that the creditor knows the names of all of its debtors and when it finds that one of those debtors has filed in bankruptcy it has the burden of getting out its files and taking whatever action is appropriate.

How explicit or dramatic must this notice be? In a 1984 case the Court of Appeals for the Tenth Circuit held that one phone call concerning the existence of a Chapter 11 case was not sufficient to create knowledge or give

---

4. 894 F.2d 778 (5th Cir.1990).

5. See also Matter of Compton, 891 F.2d 1180 (5th Cir.1990) (mere knowledge sufficient to bar the creditor's claim); Neeley v. Murchison, 815 F.2d 345 (5th Cir.1987) (Knowledge sufficient if there is enough time to file for an extension of the bar date.); In re Price, 871 F.2d 97 (9th Cir.1989) (Actual notice in time to file extension.); In re Alton, 837 F.2d 457 (11th Cir.1988).

6. The court in Sam also held that constitutional due process requires only that the creditor have notice reasonably calculated to apprise him of the pendency of the action and give him an opportunity to present his objection.

notice.[7] In a case that appears more generous to the debtor, the same court later held that at least in Chapter 7 cases, notice is enough that merely lets the creditor understand that a case exists.[8]

To whom is notice to be given? What if the creditor is an organization with multiple agents and many offices? In *United States, Small Business Admin. v. Bridges*,[9] the Court of Appeals for the Fifth Circuit held that the debtor had the burden of proving that it had given actual notice to the creditor. In that case, the knowledge of the bankruptcy had come to one branch office of the Small Business Administration. The court found that was insufficient to put the SBA "on notice" of the bankruptcy.

Doubtless there will be a continuing trickle of cases about knowledge and notice. Because there are so many factual distinctions among the cases, the stream can never be cut off entirely. We would suggest only that the courts also consider the definitions of notice and knowledge and the requirements for giving them in the Uniform Commercial Code section 1–201(25), (26), and (27). For example, section 1–201(27) gives a fairly explicit and comprehensive definition about how one might determine whether an organization had received notice:

> Notice, knowledge or a notice or notification received by an organization is effective for a particular transaction from the time when it is brought to the attention of the individual conducting that transaction, and in any event from the time when it would have been brought to his attention if the organization had exercised due diligence. An organization exercises due diligence if it maintains reasonable routines for communicating significant information to the person conducting the transaction and there is reasonable compliance with the routines. Due diligence does not require an individual acting for the organization to communicate information unless such communication is part of his regular duties or unless he has reason to know of the transaction and that the transaction would be materially affected by the information.[10]

§ 7–28 Exceptions to Discharge, Section 523, Introduction— Fraud, Defalcation and Embezzlement, Section 523(a)(4)

Section 523(a)(4),[1] one of the most concise exceptions to discharge, is also relatively easy to understand. Debts procured by fraud or defalcation while acting in a fiduciary capacity, or that arose from embezzlement or larceny,

---

7. Reliable Electric v. Olson Construction, 726 F.2d 620 (10th Cir.1984) (one phone call insufficient to give a Chapter 11 creditor sufficient notice of bankruptcy).

8. In re Green, 876 F.2d 854 (10th Cir. 1989) (Chapter 7 creditor has no right to expect notice beyond notice of existence of the case in general.).

9. 894 F.2d 108 (5th Cir.1990).

10. U.C.C. § 1–201(27).

§ 7–28

1. Section 523(a)(4) states:

(a) A discharge under section 727, 1141, 1128(a), 1228(b), or 1328(b) of this title does not discharge an individual debtor from any debt—

* * *

(4) for fraud or defalcation while acting in a fiduciary capacity, embezzlement, or larceny; * * *.

11 U.S.C.A. § 523(a)(4).

are excepted from discharge under section 523(a)(4). Because the Code does not define "fraud," "defalcation," "embezzlement," or "larceny," one must look to other federal law and to state law for definitions. Except for larceny—which is rarely alleged or proven—we deal with each. As with property settlements and support payments under section 523(a)(5)—where the courts often consult state law—the ultimate definition is federal law, but federal law relying on and arising out of state law principles.

Fraud or defalcation while acting in a fiduciary capacity is the most common of the section 523(a)(4) exceptions. Because it requires no showing of intent, the creditor is usually able to establish the nondischargeability of a debt using available objective information. First, the creditor must show that there was a fiduciary relationship, i.e., the creditor must prove a trust.[2] Second, the creditor must show that fraud or defalcation occurred while the fiduciary relationship existed.

The first of these elements is quite easy to prove. A trust will only be considered if it is an "express" or "technical" trust arising out of the relationship and not a "statutory" or "constructive" trust created by the act out of which the debt arose in the first place.[3] In other words, if there is a general trust established by state law between partners in a partnership or between an officer or director and her corporation, then a fiduciary relationship exists.[4] However, if the trust arose only by statute when the fraud or defalcation was committed, then the trust is insufficient to establish the requisite fiduciary relationship.

The requirement of express or technical trusts excludes situations that are no more than debtor-creditor relationships. Ordinary business transactions do not create "fiduciary relationships" that give rise to nondischargeable debts. The Bankruptcy Court for the Southern District of New York put it as follows:

> a distinction must be made between a true fiduciary relationship and a relationship that is in reality a debtor-creditor arrangement. The concern here is that the definition of fiduciary be narrowly construed so that it 'not reach commercial debtor-creditor transactions in which the debtor merely violated the terms of his agreement with the creditor.'[5]

---

2. Ragsdale v. Haller, 780 F.2d 794 (9th Cir.1986).

3. See Chapman v. Forsyth, 43 U.S. (2 How.) 202, 11 L.Ed. 236 (1844) (stating that for bankruptcy purposes, "fiduciary capacity" means "technical trusts, and not those implied from the contract").

4. See Ragsdale v. Haller, 780 F.2d 794 (9th Cir.1986) (while California statute literally creates trust out of wrongdoing, state courts have broadened the meaning to find a trust always existing between partners); In re Short, 818 F.2d 693 (9th Cir.1987) (a partner is a trustee of all of the assets of a partnership in favor of the other partners under Washington law); In re Decker, 36 B.R. 452 (D.N.D. 1983) (Office of corporation occupies fiduciary relationship to corporation and creditors); In re Fussell, 15 B.R. 1016 (W.D.Va.1981) (corporate officers owe fiduciary duty to corporation and creditors); but see In re Stone, 91 B.R. 589 (D. Utah 1988) (general partner owed no fiduciary duty to limited partners); In re Long, 774 F.2d 875 (8th Cir. 1985) (court will not impose fiduciary duty on stockholder-employee of corporation in absence of local rule to do so); In re Hultquist, 101 B.R. 180 (Bankr. 9th Cir. 1989) (debtor may have owed a general fiduciary duty as a corporate officer, but no pre-existing or statutorily defined "trust" existed at the time of alleged wrongdoing).

5. In re Gans, 75 B.R. 474 (Bankr. S.D.N.Y. 1987) (quoting In re Levitan, 46 B.R. 380 (Bankr. E.D.N.Y.1985)). See also Matter of Harasymiw, 97 B.R. 924 (N.D.Ill. 1989), judgment aff'd, 895 F.2d 1170 (7th Cir.1990) (contractual relationship from loan transaction is insufficient to create a trust); In re Short, 818

To separate the apples from the oranges, the courts rely on the "intention" of the parties as disclosed by the contractual and other attributes of their relationship.

Consider *In re Schneider*[6] where the court found sufficient evidence of the intention to create a trust relationship. The creditor, a church-going woman, had recently inherited a large sum of money from her mother. For help in dealing with the death of her mother, she had sought the advice and counsel of her church minister. As the debtor's status progressed from minister, counselor and therapist to lover, so too did his designs on her cash. The debtor suggested that the creditor invest her inheritance in a ranch run by the debtor and his brother, an investment that ultimately went sour. The court found that the creditor also intended the debtor to be her financial adviser and a trustee of her retirement funds.

Certain relationships will almost certainly result in a finding of a trust. An attorney can expect a trust to exist in favor of a client despite the absence of an express agreement.[7] So too could a banker or broker. Others, such as construction firms or insurance agencies, might be made into trustees by state laws recognizing trusts.[8] A trust expressly created by agreement will seldom be overturned, but one apparently created by statute may not be recognized if the parties' reasonable expectations do not suggest a trust relationship.

The second element that the creditor must establish for fiduciary fraud or defalcation is the fraud or defalcation itself. Note that defalcation and fraud are not the same thing. Fraud requires some intent; defalcation requires none. In the words of Judge Learned Hand,

> [c]olloquially perhaps the word, 'defalcation' ordinarily implies some moral dereliction, but in [the bankruptcy] context it may have included innocent defaults, so as to include all fiduciaries who for any reason were short in their accounts.[9]

Thus, defalcation requires no showing of intent, but merely a shortage of the creditor's funds and some minimal willful neglect of duty or negligence by the trustee.[10] Because of the ease with which defalcation can be established

F.2d 693 (9th Cir.1987) (ordinary commercial relationships are excluded from the reach of § 523(a)(4)); In re Phillips, 882 F.2d 302 (8th Cir.1989) (assignment of interest in proceeds was for security interest, not to grant an assignment of the full value of the contract).

6. 99 B.R. 974 (Bankr. 9th Cir.1989).

7. Kwiat v. Doucette, 81 B.R. 184 (D.Mass. 1987); Federal Deposit Insurance Corp. v. Mmahat, 907 F.2d 546 (5th Cir. 1990), cert. denied, ___ U.S. ___, 111 S.Ct. 1387, 113 L.Ed.2d 444 (1991) (actions by debtor savings and loan's general counsel urging corporation to make improper loans so he could earn fees was defalcation while in a fiduciary relationship).

8. In re Interstate Agency, Inc., 760 F.2d 121 (6th Cir.1985) (under Michigan law, insurance premiums collected by agency have status of trust fund for the benefit of insurance principal); In re Livingston, 40 B.R. 1018 (E.D.Mich.1984) (fiduciary relationship existed between insurance agent and insurance company under Michigan law for premiums collected); In re Cutler, 74 B.R. 712 (N.D.Iowa 1987) (relationship between insurance company and insurance agent was debtor-creditor and not fiduciary); Matter of Boyle, 819 F.2d 583 (5th Cir.1987) (Texas construction fund statute only prevents diversion of funds with the intent to defraud); In re Kawczynski, 442 F.Supp. 413 (W.D.N.Y. 1977) (New York statute requires segregation of funds, thus creating trust relationship).

9. Central Hanover Bank & Trust Co. v. Herbst, 93 F.2d 510 (2d Cir.1937) (interpreting § 17(a)(4), 11 U.S.C.A. § 35(a)(4), the predecessor to § 523(a)(4)).

10. In re Gonzales, 22 B.R. 58 (Bankr. 9th Cir.1982); American Ins. Co. v. Lucas, 41 B.R.

(once a fiduciary relationship is shown), few cases are prosecuted under the "fraud" theory.

A third basis for denying discharge of a debt under section 523(a)(4) is that it arose out of embezzlement. For this a fiduciary relationship need not be proven. The creditor must show only that there was a "fraudulent appropriation of property of another by a person to whom such property has been entrusted, or into whose hands it has lawfully come."[11] There must be a subjective showing of fraud-in-fact, involving either "moral turpitude" or intentional wrong. A trust need not be established.[12]

The most difficult part of the case is to show a fraudulent intent or deceit. The fraud may take many forms such as the diversion of proceeds in violation of a security agreement,[13] the disappearance of funds intended for stock market investments,[14] or a misuse of funds advanced to perform a contract.[15] However, there must be more than a showing that the debtor was not lawfully entitled to use the funds for the purposes for which they were in fact used; the creditor must show that the debtor intended to defraud the creditor. Of course fraud can often be inferred from the mere act of the debtor's use of the funds.

Matter of Weber[16] shows the creditor's hurdles. In *Weber* the creditor purchased 38 cows as a tax-avoiding investment and leased them to the debtor. The debtor, as president of the farm operation, sold the creditor's cows for $195,000, along with 92 others, to a third party without the creditor's consent. While the creditor was aware of the debtor's sale of the cows, he did not approve. Instead, the debtor continued to pay lease payments and the creditor did not report the sale on his tax return until nearly three years after they had been fully depreciated and sold. By that time, the creditor had received only $5,000 back from the sale of his cows. The court was doubtful about the debtor's intent to defraud, but the Seventh Circuit side stepped the intent issue. Instead, the court held that if the necessary intent existed, it was negated by the creditor's acquiescence in the sale. The debtor used funds with the knowledge of the creditor, who did nothing to stop him.

Where the creditor has already proved embezzlement or defalcation in a state court, his case is even easier. As long as all of the elements were established in the state court, the judgment will be given collateral estoppel effect.[17] This collateral estoppel has also been applied to settlement agree-

923 (W.D.Pa.1984) (no intentional wrong required, just misapplication of funds while fiduciary); Matter of Moreno, 892 F.2d 417 (5th Cir. 1990) (defalcation is a willful neglect of duty, even if not accompanied by fraud or embezzlement); In re Johnson, 691 F.2d 249 (6th Cir. 1982) (no mental state is required for defalcation, only need mere negligence or mistake of fact).

11. In re Belfry, 862 F.2d 661 (8th Cir. 1988); see also In re Dohm, 19 B.R. 134 (N.D.Ill. 1982).

12. See Matter of Funventures in Travel, Inc. v. Dunn, 39 B.R. 249 (E.D.Pa. 1984); In re Stephens, 51 B.R. 591 (Bankr. 9th Cir. 1985).

13. In re Littleton, 106 B.R. 632 (Bankr. 9th Cir.1985), aff'd, 942 F.2d 551 (9th Cir. 1991).

14. Matter of Michel, 74 B.R. 88 (N.D.Ohio 1986).

15. In re Belfry, 862 F.2d 661 (8th Cir. 1988) (no embezzlement where the contract did not specify what expenses were to come out of funds advanced for the restoration of a BMW).

16. 892 F.2d 534 (7th Cir.1989).

17. See In re Dohm, 19 B.R. 134 (N.D.Ill. 1982); In re Stone, 94 B.R. 298 (S.D.N.Y. 1988), aff'd, 880 F.2d 1318 (2d Cir.1989).

ments that establish the necessary elements.[18]

§ 7–29 Exceptions to Discharge, Section 523, Introduction— Alimony, Maintenance and Support, Section 523(a)(5)

Section (a)(5) is among the most important exceptions from discharge. Unlike most of the other exceptions in 523, this exception is applicable in Chapter 13 as well as the other chapters, 7, 11 and 12. It excepts from the discharge any liability for "alimony to, maintenance for, or support of" the debtor's spouse or child. The language is disarmingly simple and applies without difficulty to tens of thousands of cases a year. As we will see, there are some important exceptions and a few technical qualifications.

By far the most difficult substantive problem, one that is at the heart of almost all the disputed cases, is drawing the line between alimony, maintenance and support, on the one hand, and liabilities arising out of a property settlement on the other. If a husband and wife have accumulated some wealth and then divorce, the divorce agreement will include not only payments in the nature of alimony and support, but also a division of their property. With rare exceptions, the line between settlement and support payments will be faint, irregular and blurred. Partly this arises from the recipient's indifference to the nature of the payment. Money is money in the hands of the recipient, and (apart from possible tax consequences) the recipient has no interest in deciding whether this payment is alimony or whether it is a payment in settlement of some other property claim.

Of course, the taxability of such payments may cause parties to label them, but beyond that both husband and wife are likely to be much more interested in amount than in characterization. In any event, both are principally interested in the net economic consequence of the divorce settlement. For this reason the cases we discuss below are usually *ex post facto* attempts to characterize particular payments as one or the other.

If characterization is nothing at the time of the divorce, it is everything at the time of a later bankruptcy. That is because alimony, maintenance, and support are not discharged, but liabilities arising out of a property settlement agreement are.

Subsection (a)(5) reads in full as follows:

A discharge under section 727, 1141, 1228(a), 1228(b) or 1328(b) of this title does not discharge an individual debtor from any debt—

> (5) to a spouse, former spouse, or child of the debtor, for alimony to, maintenance for, or support of such spouse or child, in connection with a separation agreement, divorce decree or other order of a court of record, determination made in accordance with State or territorial law by a governmental unit, or property settlement agreement, but not to the extent that—

---

18. See Greenberg v. Schools, 711 F.2d 152 (11th Cir.1983) (settlement agreement entered into for full settlement of a civil action alleging fraud or defalcation); Klingman v. Levinson, 831 F.2d 1292 (7th Cir.1987) (state court consent agreement established all the elements required under section 523(a)(4) and would be given collateral estoppel effect).

(A) such debt is assigned to another entity, voluntarily, by operation of law, or otherwise (other than debts assigned pursuant to section 402(a)(26) of the Social Security Act, or any such debt which has been assigned to the Federal Government or to a State or any political subdivision of such state); or

(B) such debt includes a liability designated as alimony, maintenance, or support, unless such liability is actually in the nature of alimony, maintenance, or support[.]

One should note that this language arose out of section 17(a)(7) in the Bankruptcy Act of 1898 and it has been amended in several respects since 1978. For example, the first clause in the parenthetical expression in (a) came as an amendment in 1981. The second clause in the parenthetical expression and the phrase in paragraph (5) "or other order of a court of record" were added in 1984.[1]

Before we look at the trees, take one look at the forest. It is gender neutral; but in almost all of the appellate cases a husband has taken

§ 7–29

1. Section 17(a)(7) of the Bankruptcy Act of 1898 stated:

A discharge in bankruptcy shall release a bankrupt from all of his provable debts, whether allowable in full or in part, except such as

(7) are for alimony due or to become due, or for maintenance or support of wife or child, or for seduction of an unmarried female, or for breach of promise of marriage accompanied by seduction, or for criminal conversation; * * *

Section 4–506(a)(6) of the Kennedy Amendments read:

(a) Exceptions from Discharge, A discharge extinguished all debts of an individual debtor, whether or not allowable, except the following: * * *

(6) any liability to a spouse or child for maintenance or support, for alimony due or to become due, or under a property settlement in connection with a separation agreement or divorce decree; * * *

The Kennedy commentary stated:

12. Clause (6) of subdivision (a) overhauls § 17a(7) of the present Act. Under the proposed Act debts denied dischargeability under the clause are limited to family support obligations; debts "for seduction of an unmarried female, or for breach of promise of marriage accompanied by seduction, or for criminal conversation" are eliminated as no longer responsive to prevailing social policy. The clause is broadened, however, to include any liability to a "spouse or child * * * under a property settlement in connection with a separation agreement or divorce decree." Under the present Act such property settlements are dischargeable. The change recognizes that obligations to support family dependents in the future may take the form of either a duty to make periodic payments based on need or an obligation to pay a settlement based on the debtor's present or anticipated wealth. The choice of form frequently turns on tax considerations or other factors not directly related to the duty to provide support.

The legislative history of § 523(a)(5) accompanying the section states:

Paragraph [(5)] excepts from discharge debts to a spouse, former spouse, or child of the debtor for alimony to, maintenance for, or support of the spouse or child. This language, in combination with the repeal of section 456(b) of the Social Security Act (42 U.S.C. 656(b) [section 656(b) of Title 42, The Public Health and Welfare] by section 326 of the bill, will apply to make nondischargeable only alimony, maintenance, or support owed directly to a spouse or dependent. What constitutes alimony, maintenance, or support, will be determined under the bankruptcy law, not State law. Thus, cases such as In re Waller, 494 F.2d 447 (6th Cir.1974), are overruled, and the result in cases such as Fife v. Fife, 1 Utah 2d 281, 265 P.2d 642 (1952) is followed. The proviso, however, makes nondischargeable any debt resulting from an agreement by the debtor to hold the debtor's spouse harmless on joint debts, to the extent that the agreement is in payment of alimony, maintenance, or support of the spouse, as determined under bankruptcy law considerations as to whether a particular agreement to pay money to a spouse is actually alimony or a property settlement.

Senate Report No. 95–989. Notes of Committee on the Judiciary; see also House Report No. 95–595. Notes of Committee on the Judiciary.

bankruptcy and is appealing a bankruptcy court ruling that his liability to his wife or children is nondischargeable. Almost twenty opinions of the Courts of Appeals interpret section 523(a)(5). Of those, we have found only three cases in which the husband is the winner, and in two of those three, his victory was partial.[2] The message from the cases is quite clear. First, it shows that the Congressional judgment expressed in (a)(5) (that the wife's and child's need for alimony and support is more powerful than the husband's need for a fresh start) is shared by the courts. A husband seldom wins—even in the bankruptcy court. Second, these cases demonstrate a larger point, namely that the courts are less sympathetic to the fresh start principle and more likely to disregard it as one travels upward through the appellate system from the bankruptcy court to the Court of Appeals.

The message at all levels is quite clear: husbands seeking to escape from any liability arising out of a divorce decree or a settlement have formidable barriers. Irrespective of state law, of labels in the divorce settlement agreement, of arguments about "equity", the ex-husband seldom escapes the deal he made with his ex-wife.

a. Substantive Rule

The bankruptcy and appellate courts' responsibility under section 523(a)(5) is to determine whether the payments in question are "actually in the nature of alimony, maintenance, or support." The Congressional history shows that this determination is to be made as a matter of federal law.[3] But wait, there is no such law except as it exists in the bankruptcy court itself! Federal or not, courts must look to the law of the various states at least for analogies. The trick is to compare the particular payment in question against some template derived partly from this analogy to state law, partly from bankruptcy and appellate court decisions in bankruptcy cases and so to decide the "nature" of a payment.

The starting point is the agreement or state court decree that establishes the rights of the divorced husband or wife. If that decree or agreement identifies a particular payment as alimony, support, or maintenance, it will be determinative and no husband will convince a bankruptcy court the payment is something else and thus dischargeable.

The converse is not true. The cases are filled to overflowing with examples where the husband promised to pay lawyer's fees, to pay a debt of his former wife, to pay a lump sum, or to make some other payment not labelled alimony or support where the court held the payment to be alimony or support even though it looked like a property settlement. For example, in *In re Yates*,[4] the court disregarded an agreement of the wife to "waive" alimony and in *In re Benich*[5] the court found payments to be "in the nature of alimony" even though the only party to testify below was the husband who testified they were not so intended.

---

2. See In re Ramirez, 795 F.2d 1494 (9th Cir.1986), cert. denied, 481 U.S. 1003, 107 S.Ct. 1624, 95 L.Ed.2d 198 (1987); Tilley v. Jessee, 789 F.2d 1074 (4th Cir.1986); In re Calhoun, 715 F.2d 1103 (6th Cir.1983).

3. See legislative history to section 523(a)(5) quoted at note 1 supra.

4. 47 B.R. 460 (D.Colo.1985).

5. 811 F.2d 943 (5th Cir.1987).

We have found only one case at the Court of Appeals, *Tilley v. Jessee*[6], in which the husband has been victorious on the basis of the specific language contained in the settlement agreement. In that case the husband agreed to pay alimony of $1,000 per month until the wife's death or remarriage. In another paragraph of the agreement the husband agreed to maintain hospitalization and medical insurance. Neither party claimed that those amounts were dischargeable.

However, the husband did maintain that the payments provided in a third paragraph "property interest of wife in husband's property and estate" did constitute payments under a property settlement agreement and were dischargeable. Under the terms of that clause the husband had to pay the wife $125,000 at 7 percent interest. Notwithstanding the careful distinction and labelling, the lower courts in that case found that even the amount so labelled was a nondischargeable payment in the nature of alimony and maintenance. Contrary to the outcomes in almost all of the other cases, the husband successfully reversed the finding in the Court of Appeals.[7] *Tilley* should be regarded as the clear exception. Generally speaking, the agreement will bind the husband: anything labelled alimony or support will be so treated. The reverse is not true: labelling something as a property settlement will not protect the husband.

If the agreement is not determinative, how then is one to decide whether a payment is "in the nature of alimony and support," or is a property settlement? While there is little precision here and much to quarrel about, one can readily identify a prototype alimony or support agreement. First, it is usually an agreement that provides for periodic payments. Second, alimony is almost always limited so that it ends on the remarriage of the wife, on her death, or on the death of the husband. Third, payments for support or alimony are commonly made only in the circumstances in which there are children who need the support or in which the wife was economically dependent upon the husband and needs the payment to maintain her standard of living or to acquire the ability to support herself.

If the terms of the agreement contemplate modification, this too suggests that these terms are alimony or support. Finally, of course, one might ask whether the payments were deducted by the husband and included as income by the wife on their respective tax returns in the period after the divorce and before the bankruptcy. If they were, that indicates that they were intended as alimony. Property settlement payments do not receive such tax treatment. A representative articulation of these standards can be found in *In re Goin*[8].

> Federal courts have held that a bankruptcy court must look beyond the language of the decree to the intent of the parties and to the substance of the obligation. *Shaver v. Shaver*, 736 F.2d 1314 (9th Cir.1984). Several factors are pertinent to the bankruptcy court's determination of whether the debt is support: (1) if the agreement fails to

---

6. 789 F.2d 1074 (4th Cir.1986).
7. 789 F.2d at 1076.
8. 808 F.2d 1391 (10th Cir.1987); see also Shaver v. Shaver, 736 F.2d 1314 (9th Cir. 1984); In re Calhoun, 715 F.2d 1103 (6th Cir. 1983); Tilley v. Jessee, 789 F.2d 1074 (4th Cir.1986); In re Bedingfield, 42 B.R. 641 (S.D.Ga.1983); In re Harrell, 754 F.2d 902 (11th Cir. 1985); Sylvester v. Sylvester, 865 F.2d 1164 (10th Cir. 1989).

provide explicitly for spousal support, the court may presume that the property settlement is intended for support if it appears under the circumstances that the spouse needs support; (2) when there are minor children and an imbalance of income, the payments are likely to be in the nature of support; (3) support or maintenance is indicated when the payments are made directly to the recipient and are paid in installments over a substantial period of time; and (4) an obligation that terminates on remarriage or death is indicative of an agreement for support.

In this case, the bankruptcy court found evidence in support of all but the last of these, i.e., that the parties were married thirteen years; the wife worked part time as a beauty operator; all real and personal property was jointly owned; there were three children of the marriage; and the $350 a month child support payments were not sufficient to provide the spouse and children with the standard of living to which they had grown accustomed. Based on these specific findings, the bankruptcy court determined that the parties intended that the $80,000 was in the nature of alimony and maintenance and therefore nondischargeable.[9]

The quoted paragraphs state that the courts are applying federal not state law. Yet as one court put it, "Congress could not have intended that federal courts were to formulate the bankruptcy law of alimony and support in a vacuum, precluded from all reference to the reasoning of well established law of the states."[10] One should well understand, however, courts are still applying federal law and are looking to the state only for guidance. For example, two courts have found a father's promise to pay college expenses of adult children constituted support even though there was no state law support obligation to those children.[11] Nor did Texas law to the contrary keep the Court of Appeals for the Fifth Circuit from finding that an indefinite payment to the wife constituted a payment "in the nature of alimony."[12]

The state law issue is critical and recurrent in at least one setting. This is the question whether liabilities that originated as alimony, maintenance or support might assume a different posture in bankruptcy because of changed circumstances. It is familiar that decrees of state courts concerning alimony and support are subject to routine change and modification with the changing circumstances of the parties. Sometimes the husband's ability to pay increases, sometimes it declines; the needs of the recipients grow or diminish. In all of these circumstances it is commonplace for the state courts to modify the decrees. In a number of cases husbands have claimed that payments that were originally alimony or support should be regarded as something else and therefore be regarded as dischargeable at the time of bankruptcy because their circumstances had changed and there was no longer a need for support or no longer an ability to pay it.

9. 808 F.2d at 1392–93.
10. In re Spong, 661 F.2d 6, 9 (2d Cir.1981).
11. In re Harrell, 754 F.2d 902 (11th Cir. 1985); Boyle v. Donovan, 724 F.2d 681 (8th Cir.1984).
12. In re Benich, 811 F.2d 943 (5th Cir. 1987).

In *In re Calhoun*,[13] Judge Kennedy appears to accept this argument. In a footnote she directs the lower court on remand to consider the "debtor's current ability to pay."[14] Is the court to substitute for a state divorce court? Perhaps the purpose of this consideration is to determine if what was support is no longer, therefore what would not have been dischargeable is now dischargeable. This intimation in *Calhoun* has received uniform disapproval from the other Courts of Appeals. On various grounds the Courts of Appeals of the Second, Eighth, Tenth, and Eleventh Circuits[15] have rejected it. Among other things these courts point out that the *Calhoun* rule would put the bankruptcy courts in the position of operating as state divorce courts. Presumably the case presents the spectacle of a new trial in virtually every bankruptcy of a divorced man under which the man—who by hypothesis has fallen on bad times—might then argue that his former support and alimony obligations are now dischargeable not because they were originally property settlement payments, but because as a matter of equity, he should no longer be regarded as obliged to make such payments. Since the position of the Sixth Circuit has been rejected elsewhere, perhaps that court will retreat from it, or the Supreme Court or the Congress will be called upon to resolve the issue.[16]

Courts have been confronted by a series of technical matters in the language of (a)(5). It is commonplace in a divorce for the husband to assume certain loans that are jointly owed by the husband and wife. In some cases (as a method of indexing), the husband agrees to pay certain expenses such as health insurance.[17] For example, in *Sylvester v. Sylvester*[18] the husband was bound to pay taxes, insurance premiums and note payments on real property that had been awarded to the wife in the divorce. In addition, he was obliged to pay premiums on her life insurance policies. Finding that these payments had "the actual effect of providing support to the appellee" wife, the district court held, and the appellate court agreed, that these were in the nature of alimony or support. At least two cases from the Courts of Appeals recognize that payment of the wife's attorneys fees by the husband can constitute nondischargeable alimony or support.[19] All of these decisions that recognize payments to lawyers, insurers and other parties, who would otherwise turn to the wife for payment, seem properly to be treated as payments to the wife and, if they are in the nature of alimony or support, to be nondischargeable. To hold otherwise would make an artificial distinction that would conflict not only with common sense, but with common practice in the negotiation of divorce settlements.

There are some payments to third parties that are less obviously support or alimony. Assume, for example, that husband and wife are both liable on the note secured by the husband's car. Assume the husband keeps the car

---

13. 715 F.2d 1103 (6th Cir.1983).

14. Id. at 1110 n.11.

15. Forsdick v. Turgeon, 812 F.2d 801 (2d Cir.1987); Draper v. Draper, 790 F.2d 52 (8th Cir.1986); In re Harrell, 754 F.2d 902 (11th Cir.1985); Sylvester v. Sylvester, 865 F.2d 1164 (10th Cir.1989) rejected the argument.

16. In In re Forsdick, 812 F.2d 801 (2d Cir.1987), the court concluded that had Congress intended the debtor to escape his support and alimony obligations because of hardship, Congress could have said so as they did in § 523(a)(8) with respect to student loans.

17. Cf. Tilley v. Jessee, 789 F.2d 1074 (4th Cir.1986).

18. 865 F.2d 1164 (10th Cir.1989).

19. Matter of Seibert, 914 F.2d 102 (7th Cir.1990); In re Spong, 661 F.2d 6 (2d Cir. 1981).

and agrees to pay that note. Finally, assume that on default, lender would have the right to pursue the wife, but would be unlikely to do so after it had repossessed the car and satisfied a large part of the liability. Is such a debt nondischargeable as alimony or support? If there is a novation at the time of the divorce and the creditor agrees to release the wife from her liability, clearly the remaining obligation is not for alimony or support. Commonly there would be no novation and in theory, at least, the wife would remain liable. To the extent that the creditor would pursue the wife, the obligation should be regarded as potentially, at least, for alimony or support. But as the probability of the wife's being liable to the creditor upon the husband's default diminishes toward zero (as, for example, because they are far removed from one another, the collateral is quite valuable, or the wife herself is impecunious), it becomes less clear that the liability should be treated as nondischargeable support or alimony.

Such a holding where the wife is only theoretically liable gives the creditor something it did not earn, namely, a nondischargeable debt on a straight car loan. Only one appellate case, *In re Calhoun*[20], gives serious consideration to this question. The court's discussion of this issue is intertwined with its erroneous conclusion that the bankruptcy court can examine the needs of the parties to determine whether payment is in the nature of support. Nevertheless, it depends in part on the considerations discussed here, namely, whether payment to the third party is merely payment of the husband's debt in fact or whether in fact it is also a payment of the debt that would otherwise be collected from the wife. The court makes the following point:[21]

> Discharge of a joint debt on the bankrupt's automobile, for example, is unlikely to disrupt the dependent spouse's ability to meet daily needs when the automobile itself is available to the creditor in satisfaction of the debt.

The message here to the creditor is clear. Never agree to a novation in case of divorce because such agreement may come back to haunt you in the husband's bankruptcy.

In addition to the argument that payments to third parties are not in the nature of alimony or support, husbands initially made a second argument: even if such payments are in the nature of alimony or support, they are dischargeable merely because of their payment to third parties. The technical basis for such an argument comes from section 523(a)(5)(A). This subsection renders dischargeable a debt covered by (a)(5) if "such debt is assigned to another entity, voluntarily, by operation of law, or otherwise * * *." Presumably the theory behind the restriction is that an exception to the fresh start rule should be recognized if, but only if, the wife was the direct beneficiary of the payments. This language is a bootless attempt to strike out at the Jacobs of the world who seek to buy the wife's rights with a mess of pottage. So far as one can see from the cases, its sole consequence has been to cause confusion in the third party payment cases. Because of this subsection some husbands were able to argue that payments they had agreed to make to third parties were dischargeable, even though they might

---

20. 715 F.2d 1103 (6th Cir.1983).   **21.** Id. at 1109.

have been in the nature of alimony or support. The high point of this argument occurred in 1981 when a husband was able to convince Judge Lumbard of the Court of Appeals for the Second Circuit to dissent on that basis.[22] The argument did not prevail in the case nor has it been successful in any cases since that time.[23] None of the cases discussed above fell squarely within the exception in paragraph (A) because in none of them was the debt "assigned." Rather, the husband argued that the payment of an unassigned amount to a third party had the same consequences.

What of cases in which the obligation of the husband to the wife is in fact assigned to a third party after the divorce decree? These assignees have appeared only in the clothing of state and federal governments. It appears that the only people who routinely purchase claims against ex-husbands are the agencies of state and local governments who have made AFDC and other support payments to the husbands' former wives. The ironic consequence of the "assigned debt" rule is that the Congressional arrow aimed at the Jacobs of the world has lodged in the rump of the Congress itself. To remedy that unforeseen consequence, the Congress amended (A) in 1981 and 1984 [24] to include the parenthetical phrase that is now found there: "(other than debts assigned pursuant to section 402(a)(26) of the Social Security Act, or any such debt which has been assigned to the Federal Government or to a State or any political subdivision of such State)". As a consequence of the parenthetical expression, an assignee governmental unit can now usually pursue the husband even though he has taken bankruptcy. Such an assignment does not render the debt dischargeable.[25]

b. *Drafting Note for Divorce Lawyers*

There are some important lessons in the 523(a)(5) cases, not only for bankruptcy lawyers, but also for divorce lawyers. For bankruptcy lawyers, there is a single clear message, namely the Congress made an accurate reading of the popular will (at least as represented by bankruptcy and other federal judges) when it stigmatized ex-husbands who seek to avoid payments to or for the benefit of their children and former wives. In these cases the husbands lose all the close calls and some that *a priori* do not seem too close. Except in the quite unusual case, an argument for discharge of a liability to a wife that is not clearly identified as settlement of a property right is likely to be unavailing. The appeal of a loss by the husband at the bankruptcy court is even less likely to be productive.

The message for divorce lawyers is that they should have one eye on these cases when they draft settlement agreements or divorce decrees. It is

---

22. In re Spong, 661 F.2d 6, 11 (2d Cir. 1981).

23. See Sylvester v. Sylvester, 865 F.2d 1164 (10th Cir.1989); Tilley v. Jessee, 789 F.2d 1074 (4th Cir.1986); In re Calhoun, 715 F.2d 1103 (6th Cir.1983); Matter of Seibert, 914 F.2d 102 (7th Cir.1990). All of these cases upheld decrees that called for payment to third parties. It is not clear that the argument from Spong was made in all of them.

24. Omnibus Budget Reconciliation Act of 1981, Pub.L. No. 97–35, § 2334(b), 95 Stat. 357, 863; Bankruptcy Amendments and Federal Judgeship Act of 1984, Pub.L. No. 98–353, § 454(b), 98 Stat. 333, 376.

25. See assignment of claims under a paternity suit (unmarried mother), Matter of Stovall, 721 F.2d 1133 (7th Cir.1983) ($16,690 in child support arrearages); cf. In re Ramirez, 795 F.2d 1494 (9th Cir.1986), cert. denied, 481 U.S. 1003, 107 S.Ct. 1624, 95 L.Ed.2d 198 (1987) (payments made without a decree or order).

particularly important for the husband's lawyer clearly to distinguish alimony and support from the division of property if he is to have any hope of a discharge in a later bankruptcy.[26] Because the courts are so favorable to her, a lawyer for the wife need not be so careful, but at least one could avoid the attorneys' fees necessary to procure a victory in a bankruptcy over the husband, by a careful drafting of the divorce agreement.

§ 7–30 Exceptions to Discharge, Section 523, Introduction— Willful and Malicious Injury, Section 523(a)(6)

a. Overview

Section 523(a)(6) is composed of only 18 words and has survived substantially unchanged from the Bankruptcy Act of 1898. It reads in full as follows:

> (a) A discharge under section 727, 1141, 1228(a), 1228(b) or 1328(b) of this title does not discharge an individual debtor from any debt—
>
> (6) for willful and malicious injury by the debtor to another entity or to the property of another entity[.]

Cases that come to court under (a)(6) are not the most obvious candidates, such as liability for intentional and violent torts such as battery and the like. Why those cases do not appear is not clear. Perhaps those who commit assault, murder and mayhem wind up in the state penitentiaries where they have no need of a fresh start. Perhaps they are so confident they will lose that they do not assert the arguments under 523(a)(6). Some of them doubtless travel to Chapter 13 where even liability for willful and malicious injury can be discharged.

The largest number of cases under (a)(6) are those brought by creditors, usually secured creditors, who point to the debtor's unauthorized sale of

---

26. If a judicial lien is attached to secure the wife's portion of any divided property, it is also important to distinguish exactly what property interest is encumbered. The Supreme Court recently held that a divorced debtor's liability to his wife is not exempt under section 522(f)(1) where the judicial lien is already attached to an interest that he obtained by divorce decree. Farrey v. Sanderfoot, ___ U.S. ___, 111 S.Ct. 1825, 114 L.Ed.2d 337 (1991), on remand, 943 F.2d 679 (7th Cir. 1991). This outcome is based on the Court's finding that § 522(f)(1) requires a debtor to have possessed an interest to which a lien attached, before it attached, to avoid the fixing of the lien on that interest. Id. at ___, 111 S.Ct. at 1829, 114 L.Ed.2d at 344.

Justice White reasoned:

The gerund "fixing" [in § 522(f)] refers to a temporal event. That event—the fastening of a liability—presupposes an object onto which the liability can fasten. [§ 522(f)] defines the pre-existing object as "an interest of the debtor in property." Therefore, unless the debtor had the property interest to which the lien attached at some point before the lien attached to that interest, he or she cannot avoid the fixing of the lien under the terms of § 522(f)(1).

Id. at ___, 111 S.Ct. at 1829, 114 L.Ed.2d at 344.

This result can also be supported on another basis, that section 522(f)(1) seems to have been promulgated primarily for the purpose of protecting a debtor from creditors who attempt to nullify her exemptions by having liens attached to her property before she can file for bankruptcy. H.R. Rep. No. 595, 95th Cong., 1st Sess. 126–27, reprinted in 1978 U.S. Code Cong. & Admin. News 5963, 6087–88. It can be argued that a judicial lien imposed in order to secure the division of marital property is not one that Congress intended to void through this "race to the courthouse" provision. Rather, wife is better seen as a purchase-money lender retaining a security interest in her pre-decree property.

collateral or unauthorized use of money from sale of collateral. These acts are usually conversion under state law. They range from naive violations of security agreements in the form of good faith sales of the assets without technical permission of the creditor [1] to conniving violations in which the debtor takes money and goes to Las Vegas.[2]

The second large set of cases can be regarded as aggravated negligence suits. These are claims against physicians who have done unspeakable things to their patients, against drunk drivers (before 523(a)(9) was enacted), and against people who allow their family's pit bull to maul the four-year old children of neighbors. Because 523(a)(6) requires that the debt be for an injury that is both willful and malicious, it is surprising to find negligence suits here and yet more surprising to find that these liabilities are sometimes excepted from the discharge. The creditor wins some of these cases!

In addition there are a variety of other miscellaneous claims such as those arising out of false arrest,[3] and even out of the bringing of frivolous law suits.[4]

Although the language of (a)(6) applies alike to all of these claims, one should use some care in transporting the case involving Chrysler Credit to the case of a doctor liable for malpractice or the driver for an aggravated auto accident. We suspect that the legal judgment is influenced to a considerable degree by the court's own feeling of moral outrage. One who has been injured in a particularly grotesque way by a wealthy physician who has gone "naked" (no insurance) is much more likely to win his dischargeability claim than is someone who is merely asserting that the driver who ran into him was particularly reckless. Thus, the character of the debtor is important, and one must not stray too far from the particular facts in using the cases here.

To reiterate, most of these liabilities are dischargeable in Chapter 13. However, as we point out in Chapter 9, the court need not accept a Chapter 13 plan if it finds it was not proposed in good faith. One of the factors the court is sure to consider in determining good faith is whether the liability to be discharged would have been nondischargeable in Chapter 7. For example, in one case involving the dischargeability of a liability for false arrest, *In re Caldwell*,[5] the Court of Appeals for the Sixth Circuit held that Caldwell could not convert his case to a Chapter 13 because he was not proposing the conversion in good faith. In reality that case should be looked upon as a holding concerning the good faith of the plan that Caldwell was going to propose. Because he had hidden assets, transferred funds out of his control to his wife, proposed only a three-year as opposed to a five-year plan, and done a number of other things, the court concluded that his proposal to change to Chapter 13 was not in good faith and therefore denied it. That case also suggests that there is some danger in trying to get a discharge and in litigating that issue in a Chapter 7 before one attempts a Chapter 13.

§ 7–30

1. C.I.T. v. Posta, 866 F.2d 364 (10th Cir. 1989).

2. Chrysler Credit v. Perry Chrysler Plymouth, 783 F.2d 480 (5th Cir.1986).

3. In re Caldwell, 60 B.R. 214 (Bankr. E.D.Tenn.1986).

4. In re Wrenn, 791 F.2d 1542 (11th Cir. 1986).

5. 895 F.2d 1123 (6th Cir.1990).

Conceivably, Caldwell would not have smelled so bad to the appellate court if his original proposal had been a five year plan in Chapter 13.

b. *Willful and Malicious*

Almost all of the cases under (a)(6) deal with the definition of the two words "willful" and "malicious." Initially one might think that willful and malicious mean the same thing. If they did, Congress should have used one word and not both. Most courts feel compelled to find some different meaning for each of them. That an act is willful presents the most difficulty to a creditor in the medical malpractice and automobile cases. *A priori* one might conclude that the willful act of doing the operation by the physician or of driving the car by the defendant was not the kind of willfulness of which the statute speaks. Of course, the defendant intended to do some act. The problem is not with the act that he intended but how he did it.

In these cases, typically, the defendant has been found to have done the act (the operation on the patient or the operation of the car) negligently. Is that willful? Is that enough to constitute a willful act of the kind (a)(6) speaks? We doubt that it should be, but a number of courts have held that it is. For example, in two cases, Courts of Appeals [6] have held physician's malpractice liability not to be discharged because it was willful and malicious. In *Perkins v. Scharffe*,[7] the court found that

> Dr. Scharffe had unnecessarily injected Mrs. Perkins left foot with an unsterile needle or contaminated medication. Thereafter he failed to perform timely tests when a resultant infection was apparent. Dr. Scharffe then ignored results of belated tests that identified the offending bacteria and disclosed the appropriate drugs and drug strengths to combat them. Finally, Dr. Scharffe failed to hospitalize Mrs. Perkins when hospitalization was urgently needed.[8]

Faced with that sort of testimony the Court of Appeals reversed the lower court's decision of dischargeability. Concluding that "willful means deliberate or intentional" and, apparently mixing together the willful and malicious requirements, the court simply finds that the standards have been fulfilled. In a concurring opinion Judge Engle agrees to go along because the other circuits have ruled that way, but concludes that Judge Gilmore below was probably correct in his ruling for dischargeability. He notes "the conduct which occasioned the judgment against the bankruptcy doctor, while agreed by all to be appalling" was not "willful and malicious injury," but instead constituted "reckless disregard of a professional duty of care, the type of conduct which Congress indicated, at least in its legislative history, was even subject to dischargeability." [9]

It seems to us that Judges Engle and Gilmore probably read Congress correctly. To say that a drunk getting in his car and driving is doing a willful act and that a negligent physician is doing an act that causes willful

---

6. Perkins v. Scharffe, 817 F.2d 392 (6th Cir.1987), cert. denied, 484 U.S. 853, 108 S.Ct. 156, 98 L.Ed.2d 112 (1987); In re Franklin, 726 F.2d 606 (10th Cir.1984).

7. 817 F.2d 392 (6th Cir.1987), cert. denied 484 U.S. 853, 108 S.Ct. 156, 98 L.Ed.2d 112 (1987).

8. Id. at 393.

9. Id. at 395.

and malicious injury is to deprive the term willful of much of its meaning. Putting on our legal realist hat, we would argue that the courts are simply so offended by these cases that they reach out for whatever tools are at hand including tools that beat the language completely out of shape.

The drunk driving cases now have a place of their own in section 523(a)(9); liability arising from a drunk driver is no longer dischargeable. There too the courts were sometimes offended and at least one Court of Appeals found that such reckless behavior (driving with a .15 breathalizer, going the wrong way on a limited access highway) caused a willful and malicious injury.[10]

In summary, we question the application of § 523(a)(6) to liability that is essentially based on negligence, even liability that reaches to egregious negligence. It appears to us that Congress has made the judgment that such liability is to be discharged. As we indicate below, it appears that Congress intended to overrule an earlier Supreme Court case suggesting that willful could be read to include reckless behavior.

c. *Malicious*

The second part of the section 523(a)(6) test that the injury must be malicious has been the nub of the debate when secured creditors have argued that certain liabilities were not discharged because of conversion by the debtor—usually in the form of selling collateral "out of trust" and not remitting the proceeds. Since almost all of these cases would constitute intentional torts under state law, there is no difficulty meeting the intention requirement. When a car dealer takes ten cars, sells them, and fails to remit the proceeds, he is intentionally committing a wrong; it is not negligence.

The question is whether those acts show a maliciousness to fulfill the second part of the test. Before we return to the statutory difficulty, perhaps we should consider some of the verbal explanations of the meaning of malicious. In one case where the debtor sold property out of trust and took money to Las Vegas to bet, the court found that malicious means "without just cause or excuse."[11] In another, somewhat less heinous case, *In re Long*,[12] the Court of Appeals for the Eighth Circuit turned to the Restatement of Torts, section 8a Comment b to find that malice exists only when injury would be "certain or substantially certain" to occur.[13] Alternatively that court says there is malice when the conduct "necessarily causes injury". The court in *In re Cecchini*[14] states:

> When a wrongful act, such as conversion, is done intentionally, it necessarily produces harm and is without just cause or excuse, it is 'willful and malicious,' even absent proof of specific intent to injure.[15]

---

10. In re Adams, 761 F.2d 1422 (9th Cir. 1985); see also In re Compos, 768 F.2d 1155 (10th Cir.1985); In re Ikner, 883 F.2d 986 (11th Cir.1989).

11. Chrysler Credit Corp. v. Perry Chrysler Plymouth, 783 F.2d 480, 486 (5th Cir.1986).

12. 774 F.2d 875 (8th Cir.1985).

13. Id. at 881.

14. 780 F.2d 1440, 1443 (9th Cir.1986).

15. Id. at 1443.

That holding arose in a case where a person promoting travel for a Mexican hotel took payments from tourists and failed to remit them.

Unfortunately, the verbal articulation is of little help here. In all or almost all of these conversion cases, there is an intentional act. In those cases when the debtor sells collateral and takes the money to Las Vegas, it is, of course, quite clear that a loss will follow. That is less clear when the debtor claims ignorance of his obligations under the agreement [16] or where the money was allegedly put back in the business and used [17] or where there has been an agreement between the parties after the defalcation and where the ultimate claim is only for a breach of that agreement.[18] Thus, while the courts appear divided in the conversion area, it is not certain that a serious division will develop or last. The Court of Appeals for the Eighth Circuit in *Long* has adopted the articulation of maliciousness that is more generous to the debtor. The Courts of Appeals for Fourth, Fifth, Sixth, Ninth, and Eleventh Circuits [19] appear to have adopted the position that is more favorable to the creditor.

Whether the outcomes are attributable to the application of a different standard or whether to the fact that the appellate courts are traditionally less generous to the debtor than the bankruptcy courts, recent cases have been running more in the favor of the creditor who claims that the debtor's acts of conversion were willful and malicious and therefore were not discharged. The three most prominent recent successes have come in cases where automobile dealers have sold automobiles without remitting the proceeds and where it appears that the proceeds have either been put in other businesses, lost in Las Vegas or used for unexplained causes.[20]

This dispute over the treatment of state law conversion liability in 523(a)(6) arises from a statement in the legislative history of the 1978 act:

> To the extent that *Tinker v. Colwell* [citation omitted] held that a less strict standard is intended, and to the extent that other cases have relied on *Tinker* to apply a "reckless disregard" standard, they are overruled.[21]

Some courts have read the quoted language to apply to the "willful" portion of the test; other courts have read it to apply to the "malicious" portion of the test. If the Congressional intention is to stiffen the requirement of willfulness, then the quoted comment should cast doubt on the malpractice and automobile accident nondischarge cases. If, on the other hand, the Congressional statement is to stiffen the requirement of maliciousness, then

---

16. In re Posta, 866 F.2d 364 (10th Cir. 1989).

17. In re Long, 774 F.2d 875 (8th Cir.1985); In re Phillips, 882 F.2d 302 (8th Cir.1989).

18. In re Kimzey, 761 F.2d 421 (7th Cir. 1985).

19. Chrysler Credit Corp. v. Rebhan, 842 F.2d 1257 (11th Cir.1988); Perkins v. Scharffe, 817 F.2d 392 (6th Cir.1987), cert. denied, 484 U.S. 853, 108 S.Ct. 156, 98 L.Ed.2d 112 (1987); Ford Motor Credit Co. v. Owens, 807 F.2d 1556 (11th Cir.1987); Chrysler Credit Corp. v. Perry Chrysler Plymouth, 783 F.2d 480 (5th Cir. 1986); In re Cecchini, 780 F.2d 1440 (9th Cir. 1986); St. Paul Fire & Marine Ins. Co. v. Vaughn, 779 F.2d 1003 (4th Cir.1985).

20. Chrysler Credit Corp. v. Rebhan, 842 F.2d 1257 (11th Cir.1988); Ford Motor Credit Co. v. Owens, 807 F.2d 1556 (11th Cir.1987); Chrysler Credit Corp. v. Perry Chrysler Plymouth, 783 F.2d 480 (5th Cir.1986).

21. S. Rep. No. 95–989, 95th Cong. 2nd Sess. 1978, 1978 U.S.Code Cong. & Admin. News, 5787, 5865; H. Rep. 95–595, 95th Cong. 1st Sess. 1977, 1978 U.S.Code Cong. & Admin.News. 5963, 6320.

it should cast doubt on the cases that hold conversion liability is nondischargeable. In a 1987 case,[22] Judge Vining sorted out this debate in detail. His statement merits careful reading:

> The seminal case defining the standards applicable to the "willful and malicious injury" exception is *Tinker v. Colwell,* 193 U.S. 473, 24 S.Ct. 505, 48 L.Ed. 754 (1904), wherein the Supreme Court held that personal malevolence was not required and that a willful act was one done intentionally and voluntarily. The Court stated; "[W]e think a willful disregard of what one knows to be his duty, an act which is against good morals, and wrongful in and of itself, and which necessarily causes injury and is done intentionally, may be said to be done willfully and maliciously, so as to come within the exception." This language was subsequently interpreted to stand for two holdings.
>
> One line of cases focused on "willfulness" and interpreted *Tinker* to hold that willfulness could be established upon a finding of a reckless disregard of duty. *See, e.g., Harrison v. Donnelly,* 153 F.2d 588 (8th Cir.1946). The second line of cases focused on "malicious" and interpreted *Tinker* to hold that a finding of constructive or implied malice alone was enough to satisfy the malice requirement. No showing of special malice was necessary. *See, e.g., Bennett v. W.T. Grant Co.,* 481 F.2d 664, 664 (4th Cir.1973). Both of these earlier definitions flowed from interpretations of section 17(a)(2) of the former Bankruptcy Act, 11 U.S.C. § 35(a)(2).
>
> Congress amended the Bankruptcy Code in 1978. In the official comments appended to the changes to section 17(a)(2) which became 11 U.S.C. § 523(a)(6), Congress stated: "To the extent that *Tinker v. Colwell* [citations omitted] held that a less strict standard is intended, and to the extent that other cases have relied on *Tinker* to apply a 'reckless disregard' standard, they are overruled." Senate Report, No. 95–989, 95th Cong. 2d Sess. (1978), 1978 U.S. Code Cong. & Admin. News 5963, 6320. This official comment caused some confusion because *Tinker*'s reckless disregard standard had been incorporated in determinations of both "willful" and "malicious," and nothing in the comment revealed whether Congress intended to overrule the application of recklessness to the "willful" prong or the "malicious" prong or both; this confusion generated more divergence with respect to the holding of *Tinker.*
>
> One line of cases uncompromisingly holds that *Tinker* precluded application of the reckless disregard standard to a determination of either "willful" or "malicious." *See In re Hodges,* 4 B.R. 513 (Bankr. W.D.Va.1980). The *Hodges* court held that the "willful" requirement was satisfied by a showing that the act was committed intentionally and the "malicious" requirement was satisfied by a showing that the act was committed with an intent to harm the creditor. *Id.* at 516.
>
> Some courts were dissatisfied with the results of applying *Hodges.* By using the subjective standard of "intent to harm" to prove malice, section 523(a)(6) was eviscerated because proof of such intent was essentially impossible absent an admission by the debtor. *See In the Matter*

---

22. Chrysler Credit Corp. v. Rebhan, 842 F.2d 1257 (11th Cir.1988).

of Lewis, 17 B.R. 46 (Bankr. W.D.Ark.1981). To avoid the perceived harshness of *Hodges,* some courts began exploring avenues for reincorporating the implied or constructive malice standard that existed prior to the 1978 bankruptcy amendments.

One approach advocated essentially disregarding the legislative commentary overruling *Tinker,* since the legislative history was not always conclusive, but merely helpful, in divining legislative intent. *CreditThrift of America v. Auvenshine,* 9 B.R. 772 (Bankr. W.D.Mich. 1981).

A second approach elected to abide the legislative commentary overruling *Tinker* but then reasoned that *Hodges'* "intent to harm" standard for malice was subject to two interpretations: first, specific subjective intent to harm the creditor can establish malice, or, second, knowledge, without actual ill-will, that one's acts will harm a creditor and then acting in the face of that knowledge, could also establish malice. *Wisconsin Finance Co. v. Ries,* 22 B.R. 343 (Bankr. W.D.Wis. 1982).

Finally, the third approach held that Congress, by its legislative commentary, overruled only the application of the reckless disregard standard to the "willful" requirement. Congress did not intend to disturb the application of reckless disregard to the malice requirement. *United Bank of Southgate v. Nelson,* 35 B.R. 766, 774 (N.D.Ill. 1983). It appears that this approach now predominates.

In *United Bank of Southgate* the court noted that in the legislative commentary, immediately preceding the passage wherein Congress expressly overruled *Tinker'*s use of reckless disregard, appears the following prefatory statement: "Under this paragraph, willful means deliberate or intentional." Senate Report, No. 95-898, 95th Cong., 2d Sess. (1978), 1978 U.S. Code Cong. & Admin. News, 5787, 5865; House Report, No. 95-595, 95th Cong., 1st Sess. (1977), 1978 U.S. Code Cong. & Admin. News 5963, 6320. Based on this passage the *United Bank of Southgate* court determined that the entire legislative comment on paragraph (6) of section 523(a) defined only willful. Therefore, the court held that Congress did not alter the other interpretation of *Tinker* which allowed implied or constructive malice to satisfy the "malicious" requirement, and thereby rejected the *Hodges* approach. We hold that the approach adopted by the *United Bank of Southgate* court is the better interpretation and hereby adopt it as the law in this circuit; therefore, malice for purposes of section 523(a)(6) can be established by a finding of implied or constructive malice.[23]

The interpretation of the legislative history that is more generous to the debtor was adopted by the Court of Appeals for the Eighth Circuit in *In re Long*.[24] The majority of the appellate courts have now adopted the position

23. Id. at 1262-63.
24. 774 F.2d 875 (8th Cir.1985). The court discusses the issue as follows:

The difficulty which the lower courts are currently encountering in applying § 523(a)(6) seems attributable, at least in part, to the frequent failure to separately analyze the elements of malice and willfulness. Despite the general difficulty in applying the § 523(a)(6) exception, there is a virtual consensus of opinion that "willful," standing alone, means intentional or delib-

espoused by the Eleventh Circuit, a position that allows a debt to be held not dischargeable even in circumstances where there is no specific showing of malice.[25]

While an expansive application of the nondischargeability of conversion liability restricts the sweep of the fresh start, we do not regard it as a particularly threatening restriction. Car dealers who sell out of trust, particularly those who take the money to Las Vegas, are on the edge of and in some cases beyond the line of criminal liability. They are perfectly aware that they are violating their legal obligations when they sell out of trust. The courts should have little sympathy for them.

d. Summary

The cases under section 523(a)(6) demonstrate the importance of the peculiar factual underpinnings of those cases and of the moral outrage that attaches to certain kinds of debtors compared with others. Here we see the

erate * * *. It is the definition of malice, or the disregard of it as a separate term, which has been troublesome.

Congress tells us in § 523(a)(6) that malice and willfulness are two different characteristics. They should not be lumped together to create an amorphous standard to prevent discharge for any conduct that may be judicially considered to be deplorable. We are convinced that if malice, as it is used in § 523(a)(6), is to have any meaning independent of willful it must apply only to conduct more culpable than that which is in reckless disregard of creditors' economic interests and expectancies, as distinguished from mere legal rights. Moreover, knowledge that legal rights are being violated is insufficient to establish malice, absent some additional "aggravated circumstances," under Davis and its recent progeny.

Having determined that a heightened level of culpability must be found, going beyond recklessness and beyond intentional violation of a security interest, we turn to the task of articulating a workable standard. The bankruptcy courts have frequently attempted to define this level of culpability by speaking in terms of intentional harm. Malice is thus being given a meaning more nearly coinciding with common usage. One perceptive case turns to the Restatement (Second) of Torts, § 8A, Comment b, and uses intentional harm as a requirement for the bar to discharge, with the qualification that the expected harm must be "certain or substantially certain" to occur. * * * The Restatement observes that this is a stricter test of fault than the standard of recklessness. It is also consistent with the previously quoted Tinker language, allowing a finding of malice when conduct "necessarily causes injury." 193 U.S. at 487, 24 S.Ct. at 509. This phrase in Tinker has apparently not been criticized in the recent cases. Until a better definition can be formulated for use in this context, we accept the Restatement definition as helping to focus inquiry in applying the statutory "willful and malicious injury" requirement. When transfers in breach of security agreements are in issue, we believe nondischargeability turns on whether the conduct is (1) headstrong and knowing ("willful") and, (2) targeted at the creditor ("malicious"), at least in the sense that the conduct is certain or almost certain to cause financial harm.

This test seems to explain most of the recent cases favoring debtors when malicious conversion is alleged. It is a standard that at least partially satisfied the complaint of secured creditors who have been "done wrong" that they are faced with almost impossible obstacles in asserting nondischargeability because of actual malice. While intentional harm may be very difficult to establish, the likelihood of harm in an objective sense may be considered in evaluating intent. Use of objective information to ascertain intent to cause harm is by no means unfamiliar. Bogard v. Cook, 586 F.2d 399, 412 (5th Cir.1978), cert. denied 444 U.S. 883, 100 S.Ct. 173, 62 L.Ed.2d 113 (1979) (appraising official immunity defense); Hanek v. Global Van Lines, Inc., 533 F.2d 396, 400 (8th Cir.1976) (tort liability of moving company).

Id. at 880–81.

25. See, e.g., In re Phillips, 882 F.2d 302 (8th Cir.1989) (endorsing the view of the Eleventh Circuit). Of course, even in jurisdictions that adopt the term more generous to the creditor, courts can conclude that there is no malice.

courts bending the intent requirement quite out of shape in order to hold two physicians to their malpractice liability [26] and beating it yet more to make negligent liability for driving a car into an intentional and malicious act.[27] We suspect that there will continue to be litigation between secured creditors and debtors who sell out of trust and otherwise fail to remit proceeds or violate their security agreements. Whether the secured creditors will continue to meet with success here is unclear. The Courts of Appeals are sending a message to the bankruptcy courts to take the secured creditors' arguments seriously. Whether the sale out of trust cases or any of the other reckless tort cases make it into the statute as the drunk drivers did in (a)(9) remains to be seen.

§ 7–31 Exceptions to Discharge, Section 523, Introduction— Fines and Penalties, Section 523(a)(7)

In enacting the Bankruptcy Code of 1978, Congress made sure that debts for fines or penalties an individual owed to governmental entities, including the federal government, would not be affected by the discharge under Chapters 7 or 11. To ensure this, Congress inserted section 523(a)(7) as an exception to discharge.[1] The section provides that a debt for a fine or penalty payable to a governmental unit, as long as it is not for compensation for actual pecuniary loss, is nondischargeable. It also provides for an important tax exception to the exception.

The first question that one might ask is what is a "governmental unit." Section 101(27) is quite clear in providing that "governmental unit" means

> United States; State; Commonwealth; District; Territory; municipality; foreign state; department, agency, or instrumentality of the United States (but not a United States trustee while serving as a trustee in a case under this title), a State, a Commonwealth, a District, a Territory, a municipality, or a foreign state; or other foreign or domestic government.

Because of the latter half of the definition which covers any department, agency, or instrumentality of a governmental body, the definition is quite broad.[2] If something seems like a governmental unit, it probably is. The

---

26. Perkins v. Scharffe, 817 F.2d 392 (6th Cir.1987), cert. denied, 484 U.S. 853, 108 S.Ct. 156, 98 L.Ed.2d 112 (1987); In re Franklin, 726 F.2d 606 (10th Cir.1984).

27. In re Adams, 761 F.2d 1422 (9th Cir. 1985); cf. In re Compos, 768 F.2d 1155 (10th Cir.1985); In re Ikner, 883 F.2d 986 (11th Cir.1989).

§ 7–31

1. Section 523(a)(7) states:

(a) A discharge under section 747, 1141, 1228(a), 1228(b), or 1328(b) of this title does not discharge an individual debtor from any debt—

* * *

(7) to the extent such debt is for a fine, penalty, or forfeiture payable to and for the benefit of a governmental unit, and is not compensation for actual pecuniary loss, other than a tax penalty—

(A) relating to a tax of a kind not specified in paragraph (1) of this subsection; or

(B) imposed with respect to a transaction or event that occurred before three years before the date of the filing of the petition; * * *.

11 U.S.C.A. § 523(a)(7).

2. See In re Ellwanger, 105 B.R. 551 (Bankr. 9th Cir.1989) (private penalties are not excepted from discharge under 523(a)(7)).

exception is a debt owed to the United States trustee acting in a case under the Code.

Since the form of a fine or penalty usually mirrors its substance, there is rarely a question as to whether or not the section applies. For example, civil penalties levied upon a business by a State regulatory agency for Business Professions Code violations would be nondischargeable as long as the penalties are not compensation for actual pecuniary loss.[3] Service fees assessed by a State against an uninsured motorist to defray the costs of administration in serving notice, however, would be compensatory and thus dischargeable.[4] In at least one area—restitution obligations imposed as part of a criminal sentence—there has been dispute over the application of the exception. The Supreme Court ended the dispute by ruling in *Kelly v. Robinson*[5] that restitution obligations are not compensation for loss and are not excluded from section 523(a)(7)'s coverage.

In *Kelly,* the debtor, Carolyn Robinson, had pleaded guilty to second degree larceny for wrongful receipt of welfare benefits. Her sentence of one to three years was suspended on condition that she remain on probation for five years and make payments of $100 per month for the full five years beginning January 15, 1981. On February 5, 1981, Robinson filed a Chapter 7 petition. The State of Connecticut was notified of the petition but did not participate in the bankruptcy or in the distribution of assets. Finally, in February of 1984, Connecticut notified Robinson that it considered the monthly payments to be nondischargeable and due.

While the bankruptcy court and the district court agreed with the State, the Court of Appeals for the Second Circuit reversed. First, the court held that the obligations were a debt under bankruptcy law. Since the State failed to object to the discharge under sections 523(a)(2) or (4) for fraud or larceny, it was left with the automatic exception for governmental fines or penalties. Restitution, as the court defined it, consists of compensation to the victim of the crime for actual pecuniary loss and therefore is excluded from 523(a)(7) reach.

The Supreme Court disagreed. In an opinion which traced the history of the exception from the 1898 Act to its inclusion in the 1978 Code, the Court decided that the language of 523(a)(7) should be considered "in light of the history of bankruptcy court deference to criminal judgments and in light of the interests of the States in unfettered administration of their criminal justice systems."[6] This history reveals a clearly established judicial exception to the discharge of restitution obligations under the 1898 Act. The courts had interpreted the language of the Act as not affecting restitution obligations primarily because "[t]he right to formulate and enforce penal sanctions is an important aspect of the sovereignty retained by the States."[7]

---

3. In re Poule, 91 B.R. 83 (Bankr. 9th Cir. 1988).

4. Williams v. Motley, 925 F.2d 741 (4th Cir.1991).

5. 479 U.S. 36, 107 S.Ct. 353, 93 L.Ed.2d 216 (1986).

6. 479 U.S. at 43, 44, 107 S.Ct. at 358, 93 L.Ed.2d at 225.

7. 479 U.S. at 47, 107 S.Ct. at 360, 93 L.Ed.2d at 227.

The Court reasoned that if Congress had intended to change the established practice and encroach upon the traditional powers of the States, there would be a clear indication of such in the legislative history. Instead, the statutory history merely revealed that the phrase "not compensation for pecuniary loss" had a main purpose of preventing 523(a)(7) from being applied to tax penalties.[8]

Finally, the Court attempted to bolster its opinion by analyzing the goals of restitution. While acknowledging that restitution goes to the victim and is imposed with some reference to the harm caused, the goals are not primarily to benefit the victim. Rather, society as a whole, and hence the state, is the primary beneficiary through the penal process.

While the literal language of section 523(a)(7) leads to an almost inescapable conclusion that restitution obligations imposed as part of a criminal sentence should be discharged, the Court was probably correct in its interpretation of Congress' intent. Nothing in the legislative history indicates that Congress intended to alter the deference afforded criminal restitution obligations under the 1898 Act. However, as the dissent aptly pointed out in *Kelly*, section 523 exceptions from discharge only applied to discharges under Chapters 7, 11, 12, and 13 where the debtor did not complete payments under the plan.[9] For Chapter 13 cases where the debtor completed payments under the plan, even restitution obligations would be discharged.[10] However, Congress recently changed that result with the addition of section 1328(a)(3).[11] The amendment renders all debts "for restitution included in a sentence on the debtor's conviction of a crime" nondischargeable under section 1328(a).[12]

The reasoning of the *Kelly* Court has had a marked influence on the outcome of cases dealing with similar issues. First, courts have been reluctant to discharge the costs of a criminal trial imposed upon the defendant as part of his sentence. If the costs are part of the criminal sentence, most courts have found them nondischargeable.[13] Second, section 523(a)(7) has been interpreted to include federal criminal restitution obligations as well. Despite the fact that federalism concerns are much weaker with federal restitution obligations, the deference to the criminal process remains.[14]

---

8. S. Rep. No. 95–989, 95th Cong., 2d Sess. 79 (1978).

9. 11 U.S.C.A. § 1328(b).

10. 11 U.S.C.A. § 1328(a). In Pennsylvania Department of Public Welfare v. Davenport, 495 U.S. 552, 110 S.Ct. 2126, 109 L.Ed.2d 588 (1990), the Supreme Court held that criminal restitution obligations are "debts" within the meaning of section 101(12). As such, they were discharged under Chapter 13 where the debtor completed all payments under the plan. See also In re Heincy, 858 F.2d 548 (9th Cir.1988); In re Cancel, 85 B.R. 677 (N.D.N.Y. 1988); In re Johnson-Allen, 69 B.R. 461 (Bankr. E.D.Pa. 1987).

11. Criminal Victims Protection Act of 1990, Pub. L. No. 101–581, § 3, 104 Stat. 2865.

12. Leaving nothing to chance, the legislative history explicitly states that "this amendment will have the effect of overruling the Supreme Court's recent decision in Pennsylvania Department of Public Welfare v. Davenport * * *." S. Rep. No. 434, 101st Cong., 2d Sess. 8, reprinted in 1990 U.S. Code Cong. & Admin. News 4065, 4071.

13. In re Hollis, 810 F.2d 106 (6th Cir. 1987); Matter of Zarzynski, 771 F.2d 304 (7th Cir.1985) (costs of prosecution are a penalty even though measured by the extent of certain expenditures for trial).

14. United States v. Vetter, 895 F.2d 456 (8th Cir.1990).

§ 7–32 Exceptions to Discharge, Section 523, Introduction—Fines and Penalties, Section 523(a)(7)—Tax Penalties

One important exception to the coverage of section 523(a)(7) was left open by Congress. Certain tax penalties are dischargeable despite the fact that they are payable to or for the benefit of a government agency and are not compensation for actual pecuniary loss. Section 523(a)(7) excepts from nondischargeability

a tax penalty—

> (A) relating to a tax of a kind not specified in paragraph (1) of this subsection; or

> (B) imposed with respect to a transaction or event that occurred before three years before the date of the filing of the petition; * * *

Subsection (A) refers to penalties which relate to a tax that is not subject to nondischargeability under section 523(a)(1). Thus, if a tax is dischargeable, all penalties related to it will also be dischargeable. Subsection (B) refers to those tax penalties which relate to a "transaction or event" which occurred over three years before the petition date. While the language of each seems relatively straightforward, there is a conflict over how the two operate together.

First, it is possible to read the two tax penalty provisions in the conjunctive. Under this interpretation, a tax penalty must be related to a dischargeable tax *and* have been incurred before three years before the petition in order to qualify for discharge. Alternatively, the two sections may be read in the disjunctive, meaning that the penalty is dischargeable if either it relates to a dischargeable tax *or* it relates to an event or transaction that occurred before three years before the filing of the petition. The courts have disagreed on the proper interpretation.[1]

The Seventh Circuit Court of Appeals, in a cursory resort to the legislative history of subsection 523(a)(7)(A), decided that fraud penalties are nondischargeable if the underlying tax with respect to which the penalty was imposed is also nondischargeable.[2] In *Cassidy v. C.I.R.*,[3] where a tax penalty was assessed more than three years before the filing of the petition, the court determined that it was still nondischargeable because the underlying tax liability was nondischargeable.

While this opinion has been cited with favor by several bankruptcy and district courts, the Tenth and Eleventh Circuits have disagreed with the result. In *In re Burns*,[4] the Eleventh Circuit Court of Appeals analyzed the legislative history of subsections 523(a)(7)(A) and (B) and concluded that while some support for the conjunctive interpretation was to be found in the

---

§ 7–32

1. Compare Cassidy v. C.I.R., 814 F.2d 477 (7th Cir.1987); In re Hartman, 110 B.R. 951 (D.Kan.1990); In re Ferrara, 103 B.R. 870 (Bankr. N.D.Ohio 1989); In re Harris, 59 B.R. 545 (Bankr. W.D.Va.1986); In re Gerulis, 56 B.R. 283 (Bankr. D.Minn.1985); In re Carlton, 19 B.R. 73 (D.N.M. 1982); with In re Roberts, 906 F.2d 1440 (10th Cir. 1990); In re Burns, 887 F.2d 1541 (11th Cir. 1989).

2. Cassidy v. C.I.R., 814 F.2d 477 (7th Cir. 1987) (citing S.Rep. No. 989, 95th Cong., 2d Sess. (1978), reprinted in 1978 U.S. Code Cong. & Admin. News 5787, 5864).

3. 814 F.2d 477 (7th Cir.1987).

4. 887 F.2d 1541 (11th Cir.1989).

Joint Statement of the Conference Committee, a reliance on the legislative history is suspect. Further, the legislative history should only be consulted where there is ambiguity in the plain meaning of the statute, and none existed here. The Tenth Circuit Court of Appeals agreed in *In re Roberts*.[5]

The most conclusive example of the legislative history is the Joint Statement issued by the managers of the legislation in lieu of a conference committee report. The Joint Statement reads:

> [T]ax penalties which are basically punitive in nature are to be nondischargeable only if the penalty is computed by reference to a related tax liability which is nondischargeable or, if the amount of the penalty is not computed by reference to a tax liability, the transaction or event giving rise to the penalty occurred during the three-year period ending on the date of the petition.[6]

This statement suggests that the two subsections are to be read as applying to two different types of taxes, those computed by reference to a tax liability and those which are not so computed. Under this suggestion, the language of the subsections would be mutually exclusive thus rendering a conjunctive interpretation possible.

However, this is not clear. First, the language of 523(a)(7) contains an "or" between subsections (A) and (B). This implies that each part is to be treated as a separate exception. Second, if the two subsections were read in the conjunctive as they now stand, a tax penalty would have to be both computed by reference to a dischargeable tax *and* related to a taxable year or other taxable event occurring more than three years prior to the bankruptcy petition to be dischargeable. Such a requirement would be inconsistent with both the language and the legislative statement.

In order to carry out the meaning suggested by the legislative history, substantial change must be made to the language of 523(a)(7) as it now stands. There is presently no "computed by reference to" language in either subsection (A) or (B). Instead, as the Tenth Circuit pointed out:

> The actual language simply does not stretch that far. Subsection (A) refers, not to penalties "computed by reference" to a dischargeable tax, but rather to any penalty "relating to" such a tax. The statutory language refers to the nature of the penalty rather than the method of computing it. Likewise, the language of subsection (B) does not lend itself to the limitation which the government seeks to impose on its application. Many tax penalties are "imposed with respect to a transaction or event" and are nevertheless computed by reference to a tax liability.
>
> The government's proposed scheme, which treats penalties differently depending on whether the penalty is arithmetically computed by reference to a tax liability, is not a reasonable interpretation of the language in subsections (A) and (B); it is a different scheme altogether. However one might choose to view the relative merits of the two schemes, Congress enacted the scheme outlined by the statutory lan-

---

5. 906 F.2d 1440 (10th Cir.1990).

6. Statement of Sen. DeConcini, reprinted in 1978 U.S. Code Cong. & Admin. News 6505, 6569.

guage. Under the statutory scheme, a penalty related to a dischargeable tax is immediately dischargeable; every other penalty becomes dischargeable after three years.[7]

While the result suggested by the Seventh Circuit and other courts fits well with the legislative history, it conflicts with the language of the statute. Without the changes to the language suggested by the Tenth Circuit, even penalties relating to a dischargeable tax but less than three years old would be nondischargeable. Instead, the narrow approach taken by the Tenth Circuit is probably more appropriate given the conflict Congress created between the language of the statute and the legislative history.

§ 7–33 Exceptions to Discharge, Section 523, Introduction— Student Loans, Section 523(a)(8)

a. Overview

In section 523(a)(8) the Congress was more generous to student borrowers than it was to other pariahs, such as divorcees under (a)(5), defrauders under (a)(4), and malicious tortfeasors—but only slightly so. Under subsection 523(a)(8) educational loans are generally not dischargeable under Chapter 7; however, loans that have been outstanding for more than seven years can be discharged if enforcing them would cause "undue hardship." Until 1991, the term was five years.[1]

As in several of the other subsections of 523(a), Congress here seems accurately to have calculated the moral judgment of the courts. In interpreting the limitation on subsection (8) (for undue hardship, for example), courts have applied what one of our student assistants has characterized as "cruel strictness." "Undue hardship" has proved to be a very small hole through which only the most pitiful of bankrupt students have been able to escape from the general rule of nondischargeability.

One should note that the pressure on the court because of inability of debtors to pay student loans is likely to increase. There is considerable evidence of large default rates in the popular press and elsewhere [2]. Undergraduate and graduate students and students in trade school are borrowing to pay for their education and are borrowing in many cases far larger

---

7. In re Roberts, 906 F.2d 1440, 1443–44 (10th Cir.1990).

§ 7–33

1. Section 523(a)(8) of title 11, United States Code, is amended—

* * *

(2) by amending subparagraph (A) to read as follows:

(A) such loan, benefit, scholarship, or stipend overpayment first became due more than 7 years (exclusive of any applicable suspension of the repayment period) before the date of the filing of the petition; or[.]

Crime Control Act of 1990, Pub.L. No. 101–647, § 3621, 104 Stat. 4789, 4964–65 (effective 180 days after Nov. 29, 1990) (to be codified at 11 U.S.C.A. § 523(a)(8)(A)).

2. The current default rate on government subsidized student loans is estimated to be almost 12 percent. Quinn, Sallie Mae Takes Some Heat on Loan Delinquency Process, Wash. Post, May 26, 1991, at H3. Gross defaults increased by 350 percent from 1983 to 1989 although loan volume grew by only 83 percent during the same period. Student loan defaults now amount to over $2 billion and are expected to mushroom to nearly $3 billion sometime in 1992. Macoy, Washington Starts to Move on Student Loan Problems, Am. Banker, June 5, 1991, at 4.

amounts than would have seemed advisable or possible for prior generations. It is not uncommon to find graduate students with student loans well in excess of $40,000. A law student can have $100,000 in loans from his or her undergraduate and legal educations. Obviously, many of these students are more highly leveraged than the fabled LBO company of the 1980s. When the legal profession and the auto repair business turn down, one can expect to see many of them in bankruptcy.

With rare exceptions, those debts will not be discharged in Chapter 7. Until the 1990 amendment, discharge was possible in Chapter 13; now the same restrictions apply there. The provision on the nondischargeability of student loans was first found in the Higher Education Act of 1965[3]. It appeared almost as it does today in the Bankruptcy Commission Report and has been carried forward from 1978 to the present with only modest modifications.

Among those modifications is an expansion of its coverage. In 1978 it denied a discharge of liability to "a governmental unit or a non-profit institution of higher education for an educational loan." Now it denies discharge

> for an educational benefit overpayment or loan made, insured or guaranteed by a governmental unit, or made under any program funded in whole or in part by a governmental unit or nonprofit institution, or for an obligation to repay funds received as an educational benefit, scholarship or stipend[.]

Under the original language one could argue that a student loan owed to a trust, or one owed to a bank but guaranteed by the government would be dischargeable. Since the new language includes loans "guaranteed" by a governmental unit, the latter case is clearly included. Since the language also includes loans made under "any program" funded by any "non-profit institution", almost any loan by a trust or other organization for educational purposes is not dischargeable, at least if the courts interpret the word "institution" to include organizations such as trusts and other non-profit, non-educational organizations. Under the original language those might not have been included because the original language required that the "institution" be an institution of "higher education."

Not only has the preamble in subsection (8) been expanded to catch more fish in its nondischargeability net, but also subsection (8) has been narrowed to keep the fish from escaping through the net. First the five-year period was extended to seven. The seven-year period can be extended yet further by the parenthetical phrase found in (8)(A) "exclusive of any applicable extension of the repayment period." Thus, if one's first loan was due on January 2, 1988 and one procured a one-year forbearance from payment in 1990, the loan would fit within (8)(A)'s exception to the exception only after eight years had passed from January 2, 1988 (i.e., on January 3, 1996, not after seven years on January 3, 1995).

---

3. Pub.L. No. 89–329, § 439A, as added by Education Amendments of 1976, Pub.L. No. 94–482, § 127(a), 90 Stat. 2141 (repealed by Bankruptcy Reform Act of 1978, Pub. L. No. 95–598, § 317, 92 Stat. 2678).

b. Substantive Rules

For a loan to be denied discharge under (8) it first must be an educational loan. Doubtless there are cases lurking in the weeds that question what is and what is not educational, but they have not seen any significant action in the courts. (Since two of us make our living "educating" law students, we do not welcome a particularly searching inquiry into what is and what is not "educational.")

Nor is "loan" likely to cause much difficulty. One appellate case does address that question in the context of the scholarship program to encourage physicians to practice as primary care doctors in areas where there was a shortage. In *United States Dep't of Health and Human Services v. Smith*,[4] Mr. Smith borrowed $13,984 as a PSASP scholarship. Under the terms of the scholarship he was obliged either to repay the money with interest at the going rate or to serve one year as a primary care physician in an area where there was a doctor shortage for every year he received the scholarship. After graduation from medical school, Smith procured a four-year delay on his service while he took an ophthalmology residence (not a good sign for a prospective rural general practitioner). After he concluded his residency program, he declined to practice as a general practitioner in the back woods and, having made no payments on his loan, took Chapter 7.

Given that the present value of an ophthalmology degree is doubtless in the millions, it is hard to imagine a less appealing case. Armed with considerable gall if nothing more, Smith argued that his obligation did not constitute a "loan", but merely a "contingent scholarship". Thus, he maintained his liability was discharged because it did not fit within 523(a)(8). Remarkably he won in the bankruptcy court, but the Court of Appeals had no difficulty in concluding that his liability (which had grown to $27,841.44), constituted a debt once he had failed to fulfill the condition. One can almost hear the judge's teeth grinding and see the blood vessels standing out on his temple when he thought of Smith's avoiding this liability.

With the current language in (a)(8) there is very little room for argument that a loan procured from almost any source and used for education does not fit there. Presumably there are a few commercial loans used by students to pay their tuition, but all but a trivial part of those are in fact guaranteed by governmental agencies and thus included. In a case under the earlier language the court found that a loan funded by a private trust payable through a public college was not dischargeable.[5] This conclusion would be easier to reach under 523(a)(8) as it currently reads because loans would not only be "made by" governmental units (a state university), but also would be made under a program funded by a non-profit institution (the private trust).

---

4. 807 F.2d 122 (8th Cir.1986).

5. In re Shore, 707 F.2d 1337 (11th Cir. 1983).

c. *The Exceptions to Nondischargeability*

Each of the two exceptions, (A) and (B), presents an occasional interpretive problem. First is the question of how one measures the seven years in section 523(a)(8)(A). Courts are now agreed the period starts running on the date the first installment on the loan became due. The argument that the loan should be regarded as a series of separate installment loans and therefore that the five year period should run from the date of a particular installment has now been thoroughly discredited.[6] Assume a case in which the student debtor's obligation was to pay 36 monthly installments beginning January 2, 1988. The seven year period as to all of the installments would commence to run on January 2, 1988 and would not separate with respect to each installment. Therefore, if the debtor filed a petition in bankruptcy in Chapter 7 on January 3, 1995, the seven-year limitation would not prevent the discharge. If the debtor procures a period of forgiveness during the seven year period, that period is added to the seven years. In *Matter of Eckles*[7] the court held the same rule applied whether there was an entire suspension of payments for a period of time or merely a reduction. Relying in part upon federal regulations having to do with "forbearance", the court concluded that reduction and suspension entirely should have the same treatment and that each should extend the seven year period.

The guts of most cases under 523(a)(8) are to be found in the second part of the exception (a)(8)(B). This subsection allows the discharge only if continuing the liability would impose "an undue hardship on the debtor and the debtor's dependents." Note first a part of the section that has not received attention from any court. As the subsection reads, there must be hardship not merely to the debtor, but also to the debtor's dependents. The two nouns are connected by the conjunction "and". Hardship to one would not be enough. On a strict reading of the language, a debtor without dependents could never qualify for the exception. Apparently that argument has not been made, for it is not discussed even in cases where the courts point out that the debtor has no hardship because the debtor has no dependents.[8]

What is "undue hardship"? Undue hardship includes, but is not limited to, a consideration of the debtor's current status. Many law, medical and business students who soon will earn handsome salaries are, as students and for a period shortly thereafter, under considerable hardship. To show such short term hardship is not sufficient. The Commission on Bankruptcy recognized the problem.[9]

> In order to determine whether nondischargeability of the debt will impose "an undue hardship" on the debtor, the rate and amount of his future resources should be estimated reasonably in terms of ability to obtain, retain, and continue employment and the rate of pay that can be expected. Any unearned income or other wealth which the debtor can be expected to receive should also be taken into account. The total

---

6. Cf. United States v. Hogan, 43 B.R. 117 (D.Ariz.1984).

7. 52 B.R. 433 (E.D.Wis.1985).

8. Compare Brunner v. New York State Higher Educ. Services Corp., 831 F.2d 395 (2d Cir.1987); In re Andrews, 661 F.2d 702 (8th Cir.1981).

9. Collier on Bankruptcy, 2 Appendix at 140–41 (L. King, R. Levin & K. Klee 15th ed. 1979).

amount of income, its reliability, and the periodicity of its receipt should be adequate to maintain the debtor and his dependents, at a minimal standard of living within the management capability, as well as to pay the educational debt.

In a 1987 case, *Brunner v. New York State Higher Education (EDUC) Services* [10] the court rejected a debtor's hardship argument. Ms. Brunner had a bachelor's degree and a master's degree in social work. She had paid only a few hundred dollars on her $9,000 student loan. Bankruptcy Judge Schwartzberg found her debt dischargeable. On appeal his decision was reversed by Judge Haight in the District Court and that reversal was affirmed by the Court of Appeals *per curiam*. Judge Haight describes the debtor's status as follows:

> No specific testimony about appellee's annual expenses was elicited other than that her rent is $200 per month. At the time of the hearing she was receiving $258 per month in public assistance, $49 per month in food stamps, and Medicaid. She had been receiving this aid for approximately four months prior to the hearing. Her testimony as to her source of support prior to that time was vague. At the time of the hearing, she possessed a bank account holding $200, but two months prior to the hearing she withdrew $2,400 from her savings to purchase a used car. Upon her filing for bankruptcy four months prior to the hearing, her student loans constituted 80% of her total indebtedness.

> Appellee testified that she had sent out "over a hundred" resumes in search of employment in her chosen field of work but was unsuccessful. She noted that many of her classmates found themselves similarly unable to find such jobs. The extent to which she had attempted to find work outside her field was unclear. In response to her lawyer's inquiry as to whether she had sought clerical or other jobs, she replied, "I don't have secretarial skills, but I have applied for any position that I could find." She did not recount any specific jobs which she had sought and been refused. On cross-examination she conceded that she had done clerical work in the past. Although appellee was seeing a therapist for treatment of anxiety and depression due in part to her unemployment, she testified that she was capable of working.[11]

Rejecting Judge Schwartzberg's finding that the debtor had a psychological impairment because she was seeing a therapist, Judge Haight concluded that she was "apparently healthy, presumably intelligent, and well educated." [12] At the appellate level the Court of Appeals adopted the three part test that has been applied by Judge Haight and discussed it as follows:

> Based on legislative history and the decisions of other district and bankruptcy courts, the district court adopted a standard for "undue hardship" requiring a three-part showing: (1) that the debtor cannot maintain, based on current income and expenses, a "minimal" standard of living for herself and her dependents if forced to repay the loans; (2) that additional circumstances exist indicating that this state of affairs is likely to persist for a significant portion of the repayment period of the

10. 831 F.2d 395 (2d Cir.1987).
11. 46 B.R. at 757.
12. 46 B.R. at 757.

student loans; and (3) that the debtor has made good faith efforts to repay the loans. For the reasons set forth in the district court's order, we adopt this analysis. The first part of this test has been applied frequently as the minimum necessary to establish "undue hardship." (citations omitted) Requiring such a showing comports with common sense as well.

The further showing required by part two of the test is also reasonable in light of the clear congressional intent exhibited in section 523(a)(8) to make the discharge of student loans more difficult than that of other nonexcepted debt. Predicting future income is, as the district court noted, problematic. Requiring evidence not only of current inability to pay but also of additional, exceptional circumstances, strongly suggestive of continuing inability to repay over an extended period of time, more reliably guarantees that the hardship presented is "undue."

Under the test proposed by the district court, Brunner has not established her eligibility for a discharge of her student loans based on "undue hardship." The record demonstrates no "additional circumstances" indicating a likelihood that her current inability to find any work will extend for a significant portion of the loan repayment period. She is not disabled, nor elderly, and she has—so far as the record discloses—no dependents. No evidence was presented indicating a total foreclosure of job prospects in her area of training. In fact, at the time of the hearing, only ten months had elapsed since Brunner's graduation from her Master's program. Finally, as noted by the district court, Brunner filed for the discharge within a month of the date the first payment of her loans came due. Moreover, she did so without first requesting a deferment of payment, a less drastic remedy available to those unable to pay because of prolonged unemployment. Such conduct does not evidence a good faith attempt to repay her student loans.[13]

Presumably many debtors will be able to make a showing under the first part of the test that their current income and expenses provide only a minimal standard of living. The trouble for most will come under subsection (2). As we see in the quoted provisions, the courts are not receptive to the argument that healthy debtors with advanced degrees are unable to change their economic circumstances. At least in gross, there is a great deal of evidence that additional education improves one's income. Presumably the inference to be drawn from the statistics would be easier to overcome if one had a degree in social work than if one had a degree in plastic surgery. Nevertheless, *Brunner* shows the court's hostility even to a social worker's claims of bleak prospects.

The wild card that is likely to give the debtor a losing hand, even if she can meet subsections (1) and (2), is the good faith requirement in (3). Note that Judge Haight and the appellate court in *Brunner* were willing to draw inferences of bad faith because the debtor made no attempt to procure an extension and because she came to the bankruptcy court shortly after she was eligible for potential discharge.[14]

---

13. 831 F.2d 395, 396–97.

14. Accord In re Andrews, 661 F.2d 702 (8th Cir.1981); see also, Bryant v. Pennsylva-

Those who remain unable to find work may return to the bankruptcy court and make a motion under Rule 4007(b) to reopen the case. Under that Rule "a case may be reopened without payment of an additional filing fee for the purpose of filing a complaint to obtain a determination * * *." The court in *Brunner* notes that this option is open to debtors who after some additional period are incapable of improving their status.

d. Summary

As we have indicated above, the cases here hold little hope for a debtor. If anything, the anger of the judges at students who have been educated on subsidized debt and who later seek to avoid their student loan repayment is even greater than that of the Congress. Here the courts have narrowed, not expanded, the exception. The courts, particularly the appellate courts, are almost uniformly hostile to the debtor's claims.

§ 7–34 Exceptions to Discharge, Section 523, Introduction— Driving While Intoxicated, Section 523(a)(9)

In 1984 the political conscience of the nation in trying to deter drunk driving, stirred by such groups as Mothers Against Drunk Driving (MADD), finally reached the bankruptcy courts. At the behest of Senator John Danforth,[1] Congress enacted what may well be the most single-minded section of the Bankruptcy Code, certainly of the discharge provisions. It is section (a)(9), which originally provided that:

> (a) A discharge under section 727, 1141, 1228(a), 1228(b), or 1328(b) of this title does not discharge an individual debtor from any debt—
>
> * * *
>
> (9) to any entity, to the extent that such debt arises from a judgment or consent decree entered in a court of record against the debtor wherein liability was incurred by such debtor as a result of the debtor's operation of a motor vehicle while legally intoxicated under the laws or regulations of any jurisdiction within the United States or its territories wherein such motor vehicle was operated and within which such liability was incurred; * * *[2]

When it adopted section 523(a)(9), Congress sought three main objectives: (1) to ensure that those who caused injury by driving drunk did not

---

nia Higher Education Assistance Agency, 72 B.R. 913, 915 (Bankr. E.D.Pa. 1987); North Dakota State Board of Higher Educ. v. Frech, 62 B.R. 235 (Bankr. D.Minn.1986); Marion v. Pennsylvania Higher Education Assistance Agency (Matter of Marion), 61 B.R. 815 (Bankr. W.D.Pa.1986).

§ 7–34

1. Sen. Danforth, in introducing his legislation to amend Title 11, stated:

> Today there exists an unconscionable loophole in the bankruptcy statute which makes it possible for drunk drivers who have injured, killed, or caused property damage to others to escape civil liability for their actions by having their judgment debt discharged in Federal bankruptcy court. This loophole affords opportunities for scandalous abuse of judicial processes.

129 Cong. Rec. S1622 (daily ed. Feb. 24, 1983). Sen. Danforth then recounted the story of a drunk driver who was ordered to pay $600,000 to the families of three teenagers he had killed who then walked across the street to bankruptcy court to escape civil liability. Given this emotional language, it is no wonder Congress responded with 523(a)(9).

2. 11 U.S.C.A. § 523(a)(9) (superseded).

escape civil liability through the bankruptcy laws; (2) to protect the victims of drunk driving; and (3) to deter drunk driving.³ The drunk driving exception accomplished these objectives by excepting from discharge those "judgments or consent decrees" which were incurred as a result of the debtor's operation of a motor vehicle while intoxicated.

The original 523(a)(9) required that the creditor establish two elements. First, it had to show that the debt arose from a judgment or consent decree entered in a court of record as a result of the debtor's operation of a motor vehicle. Second, the debtor must have been operating the motor vehicle while legally intoxicated under the laws of the jurisdiction where it was operated.⁴ The first of these requirements has presented a major interpretational problem.

A literal reading of section 523(a)(9) required that a judgment or consent decree be entered in a court of record. If interpreted to mean that the creditor must have had a prepetition judgment or consent decree against the debtor before the debt would be nondischargeable, the section could be easily evaded. Debtors would be able to circumvent the nondischargeability by filing a petition in bankruptcy before an adverse judgment or consent decree is entered.⁵ That problem was addressed in the 1990 amendments. Section 523(a)(9) now provides that:

> (a) A discharge under section 727, 1141, 1228(a), 1228(b), or 1328(b) of this title does not discharge an individual debtor from any debt—
>
> * * *
>
> (9) for death or personal injury caused by the debtor's operation of a motor vehicle if such operation was unlawful because the debtor was intoxicated from using alcohol, a drug, or another substance;
> * * *⁶

This amendment was specifically designed to eliminate the "race to the courthouse" problem and to prevent debtor drivers from discharging substantial civil liability.⁷

Congressional haste to placate the anti-drunks also caused a second definitional problem. What debts arising from a judgment or consent decree were specified in (a)(9)? In *Lugo v. Paulsen*,⁸ the debtor, Lugo, was convicted of DWI in the Municipal Court of East Rutherford, New Jersey. The sentence consisted of a $250 fine, a $100 surcharge by the court, a six month revocation of Lugo's driver's license, and mandatory attendance at a twelve hour education program. Pursuant to the New Jersey Merit Rating Plan (NJMRP), the New Jersey Department of Motor Vehicles billed Lugo $3000

---

3. See In re Hudson, 859 F.2d 1418 (9th Cir.1988).

4. Whitson v. Middleton, 898 F.2d 950 (4th Cir.1990).

5. See Matter of Cain, 96 B.R. 115 (Bankr. N.D.Ohio 1988) (No state court action ever commenced to get a judgment or consent decree from a court of record, so claim discharged. Congress did not intend to have the bankruptcy courts used to try DWI cases.); In re Jackson, 77 B.R. 120 (Bankr. N.D.Ohio 1987) (Because § 523(a)(9) requires that debt be from judgment or consent decree, a civil action must at least have been commenced in state court prior to bankruptcy petition.).

6. 11 U.S.C.A. § 523(a)(9) (West Supp. 1991).

7. S. Rep. No. 434, 101st Cong., 2d Sess. 5–6, reprinted in 1990 U.S. Cong. & Admin. News 4065, 4068–70.

8. 886 F.2d 602 (3d Cir.1989), rehearing denied.

payable over three years as a surcharge to fund the New Jersey Automobile Full Insurance Underwriting Association. The surcharge is imposed upon all drivers convicted of DWI and results in a revocation of their driver's license for failure to pay. Lugo satisfied his criminal obligations but filed bankruptcy before his NJMRP surcharge was satisfied.

Judge Scirica writing for the Third Circuit Court of Appeals first had to determine if that claim was a "debt" under section 101(11). Relying on the broad definition of "debt", reinforced by the Supreme Court in *Kelly v. Robinson,* the court found the surcharge to be a debt. Since the Municipal Court judgment established liability and the surcharge statutorily arose with the conviction, the court held the debt to "arise from" a judgment or consent decree. While that interpretation was at odds with most cases that involve civil court judgments, the court could find no evidence of Congressional intent to limit the exception to civil tort liability. After a thorough analysis of the legislative history,[9] Judge Scirica found the court's interpretation to

---

9. As Judge Scirica found:

The initial legislative proposals in this area were never enacted. In 1982, Senator Danforth proposed a bill that would have added a subsection (e) to section 523:

Any injury resulting in a judgment based upon liability of the debtor where, in connection with such liability such debtor was found to have operated a motor vehicle while legally intoxicated shall be deemed to be a willful and malicious injury for purposes of subsection (a)(6) of this section.

128 Cong. Rec. 2846 (March 2, 1982). Thereafter, a version of section 523(a)(9) was introduced by Senator Dole as part of the Omnibus Bankruptcy Improvements Act of 1983 (the Omnibus Act). S. 445, 129 Cong. Rec. 9953, 9957 (April 27, 1983). After Senator Dole introduced the Omnibus Act, Senator Danforth remarked: "Subtitle D is a modified version of S. 605, a bill I introduced earlier this session * * * [which] would have defined drunk driving as a willful and malicious offense for purposes of the bankruptcy statute. The provision in the bill before us achieves the same result by specifically stating that debts arising from drunk driving shall be nondischargeable." 129 Cong.Rec. 9998 (April 27, 1983).

In his remarks accompanying the Omnibus Act, Senator Metzenbaum described the section on the dischargeability of debts incurred as a result of driving while intoxicated:

Also contained in this package is a modified version of a bill introduced by Senator Danforth which provides that a debt incurred as a result of drunk driving is not dischargeable. Under existing law, a debt resulting from a tortious act is nondischargeable only if the debt is the result of a 'willful and malicious injury' to the property or person of another. In most States, the act of drunk driver is grounded in negligence and is, thus, dischargeable. By making such debts nondischargeable, we can protect victims of the drunk driver and deter drunk driving.

129 Cong.Rec. 9974 (April 27, 1983) (statement of Senator Metzenbaum) * * * The Report of the Senate Judiciary Committee on Senator Dole's Omnibus Act, entitled "Amendments Relating to the Discharge of Debts Incurred by Persons Driving While Intoxicated," mirrors Senator Metzenbaum's statement, and concludes that "[w]here a debt was incurred by the debtor as a result of an act of drunk driving, that debt will not be dischargeable regardless of any court finding that willful, wanton, or reckless behavior was or was not involved." Sen. Rep. No. 98–65, 98th Cong., 1st Sess. 43–44 (1983).

Although the Omnibus Act was not enacted, section 523(a)(9) was eventually enacted as part of the Bankruptcy Amendments and Federal Judgeship Act of 1984, Pub.L. No. 98–353, 98 Stat. 333 (1984). Accompanying the Act is the statement of Congressman Rodino: "Subtitle D clarifies present law relating to the nondischargeability of debts incurred by drunk drivers. Debts incurred by persons driving while intoxicated are presumed to be willful and maliciously incurred under this provision." 130 Cong. Rec. H7489 (daily ed. June 29, 1984), reprinted in 1984 U.S.Code Cong. & Admin. News 576, 577.

At least one legislator's statement accompanying the [1984] version of section 523(a)(9) suggests that Congress was concerned with the dischargeability of judgments in which the debtor had been held liable for an injury resulting from an act of drunk driving. See 130 Cong.Rec. S8887 (daily ed. June 29, 1984) (remarks of Sena-

support one of the Congressional policies behind section 523(a)(9), that of deterring drunk driving. Further, the fact that the debt was owed to the State instead of an individual did not matter because section 523(a)(9) excepts debts owed to "any entity."

Although the surcharge may serve as a deterrent to drunk driving, it is not clear that Congress intended to include debts beyond civil court judgments and claims in section 523(a)(9). Senator Danforth's comments indicate that Congress was primarily concerned with protecting the tort victims of drunk drivers. The Third Circuit's reasoning is neither at odds with the express language of section 523(a)(9) nor with any expressed Congressional intent.[10]

Finally, the Bankruptcy Code does not define "motor vehicle." Automobiles, trucks, and motorcycles are motor vehicles but what about aircraft and boats? Despite Justice Holmes' decision to the contrary in *McBoyle v. United States*,[11] we suspect that the broad definition applied by one bankruptcy court in finding a motor boat to be a "motor vehicle" is appropriate for the bankruptcy section.[12]

The second element that a creditor must establish, that the debtor operated the motor vehicle while intoxicated has also created some problems for the courts. As with section 523(a)(5) dealing with support payments, the bankruptcy courts must consult state law to determine what is "drunk." The extent of that consultation is not entirely clear from the statute. A creditor may establish the intoxication element by showing a conviction on a charge of driving while intoxicated together with the civil court judgment.[13] The two judgments establish what is lacking in each of them individually.

It is not necessary for the creditor to show a civil or criminal judgment finding that the driver was under the influence of alcohol while driving.

tor Heflin), reprinted in 1984 U.S. Code Cong. & Admin. News 585 ("There is a modified version of a bill introduced by Senator Danforth which provides that a debt incurred as a result of an accident caused by drunk driving is not dischargeable.") The legislative history does not indicate, however, that this was the only type of debt that Congress intended to except from discharge under section 523(a)(9). Indeed, Congress eventually enacted a much broader exception to discharge than that originally proposed by Senator Danforth * * *. In addition, the remarks of legislators suggest that their concern with the dischargeability of debts resulting from acts of drunk driving stemmed as much from a desire to deter drunk driving as to protect the victims of accidents * * *.

886 F.2d at 609–610.

10. But see In re Gill, 93 B.R. 684 (Bankr. W.D.Mo.1988) (the fact that the debtor "totaled" his car in an accident while intoxicated does not render his debt to the seller of the car for the purchase price nondischargeable. Debt did not "arise from" the operation of the car while under the influence).

The 1990 amendments now prevent discharge under Chapter 13 of any restitution included in a sentence on a debtor's conviction of crime. 11 U.S.C.A. § 1328(a)(3) (West Supp. 1991). However, they do not speak to this larger issue.

11. 283 U.S. 25, 51 S.Ct. 340, 75 L.Ed. 816 (1931) (airplane not a motor vehicle under the National Motor Vehicle Theft Act (18 U.S.C.A. § 408 (1919))).

12. Williams v. Radivoj, 111 B.R. 361 (S.D.Fla.1989) (attempting to classify a motor boat as outside of the definition of "motor vehicle" was no safe harbor).

13. Matter of Pahule, 849 F.2d 1056 (7th Cir.1988) (guilty plea to drunk driving and civil negligence judgment satisfied 523(a)(9) requirements); In re Scholz, 111 B.R. 651 (Bankr. N.D.Ohio 1990) (pleas of "no contest" to DWI charge and default judgment alleging only negligence established exception to discharge); In re Keating, 80 B.R. 115 (Bankr. E.D.Wis.1987); In re Wright, 66 B.R. 403 (Bankr. S.D.Ind.1986) (guilty plea of public intoxication without reference to automobile usage not enough to except judgment from discharge).

Since many drunk drivers plead to lesser offenses, drunk driving charges may never be prosecuted in some cases. Where there is no DWI conviction, the creditor may show the state court judgment or consent decree and then prove to the bankruptcy court that the liability resulted from the debtor's operation of the vehicle while drunk.[14] In so doing, the bankruptcy court must rely on the law of the jurisdiction where the debtor was operating the motor vehicle to find the intoxication.[15]

In *Whitson v. Middleton*,[16] the debtor was convicted of reckless driving after driving his car into a motorcycle and causing severe injuries to the cyclist. The charge, however, did not include any reference to driving while under the influence of alcohol. In seeking to determine if the subsequent civil judgment which arose from the same circumstances was dischargeable, the Fourth Circuit looked to Virginia law on legal intoxication. The court found that " '[a]ny person who has drunk enough alcoholic beverages to so affect his manner, disposition, speech, muscular movement, general appearance or behavior, as to be apparent to observation, shall be deemed to be intoxicated' ".[17] It found that intoxication could be established from all relevant evidence; evidence of blood-alcohol content is just one method of proof. Thus, the arresting officer's testimony of the debtor's unsteadiness, bloodshot and glassy eyes, disheveled clothing, slow, slurred speech, and the strong odor of alcohol on his person all supported the bankruptcy court's conclusion that the debtor was drunk. The fact the debtor was never charged with drunk driving was not important.

In conclusion, there is little sympathy and little hope for a debtor attempting to discharge a liability arising out of drunk driving. The courts may be appropriately skeptical when there is little if any evidence of intoxication,[18] but most arguments trying to disprove causation[19] or to require a criminal conviction fail.

C. REAFFIRMATION, SECTION 524(C)
§ 7–35 Introduction and Overview of Reaffirmation

As every first-year law student learns in Contracts, the reaffirmation of a debt that has been discharged in bankruptcy is an enforceable contract at

---

14. Whitson v. Middleton, 898 F.2d 950 (4th Cir.1990) (section 523(a)(9) does not require a legal determination by a state court that liability resulted from the use of a car while intoxicated. The creditor may first show the judgment and then prove the intoxication to the bankruptcy court); In re Humphrey, 102 B.R. 629 (Bankr. S.D.Ohio 1989) (the civil judgment need not establish intoxication, the bankruptcy court can make that determination); Matter of Brunson, 82 B.R. 634 (Bankr. S.D.Ga.1988); In re Lewis, 69 B.R. 600 (Bankr. S.D.Fla.1987).

15. In re Humphrey, 102 B.R. 629 (Bankr. S.D.Ohio 1989) (ultimate issue is whether the debtor was legally intoxicated under state law); In re Vorek, 95 B.R. 599 (Bankr. S.D.Ind.1989) (evidence of two beers consumed six hours before accident not enough to prove intoxication under state law); Matter of Brunson, 82 B.R. 634 (Bankr. S.D.Ga.1988) (circumstantial evidence is enough to find intoxication under state law); Matter of Hart, 83 B.R. 840 (Bankr. M.D.Ga.1987) (not sufficient evidence of intoxication to make consent decree entered in state court nondischargeable).

16. 898 F.2d 950 (4th Cir.1990).

17. 898 F.2d at 952 (citing Va. Code § 4–2).

18. We were able to find only two decisions where the bankruptcy court found insufficient evidence of intoxication to sustain nondischargeability. See note 15 supra.

19. See In re Hodak, 119 B.R. 516 (Bankr. W.D.Pa.1990) (no need for the creditor to show that alcohol caused the accident. The result of intoxicated operation of a motor vehicle is presumed); but see In re Christiansen, 80 B.R. 481 (W.D.Mo.1987) (intoxication must be a causal factor in the collision under Missouri law).

common law. Such enforceability is given as one of the principal examples of "moral consideration." Even though the debtor was completely freed of his legal obligations by the discharge in bankruptcy, a moral obligation to pay the debt is—at common law—sufficient to bind even though the reaffirming debtor gets nothing else in the bargain.

For reasons that are not entirely clear to us, debtors who have been discharged in Chapter 7 have often chosen to reaffirm some of their debts. A debtor might reaffirm out of selfish interest, (for example, that might be the only way to keep the car that would otherwise be repossessed by a secured creditor), or one might reaffirm to settle a claim by a creditor who argued that its debt was not dischargeable because of section 523, or a debtor might wish to curry favor with a particularly important creditor and so ensure that credit would be available in the future. In all of those cases reaffirmation might be an economically sensible act.

There are also reaffirmations that are not motivated by the debtor's selfish economic interest. The debtor may feel a duty to a friend who lent him money in a time of need, or even to a commercial creditor who treated him well when he could not borrow money from others.

Reaffirmations motivated solely by the debtor's economic or moral interest are difficult to distinguish from those where the reaffirmation is motivated at least in part by lies or by threats of the creditor who benefits from the reaffirmation. For example, a reaffirmation might be stimulated by a creditor's assertion that failure to reaffirm would mean that the debtor would never again be able to borrow from him or from any other creditor. The creditor might claim that assets subject to a security interest could never be replaced at any reasonable price.

At the time of the 1978 Code, those sympathetic to the debtor's plight argued that most reaffirmations were not sensible and were in fact the result of creditor overreaching. The section proposed by the National Bankruptcy Commission in 1973 marked the high point of this sentiment. Section 4–507 stated that

> notwithstanding any other law to the contrary, a debt extinguished by discharge under [bankruptcy] shall not be revived or reaffirmed or be all or part of any bargain creating a new debt. Any judgment, whenever obtained, that a debtor is personally liable to pay a debt extinguished by discharge is null and void.[1]

The only exceptions to the rule so stated involve the possibility of redemption of collateral by the payment of its value or the settlement of a lawsuit in which the creditor attacked the dischargeability of his debt. It should not be surprising that the quoted section was the target of heavy fire from creditors, particularly consumer creditors, who often benefit from reaffirmations. Section 524(c) finally enacted in 1978 read in full as follows:

> (c) An agreement between a holder of a claim and the debtor, the consideration for which, in whole or in part, is based on a debt that is dischargeable in a case under this title is enforceable only to any extent

---

§ 7–35

1. Report of the Commission on the Bankruptcy Laws of the United States, H.R. Doc. No. 137, 93d Cong., 1st Sess., pt. II, at 142 (1973).

enforceable under applicable nonbankruptcy law, whether or not discharge of such debt is waived, only if—

>(1) such agreement was made before the granting of the discharge under section 727, 1141, or 1328 of this title;

>(2) the debtor has not rescinded such agreement within 30 days after such agreement becomes enforceable;

>(3) the provisions of subsection (d) of this section have been complied with; and

>(4) in a case concerning an individual, to the extent that such debt is a consumer debt that is not secured by real property of the debtor, the court approves such agreement as—

>>(A)(i) not imposing an undue hardship on the debtor or a dependent of the debtor; and

>>(ii) in the best interest of the debtor; or

>>(B)(i) entered into in good faith; and

>>(ii) in settlement of litigation under section 523 of this title, or providing for redemption under section 722 of this title.

One can regard section 524(c) as a tactical retreat by the debtors' advocates. Presumably they hoped to erect enough barbed wire and other obstacles around the reaffirmation that no creditor would ever be able to achieve success under 524(c). Not only must the agreement be reached before the discharge but there is a 30 day cooling off period and in the case of consumer debts the court had to approve the agreement as not imposing "undue hardship." The reaffirmation had to be found either in the "best interest of the debtor" or in a good faith settlement of litigation. In addition, the reaffirmation could be approved only if the debtor appeared in court under subsection 524(d) and was admonished by the court.

Experience under the 1978 Code has shown this defense of uncertain effect. Either because creditor overreaching is yet stronger than thought, because creditors are more aggressive and less scrupulous than first thought, or because the drafters underestimated the power of the moral compulsion to reaffirm, reaffirmations still abound despite the obstacles in subsection (c).

In accordance with the law of unintended consequences, the obstacles designed to deter the creditors and debtors from reaffirmation in fact caused difficulty for a group with no direct interest in this question, namely the bankruptcy courts. They are the principal group inconvenienced by the rule because any consumer reaffirmation required the elaborate judicial findings on undue hardship and on the best interest of the debtor. Even in circumstances where the debtor wished to reaffirm and where his counsel did not oppose that, the court still had to approve, and if it were to do its job properly, to hear evidence on undue hardship and best interest.

Emboldened partly by judicial discomfort with the courts' role, creditors pressed their attack in the 1984 amendments. That attack caused a further retreat to the position that we now see in revised 524(c) which reads in full as follows.

(c) An agreement between a holder of a claim and the debtor, the consideration for which, in whole or in part, is based on a debt that is dischargeable in a case under this title is enforceable only to any extent enforceable under applicable nonbankruptcy law, whether or not discharge of such debt is waived, only if—

(1) such agreement was made before the granting of the discharge under section 727, 1141, 1228, or 1328 of this title;

(2) such agreement contains a clear and conspicuous statement which advises the debtor that the agreement may be rescinded at any time prior to discharge or within sixty days after such agreement is filed with the court, whichever occurs later, by giving notice of rescission to the holder of such claim;

(3) such agreement has been filed with the court and, if applicable, accompanied by a declaration or an affidavit of the attorney that represented the debtor during the course of negotiating an agreement under this subsection, which states that such agreement—

(A) represents a fully informed and voluntary agreement by the debtor; and

(B) does not impose an undue hardship on the debtor or a dependent of the debtor;

(4) the debtor has not rescinded such agreement at any time prior to discharge or within sixty days after such agreement is filed with the court, whichever occurs later, by giving notice of rescission to the holder of such claim;

(5) the provisions of subsection (d) of this section have been complied with; and

(6)(A) in a case concerning an individual who was not represented by an attorney during the course of negotiating an agreement under this subsection, the court approves such agreement as—

(i) not imposing an undue hardship on the debtor or a dependent of the debtor; and

(ii) in the best interest of the debtor.

(B) Subparagraph (A) shall not apply to the extent that such debt is a consumer debt secured by real property.

Note the many changes. Now the debtor has until the time of discharge or 60 days after the reaffirmation agreement is filed with the court (whichever is later) to retract. In that sense the reaffirmation right was restricted by the 1984 amendment. In other respects it has been expanded. Under 524(c)(3) a debtor represented by a lawyer need not get court approval if the lawyer represents that the agreement is fully informed and voluntary and will not impose an "undue hardship on the debtor or a dependent of the debtor."

The consequence of the 1984 amendment was to remove the bankruptcy judge from the process of approving every single reaffirmation. In practice it removes the court from the large percentage of all reaffirmations, for in most of those the attorney for the debtor will have made the requisite representation under 524(c)(3).

What has caused this movement from the Commission's proposal in 1973 of essentially no reaffirmation to a law that has made reaffirmation almost as easy as under the Act of 1898? Does it rise exclusively from creditor self-interest? Or does it reflect a moral judgment of the people, including debtors, that certain debts should be repaid? It is possible that the Commission drafters of the proposed revision were engaging in a paternalistic judgment that debtors (and particularly consumer debtors) were completely economic people with no moral feeling, or worse that they should be forced into that mode even if they did not conform to it. In judicial judgments about "undue hardship" under section 524, one sometimes senses an expression of paternalistic superiority where, for example, the debtor desperately wants to keep the Cadillac and the judge thinks keeping a "luxury" automobile will pose an undue hardship.[2] At least one reading of the events between 1978 and 1991 is that even the poorest consumer debtors feel obligated to pay certain creditors, and are willing to go some length to fulfill those obligations by reaffirming debts. Another reading is that creditors have more political power and used it to shape the law in their favor.

§ 7–36 Procedure

In order to reaffirm, the debtor and the creditor must enter into an agreement and the agreement must not be rescinded by the debtor within the period granted by section 524. One should note that section 524(c) renders reaffirmation agreements effective "only if" the various terms described at length above in section 524(c) are followed. Absent such reaffirmation the injunction in section 524(a)(2) applies to the liability. Most, if not all, attempts to get a reaffirmation outside of the boundaries of section 524(c) would constitute a violation of that injunction. Although section 524(f) states that nothing "prevents a debtor from voluntarily repaying any debt," even the merest hints by the creditor that repayment of a discharged debt is a condition to further loans or services could constitute a violation of the injunction if those hints were regarded as an "act to collect or recover" the debt in violation of the injunction in section 524(a)(2).

In *In re Smurzynski*[1] the creditor insisted that the debtor sign papers showing an indebtedness in excess of the amount actually received on the new loan, where the debtor had been discharged in a bankruptcy in 1980 and was returning to the same creditor for a new loan in 1985. Apparently the creditor included the amount of the discharged debt in the new loan. The debtor brought suit in bankruptcy court and the court denied the creditor's motion to dismiss. Similarly, in *Matter of Hellums*[2] the court found the continuation of a postpetition wage assignment violated the stay, and would presumably violate the injunction if the discharge had been granted.

---

2. See Matter of Bryant, 43 B.R. 189 (Bankr. E.D.Mich.1984).

2. 772 F.2d 379 (7th Cir.1985).

§ 7–36

1. 72 B.R. 368 (Bankr. N.D.Ill. 1987).

That said, nothing prohibits a creditor from denying service to a debtor or refusing to lend to a debtor because that debtor had been through bankruptcy and had discharged a particular creditor's debt. Section 525(a) prohibits discrimination only by a governmental unit. If a denial of future credit or service was not tied to a recovery of a debt, there would be no violation of section 524(a)(2) injunction, even in circumstances in which the creditor might be seeking to make an example of the debtor. This causes the ironic consequence that it would not be a violation either of section 524 or of 525 for a creditor to make a complete pariah of a debtor and refuse utterly to deal with him. But it would be a violation of section 524(a)(2) to take a more generous position, namely, to agree to make a new loan to the debtor if the debtor paid off the discharged liability.

Perhaps there are cases unknown to us on the question what is a voluntary payment under section 524(f), but few of those have come to court. The ones that have come to court are mostly clumsy attempts to avoid the injunction.[3]

There are six specific conditions in section 524(c). First, the agreement must be made before the granting of the discharge. In most cases the "granting" of the discharge occurs at or shortly before a discharge hearing several months after the petition was filed. In Chapter 7 the discharge speaks as of the date of the petition, but the "granting" of that discharge is the date of the order under section 727. Second, the agreement must have a "clear and conspicuous statement" that advises the debtor of his right to rescind until the discharge or until 60 days after the agreement is filed with the court, whichever is later. Although the Bankruptcy Code has no guidelines for conspicuousness, small print in a long agreement surely will not do. Where a judge thinks there is overreaching, even relatively large print may not be satisfactory.[4]

---

3. See Matter of Hellums, 772 F.2d 379 (7th Cir.1985); In re Brinkman, 123 B.R. 611 (Bankr. N.D.Ind. 1991); In re Bowling, 116 B.R. 659 (Bankr. S.D.Ind.1990); Van Meter v. American State Bank, 89 B.R. 32 (W.D.Ark. 1988); In re Kendrick, 75 B.R. 451 (Bankr. N.D.Ga.1987); In re Smurzynski, 72 B.R. 368 (Bankr. N.D.Ill. 1987).

4. See In re Wallace, 102 B.R. 54 (Bankr. E.D.N.C.1989). The agreement that appeared to anger Judge Small in this case, which he held violated the conspicuousness requirement, reads in full as follows:

REAFFIRMATION AGREEMENT AND
DECLARATION OF DEBTOR'S
ATTORNEY: ROBERT U. JOHNSEN

This Reaffirmation Agreement made as of this 19th day of May 1989, between GENERAL ELECTRIC CAPITAL CORPORATION, as servicing agent for the GOVERNMENT NATIONAL MORTGAGE ASSOCIATION ("Creditor") and Joseph E. Wallace collectively (Debtor).

1. On April 6, 1989, a petition for relief under 11 U.S.C. Chapter 7 was filed by Debtor in the United States Bankruptcy Court for the Eastern District of North Carolina, in Cause No. 89–00895–SN7. On the date of the filing of such petition, Debtor was, and still is, indebted to Creditor for $6,904.69, pursuant to the terms of a contract dated November 30, 1977, held by Creditor for the purchase of a manufactured home 1977 Pinecrest, 60 X 24 Serial # L–1358P A & B ("the Manufactured Home"). A copy of said contract is annexed hereto.

2. Debtor desires to reaffirm the above-described debt and to retain possession of the Manufactured Home, notwithstanding the fact that Debtor may have the unsecured portion of such debt discharged pursuant to 11 U.S.C. § 727. Therefore, in good and valuable consideration, the receipt and sufficiency of which are hereby acknowledged, Debtor agrees and promises to pay Creditor the above-described debt and otherwise abide by the terms of the original contract described above and annexed hereto.

3. Debtor is of the opinion that the value of the Manufactured Home is equal to the principal balance herein reaffirmed.

4. The stay afforded by 11 U.S.C. § 362 is hereby lifted and the right of redemption un-

Third, if the debtor is represented by a lawyer, the agreement and a declaration of that lawyer must be filed with the court. The lawyer declaration must state that the agreement is made by a fully informed debtor, is voluntary and does not impose an undue hardship. The requirement that the *lawyer* certify presents an uncomfortable and potentially troublesome question for the lawyer. The lawyer must make that judgment even though his client is in no sense incapacitated and even though the client desperately wishes to reaffirm. How does the lawyer represent his client? How, for example, does the lawyer protect himself from a client who later defaults and turns on his lawyer when the creditor sues—arguing that the reaffirmation imposed an undue hardship and the lawyer should have protected him from his own folly? In reality all of this may be nothing more than a clever congressional attempt to give the appearance that an independent third party must pass on the proposed reaffirmation and thus to give the debtor greater bargaining power than he would otherwise have.

Fourth, the agreement is invalid if the debtor rescinds before the later of the discharge or 60 days after the reaffirmation is filed in court. These are important timing requirements for the creditor. A wise creditor will ensure that the 60 days have passed prior to the discharge so that the debtor is not left with a period after the discharge in which to disavow.

Section 524(c) requires, fifth, compliance with 524(d). Subsection (d) requires that the court "shall hold a hearing at which the debtor shall appear in person and at such hearing the court shall" admonish the debtor. As we indicate below, there are pitfalls here both for the creditor and the debtor. If the hearing is not held, the reaffirmation may be held invalid. If the hearing is held after the 60 day period and after the discharge it is, in the words of one judge, like giving "*Miranda* warnings after a conviction."

Finally, the reaffirmation of an individual not represented by a lawyer must be blessed by the court as in the "best interest of the debtor" and not imposing "undue hardship." That approval is not necessary to the extent the debt is a consumer debt secured by real property, i.e. a mortgage debt.

der 11 U.S.C. § 722 is hereby waived and barred.

5. Upon the occurrence of any of the following, Debtor shall immediately surrender possession of the Manufactured Home to Creditor, and in the event Debtor fails to so surrender upon demand of Creditor, Debtor shall immediately surrender same to the U.S. Marshall, who is employed and authorized to take possession of the Manufactured Home upon failure to so surrender:

(a) Debtor fails to furnish sufficient proof of insurance required by the original contract or fails to make any payment when due, or otherwise fails to comply with the terms of this Reaffirmation Agreement or the original contract subject to any right to cure which Debtor may possess under applicable state or federal law; or

(b) Debtor rescinds this Reaffirmation Agreement as provided in paragraph 8 herein before it becomes enforceable.

6. If (5)(a) or (b) occurs, then all payments made herein up to the time of said occurrence shall be considered reimbursement to Creditor for the fair rental value for the use of the Manufactured Home and will not be refundable to Debtor.

7. Debtor will make voluntary past due payments to Creditor in the sum of $–0– and begin making payments pursuant to this Reaffirmation Agreement and the original contract on July 1, 1989.

8. This Reaffirmation Agreement may be rescinded at any time prior to discharge or within sixty (60) days after this Reaffirmation Agreement is filed with the Court, whichever occurs later, by giving notice of rescission to Creditor at the following address: General Electric Credit Corporation, P.O. Box 420275, Houston, Texas 77242–0275.

IN WITNESS WHEREOF, the parties have executed this Reaffirmation Agreement as of the day and year first above written.

§ 7-37 Best Interest and Undue Hardship

Before the 1984 amendments the courts had to approve all reaffirmation agreements as not imposing undue hardship and in the best interest of the debtor. The best interest and undue hardship rules survive, but the court need address them only in a minority of the cases. But, of course, the lawyer who makes a certification under section 524(c)(3) must certify no "undue hardship."

What is in the best interest of the debtor and what is undue hardship are hopelessly subjective questions. It is not even clear that the statute speaks solely of the debtor's economic interest. It could also be speaking of the debtor's soul—peace of mind that comes because one behaves consistent with his own moral standard. Because such agreements call for inherently personal moral judgments, courts are rightfully squeamish about making them.

Presumably something is in the best interest of the debtor if it is in his economic interest. If, for example, a debtor wished to reaffirm a $5,000 debt to purchase a $5,000 pickup truck and any substitute for his pickup would cost $6,000 it would be in his interest to reaffirm. But what of the case in which he wishes to reaffirm a $10,000 debt in order to keep a pickup truck worth only $5,000, is that in his best interest? How does one factor in the possibility there are no other pickup trucks at any price available to the debtor because no one else will lend him money?

What is undue hardship? The kind of deprivation that is routinely suffered by some members of society to gratify wishes for cocaine, for a fancy car or a nice house surely subject those persons to "hardship,"—perhaps undue hardship in the eyes of others. To what extent should the lawyer or the court be influenced by the debtor's profligate but sincere choice?

In *In re McGrann*[1], the debtor sought to have a reaffirmation agreement approved for two consumer debts, $972.00 for a Magnavox color television set and $4,710.04 for a 1972 Buick Electra and a 1978 Suzuki motorcycle. The court found the present value of the items to be approximately $425.00 for the television, $600.00 for the Buick, and $2,100.00 for the motorcycle, far below the amount of the reaffirmed debt. In looking at the "best interest" of the debtors, an analysis was made of both the economics of the reaffirmations and the specific factual setting. The court agreed that the debt for the car and the motorcycle should be reaffirmed despite the fact that they appeared to reduce the debtor's wealth. Both vehicles were necessary as transportation to and from work as there was no public transportation. The court refused to reaffirm the debt for the television, however, questioning "the necessity of such an expensive television set or even the necessity of a television set at all"![2]

§ 7-37

1. 6 B.R. 612 (Bankr. E.D.Pa. 1980).

2. Id. at 613; see also In re Wallace, 102 B.R. 54 (Bankr. E.D.N.C.1989); In re Hirte, 71 B.R. 249 (Bankr. D. Ore. 1986); Matter of Malagesi, 39 B.R. 629 (E.D.Pa. 1984); In re Long, 22 B.R. 152 (Bankr. D.Me.1982); In re Leonard, 12 B.R. 91 (Bankr. D.Md.1981); In re Hinkle, 9 B.R. 283 (Bankr. D.Md.1981); In re Berkich, 7 B.R. 483 (Bankr. E.D.Pa. 1980); In re Delano, 7 B.R. 72 (Bankr. D.Me.1980); In re Jenkins, 4 B.R. 651 (Bankr. E.D.Va.1980); Matter of Avis, 3 B.R. 205 (Bankr. S.D.Ohio 1980).

One court found that a debtor's reaffirmation of a balance of $1,549 to cover certain household goods (a bed, rug and some other items) with a replacement value of $800 would impose undue hardship. Undeterred, the debtor filed a second request after the first rebuff and pointed out that her son and the godfather of the son would help to pay. Sticking to his Calvinist position, the judge found that the need for the son and the godfather to contribute *reinforced* his conclusion of hardship. While that judge seemed to be unduly paternalistic, one should note that he suggested the possibility of converting to Chapter 13 or of a redemption under 722.[3]

§ 7–38 Timing and Omission of the Admonition Hearing

Section 524(d) requires that the debtor appear, that the court hold a hearing, and that the court inform the debtor about the fact that he need not reaffirm and the effect of his doing so. In a number of cases and for reasons unexplained, the discharge has been granted without any such hearing being held. Since the 1984 amendments the court is not always required to hold a hearing at the time of discharge, rather it "may do so" if there is no reaffirmation.

What of the case in which the discharge is granted, the time for retraction of the reaffirmation passes, but there is never any admonition hearing? Several courts have held that the hearing is a *sine qua non* to reaffirmation that cannot be waived. Those courts find that a reaffirmation made without the admonishment hearing cannot be enforced.[1] One court has taken the opposite position. In *In re Richardson*[2] the debtor signed a reaffirmation and was granted a discharge without a hearing. Richardson later challenged the reaffirmation on the ground that the hearing had not been held. The court found that the debtor was estopped from challenging the reaffirmation where he had waited until the bar date on the creditor's antidischarge claim under section 523(a)(2).

At least on the face of it *Richardson* is in conflict with the other cases where there has been no hearing, but conceivably the cases can be distinguished. In *Richardson* it appears that the lawyer who represented the debtor at the time of the reaffirmation and the discharge was the one who later sued to have the reaffirmation set aside. In at least one of the cases that allowed tardy disavowal of the reaffirmation because of the lack of a hearing, the lawyer for the debtor changed between the reaffirmation and the challenge of the reaffirmation. In effect, Judge Paskay in *Richardson* may be saying that a single party, namely the lawyer, cannot manipulate the process and hope that the creditor will not insist upon a hearing so as not to avoid a reaffirmation. The rule of this case may be that a debtor and his lawyer undertake an implicit obligation to do what is necessary to make the reaffirmation valid when the debtor agrees to it. More specifically, the debtor who, represented by counsel, negotiates a reaffirmation agreement

---

3. In re Sampson, 51 B.R. 13 (Bankr. D.D.C.1984); cf. In re Wallace, 102 B.R. 54 (Bankr. E.D.N.C. 1989) (good faith); see also In re Bryant, 43 B.R. 189 (Bankr. E.D.Mich.1984); In re Long, 22 B.R. 152 (Bankr. D.Me.1982); In re Berkich, 7 B.R. 483 (Bankr. E.D.Pa. 1980).

§ 7–38

1. In re Roth, 43 B.R. 484 (N.D.Ill. 1984); In re Churchill, 89 B.R. 878 (Bankr. D. Colo. 1988).

2. 102 B.R. 254 (Bankr. M.D. Fla.1989).

should be stuck with that agreement even though there is no admonishment hearing.

In re Davis[3] presents another conundrum under the current wording of 524(c) and (d). Section 524(c) permits disavowal until the discharge or 60 days after the agreement is filed with the court, whichever occurs later, in which to disavow the reaffirmation. Assume that a reaffirmation is signed on day one and filed with the court on day two. Assume that the discharge order is signed on day 70 and on day 80 the admonishment hearing required by 524(d) is held. On the hearing date both of the events ending the right of disavowal have occurred (discharge and 60 days' passage), not so?

The second sentence of section 524(d) states that "if a discharge has been granted" then a hearing shall be held. By using the present perfect tense it sounds as though the sentence contemplates first the discharge and then the hearing. Yet that cannot be so. Presumably the whole idea for the admonishment is to give the debtor information that might lead him to disavow his reaffirmation agreement. As the court points out in *Davis*, its time for disavowal will have passed if the 60 days has run and the discharge order has been signed prior to that hearing. Congress could not have meant that. To keep it from happening, presumably the discharge order should not be signed prior to the hearing provided in 524(d). It should be up to the local rule and to the lawyers for the debtor acting within the rule to ensure that the events described in *Davis* do not occur. There the judge compared the reaffirmation warning to a *Miranda* warning given after conviction.

§ 7-39 Reaffirmation, Redemption, Negotiation and the Secured Creditor

It is clear of course that the creditor has no right to force a debtor to reaffirm. It is less clear, but also true, that the debtor has no right to force the creditor to agree to a reaffirmation. In a large share of all the reaffirmation cases the debtor is interested in reaffirming because he sees that as the only plausible way of retaining his automobile, mobile home or some other item subject to a creditor's security interest. If the debtor were able to keep the goods and pay less than the total amount due on the debt, he might be even happier. Courts generally recognize that the debtor enjoys other options in these circumstances other than reaffirmation.

First, the debtor can redeem the collateral under section 722. It enables a debtor to prevent enforcement of a lien on exempt or abandoned consumer goods securing a dischargeable consumer debt by *redeeming* the collateral, that is, by paying the creditor's allowed secured claim. In whole section 722 provides:

> An individual debtor may, whether or not the debtor has waived the right to redeem under this section, redeem tangible personal property intended primarily for personal, family, or household use, from a lien securing a dischargeable consumer debt, if such property is exempted under section 522 of this title or has been abandoned under section 554

---

3. 106 B.R. 701 (Bankr. S.D. Ala. 1989).

of this title, by paying the holder of such lien the amount of the allowed secured claim of such holder that is secured by such lien.[1]

It applies only in Chapter 7.[2]

The real significance of redemption is in the amount the debtor pays. It is the "allowed secured claim," which is not necessarily the same as the amount of the secured debt. The amount of the allowed secured claim is rather the *lesser of* the secured debt *or* the value of the collateral.[3] To the extent the debt exceeds the value, the lien is void [4] and the naked debt is an unsecured claim [5] which the bankruptcy discharges. This reduction in the secured debt is not welcomed by the secured creditor but his consent to redemption is not necessary.[6]

How the redemption amount is payable is critically important. The debtor is typically cash and credit poor. As a practical matter, therefore, the debtor can redeem only if he can do so by paying the redemption amount in installment payments. The courts nevertheless refuse to recognize redemption by installment.[7] The Sixth Circuit reasoned in *In re Bell* [8] that to construe section 722 to allow installment redemption is to read out of the Code the reaffirmation process of section 524(c) [9]. There would be no reason

§ 7–39

1. 11 U.S.C.A. § 722.

2. Section 722 resides in Chapter 7's Subchapter II which applies only in Chapter 7 cases. 11 U.S.C.A. § 103(b). A Chapter 13 debtor can nevertheless achieve the same effect. See, e.g., In re Hargis, 103 B.R. 912, 913–17 (Bankr. E.D.Tenn.1989) ("Once a debtor in a chapter 13 case pays in full the allowed amount of the secured creditor's claim, the lien on the collateral is satisfied and the debtor has in effect accomplished a redemption through deferred payments * * * " though she later converts to Chapter 7.); In re Estep, 96 B.R. 87, 88 (Bankr. E.D.Ky.1988) (debtor who paid amount of secured claim under Chapter 13 plan had redeemed); In re Tunget, 96 B.R. 89 (Bankr. W.D.Ky.1988) (lien was lost upon debtor paying Chapter 13 plan which provided for secured debt to extent the claim was an allowed secured claim); but compare Matter of Dennis, 31 B.R. 128, 131 (Bankr. M.D.Ga. 1983) (where debtor paid amount of allowed secured claim under Chapter 13 plan and then converted to Chapter 7 the debtor would not be deemed to have redeemed the collateral).

3. A claim is a "secured claim" only to the extent of the collateral's value. 11 U.S.C.A. § 506(a). In this context value usually means fair market value. In re Bell, 700 F.2d 1053, 1055 n.3 (6th Cir.1983); see also In re Polk, 76 B.R. 148, 150 (Bankr. 9th Cir.1987) ("Under this section [§ 722], a Chapter 7 debtor may redeem certain secured property by paying the creditor the approximate fair market value of the property or the amount of the lien, which is less."); compare In re King, 75 B.R. 287, 290–91 (Bankr. S.D.Ohio 1987) (value obtainable at a commercially reasonable sale). "Some bankruptcy courts have established the fair market value [for § 722] to be equivalent to the wholesale value." In re Redding, 34 B.R. 971, 973 (Bankr. M.D.Pa.1983).

The reference date for valuation is "the later of the date upon which the debtor files his request seeking to establish the amount required to redeem specific collateral or the date upon which such a request, if contested, is heard by the Court * * *." In re King, 75 B.R. 287, 290 (Bankr. S.D.Ohio 1987).

4. 11 U.S.C.A. § 506(d).

5. Id.

6. Fed. R. Bankr. P. 6008; In re Pendlebury, 94 B.R. 120, 122 (Bankr. E.D.Tenn.1988) ("Redemption may be voluntary where the debtor and secured creditor stipulate the redemption value of the secured property." Redemption can also be involuntary.).

7. In re Bell, 700 F.2d 1053, 1054–57 (6th Cir.1983); In re Avila, 83 B.R. 6, 7 (Bankr. 9th Cir.1987); In re Polk, 76 B.R. 148, 150 (Bankr. 9th Cir.1987); Edwards v. Merchants Nat'l Bank, 95 B.R. 97, 98 (S.D. Ind.1988), judgment aff'd, 901 F.2d 1383 (7th Cir.1990); In re Nikokyrakis, 109 B.R. 260, 262 (Bankr. N.D.Ohio 1989) (dicta); In re Peacock, 87 B.R. 657, 660 (Bankr. D. Colo. 1988) (dicta); In re Harp, 76 B.R. 185, 186–88 (Bankr. N.D.Fla.1987) (but debtor given 30 days to pay lump sum); In re Redding, 34 B.R. 971, 973–74 (Bankr. M.D.Pa. 1983).; Matter of Dennis, 31 B.R. 128, 131 (Bankr. M.D.Ga.1983).

8. 700 F.2d 1053 (6th Cir.1983).

9. 11 U.S.C.A. § 524(c). Reaffirmation is the process whereby the debtor makes an enforceable agreement to pay a dischargeable debt. It requires the consent of both the cred-

for a debtor to negotiate reaffirmation if he is authorized to redeem by installments over the creditor's objection.[10]

Consider an example. The principal amount of the debt outstanding is $10,000, the value of the pickup truck is $5,000. Under 722 the debtor could redeem the pickup by a payment of $5,000 lump sum. If he is to reaffirm, he must reaffirm the entire debt and thus pay $10,000 plus interest.

An additional option for the debtor is to go into Chapter 13. There he can write the debt down to the value of the collateral and, in most cases, pay it off over three to five years (together with a modest payment on the unsecured portion of the debt). In Chapter 13 the debtor can have the best of both worlds, the reduced payment and unilateral right usually associated with redemption and the installment payments associated with reaffirmations.

Many debtors have tried another alternative. They stay in Chapter 7 but do not reaffirm or redeem. Rather, the tactic is simply to continue to make the payments due under the old debt. When the debtor has not defaulted on the payments and his only breach of the security agreement is to file bankruptcy (or have rendered the creditor "insecure"), he will argue first that any clause making bankruptcy an automatic default is invalid under section 541(c) and second, that there is no reason for insecurity on the part of the creditor. The debtor will then argue that the stay (during the case) and the injunction in section 524 (after the case) prohibits repossession and permits him to retain possession as long as he continues to pay and does not violate the terms of the security agreement.

In *Matter of Edwards* [11] the Court of Appeals for the Seventh Circuit rejected this tactic. It placed substantial reliance on section 521(2) which was added as part of the 1984 amendments. Added at the urging of the consumer credit lobby, section 521(2) requires the debtor to file a statement of intention whether he intends to redeem, reaffirm the secured debt or to do neither. The debtor must make such a filing within 30 days after the filing of the petition and perform his stated intention to redeem or reaffirm within 45 days after the filing of the notice of intention. The Seventh Circuit reads this obligation of the debtor as mandatory and opines that allowing the debtor alternatively to keep the collateral by continuing payments would render "the statutory scheme set up by sections 521 and 524 * * * nugatory * * *." [12]

On the other hand, the Court of Appeals for the Tenth Circuit, in *Lowry Federal Credit Union v. West*,[13] allowed the debtor to retain the goods and enjoined repossession, even though the debtor had neither redeemed or reaffirmed. The court rejected the argument that the debtor's failure to make an election under section 521 foreclosed his retention of the collateral. This opinion is just as sensible as the opposite *Edwards*. Although 521 requires the debtor to declare his intention to reaffirm or redeem if he plans one or the other, the statute does not require the debtor to pursue either

itor and debtor and is regulated and limited by the provisions of section 524(c).
10. Id. at 1056.
11. 901 F.2d 1383 (7th Cir.1990).
12. 901 F.2d at 1387.
13. 882 F.2d 1543 (10th Cir.1989); accord In re Lawrence, 54 B.R. 1 (Bankr. D.S.C.1984).

course.¹⁴ It does not eliminate other options, such as keeping the property and paying for it when the secured party has no right to possession of it.

Where does this leave us? For the time being, installment redemption under section 722 is not permitted. Whether continued possession, a la *Lowry*, by one who has never defaulted will be permitted is less clear. Even the court in *Lowry* wondered if the outcome would be different if, as was not true in that case, the security agreement included an *ipso facto* bankruptcy default clause or a clause giving a right of repossession on discharge of personal liability. Probably, it would not matter to a court inclined to follow *Lowry*. There is substantial precedent for refusing to enforce such a clause.¹⁵

D. PROTECTION AGAINST DISCRIMINATORY TREATMENT, SECTION 525

§ 7–40 Introduction to Protection Against Discrimination

Section 525 may be considered an extension of the policies embodied in

---

14. Nothing in the Code forces a debtor who has not defaulted to reaffirm or redeem in order to retain collateral, most certainly not while the stay continues. Lowry Fed. Cr. Union v. West, 882 F.2d 1543, 1545–47 (10th Cir.1989) (debtor's continued possession of collateral, so long as she is current in payments, is not dependent upon reaffirming or redeeming, and such dependency is not the result of § 521 or the debtor's failure to comply with it); Riggs Nat'l Bank v. Perry, 729 F.2d 982, 984–85 (4th Cir.1984)(bankruptcy is not sufficient cause to lift stay); In re Avila, 83 B.R. 6, 7–8 (Bankr. 9th Cir.1987) (Debtors in bankruptcy may lawfully retain possession of secured collateral * * * [by keeping] current on their monthly payments pursuant to the security agreement." Relief from the stay is not justified merely because the value of the collateral drops below the secured debt, especially where debtor remains current on contractual payment.); In re Peacock, 87 B.R. 657, 660–61 (Bankr. D.Colo.1988) (A debtor's options are not limited to reaffirmation or redemption because she can "continue making payments on the contract, in a current and complete manner, as if the bankruptcy never occurred."); In re Cassell, 41 B.R. 737, 742 (Bankr. E.D.Va.1984) (secured party has no right to collateral if debtor is current in payments even though debtor neither reaffirms nor redeems); In re Ballance, 33 B.R. 89, 90–91 (Bankr. E.D.Va.1983) (a debtor not in default is not required to redeem or reaffirm); In re Rosenow, 22 B.R. 99, 100 (Bankr. W.D. Wash.1982) (even after discharge granted and stay lifted secured party not entitled to possession of collateral so long as debtor not in default); but compare Edwards v. Merchants Nat'l Bank, 95 B.R. 97, 98 (S.D. Ind.1988), aff'd, 901 F.2d 1383 (7th Cir.1990) (declining to follow Lowry) (debtor required to reaffirm or redeem by lump-sum payment in order to keep possession of collateral), followed in, In re Chavarria, 117 B.R. 582 (Bankr. D.Idaho 1990).

15. Riggs Nat'l Bank v. Perry, 729 F.2d 982, 984–85 (4th Cir.1984) (default upon filing clause is unenforceable, and neither it nor the bankruptcy is sufficient cause to lift stay); In re West, 101 B.R. 648 (D.Colo.1989) (debtors who are not in default are not required to reaffirm or redeem to keep possession of collateral as bankruptcy is not itself sufficient to give right to possession); In re Nikokyrakis, 109 B.R. 260, 262–63 (Bankr. N.D.Ohio 1989) (ipso facto clause does not entitle creditor to possession in case a debtor is not in default and continues to make timely payments) (dicta); In re Peacock, 87 B.R. 657, 659–61 (Bankr. D. Colo. 1988) ("A creditor cannot force a default upon a debtor by the use of the ipso facto clause of a contract solely because of a bankruptcy filing."); In re Berenguer, 77 B.R. 959, 960 (Bankr. S.D.Fla.1987) (debtor's bankruptcy and discharge of value deficiency are not sufficient grounds entitling secured creditor to repossess and creditor is enjoined from repossessing property so long as there is no other default); In re Winters, 69 B.R. 145, 146–47 (Bankr. D.Or.1986) (bankruptcy default clauses are unenforceable as a matter of federal law and are probably invalid under state law); In re Cassell, 41 B.R. 737, 740–41 (Bankr. E.D.Va.1984) (default-upon-filing clauses are unenforceable as a matter of law, and debtor's bankruptcy discharge is not sufficient basis for repossession); In re Brock, 23 B.R. 998, 1001–04 (Bankr. D. D.C. 1982) (notwithstanding termination of stay secured creditor could not repossess collateral following debtor's discharge solely because the debtor had filed bankruptcy if the debtor had not otherwise defaulted under terms of security agreement).

section 362 and in the injunction under section 524(a) against the attempt to collect a discharged debt. In its initial proposal to the Congress, the Commission on Bankruptcy Laws of the United States proposed a very broad antidiscriminatory rule. It read in full as follows:

> A person shall not be subjected to discriminatory treatment because he, or any person with whom he is or has been associated, is or has been a debtor or has failed to pay a debt discharged in a case under the Act. This action does not preclude consideration, where relevant, of factors other than those specified in the preceding sentence, such as a present and prospective financial condition or managerial ability.[1]

Like several other provisions of the Commission's bill that were particularly favorable to the debtor, this provision was considerably changed by the time it emerged from Congress as section 525 of the 1978 Bankruptcy Reform Act. At that time it read as follows:

> Except as provided in * * * a governmental unit may not deny, revoke, suspend, or refuse to renew a license, permit, charter, franchise, or other similar grant to, condition such a grant to, discriminate with respect to such a grant against, deny employment to, terminate the employment of, or discriminate with respect to employment against, a person that is or has been a debtor under this title or a bankrupt or a debtor under the Bankruptcy Act, or another person with whom such bankrupt or debtor has been associated, solely because such bankrupt or debtor is or has been a debtor under this title or a bankrupt or debtor under the Bankruptcy Act, has been insolvent before the commencement of the case under this title, or during the case but before the debtor is granted or denied a discharge, or has not paid a debt that is dischargeable in the case under this title or that was discharged under the Bankruptcy Act.

Note the protection against discrimination. First, the antidiscrimination rule applied only to "governmental units." Private parties were entirely free to discriminate against a former bankrupt. Second, the prohibited forms of discrimination were specified; even a governmental unit was permitted to discriminate against bankrupts as long as it was not "denying, revoking, suspending, or refusing to renew a license, permit, charter, franchise or other similar grant."

Third, the Congress added the adverb "solely"; it prohibited only discrimination that was stimulated "solely because a bankrupt or debtor was insolvent or had failed to pay a dischargeable debt." If there were multiple causes of the discrimination (bankruptcy and something else), the discrimination was not prohibited by section 525. What had started as a broad restriction on discrimination in the 1973 proposal wound up in 1978 as a highly restricted—almost insignificant—prohibition on discrimination.

In 1984, Congress took one step beyond its original enactment. In that year it adopted what is now section 525(b).[2] Section 525(b) for the first time applies the antidiscrimination rules to private parties, but it applies only to

§ 7–40
1. Section 4–508 of the Commission's Proposed Bankruptcy Act of 1973.

2. The old section 525 is now 525(a).

"private employers" and it prohibits only discrimination by employers with respect to employment against employees because they have been insolvent or have been bankrupt. Like subsection (a), it applies only if the discrimination was "solely because" of the debtor's bankruptcy or insolvency.

As the Commission report indicates and as the Senate Report states, section 525 is intended to "codify" the result of *Perez v. Campbell*[3]. Arizona law barred the renewal of driver's licenses by those with outstanding tort judgments against them. To purge oneself from this prohibition, a person had to pay the tort judgment; the law applied even though the judgment had been discharged in bankruptcy. Perez successfully argued that the Arizona law was an unconstitutional state encroachment on federal law.

Even a moment's thought about this statutory scheme foretells the difficulties that have confronted the courts. Because one had to pay the *discharged* liability in order to get his driver's license, the Arizona law outlawed in *Perez v. Campbell* was a direct affront to the bankruptcy discharge. But what of laws that do not require reaffirmation or payment but require only a showing of financial ability? What of laws that merely draw unfavorable inferences from one's bankruptcy and failure to pay liabilities? These are different from the Arizona law outlawed in *Perez v. Campbell,* for they are not necessarily cured by or require the payment of the discharged debt. Still such laws might run afoul of section 525.

At the outset one should note that section 525 is necessarily interrelated with several other sections. First, an act of discrimination under section 525 might also be claimed to be a violation of the injunction under section 524 or, if the case is still open, the stay under section 362. Moreover it is possible the act under section 525 will conflict with the rules under section 365 that give the debtor the right to assume and carry out certain contracts.

To see this relationship, consider a 1988 case from the Court of Appeals for the Third Circuit. In *Brown v. Pennsylvania State Employees Credit Union*[4] the Credit Union sent a letter to a member who had just taken bankruptcy. The letter read in part as follows:

> It is the Credit Union's policy to deny future services to members when any portion of the debt is discharged in bankruptcy. However, if the obligation is reaffirmed with court approval, you would remain eligible for services as though the bankruptcy had not occurred.[5]

One might view this as a not so subtle attempt to collect the debt in violation of the stay. Clearly the Credit Union would have had the right to refuse to deal with her in the future (if it did not violate section 525 by so doing) but the letter goes beyond that; it invites a reaffirmation—a collection of the debt. Ignoring the similarity between a reaffirmation and the coerced payment of an outstanding obligation, the Court of Appeals affirmed a finding that the Credit Union did not act with the purpose of collecting the debt. It discusses the relationship of sections 362, 524, and 525 as follows:

> We hold that PSECU did not violate § 362 or § 524 of the bankruptcy code merely by informing Brown of its policy. Nothing in the

---

3. 402 U.S. 637, 91 S.Ct. 1704, 29 L.Ed.2d 233 (1971).

4. 851 F.2d 81 (3d Cir.1988).

5. Id. at 82.

bankruptcy code requires this creditor to do business with this debtor. To require dealings would impermissibly extend the scope of the code's anti-discrimination provisions, and Brown fails to make out a case warranting an extension on the particular facts of this case. Because PSECU may refuse Brown services, we agree with the bankruptcy court that PSECU may inform Brown of its policy. In refusing to impose sanctions on PSECU, this court agrees with other courts of appeals which have considered the issue, and our decision does not infringe on the policies of the bankruptcy code.

The limited scope of the anti-discrimination provisions of the code demonstrates the PSECU may lawfully refuse to deal with Brown on account of her discharged debt. Section 525 bars only governmental agencies and employers from discriminating against a debtor on account of a previous bankruptcy filing * * *. Congress rejected a general anti-discrimination policy. * * * Brown has conceded, as both lower courts found, that § 525 does not bar PSECU from enforcing its policy. Yet, any refusal of future services by a present creditor has some coercive impact. If we hold that the impact itself is sufficient to violate the bankruptcy injunctions of § 362 and § 524, then a creditor—whether or not a governmental unit or employer—may be prevented from denying future services because of a prior discharged debt. The debtor could do indirectly through what she cannot accomplish directly through the anti-discrimination provision. We cannot find that Congress intended this result.[6]

One sympathetic to the debtor can easily think of half a dozen ways in which the court could have come to the opposite conclusion under sections 362, 524, or even section 525. The case is quite striking in its hostility to these sections and in its willingness to read them narrowly, contrary to the debtor's apparent interest. It may foretell a restrictive stinginess by the appellate courts in reading and applying the newer section 525(b) that sometimes (even often) marks their handling of the older 525(a).

§ 7–41 Protection Against Discrimination by Governmental Units, Section 525(a)

Section 525(a) contains several conditions. The act must be by a "governmental unit". It must be a denial, revocation, suspension, or refusal to renew "a license, permit, charter, franchise or other similar grant", or it must be a condition or discrimination with respect to such a grant. The governmental unit may not deny employment, terminate employment, or discriminate with respect to employment against a person. Any act that violates section 525(a) must have been done "solely because" the debtor has filed under the Code or the Act, or has become insolvent, or has failed to pay a debt dischargeable under the Code. Each of these three conditions presents the possibility for dispute, but most of the dispute has arisen from the last, "solely because".

---

6. Id. at 85.

a. Governmental Unit

What is a governmental unit has little troubled the courts. In *Brown v. Pennsylvania State Employees Credit Union*,[1] the court rejected the argument that a credit union whose members were governmental employees and chartered by the government was itself a governmental unit. Another court concluded that a privately owned housing unit operating under a federally regulated public housing program is not a governmental unit.[2]

In many other cases it has been indisputable that the party taking the action was a governmental unit. For example, a governmental unit would clearly include the Air Force in granting a food service contract,[3] Commodity Credit Corporation,[4] or a licensing commission.[5] The legislative history states that "governmental unit" is also broad enough to include agencies such as bar associations and medical societies that exercise licensing functions that might normally be exercised by a state agency.[6] In general there are no surprises here and little serious litigation.

b. "Solely"

Both subsections 525(a) and 525(b) require that the discriminating party's behavior be "solely because" of bankruptcy or one of the other listed events. Whether section 525 becomes a succulent piece of fruit on the debtor's plate or shrivels on the vine depends upon the courts' interpretation of this rule of causation. If the debtor is forced to prove not merely that he took bankruptcy and was then subject to discrimination by a governmental unit or by an employer who knew of the bankruptcy, but also that the discriminating party had *no other* motivation, the bankrupt is destined to lose these cases. He is likely to win them only if the burden of showing other motivation is put on the discriminating party and if the courts read the adverb "solely" in a way inconsistent with its plain meaning.

The appellate cases decided to date are not hopeful for the debtor's point of view. Representative of the cases dealing with this issue is *Laracuente v. Chase Manhattan Bank*[7]. Although that case was decided under 525(b), the same language appears in (a). Chase Manhattan won a summary judgment upholding its right to fire Ms. Laracuente. Working as a "credit department coordinator," she had participated in the procurement of several fraudulent loans by employees of her husband. In early 1984 Ms. Laracuente filed in Chapter 13; she was dismissed by Chase in August of 1985. Laracuente argued that the court should approach section 525(b) in the same way they would approach an allegation of discrimination because of race, color, religion, sex or national origin, under 42 U.S.C.A. § 2000e et seq. In such a

---

§ 7–41

1. 851 F.2d 81 (3d Cir.1988); cf. In re Callender, 99 B.R. 378 (Bankr. S.D.Ohio 1989) (credit union formed of employees of the post office might be a governmental unit).

2. In re Rosemond, 105 B.R. 8 (Bankr. W.D.Pa.1989); In re Wagner, 87 B.R. 612 (Bankr. C.D.Cal.1988).

3. In re Exquisito Services, Inc., 823 F.2d 151 (5th Cir.1987).

4. Matter of Lech, 80 B.R. 1001 (Bankr. D.Neb.1987).

5. In re Will Rogers Jockey and Polo Club, Inc., 111 B.R. 948 (Bankr. N.D. Okla. 1990); In re Anderson, 84 B.R. 426 (Bankr. E.D.Va. 1988).

6. Notes of the Committee on the Judiciary, Senate Rep. 95–989.

7. 891 F.2d 17 (1st Cir.1989).

case the bank would have had to have rebutted the presumption against it upon the proof of prima facie case by Laracuente. The bank maintained that section 525 should be limited in scope to the plain language of the statute. Under this approach, the bank asserted that "the district court properly granted summary judgment based on the uncontroverted fact that Laracuente was not fired solely because of her bankruptcy status, but for the legitimate reason that she was defrauding the bank." [8] Rejecting a lower court case in Georgia, the court makes the following finding with respect to 525(b):

> A recent district court case supports appellants' view of § 525(b). *Bell v. Sanford–Corbitt–Bruker* * * *. In *Bell*, the court suggested that "solely" within the context of § 525(b) should be defined as "played a significant role" or "but for". The court held that a narrow interpretation of the word "solely" conflicts with the policies of the Bankruptcy Act since it would be impossible for a claimant to prove that his or her employer fired the claimant due only to bankruptcy. Accordingly, the court, "in the absence of authority in the context of § 525(b), conclude[d] that burden of proof allocations for proving a discriminatory discharge due to bankruptcy should be framed by analogy to race, color, religion, sex, or national origin cases." *Bell, supra,* * * *. Under that approach, once a member of the class protected by § 525(b) makes out a prima facie case of discriminatory discharge, the employer must establish a legitimate, nondiscriminatory reason for the action.
>
> Our analysis of § 525(b) begins, as it must, with the language of the statute * * *. The ordinary meaning of words expresses the underlying legislative purpose of the statute * * *.
>
> In view of well-settled rules of statutory construction, we find that the *Bell* decision rests on tenuous grounds and we decline to follow it. Contrary to the reasoning in *Bell*, we believe that, in the absence of a clearly expressed legislative intention to the contrary, the plain language of the statute is conclusive * * *. Further, absent ambiguity in the statutory language, our inquiry is complete and ends with the plain language of the statute * * *. We decline appellants' invitation to construe § 525(b) liberally.
>
> We agree with the district court in the instant case that a fundamental element of a § 525(b) claim is that the insolvency, the filing of bankruptcy, or the discharge of a debt is the *sole reason* for discriminatory treatment by an employer.[9] [citations omitted]

Other cases come to the same conclusion. For example, in *In re Will Rogers Jockey and Polo Club, Inc.*[10] the court rejected a Chapter 11 party's claim of impermissible discrimination. It noted that the state racing commission had refused the application partly because of the lack of financial integrity of the Polo Club, but also because the horse racing market was saturated.

Note that discrimination against a bankrupt because of his weak financial state after the bankruptcy is not prohibited by section 525. It prohibits

---

8. Id. at 20.
9. Id. at 22–23.

10. 111 B.R. 948 (Bankr. N.D. Okla. 1990).

discrimination only if that discrimination is solely because the debtor has been insolvent *before* the commencement of the case and has not paid a dischargeable debt. Thus, the *Will Rogers* case would have come out the same way even if the additional reason of saturation of the racing market had not been present.

This point is made in *Stockhouse v. Hines Motor Supply (Wyoming), Inc.*[11] where the court upheld an employer's firing of an employee. It upheld that firing even though the employer had expressed pleasure with the employee's work only two months before the firing and had stated his displeasure with the filing of the bankruptcy. Noting other evidence showing the plaintiff to be a poor employee and evidence that the employer had selected a replacement even before it knew of the filing of the bankruptcy, the court concluded that the firing was not "solely" because of the filing of the petition.[12]

As a further illustration of the courts' desire to give section 525 the narrowest possible scope, consider *Duffey v. Dollison*,[13] a case quite similar to *Perez v. Campbell*. Under Ohio law, one who allowed a judgment as a result of an auto accident to go unsatisfied for 30 days is reported to the state authorities. Under the Ohio law, such person's driving privileges are revoked and they can be reinstated only by proof of financial responsibility. One proves responsibility by filing a certificate of insurance, a surety bond, a certificate of deposit, or a certificate of self-insurance.[14] In addition the liability on the judgment must either be "stayed" or satisfied in full. Unlike Arizona, Ohio treats a discharge of the liability as the equivalent of full payment after 30 days.

George and Shari Duffey were a family in need of driver training. George had an accident sometime prior to June of 1979; he suffered a judgment of $914.79 in the municipal court of Franklin County, Ohio. In the following year, Shari experienced a judgment of $1,131.90 in the same court.

After both Duffeys lost their driving privileges, they filed a voluntary joint petition in January of 1981. The bankruptcy court found the Ohio Motor Vehicle Financial Responsibility Act in conflict with the Bankruptcy Act and ordered reinstatement of their driving privileges. The district court reversed, the Court of Appeals affirmed that reversal.

The Court of Appeals held that the Ohio law was not like the Arizona law involved in *Perez v. Campbell* because in Ohio there was no requirement that the debtors pay the liability in order to have their licenses reinstated. According to the court, those who had declared bankruptcy were treated just the same as those who had paid off the judgments; for a three year period after that time they had to prove their financial ability in order to remain licensed. The court concluded that this was not a discrimination against people in bankruptcy, only a rule that applied to everyone who had suffered such a judgment; it was not a suspension "solely because". Noting how a decision on behalf of the Duffeys in this case would in fact give them greater

---

11. 75 B.R. 83 (D.Wyo.1987).

12. Id. at 85; see also In re Helms, 46 B.R. 150 (E.D.Mo.1985); but cf. In re Hopkins, 81 B.R. 491 (Bankr. W.D.Ark.1987); In re Hicks, 65 B.R. 980 (Bankr. W.D.Ark.1986).

13. 734 F.2d 265 (6th Cir.1984); accord In re Norton, 867 F.2d 313 (6th Cir.1989).

14. Ohio Rev. Code Ann. § 4509.45 Baldwin 1975.

rights than those who had in fact suffered a judgment and paid it, the court declined to read the statute in that way.

Senate Report 989 specifically observes that section 525 "does not prohibit consideration of other factors, *such as future financial responsibility or ability,* and does not prohibit imposition of requirements such as net capital rules, if applied nondiscriminatorily." * * * House Report No. 595 makes this point even more emphatically:

> [T]he prohibition [of section 525] *does not extend so far as to prohibit examination of the factors surrounding bankruptcy, the imposition of financial responsibility rules if they are not imposed only on former bankrupts,* or the examination of prospective financial condition or managerial ability * * *. [I]n those cases where the causes of a bankruptcy are intimately connected with the license, grant, or employment in question, an examination into the circumstances surrounding the bankruptcy will permit governmental units to pursue appropriate regulatory policies and take appropriate action without running afoul of bankruptcy policy.

H.R. Rep. No. 595, 95th Cong. 1st Sess. 165 *reprinted in* 1978 U.S.Code Cong. & Ad. News 5963, 6126 (emphasis added). Thus, Congress has evinced a clear intent to permit the imposition of financial responsibility requirements, so long as they are not discriminatorily applied to bankrupts.

The Ohio Financial Responsibility Act in no way discriminates against bankrupts, or penalizes them for filing in bankruptcy. The Act provides that "any person" who fails to satisfy an accident-related judgment within 30 days shall have his or her driving privileges suspended by the Registrar. Ohio Rev.Code Ann. §§ 4509.35, .37 (Baldwin 1975). The statute applies without exception to *any* person who fails to satisfy a judgment for whatever reason, whether because of unwillingness, inadvertence, or inability to pay. Once a judgment has been certified to the Registrar for nonpayment, the debtor's obligation to furnish proof of financial responsibility becomes fixed. Thereafter, neither payment of the debt, reaffirmation, nor bankruptcy can relieve the debtor of this requirement. Judgment debtors such as the Duffeys who seek relief under the bankruptcy laws are therefore treated no differently from any other judgment debtor. Indeed it is this lack of discrimination to which the Duffeys take exception. By arguing that bankrupts who have proved to be irresponsible drivers should be excused from the requirement of posting proof of financial responsibility, the Duffeys in effect ask this court "to go beyond the fresh start policy of *Perez* and * * * give a debtor a head start over persons who are able to satisfy their unpaid judgment debts without resort to a discharge in bankruptcy" *In re Cerny,* 17 B.R. 221, 224 (Bkrtcy. N.D.Ohio 1982). We do not believe that section 525 was intended by Congress to afford debtors in bankruptcy such preferential treatment.

We therefore hold that Ohio's "one-bite" approach to the imposition of financial responsibility requirements, as applied to the Duffeys, violates neither the *Perez* holding nor its statutory codification, section 525 of the Bankruptcy Act. As Judge Holschuh persuasively reasoned,

[i]t is undisputed that Ohio may require all motorists to carry liability insurance or post security before they are issued operator's licenses. * * * If the State may legitimately establish such a prerequisite to the grant of driving privileges, a less stringent requirement should *a fortiori* be valid. The challenged Ohio statutes afford individuals the opportunity of driving without any showing of financial responsibility until they incur a judgment which they are unable to pay. This "one-bite" approach undoubtedly makes it possible for many individuals who otherwise could not afford insurance to obtain driving privileges. [The Duffeys] argue that because Ohio has used this more lenient approach, it is forbidden to suspend their driving privileges, despite the fact that they have demonstrated irresponsibility as a driver coupled with an inability to satisfy a resulting judgment. [This] argument, however, ignores the potential consequences to the victims of an accident caused by an individual who is an irresponsible driver.

Duffey v. Dollison, C–2–81–1154, slip op. at 12 (S.D.Ohio Aug. 13, 1982).[15]

Cases like *Laracuente* and *Duffey v. Dollison* are correct interpretations of the "solely because" language. We presume that these courts are engaging in the kind of behavior (albeit from the right and not from the left), that Senator Kennedy and his colleagues contemplated when the Committee on the Judiciary noted: "The courts will continue to mark the contours of the antidiscrimination provision in pursuit of sound bankruptcy policy."[16]

c. Acts Prohibited

Section 525(a) does not prohibit all discrimination; it merely states that a governmental unit may not "deny, revoke, suspend, or refuse to renew, a license, permit, charter, franchise, or other similar grant, to condition such a grant to, discriminate with respect to such a grant against, deny employment to, terminate the employment of or discriminate with respect to employment against a person * * *." In some of the cases discussed above one might have argued that the act taken was not one of those enumerated.

This argument was successfully made by a New York agency in *In re Goldrich*[17]. In that case the court upheld a New York agency's refusal to grant a new student loan to one who had failed to pay an earlier one. Concluding that the grant of a new loan was not like granting a license or such, the court held denial of the future loan was not prohibited by section 525. The court found that the refusal to make new loans was not intended to "coerce payment", but merely to protect against repeated defaults. Of course, this case could also have been analyzed under the causation rules discussed above; note too the court had to address the problem of violation of the injunction under 524 and did so by examining the refusing party's motivation.[18]

---

15. 734 F.2d at 273–74.

16. Notes of the Committee of the Judiciary Sen. Rep. No. 95–989.

17. 771 F.2d 28 (2d Cir.1985); accord In re Kotter, 58 B.R. 118 (Bankr. C.D.Ill. 1986).

18. For cases in which colleges withhold transcripts, see Johnson v. Edinboro State College, 728 F.2d 163 (3d Cir.1984) (refusal okay where student loan was not dischargeable); Matter of Heath, 3 B.R. 351 (Bankr. N.D.Ill.

In re Exquisito Services, Inc.[19] is one of the few cases where the debtor won at the appellate level. The majority held that the Air Force violated section 525 by exercising an option not to renew a food service contract at Barksdale Air Force Base with a debtor in Chapter 11. In dissent Judge Jolly argued that such a contract does not constitute a license, permit, or the like and thus that any discrimination done here was not prohibited by section 525(a). We agree with the dissent; at minimum we would suggest that such a renewal should be examined under the applicable rules of section 365(b). Certainly a creditor should be free to insist upon the protections given to it under 365 in the form of cure and adequate protection of future performance. The assertion of section 365 rights should not be a violation of section 525. While we are persuaded by Judge Jolly's dissent and doubtful of the wisdom of the majority opinion here, the case holds out some hope for debtors.

d. Remedies

Because all of the cases at the core of section 525(a) involve some governmental grant (e.g., Perez's driver's license), the remedy for violation of section 525(a) is usually quite obvious, namely, an order of the court directing the governmental agency to grant the charter, license, or the like. As we will see below, section 525(b) on improper discharge from employment has already stimulated some discussion of the appropriate remedy there and is likely to provide considerably more learning over the next few years.

§ 7–42 Protection Against Discrimination by Private Employees, Section 525(b)

Because section 525(b) was enacted in 1984, few appellate cases deal with it. One should be hesitant to extrapolate from the decisions of the bankruptcy courts, because history under sections 525(a) and 523 has shown the Courts of Appeals are less generous to the debtors than are the bankruptcy courts.

Many of the issues under section 525(b) are the same as those under section 525(a); those have been discussed above. For example, the "solely because" language appears in both sections and should receive the same interpretation in (a) and (b). As we indicate above, one lower court has found that the rules of proof and presumption on discrimination found in other federal law on race and gender should be applied here to the burden of proof, but the Court of Appeals for the First Circuit has held otherwise.

In several minor respects the language of section 525(b) is different from that of section 525(a). For example, section 525(b) gives rights only to "an individual"; it is not available to a corporation who is denied a contract because it has filed in Chapter 11.[1] Note too that (a) states that one may not

---

1980); In re Ware, 9 B.R. 24 (Bankr. W.D.Mo. 1981); accord In re Kotter, 58 B.R. 118 (Bankr. C.D.Ill. 1986).

19. 823 F.2d 151 (5th Cir.1987).

§ 7–42

1. In re Madison Madison International of Illinois, P.C., 77 B.R. 678 (Bankr. E.D.Wis. 1987) (potential subcontractor for people mover at O'Hare airport, not an individual and states no claim under 525(b)).

"deny employment to, terminate the employment of, or discriminate with respect to employment against", but that section 525(b) states only that no employer "may terminate the employment or discriminate with respect to employment against." Section 525(b) does not in terms prohibit "denial." We wonder whether any difference is intended; surely the phrase "discriminate with respect to" is broad enough to include denial.[2]

Since section 525(b) contemplates "an employer", presumably it contemplates an employment contract or potential employment contract and the courts will therefore be called upon to distinguish between employees, independent contractors, joint venturers, and the like. In one Georgia case, the bankruptcy court has found that even an independent contract with certain elements of "employment" was covered.[3] The court says that the terms should be defined broadly as a matter of federal law even in circumstances in which the party would not be an employee under state law. It is not certain that this approach would be followed, as a general matter, by the Courts of Appeals.

By far the most interesting cases yet decided under section 525(b) have to do with remedies. Contrary to cases under (a) (where a license can simply be ordered), something more needs to be done if a fired employee is to be made whole.

Representative of the cases that deal with remedies under 525(b) is *In re Sweeney*[4]. After finding that Ameritrust violated section 525(b) by firing Sweeney from his job of doing tax returns, the court had to decide whether to order his reinstatement. Because he had long been out of the job and in the meantime had been doing something unrelated to his Ameritrust work, the court concluded it would be inappropriate to order a reinstatement at the old job. Nevertheless it granted him $84,592 in back pay. Several other courts have also ordered back pay in these circumstances.[5]

Problems associated with awards of back pay will be familiar to those involved in orders of reinstatement arising out of firing for racial and other prohibited discrimination. Inevitably these cases raise questions concerning the debtor's mitigation in the form of earnings enjoyed at other jobs in the meantime, and they require the courts to balance the interests of the parties in responding to the plaintiff's request for reinstatement.

Debtors here sometimes ask for attorneys fees. Finding no basis in the statute for the award of such fees, at least one court has explicitly denied them in a case where the plaintiff was victorious.[6]

The debtors in 525(b) cases will naturally seek to draw analogies to the discrimination discharge cases and will argue for the favors granted by those statutes. We believe the courts are correct in not granting all of the benefits

---

2. See In re Madison Madison International of Illinois, P.C., 77 B.R. 678 (Bankr. E.D.Wis.1987).

3. Matter of McNeely, 82 B.R. 628 (Bankr. S.D.Ga.1987).

4. 113 B.R. 359 (Bankr. N.D.Ohio 1990).

5. See In re McNeely, 82 B.R. 628 (Bankr. S.D.Ga.1987) (lost profits of $1,000 a month for five months); In re Hopkins, 81 B.R. 491 (Bankr. W.D.Ark.1987) ($13,824.50 in back pay. Net of earnings elsewhere); In re Hicks, 65 B.R. 980 (Bankr. W.D.Ark.1986).

6. In re Hopkins, 81 B.R. 491 (Bankr. W.D.Ark.1987).

conferred by those statutes (such as attorneys fees). Had Congress wished to grant such rights, it could have said so, but it did not.

E. DISMISSAL

Section 707(a) and (b) are quite different animals. Subsection (b) was enacted in 1984 at the urging of the consumer credit lobby. Section 707(a) was a part of the original 1978 Code. Section 707(a) is conventional and uncontroversial; section 707(b) is the reverse.

§ 7–43 Section 707(a)

Section 707(a) authorizes the court to dismiss a case on any one of three grounds:

>(1) unreasonable delay by the debtor that is prejudicial to creditors;

>(2) nonpayment of any fees or charges required under chapter 123 of title 28; and

>(3) failure of the debtor in a voluntary case to file, within fifteen days or such additional time as the court may allow after the filing of the petition commencing such case, the information required by paragraph (1) of section 521, but only on a motion by the United States trustee.

For several reasons, none of these three grounds is likely to produce much litigation or uncertainty. Subsection (1) allows dismissal for unreasonable delay, but only where the delay has been "prejudicial" to creditors.[1] Because delay is common, but prejudice is not, the section will be infrequently invoked. The occasions where it has been invoked seem to us to be sports that seldom arise and cause little difficulty.[2] An imaginative use of section 707(a) was in the case *In re MacFarlane Webster Associates*[3] where a junior mortgagee tried to foil the efforts of the senior mortgagee by filing an involuntary bankruptcy petition against the common debtor.[4] The senior mortgagee used section 707(a) to have the case dismissed.

Subsection (2) is conventional and completely straightforward. It should cause even less difficulty.[5]

Finally, subsection (3) has somewhat larger potential for difficulty. It was added as part of the 1984 amendments and put some teeth in the requirement that the debtor make the proper filings required by section

---

§ 7–43

1. In one such case the debtor had filed approximately two years before seeking dismissal. This had stayed the creditor's attempts at collection for the two-year time period. In addition the trustee had discovered potential assets of the estate that would have granted a substantial dividend to the unsecured creditors. In re Klein, 39 B.R. 530 (Bankr. E.D.N.Y.1984). Such discoveries by trustees and attempts by debtors to wear down creditors will result in dismissal via 707(a).

2. See, e.g., Matter of Jennings, 31 B.R. 378 (Bankr. S.D.Ohio 1983); In re Carroll, 24 B.R. 83 (Bankr. N.D.Ohio 1982); In Matter of Williams, 15 B.R. 655 (E.D.Mo.1981), aff'd, 696 F.2d 999 (8th Cir.1982); In re Wolfe, 12 B.R. 686 (Bankr. S.D.Ohio 1981); In re Wirick, 3 B.R. 539 (Bankr. E.D.Va.1980).

3. 121 B.R. 694 (Bankr. S.D.N.Y.1990).

4. See also In re Sky Group Intern., Inc., 108 B.R. 86 (Bankr. W.D.Pa.1989) (language of statute requires case by case determination as to whether an abuse constituting fraud has occurred).

5. At the time of publication we found no published opinions regarding section 707(a)(2).

521(1), (the list of creditors, schedule of assets and liabilities, the schedule of current income and current expenditures, and a statement of the debtor's financial affairs). Presumably the subsection is designed to keep a debtor who has no interest in actually liquidating from filing a petition just to get the benefit of the stay. The section is nevertheless likely to be of limited importance for two reasons. First, it is quite straightforward; one can easily determine whether the debtor has complied with 521(1). Second, the debtor can be challenged for violation of 707(a)(3) only by "the United States trustee." The United States trustee has many other things to do besides filing motions under 707(a)(3) and will do so only rarely.[6]

§ 7–44 Section 707(b)

Unlike its sister, section 707(b) is controversial. In a limited number of cases it will continue to be a battle ground between consumer debtors and consumer creditors. The subsection was first added to the Code in 1984.[1] As enacted in 1984 the section read in full as follows:

> (b) After notice and a hearing, the court, on its own motion and not at the request or suggestion of any party in interest, may dismiss a case filed by an individual debtor under this chapter whose debts are primarily consumer debts if it finds that the granting of relief would be a substantial abuse of the provisions of this chapter. There shall be a presumption in favor of granting the relief requested by the debtor.[2]

The subsection is one of the fragments that was left from an unsuccessful consumer creditor attempt to restrict substantially the power of certain consumer debtors to file in Chapter 7. The original creditor proposal would have amended section 305 with the following addition:

> (d) The court may dismiss a case under chapter 7 of this title upon the motion of any party in interest made not later than thirty days after the meeting of creditors, and after notice and a hearing, if the debtor is ineligible for relief under the provisions of section 109(f).[3]

Proposed section 109(f) contained a test to determine when Chapter 7 relief was inappropriate for a given debtor. This test provided that:

> [a]n individual may be a debtor under chapter 7 of this title only if such individual cannot pay a reasonable portion of his debts out of anticipated future income.[4]

Intermediate legislative attempts included definitions of "reasonable portion of debts" and "anticipated future income."[5] Many of these defini-

---

6. See In re MacFarlane Webster Associates, 121 B.R. 694 (Bankr. S.D.N.Y.1990); Weltman v. Independence Savings Bank, 1990 WL 96087 (S.D.N.Y.1990), aff'd, 927 F.2d 593 (2d Cir.1991), cert. denied, __ U.S. __, 111 S.Ct. 2269, 114 L.Ed.2d 721 (1991).

§ 7–44

1. Title 3 of the Bankruptcy Amendments and Federal Judgeship Act of 1984, Pub.L. No. 98–353, 98 Stat. 355.

2. In 1986 it was amended to its current form. The 1986 amendments added the language, "or on a motion by the United States Trustee" and changed the "and" to "but". Bankruptcy Judges, United States Trustee, and Family Farmer Bankruptcy Act of 1986, Pub.L.No. 99–554 § 219(b), 100 Stat. 3100.

3. H.R. 4786, 97th Cong., 1st Sess. § 3 (1981).

4. H.R. 4786, 97th Cong., 1st Sess. § 2 (1981).

5. Soon after H.R. 4786 was introduced, the Senate came up with its own set of bank-

tions were opposed by debtors' advocates. This opposition led to the compromise found in the 'substantial abuse' provision currently in section 707(b). Each camp probably agreed to the vague terminology in the hope that judicial interpretations would give their meaning to the statute.[6]

Interpreting the section is difficult for several reasons. Mainly, the conception of the section is muddled; without saying so in terms, it seems in conflict with the fresh start policy of Chapter 7. Also, the execution was

ruptcy amendments, S.2000. It proposed the following amendment to section 109:

* * * (c)(1) Subject to the provisions of paragraph (2) of this subsection, an individual may not be a debtor under chapter 7 of this title if such individual can pay a reasonable portion of his debts out of anticipated future income. For the purposes of this paragraph, the term—

(a) 'reasonable portion of debts' shall mean a substantial percentage of the total outstanding debt reflected upon the schedule of liabilities filed pursuant to section 521(1), excluding debts secured by a first mortgage or deed of trust on the debtor's principal residence;

(b) 'anticipated future income' shall mean such income, if any, that the debtor has a reasonable expectation of receiving, either from sources which—

(i) are providing actual income at the time of the filing of the petition, or

(ii) will provide income commencing upon a date certain within twelve months following the filing of the petitions, and which is not needed by the debtor for the support of himself and his dependents.

(2) The provisions of this section shall not apply in any case where the court finds that its application would impose undue hardship upon the debtor and the debtor's dependents.

S. 2000, 97th Cong., 1st Sess. § 2(c) (1981).

Compared to S.2000, H.R. 7294 demanded much more from those seeking a dismissal. That bill placed four hurdles between a creditor and a successful motion:

* * * (b)(1) Before the granting of the discharge, on motion of a creditor holding an allowed unsecured claim or one reasonably believed to be allowable, after notice and a hearing, the court shall dismiss a case under this chapter only if—

(A) the debtor is an individual;

(B) anticipated disposable income for a reasonable period after the commencement of the case equals or exceeds a reasonable portion of debts;

(C) it would be inequitable not to dismiss the case; and

(D) dismissal of the case will not impose an undue hardship on the debtor or a dependent of the debtor * * *.

H.R. 7294, 97th Cong., 2d Sess. § 308(2) (1982).

When considering these elements, the court was always to give due consideration to the primary goal of providing a fresh start to an individual debtor and to all factors—including financial—concerning the debtor. Id.

H.R. 7294 also contained slightly different formulas for determining when to dismiss a case. These were included as proposed amendments to section 101:

(3) "anticipated disposable income" means—

(A) income that the debtor has, at the time of the commencement of the case, a reasonable expectation of receiving for the reasonable future; less

(B) expenditures that the debtor has, at the time of the commencement of the case, a reasonable expectation of making to support the debtor and the debtor's dependents, and to operate any business of the debtor, for the foreseeable future, based on the level of support and operation, that the debtor generally and reasonably provided before the commencement of the case and on any change in circumstances that may affect such level;

* * *

(36) 'reasonable portion of debts' means 70 percent in amount of the debtor's debts listed on the schedule of liabilities filed under section 521(1) of this title, excluding a debt secured by a first security interest in the debtor's principal residence * * *.

H.R. 7294, 97th Cong., 2d Sess. § 301(a)(1)-(2) (1982).

In 1983, the Senate responded with an approach substantially similar to that found in S.2000. The only noticeable change was the clarification of the earlier provision's "substantial percentage" language by replacing it with the phrase "50 per centum or more." S. 445, 98th Cong., 1st Sess. § 203, Bankruptcy Improvements Act: Hearing on S. 333 and S. 445 before the Senate Comm. on the Judiciary, 98th Cong., 1st Sess. 4–6 (1983).

S. 445 was amended before it passed the Senate. One amendment replaced the old formulas with a substantial abuse test similar to that currently found in section 707(b). Id. at 8.

6. See § 7–45(c) infra regarding substantial abuse.

bungled. Note especially that the 1984 version explicitly denied any party in interest (particularly creditors) the right even to "request" or "suggest" that the court dismiss under section 707(b).

This left the bankruptcy courts with a dilemma. Should one ignore the section? Surely Congress intended something. Must the judge him or herself examine every petition to discover whether it should be dismissed? On a crowded docket, that would be wasteful at best, impossible at worst. There are no clear answers to this dilemma.

The judge's dilemma was alleviated somewhat by the 1986 amendment. In 1986 Congress authorized the United States Trustee to make a motion for dismissal under 707(b).[7] Even though the current law is more cumbersome and less certain than a law that permitted creditor motions, after 1986 creditors at least can bring cases to the attention of the United States Trustee and encourage the trustee to move for dismissal.

While the procedural difficulty is alleviated, the conceptual difficulty remains. How does section 707(b) fit with the very idea of Chapter 7, namely, that a debtor is entitled to a fresh start so that he can keep his future earnings for himself? Surely, section 707(b) is not designed to bar a discharge for the mine-run debtor who comes to bankruptcy to start over. There must be something more than that to "substantial abuse." But exactly what is it? Some might argue the person who most needs bankruptcy is the one who is likely to have some significant income after the petition is filed, for if that were not true the debtor would not need the benefit of a discharge. There is an unavoidable tension between what the creditors were hoping to achieve in 707(b) and what debtors see as the central purpose of Chapter 7.

§ 7–45 Section 707(b)—Substantive Requirements

There are only three significant substantive requirements in section 707(b). First and second, one's debts must be "primarily" "consumer". This sentence in fact contains two conditions. One is buried in the adverb "primarily" and the other in the adjective "consumer". The third and most important requirement is that any granting of relief to this debtor would be a "substantial abuse" of the provisions of Chapter 7.

a. "Primarily"

The most obvious way to define "primarily" is to compare the dollar amount of consumer debts to all of one's debts. If the consumer debt is more than fifty percent in dollar amount, the party's debts are "primarily" consumer. Some courts hold that one must look not merely at the total dollar amount of debts, but also at the total number of debts. How these courts would integrate dollar amount with number is unclear. Presumably they would hold that even when more than 50 percent of the dollar amount of the debts were consumer, the debtor would not qualify if only a small

---

7. Bankruptcy Judges, United States Trustee, and Family Farmer Bankruptcy Act of 1986, Pub.L.No. 99–554, § 219(b), 100 Stat. 3100.

§ 7-45 LIQUIDATION 579

percentage of the total debts were consumer debts.[1] In our view, introduction of the number of debts into the formula merely courts confusion and invites litigation. We would stick to dollar amounts.

b. "Consumer" Debts

What are "consumer" debts? Section 101(8) defines a consumer debt as follows: "consumer debt means debt incurred by an individual primarily for a personal, family, or household purpose". The touchstone is the debtor's *use* of the money. The nature of the collateral, the business of the creditor and the form of the loan are all irrelevant. A loan of $25,000 from a Credit Union to pay for a child's education is a consumer debt, but the same loan used to finance the opening of an accounting business is not a consumer debt. This is so irrespective of the nature of the collateral put up for the debt.

The clearest and most persuasive statement of these rules is *In the Matter of Booth*.[2] In this case a husband and wife team of physicians declared bankruptcy. They had been brought to the door of the bankruptcy court not by their inability to earn a living practicing medicine but by their foolish investments. They had borrowed money against a variety of personal and other assets and used the money to operate and finance a marina, condominium project and other real estate ventures. Even though none apparently ever turned a profit, all of these ventures were business transactions "for" profit. Under 101(8) the court correctly finds these are not consumer debts. We think the court is exactly right in looking to the purpose for which a loan is used in order to determine whether it is a consumer debt or not.

The remarks on the floor of the legislature by two of the proponents of the 1978 Code have sometimes troubled the courts in determining whether loans secured by real estate are to be treated as consumer loans. In connection with the enactment of the Code in 1978, Senator DeConcini and Congressman Edwards both stated on the floor of the Congress that a consumer debt would not include a debt to the extent that the debt was secured "by real property".[3] Responding to those statements, some courts have held that debts secured by real estate, particularly the debtor's residence, cannot be consumer debts, therefore are not to be inserted in the

---

§ 7-45

1. In re Kelly, 841 F.2d 908 (9th Cir.1988) (when more than half the dollar amount is consumer debt, statutory threshold is passed); In re Wilkes, 114 B.R. 551 (Bankr. W.D.Tenn. 1989) (court focuses on dollar amount citing Kelly and Bell favorably); In re Bell, 65 B.R. 575 (Bankr. E.D.Mich.1986) (31% of debt was consumer debt in terms of dollar amount, so dismissal denied); but cf. In the Matter of Booth, 858 F.2d 1051 (5th Cir.1988) (look to both the dollar amount and the number of creditors); In re Johnson, 115 B.R. 159 (Bankr. S.D. Ill.1990) (should look to both dollar amount and number of creditors to determine if "primarily consumer"); In re Restea, 76 B.R. 728 (Bankr. D.S.D. 1987) (consumer debts should be evaluated not only by amount, but by their relative number); In re Bryant, 47 B.R. 21 (Bankr. W.D.N.C. 1984) ("primarily consumer debts" not only aggregate amount but also the relative number of creditors).

2. 858 F.2d 1051 (5th Cir.1988).

3. "[A] consumer debt does not include a debt to any extent the debt is secured by real property", 124 Cong. Rec. 32393, 124 Cong. Rec. 17406, daily ed. October 6, 1978 (Senator DeConcini); see also 124 Cong. Rec. H. 11,090 (daily ed. Sept. 28, 1978) (statement of Congressman Edwards).

calculation to determine whether the debtor's debts are primarily consumer debts.[4]

Finding that the definition quoted above includes secured and unsecured debt, other courts have declined to follow individual statements of the Senator and the Congressman. Noting in *In re Kelly*[5] that "stray comments by individual legislators, not otherwise supported by statutory language or committee reports, cannot be attributed to the full body that voted on the bill,"[6] the Court of Appeals for the Ninth Circuit gave little weight to such statements. It found that the statutory language was more persuasive:

> The Code defines "consumer debt" as "debt incurred by an individual primarily for a personal, family, or household purpose." 11 U.S.C. § 101(7) (1982). "Debt" means "liability on a claim," 11 U.S.C. § 101(11)(1982), and "claim," in turn, is broadly defined as any "right to payment, whether or not such right is * * * *secured, or unsecured.*" 11 U.S.C. § 101(4)(A) (1982) (emphasis added). A literal reading of the Code's simple language leads inexorably to the conclusion that consumer debt includes secured debt. Indeed, section 521(2) of the Code, also added by the 1984 Act, makes special provision for "consumer debts which are secured by property of the estate," an unambiguous indication that Congress intended that the "secured or unsecured" language of the definition apply to consumer debts.
>
> Nor is there any indication that debts secured by real property are to be treated differently. To the contrary, section 524 of the Code explicitly recognizes that consumer debt may be secured by real property, making different provisions for the reaffirmation of consumer debt depending on whether or not it is "consumer debt secured by real property." 11 U.S.C. §§ 524(c)(6)(B), (d)(2) (Supp. III 1985). The statutory scheme so clearly contemplates that consumer debt include debt secured by real property that there is no room left for any other conclusion.[7]

The reasoning of *Kelly* has persuaded other courts.[8] If one could avoid the reach of section 707(b) merely by granting security in real estate, few would be subject to section 707(b). Nor does it follow that debtors will be turned away from the bankruptcy court in droves under section 707(b) simply because their debts are primarily consumer debts. Presumably most consumer debtors have debts that are primarily consumer debt. It is true, therefore, that treating debts for personal purposes but secured by real

---

4. Cf. In re Walton, 866 F.2d 981 (8th Cir. 1989) (secured part of mortgage owed to HUD was not a consumer debt); In re Circle Five, Inc., 75 B.R. 686 (Bankr. D.Idaho 1987) (court held that a consumer debt is not one secured by real estate and that for definitional purposes, the term "family" does not refer to adult children or relatives who are not part of the debtor's household); In re Green, 70 B.R. 164 (Bankr. W.D.Ark.1986) (a debt secured by real property owned by debtor's mother was considered a "nonconsumer" debt); see also In re Ikeda, 37 B.R. 193 (Bankr. D.Hawaii 1984); Matter of Nenninger, 32 B.R. 624 (Bankr. W.D.Wis.1983); In re Randolph, 28 B.R. 811 (Bankr. E.D.Va.1983); In re Stein, 18 B.R. 768 (Bankr. S.D.Ohio 1982).

5. 841 F.2d 908 (9th Cir.1988).

6. Id. at 912 n.3.

7. 841 F.2d at 912.

8. In re Higginbotham, 111 B.R. 955 (Bankr. N.D. Okla. 1990); In re Wegner, 91 B.R. 854 (Bankr. D. Minn. 1988); In re Bell, 65 B.R. 575 (Bankr. E.D.Mich.1986); In re Bryant, 47 B.R. 21 (Bankr. W.D.N.C. 1984); cf. In re Walton, 866 F.2d 981 (8th Cir. 1989) (unsecured portion of HUD mortgage consumer debt).

estate as consumer debts will bring a larger number of potential parties within section 707(b)'s reach than would otherwise be the case, but that surely was what the consumer creditors intended it to do, and, in our view, what Congress did. As we discuss below, only a handful of these debtors will have their cases dismissed under the subsection. Most will not have committed "substantial abuse."

c. Substantial Abuse

Here the rope begins to fray under the tension between section 524's fresh start and section 707(b)'s dismissal for abuse. The resolution of this tension is not helped by the fact that the Congress was divided and that the "substantial abuse" language itself may have been adopted as a knowing ambiguity to obscure true policy disagreement between the conservatives and the liberals in Congress. Earlier versions of 707(b) contained a specific formula for determining the point at which a debtor's ability to pay some debts would preclude Chapter 7 relief.[9] Because of vigorous efforts by some members of the Senate Judiciary Committee that formula was replaced with the substantial abuse phrase.[10] During the consideration and after the adoption of the 1984 amendments, representatives of both camps individually asserted their own interpretation of the substantial abuse doctrine on the floor of the Congress.[11]

Maintaining that the fresh start doctrine of Chapter 7 should leave the debtor with his postpetition income intact, the liberals argued that the amount of future income that might be earned and enjoyed by the debtor should not be considered in determining whether the filing was a substantial abuse. The conservatives maintained just the opposite, namely, that the taking of bankruptcy by the one who would enjoy high future income was the very abuse that should be punished.

---

9. See § 7-44 supra.

10. Senator Metzenbaum put up fierce resistance to the mechanical formula for future income. As a result of negotiations from both camps the formula was kept out of S.1013 and S.445 and the term "substantial abuse" took its place. For an insight into the evolution of the negotiation process see Rep. No. 65 2-4, 90-91; 130 Cong. Rec. S5358 (daily ed. April 27, 1983) (remarks of Sen. Dole), S5359 (remarks of Sen. Thurmond), S5359-S5361 (remarks of Sen. Metzenbaum); see also remarks made after enactment; 130 Cong. Rec. S5361, 5387-S5388 (daily ed. April 27, 1983) (remarks of Sen. Metzenbaum); id. at S5359 (daily ed. April 27, 1983) (remarks of Sens. Thurmond and Dole).

11. See 130 Cong.Rec. S.7624, (daily ed. June 19, 1984) ("under [the 1984 Act], the availability of bankruptcy relief would not be limited by future earnings standard") (statement of Sen. Metzenbaum); 130 Cong.Rec. H.7489, (daily ed. June 29, 1984) ("the consumer credit amendments * * * contain no threshold or future income test") (statement Representative Rodino); compare 130 Cong. Rec. H1808 (daily ed. March 21, 1984) ("I am afraid that with the 1978 changes Congress also unintentionally created incentives for individuals to invoke straight bankruptcy where other options may be available * * * [T]he changes in 5174 are badly needed and will go a long way toward curbing the increasing number of unnecessary chapter 7 straight bankruptcy filings * * *.") (statements of Rep. Roukema); 130 Cong. Rec. S6087 (daily ed. May 21, 1984) ("The bankruptcy law has become too liberal, particularly in the area of consumer credit transactions, and has provided an escape hatch for those overextended debtors, who in the long run could well afford to meet their obligations") (statements of Sen. Heflin); id. at S6090 (daily ed. May 21 1984) ("As I mentioned earlier, title III contains more than 30 amendments to insure that a fresh start does not become a head start") (statement of Sen. Hatch); 130 Cong. Rec. H.7499, (daily ed. June 29, 1984) ("no one who is capable of refinancing his debts should be discouraged from doing so.") (statement of Representative Anderson).

The committee report on the final version of Senate Bill 445 states that the rules were intended to uphold "creditors' interest in obtaining repayment where such payment would not be a burden." Moreover, the committee report suggests that when a debtor "can meet his debts without difficulty when they become due, use of Chapter 7" is a "substantial abuse." [12] Most of the cases decided under section 707(b) find that the debtor's ability to repay debts is at least a principal ingredient in determining whether there is substantial abuse.[13] Some courts, like the Ninth Circuit in *In re Kelly,* take the position that "a finding that a debtor is able to repay his debts, standing alone, supports a conclusion of substantial abuse." [14]

Even if one agrees with *Kelly,* there is still the question whether a particular debtor is truly "able" to repay his debts. This, however, is a familiar question for bankruptcy courts. It is a question they must routinely examine in passing on Chapter 13 plans where they are called upon to compare the amount of debt, the debtor's budget and the debtor's disposable income. They must do so in deciding whether to approve plans over the challenge of the creditor, whether to insist upon a five or a three year plan, whether to require that the debtor adjust her budget.

Some courts have used a potential Chapter 13 plan as a way of testing whether the debtor does have the "ability" to make repayment. If it is apparent that the debtor could have sustained a Chapter 13 plan under which most of the indebtedness would have been repaid over a five-year period, some courts have found that alone to be evidence of an ability to repay. At least one debtor has unsuccessfully argued that the availability of Chapter 13 is the principal test and because his debt was greater than the $100,000 limit contained in Chapter 13, he should be found not to have the ability to repay. That, of course, does not follow.[15]

---

12. S. Rep. No. 65, 98th Cong. 1st Sess. 53, 54, 1983.

This provision represents a balancing of two interests. It preserves the fundamental concept embodied in our bankruptcy laws that debtors who cannot meet debts as they come due should be able to relinquish non-exempt property in exchange for a fresh start. At the same time, however, it upholds the creditors' interest in obtaining repayment where such repayment would not be a burden.

Crushing debt burdens and severe financial problems place enormous strains on borrowers, and their family life, personal emotional health, or work productivity often suffer. By enabling individuals who cannot pay, the bankruptcy laws allow troubled borrowers to become productive members of the community. Nothing in this bill denies such borrowers with unaffordable debt burdens bankruptcy relief under Chapter 7. However, if a debtor can meet his debts without difficulty as they become due, use of Chapter 7 would represent a substantial abuse.

13. In re Walton, 866 F.2d 981 (8th Cir. 1989); In re Kelly, 841 F.2d 908 (9th Cir.1988);

In re Wilkes, 114 B.R. 551 (Bankr. W.D.Tenn. 1989); Matter of Strong, 84 B.R. 541 (Bankr. N.D.Ind. 1988); In re Renner, 70 B.R. 27 (Bankr. D.N.D. 1987); In re Struggs, 71 B.R. 96 (E.D.Mich.1987); Matter of Cord, 68 B.R. 5 (Bankr. W.D.Mo.1986); In re Gaukler, 63 B.R. 224 (Bankr. D.N.D. 1986); In re Kress, 57 B.R. 874 (Bankr. D.N.D. 1985); In re Hudson, 56 B.R. 415 (Bankr. N.D.Ohio 1985); In re Grant, 51 B.R. 385 (Bankr. N.D.Ohio 1985); In re Edwards, 50 B.R. 933 (Bankr. S.D.N.Y. 1985); In re White, 49 B.R. 869 (Bankr. W.D.N.C. 1985); but cf. In re Shands, 63 B.R. 121 (Bankr. E.D.Mich.1985) ("some egregious circumstances" in addition to ability to pay debts is required before dismissal); contra Matter of Antal, 85 B.R. 838 (Bankr. W.D.Mo.1988) (because § 541(a)(6) exempts future earnings from the property of Chapter 7 estate, future earnings and thus "ability to pay" may not be considered for purposes of determining "substantial abuse" and in effect § 707(b) is a "dead letter") relying on Matter of Brady, 86 B.R. 616 (W.D.Mo.1987).

14. 841 F.2d 908, 915 (9th Cir.1988).

15. In re Krohn, 886 F.2d 123 (6th Cir. 1989).

Some courts will find the need for some additional evidence of abuse beyond the ratio of the debtor's future income to the debtor's liabilities. Sometimes such evidence can be found in the debtor's dishonesty to the court.[16] In other cases, abuse might be inferred from the nature of the indebtedness and how it was incurred. We suspect that the holding in *In re Kelly* was based in part upon the fact that the debtors in that case were a lawyer and his wife who had apparently been involved in a bitter and unsuccessful dispute with a couple that had sold a house to them.

In the underlying case, the Kellys' sued the sellers for breach of contract, punitive damages, and attorney's fees. Their case against the sellers was found to be so lacking in merit that the defendant sellers were awarded attorney's fees and costs, originally in the amount of $16,369.90, amounts that later grew to more than $25,000. Moreover, in that case Kelly transferred his interest in his law firm to his partner and paid off other unsecured creditors shortly before the bankruptcy. We suspect that even courts that maintain that the only question is the ratio of future income to current indebtedness may be influenced by judgments about the fairness of the prepetition behavior of the debtors.[17]

§ 7-46 Section 707(b)—Retrospective

Because broad application of section 707(b) would conflict with the basic policy of Chapter 7 and because only a modest percentage of all Chapter 7 debtors have enough current and stable income to bail themselves out, we doubt that section 707(b) will ever become widely applied or frequently used. This judgment is supported by the quirky procedural route that must be travelled in order to bring a substantial abuse case to the court's attention. Since the creditor cannot make a motion for the court to consider section 707(b), but must either wait for the court to act *sua sponte* or must persuade

---

16. See In re Cook, 110 B.R. 544 (Bankr. N.D.Okl.1990) (debtor suffered no unforeseen calamity causing financial difficulty and had misrepresented his financial picture to the court as well as claiming unreasonable monthly expenses); but see In re Latimer, 82 B.R. 354 (Bankr. E.D.Pa. 1988) ("manipulation" of one's property to maximize exemptions is not basis for dismissal in bankruptcy cases); In re Bryant, 47 B.R. 21 (Bankr. W.D.N.C.1984) (dismissing petition where debtor was able to repay debts and had not truthfully reported his financial conditions).

17. In re Krohn, 886 F.2d 123 (6th Cir. 1989); In re Harris, 122 B.R. 744 (Bankr. D.S.D. 1990), order rev'd, 125 B.R. 254 (D.S.D. 1991) (must show more than just naked ability of debtor to repay significant amount of unsecured debts under a Chapter 13 plan; egregious behavior, such as repeated bankruptcy filings evidencing a lack of good faith, fraud, impropriety or evidence of misconduct, must also be established); In re Wheeler, 101 B.R. 39 (Bankr. N.D.Ind. 1989) (debtor's postpetition sale of a motorcycle before former spouse could exercise her rights in the same, pursuant to property settlement of divorce decree warranted denial of discharge on grounds debtor intended to hinder, delay or defraud former wife); In re Shands, 63 B.R. 121 (Bankr. E.D.Mich.1985) ("some egregious circumstance" is also required as a factor before dismissal); In re Grant, 51 B.R. 385 (Bankr. N.D.Ohio 1985) (no resolve to "tighten belt" or to incur debts with the clear intent to pay creditors grounds for dismissal as "substantial abuse"); see also In re Walton, 866 F.2d 981 (8th Cir.1989) (court may take petitioner's good faith and unique hardships into consideration in determining whether Chapter 7 petition should be dismissed on grounds of substantial abuse); Waites v. Braley, 110 B.R. 211 (E.D.Va.1990) (Neither bad faith nor fraud is element required for finding of "substantial abuse" warranting dismissal for Chapter 7 case, although courts may consider bad faith or fraud in determining whether there is "substantial abuse"); but cf. In the Matter of Belt, 106 B.R. 553 (Bankr. N.D.Ind. 1989) ("Plan may be confirmed even in face of egregious prefiling conduct if other factors suggest that plan represents debtor's good faith effort to satisfy creditors' claims.").

the United States Trustee to raise the issue, there is already a substantial procedural filter that will remove many of the doubtful cases from the stream.

F. REDEMPTION, SECTION 722

§ 7–47 Introduction and Overview of Redemption

Section 722 on redemption of goods by a debtor may be regarded as a cousin of section 524(c) on reaffirmation. In many cases a debtor's choice will be to keep his assets by redeeming under 722 or by reaffirming under 524. The successful invocation of either section by a debtor has similar but not identical consequences.

Section 722 is novel, but it presents only a small number of interpretive issues. It is a novel addition to the law because it allows redemption not by the payment of the full amount due on the debt—the kind of redemption contemplated by U.C.C. § 9–506—but by payment of the debt or the value of the collateral, *whichever is less.*

Consider how redemption under Article 9 would work as compared with redemption under 722. Assume a debt of $15,000 secured by an automobile worth $10,000. To redeem under section 9-506 the debtor must tender "fulfillment of all obligations secured by the collateral as well as expenses reasonably incurred by the secured party." In the hypothetical case, a debtor redeeming under 9–506 would have to pay $15,000 plus costs and perhaps even attorneys' fees. But the same debtor could redeem under 722 by paying only $10,000, "the amount of the allowed secured claim". Under section 506 the allowed secured claim is the lesser of the debt or the value of the collateral, here $10,000.

There are several important limitations under section 722. First it is a part of Chapter 7 and is presumably applicable only in Chapter 7 cases. Secondly, it applies only to consumer goods, "property intended primarily for personal, family, or household use." Third it applies only to liens on property exempt under section 522 or abandoned under section 554. Thus, if the trustee has not abandoned the property in question and if the state had opted out of federal exemptions and had no applicable state law exemption, no redemption would be possible.

We believe that the lion's share of all redemptions are of personal vehicles, automobiles, pickups, vans and such. Most state exemption laws cover personal automobiles. Where the federal exemption statute (section 522(d)) applies, section 522(d)(2) exempts $1,200 in value in an automobile and 522(d)(5) may grant an additional exemption of $3,750. Requirements of exemption or abandonment will rarely be an obstacle to redemption. When a valid security interest secures a debt that exceeds the value of the automobile is the very case when the trustee is likely to abandon the asset because there is nothing in it for the estate.

Since the debtor need pay only the "amount of the secured claim" and since the amount of the secured claim is defined in section 506(a) to equal "the value of such creditor's interest in the estate's interest in such property"—in words of one syllable, equal to the value of the property—the critical question is how to measure the value of the property.¹ We deal with that question at length.

An even more critical question is whether or not reducing a lien in this way, i.e., a process known as *"lien stripping,"* is possible through section 506 alone, specifically section 506(d), without resort to section 722. Section 506(d) provides, without any of the limitations of section 722, that "[t]o the extent that a lien secures a claim against the debtor that is not an allowed secured claim, such lien is void * * *." The importance of section 722 is diluted (to say the least) if Chapter 7 debtors can strip liens solely by force of section 506(d). The courts disagree, but the majority allow it.²

§ 7-47

1. Where the value of the property clearly exceeds the amount of the debt there is no valuation problem because in that case the debtor will have to pay the entire debt in order to redeem.

2. See, e.g., Matter of Folendore, 862 F.2d 1537, 1539 (11th Cir.1989) ("[W]e adopt the majority view that section 506(d) allows the voiding of a[n][unsecured] lien [even] when a court has not disallowed the claim."); Gaglia v. First Fed. Sav. & Loan Ass'n, 889 F.2d 1304, 1306–1311 (3d Cir.1989) (using § 506(d) Chapter 7 debtor can void unsecured portion of lien on residence even though debtor lacks equity in the property); Matter of Buckland, 123 B.R. 573, 575–76 (Bankr. S.D.Ohio 1991) ("[T]his court concludes that a chapter 7 debtor may bifurcate a secured creditor's claim and avoid any lien on the unsecured claim."); Matter of Crawford, 115 B.R. 381, 383 (Bankr. N.D.Ga. 1990) (Chapter 7 debtor may void an unsecured lien pursuant to § 506(d)); In re Leavell, 124 B.R. 535, 537–41 (Bankr. S.D.Ill.1991) (A Chapter 7 debtor may generally avoid excess liens under § 506(d), but not liens securing nondischargeable tax debts.); In re Kostecky, 111 B.R. 823, 825–27 (Bankr. D. Minn. 1990) (debtors could avoid liens against exempt homestead property to the extent that the liens secured debt in excess of property's value); In re Moses, 110 B.R. 962, 963–64 (Bankr. N.D. Okla. 1990) (unsecured real estate mortgage liens can be voided pursuant to § 506(d)); In re Richardson, 121 B.R. 546, 548 (Bankr. S.D. Ill.1990) ("This Court * * * adopts the view that § 506(d) is not restricted to use for a particular bankruptcy purpose and is, therefore, available for the benefit of the Chapter 7 debtor," and can be used to avoid second mortgage which exceeded the value of the real estate.); In re Zlogar, 101 B.R. 1, 3–10 (Bankr. N.D.Ill. 1989), judgment aff'd, 126 B.R. 53 (N.D.Ill.1991) (debtor can avoid unsecured liens through § 506 even though the trustee has abandoned the property and even though the purpose is to redeem or otherwise retain the property for the debtor's sole benefit); In re Garnett, 88 B.R. 123, 125–26 (Bankr.W.D.Ky.1988), aff'd sub nom., United States v. Garnett, 99 B.R. 757 (W.D.Ky.1989) (Chapter 7 debtor may use § 506(d) to void lien against debtor's real property to the extent the liens are unsecured); In re Haugland, 83 B.R. 648, 651 (Bankr. D.Minn. 1988) (in Chapter 7 case debtor avoided unsecured lien on combine using § 506(d) even though trustee had abandoned the property); cf. In re Cobb, 122 B.R. 22, 25–26 (Bankr. E.D.Pa. 1990) (Chapter 13 debtor is entitled to bifurcate mortgagee's claim under § 506(a) & (d).); In re Krahn, 124 B.R. 78, 81–82 (Bankr. D.Minn.1990) (The law in this jurisdiction is clear that liens on exempt property are subject to avoidance under § 506(d), even in a chapter 13 case and even federal tax liens.); but see In re Dewsnup, 908 F.2d 588, 589–93 (10th Cir. 1990), aff'd, ___ U.S. ___, 112 S.Ct. 733, 116 L.Ed.2d 903 (1992) (Chapter 7 debtor cannot use § 506(d) to void unsecured lien and then fully redeem the property under § 722); In re Lange, 120 B.R. 132 (Bankr. 9th Cir. 1990) (Lien avoidance under § 506(d) is not available to chapter 7 debtors.) In re Gaylor, 123 B.R. 236 (Bankr. E.D.Mich.1991) (Chapter 7 debtor cannot strip down liens under § 506.); In re Douthart, 123 B.R. 1, 3–4 (Bankr. D.N.H.1990) (Section 506 cannot be used as an avoiding power in chapter 7 cases.), In re Israel, 112 B.R. 481, 484–85 (Bankr. D. Conn. 1990) (§ 506(d) cannot be used to avoid a lien on property that is not property of the estate because it has been abandoned); In re McCullough, 122 B.R. 251 (Bankr. W.D.Pa. 1990) (A chapter 7 debtor cannot use § 506 to avoid a federal tax lien.); Matter of D'Angona, 107 B.R. 448, 449–51 (Bankr. D.Conn.1989) (Chapter 7 debtor cannot use § 506 to avoid liens on abandoned real estate); Matter of Doty, 104 B.R. 133, 135–37 (Bankr. S.D.Iowa 1989) (Chapter 7 debtor cannot use § 506(a) & (d) to avoid unsecured portion of undersecured lien on exempt real estate); cf. In re Wilks, 123 B.R. 555, 562 (Bankr. W.D.Tex.1991) (A chapter 13 plan cannot strip down a lien using § 506, which does not apply in a chapter 13 case.). For discussion of the issue, see generally Note, Can a Debtor Void a Real Property Lien that Exceeds the Value of the Collateral?: An Interpretation of Section 506(d) of the Bankruptcy Code, 45 Wash. & Lee L. Rev. 1393 (1988).

To the extent that section 722 remains useful and is applied, there are a series of pesky little questions that lie on the fringes of section 722, and that must be answered whatever the importance of section 722, such as what is property used primarily for personal, family or household use, and when has such property been abandoned or exempt under section 522 or 554. These issues have presented little controversy and we devote little space to them.

An issue of great significance is the question whether the debtor must redeem by lump sum payment or whether the court may approve an installment redemption. Although a few courts initially allowed installment redemption,[3] most courts, including two Courts of Appeals,[4] have held that section 722 requires a lump sum payment by a debtor. We believe the latter courts are correct. If the Congress had wished to grant installment redemption, it could have said so. Moreover, Congress did grant such authority in the form of Chapter 13. Thus a debtor who wishes to enjoy the benefit of unilaterally imposed installment redemption should go to Chapter 13 and will there find that he could impose such a redemption on the creditor. Alternatively, of course, the debtor can negotiate with the creditor for reaffirmation at a price roughly equivalent to the value of the collateral and, if the creditor agrees, achieve that result by agreement.[5]

In an earlier discussion we cover the relationship between 524 on reaffirmation and 722 on redemption.[6] There we note that the Court of Appeals for the Tenth Circuit in *Lowry Federal Credit Union v. West*[7]—while denying that installment redemption under 722 is possible—has in effect allowed something similar by permitting the debtor to retain his automobile after a Chapter 7 discharge and without reaffirmation. The outcome in *Lowry Federal Credit Union* is not exactly the same as an installment redemption because in *Lowry* the debtor was paying the full amount of the debt and did not seek to reduce the proposed amount to the value of the automobile.

§ 7–48 Substantive Requirements

As we indicate above, the substantive requirements for redemption are few and straightforward. They can be segregated and identified as follows: redemption is permitted of (1) tangible personal property, (2) intended primarily for personal, family or household use, (3) from a lien securing a

---

On the other hand, section 506 cannot be turned around (or inside out) and used to extinguish an oversecured creditor's equity cushion. In re Hanna, 912 F.2d 945, 948–49 (8th Cir.1990).

3. In re Carroll, 7 B.R. 907 (Bankr. D.Ariz. 1981), rev'd, 11 B.R. 725 (Bankr. 9th Cir.1981); In re Berenguer, 77 B.R. 959 (Bankr. S.D.Fla. 1987); In re Davis, 15 B.R. 118 (Bankr. C.D.Ill. 1981), rev'd in part, aff'd in part, 20 B.R. 212 (C.D.Ill. 1982).

4. Matter of Edwards, 901 F.2d 1383 (7th Cir.1990); In re Bell, 700 F.2d 1053 (6th Cir. 1983); see also In re Hart, 8 B.R. 1020 (N.D. N.Y. 1981); In re Zimmerman, 4 B.R. 739 (Bankr. S.D.Cal.1980).

5. This agreement will not be crucial for all Chapter 7 debtors. The Supreme Court recently held that a person who receives a discharge in Chapter 7 may reschedule a mortgage lien in Chapter 13. Johnson v. Home State Bank, __ U.S. __, 111 S.Ct. 2150, 115 L.Ed.2d 66 (1991), on remand, 940 F.2d 609 (10th Cir.1991). This procedure, known as a "Chapter 20," enables a debtor to write down his undersecured debt to the value of the collateral, discharge the deficiency, and then propose a Chapter 13 plan to pay the collateral's value in installments. For further discussion of "Chapter 20s," see § 9–30 infra.

6. See § 7–39 supra.

7. 882 F.2d 1543 (10th Cir.1989).

dischargeable consumer debt, (4) if the property is exempted under section 522 or has been abandoned under 554.

Since consumer debts are often used to buy personal property, the first two requirements are really one. Although one case raised the question whether a fence purchased from Montgomery Ward constituted "tangible personal property" or whether it was real estate because it had become a fixture,[1] that question is seldom at issue. Likewise there is seldom an issue whether the debt securing the obligation is a consumer debt and whether the asset is to be used for personal, family or household use. Although such an issue could arise—as for example, where a pickup truck was used for business purposes [2]—there is almost no litigation on that question either.

Exactly what is meant by the requirement that the property must be "exempted" has been the subject of some dispute. We believe that the exempted or abandoned requirement is included in section 722 to insure that no unsecured creditor has a legitimate claim against the asset to be redeemed. No unsecured creditor would have an interest if the asset would be exempt or if the trustee, acting for the unsecured creditors, abandons.

In at least one case a secured creditor successfully challenged this interpretation and used the "exempted" language to its benefit. In *In re Seguin*[3] the debtor sought to redeem a 1985 Dodge Omni. The debtor claimed the automobile was worth $2,250. Chrysler Credit, whose claim exceeded $5,000, claimed the value of the car to be $4,900. On either valuation, Chrysler's lien exceeded the value of the automobile. Chrysler argued that the Colorado exemptions were not effective against a purchase money claimant, at least where the purchase money claimant held a security interest, and therefore that the property was not "exempted" vis à vis Chrysler as provided in section 722, even though the Colorado statute would have permitted the debtor to have claimed the exemption against unsecured creditors.

The *Seguin* court accepted that argument.[4] We believe the case is an incorrect interpretation of 722; it has not been followed in other jurisdictions.[5] To read the language correctly, one should respond to Chrysler Credit's argument in *Seguin* as follows. It is enough if there is an exemption against unsecured creditors. Section 722 gives the debtor a unilateral right—without agreement of the secured creditor—to redeem the collateral for a specific payment. In almost all of the redemption cases the exemptions in 522 or in state law would not be effective against a secured creditor, yet that secured creditor is the very person against whom redemption is granted.

§ 7–48

1. In re Hall, 11 B.R. 3 (Bankr. W.D.Mo. 1980).
2. In re Pipes, 78 B.R. 981 (Bankr. W.D.Mo.1987).
3. 76 B.R. 175 (Bankr. D.Colo.1987).
4. See also In re Holcomb, 54 B.R. 59 (Bankr. D.Colo.1985).
5. See In re Williams, 9 B.R. 83 (Bankr. M.D.Tenn.1981); In re Fitzgerald, 20 B.R. 27 (Bankr. N.D.N.Y. 1982). Note that most of the cases discussed in this section by implication disagree with the outcome in Seguin, because in almost all of them the debtor is redeeming from the holder of a purchase money security interest whose claim could not be set aside under 522 or under any other provision of the Code. By implication those cases read the exempted language in 722 to protect unsecured creditors, not the secured creditor who is the subject of the redemption claim.

Note, however, that if there is *no* applicable exemption law (i.e., none effective even against unsecured creditors) and if the trustee has not abandoned, then redemption is not permitted.[6] In that case section 522 does not protect the asset from the claims of the unsecured creditors and there is no act (abandonment under 554) that demonstrates a decision by the unsecured's representative that there is no value in the asset. If the trustee is vindictive in her refusal to abandon property that has no value to the estate, the court can order the trustee to abandon the property under section 554(b). Presumably, in courts that follow *Seguin* or in cases like *Zaicek*[7], one seeking to use 722 will have to persuade the trustee to abandon or persuade the court to order the trustee to abandon under 554(b).

§ 7–49 Valuation

By a wide margin the most frequently litigated question in section 722 concerns the amount the debtor will have to pay in order to redeem the collateral. These valuation arguments sometimes ask when the collateral should be valued. Is the proper measuring point the time of the petition, the time of the redemption hearing, or some other time? The larger number of cases deal with the question, what market or what standard should be used, in order to value the property. Some of these cases involve household goods[1]; an occasional case deals with mobile homes[2] and farm machinery[3], but all of these cases may be regarded as sports.

Section 722 is about the debtor's redemption of his motor vehicle, his car, his pickup truck or his van. Far more than half of the reported opinions deal with motor vehicles and there is no reason to believe the unreported cases have any different distribution.

Sometimes the debtor will list an automobile in his original schedules as having considerable value. Later, out of expediency or because of injury to the automobile, he will maintain that it is worth much less. For example, in *In re King*[4] the debtor originally listed his Chrysler as worth $2500. Later he sought to redeem it at $500 and later yet at $200. In *In re Van Holt*[5] it appears that the debtor had an automobile accident with his car after the petition was filed but before the redemption.

In such cases the time for measuring value may be important. Usually the value is asserted to be high at the time the petition is filed and thereafter to have declined because of use, accident, or for some other reason. Faced with significantly differing values at the time the petition is filed and at the time redemption is sought, most courts now find that the collateral is to be valued at the time of the request for redemption and not at the date of the petition.[6] Most courts reach that conclusion by noting that

---

6. In re Zaicek, 29 B.R. 31 (Bankr. W.D.Ky. 1983).

7. Where there was no applicable exemption as to mobile homes.

§ 7–49

1. In re Eagle, 51 B.R. 959 (Bankr. N.D.Ohio 1985).

2. Matter of McQuinn, 6 B.R. 899 (Bankr. D.Neb.1980); In re Zaicek, 29 B.R. 31 (Bankr. W.D.Ky.1983).

3. In re Sprecher, 65 B.R. 598 (Bankr. C.D.Ill. 1986).

4. 75 B.R. 287 (Bankr. S.D.Ohio 1987).

5. 28 B.R. 577 (Bankr. W.D.Mo.1983).

6. In re King, 75 B.R. 287 (Bankr. S.D.Ohio 1987); In re Van Holt, 28 B.R. 577 (Bankr.

the creditor would not be able to get possession of the automobile and to sell it for some time after the petition is filed. The courts assume that the creditor would have to have the stay lifted or get the debtor's agreement. Thus, these courts conclude that using a value at a time later than the date of petition would most closely approximate the creditor's alternative.

All of these cases assume the presence of a bankruptcy. Had there been no bankruptcy, presumably the creditor could have repossessed and resold shortly after a default. It is not obvious why the courts applying section 722 assume the bankruptcy as part of their initial premise. Would it not be equally sensible to assume a section 9–503 repossession and a prompt section 9–504 sale?

In any event, timing is likely to be of small consequence for two reasons. First, section 521(2), enacted as part of the 1984 amendments, forces the debtor to make an early decision about redemption and, absent court extension, to redeem the automobile within two and one-half months after the petition is filed. Except in an unusual case, the value at the date of the petition and the value 75 days later should be comparable. But even if a longer time intervenes, the change in value in an automobile and a fortiori in other consumer goods is likely to be insignificant. Even in an unusual case where there is an accident with the car between the time of the petition and the time of the redemption, the court may be able to protect the creditor as it did in *In re Van Holt*.[7] There the court required the debtor to add the insurance proceeds to the amount that would otherwise be paid.

It is not yet clear how true the courts will be to the spirit of section 521(2). One court declined to deny redemption to a debtor who had violated 521. It did so on the theory that the debtor had not injured the creditor.[8] In that case the debtor had first stated his intention to reaffirm the debt securing the collateral that was later redeemed. Even though there was no timely claim for redemption, the court held that the earlier proposal to reaffirm put the creditor on notice of the debtor's intention to retain the collateral and therefore that the failure of timely notice of redemption did not cause an injury. The most obvious penalty for a debtor's failure to comply with section 521(2) is to deny the debtor the rights that he would otherwise have earned by compliance, namely, to deny him the right to redeem in these cases.

The second valuation question is well known to students of U.C.C. Article 9. The question is whether the assets, usually the automobile, should be valued at retail, wholesale, or by some other standard. The debtor can be expected to argue that the wholesale price should be used. The debtor will claim that the purpose of section 722 is to put the creditor in the same position as though there had been repossession and resale and thus that the creditor should get only the net proceeds of wholesale resale, the kind of disposition that most repossessing creditors would undertake.

W.D.Mo.1983); Matter of Pierce, 5 B.R. 346 (Bankr. D.Neb.1980); In re Zaicek, 29 B.R. 31 (Bankr. W.D.Ky.1983); but see In re Kinser, 17 B.R. 468 (Bankr. N.D.Ga.1981) (stating the time of filing the petition is the time for measuring the value. It appears from the opinion that the time of the measuring of value was not an issue between the parties.)

7. 28 B.R. 577 (Bankr. W.D.Mo.1983).

8. In re Eagle, 51 B.R. 959 (Bankr. N.D.Ohio 1985).

The creditor will take the opposite position. It will argue that if there had been repossession, debtor would have had to purchase another car at retail from some third party and thus that the gross retail price is the proper measure because that is the value to the debtor.

Neither the Code nor the statutory history resolves this dispute. Routinely courts cite the statement in section 506(a) "such value shall be determined in light of the purpose of the valuation * * * "—as though that sentence gave some guidance. At best the sentence is a rationalization for a decision made on other grounds. In our view it is empty of substance.

To the extent that the cases resolve this dispute between retail and wholesale, they favor the wholesale market. Many courts seem to be persuaded that the goal of section 722 is to put the creditor in the same position as if repossession and resale had occurred.[9] Other courts arrive at the same conclusion by a different route. For example, in *Matter of McQuinn*[10] the court stated the redemption should be for the retail value, but allowed the debtor to subtract from that value $1,000 as the overhead and other sales costs that would be associated with the retail sale which were arguably avoided. The consequence of such subtraction, of course, is to use the wholesale not retail value.

A Solomonic division is possible. The Code speaks of value, not of a creditor's or of a debtor's value. Moreover, the creditor can argue that part of his bargain is a claim upon the idiosyncratic value that this particular debtor puts on this asset. In a freely bargained deal between the debtor and the creditor, the number negotiated would be neither the wholesale nor the retail value. For both parties this transaction is more efficient than the alternative (the repossession and resale on the part of the creditor and the purchase of a new car at retail by the debtor). The efficiency gain is roughly equivalent to the difference between the wholesale and the retail prices. There is no principled reason to give that entire efficiency gain to one or to the other. Why not split the difference, 50/50?[11]

Because most of these cases involve automobiles, because there is a nationwide market that is relatively thick and efficient, the errors here are not likely to be as great as they would be with real estate or other less fungible commodities. Courts routinely use the monthly publication of the National Automobile Dealer's Used Car Guide Company or the Kelly Blue Book. Normally these books list three prices for a particular year and model of car. For example, the July 1990 Central States Edition of the NADA Official Used Car Guide shows that the average trade-in value of a 1988 V8, Cadillac DeVille is $13,275. Its original price was $23,404. The average loan value in July 1990 was $11,950 and the average retail was $15,650. Each of these numbers can be adjusted upward or downward depending upon the mileage, accessories, and various packages that are included in the car. Average loan value probably equates to a wholesale price. Solomon would add the average loan value to the retail value and

---

9. See, e.g., In re Siegler, 5 B.R. 12 (Bankr. D.Minn.1980); Matter of Pierce, 5 B.R. 346 (Bankr. D.Neb.1980); In re Van Holt, 28 B.R. 577 (Bankr. W.D.Mo.1983); cf. In re King, 75 B.R. 287 (Bankr. S.D.Ohio 1987); In re Sprecher, 65 B.R. 598 (Bankr. C.D.Ill. 1986).

10. 6 B.R. 899 (Bankr. D.Neb.1980).

11. In an analogous Chapter 13 case, that is what the court did in In re Miller, 4 B.R. 392 (Bankr. S.D.Cal.1980).

divide by two. In this case the debtor should be able to redeem his DeVille by paying $13,800.

At least for the debtor who has some assets or capacity to borrow after he has filed bankruptcy, section 722 gives the possibility of his retaining certain assets without paying far more than they are worth and without going through the inconvenience of a Chapter 13 proceeding. That said, there is no reason to benefit the debtor yet further by unreasonably low valuations of property, or, as some lower courts did, by allowing installment redemptions. Used as a negotiating tool by a lawyer representing a debtor in Chapter 7, section 722 may find its principal value in moving the creditor to agree to a more favorable reaffirmation than might otherwise be achieved.

Chapter 8

EXEMPT PROPERTY

Table of Sections

Sec.
8–1 Introduction: Meaning and Importance of Exemptions Under Nonbankruptcy Law and in Bankruptcy.
8–2 Persons Entitled to Exemptions in Bankruptcy.

A. Property That Is Exempt in Bankruptcy

8–3 Source of Law for Exemptions in Bankruptcy.

1. Exemptions of Nonbankruptcy Law

8–4 Introduction.
8–5 State Exemptions.
8–6 ____ Personal Property Exemptions.
8–7 ____ Exempt Real Property (Homestead).
8–8 ____ Applying Value Limitations on Exemptions (Centrality of the Debtor's Interest).
8–9 ____ How Far State Law Controls in Determining State Law Exemptions Under the Code.
8–10 Property Held by the Entirety.
   a. Immune Under State Law.
   b. Exempt in Bankruptcy.
8–11 Federal Exemptions (Nonbankruptcy Law).

2. Exemptions of Bankruptcy Law, Section 522(d)

8–12 Introduction.
8–13 Debtor's Residence.
8–14 Personal Property Exemptions.
8–15 ____ Goods.
8–16 ____ Income: Generally.
8–17 ____ Income: Support.
8–18 ____ Income: Losses.
8–19 ____ Life Insurance.
8–20 "Wild Card" Exemption.

3. Joint Cases, Section 522(m)

8–21 Joint Cases, Section 522(m).

4. Claiming Exemptions in Property the Trustee Recovers, Section 522(g)

8–22 Claiming Exemptions in Property the Trustee Recovers, Section 522(g).

B. Debtor's Avoidance of Transfers of Exempt Property

1. Asserting Trustee's Avoidance Powers, Section 522(h)

8–23 Asserting Trustee's Avoidance Powers, Section 522(h).

2. Debtor's Personal Powers of Avoidance, Section 522(f)

8–24 Introduction.

Sec.
8–25 Determining if the Lien Is Within the Scope of Section 522(f).
8–26 Determining if the Property Is Exempt.
8–27 Determining if the Lien Affixed to Debtor's Interest.
8–28 Determining Impairment.
8–29 Procedural Concerns.

3. Claiming Property as Exempt Upon Debtor's Avoidance (§ 522(i))

8–30 Claiming Property as Exempt Upon Debtor's Avoidance (§ 522(i)).

C. Exemption "Planning" in Anticipation of Bankruptcy

8–31 Planning by Creditors: Getting Debtors to Waive Exemptions and Related Rights.
8–32 Planning by Debtors: Converting Their Nonexempt Property to Exempt Property.

D. Pseudo-Exemptions

8–33 Property Excluded From the Estate (Herein, ERISA—Qualified Plans and Other Pension Funds).
   a. Excluding a Pension Plan From the Estate.
   b. Exempting a Pension Plan From the Estate.
   c. Enforcing Against the Estate a Pension Plan's Restrictions on Access.

---

§ 8–1 Introduction: Meaning and Importance of Exemptions Under Nonbankruptcy Law and in Bankruptcy

The common law subjects all of a debtor's property to the payment of her debts. By constitution or statute, however, all states immunize some of a debtor's personal property and, to a limited extent, the interest in her home from certain claims of creditors.[1] They cannot reach this property through judicial collection efforts. Federal nonbankruptcy law similarly shields certain property from creditors' claims.[2] A constitutional or statutory provision of state or federal law that so protects a debtor's property is known as an *exemption* law. Property covered by such a law is said to be *exempt*.

Exemption laws normally apply only in favor of debtors who are natural persons, and typically protect only property used for personal rather than business purposes. They were originally intended to protect the tax base: debtors could not produce taxable wealth if they were left destitute.[3] Today, exemption laws serve multiple purposes, including:

   To provide the debtor with property necessary for his physical survival;

   To protect the dignity and the cultural identity of the debtor;

   To enable the debtor to rehabilitate himself financially and earn income in the future;

---

§ 8–1
1. See §§ 8–5 through 8–9 infra.
2. See § 8–11 infra.

3. Woodward, Exemptions, Opting Out, and Bankruptcy Reform, 43 Ohio St.L.J. 335, 337 (1982).

To protect the debtor's family from the adverse consequences of impoverishment;

To shift the burden of providing the debtor and his family with minimal support from society to the debtors' creditors.[4]

Bankruptcy law has long provided exemptions for individual debtors because the reasons for exemptions are most compelling when a debtor is in bankruptcy. In bankruptcy, *all* of her creditors will collectively and simultaneously reach for her property to satisfy their claims. The value of the bankruptcy estate almost never equals her debts. The debtor will thus lose everything, literally everything, without the protective exemptions. Also, a pre-eminent goal of bankruptcy law is to provide the debtor a financial fresh start, and this new beginning is most meaningful if the debtor is permitted to keep some of her old assets.

Under the old Bankruptcy Act, a debtor in bankruptcy could exempt property that was exempt under local law and nonbankruptcy federal law. Bankruptcy law simply imported these exemptions and created none itself. The result was that a debtor's exemptions depended largely on the law of the state where she lived.

The Code continues this practice of importing exemptions, granting the debtor in bankruptcy whatever exemptions are available to her under local law and nonbankruptcy federal law.[5] The Code differs, however, by giving the debtor the option of exempting, alternatively, the property described in section 522(d).[6] The property listed there is exempted solely as matter of federal bankruptcy law but *only if* the debtor elects the section 522(d) exemptions and foregoes nonbankruptcy exemptions otherwise available to her. In theory, therefore, the debtor can freely choose between these two sources of law (en masse)—section 522(d) *or* state and nonbankruptcy federal law—for her exemptions.[7] She will naturally choose the source that protects more of her property.

There is a kicker. The debtor is denied the choice if her state has legislated that local debtors cannot assert the bankruptcy law exemptions of section 522(d).[8] In this event, which is commonly described as the state having "*opted out*," the debtor is stuck with the nonbankruptcy exemptions available to her under local law and nonbankruptcy federal law. She cannot chose the section 522(d) exemptions. Most states have opted out; so, in most bankruptcy cases, the source of the debtor's exemptions is nonbankruptcy law, mainly state law. *Deja vu.*

Even in these cases, however, the Code treats exemptions differently than the former law. Under the old Act exempt property never became part of the bankruptcy estate. Under the Code the debtor's exempt property passes to the bankruptcy estate along with her other property.[9] The debtor is thereafter permitted to assert her exemptions, i.e., to exempt property

---

4. Resnick, Prudent Planning or Fraudulent Transfer: The Use of Nonexempt Assets to Purchase or Improve Exempt Property on the Eve of Bankruptcy, 31 Rutgers L. Rev. 615, 621 (1978).

5. 11 U.S.C.A. § 522(b)(2).

6. See 11 U.S.C.A. § 522(b)(1) & (d). See § 8–12 infra for the list of property that section 522(d) describes.

7. 11 U.S.C.A. § 522(b)(1) & (2).

8. 11 U.S.C.A. § 522(b)(1).

9. See Practitioner Treatise, Vol. 2.

"from property of the estate," [10] by filing a list of the property that she claims as exempt.[11] "Unless a party in interest objects, the property claimed as exempt on such list is exempt." [12] The immediate consequence is that the

---

10. 11 U.S.C.A. § 522(b) (emphasis added). Exemptions cannot be claimed from other property. In re Starr, 123 B.R. 314, 316 (Bankr. S.D.Ill.1911) ("[T]he trustee does not contend that any of the settlement funds disbursed to the debtor prior to bankruptcy, or property traceable to those funds, remained in the debtor's possession at the time of his bankruptcy filing. A debtor's bankruptcy estate consists only of property in which he has an interest at the commencement of his case. Under the bankruptcy exemption provisions, an exemption is claimed as to 'property of the estate,' and a debtor cannot be said to have obtained an exemption as to property in which the debtor has no interest at the time of filing bankruptcy. Since there has been no showing here that the debtor retained any of the settlement funds disbursed prior to bankruptcy at the time he filed his petition, these funds did not become property of the estate from which his personal injury exemption could be claimed.").

11. 11 U.S.C.A. § 522(*l*). "If the debtor does not file such a list, a dependent of the debtor may file such a list, or may claim as exempt from property of the estate on behalf of the debtor." Id. The list can be amended as a matter of course at any time before the case is closed. Bankruptcy Rule 1009(a); Lucius v. McLemore, 741 F.2d 125, 127 (6th Cir.1984); Tignor v. Parkinson, 729 F.2d 977, 978 (4th Cir.1984); Redmond v. Tuttle, 698 F.2d 414, 416–17 (10th Cir.1983); Matter of Wilson, 694 F.2d 236, 238 (11th Cir.1982); In re Blaise, 116 B.R. 398, 400 (Bankr. D.Vt.1990) ("[B]y its terms Rule 1009 liberally entitles a debtor to amend at any time before the case is closed. * * * The right to amend, however, is not the same as the right to the exemption."); In re Herzog, 118 B.R. 529, 531 (Bankr. N.D.Ohio 1990) ("Rule 1009(a) permits exemptions to be amended any time before the case is closed."); In re Miller, 113 B.R. 98, 100 (Bankr. D. Mass. 1990); In re Luna, 100 B.R. 605, 606 (Bankr. S.D.Fla.1989). This right to amend is not absolute, however:

> Bankruptcy courts may deny debtors the privilege of amending their list of exempt assets where the debtor has acted in bad faith; where a party in interest may be prejudiced; and where exceptional circumstances so warrant.

In re Falconer, 79 B.R. 283, 288 (W.D.Mich. 1987) (dicta); see also In re Fabian, 122 B.R. 678, 682 (Bankr. W.D.Pa.1990); In re Vann, 113 B.R. 704, 707–09 (Bankr. D.Colo.1990); In re Jelinek, 97 B.R. 429, 430–31 (Bankr. N.D.Ill. 1989); In re Magnuson, 113 B.R. 555, 560 (Bankr. D.N.D.1989); In re Roberts, 81 B.R. 354, 362–63 (Bankr. W.D.Pa.1987). "Prejudice to creditors does not occur merely because a claimed exemption, if deemed timely, would be granted." In re Miller, 113 B.R. 98, 100 (Bankr. D.Mass.1990).

The debtor would wish to amend her list, for example, if she acquired exemptible property postpetition that became part of the estate. See 11 U.S.C.A. § 541(a)(5)-(7). This property can be exempted because any property of the estate, whenever acquired, is subject to exemption, Matter of Wilson, 694 F.2d 236, 238 (11th Cir.1982); Armstrong v. Hursman, 106 B.R. 625, 627 (D.N.D.1988) (proceeds of estate property become part of the estate and debtor can amend schedule of exemptions to claim proceeds as exempt); Cyrak v. Poynor, 80 B.R. 75, 79–81 (N.D.Tex.1987) (postpetition insurance exemptible under § 522(d)); but see In re Brown, 118 B.R. 1008, 1009 (Bankr. E.D.Mo. 1990) (monies of chapter 13 case paid to debtor after conversion to chapter 7); In re Harris, 886 F.2d 1011 (8th Cir. 1989) (debtors could not exempt postpetition estate property because lacked rights to property on date of petition), and the debtor can freely amend her list of exemptions to claim the postpetition property if she acts before the case is closed. Matter of Wilson, 694 F.2d 236, 238 (11th Cir. 1982); In re Myatt, 101 B.R. 197, 199–201 (Bankr. E.D.Cal.1989) (also conditioning amendment on debtor's good faith and lack of prejudice to party in interest, including trustee).

Even after the case is closed, the bankruptcy court enjoys the discretionary power to reopen it for the purpose of allowing the debtor to claim exemptions. Reopening the case is normally not allowed, however, if creditors will be prejudiced beyond the debtor putting additional property out of their reach. Hawkins v. Landmark Fin. Co., 727 F.2d 324, 326 (4th Cir.1984).

12. 11 U.S.C.A. § 522(*l*). For purposes of this rule, "party in interest" includes the trustee. First Nat'l Bank v. Norris, 701 F.2d 902, 904 (11th Cir.1983). With respect to objections to discharge:

> The trustee or any creditor may file objections to the list of property claimed as exempt within 30 days after the conclusion of the meeting of creditors * * * or the filing of any amendment to the list * * *.

Bankruptcy Rules 4003(b). Some courts treat this 30–day time period as fairly rigid. In re Brayshaw, 912 F.2d 1255, 1257 (10th Cir.1990) ("[A] bankruptcy court can extend the period for objections to exemptions only by acting within the original time period. There simply

property leaves the bankruptcy estate and revests in the debtor.[13]

is not room * * * to permit granting an extension of time to file objections outside the original thirty-day time limit."); compare In re Williams, 124 B.R. 864, 866 (Bankr. N.D.Fla. 1991) (The court can order an extension outside the 30-day period as long as the trustee filed for an extension within the period.); see also In re Snyder, 102 B.R. 874, 875 (Bankr. S.D.Fla.1989) (time period cannot be extended by bargaining and stipulation between the parties). On the other hand, the 30-day period runs from the meeting of creditors only with respect to exemptions properly scheduled before the meeting, In re Woodson, 839 F.2d 610, 613 (9th Cir.1988); In re Syrtveit, 105 B.R. 599, 603 (Bankr. D. Mont. 1989); and, with respect to any exemptions claimed in an amended filing, the 30-day period begins to run from the filing of the amended schedule only as to creditors who are properly notified. Id. at 615; see also In re Peterson, 929 F.2d 385 (8th Cir. 1991) (applying rule that 30-day period does not begin to run until the objecting party has actual knowledge of amendments); In re Kazi, 125 B.R. 981, 989 (Bankr. S.D.Ill.1991) (despite lack of timely objection to exemption, court would consider the objection because it concerned exemption claimed by amendment to schedules that was filed without notice to creditor).

The combination of section 522(*l*) and Rule 4003 supports the straightforward, general rule that property claimed as exempt is deemed to be exempt in the absence of an objection within the 30-day period. In re Harrigan, 74 B.R. 224, 229 (N.D.Ill. 1987) ("debtors' exemption claims are automatically permitted * * * 'unless a party in interest objects'"); In re Millsap, 122 B.R. 577, 580 (Bankr. D.Idaho 1991) ("Where no objection [to an exemption] is [timely] filed, or extension of time to object granted by the Court, the exemptions claimed by a Debtor are final."); In re Robertson, 105 B.R. 440, 445 (Bankr. N.D.Ill. 1989) ("It is well-settled that a claim of exemption to which no objection is filed is automatically allowed upon expiration of the 30-day period. * * * The effect of the automatic allowance of a claim of exemption due to the expiration of the 30-day period is, under well-settled case law, to 'revest' the property in the debt and end its status as 'property of the estate.'") (conversion of case from Chapter 11 to 7 is immaterial to operation of these rules); In re Feuerborn, 87 B.R. 173 (Bankr. D.Kan.1988) (failing timely to object gives debtor the property claimed as exempt even though court disinclined to let debtors have the property); In re Latimer, 82 B.R. 354, 359 (Bankr. E.D.Pa. 1988) (creditor waived objections to exemptions by failing timely to file within 30 days after first meeting of creditors); In re Lattimore, 81 B.R. 18, 20 (Bankr. E.D.Mo.1988) (trustee could not get nonexempt portion of pension funds from employer because trustee failed timely to object to debtor's claim of all funds as exempt and thus, by Rule 4003(b), all funds were deemed exempt).

There are, however, several caveats to the rule:

(1) The rule will also not apply if the debtor's claim of exemptions is untimely. See Bankruptcy Rule 1007(c) (schedules and statements in a voluntary case must be filed with the petition or within 15 days thereafter); In re Robertson, 105 B.R. 440, 445–50 (Bankr. N.D.Ill. 1989).

(2) Failing timely to object to an exemption does not preclude a creditor from challenging exemptibility of property if the debtor attempts through section 522(f) to avoid a lien or security interest on the property. In re Frazier, 104 B.R. 255, 258–59 (Bankr. N.D.Cal.1989); In re Caruthers, 87 B.R. 723, 726 (Bankr. N.D.Ga.1988).

(3) Rule 4003(b) does not apply to the valuation of property claimed as an exemption, so that a trustee's objection to valuation is not required within the 30-day period. In re Hyman, 123 B.R. 342, 348 (Bankr. 9th Cir.1991); see also In re Cates. 125 B.R. 222, 224 (Bankr. S.D.Ill.1991) (Trustee's failure to object timely to an exemption does not permit the debtor to exempt an amount greater than the statute allows.); but see Seifert v. Selby, 125 B.R. 174, 175–76 (E.D.Mich.1989) (Unless a timely objection is made, exempted property reverts to the debtor, meaning the whole property and not just the amount thereof that the statute exempts.).

Prior to the Supreme Court's decision in Taylor v. Freeland & Kronz, __ U.S. __, 112 S.Ct. 1644, 118 L.Ed.2d 280 (1992), many courts added another caveat: the 30-day period for objecting to exemptions does not apply if the debtor lacks a good-faith, statutory basis for claiming the exemption. In Taylor, however, the Supreme Court rejected this exception to 522(*l*) because the plain language of the statute does not provide for it. The Court also saw a policy basis for its decision: "deadlines may lead to unwelcome results, but they prompt parties to act and they produce finality."

13. If there is no timely objection to the debtor's filing that lists property she claims as exempt, the property is deemed exempted and automatically leaves the bankruptcy estate even without the trustee abandoning it. Christy v. Heights Finance Corp., 101 B.R. 542, 543–44 (C.D.Ill. 1987); see also Payne v. Wood, 775 F.2d 202, 204 (7th Cir.1985), cert. denied, 475 U.S. 1085, 106 S.Ct. 1466, 89 L.Ed.2d 722 (1986) (exempt property passes

If there is a timely objection to exemptions the debtor claims, the bankruptcy court will conduct a hearing after notice and decide the matter.[14] The person objecting to the exemptions, who is usually a creditor, "has the burden of proving that the exemptions are not properly claimed."[15]

The effect of exempting property in bankruptcy is that, whatever the source of the exemptions, the property generally *is not liable* during or after the bankruptcy for any prepetition, unsecured debts.[16] Exempt property is protected even against most nondischargeable debts.[17] The result is that "items * * * claimed as exempt * * * are subject neither to the reach of [unsecured] creditors nor to administration by the Trustee."[18] Exempt property is removed "from the bankruptcy estate and, [even] after discharge, from the claims of unsecured creditors"[19] for prepetition debts.

On the other hand, exempt property generally *is liable* for secured debts, that is, debts for which the property is collateral because of a consensual security interest or involuntary lien on the property that local law permits to pierce the exemption.[20] Most significantly, even *prepetition* secured debts are unaffected by exemptions. Neither the applicable law's description of the property as exempt, nor the debtor's claiming the exemption, dislodges the lien or prevents its enforcement so long as the lien is valid under local law and is unavoidable in bankruptcy.[21] In effect, the debtor's right to exempt the property is subordinate to the creditor's lien.

If the lien is so large that no equity exists in the property, the debtor effectively loses the exemption. If the lien is smaller than the property's value so that the debtor enjoys some equity therein, the property is exempti-

through bankruptcy, that is, it becomes part of estate and is removed by debtor claiming exemptions); In re Turner, 724 F.2d 338, 341 (2d Cir.1983) (by exempting property debtor "reclaims" it from the estate); In re Spain, 103 B.R. 286, 295 (N.D. Ala.1988) (exempting property takes it out of the estate); In re Robertson, 105 B.R. 440, 445 (Bankr. N.D.Ill. 1989) ("It is well-settled that a claim of exemption to which no objection is filed is automatically allowed upon expiration of the 30–day period. * * * The effect of the automatic allowance of a claim of exemption due to the expiration of the 30–day period is, under well-settled case law, to 'revest' the property in the debtor and end its status as 'property of the estate.'") (conversion of case from Chapter 11 to 7 is immaterial to operation of these rules); compare Matter of Sherk, 918 F.2d 1170, 1174 (5th Cir.1990) ("When a claimed exemption is upheld by the bankruptcy court, it is no longer property of the estate.").

The debtor, however, may not be entitled to immediate possession of exempted property despite its title leaving the estate and returning to her. Under appropriate circumstances the trustee can continue to hold the exempt property and not surrender it to the debtor prior to the final distribution of the estate to creditors. Greene v. Balaber-Strauss, 76 B.R. 940, 942 (S.D.N.Y. 1987), aff'd, 859 F.2d 148 (2d Cir.1988).

14. Rule 4003(c).

15. Id.; In re Magnus, 84 B.R. 976, 978 (Bankr. E.D.Pa. 1988); In re Shaffer, 78 B.R. 783, 784 (Bankr. D.S.C.1987); but see In re Eith, 88 B.R. 279, 280 (Bankr. D. Haw. 1988) ("Though the exemption provision is to be liberally construed, where there is an objection to a claimed exemption the burden is on the debtor to prove that he is entitled to the claimed exemption."). There is a middle position: any exemption that the debtor claims is prima facie valid. A person who objects to a claimed exemption must therefore carry the initial burden of producing evidence that the exemption is inappropriate. If this burden is satisfied, the debtor must produce appropriate countervailing evidence. In re Hollar, 79 B.R. 294, 296 (Bankr. S.D.Ohio 1987).

16. 11 U.S.C.A. § 522(c).

17. See Practitioner Treatise, Vol. 2.

18. In re Bistransin, 95 B.R. 29, 31 n.4 (Bankr. W.D.Pa.1989).

19. In re Duss, 79 B.R. 821, 823 (Bankr. W.D.Wis.1987).

20. See 11 U.S.C.A. § 522(c)(2).

21. See Practitioner Treatise, Vol. 2.

ble but only to the extent of the equity. The lien fully remains and is not reduced or otherwise affected by the exemption.

The debtor's exemption triumphs over the lien, however, if the lien is avoided by the trustee using her powers to undo prepetition transfers of the debtor's property.[22] Also, the Code enables the debtor herself to rid exempt property of paramount liens by (1) permitting her to assert derivatively the trustee's avoidance powers[23] and also by (2) directly giving the debtor her own limited powers of avoidance.[24]

Later we discuss in more detail these separate problems of avoiding liens that impair exemptions in property and claiming the property as exempt once avoidance has occurred. First we cover the more basic issues of who can claim exemptions and what property is exempt.

§ 8–2 Persons Entitled to Exemptions in Bankruptcy

Only an "individual debtor" can exempt property in bankruptcy,[1] that is, a real, live, breathing, natural person. This rule tracks nonbankruptcy law which also generally limits exemptions to natural people. All business entities and governmental units, such as corporations, partnerships and municipalities, are legal fictions for whom exemptions are physically and socially unnecessary.

Individual debtors can claim their exemptions in any kind of bankruptcy case for which they are eligible: Chapter 7, 11,[2] 12[3] or 13.[4] Section 522, which empowers individual debtors to claim exemptions, applies in all four kinds of cases.[5] Most typically, however, individual debtors file for liquidation under Chapter 7; so exemption issues most often arise in Chapter 7 cases.

Although exemptions are available only to natural people, their purpose has long extended beyond protecting the debtor herself. Exemptions are also intended indirectly to protect children and other individuals who depend on the debtor for support.[6] Bankruptcy law recognizes and protects these intended beneficiaries by providing that if the debtor herself fails to claim exemptions available to her in the bankruptcy case, the debtor's natural dependents may do so on the debtor's behalf.[7]

A. PROPERTY THAT IS EXEMPT IN BANKRUPTCY
§ 8–3 Source of Law for Exemptions in Bankruptcy

In theory, the debtor decides the source of law for her exemptions. Section 522(b) empowers the debtor to "exempt * * * property listed in

---

22. Ordinarily, the debtor can exempt property that the trustee frees of liens. 11 U.S.C.A. § 522(g).

23. Id. § 522(h).

24. Id. § 522(f).

§ 8–2

1. See Practitioner Treatise, Vol. 2.
2. See Practitioner Treatise, Vol. 2.
3. See Practitioner Treatise, Vol. 2.
4. See Practitioner Treatise, Vol. 2.

5. See Practitioner Treatise, Vol. 2.

6. See Practitioner Treatise, Vol. 2.

7. 11 U.S.C.A. § 522(*l*). Third persons who are not dependents cannot exercise the debtor's exemptions because they are personal to the debtor. Matter of Ross, 18 B.R. 364, 369 (N.D.N.Y.1982), aff'd sub nom., Regan v. Ross, 691 F.2d 81 (2d Cir.1982); Matter of Wickstrom, 113 B.R. 339, 348 (Bankr. W.D.Mich.1990) (creditor cannot assert debtor's exemptions).

either paragraph (1) or, in the alternative, paragraph (2) of this subsection."[1] The first option, section 522(b)(1), actually contains no list of exemptions. It rather incorporates by reference the long list of exemptions described in section 522(d),[2] commonly known as the *federal bankruptcy exemptions.*

The other option, section 522(b)(2), actually includes three categories of exemptions:

- property that is exempt under federal law other than Code section 522(d) (i.e., federal nonbankruptcy law);[3]
- property that is exempt under the state or local law where the debtor was domiciled for the longer part of the 180 days preceding bankruptcy (i.e., state law);[4] and,
- entireties or other jointly owned property that, because of the form of joint ownership, is beyond the reach of the debtor's creditors under applicable nonbankruptcy law.[5]

The exemptions provided by this option are commonly known as the *nonbankruptcy exemptions.*

The debtor chooses one of the these two options to the complete exclusion of the other option. The debtor can "use his federal exemptions, 11 U.S.C.A. § 522(d), or his state exemptions, but he cannot mix them."[6] Thus, if the debtor opts for the nonbankruptcy exemptions, she cannot exempt any property on the basis of section 522(d).[7] On the other hand, if she chooses the federal bankruptcy exemptions of section 522(d), she entirely abandons exemptions available under other federal law[8] or state and local law.

Nothing legal inhibits the debtor's free choice except the so-called "opt-out" clause of section 522(b)(1). It declares that a debtor cannot elect the federal bankruptcy exemptions of section 522(d) if the debtor's state "specifically does not so authorize,"[9] that is, the state has statutorily declared that local debtors in bankruptcy cannot choose the section 522(d) exemptions. The effect of a state "opting out" in this way is to limit the debtor to her nonbankruptcy exemptions.[10] She cannot choose the federal bankruptcy exemptions of section 522(d). They are entirely beyond the reach of a debtor who lives in a state that has "opted out" of them.

Debtors have attacked the constitutionality of the "opt-out" clause on various grounds, but all of these attacks have failed.[11] Moreover, a state that has opted out enjoys complete freedom in designing the local exemptions available to its domiciliaries in bankruptcy: "[T]he state exemptions

§ 8–3

1. 11 U.S.C.A. § 522(b).

2. By its exact terms subsection (b)(1) covers "property that is specified under subsection (d) of this section, unless the State law that is applicable to the debtor under paragraph (2)(A) of this subsection specifically does not so authorize * * * ." 11 U.S.C.A. § 522((b)(1). Subsection 522(d), is quoted in § 8–12 infra.

3. 11 U.S.C.A. § 522(b)(2)(A).

4. Id.

5. 11 U.S.C.A. § 522(b)(2)(B).

6. John T. Mather Memorial Hosp. v. Pearl, 723 F.2d 193, 194 (2d Cir.1983).

7. Hinkson v. Pfleiderer, 729 F.2d 697, 699 (10th Cir.1984).

8. See Practitioner Treatise, Vol. 2.

9. 11 U.S.C.A. § 522(b)(1). The debtor's state is the place of the debtor's domicile for the longer part of the 180–day period preceding the debtor's bankruptcy. Id. § 522(b)(2)(A).

10. See Practitioner Treatise, Vol. 2.

11. See Practitioner Treatise, Vol. 2.

* * * may be more or less generous than federal exemptions. The state exemptions need not be identical or even comparable to exemptions established under federal law." [12] Neither the Code nor the Constitution is offended by state exemptions that are less beneficial to debtors than the exemptions of section 522(d),[13] or even by a state's complete denial of exemptions with respect to certain classes of creditors.[14]

A debtor cannot avoid the consequence of her own state's opt out, or take advantage of more generous local exemptions elsewhere, by filing bankruptcy in another state. The state whose law governs the issue whether or not the debtor can elect the section 522(d) federal bankruptcy exemptions, and that also defines the local exemptions available to the debtor, is the law "at the place in which the debtor's domicile has been located for the 180 days immediately preceding the date of the filing of the petition, or for a longer portion of such 180–day period than on any other place." [15]

The key word "domicile" is not synonymous with residence. Domicile is more restrictive and means, in the case of a competent adult, the place at which a person is physically present and that she regards as her present home.[16] The physical presence must coincide with the state of mind of regarding the place as the person's present *home*. "If presence at the new place is with the intention merely to make use of favorable laws there in force or to gain other advantages without actually making a home at the new place, no domicile is acquired there." [17]

After determining the state whose law applies to the debtor, there is sometimes a further problem: the exemption laws of the state changed after the bankruptcy commenced. Either the state opted out, or the content of local exemption laws was amended. Is the debtor bound by the old or the new laws? The answer is clear: the law that applies is the "State or local law that is applicable on the date of the filing of the petition * * * ." [18] Subsequent amendments in the law are ignored [19] even if the legislature intended for them to apply retroactively.[20]

---

12. In re Golden, 789 F.2d 698, 700 (9th Cir.1986); see also In re Neiheisel, 32 B.R. 146, 168 (Bankr. D. Utah 1983) ("Nothing * * * requires states which preempt the use of federal exemptions to provide exemptions comparable to, concomitant with, or corresponding to the exemptions found in Section 522(d), either in category or amount.").

13. Rhodes v. Stewart, 705 F.2d 159, 162–64 (6th Cir.1983), cert. denied, 464 U.S. 983, 104 S.Ct. 427, 78 L.Ed.2d 361 (1983); Matter of Sullivan, 680 F.2d 1131, 1133–37 (7th Cir. 1982), cert. denied, 459 U.S. 992, 103 S.Ct. 349, 74 L.Ed.2d 388 (1982).

14. In re Ondras, 846 F.2d 33, 35–36 (7th Cir.1988) (state which had opted out placed exempt property beyond the reach of contract creditors while keeping the property within the reach of other creditors such as tort creditors).

It is a different question whether a state can validly provide for exemptions that apply only or differently in bankruptcy. There is authority that the Constitution and Code forbid such special bankruptcy exemptions because the Congress has preempted any authority in the states to create bankruptcy exemptions. In re Mata, 115 B.R. 288, 290–91 (Bankr. D.Colo. 1990) (state cannot provide for IRA exemption in bankruptcy that is not available to debtors outside of bankruptcy), relying on In re Lennen, 71 B.R. 80 (Bankr. N.D.Cal.1987).

15. 11 U.S.C.A. § 522(b)(2)(A). The section applies by identifying the state in which the debtor has been domiciled during the period. It does not require a domicile at a particular locality within the state for any period. In re Hanson, 107 B.R. 525, 527 (Bankr. W.D.Va. 1989).

16. R. Leflar, L. McDougal & R. Felix, American Conflicts Law § 10 at 20–21 (4th ed. 1986).

17. Id. at 21.

18. 11 U.S.C.A. § 522(b)(2)(A).

19. See Practitioner Treatise, Vol. 2.

20. See Practitioner Treatise, Vol. 2.

Other factors that commonly affect exemptions can also change after the debtor has filed her petition, including the debtor's use of the property; the property's value; and the debtor's business or trade. Most significantly, the property or the debtor herself may cease to exist after the bankruptcy case has commenced. Postpetition changes in these kinds of circumstances, like postpetition amendments to exemption laws, are generally ignored in determining a debtor's exemptions. The circumstances that determine the nature and size of her exemptions are the circumstances existing when she filed her bankruptcy petition.[21] If her case is later converted, most certainly when the conversion is from Chapter 11 to 7, her exemptions in the new case are controlled by the law and other circumstances existing on the date of her original bankruptcy petition in the old case.[22]

The rule that exemptions are governed by the law and circumstances existing at the time the petition is filed was carried too far in *In re Harris*.[23] In this case the debtors' farm, in which they had no equity, was foreclosed and sold after they had filed bankruptcy. The debtors were left with a right of redemption. Thereafter, while the bankruptcy was still open, the farm was leased. Local law gave the debtors the rents of the land as an incident of their redemption rights. Bankruptcy debtors generally get to keep property they acquire postpetition, but not postpetition property that is proceeds of estate property. It, too, becomes property of the estate. Thus, in the *Harris* case the debtors' right of redemption and the rents that accompanied it passed to the estate as proceeds of the farm.

The debtors then amended their schedule of exemptions to claim the rental proceeds. Their claim was based on a local "wild card" law permitting a debtor to exempt any property to a certain maximum amount. The trustee objected. The bankruptcy and district courts allowed the exemption. The appeals court reversed.

In *Harris* the Eighth Circuit reported the familiar rule that "the date of petition controls exemption eligibility,"[24] but then restated it differently as "exemption rights are determined as of the petition date."[25] The court finally reasoned that under the restated rule, the debtors could not exempt the rental proceeds because the debtors had no right to them on the date of the bankruptcy petition. "[T]he rental monies in the instant case did not exist * * *" then;[26] and the debtors' "entitlement to those rents * * * [came] from statutory redemption rights that arose postpetition * * *."[27] In sum, "no basis for the debtors' claimed exemption existed at the time of their * * * petition * * *."[28]

We disagree with *Harris* for several reasons. First, the ultimate source of the debtors' entitlement to the rents was their ownership of the farm which predated the petition.

Second, and more important, *Harris* distorts and perverts the rule that the petition date controls eligibility for exemptions. The cases behind the rule mostly say that the petition freezes an exemption to which the debtor is

---

21. See Practitioner Treatise, Vol. 2.
22. See Practitioner Treatise, Vol. 2.
23. 886 F.2d 1011 (8th Cir.1989).
24. Id. at 1013.
25. Id. at 1014.
26. Id. at 1015.
27. Id. at 1014.
28. Id. at 1016.

then entitled so that the exemption cannot be lost by a change in the circumstances that made it available.[29] The rule has mainly worked to preserve exemptions, not to deny them. Also, the rule has largely concerned the *debtor's* eligibility for the exemption, i.e., the circumstances affecting her relationship to the property. The real issue in *Harris* was *the property's* eligibility to be exempted, i.e., specifically, whether postpetition estate property, which is exemptible under local law, is subject to exemption in bankruptcy. The court misjudged the issue or used the wrong rule to resolve it.

Third, and most important, *Harris* fails to see the Code's direct and certain answer to the real issue of the case. The Code very clearly entitles a debtor to claim exemptions in postpetition property that becomes part of the estate. Section 522(b) expressly provides that a debtor "may exempt from *property of the estate*" any property that is described in section 522(d) or that is exempted by nonbankruptcy law. "Property of the estate" expressly includes certain postpetition property, such as the redemption rights in *Harris* or inheritance insurance proceeds to which the debtor becomes entitled within 180 days after the petition is filed. Thus, section 522(b) almost explicitly states that a debtor can exempt postpetition estate property; and the courts without question recognize this right with respect to postpetition insurance proceeds.[30]

Under *Harris*, however, postpetition estate property is not exemptible because the debtor lacks rights in it at the time of the petition. This conflict between *Harris* and section 522(b), which the Eighth Circuit did not even mention, is the main reason we conclude that *Harris* was wrongly decided.[31] We are confident of this conclusion because there is no good reason that the allowability of an exemption should turn, as it did in *Harris,* solely on when the property enters the estate.[32]

1. Exemptions of Nonbankruptcy Law
§ 8–4 Introduction

Although the Code provides its own schedule of exemptions in section 522(d), debtors in most states cannot claim these exemptions because the majority of states have "opted out" of section 522(d). Debtors in these states are denied the section 522(d) exemptions. Instead, they can exempt three classes of property described by nonbankruptcy law: (1) property that is exempt by state law; (2) entireties property that is immune from process under state law; and (3) property that is exempt by nonbankruptcy federal law.

§ 8–5 State Exemptions

Exemption laws are constitutional or statutory in every state, but these laws are everywhere different. The uniform state law on exemptions has been adopted only in Alaska. Every other state has its own, home-grown product. The result is wide disagreement on the exact structure and substance of exemption laws. Moreover, the courts are unusually parochial

---

29. See Practitioner Treatise, Vol. 2.

30. See Practitioner Treatise, Vol. 2.

31. See Practitioner Treatise, Vol. 2.

32. See Practitioner Treatise, Vol. 2.

in interpreting and applying local exemptions. They seldom consider how similar or comparable exemption provisions in other states are judicially construed. In short, the states are very independent with respect to the content, construction, and application of exemption laws. Wide commonality exists only at the most general levels.

§ 8–6 State Exemptions—Personal Property Exemptions

The states typically permit a debtor to exempt a certain amount of her personal property, but they go about it in several different ways:

- by *type*, e.g., the family Bible, tools of the debtor's trade, wearing apparel;
- by *value*, e.g., any personal property of a value not to exceed $5,000;[1]
- by both *type and value*, e.g., an automobile with a value of not more than $2,000;[2]
- by *type or value*, as in Mississippi where the debtor can exempt a long list of specifically identified property or any tangible personal property not exceeding $10,000 in total value.[3]

The most common method is "type and value" so that the typical exemption law lists specific items of personal property that are exemptible, but limits each exemption in terms of value. The list typically includes:

- certain goods (commonly, wearing apparel; household furnishings; tools and implements of a trade or business; and a motor vehicle);
- wages or earnings;
- certain other forms of income (such as retirement and disability payments; health and welfare assistance; workers' compensation awards; supplemental security income such as pensions and unemployment compensation; and other kinds of relief or general assistance).
- life insurance.

The basic problem in applying these exemptions is defining the property they describe. Exemption statutes typically provide no definitions of terms. Definitions come from the courts, which disagree from state to state about the meaning of the same terms. For example, there is disagreement on whether tools of the debtor's trade can ever include motor vehicles.[4] Generally, however, exemption laws are liberally construed in favor of debtors, which at least means that close issues of interpretation are resolved in favor of debtors; and the courts are especially likely to widen ancient laws to accommodate modern inventions.[5]

Defining the property that is described in exemption laws is not the only definitional problem the courts face in applying them. Many states limit exemptions of specific goods and other property, including some forms of

§ 8–6
1. See Practitioner Treatise, Vol. 2.
2. See Practitioner Treatise, Vol. 2.
3. See Practitioner Treatise, Vol. 2.
4. See Practitioner Treatise, Vol. 2.
5. See Practitioner Treatise, Vol. 2.

income, to that which is "necessary" or reasonably so. This requirement may apply instead of or in addition to a value limitation on the exemption.

"Necessary" does not necessarily mean indispensable. In *Arch Lumber Co., Inc. v. Dohm*,[6] the debtor moved to California and left some of her clothing in a Rhode Island warehouse. The creditor argued that the clothes in the warehouse were not "*necessary* wearing apparel" within the meaning of the exemption law because "defendant and her family have gotten along well in California for several months without such apparel * * * ."[7] The court rejected this argument, and affirmed the trial court's decision to exempt the clothing in storage. "The true test * * * is whether such apparel is necessary in the ordinary circumstances of family living or is a superfluous luxury. And there may be circumstances when even certain clothing which ordinarily is considered a luxury would be deemed a necessity."[8] Indeed, decisions are common that define "necessary wearing apparel" to include diamond rings and other jewelry.[9]

Deciding that "necessary" has a broader meaning than indispensable actually decides very little. It tells us that the term's boundaries are not rigidly narrow, but gives no hint as to how far they may reach. The width of the term is really determined by the perspective from which a court judges the necessity of property to a debtor. The basic choices are to apply a "reasonable person" or some similar standardized, objective test, or to judge necessity from the subjective, personalized vantage point of the particular debtor. There are cases supporting both views.[10] Disagreement on this issue, as well as local cultural differences, help to explain why an exemption of necessary household goods includes sterling silver flatware in South Carolina,[11] but excludes a VCR and lawn mower in Oklahoma.[12]

§ 8–7 State Exemptions—Exempt Real Property (Homestead)

The only real property that the states typically exempt is the debtor's home, which is commonly called the debtor's *homestead* or the *homestead exemption*. Its original purpose was "to protect helpless women and children from the improvident acts of an improvident husband" and is "founded in a wise public policy * * * [that it is] better that wives and children should have shelter and a place to live than that a creditor should have his debt * * * ."[1] A more credible justification, which better fits modern times, is that the exemption protects "the general economic welfare of all citizens,

---

6. 81 R.I. 69, 98 A.2d 840 (1953).

7. Id. at 73, 98 A.2d at 842.

8. Id. For decisions illustrating that one person's luxury is another person's necessity, see In re Westhem, 642 F.2d 1139 (9th Cir. 1981) (a $3,000 diamond is necessary wearing apparel); In re Perry, 6 B.R. 263 (Bankr. W.D.Va.1980) (a $2,500 mink coat is necessary wearing apparel). Decisions such as these are easier to understand if the law decides the issue of necessity by considering the debtor's place and standard of living and also her station in life.

9. See Practitioner Treatise, Vol. 2.

10. See Practitioner Treatise, Vol. 2.

11. In re Shaffer, 78 B.R. 783, 784–85 (Bankr. D.S.C.1987).

12. In re Miller, 101 B.R. 713 (Bankr. E.D. Okla. 1989); In re Michalak, 101 B.R. 276, 278 (W.D. Okla. 1988). On the other hand, Oklahoma's exemption of wearing apparel includes some jewelry. In re Miller, supra.

§ 8–7

1. Leonard v. Whitman, 249 Ala. 205, 209, 30 So.2d 241, 244 (1947).

creditors and debtors alike, by promoting the stability and security of our society."[2]

In most jurisdictions, a homestead is fundamentally a privilege or right to exempt certain real property from legal process, not an estate or a vested interest in the property.[3] There are, however, additional consequences of establishing a homestead that give the appearance of an estate in land. For instance, if the debtor entitled to the exemption is married, she cannot convey the property without her spouse's consent. Also, if the debtor predeceases her spouse, the homestead survives in his favor and gives him what is essentially, though not technically, a life estate in the land free of the same claims from which it was exempt while the debtor was alive. This claim of the survivor is often referred to as a *probate homestead.* In many states, surviving children are entitled during their minority to share possession of the probate homestead with the surviving spouse.

A few states provide an exemption of residential real estate for every debtor.[4] In most states, however, due to the original purpose of homestead laws to protect debtors' dependents, the homestead exemption is available only to a debtor who heads a "household" or a "family." Typically, therefore,

> [a] home is not necessarily a homestead [that is exempt], even though it is occupied as a residence and even though the person so occupying it is the owner. The crucial qualifying feature is that such resident owner must be the head of a *family* consisting of himself and at least one other person living together therein in *relationship of one family.*[5]

A family is key, and the courts generally agree on the meaning of the term:

> To constitute a "family" within the meaning of the homestead laws there must be two or more persons residing together under one head or manager, with the legal or moral obligation on the part of the person who occupies the position as head of the house or family to support one or more of the other members, and there must be a state of dependency, at least partial, on the part of the one receiving such support. The family relationship must be of a permanent and domestic character, and the living together must not be merely a temporary expedient rendered necessary or desirable by reason of temporary conditions. And one who claims a homestead right in premises * * * has the burden of establishing it.[6]

Therefore, "a mere aggregation of individuals in the same house" is not a family,[7] and a homeowner is thus not a family head simply because she shares her living quarters with others.[8]

2. Wilkinson v. Carpenter, 277 Or. 557, 565, 561 P.2d 607, 611 (1977).

3. See Practitioner Treatise, Vol. 2.

4. See Practitioner Treatise, Vol. 2.

5. In re Estate of Van Meter, 214 So.2d 639, 641 (Fla. Dist Ct.App.1968), cert. denied per curiam, 231 So.2d 524 (Fla. 1970) (emphasis in original).

6. State v. Haney, 277 S.W.2d 632, 636–38 (Mo. 1955).

7. Harbison v. Vaughan, 42 Ark. 539, 541 (1884).

8. Perez v. Pogge, 303 N.W.2d 145, 148 (Iowa 1981).

On the other hand, a homestead claim can be based on heading a family in fact as well as a family in law.[9] Thus, at least in theory, a family can consist of two friends who, though not married in the conventional sense, are committed to long-term cohabitation. One of them, however, must depend on the other for support. Mutual dependency may not suffice to establish a family because of classical doctrine that there can be only one head of a household.[10]

In most cases, a claim of homestead will be based on the relation of husband and wife or parent and child. Yet, apart from statutes providing otherwise, such a relation does not alone establish a family whose head is entitled to the homestead exemption. The element of dependency must be present. Thus, a single parent is not a family head unless a child is largely dependent on the parent's support.[11] Similarly, there is no head of household in a marriage without minor children in which the spouses live apart and each of them cares for his and her own needs.[12]

Either partner in a marriage can be the head of a family for purposes of homestead laws. Indeed, the Equal Protection Clause requires it.[13] The courts have long presumed, however, that the husband is the head of a married couple living together in a common home.[14] This presumption is sexist, outdated, and probably unlawful. Gender does not determine who heads a family and is irrelevant to the issue.

Ordinarily, a debtor can exempt as her homestead only the property that she actually occupies as a home. "It requires *both* ownership and occupancy to constitute a homestead."[15] This requirement explains the often cited maxim that a debtor cannot at the same time have two homesteads.[16] A corollary is that she cannot have "'two places, either of which at [her] election [she] may claim as [her] homestead.'"[17]

Originally, homestead laws everywhere protected only real estate and contemplated the exemption of nothing other than traditional houses and service buildings constructed on land and affixed permanently thereto. At the time, of course, there were no widely used housing alternatives. Now

---

9. Solomon v. Davis, 100 So.2d 177, 178 (Fla.1958); see also, e.g., Monroe v. Monroe, 250 Ark. 434, 465 S.W.2d 347 (1971) (homestead applies to anyone who is the head of a family whether married or not); but cf. Barker v. Lee, 337 S.W.2d 637, 639 (Tex.Civ.App. 1960) (a putative marriage relationship does not constitute a family for homestead purpose because the family does not exist by authority of law).

10. Cory v. Parks, 386 So.2d 292, 293 (Fla. Dist. Ct. App.1980), review denied, 392 So.2d 1377 (Fla.1980) (for homestead purposes there can be only one head of a family).

11. See, e.g., Scoville v. Scoville, 40 So.2d 840 (Fla.1949).

12. See, e.g., Code v. London, 27 Wash.2d 279, 178 P.2d 293 (1947).

13. U.S. Const. amend. XIV, § 1; Matter of Murrell, 588 F.2d 1207, 1209 (8th Cir.1978), cert. denied, 441 U.S. 950, 99 S.Ct. 2177, 60 L.Ed.2d 1055 (1979).

14. See, e.g., Solomon v. Davis, 100 So.2d 177, 178 (Fla.1958); Burk Royalty Co. v. Riley, 475 S.W.2d 566, 568 (Tex. 1972).

15. Lutz v. Kehr, 333 S.W.2d 61, 63 (Mo. 1960) (emphasis added); see also Automotive Supply, Inc. v. Powell, 269 Ark. 255, 256, 599 S.W.2d 735 (1980) (homestead requires actual occupancy of the land); Lutz v. Kehr, 333 S.W.2d 61, 62 (Mo.1960) (debtor must occupy land she claims as homestead); Mutual Bldg. & Inv. Co. v. Efros, 152 Ohio St. 369, 372–73, 89 N.E.2d 648, 651 (1949) (property that the debtor has never used or occupied as her residence, home, or dwelling place cannot be homestead); Security Sav. & Loan Ass'n v. Busch, 84 Wash.2d 52, 523 P.2d 1188 (1974) (applying homestead statute requiring that debtor reside on the premises).

16. See, e.g., Corcoran v. Andrews, 195 So.2d 767, 770 (La. App. 1967).

17. Horn v. Gates, 155 Neb. 667, 671, 53 N.W.2d 84, 87 (1952).

there are many forms of housing. The courts have reacted to this change by expansively interpreting existing homestead laws to include mobile homes,[18] houseboats,[19] condominiums,[20] and other forms of housing. More recently, legislatures have reacted by changing exemption statutes to cover expressly these new forms of housing.[21]

§ 8–8 State Exemptions—Applying Value Limitations on Exemptions (Centrality of the Debtor's Interest)

In many states the homestead exemption is limited in value. Also, personal property exemptions commonly carry value limitations. For example, Minnesota law exempts "one motor vehicle to the extent of a value not exceeding $2,000."[1]

In applying this or any other exemption, whether it covers personal or real property, remember that the property itself is not exempt. The exemption is rather the debtor's interest in the property.[2] Creditors can only reach their debtor's interest when they grab property in satisfaction of their claims; and exemption laws thus protect only the debtor's interest in property.

Thus, value limitations on exemptions apply to the debtor's interest in property, not to the property itself. The debtor's interest is measured by her equity in the property.[3] Her equity is determined by subtracting from the worth of the property itself, determined by its fair market value[4] free and clear of all claims, the amount of liens and security interests that encumber it and, according to most authorities, that are superior in rank to the lien (actual or potential) of the creditor attempting to execute on the property.

For example, suppose that D owns an automobile worth about $5,500. Bank has a perfected security interest in the vehicle to secure a $3,500 loan. JC wins a $2,000 judgment against D and is set to enforce the judgment through execution, levy and sale.

State law permits D to exempt a motor vehicle to the extent of $2,000 in value. This law actually means that $2,000 of D's equity in the property is exempt. JC cannot touch the car if there is no excess equity, that is, no equity exceeding $2,000.

D's equity in this case is exactly $2,000, which is computed as follows: $5,500 (vehicle's value free of liens and encumbrances) minus $3,500 security interest (which is superior to JC's claim[5]) = $2,000. This amount is fully protected by the $2,000 exemption statute; so JC cannot touch the car.[6] There is no free value to apply against her claim. The larger part of the

18. See Practitioner Treatise, Vol. 2.
19. See Practitioner Treatise, Vol. 2.
20. See Practitioner Treatise, Vol. 2.
21. See Practitioner Treatise, Vol. 2.

§ 8–8

1. Minn. Stat. § 550.37(12a) (1988).
2. See Practitioner Treatise, Vol. 2.
3. See Practitioner Treatise, Vol. 2.
4. Market value "is not what a property owner could realize at a forced sale, but the price he could obtain after reasonable and ample time, such as would ordinarily be taken by an owner to make a sale of like property." Wade v. Rathbun, 23 Cal.App.2d Supp. 758, 760, 67 P.2d 765, 766–67 (1937); see also In re Mitchell, 103 B.R. 819 (Bankr. W.D.Tex.1989) (in applying state exemption law property would be valued on basis of fair market value rather than liquidation value).

5. U.C.C. §§ 9–201 & 9–301(1)(b).
6. See Practitioner Treatise, Vol. 2.

value, $3,500, is claimed by a superior encumbrancer (the holder of the perfected security interest) and the balance which the debtor owns is immune from JC's reach by the exemption law.

When the debtor's equity in exempt property exceeds the value limitation of the exemption law, the consequence is not to deprive the debtor of the exemption altogether. Rather, the property is seized and sold under creditors' process, the debtor gets so much of the equity that is exempted, and the creditor gets the balance of the equity actually produced by the sale.[7]

§ 8–9 State Exemptions—How Far State Law Controls in Determining State Law Exemptions Under the Code

When a debtor relies on state exemptions in bankruptcy, the scope or extent of the exemptions is generally determined exclusively by state law[1] and are not expanded or restricted by federal law. Two applications of this principle are especially important. First, the reach or size of state law exemptions is not reduced, enlarged or otherwise affected by the terms of similar exemptions in section 522(d). For example, if state law completely exempts the debtor's interest in a motor vehicle or tools of trade without regard to value, the exemption is not reduced or otherwise affected by the stinginess of section 522(d) which exempts a vehicle only to the extent of $1200 and tools to the extent of $750.[2]

Second, interpretation of state exemption laws is purely a question of state law which the bankruptcy court answers solely by reference to state law.[3] For example, the meaning of "household goods" or "tools" in a state exemption law depends on how the term is or would be defined by the state legislature and state courts in line with local precedents and policy. The interpretative source and perspective are entirely state law. The federal view, which could define the same terms differently in section 522(d) or elsewhere in the Code, is not controlling.

There is a third way in which state law can define the extent of a state exemption—by prescribing that certain debts are excepted from the exemption. For example, as in Iowa, state law may create a homestead exemption but except from the exemption a claim for a particular creditor;[4] or may except a claim that arose before the homestead was acquired or recorded.[5] Even if bankruptcy honors these exceptions in theory, they probably are meaningless in practice because—absent a lien—the excepted creditor's claim will be discharged unless the claim is a debt that the Code itself excepts from discharge.[6] The discharge will forever bar the creditor from getting satisfaction after bankruptcy, and the bankruptcy itself will pay her claim only to the extent she shares in any pro rata distribution to unsecured

---

7. See Practitioner Treatise, Vol. 2.

§ 8–9

1. In re Whitney, 107 B.R. 645, 650 (Bankr. D.Minn.1989).
2. See Practitioner Treatise, Vol. 2.
3. See Practitioner Treatise, Vol. 2.
4. I.C.A. § 561.21 ("The homestead may be sold to satisfy debts of each of the following classes: * * * 3. Those incurred for work done or material furnished exclusively for the improvement of the homestead.").

5. Id. ("Those contracted prior to its acquisition, but then only to satisfy a deficiency remaining after exhausting the other property of the debtor, liable to execution.").

6. For debts generally excepted from discharge, see 11 U.S.C.A. § 523(a).

creditors.⁷ Furthermore, a judicial lien that secures the debt is vulnerable to the debtor's avoidance under 522(f), notwithstanding the state-law exception from exemption.⁸ It might be argued, however, that the exception from exemption nevertheless entitles even the creditor without a lien, as part of the bankruptcy process, to have the property applied to her debt.⁹ The argument is essentially that, *as to this creditor,* the property is not exempted, remains part of the bankruptcy estate, and should be administered for her sole benefit. This argument should fail. The effect is to exceed federal law by allowing the state to create an exception to bankruptcy discharge, or to exceed state law by forcing bankruptcy to treat the exception as a lien. In the latter case, the exception should be subject to avoidance under 522(f).

Most certainty, state law will not prevail in bankruptcy so as to except an unsecured claim from an exemption on the basis of an executory waiver of exemptions that is valid under state law.¹⁰ The Code preempts on this issue and speaks directly and clearly about it in section 522(e): "A waiver of an exemption executed in favor of a creditor that holds an unsecured claim against the debtor is unenforceable in a case under this title with respect to such claim against property that the debtor may exempt * * *." ¹¹

A recurring, related question is whether section 522(e) negates a procedural "waiver" of exemptions. Most states prescribe a procedure that a debtor must follow in order to set off or claim her exempt property once a creditor threatens it by execution or like process. Failure to comply results in the waiver of exemptions by operation of state law.¹² The courts generally hold that a debtor who has procedurally waived exemptions in this fashion cannot thereafter assert them in bankruptcy.¹³ This result flows from the broad, general principle that state law determines the scope and extent of state exemptions in bankruptcy. Section 522(e) compels no different result. It condemns only waivers that a debtor has "executed." Section 522(e) is thereby limited to contractual waivers of exemptions, and does not negate procedural waivers that result by operation of state law.

An entirely different issue is whether, upon filing bankruptcy, a debtor must comply with state procedures, which prescribe how to claim exemptions in local proccedings, in order to preserve in bankruptcy the exemptions of state law that are available to her at the time of filing. We believe that section 522(*l*) and its accompanying Bankruptcy Rules control and preempt state law on this issue. They prescribe the exclusive procedure for claiming exemptions in bankruptcy, including exemptions based on state law.¹⁴ Exemptions that are available to the debtor when she files bankruptcy cannot thereafter be lost by failing to jump procedural hurdles of state law.

On the other hand, section 522(*l*) does not negate a procedural waiver that occurred before bankruptcy.¹⁵ It applies and displaces state law only with respect to the mechanics of claiming an exemption to which there is a

---

7. Matter of Nehring, 84 B.R. 571, 577 (Bankr.S.D. Iowa 1988).
8. See 11 U.S.C.A. § 522(f)(1); Owen v. Owen, 500 U.S. ___, 111 S.Ct. 1833, 114 L.Ed.2d 350 (1991), which we discuss at § ___ infra.
9. See Practitioner Treatise, Vol. 2.
10. See Practitioner Treatise, Vol. 2.
11. 11 U.S.C.A. § 522(e).
12. See Practitioner Treatise, Vol. 2.
13. See Practitioner Treatise, Vol. 2.
14. See Practitioner Treatise, Vol. 2.
15. See Practitioner Treatise, Vol. 2.

right in bankruptcy, and has no application when the right to an exemption was lost (or never acquired) before the bankruptcy commenced.

An in-between issue is the consequence of a debtor's failure to satisfy a state exemption that, by its own terms, is effective only after the debtor has filed or recorded a public claim of exemptions. (This kind of law most commonly applies to homesteads.) The answer is clear that the exemption is unavailable to the debtor in bankruptcy.[16] This kind of filing is not merely a procedural step that a debtor must take to claim available exemptions. Rather, the filing defines who acquires the exemption or whether or not an exemption even exists. Each of these matters is controlled by state law. A postpetition filing by the debtor will not solve the problem. As a result of the terms of the exemption law itself, the filing would be effective only as against subsequent debts and not against the prepetition debts that her bankruptcy mainly concerns; also, because of federal law, the only exemptions that apply in any bankruptcy case are the exemptions applicable when the petition was filed.[17]

§ 8–10 Property Held by the Entirety

For full text of this section, see Epstein, Nickles & White, Bankruptcy, Practitioner Treatise Series, Vol. 2.

a. *Immune Under State Law*

b. *Exempt in Bankruptcy*

§ 8–11 Federal Exemptions (Nonbankruptcy Law)

For full text of this section, see Epstein, Nickles & White, Bankruptcy, Practitioner Treatise Series, Vol. 2.

2. Exemptions of Bankruptcy Law, Section 522(d)
§ 8–12 Introduction

In a state that has not "opted out," a debtor can exempt the property described in section 522(d):

> (1) The debtor's aggregate interest, not to exceed $7,500 in value, in real property or personal property that the debtor or a dependent of the debtor uses as a residence, in a cooperative that owns property that the debtor or a dependent of the debtor uses as a residence, or in a burial plot for the debtor or a dependent of the debtor.

> (2) The debtor's interest, not to exceed $1,200 in value, in one motor vehicle.

---

16. See Practitioner Treatise, Vol. 2.

17. See 11 U.S.C.A. § 522(b)(2)(A). Indeed, this federal rule is perhaps the main exception to the pre-eminence of state law in determining the scope and extent of state exemptions. The rule restricts the debtor to those exemptions "applicable on the date of the filing of the petition." Id. The rule means not only that the applicable exemption laws are those laws in existence and effect on the day bankruptcy is filed; it also means that the circumstances prevailing at the time of the filing control the application of exemption laws then in force. See discussion § 8–3 supra, and authorities cited there.

(3) The debtor's interest, not to exceed $200 in value in any particular item or $4,000 in aggregate value, in household furnishings, household goods, wearing apparel, appliances, books, animals, crops, or musical instruments, that are held primarily for the personal, family, or household use of the debtor or a dependent of the debtor.

(4) The debtor's aggregate interest, not to exceed $500 in value, in jewelry held primarily for the personal, family, or household use of the debtor or a dependent of the debtor.

(5) The debtor's aggregate interest in any property, not to exceed in value $400 plus up to $3,750 of any unused amount of the exemption provided under paragraph (1) of this subsection.

(6) The debtor's aggregate interest, not to exceed $750 in value, in any implements, professional books, or tools, of the trade of the debtor or the trade of a dependent of the debtor.

(7) Any unmatured life insurance contract owned by the debtor, other than a credit life insurance contract.

(8) The debtor's aggregate interest, not to exceed in value $4,000 less any amount of property of the estate transferred in the manner specified in section 542(d) of this title, in any accrued dividend or interest under, or loan value of, any unmatured life insurance contract owned by the debtor under which the insured is the debtor or an individual of whom the debtor is a dependent.

(9) Professionally prescribed health aids for the debtor or a dependent of the debtor.

(10) The debtor's right to receive—

(A) a social security benefit, unemployment compensation, or a local public assistance benefit;

(B) a veterans' benefit;

(C) a disability, illness, or unemployment benefit;

(D) alimony, support, or separate maintenance, to the extent reasonably necessary for the support of the debtor and any dependent of the debtor;

(E) a payment under a stock bonus, pension, profitsharing, annuity, or similar plan or contract on account of illness, disability, death, age, or length of service, to the extent reasonably necessary for the support of the debtor and any dependent of the debtor, unless—

(i) such plan or contract was established by or under the auspices of an insider that employed the debtor at a time the debtor's rights under such plan or contract arose;

(ii) such payment is on account of age or length of service; and

(iii) such plan or contract does not qualify under section 401(a), 403(a), 403(b), 408, or 409 of the Internal Revenue Code of 1954 (26 U.S.C. 401(a), 403(a), 403(b), 408 or 409).

(11) The debtor's right to receive, or property that is traceable to—

(A) an award under a crime victim's reparation law;

(B) a payment on account of the wrongful death of an individual of whom the debtor was a dependent, to the extent reasonably necessary for the support of the debtor and any dependent of the debtor;

(C) a payment under a life insurance contract that insured the life of an individual of whom the debtor was a dependent on the date of such individual's death, to the extent reasonably necessary for the support of the debtor and any dependent of the debtor;

(D) a payment, not to exceed $7,500, on account of personal bodily injury, not including pain and suffering or compensation for actual pecuniary loss, of the debtor or an individual of whom the debtor is a dependent; or

(E) a payment in compensation of loss of future earnings of the debtor or an individual of whom the debtor is or was a dependent, to the extent reasonably necessary for the support of the debtor and any dependent of the debtor.[1]

A debtor who chooses these section 522(d) exemptions thereby forfeits any and all nonbankruptcy exemptions otherwise available to her. She can only exempt property described in section 522(d); and she cannot exempt any property on the basis of exemptions provided by state law or nonbankruptcy federal law.[2] Additionally, the debtor cannot exempt entireties property (as she can when she chooses nonbankruptcy exemptions) solely on the basis that the property is immune from process under local law. Conversely, when a debtor freely chooses to rely on her nonbankruptcy exemptions instead of section 522(d), or is forced to do so because her state has opted out, she thereby altogether abandons section 522(d), and none of her property is exemptible on the basis of it.[3]

Section 522(d) resembles, in form and substance, a typical collection of state exemption laws. Its exemption of the debtor's residence is the federal counterpart to the state homestead exemption; and its long laundry list of exempt personal property includes the kinds of goods and intangibles that are usually exempted under state law. Also, like typical state law, section 522(d) actually exempts the debtor's interest in the property, and imposes value limitations on most of the exemptions.

Section 522(d) is unlike most state exemption laws in additionally providing, beyond the exemptions of specific property, an open, carte

§ 8–12

1. 11 U.S.C.A. § 522(d). This list of exemptions is not entirely original. "It is derived in large part from the Uniform Exemptions Act, promulgated by the [National Conference of] Commissioners of Uniform State Laws * * * ." H.R. Rep. No. 595, 95th Cong., 1st Sess. 361, reprinted in 1978 U.S. Code Cong. & Admin. News 5963, 6317.

2. Matter of Kochell, 732 F.2d 564, 566 (7th Cir.1984) ("That a debtor might be entitled to an exemption under some other federal law is of no consequence once the debtor has elected the exclusive list of federal exemptions outlined in the Bankruptcy Code. Other federal exemptions are only available to the debtor if he chooses the state exemptions.").

3. See, e.g., In re Barron, 85 B.R. 603, 605–06 (Bankr. N.D.Ala.1988) (debtor in opt-out state cannot claim social security exemption of § 522(d)).

blanche, or "wild card" exemption of limited value that the debtor can use to exempt her interest in "any property."

The most significant difference between state exemption laws and section 522(d) is that, despite close similarities in the two sources of law, the meaning, interpretation and application of section 522(d) are issues of federal law. State law is certainly not controlling, and is not necessarily even persuasive, in construing the federal exemptions. The only exception is that state law governs in deciding the foundational issue whether the debtor has an interest in the property that she claims as exempt under section 522(d).[4]

§ 8–13 Debtor's Residence

Section 522(d)(1) exempts the debtor's residence, that is,

[t]he debtor's aggregate interest, not to exceed $7,500 in value, in real property or personal property that the debtor or a dependent of the debtor uses as a residence, in a cooperative that owns property that the debtor or a dependent of the debtor uses as a residence, or in a burial plot for the debtor or a dependent of the debtor.[1]

It is less generous, but wider in scope and application, than the usual state homestead exemption.

Any property, real or personal, can qualify for the exemption: a traditional house, condominium, cooperative, mobile home, boat or any other form of housing can qualify. The only qualification is that the debtor or a dependent must use the property as a "residence." This term is statutorily undefined, but the courts assume that its meaning is the same as "homestead" under state law, i.e., the place that the debtor actually occupies as her home.[2] Thus, residence does not include all residential property, and specifically does not include a vacation beach house which the debtor uses only occasionally.[3]

We would agree with equating residence with the debtor's homestead or home, and would define the term basically to mean the debtor's usual, principal, or dominant dwelling place. We would caution, however, against a larger equation, that is, against equating (d)(1) with the usual state homestead exemption. The latter is not available to every debtor with an interest in a home. Rather, it is typically restricted to debtors who have families which they head. Section 522(d)(1) is not so limited. Any debtor with a home can exempt her interest in the property on the basis of (d)(1) whether or not she heads a household and even if she altogether lacks a family.

---

4. In re Russell, 80 B.R. 662, 664 (Bankr. D.Vt.1987) (federal homestead exemption of § 522(d)(1) applies only if debtor has interest in the property and that issue is decided by state law).

§ 8–13

1. 11 U.S.C.A. § 522(d)(1).

2. In re Tomko, 87 B.R. 372 (Bankr. E.D.Pa. 1988); In re Brent, 68 B.R. 893, 895 (Bankr. D.Vt.1987).

3. In re Tomko, 87 B.R. 372 (Bankr. E.D.Pa. 1988).

Like all exemptions, however, (d)(1) actually applies only to the debtor's interest in the property,[4] and the size of the exemption—compared to the typical state homestead—is quite small. It exempts only "the debtor's interest, not to exceed $7,500 in value." If the debtor's interest is larger, the trustee can sell the property to capture the debtor's excess equity above the exemption.[5] The exemption itself survives the trustee's postpetition sale and carries over into the proceeds.[6]

A wholly different issue is whether the (d)(1) exemption applies to the proceeds of a prepetition disposition of the debtor's residence. The typical state homestead exemption extends, by its express terms or by decisional rule, to the proceeds of the property for a reasonable period of time during which the debtor can invest the money into a new home.[7] The courts

---

4. The debtor's interest is determined by state law, In re Russell, 80 B.R. 662, 664 (Bankr. D.Vt.1987), and is measured in terms of the debtor's equity. See § 8–8 supra.

5. In re Johnson, 30 B.R. 467, 469 (M.D.Tenn.1983).

6. In re Sajkowski, 49 B.R. 37, 39–40 (Bankr. D.R.I.1985); In re Hoffman, 28 B.R. 503 (Bankr. D.Md.1983).

7. The prevailing rule, which is established by statute in many states, is that the proceeds from a sale of a homestead, whether the sale is voluntary or forced, are exempt from creditors' process for a reasonable period of time to allow the debtor to invest in another homestead. Sims v. McFadden, 217 Ark. 810, 813, 233 S.W.2d 375, 377 (1950) (forced sale); Orange Brevard Plumbing & Heating Co. v. La Croix, 137 So.2d 201, 306 (Fla. 1962); Millsap v. Faulkes, 236 Iowa 848, 850, 20 N.W.2d 40, 41 (1945); First Nat'l Bank v. Dempsey, 135 Kan. 608, 610, 11 P.2d 735, 736 (1932); Marcum v. Edwards, 181 Ky. 683, 686, 205 S.W. 798, 799 (1918); Harrell v. Bank of Wilson, 445 P.2d 266, 269–70 (Okla. 1968) (exemption denied because debtor had no intention to invest proceeds in a new homestead); Harrington v. Schuble, 608 S.W.2d 253, 257 (Tex.Civ.App. 1980) (forced sale); but see First Federal Savings & Loan Ass'n v. Brown, 78 A.D.2d 119, 122, 434 N.Y.S.2d 306, 310 (1980), appeal after remand, 86 A.D.2d 963, 448 N.Y.S.2d 302 (1982) (surplus proceeds arising out of foreclosure sale were not exempt under homestead law).

Some states have confirmed the general rule by statute and specify the length of the grace period during which the proceeds are exempt. See, e.g., Cal. Civ. Proc. Code §§ 704.960(a) (West Supp. 1984) (proceeds of execution sale of dwelling house homestead, and proceeds from insurance for damage thereof or destruction thereof, exempt for six months after proceeds actually received) & 704.720(b) (proceeds of voluntary sale of declared homestead exempt for six months after sale of sale); Ill. Rev. Stat. ch. 110 paragraph 12–906 (Smith–Hurd 1984) (proceeds from conveyance of homestead exempt for one year after receipt thereof); Wis. Stat. Ann. § 815.-20(1) (1977) (homestead exemption not impaired by sale and extends to proceeds which are held with the intention to procure another homestead within two years).

Because of the strong public policy favoring exemptions of all kinds, courts may occasionally exempt homestead proceeds even though there is evidence from the debtor's own mouth that she intended to use part of the money for a purpose other than securing a new homestead. See Schwanz v. Teper, 66 Wis.2d 157, 160–61, 223 N.W.2d 896, 898 (1974) (debtor planned to use portion of proceeds to pay attorney's fee). In Mississippi, the proceeds of a voluntary sale of a homestead are exempt in all circumstances without any regard whatsoever to the debtor's planned use of the money. Miss. Code Ann. § 85–3–49 (1973) (exempt property upon disposal does not become liable to debts of owner), as construed in Davis v. Lammons, 246 Miss. 624, 628–29, 151 So.2d 907, 909 (1963). Compare, however, the case of Patterson v. Adams, 245 So.2d 13 (Miss. 1971), in which the court held that proceeds of a home, from which the debtors had moved two weeks before sale of the property, were not exempt because by the time of the sale the home had already been abandoned and thus had lost its character as an exempt homestead.

In contrast, some states stingily refuse to extend the protection of homestead laws to proceeds resulting from a voluntary disposition of the property, and the debtor's intentions or plans regarding the use of the money are irrelevant. See, e.g., McLaws v. Kruger, 130 Ariz. 317, 319, 636 P.2d 95, 97 (1981); Drennen v. Wheatley, 210 Ark. 222, 225, 195 S.W.2d 43, 44–45 (1946); International Harvester Credit Corp. v. Ross, 217 Kan. 683, 687, 538 P.2d 655, 658 (1975). The claim is made in these cases that this stinginess is the general rule with respect to a voluntary disposition of a homestead. The claim is stale, however. A fresh count of authorities, including statutory provisions, suggests that, at the very least, the

disagree whether section 522(d)(1) likewise protects prepetition sale proceeds of the debtor's residence.[8] The argument against this extension of (d)(1) is that the literal letter of section 552(d)(1) covers only the debtor's *residence,* and is silent with respect to proceeds. The same silence in state homestead laws has not prevented their extension to proceeds of the property.[9] The silence of (d)(1) is quite loud, however, because section 522(d) explicitly extends other exemptions to the proceeds of the exempt property.[10] In any event, even if (d)(1) does not itself protect the prepetition sale proceeds of a debtor's residence, all or part of the money is exemptible under the wild card exemption of section 522(d).[11] Also, if exempt property is destroyed postpetition by fire or other casualty that is compensated by insurance, the insurance proceeds are exemptible in place of the exempt property itself.[12]

If the debtor owns no interest in a residence, the (d)(1) exemption is still useful to her. She can use it to exempt a "burial plot" [13]; or, as is more often done, she can use (d)(1) to enlarge the "wild card" exemption that applies to any property the debtor chooses.[14]

§ 8–14 Personal Property Exemptions

Every other exemption, except the "wild card," describes particular personal property which we classify into three groups: goods; income; and life insurance.

---

modern trend is to exempt in appropriate cases the proceeds of any sale of a homestead.

By force of decisional or statutory law, the homestead exemption ordinarily extends to proceeds paid under an insurance policy covering casualty to the property. Exchange Bank & Trust Co. v. Mathews, 267 Ark. 415, 417, 591 S.W.2d 354, 356 (1979); Reed v. Rivera, 80 Misc.2d 991, 992, 365 N.Y.S.2d 470, 472 (Sup. Ct. 1975); Home Improvement Loan Co. v. Brewer, 318 S.W.2d 673, 676–77 (Tex.Civ. App. 1958), error ref'd n.r.e.; Cal. Civ. Proc. Code § 704.710(b) (West 1987) (insurance proceeds exempt for period of six months); N.D. Cent. Code § 28–22–02(7) & (9) (1988); Tenn. Code Ann. § 26–2–304 (1980) (not exceeding $5,000); Wis. Stat. Ann. § 815.18(17) (1977). This protection of insurance proceeds may be conditioned, however, on an intent to apply the proceeds within a reasonable time toward a new or repaired homestead. Exchange Bank & Trust Co. v. Mathews, 267 Ark. 415, 417, 591 S.W.2d 354, 356 (1979).

8. Compare Matter of Healy, 100 B.R. 443, 445 (Bankr. W.D.Wis.1989) (an exemption for proceeds cannot be inferred from § 522(d)(1)); In re Hoffman, 96 B.R. 46, 48–49 (Bankr. W.D.Pa.1988) (§ 522(d)(1) does not exempt proceeds as they are not used as residence); with In re Barrett, 104 B.R. 688, 694 (Bankr. E.D.Pa. 1989), order vac'd, 111 B.R. 78 (E.D.Pa.1990), on remand, 113 B.R. 175 (Bankr.E.D.Pa.1990), decision rev'd, 118 B.R. 255 (E.D.Pa.1990), judgment aff'd, 939 F.2d 20 (3d Cir.1991) (homestead exemption of § 522(d)(1) should extend to sale proceeds); In re Linderman, 20 B.R. 826 (Bankr. W.D. Wash.1982) (court held that debtors could exempt portion of homestead proceeds under § 522(d)(1)).

9. See § 8–7 supra.

10. See 11 U.S.C.A. § 522(d)(11), which covers income from various forms of losses and also "property that is traceable to" the income.

11. See id. § 522(d)(5) ("The debtor's aggregate interest in any property, not to exceed in value $400 plus up to $3,750 of any unused amount of the exemption provided under [§ 522(d)(1)]"); In re Hoffman, 96 B.R. 46, 49 (Bankr. W.D.Pa.1988) (proceeds not exemptible under (d)(1) exempted under (d)(5); cf. In re Hawley, 24 B.R. 42 (Bankr. M.D.Pa.1982) (proceeds of residential real estate exempted under (d)(5)).

12. Payne v. Wood, 775 F.2d 202, 204 (7th Cir.1985), cert. denied, 475 U.S. 1085, 106 S.Ct. 1466, 89 L.Ed.2d 722 (1986); Lewis v. Thompson, 28 B.R. 351, 354 (Bankr. M.D.Pa.1983); cf. In re Werner, 79 B.R. 819, 820 (Bankr. W.D.Wis.1986) (debtors entitled to proceeds of postpetition sale of exempt property); but see In re Fox, 80 B.R. 753 (Bankr. W.D.Pa.1987) (postpetition proceeds of exempted property destroyed by fire are not protected because debtor did not claim fire insurance as exempt).

13. 11 U.S.C.A. § 522(d)(1).

14. See id. § 522(d)(5), which is discussed below.

§ 8–15 Personal Property Exemptions—Goods

For full text of this section, see Epstein, Nickles & White, Bankruptcy, Practitioner Treatise Series, Vol. 2.

§ 8–16 Personal Property Exemptions—Income: Generally

For full text of this section, see Epstein, Nickles & White, Bankruptcy, Practitioner Treatise Series, Vol. 2.

§ 8–17 Personal Property Exemptions—Income: Support

For full text of this section, see Epstein, Nickles & White, Bankruptcy, Practitioner Treatise Series, Vol. 2.

§ 8–18 Personal Property Exemptions—Income: Losses

For full text of this section, see Epstein, Nickles & White, Bankruptcy, Practitioner Treatise Series, Vol. 2.

§ 8–19 Personal Property Exemptions—Life Insurance

For full text of this section, see Epstein, Nickles & White, Bankruptcy, Practitioner Treatise Series, Vol. 2.

§ 8–20 "Wild Card" Exemption

Section 522(d)(5) is known as the "wild card" exemption. It allows the debtor to exempt her "aggregate interest in *any property,* not to exceed in value $400 plus up to $3,750 of any unused portion of the [§ 522(d)(1)] exemption [covering property used as a residence] * * * ."[1] Thus, using (d)(5), the debtor can enlarge the other exemptions in section 522(d); or, she can use (d)(5) to exempt property that is entirely beyond section 522(d).[2] The words "any property" in (d)(5) mean exactly that, any property.

The only restriction in (d)(5) is the value limitation. The exemption is never less than $400. It is increased by any unused portion of the (d)(1) residence exemption not to exceed $3,750. This additional amount is known as the (d)(1) *"spillover."* Its purpose is to avoid discriminating "against the nonhomeowner."[3]

The $3,750 cap limits the (d)(1) spillover, not the total (d)(5) exemption. Thus, the (d)(5) exemption can reach but never exceed $4,150. The debtor

---

§ 8–20

1. 11 U.S.C.A. § 522(d)(5) (emphasis added).

2. See, e.g., Matter of Patterson, 825 F.2d 1140, 1147 (7th Cir.1987), confirming In re Smith, 640 F.2d 888, 891–93 (7th Cir.1981) ((d)(5) is applicable to any property of the estate and is not confined to property specifically enumerated in § 522(d)); In re Rivet, 125 B.R. 704 (Bankr. D.R.I.1991) (Combining (d)(2) and (5) (both the wildcard and the spillover), the debtor exempted her interest in a truck to the extent of $5,350 and thereafter, using § 522(f), avoided a creditor's judicial lien to the extent the lien impaired the enlarged exemption.); Matter of Eldridge, 15 B.R. 594, 595 (Bankr. S.D.N.Y. 1981) (§ 522(d)(5), with spillover of (d)(1) could be used to exempt real property that was not a homestead because "any property" of (d)(5) means any property).

3. H.R. Rep. No. 595, 95th Cong., 1st Sess. 361, reprinted in 1978 U.S. Code Cong. & Admin. News 5963, 6317.

gets the spillover even if she exempts nothing under (d)(1);[4] but (d)(5) always limits the size of the spillover to $3,750 even if the unused portion of (d)(1) is a larger sum. Any unused portion of (d)(1) that exceeds $3,750 is wasted.

3. Joint Cases, Section 522(m)

§ 8–21 Joint Cases, Section 522(m)

For full text of this section, see Epstein, Nickles & White, Bankruptcy, Practitioner Treatise Series, Vol. 2.

4. Claiming Exemptions in Property the Trustee Recovers, Section 522(g)

§ 8–22 Claiming Exemptions in Property the Trustee Recovers, Section 522(g)

Ordinarily, the debtor cannot claim her exemptions in property she transferred absolutely or for security before bankruptcy. If she sold the property and retained no interest in it, there is nothing to exempt; no reason to exempt it; and no basis for doing so because exemptions are limited to estate property[1] and none of the property passed to the estate because the debtor lacked any interest in it. Property that the debtor encumbered before bankruptcy passes to the estate, but the debtor's exemptions are only effective against her interest, i.e., the equity, in the property. Exemptions themselves cannot displace security interests and liens on otherwise exemptible property, and such encumbrances generally survive the bankruptcy and remain enforceable against the collateral despite the bankruptcy.

The Code gives the trustee an arsenal of powers to undo, i.e., avoid, certain prepetition transfers of the debtor's property.[2] These avoiding powers of the trustee can be used against voluntary and involuntary transfers and transfers that are sales or that create encumbrances. Any kind of transfer is potentially avoidable. Upon avoidance of a transfer the trustee recovers the property itself or substitutional damages for the benefit of the bankruptcy estate,[3] and this recovery becomes property of the estate.[4]

If a sale or gift of property is avoided, the estate will acquire the rights in the property that the debtor transferred or their value. If an encumbrance is avoided the estate gets the freed equity in the collateral.

Because a debtor can freely claim her exemptions in property of the estate, she could exempt whatever property the trustee recovers using these avoiding powers if the Code did not restrict exemptions rights in such property through section 522(g).[5] This provision explains that the debtor

---

4. In re Duchesne, 21 B.R. 390, 392 (N.D.N.Y.1982); In re Hoffman, 96 B.R. 46, 49 (Bankr. W.D.Pa.1988).

§ 8–22

1. 11 U.S.C.A. § 522(b).

2. See, e.g., id. §§ 544, 545, 547, 548, 549, 553 & 724(a). These provision create the trustee's principal avoiding powers, to which we devote an entire unit of this book. See Chapter 6, supra.

3. 11 U.S.C.A. § 550(a).

4. Id. § 541(a)(3).

5. Id. § 522(g). This provision, together with subsections (h) and (i), "are better viewed * * * as specific restrictions on the debtor's general power to exempt estate property * * * [which] is codified in section 522(b). These restrictions only affect the debtor's ability to exempt property brought into the estate under certain of the trustee's avoiding powers."

can claim exemptions in property the trustee so recovers "to the extent that the debtor could have exempted such property * * * had [it] not been transferred," [6] *if* the transfer that the trustee avoids was:

- an involuntary transfer of property that the debtor did not conceal; or,
- a security interest that the debtor herself could have avoided under section 522(f)(2).[7]

WARNING! This rule is not an exemption itself. Rather, section 522(g) both recognizes and limits the debtor's right to claim exemptions provided by other law (either section 522(d) or nonbankruptcy law) in property that the trustee recovers under sections 550 and 551 using her avoiding powers,[8] or that she recovers under principles of equitable subordination,[9] pursuant to turnover orders,[10] or as voidable setoffs.[11]

Moreover, section 522(g) does not itself avoid claims that impair the debtor's exemption to property despite the trustee's avoidance. Section 522(g) permits the debtor to use her exemptions against recovered property

> only 'to the extent that the debtor could have exempted such property * * * if such property has not been transferred.' Thus section 522(g) adds nothing to the debtors' substantive position vis-a-vis holders of non-avoidable liens. If the property is brought into the estate by virtue of the trustee's avoidance powers, it is available for exemption, but only to the same extent as if there had been no transfer. If there had been no transfer, the debtor's exemption would apply [only] to equity in property after taking into account valid encumbrances not set aside.[12]

Accordingly, subsection (g) does not peel away liens the trustee cannot avoid on recovered property and thereby increase the debtor's exemptible interest in it.

Subsection (g) essentially applies only to property that the trustee recovers upon avoiding *involuntary* transfers[13] including: "the fixing of a

---

Matter of Wilson, 694 F.2d 236, 238 (11th Cir.1982).

6. 11 U.S.C.A. § 522(g).

7. The provision literally provides:

> Notwithstanding sections 550 and 551 of this title, the debtor may exempt under subsection (b) of this section property that the trustee recovers under section 510(c)(2), 542, 543, 550, 551, or 553 of this title, to the extent that the debtor could have exempted such property under subsection (b) of this section if such property had not been transferred, if—
> (1)(A) such transfer was not a voluntary transfer of such property by the debtor; and
> (B) the debtor did not conceal such property; or
> (2) the debtor could have avoided such transfer under subsection (f)(2) of this section.

Id. § 522(g).

8. Section 550, which is referenced in section 522(g), governs the trustee's recovery upon avoiding a transfer using any of the avoiding powers. Thus, by referring to section 550, section 522(g) indirectly refers to and incorporates all of the trustee's avoiding powers. In re Gingery, 48 B.R. 1000, 1002 (D.Colo. 1985) ("the trustee's avoiding powers * * * are incorporated in Section 550"). This answers the case, In re Smith, 105 B.R. 217 (Bankr. W.D.N.Y.1989), in which the court mistakenly opined that section 522(g) was inapplicable to a recovery of an avoidance action under section 544 because the former fails to mention the latter. Id. at 218–19.

9. 11 U.S.C.A. § 510(c)(2).

10. Id. §§ 542 & 543.

11. Id. § 553.

12. In re Simonson, 758 F.2d 103, 106 (3d Cir.1985).

13. See 11 U.S.C.A. § 522(g)(1)(A).

§ 8–22 EXEMPT PROPERTY 619

judicial lien"[14] (e.g., liens of judgment, execution, or garnishment[15]); a statutory lien[16]; setoff[17]; forced sale to enforce an encumbrance, including a consensual lien[18]; or the payment of money upon court order.[19] The debtor cannot claim her exemptions in property the trustee recovers upon avoiding any "*voluntary* transfer" such as: a freely-made payment of money;[20] an absolute transfer of other property;[21] a real estate mortgage;[22] or an Article 9 security interest in personal property,[23] except an (f)(2) security interest.[24] "[T]he transfer need only be voluntary, not * * * fraudulent, to preclude exemption."[25] Section 522(g) thereby means "to prevent the debtor from exempting property that is available to exempt only because the trustee has recovered it in spite of the debtor's having voluntarily transferred it away."[26]

For this purpose, however, a transfer is not "voluntary" simply because the debtor herself acts to accomplish it. For example, in *In re Via*[27] the debtor borrowed money from her mother in order to repay a bank loan and thereby obtain the release of a wage garnishment. The court held that the repayment was not "voluntary" and thus, upon avoidance of the transfer of the money to the bank, the debtor was permitted to exempt the recovery through section 522(g).

The court explained in *Via* that a " 'voluntary transfer' occurs 'when the Debtor, with knowledge of all essential facts and free from persuasive influence of another chooses of her own free will to transfer property to the creditors.' "[28] Yet, a debtor's transfer to a creditor is not involuntary simply because the debtor "disliked" having to make the transfer,[29] or because the

14. H.R. Rep. No. 595, 95th Cong., 1st Sess. 362, reprinted in 1978 U.S. Code Cong. & Admin. News 5963, 6318; S. Rep. No. 989, 95th Cong., 2d Sess. 76, reprinted in 1978 U.S. Code Cong. & Admin. News, 5787, 5862.

15. See Practitioner Treatise, Vol. 2.

16. See Practitioner Treatise, Vol. 2.

17. See Practitioner Treatise, Vol. 2.

18. See Practitioner Treatise, Vol. 2.

19. See Practitioner Treatise, Vol. 2.

20. See Practitioner Treatise, Vol. 2.

21. See Practitioner Treatise, Vol. 2.

22. See Practitioner Treatise, Vol. 2.

23. See Practitioner Treatise, Vol. 2.

24. See 11 U.S.C.A. § 522(g)(2), which refers to a security interest of the kind described by section 522(f)(2); Matter of Hollinsed, 54 B.R. 155, 156 (Bankr. W.D.Wis.1984) (debtors could exempt property on which trustee avoided a security interest to extent that debtors could have avoided the interest themselves under § 522(f)(2)).

25. Redmond v. Tuttle, 698 F.2d 414, 417 (10th Cir.1983).

26. In re Rollins, 63 B.R. 780, 783 (Bankr. E.D.Tenn.1986), adding this caveat with which we agree:

However, § 522(g)(1)(A) apparently was not intended to prevent the debtor from exempting equity in mortgaged property that he could have exempted even if the bankruptcy trustee had not avoided the security interest. For example, suppose the debtor has $500 equity in a car securing a $1,500 debt. The debtor can exempt the $500 equity in a bankruptcy case. [The court cites a local exemption law allowing a debtor to exempt her interest in a vehicle.] Suppose the trustee avoids the security interest. This should produce about $1,500 for the bankruptcy estate that would not otherwise have been available and which the debtor cannot exempt. But the debtor should still be able to exempt the $500 equity if the car turns out to be worth $500 more than the secured debt.

Id.; accord, In re Milcher, 86 B.R. 103, 105 (Bankr. W.D.Mich.1988) (grant of Article 9 security interest in vehicle does not meet "involuntary" requirement of § 522(g)(1), but debtors may be entitled to exempt any excess of sale proceeds over the value of the lien avoided); Matter of Curtis, 44 B.R. 416, 419–20 (Bankr. N.D.Miss.1984) (same).

27. 107 B.R. 91 (Bankr. W.D.Va.1989).

28. Id. at 94, quoting In re Hoffman, 96 B.R. 46, 47 (W.D.Pa.1988).

29. In re McQueen, 25 B.R. 592, 594 (Bankr. D.Vt.1982) (debtor made voluntary

creditor has influenced or even pressured the debtor to act so long as the debtor is not harassed [30] and is fully informed with respect to the transfer.[31] For example, a debtor acts voluntarily when, with full information, she grants a consensual lien to a lender who required the lien as a condition of the loan,[32] or when she pays a creditor to settle a pending lawsuit between them [33] or to avoid legal action against her.[34]

The real key to *Via* is that the pressure had mounted to the point that the debtor had no real choice *whether* or not the bank would be paid. The garnishment guaranteed payment unless the debtor quit her job. In paying the bank directly with the loan from her mother, instead of paying indirectly through the garnishment, the debtor exercised her free will only with respect to the means of payment. A payment made to release a garnishment is as much involuntary as a payment made through enforcement of the garnishment.[35]

A further requirement with respect to involuntary transfers is that "the debtor did not conceal" the property.[36] For this purpose concealment is broadly defined and includes verbally hiding property, that is, misrepresenting its actual or potential existence.[37] Concealment is irrelevant with respect to a voluntary transfer. The very fact that the transfer was voluntary is sufficient reason in itself (except for an (f)(2) security interest) for immunizing the property from exemptions when the trustee recovers it upon avoiding the transfer.[38]

The plain language of subsection (g) does not permit exempting just any property that the trustee recovers. By the literal terms of (g) the debtor can exempt only property the trustee recovers that could have been exempted had "*such property* not been transferred." The implication is that even when the trustee avoids a transfer that is described in (g)(1) or (2), the spoils are exemptible only if the trustee recovers the very property that was the subject of the avoided transfer. The debtor cannot exempt substitutional damages or other property that the trustee alternatively recovers in place of the transferred property itself, not even under an applicable exemption that precisely fits the substitute recovery.

We would not read (g) so tightly, and would permit its application to any property the trustee recovers. Usually, the trustee's remedy is substitutional only if the very property transferred cannot be returned by the transferee

---

transfer in allowing secured party to take and sell livestock that was collateral, and "mere fact that the Debtors disliked having to transfer the livestock for sale does not obviate the voluntariness of the transaction").

30. See Practitioner Treatise, Vol. 2.
31. See Practitioner Treatise, Vol. 2.
32. See Practitioner Treatise, Vol. 2.
33. See Practitioner Treatise, Vol. 2.
34. See Practitioner Treatise, Vol. 2.
35. See Practitioner Treatise, Vol. 2.
36. 11 U.S.C.A. § 522(g)(1)(B).
37. In re Roberts, 81 B.R. 354, 360–63 (Bankr. W.D.Pa.1987) (deliberately omitting property from bankruptcy schedules is concealment that bars exemption); In re Bidlofsky, 57 B.R. 883, 894, 899 (Bankr. E.D.Mich. 1985) (debtors could not exempt house proceeds that they concealed within meaning of § 522(g) by telling creditors that sale of house would produce no proceeds).

38. 11 U.S.C.A. § 522(g)(1)(A); In re Gingery, 48 B.R. 1000, 1004 (D.Colo.1985) ("[A] recovered asset cannot be exempted if it was transferred voluntarily regardless of whether or not such transfer was concealed."); In re Smith, 105 B.R. 217, 219 (Bankr. W.D.N.Y. 1989) ("The two conditions of § 522(g)(1) are joined by the conjunction 'and,' so that the debtor, although she did not conceal her ownership of the automobile, by voluntarily transferring a security interest in the automobile * * *, fails the test of § 522(g)(1).").

either because she never got it or no longer possesses it. There is no good reason that a debtor's right to exempt property under section 522(g) should turn on the fortuitous handling of the transferred property by the third-party defendant whom the trustee sues.

Also, our looser reading harmonizes with subsections (h) and (i). This combination of provisions (1) gives the debtor the trustee's avoiding powers to retrieve property that could have been exempted under (g) if the trustee had avoided the transfer; (2) awards the debtor the same remedies that the trustee enjoys upon avoidance, which include recovering substitutional damages for the transferred property; and (3) permits the debtor to exempt "any property" she recovers, which patently includes property other than the transferred property. In substantive terms, however, the only difference between exempting property under (g) and (h)-(i) is who avoids the transfer. There is no good reason why this difference should affect the range of recoveries subject to exemption upon avoidance. We thus believe that Congress intended the debtor's exemption rights under (g) would apply to any recovery as is true of her exemption rights under (h)-(i).

A different issue is whether a trustee's recovery of substitutional property, i.e., usually money damages, can be exempted through (g) on the basis of an exemption statute covering the transferred property. The statute strongly argues against permitting the exemption. It allows the debtor to exempt "property that the trustee recovers * * * to the extent that the debtor could have exempted *such property*." The recovery itself must be exemptible. The same is apparently true with respect to recovery under (h)-(i) because the exemption right applies to the "property *so recovered*." [39] This problem is effectively avoided, however, if another available exemption fits the recovery itself, or the applicable exemption laws protect proceeds of exempt property and the trustee's recovery is legally viewed as proceeds of the transferred property which was exempt.

B. DEBTOR'S AVOIDANCE OF TRANSFERS OF EXEMPT PROPERTY

1. Asserting Trustee's Avoidance Powers, Section 522(h)

§ 8–23 Asserting Trustee's Avoidance Powers, Section 522(h)

The debtor is usually permitted to claim her exemptions in property that the trustee recovers upon avoiding a prepetition, involuntary transfer of the debtor's property. The permission to do so is section 522(g):

> the debtor may exempt under subsection (b) of this section property that the trustee recovers * * * to the extent that the debtor could have exempted such property * * * had [it] not been transferred if—
>
> (1)(A) such transfer was not a voluntary transfer of such property by the debtor; and
>
> (B) the debtor did not conceal such property; or
>
> (2) the debtor could have avoided such transfer under subsec-

---

39. 11 U.S.C.A. § 522(i)(1) (emphasis added).

tion (f)(2) of this section.[1]

Paradoxically, the trustee is discouraged from avoiding such a transfer because the trustee's main job is representing the estate, and the estate typically gains nothing from avoidance to the extent the debtor exempts the recovery. Yet, letting the transfer stand robs the debtor of an exemption to which she would otherwise be entitled, and also effectively endorses a transfer that the Code condemns. Thus, if the trustee does not attempt to avoid the transfer, section 522(h) empowers the debtor to stand in the trustee's shoes and avoid the transfer using the trustee's avoiding powers:

> The debtor may avoid a transfer of property of the debtor or recover a setoff to the extent that the debtor could have exempted such property under subsection (g)(1) of this section if the trustee had avoided such transfer, if—
>
> (1) such transfer is avoidable by the trustee under sections 544, 545, 547, 548, 549, or 724(a) of this title or recoverable by the trustee under section 553 of this title; and
>
> (2) the trustee does not attempt to avoid such transfer.[2]

Section 522(h) is an exception to the usual rule that the trustee's avoiding powers belong exclusively to her (except where some other person substitutes for the trustee as representative of the estate). Ordinarily, no one else can exercise the trustee's avoiding powers, least of all the debtor.

This exceptional power that (h) gives debtors is available in all kinds of bankruptcy cases[3] to avoid any kind of transfer (including a lien),[4] but is really quite narrow because section 522(h) is tied to (g)(1). The debtor can use the trustee's avoiding powers through (h) only to the extent that the debtor could have exempted the property under (g)(1) if the trustee had recovered it. Because of this connection the debtor's avoidance power under section 522(h) is limited to *involuntary* transfers of property that she did not conceal and that would have been *exempt* had the property not been transferred.[5] The debtor cannot use section 522(h) as a basis for attacking any voluntary transfer of property,[6] or for attacking any involuntary transfer of nonexempt property.[7] Also, because the exemption right under (g) naturally corresponds to the size of the exemption itself, the debtor's avoidance right under (h) is correspondingly limited to the same extent.[8]

Moreover, because the debtor's right of avoidance under (h) is entirely derived from the trustee's avoiding powers, the terms of these powers, and also the Code's other restrictions on their enforcement, limit the reach of the debtor's avoidance through (h).[9] It does not empower the debtor to avoid a transfer that is unassailable by the trustee herself.

A consistent case that appears contrary is *Matter of Washkowiak*.[10] The debtors involuntarily paid an apparently long-standing judgment lien on

---

§ 8–23

1. 11 U.S.C.A. § 522(g), which we discussed in § 8–22 supra.
2. 11 U.S.C.A. § 522(h).
3. See Practitioner Treatise, Vol. 2.
4. See Practitioner Treatise, Vol. 2.
5. See Practitioner Treatise, Vol. 2.
6. See Practitioner Treatise, Vol. 2.
7. See Practitioner Treatise, Vol. 2.
8. See Practitioner Treatise, Vol. 2.
9. See Practitioner Treatise, Vol. 2.
10. 62 B.R. 884 (Bankr. N.D.Ill. 1986).

their home, and then sought through section 522(h) to recover the payment in bankruptcy. They argued that the payment was a voidable preference under section 547(b). The only sticky issue was whether the payment had a preferential effect as section 547(b)(5) requires.

Ordinarily, a payment to a fully secured creditor lacks any preferential effect and is unavoidable; but, if the creditor's encumbrance would itself have been avoidable in bankruptcy, a payment in satisfaction of the encumbrance is treated as a payment to an unsecured creditor which is preferential. In the *Washkowiak* case the debtors themselves could have avoided the judgment lien under section 522(f)(1). Therefore, their payment of the lien was preferential and avoidable by the trustee under section 547(b), and thus they could avoid the payment through section 522(h).

As reasoned by Judge Ginsberg who decided *Washkowiak:*

The usual rule is that if a lien is defeasible in bankruptcy, payments on account of that lien in advance of bankruptcy—at least within 90 days in advance of bankruptcy—are avoidable by the trustee as preferential. In effect there is a two step analysis. In step one, the lien is retroactively avoided on whatever grounds it could have been avoided had the lien not been satisfied but instead had it continued to exist at the time of the bankruptcy. In step two, the transfer of the property to the now unsecured creditor is recovered as a preference. There is no logical reason why that rule should not apply where the lien is avoidable by the debtor as well as by the trustee. In fact, that rule seems to be embodied in § 547(b)(5). Had this payment not been made, [the judgment lien creditor] would have received nothing in the Chapter 7 case by virtue of § 522(f)(1). There is no logical reason why it should get the windfall of payment in full merely because it happened to get paid within a week before the [bankruptcy] petition.[11]

Bankruptcy Judge Bentz railed against this result in an essentially identical case, *In re Ricke.*[12] He reasoned that the trustee could not avoid the payment because only a debtor can use section 522(f)(1), not a trustee.[13] Judge Bentz is correct on this narrow issue, but he misses the point. The trustee's recovery of the payment would be based on section 547(b), not section 522(f)(1). Even in relying on section 522(f)(1) to satisfy section 547(b)(5) the assumption is that the debtor would have avoided the judgment lien, not the trustee herself.

When (g)(1) and the requirements of the trustee's avoiding powers are blended together with the explicit terms of (h), the result is four very large conditions which must be satisfied before a debtor can use section 522(h) to avoid any transfer of property:

- the trustee must not have sought and must not seek to avoid the transfer;[14]
- the transfer must be avoidable by the trustee under one of her avoiding powers that subsection (h) mentions;

---

11. Id. at 888; accord, In re Hoffman, 96 B.R. 46 (Bankr. W.D.Pa.1988).

12. 84 B.R. 408 (Bankr. W.D.Pa.1988).

13. Id. at 409–10.

14. On this issue the court can take judicial notice of the contents of the file of the case. In re Pruitt, 72 B.R. 436, 440 (Bankr. E.D.N.Y.1987).

- the transfer must have been involuntary and the debtor must not have concealed the transferred property; and
- the property the debtor seeks to recover must be exemptible, and only to that extent is the transfer avoidable by the debtor under subsection (h).[15]

If any of these conditions is not met, avoidance through section 522(h) is unavailable to the debtor because "[e]very element of section 522(h) must be satisfied before the Debtor may step into the shoes of the trustee for purposes of * * * [an] avoidance action."[16]

2. Debtor's Personal Powers of Avoidance, Section 522(f)

§ 8–24 Introduction

The debtor's right to reclaim exemptible property using the trustee's avoiding powers through section 522(h) is quite narrow, but (h) is not the only source of such power for a debtor. Section 522(f) gives a debtor two avoiding powers of her own which are independent of the trustee's avoiding powers and more potent as far as they apply. It empowers the debtor to avoid, in her own right, judicial liens on any property, and nonpossessory, nonpurchase-money security interests in designated personal property, to the extent the liens or interests impair exemptions of the debtor. The whole of section 522(f) provides:

> Notwithstanding any waiver of exemptions, the debtor may avoid the fixing of a lien on an interest of the debtor in property to the extent that such lien impairs an exemption to which the debtor would have been entitled under subsection (b) of this section, if such lien is—
>
> (1) a judicial lien; or
>
> (2) a nonpossessory, nonpurchase-money security interest in any—
>
>> (A) household furnishings, household goods, wearing apparel, appliances, books, animals, crops, musical instruments, or jewelry that are held primarily for the personal, family, or household use of the debtor or a dependent of the debtor;
>>
>> (B) implements, professional books, or tools, of the trade of the debtor or the trade of a dependent of the debtor; or
>>
>> (C) professionally prescribed health aids for the debtor or a dependent of the debtor.[1]

Section 522(f) is broad in terms of general availability. It is not reserved for Chapter 7 cases. Rather, it is equally available to individual debtors in other kinds of bankruptcies, including cases under Chapters 12[2] and 13[3]. Moreover, the debtor in any case can avoid liens through section 522(f) despite an inability to do so using the trustee's avoiding powers under

---

15. This list is partly borrowed from In re Wimbish, 95 B.R. 379, 386 (Bankr. W.D.Pa. 1989), and is similar to other listings of the requirements of section 522(h) which regularly appear in the cases.

16. In re Willis, 48 B.R. 295, 299 (S.D.Tex. 1985).

§ 8–24

1. 11 U.S.C.A. § 522(f).

2. See Practitioner Treatise, Vol. 2.

3. See Practitioner Treatise, Vol. 2.

section 522(h) or the unavailability to the debtor of section 522(h) itself.[4] The two subsections operate separately. Also, a debtor can ordinarily use section 522(f) even to avoid liens for debts that are nondischargeable in bankruptcy.[5]

At the same time section 522(f) is narrow in terms of specific applicability because of four major limitations. It only works against

- two kinds of liens (i.e., the liens described in (f)(1) and (2))
- that are attached to exempt property
- in which the debtor has an interest
- and that impair the exemption.

Principally because these limitations are somewhat loosely stated but very tightly related, "the avoidance of * * * liens [under section 522(f)] is deceptively more complex than it would first appear * * *."[6]

Studying and working with section 522(f) are easier if you keep in mind why the debtor looks to section 522(f). Suppose that she owns property covered by an applicable exemption law, either section 522(d) or nonbankruptcy law. If the property were unencumbered the debtor could assert the exemption to remove the property from the bankruptcy estate and hold it free and clear of creditors' claims. It happens, however, that the property is subject to a lien or a security interest. Exemptions are generally ineffective against encumbrances on the property. Thus, the secured creditor can grab the property (consistent with the automatic stay) and apply it in satisfaction of the secured debt. The exemption is impotent, availing the debtor nothing. The encumbrance thereby *impairs the exemption,* that is, it prevents the debtor from claiming and keeping the property for herself to the extent allowed by the exemption law covering the property.

Section 522(f) allows the debtor to avoid, i.e., nullify, an encumbrance that is a judicial lien or (f)(2) security interest on exempt property. Avoiding the lien or interest removes it as an impairment on the exemption, and the debtor can thereafter claim the freed property as exempt and keep it for herself to the limits of the applicable exemption law.

§ 8–25 Determining if the Lien Is Within the Scope of Section 522(f)

Only two kinds of liens are covered by section 522(f) and avoidable thereunder by the debtor: a judicial lien on any kind of property,[1] and a nonpossessory, non-purchase-money security interest in certain goods.[2]

A judicial lien is a "lien obtained by judgment, levy, sequestration, or other legal or equitable process or proceeding."[3] It is nonconsensual and involuntary, that is, not dependent on agreement, and arises from judicial action. Good examples are judgment liens[4] and liens of garnishment.[5] A

---

4. See Practitioner Treatise, Vol. 2.
5. See Practitioner Treatise, Vol. 2.
6. In re Raymond, 103 B.R. 846 (Bankr. W.D.Ky.1989).

§ 8–25
1. 11 U.S.C.A. § 522(f)(1).
2. Id. § 522(f)(2).
3. Id. § 101(36).
4. See Practitioner Treatise, Vol. 2.

5. See note 5 on page 626.

lien that arises *solely* by force of statute (that is, without the need for judicial action) on specified circumstances or conditions is a statutory lien [6] rather than a judicial lien and is altogether beyond section 522(f). Good examples are tax liens [7] and an attorney's statutory lien.[8] Whether a lien is judicial or statutory is determined by how the lien arises.[9] If it arises without judicial action it is a statutory lien even though it is enforced through judicial proceedings; if it arises only upon judicial action it is a judicial lien even though it is based on a statute.[10] A lien that arises solely by force of common law or equity is not a statutory lien unless for rent,[11] but neither is it a judicial lien or other interest within the scope of section 522(f).[12]

Congress included judicial liens in section 522(f) as special targets for avoidance by debtors in order

> to undo the actions of creditors that bring legal action against the debtor shortly before bankruptcy. Bankruptcy exists to provide relief for an overburdened debtor. If a creditor beats the debtor into court, the debtor is nevertheless entitled to his exemptions [through § 522(f)].[13]

The courts disagree whether a lien is judicial and avoidable under section 522(f) that is embodied in a divorce decree to enforce a property division. In the normal case in which the issue arises the debtor was awarded property in species, and the non-debtor was given a lien on it to secure the value of the non-debtor's equity. Arguing against the application of (f) are three result-oriented theories: (1) the lien is, in substance, a consensual security interest rather than a judicial lien if the decree is based on a property settlement agreement between the parties;[14] (2) otherwise, the lien is essentially an equitable lien that is not a judicial lien within section 522(f)(1);[15] and (3) in any event the lien is on and secures the non-debtor's own pre-existing interest in the property and is thus unavoidable under section 522(f) because (f) works only against liens on the debtor's interest in property.[16]

The largest number of decisions on this issue are to the contrary. They generally reject these theories (most pointedly the last) and hold that a court-imposed lien to enforce a property division precisely fits the meaning of "judicial lien" and is avoidable under section 522(f) if its requirements are met.[17] This result is "consistent with Congress's policy 'that property settlements should be treated the same as other debts in bankruptcy.'"[18] Under this view, which seems to us technically correct, the non-debtor

---

5. See Practitioner Treatise, Vol. 2.

6. 11 U.S.C.A. § 101(53). The term also includes a "lien of distress for rent, whether or not statutory." Id.

7. See Practitioner Treatise, Vol. 2.

8. See Practitioner Treatise, Vol. 2.

9. See Practitioner Treatise, Vol. 2.

10. See Practitioner Treatise, Vol. 2.

11. See Practitioner Treatise, Vol. 2.

12. See Practitioner Treatise, Vol. 2.

13. H.R. Rep. No. 595, 95th Cong., 1st Sess. 126–27, reprinted in 1978 U.S. Code Cong. & Admin. News 5963, 6087–88.

14. See Practitioner Treatise, Vol. 2.

15. See Practitioner Treatise, Vol. 2.

16. See Practitioner Treatise, Vol. 2.

17. See Practitioner Treatise, Vol. 2.

18. In re Pederson, 875 F.2d 781, 784 (9th Cir.1989), quoting Boyd v. Robinson, 741 F.2d 1112, 1116 (8th Cir.1984) (Ross, J., dissenting).

A debt for alimony, maintenance or support is, however, treated differently: it is a nondischargeable debt, 11 U.S.C.A. § 523(a)(5), for which exempt property is liable. Id. § 522(c)(1). Therefore, a lien for the debt cannot be avoided under section 522(f). In re Stebbins, 105 B.R. 118, 119–20 (S.D.Fla.1989).

spouse is treated like any other creditor with a judicial lien if she is left with nothing but a judicially-secured debt for her share of the property. It is especially silly to justify a different result by reasoning that the non-debtor's lien is on her personal interest in the property rather than the debtor's interest in it: a lien to secure one's own interest in property is unnecessary and even impossible.

Clearly, however, a judicial lien for a divorce settlement, like any other judicial lien, is avoidable under section 522(f) only if the statute's other requirements are met. In *Farrey v. Sanderfoot*,[19] the debtor argued that using section 522(f), he could avoid his former wife's lien on the house that the divorce decree awarded him. The decree also created the wife's lien to secure her entitlement to one-half of the value of the marital estate. The wife did not dispute that the lien was a judicial lien, and the Supreme Court did not reach this issue. The Court held, however, that the lien was unavoidable because the lien did not "fix" on an interest of the debtor in the property, as is necessary for 522(f) avoidance.[20] This means that the debtor must "have possessed an interest to which a lien attached, *before* it attached, to avoid the fixing of the lien on that interest."[21]

The "fixing" requirement was not met in *Sanderfoot* because the husband got his interest in the house, to which the lien attached, *simultaneously* with the fixing of the lien. By state law the divorce extinguished the original joint interests of the parties; and, by the decree, created at the same time a new fee interest for the debtor and the lien on this interest for the former wife.

The Court was clear, however, that the result would have been different if local law had left the debtor with his original interest and the wife's lien had attached to it: "§ 522(f)(1) could be used to undo the encumbrance to the extent the lien fastened to any portion of Sanderfoot's previous surviving interest * * * because Sanderfoot would have possessed the interest to which that part of the lien fixed, before it fixed."[22]

A lien dependent on agreement is neither a judicial lien nor a statutory lien. It is rather a security interest [23] and is covered by and avoidable under (f) only if the interest fits within the narrow description in (f)(2).

The security interest that (f)(2) describes is:

19. 500 U.S. ___, 111 S.Ct. 1825, 114 L.Ed.2d 337 (1991), on remand, 943 F.2d 679 (7th Cir.1991).

20. The target of avoidance under § 522(f) is the "fixing of a lien on an interest of the debtor in property * * *." We discuss this requirement separately, at § 8–27 infra, which includes a fuller discussion of Sanderfoot.

21. 500 U.S. at ___, 111 S.Ct. at 1831, 114 L.Ed.2d at 347 (1991) (emphasis added).

22. Id. at ___, 111 S.Ct. at 1831, 114 L.Ed.2d at 347 (1991) (dicta, in which Justice Scalia did not join).

23. Any lien created by agreement is a security interest. 11 U.S.C.A. § 101(51); see, e.g., In re Rosol, 114 B.R. 560, 564–65 (Bankr. N.D.Ill. 1989) (to extent that wage assignment is a lien, it is a security interest rather than a judicial or statutory lien because the assignment is created by agreement) (good discussion of Code's three types of liens, emphasizing that they are mutually exclusive). Such a lien is not a judicial lien even though the creditor resorts to judicial process to enforce it. In re Underwood, 103 B.R. 849, 851 (Bankr. E.D.Mich.1989); cf. Matter of Brunson, 87 B.R. 304, 311 (Bankr. D.N.J.1988) (mortgage did not become judicial lien after judgment of foreclosure); and it is not a statutory lien even though the interest is partly dependent on or made fully effective by statute. 11 U.S.C.A. § 101(53).

a nonpossessory, nonpurchase-money security interest in any [of the following goods]—

(A) household furnishings, household goods, wearing apparel, appliances, books, animals, crops, musical instruments, or jewelry that are held primarily for the personal, family, or household use of the debtor or a dependent of the debtor;

(B) implements, professional books, or tools of the trade of the debtor or the trade of a dependent of the debtor; or

(C) professionally prescribed health aids for the debtor or a dependent of the debtor.[24]

A security interest is nonpossessory unless the parties have deliberately created a pledge, that is, it is possessory only if they structured the secured transaction so that the secured party would hold the collateral. The key is "how the lien initially attached and became enforceable against the debtor."[25] If possession before default rightfully belonged to the debtor, the interest is nonpossessory[26] and remains so even if the secured party rightly takes possession upon default to enforce the interest.[27]

Whether a security interest is purchase money or not depends on state law.[28] The Uniform Commercial Code defines purchase-money security interest to mean

(a) taken or retained by the seller of the collateral to secure all or part of its price; or

(b) taken by a person who by making advances or incurring an obligation gives value to enable the debtor to acquire rights in or the use of collateral if such value is in fact so used.[29]

Thus, a security interest is purchase money that is retained by a credit seller of a widget to secure the buyer's obligation to pay the price. Similarly, if the buyer's purchase is financed by a bank which loans her the purchase price that is paid to the seller, the bank's security interest in the widget that secures the loan is purchase money. The interest is purchase money to the extent of the principal plus finance and other charges in the cost of the collateral.[30]

The purchase-money character of the interest survives if the seller or bank assigns the interest to a third person.[31]

The courts disagree whether the purchase-money character of a security interest survives refinancing, which typically involves widening the debt beyond the original purchase price. There are basically two views. One view is that refinancing causes an automatic transformation from purchase-money to ordinary security interest which subjects the entire interest to

---

24. Id. § 522(f).

25. In re Meadows, 75 B.R. 357, 360 (W.D.Va.1987); see also In re Schultz, 101 B.R. 68, 70 (Bankr. N.D.Iowa 1989) ("[T]he court should analyze how the security interest initially attached—whether it was intended that the security interest should be possessory at that time.").

26. See Practitioner Treatise, Vol. 2.

27. See Practitioner Treatise, Vol. 2.

28. See Practitioner Treatise, Vol. 2.

29. U.C.C. § 9–107.

30. See Practitioner Treatise, Vol. 2.

31. See Practitioner Treatise, Vol. 2.

section 522(f),[32] either because the original debt for the purchase price is replaced with a fresh obligation or because a purchase-money interest is impossible that secures more than the purchase price.

The other, better and more widely-accepted view is that a substituted new debt is not certain in a refinancing and depends on the parties' intention,[33] and that a security interest can have a "dual status" that tolerates add-on debt and retains its purchase-money character to the extent collateral continues to secure its own price.[34] Under this latter view "[t]he security interest is not avoidable under section 522(f) to the extent that it is a purchase-money security interest (PMSI), but [is] avoidable to the extent it is not." [35] The creditor bears the burden, however, "to demonstrate the extent to which a security interest retains purchase money status." [36] Failing to meet this burden results in "treating the entire security interest as nonpurchase money." [37]

A security interest is avoidable under section 522(f) only if the collateral consists of goods described in (f)(2)(A)-(C). Federal law defines these classes of goods even when state law determines the debtor's exemptions.[38]

The widest terms in (2)(A) are probably "household furnishings" and "household goods." The reason Congress gave for specially protecting them through section 522(f) is to undo overreaching:

> Frequently, creditors lending money to a consumer debtor take a security interest in all of the debtor's belongings, and obtain a waiver by the debtor of his exemptions. In most of these cases, the debtor is unaware of the consequences of the forms he signs. The creditor's experience provides him with a substantial advantage. If the debtor encounters financial difficulty, creditors often use threats of repossession of all of the debtor's household goods as a means of obtaining payment.
>
> In fact, were the creditor to carry through on his threat and foreclose on the property, he would receive little, for household goods have little resale value. They are far more valuable to the creditor in the debtor's hands, for they provide a credible basis for the threat, because the replacement costs of the goods are generally high. Thus, creditors rarely repossess, and debtors, ignorant of the creditors' true intentions, are coerced into payments they simply cannot afford to make.
>
> The exemption provision allows the debtor, after bankruptcy has been filed, and creditor collection techniques have been stayed, to undo the consequences of a contract of adhesion, signed in ignorance, by permitting the invalidation of nonpurchase money security interests in

32. See Practitioner Treatise, Vol. 2.

33. See Practitioner Treatise, Vol. 2.

34. See Practitioner Treatise, Vol. 2.

35. In re Parsley, 104 B.R. 72, 74 (Bankr. S.D.Ind.1988).

36. Geist v. Converse County Bank, 79 B.R. 939, 943 (D.Wyo.1987). A local statute can control the allocation. In re Palmer, 123 B.R. 218, 221 (Bankr. N.D.Tex.1991) (following Texas U.C.C.C. provisions on retail installment contract retains its purchase money character despite commingling with other purchases).

37. Geist v. Converse County Bank, 79 B.R. 939, 943 (D.Wyo.1987); see also In re Freeman, 124 B.R. 840 (N.D.Ala.1991), aff'd, 956 F.2d 252 (11th Cir.1992) (The creditor's security interest was treated as nonpurchase-money because neither the security agreement nor statute provided an adequate allocation method.).

38. See Practitioner Treatise, Vol. 2.

household goods. Such security interests have too often been used by over-reaching creditors. The bill eliminates any unfair advantage creditors have.[39]

Despite this lengthy explanation there is no Code definition of "household furnishings" and "household goods." The courts define them. The terms do not include the debtor's residence itself[40] or all of the debtor's consumer goods,[41] but are not limited to items that are strictly necessary or essential to keeping house.[42] Courts commonly take a somewhat liberal, middle position in defining the terms so that

> household goods and furnishings includes any personal property which is normally used by and found in the residence of a debtor and his dependents or at or upon the curtilage of said residence. This definition also includes personal property that enables the debtor and his dependents to live in a usual convenient and comfortable manner or that has entertainment or recreational value and even though it is used away from the residence or its curtilage.[43]

The courts disagree whether or not to draw the line at firearms: the decisions are about evenly divided on the issue.[44] Automobiles are not covered as household furnishings or goods.[45]

Nothing that (2)(A) describes is covered, not even goods that are typically found in the household, unless the goods are "held primarily for the personal, family, or household use of the debtor or a dependent of the debtor."[46] Thus, in *In re Reid*,[47] the court refused the use of section 522(f) to avoid a security interest in paintings that hung in the debtors' home. The debtors got the paintings in payment of business debts and thereafter used them as collateral for business loans. Thus, the paintings were not covered by (2)(A) because "even though the paintings were located in debtor's home [hanging throughout the house], they were primarily used for business rather than personal, family or household purposes."[48] Similarly, although (2)(A) expressly includes "animals," it does not cover livestock raised or held commercially for business rather than for personal, family or household purposes.[49]

Goods held for business are covered only if they fit within subsection (2)(B), which includes "implements, professional books, or tools, of the trade

---

39. H.R. Rep. No. 595, 95th Cong., 1st Sess. 127, reprinted in 1978 U.S. Code Cong. & Admin. News 5963, 6088.

This problem is also regulated in other ways. For example, state law limits after-acquired security interests in consumer goods when given as additional collateral. U.C.C. § 9–204(2). Also, the Federal Trade Commission has effectively banned nonpurchase-money security interests in a consumer's household goods. 16 C.F.R. § 444.2(4).

40. See Practitioner Treatise, Vol. 2.
41. See Practitioner Treatise, Vol. 2.
42. See Practitioner Treatise, Vol. 2.
43. In re Bandy, 62 B.R. 437, 439 (Bankr. E.D.Cal.1986).
44. See Practitioner Treatise, Vol. 2.
45. See Practitioner Treatise, Vol. 2.

46. 11 U.S.C.A. § 522(f)(2)(A).
47. 757 F.2d 230 (10th Cir.1985).
48. Id. at 233. The court in In re McCain, 114 B.R. 652 (Bankr. E.D.Mo.1990), recognized another requirement to section 522(f)(2)(A): the goods must be "'necessary to the debtor's new beginning and of little resale value.'" Id. at 653, quoting Matter of Thompson, 750 F.2d 628, 631 (8th Cir. 1984).

49. Matter of Patterson, 825 F.2d 1140, 1148 (7th Cir.1987); Matter of Thompson, 750 F.2d 628, 630–31 (8th Cir.1984); but compare Matter of Simmons, 86 B.R. 160, 163–64 (Bankr. S.D.Iowa 1988) (livestock held for family's consumption as food is within § 522(f)(2)(A), at least one year's supply).

of the debtor or the trade of a dependent of the debtor."[50] We treat these terms interchangeably and refer to them individually and collectively as tools of the trade or, simply, tools.

The legislative history of section 522(f) fails to mention (2)(B). Its purpose is nevertheless obvious and clear: to free from others' claims the exempt goods that are most essential to the debtor's fresh financial start.[51]

Property usually qualifies as a tool within (2)(B) that the debtor uses in her trade[52] so long as it is reasonably necessary to her work.[53] The largest issue about section 522(f)(2)(B) is whether it can include large, costly equipment that a debtor uses in her trade or is limited to small, relatively inexpensive hand tools. The answer is:

> Congress did not place any limit on the kinds of property that may constitute a "tool" since to do so would unfairly discriminate against particular professions and undermine the fresh start policy that the Code seeks to promote.[54]

Thus, (2)(B) covers any property that is a tool of the trade and that is exempt by other applicable law on any basis, including a farmer's tractor, combine, or other expensive machinery[55]; her breeding livestock[56]; and any debtor's motor vehicle that she uses in her business.[57]

The (f)(2)(B) provision is expansively applied in this fashion, without any express or implied dollar limitation of its own,[58] even though the federal tools exemption of section 522(d)(6) has a $750 cap.[59] Even if Congress meant small tools in (d)(6), the same language in section 522(f)(2)(B) means something different.[60] Similarly, tools can include vehicles under (f) even though Congress distinguished and separated them in (d).[61]

The $750 value cap on tools in (d)(6) is itself totally irrelevant, even indirectly, to the operation of section 522(f) if the tools are exempt under state law or some other part of section 522(d) so that the size of the exemption is not determined by federal (d)(6).[62] Similarly, state law limitations (definitional or value) on tools of the trade are irrelevant to section 522(f), even when the debtor relies on state exemptions.[63] Even when the debtor claims under the federal (d)(6) or state tools exemption, section 522(d) or the local law counts under section 522(f) only to the extent of defining the property that is exempt and the exemption's size,[64] not directly in restricting or otherwise affecting the application of (f). The meaning and operation of section 522(f), which avoids rather than exempts, are in every respect always a matter of federal law even when the debtor's exemption is provided by the state; but the construction of (f) is not controlled by section 522(d) because the purposes of the two provisions are different.

---

50. 11 U.S.C.A. § 522(f)(2)(B).
51. See Practitioner Treatise, Vol. 2.
52. See Practitioner Treatise, Vol. 2.
53. See Practitioner Treatise, Vol. 2.
54. In re Walkington, 42 B.R. 67, 72 (Bankr. W.D.Mich.1984), quoted approvingly in In re Heape, 886 F.2d 280, 283 (10th Cir. 1989).
55. See Practitioner Treatise, Vol. 2.
56. See Practitioner Treatise, Vol. 2.
57. See Practitioner Treatise, Vol. 2.
58. See Practitioner Treatise, Vol. 2.
59. See Practitioner Treatise, Vol. 2.
60. See Practitioner Treatise, Vol. 2.
61. See Practitioner Treatise, Vol. 2.
62. See Practitioner Treatise, Vol. 2.
63. See Practitioner Treatise, Vol. 2.
64. See Practitioner Treatise, Vol. 2.

§ 8–26 Determining if the Property Is Exempt

Section 522(f) is limited to avoiding a lien impairing an "*exemption.*" The courts interpret this limitation to mean basically that "the only property as to which Debtors might avoid liens under * * * § 522(f)" is "property allowed as exempt,"[1] and they often generalize that, in short, subsection (f) applies only to exempt property. Thus, in applying section 522(f) the courts often begin by determining if the collateral is exempt under the applicable exemption law, which is either section 522(d) or nonbankruptcy law.

Section 522(f) is not itself an exemption law. It provides for avoiding liens on property that other law exempts. The other law is either section 522(d) or nonbankruptcy exemption law because one or the other of them is always the source of the debtor's exemptions in her bankruptcy case. The avoidance powers of section 522(f) are available to the debtor regardless of the source of the exemption law;[2] but (f) applies only to liens on property that the applicable law exempts. Thus, it is the applicable exemption law rather than section 522(f) that determines whether collateral is exempt property for purposes of (f); and there is no reason to return to section 522(f) if the exemption law does not cover the property because subsection (f) has no application whatsoever to nonexempt property.

In deciding if collateral is exempt for purposes of section 522(f), the basic question is whether the collateral is a kind or type of property that definitionally fits within the terms of the applicable exemption law. If the property does not fit there, no liens on it are avoidable under section 522(f). For example, in the case *Matter of Van Pelt*,[3] the debtor sought to avoid a security interest in a motor vehicle under (f)(2), arguing that the vehicle was a tool of his trade exempt under the local law that was the source of the debtor's exemptions. Many courts would agree that "tools of the trade", as the phrase is defined for purposes of (f)(2), can include motor vehicles; but the meaning of (f)(2) was not the issue in *Van Pelt*. Rather, the issue was whether a motor vehicle was a tool of the trade within the meaning of the applicable state exemption law. This issue was decided against the debtor. The property was therefore not exempt, and liens on it were thus immune from attack under section 522(f) which applies only to exempt property.[4]

Property may be nonexempt under local law, as to a particular debt, for the different reason that the debt owed the creditor is excepted from the exemption. Some courts have concluded that section 522(f) is inapplicable to

---

§ 8–26

1. In re Wiford, 105 B.R. 992, 1002 (Bankr. N.D. Okla. 1989).

2. Thus, section 522(f) is available even in a state that has opted out so that the debtor's exemptions are controlled by state law and federal law other than section 522(d). In re Miller, 30 B.R. 819, 821 (M.D.Tenn.1983) ("The overwhelming majority of * * * courts have similarly held that § 522(f) continues to be operative, despite the enactment of state 'opt-out' legislation and separate state exemption provisions."); O'Malley v. Rapidan River Farm, 24 B.R. 900, 903 (E.D.Va.1982) ("The power to avoid * * * in § 522(f) indeed operates independently of a state's choice regarding its exemption scheme."); Matter of Reid, 97 B.R. 472, 475–76 (Bankr. N.D.Ind.1988) (state's opt out does not impair debtor's ability to avoid liens under § 522(f)).

If the debtor can and does elect the federal bankruptcy exemptions, 11 U.S.C.A. § 522(d), she can avoid a lien using section 522(f) to the full extent of any exemption that is enlarged by adding the value of the wildcard exemption and the spillover or unused portion of the homestead exemption. 11 U.S.C.A. § 522(d)(5); In re Rivet, 125 B.R. 704 (Bankr. D.R.I.1991).

3. 83 B.R. 617 (Bankr. S.D.Iowa 1987).

4. See Practitioner Treatise, Vol. 2.

a lien for such a debt even though the exemption law describes property of the collateral's kind.[5] Because the nature of the underlying debt excepts the debtor's property from the exemption, the property is not exempt. Therefore, a lien on the property for the excepted debt is unavoidable under section 522(f) because the lien does not impair an exemption.

This conclusion is highly doubtful after the Supreme Court's decision in the slightly different case *Owen v. Owen*.[6] In *Owen,* the debtor owned a condominium to which a judicial lien attached before the property was a homestead. By the time the debtor filed bankruptcy the property qualified for the homestead exemption of local statutory law. The debtor thus asserted the exemption in the bankruptcy case and sought to avoid the judicial lien on the property under section 522(f). The creditor resisted because local decisional law had determined that the exemption did not apply against preexisting liens on the homestead, that is, liens that attached before the property acquired its homestead status.

The Eleventh Circuit sided with the creditor in *Owen,* deciding that section 522(f) was inapplicable:

> Section 522(f) allows the debtor to avoid certain liens in order to protect against impairment of an exemption to which he would otherwise be entitled. There is no impairment of an exemption here, however. Under state law, the homestead exemption precludes attachment of a judgment lien except where the lien came into existence prior to the property attaining homestead status. Where, as here, the judgment attached prior to the homestead right, there is no impairment because the exemption is specifically subject to this exception.[7]

On policy, the Eleventh Circuit court reasoned that "Congress did not intend through section 522(f) * * * to provide a federal exemption greater than that protected by state law where the exemption is created by state law."[8]

The Supreme Court reversed, focusing on the verb tense of section 522(f). By its terms a debtor can avoid a lien that impairs an exemption to which she "*would have been entitled.*"[9] The Court reasoned that because of this subjunctive tense, the issue in applying section 522(f) is "not whether the lien impairs an exemption to which the debtor is in fact entitled" under the applicable exemption.[10] Rather, the issue is whether the lien "impairs an exemption to which he would have been entitled but for the lien itself."[11]

---

5. See Practitioner Treatise, Vol. 2.

6. 500 U.S. ___, 111 S.Ct. 1833, 114 L.Ed.2d 350 (1991).

7. In re Owen, 877 F.2d 44, 46–47 (11th Cir.1989), rev'd sub nom., Owen v. Owen, 500 U.S. ___, 111 S.Ct. 1833, 114 L.Ed.2d 350 (1991); accord, Deel Rent–A–Car, Inc. v. Levine, 721 F.2d 750, 751 (11th Cir.1983); In re Stone, 119 B.R. 222 (Bankr. E.D.Wash.1990) (Lien of Hayes cannot be avoided. It is a judicial lien but the homestead exemption excepts it. The exception is inherent in the exemption, so that the lien does not impair the exemption.); In re Keenan, 106 B.R. 239, 244 (Bankr. D. Colo. 1989); but see Matter of Hershey, 50 B.R. 329, 331 (S.D.Fla.1985) ("Despite the fact that appellee's lien has priority over the homestead exemption under Florida law, this court finds that the lien may be avoided under 11 U.S.C. § 522(f)(1) because of the supremacy clause of the Constitution * * *.").

8. 877 F.2d at 47.

9. 11 U.S.C.A. § 522(f) (emphasis added).

10. Owen v. Owen, 500 U.S. ___, ___, 111 S.Ct. 1833, 1836, 114 L.Ed.2d 350, 358 (1991).

11. Id. at ___, 111 S.Ct. at 1836–37, 114 L.Ed.2d at 358.

The Supreme Court explained that the proper approach, for both federal and state-law exemptions, is to "ask first whether avoiding the lien would entitle the debtor to an exemption, and it if would, then avoid and recover the lien * * *."[12] In *Owen*, the homestead was exemptible but for the judicial lien. Therefore, the lien was avoidable under section 522(f) if the other elements of the statute were met.[13]

The Eleventh Circuit's decision in *Owen* was thus wrong both on policy and in technical analysis. The policy reasoning, that section 522(f) does not expand state-law exemptions, was wrong because the whole purpose of section 522(f) is to enlarge exemptions in bankruptcy by stripping away liens and thereby enabling exemptions that were unavailable outside of bankruptcy because the liens, enforceable there, smothered exemption value. Section 522(f) assumes that the liens suppress exemptions and its very object is to turn the tables, to allow the exemptions to suppress the liens.

The Eleventh Circuit's technical analysis in *Owen* was also wrong. The court recognized from the beginning that section 522(f) is written in the subjunctive, but posed the wrong "what if" question. Instead of correctly asking whether the property would have been exempt in the absence of the lien, the court essentially asked whether the exemption would be effective outside of bankruptcy. This approach is nonsense in light of the purpose of section 522(f) to avoid liens that trump exemptions under nonbankruptcy law.

The Supreme Court's approach in *Owen* applies equally to liens that are excepted from exemptions because of the nature of the underlying debt, and probably means that these liens, too, are avoidable under section 522(f). The main difference is that in the case of a lien that is excepted because of the nature of the debt, the underlying debt may itself be excepted from the exemption. Thus, when the "but for" test of *Owen* is applied, the answer is different than in *Owen*. There the answer was that but for the lien, the property was exemptible without condition. Here the answer is that even in the lien's absence, the property is exempt from the debt that the lien would secure.

We believe this difference is unimportant. The difference between excepting debts and liens from exemptions is merely a difference in form. Indeed, excepting a debt from an exemption is illusory. A debt is not itself a threat to property, and exemptions are not created to protect property from debts.

Exemptions exist to form a shield against liens (and process to enforce them) which threaten property by sapping the debtor's interest and permitting its sale. Thus, excepting a debt from an exemption is really intended

---

12. Id. at ___, 111 S.Ct. at 1837–38, 114 L.Ed.2d at 360. The Code's legislative history supports this interpretation and approach. The history describes section 522(f) as a means whereby the debtor can avoid a lien "to the extent that the property could have been exempted in the absence of the lien." H.R. Rep. No. 595, 95th Cong., 1st Sess. 362, reprinted in 1978 U.S. Code Cong. & Admin. News 5963, 6318.

13. The Court remanded the case for a decision as to whether or not the lien "fixed" to an interest of the debtor in property, id. at ___, 111 S.Ct. at 1838, 114 L.Ed.2d at 361, which is an additional requirement for applying section 522(f). See Farrey v. Sanderfoot, 500 U.S. ___, 111 S.Ct. 1825, 114 L.Ed.2d 337 (1991), on remand, 943 F.2d 679 (7th Cir.1991), and our discussion of this requirement at § 8–27 infra. We believe this requirement was met in Owen.

to, and is a means of, excepting a lien based on the debt. Therefore, because section 522(f) effectively ignores an exception of the exemption law for the lien that the debtor seeks to avoid, it should also ignore any exception for the debt underlying the lien.[14] Moreover, because it is the lien that impairs an exemption rather than the debt the lien secures, the *Owen* test is literally met: but for the lien the property is exemptible because the debt itself, unarmed by a lien, cannot affect the property in bankruptcy or out. Without a lien the creditor with the debt simply cannot get at the property or prevent the debtor from doing as she wishes with it.

Of course, the debt would continue and, presumably, would remain excepted from the exemption by state law. We have already explained, however, that such an exception—as applied to the debt itself—is practically meaningless in bankruptcy.[15] The exception of the debt, alone, provides no preferred treatment for an unsecured debt.

The *Owen* approach to section 522(f) also undermines, completely, a line of cases led by the Sixth Circuit's decision in *In re Pine*,[16] which permits the direct, overt, and complete subversion of section 522(f). In *Pine* the debtors exempted certain household goods on the basis of local law and sought to avoid security interests in the property on the basis of section 522(f). The property fit the definitional scope of the exemption; but the exemption expressly applied only to the debtor's interest in the property measured by the debtor's equity in it. The court inferred that in this way the local legislature "specifically declined to exempt household goods to the extent that they are encumbered by a lien."[17] (In short, any interest in the property encumbered by liens was not exempt.) The court then concluded in *Pine* that the liens were unavoidable under section 522(f), reasoning that the liens attached to a property interest that was not exempt because liens had attached to it and that section 522(f) was inapplicable to liens on nonexempt property.[18]

The circular, bootstrap reasoning of *Pine* essentially cancels section 522(f)(2) and threatens (f)(1) by honoring the exemption law's exception of secured interests. The effect is widespread. Local exemption laws everywhere, and also the exemptions of section 522(d), generally apply by force of decisional law only to the debtor's interest or equity in property. Moreover, to ensure that local creditors get the benefit of *Pine* with respect to local exemptions the states could (as some already have) expressly define their exemptions by statute to exclude property to the extent it is subject to the liens avoidable under section 522(f). *Pine* is thus a means of indirectly opting out of section 522(f).

The *Pine* case has a large following but is not universally followed[19] and is arguably wrong for three reasons. First, making the same mistake of the Eleventh Circuit in *Owen*, the court in *Pine* overlooked how section 522(f) is applied subjunctively, entitling the debtor to avoid liens impairing exemp-

---

14. See, e.g., In re Cooley, 72 B.R. 54 (N.D.Ala.1987) (although tort judgments are excepted from exemptions, a lien for such a judgment is avoidable under § 522(f)(1)).

15. See text accompanying notes 5–14 supra.

16. 717 F.2d 281 (6th Cir.1983), cert. denied, 466 U.S. 928, 104 S.Ct. 1711, 80 L.Ed.2d 183 (1984).

17. Id. at 283.

18. See Practitioner Treatise, Vol. 2.

19. See Practitioner Treatise, Vol. 2.

tions "to which the debtor would have been entitled" in the absence of the liens. The debtors in *Pine* could have exempted their equity in the household goods had the security interests not attached to it. Thus, the interests impaired an exemption to which the debtors would have been entitled so that section 522(f) applied.

Further, the option of states to opt out of federal law is extremely rare and extraordinary. Congress therefore was appropriately explicit and clear in authorizing the states to opt out of the bankruptcy exemptions of section 522(d), and in so doing was equally clear in limiting the opt out to that specific provision. There is no comparably plain language permitting the states to escape anything else in section 522, least of all subsection (f).

Finally, and most fundamentally, exemptions generally, universally, and traditionally have applied only to the debtor's equity and were so limited when Congress enacted the Code. Thus, section 522(f) (especially (f)(2)) was virtually meaningless upon enactment if *Pine* were correct.

In sum, section 522(f) is properly applied by subjunctively ignoring the lien to be avoided in deciding if the property is exempt. The statute thereby also ignores any applicable exceptions to the exemption law for liens and debts, including any exception for liens that is accomplished by defining and limiting the exemption to the debtor's unencumbered interest in the property. This interpretation applies equally whether the debtor's exemptions are controlled by section 522(d) or nonbankruptcy law. The states cannot therefore opt out of section 522(f), not even as to local exemptions, by defining exempt property (through decision or statute) to exclude encumbered property interests. The states nevertheless remain free to prevent or dilute their debtors' use of section 522(f) with respect to any or all local exemptions by entirely eliminating the exemptions, or by defining them more narrowing in terms of the nature of the property covered or the dollar size of the exemptions.

We should emphasize here that ignoring the exemption law's exception of the lien is mandated by section 522(f) because of the statute's subjunctive application, and is done for the limited purpose of deciding if the lien impairs an exemption to which the debtor would have been entitled in the lien's absence. This disregard of an aspect of the exemption law, and of the lien itself, does not include ignoring any of section 522(f)'s own limitations with respect to the liens that it covers. Obviously important in this regard are the descriptions in (f)(1) and (2) of the kinds of liens that are avoidable if they impair exemptions. Less obvious is the equally important limitation of section 522(f) that the debtor can avoid only the "fixing" of such a lien "on an interest of the debtor in property." [20]

§ 8–27 Determining if the Lien Affixed to Debtor's Interest

Section 522(f) empowers the debtor to avoid only "the fixing of a lien on an interest of the debtor in property." [1] This limitation minimally means that the debtor cannot avoid any lien on property in which she had

---

20. 11 U.S.C.A. § 522(f).

§ 8–27
1. 11 U.S.C.A. § 522(f).

absolutely no interest when the lien attached. Suppose, for example, that the debtor buys property that she later establishes as a homestead. At the time of the purchase the property is already subject to a lien securing a debt of the seller. The debtor cannot attack the lien under section 522(f). The statute by its terms can only be used to avoid "the fixing of a lien on an interest of the debtor in property."[2] The lien in this case did not affix to the debtor's interest in the property, inasmuch as the debtor owned no interest whatsoever in the property when the lien attached.[3]

The limitation also prevents using section 522(f) when the lien is created simultaneously with the debtor's interest, as in *Farrey v. Sanderfoot*.[4] In this case the debtor, Sanderfoot, and his wife, Farrey, divorced. Each of them got one-half of the marital estate. The property division was largely accomplished by the state court awarding the debtor the family house, which the couple had formerly owned jointly; and, in the same decree, giving the former wife a lien against the house for her share of the estate, which sum the debtor was personally obligated to pay. The debtor thereafter filed bankruptcy, claimed the house as his exempt homestead, and sought to avoid his former wife's lien on the property.

The Supreme Court held in *Sanderfoot* that the lien could not be avoided under section 522(f)(1). The Court reasoned that the section only avoids the "fixing of a lien on an interest of the debtor in property," which requires that the debtor "possessed the interest to which the lien fixed, before it fixed."[5] In this case, wrote Justice White,

> [t]he same decree that awarded Sanderfoot his fee simple interest simultaneously granted the lien to Farrey. * * * Sanderfoot took the interest and the lien together, as if he had purchased an already encumbered estate from a third party. Since Sanderfoot never possessed his new fee simple interest before the lien "fixed," § 522(f)(1) is not available to avoid the lien.[6]

In another case decided the same day, *Owen v. Owen*,[7] the Court questioned, but did not decide, the effect of this "fixing" limitation when a floating judicial lien automatically attaches to property the debtor acquires after the lien was established against her. The hypothetical case is this: Debtor suffers a judgment which the creditor formalizes by docketing the judgment or otherwise. This judgment creates a lien on the debtor's interest in any real estate, within the lien's reach, that the debtor then owns or later acquires. Later, the debtor buys real estate that, by state law, is automatically and immediately subjected to the judgment lien. In *Owen*, Justice Scalia speculated that in such a case, "the lien may have attached simultaneously with the acquisition of the property interest. If so, it could be

---

2. Id.

3. See, e.g., In re Brooks, 71 B.R. 6, 8–9 (W.D.Ky.1986), aff'd, 817 F.2d 104 (6th Cir. 1987); McCormick v. Mid–State Bank & Tr. Co., 22 B.R. 997, 999–1000 (W.D.Pa.1982); In re Sprick, 78 B.R. 292, 295 (Bankr. D.Kan. 1987) (dicta).

4. 500 U.S. ___, 111 S.Ct. 1825, 114 L.Ed.2d 337 (1991), on remand, 943 F.2d 679 (7th Cir. 1991).

5. Id. at ___, 111 S.Ct. at 1830, 114 L.Ed.2d at 346.

6. Id. at ___, 111 S.Ct. at 1830–31, 114 L.Ed.2d at 346–47.

7. 500 U.S. ___, 111 S.Ct. 1833, 114 L.Ed.2d

argued that the lien did not fix 'on an interest of the debtor.' "[8]

The argument that Justice Scalia suggests should fail. Liens almost always attach to peoples' interests in property, not the property itself. Thus, a debtor typically must acquire an interest in property before a lien can attach to the interest, except in the rare case in which the conveyance to the debtor is, itself, defined in terms of (and limited by) the lien. This exception covers *Sanderfoot*, where the court decree that gave the debtor his title also defined and limited the title by the former wife's lien. It also covers the case where the debtor buys property that is already encumbered by the lien: in this event the conveyance to the debtor is itself defined and limited by the preexisting lien due to the principle of derivative title.

The case that Justice Scalia hypothesizes in *Owen* is materially different. The lien arises and operates separately and independently from the creation or granting of the debtor's interest. The lien is not built into the interest that is conveyed to her; naturally, therefore, the lien can only attach to the debtor's interest after she acquires the interest. It so happens that in the case of a floating lien, the attachment of the lien follows immediately, even instantly, the debtor's acquisition of her interest; but the two events are not simultaneous. Acquisition is independent of attachment and precedes it. The lien thus meets the "fixing" limitation that Justice White describes in *Sanderfoot*. Moreover, there is no good reason to except from section 522(f)(1) floating liens that attach to the debtor's after-acquired property.

The courts further construe the "fixing" language of (f) to require additionally that the lien remains fixed to the debtor's interest at the time of bankruptcy. Thus, section 522(f) is inapplicable to any lien on property that the debtor sold before bankruptcy or in which she otherwise had no interest at the time of bankruptcy.[9]

The question that has been tough for many courts is the precise meaning of "interest." No one doubts that it includes any claim or right in property that the state recognizes in law or equity.[10] The issue is whether the meaning is restricted to so much of the interest as is unencumbered. Stated otherwise, the issue is whether the phrase "interest of the debtor in property" really means the debtor's equity in the property.

Creditors have argued for this equation in two kinds of cases. The easier case involves property that is fully encumbered either solely by the lien to be avoided or in combination with other encumbrances. The creditor makes the very wide and simple argument that section 522(f) is unavailable because the debtor lacks any equity in the property. The courts have readily rejected this argument with equally wide and simple reasoning:

> [t]here is no language in 11 U.S.C. § 522(f) that would require the debtor to have an equity interest in the property * * *. Indeed, the sole requirement is that the debtor have "an interest" in the property.

---

350 (1991).

8. Id. at ___, 111 S.Ct. at 1838, 114 L.Ed.2d at 361.

9. See Practitioner Treatise, Vol. 2.

10. See Practitioner Treatise, Vol. 2.

* * * [The argument] would clearly destroy the entire concept * * * [and] circumvent the legislative intent [behind § 522(f)].[11]

Indeed, requiring equity would contravene the aim of section 522(f) which is "to enable a debtor to *create* equity, which otherwise would not exist, by avoiding certain liens."[12]

The argument in the other kind of case is slightly more sophisticated. It is that section 522(f) is limited to avoiding a lien to the extent that the debtor had *equity* in the collateral *that the lien extinguished.* Suppose, for example, that the debtor seeks to avoid a judgment lien on her homestead which is a judicial lien within the meaning of section 522(f)(1). The property is worth $100,000, but is subject to prior, valid mortgages totalling $115,000 that trump the lien. The lien creditor argues that her lien is unavoidable under section 522(f) because no equity supports it and therefore the lien is not affixed to "an interest of the debtor in [the] property" within the meaning of the statute.

This argument is properly rejected, too. It is different from the argument of the first case but nevertheless shares the same assumption that the debtor's "interest" for purposes of section 522(f) means the debtor's equity. The courts' rejection of this definitional equation in the first case is equally fatal in the second case.[13]

In sum, for purposes of section 522(f), the debtor has an interest in property so long as she retains some right or claim that is recognized in law or equity. A lien affixes to this interest of the debtor rather than to her equity. Thus, the size of the debtor's equity in her interest is irrelevant in deciding the existence and extent of the interest and also in deciding whether or not a lien affixed to it.

The creditor in the second case can nevertheless recast and refocus the argument, claiming that the debtor's exemption is impaired only to the extent that the lien extinguished equity. Impairment is an entirely separate requirement of section 522(f). An exemption must be impaired to avoid any encumbrance under 522(f), and then avoidance is possible only to the extent of the impairment.

§ 8–28 Determining Impairment

A lien on exempt property is avoidable under section 522(f) only to the extent that the lien "impairs" the exemption.[1] Surprisingly, the cases are greatly confused about the meaning of impairment for this purpose. Disagreements among the courts abound. We frankly think that many courts have unnecessarily and artificially complicated the issue by looking away from both the sense of the statute and the plain meaning of its language.

Our approach is fairly simple. We begin with the equation that to impair means to diminish. Impairment therefore occurs within the meaning of section 522(f) when a lien diminishes an exemption. The significance of an exemption is that it gives the debtor an amount of value from the exempt

---

11. In re Brown, 81 B.R. 432, 434 (N.D.Ohio 1985).

12. Alu v. State of New York, 41 B.R. 955, 957 (E.D.N.Y.1984).

13. See Practitioner Treatise, Vol. 2.

§ 8–28

1. 11 U.S.C.A. § 522(f).

property that she can keep for herself free from creditor's claims and that, in bankruptcy, she can exclude from the estate. This amount is the *exemption value*.[2] Impairment of an exemption by a lien is basically the diminution of this value by the lien occupying otherwise exemptible equity. In sum, a lien impairs an exemption within the meaning of section 522(f) to the extent that the lien exists as a secured claim on exempt property[3] and thereby, by sapping equity, diminishes the exemption value otherwise available to the debtor in the bankruptcy case. To this extent section 522(f) strips away the lien and frees an equivalent amount of exemption value, that is, 522(f) effectively "'creates equity equal to the amount that could be exempted if the security interest did not exist.'"[4]

For example, suppose that the exempt property is unencumbered except for the lien to be avoided. The property is worth $10,000, but is exempt only to the extent of $4,000. The property is subject to a judicial lien for $6,000. This lien is safe from attack under section 522(f)(1). The lien does not impair the exemption because the exemption value in bankruptcy is unaffected by the lien. Even without the lien on the property the debtor can exempt only $4,000 of the property's value. This exemption value is not reduced by the lien because the property's value fully supports both the lien and the exemption. Notwithstanding the lien the debtor can take the full exemption. In this case, therefore, the lien does not impair the exemption.

Impairment would occur to the extent the lien exceeded $6,000 because the lien would then reduce below $4,000 the amount of the property's value available for exemption. For example, a lien for $8,000 would impair the exemption to the extent of $2,000. A $10,000 lien would impair the exemption to the full extent of the $4,000 exemption. The extent of impairment is important because a lien is avoidable under section 522(f) only to the extent that it impairs the exemption.[5]

Exemption value in bankruptcy is not the same as the market value of the property that is exempt. It is rather the amount of the property's value that the debtor can exempt from the estate on the basis of the exemption. This amount is principally limited by any dollar or other size limitation of the exemption law and by encumbrances on the exempt property.

The effect of a dollar limitation is seen in the hypothetical cases above. Even where the property that is worth $10,000 is subject to a $10,000 judicial lien, the lien impairs the exemption only to the extent of $4,000 because the exemption law limits the size of the exemption to $4,000. This limitation on the exemption thereby limits impairment and, finally, avoidance under section 522(f).[6] In no event can section 522(f) avoid a lien beyond the size of the exemption itself.

2. See Practitioner Treatise, Vol. 2.

3. See Practitioner Treatise, Vol. 2.

4. In re Weiss, 51 B.R. 224, 226 (D.Colo. 1985), quoting In re Redin, 14 B.R. 727, 729 (Bankr. D.Colo.1981); see also In re Galvan, 110 B.R. 446, 449 (Bankr. 9th Cir. 1990) (the purpose of § 522(f) is to permit the debtor "to create equity in limited instances and then to use the equity created to claim exemptions that would have otherwise been unavailable" because of the avoidance encumbrance).

5. The remaining lien can be honored in a variety of ways, including a sale of the property that divides the proceeds between the creditor and debtor or by the debtor paying the creditor the balance of the lien. In re Rivet, 125 B.R. 704, 707 (Bankr. D.R.I.1991).

6. In re Helmuth, 92 B.R. 494, 500–01 (Bankr. N.D. Okla. 1988) (§ 522(f) carries no

Exemption value is limited by encumbrances on the exempt property because, by force of exemption law, exemptions usually apply only to the debtor's equity in exempt property. This equity is generally measured by the property's market value less the amount of valid encumbrances on the property. Applying exemptions only to the debtor's equity prevents using them against the encumbrances, and is essentially a means of enforcing the law's decision to except the encumbrances from the effect of the exemptions in the first instance.

Because exemptions apply only to the debtor's equity, the only value in property that a debtor can exempt in bankruptcy is her equity in it. Thus, for purposes of section 522(f), exemption value and impairment are defined in terms of the size of the debtor's equity in the property measured by the property's value less unavoidable encumbrances.[7] In the case of an exemption that also carries a value limitation, both the value and equity limitations apply together so that the smaller of the two variables caps the exemption value.[8]

For example, suppose the debtor's homestead is worth $100,000 and is exempt without any valuation limitation. It is subject, however, to an unavoidable mortgage in the amount of $55,000 and also a judicial lien for $60,000 that attached after the mortgage. The lien is junior in priority to the mortgage by force of local law.

Whether the lien impairs the exemption in bankruptcy turns on whether the lien reduces the exemption value. Ignoring the lien, the exemption value is $45,000, which is the property's value less the amount of the mortgage, i.e., the debtor's equity. The lien exceeds this sum and thereby saps all of the exemption value. Thus, the lien impairs the exemption to the extent of $45,000 and is avoidable to the same extent under section 522(f).

Change the facts so that the homestead law limited the exemption in dollar value to $30,000. In this case the exemption value, the impairment, and the resulting avoidance under section 522(f) would be equally limited.

Implicit in this analysis is our view that a lien causes no impairment and is unavoidable under section 522(f) to the extent the lien is undersecured in the bankruptcy case.[9] We would stick to this view even in the extreme case in which the debtor's equity and thus the exemption value in the exempt property are zero because a senior, unavoidable encumbrance claims all of the property's value. In this case, there is no room or basis for applying section 522(f) to any extent to a junior lien because the lien does not impair the exemption.[10] Section 522(f) is completely inapplicable.

Before the Supreme Court's decision in *Dewsnup v. Timm*,[11] an undersecured lien that survived avoidance under 522(f) might have avoided by "lien stripping" under section 506.[12] Subsection 506(d) voids a lien to the extent

---

value limitation but can be used to avoid a lien only to the extent of the exemption that is impaired, so that avoidance under (f) is limited by any value limitation on the exemption); In re Lozano, 84 B.R. 634, 635–36 (Bankr. W.D.Mo.1988) (same).

7. See Practitioner Treatise, Vol. 2.

8. See Practitioner Treatise, Vol. 2.

9. See Practitioner Treatise, Vol. 2.

10. See Practitioner Treatise, Vol. 2.

11. __ U.S. __, 112 S.Ct. 773, 116 L.Ed.2d 903 (1992).

12. 11 U.S.C.A. § 506(a) & (d); In re Hermansen, 84 B.R. 729, 733 (Bankr. D.Colo.1988); In re Luby, 89 B.R. 120, 124 (Bankr. D.Or. 1988). In re Magosin, 75 B.R. 545, 550 n.3

that the lien secures a claim against the debtor that is not an "allowed secured claim;" 506(a) limits "allowed secured claim" to the value of the collateral. Thus, it seemed to many courts that a lien was void to the extent that the secured debt exceeded the collateral's value. *Dewsnup* disagreed. The majority could not read 506 to allow avoiding or stripping down an undersecured lien when the claim has been fully allowed.

The largest issue about impairment under section 522(f) is whether a junior encumbrance also defines exemption value and thus impairment and avoidance of a lien under section 522(f). The issue most commonly arises in this kind of case: D owns real property worth $150,000. The property has long been subject to a first mortgage for the purchase money, which now stands at $50,000. Six months before bankruptcy a judgment lien attached to the property in enforcement of a $50,000 judgment. Thereafter, D put a second mortgage on the property to secure a $50,000 debt. Under state law the priority of the encumbrances is: first mortgage; judgment lien; second mortgage. Both mortgages are properly recorded and are unavoidable on any basis in D's bankruptcy, but the judgment lien is a judicial lien that the debtor can avoid under section 522(f) to the extent the lien impairs an exemption. The property is D's homestead that is exempt to the extent of $50,000. The issue is whether the judicial lien impairs the exemption.

Arguably, the exemption value is properly calculated at $50,000: market value less the two mortgages. The lien entirely impairs the exemption value because the lien, too, equals $50,000. Therefore, because the lien impairs the exemption to the extent of $50,000, the lien is avoidable to the same extent.[13]

On the other hand, there is substantial support for a contrary holding on these facts that the lien does not impair the exemption because the second, junior mortgage should be excluded in calculating exemption value and impairment. The cases that would so hold generally take the view that a junior encumbrance is completely ignored in determining the existence and extent of impairment. The exemption value that a lien impairs under (f) is the value of the property reduced only by any senior encumbrances, not also by junior encumbrances.[14]

The courts that ignore junior encumbrances in this manner justify their approach on several grounds. Principally, they say it honors state priority rules and avoids the seemingly unfair subversion of judicial liens by debtors consensually encumbering the collateral on the eve of bankruptcy. Also, this approach arguably follows the language of section 522(f). The statute permits avoiding the "*fixing* of a lien * * * to the extent that such lien impairs an exemption * * *." If this language is read so that impairment is determined and measured as of the time the lien affixed to the collateral, then the very terms of subsection (f) dictate ignoring junior encumbrances in deciding if and the extent to which a lien impairs an exemption.[15]

(Bankr. E.D.Pa. 1987); cf. In re Galvan, 110 B.R. 446, 450–52 (Bankr. 9th Cir. 1990) (suggesting that unsecured lien that impairs exemption is avoidable either through § 522(f) or 506(d)).

13. See Practitioner Treatise, Vol. 2.

14. See Practitioner Treatise, Vol. 2.

15. See Practitioner Treatise, Vol. 2.

This approach is not entirely persuasive. The statutory language literally asks whether *the lien* impairs an exemption "to which the debtor would have been entitled under subsection (b) [§ 522(b)]." Subsection (b) provides for claiming exemptions in bankruptcy. Arguably, therefore, the proper question is whether the lien impairs an exemption at the time of bankruptcy, not before it.

The priority and fairness arguments are also doubtful. Congress determined that the liens avoidable under section 522(f) are objectionable as injurious to the debtor's "fresh start," and, in the words of Professor John Cross,

> the fact that the property is also encumbered by other liens, whether junior or senior, does not render the nonpurchase-money or judicial lien any less objectionable. The net result is the same—if the "objectionable" lien is honored, the debtor will not realize the full amount of his exemptions. Therefore, a nonpurchase-money security interest or judicial lien should be deemed to "impair" the debtor's exemption simply upon a showing that, in the absence of that lien, the debtor would receive more of his allowed exemption.[16]

Professor Cross thus endorses the view that subordinate encumbrances should be considered in determining impairment. He accordingly argues that any lien on exempt property impairs the debtor's exemption to the extent that the exemption exceeds the debtor's free equity in the property measured by the property's value less the sum of *all* secured claims against the property.[17]

This approach does not advantage an undersecured junior encumbrancer by allowing her encumbrance to spread and claim the equity formerly occupied by the avoided lien. Spreading of the encumbrance in this fashion is prevented by section 551.[18] It fictionally preserves the avoided lien in place for the very purpose of preventing "junior lienors from improving their position at the expense of the estate when a senior lien is avoided."[19] This effect works for the debtor herself rather than the estate when she avoids liens on exempt property under section 522.[20] Moreover, section 549 may confirm, in principle, that the junior encumbrance should not spread.[21] The section allows the trustee to avoid a postpetition transfer of estate property, and the debtor is sometimes authorized to use this avoiding power with respect to exempt property.[22]

---

16. Cross, The Application of Section 522(f) of the Bankruptcy Code in Cases Involving Multiple Liens, 6 Bankr. Dev. J. 309, 339 (1989).

17. He would make an exception in a case involving multiple liens that are avoidable under section 522(f). In this instance Cross would honor state law priorities and require the debtor to avoid first the junior lien. Id. at 341–42; see also In re Brantz, 106 B.R. 62, 68 (Bankr. E.D.Pa. 1989).

18. 11 U.S.C.A. § 551.

19. H.R. Rep. No. 595, 95th Cong., 1st Sess. 376, reprinted in 1978 U.S. Code Cong. & Admin. News 5963, 6332; S. Rep. No. 989, 95th Cong., 2d Sess. 91, reprinted in 1978 U.S. Code Cong. & Admin. News, 5787, 5877.

We discuss section 551 in detail elsewhere. See § 6–86 supra.

20. 11 U.S.C.A. § 522(i)(2) (transfer avoided under § 522(f) or (h) is preserved for debtor's benefit). Section 522(i) is discussed separately, infra at § 8–30.

21. 11 U.S.C.A. § 549(a).

22. See 11 U.S.C.A. § 522(h).

Conveniently, a standard formula applies to most cases that summarizes and encapsulates the proper approach to deciding impairment under section 522(f):

1. Determine the market value of the property in which the exemption is claimed.[23]

2. Subtract the sum of all other unavoidable liens and encumbrances (regardless of their priority in relation to the lien to be avoided under § 522(f)).[24]

   [a. If Figure 2 is zero or a negative number there is no impairment and no avoidance under section 522(f).]

   b. If Figure 2 is a positive number deduct from it the allowed value of the exemption (which is the market value of the property if the exemption is unlimited in value).

   i. If the difference (Figure 2.b.) is zero or a negative number there is impairment to the full extent of the lien or interest to be avoided.[25]

   ii. If the difference (Figure 2.b.) is a positive number there is impairment to the extent of the difference.

§ 8–29 Procedural Concerns

Lien avoidance by a trustee is ordinarily an adversary proceeding,[1] but avoidance by a debtor under section 522(f) is handled less formally by motion.[2] If the matter is contested the debtor generally bears the burden of establishing that the requirements of section 522(f) have been met.[3]

Debtors often have argued that the exemptibility of the collateral is a given and cannot be challenged if the creditor failed to timely object to the exemption in the first instance. The debtor asserts her exemptions by filing a list of property claimed as exempt.[4] The Code declares that "[u]nless a party in interest objects, the property claimed as exempt on such list is exempt."[5] The Bankruptcy Rules require making objections "within 30 days after the conclusion of the meeting of creditors * * *."[6] Thus, the debtor argues that a creditor who has not objected to the exemption within this 30-day period cannot do so later when the debtor invokes section 522(f) to avoid a lien on the exempt property.

The courts are divided on this issue but the trend is to reject the debtor's argument and allow the creditor's belated objection for the purpose of lien avoidance.[7] The courts that allow it disagree, however, whether the creditor or debtor then bears the burden of establishing exemptibility for this

---

23. See Practitioner Treatise, Vol. 2.
24. See Practitioner Treatise, Vol. 2.
25. See Practitioner Treatise, Vol. 2.

§ 8–29
1. Bankruptcy Rules 7001.
2. Bankruptcy Rules 4003(d); In re Galvan, 110 B.R. 446, 449 (Bankr. 9th Cir.1990); In re Windfelder, 82 B.R. 367, 369 (Bankr. E.D.Pa. 1988).

3. In re Sherwood, 79 B.R. 399, 400 (Bankr. W.D.Wis.1986) (debtor bears burden of proving § 522(f) elements).

4. 11 U.S.C.A. § 522(*l*); Bankruptcy Rule 4003(a).

5. 11 U.S.C.A. § 522(*l*).

6. Bankruptcy Rule 4003(c).

7. See Practitioner Treatise, Vol. 2.

purpose.[8] Yet, only avoidance is lost if the objection succeeds at this point, not the exemption itself.[9] Of course, the exemption is likely worthless or much diluted without avoidance.

An even more basic procedural issue is whether any time limit restricts the debtor's avoidance under section 522(f). There are statutes of limitations on avoidance by the trustee, section 546(a),[10] and on the trustee's remedies upon avoidance, section 550(e).[11] Neither these statutes nor any other statutory time limitation applies, however, to the debtor's avoidance under section 522(f).[12] Thus, a Chapter 7 debtor can make use of section 522(f) even after she gets a discharge and the case is closed.[13] Similarly, a Chapter 13 debtor can use section 522(f) even after her discharge upon completing the plan.[14] The only time limit on using section 522(f) is discretionary and equitable: the debtor cannot wait so long that the delay is prejudicial to the creditor.[15]

3. Claiming Property as Exempt Upon Debtor's Avoidance (§ 522(i))

§ 8–30 Claiming Property as Exempt Upon Debtor's Avoidance (§ 522(i))

Section 550 allows a trustee who avoids a transfer to recover the property itself or its value from an appropriate transferee.[1] By force of section 522(i) the debtor enjoys the same remedies when she avoids a lien or other transfer of exempt property using either section 522(h) or (f).[2] Typically, the transfer the debtor avoids is a lien.[3] It is fully remedied by the avoidance creating equity which the debtor then exempts. In any event, any appropriate recovery is exemptible[4] within the limits of the applicable exemption law.[5] Moreover, just as a trustee can preserve an avoided lien for the estate's benefit,[6] the debtor can preserve for her own benefit the liens she avoids on exempt property.[7] In this way debtor not only prevents the avoided transfer from going to the estate as would otherwise happen,[8] the debtor also keeps in place any unavoidable junior liens and thereby prevents

---

8. See Practitioner Treatise, Vol. 2.
9. See Practitioner Treatise, Vol. 2.
10. See Practitioner Treatise, Vol. 2.
11. See Practitioner Treatise, Vol. 2.
12. See Practitioner Treatise, Vol. 2.
13. See Practitioner Treatise, Vol. 2.
14. See Practitioner Treatise, Vol. 2.
15. See Practitioner Treatise, Vol. 2.

§ 8–30

1. 11 U.S.C.A. § 550(a).
2. Id. § 522(i)(1).
3. See Practitioner Treatise, Vol. 2.
4. 11 U.S.C.A. § 522(i)(1); In re Galvan, 110 B.R. 446, 450 (Bankr. 9th Cir.1990) ("The debtor may thus recover the avoided portion of the judicial liens, or the value thereof, * * * and then * * * exclude such value from the estate by claiming an exemption."); In re Frazier, 104 B.R. 255, 260 (Bankr. N.D.Cal. 1989) ("If the Court determines that the lien is avoidable under section 522(f), the debtor may then claim as exempt the property freed up by avoidance of the lien.").

5. 11 U.S.C.A. § 522(j).
6. 11 U.S.C.A. § 551.
7. 11 U.S.C.A. § 522(i)(2).
8. See 11 U.S.C.A. § 551 (transfers avoided under § 522 are preserved for the estate); In re Gingery, 48 B.R. 1000, 1003 (D.Colo.1985) (§ 552(i)(2) fills gaps left by § 551 which would preserve avoided transfers for estate's benefit); Beneficial Finance Co. of Virginia v. Franklin, 26 B.R. 636, 639 (W.D.Va.1983), vac'd and remanded without opinion, 714 F.2d 127 (4th Cir.1983) (§ 552(i)(2) holds avoided transfer for debtor's benefit that would otherwise automatically go to estate).

them from rising and taking the equity she has freed for exemption.[9]

C. EXEMPTION "PLANNING" IN ANTICIPATION OF BANKRUPTCY

§ 8–31 Planning by Creditors: Getting Debtors to Waive Exemptions and Related Rights

Standard form credit contracts typically provide that the debtor waives her exemptions against any claim for the debt. This form of exemption waiver, that is, any *consensual* or *contractual* waiver in favor of an *unsecured* creditor, is worthless in bankruptcy whatever its force under state or other law. The Code provides in section 522(e) that "[a] waiver of an exemption executed in favor of a creditor that holds an unsecured claim against the debtor is unenforceable * * *."[1] This provision applies "not just to federal but also to state-created exemption rights,"[2] so that such a waiver is utterly and completely ineffective in bankruptcy as a matter of overriding federal law.[3]

Two other kinds of exemption waivers are effective. A *procedural* waiver accomplished before bankruptcy under state law, because of failing to follow state procedures for claiming exemptions, is unaffected by the bankruptcy and continues there to bar the debtor's claim of the exemption to the extent provided by state law.[4]

More important, if the debtor creates a consensual lien on exempt property the practical effect, under state law, is impliedly to waive the exemption to the extent of the *secured* debt: the lien is enforceable despite the exemption.[5] The same is true in bankruptcy: exempt property is generally liable there for secured debts.[6] The implicit waiver that results from creating the lien is not negated by section 522(e). It applies to waivers of exemptions that are *un*secured.

The debtor may nevertheless avoid the lien in bankruptcy through section 522(f)(2) if it applies.[7] Notwithstanding contrary state law "a debtor can avoid a lien to the extent that such lien impairs the exempted property even though the debtor has waived the rights granted by the exemption" by creating the lien[8] or, additionally, by explicitly waiving the exemption.[9] Even an express waiver of the debtor's avoidance powers is ineffective.[10] Indeed, none of the rights that section 522 gives debtors with respect to exempt property is expressly waivable because section 522(e) not only neuters a debtor's waiver of exemptions proper, but also provides:

A waiver by the debtor of a power under subsection (f) or (h) of this section to avoid a transfer, under subsection (g) or (i) of this section to exempt property, or under subsection (i) of this section to recover

---

9. See Practitioner Treatise, Vol. 2.

§ 8–31
1. 11 U.S.C.A. § 522(e).
2. In re Blair, 79 B.R. 1, 3 (Bankr. D.Ariz. 1987).
3. See Practitioner Treatise, Vol. 2.
4. See Practitioner Treatise, Vol. 2.
5. See Practitioner Treatise, Vol. 2.
6. 11 U.S.C.A. § 522(c)(2).
7. See Practitioner Treatise, Vol. 2.
8. See Practitioner Treatise, Vol. 2.
9. See Practitioner Treatise, Vol. 2.
10. See Practitioner Treatise, Vol. 2.

property or to preserve a transfer, is unenforceable in a case under this title [i.e., in bankruptcy].[11]

Similarly, the debtor cannot waive the limited right she enjoys under section 722 to redeem exempt property.[12]

§ 8–32 Planning by Debtors: Converting Their Nonexempt Property to Exempt Property

It is not unusual for a debtor contemplating bankruptcy to increase her exempt property before filing. She converts nonexempt property to exempt property on the eve of bankruptcy by swapping (directly or indirectly) one kind for the other or by conveying solely-owned property to a form of joint ownership with a spouse that will put the property beyond creditors' reach. The debtor's lawyer may have advised her to do so as prudent "bankruptcy planning." The debtor's unsecured creditors who are thereby affected call it something else: actual fraud.

There is no simple answer whether such a conversion is right or wrong, permitted or damned in bankruptcy. The complexity begins in deciding where to look for an answer. The technically proper source of law on the propriety of a conversion may be different depending on how the issue arises, that is, the remedy that is sought. Three different remedies are possible for a conversion that is wrongful: it can amount to a fraudulent transfer that is avoidable under section 548 [1] or section 544(b) and state fraudulent conveyance law,[2] or can serve as a reason for denying an exemption provided by state or federal law or as the basis for denying her a bankruptcy discharge.[3] Properly, state law will control if the object is to avoid a transfer under local fraudulent conveyance law or to deny a state exemption. Denial of discharge, however, is always an issue that federal bankruptcy law controls.[4] For the most part, however, essentially the same analysis is followed in answering the ultimate question which is at the bottom of each remedy: did the conversion amount to actual fraud.

The larger problems that complicate the question are that the doctrine is soft and the issue in every case is very much fact-intensive. The traditional doctrine on whether or not converting assets to exempt property is actually fraudulent is easily and often stated: the conversion of nonexempt to exempt property on the eve of bankruptcy, thereby placing the property out of the reach of creditors, does not *in itself* support a finding of actual fraudulent intent [5] "even if the debtor acts with the express purpose of placing property beyond the reach of creditors and even though the debtor

---

11. 11 U.S.C.A. § 522(e).

12. Id. § 722 (by its own terms provides that the right of redemption hereunder is available "whether or not the debtor has waived the right").

§ 8–32

1. 11 U.S.C.A. § 548, which we discuss in §§ 6–47 through 6–59 supra.

2. Id. § 544(b), which we discuss in § 6–30 supra.

3. A debtor is denied a discharge if she with intent to hinder, delay or defraud * * * has transferred, removed, destroyed, mutilated, or concealed, or has permitted to be transferred, removed, destroyed, mutilated, or concealed * * * property of the debtor, within one year before the date of the filing of the petition * * *.

Id. § 727(a)(2)(A).

4. Norwest Bank v. Tveten, 848 F.2d 871, 874 (8th Cir.1988); Matter of Reed, 700 F.2d 986, 991 (5th Cir.1983).

5. See Practitioner Treatise, Vol. 2.

is insolvent at the time."[6] The reason is that the debtor is entitled to make legitimate, full use of the exemptions to which the law entitles her,[7] and is free to engage in a certain amount of "bankruptcy exemption planning."

The debtor is not allowed, however, to convert assets for fraudulent purposes. Thus, a conversion is fraudulent if extrinsic evidence, beyond the conversion itself, establishes that the debtor acted with intent to hinder, delay or defraud her creditors.[8]

It is usually rather difficult to distinguish between a lawful conversion, by which a debtor properly fully uses her legal exemptions, and an illegal conversion which is motivated by the debtor's intent to defraud her creditors. The debtor's intention is always the ultimately decisive fact, but there is seldom direct evidence of it. The courts thus typically consider a set of key circumstances that are commonly reflective of intention, that is, the courts hunt among the facts and circumstances of the case for the "badges" or "indicia of fraud" which suggest actual fraudulent intent, as they usually do in any kind of case in which actual fraud is an issue.[9] A non-exclusive list of these badges in conversion cases would include, for example:

- whether the debtor paid fair consideration for the property she got,[10] and whether the transferee of the nonexempt property paid fair value for it;
- if the money used to acquire the exempt property was borrowed[11] or was proceeds of collateral[12];
- the debtor's financial condition at the time of acquiring the property and as a result of the acquisition[13];
- whether the debtor accomplished the conversion openly or secretly,[14] and whether she lied to or misled creditors[15];
- the amount and value of the exempt property[16];
- the length of time between acquiring the property and filing bankruptcy[17];
- whether the property was acquired about the time a creditor began, or threatened to begin, collection activities[18];
- the amount of the debtor's nonexempt property involved in the conversion and remaining after it.[19]

There are many cases. Reliably reconciling them is impossible because, even though the courts' analysis is basically the same, the cases differ substantially in five very relevant respects:

- the facts;

---

6. In re Whitney, 107 B.R. 645, 650 (Bankr. D.Minn.1989).
7. See Practitioner Treatise, Vol. 2.
8. See Practitioner Treatise, Vol. 2.
9. See Practitioner Treatise, Vol. 2.
10. See Practitioner Treatise, Vol. 2.
11. See Practitioner Treatise, Vol. 2.
12. See Practitioner Treatise, Vol. 2.
13. See Practitioner Treatise, Vol. 2.
14. See Practitioner Treatise, Vol. 2.
15. See Practitioner Treatise, Vol. 2.
16. See Practitioner Treatise, Vol. 2.
17. See Practitioner Treatise, Vol. 2.
18. See Practitioner Treatise, Vol. 2.
19. See Practitioner Treatise, Vol. 2.

- the distribution of weight to various facts in the balancing process that determines the presence or absence of fraud;
- the object of finding actual fraud (e.g., to avoid a transfer as fraudulent, to deny exemptions, or to prevent a discharge);
- the source of law (state or federal); and,
- the procedural posture.

We nevertheless are tempted to generalize that, generally and basically, the dominant facts are these: whether the debtor effected the conversion openly in the ordinary course and (especially if the exemption lacks any value cap) whether the type and amount of exempt property the debtor acquired is unusual for exemption purposes. The former is important for the obvious reason that sneaky, odd conduct naturally smacks of actual fraud.

The large importance of the type and amount of exempt property is made clear by two cases decided differently by the same court on the same day. In *Norwest Bank v. Tveten* [20] the Eighth Circuit affirmed a denial of discharge. The debtor, a physician, got into financial trouble because of soured investments. In contemplation of bankruptcy, and upon his lawyer's advice, the debtor liquidated almost all of his nonexempt property (cash, IRA, profitsharing plan, house, and everything else) at market value and converted it into exempt life insurance or annuity contracts worth $700,000. These contracts were issued by a fraternal benefit association, and the applicable local exemption law exempted any and all money or other benefits payable by such an association. Because the exemption was unlimited as to value it carried "the potential for unlimited abuse," [21] and the Eighth Circuit agreed with the lower courts that the debtor in *Tveten* had abused the exemption to the extent of losing his right to a discharge: the debtor-doctor " 'did not want a mere *fresh* start, he wanted a *head* start.' " [22] In the end he got no start at all.

The contrasting companion case is *Hanson v. First Nat'l Bank*,[23] which the Eighth Circuit decided along with *Tveten*. The debtors in *Hanson* also converted property on their lawyer's advice shortly before bankruptcy, but on a much smaller scale. They did not sell everything they owned. Rather, the conversion involved about $34,000 in property. With the proceeds they bought two life insurance policies with cash values totalling $20,000 and paid $11,000 on their existing home mortgage. The applicable local law limited the insurance exemption to $20,000, and exempted the homestead. The Eighth Circuit agreed with the bankruptcy court that there were "no indicia of fraud." [24] The debtors merely "sold the property for its fair market value and then used this money to take advantage of some of the

20. 848 F.2d 871 (8th Cir.1988).
21. Id. at 876.
22. Id., quoting In re Zouhar, 10 B.R. 154, 156 (Bankr. D.N.M.1981) (emphasis in original); compare In re Johnson, 880 F.2d 78 (8th Cir. 1989), on remand, 124 B.R. 290 (Bankr. D.Minn.1991) (remanded for reconsideration whether debtor entitled to discharge where he had converted income and assets into annuities and IRAs worth about $250,000).
23. 848 F.2d 866 (8th Cir.1988).
24. Id. at 869.

limited exemptions available under [applicable] law on the advice of counsel."[25]

In truth, the only material differences between these two cases, *Tveten* and *Hanson,* are the form of the exempt property the debtors acquired and its value. Subsequently, the Eighth Circuit conceded that the cases establish

> that where an exemption, other than a homestead exemption, is not limited in amount, the amount of property converted into exempt forms and the form taken may be considered in determining whether fraudulent intent exists.[26]

The effect is judicially to limit in value the size of otherwise unlimited exemptions, taking into account the purpose of exemptions to provide "property to the debtor useful to his continuing survival."[27]

Thus, the amount of exempt property that a debtor can legitimately acquire is directly related to the property's usefulness to the debtor's survival and other exemption purposes. In the case of a homestead, the outer limit is the sky or almost as high;[28] in the case of exempt property that is functionally equivalent to cash, such as the benefits in *Tveten,* the limit is much lower.

Presumably, the courts will rarely, in this manner, limit exemptions that the legislature has already capped in value. With respect to these exemptions a policy decision has already been made as to their appropriate size. Funding them by conversion of nonexempt assets is likely to be fraudulent only if the debtor acts under cover or otherwise extraordinarily so that creditors are misled or otherwise directly harmed. There must be evidence of fraudulent intent beyond and apart from the form and value of the exempt property.

D. PSEUDO-EXEMPTIONS

§ 8-33 Property Excluded From the Estate (Herein, ERISA—Qualified Plans and Other Pension Funds

For full text of this section, see Epstein, Nickles & White, Bankruptcy, Practitioner Treatise Series, Vol. 2.

    a. Excluding a Pension Plan From the Estate

    b. Exempting a Pension Plan From the Estate

    c. Enforcing Against the Estate a Pension Plan's Restrictions on Access

---

25. Id.; compare In re Holt, 894 F.2d 1005 (8th Cir.1990) (affirmed finding of no fraud in conversion of cash into insurance policy having cash value of $10,000 where exemption statute had a value cap).

26. In re Johnson, 880 F.2d 78, 82 (8th Cir.1989), on remand, 124 B.R. 290 (Bankr. D.Minn.1991). Judge Kishel's opinion on remand is an insightful synthesis of the Eighth Circuit cases and is a model for deciding when conversion is fraudulent.

27. Id.

28. From the Eighth Circuit cases "one point is abundantly clear: the Tveten approach of considering the value of the converted assets has no application where the issue is an objection to a claim of homestead exemption." In re Whitney, 107 B.R. 645, 651 (Bankr. D.Minn.1989); see also In re Chadwick, 113 B.R. 540, 541 (Bankr. W.D.Mo.1990) (prefiling planning by debtor reducing mortgage is universally permitted in respect to homesteads).

Chapter 9

INDIVIDUAL REORGANIZATION: CHAPTERS 13 AND 12

Table of Sections

Sec.

A. Individuals With Regular Income

9–1 History.
9–2 Chapter 13 and Chapter 7 Compared.
    a. The Number of Chapter 13s.
    b. Reasons for the Chapter 13 Increase.
9–3 Eligibility.
9–4 Chapter 13 Procedure.
    a. The Opening Events: Petition, Statement, Notice, and Plan.
    b. Filing Proof of Claims.
    c. Significance of Filing Proof of Claim for Payment Under the Plan and for Discharge of the Debt.
    d. Filing and Allowance of Postpetition Claims.
    e. Secured Claims.
    f. Meeting of the Creditors.
    g. Confirmation Hearing: Form of Creditor Objections.
    h. The Chapter 13 Trustee: Appointment, Duties, and Payment.
    i. Payment to Trustee.
    j. Codebtor Stay.
9–5 The Plan: Priorities and Payment—Introduction.
9–6 Priorities and Payment—Secured Creditors and Priority Claims.
    a. Secured Creditors.
    b. Priority Claims.
9–7 General Creditor, Discrimination and the Floor.
9–8 Determining the Amount of Payments to Be Made Under the Plan: Introduction.
9–9 The Best Interest Test—In General.
9–10 ___ Computing Present Value—The Best Interest Test Applied.
9–11 Duration of the Plan and the Disposable Income Test.
9–12 ___ Section 1322(c): The Duration of the Plan.
9–13 ___ Projected Disposable Income.
9–14 Good Faith.
9–15 Modification of the Rights of Creditors—Introduction.
9–16 ___ Modification of Secured and Unsecured Claims and the Long Term Limitation.
9–17 ___ Deacceleration and Cure, Section 1322(b)(5).
9–18 ___ Restrictions on the Modification of Home Mortgages.
9–19 Feasibility, Section 1325(a)(6).
9–20 Confirmation and Discharge.
9–21 ___ Hardship Discharge.
9–22 Modification and Revocation of Confirmed Plan.

Sec.

B. Chapter 12—Family Farmers With Regular Income

9-23 History of Chapter 12.
    a. Comparison of Chapters 11 and 12.
    b. Comparison of Chapters 13 and 12.
9-24 Eligibility for Chapter 12.
    a. Farming Operation.
    b. Strategic Considerations.
    c. Retrospective.
9-25 Procedure and the Timing of Events in Chapter 12.
9-26 ___ Lessons for Chapter 11.
9-27 Conversion and Dismissal From Chapter 12.
    a. Conversion or Dismissal at Debtor's Request.
    b. Conversion or Dismissal at Creditor's Request.
    c. Retrospective.
9-28 Substantive Rules in Chapter 12.
9-29 ___ Feasibility.
9-30 Chapters 19 and 20: The Filing of a Chapter 7 Shortly Followed by a Chapter 12 or 13.

A. INDIVIDUALS WITH REGULAR INCOME

§ 9-1 History

The history of Chapter 13 begins at the turn of the century with the Bankruptcy Act of 1898.[1] Section 12 of that Act contained a provision for relief to the wage earner,[2] but according to Justice Clark, it was not particularly salubrious for most individual bankrupts:

> Section 12 proceedings, which were primarily adaptable for use by business entities, were disproportionately expensive in view of the small sums ordinarily involved in wage-earner cases; they lacked flexibility; and they did not provide for jurisdiction of the court subsequent to confirmation.[3]

The next stage in the development of consumer plans occurred during the Great Depression. In 1933, Congress adopted Section 74; it authorized extended proceedings and granted post-confirmation jurisdiction to the courts.[4] Bankruptcy Referees Charles True Adams of Chicago and Valentine Nesbitt of Birmingham, Alabama used Section 74 to implement the first real wage-earner plans.[5] Many of these first plans were successful; however, they involved some procedures that were cumbersome and others not sanctioned by the act.[6] Moreover, because confirmation was conditioned

---

§ 9-1

1. Act of July 1, 1898, 30 Stat. 544-66 (1898) (hereinafter the "Act of 1898").

2. Act of 1898, c. 541, § 12, 30 Stat. 549; see Perry v. Commerce Loan Co., 383 U.S. 392, 394, 86 S.Ct. 852, 15 L.Ed.2d 827 (1966), reh'g denied, 384 U.S. 934, 86 S.Ct. 1441, 16 L.Ed.2d 535 (1966).

3. Perry v. Commerce Loan Co., 383 U.S. 392, 394, 86 S.Ct. 852, 15 L.Ed.2d 827 (1966), reh'g denied, 384 U.S. 934, 86 S.Ct. 1441, 16 L.Ed.2d 535 (1966).

4. Act of March 3, 1933, Pub. L. No. 72-420, 47 Stat. 1467 (1933).

5. See Allgood, Operation of the Wage Earners' Plan in the Northern District of Alabama, 14 Rutgers L. Rev. 578, n.2 (1960). These wage-earner plans were creations of the Bankruptcy Referees. Bankruptcy law did not permit payment of prepetition debts with postpetition income.

6. Allgood, Operation of the Wage Earners' Plan in the Northern District of Alabama, 14 Rutgers L. Rev. 578 (1960).

upon the debtor's depositing cash in advance to cover proceeding costs and all priority claims, Section 74 was of limited use to many individual debtors.

In 1938, the Chandler Act and Chapter XIII replaced Section 74.[7] Chapter XIII provided a way of using future earnings to pay off debts under court protection, and free from creditor harassment. For the first time American Bankruptcy law explicitly sanctioned use of future earnings for postpetition payment of prepetition debts.

Use of Chapter XIII varied greatly among the federal districts. By 1968, Chapter XIII accounted for 76% of all voluntary individual bankruptcies in Northern Alabama, compared to 7% in Northern Ohio and 11% in Southern California.[8]

Like the statutes that came before it, Chapter XIII eventually needed revision.[9] Individuals who were self employed were often excluded from relief because Chapter XIII was limited to those earning income from wages, salary, or commissions.[10] Discharge due to hardship was not available to a debtor unless he participated under the plan for three years.[11] Joint petitions by husband and wife were not permitted. Approval of the debtor's plan by a majority of the unsecured creditors was necessary for confirmation.[12] The debtor's cosigners were not granted any relief from his creditors under Chapter XIII.[13] The role of the trustee in Chapter XIII was uncertain.[14] No restrictions were placed on the duration of a Chapter XIII plan [15] and Chapter XIII did not treat secured creditors consistently.[16]

Finding that Chapter XIII was "overly stringent and too formalized,"

---

7. Act of June 22, 1938, Pub. L. No. 74-696, 52 Stat. 840-940 (1938).

8. See Boren, An Analysis of Changes in the Use of Chapter 13 Since the Enactment of the Bankruptcy Reform Act of 1978, 23 Am. Bus. L.J. 451, 458 (1985); see also Ginsberg, Introduction to the Symposium: Bankruptcy Reform Act of 1978—A Primer, 28 De Paul L. Rev. 923, 930 (1979).

9. See Kaplan, Chapter 13 of the Bankruptcy Reform Act of 1978: An Attractive Alternative, 28 DePaul L. Rev. 1045 (1979), where the author calls Chapter XIII "[o]ne of the least understood and most erratically applied of the federal bankruptcy statutes * * *." (footnotes omitted).

10. Act of 1898, c. 541, § 606(8), as added June 22, 1938, c. 575, § 1, 52 Stat. 930, and amended Dec. 29, 1950, c. 1193, 64 Stat. 1134; May 13, 1959, Pub. L. No. 86-24, § 1, 73 Stat. 24, 11 U.S.C.A. § 1006(8) (1970). However, "courts have fudged on that definition in their decisions; the courts have held that social security recipients are eligible and that a self employed carpenter is eligible." Lee, Chapter 13 Cases in The Bankruptcy Act of 1978 160 (A. Holmes ed. 1979).

11. Act of 1898, c. 541, § 661, as added June 22, 1938, c. 575, § 1, 52 Stat. 936, and amended July 7, 1952, c. 579, § 52, 66 Stat. 437, 11 U.S.C.A. § 1061 (Supp. 1970).

12. Act of 1898, c. 541, § 661, as added June 22, 1938, c. 575, § 1, 52 Stat. 936, and amended July 7, 1952, c. 579, § 52, 66 Stat. 437, 11 U.S.C.A. § 1061 (Supp. 1970) and Act of 1898, c. 541, § 652, as added June 22, 1938, c. 575, § 1. 52 Stat. 934, 11 U.S.C.A. § 1052 (1970).

13. See S. Rep. 989, 95th Cong., 2d Sess. 12, reprinted in 1978 U.S. Code Cong. & Ad.News 3, at 13; see also H.R. Rep.595, 95th Cong., 1st Sess. 121-22, reprinted in 1978 U.S. Code Cong. & Ad.News 5963, 6082-83, cited in Kaplan, supra note 9 at 1047; Lee, supra note 10, at 171, where Judge Lee describes a firefighter who filed for Chapter XIII, owing a debt cosigned by fellow workers. When the co-workers discovered that the debtor had filed in bankruptcy, "[t]hey took him out behind the firehouse and beat him up."

14. 5 Collier on Bankruptcy 1300.01 at 1300-14 (15th ed. 1979); see generally Tselikis, The Chapter XIII Trustee: "Trustee or Dispersing Agent?", 21 Me. L. Rev. 53 (1969).

15. 5 Collier On Bankruptcy 1300.01 at 1300-14 (15th ed. 1979).

16. Bankruptcy Act § 606(1); 11 U.S.C.A. § 1006(1). Plans could not cover secured claims in real property, involving the debtor's home.

Congress replaced it with Chapter 13 in the 1978 Bankruptcy Reform Act.[17] Chapter 13 plans were to cure the problems inherent in Chapter XIII and create a means for debtors to obtain a financial "fresh start."[18] In order to encourage use of Chapter 13, Congress included a spoonful of sugar.[19] For example, Chapter 13 is now available not just to wage earners but to any debtor with regular income.[20] The automatic stay protects codebtors from the actions of creditors.[21] Confirmation of the plan is no longer contingent on approval by a majority of the unsecured creditors,[22] and secured creditors are subject to the "cram-down" provisions, that is, their rights may be modified in certain ways without their agreement.[23] Moreover, Chapter 13 plans are limited in duration to five years and normally are limited to three years.[24] If difficulties arise, a hardship dismissal is permitted under certain conditions.[25]

§ 9–2 Chapter 13 and Chapter 7 Compared

In theory Chapter 13 gives the individual debtor a number of advantages over Chapter 7.[1] In practice those advantages are more limited than it may seem at first. An apparently significant advantage is that Chapter 13 debtors may retain their assets and pay creditors out of postpetition earnings.[2] Conversely, Chapter 7 debtors liquidate their assets and pay their creditors out of liquidated funds.[3] Considering the entire universe of Chapter 7 and Chapter 13, one distinguishing the two on that ground would doubtless be mistaken. Many Chapter 7 cases are "no assets" cases, at least in the sense that there are no assets after exemptions are accounted for that are not subject to security interests. In such cases no assets are "turned over" to the trustee for liquidation. The Chapter 7 debtor retains the exempt assets and holds assets subject to security interests, at least if he can negotiate deferred payments with his secured creditors.

To put the point a slightly different way, Chapter 13 gives debtors bargaining power, particularly with their secured creditors, that they do not enjoy in a Chapter 7. Assume, for example, that a debtor has defaulted on her car loan and on her mortgage and that the two secured creditors are

---

17. Bankruptcy Reform Act of 1978, Pub. L. No. 95–598, 92 Stat. 2549, 11 U.S.C.A. § 1301 et seq.

18. See S. Rep. 989, 95th Cong., 2d Sess. 12–13, reprinted in 1978 U.S. Code Cong. & Ad.News 5787, 5798–99; H.R. Rep. 595, 95th Cong., 1st Sess. 118 (1977), reprinted in 1978 U.S. Code Cong. & Ad.News 5963, 6097.

19. In addition to the provisions mentioned here, see also § 9–2 infra.

20. 11 U.S.C.A. § 109(e).

21. Id. § 1301(a).

22. Id. § 1325.

23. Id. § 1327(a).

24. Id. § 1322(c).

25. Id. § 1328.

§ 9–2

1. For a discussion on whether a debtor should file in Chapter 7 or Chapter 13, see E. Warren & J. Westbrook, The Law of Debtors and Creditors: Text, Cases, and Problems 335–369 (1986).

2. 11 U.S.C.A. § 1306(b).

3. Id. § 704. However, the Chapter 7 debtor can keep exempt property under § 522(d); 11 U.S.C.A. § 541(c)(2); see generally D. Epstein, J. Landers & S. Nickles, Debtors & Creditors: Cases and Materials 710 (3rd ed. 1987). Chapter 13 debtors have substantially less unsecured debt and substantially more secured debt than Chapter 7 debtors. Moreover, 50% of the Chapter 13 debtors are homeowners compared to 25% of the Chapter 7 debtors. See Report of the Comptroller General to the Chairman of the Committee on the Judiciary, House of Representatives 47 (1983) cited in Jordan and Warren, Bankruptcy 625 (1987).

threatening, one to repossess the car and the other to foreclose on the home. If the debtor files in Chapter 7 the debts, but not the security claim, will be discharged, and the debtor will have to undertake negotiation with the two creditors to keep them from asserting their security interests against the two assets. If the secured creditors refuse to renegotiate their loans, the debtor will have to give up the assets to them if she cannot pay off the accelerated loans in full.

Conversely, in Chapter 13 the debtor can "deaccelerate" the loans, pay the arrearage on the home mortgage over the three-year life of the plan and continue current monthly payments on her home mortgage outside of the plan. If the debtor can make such payments, the secured creditor is helpless to oppose it, for the court will undo the acceleration even over the creditor's objection.

In the auto loan case, the debtor will be permitted to write the loan down to the present value of the car as a secured loan, pay that secured loan over the three to five year life of the plan and then pay off the remaining, unsecured portion at a fraction of its face value. Within the limits that we will discuss below, this plan too can be imposed on a non-consenting creditor.

Thus, to say that a Chapter 13 allows the individual debtor to "keep" assets that would be put up for auction in Chapter 7 is to overstate the case. Even in Chapter 7 there will be negotiation with various creditors, and even there (because of the exemption laws) the debtor will keep many assets free of any creditor's claim. However, these negotiations are facilitated by the rules in Chapter 13 that in effect authorize debtors to procure a unilateral loan from their existing creditors for a three to five year period simply by proposing a plan.

Second, Chapter 13 appeals to debtors who owe significant debts that would not be dischargeable under Chapter 7. Traditionally, the Chapter 13 debtor could discharge all prepetition debts except those for alimony, maintenance and child support payments.[4] Courts have held that the debtor is entitled to a discharge in Chapter 13 from listed[5] prepetition obligations arising from grand larceny of insurance money,[6] welfare fraud,[7] and willful and malicious injury to property.[8] Prior to the 1990 amendments,[9] discharge was possible for liabilities arising from student loans,[10] "criminal restitu-

4. 11 U.S.C.A. § 1328(a); see Memphis Bank & Trust Co, v. Whitman, 692 F.2d 427 (6th Cir.1982). Accord Ravenot v. Rimgale, 669 F.2d 426 (7th Cir.1982); In re Riggleman, 76 B.R. 111 (Bankr. S.D.Ohio 1987); Matter of Cruz, 75 B.R. 56 (Bankr. D.P.R.1987); In re Walsey, 7 B.R. 779 (Bankr. N.D.Ga.1980) (Debt based on materially false financial statement is dischargeable in Chapter 13.); but see In re McMinn 4 B.R. 150 (Bankr. D.Kan.1980).

5. See In re Gamble, 85 B.R. 150 (Bankr. N.D.Ala.1988)(Certain debts held nondischargeable in Chapter 13, where the debtor failed to list all aliases used within six years of filing which resulted in certain creditors filing no proof of claims).

6. In re Kazzaz, 62 B.R. 308 (Bankr. E.D.Va.1986).

7. In re Davenport, 83 B.R. 309 (Bankr. E.D.Pa. 1988), order rev'd, 89 B.R. 428 (E.D.Pa.1988).

8. In re Riggleman, 76 B.R. 111 (Bankr. S.D.Ohio 1987).

9. Omnibus Budget Reconciliation Act of 1990, Pub. L. No. 101–508, § 3007(b), 1991 U.S. Code Cong. & Admin. News (104 Stat.) 1388–90; Criminal Victims Protection Act of 1990, Pub. L. No. 101–581, 1991 U.S. Code Cong. & Admin. News (104 Stat.) 2865; Crime Control Act of 1990, Pub. L. No. 101–647, §§ 3102(b)–3103, 1991 U.S. Code Cong. & Admin. News (104 Stat.) 4916.

10. Education Assistance Corp. v. Zellner, 827 F.2d 1222 (8th Cir.1987); United States v. Estus, 695 F.2d 311 (8th Cir.1982); Phoenix Institute of Technology v. Klein, 57 B.R. 818

tion,"[11] and judgments for personal injuries caused by drunk driving.[12] The amendments preclude discharge of almost all debts of those types. In Chapter 7 most of these debts could not have been discharged if the creditor objected.[13]

Third, a debtor in Chapter 7 is taking a higher, though modest, risk that discharge will be denied in toto. In Chapter 7, discharge can be denied on any one of ten different grounds.[14] These provisions are not applicable to the debtor in Chapter 13.

Fourth, Chapter 13 stays suit against certain codebtors;[15] a Chapter 7 filing would leave the creditor free to sue the cosigner. This provision frees the debtor from worrying that his cosigning associates will use extra legal coercion when they discover that he has filed in bankruptcy and that they must pay *his* debt.

Fifth, debtors who cannot file in Chapter 7 because they have received a discharge in bankruptcy within 6 years, can use Chapter 13. Receiving a discharge under any of the bankruptcy chapters bars a debtor from filing in Chapter 7 case for six years.[16] Chapter 13 debtors are not subject to any similar limitation. They can file successive Chapter 13 petitions, limited in time only by the provision requiring the debtor to wait 180 days after *certain* dismissals.[17]

Finally, Chapter 13 may offer some balm to one who feels it is reprehensible to fail to pay one's debts. The rising rate of consumer bankruptcies has suggested to some that the moral obligation once felt by many debtors has disappeared, yet some debtors feel a moral as well as a legal obligation to pay their debts. For them a Chapter 13 plan that entails payment of all or substantially all of their debt over a period of time is more acceptable than a Chapter 7 discharge.[18] Moreover, some people believe that creditors who would not lend to a recent Chapter 7 debtor may be more willing to lend money to a recent Chapter 13 graduate.[19]

(Bankr. 9th Cir.1985); In re Reese, 38 B.R. 681 (Bankr. N.D.Ga.1984); but see In re Owens, 82 B.R. 960 (Bankr. N.D.Ill. 1988)(Public Health Service Act controls over Article 13 provisions); Matter of Johnson, 787 F.2d 1179 (7th Cir.1986) (Health Education Assistance loans held not dischargeable in Chapter 13 under 42 U.S.C.A. § 294f(g)); accord In re Gronski, 65 B.R. 932 (Bankr. E.D.Pa. 1986); contra United States v. Lee, 71 B.R. 833 (Bankr. N.D.Ga. 1987), judgment aff'd in part, rev'd in part, 89 B.R. 250 (N.D.Ga.1987), judgment aff'd, 853 F.2d 1547 (11th Cir.1988) (Dischargeability of HEAL loan is governed by 11 U.S.C.A. § 1328(a)).

11. Pennsylvania Dep't of Public Welfare v. Davenport, 495 U.S. 552, 110 S.Ct. 2126, 109 L.Ed.2d 588 (1990); California v. Heincy, 78 B.R. 246 (Bankr. 9th Cir.1987), decision rev'd, 858 F.2d 548 (9th Cir.1988); Dep't of Public Welfare v. Johnson–Allen, 69 B.R. 461 (Bankr. E.D.Pa. 1987); Cullens v. District Court of Colorado, 77 B.R. 825 (Bankr. D.Colo.1987); Everett C. Turner Realtors v. Carroll, 61 B.R. 178 (Bankr. D. Ore. 1986); contra In re Cancel, 82 B.R. 674 (N.D.N.Y.1988), rev'd, 85 B.R. 677 (Bankr. N.D.N.Y.1988); In re Johnson 32 B.R. 614 (Bankr. D. Colo. 1983); see United States v. Jacobson, 35 B.R. 40 (Bankr. D.Ariz. 1983) (criminal fine imposed by the United States district court is not dischargeable).

12. In re Sturgeon, 51 B.R. 82 (Bankr. S.D.Ind.1985).

13. 11 U.S.C.A. § 523.

14. Id. § 727(a)(1)–(10).

15. Id. § 1301.

16. Id. § 727(a)(8) & (9).

17. Id. § 109(g)(1) & (2).

18. See E. Warren & J. Westbrook, The Law of Debtors and Creditors: Text, Cases, and Problems 360–369 (1986).

19. On the one hand, the Chapter 13 graduate has established an ability and desire to pay off her obligations. In addition, at least in theory, the Chapter 13 graduate will have more unencumbered assets than the Chapter 7 debtor with which to secure new credit. On the other hand, the Chapter 7 debtor cannot

a. *The Number of Chapter 13s*

Since 1978 the number of individual bankruptcy petitions filed under both 7 and 13 has dramatically increased. In 1978 the total number of voluntary 7 and 13 petitions filed was 249,242; in 1982 the number was to 352,472.[20] Chapter 7 filings between 1975 and 1982 rose from 208,064 to 253,767; an increase of 22 percent.[21] For the same period Chapter 13 filings grew from 41,178 to 98,705; an increase of 140 percent.[22]

The growth rate of Chapter 13 petitions continues to be slightly higher than the growth in Chapter 7 filings. Between 1982 and 1988 the number of Chapter 13 filings has grown at a rate of approximately 66 per cent and the number of Chapter 7 filings at a rate of approximately 60 percent.[23] In 1990 there were 660,796 new personal bankruptcy cases. Of those cases, 2,116 were under Chapter 11, 468,171 were Chapter 7 liquidations, and 190,509 filings were under Chapter 13.[24]

The differences between Chapter 7 and Chapter 13 debtors are few. Generally they are of similar age, education, and income levels.[25] Perhaps the most significant difference between the two groups is that Chapter 13 debtors are twice as likely to own their home as those in Chapter 7.[26] One might speculate that a large number of Chapter 13s are filed specifically to stop a threatened home foreclosure. Additionally, debtors in Chapter 13 are more likely to be blue collar workers; those in 7 are more likely to be white

immediately refile in Chapter 7 and so one might expect that creditors would be less apprehensive about extending credit to these particular debtors.

In fact, however, empirical evidence suggests that creditors view Chapter 13 and Chapter 7 debtors alike—with contempt. E. Warren & J. Westbrook, The Law of Debtors and Creditors: Text, Cases, and Problems 364 (1986). Warren and Westbrook explain how a Phoenix attorney investigated the issue of whether filing in Chapter 13 would result in a more favorable credit rating for the client:

> I found out from the Phoenix Credit Bureau that when they rate you with credit points that not paying the debt off is the same—whether it is in chapter 7 or chapter 13 or not in bankruptcy. They don't make any real distinction. Chapter 13 wasn't going to help this lady at all.

Other credit reporting firms and several bankruptcy judges across the country confirmed this finding. Id.

20. Tables of Bankruptcy Statistics, during the twelve-month period ended June 30, 1975 and 1982, Table F-2 Administrative Office of the United States Courts, Washington, D.C. cited in Boren, An Analysis of Changes in the Use of Chapter 13 Since the Enactment of the Bankruptcy Reform Act of 1978, 23 Am.Bus L.J. 451, 457 (1985).

21. Id.

22. Id.

23. See Administrative Office of the United States Courts, Tables 10 and F-2, Tables of Bankruptcy Statistics, during the twelve month period ended June 30, 1987, and Tables of Bankruptcy Statistics, during the twelve month period ended June 30, 1988. Chapter 13 filings had been growing at a rate significantly higher than Chapter 7 filings. Between 1987 and 1988, however, Chapter 7 personal liquidations accounted for the chief source of increased bankruptcy filings. Chapter 7 personal filings rose 10% between 1987 and 1988.

24. Wall St. J., June 14, 1991, at A2, col. 4.

25. Id. The bulk of debtors in both chapters are between ages 25 and 34, with the next largest group being those between 35 and 44 years of age. Of the debtors in Chapter 7, 32% were high school graduates and 35% had at least some college. Similarly, of the debtors in Chapter 13, 34% were high school graduates and 32% had some college. The annual income for 69% of the debtors in either chapter was less than $20,000. Id. at 12–13.

26. Id. at 20, 47.

collar workers.[27]

b. Reasons for the Chapter 13 Increase

Most attribute the increase in Chapter 13 filings to the 1978 changes in the law.[28] Some commentators, however, believe that Code changes are not primarily responsible for the increased use of Chapter 13.[29] Instead, they suggest that social and economic forces are the cause of the increase. Not surprisingly there are high correlations between the number of debtors (adjusted filings) and selected social and economic variables such as financial problems, divorce, unemployment, and mortgage delinquency.[30]

Even a cursory examination of the statistics both before and after the enactment of the Code tells one that the legal distinction between Chapters 7 and 13 is only one of the reasons for a particular debtor's choice of one chapter or the other. During the late 1960s, Chapter XIII was practiced widely in Northern Alabama and Maine, but in few other jurisdictions. With the passage of the Code, Chapter 13 is used a great deal more in some states than in others. These differences are attributable to the predilection of the local bankruptcy judges, and to a lesser degree, of the bar and the community at large. A judge who encourages and welcomes Chapter 13s, and who prefers that debtors use 13 rather than Chapter 7, will have an impact upon the lawyers' views and the lawyers will in turn influence their debtors' choice of chapters.

Given the merits of Chapter 13 that were pointed out above and will be considered below, one might ask why Chapter 13 filings do not take an even larger percentage of all consumer bankruptcies than they do. One answer to that question may be certain judges' impatience with Chapter 13. Other explanations may have to do with the skill and efficiency of the local Chapter 13 trustee and with lawyers' selfish interests. Unless there is an effective trustee and unless a lawyer has set up an "assembly line," it seems likely that a Chapter 13 will produce a lower return per hour for a lawyer than will a Chapter 7. If that is so, and if the differences between Chapters 7 and 13 for most debtors are marginal, one would expect the lawyers to use Chapter 7 more frequently than Chapter 13. On the other hand, a client

---

27. Id. at 20. White collar workers made up 34% of the Chapter 7 debtors while only 25% of the Chapter 13 debtors. Id. at 13.

28. See Boren, supra note 20 at 451–456; Cooper, A Statistical Analysis of Chapter 13 Usage Before and After the Bankruptcy Reform Act of 1978, 1985 Annual Survey of Bankruptcy Law 351, 373–4 (1985); Carter, The Surge in Bankruptcies: Is the New Law Responsible? Econ. Rev., Jan. 1982, 20 (the Code is responsible for as much as three-fourths of the increase); Dunkelberg, Bankruptcy in the United States, Fam. Econ. Rev., Spring 1982, 16, 18 (the Code encourages consumers to declare bankruptcy), cited in Comment, Home Foreclosures Under Chapter 13 of the Bankruptcy Reform Act, 30 UCLA L. Rev. 637, 639 n.11 (1983).

29. "[T]he implementation of the Code may have contributed no more than 6 percent of the total adjusted filings and 13 percent of the number of debtors, who filed in fiscal year 1982." Report of the Comptroller General to the Chairman of the Committee on the Judiciary, House of Representatives 16 (1983).

30. Id. at 18. Moreover, Chapter 13 debtors indicated that the most significant factors causing them to file were increased cost of living (72%), periods of unemployment (34%), too many debts, and ease of credit availability. Additional factors mentioned by less than 20% of the debtors include accidents, increased family size, and emotional problems related to drugs or alcohol. Id. at 15.

§ 9-3 Eligibility

Section 109(e) states who is eligible for Chapter 13 relief:

Only an individual with regular income that owes, on the date of the filing of the petition, noncontingent, liquidated, unsecured debts of less than $100,000 and noncontingent, liquidated, secured debts of less than $350,000, or an individual with regular income and such individual's spouse, except a stockbroker or a commodity broker, that owe, on the date of the filing of the petition, noncontingent, liquidated, unsecured debts that aggregate less than $100,000 and noncontingent, liquidated, secured debts of less than $350,000 may be a debtor under chapter 13 of this title.[1]

Determining eligibility is occasionally tricky. The bankruptcy judge must first determine whether the debtor is "an individual," who has "regular income," and whether debtor's "noncontingent" and "liquidated" debts exceed the statutory limits. Moreover, the judge must determine which debts are "secured" and "unsecured," whether claims means the same thing as debts, and a host of additional eligibility questions.

Section 101(30) defines "individual with regular income":

"individual with regular income" means individual whose income is sufficiently stable and regular to enable such individual to make payments under a plan under chapter 13 of this title, other than a stock or a commodity broker.[2]

Use of the word "individual" excludes partnerships,[3] single shareholder corporations,[4] and estates.[5]

Congress' requirement of "regular income" was to encourage use of Chapter 13 by enlarging Chapter XIII's rule that income be derived from wages, salary or commissions. As a result of this change the source of the debtor's income is seldom an issue.[6]

---

§ 9-3

1. 11 U.S.C.A. § 109(e). There is no involuntary Chapter 13. 11 U.S.C.A. § 303(a). To the extent a debtor is avoiding an involuntary petition, however, the voluntariness of filing in Chapter 13 is illusory.

2. 11 U.S.C.A. § 101(30); see also In re Berry, 22 B.R. 950 (Bankr. N.D.Ohio 1982) (stockbroker without customers is eligible).

3. Fisk v. Allis Chalmers Credit Corp., 36 B.R. 924 (Bankr. W.D.Mich.1984); Matter of Monaco, 36 B.R. 882 (Bankr. M.D. Fla.1983); Miami Valley Production Credit Ass'n v. Tegtmeyer, 31 B.R. 555 (Bankr. S.D.Ohio 1983).

4. Forestry Products, Inc. v. Hope, 34 B.R. 753 (M.D.Ga.1983); see Matter of LaCache Land Co., Inc., 54 B.R. 629 (E.D.La.1985).

5. Matter of Jarrett, 19 B.R. 413 (Bankr. M.D.N.C.1982) (deceased debtor's estate is not an individual with regular income).

6. See United States v. Devall, 704 F.2d 1513 (11th Cir.1983), reh'g denied, 714 F.2d 1068 (11th Cir.1983); Regan v. Ross, 691 F.2d 81 (2d Cir.1982) (state pension benefits); In re Hammonds, 729 F.2d 1391 (11th Cir.1984) (AFDC benefits); In re Smith, 51 B.R. 273 (Bankr. D. D.C. 1984) (sale of property); In re Campbell, 38 B.R. 193 (Bankr. E.D.N.Y.1984) (family contributions under special circumstances); In re Monaco, 36 B.R. 882 (Bankr. M.D.Fla.1983); In re Tucker, 34 B.R. 257 (Bankr. W.D. Okla. 1983) (disability benefits); Margraf v. Oliver, 28 B.R. 420 (Bankr. S.D.Ohio 1983); In re Wood, 23 B.R. 552 (Bankr. E.D.Tenn.1982) (ERISA benefits); In re Overstreet, 23 B.R. 712 (Bankr. W.D.La. 1982) (unemployment benefits); Matter of Moore, 17 B.R. 551 (Bankr. M.D. Fla.1982) (supplementing income with odd jobs); In re Taylor, 15 B.R. 596 (Bankr. D. Ariz. 1981) (child support payments); In re Wilhelm, 6

Often at issue, however, is the question *when* the debtor must have "regular income." If the debtor has the same job at the time the plan is filed at the first meeting of the creditors and when the plan is confirmed, surely the debtor meets the "regular income" requirement. But what of the debtor who has a job at the time of filing, but not at confirmation or vice versa? Confirmation typically occurs several months after the filing and that is the time when the courts normally measure this requirement.[7] Since it is then that the plan's feasibility is determined, it makes sense to require that the debtor have regular income at confirmation. If the debtor does not have regular income then, it is hard to see how a feasible plan can be proposed. In effect, denial of a plan on the ground that the debtor is not eligible for want of regular income may be no different from a denial on the ground the plan is not feasible.[8]

Unsecured debts [9] cannot exceed $100,000 and secured debts [10] cannot exceed $350,000. In either case, however, only debts that are "noncontingent" and "liquidated" are included in this limitation. For this reason, debtors wishing to file in Chapter 13 who have large debts sometimes argue that a particular debt is contingent or unliquidated and therefore not to be counted against the $100,000 or $350,000.

A debt is contingent "[i]f the debtor's legal duty to pay, i.e., his liability, does not come into existence until triggered by the occurrence of a future event that was reasonably within the presumed contemplation of the parties

---

B.R. 905 (Bankr. E.D.N.Y.1980) (income from self employment); In re Ballard, 4 B.R. 271 (Bankr. E.D.Va.1980); In re Cole, 3 B.R. 346 (Bankr. S.D.W.Va.1980) (income from odd jobs); compare to the following which were held not to constitute regular income: In re Buren, 725 F.2d 1080 (6th Cir.1984), cert. denied, 469 U.S. 818, 105 S.Ct. 87, 83 L.Ed.2d 34 (1984) (social security benefits); In re Hogue, 78 B.R. 867 (Bankr. S.D.Ohio 1987) (sale of property alone); In re Cregut, 69 B.R. 21 (Bankr. D. Ariz. 1986) (family contributions); In re Corey, 19 B.R. 76 (Bankr. S.D.Ala.1982) (income from flea market).

Quaere whether one who is undertaking a "liquidating Chapter 13" should be required to have any significant income in order to qualify.

7. Matter of Cole, 3 B.R. 346 (Bankr. S.D.W.Va.1980); see In re Donohue, 81 B.R. 714 (Bankr. S.D. Fla.1987) (debtor who lost job by the time of confirmation hearing was ineligible, even with prospects of a job within two months); In re McMonagle, 30 B.R. 899 (Bankr. D.S.D.1983) (debtor employed at time of filing but unemployed and receiving unemployment compensation at time of confirmation is eligible); compare Matter of Moore, 17 B.R. 551 (Bankr. M.D.Fla.1982) (determine whether debtor has regular income at time most favorable to debtor, not necessarily the date of petition).

8. In re Mozer, 1 B.R. 350 (Bankr. D.Colo. 1979); Tenney v. Terry, 630 F.2d 634 (8th Cir. 1980); Georgia Federal Savings & Loan Ass'n v. Anderson, 21 B.R. 443 (Bankr. N.D.Ga. 1981); In re Dant, 9 B.R. 117 (Bankr. E.D.Va. 1981); Matter of Wiggles, 7 B.R. 373 (Bankr. N.D.Ga.1980); In re Burns, 6 B.R. 286 (Bankr. D. Colo. 1980); In re Seman, 4 B.R. 568 (Bankr. S.D.N.Y. 1980).

9. For purposes of 11 U.S.C.A. § 109(e), priority claims are considered unsecured debts. In re Tashman, 13 B.R. 549 (Bankr. D.Vt.1981).

10. Undersecured claims are calculated as being equal to the value of the security. In re Ballard, 4 B.R. 271 (Bankr. E.D.Va.1980).

Because section 109(e) refers to "debts," secured and unsecured and not to "claims," arguably § 506 (that provides a rule for determining what "claims" are secured and what "claims" are unsecured) is not applicable. For example, under § 506, liability of $150,000 secured by a mortgage on property worth $20,000 would be treated as an unsecured claim to the extent of $130,000 and a secured claim only to the extent of $20,000. Distinguishing § 506, one could argue the entire "debt" under § 109(e) is a secured debt and thus fits under the $350,000 limit and not under the $100,000 limit. We doubt the drafters were as careful as we have suggested and we suspect that the use of the word "debt" in § 109(e) does not reflect a conscious intention of the Congress to exclude the use of § 506 in determining what is and what is not secured.

at the time the original relationship between the parties was created." [11] Simply because a debt is disputed, however, does not mean that it is contingent or unliquidated.[12] In *In re Michaelsen*,[13] buyers advanced $98,000 on contracts to purchase unimproved land from the debtor. They claimed that the debtor had breached the contract because the land was encumbered. The debtor argued the advance was a "deposit" for the homes to be built on the property and not a "debt" under section 109(e). Concluding that misappropriation of the money was a breach of the contract, the court found that a "claim for breach of contract * * * is not contingent, although it may be disputed." [14]

Examples of debts that are not contingent include a workers' compensation judgment requiring weekly payments by the debtor,[15] a judgment fixing debtor's personal liability for corporate debts,[16] guarantees where default occurred prepetition,[17] breach of contract claims,[18] and judgments on appeal.[19]

In contrast a liquidated debt [20] must be certain both as to "amount and liability." [21] In *Matter of Vaughan*,[22] the debtor argued that his $87,000

11. In re Lambert, 43 B.R. 913 (Bankr. D. Utah 1984) citing In re All Media Properties, Inc., 5 B.R. 126 (Bankr. S.D.Tex.1980), aff'd per curiam 64 F.2d 193 (5th Cir.1981); see Brockenbrough v. C.I.R., 61 B.R. 685 (W.D.Va. 1986); Matter of Ramus, 37 B.R. 723 (Bankr. N.D.Ga.1984) (personal shareholder liability is contingent); Norman v. Norman, 32 B.R. 562 (Bankr. W.D.Mo.1983) (personal partnership liability is contingent); contra, In re Anderson, 51 B.R. 532 (Bankr. D.S.D.1985) (all partnership debts are noncontingent); In re Ashline, 37 B.R. 136 (Bankr. N.D.N.Y.1984); Miami Valley Production Ass'n v. Tegtmeyer, 31 B.R. 555 (Bankr. S.D.Ohio 1983); In re Kelsey, 6 B.R. 114 (Bankr. S.D.Tex.1980). Matter of Brown, 7 B.R. 529 (Bankr. S.D.N.Y. 1980) (auto accident claims); see In re Albano, 55 B.R. 363 (Bankr. N.D.Ill. 1985); In re Martinez, 51 B.R. 944 (Bankr. D. Colo. 1985) (state court judgment on appeal).

12. Disputed debts are not excluded by the limitations imposed by section 109(e) for calculating eligibility. Sylvester v. Dow Jones and Co., Inc., 19 B.R. 671 (Bankr. 9th Cir.1982); In re Henstra, 75 B.R. 260 (Bankr. D.Minn.1986); In re Crescenzi, 69 B.R. 64 (S.D.N.Y. 1986); In re Hutchens, 69 B.R. 806 (Bankr. E.D.Tenn. 1987); In re Albano, 55 B.R. 363 (Bankr. N.D.Ill. 1985); In re Williams, 51 B.R. 249 (Bankr. S.D. Ind.1984); Vaughan v. Central Bank of the South, 36 B.R. 935 (N.D.Ala.1984), aff'd, 741 F.2d 1383 (11th Cir.1984); In re Carson, 32 B.R. 27 (Bankr. S.D.Fla.1983); In re McMonagle, 30 B.R. 899 (Bankr. D.S.D. 1983); In re King, 9 B.R. 376 (Bankr. D. Ore. 1981); compare In re Burgat, 68 B.R. 408 (Bankr. D. Colo. 1986) (a disputed claim should not be included where the dispute goes to the essential question whether there is a right to payment).

13. 74 B.R. 245 (Bankr. D.Nev.1987).

14. Id. at 250.

15. Matter of Perry, 56 B.R. 663 (Bankr. M.D.Ga.1986).

16. In re Albano, 55 B.R. 363 (Bankr. N.D.Ill. 1985).

17. Dekalb Bank v. Flaherty, 10 B.R. 118 (Bankr. N.D.Ill. 1981); In re Williams, 51 B.R. 249 (Bankr. S.D.Ind.1984); see In re Walters, 11 B.R. 567 (Bankr. S.D.W.Va.1981); contra In re Michaelsen, 74 B.R. 245 (Bankr. D.Nev. 1987); Matter of Fox, 64 B.R. 148 (Bankr. N.D.Ohio 1986); In re Lambert, 43 B.R. 913 (Bankr. D. Utah 1984).

18. In re Michaelsen, 74 B.R. 245 (Bankr. D.Nev.1987).

19. See In re Albano, 55 B.R. 363 (Bankr. N.D.Ill. 1985).

20. Liquidated debts are debts "whose dollar amount (1) is determined, fixed, settled, adjusted, and made certain mathematically and with precision, (2) is agreed upon, or (3) is fixed by operation of law." In re Lambert, 43 B.R. 913, 921 (Bankr. D. Utah 1984) citing In re King, 9 B.R. 376 (Bankr. D. Ore. 1981).

21. In re Lambert, 43 B.R. 913, 921 (Bankr. D. Utah 1984); see In re Albano, 55 B.R. 363 (Bankr. N.D.Ill. 1985). For examples of liquidated debts see Vaughan v. Central Bank of the South, 36 B.R. 935 (Bankr. N.D.Ala.1984), aff'd, 741 F.2d 1383 (11th Cir.1984); In re Michaelsen, 74 B.R. 245 (Bankr. D.Nev.1987) (amount is ascertained by referring to the contract); In re Crescenzi, 53 B.R. 374 (Bankr. S.D.N.Y. 1985), aff'd, 69 B.R. 64 (S.D.N.Y. 1986) (prepetition judgment); In re Furey, 31 B.R. 495 (Bankr. E.D.Pa. 1983); In re Troyer, 24 B.R. 727 (Bankr. N.D.Ohio 1982) (conversion of assets).

22. See note 22 on page 662.

bank loan was "disputed" and therefore either unliquidated or contingent. Following *McCormick on Damages*,[23] the court found a claim to be liquidated "if the evidence furnishes data which, if believed makes it possible to compute the amount with exactness, without reliance upon opinion or discretion." Moreover, it pointed out that pre-trial tort claims are commonly regarded as unliquidated whereas pre-trial contract claims, even though subject to setoff or defenses, are commonly regarded as "liquidated." Correctly the court noted that if every dispute, however small, rendered a claim either contingent or unliquidated, the eligibility requirements set forth in section 109(e) would be no barrier to debtors with enormous debts who chose to "dispute" their debts only to find that they are not eligible for Chapter 13 when the disputes evaporated after substantial delay. Little is to be gained by extended litigation over these terms. We applaud a court's willingness to draw bright, if somewhat harsh lines, between the cases that are properly in Chapter 13 and those that must go either to Chapter 7 or to Chapter 11.

Initially one determines eligibility from the dollar amount of debt shown on the debtor's statement.[24] If before confirmation the court finds that debts exceed the 109(e) limitations, the debtor is ineligible and the case must be dismissed or converted.[25] Some courts hold that the case must be dismissed even if this discovery is first made after confirmation.[26] Other courts hold that 109(e) is not jurisdictional and that a confirmed plan should not be dismissed on the basis of ineligibility.[27] We agree with the latter cases. After the debtor, the trustee and the court have travelled the Chapter 13 road all the way to confirmation of a plan, we see little to be gained in allowing a disgruntled creditor who belatedly raises his head to attack the court's jurisdiction. Only modest injury is likely to be done to any given creditor by allowing even an ineligible case to be heard under Chapter 13. It is better to force those who wish to speak up to do so early in the transaction or forever hold their peace.

The final eligibility requirement relates to debtor misuse of the bankruptcy system. Section 109(g) denies eligibility to anyone who, in the preceding 180 days,[28] has been a debtor under the Bankruptcy Code *if*:

(1) the case was dismissed by the court for willful failure of the debtor to abide by orders of the court, or to appear before the court in proper prosecution of the case; or

(2) the debtor requested and obtained the voluntary dismissal of the case following the filing of a request for relief from the automatic stay provided by section 362 of this title.[29]

22. 36 B.R. 935 (N.D.Ala.1984), aff'd, 741 F.2d 1383 (11th Cir.1984).

23. McCormick on Damages § 54 at 213 (1935).

24. See Matter of Pearson, 773 F.2d 751 (6th Cir.1985); In re Lambert, 43 B.R. 913 (Bankr. D. Utah 1984).

25. See In re Edwards, 51 B.R. 790 (Bankr. D.N.M.1985).

26. Mercantile Holdings, Inc. v. Dobkin, 12 B.R. 934 (Bankr. N.D.Ill. 1981).

27. In re Jarvis, 78 B.R. 288 (Bankr. D. Ore. 1987), citing In re Republic Trust and Sav. Co., 59 B.R. 606 (Bankr. N.D. Okla. 1986).

28. The 180 day bar is counted from the date of the court's order dismissing the debtor's most recent case. See McIver v. Phillips, 78 B.R. 439 (D.S.C.1987).

29. 11 U.S.C.A. § 109(g).

Under subparagraph (1), the objecting party must generally establish debtor's unexplained failure to attend court or mandatory creditor meetings.[30] In *In re Bono*,[31] the debtor filed three successive Chapter 13 petitions in response to the mortgagee's attempts to foreclose on debtor's home. Petition one was dismissed after the debtor neglected to pay the trustee and failed to attend a hearing. Under identical circumstances petition two was dismissed for "willful failure to make payments * * * and to appear * * *." Before petition two proceedings were completed the debtor filed again. It is no surprise that the court dismissed petition three.

In *In re Keul*,[32] the debtor voluntarily dismissed his first petition after a creditor's request for relief from the stay was granted. Debtor refiled within 180 days. The court states that by "dismissing and then refiling, a debtor could avoid the consequences of a creditor's obtaining relief from the stay because refiling once again brings into play the automatic stay provisions of section 362(a)." In dismissing the Chapter 13, this court stated that "this is the very ill" section 109(g)(2) was designed to cure. The court noted, however, that section 109(g)(2) is not applicable to refilings where the creditor is not adversely affected. We interpret this to mean that ineligibility requires at least a belief that the voluntary dismissal and the request for relief from the stay are causally connected.

If the debtor is able to comply with all of these requirements, the debtor is eligible for Chapter 13 relief. If, however, the debtor fails one or more of these standards, the bankruptcy court has the jurisdiction to convert the case to a Chapter for which the debtor is eligible.[33] One should appreciate that debtors eligible for Chapter 13 may choose to participate in those other chapters voluntarily. In *Toibb v. Radloff*,[34] the Supreme Court held that the plain language of section 109(d) permits nonbusiness individual debtors that qualify for Chapter 7 relief to file for Chapter 11 reorganization. To the extent that Chapter 13 debtors qualify under Chapter 7, this holding should extend to those individuals as well.

Although most consumer debtors will not file in Chapter 11 due to greater expense, increased complexity and the bankruptcy court's discretion to dismiss a Chapter 11 case based on an untenable plan, we see at least two reasons that may convince consumer debtors to choose Chapter 11. First, a debtor expecting high earnings may choose to stay out of Chapter 13 to protect his disposable income while simultaneously avoiding Chapter 7 to prevent the liquidation of his assets, especially those found to be nonexempt. The other reason for choosing Chapter 11 deals with the debtor's home mortgage. As we discuss in more detail later,[35] a Chapter 13 debtor may not modify the rights of his residential mortgagee as he could those of secured

---

30. Clinton State Bank v. Ward, 78 B.R. 914 (Bankr. E.D.Ark.1987); In re Correa, 58 B.R. 88 (Bankr. N.D.Ill. 1986); In re Ellis, 48 B.R. 178 (Bankr. E.D.N.Y.1985); In re Nelkovski, 46 B.R. 542 (Bankr. N.D.Ill. 1985) (repetitive filing).

31. 70 B.R. 339 (Bankr. E.D.N.Y.1987).

32. 76 B.R. 79 (Bankr. E.D.Pa. 1987); see also In re Denson, 56 B.R. 543 (Bankr. N.D.Ala.1986).

33. See In re Tatsis, 72 B.R. 908 (Bankr. W.D.N.C.1987); In re Hutchens, 69 B.R. 806 (Bankr. E.D.Tenn.1987); contra Matter of Wulf, 62 B.R. 155 (Bankr. D.Neb.1986) (ineligible Chapter 13 debtor has no case to convert); see Matter of Koehler, 62 B.R. 70 (Bankr. D.Neb.1986).

34. ___ U.S. ___, 111 S.Ct. 2197, 115 L.Ed.2d 145 (1991).

35. See § 9–18 infra.

creditors. Rather, the debtor is limited to curing any default and deaccelerating the residential debt. There is no such restriction on debtors in Chapter 11.

§ 9–4 Chapter 13 Procedure

a. *The Opening Events: Petition, Statement, Notice, and Plan*

One needs to understand the opening moves in a Chapter 13 proceeding because those moves may have a significant impact on the concluding events. Specifically, what debts are discharged at the end of the case may depend upon the disclosures and filings made at the beginning of the case.

Under Rule 1002, the debtor commences a case by filing a petition. Under Rule 1007(a) and (b)(2) the debtor must file a Chapter 13 "statement" with the petition. The statement must conform to official form number 10. Among other things, it contains a complete listing of the debtor's secured and unsecured creditors together with addresses. It also provides other information that may be useful to the trustee and ultimately to the court in deciding whether to confirm a plan.

The list of creditors is critical, for it is to the persons on this list that the clerk of the court will give notice of the meetings of creditors under section 341 and of other important events. As we will see, if the debtor omits a creditor from the statement, and the clerk fails to give notice to that creditor, the creditor's debt may not be discharged.[1]

After the filing of the petition, a Chapter 11 case is likely to amble on for months or even years at a leisurely pace without the filing of a plan, and, of course, without any payment to creditors. That is not true in Chapter 13. Rule 3015 authorizes the filing of a plan with a petition and requires that a plan be filed within 15 days after the petition unless the court grants a greater time. Under section 1326, the debtor "shall commence making the payments proposed by a plan within 30 days after the plan is filed." Thus, in many Chapter 13s the debtor's first payment will be due only a month after the petition has been filed.[2]

b. *Filing Proof of Claims*

Rule 3002(c) requires creditors to file their proof of claim within 90 days after the first date set for the meeting of the creditors pursuant to section 341(a). In the usual case the meeting of creditors must be not less than 20 nor more than 40 days after the time the petition is filed.[3] This means that the creditor's right to file a claim under Rule 3002(c) (90 days after the first date set for the 341 meeting) may expire as early as four months after the petition was filed. If the creditor fails to file within its period under Rule 3002, the debtor or trustee may file on the creditor's behalf within the 30

---

§ 9–4

1. See Bankr. R. 2002.

2. See Matter of Casteel, 85 B.R. 741 (Bankr. W.D.Mich.1988); In re Bracey, 89 B.R. 6 (Bankr. D.Md.1988).

3. Bankr. R. 2003.

c. Significance of Filing Proof of Claim for Payment Under the Plan and for Discharge of the Debt

Whether there is to be payment to a particular creditor under a Chapter 13 plan and whether a particular debt is to be discharged is interrelated in a complex way with the debtor's listing of the creditor in its statement and with the creditor's filing of a claim under Rule 3002. This relationship becomes particularly complex when one begins to consider secured creditors with unavoidable security interests and creditors such as the Internal Revenue Service, who may have sizable claims for past income taxes but in undetermined amount.[5]

Consider first the case in which the debtor fails to list the creditor in his Chapter 13 statement. Because of that, the clerk will not send notice to the creditor. If the creditor does not procure notice of the debtor's bankruptcy in some other way, its debt will not be discharged irrespective of the plan and notwithstanding the statement in 1328 that confirmation of the plan and payment of the debts in it entitle the debtor to "a discharge of all debts provided for by the plan * * *."

In 1984 the Court of Appeals for the Tenth Circuit[6] affirmed a finding that the comparable provision of Chapter 11 (section 1141) did not discharge the debt of a creditor who was omitted from the schedules and had never received notice. The court found that it would be a violation of the due process clause of the United States Constitution to hold otherwise. Moreover, it reached that conclusion despite the fact that the creditor's lawyer had received informal notice that the debtor was in Chapter 11 proceedings.[7]

Moving to the filing of proof of claim, assume that the creditor receives notice, but fails to file a proof of claim. Can the creditor preserve its debt from discharge by failing to file? Surely not, but consider the statutes and rules to see why. First, under Rule 3004 the debtor or trustee may choose to file on behalf of the creditor. Second, failure to discharge the debt of a creditor who knows of the bankruptcy but fails to file would give exactly the wrong incentives. Debts held by knowing non-filers are discharged.

Either the creditor, the trustee or debtor must file a claim on behalf of the creditor if there is to be a payment in the plan to that creditor.[8] This outcome arises from Rule 3002(2)(a) which reads as follows:

> Necessity for a filing. An unsecured creditor * * * must file a proof of claim * * * in accordance with this rule for the claim * * * to be

---

4. Id. 3004.

5. Consider, for example, the debtor who has filed unaudited tax returns that understate his income.

6. Reliable Electric Co. v. Olson Construction Co., 726 F.2d 620 (10th Cir.1984).

7. Accord In re Doane, 19 B.R. 1007 (W.D.Va.1982) (general creditor's interest is not discharged where debtor fails to schedule the general creditor); In re Martinez, 51 B.R. 944 (Bankr. D.Colo.1985) (creditor must be given notice of all vital steps in the debtor's bankruptcy proceeding); see also In re Ryan, 78 B.R. 175 (Bankr. E.D.Tenn.1987) (a creditor receiving no notice of debtor's bankruptcy and who is not scheduled is not discharged).

8. Presumably the debtor could waive provision of Bankruptcy Rule 3002(a) by including the creditor in the plan at a specific amount.

allowed * * *.[9]

Section 502 deals at length with "allowance" of claims and section 1325 speaks of payments for "allowed unsecured claims."[10] Except by implication, Chapter 13 does not say that there is no payment for claims that are "not allowed" or that there is to be payment for claims that are "allowed." That surely is the meaning of these sections, however, and that implication is supported by the history under the Act of 1898. In effect, therefore, Rule 3002(a) on "[n]ecessity for filing" is telling the creditor that the creditor will be entitled to no payment unless it, or the debtor or the trustee on its behalf, files a proof of claim.[11] Rule 3002(a) speaks of an "unsecured creditor;" we deal with secured creditors later.

At this point one might properly ask, how can a creditor who does not file a proof claim (and for whom one is not filed by someone else) be "provided for by the plan" and so subject to discharge under section 1328(a)? First, of course, it is possible that the debtor or trustee will list the creditor's claim at a lower value than the creditor believes is proper. But more likely the plan could provide for the creditor's claim generically without any specific reference to a particular creditor's claim. For example, the plan might provide for "full payment, in deferred cash payments, of all claims entitled to priority under [Bankruptcy Code] section 507."[12] In *In re Ryan*[13] the court found that certain claims for income tax for years prior to the Chapter 13 petition were totally discharged even though the Internal Revenue Service filed a proof of claim for only a portion of those taxes. In that case the debtor had not listed the Internal Revenue Service as a creditor, but according to the rules then in force, the clerk routinely gave notice of a Chapter 13 filing to the IRS. The court found that the IRS had an obligation to determine the debtor's tax liability when it received notice and that the provision for payment of priority claims in full "provided for" the Internal Revenue Service and thus discharged its entire claim.

Although we are modestly uncomfortable with Judge Kelley's conclusion in the *Ryan* case, we agree with his basic premise. The premise is that a creditor should not be free to avoid a discharge simply by its failure to file a proof of claim. On the other hand, it seems to us that debtors walk a narrow line between their own ignorance and unfairness when they or their lawyers intentionally include a group of creditors in a generic description, choose not to file a claim on behalf of those creditors and then argue that the creditors are discharged because they have "been provided for in the plan."

Where it could be shown that the debtor had evidence of the amount of the claim yet failed to file a proof of claim under Rule 3004, we believe a different outcome might be appropriate. In that case it would seem proper for the court to read the "provided for" language in 1328 more narrowly and to find that a plan by a debtor who declines to file a proof of claim for a debt that he knows he owes, does not "provide for" the debt.

9. Bankr. R. 3002(a).

10. 11 U.S.C.A. § 1325(a)(4).

11. See In re Daniel, 107 B.R. 798 (Bankr. N.D.Ga.1989) (Federal tax debt for which claim was never filed was "provided for" under Chapter 13 plan, and thus discharged upon completion of plan, in that plan provided for payment of priority claims; debtor was not required to file proof of claim on behalf of Government.); see also In re Griffin, 108 B.R. 717 (Bankr. W.D.Mo.1989).

12. 11 U.S.C.A. § 1322(a)(2).

13. 78 B.R. 175 (Bankr. E.D.Pa. 1987).

d. Filing and Allowance of Postpetition Claims

Since the debtor's statement is filed simultaneously with or shortly after the petition, it necessarily fails to list postpetition creditors. Congress may have believed that filing a Chapter 13 petition was a resurrection of the debtor and that this person, now so burdened with debt, was never again to incur debt. Of course, such a belief is not true to life. What of debts that arise after the filing of the petition, but before confirmation or final payment?

Section 1305 authorizes filing of proof of claims for certain postpetition claims and, by implication, their inclusion in the plan and discharge under 1328. Consider first the problem of income taxes. Because a debtor may have substantial, but undisclosed tax liability, for periods both prior to and after the filing of the petition, the courts have dealt at considerable length with these questions.[14] Since these are priority claims that must be paid in full if the plan is to be confirmed, the debtor seldom avoids the liability, but he may wish to stretch them out and to deprive the Internal Revenue Service of the right to assert its lien and seize his assets. Under 502(i) and 1305(a)(1), it is clear that the Internal Revenue Service may file a proof of claim for prepetition taxes where the amount owing is determined after the petition, and also for taxes owed for periods after the petition is filed.

But what if the IRS would like to assert its lien and proceed by state collection activity in disregard of the Chapter 13? May the debtor or taxpayer require that a proof of claim be filed under section 1305(a)? The answer with respect to taxes owed for periods after the petition is filed is no. In *In re Dickey*[15] the debtor's plan was confirmed in March of 1982. Thereafter the debtor sought to file a proof of claim for his 1982 and 1983 income tax liability even though the IRS had not done so. The court found that neither section 502(i) nor section 1305(a) allowed the debtor to file a proof of claim on behalf of the IRS. Apparently the court concluded as to section 1305 that the debtor himself could not be "any entity that holds a claim."

---

14. Treatment of tax liability in Chapter 13 cases by the courts has been generally consistent and relatively clear. Where a tax year has ended and the debtor has filed a return for that year before filing for Chapter 13 relief, the tax liability is considered prepetition even though the IRS completes its audit after the debtor files. In re Easton, 59 B.R. 714 (Bankr. C.D.Ill. 1986); In re Overly–Hautz Co., 57 B.R. 932 (Bankr. N.D.Ohio 1986), decision aff'd, 81 B.R. 434 (N.D.Ohio 1987); In re Starkey, 49 B.R. 984 (D. Colo. 1984); In re Pennetta, 19 B.R. 794 (Bankr. D.Colo.1982).

If the debtor provides for the IRS as a priority or general unsecured claim or both and the debtor fails to make any payments to the IRS because the IRS fails to file a timely proof of claim, the debtor will receive a discharge from the IRS's claim upon completion of the plan. In re Richards, 50 B.R. 339 (E.D.Tenn.1985); accord In re Goodwin, 58 B.R. 75 (Bankr. D.Me.1986).

Alternatively, where the debtor incurs additional tax liability after filing a Chapter 13 petition, the debtor cannot compel the government to receive payment under the plan. The government has the choice of collecting either under the plan or after discharge. In re Hester, 63 B.R. 607 (Bankr. E.D.Tenn.1986).

What is unclear to the courts, however, is how to treat tax liability when the debtor files a late return after filing a Chapter 13 petition. In re Moseley, 74 B.R. 791 (Bankr. C.D. Cal. 1987), order vac'd, appeal dism'd, 101 B.R. 608 (Bankr. 9th Cir.1989); Matter of Hazel, 68 B.R. 287 (Bankr. E.D.Mich.1986), order aff'd, 95 B.R. 481 (E.D.Mich.1988); In re Owens, 67 B.R. 418 (Bankr. E.D.Pa. 1986), order aff'd, 84 B.R. 361 (E.D.Pa.1988).

15. 64 B.R. 3 (Bankr. E.D.Va.1985).

e. Secured Claims

Recall that Rule 3002 states only that it is necessary for an "unsecured creditor" to file a proof of claim in order for that claim to be allowed. What of a creditor who holds a secured claim where the security cannot be avoided? In *In re Simmons* [16] the court found that a creditor's unavoidable construction lien under Mississippi law carried through the confirmation of the debtor's Chapter 13 plan even though the creditor failed to object to the confirmation and even though the plan listed the creditor as unsecured. Because the creditor in that case in fact filed his claim as a secured claim, the case is not a square holding that a completely silent secured creditor nevertheless carries over his security interest, but we believe that is the meaning of the case and agree with it. There the creditor checked the box that he "accepted" the plan, but then wrote on the acceptance form a typewritten objection of the scheduling of his claim as unsecured. Following *In re Tarnow* [17] the court concluded that section 506(d) did not invalidate the lien of the creditor. It found that section 506(d) contemplated the invalidation of such a lien only where there was a finding of the lien's invalidity, but not because of a failure of the creditor to make a timely filing of proof of claim.[18] Presumably in such cases the debtor's personal liability will be discharged, but the creditor's security interest will continue against the assets of the debtor to which the security had previously attached to the value of those assets.[19]

f. Meeting of the Creditors

Code section 341 requires that a creditor meeting be conducted:

(a) Within a reasonable time after the order for relief in a case under this title, the United States trustee shall convene and preside at a meeting of creditors.[20]

The creditor meeting is to be held no sooner than 20 days and no later than

---

16. 765 F.2d 547 (5th Cir.1985).

17. 749 F.2d 464 (7th Cir.1984).

18. In Matter of Tarnow, 749 F.2d 464 (7th Cir.1984), the court held that a late filing of a proof of claim by the creditor with a valid lien barred the creditor from participating in the debtor's Chapter 11 reorganization plan. This did not, however, prevent the creditor from ignoring the bankruptcy proceeding and looking to the lien for satisfaction of the debt. See also In re Rogers, 57 B.R. 170 (Bankr. E.D.Tenn.1986), where the court rejected the argument that Bankruptcy Rule 3002(a) does not require a proof of a secured claim for its allowance. The court indicated that the Chapter 13 trustee with more than 3,000 Chapter 13 cases pending could not operate efficiently if he were required to make payments on claims for which no proof of claim had been filed. As in Tarnow, the court did not suggest that a creditor's valid security interest is dischargeable where the creditor fails to file a proof of claim. Rather, the court suggested that the tardy secured creditor has no right to participate in the debtor's Chapter 13 reorganization.

19. What is the value of a creditor's claim where payments within the Chapter 13 have discharged a superior lien? It seems to us the subordinate creditor with the non-recourse liability would be saved only to the extent there was value at the time the petition was filed. Otherwise the payments under the plan would be resurrecting his now discharged unsecured claim.

20. 11 U.S.C.A. § 341(a).

40 days after the debtor files a petition.[21] Section 343 requires the debtor's attendance at the meeting.

> The debtor shall appear and submit to examination under oath at the meeting of the creditors under section 341(a) of this title. Creditors, any indenture trustee, any trustee or examiner in the case, or the United States trustee may examine the debtor * * *.[22]

The bankruptcy judge, however, is forbidden from attending the 341 meeting.

As section 343 suggests, the principal purpose of the 341 meeting is to examine the debtor.[23] Creditors can use this opportunity to find out about the debtor's discharge and the dischargeability of certain debts. They may also attempt negotiations regarding debt reaffirmation or the disposition of collateral, even though this activity may violate the automatic stay. The 341 meeting also allows the trustee an opportunity to examine the possibility of avoiding some prebankruptcy transfers.

Because section 343 directs "the debtor shall appear and submit to examination," one would think that the debtor's presence at the meeting was mandatory. In fact, most courts hold that confirmation of the debtor's plan can be denied until the debtor attends the meeting.[24] Other courts read the section more generously; if, for example, the debtor is ill or in jail, his absence may be overlooked.[25] Moreover, only repeated absences give rise to an inference of "willfulness" of the kind necessary to bar a subsequent filing under section 109(g)(1).[26]

One suspects that the statutory vision of the first meeting of creditors is quite inconsistent with the reality. Particularly in jurisdictions where a single Chapter 13 trustee must supervise thousands of Chapter 13 cases, we suspect that the typical meeting of creditors is an entirely perfunctory arrangement, seldom attended by any creditor at all, and accompanied by little searching inquiry into the status of the debtor's finances. On the other hand, the significant number of cases in which creditors object to confirmation and carry their arguments even to the appellate level tell that there are at least a minority of cases in which one creditor has enough at stake in the Chapter 13 (or enough anger at a particular debtor) to attend, question, and object. The student should understand what the lawyer knows, namely, that the real events that occur in a 341 meeting are likely to vary greatly from place to place and to be more or less formal, depending upon the inclination of the standing trustee, of the judges, and of the workload of the parties.

---

21. If the meeting place is not regularly staffed by a clerk, the meeting must be held within 60 days from debtor's filing. Bankr. R. 2003(a).

22. 11 U.S.C.A. § 343.

23. Liberal questioning is permitted regarding the debtor's financial affairs, the debtor's discharge, and the estate's administration. Bankr. R. 2004(b).

24. See In re Perskin, 9 B.R. 626, 629 (Bankr. N.D.Tex.1981).

25. See In re Vilt, 56 B.R. 723 (Bankr. N.D.Ill. 1986).

26. In re Nelkovski, 46 B.R. 542 (Bankr. N.D.Ill. 1985); accord Matter of Haggerty, 57 B.R. 384 (S.D.Miss.1986).

g. Confirmation Hearing: Form of Creditor Objections

Except for the ministerial event of granting the discharge after the payments have been made under the plan, the concluding formal event in a Chapter 13 is the "confirmation hearing." Section 1324 directs the court to hold a hearing and provides that any party in interest may object to confirmation at that time.[27] If there are objections to the plan, presumably there will be testimony during the confirmation hearing concerning those objections and argument concerning their legal validity. If there is no objection, we suspect that the hearing will be perfunctory and that numerous hearings might "occur" in a minute's time in a single court room.

The Code is silent about the timing of a hearing. Since the debtor must commence payment shortly after the plan is filed, there is no pressing need for early confirmation. For that reason it seems sensible to await the bar date for filing of creditors' proof claims before the hearing is held. Although one sees the occasional argument that the hearing was set too early, timing problems have not been significant.[28]

Rules 3020 and 9014 govern the making of objections to the confirmation of a plan. Once a creditor receives notice of the confirmation, it is the creditor's responsibility to serve the debtor, the trustee and any committee with its objection. Under Rule 9014 the case then follows the usual rules for contested matters to make certain that everyone knows the basis for the objection and that the debtors and others have an opportunity to respond. Many of the cases discussed in this chapter arise in exactly this context, when a creditor objects to confirmation of the plan. It is here that the law under sections 1322 and 1325 is made.

The objecting creditor has the burden of going forward, but some courts have held that the debtor has the "ultimate burden of persuasion."[29] Exactly what these statements on burden of proof add to the requirement in the rules that the creditor give notice of its particular objection is not clear. Presumably, if the creditor's objection is based upon some fact, the creditor will have to give evidence of that fact or show that it has been admitted by the debtor in his statement or otherwise in court.[30]

If there is no objection to the plan, Rule 3020(b)(2) authorizes the court to "determine that the plan has been proposed in good faith and not by any means forbidden by law without receiving evidence."[31] Does one infer from that statement that the court must hear evidence on other issues of 1322 and 1325 such as feasibility, for example? Since by hypothesis we are speaking of cases where there is no objection, one would expect this issue to be seldom

---

27. 11 U.S.C.A. § 1324.

28. In re Robinson, 22 B.R. 497 (W.D.Va. 1982); see also In re Minick, 63 B.R. 440 (Bankr. D. D.C. 1986).

29. In re Fries, 68 B.R. 676 (Bankr. E.D.Pa. 1986).

30. Once the creditor meets the initial burden of producing evidence, the ultimate burden of persuasion arises. In a Chapter 13 contest, the burden of persuasion is on the debtor. In re Fries, 68 B.R. 676 (Bankr. E.D.Pa. 1986). Other courts, however, hold that after the creditor meets its burden of producing evidence, only the burden of production shifts to the debtor. If the debtor is able to meet its burden of producing evidence, confirmation turns on the success of the party who has the burden of persuasion—the party raising the objection. See In re Mendenhall, 54 B.R. 44 (Bankr. W.D.Ark.1985) (at confirmation the burden of persuasion lies with the creditor, and where both debtor and creditor fail to shift the burden of proof, the plan is confirmed); accord In re Flick, 14 B.R. 912 (Bankr. E.D.Pa. 1981).

31. Bankr. R. 3020(b)(2).

raised, even if the courts were doing things completely forbidden by the statute. For that reason and possibly for others, there is little case law on this question. Indeed, some courts seem to say that no hearing is necessary where there is no objection to the plan.[32] At least one judge has stated that the court has an independent duty to determine that each plan meets the requirements of section 1325 and that such a duty can be fulfilled only by holding a hearing.[33] As we indicated above, we suspect the practice varies greatly from jurisdiction to jurisdiction. In courts that are overflowing with Chapter 13 cases, and particularly in those where there is an efficient and reliable Chapter 13 trustee in whom the judge has confidence, we doubt the courts often make an independent evaluation of the merits of the confirmability of a plan under 1325 where the trustee is satisfied and where there are no creditor objections. In such cases we see no reason why valuable judicial time should be so used.

h. The Chapter 13 Trustee: Appointment, Duties, and Payment

Under 28 U.S.C.A. § 586, a federal official, the United States trustee, may "appoint one or more individuals to serve as standing trustee" in Chapter 12 and 13 cases if the number of cases warrant such appointment.[34] In the few federal districts where there is no United States trustee, this section does not apply.[35] Because it contemplates the possibility that there will be such a small number of Chapter 12 or Chapter 13 cases in some districts that there will be no need for a standing trustee, the possibility also

---

32. Cf. In re Hartdegen, 67 B.R. 230 (Bankr. N.D.Ala.1986); see also In re Powell, 15 B.R. 465 (Bankr. N.D.Ga.1981).

33. In re Hartdegen, 67 B.R. 230 (Bankr. N.D.Ala.1986).

34. 28 U.S.C.A. § 586(b).

35. In jurisdictions where the United States trustee is not yet in operation, sections 1302(a), (d), and (e), which were repealed in 1986 as to restrictions with United States trustees, still govern appointment. It reads as follows:

(a) If the court has appointed an individual under (d) of this section to serve as standing trustee in cases under this chapter and if such individual qualifies under section 322 of this title, then such individual shall serve as trustee in the case. Otherwise, the court shall appoint a person to serve in the case.

* * *

(d) If the number of cases under this chapter commenced in a particular judicial district so warrant, the court may appoint one or more individuals to serve as standing trustee for such district in cases under this chapter.

(e)(1) A court that has appointed an individual under subsection (d) of this section to serve as standing trustee in cases under this chapter shall fix—

(A) a maximum annual compensation for such individual, not to exceed the lowest annual rate of basic pay in effect for grade GS–16 of the General Schedule prescribed under section 5332 of title 5; and

(B) a percentage fee, not to exceed ten percent, based on such maximum annual compensation and the actual, necessary expenses incurred by such individual as standing trustee.

(2) Such individual shall collect such percentage fee from all payments under plans in the cases under this chapter for which such individual serves as standing trustee. Such individual shall pay annually to the Treasury—

(A) any amount by which the actual compensation of such individual exceeds five percent upon all payments under plans in cases under this chapter for which such individual serves as standing trustee; and

(B) any amount by which the percentage fee fixed under paragraph (1)(B) of this subsection for all such cases exceeds—

(i) such individual's actual compensation for such cases, as adjusted under subparagraph (A) of this paragraph; plus

(ii) the actual, necessary expenses incurred by such individual as standing trustee in such cases.

exists that there will be no standing trustee even when there is a United States trustee.

In most districts a standing trustee handles all Chapter 13 cases. The trustee's obligations have not been a source of controversy. They are spelled out in section 1302(b). The trustee has a broad mandate and one suspects that the trustee's role is what the trustee makes it. Not only is the trustee instructed to "advise * * * and assist the debtor," but also to insure that the debtor commences making payments and to appear and be heard at critical points when the plan is under consideration. In a sense the trustee is at once a collection agency, a debt counselor and adviser concerning the intricacies of bankruptcy practice and the idiosyncracies of the local judges and rules.

i. Payment to Trustee

While the trustee's general powers have been noncontroversial, how and what trustees are to be paid has been an issue of considerable controversy. Section 28 U.S.C.A. § 586(e) governs payment for Chapter 12 and 13 trustees.[36] If one stands back from the intricacies of 586(e), one sees the general rule, namely, that the trustee's salary and other expenses are to be borne by the debtors (more likely the creditors) in the form of a percentage levy on the amounts paid through the Chapter 13 and Chapter 12 process. In general, the trustee collects 10 percent of the amounts paid through a Chapter 13 plan and a scaled percentage (from 10 down to 3 percent) in Chapter 12 cases.

---

36. The statute provides

(1) The Attorney General, after consultation with a United States trustee that has appointed an individual under subsection (b) of this section to serve as standing trustee in cases under chapter 12 and 13 of title 11, shall fix—

(A) a maximum annual compensation for such individual, not to exceed the annual rate of basic pay in effect for step 1 grade GS–16 of the General Schedule prescribed under section 5332 of title 5; and

(B) a percentage fee not to exceed—

(i) in the case of a debtor who is not a family farmer, ten percent; or

(ii) in the case of a debtor who is a family farmer, the sum of

(I) not to exceed ten percent of the payments made under the plan of such debtor, with respect to payments in an aggregate amount not to exceed $450,000; and

(II) three percent of payments made under the plan of such debtor, with respect to payments made after the aggregate amount of payments made under the plan exceeds $450,000;

based on such maximum annual compensation and the actual, necessary expenses incurred by such individual as standing trustee.

(2) Such individual shall collect such percentage fee from all payments received by such individual under plans in the cases under chapter 12 or 13 of title 11 for which such individual serves as standing trustee. Such individual shall pay to the United States trustee, and the United States trustee shall deposit in the United States Trustee System Fund—

(A) any amount by which the actual compensation of such individual exceeds 5 per centum upon all payments received under plans in cases under chapter 12 or 13 of title 11 for which such individual serves as standing trustee; and

(B) any amount by which the percentage for all such cases exceeds—

(i) such individual's actual compensation for such cases, as adjusted under subparagraph (A) of paragraph (1); plus

(ii) the actual, necessary expenses incurred by such individual as standing trustee in such cases. Subject to the approval of the Attorney General, any or all of the interest earned from the deposit of payments under plans by such individual may be utilized to pay actual, necessary expenses without regard to the percentage limitation contained in subparagraph (d)(1)(B) of this section.

28 U.S.C.A. § 586(e).

These fees go into three pockets. First they pay the trustee's salary. That salary is set by the Attorney General in consultation with the United States trustee; it may not exceed the salary for step 1 in GS–16. Second, the percentage fee pays the "actual, necessary expenses incurred" by the standing trustee. These fees would pay office rent, secretarial and other clerical help, computer costs, and any other appropriate expenses. The third beneficiary of the fee is the "United States Trustee System Fund," a fund to pay for the United States trustee portion of the system and for that trustee's office.

If the court finds the amounts collected in a particular case are too high, the court can reduce the fee to correspond with the trustee's actual efforts.[37] In some cases the trustee can receive more than 10 percent where the distributions under the plan are quite low.[38] Where a trustee is appointed for a particular case, the court under section 326(b) may set an appropriate fee "not to exceed five percent on all payments under the plan." [39]

Section 1326(c) provides that the trustee, not the debtor, makes the payments under the plan to particular creditors:

(c) Except as otherwise provided in the plan or in the order confirming the plan, the trustee shall make payments to creditors under the plan.[40]

In the typical case the debtor might pay $1,000 per month to the trustee, the trustee will subtract his $100 and pay the remaining $900 to various creditors. When the system operates in that fashion, there is little difficulty—at least from the trustee's point of view. The trustee takes his 10 percent off the top and distributes the rest.

Seeking to avoid this 10 percent haircut, some debtors have proposed payments directly to particular creditors.[41] For example, it is common for Chapter 13 debtors to propose to pay mortgage arrearages within the plan and through the hands of the trustee, but to continue to make current payments on a mortgage outside the plan by direct payment to the mortgagee.

Prior to 1986, percentage payments were governed by section 1302(e) which provided that the percentage fee should be paid "from all payments under plans." Trustees argued that payments directly to a mortgagee were in fact payments "under the plan," even though the payments did not pass through the trustee's hands. Therefore, the trustees argued they had a right to a percentage fee based on those payments as well as to those that did pass through their hands. On substantially those facts, the Court of Appeals for the Fifth Circuit concluded that the trustee had a right to some part of such payments in *Matter of Foster*.[42] In *dictum* the court intimated that "fully secured" claims would be dealt with outside the plan, but presumably all others were "under the plan" even if the money never touched the trustee's palms.

37. See Matter of Eaton, 1 B.R. 433 (Bankr. N.D.N.C.1979); In re Sousa, 46 B.R. 343 (Bankr. D.R.I.1985).

38. 11 U.S.C.A. § 330(c).

39. 11 U.S.C.A. § 326(b).

40. Id. § 1326(c).

41. Some courts have said that there is a presumption that the trustee should disburse payments made to creditors under a confirmed plan. See In re Jutila, 111 B.R. 621 (W.D.Mich.1989).

42. 670 F.2d 478 (5th Cir.1982).

Of course, in any case in which the debtor seeks to "deaccelerate" a mortgage loan and to pay the arrearages within the plan, the filing of a Chapter 13 has a critical impact on the entire mortgage debt. It is only through the Chapter 13 that the lump sum can be deaccelerated and that the term payments can be reinstated. The same would be true of any unsecured debt that was not going to be paid in full. For those reasons, the Court of Appeals allowed the trustee to collect some percentage of the payments made directly to the mortgagee. The court concluded, however, that such payment might properly be reduced because the expense of the trustee would be reduced. On varying grounds other courts have generally agreed with *Foster*.[43]

After 1986 the percentage payments of trustees was no longer determined by 1302, but by 28 U.S.C.A. 586(e)(2).[44] The language of section 586(e)(2) authorizes the trustee to collect a percentage fee "from all payments received" by the trustee. Although there is no indication that Congress intended to overrule the decision in *Foster,* one court has found that the new language changes the outcome.

In *In re Wright*[45] the debtor proposed to pay its mortgagee, a jeweler with a secured claim, and a purchase money lender with a secured claim outside the plan, and to pay only $75 per month inside the plan to unsecured creditors. Acknowledging the need for some funds to operate the system and recognizing that Congress intended the lion's share of Chapter 13 payments to pass through the hands of the trustee, the court nevertheless concluded that payments made directly to creditors are not subject to the percentage payment. The court intimated that it could deny confirmation of plans where the debtor proposed that most of the payments go directly to the creditors and not through the hands of the trustee. In the case before it, the court in effect modified the plan to require the debtor to pay two of the secured creditors through the trustee, but it allowed the debtor to make payment to the mortgagee outside of the plan.

We cannot quarrel with Judge Pearson's interpretation of the statute. At the time when Congress enacted the language "all payments received," this issue was well known and had been an issue in many cases. Like the rest of us, Congress should be bound by what it said.

---

43. See also In re Waldman, 75 B.R. 1005 (Bankr. E.D.Pa. 1987) (Debtor opting to deal with creditor "outside the plan" must forbear use of the Code to affect the rights of the secured creditor in any other way); In re Carson, 85 B.R. 460 (Bankr. S.D.Ohio 1988) (Assumption of executory contract by the debtor is "under the plan" and entitles trustee to percentage fee where debtor is the disbursing agent); In re Mascari, 70 B.R. 325 (Bankr. N.D.N.Y.1987)("[I]rrespective of the terminology employed by the parties or the plan itself, when any portion of any obligation on a secured claim is provided for under a Chapter 13 plan, payment thereon from whatever source subjects the payments to the Chapter 13 trustee's percentage fee."); Matter of Harris, 107 B.R. 204 (Bankr. D.Neb.1989) (Generally debts provided for by the Chapter 13 plan must be paid for through the Chapter 13 standing trustee. On the other hand, some payments, particularly those dealing with residential mortgages, may be made outside the plan and when so made, no trustee's fee is due.).

44. Section 586(e)(2) reads in pertinent part:

> Such individual shall collect such percentage fee from all payments received by such individual under plans in the cases under chapter 12 or 13 of title 11 for which such individual serves as standing trustee.

45. 82 B.R. 422 (Bankr. W.D.Va.1988).

Ultimately there is a larger question here. The debtor in the *Wright* case learned a lesson well known to bankruptcy lawyers, namely, bankruptcy is expensive. To the extent that those expenses and costs can be reduced, they should be. To the extent they cannot be reduced, they should be borne by those who use the system. In the *Wright* case the debtor was going to bear those costs because he was making a 100 percent plan. In other cases, the creditors will bear that cost and, presumably, the costs will be added to other costs of doing business and included in the interest rate that is charged to potential beneficiaries of Chapter 13. We regard this as sensible and fair. Accordingly we think it appropriate for courts to deny confirmation of plans that propose only insignificant payment through the trustee and propose much larger payments directly to the creditors. Such debtors have reaped the benefits of Chapter 13 without paying their fair share.

Of course, this problem is not likely to grow to gigantic proportions since most debtors wish to modify their obligations; to do so their modified debts must be included within the plan and be subject to the confirmation order. Should our predictions about the magnitude of the problem be wrong, Congress should reexamine section 586.

j. Codebtor Stay

Normally the automatic stay of section 362 protects only the debtor, the debtor's property, and property of the estate.[46] If a second party not in bankruptcy is also liable on the debt, the stay does not normally prohibit creditor from pursuing that person. Section 1301 is an exception to this rule that applies in Chapter 13 cases. It extends the stay to certain codebtors liable on consumer debt with the Chapter 13 debtor. It reads in part as follows:

(a) Except as provided in subsections (b) and (c) of this section, after the order for relief under this chapter, a creditor may not act, or commence or continue any civil action, to collect all or any part of a consumer debt of the debtor from any individual that is liable on such debt with the debtor, or that secured such debt, unless—

(1) such individual became liable on or secured such debt in the ordinary course of such individual's business; or

(2) the case is closed, dismissed, or converted to a case under chapter 7 or 11 of this title.

* * *

(c) On request of a party in interest and after notice and a hearing, the court shall grant relief from the stay provided by subsection (a) of this section with respect to a creditor, to the extent that—

(1) as between the debtor and the individual protected under subsection (a) of this section, such individual received the consideration for the claim held by such creditor;

(2) the plan filed by the debtor proposes not to pay such claim; or

---

46. 11 U.S.C.A. § 362(a).

(3) such creditor's interest would be irreparably harmed by continuation of such stay.[47]

Section 1301 has not been the subject of much litigation but has posed a few issues for the courts. We discuss the section and its issues in our Chapter 3 on the automatic stay, together with other exceptions to the usual rule that the stay protects only the debtor.[48]

§ 9–5 The Plan: Priorities and Payment—Introduction

Priority rules under Chapter 13 are essentially the same as those under the other chapters.[1] In Chapter 13, as in the other chapters, the value and amount of the secured creditor's claim is determined under 506; here, as elsewhere, the perfected secured creditor gets the benefit of its security. The best interest test (discussed below) means that the secured creditor must be paid under the plan the present value of its collateral. If that is done, the debtor may keep and use the collateral.

Section 1326(b)(1) requires that administrative expenses be paid in full "before or at the time of each payment to creditors."[2] Presumably this means that administrative expenses incurred prior to the first payment under the plan must be paid in full as part of the payment before any payment may be made under the plan to creditors. This treatment is generally consistent with section 1129(a)(9)(A) which requires payment in cash of administrative expenses on the effective date of the plan.

Other priority claims must be paid in full in deferred cash payments under section 1322(a)(2). Under section 1322 the holder of a particular claim can agree to accept less than full payment.[3] Note, too, that the requirement is merely for "full payment," not for payment of present value equal to the total claimed. If, for example, the debtor's unpaid income tax liability under section 507(a)(7) for the three years prior to the filing of the petition was $10,000, that amount could be paid over the life of the plan (payments totaling $10,000) even though the present value of those payments would be substantially less than $10,000.

Finally, the unsecured creditors are to be paid over the life of the plan. As we will see, the unsecured creditor's principal protection is the best interest test, namely, the right to receive payments with a present value equal to the liquidation value of their interest in the debtor's estate if the debtor were liquidated.

Section 1322(b)(1) explicitly authorizes the debtor separately to classify claims for consumer debt in which there is a co-signer. The section specifically authorizes the debtor to treat such debts "differently than other unsecured claims."[4] Although it does not say so in so many words, this section authorizes the debtor to give radically better treatment to the co-signed debt than to others. In the 1984 amendment, Congress recognized

---

47. 11 U.S.C.A. § 1301.
48. See § 3–10(c) supra.

§ 9–5

1. For a discussion of priorities in Chapter 13, see §§ 9–5 & 9–6 supra. For a discussion of priorities in the other chapters, see §§ 10–16, 10–23 through 10–28 infra (Chapter 11), and §§ 7–9 through 7–13 supra (Chapter 7).
2. 11 U.S.C.A. § 1326(b)(1).
3. 11 U.S.C.A. § 1322(a)(2).
4. 11 U.S.C.A. § 1322(b)(1).

the difficulties that face a debtor who was discharged from a debt that was co-signed by a friend or co-worker. Apparently out of sympathy for such debtors, the drafters authorized separate treatment of such debt and apparently intended that such debts could be paid in full even in circumstances in which other unsecured creditors received little or nothing.[5] We think this reading of section 1322 is fair even though it says so only by implication.

Whether a debtor in Chapter 13 can use other means to prefer one unsecured creditor over another is the same question as that faced above with respect to Chapter 11. By adopting the rules of section 1122 from Chapter 11, section 1322(b)(1) authorizes separate classes. It specifically provides that the debtor may not "discriminate unfairly against any class so designated,"[6] and 1325 requires that any plan be proposed "in good faith."[7] Theoretically, all of this leaves us in the same position as we find ourselves in Chapter 11; in fact, debtors have proposed and courts have approved many forms of discrimination between classes of unsecured creditors. We discuss those issues below.[8]

§ 9–6. Priorities and Payment—Secured Creditors and Priority Claims

a. Secured Creditors

In Chapter 13, as elsewhere in bankruptcy, section 506 determines who is a secured creditor. One is secured only to the extent that the value of that person's collateral and irrespective of the face amount of the claim. Thus a mortgage on property worth $500,000 securing an outstanding debt of $1,000,000 represents a $500,000 secured claim and a $500,000 unsecured claim. In Chapter 13, as in Chapters 11 and 7, the claims will be split and the parts treated separately.

For the most part there are no surprises for secured creditors here. Chapter 13 differs from Chapter 11 in that there are no votes and no absolute priority rule; thus a "cramdown" can be imposed on creditors without the necessity of a vote and without the protection of the absolute priority (section 1129(b)(2)). But the basic protection for a secured creditor in Chapter 13 is the same as that in Chapter 11, namely, the best interest test. With respect to secured creditors the test is stated as follows in section 1325(a)(5):

> [the court shall confirm if] with respect to each allowed secured claim provided for by the plan—
>
> (A) the holder of such claim has accepted the plan;

---

5. In re Perkins, 55 B.R. 422 (Bankr. N.D. Okla. 1985) (plan confirmed which pays 100% to co-signed claim holder and 22% to all other unsecured claim holders); In re Todd, 65 B.R. 249 (Bankr. N.D.Ill. 1986) (100% to claim cosigned by police partner and 26% to other unsecured creditors); see also In re Diaz, 97 B.R. 903 (Bankr. S.D.Ohio 1989) (co-signed claim cannot be treated worse than other unsecured creditors); accord In re Dondero, 58 B.R. 847 (Bankr. D. Ore. 1986); but see In re Easley, 72 B.R. 948 (Bankr. M.D.Tenn.1987); In re Gonzalez, 73 B.R. 259 (Bankr. D. P. R. 1987) (confirmation denied where preferential treatment to codebtor resulted in remaining unsecured creditors receiving less than they would in liquidation).

6. 11 U.S.C.A. § 1322(b)(1).

7. 11 U.S.C.A. § 1325(a)(3).

8. See § 9–7 infra.

(B)(i) the plan provides that the holder of such claim retain the lien securing such claim; and

(ii) the value, as of the effective date of the plan, of property to be distributed under the plan on account of such claim is not less than the allowed amount of such claim; or

(C) the debtor surrenders the property securing such claim to such holder.[1]

In effect, the best interest test in this setting assures that the secured creditor will get the value of its collateral either through secured payments with a present value equal to the collateral or by the debtor's surrender of the property to secured creditor.

Although there is no provision in Chapter 13 for a vote, note that section 1325(a)(5)(A) provides for secured creditors' "acceptance" and, in that circumstance, the secured creditor need not be given payment with a present value equal to its collateral. How the secured creditor "accepts" the plan is not clear.[2]

In addition to the fact that secured and unsecured creditors have no vote under Chapter 13 and thus cannot use that practical and strategic power, Chapter 13 differs in one other important way from Chapter 11. There is no Chapter 13 analog to 1111(b) which in effect allows a secured creditor to continue its security interest in the asset to the full amount of its claim, both secured and unsecured. In the words of 1111(b), it treats the entire claim as "secured." The typical case in which the secured creditor would wish to exercise this right is one where the creditor believes the collateral (such as real estate) will increase rapidly in value after the plan is confirmed. Accordingly the electing secured creditor foregoes any present payment on the unsecured portion of its claim in return for continuing its full claim as "secured" by the property against the prospect of the increased value of that collateral. There is no such right under Chapter 13.

In general, one understanding the priorities and rights of a secured creditor in Chapter 11 will feel comfortable with the rules in Chapter 13.[3]

b. *Priority Claims*

Section 1322(a)(2) requires "full payment, in deferred cash payments," of all priority claims under section 507.[4] This means that a priority claimant who has not agreed to a lesser payment is likely to receive substantially greater payment under Chapter 13 than a claimant would receive in many Chapter 7 cases where proceeds often fall short of paying all the priority claims in full.

§ 9–6
1. 11 U.S.C.A. § 1325(a)(5).
2. Bankruptcy Form 30 is a ballot apparently designed for use in Chapter 11, not in Chapters 12 or 13.
3. One difference that may not be significant between section 1129 and section 1325 is that section 1129(b)(2)(A)(ii) requires deferred "cash payments" of the present value equal to the secured claim for a cramdown under that subsection. The comparable section of 1325, section 1325(a)(5)(B)(ii), requires only that "property" distributed under the plan have a present value. It does not require the distribution of cash.

4. 11 U.S.C.A. § 1322(a)(2).

Section 1326(b) requires that administrative expenses (priority claims listed in section 507(a)(1)) be paid "[b]efore or at the time of each payment to creditors."[5] Presumably this means that all existing administrative expenses must be paid before the first payment is made to creditors. If one assumes that the administrative expenses are largely incurred at the beginning of the plan, this means that at the beginning the debtor will have to make a lump sum available in order to meet those payments unless the claimants agree to some other treatment. To the extent the plan incurs administrative expenses as it goes along, and to the extent there are payments due to the standing trustee under section 1326(b)(2), those too must be paid from time to time ahead of any payments to creditors.

Priority claims under section 507 that are not administrative expenses under (a)(1) need not be paid in cash at the outset of the plan. However such claims must be paid in full because of section 1322(a)(2). Because of the best interest rule under section 1325(a)(4), the debtor may have to pay not only the full amount of the priority claim, but also an additional amount to raise this stream of payments to a present value equal to the amount that would be distributed on liquidation. If the priority claims would be fully paid on liquidation in Chapter 7, and they are to be paid over time in the Chapter 13 plan, they must be paid the full amount plus an additional percentage to make up for the time discount.

§ 9–7 General Creditor, Discrimination and the Floor

Litigation concerning general creditor priority and treatment in a Chapter 13 plan takes two forms. First, an unsecured creditor sometimes argues that the total payment to him is less than he deserves under the best interest test. That argument is based on section 1325(a)(4); we deal with it below. Second, unsecured creditors sometimes object to their treatment on the ground that they are the object of "unfair discrimination" and thus that the plan violates section 1322(b)(1). In this section we consider that challenge.

For reasons that are sometimes obvious and sometimes not, a debtor often proposes a large payment to certain unsecured creditors and a modest payment to others. When each of the creditors would have a claim with the same priority against the debtor's assets and thus realize the same percentage of its claim in a Chapter 7 case, a creditor who is receiving the worse of it in Chapter 13 argues alternatively that the plan cannot be approved because of section 1322(b) ("discriminates unfairly"), or because of section 1325(a)(3) (not proposed in good faith, or proposed "by * * * [a means] forbidden by law").

Unlike Chapter 11 where the issue of discrimination between classes of unsecured creditors is occasionally discussed but is rarely a central issue, there are many Chapter 13 cases where discrimination between classes is a fighting issue. It is through these Chapter 13 cases that one can appreciate the uncertainty in the law about the debtor's right to discriminate not only in Chapter 13, but also in Chapter 11.

---

5. Id. § 1326(b).

One should appreciate that every classification is likely to result in some discrimination in favor of one creditor and against another. Because section 1325(b) requires that the debtor give up all of his disposable income in most cases, there is no "extra money" that will go to creditor A which does not come from creditor B. Put another way, modification of a debtor's plan is likely to be a zero sum game in which gains that go to one creditor because of classification or for other reasons, come out of the pockets of other creditors. (Plus one for creditor A is minus one for creditor B and the sum is zero.) That being the case, Congress must have intended that a certain level of discrimination is to be expected and is acceptable.

Chapter 13 explicitly provides for two forms of discrimination between unsecured creditors. First, section 1322(b)(1) authorizes the designation of classes as provided in section 1122. Section 1122 in turn authorizes establishing a separate class of claims "consisting only of every unsecured claim that is less than or reduced to an amount that the court approves as reasonable and necessary for administrative convenience." In Chapter 11 this provision is used to dispose of small claims by paying them in full, even in circumstances where other unsecured creditors with larger claims will receive much less than full payment. Presumably a Chapter 13 plan that fully paid every claim under $50 but paid only 60 percent of claims over $50 would be permissible under section 1322(b)(1).[1]

In the 1984 amendments to section 1322(b), Congress endorsed a second specific form of discrimination. Post–1984, the section provides that "such plan may treat claims for a consumer debt of the debtor if an individual is liable on such consumer debt with the debtor differently than other unsecured claims."[2] If, for example, a friend who is not in bankruptcy has co-signed a loan, section 1322(b)(1) in effect authorizes the debtor to pay that debt in full, even while the debtor is paying far less than that to all other unsecured creditors. This subsection is a recognition of the debtor's desire to pay off co-signed debt and is, we suppose, a legislative bow to the pitiful state of consumer guarantors, mostly parents, spouses, and friends. One reading the cases should be careful to distinguish between the post–1984 and the pre–1984 decisions. Many of the pre–1984 cases that raised the discrimination question are guarantee cases that would now be covered explicitly by (b)(1).

The small claimant case under section 1122(b) and the co-signer case under section 1322(b)(1) will take up only a small part of the universe in which the debtor seeks to treat one creditor or group of creditors better than others who have similar or identical legal rights. The debtor will be stimulated to discriminate in favor of one set of creditors in a variety of circumstances. For example, the debtor may choose to treat creditors with whom he will have a continuing relationship (physicians, business suppliers, utilities) differently than others with whom he has no intention of dealing in

§ 9–7

1. Some courts favor a requirement: "necessity for performance of the plan" as the only good reason for allowing the debtor to favor some non-priority unsecured claims over others. In re Girardeau, 35 B.R. 9 (Bankr. D.S.C.1983); In re Hosler, 12 B.R. 395 (Bankr. S.D.Ohio 1981); In re S & W Enterprise, 37 B.R. 153 (Bankr. N.D.Ill. 1984) (all general unsecured claims must be placed in the same class unless separate classification is necessary or reasonable for administrative convenience).

2. 11 U.S.C.A. § 1322(b)(1).

the future (a hospital that is no longer used, a car dealer, or financial institution where the debtor no longer borrows). If the debtor has local creditors and creditors at some distance whom he will never see, that may stimulate him to pay the local and to ignore the more distant. If the debtor plans to go back to his college and is fearful that he will not receive a student loan, he may wish to pay off the student loan in full even while he stiffs others.[3] When a third person has put up collateral to secure the debtor's debt, the debtor may well seek to pay that debt and to exclude others; this is merely a variant of the co-signer situation.

Although the reasons for favoring one creditor over another appear to be diverse, they all rest upon the debtor's selfish interest. Where the particular creditor or a third party (co-signer) has a hook in the debtor, the debtor sees it in his interest to pay that creditor while he refuses to pay others. The question for the courts in interpreting Chapter 13 is the extent to which they will allow the debtor to pursue that selfish interest.[4]

In the early days, a few cases, such as *In re Iacovoni*,[5] took the position that Chapter 13 prohibited all such discrimination between creditors who had claims of equal legal status except where Chapter 13 specifically provided otherwise or where the creditors did not object.[6] This interpretation of Chapter 13 conflicts with the language of section 1322(b)(1). Recall that that section provides the debtor "may not discriminate unfairly." The implication is that the debtor may do some "discrimination" as long as it is not "unfair." In fact, this section implies that identical treatment is not necessary even for those who are similarly situated. Section 1325(a)(3) is of slight help in resolving this issue because of the inherent ambiguity in the meaning of "good faith."

Other courts held that the debtor could discriminate among creditors who were similarly situated as long as each of them received more than he would receive in a Chapter 7. This was the holding in *In re Sutherland*.[7] In effect, the *Sutherland* decision finds that as long as the best interest test of section 1325(a)(4) is met there is no requirement of equal treatment of

---

3. See In re Freshley, 69 B.R. 96 (Bankr. N.D.Ga.1987) (plan proposing to pay 100% to debtor's college does not unfairly discriminate against unsecured creditors receiving 1%, where paying off student loan will enable debtor to return to school); In re Davidson, 72 B.R. 384 (Bankr. D.Colo.1987) (court recognizes that classifying nondischargeable child support separately is reasonable and should be permitted); contra In re Stewart, 52 B.R. 281 (Bankr. W.D.N.Y.1985).

4. For cases declining to confirm because of lack of good faith or unfair discrimination, see In re Mielke, 39 B.R. 556 (Bankr.D. N.D. 1984); In re Gunn, 37 B.R. 432 (Bankr. D. Ore. 1984); In re Gaskin, 79 B.R. 388 (Bankr. C.D.Ill. 1987); In re Green, 70 B.R. 164 (Bankr. W.D.Ark.1986); In re Harris, 62 B.R. 391 (Bankr. E.D.Mich.1986); In re Wolff, 22 B.R. 510 (Bankr. 9th Cir.1982); In re Bowles, 48 B.R. 502 (Bankr. E.D.Va.1985); In re Dziedzic, 9 B.R. 424 (Bankr. S.D.Tex.1981).

For cases where plan was confirmed or conditionally approved despite a claim of unfair discrimination or lack of good faith, see In re Terry, 78 B.R. 171 (Bankr. E.D.Tenn.1987); In re Freshley, 69 B.R.96 (Bankr. N.D.Ga.1987); In re Sutherland, 3 B.R. 420 (Bankr. W.D. Ark.1980); In re Kovich, 4 B.R. 403 (Bankr. W.D.Mich.1980).

5. 2 B.R. 256 (Bankr. D. Utah 1980).

6. See In re Iacovoni, 2 B.R. 256 (Bankr. D. Utah 1980) and the concurring opinion of Judge Hughes in In re Wolff, 22 B.R. 510 (Bankr. 9th Cir. 1982); In re McKenzie, 4 B.R. 88 (Bankr. W.D.N.Y.1980) (unsecured claims on which there is a codebtor must be treated the same as other unsecured claims); accord In re Montano, 4 B.R. 535 (Bankr. D. D.C. 1980), aff'd in part, remanded in part, 13 B.R. 997 (D.D.C.1981). Note that these cases have been statutorily reversed by section 1322(b)(1) discussed earlier.

7. 3 B.R. 420 (Bankr. W.D.Ark.1980).

similarly situated creditors. This interpretation also conflicts with section 1322(b)(1). Surely the drafters intended that the phrase "may not discriminate unfairly" to have some meaning, and if no discrimination is prohibited as long as each creditor receives more than it would receive in a Chapter 7, that language has none.

The judge who is not comfortable either in *Sutherland*'s debtor's wing or *Iacovoni*'s creditor's wing must somehow interpret the "may not discriminate unfairly" language of section 1322. It is essentially the same language that appears in section 1129(b)(1).

In *In re Kovich*,[8] Judge Howard first set down four rules to test what discrimination is permitted and what is not. In a slightly varying form these rules have now been adopted by more than a score of cases and have become the standard articulation of the rule concerning discrimination among unsecured creditors. The four tests have become a shibboleth routinely uttered by judges even in circumstances where they seem to have lost the meaning given them by Judge Howard, and where they could have as easily pointed one way as the other.

To understand the rules' source consider the two cases that make up *In re Kovich*. In the first case the debtor proposed a five percent payment to most of his unsecured creditors and 100 percent payment to the unsecured creditor whose claim was co-signed. In the second plan the debtor proposed to pay most unsecured creditors a ten percent dividend, but to pay one, the landlord, in full. The first case is now resolved by the explicit provision on co-signed debts in section 1322, but that was not true at the time the case was decided in 1980, and it would still not be true of the landlord. In *Kovich* the court concluded that full payment to one and only ten percent to others in a circumstance in which a smaller payment would force the debtor into Chapter 7 might render such treatment "fair." In *Kovich*, the first test is whether such discrimination was "necessary" for the debtor to avoid Chapter 7.

The second test is whether the debtor would be able to perform the Chapter 13 plan without the classification. If, for example, the debtor could pay a larger dividend to all of the creditors, presumably the debtor could perform the plan "without the classification" and the discrimination is unfair. Essentially the court is asking whether the debtor has additional assets that might be put into the plan. Such assets might be found either by reducing the amount of assets to be withheld by the debtor for his or her own personal living expenses or, alternatively, by extending the plan for additional time. If one limits the reasonable basis for the classification rules to cases in which a conversion to Chapter 7 would be the result from any larger payment, then tests one and two in Judge Howard's list come to the same thing.

The third test is whether the debtor has acted in good faith.[9] The court in *Kovich* commented that "certainly the debtor should not be permitted to pay a creditor less because of ill will."[10] By this test Judge Howard seems to be excluding only cases where the debtor pays one creditor less than others

---

8. 4 B.R. 403 (Bankr. W.D.Mich.1980).
9. 11 U.S.C.A. § 1325(a)(3).
10. Id. at 407.

out of vindictiveness. Notwithstanding many creditors' belief to the contrary, vindictive refusal to pay is surely infrequent.

The final test is whether other creditors are "receiving a meaningful payment, or is the plan just a sham." [11] The judge in *Kovich* said that he would not comment on the proposed payments of five and ten percent since the payments in that case to the other creditors were not an issue. In effect, the fourth requirement seems to invite the court to refuse plans where there are very small dividends paid to the other unsecured creditors.

The many courts that follow *Kovich* apply Judge Howard's four rules in quite different settings and in thoroughly unpredictable ways.[12] It is clear that many judges use these tests simply to indulge their own views about what is fair and what is not. It is also clear that the language does not mean the same thing to any two judges and that cases often stray far from the ideas Judge Howard appeared to have in the *Kovich* case.

Consider some cases that have applied the *Kovich* test. In *In re Mielke*,[13] the court refused to confirm the debtor's plan where the debtor had established two unsecured classes. He proposed to pay those with claims of less than $1,000 one hundred percent, and those with claims over $1,000 ten percent. But there was only one claim for more than $1,000, namely, the bank's. The court found that this method of discrimination was simply a way to treat the bank worse than the other creditors. On the other hand, Judge Kelly in *In re Terry* [14] confirmed a plan even though it paid twelve of the debtor's thirteen creditors in full and paid Credit Thrift about twenty-three percent of its $7,000 claim. In discussing the tests and Credit Thrift's complaint, the court seems to embrace the debtor's argument of expediency: "The majority of the claims in number and amount is still held by doctors, a drug store, a dentist, a service station, a hospital, and a veterinarian. AT & T is not a local creditor, but it is much like a national utility that the debtors are likely to deal with in the future. The use of a cutoff * * * [to establish a class] may not always be appropriate, but is accurate enough in this case." [15]

One wonders why it is so obvious that the debtor was acting in bad faith and unfairly discriminating in *Mielke*, but was not doing so in *Terry*. The difference may lie not so much in the law, but in the judge's internal and *a priori* judgment about what is and what is not fair.

Note that the debtor cannot evade the discrimination rule by proposing to pay certain creditors outside the plan. In *In re Gunn* [16] the joint debtors proposed to pay two debts secured by automobiles outside of the plan. The total payments would have exceeded the value of the automobiles by several

---

11. Id.

12. See In re Lawson, 93 B.R. 979 (Bankr. N.D.Ill. 1988); In re Atlanta West VI, 91 B.R. 620 (Bankr. N.D.Ga.1988); In re Bowles, 48 B.R. 502 (Bankr. E.D.Va.1985); In re Ratledge, 31 B.R. 897 (Bankr. E.D.Tenn.1983); In re Dziedzic, 9 B.R. 424 (Bankr. S.D.Tex.1981). For decisions which note difficulties with the four factor test, see In re Furlow, 70 B.R. 973 (Bankr. E.D.Pa. 1987); In re Green, 70 B.R. 164 (Bankr. W.D.Ark.1986).

13. 39 B.R. 556 (Bankr. D.N.D.1984).

14. 78 B.R. 171 (Bankr. E.D.Tenn.1987).

Another variation on the unfair discrimination rule is to conclude that a plan that discriminates may be approved only if there is "absolute necessity," i.e., if there must be such discrimination for any sort of a Chapter 13 to go forward. In re Girardeau, 35 B.R. 9 (Bankr. D.S.C.1983); In re Hosler, 12 B.R. 395 (Bankr. S.D.Ohio 1981).

15. 78 B.R. at 174.

16. 37 B.R. 432 (Bankr. D. Ore. 1984).

thousand dollars. The court rejected a plan that would have paid the unsecured creditors three percent within the plan, but would have paid GMAC the full $9,600 owing on a Firebird that was worth approximately $4,000.

One basis for discrimination that seems appropriate and was accepted by one court is that found in section 523. While the 1990 amendments to section 1328 now explicitly prevent discharge in most student loan situations, *In re Freshley* [17] demonstrates that discrimination in favor of a creditor who is covered by section 523(a) may be acceptable. In that case the debtor proposed to pay 100 percent of a student loan and only one percent of his other $5,314 of unsecured debts. The trustee challenged the plan as not in good faith, yet the court approved it. The court specifically recognized that in Chapter 7 the student loan would be excepted from the discharge under section 523(a)(8). The court recognized that the debtor had an expedient reason to pay that debt in full (he wanted to go back to school at the same place), but it noted that Congress had in effect set apart this kind of creditor from others and had given it an elevated position in section 523(a)(8).

Where the debtor is engaged in dubious activity, courts read the standards more narrowly and seem more likely to refuse to confirm a plan. For example, in *In re Gaskin* [18] the court declined to confirm a plan where the debtor was going to pay GMAC outside the plan more than the value of the collateral. The court noted that the debtor had just been through Chapter 7 and that part of the motivation to pay outside the plan was an attempt to avoid payment of fees to the trustee. *In re Bowles* [19] is a similar case. There the debtor and his spouse had been in Chapter 7 shortly before the Chapter 13. The discharge in the earlier bankruptcy had been revoked under 727 for failure of the debtor to disclose certain assets. The debtor proposed to pay 100 cents on his restitution obligation that had arisen out of a criminal plea on the ground that he would go to jail if he did not make full payment of that amount. Even though he was faced with jail, the court found that the 100 percent payment unfairly discriminated and held that the plan was not proposed in good faith.

In summary we return to the four tests proposed originally by Judge Howard:

    1) Whether the discrimination has a reasonable basis;

    2) Whether the debtor can carry out a plan without such discrimination;

    3) Whether such discrimination is proposed in good faith; and

    4) The treatment of the class discriminated against.

As indicated above, we are doubtful that this list gives truly significant guidance except in the unusual case. In the hands of a generous judge, test one is simply a measure of the debtor's selfish interest. Invariably the debtor wishes to make payment to the creditor who makes the largest threat or who commands the debtor's greatest love. In a rare case, such as a creditor belonging to a class enumerated in section 523(a), one can conclude that Congress intended certain debts to be paid before others, and can

---

17. 69 B.R. 96 (Bankr. N.D.Ga.1987).
18. 79 B.R. 388 (Bankr. D. Ill. 1987).
19. 48 B.R. 502 (Bankr. E.D.Va.1985).

perhaps justify the discrimination on that basis. But short of that we find test one to be rarely helpful.

Test two is almost always met if it requires only that a court ask whether the debtor has the financial ability to make payments to all creditors equal to those proposed for the most favored creditor. The answer to that will almost always be no, and therefore that test will almost always be met.

If test three means only that the debtor should not be vindictive in his discrimination (as Judge Howard seemed to suggest), it too can easily be met in the usual case. Often one suspects there is a little anger or vindictiveness mixed with the debtor's expedient judgment, but it would take fancy Freudian analysis to determine when a debtor is motivated by ill will against a particular creditor and when not.

The final test could have some bite. If, for example, one read it to mean that the discrimination between the highest paid and the lowest can only be a certain number (e.g., only twenty percentage points) or that no plan can be approved where the payment to those who are being discriminated against is quite small (e.g., none under 10 percent), it would rule out a wide range of plans. From the cases decided so far, we cannot say that the fourth test is playing that role.

Ultimately we suspect one can do no better with these questions than the court did in *In re Harris*.[20] The judge declined to confirm a plan which paid little to the debtors' business creditors (lenders to a failed bookstore), and one hundred percent to the debtors' personal creditors. The court suggests that there should be a presumption "of equal treatment" and that the debtor should bear the burden of persuading the court why there should not be equal treatment. At least this ruling puts the burden in the right place and starts from the right point. It does not draw a clear line between cases where discrimination is permitted and those where it is not, but it has the virtue at least of informing the parties as to who must convince the judge to exercise discretion.

Ultimately we throw up our hands here. Like other lawyers, we read the cases and like many of those, we do not find the cases to be a particularly satisfactory description of how any decision has been arrived at or of what this or another judge will do in the next case.

We believe the norm should be one of non-discrimination, and that the courts should pay more respect to the general bankruptcy policy which says similarly situated creditors under state law have the same status under bankruptcy law. We would read the authorization for discrimination among creditors quite narrowly and would rest that conclusion not only on the negative implication from the language of section 1322 (where the Congress has explicitly authorized some forms of discrimination), but also on general bankruptcy policy.

§ 9–8 Determining the Amount of Payments to Be Made Under the Plan: Introduction

Some debtors make the smallest possible payments under their Chapter 13 plans; others make payments well in excess of the minimum that might

---

20. 62 B.R. 391 (Bankr. E.D.Mich.1986).

be required by the rules in Chapter 13. Here we are concerned exclusively with the former group of debtors and we consider the statutory provisions and the case law under them that establish the minimum amount that a debtor can pay and still have his or her plan confirmed. For the purpose of all of the following discussion, we are assuming that either the standing trustee or some creditor objects to the plan. If all are silent, there is no practical restriction on what the debtor can do.

There are at least three legal principles in Chapter 13 that a creditor can claim to be a floor on the amount that may be paid. By far the most significant of these is a rule well known to students of other chapters, the *best interest rule*. That rule, found in section 1325(a)(4), says essentially that each creditor must receive property with a present value under the plan at least equal to the amount that that creditor would receive if the debtor's assets were liquidated under Chapter 7. Thus, if the debtor has $10,000 of nonexempt assets that would go to his creditors in Chapter 7, payments under his plan must have a present value of $10,000 for the same creditors under Chapter 13. The rule is stated in full in section 1325(a)(4):

> the value, as of the effective date of the plan, of property to be distributed under the plan on account of each allowed unsecured claim is not less than the amount that would be paid on such claim if the estate of the debtor were liquidated under chapter 7 of this title on such date.[1]

One can regard the rule as an algebraic equation in which the value of the property that would be distributed in Chapter 7 is on one side; the amount on the other side is the present value of the payments to be made under the plan.

From this test springs a large headache, not only for the trustee and lawyers, but also for the courts, namely, how does one compute present value. We will devote considerable space to that question which ultimately boils down to a determination of the proper "discount" or interest charge attributable to future payments. The question is easy to pose, but hard to answer. What set of payments over three years, for example, is precisely equal to $1,000 in hand today? The answer to that question will depend upon the creditworthiness of the debtor, upon the credit market and on the attendant alternative investments that might be available to one who had the $1,000 in hand. Where the payment is made in property other than dollars, it would depend even upon an estimation of the value of the property. The best interest test is the most important legally and the most thorny factually. It is the mainline defense of a creditor who believes that he is being underpaid.

The second legal principle that sometimes forms a floor on the debtor's permissible payments is the requirement in section 1325(b)(1)(B) that the debtor give up all of his or her *"disposable income"* for three years if there are objecting creditors.[2] To see how this rule might apply to require greater payments than the best interest rule would, consider a debtor with no unencumbered assets, but with $100,000 of unsecured debt and a yearly

§ 9–8
1. 11 U.S.C.A. § 1325(a)(4).

2. For an extended discussion of the disposable income test see § 9–13 infra.

income of $70,000. Because there are no assets and because future income need not be paid out in Chapter 7, but is kept entirely by the debtor, such a debtor could meet the best interest tests in section 1325(a)(4) with a plan that paid nothing to unsecured creditors. Nevertheless, such a debtor might have substantial disposable income, and thus might be required under section 1325(b)(1)(B) to make substantial payments over the three year period.

The disposable income requirement was added in 1984 at the urging of creditors who put forward the examples of just the kind suggested, where there were few assets but relatively large incomes. We suspect that the rule has bite in many cases, but that those cases are fewer than the cases where the best interest rule sets the floor.

Yet less important is a third legal requirement sometimes put forward by creditors. This is the requirement in section 1325(a)(3) that the plan be proposed in "*good faith.*" In the early days of Chapter 13 many creditors argued, some successfully, that plans which paid only small amounts were not made in good faith and thus could not be confirmed even though they complied with the best interest test. For the most part those cases have gone against the creditor and the courts are now willing to approve even relatively small payouts (provided the plans meet the other tests) as being in good faith.

§ 9–9 The Best Interest Test—In General

Before one turns to the right-hand side of the algebraic equation and determines the present value of the proposed payments, he has to consider the left-hand side of the equation and decide what amount would be paid "on such claim if the estate of the debtor were liquidated under chapter 7." To do that one must determine the liquidation value of the debtor's unencumbered assets, subtract the amount that the debtor could claim as exempt under section 522 (and could therefore be kept by him and not given to the creditors), then divide the available assets among the claims to be made and so determine what a particular creditor would receive under Chapter 7. This is the main reason, usually the only reason, that the exemption laws incorporated into bankruptcy by section 522 and discussed in our Chapter 8 are relevant in a bankruptcy Chapter 13. Obviously one has to make some assumptions about what exemptions would be claimed and how they would be applied in order to arrive at the result. Obvious too is the fact that one must know exactly what claims have been made, which are to be disallowed and which are to be reduced in value, in order to determine what a particular claim would have received under Chapter 7. These calculations may be tedious, occasionally crude and imprecise, but they offer no significant legal issues.

One issue early raised in the cases and soon put to bed is the question how one deals with claims that could not have been discharged under section 523 (because, for example, they arose out of student loans or fraud). Of course one of the reasons debtors choose Chapter 13 over 7 is to be discharged from such debts that they could not escape in Chapter 7.

In the early days of Chapter 13, creditors often argued that plans proposed by such debtors could not be approved under the best interest rule of section 1325(a)(4). Creditors maintained that under Chapter 7 they would be paid in full (because their particular debt was not dischargeable) and—they argued—unless they received full payment under the Chapter 13 plan, the best interest test was not met.

Of course, the difficulty with this argument is that it deprives the Chapter 13 debtor of the very spoonful of sugar that was offered by the Congress to induce the debtor to elect Chapter 13, namely, the "super-discharge." While the 1990 amendment to section 1328(a) does not eliminate the "super-discharge," it does make the "sugar-spoon" smaller. If the creditor's argument prevailed, no plan paying less than 100 cents on the dollar in Chapter 13 could be approved under section 1325; thus, the obvious Congressional intention would have been frustrated. Uniformly courts found that Congress could not have intended section 1325(a)(4) to be so read.

In addition, some courts found that section 1325(a)(4) was not violated by a plan that paid only a small amount on a dischargeable debt because all that section 1325 required was a present value payment under the plan to be no less than the amount "that would be paid on such claim" in a Chapter 7. These courts pointed out the payment in the Chapter 7 would be no greater than the present value payment under Chapter 13, even though the debt were not discharged and although the creditor would thereafter pursue the debtor in state court and collect the remainder of the debt out of the debtor's post-bankruptcy income. This non-bankruptcy recovery—these courts argued—was not a payment on such claim and thus was not contemplated under section 1325(a)(4).[1]

Whether one relies on the policy or upon the narrow reading of the language in section 1325(a)(4), courts are now in agreement that a creditor whose debt would be excluded from the discharge under section 523 in a Chapter 7 cannot for that reason bar confirmation of a plan under section 1325(a)(4) because it pays less than 100 cents on the dollar.[2]

§ 9–10 The Best Interest Test—Computing Present Value—The Best Interest Test Applied

Every Chapter 13 plan that conforms to the requirements of section 1325 calls for the calculation of the present value of the stream of payments to be made under that plan. The best interest test embodied in section 1325(a)(4) promises "the value, as of the effective date of the plan, of property to be distributed under the plan," be not less than the amount "that would be paid on such claim on liquidation in chapter 7." If, therefore, a liquidation of the debtor in Chapter 7 would produce a check from the trustee to the creditor of $1,200, the payments under Chapter 13 (over a period that may be as long as five years) must have a present value of $1,200.

§ 9–9

1. See In re Klein, 57 B.R. 818 (Bankr. 9th Cir.1985).

2. Matter of Hawkins, 33 B.R. 908 (Bankr. S.D.N.Y. 1983); Education Assistance Corp. v. Zellner, 827 F.2d 1222 (8th Cir.1987); In re Kazzaz, 62 B.R. 308 (Bankr. E.D.Va.1986); In re Klein, 57 B.R. 818 (Bankr. 9th Cir. 1985); In re McAloon, 44 B.R. 831 (Bankr. E.D.Va. 1984); In re Crawford, 10 B.R. 815 (Bankr. M.D.Ala.1981).

Section 1325(a)(5)(B)(ii) establishes the same rule for secured creditors. There the comparison is not the distribution under Chapter 7 to an unsecured creditor, but the value of the underlying collateral which in turn establishes "the allowed amount of such claim" under section 506. If, therefore, the debtor's car is subject to a valid security interest and it could be liquidated for a net amount of $1200, the payment to the secured creditor under the plan must have a present value of $1,200.

The courts are in agreement that the word "value" in (a)(4) and (a)(5) means present value and that somehow one must apply a discount factor or an interest charge to payments made over time in order to give them the present value that has been derived by an appraisal of the collateral and a calculation of a Chapter 7 distribution. No one would dispute the proposition that payments of $100 in each month for one year have a lower present value than a current payment of $1,200.

Consider why the stream of payments totalling $1200 has a lower present value than a single payment of $1200. Even if one assumed that there was no risk of non-payment and no possibility of inflation, the current payment would have more value than payments over twelve months because the payee could invest the $1,200 and earn a return on it for that period. If one adds inflation so that $100 twelve months from now will not buy what $100 will today and, further, the possibility of default, it is easy to imagine a case in which the payments would have to be radically greater than $1,200 to have a present value equal to $1,200.

Everything that we have said so far is quite elementary. At this point any self-respecting economist or accountant would have passed on to other things, confident that there is nothing here of even passing intellectual interest.

One who has read even a handful of the cases under Chapter 13 will realize, however, that the mode of calculating present value is a hotly debated, and frequently litigated issue.[1] Moreover, it is an area in which the bankruptcy judges have not distinguished themselves and where the commentators have stumbled. In fact, there is a great deal of nonsense, both in the decided opinions and in the commentaries on this question.

While we believe that many of the cases are not well reasoned, we acknowledge that there are some legitimate difficulties and some questions on which reasonable people could differ. First, to what extent should a court consider the circumstances of a particular debtor and a particular debt in determining the interest rate that must be applied to the stream of payments in order to give the creditor its present value? Should the court take into account the value of the collateral, the credit worthiness of the particular debtor, the length of time for the payments, the type of loan? Presumably, a creditor making a bargain with a debtor would consider all of those factors in determining the interest rate. What of the market for funds that now fluctuates substantially from month to month and year to year? To what extent should such fluctuations be taken into account?

§ 9–10

1. For a collection of the different methods used by courts to calculate present value, see In re Evans, 20 B.R. 175 (Bankr. E.D.Pa. 1982).

Secondly, one can wonder the extent to which one should consider the particular circumstances of the creditor. The present value of a dollar is greater to some creditors than to others. Assume, for example, a creditor with a large clientele of VISA credit card borrowers who are willing to pay 18 percent. Assume another whose borrowers are all mortgagors in a mortgage market where the norm is 11 percent. Assume for the purpose of the argument that the markets are to some extent segmented so that creditor number one cannot enter creditor number two's market. Would it not be logical for creditor one to pay a higher price (to acquire dollars and lend them at 18 percent) than creditor two would pay (to lend at 11 percent)? That dollars, in fact, have different values to creditors even in the same market is demonstrated by any local market for certificates of deposit. Some creditors will issue nine percent certificates of deposit while others will offer CDs for only eight percent at the same time in the same market. This interest differential cannot be a function of the credit worthiness of the borrower bank for both CDs, if less than $100,000 will be guaranteed by the federal government.

Should the courts consider this differential value of the dollar to the various creditors? We think not. We read section 1325 to treat the present value of a dollar as a dollar and to ignore the fact that a particular dollar might be worth only 98 cents to one party and $1.04 to another. By assuming in our example that the present value of a $1,200 payment today is $1,200 for all creditors, we have assumed away the fact that some might be willing to pay a higher price to acquire those $1,200 than others.

The final question that lies beneath the surface in some cases and is discussed in others is the question whether, for administrative convenience, the courts should adopt standards that would estimate the proper discount rate only in fairly crude and approximate ways. For example, the court might concede that a true present value calculation should consider the debtor's status, the length of the loan, the security given, and yet conclude that some number tied to an index such as Treasury Bill rates, is an adequate approximation. We would not argue with such attempts, at least if the court openly makes such assumptions.

In our view the proper way of calculating the present value (of determining the appropriate interest or discount rate) is to assume that the Chapter 13 plan constitutes a new loan by this creditor to this debtor and then to ask what the market would charge for such a loan. In *Memphis Bank & Trust Co. v. Whitman*[2] Judge Merritt correctly and succinctly stated both the rule and the reason for it as follows:

> Rather than tying the interest rate to an arbitrary ten per cent rate, the Bankruptcy Court's solution, or some other arbitrary rate, we hold that in the absence of special circumstances bankruptcy courts should use the current market rate of interest used for similar loans in the region. Bankruptcy courts are generally familiar with the current conventional rates on various types of consumer loans. And where parties dispute the question, proof can easily be adduced.

2. 692 F.2d 427 (6th Cir.1982).

The reason we do not use an arbitrary rate is that such a rate may vary widely from the current market rate. The theory of the statute is that the creditor is making a new loan to the debtor in the amount of the current value of the collateral. Under this theory, the most appropriate interest rate is the current market rate for similar loans at the time the new loan is made, not some other unrelated arbitrary rate.[3]

The choice of a particular market at the time of the confirmation for a particular kind of loan seems the best approximation of an interest rate for calculating present value. This market would necessarily take account of the security to be given, of the general rates prevailing in the market (thus of judgments about inflation or deflation) of the length of the loan, and possibly too of creditworthiness, at least of the general class of creditors in that particular market who procure that particular kind of loan.

Consider the other rate setting possibilities to see why they are less satisfactory than the current market rate. First is the suggestion that the court should use "the creditor's cost of funds in its business":

> Thus, contrary to the holdings of a number of courts, it is rarely appropriate to select the rate charged to the debtor in the original transaction as the present value discount rate. Treating the chapter 13 deferral of payments like a new loan transaction, as those courts have done, provides the holder of the allowed secured claim with not only the cost of the funds it would lend but also the costs of a new loan transaction, which would not be incurred, and the profit that would be earned in that transaction. Neither of these latter two amounts would be received if the collateral were surrendered; the lender would have to incur new transaction costs to earn an additional profit. To include them in the present value discount rate would give the holder of an allowed secured claim more than the equivalent of immediate payment of that claim in full.[4]

This is wrong. First, the creditor is not likely to *avoid* the "costs of a new loan transaction," for negotiating a Chapter 13 plan with a debtor is likely to cost at least as much as making a new loan. In many cases the cost of a new loan is *de minimis*. Consider, for example, an extension of credit on a credit card. If, in our hypothetical case above, the creditor were to use the $1,200 in a loan to one of its existing VISA customers, the cost of making that loan is surely less than the cost of negotiating a Chapter 13 plan even if there were no lawyer time involved in such a negotiation.

While the transaction cost assumption is at least plausible, the claim that the creditor is not entitled to a profit on the new loan is simply wrong. Is it assumed that our hypothetical creditor who receives $1,200 in hand will not reinvest the money? What creditor willingly fails to invest its money and what creditor willingly reinvests its money at its own cost of funds? No creditor reinvests its money at its own cost of funds. The only reason a creditor will borrow money (and incur costs of funds) is because it can lend

---

3. Id. at 431. In a later case, In re Colegrove, 771 F.2d 119 (6th Cir.1985), the Sixth Circuit appears to retreat somewhat from the market value standard, at least to the extent that it puts a cap on the rate at the contract rate where the debt is secured by a home mortgage that is being deaccelerated.

4. 5 Collier On Bankruptcy ¶ 1325.06, at 1325–37 to 1325–40 (15th ed. 1987).

that money at a higher interest rate to a third party and make a profit. The proper assumption is that the $1,200 which is in hand will be reinvested at a profit by the lender. If the stream of payments is to equal that $1,200 in hand, the stream must include that profit. One should understand that this is not a matter of discretion. The court must order a stream of payments large enough to have a present value equal to the amount that would be received on liquidation. For two reasons, therefore, because it makes an inaccurate empirical assumption about the cost of making the new loan and because it fails to perceive the need for a profit on reinvestment, the formulation of the cost of funds as a proper discount will always exaggerate the present value of the stream of payments.[5]

A second way of calculating present value is to use the contract rate to which the parties had agreed at the time of the original loan. When rates have fallen between the time of the loan and the time of the Chapter 13, the debtor will invariably argue for use of the market rate as opposed to the contract rate, and the creditor will argue the opposite. When rates on comparable loans have risen, the positions will be reversed, the creditor arguing for the market and the debtor for the contract rate. In our view, the contract rate is persuasive only if one recognizes it is a crude proxy for the market. Particularly in highly variable long-term rates (such as mortgage rates), the contract rate may be far out of line with the current market and thus may be a quite inaccurate way to establish the appropriate discount rate for determining present value. For that reason we believe the contract rate normally should not be used. It may serve as an indication of the market for a particular loan, but it should always be subject to amendment because rates have risen or declined between the date of the loan and the time of the Chapter 13 filing.[6]

Other courts have used the rate that is applied by the Internal Revenue Service for delinquent tax payment or some variation of the Treasury Bill rate. At best these can be defended as crude attempts at determining present value by courts that are unwilling to consider more precise and sophisticated formulae.[7] Of course, use without adjustment of a rate paid by the federal government as the borrower is necessarily too low, for the federal government is the most reliable and creditworthy of all debtors. Few citizens, much less bankrupt citizens, can claim similar creditworthiness.

Finally, some courts have held that the market rate is capped by the contract rate.[8] In effect, these courts conclude that the discount rates should be the market rate or the contract rate, whichever is lower. We see

---

5. Two courts have already missed this point and reached the wrong decision on this issue. In re Mitchell, 77 B.R. 524 (Bankr. E.D.Pa. 1987) (Judge Scholl recants on his earlier and correct decisions applying market rate); cf. In re Cassell, 107 B.R. 536 (Bankr. W.D.Va.1989), rev'd, 119 B.R. 89 (W.D.Va. 1990).

6. For cases relying at least in part on the contract rate to establish the proper discount, see In re Smith, 42 B.R. 198 (Bankr. N.D.Ga. 1984); In re Frey, 34 B.R. 607 (Bankr. M.D.Pa. 1983); In re Thorne, 34 B.R. 428 (Bankr. E.D.Tenn.1983); see also In re Einspahr, 30 B.R. 356 (Bankr. E.D.Pa. 1983), affirming its earlier opinion in In re Evans, 20 B.R. 175 (Bankr. E.D.Pa. 1982), holding that the rate of interest is the rate provided in the debtor's written obligation.

7. See, e.g., In re Frost, 47 B.R. 961 (D.Kan.1985); In re Mitchell, 77 B.R. 524 (Bankr. E.D.Pa. 1987) (rate, however, is justified as an attempt at reaching cost of funds).

8. In re Wilkins, 71 B.R. 665 (Bankr. N.D.Ohio 1987); In re Colegrove, 771 F.2d 119 (6th Cir.1985).

no basis for this conclusion. Section 1325 directs the debtor to pay the creditor "the value," it does not direct payment of the value "but not more than the contract rate." As we have noted above, the contract rate may be too low or too high, not merely because of the change in circumstances of the debtor, but because the market itself has shifted since the loan was originally written. Where the debtor chooses to cure under section 1322(a)(3) and thus to deaccelerate the loan, Congress has explicitly authorized the court to recognize a plan under which a creditor may be receiving substantially less than present value (as, for example, when a six percent mortgage loan is reinstated by cure at a time when the going market rate is 12 percent). That is not what the Congress authorized in section 1325, and the courts have no authority to read it there. One should note that the *Colegrove* [9] case (where the Court of Appeals for the Sixth Circuit stated that limitation) was a case in which the debtor was apparently curing a mortgage. However, the court in that case was discussing not the cured mortgage itself, but the cure payments within the plan. We believe that the court erred in holding that the interest rate should not be greater than the contract rate.[10]

In summary, we endorse Judge Merritt's position in the *Memphis Bank* [11] case. Congress has directed the courts to calculate the present value and that value depends not merely upon the market at the time of confirmation, but also upon the length of the loan, the collateral available and the creditworthiness of the debtor. We are sympathetic with the courts who choose various indices as an administrative convenience to approximate the appropriate discount rate, but we wonder if such courts exaggerate the difficulty of calculating a more precise rate, and we suspect that a few courts may be following their own judgment, not that of the market. In addition to the Sixth Circuit, the Court of Appeals for the Eighth and Eleventh Circuits have spoken on this question as has the Bankruptcy Appellate Panel in the Ninth Circuit.[12] All three of those courts rejected lower court decisions that relied upon some form of fixed legal or governmental rate to establish the proper discount rate.[13] Although only the Bankruptcy Appellate Panel in the Ninth Circuit specifically indorsed the market rate, both the Eighth and Eleventh Circuits directed the lower courts to consider factors such as the length of the payment period, the quality of the security, and the risk of default in determining the proper discount. Though these decisions do not indorse the market rate in so many words, we read them to do almost exactly that. If the other circuits follow their lead, we see hope of escaping from the chaotic state that currently characterizes the bankruptcy court decisions on this issue.

9. In re Colegrove, 771 F.2d 119 (6th Cir. 1985).

10. For cases holding that anything other than the contract rate (in the home mortgage setting) would be an impermissible modification, see Matter of Stratton, 30 B.R. 44 (Bankr. W.D.Mich.1983); In re Einspahr, 30 B.R. 356 (Bankr. E.D.Pa. 1983); In re Frey, 34 B.R. 607 (Bankr. M.D.Pa.1983); In re Simpkins, 16 B.R. 956 (Bankr. E.D.Tenn.1982).

11. Memphis Bank & Tr. Co. v. Whitman, 692 F.2d 427 (6th Cir.1982).

12. United States v. Neal Pharmacal Co., 789 F.2d 1283 (8th Cir.1986); Matter of Southern States Motor Inns, Inc., 709 F.2d 647 (11th Cir.1983), cert. denied, 465 U.S. 1022, 104 S.Ct. 1275, 79 L.Ed.2d 680 (1984); In re Welco Indust., 60 B.R. 880 (Bankr. 9th Cir.1986).

13. For cases holding that the proper rate is the legal rate, see In re Marx, 11 B.R. 819 (Bankr. S.D.Ohio 1981); In re Crockett, 3 B.R. 365 (Bankr. N.D.Ill. 1980).

§ 9–11 Duration of the Plan and the Disposable Income Test

Major battles on confirmation of Chapter 13 plans are fought out under section 1325(a)(4) and (a)(5) discussed above. At least in the negotiations over a Chapter 13 plan, and to a lesser extent in court, the length of the plan and the percentage of the debtor's income that is paid into the plan at each payday will also be items of dispute between debtor and creditors. Since the debtor has the exclusive power to propose a plan,[1] the debtor controls the length of the plan. Under section 1322, the plan "may not provide for payments over a period that is longer than three years unless the court, for cause, approves a longer period * * *."

Nothing in section 1322 or elsewhere explicitly prohibits the debtor from proposing a plan that is shorter than three years, but, of course, too short a stream of payments might have a present value less than the value of assets that would be distributed in a Chapter 7, and thus fail the best interests test in 1325. No plan may be longer than five years and if the plan is more than three, but less than five, the court must approve.[2] Normally it is in the debtor's economic interest to have the shortest possible plan and in the creditors' interest to have the longest possible plan. Particularly if debtor has substantial and rising income, an extension of the plan for one or two years may increase the total payments dramatically.

Because establishing the length of the plan is within the exclusive control of the debtor (except as it is subject also to court supervision between three and five years), one might ask how a creditor is to influence that decision. The answer doubtless lies in the leverage the creditor might derive from arguing that a short plan fails the best interest test, the three-year disposable income rule in section 1325(b)(1)(B), or that it is not proposed in good faith.[3] The creditor may also have leverage arising from the debtor's need for a new loan from a particular creditor.

A related but different question involves the determination of the percentage of the debtor's income that will be paid into the plan during its pendency. In certain circumstances section 1325(b) requires that the debtor give all of his or her "projected disposable income to be received in the three year period beginning on the date" of the first payment under the plan.[4]

This section was added as part of the 1984 amendments and may be regarded as a poor cousin of the absolute priority rule set out in section 1129(b)(2). The absolute priority rule says that a debtor must either pay his objecting unsecured creditors in full or get the vote of their class, or not retain any interest in the Chapter 11 property. The effect of this provision is to give classes who vote against a plan the power to bar a Chapter 11 debtor from ownership of the assets that are subject to the plan. This is a powerful restriction upon the debtor's behavior, particularly in the usual case in which the debtor is in Chapter 11 for the very reason that he wishes to continue to operate a business.

§ 9–11

1. There is nothing in Chapter 13 analogous to section 1121(c) that authorizes non-debtor parties in interest to file plans in certain circumstances in Chapter 11.

2. 11 U.S.C.A. § 1322(c).

3. For a discussion of good faith, see § 9–14 infra.

4. 11 U.S.C.A. § 1325(b)(1)(B).

There is nothing exactly comparable to the absolute priority rule in Chapter 13; indeed, there is no provision for a vote on the plan. To the extent the three-year disposable income requirement in section 1325(b) may require a payment greater than the best interest test, that subsection has a restrictive effect somewhat like the absolute priority rule in Chapter 11.

It is easy to think of cases in which the disposable income test would require a much larger payment than would be required under the best interest test. Assume, for example, a professional athlete with large debts, small assets, and a large income. Considering only the best interest test, a plan could be confirmed that would pay only a small percentage dividend on the outstanding indebtedness. If, on the other hand, the athlete were required to give up all of his disposable income from a $400,000 annual salary for three years, payments would greatly exceed what would be required under the best interest test. We are certain that the professional athlete is the rare exception and we suspect it is a rare case where the disposable income test will add more than a modest dividend over and above what would be required under the best interest rule.

§ 9–12 Duration of the Plan and the Disposable Income Test— Section 1322(c): The Duration of the Plan

If the plan is to last for more than three years, "the court, for cause," must approve such "longer period."[1] An initial reading of this subsection leaves one with many questions. First, must the court *sua sponte* examine each plan of more than three years, or must that be done only if there is a question by the trustee, the debtor, or a creditor? Second, does the section authorize the court to deny approval of a plan that is only three years at the request of a creditor who seeks a longer period? Third, if the debtor wishes a period longer than three years, but less than five and some other party complains, may the court decline to approve despite the debtor's desire for a longer period? Finally, how procedurally do these questions come to the court's attention where there is no complaint by the creditor or trustee?

A reasonable case can be made that the five-year limitation in section 1322 was put there by Congress to protect the debtors from their own foolishness. Under Chapter XIII of the Act of 1898, apparently some debtors were stuck with very long plans. Apparently Congress thought it inappropriate to permit a debtor to be so indentured to creditors. Partly, therefore, the section is here to protect the debtor against his own willingness to pay his debts or perhaps to protect the debtor from creditors' pressure to do so.[2]

§ 9–12

1. 11 U.S.C.A. § 1322(c).

2. For the legislative reasoning behind the enactment of the section 1322(c) time restriction, see H.R. Rep. No. 595, 95th Cong., 1st Sess. 117 (1977), reprinted in 1978 U.S. Code Cong. & Admin. News 5787, 6078:

On the other hand in certain areas of the country inadequate supervision of debtors attempting to perform under the wage earner plans have (sic) made them a way of life for certain debtors. Extensions on plans, new cases, and newly incurred debts put some debtors under court supervised repayment plans for seven (7) to ten (10) years. This has become the closest thing there is to involuntary servitude * * * .

Cited in In re Poff, 7 B.R. 15 (Bankr. S.D.Ohio 1980) and In re Black, 78 B.R. 840 (Bankr. S.D.Ohio 1987).

For cases which deny confirmation of a plan exceeding three years on the basis that the debtor is unable to meet its burden of proof, see In re Fizer, 1 B.R. 400 (Bankr. S.D.Ohio 1979); In re Nickels, 4 B.R. 481 (Bankr. S.D.Ohio 1980); see also In re Cadogan, 4 B.R.

May the court refuse to approve a three year plan under section 1322(c) on the ground that it should be a longer? We believe the answer to that question is no. The timing of the plan is within the control of the debtor.³ We do not see anything in section 1322(c) that gives the court the right to tell the debtor that he or she should have chosen a longer time. On the other hand, the court doubtless has this power where it finds that the plan proposed is not in good faith under section 1325 or it does not pay out the projected disposable income under section 1325(b)(1)(B). In those cases, the court's power is limited to denial of confirmation, but the consequence of such denial may be a newly negotiated plan that is longer than three years. In some cases the court issuing such a denial invites the debtor to present a longer plan.⁴

Rejecting the debtor's laudable instincts, several courts have denied the debtor's request for approval of a plan that goes beyond the three years. In summarizing the cases in *In re Greer*,⁵ Judge Bufford recites reasons that have been regarded as "cause" for extension beyond three years. The first is to enable the debtor to pay 70 or 100 percent of his debts and so fit within section 727(a)(9) and be entitled to a discharge in Chapter 7 within six years after the Chapter 13 discharge. The second reason recognized by Judge Bufford is that there has been a suspension of payments during the Chapter 13 plan and thus a need to extend so there would be a total of three years of payments. Many courts state that the mere desire to pay more to one's creditors is not "cause" under section 1322(c).⁶

We are puzzled at this judicial concern that the debtor pay too much. We would have expected the courts to accept almost any reason as "cause" if the debtor chose to extend the plan unless there was evidence that a threatening creditor stimulated the debtor's wish. In our view the absolute limit of five years is a sufficient protection against creditor overreaching. We share Judge Cole's conclusion in *In re Pierce*⁷ that the debtor's unforced "desire to extend his or her plan beyond three years in order to increase the dividend to his unsecured creditors without more" is adequate cause under section 1322(c).⁸

---

598 (Bankr. W.D.La.1980) where the court denied confirmation because the debtor failed to procure the court's permission before proposing a plan exceeding three years.

3. See In re Vensel, 39 B.R. 866 (Bankr. E.D.Va.1984); In re Gathright, 67 B.R. 384 (Bankr. E.D.Pa. 1986), appeal dism'd, 71 B.R. 343 (E.D.Pa.1987).

4. In re Kitson, 65 B.R. 615 (Bankr. E.D.N.C.1986) (in denying confirmation the court states that it is unlikely to approve any plan that pays less than 100 cents on the dollar and suggests a four or a three year plan that would meet with its approval).

5. 60 B.R. 547 (Bankr. C.D.Cal.1986).

6. In re Festa, 65 B.R. 85 (Bankr. S.D.Ohio 1986), citing H.R. Rep. No. 595 95th Cong., 1st sess. 117 (1977), reprinted in U.S. Code & Admin. News 1978 5787, 6078; In re Rogers, 65 B.R. 1018 (Bankr. E.D.Mich.1986); cf. In re Mothershed, 62 B.R. 113 (Bankr. E.D. Ark. 1986); contra In re Red, 60 B.R. 113 (Bankr. E.D.Tenn.1986) ("[C]ause" is established when debtor simply wishes to pay a higher dividend to unsecured creditors by extending his or her plan longer than three years. Counsel submits that his client's request is unforced and that a three to five year plan, voluntarily proposed, does not amount to involuntary servitude.); In re Pierce, 82 B.R. 874 (Bankr. S.D.Ohio 1987) (desire to extend plan beyond three years to increase dividend to unsecured creditor is cause justifying extension).

7. 82 B.R. 874 (Bankr. S.D.Ohio 1987).

8. See also In re Fries, 68 B.R. 676 (Bankr. E.D.Pa. 1986); In re Eury, 11 B.R. 397 (Bankr. N.D.Ga.1981); In re Colston, 11 B.R. 251 (Bankr. N.D.Ga.1981) (all allowing or contemplating payment over a period longer than three years based principally upon the debtor's desire).

Ironically, in some of the cases in which the debtor has proposed a plan for more than three years, specific creditors have opposed an extension for various reasons. For example, in *In re Frank*[9] the debtor proposed a 57-month plan under which almost all of the payments would go to priority tax payments and to secured creditors. Thorp, a small loan company, objected to the length of the plan. Apparently it did so in the belief that a three-year Chapter 13 plan could not be approved (because the income would be insufficient to pay off the entire $8,000 of priority tax claims), thus the debtor would be thrown into Chapter 7. There Thorp could argue that its debt was not dischargeable because it had been procured by a false financial statement. Similar factors may have been at work in *In re Rogers*,[10] in which the objecting credit union argued that the debtor had proposed a 42 month period merely to "lull the other creditors" to sleep. Conceivably the credit union's complaint was part of a strategy to force the debtor to sell her two-year old Corvette and so put more money into the plan that might have gone to satisfy the credit union's claim.[11]

Although most of the litigation has concerned the debtor's right to a plan of more than three but less than five years, questions concerning the five-year limitation arise occasionally. For example, in *In re Hildebran*[12] the debtor proposed to amortize a mortgage over 25 years. The mortgage liability had been represented by a three-year note prior to the filing and the creditor objected to its extension to 25 years. The court held that the proposal to extend the payment period beyond five years violated section 1322(c) even though the debtor argued that the payment was not "under the plan." So applied, section 1322(c) is a substantial limitation on the power granted by section 1322(b)(2) to "modify the rights of holders of secured claims."[13] We consider that question below.[14]

In summary, we are uneasy with the cases under section 1322(c). In some cases, the courts, apparently angered by what they regard as inappropriate debtor action, refuse plans that go beyond three years even when such plans are clearly in the economic interest of the debtors. In other cases, the courts squelch what appear to be debtors' good intentions in making more substantial payments on their debts. In both cases we would be more generous in finding "cause" for extension beyond three years and would be inclined to approve such plans any time they are proposed by a debtor who is

---

9. 69 B.R. 129 (Bankr. C.D.Ill. 1986).
10. 65 B.R. 1018 (Bankr. E.D.Mich.1986).
11. Cf. In re Fries, 68 B.R. 676 (Bankr. E.D.Pa. 1986) (bank objects to extension, but unclear why it does so, for it would apparently get nothing in a shorter plan); In re DeMoss, 59 B.R. 90 (Bankr. W.D.La.1986) (debtor could not get financing for a proposed balloon payment and so could not comply with original plan is not cause to extend the term beyond 36 months).
12. 54 B.R. 585 (Bankr. D. Ore. 1985).
13. For example, In the Matter of Foster, 61 B.R. 492 (Bankr. N.D.Ind. 1986), the debtors owed $141,623 on land with a value of $104,650. They proposed to cramdown the debt (i.e., to reduce the secured debt to $104,650, and to pay it over the life of the original mortgage that went well beyond five years).

The court concluded that the debtor could have cured the arrearages within the plan and then paid according to the original agreement. Following In re Hildebran, 54 B.R. 585 (Bankr. D. Ore. 1985), the court then found that to modify the long term mortgage would be to propose a plan that extended beyond the § 1322(c) five year period. In such cases the debtors will be forced to use Chapters 12 or 11.

14. See §§ 9–11 and 9–12 infra. The five-year limitation of § 1322(c) was also an issue in In re Black, 78 B.R. 840 (Bankr. S.D.Ohio 1987). There the court held that § 1322(c) was not a basis for dismissing a properly confirmed plan which eventually took more than five years to complete.

represented by competent counsel. We believe the five-year limit and the presence of counsel adequately protects the debtor from creditor overreaching.

Except to the extent that the court finds a three-year plan to be in violation of some other section of Chapter 13 (such as the rule on good faith in section 1325), we see no power in the court to require a debtor to increase the length of a proposed plan. Thus, except by moral suasion, we do not believe section 1322(c) offers any opening for the creditors to procure a court order for an extended period.

§ 9-13 Duration of the Plan and the Disposable Income Test— Projected Disposable Income

A second variable that will affect the amount to be paid under a plan is the projected disposable income limitation set out in section 1325(b). The section was added as a part of the 1984 amendments to the Code. It reads in full as follows:

> (b)(1) If the trustee or the holder of an allowed unsecured claim objects to the confirmation of the plan, then the court may not approve the plan unless, as of the effective date of the plan—
>
> > (A) the value of the property to be distributed under the plan on account of such claim is not less than the amount of such claim; or
> >
> > (B) the plan provides that all of the debtor's projected disposable income to be received in the three-year period beginning on the date that the first payment is due under the plan will be applied to make payments under the plan.
>
> (2) For purposes of this subsection, "disposable income" means income which is received by the debtor and which is not reasonably necessary to be expended—
>
> > (A) for the maintenance or support of the debtor or a dependent of the debtor; and
> >
> > (B) if the debtor is engaged in business, for the payment of expenditures necessary for the continuation, preservation, and operation of such business.[1]

As we have indicated above, Congress adopted the disposable income test at least in part to capture the debtor who has limited assets (and thus would be required to make only a limited payout by the best interest test), but has a large current disposable income. Requiring more to be paid into the plan has the same practical consequence as an extension of the plan, namely, to increase the total payments to the creditors. In that sense this provision is analogous to the rule under section 1322(c) that the plan can be extended beyond three years for cause. In most other respects this rule is not analogous. To pay one's projected disposable income is not a matter of discretion with the debtor; it is something that the debtor must do if there is a complaint from the trustee or an unpaid unsecured creditor (unless the plan is going to pay such claims in full). Because most plans do not provide

§ 9-13
1. 11 U.S.C.A. § 1325(b).

for full payment, most are at least theoretically subject to challenge under section 1325(b)(1)(B).[2]

Obviously the amount of a debtor's disposable income is an item about which reasonable people can differ even if they accept the same legal definition of that term.[3] Section 1325(b)(2) tells us that this is income, which is "not reasonably necessary * * * for the maintenance or support of the debtor or a dependent." There is not space in this book to deal with every possible case under section 1325(b)(2), but we will examine a few of the larger issues and one or two of the reported opinions.

First, what of the spouse's income? Must a debtor include his or her spouse's income in the budget in order to determine what income is disposable and what is not? Of course, if this is not done, there is great potential for hanky panky; on the other hand, if it is done, the debtor may be treated as having more money than the debtor in fact can claim from a recalcitrant spouse. In general, the courts have required that the spouse's income be included in the debtor's budget on the theory that such money will go into a common pot and will in fact be shared by the debtor—absent concrete proof of separation or the institution of divorce proceedings.[4]

Second, one might ask whether the section contemplates a change in lifestyle of a debtor under Chapter 13. Consider, for example, debtor Arthur and debtor Louise. Louise has been frugal yet she has had to file in Chapter 13. Arthur, on the other hand, has been a wastrel. He has lived in a large house, driven fancy cars, and had an extravagant lifestyle. If Arthur is to comply with section 1325(b), should we apply the same disposable income test to him as we would apply to Louise? Put another way, does 1325 insist that Arthur substantially modify his lifestyle by disposing of his house and cars and acquiring less expensive substitutes, or does the Code take him as it finds him?

There have been only a limited number of decisions interpreting section 1325(b)(2), but they are in agreement that the "reasonably necessary" language requires the spendthrift debtor to change his ways. It requires not merely that the debtor reduce his expenditures for consumable items, but also that he or she dispose of capital assets such as automobiles and houses.[5] In re Jones[6] is instructive on several grounds. There Judge Mahoney denied confirmation of a plan on the ground that the debtor had not given up her disposable income for three years. Quoting the Senate Report, Judge Maho-

---

2. Absent an objection the court need not pass on the disposable income test for a plan that otherwise satisfies § 1325(a). Education Assistance Corp. v. Zellner, 827 F.2d 1222 (8th Cir.1987); In re Fries, 68 B.R. 676 (Bankr. E.D.Pa. 1986); In re March, 83 B.R. 270 (Bankr. E.D. Pa 1988). In this respect the disposal income test is different from the other requirements found in § 1325. See In re Lattimore, 69 B.R. 622 (Bankr. E.D.Tenn. 1987).

3. See, e.g., Matter of Killough, 900 F.2d 61 (5th Cir.1990) (pay for projected overtime excluded).

4. Matter of Belt, 106 B.R. 553 (Bankr. N.D.Ind. 1989). See Matter of Strong, 84 B.R. 541 (Bankr. N.D.Ind. 1988); Matter of Saunders, 60 B.R. 187 (Bankr. N.D.Ohio 1986); In re Sellers, 33 B.R. 854 (Bankr. D. Colo. 1983); see also In re Kern, 40 B.R. 26 (Bankr. S.D.N.Y. 1984); In re Kull, 12 B.R. 654 (S.D.Ga.1981), aff'd sub nom. In re Kitchens, 702 F.2d 885 (11th Cir. 1983); cf. In re Bryant, 47 B.R. 21 (Bankr. W.D.N.C.1984); In re Lezer, 21 B.R. 783 (Bankr. N.D.N.Y.1982); In re Bagley, 4 B.R. 248 (Bankr. D. Ariz. 1980).

5. In re Jones, 55 B.R. 462 (Bankr. D.Minn. 1985); In re Kitson, 65 B.R. 615 (Bankr. E.D.N.C.1986); In re Rogers, 65 B.R. 1018 (Bankr. E.D.Mich.1986); In re Reyes, 106 B.R. 155 (Bankr. N.D.Ill. 1989).

6. 55 B.R. 462 (Bankr. D.Minn.1985).

ney concluded that "Chapter 13 * * * 'contemplates a substantial effort by the debtor to pay his debts' and furthermore [s]uch an effort may require some sacrifices by the debtor.'"[7] In defining the phrase "reasonably necessary" the court adopts a definition of an analogous phrase from *In re Taff*[8]:

> "The reasonably necessary standard requires that the Court take into account other income and exempt property of the debtor, present and anticipated * * * and that the appropriate amount to be set aside for the debtor ought to be sufficient to sustain basic needs not related to [the debtor's] former status in society or the lifestyle to which he is accustomed."[9]

Applying those rules to the case before her, Judge Mahoney concludes that the expenditure of $500 per month for private college tuition and $500 per month for secondary school expenses were excessive and would not be counted toward reasonably necessary living expenses. Although the creditor had objected only to those two items, Judge Mahoney found that other items violated the standard as well. She concluded that the $515 per month as food for a family of four was too high, and that a monthly house payment of $989 was well above "the amount necessary to provide adequate housing for a family of four."[10] In effect, the judge directed the debtor to sell her house or to rent or to buy a less expensive one.

In *In re Kitson*,[11] Judge Small came to a similar conclusion. There the husband and wife debtors had a combined income of approximately $100,000. Among other expenses was the cost of maintaining two cars and paying principal and interest on a $170,000 mortgage, secured by a $180,000 house. Obviously uncomfortable at having to make fundamental judgments about another person's expenditures, Judge Small nevertheless concluded that the plan could not be confirmed because of section 1325(b). The judge stated that he would be reluctant to approve any plan that did not pay 100 cents on the dollar within four years.

The decisions by Judges Mahoney and Small seem correct. It would be fruitless for us to attempt to canvas hundreds of different decisions that will be cascading down under section 1325(b). However distasteful the task, Congress has directed the courts to use the disposable income test as a way of policing debtors' predilections.

In conclusion, one should note the possible effect of section 1325(b)'s enactment on the good faith requirement in section 1325(a)(3). As we discuss more fully below, some courts have concluded that the disposable income test in section 1325(b) removes the need to determine whether the amount paid under the plan violates the good faith requirement in section 1325(a)(3).[12]

7. Id. at 685, quoting from S. Rep. No. 65, 98th Cong. 1st Sess. 22 (1983).

8. 10 B.R. 101 (Bankr. D.Conn.1981).

9. In re Jones, 55 B.R. 462, 466 (Bankr. D.Minn.1985), quoting Matter of Taff, 10 B.R. 101 (Bankr. D.Conn.1981).

10. Id. at 467.

11. 65 B.R. 615 (Bankr. E.D.N.C.1986).

12. In re Red, 60 B.R. 113 (Bankr. E.D.Tenn.1986); In re Ashton, 85 B.R. 766 (Bankr. S.D.Ohio 1988) (objection reserved until debtor makes more extensive disclosure of income and expenses); In re Greer, 60 B.R. 547 (Bankr. C.D.Cal.1986); see In re Reyes, 106 B.R. 155 (Bankr. N.D.Ill. 1989); contra Matter of Hale, 65 B.R. 893 (Bankr. S.D.Ga. 1986); In re Warren, 89 B.R. 87 (Bankr. 9th Cir. 1988) (Appellate panel remanded with

§ 9–14 Good Faith

The final term in section 1325 that might affect the amount that a debtor must pay in order to have a plan confirmed is section 1325(a)(3) which requires that "the plan has been proposed in good faith and not by any means forbidden by law."[1] In a world where one person's terrorism is another's patriotism, we are not likely to get agreement on the meaning of a term such as "good faith." Here the phrase carries all of the definitional baggage it has in Article 2 of the U.C.C. and in the common law. Because of the history of Chapter 13, the term good faith in section 1325(a)(3) bears an additional burden.

To understand why this is so, consider some of the history to the section. Under Chapter XIII of the Bankruptcy Act of 1898, almost all plans proposed full payment.[2] Occasionally a plan would pay less than 100 percent, but such plans invariably paid a very high percentage of the total indebtedness, surely more than 70 percent.[3] Perhaps because they knew that history too well, members of the Bankruptcy Commission and the persons who succeeded them in Congress sought ways to encourage debtors to use Chapter 13. Creditors welcomed such suggestions, for they contemplated full or high percentage payouts, in the new Chapter 13. With the concurrence of the creditors, the drafters made almost every debt, including many not dischargeable in Chapter 7, to be dischargeable in Chapter 13. They removed the possibility of a creditors' vote to turn down a Chapter 13 plan and they granted the debtor wide powers to modify secured credit. All of these rules were designed to entice the debtor to use Chapter 13 where, it was thought, all would be better off.

Promptly upon the passage of the Code in 1978, this description of Chapter 13 was shown to be a shimmering mirage; the brutal reality of Chapter 13 was something quite different. Debtors began to file plans under which they enjoyed all the benefits of Chapter 13—particularly the "super discharge" that freed one not only from most ordinary debts, but also from civil liability for assault and battery, for child molestation, and for other less morally depraved acts. But the debtors reaped these benefits of Chapter 13 in plans that proposed the payment of only a small percentage of their debts, in some cases zero percentage. These plans did not violate the best interest rule, for the debtors often had little or no nonexempt property.

Of course, these plans were in direct conflict with the creditors' vision of Chapter 13 and also with that of some of the judges. Yet there was no

---

instructions that the lower court must hold evidentiary hearing to determine that the good faith requirement had been met. The court assumed that the best efforts test had been met under § 1325(b), but concluded nevertheless that there must be evidence to show good faith.).

§ 9–14

1. 11 U.S.C.A. § 1325(a)(3).

2. See D. Stanley & M. Girth, Bankruptcy: Problem, Process, Reform 94 (1971), where only one percent of the chapter XIII cases surveyed by the authors proposed less than full payment. See also Epstein, Chapter 13: Its Operation, Its Statutory Requirements as to Payments and to Classification of Unsecured Claims, and Its Advantages, 20 Washburn L.J. 1, 8 (1980).

3. See H.R. Rep. No. 595 at 123, reprinted in 1978 U.S. Code Cong. & Admin. News 5963, 6084 ("Under present law, the consent requirement often prevents a debtor from making a legitimate offer of less than full payment, for fear that the offer will not obtain the requisite consents. Instead, the debtor unable to pay his debts in full within a reasonable period will opt for liquidation.").

specific provision of Chapter 13 that made the pre-Code practice of full or large payment a requirement in Chapter 13. To argue that such minimal payment plans were not permissible under Chapter 13, creditors claimed that they were not proposed in "good faith" under section 1325(a)(3). Initially the creditors had some success,[4] but ultimately nearly all courts agreed that the mere fact that the debtor made only a small percentage (or no payment at all) to his general creditors was not itself a lack of good faith.[5] Most of the courts were unwilling to say that the percentage of payment was irrelevant; they held only that it alone was not enough to show bad faith. Usually courts held that the level of payment could be considered among other factors in determining whether a plan was proposed in good faith.

Even this limited use of the level of payments as an element in the good faith test was called into question by the 1984 Congressional amendments to section 1325. As part of that act Congress added section 1325(b), the "disposable income test". Recall that it requires the debtor to pay all of his or her disposable income over a three-year period if there is any complaint about the proposed plan by an unsecured creditor who is not to be fully paid. Since 1984, some courts have held that section 1325(b) is the only standard by which to test the percentage of payment.[6] Other courts have found that the percentage of payment remains a factor in determining whether the plan has been proposed in good faith even after the 1984 amendments.[7]

The upshot of this history is that judges now have the maddening job of deciding what debtors are to enjoy the Chapter 13 benefits and what debtors are to be excluded. Congress' enactment of the disposable income test in section 1325(b) at the behest of the consumer creditors in 1984 has not resolved the issue. Those who read the 1984 act as a Congressional endorsement of the proposition that the amount of payment is not relevant to the good faith question probably read too much into the enactment of 1325(b). The conundrum that faces the court who is honestly attempting to carry out congressional wishes is well demonstrated by the following quotation from the Ninth Circuit Bankruptcy Appellate Panel in *In re Warren*.[8] There the debtor sought to escape an embezzlement liability of $40,595.88 by a 36 month plan with a 2 percent payout. In reversing the lower court's confirmation of the plan, the Appellate Panel made the following observations:

> The super discharge of Chapter 13 was provided by Congress as an incentive for the debtor to commit to a repayment plan under Chapter 13, as an alternative to providing creditors nothing under Chapter 7. Given a proper case, the court need not, and should not, neutralize that

---

4. See In re Iacovoni, 2 B.R. 256 (Bankr. D. Utah 1980); In re Cole, 3 B.R. 346 (Bankr. S.D.W.Va.1980); Matter of Cook, 3 B.R. 480 (Bankr. S.D.W.Va.1980); In re Seman, 4 B.R. 568 (Bankr. S.D.N.Y. 1980); In re Hobday, 4 B.R. 417 (Bankr. N.D.Ohio 1980).

5. In re Kitchens, 702 F.2d 885 (11th Cir. 1983); In re Estus, 695 F.2d 311 (8th Cir.1982); Deans v. O'Donnell, 692 F.2d 968 (4th Cir. 1982); Barnes v. Whelan, 689 F.2d 193 (D.C. Cir. 1982); In re Goeb, 675 F.2d 1386 (9th Cir.1982); In re Rimgale, 669 F.2d 426 (7th Cir.1982); Matter of Belt, 106 B.R. 553 (Bankr. N.D.Ind. 1989).

6. In re Greer, 60 B.R. 547 (Bankr. C.D.Cal. 1986); In re Red, 60 B.R. 113 (Bankr. E.D.Tenn.1986); cf. Education Assistance Corp. v. Zellner, 827 F.2d 1222 (8th Cir.1987).

7. Matter of Hale, 65 B.R. 893 (Bankr. S.D.Ga.1986); In re Warren, 89 B.R. 87 (Bankr. 9th Cir. 1988); cf. In re Kitson, 65 B.R. 615 (Bankr. E.D.N.C.1986).

8. 89 B.R. 87 (Bankr. 9th Cir.1988).

incentive by confirming Chapter 13 plans that are in essence veiled Chapter 7 cases.

Logic requires there be an articulated standard distinguishing entitlement to dischargeability under Chapter 13 vis-à-vis Chapter 7. To put it otherwise, there must be criteria which preclude by-pass of nondischargeability under Chapter 7 simply by detouring or converting to Chapter 13. Where there is an absence of any significant factual element distinguishing the circumstances of a Chapter 13 petition, the debtor should not be permitted to nullify major provisions of 11 U.S.C. § 523 merely by paying an insignificant portion of the nondischargeable debt. Congress in Chapter 7 does not allow "best effort" to discharge certain debts. Neither should best effort alone discharge them in Chapter 13. Good faith requires more.

We hold that the good faith requirement under 11 U.S.C. § 1325(a)(3) is separate and distinct from the best effort requirement of 11 U.S.C. § 1325(b)(1)(B). The court should conduct more than a ministerial review related to payments in order that it may make an informed and independent judgment concerning whether a plan was proposed in good faith. Although the trial court's finding of good faith in the context of a Chapter 13 plan normally should not be overturned, the procedural history of this case indicates that no actual inquiry into the totality of the circumstances was made by the court below. When factors of minimal repayments and a non-dischargeable debt are present, particular scrutiny by the court is required and the debtor has the burden of producing more than simply evidence of best effort.[9]

We are all over the boards on this issue. One of us is persuaded by the bankruptcy appellate panel's position; another believes that the court is wrong and that the best efforts rule appropriated the field. The first believes that the percentage payment is not merely one of the factors to be considered in measuring the good faith of a plan, but the most important one. The third of us is in the middle. He believes that percentage payment counts in measuring good faith but only marginally, its significance having been diluted for purposes of (a)(3) by the best-efforts rule of (b)(1)(B).

Under the rules that are now applied by almost all of the appellate courts, good faith is to be measured by a long list of factors in addition to the percentage of payment. Like all attempts to find good faith, these make a pretty watery gruel.

The Court of Appeals for the Eighth Circuit in *In re Estus*[10] stated a list of eleven factors that have been widely quoted by other courts:

(1) the amount of the proposed payments and the amount of the debtor's surplus;

(2) the debtor's employment history, ability to earn and likelihood of future increases in income;

(3) the probable or expected duration of the plan;

---

9. Id. at 95.

10. 695 F.2d 311 (8th Cir.1982).

(4) the accuracy of the plan's statements of the debts, expenses and percentage repayment of unsecured debt and whether any inaccuracies are an attempt to mislead the court;

(5) the extent of preferential treatment between classes of creditors;

(6) the extent to which secured claims are modified;

(7) the type of debt sought to be discharged and whether any such debt is non-dischargeable in Chapter 7;

(8) the existence of special circumstances such as inordinate medical expenses;

(9) the frequency with which the debtor has sought relief under the Bankruptcy Reform Act;

(10) the motivation and sincerity of the debtor in seeking Chapter 13 relief; and

(11) the burden which the plan's administration would place upon the trustee.[11]

Perhaps because we have become jaded and cynical from having read too many cases about good faith, we are somewhat suspicious about the utility of such lists. At least to vary the style, let us consider some of these factors from the rear. Let us focus on which of the debtor's acts might be regarded as acts of "bad faith." Conceivably this perspective will give us greater insight.

The first indicia of bad faith is a small payment. Where the payments are small or nonexistent, courts such as *Warren* take the position which we endorse, namely, that these small payments are themselves an indicia of bad faith. A central part of Chapter 13 is a significant payment to creditors.[12]

A short plan shows bad faith. If the term is under three years, the plan may fail the disposable income test in section 1325(b) and so never present a good faith issue. Plans making a small payment over only three years are

---

11. Id. at 317.

12. See In re Lattimore, 69 B.R. 622 (Bankr. E.D.Tenn.1987) quoting H.R. Rep. No. 595, 95th Cong. 1st Sess. 118, reprinted in 1978 U.S. Code Cong. & Admin. News 5787, 5963, 6079:

> The purpose of chapter 13 is to enable an individual, under court supervision and protection, to develop and perform under a plan for the repayment of his debts over an extended period. In some cases, the plan will call for full repayment. In others, it may offer creditors settlement. During the repayment period, creditors may not harass the debtor or seek to collect their debts. They must receive payments only under the plan. This protection relieves the debtor from indirect and direct pressures from creditors, and enables him to support himself and his dependents while repaying his creditors at the same time.

> The benefit to the debtor of developing a plan of repayment under chapter 13, rather than opting for liquidation under chapter 7, is that it permits the debtor to protect his assets. In a liquidation case, the debtor must surrender his nonexempt assets for liquidation and sale by the trustee. Under chapter 13, the debtor may retain his property by agreeing to repay his creditors. Chapter 13 also protects a debtor's credit standing far better than a straight bankruptcy, because he is viewed by the credit industry as a better risk. In addition, it satisfies many debtors' desire to avoid the stigma attached to straight bankruptcy and to retain the pride attendant on being able to meet one's obligations. The benefit to creditors is self-evident: their losses will be significantly less than if their debtors opt for straight bankruptcy.

69 B.R. at 625.

sometimes suspect.¹³ On the other hand, most courts take the position that since Congress chose the three-year period and reaffirmed it in section 1325(b), one should not draw any inference of bad faith solely because a plan lasts only three years.¹⁴ We, however, see no reason why a debtor should not be asked to pay for five years if that is necessary to make a substantial payment, or why, in a proper case, a refusal to do so should not be regarded as bad faith.

The debtor's dishonesty in dealing with the bankruptcy court is the darkest form of bad faith.¹⁵ The debtor may get away with lying to a creditor to get a loan, but the risks and costs are much higher and more certain of lying to creditors and the court on one's bankruptcy filing. To do so is bright indicia of bad faith.

Treating some creditors substantially worse than others may be an indicia of bad faith. If, for example, the debtor pays 100 cents on the dollar to all creditors but one and pays that creditor 2 cents on the dollar, some courts will find that to be bad faith.

Above we have discussed the debtor's right to discriminate between creditors. Assuming the law permits such discrimination—at least where it is "fair"—why then should that be an indicia of bad faith? Perhaps there is an unspoken thought here that the plan should not show the debtor to be vindictive, but should show him to deal with all of his children with an even hand.

The same notion may stand behind the standard that says it is evidence of bad faith when one grossly modifies the rights of the secured creditors. But why? If, in fact, the debtor has done no more than is permitted under 506 and the other provisions of the Bankruptcy Code, that should not offend.

Has the debtor filed repeated bankruptcies? If it appears that the debtor has repeatedly filed and dismissed when the stay was about to be lifted, this will be particularly damning.¹⁶ Everyone would agree that such

---

13. In re Keiser, 35 B.R. 496 (Bankr. D.Del. 1983) (plan paying less than 6.5% of unsecured debt denied confirmation, where debtor's budget showed a surplus of $1,115.35, and debtor did not seek to extend plan to five years); see also In re Williams, 42 B.R. 474 (Bankr. E.D. Ark.1984); In re Hale, 65 B.R. 893 (Bankr. S.D.Ga.1986); In re Rogers, 65 B.R. 1018 (Bankr. E.D.Mich.1986). Historically three year plans were apparently suspect because they did not comply with the disposable income test. For cases where courts refused to confirm plans providing for low payments, because the debtor's budget showed that higher payments could be made, see In re Sellers, 33 B.R. 854 (Bankr. D. Colo. 1983); In re Brown, 29 B.R. 360 (Bankr. N.D.Ohio 1983); or because they proposed zero or minimal payments to unsecured creditors, see In re Burrell, 2 B.R. 650 (Bankr. N.D.Cal.1980); In re Iacovoni, 2 B.R. 256 (Bankr. D. Utah 1980).

Courts now generally recognize that a three year plan is the rule and that confirmation will not be denied for bad faith solely on this ground or solely because the plan proposes zero or minimal payments. See In re Greer, 60 B.R. 547 (Bankr. C.D.Cal.1986); Flygare v. Boulden, 709 F.2d 1344 (10th Cir.1983); In re Hines, 723 F.2d 333 (3d Cir.1983); In re Kitchens, 702 F.2d 885 (11th Cir.1983); Deans v. O'Donnell, 692 F.2d 968 (4th Cir.1982); In re Estus, 695 F.2d 311 (8th Cir.1982); In re Goeb, 675 F.2d 1386 (9th Cir.1982); In re Rimgale, 669 F.2d 426 (7th Cir.1982); Barnes v. Whelan, 689 F.2d 193 (D.C. Cir. 1982).

14. In re Carver, 110 B.R. 305 (Bankr. S.D.Ohio 1990); Matter of Belt, 106 B.R. 553 (Bankr. N.D.Ind. 1989) (debtor need not propose a 60 month plan, but length of plan is relevant to good faith—relates to state of mind and intentions).

15. See In re Estus, 695 F.2d 311 (8th Cir. 1982).

16. In re Pappalardo, 109 B.R. 622 (Bankr. S.D.N.Y. 1990) (successive Chapter 13 filings alone are not enough to establish bad faith manipulation of Bankruptcy Code); Matter of Gates, 42 B.R. 4 (Bankr. N.D.Ga.1983); see In re Felts, 60 B.R. 736 (Bankr. W.D.Ky.1986);

action is bad faith. On the other hand, the mere filing in Chapter 7 followed by a filing in 13 is a right given the debtor by the Congress. One suspects the courts of making an unspoken judgment that people who act in good faith use bankruptcy less often than the law permits.[17]

Several courts correctly examine pre-bankruptcy behavior to find evidence of bad faith.[18] If, for example, the court concludes the debtor incurred one of the principal debts without any intention to repay, but with the concurrent intention to go into bankruptcy,[19] that act alone is regarded as an element of bad faith. Other courts find that prepetition activity of that kind is not relevant.[20]

An attempt to escape a debt in Chapter 13 that is not dischargeable in Chapter 7 is evidence of bad faith.[21] Since Congress has used the very device of the "superdischarge" to beckon debtors into Chapter 13, it is not clear to us why acceptance of Congress' offer should be bad faith.

Nevertheless it is quite clear that the probability of denial of a confirmation of a Chapter 13 plan is directly proportional to the heinousness of the act from which the non-dischargeable debt arose. In *Warren* the court dealt

but see Matter of Metz, 820 F.2d 1495 (9th Cir. 1987); In re Johnson, 708 F.2d 865 (2d Cir. 1983).

For a discussion on abusive dismissals and refilings see § 9–13 supra, note 32 and accompanying text.

17. Neufeld v. Freeman, 794 F.2d 149 (4th Cir.1986), on remand, 66 B.R. 610 (Bankr. W.D.Va.1986); In re Chinichian, 784 F.2d 1440 (9th Cir.1986); In re Johnson, 708 F.2d 865 (2d Cir.1983); cf. In re Gathright, 67 B.R. 384 (Bankr. E.D.Pa. 1986), appeal dism'd, 71 B.R. 343 (E.D.Pa.1987).

18. See, e.g., Memphis Bank & Trust Co. v. Whitman, 692 F.2d 427 (6th Cir.1982); In re Caldwell, 895 F.2d 1123 (6th Cir.1990); In re LeMaire, 898 F.2d 1346 (8th Cir.1990); but see In re Rasmussen, 888 F.2d 703 (10th Cir.1989).

19. In re Chase, 43 B.R. 739 (D.Md.1984); Memphis Bank & Trust Co. v. Whitman, 692 F.2d 427 (6th Cir.1982); Neufeld v. Freeman, 794 F.2d 149 (4th Cir.1986), on remand, 66 B.R. 610 (Bankr.W.D.Va.1986); In re Easley, 72 B.R. 948 (Bankr. M.D.Tenn.1987); see also In re Nittler, 67 B.R. 217 (D.Kan.1986).

20. In re Trigwell, 67 B.R. 808 (Bankr. C.D. Cal.1986); see In re Okoreeh–Baah, 836 F.2d 1030 (6th Cir.1988) (court should not focus solely on pre-plan conduct).

21. Discharge of an obligation that would not be dischargeable in Chapter 7, however, is not alone enough to support a finding of bad faith under § 1325. Matter of Belt, 106 B.R. 553 (Bankr. N.D.Ind. 1989); In re Stewart, 109 B.R. 998 (D.Kan.1990) (including student loan obligations not dischargeable in a Chapter 7 does not per se bar confirmation, but such factor is entitled to great weight in determining whether debtor's plan is proposed in good faith); In re Lincoln, 30 B.R. 905 (Bankr. D. Colo. 1983); In re Jonson, 17 B.R. 78 (Bankr. S.D.Ind.1981); In re Terry, 9 B.R. 314 (Bankr. D. Colo. 1981); but see In re Rasmussen, 888 F.2d 703 (10th Cir. 1989); In re Davidson, 72 B.R. 384 (Bankr. D.Colo.1987) (it is a lack of good faith to fail to pay back child support in full where that claim would not be dischargeable either in Chapter 7 or Chapter 13).

For cases where creditors on student loans have argued bad faith and have failed, see In re Rowe, 17 B.R. 870 (Bankr. E.D.Va.1982) (32 percent dividend to unsecured creditors where 80 percent of the unsecured debt was a student loan); Matter of Lambert, 10 B.R. 223 (Bankr. E.D.N.Y.1981) (26 percent dividend and 65 percent of the unsecured debt consisted of student loan obligations); In re Vensel, 39 B.R. 866 (Bankr. E.D.Va.1984) (53 percent of debt student loans, 11 percent dividends); In re Gathright, 67 B.R. 384 (Bankr. E.D.Pa. 1986), appeal dism'd, 71 B.R. 343 (E.D.Pa.1987) (that student loan is not dischargeable in a Chapter 7 is irrelevant in determining good faith under § 1325). For other cases dealing with student loans and allowing their discharge in Chapter 13, see Matter of Bear, 789 F.2d 577 (7th Cir. 1986); In re Rushton, 58 B.R. 36 (Bankr. M.D.Ala.1986); In re McAloon, 44 B.R. 831 (Bankr. E.D.Va.1984); In re Powell, 29 B.R. 346 (Bankr. D.Colo.1983). For cases rejecting confirmation based in part upon debtor's attempt to avoid student loans, see In re Vance, 49 B.R. 973 (Bankr. D.Minn. 1985); In re Dalby, 38 B.R. 107 (Bankr. D. Utah 1984).

In cases commencing after the 1990 amendments, the bad faith argument regarding student loans will not arise. Those amendments prevent discharge in Chapter 13 of student loans that are not dischargeable under Chapter 7.

§ 9–15   INDIVIDUAL REORGANIZATION   707

with an embezzling car salesman.[22] Avoiding parking tickets in bankruptcy is a no-no.[23] Even more reprehensible, is one who seeks to avoid liability for assault and battery after his criminal conviction and with no display of remorse.[24]

The most obvious case of bad faith involves a debtor who was convicted of a sexual assault on a neighbor girl and on his own daughter. After his conviction, he sought to avoid a $25,000 civil liability to the neighbor girl. This case was so repugnant to the court that it found the debtor to be in bad faith despite his proposal to pay a considerable sum ($9,750 over five years).[25]

In addition to the routine factors on bad faith, the court sometimes includes standards that are wholly opaque. For example, the court in *In re Estus* [26] lists "the motivation and sincerity of the debtor in seeking Chapter 13 relief." We are doubtful that a court can make a reliable judgment about the debtor's motivation and sincerity. Either this is merely a reiteration of other standards (e.g., is this person contrite about the crime he committed) or it suggests some test that we do not understand. Presumably the motivation of a debtor who goes into Chapter 13 is to avoid payment of certain of his debts. If that is offensive, so be it, but it is nevertheless an act permitted by the law. We doubt Congress intended to allow the court to deny confirmation because the debtor has his fingers crossed behind his back. The same point, of course, could be made about many of the *Estus* factors set out above.

The real difficulty arises from the history that we described above. By apparently proceeding on the assumption of large payments as a quid pro quo for the superdischarge and by declining to establish clear standards in the 1984 amendments, Congress has left the courts in doubt about the Congressional will. Some, like the Bankruptcy Appellate Panel in the Ninth Circuit, say Congress must have intended some difference between the low payout liquidation under which certain debts are not discharged in Chapter 7 and the same transaction in Chapter 13 where those debts are discharged. It is Congress' failure to state its own mind clearly that has left the courts fumbling through these various factors and apparently contradicting what Congress directed while attempting to do what Congress intended.[27]

§ 9–15 Modification of the Rights of Creditors—Introduction

Section 1322(b)(2) provides that the plan may "modify the rights of holders of secured claims, other than a claim secured only by a security

---

22. In re Warren, 89 B.R. 87 (Bankr. 9th Cir.1988).

23. In re Meltzer, 11 B.R. 624 (Bankr. E.D.N.Y.1981).

24. In re Kourtakis, 75 B.R. 183 (Bankr. E.D.Mich.1987).

25. In re Chase, 43 B.R. 739 (D.Md.1984).

26. 695 F.2d 311 (8th Cir.1982).

27. We have focused on the items that constitute bad faith. At least one of the factors can only constitute good faith. This is the "existence of special circumstances such as inordinate medical expenses." In re Estus, 695 F.2d 311, 317 (8th Cir.1982). Presumably the norm in Chapter 13 is a debt voluntarily, but perhaps unwisely incurred by the debtor. Where the liability is focused on the debtor, as by the urgent need for medical treatment, and an honest debtor is tipped over the edge, the court suggests that that should be evidence of good faith and should explain or overcome contrary elements such as small payments.

interest in real property that is the debtor's principal residence * * *."[1] Subsection (b)(3) authorizes the plan to "provide for the curing or waiving of default."[2] Read alone these sections seem to authorize any modification that appeals to the whim of the debtor. But as we have already discussed,[3] the creditor's first line of protection against such an interpretation is the best interest rule in section 1325(a)(5). A non-accepting secured creditor must either (1) receive its collateral or (2) retain its lien and be provided payments in the plan with a value equal to the "allowed amount of such [the creditor's] claim."

To understand the limitations that Chapter 13 puts upon the power of the debtor to modify a secured creditor's rights, compare the right of a debtor in possession (DIP) in Chapter 11. First, in Chapter 11 the DIP will divide a loan into two claims, a secured claim equal to the value of the collateral and an unsecured claim. The Chapter 11 plan may pay only a few cents on the dollar, but it will pay 100 cents on the secured portion. As part of the Chapter 11 plan, the debtor in possession will add interest to the stream of payments, but the rate used will not necessarily be the same as the rate in the loan contract. The rate must be adequate to give the stream of payments a present value equal to the value of the collateral.

Also, in Chapter 11 the debtor in possession will sometimes propose the sale of the asset free of security or the substitution of one piece of collateral for another. It would be common for a debtor in possession to change the term of the loan and the amount of each installment. Thus a loan payable in 12 annual payments might be changed to provide for payments over 14 or 15 years.

Finally, a debtor in possession in a Chapter 11 may choose to "deaccelerate" a loan on which there has been a default and acceleration of the debt. Section 1124(2) says that a creditor holding an accelerated claim is not impaired (and is therefore deemed to have accepted the plan) if debtor cures any default and reinstates the former maturity. Assume, for example, that a debtor had missed two payments on a $1,000,000 note payable in $100,000 installments. Even if the debt had been accelerated (so that $1,000,000 was due in one lump sum), section 1124 would permit the debtor to pay the missed payments within a reasonable period of time (cure) to undo the acceleration and continue to pay $100,000 per installment over the term of the loan. Section 1124 invites such a transaction.

Turn now to Chapter 13. For at least three reasons the debtor's power to modify a secured creditor's rights in Chapter 13 is more restricted than would be true under Chapter 11. The most obvious limitation arises from the "other than" clause in section 1322(b)(2). That clause excludes modification of mortgages on the debtor's principal residence. Because a Chapter 13 debtor's principal secured loan is likely to be one secured by his home, that exclusion is significant. Second, section 1322(c) contemplates three-year plans as the norm and prohibits any plans that are longer than five years. Because a plan cannot extend beyond five years, courts have found that the

§ 9–15

1. 11 U.S.C.A. § 1322(b)(2).
2. Id. § 1322(b)(3).
3. See § 9–9 supra.

Chapter 13 debtor has no power to modify the rights of a secured creditor whose debt is payable over a term longer than five years. A final potential restriction that has been largely avoided by the courts' interpretation of Chapter 13 arises from the absence from Chapter 13 of anything quite comparable to the rule in 1124 (that cure and deacceleration are not a modification or impairment).

To summarize, the apparently large power in Chapter 13 to modify the rights of secured creditors is in fact smaller than first appears. Here, as in Chapters 11 and 12, the principal limitation upon the power to modify the rights is the best interest test—the rule that the creditor must receive no less than it would have received on liquidation. In addition, home mortgagees and certain other creditors holding long term liabilities are protected by the exclusion for mortgages on principal residences and by the fact that Chapter 13 plans can neither have terms longer than five years nor provide for the discharge of debts due beyond the plan's term.

§ 9–16 Modification of the Rights of Creditors—Modification of Secured and Unsecured Claims and the Long Term Limitation

Section 1322(b)(2) specifically authorizes the debtor to "modify" the rights of secured creditors. Section 1322(b)(1) implicitly authorizes the same with respect to the rights of unsecured creditors. The standard modification of an unsecured claim is to write it down to an amount no lower than an amount that would be paid in a Chapter 7 and then to pay that value (plus interest) over the life of the plan.

The typical modification of a secured loan whose final payment date is within the plan period can be illustrated with an automobile loan. Assume that a car worth $10,000 secures a loan with a face value of $13,000. Under section 506 the debtor can write the loan down to the value of the car, $10,000, and treat the remaining $3,000 as an unsecured debt.

The unsecured portion must be paid at the same level that would be required on liquidation under the best interest test and thus may receive only a few cents on the dollar. The secured portion, on the other hand, must receive similar treatment, which in this case would be 100 cents on the dollar. In the typical case the debtor could pay the $10,000 in monthly installments over a three to five-year period together with an appropriate interest rate. In general the creditor has no control over this question; its only recourse is to complain to the court that the car is worth more than $10,000 or that the interest rate is too low. In effect, section 1322(b)(2) allows the debtor to force the creditor to make a five-year loan against the automobile whether the creditor likes it or not.

The two important exceptions to the rules on modification of claims are not particularly novel or complicated. The two exceptions have to do with loans against the debtor's principal residence, a topic dealt with in the next subsection, and with debt amortized for a period longer than the period of the plan.

As we have indicated above, at least two provisions suggest that modification of long term loans are beyond the power of the Chapter 13 debtor. First, section 1322(c) prohibits plans for longer than five years. Second, section 1328(a)(1) states that there is no discharge for loans "provided for under 1322(b)(5)."

The most obvious way to interpret the phrase loans "provided for under section 1322(b)(5)"[1] is as a reference to all loans (whether or not they are to be cured) "on which the last payment is due after the date on which the final payment under the plan is due * * *."[2]

Relying principally on section 1322(c), several courts have held the debtor has no right to modify a debt whose last payment is due after the end of its proposed plan.[3] In *Matter of Foster*,[4] the debtor proposed to cramdown a long-term mortgage. The mortgage debt was $141,623; the value of the mortgaged land was $104,650. The life of the mortgage went well beyond the five years and the debtor sought to amortize the $104,650 over the original term of the mortgage. He proposed to pay off a small percentage of the remaining $37,000 of unsecured debt within the plan and to discharge the rest. The court held that it could not approve such a plan because the "plan" would have a term longer than five years. As a consequence of this conclusion shared by other courts who have faced the question, debtors such as the Fosters, who wish to modify long-term liabilities must file in Chapters 11 or 12.

This conclusion is likely to have little significance for Chapter 13 debtors in inflationary times. Most Chapter 13 debtors' liability will be under five years and thus subject to modification despite section 1322(c). The only common exception to that rule is the debtor's home mortgage. When the value of the home exceeds the amount of the debt, most debtors are satisfied to cure the default under section 1322(b)(5), by "deaccelerating" the loan and continuing to make payments under the reinstated mortgage.

In a period of deflation of real estate values, the debtor's interest might be quite different. When the value of the property has declined below the principal of the debt, the debtor will wish to do what was proposed in *Foster*, to divide the debt into secured and unsecured portions and pay off the latter in cents on the dollar. Under the three cases cited above, the debtor will not be able to do that in Chapter 13. Moreover, if the collateral was the debtor's principal residence, the debtor might be prevented from doing it by section 1322(b)(2) even if courts ultimately come to a different conclusion about the meaning of section 1322(c).

§ 9–16

1. Section 1322(b) provides:

    Subject to subsections (a) and (c) of this section, the plan may—

    * * *

    (5) notwithstanding paragraph (2) of this subsection, provide for the curing of any default within a reasonable time and maintenance of payments while the case is pending on any unsecured claim or secured claim on which the last payment is due after the date on which the final payment under the plan is due.

    11 U.S.C.A. § 1322(b)(5).

2. The other way to read the reference of section 1328 is to loans where the last payment is due after the plan and the loan is to be cured.

3. In re Ramirez, 62 B.R. 668 (Bankr. S.D.Cal.1986); Matter of Foster, 61 B.R. 492 (Bankr. N.D.Ind. 1986); In re Hildebran, 54 B.R. 585 (Bankr. D. Ore. 1985).

4. 61 B.R. 492 (Bankr. N.D.Ind. 1986).

For the time being the law seems clear.[5] If a debt's last installment is due after the final payment under the plan, the debtor can do no more than to cure it and reinstate the debt. If the debtor wishes to write down a long-term secured liability and pay off the unsecured portion in pennies on the dollar, the debtor must file in Chapters 11 or 12.

§ 9–17 Modification of the Rights of Creditors—Deacceleration and Cure, Section 1322(b)(5)

One of the important reasons that debtors come to Chapter 13 is to avoid the loss of their homes in a threatened foreclosure of a long term mortgage. Almost always these debtors are in arrears on their payments and they wish to undo the acceleration of the debt and reinstate the monthly amortization. Section 1322 specifically provides for the curing of defaults (section 1322(b)(3)) and section 1322(b)(5) seems specifically to contemplate our debtor in default on the mortgage:

> notwithstanding paragraph (2) of this subsection, [the plan may] provide for the curing of any default within a reasonable time and maintenance of payments while the case is pending on any unsecured claim or secured claim on which the last payment is due after the date on which the final payment under the plan is due.[1]

The scenario, repeated now in thousands of cases, is for the debtor to propose to reestablish the mortgage and to continue the monthly payments outside of the plan for the life of the mortgage in accordance with the mortgage contract. Typically the debtor proposes to pay the arrearages within the Chapter 13 plan in three to five years.

Mortgagees frequently oppose the confirmation of such plans. A mortgagee might be opposed to such a plan for several reasons. First, the mortgage might have been originally written when interest rates were low and reinstatement of the mortgage forces the mortgagee to continue to lend the money over the life of the mortgage at a rate that is now less than the market rate. Second, the debtor may owe substantial arrearages and may propose their payment in the plan without interest. (This means that the present value of the cure payments will be less than the value of a cash cure.) Third, the mortgagee, having lost patience with the debtor, may have concluded that the debtor is incapable of paying the debt, in or out of bankruptcy. Such a creditor would view the bankruptcy as merely an extension of an intolerable situation, that in the creditor's view will inevitably result in default and foreclosure.

Mortgagees who oppose cure and deacceleration plans have concentrated on three statutory arguments. Initially they argued that the prohibition on

---

5. Perhaps one should not be too sanguine about the clarity of the law. In several recent cases courts have allowed the division of home mortgage liabilities into secured and unsecured portions and have permitted the Chapter 13 plans to modify the unsecured portions. Several of the courts that have done this have not specified that the unsecured portion has an amortization period of less than five years. If, in fact, these courts are permitting modification of debts calling for payments longer than five years, they are disregarding the section 1322(c) limitation. See, e.g., In re Hougland, 886 F.2d 1182 (9th Cir.1989); Wilson v. Commonwealth Mortgage, 895 F.2d 123 (3d Cir.1990).

§ 9–17

1. 11 U.S.C.A. § 1322(b)(5).

the modification of mortgages on the debtor's principal residence under section 1322(b)(2) was violated by the proposal to deaccelerate the mortgage and pay the arrearages within the plan. Secondly, mortgagees argued that when a foreclosure judgment occurred under state law, the mortgage debt was "merged" into the judgment and no debt existed that would qualify for deacceleration under section 1322(b)(5), for section 1322(b)(5) requires a debt on which the last payment was due after the end of the plan. Since the judgment and debt are now merged and all are currently due, there is no payment due after the plan and thus (b)(5) does not apply—so the argument goes.

The final argument deals with the debtor's obligation to pay interest during the plan on the arrearages (cure). Mortgagees have argued that failure to pay interest on that amount is a violation of section 1325(b)(5)'s best interest rule. The first of these creditor arguments has been rejected universally. The second has been rejected for the most part, and the third has produced an almost even division in the courts.

First, is the common deacceleration and cure proposal a violation of section 1322(b)(2)? Is it an impermissible modification of a mortgagee's rights on a debt secured solely by the debtor's principal residence? At least to the simple-minded, like us, the answer to that is clearly no; the answer is found in section 1322(b)(5) which begins with the phrase "notwithstanding paragraph (2) of this subsection." For us that is enough. Congress has told us that despite the limiting language of subsection (2), the acceleration may be undone and the payments resumed according to the original amortization schedule. This is not a modification. All Courts of Appeals that have spoken on the issue agree;[2] we believe the issue has been put to rest.

The second argument (that the debt has been merged in the judgment, thus no payments are due after the plan and, therefore, (b)(5) is not met) has been accepted by some courts.[3] We regard this as a technical and incorrect reading of section 1322(b)(5). At some point in the foreclosure process, presumably the right to cure has ended, but we doubt Congress intended to hold out hope of deacceleration in the form of (b)(5) only to have it withdrawn because the acceleration and a prompt default judgment merged the debt into the judgment.

In our view the best answer to this question is to be found in *In re Glenn*.[4] That court concluded that the debtor retained a right to undo an acceleration and to cure until the time of the foreclosure sale. In the court's view this allowed the debtor a reasonable time to arrange for alternative financing, but it also respected the rights of parties who might buy at the

---

2. In re Taddeo, 685 F.2d 24 (2d Cir.1982); In re Glenn, 760 F.2d 1428 (6th Cir.1985), cert. denied, 474 U.S. 849, 106 S.Ct. 144, 88 L.Ed.2d 119 (1985); Grubbs v. Houston First American Savings Ass'n, 730 F.2d 236 (5th Cir.1984) (en banc); Matter of Clark, 738 F.2d 869 (7th Cir.1984); contra, Matter of Wilson, 11 B.R. 986 (Bankr. S.D.N.Y. 1981); Matter of Lapaglia, 8 B.R. 937 (Bankr. E.D.N.Y.1981); In re Allen, 17 B.R. 119 (Bankr. N.D.Ohio 1981) (in light of the subsequent decisions in the Second and Sixth Circuits the contra cases are probably overruled).

3. See Percy Wilson Mortgage & Finance Corp. v. McCurdy, 21 B.R. 535 (Bankr. S.D.Ohio 1982); In re Maiorino, 15 B.R. 254 (Bankr. D. Conn. 1981); In re Pearson, 10 B.R. 189 (Bankr. E.D.N.Y.1981); In re Canady, 9 B.R. 428 (Bankr. D. Conn. 1981).

4. 760 F.2d 1428 (6th Cir.1985), cert. denied, 474 U.S. 849, 106 S.Ct. 144, 88 L.Ed.2d 119 (1985); see also In re Kohler, 107 B.R. 167 (Bankr. S.D.Ill.1989) (can cure until sale confirmed).

foreclosure sale. In the court's view, to allow for a shorter cutoff would be to render (b)(5) meaningless. Several lower courts[5] have now adopted *In re Glenn* and we think it the right outcome. An added virtue of that interpretation is that it does not depend on state law and therefore may produce consistency across state lines even in the face of differing state mortgage foreclosure rules.

In conclusion, we believe courts should reject the argument that a mere judgment of foreclosure extinguishes the mortgage debt and thus rules out its cure and reinstatement under (b)(5). On the other hand, the time of foreclosure sale is an appropriate time to regard the debtor's interest as so attenuated that there is nothing left to be cured.[6]

The third question (whether the debtor need pay interest on the cured arrearage within the plan) has divided the courts almost evenly. Two Courts of Appeals have concluded that there is no need to pay interest unless the mortgage contract so provides.[7] One court, correctly in our view, has held that interest is due regardless of the contract's provisions.[8] The argument for not paying interest is that the deacceleration and payment within the plan is not a modification of the liability and is not the "treatment of the claim" as a secured claim within the bankruptcy proceeding, but it is something else, apparently simply the reinstatement of the old obligation.

It is clear, of course, that a mortgagee whose mortgage is deaccelerated has no right to the present value of the stream of payments *under* that mortgage (as when the current market rates are higher than the contract rate). Clearly, Congress intended the mortgagee to absorb that loss under section 1322, and section 1124, but it does not follow that Congress intended the creditor to absorb losses because the *cure* is paid over time. For example, the Chapter 11 analogue simply provides that if a mortgage is to be reinstated, the debtor must "cure" any default.[9]

If, as we believe, Congress contemplated the normal cure to be an immediate cash payment, the time-payment equivalent of a cash payment must bear an appropriate rate of interest. If section 1322(b)(5)'s phrase "the curing of any default within a reasonable time" contemplates cure by full

---

5. In re Thomas, 59 B.R. 758 (Bankr. N.D.Ohio 1986); In re Threet, 60 B.R. 87 (Bankr. N.D.Ohio 1986); In re Prange Foods, Corp., 63 B.R. 211 (Bankr. W.D.Mich.1986); In re Ashton, 63 B.R. 244 (Bankr. D.N.D.1986); In re Ruespin Corp., 85 B.R. 630 (Bankr. S.D. Fla.1988) (Chapter 7); In re Klein, 106 B.R. 396 (Bankr. E.D.Pa. 1989); see also Transouth Financial Corp. v. Hill, 106 B.R. 145 (W.D.Tenn.1989) (credit life and disability insurance).

6. In some cases the debtor will have a right after that time to redeem, but redemption requires full cash payment of the amount owing.

7. See In re Capps, 836 F.2d 773 (3d Cir. 1987); In re Terry, 780 F.2d 894 (11th Cir. 1985); In re Kooker, 106 B.R. 233 (Bankr. D.Nev.1989); In re Morgan, 106 B.R. 449 (Bankr. E.D.Va.1989). For cases agreeing with Terry and denying interest, see In re Carr, 36 B.R. 381 (Bankr. N.D.Ga.1984); In re Small, 65 B.R. 686 (Bankr. E.D.Pa. 1986), decision aff'd and adopted, 76 B.R. 390 (E.D.Pa. 1987); In re Harmon, 72 B.R. 458 (Bankr. E.D.Pa. 1987); In re Ward, 73 B.R. 119 (Bankr. N.D.Ga.1987); Matter of Christian, 35 B.R. 229 (Bankr. N.D.Ga.1983).

8. In re Colegrove, 771 F.2d 119 (6th Cir. 1985). For cases agreeing with the Sixth Circuit view expressed in Colegrove, see In re Nesmith, 57 B.R. 348 (Bankr. E.D.Pa. 1986); In re Trigwell, 67 B.R. 808 (Bankr. C.D.Cal. 1986); In re Van Gordon, 69 B.R. 545 (Bankr. D. Mont. 1987); In re Gincastro, 48 B.R. 662 (Bankr. D.R.I.1985); In re Einspahr, 30 B.R. 356 (Bankr. E.D.Pa. 1983); Matter of Stratton, 30 B.R. 44 (Bankr. W.D.Mich.1983).

9. 11 U.S.C.A. § 1124(2)(A).

payment at once or within a few weeks then cure by payment over three to five years of monthly payments in the plan must bear interest if the two are to be equivalent. Thus, we indorse the decision of Judge Wellford in *Colegrove*. We believe that the Courts of Appeals for the Third and Eleventh Circuits and like-minded commentators misread the definition of cure and the requirement of a reasonable time.

§ 9–18 Modification of the Rights of Creditors—Restrictions on the Modification of Home Mortgages

Section 1322(b)(2) authorizes the debtor to "modify the rights of holders of secured claims."[1] But the section authorizes modification only of "claims, other than a claim secured only by a security interest in real property that is the debtor's principal residence * * *."[2] The quoted clause crept into section 1322 unannounced in the later stages of the Bankruptcy Code's consideration by Congress. Presumably it was put forward by the mortgage bankers. It may have been designed to forestall the kind of manipulation of mortgage debt that occurred in the 1930's under state law and under the Frazier–Lemke Act.[3] But all of this is speculation. Where exactly the language came from and what exactly it is to do is the subject of debate in the courts.

To grasp the consequences that almost all believe flow from the clause, consider a typical case. Frequently debtors come to Chapter 13 after a judgment of foreclosure on their homes, but before the sale has occurred. Invariably these debtors are in default on several installments. Usually the total amount of the debt is less than the value of the home and the debt is commonly amortized over many years, well beyond the normal three or five year term of a Chapter 13 plan.

But for the clause that prohibits modification such a debtor might propose to extend the term of the loan, reduce the amount of the installments and change the interest rate. If, for example, the mortgage had been written at a time when interest rates of 12 percent were common, but the rates had fallen in the meantime to 9 percent, one can expect that the debtor would propose that the interest rate be reduced on the ground that a lower interest rate would create the present value that would have to be given to the creditor. The clause prohibits all of these acts. To reduce the interest rate is a modification; equally clear, the extension of the term or the reduction of the payments is a modification.[4]

Note the ironic consequence that follows from the non-modification exception for home mortgages in section 1322(b)(2). It means that the

---

§ 9–18

1. 11 U.S.C.A. § 1322(b)(2).

2. Id.

3. The provisions commonly referred to as the Frazier–Lemke Act constituted parts of § 75 of the Bankruptcy Act. In 1933 Congress enacted section 75(a)–75(r) in 47 Stat. 1470 (1933), 11 U.S.C.A. § 203. In 1934, Congress added section 75(s) in 48 Stat. 1289, 11 U.S.C.A. § 203(s). After the Supreme Court held 75(s) to be unconstitutional, Congress replaced it in 49 Stat. 943 (1935), 11 U.S.C.A. § 203(s).

4. What does the debtor hope to get from Chapter 13? Typically the debtor asks that the debt be "deaccelerated" and that he be permitted to pay the arrearage during the term of the plan. Almost all courts now agree that such a cure and reestablishment of the normal amortization schedule is permitted under section 1322(b)(5) and is not prohibited by the non-modification clause. We discuss that question above in § 9–17 supra.

consumer debtor is denied certain rights against his home mortgagee that are routinely enjoyed by debtors in Chapters 11 and 12. Appreciating that irony, a number of courts have bent and twisted the clause in the debtor's favor.

It is important to read the rules on modification together with sections 1322(c) and 1322(b)(5). The former section limits plans to five years. The latter permits cure and deacceleration of debts in which the last payment is due after the date on which the final payment under the plan is due. All courts that have explicitly considered the question have held that section 1322(c), aided by the implication in section 1322(b)(5), prohibits the debtor from dealing with a debt whose last payment is more than five years distant except by deacceleration and cure. If that interpretation of sections 1322(c) and 1322(b)(5) stands, the non-modification clause in section 1322(b)(2) will have more limited impact because any mortgage on which the last payment was due more than five years after the petition was filed will already be beyond the power of the debtor to change in a Chapter 13 plan. This means that the non-modification clause will apply exclusively to mortgages with less than five years to run and to other short-term consumer loans where the creditor takes a mortgage on the debtor's home in lieu of a mortgage on the debtor's personal property.

Limiting one's consideration to debts due within five years, a number of questions remain. First, which loans are those "secured only by security interest in real property that is the debtor's principal residence"?[5] If the creditor takes a security interest not only in the principal residence, but also on other specific tangible property such as debtor's automobile, the creditor loses the protection of the non-modification clause.[6] Where the "other collateral" is less concrete, several courts have refused to find that its presence removes the application of the non-modification clause. For example, in *In re Hemsing*[7] the debtor argued that a third party guaranty constituted "other security" and so made the non-modification rule inapplicable. Finding that a guaranty is not a "security interest" and that a security interest was required, the court held that the non-modification rule applied. Other courts have found that the presence of credit life policies insuring the debtor's life on behalf of the creditor constitute other collateral that removes the case from the protection of section 1322(b)(2).[8]

A line of cases in the bankruptcy court in Pennsylvania has held that routine boilerplate in Pennsylvania land mortgages claiming security in "buildings and improvements on said premises as well as all alterations, additions, or improvements * * * and any and all appliances, machinery, furniture and equipment, whether fixtures or not * * *" constitute a securi-

---

5. A creditor who perfects its interest in a mobile home by use of personal property security law in Texas is not protected by the non-modification clause. The court implies the creditor would be protected had it chosen the Texas alternative of a real property perfection. See In re Thurston, 73 B.R. 138 (Bankr. N.D. Texas 1987).

6. In re Reeves, 65 B.R. 898 (N.D.Ill. 1986); In re Johnson–Allen, 67 B.R. 968 (Bankr. E.D. Pa.1986); In re Lapp, 66 B.R. 67 (Bankr. D.Colo.1986); In re Leazier, 55 B.R. 870 (Bankr. N.D.Ind. 1985); In re Brantley, 6 B.R. 178 (Bankr. N.D.Fla.1980); but see In re Williams, 109 B.R. 36 (Bankr. E.D.N.Y.1989).

7. 75 B.R. 689 (Bankr. D.Mont.1987).

8. In re Wilson, 91 B.R. 74 (Bankr. W.D.Mo.1988); Transouth Financial Corp. v. Hill, 106 B.R. 145 (W.D.Tenn.1989); In re Stiles, 74 B.R. 708 (Bankr. N.D. Ala.1987); but see In re Diquinzio, 110 B.R. 628 (Bankr. D.R.I.1990).

ty interest in personal property that removes the mortgage from the protection of the non-modification clause.[9] In our view these judges have gone too far. If, as we believe to be the case, clauses of the kind just quoted are found in mortgages in many parts of the country, Congress could not have intended that the presence of such language would deprive the mortgagee of the protection specifically granted by section 1322(b)(2).

A yet more questionable interpretation of section 1322(b)(2) is the holding in several cases that the non-modification rule is limited to long-term purchase-money mortgages and that it does not apply to short-term consumer debt that happens to be secured only by a mortgage on the debtor's principal residence.[10] So far as we can tell, these cases arise exclusively from judicial speculation about the purpose of section 1322(b)(2). The language of the statute makes no mention of the length of the liability, whether it is amortized over a period of years or whether it was a purchase money obligation. If Congress had intended to limit the non-modification rule to long-term purchase money mortgages, it could have said so, but it did not.

We are persuaded by the decision in *In re Bradshaw*.[11] There the court notes that a creditor who chooses to take security only in the debtor's residence in order to achieve the protection of section 1322(b)(2) may well forfeit other protection such as a claim on the debtor's automobile or household furniture. More importantly, the court concludes "section 1322(b)(2) is unambiguous. Accordingly, the appellees plan cannot be allowed to modify the contract interest rate on the * * * claim." [12]

Two remaining questions have divided the courts about the application of the modification rule. The first has to do with the division of the debt into secured and unsecured and with the treatment of the two debts. The second has to do with debts that become due without acceleration prior to the filing of the petition in Chapter 13.

To understand the first question, consider an example in which the debtor's residence is worth $70,000 and the mortgage debt stands at $90,000. In a routine Chapter 11 proceeding the debtor would divide the liability into a $70,000 secured debt and a $20,000 unsecured debt. Typically in the plan the $20,000 would be paid off at a small percentage of its total value, the $70,000 would be paid in full together with interest. May the debtor make

---

9. In re Caster, 77 B.R. 8 (Bankr. E.D.Pa. 1987); In re Crompton, 73 B.R. 800 (Bankr. E.D.Pa. 1987); In re Jablonski, 70 B.R. 381 (Bankr. E.D.Pa. 1987), aff'd in part and remanded, 88 B.R. 652 (E.D.Pa.1988); contra In re Ross, 107 B.R. 759 (Bankr. W.D. Okla. 1989).

10. See In re Williams, 109 B.R. 36 (Bankr. E.D.N.Y.1989); In re Bruce, 40 B.R. 884 (Bankr. W.D.Va.1984); In re Morphis, 30 B.R. 589 (Bankr. N.D.Ala.1983); In re Paige, 13 B.R. 713 (Bankr. S.D.Ohio 1981); In re Neal, 10 B.R. 535 (Bankr. S.D.Ohio 1981); In re Brantley, 6 B.R. 178 (Bankr. N.D.Fla.1980); In re Shaffer, 84 B.R. 63 (Bankr. W.D.Va.1988), decision aff'd in part, remanded in part, 116 B.R. 60 (W.D.Va.1988), appeal dism'd, 912 F.2d 749 (4th Cir.1990); contra Matter of Marrero, 111 B.R. 384 (Bankr. D.P.R.1990); In re Ross, 107 B.R. 759 (Bankr. W.D. Okla. 1989); In re Diquinzio, 110 B.R. 628 (Bankr. D.R.I.1990).

11. 56 B.R. 742 (S.D.Ohio 1985), overruling In re Paige, 13 B.R. 713 (Bankr. S.D.Ohio 1981).

12. 56 B.R. at 474. For other decisions agreeing with Bradshaw, see Matter of Stratton, 30 B.R. 44 (Bankr. W.D.Mich.1983); In re Allen, 75 B.R. 344 (Bankr. S.D.Ohio 1987); In re Coffey, 52 B.R. 54 (Bankr. D.N.H.1985); In re Hubbard, 30 B.R. 39 (Bankr. W.D.Mo.1983); In re Simpkins, 16 B.R. 956 (Bankr. E.D.Tenn. 1982); see also In re Hobaica, 65 B.R. 693 (Bankr. N.D.N.Y.1986).

such a division and give favored treatment only to the secured portion under Chapter 13? As we saw above, if the last payment on the mortgage is due more than five years after the petition is filed, the answer is no, not because of section 1322(b)(2), but because to do so would violate the five-year limitation in section 1322(c).

A growing majority of the courts, including the Third and the Ninth Circuits, has now held that the debt can be divided under section 506 and that only the secured portion is entitled to the protection of the non-modification clause in (b)(2).[13] These courts find that (b)(2) only prohibits modification "in the plan" and not by other procedures under the Bankruptcy Code. An alternative reading would be to say that (b)(2) protects only secured claims from modification and that one must look to section 506 for a definition of what is and what is not a secured claim. But for such a conclusion, a creditor can take a security interest in the debtor's residence (even though the debtor has no equity and it is "under water" because of other mortgages) and then avoid any modification under Chapter 13. We doubt Congress intended to permit that and we would read the words "secured claims" of section 1322(b)(2) to require applying section 506 to determine what part of a claim is secured.

Other courts have concluded that sections 506 and 1322(b)(2) are in conflict and that section 1322(b)(2), the most directly applicable and specific section, should govern.[14] In effect, these courts make the judgment that Congress intended to give mortgagees an expansive shield against attack. In their view, to write the mortgage debt down to the value of the underlying collateral is the very thing that Congress intended to avoid. Anyone who has read even a few bankruptcy cases understands the power of the bankruptcy court to manipulate outcomes by choosing from quite differing appraisals offered by the parties. In effect, these courts are saying that Congress intended to remove that discretion from the bankruptcy court and to allow the mortgagee to assert the full amount of its debt.

Although we appreciate the argument of these courts, we see no true conflict between sections 1322(b)(2) and 506, and we believe the definition of secured claim calls for the application of both sections.

The proliferation of second and third mortgages in the form of "home equity loans" (written to enjoy the deductibility of consumer interest payments not otherwise deductible), and the recent deflation in real estate values will make this issue more and not less significant. Although we

---

13. Wilson v. Commonwealth Mortgage Corp., 895 F.2d 123 (3d Cir.1990); In re Hougland, 886 F.2d 1182 (9th Cir.1989); In re Honett, 116 B.R. 495 (Bankr. E.D.Tex.1990); In re McNair, 115 B.R. 520 (Bankr. E.D.Va.1990); In re Gadson, 114 B.R. 453 (Bankr. E.D.Va. 1990); In re Moore, 113 B.R. 239 (Bankr. E.D.Va.1990); In re Marshall, 111 B.R. 325 (Bankr. D.Mont.1990); In re Hayes, 111 B.R. 924 (Bankr. D.Or.1990); In re Hyden, 110 B.R. 46 (Bankr. W.D. Okla. 1990); In re Brouse, 110 B.R. 539 (Bankr. D. Colo. 1990); In re Demoff, 109 B.R. 902 (Bankr. N.D.Ind. 1989); In re Ross, 107 B.R. 759 (Bankr. W.D. Okla. 1989); In re Kehm, 90 B.R. 117 (Bankr. E.D.Pa. 1988); In re Simmons, 78 B.R. 300 (Bankr. D.Kan.1987) (applies only to fully secured claims); In re Caster, 77 B.R. 8 (Bankr. E.D.Pa. 1987); In re Jablonski, 70 B.R. 381 (Bankr. E.D.Pa. 1987), aff'd, 88 B.R. 652 (E.D.Pa. 1988); In re Spadel, 28 B.R. 537 (Bankr. E.D.Pa. 1983).

14. In re Sauber, 115 B.R. 197 (Bankr. D.Minn.1990); In re Brown, 91 B.R. 19 (Bankr. E.D.Va.1988); Matter of Smith, 63 B.R. 15 (Bankr.D.N.J.1986); In re Simpkins, 16 B.R. 956 (Bankr. E.D.Tenn.1982); see also In re Schum, 112 B.R. 159 (Bankr. N.D.Tex.1990) (§ 1322(b)(2) prevents bifurcation where claim is secured only by principal residence).

endorse the former set of cases which hold that the debt can be split and that only the secured portion is protected by section 1322(b), we are unclear how these courts are to face the conclusion arising out of sections 1322(c), 1325(b)(5), and 1328(a)(1) that debts extending beyond the plan's life are not discharged.[15] If the debtor is successful in persuading the bankruptcy court to divide the mortgage debt into a secured and unsecured portion, how does that same debtor avoid the five-year limitation in 1322(c)? If the mortgage has more than five years left to run, even the unsecured portion of the debt would be due more than five years after the petition. Moreover, even if such a plan was confirmed, the creditor arguably could wait for the expiration of the five-year period and then sue on the debt. Creditor would argue, of course, that section 1328(a)(1) excepts from the discharge any debt whose last payment is due beyond the last date in the plan.[16] Neither of the court of appeals cases that allows the loan to be divided discusses this limitation. It is possible that both of those cases involve loans written for less than five years, but that seems unlikely, and that certainly does not appear from the opinions. Are these courts also silently amending section 1322(c) and overruling the cases cited above?

Note, too, that there may be disputes about the "term" of some home equity mortgages. Many home equity loans are written like lines of credit and do not have explicit termination dates. Some give the creditor authority to call the loan even though most are amortized over a certain period of time with the expectation that many will be paid off long before that amortization period is over. In all of those cases there will be an initial question whether the section 1328(a)(1) prohibition referring to section 1322(b)(5) applies because "the last payment is due after the date on which the final payment under the plan is due." As we have said above, if one concludes that section 1328(a)(1) bars the discharge of debts due more than five years after the confirmation, dividing a long-term mortgage debt into secured and unsecured portions will do little or nothing for the typical Chapter 13 debtor.

The final set of cases that has troubled the courts is those in which the mortgage debt becomes due not because of default or acceleration, but because of its terms, either before the Chapter 13 plan is filed or during the plan's term. In these cases debtors have argued for some form of cure under section 1322(b)(5) or (b)(3). But truly they are asking for more than cure since, by hypothesis, even a cured debt would still be due in full according to

---

15. For cases holding that there is no right to modify a loan that extends beyond the five-year term of the plan, see In re Ramirez, 62 B.R. 668 (Bankr. S.D.Cal.1986); Matter of Foster, 61 B.R. 492 (Bankr. N.D.Ind. 1986); In re Hildebran, 54 B.R. 585 (Bankr. D. Ore. 1985).

16. A potential solution for the debtor might be to file a "Chapter 20", that is to say, the debtor might file a Chapter 7, use § 506 to divide the mortgage into a secured and unsecured portion and discharge the unsecured portion. He could then file a Chapter 13 in order to deal with the arrearages and would not have the bothersome unsecured portion yet to deal with. The Supreme Court has specifically approved of "Chapter 20" bankruptcies. Johnson v. Home State Bank, ___ U.S. ___, 111 S.Ct. 2150, 115 L.Ed.2d 66 (1991), on remand, 940 F.2d 609 (10th Cir.1991), on remand, ___ B.R. ___ (D.Kan.1991); but see In re Honett, 116 B.R. 495 (Bankr. E.D.Tex.1990); In re Hyden, 110 B.R. 46 (Bankr. W.D. Okla. 1990); see also In re Edwards, 87 B.R. 671 (Bankr. W.D. Okla. 1988); In re Klapp, 80 B.R. 540 (Bankr. W.D. Okla. 1987).

For a discussion of "Chapter 20", see 9–30 infra.

its own terms. The leading case, *In re Seidel*,[17] held flatly that any extension of such debt would be an impermissible modification under section 1322(b)(2) and could not be approved. We believe that to be a correct reading even though it may have severe consequences for some debtors.[18]

This conclusion, of course, means that if a creditor chooses to write its mortgages as a series of three or five year obligations with balloon payments, they will be subject to the protection of section 1322(b)(2), and the creditor will be protected from a cure and extension of a low-interest mortgage under section 1322(b)(5). On the other hand, there are good reasons why such mortgages will not become commonplace. Many mortgagees will want protection from the costs of renegotiating and rewriting mortgages every three years and from the risks that their debtors will borrow elsewhere at the end of the three-year term if the rates are lower then than they were when the mortgage was written.

To summarize the status of the mortgagor in Chapter 13, think again of the common case in which the debtor has defaulted, and the home is worth more than the amount of the debt. In the usual case the debtor will be able to cure and reinstate the mortgage under section 1322(b)(5). If the value of the home has fallen, and if it is a short term debt, the debtor may be successful in writing down the secured amount to the value of the home. Some courts, however, would prohibit that and all courts (that have spoken explicitly) deny the debtor that right (because of section 1322(c)) if the term of the mortgage is more than five years at the time of the filing.

§ 9–19 Feasibility, Section 1325(a)(6)

For a plan to be confirmed a court must find "the debtor will be able to make all payments under the plan and to comply with the plan."[1] This is known as the "feasibility" test, determining whether it is feasible for the debtor to carry out the plan. The cases that rely on section 1325(a)(6) are sparse and unremarkable. As one might expect, it is the unusual debtor who needs to be told that he is attempting too much, that what he proposes to pay under the plan is more than he can afford, and that he should propose a more modest plan. In most of the cases where a creditor challenges the feasibility of the plan, presumably the creditor does not contemplate the confirmation of a less generous plan, but rather the confirmation of no plan at all. In such cases the creditor hopes either that the creditor will leave bankruptcy altogether and thus be subject to the creditor's state law claim, or that the debtor with substantial assets will be forced into selling and thereby be required to give up the assets to the creditors.

One subset of feasibility cases involves debtors who propose plans with balloon payments. These debtors propose funding the balloon payments either by the sale of their assets (such as their residences) or by refinancing

---

17. 752 F.2d 1382 (9th Cir.1985).

18. For cases agreeing with Seidel, see In re Sennhenn, 80 B.R. 89 (Bankr. N.D.Ohio 1987), aff'd, 80 B.R. 93 (N.D.Ohio 1987); In re Davis, 91 B.R. 477 (Bankr. N.D.Ill. 1988); contra In re Spader, 66 B.R. 618 (W.D.Mo.1986); Grubbs v. Houston First American Savings Ass'n, 730 F.2d 236 (5th Cir. 1984); Larkins v. Commercial Bank of Dawson, 50 B.R. 984 (W.D.Ky.1985); In re Minick, 63 B.R. 440 (Bankr. D. D.C. 1986).

§ 9–19

1. 11 U.S.C.A. § 1325(a)(6).

existing debt. In general, the courts have found these plans not feasible. For example, in *In re Hogue*,[2] the court found such a plan not to be feasible where the debtor had produced no evidence that sale or refinancing was "reasonably likely to occur at the time specified in the plans." The court went on to state that it was difficult to imagine any testimony at the outset of a plan by a debtor that would satisfy the court about the feasibility of a plan which was dependent upon the sale of an illiquid asset such as residence, three or four years later.[3]

Other cases under the feasibility standard are nothing more than quibbling contests between debtors and creditors over the nature and amount of expenses, and revenues to be derived from the debtor's activities. For example, in *In re Fiegi*[4] the court found a plan feasible, despite the fact that the farm debtor proposed only one annual payment of $29,400 in each of the five years of the plan. There the debtor adequately responded to the creditor's complaint that the plan did not contemplate irrigation payments, payments of real property taxes and a claim that the expenses were unreasonably low.[5]

A final class of plans found to be unfeasible are those that do not propose full payment of nondischargeable liability which could then be asserted against the debtor. In *In re Davidson*,[6] the court rejected as not feasible three plans that dealt in various ways with child support obligations. The court concluded first that such obligations could not be modified in the plan, and found if the unmodified obligations were asserted against the debtor, the plans would not be feasible because they did not provide for payment at the level that would be required under state law outside of bankruptcy.[7]

One suspects that most creditors' feasibility arguments are in fact strategic devices to drive the debtor either to Chapter 7 or outside of bankruptcy entirely, and are made by creditors who believe for one reason or another that they will fare better in those regimes than they will in Chapter 13. For this reason the reported feasibility cases seem to be weird outgrowths of the bankruptcy system. Presumably most true feasibility issues are worked out in negotiations among the creditors, the trustee, and the debtor. In most cases the debtor and the debtor's lawyer will have made a judgment about the feasibility before they propose a plan. Certainly the debtor's selfish bias to understate the amount that he is willing to pay minimizes any feasibility problems that exist, therefore one should recognize the feasibility standard as an important rule in determining what the lawyer will advise and the trustee will approve, but it is not a standard likely to be important for the typical creditor or to become the central issue in bona fide confirmation litigation.

2. 78 B.R. 867 (Bankr. S.D.Ohio 1987).

3. See also In re Gavia, 24 B.R. 216 (Bankr. E.D.Cal.1982), aff'd, 24 B.R. 573 (Bankr. 9th Cir.1982).

4. 61 B.R. 994 (Bankr. D. Ore. 1986).

5. See In re Schyma, 68 B.R. 52 (Bankr. D.Minn.1985) (plan feasible even though breeding and raising horses had not made money in the past and the plan did not include expenses likely to be suffered in raising horses); In the Matter of Truxon, 71 B.R. 28 (Bankr. D.Del.1987) (plan not feasible where it counted on larger rental payments from the restaurant business to debtor as landlord than the restaurant business could sustain).

6. 72 B.R. 384 (Bankr. D.Colo.1987).

7. See also In re Huber, 80 B.R. 531 (Bankr. D.Colo.1987).

§ 9-20 Confirmation and Discharge

Section 1327 states the effect of confirmation as follows:

(a) The provisions of a confirmed plan bind the debtor and each creditor, whether or not the claim of such creditor is provided for by the plan, and whether or not such creditor has objected to, has accepted, or has rejected the plan.

(b) Except as otherwise provided in the plan or the order confirming the plan, the confirmation of a plan vests all of the property of the estate in the debtor.

(c) Except as otherwise provided in the plan or in the order confirming the plan, the property vesting in the debtor under subsection (b) of this section is free and clear of any claim or interest of any creditor provided for by the plan.[1]

The basic discharge rules are the following in section 1328(a):

(a) As soon as practicable after completion by the debtor of all payments under the plan, unless the court approves a written waiver of discharge executed by the debtor after the order for relief under this chapter, the court shall grant the debtor a discharge of all debts provided for by the plan or disallowed under section 502 of this title, except any debt—

(1) provided for under section 1322(b)(5) of this title; or

(2) of the kind specified in section 523(a)(5) or (8) of section 523(a) or 523(a)(9) of this title.

(3) for restitution included in a sentence on the debtor's conviction of a crime.[2]

---

§ 9-20

1. 11 U.S.C.A. § 1327.
2. Id. § 1328(a). The remainder of § 1328 reads as follows:

(b) At any time after the confirmation of the plan and after notice and a hearing, the court may grant a discharge to a debtor that has not completed payments under the plan only if—
(1) the debtor's failure to complete such payments is due to circumstances for which the debtor should not justly be held accountable;
(2) the value, as of the effective date of the plan, of property actually distributed under the plan on account of each allowed unsecured claim is not less than the amount that would have been paid on such claim if the estate of the debtor had been liquidated under chapter 7 of this title on such date; and
(3) modification of the plan under section 1329 of this title is not practicable.

(c) A discharge granted under subsection (b) of this section discharges the debtor from all unsecured debts provided for by the plan or disallowed under section 502 of this title, except any debt—
(1) provided for under section 1322(b)(5) of this title; or
(2) of a kind specified in section 523(a) of this title.

(d) Notwithstanding any other provision of this section, a discharge granted under this section does not discharge the debtor from any debt based on an allowed claim filed under section 1305(a)(2) of this title if prior approval by the trustee of the debtor's incurring such debt was practicable and was not obtained.

(e) On request of a party in interest before one year after a discharge under this section is granted, and after notice and a hearing, the court may revoke such discharge only if—
(1) such discharge was obtained through fraud; and
(2) the requesting party did not know of such fraud until after such discharge was granted.

Id. § 1328(b-c).

The 1990 amendments to section 1328(a) prevent discharge in three situations previously allowed in Chapter 13. In addition to the previous exemption for alimony, maintenance and child support payments, section 1328(a)(2) now makes most obligations due to educational benefit overpayments or student loans non-dischargeable. Additionally, this section now disallows discharge for judgments against the debtor for liabilities due to driving while intoxicated. This exemption includes intoxication caused by drug usage as well as by consumption of alcohol. The drunk driving amendment was supported by various lawyers, bankruptcy judges and victims rights organizations.[3] Finally, the 1990 amendments created a new section, 1328(a)(3), which exempts criminal restitution from Chapter 13 discharge. Section 1328(a)(3) overturned the rule in *Pennsylvania Dep't of Pub. Welfare v. Davenport*.[4] The criminal restitution provision, formally endorsed by the National Association of Attorneys General, was meant to prevent federal bankruptcy courts from invalidating the results of state criminal proceedings.[5]

The application of section 1327, together with section 1328, is ordinarily quite straightforward. Assume a creditor with a $1,000 claim, who files a proof of claim that is included in a plan which provides for a 50 percent dividend. On confirmation of the plan this creditor has a right to total payments equal to a present value of 50 percent of its claim over the life of the plan, and if it receives those payments, it will have no right after the confirmation and before discharge to ask for anything more. Clearly, this is the meaning of section 1327(a), that the plan "binds" the parties. If payment is made in full, the debt will be discharged at the end of the plan under 1328 and the creditor, having received $500 plus interest, will see its $1,000 claim completely discharged.

The outcome would be the same if our hypothetical creditor held security worth $500 and the plan provided for payment of secured creditors in full and for no payment of unsecured creditors. Having received its $500, the liability would be discharged and the asset would be free of the creditor's claim. Pending the discharge, the creditor would retain its security interest in accordance with the terms of the plan.

Sometimes, the effect of sections 1327 and 1328 is unclear. We earlier discussed the creditor who is not scheduled and who never receives any other adequate notice of the bankruptcy. This creditor's claim is not discharged. More difficult is the case of the creditor whose debt is scheduled in the debtor's statement who receives formal notice, but who fails ever to file proof of claim. Under Chapter 11, section 1111(a) would treat such a creditor as though he had filed a proof of claim, if the debt were listed and there were no dispute. There is no comparable provision in Chapter 13 and if neither the debtor nor the trustee files on behalf of the creditor, the courts are left to dig through sections 1327 and 1328 to determine the effect of a confirmation and the discharge on such a debt.

---

3. S. Rep. No. 434, 101st Cong., 2d Sess. 4, reprinted in 1991 U.S. Code Cong. & Admin. News 4065, 4069.

4. 495 U.S. 552, 110 S.Ct. 2126, 109 L.Ed.2d 588 (1990).

5. S. Rep. No. 434, 101st Cong., 2d Sess. 8, reprinted in 1991 U.S. Code Cong. & Admin. News 4065, 4071.

This issue might first arise after the confirmation and before the discharge when the creditor is suddenly aroused from its sleep. The creditor may then try to collect its debt under state law or to ask the bankruptcy court for some form of relief (lifting the stay, allowing it to file a tardy claim). If there is no term in the plan to deal with this debt, section 362(a) presumably continues to stay any collection effort by the creditor. If the creditor asks for the stay to be lifted, it is not likely to meet with the court's approval, for, by hypothesis, the creditor has slept on its rights.

If the plan can be said in some sense to have "provided for" the claim, the creditor may be in even worse shape. Presumably in that case one would read section 1327(a) to give the creditor what the plan states he gets and no more. At the end of the payments under the plan, the debts will be discharged under section 1328(a) as a debt "provided for" under section 1328(a). It might seem impossible that a debt could be both "provided for" and yet receive no payment under the plan, but that is exactly what some courts have held possible. For example, in cases in which the plan provides for "payment of all priority claims in full," or payment of a 20 percent "dividend on all unsecured claims" but on which there is no payment to a particular creditor because no proof of claim has been filed, several courts have held that the debt is provided for, that the creditor is bound by the confirmation and the debt is discharged.[6]

We are uncertain about the fairness of this outcome. In Chapter 11 it would be the responsibility of the debtor to treat the debt as though a proof of claim had been filed and thus to include it within one of the classes and to pay it. One might distinguish Chapter 13 cases on the ground that a Chapter 13 debtor is less sophisticated and that it is unfair to expect such a debtor to determine the exact amount owing to a creditor, so to file a claim and include that amount. On the other hand, there may be cases in which the debtor's statement shows that a debtor fully understands that a debt is due, understands the approximate amount of the debt, yet where the debtor would be freed from the obligation with no payment if he could propose a plan which "provides for that debt" without any payment.

If the debt is not "provided for" (if, for example, the court finds that the language of the plan does not deal with a particular debt at all), presumably the creditor may pursue its debt after the discharge under 1328. This, of course, produces a result that is quite senseless. It means that the creditor's claim is stayed by section 362 during the three to five years of the plan, but at the end of that time (when the stay is lifted by the discharge) it may proceed against the assets of the debtor. Apart from questions such as the running of the statute of limitations and its tolling, it makes no sense to us to say that the creditor held at bay for three years should now be allowed to attack the debtor with full force. It seems better to us to say that the debt is dead for all times or to include it by allowing a delayed filing or for a modification of the plan.

---

6. See In re Gleason, 89 B.R. 177 (Bankr. N.D.Ala.1988), judgment rev'd, 95 B.R. 801 (N.D.Ala.1988); In re Ryan, 78 B.R. 175 (Bankr. E.D.Tenn.1987) ("Actual payment of the debt as provided in the plan depends on the filing of a proof of claim, which is the creditor's obligation."); see also In re Richards, 50 B.R. 339 (E.D.Tenn.1985); In re Goodwin, 58 B.R. 75 (Bankr. D.Me.1986); United States v. Vlavianos, 71 B.R. 789 (Bankr. W.D.Va.1986).

All of this becomes yet more difficult for the courts when the creditor has an unavoidable security interest. In *In re Simmons*,[7] the Court of Appeals for the Fifth Circuit has found that such a security interest survives under section 506(d) and that it may be asserted after the discharge. Another court has concluded that the language in section 1327(c) (which provides that the assets to which the security interest formerly attached, passes "free and clear" to the debtor upon confirmation) frees the assets even from valid security interests.[8] That court would presumably hold not only that the asset was free and clear, but that the discharge would discharge the liability and thus that the debtor would have to pay no part of the debt but would be free to keep the asset.

We favor the decision in the *Simmons* case. We believe that 506(d) was intended to allow the security interest to ride through and to continue as a nonrecourse liability. Although the clause in 1327(c) (granting the asset "free and clear of any claim or interest") can be regarded as freeing the asset from the security interest, the Court of Appeals in *Simmons* concluded that "claim and interest" were used in a technical sense in section 1327 and were not intended to apply to liens and security interests. The effect of allowing the security to carry through would be to require the debtor and the debtor's lawyer to insure that a proof of claim is filed on behalf of the creditor. That would not be a bad thing; it should be a rare case in which neither the creditor, the trustee, nor the debtor files a proof of claim.

A final question concerning the effect of confirmation arises when the debtor defaults on a provision of the plan or when a postpetition liability is created and not paid. Consider the facts of *In re Walker*[9] and *In re Clark*.[10] In each of those cases the debtor incurred a liability after his Chapter 13 plan had been confirmed. In each case the new creditor sought to satisfy the debt out of the assets under the debtor's control. In each case the debtor argued the stay prohibited the recovery. Because it was conceded that each of the debts arose after the petition, neither was stayed by section 362(a)(6) which applies only to debts that arise before the commencement of the case. Collection of these claims could be stayed only if they violated section 362(a)(4) or (3) as an act against "property of the estate."

One would have thought that whether assets owned by the debtor after confirmation, but before discharge, are "property of the estate" would have been long settled. One who thought that would be wrong. The court in *Walker* concluded that such assets are no longer property of the estate. It found that section 1327(b) dissolved the estate by its statement that the confirmation "vests all of the property of the estate in the debtor." Accordingly, that court concluded that the postpetition debt could be enforced against the property owned by the debtor that was formerly property of the estate.

Relying in important part on section 1306, Judge Scholl comes to the opposite conclusion in the *Clark* case. In *Clark* the court points out that

---

7. 765 F.2d 547 (5th Cir.1985).

8. In re Gleason, 89 B.R. 177 (Bankr. N.D.Ala.1988), judgment rev'd, 95 B.R. 801 (N.D.Ala.1988).

9. 84 B.R. 888 (Bankr. D. D.C. 1988).

10. 71 B.R. 747 (Bankr. E.D.Pa. 1987).

section 1306(a)(1) adds to the estate certain property acquired "after the commencement of the case, but before the case is closed."

So, there you have it. Some courts find that section 1327 dissolves the estate and puts the property into the hands of the debtor where it is subject at least to the claims based on debts that have not been provided for and that have arisen after the filing of the petition.[11] Others find section 1306 to be paramount and to retain the property as part of the estate under the stay's protection.[12] We discuss this specific problem with a bit more detail in our Chapter 3 on the stay.[13]

The final question on the post-confirmation phase has to do with debtor default on liabilities that are explicitly provided for in the plan. By definition these liabilities have arisen prior to the petition (except for those few that might have been added by modification afterwards) and are, in that sense, prepetition liabilities. On the other hand, most have been substantially modified by the plan itself and are, in that sense, postpetition liabilities. When the debtor defaults, are these obligations to be considered prepetition liabilities subject to the stay, or are they to be considered postpetition liabilities, possibly not subject to the stay?

In *In re Nicholson*[14] the court found that a confirmed plan created a new set of obligations and when one of those obligations was violated, the debtor was no longer protected by section 362. The court reasoned that section 362 did not apply to postpetition liabilities,[15] therefore permitted the creditor to proceed under state law to enforce its mortgage. In *In re Broman*[16] another Colorado bankruptcy judge has come to the opposite conclusion. There the court found that the stay continued and that the only option open to a mortgagee whose debt was in default was to move that the Chapter 13 be dismissed so the creditor could proceed under state law.

Although these seem to be the only two cases that have directly faced the question, analogous cases are more in general agreement with *Broman*.[17] To the extent that the *Nicholson* case depends upon a conclusion that confirmation wipes out the old debt and leaves the creditor only with the new one, we disagree with it.[18] Several provisions of Chapter 13 make it clear that the drafters intended that some attributes of the old debt continue. For example, section 1307 provides for dismissal of a Chapter 13 plan under section 1307(c)(6) upon "material default by the debtor with respect to a term of a confirmed plan."[19] Surely the drafters did not intend that on

---

11. In re Adams, 12 B.R. 540 (Bankr. D. Utah 1981); In re Dickey, 64 B.R. 3 (Bankr. E.D.Va.1985); In re Severson, 53 B.R. 8 (Bankr. D. Ore. 1985); In re Korgan, 52 B.R. 557 (Bankr. D. Ore. 1985); In re Johnson 36 B.R. 958 (Bankr. D. Utah 1983); In re Mason, 51 B.R. 548 (D. Ore. 1985); In re Root, 61 B.R. 984 (Bankr. D. Colo. 1986) (dictum); In re Aneiro, 72 B.R. 424 (Bankr. S.D.Cal.1987).

12. In re Clark, 71 B.R. 747 (Bankr. E.D.Pa. 1987); see also In re Broman, 82 B.R. 581 (Bankr. D.Colo.1988), citing In re Garcia, 42 B.R. 33 (Bankr. D.Colo.1984).

13. See § ___ supra.

14. 70 B.R. 398 (Bankr. D. Colo. 1987).

15. Presumably the court also assumes that these assets, subject to the creditor's mortgage, were no longer part of the estate.

16. 82 B.R. 581 (Bankr. D.Colo.1988).

17. See, e.g, In re McCollum, 76 B.R. 797 (Bankr. D. Ore. 1987); see also In re Vanasen, 81 B.R. 59 (D. Ore. 1987).

18. For a recitation of the unusual circumstances that would come about if Nicholson were rigorously followed, see In re McCollum, 76 B.R. 797 (Bankr. D. Ore. 1987); see also In re Ford, 84 B.R. 40 (Bankr. E.D.Pa. 1988).

19. 11 U.S.C.A. § 1307(c)(6).

dismissal the creditor's only claim is the one that had previously been spelled out in the confirmed plan.

More to the point is section 1328(a) which specifies that a discharge in Chapter 13 occurs not at confirmation, but only after all payments have been made under the plan. By its very terms, section 1328(a) seems to keep the prepetition debts alive until that time. The finding that all debts have life only in the confirmed plan would produce a variety of other unexpected and bizarre results, such as the elevation of a subordinate claim that was not provided for in the plan over one that was, or the recovery of only 50 percent of one party's debt were it so reduced in the plan, and the recovery of the full amount by one whose claim was not so reduced.

§ 9–21 Confirmation and Discharge—Hardship Discharge

Section 1328(b) states the requirements necessary for a debtor to obtain a hardship discharge:

> (b) At any time after the confirmation of the plan and after notice and a hearing, the court may grant a discharge to a debtor that has not completed payments under the plan only if—
>
> (1) the debtor's failure to complete such payments is due to circumstances for which the debtor should not justly be held accountable;
>
> (2) the value, as of the effective date of the plan, of property actually distributed under the plan on account of each allowed unsecured claim is not less than the amount that would have been paid on such claim if the estate of the debtor had been liquidated under chapter 7 of this title on such date; and
>
> (3) modification of the plan under section 1329 of this title is not practicable.[1]

Hardship discharges usually arise from post-confirmation economic problems. Often the debtor loses his job or the debtor's spouse dies, leaving little income to feed the plan.

A classic example of such hardship is *In re McNealy*.[2] After the plan was confirmed and the debtors began making payments, Mr. McNealy died. Mrs. McNealy was left with only her social security benefits, $500 per month. Even though the court recognized that the debtor was suffering economic hardship which was out of her control, it did not grant the discharge because it believed that a 1329 modification was possible by liquidation of nonexempt real and personal property.

The most common issue in recent hardship cases is whether the debtor seeking the discharge has distributed enough under the plan to comply with the best interest test. If, as in *In re Moore*,[3] the debtor meets (b)(1) and (b)(3) but is unable to establish that unsecured creditors have been paid the minimum required by the best interest test, discharge will be denied. At confirmation in *Moore*, the court determined that $1,974.98 was the mini-

---

§ 9–21
1. 11 U.S.C.A. § 1328(b).
2. 31 B.R. 932 (Bankr. S.D.Ohio 1983).
3. 87 B.R. 499 (Bankr. S.D.Ohio 1988).

mum amount necessary to satisfy the best interest test. Subsequently the debtor was divorced, hospitalized, and her mother died. The court, however, refused to grant a hardship discharge because only $858.26 had been distributed to unsecured creditors.

Section 1328(c) limits the discharge in hardship cases by excluding long-term liabilities from section 1322(b)(5) and by excluding from the discharge debts that would be excluded under section 523(a) in a Chapter 7 proceeding.

Finally, any party considering a hardship discharge should consider the possibility of a modification discussed in the next section. Such a modification may well be easier to accomplish and may offer all of the benefit and none of the detriments of a hardship discharge.

§ 9–22 Modification and Revocation of Confirmed Plan

Prior to the amendments of 1984, the general rule was that only the debtor could move to modify a confirmed plan.[1] Even today, plans confirmed on or before October 8, 1984, can be modified only by the debtor.[2] Any plans confirmed after that date, however, are subject to section 1329 as amended. Section 1329(a) states that:

(a) At any time after confirmation of the plan but before the completion of payments under such plan, the plan may be modified upon request of the debtor, the trustee, or the holder of an allowed unsecured claim, to—

(1) increase or reduce the amount of payments on claims of a particular class provided for by the plan;

(2) extend or reduce the time for such payments; or

(3) alter the amount of the distribution to a creditor whose claim is provided for by the plan to the extent necessary to take account of any payment of such claim other than under the plan.[3]

While the trustee and allowed unsecured claim holders are now permitted to move for modification, some limitations are imposed. Modification is granted to the moving party only if there is a significant change in circumstances affecting the debtor's ability to make future payments. In *In re Gronski*,[4] a joint motion to modify the debtor's plan was brought by the trustee and an unsecured creditor. They alleged, as grounds for modification, modest increments in debtor's income, intentional expense understatements by debtor at the original confirmation, and a subsequent decrease in debtor's living expenses from $355 to $225 monthly. The movants claimed that any one of the three grounds was independently enough to justify modification. The court, however, held that only the last ground—decrease in living

§ 9–22

1. In re Boone, 53 B.R. 78 (Bankr. E.D.Va. 1985) (Trustee lacks standing to invoke 1329); Matter of Nelson, 27 B.R. 341 (Bankr. M.D.Ga. 1983); In re Fluharty, 23 B.R. 426 (Bankr. N.D.Ohio 1982) (Creditor lacks standing to invoke 1329); but see In re Koonce, 54 B.R. 643 (Bankr. D.S.C.1985) (Trustee permitted to move for increase in debtor's payments, after debtor won lottery increasing annual income by $49,000.).

2. In re Cherry, 85 B.R. 11 (Bankr. W.D.N.Y.1988); see In re Moseley, 74 B.R. 791 (Bankr. C.D. Cal.1987), order vac'd, appeal dism'd, 101 B.R. 608 (Bankr.9th Cir.1989).

3. 11 U.S.C.A. § 1329(a).

4. 86 B.R. 428 (Bankr. E.D.Pa. 1988).

expenses—justified modifying the plan to increase the debtor's monthly payments from $85 to $200.

Second, section 1329(b)(1) states that "[s]ections 1322(a), 1322(b), and 1323(c) of this title and the requirements of section 1325(a) of this title apply to *any modification* under subsection (a) of this section."[5] The court in *In re Stage*[6] held that only the portions of the plan proposed to be changed are subject to section 1329(b)(1). That is to say, if the debtor does not propose to change the rights of a creditor as they existed in the original plan, that creditor has no standing to object to modification. Any other position would produce the burdensome result of reopening every issue that was or could have been considered at the original confirmation.

Third, a motion to modify must be brought "before the completion of payments under such plan * * *." In *In re Moss*,[7] the Chapter 13 debtor, an attorney, proposed a 36 month plan to pay unsecured creditors a dividend of about 36 percent. The plan was confirmed without objection. The debtor completed the plan about seven months early and the trustee subsequently objected to the debtor's discharge, complaining that the debtor failed to comply with the disposable income test of section 1325(b)(1)(B). The court held that once all of the payments contemplated by the plan are paid to the trustee, modification is not permissible.

Similarly, in *In re Chancellor*,[8] the debtor completed payments to the unsecured creditors according to the confirmed plan. Because the plan called for 46 more payments to secured creditors, the unsecured creditors claimed the right to modify. The court, however, held that the words "completion of payments" in section 1329 referred to the point at which the debtor completed payment to each class of creditors under the plan. Because the unsecured creditors had been fully paid under the plan, they could not receive modification of the plan, even though payments were still due other classes of creditors.

Finally, modification cannot be used by the debtor to draw out the length of time to pay under the plan, except "for cause." In no case, however, is the court empowered to extend the time for payment under a modified plan beyond five years from the first payment due under the original confirmed plan.[9]

If the court denies a motion for modification, the final attempt at defeating a confirmed plan is to seek a revocation of the confirmation order. Revocation is governed by section 1330, which states,

> (a) On request of a party in interest at any time within 180 days after the date of the entry of an order of confirmation under section 1325 of this title, and after notice and a hearing, the court may revoke such order if such order was procured by fraud.[10]

---

5. 11 U.S.C.A. § 1329(b)(1) (emphasis added).
6. 79 B.R. 487 (Bankr. S.D.Cal.1987).
7. 91 B.R. 563 (Bankr. C.D.Cal.1988).
8. 78 B.R. 529 (Bankr. N.D.Ill. 1987).
9. 11 U.S.C.A. § 1329(c); West v. Costen, 826 F.2d 1376 (4th Cir.1987) (payment by debtor under the modified plan is permissible for five years from the date payment was first due under the original plan); accord In re Stage, 79 B.R. 487 (Bankr. S.D.Cal.1987).
10. 11 U.S.C.A. § 1330(a).

The movant requesting revocation must be a "party in interest." All creditors provided for under the plan and the trustee are parties in interest. Beyond them it is unclear who are included. In *In re Hicks*,[11] the court held that a party claiming breach of a postpetition contract was not included.

The motion must be made within 180 days of the confirmation order. The 180 day time limit will, however, be tolled if it does not appear that the party knew or should have known of the debtor's deception.[12]

The crucial issue on a revocation motion, however, will be proving that the debtor procured the confirmation order by means of fraud. If the movant fails either to claim [13] or prove [14] fraud the revocation request will be denied.

The court in *In re Scott*,[15] shows how a debtor might commit fraud. The documents filed by the debtor failed accurately to list the number of previous bankruptcies filed by the debtor, the different aliases and social security numbers used, the previous addresses and lengths of stay, and the present job and length of time held. Moreover, the court found that the debtor made these representations with the intent to mislead the court and creditors.

B. CHAPTER 12—FAMILY FARMERS WITH REGULAR INCOME

§ 9–23 History of Chapter 12

For full text of this section, see Epstein, Nickles & White, Bankruptcy, Practitioner Treatise Series, Vol. 2.

   a. Comparison of Chapters 11 and 12

   b. Comparison of Chapters 13 and 12

§ 9–24 Eligibility for Chapter 12

For full text of this section, see Epstein, Nickles & White, Bankruptcy, Practitioner Treatise Series, Vol. 2.

   a. Farming Operation

   b. Strategic Considerations

   c. Retrospective

---

11. 79 B.R. 45 (Bankr. N.D.Ala.1987).

12. In re Moseley, 74 B.R. 791 (Bankr. C.D.Cal.1987), order vac'd, appeal dism'd, 101 B.R. 608 (Bankr. 9th Cir.1989).

13. United States v. Hochman, 89 B.R. 250 (N.D.Ga.1987), judgment aff'd, 853 F.2d 1547 (11th Cir.1988).

14. In re Bruce, 80 B.R. 927 (Bankr. C.D.Ill. 1987), order rev'd after district court affirmance, 877 F.2d 594 (7th Cir.1989); see In re Moseley, 74 B.R. 791 (Bankr. C.D.Cal.1987), order vac'd, appeal dism'd, 101 B.R. 608 (Bankr.9th Cir.1989), citing Stamford Municipal Employees' Credit Union v. Edwards, 67 B.R. 1008, 1010 (Bankr. D. Conn. 1986) (Deceit requires proving (1) that the debtor made a representation regarding compliance with § 1325 which is materially false; (2) that the representation was either known by the debtor to be false, or was made without belief in its truth, or was made with reckless disregard for the truth; (3) that the representation was made to induce the court to rely upon it; (4) that as a consequence of such reliance, the court entered the confirmation order.).

15. 77 B.R. 636 (Bankr. N.D.Ohio 1987).

§ 9-25 Procedure and the Timing of Events in Chapter 12

For full text of this section, see Epstein, Nickles & White, Bankruptcy, Practitioner Treatise Series, Vol. 2.

§ 9-26 Procedure and the Timing of Events in Chapter 12—Lessons for Chapter 11

For full text of this section, see Epstein, Nickles & White, Bankruptcy, Practitioner Treatise Series, Vol. 2.

§ 9-27 Conversion and Dismissal From Chapter 12

For full text of this section, see Epstein, Nickles & White, Bankruptcy, Practitioner Treatise Series, Vol. 2.

a. Conversion or Dismissal at Debtor's Request

b. Conversion or Dismissal at Creditor's Request

c. Retrospective

§ 9-28 Substantive Rules in Chapter 12

For full text of this section, see Epstein, Nickles & White, Bankruptcy, Practitioner Treatise Series, Vol. 2.

§ 9-29 Substantive Rules in Chapter 12—Feasibility

For full text of this section, see Epstein, Nickles & White, Bankruptcy, Practitioner Treatise Series, Vol. 2.

§ 9-30 Chapters 19 and 20: The Filing of a Chapter 7 Shortly Followed by a Chapter 12 or 13

For full text of this section, see Epstein, Nickles & White, Bankruptcy, Practitioner Treatise Series, Vol. 2.

Chapter 10

BUSINESS REORGANIZATION: CHAPTER 11

Table of Sections

Sec.
10–1 History and Introduction.
10–2 ____ Nature of the Chapter 11 Process.
10–3 ____ Roadmap.

A. Operating the Business After the Chapter 11 Filing

10–4 Debtor in Possession Usually Operates.
10–5 Limits on Conducting Business.
10–6 Discretion in Operating Business.
10–7 Effect on Corporate Governance.

B. The Trustee, Examiners, Committees

10–8 Grounds for Appointment of Trustee.
10–9 ____ Powers of the Trustee.
10–10 Examiners.
10–11 Committees and Their Operation.
10–12 ____ Composition of the Committee.
10–13 ____ Powers and Duties of a Committee.
10–14 ____ Who Pays and How.

C. The Plan of Reorganization

10–15 A Practical Overview.
10–16 The Basic Contents of the Plan of Reorganization: Best Interest, Cramdown, and Absolute Priority.
10–17 ____ Acceptance Requirements.
10–18 ____ Best Interest Test.
10–19 ____ Requirements for Cramdown Under Section 1129(b).
10–20 ____ Fair and Equitable Treatment—Secured Claims.
10–21 ____ The Absolute Priority Rule—Unsecured Claims.
10–22 ____ Unfair Discrimination.

D. Claims

10–23 Impairment of Claims.
10–24 Manipulation of Classes.
10–25 Special Rules for Secured Claims in Chapter 11.
10–26 ____ Section 1111(b): Right of Recourse.
10–27 ____ Section 1111(b)(2).
10–28 ____ Exceptions to 1111(b)(2).

Sec.

E. Post-Confirmation Issues

10–29 Return of Property to the Debtor.
10–30 Discharge of the Debtor.
10–31 Binding Effect of the Plan of Reorganization.
10–32 Implementation, Adjustment, and Modification.
10–33 Revocation and Modification.

F. Retrospective

10–34 Retrospective: The Unpractical View.

§ 10–1 History and Introduction

The Chapter 11 one sees in the Bankruptcy Reform Act of 1978 is the product of 80 years of experience under the Bankruptcy Act of 1898.[1] The latter Act contained three reorganization provisions that are directly relevant to the current Chapter 11. Those were Chapters X, XI, and XII.[2] Chapter XII was designed for real estate reorganizations and we need not concern ourselves with it. Chapters X and XI overlapped. Chapter XI was designed for the reorganization of comparatively small businesses that did not have publicly traded securities. Under Chapter XI the existing management of the debtor continued to run the business, to hire the lawyers and otherwise to control the reorganization.[3] Chapter XI differed principally from the current Chapter 11 in that the bankruptcy court and the debtor in possession had substantially more limited powers than they do now. In theory, the Chapter XI debtor in possession had no power to modify the rights of unconsenting secured creditors. That was probably not true in practice, but clearly the power of the court and of the debtor over nonconsenting secured creditors was much smaller under Chapter XI.[4]

Chapter X required the appointment of a trustee to operate the business; this trustee ousted current management. This ouster was necessary because Chapter X was designed for the company with publicly held shares and

---

§ 10–1

1. The previous law was the Bankruptcy Act of 1898, ch. 541, 30 Stat. 544, as amended by Chandler Act of 1938, Pub.L.No. 95–598, § 402(a), 92 Stat. 2682. The Reform Act clarifies, simplifies, and modernizes the previous law, which did not deal with vast twentieth-century changes in the amount and kind of debt. In 1970 Congress established the Commission on the Bankruptcy Laws of the United States. In July 1973 the Commission reported its findings and recommendations to Congress, including the text of a suggested bankruptcy code. For a concise historical background to Chapter 11 see, Klee, The New Bankruptcy Act of 1978, 64 A.B.A. 1865, 1866 (1978); see also Comment, Business Reorganization Under the Bankruptcy Reform Act of 1978: An Analysis of Chapter 11, 1979 B.Y.U. L. Rev. 961, 961–65; House Comm. on the Judiciary, Report of the Commission on the Bankruptcy Laws of the United States, H.R. No. 137 (pt. 1), 93rd Cong., 1st Sess., at 1 (1973)[hereinafter cited as Report of the Commission on Bankruptcy Laws]. For an in depth analysis of the pre-Code law see The Institute of Continuing Legal Education, Bankruptcy and the Chapter Proceedings, 1976.

2. 11 U.S.C.A. §§ 501–676 (Chapter X), 701–799 (Chapter XI), 801–926 (Chapter XII) (1976) (repealed 1978).

3. See Comment, supra note 1, at 965–8 for comparison of Chapters X, XI, and XII; see also Report of the Commission on Bankruptcy Laws, supra note 1, at 237–48.

4. For comparison with the current Chapter 11 see King, Chapter 11 of the 1978 Bankruptcy Code, 53 Am. Bankr. L.J. 107 (1979). For an analysis of secured creditors under Chapter 11, see Orr and Klee, Secured Creditors Under the New Bankruptcy Code, 11 U.C.C. L.J. 312 (1979). There has, however, been some skepticism as to whether Chapter XI effectively limited the debtor's power over secured creditors: "Lawyers who specialize in business reorganization have had little difficulty in overcoming the limitations of Chapter XI—the inability to affect secured creditors or equity security interests. Case law has evolved to the point that as a matter of course secured creditors are enjoined from realizing on their security during the pendency of the proceeding." Report of the Commission on Bankruptcy Laws, supra note 1, at 247.

provided a significant role for the SEC in the reorganization. Chapter X gave the trustee and the bankruptcy courts substantially greater power to impose solutions contrary to desires of the creditors than did Chapter XI. Because there was no explicit dividing line between Chapters X and XI and because the debtor frequently wished to be in XI even though he should have been in X, there was much litigation prior to 1978 on the question whether a particular debtor belonged in Chapter X or XI. Typically the debtor wished to be in Chapter XI because that left him in control of the business; it did not pass it to a third-party trustee. Not surprisingly, the debtor's lawyer felt exactly the same way because a third-party trustee could normally be expected to hire someone else as his lawyer. Many cases that the drafters would have placed in Chapter X wound up in Chapter XI and much time and money was spent litigating over the proper chapter for a particular bankruptcy and reorganization.[5] To avoid these kinds of jurisdictional disputes and out of a belief that third-party intervention by a trustee and by the SEC was more costly than it was valuable,[6] the drafters produced only one business reorganization chapter in the 1978 Act, Chapter 11. Close examination of Chapter 11 shows traces of Chapters X, XI and XII, but probably the closest analogy is to Chapter XI as it lived in the courts just prior to 1978.

Chapter 11 has separate and specific provisions for two unique forms of reorganization, those dealing with railroads and those dealing with stockbrokers. In 1985, Chapter 11 was joined by Chapter 12,[7] a reorganization chapter designed exclusively for farmers which we discuss in our preceding Chapter 9.

§ 10–2 History and Introduction—Nature of the Chapter 11 Process

The goal of this discussion of Chapter 11 is twofold. First we hope to introduce the student and lawyer to the critical sections in Chapter 11 and to explain their technical operation. Second we intend to give the reader a feeling of the Chapter 11 process. A person reading the Chapter 11 sections without any knowledge of the practical might expect routine litigation covering each of the many requirements in section 1129 and other complex sections of Chapter 11.

Although there are cases interpreting nearly every section of Chapter 11, it would be wrong to think of the Chapter 11 process as primarily a

---

5. One court deciding a dispute over which chapter was appropriate commented that the patient would probably die while the doctors argued about which operating table he should be on. Securities & Exchange Commission v. Canandaigua Enterprises Corp., 339 F.2d 14, 19 (2d Cir.1964).

6. The 1978 Act increased the flexibility of the bankruptcy courts to save large amounts of money over the strict and often overly protective requirements of the SEC under Chapter X. See Comment, supra note 1, at 978. For a full analysis of pre-Code SEC involvement and a comparison to the SEC role under the Code, see Hooton, The Role of The Securities and Exchange Commission under Chapter X, Chapter XI and Proposed Amendments to the Bankruptcy Act, 18 B.C. Ind. & Comm. L. Rev. 427 (1977).

7. 11 U.S.C.A. §§ 1201–1231. For discussion and analysis of Chapter 12, see Note, An Analysis of the Family Farmer Bankruptcy Act of 1986, 15 Hofstra L. Rev. 353 (1987); Shepard, Farm Bankruptcy: The New Chapter 12, 48 Ala. L.Rev. 10 (1987). For one critical view of the chapter, see White, Taking From Farm Lenders and Farm Debtors: Chapter 12 of the Bankruptcy Code, 13 J. Corp. Law 1, 1–31 (1987).

litigated, judge-ruled adversarial process. Plans proposed and adopted in Chapter 11 almost always have been produced by negotiation, not by litigation.[1] Whether a Chapter 11 plan can be proposed or whether the debtor must transfer into Chapter 7 and liquidate is itself typically determined by negotiation, not by litigation. These facts do not diminish the importance of the law. All the negotiation occurs with one eye on the statutory rules and the other on the judge's likely reaction to a particular issue under those statutory rules. Presumably a creditor, shareholder or debtor who is granted certain rights by Chapter 11 will concede those rights in negotiation only in return for some quid pro quo. Always the negotiators should have their eyes on the alternative of a court resolution under the various sections of Chapter 11. Thus the negotiations go on very much in the shadow of bankruptcy law, and one can effectively represent his client only if he has a thorough knowledge of that law.

Sketchy as they are, the data on success and failure of Chapter 11 and on its operation suggest that one should divide the Chapter 11 universe in two.[2] Small and medium size companies populate one part of that universe, companies that are typically closely held and range in size from several millions of dollars in assets down to hundreds of thousands. These would encompass not only the small retail stores or real estate developments, but also the small manufacturing or service organizations. Large, publicly held companies populate the other part of the universe. Recent examples of this latter group are LTV,[3] Johns–Manville,[4] White Motor[5] and Revere Copper.[6] For reasons that are not too clear to us, the latter group (the large companies) almost always produce reorganization plans that are successful at least in the sense that some existing business enterprise carries on the old business after the conclusion of the Chapter 11 bankruptcy.[7] The norm with respect to small businesses is the failure of the business to achieve a confirmed plan; in many cases none is even proposed. The fate of the small business who enters Chapter 11 is to exit not through a confirmed plan but by conversion to Chapter 7 and liquidation. Thus, it is probably fair to look at the Chapter 11 of the small and medium size business as a step that leads almost certainly to its liquidation. On the contrary, the Chapter 11 of a big business usually leads to some form of reorganization of the company that is

§ 10–2

1. This also seems to have been the case in pre-Code reorganizations as evidenced by Congress' assertion that "[m]ost business arrangements, that is, extensions or compositions (reduction) of debts, occur out of court." H.R. Rep. No. 595, 95th Cong., 1st Sess. 220 (1977).

2. There is actually a third sphere, although it is barely visible. The Supreme Court recently found that there is no ongoing business requirement for reorganization under Chapter 11. As a result, the Court resolved a split among the circuits by holding that non-business individuals may file for relief under Chapter 11. Toibb v. Radloff, ___ U.S. ___, 111 S.Ct. 2197, 115 L.Ed.2d 145 (1991).

3. In re Chateaugay Corp., 838 F.2d 59 (2d Cir. 1988), 80 B.R. 279 (S.D.N.Y.1987), 76 B.R. 945 (S.D.N.Y.1987), 64 B.R. 990 (S.D.N.Y. 1986).

4. In re Johns–Manville Corp., 824 F.2d 176 (2d Cir. 1987), 45 B.R. 833 (S.D.N.Y.1984), 42 B.R. 651 (S.D.N.Y.1984), 39 B.R. 234 (S.D.N.Y.1984).

5. In re White Farm Equipment Co., 788 F.2d 1186 (6th Cir. 1986); In re White Motor Credit, 761 F.2d 270 (6th Cir. 1985), 37 B.R. 631 (E.D.Ohio 1984).

6. In re Revere Cooper and Brass Inc., 78 B.R. 17 (S.D.N.Y.1987); Matter of Revere Copper & Brass, Inc., 652 F.Supp. 80 (N.D.Ala. 1986).

7. See Lopucki, The Debtor in Full Control—Systems Failure under Chapter 11 of the Bankruptcy Code? 57 Am. Bankr. L.J. 99, 108–09 (1983).

"successful" at least in the sense that some part of the business continues as a going concern.

One can speculate about the reasons for this dichotomy. Many of the small Chapter 11's belonged in Chapter 7 from the beginning and never had any hope of a successful reorganization. They began in Chapter 11, not in Chapter 7, in part because the owners of the business might not have been ready to concede what was obvious to others and because there is no cost to the owners in trying Chapter 11, and, at least for them, there may be considerable gain. For example, management may retain their jobs for a longer period by filing a Chapter 11 petition. They receive payment of their wages for a longer period of time, and thus take more for themselves than if a petition were filed in Chapter 7 and a trustee were appointed.

Surely a second reason for the difference between the large and small business is the cost of a Chapter 11 proceeding. Operating a business within Chapter 11 is necessarily more expensive than normal operations. This cost arises from the necessity of hiring lawyers and accountants, going to court for approvals and for bargaining endlessly under the umbrella of Chapter 11 with various other parties. Perhaps because there are some economies of scale, a large business can bear this burden more readily than a small one.

Doubtless there are other reasons explaining some of the differences between large and small reorganizations.[8] For example, the motivation of the banks and other creditors in a large business may be different than in a small one; they may see it in their interest to sink more money into a large business in hopes of avoiding a catastrophic loss. It is possible too that the principal causes of insolvency in large businesses are different from those in small. But all of this is speculation. In any event one should understand that only a limited percentage of small and medium size businesses entering Chapter 11 are likely to emerge with an approved plan. Most will be liquidated in Chapter 7. In comparison, large businesses usually produce plans that are successful.[9]

§ 10–3 History and Introduction—Roadmap

We turn now to a roadmap of the basic sections in Chapter 11. If one excludes railroad reorganization, there are only twenty-nine sections in Chapter 11. Sections 1101 through 1113 deal mostly with non-substantive matters having to do with administration of the estate, the appointment and duties of various of the parties such as the committees, the trustee and the examiner. The guts of Chapter 11 are to be found in sub-chapter two on "the plan," particularly the provisions concerning (1) who can proposed a plan; (2) the contents of a plan; (3) creditor approval of plans; and (4) court approval of plans.

Section 1121 provides the debtor an exclusive period of 120 days in which to file a plan. If the debtor files within that period, no other party is

---

8. For a discussion on why certain types of debtors succeed see Lopucki, id. at 113.

9. In 1987, 41 percent of the companies that sought protection from creditors under Chapter 11 had annual revenue up to $25 million. Of those, only 30 percent were successful. On the other hand, 7 percent of those filed had revenues of $100 million or more and 69 percent of those companies were successful. Brown, "For Small Firms, Perils Lie in Chapter 11," Wall St. J., July 14, 1988, at 25, col. 3–4.

permitted to file a plan for an additional 60 days. Routinely the 120 and 180-day period of exclusivity are extended at the request of the debtor.

Section 1122 provides that one can classify claims or interests together "only if" they are "substantially similar to the other claims or interests of such class." The section and the case law interpreting it limit the debtor's power to gerrymander the class in a way that might enable the debtor either to prefer one set of creditors over another or to nullify the vote of one set of creditors or shareholders.

Section 1123 is an analog to section 1129 in that it specifies certain things that must be in the plan. It directs, for example, that the plan designate various classes, that it set out how each class is to be treated, that it signify how the plan is to be carried out, etc.

Section 1124 defines which claims are "impaired" and which not. Impairment is important, for any class that is unimpaired is deemed to have accepted the plan even though the class members may be rabidly opposed to it. Moreover the section defines how a claim may be left "unimpaired." Specifically it provides for unimpairment by curing a default (de-accelerating), by full payment in cash or by leaving the claimant's right unaltered.

Section 1125 on postpetition disclosure and solicitation will be important to any party who is representing a debtor in Chapter 11. Obviously there must be some means by which the provisions of a plan are communicated to the various creditors and shareholders who are expected to vote on the plan.

Section 1126 tells, among other things, that a class of creditors accepts a plan only if two-thirds in amount and more than one-half in number of those creditors in the class who vote accept the plan. This means that a single creditor holding a claim composing more than one-third of the sum of the claims in the class can cause the class to reject a plan by a single negative vote.[1]

Section 1127 provides for modification of a previously proposed plan. Section 1128 provides merely that there should be a confirmation hearing and that parties can oppose confirmation. Section 1129 sets out the factors that a court is to consider in approving a plan, i.e., the requirements for confirmation. The requirements of paragraph (a) of section 1129 are always applicable. Even if every class of claims and interests accepts a plan, a court still must apply the various requirements of section 1129(a).

Law students and lawyers need to be aware of these requirements and be aware of the "popular" names of two of these requirements. Courts and commentators frequently refer to the requirement of section 1129(a)(11) that "confirmation is not likely to be followed by the liquidation * * *" as a *feasibility requirement*. The *best interests of creditors test* refers to the requirement of section 1129(a)(7) that each nonassenting creditor must receive "not less than the amount that such holder would receive or retain if the debtor were liquidated under chapter 7 * * *."

§ 10–3

1. The Notes of Committee on the Judiciary, Senate Report No. 95–989 state that "The amount and number are computed on the basis of claims actually voted for or against the plan, not as under Chapter X [former section 501 et seq. of this title] on the basis of the allowed claims in the class." 11 U.S.C.A. § 1126(c) Historical and Revision Notes.

While paragraph (a) of section 1129 is always applicable, paragraph (b) is applicable only if the plan (1) was accepted by at least one class of claims impaired under the plan but (2) not accepted by all classes of claims or interests impaired by the plan. Confirmation under section 1129(b) is sometimes referred to as a *cram down,* and the requirement of section 1129(b)(2)(B)(ii) as the *absolute priority rule.* We consider cram down and absolute priority in detail below.

The most important section of subchapter 3 on post confirmation matters, for the purpose of this book, is section 1141 "Effect of Confirmation." This section provides among other things that parties are bound by a confirmed plan, the property of the estate is returned to the debtor after the confirmation, and the property "dealt with by the plan" is free and clear of all claims and interests except as provided in the plan. Moreover, the confirmation discharges the debtor from any debt, with certain exceptions, that arose prior to the date of the confirmation. In effect, section 1141 is the discharge provision of Chapter 11 and one looks to it to see the legal effect of the various obligations owed by the debtor as a result of the confirmation of a particular plan.

A. OPERATING THE BUSINESS AFTER THE CHAPTER 11 FILING

§ 10–4 Debtor in Possession Usually Operates

Filing a petition in Chapter 11 always alters and sometimes tears asunder the web of contractual and state law relationships among the various parties with an interest in the corporation. Prior to bankruptcy the typical publicly held corporation is usually "run" by management. Creditors, particularly creditors whose debt is in default, have specific but generally quite crude rights. These rights may arise because of judgments they have procured in state court proceedings and because of promises that the corporation has made in its debt instruments, typically about incurring other debt, defaulting on debt and the like. Shareholders, of course, have the theoretical power to vote management out, but that power is infrequently exercised and even the threat of its use is normally quite remote, unless a particularly nettlesome and powerful shareholder has acquired a large block of stock with the intention of challenging management.

By imposing on the corporation all of the limitations that we discuss above in our Chapters 3 and 4, filing inevitably diminishes the discretion of management, and usually reduces the power of the shareholder and alters, sometimes for the better and sometimes for the worse, the position of the creditors. Indeed, it is possible that a Chapter 11 filing will diminish the power of all the pre-filing actors and will transfer that power to the trustee, to an examiner, or to the court itself.

In most cases the person who will operate the corporation after the petition is filed is called the debtor in possession ("DIP" for short).[1] The person sitting in the president's chair the day before the petition is filed will

§ 10–4

1. The Code requires the appointment of a trustee on request of a party in interest (1) for cause, such as fraud or incompetency, 11 U.S.C.A. § 1104(a)(1), or (2) if it is in the interest of creditors or equity security holders, 11 U.S.C.A. § 1104(a)(2).

be the same person sitting there the day after. He will now be called or will represent the debtor in possession. As we will see, it is quite unusual to have a trustee or even an examiner selected by the court in a Chapter 11. Nevertheless the court itself, stimulated perhaps by creditors' committees, may veto certain acts of the corporate management. We also will see that even in large Chapter 11s there is inevitably one or several creditors' committees who theoretically have power to influence the operations of the company. These committees may have substantial influence particularly over significant decisions with important economic consequences. Thus, although in theory those operating a corporation in Chapter 11 are the same the day after petition as the day before, in practice they may have less power. The DIP's power, on the other hand, may be increased vis à vis certain people such as creditors who have received judgment liens or other transfers that may be voidable in bankruptcy.

§ 10–5 Limits on Conducting Business

Within limits, a debtor in possession of an operating business retains control over the business's assets. The assets might constitute, for example, an ownership or leasehold interest in the debtor's premises; machinery, equipment or fixtures used in the business; inventory; notes, chattel paper, accounts receivable and other forms of accrued income; and cash on hand. Creditors will also hold direct or indirect interests in these same assets. At least in theory a debtor's opportunity to stay in business and reorganize must not come at the expense of creditor interests. A DIP operates its business under essentially the same rights and restrictions as a Chapter 11 trustee.[1] Significant limits on business operations derive from the administrative powers section of the Bankruptcy Code.[2] The court may condition or prohibit use of various forms of collateral including buildings, machinery, equipment, fixtures, inventory, or cash and accounts receivable generated by the business; pass on certain business decisions of the debtor; and approve or disapprove financing arrangements and credit transactions made outside of the ordinary course of business.

Frequently, a secured creditor foreclosing on collateral, declaring a loan in default or accelerating a debt precipitates the Chapter 11 petition. Once a Chapter 11 petition has been filed, however, the automatic stay[3] bars the creditors from seizing collateral or taking other collection action against the debtor. The concept of adequate protection conserves the rights of secured creditors during the automatic stay period.[4] In addition, if the debtor uses, sells or leases property in which a creditor holds an interest, the creditor

---

§ 10–5

1. The debtor in possession's duties are set forth in 11 U.S.C.A. § 1107(a). These include the duty to account for all property received; examine and object to claims if any purpose would be served by so doing; furnish information requested by a party in interest with regard to the estate and its administration; and if the business is to be operated, file reports, including statements of receipts and disbursements, with the court and relevant taxing agencies. 11 U.S.C.A. §§ 1106(a)(1); 704(2), (5), (7), (8) & (9). The debtor in possession is not entitled to compensation as a trustee, see, 11 U.S.C.A. § 330, nor is it required to investigate the conduct of the debtor's business or file a statement of any such investigation. 11 U.S.C.A. §§ 1107(a) & 1106(a)(3) & (4).

2. Id. §§ 361–365.

3. See id. § 362, discussed in our Chapter 3 supra.

4. See discussion of 11 U.S.C.A. §§ 361, 362(d) & 363(e) in our Chapters 3 and 4 supra.

may request that the court prohibit or condition the use or sale.[5] Unless creditors holding an interest consent, or the court after notice and hearing approves, the debtor may not use its cash collateral.[6]

To see how these rules might work in a real case, consider a typical corporate debtor who produces parts for use by other manufacturers. Two outstanding loans, a revolving credit agreement secured by inventory and receivables, and a term loan secured by the equipment and machinery finance operations. The debtor defaulted on both loans. Just prior to the Chapter 11 filing, the bank accelerated the loans and threatened to seize its collateral.

Unless the bank seeks relief, section 362's automatic stay prevents the bank from taking further action to realize on its collateral once the Chapter 11 petition is filed.

If the debtor continues to use equipment and machinery securing the term loan, the bank may request adequate protection of its interest in that property.[7] The balance of power shifts somewhat in this context as the debtor need not seek court approval prior to using equipment in the ordinary course of business.[8] Adequate protection of a security interest in equipment might include insuring equipment, paying accruing interest or depreciation, and maintaining equipment in good working order.

Once a petition is filed the debtor may lack funds to pay its suppliers and employees or otherwise continue day-to-day operations. The Code prohibits use of cash collateral, i.e., proceeds of inventory and receivables (the debtor's only likely source of revenue) without bank consent or the court authorization. Continued operation of the debtor's business, however, depends on obtaining use of cash collateral. Although the debtor may seek financing from other sources,[9] it is unlikely to receive the necessary cash within the time required. Section 363(c)(3) provides that a cash collateral hearing "shall be scheduled in accordance with the needs of the debtor." This allows the debtor to obtain use of cash promptly and avoid damage to its business from disruption of supplies to customers.[10]

In addition to constraints arising from interests of secured creditors, other limits on a debtor in possession's authority to operate its business exist. Before using, selling or leasing property of the estate outside the ordinary course of business, the debtor must obtain court approval after notice and a hearing.[11] The debtor's use of unsecured or secured credit

---

5. 11 U.S.C.A. § 363(e).

6. "'Cash collateral' means cash, negotiable instruments, documents of title, securities, deposit accounts, or other cash equivalents whenever acquired in which the estate and an entity other than the estate have an interest and includes the proceeds, products, offspring, rents, or profits of property subject to a security interest as provided in section 552(b) of this title, whether existing before or after the commencement of a case under this title." Id. § 363(a); see also id. § 363(c)(2). To authorize use, the court must condition or limit use as necessary to provide adequate protection of creditors' interests. Id. § 363(e).

7. Id. § 363(e).

8. Id. § 363(c)(1).

9. See id. § 364.

10. See discussion of the automatic stay and adequate protection in our Chapter 3 supra.

11. 11 U.S.C.A. § 363(b). For cases considering debtor's proposals in non-ordinary course, see In re Continental Air Lines, 780 F.2d 1223 (5th Cir.1986) (reversal of lower court to permit a DIP's motion to enter into lease agreements outside the ordinary course of business for two jet aircraft for use on profitable routes); In re American Develop-

outside of the ordinary course requires court approval.[12] No court review of ordinary credit transactions, as where suppliers ship under "net 30" terms, is needed.[13]

§ 10–6 Discretion in Operating Business

Within parameters set by creditor interests in property of the estate and the need for court supervision of extraordinary transactions, the debtor holds broad discretion to operate its business. Normally the court will not scrutinize or entertain objections to ordinary course transactions[1] nor will the court substitute its judgment of business risk for that of the debtor.[2] However, allegations of self dealing by insiders may stimulate court intervention.[3]

Section 363(c)(1) allows the debtor to conduct its business in the ordinary course without court review. What constitutes the "ordinary course of business" varies from case to case, and depends upon the debtor's history, the nature of its prepetition business, and general practice for businesses of the same type and size.[4] So, for example, a large, multi-national corporate debtor's retention of non-lawyer lobbyists to monitor and lobby for legislation related to asbestos compensation and bankruptcy reform qualifies as a transaction in the ordinary course of business. The debtor need not obtain court approval for such a transaction where the debtor retained lobbyists prior to filing Chapter 11, and other similar corporations also engage in such activity. Clearly, a smaller corporation's hiring of lobbyists would fall outside the ordinary course of business.

Even where the Code requires notice and hearing to authorize a transaction, courts generally refrain from interfering in the debtor's exercise of

---

ment Corp., 95 B.R. 735 (Bankr. C.D.Cal.1989) (list of appropriate factors in deciding on a debtor's request for approval of a transaction that is not in the ordinary course of business); In re Ionosphere Clubs, Inc., 100 B.R. 670 (Bankr. S.D.N.Y. 1989) (debtor bears the burden of demonstrating that the sale of property out of the ordinary course of business will aid the debtor's reorganization and is supported by good justification); see also In re Lionel Corp., 722 F.2d 1063 (2d Cir.1983) where the court denied DIP's motion to sell its ownership of a large share of stock in a subsidiary corporation outside of plan.

12. 11 U.S.C.A. § 364(b) & (c).

13. "Net 30" is a standard trade term under which the buyer is given 30 days to pay. At the end of the 30 days total payment will be due.

§ 10–6

1. In re Johns–Manville Corporation, 60 B.R. 612 (Bankr. S.D.N.Y. 1986) (Multinational corporate debtor's hiring of lobbyist is a transaction in the ordinary course of business, where corporation hired lobbyists before filing petition and such employment is common industry practice).

2. In re Simasko Production Company, 47 B.R. 444 (D.Colo.1985) (court would not entertain objections to debtor's financing order on basis that financing would be used to fund a business program which posed a bad economic risk).

3. In re Rittenhouse Carpet, Inc., 56 B.R. 131 (Bankr. E.D.Pa. 1985) (debtor's proposed sublease to corporation whose sole shareholder also owned a significant interest in the debtor could not be approved unless debtor showed transaction fair to all parties).

4. In re American Development Corp., 95 B.R. 735 (Bankr. C.D.Cal.1989) (a transfer of all the assets of a corporate debtor to a subsidiary is not a matter in the "ordinary course of business"); In re Johns–Manville Corporation, 60 B.R. 612 (Bankr. S.D.N.Y. 1986); In re Waterfront Companies, Inc. v. Johnston, 56 B.R. 31 (Bankr. D. Minn. 1985) (entering into an indemnity agreement not in the ordinary course of business); In re DeLuca Distributing Co., 38 B.R. 588 (Bankr. N.D.Ohio 1984) (postpetition collective bargaining agreement is a transaction in the ordinary course of business); In re James A. Phillips, Inc., 29 B.R. 391 (S.D.N.Y. 1983) (court defines "ordinariness").

business judgment. In *In re Simasko Production Company,*[5] the debtor, a company engaged in development and production of oil and gas, sought approval of an interim financing arrangement. A creditor objected that the proposed drilling program posed a bad economic risk. Without considering the degree of risk, the court approved the financing and stated that business judgments should be made in the board room and not in the courtroom.

Where the debtor is dealing with a related party, the debtor may have to show that the proposed transaction is fair to all parties. A court refused to approve revision of a sublease on this basis in *In re Rittenhouse Carpet, Inc.*[6] In this case the debtor subleased a portion of its premises. The debtor's sole shareholder also owned 45 percent of the sublessee's stock, and exercised significant control over both corporations. In declining to approve a new sublease that would have allowed the offset of building repairs against rents due, the court noted that for a contract tainted with self dealing, the contract will be approved only if the debtor shows that the transaction is fair to all parties. Transactions that benefit insiders at the expense of the debtor should not be approved.

§ 10–7 Effect on Corporate Governance

The question of corporate governance, discussed as a theoretical matter in academic literature, sometimes becomes a matter of intense and practical debate in Chapter 11 bankruptcies. A split in interests is recognized between management of public companies and shareholders of those companies. It has been suggested that management sometimes cares too much for its own interests and little for those of the shareholders. If that is true in solvent corporations, it is much more likely to be so in the corporation on the edge of insolvency. In a Chapter 11 case, where the corporation may be on its last legs, and the shareholders' interest is likely to be diminished in any reorganization, the split is likely to be exacerbated. It is only normal to anticipate a decline in management loyalty to shareholders when management sees the shareholders preparing the corporate equivalent of the guillotine for them.

Let us review the strengths and weaknesses of the players. First, the shareholders themselves are not without power. Filing of a Chapter 11 petition of a large publicly traded corporation may well bring about massive changes in the identity of the shareholders. One imagines four years after Manville filed its Chapter 11, many of the retirees from Atlanta had sold their stock and that much of the stock had been assembled into the hands of sophisticated investors in the hope that the market would be unduly pessimistic and in anticipation of influencing a plan to their benefit. Such sophisticated shareholders are not likely to be passive; in *Manville* the shareholders argued for and ultimately appealed to the Court of Appeals for the Second Circuit to force a shareholders' meeting. At the meeting they

---

5. 47 B.R. 444 (D.Colo.1985) (involving 364 refinancing rather than 363 operating); see also, Matter of Lifeguard Industries, Inc., 37 B.R. 3 (Bankr. S.D.Ohio 1983) (not the court's responsibility to determine what business decisions a company should follow); In re Curlew Valley Associates, 14 B.R. 506 (Bankr. D. Utah 1981) ("[d]isagreements over business policy are not amenable to judicial resolution * * *.").

6. 56 B.R. 131 (Bankr. E.D.Pa. 1985).

apparently hoped to oust the board of directors and the management and to install persons more favorable to their interests.

Shareholders interests are weakened not only by the fact that management may be at cross purposes to them and may perceive its future to lie in the hands of the creditors, but also because shareholders of a truly insolvent corporation arguably have no interest that is entitled to recognition. In granting the petition for a shareholders meeting, the Court of Appeals for the Second Circuit in *Manville* suggested that no meeting needed to be held if it were shown that the corporation were solvent. In theory, if the corporation is solvent (if its liabilities are less than the value of its assets), the shareholders retain all their normal state law rights, except for those that might conflict with the rules in 362 and 363 and other creditor protection provisions. But if the corporation is insolvent, presumably they forfeit many of those rights.

Knowing whether a corporation in Chapter 11 is solvent or not is like knowing whether a match will light when it is struck on the matchbox. Only by destroying the match can you tell whether it will light. Only by dissolving the corporation and selling off the assets and paying the debts can one tell whether it is truly insolvent. Thus, when we speak of insolvency in the bankruptcy context we are speaking about opinions: opinions given by experts on both sides and opinions of the court in some cases. Inevitably, therefore, the negotiation on these questions takes place in uncertainty about the true rights and interests of the shareholders because none of the players is anxious to risk consequences of an adverse finding, and because the court does not welcome a long and expensive hearing about the solvency of a large company. Commonly such issues are pushed aside while the plan is negotiated between representatives of shareholders and representatives of the creditors. The issues, however, continue to play a part in the negotiation process.

Courts are not receptive to investors who use the demand for a shareholders' meeting merely as a ploy to gain leverage in the negotiation. A court cynical about shareholder motives is likely to pay lip service to the authority of corporate state laws after a Chapter 11 filing, but will construe those laws in such a way as to limit or restrain shareholder power consistent with the court's view of how Chapter 11 should operate. To some extent the court is aided by the explicit rules of the Bankruptcy Code to limit corporate power.[1]

Central to the corporate governance analysis is the shareholder's ability to assert direct control over the debtor in possession. The owners' right to choose and control management is clear prior to bankruptcy; however, when the bankruptcy petition is filed, the owner's ability to control management becomes more difficult. The debtor in possession no longer stands in a fiduciary relationship with the owners, but rather, his fiduciary obligations run to "the estate."[2] Thus, the debtor in possession has the responsibility to

§ 10–7

1. See 11 U.S.C.A. §§ 362, 363, 364.

2. In re Pacific Forest Indus., Inc., 95 B.R. 740 (Bankr. C.D.Cal.1989) (a debtor in possession is a fiduciary to the estate); In re N.S. Garrott & Sons, 63 B.R. 189 (Bankr. E.D.Ark. 1986) (a debtor in possession is a fiduciary who owes undivided loyalty to the estate); In re Coastal Equities, Inc., 39 B.R. 304 (Bankr. S.D.Cal.1984) (a debtor in possession owes un-

act in the best interest of the estate as a whole. This entails protecting and treating fairly the various groups with claims against the estate.

The change in fiduciary duty will inevitably result in decisions by the DIP that are not welcomed by the shareholders. For example, in *In re Johns–Manville Corp.*[3] the debtor's proposed plan would have diluted shareholder's stock by 90 percent or more.

Nonetheless, the owners do have several options in attempting to assert direct control over the debtor in possession. First, they can attempt to influence the DIP by acting through a committee appointed to represent their interests.[4] Second, they can request the appointment of a trustee;[5] however, this is an extraordinary remedy and is used sparingly by the courts.[6] Third, owners can call a shareholders' meeting and attempt to replace management. Although this last tactic threatens the independence of the DIP, the shareholders' right to call a shareholders' meeting has been expressly recognized by several courts.[7] However, limitations on this right have been recognized where the DIP argues that such requests are really attempts to sabotage the reorganization process.[8]

To see how the corporate governance game might be played, consider *In re Johns–Manville Corporation.*[9] Shortly after the debtor and certain creditors announced a tentative agreement on a reorganization plan, the equity security holders' committee filed suit in state court for an order allowing a shareholders' meeting. The bankruptcy and district courts enjoined the state court proceeding. The Second Circuit reversed. The court held that the federal courts could not restrict shareholders' rights absent some clear abuse by the committee in attempting to call the meeting. The court concluded that the desire to obtain bargaining power in the negotiation and to derail a specific organization plan was not a clear abuse. The court suggested, however, that an attempt to destroy all prospects of reorganization might constitute such abuse. Although it reversed the lower court, the Second Circuit suggested that the shareholders' meeting might be enjoined if the lower court found that Manville was insolvent and thus the shareholders

---

divided loyalty to the estate); see, Nimmer and Feinberg, Chapter 11 Business Governance: Fiduciary Duties, Business Judgment, Trustees, and Exclusivity, 6 Bankr. Dev. J. 1 (1989).

3. 801 F.2d 60, 63 (2d Cir.1986), on remand, 66 B.R. 517 (Bankr.S.D.N.Y.1986).

4. 11 U.S.C.A. § 1102.

5. Id. § 1104.

6. See § 10–8 note 3 infra.

7. See In re Bush Terminal Co., 78 F.2d 662 (2d Cir.1935); In re Saxon Indus., 39 B.R. 49 (Bankr. S.D.N.Y. 1984); In re Lionel Corp., 30 B.R. 327 (Bankr. S.D.N.Y. 1983).

8. In re Potter Instrument Co., 593 F.2d 470 (2d Cir.1979) (the bankruptcy court and the district court were justified in denying appellant's petition for a special meeting to elect new directors in view of the finding that such an election might result in unsatisfactory management and would probably jeopardize the debtor's reorganization and the rights of creditors and stockholders); In re J.P. Linahan, Inc., 111 F.2d 590 (2d Cir.1940) (right of the majority stockholders to be represented by directors is paramount and will not be disturbed unless a clear case of abuse is made out); but see, In re Johns–Manville Corp., 801 F.2d 60 (2d Cir.1986), on remand, 66 B.R. 517 (Bankr.S.D.N.Y.1986) (the right of a shareholder's committee to compel a shareholder meeting can be enjoined only if there is a showing of clear abuse that causes irreparable injury. The determination whether the committee is guilty of clear abuse turns on whether rehabilitation will be seriously threatened, rather than merely delayed).

9. 801 F.2d 60 (2d Cir.1986), on remand, 66 B.R. 517 (Bankr.S.D.N.Y.1986).

had no interest to be protected.[10]

Resignations or vacancies in the board of directors or corporate management also may cause courts to circumvent state law for replacing management. Courts find authority for this procedure under both the Bankruptcy Code and state corporation laws.[11] In *In re FSC Corporation*,[12] the board of directors resigned just prior to entry of the Chapter 11 order for relief. The court appointed an officer to perform the duties and exercise the rights of the debtor in possession. A later order authorized the officer to vote shares in subsidiaries, to elect directors, and take other action controlled by shareholder vote. Debtor's shareholders challenged this order as a denial of their state law rights. Paying lip service to the notion that the Bankruptcy Code leaves state corporation law unaffected, the court found that its appointment of the responsible officer to vote shares was authorized under state law. This law allowed appointment of a custodian or receiver where vacancies exist in corporate management, or a deadlock prevents a divided board from taking action. The court found additional authority for its order under section 1107 which gives DIPs the rights and powers of a Chapter 11 trustee and under section 105 which authorizes the court to issue orders as necessary to carry out provisions of the Code.

In other instances, particularly cases of insider abuse, courts abandon the pretext of finding authorization under state law and openly acknowledge that policies of the Bankruptcy Code may override shareholders' rights, even in areas of "business judgment." For example, in *In re Lifeguard Industries*,[13] following a heated contest for control among shareholders, a newly elected board of directors sought to replace management with new officers of "uncertain qualifications." Citing its responsibility to protect creditor interests from actions of inexperienced, incapable or foolhardy management, the court allowed installation of the new board, but prohibited them from replacing management until after confirmation of a plan. The court's prohibition against replacing management because of doubts surrounding the "uncertain qualifications" of the new management seems in direct conflict with the rule of noninterference concerning debtors' business judgment.

Chapter 11 might be regarded as the laboratory in which the ideas of corporate governance are tested. Outside of bankruptcy such issues are mostly the province of academic theorists. In bankruptcy the interests of the various parties come into direct conflict and sometimes call for an explicit judicial judgment about corporate governance. Bankruptcy decisions and the Bankruptcy Code provide inadequate guidance. Except to the extent that the Code gives explicit powers to the trustee, and provides

---

10. See In re Johns–Manville Corporation, 801 F.2d 60, 65 n.6 (2d Cir.1986), on remand, 66 B.R. 517 (Bankr.S.D.N.Y.1986) ("[I]f Manville were determined to be insolvent so that the shareholders lacked equity in the corporation, denial of the right to call a meeting would likely be proper, because the shareholders would no longer be real parties in interest.").

11. See Matter of Gaslight Club, Inc., 782 F.2d 767 (7th Cir.1986) (In light of allegations of improprieties by debtor corporation's president and majority shareholder, grant of creditor committee's request to replace president as person exercising DIP powers is not a circumvention of trustee appointment procedures); Matter of FSC Corp., 38 B.R. 346 (Bankr. W.D.Pa.1983).

12. 38 B.R. 346 (Bankr. W.D.Pa.1983).

13. 37 B.R. 3 (Bankr. S.D.Ohio 1983).

administrative rules such as those in sections 362 and 364, it fails to address directly the conflicting rules of governance. The presence of strong but conflicting policies, evidenced in the case law, has impeded the development of clear rules for corporate control.

Because Congress has authorized bankruptcy procedures for removing the shareholders or managers from control (such as the appointment of a trustee or examiner for the conversion of a case to Chapter 7), a court unwilling to adopt those procedures should be hesitant to make up its own rules of corporate control in the form of prohibitions on shareholder meetings and the like. If Congress intended to free a reorganizing corporation from all of the rules of state corporate law, it could have clearly stated that intent.

In general we believe that the bankruptcy courts should stay out of corporate governance. Short of a finding that there should be a trustee or an examiner, or that the case should be converted, we believe that the court should generally allow the shareholders to stay in control, to exert their influence over management and to make decisions, even stupid ones. Both the creditors and the employees are capable of looking out for themselves in negotiation or litigation, and the court should let them do so.

B. THE TRUSTEE, EXAMINERS, COMMITTEES
§ 10–8 Grounds for Appointment of Trustee

Ordinarily the debtor, as debtor in possession (DIP), remains in possession of the estate. Section 1104 of the Bankruptcy Code authorizes the court [1] to enter an order appointing a trustee at any time after commencement of the case and before confirmation of the plan.[2] Appointment of a trustee is extraordinary, and the requesting party must establish the grounds for appointment by clear and convincing evidence.[3] Two separate bases support appointment of a trustee. The Code requires appointment

§ 10–8

1. It is not clear whether the court may act sua sponte to appoint a trustee. See Cournoyer v. Town of Lincoln, 53 B.R. 478 (D.R.I.1985), aff'd, 790 F.2d 971 (1st Cir. 1986) (a bankruptcy court is not a "party in interest" and therefore lacks the authority sua sponte to order the appointment of a trustee); In re Gurwitch, 1 C.B.C.2d 762 (Bankr. S.D.Fla.1980) (Bankruptcy court has no discretion to appoint a trustee absent a request by a party in interest); but see In re Landscaping Services, Inc., 39 B.R. 588 (Bankr. E.D.N.C.1984) (if appointment of a trustee or examiner is necessary or appropriate to carry out provisions of the Bankruptcy Code, the court itself may initiate a request for appointment).

The bankruptcy court's ability sua sponte to order the appointment of a trustee under the court's general equitable powers of section 105(a) is limited by the legislative history accompanying section 105(b).

2. A trustee should not be appointed at the time a plan is confirmed; a liquidating and disbursing agent is the appropriate entity for carrying out a liquidating plan of reorganization. In re Schultz, 69 B.R. 629 (D.S.D.1987), cause dism'd, 837 F.2d 481 (8th Cir. 1987).

3. In re Microwave Products of America, 102 B.R. 666 (Bankr. W.D.Tenn.1989); In re Stein & Day, Inc., 87 B.R. 290 (Bankr. S.D.N.Y. 1988); In re Nautilus of New Mexico, Inc., 83 B.R. 784 (Bankr. D.N.M.1988); In re William A. Smith Const. Co., Inc., 77 B.R. 124 (Bankr. N.D.Ohio 1987); In re McCorhill Publ., Inc., 73 B.R. 1013 (Bankr. S.D.N.Y. 1987); In re Fisher & Son, 70 B.R. 7 (Bankr. S.D.Ohio 1986); In re St. Louis Globe–Democrat, Inc., 63 B.R. 131 (Bankr. E.D.Mo.1985); In re Evans, 48 B.R. 46 (Bankr. W.D.Tex.1985); In re GHR Companies, Inc., 43 B.R. 165 (Bankr. D. Mass.1984); In re General Oil Distributors, Inc., 42 B.R. 402 (Bankr. E.D.N.Y. 1984); In re Ford, 36 B.R. 501 (Bankr. W.D.Ky.1983); In re Harlow, 34 B.R. 668 (Bankr. E.D.Pa. 1983); In re Tyler, 18 B.R. 574 (Bankr. S.D.Fla.1982); Matter of McCordi Corp., 6 B.R. 172 (Bankr. S.D.N.Y. 1980); Matter of Anchorage Boat Sales, 4 B.R. 635 (Bankr. E.D.N.Y.1980).

"for cause, including fraud, dishonesty, incompetence, or gross mismanagement of the affairs of the debtor by current management, either before or after the commencement of the case, or similar cause."[4] A second standard allows the court to appoint a trustee if it is in the interests of creditors, equity security holders and other interests of the estate, without regard to the number of security holders or the amount of assets and liabilities of the debtor.[5]

It should come as no surprise that courts have not clearly defined the "cause" sufficient to warrant appointment of a trustee under section 1104(a)(1).[6] Misconduct of the debtor which diminishes the value of secured claims or depletes assets of the estate, combined with records that fail adequately to reflect such transactions may be enough.[7] However, allegations of mismanagement of the debtor's business alone will not normally warrant appointment of a trustee. In most Chapter 11 cases, some form of mismanagement, incompetence or bad business judgment brings about the filing.[8]

For example, in *Matter of Anchorage Boat Sales, Inc.*[9] the court found sufficient cause for appointment of a trustee. There, the debtor, a boat retailer, sold inventory free of a security interest yet failed to apply the proceeds to a secured loan as was required under the security agreement. In addition, the debtor's books and records failed accurately to reflect the sales. The court found the debtor's actions amounted to more than simple misconduct, and in fact so adversely reflected upon the abilities and integrity of management as to warrant appointment of a trustee.

In contrast, the court in *In re Crescent Beach Inn, Inc.*,[10] denied a request for appointment of a trustee, despite the existence of debtor misconduct. In that case the debtor's sole shareholder had purchased the company two years prior to filing with money borrowed from his mother. The debtor corporation had assumed the shareholder's obligation by issuing a promissory note secured by a mortgage. The debtor's books and records did not clearly

---

4. 11 U.S.C.A. § 1104(a)(1). Note, however, that when the reasons for appointing a trustee no longer exist, the court may terminate the appointment and restore the debtor to possession. See 11 U.S.C.A. § 1105; In re Eastern Consolidated Utilities, Inc., 3 B.R. 591 (Bankr. E.D.Pa. 1980) (where the major cause for appointment of trustee was ill-advised legal counsel, hiring of new counsel along with debtor's stated intention to comply with Code obviates need for trustee).

5. 11 U.S.C.A. § 1105(a)(2).

6. See, Berdan & Arnold, Displacing the Debtor in Possession: The Requisites For and Advantages Of the Appointment of a Trustee in Chapter 11 Proceedings, 67 Marq. L. Rev. 457 (1984) for a more detailed discussion of the grounds for appointment of a trustee.

7. In re Main Line Motors, Inc., 9 B.R. 782 (Bankr. E.D.Pa. 1981) (Transfer of over $300,000 to related corporations without supporting documents, security or an obligation to pay interest, which is not accurately reflected in the debtor's books and records warrants appointment of trustee); Matter of Anchorage Boat Sales, Inc., 4 B.R. 635 (Bankr. E.D.N.Y. 1980) (Sales out of trust combined with misapplication of collateral proceeds, confusion in accounting system and failure to supervise bookkeeper constitutes case for appointment of a trustee); see also In re St. Louis Globe–Democrat, 63 B.R. 131 (Bankr. E.D.Mo.1985) (trustee was appointed on grounds that the debtor withheld money in excess of $300,000 from its employees in the form of union dues, taxes, and charitable contributions, but did not forward the withheld funds to the appropriate authorities); In re Caroline Desert Disco, 5 B.R. 536 (Bankr. C.D.Cal.1980) (debtor failed to comply with the court's orders on business operating controls, insurance and reports to the U.S. Trustee).

8. In re Crescent Beach Inn, Inc., 22 B.R. 155 (Bankr. D.Me.1982).

9. 4 B.R. 635 (Bankr. E.D.N.Y.1980).

10. 22 B.R. 155 (Bankr. D.Me.1982).

reflect the assumption of the shareholder's debt. In addition to the discrepancies, schedules of assets and liabilities filed with the Chapter 11 petition failed to disclose the shareholder's receipt of free gas and meals at the debtor's hotel and restaurant. The court found the principal's conduct fell short of gross mismanagement, and therefore, that a trustee need not be appointed. Because some degree of mismanagement exists in virtually every insolvency case, appointment of a trustee based on mere mismanagement would defeat the Chapter 11 philosophy of giving the debtor a second chance.

Apart from cases where "cause" for appointing a trustee exists, section 1104(a)(2) authorizes a trustee, "if such appointment is in the interests of creditors, any equity security holders, and other interests of the estate." Theoretically this is an alternate standard for appointment; practically courts rarely order a trustee where no elements of fraud, dishonesty or gross mismanagement exist.[11]

A few examples of trustee appointment under section 1104(a)(2) do exist. One court appointed a trustee "in the interests of creditors," even though it specifically found no "cause" for appointment under subsection 1104(a)(1). In *In re L.S. Good & Co.*,[12] the court, relying on numerous intercompany transactions between related corporate debtors and the finding of prospects for successful rehabilitation remote, appointed a trustee. The court held that continuation of management posed a serious potential conflict of interest.

Perhaps with good reason courts wander through and around rules for appointing trustees. Chapter 11 embodies a policy in favor of reorganization and rehabilitation of businesses, at least where creditors, equity security holders, the debtor and others can expect to receive more through preservation of an ongoing business than through liquidation. Rather than developing hard and fast rules determining when "cause" exists, it makes more sense to evaluate the need for a trustee in light of its potential effect on the reorganization's success or failure. This in turn requires courts to balance several competing and conflicting interests.

First, the displacement of management with a trustee will remove whatever expertise is available to the business at the time of the filing. Second, the trustee and the trappings that he brings with him are likely to be substantially more expensive than existing management. Not only will the trustee have to invest time and money in learning the ropes but, because his position is short term, the trustee may insist on premium pay for his lack of tenure. On the other hand, the trustee may be able to get the parties to

---

11. The tendency to require "cause" before ordering appointment of a trustee is exacerbated by authority which indicates that a trustee should be appointed only if shareholders do not support current management. See 5 Collier on Bankruptcy ¶ 1104.01[7][d]; In re St. Louis Globe–Democrat, Inc., 63 B.R. 131, 138 n.9 (Bankr. E.D.Mo.1985) (Section 1104(a)(2) requires finding that appointment of trustee is in interest of creditors, any equity security holders AND other interests of estate).

12. 8 B.R. 312 (Bankr. N.D.W.Va.1980); see also In re Advanced Electronics, Inc., 99 B.R. 249 (Bankr. M.D.Pa.1989) (a deadlock among the board of directors of the debtor warranted appointment of a trustee: "We note at the outset that such an appointment would not be grounded on fraud, gross mismanagement or any 'cause' mentioned in § 1104(a)(1), rather the following § 1104(a)(2) is relied upon. This permits the court to order the appointment of a trustee in the best interests of the estate").

work together where existing management could not, particularly in circumstances in which the various parties are antagonistic to one another.

§ 10–9 Grounds for Appointment of Trustee—Powers of the Trustee

Basically, the trustee exercises all the rights of a DIP, including authority to operate the business.[1] The Code also requires the trustee to conduct an investigation of the debtor's financial condition and operations. Indeed, the Supreme Court has held that the trustee even controls the corporate attorney-client privilege.[2]

§ 10–10 Examiners

As an alternative to appointing a Chapter 11 trustee, the court may appoint an examiner to investigate the debtor's affairs.[1] Section 1104(b) provides:

> (b) If the court does not order the appointment of a trustee under this section, then at any time before the confirmation of a plan, on request of a party in interest or the United States trustee, and after notice and a hearing, the court shall order the appointment of an examiner to conduct such an investigation of the debtor as is appropriate, including an investigation of any allegations of fraud, dishonesty, incompetence, misconduct, mismanagement, or irregularity in the management of the affairs of the debtor of or by current or former management of the debtor, if—
>
>> (1) such appointment is in the interests of creditors, any equity security holders, and other interests of the estate; or
>>
>> (2) the debtor's fixed, liquidated, unsecured debts, other than debts for goods, services, or taxes, or owing to an insider, exceed $5,000,000.

Although section 1104(b)(1) specifies an examiner "shall" be appointed to conduct an investigation when such appointment is in the interest of creditors, equity security holders and other interests of the estate, this first basis for appointing an examiner contemplates judicial consideration of the

---

§ 10–9

1. Section 321 sets forth the basic qualifications for a trustee. A trustee may be an individual or a corporation authorized by its charter to act as trustee. A person who served as an examiner in the case is not eligible to serve as trustee, 11 U.S.C.A. § 321(b), nor may that person be employed by the trustee. 11 U.S.C.A. § 327(f); see also 11 U.S.C.A. §§ 1106(a) & 1108.

2. Commodity Futures Trading Comm'n v. Weintraub, 471 U.S. 343, 105 S.Ct. 1986, 85 L.Ed.2d 372 (1985), on remand, 776 F.2d 1049 (7th Cir. 1985).

§ 10–10

1. The number of reported cases suggests examiners are infrequently appointed. See In re Jartran, Inc., 78 B.R. 524 (Bankr. N.D.Ill. 1987); In re Florida Peach Corp. of America, Int., 63 B.R. 833 (Bankr. M.D.Fla.1986); In re Carnegie International Corp., 51 B.R. 252 (Bankr. S.D.Ind.1984); In re John Peterson Motors, Inc., 47 B.R. 551 (Bankr. D. Minn. 1985); In re Gilman Services, Inc., 46 B.R. 322 (Bankr. D.Mass.1985); In re Baldwin United Corp., 46 B.R. 314 (Bankr. S.D.Ohio 1985); In re Shelter Resources Corp., 35 B.R. 304 (Bankr. N.D.Ohio 1983); In re Tyler, 18 B.R. 574 (Bankr. S.D.Fla.1982); Matter of Burnside, Lee & Harris Diamond Co., 17 B.R. 104 (Bankr. Fla.1981); Matter of Liberal Market, Inc., 11 B.R. 742 (Bankr. S.D.Ohio, 1981); In re 1243 20th Street, Inc., 6 B.R. 683 (Bankr. D. D.C. 1980); In re Lenihan, 4 B.R. 209 (Bankr. D.R.I.1980); In re Bel Air Associates, Ltd., 4 B.R. 168 (Bankr. W.D. Okla. 1980).

need for an examiner.[2] Further, naked allegations of misconduct will not suffice; appointment of an examiner requires presentment of evidence of misconduct. In *In re Lenihan*,[3] the United States Trustee tested section 1104(b)(1) by seeking appointment of an examiner and refusing to present evidence supporting his assertions of fraud. The U.S. Trustee contended the Code only requires allegations of misconduct for appointment of an examiner, not evidence. Rejecting that position, the court noted section 1104(b)(1)'s notice and hearing requirement becomes superfluous unless the Code contemplates judicial consideration of the issue after evidence.[4]

The Code also couches the second basis for an examiner in mandatory language, requiring such an appointment when "the debtor's fixed, liquidated, unsecured debts other than debts for goods, services, or taxes, or owing to an insider, exceed $5,000,000."[5] Some courts nevertheless hold that even in cases that satisfy this debt requirement, the appointment of an examiner requires some further reason or purpose. In *In re Shelter Resources Corp.*,[6] the SEC and two secured creditors moved for appointment of an examiner because matters relating to a shareholder derivative action needed investigation and because the debtor's unsecured debts exceeded $5,000,000. After a hearing on the request, both the state and bankruptcy courts approved settlement of the derivative action. The bankruptcy court then refused to appoint an examiner. Acknowledging that the debtor met the $5,000,000 debt requirement in 1104(b)(2), the court nevertheless found the circumstances did not warrant the cost and expense of an examiner since nothing remained to investigate.

Section 1106(b) defines somewhat the role of the examiner. The section requires examiners to investigate the debtor's affairs; file a statement of the investigation with the court; and perform any other duties of the trustee that the court orders the DIP not to perform. Courts have used the latter item, giving the examiner powers withheld from the DIP, to create a hybrid between trustees and examiners. In *In re John Peterson Motors, Inc.*[7] the debtor, an automobile dealer, sold cars out of trust (free of a security interest in inventory without remitting proceeds to the secured creditor) and engaged in other conduct warranting appointment of a trustee. However, the debtor previously filed suit alleging antitrust and racketeering violations against the creditor requesting the trustee. Concerned that the creditor might effectively oust its opponent in the antitrust suit through appointment of a trustee, the court instead appointed an examiner with most of the powers of a trustee. The debtor, however, retained authority to pursue the antitrust action. While this trustee-examiner hybrid arguably subverts trustee ap-

2. In re Revco D.S., Inc., 93 B.R. 119 (Bankr. N.D.Ohio 1988), decision rev'd, 898 F.2d 498 (6th Cir. 1990) (the word "shall" does not impose a mandatory duty upon the court to appoint an examiner when the debt limit is reached); In re Lenihan, 4 B.R. 209 (Bankr. D.R.I.1980).

3. 4 B.R. 209 (Bankr. D.R.I.1980).

4. See also In re Revco D.S., Inc., 93 B.R. 119 (Bankr. N.D.Ohio 1988), decision rev'd, 898 F.2d 498 (6th Cir. 1990); In re Bel Air Associates, Ltd., 4 B.R. 168 (Bankr. W.D. Okla. 1980).

5. 11 U.S.C.A. § 1104(b)(2); see 5 Collier on Bankruptcy ¶ 1104.03[4][a].

6. 35 B.R. 304 (Bankr. N.D.Ohio 1983); see also In re Revco D.C., Inc., 93 B.R. 119 (Bankr. N.D.Ohio 1988), decision rev'd, 898 F.2d 498 (6th Cir. 1990); In re GHR Companies, Inc., 43 B.R. 165 (Bankr. D. Mass. 1984), aff'd, 792 F.2d 476 (5th Cir. 1986) (appointment of examiner not mandatory); but see In re Revco DS, Inc., 898 F.2d 498 (6th Cir. 1990), rev'g, 93 B.R. 119 (Bankr. N.D.Ohio 1988).

7. 47 B.R. 551 (Bankr. D.Minn.1985).

pointment procedures, it also provides courts with a great deal of flexibility to assure that corporate management arrangements serve the best interest of all parties in interest.

§ 10–11 Committees and Their Operation

Aside from the debtor in possession and any trustee or examiner appointed, the other significant actors in a Chapter 11 reorganization are committees of creditors and equity security holders.[1] Official committees wield substantial bargaining power in reorganization proceedings. Committees consult with the trustee and debtor in possession concerning administration; investigate the debtor and other relevant matters; participate in formulating a plan of reorganization; and make recommendations on plan acceptance or rejection to the creditors or interests represented. A committee may request appointment of a trustee or examiner; perform other services in the interest of those represented;[2] and in certain circumstances propose a plan.[3] These powers allow a committee to play a large role in the debtor's reorganization.

Having spelled out the statutory duties in detail, we confess that the committee retains some of the mystery of the institutions in a Kafka novel. We know they are important but we do not see them at work. If there is ever to be a negotiated accommodation of the competing interest in the reorganization of a sizeable business, it is obvious various parties, each composed of multiple subparties, must have some representative with power to speak for them. Thus, we have the creditors' committee, in some cases the secured creditors' committees, and occasionally a shareholders' committee as well. The principal role of the committee is to speak and negotiate for the larger group which it represents. Because most bankruptcy negotiations occur behind closed doors and beyond the court's view—through discussion, cajole, and threat—one can rarely say how the negotiations occurred or how a particular reorganization deal was reached. In many cases, the impact of the committee is not clear. In some bankruptcies one guesses the committee plays an active role in shaping the plan and determining the interim performance of the debtor; in others, one suspects the committee is almost totally passive and in small cases there may be no committee, notwithstanding the statutory direction.

§ 10–12 Committees and Their Operation—Composition of the Committee

The Code requires the United States Trustee to appoint a committee of creditors holding unsecured claims as soon as practicable after filing of the Chapter 11 petition. Additional committees of creditors or equity security

---

§ 10–11

1. See 11 U.S.C.A. § 1102(a). For a more detailed discussion of the role of creditors' committees in Chapter 11 reorganization proceedings, see Blain & Erne, Creditors' Committees Under Chapter 11 of the United States Bankruptcy Code: Creation, Composition, Powers and Duties, 67 Marq. L. Rev. 491 (1984); Meir & Brown, Representing Creditors' Committees Under Chapter 11 of the Bankruptcy Code, 56 Am. Bankr. L.J. 217 (1982).

2. See 11 U.S.C.A. § 1103(c).

3. See id. § 1121.

holders may also be appointed.[1] A committee ordinarily consists of persons willing to serve, that hold the seven largest claims or amounts of equity securities of the kind represented.[2] To serve on a committee of unsecured creditors appointed under section 1102(a)(1), the entity appointed must: (1) be a "person,"[3] (2) who holds a claim against the estate,[4] (3) that is unsecured.[5]

Apart from the committee of unsecured creditors, the United States Trustee or bankruptcy court may appoint additional committees of creditors or equity security holders.[6] In theory the decision whether to appoint additional committees depends principally on whether such committees are "necessary" to provide adequate additional representation to the other interests. We suspect more practical considerations displace these theoretical grounds for appointing additional committees. For companies with ownership separated from management (i.e., most publicly traded debtors), shareholder interests may run contrary not only to creditors' interests, but also to management's. Further, a respectable body of thought advances the position that in bankruptcy, managers represent creditors' interests as well as those of the shareholders.[7] These factors exacerbate any selfish tendency of management. Interests of shareholders and creditors obviously conflict; the more one examines any particular case, the more intense and deep the tension appears. For all these reasons additional committees should be the norm, not the exception in a cost-free society. But multiplying the number

§ 10–12

1. See 11 U.S.C.A. § 1102(a).

2. Id. § 1102(b).

3. A governmental unit is not a person eligible to serve on a committee unless it acquired its claim against the debtor through a loan guaranty agreement or as a receiver or liquidating agent of a person. See 11 U.S.C.A. § 101(33); Matter of Baldwin–United Corp., 38 B.R. 802 (Bankr. S.D.Ohio 1984) (FDIC precluded as a governmental unit from serving on creditor's committee); In re American Atomics Corp., 2 B.R. 526 (Bankr. D. Ariz. 1980) (School district holding contingent claim not a person within meaning of Bankruptcy Code and therefore not eligible to serve on creditors' committee; cf. In re VTN, Inc., 65 B.R. 278 (Bankr. S.D.Fla.1986) (fact that governmental body performs proprietary rather than purely governmental functions is not sufficient to change characterization to person eligible to serve on creditors' committee).

4. Any holder of a claim against the estate may be eligible to serve on a committee, including a union representing employees of the debtor under a collective bargaining agreement. The fact that the claim may be disputed or the creditor unsympathetic to the debtor's reorganization efforts, or the debtor has made yet unproven allegations of fraud against the creditor, does not limit eligibility to serve. See In re Altair Airlines, Inc., 727 F.2d 88 (3d Cir.1984) (union who has right to seek enforcement of collective bargaining agreement for employees' unpaid wages is a creditor eligible to serve); In re Richmond Tank Car Co., 93 B.R. 504 (Bankr. S.D.Tex. 1988) (a disputed claim being litigated in state court did not nullify a creditor's status as an unsecured creditor and creditor retained ability to serve); In re Public Service Co. of New Hampshire, 89 B.R. 1014 (Bankr. D.N.H.1988) (strong and diverse views are not a per se disqualification for service on a creditor's committee); Matter of Enduro Stainless, Inc., 59 B.R. 603 (Bankr. N.D.Ohio 1986) (a union filing proof of claims for unpaid life, health, and supplemental unemployment premiums on behalf of debtor's workers is a creditor eligible to serve); In re M.H. Corporation, 30 B.R. 266 (Bankr. S.D.Ohio 1983) (nothing in Bankruptcy Code prevents service of creditor on committee who is unsympathetic to debtor's reorganization effort); In re Bennett, 17 B.R. 819 (Bankr. D.N.M.1982) (creditor not barred from serving on committee by debtor's unproven allegations of fraud); In re Grynberg, 10 B.R. 256 (Bankr. D. Colo. 1981) (person holding a disputed claim is still a creditor of the debtor and therefore eligible to serve on committee).

5. In re Bennett, 17 B.R. 819 (Bankr. D.N.M.1982).

6. 11 U.S.C.A. § 1102(a)(2).

7. In re Pacific Forest Industries, Inc., 95 B.R. 740 (Bankr. C.D.Cal.1989); In re N.S. Garrott & Sons, 63 B.R. 189 (Bankr. E.D.Ark. 1986); In re Coastal Equities, Inc., 39 B.R. 304 (Bankr. S.D.Cal.1984).

of players in the game costs money, sometimes lots of money and may increase the complexity of the reorganization.

Appointment of additional committees might diminish the power of the judge, or other parties, to control the reorganization procedure. The judge may already find himself astride an unruly horse and may not relish the thought of yet another actor to spook his mount. Even more important, additional committees, and the lawyers and accountants that come with them, are expensive. If only one plausible mode of reorganization exists, or there is no potential for successful reorganization, additional committees add only cost. For these reasons we suspect courts infrequently appoint additional committees in modest-sized cases, and do so less frequently than might be theoretically appropriate in large cases.

In large, complex Chapter 11 cases the sharply differing interests between various creditor groups will more likely override the practical difficulties involved, to allow appointment of additional committees. For example, *In re McLean Industries, Inc.*[8] involved four jointly administered but not consolidated debtor companies with complicated debt structures. Debentures constituted a major portion of the companies' debt. The United States Trustee appointed a single unsecured creditors' committee to represent both trade creditors and debenture holders. In ordering a separate committee for debenture holders, the court considered the ability of the committee to function, the nature of the case, and the standing and desires of the various constituencies. Although potential conflicts of interest between groups represented by a committee may not always require separate committees, over-representation of one set of interests may call for appointment of additional committees.

In some cases, however, practical considerations may militate against appointing additional committees, even for large, complex corporate debtors. In *In re Johns–Manville Corp.*[9] the district court upheld the bankruptcy court's refusal to appoint separate committees to represent common and preferred shareholders. The court found that with the reorganization in its final stages, an official committee's potential for meaningful participation in the reorganization had passed, so that the interest in assuring adequate representation did not require appointment of a separate committee.

Conflicts of interest between creditors, apart from providing a basis for appointing a separate committee, may also furnish grounds for barring a particular creditor from serving on a committee.[10] The 1986 amendments to the Bankruptcy Code repealed section 1102(c), which authorized courts to change committee membership to assure adequate representation.[11] Courts

---

8. 70 B.R. 852 (Bankr. S.D.N.Y. 1987).

9. 68 B.R. 155 (S.D.N.Y. 1986).

10. See Blain & Erne, supra note 1.

11. The court in In re Drexel Burnham Lambert Group, Inc., 118 B.R. 209 (Bankr. S.D.N.Y. 1990), denied the motion of two creditors to be added to the creditors' committee. The court relied on the deletion of section 1102(c) in concluding that it no longer had the authority to change the composition of a creditors' committee. On the other hand, the court in In re Public Service Company of New Hampshire, 89 B.R. 1014 (Bankr. D.N.H.1988), added members to a creditors' committee. The court reasoned that since it had authority under section 1102(a)(2) to order the appointment of additional committees, it had "the inherent power to provide a 'lesser included remedy' of simply directing the expansion of the existing committee." 89 B.R. at 1021. We are comfortable with citing section 1102(a)(2) to justify increasing the number of committee members; we are more comforta-

however, retained the ultimate authority to determine adequate representation issues. Prior to repeal of section 1102(c), courts frequently prohibited service on committees by insiders whose entanglement with the debtor rendered them unfit to monitor, scrutinize or negotiate with the debtor, or act as a creditor representative.[12] Similar bars prevent security holders from sitting on committees of unsecured creditors.[13]

Insiders are not the only creditors whose service on a committee may pose a conflict of interest. A business competitor's participation in a committee may also hamper a committee's ability to function properly. Members of a creditors' committee may receive a great deal of secret business information concerning the debtor. This material might include analyses of weaknesses in the debtor's administration; production or marketing structure and proposed changes or remedies; business plans for developing additional markets or customers; or, data on bids or future contracts or agreements in the works. Disclosure of this could prove extremely useful to a competitor and damaging to the debtor.

Two alternatives exist for dealing with this problem: the court can bar competitors from serving on any committee, or it can appoint a separate committee of competitors and limit their access to confidential business materials. *In re Wilson Foods Corp.*[14] adopted the first approach. There, one of the debtor's twenty largest creditors, a business competitor, sought appointment to the unsecured creditor's committee. The court denied the request, noting the conflict between a committee member's duty to the debtor and other creditors, and the competitor's duty to its own shareholders to maximize profits. Where business competitors comprise a significant portion of the debtor's creditors, appointing a separate committee with limited access to confidential business data may be necessary to protect both the debtor's operations and to assure adequate representation. *In re Texaco*[15] followed the second approach and allowed appointment of a separate committee of industry creditors. The Industry Creditors Committee initially received only limited access to business information concerning the debtor. Later, after resolution of most of those claims against the debtor and the resignation of several committee members, the court ordered the separate committees merged. The court found the committees received virtually all the same information, and therefore the marginal benefits derived from separate committees did not justify the additional cost.

§ 10–13 Committees and Their Operations—Powers and Duties of a Committee

Official committees consult with the debtor or trustee concerning administration of the case; investigate the debtor's business and financial condi-

---

ble with citing section 105 to justify specifying the new committee members.

12. In re Swolsky, 55 B.R. 144 (Bankr. N.D.Ohio 1985); In re Penn–Dixie Industries, Inc., 9 B.R. 941 (Bankr. S.D.N.Y. 1981); but cf. In re Vermont Real Estate Inv. Trust, 20 B.R. 33 (Bankr. D.Vt.1982) (fact that creditor is an insider because married to debtor's former president alone will not prevent creditor from serving on committee, but creditor must disqualify self from participating where a conflict of interest may be present).

13. In re The Charter Co., 44 B.R. 256 (Bankr. M.D.Fla.1984) (holder of preferred, convertible stock not eligible to serve on creditors' committee).

14. 31 B.R. 272 (Bankr. W.D. Okla. 1983).

15. 79 B.R. 560 (Bankr. S.D.N.Y. 1987).

tion; participate in formulating a plan of reorganization; make recommendations to their constituencies regarding any plan proposed; request appointment of a trustee or examiner; and perform other services.[1] As a party in interest, the committee may appear and be heard on any issue in the Chapter 11 case.[2] The Code also authorizes committees to retain accountants, attorneys and other agents to represent the committee and assist it in carrying out its functions.[3]

Committees hold significant leverage in plan negotiations even where unsecured creditors would receive little or no distribution in liquidation. Creditors with "impaired"[4] claims vote on the proposed plan during the confirmation process.[5] Unless at least one-half in number, and two-thirds in amount of each class, vote to accept, the plan of reorganization cannot be confirmed except through the "cramdown"[6] procedures of section 1129(b). Debtors wisely avoid cramdowns where they can. Preparation for and participation in cramdown litigation diverts management attention from the needs of the business, and the surrounding adverse publicity may drive customers away. Equally important, interests junior to a rejecting class cannot receive anything on account of their claims or interests under a cramdown plan. This means shareholders, which may include the debtor's officers and managers, may not retain any interest under the plan. To avoid disruption and to assure that the current owners retain control after Chapter 11, the owners will make significant concessions to the creditors in order to get their vote and avoid the cramdown.

The debtor in possession's authority to remain in possession of the estate and operate its business sets parameters for other committee powers.[7] For example, in *In re UNR Industries, Inc.*,[8] the court denied a request for modification of the debtor's operating order as unduly interfering with the debtor's day-to-day operations. The trade creditors' committee requested entry of an order requiring the debtor to give prior written notice to the committee of certain proposed salary increases, capital expenditures, commitments to purchase inventory and lease agreements. A broad range of business activities, including preparation of future budgets, budget revisions and forecasts of future operations would have required prior consultation with the committee under the proposed order. The court rejected the committee's request because the debtor's authority to conduct business as usual after the Chapter 11 implicitly excluded day-to-day meddling by

§ 10–13

1. 11 U.S.C.A. § 1103(c).

2. Id. § 1109.

3. Id. § 1103(a). However, an attorney or accountant employed by a committee may not represent any other entity having an adverse interest in connection with the case while employed by the committee. Representation of one or more creditors of the class represented by the committee is not per se representation of an adverse interest. Id. § 1103(b).

4. An unsecured claim is "impaired" under a plan unless the plan leaves unaltered the legal, equitable and contractual rights to which the holder of the claim is entitled or provides that on the effective date of the plan the creditor receives cash equal to the allowed amount of its claim. See Id. § 1124.

5. See our discussion of confirming a plan of reorganization, § 10–17 infra.

6. Cramdown procedures allow for the acceptance of a reorganization plan despite the rejection of the plan by certain creditors. See our discussion of section 1129(b), § 10–19 infra.

7. Note, however, that a state law accountant-client privilege cannot be used to deny a creditors' committee access to financial information and documentation in the hands of the debtor's accountants. Matter of International Horizons, Inc., 689 F.2d 996 (11th Cir.1982).

8. 30 B.R. 609 (Bankr. N.D.Ill. 1983).

creditors. Similarly, the court in *In re Calvary Temple Evangelistic Association*,[9] held a creditors' committee did not have standing to bring a motion for authority to sell the debtor's real estate, because the committee's sections 1109(b) or 1103(c)(5) powers did not extend to proceedings involving the ongoing operations and business judgment of the debtor.

Although a committee cannot interfere with the debtor's ongoing operations and business judgment, committees can take certain steps when the debtor fails to pursue potential assets of the estate. As discussed in our Chapter 6, the Code gives a DIP substantial powers to avoid unperfected security interests,[10] preferential transfers,[11] and fraudulent conveyances.[12] Potential recoveries under these sections often represent a significant asset of the estate and source of funds for payments to creditors. Because the creditor who received the voidable transfer may be uniquely important to the continued operation of the business, the debtor may choose not to avoid the preference. The short-term interests of some or all of the creditors in maximizing the current assets of the estate arguably conflict with the long-term interests of other creditors, with the debtor in possession and with others such as the employees. Courts sometimes side with the debtor in possession to bar the creditors' committee from pursuing avoidance actions. Typically the court will allow the creditors' committee to pursue the avoidance action only after a hearing and upon a finding the debtor has been asked and has refused to pursue the action, and after concluding that the debtor's refusal is an abuse of discretion.[13]

§ 10–14 Committees and Their Operations—Who Pays and How

Just underneath the surface of legal issues surrounding the question of who operates or controls the debtor's estate after a Chapter 11 filing, runs a more practical and perhaps more important consideration—who pays and how? Each actor in the Chapter 11 proceeding hires its own set of attorneys and accountants (sometimes business or financial consultants as well).[1]

Section 327 authorizes the trustee "with the court's approval" to employ "one or more attorneys, accountants, appraisers, auctioneers, or other professional persons * * *." Section 328 authorizes any "committee appointed under section 1102" to employ a professional person on "any reasonable terms and conditions of employment * * *." Although neither section 327 nor 328 states that the fees of such lawyers and accountants will be paid out

9. 47 B.R. 520 (Bankr. D.Minn.1984).

10. 11 U.S.C.A. § 544(a).

11. Id. § 547.

12. Id. §§ 548 & 544(b).

13. See In re Amarex, Inc., 36 B.R. 59 (Bankr. W.D. Okla. 1984) (creditors' committee did not have standing to bring suit to avoid preferential transfer, where it did not seek court approval prior to filing action and debtor was involved in settlement negotiations with creditors over possible preferential transfers); In re Toledo Equipment Co., Inc., 35 B.R. 315 (Bankr. N.D.Ohio 1983) (creditors committee lacked standing to bring suit to avoid preferential transfer where no assertion made that the committee had requested the DIP to bring suit or that the DIP's inaction was unjustifiable).

For a full discussion of the issue who can assert the avoiding powers, see § 6–2 supra.

§ 10–14

1. The Code authorizes the trustee and the debtor in possession (which has the powers of a trustee pursuant to 11 U.S.C.A. § 1107) to retain attorneys, accountants and other professional persons under section 327.

of the assets of the estate, that is the rule.² Moreover, these fees are "administrative expenses" that are recoverable under section 503 from the assets of the estate prior to the payment of claims of general creditors.³ These expenses—substantially in addition to and not in lieu of the ordinary expenses of operating the business—are surely one of the reasons why many small businesses die in Chapter 11. They are a reason why even larger businesses seek to avoid it. For example, in *In re Texaco,* the *Texaco* bankruptcy lasted four years; it was reported that lawyers were permitted to file applications for legal services not to exceed $10 million.⁴ As indicated above, these expenses and the cost to the estate are the strongest reason for refusing the appointment of multiple committees and multiple lawyers and accountants to represent adverse interests.

C. THE PLAN OF REORGANIZATION
§ 10–15 A Practical Overview

The debtor's ultimate goal in Chapter 11 proceedings is formulating and confirming a plan of reorganization. Code sections staying acts against the debtor,¹ authorizing operation of the debtor's business,² use, sale or lease of property,³ and obtaining credit,⁴ provide breathing space for the debtor to determine how best to reorganize⁵ and preserve its going-concern value.

Developing a plan of reorganization requires the debtor to evaluate its current financial situation and resources, determine the changes and resources necessary to conduct future operations on a profit-making basis, and reconcile these items with creditor demands. This brief laundry list of what reorganization "requires" the debtor to do belies the difficulty and complexity of the task. Reorganization is a process of negotiation, accommodation and compromise, carried on for the most part outside of the courtroom. Almost by definition, claims against the debtor exceed available assets.⁶ Tensions between various groups asserting claims against or interests in the debtor, their expectations about "what they can get out of the debtor" and the financial resources available, play a significant role in shaping the reorganization. Code provisions do set limits, and parties may opt to battle it out in court if an impasse occurs. Even so, a real understanding of the reorganization process requires some appreciation of the parties involved,

---

2. 11 U.S.C.A. § 328.

3. In re Glade Springs, Inc., 77 B.R. 184 (Bankr. E.D.Tenn.1987) (appraisal fees permitted as allowable administrative expense); Matter of Malaspina, 30 B.R. 267 (Bankr. W.D.Pa.1983) (attorney fees are permitted as an allowable administrative expense and warrant priority).

4. In re Texaco, 84 B.R. at 898. Judge Schwartzberg awarded fees and disbursements totaling $518,430.84. See In re Texaco, 92 B.R. 38 (S.D.N.Y.1988) (citing In re Texaco, Nos. 897 B, 20142, 20143, and 20144 (Bankr. S.D.N.Y. 1988)). An abstract in the Wall Street Journal, dated August 19, 1988, stated that a federal bankruptcy court awarded fees of $382,800 (or 3.5% of the $10 million that the attorneys had requested).

§ 10–15

1. 11 U.S.C.A. § 362.
2. Id. § 1108.
3. Id. § 363.
4. Id. § 364.

5. Reorganization may involve either a change in business or management practices with the debtor continuing in business or a sale of all or substantially all of the assets. See id. § 1123(b)(4). For a detailed discussion of liquidating plans of reorganization see, Anderson & Wright, Liquidating Plans of Reorganization, 56 Am. Bankr. L.J. 29 (1982).

6. Although a debtor need not be insolvent to file a petition in bankruptcy, see 11 U.S.C.A. § 109, solvent debtors are the exception, not the rule.

their interests and goals, and the "fighting" issues which give parties leverage in negotiations.

To illustrate these points, consider a routine reorganization. The parent, a publicly held, small corporation, owned 100 percent of the stock of two separate "high tech" subsidiaries. The second of the subsidiaries, the debtor, manufactured plastic parts, had revenues of several million dollars per year, and employed 20 to 30 people. The debtor's primary assets consisted of patents, trademarks and manufacturing equipment. As frequently occurs, the companies suffered from a severe cash shortage, fell behind in their payments to creditors, and owed the IRS a substantial amount for back taxes. A threatened IRS tax levy and an involuntary petition filed against the first subsidiary precipitated the Chapter 11 filing. In a race to the courthouse the involuntary petition (filed in another state) beat the voluntary petitions by a matter of minutes, and the parties agreed to transfer the second subsidiary's reorganization proceedings to the state where the involuntary petition was filed. Who are the actors involved and what do they want?

Secured creditors stand first in line in Chapter 11 proceedings. The secured creditor in this case, a venture capital firm, held a security interest in virtually all the debtor's assets, including the patents, trademarks, equipment, machinery and accounts. In exchange for providing additional working capital through a capital contribution as well as existence financing (financing necessary to fund both the plan and subsequent operations) the venture capital firm wanted a 100 percent ownership interest in the debtor. More commonly, the secured creditor (a bank or finance company) cares only about collecting the full amount of its debt. For a fully secured creditor with a below-market-rate of interest on its loan, that means realizing on its collateral as soon as possible. An undersecured creditor, whose claim exceeds the value of its collateral, may be more willing to accommodate reorganization attempts in hopes of maximizing recovery on the unsecured portion of its claim. On the other hand, if the collateral is likely to decline in value, or if no prospects for a successful reorganization exist, an undersecured creditor may oppose any attempt to reorganize out of a belief that the value of its collateral will decline during unsuccessful reorganization efforts.

Behind secured creditors are administrative expense claims, involuntary gap creditors,[7] certain employee wage and benefit claims, certain claims against grain storage or fish storage and processing facilities, consumer deposit claims, and tax claims.[8] In general, creditors holding these types of claims do not play a substantial role in plan negotiations. Section 1129(a)(9) specifies preferred treatment for these groups and leaves little leeway for the debtor. Each party claiming administrative expense and each involuntary gap creditor has a right to cash on the effective date of the plan unless the *individual creditor* agrees to take something else. Other priority claims such as employee wages and benefits, consumer deposits, must be paid in cash on the effective date only if their *class* votes against the plan. If their class accepts the plan they may receive other property with present value

---

7. Creditors whose claims arise in an involuntary proceeding, after commencement of the case, but before filing of the order for relief or appointment of a trustee. See id. § 502(f).

8. See id. § 507(a).

equal to the claim on the date of the petition. The debtor can pay the present value of priority tax claims over a period of up to six years.[9]

After priority claimants come unsecured creditors represented by the committee whose rights and duties were discussed in the earlier section. In a game where payment in full is winning, creditors want to minimize their losses. The means of achieving this vary, depending on creditors' prospects for profiting from business with the debtor in the future; creditors' views on the potential for successful reorganization; and the amount creditors expect to receive upon liquidation. Creditors who expect to recoup losses through future transactions with the debtor may happily accept a small distribution under a plan. If creditors view the setbacks precipitating the Chapter 11 filing as temporary, they may risk delayed payment for a larger distribution, particularly if the plan ties the amount of payments to future profits. When unsecured creditors would receive nothing under a liquidation, they suffer the debtor's reorganization attempts because they have nothing more to lose.

In the example case, the unsecured creditors through their committee demanded an extremely high distribution. Despite the fact that the debtor's liquidation analysis showed they would receive nothing in a Chapter 7 case, the committee rejected debtor's offer of a 10 percent distribution (over time) as "not enough." This position is not atypical of unsecured creditors.

Particularly with larger, publicly held corporations, a second distinct group of unsecured creditors, bond and debenture holders, sometimes play a role in reorganization proceedings. Their objectives in reorganization basically track those of other unsecured creditors, except they do not expect to recoup losses through future transactions. Because debenture holders' claims arise from an investment and not a current transaction, they may be more amenable to a deferred payment plan.

Shareholders are at the bottom of the pecking order for persons holding claims or interests in the debtor. Shareholders' objectives in the reorganization depend on the extent of the debtor's insolvency (i.e., does the value of the debtor's projected earnings leave anything for shareholders after creditors receive payment) and whether the shareholders participate in management.

In the example case, clearly nothing was left for equity, and consequently the shareholders played no significant role. For less resoundingly insolvent debtors, equity committees may participate extensively in negotiating the plan and may attempt to preserve at least a share of the business for themselves. Where the owners also operate the business, a successful reorganization may depend on their continued interest.

Two other groups of actors, who do not hold claims or interests in the estate, deserve mention—management and attorneys. As noted above,[10] for companies with management separated from ownership (most publicly traded debtors) management may possess and act on interests sharply different from those of either shareholders or creditors. We suspect that in addition to its other duties, management works to preserve both their jobs and professional reputation in the business community.

9. Id. § 1129(a)(9).

10. See our discussion on appointment of additional committees, § 10–11 supra.

Lawyers also play a substantial role in shaping the reorganization. Because the process is primarily one of negotiation, the negotiating skill of the lawyer or other representative affects the deal ultimately available to the client. Furthermore, the bankruptcy specialist's experience with financially troubled companies may shift some responsibility for making business decisions (which in other contexts rests on the client) away from the client to the lawyer.

§ 10–16 The Basic Contents of the Plan of Reorganization: Best Interest, Cramdown, and Absolute Priority

The debtor usually proposes the plan. After an exclusivity period, one of the other parties in interest may propose a plan of reorganization.[1] In general a plan must:[2] designate classes of claims and interests,[3] specify which classes of claims and interests remain unimpaired,[4] and explain the proposed treatment of any class of impaired claims. The Code requires that all claims or interests within a particular class receive equal treatment unless an individual claimholder agrees to accept less.[5] In deciding whether to confirm, the court also considers feasibility, i.e., whether the plan will likely be followed by liquidation or the need for further financial reorganization.[6] Many of the confirmation standards are straightforward; either the plan meets them or it does not.

The feasibility requirement, however, provides ample fodder for disputes. How does the debtor establish feasibility? It does so through business projections, and by putting the chief financial officer, accountants, business consultants or other experts on the witness stand to explain why a new and sunny day is dawning. Business projections are inexact at best, and creditors can easily cast doubt on feasibility by challenging the debtor's assumptions and by presenting their own skeptical witnesses.

§ 10–16

1. In general, the debtor has an exclusive right to file a plan for a period of 120 days following the filing of the Chapter 11 petition. See 11 U.S.C.A. § 1121(b) & (d). Other parties in interest may file a plan only if: (i) a trustee has been appointed; (ii) the debtor has not filed a plan within the 120 day period and that time has not been extended; or (iii) a plan filed by the debtor has not been accepted by each class of impaired claims within 180 days after the Chapter 11 filing. 11 U.S.C.A. § 1121(c). For further discussion of non-debtor plans, see Rosen & Rodriguez, Section 1121 and Non–Debtor Plans of Reorganization, 56 Am. Bankr. L.J. 349 (1982).

2. Standards for confirmation of a plan are set forth in section 1129: (i) the proponent of a plan must comply with all provisions of the Bankruptcy Code, including the restrictions on disclosure and solicitation of acceptances for the plan under 11 U.S.C.A. § 1125; (ii) the plan must be proposed in good faith; (iii) the plan must approve as reasonable, payments by the proponent, the debtor or a person issuing securities or acquiring property under the plan for services; costs or expenses in connection with the plan or case must be subject to court approval as reasonable; and (iv) the identity and compensation of any insider that will be employed or retained by the reorganized debtor must also be disclosed, as well as the identity and affiliation of individuals involved in management after confirmation. For a detailed discussion of disclosure requirements, see Note, Disclosure of Adequate Information in a Chapter 11 Reorganization, 94 Harv.L.Rev. 1808 (1981); Phelan & Cheatham, Would I Lie to You? Disclosure in Bankruptcy Reorganizations, 9 Sec. Reg. L.J. 146 (1981); Thimmig, Adequate Disclosure under Chapter 11 of the Bankruptcy Code, 53 S.Cal. L. Rev. 1527 (1980).

3. See our discussion of classification of claims, § 10–24 infra.

4. See our discussion of impairment of claims, § 10–23 infra.

5. 11 U.S.C.A. § 1123(a)(4).

6. Id. § 1129(a)(11).

Apart from these general acceptance requirements, several confirmation standards merit separate attention. The best interest test sets a floor on treatment of non-consenting *individual* claimants. The "fair and equitable" standards for cramdown under section 1129(b) set a floor on treatment of non-consenting *classes* of creditors.

§ 10–17 The Basic Contents of the Plan of Reorganization: Best Interest, Cramdown, and Absolute Priority— Acceptance Requirements

Chapter 11 both requires and encourages negotiation and compromise among parties affected by a plan of reorganization. Section 1129(a)'s acceptance requirements and the alternative section 1129(b), which allows confirmation despite a class's failure to accept, both set the stage and provide the tools for making a plan. Absent a cramdown, each class of claims or interests must either be unimpaired,[1] or accept the plan if there is to be confirmation.[2] Debtors rarely possess sufficient resources to leave all creditors unimpaired, e.g., by payment in full, and therefore must negotiate with creditors for acceptance. Even where the debtor attempts a cramdown[3] under section 1129(b), the Code requires acceptance by at least one impaired class.[4]

Apart from the acceptance requirements, creditors' primary negotiating tools are delay and the threat of successful legal challenge. Financing arrangements may require confirmation of a plan within a relatively short time, and protracted confirmation proceedings encourage customers to take their business elsewhere. Furthermore, the debtor may not want to risk losing the business if it loses in court. Conversely, the threat of cramdown gives the debtor the most effective tool in its belt.[5] Section 1129(b) allows confirmation, despite a class's nonacceptance, so long as the plan provides

---

§ 10–17

1. A class that is not impaired under the plan, and each holder of an unimpaired claim or interest is conclusively presumed to have accepted the plan. 11 U.S.C.A. § 1126(f). 11 U.S.C.A. § 1124 defines "impairment." See our discussion of impairment of claims, § 10–23 infra.

2. 11 U.S.C.A. § 1129(a)(8).

3. Cramdown implies confirmation, despite a class's nonacceptance, so long as the plan provides certain minimal treatment for the dissenting class.

4. 11 U.S.C.A. § 1129(a)(10). See In re Ruti–Sweetwater, Inc., 836 F.2d 1263, 1267 (10th Cir.1988) ("Once a single noninsider class has accepted, plan may be 'crammed down' on every other class of creditors."); Hanson v. First Bank of South Dakota, N.A., 828 F.2d 1310 (8th Cir.1987) (actual acceptance by at least one impaired class is necessary for confirmation of a plan under § 1129(a)(10)); In re Gilbert, 104 B.R. 206 (Bankr. W.D.Mo.1989) ("only one impaired non-insider class need vote to accept a plan for purposes of confirmation under Section 1129(a) or (b)"); In re Douglas Hereford Ranch, Inc., 76 B.R. 781 (Bankr. D.Mont.1987) (one class of creditors must affirmatively accept; silence is inadequate to constitute acceptance); see also In re Perdido Motel Group, Inc., 101 B.R. 289 (Bankr. N.D.Ala.1989) (priority tax claims are not a class of impaired claims and the government's acceptance as a class would not satisfy § 1129(a)(10) confirmation requirement); In re Pine Lake Village Apartment Co., 19 B.R. 819 (Bankr. S.D.N.Y. 1982) (production of one accepting class which has been deemed accepted does not meet the requirements of § 1129(a)(10)).

The requirement that at least one impaired class accept applies even to Chapter 11 liquidating plans. In re Russell, 44 B.R. 452 (Bankr. E.D.N.C.1984). For purposes of determining whether at least one impaired class has accepted, acceptances of insiders are excluded from consideration. 11 U.S.C.A. § 1129(a)(10); In re Aztec Co., 107 B.R. 585 (Bankr. M.D.Tenn.1989) (impaired class deemed to have accepted even though class contained insiders, where non-insiders voted overwhelmingly to accept).

5. For a discussion of section 1129(b) and its effect of settlement negotiations, see Booth,

certain minimal treatment for the dissenting class. The power of a class to bind all of its members prevents a few intractable creditors from blocking a plan.[6]

Whether the debtor (and creditors) settle or hold out and try their luck in court depends on estimates of the strengths and weaknesses of each side's case, the financial flexibility of the debtor, its willingness to risk losing, and the quality of counsel. In the example case, the unsecured creditor's committee rejected treatment offered under the plan (10 percent) as "not enough" even though it met the section 1129(b) standards.[7] The debtor refused to reconsider its offer. Debtors in this situation sometimes compromise by offering creditors a piece of the hoped for profits in exchange for agreement (i.e., making distributions under the plan a percentage of post-confirmation profits). This debtor rejected that alternative for three reasons. First, the company was too thin; sharing profits with creditors would deprive the new capital investor of any return on its investment. Second, the debtor believed it could beat the creditors in court. Finally, the debtor was willing to risk losing its company. We can only speculate on the reasons behind the committee's "no compromise" position. Most likely it felt that by hanging tough, the debtor would cave in and give it something extra. The committee guessed wrong and the debtor won confirmation.

§ 10–18 The Basic Contents of the Plan of Reorganization: Best Interest, Cramdown, and Absolute Priority— Best Interest Test

Section 1129(a)(7)'s best interest test protects individual dissenting claims[1] by requiring that each claimholder receive property equal in value to the amount the creditor would receive in a Chapter 7 liquidation of the debtor. A plan proponent demonstrates compliance with the best interest test through a liquidation analysis showing the value of the debtor's assets, the secured claims against those assets, projected Chapter 11 and Chapter 7 administrative expenses, priority claims and unsecured claims, and a calculation of the percent of distribution to each type of claim. Like business projections, liquidation analyses may be quite subjective.

In the example case, the debtor's liquidation analysis showed unsecured creditors would receive nothing upon liquidation; claims of secured creditors, administrative expenses and priority claims depleted the entire estate.

The Cramdown on Secured Creditors: An Impetus Toward Settlement, 60 Am. Bankr. L.J. 69 (1986); Broude, Cramdown and Chapter 11 of the Bankruptcy Code: The Settlement Imperative, 39 Bus. Law. 441 (1984).

6. Section 1126 controls acceptance. A class of claims has accepted the plan if creditors holding at least one-half in number and two-thirds in amount of the claims voting, vote to accept. 11 U.S.C.A. § 1126(c). A class of interests accepts if, of those voting, at least two-thirds in amount vote to accept. Id. § 1126(d). A class vote in favor of acceptance binds dissenting members, except to the extent treatment proposed under the plan does not meet the best interest test. See id. § 1129(a)(8); cf. id. § 1129(a)(7); see also In re Friese, 103 B.R. 90 (Bankr. S.D.N.Y.1989) ("Court cannot deem an impaired class to have accepted a plan if no creditors in that class have voted"); but see In re Ruti–Sweetwater, Inc., 836 F.2d 1263 (10th Cir. 1988) (Nonvoting and nonobjecting members of class can be deemed to have accepted reorganization plan for purposes of § 1129(b)); In re Campbell, 89 B.R. 187 (Bankr. N.D.Fla.1988) (same).

7. See this discussion in the next section, § 10–18 infra.

§ 10–18

1. The acceptance requirements of § 1129(a)(8) and (10) apply to classes of claims, as do the fair and equitable and no unfair discrimination standards of § 1129(b).

The creditors' committee formally accepted the debtor's liquidation analysis, even though it included appraisals of patents and trademarks—assets whose valuation is highly problematic. Because of this stipulation, the proposed 10 percent payment to unsecured creditors satisfied the best interest test. Creditors received more under the plan than they would in liquidation. Had creditors persuaded the court to adopt a higher value for the trademarks and patents, failure to comply with the best interest test might have prevented confirmation over creditors' objections. For this reason, a creditor who wishes to prevent confirmation should seldom stipulate to the debtor's liquidation analysis. *Note that the best interest test applies to creditors, irrespective of class votes. If liquidation will bring 10 percent, each nonconsenting creditor must get 10 percent or the plan fails even if such creditor's class votes for the plan.*

§ 10–19 The Basic Contents of the Plan of Reorganization: Best Interest, Cramdown, and Absolute Priority—Requirements for Cramdown Under Section 1129(b)

On request of the plan proponent, section 1129(b) allows confirmation despite the rejection of one or more classes, "if the plan does not discriminate unfairly, and is fair and equitable, with respect to each class of claims or interests that is impaired under, and has not accepted, the plan."[1] Paragraphs (A), (B), and (C) of section 1129(b)(2) deal with what is "fair and equitable" for holders of secured claims, holders of unsecured claims, and equity holders. Note that the verb preceding these paragraphs is "includes." The Fifth Circuit focused on this word in *In re D & F Const. Inc.*,[2] to conclude that a plan that complied with section 1129(b)(2)(B) was not "fair and equitable."

In *D & F*, the debt was approximately $7 million and the collateral had a value of about $5 million. The plan proposed to pay the creditor the $5 million present value of its collateral over a fifteen year period at ten percent interest with a final balloon payment of over $4.7 million. Under this schedule, the amount owed would not fall below $5 million until the end of the twelfth year. In reversing the confirmation of the plan, Judge Clark wrote, "A plan which does not meet the standards set forth in section 1129(b)(2) cannot be 'fair and equitable.' However, technical compliance with all the requirements in section 1129(b)(2) does not assure that the plan is fair and equitable."[3]

§ 10–20 The Basic Contents of the Plan of Reorganization: Best Interest, Cramdown, and Absolute Priority—Requirements for Cramdown Under Section 1129(b)—Fair and Equitable Treatment—Secured Claims

Section 1129(b)(2)(A) provides three alternate standards for cramdown of

§ 10–19
1. 11 U.S.C.A. § 1129(b)(1).
2. 865 F.2d 673 (5th Cir.1989).
3. Id. at 575. The court added, "We do not hold that there can never be an occasion when negative amortization would be fair and equitable. We do say this plan is not fair and equitable." Id. at 676. See generally Schermer & Burtz, Negative Amortization and Plan Confirmation, 8 Bankr. Dev. J. (1991).

a plan over the objection of a class of secured creditors.[1] The first standard permits cramdown if the members of the class retain their lien on the secured property,[2] and receive cash payments, with face amounts of at least the allowed amount of the secured claim[3] and a present value equal to the value of their collateral.[4] This allows the debtor to do more than simply cure defaults and reinstate the loans. The debtor may extend payments beyond the security agreement's original maturity date. Further, present value calculations use a market rather than contract rate of interest.[5] This is a boon to debtors who originally borrowed at a time of high interest rates. Conversely, for debtors who previously paid interest at a low rate, it represents a cost of extending the loan's maturity date.

Confirmation is also possible over a secured creditor's dissent if the plan provides that each member of the class will realize the "indubitable equivalent" of its allowed secured claim.[6] This language comes from *In re Murel Holding Corp.*,[7] where Judge Learned Hand indicated that whether the plan provides a secured creditor with the indubitable equivalence of its original security depends on:

(i) whether the substituted security completely compensates the debtor; and,

(ii) the likelihood the creditor will receive payment.

In what instances will payment in property other than cash constitute an "indubitable equivalent"? The court in *In re San Felipe Voss, Ltd.*[8] considered the question. There, the court held that equity securities of a third-party purchaser can form the indubitable equivalent of a secured creditor's claim.[9] The court interpreted the language of section 1129 as prohibiting only the use of equity securities of the newly reorganized debtor in satisfying a secured party's claim. In deciding this case, the court in *San Felipe* rejected the holding of an earlier case, *In re Future Energy Corp.*,[10] which held "a transfer of property satisfies the 'indubitable equivalent' standard only if that property is the equivalent of cash."[11] The *San Felipe* court noted that bankruptcy courts had a responsibility to review the

§ 10-20

1. Ordinarily, the holder of an allowed secured claim against specific property of the debtor will be placed in a separate class. 5 Collier on Bankruptcy ¶ 1122.03[6].

2. The plan may be crammed down even though the property is transferred to another entity, as long as the creditor retains its lien. 11 U.S.C.A. § 1129(b)(2)(A)(i)(I).

3. Pursuant to section 506(a), a claim secured by a lien on property in which the debtor has an interest, is secured to the extent of the value of the collateral, and unsecured to the extent the claim amount exceeds that value. For secured creditors the allowed amount of the claim will be (i) the amount of the claim or (ii) the value of the collateral, whichever is smaller, unless the creditor is an undersecured creditor to whom the § 1111(b)(2) election is available. For a discussion of the treatment of undersecured creditors, see § 10-20 infra.

4. 11 U.S.C.A. § 1129(b)(2)(A)(i).

5. See Klee, All You Ever Wanted to Know about Cram Down Under the New Bankruptcy Code, 53 Am. Bankr. L.J. 133, 158 (1979); see also our Chapter 9, supra, for a discussion of Chapter 13 cases.

6. 11 U.S.C.A. § 1129(b)(2)(A)(iii); see also the discussion of the "indubitable equivalence" standard as it relates to adequate protection under section 362.

7. 75 F.2d 941 (2d Cir.1935).

8. 115 B.R. 526 (Bankr. S.D.Tex.1990).

9. Id. at 529.

10. 83 B.R. 470 (Bankr. S.D.Ohio 1988).

11. Id. at 495-96.

stability and liquidity of all securities offered as part of a reorganization plan.[12]

The Fifth Circuit, in *Matter of Sandy Ridge Development Corp.*,[13] acknowledged that the abandonment of the collateral to the creditor, for a credit to the extent of the fair market value of the property, also satisfies the "indubitable equivalence" standard.[14] The granting of a replacement lien on similar collateral with a value equal to or greater than its original collateral, may also satisfy this standard.[15]

Sale of the property [16] free and clear, with the creditor's liens attaching to proceeds of the sale provides the third means for cramdown. Payment of the claim secured by those liens must then follow either the present value standard or the indubitable equivalent standard for cramdown.[17]

§ 10–21 The Basic Contents of the Plan of Reorganization: Best Interest, Cramdown, and Absolute Priority—Requirements for Cramdown Under Section 1129(b)—The Absolute Priority Rule—Unsecured Claims

The absolute priority rule is the name of the standard for fair and equitable treatment of dissenting classes of unsecured claims. If a class of unsecured claims dissents, the plan must eliminate junior claims and interests unless the dissenting class receives property [1] with a present value equal to the allowed amount of their claims.[2] The debtor may pay creditors over time as long as the present value of the time payment at least equals the allowed amount of the claim.

To understand what we have just said consider the following case. Assume an unsecured claimant with a note for $100,000 on which there had been no payments. Assume that the liquidation value is 33 percent; thus on liquidation of the corporation the creditor would receive $33,333. Assume further that the unsecured claimant has objected to the confirmation plan. Now consider three possibilities. First is a payment of $33,333 over five years with no interest. Second is a payment of $33,333 with a market rate of interest over five years. Finally is the payment of $100,000 with interest over five years. The first proposal, the payment of $33,333 over five years with no interest, meets neither the best interest nor the absolute priority tests. Since the present value of payment over five years would be signifi-

---

12. 115 B.R. at 530.

13. 881 F.2d 1346 (5th Cir.1989), reh'g denied, 889 F.2d 663 (5th Cir. 1989).

14. 881 F.2d at 1350 (noting that when a secured creditor "will receive the actual property underlying its secured claim * * * it is clear that it will receive the indubitable equivalent of its secured claim."); see also In re Western Real Estate Fund, Inc., 109 B.R. 455 (Bankr. W.D. Okla. 1990) (the transfer of property meets the requirements of § 1129(b)(2)(A)(iii) because property is the indubitable equivalent of itself).

15. 124 Cong. Rec. H. 11,104 (Sept. 28, 1978); 124 Cong. Rec. S. 17, 420 (Oct. 6, 1978).

16. The sale may be under 11 U.S.C.A. § 363(k), which allows a creditor holding a lien to bid at the sale and offset its claims, both the secured and unsecured portions, against the sale price.

17. 11 U.S.C.A. § 1129(b)(2)(A)(ii).

§ 10–21

1. Property received may be tangible or intangible, including securities of the debtor or a successor to the debtor under a plan of reorganization. H. Rep. 595, 95th Cong., 1st Sess. 414 (1977).

2. 11 U.S.C.A. § 1129(b)(2)(B).

cantly less than $33,333 (the amount that would be received on liquidation), the proposal flunks the best interest test. The second proposal meets the best interest test but fails the absolute priority rule because the absolute priority rule requires present value equal not to the amount that would be received on liquidation, but to the amount of the allowed claim. That amount is $100,000. Only the third proposal meets both tests, as would a proposal to pay $100,000 on confirmation of the plan.

Mostly we have concentrated on "claims" and have ignored "interests." Interests are the rights of shareholders (common and preferred), of partners in partnerships, and conceivably those of other parties whose rights do not rise to the level of creditors. Typically, therefore, there will be junior and subordinate classes of interests only in corporations that have complex financial structures that include both common and preferred stockholders.[3]

To cram down over a dissenting class of interests, junior interest holders must be eliminated, unless each interest holder receives property with a present value, as of the effective date of the plan, equal to the greater of the allowed amount of any fixed liquidation preference, fixed redemption price, or the value of such interest.[4]

The absolute priority rule applies to each dissenting class—if a junior class receives anything at all, the plan must pay the dissenting class in full. A plan may propose that a senior class give up value to junior claims or interests, but the dissent of a senior or intermediate class will prevent confirmation.[5] For example, a plan might divide its unsecured creditors into two separate classes, one comprised of a secured creditor's unsecured deficiency claim, and the other of trade creditors. Even if the trade creditor class agreed to give equity an interest in the reorganized company, the deficiency claimant's objection would preclude confirmation because a junior class receives property under the plan.

The absolute priority rule provides unsecured creditors with a significant bargaining chip against the debtor—the ability to insist on elimination of ownership interests. This power, however, may present a serious obstacle to reorganization in instances where the debtor is a sole proprietor, such as a farmer, or where a majority shareholder's management skills and expertise would greatly enhance the debtor's prospects for success. In those circumstances, a particularly recalcitrant class of creditors or interest holders, or a creditor with a grudge (and a large enough claim) could completely derail a debtor's reorganization attempts. It might occur even where there are favorable business prospects.

---

3. See Klee, All You Ever Wanted to Know About Cram Down Under the New Bankruptcy Code, 53 Am. Bankr. L.J. 133, 147 (1979).

4. 11 U.S.C.A. § 1129(b)(2)(C). But note that the fair and equitable standard also prevents senior classes from receiving more than payment in full if a junior class of claims or interests objects. H. Rep. 595, 95th Cong., 1st Sess. 414 (1977). This requirement gives negotiating leverage to ownership interests. If the property distributed to senior classes of claims and interests is stock of the debtor, valuation of the business will be required to determine whether any class received more than the present value of the allowed amount of their claims or interests. Senior classes may often give up value to obtain consent to the plan and avoid a costly valuation. Klee, All You Ever Wanted to Know About Cram Down Under the New Bankruptcy Code, 53 Am. Bankr. L.J. 133, 145 (1979).

5. Klee, supra note 4, at 144.

What of the case in which the shareholders propose to keep the equity interest in the reorganized corporation not as shareholders, but as contributors of new capital? Does the absolute priority rule stigmatize these very people so they may never again be shareholders of the corporation unless they are welcomed by the creditors? The government took this position in the Supreme Court case *Norwest Bank Worthington v. Ahlers*.[6]

In *Ahlers* a farm couple proposed to keep their equity in their farm despite the fact they did not meet the absolute priority rule on the ground that they would contribute "sweat equity" and thus earn the right to the ownership of the property. By a split decision the Court of Appeals for the Eighth Circuit accepted that argument; the Supreme Court reversed. Justice White found that Congress did not intend for any such sweat-equity exception to the absolute priority rule. He pointed out a similar proposal had been made to Congress and had been rejected. Of course, lurking in the wings of granting any such exception is the possibility that the absolute priority rule could be driven completely off stage. If sweat equity were enough, equity holders could propose they would "work extra hard" for five years and upon a finding that the value of that sweat was equal to their equity interest, the court could approve a plan over the objection of a class of creditors despite those creditors' failure to be paid in full. Necessarily the value of such labor is difficult to measure; indeed, the idea that there is any increment of labor over and above the normal obligation that the debtor would otherwise have is problematical. Accordingly, the Court rejected the argument in *Ahlers*. Note, however, that the Congress has accepted the idea for a limited number of farm bankruptcy cases by its enactment of Chapter 12.

What does the *Ahlers* case mean if the existing shareholders propose not the addition of sweat equity, but the payment of cash or contribution of property with a fixed value as their payment for an equity interest in the reorganized corporation? Prior to 1978, such acquisition by payment was known as the *Los Angeles Lumber*[7] exception to the absolute priority rule. We discuss the new value exception at greater length in our Chapter 11.[8] As this book is written, several courts, including the Court of Appeals for the Sixth and Seventh Circuits,[9] have agreed that there is a "new value" exception from the absolute priority rule. These courts have found that shareholders, partners, or other holders of junior interests can retain those interests if they pay new value that meets three requirements. These requirements come from a pre-Code case, *Case v. Los Angeles Lumber Products Co.*[10] They are the following: (1) the new value must be contributed in money or money's worth; (2) the contribution from the shareholders or other junior interests must be "necessary"; and (3) the contribution must be substantial or, as the rule is sometimes stated, must equal or exceed the going-concern value of the company.

---

6. 485 U.S. 197, 108 S.Ct. 963, 99 L.Ed.2d 169 (1988), on remand, 844 F.2d 587 (8th Cir. 1988).

7. See Case v. Los Angeles Lumber Products Co., 308 U.S. 106, 60 S.Ct. 1, 84 L.Ed. 110 (1939), reh'g denied, 308 U.S. 637, 60 S.Ct. 258, 84 L.Ed. 529 (1939).

8. See § 11–25 infra.

9. See In re U.S.Truck Co., Inc., 800 F.2d 581 (6th Cir.1986); In re Potter Material Service, Inc., 781 F.2d 99 (7th Cir.1986).

10. 308 U.S. 106, 60 S.Ct. 1, 84 L.Ed. 110 (1939), reh'g denied, 308 U.S. 637, 60 S.Ct. 258, 84 L.Ed. 529 (1939).

Other courts have concluded that the new value exception did not survive the Code's enactment. The two Courts of Appeals decisions that have approved plans based on the new value exception were both decided prior to the *Ahlers* case in the Supreme Court, at a time when there seemed to be little or no argument about the existence of the new value exception and when all of the arguments went to the question whether the exception had been satisfied in a particular case. As we indicate in greater detail in our Chapter 11, some doubt the wisdom of the new value exception and argue that it did not survive enactment of the 1978 Code.

§ 10–22 The Basic Contents of the Plan of Reorganization: Best Interest, Cramdown, and Absolute Priority—Requirements for Cramdown Under Section 1129(b)—Unfair Discrimination

A second condition for cramming down a plan on a non-consenting class is that it not "discriminate unfairly." [1] Unfair discrimination is not defined in the Code. The legislative history suggests that this criterion is to protect creditors from unfair discrimination between classes of claims with equal priority:

> From the perspective of unsecured trade claims, there is no unfair discrimination as long as the total consideration given all other classes of equal rank does not exceed the amount that would result from an exact aliquot distribution.
>
> * * *
>
> The criterion of unfair discrimination is not derived from the fair and equitable rule or from the best interests of creditors test. Rather it preserves just treatment of a dissenting class from the class's own perspective.[2]

To understand how the unfair discrimination rule might work consider the case in which there are three classes of debt: trade creditors, unsecured debenture holders and bank debt that by agreement is subordinated to the debentures, but not to the trade creditors. If the appropriate dividend for the entire group would be 30 cents on the dollar for each unsecured creditor, trade creditors could be paid 30 cents, debenture holders 60 cents, and the subordinated bank debt nothing. In effect the subordination agreement cedes the bank's claim to the debenture holders but promises nothing to the other unsecured creditors. By allowing the distribution described above the plan carries out that agreement. In addition, the trade creditors who did not negotiate for such a subordination cannot now complain simply because they were not involved in the negotiation.

An example like the one given above is contained in the legislative history as the only explicit illustration of the operation of the unfair discrimination rule. The rule might also be used to prohibit discriminatory treatment of a dissenting class in comparison with other classes having the same priority. Assume again that a pro rata distribution on liquidation would give each of the creditors 30 cents on the dollar but that there is no

---

§ 10–22

1. 11 U.S.C.A. § 1129(b)(1).

2. H. Rep. No. 595, 95th Cong., 1st Sess. 417 (1977).

subordination agreement. Assume that the plan proposes the payment of 30 cents to dissenting trade creditors, 35 cents to the debenture holders and to the unsecured bank debt. None could complain under the best interest rule because each receives more than he would on liquidation, but the trade creditors could certainly argue that they were unfairly discriminated against.

Creditors often base their unfair discrimination arguments on the classification of claims under section 1122. A debtor wishing to discriminate in favor of one creditor may separate claims which appear similar. For example, a debtor may wish to favor local creditors, creditors with which the debtor plans to have a continuing relationship, or a creditor from whom the debtor seeks new funds. In addition, the debtor may seek to separate claims in order to ensure that one impaired class votes for the reorganization plan, thereby making it eligible for cramdown. Section 1122(a) provides that a plan "may place a claim or an interest in a particular class only if such claim or interest is substantially similar to the other claims or interests of such class."[3] It is unclear from the wording of this section whether similar claims *must* be placed in the same class. Some creditors argue that the separation of similar claims results in "unfair discrimination."

In response to this argument, some courts restrict the unfair discrimination standard to cases involving subordination agreements.[4] Other courts follow a strict mechanical rule requiring all similar claims to be in one class.[5]

The Sixth Circuit has rejected strict mechanical rules for determining when separate classification is justified. The court in *In re U.S. Truck*[6] considered the question when a debtor can keep a creditor out of a class of similarly impaired claims. While the court recognized that Congress intentionally did not impose a strict requirement on the classification of similar claims, it held the debtor did not have unlimited power to manipulate classes to ensure confirmation. Instead, the courts should exercise broad discretion to determine whether proper classification, based on the circumstances, had occurred. The focus of the inquiry should be whether two similar claims have been treated differently.[7]

---

3. 11 U.S.C.A. § 1122(a). A dissenting member of an assenting class can challenge the legality of the division of unsecured claims and classes under section 1129(a)(1). Absent a dissenting class, however, a creditor cannot invoke the "unfair discrimination" language of section 1129(b).

4. See S. Rep. No. 595, 95th Cong., 1st Sess. 416 reprinted in 1978 U.S. Code Cong. & Admin. News 5787, 6372; In re Acequia, Inc., 787 F.2d 1352 (9th Cir.1986); In re Martin, 66 B.R. 921 (Bankr. D.Mont.1986).

5. Granada Wines, Inc. v. New England Teamsters and Trucking Industry Pension Fund, 748 F.2d 42, 46 (1st Cir.1984) (limitation on liability affects only the allowable amount of a claim and is not sufficient grounds for separate classification); In re Fantastic Homes Enterprises, Inc., 44 B.R. 999 (M.D.Fla. 1984) (Congress intended all claims of similar nature to be in one class, unless authorized by section 1122(b)); In re S & W Enterprise, 37 B.R. 153 (Bankr. N.D.Ill. 1984); In re Pine Lake Village Apt. Co., 19 B.R. 819 (Bankr. S.D.N.Y. 1982).

6. 800 F.2d 581 (6th Cir.1986).

7. Hanson v. First State Bank of South Dakota, N.A., 828 F.2d 1310 (8th Cir.1987) (while all substantially similar claims do not have to be included in the same class, the debtor's discretion in forming the classes is not unlimited. Classes specifically designed to manipulate class voting must be carefully scrutinized); Matter of Jersey City Medical Center, 817 F.2d 1055 (3d Cir.1987) (separate classification of physicians, medical malpractice victims, employee benefit plan participants, and trade creditors did not amount to unfair discrimination); In re AOV Industries, Inc., 792 F.2d 1140 (D.C. Cir. 1986); Matter of

Many courts, in looking at the facts and circumstances of each case have followed a four-part test enunciated for Chapter 13 bankruptcies in *In re Dziedzic*.[8] This test assumes that discrimination in bankruptcy was anticipated by Congress as an obvious result of separate classification. The following factors are considered to ensure that the natural discrimination is not unfair:

1. Whether the discrimination has a reasonable basis;
2. Whether the debtor can carry out a plan without such discrimination;
3. Whether such discrimination is proposed in good faith; and
4. The treatment of the class discriminated against.

As we say in our discussion of Chapter 13 bankruptcies, we doubt that these criteria give significant guidance except in an unusual case. We see the first test as merely identifying the debtor's selfish interests in favoring one creditor over another. Tests two and three can easily be met since it is doubtful the debtor can provide treatment for all creditors equal to the terms reached with the most favored creditor and since vindictiveness on the part of the debtor is difficult to determine. Test four may have some strength but is untested by substantive case law.

We believe that the better rule would be a presumption of equal treatment, with the burden on the debtor of persuading the court when equal treatment does not occur. In the example at the beginning of this section then, the rule would be violated and the suggested plan could not be approved over the trade creditors' dissent. Presumably the unfair discrimination rule would not prohibit giving different maturities to the obligations to each of the different classes in accordance with their interests if the present value of each set of payments was the same. Such a narrow reading of section 1129 rests on general bankruptcy policy.

D. CLAIMS

§ 10–23 Impairment of Claims

"Impairment" triggers important rights in Chapter 11. A plan must

---

LeBlanc, 622 F.2d 872 (5th Cir.1980), reh'g denied, 627 F.2d 239 (5th Cir. 1980) (the discrimination of unsecured insiders receiving nothing under a plan which gave 40% to unsecured trade creditors was not unfair based on the insiders knowledge of the financial condition and risk of investing with the debtor); In re Greystone III Joint Venture, 102 B.R. 560 (Bankr. W.D.Tex.1989), opinion aff'd, 127 B.R. 138 (W.D.Tex.1990), judgment rev'd, 948 F.2d 134 (5th Cir.1991) (marked legal and economic differences justify separate classification of Code-created deficiency claim and trade creditors); In re AG Consultants Grain Div., Inc., 77 B.R. 665 (Bankr. N.D.Ind. 1987); In re Northeast Dairy Coop Federation, Inc., 73 B.R. 239 (Bankr. N.D.N.Y. 1987) (court may not condone classification of claims for purposes of defeating goal of equal treatment of similarly situated creditors).

8. 9 B.R. 424 (Bankr. S.D.Tex.1981). Although this case involved a Chapter 13 bankruptcy, the analysis is applicable to Chapter 11 bankruptcies since section 1322, which addresses unfair discrimination, authorizes the designation of classes as provided in section 1122; see also In re 11,111, Inc., d/b/a Energy Conservation Consultants, 117 B.R. 471 (Bankr.D.Minn.1990); In re Aztec Co., 107 B.R. 585 (Bankr. M.D.Tenn.1989) (contains list of cases in which the court follows the four-part test by looking at other facts and circumstances); In re Storberg, 94 B.R. 144 (Bankr. D. Minn. 1988). Also review our discussion of section 1322 in Chapter 9.

propose treatment for every class of "impaired" claims or interests.[1] Only impaired creditors may vote on the plan. The Code establishes a conclusive presumption that classes of unimpaired claims accept the plan.[2] The right to vote gives the class power to reject the plan and so to invoke the protections of cramdown.[3]

Section 1124 of the Code defines a claim as "impaired" unless it fits within one of three narrow exceptions. The first exception applies if the plan does not alter the legal, equitable or contractual rights of the holder. Examples of alteration of the rights of a creditor are the changing of the amount of principal, changing the interest rate, altering the maturity, and changing the form or amount of collateral. In one sense a creditor's rights are like Humpty Dumpty: after a two or three year Chapter 11 proceeding there is no way to put them back together again. Presumably that kind of alteration is not the alteration spoken of in section 1124. A plan could propose to put a creditor in the same position as the creditor was in at the time the petition was filed by granting a security interest with identical collateral. That would leave the creditor technically unimpaired, even though practically in a much worse position than if the Chapter 11 had never been filed. Even an alteration that enhances the value of the creditor's claim impairs it.

The second way to leave a creditor unimpaired is to cure a default and reinstate the maturity date under the original agreement. The most obvious application of this rule allows a debtor to undo an acceleration clause in a mortgage—possibly even after a judgment or foreclosure as long as state law has not merged the judgment and mortgage.[4] Such cases are routine in Chapter 13. There the debtor continues to pay the unaccelerated amount and pays the missed installments with interest over the life of the plan, usually three years. By rendering the creditor unimpaired the debtor can retain the benefit of a favorable interest rate on a defaulted loan.[5]

Cash payment of the amount of the claim on the effective date of the plan is a third method of leaving a creditor unimpaired. An interest (e.g., a holder of preferred or common stock) may be rendered "unimpaired" by a

§ 10–23

1. 11 U.S.C.A. § 1123(a)(3).
2. Id. § 1126(f).
3. In re Wilhelm, 101 B.R. 120 (Bankr. W.D.Mo.1989) (even the slightest impairment entitles a creditor to vote on confirmation).
4. Matter of Madison Hotel Associates, 749 F.2d 410 (7th Cir.1984) (because under state law a judgment of foreclosure merely determines the amount and does not merge into the mortgage and no foreclosure sale has occurred, the creditor holding a foreclosure judgment is not impaired by cure under § 1124); In re Hewitt, 16 B.R. 973 (Bankr. D. Alaska 1982) (§ 1124 applies to allow reversal of a contractual acceleration which has been reduced to a foreclosure judgment prior to a Chapter 11 petition); contra In re Monroe Park, 18 B.R. 790 (Bankr. D.Del.1982) (cure of default and reinstatement of maturity date under mortgage not possible after entry of judgment of foreclosure); In re Saint Peter's School, 16 B.R. 404 (Bankr. S.D.N.Y.1982) (when bank obtains judgment of foreclosure before Chapter 11 filing, a debtor cannot cure or achieve a deacceleration of the prepetition mortgage).

5. See In re Kuljis Seafood Co., Inc., 73 B.R. 659 (Bankr. S.D.Miss.1986) (contract rate is appropriate when resumption of payment is called for under reorganization plan); In re Victory Construction Company, Inc., 42 B.R. 145 (Bankr. C.D. Calif. 1984) (if a claim is unimpaired under § 1124, the plan need not provide for interest at the market rate, but may reinstate the contract rate of interest); but see In re Bear Creek Ministorage, Inc., 49 B.R. 454 (Bankr. S.D.Tex.1985) (appropriate interest rate is the creditor's current lending rate).

cash payment only if the security provides for a fixed liquidation, preference, or redemption price.[6]

§ 10–24 Manipulation of Classes

A debtor may attempt to nullify a dissenting creditor's ability to invoke the protections of section 1129(b) by including that creditor within a larger class. Assume a corporate debtor with four creditors: an undersecured bank holding a secured claim of $400,000 and an unsecured claim of $100,000;[1] and three suppliers holding claims totalling $300,000. The plan proposes payment of the bank's secured claim in installments with a present value of $400,000, and a distribution to unsecured creditors equal to 20 percent of their claims (the amount creditors would otherwise receive on liquidation). The debtor's president and sole shareholder retains equity in the reorganized debtor.

Because suppliers expect to recoup their losses in future transactions with the debtor, they vote for acceptance. The bank votes both its secured and unsecured claims for rejection. Grouping the unsecured claims in a single class allows confirmation. An impaired class, the unsecured creditors, accepted the plan.[2] Treatment proposed for the bank's secured claim meets the fair and equitable standard for cramdown.[3] On the other hand, classifying the unsecured portion of the bank's claim separately requires elimination of the shareholder's interest if confirmation is to occur.[4]

Section 1122(a) restricts a debtor's ability to lump dissimilar claims into the same class. "[A] plan may place a claim or an interest in a particular class only if such claim or interest is substantially similar to the other claims or interests of such class."[5] This prevents the debtor from diluting voting rights of a creditor who holds greater rights than other creditors by including the creditor's claim in a much larger class of dissimilar claims.[6]

---

6. 11 U.S.C.A. § 1124(3)(B).

§ 10–24

1. An undersecured creditor's claim is bifurcated into secured and unsecured claims under 11 U.S.C.A. § 506(a). See S. Rep. No. 989, 95th Cong., 1st Sess. 68 reprinted in 1978 U.S. Code Cong. & Admin. News 5787; United States v. Ron Pair Enterprises, Inc., 489 U.S. 235, 109 S.Ct. 1026, 103 L.Ed.2d 290 (1989), on remand, 872 F.2d 778 (6th Cir.1989) (subsection (a) of § 506 provides that a claim is secured only to the extent of the value of the property on which the lien is fixed; the remainder of that claim is considered unsecured); United Savings Ass'n of Texas v. Timbers of Inwood Forest Assoc., 484 U.S. 365, 370, 108 S.Ct. 626, 98 L.Ed.2d 740 (1988) (the value of an undersecured creditor's secured claim is the value of the underlying collateral).

2. Claims totalling at least 2/3 in amount and 1/2 in number voted for the plan. See 11 U.S.C.A. § 1126(c).

3. The treatment of the secured claim is fair and equitable under the standards of section 1129(b)(2)(A).

4. In order to cram down over the dissent of a class of impaired unsecured claims, a plan must either provide for payment in full, or that no junior class receive any property. 11 U.S.C.A. § 1129(b)(2)(B).

5. Id. § 1122(a). See unfair discrimination we discuss in § 10–22 supra.

6. See In re AOV Industries, Inc., 792 F.2d 1140 (D.C. Cir.1986) (in classifying claims, the nature of the claims being classified, and not the nature of other claims or interests that the creditor may hold, determines whether the claims are "substantially similar." A plan cannot, however, provide for unequal treatment by requiring one member of a class to release its direct claim against a third party where other members of the class are only required to release derivative claims).

Various factors may impact classification of claims. See, e.g., In re AOV Industries, Inc., 792 F.2d 1140 (D.C. Cir. 1982) (focus of classification is relationship of claim to the assets of the debtor; third party guarantors are therefore irrelevant); In re Waterways Barge Partnership, 104 B.R. 776 (Bankr. N.D.Miss.1989) (size of claims does not, standing alone,

Aside from dumping diverse claims into a single class, the debtor might also want to split similar claims of equal priority into smaller classes. Although section 1122 does not prohibit this tactic,[7] such splitting holds the potential for abuse. For example, a debtor might devise a friendly but theoretically impaired class by giving full payment but delaying it for 30 days, and then cramdown against all significant creditors of the estate. Alternatively the debtor might generate the classes to nullify some votes. Responding to this potential for unfairness and to section 1122's silence on the question,[8] several courts[9] and one commentator[10] have maintained that there should be a single class for unsecured claims of a similar nature.

Reading the cases and thinking about statutory rules on classification confronts one starkly with the question whether the debtor is ever permitted to treat one class of creditors better than another despite the fact that both would be treated the same on liquidation. First consider a clear case: a debt carrying a below market rate of interest on which there has been a default. Assume, for example, that the debtor has defaulted on a mortgage that bears interest at 6 percent when the current rate is 11 percent. The Code explicitly contemplates that the debtor can separately classify the mortgage, cure the default, and so leave the mortgagee unimpaired to carry merrily on for the next 20 years of the term at 6 percent. That particular creditor will be substantially worse off than other creditors who must receive *present value* equal to the allowed amount of their claims. In the case of our hypothetical mortgagee, the present value of its claim will substantially exceed the amount it is to be paid over the time because the contract interest rate (6%) is lower than would be used to compute the present value of an impaired, dissenting claim (here 11%).

Second is the possibility of manipulating the present value findings in such a way as to favor one set of creditors over another while apparently giving each of them the same thing. Consider the proposal to pay trade creditors in cash, paying others an identical "present value" over five years.

amount to a distinguishable dissimilarity justifying separate classification).

7. Section 1122(a) merely provides that: "a plan may place a claim or an interest in a particular class only if such claim or interest is substantially similar to the other claims or interests of such class."

8. The basic argument is that the specific administrative convenience exception of section 1122(b) implies the non-existence of other exceptions.

9. In re Lettick Typografic, Inc., 103 B.R. 32 (Bankr. D.Conn.1989) (creation of an artificially impaired class distorts the meaning and purpose of § 1129(a)(10). The purposes of section 1129(a)(10) include a) to provide indicia of support by affected creditors and b) to prevent confirmation when support is lacking); In re Fantastic Homes Enterprises, Inc., 44 B.R. 999 (M.D.Fla.1984) (section 1122(a) and the section 1122(b) administrative convenience exceptions, when read together, indicate Congress intended all unsecured claims of a similar nature to be included in the same class); In re S & W Enterprise, 37 B.R. 153 (Bankr. N.D.Ill. 1984) (all general unsecured claims must be placed in the same class unless separate classification is necessary or reasonable for administrative convenience); but see Barnes v. Whelan, 689 F.2d 193 (D.C. Cir. 1982) ("Section 1122(a) * * * does not require that similar claims must be grouped together, but merely that any group created must be homogeneous."); In re Meadow Glen, Ltd., 87 B.R. 421 (Bankr. W.D.Tex.1988) (classification of similar claims in different classes is permissible but treatment must meet "fair and equitable", nondiscrimination, and good faith standards); In re AG Consultants Grain Div., Inc., 77 B.R. 665, n.16 (Bankr. N.D.Ind. 1987) (list of cases in which the court permitted separate classification of similar claims). In re Atlanta West VI, 91 B.R. 620 (Bankr. N.D.Ga.1988) contains an extensive list of cases both supporting and disputing the requirement that similar claims must be in the same class.

10. 3 W. Norton, Bankruptcy Law and Practice 60.05 (1987).

As a matter of theory, this is not discrimination, for by hypothesis the promise to pay over five years has an identical value to the cash payment today. One suspects that the theory and the practice diverge here. Faced with the choice of $50,000 cash on the date of confirmation of the plan or of the possibility of receiving $50,000 with even a generous interest payment over five years, most would grasp the former.

A third case permitting distortion arises in section 1122 itself. Section 1122(b) explicitly authorizes establishing a separate set of claims that are below a certain amount. Implicitly this authorization invites separate treatment for that class, usually more favorable treatment.

The fourth way of favoring one set of creditors over another arises from the operation of the business. There is nothing to prevent the debtor from directing a larger share of its business to a creditor it wishes to favor than would otherwise be directed to that creditor. Likewise there is nothing that prohibits the debtor from negotiating higher prices for goods purchased from that creditor. To the extent that this creditor gets additional business at higher prices than it would receive if it were not a creditor, it is receiving a *de facto* premium payment on its preexisting debt. Although judicial references to such behavior are rare, we have no doubt they occur, and we suspect they occur frequently.

The fifth possibility is closely allied to the fourth. This would involve simply making payments to one prepetition creditor while declining to make similar payments to other creditors. This occurred in *In re James A. Phillips, Inc.*,[11] which we discuss earlier, where the debtor made payments to a creditor who had a mechanics lien on an ongoing building project and who threatened to withhold future deliveries. With some difficulty the court in that case approved the payments.

The question remains whether the debtor can overtly treat one group of creditors not covered by any of the above exceptions better than another group by separate classification when both sets of creditors would receive the same percentage payment on liquidation. Except as discussed above, nothing in the Code explicitly authorizes such treatment and, as suggested above, much implies that such preference is improper. Yet there are strong utilitarian arguments for the more favorable treatment of one creditor compared with another. Imagine a case in which a particular financial or trade creditor is critical for the continuing existence of the business, and another creditor is completely unimportant because that creditor's loan dealt only with a division that is to be liquidated under the plan. On these facts, the continuing creditor, shareholders, and employees will wish to favor the powerful creditor on purely utilitarian grounds. The real question is whether there is any right under the Code to do so beyond some of the cases discussed above. We are uncertain and divided on the answer.

Professor Riesenfeld has suggested a middle ground, which is that the Code permits differential treatment as long as the treatment is not "unfairly discriminatory."[12] In effect, he suggests that a little bit of discrimination is

---

11. 29 B.R. 391 (S.D.N.Y.1983).

12. Riesenfeld, Classification of Claims and Interests in Chapter 11 and 13 Cases, 75 Calif.L.Rev. 391, 401 (1987). As the title suggests, Professor Riesenfeld's article deals with classification of claims in both Chapters 11 and 13.

not bad where a lot might be. Even if there is a principle against this discrimination, utilitarianism justifies small deviations.

§ 10–25 Special Rules for Secured Claims in Chapter 11

When the secured creditor is "oversecured" (i.e., when the value of the collateral exceeds the amount of the debt), permissible treatment under Chapter 11 is fairly straightforward. If the creditor is recalcitrant, the debtor has the option of leaving the creditor unimpaired under section 1124 or of granting one of the alternatives under section 1129(b)(2). These alternatives include the sale of the collateral and granting a lien on the proceeds, providing for the realization of the "indubitable equivalent", or allowing the creditor to retain its lien and giving "deferred cash payments totalling at least the allowed amount of such claim" with a present value of the claim. Of course, the plan may provide any other treatment to which the creditor agrees.

When the creditor is undersecured (i.e., the value of the collateral is less than the amount of the debt), there is additional complexity. Under section 506(a) the creditor is treated as a secured creditor up to the value of the collateral [1] and as an unsecured creditor to the extent the debt exceeds the value of the collateral.[2] Except to the extent that section 1111(b)(2) permits and requires different treatment,[3] the plan may treat these two claims, one secured and the other unsecured, like any other similar claims.[4]

Nonrecourse secured claims, claims on which there is no personal liability on the underlying debt and where the creditor's only right is to pursue the collateral, present different questions. Under Chapter 7, nonrecourse claimants get exactly what they would get outside of bankruptcy, namely the right to the value of the collateral. Section 502(b)(1) disallows the unsecured (or "deficiency" portion) of the claim because it is unenforceable against the debtor under the terms of the original loan.[5]

If nonrecourse loans were given similar treatment under Chapter 11, there would be considerable opportunity for bad faith debtors who could file in Chapter 11 at a time when the value of the collateral was temporarily depressed. If the effect of such filing were to dismiss the unsecured portion of the nonrecourse loan, the debtor could conceivably emerge from bankruptcy with a scaled down loan and so keep for itself the subsequent increase in

The article acknowledges that classification of claims presents different problems in Chapter 11 cases and discusses each chapter separately. Section 1322(b)(1) governs classification of claims in Chapter 13 cases; section 1322(b)(1) requires that the classification not "discriminate unfairly." Section 1122 governs classification of claims in Chapter 11 cases; it does not expressly require that the classification not "discriminate unfairly." Chapter 11's language regarding unfair discrimination is in section 1129(b); in Chapter 11 cases, cram down, not classification, triggers an inquiry into whether there has been unfair discrimination.

§ 10–25

1. Section 506(a) refers to the "creditor's interest in the estate's interest in such property" rather than collateral. See United Savings Assn. of Texas v. Timbers of Inwood Forest Assoc., 484 U.S. 365, 108 S.Ct. 626, 98 L.Ed.2d 740 (1988).

2. 11 U.S.C.A. § 506(a).

3. See "Section 1111(b)(2) Election," § 10–27 infra.

4. See our overview of Chapter 11, §§ 10–1 & 10–2 supra.

5. 11 U.S.C.A. § 502(b)(1).

the value of the collateral. Such abusive use of bankruptcy would be particularly inviting where the collateral was real estate in a cyclical market that could reasonably be expected to regain its value. To minimize the possibility described above, Congress enacted section 1111(b).

§ 10–26 Special Rules for Secured Claims in Chapter 11—Section 1111(b)(1): Right of Recourse

Section 1111(b)(1) treats nonrecourse creditors as if they held a right of recourse against the debtor.[1] In Chapter 11, undersecured creditors with nonrecourse claims possess the basic rights of recourse creditors;[2] they hold a secured claim for the value of the collateral and an unsecured claim for the balance which can be referred to as a deficiency claim. Two exceptions to the general rule of section 1111(b)(1) exist. First, the Code denies recourse status to a creditor whose collateral is sold.[3] The creditor receives the benefit of its original bargain through its right to bid at a sale and offset its claim against the price.[4] Neither the Code nor practical considerations require further protection. Second, recourse is denied when the creditor makes the section 1111(b)(2) election described below.

§ 10–27 Special Rules for Secured Claims in Chapter 11—Section 1111(b)(2)

Section 1111(b)(2) allows an undersecured claim to be treated as a "secured claim * * * notwithstanding section 506(a)." Thus a creditor, with a mortgage on a piece of property worth $5,000,000 securing a debt of $10,000,000 who makes the section 1111(b)(2) election, will be treated as "secured" to the full extent of the $10,000,000, not just to the value of the underlying collateral as would otherwise be the case under section 506(a).

The provision was apparently designed to bar the debtor from doing

§ 10–26

1. Section 1111(b)(1)(A) provides: "A claim secured by a lien on property of the estate shall be allowed or disallowed under section 502 of this title the same as if the holder of such claim had recourse against the debtor on account of such claim, whether or not such holder has recourse * * *." See Matter of Tampa Bay Associates, Ltd., 864 F.2d 47 (5th Cir.1989) (foreclosure sale does not provide an exception to the recourse status afforded nonrecourse creditors); In re Western Real Estate Fund, Inc., 109 B.R. 455 (Bankr. W.D. Okla. 1990) ("The purpose of § 1111(b) was to restore the non-recourse secured creditor the benefit of his bargain * * * [and to prevent the debtor from paying such creditor] only the then value of the property securing the debt, thus preserving to itself all potential future appreciation * * *."); Matter of N.R.G. Investments, Inc., 99 B.R. 475 (Bankr. M.D. Fla. 1989) ("Whether the nonrecourse indebtedness arises by agreement or by law * * *, such indebtedness can be handled within the context of the Chapter 11 plan.").

2. As the holder of an unsecured deficiency claim, the nonrecourse creditor may vote on the plan, and if its class dissents, obtain the protections of section 1129(b). Unlike creditors with recourse, however, the dissenting nonrecourse creditor who is a member of an accepting class receives no additional protection from the best interest test of section 1129(a)(7). If the debtor were liquidated under Chapter 7, the nonrecourse creditor would receive nothing on account of its deficiency claim.

3. 11 U.S.C.A. § 1111(b)(1)(A)(ii). Sale may be under the plan or under section 363.

4. See id. § 363(k), which provides that if property subject to a lien which secures an allowed claim is sold, unless the court for cause orders otherwise, the holder of the claim may bid at sale and offset its claim against the purchase price. This section applies when property is sold under § 363 or if property subject to a lien is sold under the plan and the lienholder dissents. See id. § 1129(b)(2)(A).

what the debtor did in *In re Pine Gate Associates, Ltd.*[1] Pine Gate was a limited partnership whose only asset was an apartment complex. While the Georgia real estate market was depressed, debtor used its bankruptcy cramdown powers to "cash out" an undersecured mortgagee at an amount equal to the current value of the apartment property. Mortgagee received only a small percentage of the principal balance of its debt and, apparently, the apartment complex rose substantially in value shortly after the confirmation when the real estate market made a strong recovery. The consequence of this transaction was that the debtor liquidated his debts at far less than face value, yet retained for himself almost all of the appreciation in the property. In theory section 1111(b)(2) would prevent a recurrence of *Pine Gate*. As we will see, the theory does not match the practice.

In the words of the Judiciary Committee, section 1111(b)(2) was added with the following intention:

> If section 1111(b)(2) applies, then the "electing" class is entitled to have the entire allowed amount of the debt related to such property secured by a lien even if the value of the collateral is less than the amount of the debt. In addition, the plan must provide for the holder to receive, on account of the allowed secured claims, payments, either present or deferred, of a principal face amount equal to the amount of the debt and of a present value equal to the value of the collateral.
>
> * * * [I]f a creditor loaned $15,000,000 to a debtor secured by real property worth $18,000,000 and the value of the real property had dropped to $12,000,000 by the date when the debtor commenced a proceeding under chapter 11, the plan could be confirmed notwithstanding the dissent of the creditor as long as the lien remains on the collateral to secure a $15,000,000 debt, the face amount of present or extended payments to be made to the creditor under the plan is at least $15,000,000 and the present value of the present or deferred payment is not less than $12,000,000 * * *.[2]

To understand how section 1111(b)(2) works, consider the following example.[3] Assume a debtor with a first mortgage debt of $10,000,000. At the time of the bankruptcy petition the court determines that the value of the mortgage real estate is $7,500,000, and thus that the secured creditor is undersecured to the extent of $2,500,000. If the creditor fails to make the section 1111(b)(2) election, one can anticipate a plan under which the creditor would be paid a very small percentage of the $2,500,000 as one of the unsecured creditors and that it would receive a promise as part of the confirmation of the plan with a present value of $7,500,000 secured by the existing real estate. If the real estate shot up in value to $12,000,000 one year after the

§ 10–27

1. 2 B.C.D. 1478 (Bankr. N.D.Ga.1976).
2. 124 Cong. Rec. H32407 (1978).
3. There are several procedural questions presented by the § 1111(b)(2) election. First one makes the election under Rule 3014 (of the Rules of Practice and Procedure in Bankruptcy) as follows:

"An election of application of section 1111(b)(2) of the Code by a class of secured creditors in a chapter 9 or 11 case may be made at any time prior to the conclusion of the hearing on the disclosure statement or within such later time as the court may fix. The election shall be in writing and signed unless made at the hearing on the disclosure statement. The election, if made by the majorities required by section 1111(b)(1)(A)(i), shall be binding on all members of the class with respect to the plan."

plan's confirmation, the mortgagee would be paid $7,500,000 and the remainder of the gain would go to the debtor.

If the creditor makes the section 1111(b)(2) election, the entire $10,000,000 claim is treated as secured. One cost to the creditor of such an election is that the creditor now has no unsecured claim and therefore, no power to vote against a plan as an unsecured creditor and to insist upon observation of the absolute priority rule under section 1129(b). Of smaller concern to the creditor is that it will receive no distribution as an unsecured creditor. If the distribution is to be insignificant to unsecured creditors, that will be of no consequence whatsoever. The benefit to the creditor is obvious if the property appreciates in value and is sold shortly after the plan. Because the creditor must be treated in the plan as having a $10,000,000 secured claim, it would have to be paid the lesser of the net sale price or $10,000,000 on the sale and thus could reap an additional $2,500,000 from the appreciated value of the real estate. That, at least, is the theory.

To see how this loan must be treated, consider section 1129(b)(2)(A)(i)(II). It requires an electing *secured* creditor receive

> on account of such claim deferred cash payments totaling at least the allowed amount of such claim, of a value, as of the effective date of the plan, of at least the value of such holder's interest and the estate's interest in such property.

This means that the total payments under the plan must be $10,000,000 (the allowed amount of the secured claim after the election) and that the payments must have a present value of $7,500,000 (the value of the estate's interest in the real estate).

Note one consequence of this rule: the interest payment is doing double duty. First, the interest on the $7,500,000 is what gives time payment of $7,500,000 a present value of $7,500,000. Second, the interest payments themselves make up the remainder of the "payments" under the plan so that the "total payments" will equal $10,000,000.

Note how this fact diminishes the value of section 1111(b)(2) as a creditor protection. If the payments of the $7,500,000 in our hypothetical case are sufficiently extended in the plan so the total interest on the $7,500,000 will equal $2,500,000, sections 1129(b) and 1111(b)(2) are satisfied.

Did Congress intend that the interest payments count twice here? All the writers seem to assume so,[4] and it is hard to argue otherwise by reading section 1129(b)(2)(A)(i)(II). Yet, such a rule seems at odds with the policy of section 1111(b)(2). Note that Congress, in the House Report quoted above, speaks of payments of a "principal face amount equal to the amount of the debt." One might argue that the use of the words "principal" and "face amount" was to express a congressional intention to require payments of that amount at least and not to permit interest payments to be used both to maintain the present value and to reduce the principal obligation.

---

4. See, for example, Pusateri, et al., Section 1111(b) of the Bankruptcy Code: How Much Does the Debtor Have to Pay and When Should the Creditor Elect?, 58 Am. Bankr. L.J. 128, 137–39 (1984) and Klee, All You Ever Wanted to Know About Cram Down Under the New Bankruptcy Code, 53 Am. Bankr. L.J. 133, 157–58 (1979).

To understand the problem, assume that a plan is proposed in our hypothetical case with a ten percent interest rate. Assume further that the plan contemplates equal monthly payments over ten years and that the property is sold for $9,500,000 at the end of two years. Using normal rules for allocation of interest and principal, one would conclude that $1,410,486 of interest and $986,250 of principal had been paid on the $7,500,000 debt at the end of two years. What amount must be given to the secured creditor? One might find that the secured creditor still has a debt against the property equal to $10,000,000 less principal payment of $968,250 or $9,031,750. But that calculation gives only single coverage to the interest payment. If one is to treat them as also reducing the undersecured $2,500,000 portion then the secured creditor gets only $7,621.264.

The implication from section 1129 is that the interest payments really do double duty and that those payments have not only satisfied the present value requirement, but also should be used to reduce the principal amount of the mortgage. We think that is unfair and is in conflict with the policy of section 1111(b)(2), but we see no clear way to escape that outcome. If that were not true, the plan that we have proposed could not have been approved because at the end of the plan there would still be an outstanding balance of $2,500,000 (if none of the interest was treated as reducing the principal balance). Thus, it would be inconsistent to say the plan we have suggested with total payments of more than $10,000,000 and a present value of $7,500,000 could be approved and yet that the interest payments would not go to reduce the principal balance of $10,000,000. This fact renders section 1111(b)(2) worthless except in the case in which the collateral will be sold shortly after the confirmation.[5]

Yet other traps and snares await the electing creditor. Assume again that our creditor makes the election and so is left after confirmation with a $10,000,000 mortgage. Just as he predicted, real estate values reverse themselves and the debtor makes an agreement to sell the property for $12,000,000 to a third party. When the creditor appears at the closing to receive its $10,000,000, the debtor says: "Not so fast. I have sold the property subject to the mortgage. You will continue to get your payments because my purchaser has assumed the mortgage and I remain liable on it, but the only cash available is the $2,000,000 above the $10,000,000 and that goes to me." To make section 1111(b)(2) even remotely fair, this sort of activity should be prohibited. Surely the policy behind section 1111(b)(2) demands that the court infer a "due on sale" clause in any such mortgage whether one exists or not. Needless to say, a well-counseled secured creditor

---

5. Making the election might also benefit the creditor if the debtor will be unable to put together any set of payments during the time permitted by the court that total the amount of the debt. Consider, for example, In re Kvamme, 93 B.R. 698 (Bankr. D.N.D.1988). In Kvamme, the court would not confirm the debtors' plan because it failed to meet the requirements stemming from the § 1111(b)(2) election. The creditor (FmHA) made the § 1111(b)(2) election and therefore, must receive the greater of (1) the present value of the collateral or (2) total payments equal to at least the total amount of its allowed secured claim. The plan proposed by the debtors was to pay FmHA a total of $92,272.74 over 15 years (payments including 9% interest on the value of the collateral which was $51,000.00). This plan failed to meet the second requirement because it provided FmHA with less than its total secured claim of $174,234.72 and therefore, was not confirmed by the court. Kvamme, 93 B.R. at 700.

should insist on such a clause and should readily be given one if section 1111(b)(2) has any meaning.

There is nothing in section 1129 to prohibit an undersecured creditor from striking a bargain with the debtor that would cause the mortgage to be resurrected for its full amount in any case in which the underlying collateral were sold at any time prior to the expiration of the plan. Thus, in our hypothetical case, the secured creditor might choose not to make the section 1111(b)(2) election, but rather to negotiate an agreement to be incorporated in the plan that would give him present value of $7,500,000 and a right to recover as much as an additional $2,500,000 if the collateral were sold anytime within a specified period for more than $7,500,000. If there were junior dissenting classes, they might make the argument that terms of that sort would not be fair and equitable because they would give the secured creditor more than 100 percent of his value. We are unpersuaded by such objections when the secured creditor sees its debt written down to $7,500,000 and receives in return an option of uncertain value. Any option on appreciation of collateral has an highly uncertain value.

§ 10–28 Special Rules for Secured Claims in Chapter 11—Exceptions to 1111(b)(2)

Undersecured creditors may not elect section 1111(b)(2) treatment if: (1) the debtor sells the collateral in a sale where the creditor can bid the amount of its claim;[1] or (2) the collateral has only inconsequential value.[2] The first exception to section 1111(b)(2) parallels the denial of deficiency claims to nonrecourse creditors upon sale of the collateral. Similar justifications apply. The creditor can protect its interest in property sold under either section 363 or the plan, by bidding at the sale and offsetting its claim against the purchase price. This assures the creditor the benefits of its original bargain.

In addition, section 1111(b)(1)(B) denies the election to creditors whose interest in the collateral is of "inconsequential value."[3] No definition of this term appears in the Code. Where senior claims total more than the collateral's value, the junior creditor's interest is clearly inconsequential.[4] Consider the case in which the value of the collateral is $2 million, the first mortgage secures a debt of $3 million and there is a second mortgage of $500,000. In such case the collateral will almost certainly be used up to satisfy the first mortgage; the second mortgage is already "under water" to the extent of $1,000,000. Clearly the collateral is of "inconsequential value" vis à vis the second mortgage.

More difficult questions are posed where there is some value left for the electing creditor, but that value is quite small by comparison to the amount of the debt.

§ 10–28

1. In re Waterways Barge Partnership, 104 B.R. 776 (Bankr. N.D.Miss.1989) (undersecured recourse creditor not permitted to credit bid its claim is entitled to § 1111(b)(2) election; failure to make election does not conversely entitle creditor to bid).

2. See 11 U.S.C.A. § 1111(b)(1)(B).

3. Id. § 1111(b)(1)(B)(i).

4. But see In re Wandler, 77 B.R. 728, 733 (Bankr. D.N.D.1987) (criticizing In re Baxley and holding that inconsequential value does not mean zero collateral value. Found interest in 4% of a $390,000 claim inconsequential).

Consider *In re Baxley*,[5] where the first mortgage holder, Federal Land Bank, had a claim of almost $430,000 against property of approximately the same value. The second mortgagee, the Farmers' Home Administration, had a $362,000 claim that constituted a second mortgage on the assets covered by the Federal Land Bank, but also constituted a first claim on the debtor's hog herd worth $28,500. Farmers' Home Administration was not willing to consent to the proposed plan and thus any plan would have required a section 1129(b) cramdown. Holding that FmHA's interest was not inconsequential, the court allowed the Farmers' Home Administration to make the section 1111(b)(2) election. The consequence of that election was that on resale of the farm at a price in excess of $430,000, the Farmers' Home Administration would take the excess. If the Farmers' Home argument had been rejected, it could have been treated as an unsecured creditor, crammed down in reorganization, and could have received little or nothing thereafter.[6]

E. POST–CONFIRMATION ISSUES

§ 10–29 Return of Property to the Debtor

For full text of this section, see Epstein, Nickles & White, Bankruptcy, Practitioner Treatise Series, Vol. 3.

§ 10–30 Discharge of the Debtor

For full text of this section, see Epstein, Nickles & White, Bankruptcy, Practitioner Treatise Series, Vol. 3.

§ 10–31 Binding Effect of the Plan of Reorganization

For full text of this section, see Epstein, Nickles & White, Bankruptcy, Practitioner Treatise Series, Vol. 3.

§ 10–32 Implementation, Adjustment, and Modification

For full text of this section, see Epstein, Nickles & White, Bankruptcy, Practitioner Treatise Series, Vol. 3.

§ 10–33 Revocation and Modification

For full text of this section, see Epstein, Nickles & White, Bankruptcy, Practitioner Treatise Series, Vol. 3.

F. RETROSPECTIVE

§ 10–34 Retrospective: The Unpractical View

For full text of this section, see Epstein, Nickles & White, Bankruptcy, Practitioner Treatise Series, Vol. 3.

---

5. 72 B.R. 195 (Bankr. D.S.C.1986).

6. See also In re Rideout, 75 B.R. 104 (Bankr. N.D.Ohio 1987) (with no discussion of the amount of the secured creditor's claim, the court held where the interest to which the lien could attach was valued at $39,000, interest is not of inconsequential value and therefore the section 1111(b)(2) election could be made).

Chapter 11

SELECTED TOPICS IN CHAPTER 11 PROCEEDINGS

Table of Sections

Sec.

A. Claims

11–1 Significance and Overview of Problems.
11–2 What Is a Claim (Section 101(5))?
11–3 When Does a Claim Arise?
11–4 Filing Claims in Bankruptcy.
11–5 Estimating Claims (Section 502(c)).
11–6 ____ Estimation for Voting Purposes.
11–7 ____ Estimation for Distribution Purposes.

B. Mega–Claims

11–8 Bankruptcy and Mass Torts.
11–9 Claims for Environmental Cleanup in Chapters 11 and 7.
11–10 ____ Relative Priority Under the Code.
11–11 ____ Cleanup Expenses as Secured Claims.
11–12 ____ Retrospective: The Better Judicial and Legislative Answers.

C. Waiting for the Debtor's Plan: The "Exclusivity Period," Section 1121(d)

11–13 Introduction: Exclusivity and Delay.
11–14 Procedure for Extending the Period.
11–15 Cause for Extension.

D. Disclosure and Plan Approval

11–16 Overview.
11–17 Standards for Adequate Information.
11–18 Solicitation of Rejection or Acceptance of Competing Plans.
11–19 Voting Agreements.
11–20 Voting in Multiple Plan Cases, Rule 3016.
11–21 Pre-packaged Plans.
11–22 ____ Prepetition Disclosure.
11–23 ____ Prepetition Solicitation.
11–24 ____ Why Use Prepackaged Plans.
    a. Advantages of Prepackaged Plan Over Nonbankruptcy Workout.
       Binds All Creditors.
       Tax Benefits.
       Original Issue Discount.
    b. Advantages of Prepackaged Chapter 11 Over Ordinary Chapter 11.
    c. Disadvantage of Prepackaged Chapter 11.

Sec.

E. Absolute Priority and New Value

11–25 Overview of "Absolute Priority" Rule.
11–26 Origin and Development of the "New Value" Exception.
11–27 The "New Value" Exception Under the Code.
11–28 Applying the Exception.
11–29 ____ The Cases.
    In re Greystone III Joint Venture.
    In re Marston Enterprises Inc.
    Potter Material Services, Inc.
    Jartran.
11–30 ____ Arguing Against the Exception.

F. Bankruptcies Involving Partnerships

11–31 Introduction.
11–32 Liability of Partnerships and General Partners to the Creditors of Each.
11–33 Priority.
11–34 Staying Creditors.
11–35 ____ Automatic Stay, Section 362.
11–36 ____ Injunctions, Section 105.
11–37 Partner Bankruptcy Effects on the Enforcement of the Partnership Agreement.
11–38 ____ Assumption, Assignment and Rejection, Sections 365(c) and 365(e).
11–39 ____ Partner's Settlement and Contribution.

G. Substantive Consolidation

11–40 Meaning and Reasons.
11–41 Cases and Rules.

A. CLAIMS

§ 11–1 Significance and Overview of Problems

The determination what is a claim is pivotal in bankruptcy law. Only "claims" can be addressed in the bankruptcy case, and only "claims" can be discharged in bankruptcy.[1] To the extent that a debtor's obligations are not discharged, he is deprived of the "fresh start" that underlies much of the purpose and design of the Bankruptcy Code.[2] Chapter 11 "claimants" without "claims" cannot vote on the plan of reorganization and may be

---

§ 11–1

1. In re Edge, 60 B.R. 690, 694 (Bankr. M.D.Tenn.1986); Kesner, Future Asbestos Related Litigants as Holders of Statutory Claims Under Chapter 11 of the Bankruptcy Code and Their Place in the Johns–Manville Reorganization (First Installment), 62 Am.Bankr. L.J. 69, 83 n.4 (1988)[hereinafter Future Asbestos Related Litigants], citing 3 Collier on Bankruptcy ¶¶ 501.01, 501.02, 502.01 (15th ed.).

2. Ohio v. Kovacs, 469 U.S. 274, 282, 105 S.Ct. 705, 709, 83 L.Ed.2d 649 (1985); Local Loan Co. v. Hunt, 292 U.S. 234, 244, 54 S.Ct. 695, 78 L.Ed. 1230 (1934); Matter of Gary Aircraft, 698 F.2d 775, 783 n.5 (5th Cir.1983), cert. denied, 464 U.S. 820, 104 S.Ct. 82, 78 L.Ed.2d 92 (1983) (applying principles of former Bankruptcy Act); In re Baldwin–United Corp., 55 B.R. 885, 897 (Bankr. S.D.Ohio 1985); S.Rep.No. 1106, 95th Cong., 2d Sess. 1 (1977); 123 Cong.Rec. 35, 452 (1977); see also Kesner, Future Asbestos Related Litigants as Holders of Statutory Claims Under Chapter 11 of the Bankruptcy Code and Their Place in the Johns–Manville Reorganization (Second Installment), 62 Am.Bankr. L.J. 159, 162 (1988)[hereinafter Future Asbestos Related Litigants]; Comment, Bankruptcy, Hazardous Waste and Mass Tort: A Top Priority Review, 23 Hous.L.Rev. 1243, 1252 (1986); but see Bibler, The Status of Unaccrued Tort Claims in Chapter 11 Bankruptcy Proceedings, 61 Am. Bankr.L.J. 145, 157 (1987); T. Jackson, The Logic and Limits of Bankruptcy Law 4–5 (1986) (fresh start principles apply to individuals, but not to corporations).

§ 11–1 SELECTED TOPICS IN CHAPTER 11 783

barred from distribution from the estate,[3] perhaps preventing forever any chance of recovery from the debtor.[4]

Bankruptcy laws have steadily expanded the scope of claims that participate in bankruptcy cases. The Bankruptcy Act of 1898, which originally dealt only with liquidations, contained allowability and provability requirements that barred contingent[5] and unliquidated claims from bankruptcy cases. That act thereby excluded almost all tort claims, as well as other claims where the value of the claim was uncertain.[6]

Congress provided for a broader definition of claim for reorganizations when it added provisions for railroad and corporate reorganizations in 1933 and 1934, respectively. The reorganization amendments, contained in sections 77A and 77B of the Act, discarded the provability requirement and focused instead on whether a claim existed.[7] Even after this change, however, creditors still had to hurdle the "allowability" requirement of section 57(d), which "disallowed" claims if the court determined the claim was "not capable of liquidation or of reasonable estimation or that such liquidation or estimation would unduly delay the administration of the estate or any proceeding under this Act."[8] The result was that contingent and unliquidated claims were treated in a haphazard manner by the bankruptcy courts, with "[t]he net effect [of] an unequal distribution, as creditors holding disallowed claims might later recover in full, while other creditors with provable claims were limited to a share in the distribution from the estate."[9] In addition, the Bankruptcy Act remained silent as to the status of contingent tort claims, and those claims were still held to be unallowable.[10] In 1938 the Chandler Act expanded the scope of provable claims for

---

3. Bankr. R. 3003(c)(2). The mass tort cases, however, have characterized future claimants as "parties in interest" under § 1109(b) and included provisions for distribution for these claimants under the plan of reorganization. See § 11–8 infra.

4. In re Baldwin–United Corp., 55 B.R. at 897. But in cases where a viable organization remained subsequent to the bankruptcy, the "creditor" without a "claim" could actually be better off for not having been allowed in the bankruptcy proceeding, because he could seek full recovery from the debtor's post-confirmation assets. This had the negative effect, however, of depriving the debtor of a "fresh start." See note 2 supra; see also In re Pettibone Corp., 90 B.R. 918, 922–23 (Bankr. N.D.Ill. 1988).

5. "A contingent claim has been described as one in which 'the debtor's legal duty to pay does not come into existence until triggered by the occurrence of a future event and such future occurrence was within the actual or presumed contemplation of the parties at the time the original relationship of the parties was created.'" In re Chateaugay Corp., 112 B.R. 513, 520 (S.D.N.Y. 1990), judgment aff'd, 944 F.2d 997 (2d Cir.1991), quoting In re All Media Properties, Inc., 5 B.R. 126, 133 (Bankr. S.D.Tex.1980), aff'd, 646 F.2d 193 (5th Cir. 1981).

6. See generally Matter of Wood, 825 F.2d 90, 91 (5th Cir.1987), on remand, 84 B.R. 432 (S.D.Miss.1988); Matter of UNR Industries, Inc., 725 F.2d 1111, 1116 (7th Cir.1984); In re Johns–Manville Corp., 36 B.R. 727, 740 (Bankr. S.D.N.Y. 1984), appeal denied, 39 B.R. 234 (D.N.Y.1984); see also Future Asbestos Related Litigants, 62 Am.Bankr.L.J. at 77–86.

7. Vanston Bondholders Protective Committee v. Green, 329 U.S. 156, 170, 67 S.Ct. 237, 243, 91 L.Ed. 162 (1946) (Frankfurter, J., concurring), reh'g denied, 329 U.S. 156, 67 S.Ct. 497, 91 L.Ed. 706 (1947) (Chapter X case); see also Future Asbestos Related Litigants, 62 Am.Bankr.L.J. at 79, 84.

8. In re Pettibone Corp., 90 B.R. at 923; see also Future Asbestos Related Litigants, 62 Am.Bankr.L.J. at 161.

9. In re Pettibone Corp., 90 B.R. at 923; see also In re Edge, 60 B.R. at 694 ("The basic irrationality of admitting to proof claims based on contract but excluding most claims based on tort lead to many convoluted exceptions to the nonprovability of tort claims and eventually to the abandonment of the rule").

10. In re Magnavox Co., 627 F.2d 803, 805 (7th Cir.1980); In re Pettibone Corp., 90 B.R. at 923; In re Johns–Manville Corp., 36 B.R. at 740.

liquidation cases by including "contingent debts and contingent contractual liabilities."[11]

The 1978 Bankruptcy Reform Act continued the expansion of claims admitted in bankruptcy by providing a broad definition of "claim" for all bankruptcy cases;[12] by eliminating the concept of provable claims; and by requiring the estimation of all contingent and unliquidated claims.[13] The combined effect of these provisions was to provide for the discharge of contingent tort claims and other claims of uncertain value that had never before been addressed in bankruptcy proceedings.[14] These changes raise a variety of issues that are the subject of controversy among legal scholars and practitioners. We focus on four major points in the discourse on what constitutes a "claim" in bankruptcy law.

First, questions have arisen as to the precise scope of the term "claim" since the Bankruptcy Reform Act of 1978, and any meaningful discussion of the term must necessarily begin with an understanding of how the courts define "claim." Second, we give an overview of the filing and allowability of Chapter 11 claims. Third, we discuss the estimation requirement and the various interpretations courts have given that requirement. Finally, we consider mass tort litigation in bankruptcy, which is a new and unexpected development arising from the changes made in the 1978 Bankruptcy Reform Act. The mass tort cases stretch the Bankruptcy Code to its outer limits and thus provide an opportunity to test the rules against the practicalities of bankruptcy litigation and the constitutional underpinnings of our entire legal structure.

§ 11–2 What Is a Claim (Section 101(5))?

Consistent with Congress' goal that "all legal obligations of the debtor, no matter how remote or contingent, will be able to be dealt with in the bankruptcy case,"[1] the Code provides broad relief for debtors. It is limited only by the requirement that there be a "right to payment" as described in the Code's definition of the term "claim" in section 101(5). It means:

> (A) right to payment, whether or not such right is reduced to judgment, liquidated, unliquidated, fixed, contingent, matured, unmatured, disputed, undisputed, legal, equitable, secured, or unsecured; or

> (B) right to equitable remedy for breach of performance if such breach gives rise to a right of payment, whether or not such right to an equitable remedy is reduced to judgment, fixed, contingent, matured, unmatured, disputed, undisputed, secured, or unsecured.[2]

---

11. Bankruptcy Act of 1898 § 63a(8).

12. 11 U.S.C.A. § 101(5) (formerly § 101(4)).

13. 11 U.S.C.A. § 502(c).

14. In re Amatex Corp., 110 B.R. 168, 171 (Bankr. E.D.Pa. 1990) ("One of the principles of section 502 is that certain contingent claims * * * can be allowed, estimated, and the obligations of same discharged in a bankruptcy case").

§ 11–2

1. H.R.Rep.No. 595, 95th Cong., 1st Sess. 309 (1977); S.Rep.No. 989, 95th Cong., 2d Sess. 21–1 (1978), reprinted in 1978 U.S. Code & Admin. News 5968, 6866; 5787, 5807–08.

2. 11 U.S.C.A. § 101(5). Subsection (A) is discussed fully later. Subsection (B) issues arise in Chapter 7 environmental cases which present the question whether an injunction to clean-up hazardous waste is a § 101(5)(B) "right of payment." See our earlier discussion in § 7–8 supra.

The courts and commentators have recognized the broad meaning of "claim" encompassed by the Code.[3] They disagree as to the scope of that term, especially on the question of the precise moment a claim arises under bankruptcy law.[4]

To begin, it is clearest from section 101(5)(A) that any right to payment is a "claim." Suppose, for example, that D borrows money from C and G guarantees D's payment. Both C and G have claims.

Section 101(5)(B) dealing with rights to equitable remedies is less clear. Legislative history provides the example of a contract for the sale of unique property. If under state law the seller's specific performance obligation may be satisfied by payment, the buyer has a "claim" in bankruptcy. Its test is whether the right to an equitable remedy "gives rise to a right to payment."[5] Similarly, if D breached her covenant not to compete with C, C would have not only a right to equitable injunctive relief but also a right to payment, i.e., C would have a "claim."

The "gives rise to a right to payment" test suggests that some equitable remedies are not "claims" and so do not participate in the bankruptcy distribution and are not affected by the automatic stay or a bankruptcy discharge.[6] For example courts are currently divided as to which environmental injunctions are "claims" under section 101(5)(B). A comparison of the district court and Second Circuit decisions in the LTV bankruptcy illustrates the division.

The district court focused on the statutory enforcement scheme rather than the actual injunctive order that was obtained.[7] According to the district court, application of the phrase "gives rise to a right of payment" requires a reference to the statutory enforcement scheme and a determination whether the EPA had a right to seek payment. The district court held that injunctive relief, where there was an option to receive payment, falls within the broad definition of the term "claim," "and the fact that the EPA

---

3. Ohio v. Kovacs, 469 U.S. 274, 105 S.Ct. 705, 709, 83 L.Ed.2d 649 (1985); In re Edge, 60 B.R. 690, 692–93 (Bankr. M.D.Tenn.1986); Matter of Baldwin-United Corp., 48 B.R. 901, 903 (Bankr.S.D. Ohio 1985); In re Johns-Manville Corp., 36 B.R. 743, 754 n.6 (Bankr. S.D.N.Y. 1984), appeal denied, 39 B.R. 234 (S.D.N.Y.1984); see also Future Asbestos Related Litigants, 62 Am.Bankr.L.J. at 84; Matthews, The Scope of Claims Under the Bankruptcy Code, 57 Am.Bankr.L.J. 221, 223 (1983).

4. The determination of when a claim arises is critical to several Code provisions. A claim may arise either prepetition, postpetition, preconfirmation, postconfirmation or after consummation.

A claimant must hold a prepetition claim in order to file a claim under section 502(b) unless it falls under one of the exceptions of § 501(d), which allows certain postpetition claims to be filed under that section "the same as if such claim * * * had arisen before the date of the filing of the petition." (See § ___ infra.) The automatic stay provision (11 U.S.C.A. § 362(a)) is also limited to prepetition claims.

On the other hand, the term "creditor" is defined by section 101(10)(A) to include any entity holding a preconfirmation claim against the debtor; and the discharge provision of 1141 applies to preconfirmation claims. Section 502(f) bridges the postpetition-preconfirmation gap for involuntary bankruptcy cases by equating most of those claims with prepetition claims, and specifies that those claims are to be allowed "the same as if such claim had become fixed before the date of the filing of the petition."

5. See 124 Cong. Rec. 32392 (1978) (remarks of Representative Edwards); cf. In re Bluman, 1991 WL 45826 (Bankr. E.D. N.Y. 1991) (covenant not to compete).

6. See In re Villarie, 648 F.2d 810, 812 (2d Cir.1981).

7. In re Chateaugay Corp., 112 B.R. 513 (S.D.N.Y. 1990), judgment aff'd, 944 F.2d 997 (2d Cir.1991).

may not choose to exercise that option in no way negates the existence of that right."[8]

The Second Circuit opinion seems to focus on the actual order by the environmental agency rather than the statutory opinions available to the agency.[9] For example, the opinion states that an EPA order is not a claim that "requires LTV to take any action that ends or ameliorates current pollution," even though the EPA could have, under the CERCLA enforcement scheme, cleaned up the problem itself and sought repayment of costs.

Since almost all rights to "payment" and other "claims" identified under section 101(5)(A) arise out of state law (the law of contract, tort, etc.), bankruptcy law looks to the state or to other federal law to determine the existence of a "claim." By the same token, bankruptcy law looks to the law of the state or other federal law to determine whether a claim that clearly exists is "allowable" under section 502(b). Even a claim that exists (or once existed) under state law might be (or have become) unenforceable because of some defense. Under those circumstances it would not be allowable under section 502(b)(1) because it would be "unenforceable against the debtor and property of the debtor." Even though the idea of a claim's existence and its allowability are conceptually similar, they are housed under different roofs in the Bankruptcy Code.

To understand the problem, assume a case in which a debtor does the same act in Minnesota and in California. Assume that the act gives rise to a cause of action under the law of Minnesota, but that it is neither a breach of contract nor a tort nor the basis for any other civil liability under the law of California. If our debtor goes into bankruptcy, the allegedly injured parties in Minnesota would have a "claim," but there would be no claim by those allegedly injured in California. This is because the "claim" rises or falls on the state law.

Change the facts so there is a cause of action by those in California and those in Minnesota. Assume, however, that the statute of limitations has run in California, but not in Minnesota. Now both sets of parties allegedly injured would have "claims" under section 101(5)(A), but those asserted by the Californians would not be allowable because they would be "unenforceable against the debtor * * * under * * * applicable law."[10] The Minnesotans would face no such limitations.

The point is simple. For most purposes one must look to state law and to other non-bankruptcy federal law to determine the vitality of a right that a creditor purports to assert. Sometimes the right will not be recognized at all under the applicable nonbankruptcy law and in such case we would say that there is no "claim." Sometimes there is a claim but it is barred by a defense; in such cases we would say there is no "allowable claim" under section 502(b). Each conclusion leads to the same result, namely no distribution in this bankruptcy to the purported creditor.

---

8. Id. at 523.
9. In re Chateaugay, 944 F.2d 997 (2d Cir. 1991).
10. 11 U.S.C.A. § 502(b)(1).

§ 11–3 When Does a Claim Arise?

There are several reasons to know when a claim arises. First, the automatic stay bars non-bankruptcy litigation on prepetition claims, but does not always bar that litigation on postpetition claims.[1] Second, claims that arise prior to the petition that are unsecured will be lumped together with a large variety of other unsecured claims and will receive, in general, the lowest level of treatment in the bankruptcy distribution. On the other hand, claims of an identical type that arise after the petition and before the confirmation of a plan may be treated as administrative "expenses" (not as "claims" at all), and receive one of the highest priorities in distribution. Finally, only "claims" that exist prior to the confirmation are discharged. If a person's putative rights do not even rise to the level of a "claim" prior to the time of confirmation, those rights are not cut off by the discharge under section 1141, they receive no distribution, and they may be asserted against the debtor notwithstanding the discharge.

While the Third Circuit has determined that a claim arises only at the time that a state cause of action manifests,[2] most other courts hold there can be a "claim" for the purposes of section 101(5)(A) even though the plaintiff would not yet have a cause of action against the debtor under state law. This majority rule is justified on the basis of the policies of the bankruptcy law (the granting of debtor's discharge, debtor's fresh start, and treating all debtors fairly). Some people would criticize the majority rule as conflicting with the idea that federal bankruptcy law does not decide the existence of a claim and that all claims essentially are either state law claims or are based on rights arising under other federal law. A response to this criticism is that the conflict they see is false. Even if state law determines the existence of a claim (i.e., *if* a claim exists), it is entirely appropriate for federal bankruptcy law to determine, for bankruptcy purposes, *when* the claim arises. In any event, federal law should ultimately control, as it does in deciding what is property, to advance the peculiar, overriding policies of bankruptcy law.

Although this dispute typically arises in the context of tort litigation,[3]

---

§ 11–3

1. Section 362(a) provides:

(a) Except as provided in subsection (b) of this section, a petition filed under sections 301, 302, or 303 of this title * * * operates as a stay, applicable to all entities, of—

(1) the commencement or continuation, including the issuance or employment of process, of a judicial, administrative, or other action or proceeding against the debtor that was or could have been commenced before the commencement of the case under this title, or to recover a claim against the debtor that arose before the commencement of the case under this title * * *.

11 U.S.C.A. § 362(a); see also Taylor v. First Federal Sav. & Loan Ass'n of Monessen, 843 F.2d 153, 154 (3d Cir.1988) ("the automatic stay is not intended to bar proceedings for postpetition claims that could not have been commenced before the petition was filed."); In re Pettibone Corp., 90 B.R. 918, 922–23, 932–33 (Bankr. N.D.Ill. 1988).

2. Matter of M. Frenville Co., 744 F.2d 332 (3d Cir.1984), cert. denied, 469 U.S. 1160, 105 S.Ct. 911, 83 L.Ed.2d 925 (1985).

3. Tort cases frequently present definitional issues for bankruptcy courts. One of the reasons for this is that one element of a tort cause of action is harm to the victim. For a legal cause of action to exist, therefore, a plaintiff must have manifested some sort of injury. This is not a harsh rule in the non-bankruptcy world, where compensation is expected to be available should injury occur in the future. In the world of bankruptcy, however, the debtor will either be liquidated under Chapter 7, leaving nothing for future creditors; or will be reorganized under Chapter 11, where the discharge of debt and the "fresh start" of the debtor are primary goals of the

the leading Third Circuit case, *Matter of M. Frenville Co.*[4] involved an action by the accounting firm Avellino & Bienes (A & B), for relief from the automatic stay, section 362(a), against M. Frenville Co., Inc., a company in involuntary Chapter 7 bankruptcy proceedings. Fourteen months after the filing of the bankruptcy petition, several banks brought suit against A & B for their allegedly negligent and reckless preparation of Frenville's financial statements. A & B sought relief from the automatic stay in order to include Frenville as a third party defendant for indemnity or contribution, thereby raising the issue of whether a creditor holds a prepetition claim for purposes of the automatic stay when the debtor's harmful act occurred prepetition but the creditor did not have a legal cause of action until postpetition.[5]

In equating a bankruptcy claim with a prepetition cause of action under non-bankruptcy law, the Third Circuit has been criticized for effectively barring contingent tort claims from bankruptcy proceedings,[6] and "reinstitut[ing] the provability concept of claims, which the drafters of the Code specifically intended to abolish".[7] Contract claims differ from other types of claims under the Third Circuit's analysis because of the existence of a pre-existing legal relationship between the parties which creates a "right to payment" between those parties.[8] That "right" becomes effective for bankruptcy purposes at the time the contract becomes legally binding.[9] If the debtor files in bankruptcy and the payment of the debt depends on some future event, then the right to payment is a contingent claim. Other types of claims are not valid under the Third Circuit's analysis until some sort of legal relationship has been established. Since an essential element of tort claims is injury to the victim, for example, this view holds there can be no tort claim in bankruptcy if there is no prepetition manifestation of injury.[10]

The parties in *Frenville* did not have a contractual indemnification agreement, and thus lacked the preexisting legal relationship that would have given A & B a prepetition claim against Frenville. Since the banks did not sue A & B until 14 months after the filing of the bankruptcy petition, A & B did not have a legal cause of action against Frenville until that time.

---

bankruptcy courts. In order to protect the interests of both the debtor and his creditors, it is therefore imperative for the bankruptcy court to consider the interests of not only present claimants, but potential future claimants as well.

4. 744 F.2d 332 (3d Cir.1984), cert. denied, 469 U.S. 1160, 105 S.Ct. 911, 83 L.Ed.2d 925 (1985).

5. Id. at 334.

6. Grady v. A.H. Robins Co., 839 F.2d 198, 202 (4th Cir.1988), cert. dism'd, 487 U.S. 1260, 109 S.Ct. 201, 101 L.Ed.2d 972 (1988).

7. In re Johns–Manville Corp., 57 B.R. 680, 690 (Bankr. S.D.N.Y. 1986).

8. Matter of M. Frenville Co., 744 F.2d at 337; Schweitzer v. Consolidated Rail Corp. (Conrail), 758 F.2d 936, 943 (3d Cir.1985), cert. denied, 474 U.S. 864, 106 S.Ct. 183, 88 L.Ed.2d 152 (1985).

9. Matter of M. Frenville Co., 744 F.2d at 337; In re Service Decorating Co., 105 B.R. 859, 864 (N.D.Ill. 1989). In the latter case the court notes there are few contract cases involving the issue of when a claim arises, and cites In re Peltz, 55 B.R. 336 (Bankr. M.D.Fla. 1985) as one other contracts case. Id. Both cases conclude that a claim for bankruptcy purposes occurs at the time the contract is signed, regardless of whether the creditor is aware of damages or is able to calculate the amount of damages. Id. at 865.

10. Schweitzer v. Consolidated Rail Corp., 758 F.2d 936, 943 (3d Cir.1985), cert. denied, 474 U.S. 864, 106 S.Ct. 183, 88 L.Ed.2d 152 (1985) ("There is no legal relationship * * * between a tortfeasor and a tort victim until a tort actually has occurred * * * [and] there is no tort under F.E.L.A. until injury manifests itself"). Interestingly, the Third Circuit did allow "future claimants" of asbestos-related diseases to be represented as "parties in interest" by a legal representative in In re Amatex Corp., 755 F.2d 1034, 1043 (3d Cir.1985).

The court noted that if there had been a contractual relationship between the parties, the claimant would have had a contingent prepetition claim.

Central to the Third Circuit's analysis is the proposition that in the absence of controlling federal law, the bankruptcy court must turn to state law in determining whether a non-bankruptcy cause of action existed prepetition.[11] This view has been widely criticized.[12]

Most courts disagree with the Third Circuit's conception of the term claim, and hold that a claim arises at "the time when the acts giving rise to the alleged liability were performed." [13] Under this analysis, a claim may exist in bankruptcy even if it is not a cognizable cause of action under state law at the time the bankruptcy petition is filed.[14] The court in *In re Edge* thus concluded: "This is a foundation principle of the 1978 Code: creditors may be entitled to allowable claims in bankruptcy even though remedies are not yet (and may never be) available under nonbankruptcy law." [15]

The court in *Grady v. A.H. Robins Co.* thus determined that Mrs. Grady had a bankruptcy "claim," because of her prepetition exposure to the Dalkon Shield, an allegedly defective intrauterine birth control device, even though manifestation of injury did not occur until postpetition.[16] The same result has been found in non-tort cases as well, with one court taking precisely the opposite view of the *Frenville* court on a similar issue, stating: "[r]egardless of when the principals' cause of action for indemnification might have accrued under state law, their 'right to payment' arose at the 'time when the acts giving rise to the alleged liability were performed.' " [17]

Arguably, the characterization of "claims" as accruing at the time of the debtor's harmful act not only protects the distribution rights of creditors

---

11. Id. at 337, citing Vanston Bondholders Protective Committee v. Green, 329 U.S. 156, 67 S.Ct. 237, 91 L.Ed. 162 (1946), reh'g denied, 329 U.S. 833, 67 S.Ct. 497, 91 L.Ed. 706 (1947); but see In re Yanks, 49 B.R. 56, 58 (Bankr. S.D.Fla.1985) (suggests Frenville court misapplied the Vanston holding).

12. In re Service Decorating Co., 105 B.R. at 864 n.2; In re Edge, 60 B.R. at 696 n.4; In re Baldwin-United Corp., 48 B.R. at 903; Mabey and Jarvis, In re Frenville: A Critique by the National Bankruptcy Conference's Committee on Claims and Distributions, 42 Bus. Law 675, 704-07 (1987); but see In re White Motor Credit Corp., 75 B.R. 944, 949 (Bankr. N.D.Ohio 1987) (in dicta, the court states that if the question presented were the issue of when the claim arose, "this court favors limited construction of tort claims based on state law concepts.").

13. See, e.g., In re Johns-Manville Corp., 57 B.R. 680, 690 (Bankr. S.D.N.Y. 1986), aff'd on other grounds sub nom., Pension Benefit Guaranty Corp. v. LTV Corp., 875 F.2d 1008 (2d Cir.1989), rev'd on other grounds, 496 U.S. 633, 110 S.Ct. 2668, 110 L.Ed.2d 579 (1990), on remand, 122 B.R. 863 (S.D.N.Y.1990).

14. Grady v. A.H. Robins Co., 839 F.2d 198, 202-03 (4th Cir.1988), cert. dism'd, 487 U.S. 1260, 109 S.Ct. 201, 101 L.Ed.2d 972 (1988); Matter of Hi-Lo Powered Scaffolding, Inc., 70 B.R. 606, 610 (Bankr. S.D.Ohio 1987); In re Dennis Ponte, Inc., 61 B.R. 296, 299 (Bankr. 9th Cir.1986); In re Edge, 60 B.R. at 694; In re Johns-Manville Corp., 36 B.R. 743, 754-55 n.6 (Bankr. S.D.N.Y. 1984), appeal denied, 39 B.R. 234 (S.D.N.Y.1984).

15. In re Edge, 60 B.R. at 694-95. (The court goes on to hold that the Code "recognizes a 'right to payment' at the earliest point in the relationship between victim and wrongdoer," even though the victim may not have access to other courts); but see Bibler, The Status of Unaccrued Tort Claims in Chapter 11 Bankruptcy Proceedings, 61 Am.Bankr. L.J. 145, 156 (1987) (author concludes "the bankruptcy court has no authority, actual or inherent, to create claims that do not exist under federal or state law.").

16. Grady v. A.H. Robins Co., 839 F.2d at 202-03. The Grady court left open the questions whether the claim was an administrative expense or whether the claims of "Future Tort Claimants" were dischargeable in the bankruptcy proceeding.

17. In re Hi-Lo Powered Scaffolding, Inc., 70 B.R. 606, 610 (Bankr. S.D.Ohio 1987), quoting In re Johns-Manville Corp., 57 B.R. 680, 690 (Bankr. S.D.N.Y. 1986).

who may not manifest injury until postpetition or postconfirmation;[18] but also the debtor's opportunity for a "fresh start" by addressing all possible claims in the bankruptcy proceedings.[19]

Difficulties arise, however, when a debtor is faced with liability to an unidentifiable class of claimants, unknown because they have not yet manifested injury after exposure to the debtor's product.[20] Courts are especially concerned about the dischargeability of those claims, given the broad discharge provision of section 1141.[21] If the identity of these claimants is unknown to both the debtor and the claimants themselves, how can they be "creditors"[22] under the Bankruptcy Code, and how can they be subject to discharge under section 1141? One court describes the constitutional issues presented by this characterization of the term "claim":

> The theory of claims herein adopted, admits of the possibility that a victim of the debtor's prepetition misconduct has a claim in bankruptcy notwithstanding that the victim knows not of any injury and may be known to the debtor only as a member of a class. Acknowledging that victims of prepetition torts have claims implicates the need to develop methods to identify claimholders and to give notice, and the need to design systems to compensate "future claimants." *See UNR Industries, Inc.,* 725 F.2d 1111, 1119 (7th Cir.1984). If notice and participation

---

18. See § 11–8 supra.

19. See § 11–1, note 2 supra.

20. See § 11–8 infra, regarding bankruptcy and mass torts.

21. 11 U.S.C.A. § 1141 provides:

(d)(1) Except as otherwise provided in this subsection, in the plan, or in the order confirming the plan, the confirmation of a plan—

(A) discharges the debtor from any debt that arose before the date of such confirmation * * * whether or not—

(i) a proof of the claim based on such debt is filed or deemed filed under section 501 of this title;

(ii) such claim is allowed under section 502 of this title; or

(iii) the holder of such claim has accepted the plan * * *.

In general, all claims are discharged under 11 U.S.C.A. § 1141(d)(1)(A) unless alternate provisions are specified, In re Service Decorating Co., 105 B.R. at 862; In re Pettibone Corp., 90 B.R. at 922; In re White, 75 B.R. at 949; In re Hi–Lo Powered Scaffolding, 70 B.R. at 611, or other exceptions apply. 11 U.S.C.A. § 523 (provides for exceptions to discharge for individual debtors).

The discharge may be effective even if the claimant did not participate in the bankruptcy proceeding, In re Siouxland Beef Processing Co., 55 B.R. 95, 100 (Bankr. N.D.Iowa 1985) (court notes one "case-law-created exception" for those cases where the debtor failed to provide notice to a known creditor and that creditor did not have actual knowledge of the bankruptcy proceeding in time to file a proof of claim). Several courts have held it would be unconstitutional to apply section 1141 to certain creditors who lack knowledge of the bankruptcy proceedings. In re General Oil Distributors, Inc., 68 B.R. 603 (Bankr. E.D.N.Y.1986) ("Four circuit courts have held [section 1141(d)(1)(A)] unconstitutional" where the creditor did not have actual knowledge of the proceeding; cites Broomall Industries v. Data Design Logic Systems, Inc., 786 F.2d 401 (Fed. Cir.1986), Reliable Electric Co., Inc. v. Olson Construction Co., 726 F.2d 620, 622 (10th Cir.1984); In re Intaco Puerto Rico, Inc., 494 F.2d 94 (1st Cir.1974); In re Harbor Tank Storage Co., 385 F.2d 111 (3d Cir.1967)); see also Acevedo v. Van Dorn Plastic Machinery Co., 68 B.R. 495, 499 (Bankr. E.D.N.Y. 1986); In re Spring Valley Farms, Inc., 68 B.R. 756, 761 (Bankr. N.D.Ala.1986), decision aff'd, 85 B.R. 593 (N.D.Ala.1988).

For Supreme Court rulings on notice issues, see generally, City of New York v. N.Y., N.Y. & H.R. Co., 344 U.S. 293, 73 S.Ct. 299, 97 L.Ed. 333 (1953), motion denied, 345 U.S. 901, 73 S.Ct. 639, 97 L.Ed. 1339 (1953); Mullane v. Central Hanover Bank & Trust Co., 339 U.S. 306, 314, 70 S.Ct. 652, 657, 94 L.Ed. 865 (1950); see also In re Charter Co., 93 B.R. 281 (Bankr. M.D.Fla.1988), rev'd, 113 B.R. 725 (M.D.Fla. 1990); In re Edge, 60 B.R. at 691–92 n.1.

22. 11 U.S.C.A. § 101(9)(A) defines "creditor" as an "entity that has a claim against the debtor that arose at the time of or before the order for relief concerning the debtor."

cannot be provided, then difficult questions are presented whether a claim held by someone who cannot timely and reasonably be given notice is dischargeable.[23]

These questions have been raised most dramatically in the *Johns–Manville* reorganization case, where thousands of unknown "future claimants" were given the status of "parties in interest" under section 1109(b), were represented by a court-appointed legal representative, and subsequently enjoined from suing the reorganized Manville corporation. Those claimants were forced to litigate against a trust fund designed to settle all Johns–Manville asbestos-related personal injury claims. When the trust fund was depleted far sooner than anticipated, the question of the rights of these future claimants once again rose to the forefront. The answers to the questions raised by these cases are still being forged. Later in this chapter we take a closer look at the *Johns–Manville* case and other mass tort litigation.[24]

Environmental litigation also often involves questions of when a claim arises. Cases and commentators are divided on whether a "claim" arises for bankruptcy purposes at the time of (1) the debtor's action that is detrimental to the environment, (2) the release or threatened release of hazardous materials, (3) the environmental agency's awareness of the problem, or (4) the agency's response to it.[25] At least one court has held that if there is no prepetition tort (such as release or threatened release of hazardous waste) *and* no contractual relationship between the debtor and those who may wish to sue him in the future, their claims are not dischargeable in bankruptcy.[26]

§ 11–4 Filing Claims in Bankruptcy

The filing of proofs of claims or interests is permissive. No creditor or party in interest is required to file a claim, but filing is a prerequisite to receiving distribution under Chapters 7 and 13.[1] Chapters 9 and 11 do not require any filing of a proof of claim if the claim is listed properly on the debtor's schedule. If the claim is listed incorrectly, however, or is listed as disputed, contingent or unliquidated, the creditor or equity security holder must file a proof of claim or lose its voting and distribution rights.[2]

Creditors and indenture trustees may file a proof of claim.[3] Equity security holders may file a proof of interest.[4] Filing deadlines are determined by the court in Chapter 9 and 11 cases,[5] and are set at 90 days after the first meeting date for the creditors in Chapter 7 and 13 cases.[6] If a

---

23. In re Edge, 60 B.R. at 692 n.1.

24. See § 11–8 infra.

25. See generally Aaron, Chateaugay Appeal—The Crash at the Intersection of Bankruptcy and Environmental Law, 3 BNA Bankruptcy Law Reporter 1129 (1991).

26. In re Chateaugay Corp., 112 B.R. 513, 521 (S.D.N.Y. 1990), aff'd, 944 F.2d 977 (2d Cir.1991) ("before a contingent claim can be discharged, it must result from prepetition conduct fairly giving rise to that contingent claim").

§ 11–4

1. Bankr. R. 3002.
2. Id. 3003(c)(2).
3. 11 U.S.C.A. § 501(a); see also Bankr. R. 3001(a).
4. 11 U.S.C.A. § 501(a).
5. Bankr. R. 3003(c)(3).
6. Id. 3002(c).

creditor fails to file a proof of claim, the creditor's co-debtor, surety, guarantor or debtor may file a proof of claim on his behalf,[7] but must do so within 30 days of the creditor's filing deadline.[8]

In addition, section 501(d) provides that certain claims must be treated as prepetition claims even though they arose postpetition. Specifically, claims which do not become fixed or do not arise until after the commencement of the case are treated the "same as if such claim were a claim against the debtor and had arisen before the date of the filing of the petition."[9] Thus, claims for reimbursement or contribution,[10] rejected executory contracts,[11] recovery of property,[12] priority taxes,[13] as well as certain postpetition claims in involuntary cases,[14] are treated as prepetition claims even if they arose postpetition. Many other postpetition claims are administrative expenses,[15] and thus have priority in payment over prepetition claims.[16]

A proof of claim or interest filed under section 501 constitutes "prima facie evidence of the validity and amount of the claim,"[17] and is deemed allowed unless objected to by a party in interest.[18] The value of a disputed claim is determined by the court,[19] subject to disallowance of unenforceable claims,[20] claims for unmatured interest,[21] excessive property taxes,[22] unreasonable attorney or insider fee claims,[23] unmatured debts excepted from section 523(a)(5) discharge,[24] lease termination claims,[25] and certain employee claims.[26]

7. 11 U.S.C.A. § 501(b)-(c); In re A.H. Robins Co., Inc., 88 B.R. 742, 752 (E.D.Va.1988), order aff'd, 880 F.2d 694 (4th Cir.1989), cert. denied, 493 U.S. 959, 110 S.Ct. 376, 107 L.Ed.2d 362 (1989); In re White Motor Credit Corp., 75 B.R. 944, 950 (Bankr. N.D.Ohio 1987) ("A debtor's fresh start is affected by the discharge of all debts arising prior to confirmation."); In re Edge, 60 B.R. 690, 691 (Bankr. M.D.Tenn.1986); In re Johns–Manville, 57 B.R. 680, 692 N.6 (Bankr. S.D.N.Y. 1986); In re Baldwin–United Corp., 55 B.R. 885, 898 (Bankr. S.D.Ohio 1985) (" * * * Congress has insured that the debtor will receive a complete discharge of his debts and a real fresh start, without the threat of lingering claims 'riding through' the bankruptcy.").

8. Bankr. R. 3004.

9. 11 U.S.C.A. § 501(d); see also In re A.H. Robins Co., Inc., 63 B.R. 986, 992 (Bankr. E.D.Va.1986) (even claims that "accrued" postpetition actually "existed" prepetition); but see In re Pettibone Corp., 90 B.R. 918, 933 (Bankr. N.D.Ill. 1988) (not all postpetition claims entitled to administrative priority).

10. Id. § 502(e)(2).

11. Id. § 502(g).

12. Id. § 502(h).

13. Id. § 502(i).

14. Id. § 502(f).

15. Id. § 503(b)(1)(A); see also In re Dennis Ponte, Inc., 61 B.R. 296, 298 (Bankr. 9th Cir. 1986) ("damages for a postpetition tort become an administrative expense under 11 U.S.C.A. § 503(b)(1)(A)"); In re Alan Wood Steel Co., 2 B.R. 161, 163 (Bankr. E.D.Pa. 1980) (applying former Bankruptcy Act, citing Reading Co. v. Brown, 391 U.S. 471, 88 S.Ct. 1759, 20 L.Ed.2d 751 (1968)); but see In re White Motor Credit Corp., 75 B.R. at 951 ("Postpetition claims based on prepetition activity are not intrinsically administrative expenses. Elevating product liability claims through successor liability subverts the Code established priorities.").

16. 11 U.S.C.A. §§ 503(b) & 507(a); see also Kesner, Future Asbestos Related Litigants as Holders of Statutory Claims Under Chapter 11 of the Bankruptcy Code and Their Place in the Johns–Manville Reorganization (Second Installment), 62 Am.Bankr. L.J. 159, 173–78 (1988).

17. Bankr. R. 3001(f).

18. 11 U.S.C.A. § 502(a).

19. Id. § 502(b).

20. Id. § 502(b)(1).

21. Id. § 502(b)(2).

22. Id. § 502(b)(3).

23. Id. § 502(b)(4).

24. Id. § 502(b)(5).

25. Id. § 502(b)(6).

26. Id. § 502(b)(7–8).

Contingent claims are allowable under section 502(c).[27] If a contingent claim is a claim for reimbursement or contribution, it must also hurdle the requirements of sections 502(e) and 509.[28] Claims for reimbursement or contribution become interesting when a co-obligor asserts a claim against the debtor. The basic rule is that "the scope of section 502(e)(1)(B), in conjunction with section 509(a), operates to disallow any contingent co-liability, even if the co-liability has not been judicially established, unless the co-obligor pays the liability and becomes subrogated to the rights of the underlying creditor therefore." [29]

The result of the interaction of sections 502(e) and 509 is that "[a] claim for reimbursement or contribution 'is entitled to no better status than the claim of a creditor assured by such surety.'" [30] Thus, if the underlying creditor's claim is disallowed, the claim of the indemnitor or contributor is disallowed under section 502(e)(1)(A), and if the indemnitor or contributor's claim is allowed, it is subordinated to the creditor's claim under section 509(c). If the indemnitor or contributor pays the underlying creditor, then it is subrogated to the creditor's rights under sections 502(e)(1)(C) and 509(a), thereby gaining the same rights as the creditor would have had.[31]

---

27. For a full discussion of section 502(c), see § 11-5 infra.

28. Those provisions provide:

(e)(1) Notwithstanding subsections (a), (b), and (c) of this section and paragraph (2) of this subsection, the court shall disallow any claim for reimbursement or contribution of an entity that is liable with the debtor on or has secured the claim of a creditor, to the extent that—

   (A) such creditor's claim against the estate is disallowed;

   (B) such claim for reimbursement or contribution is contingent as of the time of allowance or disallowance of such claim for reimbursement or contribution; or

   (C) such entity asserts a right of subrogation to the rights of such creditor under section 509 of this title.

(2) A claim for reimbursement or contribution of such an entity that becomes fixed after the commencement of the case shall be determined, and shall be allowed under subsection (a), (b), or (c) of this section, or disallowed under subsection (d) of this section, the same as if such claim had become fixed before the date of the filing of the petition.

11 U.S.C.A. § 502.

(a) Except as provided in subsection (b) or (c) of this section, an entity that is liable with the debtor on, or that has secured, a claim of a creditor against the debtor, and that pays such claim, is subrogated to the rights of such creditor to the extent of such payment.

(b) Such entity is not subrogated to the rights of such creditor to the extent that—

   (1) a claim of such entity for reimbursement or contribution on account of such payment of such creditor's claim is—

     (A) allowed under section 502 of this title;

     (B) disallowed other than under section 502(e) of this title; or

     (C) subordinated under section 510 of this title; or

   (2) as between the debtor and such entity, such entity received the consideration for the claim held by such creditor.

(c) The court shall subordinate to the claim of a creditor and for the benefit of such creditor an allowed claim, by way of subrogation under this section, or for reimbursement or contribution, of an entity that is liable with the debtor on, or that has secured, such creditor's claim, until such creditor's claim is paid in full, either through payment under this title or otherwise.

Id. § 509.

29. In re Amatex Corp., 110 B.R. 168 (Bankr. E.D.Pa. 1990).

30. Id. at 170, quoting 124 Cong. Rec. S17410-11 (daily ed. Oct. 6, 1987); Cong. Rec. H11094 (daily ed. September 28, 1978).

31. 110 B.R. at 171; see also In re Spirtos, 103 B.R. 240 (Bankr. C.D.Cal.1989) (insurer may be subrogated to rights of insured); In re Watkins Oil Service, Inc., 100 B.R. 7 (Bankr. D. Ariz. 1989) (claimant may be subrogated to rights of IRS); Matter of Baldwin–United Corp., 55 B.R. 885 (Bankr. S.D.Ohio 1985) (claim for contribution and indemnity disallowed).

§ 11–5 Estimating Claims (Section 502(c))

If contingent claims are to be treated and discharged in bankruptcy, somehow their value must be estimated and they must be included in and provided for in the bankruptcy plan. Although section 502(c) provides for such estimation, it does not specify how that estimation must occur. Section 502(c) provides:

> (c) There shall be estimated for purpose of allowance under this section—
>
> (1) any contingent or unliquidated claim, the fixing or liquidation of which, as the case may be, would unduly delay the administration of the case; or
>
> (2) any right to payment arising from a right to an equitable remedy for breach of performance.

One should be clear about the consequences of "estimation." If the court decides it will "estimate the value" of the claim for all purposes, then the creditor has a right to vote only to the extent of the value of that estimated claim; the creditor will be included in the plan only to that amount, and will get a distribution based upon that estimated value. Absent an appeal of such a finding, "estimation" is in fact a final determination of the value of the claim that substantially affects the rights of the creditor.[1] Because of the inherent difficulties of ascertaining the value of these claims, however, estimation requires only that the court "arrive at a reasonable estimate of the probable value of the claim."[2]

Estimation is required to ascertain the value of a claim for voting, distribution and confirmation purposes.[3] Many courts have held that the word "shall" creates an affirmative duty on the part of the bankruptcy court to estimate a contingent or unliquidated claim for purposes of confirmation,[4] and voting,[5] although at least one court has refused to estimate for voting purposes.[6] Another case holds the court has no affirmative duty to estimate

---

§ 11–5

1. See In re Amatex Corp., 110 B.R. 168, 171 (Bankr. E.D.Pa.1990); Note, The Manville Bankruptcy: Treating Mass Tort Claims In Chapter 11 Proceedings, 96 Harv.L.Rev. 1121, 1128 n.41 (1983) ("the legislative history of section 502(c) indicates that the term 'estimation' is synonymous with 'liquidation' ").

2. Matter of Baldwin–United, 55 B.R. at 898; see also In re Nova Real Estate Inv. Trust, 23 B.R. 62, 66 (Bankr. E.D.Va.1982).

3. The courts have not deemed it necessary to value a claim at a single amount for voting, distribution and confirmation. In cases where the estimation process itself would cause undue delay, some courts have assigned a nominal value for purposes of voting and confirmation with the expectation that the distribution amount (to be determined in another court) would be significantly higher. Kane v. Johns–Manville Corp., 843 F.2d 636, 641 (2d Cir.1988); In re A.H. Robins Co., 88 B.R. 742, 746–47 (E.D.Va.1988), order aff'd, 880 F.2d 694 (4th Cir.1989), cert. denied, 493 U.S. 959, 110 S.Ct. 376, 107 L.Ed.2d 362 (1989); Matter of Johns–Manville Corp., 68 B.R. 618, 631 (Bankr. S.D.N.Y. 1986), decision aff'd in part, rev'd in part, 78 B.R. 407 (S.D.N.Y.1987), judgment aff'd, 843 F.2d 636 (2d Cir.1988).

4. In re Dennis Ponte, Inc., 61 B.R. 296, 300 (Bankr. 9th Cir.1986); Matter of Pizza of Hawaii, Inc., 40 B.R. 1014, 1015 (D.Hawaii 1984), order aff'd, 761 F.2d 1374 (9th Cir.1985); In re Unit Parts Co., 9 B.R. 386, 390 (W.D. Okla. 1981).

5. In re TransAmerican Natural Gas Corp., 79 B.R. 663, 665 (Bankr. S.D.Tex.1987); In re Continental Airlines Corp., 60 B.R. 903 (Bankr. S.D.Tex.1986).

6. Moody v. Security Pacific Business Credit, Inc., 85 B.R. 319, 352 (W.D.Pa.1988), order vac'd, 858 F.2d 137 (3d Cir.1988), cert. denied, 489 U.S. 1078, 109 S.Ct. 1529, 103 L.Ed.2d 835 (1989).

until the "undue delay" requirement has been met.[7]

The ability of the court to estimate for distribution purposes was curtailed somewhat under the 1984 Bankruptcy Amendments and Judiciary Reform Act, section 157. It introduces new language into bankruptcy law by distinguishing "core" from "non-core" proceedings.[8] The section gives the bankruptcy courts jurisdiction over all core proceedings,[9] and limited jurisdiction over non-core proceedings (subject to *de novo* review by the district court).[10]

The major effect of the section is to bar bankruptcy courts from determining distribution estimates for personal injury tort or wrongful death cases.[11] This limitation applies solely to distribution issues.[12] Even cases which do not fall under the tort rubric, however, are often not estimated for distribution purposes, as we discuss later.[13]

§ 11–6 Estimating Claims (Section 502(c))—Estimation for Voting Purposes

Unfortunately, the Code offers no guidance on the question how courts should estimate claims.[1] On a substantive level, courts have accepted the "ultimate merits" test of *Bittner v. Borne Chemical Co.*,[2] and prefer it over the "present value" theory proposed by the claimants in that case.[3] In *Bittner,* the court assigned a value of zero to the claims of the Rolfite stockholders on the basis that their claim lacked legal merit.[4] The Court of Appeals for the Third Circuit affirmed the bankruptcy court, saying: "[f]aced with only the remote possibility that the state court would find otherwise, the bankruptcy court correctly valued the claims at zero."[5] The claimants had a different standard in mind:

---

7. In re Apex Oil Co., 107 B.R. 189, 193 (Bankr. E.D.Mo.1989).

8. A.H. Robins Co., Inc. v. Piccinin, 788 F.2d 994, 1012–13 (4th Cir.1986), ccrt. denied, 479 U.S. 876, 107 S.Ct. 251, 93 L.Ed.2d 177 (1986); Matter of Hughes–Bechtol, Inc., 107 B.R. 552, 556–57 (Bankr. S.D.Ohio 1989), citing Granfinanciera, S.A. v. Nordberg, 492 U.S. 33, 109 S.Ct. 2782, 2798, 106 L.Ed.2d 26 (1989).

9. 28 U.S.C.A. § 157(b)(1); see also A.H. Robins Co., Inc. v. Piccinin, 788 F.2d at 1011. For a discussion on congressional intent regarding section 157, see Matter of Poole Funeral Chapel, Inc., 63 B.R. 527, 532 (Bankr. N.D.Ala.1986); see also In re Hudgins, 102 B.R. 495, 497 (Bankr. E.D.Va.1989); In re Towner Petroleum Co., 48 B.R. 182 (Bankr. W.D. Okla.1985).

10. 28 U.S.C.A. § 157(c)(1).

11. 28 U.S.C.A. § 157(b)(2)(B). In addition, 28 U.S.C.A. section 1411 provides for a jury trial for personal injury or wrongful death claims. See also Granfinanciera S.A. v. Nordberg, 492 U.S. 33, 64, 109 S.Ct. 2782, 2802, 106 L.Ed.2d 26 (1989); Matter of Hughes–Bechtol, 107 B.R. at 571 (" * * * it is difficult for this court to conclude that Congress intended, by any presently existing legislation, to permit bankruptcy courts to conduct jury trials.").

12. A.H. Robins Co., Inc. v. Piccinin, 788 F.2d at 1012, n.16, citing Roberts v. Johns–Manville Corp., 45 B.R. 823, 825–26 (Bankr. S.D.N.Y. 1984); Matter of Poole Funeral Chapel, Inc., 63 B.R. at 532; In re Aquaslide "N" Dive Corp., 85 B.R. 545 (Bankr. 9th Cir. 1987).

13. See § 11–7 infra.

§ 11–6

1. Bittner v. Borne Chemical Co., 691 F.2d 134, 135 (3d Cir.1982); Matter of Baldwin–United Corp., 55 B.R. 885, 899 (Bankr. S.D.Ohio 1985).

2. 691 F.2d 134 (3d Cir.1982).

3. Id. at 136; In re The Bible Speaks, 65 B.R. 415, 427 (Bankr. D.Mass.1986); In re Ram Mfg., Inc. 36 B.R. 822, 825 (Bankr. E.D.Pa.1984); but see T. Jackson, The Logic and Limits of Bankruptcy Law 46–47 (1986) (zero valuation is improper).

4. 691 F.2d at 139.

5. Id.

According to Rolfite stockholders, the estimate which section 502(c)(1) requires is the present value of the probability that appellants would be successful in their state court action. Thus, if the bankruptcy court should determine as of this date that the Rolfite stockholders' case is not supported by a preponderance or 51% of the evidence but merely 40%, they apparently would be entitled to have 40% of their claims allowed during the reorganization proceedings, subject to modification if and when the claims are liquidated in state court.[6]

In affirming the bankruptcy court's determination, the Court of Appeals found the decision was consistent with the Code's goal of quick and efficient reorganizations.[7] In addition, a valuation of the claim based on the claimants' definition of "present value" would have resulted in the stockholders acquiring "a significant, if not controlling, voice in the reorganization proceedings," in spite of the fact that their chances of success at the state court level were highly uncertain.[8]

The *Bittner* court protected the stockholders' distribution rights by requiring Borne to waive the discharge of the Rolfite claims.[9] In effect, the court made the case easy for itself by denying the Rolfite creditors the right to vote but by allowing them to establish their right to distribution under the plan through the state court action. The court did this by denying a discharge to these claims in the bankruptcy proceeding. In effect, the issues are much more simple when the court is merely passing on the creditor's right to vote than when the court is deciding, for example, to discharge the creditor's claim entirely by an estimate of its value at zero for the purpose of inclusion in the plan.

The *Bittner* court's zero valuation has been used in other cases estimating claims for voting purposes,[10] but *Bittner*'s "ultimate merits" analysis can be construed to include values other than zero (in cases where the "ultimate merits" may predict partial success);[11] or the assignment of even a nominal value for purposes of voting.[12] In addition, the court does not expressly limit distribution decisions to liquidation in another forum. On the contrary, Bittner's language seems to allow for great flexibility by the bankruptcy courts in making estimations in whatever manner and in whatever amount the courts determine is appropriate, within the confines of the principles of

6. Id. at 136.
7. Id. at 137.
8. Id.
9. Id. at 135.
10. In re Corey, 892 F.2d 829, 834 (9th Cir.1989), cert. denied, ___ U.S. ___, 111 S.Ct. 56, 112 L.Ed.2d 31 (1990); In re Continental Airlines Corp., 60 B.R. 903, 906 (Bankr. S.D.Tex.1986).
11. In re TransAmerican Natural Gas Corp., 79 B.R. 663, 668 (Bankr. S.D.Tex.1987) (court estimates value of claim at $10,569,-105.74) where the debtor had estimated the claim to be worthless, and the creditor had estimated the claim to be worth over $38,000,-000.); In re Lane, 68 B.R. 609, 613 (Bankr. D.Hawaii 1986) (court estimates value of claim at $550,000 where claimants are seeking $5,000,000 in a state court action). Both of the courts expressly limit their estimation to voting purposes only.

12. Kane v. Johns–Manville Corp., 843 F.2d 636, 641 (2d Cir.1988); In re A.H. Robins Co., Inc., 88 B.R. 742, 746–47 (E.D.Va.1988), order aff'd, 880 F.2d 694 (4th Cir.1989), cert. denied, 493 U.S. 959, 110 S.Ct. 376, 107 L.Ed.2d 362 (1989); In re Johns–Manville Corp., 68 B.R. 618, 631 (Bankr. S.D.N.Y. 1986), decision aff'd in part, rev'd in part, 78 B.R. 407 (S.D.N.Y.1987), order aff'd, 843 F.2d 636 (2d Cir.1988).

the Code and other legal doctrines. Other courts have agreed with this analysis.[13]

§ 11-7 Estimating Claims (Section 502(c))—Estimation for Distribution Purposes

Ultimately, there are several options open to the court attempting to estimate claims. They include:

accepting the claimant's claim at face value, estimating the claim at zero and waiving discharge of the claim under section 1141(d), arriving at its independent estimation of the claim, or utilizing a jury trial to obtain an accurate estimation."[1]

Other options also exist, including estimating the claim at zero (or any other number) and *not* waiving the discharge, thus providing an estimation for both voting and distribution purposes from the bankruptcy court.[2]

Bankruptcy courts have been cautious in their use of section 502(c) to estimate for purposes of distribution. As was seen in *Bittner,* estimation for voting and confirmation purposes is of lesser moment than estimation for distribution purposes. There is a reluctance on the part of the courts to make this determination, in spite of the criticisms that liquidation in another forum may cause "delay and uncertainty,"[3] and that a waiver of discharge allows the creditor a full recovery after the plan has been confirmed,[4] thus denigrating the "fresh start" policy of the Bankruptcy Code.[5]

The initial reluctance of courts to estimate for purposes of distribution is beginning to wane, however. It had already been generally established under the 1898 Bankruptcy Act that "[t]he bankruptcy court normally supervises the liquidation of claims,"[6] but liquidation in nonbankruptcy forums had been held to be appropriate "to avoid duplicative litigation, to prevent waste of scant federal resources, or to allow a court of special

---

13. In re Corey, 892 F.2d 829 (9th Cir. 1989), cert. denied, ___ U.S. ___, 111 S.Ct. 56, 112 L.Ed.2d 31 (1990); In re TransAmerican Natural Gas Corp., 79 B.R. at 666; In re Baldwin-United Corp., 55 B.R. at 899. Procedurally, courts have held estimation hearings, id., heard testimony on the estimation question, In re Nova Real Estate Inv. Trust, 23 B.R. 62, 65 (Bankr. E.D.Va.1982), made an objective evaluation of the claim, In re TransAmerican Natural Gas Corp., 79 B.R. at 667, and contemplated in dicta "something approaching a complete trial." In re The Bible Speaks, 65 B.R. 415, 427 (Bankr. D.Mass.1986).

§ 11-7

1. In re Federal Press Company, 116 B.R. 650, 653 (Bankr. N.D.Ind. 1989).

2. In re Apex Oil Co., 92 B.R. 843, 844 (Bankr. E.D.Mo.1988) (court develops procedure for estimation of claims for both liquidation and distribution purposes); In re Continental Airlines Corp., 64 B.R. 865, 874 (Bankr. S.D.Tex.1986), vacated, remanded, 901 F.2d 1259 (5th Cir.1990) (original zero valuation of claims by bankruptcy court was determined to be incorrect value, remanded to determine correct amount; but propriety of bankruptcy court making that valuation not questioned).

3. In re The Bible Speaks, 65 B.R. at 427.

4. In re Baldwin-United, 55 B.R. at 901 n.17, citing B. Weintraub & A. Resnick, Treatment of Contingent and Unliquidated Claims Under the Bankruptcy Code, 15 U.C.C. L. J. 373, 377 (1983).

5. See § 11-3 supra.

6. Nathanson v. National Labor Relations Board, 344 U.S. 25, 30, 73 S.Ct. 80, 97 L.Ed. 23 (1952). For further authority on the bankruptcy courts' exclusive jurisdiction over the liquidation and allowance of claims, see generally, Granfinanciera, S.A. v. Nordberg, 492 U.S. 33, 109 S.Ct. 2782, 106 L.Ed.2d 26 (1989); Katchen v. Landy, 382 U.S. 323, 86 S.Ct. 467, 15 L.Ed.2d 391 (1966); Pepper v. Litton, 308 U.S. 295, 304, 60 S.Ct. 238, 244, 84 L.Ed. 281 (1939).

expertise to resolve a dispute within its purview."[7] More recent cases are beginning to recognize the expanded ability of the bankruptcy courts to estimate virtually any claim for distribution purposes.[8]

Two courts have found a middle ground by estimating for purposes of both voting and distribution, but also lifting the automatic stay to allow liquidation in another court, advising in dicta that either party could seek a readjustment of the claim under section 502(j)[9] if the state court awarded an amount greatly in excess of, or less than, the amount estimated by the bankruptcy court.[10]

In deciding whether to grant relief from the automatic stay, the most important factor to consider, in one court's opinion, is "the effect of such litigation on the administration of the estate."[11] The "effect on the estate" is mostly a function of two matters. One is the question how fast will the state case be resolved and the second is how large is the claim. If the claim is insignificant by comparison with the value of the estate and the amount of the other claims, it can safely be put off indefinitely with the understanding that any payment to be made will not materially alter the plan. By the same token, if the claim will be resolved by the state court, so that there will be a final judgment in a matter of weeks or months, there will be no significant interference with the administration of the bankruptcy case and

---

7. In re Comstock Financial Services, Inc., 111 B.R. 849, 855 (Bankr. C.D.Cal.1990); see also Nathanson v. NLRB, 344 U.S. at 30, 73 S.Ct. at 83 ("where the matter in controversy has been entrusted by Congress to an administrative agency, the bankruptcy court should normally stay its hand pending an administrative decision."); In re Gary Aircraft Corp., 698 F.2d 775 (5th Cir. 1983), cert. denied, 464 U.S. 820, 104 S.Ct. 82, 78 L.Ed.2d 92 (1983) (under former Bankruptcy Act, liquidation of government contract claim should be deferred to the Armed Services Board of Contract Appeals because of the "technical and esoteric" nature of the litigation); In re Compton Corp., 90 B.R. 798, 807 (N.D.Tex.1988), appeal dism'd, 889 F.2d 1104 (Em.App.1989); In re Misener Industries, Inc., 54 B.R. 89, 90 (Bankr. M.D.Fla. 1985); but see, In re Gary Aircraft Corp., 92 B.R. 1023 (Bankr. W.D.Tex.1988) (claimants waiting over 12 years for distribution cannot be paid until "the Board acts.").

8. In re Continental Airlines Corp., 60 B.R. 472, 479 (Bankr. S.D.Tex.1986) (distinguishes Gary, mentioned in the preceding note, on the basis that it was decided under the 1898 Bankruptcy Act which did not have the expanded subject matter jurisdiction available to bankruptcy courts under the 1978 Bankruptcy Reform Act, and did not have the estimation requirement of 11 U.S.C.A. § 502(c)); In re T.D.M.A., Inc., 66 B.R. 992 (Bankr. E.D.Pa. 1986); Matter of Page–Wilson Corp., 37 B.R. 527, 529 (Bankr. D.Conn.1984); Matter of Cott Corp., 26 B.R. 332, 336 (Bankr. D.Conn.1982) (distinguishes Nathanson on grounds that the complexities of that case required the special expertise of the NLRB).

9. Section 502(j) provides:

A claim that has been allowed or disallowed may be reconsidered for cause. A reconsidered claim may be allowed or disallowed according to the equities of the case. Reconsideration of a claim under this subsection does not affect the validity of any payment or transfer from the estate made to a holder of an allowed claim on account of such allowed claim that is not reconsidered, but if a reconsidered claim is allowed and is of the same class as such holder's claim, such holder may not receive any additional payment or transfer from the estate on account of such holder's claim until the holder of such reconsidered and allowed claim receives payment on account of such claim proportionate in value to that already received by such holder. This subsection does not alter or modify the trustee's right to recover from a creditor any excess payment or transfer made to such creditor.

11 U.S.C.A. § 502(j).

10. In re Lane, 68 B.R. 609, 613 (Bankr. D.Hawaii 1986); In re Nova Real Estate Inv. Trust, 23 B.R. at 66; see also, In re Perpetual Corp., 112 B.R. 27, 30 n.4 (Bankr. M.D.Tenn. 1990); In re Monument Record Corp., 71 B.R. 853 (Bankr. M.D.Tenn.1987); In re Turchon, 62 B.R. 461, 464 n.3 (Bankr. E.D.N.Y.1986); In re Baldwin–United, 55 B.R. at 898 ("estimated claims are covered by the debtor's discharge, subject only to a section 502(j) motion for reconsideration at a later time.").

11. In re Towner Petroleum Co., 48 B.R. 182, 190 (Bankr. W.D. Okla. 1985).

it can safely await that time. On the other hand, when the amount may be large and the time extended, there is greater need for the bankruptcy court itself to make a decision and for it to take the power away from the state court.

This issue of lifting the stay to permit nonbankruptcy litigation is also explored in our chapter on the stay, Chapter 3.[12]

Creating yet another method of distribution, an Ohio court chose not to estimate personal injury claims, but to pay those claimants out of a "contingent fund" equal to the net value of the debtor, to be funded by the debtor in monthly installments until the total net value was realized. Following liquidation of all the claims, the fund would be divided pro rata among those claimants.[13]

B. MEGA–CLAIMS
§ 11–8 Bankruptcy and Mass Torts

In broadening the scope of claims allowable in bankruptcy and mandating the estimation of contingent and unliquidated claims, Congress unwittingly opened the door to an entirely new and uncharted area of law—bankruptcy and mass tort litigation. The Bankruptcy Reform Act of 1978 suddenly made it possible for otherwise solvent companies facing crippling present and future products liability to file for Chapter 11 reorganization.[1] The additional protection afforded the debtor by the automatic stay provided these corporations with the necessary time to work out plans of reorganization that may be capable of determining the voting and distribution rights of both present and future claimants.[2] In so doing, the bankruptcy courts pioneered new territory by approving the appointment of legal representatives to represent the interests of future claimants, and by using trust funds to provide for the distribution of assets to claimants decades into the future. Whether the methods used by the bankruptcy courts create insurmountable due process issues that will ultimately result in the failure of the reorganization plans remains an unanswered question.

The largest and best known of the bankruptcy and mass tort litigation cases involve three asbestos manufacturers who faced massive present and future tort liability in the early 1980s. Asbestos emerged as a serious public health threat in the 1970s with the realization that exposure to asbestos fibers can cause serious illness and death. A latency period of as much as thirty years may separate the victim's exposure to asbestos from the onset of an asbestos-related disease, with the result that thousands of people were seriously exposed to the product before its dangers were recognized by the American public. By the time Johns–Manville, one of the largest asbestos

---

12. See § 3–30 supra.
13. In re Hi–Lo Powered Scaffolding, Inc., 70 B.R. 606, 607 (Bankr. S.D.Ohio 1987).

§ 11–8
1. In re Johns–Manville, 36 B.R. 727 (Bankr. S.D.N.Y. 1984), appeal denied, 39 B.R. 234 (S.D.N.Y.1984) (court discusses propriety of solvent company filing for Chapter 11 bankruptcy); see also Note, The Manville Bankruptcy: Treating Mass–Tort Claims in Chapter 11 Proceedings, 96 Harv.L.Rev. 1121 (1983).

2. A future claimant is a person with pre-petition exposure to a product manufactured by a debtor who has not yet filed a claim against that debtor. In re Johns–Manville Corp., 36 B.R. 743, 744–45 (Bankr. S.D.N.Y. 1984), appeal denied, 39 B.R. 234 (S.D.N.Y. 1984).

producers, filed for bankruptcy in 1982, the corporation faced 16,000 asbestos-related lawsuits. Another 6,000 lawsuits were filed during the next 16 months,[3] and an additional 32,000 were expected to be filed by the year 2001, to create a combined liability of at least $1.9 billion.[4] While other asbestos manufacturers sought congressional intervention to help provide relief to the millions of victims of asbestos exposure,[5] three manufacturers—Johns-Manville, UNR, and Amatex—sought relief by filing Chapter 11 bankruptcy petitions.

The filing of a Chapter 11 bankruptcy petition by a mass tort debtor serves a variety of interests. The debtor benefits from the opportunity for a "fresh start," to enable it to continue as a viable entity. Society benefits from the continuation of a successful corporation if the corporation has going concern value or is more valuable alive than liquidated. This is especially true for future claimants, who may have no assets from which to recover if the corporation is liquidated and its assets distributed before those claimants even become aware they have claims against the corporation. The liquidation of these corporations might "preclude just compensation of some present asbestos victims and all future asbestos claimants."[6]

With thousands of future claimants creating billions of dollars of future liability, the asbestos corporations could not hope to develop any successful plan of reorganization without the inclusion of those claimants.[7] But to include the future claimants meant bringing to the forefront seemingly intractable due process issues. A holding that future claimants were "creditors" with "claims" would make them subject to discharge under section 1141. As noted earlier, several courts have already held applications of this provision to be unconstitutional when adequate notice is not provided to claimants.[8] When the issue first arose in the context of the debtor's request to assign a legal representative to represent the future claimants, the initial response by the *Amatex* and *UNR* courts was to deny this request.[9]

When Johns-Manville made the same request, however, Judge Lifland granted it, characterizing future claimants as "parties in interest" under 1109(b),[10] thereby avoiding the dischargeability and due process issues raised

---

3. Id. at 729.

4. Kesner, Future Asbestos Related Litigants as Holders of Statutory Claims Under Chapter 11 of the Bankruptcy Code and Their Place in the Johns-Manville Reorganization (First Installment), 62 Am.Bankr. L.J. 69, 73 (1988). This figure has since proven to be woefully short of Johns Manville's true liability. By 1990, 130,000 claimants had filed suit against Johns-Manville, and the corporation's total liability was reestimated to be at least $8.8 billion.

5. See generally Comment, Relief for Asbestos Victims: A Legislative Analysis, 20 Harv. J. on Legis. 179 (1983).

6. In re Johns-Manville Corp., 36 B.R. at 736.

7. In re Johns-Manville, 36 B.R. at 746 ("[A] resolution of the interests of future claimants is a central focus of these reorganization proceedings. Any plan emerging from this case which ignores these claimants would serve the interests of neither the debtor nor any of its other creditor constituencies in that the central short and long term economic drain on the debtor would not have been eliminated."); see also In re UNR Industries, Inc., 725 F.2d 1111, 1119 (7th Cir.1984).

8. See § 11–3 supra.

9. In re Amatex Corp., 30 B.R. 309 (Bankr. E.D.Pa. 1983), order rev'd, 755 F.2d 1034 (3d Cir.1985); In re UNR Industries, Inc., 29 B.R. 741, 748 (N.D.Ill. 1983), appeal dism'd, 725 F.2d 1111 (7th Cir.1984) (debtor's fresh start not as important as statutory and constitutional rights of future claimants).

10. Section 1109(b) provides that:

A party in interest, including the debtor, the trustee, a creditors' committee, an equity security holders' committee, a creditor, an equity security holder, or any indenture

by being termed a "creditor" holding a "claim" under the Bankruptcy Code. The court held:

> Any meaningful plan will either provide funding for future claimants directly or provide for the continuation of some form of responsive, ongoing entity post-confirmation, from which to glean assets with which to pay them. If they are denied standing as parties in interest, they will be denied all opportunity either to help design the ship that sails away from these reorganization proceedings with their cargo on board or to assert their interests during a pre-launching distribution.[11]

Manville probably represents the most sophisticated approach to this problem to date. In this case Judge Lifland appointed a Wall Street lawyer to represent the unknown claimants in much the same way as one would represent unborn heirs in a probate proceeding. The lawyer negotiated on behalf of the claimants and ultimately there was an agreement under which specific parts of the assets of Johns–Manville and its profits were to be put into a trust fund and ultimately to be paid out both to the existing and to the future claimants.[12] Although the judge was careful not to identify the

---

trustee, may raise and may appear and be heard on any issue in a case under this chapter.

11 U.S.C.A. § 1109(b); see also In re Amatex Corp., 755 F.2d 1034, 1043 (3d Cir.1985); In re UNR Industries, Inc., 46 B.R. 671, 675 (Bankr. N.D.Ill. 1985); In re Johns–Manville Corp., 36 B.R. at 747–49. For an analysis of the limitations of § 1109(b) by Chief Judge Lifland, see In re Ionosphere Clubs, Inc., 101 B.R. 844, 849 (Bankr. S.D.N.Y. 1989) ("[a]lthough § 1109(b) ought to be construed broadly, if a party is not affected by the reorganization process it should not be considered a party in interest"). For arguments disfavoring the discharge of these claims, see Bibler, The Status of Unaccrued Tort Claims in Chapter 11 Bankruptcy Proceedings, 61 Am.Bankr.L.J. 145, 150 (1987).

11. In re Johns–Manville, 36 B.R. at 749. (The Manville court continued: " * * * it is unnecessary for this Court to face the dischargeability issue at this time in order to decide whether these claimants are parties in interest. In fact, this Court may never be faced with deciding the dischargeability issue since Manville's currently proposed nonconsensual plan intends to treat future claims as non-dischargeable." Id. at 754. The court goes on to suggest in dicta that future claims may in fact be dischargeable, and the problem of notice is not insurmountable. Id. at 754–56 n.6. In In re Johns–Manville Corp., 68 B.R. 618 (Bankr. S.D.N.Y. 1986), decision aff'd in part, rev'd in part, 78 B.R. 407 (S.D.N.Y.1987), order aff'd, 843 B.R. 2d 636 (2d Cir.1988), the court determined that the claims of future claimants would not be discharged, but would be subject to the injunction channeling claims to the Trust rather than to the reorganized entity. The court again avoided the issue of whether the future claimants had "claims," saying: "whether these parties in interest have claims that are cognizable in a reorganization proceeding * * * is not an issue which needs to be determined in order to confirm this Plan." Id. at 628.

Both the Amatex and UNR courts later found this characterization acceptable, and followed the Johns–Manville example of appointing a legal representative, but also specifically left open questions regarding the future rights of these "parties in interest." See In re Amatex Corp., 755 F.2d at 1043 ("we do not know whether future claimants can or should be considered 'creditors' under the Code, whether constitutionally adequate notice can be provided to such a class, and how best to solve a whole host of other problems which have not been briefed"); In re UNR Industries, Inc., 46 B.R. at 676 ("[t]he determination of whether putative asbestos disease victims are creditors of these estates, or whether their interests could be represented in these proceedings in a manner analogous to a class action, or whether these parties would be entitled to vote on a plan of reorganization, or whether their claims might be discharged in this bankruptcy proceedings, are all questions which can properly be addressed after putative asbestos disease victims commence actual participation in these cases," citing In re UNR Industries, Inc., 725 F.2d 1111, 1118 (7th Cir. 1984)).

12. Distribution in mass tort cases has revolved around a Trust Fund from which present and future litigants will be paid the value of their claim. As noted earlier, 28 U.S.C.A. § 157(b) bars bankruptcy courts from estimating personal injury claims for purposes of distribution, but the formation of a trust presumably is not barred by that requirement.

future claimants as "creditors" and was careful not to say their claims were "discharged," as we see above, he did identify them as "parties in interest," and by granting a permanent injunction that prohibited any claims by them against the other assets of Johns–Manville, he gave the debtor something close to a discharge as to those potential claims. This order was tested on appeal to the Second Circuit in the case *Kane v. Johns–Manville Corp.*[13] There the court declined to pass on the constitutionality of Judge Lifland's reorganization plan.[14] Judge Newman of the Second Circuit pointed out that those challenging the order, namely the representative of the existing creditors, had a conflict of interest and that, in any case, the issue was not yet ripe.

At this writing the Manville Trust appears to be in deep trouble. Although the parties anticipated the possibility that it would be illiquid only in its early years, the trust has run short of cash more quickly than was anticipated and the prospects for payment to various tort claimants now appear much more bleak than they did at the time of confirmation. Partly this is a consequence of the fact there are many more asbestos claimants than was anticipated. It may also stem from the fact that the assumptions about Manville's earning capacity were exaggerated. This problem demonstrates one of the inevitable consequences of setting a plan today that will govern the rights of parties tomorrow. If we are to preserve the going-concern value of a company like Manville, we must somehow free it from the cloud of an indefinite and indeterminate potential liability. If that cannot be done, the market for ownership of such companies will dry up and the potential going-concern value will never be realized.

This irony is illustrated by the *Manville* case itself. If it exercises its rights to convert preferred stock to common, the Manville Trust will own 80 percent of the company; yet every time a court or somebody else asserts a right to reopen the Trust and redo the plan, the value of the stock declines. Investors fear that, for future creditors, a claim will be made to a portion of the remaining 20 percent of the company that investors thought they had purchased free and clear. Indeed, we suspect that opening the plan has the potential for doing injury not only to the creditors of Manville, but also to the capacity of the Bankruptcy Court to write discharges in similar cases that will satisfy future investors.

Mass tort claims with long latency periods present difficult problems for bankruptcy courts. The Third Circuit approach in *Schweitzer v. Consolidat-*

See In re Amatex Corp., 107 B.R. 856, 862 (E.D.Pa. 1989); In re A.H. Robins Co., 88 B.R. 742, 751 (E.D.Va.1988), order aff'd, 880 F.2d 694 (4th Cir.1989), cert. denied, 493 U.S. 959, 110 S.Ct. 376, 107 L.Ed.2d 362 (1989); In re Johns–Manville Corp., 68 B.R. at 621–22. The trusts typically define a liquidation procedure which includes a variety of options to liquidate a claim, starting with mandatory negotiation, to be followed, if necessary, by the claimant's choice of mediation, arbitration or traditional tort litigation. Kane v. Johns–Manville Corp., 843 F.2d 636, 640 (2d Cir. 1988); In re A.H. Robins Co., 880 F.2d 709, 722 (4th Cir. 1989). The amount of distribution as a percentage of the liquidated amount varies from 100%, In re Johns–Manville Corp.; In re A.H. Robins Co., 88 B.R. at 751 (but Johns–Manville's may not succeed in its attempt to provide fully for all future claimants), to 15%, In re Amatex, 107 B.R. at 862, and punitive damages are generally disallowed. In re A.H. Robins Co., 89 B.R. 555 (E.D.Va.1988); In re Johns–Manville Corp., 68 B.R. 618, 627 (Bankr. S.D.N.Y. 1986), decision aff'd in part, rev'd in part, 78 B.R. 407 (S.D.N.Y.1987), aff'd, 843 F.2d 636 (2d Cir.1988).

13. 843 F.2d 636 (2d Cir.1988).

14. Id. at 639.

ed Rail Corp.,¹⁵ that such plaintiffs do not have claims and are not discharged leaves the debtor incapable of being reorganized. Such a ruling may cause mass tort debtors either to waste away (as many smaller companies appear to be doing under the asbestos claims today) or to go through Chapter 7 liquidation that destroys the going-concern value and allows the assets to be used to satisfy the existing creditors. The *Manville* approach seems preferable to that, yet it will not work unless some mechanism can be designed that will free the reorganized corporation from newly found claims. If the reorganization can be continually reopened and additional assets seized by the newly found creditors, then the *Manville* solution comes to nothing more than the Third Circuit proposal, namely a company with continuing and unknown liabilities. We hope, therefore, that the courts will work out sensible ways, such as that attempted in *Manville,* in which unknown plaintiffs can be represented by legal representatives, and further that the courts will have the steel to stick to deals that were fairly bargained in such circumstances, notwithstanding subsequent events.

§ 11–9 Claims for Environmental Cleanup in Chapters 11 and 7

In the past ten years, two Supreme Court cases, a handful of appellate cases, and a larger number of bankruptcy cases have dealt in one way or another with the priority of claims for environmental cleanup in bankruptcy. Many of these cases have focused on the question whether a trustee in bankruptcy can abandon property under section 554 that is rendered worthless because of the presence of hazardous or toxic waste. Some have dealt with the question whether large environmental claims should call for dismissal of the case; only a few have focused directly on the relative priority of the environmental claim.

To the extent that these cases talk about section 554 on abandonment, about section 959 of Title 28, or about the rules concerning exceptions from discharge under section 523, the courts are not focusing on the true issue here. In fact, some of the opinions read like an allegorical play written by a dissident author under a despotic regime who must obscure the true identities of the objects of his criticism. Like such allegorical criticisms, these cases leave the reader to draw inferences about the law from their treatment of other issues.

In our view there is one and only one significant issue in all of these cases. It is the priority of a claim for environmental cleanup in relation to other claims against the estate. To understand the allegorical quality of these cases, consider the two that have come to the Supreme Court in the past decade. First was *Ohio v. Kovacs.*¹ Kovacs was the chief executive officer of Chem–Dyne, the operator of an industrial waste site in Ohio. To settle claims that Chem–Dyne had violated state environmental laws, Chem–Dyne and Kovacs entered a settlement agreement with Ohio. The settlement agreement required the company and Kovacs to remove certain wastes and to pay $75,000. When Kovacs and the company failed to comply with

---

15. 758 F.2d 936, 942–44 (3d Cir.1985), cert. denied, 474 U.S. 864, 106 S.Ct. 183, 88 L.Ed.2d 152 (1985).

§ 11–9

1. 469 U.S. 274, 105 S.Ct. 705, 83 L.Ed.2d 649 (1985).

the agreement, Ohio caused a receiver to be appointed to take possession of the property in order to comply with the judgment. Kovacs then filed personal bankruptcy, and the state of Ohio cleaned up the waste site. Ohio argued that Kovacs should not be discharged from his liability to the state because its right against him did not amount to a "claim" under section 101(5)(B):

> the injunction it has secured is not a claim against Kovacs for bankruptcy purposes because (1) Kovacs' default was a breach of the statute, not a breach of an ordinary commercial contract which concededly would give rise to a claim; and (2) Kovacs' breach of his obligation under the injunction did not give rise to a right to payment within the meaning of § 101(5)(B).

The Supreme Court found that Ohio's right did constitute a claim, and further, that the claim was dischargeable in bankruptcy. Since Kovacs was dispossessed, and the state had been in possession of the property, the Court found that payment of money was the only remedy that would satisfy Ohio and that, it held, was clearly a dischargeable obligation. The Court suggested that the state of Ohio might have fared better had it brought civil or criminal contempt proceedings against Kovacs and had it not stepped in to take possession of the property itself. Although it is often billed as the first round in a fifteen round championship fight between the environmentalists and a debtor in bankruptcy, *Kovacs* ultimately comes to nothing more than a rather routine judgment about dischargeability, with some implications about the stay.

The second Supreme Course case, *Midlantic National Bank v. New Jersey Department of Environmental Protection*[2] comes a step closer to the real issue. The environmental protection authorities in New Jersey and New York found environmental violations by Quanta Resources Corporation ("Quanta"), a waste oil processor, in both states. During the negotiation of the terms of the cleanup, Quanta filed in Chapter 11. Ultimately Quanta converted to a Chapter 7 and the trustee sought to abandon the property under 554(a). It did this because the cleanup costs together with the mortgages on the real estate exceeded the property's value.

Over the objection of the environmental authorities, the bankruptcy court authorized the abandonment. The district court affirmed the abandonment and the Court of Appeals for the Third Circuit reversed. In a 5–4 decision the Supreme Court affirmed the Third Circuit; it held that the trustee in bankruptcy could not in these circumstances abandon the property under 554(a). The majority first concluded that section 554(a) was a codification of judge-made law that had certain exceptions. It relied upon three pre-Code cases[3] to support the proposition that the trustee's abandonment power was limited by state law and by safety concerns. It relied in part upon the requirements of related law, 28 U.S.C.A. section 959(b), to the effect that the trustee must "manage and operate property in his possession

---

2. 474 U.S. 494, 106 S.Ct. 755, 88 L.Ed.2d 859 (1986), reh'g denied, 475 U.S. 1090, 106 S.Ct. 1482, 89 L.Ed.2d 736 (1986).

3. Ottenheimer v. Whitaker, 198 F.2d 289 (4th Cir.1952); In re Chicago Rapid Transit Co., 129 F.2d 1 (7th Cir.1942), cert. denied, 317 U.S. 683, 63 S.Ct. 205, 87 L.Ed. 547 (1942); In re Lewis Jones, Inc., 1 B.C.D. 277 (Bankr. E.D.Pa. 1974).

according to the requirements of valid laws in the state." Finally the court concluded:

> In light of the bankruptcy trustee's restricted pre–1978 abandonment power and the limited scope of other Bankruptcy Code provisions, we conclude that Congress did not intend for section 554(a) to pre-empt all state and local laws. The Bankruptcy Court does not have the power to authorize the abandonment without formulating conditions that will adequately protect the public's health and safety. Accordingly, without reaching the question whether certain state laws imposing conditions on abandonment may be so onerous as to interfere with the bankruptcy adjudication itself, we hold that a trustee may not abandon property in contravention of a state statute or regulation that is reasonably designed to protect the public health or safety from identified hazards.[4]

That opinion drew a strong dissent from Justice Rehnquist, who was joined by Chief Justice Burger and Justices White and O'Connor. The dissenters would clearly allow the trustee to abandon the property. They suggest that the three cases that form the basis for 554 hardly justify a conclusion that there is an exception to it. In his concluding paragraphs, Justice Rehnquist identifies the true issue:

> What the court fails to appreciate is that respondent's interest in these cases lies not in just protecting public health and safety, but also in protecting the public fisc * * *. The New Jersey Department of Environmental protection * * * apparently seeks to undo the abandonment and force the trustee to expend the estate's remaining assets cleaning up the site, thereby reducing the cleanup cost that must ultimately be borne by the State.[5]

Here, of course, is the issue, not merely in *Midlantic*, but in all of these cases, namely, who bears the cost of the cleanup. Is the cost to be borne exclusively by the citizens of the state? Should the unsecured creditors share? Or perhaps the unsecured creditors should be completely subordinated (by making this an administrative expense), or the secured creditors given a slug. Who pays? This is the real question.

§ 11–10 Claims for Environmental Cleanup in Chapters 11 and 7—Relative Priority Under the Code

Most of the cases that have squarely faced the issue have held that environmental cleanup costs that were not paid prior to the filing of the petition are administrative expenses. In order for something to qualify as an administrative expense under section 503(b)(1)(A) it must constitute part of the "actual, necessary cost and expenses of preserving the estate * * *." There are two requirements buried in the quoted language. First, the amount must normally be expended (the claim must arise) after the petition has been filed. Money spent prior to the petition is spent when there is no estate and it is hard to see how they could be spent to "preserve" this nonexistent estate. Even postpetition expenses must be the actual necessary costs of preserving the estate. Some expenses might be so unrelated to the

---

4. 474 U.S. at 506–7, 106 S.Ct. at 762, 88 L.Ed.2d at 869.

5. 474 U.S. at 516, 106 S.Ct. at 767, 88 L.Ed.2d at 875.

business of the estate or to the maintenance of the property of the estate that they would not be construed as necessary for its preservation.[1]

In a typical environmental case both of those arguments might be used by one who seeks to make a cleanup expenditure into something less than an administrative expense. If, for example, the entire cleanup had been done on credit before the petition was filed, presumably the unpaid claim of the contractor would not be an administrative expense and the one with the claim would simply share as an unsecured creditor. Even if the cleanup had not been completed at the time the petition was filed, one might argue that the one undertaking the cleanup, or the one with the liability for doing so, had a contingent claim that existed prior to the petition and should thus be treated as a simply unsecured claimant. By and large the courts have glossed over the timing problem or have concluded that the *Midlantic* opinion transposes all unfulfilled cleanup obligations into postpetition administrative claims by that case's recognition of their importance.

Unsecured creditors of the estate will press the second argument. They will maintain that section 503(b)(1) expenditures are to "preserve the estate", namely to preserve some assets to be distributed to them, the unsecured creditors. If there is a $2,000,000 environmental claim and there are $2,000,000 of unencumbered assets in the estate, it is hard to see how the expenditure of those $2,000,000 for cleaning up an environmental spill will "preserve" anything for the unsecured creditors. In fact, it will do just the opposite, for it will take the $2,000,000, transfer that $2,000,000 to the waste disposal party and leave no estate whatsoever for distribution to the unsecured creditors. Is the Court in *Midlantic* (no abandonment "in contravention of a state statute or regulation that is reasonably designed to protect the public health or safety from identified hazards"[2]), really saying that such expenditures are "necessary" for the "preservation" of the estate? If that is what the Court meant, it should have said so.

§ 11–10

1. Section 503 should be narrowly construed. Grantham v. Eastern Marine, Inc., 93 B.R. 752 (Bankr. N.D.Fla.1988). A claim should be granted administrative priority as actual and necessary cost of preserving debtor's estate only under extraordinary circumstances, when claimant sustains statutory burden of proof. In re Amfesco Industries, Inc., 81 B.R. 777 (Bankr. E.D.N.Y.1988).

The fact that the claim arises postpetition does not necessarily entitle claimant to administrative priority. In re Pettibone Corp., 90 B.R. 918 (Bankr. N.D.Ill. 1988); In re Photo Promotion Associates, Inc., 87 B.R. 835 (Bankr. S.D.N.Y. 1988). In addition, for a claim to be granted administrative priority as actual and necessary cost of preserving debtor's estate it must: (1) arise from a transaction with debtor in possession, In re Amfesco Industries, Inc., 81 B.R. 777 (Bankr. E.D.N.Y. 1988); In re Precision Carwash Corp., 90 B.R. 34 (Bankr. E.D.N.Y.1988), and (2) be beneficial to the debtor in possession in its operation of business. In re Amfesco Industries, Inc., 81 B.R. 777 (Bankr. E.D.N.Y.1988).

For examples of expenses that are not actual and necessary to preservation of estate, see In re Jartran, Inc., 87 B.R. 525 (N.D.Ill. 1988), judgment aff'd, 886 F.2d 859 (7th Cir.1989) (creditor's costs of marshaling and repossessing leased equipment to preserve creditor's property); Matter of Zook, 83 B.R. 447 (Bankr. W.D.Mich.1988) (rent owed to lessor of farm equipment where the equipment was not used, even though no motion to reject lease was made); Guaranty Nat. Ins. Co. v. Greater Kansas City Transp., Inc., 90 B.R. 461 (D.Kan. 1988) (insurer's postpetition payments of prepetition claims does not benefit the debtor in possession; In re Amfesco Industries, Inc., 81 B.R. 777 (Bankr. E.D.N.Y.1988) (indemnification claims by directors and former directors against corporate debtors, based on prepetition indemnification agreement).

2. 474 U.S. at 505, 106 S.Ct. at 762, 88 L.Ed.2d at 868.

At least in cases where there is a CERCLA liability under section 107 (i.e., where the bankruptcy estate itself has joint and several liability for the cleanup) one can argue more readily that this is an administrative expense under section 503(b)(1) or that, in effect, it is a tax.

To see how these rules operate in practice, consider *In re Stevens*[3]. In that case Judge Cyr held that the postpetition removal costs ($7,572.20) of some barrels of contaminated oil was an administrative expense of the estate. A trustee had been appointed; she first refused to remove the contaminated oil. Accordingly the state Department of Environmental Protection did so and sought reimbursement. The state argued that these expenditures conferred a benefit on the estate "by bringing the estate into compliance with the cleanup mandate of state and federal law and by protecting the estate from increased liability, which would result in event of a spill." The court did not accept that argument. Rather it concluded that the language quoted above from the majority opinion in *Midlantic* alters the "criteria for determining the allowance for administrative expenses under the Bankruptcy Code section 503(b)(1)(A) * * *." In effect, the court concluded that the Supreme Court has altered the language and meaning of section 503(b) as though an additional subsection were inserted in section 503(b) that granted priority status not merely to administrative costs, taxes, etc., but also to postpetition environmental cleanup costs.[4] While we are sympathetic with Judge Cyr's difficulty in reading of the mysterious *Midlantic* statement, it does not necessarily follow that *Midlantic* requires the bankruptcy estate to undertake the full cost of a cleanup and to grant that cost administrative expense status.

For example, the Court of Appeals for the Fourth Circuit has read *Midlantic* to permit abandonment where there is no "imminent danger".[5] Yet even that court says *in dictum,* that had there been unencumbered assets, it would have been appropriate for the bankruptcy court to have required cleanup before abandonment and to have allowed the cleanup expenses as an administrative expense.

In a case decided prior to *Midlantic*, Judge Bare comes to the opposite conclusion. In *In re Wall Tube and Metal Products Co.,*[6] he refused administrative expense treatment even for costs incurred by the state in connection with certain drums and tanks of hazardous waste owned by the debtor. The court summarizes the question as follows:

> The question before this court is not whether public policy might justify the enactment of well-considered and carefully crafted legislation affording some type of priority treatment to environmental cleanup expenses. The question is whether the particular expenses claimed in this proceeding come within the language and purpose of the current statute. This court believes that they do not. There are dangers to judicially legislating here by stretching § 503(b) beyond its intended scope—among them, the potential for unwittingly creating an incentive

---

3. 68 B.R. 774 (D.Me.1987).

4. See, In re Pierce Coal & Construction, Inc., 65 B.R. 521 (Bankr. N.D.W.Va.1986).

5. In re Smith–Douglass, Inc., 856 F.2d 12 (4th Cir.1988); accord In re Purco, 76 B.R. 523 (Bankr. W.D.Pa.1987); In re Franklin Signal Corp., 65 B.R. 268 (Bankr. D.Minn.1986); cf. In re Peerless Plating Co., 70 B.R. 943 (Bankr. W.D.Mich.1987).

6. 56 B.R. 918 (Bankr. E.D.Tenn.1986).

for governmental authorities to postpone environmental cleanup activities for financially strategic reasons in order to gain the advantage of priority treatment in a bankruptcy context. In addition, there is the danger of dissipating and depleting those funds which under the current statutory design are essential for an effective administration of the estate * * *. This court's function is to interpret, not to legislate. Since the expenses claimed here do not come within § 503(b), the State's claim for administrative expense priority must be denied.[7]

Comparing Judge Bare's conclusion with Judge Cyr's reading of *Midlantic* presents an interesting jurisprudential conundrum. If Judge Bare is right, these expenses can be elevated to administrative status only by judicial legislation. Yet, if the Supreme Court in *Midlantic* has engaged in that kind of judicial legislation, are the lower courts not bound to follow it? If they are and if Judge Cyr's reading of *Midlantic* is correct, then his outcome is correct too—albeit regrettable.

One should be particularly hesitant to draw the inference that Judge Cyr does in view of footnote 2 in *Midlantic* where the court explicitly states that New York's right to have its claim treated as an administrative expense "is not before us." Because the Supreme Court did not say in terms that such expenses are administrative expenses and because it might say something different in the future, we cling to the hope that the Court might recognize the wisdom of Judge Bare's position. Therefore we think it appropriate for courts still to take Judge Bare's position until the Supreme Court speaks again.

Note too that section 28 U.S.C.A. § 959 does not require a finding that the expenses are administrative expenses. As a number of courts point out, that section is most sensibly limited to cases in which the trustee or debtor can be said to be "carrying on business". The most sensible meaning of that phrase—which is the heart of section 959(a)—is to refer to a business in Chapter 11 or in Chapter 7 that is being maintained and operated. Were a business operated in Chapter 11 for a period, presumably section 959(a) would apply, but that is not true in many of these cases in which all business operations ceased before the petition was filed.

The foregoing cases and section 959(b) involve state environmental law. Where there is federal CERCLA liability, the timing issue is necessarily resolved.

In *In re T.P. Long Chemical, Inc.*[8] the court concluded that a postpetition cleanup expense was an administrative expense. In that case the estate had been the owner of a piece of property where drums containing hazardous waste were buried. As owner it had liability under section 107(a) of CERCLA[9]. That section makes *any* owner or operator of a hazardous waste facility jointly and severally liable for all costs of cleanup. Thus, under CERCLA, the bankruptcy estate itself as the owner of the hazardous waste facility had joint and several liability with the prepetition debtor and with other owners. The court correctly concluded that it was beside the point whether the estate could abandon the property since the CERCLA liability

---

7. Id. at 927.
8. 45 B.R. 278 (Bankr. N.D.Ohio 1985).
9. 42 U.S.C.A. § 9607(a).

would continue irrespective of its transfer of the property. This necessarily made the claim a postpetition claim and there was only the question whether this claim was an actual and necessary expense of preserving the estate. The court concluded that it was a necessary cost only because the cost incurred in discharging the liability "could not be avoided." Of course, that conclusion does not follow. Clearly this is a postpetition claim, yet if there is no estate to be preserved, why must one conclude its payment "necessary" for such preservation? Although Judge White's analysis under CERCLA seems persuasive, his conclusion ultimately runs upon the rock suggested by Chief Justice Rehnquist and by Judge Bare.

In conclusion, we understand the arguments of Judge Cyr and we appreciate those who argue that the Supreme Court in *Midlantic* must have intended that cleanup expenditures be granted administrative expense treatment. Given that the Supreme Court has not explicitly so held and because such a conclusion would effectively add a new subsection to sections 503 or 507, we would still side with Judge Bare and would argue that these expenses are not necessarily "actual and necessary costs and expenses of preserving the estate." We think it fair at least to demand that the Supreme Court spell out its "legislation." Nevertheless we concede that after *Midlantic,* most courts have concluded and may continue to conclude they are required to treat postpetition cleanup costs as administrative expenses.

§ 11–11 Claims for Environmental Cleanup in Chapters 11 and 7—Cleanup Expenses as Secured Claims

There are at least three ways in which one doing an environmental cleanup might argue for secured status in the ensuing bankruptcy. A lawyer with sufficient chutzpah might simply argue that the critical language from *Midlantic* ("a trustee may not abandon property in contravention of a state statute and regulation that is reasonably designed to protect the public health or safety from identified hazards,"[1]) itself requires such priority. Conclusions in favor of administrative expense treatment have rested on that language. If it is nice to subordinate claims of unsecured creditors to environmental costs, why is it not even nicer to subordinate administrative expense claims and possibly even secured claims? Apparently that idea is simply so outrageous that the courts cannot contemplate it.[2]

A second argument—not strictly speaking an argument for security—has the same effect. It is based on section 506(c). That section allows the trustee to recover from a secured creditor's collateral "the reasonable, necessary costs and expenses of preserving, or disposing of, such property to the extent of any benefit to the holder of such claim." The section 506(c) argument was rejected in *In re T.P. Long Chemical, Inc.*[3] There the EPA argued that its cleanup benefitted Bank Ohio who had a security interest in certain of the debtor's assets and also in the real estate to be cleaned up.

---

§ 11–11
1. Midlantic Nat. Bank v. New Jersey Dept. of Environmental Protection, 474 U.S. 494, 507, 106 S.Ct. 755, 762, 88 L.Ed.2d 859, 869 (1986), reh'g denied, 475 U.S. 1090, 106 S.Ct. 1482, 89 L.Ed.2d 736 (1986).

2. See In re Smith–Douglass, Inc., 856 F.2d 12 (4th Cir.1988); In re Stevens, 68 B.R. 774 (D.Me.1987).

3. 45 B.R. 278 (Bankr. N.D.Ohio 1985).

Bank Ohio apparently proposed to make no claim against the real estate, but to take the other collateral. The EPA argued that Bank Ohio must aggregate all of its collateral and when so aggregated it received a benefit from the EPA's cleanup of the property that Bank Ohio wished to discard. The court rejected the argument.

Where real estate had substantial value after the cleanup and where a mortgagee sought to enjoy that value, there would be a benefit to the secured creditor and there should be some sort of division of the value between the party cleaning up and the secured creditor. The more common result, particularly since CERCLA, is that the secured creditor holding the mortgage will give the property up for fear of itself incurring direct liability as an "owner or operator" under CERCLA for joint and several liability of the entire cleanup expense. Thus, section 506(c) will usually not be available to the party doing the cleanup, but that is not always so.[4]

The final possibility for secured status lies in the liens granted for cleanup under the laws of a small number of states or under CERCLA. For example, New Jersey law that would have been applicable in the *Midlantic* case now provides that any expenditures to clean up hazardous waste are debts with first priority "over all other claims or liens which are or have been filed against the property."[5] CERCLA has been amended to provide a federal lien for the United States or a state or any other person who removes waste or undertakes remedial action in certain circumstances.[6] These claims constitute a lien on all real property that belongs to the polluter that is "subject to the removal or remedial action under section 107." The federal lien's priority, however, is substantially lower than that of the state liens. Typically it does not take priority over liens perfected before notice of the federal lien is filed in the appropriate state office.

The best hope for the cleaner is to make a claim under one of the state statutes. Under those statutes expenditures typically achieve priority at least as to the real estate that has been cleaned up. In some cases that will be a considerable benefit and in others it will be insignificant. If those statutes are not enacted beyond a few states, the only other significant chance of sharing in the wealth is for the party doing the cleanup to assert a claim under section 506(c). Where the property has substantially positive value after the cleanup and that value was achieved by the cleanup, we can see no reason why the party doing the cleaning should not get a claim

---

4. There is a remote possibility that the cleanup cost could achieve secured status under section 364(d), at least if there is other adequate collateral from which the court could grant adequate protection to the existing secured creditors. This seems a remote possibility in most cases, but it surely is possible. One case where that was apparently done is In re Berg Chemical, No. 82–B12052(HB) (Bankr. S.D. N.Y July 9, 1984) as cited in Cosetti & Friedman, Bankruptcy Code and State Environmental Law, 7 J. Law & Com. 65, 93 (1987).

5. 58 N.J. Stat. Ann. 10–23.11(f) (West 1986) (debtor causing pollution is also subject to the lien, but the latter lien has priority only from the date of the filing). It is reported, by Cosetti & Friedman, supra note 4, at 92 n.147, that there are similar laws in Massachusetts, Oil and Hazardous Materials Release Prevention and Response Act, Mass. Gen. Laws Ann., ch. 21E (West 1983); New Hampshire, Solid and Hazardous Waste Management Act, N.H. Rev. Stat. Ann. § 147–B:10 (Supp. 1983); Arkansas Emergency Response Fund Act and Remedial Action Trust Fund Act, Ark. Stat. Ann. §§ 82–4709, 82–4720 (Supp. 1986); Tennessee Hazardous Waste Management Act, Tenn. Code Ann. § 68–42–209 (Supp. 1986); Connecticut Hazardous Waste Act Conn. Gen. Stat. Ann. § 22a–452a (West 1986).

6. 42 U.S.C.A. § 9607(a), (b) (1982).

against the asset. If, on the other hand, the ultimate value of the cleaned up property is small, there is really no benefit to the secured party and there should be no payment. To the extent that the cleanup cost is an administrative expense and otherwise a claim against the estate, there is no benefit to the secured party to the extent there are assets in the estate. To hold otherwise would subordinate the secured creditor to the interest of other administrative claimants and of the general creditors.

§ 11–12 Claims for Environmental Cleanup in Chapters 11 and 7—Retrospective: The Better Judicial and Legislative Answers

We come out where we went in. The question is what is the proper priority for costs of environmental cleanup? By focusing on section 554 and not on sections 503 and 507, the Supreme Court in *Midlantic* has left the lower courts uncertain about the answer to the question. While we believe the claim should normally rank no better than ordinary unsecured claims, most courts have read *Midlantic* to require administrative expense treatment. Correctly, in our view, the courts have rejected the argument that these claims are equal or superior to the claims of secured creditors. If the federal government or the states wish to achieve that result, they can surely do so by legislation.

What should be the outcome in these cases? From the point of view of the lower courts, we have stated our preference above. Left to our own devices, we would read *Midlantic* as not requiring administrative expense treatment and would therefore treat most of the claimants as general creditors. If one were to ask the question not as a court, but as a federal or state legislator, the proper answer might be different. To some extent the answer to that question should depend on who can most cheaply monitor these problems and upon the consequences to the conventional credit markets of subordination of certain conventional claims. For example, it would be a foolish legislative decision to grant priority to environmental cleanup if such grant of priority would cause any significant number of lenders to pull out of the mortgage market. The economic cost of such a dislocation would surely be greater than the cost to the state itself of bearing the cleanup expenses. Yet, one cannot be certain what creditors would do in face of a higher priority for such cleanup expenses. The creditors' own assertions about their future behavior in the face of such legislation should seldom be taken at face value. Thus, the economic calculation is a difficult one and is likely to depend upon highly uncertain predictions about the behavior of the relevant actors in the face of such new legislation.

In general we believe that the legislatures should go slowly here. The imposition of joint and several liability on every potential owner or operator of a waste site has already caused some significant dislocation and prompts bizarre behavior when the deepest pocket who owns the smallest share bears the greatest loss. Surely any subordination should not go beyond the subordination of the creditor who holds security in the very asset that is to be cleaned up. That subordination might be defended on the ground the secured creditor is a better, less expensive preventer of pollution than is a state agency or other party. On the other hand, granting administrative expense priority places the monitoring cost on the parties who are least likely of any to do monitoring, namely, the trade and other unsecured creditors. Can the plumber, the electrician, or supplier do an EPA inspection? To protect themselves against subordination in bankruptcy, that is exactly what they would have to do. We doubt they have the will or the ability to do that.

In summary, it seems likely that the Congress or the Supreme Court will have to return yet again to the questions posed here. If the current trend continues and environmental cleanup expenses enjoy administrative expense treatment in bankruptcy, that ultimate result may be achievable without the Supreme Court speaking again. If, however, the Court agrees with us or if other courts follow Judge Bare to the conclusion these are not administrative expenses, then either the courts or the Congress will ultimately have to resolve the dispute.

C. WAITING FOR THE DEBTOR'S PLAN: THE "EXCLUSIVITY PERIOD," SECTION 1121(D)

§ 11–13 Introduction: Exclusivity and Delay

Section 1121 of the Bankruptcy Code gives the debtor an exclusive right to file a Chapter 11 reorganization plan within 120 days after the order for relief. The debtor then has 180 days from the order for relief to have its plan accepted by each class of claims or interest that is impaired under the plan.[1] This time period is commonly referred to as the "exclusivity period". Upon request by a party in interest, the bankruptcy court may increase or decrease this period upon a showing of cause by the moving party.[2] In practice most Chapter 11 debtors request and are routinely granted extensions of the exclusivity period.[3]

In promulgating section 1121, Congress sought a compromise between Chapters X and XI of the 1898 Bankruptcy Act.[4] Filing under the old Chapter X meant the appointment of an independent trustee who would run the business and allowed any party in interest to propose a reorganization plan. If the debtor filed under the old Chapter XI, he enjoyed indefinitely

---

§ 11–13

1. 11 U.S.C.A. § 1121.

2. Id. § 1121(d).

3. For cases where extensions of exclusivity were granted see, e.g., In re Public Service Co. of New Hampshire, 88 B.R. 521 (Bankr. D.N.H.1988); In re Texaco Inc., 76 B.R. 322 (Bankr. S.D.N.Y. 1987); In re Perkins, 71 B.R. 294 (W.D.Tenn.1987); In re Pine Run Trust, 67 B.R. 432 (Bankr. E.D.Pa. 1986); In re UNR Industries, 72 B.R. 789 (Bankr. N.D.Ill. 1987); In re McLean Industries, Inc., 87 B.R. 830 (Bankr. S.D.N.Y. 1987); In re Manville Forest Products Corp., 31 B.R. 991 (S.D.N.Y.1983); In re United Press International, Inc., 60 B.R. 265 (Bankr. D.Colo.1986); In re Gibson & Cushman Dredging Corp., 101 B.R. 405 (E.D.N.Y.1989); In re Swatara Coal Co., 49 B.R. 898 (Bankr. E.D.Pa. 1985). For cases where motion for extension of exclusivity was denied see, e.g., In re Ravenna Industries, Inc., 20 B.R. 886 (Bankr. N.D.Ohio 1982); In re Tony Downs Foods Co., 34 B.R. 405 (Bankr. D.Minn.1983); Matter of Gagel & Gagel, 24 B.R. 674 (Bankr. S.D.Ohio 1982); Matter of Am. Federation of T.V. & Radio Artists, 30 B.R. 772 (Bankr. S.D.N.Y. 1983); In re Washington–St Tammany Elec. Co–op., Inc., 97 B.R. 852 (E.D. La.1989); Matter of Lake in the Woods, 10 B.R. 338 (E.D.Mich.1981); In re Parker St. Florist & Garden Center, Inc., 31 B.R. 206 (Bankr. D. Mass. 1983); In re Sharon Steel Corp., 78 B.R. 762 (Bankr. W.D.Pa.1987); In re Southwest Oil Co. of Jourdanton, Inc., 84 B.R. 448 (Bankr. W.D.Tex.1987); In re Barker Estates, Inc., 14 B.R. 683 (Bankr. W.D.N.Y. 1981); In re Trainer's Inc., 17 B.R. 246 (Bankr. E.D.Pa. 1982).

4. H.R. Rep. No. 595, 95 Cong., 1st Sess. 231 (1977), reprinted in 1978 U.S. Code Cong. & Admin. News 5963, 6191.

the exclusive right to file a reorganization plan. Not surprisingly, the majority of debtors who filed under the Act filed in Chapter XI.[5] Congress noted that a debtor with an indefinite exclusive right to file a plan could delay the filing until creditors, faced with the increasing cost of continued delay, acquiesced to an unfavorable plan.[6] By limiting the period to 120 days, section 1121 was intended to put a certain amount of pressure on the debtor while it recognized the need for the debtor to remain in control of the reorganization process. Congress also recognized the creditors' interest in expediting the bankruptcy proceedings. A routine granting of extensions of the exclusivity period can destroy the balance that Congress intended; some creditors would claim that such extensions have destroyed that balance.

The cost of a long drawn out bankruptcy proceeding is borne by the creditors. While it is unfair to suggest that debtors in bankruptcy grow wealthy there, the disadvantages to the debtor are offset by its ability to keep prepetition creditors at bay while continuing to run its business, albeit under court scrutiny.[7] Conversely, delay can cause the creditors irreparable harm. The longer the case the greater the cost to the creditor who must pay legal fees[8] and suffer unreasonable opportunity costs,[9] while he watches administrative claims of various kinds diminish the value of his own claim.[10] Since the majority of Chapter 11 cases produce no reorganization plan, or, at least a plan of partial or total liquidation,[11] the debtor has often done no

---

5. The history is:

Chapters X and XI of current law permit different entities to propose plans of reorganization. Under Chapter X, because an independent trustee has been appointed, the debtor has lost control of the business, and the financial standard rules restrict the possibilities for negotiation in the formulation of a plan, any party in interest, including the trustee creditors, and the debtor, may propose a plan. This feature has been heavily disfavored by debtors when choosing a reorganization chapter, because they lose control over the future of the enterprise.

Id.

6. Ray & Schreve, Request for Extensions of the Debtor's Exclusivity Period for Filing a Plan: Section 1121 Since In re Timbers of Inwood Forest Associates, 29 S. Tex.L.Rev. 563–76 (1988).

7. As Professor LoPucki reports:

In most cases it is in the best interest of the debtor to delay filing a plan for as long as possible. Without a plan there can be no confirmation. Until confirmation the debtor need make no payments to unsecured creditors, interest does not accrue on the unsecured debt and the debtor can also suspend payments to secured creditors, at least until they obtain a ruling from the court providing them with payments as "adequate protection."

L.M. LoPucki, The Debtor in Full Control—Systems Failure Under Chapter 11 of the Bankruptcy Code?, 57 Am. Bankr. L.J. 99, 263 (1983).

8. In the Drexel Burnham bankruptcy case, Judge Howard Buschman III harshly criticized the lawyers working on the case for charging excessive legal fees. Judge Buschman went on to say that fees were a major concern in bankruptcy cases and that they need to be controlled. The Judge then went on to reduce the requested legal fees for the first three months of the case from $8.1 million to $7.6 million, or about 15%. Wall Street Journal, August 16, 1990, at B2, col.1.

9. Lost opportunity costs are the cost to creditors when they are prevented from liquidating their debts and reinvesting the proceeds at interest. The Supreme Court, in affirming the Fifth Circuit en banc decision in In re Timbers of Inwood Forest Associates, Ltd., held that unsecured creditors are not entitled to adequate protection payments to defray their lost opportunity cost. See In re Timbers of Inwood Forest Assoc., Ltd., 808 F.2d 363 (5th Cir.1987), aff'd, 484 U.S. 365, 108 S.Ct. 626, 98 L.Ed.2d 740 (1988).

10. Ray & Schreve, supra note 6, at 563–85.

11. As one judge wrote:

The court also takes judicial notice that, since the effective date of the Code, only three and one-half percent of the hundreds of Chapter 11 cases filed in this District have resulted in confirmed plans; and that most of the cases confirmed involved partial or total liquidation as opposed to reorganization and the continuation of the business.

In re Petur U.S.A. Instrument Co., Inc., 35 B.R. 561 (Bankr. W.D. Wash.1983).

more than delay the inevitable, but at some cost to the creditors.[12] The creditor's most effective relief may be to secure confirmation of its own plan of reorganization, yet that cannot happen until the exclusivity period expires. Yet if the debtor is successful in obtaining extensions of the period, the creditor is powerless.[13]

§ 11-14 Procedure for Extending the Period

An extension or reduction of the exclusivity period can only be granted after notice and a hearing by the bankruptcy court.[1] In *In re Westgate General Partnership*[2], a Pennsylvania bankruptcy court read section 1121(d) as permitting only one extension of the exclusivity period. Sadly, that court stands alone in its interpretation of section 1121(d). Most courts read section 1121(d) as allowing extensions of the exclusivity period after the initial statutory period (the initial 120 days), provided it is made during pendency of a previously granted extension.[3]

Any motion for extension much after the expiration of the prior period is a request for a *nunc pro tunc* order.[4] Rule 9006 of the Code allows the court to grant such an order upon the showing of "excusable neglect." However, bankruptcy courts are unanimous in their refusal to grant nunc pro tunc motions which extend the exclusivity period.[5] In denying those motions, the bankruptcy courts point out that the debtor is not necessarily prejudiced since he loses only his monopoly, not his right to file a plan.

Courts have disagreed about the effect on the 180 day period of an extension of the 120 day period. In *In re Barker Estates, Inc.*[6] and *In re*

---

12. The court in In re Public Service Co. of New Hampshire, 88 B.R. 521 (Bankr. D.N.H. 1988), took judicial notice of the cost of delay in its decision on a § 1121(d) motion.

> As for the effect of these reorganization proceedings upon the debtor and other parties in interest, and the effect of delay herein, it can be noted that professional fees and expense unique to the reorganization may well exceed one million dollars per month. It can also be noted as a functional 'administrative cost of delay' that the unsecured creditors are losing perhaps in excess of ten million dollars per month in lost interest on their moneys because they will not be paid interest under reorganization law.

Id. at 526.

13. Indeed, it was the prospect of such a long, drawn out proceeding that convinced the creditors of Donald Trump to lend him over $20 million in loans when he was about to default on a $43 million dollar bond payment, an "out-of-court bankruptcy" if you will. Wall Street Journal, June 27, 1990, at A2, col.2.

§ 11-14

1. 11 U.S.C.A. § 1121(d).

2. 55 B.R. 562 (Bankr. E.D.Pa. 1985). Judge E.F. Goldhaber read § 1121 as prohibiting a debtor any extension of the exclusivity period after the initial 120-day and 180-day periods had run, even if the request was made during pendency of a previously granted extension. This sort of reading of § 1121 would therefore prohibit any but an initial request for the extension of the exclusivity period. The holding in Westgate has been criticized as illogical and unfair. See In re Perkins, 71 B.R. 294 (Bankr. W.D.Tenn.1987); In re First American Bank, 64 B.R. 963 (Bankr. D.Del. 1986). Two years after Westgate, Judge Goldhaber's own court respectfully declined to follow his reasoning in Westgate, viewing it as harsh and questionable. See In re Nicolet, Inc., 80 B.R. 733 (Bankr. E.D.Pa. 1987).

3. In re Perkins, 71 B.R. 294 (Bankr. W.D.Tenn.1987); In re First American Bank, 64 B.R. 963 (D.Del.1986); In re Nicolet, Inc., 80 B.R. 733 (Bankr. E.D.Pa. 1987).

4. Bankr. Rule 9006(b).

5. In re Parker St. Florist & Garden Center, Inc., 31 B.R. 206 (Bankr. D.Mass.1983) (motion denied); In re Reetz, 61 B.R. 412 (Bankr. W.D.Wis.1986) (motion denied); In re Cramer, Inc. 105 B.R. 433 (Bankr. W.D.Tenn. 1989) (motion denied); (In re Ravenna Industries, Inc., 20 B.R. 886 (Bankr. N.D.Ohio 1982) (motion denied).

6. 14 B.R. 683 (Bankr. W.D.N.Y.1981).

Trainer's Inc.,[7] courts held that the 120 day and the 180 day period run from the date the order of relief is granted and are exclusive of each other. Therefore, the granting of an extension of one period does not automatically extend the other. This reading of section 1121 means that the debtor who requested and was granted an extension of the exclusive time to file a plan would lose that right if he neglected to move for the extension of the 180-day period.

Such a narrow reading of section 1121 has come under attack in *In re United Press International, Inc.*,[8] and *In re Ravenna Industries, Inc.*[9] In *United Press International*, the bankruptcy court labeled as "anomalous" a result that caused the debtor to lose its right to exclusivity even though it has shown cause. The court noted that it would be impossible for the debtor to attempt to get a plan accepted within the 180-day period when no plan had yet been filed. Both courts found that the 120-day period and the 180-day period were in fact separate, but unless the first act takes place (the filing of the plan), the second act (solicitation of acceptances) and its time period do not come into play. This seems more sensible.

Creditors who seek to challenge a bankruptcy court's grant of an extension of the exclusivity period face large obstacles. If the district court reviews such an order as merely interlocutory, it need not hear the appeal at all. Since an extension of the exclusivity period is more like being nibbled to death by ducks than suffering the guillotine, it is difficult to convince a court that such a judgment is final and will, if not overturned, end the litigation. Even though the standard is more generous in bankruptcy,[10] most of the courts that have faced this question have held that the request is interlocutory.[11] Reasoning that the exclusivity period merely "postponed" the creditor's right to propose a plan and did not end it, the Delaware district court found an extension of the period was not a final order.[12]

Yet, even if the courts view the order as interlocutory, they can still grant an appeal under 28 U.S.C.A. section 1292(b) if there is a "question of law" and an immediate appeal may "materially advance" the litigation. In line with our view that, in bankruptcy, substance is little and time is everything, we would urge the district courts to take such appeals, and would urge then to send a message to the bankruptcy judge that extensions are inappropriate. This will do more to clear the bankruptcy docket than rulings on a hundred substantive issues.

Realistically, even if the district court chooses to hear the appeal, the creditor is still far from his goal. The district judge is likely to be generous

---

7. 17 B.R. 246 (Bankr. E.D.Pa. 1982).

8. 60 B.R. 265 (Bankr. D.D.C.1986).

9. 20 B.R. 886 (Bankr. N.D.Ohio 1982).

10. "[A] bankruptcy order need not dispose of all aspects of a case in order to be final. An order which disposes of a "discrete dispute within the larger case" will be considered final and appealable." Ray & Schreve, Request for Extensions of the Debtor's Exclusivity Period for Filing a Plan: Section 1121 Since In re Timbers of Inwood Forest Associates, 29 S.Tex.L.Rev. 563, 582 (1988), quoting In re American Colonial Broadcasting Corp., 758 F.2d 794, 801 (lst Cir.1985).

11. "Such an order does not finally dispose of an estate's assets nor does it finally and irrevocably decide the rights of any party to the bankruptcy." In re Gibson & Cushman Dredging Corp., 101 B.R. 405, 408 (Bankr. E.D.N.Y.1989); see also First American Bank of New York v. Century Glove, 64 B.R. 958 (D.Del.1986).

12. First American Bank of New York v. Century Glove, 64 B.R. 958 (D.Del.1986).

to the bankruptcy judge here and to find that decisions on section 1121 lie within the discretion of the bankruptcy court that, after all, must handle the case.[13]

§ 11–15 Cause for Extension

To earn an extension of the exclusivity period, the debtor must show "cause."[1] The Code does not define "cause" but the legislative history provides some suggestions.[2] Because of the general language used in section 1121, courts have inferred that Congress intended to leave the question of "cause" to the bankruptcy court in the exercise of its discretion and to promote flexibility to suit various types of reorganization proceedings.[3]

The most popular reason advanced by debtors seeking an extension of exclusivity is that the case is large and complex. Bankruptcy courts have routinely based extension on this argument. Debtors in well known bankruptcy cases such as those involving Texaco, Public Service of New Hampshire and Johns–Manville have won successive extensions by using the size and complexity arguments. In many cases it has been sufficient for the debtor to use only the size and complexity arguments in order to get not one, but many, extensions of the exclusivity period. However, there are now signs, after the *Timbers of Inwood*[4] case that the courts are becoming more stringent. In our view the courts have been too generous to debtors. Such generosity inevitably costs all parties; we suspect it rarely provides for a better plan than could be arranged in a shorter time.

---

13. In re Washington–St. Tammany Elec. Co-op., Inc., 97 B.R. 852 (Bankr. E.D.La.1989); In re Sharon Steel Corp., 78 B.R. 762 (Bankr. W.D.Pa.1987). But consider Matter of Lake in the Woods, 10 B.R. 338, 342–3 (E.D.Mich. 1981):

> This court rejects the appellee's contention that the finding of cause to extend the debtor's exclusive period under Section 1121(d) is commended to the bankruptcy court's discretion and thus subject to reversal only if the reviewing court finds abuse. Unlike Rule 906 of the Rules of Bankruptcy Procedure under the old Act, which allows the bankruptcy court in its discretion to reduce or extend time periods for cause shown, Section 1121(d) does not refer to the discretion of the bankruptcy court. This court finds the absence of reference to the bankruptcy court's discretion in Section 1121(d) to be significant and indicative of congressional intent to require a higher standard of review by the district court than would be the case were an exercise of discretion by the bankruptcy court on appeal.

For cases where grants of extension have been reversed, see In re Huebner, 58 B.R. 600 (W.D.Wis.1986); In re Washington–St. Tammany Elec. Co-op., Inc., 97 B.R. 852 (Bankr. E.D.La.1989); Matter of Lake in the Woods, 10 B.R. 338 (E.D.Mich.1981); see also Ray & Schreve, supra note 10, at 563.

§ 11–15

1. 11 U.S.C.A. § 1121(d).

2. The House Report states: "Finally, subsection (d) permits the court, for cause, to increase or reduce the 120–day and 180–day periods specified. Cause might include an unusually large or unusually small case, delay by the debtor, or recalcitrance among creditors." H.R. Rep. No. 695, 95th Cong., 1st Sess. 406 (1977), reprinted in 1978 U.S. Code Cong. & Admin. News 5963, 6362. In addition, the Senate Report contained the following language relating to § 1121(d): "Subsection (d) permits the court, for cause, to increase or reduce the 120–day and 180–day periods specified. Since, the debtor has an exclusive privilege for six months during which others may not file a plan, the granted extension should be based on a showing of some promise of probable success. An extension should not be employed as a tactical device to put pressure on parties in interest to yield to a plan they consider unsatisfactory. S. Rep. No. 989, 95 Cong., 2d Sess. 118, reprinted in 1978 U.S. Code Cong. & Admin. News 5785, 5904.

3. In re Public Service Co. of New Hampshire, 88 B.R. 521 (Bankr. D.N.H.1988).

4. In re Timbers of Inwood Forest Assoc., Ltd., 808 F.2d 363 (5th Cir.1987), aff'd, 484 U.S. 365, 108 S.Ct. 626, 98 L.Ed.2d 740 (1988).

To understand our argument, consider several cases. First is *In re Texaco Inc.*[5] The company filed a Chapter 11 proceeding on April 12, 1987. It did so exclusively to stay a $10.3 billion judgment in favor of Pennzoil. Although *Texaco* was a very large bankruptcy, it was not really a complex one. Texaco was among the ten largest corporate enterprises in the United States with approximately $25.5 billion in assets. Yet the entire bankruptcy was caused by the Pennzoil judgment and its resolution depended almost exclusively upon the negotiation of an agreement between Pennzoil and Texaco about the handling of the judgment. Despite the simplicity of the bankruptcy, the court granted an extension. Ultimately a reorganization plan was confirmed in just under one year.

In re Public Service Co. of New Hampshire[6] surely qualifies as large and complex if any case does. Ultimately, Public Service of New Hampshire was purchased by Northeast Utilities. The settlement of the case required independent negotiation with an agreement by a New Hampshire agency that sets rates. Because such negotiations were necessary and because there were several potential bidders for the utility, the court granted one extension, but ultimately it denied a second extension. Notwithstanding the size and complexity argument the court concluded there should not be a second extension because, it concluded, the need for time did not arise out of the size and complexity of the case, but because the negotiations were stalemated. The suspicion apparently held by the court, that removal of the exclusivity period might stimulate negotiation, proved accurate and ultimately a deal was reached.

Representative of cases where courts have allowed the debtor to abuse the process by repeated extensions is *In re Perkins.*[7] This modest-sized debtor has enjoyed more than six years of exclusivity even though his bankruptcy appears to be a relatively routine case.

In summary, we believe the courts should not routinely grant extensions upon the exhortation by the debtor that the case is large and complex. Even very large cases, such as *Texaco,* are not necessarily complex. Moreover, even large and complex cases can often be speeded to a satisfactory conclusion more effectively by a denial of extension than by a granting of one.

A second argument that is sometimes given for an extension might be called the "almost home" argument. This is the argument that negotiations have gone a long way toward a conclusion and that they are now at a sensitive point and that continuation of the exclusivity period will insure that they proceed to a successful culmination. This argument was successfully made in *Pine Run Trust*[8] on two occasions in 1986 and early 1987. The court, however, denied the third extension on May 7, 1987 and allowed the creditor who had opposed all the extensions to submit his own plan. Aided by the possibility of the approval of creditors, the parties reached agreement.

Although we doubt the almost home argument should ever be regarded as persuasive, we endorse the idea that the court should consider likely impact on negotiation of its granting or denial of an extension. For a

---

5. 76 B.R. 322 (Bankr. S.D.N.Y. 1987).
6. 88 B.R. 521 (Bankr. D.N.H.1988).
7. 71 B.R. 294 (W.D.Tenn.1987).
8. In re Pine Run Trust, Inc., 67 B.R. 432 (Bankr. E.D.Pa. 1986).

variety of reasons most creditors are unlikely to propose a comprehensive plan that will compete against a debtor's plan. This is because a typical creditor either has too little at stake to invest the time in proposing a plan or has too little information to control an effective one. Thus, the likely consequence of the denial of the extension of the exclusivity period is not that creditor plans will be proposed and approved, but that the threat of such plans will cause the debtor to come forward more quickly than he might otherwise.[9]

The final "cause" that is sometimes offered as a basis for extension is that the debtor is engaged in litigation that must be concluded before a plan can be proposed. Rejecting that argument, the court in *In re Southwest Oil Co. of Jourdanton, Inc.*[10] concluded that almost every Chapter 11 debtor brings litigation with it. In that case the courts rejected the request for an extension concluding that Southwest Oil "should not be allowed to foster litigation and the request an extension of the exclusivity period on the grounds of the pending litigation."[11] Similarly, in *In re Parker Street Florist & Garden Center, Inc.,*[12] the court denied the extension and pointed out that the debtor could propose a plan that took into consideration all of the possible outcomes of the litigation.

There is at least one set of circumstances that might be regarded as cause for not extending the exclusivity period. This is evidence of the deterioration of the debtor's business. For example, in *In re Sharon Steel Corp.*[13] the court noted the debtor's inability to improve its business. In that case the creditors' committee had argued that Sharon Steel's processing plant was in danger of permanent closure. If the creditor can present credible evidence of deteriorating business activities, the court should listen to such testimony and hasten the proposal of a plan by denying any extension. Conversely, when the debtor appears to be turning around its business while it is in Chapter 11, the court may be influenced (though we doubt correctly) by that fact to grant additional extensions.[14]

Although it is too soon to be certain, the cases may now be turning in the creditors' favor. Particularly since the decision by the Court of Appeals for the Fifth Circuit in *In re Timbers of Inwood Forest*[15], a number of courts have denied extensions on the basis of the court's dicta. There the Fifth Circuit urged bankruptcy courts to "avoid reinstituting the imbalance between debtor and creditors that characterized proceedings under the old Chapter XI."[16] The dicta has now appeared in a number of cases, and we believe and hope that it shows a new skepticism on the part of the bankruptcy courts both about the beneficial effects of granting additional exclusivity and about the court's authority to do so.[17] Moreover, if it is true,

---

9. Examples of debtor's plans that were apparently stimulated by and produced earlier than might otherwise be the case because the courts denied extension are In re Tony Downs Foods Co., 34 B.R. 405 (Bankr. D.Minn.1983), and In re Ravenna Industries Inc., 20 B.R. 886 (Bankr. N.D.Ohio 1982).

10. 84 B.R. 448 (Bankr. W.D.Tex.1987).

11. Id. at 453.

12. 31 B.R. 206 (Bankr. D.Mass.1983).

13. 78 B.R. 762 (Bankr. W.D.Pa.1987).

14. See, e.g., In re United Press International, Inc., 60 B.R. 265 (Bankr. D.D.C.1986).

15. 808 F.2d 363 (5th Cir.1987), aff'd, 484 U.S. 365, 108 S.Ct. 626, 98 L.Ed.2d 740 (1988).

16. 808 F.2d at 372.

17. Cases discussing section 1121(d) and citing Timbers are: In re Washington–St. Tammany Elec. Co-op., Inc., 97 B.R. 852 (E.D.La.1989); In re Perkins, 71 B.R. 294

as we believe, that most corporate debtors are dead the day they file the petition in Chapter 11 and will emerge from bankruptcy in a pine box rather than a limousine, better to hasten that death than to make it an expensive and wasteful process. Thus, we applaud the courts that follow the dicta of *Timbers of Inwood* and are beginning to cast a skeptical eye on requests for extension.[18]

D. DISCLOSURE AND PLAN APPROVAL

§ 11–16 Overview

One of the prices that a debtor pays for entering the gates to bankruptcy is to make disclosure to its creditors of a large variety of facts and information that are normally private. The purpose of this disclosure is severalfold. First, it may be useful to enable a trustee or one of the creditors to pursue and avoid payments that have been made to other creditors, to insiders, or to other friends of the debtor.[1] Second, this information enables the creditors to shape their behavior pending the proposal of a plan of reorganization or liquidation. For example, a secured creditor who is contemplating the possibility of having the stay lifted might be interested in knowing the nature of free assets that would be available and would welcome information that would enable him to determine the probability of a successful reorganization. Finally, and most important for our purposes, the disclosures enable the creditor to bargain over a plan and ultimately to decide whether to vote for or against such a plan.[2]

By focusing here on the limited number of Chapter 11 cases where a plan is in fact proposed and ultimately voted upon, we do not intend to ignore the majority of cases where no plan is ever proposed or the business sinks into some form of liquidation. Nevertheless, our concern here is with a limited number of quite important cases where some plan is proposed and successfully negotiated under the shadow of a cramdown or a vote, and where there ultimately is a vote, either on a consensual plan or on one to be crammed down.

Because our focus is on approval of the plan at the later stages of the Chapter 11, we do not devote extensive consideration to the prior disclosures. Yet it is important to note those disclosures in passing and the impact on the disclosures that are required under section 1125 in connection with the

---

(W.D.Tenn.1987); In re Public Service Co. of New Hampshire, 88 B.R. 521 (Bankr. D.N.H. 1988); In re UNR Industries, Inc., 72 B.R. 789 (Bankr. N.D.Ill. 1987); In re Nicolet, Inc., 80 B.R. 733 (Bankr. E.D.Pa. 1987); In re Southwest Oil of Jourdanton, Inc., 84 B.R. 448 (Bankr. W.D.Tex.1987).

18. As one researcher has reported:

Corporations do not ordinarily fail because of lack of current capital; rather the appearance of a lack of current capital is an outward sign of more fundamental difficulties. As in the case of railroad failures the real cause of industrial failure is not likely to be a difficulty in securing credit due to sudden tightening of the money market, although this cause will be alleged if there is any plausible justification. The real reason underlying the difficulty in securing further bank loans is not the obstinacy of the banks but the inherent and continued lack of earning capacity of the corporation itself. Behind this is the failure of management.

L.M. LoPucki, The Debtor in Full Control—Systems Failure Under Chapter 11 of the Bankruptcy Code?, 57 Am. Bankr. L.J. 99, 263 n.7, quoting Dewing, Financial Policy of Corporations 1282–83 (5th ed. 1953).

§ 11–16

1. See M. Bienenstock, Bankruptcy Reorganization 261 (1987).

2. See H.R. Rep. No. 595, 95th Cong., 1st Sess. 226, reprinted in 1978 U.S. Code Cong. & Admin. News 5963, 6185–86.

approval or rejection of a plan. As a basis for understanding them, consider the earlier disclosures.

The first disclosure in a Chapter 11 is under Rule 1007.[3] It requires the debtor to file with the petition or shortly thereafter not only a list of its creditors but also a general schedule of assets and liabilities, current income and expenditures and in some cases a "statement of financial affairs." Under Rule 1007, these must all conform more or less to Official Forms 6, 7, and 8, and the debtor must submit to examination as provided in section 343 at the meeting of creditors that is provided for under section 341(a). The courts have been quite insistent upon the appearance of the debtor at this meeting and upon his submission to examination under oath.[4] A third important source of information is the Rule 2004 examination. It authorizes the broadest possible kind of deposition: "on motion of any party in interest, the court may order the examination of any entity."[5] It is well beyond our

---

3. Bankr. R. 1007.

4. See e.g, In re O'Donnell, 43 B.R. 679 (Bankr. E.D.Pa. 1984)(debtor's attendance required at the meeting of creditors even though debtor executed power of attorney authorizing her sister to institute the bankruptcy proceedings, since debtor's illness was unsubstantiated); In re Rust, 1 B.R. 656 (Bankr. M.D.Tenn. 1979) (husband still required to attend meeting of creditors even though no creditors wanted to examine him, and even though the trustee was satisfied with examining only the wife, because often the mere physical presence of the bankrupt under the former Act leads to additional recovery of the estate).

In enacting both the Bankruptcy Code and the Bankruptcy Act of 1898, Congress had contemplated that as a condition of the substantial relief that bankruptcy law makes available to a debtor, the debtor should be compelled to make this public appearance at the meeting of creditors at least once. In re Rust, 1 B.R. at 657 (citing In re Shanker, 138 Fed. 862, 864 (M.D.Pa.1905)("If hardship [to the debtor because of the creditor's examinations of it] seems to result, it is to be remembered that a discharge of the bankrupt from his debts is a large privilege, and, while it cannot be refused, where the law has been complied with, except upon the grounds there mentioned, yet the steps leading up to it must be followed before it can be claimed of right.")

Section 343 of the Bankruptcy Code requires, in unambiguous terms, the debtor's appearance at the § 341 meeting of creditors. In re O'Donnell, 43 B.R. at 680. This has been referred to as the debtor's "command performance." Id. at 680. Creditors may examine the debtor at the meeting of creditors for information concerning the debtor's acts, financial condition, or any matter which may affect the administration of the debtor's estate or right to discharge. In re Nixon Electric Supply, 85 B.R. 988 (Bankr. W.D. Tex.1988); Bankr. R. 2004(b). The scope of this examination is broad. See In re Foxcroft Bldg. Corp., 13 B.R. 837 (Bankr. S.D. Fla.1981)(citing 11 U.S.C.A. § 343 and 2 Collier on Bankruptcy ¶ 373.05 (15th ed.) for the proposition that the scope of the creditors' examination is broad).

Note that since § 343 refers to the examination of the debtor at the § 341 meeting, Rule 2004(b) applies to both Rule 2004 examinations and § 341 examinations.

5. Bankruptcy Rule 2004 reads as follows:

(a) Examination on Motion. On motion of any party in interest, the court may order the examination of any entity.

(b) Scope of Examination. The examination of an entity under this rule or of the debtor under § 343 of the Code may relate only to the acts, conduct, or property or to the liabilities and financial condition of the debtor, or to any matter which may affect the administration of the debtor's estate, or to the debtor's right to a discharge. In an individual's debt adjustment case under chapter 13 or a reorganization case under chapter 11 of the Code, other than for the reorganization of a railroad, the examination may also relate to the operation of any business and the desirability of its continuance, the source of any money or property acquired or to be acquired by the debtor for purposes of consummating a plan and the consideration given or offered therefor, and any other matter relevant to the case or to the formulation of the plan.

(c) Compelling Attendance and Production of Documentary Evidence. The attendance of an entity for examination and the production of documentary evidence may be compelled in the manner provided in Rule 9016 for the attendance of witnesses at a hearing or trial.

(d) Time and Place of Examination of Debtor. The court may for cause shown and on terms as it may impose order the debtor to be examined under this rule at any time or place it designates, whether

purpose to examine the outer limits of the Rule 2004 examination.[6] While one can expect a continuing flow of cases about the limits of such hearings, it is quite clear that the range of examinations that can be held under 2004 is very broad and that no court is likely to limit them in any very significant way.

within or without the district wherein the case is pending.

(e) Mileage. An entity other than a debtor shall not be required to attend as a witness unless lawful mileage and witness fee for one day's attendance shall first be tendered. If the debtor resides more than 100 miles from the place of examination when required to appear for an examination under this rule, the mileage allowed by law to a witness shall be tendered for any distance more than 100 miles from the debtor's residence at the date of the filing of the first petition commencing a case under the Code or the residence at the time the debtor is required to appear for the examination, whichever is the lesser.

6. For a discussion of those limits see e.g., In re Johns–Manville Corp., 42 B.R. 362 (S.D.N.Y. 1984) (facilitation of negotiations is not a proper ground on which a bankruptcy judge may compel a production of documents using Rule 2004); In re Wilcher, 56 B.R. 428 (Bankr. N.D.Ill. 1985)(subpoena for Rule 2004 examination of a non-debtor third party quashed partly because third party was not sufficiently involved with the debtor and partly because party requesting examination failed sufficiently to substantiate reason for examination).

The primary purpose of the Rule 2004 examination is to permit the trustee, a newcomer in the debtor's affairs, to ascertain quickly the extent and location of the estate's assets. In re Wilcher, 56 B.R. at 433; see also In re Good Hope Refineries, Inc., 9 B.R. 421, 423 (Bankr. D.Mass.1981)(discussion of former Rule 205). Consequently, courts have regarded examinations under Bankruptcy Rule 2004 to be "fishing expeditions" into the financial affairs of the debtor. See In re Vantage Petroleum Corp., 34 B.R. 650, 651 (Bankr. E.D.N.Y.1983) and cases cited therein. However, bankruptcy judges have exercised their discretion to deny such examinations if the "party in interest" that wishes to conduct the examination fails to show that the potential examinees have knowledge of the debtor's financial acts and affairs. In re GHR Energy Corp., 35 B.R. 534, 536 (Bankr. D. Mass. 1983), citing Cameron v. United States, 231 U.S. 710, 34 S.Ct. 244, 58 L.Ed. 448 (1914).

Courts have required that the party moving for a Rule 2004 examination show that a causal connection exists between the financial affairs of the debtor relevant to the bankruptcy proceeding and the information sought by the parties moving for examinations. See In re Johns–Manville Corp., 42 B.R. at 362. By refusing to grant an order to examine non-debtors, courts have also acknowledged the right that creditors and third parties have to privacy in their business affairs. See In re Wilcher, 56 B.R. at 428. The Federal Rules of Civil Procedure offer further protections to creditors and third parties in certain bankruptcy contexts. In re GHR Energy Corp., 35 B.R. at 538 (citing In re duPont Walston, Inc., 4 B.C.D. 61 (Bankr. S.D.N.Y. 1978), and In re Western Pork Packers, Inc., 5 B.C.D. 396 (Bankr. S.D.N.Y. 1978)).

Bankruptcy Rule 2004 authorizes broad examinations simply because the logistics of the examination at the § 341 meeting of creditors prevents the creditors from comprehensively examining the debtor. As a practical matter, creditors have a limited opportunity to ask the debtor questions at the meeting of creditors because the meetings are short. Bienenstock, supra note 1, at 267–68 (1987). See also In re Nixon Electric Supply, 85 B.R. 988, 989 (Bankr. W.D. Tex.1988), citing 8 Collier on Bankruptcy ¶ 2003.04[c] (15th ed. 1988) ("If a creditor attempts to go into great detail at a meeting of creditors, the result may well be that other creditors will not have adequate opportunities to ask relevant questions.").

Courts have been reluctant to allow debtors to avail themselves of these "fishing expedition" examinations because the Rule was primarily meant to give the only the trustee and the creditors an easier procedural time in getting the debtor to disclose information. See e.g., In re Wilcher, 56 B.R. at 433; In re GHR Energy Corp., 35 B.R. at 537; Matter of Georgetown of Kettering, 17 B.R. 73, 75 (Bankr. S.D.Ohio 1981)(Rule 2004 examinations are not proper when it appears to the court that the debtor merely wishes to exploit the procedural ease of the examinations); In re Interpictures, 86 B.R. 24 (Bankr. E.D.N.Y.1988)(debtor's shareholders' motion to examine other party is denied because the shareholders aren't "parties in interest"); In re Good Hope Refineries, 9 B.R. 421 (Bankr. D.Mass.1981) (improper for post-confirmation debtor to use Rule 205(a) examination under the Act to obtain a strategic advantage in fishing for potential private litigation); but see e.g., In re Arkin–Medo, Inc., 44 B.R. 138 (Bankr. S.D.N.Y. 1984)(debtor allowed to examine large claimholder on matters bearing directly on the validity of the claim; assertion that a party to be examined lacks knowledge is insufficient to vacate the examination order).

Finally, one should understand that the largest creditors in a sizeable Chapter 11 case will come to the table with a great deal of information that they have acquired privately both before and after the Chapter 11 filing. Large secured creditors will have received substantial documentation about the debtor's financial affairs at the time they made their loan, and if they have done their job, will have received updates as the debtor slid toward Chapter 11. The large creditors, particularly those sitting on secured and unsecured committees during the bankruptcy, will also have received direct information from the debtor in possession about the value of various assets, their sale and use, and the revenues and expenditures of the business.

In some settings and for some creditors a disclosure statement at the time of the plan is almost superfluous. The creditors will have collected a huge body of information, both prepetition and postpetition, from voluntary disclosures in the documents filed with the petition, from Rule 2004 hearings, and from informal negotiations over proposed plans. On the other hand, smaller creditors in large cases and most creditors in small cases with few assets may be completely in the dark. Presumably the small creditors in the large cases hope to stand in line with their larger brethren and get the same handout. They hope to be protected by an active creditors' committee formed of larger creditors who share their own interests. Where the creditors' committee is not active, that is no solution. Nor is it a reliable solution where the small creditors' interests diverge from those of the large creditors.

So one comes to section 1125, postpetition disclosure and solicitation. It explicitly recognizes a substantial difference in the knowledge and need for information of the various parties. Its key language, in section 1125(b), requires that the potential voter receive "adequate information":

> An acceptance or rejection of a plan may not be solicited after the commencement of the case under this title from a holder of a claim or interest with respect to such claim or interest, unless, at the time of or before such solicitation, there is transmitted to such holder the plan or a summary of the plan, and a written disclosure statement approved, after notice and a hearing, by the court as containing adequate information. The court may approve a disclosure statement without a valuation of the debtor or an appraisal of the debtor's assets.

Subsection (a) defines "adequate information" as:

> information of a kind, and in sufficient detail, as far as is reasonably practicable in light of the nature and history of the debtor and the condition of the debtor's books and records, that would enable a hypothetical reasonable investor typical of holders of claims or interests of the relevant class to make an informed judgment about the plan, but adequate information need not include such information about any other possible or proposed plan[.]

Subsection (c) explicitly recognizes the difference in the need for information of the various claimants. Although it requires that the same disclosure statement be transmitted to each member of a particular class, it authorizes different disclosure statements "differing in amount, detail, or kind of information, as between classes."

Rules 3016 and 3017 implement the provisions of section 1125. Rule 3017 contemplates a hearing 25 days or more after the disclosure statement is prepared and parties are given notice. Even if no one objects or otherwise asks for a hearing, a disclosure statement hearing must be held.[7] An objection to the disclosure statement will provide an additional occasion for dissatisfied creditors to argue for better treatment and to litigate over the debtor's failure to give it, albeit in the guise of complaining about the form of disclosure.

The first general question presented in section 1125 is what should be disclosed in order to give the other parties "adequate information." The description in section 1125(a) is generic and fails to give any explicit idea about the specific kinds of information that must be disclosed in a particular case.

A second issue, obviously posed by the disclosure requirement, concerns strategic behavior by creditors. Few creditors are above complaining about a disclosure statement even though their real complaint is with the plan and their treatment under the plan, not with the disclosure ("Sir, you refer to the guillotine for me. What really does that mean?"). We suspect that many creditors who complain about the disclosure are in fact trying to sabotage the confirmation proceeding in the hope that their sabotage will earn them more favorable treatment in another plan. In effect, these are sub rosa attacks upon the negotiation or they are complaints that should be directed at the plan and at its failure to conform to the provisions of section 1129. How to distinguish legitimate complaints about inadequate disclosure from those that are illegitimate is a continuing problem for the courts in such cases.

Finally is the intriguing question of the effect of the disclosure requirement on one who has a competing plan that cannot be brought out from under wraps because of the exclusivity period or who, with or without a competing plan, wishes to solicit a rejection.[8] Note that section 1125(b) states:

> an acceptance or rejection of a plan may not be solicited after the commencement of the case * * * unless at the time of or before such solicitation, there is transmitted to such holder * * * a written disclosure statement approved after notice and a hearing by the court containing adequate information.

---

7. Although the "after notice and hearing" language in §§ 102(1) and 1125(b) of the Code may seem to indicate that a disclosure statement hearing is required only when an objection to its adequacy has been filed, Rule 3017(a) requires that a disclosure statement hearing be held regardless of whether there are objections. See Bankr. R. 3017(a) and advisory committee note; see also Merrick, The Chapter 11 Disclosure Statement in a Strategic Environment, 44 Bus. L. 103, 109 (1988), citing H.R. Rep. No. 595, 95th Cong., 1st Sess. at 227, 229 ("[the disclosure statement hearing would] be one of, if not the major procedural hearing in a reorganization case * * *. The disclosure hearing is the central hearing in the case, and in a case of any size will be a relatively long process."); cf. In re Forrest Hills Assocs., Ltd., 18 B.R. 104, 105 (Bankr. D.Del.1982) (dictum in case pre-dating the adoption of Bankruptcy Rule 3017(a) in 1983 stating that if no objections are filed to the disclosure statement information nor any requests that a disclosure statement hearing be held, the notice and hearing requirements of § 1125 are met and an actual hearing is unnecessary).

8. Compare Bankruptcy Rule 3016(a) with Code section 1121. The former provides for exclusivity on approval of a disclosure statement beyond the exclusivity provided by the latter.

If the debtor solicits a plan and distributes a disclosure statement and a creditor wishes to solicit a rejection based in part upon defects in the debtor's plan and in part upon the prospect of his own plan, must that creditor also have a second disclosure statement? And what of the creditor who wants to solicit a rejection even before the debtor submits and distributes a disclosure statement? Are whispered meetings in the halls of bankruptcy court prohibited by section 1125(b)?

After all of this, we discuss pre-packaged Chapter 11 plans. We do so here because the thorniest problems with these plans are problems of disclosure and related issues.

§ 11-17 Standards for Adequate Information

One way to determine the appropriate standard for measuring adequate information is to ask what a voting creditor would wish to know. Presumably a creditor or other party who is to vote on a plan is entitled to some assurance that the plan meets the requirements of section 1129. The principal protection in section 1129 is the best interest test in section 1129(a)(7) that bars the confirmation of any plan that fails to give each non-consenting creditor as much as he would receive in Chapter 7. At the outset, therefore, the disclosure statement should show or give data from which one could calculate the kind of payment that he would expect upon liquidation. The disclosure statement data would thus show the amount and priority of all of the claims and estimate the liquidated value after all the assets had been sold. Recognizing the importance of a liquidation analysis, a number of courts have required its disclosure.[1] For example, in *In re A.C. Williams Co.* the judge explicitly found that the facts set forth in the exhibits to the disclosure statement indicated the liquidation value of the assets and stated the amount that could be expected to be paid on liquidation to the creditors as a group. In that case the court approved the disclosure statement providing certain limited modifications were made to it. It bears mentioning that the financial statements alone are likely to give no clue about the liquidation value of a company. This is so because some of the assets may be carried on the balance sheet at far less than their true value and others may be carried at substantially more than the value at which they could be sold. That difficulty must somehow be overcome by showing a reasonable estimate of current value.

Of course, one cannot determine if he will receive more under the plan than on liquidation simply by knowing the liquidation value. Somehow the disclosure must show facts on which one can estimate the present value of the payments or other transfers that are to be made under the plan. To put a number on this side of the equation under section 1129(a)(7) the creditor may need to know not merely a description of what it is to receive but also the probability that the reorganized debtor will be able to pay the amount. This showing would require some disclosure of projections of cash flow,

§ 11-17

1. See e.g., In re Malek, 35 B.R. 443 (Bankr. E.D.Mich.1983) (individual debtor neglected to include liquidation analysis); In re A.C. Williams Co., 25 B.R. 173 (Bankr. N.D.Ohio 1982).

business prospects and income. Not surprisingly a number of courts require exactly this kind of information.[2]

Other important requirements in section 1129 protect against debtor self-dealing. For example, section 1129(a)(5) requires disclosure of positions to be held by insiders or affiliates. The absolute priority rule in section 1129(b)(2)(B) prohibits the junior claim or interest holders from keeping any interest in the reorganized company unless those above them have agreed to the plan or have been paid in full. For that reason, too, it is important to know what the debtor or shareholders or other junior parties expect to reap in the plan. The creditor should have an opportunity to make an evaluation whether the plan is feasible under section 1129(a)(11) or is "likely to be followed by liquidation." For this the creditor needs not only current financial information, but also some information about the projected business and its prospects.

It will sometimes be difficult to distinguish creditors who are honestly seeking information from the creditors who are trying to derail a confirmation. By testing the creditor's request for additional information against his likely behavior and against his rights under section 1129, one may be able to distinguish the honestly troubled creditor from the disingenuous.[3]

Considering a specific case in detail provides a better grasp on what is required. *In re Metrocraft Publishing Servs. Inc.*[4] is a good example. There Judge Drake refused to approve a disclosure statement. The creditors' committee had complained about the disclosure on a variety of grounds. The debtor was a medium-sized business with some prospect for reorganization.

It is with such medium-sized business that the need for disclosure is greatest. If the business is larger, there is likely to be an active creditors' committee that will know all and can guide others. If the business is smaller, Chapter 7 doubtless awaits it and there is no need for a description of the meager flesh to be found on its bones.

---

2. See, e.g., In re Jeppson, 66 B.R. 269, 292 (Bankr. D. Utah 1986); In re Weiss–Wolf, Inc., 59 B.R. 653, 656 (Bankr. S.D.N.Y. 1986);In re Malek, 35 B.R. 443,444 (Bankr. E.D.Mich. 1983); In re Metrocraft Publishing Servs., 39 B.R. 567, 568 (Bankr. N.D.Ga.1984); In re A.C. Williams Co., 25 B.R. at 176; In re Pappas, 17 B.R. 662, 667 (Bankr. D.Mass.1982); In re Adana Mortgage Bankers, 14 B.R. 29, 30 (Bankr. N.D.Ga.1981); In re Hughes Marina, Inc., 16 B.R. 6 (Bankr. W.D.N.Y.1980).

3. For cases in which the creditor may have acted disingenuously in objecting to the adequacy of a disclosure statement, see, e,g, In re Valley Nat'l Bank of Arizona, 609 F.2d 1274 (9th Cir.1979), cert. denied, 444 U.S. 1015, 100 S.Ct. 667, 62 L.Ed.2d 645 (1980), reh'g denied, 444 U.S. 1103, 100 S.Ct. 1072, 62 L.Ed.2d 790 (1980); In re Bel Air Assocs., Ltd., 4 B.R. 168 (Bankr. W.D. Okla. 1980); Matter of Northwest Recreational Activities, Inc., 8 B.R. 10 (Bankr. N.D.Ga.1980); In re A.C. Williams Co., 25 B.R. 173 (Bankr. N.D.Ohio 1982); In re Brandon Mill Farms, 37 B.R. 190 (Bankr. N.D.Ga.1984); In re Texas Extrusion Corp., 844 F.2d 1142 (5th Cir. 1988), cert. denied, 488 U.S. 926, 109 S.Ct. 311, 102 L.Ed.2d 330 (1988); In re J.E. Jennings, Inc., 46 B.R. 167 (Bankr. E.D.Pa. 1985); Matter of Snyder, 56 B.R. 1007 (N.D.Ind. 1986); Matter of Johns–Manville Corp., 68 B.R. 618 (Bankr. S.D.N.Y. 1986), decision aff'd in part, rev'd in part, 78 B.R. 407 (S.D.N.Y.1987), order aff'd, 843 F.2d 636 (2d Cir.1988); In re Waterville Timeshare Group, 67 B.R. 412 (Bankr. D.N.H. 1986); In re Future Energy Corp., 83 B.R. 470 (Bankr. S.D.Ohio 1988). For a case involving a debtor who may have acted disingenuously, see, e.g., In re Nerlich, N.V., 72 B.R. 181 (Bankr. D.S.C.1986). See also In re Sweetwater, 57 B.R. 354 (D. Utah 1985)(creditor's appeal from bankruptcy court order confirming plan is denied in part because additional disclosure in disclosure statement would not have affected creditor's vote).

4. 39 B.R. 567 (Bankr. N.D.Ga.1984).

In response to the creditors' committee's complaint, Judge Drake set out a list of 19 facts to be disclosed that he had gleaned from other cases, from the statute and from the case before him. They are as follows:

(1) the events which led to the filing of a bankruptcy petition; (2) a description of the available assets and their value; (3) the anticipated future of the company; (4) the source of information stated in the disclosure statement; (5) a disclaimer; (6) the present condition of the debtor while in Chapter 11; (7) the scheduled claims; (8) the estimated return to creditors under a Chapter 7 liquidation; (9) the accounting method utilized to produce financial information and the name of the accountants responsible for such information; (10) the future management of the debtor; (11) the Chapter 11 plan or a summary thereof; (12) the estimated administrative expenses, including attorneys' and accountants' fees; (13) the collectibility of accounts receivable; (14) financial information, data, valuations or projections relevant to the creditors' decision to accept or reject the Chapter 11 plan; (15) information relevant to the risks posed to creditors under the plan; (16) the actual or projected realizable value from recovery of preferential or otherwise voidable transfers; (17) litigation likely to arise in a nonbankruptcy context; (18) tax attributes of the debtor, and (19) the relationship of the debtor with affiliates.[5]

A list like Judge Drake's appears in other cases and in many variations.[6] Here the court found many deficiencies in the debtor's disclosure. Impor-

---

5. Factors (1) through (11) are taken from the case of In re A.C. Williams Co., 25 B.R. 173 (Bankr. N.D.Ohio 1982). Factors (12) through (13) and (14) through (15) appear in In re William F. Gable Co., 10 B.R. 248 (Bankr. N.D.W.Va.1981), and In re Adana Mortgage Bankers, Inc., 14 B.R. 29 (Bankr. N.D.Ga. 1981), respectively. Judge Drake adds factors (16) through (19) in response to objections raised in the Metrocraft case.

6. See In re S.E.T Income Properties, III, 83 B.R. 791 792 (Bankr. N.D. Okla. 1988); In re Jeppson, 66 B.R. at 292; In re Malek, 35 B.R. at 443–44; In re A.C. Williams Co., 25 B.R. at 176; In re Adana Mortgage Bankers, 14 B.R. at 30–31; In re William F. Gable Co., 10 B.R. at 249–50. For an encompassing listing of disclosures suggested by these cases, see Merrick, The Chapter 11 Disclosure Statement in a Strategic Environment, 44 Bus. Law 103, 114 (1988):

(i) A history of the debtor and a description of the debtor's business(es);

(ii) A recitation of the events precipitating the chapter 11 filing;

(iii) A description of the debtor's assets and an estimate of their current value;

(iv) A statement of the anticipated future operations of the debtor;

(v) Identification of the source of the information contained in the disclosure statement;

(vi) A disclaimer;

(vii) A statement describing the present condition of the debtor;

(viii) A schedule of claims;

(ix) An estimate of the return to interested parties in a chapter 7 liquidation;

(x) A statement of the accounting method utilized to produce the financial information contained in the disclosure statement and an identification of the accountant(s) responsible for deriving the information;

(xi) An identification of future management of the debtor and the compensation to be received by that management;

(xii) The chapter 11 plan or a summary of it;

(xiii) A statement as to how the plan is to be executed;

(xiv) An estimate of administrative expenses, including professional fees;

(xv) An estimate of the collectibility of the debtor's accounts receivable;

(xvi) Financial data, going-concern valuations, and projections;

(xvii) Information concerning the risks posed to creditors and equity interest holders under the proposed plan;

(xviii) The actual or projected realizable value from the recovery of avoidable transfers;

(xix) Information as to pending and contemplated litigation by the debtor;

tant among those was the failure to comply with number 7 on the list, showing scheduled claims.

The Committee raises a number of objections relating to the disclosure of claims. First, the Committee points out that the plan proposes to pay claims held by Compugraphic Corporation, Rockwell International Corporation and General Electric Credit Corporation, yet these claims are not scheduled. It is imperative that creditors be informed of the nature of these claims, the principal amount due on these claims and the monthly payments specified in the agreements under which these claims arise. Second, the Committee strongly desires to know the amount of unsecured claims so that some calculation can be made as to the percentage at which such claims shall be paid under the proposed pro rata distribution of $48,000.00. The debtor argues that the amount of unsecured claims is subject to the Court's determination of which claims are allowable. In addition, the debtor asserts that certain claims may be offset by preferential transfers. The Court concludes that the debtor cannot avoid all disclosure regarding unsecured claims simply because their exact amount cannot be determined at this time. Some discussion of the nature of unsecured claims, their approximate value and the approximate amount by which such claims may be subject to setoff for settlement purposes shall be disclosed to creditors. Third, the Committee objects that the disclosure statement fails to indicate the sums to be paid to other creditors, both on a monthly basis and in total amount. The Court agrees that disclosure in this regard is necessary to evaluate, *inter alia,* the debtor's cash flow and the amount of money being diverted to creditors which might be available to pay unsecured claims. Fourth, the Chapter 11 plan provides for payment of wage priority claims notwithstanding the fact that no such claims have been scheduled. The debtor argues that no disbursements are intended to be made to priority wage claimants, but that the wage priority provision was included in the plan to assure that the plan complies with the Bankruptcy Code. Rather than force creditors to ponder the discrepancy between the schedule and the plan, a short statement explaining why the wage priority provision is in the plan shall be provided to eliminate any confusion.[7]

In this case the creditors found a sympathetic ear. Note how carefully the judge identified the ways in which the information might be used by a creditor in deciding to vote. We think Judge Drake's analysis is sensible and appropriate.[8]

(xx) A statement of the tax attributes of the debtor and the tax consequences of the plan;

(xxi) Identification of the relationship between the debtor and its affiliates; and

(xxii) Disclosure of transactions with insiders.

7. 39 B.R. at 569–70.

8. For other cases with good disclosure statement analysis, see, e.g., In re The Stanley Hotel, Inc., 13 B.R. 926 (Bankr. D.Colo.1981); In re New Haven Radio, Inc., 18 B.R. 977 (Bankr. D.Conn.1982); In re Genesee Cement, Inc., 31 B.R. 442 (Bankr. E.D.Mich.1983); In re Malek, 35 B.R. 443 (Bankr. E.D.Mich.1983); In re William F. Gable Co., 10 B.R. 248 (Bankr. N.D.W.Va.1981); In re Feldman, 53 B.R. 355 (Bankr. S.D.N.Y. 1985); In re Weiss–Wolf, Inc., 59 B.R. 653 (Bankr. S.D.N.Y. 1986); In re McGrew, 60 B.R. 276 (Bankr. W.D.Ark.1986); In re Copy Crafters Quickprint, Inc., 92 B.R. 973 (Bankr. N.D.N.Y.1988); Kirk v. Texaco, 82 B.R. 678 (S.D.N.Y. 1988); In re Diversified Investors Fund XVII, 91 B.R. 559 (Bankr. C.D.Cal.1988); In re Seneca Oil Co., 65 B.R.

In general, we think the courts are coming to sensible conclusions in defining "adequate information." Most courts properly look to the information needed to make a decision under section 1129. There are surely cases in which the debtor is attempting to pull the wool over the creditors' eyes by an inadequate disclosure—where he is attempting to disguise the transfer of assets to friends and neighbors. We suspect, however, that the majority of the arguments against disclosure statements are in fact strategically motivated attempts to forestall a plan that does not favor the objecting creditor. We believe the courts should approach such claims with considerable skepticism and feel quite free to dismiss them.

§ 11–18 Solicitation of Rejection or Acceptance of Competing Plans

There are two limitations on those who wish to propose plans in competition with the debtor. First is the exclusivity period in section 1121 (and arguably Bankruptcy Rule 3016(a)). Normally only the debtor may file a plan within the 120 days after the date of the petition. If the debtor files a plan within the 120 days, the exclusivity period is extended an additional 60 days (to a total of 180). Thus in virtually all cases the debtor has an unencumbered period of 4 months. In reality, the exclusivity period is routinely extended for months, sometimes for years.[1] During that period no competitor "may file a plan".

The second limitation is contained in section 1125(b). The competitor may not solicit a rejection of the debtor's plan (in anticipation of proposing a competing plan) until the debtor's written disclosure statement is approved and transmitted. A fair reading of section 1125(b), which fails to say so explicitly, is that a creditor with a competing plan must send his own disclosure statement.[2] Subsection (b) requires the distribution of only "the

---

902 (Bankr. W.D. Okla. 1986); In re Scioto Valley Mortgage Co., 88 B.R. 168 (Bankr. S.D.Ohio 1988); In re Monroe Well Serv., Inc., 80 B.R. 324 (Bankr. E.D.Pa. 1987).

§ 11–18

1. See, e.g., In re Perkins, 71 B.R. 294, 296 (W.D.Tenn.1987) (nearly two years); In re Ravenna Inds., Inc., 20 B.R. 886, 890 (Bankr. N.D.Ohio 1982)(about one year); In re Texaco Inc., 76 B.R. 322, 327 (Bankr. S.D.N.Y. 1987)(120 days); In re Kanawha Trace Development Partners, 87 B.R. 892, 895 (Bankr. E.D.Va.1988)(about six months); In re Swatara Coal Co., 49 B.R. 898, 900 (Bankr. E.D.Pa. 1985)(five months); In re Trainer's Inc., 17 B.R. 246, 247 (Bankr. E.D.Pa. 1982)(four months); In re United Press Int'l, Inc., 60 B.R. 265, 269 (Bankr. D. D.C. 1986) (ninety days); In re Pine Run Trust, Inc., 67 B.R. 432, 435 (Bankr. E.D.Pa. 1986)(ninety days); In re UNR Indus., Inc., 72 B.R. 789, 796 (Bankr. N.D.Ill. 1987)(sixty days). For cases which denied a debtor's motion for an extension of the period after an extension had already been granted, see, e.g., Matter of Lake in the Woods, 10 B.R. 338 (E.D. Mich. 1981) (1½ years); In re Westgate Gen. Partnership, 55 B.R. 562, 563 (Bankr. E.D.Pa. 1985)(about three months); In re Barker Estates, Inc., 14 B.R. 683 (Bankr. W.D.N.Y.1981)(about 1½ years).

2. For policy bases which support reading section 1125(b) to require that creditors with competing plans have their own plans for approval, see Glassman, Solicitation of Plan Rejections Under the Bankruptcy Code, 62 Am. Bankr. L. J. 261 (1988)(One, since a reorganization resembles a proxy solicitation inasmuch as groups advocating rejection of the plan are indirectly proposing that the reorganization electorate forego the opportunities offered by the proposed plan in favor of a competing plan, the same rationale for requiring disclosure by a plan's proponents supports requiring disclosure by the plan's dissenters; two, requiring disclosure as a precondition to soliciting rejections reduces the dissenter's ability to use the hearing on adequate information to derail the plan).

However, Glassman concludes that the most plausible reading of section 1125(b) is that the section does not require separate disclosure because of countervailing policies. Requiring

plan or a summary of the plan" and a written disclosure statement approved by the court containing "adequate information." A creditor could argue that he could distribute his own plan and that he need not distribute a disclosure statement if one had already been distributed concerning the debtor's plan. Yet, the language of section 1125(a)(1) requires information "to make an informed judgment about *the* plan * * *."[3] The implication is that the adequate information refers to the particular plan under consideration.

Consider the restraints that these rules put on one who is seeking the rejection of the debtor's plan and who may or may not have a competing plan in his pocket. Conceivably one could read section 1121 to prohibit any solicitation for or consideration of a competing plan during the exclusivity period. Of course, that is not what section 1121 says. It merely prohibits the "filing" of a plan; it does not prohibit discussion or dissemination of a competing plan.

How should section 1121 be read? We think a proper reading of the statute would prohibit only a formal and widespread distribution of a plan.[4] The policy of section 1121 is to give the debtor at least a running start and if a formal competing plan was widely disseminated at the time the debtor was disseminating his own plan, the policy of the statute might be frustrated. On the other hand, we see no reason why competing plans ought not be informally disseminated and considered by various creditors. Inevitably the debtor's plan will engender comparisons. As long as the debtor is not made to fight down competing plans in court or to confront them in a formal distribution, we think it unwise and unrealistic to read section 1121 to bar the drafting and even extensive informal dissemination of competing plans.

Does section 1125(b)'s requirement ("acceptance or rejection of a plan may not be solicited after the commencement of the case * * * unless" a disclosure statement has been distributed) prohibit even a discouraging

dissenters to disclose fails to accord with Chapter 11's rejection of Chapter X's cumbersome procedural requirements, and causes unnecessary delay which would chill bona fide opposition to the plan. Glassman further argues that if one reads § 1125(b) literally, it requires only that one court-approved disclosure statement be disseminated by the plan proponent to claimholders before a plan opponent may solicit plan rejections. This view of not requiring further court approval (which may include further disclosure) before plan opponents may solicit plan rejections is also supported by the Code's anticipating further "disclosure" in the form of continuing communication between the parties after the plan proponent has disseminated its disclosure statement. Section 1125(a)(2)(C) defines a typical investor as one with "such ability to obtain * * * information from sources other than the disclosure required by this section as holders of claims or interests in such class generally have." Section 1103(c)(3) requires a creditors' committee to "advise those represented by such committee of such committee's recommendations as to any plan formulated

* * *." Sections 1106(a)(1) and 704(7) require a trustee or a debtor in possession to "furnish such information concerning the estate * * * as is requested by a party in interest." Section 1106(a)(3) and (4) require a trustee to conduct an investigation of the debtor's business and both file and transmit a report of this investigation to creditors. Glassman, supra; see also Century Glove Inc. v. First Amer. Bank of New York, 860 F.2d 94, 101 (3d Cir.1988)("Once adequate information has been provided a creditor, section 1125(b) does not limit communication between creditors. It is not an antifraud device. Thus, the bankruptcy court erred in holding that [the creditor] had violated section 1125(b) by communicating with other materials and the district court properly reversed on this issue.").

3. 11 U.S.C.A. § 1125(a)(1) (emphasis added).

4. See Century Glove, Inc. v. First Am. Bank of New York, 860 F.2d 94 (3d Cir.1988)(section 1121(b) does not state that debtor has right to have plan considered exclusively).

word? We think not. Any hope of reorganization in even the simplest Chapter 11 business requires negotiation. A plan of reorganization is not simply a fixed commodity to be put up for bids. The plan takes account of many constituencies—secured creditors, unsecured creditors, trade creditors, long-term creditors and shareholders. Only by negotiation and discussion can the various interests be properly adjusted. Were the law to prohibit a creditor's argument against an existing debtor's plan and informal negotiation among creditors considering that plan and alternatives, the possibility of movement toward the most efficient settlement would be stultified and, of course, any such rule would be impossible to enforce.[5] For these reasons we would read "solicitation of acceptance or rejection" quite narrowly. We would find it perfectly appropriate and indeed admirable for creditors to say, "Here is my plan; consider it," even though the implication of such consideration would be a proposed rejection of the debtor's plan. Moreover, we would think it appropriate for interested creditors to distribute information that might lead one to a rejection, and we think it excessive to ask for such distributions to be approved by the court. There is, of course, some risk that the creditors will play fast and loose with the facts, but there are remedies for such behavior and the court surely has the power to enforce them by way of injunction, penalty, or subordination.

To put the issues in context, consider *Century Glove v. First American Bank of New York*.[6] In this case the debtor filed a reorganization plan together with a draft of the disclosure statement on August 1, 1986. The creditor, First American Bank, gave a copy of its alternative plan to the unsecured creditors' committee, told them it would seek court approval of its plan as soon as possible and apparently encouraged rejection of the debtor's plan. Nevertheless, the creditors' committee approved the debtor's plan. Shortly after the debtor's disclosure statement had been approved, a lawyer for the bank solicited other creditors to find out what they thought of the proposed reorganization and to convince them to vote against the plan. Conceding that there was no other plan approved for presentation, he said that the bank had drafted the plan and tried to file it. The creditors' lawyers asked for a copy of the plan and the lawyer for the bank provided it. Copies of the proposed plan were marked "Draft" and the covering letter stated they were submitted to the creditors for their comments. Motivated at least in part by the competing plan, the creditors voted against the debtor's plan. Holding that the bank had violated section 1125(b), the court disallowed the bank's vote and the vote of one set of creditors. It found that the bank had violated the spirit of section 1121(b) and that section 1125(b) required that any written solicitations by a creditor had to be "court approved."

The bankruptcy judge's decision was reversed by the district court, and the Court of Appeals for the Third Circuit affirmed. The Court of Appeals concluded that the word "solicitation" in section 1125 must be read narrowly. It could find no reliable distinction between negotiation and solicitation of future acceptances.[7] It concluded that a narrow definition of solicitation

---

5. See In re Gulph Woods Corp., 83 B.R. 339, 342 (Bankr. E.D.Pa.1988).

6. 860 F.2d 94 (3d Cir.1988).

7. Id. at 101.

did not "offend the language or policy of" section 1121(b), because that section dealt with "filing" and not with "consideration."

In our view, the case is right; we endorse it. We believe that almost anything that increases the speed of a Chapter 11 case and enlivens the bidding is desirable. The Chapter 11 case is surely speeded up by limitations on the exclusivity period and by encroachments that might be made by having a threatening creditor's plan waiting in the wings. Better to have the complexity associated with several plans than to have an unlimited period of quiescence in which no creditor can successfully challenge the debtor because none can propose a plan.[8]

An expansive definition of "solicitation" of acceptances or rejections in section 1125 could have two deleterious consequences. First, it would increase the cost of Chapter 11 by unnecessarily bringing creditors to court for approval of their materials. Second, it might chill negotiation (and ultimately the bidding) of the kind that is necessary to produce the most efficient possible reorganization in a setting where there are many variables. Even though it presents the possibility that a creditor may disseminate information later found to be inaccurate and that the creditor may enjoy certain advantages not enjoyed by the debtor (in the sense that the creditor can distribute unapproved material), we think the *Century Glove* decision is correct and in the long-term interest of all Chapter 11 participants.

Ironically, the debtor may be held to higher standards than creditors who harbor alternative plans or who are challenging the debtor's plan. For example, in *In re Media Central, Inc.*[9] the debtor, an operator of nine television stations, had received court approval for the distribution of a plan and a disclosure statement. Thereafter, in negotiation with various of the creditors, it came upon at least two alternatives not considered in its plan. When it distributed the disclosure statement and the plan, it included information on those alternatives and solicited a vote which gave the creditors the opportunity to accept or reject the plan or to accept the plan if "amended to include the pooling arrangement" or, alternatively, if "amended to include both the pooling arrangement and the revision for payment to include participation by holders of claims on rejected contracts." One creditor successfully objected to the solicitation on the ground that the alternatives had not been approved by the court nor had the description of the alternatives. The court voided the vote and required the debtor to come back for approval of yet another disclosure statement. It found that the

---

8. See In re Gilbert, 104 B.R. 206, 214 (Bankr. W.D.Mo.1989) (a broad definition of "solicitation" for § 1125 purposes would inhibit the creditors' meaningful participation in the debtor's reorganization); Century Glove, Inc. v. First Am. Bank of New York, 860 F.2d at 97; First Am. Bank v. Century Glove, Inc., 81 B.R. 274, 280 (D.Del.1988); In re Gulph Woods Corp., 83 B.R. at 342; In re Snyder, 51 B.R. 432, 437 (Bankr. D. Utah 1985)(if discussions, exchanges of information, negotiations, or tentative contracts made by the various parties in interest were prohibited, meaningful creditor participation would cease to exist). But see In re Gulph Woods Corp., 83 B.R. at 343 (some limit is needed on communications so that the entire process of requiring court approval of disclosure statements is not undermined).

For a thorough discussion of the legislative history of the Bankruptcy Code and its emphasis on creditor participation in the reorganization process, see In re Jeppson, 66 B.R. 269 (Bankr. D. Utah 1986).

9. 89 B.R. 685 (Bankr. E.D.Tenn.1988).

debtor had violated section 1125.[10]

How is this behavior different from that approved by the Court of Appeals for the Third Circuit in *Century Glove?* The most important difference lies in the fact that it was the debtor and not a creditor who violated section 1125 in the case. Here the debtor had the right and the power to propose and get the approval of a disclosure statement, a right and power that no creditor enjoys during the exclusivity period. The second distinction is that these documents were included in and an integral part of an actual "solicitation." Indeed, the four alternatives offered for vote were listed one after the other for a vote; they could not be said to have been merely bases for negotiation of alternatives.

The cautious creditor may, of course, wish to have its own documents approved by the court before they are sent out. We think this is a waste of judicial time and effort and adds unnecessary cost, but we understand the reason a cautious creditor may wish to do it in any event. Approval by the court of the creditor's competing statement would avoid any possibility that the creditor violated section 1125 or that the subsequent vote will be overturned on that basis.[11]

§ 11–19 Voting Agreements

In *In re Texaco Inc.,*[1] Pennzoil agreed not to "vote for, consent to, support or participate in the formulation of any other plan." This language was in a stipulation entered into between Pennzoil and Texaco as part of the settlement of their lawsuit. Because this stipulation and the associated agreement to vote for Texaco's plan occurred before there was a disclosure statement, other creditors argued that it violated section 1125(b). An agreement between Pennzoil and Texaco concerning Pennzoil's $10.3 billion judgment (ultimately reduced to $3 billion) was necessary before any plan of reorganization could be proposed to others. If Pennzoil could not be bound to a number smaller than $10.3 billion, any other negotiation about a plan would be meaningless. The court supported this sensible conclusion by reading section 1125(b) narrowly. It concluded first that the agreement *not* to vote for any other plan did not bind Pennzoil to *vote for* the Texaco plan. In the words of the court it was not bound "to cast any ballot at all." The agreement not to vote for any other plan did not violate section 1125(b) because section 1125(b) related only to the voting process with respect to "filed plans." Reading the section quite technically, the court held that this agreement could not amount to a solicitation of rejection of a plan since there was no plan. While one might not agree with such a technical reading of section 1125, surely the court's common-sense approach is sound; in a case like this, no other party should be heard to claim injury because one highly

---

10. Id. at 689; see also In re Temple Retirement Community, Inc., 80 B.R. 367 (Bankr. W.D.Tex.1987) (indentured trustee need not, as part of his § 1125(b) solicitation, state the position of dissenting bondholders and put forward the statement that those dissenters would like to propose an alternative).

11. See Glassman, supra note 2, at 277–83; see also In re Gulph Woods Corp., 83 B.R. 339, 342 (Bankr. E.D.Pa. 1988)("It is hoped that parties desiring to make communications will opt to seek out court approval in any doubtful cases").

§ 11–19
1. 81 B.R. 813 (Bankr. S.D.N.Y. 1988).

sophisticated creditor, holding by far the largest claim agreed to give up some its rights in hard fought negotiation with the debtor.

Section 1125(b) is not there to protect other creditors, but to protect the person whose vote is being solicited. Surely Pennzoil did not need help from Carl Ichan in deciding whether to forego its right to vote. For the court to have granted Ichan's request would be to allow one creditor to manipulate the rule in a strategic way for his own benefit and not for the benefit of the party for whom section 1125(b) was written.

§ 11–20 Voting in Multiple Plan Cases, Rule 3016

Where two or more plans are being proposed, complications in the disclosure statements and their modifications can arise. Consider, for example, *In re Cramer, Inc.*[1] The debtor was a medium-sized manufacturer of furniture and office equipment. In January 1989 the debtor and a shareholder proposed competing plans. The court approved each disclosure statement for distribution and voting. Subsequently the debtor renegotiated some elements of its plan with the unsecured creditors' committee and made limited, but potentially significant changes with respect to some creditors. When the competing shareholder got wind of the changes in the debtor's plan, he moved to prohibit solicitation and acceptance and to order voting on his (the shareholder's) plan alone. The debtor, the unsecured creditors' committee, and the bank sought to allow the confirmation hearing to go forward on the ground that no prejudice had resulted to any creditors. Apparently both plans had been submitted for voting but the ballots had never been accepted by the court. Proponents of the debtor's plan maintained that the other shareholder was merely an officious claimant who was not himself affected by the changes in debtor's plan. In fact, they were charging him of using the disclosure requirement as a strategic basis on which to prevent fair consideration of the competing plan.

Judge Pusateri conceded the merit of the creditors' argument but ultimately rejected it in this case. When there are competing plans, he reasoned that one competitor should not be able to see his opponent's plan, conduct new negotiations, and then send a new plan and disclosure statement that presumably took advantage of the weakness of the competing plan—all while a similar opportunity was not available to the other party. Therefore, the court proposed that each of the parties submit new plans and disclosure statements simultaneously for the court's approval and it invalidated any votes that had been taken on the original plans. We are persuaded by Judge Pusateri's argument in the setting in which the complaining party is himself proposing a plan. The Judge distinguished cases such as *In re American Solar King Corp.*[2] where there was a renegotiation, no competing plan, and ultimate approval of the modified plan, even though the newly modified plan had not been voted on as such. Note that section 1129(d) contemplates the possibility that a modified plan can be confirmed without further vote, at least if there is an opportunity for such a vote.

§ 11–20
1. 100 B.R. 63 (Bankr. D.Kan.1989).

2. 90 B.R. 808 (Bankr. W.D.Tex.1988).

In re Public Serv. Co. of New Hampshire[3] illustrates the difficulties that might occur if there were multiple plans to be submitted to the creditors. In that case Judge Yacos contemplated the possibility that "six or seven" plans would be submitted. He considered the "chaos" that might arise upon submission of such a large number of competing plans.[4] Consider how chaotic it might be. First, presumably, each of the plans would have to be frozen at some point to allow each of the other proponents to make realistic statements and comparisons between their plan and the others. Second, some means of voting would have to be devised and it is not clear exactly what that would be. Does one eliminate the bottom five and then have a run off? It is conceivable and even likely that one class of creditors would prefer a particular plan and another class of creditors would prefer another. If two plans are "accepted" and meet the tests of section 1129, does the court then choose the one to implement? Of course the practical and important question is how one facilitates negotiation among the interested parties after the various plans have been proposed. None of those questions has yet been answered.

§ 11–21 Pre-packaged Plans

Perhaps the most significant bankruptcy development of the early 1990's has been the use of prepackaged plans.[1] A prepackaged plan is a plan that is negotiated with and accepted[2] by creditors prior to the filing of any bankruptcy petition.

The Bankruptcy Code recognizes creditor acceptances of a Chapter 11 plan obtained prior to the filing of the Chapter 11 case if the solicitation of the acceptances meets the requirements of section 1126. These provisions for prepetition solicitation have been a part of the Bankruptcy Code since its enactment in 1979. Even earlier, prepetition solicitation was possible under Chapter XI of the old Bankruptcy Act.[3]

While the prepackaged Chapter 11 plan is not a product created *in* the 1990's, it has proved to be a product created *for* the 1990's. Leveraged buyouts in the 1980's resulted in numerous businesses with too much public debt. A prepackaged Chapter 11 is often the most efficient way to restructure that debt.

---

3. 88 B.R. 521 (Bankr. D.N.H.1988).
4. Id. at 538.

§ 11–21

1. See generally Case & Harwood, Current Issues in Prepackaged Chapter 11 Plans of Reorganization and Using the Declaratory Judgment Act for Instant Reorganizations, 1991 Annual Survey of American Law 75; Epling, Exchanges Offers, Defaults, and Insolvency: A Short Primer, 8 Bankr. Dev. J. 15 (1991); Kirschner, Kusnetz, Solarsh, Gatarz, Prepackaged Plans: The Deleveraging Tool of the '90's in the Wake of OID and Tax Concerns, 21 Seton Hall L. Rev. 643 (1991).

2. We distinguish prepackaged plans in which solicitation of creditor and shareholder acceptance of the plan occurs prior to the bankruptcy filing from "prenegotiated" plans in which the structure and perhaps even the language of the plan and disclosure statement are negotiated prior to a bankruptcy filing but the actual solicitation of acceptance is delayed until after the bankruptcy filing. By "prenegotiating" but not "pre-soliciting", the plan proponent avoids SEC review of its disclosure documents. See 11 U.S.C.A. § 1125(e); cf. 15 U.S.C.A. § 77a. For a general discussion of the SEC rules governing exchange offers, see Epling, supra note 1, at 18–30.

3. See Campbell v. Alleghany Corp., 75 F.2d 947 (4th Cir.1935), cert. denied, 296 U.S. 581, 56 S.Ct. 92, 80 L.Ed. 411 (1935).

§ 11-22 Pre-packaged Plans—Prepetition Disclosure

A prepackaged Chapter 11, like an "ordinary" Chapter 11 case, requires disclosure to those who vote on the plan. The disclosure differences between prepackaged and ordinary Chapter 11 cases are (i) the time that the bankruptcy court reviews the adequacy of the disclosure and (ii) possibly the standard by which the disclosure is tested.

In the "ordinary" Chapter 11 case, a plan proponent cannot seek or obtain creditor and shareholder approval of its plan until impaired holders of claims and interests have received a copy of a disclosure statement that has been approved by the bankruptcy court, after notice and hearing, as containing "adequate information." First, court approval of the disclosure statement, then solicitation of acceptances.

In the prepackaged Chapter 11, this order is reversed. In other words, first, solicitation of acceptances, then court approval of the disclosure.

The proponent of a prepackaged plan seeks and obtains creditor and shareholder approval of its plan prior to any bankruptcy filing and any bankruptcy court review of its disclosure statement. After the solicitation and the filing of a bankruptcy petition, the bankruptcy court will test the adequacy of the disclosure by the standards of section 1126(b).

Section 1126(b) sets out two alternate standards. The first alternative, section 1126(b)(1), requires "compliance with any applicable nonbankruptcy law, rule, or regulation governing the adequacy of disclosure in connection with such solicitation." The "applicable nonbankruptcy law" Congress had in mind was the Securities Exchange Act of 1934. More specifically, section 14 of that Act dealing with proxy solicitation. Prepackaged plans for companies with public debt usually offer new securities to the old debt holders. Under the securities laws, such an "exchange offer" is subject to the requirements of section 14 of the Securities Exchange Act.

To date, none of the prepackaged plan cases and none of the commentators writing about prepackaged plans have suggested any other "applicable nonbankruptcy law" that satisfies the disclosure requirement of section 1126(b)(1). Indeed, it can be argued that even compliance with the proxy rules of section 14 of the Securities Exchange Act of 1934 should not satisfy the Bankruptcy Code's disclosure requirements. Recall that under section 1125, the bankruptcy court determines that the disclosure statement contains "adequate information." The SEC does not make a similar determination with respect to proxy statements.[1] SEC Rule 501(c)(5)[2] requires that a prospectus include a statement in bold print that the SEC has not "passed upon the * * * adequacy of the information contained in this document." So, there is at least a question as to whether federal securities laws qualify under the language of section 1126(b)(1)—whether the Securities Exchange Act of 1934 is a "law * * * *governing the adequacy of disclosure.*"

In the absence of an "applicable nonbankruptcy law," section 1126(b)(2) requires that the bankruptcy court determine whether the disclosure provid-

§ 11-22
1. 15 U.S.C.A. § 77w.

2. 17 C.F.R. § 229.501(c)(5).

ed creditors and shareholders with "adequate information" as defined in section 1125, which we discuss earlier.

§ 11–23 Pre-packaged Plans—Prepetition Solicitation

Section 1126(b) needs to be read together with Rule 3018(b) which sets out two procedural requirements for prepetition solicitation.

The first requirement of Rule 3018(b) focuses on to whom the plan was transmitted—"all creditors and equity holders of the same class." It is not necessary that the plan be provided to all members of all classes. If, as in *TIE/Communications, Inc.*,[1] the debtor does a partial "pre-pack," it can transmit the plan to and solicit acceptances from the one class of creditors such as secured senior debt prior to filing a bankruptcy petition but wait until after filing to solicit acceptances from other classes of creditors and shareholders.

Second, Rule 3018(b) looks to the amount of time that creditors and shareholders had to accept or reject the plan—it cannot be "an unreasonably short time." Courts should consider the twenty-five day notice requirement for objections to disclosure statements in "ordinary" Chapter 11 cases[2] in determining what is "an unreasonably short time" in a prepackaged case.

Judge Abrahamson dealt with Rule 3018(b)'s two procedural requirements for prepetition solicitation in *In re Southland Corp.*[3] The debtor in *Southland* sent solicitation materials to record holders of claims and interests, including broker-dealers who held securities in the street name. While Rule 3018(b) requires solicitation of record holders, section 1126 refers to "holders of claims", "claims", "interests" and "creditors"; there is no mention of "record holders" in section 1126. Judge Abrahamson concluded that to the extent that Rule 3018(b)(2) substituted record holders for beneficial owners, it was as invalid as a change of substantive law. He ordered a resolicitation in which the record holders supplied lists of beneficial owners and each voter affirmed its authority to cast its vote.

In *Southland*, the debtor began distributing solicitation materials on October 8, and the offer expired on October 23. The materials took a week to get to the beneficial holders. The *Southland* solicitation presents two questions about time: (1) If a prepetition solicitation is made pursuant to section 1126(b)(1) and complies with "applicable nonbankruptcy law" time requirements, does a bankruptcy court still apply the "unreasonably short time" test of Rule 3018(b) and (2) if so, was the time in *Southland* "unreasonably short." The debtor in *Southland* argued that it satisfied the relevant SEC time requirements. Judge Abrahamson found that bankruptcy law controls and the bankruptcy test of not "unreasonably short time" was not met.[4]

---

§ 11–23

1. Nos. 91–362 to 91–386 (Bankr. D.Del.)(filed April 8, 1991, and confirmed June 20, 1991).

2. Bankr. R. 2002(b)(2).

3. 124 B.R. 211 (Bankr. N.D.Tex.1991).

4. Judge Abrahamson's opinion in Southland also deals with other issues such as the form of the ballot, id. at 222, and solicitation fees. Id. at 220–21.

§ 11-24 Pre-packaged Plans—Why Use Prepackaged Plans

While a law student or lawyer needs to understand the legal differences in disclosure and solicitation between an "ordinary" and a prepackaged Chapter 11, she also needs to understand that these differences generally do not drive the decision to use a "prepackaged" Chapter 11. In deciding whether to use a prepackaged Chapter 11, a debtor generally considers

(1) the legal advantages of a prepackaged Chapter 11 over a nonbankruptcy workout;

(2) the business advantages of a prepackaged Chapter 11 over an "ordinary" Chapter 11; and

(3) the disadvantages of a prepackaged Chapter 11.

a. *Advantages of Prepackaged Plan Over Nonbankruptcy Workout*

Binds All Creditors

Except for the disclosure requirements of section 1126 and the solicitation requirements of Rule 3018, the Bankruptcy Code and the Federal Rules of Bankruptcy Procedure do not distinguish between prepackaged Chapter 11 cases and "ordinary" Chapter 11 cases. Under section 1141(a), a confirmed Chapter 11 plan binds all creditors—even dissenting creditors. Outside of bankruptcy, an exchange offer or other workout is binding only on those that assent thereto.

Tax Benefits

Under section 382 of the Internal Revenue Code, a change in the ownership of a corporation severely restricts its ability to use net operating loss carry forwards to shield future income from taxation. If a nonbankruptcy debt restructuring results in creditors receiving 51% or more of the common stock of the corporation, a section 382 change in ownership is deemed to have occurred. There is a bankruptcy exception to this change in ownership rule. Stock issued to creditors under a Chapter 11 plan is not counted in calculating a section 382 change in ownership as to creditors who have held their claims for more than 18 months prior to the Chapter 11 filing.[1]

Original Issue Discount

Bondholders who agree to a nonbankruptcy exchange offer may confront "original issue discount" problems if the debtor later files for bankruptcy.

The Bankruptcy Code nowhere uses the phrase "original issue discount." Original issue discount is a business or economic term that describes the difference between the amount received by the issuer of a debt instrument and the face amount of that instrument. In Bankruptcy Code terms,

---

§ 11-24

1. See generally, Jacobs, The Chapter 11 Corporate Tax Survival Kit or How to Succeed as Guardian Ad Litem of a Corporate Debtor's NOL's, 42 Tax law 3 (Fall 1988).

original issue discount is "unmatured interest." Under section 502(b)(2), a bankruptcy court is to disallow any part of any claim that is unmatured interest. If C advances $900 to D and receives a $1,000 note, the $100 difference between C's advance and the face amount of the loan is the original issue discount and would be treated as unmatured interest and thus would be disallowed if D filed a bankruptcy petition later that day.[2]

The bankruptcy court in *In re Chateaugay*[3] applied the original issue discount concept to a nonbankruptcy exchange offer. There LTV entered into a nonbankruptcy exchange offer in which its bondholders received new bonds with the same face amount but lower interest rate and earlier maturity. Shortly thereafter, LTV filed for Chapter 11 relief. Judge Lifland then disallowed a portion of the claims of the holders of these new debt securities on the grounds that their claims included "unmatured interest" under section 502(b)(2). The bankruptcy court held that the difference between the face amount of the new securities and the "value" of the old securities was unmatured interest in the form of original issue discount. Thus, as a result of the nonbankruptcy exchange offer, the claims of the holders of the new securities were reduced to the fair market value of the securities at the time of the exchange.[4] While Judge Lifland's decision was cited approvingly by other bankruptcy courts, the Second Circuit reversed. In concluding that no original issue discount arose from the exchange, the court emphasized the importance of out-of-court workouts.

b. Advantages of Prepackaged Chapter 11 Over Ordinary Chapter 11

The primary advantages of a prepackaged Chapter 11 over an ordinary Chapter 11 are differences in time in bankruptcy and business and legal risks from bankruptcy. An ordinary Chapter 11 can take months if not years to complete, and a debtor in Chapter 11 faces not only the business risks of loss of customers and suppliers but the legal risk of loss of assets and even loss of control to creditors during the course of the Chapter 11. Prepackaged Chapter 11 cases have been completed in less than two months. Through the use of a prepackaged Chapter 11 plan, a business can at least reduce the business and legal risks of Chapter 11.

c. Disadvantage of Prepackaged Chapter 11

The primary advantage of a prepackaged Chapter 11, less time in bankruptcy, is also its greatest disadvantage. Because a debtor is using a prepackaged Chapter 11 to spend less time in bankruptcy, it will generally forego aspects of potentially enriching bankruptcy relief that are likely to

---

2. H.R. Rep. No. 595, 95th Cong., 2d Sess., 352–53 (1977), reprinted in 1978 U.S. Code Cong. & Admin. News 5963, 6308–09; In re Allegheny International Inc., 100 B.R. 247, 250 (Bankr. W.D.Pa.1989); see generally Kirschner, Kusnetz, Solarsh & Gatarz, Prepackaged Bankruptcy Plans: The Deleveraging Tool of the '90s in the Wake of OID and Tax Concerns, 21 Seton Hall L. Rev. 643, 650–59 (1991).

3. 109 B.R. 51 (Bankr. S.D.N.Y. 1990), affirmed, 130 B.R. 403 (S.D.N.Y. 1991), rev'd 961 F.2d 378 (2d Cir.1992).

4. See Klein, Chateaugay—The Bankruptcy Death Knell for Bondholder Workouts, New York Law Journal, Aug. 1, 1991 at 1.

result in litigation or otherwise delay the confirmation plan such as (i) avoidance actions, (ii) challenges to claims, and (iii) rejection of contracts and leases. And, because time in bankruptcy is obviously a premium to a debtor who is negotiating a prepackaged plan with its creditors, disgruntled creditors attempt to gain concessions by threatening to take action that will delay the confirmation of the Chapter 11 plan. Requesting an examiner is a common threat.[5]

E. ABSOLUTE PRIORITY AND NEW VALUE
§ 11–25 Overview of "Absolute Priority" Rule

The absolute priority rule is a specific application of the broader doctrine that reorganization plans must be "fair and equitable". Both have their origins in the railroad reorganization cases of the early 20th century.[1] The general doctrine is now codified in section 1129(b)(2) and the rule is codified in subsection 1129(b)(2)(B)(ii) which provides that the debtor must pay a nonconsenting class of unsecured creditors in full or "the holder of any claim or interest that is junior to the claims of such class will not receive or retain under the plan on account of such junior claim or interest any property." At least when it is applied rigorously, this simple rule is a powerful brake on the debtor's behavior and a strong influence on the negotiation that is likely to occur over a reorganization plan.

It means that the shareholders of the debtor (whether a small closely held company or a large publicly held one), or the partners of a partnership, or the debtors who own the farm cannot keep anything unless they either pay the unsecured creditors in full or get the agreement of all of the unsecured creditor classes. Because the rule is a part of section 1129(b), it need not be satisfied unless the plan is to be "crammed down", that is to say, unless there is a class of creditors that has not accepted the plan under section 1129(a)(8)(A). Because the most obvious escape from the rule is to negotiate with the creditor class that objects and procure its acceptance (by a vote of more than one-half in number and at least two-thirds in amount), the initial consequence of the rule is to make the debtor more willing to negotiate. In fact, the rule protects against a multitude of evils.

Assume, for example, that the debtor procures a particularly persuasive appraiser who appears before a sympathetic judge. The appraiser and debtor convince the court that the value of the property in the bankruptcy estate is much lower than the creditors believe it to be. But for the absolute priority rule, the creditors would have no recourse. Being stuck with the court's finding about the value, the best interest rule in section 1129(a)(7)(A)(ii) (promising them only as much as they would get on a hypothetical liquidation based on the low estimation) would assure them only a small recovery. With the absolute priority rule, each class can protect itself by vetoing the plan.

---

5. Under section 1104(b), the bankruptcy court must appoint an examiner on request of a party in interest if the debtor has more than $5,000,000 of unsecured claims other than trade debt.

§ 11–25

1. See Northern Pacific R. Co. v. Boyd, 228 U.S. 482, 33 S.Ct. 554, 57 L.Ed. 931 (1913); Kansas City Terminal Ry. Co. v. Central Union Trust Co., 271 U.S. 445, 46 S.Ct. 549, 70 L.Ed. 1028 (1926).

Assume alternatively that the proposed plan uses a present value discount rate that is unacceptable to the creditors or that the plan puts unacceptable contingencies on the payments to be made under it. Against all of these manipulations stands the absolute priority rule.

Of course, strict application of the absolute priority rule on behalf of a stubborn, vindictive, or ignorant class of creditors could forestall what might be the most efficient plan. If, for example, the debtor was in fact the most efficient operator of the business to be reorganized and if the reorganization plan would truly produce more than might be gained on liquidation by the creditors, a stubborn or ignorant creditor class insisting upon full payment might cause the debtor to abandon such a plan and so leave all parties in a worse position than if the plan had been adopted. The former problem (improper debtor manipulation) is probably more significant than the latter (creditor ignorance and vindictiveness), but no one is sure.

This wall, the absolute priority rule, has protected reorganization creditors quite effectively against debtor onslaught for nearly 80 years. However, in the past decade debtors have successfully breached the wall in a handful of cases under the banner of "new value." In these cases the junior claimants (usually shareholders of a debtor corporation or partners of a debtor partnership) have argued they may retain a stake in the reorganized company without making full payment to unconsenting creditor classes because they are contributing "new value" and thus are not merely junior claimants "retaining" their interest "on account of such junior claim." Whether the wall can be repaired against this attack or whether it will be routinely and continuously subject to breach because of the new value rule remains to be seen. Some courts embrace the new value exception while others completely deny its validity.

§ 11–26 Origin and Development of the "New Value" Exception

The doctrine that a reorganization must be "fair and equitable" was itself originally a judge-made rule. It is commonly traced to the case of *Northern Pacific Railway Co. v. Boyd*.[1] Boyd was a creditor of the original railroad that had gone through an equity reorganization. In that reorganization the old bondholders and stockholders, mostly the same people, used the reorganization in effect to "squeeze out" the intermediate unsecured debt. Because the senior creditors and the shareholders were the same people, the senior creditors' agreement to a plan that favored the shareholders said nothing about its fairness to creditors who were not also shareholders. Ultimately Boyd, a squeezed intermediate creditor, won in a Supreme Court decision that established that such a squeeze out was impermissible because it was not "fair and equitable."

Professor Ayer has described the next major set of Supreme Court developments, those occurring shortly before World War II:

§ 11–26
1. 228 U.S. 482, 33 S.Ct. 554, 57 L.Ed. 931 (1913).

That was the situation as it stood when the Supreme Court decided *Case v. Los Angeles Lumber Products Co.*[2] in 1939. The facts of *Case* are simple: the debtor holding company had liabilities of $3.8 million and held a subsidiary that owned the Los Angeles Shipyard and Drydock—an asset valued at $830,000. The plan was to cancel old securities and issue new ones in their place. Some twenty-three percent of the new securities would go to the former stockholders. Both lower courts confirmed the plan, but a unanimous Supreme Court reversed.

The case is both historically and doctrinally important. In terms of political history, the case marks a milestone in the career of Justice William O. Douglas, who wrote the opinion for the unanimous Court. Douglas had served on the Court less than a year at the time of the decision, having come from the chairmanship of the Securities and Exchange Commission. At the SEC, he was one of the principal architects of the New Deal corporate law reforms, and one of the authors of Chapter X of the Bankruptcy Act. His opinion adopts much of the substance of an *amicus* brief filed by the SEC.

As an instance of decisionmaking strategy, the case is noteworthy because it is the first major absolute priority case in which the Court interprets a statute. And indeed, Justice Douglas' interpretation has become so rooted in the culture of the law that it is a surprise to note just how attenuated it is. For the statute—Bankruptcy Act, section 77B, the precursor of Chapter X—nowhere states that claims must be paid by a principle of absolute priority. Instead, Justice Douglas deploys a provision in subsection (f), which provides that a plan must be "fair and equitable." These words, Justice Douglas writes, "are words of art which prior to the advent of Section 77B had acquired a fixed meaning through judicial interpretations in the field of equity receivership reorganizations." Strictly speaking, this is poppycock, and Justice Douglas knew it. None of the Supreme Court's absolute priority cases used that particular phrase in that particular way. Indeed, Justice Douglas himself cites only one prior use of the term in case law, and that is in an appellate opinion which the Supreme Court later overturned. On the other hand, the question was at least open, and it was reasonable to infer that the drafters intended to import at least some kind of absolute priority rule into section 77B.

But what kind of rule? Substantively, the remarkable fact about *Case* is that over ninety percent of all bondholders had accepted the plan. Justice Douglas held that this fact was "immaterial on the basic issue of its fairness." The only possible inference was that this time, the Supreme Court meant business.

Case interpreted old section 77B, already superseded before the Supreme Court issued its opinion. But the Court soon made clear that the "fair and equitable" language also applied under the superseding Chapter X. The Court also articulated one further principle necessary to make the absolute priority rule work in practice. Thus, in *Consolidated Rock Products Co. v. Du Bois,* the Court held that in order to apply the absolute priority rule, a finding as to the value of the reorganized enterprise must be made. On

---

2. 308 U.S. 106, 60 S.Ct. 1, 84 L.Ed. 110 (1939), reh'g denied, 308 U.S. 637, 60 S.Ct. 258, 84 L.Ed. 529 (1939).

reflection, this seems obvious. If the creditors hold claims worth $10 and the debtor is worth $8, then it violates the absolute priority rule to leave any interest with the debtor; if the debtor is worth $12, then it does not. Nevertheless, this obvious truth seems to have eluded a number of earlier courts. *Consolidated Rock Products* also established that the criterion of "value" for purposes of the rule was not merely the value of the enterprise in liquidation. Rather, it was the (presumably higher) value of the business as a going concern."[3]

In *Case*, Justice Douglas rejected the argument of the old shareholders who sought to receive shares of the reorganized corporation; these shareholders had argued that their "familiarity with the operation of the business" and financial standing and influence constituted new value that would entitle them to shares in the new corporation. Nevertheless Justice Douglas stated in *dictum* that payment of proper "new value" would entitle the shareholders to a piece of the reorganized company. He found it "clear that there are circumstances under which stockholders may participate in a plan of reorganization of an insolvent debtor."[4] He noted that the old stockholders could share where there was "necessity" to make "a fresh contribution and receive in return a participation reasonably equivalent to their contribution * * *."[5] All of this, of course, was *dictum*, for the holding rejected the plan as violating the absolute priority rule. Justice Douglas quoted at length from and relied upon an earlier and confusing Supreme Court case *Kansas City Terminal Railway Co. v. Central Union Trust Co. of New York*.[6] That case permitted a plan under which a creditor would receive certain securities of the new corporation and shareholders would receive similar securities only if they paid a specific assessment. Professor Ayer summarizes the case as follows:

> The gist of this analysis is that Justice McReynolds' opinion in *Kansas City Terminal,* while it does indeed contain intimations of an absolute priority rule and also of a new value exception, is equivocal at best, and can be read as supporting something quite different. All this is captious or fanciful in the absence of evidence that the opinion was actually (mis)read this way. Fortunately, evidence was already at hand in the interpretation by the lower court on remand, approving a revised reorganization plan. The plan allocated value to all classes, including equity. Since neither absolute priority nor its recently-hatched new value corollary guided the Court, the governing principles of the case are obscure. There was no pretense of a valuation, no pretense of an allocation of value in terms of claims, and no pretense that shareholders were being compensated according to their contribution. The plan was simply confirmed, and the Supreme Court denied *certiorari*.
>
> The point of all this is that neither of the cases taken as seminal for the new value doctrine can be read as an application of the new value doctrine. *Kansas City Terminal* "states" it, but in a self-contradictory manner, and accepts the ruling of the lower court when that court chose

---

3. J. Ayer, Rethinking Absolute Priority After Ahlers, 87 Mich.L.Rev. 963, 974–76 (1989).

4. 308 U.S. at 121, 60 S.Ct. at 10, 84 L.Ed. at 123.

5. Id.

6. 271 U.S. 445, 46 S.Ct. 549, 70 L.Ed. 1028 (1926).

not to apply it. *Case* "states" it well enough (indeed, one is tempted to say that Justice Douglas understood Justice McReynolds' opinion far better than Justice McReynolds understood it himself) but then refuses to apply it on the particular facts.[7]

§ 11–27 The "New Value" Exception Under the Code

The next event in the history of the new value exception is the passage of the Bankruptcy Reform Act of 1978. As we see above, the absolute priority rule for the first time appears in section 1129(b)(2)(B)(ii) of the Code. What started as a rule of equity in *Boyd,* and cases like it, has now become a rule of statutory law explicitly adopted by the Congress. Note, too, that there is no mention of a new value exception to the absolute priority rule. What inference does one draw from that? One possibility is illustrated by the opinion of Bankruptcy Judge Clark in *In re Greystone III Joint Venture*[1]. There, Judge Clark states:

> [i]t is fair to assume that Congress was aware of *Case* when it passed the Bankruptcy Code. That Congress did not expressly codify *Case*'s holding should be of no moment, as the term of art carried with it the judicial glosses that had been placed upon it * * *. It is a time-honored principle of statutory construction that legislators are presumed to be aware of judicial glosses placed on prior statutory enactments, and that subsequent amendments and codifications are presumed to have been carried into the new statute unless expressly repudiated.[2]

In *In re Winters,*[3] Judge Bentz draws the opposite inference. First the judge quotes from the House Report that describes the absolute priority rule's application as follows:

> "If the debtor is unable to obtain the consents of all classes of creditors and stockholders, then the court may confirm the plan anyway on the request of the plan's proponent if the plan treats the non-consenting classes fairly. The bill defines 'fairly' in terms of the relative rights among the classes. Simply put, the bill requires that the plan pay any dissenting class in full before any class junior to the dissenter may be paid at all. The rule is a partial application of the absolute priority rule now applied under Chapter X and requires a full valuation of the debtor as the absolute priority does under current law."[4]

Noting that absolute priority is brought into play in the current law only if the class—as opposed to an individual creditor—votes against the plan, the court points out that the Congress made several changes in the court-made rule. Judge Bentz then concludes:

> Congress, with apparent deliberation, did not mention the 'infusion of new capital' as a consideration in applying the fair and equitable test. Thus, the discussion in *Los Angeles Lumber Products Co.* about 'infusion

---

7. Ayer, supra note 3, at 1006–07.

§ 11–27

1. 102 B.R. 560 (Bankr. W.D.Tex.1989), opinion aff'd, 127 B.R. 138 (W.D.Tex.1990), judgment rev'd, 948 F.2d 134 (5th Cir.1991).

2. Id. at 575 n.20.

3. 99 B.R. 658 (Bankr. W.D.Pa.1989).

4. Id. at 662, quoting H.R. Rep. No. 595, 95th Cong., 2d Sess. 221–24, reprinted 1978 U.S. Code and Cong. Ad. News 5963, 6181–84.

of new capital' is no longer an element to be considered a 'fair and equitable' issue for confirmation under 11 U.S.C. § 1129(b)(2)(B).[5]

What does one do in the face of such diametrically opposed inferences drawn by sensible persons from the same Congressional enactment? Perhaps neither the language of 1129 nor the statutory history gives an unequivocal answer to the Congressional intention. Whether the "words speak for themselves" in omitting mention of new value or whether these same words are covered by the invisible judicial gloss of *Los Angeles Lumber v. Case*, we do not know. Striking, however, is Judge Pusateri's point that the Congress did not merely invoke the "fair and equitable standard" but in fact included a series of subsections that specifically defines the fair and equitable standard in several circumstances.[6] Having taken one large step beyond a mere statement of the fair and equitable rule by its statement of 1129(b)(2), why did the Congress not go the next small step and spell out the new value exception if it intended the exception to exist? The omission gives at least a breath of support for the inference that Congress did not intend the new value exception to continue.

Additional support for that position rests in the disparate application of the fair and equitable standard announced in *Boyd* (as codified in section 77B(f) of the Bankruptcy Act) and section 1129(b)(2)(B)(ii) of the Bankruptcy Reform Act of 1978. The absolute priority rule is now applicable only when the plan proponent is seeking a "cramdown" on an impaired class that rejected the plan. If the requisite majority of creditors (at least two-thirds in amount and more than one-half in number, section 1126(c)) in each class has accepted the plan, then the plan can be approved even though some junior parties take and some senior parties are not paid. The absolute priority rule does not apply. In contrast, confirmation under 77B(f) required class approval *and* compliance with the fair and equitable standard (including the absolute priority rule).

When one considers the "new value" exception to the absolute priority rule, this distinction is important. Since the absolute priority rule was a threshold condition for confirmation of any plan under section 77B(f), the judge-made "new value" exception found in *Case* gave plan proponents some leverage when dealing with an obstinate *minority* of creditors who could otherwise block confirmation.[7]

Today, obstinate inflexible minority creditors within an accepting class cannot demand plan compliance with the absolute priority rule, for section 1129(b)(2)(B)(ii) applies only when the class as a whole has rejected the plan. Thus, to the extent one views the new value exception as a means of silencing minority creditors within an accepting class, there is no longer any

---

5. 99 B.R. at 663; see also In re Drimmel, 108 B.R. 284 (Bankr. D.Kan.1989), decision aff'd, 135 B.R. 410 (D.Kan.1991).

6. In re Drimmel, 108 B.R. 284, 289 (Bankr. D.Kan.1989), decision aff'd, 135 B.R. 410 (D.Kan.1991).

7. The U.S. Supreme Court noted that the " 'new value would be used' not only to provide new working capital but also to pay dissenting creditors." Case v. Los Angeles Lumber Products Co., 308 U.S. 106, 121 n.15, 60 S.Ct. 1, 10 n. 15, 84 L.Ed. 110, 123 n. 15 (1939), reh'g denied, 308 U.S. 637, 60 S.Ct. 258, 84 L.Ed. 529 (1939). Minority creditors are those creditors within an accepting class which have rejected the plan (less than two-thirds in amount and no more than one-half in number in their class).

need for such an exception under the Bankruptcy Reform Act of 1978, given the revised confirmation standard of section 1129.[8]

There is one additional statutory argument for the new value exception. It is very simple:

> Section 1129(b) prohibits owners from retaining or receiving any property "on account" of their prior interests unless creditors receive full value. In a new capital case, however, the source of the owners' interest in the reorganized company is their new contribution. Ownership is not retained "on account" of the prior interest.[9]

An answer to this argument is that to the extent current equity holders are able to retain interests in existing reorganized corporations, it is because only they can propose plans under § 1121's exclusivity rule or because of insiders' knowledge of the reorganized corporation. They do receive a benefit "on account of such junior claim or interest" because it is their very status and role as debtor in possession that entitles them to the exclusivity period (holding competitors at bay) and that grants them the knowledge sufficient to make a plan. Contributing new value does not erase this benefit. The statutory argument based on the preposition ("on account of") is not totally convincing.[10]

Since 1978, three Courts of Appeal—the Sixth, Seventh, and Eighth—have applied the new value exception.[11] They mostly assume the existence of the exception, especially the Sixth and Seventh. The main Eighth Circuit case was reversed by the Supreme Court, though not because the Court decided against the exception. In a recent Seventh Circuit case,[12] Judge Posner has made clear that the earlier Seventh Circuit application of the new value exception in *Potter Material Service* should not be read to bind the Seventh Circuit to that position. "We emphasize, however, that the issue is an open one in this circuit, *Potter* notwithstanding * * *. A point of law merely assumed in an opinion, not discussed, is not authoritative." [13]

The Court of Appeals decisions applying the new value exception are yet less persuasive than they might otherwise be because they were decided prior to the Supreme Court decision in *Norwest Bank Worthington v. Ahlers*[14]. The Court in *Ahlers* held that "sweat equity"—the addition of extra labor—is not sufficient to satisfy the new value requirement, assuming arguendo that the new value exception exists. In an amicus brief in that case the Solicitor General had argued that the new value exception did not

---

8. It is important to note that if Case v. Los Angeles Lumber were decided today under § 1129 the plan would have been confirmed since over 90 percent of the objecting creditors' class had accepted the plan.

9. Nimmer, Negotiated Bankruptcy Reorganization Plans: Absolute Priority and New Value Contributions, 36 Emory L. J. 1009, 1051 (1987).

10. The argument was rejected in In re Drimmel, 108 B.R. 284, 290 (Bankr. D.Kan. 1989), decision aff'd, 135 B.R. 410 (D.Kan. 1991).

11. In re Ahlers, 794 F.2d 388 (8th Cir. 1988), rev'd sub nom., Norwest Bank Worthington v. Ahlers, 485 U.S. 197, 108 S.Ct. 963, 99 L.Ed.2d 169 (1988), on remand, 844 F.2d 587 (8th Cir.1988); In re U.S. Truck Co., Inc., 800 F.2d 581 (6th Cir.1986); In re Potter Material Service, 781 F.2d 99 (7th Cir.1986); cf. In re Anderson, 913 F.2d 530 (8th Cir.1990).

12. In the Matter of Stegall, 865 F.2d 140 (7th Cir.1989); see also Kham & Nate's Shoes No. 2, Inc. v. First Bank of Whiting, 908 F.2d 1351 (7th Cir.1990) (Judge Easterbrook rejecting new value on facts of that case).

13. 865 F.2d at 142.

14. 485 U.S. 197, 108 S.Ct. 963, 99 L.Ed.2d 169 (1988), on remand, 844 F.2d 587 (8th Cir. 1988).

survive the 1978 enactment and urged the Court to decide the case on that basis. The Court declined that offer, but it makes clear that one should not draw an inference that the new value exception continues to exist from its refusal to deny its existence:

> Thus, our decision today should not be taken as any comment on the continuing vitality of the *Los Angeles Lumber* exception—a question which has divided the lower courts since passage of the Code in 1978 * * *. Rather, we simply conclude that even if "an infusion of 'money' or 'money's worth'" exception to the absolute priority rule has survived the enactment of 1129(b), respondents' proposed contribution to the reorganization plan is inadequate to gain the benefit of this exception." [15]

Since *Ahlers* was decided, the Fifth and Fourth Circuits have spoken on the question. In *Matter of Greystone III Joint Venture* [16] the Court of Appeals for the Fifth Circuit first found that new value was not an exception to the absolute priority rule under the Code; on rehearing the court reversed itself and vacated its earlier opinion as it applies to the new value exception. It now expresses "no view whatever" on the new value exception.

In *Traveler's Insurance Co. v. Bryson Properties* [17] the Court of Appeals for the Fourth Circuit rejected a proposed plan as not fair and equitable. The court found that even if the new value exception survived the enactment of the Bankruptcy Code to a limited extent, it should not be applied to a single asset real estate case.

Since *Ahlers,* the new value exception appears to be in decline, but it is hardly dead. It is important therefore to continue to understand how it might be applied.

§ 11–28 Applying the Exception

If and where the "new value" rule lives, how is it applied? Because the new value rule is not codified and must therefore be drawn from language of several Supreme Court cases, the precise shape of the rule is uncertain. Reading Justice Douglas' *dicta* in *Case v. Los Angeles Lumber,* most authorities find three requirements for applying it. First, the new value must be given in cash or something roughly equivalent to cash; second, the new value must be a "necessity" for reorganization; and third, the payment must be roughly equivalent to the going-concern value of the business. Since Justice Douglas held that the proposal in *Case* did not meet the new value test, we can only guess from his opinion what would meet it.

The requirement that any new value be contributed in the form of cash or something equivalent to cash has real bite. Part of the reason Justice Douglas rejected the proposal in *Case* was that the new value was to be

---

15. 485 U.S. at 203, 204 n.3, 108 S.Ct. at 966 n.3, 99 L.Ed.2d at 177 n.3.

16. 948 F.2d 134 (5th Cir.1991), vac'd in part, 1992 WL 35878 (Feb. 27, 1992).

17. 961 F.2d 496 (4th Cir.1992). See also In re Triple R Holdings, Ltd. Partnership, 134 B.R. 382 (Bankr. N.D.Cal.1991) and Penn Mutual Life Ins. Co. v. Woodscape Ltd. Partnership, 134 B.R. 165 (Bankr. D.Md.1991).

composed in part of the connections and business acumen of the existing shareholders. More than any of the other requirements, the requirement of cash or equivalent stands on a firm footing in *Case v. Los Angeles Lumber*.

It has been further strengthened in the Supreme Court's 1989 decision in *Norwest Bank Worthington v. Ahlers* [1] and by a recent decision of Judge Easterbrook in the Seventh Circuit. In effect, the Ahlers suggested that they would add new value that would go to the benefit of the creditors by working longer hours or more productively than they would otherwise work. By its reversal of the decision of the Court of Appeals for the Eighth Circuit, the Supreme Court flatly rejected sweat equity as satisfying the new value exception.

Several decisions have accepted shareholders' or managers' guarantees as contributions of new value to the plan. In *Kham & Nate's Shoes No. 2, Inc. v. First Bank of Whiting*,[2] Judge Easterbrook rejected the guarantee of the debtor's obligation as a contribution of new value. In that decision he concluded that *Ahlers* by implication also rejected such a contribution. He analogized the contribution of new value to the purchase of stock in an existing corporation and pointed out that under Illinois law, one could not purchase new stock by promising to perform services. Moreover, he noted that the guarantee of a shareholder is of uncertain value (for it depends upon the creditworthiness of the guarantor) and that it does not become an asset on the balance sheet of the debtor nor is it alienable. All of these factors make its value uncertain. A guarantee lacks many of the usual characteristics of an asset that might be used as collateral, be sold to raise money or form the basis of the satisfaction of a debt.

The combination of Justice Douglas's original decision with *Ahlers* and cases like *Kham & Nate* shows that the courts are serious in requiring money or money's worth. They will not accept assets of indeterminate or uncertain value or assets that have significant limitations on their alienability.

The second requirement—that the new value coming from the shareholders be a "necessity"—does not carry a clear message. What is "necessary"? First, a payment from the shareholders could be necessary because no others will pay the same amount. Yet that hardly seems to fit the conventional meaning of the word. Second, the payment could be necessary (1) because no one else would pay any amount and (2) if there is no payment, the debtor will have to be liquidated. Of course, that idea is inconsistent with the thought that there is a going-concern value that is to be protected by the reorganization and that would otherwise be lost on a liquidation. How can one say there is a going-concern value when no one but the existing shareholders will make any payment for it?

To the extent that "necessity" means that liquidation will occur unless there is a capital contribution to pay existing creditors (suppliers and such), the necessity requirement is itself in conflict with other ideas in the new

§ 11-28

1. 485 U.S. 197, 108 S.Ct. 963, 99 L.Ed.2d 169 (1988), on remand, 844 F.2d 587 (8th Cir. 1988).

2. 908 F.2d 1351 (7th Cir.1990).

value rule. For example, if, as Professors Baird and Jackson have argued [3] and as Judge Easterbrook has held,[4] the existing creditors are to be treated as "owners" and the new value is to be treated as a "purchase" of the company from them as the owners, that payment should go into the pocket of those creditors. If instead of going into their pockets, it is to be used as working capital of the debtor, ultimately paid out to other existing and new creditors for current operations, it cannot properly be regarded as a payment to the existing creditors for the going-concern value "owned" by them. Thus, to the extent that the necessity requirement carries the implication of a need for a quick capital infusion to be paid out to new and existing trade creditors, it conflicts with the most sophisticated articulation of the rule, namely, that the new value is a purchase of the company from the existing creditors.

If the necessity requirement is to have any meaning and practical application, it is not exactly clear how it is to be applied. Perhaps the court in *In re Jartran*[5] is talking about this requirement when it recites how parties have attempted over a period of time to sell the company and that no one but the shareholders were willing to bid for it. If that is the meaning, then cases like *Greystone*[6] violate the necessity requirement, for in that case Judge Clark explicitly states that he will not conduct an auction for the company and implicitly states that he is going to prefer the existing shareholders' plan over the secured creditor's plan by allowing the exclusivity period to bar the secured creditors from presenting a competing bid.

In summary, we are doubtful about the meaning of the necessity requirement. Perhaps it should be disregarded. It may simply have been Justice Douglas' admonition in *Case* to other courts that the new value exception should be rarely applied and that normally one would expect the shareholders to be wiped out and for others to own the company after the reorganization.

Third, the new value given must roughly equal the going-concern value of the business. In *In re Jartran*[7] the court uses the testimony of several sophisticated financial analysts to determine the going-concern value of the business and thus to decide whether the contribution of the shareholders equals this value. In other cases the courts are less true to this rule and sometimes simply state there is no going concern and therefore anything to be paid equals or exceeds it.[8]

It is somewhat ironic that this portion of the new value exception invites the court to make the very error that the fair and equitable doctrine is designed to protect against. That is, a principal reason for the fair and

---

3. Baird & Jackson, Bargaining After the Fall and the Contours of the Absolute Priority Rule, 55 U.Chi.L.Rev. 738 (1988).

4. Kham & Nate's Shoes No. 2, Inc. v. First Bank of Whiting, 908 F.2d 1351, 1360–63 (7th Cir.1990).

5. 44 B.R. 331 (Bankr. N.D.Ill. 1984).

6. In re Greystone III Joint Venture, 102 B.R. 560 (Bankr.W.D.Tex.1989), aff'd, 127 B.R. 138 (W.D.Tex.1990), rev'd, 948 F.2d 134 (5th Cir.1991).

7. 44 B.R. 331 (Bankr. N.D.Ill. 1984).

8. In re Aztec Co., 107 B.R. 585 (Bankr. M.D.Tenn.1989); In re Greystone III Joint Venture, 102 B.R. 560 (Bankr. W.D.Tex.1989), opinion aff'd, 102 B.R. 560 (W.D.Tex.1990), judgment rev'd, 948 F.2d 134 (5th Cir.1992); In re Jartran, 44 B.R. 331 (Bankr. N.D.Ill. 1984); In re Landau Boat Co., 13 B.R. 788 (Bankr. W.D.Mo.1981); In re Marston Enterprises, Inc., 13 B.R. 514 (Bankr. E.D.N.Y.1981).

equitable doctrine is to keep the courts from making unfairly low valuations of the assets and so undermining the rights of the creditors. Yet here we return to the same forum to ask for valuation of the same property in applying the new value exception.

We believe that the third requirement is likely to be an empty rule. Only by arranging for others to investigate the value of the concern and allowing them to bid against the shareholders on a fair basis is one likely to determine the true going-concern value. Even experts as sophisticated as those in *Jartran* can make only educated guesses.[9]

As one sees when reading the cases discussed below, the three rules distilled from *Case* are rather open and soft. They leave some worry that the new value exception will tear a large hole in the fair and equitable rule and will invite the very same abuses that the fair and equitable rule is to prevent. On the other hand, some of the cases show reasons why the rule might help to produce efficiencies that could not otherwise be achieved.

§ 11-29 Applying the Exception—The Cases

The Code cases that consider the new value exception can be divided chronologically or by representative fact pattern.[1] Chronologically, *Ahlers* may be a milestone. By striking down a particular application of the new value exception, *Ahlers* also caused courts to be more critical about the kind

---

9. If one reads into the going concern equivalence requirement the implication that that value should go into the hands of the "owning creditors," and should not be used for continuing operation of the business, there might be some bite to the requirement. The objection of the Supreme Court in Ahlers and of Judge Easterbrook of the Seventh Circuit in Kham & Nate's Shoes to "certain payments" as new value might ultimately rest on the proposition that these are not new value not because they are not new value to the debtor, but because they are not payments to the existing creditors as a purchase for their rights in the company. If, ultimately that is the interpretation placed on Ahlers and Kham & Nate's Shoes and by them upon the third requirement, it will have clarified the law and produced a desirable outcome.

§ 11-29

1. The cases that deal at length with the new value exception fall into four categories. First are those who have accepted the existence of the new value exception and have applied it. Second are cases that accept the proposition but, for one reason or another, do not approve the debtor's plan. Third are cases that do not accept the plan and express doubt about the continuing vitality of the rule. Finally are cases that do not accept the plan and find that the new value exception did not survive the 1978 enactment of the Code.

Accepted and applied: In re U.S. Truck Co., Inc., 800 F.2d 581 (6th Cir.1986); In re Potter Material Service, 781 F.2d 99 (7th Cir.1986); In re Landau Boat Co., 13 B.R. 788 (Bankr. W.D.Mo.1981); In re Greystone III Joint Venture, 102 B.R. 560 (Bankr. W.D.Tex.1989), opinion aff'd, 127 B.R. 138 (W.D.Tex.1990), judgment rev'd, 948 F.2d 134 (5th Cir.1991); In re Jartran, 44 B.R. 331 (Bankr. N.D.Ill. 1984).

New value exception accepted but not applied: In re Marston Enterprises, Inc., 13 B.R. 514 (Bankr. E.D.N.Y.1981); In re Aztec Co., 107 B.R. 585 (Bankr. M.D.Tenn.1989); In re Sawmill Hydraulics, Inc., 72 B.R. 454 (Bankr. C.D.Ill. 1987); In re Pullman Construction Industries, Inc., 107 B.R. 909 (Bankr. N.D.Ill. 1989); In re Mortgage Investment Company of El Paso, Texas, 111 B.R. 604 (Bankr. W.D.Tex. 1990).

New value exception not applied and doubt expressed about its vitality: Norwest Bank Worthington v. Ahlers, 485 U.S. 197, 108 S.Ct. 963, 99 L.Ed.2d 169 (1988), on remand, 844 F.2d 587 (8th Cir.1988); Kham & Nate's Shoes No. 2, Inc. v. First Bank of Whiting, 908 F.2d 1351 (7th Cir.1990); In the Matter of Stegall, 865 F.2d 140 (7th Cir.1989); In re Ashton, 107 B.R. 670 (Bankr. D.N.D. 1989).

New value exception abolished by the Congressional enactment of the 1978 Code: In re Drimmel, 108 B.R. 284 (Bankr. D.Kan.1989), decision aff'd, 135 B.R. 410 (D.Kan.1991); In re Winters, 99 B.R. 658 (Bankr. W.D.Pa.1989).

of contribution by the shareholders that could be recognized as new value.[2] If the farmer's sweat equity was not new value, what did that tell about guarantees by the shareholder, payment of lawyers fees and other debts or promises of future payment to new creditors of the existing business? It is possible that we have seen the high point of the new value exception, and that the courts will increasingly conclude that it did not survive the 1978 enactment. At minimum, the *Ahlers* decision has caused a searching

---

2. Representative of these post-*Ahlers* cases, that show skepticism about the continued existence of the exception and also restrict the kind of contribution that constituted new value, is Judge Easterbrook's decision in Kham & Nate's Shoes No. 2, Inc. v. First Bank of Whiting, 908 F.2d 1351 (7th Cir.1990). There Judge Easterbrook commented as follows on the exception:

Bank asks us to hold that the new value exception vanished in 1978. We stop short of the precipice, as the Supreme Court did in Ahlers, 485 U.S. at 203–04 n.3, 108 S.Ct. 967–68 n. 3, for two reasons: first, the consideration for the shares is insufficient even if the new value exception retains vitality; second, although Bank vigorously argues the merits of the new value exception in this court, it did not make this argument in the bankruptcy court. Despite Bank's failure to preserve its argument, the history and limits of the rule before 1978 are pertinent to our analysis because, as the Court held in Ahlers, 485 U.S. at 205–06, 108 S.Ct. at 968–69, at a minimum the Code forbids any expansion of the exception beyond the limits recognized in Case.

Case rejected the argument that continuity of management plus financial standing that would attract new investment is "new value". According to the Court, only an infusion of capital in "money or money's worth" suffices. Ahlers reinforces the message, holding that a promise of future labor, coupled with the managers' experience and expertise, also is not new value. It remarked that the promises of the managers in Case "[n]o doubt * * * had 'value' and would have been of some benefit to any reorganized enterprise. But ultimately, as the Court said * * *, '[t]hey reflect merely vague hopes or possibilities.' The same is true of respondents' pledge of future labor and management skills." 485 U.S. at 204, 108 S.Ct. at 967 (citations omitted). The Court observed, ibid, again quoting from Case, that the promise was "intangible, inalienable, and, in all likelihood, unenforceable. It 'has no place in the asset column of the balance sheet of the new [entity]'."

Guarantees are no different. They are intangible, inalienable, and unenforceable by the firm. Beard and Parker may revoke their guarantees or render them valueless by disposing of their assets; although a lender may be able to protest the revocation, the debtor cannot compel the guarantor to maintain the pledge in force. Guarantees have "no place in the asset column" of a balance sheet. We do not know whether these guarantees have the slightest value, for the record does not reveal whether Parker and Beard have substantial unencumbered assets that the guarantees would put at risk. If Beard and Parker were organizing a new firm in Illinois, they could not issue stock to themselves in exchange for guarantees of loans. Illinois requires the consideration for share to be money or other property, or "labor or services actually performed for the corporation," Ill. Rev. Stat. ch. 32 ¶ 6.30. So Beard and Parker could subscribe for shares against a promise of labor, but the firm could not issue the shares until the labor had been performed. A guarantee does not fit into any of the statutory categories, and there is no reason why it should. One who pays out on a guarantee becomes the firm's creditor, a priority higher than that of stockholder. A guarantor who has not paid has no claim against the firm. Promises inadequate to support the issuance of shares under state law are also inadequate to support the issuance of shares by a bankruptcy judge over the protest of the creditors, the real owners of the firm.

Debtor relies on In re Potter Material Service, Inc., 781 F.2d 99 (7th Cir.1986), but it does not support the bankruptcy judge's decision. The new value in Potter was a combination of $34,800 cash plus a guarantee of a $600,000 loan. If Beard and Parker had contributed substantial cash, we would have a case like Potter. They didn't, and we don't. To the extent Potter implies that a guarantee alone is "new value", it did not survive Ahlers. Potter observed that the guarantor took an economic risk, 781 F.2d at 103. Ahlers holds that detriment to the shareholder does not amount to "value" to the firm; there must be an infusion of new capital. See John D. Ayer, Rethinking Absolute Priority after Ahlers, 87 Mich.L.Rev. 963 (1989). A guarantee may be costly to the guarantor, but it is not a balance-sheet asset, and it therefore may not be treated as new value. The plan of reorganization should not have been confirmed over Bank's objection.

Id. at 1361–1363.

skepticism in the lower courts about the meaning of the rule and the modes of satisfying it.

As a basis for considering how the rule is justified and applied where the courts conclude that it lives, consider the facts of four cases. In each case the shareholders or partners proposed plans based on the application of the rule. In all four of these cases the lower courts found the rule was applicable and satisfied, but in one of them the court rejected the plan for other reasons. In another of the cases, the court of appeals ultimately decided against the plan on the basis that the new value rule is altogether dead. The lower court's decision in this case is nevertheless useful in examining how the rule could work where it is available.

Here we mean to direct the reader's consideration to the application of the rule to specific and generic sets of facts. The first two cases, *Greystone*[3] and *Marston*,[4] are known in the bankruptcy trade as "single asset" cases. In both, the debtor's single asset was a piece of developed real estate. In *Marston* it was an apartment complex of 184 units; in *Greystone* it was a commercial building in Austin, Texas. The fourth case is *Jartran*.[5] *Jartran* lies at the opposite end of the complexity spectrum from *Greystone* and *Marston*. It involved the operation of a large, nationwide going-concern that was operated in Chapter 11 for almost three years by the purchasing shareholder. Only the third modification of the fifth plan was approved in *Jartran* and that case required the negotiation with and the agreement of many different creditors—secured, trade, general unsecured and unsecured holding claims such as lawsuits. The third case, *Potter Material*,[6] lies somewhere between the others. Potter was a modest operating business. A controlling shareholder operated the business, proposed the plan and was the beneficiary of the new value exception. We will first recount the facts of each of the four cases and then use them as a basis for considering the theoretical arguments in favor of and against the new value exception to the absolute priority rule.

In re Greystone III Joint Venture[7]

In *Greystone* the bankruptcy and district courts approved a plan over the objection of Phoenix Mutual Life Insurance Company, the mortgagee on a commercial building. The plan proposed to give Phoenix the present value of the mortgaged premises and in addition to pay three cents on the dollar to the trade debt and on Phoenix's $3,475,000 deficiency. The plan would also pay taxes of more than $108,000 and "assure payment" of 75 percent of the tenants' security deposit claims. The partners proposed to keep their interest by making a contribution of $500,000 to the estate. This new value was to be used to pay the items specified above, including the 3 percent dividend to Phoenix. Phoenix objected that the plan was not fair and equitable.

---

3. In re Greystone III Joint Venture, 102 B.R. 560 (Bankr.W.D.Tex.1989), aff'd, 127 B.R. 138 (W.D.Tex.1990), rev'd, 948 F.2d 134 (5th Cir.1991).

4. 13 B.R. 514 (Bankr. E.D.N.Y.1981).

5. 44 B.R. 331 (Bankr. N.D.Ill. 1984).

6. 781 F.2d 99 (7th Cir.1986).

7. 102 B.R. 560 (Bankr.W.D.Tex.1989), aff'd, 127 B.R. 138 (W.D.Tex.1990), rev'd, 948 F.2d 134 (5th Cir.1991).

In finding that the new value exception was satisfied, the bankruptcy court rejected Phoenix's argument. It made no findings about the going-concern value of the partnership. The court noted Phoenix had indicated its willingness to pay off the unsecured creditors, complete the tenant "finish out obligations", but found that it was not a source of "working capital" because Phoenix would not make any such payment unless it could take over ownership of the property. In a telling footnote, Judge Clark emphatically rejects the theory under which Judge Easterbrook and other commentators have proceeded, namely, the theory that the existing owners were "purchasing" the company for the new value and that they have a right to do so only to the extent that they give greater new value than others would give. Judge Clark responds to that suggestion as follows:

> It is important to emphasize that, due to the nature of the *Case* capital infusion exception, it is inappropriate to approach the problem as though the ownership of the entire enterprise were up for sale. That is simply not the issue at all. Instead the question is whether there is an available source of capital to fund the plan * * *. In other words, the issue of where to get the cash to make the plan work is not an opportunity to undermine the plan. Instead, if the plan *fails*, then another party in the case with standing may propose an alternative plan.[8]

The district court agreed with Judge Clark but, in the end, the court of appeals reversed, finding that the new value rule did not survive enactment of the Code.[9] We consider the Judge Clark's opinion anyway, as an example of how the rule can be applied where it is law.

In re Marston Enterprises, Inc.[10]

The shareholders[11] proposed to purchase the sole asset of Marston Enterprises, an apartment complex containing 184 units. They proposed to pay $900,000 for the complex and to take title to it. The payment was to go to the holder of the first mortgage for a mortgage debt of $2,300,000. The unsecured portion of the mortgage debt, $1,400,000, was to be discharged with no payment, as were the claims of other unsecured creditors. The new value apparently constituted the $900,000 together with some other undetermined contribution to future operating expenses allegedly equal to $300,000 to $400,000. The plan was rejected because the shareholders had not been clever enough to construct even one class who would vote for the plan, and thus it did not qualify under section 1129(a)(10). In *dictum*, the court, nevertheless, concluded that the new value exception had been met and presumably would have approved the plan but for the failure of an impaired class to vote for it. Had the plan been approved, the mortgagor would successfully have written the mortgage down to the amount found by the court to be the value of the property. Having discharged all of its unsecured

---

8. Id. at 577 n.22.
9. 948 F.2d 134, rev'g, 127 B.R. 138 (W.D.Tex.1990), aff'g, 102 B.R. 560 (Bankr. W.D.Tex.1989).
10. 13 B.R. 514 (Bankr. E.D.N.Y.1981).
11. The parties were actually shareholders of a co-debtor but were found to be the "shareholders."

debt with no payment, the debtor would have kept for itself the going-concern value, if any, over the $900,000. Here one might regard this "value" as a call option on any increase in value of the real estate.

Potter Material Service, Inc.[12]

In *Potter Material* the debtor proposed a payment of 3 percent to the unsecured creditors. The controlling shareholder proposed to keep the equity in the company by guaranteeing certain debt and by contributing $34,800 of new value. Twenty thousand of this new value was to pay off the debtor's lawyer for his representation of the debtor in bankruptcy and the other $14,800 was to fund the 3 percent payment to the unsecured creditors.

The Court of Appeals for the Seventh Circuit affirmed a finding that the new value exception had been satisfied. The court concluded that this payment equalled the going-concern value of the company. There is no finding whether the going-concern value was considered in setting the 3 percent payment to the unsecured creditors or whether that number was arrived at by determining liquidation value of the company. In its brief, the creditors' committee complained that the controlling shareholder had drawn excessive payments out of the company before the bankruptcy and argued that he would do so afterwards. In effect, the creditors argued that the shareholder took the going-concern value for himself in the form of salary and personal expense payments.

Jartran[13]

Jartran Truck and Trailer Rental Company competed with U-Haul, Ryder Systems, and Hertz in the market for rental of trucks and of trailers to be pulled by automobiles. Formed in 1978, the company began having economic difficulties as early as 1980. The difficulties intensified in 1981 and the owners sought a joint venture or a buyout partner. Early in 1981 the controlling shareholders signed a letter of intent to sell the company to Ameribond Securities Associates. That transaction contemplated the sale of a majority interest for a "capital infusion" of possibly $20 million. Ultimately the Ameribond deal fell through. In December of 1981 the Jartran shareholders struck a deal with Frank B. Hall and Co. Inc. Under the terms of the December 31, 1981 agreement, Hall agreed to purchase most of the shares of Jartran from the various shareholders. Although Hall acquired the stock on that date, most of the payments for the stock were deferred and contingent. On the same day (and presumably at Hall's direction) Jartran filed a petition under Chapter 11. For approximately three years Hall ran the company, negotiated with the creditors and proposed various Chapter 11 plans. On September 29, 1984, Judge Fisher confirmed the third modification of Hall's fifth plan.[14] Hall's principal antagonist was U-Haul who presumably had various legitimate and perhaps some illegitimate interests in Jartran's future. In an opinion of more than 80 pages, Judge Fisher confirmed the plan over a multitude of objections by U-Haul.

12. 781 F.2d 99 (7th Cir.1986).
13. 44 B.R. 331 (Bankr. N.D.Ill. 1984).
14. In re Jartran, 44 B.R. 331 (Bankr. N.D.Ill. 1984).

The opinion well demonstrates the complexity of such a plan and the difficult judgments that have to be made in applying the best interest rule, the absolute priority rule, and other provisions of section 1129.

Among other things U–Haul complained that Hall, as the principal shareholder, did not meet the new value exception in the case.[15] Aided by extensive and expert testimony from various financial experts, the court made explicit findings not only about the liquidation value of the company, but also about its going-concern value and the value of the shareholders' equity. The court addressed the new value exception as follows:

> The Court's estimate of the updated value of shareholders' equity is negative $18,500,000, being the difference between the $52,500,000 going concern value and the $71,000,000 value of debt. Accordingly, one aspect of the *Los Angeles Lumber* test is satisfied. Inasmuch as the shareholders' equity is valueless, any contribution by Hall will necessarily be equal to or greater than the value of its 100% ownership interest.
>
> The Court further finds that Hall is the most feasible source of the new capital and that its contribution is necessary to assure the viability of reorganized Jartran. As explained in greater detail *infra* in connection with U–Haul's contentions concerning § 1129(a)(3), the company was marketed for a substantial period prior to the filing of the petition herein. Other than the proposed Hall acquisition, no firm commitment for financing was obtained. Nor has Debtor received any such commitments since the filing of the petition on December 31, 1981. After a review of the entire record, the Court is satisfied that the Hall contribution is necessary to Jartran's successful reorganization within the purview of the *Los Angeles Lumber* decision.[16]

To support its position the court noted that debtor engaged in a "thorough marketing effort, wherein the tax attributes were disclosed and highlighted. No viable offers materialized other than that of Hall." [17]

Hall's contribution of new value constituted several million dollars of guarantees, a $5,000,000 equity contribution, and a commitment to an investment of $52,000,000 to acquire certain secured claims. Apparently the $52,000,000 "investment" was Hall's purchase of the position of two of the secured creditors, Ford and Chrysler. In effect this constituted a $52,000,000 loan to Jartran by Hall. The court approved the plan.

§ 11–30 Applying the Exception—Arguing Against the Exception

For full text of this section, see Epstein, Nickles & White, Bankruptcy, Practitioner Treatise Series, Vol. 3.

F. BANKRUPTCIES INVOLVING PARTNERSHIPS
§ 11–31 Introduction

For full text of this section, see Epstein, Nickles & White, Bankruptcy, Practitioner Treatise Series, Vol. 3.

---

15. The absence of any discussion of the question whether the new value exception had survived passage of the 1978 Code suggests that that argument was not made by U–Haul.

16. Id. at 379.

17. 44 B.R. at 381 n.114.

§ 11–32 Liability of Partnerships and General Partners to the Creditors of Each

For full text of this section, see Epstein, Nickles & White, Bankruptcy, Practitioner Treatise Series, Vol. 3.

§ 11–33 Priority

For full text of this section, see Epstein, Nickles & White, Bankruptcy, Practitioner Treatise Series, Vol. 3.

§ 11–34 Staying Creditors

For full text of this section, see Epstein, Nickles & White, Bankruptcy, Practitioner Treatise Series, Vol. 3.

§ 11–35 Staying Creditors—Automatic Stay, Section 362

For full text of this section, see Epstein, Nickles & White, Bankruptcy, Practitioner Treatise Series, Vol. 3.

§ 11–36 Staying Creditors—Injunctions, Section 105

For full text of this section, see Epstein, Nickles & White, Bankruptcy, Practitioner Treatise Series, Vol. 3.

§ 11–37 Partner Bankruptcy Effects on the Enforcement of the Partnership Agreement

For full text of this section, see Epstein, Nickles & White, Bankruptcy, Practitioner Treatise Series, Vol. 3.

§ 11–38 Partner Bankruptcy Effects on the Enforcement of the Partnership Agreement—Assumption, Assignment and Rejection: Sections 365(c) and 365(e)

For full text of this section, see Epstein, Nickles & White, Bankruptcy, Practitioner Treatise Series, Vol. 3.

§ 11–39 Partner Bankruptcy Effects on the Enforcement of the Partnership Agreement—Partner's Settlement and Contribution

For full text of this section, see Epstein, Nickles & White, Bankruptcy, Practitioner Treatise Series, Vol. 3.

G. SUBSTANTIVE CONSOLIDATION

§ 11–40 Meaning and Reasons

For full text of this section, see Epstein, Nickles & White, Bankruptcy, Practitioner Treatise Series, Vol. 3.

§ 11–41 Cases and Rules

For full text of this section, see Epstein, Nickles & White, Bankruptcy, Practitioner Treatise Series, Vol. 3.

Chapter 12

JURISDICTION AND PROCEDURE

Table of Sections

Sec.

A. Jurisdiction and Allocation of Judicial Power

12–1 Introduction and Overview.
12–2 *Marathon* and the Core Proceeding.
12–3 ____ Related Proceedings.
12–4 Personal Injury Cases.
12–5 Abstention.

B. Venue

12–6 Venue of Cases, Section 1408(1).
12–7 ____ Affiliates, Section 1408(2).
12–8 Venue of Proceeding, Section 1409.
12–9 Change of Venue, Section 1412.
12–10 ____ Proper Venue.
12–11 ____ Improper Venue.

C. Appeals

12–12 Appeals.

D. Jury Trial

12–13 The Right to Jury Trial.
12–14 ____ *Granfinanciera*.
12–15 ____ Jury Cases After *Granfinanciera*.
12–16 Which Judge Presides.

A. JURISDICTION AND ALLOCATION OF JUDICIAL POWER

§ 12–1 Introduction and Overview

The basic grant of jurisdiction in bankruptcy cases by the Congress is 28 U.S.C.A. § 1334. The principal subsections, (a) and (b), read in full as follows:

(a) Except as provided in subsection (b) of this section, the district courts shall have original and exclusive jurisdiction of all cases under title 11.

(b) Notwithstanding any Act of Congress that confers exclusive jurisdiction on a court or courts other than the district courts, the district courts shall have original but not exclusive jurisdiction of all civil proceedings arising under title 11, or arising in or related to cases under title 11.

One might think that the grant of jurisdiction in a specialized area such as bankruptcy would be a simple matter attended by little confusion and no serious conflict. The first reading of the two subsections above should begin to give one doubt about that conclusion. Note, first, that they grant jurisdiction not to the bankruptcy court and the bankruptcy judge where we all know most cases are heard and decided, but to the "district courts." Can it be that all one has read in the papers about the decisions by people called "bankruptcy judges" is fictitious? One's doubt about the certainty and meaning of the language becomes more profound as he compares subsections (a) and (b). The first grants "original and exclusive jurisdiction of all cases"; the second says the district court shall have "original but not exclusive jurisdiction of all civil proceedings * * *." How can the district court have original and exclusive jurisdiction and original, but not exclusive jurisdiction at the same time?

The quoted sections and the resulting rules that we will study in this chapter are the stinking broth composed of a long history in which the bankruptcy court grew from a purely administrative arm of the district court, supervised by persons called "referees", into a recognized and fixed court supervised by people called bankruptcy judges who behave in all respects like other judges. This history has been spiced with a 1982 Supreme Court case *Northern Pipeline Constr. Co. v. Marathon Pipe Line Co.*[1] in which the Supreme Court found that bankruptcy judges, as Article I judges, could not hear cases like *Marathon* under the Constitution. To hear these cases required the life tenure of an Article III judge. In effect, *Marathon* destroyed the 1978 act's jurisdictional basis. That history and the lessons of the *Marathon* case have been combined with substantial parts of national and judicial politics to provide 28 U.S.C.A. § 157, the section to which we will soon turn.

After *Marathon*, Congress was strongly affected by several political forces that were pulling on it. Some in Congress wished to make bankruptcy judges Article III judges and so solve the problem. Others in Congress did not wish to grant President Reagan the power to give lifetime appointment to the large number of bankruptcy judges that had to be appointed. The existing Article III judges, always jealous of their prerogatives, were also not receptive to the idea that bankruptcy judges would be elevated to their level or, indeed, to the idea that the President should continue to appoint them. Rather they wished to have the power to appoint bankruptcy judges, power they had had prior to 1978, as an item of local political patronage.

In an attempt to solve the Article I/Article III issue presented by *Marathon,* the Congress gave bankruptcy jurisdiction not directly to the bankruptcy court, but apparently (as we have seen in 28 U.S.C.A. § 1334) to the district court. Under a section ingenuously labeled "Procedures," 28 U.S.C.A. § 157, the Congress provided as follows:

> (a) Each district court may provide that any or all cases under title 11 and any or all proceedings arising under title 11 or arising in or

§ 12–1

1. 458 U.S. 50, 102 S.Ct. 2858, 73 L.Ed.2d 598 (1982), judgment stayed, 459 U.S. 813, 103 S.Ct. 199, 74 L.Ed.2d 160 (1982).

related to a case under title 11 shall be referred to the bankruptcy judges for the district.

In effect the Congress was saying the district court had jurisdiction, but that the district court in one way or another could delegate some parts of this to the bankruptcy judges.[2] Many who wrote on the issue doubted that Congress thereby solved the Article I/Article III issue raised by *Marathon*,[3] but it seems likely that the Supreme Court has tired of the question and does not wish to throw the courts into chaos one more time. Conceivably we have seen a de facto reversal of the *Marathon* decision.[4]

That still does not explain why subsection (a) gives exclusive and original jurisdiction while subsection (b) seems to give original, but not exclusive jurisdiction to the same courts. A closer reading of the two subsections will show that subsection (a) applies to "all cases under title 11" while subsection (b) applies to "all civil proceedings arising under title 11 or arising in or related to cases under title 11." One might ask how could it be that these are different? Is not a bankruptcy case, whether in Chapter 7 or Chapter 11, a bankruptcy case which is to be filed in all cases in the bankruptcy court? The answer is yes and no. The bankruptcy case itself, described under 28 U.S.C.A. § 1334(a), is filed in the bankruptcy court (under the delegation provisions from the district court) but it is a mistake to regard a "bankruptcy case" to be the same as a conventional criminal or civil law "case." In fact, a large bankruptcy may constitute a single case, but it is a case which includes as sub-plots, tens or possibly even hundreds or thousands of other "proceedings" that are themselves civil disputes between various parties.

Consider the famous *Manville* case. Manville filed bankruptcy because it was being beset by tens of thousands of plaintiffs in asbestos cases. Each of those plaintiffs had a "claim" against Manville and had Manville gone through a routine bankruptcy, each would have had to have been admitted or proved by the plaintiff in an individual "proceeding." During the course

---

2. Congress attempted to ameliorate the Constitutional problem somewhat by allowing the district court to withdraw the reference of cases and proceedings from the bankruptcy court. 28 U.S.C.A. § 157(d). See Holland America Insurance Co. v. Succession of Roy, 777 F.2d 992 (5th Cir.1985). Congress went further in the second sentence of § 157(d) to require mandatory withdrawal of reference "if the court determines that resolution of the proceeding requires consideration of both title 11 and other laws of the United States regulating organizations or activities affecting interstate commerce." There has, however, been little agreement as to the interpretation of the mandatory withdrawal clause. See generally 1 Collier on Bankruptcy ¶ 3.01 at 3–61–69 (15th ed. 1979).

3. Countryman, The Bankruptcy Judges: Jurisdiction By Neglect, 92 Com. L.J. 1 (1987); King, A Chart of Bankruptcy Jurisdiction for Admiralty Lawyers, 59 Tulane L. Rev. 1264, 1275 (1985).

4. One consequence of Marathon has been the doubt cast upon the contempt power of the bankruptcy judge under the Constitution. After the 1984 amendments there was nothing left in the legislation that dealt directly with the contempt power. While some courts have construed section 105 of the Code as granting civil contempt authority, others have denied such grant and held further that, since they are not Article III judges, bankruptcy judges have no inherent power to punish for contempt. See In re Walters, 868 F.2d 665 (4th Cir.1989), where it was held that a bankruptcy judge was authorized to hold an attorney in civil contempt pursuant to § 105 where the attorney had failed to comply with an order of the court. The court also found that there was no separation of powers problem with a bankruptcy judge exercising civil contempt powers. But see In re Sequoia Auto Brokers Ltd., Inc., 827 F.2d 1281 (9th Cir.1987), where bankruptcy judges were found to possess neither the statutory nor inherent authority to exercise the power of contempt.

§ 12–1   JURISDICTION AND PROCEDURE   859

of a bankruptcy like *Manville,* there would be tens or hundreds of cases in which the debtor in possession would seek to lease goods, sell them, or make other specific investment or incur indebtedness. Various creditors and possibly shareholders might object to such proposals. Each time there was such an objection to the extent it was to be heard by the bankruptcy judge, it too would constitute an independent "proceeding," a sub-plot in the *Manville* play.

Particularly in a large Chapter 11 case, therefore, it is not accurate to think of the case as an individual civil case, but rather to think of it as a combination of cases involving a variety of issues concerning the operation of the business, the interpretation of the Bankruptcy Code and its application to the particular facts and the interpretation and application of state law rules on contract, priorities, and other matters. That explains why there is "original and exclusive" jurisdiction of all "cases" but only original and not exclusive jurisdiction of "civil proceedings."

What we have said above still does not explain why there is any jurisdictional confusion. Why is not all litigation now heard in the bankruptcy court (at least if the district court delegates); why does that not end the jurisdictional question? We return to section 1334(b). Note that it does not provide for all proceedings to be heard in the bankruptcy court, only those "arising under title 11 or arising in or related to cases under title 11." The three descriptions, *arising under, arising in, and related,* are themselves terms of art. Although it is quite unclear which cases are to be excluded from bankruptcy court jurisdiction, it is clear that there must be some such cases after *Marathon.*

In general, cases arising under or arising in might be regarded as more central to the bankruptcy adjudication than those that are merely "related to" the case. Thus, for example, determination whether a particular creditor actually had a claim against the debtor's estate surely "arises under or in" the case. On the other hand, a debtor's right to recover damages for a tort committed by a third party prior to the bankruptcy would at most be "related to". Or, for example, litigation over the status of a trucking company's continuing rights under its license would be merely "related."

Although we will grapple with the problem of distinction among these proceedings, we will see that the problem gets more, not less, complex when one looks at 28 U.S.C.A. § 157. That subsection introduces the idea of "core" versus "non-core" proceedings. In our view, core is generally synonymous with "arising under" and "arising in," and the finding that a proceeding "arises under" or is a "core proceeding" has the same practical consequence.

What is that practical consequence? If the matter is a core proceeding or one arising under or in a Chapter 11, the debtor in possession can normally force the proceeding to be heard in the bankruptcy court even though the other party objects. If the matter is not a core proceeding and the other party seeks to have the case heard outside of the bankruptcy court, that party will often be successful even over the objection of the debtor in possession.

§ 12–2 Marathon and the Core Proceeding

In *Northern Pipeline Constr. Co. v. Marathon Pipe Line Co.*,[1] the debtor in possession sought to sue Marathon Pipe Line for breach of a prepetition contract. Thus, the debtor in possession was the plaintiff and the third party the defendant. The debtor in possession brought the action in the bankruptcy court. The defendant maintained that there was no proper jurisdiction in the bankruptcy court and furthermore that Congress lacked the power to authorize the bankruptcy court to hear such a case. The Supreme Court agreed with the defendant and held that Congress lacked the authority to grant jurisdiction to an Article I court to hear a proceeding as remote from the bankruptcy case itself as this one.[2] Note, this was not a case in which the defendant had itself asserted a claim against the bankruptcy estate (so that the debtor in possession's suit might be regarded as a counterclaim) nor was it a case in any way directly related to the bankruptcy case, such as a claim about preferences, a challenge to a security interest, or a question concerning the administration of the assets of the debtor in possession.

As we have indicated above, the *Marathon* decision left the courts in chaos and the Congress in a state of indecision. After two years Congress sought to solve the problem first by granting jurisdiction generally to an Article III court, namely the district court, and then authorizing (by section 157) that the jurisdiction be delegated to the bankruptcy court. The Congress apparently recognized still that under *Marathon* some cases should not be handled even by a federal district judge. Accordingly it enacted 28 U.S.C.A. § 1334(c)(2) which provided that even the district court, and *a fortiori* the bankruptcy court, should abstain from exercising jurisdiction in a proceeding based upon a state law cause of action:

> "related to * * * but not arising under * * * or arising in title 11 with respect to which an action could not have been commenced in a court of the United States absent jurisdiction under this section, * * * if an action is commenced, and can be timely adjudicated in a state forum or appropriate jurisdiction."

The conditions under which the district courts are required to abstain are so narrow that it is doubtful that many such cases exist.[3] Indeed, it is unclear what would happen if the *Marathon* case were reincarnated. In *Marathon* it is not clear that an action had been "commenced" when the claim was asserted in bankruptcy court.

Using language that first appeared in the *Marathon* case, the Congress defined the cases within the bankruptcy court jurisdiction as "core proceedings arising in a case under title 11" and defined the others as non-core proceedings. As we have indicated above, core is roughly equivalent to

---

§ 12–2

1. 458 U.S. 50, 102 S.Ct. 2858, 73 L.Ed.2d 598 (1982), judgment stayed, 459 U.S. 813, 103 S.Ct. 199, 74 L.Ed.2d 160.

2. Justice Brennan announced the Court's judgment and delivered an opinion in which Justices Marshall, Blackmun and Stevens joined. Justice Rehnquist filed an opinion concurring in the judgment in which Justice O'Connor joined. Chief Justice Burger filed a dissenting opinion. Justice White filed a dissenting opinion in which Chief Justice Burger and Justice Powell joined. The constitutional question regarding Article III, therefore, represents only a plurality, while the judgment itself was affirmed by the majority.

3. For a discussion of abstention issues and case law see infra at § 12–5.

arising in or arising under in the old vernacular, and non-core to those *not* arising in or arising under but "related." Section 157(b)(2) of 28 U.S.C.A. defines core proceedings to include the following:

(A) matters concerning the administration of the estate;

(B) allowance or disallowance of claims against the estate or exemptions from property of the estate, and estimations of claims or interest for the purposes of confirming a plan under chapter 11, 12, or 13 of title 11 but not the liquidation or estimation of contingent or unliquidated personal injury tort or wrongful death claims against the estate for purposes of distribution in a case under title 11;

(C) counterclaims by the estate against persons filing claims against the estate;

(D) orders in respect to obtaining credit;

(E) orders to turn over property of the estate;

(F) proceedings to determine, avoid, or recover preferences;

(G) motions to terminate, annul or modify the automatic stay;

(H) proceedings to determine, avoid, or recover fraudulent conveyances;

(I) determinations as to the dischargeability of particular debts;

(J) objections to discharges;

(K) determinations of the validity, extent, or priority of liens;

(L) confirmations of plans;

(M) orders approving the use or lease of property, including the use of cash collateral;

(N) orders approving the sale of property other than property resulting from claims brought by the estate against persons who have not filed claims against the estate; and

(O) other proceedings affecting the liquidation of the assets of the estate or the adjustment of the debtor-creditor or the equity security holder relationship, except personal injury tort or wrongful death claims.

If the proceeding is not listed in section (b)(2) and not otherwise included as "core" by some other unarticulated principle, the bankruptcy judge is not permitted to "hear and determine" the case unless the parties consent to the court's jurisdiction under 28 U.S.C.A. § 157(c)(2). If the parties do not consent, the bankruptcy judge's authority under section 157(c)(1) is merely to "submit proposed findings of fact and conclusions of law to the district court" with the understanding that the judgment will be entered by the district judge after considering those findings and conclusions. The Supreme Court's recent holding that a jury trial is appropriate in a core proceeding has, however, partially undermined the importance of deeming a proceeding as "core." [4]

---

4. Granfinanciera v. Nordberg, 492 U.S. 33, 109 S.Ct. 2782, 106 L.Ed.2d 26 (1989). For a full discussion of this case, see our § 12-14 infra. The Court granted a jury trial under the Seventh Amendment to a defendant in a fraudulent conveyance action even though the

Let us now turn to the examples of core proceedings listed in section 157(b)(2). A large number of all of the actions in a given day or week of the bankruptcy judge will fit within and be authorized by subsection (A) "matters concerning administration of the estate." Those would include things such as setting attorneys' fees, approving reports of creditors' committees, making findings on the use of property under 363, and proposals for borrowing under 364.

In addition, subparagraph (A) has been used to authorize actions further removed than those described in the last paragraph. For example, it has been used to support finding that a motion to enjoin a state court is a core proceeding,[5] as well as a proceeding to determine if the automatic stay has been violated [6] and a motion to reject an executory contract.[7] The general administrative authorization in (A) is supplemented by more specific administrative provisions in (D)(the automatic stay), (L)(confirmation of plans), and (I)(power to determine dischargeability of debts).

Even so, some sections of (b)(2) are an expansion of the bankruptcy court's powers as they existed prior to 1978. Under the Act of 1898 the avoidance of fraudulent conveyances and preferences was not a part of the bankruptcy court's "summary jurisdiction" unless the property involved was in the actual or constructive possession of the court or unless the defendant had submitted itself to the bankruptcy court's jurisdiction. Since the actions in (F) and (H) are based on rights emanating directly from the Code, there is no reason why they should not be considered to be core or why they should be found without the constitutional limitations set down in *Marathon*.[8]

Other provisions in the list allow the court to exercise full authority over property in the estate. These provisions are subparagraphs (E), which allows for turnover of property of the estate, (K), which allows the bankruptcy judge to determine "the validity, extent, or priority of liens," (M) which provides for core status in hearings for approving the use or lease of property, including the use of cash collateral, and (N), which deals with the sale of property. Here one begins to see an interplay of state rights and rights arising out of the Bankruptcy Code. For example, a determination of the validity or priority of a lien is likely to depend not merely on state law, but also upon federal law.

---

proceeding was core. The practical significance of this is, of course, that the jury, and not the bankruptcy judge will issue the final order in the proceeding. While the Supreme Court did impose some limitations on the exercise of this jury trial right, bankruptcy courts have already extended it to other core actions. See, e.g., In re Paris Industries Corporation, 106 B.R. 344 (Bankr. D.Me.1989) (applied to preference); In re Kroh Bros. Development Co., 108 B.R. 710 (Bankr. W.D.Mo.1989) (applied to preference); In re Owensboro Distilling Co., 108 B.R. 572 (Bankr. W.D.Ky.1989) (applied to trustee's section 723 action to recover personal assets from general partners).

5. In re Johns–Manville Corp., 801 F.2d 60 (2d Cir.1986), on remand, 66 B.R. 517 (Bankr. S.D.N.Y.1986), relying on subparagraph (A) to find a motion to have a state court enjoined from forcing debtor in possession to call a shareholder meeting a core proceeding; In re Davis, 730 F.2d 176, 183–184 (5th Cir.1984).

6. In re Turbowind, Inc., 42 B.R. 579 (Bankr. S.D.Cal.1984).

7. Id.

8. In re Associated Grocers of Nebraska Coop., Inc., 62 B.R. 439 (D.Neb.1986), holding subparagraph (F) constitutional; accord In re Northwest Cinema Corp., 49 B.R. 479 (Bankr. D.Minn.1985); In re Acme–Dunham, Inc. 45 B.R. 227 (Bankr. D.Me.1984); but see In re TWI, Inc., 51 B.R. 470 (Bankr. E.D.Va.1985), judgment rev'd, 68 B.R. 487 (Bankr. E.D.Va. 1986), holding that fraudulent conveyance was based on state law and therefore section 157 is afoul of Marathon, for it cannot "cover the sins" of the former legislation by simply making referral discretionary.

Among these provisions subparagraph (E) allowing orders to "turn over property of the estate" has been the center of significant controversy. Carried to its absolute extreme this subparagraph would allow the bankruptcy court to decide virtually all state law claims. If, for example, one defined a contract claim by the debtor in possession against a third party to be "property of the estate," then subparagraph (E) would authorize the bankruptcy court to hear the "turnover" case and do the very thing that was prohibited in *Marathon*. The courts thus far have been unwilling to classify mere contract claims as core.[9] However, some courts have said that matured accounts receivable are "property" of the kind described in the order for their turnover as a core proceeding.[10] In effect, these courts define the word "property," for purposes of subparagraph (E), by drawing the line between something which is sufficiently fixed and of recognized value to be described as property and something else which is sufficiently contingent that it should be called merely a contract claim which does not constitute property. Given that an action to collect an account receivable is virtually nothing more nor less than a contract claim, we doubt the utility of drawing such distinction, but see little way to avoid such arguments in the face of *Marathon* and section 157(b)(2)(E).

Subparagraph (C), without the benefit or the burden of history, would suggest that all counterclaims brought by the debtor in possession against those who have filed claims against the bankruptcy estate are themselves core proceedings and can be heard by the bankruptcy judge. Under the Act of 1898, the filing of a proof of claim was deemed to be a consent to the bankruptcy court's jurisdiction, but only as to compulsory counterclaims or as to those arising out of the same transaction or occurrence as the original claim. Under the Act of 1898 the courts never reached a consensus on the question whether permissive counterclaims could be filed by the trustee under the bankruptcy court's jurisdiction.[11]

9. In re World Solar Corp., 81 B.R. 603 (Bankr. S.D.Cal.1988), holding that bankrupt's claims of breach of contract, declaratory relief, interference with prospective economic advantage, and bad faith breach of contract were non-core; see also In re Republic Reader's Service, Inc., 81 B.R. 422 (Bankr. S.D.Tex. 1987).

10. In re Total Transportation, Inc., 87 B.R. 568 (Bankr. D.Minn.1988), which held that pre-petition undercharges were matured debts owed to the estate under 11 U.S.C.A. § 542(b). As such, an action to turnover these amounts owed was a core proceeding under § 157(b)(2)(E); cf. In re Cassidy Land & Cattle Co., Inc. (Craig v. McCarthy Ranch Trust), 836 F.2d 1130 (8th Cir.1988), cert. denied, 486 U.S. 1033, 108 S.Ct. 2016, 100 L.Ed.2d 603 (1988); but see, St. George Island, Ltd. v. Pelham, 104 B.R. 429 (Bankr. N.D.Fla.1989), which held that an action to collect a prepetition note receivable was similar to the action the Supreme Court addressed in Marathon, see supra, and thus was noncore. The court adopted an approach which would treat all actions to recover prepetition debts as non-core. In general, the court felt compelled to take a restrictive view of actions that could be characterized as core. This restrictive view was based upon the reaffirmation of "Marathon's restrictions on the power of the Bankruptcy judge" by the Supreme Court in Granfinanciera v. Nordberg, 492 U.S. 33, 109 S.Ct. 2782, 106 L.Ed.2d 26 (1989). For a full discussion of the Granfinanciera case, see, infra at 12–14. See also Christison v. Caterpillar, Inc., 74 B.R. 373 (Bankr. C.D.Ill. 1987); In re Maislin Indus., U.S., Inc., 50 B.R. 943 (Bankr. E.D.Mich.1985). For a discussion of accounts receivable, see infra at note 19.

11. For examples of cases which held that consent only subjects compulsory counterclaims to the bankruptcy court's jurisdiction, see, Inter-State National Bank of Kansas City v. Luther, 221 F.2d 382 (10th Cir.1955), cert. granted, 350 U.S. 810, 76 S.Ct. 77, 100 L.Ed. 726 (1955); Katchen v. Landy, 382 U.S. 323, 86 S.Ct. 467, 15 L.Ed.2d 391 (1966). For examples of cases which held that bankruptcy jurisdiction through consent encompassed both compulsory and permissive counterclaims, see, Cherno v. Engine Air Service, Inc., 330 F.2d

Although subparagraph (C) would seem to endorse the extension of bankruptcy court jurisdiction to permissive as well as compulsory counterclaims, that is not clear. Surely subsection (C) should not be read to give more limited powers to the bankruptcy court than recognized by pre-1978 bankruptcy judges. But several courts have held that permissive counterclaims not related to the claim itself cannot be asserted under the core authority of the bankruptcy court.[12] These cases seem wrong to us; we see no reason not to indulge the fiction that the party filing a claim consents not merely to compulsory counterclaims but also to other counterclaims that are not directly related and are not necessarily compulsory.[13]

The catchall provision in (b)(2)(O) that authorizes as core all proceedings "affecting the liquidation of the assets of the estate or the adjustment of the debtor, creditor, or equity security holder relationship" is broad enough to swallow up almost every conceivable non-core proceeding and to transform it into a core proceeding. Recognizing this fact, some courts have cautioned that it should be read in a fairly limited fashion.[14] Others, however, have used it to hear and decide proceedings which were seemingly prohibited by *Marathon*. For example, in *In re Lion Capital Group*[15] the court found that (O) authorized the bankruptcy court to collect capital contributions from a limited partner because the limited partners should be considered to be "equity security holders." Another court used the subsection to authorize the collection of a prepetition account receivable.[16] A final example involved the use of (O) by a bankruptcy court to rule that an action against former directors, officers and professionals for breach of fiduciary duty was core.[17] These cases come perilously close to a complete rejection of the principles in *Marathon*.[18]

While earlier we expressed skepticism over the utility of distinguishing accounts receivable from a contract claim because of their virtual equality, courts have seemingly placed accounts receivable teetering on the line that divides core and non-core proceedings. For this reason they are given

191 (2d Cir.1964); In re Carnell Constr. Co., 424 F.2d 296 (3d Cir.1970), cert.denied, 400 U.S. 828, 91 S.Ct. 56, 27 L.Ed.2d 58 (1970); see generally 2 Collier on Bankruptcy ¶ 23.08 at 557 (14th ed. 1976).

12. See, e.g., In re Oxford Marketing, Ltd., 444 F.Supp. 399, 402 (N.D.Ill. 1978); In re Aerni, 86 B.R. 203, 205 (Bankr. D.Neb.1988) (a bankruptcy court has subject matter jurisdiction to adjudicate a counterclaim in an adversary proceeding if there is an independent jurisdictional basis for the counterclaim, or if the counterclaim is compulsory and the court has ancillary power under 28 U.S.C.A. § 1334).

13. See Macon Prestressed Concrete Co. v. Duke, 46 B.R. 727 (M.D.Ga.1985); contra In re Lombard–Wall, Inc., 48 B.R. 986 (S.D.N.Y. 1985) (which suggests that consent may only be implied as to compulsory counterclaims); In re Illinois–California Express, Inc., 50 B.R. 232 (Bankr. D. Co. 1985); In re Nanodata Computer Corp., 52 B.R. 334 (Bankr. W.D.N.Y. 1985), aff'd, 74 B.R. 766 (W.D.N.Y. 1987).

14. In re Wood, 825 F.2d 90 (5th Cir.1987), on remand, 84 B.R. 432 (Bankr. S.D.Miss. 1988); In re Cassidy Land and Cattle Co., Inc., 836 F.2d 1130 (8th Cir.1988), cert. denied sub nom., McCarty Ranch Trust v. Craig, 486 U.S. 1033, 108 S.Ct. 2016, 100 L.Ed.2d 603 (1988); St. George Island, Ltd. v. Pelham, 104 B.R. 429 (Bankr. N.D.Fla.1989).

15. 46 B.R. 850 (Bankr. S.D.N.Y.1985).

16. In re All–American of Ashburn, Inc., 49 B.R. 926 (Bankr. N.D.Ga.1985).

17. In re DeLorean Motor Co., 49 B.R. 900 (Bankr. E.D.Mich.1985).

18. In fact one commentator believes that the foregoing cases decided under (O) are flatly wrong. See 1 Collier on Bankruptcy 3.01 at 3–45 (15th ed. 1979). Several courts have recognized that claims delineated as "contract" cannot be brought under (O). See Mohawk Ind., Inc. v. Robinson Ind., Inc., 46 B.R. 464 (Bankr. D.Mass.1985); In re Morse Elec. Co., 47 B.R. 234 (Bankr. N.D.Ind. 1985); In re Castlerock Properties, 781 F.2d 159 (9th Cir. 1986).

special attention here.[19] In the case of *In re Arnold Print Works, Inc.*[20] the court notes the agreement of the vast majority of opinions that claims based on postpetition accounts receivable ("postpetition claims") are core. *Marathon* is distinguished by the court on the ground that it involved a prepetition claim. Moreover, the *Arnold* court convincingly argues that postpetition claims fall within the literal meaning of subparagraphs (A) and (O) of section 157(b)(2), while plausible arguments can be made for coverage by other subparagraphs including (E).[21] The argument that these actions are core has probably been weakened somewhat by *Granfinanciera v. Nordberg*[22] where the Supreme Court granted a jury right in a core proceeding and implicitly reaffirmed some of the ideas in *Marathon*. In the face of this reaffirmance, lower courts should be hesitant to expand the definition of "core" too far.

For most purposes, and perhaps for all, we assume that "core" encompasses both "arising in" and "arising under." As we have indicated above, the word core has recently crept in and has further complicated an already messy nomenclature. The basic jurisdictional grant of 28 U.S.C.A. § 1334 does not mention core; it speaks only of arising in and arising under and related cases, whereas section 157(b) speaks of "core proceedings" arising under and arising in. It is conceivable that Congress intended some difference. If they did, we do not know what it was and accordingly we proceed in the belief that core is equal to the sum of arising in and arising under.

To summarize and reiterate, if a case is a core proceeding and thus "arising in" or "arising under," there is jurisdiction in the district court and section 157(b)(1) authorizes that court to refer such cases to the bankruptcy judges for hearing and decision.

§ 12–3 Marathon and the Core Proceeding—Related Proceedings

The next set of proceedings are one step removed from core, but still with some relationship to the bankruptcy case. These are "related" proceedings. By inference "related" proceedings are excluded from the core definition by 28 U.S.C.A. § 157(b)(1). This section gives jurisdiction to the district court for proceedings "related to" cases under title 11, but does not authorize the district court to grant the bankruptcy court judges power to hear such cases. These cases are governed by section 157(c)(1) which states:

---

19. Evidence that accounts receivable have, and continue to be, a unique problem for courts is seen in the number of conflicting decisions. In the context of a suit based on prepetition accounts receivable ("prepetition claims") authority can be cited for either proposition—that the suit is core or non-core. For a list of cases which hold that a suit to collect a prepetition account receivable is a core proceeding and another list which says it is not, see, In re Total Transportation, Inc., 87 B.R. 568, 572 (D.Minn.1988). The court in Total adopted the position that collection of prepetition accounts receivable was core. For another list of cases and contra holding, see, St. George Island, Ltd. v. Pelham, 104 B.R. 429, 431 (Bankr.N.D. Fla. 1989); see also Note, Jurisdiction of Bankruptcy Courts in Accounts Receivable Actions, 4 Bankr. Dev. J. 257 (1987).

20. 815 F.2d 165 (1st Cir.1987); see also Valley Forge Plaza Associates v. Fireman's Fund Ins. Companies, 107 B.R. 514 (E.D.Pa. 1989) (extending Arnold to other postpetition contract claims).

21. 815 F.2d at 168; 1 Collier on Bankruptcy 3.01 at 3–48 (15th ed. 1979).

22. 492 U.S. 33, 109 S.Ct. 2782, 106 L.Ed.2d 26 (1989). For a full discussion, see § 12–14 infra.

A bankruptcy judge may hear a proceeding that is not a core proceeding but that is otherwise related to a case under title 11. In such proceeding, the bankruptcy judge shall submit proposed findings of fact and conclusions of law to the district court, and any final order or judgment shall be entered by the district judge after considering the bankruptcy judge's proposed findings and conclusions and after reviewing de novo those matters to which any party has timely and specifically objected.

Section 157(c)(2), however, makes it clear that a bankruptcy judge may hear a related case in exactly the same way as the judge could hear a core case, if all of the parties consent to the proceeding. Thus, in many cases where the parties agree (or where there is no objection if the rules so provide) the bankruptcy judge may hear a related case in exactly the same way as if it were a core case. Absent such consent, the bankruptcy judge operates as a kind of finder of fact and proposer of legal conclusions under (c)(1).

Under the local rules by which some of the district courts have referred cases to the bankruptcy court, the parties are deemed to have consented to the bankruptcy judge's jurisdiction unless they affirmatively challenged the bankruptcy judge's authority. Consider, for example, this local rule of the Eastern District of Michigan: [1]

> A party shall indicate whether or not it consents to the authority of the bankruptcy judge in * * * the first pleading it files * * *. *Failure to so indicate shall be deemed consent.*"

Section 157(c)(2) takes on considerable meaning in those districts where sneezing is consent to the bankruptcy judge's jurisdiction to hear related cases.

Where there is no express or implied consent, it will occasionally be necessary to determine whether a proceeding is core or merely "related." How? The verbal articulations are nearly worthless in distinguishing between the two kinds of cases; yet, like the person called upon to decide where the dog's tail begins and where his back ends, the lawyer must decide. Note that there are two boundaries to related cases. There are those so close to the bankruptcy proceeding that they are core proceedings and those so far removed that they are not even related cases. For example, the divorce proceeding of the secretary to the president of a corporation in Chapter 11 would not only not be core, it would not be related. For now, let us attempt to draw the line between related and core.

Consider *Marathon*[2] itself. There the debtor in possession sought to assert a cause of action against a third party. Money received in that lawsuit would have gone into the bankruptcy estate and in that sense it was clearly related to the bankruptcy. Yet, the court found it was not a core proceeding. Thus, we can probably start with the proposition that a contested claim held by the debtor in possession against a third party, which has

§ 12–3

1. Local Bankr. R. 33(a)(3)(C)(i) (E.D. Mich.) (emphasis added).
2. Northern Pipeline Constr. Co. v. Marathon Pipe Line Co., 458 U.S. 50, 102 S.Ct. 2858, 73 L.Ed.2d 598 (1982), judgment stayed, 459 U.S. 813, 103 S.Ct. 199, 74 L.Ed.2d 160 (1982).

not itself filed a claim against the estate, is a related though not necessarily a core proceeding.[3] Similarly, the court in *Maryland National Industrial Finance Corp. v. Gold Dust Coal Co.*[4] found that a secured creditor's suit against the creditors of the debtor's wholly owned subsidiary was related. The court found that although the suit did not directly involve the estate of the debtor, and was not congressionally created, it did have a relation to and an impact upon the bankruptcy decision. Other "related" cases involve an action against guarantors of corporate debtors' note[5] and an action for tortious interference with a contract.[6]

We are doubtful that we can give useful guidance about how to distinguish core from related and related from unrelated except by giving examples. Time and an accretion of case law will ultimately define the line for most of the important cases. We offer a footnote to aid the student and the lawyer in their research,[7] but it represents only a drop in the bucket of hundreds of cases that might be cited. Most of these suits somehow affect the bankruptcy cases in the sense that the proceeds of the suit might be brought into the estate or it might affect the rights of creditors to the estate. Most of them are also suits that could have been brought in state or federal court even when there had never been a bankruptcy case. They arise out of disputes that are not dependent upon the debtor being in bankruptcy.

§ 12–4 Personal Injury Cases

Several of the most notorious Chapter 11 cases in the early 1980's were filed by defendants who were the subject of large numbers of tort suits. The

---

3. In re Freudenmann, 76 B.R. 600 (Bankr. S.D.Tex.1987). The reason that the claim held by the debtor in possession is "related," is because its disposition will affect the property of the estate.

4. 49 B.R. 288 (Bankr. N.D.Ill. 1985).

5. In re Red Ash Coal & Coke Corp., 83 B.R. 399 (W.D.Va.1988).

6. In re Bokum Resources Corp., 49 B.R. 854 (Bankr. D.N.M.1985).

7. To determine whether a proceeding is in fact core one must consider the form and substance of the underlying claim. See In re Wood, 825 F.2d 90 (5th Cir.1987), on remand, 84 B.R. 432 (Bankr. S.D.Miss.1988); In re BTS, Inc., 104 B.R. 1009 (Bankr. W.D.Mo.1989); Meadowlands Communications, Inc. v. Banker's Trust Co., New York, 79 B.R. 198 (D.N.J. 1987); In re Nanodata Computer Corp., 74 B.R. 766 (W.D.N.Y.1987). Some courts have characterized core proceedings as those which generally do not arise under state law and which have no life outside of bankruptcy. Matter of Oliver's Stores, Inc., 107 B.R. 40 (D.N.J.1989); Matter of Honeycomb, Inc., 72 B.R. 371 (Bankr. S.D.N.Y. 1987); Matter of Wood, 825 F.2d 90 (5th Cir.1987), on remand, 84 B.R. 432 (Bankr. S.D.Miss.1988); Holloway v. HECI Exploration Co. Employees' Profit Sharing Plan, 76 B.R. 563 (N.D.Tex.1987), aff'd, 862 F.2d 513 (5th Cir.1988). Although these elements may be sufficient to make a proceeding core, we have already seen (at least in the context of post-petition accounts receivable actions) that they are not necessary. The fact that the claim raises state rather than federal issues may not be determinative. See § ___ supra, and our discussion of In re Arnold Print Works, Inc., 815 F.2d 165 (1st Cir.1987).

The general test articulated for determining whether a case is "related" is whether its outcome could conceivably have any effect on the bankruptcy estate. In re Grell, 83 B.R. 652 (Bankr. D.Minn.1988); In re Petrolia Corp. 79 B.R. 686 (Bankr. E.D.Mich.1987); In re Freudenman, supra; Matter of Wood, supra; In re Red Ash, supra. This broad definition has been accepted by the Third Circuit. See, Brock v. Morysville Body Works, Inc., 829 F.2d 383, 385 (3d Cir.1987) ("an action is related to bankruptcy if the outcome could alter the debtor's rights, liabilities, options, or freedom of action (either positively or negatively) and which in any way impacts upon the handling and administration of the bankrupt estate."). But compare the narrow definition adopted by the Seventh Circuit. See, In re Kubly, 818 F.2d 643, 645 (7th Cir.1987); In re Xonics, Inc., 813 F.2d 127 (7th Cir.1987) (disputes among creditors come within federal bankruptcy jurisdiction only if they involve property of the estate or if resolution of the disputes will affect the recovery of another creditor).

best examples are the Johns Manville company and the A.H. Robins Company. Although one cannot be certain, it is likely that each hoped to consolidate all of the tort cases against it and probably to minimize the total recovery that might otherwise be had by plaintiffs and by the plaintiffs' lawyers in piecemeal tort suits around the country. The plaintiffs (and the plaintiffs' lawyers) were upset at the prospect of being deprived of a jury, particularly a jury in certain forums known to be quite sympathetic to plaintiffs' claims that would be expected to grant large awards against solvent defendants. If all of these cases were to be turned into administrative proceedings in front of a judge or other bankruptcy official, one could imagine that the awards on average would decline and that there would likely be a leveling effect under which those who would otherwise receive a large amount in a favorable plaintiff's jurisdiction, would get substantially less, and those who might receive little or nothing in a strong defendant's jurisdiction would receive somewhat more. Surely the lawyer would get less from a stingy bankruptcy judge than under a contingent fee arrangement in multiple state court actions.

In partial response to the cries of the plaintiffs' lawyers, we now have section 157(b)(2)(B) which tells us that core proceedings do not include:

> "the liquidation or estimation of contingent unliquidated personal injury tort or wrongful death claims against the estate for the purpose of distribution * * *."

Moreover, (b)(5) states that the district court

> "shall order that personal injury tort and wrongful death claims shall be tried in the district court in which the bankruptcy case is pending, or in the district court in the district in which the claim arose, as determined by the district court in which the bankruptcy case is pending."

Presumably, these provisions are intended to preserve the plaintiff's jury trial, but it is unclear how they will operate in practice.

Reading *A.H. Robins Co., Inc. v. Piccinin*[1] leads one to doubt their ability to preserve the jury trial. From 1971 until 1974, the A.H. Robins Company ("Robins") manufactured an intrauterine contraceptive device known as the Dalkon Shield. It discontinued manufacture and sale of the device due to mounting complaints and suits in 1974, but did not recall the product until 1984. By the middle of 1985 the number of suits arising out of the use of the Dalkon Shield grew to approximately 5,000. In the face of these suits the company filed in Chapter 11 bankruptcy in the Eastern District of Virginia in August of 1985.

The filing naturally stayed all suits against Robins. At Robins' request the court transferred all suits to the Eastern District of Virginia for trial. The Court of Appeals for the Fourth Circuit declined to overturn the transfer. The plaintiffs argued that although the language of section 157(b)(5) gave the district court the power to determine and transfer trial venue for personal injury cases, the legislative purpose was to permit trials

§ 12–4 (1986).
1. 788 F.2d 994 (4th Cir.1986), cert. denied, 479 U.S. 876, 107 S.Ct. 251, 93 L.Ed.2d 177

where they were filed. Stating that "Unquestionably the district court in this case had the power under the statute to fix the trial venue in its district for all the Dalkon Shield cases", the court rejected this contention.[2] To support centralization, the court cited the facilitation of a plan of reorganization of the bankrupt and the assurance of a "fair and non-preferential resolution of the Dalkon Shield claims."

In keeping with these policies, the court read section 157(b) in a way that thwarted efforts to give each plaintiff a jury trial. It found that section 157(b)(2)(B) prohibited the bankruptcy court from estimating personal injury claims against the estate for purposes of *distribution,* but held that it did not prohibit the bankruptcy court from doing so for purposes of determining the feasibility of reorganization. Moreover, the estimation of the contingent claims was to precede any jury trials on the claims.[3] The final blow to the jury trial was delivered by the settlement plan.[4] The plan establishes a trust which acts as defendant and payor of all claims. Adopting a carrot and stick approach, the plan ensures that very few claimants will pursue trial. Claimants who forego trial receive the benefit of lower proofs,[5] fewer obstacles,[6] and quicker recovery.[7] Alternatively, claimants that attempt to exercise their right to trial by jury face a hostile defendant who will use all defenses, oppose any transfer motions and any motions for jury trial in another jurisdiction.[8]

2. In so holding, the court rejected the idea that section 1412, which permits only the court where a suit is pending to transfer it to another jurisdiction, somehow limited the section 157(b)(5) power to take away from another court a personal injury case.

3. The court reasoned that:

It is impossible to anticipate the huge costs that would be involved if all the claims had to be tried. If the claimants as a whole are to realize reasonable compensation for their claims, it is obviously in the interest of the class of claimants as a whole to avoid the expense of trying these cases separately. If the bankruptcy court could arrive at a fair estimation of the value of all the claims and submit a fair plan of reorganization based on such estimation, with some mechanism for dispute resolution and acceptable to all interested parties, great benefit to all the claimants could be achieved and the excessive expenses of innumerable trials, stretching over an interminable time, could be avoided.

Robins, 788 F.2d at 1013.

4. In re A.H. Robins Co., Inc., No. 85-01307-R United States Bankruptcy Court for the Eastern District of Virginia, (The Claims Resolution Facility, April 16, 1987, J. Merhige) ("The Plan").

The Plan is divided into five "steps": (1) The Claim Affidavit; (2) Initial Evaluation; (3) In Depth Review; (4) Binding Arbitration, and (5) Trial by Jury. Except for the trial option, the claimant must meet a number of conditions to pass from one step to the next if not satisfied with the settlement offered at that step. If satisfied, the claimant must respond affirmatively and execute a "General Release" within a specified time in order to avoid loss of the claim.

5. For example, at Step 1 a claimant is able to receive payment of $100 by electing the "First Option" which requires only attesting to use of the Dalkon Shield and the belief that it caused injury. The Plan, at 7. In Step 1, "Second Option" the claimant can recover set amounts by claiming a particular injury and showing only use of the Dalkon Shield. The Plan, at 9. At steps 2 and 3 the claimant is permitted a percentage of the full claim for an injury if she does not submit medical records of Dalkon Shield use but does submit medical evidence of Dalkon Shield use. The Plan, at 12 and 14).

6. For example, see Step 1, First Option. If this option is properly selected and its "informational and other requirements met, the Trust waives all defenses to the claim, other than challenges based on duplication of the claim, previous payments, or late filing, as described below." The Plan, at 7.

Moreover, claims to be processed under Option 1 and Option 2 are given priority over all other claims, regardless of when received. The Plan, at 3.

7. A claimant who agrees to settlement will receive a check as quickly as 20 days after proper execution of the General Release. The Plan, at 8.

8. The Plan, at 17.

By granting a right to jury trial, Congress gave something fundamentally inconsistent with the rules and purposes of bankruptcy. The *Robins* court correctly recognized that any efforts to reorganize and treat claimants fairly will be stifled by permitting thousands of trials across the country.[9] This, of course, would not be the first time that Congress has amended an existing statute in response to the pressure of an intensely interested group, but in a way that is fundamentally inconsistent with the basic policy of the original law. We endorse the Fourth Circuit's decision and believe that the court correctly resolved the conflict between the amended 157 and the basic policy.

§ 12–5 Abstention

When the district court, and therefore a bankruptcy court, must abstain from hearing a proceeding is a question that arises inevitably from the overlapping jurisdiction. By hypothesis all related and some core claims could and likely would have arisen and been heard outside the bankruptcy court if the bankruptcy had not been filed. As indicated above, these are often disputes that arise out of the business operations of a Chapter 11 debtor, the kind that every business suffers whether it is in Chapter 11 or not. In many circumstances such claims might thus be heard in state court and, as *Marathon*[1] showed, some of them cannot constitutionally be heard by a federal judge who only possesses Article I powers.

Thus, on the one hand, there is the large and continuing question, when *should* the bankruptcy court in its discretion abstain from hearing the proceeding and allow it to be heard in the state court or possibly in another federal court. Second, there is the more intricate, but ultimately less significant question, when *must* the bankruptcy and federal district court abstain because of the mandatory abstention provisions under 1334(c)(2). The latter question seems mostly an artifact of the *Marathon* decision. We devote only a little time to it here.

Section 1334(c)(2) states that in a proceeding based upon a state law claim or state law cause of action related to but not arising in or under with respect to an action that could not have been commenced in a court of the United States absent jurisdiction under section 1334, the district court "shall abstain" when the action is commenced and can be timely adjudicated in a state forum. This clumsy attempt to deprive the federal district court of certain jurisdiction (the kind of jurisdiction that *Marathon* said a bankruptcy court could not have) raises many issues. Note, first, that it applies only to related but not core cases. Second, it applies only with respect to actions for which there is no independent federal jurisdiction. Third, it applies only "if an action is commenced" and can be "timely adjudicated." One way to read the section is that it does not apply at all unless the related suit (almost invariably a suit by the debtor in possession against a third party) had been

---

9. Under the plan the value of each claim will take into account how the claimant would have fared in his original forum. Any claimant requesting a jury trial can attempt to transfer back to her original jurisdiction. This motion will be opposed by the Trustee.

§ 12–5

1. Northern Pipeline Constr. Co. v. Marathon Pipe Line Co., 458 U.S. 50, 102 S.Ct. 2858, 73 L.Ed.2d 598 (1982), judgment stayed, 459 U.S. 813, 103 S.Ct. 199, 74 L.Ed.2d 160 (1982).

commenced prior to the bankruptcy in state court.[2]

What is "timely adjudication" in (c)(1) is also not clear. All claims must be resolved before there can be a final distribution. If a particular bankruptcy is likely to last four years, conceivably a "timely adjudication" in state court would encompass a lawsuit that might not be concluded for several years. Conversely, if the Chapter 11 is likely to be concluded in six months, even a relatively speedy state court trial might not be timely. Moreover, if the parties to the action are of diverse citizenship, there would thus be diversity jurisdiction, and the abstention provision would not apply.[3]

Finally, the statute itself speaks to the district court, not to the bankruptcy court. These presumably are the cases which the bankruptcy court could not hear except by consent of the parties, but *Marathon* would not appear to require their withdrawal from the district court as opposed to the bankruptcy court. Nevertheless, if abstention is required of the district court, *a fortiori* it would be required of the bankruptcy court. Section (c)(2), which has aroused the fury of the law scholars,[4] will soon become a dead letter. The section is so full of weasel words and so obviously subject to narrow interpretation by a court that wishes to retain jurisdiction, we doubt it will be frequently applied.[5]

Substantially more significant in the long run will be the discretionary abstention rules in (c)(1). First, (c)(1) applies not merely to related cases, but also to core cases. Thus, the court need not face the question whether a particular proceeding is core or not. It seems unlikely that a bankruptcy

---

2. See Matter of Foster, 105 B.R. 746 (Bankr. M.D.Ga.1989); In re Container Transport, 86 B.R. 804 (E.D.Pa. 1988); Williams v. Heller Financial, Inc., 82 B.R. 823 (E.D.La. 1988); In re Landbank Equity Corp., 77 B.R. 44 (E.D.Va.1987); In re Boughton, 60 B.R. 373 (N.D.Ill. 1986); In re World Financial Services Center, Inc., 64 B.R. 980 (Bankr. S.D.Cal.1986), aff'd, 860 F.2d 1090 (1989); Ram Construction Co. v. Port Authority of Allegheny County, 49 B.R. 363 (W.D.Pa.1985); In re Excelite Corp., 49 B.R. 923 (Bankr. N.D.Ga.1985); In re Illinois–California Express, Inc., 50 B.R. 232 (Bankr. D. Col. 1985); but see, In re P & P Oilfield Equipment, Inc., 71 B.R. 621 (Bankr. D. Col. 1987), holding that the "is commenced" requirement is a technical nicety, but not an essential requirement when all the other criteria for mandatory abstention are met; In re World Solar Corp., 81 B.R. 603 (Bankr. S.D.Cal.1988).

3. Gorse v. Long Neck, Ltd., 107 B.R. 479 (D.Del.1989); In re Elegant Concepts, Ltd., 61 B.R. 723 (Bankr. E.D.N.Y.1986), in which all criteria were met, except that the parties were of diverse citizenship; In re Republic Oil Co., 51 B.R. 355 (Bankr. W.D.Wis.1985); Macon Prestressed Concrete Co. v. Duke, 46 B.R. 727 (M.D.Ga.1985); Maryland National Industrial Fin. Corp. v. Gold Dust Coal Co., 49 B.R. 288, 292 n.6 (Bankr. N.D.Ill. 1985).

4. See M. Bienenstock, Bankruptcy Reorganization 755 (1987) where the author states that "[i]n any event, the mandatory abstention provisions thwart any hope of coordinated and efficient administration of bankruptcy cases."

5. For examples of courts refusing to apply mandatory abstention, see In the Matter of Foster, 105 B.R. 746 (Bankr. M.D.Ga.1989) (mandatory abstention not required with respect to Chapter 13 debtor's claim that mortgage foreclosure sale was not properly advertised and was void under Georgia law, where no legal action had been commenced in state court tribunal); In re World Solar Corp., 81 B.R. 603 (S.D.Cal.1988) (suits by debtor for contract arrearages was not subject to mandatory abstention when accelerated bankruptcy court calendar afforded quicker settlement); J.D. Marshall Internat'l, Inc. v. Redstart, Inc., 74 B.R. 651 (N.D.Ill. 1987) (action to reduce arbitration award to judgment need not be mandatorily abstained from where state adjudication would impair administration or liquidation of the estate); In re Pacor, Inc., 72 B.R. 927 (Bankr. E.D.Pa. 1987), aff'd, 86 B.R. 808 (E.D.Pa. 1987) (debtor's suit on the contract with its insurance company was not subject to mandatory abstention where untimely adjudication would stifle administration of the estate); In re Earle Industries, Inc., 72 B.R. 131 (Bankr. E.D.Pa. 1987) (mandatory abstention not required for breach of contract claim where no showing of any pending state action or that one could timely be adjudicated).

court will abstain in many core proceedings. The most obvious candidate for a core abstention would be a case in which a third party had brought a suit against the debtor in possession (which would require a trial and could be best heard in a state court).

In summary, if the issue to be litigated is not core,[6] courts faced with the claim that they should mandatorily abstain have generally applied a six or seven point test.[7] Whether the court in fact abstains on the grounds of (c)(2) usually turns on the following factors: (1) backlog of the state court's calendar; (2) status of the bankruptcy proceeding; (3) complexity of the issues; and (4) whether the state court proceeding would prolong the administration of the estate.[8] As indicated in (c)(2), any decision to mandatorily abstain is not reviewable by appeal or otherwise.[9]

If, however, a party is seeking voluntary abstention, it is seeking an "extraordinary exception to the general rule that courts should adjudicate matters properly before them and, as such, 'should be exercised sparingly and cautiously.'"[10] Because most bankruptcy courts believe that they can rule on the state issue more quickly than the alternative state court, they are generally unwilling to abstain voluntarily. However, a litmus test has developed which helps to determine when abstention under (c)(1) is appropriate. When the state issue is of substantial public importance, abstention would not hinder reorganization, and little or no state precedent exists to help guide the bankruptcy court, abstention is particularly appropriate.[11]

B. VENUE

§ 12–6 Venue of Cases, Section 1408(1)

To determine whether venue is proper in bankruptcy requires distinguishing between "cases" on the one hand and "proceedings" on the other. The "case" is the entire bankruptcy; to ask what is proper venue of the case

---

6. In re Baptist Medical Center of New York, 80 B.R. 637 (Bankr. E.D.N.Y.1987); In re Cossett, 75 B.R. 766 (Bankr. S.D.Ohio 1987); In re United Church of the Ministers of God, 74 B.R. 271 (Bankr. E.D.Pa. 1987).

7. The elements include: (1) A timely motion; (2) a purely state law question; (3) a non-core proceeding (section 157(c)(1)); (4) a lack of independent federal jurisdiction absent the petition under title 11; (5) that an action is commenced in a state court; (6) that the state court action may be timely adjudicated; (7) a state forum of appropriate jurisdiction exists. In re World Solar Corp., 81 B.R. 603, 606 (S.D.Cal.1988); In re Consulting Actuarial Partners, Ltd. Ptn., 72 B.R. 821 (S.D.N.Y. 1987).

8. J.D. Marshall Intern., Inc. v. Redstart, Inc., 74 B.R. 651, 654 (N.D.Ill. 1987), citing In re DeLorean Motor, 49 B.R. 900, 911 (Bankr. E.D.Mich.1985); In re Boughton, 49 B.R. 312, 315–16 (Bankr. N.D.Ill. 1985), aff'd, 60 B.R. 373 (N.D.Ill. 1986).

9. While a decision to abstain under (c)(2) is not reviewable, a decision not to abstain under (c)(2) is. Moreover, a decision made either way under (c)(1) is reviewable. Kind, A Chart of Bankruptcy Jurisdiction for Admiralty Lawyers, 59 Tulane L. Rev. 1264 (1985); see also California State Board of Equalization v. Sierra Summit (In re China Peak Resort), 847 F.2d 570 (9th Cir.1988), judgment vac'd, 490 U.S. 844, 109 S.Ct. 2228, 104 L.Ed.2d 910 (1989).

10. In re Ionosphere, Inc., 108 B.R. 951 (Bankr. S.D.N.Y.1989); In re Kolinsky, 100 B.R. 695 (Bankr. S.D.N.Y.1989); In re Charter Co., 82 B.R. 602, 603 (Bankr. M.D. Fla.1988); Ronix Corporation v. City of Philadelphia, 82 B.R. 19, 20 (E.D.Pa. 1988).

11. In re Titan Energy, Inc., 837 F.2d 325 (8th Cir.1988); In re Naugatuck Dairy Ice Cream Co., Inc., 106 B.R. 24 (Bankr. D.Conn. 1989); In the Matter of Oliver's Stores, 107 B.R. 40 (D.N.J.1989); In re Charter Co., 82 B.R. 602 (Bankr. M.D.Fla.1988); State ex rel. Roberts v. Mushroom King, Inc., 77 B.R. 813 (D. Ore. 1987); In re Stephen Smith Home For the Aged, Inc., 80 B.R. 678 (Bankr. E.D.Pa. 1987); In re Landbank Equity Corp., 77 B.R. 44 (E.D.Va.1987).

is to ask the question in which bankruptcy court should the petition be filed. Once that petition has been filed, most, but not all, of the "proceedings" (that is, the subplots within the larger play) will have the same venue. Some proceedings that are no more than lawsuits that arise between a going concern and a third party will properly find venue in other courts or outside the bankruptcy system entirely. The proper venue of "cases" is defined by 28 U.S.C.A. § 1408. Section 1409 defines venue of proceedings.

The basic grant of venue under section 1408(1) for cases is as follows:

"In the district * * * in which the domicile, residence, principal place of business in the United States, or principal assets in the United States * * * have been located for the longer portion of * * * the 180 day period preceding the filing."

Most of the venue issues are fairly straightforward. At the outset one should understand that a typical case may have proper venue in several different districts. It is conceivable, for example, that a person could have a domicile in Ohio, be residing in Florida, operating a sole proprietorship whose principal place of business is in Georgia, and whose principal assets are an apartment complex in Mississippi. In that case venue would be proper in any one of the four jurisdictions.

It should also be apparent that some of the words fit more comfortably with some entities than with others. For example, we know that an individual can be domiciled in one place and reside in another; it is not so obvious that the same can be true of a corporation. Yet a corporation clearly could be domiciled in one place and have a principal place of business or its principal assets in another.

To understand the operation of section 1408(1), first consider a corporation.[1] One can imagine arguments on the question whether a Delaware corporation that has plants in several states has its principal place of business in one or another of those plants. For most purposes the Uniform Commercial Code defines the principal place of business as the place of the corporation's chief executive office.[2] That definition might also work in many cases presented to the bankruptcy court. Some cases addressing that question have said that the principal place of business is the "nerve cen-

§ 12–6

1. It is conceivable that a bankruptcy case by or against a corporation could be properly venued in the district where it is incorporated, because the district which includes the state of incorporation would be the corporation's domicile. This possibility for venue exists despite the fact that many corporations have no further contact with the states of their incorporation than the simple fact of their having been incorporated there. Several courts have indicated that domicile would be a proper venue for corporations without further connections to the forum. See Matter of Ofty Corp., 44 B.R. 479 (Bankr. D.Del.1984); In the Matter of Landmark Capital Company, 19 B.R. 342 (Bankr. S.D.N.Y.1982), aff'd, 20 B.R. 220 (S.D.N.Y.1982); see generally LoPucki, Venue Choice and Forum Shopping in the Bankruptcy Reorganization of Large Publicly Held Companies, 1991 Wis.L.Rev. 11.

2. U.C.C. § 9–103(3)(d) states:

A debtor shall be deemed located at his place of business if he has one, at his chief executive office if he has more than one place of business, otherwise at his residence. If, however, the debtor is a foreign air carrier under the Federal Aviation Act of 1958, as amended, it shall be deemed located at the designated office of the agent upon whom service of process may be made on behalf of the foreign air carrier.

ter."[3] One court found that to be "where those interested in [the corporation] choose primarily to conduct its business."[4] Presumably this place will usually be the place of the chief executive offices or at least where most of the administration of the corporation is to be done. Consider, for example, *In the Matter of Commonwealth Oil Refining Co., Inc.*,[5] decided under Rule 116(a)(2), which had similar language, but preceded section 1408(1). The debtor's corporate headquarters were in San Antonio, Texas; its principal asset, a refinery, and its manufacturing activities and the bulk of its sales all were in Puerto Rico. The Puerto Rican government argued that the case should be heard in Puerto Rico because of its extensive application of Spanish civil law and because the refinery and the sales were there. The Court of Appeals for the Fifth Circuit upheld the bankruptcy judge's decision that the case should be heard in Texas. Even though it was conceded that the principal assets were in Puerto Rico, the principal place of business was in Texas and therefore venue was proper. Other courts have come to similar conclusions.[6] To say that venue is proper at the principal place of business does not deny the proposition that it might also be proper where the principal assets are located, or indeed that it might be appropriate in certain circumstances to transfer the case despite proper venue where filed to another place where venue is even more appropriate.[7]

Partnerships present somewhat more difficult venue questions. Partnerships are distinct entities from their general partners yet the general partners, who bear the ultimate partnership liability, represent the partnership entity in a much more fundamental way than shareholders represent the corporate entity. However, at least one court has found "it is difficult to see how a partnership can be said to have a residence or domicile * * *. Therefore the only meaningful test for venue with respect to a partnership is the district in which it has its principal place of business or its principal assets."[8] Thus, if a California partnership has its principal place of business and chief executive office in Sacramento but owns nothing but apartment buildings in Dallas, Texas, venue would be proper either in California or in Texas. Whether a court in one jurisdiction should transfer the case to the other would depend in substantial degree upon the convenience to the creditors and to the debtor.

In theory at least the place of residence of the general partners has nothing to do with the proper venue of the partnership itself. In practice that is not true, but only because of the application of section 1408(2), which authorizes venue of a partnership in any district where "there is pending a case * * * concerning such person's * * * general partner." Thus, if the general partner in Nebraska went into bankruptcy in Omaha, that would be

3. In re Dock of the Bay, Inc., 24 B.R. 811, 814–15 (Bankr. E.D.N.Y.1982); In re Lakeside Utilities, 18 B.R. 115 (Bankr. D.Neb.1982).

4. In re Portex Oil Co., 30 F.Supp. 138 (D. Ore. 1939), aff'd sub nom., Clark Bros. Co. v. Portex Oil Co., 113 F.2d 45 (9th Cir.1940).

5. 596 F.2d 1239 (5th Cir.1979), cert. denied, 444 U.S. 1045, 100 S.Ct. 732, 62 L.Ed.2d 731 (1980).

6. In re Holiday Towers, Inc., 18 B.R. 183 (Bankr. S.D.Ohio 1982); In re Baltimore Food Systems, Inc., 71 B.R. 795 (Bankr. D.S.C. 1986); cf. In re Eleven Oak Tower Ltd. Partnership, 59 B.R. 626 (Bankr. N.D.Ill. 1986).

7. Unincorporated associations are treated like incorporated associations for venue purposes.

8. In re 1606 New Hampshire Avenue Associates, 85 B.R. 298 (Bankr. E.D.Pa. 1988); In re Greenridge Apartments, 13 B.R. 510 (Bankr. D.Hawaii 1981).

a proper venue for the bankruptcy of the partnership even if the partnership's principal place of business was in Atlanta and its principal assets were in Georgia.[9]

The issues with respect to natural persons add little to the questions discussed above concerning partnerships and corporations. An occasional case can present the familiar, although difficult, question whether a particular person is "domiciled" where he "resides." For example, in *In re MacDonald*,[10] the debtor argued that he was domiciled in Ohio even though he lived in Massachusetts. Upon proof that the debtor intended to retire to Canada and not to return to Ohio, the court found that Massachusetts, where he had been recently employed and had spent most of his time, was his "residence" and was therefore the proper venue.

§ 12-7 Venue of Cases, Section 1408(1)—Affiliates, Section 1408(2)

Section 1408(2) deals not merely with the partners discussed above, but also provides that venue is proper in any case where a "person's affiliate has a case pending." The term "affiliate" is quite broadly defined by 101(2). It includes subsidiary, parent, and sibling corporations. Moreover, it includes a series of parent and subsidiary corporations which own as little as 20 percent of one another's stock. In addition, it includes certain entities which are related because the debtor leases "substantially all" of the debtor's property, and vice versa. Consider for a moment the consequences of this section. This means that LTV, a multi-billion dollar corporation, headquartered in Dallas, finds proper venue in New York City because of an insignificant and formally unknown subsidiary that owns a couple of ships.[1] The purpose of the provision should be obvious. If the bankruptcy court is to supervise a reorganization of a complex economic organization that is composed of a series of related corporations, it is desirable that the administration take place in only one place and not be done piecemeal in a series of courts. Yet, cases such as LTV show that a large corporation will find venue in any of a large number of districts.[2]

---

9. But see In re Nantucket Apartments Associates, 80 B.R. 154 (Bankr. E.D.Mo.1987), where the court held that where the debtor was a limited partnership the domicile or residence of the individual general or limited partners was irrelevant. The Missouri limited partnership's chapter 11 case was not properly venued in Missouri where its only place of business, management, and sole asset was located in Louisiana. See also In re Spicer Oaks Apartments, Ltd., 80 B.R. 142 (Bankr. E. D. Mo. 1987); also, see In re Phoenix Piccadilly, Ltd., 849 F.2d 1393 (11th Cir.1988), where venue chosen by partnership debtor was over 700 miles from partnership's sole asset, employees, secured and unsecured creditors, and pending state action. This choice of venue, though technically proper, supported a finding that Chapter 11 case was filed in bad faith and therefore could be dismissed pursuant to section 1112.

10. 73 B.R. 254 (Bankr. N.D.Ohio 1987).

§ 12-7

1. In re Chateaugay Corporation, 102 B.R. 335 (Bankr. S.D.N.Y.1989).

2. Section 109(a) of title 11 establishes that "[o]nly a corporation that resides or has a domicile, place of business, or property in the United States * * * may be a debtor under the bankruptcy code." The recent case Atlanta Shipping Corp. v. Chemical Bank, 631 F.Supp. 335 (1986), aff'd, 818 F.2d 240 (2d Cir.1987), makes it clear that "[o]nce a court has found that a particular (entity), who may be an alien, is eligible to be a debtor under the Code, because that individual has a place of business or property in the United States, and therefore the bankruptcy court can entertain the petition, (28 U.S.C.A. 1408(1)) indicates the appropriate venue for that proceeding." In Atlanta Shipping, the debtor did not allege maintenance of its principal place of business in the United States. It maintained some

A detailed empirical study[3] has shown that virtually every major reorganization case presents several venue options, and that a significant amount of "forum shopping" goes on in selecting the district in which to file the petition. New York City appears to be the most popular choice, and some companies have gone to considerable trouble to make a filing in New York City feasible. Johns–Manville, a company with assets of over $2 billion, 27,000 employees, and significant holdings throughout the United States, filed in New York City, even though New York was one of the few states in which Johns–Manville did *not* have significant assets or operations.[4] Similarly, although virtually all of Towle Manufacturing's assets and offices were in Massachusetts, it filed in New York City, basing its venue claim on 60,000 square feet of leased showroom space.[5]

There are a number of explanations for New York City's status as the venue of choice for large Chapter 11 cases. Convenience is certainly one of the most important: many highly regarded bankruptcy attorneys are located in New York, as are large banks, experienced accountants and investment bankers. Of course, the extensive experience of judges and staff with large reorganizations in the New York City bankruptcy courts makes that district attractive to parties, both because of their knowledge of the procedures involved and because of the large body of precedent available. Less legitimate motives also intrude, alas; among these are the New York City courts' liberal policies regarding extensions of exclusivity periods and their generous awards of attorney fees.[6]

§ 12–8 Venue of Proceeding, Section 1409

Section 1409 of title 28 covers venue of proceedings. Subsection (a) sets out the general provisions for venue of a proceeding in a bankruptcy case, while subsections (b) through (e) offer alternatives and exceptions. Subsection (a) provides:

> (a) Except as otherwise provided in subsection (b) and (d), a proceeding arising under title 11 or arising in or related to a case under title 11 may be commenced in the district court in which such case is pending.

This section provides that proceedings "may" be commenced where the case is filed, not that they "must" be commenced there. Apparently the "may" of section 1409(a) distinguishes it from its exceptions in subsections (b) and (d) which use the mandate "only." However, the exhortation of section 1409(a) is stronger than it first appears, particularly in circumstances in which a litigant cannot find any other subsection of 1409 that grants venue. In such case, the "may" becomes "must." Thus, one might wish to think of section 1409(a) as stating the proposition that all proceedings "arising under", "in", or "related to" should presumptively be held before the bankruptcy court

---

assets, including accounts receivable in the United States. The maintenance of property or assets in the United States is enough to confer jurisdiction under title 11. Once such contacts with the United States have been established, venue will be determined in the same manner as it would be in any other case.

3. LoPucki & Whitford, *Venue Choice and Forum Shopping in the Bankruptcy Reorganization of Large, Publicly Held Companies*, 1991 Wis.L.Rev. 11 (1991).
4. Id. at 27 n.56.
5. Id., n.57.
6. Id. at 29–33.

where the petition is filed. Having said that, consider the alternatives where other venue is possible or required.

As we have already pointed out, subsection (b) differs from subsection (a) in that it is mandatory. Where the trustee or debtor in possession seeking to recover a money judgment or property worth less than $1,000 or a consumer debt of less than $5,000 the proper venue exists only in the district in which the defendant resides. Subsection (b) governs only those proceedings initiated by the DIP or the trustee. If a similar claim of less than $1,000 (or $5,000 in the case of a consumer debt) were commenced by a third party against the trustee, venue could be proper in the bankruptcy court where the case was filed.

The intent of the drafters in adopting section 1409(b) is clear. The House Report on section 1473(b) (which preceded section 1409(b) and had identical language) stated that the "section prevents unfairness to distant debtors of the estate, when the cost of defending would be greater than the cost of paying the debt owed."[1] A similar unfairness would occur if, for reasons of venue, the trustee were forced to travel great distances, at an expense beyond the estate's capacity, in order to litigate a small claim brought by a third party.

Assume a petition is filed in New York, and that a party residing in Fort Worth allegedly owes the debtor $800. If one considered only section 1409(a), venue would be proper in New York and would require the Texas debtor to travel to New York to present any defense he might have to the $800 claim against him. Congress regarded that situation as unfair and accordingly has required the trustee to go to Fort Worth to bring suit.

Subsection (c) provides an alternative venue for a proceeding based upon the trustee's avoidance power under section 544(b), or power to claim specific property of the estate. It authorizes the debtor in possession to seek assets claimed under sections 541 or 544(b) in any district where a case could have commenced had a title 11 case not been filed. Thus, in many cases in which the debtor in possession is seeking the return of assets that allegedly belong to the estate under section 541 or assets that were improperly conveyed and can be recovered under section 544(b), the trustee will have the alternative of bringing the case where the petition is filed or at the place of residence of the one possessing the property or, conceivably, where the property is located. It is an alternative section, but it applies only to proceedings brought by the trustee or the debtor in possession, not to those where the trustee or debtor in possession is the defendant.

Subsections (d) and (e) respond to a unique problem of operating the continuing business under Chapter 11. It is familiar but ironic that one's capacity to do business is enhanced by his ability to be sued. If parties are amenable to suit in the local court, locals are more likely to deal with them than if they must go to a distant place to sue. If all disputes between a Chapter 11 business and third parties had to be resolved in the bankruptcy court where the case is filed, that might deter merchants and others from dealing with Chapter 11 debtors who have far-flung business interests. Accordingly, subsections (d) and (e) say that claims arising "after the

---

§ 12-8
1. H.Rep. No. 595, 95th Cong., 1st Sess. 446 (1977).

commencement of such case" require that the trustee as plaintiff go to the district court where the case could have been brought absent bankruptcy in order to pursue its suit and permit the third party as plaintiff either to sue the debtor in possession in the district court where there would have been non-bankruptcy jurisdiction or in the district court where the case is pending. That means, in the case of LTV which filed its petition in New York and has continuing business operations in Pennsylvania, Ohio, and Texas, among other states, that as to any dispute that arose after the commencement of the case, the LTV debtor in possession must pursue third parties in the district court in Pennsylvania, Ohio, or Texas respectively, but that those wishing to sue LTV on transactions arising after the case, have the choice of proceeding in Texas, Ohio, or Pennsylvania, or in the main bankruptcy case in New York City.

Note, that in all these cases, venue is in "the district court." Under local rules that usually means in "the bankruptcy court." Thus, the bankruptcy at least forecloses a state court action unless the bankruptcy court chooses to abstain. In the words of the court in *In re Cox Cotton Co.*,[2] these subsections "afford protection to those entities who in good faith dealt with the trustee or debtor in possession after the order for relief and in regards to the administration of the estate."[3] In effect, (d) and (e) prohibit the debtor in possession from using its section 1409(a) hometown venue for claims that arise after the petition was filed unless there would have been venue in that district absent the bankruptcy.

The general policies and rules in section 1409 seem fairly straightforward and unexceptional. One would expect most proceedings to be heard in the same court where the petition is filed, yet one can easily see why certain cases such as those in (b) or occasionally in (d) or (e) should be heard elsewhere.

§ 12–9 Change of Venue, Section 1412

Perhaps the most important provision in the collection of venue statutes and rules is section 1412 which provides for transfer of venue:

> "A district court may transfer a case or proceeding under title 11 to a district court for another district, in the interest of justice or for the convenience of the parties."[1]

Disputes over change of venue are generally held to be core.[2]

§ 12–10 Change of Venue, Section 1412—Proper Venue

Section 1412 covers both cases and proceedings. Rule 1014 implements its provisions concerning cases and Rule 1014(a)(1) deals with transfer of cases where original venue is proper:

2. 8 B.R. 682 (Bankr. E.D.Ark.1981).
3. Id. at 684.

§ 12–9

1. 28 U.S.C.A. § 1412. Note that the court in A.H. Robins held that section 1412 was limited by section 157(b)(5). The court held that the district court's power to transfer could not hinder another court's power to consolidate and pull together personal injury claims filed against the bankrupt. See § 12–4 note 2 supra.

2. In re Ridgely Communications, Inc., 107 B.R. 72 (Bankr. D.Md.1989); In re Texaco Inc., 89 B.R. 382 (Bankr. S.D.N.Y.1988); In re D'Angona, 74 B.R. 577 (Bankr. D.R.I. 1987), transferred, 107 B.R. 448 (Bankr.D.Conn. 1989); In re Whilden, 67 B.R. 40 (Bankr. M.D. Fla.1986); contra In re HME Records, Inc., 62 B.R. 611 (Bankr. M.D.Tenn.1986).

"If a petition is filed in a proper district, on timely motion of a party in interest, and after hearing on notice to the petitioners, the United States Trustee, and other entities as directed by the court, the case may be transferred to any other district if the court determines that the transfer is in the interest of justice or for the convenience of the parties."

When venue is proper as it stands, the burden is on the moving party to demonstrate with a preponderance of evidence that transfer is "in the interest of justice or the convenience of the parties." [1] As one might expect, the courts have developed a set of criteria for balancing interests in decisions on transfer. This list varies in content from case to case, but six factors recur: (1) the relative economic harm to debtors and creditors if transfer is granted; (2) the location of the assets; (3) the economic administration of the estate; (4) the necessity for ancillary administration if liquidation should result; (5) the effect on parties' (including witnesses') willingness or ability to participate in the case or proceeding; (6) the existence of any intertwined relationship with another bankruptcy case under section 1408(2).[2]

The list of factors is sufficiently diffuse that it can be arranged to defend almost any decision that appeals to the bankruptcy judge. Nevertheless, it appears that some of the factors weigh more heavily and are more likely to influence the judge than others. The most important of these factors involves the economic administration of the case.[3] All of the factors are subsumed within this one, but in addition, it takes into account the ability of the trustee or debtor in possession to manage the debtor's business affairs. For example, the Fifth Circuit in *In the Matter of Commonwealth Oil Refining Co., Inc.*,[4] affirmed the bankruptcy court's decision that venue should lie in San Antonio, the principal place of business, rather than Puerto Rico, the site of production and the location of principal assets. Both venues would be proper. But the Fifth Circuit approved the bankruptcy court determination that venue at the site of production would be administratively inefficient, by comparison to the existing venue at the location of corporate headquarters where the actual management of the business had been taking place. The economic administration of the case is an especially pertinent factor in a reorganization case, where it is vital that the business affairs of the debtor be well managed if the debtor is to be successful in its reorganization.

Another important factor is location of the debtor's assets.[5] This factor is especially important in cases where the debtor is in liquidation or where

§ 12–10

1. In re Jolly, 106 B.R. 299 (Bankr. M.D.Fla.1989); Matter of Windtech, Inc., 73 B.R. 448 (Bankr. D. Conn. 1987); In re Legend Industries, Inc., 49 B.R. 935 (Bankr. E.D.N.Y. 1985).

2. See In re Commonwealth Oil Refining Co., Inc., 596 F.2d 1239 (5th Cir.1979), cert. denied, 444 U.S. 1045, 100 S.Ct. 732, 62 L.Ed.2d 731 (1980); In re Jolly, 106 B.R. 299 (Bankr. M.D.Fla.1989); In re Waits, 70 B.R. 591, 594–595 (Bankr. S.D.N.Y. 1987); In re 19101 Corp., 74 B.R. 34 (Bankr. D.R.I. 1987); McLemore v. Thomasson (In re Thomasson), 60 B.R. 629 (Bankr. M.D.Tenn.1986); In re Butcher, 46 B.R. 109, 112 (Bankr. N.D.Ga. 1985).

3. Matter of Windtech, 73 B.R. 448 (Bankr. D.Conn.1987); In re Baltimore Food Systems, Inc., 71 B.R. 795 (Bankr. D.S.C. 1986).

4. 596 F.2d 1239 (5th Cir.1979), cert. denied, 444 U.S. 1045, 100 S.Ct. 732, 62 L.Ed.2d 731 (1980).

5. The court in HME Records, 62 B.R. 611 (Bankr. M.D.Tenn.1986) held that venue was proper in Tennessee because debtor's principal

the assets are real property.[6] Note that even where venue is proper at debtor's management office, authority indicates that venue should be transferred to the place of debtor's realty if the creditors request it.[7]

One problem in cases involving individual debtors arises when assets and creditors are located far from the debtor's residence so that that venue would be burdensome for the debtor.[8] In such a case the balancing of relative economic harm to the debtor and the creditors is the most important factor. If, however, most of the assets and most of the creditors are in a venue remote from the debtor's residence, the balance is tipped in favor of transfer, and the debtor will and should be forced to travel the distance.[9] An example is *In re Almeida* [10] in which the court transferred a Chapter 7 case from Pennsylvania to California because the creditors, assets, and witnesses were all located there, although the cost of the debtor's travel to and from California was recognized as a significant concern.

§ 12–11 Change of Venue, Section 1412—Improper Venue

As originally enacted, the Bankruptcy Reform Act of 1978 explicitly authorized a court to retain or transfer a case or proceeding even though it had been filed in a court where venue was improper:

> The bankruptcy court of a district in which is filed a case or proceeding laying venue in the wrong division or district may, in the interests of justice and for the convenience of the parties, retain such case or proceeding, or may transfer, * * * such case or proceeding to another district or division.

Under this rule, which was 28 U.S.C.A. § 1477, the court was without authority to dismiss a case or proceeding. In 1984 the quoted section was repealed and was replaced by section 1412. Section 1412 merely refers to a transfer or change of venue in the interest of justice or for the convenience of the parties, but it makes no reference to improper venue. Although it is not clear whether transfer is mandatory under section 1412, the section does not authorize dismissal.[1] Moreover Bankruptcy Rule 1014(a)(2) implicitly

---

assets (400 tape recordings) were located there, even though over 200 unsecured creditors and three out of five of debtor's directors were located in New York.

6. In re Sundance Corp., 84 B.R. 699 (Bankr. D.Mont.1988); In re 19101 Corp., 74 B.R. 34 (Bankr. D.R.I. 1987); In re Wood Family Interests, Ltd., 78 B.R. 434 (Bankr. E.D.Pa. 1987); In re Pickwick Place, Ltd., 63 B.R. 290 (Bankr. N.D.Ill. 1986); In re Eleven Oak Tower Ltd., 59 B.R. 626 (Bankr. N.D.Ill. 1986); In re Old Delmar Corp., 45 B.R. 883 (D.C.N.Y. 1985), in which the court stated that the existence of real property assets overwhelmingly militates in favor of laying venue at their location.

7. See In re Boca Raton Sanctuary Associates, 105 B.R. 273 (Bankr. E.D.Pa. 1989); In re Spicer Oaks Apartments, Ltd., 80 B.R. 142 (Bankr. E.D.Mo.1987); In re 19101 Corp., 74 B.R. 34 (Bankr. D.R.I. 1987); In re Landmark Capital Co., 19 B.R. 342 (Bankr. S.D.N.Y.1982), aff'd, 20 B.R. 220 (S.D.N.Y.1982).

8. See In re Walter, 47 B.R. 240 (Bankr. M.D.Fla.1985); In re Ocheltree, 71 B.R. 1 (Bankr. D.N.M. 1983) (in no-asset chapter 9 bankruptcy, ill debtor's district was proper place to transfer venue).

9. Graham v. Lennington, 74 B.R. 963 (S.D.Ind.1987); In re Ofia Realty Corp., 74 B.R. 574 (Bankr. S.D.N.Y. 1987); In re D'Angona, 74 B.R. 577 (Bankr. D.R.I. 1987), transferred, 107 B.R. 448 (Bankr.D.Conn.1989).

10. 37 B.R. 186 (Bankr. E.D.Pa. 1984).

§ 12–11

1. In re Great American Resources, Inc., 85 B.R. 444 (Bankr. N.D.Ohio 1988) (improper venue was not grounds for dismissing the case); see also 1 Collier Bankruptcy Manual 3.02 at 3–153 (3rd ed. 1988); contra In re Greiner, 45 B.R. 715 (Bankr. D.N.D. 1985).

authorized the retention of jurisdiction in an improper venue until 1987 when the rule was changed in response to the repeal of section 1477(a). Now the rule reads:

> If a petition is filed in an improper district, on timely motion of a party in interest and after hearing or notice to the petitioners, the United States Trustee, and other entities as directed by the court, the case may be dismissed or transferred to any other district if the court determines that transfer is in the interest of justice or for the convenience of the parties.[2]

Where does this leave us? Under the laws existing between 1978 and 1984, it was clear that a court could retain jurisdiction even though venue was improper if it was in the interest of justice and the parties.

Under the current law it is unclear whether a court can retain a case or proceeding in an improper venue absent waiver by the parties. This lack of clarity arises partly because it is uncertain whether Congress' replacement of section 1477 with section 1412 was intended to withdraw the power previously exercised by the courts to hear cases in improper venues. At least one case, *In re Greiner*,[3] holds that a court is now foreclosed from hearing a case when venue is improper. A number of courts have disagreed with the conclusion in *Greiner* and have found power to hear a case in an improper venue despite section 1477's repeal even though there is no explicit authority in section 1412.[4] An argument that these courts made for the retention of cases where venue is improper is that section 1412 contains no explicit requirement of transfer to a jurisdiction where venue is proper. If a court where venue is improper can transfer to another court where venue is also improper, then, the argument goes, there is no reason why the first court should not be able to retain the case.[5]

In re Boeckman[6] illustrates the problem. In that case the debtor had a trucking business and did some farming in Nebraska. Nearly all of his assets were located there. Some creditors were in Nebraska and some in South Dakota; the debtor lived closer to Sioux Falls, the seat of the South Dakota bankruptcy court, than he did to Omaha, the seat of the Nebraska bankruptcy court. Debtor filed in Sioux Falls where venue was not proper.

---

2. Bankr. R. 1014(a)(2).

3. 45 B.R. 715 (Bankr. D.N.D.1985).

4. In re Lazaro, 128 B.R. 168 (Bankr. W.D.Tex.1991); In re U.S. Aviex Co., Inc., 96 B.R. 874 (Bankr. N.D.Ind. 1989); Baltimore Food Systems, Inc., 71 B.R. 795 (Bankr. D.S.C. 1986); In re Leonard, 55 B.R. 106 (Bankr. D.D.C. 1985); In re Boeckman, 54 B.R. 110 (Bankr. D.S.D. 1985); In re Osage Exploring Company, 39 B.R. 966 (Bankr. S.D.N.Y. 1984), on remand, 104 F.R.D. 45 (S.D.N.Y.1984).

5. In re Leonard, 55 B.R. 106 (Bankr. D.D.C.1985); In re Boeckman, 54 B.R. 110 (Bankr. D.S.D. 1985). This argument finds its roots in the text of section 1412 which simply allows transfer "to a district court for another district, in the interest of justice or for the convenience of the parties." The general venue statutes for district courts, 28 U.S.C.A. §§ 1404 & 1406, on the other hand, require that transfer can only be made "to any other district or division where it might have been brought." The contrast was even more distinct in section 1477 which allowed transfer from an improper venue, under section 1475, to "any other district or division." Section 1475, which pertained to transfer from a proper venue, contained language similar to § 1412. See generally 1 Collier on Bankruptcy at 3–153–164 (15th ed. 1989); M. Bienenstock, Bankruptcy Reorganization 49 (1985). Bear in mind, that the argument which allows retention because improper districts can transfer to improper district leads, somewhat unfortunately, to the converse conclusion that transfer may be made from a district where venue is proper to one where it is improper.

6. 54 B.R. 110 (Bankr. S.D.N.Y.1985).

Over a Nebraska creditor's objection, the South Dakota court retained jurisdiction and refused to transfer the court to the proper venue in Nebraska.[7]

In re Townsend[8] presents a well-reasoned opinion on this issue. There the case was improperly filed in the northern district of Florida, a place with no connection to the debtor. Relying on Bankruptcy Rule 1014(a)(2) and the accompanying Advisory Committee Note,[9] the court stated that "once the Court has made a determination that venue is not proper, it no longer has discretion to retain the case. The only issue left for determination is whether the case should be transferred or dismissed."[10]

Note finally that parties may waive their right to challenge proper venue, a topic with which rule 1014 deals. Exactly what acts constitute waiver are too detailed to consider here, but lawyers should be aware of that possibility and should carefully examine rule 1014 and the cases if they hope to challenge venue.

C. APPEALS

§ 12–12 Appeals

Historically appeals from the bankruptcy court have gone to the district court where the bankruptcy court sits. For a brief period between 1978 and 1984 it appeared as though a large share of such appeals would go either directly to the Courts of Appeals or to bankruptcy appellate panels established in each of the circuits. Because most of the circuits did not establish bankruptcy appellate panels and because the direct appeal possibility was substantially reduced in the 1984 act, we are now back roughly where we started prior to 1978 with most appeals going to the district court judges.[1]

---

7. In another example, the debtor had clearly filed in a district which constituted improper venue. In re Great American Resources, Inc., 85 B.R. 444 (Bankr. N.D.Ohio 1988). Venue was improper in Ohio because the debtor had only been there for three weeks prior to filing in Chapter 11. Venue would have been proper in Southern California, where debtor had spent the majority of the 180 days prior to filing, under section 1408(1). Relying on In re Holiday Towers, Inc., 18 B.R. 183 (Bankr. S.D.Ohio 1982), the court held that dismissal was not appropriate. However, the number of creditors located in the proper venue and the amounts owed to them were "negligible," and thus, even though the debtor had no legitimate reasons for retaining the improper venue, the court refused to transfer. It believed that when there were no compelling arguments for retaining or transferring venue even an improper venue should go undisturbed. See also In re U.S. Aviex Co., Inc., 96 B.R. 874 (Bankr. N.D.Ind. 1989).

8. 84 B.R. 764 (Bankr. N.D.Fla.1988).

9. The court quoted the 1987 Advisory Committee Note to Rule 1014 which states in relevant part:

Both paragraphs 1 and 2 of subdivision (a) are amended to conform to the standard for transfer in 28 U.S.C. 1412. Formerly 28 U.S.C. 1477 authorized a court either to transfer or retain a case which had been commenced in a district where venue was improper. However, 28 U.S.C. 1412, which supercedes 28 U.S.C. 1477, authorizes only the transfer of a case. The rule is amended to delete the reference to retention of a case commenced in an improper district. Dismissal of a case commenced in the improper district as authorized by 28 U.S.C. 1406 has been added to the rule. If a timely motion to dismiss for improper venue is not filed, the right to object to venue is waived * * *."

Id. at 766.

10. Id. at 767; see also In re Pick, Jr., 95 B.R. 712 (Bankr. D.S.D. 1989).

§ 12–12

1. The ability to appeal has been reduced in a number of ways by the 1984 act. The option of appealing directly to the Court of Appeals without bankruptcy or district court approval under 28 U.S.C.A. § 1293(b) no longer exists. Moreover, the only alternative to an appeal to the district court is appeal to the bankruptcy appellate panel. Under § 158(b)(1) establishing such panels is at the

To the extent that a bankruptcy judge's decision is on a non-core, related matter, and thus constitutes only proposed findings of fact and conclusions of law to the district court, there is in effect a direct appeal and a "de novo" review under section 157(c)(1). In core proceedings, section 158(a) states that the district court shall hear appeals "from final judgments, orders and decrees and, with leave of court * * *." These are heard not de novo, but in the form of regular appeals.

Section 158(b) authorizes the establishment of bankruptcy appellate panels by the judicial council of a circuit. If such a panel is established, such appeals may be taken to it, but only if all the parties consent and only if the district judges in a particular district within the circuit authorize appeals to the panel. At this writing only the Ninth Circuit has such a panel.[2] It seems doubtful that such panels or their authority will become widespread. As indicated above, district judges, ever jealous of their prerogatives, apparently saw to it that the panels which had somewhat wider authority under the pre-1984 law were brought back under the control of the district judges in the 1984 act.[3]

Appeals from the district courts' decisions and from the bankruptcy appellate panel decisions are taken to the Courts of Appeals.

In bankruptcy practice the more troublesome question is what orders and decisions can be appealed rather than to what courts appeals are made. Section 158 explicitly authorizes appeals of "final judgments, orders, and decrees" and, in the discretion of the court, "from interlocutory orders and decrees". Volumes could be written about the question whether a decision is interlocutory or final;[4] it may be even more difficult to tell the difference between final and interlocutory orders in bankruptcy law than it is in general. Any order that will have the effect of foreclosing on a right is final. Orders that merely delay the decision on or realization of a right are interlocutory. Because many orders in a bankruptcy case involve postponement rather than an immediate foreclosure of rights, the line between finality and interlocutory status is especially blurred.

On the other hand, the courts in bankruptcy cases have been liberal in finding orders final. This is in part due to a history of providing greater

---

total discretion of the judicial council of each circuit and the consent of all parties is needed to appeal to the panel. Section 158(b)(2) states that "no appeal be referred to a panel * * * unless the district judges for the district, by majority vote, authorize such referral of appeals originating within the district." Finally, § 158(b)(3) states that no judge sitting on the panel can be from the same district from which the order is being appealed. At this writing only the Ninth Circuit has such a panel.

2. Two issues arise when applying the panel in the Ninth Circuit. First, the parties are deemed to have consented to the panel if they do not object within the prescribed period. This may well raise constitutional questions as to the right to a hearing by an Article III judge. Second, at least one court has held that a decision by the panel is binding on the entire Ninth Circuit because all the districts authorized appeals to the panel. In re Windmill Farms, Inc., 70 B.R. 618 (Bankr. 9th Cir. 1987), rev'd on other grounds, 841 F.2d 1467 (9th Cir.1988), on remand, 116 B.R. 755 (Bankr.S.D.Cal.1990).

3. The National Conference of Bankruptcy Judges recently recommended that BAPs be established in all circuits to hear first-level appeals from decisions of bankruptcy judges. For an exhaustive analysis of the Ninth Circuit's experience with a BAP, see Bermant & Sloan, Bankruptcy Appellate Panels: the Ninth Circuit Experience, 21 Ariz. St. L.J. 181 (1989).

4. See Moore's Federal Practice 110.08–.22 (2d ed. 1986) for an exhaustive analysis; 15 C. Wright, A. Miller, & E. Cooper Federal Practice and Procedure §§ 3905–3918 (1st ed. 1976).

opportunity to appeal in bankruptcy while a case is pending. As the First Circuit has stated:

> Were this not a bankruptcy case, we doubt that the kind of order before us would be considered 'final.' * * * Congress has long provided that orders in bankruptcy cases may be immediately appealed if they finally dispose of *discrete disputes within the larger case* * * *.[5]

The usual formulation is in the so-called *Cohen* rule. An order will be final in bankruptcy when it falls into that

> class which finally determine claims of right separable from, and collateral to, rights asserted in the action, too important to be denied review and too independent of the cause itself to require that appellate consideration be deferred until the whole case is adjudicated.[6]

Another test that the courts apply is simply whether the order requires further proceedings before its outcome can be fully evaluated. If the order requires no further action than simple "managerial" or "mechanical" proceedings, then the order is final; but if significant further proceedings are required, the order is interlocutory.[7]

Some examples of final orders are an order allowing a claim, even if the actual amount to be realized by the claim is undetermined,[8] an order dismissing an objection to discharge,[9] an order to sell property of the estate,[10] an order by the district court to vacate a bankruptcy court's confirmation of a plan,[11] an order disallowing or allowing a homestead exemption,[12] an order for the turnover of property,[13] an order granting relief from the automatic stay,[14] and an order fixing venue.[15]

Examples of orders which are not final include an order granting

---

5. In re Saco Local Development Corp., 711 F.2d 441, 443–44 (1st Cir.1983).

6. Cohen v. Beneficial Industrial Loan Corp., 337 U.S. 541, 546, 69 S.Ct. 1221, 1225, 93 L.Ed. 1528 (1949); Coopers & Lybrand v. Livesay, 437 U.S. 463, 468, 98 S.Ct. 2454, 2457, 57 L.Ed.2d 351 (1978); 1 Collier on Bankruptcy 3.03 at 3–171 (15th ed. 1983); 9 Moore's Federal Practice 110.10 (2d ed., 1986). For treatment of interlocutory review of bankruptcy appeals, see 16 C. Wright, A. Miller & E. Cooper, Federal Practice and Procedure § 3926 (1st ed. 1976).

7. City of Louisa v. Levi, 140 F.2d 512, 514 (6th Cir.1944). Another test lists the factors used in deciding finalities as the extent to which (1) the order leaves the bankruptcy court nothing to do but execute the order; (2) delay in obtaining review would prevent the aggrieved party from obtaining effective relief; and (3) a later reversal on that issue would require recommencement of the entire proceeding. In re Apex Oil Co., 884 F.2d 343 (8th Cir.1989).

8. In the Matter of Fox, 762 F.2d 54 (7th Cir.1985); but see In re Hospital General San Carlos, Inc., 83 B.R. 870 (D. Puerto Rico 1988).

9. In the Matter of Riggsby, 745 F.2d 1153 (7th Cir.1984); In re Daley, 776 F.2d 834 (9th Cir.1985), cert. denied, 476 U.S. 1159, 106 S.Ct. 2279, 90 L.Ed.2d 721 (1986).

10. In re Sax, 796 F.2d 994 (7th Cir.1986).

11. In the Matter of Pizza of Hawaii, Inc., 761 F.2d 1374 (9th Cir.1985).

12. In re Sumy, 777 F.2d 921 (4th Cir. 1985); In re White, 727 F.2d 884 (9th Cir. 1984).

13. In re Moody, Jr., 817 F.2d 365 (5th Cir.1987), appeal after remand, 899 F.2d 383 (5th Cir.1990); In re Cash Currency Exchange, Inc., 762 F.2d 542 (7th 1985).

14. In re Kemble, 776 F.2d 802 (9th Cir. 1985); but cf cases holding that orders denying relief from stay were not final, Bowers v. Connecticut National Bank, 847 F.2d 1019 (2d Cir.1988); Promenade National Bank v. Phillips (In the Matter of Phillips), 844 F.2d 230 (5th Cir.1988); Quinn v. CGR, 828 F.2d 1463, 1465–67 (10th Cir.1987); contra In re Apex Oil Co., 884 F.2d 343 (8th Cir.1989).

15. A.H. Robins Company, Inc. v. Piccinin, 788 F.2d 994 (4th Cir.1986), cert. denied, 479 U.S. 876, 107 S.Ct. 251, 93 L.Ed.2d 177 (1986).

summary judgment for debtor against city for postpetition services,[16] an order by the bankruptcy court permitting debtor in possession to recover amounts paid on a mortgage,[17] an order denying a motion to bar experts,[18] and a bankruptcy court's determination on the validity of a disclosure statement.[19]

Even if an order is not final, section 158(a) provides that interlocutory appeals are available with leave from the court:

> The district courts * * * shall have jurisdiction to hear appeals * * * with leave of the court, from interlocutory orders and decrees, of bankruptcy judges entered in cases and proceedings referred to the bankruptcy judges under section 157 of this title.[20]

Section 158(a) is not instructive on the standard for interlocutory appeals like its repealed forerunner, section 1292.[21] As a result some courts have continued to use the 1292(b) standard as the appropriate one for use under section 158.[22] This standard permits appeal:

> where there are substantial grounds for difference of opinion as to the controlling questions of law, and where an immediate appeal from the order may materially advance the ultimate termination of the litigation.[23]

Some examples of interlocutory orders when appeal was granted[24] are orders compelling production of documents,[25] orders determining creditor's interest adequately protected by debtor's security deposit,[26] order denying a motion for summary judgment,[27] an order allowing a claim when the amount of that claim (versus the realizable value of the claim) is uncertain,[28] and a district court order to remand to the bankruptcy court for further proceedings to determine sanctions for violation of the automatic stay.[29]

Examples of orders where courts declined to allow interlocutory appeal include an order refusing to approve trustee's proposed settlement with creditor,[30] and an order denying a demand for jury.[31]

---

16. Matter of Berke, 837 F.2d 293 (7th Cir.1988).

17. In re White Beauty View, Inc., 841 F.2d 524 (3d Cir.1988).

18. In re Forseen Inc., 81 B.R. 903 (N.D.Ill. 1987).

19. In re Elsinore Shore Associates, 82 B.R. 339 (D.N.J.1988).

20. 28 U.S.C.A. § 158(a).

21. 28 U.S.C.A. § 1292 (repealed).

22. In the Matter of Bertoli, 58 B.R. 992, 993 (D.N.J.1986), aff'd, 812 F.2d 136 (3d Cir. 1987); In re Manville Forest Products Corp., 31 B.R. 991, 995 n.5 (S.D.N.Y.1983).

23. In re Matter of Bertoli, 58 B.R. at 995.

24. For an example of the mess which can result from appealing interlocutory orders which later become final, see In re Tveten, 97 B.R. 541 (Bankr. D.Minn.1989).

25. Butcher v. Bailey, 753 F.2d 465 (6th Cir.1985), in which it was held that the only way to appeal such an order would be to refuse to comply and then appeal the court sanctions. In this case the would-be appellant had already complied with the order, rendering the issue moot. This view is reflected in other opinions as well. See In the Matter of International Horizons, Inc., 689 F.2d 996, 1000–1001 (11th Cir.1982), which citing other cases states that orders concerning discovery are not generally appealable.

26. In re Alchar Hardware, 730 F.2d 1386 (11th Cir.1984).

27. In re Smith, 735 F.2d 459 (11th Cir. 1984).

28. In the Matter of Fox, 762 F.2d 54 (7th Cir.1985).

29. In re Brown, 803 F.2d 120 (3d Cir. 1986), in which it was held that the order would not be final and appealable until liability and damages had been established.

30. In re Neshaminy Office Bldg. Associates, 81 B.R. 301 (E.D.Pa. 1987).

---

31. See note 31 on page 886.

D. JURY TRIAL
§ 12–13 The Right to Jury Trial

Does the jury live in bankruptcy? To help the analysis, we divide the question into two parts. First, when is there a right to a jury trial in a proceeding arising in, under, or related to a bankruptcy case? Second, can a bankruptcy judge hear a jury trial or must the trial be heard by a district court judge?

To begin, understand that the bankruptcy court has routinely and long been characterized as a "court of equity." "The Bankruptcy Act, passed pursuant to the power given to Congress by Art[icle] I, s[ection] 8, of the Constitution to establish uniform laws on the subject of bankruptcy, converts the creditor's legal claim into an equitable claim to a pro rata share of the res."[1] In *Barton v. Barbour*,[2] the Supreme Court states the consequence of this conversion:

> [T]he fundamental principle [is] that the right of trial by jury, considered as an absolute right, does not extend to cases of equity jurisdiction. If it be conceded or clearly shown that a case belongs to this class, the trial of questions involved in it belongs to the court itself, no matter what may be its importance or complexity.
>
> * * *
>
> So, in cases of bankruptcy, many incidental questions arise in the course of administering the bankrupt estate, which would ordinarily be pure cases at law, and in respect of their facts triable by jury, but, as belonging to the bankruptcy proceedings, they become cases over which the bankruptcy court, which acts as a court of equity, exercises exclusive control. Thus, a claim of debt or damages against the bankrupt is investigated by chancery methods * * *.

Because it is a "court of equity," the lion's share of all proceedings before the bankruptcy court are equitable and neither party has a right to a jury in those proceedings. But as we have seen above, many of the proceedings in a bankruptcy case are themselves identical to conventional civil cases where the parties would have a right to a jury but for the happenstance that one party to the civil case is in Chapter 11. Are those cases converted to equitable cases because one party is in Chapter 11? Are the parties thus deprived of their right to a jury? The answer is yes, but only some of the time.

The 1989 Supreme Court case *Granfinanciera, S.A. v. Nordberg*[3] is the most authoritative comment on this question, but to understand that case one needs to examine the law before and after 1978. Prior to 1978 and under the Act of 1898, the courts had generally drawn the line between

---

31. T.O.S. Industries, Inc. v. Ross Hill Controls Corp., 72 B.R. 749 (S.D.Tex.1987).

§ 12–13

1. Katchen v. Landy, 382 U.S. 323, 336, 86 S.Ct. 467, 476, 15 L.Ed.2d 391 (1966), quoting Gardner v. State of New Jersey, 329 U.S. 565, 573–4, 67 S.Ct. 467, 471–72, 91 L.Ed. 504, 514–15 (1947), reh'g denied, 330 U.S. 853, 67 S.Ct. 768, 91 L.Ed. 1296 (1947).

2. 104 U.S. (14 Otto) 126, 133–34, 26 L.Ed. 672 (1881).

3. 492 U.S. 33, 109 S.Ct. 2782, 106 L.Ed.2d 26 (1989).

equity and law along the same border that divided "summary" from "plenary" jurisdiction. Then the bankruptcy court had only summary jurisdiction and, absent the agreement of the parties, could not hear cases that required "plenary" consideration. Thus, those requiring plenary jurisdiction (an example might be a case in which property, in the possession of a third party and not subject to the actual or constructive control of the debtor, was claimed by the trustee) would be heard in state or federal court as part of a separate proceeding and not in the bankruptcy court. Because those cases were heard as ordinary civil suits, they carried with them all the normal civil rules including the right to a jury trial. If an action was brought in federal court, it was consequently governed by the Seventh Amendment and possibly concurrent or supplemental federal statutes and rules. If brought in a state court, it was likewise governed by the state constitution and that state's statutes or rules.[4]

The right to a jury trial under an exercise of summary jurisdiction was limited. The Bankruptcy Act of 1898 did grant a statutory right to jury trial before the bankruptcy court on behalf of "a person against whom an involuntary petition has been filed."[5] In such cases only the issues of insolvency and whether an act of bankruptcy had been committed had to be heard by a jury.

The most prominent Supreme Court case on the pre-1978 right to a jury in bankruptcy is *Katchen v. Landy*.[6] In finding summary jurisdiction to recover a voidable preference from a creditor (at least in the case in which that creditor had previously filed a claim against the bankruptcy estate), the Supreme Court held that there was no right to a jury trial on the issues involving preferences. It so held even though the identical issues in a preference case where the assets were in the hands of a third party who had not filed a claim in the bankruptcy estate, would have required a plenary hearing, would have been outside the bankruptcy court, and would therefore have allowed either of the parties to insist upon a jury trial.

When the 1978 act was passed, the distinction between plenary and summary jurisdiction was abolished. The effect of this was that many plenary cases that would formerly have been heard by federal district courts or by state courts would be heard by the bankruptcy court. Accordingly, Congress had to decide whether juries would be available in those cases. To solve that problem Congress enacted 28 U.S.C.A. § 1480(a) which reads as follows:

> This chapter and title 11 do not affect any right to trial by jury, in a case under title 11 or in a proceeding arising under title 11 or arising in or related to a case under title 11, that is provided by statute in effect on September 30, 1979.

The most obvious reading of 1480(a) is to tell the parties that in cases that would have been "plenary," and so would have required trial before juries outside of bankruptcy court prior to 1978, there would be a right to a jury trial in the bankruptcy court after 1978. Subsection (b) of section 1480 also provided that the bankruptcy court could order the issues arising under

4. 5 Moore's Federal Practice para. 38.-30[4] at 224.3 (2d ed. 1978).

5. Bankruptcy Act § 19.

6. 382 U.S. 323, 86 S.Ct. 467, 15 L.Ed.2d 391 (1966).

section 303 of title 11 (involuntary cases) to be triable without a jury. The effect of this was to place the issues of involuntary petitions, some of which had been triable by jury as of right under the Act (see above), within the discretion of the bankruptcy judge.

In 1982, the *Marathon*[7] case came along to disrupt the jurisdictional grant to the bankruptcy courts. One of the several bases for finding that the bankruptcy court was an Article I court impermissively exercising Article III power was the fact that the bankruptcy court could hear jury trials.[8] As part of the 1984 act solving the *Marathon* conundrum, Congress passed 28 U.S.C.A. § 1411, titled "Jury Trials." Subsection (a) of section 1411 reads as follows:

> Except as provided in subsection (b) of this section, this chapter and title 11 do not affect any right to trial by jury that an individual has under applicable non-bankruptcy law with regard to a personal injury or wrongful death tort claim.

Most have concluded that section 1480 quoted above was implicitly repealed by section 1411 which has quite similar language.[9] Some have argued that the implication of 1411 is not only that section 1480 is repealed, but also that the right to jury trial in bankruptcy proceedings is (to the extent permitted by the Seventh Amendment) limited to cases heard by the district court (as mandated by section 157(b)(5)) involving personal injury or wrongful death tort claims. In other words, some might say that the passage of section 1480, the repeal of section 1480 and the passage of 1411 have narrowed the statutory right to jury trial to personal injury or wrongful death tort claims.[10] All would concede that there must be some other cases or proceedings in a bankruptcy case where the Seventh Amendment would demand a jury trial, but prior to *Granfinanciera* there was very little agreement on the scope of the Seventh Amendment's demand.[11]

It should come as no surprise to the reader to know that the decisions leading up to *Granfinanciera* were in disagreement over the effect of the 1984 amendments. One line of cases can be illustrated by *Matter of McLouth Steel.*[12] In that case two parties who had filed claims in the McLouth Chapter 11 case sought jury trials in response to the debtor in possession's suit for the return of a voidable preference. The case is almost identical to *Katchen v. Landy*. Judge Pratt found that *Katchen v. Landy* was good law, at least until the enactment of 1411 and appeared to adopt the

---

7. Northern Pipeline Constr. Co. v. Marathon Pipe Line Co., 458 U.S. 50, 102 S.Ct. 2858, 73 L.Ed.2d 598 (1982), judgment stayed, 459 U.S. 813, 103 S.Ct. 199, 74 L.Ed.2d 160 (1982).

8. 458 U.S. at 85, 102 S.Ct. at 2878–79, 73 L.Ed.2d at 624.

9. In re Chase & Sanborn Corp., 835 F.2d 1341, 1348 (11th Cir.1988), rev'd on other grounds, Granfinanciera v. Nordberg, 492 U.S. 33, 109 S.Ct. 2782, 106 L.Ed.2d 26 (1989) ("Section 1480 was repealed, however, by the enactment of Section 1411 of the Bankruptcy Amendments * * *."); In re Riggsby, 745 F.2d 1153 (7th Cir. 1984).

10. See King, Jurisdiction and Procedure, 38 Vand.L.Rev. 675, 702 (1985), where it is argued that no right to a jury trial exists in the bankruptcy court because it is a court of equity. Personal injury cases are not equity cases and are brought in the first instance to the district court. All other cases in the bankruptcy court, whether core or non-core, are without the right to jury.

11. It should be noted that § 1411(b) grants the discretion to decide whether a jury is appropriate in a § 303 involuntary case to the district court and not the bankruptcy court unlike § 1480(b) did.

12. 55 B.R. 357 (E.D.Mich.1985).

proposition that core proceedings should be treated the same way as the old "summary proceedings" and non-core proceedings should be treated like old "plenary proceedings." Although the case did not call for such a decision, apparently Judge Pratt and those following *McLouth* would say there is no right to a jury trial as long as a proceeding is a core proceeding,[13] but that there might be such a right if the proceeding is not a core proceeding. In *McLouth* the judge simply concluded there was no Seventh Amendment right or statutory right to a jury and followed *Katchen v. Landy.*

A case representing the opposing position is *In re Wolfe.*[14] In that case the debtor challenged the validity of creditor's lien under the Texas constitution and also claimed certain homestead rights under Texas law. The creditor demanded a jury trial and the court concluded that the dispute over validity of the creditor's lien in light of the Texas homestead law required a jury trial. The court made that finding despite the fact that the creditor had stipulated that the challenge to its lien was a core proceeding.

In finding there was a right to a jury trial despite the fact that the issue arose in a core proceeding as identified under section 157, the court made several points. First, it recited that many of the summary proceedings prior to 1978 in fact rested on the consent of the parties for the finding that they were "summary" instead of "plenary." Because the court's jurisdiction in those proceedings rested on the litigants' assent, including implicit assent to denial of a jury trial, one should not draw inferences about rights to juries of non-consenters. Secondly, the court disagreed with the dictum in *McLouth Steel* concerning section 1411. It concluded that Congress intended merely to make it clear that the right to a jury trial would be preserved in personal injury or wrongful death court cases, but did not intend to withdraw the statutory authority for all other jury trials.

Finally, the court concluded that one should not look at cases such as *Katchen v. Landy,* and at the pre-1978 summary/plenary distinction, but rather look more generally at the issues and decide whether they should be characterized as "equitable" or "legal" under traditional Seventh Amendment analysis that would be undertaken in any United States court.

§ 12–14 The Right to Jury Trial—Granfinanciera

So sat the law until 1989. In that year the Supreme Court decided *Granfinanciera v. Nordberg;*[1] the case exceeded the wildest dreams of jury advocates. Apart from a few subtleties, the Court adopted a traditional Seventh Amendment analysis for determining when jury trials are appropriate in bankruptcy.

The case arose out of the bankruptcy of the Chase & Sanborn Corporation ("C & S") which filed a petition on May 18, 1983. In 1985, Nordberg, the trustee for Chase & Sanborn's estate, commenced an action in the district court to void three allegedly fraudulent transfers made to Granfinan-

---

13. But see St. Paul Fire & Marine Ins. v. Vaughn, 779 F.2d 1003 (4th Cir.1985) (creditor successfully removed case to the District Court in order to have a jury trial on exemption or discharge under the willful and malicious rule, section 543(a)(6)).

14. 68 B.R. 80 (Bankr. N.D.Tex.1986), appeal denied, 67 B.R. 260 (N.D.Tex.1986).

§ 12–14

1. 492 U.S. 33, 109 S.Ct. 2782, 106 L.Ed.2d 26 (1989).

ciera, S.A. and Medex, Ltd. The district court referred the case to the bankruptcy court where it was first heard. The transfers consisted of: (1) a $1,500,000 wire transfer on October 21, 1982 from a C & S bank account to a Granfinanciera bank account; (2) a cashier's check for $100,000 dated December 15, 1982, purchased by C & S and deposited in a Medex bank account; and (3) another cashier's check for $80,000 dated December 16, 1982, purchased by C & S and also deposited in a Medex bank account. The complaint alleged that at the time of the transfers, C & S was insolvent and that C & S received no consideration or less than a reasonably equivalent value in exchange for the transfers. Therefore, Nordberg alleged, the transfers were fraudulent conveyances which could be avoided under section 548(a)(2) and recovered for the benefit of the estate pursuant to section 550(a). In answer to the complaint, Granfinanciera and Medex requested a jury trial. Neither Granfinanciera nor Medex submitted a proof of claim against the estate.[2]

Reasoning that a suit to recover a fraudulent transfer was a "core action" that presented a non-jury issue under English common law, the bankruptcy judge denied the request for a jury trial.[3] The District Court affirmed without discussion of the jury issue and the Court of Appeals for the Eleventh Circuit affirmed, noting that section 1411 only provides for a jury trial in personal injury or wrongful death suits. That court also ruled that the Seventh Amendment preserved no rights since fraudulent conveyance actions were equitable in nature even when the plaintiff sought only a monetary recovery.

Holding that petitioners were entitled to a jury trial under the Seventh Amendment, the Supreme Court reversed and remanded. Justice Brennan admonished Congress for the ambiguity of the current statutory scheme (sections 1411 and 1480) and indicated that in the absence of special legislation, a right to jury in bankruptcy "must necessarily be predicated entirely on the Seventh Amendment."[4] Notwithstanding the Court's disapproval of the ambiguity in section 1411, it failed to give any interpretation of that section and stressed that the holding did no more than preserve a jury right based upon the Seventh Amendment.

> In pertinent part the Seventh Amendment provides: In Suits at common law, where the value in controversy shall exceed $20, the right of trial by jury shall be preserved * * *.[5]

---

2. For facts of proceeding see In re Chase & Sanborn Corp., 835 F.2d 1341 (11th Cir. 1988), cert. granted, 486 U.S. 1054, 108 S.Ct. 2818, 100 L.Ed.2d 920 (1988); Granfinanciera v. Nordberg, 492 U.S. at 36, 109 S.Ct. at 2787, 106 L.Ed.2d at 37.

3. Hereinafter, for reasons of simplicity, the creditors will be referred to only as "Granfinanciera." For the issues resolved by the Court, Granfinanciera and Medex were treated similarly. The trustee attempted to persuade the Court that Granfinanciera—though not Medex—was not entitled to a jury trial because when the jury request was made Granfinanciera was a commercial instrumentality of the Columbian government. Being as such, foreign sovereigns could only be sued in accordance with the Foreign Sovereign Immunities Act which, the trustee argued, prohibited trial by jury. The Court declined to address the argument because it had neither been raised below nor adequately briefed and argued. Granfinanciera, 492 U.S. at 38, 109 S.Ct. at 2788, 106 L.Ed.2d at 38.

4. Granfinanciera, 492 U.S. at 41 n.3, 109 S.Ct. at 2789–90 n.3, 106 L.Ed. 2d at 40 n.3.

5. 492 U.S. at 64, 109 S.Ct. at 2802, 106 L.Ed. 2d at 55.

Under the analysis applied by Justice Brennan in *Granfinanciera,* there are only three ways in which a litigant in bankruptcy court can be deprived of its right to jury trial. First, there is no right to a jury trial if the claim is "equitable" and not "legal" or in the terms of the amendment not "at common law". Courts today must distinguish equitable from legal claims by imagining that they are the courts of England in the year 1791 and by then deciding whether an English court—if it were faced with the modern day cause of action—would cause it to be heard in a court of equity or in a court of law. Second, there is no right to a jury trial if the claim of right asserted is a "public right" and Congress assigned it to a tribunal (such as an administrative agency) that does not hold jury trials or a specialized court of equity. Third, one who submits to the jurisdiction of the court of equity (as by filing a claim in bankruptcy court) loses his right to a jury trial.

When the Court referred to the analysis of the cause of action as legal or equitable as "familiar", it may have been a bit loose with that term. One of the amusing byproducts of the requirement that a modern-day judge transport himself to 1791 and then determine whether the case before him would be legal or equitable is to find grown and sensible men, in this case Justices Brennan and White, quarreling in print over the writings of obscure 19th century legal scholars such as O. Bump (writing on Conveyances Made By Debtors to Defraud Creditors in 1890) and W. Roberts (writing on Voluntary and Fraudulent Conveyances in 1845). Justice White cites Roberts' 1845 treatise with approval; Justice Brennan dismisses that treatise as "obscure and not speaking squarely to the question whether 18th century English courts of equity would hear cases where legal remedies were sufficient." [6]

The Court relied on *Tull v. United States* [7] as one basis for the Seventh Amendment analysis it applied. In that case, the Court granted a jury trial to the defendant in a Clean Water Act enforcement action. There Justice Brennan found that a jury trial is required in "actions that are analogous to 'suits at common law'" with the purpose of the analysis being "[t]o determine whether a statutory action is more similar to cases that were tried in courts of law than to suits tried in courts of equity." [8] He noted that the determination required both a comparison of the action to 18th century analogues and a characterization of the remedy as either legal or equitable. [9] While the Court in *Tull* accepted that the enforcement proceeding could be analogized to either an 18th-century action in debt (law) or public nuisance (equity), it stressed that the conclusion need not rest "on what has been called an 'abstruse historical' search for the nearest 18th-century analogue * * * characterizing the relief sought as '[m]ore important' than finding a precisely analogous common law cause of action." [10] In a footnote on the same page, the Court indicated that both the cause of action and the remedy need not be legal for the jury right to be available, but that the search was

---

6. 492 U.S. at 47 n.6, 109 S.Ct. at 2793 n.6, 106 L.Ed. 2d at 44 n.6.

7. 481 U.S. 412, 417–18, 107 S.Ct. 1831, 1835, 95 L.Ed.2d 365 (1987).

8. Id. at 417, 107 S.Ct. at 1835, 95 L.Ed.2d at 373.

9. Id.

10. Id. at 421, 107 S.Ct. at 1837, 95 L.Ed.2d at 375.

for a "single historical analogue," using both characterizations as important factors.[11]

In effect, the *Tull* case suggests there are two parts to the equity-legal template. First, one looks at the cause of action in general to determine whether it would traditionally have been regarded as legal or equitable. Second, and more important, one determines the equitable or legal nature by the nature of the remedy. In effect these are merely two attributes of the cause of action. It seems sensible, as the Court suggests, to rely upon the relief requested as the most important of the two. In applying those standards to the facts in *Granfinanciera*, the Court pointed out that the trustee was seeking only a money judgment from the defendant, which clearly pointed toward the legal and not the equitable side. It also found that actions to recover fraudulent transfers were in fact heard at law in 18th century England.

With that finding, the plaintiff was entitled to a jury unless it could be found that his was a "public right" assigned to a tribunal which was not intended by Congress to hear cases by jury. Although Justice Brennan rejected the narrow definition of "public rights" suggested by Justice Scalia in a concurring opinion[12], he found that *Granfinanciera* involved private and not public rights. Most public rights are those asserted against the United States or some other governmental agency. In *Granfinanciera*, a representative of the creditors' private interests was suing another private party for the recovery of money. Justice Brennan found that such rights were private and not public. In reaching this decision Justice Brennan disavowed the inference that might have been drawn from the statement in *Northern Pipeline Construction Co. v. Marathon Pipe Line Co.*[13] that almost any restructuring of debtor-creditor relations might be a "public right."[14] By pointing out that fraudulent conveyances are not proceedings "in" bankruptcy but merely "arising out of" bankruptcy, the Court left some room for the recognition of some bankruptcy claims as "public" and so capable of release by Congress from the grasp of the Seventh Amendment.

Justice Brennan distinguished *Katchen v. Landy*, an earlier preference case where jury trial was denied, by pointing out that it involved a creditor who had submitted a claim in the bankruptcy court. In a complicated discussion of *Katchen* and of other cases, Justice Brennan maintained that one who submits a claim is not waiving his right to a jury trial as such, but is rather submitting to the "process of allowance and disallowance of claims" which is itself a process in equity. While the reasoning is rather finespun,

---

11. Id. at 421 n.6, 107 S.Ct. at 1837 n.6, 95 L.Ed.2d at 375 n.6.

12. The Court rejected the view that public rights require the government to be a party to the dispute. Public rights are also involved, the majority indicated, when Congress in delegating the cause of action to a non-jury tribunal "[has] create[d] a seemingly 'private' right that is so closely integrated into a public regulatory scheme as to be a matter appropriate for agency resolution with limited involvement by the Article III judiciary." Granfinanciera at 2797, quoting, Thomas v. Union Carbide Agricultural Products Co., 473 U.S. 568, 593–594, 105 S.Ct. 3325, 3339–3340, 87 L.Ed.2d 409 (1985).

13. 458 U.S. 50, 71, 102 S.Ct. 2858, 2871, 73 L.Ed.2d 598 (1982), judgment stayed, 459 U.S. 813, 103 S.Ct. 199, 74 L.Ed.2d 160 (1982).

14. Granfinanciera, 492 U.S. at 55 n.11, 109 S.Ct. at 2797 n.11, 106 L.Ed. at 50 n.11.

the conclusion is solid: if the creditor submits a claim, he loses his right to a jury trial on the issues of fraudulent conveyance and preference.[15]

Where do we stand after *Granfinanciera?* First, it seems clear that Justice Brennan and the majority, and *a fortiori* Justice White and the other dissenters, believe that the Seventh Amendment does *not* require a jury in the large bulk of bankruptcy proceedings. Presumably no jury is required in proceedings such as those on the allowance or disallowance of claims in sections 502 and 506, the valuation of assets in the bankruptcy estate, determinations concerning adequate protection under 362 and 364, questions about loans under 364 and sales under 363, and a host of other things having to do with everyday disputes in the administration of bankruptcy estates. These details of administration are beyond the Seventh Amendment for one of three reasons.

First, one might conclude that they are inherently equitable and not legal. If there was no bankruptcy in 1791, presumably no bankruptcy case concerning the automatic stay or discharge could have been heard in the common law courts of England in that year. Therefore, presumably they are not legal, but equitable.[16] We read the Court as applying the test which says that a jury is required only if the action could be heard at law. If the action is nothing that would be recognized by an English court of any kind at that time, there is no requirement of a jury.

A second route to the conclusion that no jury is required in routine bankruptcy administrative cases is to conclude that those central parts of bankruptcy administration are themselves public rights established under the bankruptcy clause by the Congress and designated as non-jury issues. That is a proposition with which Justice Scalia would certainly not agree and it is not one that either the majority or the dissent emphasized.

As time passes, however, we suspect the Court may be driven to a conclusion that much of bankruptcy is a "public right." One should note the significance of the route by which one concludes there is no right to a jury. If that conclusion rests upon the proposition that the cause of action is equitable, that it would not have been heard by a court of law in 1791, or vice versa, it is a conclusion that cannot be altered by the Congress because it arises exclusively from an interpretation of the Seventh Amendment. If, on the other hand, the conclusion of no jury right rests upon the proposition that the right at issue is a "public right" established by Congress and assigned to a non-jury tribunal, then Congress is left with the power to change or alter it, to establish different procedures and to tune the system to meet the society's needs. To give Congress that flexibility, the Court may

---

15. The Court did not find it important that Katchen was decided before 1984 when a creditor who had not submitted a claim in bankruptcy court was subject to a preference proceeding only in a plenary action in district court where the creditor would have been entitled to a jury. See Schoenthal v. Irving Trust Co., 287 U.S. 92, 53 S.Ct. 50, 77 L.Ed. 185 (1932). After the 1984 Amendments, a bankruptcy court could hear a preference proceeding regardless of whether a creditor had submitted a claim since such proceedings had been deemed core.

16. We have assumed that everything that is not an action to be heard at law in 1791 is not entitled to a jury. Of course one could take the opposite position, namely there is a jury unless an action is found to be equitable. The metaphysical nature of this inquiry makes that assumption important. Because there would be no possibility in 1791 of considering lifting the stay under sections 362 and 361, there could neither be a hearing at law or at equity and the right to a jury trial would depend upon which test one applied.

ultimately be driven to recognize larger "public rights" than at least the majority now seems disposed to grant.

Third, the Court's extensive discussion of *Katchen v. Landy* and its distinguishing of that case on the ground that the creditor there filed a claim means that almost any creditor who has filed a claim in bankruptcy has lost the opportunity to demand a jury trial under the Seventh Amendment. Note that the same is not necessarily true of the creditor who is merely listed as a claimant or for whom the trustee or the debtor in possession files a claim. While we would be quite willing to recognize such filing as a submission to equitable jurisdiction, we are doubtful that the Court would go that far.[17]

What cases does this leave for jury trials that would have not commanded jury trials before? First are fraudulent conveyance cases where the defendant has filed no claim and where the trustee seeks a money recovery. Second are preference cases that have the same characteristics.[18] Throughout *Granfinanciera* the Court used fraudulent conveyance and preference interchangeably.[19] Even though one might distinguish fraudulent conveyance from preferences on the ground that the latter are uniquely a child of bankruptcy and thus did not exist in 1791, it seems clear that the Supreme Court does not intend to draw this distinction.[20]

---

17. A list of creditors filed by the debtor pursuant to 11 U.S.C.A. § 521(1) or by the trustee pursuant to 11 U.S.C.A. § 1106(a)(2) is deemed a proof of claim under 11 U.S.C.A. § 1111(a). The trustee or co-debtor may also file a proof of claim in the name of a creditor under 11 U.S.C.A. § 501(b) and (c). See Bankr. R. 3001, et seq. All of these types of filing can be superseded, however, by the creditor's own later filing. Bankr. R. 3003(c)(4), 3004.

A proof of claim as evidence of consent has been used before by courts to find bankruptcy court jurisdiction over related counterclaims. See Northwestern Mutual Life Ins. Co. v. Axton (In re Axton), 641 F.2d 1262, 1268 (9th Cir.1981); Peters v. Lines, 275 F.2d 919, 925 (9th Cir.1960). Some courts, however, have indicated that such filings indicate consent only to the extent that they are evidence of a voluntary, consenting action by the creditor. See Piombo Corp. v. Castlerock Properties (In re Castlerock Properties), 781 F.2d 159 (9th Cir.1986) (no consent to bankruptcy jurisdiction in related proceedings where creditor forced to file as defensive maneuver); cf. Dexter v. Gilbert (Matter of Kirchoff Frozen Foods, Inc.), 496 F.2d 84, 86 (9th Cir.1974) (no consent when no relief sought in bankruptcy court "save in the event the trustee first prevailed in the dispute initiated by him"); Cline v. Kaplan, 323 U.S. 97, 99, 65 S.Ct. 155, 156, 89 L.Ed. 97 (1944) (no consent where claimant resisted petition for turnover order and made formal protest against exercise of summary jurisdiction).

18. It should be noted, however, that in separate footnotes the court left open the door as to whether preferences (Granfinanciera, 492 U.S. at 58 n.13, 109 S.Ct. at 2799 n.13, 106 L.Ed.2d at 51 n.13) and fraudulent conveyance (Id. at 49 n.7, 109 S.Ct. at 2794 n.7, 106 L.Ed.2d at 45 n.7) would be considered equitable in nature if the recovery sought could not be satisfied by a fixed sum of money. A request for an accounting or some other specifically equitable form of relief were noted as factors which could make a fraudulent conveyance equitable in nature. Id.

19. Granfinanciera, 492 U.S. at 48, 109 S.Ct. at 2793, 106 L.Ed.2d at 45. The Court cited Schoenthal v. Irving Trust Co., 287 U.S. 92, 53 S.Ct. 50, 77 L.Ed. 185 (1932), a case involving both preferences and fraudulent conveyances to support the finding that fraudulent conveyance actions were legal in nature. The Court cited Katchen v. Landy, 382 U.S. 323, 86 S.Ct. 467, 15 L.Ed.2d 391 (1966), a case involving preferences to show that fraudulent conveyances involve private rights. 492 U.S. at 57, 109 S.Ct. at 2798–99, 106 L.Ed.2d at 50.

20. Shortly after deciding Granfinanciera, the Court vacated and remanded a preference claim for a sum certain of money where a creditor, who had not filed a claim, was denied a jury. Huffman v. Perkinson (In re Harbour), 840 F.2d 1165 (4th Cir.1988), vacated, 492 U.S. 913, 109 S.Ct. 3234, 106 L.Ed.2d 582 (1989).

Bankruptcy courts have already accepted that fraudulent conveyances and preferences will receive the same treatment. In re Paris Industries Corporation, 106 B.R. 344, 344 (Bankr. D.Me.1989) (court accepted that Granfinanciera analysis applied as well to prefer-

In addition to the preference and fraudulent conveyance cases, it appears that *Granfinanciera* would resolve all doubt in favor of a jury for cases that might have been thought on the border that was established in the *Marathon* case. For example, any case in which a debtor or trustee was attempting to collect an account receivable from a party who had not filed a claim would seem to be a case well within *Granfinanciera*'s holding. That would also be true for any case in which a trustee or debtor in possession was asserting essentially a common law claim against a third party who had not filed a claim in the estate. Of course, many of those cases would already have been outside the bankruptcy court's consideration under *Marathon*, and would, if the defendant so wished, have been tried outside of bankruptcy. To the extent that section 1334 does not take them outside of bankruptcy, they will still enjoy a jury trial within.

Doubtless there are other cases that we do not consider where the outcome is not so clear. These would be cases in which the trustee or debtor in possession was the plaintiff and the defendant did not file a claim, but where the trustee is asserting a claim with a common law analogue that arises out of the Bankruptcy Code.

§ 12–15 The Right to Jury Trial—Jury Cases After Granfinanciera

The courts have already been at work interpreting *Granfinanciera*. They read *Granfinanciera*, as we expected, to mean that the filing of a claim is the death knell to a jury trial claim.[1] The courts have had somewhat more difficulty when the creditor has done some other act such as filing a counterclaim.[2]

---

ences); In re Kroh Bros. Development Co., 108 B.R. 710, 712 (Bankr. W.D.Mo.1989) (court characterized Granfinanciera holding as applicable to fraudulent conveyances and preferences, and accordingly granted jury in preference case where creditor had not submitted claim).

§ 12–15

1. See, e.g., Langenkamp v. Culp, ___ S.Ct. ___, 111 S.Ct. 330, 112 L.Ed.2d 343 (1990), reh'g denied, ___ U.S. ___, 111 S.Ct. 721, 112 L.Ed.2d 709 (1991) (creditors who filed claims had no right to jury trail in trustee's preference action against them); In re Friedberg, 106 B.R. 50, 55 (Bankr. S.D.N.Y.1989), order rev'd, 131 B.R. 6 (S.D.N.Y.1991) ("After Granfinanciera, there can be no doubt as to the preclusive effect a filing of a proof of claim has on a party's right to a jury trial"); In re Wheeling-Pittsburgh Steel Corp., 108 B.R. 82, 85 (Bankr. W.D.Pa.1989) (creditor lost jury right to debtor's counterclaims by filing proof of claims in debtor's bankruptcy case); In re Fort Lauderdale Hotel Partners, Ltd., 103 B.R. 335, 336 (Bankr. S.D.Fla.1989) (expressly adopting as a component of the jury trial analysis "whether the defendant has submitted to the jurisdiction of this Court by submitting a Proof of Claim"); In re Paris Industries Corp., 106 B.R. 344 (Bankr. D.Me.1989) (defendant's jury request denied in preference action where had filed proof of claim).

2. For cases limiting exception to when "proof of claim" is filed by creditor, see In re Industrial Supply Corp., 108 B.R. 799, 801–2 (Bankr. M.D.Fla.1989) (filing of complaint for reclamation of goods by seller pursuant to section 546(c) held not to constitute filing of claim such as would deprive seller of jury right since filing was not of type contemplated by reasoning underlying Granfinanciera); but cf. In re Kaiser Steel Corp., 109 B.R. 968 (D. Colo. 1989) (Bankruptcy court had held below that creditor had lost jury right because it had filed counterclaims which were only in response to adversary proceeding initiated by debtor. The district court questioned whether bankruptcy court ruling which disallowed jury was contradictory to rationale of Granfinanciera, but still affirmed noting absence of law in the area).

For cases expanding the exception, see In re Kaiser, supra, (where creditor held to have consented by filing counterclaims in bankruptcy court, even though such claims were only in response to adversary proceeding initiated by debtor); In re Friedberg, 106 B.R. 50,

A related and yet unanswered question concerns the debtor's right to seek a jury. Presumably the debtor's filing of the petition is a more significant and overt concession to the Court's equitable jurisdiction even than a creditor's filing a claim and thus should be read as a forfeiture of all rights to a jury. However, if one reads the Supreme Court's language as limited strictly to "claims", he might come to the opposite conclusion. We believe one who has filed a voluntary petition in bankruptcy is never entitled to a jury trial in that court.

Exactly how the lower courts are going to respond to the Supreme Court's invitation that they examine the English law of 1791 is not yet clear. In *In re Brown*,[3] Judge Schneider denied a jury trial to a creditor who was challenging the dischargeability of a debt. Without canvassing 18th century precedent, the court pushed aside the request like a troublesome child: "the administration of a bankruptcy estate by the bankruptcy court in an exercise of its traditional equity jurisdiction and adjustment of a debtor creditor relationship" did not require a jury. We expect many courts to give equally short shrift to such claims, particularly where the issue is central to bankruptcy administration.

When a court makes a more faithful attempt to follow the rules laid down in *Granfinanciera*, the goblins appear. In *In re Friedberg*,[4] a prospective purchaser sought recovery of a prepetition deposit from the debtor in connection with a sale which the purchaser chose not to close because of alleged fraudulent misrepresentations. The court denied the purchaser's request for a jury by characterizing both the nature and the remedy as equitable in nature. The court was not fazed by arguments that the action was legal in nature because it was based on "fraud, breach of contract, conversion and unfair trade practices." Instead the court viewed the essence of the action as being a "rescission of the Agreement" and thus equitable.[5] The court was equally unmoved by the argument that a request for monetary damages was legal, and reasoned that money recovered in an equitable action would not bring with it a right to a jury trial.[6] The court could have easily ruled differently. It might have followed the purchaser's "legal" analogue or it could have focused on the monetary nature of the remedy. The Supreme Court stressed the reigning importance of the remedy characterization in both *Tull* and *Granfinanciera*, and in the latter specifically stressed the legal nature of relief in the form of judgment for a certain sum of money.

The *Friedberg* decision gives a glimpse of the kind of indeterminacy and uncertainty that may encourage parties too frequently to litigate the jury question. Although the court denied the request for a jury in that case, the case seems at least as "legal" as a fraudulent conveyance claim and perhaps

55–56 (Bankr. S.D.N.Y 1989), order rev'd, 131 B.R. 6 (S.D.N.Y.1991) (prospective purchaser, by seeking bankruptcy court's approval to proposed sale, invoked bankruptcy court's equitable jurisdiction and thus forfeited right to jury on all issues arising out of transaction, including fraudulent misrepresentation claims); Bayless v. Crabtree Through Adams, 108 B.R. 299, 304–05 (W.D. Okla. 1989), aff'd, 930 F.2d 32 (10th Cir.1991) (defendants to trustee's proceeding to turn over property submitted to equitable jurisdiction of bankruptcy judge by filing counterclaim).

3. 103 B.R. 734 (Bankr. D.Md.1989).

4. 106 B.R. 50 (Bankr. S.D.N.Y.1989), order rev'd, 131 B.R. 6 (S.D.N.Y.1991).

5. In re Friedberg, 106 B.R. at 54.

6. Id. at 55.

more so, yet the court ignores the Supreme Court's admonition and chooses the obscure equitable analogue of "rescission" instead of more obvious legal analogues such as breach of contract.

Judge Stosberg in *In re Owensboro Distilling Company Co.* was more faithful to *Granfinanciera*. He concluded that *Granfinanciera* required a jury trial of a trustee's action under section 723 against the general partners of a bankrupt partnership because the proceeding "does scarcely more than create a conduit for the trustee to serve as the plaintiff in a contract action." [7]

Of course, bankruptcy judges and bankruptcy lawyers are not potted plants. If some judges regard demands for jury trial as challenges to their authority, they and their lawyer allies have the power to manipulate the procedure and to characterize the issues in a way that diminishes the requesting party's chance for a jury. Consider *In re Otasco* [8]. In that case the debtor had an insurance contract for the years 1984 and 1985 with Kemper. There was a $50,000 deductible and when Kemper paid the deductible amount to claimant (as it apparently did), it had a claim against Otasco for that amount. To get cash to reimburse Kemper for the deductible payment, Otasco got AmeriTrust to issue a letter of credit under which Otasco was the customer and Kemper was the beneficiary. Since AmeriTrust had a perfected security interest in all of Otasco's assets, payments to Kemper under the letter of credit turned an unsecured or administrative expense claim into a secured claim. In effect, this transaction converted unsecured tort claims into secured bank claims. This transformation was from the lowest to the highest and it subordinated all with claims in between.

The debtor in possession challenged the transaction. In a complaint filed in several counts, the debtor in possession asserted first that the transaction should be undone, and it asked for injunctive relief to stop further operation of the transaction. Second, it asked for equitable subordination of the claims of Kemper (and perhaps of AmeriTrust). Third, it sought avoidance and recovery of unauthorized post petition transfers under section 549. Finally, it asked for money damages as a result of violations of several Bankruptcy Code sections and for breach of prepetition insurance contracts.

Finding that the first three causes of action were equitable, the court concluded that even the money damage portion was an "integral part of administration of the case and estate." Therefore, the court concluded that even the fourth cause of action depended upon the "exercise of equity jurisdiction" and so did not qualify for a jury trial.

Consider how an adroit counsel like the one in *Otasco* can minimize the possibility of a jury trial by careful selection of the claim and of the request for relief. In another time and place the claim in *Otasco* might have been merely an action for breach of Kemper's insurance contract. Yet counsel dressed the claim as though the breach of the insurance contract was an incidental afterthought. If other courts find that the presence of several equitable claims make the combination "equitable" even when individually

---

7. 108 B.R. 572, 574 (Bankr. W.D.Ky.1989).   8. 110 B.R. 964 (Bankr. N.D. Okla. 1990).

such claims might be described as "legal", or if they conclude that even claims seeking legal relief are equitable because they are deeply integrated in the process of bankruptcy determination and distribution, there will be little or no hope for the person seeking a jury trial.

But Judge Wilson was not content with characterizing Kemper's claim as equitable. He went on to describe how Kemper had participated in the Chapter 11 process in a number of ways. Among other things, it had joined in a motion for relief from the stay for the parties who had claims against Otasco. It filed a brief in that proceeding and asked the bankruptcy court to determine the parties' rights. Moreover, it and Otasco had filed a joint motion for approval of a settlement agreement under which the court was to approve certain of Kemper's claims against Otasco. Thus in the judge's eyes it had submitted to the bankruptcy court's equitable jurisdiction.

Any creditor who has a continuing business relationship with a debtor in Chapter 11 will find repeated occasions in which it needs to seek orders from the bankruptcy court. These trips to court may later be found to be submission to the court's jurisdiction. If other courts follow *Otasco* and draw the inference of consent from these acts, such creditors will have little hope of ever receiving a jury trial, even in circumstances in which they never file a claim.[9]

Fundamentally we regard *Granfinanciera* as a mischievous event. It offers the opportunity to every clever lawyer to forum shop, between the bankruptcy judge on the one hand and the jury on the other. Even if that lawyer is not successful in forum shopping, mere litigation over the forum will create delay in many Chapter 11 cases. Worse than that is the consequence of the constitutional nature of the rule; by finding this doctrine hidden in the Seventh Amendment, and by narrowing the scope of "public rights", the Court has hobbled any congressional attempt at curing the difficulty.

The best that can be hoped from this mess is that other courts will follow Judges Wilson and Schneider who cast a blind eye on the logical but not sensible deductions from the reasoning in *Granfinanciera*. Perhaps some of the damage can be cured by the lower courts' pretending that those implications do not lie in *Granfinanciera* and eventually, by the Court's permitting an erosion and even a silent overturning of the case.

§ 12–16 Which Judge Presides

Once one has decided that there is a right to a jury trial, there remains the question whether the jury trial is to be heard by the bankruptcy judge or

---

9. A creditor that manages to avoid these pitfalls may nonetheless find itself submitting to the equitable jurisdiction of the bankruptcy court. A recent case holds that even if a creditor has a jury trial and risks losing it, the bankruptcy judge has the discretion not to exempt the creditor from the bar date for filing a claim. In re Hooker Investments, Inc., 122 B.R. 659, 663–64 (S.D.N.Y.1991), aff'd, 937 F.2d 833 (2d Cir.1991).

by the district judge.¹ The Supreme Court explicitly stated in *Granfinanciera* that it did not decide whether jury trials could be held in bankruptcy courts.²

At least where the parties agree, there is no reason why a bankruptcy judge cannot hear a jury trial.

If one party does not consent to the bankruptcy judge's sitting, but there is to be a jury trial, one is back to drawing inferences from sections 1480 and 1411 quoted above. Conceivably section 1480, sitting as it was among the jurisdictional requirements of the bankruptcy court, was implicit authorization not only for the jury trial to be heard in the bankruptcy proceeding, but also for the bankruptcy judge to be sitting at the bench. On the other hand, one can argue that the *Marathon* case stands for the proposition that no Article I court can hear a jury trial. But this stretches the holding in that case; the jury question was only one of the reasons for the finding that the bankruptcy judge is merely an Article I animal. Several courts, including the Second Circuit Court of Appeals, have held that bankruptcy judges themselves have the power to hear jury trials.³ The Court of Appeals found statutory authority for jury trials in bankruptcy in 28 U.S.C.A. sections 151 and 157(b), even though no specific provision or Bankruptcy Rule addresses such right.⁴ The court further found that jury trials in core proceedings held in the bankruptcy court do not violate the Seventh Amendment or Article III of the Constitution.⁵ The Eighth Circuit, however, disagreed with the Second Circuit in *In re United Missouri Bank of Kansas City, N.A.*⁶ The court found that Congress had neither expressly nor impliedly granted statutory authority to bankruptcy judges to conduct jury trials, and that any such trial arising in a bankruptcy case must be conducted by the district judge. Having found no statutory authority for bankruptcy judges to conduct jury trials, the Eighth Circuit did not reach the constitutional issues discussed by the Second Circuit.⁷

Although it appeared that the inter-circuit conflict regarding jury trials by bankruptcy judges would be resolved when the Supreme Court granted certiorari in *Ben Cooper*,⁸ the Court merely vacated and remanded the case to the Second Circuit for a determination as to whether the case was

§ 12–16

1. For an analysis of this issue, see Cyr, "The Right to Trial in Bankruptcy: Which Judge is To Preside?," 63 Am. Bankr. L.J. 53–63 (1989).

2. Granfinanciera, 492 U.S. at 64, 109 S.Ct. at 2802, 106 L.Ed.2d at 55.

3. In re Ben Cooper, Inc., 896 F.2d 1394 (2d. Cir.1990), vacated and remanded, ___ U.S. ___, 111 S.Ct. 425, 112 L.Ed.2d 408 (1990); reinstated, 924 F.2d 36 (2d Cir.1991); cert. denied, ___ U.S. ___, 111 S.Ct. 2041, 114 L.Ed.2d 126 (1991) (court held that bankruptcy court had the statutory and constitutional authority to conduct jury trials in core proceeding); see also Dailey v. First Peoples Bank of New Jersey, 76 B.R. 963 (D.N.J.1987); Matter of Honeycomb, Inc., 72 B.R. 371 (Bankr. S.D.N.Y. 1987); contra In re United Missouri Bank of Kansas City, N.A., 901 F.2d 1449 (8th Cir. 1990); In re Owensboro Distilling Company, 108 B.R. 572 (Bankr. W.D.Ky.1989); In re Smith, 84 B.R. 175 (Bankr.D.Ariz.1988); In re Mark Jay Kaufman, P.A., 78 B.R. 309 (Bankr. N.D.Fla.1987); In re Brown, 56 B.R. 487 (Bankr. D.Md.1985).

4. Ben Cooper, 896 F.2d at 1402.

5. Id. at 1403.

6. 901 F.2d 1449 (8th Cir.1990). The Tenth and the Sixth Circuits have sided with the Eighth Circuit. In re Baker & Getty Financial Services Inc., 954 F.2d 1169 (6th Cir. 1992); Kaiser Steel Corp. v. Frates, 911 F.2d 380 (10th Cir. 1990).

7. See Ben Cooper, supra note 3.

8. ___ U.S. ___, 110 S.Ct. 3269, 111 L.Ed.2d 779 (1990).

properly before it. The Second Circuit decided that it was and reinstated its previous opinion.[9] The Supreme Court refused to grant certiorari a second time.[10] As a result, it does not appear that the conflict as to whether jury trials may be conducted by bankruptcy judges will be resolved in the near future.

An alternative, surely within the power of the district courts, is to pass a local rule which specifies that such trials will be held before a district judge and which allocates the pre-trial duties between the bankruptcy judges and the district judges. An example of such local rule is one formerly in effect in the Eastern District of Michigan where all jury trials, except for those where there is consent of all, were to be heard by the district judges, not by the bankruptcy judges. Under the rule the bankruptcy judge had the responsibility of preparing the case for trial and the rule explicitly provided there was to be no second jury trial even in cases where there was *de novo* review.[11]

If bankruptcy judges eventually are found to have the power to conduct jury trials, that finding may have an impact on the question discussed earlier, namely on the right of parties to have juries determine issues in bankruptcy cases and proceedings. Part of the justification for denying a jury in a public rights setting is the recognition that Congress should have a right to establish certain rights and to assign them to tribunals (such as administrative agencies) that do not use jurors as fact finders. If, after *Granfinanciera*, the argument against juries in bankruptcy still rests at all on the notion that bankruptcy is a public right heard in an administrative agency that argument will be weakened when bankruptcy judges themselves begin to hear jury trials. No longer will one be able to say that bankruptcy court is merely an "agency" that does not have the capacity of deciding cases by jury trial. Thus, the public right rationale will be further undermined and will become a yet weaker basis for denying juries.

---

9. 924 F.2d 36 (2d Cir.1991), reinstating 896 F.2d 1394 (2d Cir.1990).

10. ___ U.S. ___, 111 S.Ct. 2041, 114 L.Ed.2d 126 (1991).

11. Here is the local rule:

(c) Jury Trial. (1) Jury Trial Before a Bankruptcy Judge. In any case or proceeding under this Rule in which a jury trial is demanded, the party making the demand shall state whether it consents to a jury trial conducted by the Bankruptcy Judge. If such consent is given, each additional party to the case or proceeding shall then state whether it consents to a jury trial by the Bankruptcy Judge in the next pleading it files, or, if no pleading is required, within ten days after service of the jury demand. The failure of a party to so indicate shall be deemed a refusal to consent. If all parties consent, and if the case is properly triable by a jury, the Bankruptcy Judge shall conduct the jury trial. Matters determined in a jury trial before a Bankruptcy Judge shall not be reexamined by another jury, notwithstanding any implication to the contrary in subparagraph (a)(3)(B).

(2) Jury Trial Before a District Judge. In any case or proceeding in which a demand for a jury trial is properly made and in which the parties have not consented to a jury trial conducted by the Bankruptcy Judge, the proceeding shall be administered by the Bankruptcy Judge until it is ready for a final pretrial conference before a District Judge. The Bankruptcy Judge shall prepare written recommendations concerning the effect of the proceeding upon the disposition of the underlying bankruptcy petition and whether the trial of the proceeding should be expedited, copies of which shall be mailed to the parties in accordance with the procedures set forth in subparagraph (a)(3)(B). The District Judge shall conduct the jury trial of the case or proceeding.

Local Bankr. R. 33 (E.D. Mich.) (Bankruptcy Cases and Proceedings).

Table of Cases

EDITORIAL NOTE: A number of entries in this shared table relate to material appearing only on the three volume edition of this work. In those instances, see Epstein, Nickles and White, Bankruptcy, Practitioner Treatise Series.

A

AAA Produce Co., Inc., In re—§ 4-12, n. 3; § 4-13, n. 6; § 4-16, n. 4.
Aab v. Loehmann's, Inc.—§ 4-3, n. 2.
Abbott, Matter of—§ 8-33, n. 20.
Abbott v. Blackwelder Furniture Co. of Statesville, Inc.—§ 6-36, n. 12.
Abbotts Dairies of Pennsylvania, Inc., In re—§ 4-4, n. 7, 15, 27; § 4-17, n. 11.
Abdallah, In re—§ 8-10, n. 8.
Abdul–Hasan, In re—§ 6-72, n. 1.
Abernathy, In re—§ 6-77, n. 7.
A & B Homes, Ltd., In re—§ 6-40, n. 6; § 6-43, n. 3.
Aboussie Bros. Const. Co., In re—§ 11-35; § 11-35, n. 3; § 11-36, n. 8.
Abraham, Matter of—§ 6-49, n. 35; § 6-60, n. 20.
Abrams, In re—§ 3-14, n. 15; § 3-33, n. 13, 45.
Abramson v. Lakewood Bank and Trust Co.—§ 6-54, n. 7.
Academy Answering Service, Inc., In re, 100 B.R. 327—§ 3-33, n. 6, 24; § 3-34, n. 9.
Academy Answering Services, Inc., In re, 90 B.R. 294—§ 6-39, n. 20; § 6-42, n. 2; § 6-43, n. 4, 15, 19.
Acadiana Elec. Service, Inc., In re—§ 6-9, n. 11; § 6-88, n. 34.
Accardi v. Pennsylvania R. Co.—§ 6-40, n. 16.
Acequia, Inc., In re—§ 10-22, n. 4.
Acevedo v. Van Dorn Plastic Machinery Co.—§ 11-3, n. 21.
Acme–Dunham Inc., In re, 50 B.R. 734—§ 6-17, n. 10.
Acme–Dunham, Inc., In re, 45 B.R. 227—§ 12-2, n. 8.
Acorn Investments, In re—§ 3-28, n. 13.
Acquafredda, Matter of—§ 6-48, n. 17; § 6-60, n. 29; § 6-87, n. 8, 18; § 6-88, n. 21, 30.
Acquisition Corp. of America v. Federal Sav. & Loan Ins. Corp.—§ 3-25, n. 32; § 3-29, n. 1, 11.
Action Drug Co., Inc. v. Overnite Transp. Co.—§ 3-6, n. 48.
Action Industries, Inc. (Dollarama) v. Dixie Enterprises, Inc.—§ 6-66, n. 2, 7; § 6-67, n. 10.
A.C. Williams Co., In re—§ 11-17; § 11-17, n. 1, 3, 5.
Adams, In re, 761 F.2d 1422—§ 7-30, n. 10, 27.
Adams, In re, 102 B.R. 271—§ 6-7, n. 1; § 6-16, n. 1; § 6-20, n. 20.
Adams, In re, 86 B.R. 867—§ 6-72, n. 2.
Adams, In re, 65 B.R. 646—§ 5-10, n. 16.
Adams, In re, 12 B.R. 540—§ 3-12, n. 18; § 9-20, n. 11.
Adams Apple, Inc., In re—§ 4-15; § 4-15, n. 11, 15; § 4-17; § 4-17, n. 5, 7.
Adamson Co., Inc., In re—§ 4-16, n. 4.
Adana Mortg. Bankers, Inc., In re, 14 B.R. 29—§ 11–17, n. 2, 5.
Adana Mortg. Bankers, Inc., In re, 12 B.R. 977—§ 5–13; § 5–13, n. 1.
A & D Care, Inc., In re—§ 3-30, n. 27.
Addario, In re—§ 4-9, n. 10.
Adeeb, In re—§ 7-19, n. 9.
Adelman, In re—§ 7-26, n. 60.
Adkinson, In re—§ 2-15, n. 26.
Adolphsen, In re—§ 5-4, n. 14.
Advanced Aviation, Inc., In re—§ 6-61, n. 16, 77.
Advanced Electronics, Inc., In re, 107 B.R. 503—§ 7-25, n. 1.
Advanced Electronics, Inc., In re, 99 B.R. 249—§ 10–8, n. 12.

Advanced Professional Home Health Care Inc., In re—§ 5-25, n. 7.
Advanced Ribbons and Office Products, Inc., In re—§ 3-5, n. 6; § 3-8, n. 2; § 3-10, n. 6; § 3-32, n. 4.
Advance Glove Mfg. Co., Matter of—§ 6-19, n. 17.
Advertising Associates, Inc., In re—§ 6-28, n. 2.
Adwar, In re—§ 6-56, n. 17, 41.
A.E.F.S., Inc., In re—§ 6-33, n. 15.
AEG Acquisition Corp., In re—§ 6-10, n. 13; § 6-61, n. 16.
Aegean Fare, Inc., In re—§ 2-8, n. 2.
Aerco Metals, Inc., In re—§ 6-10, n. 15; § 6-17, n. 8; § 6-88, n. 54.
Aerni, In re—§ 12-2, n. 12.
Aerosmith Denton Corp., In re—§ 6-77, n. 1, 7.
Aetna Finance Co. v. Antoine—§ 8-31, n. 5.
AFCO Development Corp., In re—§ 6-11, n. 6; § 6-73, n. 4; § 6-83, n. 16.
Affiliated Food Stores, Inc., In re—§ 6-40, n. 6.
A.F. Walker & Son, Inc., In re—§ 6-60, n. 17.
Agard v. People's Nat. Bank of Shakopee—§ 6-38, n. 10.
AG Consultants Grain Div., Inc., In re—§ 10-22, n. 7; § 10-24, n. 9.
Agnew, Matter of—§ 7-19, n. 1.
Agricultural Research and Technology Group, Inc., In re—§ 6-60, n. 4, 7; § 6-87, n. 14.
Ahead By A Length, Inc., In re—§ 6-82, n. 6; § 6-84, n. 3.
Ahlers, In re—§ 11-27, n. 11.
Ahrens Aircraft, Inc. v. N.L.R.B.—§ 3-21, n. 27, 70.
A.H. Robins Co., Inc., In re, 880 F.2d 709—§ 11–8, n. 12.
A.H. Robins Co., Inc., In re, 880 F.2d 694—§ 3–22, n. 4, 5, 24.
A.H. Robins Co., Inc., In re, 846 F.2d 267—§ 3-5, n. 7; § 3-10, n. 11.
A.H. Robins Co. Inc., In re, 828 F.2d 1023—§ 3-22, n. 5, 17.
A.H. Robins Co., Inc., In re, 89 B.R. 555—§ 11–8, n. 12.
A.H. Robins Co., Inc., In re, 88 B.R. 742—§ 11-4, n. 7; § 11-5, n. 3; § 11-6, n. 12.
A.H. Robins Co., Inc., In re, 63 B.R. 986—§ 11–4, n. 9.
A.H. Robins Company, Inc., In re, No. 85–01307–R—§ 12-4, n. 4.
A.H. Robins Co., Inc. v. Piccinin—§ 2-8, n. 21; § 3-10; § 3-10, n. 5, 7, 8, 10, 12, 24, 26, 31; § 3-22; § 3-22, n. 1, 11; § 11-5, n. 8; § 12-4; § 12-4, n. 1; § 12-12, n. 15.
AIC Photo, Inc., Matter of—§ 6-65, n. 9; § 6-66, n. 11.
Aikens, In re, 100 B.R. 729—§ 6–89, n. 20.
Aikens, In re, 94 B.R. 869—§ 6–62, n. 12, 22, 26, 28; § 8–23, n. 3.
Aikens, In re, 87 B.R. 350—§ 8–25, n. 7.
Aikens v. City of Philadelphia—§ 8-23, n. 5.
Air Atlanta, Inc., In re—§ 3-15, n. 5.
Air Atlanta, Inc. v. National Bank of Georgia, Inc.—§ 3-15, n. 6; § 6-38, n. 21, 22; § 6-39, n. 2, 38; § 6-43, n. 3, 29.
Air Conditioning, Inc. of Stuart, In re—§ 6-7, n. 5; § 6-9, n. 10; § 6-20, n. 23; § 6-25, n. 13; § 6-88, n. 46.
Air Florida System Inc., In re—§ 6-77, n. 1, 7.
Airlift Intern., Inc., In re, 761 F.2d 1503—§ 3–17, n. 17.
Airlift, Intern., Inc., In re, 97 B.R. 664—§ 6-93, n. 66.
Airlift Intern., Inc., In re, 70 B.R. 935—§ 3–17, n. 7.
Air Nat. Aircraft Sales and Service, Inc., In re—§ 3-17, n. 16.
Air One, Inc., In re, 80 B.R. 145—§ 6-31, n. 15.
Air One, Inc., In re, 75 B.R. 998—§ 6-2, n. 32.
Airport–81 Nursing Care, Inc., In re—§ 6-94, n. 5.
Air Vermont, Inc., In re, 761 F.2d 130—§ 3–17, n. 20.
Air Vermont, Inc., In re, 45 B.R. 817—§ 6–24, n. 6.
Airwest Intern., In re—§ 6-38, n. 9.
Akin, In re—§ 6-60, n. 4.
Alabama Fuel Sales Co., Inc., In re—§ 10-29; § 10-29, n. 4, 5.
Alagna, In re—§ 8-11, n. 18; § 8-33, n. 4, 17, 18, 24, 34.
Alan Wood Steel Co., In re—§ 11-4, n. 15.
Alaqua v. Mayfield—§ 3-21, n. 8, 17.
Albano, In re—§ 9-3, n. 11, 12, 16, 19, 21.
Albany Partners, Ltd., In re—§ 3-25, n. 32; § 3-32, n. 10, 20.
Alberto, In re, 823 F.2d 712—§ 3–18, n. 21.
Alberto, In re, 121 B.R. 527—§ 3–6, n. 24.
Alberto, In re, 119 B.R. 985—§ 3–33, n. 13, 18, 27, 29; § 3–35, n. 7.
Alberto, Matter of—§ 3-11, n. 14; § 6-61, n. 59.
Albrecht, In re—§ 8-17, n. 7; § 8-18, n. 3.
Albrecht v. Robison—§ 6-83, n. 15.
Alchar Hardware, In re—§ 12-12, n. 26.

TABLE OF CASES

Aldridge, In re—§ 6-9, n. 5; § 6-10, n. 15; § 6-31, n. 15, 19; § 6-88, n. 54.
Alexander, In re—§ 8-30, n. 3.
Alexander Dispos-Haul Systems, Inc., In re—§ 6-50, n. 36; § 6-51, n. 22, 24, 40.
Alfar Dairy, Inc., In re—§ 5-1, n. 1.
Algeran, Inc. v. Advance Ross Corp.—§ 3-32, n. 10.
Alithochrome Corp., In re—§ 6-83, n. 12; § 6-84, n. 5.
Alkap, Inc., Matter of—§ 6-36, n. 12, 14.
All-American Auxiliary Ass'n, In re—§ 6-93, n. 32, 37.
All American of Ashburn, Inc., In re, 56 B.R. 186—§ 4-10; § 4-10, n. 3.
All American of Ashburn, Inc., In re, 49 B.R. 926—§ 12-2, n. 16.
All American of Ashburn, Inc., Matter of, 95 B.R. 251—§ 6-16, n. 1; § 6-31, n. 16.
All American of Ashburn, Inc., Matter of, 92 B.R. 551—§ 6-84, n. 2.
Alla-Ohio Valley Coals, Inc., In re—§ 6-65, n. 12.
Allbrand Appliance & Television Co., Inc., In re—§ 6-84, n. 2.
Allbrand Appliance & Television Co., Inc., Matter of—§ 6-39, n. 6; § 6-41, n. 18; § 6-42, n. 2; § 6-43, n. 7.
All-Brite Sign Service Co., Inc., In re—§ 6-40, n. 4; § 6-77, n. 1, 21.
Allegheny Intern., Inc., In re, 118 B.R. 282—§ 6-93, n. 61.
Allegheny Intern., Inc., In re, 100 B.R. 247—§ 11-24, n. 2.
Allegheny Intern., Inc., In re, 93 B.R. 903—§ 6-2, n. 9, 28.
Allegheny Nursing Service, Inc., Matter of—§ 6-62, n. 40.
Allen, In re, 888 F.2d 1299—§ 6-25, n. 32.
Allen, In re, 75 B.R. 572—§ 6-61, n. 21, 55.
Allen, In re, 75 B.R. 344—§ 9-18, n. 12.
Allen, In re, 69 B.R. 867—§ 3-9, n. 29.
Allen, In re, 65 B.R. 752—7-26, n. 35.
Allen, Matter of, 725 F.2d 290—§ 8-26, n. 18.
Allen, Matter of, 17 B.R. 119—§ 9-17, n. 2.
Allenwear & Associates, In re—§ 6-61, n. 41.
Allgeier & Dyer, Inc., In re—§ 6-62, n. 17, 26, 27.
Allied Mechanical Services, Inc., In re—§ 7-5, n. 2.
Allied Sheet Metal Fabricators, Inc. v. Peoples National Bank of Washington—§ 6-38, n. 14.
All Media Properties, Inc., In re—§ 2-5; § 2-5, n. 10, 26; § 9-3, n. 11; § 11-1, n. 5.
All Products Co., Matter of—§ 6-93, n. 29.
All Seasons Resorts, Inc., In re—§ 3-5, n. 12; § 3-10, n. 11; § 3-22, n. 21, 24.
Allstar Bldg. Products, Inc., In re—§ 3-31, n. 77.
Alltop v. Alltop—§ 3-20, n. 11.
All-Way Services, Inc., Matter of—§ 6-40, n. 6.
Almarc Corp., In re—§ 10-32, n. 1.
Almeida, In re—§ 12-10; § 12-10, n. 10.
Almendinger, In re—§ 3-10, n. 46.
Alpco, Inc., In re—§ 5-25, n. 6; § 6-45, n. 2, 3, 6, 7, 10, 22.
Alpha Industries, Inc., In re—§ 4-4, n. 8.
Alpha & Omega Realty, Inc., In re—§ 11-40, n. 1.
Alsop, In re—§ 6-21, n. 5, 8; § 6-50, n. 27; § 6-54, n. 2; § 6-55, n. 3.
Alston, In re—§ 6-15, n. 5; § 6-47, n. 8; § 6-49, n. 34; § 8-23, n. 9.
Alt, Matter of—§ 6-83, n. 18.
Altair Airlines, Inc., In re—§ 10-12, n. 4.
Alta Title Co., In re—§ 2-5, n. 22.
Altchek, In re—§ 2-8, n. 33; § 3-20, n. 11, 14.
Altek Systems, Inc., In re—§ 6-39, n. 3; § 6-41, n. 18, 22.
Alten, In re—§ 3-20; § 3-20, n. 7, 23, 33, 34.
Alternate Energy Management Corp. v. Goodman—§ 3-23, n. 45.
Altimaro v. Bohn—§ 8-33, n. 15.
Alton, In re, 837 F.2d 457—§ 7-27, n. 5.
Alton, In re, 81 B.R. 97—§ 11-33, n. 1.
Alu v. State of N.Y., Dept. of Taxation & Finance—§ 8-27, n. 11, 12; § 8-28, n. 3.
Alvarado, In re—§ 8-25, n. 17.
Alves, In re—§ 4-4, n. 5, 8.
Alvey, In re—§ 4-6, n. 8.
Alyeska Pipeline Service Co. v. Wilderness Soc.—§ 3-34, n. 7.
Amarex, Inc., In re, 96 B.R. 330—§ 6-2, n. 32.
Amarex, Inc., In re, 88 B.R. 362—§ 6-31, n. 16; § 6-34, n. 7, 17, 19.
Amarex, Inc., In re, 78 B.R. 605—§ 6-93, n. 33.
Amarex, Inc., In re, 74 B.R. 378—§ 6-34, n. 26.
Amarex, Inc., In re, 36 B.R. 59—§ 10-13, n. 13.
Amatex Corp., In re, 755 F.2d 1034—§ 11-3, n. 10; § 11-8, n. 10.
Amatex Corp., In re, 110 B.R. 168—§ 11-1, n. 14; § 11-4, n. 29; § 11-5, n. 1.

Amatex Corp., In re, 107 B.R. 856—§ 11-8, n. 12.
Amatex Corp., In re, 30 B.R. 309—§ 11-8; § 11-8, n. 9.
Amato, In re—§ 6-89, n. 9, 24.
Ambassador Riverside Inv. Group, In re—§ 6-93, n. 41.
Amco Products, Inc., In re—§ 6-38, n. 5, 7.
Amcor Funding Corp., In re—§ 3-15, n. 9.
Americana Apparel, Inc., In re—§ 6-93, n. 32.
American Ambulance Service, Inc., In re—§ 6-35; § 6-35, n. 41, 44.
American Atomics Corp., In re—§ 10-12, n. 3.
American Bicycle Ass'n, In re—§ 3-22, n. 5.
American Cent. Airlines, Inc., In re—§ 6-39, n. 39; § 6-40, n. 2; § 6-43, n. 4; § 6-45, n. 2, 5, 6, 7.
American Colonial Broadcasting Corp., In re—§ 11-14, n. 10.
American Continental Corp., In re—§ 6-77, n. 19.
American Development Corp., In re—§ 10-5, n. 11; § 10-6, n. 4.
American Federation of Television and Radio Artists, Matter of—§ 11-13, n. 3.
American Gypsum Co., In re—§ 6-69, n. 13; § 6-71, n. 9, 21.
American Hardwoods, Inc., In re—§ 3-22, n. 4, 7.
American Healthcare Management, Inc., Matter of—§ 5-10; § 5-10, n. 9.
American Home Assur. Co. v. L & L Marine Service, Inc.—§ 3-6, n. 41.
American Ins. Co. v. Lucas—§ 7-28, n. 10.
American Lumber Co., In re—§ 6-17, n. 18; § 6-93; § 6-93, n. 50, 57.
American Mariner Industries, Inc., In re—§ 3-27, n. 30; § 9-23, n. 4.
American Motor Home Rentals, Inc., Matter of—§ 6-40, n. 1.
American Precision Vibrator Co. v. National Air Vibrator Co.—§ 3-6, n. 30.
American Properties, Inc., In re—§ 6-48, n. 16, 17, 19; § 6-49, n. 46; § 6-59, n. 11.
American Solar King Corp., In re—§ 11-20; § 11-20, n. 2.
American Sunlake Ltd. Partnership, Matter of—§ 6-43, n. 7; § 6-45, n. 13.
American Trading and Shipping, Inc., Matter of—§ 6-49, n. 49, 52; § 6-51, n. 24, 33.
Ameritech Homes, Inc., In re—§ 6-7, n. 5.
Ames Dept. Stores, Inc., In re, 127 B.R. 744—§ 5-20, n. 11.
Ames Dept. Stores, Inc., In re, 121 B.R. 160—§ 5-20, n. 5.
Ames Trust and Sav. Bank v. Reichardt—§ 6-38, n. 8.
Amfesco Industries, Inc., In re—§ 11-10, n. 1.
Amici, In re—§ 8-10, n. 5, 26.
Amigoni, In re—§ 10-29, n. 14.
AMWC, Inc., In re—§ 6-16, n. 1.
Ananko, In re—§ 6-50, n. 23.
Ananko v. Harsanyi—§ 6-54, n. 10; § 6-55, n. 9; § 6-56, n. 17, 41, 50.
Anchorage Boat Sales, Inc., Matter of—§ 10-8; § 10-8, n. 3, 7, 9.
Anchorage Marina, Inc., In re—§ 6-10, n. 14; § 6-48, n. 12, 19; § 6-50, n. 12, 15, 18, 19; § 6-52, n. 22; § 6-88, n. 35, 38.
Anders, In re—§ 6-19, n. 16.
Anderson, In re, 913 F.2d 530—§ 3-25, n. 56; § 11-27, n. 11.
Anderson, In re, 84 B.R. 426—§ 7-41, n. 5.
Anderson, In re, 51 B.R. 532—§ 9-3, n. 11.
Anderson, In re, 50 B.R. 728—§ 6-77, n. 19.
Anderson, In re, 30 B.R. 995—§ 6-86, n. 19.
Anderson, In re, 23 B.R. 174—§ 3-6, n. 62.
Anderson Industries, Inc., In re—§ 6-52, n. 13.
Anderson Oaks (Phase I) Ltd. Partnership, In re—§ 3-25, n. 51.
Andrews, In re—§ 7-33, n. 8, 14.
Aneiro, In re—§ 9-20, n. 11.
Angeles Real Estate Co. v. Kerxton—§ 6-61, n. 42, 53, 79.
Anglemyer v. United States—§ 3-8, n. 17; § 3-32, n. 1, 3, 7, 34.
Anheuser-Busch, Inc. v. Miller—§ 6-40, n. 6.
Anje Jewelry Co., Inc., In re—§ 11-35, n. 2.
Ankeny v. Moffett—§ 11-39, n. 3.
Anoai, In re—§ 3-20, n. 11, 13, 26.
Answerfone, Inc., In re—§ 6-93, n. 6, 8, 41.
Antal, Matter of—§ 7-45, n. 13; § 8-11, n. 3.
Antico Mfg. Co., Inc., In re—§ 4-15, n. 6.
Antinarelli Enterprises, Inc., In re, 107 B.R. 410—§ 6-77, n. 1.
Antinarelli Enterprises, Inc., In re, 94 B.R. 227—§ 6-86, n. 10.
Antinarelli Enterprises, Inc., In re, 76 B.R. 247—§ 6-28, n. 2; § 6-31, n. 4, 17; § 6-34, n. 6, 23.
Antoine's Industries, Inc., Matter of—§ 6-93, n. 32.
Antweil, In re, 931 F.2d 689—§ 6-16, n. 1.
Antweil, In re, 97 B.R. 69—§ 6-16, n. 1.
Antweil, In re, 97 B.R. 63—§ 6-11, n. 7.

Anzman, In re—§ **7-26, n. 37.**
A–1 Hydro Mechanics Corp., In re—§ **6-45, n. 7.**
AOV Industries, Inc., In re, 792 F.2d 1140—§ **10–22, n. 7**; § **10–24, n. 6.**
AOV Industries, Inc., In re, 85 B.R. 183—§ **6–20, n. 12**; § **6–32, n. 8.**
APC Const., Inc., In re—§ **6-36, n. 3**; § **6-61, n. 58, 60**; § **6-62, n. 5, 17.**
Apex Oil Co., In re, 884 F.2d 343—§ **12–12, n. 7, 14.**
Apex Oil Co., In re, 122 B.R. 559—§ **3–6, n. 6**; § **3–8, n. 20**; § **3–21, n. 69.**
Apex Oil Co., In re, 118 B.R. 683—§ **6–93, n. 66.**
Apex Oil Co., In re, 107 B.R. 189—§ **11–5, n. 7.**
Apex Oil Co., In re, 92 B.R. 847—§ **4–4, n. 3, 20.**
Apex Oil Co., In re, 92 B.R. 843—§ **11-7, n. 2.**
Apex Oil Co., In re, 85 B.R. 538—§ **3–26, n. 10.**
AP Industries, Inc., In re—§ **3-10, n. 22**; § **3-14, n. 29, 31**; § **3-22, n. 5, 26, 27, 29**; § **3-33, n. 13.**
Apollo Hollow Metal and Hardware Co., Inc., In re—§ **6-17, n. 15**; § **6-53, n. 4, 8**; § **6-87, n. 8.**
Appalachian Energy Industries, Inc., In re—§ **6-86, n. 2, 10.**
Appeal of (see name of party)
Applied Logic Corp., In re—§ **6-42, n. 2.**
Aquaslide 'N' Dive Corp., In re—§ **11-5, n. 12.**
Aquasport, Inc., In re—§ **6-40, n. 2**; § **6-44, n. 5.**
Archer, In re—§ **6-43, n. 18**; § **6-44, n. 1.**
Archer v. Macomb County Bank—§ **3-33, n. 26.**
Archer Daniels Midland Co. v. Charter Intern. Oil Co.—§ **6-65, n. 7**; § **6-67, n. 1.**
Arch Lumber Co. v. Dohm—§ **8-6**; § **8-6, n. 6.**
Arctic Enterprises, Inc., In re, 35 B.R. 978—§ **10–32**; § **10–32, n. 3.**
Arctic Enterprises, Inc., In re, 17 B.R. 839—§ **6–40, n. 4, 14.**
Arcuri, In re—§ **7-21, n. 3, 5, 6.**
Arena, In re—§ **2-2, n. 21.**
Arizona Laborers, Teamsters, and Cement Masons, Local 395 Pension Trust Fund v. Nevarez—§ **8-33, n. 15.**
Arkin–Medo, Inc., In re—§ **11-16, n. 6.**
Armory Hotel Associates, United States v.—§ **3-21, n. 23, 44, 45.**
Armstrong, Matter of, 812 F.2d 1024—§ **9–24**; § **9–24, n. 6, 20.**
Armstrong, Matter of, 97 B.R. 565—§ **8–32, n, 5, 8, 9, 18.**
Armstrong v. Hursman—§ **8-1, n. 11.**
Arnett, In re—§ **6-27, n. 11, 13.**
Arnold, In re, 908 F.2d 52—§ **6–69, n. 2.**
Arnold, In re, 806 F.2d 937—§ **3–29, n. 7.**
Arnold, In re, 88 B.R. 917—§ **6–62, n. 39.**
Arnold Print Works, Inc., In re—§ **12-2**; § **12-2, n. 20**; § **12-3, n. 7.**
Aronsohn & Springstead v. Weissman—§ **8-33, n. 16.**
Arrowhead Gardens, Inc., In re—§ **6-18, n. 18.**
Art Metal U.S.A., Inc., In re—§ **6-40, n. 29.**
Art Shirt Ltd., Inc., In re—§ **6-18, n. 11**; § **6-87, n. 14.**
Arundel Housing Components, Inc., In re—§ **6-10, n. 15.**
Ashe, In re—§ **8-25, n. 4.**
Asheville Bldg. Associates v. Carlyle Real Estate Ltd. Partnership, VIII—§ **3-31, n. 103.**
Ashgrove Apartments of DeKalb County, Ltd., In re—§ **3-25**; § **3-25, n. 45, 50.**
Ashley, In re—§ **6-12, n. 11.**
Ashline, In re—§ **9-3, n. 11.**
Ashton, In re, 107 B.R. 670—§ **11–29, n. 1.**
Ashton, In re, 85 B.R. 766—§ **9–13, n. 12.**
Ashton, In re, 63 B.R. 244—§ **9–17, n. 5.**
Ashton, Matter of—§ **7-26, n. 50.**
ASI Reactivation, Inc., In re—§ **3-25, n. 6, 9**; § **3-31, n. 56**; § **6-93, n. 29.**
Aspen Data Graphics, Inc., In re—§ **6-15, n. 8**; § **6-39, n. 13.**
Assman v. J.I. Case Credit Corp.—§ **6-56, n. 1.**
Associated Grocers of Nebraska Co-op., Inc., Matter of—§ **12-2, n. 8.**
Association of St. Croix Condominium Owners v. St. Croix Hotel Corp.—§ **3-6, n. 30, 31.**
Assured Fastener Products Corp., Matter of—§ **6-39, n. 25**; § **6-41, n. 11.**
Asters, In re—§ **3-35, n. 1.**
Atallah, In re—§ **8-17, n. 13**; § **8-33, n. 39.**
Atchison, In re—§ **6-47, n. 7.**
Atlanta Shipping Corp., Inc. v. Chemical Bank—§ **12-7, n. 2.**
Atlanta West VI, In re—§ **9-7, n. 12**; § **10-24, n. 9.**
Atlantic Business and Community Corp., In re—§ **3-14, n. 64, 65**; § **3-33, n. 6, 12, 15, 20, 21, 39.**
Atlantic Fish Market, Inc., In re—§ **6-31, n. 10, 17, 19.**
Atlantic Mortg. Corp., In re—§ **6-61, n. 38, 79.**
Atlantic Sav. Bank v. Metropolitan Bank and Trust Co.—§ **8-31, n. 5.**

AT of Maine, Inc., In re—§ 2-16; § 2-16, n. 16.
Atreus Enterprises, Ltd., In re—§ 3-6, n. 36; § 6-69, n. 9.
Atwood, In re—§ 2-5, n. 18.
Aubrey, In re—§ 7-19; § 7-19, n. 1, 2; § 7-21, n. 5.
Audio Data Corp. v. Monus—§ 3-10, n. 23; § 3-32, n. 10, 38.
Augie/Restivo Baking Co., Ltd., In re—§ 6-2, n. 5, 30; § 6-49, n. 39, 49, 51; § 6-51, n. 24, 29, 40; § 11-40; § 11-40, n. 3; § 11-41; § 11-41, n. 10.
Augustine v. United States—§ 8-21, n. 4; § 8-25, n. 55, 62.
Aulick v. Largent—§ 6-9, n. 7.
Au Natural Restaurant, Inc., In re—§ 4-13, n. 1.
Austin v. Unarco Industries, Inc.—§ 3-5, n. 19; § 3-6, n. 20.
Automotive Supply, Inc. v. Powell—§ 8-7, n. 15.
Auto–Pak, Inc., In re—§ 6-88, n. 14, 21.
Auto–Train Corp., Inc., In re, 810 F.2d 270—§ 11-41, n. 16.
Auto–Train Corp., In re, 49 B.R. 605—§ 6-35; § 6-35, n. 38, 44.
Auxano, Inc., In re, 96 B.R. 957—§ 6–71, n. 2; § 6–72, n. 3, 13.
Auxano, Inc., In re, 87 B.R. 72—§ 6–2, n. 5, 24.
Avair, Inc., In re—§ 6-61, n. 16.
Avco Financial Service of New York Inc., State v.—§ 8-31, n. 5.
Avila, In re—§ 7-39, n. 7, 14.
Avis, Matter of—§ 7-37, n. 2.
Axona Intern. Credit & Commerce Ltd., Matter of—§ 2-6, n. 2; § 2-10, n. 1.
Axvig, In re—§ 6-40, n. 14.
Ayscue, In re—§ 2-8, n. 2.
Aztec Co., In re—§ 10-17, n. 4; § 10-22, n. 8; § 11-28, n. 8; § 11-29, n. 1.

B

Babcock, In re—§ 8-18, n. 6.
Babcock Dairy Co. of Ohio, Inc., In re—§ 6-17; § 6-17, n. 10, 12, 23.
Bacher, In re—§ 6-2, n. 24, 29.
Bacigalupi, Inc., In re—§ 6-39, n. 12; § 6-40, n. 27; § 6-42, n. 2, 4.
Badger Freightways, Inc., In re—§ 6-17, n. 11; § 6-93, n. 38, 53.
Badger Mountain Irr. Dist., In re—§ 6-62, n. 28.
Bagley, In re—§ 9-13, n. 4.
Bailey, In re, 111 B.R. 151—§ 3–22, n. 4.
Bailey, In re, 84 B.R. 608—§ 8–18, n. 9.
Bailey, Matter of—§ 3-12, n. 25.
Bailey v. Glover—§ 6-84, n. 3.
Bain, In re—§ 6-61, n. 60.
Baird, In re—§ 6-11, n. 6.
Baker, In re, 108 B.R. 663—§ 3–10, n. 9.
Baker, In re, 86 B.R. 234—§ 3–6, n. 36.
Baker, In re, 17 B.R. 392—§ 6–60, n. 29; § 6–87, n. 8, 10, 11, 17.
Baker v. Bloom—§ 3-32, n. 38.
Baker v. Gold Seal Liquors, Inc.—§ 6-40, n. 4.
Baker & Getty Financial Services, Inc., In re, 954 F.2d 1169—§ 12–16, n. 6.
Baker & Getty Financial Services, Inc., In re, 98 B.R. 300—§ 6–11, n. 7; § 6–50, n. 10; § 6–88, n. 30, 36.
Baker & Getty Financial Services, Inc., In re, 88 B.R. 792—§ 6–17, n. 8; § 6–30, n. 6; § 6–87, n. 14.
Balay, In re—§ 8-3, n. 19; § 8-17, n. 13; § 8-33; § 8-33, n. 24, 38.
Balber, In re—§ 8-10, n. 26.
Balducci Oil Co., Inc., In re—§ 6-38, n. 18; § 6-40, n. 22.
Baldwin, In re, 84 B.R. 394—§ 8–28, n. 14.
Baldwin, In re, 70 B.R. 612—§ 8–21, n. 9.
Baldwin v. Avco Financial Services—§ 8-24, n. 3.
Balwin–United Corp., Matter of, 55 B.R. 885—§ 11-1, n. 2; § 11-4, n. 7, 31; § 11-6, n. 1, 3.
Baldwin–United Corp., Matter of, 48 B.R. 901—§ 11-2, n. 3.
Baldwin–United Corp., Matter of, 48 B.R. 49—§ 6-40, n. 30.
Baldwin United Corp., Matter of, 46 B.R. 314—§ 10-10, n. 1.
Baldwin United Corp., Matter of, 43 B.R. 888—§ 4-4; § 4-4, n. 15, 20.
Baldwin–United Corp., Matter of, 38 B.R. 802—§ 10-12, n. 3.
Baldwin-United Corp. Litigation, In re—§ 3-21, n. 27.
Ballance, In re—§ 7-39, n. 14.
Ballard, In re, 100 B.R. 526—§ 6–61, n. 12, 16.

TABLE OF CASES

Ballard, In re, 4 B.R. 271—§ 2-2, n. 12; § 9-3, n. 6, 10.
Ballentine Bros., Inc., Matter of—§ 3-21, n. 69.
Baltimore Food Systems, Inc., In re—§ 12-6, n. 6; § 12-10, n. 3; § 12-11, n. 4.
BA Mortg. and Intern. Realty Corp. v. American Nat. Bank and Trust Co. of Chicago—§ 6-93, n. 44.
BancOhio Nat. Bank v. Walters—§ 8-19; § 8-19, n. 16.
B and B Associates v. Fonner—§ 3-5, n. 19.
Bandy, In re—§ 8-25, n. 43.
Bank Center, Ltd., In re—§ 11-36, n. 8.
Bank of Celina, United States v.—§ 6-38, n. 12.
Bank of Guntersville v. Crayter—§ 6-38, n. 12.
Bank of Marin v. England—§ 6-74; § 6-74, n. 6, 13.
Bank of Oklahoma, N.A. v. Fidelity State Bank and Trust Co., Dodge City, Kansas—§ 6-92, n. 9.
Bankwest Boulder Indus. Bank, In re—§ 2-2, n. 3.
Baptist Medical Center of New York, In re—§ 12-5, n. 6.
Barash v. Farmers & Merchants Bank—§ 6-19, n. 16.
Barash v. Public Finance Corp.—§ 6-32, n. 1.
Barber v. Emporium Partnership—§ 3-16, n. 20.
Barbour, In re—§ 6-82, n. 1; § 6-88, n. 14; § 6-90, n. 4.
Barfknecht, In re—§ 6-39, n. 11; § 6-40, n. 3.
Barge v. Beneficial Indus. Loan Corp.—§ 12-12, n. 6.
Barge, Matter of—§ 6-8, n. 6; § 6-19, n. 4.
Barger, In re—§ 7-26, n. 50.
Bari, In re—§ 8-17, n. 48.
Barker v. Lee—§ 8-7, n. 9.
Barker Estates, Inc., In re—§ 11-13, n. 3; § 11-14; § 11-14, n. 6; § 11-18, n. 1.
Barnes, In re, 125 B.R. 484—§ 3-27, n. 21.
Barnes, In re, 117 B.R. 842—§ 8-25, n. 43, 44.
Barnes v. Whelan—§ 9-14, n. 5, 13; § 10-24, n. 9.
Barrett, In re, 118 B.R. 255—§ 6-56, n. 39.
Barrett, In re, 105 B.R. 385—§ 9-30, n. 8.
Barrett, In re, 104 B.R. 688—§ 6-49, n. 22, 24; § 6-50, n. 23, 28; § 8-13, n. 8.
Barnett, Matter of—§ 6-80, n. 11, 12.
Barnett v. Stern—§ 6-61, n. 8.
Barnette v. Evans—§ 3-20, n. 33.
Barney, In re—§ 7-19, n. 9.
Barnhill v. Johnson—§ 6-16; § 6-16, n. 2.
Barrett, In re—§ 6-49, n. 22, 24; § 6-50, n. 23, 28; § 6-56, n. 39; § 8-13, n. 8; § 9-30, n. 8.
Barrett v. Commonwealth Federal Sav. and Loan Ass'n, 939 F.2d 20—§ 6-56, n. 24.
Barrett v. Commonwealth Federal Sav. and Loan Ass'n, 111 B.R. 78—§ 6-56, n. 54.
Barrick, In re—§ 8-25, n. 43, 44.
Barron, In re—§ 8-12, n. 3.
Barrow, In re—§ 8-28, n. 23.
Barry, In re—§ 6-36, n. 3, 7; § 6-62, n. 4, 5, 22; § 6-86, n. 2, 4.
Barsky, In re—§ 7-3, n. 7.
Barthol, In re—§ 7-26, n. 50.
Bartlett, In re, 67 B.R. 455—§ 8-17, n. 49.
Bartlett, In re, 24 B.R. 605—§ 2-8, n. 8.
Bartlett, Matter of—§ 8-33; § 8-33, n. 20, 45, 46.
Bartlett Co-op. Ass'n v. Patton—§ 8-33, n. 16.
Bartley Lindsay Co., In re—§ 6-69, n. 14.
Barton v. Barbour—§ 12-13; § 12-13, n. 2.
Bashour, In re—§ 6-2, n. 5.
Basin Elec. Power Co-op. v. Midwest Processing Co.—§ 2-5, n. 22.
Bassin, In re—§ 8-3, n. 18.
Bass Mechanical Contractors, Inc., In re, 88 B.R. 201—§ 6-41, n. 38.
Bass Mechanical Contractors, Inc., In re, 84 B.R. 1009—§ 6-40, n. 13; § 6-41, n. 47; § 6-43, n. 29; § 6-44, n. 2.
Bateman, In re—§ 7-19, n. 5.
Bates, In re, 123 B.R. 38—§ 8-18, n. 9, 16.
Bates, In re, 32 B.R. 40—§ 6-49, n. 39, 62; § 6-53, n. 6.
Baum, In re—§ 3-11, n. 26; § 6-15, n. 9; § 8-31, n. 3, 9.
Baum v. Earl Millikin, Inc.—§ 7-22, n. 7.
Baumgold Bros., Inc., In re—§ 6-34, n. 11.
Baxley, In re—§ 10-28; § 10-28, n. 5.
Bayless v. Crabtree Through Adams—§ 12-15, n. 2.
Bay State Yacht Sales, Inc., In re—§ 6-62, n. 3, 5, 26, 28, 29.
B.B.S.I., Ltd., In re—§ 2-5, n. 12.

B C & K Cattle Co., In re—§ 2-5, n. 9.
B. Cohen & Sons Caterers, Inc., In re—§ 3-31, n. 93; § 3-33, n. 13, 35, 36.
Beacon Health, Inc., In re—§ 2-2, n. 9.
Bear, Matter of—§ 9-14, n. 21.
Bear Creek Ministorage, Inc., In re—§ 10-23, n. 5.
Beard v. Braunstein—§ 3-30, n. 29.
Bearhouse, Inc., In re, 99 B.R. 926—§ 6-61, n. 53, 67.
Bearhouse, Inc., In re, 84 B.R. 552—§ 6-61, n. 11, 53; § 6-65, n. 11.
Beattie, In re—§ 6-35, n. 5, 23, 44; § 6-49, n. 34.
Beaucrest Realty Associates, Matter of—§ 2-5, n. 27.
Beck, In re, 96 B.R. 161—§ 6-40, n. 4, 14.
Beck, In re, 25 B.R. 947—§ 6-19, n. 17.
Beck, Matter of—§ 6-77, n. 1; § 6-78, n. 14.
Beck v. General Acc. Ins.—§ 6-7, n. 4, 5, 9, 10.
Becker, In re—§ 7-13; § 7-13, n. 11.
Beckman, In re—§ 6-49, n. 46; § 6-58, n. 1; § 8-32, n. 8, 13, 14, 16, 17, 19.
Beck Rumbaugh Associates, Inc., In re—§ 6-93, n. 41.
Bedingfield, In re—§ 7-29, n. 8.
Begier v. I.R.S.—§ 6-7, n. 4.
Begley v. Philadelphia Elec. Co.—§ 3-9, n. 33, 35.
Behm, Matter of—§ 3-35, n. 1.
Behr Contracting, Inc., Matter of—§ 6-50, n. 5; § 6-52, n. 49; § 6-88, n. 51.
Behrens, In re—§ 3-23, n. 18, 40; § 7-7, n. 2.
Behrens v. Woodhaven Ass'n—§ 3-23, n. 7.
Behring Intern., Inc. v. Greater Houston Bank—§ 6-38, n. 7.
Beker Industries Corp., In re, 63 B.R. 474—§ 4-7; § 4-7, n. 11, 18, 19.
Beker Industries Corp., In re, 58 B.R. 725—§ 4-14, n. 5; § 4-15, n. 15.
Bel Air Associates, Ltd., In re—§ 2-2, n. 20; § 10-10, n. 1, 4; § 11-17, n. 3.
Bel Air Chateau Hosp., Inc., In re—§ 3-21, n. 70.
Belco, Inc., In re—§ 6-17, n. 11, 13.
Belfry, In re—§ 7-28, n. 11, 15.
Belisle v. Plunkett—§ 6-61; § 6-61, n. 28, 35, 74.
Belize Airways Ltd., In re, 7 B.R. 601—§ 3-17, n. 12.
Belize Airways, Ltd., In re, 5 B.R. 152—§ 5-20, n. 8.
Belknap, Inc., In re, 909 F.2d 879—§ 6-16, n. 1.
Belknap, Inc., In re, 96 B.R. 108—§ 6-16, n. 1.
Bell, In re, 700 F.2d 1053—§ 3-11, n. 14; § 7-39; § 7-39, n. 3, 7, 8; § 7-47, n. 4.
Bell, In re, 181 F.Supp. 387—§ 8-7, n. 19.
Bell, In re, 119 B.R. 783—§ 8-17, n. 35, 36.
Bell, In re, 80 B.R. 104—§ 4-9, n. 12, 14.
Bell, In re, 80 B.R. 97—§ 8-17, n. 33.
Bell, In re, 65 B.R. 575—§ 7-45, n. 1, 8.
Bellanca Aircraft Corp., In re, 850 F.2d 1275—§ 6-34, n. 7; § 6-84, n. 2; § 6-93, n. 16, 37, 48.
Bellanca Aircraft Corp., In re, 96 B.R. 913—§ 6-7, n. 4.
Bellanca Aircraft Corp., In re, 56 B.R. 339—§ 6-17; § 6-17, n. 14.
Bell & Beckwith, In re, 70 B.R. 725—§ 6-87, n. 18.
Bell & Beckwith, In re, 64 B.R. 620—§ 6-47, n. 7, 9; § 6-48, n. 19, 21; § 6-50, n. 6, 19; § 6-88, n. 33.
Bell & Beckwith, In re, 44 B.R. 656—§ 6-49, n. 12.
Bellman Farms, Inc., In re—§ 3-23, n. 27.
Bell Tower Associates, Ltd., In re—§ 2-15, n. 23.
Bellucci, In re—§ 3-6, n. 30; § 3-30, n. 3, 5, 27; § 3-31, n. 1.
Belme, In re—§ 6-7, n. 12, 13.
Belmont Realty Corp., In re—§ 3-25, n. 58; § 3-26, n. 8.
Belt, Matter of—§ 7-45, n. 17; § 9-13, n. 4; § 9-14, n. 5, 14, 21.
Ben Cooper, Inc., In re, 924 F.2d 36—§ 12-16, n. 9.
Ben Cooper, Inc., In re, 896 F.2d 1394—§ 3-30, n. 29; § 12-16, n. 3.
Benedict, Matter of—§ 7-26, n. 55.
Beneficial Finance Co. of Colorado v. Schmuhl—§ 8-31, n. 5.
Beneficial Finance Co. of Virginia v. Franklin—§ 6-80, n. 14, 17; § 8-30, n. 8.
Beneficial Finance Co. of Virginia v. Lazrovitch—§ 6-80, n. 11; § 8-29, n. 12, 13.
Benefield, In re—§ 6-72, n. 4.
Benich, Matter of—§ 7-29; § 7-29, n. 5, 12.
Benjamin v. Diamond (Matter of Mobile Steel Co.—§ 6-93, n. 63.
Bennett, In re, 35 B.R. 357—§ 6-6, n. 3, 7.
Bennett, In re, 17 B.R. 819—§ 10-12, n. 4, 5.
Bennett Co., Inc., In re—§ 6-39, n. 18.
Benny, In re—§ 2-5, n. 2.

Bensar Co., Inc., Matter of—§ **6-67, n. 10.**
Benson, In re—§ **3-28, n. 12.**
Bentson, In re—§ **9-25;** § **9-25, n. 8.**
Berenguer, In re—§ **7-39, n. 15;** § **7-47, n. 3.**
Berg Chemical, In re—§ **11-11, n. 4.**
Berge, Matter of—§ **6-53, n. 9;** § **6-54, n. 3, 10;** § **6-55, n. 22;** § **6-56, n. 5, 23, 52.**
Berke, Matter of—§ **12-12, n. 16.**
Berkich, In re—§ **7-37, n. 2, 3.**
Berkland, In re Marriage of—§ **6-2, n. 1.**
Berkley Multi–Units, Inc., In re—§ **6-69, n. 9;** § **6-72, n. 16.**
Berkley Multi–Units, Inc., Matter of—§ **6-69, n. 9.**
Berkshire Manor Apartments, Ltd., In re—§ **3-29, n. 14.**
Berman, In re—§ **6-4, n. 9;** § **6-24, n. 2;** § **6-33, n. 7.**
Bernard, In re—§ **6-72, n. 1, 7, 10;** § **6-73, n. 22.**
Berndt, In re—§ **2-14, n. 2.**
Bernstein, In re—§ **7-22, n. 3, 6.**
Bernstein v. IDT Corp.—§ **6-44, n. 2.**
Berry, In re, 30 B.R. 36—§ **6-2, n. 22.**
Berry, In re, 22 B.R. 950—§ **9-3, n. 2.**
Berry Estates, Inc., In re—§ **3-6, n. 45;** § **3-21, n. 24, 82, 112.**
Bertholet Enterprises, Inc., In re—§ **6-61, n. 74.**
Bertoli, Matter of—§ **12-12, n. 22.**
Bessent, In re—§ **8-26, n. 18.**
Best v. Yerkes—§ **11-39, n. 3.**
Best Buy Drugs, Inc., In re—§ **6-66, n. 11.**
Best Corp. v. Gibson Chemical & Oil Corp.—§ **6-34, n. 4, 17.**
Bethune, In re—§ **6-60, n. 17.**
Better–Brite Plating, Inc., In re—§ **3-21, n. 110.**
Better Care, Ltd., In re—§ **6-39, n. 8;** § **6-40, n. 18, 27.**
Betts, In re—§ **3-10, n. 56, 70, 82.**
Beverages Intern. Ltd., In re—§ **6-17, n. 18;** § **6-93, n. 8, 16, 17, 21, 29, 31, 32, 50, 51.**
Beverly, In re—§ **7-26, n. 19.**
Bevill, Bresler & Schulman Asset Management Corp., Matter of—§ **3-15, n. 10;** § **6-39, n. 4;** § **6-40, n. 19.**
Bevill, Bresler & Schulman Asset Management Corp. v. Spencer Sav. & Loan Ass'n—§ **3-15, n. 11;** § **6-85, n. 11.**
Bevill, Bresler & Schulman, Inc., Matter of—§ **6-69, n. 10.**
BGNX, Inc., In re—§ **6-48, n. 2, 6.**
Bialac, In re, 712 F.2d 426—§ **3-10, n. 21;** § **3-13, n. 6;** § **3-16, n. 10, 11;** § **3-25, n. 2.**
Bialac, In re, 694 F.2d 625—§ **3-31, n. 60.**
Bible, In re—§ **3-12;** § **3-12, n. 5, 12;** § **3-20, n. 11;** § **3-30, n. 10, 12, 14, 15, 17, 18, 19.**
Bickleman, In re—§ **8-30, n. 9.**
Bicoastal Corp., In re—§ **3-21, n. 59.**
Bicro Corp., In re—§ **3-20, n. 21.**
Bidlofsky, In re—§ **8-22, n. 37.**
Bigalk, In re—§ **3-10, n. 38, 46, 47, 58, 59.**
Big Apple Scenic Studio, Inc., In re—§ **6-69, n. 9;** § **6-88, n. 45.**
Big Hook Land & Cattle Co., In re, 81 B.R. 1001—§ **6–77, n. 22.**
Big Hook Land & Cattle Co., In re, 77 B.R. 793—§ **9–29, n. 2.**
Big Squaw Mountain Corp., In re—§ **3-14, n. 39;** § **3-32, n. 32;** § **6-61, n. 11, 54.**
Big Three Transp., Inc., In re—§ **6-10, n. 13, 18;** § **6-88, n. 54.**
Billerman, In re—§ **8-3, n. 21;** § **8-27, n. 9.**
Billick, Matter of—§ **6-70, n. 3.**
Billings, In re—§ **8-25, n. 28, 33.**
Binek v. Ziebarth—§ **3-6, n. 30.**
Biniecki Bros., Matter of—§ **6-19, n. 17, 18.**
Binstock, In re—§ **3-10, n. 66, 67, 73.**
Birch, In re—§ **2-3;** § **2-3, n. 4.**
Bird, In re—§ **8-28, n. 3.**
Bird, Matter of—§ **9-27;** § **9-27, n. 6.**
Bird v. Plains State Bank—§ **6-76, n. 2.**
Bird Engineering, Inc., Matter of—§ **6-92, n. 8.**
Birdview Satellite Communications, Inc., In re—§ **6-61, n. 60.**
Birk v. Simmons—§ **3-20, n. 18, 33.**
Birmingham Trust Nat. Bank v. Case—§ **7-26;** § **7-26, n. 54.**
Bishop, In re—§ **6-92, n. 3.**
Bishop, Baldwin, Rewald, Dillingham & Wong, Inc., Matter of—§ **6-30, n. 3, 6.**
Bistransin, In re—§ **6-4, n. 17;** § **6-62, n. 15;** § **8-1, n. 18;** § **8-22, n. 16;** § **8-23, n. 5.**

TABLE OF CASES

Bittner v. Borne Chemical Co., Inc.—§ 11-6; § 11-6, n. 1, 2.
BKW Systems, Inc., In re—§ 3-30, n. 26.
Black, In re, 787 F.2d 503—§ 7-26, n. 5.
Black, In re, 78 B.R. 840—§ 9-12, n. 2, 14.
Black, In re, 19 B.R. 468—§ 6-69, n. 13; § 6-72, n. 17.
Blackburn, In re—§ 7-26, n. 49, 52.
Blackburn, Matter of—§ 6-12, n. 8; § 6-24, n. 2; § 6-29, n. 11; § 6-87, n. 10; § 6-88, n. 36.
Black & Geddes, Inc., In re—§ 6-88, n. 35.
Black & White Cattle Co., In re—§ 6-80, n. 20; § 6-88, n. 14; § 6-89, n. 8, 12, 29.
Blaine Richards & Co., Inc., In re—§ 2-5, n. 18.
Blair, In re—§ 8-31, n. 2, 3.
Blair v. Trafco Products, Inc.—§ 6-38, n. 10.
Blaise, In re—§ 8-1, n. 11.
Bland, In re—§ 8-1, n. 20; § 8-24, n. 3.
Blanks, In re—§ 6-86, n. 2, 4, 5.
Blanton, In re, 105 B.R. 321—§ 6-39, n. 31; § 6-85, n. 6, 11.
Blanton, In re, 78 B.R. 442—§ 3-26, n. 11; § 3-27, n. 26.
Blanton Smith Corp., In re—§ 6-88, n. 37.
Blanton-Smith Corp., In re—§ 10-31, n. 2.
Blauvelt v. Village of Nyack—§ 11-39, n. 1.
Blecker, In re—§ 8-7, n. 20.
Blehm Land & Cattle Co., In re—§ 7-13; § 7-13, n. 6.
B & L Laboratories, Inc., In re—§ 6-93, n. 31.
B & L Oil Co., In re—§ 6-45; § 6-45, n. 5, 6, 7, 8, 23.
Blondheim Real Estate, Inc., In re—§ 6-93, n. 33.
Bloom, In re, 875 F.2d 224—§ 3-6, n. 24; § 3-33, n. 12, 15, 21, 33, 38.
Bloom, In re, 91 B.R. 445—§ 8-17, n. 35, 36, 48, 49.
Blue, Matter of—§ 8-31, n. 3.
Blueberry Hill Apartments, Ltd., In re—§ 3-29, n. 14.
Blue Coal Corp., In re—§ 6-86, n. 10.
Blue Point Carpet, Inc., In re—§ 6-17, n. 6; § 6-18, n. 21; § 6-20, n. 17.
Bluestone, In re—§ 6-2, n. 24.
Bluford, Matter of—§ 6-47, n. 10.
Blum, In re—§ 8-10, n. 26; § 8-21, n. 15.
Bluman, In re—§ 11-2, n. 5.
Bluridg Farms, Inc., Matter of—§ 3-23, n. 38; § 9-27, n. 11; § 9-29; § 9-29, n. 4.
BNT Terminals, Inc., In re—§ 3-14, n. 9; § 3-32, n. 8; § 6-69, n. 8.
Board of County Com'rs of County of Archuleta v. Fairfield Communities, Inc.—§ 3-21, n. 69.
Board of Governors v. MCorp Financial, Inc.—§ 3-21, n. 14, 87.5, 87.10.
Board of Trade of City of Chicago v. Johnson—§ 2-8; § 2-8, n. 4, 41.
Boardwalk Development Co., Inc., In re—§ 6-61, n. 29.
Bob Grissett Golf Shoppes, Inc., In re, 78 B.R. 787—§ 6-31, n. 15; § 6-34, n. 17.
Bob Grissett Golf Shoppes, Inc., In re, 58 B.R. 996—§ 6-83, n. 15.
Bobilin, In re—§ 6-61, n. 53.
Bobroff, In re—§ 3-27; § 3-27, n. 28; § 4-7, n. 12.
Bobroff, Matter of—§ 7-21, n. 5.
Bob's Supermarket's Inc., In re—§ 3-7, n. 7.
Boca Raton Sanctuary Associates, In re—§ 12-10, n. 7.
Bodine, In re—§ 2-16, n. 26.
Boeckman, In re—§ 12-11; § 12-11, n. 4, 5, 6.
Boerne Hills Leasing Corp., In re—§ 3-3, n. 4; § 3-16, n. 3, 6; § 3-18, n. 20; § 6-61, n. 59; § 6-62, n. 26; § 6-86, n. 10.
Boggess, In re—§ 8-25, n. 17.
Boggs, Inc., Matter of—§ 6-92, n. 5; § 6-93, n. 42.
Bogstad, Matter of—§ 7-26, n. 37.
Bohlen Enterprises, Ltd., In re, 859 F.2d 561—§ 6-7, n. 7, 8; § 6-38, n. 18; § 6-41, n. 20.
Bohlen Enterprises, Ltd., In re, 78 B.R. 556—§ 6-7, n. 10; § 6-41, n. 23, 26, 46.
Bohne, In re—§ 6-77, n. 1; § 6-78, n. 17.
Bokum Resources Corp., In re—§ 12-3, n. 6.
Bond, In re—§ 6-77, n. 20.
Bonded Financial Services, Inc. v. European American Bank—§ 6-46, n. 9; § 6-50, n. 34, 35; § 6-88, n. 14, 21, 23, 24, 27, 35, 37, 39, 42, 48, 49.
Bond Enterprises, Inc., In re—§ 6-61, n. 66.
Bonhiver v. State Bank of Clearing—§ 6-38, n. 7.
Bonnett, Matter of—§ 7-26, n. 46.
Bono, In re—§ 9-3; § 9-3, n. 31.
Booker, In re—§ 6-62, n. 26.
Bookman, In re—§ 8-10, n. 25.

Bookout Holsteins, Inc., In re—§ **6-73, n. 4, 23, 26.**
Boomgarden, Matter of—§ **3-27, n. 6;** § **3-31, n. 45, 96.**
Boon, Matter of—§ **8-17, n. 17, 35, 36, 48;** § **8-33, n. 27.**
Boone, In re—§ **9-22, n. 1.**
Booth, In re—§ **5-4;** § **5-4, n. 13.**
Booth, Matter of—§ **2-14, n. 2;** § **7-45;** § **7-45, n. 1, 2.**
Booth Tow Services, Inc., United States v.—§ **6-76, n. 5.**
Borbidge, In re—§ **3-28, n. 3.**
Borg, In re—§ **9-29, n. 2.**
Borkman, In re—§ **6-40, n. 27.**
Borman, In re—§ **8-25, n. 15.**
Borman's, Inc. v. Allied Supermarkets, Inc.—§ **5-8, n. 10.**
Borne Chemical Co., Inc., Matter of—§ **4-15, n. 15.**
Borste, In re—§ **7-26, n. 21, 28.**
Bosler Supply Group, Matter of—§ **6-67;** § **6-67, n. 12.**
Boston v. Schapiro (In re Kansas City Journal-Post Co.)—§ **6-93, n. 2.**
Boughton, Matter of, 60 B.R. 373—§ **12-5, n. 2.**
Boughton, Matter of, 49 B.R. 312—§ **12-5, n. 8.**
Bourgeois, In re—§ **6-32, n. 5;** § **6-35, n. 40.**
Bovay, In re—§ **8-27, n. 11;** § **8-28, n. 7.**
Bowen, In re—§ **8-11, n. 18;** § **8-33, n. 34.**
Bowers v. Connecticut Nat. Bank—§ **12-12, n. 14.**
Bowles, In re—§ **9-7;** § **9-7, n. 4, 12, 19.**
Bowling, In re—§ **7-36, n. 3.**
Boyd, In re, 121 B.R. 622—§ **8–10, n. 26, 27.**
Boyd, In re, 96 B.R. 694—§ **6-45, n. 3.**
Boyd, In re, 11 B.R. 690—§ **6-6, n. 4, 7.**
Boyd v. Martin Exploration Co.—§ **6-2, n. 24.**
Boyd v. Robinson—§ **8-25, n. 16, 18.**
Boyd Elevator, Inc., In re—§ **6-77, n. 8.**
Boyette, In re—§ **6-2, n. 20.**
Boyle, Matter of—§ **7-28, n. 8.**
Boyle v. American Sec. Bank—§ **6-38, n. 6.**
Boyle v. Donovan—§ **7-29, n. 11.**
Bracey, In re—§ **9-4, n. 2.**
Bradley, Matter of—§ **3-10, n. 72.**
Bradlow, In re—§ **8-28, n. 3;** § **8-29, n. 7.**
Bradshaw, In re—§ **9-18;** § **9-18, n. 11.**
Bradt, In re—§ **3-16, n. 8.**
Brady, Matter of—§ **7-45, n. 13;** § **8-11, n. 3.**
Brady, Texas, Mun. Gas Corp., Matter of—§ **3-23, n. 34.**
Braen, In re—§ **7-26, n. 6.**
Brandon Mill Farms, Ltd., In re—§ **11-17, n. 3.**
Braniff Airways, Inc., In re, 700 F.2d 935—§ **4-4;** § **4-4, n. 18, 27;** § **11-41;** § **11-41, n. 15.**
Braniff Airways, Inc., In re, 42 B.R. 443—§ **6-39, n. 1, 39;** § **6-40, n. 4, 6, 16, 28, 33;** § **6-42, n. 2, 3;** § **6-94, n. 6.**
Braniff Airways, Inc., In re, 21 B.R. 181—§ **3-21, n. 113.**
Braniff Airways, Inc. v. Exxon Co., U.S.A.—§ **6-20, n. 20;** § **6-39, n. 35, 39;** § **6-40, n. 6, 7, 27;** § **6-41, n. 38, 44, 45.**
Braniff Airways, Inc. v. Midwest Corp.—§ **6-31, n. 16.**
Braniff, Inc., In re, 118 B.R. 819—§ **3-17, n. 7, 20.**
Braniff, Inc., In re, 113 B.R. 745—§ **6-65, n. 9;** § **6-66, n. 5;** § **6-67, n. 3.**
Braniff, Inc., In re, 110 B.R. 980—§ **3-17, n. 9, 10, 18.**
Brantley, In re—§ **9-18, n. 6, 10.**
Brantz, In re—§ **6-48, n. 6;** § **8-28, n. 7, 17, 25;** § **8-29, n. 7.**
Brasby, In re—§ **6-56, n. 50, 52.**
Braten, In re—§ **2-5, n. 21.**
Brayshaw, In re—§ **8-1, n. 12.**
Breen, In re—§ **8-25, n. 57.**
Breezewood Acres, Inc., In re—§ **6-93, n. 29, 44.**
Brendern Enterprises, Inc., In re—§ **6-40, n. 14.**
Brent, In re—§ **8-13, n. 2.**
Brent Explorations, Inc., In re—§ **6-62, n. 26.**
Bresler, In re—§ **3-2, n. 6;** § **3-32, n. 11, 30.**
Breuer, In re—§ **8-32, n. 5.**
Brewer, In re—§ **8-25, n. 17.**
Brewood, In re—§ **7-26, n. 55.**
BRI Corp., In re—§ **6-61, n. 33.**

Briden v. Foley—§ 6-18, n. 4.
Bridge, In re—§ 6-48, n. 5, 8.
Bridgeport Co., Inc. v. U.S. Postal Service—§ 6-38, n. 9, 18; § 6-40, n. 14; § 6-43, n. 3, 4, 15.
Bridges, In re—§ 6-2, n. 3, 24.
Bridges Enterprises, Inc., In re—§ 6-69, n. 7.
Bridges Enterprises, Inc., Matter of—§ 6-19, n. 18; § 6-69, n. 13.
Briggs v. Southern Bakeries Co.—§ 6-38, n. 7.
Brighton Co., In re—§ 3-25, n. 6.
Brinkman, In re, 123 B.R. 611—§ 7-36, n. 3.
Brinkman, In re, 123 B.R. 318—§ 3-20, n. 42, 43, 44, 47.
Brints Cotton Marketing, Inc., In re—§ 6-19, n. 17, 18.
Brissette, Matter of—§ 8-11, n. 27.
Bristol Industries, In re—§ 6-16, n. 1.
Bristol Industries Corp., Matter of—§ 6-88, n. 19, 33.
Brittain, In re—§ 6-4, n. 17; § 6-36, n. 11; § 6-62, n. 15, 23, 39.
Britton, In re, 83 B.R. 914—§ 6-38, n. 16; § 6-39, n. 15; § 6-40, n. 36; § 6-44; § 6-44, n. 3.
Britton, In re, 66 B.R. 572—§ 6-82, n. 2; § 6-83, n. 12.
Britts, In re—§ 3-10, n. 56, 70, 82.
Broadcast Corp. of Georgia v. Broadfoot—§ 7-11, n. 6.
Broadcast Music, Inc. v. Game Operators Corp.—§ 3-6, n. 40, 52.
Broad Nat. Bank v. Kadison—§ 7-20, n. 2.
Broadnax, In re—§ 3-9, n. 6.
Brock, In re—§ 7-39, n. 15.
Brock, Matter of—§ 3-12, n. 15.
Brock v. Morysville Body Works, Inc.—§ 3-21, n. 20, 90, 99, 104; § 12-3, n. 7.
Brock v. Rusco Industries, Inc.—§ 3-21, n. 8, 19, 73, 82, 112.
Brockenbrough v. C.I.R.—§ 9-3, n. 11.
Broman, In re—§ 3-23, n. 35, 46; § 9-20; § 9-20, n. 12, 16.
Bronner v. Exchange State Bank—§ 6-94, n. 8.
Brooks, In re, 871 F.2d 89—§ 3-11, n. 17; § 3-32, n. 6.
Brooks, In re, 79 B.R. 479—§ 6-73, n. 8, 10, 11.
Brooks, In re, 71 B.R. 6—§ 8-27, n. 3.
Brooks, In re, 26 B.R. 210—§ 3-10, n. 60.
Brooks, Matter of, 844 F.2d 258—§ 8-33, n. 17, 27.
Brooks, Matter of, 44 B.R. 963—§ 6-18, n. 30.
Brooks Farms, In re—§ 6-38, n. 18; § 6-39, n. 15; § 6-41, n. 10, 17, 18, 23, 51.
Brooks & Woodington, Inc., In re—§ 5-23, n. 3.
Broomall Industries, Inc. v. Data Design Logic Systems, Inc.—§ 10-31, n. 6; § 11-3, n. 21.
Brosamer v. Mark—§ 8-33, n. 15.
Brothers, In re—§ 8-25, n. 17.
Brouse, In re—§ 9-18, n. 13; § 11-30, n. 11.
Brower, In re—§ 6-20, n. 22; § 6-61, n. 16.
Brown, In re, 803 F.2d 120—§ 12-12, n. 29.
Brown, In re, 734 F.2d 119—§ 8-1, n. 20; § 8-27, n. 11.
Brown, In re, 126 B.R. 481—§ 6-56, n. 50.
Brown, In re, 118 B.R. 1008—§ 8-1, n. 11.
Brown, In re, 118 B.R. 57—§ 6-87, n. 8, 10, 11.
Brown, In re, 113 B.R. 318—§ 8-23, n. 6.
Brown, In re, 105 B.R. 531—§ 3-20, n. 21, 24.
Brown, In re, 104 B.R. 609—§ 6-54, n. 10; § 6-55, n. 13; § 6-56, n. 54.
Brown, In re, 103 B.R. 734—§ 12-15; § 12-15, n. 3.
Brown, In re, 91 B.R. 19—§ 9-18, n. 14.
Brown, In re, 88 B.R. 280—§ 2-9, n. 2.
Brown, In re, 81 B.R. 432—§ 8-27, n. 11; § 8-28, n. 3.
Brown, In re, 56 B.R. 487—§ 12-16, n. 3.
Brown, In re, 51 B.R. 51—§ 3-20, n. 21.
Brown, In re, 33 B.R. 219—§ 6-86, n. 3; § 8-10, n. 11, 21.
Brown, In re, 29 B.R. 360—§ 9-14, n. 13.
Brown, In re, 12 B.R. 885—§ 3-10, n. 58, 59, 62.
Brown, Matter of, 123 B.R. 260—§ 8-28, n. 3.
Brown, Matter of, 73 B.R. 740—§ 8-1, n. 20; § 8-22, n. 23; § 8-23, n. 6.
Brown, Matter of, 7 B.R. 529—§ 9-3, n. 11.
Brown v. First Nat. Bank in Lenox—§ 5-4, n. 14.
Brown v. First Nat. Bank of Little Rock, Ark.—§ 6-7, n. 5.
Brown v. Pennsylvania State Employees Credit Union—§ 3-8, n. 10, 34; § 7-40; § 7-40, n. 4; § 7-41; § 7-41, n. 1.
Brown v. Vanguard Holding Corp.—§ 6-56, n. 54.
Browner v. Rosen—§ 6-39, n. 30; § 6-40, n. 27.

TABLE OF CASES

Brown Family Farms, Inc., In re—§ 6-27; § 6-27, n. 4; § 6-34, n. 15; § 6-61, n. 21, 70; § 6-89, n. 9, 16, 24, 25.
Browning, In re—§ 6-92, n. 9.
Browning v. Navarro—§ 3-22, n. 4; § 3-30, n. 2.
Brown Iron & Metal, Inc., In re—§ 6-89, n. 9, 16, 20, 24, 25.
Brownlee, Matter of—§ 2-17, n. 5.
Brown Transport Truckload, Inc., Matter of—§ 3-14, n. 80; § 3-25, n. 5; § 3-31; § 3-31, n. 7.
Bruce, In re, 96 B.R. 717—§ 6-2, n. 3, 16, 22, 28, 30; § 8-22, n. 22; § 8-23, n. 3, 6.
Bruce, In re, 80 B.R. 927—§ 9-22, n. 14.
Bruce, In re, 40 B.R. 884—§ 9-18, n. 10.
Brumlow, In re, 96 B.R. 375—§ 3-23, n. 35.
Brunell, In re, 76 B.R. 64—§ 8-22, n. 18.
Brunell, In re, 47 B.R. 830—§ 6-49, n. 73; § 6-56, n. 50.
Bruning v. United States—§ 7-25; § 7-25, n. 12.
Brunner v. New York State Higher Educ. Services Corp.—§ 7-33; § 7-33, n. 8, 10.
Brunson, Matter of, 87 B.R. 304—§ 8-25, n. 23.
Brunson, Matter of, 82 B.R. 634—§ 7-34, n. 14, 15.
Bryant, In re, 103 B.R. 95—§ 6-72, n. 1.
Bryant, In re, 95 B.R. 856—§ 3-23, n. 11, 22, 32.
Bryant, In re, 47 B.R. 21—§ 7-45, n. 1, 8, 16; § 9-13, n. 4.
Bryant, Matter of, 43 B.R. 189—§ 7-35, n. 2; § 7-37, n. 3.
Bryant, Matter of, 28 B.R. 362—§ 2-13, n. 8.
Bryant v. General Elec. Credit Corp.—§ 8-25, n. 5, 6.
Bryant v. Pennsylvania Higher Education Assistance Agency—§ 7-33, n. 14.
Bryson Properties, XVIII, In re—§ 11-27; § 11-27, n. 17.
B. Siegel Co., Matter of—§ 5-12; § 5-12, n. 9.
BTS, Inc., In re—§ 12-3, n. 7.
Buchanan, In re—§ 6-60, n. 20.
Buckenmaier, In re—§ 6-40, n. 7; § 6-43, n. 3.
Buckland, Matter of—§ 7-47, n. 2.
Buckley & Associates Ins., Inc., In re—§ 6-40, n. 4; § 6-45, n. 3, 17.
Budget Service Co. v. Better Homes of Virginia, Inc.—§ 3-33, n. 6, 18.
Builders Supply of Wilmington, Inc., Matter of—§ 6-88, n. 37, 45, 46.
Bulger, In re—§ 8-25, n. 52, 57.
Bullion Reserve of North America, In re, 922 F.2d 544—§ 6-88, n. 14, 37.
Bullion Reserve of North America, In re, 836 F.2d 1214—§ 6-7, n. 1, 4; § 6-19, n. 4, 18; § 6-27, n. 3; § 6-30, n. 6.
Bulson, In re—§ 3-8, n. 4; § 3-33, n. 15; § 3-34, n. 7, 20.
Bumper Sales, Inc., In re—§ 6-77, n. 7, 22.
Bunch, In re—§ 3-15, n. 6; § 3-33, n. 13.
Bundles v. Baker—§ 1-3, n. 8.
Bundles, Matter of—§ 6-49, n. 73, 74; § 6-54, n. 2, 10; § 6-56; § 6-56, n. 12, 17, 18, 20, 21, 24, 27, 42, 56.
Bunker Exploration Co., In re—§ 6-93, n. 10, 11.
Burbank Generators, Inc., In re—§ 6-49, n. 46, 49.
Burden v. United States—§ 6-93, n. 66.
Buren, In re—§ 8-11, n. 3; § 9-3, n. 6.
Burgat, In re—§ 9-3, n. 12.
Burk v. Emmick—§ 6-63, n. 2, 3.
Burke, In re—§ 6-71, n. 12.
Burk Royalty Company v. Riley—§ 8-7, n. 14.
Burner, In re—§ 6-18, n. 21; § 6-93, n. 53.
Burnette, In re—§ 6-33, n. 15.
Burns, In re, 887 F.2d 1541—§ 7-32; § 7-32, n. 1, 4.
Burns, In re, 108 B.R. 308—§ 8-33, n. 17, 24, 34.
Burns, In re, 6 B.R. 286—§ 9-3, n. 8.
Burns, Matter of—§ 4-10, n. 8.
Burnside, Lee & Harris Diamond Co., Matter of—§ 10-10, n. 1.
Buroker v. Raybourn—§ 8-2, n. 2.
Burrell, In re—§ 9-14, n. 13.
Burrow, In re—§ 6-43, n. 32.
Burstein-Applebee Co., Matter of—§ 6-73, n. 4; § 6-84, n. 2.
Busenlehner, In re—§ 6-13, n. 4; § 6-33; § 6-33, n. 12.
Bush v. Taylor, 912 F.2d 989—§ 7-5, n. 2; § 7-6; § 7-6, n. 4.
Bush v. Taylor, 893 F.2d 962—§ 3-12, n. 26.
Bush Terminal Co, In re—§ 10-7, n. 7.
Busick, Matter of—§ 2-5, n. 12.
Buske, In re—§ 6-39, n. 15; § 6-40, n. 6.

Butcher, In re, 829 F.2d 596—§ 6-83, n. 4.
Butcher, In re, 79 B.R. 741—§ 6-41, n. 18, 21.
Butcher, In re, 75 B.R. 441—§ 8-3, n. 21.
Butcher, In re, 72 B.R. 447—§ 6-49, n. 13, 36, 43; § 6-88, n. 17.
Butcher, In re, 62 B.R. 162—§ 2-17, n. 8.
Butcher, In re, 58 B.R. 128—§ 6-49, n. 39, 46, 69.
Butcher, In re, 51 B.R. 61—§ 6-49, n. 78.
Butcher, In re, 46 B.R. 109—§ 12-10, n. 2.
Butcher v. Bailey—§ 12-12, n. 25.
Butler, In re, 97 B.R. 508—§ 6-76, n. 2.
Butler, In re, 85 B.R. 34—§ 6-32, n. 2.
Butler, In re, 75 B.R. 528—§ 6-50, n. 27; § 8-23, n. 5.
Butler, In re, 61 B.R. 790—§ 6-39, n. 38; § 6-44, n. 2, 6, 9.
Butler, In re, 14 B.R. 532—§ 3-6, n. 11.
Butler v. Lomas and Nettleton Co.—§ 6-55; § 6-55, n. 17.
Butner v. United States—§ 2-8, n. 5; § 5-7, n. 17; § 6-77, n. 19, 20.
Butts, In re—§ 6-58, n. 4; § 8-32, n. 5.
Butz, Matter of, 104 B.R. 128—§ 6-43, n. 7.
Butz, Matter of, 86 B.R. 595—§ 6-39, n. 15.
Butz v. Pingel—§ 6-49, n. 32.
Butz v. Wheeler—§ 6-48, n. 11; § 6-49, n. 12, 40.
Buyer's Club Markets, Inc., In re, 123 B.R. 895—§ 6-20, n. 5, 17; § 6-31, n. 10.
Buyer's Club Markets, Inc., In re, 100 B.R. 37—§ 6-67, n. 3.
Buyer's Club Market, Inc., In re, 100 B.R. 35—§ 6-65, n. 9.
Buzzell, In re—§ 6-6, n. 7; § 8-23, n. 9; § 8-24, n. 4.
B & W Enterprises, Inc., Matter of, 713 F.2d 534—§ 6-93, n. 65.
B & W Enterprises, Inc., Matter of, 19 B.R. 421—§ 4-15; § 4-15, n. 4.
B & W Tractor Co., Inc., In re—§ 4-15, n. 15; § 7-13, n. 8.
By-Rite Distributing, Inc., In re—§ 6-69, n. 7, 13.

C

Cabrillo, In re—§ 3-25, n. 5; § 3-31, n. 67; § 6-40, n. 13; § 6-41, n. 47; § 6-42, n. 2, 3; § 8-1, n. 20.
Caceres Johnson P.R., Inc., In re—§ 6-19, n. 17.
Caddell, United States v.—§ 3-20; § 3-20, n. 10, 16.
Cadogan, In re—§ 9-12, n. 2.
CAE Industries Ltd. v. Aerospace Holdings Co.—§ 3-5, n. 12, 19; § 3-10, n. 16.
Cafe Partners/Washington 1983, A New York Ltd. Partnership, In re—§ 5-24, n. 3.
Cain, In re—§ 8-17, n. 7.
Cain, Matter of—§ 7-34, n. 5.
Calandriello, In re—§ 8-28, n. 3.
Calatayud, In re—§ 6-47, n. 13; § 6-49, n. 47, 49; § 6-51, n. 33.
Calder, In re, 907 F.2d 953—§ 3-32, n. 18.
Calder, In re, 94 B.R. 200—§ 2-8, n. 14.
Caldwell, In re, 895 F.2d 1123—§ 7-30; § 7-30, n. 5; § 9-14, n. 18.
Caldwell, In re, 60 B.R. 214—§ 7-30, n. 3.
Calhoun, In re—§ 7-29; § 7-29, n. 2, 8, 13, 20, 23.
California v. Heincy—§ 9-2, n. 10.
California Canners and Growers, In re—§ 6-45; § 6-45, n. 19, 29.
California Devices, Inc., In re—§ 3-27, n. 45.
California State Board of Equalization v. Sierra Summit (In re China Peak Resort)—§ 12-5, n. 9.
California Trade Technical Schools, Inc., In re—§ 6-7, n. 4; § 6-88, n. 17, 36, 37.
Callender, In re—§ 7-41, n. 1.
Calmenson Clothing Co. v. First Nat. Bank & Trust Co. of Aberdeen—§ 6-38, n. 12.
Calvary Temple Evangelistic Ass'n, In re—§ 10-13; § 10-13, n. 9.
Calvo, In re—§ 7-26, n. 37.
Camacho, Matter of—§ 6-21, n. 5, 8.
Camacho v. Martin—§ 7-19, n. 3.
Camarda v. Danziger, Bangser & Weiss—§ 6-52, n. 14.
Cambria Clover Mercantile Co., Inc., In re—§ 6-77, n. 1, 7; § 6-78, n. 3.
Cambridge Properties, Inc., In re—§ 3-26, n. 11; § 3-27, n. 26.
Cambron Corp., In re—§ 6-62, n. 3, 27.
Camden Nursery, Inc., Matter of—§ 6-17, n. 8, 15; § 6-48, n. 10; § 6-59, n. 3.
Camellia Court Apartments, Ltd., In re—§ 3-25, n. 13; § 3-27, n. 23.
Camelot Associates Ltd. Partnership, In re—§ 6-77, n. 8, 11, 15.
Camelot Motors Corp., In re—§ 6-34, n. 18.

TABLE OF CASES

Cameron v. United States—§ 11-16, n. 6.
Campbell, In re, 89 B.R. 187—§ 10–17, n. 6.
Campbell, In re, 63 B.R. 702—§ 2–14, n. 1.
Campbell, In re, 38 B.R. 193—§ 9–3, n. 6.
Campbell v. Alleghany Corp—§ 11-21, n. 3.
Campbell v. Lauigan—§ 3-32, n. 6.
Camp Rockhill, Inc., In re—§ 6-17, n. 23, 29.
Canady, In re—§ 9-17, n. 3.
Canal Place Ltd. Partnership, Matter of—§ 3-25, n. 36, 59; § 3-26, n. 8.
Can-Alta Properties, Ltd., In re—§ 3-29, n. 14.
Cancel, In re, 85 B.R. 677—§ 7–31, n. 10.
Cancel, In re, 82 B.R. 674—§ 9–2, n. 11.
Candor Diamond Corp., In re—§ 6-18, n. 22, 27; § 6-40, n. 23, 27; § 6-49, n. 46, 69; § 6-50, n. 7, 12, 34, 35; § 6-84, n. 3; § 6-88, n. 23.
Cantrup, In re—§ 6-62, n. 25.
Caplin v. Marine Midland Grace Trust Co. of New York—§ 6-61, n. 8.
Capodanno, In re—§ 3-10, n. 81.
Capps, Appeal of—§ 9-17, n. 7.
Carco Partnership, In re—§ 3-29, n. 12.
Cardell, Matter of—§ 3-25, n. 9.
Cardinal Enterprises, In re—§ 6-55, n. 3.
Cardinal Industries, Inc., In re—§ 5-15, n. 10; § 11-38; § 11-38, n. 4, 9.
Cardinal Mine Supply, Inc., United States v.—§ 7-3; § 7-3, n. 4; § 7-15; § 7-15, n. 11, 18.
Care Givers, Inc., In re—§ 5-10, n. 3.
Carey, In re, 96 B.R. 336—§ 8–32, n. 5.
Carey, In re, 36 B.R. 194—§ 8–11, n. 3.
Carib-Inn of San Juan Corp., In re—§ 3-21, n. 8, 70, 126.
Carley Capital Group, In re—§ 6-2, n. 24.
Carley Capital Group v. Fireman's Fund Ins. Co.—§ 3-6, n. 32, 33.
Carlsen, In re—§ 6-15, n. 3; § 6-40, n. 27.
Carlson, In re—§ 8-18, n. 6.
Carlson, Matter of—§ 6-70, n. 3.
Carlson's for Music, Inc. v. Gould—§ 1-3, n. 1.
Carl Subler Trucking, Inc., In re—§ 6-11, n. 7.
Carlton, In re—§ 7-32, n. 1.
Carlton Fruit Co., In re—§ 3-21, n. 9, 46, 109.
Carlyle, In re—§ 6-61, n. 74.
Carmel, In re—§ 6-73, n. 4.
Carnegie Intern. Corp., In re—§ 10-10, n. 1.
Carnell Const. Corp., In re—§ 12-2, n. 11.
Carolina Parachute Corp., In re—§ 5-15, n. 5.
Carolina Parachute Corp., United States v.—§ 3-22, n. 7, 29; § 3-23, n. 34; § 10-29, n. 9.
Carolina Resort Motels, Inc., In re—§ 6-36, n. 3, 7; § 6-62, n. 5.
Carolin Corp. v. Miller—§ 2-15; § 2-15, n. 9, 12, 24.
Caroline Desert Disco Inc., In re—§ 10-8, n. 7.
Caro Products, Inc., Matter of—§ 6-19, n. 17, 18.
Carousel Candy Co., Inc., In re—§ 6-18, n. 18; § 6-69, n. 9.
Carpenter, In re—§ 6-38, n. 21, 22; § 6-43, n. 29; § 6-74, n. 11.
Carpenter, Matter of—§ 7-26, n. 25.
Carper, In re—§ 6-35, n. 23.
Carr, In re, 36 B.R. 381—§ 9–17, n. 7.
Carr, In re, 34 B.R. 653—§ 6–2, n. 20; § 6–50, n. 4, 23; § 6–53, n. 3, 9; § 6–55, n. 13; § 6–56, n. 52; § 6–88, n. 30; § 6–89; § 6–89, n. 8.
Carroll, In re, 903 F.2d 1266—§ 3–14, n. 34, 40; § 3–33, n. 12.
Carroll, In re, 24 B.R. 83—§ 7–43, n. 2.
Carroll, In re, 7 B.R. 907—§ 7–47, n. 3.
Carroll, Matter of—§ 8-1, n. 20; § 8-22, n. 23; § 8-23, n. 6.
Carson, In re, 119 B.R. 264—§ 6–27, n. 8.
Carson, In re, 85 B.R. 460—§ 9–4, n. 43.
Carson, In re, 82 B.R. 847—§ 8–18, n. 5, 16.
Carson, In re, 32 B.R. 27—§ 9–3, n. 12.
Carter, In re—§ 6-2, n. 16.
Carter, Matter of—§ 3-35, n. 4.
Cartledge v. Miller—§ 8-33, n. 15.
Caruthers, In re—§ 8-9, n. 14; § 8-25, n. 43.
Carver, In re—§ 9-14, n. 14.
Casa Loma Associates, In re—§ 2-16; § 2-16, n. 24.
Casbeer, In re—§ 4-6, n. 1; § 6-61, n. 53, 58, 77; § 6-77, n. 7, 19.

Cascade Oil Co., Inc., In re—§ 6-61, n. 38.
Case v. Los Angeles Lumber Products Co.—§ 10-21; § 10-21, n. 7, 10; § 11-26; § 11-26, n. 2; § 11-27, n. 8; § 11-28.
Cash Currency Exchange, Inc., In re—§ 6-48, n. 18; § 6-49, n. 46.
Cash Currency Exchange, Inc., Matter of—§ 12-12, n. 13.
Casperone v. Landmark Oil & Gas Corp.—§ 3-6, n. 3, 39; § 3-30, n. 33.
Cass, In re—§ 8-25, n. 41, 52; § 8-26, n. 4.
Cassell, In re, 107 B.R. 536—§ 9-10, n. 5.
Cassell, In re, 41 B.R. 737—§ 7-39, n. 14, 15.
Cassidy v. Commissioner—§ 7-32; § 7-32, n. 1, 2, 3.
Cassidy Land and Cattle Co., Inc. (Craig v. McCarthy Ranch Trust), In re—§ 12-2, n. 10, 14.
Casteel, Matter of—§ 9-4, n. 2; § 9-27, n. 11.
Caster, In re—§ 9-18, n. 9, 13.
Castillo, In re—§ 6-7, n. 5.
Castlerock Properties, In re—§ 3-30, n. 30; § 3-31, n. 98; § 12-2, n. 18.
Castleton, In re—§ 6-88, n. 17, 18.
Catamount Dyers, Inc., In re—§ 6-61, n. 66.
Cates, In re—§ 8-33, n. 6.
Cathey v. Johns–Manville Sales Corp.—§ 3-6, n. 30, 38.
Caucus Distributors, Inc., In re—§ 2-5, n. 3, 4.
Causa, In re—§ 3-30, n. 17.
Cavalier Homes of Georgia, Inc., Matter of—§ 6-9, n. 5; § 6-10, n. 13; § 6-17, n. 6, 11, 28; § 6-19, n. 4, 10, 18; § 6-20, n. 14, 17; § 6-49, n. 32, 47, 72; § 6-88, n. 54.
Cecchini, In re—§ 7-30; § 7-30, n. 14, 19.
Cedar Rapids Meats, Inc., In re—§ 6-4, n. 9; § 6-7, n. 4; § 6-20, n. 20.
Cedar Tide Corp., In re—§ 4-4, n. 15, 27.
Celco, Inc. of America v. Davis Van Lines, Inc.—§ 8-9, n. 10.
C.E.N., Inc., In re—§ 4-12, n. 2.
Center Wholesale, Inc., In re—§ 4-14, n. 5; § 4-16, n. 4; § 6-61, n. 8.
Central Florida Fuels, Inc., In re—§ 5-8, n. 8.
Central Foundry Co., In re—§ 6-82, n. 1.
Central Hanover Bank & Trust Co. v. Herbst—§ 7-28, n. 9.
Central Pacific Boiler & Piping, Ltd., In re—§ 6-17, n. 18; § 6-93, n. 29.
Central Trust Co of Illinois v. Chicago Auditorium Ass'n—§ 5-4, n. 2.
Centre De Tricots De Gaspe, In re—§ 6-72, n. 1.
CenTrust Services, Inc. v. Guterman—§ 3-5, n. 19.
Century Brass Products, Inc., Matter of, 127 B.R. 720—§ 6-83, n. 12.
Century Brass Products, Inc., Matter of, 121 B.R. 136—§ 6-31, n. 17, 19.
Century Brass Products, Inc., Matter of, 97 B.R. 152—§ 6-38, n. 21, 22; § 6-39, n. 2; § 6-40, n. 2; § 6-42, n. 2; § 6-44, n. 5.
Century Glove, Inc. v. First American Bank of New York—§ 11-18; § 11-18, n. 2, 4, 6.
Century Inns, Inc., In re—§ 6-93, n. 47.
Certain, In re—§ 6-15, n. 5.
Chabot, In re—§ 3-23, n. 32; § 6-2, n. 25; § 8-28, n. 9.
Chadborne Industries, Ltd., In re—§ 6-50, n. 21.
Chadwick, In re—§ 6-6, n. 3; § 8-3, n. 21; § 8-32, n. 28.
Chaffin, Matter of—§ 2-16, n. 6.
Chalik, In re—§ 7-21; § 7-21, n. 5, 6, 10; § 7-22, n. 2, 7.
Challinor, In re—§ 8-9, n. 2; § 8-25, n. 26, 27, 32, 55, 58, 62; § 8-27, n. 11.
Chambers, In re—§ 6-20, n. 20.
Chamblin, In re—§ 6-39, n. 35; § 6-41, n. 39.
Champion, In re—§ 8-25, n. 44.
Chancellor, In re—§ 9-22; § 9-22, n. 8.
Chandler, In re, 805 F.2d 555—§ 7-6, n. 5.
Chandler, In re, 89 B.R. 1002—§ 2-9, n. 2.
Channel One Communications, Inc., In re—§ 6-93, n. 66.
Channel 64 Joint Venture, In re—§ 2-2, n. 18.
Chapel Gate Apartments, Ltd., In re—§ 1-4, n. 6.
Chapman, In re, 113 B.R. 561—§ 6-4, n. 16; § 6-61, n. 16; § 6-87, n. 8.
Chapman, In re, 51 B.R. 663—§ 6-2, n. 20.
Chapman v. Forsyth—§ 7-28, n. 3.
Chapman Parts Warehouse, Inc. v. Guderian—§ 6-63, n. 2.
Charisma Inv. Co., N.V. v. Air Florida System, Inc.—§ 6-25, n. 11, 13.
Charrington Worldwide Enterprise, Inc., In re 110 B.R. 973—§ 5-13, n. 3.
Charrington Worldwide Enterprises, Inc., In re, 98 B.R. 65—§ 5-13, n. 4; § 5-14, n. 2.
Charter Co., In re, 103 B.R. 302—§ 6-43, n. 16; § 6-44, n. 16.
Charter Co., In re, 93 B.R. 281—§ 11-3, n. 21.
Charter Co., In re, 86 B.R. 280—§ 6-40, n. 4; § 6-42, n. 2; § 6-43, n. 5.

Charter Co., In re, 82 B.R. 602—§ 12-5, n. 10, 11.
Charter Co., In re, 63 B.R. 568—§ 6-39, n. 1; § 6-40, n. 6.
Charter Co., In re, 54 B.R. 91—§ 6-67, n. 3.
Charter Co., In re, 52 B.R. 263—§ 6-66, n. 4; § 6-67, n. 10.
Charter Co., In re, 44 B.R. 256—§ 10-12, n. 13.
Charter First Mortg., Inc., In re, 56 B.R. 838—§ 6-78, n. 6.
Charter First Mortg., Inc., In re, 42 B.R. 380—§ 3-21, n. 22.
Chase, In re, 43 B.R. 739—§ 9-14, n. 19, 25.
Chase, In re, 37 B.R. 345—§ 8-22, n. 23; § 8-23, n. 6.
Chaseley's Foods, Inc., In re—§ 6-61, n. 66.
Chaseley's Foods, Inc., Matter of—§ 6-61, n. 66; § 6-77, n. 7; § 6-78, n. 3.
Chase & Sanborn Corp., In re, 904 F.2d 588—§ 6-25, n. 3; § 6-49, n. 13; § 6-51, n. 11; § 6-88, n. 17, 39, 46.
Chase & Sanborn Corp., In re, 848 F.2d 1196—§ 6-88, n. 35.
Chase & Sanborn Corp., In re, 835 F.2d 1341—§ 12-13, n. 9; § 12-14, n. 2.
Chase & Sanborn Corp., In re, 813 F.2d 1177—§ 6-2, n. 32; § 6-47, n. 8.
Chase & Sanborn Corp., In re, 127 B.R. 903—§ 6-87, n. 14.
Chase & Sanborn Corp., In re, 124 B.R. 371—§ 6-40, n. 4.
Chase & Sanborn Corp., In re, 55 B.R. 451—§ 6-93, n. 31.
Chase & Sanborn Corp., In re, 51 B.R. 739—§ 6-48, n. 18; § 6-49, n. 46, 49; § 6-50, n. 6, 19.
Chastant, Matter of—§ 7-19, n. 1, 5.
Chateaugay Corp., In re, 944 F.2d 997—§ 7-7; § 7-7, n. 8; § 7-8, n. 6; § 11-2, n. 9.
Chateaugay Corp., In re, 920 F.2d 183—§ 3-33, n. 5.
Chateaugay Corp., In re, 838 F.2d 59—§ 10-2, n. 3.
Chateaugay Corp., In re, 118 B.R. 19—§ 3-6, n. 59; § 3-21, n. 39; § 3-22, n. 2.
Chateaugay Corp., In re, 115 B.R. 760—§ 6-69, n. 6; § 6-76, n. 5.
Chateaugay Corp., In re, 115 B.R. 28—§ 3-21, n. 59.
Chateaugay Corp., In re, 112 B.R. 526—§ 3-6, n. 1; § 3-33, n. 13, 15, 17, 22, 25, 28.
Chateaugay Corp., In re, 112 B.R. 513—§ 7-5, n. 2; § 7-7; § 7-7, n. 4; § 7-8, n. 5, 6; § 11-1, n. 5; § 11-2, n. 7; § 11-3, n. 26.
Chateaugay Corp., In re, 109 B.R. 613—§ 3-22, n. 5, 19, 26, 30.
Chateaugay Corp., In re, 109 B.R. 51—§ 11-24; § 11-24, n. 3.
Chateaugay Corp., In re, 104 B.R. 617—§ 3-23, n. 45.
Chateaugay Corp., In re, 102 B.R. 335—§ 12-7, n. 1.
Chateaugay Corp., In re, 87 B.R. 779—§ 3-6; § 3-6, n. 65; § 3-14; § 3-14, n. 19; § 3-21, n. 6, 8, 18, 73, 102, 116.
Chateaugay Corp., In re, 86 B.R. 40—§ 6-40, n. 23.
Chateaugay Corp., In re, 80 B.R. 279—§ 10-2, n. 3.
Chateaugay Corp., In re, 76 B.R. 945—§ 10-2, n. 3.
Chateaugay Corp., In re, 64 B.R. 990—§ 10-2, n. 3.
Chateaugay Corp., Reomar, Inc., In re—§ 3-6, n. 38, 40; § 3-22, n. 26, 27.
Chatman Elec. Services, Inc., United States v.—§ 3-5, n. 12; § 3-22, n. 5.
Chattanooga Wholesale Antiques, Inc., In re—§ 6-20, n. 17; § 6-69, n. 11; § 6-70, n. 2; § 6-87, n. 14.
Chavarria, In re—§ 7-39, n. 14.
Cheatham, In re—§ 3-27, n. 45; § 7-13; § 7-13, n. 2.
Chech, In re—§ 7-26, n. 21.
Checkmate Stereo and Electronics, Ltd., In re—§ 6-48, n. 13, 17; § 6-49, n. 12, 46; § 6-87, n. 16, 17.
Checkmate Stereo & Electronics, Ltd., In re—§ 6-60, n. 29; § 6-88, n. 46.
Cheek, In re—§ 8-27, n. 11.
Cheeseman v. Nachman—§ 8-21, n. 9.
Chemical Bank New York Trust Co. v. Kheel—§ 11-41; § 11-41, n. 4, 7, 8.
Chemical Separations Corp., In re—§ 6-2, n. 28, 30.
Chemold Systems, Inc., In re—§ 6-2, n. 9.
Cheng v. Commissioner—§ 3-6, n. 33.
Chenich, In re—§ 6-12, n. 10; § 6-27, n. 11; § 6-61, n. 28, 41.
Chequers, Ltd., In re—§ 6-83, n. 7, 8.
Chernicky Coal Co., Inc., In re—§ 3-23, n. 6; § 6-70, n. 2.
Cherno v. Engine Air Service, Inc.—§ 12-2, n. 11.
Cherry, In re—§ 9-22, n. 2.
Chestnut Co., Inc., In re—§ 6-38, n. 21, 22; § 6-39, n. 2; § 6-40, n. 2, 16, 36; § 6-43, n. 3, 13.
Chevy Devco, In re—§ 4-14; § 4-14, n. 6, 7.
CHG Intern., Inc., Matter of—§ 6-19, n. 16; § 6-32, n. 5, 8.
Chicago, Missouri & Western Ry. Co., In re, 127 B.R. 839—§ 6-16, n. 1.
Chicago, Missouri & Western Ry. Co., In re, 124 B.R. 769—§ 6-10, n. 13; § 6-49, n. 46, 50; § 6-51, n. 26.
Chicago, Missouri and Western Ry. Co., In re, 90 B.R. 344—§ 4-14, n. 5.

Chicago Music Corp., In re—§ 6-49, n. 12; § 6-60, n. 10.
Chicago Rapid Transit Co., In re—§ 5-8, n. 3; § 11-9, n. 3.
Chicago, Rock Island and Pacific R. Co., Matter of—§ 7-11; § 7-11, n. 11.
Chicora Group, In re—§ 6-12, n. 10; § 6-24, n. 2.
Chief Charley's, Inc., Matter of—§ 3-18, n. 24.
Chinichian, In re—§ 9-14, n. 17.
Chipin Cliveden Associates, Inc., In re—§ 6-93, n. 29.
Chisum, In re—§ 2-16, n. 6.
Choice Vend, Inc., Matter of—§ 3-23, n. 14; § 6-83, n. 12, 15.
Chorus Data Systems, Inc., In re—§ 3-30, n. 23.
Chrisman, In re—§ 3-10, n. 47.
Christ Hospital v. Greenwald—§ 8-33, n. 15.
Christian, In re—§ 6-47, n. 7; § 6-54, n. 2, 10; § 6-55, n. 13, 22.
Christian, Matter of, 51 B.R. 118—§ 2-14, n. 1.
Christian, Matter of, 35 B.R. 229—§ 9-17, n. 7.
Christian Life Center, In re—§ 6-93, n. 33, 40.
Christiansen, In re—§ 7-34, n. 19.
Christison v. Caterpillar, Inc.—§ 12-2, n. 10.
Christy, In re—§ 9-27; § 9-27, n. 3, 4.
Christy v. Heights Finance Corp.—§ 8-1, n. 9, 13.
Chrysler Credit Corp. v. Perry Chrysler Plymouth, Inc.—§ 7-30, n. 2, 11, 19, 20.
Chrysler Credit Corp. v. Rebhan—§ 7-26, n. 5; § 7-30, n. 19, 20, 22.
C. H. Stuart, Inc., In re—§ 6-62, n. 25.
Church Bldgs. and Interiors, Inc., In re—§ 6-10, n. 15; § 6-88, n. 54.
Churchfield Management & Inv. Corp., In re—§ 6-2, n. 32.
Churchill, In re—§ 7-38, n. 1.
Ciavarella, In re—§ 6-2, n. 24.
Ciccarello, In re—§ 8-10, n. 25.
Cilek, In re—§ 6-93, n. 41, 50; § 8-17, n. 17, 31, 35, 36, 49.
Cimmaron Oil Co., Inc., In re—§ 6-16, n. 1.
Cimmaron Oil Co., Inc. v. Cameron Consultants, Inc.—§ 6-25, n. 13; § 6-36, n. 14.
Cinderella Clothing Industries, Inc., In re—§ 10-32, n. 2.
Cinematronics, Inc., In re—§ 3-30, n. 29.
Cipa, Matter of—§ 8-10, n. 25, 26.
Circle Five, Inc., In re—§ 3-10, n. 46, 47, 49; § 7-45, n. 4.
Circle K Corp., In re—§ 3-10, n. 33; § 3-14, n. 4, 36; § 3-22, n. 5, 24.
Circleville Distributing Co., In re—§ 6-26, n. 2; § 6-31, n. 15.
Cirineo, In re—§ 7-26, n. 21.
Cissell v. First Nat. Bank of Cincinnati—§ 6-39, n. 35.
Cissne v. Robertson—§ 3-32, n. 38.
C.I.T. v. Posta—§ 7-30, n. 1.
Citibank (New York State), N.A. v. Interfirst Bank of Wichita Falls, N.A.—§ 6-38, n. 10.
Citizens Bank of Roseville v. Taggart—§ 6-63, n. 4.
Citizens State Bank v. Peoples Bank—§ 6-92, n. 5.
Citrowske, In re—§ 9-29, n. 2.
City of (see name of city)
Claar, Matter of—§ 7-26, n. 50, 53.
Clark, In re, 927 F.2d 793—§ 2-14, n. 1.
Clark, In re, 711 F.2d 21—§ 8-17; § 8-17, n. 11, 35.
Clark, In re, 112 B.R. 226—§ 6-12, n. 8.
Clark, In re, 99 B.R. 955—§ 6-53, n. 6; § 6-56, n. 39.
Clark, In re, 79 B.R. 723—§ 6-73, n. 8.
Clark, In re, 71 B.R. 747—§ 9-20; § 9-20, n. 10, 12.
Clark, In re, 47 B.R. 88—§ 6-77, n. 1.
Clark, Matter of—§ 9-17, n. 2.
Clark Pipe and Supply Co., Inc., Matter of, 893 F.2d 693—§ 6-35, n. 45, 50; § 6-93, n. 16, 46, 56.
Clark Pipe & Supply Co., Inc., Matter of, 870 F.2d 1022—§ 6-93, n. 9.
Clarkson v. Selected Risks Ins. Co.—§ 6-38, n. 11.
Classe v. Classe—§ 3-6, n. 45.
Classic Drywall, Inc., In re, 127 B.R. 874—§ 6-87, n. 8.
Classic Drywall, Inc., In re, 121 B.R. 69—§ 6-31, n. 17, 19.
Claussen, In re—§ 3-3, n. 4, 8; § 3-16, n. 3, 6; § 3-18, n. 20; § 6-61, n. 59; § 6-62, n. 18, 26, 28.
Clavis Smith Bldg., Inc., In re—§ 5-4, n. 16.
Claxton, In re—§ 6-93, n. 16, 49.
Claybrook Drilling Co. v. Divanco, Inc.—§ 10-32, n. 1.
C-L Cartage Co., Inc., In re—§ 6-9, n. 2; § 6-10, n. 13; § 6-20, n. 20.
Clemons, In re—§ 6-89, n. 8.
Cleveland Graphic Reproduction, Inc., In re—§ 6-31, n. 7; § 6-36, n. 15; § 6-62, n. 22.

TABLE OF CASES

Cliff's Ridge Skiing Corp., Matter of—§ 6-92, n. 10.
Clifton, In re—§ 6-61, n. 18.
Cline, Matter of—§ 3-12, n. 25.
Cline v. Kaplan—§ 12-14, n. 17, 18.
Clinton State Bank v. Ward—§ 9-3, n. 30.
Closson, In re—§ 6-11, n. 6.
Clover Donut of White Plains Corp., Matter of—§ 6-47, n. 9.
Cloverleaf Farmer's Co-op., In re—§ 6-39, n. 15; § 6-42, n. 3, 4; § 6-77, n. 21.
Clowards, Inc., In re—§ 6-45, n. 2, 3, 6, 7, 9, 10.
Club Development & Management Corp., In re—§ 4-12; § 4-12, n. 3.
Coachlight Dinner Theatre of Nanuet, Inc., In re—§ 3-8, n. 35.
Coal-X Ltd., '76', In re—§ 6-86, n. 4, 8, 9.
Coan, In re—§ 6-82, n. 4.
Coan, Matter of—§ 6-62, n. 34.
Coastal Alaska Lines, Inc., In re—§ 7-3, n. 3; § 7-15, n. 4, 8.
Coastal Cable T.V., Inc., In re—§ 3-27, n. 3.
Coastal Dry Dock & Repair Corp., In re—§ 3-9, n. 23.
Coastal Equities, Inc., In re—§ 10-7, n. 2; § 10-12, n. 7.
Coastal Group, Inc., Matter of—§ 6-83, n. 12.
Coastal Industries, Inc., In re—§ 4-4, n. 3.
Coastal Industries, Inc., Matter of—§ 5-10, n. 5.
Coastal Petroleum Corp., In re—§ 6-9, n. 5; § 6-10, n. 13; § 6-88, n. 54.
Coast Trading Co., Inc., In re—§ 6-65, n. 10; § 6-67, n. 3, 10.
Coated Sales, Inc., In re, 124 B.R. 17—§ 3-18, n. 19, 23; § 6-61, n. 60.
Coated Sales, Inc., In re, 119 B.R. 452—§ 6-87, n. 5.
Cobb, In re, 122 B.R. 22—§ 3-25, n. 8, 31; § 7-47, n. 2.
Cobb, In re, 76 B.R. 557—§ 2-2, n. 15.
Cockreham, In re—§ 6-4, n. 17; § 6-88, n. 36.
Coco, In re—§ 6-4, n. 9; § 6-11, n. 6; § 6-18, n. 29; § 6-69, n. 2; § 6-84, n. 5.
Code v. London—§ 8-7, n. 12.
Codfish Corp., In re—§ 3-5, n. 6; § 3-22, n. 5, 21, 23, 24.
Cody v. Riecker—§ 8-33, n. 15.
Coffey, In re, 52 B.R. 54—§ 9-18, n. 12.
Coffey, In re, 21 B.R. 804—§ 8-21, n. 4.
Cohoes Indus. Terminal, Inc., In re—§ 6-61, n. 10.
Colandrea, In re—§ 6-2, n. 16; § 6-86, n. 4.
Cole, In re—§ 6-50; § 6-50, n. 11, 28, 32; § 6-53, n. 3, 6; § 6-56, n. 5, 50, 51.
Cole, Matter of—§ 9-3, n. 6, 7; § 9-14, n. 4.
Cole v. Cole—§ 8-7, n. 3.
Colegrove, In re—§ 9-10; § 9-10, n. 3, 8, 9; § 9-17, n. 8.
Coleman, In re, 52 B.R. 1—§ 6-39, n. 28, 38; § 6-40, n. 2; § 6-42, n. 2.
Coleman, In re, 21 B.R. 832—§ 6-53, n. 4, 6; § 6-56, n. 5, 52; § 6-88, n. 24, 28; § 8-23, n. 3.
Colin, Matter of—§ 6-93, n. 66.
Colin, Hochstin Co., In re—§ 3-21; § 3-21, n. 35.
Collins, In re—§ 3-30, n. 32.
Colombian Coffee Co., Inc., In re—§ 6-88, n. 35.
Colonial Ford, Inc., In re—§ 2-10, n. 5.
Colonial Manor Associates, Ltd., In re—§ 3-29, n. 2, 11.
Colonial Mortg. Bankers Corp., In re—§ 6-40, n. 2, 24.
Colonial Realty Co., Matter of—§ 3-14; § 3-14, n. 20, 37.
Colston, In re, 87 B.R. 193—§ 8-10, n. 25.
Colston, In re, 11 B.R. 251—§ 9-12, n. 8.
Colter, Inc., In re—§ 6-77, n. 11, 19.
Columbia Data Products, Inc., In re, 892 F.2d 26—§ 6-88, n. 35, 36.
Columbia Data Products, Inc., In re, 99 B.R. 682—§ 6-88, n. 37, 49, 50.
Columbus Typewriter Co., Inc., In re—§ 6-61, n. 12.
Comark, In re, 124 B.R. 806—§ 6-85, n. 11, 20.
Comark, In re, 53 B.R. 945—§ 11-36, n. 7.
Combs v. Richardson—§ 7-26, n. 6.
Combustion Equipment Associates, Inc., In re—§ 7-7, n. 18.
Comcoach Corp., In re—§ 3-25, n. 5; § 3-31; § 3-31, n. 2.
Comer, In re—§ 3-10, n. 9.
Comerica Bank-Midwest v. Kouloumbris—§ 7-26, n. 23.
Commerce Oil Co., In re—§ 3-21; 3-21, n. 7, 45, 50, 51, 74.
Commercial Candy Co., Matter of—§ 6-17, n. 6; § 6-49, n. 40; § 6-88, n. 32.
Commercial Discount Corp. v. Milwaukee Western Bank—§ 6-38, n. 10.
Commercial Investments, Ltd., In re—§ 6-93, n. 39, 47.
Commercial Mortg. Ins. Inc. v. Citizens Nat. Bank of Dallas—§ 8-11, n. 19; § 8-33, n. 15.

Commercial Reprographics, Inc., In re—§ 6-39, n. 10; § 6-40, n. 3, 16.
Commerzanstalt v. Telewide Systems, Inc.—§ 3-6, n. 30, 38.
Commodity Futures Trading Commission v. Incomco, Inc.—§ 3-21, n. 15.
Commodity Futures Trading Com'n v. Co Petro Marketing Group, Inc.—§ 3-21, n. 15, 44, 109.
Commodity Futures Trading Com'n v. Weintraub—§ 10-9, n. 2.
Commonwealth Companies, Inc., In re—§ 3-21; § 3-21, n. 45, 57, 58, 60, 61, 67, 68, 74, 85, 116.
Commonwealth Elec. Co., Matter of—§ 6-39, n. 14.
Commonwealth Oil Refining Co., Inc., Matter of, 805 F.2d 1175—§ 3-21, n. 7, 57, 100, 104; § 3-22, n. 29.
Commonwealth Oil Refining Co., Inc., Matter of, 596 F.2d 1239—§ 12-6; § 12-6, n. 5; § 12-10; § 12-10, n. 2, 4.
Communicall Cent., Inc., In re—§ 6-39, n. 13.
Communications Co. of America, Inc., In re—§ 6-61, n. 16.
Community Hosp. of Rockland County, Matter of—§ 6-36, n. 19.
Compos, In re—§ 7-30, n. 10, 27.
Comprop Inv. Properties, Ltd., Matter of—§ 6-38, n. 5, 21, 22; § 6-39, n. 2, 38; § 6-43, n. 3, 4.
Compton Corp., In re, 90 B.R. 798—§ 3-21, n. 45, 74, 90; § 3-22, n. 7, 29; § 11-7, n. 7.
Compton Corp., In re, 22 B.R. 276—§ 6-39, n. 38; § 6-41, n. 38, 41; § 6-43, n. 3.
Compton, Matter of—§ 7-27, n. 5.
Compton Corp., In re—§ 3-21, n. 45, 74, 90; § 3-22, n. 7, 29; § 6-39, n. 38; § 6-41, n. 38, 41; § 6-43, n. 3; § 11-7, n. 7.
Compton Corp., Matter of—§ 6-9, n. 3, 7, 10; § 6-10, n. 16, 18.
Computer Communications, Inc., In re—§ 3-14, n. 40, 42, 43; § 5-5; § 5-5, n. 6; § 5-22, n. 6.
Computer Universe, In re—§ 6-49, n. 46, 49; § 6-87, n. 8, 10, 11.
Comstock Financial Services, Inc., In re—§ 3-10, n. 9; § 7-15, n. 2; § 11-7, n. 7.
Comtec Industries, Inc., In re—§ 6-93, n. 29, 32.
Conco Bldg. Supplies, Inc., In re—§ 6-83, n. 7.
Concord Sr. Housing Foundation, In re—§ 6-88, n. 14, 21, 27.
Concrete Pumping Service, Inc., In re—§ 2-5; § 2-5, n. 16.
Confederation Life Ins. Co. v. Beau Rivage Ltd.—§ 3-27, n. 23.
Conley, Matter of—§ 6-80, n. 12.
Connally, In re—§ 8-3, n. 19, 21; § 8-33, n. 24.
Connelly v. Marine Midland Bank, N.A.—§ 6-86, n. 10.
Connelly v. Roach—§ 8-3, n. 30.
Conner, In re—§ 6-15, n. 8.
Connor v. Great Western Sav. & Loan Ass'n—§ 6-93, n. 44.
Conquest Offshore Intern., Inc., In re—§ 2-15, n. 27.
Conroy, In re, 110 B.R. 492—§ 8-33, n. 9, 17, 20, 34.
Conroy, In re, 99 B.R. 113—§ 7-26, n. 21.
Consolidated Lewis Inv. Corporation-Limited Partnership, In re—§ 3-30, n. 27.
Consolidated Rock Products Co. v. Du Bois—§ 11-26; § 11-30; § 11-30, n. 1.
Consolidated Southeastern Group, Inc., In re—§ 5-20, n. 9; § 6-61, n. 12, 24.
Constable Plaza Associates, L.P., In re—§ 6-77, n. 11.
Consulting Actuarial Partners, Ltd. Partnership, In re—§ 12-5, n. 7.
Container Transport, Inc., In re—§ 12-5, n. 2.
Conti, In re—§ 6-39, n. 19; § 6-43, n. 3; § 6-44, n. 9.
Continental Airlines Corp., In re, 64 B.R. 865—§ 11-7, n. 2.
Continental Airlines Corp., In re, 60 B.R. 903—§ 11-5, n. 5; § 11-6, n. 10.
Continental Airlines Corp., In re, 60 B.R. 472—§ 11-7, n. 8.
Continental Airlines Corp., In re, 59 B.R. 782—§ 6-2, n. 30.
Continental Airlines Corp., In re, 57 B.R. 854—§ 3-17, n. 5, 14.
Continental Airlines Inc., In re, 932 F.2d 282—§ 3-17, n. 6, 9, 10, 11.
Continental Air Lines Inc., In re, 780 F.2d 1223—§ 4-4; § 4-4, n. 1, 15, 22, 24, 27; § 10-5, n. 11.
Continental Airlines, Inc., Matter of—§ 6-65, n. 9.
Continental Casing Corp. v. Samedan Oil Corp.—§ 3-32, n. 38.
Continental Commodities, Inc., In re—§ 6-31, n. 16.
Continental Country Club, Inc., In re, 108 B.R. 327—§ 6-3, n. 11; § 6-20, n. 17.
Continental Country Club, Inc., In re, 64 B.R. 177—§ 6-61, n. 60; § 6-62, n. 17, 26.
Continental Experts Enterprises, Inc., In re—§ 6-39, n. 22.
Continental Marine Corp., In re—§ 4-6; § 4-6, n. 5.
Continental Vending Mach. Corp., In re—§ 11-41, n. 9.
Control Elec., Inc., In re—§ 6-32, n. 5, 7.
Control Elec., Inc., Matter of—§ 6-25, n. 13.
Cook, In re—§ 7-45, n. 16.
Cook, Matter of, 43 B.R. 996—§ 8-33, n. 24.
Cook, Matter of, 3 B.R. 480—§ 9-14, n. 4.
Cooke, In re—§ 3-16, n. 11.
Cook United, Inc., In re, 117 B.R. 884—§ 6-3, n. 13; § 6-31, n. 15.

Cook United, Inc., In re, 117 B.R. 881—§ **6-83, n. 5.**
Cook United, Inc., In re, 117 B.R. 301—§ **6-87, n. 9.**
Cooley, In re, 87 B.R. 432—§ **2-8, n. 33;** § **9-27, n. 2.**
Cooley, In re, 72 B.R. 54—§ **8-26, n. 5, 14.**
Coombs, In re—§ **4-9, n. 10, 11.**
Coons, In re—§ **3-9, n. 8;** § **3-33, n. 13.**
Coonse, In re—§ **8-25, n. 40.**
Cooper, In re—§ **3-10, n. 70.**
Cooper v. State Bar of California—§ **3-21, n. 9, 43, 109.**
Cooper-Jarrett, Inc. v. Central Transport, Inc.—§ **6-40, n. 4.**
Coopers & Lybrand v. Livesay—§ **12-12, n. 6.**
Coors of North Mississippi, Inc., In re, 66 B.R. 845—§ **6-17, n. 10, 29;** § **6-49, n. 13, 47, 49, 50;** § **6-60, n. 17, 20.**
Coors of North Mississippi, Inc., In re, 27 B.R. 918—§ **5-19;** § **5-19, n. 1.**
Copeland v. Stevens—§ **5-5;** § **5-5, n. 1.**
Coppie, Matter of—§ **6-15, n. 5.**
Copter, Inc., In re—§ **6-60, n. 23.**
Copy Crafters Quickprint, Inc., In re—§ **11-17, n. 8.**
Corbett, In re—§ **6-50, n. 23, 28;** § **6-53, n. 3, 6;** § **6-56, n. 5;** § **8-23, n. 5.**
Corbo, Matter of—§ **3-20, n. 6, 9.**
Corcoran v. Andrews—§ **8-7, n. 16.**
Cord, Matter of—§ **7-45, n. 13.**
Corey, In re, 892 F.2d 829—§ **11-6, n. 10, 13.**
Corey, In re, 19 B.R. 76—§ **9-3, n. 6.**
Corky Foods Corp., In re—§ **11-37, n. 3.**
Cormarc, Inc., In re—§ **6-92, n. 10;** § **6-93, n. 47.**
Corner Pockets of the Southwest, Inc., In re—§ **3-31, n. 21.**
Coronado, In re—§ **3-11, n. 14.**
Corporacion de Servicios Medicos Hospitalarios de Fajardo, In re, 805 F.2d 440—§ **3-6, n. 39;** § **3-21, n. 69;** § **3-30, n. 33.**
Corporacion de Servicios Medico-Hospitalarios de Fajardo, In re, 96 B.R. 639—§ **6-4, n. 17.**
Corporate Jet Aviation, Inc., In re—§ **6-49, n. 39, 44;** § **6-52, n. 49.**
Correa, In re—§ **9-3, n. 30.**
Cory v. Parks—§ **8-7, n. 10.**
Cosmopolitan Aviation Corp., In re—§ **6-11, n. 7;** § **6-61, n. 6, 53.**
Cosner, In re—§ **6-40, n. 14.**
Cosper, In re—§ **6-13, n. 2;** § **6-20, n. 21.**
Cossett, In re—§ **12-5, n. 6.**
Costa and Head Land Co., In re—§ **11-36;** § **11-36, n. 2, 4.**
Costell, In re—§ **6-61, n. 23.**
Cothran v. United States—§ **4-6, n. 9.**
Cott Corp., Matter of—§ **11-7, n. 8.**
Cottrell, In re—§ **8-33, n. 2.**
Cottrill, In re—§ **6-49, n. 38, 39, 49.**
Coulter v. Blieden—§ **4-7, n. 13.**
Council, In re—§ **8-17, n. 13;** § **8-33, n. 39.**
Countdown of Connecticut, Inc., In re—§ **6-49, n. 32, 35, 64, 71, 72.**
Counties Contracting and Const. Co. v. Constitution Life Ins. Co., 855 F.2d 1054—§ **3-16, n. 14.**
Counties Contracting & Const. Co. v. Constitution Life Ins. Co., 81 B.R. 306—§ **3-14, n. 46.**
Counts, In re—§ **6-45, n. 2.**
Cournoyer v. Town of Lincoln, 790 F.2d 971—§ **3-21, n. 12, 104, 109, 116.**
Cournoyer v. Town of Lincoln, 53 B.R. 478—§ **3-21, n. 113, 116;** § **10-8, n. 1.**
Courtney, In re—§ **8-25, n. 43, 44.**
Coury, In re—§ **3-9, n. 22.**
Cove Patio Corp., In re—§ **6-10, n. 15;** § **6-88, n. 54.**
Cowart, Matter of—§ **3-34, n. 9.**
Cox, In re, 904 F.2d 1399—§ **7-20, n. 6.**
Cox, In re, 68 B.R. 788—§ **6-61, n. 28.**
Cox Cotton Co., In re, 24 B.R. 930—§ **4-7, n. 20.**
Cox Cotton Co., In re, 8 B.R. 682—§ **12-8;** § **12-8, n. 2.**
Crabtree, In re, 871 F.2d 36—§ **6-61, n. 42.**
Crabtree, In re, 51 B.R. 521—§ **6-77, n. 7.**
Crabtree, In re, 49 B.R. 806—§ **6-87, n. 12;** § **6-88, n. 30;** § **6-89, n. 31.**
Crabtree, In re, 39 B.R. 718—§ **11-40, n. 1.**
Crabtree, In re, 14 B.R. 601—§ **6-62, n. 3.**
Craddock-Terry Shoe Corp., In re—§ **6-39, n. 34;** § **6-41, n. 42, 46, 51;** § **6-43, n. 29.**
Craig, Matter of—§ **6-20, n. 8;** § **6-25, n. 13, 14, 40;** § **6-48, n. 8;** § **6-59, n. 11.**
Craig Oil Co., Matter of—§ **6-87, n. 14;** § **6-88, n. 17.**

Cramer, Inc., In re, 105 B.R. 433—§ 11-14, n. 5.%
Cramer, Inc., In re, 100 B.R. 63—§ 11-20; § 11-20, n. 1.
Crane, In re—§ 6-49, n. 34.
Craner, In re—§ 6-76, n. 2; § 6-77, n. 21.
Cravey, In re—§ 8-27, n. 10, 11.
Crawford, In re, 95 B.R. 491—§ 3-23, n. 34.
Crawford, In re, 10 B.R. 815—§ 9-9, n. 2.
Crawford, Matter of—§ 7-47, n. 2.
Crawford County State Bank v. Doss—§ 6-59, n. 2.
Crawley, In re—§ 3-14, n. 3, 66; § 3-16, n. 11.
Crazy Eddie Securities Litigation, In re—§ 3-5, n. 19; § 3-6, n. 40; § 3-10, n. 11.
Creasy v. Coleman Furniture Corp.—§ 8-11, n. 18.
Creative Media Productions, Inc., In re—§ 3-20, n. 7, 23.
Credit Alliance Corp. v. Williams—§ 3-5, n. 6; § 3-10, n. 13.
Credit Managers Ass'n of Southern California v. Federal Co.—§ 6-52, n. 7, 8, 11, 34, 35.
Creel, In re—§ 6-12, n. 7; § 6-87, n. 6.
Cregut, In re—§ 9-3, n. 6.
Crenshaw, In re—§ 8-33, n. 17, 18, 20.
Crenshaw, Matter of—§ 8-11, n. 18.
Crescent Beach Inn, Inc., In re—§ 10-8; § 10-8, n. 8, 10.
Crescenzi, In re, 69 B.R. 64—§ 9-3, n. 12.
Crescenzi, In re, 53 B.R. 374—§ 9-3, n. 21.
Cress, Matter of—§ 8-33, n. 17, 21, 24.
Crevier, In re—§ 6-68, n. 2.
Crisp, Matter of—§ 6-92, n. 5.
Crispell, In re—§ 3-15, n. 5; § 6-43, n. 29; § 6-44, n. 1.
Crockett, Matter of—§ 9-10, n. 13.
Crompton, In re—§ 9-18, n. 9.
Cross Baking Co., Inc., In re—§ 4-15, n. 14; § 6-77, n. 21; § 6-78, n. 6, 9.
Crouch, In re, 51 B.R. 331—§ 6-77, n. 1; § 6-78, n. 14, 17.
Crouch, In re, 33 B.R. 271—§ 8-10, n. 25.
Crouse Group, Inc., In re—§ 4-12, n. 3; § 4-13; § 4-13, n. 4.
Crow v. Long—§ 8-1, n. 20.
Crowthers McCall Pattern, Inc. v. Lewis—§ 6-52, n. 10, 13.
Cruickshank, In re—§ 8-32, n. 8, 9.
Crutcher Resources Corp., In re—§ 4-4; § 4-4, n. 19.
Cruz, Matter of—§ 9-2, n. 4.
Crysen/Montenay Energy Co., In re—§ 3-14, n. 22, 24, 26, 27, 28; § 3-33, n. 12, 19, 32.
CS Associates, In re—§ 3-13, n. 6.
C-T of Virginia, Inc., In re—§ 6-49, n. 46; § 6-51, n. 26, 27; § 6-60, n. 17.
C-T of Virginia, Inc. v. Euroshoe Associates Ltd. Partnership—§ 6-52, n. 7.
CTS Truss, Inc., Matter of—§ 6-93; § 6-93, n. 22, 31, 42.
Cucinotta v. Saljon Enterprises, Ltd.—§ 3-5, n. 11.
Cullens v. District Court of Colorado—§ 9-2, n. 11.
Culmer, Matter of—§ 2-6, n. 8.
Cummings, In re—§ 8-8, n. 6.
Cummings General Tire Co. v. Volpe Const. Co.—§ 6-15, n. 2.
Cunningham, In re—§ 6-61, n. 29.
Curlew Valley Associates, In re—§ 10-6, n. 5.
Currie, In re—§ 8-2, n. 6; § 8-3, n. 21; § 8-25, n. 52, 57.
Curry and Sorensen, Inc., In re—§ 6-2, n. 5, 24, 27, 30.
Curtina Intern., Inc., Matter of—§ 4-3, n. 2; § 6-49, n. 39, 74; § 6-50, n. 5; § 6-60, n. 10, 29; § 6-87, n. 8, 10; § 6-88, n. 19.
Curtis, In re—§ 3-30; § 3-30, n. 6.
Curtis, Matter of—§ 8-22, n. 23, 26.
Cusanno, In re—§ 8-21, n. 4.
Cusanno v. Fidelity Bank—§ 6-43, n. 29.
Custom Millwork, Inc., Matter of—§ 5-7, n. 17.
Cutler, In re—§ 7-28, n. 8.
Cutler-Owens Intern. Ltd., In re—§ 6-94, n. 5.
Cutters, Inc., In re—§ 5-4, n. 15.
Cyrak v. Poynor—§ 8-1, n. 9, 11; § 8-3, n. 30; § 8-19, n. 4, 15, 20.

D

Dahlberg, Matter of—§ 6-42, n. 2.

TABLE OF CASES

Dahlquist, In re—§ 3-27, n. 18.
Dailey v. First Peoples Bank of New Jersey—§ 12-16, n. 3.
Dakota Country Store Foods, Inc., In re—§ 6-28, n. 2; § 6-87, n. 8; § 6-93, n. 50, 58.
Dakota Lay'd Eggs, In re—§ 9-24; § 9-24, n. 16, 19.
Dakota Nat. Bank of Fargo v. Salzwedel—§ 8-9, n. 12.
Dalby, In re—§ 9-14, n. 21.
Daley, In re—§ 12-12, n. 9.
Dallam, In re—§ 7-26, n. 3, 11, 16.
Dallas v. S.A.G., Inc.—§ 3-31, n. 77; § 6-62, n. 39.
Dallas Ceramic Co. v. Morgan—§ 8-8, n. 3.
Dalton, In re—§ 6-61, n. 9, 28.
Damason Const. Corp., In re—§ 6-49, n. 28, 67.
Damo Corp, In re—§ 6-48, n. 5; § 6-88, n. 17.
Dana Molded Products, Inc. v. Brodner—§ 6-2, n. 24.
Dandi–Line Plants, Inc., In re—§ 3-9, n. 29.
D'Angona, In re—§ 12-9, n. 2; § 12-10, n. 9.
D'Angona, Matter of—§ 7-47, n. 2.
Dan Hixson Chevrolet Co., In re—§ 3-21, n. 43, 50.
Dania Corp., In re—§ 4-4; § 4-4, n. 11.
Daniel, In re, 771 F.2d 1352—§ 8-11, n. 12, 18; § 8-33, n. 17, 34.
Daniel, In re, 107 B.R. 798—§ 9-4, n. 11.
Daniele Laundries, Inc., Matter of—§ 6-2, n. 24.
D'Annies Restaurant, Inc., In re—§ 3-11, n. 13, 14.
Dant, In re—§ 9-3, n. 8.
Dant & Russell, Inc., In re—§ 4-3, n. 7; § 6-70, n. 2; § 7-11, n. 6.
Dan-Ver Enterprises, Inc., In re—§ 6-92, n. 4; § 6-93, n. 31, 32, 43.
Dargis, In re—§ 8-23, n. 6.
Dartmouth House Nursing Home, Inc., In re—§ 6-42, n. 2; § 6-43, n. 4, 7, 10, 13, 14, 18.
Darwin, In re—§ 5-3, n. 4.
Dascoli's, Inc., In re—§ 3-28, n. 13.
DaShiell, In re—§ 3-33, n. 12, 32.
Daugherty, Matter of—§ 3-1, n. 19; § 3-12; § 3-12, n. 5, 8, 27.
Daugherty v. Central Trust Co. of Northeastern Ohio, N.A.—§ 6-38, n. 6.
Dave Noake, Inc., In re—§ 6-69, n. 13; § 6-70, n. 2.
Davenport, In re—§ 9-2, n. 7.
Davenport, Matter of—§ 6-48, n. 1.
David, In re—§ 3-23, n. 21.
David A. Rosow, Inc., Matter of—§ 6-93, n. 65.
Davidovich, In re—§ 6-39, n. 33; § 6-40, n. 4, 14; § 6-44, n. 2; § 6-45, n. 7, 11, 22.
Davidson, In re, 120 B.R. 777—§ 3-15, n. 6.
Davidson, In re, 72 B.R. 384—§ 9-7, n. 3; § 9-14, n. 21; § 9-19; § 9-19, n. 6.
Davidson Lumber Co., In re—§ 6-67, n. 10.
Davidson Rehab Associates, In re—§ 6-61, n. 74.
Davies, In re—§ 5-7, n. 16.
D'Avignon v. Palmisano—§ 8-10, n. 26; § 8-21, n. 15.
Davis, In re, 936 F.2d 771—§ 7-3, n. 3; § 7-15, n. 4, 8, 17.
Davis, In re, 734 F.2d 604—§ 6-24, n. 2, 4; § 6-33, n. 15.
Davis, In re, 730 F.2d 176—§ 2-8, n. 21; § 3-10, n. 25; § 12-2, n. 5.
Davis, In re, 125 B.R. 242—§ 8-17, n. 47, 49; § 8-33, n. 24.
Davis, In re, 120 B.R. 823—§ 6-18, n. 11, 13, 14.
Davis, In re, 109 B.R. 633—§ 6-61, n. 74.
Davis, In re, 108 B.R. 95—§ 7-15, n. 7.
Davis, In re, 106 B.R. 701—§ 7-38; § 7-38, n. 3.
Davis, In re, 105 B.R. 288—§ 8-3, n. 21; § 8-18, n. 24.
Davis, In re, 97 B.R. 292—§ 8-26, n. 5.
Davis, In re, 91 B.R. 477—§ 9-18, n. 18.
Davis, In re, 91 B.R. 470—§ 3-30, n. 26.
Davis, In re, 56 B.R. 120—§ 7-26, n. 50, 51.
Davis, In re, 22 B.R. 523—§ 6-62, n. 4, 38.
Davis, In re, 15 B.R. 118—§ 7-47, n. 3.
Davis, Matter of, 691 F.2d 176—§ 3-20, n. 21, 33, 39; § 3-22, n. 5.
Davis, Matter of, 18 B.R. 701—§ 3-20, n. 7, 12, 19.
Davis v. Broad Street Garage—§ 11-39, n. 3.
Davis v. Johns–Manville Products—§ 3-6, n. 5.
Davis v. Lammons—§ 8-13, n. 7.
Davis v. Lawrence–Cedarhurst Bank—§ 4-3, n. 2.
Dawson, In re—§ 8-10, n. 21.
Daylight Dairy Products, Inc., In re—§ 6-61, n. 70.

Day Telecommunications, Inc., In re—§ 6-18, n. 29; § 6-31, n. 3.
Dayton Circuit Courts No. 2, Matter of—§ 6-38, n. 18; § 6-41, n. 20.
Dean v. Davis—§ 6-27; § 6-27, n. 6; § 6-59; § 6-59, n. 4, 5, 6, 11.
Deans v. O'Donnell—§ 9-14, n. 5, 13.
De Berry, In re—§ 6-73, n. 20.
Debmar Corp., In re—§ 6-36, n. 19; § 6-62, n. 34.
Decatur Contracting v. Belin, Belin & Naddeo—§ 6-12, n. 12; § 6-14, n. 2.
Decker, In re—§ 7-28, n. 4.
Deeb, In re—§ 6-5, n. 6.
Deel Rent-A-Car, Inc. v. Levine—§ 6-4, n. 17; § 6-6, n. 3, 8; § 8-23, n. 5; § 8-26, n. 7.
Deephouse Equipment Co., Inc., Matter of—§ 6-65, n. 12; § 6-66, n. 4; § 6-67, n. 3.
Defense Services, Inc., In re—§ 6-39, n. 17.
De Feo Fruit Co., Inc., Matter of—§ 6-93, n. 29.
DeFranco, In re—§ 6-78, n. 3.
Dehmer v. Temple—§ 6-2, n. 24; § 6-48, n. 11; § 6-60, n. 17.
Deiter, Matter of—§ 3-9, n. 23.
de Jesus Saez, In re—§ 3-16, n. 5; § 3-23, n. 27.
Dekalb Bank v. Flaherty—§ 9-3, n. 17.
DeLancey, Matter of, 94 B.R. 311—§ 6-61, n. 51; § 6-86, n. 5, 9, 10.
DeLancey, Matter of, 77 B.R. 424—§ 6-61, n. 44.
Delano, In re, 50 B.R. 613—§ 7-26, n. 37.
Delano, In re, 7 B.R. 72—§ 7-37, n. 2.
Delaware & Hudson Ry. Co., Matter of—§ 3-15, n. 6.
DeLay, In re—§ 3-20, n. 14.
Delbridge, In re—§ 6-76, n. 2; § 6-77, n. 1, 21, 23; § 6-78, n. 15.
Delbridge v. Production Credit Ass'n and Federal Land Bank—§ 6-76, n. 2; § 6-77, n. 24; § 6-78, n. 15.
De Leonard, In re—§ 6-69, n. 3.
Del Mission Ltd., In re—§ 6-93, n. 66.
DeLorean Motor Co., In re—§ 12-2, n. 17; § 12-5, n. 8.
Delta Energy Resources, Inc., In re—§ 6-39, n. 39; § 6-40, n. 2, 7; § 6-41, n. 38, 41.
Delta Sav. & Loan Ass'n, Inc. v. I.R.S.—§ 3-6, n. 37.
Delta Smelting & Refining Alaska, Inc., In re—§ 6-93, n. 29, 32, 41.
Delta Towers, Ltd., Matter of—§ 3-9, n. 31.
DeLuca Distributing Co., In re—§ 10-6, n. 4.
Deluxe Sheet Metal, Inc. v. Plymouth Plastics, Inc.—§ 3-5, n. 8.
Demaree, In re—§ 3-10, n. 47.
Demoff, In re—§ 9-18, n. 13.
DeMoss, In re—§ 9-12, n. 11.
Demp, In re—§ 3-9, n. 22, 33.
Dempster, Matter of—§ 6-18, n. 25.
Denby Stores, Inc., In re—§ 3-6, n. 60; § 6-39, n. 24; § 6-40, n. 14, 27; § 6-41, n. 16; § 6-44, n. 2, 7; § 6-45, n. 3, 11.
Denn, In re—§ 3-11, n. 10; § 3-12, n. 11.
Dennis, Matter of—§ 7-39, n. 2, 7.
Dennis v. A.H. Robins Co., Inc.—§ 3-6, n. 26; § 3-22, n. 5.
Dennis Ponte, Inc., In re—§ 11-3, n. 14; § 11-4, n. 15; § 11-5, n. 4.
Denson, In re—§ 9-3, n. 32.
Dent v. Martin, 104 B.R. 477—§ 6-17, n. 8; § 6-18, n. 4.
Dent v. Martin, 86 B.R. 290—§ 6-12, n. 12; § 6-17; § 6-17, n. 8, 34.
Department of Public Welfare v. Johnson-Allen—§ 9-2, n. 11.
Depew, Matter of—§ 2-16, n. 20.
Deposit Guar. Nat. Bank v. B.N. Simrall & Son, Inc.—§ 6-38, n. 6, 12.
Depositors Trust Co. of Augusta v. Frati Enterprises, Inc.—§ 6-39, n. 25.
DePoy, Matter of—§ 3-35, n. 1.
Deppe, In re—§ 3-28, n. 11, 15.
Dervaes, In re—§ 3-20, n. 11, 21; § 3-21, n. 50.
Design Builders, Inc., Matter of—§ 6-61, n. 60.
Design Spectrum, Inc. v. First Nat. Bank of Atlanta—§ 6-38, n. 6.
Destro, In re—§ 6-61, n. 42.
Dettman, In re—§ 6-77, n. 1.
Dettman, Matter of—§ 8-25, n. 40.
Devall, United States v.—§ 8-11, n. 3; § 9-3, n. 6.
Devers, In re—§ 7-19; § 7-19, n. 4.
DeVito, In re—§ 6-48, n. 4.
DeWeese, In re—§ 8-17, n. 13; § 8-33, n. 39.
Dewsnup, In re—§ 7-10, n. 2; § 7-47, n. 2; § 11-30, n. 7, 11.
Dewsnup v. Timm, 112 S.Ct. 773—§ 8-1, n. 20; § 8-28; § 8-28, n. 11.

Dewsnup v. Timm, 908 F.2d 588—§ **9-30**; § **9-30, n. 13**.
Dexter, Matter of—§ **3-12, n. 20**.
Dexter v. Gilbert (Matter of Kirchoff Frozen Foods, Inc.)—§ **12-14, n. 17, 18**.
D & F Const. Inc., Matter of—§ **10-19**; § **10-19, n. 2**.
D. H. Overmyer, Co., Inc., In re—§ **5-12, n. 1**.
D.H. Overmyer Telecasting Co., Inc., In re—§ **6-48, n. 7, 8**.
Diamond Hill Inv. Co. v. Shelden—§ **3-6, n. 18**.
Diamond Lumber, Inc., In re—§ **6-66, n. 11**.
Diamond Mfg. Co., Inc., In re—§ **6-62, n. 29**.
Diamond Mortg. Corp. of Illinois, Matter of—§ **6-27, n. 3, 11**; § **6-30, n. 4**.
Diasonics, Inc. v. Ingalls—§ **6-93, n. 32, 35**.
Diaz, In re—§ **9-5, n. 5**.
Dibbern, Matter of—§ **3-31, n. 92, 93**.
DiBona, In re—§ **6-94, n. 2**.
Dickey, In re—§ **9-4**; § **9-4, n. 15**; § **9-20, n. 11**.
Dick Henley, Inc., In re—§ **6-25, n. 20**.
Dickson, In re—§ **8-33, n. 24**.
DiDomizio, Matter of—§ **3-10, n. 65**.
Dietz, In re, 914 F.2d 161—§ **6-88, n. 18**.
Dietz, In re, 94 B.R. 637—§ **6-69, n. 9**; § **6-88, n. 14, 21, 35**.
Dilbert's Quality Supermarkets, Inc., In re—§ **10-32, n. 1**.
Dillard Ford, Inc., In re—§ **6-41, n. 44**.
Dilley, In re—§ **2-11, n. 4**.
DiMarco, In re—§ **7-26, n. 37**.
Dino & Artie's Automatic Transmission Co., Inc., In re—§ **6-93, n. 33, 40**.
Diodati, In re—§ **7-21, n. 9**.
Diorio v. Kreisler-Borg Const. Co.—§ **7-21, n. 11**.
Dipalma, In re—§ **8-25, n. 40**.
Diquinzio, In re—§ **9-18, n. 8, 10**.
Diversa-Graphics, Inc. v. Management & Technical Services Co.—§ **6-40, n. 4**.
Diversified Investors Fund XVII, In re—§ **11-17, n. 8**.
Diversified World Investments, Ltd., In re—§ **6-15, n. 3**.
Dixie Broadcasting, Inc., In re—§ **3-29**; § **3-29, n. 1, 6, 8, 19**.
Dixon, In re—§ **8-26, n. 18**; § **8-28, n. 3**.
Dixon, Matter of—§ **8-24, n. 3**; § **8-28, n. 3, 7, 25**.
D. M. Barber, Inc., In re—§ **3-21, n. 8**.
D. M. Christian Co., In re—§ **4-4, n. 14**.
Doane, In re—§ **9-4, n. 7**.
Dockery, In re—§ **6-61, n. 18**.
Dock of the Bay, Inc., In re—§ **12-6, n. 3**.
Doctors Hospital, Inc., In re—§ **6-40, n. 27**.
Dodd, In re—§ **7-3, n. 6**.
Dohm, In re—§ **7-28, n. 11, 17**.
Dole v. Hansbrough—§ **3-21, n. 8, 21, 73**; § **3-22, n. 7, 29, 30**.
Dolin, In re—§ **7-20, n. 6**.
Dominelli, In re—§ **6-94, n. 2**.
Dominguez, In re—§ **6-40, n. 7**; § **6-44, n. 2**.
Dominion Bank of Cumberlands, NA v. Nuckolls—§ **8-21, n. 4**; § **8-25, n. 32**; § **8-31, n. 9**.
Donaghy, In re—§ **8-17, n. 10**.
Donahue, In re—§ **8-1, n. 20**.
Donato, In re—§ **6-39, n. 2**; § **6-40, n. 2, 4**.
Dondero, In re—§ **9-5, n. 5**.
D-1 Enterprises, Inc. v. Commercial State Bank—§ **3-31, n. 54, 56**.
Don & Lin Trucking Co., Inc., In re—§ **5-7, n. 20**.
Donohue, In re—§ **9-3, n. 7**.
Donut Queen, Ltd., In re—§ **11-41, n. 13**.
Dore, In re—§ **8-28, n. 7, 8, 14, 23**.
Dorner, In re—§ **3-23, n. 40**.
Dorsey, In re—§ **7-26, n. 21, 22**.
Doty, Matter of—§ **7-47, n. 2**.
Dougherty, In re—§ **7-26**; § **7-26, n. 5, 19, 21, 23, 26**.
Douglas Hereford Ranch, Inc., In re—§ **10-17, n. 4**.
Douthart, In re—§ **7-47, n. 2**.
Dowdy, In re—§ **8-22, n. 15, 33**; § **8-23, n. 6**.
Drabkin v. A.I. Credit Corp.—§ **6-25, n. 13**; § **6-34, n. 7**.
Drabkin v. District of Columbia—§ **6-7, n. 4**.
Draper v. Draper—§ **7-29, n. 15**.

Draughon Training Institute, Inc., In re—§ 3-14, n. 80, 82; § 3-21, n. 9, 113, 120; § 3-32, n. 1; § 3-34, n. 5, 6.
Drennen v. Wheatley—§ 8-13, n. 7.
Drewes, In re—§ 6-76, n. 2; § 6-77, n. 21.
Drexel Burnham Lambert Group Inc., In re, 120 B.R. 724—§ 2-8, n. 4; § 3-6, n. 8; § 3-30, n. 21; § 3-33, n. 20.
Drexel Burnham Lambert Group, Inc., In re, 118 B.R. 209—§ 10-12, n. 11.
Drexel Burnham Lambert Group, Inc., In re, 113 B.R. 830—§ 3-30, n. 8, 33; § 3-31; § 3-31, n. 74, 78; § 6-40, n. 2, 4, 14, 19; § 6-43, n. 31; § 6-45, n. 1, 7, 33, 35.
Drexel Burnham Lambert Group, Inc., In re, 1992 WL 36294—§ 5-7, n. 12.
Drexel Burnham Lambert Group Inc. v. Galadari—§ 2-6, n. 8.
D.R. Goris Plumbing, Inc., Matter of—§ 6-36, n. 3, 14; § 6-62, n. 3, 17.
Drimmel, In re—§ 11-27, n. 5, 6, 10; § 11-29, n. 1.
Driscoll, Matter of—§ 6-2, n. 16, 22; § 6-62, n. 22; § 8-23, n. 7.
Drislor Associates, In re—§ 3-29, n. 1, 13; § 3-31, n. 50, 51, 103.
DRW Property Co. 82, In re—§ 11-41; § 11-41, n. 14.
Dry Wall Supply, Inc., In re—§ 6-60, n. 26; § 6-82, n. 6; § 6-93, n. 38, 49.
DuBay v. Williams—§ 6-14; § 6-14, n. 3; § 6-35, n. 3.
Duchesne, In re—§ 8-20, n. 4; § 8-25, n. 51, 52.
Ducker v. Lohrey—§ 6-39, n. 38; § 6-40, n. 19, 21, 27; § 6-43, n. 3.
Dudley, In re—§ 6-56, n. 17, 50; § 8-23, n. 3.
Duffey v. Dollison—§ 7-41; § 7-41, n. 13.
Duffy, Matter of—§ 6-25, n. 8, 13.
Dumas, In re—§ 3-20, n. 11.
Dun & Bradstreet, Inc. v. Greenmoss Builders, Inc.—§ 3-8, n. 9.
Duncan, In re, 107 B.R. 754—§ 8-3, n. 19.
Duncan, In re, 85 B.R. 80—§ 8-25, n. 17.
Duncan, In re, 10 B.R. 13—§ 6-41, n. 46, 49.
Dunckle Associates, Inc., In re—§ 4-14, n. 6.
Dunes Casino Hotel, In re—§ 4-14, n. 5.
Dunlop v. First Nat. Bank of Arizona—§ 8-11, n. 28.
Dunn, In re, 109 B.R. 865—§ 8-25, n. 14.
Dunn, In re, 56 B.R. 275—§ 6-15, n. 3.
DuPont Walston, Inc., In re—§ 11-16, n. 6.
Dunwell Heating & Air Conditioning Contractors Corp., In re—§ 6-62, n. 42.
Duque Rodriguez, In re, 77 B.R. 944—§ 6-49, n. 39, 46, 49, 51.
Duque Rodriguez, In re, 77 B.R. 942—§ 6-47, n. 8; § 6-49, n. 46.
Duque Rodriguez, In re, 75 B.R. 829—§ 6-49, n. 23.
Durant's Rental Center, Inc., In re—§ 6-19, n. 13; § 6-25, n. 14; § 6-31, n. 10.
Durham, Matter of, 100 B.R. 711—§ 6-77, n. 8.
Durham, Matter of, 56 B.R. 145—§ 6-2, n. 20.
Durham v. SMI Industries Corp.—§ 6-38, n. 18; § 6-39, n. 3, 35.
Durrett v. Washington Nat. Ins. Co.—§ 6-54, n. 4; § 6-55; § 6-55, n. 10, 12; § 6-56; § 6-56, n. 2, 51.
Duss, In re—§ 8-1, n. 19, 20; § 8-25, n. 55, 58, 62.
Duvall v. Gleason—§ 3-6, n. 20; § 3-10, n. 11, 32.
Dyer v. Weedon—§ 3-6, n. 46.
Dyke, In re—§ 8-11, n. 18.
Dykstra, In re—§ 8-24, n. 2.
Dynamic Technologies Corp., In re—§ 6-65, n. 12.
Dziedzic, In re—§ 9-7, n. 4, 12; § 10-22; § 10-22, n. 8.

E

Eads, In re—§ 6-61, n. 26, 28.
Eagle, In re—§ 7-49, n. 1, 8.
Earle Industries, Inc., In re—§ 12-5, n. 5.
Earley, In re—§ 10-33, n. 2.
Earl Roggenbuck Farms, Inc., In re—§ 6-47, n. 10.
Ear, Nose and Throat Surgeons of Worcester, Inc., In re—§ 6-49, n. 13, 46, 49, 51, 58, 60; § 6-51, n. 33.
Easebe Enterprises, Inc., In re—§ 5-13; § 5-13, n. 7; § 5-14; § 5-14, n. 1.
Easley, In re—§ 9-5, n. 5; § 9-14, n. 19.
Easterly, In re—§ 7-26, n. 55.
Eastern Consol. Utilities, Inc., In re—§ 10-8, n. 4.
Eastgroup Properties v. Southern Motel Assoc., Ltd.—§ 2-4, n. 4.
Easton, In re, 883 F.2d 630—§ 9-24; § 9-24, n. 14.

TABLE OF CASES

Easton, In re, 882 F.2d 312—§ **3-16, n. 11.**
Easton, In re, 59 B.R. 714—§ **9-4, n. 14.**
East Texas Steel Facilities, Inc., In re—§ **6-65, n. 9.**
East-West Associates, Matter of—§ **3-25, n. 9, 37, 42, 44;** § **3-27, n. 21, 24;** § **3-29, n. 5.**
Eaton, Matter of, 41 B.R. 800—§ **7-26, n. 60.**
Eaton, Matter of, 1 B.R. 433—§ **9-4, n. 37.**
Ebbler Furniture and Appliances, Inc., In re—§ **6-35;** § **6-35, n. 12, 14, 46, 47, 48.**
Ebenger, In re—§ **6-60, n. 4.**
Echoles, In re—§ **6-2, n. 21.**
Eckles, Matter of—§ **7-33;** § **7-33, n. 7.**
EDC Holding Co., Matter of—§ **4-17;** § **4-17, n. 6, 9.**
EDC, Inc., Matter of—§ **6-20, n. 20;** § **6-25, n. 15, 20;** § **6-93, n. 45, 49.**
Eddingfield, In re—§ **6-62, n. 39.**
Eddleman v. United States Dept. of Labor—§ **3-21, n. 8, 50, 70, 82, 90, 116;** § **3-31, n. 96.**
Edelsberg, In re—§ **6-44, n. 5;** § **6-85, n. 16.**
Edge, In re—§ **7-7, n. 5;** § **11-1, n. 1;** § **11-2, n. 3;** § **11-3;** § **11-4, n. 7.**
Edgerton, In re—§ **3-30, n. 23.**
Edgewater Motel, Inc., In re—§ **6-93, n. 41.**
Edgins, In re—§ **6-43, n. 29.**
E.D. Presley Corp. Ltd., In re—§ **6-49, n. 8, 46;** § **6-60, n. 29.**
Education Assistance Corp. v. Zellner—§ **9-2, n. 10;** § **9-9, n. 2;** § **9-13, n. 2;** § **9-14, n. 6.**
Edward Harvey Co., Inc., In re—§ **6-47, n. 7;** § **6-49, n. 44.**
Edward M. Johnson & Associates, Inc., In re—§ **6-49, n. 34, 47, 50, 52.**
Edwards, In re, 87 B.R. 671—§ **2-16, n. 7;** § **9-18, n. 16.**
Edwards, In re, 56 B.R. 582—§ **6-48, n. 11;** § **8-32, n. 8.**
Edwards, In re, 51 B.R. 790—§ **9-3, n. 25.**
Edwards, In re, 50 B.R. 933—§ **7-45, n. 13.**
Edwards, In re, 5 B.R. 663—§ **6-73, n. 22.**
Edwards, Matter of—§ **7-39;** § **7-39, n. 11;** § **7-47, n. 4.**
Edwards v. Henry—§ **8-11, n. 28.**
Edwards v. Merchants Nat. Bank—§ **7-39, n. 7, 14.**
Edwards v. United States—§ **3-34, n. 7.**
Edwards Mobile Home Sales, Inc., Matter of—§ **3-14, n. 43;** § **3-21, n. 9, 46, 109.**
Edwardson, In re—§ **9-25;** § **9-25, n. 10.**
E.E.O.C. v. Hall's Motor Transit Co.—§ **3-21, n. 8.**
EEOC v. McLean Trucking Co.—§ **3-21, n. 8, 73, 74.**
E.E.O.C. v. Rath Packing Co.—§ **3-21, n. 8, 48, 73;** § **3-22, n. 1, 30.**
E.F. Hutton & Co., Inc. v. Hadley—§ **6-61, n. 8.**
Eggemeyer, In re—§ **6-39, n. 19;** § **6-40, n. 5;** § **6-44, n. 9.**
Eggleston, In re—§ **6-15, n. 1, 3.**
Ehring, In re, 900 F.2d 184—§ **6-21, n. 4, 10;** § **6-55;** § **6-55, n. 14.**
Ehring, In re, 91 B.R. 897—§ **6-21, n. 5, 8;** § **6-55, n. 3, 9.**
18th Ave. Development Corp., In re, 29 B.R. 589—§ **6-40, n. 23.**
18th Ave. Development Corp., In re, 14 B.R. 862—§ **4-7, n. 20.**
18th Ave. Development Corp., In re, 12 B.R. 10—§ **6-40, n. 22.**
8th Street Village Ltd. Partnership, In re—§ **3-25, n. 35.**
EI Intern., In re—§ **5-7, n. 16.**
Eiland, In re—§ **8-26, n. 18.**
Einoder, Matter of—§ **6-2, n. 20;** § **6-61, n. 80;** § **8-23, n. 3, 8.**
Einspahr, In re—§ **9-10, n. 6, 10;** § **9-17, n. 8.**
Eisenberg v. Village of Mineola—§ **3-21, n. 56.**
Eith, In re—§ **8-1, n. 15.**
El-Amin, In re—§ **3-12, n. 18;** § **3-30, n. 12, 14.**
Elcona Homes Corp., Matter of—§ **6-39, n. 39;** § **6-40, n. 14;** § **6-41, n. 9.**
Elder, In re—§ **3-11, n. 26.**
Eldridge, Matter of—§ **8-20, n. 2.**
Electrical Workers, Local No. 1 Credit Union v. IBEW- NECA Holiday Trust Fund—§ **8-33, n. 15.**
Electronic Metal Products, Inc., In re—§ **6-25, n. 12;** § **6-62, n. 26.**
Electronic Metal Products, Inc. v. Honeywell, Inc.—§ **6-45, n. 3, 5, 15.**
Electronic Theatre Restaurants Corp., Matter of—§ **3-10, n. 3.**
Elegant Concepts, Ltd., In re—§ **12-5, n. 3.**
Eleven Oak Tower Ltd. Partnership, In re—§ **12-6, n. 6;** § **12-10, n. 6.**
11,111, Inc. d/b/a Energy Conservation Consultants, In re—§ **10-22, n. 8.**
Elias, In re—§ **7-7, n. 2.**
Elin v. Buscha—§ **6-86, n. 19.**
Elizarraras v. Bank of El Paso—§ **6-38, n. 7, 13.**
Eljay Jrs., Inc., In re—§ **6-19, n. 7.**

Elkins, In re—§ 8-32, n. 8.
Ellingsen MacLean Oil Co., Inc., In re—§ 4-15, n. 15.
Ellingsen MacLean Oil Co., Inc., Matter of—§ 4-13; § 4-13, n. 6; § 4-16; § 4-16, n. 3, 4; § 4-17; § 4-17, n. 1.
Ellingson, In re—§ 8-26, n. 5.
Elliott, In re, 81 B.R. 460—§ 6-72, n. 6; § 6-73, n. 6, 23.
Elliott, In re, 79 B.R. 944—§ 8-32, n. 5.
Ellis, In re, 66 B.R. 821—§ 3-21, n. 69.
Ellis, In re, 48 B.R. 178—§ 9-3, n. 30.
Ellis, In re, 40 B.R. 760—§ 6-72, n. 5; § 6-73, n. 10.
Ellis v. Chicago & N. W. Ry. Co.—§ 11-39, n. 3.
Ellis v. Consolidated Diesel Elec. Corp.—§ 3-6, n. 23; § 3-32, n. 1, 7, 10.
Ellis v. Dillon—§ 8-7, n. 18.
Ellison v. Northwest Engineering Co.—§ 3-6, n. 30, 38.
Ellwanger, In re—§ 7-31, n. 2.
Elmhurst Transmission Corp., In re—§ 5-7, n. 3.
Elm Inn, Inc., In re—§ 5-10, n. 15.
Elmore, In re—§ 3-23, n. 48.
Elrod, Matter of—§ 3-6, n. 14; § 6-61, n. 28.
Elsea, In re—§ 8-33, n. 20.
Elsinore Shore Associates, In re, 91 B.R. 238—§ 6-93, n. 29, 32.
Elsinore Shore Associates, In re, 82 B.R. 339—§ 12-12, n. 19.
Elsinore Shore Associates, In re, 67 B.R. 926—§ 6-38, n. 5, 21, 22; § 6-39, n. 2; § 6-40, n. 6; § 6-43, n. 3; § 6-73, n. 26.
Elsub Corp., Matter of—§ 11-32, n. 3.
EMB Associates, Inc., In re, 100 B.R. 629—§ 6-93, n. 5, 8, 9, 31.
EMB Associates, Inc., In re, 92 B.R. 9—§ 6-93, n. 2, 5, 21, 31, 35, 37, 38.
Embassy Enterprises of St. Cloud, In re—§ 3-25, n. 9, 56, 60.
Emerald Hills Country Club, Inc., Matter of—§ 6-49, n. 13, 15, 62; § 6-51, n. 16, 33; § 6-52, n. 8.
Emerald Oil Co., In re—§ 6-47, n. 13.
Emergency Beacon Corp., In re—§ 10-31, n. 1.
Emple Knitting Mills, Inc., In re—§ 5-7, n. 17.
Emrick, In re—§ 6-12, n. 8; § 6-27, n. 11.
Encinas, In re—§ 6-77, n. 1.
Endicott, Matter of—§ 3-12, n. 5, 10.
Endrex Exploration Co., In re—§ 3-25, n. 24, 36, 52.
Enduro Stainless, Inc., Matter of—§ 10-12, n. 4.
Energetics, Inc. v. Allied Bank of Texas—§ 6-38, n. 10.
Energy Co-op., Inc., In re, 832 F.2d 997—§ 6-19, n. 4, 17, 18; § 6-25, n. 2, 14; § 6-30, n. 7, 8.
Energy Co-op., Inc., In re, 103 B.R. 171—§ 6-31, n. 14.
Energy Co-op., Inc., In re, 100 B.R. 992—§ 6-41, n. 38.
Energy Co-op., Inc., In re, 97 B.R. 388—§ 6-19, n. 17.
Energy Co-op., Inc., In re, 94 B.R. 975—§ 6-66, n. 4; § 6-67, n. 10.
Energy Co-op., Inc., In re, 80 B.R. 921—§ 6-27, n. 3.
Energy Co-op., Inc., In re, 32 B.R. 680—§ 6-39, n. 3; § 6-40, n. 4; § 6-42, n. 2; § 6-43, n. 7.
Energy Co-op., Inc., Matter of, 886 F.2d 921—§ 3-22, n. 29.
Energy Co-op., Inc., Matter of, 814 F.2d 1226—§ 6-39, n. 35.
Energy Sav. Center, Inc., In re—§ 6-49, n. 46; § 6-50, n. 16, 35; § 6-52, n. 22; § 6-88, n. 14, 18.
Engel, In re—§ 6-15, n. 3; § 6-35, n. 5.
Engler, In re—§ 7-26, n. 35.
Englestein v. Mackie—§ 11-37, n. 5.
English, In re—§ 6-61, n. 77; § 6-62, n. 28.
Engstrom, In re—§ 6-77, n. 19.
Enterprise Fabricators, Inc., In re—§ 6-11, n. 7.
Environmental Waste Control, Inc., Matter of—§ 3-21, n. 110.
Equibank, N.A. v. Wheeling–Pittsburgh Steel Corp.—§ 3-1, n. 20; § 3-16, n. 5; § 3-18, n. 20; § 4-7, n. 7.
E.R. Fegert, Inc., In re—§ 6-25, n. 7, 15.
Erickson, In re—§ 3-20, n. 33.
Erickson, Matter of—§ 8-6, n. 5.
Erickson v. Federal Land Bank of Omaha—§ 3-25, n. 52.
Erickson v. Polk—§ 3-14, n. 77.
Erie Hilton Joint Venture, In re—§ 3-11, n. 12; § 3-23, n. 34, 48.
Erin Food Services, Inc., In re—§ 6-9, n. 5; § 6-25, n. 11.
Ernest and Associates, Inc., In re—§ 6-62, n. 26.
Ernst, In re—§ 10-29, n. 9.
Errington, In re—§ 10-33, n. 1.
E & S Comfort, Inc., In re—§ 6-7, n. 4.

Escondido West Travelodge, Matter of—§ 5-3, n. 4.
Esgro, Inc., Matter of—§ **6-40, n. 20.**
Espino, In re—§ **7-19, n. 10.**
Espinoza, In re—§ **6-18, n. 6.**
Esser, In re—§ **3-11, n. 18.**
Estate of (see name of party)
Estep, In re—§ 7-39, n. 2; § 8-26, n. 18.
Estus, In re—§ 9-2, n. 10; § 9-14; § 9-14, n. 5, 10, 13, 15, 26, 27.
Etch–Art, Inc., In re—§ 4-6; § 4-6, n. 6; § 6-77, n. 21.
Euerle Farms, Inc., In re—§ 9-27; § 9-27, n. 10; § 9-29; § 9-29, n. 1.
Euro–Swiss Intern. Corp., In re—§ 6-48, n. 21, 22; § 6-49, n. 28, 64.
Eury, In re—§ 9-12, n. 8.
Evans, In re, 88 B.R. 813—§ **6-61, n. 11, 38, 42.**
Evans, In re, 48 B.R. 46—§ **10-8, n. 3.**
Evans, In re, 20 B.R. 175—§ 9-10, n. 1, 6.
Evans, In re, 16 B.R. 731—§ 6-15, n. 3.
Evans, Matter of—§ 8-17, n. 7; § 8-18, n. 3.
Evans Potato Co., Inc., Matter of—§ **6-49, n. 49, 52.**
Evans Temple Church of God in Christ and Community Center, Inc., Matter of—§ **6-19, n. 15.**
Evatt, In re, 112 B.R. 417—§ **6-39, n. 15.**
Evatt, In re, 112 B.R. 405—§ **6-39, n. 15;** § **6-43, n. 4, 7, 10.**
Eveland, In re—§ **8-25, n. 38, 41.**
Everett, In re—§ 3-34, n. 9.
Everett v. Pape Bros., Inc.—§ 8-8, n. 3.
Everett C. Turner Realtors v. Carroll—§ 9-2, n. 11.
Evergreen Valley Resort, Inc., In re—§ 6-2, n. 28.
Everhart, In re—§ 6-6, n. 3, 4, 8; § 8-17, n. 34.
E.W. Shields, Inc., In re—§ **6-36, n. 3, 14.**
Excel Enterprises, Inc., In re—§ **6-34, n. 18.**
Excelite Corp., In re—§ 12-5, n. 2.
Excellair, Inc., United States v.—§ **6-56, n. 1.**
Excello Press, Inc., In re—§ **6-18, n. 4, 10, 27, 29;** § **6-31, n. 17.**
Exchange Bank & Trust Co. v. Mathews—§ 8-13, n. 7.
Executive Air Services, In re—§ 4-13, n. 3.
Executive House Associates, In re—§ **6-61, n. 53;** § **6-77, n. 1, 6, 11, 12.**
Executive Square, Ltd., In re—§ **6-77, n. 15.**
Express Liquors, Inc., In re—§ **6-60, n. 25.**
Expressway Texaco Service, Inc. v. Orgeron—§ 3-6, n. 35.
Exquisito Services, Inc., In re—§ 7-41; § 7-41, n. 3, 19.
Eyde Const. Co. v. Public Data Associates—§ **6-35, n. 3.**
Eye Contact, Inc., Matter of—§ **6-82, n. 4;** § **6-83, n. 16.**

F

Faber, Coe & Gregg, Inc. v. First Nat. Bank of Chicago—§ **6-38, n. 7.**
Fabian, In re—§ 8-1, n. 11.
Fabricators, Inc., In re—§ **6-93, n. 32.**
Fabricators, Inc., Matter of—§ **6-93, n. 5, 29, 31, 32, 36, 63.**
Fabric Buys, In re—§ **6-65, n. 17.**
Fabric Buys of Jericho, Inc., In re—§ **6-88, n. 35.**
Factory Tire Distributors, Inc., In re—§ **6-47, n. 7;** § **6-48, n. 12;** § **6-49, n. 40.**
Fairchild v. Lebanon Production Credit Ass'n—§ 6-5; § 6-5, n. 1, 2, 3, 5; § **6-35, n. 25, 44.**
Falconer, In re—§ 8-1, n. 11.
Family Health Services, Inc., In re—§ 2-2, n. 9.
Family Investments, Inc., In re—§ 3-27, n. 42; § 43.
Famous State Fair Meat Products, Inc., In re—§ **6-49, n. 18.**
Fandrich, In re—§ 4-7; § 4-7, n. 4.
Fantastic Homes Enterprises, Inc., In re—§ **10-22, n. 5;** § **10-24, n. 9.**
F.A. Potts & Co., Inc., In re, 115 B.R. 66—§ **6-93, n. 16.**
F.A. Potts & Co., Inc., In re, 114 B.R. 92—§ **6-93, n. 66.**
Fargo Biltmore Motor Hotel Corp., In re—§ **6-54, n. 3;** § **6-55, n. 13, 22;** § **6-56, n. 17, 41, 52.**
Fargo Financial, Inc., In re—§ **6-93, n. 11, 12, 42, 44, 50.**
Farmer, In re—§ 3-23, n. 45.
Farmers Co-op. Ass'n of Talmage, Kan. v. Strunk—§ **7-19, n. 6;** § **7-21, n. 11.**
Farmers Markets, Inc., In re—§ 2-8; § 2-8, n. 42, 44; § 3-8; § 3-8, n. 25, 27.
Farrey v. Sanderfoot—§ **7-29, n. 26;** § **8-25;** § **8-25, n. 19;** § **8-26, n. 13;** § **8-27;** § **8-27, n. 4.**

Far West Corp. of Shasta County, In re—§ 5-23, n. 3.
Fasano/Harriss Pie Co., In re—§ 6-28, n. 1, 2.
Fasano/Harriss Pie Co., Matter of, 43 B.R. 871—§ 6-27, n. 15.
Fasano/Harriss Pie Co., Matter of, 43 B.R. 864—§ 6-40, n. 16.
Fashion World, Inc., In re—§ 6-47, n. 7.
Fassnacht & Sons, Inc., In re—§ 6-17, n. 9.
Fastrax, Inc., In re—§ 5-15, n. 4, 10.
Fauchier, In re—§ 7-27, n. 2, 3.
Faulk, In re—§ 7-26, n. 24, 50.
Fax Station, Inc., In re—§ 2-10, n. 5.
F & C Services, Inc., In re—§ 6-48, n. 8, 12.
FCX, Inc., In re, 62 B.R. 315—§ 6-65, n. 10; § 6-67, n. 10.
FCX, Inc., In re, 60 B.R. 405—§ 6-93, n. 64.
FCX, Inc., In re, 54 B.R. 833—§ 4-13, n. 6; § 4-15, n. 15; § 4-16, n. 4; § 4-17, n. 4.
F.D. Roberts Securities, Inc., Matter of—§ 6-93, n. 66.
Featherworks Corp., In re—§ 6-93, n. 31, 55.
Feature Homes, Inc., In re—§ 3-8, n. 26; § 3-14, n. 80.
Federal Deposit Ins. Corp. v. Davis—§ 6-2, n. 25.
Federal Deposit Ins. Corp. v. Key Biscayne Development Ass'n—§ 6-93, n. 44.
Federal Deposit Ins. Corp. v. Mmahat—§ 7-28, n. 7.
Federal Ins. Co. v. Fifth Third Bank—§ 6-38, n. 10.
Federal Land Bank of Columbia v. McNeal—§ 9-24, n. 17.
Federal Land Bank of Spokane v. Stiles—§ 3-5, n. 6, 19.
Federal Life Ins. Co. (Mut.) v. First Finance Group of Texas, Inc.—§ 11-35, n. 5.
Federal Press Co., Matter of—§ 11-7, n. 1.
Federal's Inc. v. Edmonton Inv. Co. § 5-1, n. 1.
Federated Department Stores, Inc., In re—§ 5-15, n. 10; § 5-16, n. 2.
Federated Marketing, Inc., In re—§ 6-31, n. 6, 15; § 6-87, n. 14.
Feely, In re—§ 2-18; § 2-18, n. 4.
Feldhahn, Matter of—§ 6-2, n. 3, 24, 30.
Feldman, In re—§ 11-17, n. 8.
Felts, In re, 114 B.R. 131—§ 8-11, n. 18; § 8-33, n. 24, 34.
Felts, In re, 60 B.R. 736—§ 9-14, n. 16.
Feola, Matter of—§ 8-10, n. 11.
Ferguson, In re, 83 B.R. 676—§ 6-39, n. 19; § 6-40, n. 16.
Ferguson, In re, 15 B.R. 439—§ 8-21, n. 4.
Fernandes Super Markets, Inc., In re—§ 6-40, n. 25.
Fernandez, Matter of, 855 F.2d 218—§ 8-6, n. 9.
Fernandez, Matter of, 125 B.R. 317—§ 3-11, n. 26; § 3-34, n. 9, 19.
Fernwood Markets, In re—§ 4-16, n. 2.
Ferrara, In re—§ 7-32, n. 1.
Festa, In re—§ 9-12, n. 6.
Feuerborn, In re—§ 8-1, n. 12.
Feyline Presents, Inc., In re—§ 5-22; § 5-22, n. 4.
F.H.L., Inc., In re—§ 6-16, n. 1; § 6-17, n. 29; § 6-18, n. 4.
Fichter, In re—§ 8-17; § 8-17, n. 35, 36, 37.
Fidelity Sav. & Inv. Co. v. New Hope Baptist—§ 6-32, n. 7.
Fidelity Standard Mortg. Corp., Matter of—§ 6-61, n. 67.
Fiegi, In re—§ 9-19; § 9-19, n. 4.
Field, In re—§ 6-20, n. 22; § 6-77, n. 7.
Fields, In re—§ 3-25; § 3-25, n. 25, 28, 31.
Fields v. Demint—§ 3-2, n. 6; § 3-6, n. 1, 2, 5; § 3-32, n. 1, 8.
Fiero Production, Inc., In re—§ 6-45, n. 3, 5, 7, 29.
Fifth Ave. Originals, In re—§ 5-20, n. 9.
Figearo, In re—§ 6-50, n. 22; § 6-76, n. 2; § 6-77, n. 1.
Figge, In re—§ 7-26, n. 36.
Figgers, In re—§ 3-2, n. 6; § 3-8; § 3-8, n. 28; § 3-11, n. 20; § 6-40, n. 4; § 6-76, n. 2.
Figueroa Ruiz, In re—§ 3-25, n. 15, 16, 19.
Fill, In re, 84 B.R. 332—§ 8-3, n. 19; § 8-17, n. 17, 35, 36, 49.
Fill, In re, 82 B.R. 200—§ 6-87, n. 16, 18; § 6-88, n. 30.
Financial Partners, Ltd., In re, 116 B.R. 629—§ 6-19, n. 4, 14; § 6-30, n. 6.
Financial Partners, Ltd., In re, 94 B.R. 537—§ 6-31, n. 19.
Fine, In re—§ 8-32, n. 5, 9.
Finelli Jewelry Co., Inc., In re—§ 6-25, n. 27.
Fingado, In re—§ 8-3, n. 21.
Fink, In re—§ 3-10, n. 65.
Finn, In re, 909 F.2d 903—§ 6-9, n. 5; § 6-30, n. 3; § 6-32, n. 2, 7.
Finn, In re, 86 B.R. 902— 6-20, n. 3, 5, 12.

Finn, Matter of—§ 6-17, n. 9.
Finn v. Meighan—§ 5-12, n. 1.
Fiore, Matter of—§ 8-28, n. 15.
Fiorillo & Co., Matter of—§ 6-61, n. 58.
First American Bank of New York, In re—§ 11-14, n. 2, 3.
First American Bank of New York v. Century Glove, Inc.—§ 11-14, n. 11, 12.
First American Bank of New York (FAB) v. Century Glove, Inc.—§ 11-18, n. 8.
First Bank of Whiting v. Sisters of Mercy Health Corp.—§ 3-6, n. 22; § 3-32, n. 38.
First Baptist Church, Inc., Matter of—§ 4-16, n. 2.
First Barnstable Corp., In re—§ 3-25, n. 19.
First Capital Mortg. Loan Corp., In re—§ 6-77, n. 1.
First City Mortg. Co., In re—§ 6-61, n. 68; § 6-77, n. 11; § 6-78, n. 3.
First City Nat. Bank of Oxford v. Long-Lewis Hardware Co.—§ 6-38, n. 9.
First Connecticut Small Business Inv. Co., In re—§ 3-15, n. 5, 6; § 3-31, n. 84.
Firstcorp, Inc., In re—§ 3-3, n. 8; § 3-5, n. 13; § 3-14, n. 21; § 3-21, n. 14, 113.
First Federal of Michigan v. Barrow—§ 6-7, n. 4; § 6-31, n. 19.
First Federal Sav. and Loan Ass'n of Rochester v. Brown—§ 8-13, n. 7.
First Federal Sav. & Loan Ass'n of Warner Robbins v. Standard Bldg. Associates, Ltd.—§ 6-20, n. 20; § 6-21; § 6-21, n. 5, 6; § 6-53, n. 6; § 6-56, n. 5, 51.
First Intern. Services Corp., In re—§ 4-16, n. 2.
First Nat. Bank of Abbeville v. Capps—§ 6-38, n. 11.
First Nat. Bank of Denver v. Turley—§ 6-61, n. 16, 51, 55.
First Nat. Bank of Everett v. Tiffany—§ 8-31, n. 5.
First Nat. Bank of Manhattan v. Dempsey—§ 8-13, n. 7.
First Nat. Bank of Mobile v. Norris—§ 8-1, n. 12; § 8-3, n. 18; § 8-21, n. 9, 11.
First Nat. Bank of Mobile v. Roddenberry—§ 7-26, n. 25.
First Nat. Bank of Park Falls v. Maley—§ 8-29, n. 13.
First Republicbank Dallas v. Gargyle Corp.—§ 3-31, n. 13.
First Sec. Bank of Utah, N.A. v. Wright—§ 6-92, n. 9.
First Software Corp., In re, 85 B.R. 669—§ 6-31, n. 16, 17.
First Software Corp., In re, 84 B.R. 278—§ 6-20, n. 2, 12, 13; § 6-31, n. 15; § 6-87, n. 11, 14.
First Software Corp., In re, 81 B.R. 211—§ 6-31, n. 16, 17.
First Software Corp., In re, 72 B.R. 403—§ 6-65, n. 12; § 6-66, n. 2.
First Software Corp. v. Micro Educ. Corp. of America—§ 6-31, n. 14, 17.
First State Bank of Denton v. Vestal & Naugle—§ 6-38, n. 11.
First State Bank of Ringling v. Hunt—§ 6-38, n. 12.
First Texas Savings Assoc., Inc. v. Reed—§ 7-19, n. 1.
Fisher, In re, 117 B.R. 191—§ 8-28, n. 25.
Fisher, In re, 100 B.R. 351—§ 6-20, n. 17; § 6-22, n. 5.
Fisher, In re, 67 B.R. 666—§ 3-30, n. 12, 14, 16, 17, 18.
Fisher, Matter of—§ 6-47, n. 10.
Fisher & Son, Inc., In re—§ 10-8, n. 3.
Fisk, In re—§ 8-24, n. 3; § 9-3, n. 3.
Fisk v. Allis Chalmers Credit Corp.—§ 9-3, n. 3.
Fitak, In re—§ 6-2, n. 20.
Fitch, In re—§ 3-21, n. 9.
Fitness Connection, Inc., In re—§ 6-61, n. 12, 59.
Fitterer Engineering Associates, Inc., Matter of—§ 6-35, n. 33, 44; § 6-76, n. 5.
Fitzgerald, In re—§ 7-48, n. 5.
Fitzgerald v. Critchfield—§ 3-6, n. 45.
Fitzgerald v. Davis—§ 8-28, n. 7.
Fitzpatrick, Matter of—§ 6-50, n. 16, 18; § 6-52, n. 22; § 6-87, n. 8.
Fitzsimmons, In re—§ 2-8; § 2-8, n. 31.
550 Les Mouches Fashions, Ltd., In re—§ 6-49, n. 32, 35.
523 East Fifth Street Housing Preservation Development Fund Corp., In re—§ 4-7; § 4-7, n. 5; § 4-10; § 4-10, n. 6.
Fizer, In re—§ 9-12, n. 2.
Flagg Bros., Inc. v. Brooks—§ 6-38, n. 14.
Flagler-at-First Associates, Ltd., In re—§ 6-77, n. 1.
Flagstaff Foodservice Corp., In re, 56 B.R. 910—§ 6-66, n. 2.
Flagstaff Foodservice Corp., In re, 56 B.R. 899—§ 6-65, n. 12; § 6-66, n. 11; § 6-67, n. 1.
Flanagan Bros., Inc., In re—§ 6-39, n. 24, 38; § 6-41; § 6-41, n. 14.
Flanzbaum, Matter of—§ 6-48, n. 17.
Fleeman, Matter of—§ 6-61, n. 18, 55.
Fleet Factors Corp., United States v.—§ 3-21, n. 110.
Fleming-Roberts Corp., Ltd., In re—§ 6-73, n. 26.
Fletcher v. Rhode Island Hospital Trust Nat. Bank—§ 6-38, n. 14.
Fletcher Oil Co., Inc., In re—§ 6-2, n. 9; § 6-61, n. 74.

Flexible Artcraft Graphics Unlimited, Inc., In re—§ **6-82**, n. 7.
Flick, In re—§ **9-4**, n. 30.
Flick v. United States—§ **8-25**, n. 52.
Flight Management, Inc., In re—§ **6-30**, n. 4.
Flindall, In re—§ **8-33**, n. 24, 34.
Flip Mortg. Corp. v. McElhone—§ **6-2**, n. 24.
Floater Vehicle, Inc., In re—§ **6-61**, n. 18.
Flooring Concepts, Inc., In re—§ **6-69**, n. 2.
Flora Mir Candy Corp., In re—§ **11-41**; § **11-41**, n. 6.
Florida Nat. Bank of Gainesville v. Sherouse—§ **6-48**, n. 9.
Florida Peach Corp. of America, Int., In re—§ **10-10**, n. 1.
Flue Gas Resources, Inc., In re—§ **6-62**, n. 28.
Fluge, In re—§ **6-77**, n. 6, 12, 19.
Fluharty, In re—§ **9-22**, n. 1.
Flygare v. Boulden—§ **9-14**, n. 13.
Flygstad, In re—§ **8-17**, n. 17, 18, 33, 47, 49.
Fogarty, In re—§ **6-2**, n. 9; § **6-70**, n. 3; § **10-29**, n. 3.
Folendore, Matter of—§ **7-10**, n. 2; § **7-47**, n. 2; § **11-30**, n. 11.
Foley, In re—§ **8-7**, n. 18.
Fonda Group, Inc., In re—§ **6-16**, n. 1; § **6-19**, n. 10, 14; § **6-31**, n. 4; § **6-34**, n. 10.
Food City, Inc., In re, 110 B.R. 808—§ **10-31**, n. 1.
Food City, Inc., In re, 94 B.R. 91—§ **5-8**, n. 13.
Food Fair, Inc., In re—§ **11-41**; § **11-41**, n. 11.
Ford, In re, 773 F.2d 52—§ **8-32**, n. 8.
Ford, In re, 98 B.R. 669—§ **6-25**, n. 13; § **6-34**, n. 10, 20.
Ford, In re, 84 B.R. 40—§ **9-20**, n. 18.
Ford, In re, 53 B.R. 444—§ **7-19**, n. 1, 8; § **8-32**, n. 8, 18.
Ford, In re, 36 B.R. 501—§ **10-8**, n. 3.
Ford, Matter of—§ **2-17**, n. 20; § **6-70**, n. 2.
Ford Concepts, Inc., In re—§ **6-11**, n. 6; § **6-47**, n. 10; § **6-74**, n. 13.
Forde v. Kee–Lox Mfg. Co., Inc.—§ **4-10**, n. 4.
Ford Motor Co. v. Transport Indem. Co.—§ **6-39**, n. 9.
Ford Motor Credit Co. v. Owens—§ **7-30**, n. 19, 20.
Fordson Engineering Corp., Matter of—§ **6-40**, n. 4.
Forestry Products, Inc. v. Hope—§ **9-3**, n. 4.
Formaggio Mfg., Inc., In re—§ **6-48**, n. 19; § **6-49**, n. 43; § **6-59**, n. 3.
Forrest Hills Associates, Ltd., In re—§ **11-16**, n. 7.
Forsdick v. Turgeon—§ **7-29**, n. 15, 16.
Forseen, Inc., In re—§ **3-31**, n. 21, 22, 26, 27; § **12-12**, n. 19.
Fortier v. Dona Anna Plaza Partners—§ **3-5**, n. 19.
Fort Lauderdale Hotel Partners, Ltd., In re—§ **12-15**, n. 1.
Fortunato, Matter of—§ **8-19**, n. 10.
48th Street Steakhouse, Inc., In re—§ **3-10**, n. 21; § **3-14**, n. 20, 64, 65; § **3-32**, n. 1, 2.
Fosco, In re—§ **7-26**, n. 32.
Fossey, In re—§ **3-23**, n. 20.
Foster, In re, 79 B.R. 906—§ **9-29**, n. 2.
Foster, In re, 19 B.R. 28—§ **4-16**, n. 2.
Foster, Matter of, 670 F.2d 478—§ **9-4**; § **9-4**, n. 42.
Foster, Matter of, 105 B.R. 746—§ **12-5**, n. 2, 5.
Foster, Matter of, 61 B.R. 492—§ **9-12**, n. 13; § **9-16**; § **9-16**, n. 3, 4; § **9-18**, n. 15.
Foster v. City Loan and Sav. Co.—§ **8-26**, n. 18.
Foster v. North Texas Production Credit Association—§ **2-13**, n. 17.
Fountain, Matter of—§ **6-21**, n. 4.
4–S Corp., In re—§ **6-4**, n. 14; § **6-35**, n. 5, 44; § **6-41**, n. 47.
Four Winds Enterprises, Inc., In re, 100 B.R. 24—§ **6-29**, n. 11.
Four Winds Enterprises, Inc., In re, 94 B.R. 694—§ **6-12**, n. 7; § **6-19**, n. 13.
Fox, In re, 16 F.Supp. 320—§ **8-8**, n. 6.
Fox, In re, 83 B.R. 290—§ **5-4**, n. 14.
Fox, In re, 80 B.R. 753—§ **2-8**, n. 21; § **8-13**, n. 12.
Fox, In re, 62 B.R. 432—§ **6-41**, n. 44, 46; § **8-23**, n. 5.
Fox, In re, 29 B.R. 46—§ **8-2**, n. 4.
Fox, In re, 1989 WL 112790—§ **3-23**, n. 32.
Fox, Matter of, 762 F.2d 54—§ **12-12**, n. 8, 28.
Fox, Matter of, 64 B.R. 148—§ **9-3**, n. 17.
Fox v. Western New York Motor Lines—§ **11-39**, n. 1.
Foxcroft Bldg. Corp. Foxcroft Ltd., In re—§ **11-16**, n. 4.
Fox Hill Office Investors, Ltd., In re—§ **6-49**, n. 46; § **6-61**, n. 18; § **6-93**, n. 41.
Foxhill Place Associates, In re—§ **6-77**, n. 12.

TABLE OF CASES

Fragapane, In re—§ 8-23, n. 8.
Francis, In re—§ 3-10, n. 58.
Frank, In re—§ 9-12; § 9-12, n. 9.
Frank, Matter of—§ 6-50, n. 35; § 6-53, n. 3, 8; § 6-55, n. 13, 22; § 6-56, n. 17.
Franklin, In re, 726 F.2d 606—§ 7-30, n. 6, 26.
Franklin, In re, 111 B.R. 582—§ 3-31, n. 54, 59.
Franklin Bank and Trust Co. v. Mithoefer—§ 3-32, n. 6.
Franklin Computer Corp., In re—§ 6-40, n. 4.
Franklin Signal Corp., In re—§ 11-10, n. 5.
Franview Drug Corp., In re—§ 6-93, n. 29.
Frascatore, In re—§ 6-56, n. 1; § 6-60, n. 8; § 6-82, n. 6; § 6-83, n. 10; § 6-84, n. 2.
Frazier, In re, 116 B.R. 675—§ 8-17, n. 10.
Frazier, In re, 104 B.R. 255—§ 8-29, n. 7, 8; § 8-30, n. 4.
Frazier v. Marine Midland Bank, N.A.—§ 6-38, n. 6.
Frederick, Matter of—§ 6-38, n. 5, 18; § 6-39, n. 2; § 6-40, n. 16, 36; § 6-41, n. 44, 46, 51.
Fred Sanders Co., Matter of, 33 B.R. 310—§ 6-39, n. 28; § 6-40, n. 5, 7.
Fred Sanders Co., Matter of, 22 B.R. 902—§ 5-23, n. 10.
Fred Swain, Inc., In re—§ 5-23, n. 3.
Freeborn, In re—§ 6-42, n. 2; § 6-43, n. 3.
Freedlander, Inc., In re—§ 6-12, n. 10.
Freeman, In re, 124 B.R. 840—§ 8-25, n. 37.
Freeman, In re, 72 B.R. 850—§ 6-2, n. 20; § 6-61, n. 12.
Freeman v. Commissioner—§ 3-6, n. 33.
Freewerth Enterprises, Inc., In re—§ 6-9, n. 5; § 6-10, n. 13; § 6-32, n. 2.
Freshley, In re—§ 9-7; § 9-7, n. 3, 4, 17.
Freshman v. Atkins—§ 2-16; § 2-16, n. 25.
Freudenmann, In re—§ 12-3, n. 3.
Frey, In re—§ 9-10, n. 6, 10.
FRG, Inc., In re—§ 3-6, n. 36.
FRG, Inc. v. Manley—§ 3-31, n. 100.
Friedberg, In re—§ 12-15; § 12-15, n. 1, 2, 4.
Friedman, In re, 126 B.R. 63—§ 6-17, n. 11; § 6-93, n. 45.
Friedman, In re, 38 B.R. 275—§ 8-21, n. 4.
Friendship College, Inc., United States v.—§ 5-23, n. 3.
Friends of Sakonnet v. Dutra—§ 3-21, n. 109.
Frieouf, In re—§ 2-11; § 2-11, n. 5, 7.
Frierson v. United Farm Agency, Inc.—§ 6-38, n. 7.
Fries, In re—§ 9-4, n. 29, 30; § 9-12, n. 8, 11; § 9-13, n. 2.
Friese, In re—§ 10-17, n. 6.
Fritz, In re—§ 6-2, n. 24.
Fritz–Mair Mfg. Co., In re—§ 6-24, n. 6.
Froid, In re—§ 2-8, n. 23; § 6-76, n. 2.
Frost, In re, 111 B.R. 306—§ 8-25, n. 7.
Frost, In re, 47 B.R. 961—§ 9-10, n. 7.
Fry, In re, 122 B.R. 427—§ 3-33, n. 35, 38, 42; § 3-35, n. 1.
Fry, In re, 83 B.R. 778—§ 8-28, n. 3.
Fryar, In re, 99 B.R. 747—§ 11-38, n. 4.
Fryar, In re, 93 B.R. 101—§ 6-39, n. 15; § 6-40, n. 2, 3, 16.
Fry, In re—§ 3-33, n. 35, 38, 42; § 3-35, n. 1; § 8-28, n. 3.
Fryar, In re—§ 6-39, n. 15; § 6-40, n. 2, 3, 16; § 11-38, n. 4.
FSC Corp., Matter of—§ 10-7; § 10-7, n. 11, 12.
F & S Cent. Mfg. Corp., In re—§ 6-17; § 6-17, n. 15, 30.
F.T.C. v. R.A. Walker & Associates, Inc.—§ 3-21, n. 44.
Ft. Dodge Creamery Co., In re—§ 6-69, n. 12; § 6-71, n. 17.
Fuel Oil Supply and Terminaling, Inc., In re—§ 3-32, n. 6; § 6-73, n. 8, 10.
Fuel Oil Supply & Terminaling, Inc., Matter of—§ 6-25; § 6-25, n. 7, 15, 18.
Fugazy Exp., Inc., Matter of, 124 B.R. 426—§ 3-14, n. 80; § 3-21, n. 60, 118; § 3-33, n. 11; § 6-87, n. 15.
Fugazy Exp., Inc., Matter of, 114 B.R. 865—§ 6-87, n. 3, 19.
Fukutomi v. Siegel—§ 3-6, n. 16; § 3-14, n. 15.
Fulghum Const. Corp., In re, 872 F.2d 739—§ 6-30, n. 2; § 6-31, n. 19.
Fulghum Const. Corp., In re, 45 B.R. 112—§ 6-87, n. 14.
Fulghum Const. Corp., In re, 23 B.R. 147—§ 6-39, n. 14, 38; § 6-43, n. 3; § 6-44, n. 2.
Funding Systems Asset Management Corp., In re—§ 6-20, n. 22; § 6-61, n. 16; § 6-77, n. 21.
Funventures In Travel, Inc. v. Dunn—§ 7-28, n. 12.
Furey, In re—§ 9-3, n. 21.
Furkes, In re—§ 8-10, n. 10, 12; § 8-33, n. 2.
Furlow, In re—§ 9-7, n. 12.

Furniture Den, Inc., Matter of—§ 6-89, n. 14, 24.
Furniture Discount Stores, Inc., In re—§ 6-35, n. 35; § 6-62, n. 39.
Furniture Distributors, Inc., In re—§ 6-66, n. 11.
Fussell, In re, 928 F.2d 712—§ 3–20, n. 33, 39, 40.
Fussell, In re, 15 B.R. 1016—§ 7-28, n. 4.
Future Energy Corp., In re—§ 6-93, n. 29, 32, 38; § 10-20; § 10-20, n. 10; § 11-17, n. 3.
Future Growth Enterprises, Inc., In re—§ 3-28, n. 12.
Future Time, Inc. v. Yates—§ 7-19, n. 6.

G

Gabel, In re—§ 4-7; § 4-7, n. 8; § 4-17, n. 11.
Gadson, In re—§ 9-18, n. 13.
Gagel & Gagel, Matter of—§ 11-13, n. 3.
Gaglia, In re—§ 7-10, n. 2; § 11–30; § 11–30, n. 7, 11, 14.
Gaglia v. First Federal Sav. & Loan Ass'n—§ 7-47, n. 2.
Gaildeen Industries, Inc., In re—§ 6-27, n. 15.
Gailey, Inc., In re—§ 6-49, n. 46, 59.
Gaines, In re, 121 B.R. 1015—§ 8–33, n. 34.
Gaines, In re, 82 B.R. 105—§ 6-50, n. 23; § 6-53, n. 6.
Galizia, In re—§ 7-26, n. 37.
Gallagher, In re—§ 8-17, n. 49; § 8-33, n. 24.
Gallo, In re—§ 8-3, n. 21; § 8-21, n. 4.
Galvan, In re—§ 8-24, n. 3; § 8-28, n. 2, 4, 8, 9, 12; § 8-29, n. 2; § 8-30, n. 4.
Gamble, In re—§ 9-2, n. 5.
Gamest, Inc., In re—§ 6-9, n. 11; § 6-10, n. 7.
Ganakes, Matter of—§ 8-27, n. 11.
Gancarz, In re—§ 8-28, n. 3.
Gander Mountain, Inc., In re—§ 6-2, n. 28.
Gans, In re—§ 7-28, n. 5.
Garafano, In re—§ 8-10, n. 25.
Garcia, In re, 109 B.R. 335—§ 3–16, n. 3; § 3–32, n. 1, 27, 37; § 6–73, n. 11.
Garcia, In re, 42 B.R. 33—§ 9–20, n. 12.
Garcia, In re, 23 B.R. 266—§ 6–40, n. 4.
Garden Manor Associates, L.P., In re—§ 2-15, n. 23.
Gardinier, Inc., In re—§ 5-4; § 5-4, n. 15.
Gardner, In re—§ 8-33, n. 317.
Gardner v. State of New Jersey—§ 12-13, n. 1.
Gardner Matthews Plantation Co., In re—§ 6-31, n. 17.
Garland Coal & Min. Co., In re—§ 2-5, n. 12.
Garland Coal & Min. Co. v. United Mine Workers of America—§ 3-30, n. 23.
Garman, Matter of—§ 7-26, n. 42.
Garner, In re—§ 8-10, n. 6.
Garner v. Strauss—§ 8-10, n. 25.
Garnett, In re—§ 7-47, n. 2.
Garrett, In re—§ 3-10, n. 65, 68.
Garrett Marine, Inc., In re—§ 6-61, n. 28, 41.
Garris, In re—§ 8-23, n. 9.
Garrison, In re, 56 B.R. 528—§ 6-56, n. 17, 35, 36, 37, 53.
Garrison, In re, 48 B.R. 837—§ 6–53, n. 6; § 6–54, n. 10; § 6–56; § 6–56, n. 17, 20, 25, 26, 28, 41, 47, 52.
Gartrell, In re—§ 8-1, n. 17.
Gary Aircraft Corp., In re—§ 11-7, n. 7.
Gary Aircraft Corp., Matter of—§ 11-1, n. 2; § 11-7, n. 7.
Gaskin, In re—§ 9-7; § 9-7, n. 4, 18.
Gaslight Club, Inc., Matter of—§ 10-7, n. 11.
Gates, In re—§ 3-20, n. 7, 40.
Gates, Matter of—§ 9-14, n. 16.
Gates Community Chapel of Rochester, Inc., In re—§ 6-9, n. 7.
Gathright, In re—§ 9-12, n. 3; § 9-14, n. 17, 21.
Gatlinburg Motel Enterprises, Ltd., In re—§ 6-61, n. 18.
GATX Aircraft Corp. v. M/V Courtney Leigh—§ 3-5, n. 6; § 3-22, n. 24.
Gaudet, In re—§ 2-13, n. 14.
Gaukler, In re—§ 7-45, n. 13.
Gavia, In re, 24 B.R. 573—§ 2–2, n. 11.
Gavia, In re, 24 B.R. 216—§ 9–19, n. 3.

TABLE OF CASES

Gaylor, In re—§ 7-47, n. 2; § 8-8, n. 2.
Geauga Trenching Corp., In re—§ 6-44, n. 2.
Gee, In re—§ 3-31, n. 79.
Gefen, In re—§ 6-60, n. 17; § 8-32, n. 8.
Gehrke, In re—§ 3-9, n. 7.
Geis, In re—§ 8-18, n. 2, 10.
Geist v. Converse County Bank—§ 8-25, n. 34, 36, 37.
Gelking, In re—§ 6-61, n. 53.
Geller, In re—§ 2-13, n. 6.
Gelwicks, In re—§ 6-77, n. 11, 19.
General Coffee Corp., In re—§ 6-61, n. 38, 42, 67, 79.
General Elec. Credit Corp. v. Nardulli & Sons, Inc.—§ 2-17, n. 19; § 6-61, n. 51, 66.
General Industries, Inc., In re—§ 6-50, n. 23, 27; § 6-53, n. 3, 6, 7; § 6-54, n. 10; § 6-55, n. 9; § 6-56, n. 27, 54; § 6-87, n. 6, 8; § 6-89, n. 9, 19, 25, 27.
General Motors Corp. v. Buha—§ 8-11, n. 19; § 8-33, n. 9, 15.
General Office Furniture Wholesalers, Inc., In re, 42 B.R. 232—§ 6-69, n. 2.
General Office Furniture Wholesalers, Inc., In re, 37 B.R. 180—§ 6-11, n. 6.
General Oil Distributors, Inc., In re, 68 B.R. 603—§ 11-3, n. 21.
General Oil Distributors, Inc., In re, 42 B.R. 402—§ 10-8, n. 3.
General Oil Distributors, Inc., In re, 20 B.R. 873—§ 4-15, n. 15.
Genesee Cement, Inc., In re—§ 11-17, n. 8.
Gentile, In re—§ 6-29, n. 10, 12.
Geoghegan, Matter of—§ 8-10, n. 25, 26.
George, In re, 78 B.R. 886—§ 6-77, n. 1; § 6-78, n. 7.
George, In re, 62 B.R. 671—§ 6-78, n. 14.
George Rodman, Inc., In re, 792 F.2d 125—§ 6-25; § 6-25, n. 28.
George Rodman, Inc., In re, 39 B.R. 855—§ 6-25, n. 1, 7, 8, 27, 29.
George's Radio v. Capital Transit Co—§ 11-39, n. 3.
Georgetown of Kettering, Matter of—§ 11-16, n. 6.
Georgia Federal Savings & Loan Ass'n v. Anderson—§ 9-3, n. 8.
Georgia Steel, Inc., Matter of—§ 6-19, n. 17; § 6-25, n. 13.
Gerbig v. White Motor Credit Corp.—§ 3-6, n. 59.
Gerdes, In re—§ 4-7, n. 20.
Gerlach, In re—§ 7-26; § 7-26, n. 9, 15, 57, 61.
Gerulis, In re—§ 7-32, n. 1.
GHR Companies, Inc., In re—§ 10-8, n. 3; § 10-10, n. 6.
GHR Energy Corp., In re—§ 11-16, n. 6.
Gianakas, In re, 917 F.2d 759—§ 3-12, n. 29.
Gianakas, In re, 112 B.R. 737—§ 3-12, n. 5, 28.
Gibbs, In re—§ 3-10, n. 9.
Gibbs, Matter of—§ 3-21, n. 69, 113.
Gibson, In re—§ 3-11, n. 14.
Gibson v. General Motors Acceptance Corp.—§ 6-12, n. 7; § 6-24, n. 2; § 6-33, n. 10.
Gibson & Cushman Dredging Corp., In re—§ 11-13, n. 3; § 11-14, n. 11.
Gibson Distributing Co., Inc.–Permian Basin, In re—§ 6-65, n. 12; § 6-66, n. 4.
GIC Government Securities, Matter of—§ 6-66, n. 1, 8.
Giesing, In re—§ 6-42, n. 1; § 6-45, n. 2, 3, 6.
Gilbert, In re, 104 B.R. 206—§ 10-17, n. 4; § 11-18, n. 8.
Gilbert, In re, 74 B.R. 1—§ 8-17, n. 24.
Gilbertson, In re—§ 6-18, n. 29; § 6-20, n. 23; § 6-30, n. 7.
Gilchrist Machinery Co., Inc., In re—§ 6-25, n. 20.
Gilda Gradenigo, Inc., Matter of—§ 6-92, n. 10.
Gill, In re—§ 7-34, n. 10.
Gilliam, In re—§ 3-20, n. 15, 33.
Gillie, In re—§ 8-25, n. 28, 32.
Gillman, In re—§ 6-47, n. 8.
Gilman, In re—§ 8-31, n. 3.
Gilman Services, Inc., In re—§ 10-10, n. 1.
Gilmore, In re—§ 6-55, n. 22; § 6-56, n. 8.
Gincastro, In re—§ 9-17, n. 8.
Gingery, In re—§ 8-22, n. 8, 21, 38; § 8-30, n. 8.
Giorgio, In re—§ 6-93, n. 16, 38, 64; § 6-94, n. 8.
Girardeau, In re—§ 9-7, n. 1, 14.
Gitex, In re—§ 7-11; § 7-11, n. 9.
Gitts, In re—§ 8-9, n. 16.
Glade Springs, Inc., In re—§ 10-14, n. 3.
Glanzer v. St. Joseph Indian School—§ 3-5, n. 6, 15.
Glaser, In re—§ 7-22, n. 5, 7.

Glass, Matter of—§ 4-9, n. 9.
Glassley, In re—§ 6-7, n. 1.
Gleason, In re—§ 9-20, n. 6, 8.
Glenco Intern. Corp., In re—§ 6-83, n. 15.
Gleneagles Inv. Co., Inc., United States v.—§ 6-52, n. 7, 10, 43, 47.
Glenn, In re, 760 F.2d 1428—§ 3-16, n. 11; § 9-17; § 9-17, n. 2, 4.
Glenn, In re, 108 B.R. 70—§ 6-2, n. 24.
Global Distribution Network, Inc., In re—§ 6-16, n. 1; § 6-31, n. 15, 19.
Global Intern. Airways Corp., Matter of, 80 B.R. 990—§ 6-31, n. 16.
Global Intern. Airways Corp., Matter of, 80 B.R. 983—§ 6-31, n. 16; § 6-34, n. 4, 17.
Globe Inv. and Loan Co., Inc., In re—§ 3-32, n. 6.
Gloria Mfg. Corp., In re, 65 B.R. 341—§ 4-13, n. 6.
Gloria Mfg. Corp., In re, 47 B.R. 370—§ 4-12, n. 3.
Gloria Mfg. Corp. v. International Ladies' Garment Workers' Union—§ 5-4, n. 9.
G-N Partners, In re—§ 2-10, n. 5.
Godfrey, In re, 102 B.R. 769—§ 3-2, n. 2.
Godfrey, In re, 93 B.R. 451—§ 8-9, n. 9.
Goeb, In re—§ 9-14, n. 5, 13.
Goerg, In re—§ 2-6; § 2-6, n. 5.
Goering, In re—§ 8-21, n. 9.
Goff, Matter of—§ 8-11, n. 18; § 8-33, n. 17, 18, 24, 34.
Goin, In re—§ 7-29; § 7-29, n. 8.
Goldberg, In re—§ 8-19, n. 5, 20.
Goldblatt Bros., Inc., In re—§ 5-23, n. 3.
Goldblatt Bros., Inc., Matter of—§ 5-20, n. 5.
Gold Coast Seed Co., In re—§ 6-19, n. 17.
Golden, In re—§ 8-3, n. 12, 21.
Golden v. Tomiyasu—§ 6-56, n. 1.
Golden Distributors, Ltd., In re—§ 3-14; § 3-14, n. 20, 47.
Golden Plan of California, Inc., In re, 39 B.R. 551—§ 6-72, n. 6.
Golden Plan of California, Inc., In re, 37 B.R. 167—§ 3-21, n. 126; § 3-22, n. 29.
Gold Key Properties, Inc., In re—§ 6-61, n. 11, 16.
Gold Leaf Corp. v. Hamilton Projects, Inc.—§ 6-45, n. 4, 11, 12.
Goldman, In re—§ 6-57, n. 3, 5; § 8-22, n. 21.
Goldman v. Haverstraw Associates (In re R.H.N. Realty Corp.)—§ 11-40, n. 1.
Goldman v. Mitchell-Fletcher Co.—§ 11-39, n. 3.
Goldrich, In re—§ 3-8, n. 34; § 7-41; § 7-41, n. 17.
Goldstein v. Madison Nat. Bank of Washington, D.C.—§ 6-15, n. 5.
Gonic Realty Trust, In re—§ 2-13, n. 9.
Gonshorowski, In re—§ 8-25, n. 43, 44.
Gonzales, In re—§ 7-28, n. 10.
Gonzalez, Matter of—§ 9-5, n. 5.
Good Hope Refineries, Inc., In re—§ 11-16, n. 6.
Goodman, In re—§ 7-18; § 7-18, n. 1.
Goodman Industries, Inc., In re—§ 6-51, n. 33; § 6-93, n. 29, 32.
Goodstein, United States v.—§ 4-3, n. 9.
Good Time Charlie's Ltd., In re—§ 3-9, n. 5, 11.
Goodwin, In re, 115 B.R. 674—§ 6-88, n. 21, 27.
Goodwin, In re, 82 B.R. 616—§ 8-26, n. 5; § 8-28, n. 3.
Goodwin, In re, 58 B.R. 75—§ 9-4, n. 14; § 9-20, n. 6.
Gore, In re, 124 B.R. 75—§ 6-39, n. 15.
Gore, In re, 113 B.R. 504—§ 3-23, n. 38.
Gorse v. Long Neck, Ltd.—§ 12-5, n. 3.
Gouker, Matter of—§ 8-33, n. 20, 52.
Gould & Eberhardt Gear Machinery Corp., In re—§ 7-25, n. 2.
Goulding Place Developers, Inc., In re—§ 3-29, n. 11.
Goydoscik, In re—§ 6-80, n. 11; § 8-29, n. 12, 13.
Grabill Corp., In re—§ 6-49, n. 46, 49, 50, 68; § 6-51, n. 24.
Grady v. A.H. Robins Co., Inc.—§ 3-6, n. 55, 57, 58, 59; § 3-22, n. 2; § 7-5, n. 2; § 7-7; § 7-7, n. 5; § 11-3; § 11-3, n. 6, 14.
Graettinger, In re—§ 8-25, n. 38, 57.
Graf Bros. Inc., In re—§ 7-15, n. 1.
Graham, In re, 726 F.2d 1268—§ 8-1, n. 9; § 8-11, n. 18, 20, 21; § 8-33, n. 2, 5, 17, 30, 34.
Graham, In re, 122 B.R. 447—§ 7-26, n. 21.
Graham, In re, 110 B.R. 408—§ 6-61, n. 55, 71, 74.
Graham, In re, 35 B.R. 15—§ 6-72, n. 10.
Graham, In re, 24 B.R. 305—§ 8-11, n. 18.
Graham, In re, 14 B.R. 246—§ 3-30, n. 11.

TABLE OF CASES 937

Graham v. Lennington—§ 12-10, n. 9.
Grain Merchants of Indiana, Inc., In re—§ 6-14; § 6-14, n. 4; § 6-35, n. 3.
Grambling, In re, 99 B.R. 515—§ 6-9, n. 5.
Grambling, In re, 85 B.R. 675—§ 6-83, n. 16.
Granada, Inc., In re, 115 B.R. 702—§ 6-9, n. 5; § 6-10, n. 13; § 6-88, n. 35, 36.
Granada, Inc., In re, 110 B.R. 548—§ 6-88, n. 36, 41.
Granada, Inc., In re, 92 B.R. 501—§ 6-61, n. 28, 34, 38, 41, 74.
Granada Wines, Inc. v. New England Teamsters and Trucking Industry Pension Fund—§ 10-22, n. 5.
Grand Builders, Inc., In re—§ 6-93, n. 31.
Grand Sports, Inc., In re—§ 3-25, n. 48.
Granfinanciera, S.A. v. Nordberg—§ 3-30, n. 28; § 11-5, n. 8, 11; § 11-7, n. 6; § 12-2; § 12-2, n. 4, 10, 22; § 12-13; § 12-13, n. 3; § 12-14; § 12-14, n. 1; § 12-15; § 12-16.
Granger, In re—§ 8-21, n. 9, 12.
Grant, In re, 51 B.R. 385—§ 7-45, n. 13, 17.
Grant, In re, 40 B.R. 612—§ 8-17, n. 51.
Grantham v. Eastern Marine, Inc.—§ 11-10, n. 1.
Grassmueck, In re—§ 6-20, n. 23; § 6-25, n. 27.
Grassridge Industries, Inc., In re—§ 6-77, n. 1.
Graven, In re—§ 2-13; § 2-13, n. 15.
Gray, In re—§ 8-25, n. 44; § 8-27, n. 11.
Gray v. Giant Wholesale Corp.—§ 6-61, n. 53.
Gray v. Snyder—§ 6-49, n. 36; § 6-56, n. 14.
Grayhall Resources, Inc., In re—§ 5-18; § 5-18, n. 3; § 5-19; § 5-19, n. 3.
G & R Builders, Inc., In re—§ 6-61, n. 28, 71.
Great American Resources, Inc., In re—§ 12-11, n. 1, 7.
Greater Louisville Auto Auction, Inc. v. Ogle Buick, Inc.—§ 6-67, n. 3.
Green, In re, 934 F.2d 568—§ 2-14; § 2-14, n. 6.
Green, In re, 876 F.2d 854—§ 7-27, n. 8.
Green, In re, 123 B.R. 327—§ 8-17, n. 13; § 8-33, n. 24, 39.
Green, In re, 115 B.R. 1001—§ 8-17, n. 49; § 8-33, n. 24, 34.
Green, In re, 70 B.R. 164—§ 7-45, n. 4; § 9-7, n. 4, 12.
Green, In re, 64 B.R. 462—§ 8-28, n. 13.
Greenbelt Co-op., Inc., In re—§ 6-61, n. 16, 77.
Greenberg v. Fincher & Son Real Estate, Inc.—§ 3-6, n. 30; § 3-10, n. 6.
Greenberg v. Schools—§ 7-28, n. 18.
Greenblatt v. Ford—§ 8-10, n. 6.
Greenbrook Carpet Co., Inc., In re, 722 F.2d 659—§ 6-49, n. 46; § 6-52, n. 10.
Greenbrook Carpet Co., Inc., In re, 22 B.R. 86—§ 6-88, n. 24, 30; § 6-93, n. 31.
Greene, In re—§ 7-26, n. 36, 37.
Greene v. Balaber-Strauss—§ 8-1, n. 13.
Greene & Kellogg, Inc. v. Oxford Hosp., Inc.—§ 3-5, n. 14, 19.
Greenhaven Village Apartments of Burnsville Phase II Ltd. Partnership, In re—§ 6-61, n. 53; § 6-77, n. 1, 6, 11, 12.
Greenhill, In re—§ 8-28, n. 3.
Green Lantern, Inc., In re—§ 6-61, n. 38.
Greenley Energy Holdings of Pennsylvania, Inc., In re—§ 10-32, n. 1, 2.
Greenridge Apartments, In re—§ 12-6, n. 8.
Greenspoint Palms, Ltd. v. Greenspoint Co.—§ 3-6, n. 30.
Greenwald, In re—§ 3-21, n. 56, 69.
Greer, In re, 89 B.R. 757—§ 3-23, n. 4, 27.
Greer, In re, 60 B.R. 547—§ 9-12; § 9-12, n. 5; § 9-13, n. 12; § 9-14, n. 6, 13.
Greetis, In re—§ 3-2, n. 9.
Gregg's Custom Vans, In re—§ 3-14, n. 64.
Greiman, In re—§ 3-31, n. 68.
Greiner, In re—§ 12-11; § 12-11, n. 1, 3.
Grell, In re—§ 6-2, n. 24; § 12-3, n. 7.
Greseth, In re—§ 6-39, n. 15; § 6-40, n. 6; § 9-25, n. 11.
Greylock Glen Corp. v. Community Sav. Bank—§ 3-31, n. 103.
Greystone III Joint Venture, In re—§ 10-22, n. 7; § 11-27; § 11-27, n. 1; § 11-28; § 11-28, n. 6, 8; § 11-29; § 11-29, n. 1, 3, 7; § 11-30; § 11-30, n. 2, 16.
Greystone III Joint Venture, Matter of—§ 5-1, n. 1; § 5-10, n. 4; § 11-27; § 11-27, n. 16; § 11-29, n. 9.
Gribben, In re—§ 8-33, n. 17, 24, 34.
Grieshop, Matter of—§ 3-29, n. 13.
Griffin, In re—§ 9-4, n. 11.
Griffin Retreading Co., Matter of—§ 6-65, n. 9.
Grigsby, Matter of—§ 3-10, n. 56.

Grimes, In re—§ 2-16, n. 27.
Groetken, In re—§ 7-25; § 7-25, n. 3.
Grogan v. Garner—§ 3-10, n. 9; § 6-48, n. 4; § 7-26; § 7-26, n. 4, 13.
Gronski, In re, 86 B.R. 428—§ 9–22; § 9–22, n. 4.
Gronski, In re, 65 B.R. 932—§ 9–2, n. 10.
Grosse, In re—§ 3-35, n. 2, 4.
Gross–Feibel Co., Inc., Matter of—§ 6-77, n. 21.
Grosslight, Matter of—§ 8-10, n. 25.
Grossman, In re—§ 8-17, n. 35, 36.
Grosso, In re—§ 6-6, n. 7; § 8-28, n. 14.
Groves, In re—§ 8-33, n. 18, 24.
Grubbs v. Houston First American Sav. Ass'n—§ 9-17, n. 2; § 9-18, n. 18.
Grudoski, In re—§ 5-17, n. 7; § 5-20, n. 9.
Grundy Nat. Bank v. Rife—§ 3-31, n. 21.
Grunzke v. Security State Bank of Wells—§ 6-77, n. 8.
Grynberg, In re—§ 10-12, n. 4.
Grynberg v. Bancroft, Avery, and McAlister—§ 6-40, n. 16.
G & S Business Services, Inc. v. Fast Fare, Inc.—§ 3-6, n. 18.
Guaranty Nat. Ins. Co. v. Greater Kansas City Transp., Inc.—§ 11-10, n. 1.
Guardian Loan Co., Inc. v. Early—§ 6-56, n. 1.
Guerrero, In re—§ 8-1, n. 9.
Gugenhan, In re—§ 6-62, n. 14.
Guinnane, In re—§ 9-24, n. 12, 19.
Gulf Tampa Drydock Co., Matter of—§ 3-14, n. 34, 39, 46.
Gull Air, Inc., In re, 890 F.2d 1255—§ 3–6, n. 25, 44, 52; § 3–14, n. 46.
Gull Air, Inc., In re, 90 B.R. 10—§ 6–14, n. 2; § 6–15, n. 1, 3; § 6–31, n. 4.
Gull Air, Inc., In re, 82 B.R. 1—§ 6–30, n. 7, 9; § 6–31, n. 5.
Gulph Woods Corp., In re—§ 11-18, n. 5, 11.
Gunn, In re—§ 9-7; § 9-7, n. 4, 16.
Gunter, In re—§ 8-21, n. 4; § 8-27, n. 11.
Gunter Hotel Associates, In re—§ 5-23, n. 8.
Gurs, In re—§ 6-61, n. 69.
Gurst, In re—§ 3-9, n. 24.
Gurwitch, In re—§ 10-8, n. 1.
Gusam Restaurant Corp., In re—§ 2-9, n. 2.
Gustafson, In re, 934 F.2d 216—§ 3–34, n. 6.
Gustafson, In re, 111 B.R. 282—§ 3–8, n. 36; § 3–12, n. 2.
Guterl Special Steel Corp., Matter of—§ 3-3, n. 4, 7; § 3-16, n. 3; § 3-18, n. 20; § 3-32, n. 1.
Gutterman v. First Nat. Bank of Anchorage—§ 8-8, n. 7.

H

Habinger, Inc. v. Metropolitan Cosmetic and Reconstructive Surgical Clinic, P.A.—§ 6-70, n. 2.
Hable, In re—§ 7-26, n. 19.
Hackney, In re—§ 6-88, n. 18.
Haga, In re—§ 8-18, n. 10, 19.
Hagan, In re—§ 8-11, n. 3.
Hagberg, Matter of—§ 2-16, n. 4.
Hagen, In re—§ 6-14; § 6-14, n. 5; § 6-20, n. 20.
Hager, In re—§ 8-2, n. 4; § 8-24, n. 3.
Haggerty, Matter of—§ 9-4, n. 26.
Haider, In re—§ 6-56, n. 39, 50, 52, 54.
Haile v. New York State Higher Educ. Services Corp.—§ 3-35, n. 2, 4.
Haines v. Bero Engineering Const. Corporation—§ 11-39, n. 1.
Haines & Baker Excavating, Inc., In re—§ 6-87, n. 8; § 6-90, n. 4.
Hale, In re—§ 3-31, n. 16, 29, 39.
Hale, Matter of—§ 9-13, n. 12; § 9-14, n. 7, 13.
Haley, In re, 100 B.R. 13—§ 4–9, n. 14.
Haley, In re, 41 B.R. 44—§ 6–40, n. 27.
Hall, In re, 752 F.2d 582—§ 8–26, n. 19.
Hall, In re, 101 B.R. 781—§ 7–26, n. 21.
Hall, In re, 31 B.R. 42—§ 6–58, n. 4; § 8–32, n. 8.
Hall, In re, 15 B.R. 913—§ 2–13; § 2–13, n. 4.
Hall, In re, 11 B.R. 3—§ 7–48, n. 1.
Hall, Matter of, 51 B.R. 1002—§ 7–6; § 7–6, n. 1.
Hall, Matter of, 26 B.R. 10—§ 6–2, n. 16.

Hall v. Vance—§ 2-13, n. 9.
Halliburton Co. v. Mor—§ 8-33, n. 16.
Hall's Motor Transit Co., In re—§ 10-29, n. 6.
Hamilton, In re, 100 B.R. 385—§ 3-31, n. 6.
Hamilton, In re, 32 B.R. 337—§ 8-10, n. 7.
Hamilton, In re, 18 B.R. 868—§ 6-76, n. 2; § 6-77, n. 21.
Hamilton, Matter of—§ 6-13, n. 4; § 6-33, n. 11.
Hammett, In re—§ 6-84, n. 2.
Hammonds, In re—§ 2-2, n. 12; § 9-3, n. 6.
Hampton, In re—§ 8-24, n. 5.
Hancock, In re—§ 3-25, n. 6; § 3-27, n. 21.
Hancock Bank v. Jefferson—§ 6-2, n. 21.
Hancock-Nelson Mercantile Co., Inc., In re—§ 6-31, n. 15, 19; § 6-34, n. 26.
Handy, In re—§ 6-39, n. 33; § 6-44, n. 9.
Haney, State v.—§ 8-7, n. 6.
Hankins, In re—§ 8-10, n. 16.
Hanley, In re—§ 3-25, n. 10, 18, 52.
Hanna, In re, 912 F.2d 945—§ 7-47, n. 2.
Hanna, In re, 872 F.2d 829—§ 7-25; § 7-25, n. 11.
Hanna v. United States—§ 7-25, n. 13.
Hanratty, In re—§ 3-9, n. 29, 30.
Hanratty v. Philadelphia Elec. Co.—§ 3-9, n. 32.
Hansen, In re, 85 B.R. 821—§ 8-25, n. 33.
Hansen, In re, 48 B.R. 107—§ 3-20; § 3.20, n. 27.
Hanson, In re—§ 8-3, n. 15.
Hanson v. First Bank of South Dakota, N.A.—§ 10-17, n. 4; § 10-22, n. 7.
Hanson v. First Nat. Bank in Brookings—§ 8-32; § 8-32, n. 5, 23.
Harasymiw, Matter of, 895 F.2d 1170—§ 7-26, n. 36.
Harasymiw, Matter of, 97 B.R. 924—§ 7-28, n. 5.
Harbison v. Vaughan—§ 8-7, n. 7.
Harbor Tank Storage Co., In re—§ 11-3, n. 21.
Harbour, In re—§ 6-88, n. 38.
Harbour Town Associates, Ltd., In re—§ 6-61, n. 32, 55, 59; § 6-77, n. 11, 20; § 6-78, n. 3.
Hardware Products, Inc., Matter of—§ 6-40, n. 4.
Hargis, In re—§ 7-39, n. 2.
Hargis, Matter of—§ 6-69, n. 3.
Harley, In re—§ 6-33, n. 15; § 6-88, n. 36.
Harline, In re—§ 8-33, n. 17.
Harlow, In re—§ 10-8, n. 3.
Harmon, In re—§ 9-17, n. 7.
Harms, In re—§ 5-4, n. 10; § 11-37, n. 3; § 11-38; § 11-38, n. 2.
Harp, In re—§ 7-39, n. 7.
Harrell, In re, 754 F.2d 902—§ 7-29, n. 8, 11, 15.
Harrell, In re, 72 B.R. 107—§ 8-6, n. 4, 5.
Harrell, In re, 57 B.R. 88—§ 3-11, n. 12.
Harrell, In re, 55 B.R. 203—§ 6-62, n. 23, 39.
Harrell v. Bank of Wilson—§ 8-13, n. 7.
Harrigan, In re—§ 8-1, n. 12.
Harrington, In re—§ 6-15, n. 8.
Harrington v. Schuble—§ 8-13, n. 7.
Harris, In re, 886 F.2d 1011—§ 8-1, n. 11; § 8-3; § 8-3, n. 23, 32; § 8-19, n. 15.
Harris, In re, 122 B.R. 744—§ 7-45, n. 17.
Harris, In re, 120 B.R. 142—§ 8-28, n. 14, 23.
Harris, In re, 101 B.R. 210—§ 6-47, n. 13.
Harris, In re, 85 B.R. 858—§ 3-30, n. 35.
Harris, In re, 62 B.R. 391—§ 9-7; § 9-7, n. 4, 20.
Harris, In re, 59 B.R. 545—§ 7-32, n. 1.
Harris, In re, 16 B.R. 371—§ 3-10, n. 44, 57.
Harris, Matter of, 115 B.R. 376—§ 3-31, n. 73, 76.
Harris, Matter of, 107 B.R. 204—§ 9-4, n. 43.
Harris, Matter of, 50 B.R. 157—§ 8-18, n. 16.
Harris, Matter of, 7 B.R. 456—§ 6-49, n. 40.
Harris v. Fort Oglethorpe State Bank—§ 3-10, n. 66, 80.
Harrison, In re, 117 B.R. 570—§ 5-4; § 5-4, n. 17.
Harrison, In re, 82 B.R. 557—§ 3-10, n. 47.
Harris Pine Mills, In re—§ 5-2, n. 5; § 5-10, n. 2.
Harry Kaiser Associates, Inc., In re—§ 6-60, n. 17, 20.
Hart, In re, 76 B.R. 774—§ 3-23; § 3-23, n. 17.

Hart, In re, 50 B.R. 956—§ 6-40, n. 2, 6; § 8-22, n. 15; § 8-23, n. 6.
Hart, In re, 8 B.R. 1020—§ 7-47, n. 4.
Hart, Matter of—§ 7-34, n. 15.
Hartdegen, In re—§ 9-4, n. 32, 33.
Hartec Enterprises, Inc., In re—§ 5-15, n. 10, 11.
Hartley, In re, 825 F.2d 1067—§ 6-7, n. 13.
Hartley, In re, 52 B.R. 679—§ 6-49, n. 31; § 6-59, n. 2; § 6-93, n. 40, 47.
Hartman, In re, 110 B.R. 951—§ 7-25; § 7-25, n. 8; § 7-32, n. 1.
Hartman, In re, 102 B.R. 90—§ 6-2, n. 13; § 6-61, n. 16.
Hartman Paving, Inc., In re—§ 6-61, n. 77.
Hartwig Poultry, Inc., In re—§ 6-31, n. 16.
Harvard Mfg. Corp., In re—§ 6-3, n. 12, 13; § 6-19, n. 10; § 6-31, n. 12.
Harvest Milling Co., In re—§ 6-93, n. 20.
Harvey, In re—§ 3-23, n. 40.
Haschke, Matter of—§ 9-24, n. 21.
Hatch, In re—§ 6-83, n. 2.
Hatfield, In re—§ 8-25, n. 34.
Hatfield Elec. Co., In re—§ 6-25, n. 2, 7, 8, 20; § 6-36, n. 12, 15.
Hatfield Homes, Inc., In re—§ 4-7, n. 12, 18.
Hathaway Ranch Partnership, In re—§ 6-61, n. 28, 38.
Hatton v. Barnett Bank of Palm Beach County—§ 3-23, n. 27.
Haugen Const. Service, Inc., In re, 104 B.R. 233—§ 6-2, n. 5.
Haugen Const. Service, Inc., In re, 88 B.R. 222—§ 6-73, n. 4, 12; § 6-80, n. 20; § 6-82, n. 3.
Haugland, In re—§ 7-47, n. 2.
Hausman, In re—§ 6-6, n. 2.
Haute Cuisine, Inc., Matter of—§ 5-20, n. 9.
Havee v. Belk—§ 6-60, n. 24; § 6-61, n. 11.
Hawkins, Matter of—§ 9-9, n. 2.
Hawkins v. Landmark Finance Co.—§ 8-1, n. 11.
Hawley, In re—§ 8-13, n. 11.
Hawley, Matter of—§ 8-22, n. 23.
Hayball Trucking, Inc., In re—§ 10-33; § 10-33, n. 2, 3.
Hayes, In re—§ 9-18, n. 13.
Hayes, Matter of—§ 7-11; § 7-11, n. 7.
Haynes, Matter of—§ 2-8; § 2-8, n. 24.
Haynie Grain Services, Inc., In re—§ 6-61, n. 34.
Hazard, In re—§ 8-28, n. 13.
Hazel, Matter of—§ 9-4, n. 14.
Hazelton, Matter of—§ 6-39, n. 15; § 6-40, n. 2, 5; § 6-42, n. 2; § 6-43, n. 7.
Hazen First State Bank v. Speight—§ 3-14, n. 46.
HBA East, Inc., In re—§ 3-29, n. 12, 18.
HBG Servicenter, Inc., In re—§ 3-20, n. 33, 40.
Head, In re—§ 6-19, n. 16.
Heafitz, In re—§ 6-45, n. 7, 9, 36.
Healthcare Services, Inc., In re, 85 B.R. 913—§ 6-4, n. 17.
Healthcare Services, Inc., In re, 80 B.R. 563—§ 6-20, n. 11, 12, 20; § 6-36, n. 19.
Health Gourmet, Inc., In re—§ 6-49, n. 46, 52; § 6-50, n. 6, 15, 17; § 6-52, n. 22; § 6-59, n. 11.
Healy, Matter of—§ 8-3, n. 21; § 8-13, n. 8.
Heape, In re—§ 8-25, n. 38, 51, 52, 54, 56, 64.
Heard, In re—§ 3-9, n. 4, 10, 22, 30.
Hearing of Illinois, Inc., In re—§ 6-36, n. 15; § 6-62, n. 34.
Heartland Chemicals, Inc., In re—§ 6-93, n. 50.
Heath, Matter of—§ 7-41, n. 18.
Hecht, In re—§ 6-60, n. 10, 20, 23.
Hecht, Matter of, 54 B.R. 379—§ 6-84, n. 5.
Hecht, Matter of, 41 B.R. 701—§ 6-38, n. 5, 7; § 6-41, n. 46, 48.
Heckler Land Development Corp. v. Montgomery—§ 3-21, n. 69.
Heide, In re—§ 6-61, n. 79.
Heims, Matter of—§ 6-77, n. 1, 7, 22; § 6-78, n. 3.
Heincy, In re—§ 7-31, n. 10.
Heins, Matter of—§ 8-19, n. 14.
Heinzeroth, In re—§ 3-27, n. 21.
Heisey, In re—§ 8-17, n. 13.
Helen Gallagher Enterprises, Inc., In re—§ 6-9, n. 5; § 6-10, n. 7, 13; § 6-32, n. 5.
Hellums, Matter of—§ 3-8; § 3-8, n. 30; § 3-11, n. 25; § 7-36; § 7-36, n. 2, 3.
Helms, In re—§ 7-41, n. 12.
Helmsley-Spear, Inc. v. Winter—§ 8-33, n. 15.
Helmuth, In re—§ 8-28, n. 6.

Hemingson, In re—§ 8-25, n. 28, 33, 34.
Hemphill, Matter of—§ 6-18, n. 18; § 6-49, n. 13, 31, 62; § 6-51, n. 16.
Hemsing, In re—§ 9-18; § 9-18, n. 7.
Henderson, In re—§ 6-17, n. 11, 29.
Henderson, Matter of—§ 6-39, n. 1.
Henderson Ranches, In re—§ 9-24, n. 24.
Hendleman, In re—§ 6-61, n. 28, 80.
Hendrickson v. Philadelphia Gas Works—§ 3-9, n. 6.
Hennen v. Dayton Power & Light Co.—§ 3-9, n. 23, 34.
Hensley, In re—§ 6-12, n. 19.
Henson, In re—§ 3-10, n. 60.
Henstra, In re—§ 9-3, n. 12.
Herberman, In re—§ 2-8; § 2-8, n. 33, 35, 37.
Herd, In re—§ 10-31, n. 6.
Heritage House Interiors, Inc., In re—§ 6-61, n. 52.
Heritage Village Church and Missionary Fellowship, Inc., In re—§ 3-8, n. 11; § 3-14, n. 80; § 3-21, n. 46, 69, 122.
Herman, In re, 120 B.R. 127—§ 8-28, n. 3.
Herman, In re, 95 B.R. 504—§ 8-25, n. 12.
Hermansen, In re—§ 8-28, n. 9, 12.
Herndon, Matter of—§ 8-17, n. 13.
Herr, In re, 79 B.R. 793—§ 6-61, n. 29, 67, 77.
Herr, In re, 28 B.R. 465—§ 3-21, n. 25, 47, 50, 66, 76, 122.
Hershey, Matter of—§ 8-26, n. 7.
Hertz, In re—§ 10-33, n. 1.
Herzig, In re—§ 6-83, n. 18, 19.
Herzog, In re—§ 8-1, n. 11; § 8-17, n. 49.
Hester, In re, 63 B.R. 607—§ 9-4, n. 14.
Hester, In re, 14 B.R. 647—§ 6-49, n. 40.
Hewitt, In re—§ 10-23, n. 4.
H & H Beverage Distributors v. Department of Revenue of Com. of Pa., 85 F.2d 165—§ 3-8, n. 19, 20, 21.
H & H Beverage Distributors, Inc. v. Department of Revenue of Com. of Pa., 79 B.R. 205—§ 3-33, n. 13.
H.I.A. of Mt. Vernon, In re—§ 6-73, n. 4; § 6-82, n. 3.
Hickey v. Nightingale Roofing, Inc.—§ 6-30, n. 7, 8; § 6-32, n. 3.
Hickory Point Industries, Inc., In re—§ 5-3, n. 2.
Hicks, In re, 79 B.R. 45—§ 9-22; § 9-22, n. 11.
Hicks, In re, 65 B.R. 980—§ 7-41, n. 12; § 7-42, n. 5.
Higginbotham, In re—§ 7-45, n. 8.
High Sierra Transport, Inc., In re—§ 6-40, n. 4.
Highway Truck Drivers and Helpers Local Union 107, Matter of—§ 3-30, n. 5; § 3-31, n. 98, 101.
Hildebran, In re—§ 9-12; § 9-12, n. 12, 13; § 9-16, n. 3; § 9-18, n. 15.
Hild Floor Machine Co. v. Rudolph—§ 8-9, n. 12.
Hill, In re, 102 B.R. 804—§ 3-30, n. 12; 3-31, n. 98.
Hill, In re, 95 B.R. 293—§ 8-3, n. 21.
Hill, In re, 39 B.R. 894—§ 6-21, n. 5, 8.
Hill, In re, 19 B.R. 375—§ 6-39, n. 15.
Hill, In re, 5 B.R. 518—§ 8-18, n. 7, 16.
Hiller's Estate, In re—§ 2-6, n. 6.
Hilligoss, In re—§ 6-62, n. 23, 39, 42.
Hill Petroleum Co., In re—§ 6-40, n. 16, 22.
Hillsborough Holdings Corp., In re—§ 3-22, n. 5, 23, 29.
Hi-Lo Powered Scaffolding, Inc., Matter of—§ 11-3, n. 14, 17; § 11-7, n. 13.
Hilsen v. Hilsen—§ 3-12, n. 5.
Hilyard Drilling Co., Inc., In re—§ 4-3; § 4-3, n. 10.
Hines, In re, 723 F.2d 333—§ 9-14, n. 13.
Hines, In re, 3 B.R. 370—§ 6-36, n. 11; § 6-62, n. 15.
Hinkle, In re—§ 7-37, n. 2.
Hinkson v. Pfleiderer—§ 8-3, n. 7.
Hinman, In re—§ 7-26, n. 21, 24.
Hinshaw, In re—§ 8-11, n. 18.
Hinson, In re—§ 6-4, n. 13; § 8-22, n. 17; § 8-23, n. 5.
Hipp, Inc., Matter of—§ 3-35, n. 1.
Hipps, Matter of—§ 8-25, n. 32.
Hirte, In re—§ 7-37, n. 2.
H.L. Murry Drilling Co., In re—§ 6-7, n. 4.
HME Records, Inc., In re—§ 12-9, n. 2; § 12-10, n. 5.

Hobaica, In re, 77 B.R. 392—§ **6–20, n. 5, 12, 16, 17.**
Hobaica, In re, 65 B.R. 693—§ **9–18, n. 12.**
Hobbs, In re—§ **3-9, n. 5, 22.**
Hobbs v. Hurley—§ **11-39, n. 3.**
Hobday, In re—§ **9-14, n. 4.**
Hochman, United States v.—§ **9-22, n. 13.**
Hodak, In re—§ **7-34, n. 19.**
Hodgson, In re—§ **2-8, n. 23.**
Hoffman, In re, 96 B.R. 46—§ **6–20, n. 20;** § **8–13, n. 8, 11;** § **8–20, n. 4;** § **8–22, n. 28, 35;** § **8-23, n. 5, 11.**
Hoffman, In re, 65 B.R. 985—§ **2–8, n. 42.**
Hoffman, In re, 51 B.R. 42—§ **3–15, n. 5;** § **6–38, n. 21, 22;** § **6–40, n. 6, 13;** § **6–43, n. 13, 29.**
Hoffman, In re, 28 B.R. 503—§ **8–13, n. 6.**
Hoffman v. Cheek—§ **6-47, n. 10;** § **6-54, n. 3, 10;** § **6-55, n. 22.**
Hoffman v. Connecticut Dept. of Income Maintenance—§ **3-3, n. 5;** § **3-34;** § **3-34, n. 2, 4, 12;** § **6-87, n. 9;** § **6-88, n. 4.**
Hofstee, In re—§ **6-77, n. 1;** § **6-78, n. 7, 14.**
Hogan, United States v.—§ **7-33, n. 6.**
Hoggarth, In re—§ **2-17, n. 19;** § **6-11, n. 6.**
Hogue, In re—§ **9-3, n. 6;** § **9-19;** § **9-19, n. 2.**
Holcomb, In re—§ **7-48, n. 4.**
Holder, In re, 892 F.2d 29—§ **6-24, n. 2.**
Holder, In re, 94 B.R. 395—§ **6-13, n. 4.**
Holder, In re, 94 B.R. 394—§ **6-24, n. 2.**
Holdway, In re—§ **6-15, n. 3, 8;** § **8-23, n. 9.**
Holford, Matter of—§ **3-15, n. 6;** § **6-45, n. 10, 36.**
Holiday Meat Packing Inc., Matter of—§ **6-66, n. 5.**
Holiday Rambler Corp. v. First Nat. Bank and Trust Co. of Great Bend, Kan.—§ **6-63, n. 4.**
Holiday Towers, Inc., In re—§ **12-6, n. 6;** § **12-11, n. 7.**
Holland, In re—§ **6-20, n. 12, 20.**
Holland America Ins. Co. v. Succession of Roy—§ **3-6, n. 52;** § **3-10, n. 25, 34;** § **3-14, n. 15;** § **12-1, n. 2.**
Hollander, In re—§ **6-49, n. 12.**
Hollar, In re—§ **8-1, n. 15.**
Hollar, Matter of—§ **6-17, n. 5, 23.**
Hollie, Matter of—§ **6-77, n. 1, 22;** § **6-78, n. 18.**
Hollinrake, Matter of—§ **6-77, n. 1, 6, 11, 12;** § **6-78, n. 18;** § **6-86, n. 10.**
Hollinsed, Matter of—§ **6-6, n. 3, 6;** § **8-22, n. 24.**
Hollis, In re—§ **7-31, n. 13.**
Holloway v. HECI Exploration Co. Employees' Profit Sharing Plan—§ **12-3, n. 7.**
Holly, Matter of—§ **8-22, n. 19.**
Holly Hill Medical Center, Inc., In re—§ **6-49, n. 49, 52.**
Hollytex Carpet Mills v. Tedford, 691 F.2d 392—§ **8–2, n. 4.**
Hollytex Carpet Mills v. Tedford, 24 B.R. 197—§ **8–3, n. 19.**
Holmes, In re—§ **3-10, n. 65.**
Holt, In re, 894 F.2d 1005—§ **8–32, n. 5, 11, 13, 15, 16, 25.**
Holt, In re, 97 B.R. 997—§ **8–32, n. 14.**
Holt, In re, 84 B.R. 991—§ **8–3, n. 11.**
Holtkamp, Matter of—§ **3-30, n. 30, 33, 35;** § **3-31, n. 98.**
Holtzhauser, Matter of—§ **8-25, n. 16.**
Holyfield, In re—§ **6-6, n. 7;** § **6-37, n. 4.**
Holywell Corp., In re—§ **6-93, n. 35.**
Home America, Inc. v. T & J Paving, Inc.—§ **3-6, n. 26.**
Home Co., In re—§ **6-16, n. 1.**
Home Imp. Loan Co. v. Brewer—§ **8-13, n. 7.**
Home Life Ins. Co. v. Abrams Square II, Ltd.—§ **3-31, n. 94.**
Homer Nat. Bank v. Namie—§ **3-16, n. 7;** § **3-32, n. 5;** § **3-33, n. 3, 13, 16, 23.**
Homes of Port Charlotte, Florida, Inc., In re—§ **6-31, n. 15, 17.**
Home State Bank v. Johnson—§ **9-30, n. 2.**
Honett, In re—§ **9-18, n. 13, 16.**
Honeycomb, Inc., Matter of—§ **12-3, n. 7;** § **12-16, n. 3.**
Honeycutt Grain Co., Inc., In re—§ **6-44, n. 2.**
Hood, In re, 118 B.R. 417—§ **6–7, n. 5, 6.**
Hood, In re, 92 B.R. 648—§ **6–49, n. 74.**
Hooker Investments, Inc., In re—§ **12-15, n. 9.**
Hooton, In re—§ **6-47, n. 7;** § **6-49, n. 35.**
Hoover, In re—§ **2-5, n. 18.**
Hopkins, In re—§ **7-41, n. 12;** § **7-42, n. 5, 6.**

Horath, In re—§ 8-32, n. 5.
Horn v. Gates—§ 8-7, n. 17.
Horton, In re, 87 B.R. 650—§ 7–7, n. 1.
Horton, In re, 31 B.R. 464—§ 6–39, n. 32.
Horton, Matter of—§ 7-20, n. 6.
Hosler, In re—§ 9-7, n. 1, 14.
Hospital General San Carlos, Inc., In re—§ 12-12, n. 8.
Hotchkiss, In re, 93 B.R. 546—§ 8–17, n. 17, 49.
Hotchkiss, In re, 75 B.R. 115—§ 8–17, n. 32, 49, 51.
Houdashell, Matter of—§ 6-43, n. 16, 19.
Hougland, In re—§ 9-16, n. 5; § 9-18, n. 13.
House of Deals of Broward, Inc., In re—§ 5-10, n. 5.
Houtman, In re—§ 7-26, n. 39.
Houts, In re—§ 6-61, n. 60.
Howard, In re, 73 B.R. 694—§ 7–26, n. 35.
Howard, In re, 43 B.R. 135—§ 6–62, n. 3, 5, 18, 38.
Howard v. Allard—§ 3-20; § 3-20, n. 20; § 3-22, n. 3, 5.
Howard's Appliance Corp., In re, 874 F.2d 88—§ 6-61, n. 38, 42, 79.
Howards Appliance Corp., In re, 91 B.R. 204—§ 6-2, n. 9.
Howe, In re—§ 5-17, n. 3.
Howe, Matter of—§ 3-31, n. 51.
Howell, In re, 84 B.R. 834—§ 10–31, n. 1.
Howell, In re, 51 B.R. 1015—§ 8–9, n. 13, 15; § 8–31, n. 4.
Howland, In re—§ 8-3, n. 30; § 8-19, n. 15, 20.
Hoyos Precsas, Matter of—§ 6-2, n. 9, 20.
Hoyt, Matter of—§ 3-23, n. 45.
H.P. King Co., Inc., In re—§ 6-87, n. 14.
HRT Industries, Inc., In re—§ 6-65, n. 12.
H & S Transp. Co., Inc., In re, 939 F.2d 355—§ 6–10, n. 9.
H & S Transp. Co., Inc., In re, 80 B.R. 441—§ 6–25, n. 20; § 6–34, n. 11.
H & S Transp. Co., Inc., In re, 42 B.R. 164—§ 6–62, n. 11, 19, 41.
Hubbard, In re—§ 9-18, n. 12.
Hubbard Mill. Co. v. Citizens State Bank—§ 6-92, n. 3, 5.
Huber, In re—§ 9-19, n. 7.
Hubka, Matter of—§ 9-27, n. 5, 8.
Hubler, United States v.—§ 3-21, n. 7, 101; § 7-8, n. 5.
Hucke, In re—§ 3-20, n. 18.
Huddleston v. Texas Commerce Bank–Dallas, N.A.—§ 3-32, n. 7, 34.
Hudgins, In re—§ 11-5, n. 9.
Hudson, In re, 859 F.2d 1418—§ 7–34, n. 3.
Hudson, In re, 56 B.R. 415—§ 7–45, n. 13.
Hudson Feather & Down Products, Inc., Matter of—§ 10-32, n. 1.
Hudson Oil Co., Inc., In re—§ 6-39, n. 1.
Huebner, In re—§ 11-14, n. 13.
Huffman v. Perkinson (In re Harbour)—§ 12–14, n. 20.
Hughes, In re—§ 3-21, n. 11.
Hughes, Matter of—§ 6-62, n. 26.
Hughes–Bechtol, Inc., Matter of, 117 B.R. 890—§ 3–1, n. 20; § 3–14, n. 4, 38.
Hughes–Bechtol, Inc., Matter of, 107 B.R. 552—§ 11–5, n. 8.
Hughes Marina, Inc., In re—§ 11-17, n. 2.
Hughson, In re—§ 6-15, n. 3.
Hugo, In re, 58 B.R. 903—§ 6–77, n. 7, 22, 26; § 6–78, n. 3.
Hugo, In re, 50 B.R. 963—§ 6–77, n. 7.
Huizar, In re—§ 6-17, n. 11; § 6-93, n. 28.
Hulk, Matter of—§ 6-49, n. 34.
Hulm, In re—§ 6-4, n. 2; § 6-21, n. 1, 8; § 6-53, n. 6; § 6-54, n. 2, 10; § 6-56; § 6-56, n. 40.
Hultquist, In re—§ 7-28, n. 4.
Hulvey, In re—§ 3-6, n. 2; § 3-12, n. 2; § 8-24, n. 5; § 8-27, n. 9.
Humble Place Joint Venture, In re—§ 3-29, n. 5.
Humphrey, In re—§ 7-34, n. 14, 15.
Humphreys, In re—§ 2-17, n. 15.
Hundley, In re—§ 2-11, n. 4; § 3-29, n. 13.
Hunerdosse, Matter of—§ 6-77, n. 8; § 8-2, n. 3; § 8-24, n. 2.
Hunsucker, In re—§ 8-17, n. 35, 36.
Hunt, In re—§ 3-21, n. 126; § 3-22, n. 29.
Hunt v. Bankers Trust Co.—§ 3-6, n. 40.
Hunt Energy Co., Inc., In re—§ 4-7, n. 6, 18.
Hunter, In re—§ 7-26, n. 5.

Hunter, Matter of—§ 8-10, n. 26.
Hunters Run Ltd. Partnership, In re—§ 6-61, n. 60.
Hurricane Elkhorn Coal Corp. II, In re—§ 6-43, n. 4, 15.
Hurst Lincoln–Mercury, Inc., In re—§ 5-10, n. 15.
Hussey, In re—§ 7-26, n. 50, 53.
Hutchens, In re—§ 9-3, n. 12, 33.
Hutchinson, In re—§ 8-31, n. 9.
H. Wolfe Iron & Metal Co., In re—§ 6-40, n. 25; § 6-45, n. 12.
Hyden, In re—§ 9-18, n. 13, 16.
Hydraulic Indus. Products, Co., In re—§ 6-17, n. 5, 7.
Hyman, In re, 123 B.R. 342—§ 8-8, n. 2, 3.
Hyman, In re, 82 B.R. 23—§ 9-27; § 9-27, n. 11, 14.

I

Iacovoni, In re—§ 9-7; § 9-7, n. 5, 6; § 9-14, n. 4, 13.
Ian Homes, Inc., In re—§ 3-18, n. 21; § 6-61, n. 24.
I.C.C. v. Holmes Transp., Inc.—§ 3-1, n. 7.
IDK Logging, Inc., In re—§ 6-61, n. 16.
Ikeda, In re—§ 3-10, n. 50; § 7-45, n. 4.
Ikner, In re—§ 7-30, n. 10, 27.
Illinois v. Electrical Utilities—§ 3-21, n. 39.
Illinois–California Exp., Inc., In re—§ 12-2, n. 13; § 12-5, n. 2.
IML Freight, Inc., In re—§ 6-39, n. 17, 39; § 6-40, n. 16; § 6-42, n. 2, 4; § 6-43, n. 7; § 6-45, n. 2.
Income Property Builders, Inc., In re—§ 3-23, n. 23, 25, 27, 28, 30.
Independence Bank v. Heller—§ 8-6, n. 10.
Independent Clearing House Co., In re—§ 6-50, n. 5, 9, 10, 11, 12, 15, 18, 21; § 6-52, n. 22.
Indri, In re—§ 5-3, n. 3; § 6-47, n. 7.
Industrial Distribution Services, Inc., In re—§ 6-4, n. 17; § 6-15, n. 9.
Industrial & Mun. Engineering, Inc., In re—§ 6-30, n. 3; § 6-87, n. 14.
Industrial Supply Corp., In re, 109 B.R. 484—§ 6-31, n. 9; § 6-34, n. 10.
Industrial Supply Corp., In re, 108 B.R. 799—§ 12-15, n. 2.
Industrial Valley Refrigeration and Air Conditioning Supplies, Inc., In re—§ 4-4; § 4-4, n. 1, 2, 6.
Indvik, In re—§ 8-28, n. 9; § 8-29, n. 7, 8.
Infosystems Technology, Inc. v. Logical Software, Inc.—§ 5-8, n. 12.
Ingersoll, In re—§ 6-40, n. 2, 16, 22, 37; § 7-21, n. 3.
Ingersoll–Rand Financial Corp. v. Miller Min. Co., Inc.—§ 3-5, n. 6; § 3-6, n. 30, 35.
Ingersoll–Rand Financial Corp. v. Nunley—§ 6-61, n. 11, 53.
Innis, In re—§ 8-17, n. 13, 35, 36.
In re (see name of party)
Inslaw, Inc., In re—§ 6-39, n. 13, 38; § 6-42, n. 2.
Inslaw, Inc., United States v., 932 F.2d 1467—§ 3-14, n. 7, 15.
Inslaw, Inc., United States v., 113 B.R. 802—§ 3-33, n. 6; § 3-34; § 3-34, n. 15.
Installation Services, Inc., Matter of—§ 6-10, n. 13; § 6-25, n. 13; § 6-88, n. 54.
Insurance Co. of Pa. v. Ben Cooper, Inc.—§ 12-16, n. 10.
Insurance Co. of State of Pennsylvania v. Ben Cooper, Inc.—§ 12-16; § 12-16, n. 8.
Intaco Puerto Rico, Inc., In re—§ 10-31, n. 6; § 11-3, n. 21.
Integrated Petroleum Co., Inc., In re—§ 3-28, n. 12.
Integrated Testing Products Corp., In re—§ 6-77, n. 1, 8; § 6-86, n. 4.
Intercity Oil Co., Inc., In re—§ 6-67, n. 10.
Intermagnetics America, Inc., In re—§ 6-70, n. 3.
Intermountain Porta Storage, Inc., In re—§ 6-38, n. 18; § 6-39, n. 34; § 6-41, n. 47.
International Airport Inn Partnership, In re—§ 2-13; § 2-13, n. 5.
International Club Enterprises, Inc., In re—§ 6-7, n. 7.
International Gold Bullion Exchange, Inc., Matter of—§ 6-85, n. 16.
International Harvester Credit Corp. v. Ross—§ 8-13, n. 7.
International Harvester Emp. Credit Union, Inc. v. Daniel—§ 3-10, n. 65.
International Horizons, Inc., Matter of—§ 10-13, n. 7; § 12-12, n. 25.
International Radiator Co., In re—§ 6-52, n. 49.
International Shoe Co. v. Pinkus—§ 1-3, n. 1.
International Ski Service, Inc., In re—§ 6-87, n. 6.
International Teldata Corp., Matter of—§ 6-71, n. 11.
International Trade Admin. v. Rensselaer Polytechnic Institute—§ 5-2, n. 7.
International Union v. Miles Machinery Co.—§ 5-1, n. 1.
Interpictures, Inc., In re—§ 11-16, n. 6.
Interstate Agency, Inc., In re—§ 7-28, n. 8.

TABLE OF CASES

Inter-State National Bank of Kansas City v. Luther—§ 12-2, n. 11.
Invesco Intern. Corp., Matter of—§ 3-20, n. 37.
Iola State Bank v. Bolan—§ 6-38, n. 10.
Ionosphere Clubs, Inc., In re, 922 F.2d 984—§ 3-7; § 3-7, n. 3, 5, 8; § 3-22, n. 7.
Ionosphere Clubs Inc., In re, 124 B.R. 635—§ 3-6, n. 61, 62; § 3-22, n. 5, 25; § 3-33, n. 5.
Ionosphere Clubs, Inc., In re, 123 B.R. 166—§ 3-17, n. 4, 5.
Ionosphere Clubs, Inc., In re, 114 B.R. 379—§ 3-22, n. 22.
Ionosphere Clubs, Inc., In re, 108 B.R. 951—§ 12-5, n. 10.
Ionosphere Clubs, Inc., In re, 101 B.R. 844—§ 11-8, n. 10.
Ionosphere Clubs, Inc., In re, 100 B.R. 670—§ 10-5, n. 11.
Ionosphere Clubs, Inc., In re, 98 B.R. 174—§ 4-4, n. 1.
Iowa-Missouri Realty Co., Inc., In re—§ 6-2, n. 9; § 6-61, n. 18, 29, 77.
Iowa Premium Service Co., Inc., In re—§ 6-19, n. 16; § 6-32, n. 8.
IPI Liberty Village Associates, In re—§ 6-56, n. 5, 52.
Ipswich Bituminous Concrete Products, Inc., In re, 82 B.R. 661—§ 6-47, n. 8.
Ipswich Bituminous Concrete Products, Inc., In re 79 B.R. 511—§ 6-49, n. 23, 28; § 6-52, n. 49.
Irvine, In re—§ 6-37, n. 8, 9; § 8-25, n. 5, 6.
Isakson, Matter of—§ 8-18, n. 10.
Isbell, Matter of—§ 6-40, n. 5.
Isis Foods, Inc., Matter of—§ 6-38, n. 21, 22; § 6-39, n. 2; § 6-40, n. 5, 9; § 6-42, n. 2; § 6-69, n. 7.
Island Club Marina, Ltd., In re—§ 3-21, n. 56.
Island Helicopter Corp., In re—§ 6-78, n. 2.
Israel, In re—§ 7-47, n. 2.
Italiano, In re—§ 6-61, n. 30, 67.
I.T.T. Small Business Finance Corp. v. Frederique—§ 3-16, n. 14.
Iverson, In re—§ 7-26, n. 37.
Ivy, In re—§ 9-25; § 9-25, n. 11, 12.

J

Jablonski, In re—§ 9-18, n. 9, 13.
Jackels, In re—§ 6-76, n. 2.
Jackson, In re, 115 B.R. 286—§ 8-27, n. 11.
Jackson, In re, 105 B.R. 15—§ 6-47, n. 8.
Jackson, In re, 86 B.R. 251—§ 8-28, n. 3.
Jackson, In re, 90 B.R. 793—§ 6-32, n. 5.
Jackson, In re, 77 B.R. 120—§ 7-34, n. 5.
Jackson, In re, 48 B.R. 616—§ 3-12, n. 5, 8.
Jackson Brewing Co., Matter of—§ 5-8, n. 4.
Jackson County Escrow Services, Inc., In re—§ 3-30, n. 35.
J.A. Clark Mechanical, Inc., In re—§ 6-40, n. 14, 16, 26, 32.
Jacobs, In re, 60 B.R. 811—§ 6-47, n. 13; § 6-48, n. 8, 22; § 6-50, n. 6, 16, 19.
Jacobs, In re, 43 B.R. 971—§ 2-13, n. 14.
Jacobsen, In re—§ 3-10, n. 65.
Jacobson, In re—§ 6-49, n. 8; § 6-56, n. 5, 52.
Jacobson, United States v.—§ 9-2, n. 11.
James, In re, 940 F.2d 46—§ 3-21, n. 5, 10.
James, In re, 126 B.R. 360—§ 8-33, n. 20.
James, In re, 120 B.R. 802—§ 3-2, n. 6; § 3-3, n. 4; § 3-6, n. 4; § 3-34, n. 9; § 6-94, n. 8.
James, In re, 112 B.R. 687—§ 6-94, n. 8.
James A. Phillips, Inc., In re—§ 4-3; § 4-3, n. 4, 5; § 4-12; § 4-12, n. 1; § 4-15; § 4-15, n. 2; § 10-6, n. 4; § 10-24; § 10-24, n. 11; § 10-34; § 10-34, n. 2.
James B. Downing & Co., In re, 94 B.R. 515—§ 3-27, n. 45.
James B. Downing & Co., In re, 74 B.R. 906—§ 6-69, n. 10.
Jameson's Foods, Inc., In re—§ 6-87; § 6-88, n. 24, 30, 32, 37, 40.
Jamison, In re, 93 B.R. 595—§ 8-28, n. 7, 25.
Jamison, In re, 21 B.R. 380—§ 6-49, n. 62, 69.
Janesofsky, In re—§ 8-21, n. 4.
Janis, In re—§ 3-6, n. 4; § 3-32, n. 32.
Janovski, In re—§ 3-30, n. 14.
Janssen, In re—§ 6-62, n. 3.
Jardine, In re—§ 6-2, n. 16; § 8-23, n. 8.
Jarrett, Matter of—§ 9-3, n. 5.
Jartran, Inc., In re, 886 F.2d 859—§ 2-16; § 2-16, n. 18.
Jartran, Inc., In re, 87 B.R. 525—§ 11-10, n. 1.
Jartran, Inc., In re, 78 B.R. 524—§ 10-10, n. 1.

Jartran, Inc., In re, 71 B.R. 938—§ **2-16**; § **2-16, n. 19**; § **2-17, n. 20**.
Jartran, Inc., In re, 44 B.R. 331—§ **11-28**; § **11-28, n. 5, 7, 8**; § **11-29**; § **11-29, n. 1, 5, 13, 14**; § **11-30**; § **11-30, n. 2, 3, 17**.
Jarvis, In re—§ **9-3, n. 27**.
Jarvis Kitchenware of D.C., Inc., In re—§ **6-39, n. 13**; § **6-94, n. 6**.
J.A.S. Markets, Inc., In re—§ **6-11, n. 7**; § **6-35, n. 7, 19**.
J.B. Winchells, Inc., In re—§ **6-62, n. 22, 26**.
J. Catton Farms, Inc. v. First Nat. Bank of Chicago—§ **6-77, n. 1**; § **6-78, n. 11**.
J.D. Marshall Intern., Inc. v. Redstart, Inc.—§ **12-5, n. 5, 8**.
Jeanes Mechanical Contractors Inc., In re—§ **6-65, n. 12**; § **6-66, n. 4**.
Jeens of Puerto Rico, Inc., Matter of—§ **3-20, n. 7**.
Jefferson, In re—§ **6-2, n. 5, 21**.
Jefferson Mortg. Co., Inc., Matter of—§ **6-17, n. 11**; § **6-35, n. 33**.
Jeffrey Bigelow Design Group, Inc., In re—§ **6-19, n. 16**; § **6-32, n. 9**; § **6-49, n. 50**.
J.E. Jennings, Inc., In re—§ **6-2, n. 32**; § **6-83, n. 12**; § **6-84, n. 5**; § **11-17, n. 3**.
Jelinek, In re—§ **8-1, n. 11**.
Jenkins, In re, 664 F.2d 184—§ **2-5, n. 4**.
Jenkins, In re, 74 B.R. 440—§ **6-61, n. 22**.
Jenkins, In re, 4 B.R. 651—§ **7-37, n. 2**.
Jennings, In re—§ **3-20, n. 7, 13, 26**.
Jennings, Matter of—§ **7-43, n. 2**.
Jensen, In re—§ **7-7**; § **7-7, n. 10, 14**.
Jensen v. State Bank of Allison—§ **6-38, n. 13**.
Jeppson, In re—§ **11-17, n. 2**; § **11-18, n. 8**.
Jermoo's Inc., Matter of—§ **6-2, n. 28, 30**; § **6-47, n. 7**.
Jerry–Sue Fashions, Inc., In re, 91 B.R. 1006—§ **6-31, n. 17**.
Jerry–Sue Fashions, Inc., In re, 89 B.R. 995—§ **6-31, n. 17**.
Jersey City Medical Center, Matter of—§ **10-22, n. 7**.
Jessen, Matter of—§ **9-27, n. 11**.
Jet Florida Systems, Inc., In re, 841 F.2d 1082—§ **6-25, n. 7, 11**.
Jet Florida Systems, Inc., In re, 105 B.R. 137—§ **6-88, n. 37**.
Jet Florida Systems, Inc., In re, 80 B.R. 544—§ **6-39, n. 1**.
Jet Florida Systems, Inc., In re, 73 B.R. 552—§ **6-83, n. 12**; § **6-88, n. 36**.
Jet Florida Systems, Inc., In re, 69 B.R. 83—§ **6-88, n. 35**.
Jewelers Shipping Ass'n, In re—§ **3-23, n. 40**.
J.F. Hink & Son, In re—§ **5-17, n. 4**.
J.I.C. Installations, Inc., In re—§ **6-16, n. 1**.
Jim Nolker Chevrolet-Buick-Oldsmobile, Inc., In re—§ **3-33, n. 6**; § **3-35, n. 2**.
J. J. Bradley & Co., Inc., Matter of—§ **3-21, n. 37**.
JJ's Home Style Laundry, Inc., In re—§ **6-61, n. 77, 79**.
J.L. Graphics, Inc., In re—§ **4-15, n. 14**; § **6-77, n. 22**.
J & L Transport, Inc., Matter of—§ **3-14, n. 39**.
J.M. Fields, Inc., In re—§ **10-32, n. 1**.
Joe Flynn Rare Coins, Inc., In re—§ **6-2, n. 28**; § **6-18**; § **6-18, n. 4, 9**; § **6-20, n. 23**; § **6-35, n. 47, 49**.
Joe T. Dehmer Distributors, Inc. v. Temple—§ **6-60, n. 17**.
John Deere Co. v. Alamosa Nat. Bank—§ **3-16, n. 20**.
John Deskins Pic Pac, Inc., In re—§ **6-62, n. 11, 39, 41**.
John I. Paulding, Inc., In re—§ **6-86, n. 13, 15**.
John L. Motley Associates, Inc. v. Rumbaugh—§ **6-94, n. 8**.
John O. Melby & Co. Bank v. Anderson—§ **8-11, n. 28**.
John Peterson Motors, Inc., In re—§ **10-10**; § **10-10, n. 1, 7**.
Johns–Manville Corp., In re, 837 F.2d 89—§ **3-22, n. 8**.
Johns–Manville Corp., In re, 824 F.2d 176—§ **10-2, n. 4**.
Johns–Manville Corp., In re, 801 F.2d 60—§ **10-7**; § **10-7, n. 3, 8, 9, 10**; § **12-2, n. 5**.
Johns–Manville Corp., In re, 68 B.R. 155—§ **10-12**; § **10-12, n. 9**.
Johns–Manville Corp., In re, 60 B.R. 612—§ **4-3, n. 3**; § **10-6, n. 1, 4**.
Johns–Manville Corp., In re, 57 B.R. 680—§ **3-6, n. 67**; § **7-7, n. 16**; § **11-3, n. 7, 13, 17**; § **11-4, n. 7**.
Johns–Manville Corp., In re, 45 B.R. 833—§ **10-2, n. 4**.
Johns–Manville Corp., In re, 42 B.R. 651—§ **10-2, n. 4**.
Johns–Manville Corp., In re, 42 B.R. 362—§ **11-16, n. 6**.
Johns–Manville Corp., In re, 39 B.R. 234—§ **10-2, n. 4**.
Johns–Manville Corp., In re, 36 B.R. 743—§ **11-2, n. 3**; § **11-3, n. 14**; § **11-8, n. 2**.
Johns–Manville Corp., In re, 36 B.R. 727—§ **2-2, n. 1**; § **2-15**; § **2-15, n. 14**; § **11-1, n. 6**; § **11-8, n. 1**.
Johns–Manville Corp., Matter of—§ **11-5, n. 3**; § **11-6, n. 12**; § **11-8, n. 11, 12**; § **11-17, n. 3**.
Johnson, In re, 904 F.2d 563—§ **9-30, n. 4**.

Johnson, In re, 880 F.2d 78—§ 8–32, n. 16, 22, 26, 27.
Johnson, In re, 756 F.2d 738—§ 3–31, n. 58.
Johnson, In re, 708 F.2d 865—§ 9–14, n. 16, 17.
Johnson, In re, 691 F.2d 249—§ 7–28, n. 10.
Johnson, In re, 120 B.R. 992—§ 8–33, n. 27.
Johnson, In re, 115 B.R. 159—§ 7–45, n. 1.
Johnson, In re, 105 B.R. 352—§ 6–61, n. 16.
Johnson, In re, 101 B.R. 280—§ 8–6, n. 4, 5; § 8–25, n. 34.
Johnson, In re, 96 B.R. 326—§ 9–30, n. 3.
Johnson, In re, 90 B.R. 973—§ 3–31, n. 84.
Johnson, In re, 53 B.R. 919—§ 6–6, n. 7; § 6–37, n. 4; § 8–23, n. 9.
Johnson, In re, 39 B.R. 358—§ 6–61, n. 55.
Johnson, In re, 36 B.R. 958—§ 9–20, n. 11.
Johnson, In re, 36 B.R. 54—§ 8–17, n. 33, 51.
Johnson, In re, 32 B.R. 614—§ 9–2, n. 11.
Johnson, In re, 30 B.R. 467—§ 8–13, n. 5.
Johnson, In re, 26 B.R. 381—§ 6–2, n. 14.
Johnson, In re, 25 B.R. 889—§ 6–36, n. 17.
Johnson, In re, 13 B.R. 342—§ 2–5, n. 4.
Johnson, In re, 12 B.R. 894—§ 3–10, n. 72.
Johnson, Matter of, 787 F.2d 1179—§ 9–2, n. 10.
Johnson, Matter of, 724 F.2d 1138—§ 8–33, n. 24.
Johnson, Matter of, 47 B.R. 204—§ 6–77, n. 1, 23; § 6–78, n. 2.
Johnson v. Dutch Mill Dairy—§ 6-15, n. 2.
Johnson v. Edinboro State College—§ 7-41, n. 18.
Johnson v. Fairco Corp.—§ 5-8; § 5-8, n. 7.
Johnson v. First Nat. Bank—§ 6-49, n. 31, 39, 49, 51, 62; § 6-51, n. 24, 25.
Johnson v. First Nat. Bank of Montevideo, Minn.—§ 3-16, n. 11, 13.
Johnson v. Home State Bank—§ 2-2; § 2-2, n. 23; § 2-16; § 2-16, n. 8; § 7-47, n. 5; § 9-18, n. 16; § 9-30; § 9-30, n. 1, 5, 11.
Johnson v. Philadelphia Elec. Co.—§ 3-9, n. 33, 34.
Johnson v. Star—§ 1-3, n. 1.
Johnson–Allen, In re, 871 F.2d 421—§ 6-19, n. 4.
Johnson–Allen, In re, 69 B.R. 461—§ 7-31, n. 10; § 8-22, n. 19; § 8-23, n. 5.
Johnson–Allen, In re, 67 B.R. 968—§ 9-18, n. 6.
Johnson, Wilson and Dillon, In re—§ 6-77, n. 19.
Johnston Hawks, Ltd., In re—§ 2-5, n. 12.
John T. Mather Memorial Hosp. of Port Jefferson, Inc. v. Pearl—§ 8-3, n. 6; § 8-21, n. 4.
Joing v. O & P Partnership—§ 6-56, n. 52; § 8-23, n. 5.
Join–In Intern. (U.S.A.) Ltd., In re—§ 6-49, n. 49, 65, 66, 70; § 6-51, n. 11.
Jolly, In re, 574 F.2d 349—§ 5-4, n. 12.
Jolly, In re, 106 B.R. 299—§ 12-10, n. 1, 2.
Jolly N, Inc., In re—§ 6-16, n. 1; § 6-25, n. 11; § 6-28, n. 1, 2; § 6-34, n. 10, 17, 18, 20.
Jones, In re, 908 F.2d 859—§ 6-76, n. 2.
Jones, In re, 121 B.R. 122—§ 3-5, n. 16; § 3-13, n. 7; § 3-14, n. 21.
Jones, In re, 116 B.R. 810—§ 8-25, n. 7.
Jones, In re, 112 B.R. 770—§ 2-5, n. 2.
Jones, In re, 107 B.R. 888—§ 6-40, n. 16, 23.
Jones, In re, 106 B.R. 33—§ 3-10, n. 58.
Jones, In re, 87 B.R. 738—§ 8-3, n. 21; § 8-25, n. 32, 52, 55, 58, 62.
Jones, In re, 77 B.R. 541—§ 6-61, n. 41.
Jones, In re, 55 B.R. 462—§ 9-13; § 9-13, n. 5, 6, 9.
Jones, In re, 37 B.R. 969—§ 6-2, n. 28, 30; § 6-49, n. 49, 50, 52; § 6-51, n. 24, 29.
Jones, In re, 20 B.R. 988—§ 6-50, n. 37; § 6-53, n. 3, 6; § 6-54, n. 10; § 6-56, n. 17; § 6-72, n. 10; § 6-88, n. 14; § 6-89, n. 4, 9, 15, 16, 24.
Jones, Matter of, 119 B.R. 996—§ 3-25, n. 2, 8, 10, 31, 37.
Jones, Matter of, 68 B.R. 483—§ 6-47, n. 7; § 6-48, n. 8; § 6-88, n. 17; § 6-89, n. 8.
Jones, Matter of, 43 B.R. 1002—§ 8-33, n. 17, 20.
Jones v. Harrell—§ 6-68, n. 2; § 6-74, n. 12.
Jones & Lamson Mach. Co., Inc., In re—§ 6-2, n. 1, 24; § 6-61, n. 58; § 6-62, n. 25.
Jones & Laughlin Steel Corp., United States v.—§ 3-21, n. 7, 44, 82.
Jonson, In re—§ 9-14, n. 21.
Jorges Carpet Mills, Inc., In re, 50 B.R. 84—§ 6-88, n. 14, 21.
Jorges Carpet Mills, Inc., In re, 41 B.R. 60—§ 6-71, n. 7, 16, 21.
Joseph M. Eaton Builders, Inc., In re, 84 B.R. 56—§ 6-20, n. 22; § 6-25, n. 23.
Joseph M. Eaton Builders, Inc., In re, 82 B.R. 775—§ 6-4, n. 17; § 6-7, n. 7.
Josephs, In re—§ 3-16, n. 9, 10.
Joshua Slocum Ltd., In re, 922 F.2d 1081—§ 5-20; § 5-20, n. 4, 9, 10.

Joshua Slocum, Ltd., In re, 103 B.R. 610—§ **6-16, n. 1**; § **6-17, n. 29**; § **6-52, n. 49**.
Joshua Slocum, Ltd., In re, 99 B.R. 261—§ **4-4, n. 4**.
Joy, In re—§ **6-86, n. 4**.
Joyanna Holitogs, Inc., Matter of—§ **6-2, n. 28**.
J.P. Fyfe, Inc. of Florida v. Bradco Supply Corp.—§ **6-31, n. 10**.
J.P. Linahan, Inc., In re—§ **10-7, n. 8**.
J. R. Nieves & Co., In re—§ **6-62, n. 28**.
JRT, Inc., Matter of—§ **5-7, n. 19**.
J. T. Gerken Trucking, Inc., In re—§ **10-32, n. 1**.
Jug End in the Berkshires, Inc., In re—§ **3-31, n. 68**.
Julien Co., In re, 127 B.R. 604—§ **6-20, n. 20**.
Julien Co., In re, 120 B.R. 930—§ **2-4, n. 2**.
Julien Co., In re, 116 B.R. 623—§ **3-15, n. 6**; § **6-39, n. 15**.
Julien J. Studley, Inc. v. Lefrak—§ **6-52, n. 48**.
Juneau's Builders Center, Inc., In re—§ **3-10, n. 3, 4**.
Just for the Fun of It of Tennessee, Inc., In re—§ **6-93, n. 41**.
Justus, In re—§ **6-31, n. 19**.
Justus Hospitality Properties, Ltd., In re—§ **2-19, n. 5**.
Jutila, In re—§ **9-4, n. 41**.
J. Woodson Hays, Inc., Matter of—§ **3-10, n. 65**.

K

Kachanizadeh, In re—§ **6-56, n. 8**.
Kaczorowski, Matter of—§ **6-49, n. 36**; § **6-56, n. 14**; § **6-87, n. 8**.
Kadison, In re—§ **7-20, n. 8**.
Kaelin Associates Elec. Const., Inc., In re—§ **6-83, n. 1, 2, 4, 12**.
Kain, Matter of—§ **6-77, n. 1**; § **6-78, n. 17**.
Kaiser, In re—§ **6-48, n. 7, 8**; § **7-19, n. 5**.
Kaiser Steel Corp., In re, 952 F.2d 1230—§ **6-52**; § **6-52, n. 32, 51**; § **6-85, n. 13**.
Kaiser Steel Corp., In re, 911 F.2d 380—§ **3-30, n. 29**; § **12-16, n. 6**.
Kaiser Steel Corp., In re, 110 B.R. 514—§ **6-85, n. 14**; § **6-88, n. 35**.
Kaiser Steel Corp., In re, 110 B.R. 20—§ **6-40, n. 27**.
Kaiser Steel Corp., In re, 109 B.R. 968—§ **12-15, n. 2**.
Kaiser Steel Corp. v. Charles Schwab & Co., Inc.—§ **6-52, n. 33**; § **6-85**; § **6-85, n. 11, 12**.
Kam Kuo Seafood Corp., In re—§ **6-84, n. 2**.
Kan-Ag Grain Terminal Co., In re—§ **6-31, n. 17**.
Kanawha Trace Development Partners, In re—§ **11-18, n. 1**.
Kane v. Johns-Manville Corp.—§ **10-31**; § **10-31, n. 7**; § **11-5, n. 3**; § **11-6, n. 12**; § **11-8**; § **11-8, n. 12, 13**.
Kangas, In re—§ **6-54, n. 3, 10**; § **6-55, n. 22**.
Kannry & Morton, Inc., In re—§ **6-7, n. 4**.
Kansas City Terminal Ry. Co. v. Central Union Trust Co.—§ **11-25, n. 1**; § **11-26**; § **11-26, n. 6**.
Kantack v. Kreuer—§ **6-56, n. 1**.
Kanterman, In re—§ **6-88, n. 8, 27, 37**.
Kaplan, In re—§ **8-3, n. 22**; § **8-33, n. 17, 24**.
Kapler v. Atkinson—§ **4-9, n. 12**.
Karelin, In re—§ **7-26**; § **7-26, n. 17, 18**.
Karpe, In re—§ **4-4**; § **4-4, n. 4**; § **4-17, n. 11**.
Karsh Travel, Inc., In re—§ **3-33, n. 8, 12, 18, 21**.
Katchen v. Landy—§ **11-7, n. 6**; § **12-2, n. 11**; § **12-13**; § **12-13, n. 1, 6**; § **12-14**; § **12-14, n. 19**.
Kaveney, In re—§ **11-32**; § **11-32, n. 4**.
Kawczynski, Matter of—§ **7-28, n. 8**.
Kazi, In re—§ **8-1, n. 12**; § **8-33, n. 17, 24**.
Kazzaz, In re—§ **9-2, n. 6**; § **9-9, n. 2**.
K.B. Oil Co. v. Ford Motor Credit Co., Inc.—§ **6-56, n. 1**.
Kearney Hotel Partners, In re—§ **6-77, n. 11**.
Keating, In re—§ **7-34, n. 13**.
Keen, In re—§ **2-16, n. 26**.
Keenan, In re, 106 B.R. 239—§ **8-23, n. 9**; § **8-26, n. 7**; § **8-29, n. 12**.
Keenan, In re, 96 B.R. 197—§ **6-61, n. 21, 74**.
Keenen, Matter of—§ **6-48, n. 11**; § **6-50, n. 12**; § **6-87, n. 6**.
Kehm, In re—§ **9-18, n. 13**.
Keinath, In re—§ **8-27, n. 9**.
Keiser, Matter of—§ **9-14, n. 13**.
Kelley, In re, 22 B.R. 150—§ **3-10, n. 81**.

Kelley, In re, 7 B.R. 384—§ 6-47, n. 13; § 6-49, n. 35.
Kelly, In re, 841 F.2d 908—§ 2-14, n. 4; § 6-37, n. 15; § 7-45; § 7-45, n. 1, 5, 13, 14.
Kelly, In re, 125 B.R. 301—§ 3-25, n. 6; § 3-26, n. 10; § 3-30, n. 10, 19.
Kelly v. Robinson—§ 3-20, n. 45; § 7-31; § 7-31, n. 5; § 7-34.
Kelsey, In re—§ 9-3, n. 11.
Kelton Motors Inc., In re—§ 3-10, n. 11; § 6-93, n. 50.
Kel-Wood Timber Products Co., In re—§ 6-20, n. 17.
Kemble, In re—§ 3-30, n. 30; § 12-12, n. 14.
Kenderdine, In re—§ 6-45, n. 7.
Kendrick, In re—§ 7-36, n. 3.
Ken Gardner Ford Sales, Inc., In re—§ 6-35, n. 18.
Kenitra, Inc., In re—§ 6-88, n. 14.
Kennedy, In re—§ 7-3, n. 6.
Kennedy Mortg.Co., Matter of—§ 6-38, n. 21, 22.
Kennesaw Mint, Inc., Matter of—§ 6-69, n. 13.
Kenny, Matter of—§ 6-93, n. 40.
Kentech Corp., In re—§ 3-9, n. 14, 32.
Kent Holland Die Casting & Plating, Inc., In re—§ 6-84, n. 2.
Kentucky Flush Door Corp., In re—§ 6-65, n. 12; § 6-66, n. 5; § 6-67, n. 3.
Kenval Marketing Corp., In re—§ 6-59, n. 2; § 6-60, n. 8, 22.
Kern, In re—§ 9-13, n. 4.
Kerr, In re—§ 8-11, n. 18; § 8-17, n. 17.
Kershaw v. Behm—§ 7-23; § 7-23, n. 1.
Kervin, In re—§ 2-8, n. 23.
Ketelsen, In re—§ 3-33, n. 34, 40.
Ketelsen, United States v.—§ 3-15, n. 6; § 3-33, n. 33, 35, 37; § 3-34, n. 21; § 3-35, n. 2; § 6-43, n. 15.
Keul, In re—§ 9-3; § 9-3, n. 32.
Keydata Corp., In re, 37 B.R. 324—§ 6-18, n. 25.
Keydata Corp., In re, 12 B.R. 156—§ 3-9, n. 19, 22.
Keyworth, In re—§ 8-18, n. 6.
Keziah, In re—§ 2-2, n. 22.
Kham & Nate's Shoes No. 2, Inc., In re—§ 3-22, n. 5, 26.
Kham & Nate's Shoes No. 2, Inc. v. First Bank of Whiting—§ 6-93, n. 42, 46; § 11-27, n. 12; § 11-28; § 11-28, n. 2, 4; § 11-29, n. 1, 2.
Kidder Skis Intern. v. Williams—§ 6-48, n. 21; § 6-50, n. 10, 16; § 6-59, n. 3; § 6-87, n. 8.
Killian Const. Co., Inc., Matter of—§ 6-83, n. 7.
Killough, Matter of—§ 9-13, n. 3.
Kimble, In re—§ 2-13, n. 6.
Kimzey, In re—§ 7-26; § 7-26, n. 5, 29, 33; § 7-30, n. 18.
Kincaid, In re, 917 F.2d 1162—§ 8-33, n. 18, 20.
Kincaid, In re, 96 B.R. 1014—§ 8-3, n. 19.
King, In re, 75 B.R. 287—§ 7-39, n. 3; § 7-49; § 7-49, n. 4, 6, 9.
King, In re, 9 B.R. 376—§ 9-3, n. 12, 20.
King, Matter of—§ 6-72, n. 1; § 6-73, n. 10.
King Arthur Clock Co., Inc., In re—§ 6-20, n. 20; § 6-87, n. 8, 10.
King Memorial Hosp., Inc., In re—§ 3-21, n. 56.
King-Porter Co., In re—§ 6-35, n. 3.
Kinnan & Kinnan Partnership v. Agristor Leasing—§ 5-23, n. 11.
Kinney, In re—§ 3-29, n. 13.
Kinser, In re—§ 7-49, n. 6.
Kiriluk, In re—§ 3-9, n. 9, 11.
Kirk v. Texaco, Inc.—§ 11-17, n. 8.
Kitchens, In re—§ 9-14, n. 5, 13.
K.I.T. Motor Exp., Inc., In re—§ 6-39, n. 9, 34.
Kitson, In re—§ 9-12, n. 4; § 9-13; § 9-13, n. 5, 11; § 9-14, n. 7.
Kittrell, In re—§ 6-20, n. 20; § 6-36, n. 12; § 6-38, n. 18; § 6-41, n. 19; § 6-62, n. 38.
Kjeldahl, In re, 52 B.R. 926—§ 6-56, n. 52.
Kjeldahl, In re, 52 B.R. 916—§ 6-54, n. 2.
Klapp, In re—§ 9-18, n. 16.
Kleckner, In re, 93 B.R. 143—§ 6-4, n. 2; § 6-15, n. 5; § 6-61, n. 53.
Kleckner, In re, 81 B.R. 464—§ 6-61, n. 28, 41.
Klein, In re, 114 B.R. 778—§ 7-21, n. 12.
Klein, In re, 106 B.R. 396—§ 9-17, n. 5.
Klein, In re, 57 B.R. 818—§ 9-9, n. 1, 2.
Klein, In re, 39 B.R. 530—§ 7-43, n. 1.
Klein's Dept. Store, Inc., Matter of—§ 6-69, n. 2.
Klingbeil, In re—§ 8-23, n. 5.

Klingberg Schools, In re—§ 6-43, n. 14; § 6-45, n. 3, 4, 36.
Klingman v. Levinson—§ 7-28, n. 18.
Knapp, In re—§ 6-7, n. 3.
Knapp v. Cowell—§ 6-38, n. 12.
Knapp v. Johnson—§ 8-33, n. 15.
Knaus, In re—§ 3-14; § 3-14, n. 6, 13, 14, 15; § 3-33, n. 13, 34, 42, 46.
Knights Athletic Goods, Inc., In re—§ 6-62, n. 22, 38.
Knightsbridge Development Co. Inc., In re—§ 3-6, n. 7, 22, 41, 43; § 3-14; § 3-14, n. 16; § 3-32, n. 1.
KNM Roswell Ltd. Partnership, In re—§ 6-77, n. 11.
Knoware, Inc., In re—§ 6-62, n. 26.
Knowles, In re—§ 8-33, n. 20, 24, 34.
Knox Kreations, Inc., In re—§ 6-51, n. 11; § 6-52, n. 8, 34, 35.
Knoxville Teachers Credit Union v. Parkey—§ 7-26, n. 14, 39, 40, 46.
Knudsen, In re—§ 8-3, n. 21.
Knudson, In re—§ 6-38, n. 18; § 6-70, n. 3.
Kochell, Matter of, 732 F.2d 564—§ 8-3, n. 8; § 8-12, n. 2; § 8-17, n. 44.
Kochell, Matter of, 26 B.R. 86—§ 8-17, n. 49.
Koch Refining v. Farmers Union Cent. Exchange, Inc.—§ 2-8, n. 6.
Koehler, Matter of, 62 B.R. 70—§ 2-2; § 2-2, n. 3, 4; § 9-3, n. 33.
Koehler, Matter of, 6 B.R. 203—§ 8-10, n. 25.
Kohler, In re—§ 9-17, n. 4.
Kohls, In re—§ 6-77, n. 1.
Kohn v. Hursa—§ 3-30, n. 27.
Kohr, In re—§ 3-20, n. 5, 15.
Kokoszka v. Belford—§ 2-8, n. 13; § 8-11, n. 27.
Kolinsky, In re—§ 12-5, n. 10.
Komet, In re—§ 8-11, n. 18; § 8-33, n. 9, 34.
Kommanditselskab Supertrans v. O.C.C. Shipping, Inc.—§ 3-10, n. 22; § 3-14, n. 29.
Konowitz, In re—§ 6-72, n. 8, 11.
Kooker, In re—§ 9-17, n. 7.
Koonce, In re—§ 2-8, n. 15; § 9-22, n. 1.
Koran Enterprises, Inc., Matter of—§ 4-6; § 4-6, n. 10.
Korff, In re—§ 8-10, n. 25.
Korgan, In re—§ 9-20, n. 11.
Korhumel Industries, Inc., Matter of—§ 10-29, n. 6.
Koro Corp., In re—§ 6-65, n. 13; § 6-67, n. 3.
Kors, Inc., In re—§ 6-61, n. 11, 16, 67; § 6-86; § 6-86, n. 14.
Korvettes, Inc., In re, 67 B.R. 730—§ 6-83, n. 12, 13; § 6-84, n. 4.
Korvettes, Inc., In re, 42 B.R. 217—§ 3-23, n. 14.
Kosenka, In re—§ 2-16, n. 27.
Kost, In re—§ 3-27; § 3-27, n. 39.
Kostecky, In re—§ 7-47, n. 2.
Kotter, In re—§ 7-41, n. 17, 18.
Koubourlis, In re—§ 6-18, n. 3, 22, 30.
Kourtakis, In re—§ 9-14, n. 24.
Kovacs, In re—§ 3-21; § 3-21, n. 93.
Kovich, In re—§ 9-7; § 9-7, n. 4, 8.
Kragness, In re—§ 7-15; § 7-15, n. 8, 9.
Krahn, In re—§ 7-47, n. 2.
Kranich, In re—§ 6-48, n. 9, 17.
Krantz, In re—§ 6-58, n. 4; § 8-3, n. 19; § 8-32, n. 8, 9, 10, 16.
Kras, United States v.—§ 2-2, n. 24.
Kress, In re—§ 7-45, n. 13.
Krilich, In re—§ 3-29, n. 14.
Krisle, In re—§ 3-31, n. 84; § 4-6; § 4-6, n. 3, 4, 13.
Krivo Indus. Supply Co. v. National Distillers & Chemical Corp.—§ 6-93, n. 52.
K & R Min., Inc., Matter of—§ 6-12, n. 5, 10; § 6-17, n. 28, 29; § 6-18, n. 7, 10, 16.
Kroh Bros. Development Co., In re, 115 B.R. 1011—§ 6-9, n. 5.
Kroh Bros. Development Co., In re, 108 B.R. 710—§ 12-2, n. 4; § 12-14, n. 20.
Kroh Bros. Development Co., In re, 104 B.R. 182—§ 6-34, n. 27.
Kroh Bros. Development Co., In re, 101 B.R. 114—§ 6-38, n. 23; § 6-40, n. 5, 13; § 6-43, n. 16, 19.
Kroh Bros. Development Co., In re, 100 B.R. 487—§ 6-2, n. 32.
Kroh Bros. Development Co., In re, 86 B.R. 186—§ 6-4, n. 14; § 6-20, n. 18; § 6-38, n. 18; § 6-41, n. 20, 26, 47.
Kroh Bros. Development Co., Matter of—§ 6-34, n. 17, 26, 29.
Krohn, In re—§ 7-45, n. 15, 17.

Kruger v. Wells Fargo Bank—§ **6-38, n. 14**.
Krump, In re—§ **6-62, n. 22**.
Krumpe, In re—§ **6-15, n. 3**.
Kruse, In re—§ **6-76, n. 2**; § **6-77, n. 1**.
Kruse, Matter of—§ **8-25, n. 34**.
Kubly, Matter of—§ **12-3, n. 7**.
Kucera, Matter of—§ **6-76, n. 4**.
Kucharek, Matter of—§ **6-17, n. 10, 23**; § **6-18, n. 18**.
Kuck, In re—§ **3-21, n. 50**.
Kuhns, In re—§ **6-48, n. 11, 20**; § **6-69, n. 8**.
Kuljis Seafood Co., Inc., In re—§ **10-23, n. 5**.
Kull, Matter of—§ **9-13, n. 4**.
Kumar Bavishi & Associates, In re—§ **6-7, n. 7**; § **6-25, n. 3, 20, 22**.
Kuntz v. Lake Placid Olympic Organizing Committee of 1980, Inc.—§ **3-6, n. 49**.
Kupetz v. Continental Illinois Nat. Bank and Trust Co. of Chicago—§ **6-47, n. 8**.
Kupetz v. Wolf—§ **6-52, n. 3, 11, 13, 17, 21, 34, 38**.
Kurth Ranch, In re—§ **6-77, n. 20**.
Kvamme, In re—§ **10-27, n. 5**.
Kwiat v. Doucette—§ **7-28, n. 7**.

L

LaBelle, In re—§ **8-17**; § **8-17, n. 6**; § **8-18, n. 3**.
LaBonne, Matter of—§ **6-40, n. 33**.
LaBuda, Matter of—§ **7-26, n. 19**.
LaCache Land Co., Inc., Matter of—§ **3-31, n. 84**; § **9-3, n. 4**.
Lackawanna Detective Agency, Inc., Matter of—§ **7-25, n. 2**.
Lackow Bros., Inc., Matter of, 752 F.2d 1529—§ **6-35, n. 51**.
Lackow Bros., Inc., Matter of, 19 B.R. 601—§ **6-35, n. 5, 18**.
Lady Liberty Tavern Corp., In re—§ **3-14, n. 66**.
La Fata, Matter of—§ **8-11, n. 19**; § **8-17**; § **8-17, n. 35, 36, 40**.
Lafayette Dial, Inc., Matter of—§ **3-26, n. 11**; § **3-27, n. 26, 44**.
Lafayette Radio Electronics Corp., In re—§ **5-6, n. 2**.
La Flamme, In re—§ **3-10, n. 47**.
LaFollette Sheet Metal, Inc., In re—§ **6-39, n. 14**.
LaFond, In re—§ **8-25, n. 51, 52, 53, 55**.
Lahman Mfg. Co., Inc., In re—§ **11-36**; § **11-36, n. 11**.
Lake Austin Centre Joint Venture, In re—§ **6-77, n. 19**.
Lake in the Woods, Matter of—§ **11-13, n. 3**; § **11-14, n. 13**; § **11-18, n. 1**.
Lakeside I Corp., In re—§ **6-61, n. 77**.
Lakeside Utilities, Matter of—§ **12-6, n. 3**.
Lakeview Inv. Group, Inc., Matter of—§ **6-54, n. 3, 10**; § **6-55, n. 13**.
La Lone v. Carlin—§ **11-39, n. 1**.
Lam, In re—§ **2-3, n. 1**.
Lambert, In re, 64 B.R. 170—§ **7–26, n. 36, 37**.
Lambert, In re, 43 B.R. 913—§ **9–3, n. 11, 17, 20, 21, 24**.
Lambert, In re, 9 B.R. 799—§ **8–17**; § **8–17, n. 4**.
Lambert, Matter of—§ **9-14, n. 21**.
Lamons, In re—§ **6-19, n. 10, 14, 16**; § **6-33, n. 9**.
Lampkin, In re—§ **3-32, n. 1, 7, 10, 27, 34**.
Landau Boat Co., In re—§ **11-28, n. 8**; § **11-29, n. 1**; § **11-30, n. 2**.
Landbank Equity Corp., In re, 83 B.R. 362—§ **6-17, n. 8, 26**; § **6-60, n. 17**; § **6-87, n. 16**.
Landbank Equity Corp., In re, 77 B.R. 44—§ **12–5, n. 2, 11**.
Landen, In re—§ **7-26, n. 21**.
Landmark Air Fund II, In re—§ **11-36, n. 3**.
Landmark Capital Co., Matter of—§ **12-6, n. 1**; § **12-10, n. 7**.
Landmark Park & Associates, United States v.—§ **6-77, n. 11**.
Landmeier v. Hanna—§ **8-31, n. 5**.
Landscaping Services, Inc., In re—§ **10-8, n. 1**.
Landy Beef Co., Inc., In re—§ **6-67, n. 1, 3, 10**.
Lane, In re, 103 B.R. 816—§ **8–31, n. 3**.
Lane, In re, 68 B.R. 609—§ **11–6, n. 11**; § **11–7, n. 10**.
Lanford, In re—§ **3-9, n. 7, 8**.
Lange, In re, 120 B.R. 132—§ **7–47, n. 2**.
Lange, In re, 75 B.R. 154—§ **6-55, n. 13**; § **6-56, n. 8**.
Lange, In re, 35 B.R. 579—§ **6-49, n. 44**; § **6-56, n. 14**.

Langenkamp v. Culp—§ 12-15, n. 1.
Lansford, In re—§ 7-26, n. 35, 40.
Lantana Motel, In re—§ 6-92, n. 10.
Lapaglia, Matter of—§ 9-17, n. 2.
Lapp, In re—§ 9-18, n. 6.
Laracuente v. Chase Manhattan Bank—§ 7-41; § 7-41, n. 7.
Lare, Matter of—§ 3-20, n. 8, 33.
Lario, Matter of—§ 6-25, n. 13.
Larkins v. Commercial Bank of Dawson—§ 9-18, n. 18.
Larrymar Corp., Matter of—§ 6-39, n. 9.
Larsen, In re—§ 6-73, n. 4; § 6-82, n. 4; § 6-90, n. 4.
Larson, In re—§ 6-15, n. 3, 8; § 6-35, n. 29.
Larson, Matter of—§ 7-25; § 7-25, n. 10.
LaSalle Rolling Mills, Inc., Matter of—§ 3-22, n. 5.
Lashley, In re—§ 3-31, n. 103.
Laska, In re—§ 3-10, n. 56, 65.
Lassiter, Matter of—§ 8-1, n. 20; § 8-2, n. 4.
Latham, Matter of—§ 6-15, n. 8.
Latimer, In re—§ 7-45, n. 16; § 8-1, n. 12.
Lattimore, In re, 81 B.R. 18—§ 8-1, n. 12.
Lattimore, In re, 69 B.R. 622—§ 9–13, n. 2; § 9–14, n. 12.
Lauer, In re—§ 6-2, n. 24.
Laues, In re—§ 8-1, n. 20; § 8-31, n. 3.
Laughlin, Matter of—§ 6-50, n. 2, 16, 25, 38; § 6-88, n. 30, 31.
Laughlin v. United States I.R.S., 912 F.2d 197—§ 3–5, n. 18; § 3–22, n. 5.
Laughlin v. United States I.R.S., 98 B.R. 494—§ 3–23, n. 47, 48.
Lausch, In re—§ 8-3, n. 11.
Laventhol, Krekstein, Horwath & Horwath v. Horwitch—§ 11-39, n. 5.
Lavonia Mfg. Co. v. Emery Corp.—§ 6-67, n. 10.
Law Clinic of Mott & Gray, P.C., In re—§ 3-28, n. 15.
Lawless, In re—§ 9-25; § 9-25, n. 6, 14; § 9-27; § 9-27, n. 5, 13, 16.
Lawrence, In re, 57 B.R. 727—§ 8–17, n. 17, 19, 35, 36, 49.
Lawrence, In re, 56 B.R. 727—§ 6–78, n. 14.
Lawrence, In re, 54 B.R. 1—§ 7–39, n. 13.
Lawrence, In re, 41 B.R. 36—§ 6–77, n. 23.
Lawrence, In re, 19 B.R. 627—§ 6–39, n. 20.
Lawrence, Matter of—§ 6-20, n. 17, 19.
Lawrence Paperboard Corp., In re, 76 B.R. 866—§ 6–49, n. 39, 49, 51, 52, 58, 60; § 6–51, n. 2, 22, 24, 29, 33.
Lawrence Paperboard Corp., In re, 52 B.R. 907—§ 6–65, n. 10; § 6–66, n. 2; § 6–67, n. 1, 3, 10, 16.
Lawson, In re—§ 9-7, n. 12.
Lawson v. Liberty Nat. Bank and Trust Co.—§ 8-3, n. 21.
Lawson Burich Associates, Inc., In re—§ 3-21, n. 116, 120.
Laymon, In re—§ 3-27, n. 15.
Layton, Matter of—§ 8-33, n. 26.
Lazar, In re—§ 6-60, n. 4, 17, 18.
Lazaro, In re—§ 12-11, n. 4.
Lazerow, In re—§ 3-5, n. 5.
LCO Enterprises, In re—§ 6-31, n. 10.
L.D. Patella Const. Corp., In re—§ 6-61, n. 42, 53, 54.
Leach, In re, 92 B.R. 483—§ 2–5, n. 12.
Leach, In re, 15 B.R. 1005—§ 6-62, n. 26, 27.
Leaird, In re—§ 7-26, n. 21.
Leamon, In re—§ 8-33, n. 17.
Learn, In re—§ 6-38, n. 5, 21, 22; § 6-39, n. 2, 38; § 6-40, n. 16; § 6-43, n. 3, 29, 30.
Leasing Service Corp., In re—§ 5-7, n. 7.
Leathers v. Prime Leather Finishes Co.—§ 6-34, n. 10.
Leavell, In re—§ 7-47, n. 2.
Leazier, Matter of—§ 9-18, n. 6.
LeBlanc, Matter of—§ 10-22, n. 7.
Lech, Matter of—§ 7-41, n. 4.
Leck, In re—§ 8-33, n. 2.
Ledgemere Land Corp., In re—§ 3-25; § 3-25, n. 27, 37, 40; § 3-27, n. 20, 23, 35.
Lee, Matter of, 119 B.R. 833—§ 8–33, n. 34.
Lee, Matter of, 40 B.R. 123—§ 6-43, n. 16, 29, 31.
Lee, Matter of, 35 B.R. 452—§ 3–14, n. 40.
Lee, United States v., 71 B.R. 833—§ 9-2, n. 10.

TABLE OF CASES

Lee v. Schweiker—§ 3-15, n. 6; § 6-38, n. 18; § 6-39, n. 34; § 6-41, n. 36; § 6-45, n. 3, 6, 8, 9, 11.
Lee Way Holding Co., In re—§ 6-38, n. 18; § 6-40, n. 19.
LeFeber, Matter of—§ 8-17, n. 13; § 8-33, n. 20, 39.
Legend Industries, Inc., In re—§ 12-10, n. 1.
Leger, Matter of—§ 3-10, n. 65.
Lehan Bros., Inc., Matter of—§ 6-73, n. 26.
Lehman v. Nakshian—§ 3-34, n. 7.
Leinheiser, In re—§ 6-49, n. 18; § 6-60, n. 4, 29.
Lellock, Estate of v. Prudential Ins. Co. of America—§ 8-1, n. 20; § 8-19, n. 5.
LeMaire, In re—§ 9-14, n. 18.
Lemco Gypsum, Inc., Matter of, 911 F.2d 1553—§ 6-93, n. 31, 35, 36.
Lemco Gypsum, Inc., Matter of, 108 B.R. 831—§ 6-93, n. 5, 8.
Lemley Estate Business Trust, In re—§ 6-35, n. 24; § 6-77, n. 26; § 6-78, n. 3.
Lemons & Associates, Inc., In re—§ 6-61, n. 38.
Lendvest Mortg., Inc., In re, 123 B.R. 623—§ 6-3, n. 7; § 6-88, n. 33.
Lendvest Mortg., Inc., In re, 119 B.R. 199—§ 6-61, n. 16.
Lenihan, In re—§ 10-10; § 10-10, n. 1, 2, 3.
Lennen, In re—§ 8-3, n. 14.
Lennon, In re—§ 2-17, n. 6.
Lenox, In re—§ 8-21, n. 9.
Lenz, In re—§ 6-40, n. 4.
Leonard, In re, 866 F.2d 335—§ 8-26, n. 19.
Leonard, In re, 55 B.R. 106—§ 12-11, n. 4, 5.
Leonard, In re, 12 B.R. 91—§ 7-37, n. 2.
Leonard v. Whitman—§ 8-7, n. 1.
Lerch v. Federal Land Bank of St. Louis—§ 2-11, n. 8.
Leslie, In re—§ 6-62, n. 38; § 8-1, n. 20.
Lessig Const., Inc., In re—§ 6-40, n. 6, 7; § 6-43, n. 4, 5, 15.
Lettick Typografic, Inc., In re—§ 10-24, n. 9.
Levenhar, In re—§ 4-9, n. 3, 8; § 8-10, n. 11.
Leverette, In re—§ 3-16, n. 7; § 3-33, n. 42.
Levine, In re, 100 B.R. 537—§ 4-4, n. 7.
Levine, In re, 6 B.R. 54—§ 7-26, n. 37.
Levinsky, Matter of—§ 2-15, n. 27.
Levit v. Ingersoll Rand Financial Corp.—§ 6-10; § 6-10, n. 2, 18; § 6-20, n. 25; § 6-88, n. 54.
Levitan, In re—§ 7-28, n. 5.
Lewellyn, Matter of—§ 11-41, n. 16.
Lewellyn & Co., Inc., In re—§ 6-25, n. 2.
Lewis, In re, 116 B.R. 54—§ 6-15, n. 4; § 6-37, n. 8, 9.
Lewis, In re, 94 B.R. 789—§ 6-18, n. 6.
Lewis, In re, 70 B.R. 699—§ 6-62, n. 2, 26.
Lewis, In re, 69 B.R. 600—§ 7-34, n. 14.
Lewis v. Diethorn—§ 6-19, n. 9; § 6-20, n. 20; § 6-25, n. 15; § 6-61, n. 42.
Lewis v. Marsh—§ 6-5, n. 6.
Lewis v. Thompson—§ 8-3, n. 21.
Lewis Jones, Inc., In re—§ 11-9, n. 3.
Lewis W. Shurtleff, Inc., In re—§ 6-20, n. 2.
Lezer, In re—§ 9-13, n. 4.
L.F. Rothschild & Co., Inc. v. Angier—§ 7-5, n. 2.
Liberal Market, Inc., Matter of—§ 10-10, n. 1.
Lichstrahl, In re—§ 8-11, n. 18, 21; § 8-33, n. 17, 18, 24, 34.
Liebe, In re—§ 6-76, n. 2; § 6-77, n. 21.
Liebowitz v. Columbia Packing Co.—§ 6-93, n. 33.
Lifeguard Industries, Inc., Matter of—§ 10-6, n. 5; § 10-7; § 10-7, n. 13.
Life Imaging Corp., In re—§ 6-36, n. 3.
Life Science Church of River Park, Matter of—§ 6-48, n. 13.
Liggett, In re, 118 B.R. 219—§ 6-2, n. 9.
Liggett, In re, 118 B.R. 213—§ 3-14, n. 66; § 3-16, n. 9; § 3-32, n. 6.
Lile, In re—§ 3-33, n. 30.
Lilienthal, Matter of—§ 8-17, n. 35, 36.
Lill, In re—§ 6-7, n. 1; § 6-16, n. 1; § 6-20, n. 20; § 6-83, n. 12.
Liming, In re—§ 7-26; § 7-26, n. 40, 46, 64; § 8-24, n. 5; § 8-25, n. 52, 55, 62.
Lincoln, In re—§ 9-14, n. 21.
Lincoln Nat. Bank v. Conti—§ 6-61, n. 79.
Lindamood, In re—§ 3-10, n. 40, 47.
Lindberg, In re—§ 2-17; § 2-17, n. 5, 9; § 8-3, n. 22.
Linderman, In re—§ 8-13, n. 8.
Lindley, In re—§ 6-60, n. 17; § 6-87, n. 8; § 6-88, n. 24.

Lindsay, In re—§ 6-54, n. 10; § 6-55, n. 13; § 6-56, n. 54.
Lindsey, Matter of—§ 11-30, n. 7, 11.
Lineas Areas de Nicaragua, S. A., In re, 13 B.R. 779—§ 2-6; § 2-6, n. 7, 9.
Lineas Aereas De Nicaragua S.A., In re, 10 B.R. 790—§ 2-6; § 2-6, n. 7.
Lineberry, In re—§ 7-21, n. 11.
Linen Warehouse, Inc., In re—§ 6-88, n. 23, 24.
Lines v. Frederick—§ 2-8; § 2-8, n. 26, 30.
Lion Capital Group, In re—§ 12-2; § 12-2, n. 15.
Lionel Corp., In re, 722 F.2d 1063—§ 4-4; § 4-4, n. 1, 15, 21, 27; § 10-5, n. 11.
Lionel Corp., In re, 30 B.R. 327—§ 10-7, n. 7.
Lippman, In re—§ 5-10, n. 3.
Liquidating Committee of Papeleras Reunidas, S.A., In re Application of the—§ 2-6, n. 8.
Lite Coal Min. Co., In re—§ 3-11, n. 23; § 3-16, n. 8.
Littke, In re—§ 3-23, n. 35, 46; § 3-33, n. 40.
Little Creek Development Co., Matter of—§ 3-26, n. 4; § 3-29; § 3-29, n. 1, 3, 10; § 3-31, n. 1.
Littleton, In re, 888 F.2d 90—§ 6-54, n. 10; § 6-56; § 6-56, n. 17, 19, 39, 41, 44, 45, 46, 53.
Littleton, In re, 106 B.R. 632—§ 7-28, n. 13.
Littleton, Matter of—§ 6-49, n. 13; § 6-56, n. 5, 6.
Livingston, In re—§ 7-28, n. 8.
LJP, Inc., In re—§ 5-12, n. 10.
Lloyd v. Champaign Telephone Co.—§ 3-9, n. 22, 29, 34.
Local Loan Co. v. Hunt—§ 1-3; § 1-3, n. 15; § 11-1, n. 2.
Lockard, Matter of—§ 3-5, n. 6; § 3-10; § 3-10, n. 14, 17, 29.
Lockspur, Inc., Matter of—§ 5-13, n. 3.
Lockwood, In re—§ 6-93, n. 41.
Lockwood v. Exchange Bank of Fort Valley—§ 2-8, n. 39; § 6-6, n. 1.
Loe, In re, 83 B.R. 641—§ 8-17, n. 13; § 8-33; § 8-33, n. 39, 40.
Loe, In re, 63 B.R. 259—§ 8-17, n. 49.
Lomas Financial Corp., In re—§ 3-10, n. 11.
Lombard–Wall Inc., In re—§ 12-2, n. 13.
London, Inc., Matter of—§ 4-13, n. 3.
Long, In re, 774 F.2d 875—§ 7-28, n. 4; § 7-30; § 7-30, n. 12, 17, 24.
Long, In re, 22 B.R. 152—§ 7-37, n. 2, 3.
Longardner & Associates, Inc., In re—§ 10-31, n. 6.
Longhorn 1979–II Drilling Program, In re—§ 2-5, n. 47.
Long Island Jewish Hillside Medical Center v. Prendergast—§ 8-33, n. 16.
Long Island Lighting Co. v. Bokum Resources Corp.—§ 6-93, n. 44.
Longua, Matter of—§ 5-23, n. 2.
Looney, In re, 823 F.2d 788—§ 3-31, n. 21, 22, 27, 41, 46, 48.
Looney, In re, 90 B.R. 217—§ 2-13, n. 13.
Loop Hosp. Partnership, In re—§ 6-93, n. 6, 41.
Lopez–Soto, In re—§ 3-27, n. 10; § 3-31, n. 11.
Lorandos, Matter of—§ 6-33, n. 15.
Lorenz, In re—§ 6-77, n. 21.
Loretto Winery Ltd., In re, 898 F.2d 715—§ 6-62, n. 27, 29.
Loretto Winery, Ltd., In re, 107 B.R. 707—§ 6-31, n. 19.
Los Angeles Finance Co. v. Flores—§ 8-6, n. 10.
Losieniecki, In re—§ 6-86, n. 5, 17, 19; § 8-30, n. 9.
Lott, In re—§ 6-38, n. 18; § 6-39, n. 23, 38; § 6-40, n. 4, 6, 13, 27; § 6-42, n. 2; § 6-43, n. 3.
Lough, In re—§ 2-5; § 2-5, n. 11.
Louisa, City of v. Levi—§ 12-12, n. 7.
Louisiana Indus. Coatings, Inc., In re—§ 6-17, n. 6, 15.
Louisiana Indus. Coatings, Inc., Matter of—§ 6-39, n. 14; § 6-40, n. 5, 14; § 6-45, n. 2.
Louisiana World Exposition, Inc., In re—§ 3-10, n. 33.
Louis L. Lasser & Stanley M. Kahn, In re—§ 6-47, n. 7; § 6-53, n. 8; § 6-54, n. 10.
Love, In re—§ 8-28, n. 3.
Lovelady, In re—§ 6-77, n. 22.
Lovett, In re—§ 6-19, n. 6.
Lovett, Matter of—§ 8-27, n. 11.
Lovett v. Honeywell, Inc.—§ 3-33, n. 27, 28.
Lovett v. St. Johnsbury Trucking—§ 6-31, n. 17.
Lovitt, In re—§ 5-5; § 5-5, n. 4.
Lowe, In re—§ 8-17, n. 13, 35, 36.
Lower Brule Const. Co. v. Sheesley's Plumbing & Heating Co., Inc.—§ 3-14, n. 59.
Lower Downtown Associates, L.P. v. Brazosbanc Sav. Ass'n of Texas—§ 6-55, n. 9; § 6-56, n. 12, 17, 25, 29, 30, 31, 32, 33.
Lowe's of Virginia, Inc. v. Thomas—§ 7-21, n. 5; § 7-22, n. 7.
Lowry Federal Credit Union v. West—§ 7-39; § 7-39, n. 13, 14; § 7-47; § 7-47, n. 7.

Lozano, In re—§ 8-28, n. 6.
L.P. Maun, M.D., Ltd., In re—§ 6-40, n. 14.
L.P. Maun, M.D., Ltd. v. Salyapongse—§ 6-40, n. 19, 27.
L.S. Good & Co., In re—§ 10-8; § 10-8, n. 12.
L.T.S., Inc., In re—§ 6-65, n. 12; § 6-66, n. 5.
L & T Steel Fabricators, Inc., In re—§ 6-20, n. 20; § 6-61, n. 16; § 6-87, n. 8.
Lubbers, In re—§ 9-25; § 9-25, n. 6.
Lubrizol Enterprises, Inc. v. Richmond Metal Finishers, Inc.—§ 5-7; § 5-7, n. 8, 13; § 5-26; § 5-26, n. 19.
Luby, In re—§ 8-28, n. 10, 12.
Lucar Enterprises, Inc., In re—§ 6-59, n. 2.
Lucas, In re, 924 F.2d 597—§ 8–33, n. 17.
Lucas, In re, 107 B.R. 332—§ 6–15, n. 5.
Lucas, In re, 100 B.R. 969—§ 6–73, n. 25; § 6–74, n. 10; § 6–82, n. 1; § 6–88, n. 17; § 6–90, n. 4; § 8–3, n. 19.
Lucas, In re, 21 B.R. 794—§ 6–49, n. 35.
Luchenbill, In re—§ 9-23, n. 1.
Lucius v. McLemore—§ 8-1, n. 11.
Ludford Fruit Products, Inc., In re—§ 6-7, n. 6, 7; § 6-20, n. 5, 23; § 6-77, n. 1, 2, 7, 8.
Ludwig Honold Mfg. Co., In re—§ 6-93, n. 11.
Ludwig Honold Mfg. Co., Inc., In re—§ 6-93, n. 45, 46, 53.
Luftek, Inc., Matter of—§ 2-5, n. 46.
Lugo v. Paulsen—§ 7-34; § 7-34, n. 8.
Lumber Exchange Ltd. Partnership, In re—§ 3-25, n. 45.
Luna, In re, 100 B.R. 605—§ 8–1, n. 11; § 8–10, n. 9.
Luna, In re, 73 B.R. 999—§ 2–17, n. 4.
Lunday, In re—§ 8-32, n. 5, 15.
Lundell Farms, Matter of—§ 6-39, n. 15; § 6-40, n. 5, 6, 7, 16, 27.
Lusk, In re—§ 8-27, n. 11.
Lutz v. Kehr—§ 8-7, n. 15.
Lynch v. Johns–Manville Sales Corp.—§ 3-5, n. 19; § 3-22, n. 26, 35.
Lyn–Dee Dairy Farm, Inc., In re—§ 6-61, n. 16.
Lynn, Matter of—§ 8-18, n. 7, 9.
Lyons, In re—§ 8-3, n. 20.

M

Maanum, In re—§ 3-16, n. 11, 15.
Mableton–Booper Associates, Matter of—§ 3-29, n. 13.
MacArthur Co. v. Johns–Manville Corp.—§ 3-10, n. 25.
MacDonald, In re, 755 F.2d 715—§ 3–30, n. 11, 12.
MacDonald, In re, 73 B.R. 254—§ 2–13, n. 1; § 12–6; § 12–6, n. 10.
Mace, In re—§ 7-6, n. 2.
Mace Electronics of Ohio, Inc., In re—§ 6-93, n. 16.
Mace Levin Associates, Inc., In re—§ 6-39, n. 13.
MacFarlane Webster Associates, In re—§ 7-43; § 7-43, n. 3, 6.
Machinery and Steel Service, Inc., In re—§ 6-88, n. 35.
Mack, In re, 93 B.R. 695—§ 6–61, n. 16.
Mack, In re, 46 B.R. 652—§ 3–12, n. 2, 10, 18.
Mack v. Newton—§ 6-40, n. 27.
Mackey v. Lanier Collection Agency & Service, Inc.—§ 8-33, n. 15.
MacLochlan, In re—§ 7-15; § 7-15, n. 7, 14.
Macon Prestressed Concrete Co. v. Duke—§ 12-2, n. 13; § 12-5, n. 3.
Madcat Two, Inc., In re—§ 6-36, n. 3; § 6-38, n. 18; § 6-62, n. 5, 29.
Maddox, In re—§ 8-26, n. 19.
Madison Hotel Associates, Matter of—§ 10-23, n. 4.
Madison Madison Intern. of Illinois, P.C., In re—§ 7-42, n. 1, 2.
Madrid, In re, 725 F.2d 1197—§ 6–54, n. 7; § 6–55; § 6–55, n. 2, 4, 11; § 6–56.
Madrid, In re, 21 B.R. 424—§ 6–56; § 6–56, n. 7, 9.
Madrid, In re, 10 B.R. 795—§ 6–56, n. 52.
Magallanes, In re—§ 8-3, n. 22.
Magic Circle Energy Corp., In re—§ 6-30, n. 7, 8; § 6-31, n. 3, 19.
Magnavox Co., Matter of—§ 11-1, n. 10.
Magnus, In re—§ 8-1, n. 15; § 8-3, n. 21; § 8-21, n. 4.
Magnuson, In re—§ 8-1, n. 11.
Magosin, In re—§ 8-28, n. 9, 12, 13, 25.

Mahaffey v. E–C–P of Arizona, Inc.—§ **11-36, n. 8.**
Mahloch, Matter of—§ **6-77, n. 19;** § **6-78, n. 3.**
Maike, In re—§ **9-24;** § **9-24, n. 4, 12.**
Mailbag Intern., Inc., In re—§ **6-11, n. 7.**
Main, In re—§ **6-47, n. 7;** § **6-53, n. 9;** § **6-54, n. 10;** § **6-55, n. 9, 13, 20.**
Maine, In re—§ **6-45, n. 4, 7, 9, 36.**
Maine Nat. Bank v. Jopet Jewelers, Inc.—§ **6-56, n. 1.**
Main Line Motors, Inc., In re—§ **10-8, n. 7.**
Maiorino, In re—§ **9-17, n. 3.**
Maislin Industries, United States, Inc., In re—§ **12-2, n. 10.**
Maitland, In re—§ **11-30, n. 11.**
Majesto Electro Industries, Ltd., In re—§ **6-73, n. 4;** § **6-82, n. 3.**
Major Funding Corp., In re—§ **6-47, n. 10;** § **6-48, n. 4, 5, 8, 10;** § **6-49, n. 46;** § **6-60, n. 20.**
Majul, In re—§ **8-33, n. 17, 34.**
Makarewicz, In re—§ **3-30, n. 8.**
Mako, Inc., In re—§ **6-80, n. 5;** § **6-88, n. 2.**
Makoroff v. City of Lockport, N.Y.—§ **3-18, n. 20;** § **6-61, n. 59.**
Malagesi, Matter of—§ **7-37, n. 2.**
Malaspina, Matter of—§ **10-14, n. 3.**
Malek, In re—§ **11-17, n. 1, 2, 8.**
Malmart Mortg. Co., Inc., In re—§ **6-7, n. 4.**
Malone, In re—§ **2-3, n. 1.**
Maloney Enterprises, Inc., In re—§ **6-66, n. 2.**
Mammoth Mart, Inc., In re—§ **5-8, n. 10.**
Manchester Center, In re—§ **3-27, n. 25.**
Manchester Hides, Inc., In re—§ **6-39, n. 3.**
Mandalay Shores Co-op. Housing Ass'n, Inc., In re—§ **2-16, n. 2.**
Mandrell, In re—§ **6-84, n. 5.**
Mann, In re—§ **3-16, n. 9, 11;** § **3-31, n. 103.**
Manners, In re—§ **7-6, n. 2.**
Manning, In re, 831 F.2d 205—§ **4–10;** § **4–10, n. 1.**
Manning, In re, 126 B.R. 984—§ **2–14, n. 2.**
Manning, In re, 37 B.R. 755—§ **4–7, n. 6, 20;** § **11–38, n. 1.**
Manring Auto Sales, Inc., In re—§ **6-60, n. 4.**
Mansfield Tire and Rubber Co., In re—§ **3-21, n. 17, 73, 90.**
Mansfield Tire & Rubber Co., Matter of—§ **6-93, n. 66.**
Manson Billard, Inc., In re—§ **6-11, n. 6.**
Manufacturers Acceptance Corp., In re—§ **6-47, n. 8.**
Manville Forest Products Corp., In re—§ **11-13, n. 3;** § **12-12, n. 22.**
M.A.P.P., Inc., In re—§ **6-62, n. 24, 40, 41.**
Maralak, Ltd., In re—§ **5-4, n. 9.**
March, In re—§ **9-13, n. 2.**
Marcum v. Edwards—§ **8-13, n. 7.**
Marcus, In re, 128 B.R. 294—§ **2–17, n. 8, 9, 15.**
Marcus, In re, 45 B.R. 338—§ **6-48, n. 18;** § **6-59, n. 2, 11;** § **7-19, n. 5.**
Marcus, Stowell & Beye Government Securities, Inc. v. Jefferson Inv. Corp.—§ **3-5, n. 17, 19;** § **3-6, n. 30, 35.**
Marengo State Bank v. West—§ **6-15, n. 2.**
Margraf v. Oliver—§ **9-3, n. 6.**
Marie Pastor's Morningstar Management, Ltd., In re—§ **3-30, n. 26, 27, 28, 32.**
Marina Enterprises, Inc., In re—§ **3-29, n. 16.**
Marin Aviation, Inc., Matter of—§ **6-2, n. 29.**
Marine Charter & Storage, Ltd., Inc. v. Lloyds of London—§ **3-6, n. 33.**
Marine Optical, Inc., In re—§ **3-27, n. 45.**
Marine Pollution Service, Inc., In re—§ **3-7, n. 7.**
Marine Power & Equipment Co., Inc., In re—§ **3-31, n. 20, 21, 41, 51.**
Marin Motor Oil, Inc., Matter of—§ **6-66, n. 2.**
Marino, In re—§ **6-61, n. 6, 11, 25.**
Marion v. Pennsylvania Higher Education Assistance Agency (Matter of Marion)—§ **7-33, n. 14.**
Marion Steel Co., In re—§ **3-9, n. 18, 22, 23, 27, 29, 31, 32, 33.**
Marketing Resources Intern. Corp., In re—§ **6-40, n. 7, 27.**
Mark Jay Kaufman, P.A., In re—§ **12-16, n. 3.**
Mark Twain Marine Industries, Inc., In re—§ **6-77, n. 7.**
Markunes, In re—§ **3-30, n. 19.**
Marlar, In re—§ **6-73, n. 4.**
Marley Orchards Income Fund I, Ltd. Partnership, In re—§ **3-5, n. 15;** § **3-22, n. 5, 26, 29.**
Marlin Oil Co., In re—§ **6-62, n. 26.**
Marlow, United States v.—§ **8-1, n. 20.**

Marrero, Matter of—§ 9-18, n. 10.
Marriage of (see name of party)
Marsh, Matter of—§ 8-29, n. 12, 13.
Marshall, In re—§ 9-18, n. 13.
Marshall, Matter of—§ 6-53, n. 6; § 6-54, n. 10.
Marsowicz, In re—§ 3-10, n. 9.
Marston Enterprises, Inc., In re—§ 11-28, n. 8; § 11-29; § 11-29, n. 1, 4, 10; § 11-30; § 11-30, n. 15.
Marta Group, Inc., In re—§ 6-40, n. 2, 16.
Marta Group, Inc. v. County Appliance Co., Inc.—§ 6-40, n. 4, 16, 28.
Martec Corp., In re—§ 6-32, n. 9.
Martin, In re, 761 F.2d 1163—§ 7-26; § 7-26, n. 38, 39, 40, 46.
Martin, In re, 761 F.2d 472—§ 3-27, § 3-27, n. 4, 30, 31, 33, 34.
Martin, In re, 698 F.2d 883—§ 7-22, n. 2, 4.
Martin, In re, 124 B.R. 69—§ 6-2, n. 24, 30.
Martin, In re, 119 B.R. 297—§ 8-33, n. 17, 24, 34.
Martin, In re, 117 B.R. 243—§ 6-12, n. 7.
Martin, In re, 88 B.R. 319—§ 7-19, n. 1; § 7-21, n. 6, 8, 9.
Martin, In re, 66 B.R. 921—§ 10-22, n. 4.
Martin v. First Nat. Bank of Opelika—§ 8-31, n. 5.
Martin Bros. Toolmakers, Inc., In re—§ 5-2, n. 7; § 5-4, n. 12.
Martin County Custom Pools Inc., In re—§ 6-87, n. 8.
Martin Exploration Co., Matter of—§ 3-22, n. 4; § 3-31, n. 28, 41.
Martinez, In re, 92 B.R. 916—§ 3-9, n. 31.
Martinez, In re, 51 B.R. 944—§ 9-3, n. 11; § 9-4, n. 7.
Martin Marietta Corp. v. New Jersey Nat. Bank—§ 4-3, n. 2.
Martin Specialty Vehicles, Inc., In re—§ 6-39, n. 21; § 6-93, n. 42, 63.
Martin-Trigona v. Champion Federal Sav. and Loan Ass'n—§ 3-6, n. 34, 45, 49; § 3-33, n. 7.
Martin-Trigona v. Gouletas—§ 3-20, n. 11.
Marx, In re—§ 9-10, n. 13.
Mary Freese Farms, Inc., In re—§ 9-24; § 9-24, n. 7.
Maryland Nat. Bank v. Mayor and City Council of Baltimore—§ 6-62, n. 25.
Maryland Nat. Indus. Finance Corp. v. Gold Dust Coal Co.—§ 12-3; § 12-3, n. 4; § 12-5, n. 3.
Mascari, In re—§ 9-4, n. 43.
Maschke, to Use of Ehnes v. O'Brien—§ 8-8, n. 7.
Mason, In re, 79 B.R. 786—§ 6-39, n. 16, 38; § 6-41, n. 38; § 6-43, n. 3, 13.
Mason, In re, 69 B.R. 876—§ 6-6, n. 3, 7; § 8-22, n. 19; § 8-23, n. 5.
Mason, In re, 51 B.R. 548—§ 9-20, n. 11.
Mason, In re, 18 B.R. 817—§ 3-21, n. 126, 127.
Mason and Dixon Lines, Inc., In re—§ 6-25, n. 15.
Massenzio, In re—§ 3-6, n. 12; § 3-21, n. 50; § 3-32, n. 1.
Mast, Matter of—§ 6-2, n. 16.
Mastroeni, In re—§ 6-38, n. 9; § 6-40, n. 16, 19.
Mata, In re—§ 8-3, n. 14.
Matera, In re—§ 7-26, n. 39.
Matheson, In re—§ 6-47, n. 10; § 6-54, n. 10; § 6-70, n. 3.
Matos, In re—§ 6-61, n. 67, 77.
Mattern, In re—§ 3-12, n. 5.
Matter of (see name of party)
Matters, In re—§ 6-31, n. 17.
Matteson, In re—§ 8-33, n. 17, 18, 20.
Matthews, In re, 724 F.2d 798—§ 8-25, n. 32.
Matthews, In re, 65 B.R. 24—§ 8-17, n. 35, 36.
Matthews v. Rosene—§ 3-32, n. 19, 20.
Matthieson, Matter of—§ 6-39, n. 15; § 6-40, n. 5, 6.
Mattiace Industries, Inc., United States v.—§ 3-21, n. 7.
Mattice, Matter of—§ 6-77, n. 21.
Mattis, In re—§ 8-1, n. 20; § 8-23, n. 7.
Matula, In re—§ 3-10, n. 65.
Maus v. Maus—§ 8-25, n. 15.
Max Sugarman Funeral Home, Inc. v. A.D.B. Investors, 926 F.2d 1248—§ 6-48, n. 5, 9; § 6-88, n. 24, 30, 37; § 6-93, n. 5.
Max Sugarman Funeral Home, Inc. v. A.D.B. Investors, 127 B.R. 508—§ 6-93, n. 2, 9, 21, 31, 35, 37, 38.
Mayhugh v. Coon—§ 8-9, n. 10.
Mayo, In re—§ 6-93, n. 11, 41, 62.
Mayo v. Pioneer Bank & Trust Company—§ 6-51, n. 40.
May Reporting Services, Inc., In re—§ 6-76, n. 5.
Mayville Feed & Grain, Inc., In re, 123 B.R. 245—§ 7-15; § 7-15, n. 15.

Mayville Feed & Grain, Inc., In re, 96 B.R. 755—§ **6–61, n. 33.**
M.B.K., Inc., In re—§ **6-4, n. 9.**
McAloon, In re—§ **9-9, n. 2;** § **9-14, n. 21.**
McBee, In re—§ **6-61, n. 53.**
McBoyle v. United States—§ **7-34;** § **7-34, n. 11.**
McCabe, In re—§ **8-17, n. 24.**
McCadams v. Bank of Lenox—§ **3-6, n. 5.**
McCain, In re—§ **8-25, n. 44, 48.**
McCall, In re—§ **8-25, n. 30, 34.**
McCannon v. Marston—§ **6-61, n. 74.**
McCarthy v. McCabe—§ **8-6, n. 10.**
McCarty Ranch Trust v. Craig—§ **12-2, n. 14.**
McCauley, In re—§ **6-72, n. 16;** § **6-88, n. 17, 19, 33.**
McClintock, In re—§ **6-53, n. 4, 6;** § **6-56, n. 53;** § **6-87, n. 8.**
McCollum, In re—§ **9-20, n. 17, 18.**
McCollum v. Parkdale State Bank—§ **6-38, n. 8.**
McCombs, Matter of—§ **8-25, n. 32.**
McConchie, In re—§ **8-10, n. 10, 12.**
McConnell, In re—§ **6-40, n. 27;** § **6-45, n. 14.**
McCordi Corp., Matter of—§ **10-8, n. 3.**
McCorhill Pub., Inc., In re, 92 B.R. 74—§ **6–77, n. 1;** § **6–78, n. 2.**
McCorhill Pub., Inc., In re, 86 B.R. 783—§ **6–86, n. 10;** § **6–94, n. 3.**
McCorhill Pub., Inc., In re, 73 B.R. 1013—§ **10–8, n. 3.**
McCormick v. Mid–State Bank & Trust Co.—§ **8-27, n. 3.**
McCoy, In re, 92 B.R. 750—§ **4–9, n. 10.**
McCoy, In re, 46 B.R. 9—§ **6–4, n. 17.**
McCracken, In re—§ **3-30, n. 19.**
McCracken v. Brown—§ **3-31, n. 101.**
McCulloch & Son, Inc., In re—§ **8-19, n. 5.**
McCullough, In re—§ **7-47, n. 2.**
McDaniel, In re—§ **6-40, n. 19.**
McDaniel v. Nationwide—§ **6-6, n. 7;** § **6-37;** § **6-37, n. 12.**
McDonald Trucking Co., Inc., In re—§ **2-5, n. 22.**
McDowell, In re—§ **6-60, n. 10, 20, 24, 25.**
McElveen, In re—§ **2-16;** § **2-16, n. 3.**
McEvoy v. Ron Watkins, Inc.—§ **6-61, n. 18, 24, 70, 74.**
McFarlin's, Inc., In re—§ **6-93, n. 31, 32.**
McGinty, In re—§ **3-6, n. 2;** § **3-14, n. 4;** § **3-33, n. 10;** § **3-35, n. 7.**
McGoldrick, In re—§ **6-82, n. 6;** § **6-84, n. 3, 4.**
McGowan, In re—§ **6-72, n. 1.**
McGoy, In re—§ **8-17, n. 10.**
McGrann, In re—§ **7-37;** § **7-37, n. 1.**
McGrew, In re—§ **11-17, n. 8.**
McGuirt, In re—§ **3-30, n. 27.**
McIntosh, In re—§ **8-33, n. 24, 34.**
McIver v. Phillips—§ **9-3, n. 28.**
McKaskle, In re—§ **8-29, n. 7.**
McKeag, In re—§ **8-3, n. 19, 20.**
McKenna, In re—§ **8-17, n. 17.**
McKenzie, In re—§ **9-7, n. 6.**
McKillips, In re—§ **9-24, n. 5, 12.**
McLamb, In re—§ **8-3, n. 10;** § **8-9, n. 13.**
McLaughlin, In re—§ **11-30, n. 11.**
McLaws v. Kruger—§ **8-13, n. 7.**
McLean, In re, 97 B.R. 789—§ **6–61, n. 55, 59;** § **6–62, n. 26;** § **6–89, n. 20.**
McLean, In re, 41 B.R. 893—§ **8–17, n. 13; 8–33, n. 39.**
McLean v. City of Philadelphia, Water Revenue Bureau—§ **6-61, n. 24.**
McLean Industries, Inc., In re, 884 F.2d 1566—§ **3-31, n. 84.**
McLean Industries, Inc., In re, 96 B.R. 440—§ **5–22, n. 5.**
McLean Industries, Inc., In re, 90 B.R. 614—§ **6–40, n. 2;** § **6–44, n. 1.**
McLean Industries, Inc., In re, 84 B.R. 340—§ **6–61, n. 6.**
McLean Industries, Inc., In re, 87 B.R. 830—§ **11–13, n. 3.**
McLean Industries, Inc., In re, 70 B.R. 852—§ **10–12;** § **10–12, n. 8.**
McLean Thomas, Inc. v. FLR Co., Inc.—§ **3-22, n. 4;** § **3-31, n. 41.**
McLemore v. Thomassen (In re Thomasson)—§ **12-10, n. 2.**
McLouth Steel Corp., Matter of—§ **12-13;** § **12-13, n. 12.**
McMahon, In re—§ **6-6, n. 3, 7;** § **8-23, n. 5.**
McManus, Matter of—§ **8-26, n. 18.**

TABLE OF CASES

McMinn, In re—§ 9-2, n. 4.
McMonagle, In re—§ 9-3, n. 7, 12.
McNair, In re—§ 9-18, n. 13.
McNealy, In re—§ 9-21; § 9-21, n. 2.
McNeely, In re—§ 6-62, n. 15, 16.
McNeely, Matter of—§ 7-42, n. 3, 5.
McNierney, In re—§ 7-6, n. 5.
McNutt, In re—§ 8-25, n. 57, 62.
MCorp Financial, Inc., In re—§ 5-2, n. 5.
McPeck, United States v.—§ 3-3, n. 4; § 3-34; § 3-34, n. 8, 11, 18.
McQueen, In re, 25 B.R. 592—§ 6-6, n. 9; § 8-22, n. 29.
McQueen, In re, 21 B.R. 736—§ 8-10, n. 25.
McQuinn, Matter of—§ 7-49; § 7-49, n. 2, 10.
Mead, In re—§ 8-33, n. 18, 24.
Meadow Glen, Ltd., In re—§ 10-24, n. 9.
Meadowlands Communications, Inc. v. Banker's Trust Co., New York—§ 12-3, n. 7.
Meadows, In re—§ 8-25, n. 25, 27, 52, 56.
Mechanical Maintenance, Inc., In re—§ 2-13; § 2-13, n. 10.
Media Cent., Inc., In re—§ 11-18; § 11-18, n. 9.
Medical Cost Management, Inc., In re—§ 6-88, n. 21, 35.
Medical Equities, Inc., In re—§ 6-17, n. 18; § 6-93, n. 29.
Medomak Canning, In re—§ 6-93, n. 11.
Mehrer, Matter of—§ 6-58, n. 4; § 8-32, n. 8, 9.
Mehrhoff, Matter of—§ 6-39, n. 15; § 6-40, n. 16.
Meinhardt Mechanical Service Co., Inc., In re—§ 6-20, n. 5, 17, 19.
Meinke, Peterson & Damer, P.C., In re—§ 3-14, n. 45.
Mellon Bank, N.A. v. Lee—§ 3-6, n. 25; § 3-8, n. 10.
Mellor, In re—§ 3-25, n. 2, 10; § 3-27, n. 22, 38.
Melon Produce, Inc., In re—§ 6-20, n. 20.
Meltzer, In re—§ 9-14, n. 23.
Meltzer, Matter of—§ 6-47, n. 10.
Melvin Liquid Fertilizer Co., Inc., Matter of—§ 6-67, n. 10.
Memorial Hosp. of Iowa County, Inc., In re—§ 3-6, n. 36; § 3-14, n. 80; § 3-15, n. 6; § 3-35, n. 2; § 5-25, n. 6.
Memphis Bank & Trust Co. v. Whitman—§ 9-2, n. 4; § 9-10; § 9-10, n. 2, 11; § 9-14, n. 18, 19.
Memphis-Friday's Associates, In re—§ 3-28, n. 13.
Mendenhall, In re, 54 B.R. 44—§ 9-4, n. 30.
Mendenhall, In re, 4 B.R. 127—§ 8-17, n. 35, 36.
Mercantile Holdings, Inc. v. Dobkin—§ 9-3, n. 26.
Merchants and Mechanics Federal Sav. and Loan Ass'n v. Lewis—§ 3-31, n. 84.
Merchants & Farmers Bank of Dumas, Ark. v. Hill—§ 3-6, n. 46, 47.
Merchants' Nat. Bank v. McAnulty—§ 11-39, n. 1.
Mercier v. Partlow—§ 8-8, n. 3.
Mercon Industries, Inc., In re—§ 6-10, n. 15; § 6-88, n. 46, 54.
Meredith Manor, Inc., In re—§ 6-34, n. 10.
Merritt Dredging Co., Inc., In re—§ 6-61, n. 16.
Merwede, In re—§ 6-93, n. 66.
Mesa Business Park Partnership, In re—§ 3-32, n. 11.
Mesa Refining, Inc., In re—§ 5-23, n. 3.
Messing, In re—§ 8-11, n. 18; § 8-33, n. 34.
Metal Center, Inc., In re—§ 3-10, n. 9.
Met-L-Wood Corp., Matter of—§ 4-4, n. 1.
Metro Communications, Inc., In re, 115 B.R. 849—§ 6-9, n. 10.
Metro Communications, Inc., In re, 95 B.R. 921—§ 6-12, n. 7; § 6-49, n. 58; § 6-51, n. 17, 25; § 6-52, n. 6, 13.
Metrocraft Pub. Services, Inc., In re—§ 11-17; § 11-17, n. 2, 4.
Metropolitan Cosmetic and Reconstructive Surgical Clinic, P.A., In re—§ 6-70, n. 2.
Metropolitan Cosmetic Reconstructive Surgery P.A., In re—§ 6-60, n. 3; § 6-73, n. 4.
Metropolitan Hosp., In re—§ 6-40, n. 7, 23.
Metropolitan Intern., Inc., In re—§ 6-44, n. 1.
Metro Produce, Inc., In re—§ 6-31, n. 16.
Metro Shippers, Inc., In re—§ 6-83, n. 5, 8.
Metro Square, In re—§ 6-77, n. 11.
Metz, Matter of—§ 2-16, n. 7; § 9-14, n. 16; § 9-30; § 9-30, n. 7, 8.
Metzeler, In re—§ 6-84, n. 2, 4.
Meyer, In re—§ 6-39, n. 29; § 6-40, n. 17.
Meyer, Matter of—§ 7-26, n. 36.
Meyer v. Idaho First Nat. Bank—§ 6-38, n. 14.

Meyer–Midway, Inc., In re—§ **6-65, n. 15**; § **6-66, n. 2**.
Meyers v. Postal Finance Co.—§ **6-93, n. 44**.
Meyerson v. Werner—§ **3-20, n. 11**.
M. Frenville Co., Inc., Matter of—§ **3-6, n. 54, 58, 60**; § **7-5**; § **7-5, n. 1**; § **11-3**; § **11-3, n. 2, 4**.
MGS Marketing, In re—§ **6-65, n. 14**; § **6-67, n. 3**.
M.H. Corp., In re—§ **10-12, n. 4**.
M.H. Gordon & Son, Inc. v. Debtor and Committee of Unsecured Creditors—§ **6-93, n. 12**.
Miami Center Ltd. Partnership v. Bank of New York—§ **3-31, n. 103**.
Miami General Hosp., Inc., In re, 124 B.R. 383—§ **6-49, n. 49, 51**; § **6-51, n. 27**.
Miami General Hosp., Inc., In re, 81 B.R. 682—§ **4-8**; § **4-8, n. 1**.
Miami General Hosp., Inc., Matter of—§ **6-93, n. 31**.
Miami Valley Production Credit Ass'n v. Tegtmeyer—§ **9-3, n. 3, 11**.
Michaelsen, In re—§ **9-3**; § **9-3, n. 13, 17, 18, 21**.
Michalak, In re—§ **8-6, n. 12**; § **8-26, n. 4**.
Michel, Matter of—§ **7-28, n. 14**.
Micro Design, Inc., In re—§ **3-6, n. 45**; § **3-30, n. 24, 25, 27**.
Microfab, Inc., In re—§ **3-21, n. 69, 113**; § **6-61, n. 59**.
Microwave Products of America, Inc., In re, 118 B.R. 566—§ **6-25, n. 22**.
Microwave Products of America, Inc., In re, 102 B.R. 666—§ **10-8, n. 3**.
Microwave Products of America, Inc., In re, 94 B.R. 967—§ **6-63, n. 4, 6**; § **6-65, n. 10**.
Mid–America Petroleum, Inc., In re—§ **6-61, n. 77**.
Mid–Atlantic Fuels, Inc., In re—§ **3-21, n. 110**; § **3-27**; § **3-27, n. 36, 44**.
Mid Atlantic Fund, Inc., Matter of—§ **6-82, n. 4**.
Middleton v. Farmers State Bank of Fosston—§ **8-3, n. 21**; § **8-25, n. 52, 55**.
Middletown, City of v. Holiday Syrups, Inc.—§ **3-32, n. 38**.
Midlantic Nat. Bank v. New Jersey Dept. of Environmental Protection—§ **2-8, n. 39**; § **11-9**; § **11-9, n. 2**; § **11-10**; § **11-11**; § **11-11, n. 1**; § **11-12**.
Mid–South Cabinet & Millwork, Inc., In re—§ **6-31, n. 9**; § **6-34, n. 10, 21**.
Midwest Emery Freight System, Inc., In re—§ **3-7, n. 9**.
Midwestern Companies, Inc., Matter of—§ **6-10, n. 15**; § **6-88, n. 54**.
Midwest Properties No. Two v. Big Hill Inv. Co., Inc.—§ **4-6**; § **4-6, n. 3, 7, 11, 12**.
Midwest Service and Supply Co., Inc., In re—§ **6-45, n. 3, 7, 29, 36**.
Mielke, In re—§ **9-7**; § **9-7, n. 4, 13**.
Miera, In re—§ **6-57, n. 3**.
Mihalko, In re—§ **6-92, n. 7, 10**.
Milam, Matter of—§ **6-2, n. 3, 4, 24**.
Milano Textiles, Inc., In re—§ **6-38, n. 9, 10**.
Milcher, In re—§ **6-61, n. 16**; § **8-22, n. 23, 26**; § **8-23, n. 6**.
Mile Hi Metal Systems, Inc., In re—§ **3-7, n. 3**.
Mill Concepts Corp., In re—§ **6-61, n. 38**.
Miller, In re, 123 B.R. 46—§ **6-20, n. 26**.
Miller, In re, 113 B.R. 98—§ **8-1, n. 11**; § **8-32, n. 5**.
Miller, In re, 103 B.R. 353—§ **3-28, n. 11, 14**.
Miller, In re, 101 B.R. 713—§ **8-6, n. 12**; § **8-26, n. 4**.
Miller, In re, 98 B.R. 110—§ **3-6, n. 2**; § **3-11, n. 4**; § **3-12, n. 2**; § **8-1, n. 21**.
Miller, In re, 68 B.R. 385—§ **2-8, n. 42**.
Miller, In re, 36 B.R. 420—§ **8-18**; § **8-18, n. 16, 22**.
Miller, In re, 33 B.R. 549—§ **8-17**; § **8-17, n. 14, 28, 49, 51**.
Miller, In re, 30 B.R. 819—§ **8-26, n. 2**.
Miller, In re, 16 B.R. 790—§ **8-17, n. 24, 26**.
Miller, In re, 4 B.R. 392—§ **7-49, n. 11**.
Miller v. Dixon—§ **8-8, n. 7**.
Millerburg, In re—§ **4-7, n. 15**; § **8-22, n. 23**.
Miller's Auto Supplies, Inc., In re—§ **6-7, n. 4**.
Millsap, In re—§ **8-1, n. 12**.
Millsap v. Faulkes—§ **8-13, n. 7**.
Mill Street, Inc., In re—§ **6-88, n. 39**.
Milwaukee County Conservation and Public Service Corp., Matter of—§ **6-88, n. 20**.
Mimi's of Atlanta, Inc., Matter of—§ **5-3, n. 2**.
Miner Industries, Inc., In re—§ **6-29, n. 17**.
Minichello, In re—§ **6-61, n. 16**; § **6-82, n. 4**.
Minick, In re—§ **9-4, n. 28**; § **9-18, n. 18**.
Miniscribe Corp., In re—§ **6-2, n. 9**; § **6-16, n. 1**; § **6-18, n. 24**; § **6-19, n. 10, 14, 17**; § **6-20, n. 17**; § **6-25, n. 11**; § **6-31, n. 9, 17**.
Minnehoma Financial Co. v. Ditto—§ **8-7, n. 18**.
Minnesota Kicks, Inc., In re—§ **6-93, n. 39, 43**.
Minnesota Utility Contracting, Inc., In re—§ **6-19, n. 8**; § **6-24, n. 2**; § **6-27, n. 8, 9, 11**; § **6-49, n. 25**; § **6-51**; § **6-51, n. 37**.

TABLE OF CASES

Minoco Group of Companies, Ltd., In re—§ 3-2, n. 5; § 3-14, n. 39.
Minton Group, Inc., In re, 28 B.R. 789—§ 6-36, n. 11.
Minton Group, Inc., In re, 28 B.R. 774—§ 6-61, n. 59.
Minton Group, Inc., Matter of—§ 11-36; § 11-36, n. 12.
Miranda Soto, In re—§ 6-76, n. 2.
Miranne, In re—§ 3-30, n. 33; § 3-31, n. 92, 93.
Mirolla v. Mendez—§ 8-8, n. 6.
Misco Supply Co., In re—§ 6-62, n. 28.
Misener Industries, Inc., In re—§ 11-7, n. 7.
Mission Indians v. American Management & Amusement, Inc.—§ 3-6, n. 3; § 3-30, n. 4.
Missionary Baptist Foundation of America, Inc., In re—§ 6-48, n. 2, 5, 14; § 6-49, n. 12, 40, 45, 62; § 6-59, n. 2.
Missionary Baptist Foundation of America, Matter of, 818 F.2d 1135—§ 6-93, n. 16.
Missionary Baptist Foundation of America, Inc., Matter of, 796 F.2d 752—§ 3-15, n. 6; § 6-20, n. 20; § 6-35, n. 47, 52.
Missionary Baptist Foundation of America, Inc., Matter of, 712 F.2d 206—§ 6-93, n. 29, 37.
Missouri River Sand & Gravel, Inc., In re—§ 6-73, n. 4, 20; § 6-76, n. 6; § 6-80, n. 20; § 6-83, n. 8.
Missouri, State of v. United States Bankruptcy Court for E. D. of Arkansas—§ 3-21; § 3-21, n. 69, 78, 108.
Mitchell, In re, 103 B.R. 819—§ 8-6, n. 9; § 8-8, n. 4.
Mitchell, In re, 80 B.R. 372—§ 8-29, n. 7.
Mitchell, In re, 80 B.R. 350—§ 6-61, n. 74.
Mitchell, In re, 77 B.R. 524—§ 9-10, n. 5, 7.
Mitchell v. Huntsville Wholesale Nurseries, Inc.—§ 9-24, n. 15.
Mitsubishi Motors Corp. v. Soler Chrysler-Plymouth, Inc.—§ 3-31, n. 46.
ML Barge Pool VII Partners Series A, In re—§ 3-22, n. 3, 29.
M. Miller Ltd., In re—§ 3-9, n. 7.
Mobile Steel Co., Matter of—§ 6-93, n. 16, 17.
Modern Mix, Inc., In re—§ 6-83, n. 7.
Modern Settings, Inc., Matter of—§ 6-61, n. 55.
Modern Settings, Inc. v. Prudential-Bache Securities, Inc.—§ 6-40, n. 27.
Moesel, In re—§ 3-20; § 3-20, n. 33, 38.
Moffat, In re—§ 8-19, n. 20.
Mohawk Industries, Inc., In re—§ 6-39, n. 15; § 6-40, n. 4; § 6-45, n. 2, 3, 6, 7.
Mohawk Industries, Inc. v. Robinson Industries, Inc.—§ 12-2, n. 18.
Mold Makers, Inc., In re—§ 3-23; § 3-23, n. 12, 16.
Momentum Computer Systems Intern., In re—§ 6-15, n. 5.
Monach Circuit Industries, Inc., In re—§ 4-15; § 4-15, n. 14; § 4-16, n. 4.
Monaco, Matter of—§ 9-3, n. 3, 6.
Monarch Tool & Mfg. Co., In re—§ 5-8, n. 12.
Monex Corp., In re—§ 6-39, n. 24; § 6-44, n. 2.
Monroe, In re—§ 6-62, n. 42.
Monroe v. Monroe—§ 8-7, n. 9.
Monroe Park, In re—§ 10-23, n. 4.
Monroe Well Service, Inc., In re, 83 B.R. 317—§ 3-9, n. 14.
Monroe Well Service, Inc., In re, 80 B.R. 324—§ 11-17, n. 8.
Monroe Well Service, In re, 69 B.R. 58—§ 3-9, n. 25.
Monsour Medical Center, Matter of—§ 6-2, n. 28.
Montanino, Matter of—§ 6-17; § 6-17, n. 24.
Montano, In re—§ 9-7, n. 6.
Montavon, In re—§ 8-17, n. 35, 36, 49.
Montford v. Grohman—§ 8-31, n. 5.
Montgomery, In re, 123 B.R. 801—§ 6-19, n. 4, 20; § 6-27, n. 2; § 6-31, n. 13.
Montgomery, In re, 104 B.R. 112—§ 8-33, n. 26.
Montgomery, In re, 80 B.R. 385—§ 8-29, n. 7, 8, 9.
Montgomery Mall Ltd. Partnership, In re—§ 3-31, n. 84.
Montney, Matter of—§ 6-82, n. 3; § 8-29, n. 12, 13.
Montoya, In re—§ 7-7, n. 2.
Monument Record Corp., In re—§ 11-7, n. 10.
Moody, In re, 817 F.2d 365—§ 12-12, n. 13.
Moody, In re, 97 B.R. 605—§ 8-25, n. 33.
Moody, In re, 77 B.R. 580—§ 8-3, n. 22.
Moody, In re, 77 B.R. 566—§ 6-61, n. 8; § 6-83, n. 16.
Moody v. Amoco Oil Co.—§ 5-11; § 5-11, n. 1; § 5-19, n. 6.
Moody v. Security Pacific Business Credit, Inc., 127 B.R. 958—§ 6-49, n. 8, 23; § 6-51, n. 27; § 6-52, n. 7, 8, 9, 13.
Moody v. Security Pacific Business Credit, Inc., 85 B.R. 319—§ 11-5, n. 6.
Mooney Aircraft, Inc., Matter of—§ 4-10, n. 4.

Moore, In re, 907 F.2d 1476—§ 8–33, n. 17.
Moore, In re, 113 B.R. 239—§ 9–18, n. 13.
Moore, In re, 87 B.R. 499—§ 9–21; § 9–21, n. 3.
Moore, In re, 73 B.R. 607—§ 9–27, n. 9, 11.
Moore, In re, 54 B.R. 781—§ 6–61, n. 79.
Moore, In re, 39 B.R. 571—§ 6–47, n. 7.
Moore, Matter of, 22 B.R. 200—§ 3–12, n. 2, 18.
Moore, Matter of, 17 B.R. 551—§ 9–3, n. 6, 7.
Moore v. Bay—§ 6-60, n. 28.
Moralez, In re—§ 3-30, n. 13.
Moran, In re—§ 3-23, n. 32.
Moreggia & Sons, Inc., In re—§ 5-2, n. 5, 7; § 5-10, n. 2.
Moreno, Matter of—§ 7-28, n. 10.
Morgan, In re, 106 B.R. 449—§ 9–17, n. 7.
Morgan, In re, 96 B.R. 615—§ 6–61, n. 18.
Morgan, In re, 77 B.R. 81—§ 6–4, n. 13; § 6–38, n. 18; § 6–39, n. 28, 34; § 6–40, n. 6; § 6–44, n. 9.
Morgan, In re, 44 B.R. 516—§ 3–12, n. 2.
Morgan Guar. Trust Co. of New York v. American Sav. and Loan Ass'n—§ 3-8; § 3-8, n. 12.
Morin, In re—§ 3-12, n. 2.
Morningstar Enterprises, Inc., In re—§ 3-15, n. 6.
Morphis, In re—§ 9-18, n. 10.
Morren Meat and Poultry Co. Inc., In re—§ 6-31, n. 3, 19.
Morris, In re—§ 3-9, n. 6.
Morris Communications NC, Inc., In re, 914 F.2d 458—§ 6–49, n. 66, 68.
Morris Communications NC Inc., In re, 75 B.R. 619—§ 6–49, n. 13, 63, 66, 73; § 6–50, n. 23; § 6–87, n. 6, 12; § 6–89; § 6–89, n. 9, 30.
Morristown & Erie R. Co., In re—§ 3-22, n. 6.
Morristown Lincoln–Mercury, Inc., In re, 42 B.R. 413—§ 6–38, n. 8; § 6–40, n. 6, 9.
Morristown Lincoln–Mercury, Inc., In re, 42 B.R. 411—§ 6–38, n. 21, 22; § 6–39, n. 2.
Morrow, In re—§ 8-33, n. 17, 24, 34.
Morse, In re—§ 6-61, n. 72, 73, 74.
Morse Elec. Co., Inc., In re—§ 12-2, n. 18.
MortgageAmerica Corp., In re, 831 F.2d 97—§ 6–83, n. 15.
MortgageAmerica Corp., In re, 714 F.2d 1266—§ 3–10, n. 22, 23; § 3–14, n. 25, 29, 30; § 6–2, n. 24.
Mortgage Inv. Co. of El Paso, Tex., In re—§ 11-29, n. 1.
Morton, In re—§ 3-16, n. 18, 19, 20.
Morton, Matter of—§ 6-15, n. 3, 8.
Moseley, In re—§ 9-4, n. 14; § 9-22, n. 2, 12, 14.
Moses, In re—§ 7-47, n. 2; § 11-30, n. 11.
Moses, Matter of, 91 B.R. 994—§ 6–39, n. 16; § 6–40, n. 2, 14; § 6–41, n. 11, 18, 36.
Moses, Matter of, 59 B.R. 815—§ 6–49, n. 13, 40, 43, 45.
Moskowitz, In re—§ 6-88, n. 35.
Mosley, In re—§ 8-33, n. 17, 34.
Moss, In re—§ 9-22; § 9-22, n. 7.
Mothershed, In re—§ 9-12, n. 6.
Mott Signs, Inc., In re—§ 6-61, n. 77.
Moulton, In re Estate of—§ 8-33, n. 7.
Moyer v. International State Bank of International Falls, Minn.—§ 8-31, n. 5.
Mozer, In re—§ 9-3, n. 8.
M. Paolella & Sons, Inc., In re—§ 6-93, n. 11.
Mr. Grocer, Inc., In re—§ 5-17, n. 2.
M.R.R. Traders, Inc. v. Cave Atlantique, Inc.—§ 4-16, n. 2.
M.S.V., Inc., In re—§ 6-73, n. 25.
Mueller, In re—§ 6-58, n. 4; § 8-32, n. 8.
Mueller, Matter of—§ 3-26, n. 12; § 3-27, n. 20.
Muleshoe State Bank, Muleshoe, Tex. v. Black—§ 7-26, n. 60.
Mullane v. Central Hanover Bank & Trust Co.—§ 10-31; § 10-31, n. 3; § 11-3, n. 21.
Mullen v. United States—§ 3-15, n. 6.
Mullet, In re—§ 7-26, n. 29.
Multi–Group III Ltd. Partnership, In re—§ 6-77, n. 8, 11, 20.
Multiponics, Inc., Matter of, 622 F.2d 725—§ 6–38, n. 9.
Multiponics, Inc., Matter of, 622 F.2d 709—§ 6–93, n. 32.
Muncrief, In re—§ 6-7, n. 12.
Munford, Inc., Matter of—§ 2-4, n. 2.
Munoz, In re—§ 3-27, n. 6.
Munroe v. Lasch—§ 3-20, n. 33.

Munsey Corp., In re—§ 3-11, n. 14; § 6-61, n. 55.
Murel Holding Corp., In re—§ 10-20; § 10-20, n. 7.
Murphy, In re—§ 4-7, n. 12.
Murray, In re, 128 B.R. 517—§ 3-21, n. 14.
Murray, In re, 105 B.R. 576—§ 8-28, n. 14.
Murray, In re, 89 B.R. 533—§ 3-8, n. 10.
Murray, In re, 31 B.R. 499—§ 3-30, n. 10, 12, 15, 17, 18.
Murray, In re, 27 B.R. 445—§ 6-33, n. 15.
Murray, In re, 5 B.R. 732—§ 6-72, n. 1; § 6-73, n. 10.
Murray Industries, Inc., In re, 125 B.R. 314—§ 6-87, n. 9.
Murray Industries, Inc., In re, 121 B.R. 635—§ 3-30, n. 30, 33.
Murrell, Matter of—§ 8-7, n. 13.
Muscatell, In re—§ 7-21, n. 3.
Musgrove, In re—§ 8-18, n. 2.
Mushroom King, Inc., State ex rel. Roberts v.—§ 12-5, n. 11.
Mushroom Transp. Co., Inc., In re—§ 5-5, n. 8; § 5-10, n. 6.
Music House, Inc., In re—§ 6-35, n. 44.
Musser, In re—§ 8-31, n. 3.
Musurlian, Matter of—§ 6-71, n. 16; § 6-88, n. 39.
Mutchler, In re—§ 2-17, n. 8.
Mutual Building & Investment Co. v. Efros—§ 8-7, n. 15.
Myatt, In re—§ 8-1, n. 11.
Myerson & Kuhn, In re—§ 3-22, n. 5, 23.

N

Nacol, Matter of—§ 6-49, n. 28; § 6-50, n. 6, 23.
Nancant, Inc., Matter of—§ 2-15, n. 22.
Nance, In re—§ 6-49, n. 12, 73, 76; § 6-87, n. 8.
Nanodata Computer Corp., In re, 74 B.R. 766—§ 12-3, n. 7.
Nanodata Computer Corp., In re, 52 B.R. 334—§ 12-2, n. 13.
Nantucket Apartments Associates, In re—§ 12-6, n. 9.
Napco Graphic Arts, Inc., In re—§ 3-16, n. 3; § 3-21, n. 82.
Napco Graphic Arts, Inc., Matter of—§ 6-62, n. 18, 26, 38.
Napotnik v. Equibank and Parkvale Sav. Ass'n—§ 2-8, n. 11; § 8-10, n. 5, 6, 25; § 8-33, n. 2.
Nardulli & Sons Co., Inc., In re—§ 10-29, n. 3.
Naron & Wagner, Chartered, In re—§ 4-4, n. 1, 15.
Nasco P.R., Inc., In re—§ 3-31, n. 17, 21, 41, 42.
Nashawaty, In re—§ 3-20, n. 9, 46.
Nash Phillips/Copus, Inc., In re—§ 6-61, n. 60.
Nashville White Trucks, Inc., In re—§ 3-3, n. 4; § 3-16, n. 3.
Nasr, In re—§ 6-94, n. 2.
Nathanson v. National Labor Relations Board—§ 11-7, n. 6.
National Ass'n for Advancement of Colored People v. Civiletti—§ 3-34, n. 7.
National Bank of Georgia v. Weiner—§ 6-38, n. 10.
National Bank of Newport v. National Herkimer County Bank of Little Falls—§ 6-9, n. 3.
National City Bank of New York v. Hotchkiss—§ 6-28, n. 3.
National Environmental Systems Corp., In re—§ 6-53, n. 6; § 6-56, n. 17, 27, 54.
National Equipment & Mold Corp., In re—§ 6-73, n. 26.
National Financial Alternatives, Inc., In re—§ 6-76, n. 5; § 6-77, n. 1.
National Hosp. and Institutional Builders Co., Matter of—§ 3-21, n. 5; § 3-22, n. 3.
National Office Products, Inc., In re—§ 6-31, n. 14, 17.
National Quick Print, Inc., In re—§ 6-4, n. 17.
National Real Estate Ltd. Partnership–II, In re, 104 B.R. 958—§ 6-77, n. 19.
National Real Estate Ltd. Partnership II, In re, 87 B.R. 986—§ 3-25, n. 42.
National Safe Northeast, Inc., Matter of—§ 6-48, n. 4; § 6-49, n. 15, 18, 43; § 6-88, n. 46.
National Service Corp., Matter of—§ 3-8, n. 9.
National Structures, Inc., In re—§ 6-40, n. 17, 27.
National Sugar Refining Co., In re—§ 6-65, n. 17.
National Sur. Corp. v. Gillette—§ 6-15, n. 2.
National Westminster Bank v. Ross—§ 3-31, n. 56, 57.
Nationwide Finance Corp. v. Wolford—§ 8-9, n. 12.
Natural Land Corp., In re—§ 3-29, n. 5.
Nat Warren Contracting Co., Inc., In re—§ 6-40, n. 2.
Naudain, Inc., In re—§ 6-41; § 6-41, n. 30.
Naugatuck Dairy Ice Cream Co., Inc., In re—§ 12-5, n. 11.

Nautilus of New Mexico, Inc., In re—§ **10-8, n. 3.**
Nazareth Nat. Bank v. Trina–Dee, Inc.—§ **3-25, n. 9.**
Ndosi, In re—§ **7-25, n. 2.**
N & D Properties, Inc., In re, 799 F.2d 726—§ **6–47, n. 8;** § **6–93, n. 16, 31, 32, 37, 38, 62.**
N & D Properties, Inc., In re, 54 B.R. 590—§ **6–49, n. 34.**
Neal, In re, 113 B.R. 607—§ **7–26, n. 53.**
Neal, In re, 10 B.R. 535—§ **9–18, n. 10.**
Nealis, In re—§ **6-15, n. 3;** § **8-23, n. 5.**
Neal Pharmacal Co., United States v.—§ **9-10, n. 12.**
Neavear, Matter of—§ **8-11, n. 3.**
Nebraska State Bank v. Jones—§ **6-2;** § **6-2, n. 24, 26;** § **6-82, n. 8.**
Neeley v. Murchison—§ **7-27, n. 5.**
Nehring, Matter of—§ **8-9, n. 7.**
Neiheisel, In re—§ **8-3, n. 12.**
Nejberger, In re—§ **3-14, n. 80.**
Nelkovski, In re—§ **9-3, n. 30;** § **9-4, n. 26.**
Nelsen, In re—§ **6-51, n. 22, 40.**
Nelson, In re, 123 B.R. 993—§ **3–8, n. 4;** § **3–21, n. 69.**
Nelson, In re, 92 B.R. 837—§ **8–1, n. 20.**
Nelson, In re, 73 B.R. 363—§ **2–2, n. 15.**
Nelson, In re Estate of—§ **3-6, n. 15.**
Nelson, Matter of, 66 B.R. 231—§ **2–15, n. 26.**
Nelson, Matter of, 27 B.R. 341—§ **9–22, n. 1.**
Nelson v. Bennett—§ **11-39;** § **11-39, n. 4.**
Nelson Co., In re—§ **6-4, n. 17;** § **6-11, n. 7;** § **6-20, n. 21.**
Nemacolin, Inc., In re—§ **6-61, n. 18, 21.**
Nemeti, In re—§ **6-47, n. 10.**
Nenninger, Matter of—§ **7-45, n. 4.**
Nentwick, In re—§ **6-62, n. 3, 38;** § **8-25, n. 7.**
NEPSCO, Inc., In re, 55 B.R. 574—§ **6–39, n. 35;** § **6–40, n. 14.**
NEPSCO, Inc., In re, 36 B.R. 25—§ **4–4, n. 8.**
Neptune World Wide Moving, Inc., In re—§ **10-29, n. 3.**
Nerlich, N.V., In re—§ **11-17, n. 3.**
Neshaminy Office Bldg. Associates, In re—§ **12-12, n. 30.**
Nesmith, In re—§ **9-17, n. 8.**
Network 90(degree), Inc., In re—§ **6-7, n. 6;** § **6-69, n. 3.**
Neufeld v. Freeman—§ **9-14, n. 17, 19.**
Neuman, In re—§ **3-22, n. 27.**
Neusteter Realty Co., In re—§ **3-14, n. 46;** § **3-16, n. 14.**
Neutgens, In re—§ **6-61, n. 55;** § **8-6, n. 4, 5;** § **8-9, n. 16.**
Neuton, In re—§ **8-33, n. 26.**
Nevada Implement Co., Matter of—§ **6-88, n. 30.**
Neville, In re—§ **3-14, n. 77.**
Newberry Corp. v. Fireman's Fund Ins. Co.—§ **6-9, n. 5;** § **6-25, n. 15.**
Newcomb, Matter of—§ **6-4;** § **6-4, n. 6;** § **6-17, n. 11;** § **6-61, n. 53;** § **6-93, n. 28.**
New Commonwealth Pub. Co., Inc., In re—§ **6-49, n. 49;** § **6-93, n. 45.**
New Concept Realty and Development, Inc., Matter of—§ **6-61, n. 53.**
Newell, In re, 117 B.R. 323—§ **3–8, n. 4.**
Newell, In re, 71 B.R. 672—§ **8–23, n. 9.**
New England Fish Co., In re—§ **4-10, n. 4.**
New Era Co., In re—§ **3-25;** § **3-25, n. 9, 10, 20.**
New Haven Radio, Inc., In re—§ **11-17, n. 8.**
Newman, In re—§ **6-60, n. 20.**
Newman, Matter of, 875 F.2d 668—§ **6–68, n. 2.**
Newman, Matter of, 64 B.R. 125—§ **6–87, n. 14;** § **6–88, n. 33.**
Newman, Matter of, 59 B.R. 670—§ **6–69, n. 13;** § **6–74, n. 8;** § **6–87, n. 8, 10;** § **6–88, n. 18, 20.**
Newman Companies, Inc., In re—§ **6-16, n. 1, 10;** § **6-27, n. 15.**
Newport Nat. Bank v. Adair—§ **8-6, n. 10.**
Newport Offshore, Ltd., In re—§ **6-44, n. 16.**
New York, City of v. Exxon Corp.—§ **3-21, n. 7, 74.**
New York, City of v. New York, N.H. & H.R. Co.—§ **10-31, n. 5;** § **11-3, n. 21.**
New York City Shoes, Inc., In re, 880 F.2d 679—§ **6–34, n. 17.**
New York City Shoes, Inc., In re, 98 B.R. 725—§ **6–7, n. 9.**
New York City Shoes, Inc., In re, 78 B.R. 426—§ **6–43, n. 29.**
New Yorketown Associates, In re—§ **6-54, n. 10;** § **6-55, n. 13;** § **6-56, n. 50.**
New York Investors Mut. Group, Inc., In re—§ **5-7, n. 13;** § **5-8, n. 3.**
New York Life Ins. Co. v. Bremer Towers—§ **3-16, n. 5.**
Nicholas, Inc., Matter of—§ **3-21, n. 70.**

TABLE OF CASES

Nichols, Matter of—§ 8-11, n. 18.
Nicholson, In re, 70 B.R. 398—§ 3–11; § 3–11, n. 11, 14; § 9–20; § 9–20, n. 14.
Nicholson, In re, 57 B.R. 672—§ 6-61, n. 59; § 6-62, n. 18, 26.
Nickels, In re—§ 9-12, n. 2.
Nickerson & Nickerson, Inc., Matter of—§ 6-40, n. 5, 25; § 6-45, n. 3, 7, 12.
Nicolet, Inc., In re—§ 11-14, n. 2, 3; § 11-15, n. 17.
Nicolet, Inc., United States v.—§ 3-21, n. 7, 45, 50, 57, 74, 90; § 3-31, n. 96.
Niedermayer v. Adelman—§ 8-18, n. 6.
Nield, In re—§ 3-23, n. 35.
Nielsen, In re—§ 6-77, n. 1, 23.
Nielson, In re—§ 6-39, n. 15; § 6-40, n. 4; § 6-42, n. 2, 3.
Nikokyrakis, In re—§ 7-39, n. 7, 15.
905 Intern. Stores, Inc., In re—§ 5-20, n. 5.
19101 Corp., In re—§ 12-10, n. 2, 6, 7.
Nittler, In re—§ 9-14, n. 19.
Nivens, In re—§ 6-35, n. 24, 26.
Nixon Elec. Supply, Inc., In re—§ 11-16, n. 4, 6.
N.L.R.B. v. Better Bldg. Supply Corp.—§ 7-18, n. 2.
N.L.R.B. v. Bildisco and Bildisco—§ 1-4, n. 6; § 3-7; § 3-7, n. 1; § 5-1, n. 1; § 5-8; § 5-8, n. 6; § 5-15; § 5-15, n. 2; § 5-22, n. 5; § 6-39, n. 15.
N.L.R.B. v. Brada Miller Freight Systems, Inc.—§ 3-21, n. 126.
N.L.R.B. v. Continental Hagen Corp.—§ 3-21, n. 8, 34, 45, 70, 90, 92.
N.L.R.B. v. Edward Cooper Painting, Inc.—§ 3-6, n. 5, 40; § 3-7, n. 4; § 3-21; § 3-21, n. 6, 27, 45, 49, 70, 71, 74, 76, 90.
N.L.R.B. v. Evans Plumbing Co.—§ 3-21, n. 8, 27, 44, 45, 70.
N.L.R.B. v. Laborers' Intern. Union of North America, AFL–CIO—§ 7-18, n. 2.
N.L.R.B. v. Martin Arsham Sewing Co.—§ 6-2, n. 25.
N.L.R.B. v. P*I*E Nationwide, Inc.—§ 3-21, n. 45, 70, 90, 92.
N.L.R.B. v. Twin Cities Elec.—§ 3-21, n. 8, 70.
NLT Computer Services Corp. v. Capital Computer Systems, Inc.—§ 3-2, n. 4; § 3-6, n. 3, 16, 38.
N.N. Elec. Co., Inc., In re—§ 6-39, n. 14, 38.
Noble v. Yingling, 37 B.R. 647—§ 8–29, n. 12.
Noble v. Yingling, 29 B.R. 998—§ 8–1, n. 20.
Noco, Inc., In re—§ 5-7, n. 20.
Nogami, In re—§ 7-26, n. 21.
Nohinek v. Logsdon—§ 8-6, n. 10.
Nolen, In re—§ 8-22, n. 21.
Noli v. Commissioner—§ 3-30, n. 20, 33.
Norco Food Systems, Inc., In re—§ 6-88, n. 15.
Nordbrock, In re—§ 2-5, n. 15.
Nordic Village, Inc., In re—§ 6-88, n. 22, 26, 27.
Nordic Village, Inc., United States v.—§ 3-34; § 3-34, n. 7.5; § 6-87, n. 9; § 6-88, n. 4.
Norfolk, In re—§ 3-12, n. 5.
Norman, In re, 32 B.R. 562—§ 8–19, n. 12.
Norman, In re, 13 B.R. 894—§ 3–10, n. 47.
Norman v. Norman—§ 9–3, n. 11.
Normandin, In re—§ 4-10, n. 1.
Norquist, In re—§ 11-38, n. 1.
North, In re—§ 3-6, n. 6; § 3-11, n. 26; § 3-14, n. 46, 80; § 3-21, n. 69.
Northampton Corp., In re—§ 2-16; § 2-16, n. 15.
North County Place, Ltd., In re—§ 6-78, n. 9.
North Dakota State Board of Higher Educ. v. Frech—§ 7-33, n. 14.
Northeast Chick Services, Inc., In re—§ 6-76, n. 2; § 6-77, n. 1, 21; § 6-78, n. 17.
Northeast Dairy Co-op. Federation, Inc., In re—§ 10-22, n. 7.
Northeastern Intern. Airways, Inc., In re—§ 6-39, n. 13; § 6-43, n. 3; § 6-44, n. 5.
Northern Pac. R. Co. v. Boyd—§ 11-25, n. 1; § 11-26; § 11-26, n. 1; § 11-27.
Northern Pipeline Const. Co. v. Marathon Pipe Line Co.—§ 12-1; § 12-1, n. 1; § 12-2; § 12-2, n. 1; § 12-3; § 12-3, n. 2; § 12-5; § 12-5, n. 1; § 12-13; § 12-13, n. 7; § 12-14; § 12-14, n. 13.
Northgate Terrace Apartments, Ltd., In re—§ 3-25, n. 46, 49.
North Indianapolis Venture, In re—§ 3-29, n. 14.
Northlake Bldg. Partners, In re—§ 11-36; § 11-36, n. 3, 10.
North Star Contracting Corp., In re—§ 3-10, n. 11.
Northwest Aggregate & Const. Co., Inc., In re—§ 3-31, n. 20.
Northwest Airlines, Inc. v. Roemer—§ 8-33, n. 15.
Northwest Cinema Corp., In re—§ 12-2, n. 8.
Northwestern Mutual Life Ins. Co. v. Axton (In re)—§ 12-14, n. 17, 18.
Northwest Recreational Activities, Inc., Matter of, 8 B.R. 10—§ 11-17, n. 3.
Northwest Recreational Activities, Inc., Matter of, 4 B.R. 36—§ 2–15; § 2–15, n. 6.

Northwest Wholesale Lumber, Inc. v. Citadel Co.—§ 3-18, n. 24; § 3-32, n. 6.
Norton, In re—§ 7-41, n. 13.
Norton v. Brokerage Oil Co.—§ 8-9, n. 13.
Norton, United States v.—§ 3-15, n. 6; § 6-40, n. 2; § 6-42, n. 2; § 6-43, n. 4, 14, 15, 32.
Norwegian Health Spa, Inc., In re—§ 5-5, n. 8.
Norwesco Development Corp., In re—§ 3-21, n. 103.
Norwest Bank Nebraska, N.A. v. Tveten—§ 8-9, n. 3; § 8-32; § 8-32, n. 4, 8, 19, 20.
Norwest Bank Worthington v. Ahlers—§ 10-21; § 10-21, n. 6; § 11-27; § 11-27, n. 14; § 11-28; § 11-28, n. 1; § 11-29; § 11-29, n. 1.
Novak, In re, 121 B.R. 18—§ 3-27, n. 41.
Novak, In re, 103 B.R. 403—§ 3-31, n. 5.
Nova Real Estate Inv. Trust, In re—§ 11-5, n. 2; § 11-6, n. 13.
Nowak, In re—§ 8-25, n. 57.
N.R.G. Investments, Inc., Matter of—§ 10-26, n. 1.
N.R. Guaranteed Retirement, Inc., In re—§ 3-29, n. 5, 9, 12.
N.S. Garrott & Sons, In re—§ 10-7, n. 2; § 10-12, n. 7.
NTG Industries, Inc., In re—§ 6-39, n. 27; § 6-40, n. 5, 6; § 6-43, n. 3.
Nucorp Energy, Inc., In re, 902 F.2d 729—§ 6-36, n. 12; § 6-61, n. 60; § 6-62, n. 5.
Nucorp Energy, Inc., In re, 102 B.R. 204—§ 6-20, n. 7.
Nucorp Energy, Inc., In re, 92 B.R. 416—§ 6-16, n. 1.
Nucorp Energy, Inc., In re, 80 B.R. 517—§ 6-25; § 6-25, n. 7, 13, 15, 24, 35.
Nucorp Energy Securities Litigation, In re—§ 11-39, n. 5.
Null's Service, Inc., In re—§ 6-39, n. 14.
Nunally, In re—§ 8-25, n. 5, 6; § 8-27, n. 9.
Nunley, In re—§ 8-10, n. 26; § 8-28, n. 25.
Nu-Process Brake Engineers, Inc., In re—§ 3-8, n. 26.
Nutting, In re—§ 8-23, n. 6.
Nuttleman, Matter of—§ 8-33, n. 2, 24.
NWFX, Inc., In re—§ 6-40, n. 19; § 6-42, n. 1; § 6-45, n. 3, 5, 12; § 6-74, n. 9.

O

Oak Creek Florists, Matter of—§ 6-61, n. 77.
Oberlies, In re—§ 4-9, n. 13; § 8-3, n. 21; § 8-10, n. 25, 26.
Oberst, In re—§ 8-32, n. 8, 17, 18.
O'Brien, In re, 67 B.R. 317—§ 8-19, n. 1, 2; § 8-32, n. 5.
O'Brien, In re, 50 B.R. 67—§ 8-11, n. 18.
O'Brien, Matter of—§ 8-33, n. 17, 24, 34.
O'Brien v. Fischel—§ 3-20, n. 11; § 3-21; § 3-21, n. 40, 44.
Obshatkin, In re—§ 6-6, n. 9.
Ocean Beach Club, Inc., In re—§ 6-94, n. 3, 5.
Ocean Developments of America, In re, 29 B.R. 129—§ 6-49, n. 40.
Ocean Developments of America, Inc., In re, 22 B.R. 834—§ 6-49, n. 78.
Ocheltree, In re—§ 12-10, n. 8.
O'Connell, In re—§ 6-12, n. 7; § 6-17, n. 23; § 6-89, n. 8.
Octagon Roofing, In re, 124 B.R. 522—§ 6-9, n. 5; § 6-17, n. 11.
Octagon Roofing, In re, 123 B.R. 583—§ 6-10, n. 13; § 6-49, n. 46.
O'Day Corp., In re—§ 6-52, n. 7, 8, 10, 13; § 6-93, n. 5, 50.
O'Donnell, In re—§ 11-16, n. 4.
O'Donnell, United States v.—§ 7-21, n. 11.
O'Farrell, In re—§ 9-25, n. 11; § 9-29, n. 3.
Official Creditors' Committee v. Liberal Market, Inc.—§ 6-2, n. 28.
Ofia Realty Corp., In re—§ 12-10, n. 9.
Ofty Corp., Matter of—§ 12-6, n. 1.
Ohio v. Kovacs—§ 3-21; § 3-21, n. 106; § 7-8; § 7-8, n. 1, 2; § 11-1, n. 2; § 11-2, n. 3; § 11-9; § 11-9, n. 1.
Ohio Corrugating Co., In re—§ 6-49, n. 13, 23, 39, 46; § 6-52; § 6-52, n. 7, 8, 13, 15, 27.
Ohio Corrugating Co., Matter of—§ 6-49, n. 49, 57, 69; § 6-52, n. 28; § 6-88, n. 45, 51.
Ohning, In re—§ 6-45, n. 18, 36.
O-Jay Foods, Inc., In re—§ 3-28, n. 5, 13.
Oklahoma Associates, In re—§ 6-77, n. 12.
Oklahoma P.A.C. First Ltd. Partnership, In re—§ 3-25, n. 43, 59; § 3-29, n. 1, 12.
Oklahoma Plaza Investors, Ltd., In re—§ 5-10, n. 4.
Okoreeh-Baah, In re—§ 9-14, n. 20.
Old Delmar Corp., In re—§ 12-10, n. 6.
Old World Cone Co., In re—§ 6-18, n. 21, 23.

TABLE OF CASES

Oliphant, In re—§ 6-40, n. 4.
Oliver, In re, 66 B.R. 426—§ 6-77, n. 5, 21.
Oliver, In re, 44 B.R. 989—§ 6-58, n. 1.
Oliver, In re, 38 B.R. 245—§ 6-73, n. 8.
Oliver v. Milford—§ 8-7, n. 3.
Oliver Rubber Co. v. Griffin Retreading Co., Inc.—§ 6-67; § 6-67, n. 14.
Oliver's Stores, Inc., Matter of, 112 B.R. 671—§ 6-7, n. 6.
Oliver's Stores, Inc., Matter of, 107 B.R. 40—§ 12-3, n. 7; § 12-5, n. 11.
Olive Street Investments, Inc., In re—§ 3-31, n. 103.
Olivier, In re—§ 7-19, n. 10, 11.
Ollada, In re—§ 6-82, n. 1; § 6-83, n. 8.
Ollag Const. Equipment Corp., Matter of—§ 6-18, n. 18; § 6-51, n. 16.
Oller v. Sonoma County Land Title Co.—§ 6-56, n. 1.
Olm Associates, In re—§ 6-40, n. 16.
Olmstead, In re—§ 8-3, n. 21.
Olsen, In re, 861 F.2d 188—§ 10-33, n. 2.
Olsen, In re, 87 B.R. 148—§ 4-14, n. 5.
Olson, In re, 916 F.2d 481—§ 7-21; § 7-21, n. 4.
Olson, In re, 45 B.R. 501—§ 8-32, n. 5.
Olson, Matter of—§ 6-73, n. 8.
Olympic Foundry Co., In re—§ 6-26, n. 2.
Omaha Midwest Wholesale Distributors, Inc., Matter of—§ 2-17, n. 19; § 6-11, n. 6; § 6-71, n. 13.
O'Malley, In re—§ 3-20, n. 22, 25.
O'Malley v. Rapidan River Farm—§ 8-26, n. 2.
Omega Lithographers, Inc., In re—§ 6-93, n. 29.
Omni Graphics, Inc., In re—§ 3-16, n. 7; § 3-32, n. 27, 28; § 3-33, n. 28, 34; § 6-93, n. 62.
Omni Mechanical Contractors, Inc., In re—§ 6-20, n. 5, 17; § 6-60, n. 10, 17.
Ondras, In re—§ 8-3, n. 14.
151-69 Nagle Ave. Associates v. Jiminez—§ 3-6, n. 47.
134 Baker Street, Inc. v. State—§ 3-20, n. 5, 15.
O'Neill, In re—§ 6-83, n. 5.
O'Neill v. Nestle Libbys P.R., Inc.—§ 6-31, n. 16.
One Marketing Co., Inc., In re—§ 6-83, n. 12.
1438 Meridian Place, N. W., Inc., In re—§ 11-40, n. 1.
1726 Washington, D.C. Partners, In re—§ 6-77, n. 11, 15.
1606 New Hampshire Ave. Associates, In re—§ 12-6, n. 8.
1301 Connecticut Ave. Associates, In re, 126 B.R. 1—§ 6-77, n. 11.
1301 Connecticut Ave. Associates, In re 117 B.R. 2—§ 6-77, n. 19.
1243 20th Street, Inc., In re—§ 10-10, n. 1.
Onio's Italian Restaurant Corp., In re—§ 3-14, n. 67, 68.
Onouli-Kona Land Co., In re—§ 3-31, n. 103; § 4-4, n. 7; § 4-17, n. 11.
Ontario Locomotive & Indus. Ry. Supplies (United States) Inc., In re—§ 5-15, n. 10, 11.
Ophaug, In re—§ 7-26; § 7-26, n. 3, 12, 30.
O.P.M. Leasing Services, Inc., In re, 40 B.R. 380—§ 6-49, n. 39, 46, 49.
O.P.M. Leasing Services, Inc., In re, 35 B.R. 854—§ 6-40, n. 27; § 6-48, n. 8.
O.P.M. Leasing Services, Inc., In re, 32 B.R. 199—§ 6-60, n. 17, 29; § 6-88, n. 30.
O.P.M. Leasing Services, Inc., In re, 28 B.R. 740—§ 6-49, n. 46; § 6-60, n. 10.
O.P.M. Leasing Services, Inc., In re, 23 B.R. 104—§ 5-7, n. 13, 16; § 6-87, n. 15.
O.P.M. Leasing Services, Inc., Matter of—§ 6-4, n. 9.
Orah Wall Financial Corp., In re—§ 6-93, n. 39, 42, 47.
Orange Brevard Plumbing & Heating Co. v. La Croix—§ 8-13, n. 7.
Orecchio, In re—§ 7-26, n. 50.
Orient River Investments, Inc., In re—§ 6-40, n. 4, 7.
Originala Petroleum Corp., In re—§ 6-47, n. 8.
Orion Investments, Inc. v. Dunaway and Associates, Inc.—§ 3-6, n. 26.
Oro Import Co., Inc., In re—§ 6-83, n. 4.
Orsa Associates, In re—§ 6-17, n. 11; § 6-49, n. 46; § 6-50, n. 28; § 6-53, n. 9.
Orsa Associates, Inc., In re—§ 6-50, n. 33; § 6-89, n. 17, 18, 28.
Ortiz Vega, In re—§ 8-23, n. 3.
Orvco, Inc., In re—§ 5-23, n. 4.
Osage Crude Oil Purchasing, Inc., In re—§ 6-49, n. 46, 47.
Osage Exploration Co., In re—§ 12-11, n. 4.
Osborn v. Charles E. Scott Co., Inc.—§ 3-6, n. 30.
Osborne, In re—§ 6-93, n. 39, 41, 53.
Osbourne, In re—§ 6-48, n. 4, 5.
Osburn, Matter of—§ 8-11, n. 16, 18; § 8-17, n. 33, 34.
Osner & Mehlhorn v. Loewe—§ 6-56, n. 1.
Oswald, In re—§ 4-9, n. 10; § 8-10, n. 11, 21.

Otasco, Inc., In re—§ 12-15; § 12-15, n. 8.
Otis & Edwards, P.C., In re—§ 6-52, n. 49; § 6-60, n. 4; § 6-93, n. 16, 21, 31, 33, 35.
Otoe County Nat. Bank v. W & P Trucking, Inc.—§ 3-5, n. 6.
Ottaviano, Matter of—§ 6-2, n. 20; § 6-47, n. 7; § 6-49, n. 44; § 6-56, n. 14.
Ottawa Cartage, Inc., In re—§ 6-36, n. 11.
Ottenheimer v. Whitaker—§ 11-9, n. 3.
Oulman v. Rolling Green, Inc.—§ 3-16, n. 12.
Our Distribution Co., Inc., In re—§ 6-87, n. 10.
Outlook/Century, Ltd., In re—§ 3-25, n. 32, 45.
Ouverson, In re—§ 3-29, n. 13.
Overbey v. Murray—§ 3-6, n. 2; § 3-32, n. 38.
Overly–Hautz Co., In re—§ 9-4, n. 14.
Overstreet, In re—§ 9-3, n. 6.
Owen, In re, 877 F.2d 44—§ 8–26, n. 7.
Owen, In re, 104 B.R. 929—§ 6–6, n. 3.
Owen v. Owen—§ 8-9, n. 8; § 8-26; § 8-26, n. 6, 10; § 8-27; § 8-27, n. 7.
Owens, In re, 82 B.R. 960—§ 9–2, n. 10.
Owens, In re, 67 B.R. 418—§ 9–4, n. 14.
Owensboro Distilling Co., In re—§ 12-2, n. 4; § 12-15; § 12-15, n. 7; § 12-16, n. 3.
Owens–Peterson, In re—§ 6-42, n. 2; § 6-43, n. 7, 29.
Owners of Harvey Oil Center, In re—§ 6-74, n. 11, 14.
Oxford Marketing, Ltd., In re—§ 12-2, n. 12.
Ozark Restaurant Equipment Co., Inc., In re, 850 F.2d 342—§ 6–49, n. 63, 73, 76; § 6–88, n. 51.
Ozark Restaurant Equipment Co., Inc., In re, 816 F.2d 1222—§ 2–4, n. 2; § 2–8, n. 6; § 6–61, n. 7, 8.
Ozark Restaurant Equipment Co., Inc., In re, 77 B.R. 686—§ 6–84, n. 2.
Ozark Restaurant Equipment Co., Inc., Matter of—§ 6-49, n. 3.
Ozias v. Renner—§ 6-56, n. 1.

P

Pacana, In re—§ 3-12, n. 10.
Pacific Exp., Inc., In re—§ 6-61, n. 12, 16; § 6-93, n. 39, 44, 46.
Pacific Forest Industries, Inc., In re—§ 10-7, n. 2; § 10-12, n. 7.
Pacileo, In re—§ 6-20, n. 22.
Packer, In re—§ 8-28, n. 3.
Pacor, Inc., In re—§ 12-5, n. 5.
Page–Wilson Corp., Matter of—§ 11-7, n. 8.
Pagoda Intern., Inc., In re—§ 3-28, n. 13.
Pahule, Matter of—§ 7-34, n. 13.
Paige, In re—§ 9-18, n. 10, 11.
Pako Corp. v. Citytrust—§ 10-29, n. 3, 11.
Palmer, In re—§ 8-25, n. 34, 36.
Palmieri, In re—§ 6-40, n. 36.
Panache Development Co., Inc., In re—§ 2-15, n. 22.
Pan Am Corp., In re, 128 B.R. 59—§ 3–24, n. 1.
Pan Am Corp., In re, 124 B.R. 960—§ 3–17, n. 5, 7, 9, 10, 13, 14, 18, 19, 21.
Pancho's Intern., Inc., Matter of—§ 6-93, n. 32, 33.
Panholzer, In re—§ 2-8, n. 10.
Pan Trading Corp., S.A., In re—§ 6-19, n. 16; § 6-25, n. 13; § 6-31, n. 9; § 6-69, n. 11.
Papercraft Corp., In re—§ 6-40, n. 4; § 6-94, n. 6.
Pappalardo, In re—§ 9-14, n. 16.
Pappas, In re, 106 B.R. 268—§ 3-23, n. 40.
Pappas, In re, 17 B.R. 662—§ 11–17, n. 2.
Paradise Hotel Corp. v. Bank of Nova Scotia—§ 2-5, n. 13.
Paradise Valley Country Club, In re—§ 10-29, n. 9.
Paralelo 42 Corp., In re—§ 6-74, n. 11.
Parham, In re—§ 6-77, n. 12.
Paris Industries Corp., In re, 106 B.R. 344—§ 12-2, n. 4; § 12–14, n. 20; § 12–15, n. 1.
Paris Industries Corp., In re, 80 B.R. 2—§ 3–21, n. 110.
Park at Dash Point L.P., In re—§ 3-27, n. 35; § 6-77, n. 1, 12.
Parker, In re—§ 6-45, n. 7.
Parker Montana Co., In re—§ 6-93, n. 11.
Parker Street Florist & Garden Center, Inc., In re—§ 11-13, n. 3; § 11-14, n. 5; § 11-15; § 11-15, n. 12.
Park North Partners, Ltd., In re—§ 6-20, n. 13.

TABLE OF CASES

Park North Partners, Ltd., Matter of—§ 6-21, n. 6.
Park Terrace Townhouses v. Wilds—§ 4-3, n. 3.
Parkway Calabasas Ltd., In re—§ 2-4, n. 5; § 6-20, n. 20.
Paroline v. Doling—§ 2-5, n. 15.
Parrish, In re—§ 6-39, n. 15; § 6-40, n. 5.
Parr Meadows Racing Ass'n, Inc., In re, 880 F.2d 1540—§ 3-18, n. 20.
Parr Meadows Racing Ass'n, Inc., In re, 92 B.R. 30—§ 3-3, n. 4; § 3-16, n. 3; § 3-21, n. 69.
Parsley, In re—§ 8-25, n. 31, 33, 34, 35.
Patch Graphics, Matter of—§ 4-12, n. 3.
Patch Press, Inc., Matter of—§ 6-70, n. 2.
Pat Freeman, Inc., Matter of—§ 6-93, n. 6, 42.
Patterson, In re—§ 3-15, n. 6.
Patterson, Matter of—§ 8-3, n. 21; § 8-20, n. 2; § 8-25, n. 49, 56.
Patterson v. Adams—§ 8-13, n. 7.
Patterson v. Shumate—§ 8-11; § 8-11, n. 22; § 8-33; § 8-33, n. 19.
Patton, Matter of—§ 2-2, n. 22.
Paul, In re—§ 8-24, n. 4.
Paul v. Monts—§ 10-31, n. 1.
Paul Pack Steel Erection, Co., Inc., In re—§ 6-39, n. 14.
Pauquette, In re—§ 8-17, n. 35, 36, 51.
Payment Plans, Inc. v. Strell—§ 6-61, n. 16.
Payne, In re—§ 2-17, n. 4.
Payne v. Wood—§ 8-1, n. 9, 13; § 8-13, n. 12.
PCH Associates, In re, 804 F.2d 193 (2nd Cir.1986)—§ 5-2; § 5-2, n. 6.
PCH Associates, In re, 122 B.R. 181 (Bkrtcy.S.D.N.Y.1990)—§ 3-14, n. 40.
PDQ Copy Center, Inc., In re—§ 6-36, n. 17, 19.
Peacock, In re, 119 B.R. 605—§ 8-3, n. 18, 20.
Peacock, In re, 87 B.R. 657—§ 7-39, n. 7, 14, 15.
Pearl, Matter of—§ 8-21, n. 4.
Pearson, In re, 917 F.2d 1215—§ 3-3, n. 4; § 3-34, n. 8, 9.
Pearson, In re, 10 B.R. 189—§ 9-17, n. 3.
Pearson, Matter of—§ 9-3, n. 24.
Pearson v. Salina Coffee House, Inc.—§ 6-61, n. 16.
Peck, In re—§ 8-28, n. 3.
Peck v. Augustin Bros. Co.—§ 6-63, n. 2.
Pederson, In re—§ 8-25, n. 17, 18.
Peeples, In re—§ 6-47, n. 8.
Peerless Plating Co., In re—§ 11-10, n. 5.
Peltz, In re—§ 11-3, n. 9.
Pembroke Development Corp., In re, 124 B.R. 398—§ 6-18, n. 10; § 6-49, n. 49, 51.
Pembroke Development Corp., In re, 122 B.R. 610—§ 6-18, n. 26, 30.
Pendlebury, In re—§ 7-39, n. 6.
Penfil, In re—§ 6-72, n. 4.
Penn-Dixie Industries, Inc., In re—§ 10-12, n. 12.
Pennetta, In re—§ 9-4, n. 14.
Penn Jersey Corp., In re—§ 3-9; § 3-9, n. 20, 31.
Pennsylvania Dept. of Public Welfare v. Davenport—§ 3-1, n. 20; § 6-19, n. 4; § 7-31, n. 10; § 9-2, n. 11; § 9-20; § 9-20, n. 4.
Pennsylvania Tire Co., Matter of—§ 6-45, n. 3, 6, 7, 10.
Penn Terra Ltd. v. Department of Environmental Resources, Com. of Pa.—§ 3-21; § 3-21, n. 7, 74, 92, 95, 105.
Penthouse Travelers of Aripeka, Inc., In re—§ 6-67, n. 1.
Peoples Finance Co. v. Saffold—§ 8-33, n. 15.
Pepenella, In re, 103 B.R. 299—§ 8-10, n. 26.
Pepenella, In re, 79 B.R. 76—§ 8-10, n. 24.
Pepper v. Litton—§ 6-93; § 6-93, n. 25, 27; § 11-7, n. 6.
Pepsico, Inc. v. Burden—§ 3-5, n. 6, 14.
Percy Wilson Mortg. and Finance Corp. v. McCurdy—§ 9-17, n. 3.
Perdido Bay Country Club Estates, Inc., In re—§ 6-49, n. 12; § 6-53, n. 9; § 6-56, n. 5.
Perdido Motel Group, Inc., In re, 108 B.R. 316—§ 6-7, n. 5.
Perdido Motel Group, Inc., In re, 101 B.R. 289—§ 10-17, n. 4.
Pereau, In re—§ 6-18, n. 15.
Peregrine Entertainment, Ltd., In re—§ 6-61, n. 16, 69.
Perez, In re—§ 6-2, n. 3, 21.
Perez v. Campbell—§ 7-40; § 7-40, n. 3; § 7-41.
Perez v. Pogge—§ 8-7, n. 8.
Perez, United States v.—§ 6-40, n. 12.
Perfectlite Co., In re—§ 5-10; § 5-10, n. 12, 13.

Performance Communications, Inc., In re—§ 6-10, n. 15.
Performance Papers, Inc., In re—§ 6-67, n. 3.
Perkins, In re, 71 B.R. 294—§ 11–13, n. 3; § 11–14, n. 2, 3; § 11–15; § 11–15, n. 7, 17; § 11–18, n. 1.
Perkins, In re, 55 B.R. 422—§ 9–5, n. 5.
Perkins v. Scharffe—§ 7-30; § 7-30, n. 6, 7, 19, 26.
Pernie Bailey Drilling Co., Inc., In re—§ 6-88, n. 23, 30; § 6-93, n. 13.
Pero Bros. Farms, Inc., In re—§ 2-18, n. 2.
Perpetual Corp., In re—§ 11-7, n. 10.
Perrin's Marine Sales, Inc., In re—§ 6-61, n. 67, 74.
Perry, In re, 124 B.R. 50—§ 3-33, n. 12.
Perry, In re, 90 B.R. 565—§ 6–2, n. 16, 22; § 8–1, n. 20; § 8–23, n. 7.
Perry, In re, 48 B.R. 591—§ 6–15, n. 3; § 8–23, n. 5.
Perry, In re, 29 B.R. 787—§ 3–11, n. 14.
Perry, In re, 26 B.R. 599—§ 6–43, n. 13, 31.
Perry, In re, 6 B.R. 263—§ 8–6, n. 8.
Perry, Matter of—§ 9-3, n. 15.
Perry v. Commerce Loan Co.—§ 9-1, n. 2, 3.
Perry, Adams and Lewis Securities, Inc., Matter of—§ 6-40, n. 6; § 6-42, n. 2, 3; § 6-49, n. 49, 50.
Perskin, In re—§ 9-4, n. 24.
Persky, In re—§ 4-9, n. 10; § 8-10, n. 19, 21.
Personal Designs, Inc. v. Guymar, Inc.—§ 3-5, n. 17.
Personalized Air Conditioning, Inc. v. C.M. Systems of Pinellas County, Inc.—§ 3-6, n. 27.
Pester Refining Co., Matter of, 845 F.2d 1476—§ 6–73, n. 26.
Pester Refining Co., Matter of, 66 B.R. 801—§ 6–67, n. 10.
Pestritto, Matter of—§ 3-5, n. 10; § 3-22, n. 24.
Peters v. Lines—§ 12-14, n. 17, 18.
Peterson, In re, 929 F.2d 385—§ 8–1, n. 12.
Peterson, In re, 897 F.2d 935—§ 8–3, n. 21.
Peterson, In re, 118 B.R. 801—§ 3–1, n. 21; § 3–23, n. 40.
Peterson, In re, 116 B.R. 247—§ 3–30, n. 33, 34; § 3–31, n. 98.
Peterson, In re, 106 B.R. 229—§ 8–9, n. 3, 16.
Peterson, In re, 80 B.R. 167—§ 6–61, n. 30.
Peterson's Ltd., Inc., In re—§ 5-20, n. 9.
Petrolia Corp., In re—§ 12-3, n. 7.
Petruccelli, In re—§ 3-23, n. 48.
Pettibone Corp., In re, 110 B.R. 848—§ 3–32, n. 1, 10, 11, 34.
Pettibone Corp., In re, 90 B.R. 918—§ 7–7, n. 5; § 11–1, n. 4: § 11–3, n. 1; § 11–4, n. 9; § 11–10, n. 1.
Pettibone Corp. v. Easley—§ 3-23, n. 34.
Pettigrew, In re—§ 8-3, n. 10, 19.
Pettit, In re, 61 B.R. 341—§ 8–17, n. 31.
Pettit, In re, 57 B.R. 362—§ 8–17, n. 19.
Pettit, Matter of—§ 8-17, n. 23.
Pettitt v. Baker—§ 3-33, n. 7.
Petty, In re—§ 6-83, n. 18; § 6-84, n. 5.
Petur U.S.A. Instrument Co., Inc., In re—§ 5-8, n. 12; § 11-13, n. 11; § 11-36, n. 9.
Pfingsten, In re—§ 8-25, n. 16.
Pharmadyne Laboratories, Inc., Matter of—§ 5-23, n. 3.
Philadelphia Light Supply Co., In re—§ 6-2, n. 28.
Philippe v. Anderson—§ 3-32, n. 38.
Phillips, In re, 882 F.2d 302—§ 7–28, n. 5; § 7–30, n. 17, 25.
Phillips, In re, 804 F.2d 930—§ 7–26, n. 3, 5, 13, 35.
Phillips, In re, 104 B.R. 499—§ 6–60, n. 4.
Phillips, In re, 103 B.R. 893—§ 6–12, n. 7; § 6–24, n. 2; § 6–33, n. 10.
Phillips, In re, 45 B.R. 529—§ 8–17, n. 33.
Phillips, In re, 24 B.R. 712—§ 6–35, n. 40.
Phillips, Matter of—§ 2-2, n. 22.
Phillos, In re—§ 8-10, n. 8, 11.
Phoenix Institute of Technology v. Klein—§ 9–2, n. 10.
Phoenix Piccadilly, Ltd., In re—§ 2-15; § 2-15, n. 8, 21; § 3-29, n. 1, 2, 11; § 12-6, n. 9.
Phoenix Steel Corp., In re—§ 4-13, n. 1; § 4-14; § 4-14, n. 3, 6.
Phoenix Steel Corp., Matter of, 82 B.R. 334—§ 4–14, n. 4.
Phoenix Steel Corp., Matter of, 76 B.R. 373—§ 6–20, n. 20; § 6–25, n. 15.
Photo Promotion Associates, Inc., In re, 881 F.2d 6—§ 6–69, n. 14.
Photo Promotion Associates, Inc., In re, 87 B.R. 835—§ 11–10, n. 1.
Photo Promotion Associates, Inc., In re, 61 B.R. 936—§ 6–78, n. 16.
Photo Promotion Associates, Inc., In re, 53 B.R. 759—§ 6–76, n. 2.

TABLE OF CASES

Picco v. Global Marine Drilling Co.—§ 3-6, n. 40; § 3-32, n. 30.
Piche, In re—§ 6-47, n. 7; § 6-48, n. 8; § 6-60, n. 17.
Pick, In re—§ 12-11, n. 10.
Pickwick Place Ltd. Partnership, In re—§ 12-10, n. 6.
Pierce, In re, 809 F.2d 1356—§ 6-62, n. 26.
Pierce, In re, 82 B.R. 874—§ 9-12; § 9-12, n. 6, 7.
Pierce, In re—§ 6-62, n. 26; § 9-12; § 9-12, n. 6, 7.
Pierce, Matter of—§ 7-49, n. 6, 9.
Pierce Coal and Const., Inc., In re—§ 11-10, n. 4.
Pieri, In re—§ 6-40, n. 2; § 6-42, n. 2; § 6-43, n. 3.
Pigeon, In re—§ 6-77, n. 23.
Pilkington, In re—§ 8-33, n. 24.
Pine, In re—§ 8-26; § 8-26, n. 16.
Pine Gate Associates, Ltd., In re—§ 10-27; § 10-27, n. 1.
Pine Lake Village Apartment Co., In re, 19 B.R. 819—§ 10-17, n. 4; § 10-22, n. 5.
Pine Lake Village Apartment Co., In re, 16 B.R. 750—§ 2-10; § 2-10, n. 4.
Pine Run Trust, Inc., In re—§ 11-13, n. 3; § 11-15; § 11-15, n. 8; § 11-18, n. 1.
Pinetree, Ltd., Matter of—§ 3-32, n. 18.
Pinetree Partners, Ltd., Matter of—§ 6-49, n. 13, 34; § 6-93, n. 32, 35, 37, 39, 44, 46, 53.
Pinkert, In re—§ 6-39, n. 15; § 6-41, n. 38; § 6-78, n. 18.
Pinkstaff, In re—§ 3-34, n. 9; § 3-35, n. 6; § 6-2, n. 20; § 6-62, n. 26.
Pin Oaks Apartments, In re—§ 5-6, n. 3.
Pinto, In re, 98 B.R. 200—§ 6-87, n. 8.
Pinto, In re, 89 B.R. 486—§ 6-49, n. 8.
Pinto Trucking Service, Inc., In re—§ 6-48, n. 2, 4, 6, 18; § 6-49, n. 13, 18, 44; § 6-52, n. 49.
Piombo Corp. v. Castlerock Properties—§ 3-30, n. 27; § 12-14, n. 17, 18.
Pioneer Commercial Funding Corp. v. United Airlines, Inc.—§ 3-5, n. 9; § 3-6, n. 19; § 3-22, n. 32.
Pioneer Ford Sales, Inc., In re—§ 4-4, n. 18; § 5-16; § 5-16, n. 1.
Pioneer Technology, Inc., In re—§ 6-18, n. 26.
Pipes, In re—§ 7-48, n. 2.
Pippin, In re—§ 6-19, n. 16.
Pitman, In re—§ 6-24, n. 6; § 6-26, n. 7; § 6-27, n. 11.
Pitrat v. Garlikov—§ 8-33, n. 36.
Pitts v. Unarco Industries, Inc.—§ 3-5, n. 19.
Pittsburgh Cut Flower Co., Inc., In re—§ 6-17, n. 5, 23; § 6-30, n. 3; § 6-93, n. 38, 46.
Pizza of Hawaii, Inc., Matter of, 761 F.2d 1374—§ 12-12, n. 11.
Pizza of Hawaii, Inc., Matter of, 40 B.R. 1014—§ 11-5, n. 4.
Placid Oil Co., In re—§ 4-6, n. 2.
Planned Systems, Inc., In re—§ 3-31, n. 70; § 4-4, n. 5.
Playa Development Corp., In re—§ 3-31, n. 68.
Plaza Family Partnership, Matter of—§ 4-4, n. 1.
Plaza Hotel Corp., In re—§ 6-16, n. 1; § 6-69, n. 7.
Plihal, Matter of—§ 6-18, n. 3, 4, 10; § 6-62, n. 15; § 6-76, n. 5.
Plumlee, In re—§ 8-25, n. 8, 10.
Plunkett, Matter of—§ 6-61, n. 38.
P.M.G. Properties, Matter of—§ 6-77, n. 12.
PM-II Associates, Inc., In re—§ 6-19, n. 10.
Pody, In re—§ 3-35, n. 1.
Poff, In re—§ 9-12, n. 2.
Pointer, In re—§ 3-23, n. 45.
Polanco v. 21 Arden Realty Corp.—§ 3-5, n. 12.
Polar Chips Intern., Inc., In re—§ 6-50, n. 16, 17, 18.
Polk, In re, 125 B.R. 293—§ 6-17; § 6-17, n. 5, 21.
Polk, In re, 76 B.R. 148—§ 7-39, n. 3, 7.
Polries Bros., In re—§ 3-26, n. 11; § 3-27, n. 26.
Poole Funeral Chapel, Inc., Matter of—§ 11-5, n. 9.
Pope v. Manville Forest Products Corp.—§ 3-6, n. 27, 28.
Porta-Kamp Mfg. Co., Inc. v. Atlanta Maritime Corp.—§ 3-6, n. 45.
Porter, In re, 112 B.R. 979—§ 8-25, n. 17; § 8-28, n. 7, 9.
Porter, In re, 50 B.R. 510—§ 6-93, n. 62.
Porter, In re, 42 B.R. 61—§ 3-21, n. 113.
Porter, In re, 37 B.R. 56—§ 6-18, n. 18; § 6-48, n. 10, 11; § 6-49, n. 41; § 6-60, n. 4.
Porter v. Yukon Nat. Bank—§ 6-18, n. 4; § 6-20, n. 23.
Portex Oil Co., In re—§ 12-6, n. 4.
Portjeff Development Corp., In re—§ 6-7, n. 4.
Port Side Transport, Inc. v. Van Huffel Tube Corp.—§ 6-7, n. 7, 11.
Posadas De Puerto Rico Associates v. Tourism Co. of Puerto Rico—§ 3-8, n. 9.
Posta, In re—§ 7-30, n. 16.

TABLE OF CASES

Postle Enterprises, Inc., In re—§ 5-13, n. 3.
Potter, In re—§ 6-77, n. 22.
Potter Instrument Co., Inc., In re—§ 10-7, n. 8.
Potter Material Service, Inc., In re—§ 10-21, n. 9; § 11-27; § 11-27, n. 11; § 11-29; § 11-29, n. 1, 6, 12; § 11-30; § 11-30, n. 2, 18.
Poule, In re—§ 7-5, n. 2; § 7-31, n. 3.
Powell, In re, 29 B.R. 346—§ 9–14, n. 21.
Powell, In re, 15 B.R. 465—§ 9–4, n. 32.
Powerine Oil Co., In re—§ 6-29, n. 8.
Powers, In re, 98 B.R. 577—§ 8–17, n. 24, 25.
Powers, In re, 88 B.R. 294—§ 6–72, n. 13.
Powers, In re, 28 B.R. 86—§ 6–39, n. 19, 38; § 6–43, n. 13, 31.
P & P Oilfield Equipment, Inc., In re—§ 12-5, n. 2.
Pracht v. Oklahoma State Bank—§ 6-38, n. 6.
Practical Inv. Corp., In re—§ 6-12, n. 10; § 6-17, n. 11; § 6-50, n. 16, 22, 23, 24, 25; § 6-61, n. 53; § 6-62, n. 14.
Prairie Trunk Ry., In re, 125 B.R. 217—§ 3–33, n. 5; § 3–35, n. 2, 3.
Prairie Trunk Ry., In re, 112 B.R. 924—§ 3–32, n. 6.
Prange Foods, Corp., In re—§ 9-17, n. 5.
Precision Carwash Corp., In re—§ 11-10, n. 1.
Prejean, In re—§ 8-23, n. 7.
Prescott, Matter of—§ 6-88, n. 46.
Presidents Mortg. Indus. Bank, In re—§ 6-20, n. 20.
Presidio Bridge Co., Inc., In re—§ 3-23, n. 4, 11.
Presque Isle Apartments, L.P., In re—§ 6-39, n. 1.
Pressimone, In re—§ 3-10, n. 47.
Pressimone v. Internal Revenue Service—§ 3–10, n. 51.
Preston, In re—§ 6-86, n. 4.
Pretner, In re—§ 7-26, n. 37.
Previs, In re—§ 6-82, n. 4; § 6-86, n. 4.
Price, In re, 871 F.2d 97—§ 7–27, n. 5.
Price, In re, 103 B.R. 989—§ 3–16, n. 3.
Price, In re, 97 B.R. 264—§ 6-61, n. 18; § 6–86, n. 4, 9.
Price Chopper Supermarkets, Inc., In re—§ 6-7, n. 5.
Prichard Plaza Associates Ltd. Partnership, In re—§ 6-77, n. 20.
Priestly, In re, 94 B.R. 195—§ 6-69, n. 9.
Priestly, In re, 93 B.R. 253—§ 11–38; § 11–38, n. 7.
Primack, In re, 89 B.R. 954—§ 6–60, n. 17, 20; § 8–32, n. 5.
Primack, In re, 81 B.R. 711 § 6 2, n. 24.
Prime, Inc., In re—§ 5-14, n. 2.
Prime Motor Inns, In re—§ 5-8, n. 10.
Princess Baking Corp., In re—§ 6-40, n. 4, 13; § 6–43, n. 13; § 6–44, n. 1.
Pristas v. Landaus of Plymouth, Inc.—§ 8-25, n. 34.
Pritchard, In re—§ 8-11; § 8-11, n. 12, 13, 29.
Probasco, In re—§ 4-9, n. 12; § 6-61, n. 74, 77.
Production Credit Ass'n of St. Cloud v. LaFond—§ 8-25, n. 52.
Production Steel, Inc., In re—§ 6-66, n. 6.
Professional Sales Corp., In re—§ 3-34, n. 7.
Professional Technical Services, Inc., In re—§ 6-39, n. 10.
Proffitt Const. Co., Inc., In re—§ 6-12; § 6-12, n. 15, 18, 21.
Promenade Nat'l Bank v. Phillips—§ 2–2, n. 6; § 12–12, n. 14.
Proper v. Don Conolly Const. Co., Inc.—§ 3-6, n. 29.
Propps, In re—§ 6-69, n. 2.
Provident Hosp. & Training Ass'n, In re—§ 6-60, n. 24.
Proyectos Electronicos, S.A. v. Alper—§ 3-14, n. 5.
Prudential Ins. Co. of America v. Colony Square Co.—§ 2-16, n. 26.
Prudential Ins. Co. of America v. Ryan Place Joint Venture—§ 3-31, n. 21.
Prudential Lines Inc., In re, 928 F.2d 565—§ 2–8, n. 13; § 3–14, n. 20; § 3–22, n. 8.
Prudential Lines Inc., In re, 119 B.R. 430—§ 3–22, n. 4.
Pruitt, In re, 829 F.2d 1002—§ 8–21, n. 10.
Pruitt, In re, 72 B.R. 436—§ 6–2, n. 16, 22; § 6–53, n. 6; § 6–54, n. 3, 10; § 6–55, n. 13; § 6–56, n. 17, 41, 48, 52; § 8–23, n. 3, 5, 14.
Pruitt, In re, 30 B.R. 330—§ 8–33, n. 17.
Pruitt; In re, Civ.Action No. 83-JM-212—§ 8–9, n. 2.
Ptacek, In re—§ 8-2, n. 3; § 8-24, n. 2.
Pub Dennis of Mineral Spring Ave., Inc., In re—§ 3-21, n. 69.
Public Service Co. of New Hampshire, In re, 884 F.2d 11—§ 5–22, n. 5; § 6–40, n. 2; 6–44, n. 1.
Public Service Co. of New Hampshire, In re, 107 B.R. 441—§ 6–45, n. 7, 35.

Public Service Co. of New Hampshire, In re, 89 B.R. 1014—§ 10–12, n. 4, 11.
Public Service Co. of New Hampshire, In re, 89 B.R. 1012—§ 6–40, n. 6; § 6–42, n. 2, 3; § 6–43, n. 7.
Public Service Co. of New Hampshire, In re, 88 B.R. 521—§ 11–13, n. 3, 12; § 11–15; § 11–15, n. 3, 6, 17; § 11–20; § 11–20, n. 3.
Pullman Const. Industries Inc., In re—§ 11-29, n. 1.
Purco, In re—§ 6-59, n. 3; § 6-60, n. 4, 8; § 6-93, n. 31; § 11-10, n. 5.
Purity Ice Cream Co., Inc., In re—§ 3-31, n. 76.
Purnell, In re—§ 6-72, n. 4, 7; § 6-73, n. 10.
Pursifull v. Eakin—§ 3-31, n. 98.
Putnam County Canning Co., In re—§ 6-62, n. 3.

Q

Q.T., Inc., In re—§ 3-28, n. 13, 15.
Quaal, In re—§ 6-78, n. 3.
Quackenbos, In re—§ 6-82, n. 3; § 8-29, n. 13, 15.
Quade, In re, 108 B.R. 681—§ 6-27, n. 7.
Quade, In re, 108 B.R. 674—§ 6-25, n. 16.
Quality Holstein Leasing, Matter of—§ 6-61, n. 16, 38, 67.
Quality Interiors, Inc., In re—§ 3-15, n. 5, 6; § 6-43, n. 29.
Quality Sign Co., Inc., In re—§ 6-93, n. 66.
Quality Takes Time, Inc., In re—§ 6-10, n. 13.
Qual Krom South, Inc., Matter of—§ 3-14, n. 45.
Quatray v. Wicker—§ 11-39, n. 3.
Queen City Grain, Inc., In re—§ 6-47, n. 7; § 6-88, n. 21, 24, 25, 37.
Queens Boulevard Wine & Liquor Corp. v. Blum—§ 5-12; § 5-12, n. 3.
Quinn, Matter of—§ 3-10, n. 81.
Quinn v. CGR—§ 12-12, n. 14.
Quinn Wholesale, Inc. v. Northen—§ 6-69, n. 7.
Quirk, In re—§ 6-61, n. 11, 13, 44.

R

Raanes, In re—§ 6-39, n. 2; § 6-43, n. 4, 16, 19; § 6-45, n. 2.
Rab v. Safeco Ins. Co. of America—§ 3-31, n. 87, 88.
Rabai v. Rabai—§ 3-6, n. 33.
R.A. Beck Builder, Inc., Matter of—§ 6-10, n. 15; § 6-88, n. 46, 54.
Racca, In re—§ 8-22, n. 23.
Ragsdale, In re—§ 8-10, n. 26; § 8-21, n. 15.
Ragsdale v. Haller—§ 7-28, n. 2, 4.
RAI Marketing Services, Inc., In re—§ 2-10, n. 3.
Ralph A. Veon, Inc., Matter of—§ 6-89, n. 12.
Ramage, In re—§ 3-12, n. 20.
Ramco American Intern., Inc., Matter of—§ 6-12; § 6-12, n. 16.
Ramco/Fitzsimons Steel Co., Inc., In re—§ 6-31, n. 15.
Ram Const. Co., Inc. v. American States Ins. Co.—§ 6-40, n. 4; § 6-77, n. 21.
Ram Const. Co., Inc. v. Port Authority of Allegheny County—§ 12-5, n. 2.
Rames v. Norbraten—§ 8-9, n. 12.
Ramirez, In re, 795 F.2d 1494—§ 7–29, n. 2, 25.
Ramirez, In re, 62 B.R. 668—§ 9–16, n. 3; § 9–18, n. 15.
Ram Mfg., Inc., In re—§ 11-6, n. 3.
Ramm Industries, Inc., In re—§ 2-5, n. 12.
Ramus, Matter of—§ 9-3, n. 11.
Rancourt, In re—§ 6-77, n. 12.
Randall, In re—§ 6-76, n. 2; § 6-77, n. 1; § 6-78, n. 17.
Randolph, In re—§ 7-45, n. 4.
Rankin, In re, 102 B.R. 439—§ 2–8, n. 23.
Rankin, In re, 49 B.R. 565—§ 6–77, n. 1, 23.
Rappaport, In re—§ 8-21, n. 4.
Rare Coin Galleries of America, Inc., In re, 862 F.2d 896—§ 6–94, n. 8.
Rare Coin Galleries of America, Inc., In re, 72 B.R. 415—§ 5–23, n. 2.
Rasmussen, In re—§ 9-14, n. 18, 21.
Rassi, Matter of—§ 2-5, n. 18.
Ratledge, In re—§ 9-7, n. 12.

Ratliff, In re—§ 6-39, n. 15; § 6-40, n. 5.
Rausch Mfg. Co., Inc., In re—§ 4-4, n. 15.
Ravenna Industries, Inc., In re—§ 11-13, n. 3; § 11-14; § 11-14, n. 4, 9; § 11-15, n. 9; § 11-18, n. 1.
Ravenot v. Rimgale—§ 9–2, n. 4.
Ravick Corp., In re—§ 3-29, n. 5, 9.
Rawson Food Service, Inc., In re—§ 6-67, n. 1.
Ray, In re, 104 B.R. 217—§ 8–28, n. 3.
Ray, In re, 83 B.R. 670—§ 8–25, n. 43, 44.
Ray, Matter of—§ 4-9, n. 11.
Ray v. Dawson—§ 8-10, n. 5, 10, 12.
Raymond, In re, 103 B.R. 846—§ 8–3, n. 10; § 8–24, n. 6; § 8–25, n. 43; § 8–26, n. 18.
Raymond, In re, 99 B.R. 819—§ 3–27, n. 6; § 3–31; § 3–31, n. 67, 69.
Raymond, In re, 71 B.R. 628—§ 8–17, n. 27.
R. Bastyr and Associates, Inc., In re—§ 6-39, n. 1.
RBS Industries, Inc., In re—§ 6-77, n. 1.
R. C. I. Enterprises Inc., In re—§ 6-42, n. 2; § 6-43, n. 10, 13.
RDC Corp., In re—§ 6-32, n. 5.
Reading Co. v. Brown—§ 11-4, n. 15.
Reading Tube Industries, In re—§ 4-13, n. 3; § 4-14, n. 6.
Reaves, In re—§ 6-49, n. 46; § 6-50, n. 13; § 8-22, n. 30, 31.
Rebeor, In re, 93 B.R. 16—§ 4–4, n. 1.
Rebeor, In re, 89 B.R. 314—§ 2–13, n. 13.
Rebuelta, In re—§ 3-10, n. 65.
Red, In re—§ 9-12, n. 6; § 9-13, n. 12; § 9-14, n. 6.
Red Ash Coal & Coke Corp., In re—§ 3-6, n. 22; § 3-33, n. 24; § 3-35, n. 2; § 12-3, n. 5.
Redding, In re—§ 7-39, n. 3, 7.
Reddington/Sunarrow Ltd. Partnership, In re—§ 3-27, n. 12, 15, 18.
Redfearn, In re—§ 7-20, n. 6.
Redin, In re—§ 8-28, n. 4.
Redmond, In re—§ 8-10, n. 10, 12.
Redmond v. Mendenhall—§ 6-12, n. 22; § 6-14, n. 2.
Redmond v. Tuttle—§ 6-57, n. 5; § 8-1, n. 11; § 8-22, n. 20, 25.
Red Oak Farms, Inc., In re—§ 4-7; § 4-7, n. 6, 12, 17.
Red Way Cartage Co., Inc., Matter of—§ 6-30, n. 7; § 6-31, n. 15.
Reed, In re, 951 F.2d 1046—§ 8–33, n. 17.
Reed, In re, 94 B.R. 48—§ 3–30, n. 27.
Reed, In re, 89 B.R. 100—§ 3–23, n. 8, 18.
Reed, In re, 11 B.R. 683—§ 8–32, n. 8.
Reed, Matter of—§ 7-21, n. 8; § 8-32, n. 4, 8.
Reed v. Rivera—§ 8-13, n. 7.
Reeder, In re—§ 8-21, n. 4.
Reese, In re—§ 9-2, n. 10.
Reese v. Beacon Hotel Corporation—§ 10-32, n. 1.
Reetz, In re—§ 11-14, n. 5.
Reeves, In re—§ 9-18, n. 6.
Regal Const. Co., Inc., In re—§ 3-6, n. 46.
Regan v. Ross—§ 9-3, n. 6.
Regency Architectural Metals Corp., Matter of—§ 6-61, n. 31.
Regency Woods Apartments, Ltd., In re—§ 3-31, n. 50.
Rego Crescent Corp., Matter of—§ 6-2, n. 28; § 6-93, n. 29, 32.
Reice, In re—§ 3-28, n. 3; § 3-31, n. 71; § 5-24, n. 3.
Reid, In re, 757 F.2d 230—§ 8–3, n. 21; § 8–25; § 8–25, n. 47.
Reid, In re, 121 B.R. 875—§ 8–25, n. 43.
Reid, Matter of—§ 8-25, n. 42, 43; § 8-26, n. 2.
Reilly v. First Nat. Bank & Trust Co.—§ 6-92, n. 3, 5, 6.
Reinboldt, In re—§ 6-54, n. 7.
Reinhardt, In re—§ 6-61, n. 58; § 6-62, n. 25.
Reininger-Bone, Matter of—§ 6-48, n. 2, 10, 11; § 6-60, n. 4.
Reisnour, In re—§ 8-21, n. 9.
Reiter, In re—§ 3-10, n. 21, 48; § 3-33, n. 22.
Reitz, In re—§ 7-20, n. 6.
Reliable Elec. Co., Inc. v. Olson Const. Co.—§ 7-27, n. 7; § 9-4, n. 6; § 10-31; § 10-31, n. 6; § 11-3, n. 21.
Renges, Inc. v. PAC Financial Corp.—§ 3-6, n. 30.
Renner, In re—§ 7-45, n. 13.
Rent-A-Tainment, Inc./Mail 'N Things v. United States on Behalf of U.S. Postal Service—§ 3-21, n. 44, 69.
Replogle, In re—§ 3-6, n. 35.

Republican Valley Bank v. Security State Bank—§ 6-38, n. 10.
Republic Financial Corp., In re, 75 B.R. 840—§ 6-85, n. 16; § 6-87, n. 14.
Republic Financial Corp., In re, 47 B.R. 766—§ 6-39, n. 25; § 6-40, n. 34.
Republic Nat. Bank of New York v. Greenwald—§ 6-51, n. 25.
Republic Oil Corp., Matter of—§ 12-5, n. 3.
Republic Reader's Service, Inc., In re—§ 3-30, n. 27, 31; § 12-2, n. 9.
Republic Trust & Sav. Co., In re—§ 6-25, n. 14, 40; § 6-29, n. 7; § 9-3, n. 27.
Resendez v. Lindquist—§ 8-22, n. 19, 20.
Reserves Development Corp., Matter of, 821 F.2d 520—§ 3-23, n. 45.
Reserves Development Corp., Matter of, 78 B.R. 951—§ 3-3, n. 4; § 3-16, n. 3, 4; § 3-21, n. 69, 82, 113; § 3-32, n. 5.
Reserves Development Corp., Matter of—§ 3-3, n. 4; § 3-16, n. 3, 4; § 3-21, n. 69, 82, 113; § 3-23, n. 45; § 3-32, n. 5.
Resolution Trust Corp. v. Security Town Co.—§ 3-5, n. 16; § 3-10; § 3-10, n. 1.
Ressler, In re—§ 6-4, n. 17; § 6-36, n. 11; § 6-62, n. 15.
Restea, In re—§ 7-45, n. 1.
Retirement Fund Trust of Plumbing v. Franchise Tax Bd.—§ 8-33, n. 15.
Re–Trac Corp., In re—§ 5-10, n. 16.
Rettemnier, Matter of—§ 8-25, n. 5, 6.
Rett White Motor Sales Co. v. Wells Fargo Bank—§ 3-6, n. 16, 45, 50; § 3-14, n. 15.
Revco D.S., Inc., In re, 989 F.2d 498—§ 10–10, n. 6.
Revco D.S., Inc., In re, 111 B.R. 631—§ 6-40, n. 14, 19.
Revco D.S., Inc., In re, 99 B.R. 768—§ 3-26, n. 2; § 3-30, n. 2, 27, 30, 33; § 3-31, n. 91.
Revco D.S., Inc., In re, 93 B.R. 119—§ 10–10, n. 2, 4, 6.
Revere Copper and Brass, Inc., In re, 78 B.R. 17—§ 10-2, n. 6.
Revere Copper and Brass, Inc., In re, 29 B.R. 584—§ 3-21; § 3-21, n. 38.
Revere Copper & Brass, Inc., Matter of—§ 10-2, n. 6.
Rex Group, Inc., In re—§ 3-31, n. 76.
Reyes, In re—§ 9-13, n. 5, 12.
Reynolds, United States v.—§ 3-15, n. 6; § 6-43, n. 32.
R.H.N. Realty Corp., In re—§ 3-10, n. 23.
Rhodes, In re—§ 3-10, n. 61, 62.
Rhodes v. Stewart—§ 8-3, n. 11, 13.
Rice, In re, 109 B.R. 405—§ 7-19, n. 7.
Rice, In re, 83 B.R. 8—§ 6-50, n. 5; § 6-69, n. 15; § 6-72, n. 17; § 6-88, n. 8, 17, 19.
Richard, In re—§ 6-53, n. 8; § 6-56, n. 17.
Richard v. City of Chicago—§ 3-2, n. 6; § 3-3, n. 4; § 3-16, n. 11; § 3-32, n. 1, 7, 27; § 6-73, n. 7.
Richards, In re, 92 B.R. 369—§ 6-4, n. 3.
Richards, In re, 58 B.R. 233—§ 6-49, n. 35, 46, 49.
Richards, In re, 50 B.R. 339—§ 9-4, n. 14; § 9-20, n. 6.
Richards, In re, 43 B.R. 554—§ 8-3, n. 22.
Richardson, In re, 121 B.R. 546—§ 7-47, n. 2.
Richardson, In re, 102 B.R. 254—§ 7-38; § 7-38, n. 2.
Richardson, In re, 94 B.R. 56—§ 6-30, n. 7; § 6-31, n. 18, 19.
Richardson, In re, 75 B.R. 601—§ 6-61, n. 74.
Richardson, In re, 23 B.R. 434—§ 6-49, n. 62, 79; § 6-50, n. 4, 23, 37; § 6-53, n. 3; § 6-55, n. 13; § 6-56; § 6-56, n. 15, 52; § 6-88, n. 18.
Richardson, Matter of—§ 6-77, n. 1.
Richardson v. TIAA/CREF—§ 8-33, n. 24.
Richardson Builders, Inc., In re—§ 3-1, n. 8; § 3-6, n. 18; § 3-10, n. 21; § 3-18, n. 24.
Richmond Leasing Co. v. Capital Bank, N.A.—§ 5-20, n. 7.
Richmond Metal Finishers, Inc., In re, 38 B.R. 341—§ 5-7, n. 8.
Richmond Metal Finishers, Inc., In re, 34 B.R. 521—§ 5-7, n. 8.
Richmond Produce Co., Inc., In re—§ 6-88, n. 48, 49, 52.
Richmond Tank Car Co., In re—§ 10-12, n. 4.
Richton Intern. Corp., In re—§ 11-41, n. 16.
Ricke, In re—§ 8-22, n. 35; § 8-23; § 8-23, n. 6, 9, 12.
Ricks, In re—§ 6-82, n. 3; § 8-29, n. 13, 15.
Riddell, Matter of—§ 8-27, n. 9; § 8-28, n. 10.
Riddervold, In re—§ 6-15, n. 5; § 6-36, n. 11; § 6-62, n. 16; § 8-23, n. 9.
Ridenour, In re—§ 6-47, n. 13; § 6-49, n. 44; § 6-56, n. 14.
Rideout, In re, 86 B.R. 523—§ 10-33, n. 1.
Rideout, In re, 75 B.R. 104—§ 10-28, n. 6.
Ridgely, In re—§ 2-18; § 2-18, n. 3.
Ridgely Communications, Inc., In re—§ 12-9, n. 2.
Ridgemont Apartment Associates, Ltd. v. Atlanta English Village, Ltd.—§ 3-27, n. 24.
Ridgley, In re—§ 7-25, n. 2; § 8-23, n. 4, 7.
Ridley, In re—§ 7-20; § 7-20, n. 9.

Riebow, In re—§ 8-21, n. 11.
Rigby Corp. v. Boatmen's Bank and Trust Co.—§ 6-38, n. 6.
Riggleman, In re—§ 9-2, n. 4, 8.
Riggsby, In re—§ 6-6, n. 7; § 8-22, n. 17.
Riggsby, Matter of—§ 12-12, n. 9; § 12-13, n. 9.
Riggs Nat. Bank of Washington, D.C. v. Perry—§ 3-25, n. 5; § 3-27, n. 23; § 7-39, n. 14, 15.
Riley, Matter of—§ 6-62, n. 3, 22.
Rimgale, In re—§ 9-14, n. 5, 13.
Rimmer Corp., In re—§ 6-7, n. 4; § 6-20, n. 10, 11, 20.
Rinehart, United States v.—§ 6-38, n. 16; § 6-39, n. 15; § 6-42, n. 2, 4; § 6-43, n. 4, 32.
Rink v. Timbers Homeowners Ass'n I, Inc.—§ 7-7, n. 1.
Rinker, Matter of—§ 9-24; § 9-24, n. 23.
Rio v. Army Aviation Center Federal Credit Union—§ 3-15, n. 6; § 6-43, n. 29.
Ripley v. Mulroy—§ 3-5, n. 12.
Riso, In re—§ 6-56, n. 14.
Ristich, In re—§ 6-49, n. 13; § 6-54, n. 2, 10; § 6-55, n. 13; § 6-56, n. 8, 52, 53.
Rittenhouse, In re—§ 8-25, n. 16.
Rittenhouse Carpet, Inc., In re—§ 10-6; § 10-6, n. 3, 6.
Ritz–Carlton of D.C., Inc., In re—§ 3-25, n. 37, 42, 44, 48.
Rivera Feliciano v. Sistema de Retiro del E.L.A., Asoc.—§ 6-76, n. 2; § 8-33, n. 24.
Rivera Sanchez, In re—§ 9-27, n. 11.
Riverfront Food and Beverage Corp., In re—§ 6-36, n. 11, 19.
River Hills Apartments Fund, In re—§ 3-31; § 3-31, n. 14, 23, 24, 29, 30, 46.
Rivet, In re—§ 8-20, n. 2; § 8-26, n. 2; § 8-28, n. 5.
Rizzo, In re—§ 8-21, n. 4.
R & J Const. Co., Inc., In re—§ 6-86, n. 4.
R. & L. Cartage & Sons, Inc., In re—§ 3-14, n. 8; § 6-73, n. 11, 20.
Roach, Matter of—§ 3-16, n. 11.
Roamer Linen Supply, Inc., In re—§ 4-14, n. 6.
Roanoke Iron & Bridge Works, Inc., In re—§ 6-71, n. 7, 11, 21, 22.
Robbins, In re, 119 B.R. 1—§ 3-27, n. 9, 24.
Robbins, In re, 91 B.R. 879—§ 6-72, n. 3; § 6-82, n. 7; § 6-88, n. 28, 29, 30, 36.
Roberson, Matter of—§ 6-6, n. 3, 7.
Roberts, In re, 906 F.2d 1440—§ 7-32; § 7-32, n. 1, 5, 7.
Roberts, In re, 81 B.R. 354—§ 6-48, n. 8, 11; § 6-57, n. 5; § 7-19, n. 3; § 8-1, n. 11; § 8-22, n. 37.
Roberts, In re, 78 B.R. 536—§ 9-24, n. 24.
Roberts, In re, 38 B.R. 128—§ 6-86, n. 4, 9.
Roberts, In re, 29 B.R. 808—§ 3-9, n. 11.
Roberts v. Johns-Manville Corp.—§ 11-5, n. 12.
Roberts, State ex rel. v. Mushroom King, Inc.—§ 12-5, n. 11.
Roberts Hardware Co., In re—§ 6-67, n. 10.
Roberts, Inc., In re—§ 6-93, n. 41.
Robertson, In re—§ 8-1, n. 12, 13.
Robinson, In re, 114 B.R. 716—§ 8-28, n. 3.
Robinson, In re, 80 B.R. 455—§ 6-2, n. 20; § 6-49, n. 73.
Robinson, In re, 46 B.R. 136—§ 7-8, n. 4.
Robinson, In re, 44 B.R. 292—§ 8-21, n. 9.
Robinson, In re, 22 B.R. 497—§ 9-4, n. 28.
Robinson v. Michigan Consol. Gas Co. Inc.—§ 3-9, n. 29, 33, 35.
Robinson v. Olin Federal Credit Union—§ 8-1, n. 20.
Robinson Bros. Drilling, Inc., In re, 892 F.2d 850—§ 6-10, n. 13.
Robinson Bros. Drilling, Inc., In re, 877 F.2d 32—§ 6-25, n. 27.
Robinson Bros. Drilling, Inc., In re, 97 B.R. 77—§ 6-88, n. 54.
Robinson Ranch, Inc., In re—§ 3-10, n. 49.
Roblin Industries, Inc., In re, 127 B.R. 722—§ 6-16, n. 1.
Roblin Industries, Inc., In re, 52 B.R. 241—§ 4-15, n. 15.
Rocchio, In re—§ 3-28, n. 11.
Rockefeller, In re—§ 8-18, n. 8, 23.
Roco Corp., In re, 701 F.2d 978—§ 6-18, n. 27; § 6-48, n. 19; § 6-49, n. 69; § 6-50, n. 7, 8, 13; § 6-52, n. 49.
Roco Corp., In re, 37 B.R. 770—§ 6-93, n. 31.
Roco Corp., In re, 21 B.R. 429—§ 6-52, n. 21, 34, 36, 43.
Roco Corp., In re, 15 B.R. 813—§ 6-17, n. 8.
Rodemeyer, In re—§ 8-32, n. 12.
Rodgers, In re, 115 B.R. 678—§ 7-26, n. 19.
Rodgers, In re, 68 B.R. 17—§ 8-26, n. 18.
Rodgers, United States v.—§ 4-9; § 4-9, n. 6.

TABLE OF CASES

Rodriguez, In re—§ 6-49, n. 46; § 6-51, n. 25.
Roehrich, In re—§ 6-16, n. 1.
Roemig, In re—§ 6-25, n. 11; § 6-31, n. 11.
Roete, In re—§ 3-8, n. 14.
Rogers, In re, 127 B.R. 844—§ 6-32, n. 5.
Rogers, In re, 65 B.R. 1018—§ 9-12; § 9-12, n. 6, 10; § 9-13, n. 5; § 9-14, n. 13.
Rogers, In re, 57 B.R. 170—§ 9-4, n. 18.
Rogers Refrigeration, Inc., In re—§ 6-36, n. 19.
Rolain, In re—§ 6-61, n. 11, 53.
Roland, In re—§ 7-26, n. 36, 37.
Rolland, In re—§ 3-10, n. 70.
Rollins, In re—§ 8-22, n. 22, 26.
Romano, Matter of—§ 6-39, n. 32; § 6-40, n. 16.
Rondeau, In re—§ 3-10, n. 65.
Ronix Corp. v. City of Philadelphia—§ 12-5, n. 10.
Ron Pair Enterprises, Inc., United States v.—§ 1-3; § 1-3, n. 9; § 2-11; § 2-11, n. 6; § 3-27, n. 13, 14; § 10-24, n. 1.
Rook, In re—§ 3-6, n. 14; § 3-20, n. 11.
Rooster, Inc., In re—§ 6-19, n. 7; § 6-45, n. 7, 36.
Root, In re—§ 9-20, n. 11.
Ropietski, In re—§ 3-20, n. 7, 33.
Rosa v. Colonial Bank—§ 6-38, n. 6.
Rose, In re, 113 B.R. 534—§ 3-32, n. 8.
Rose, In re, 86 B.R. 193—§ 6-4, n. 17; § 6-12, n. 11; § 6-18, n. 4, 18, 22, 25, 28; § 6-20, n. 18.
Rose, In re, 25 B.R. 744—§ 6-69, n. 9.
Rosebud Corp. v. Boggio—§ 6-52, n. 48.
Rosemond, In re—§ 7-41, n. 2.
Rosen, In re—§ 8-17, n. 35, 36.
Rosen v. Barclays Bank of New York—§ 6-49, n. 65.
Rosenberg, In re—§ 6-47, n. 8; § 6-49, n. 11.
Rosenow, In re—§ 7-39, n. 14.
Rosenow v. State of Ill., Dept. of Revenue—§ 7-25; § 7-25, n. 5.
Rosenquist, In re—§ 8-33, n. 18, 24, 34.
Rosenthal, In re—§ 6-41, n. 46; § 8-23, n. 5.
Rose Way, Inc., Matter of—§ 6-61, n. 11.
Rosol, In re—§ 8-25, n. 23; § 8-27, n. 9.
Ross, In re, 122 B.R. 462—§ 7-25, n. 2.
Ross, In re, 107 B.R. 759—§ 9-18, n. 9, 10, 13.
Ross, In re, 104 B.R. 171—§ 3-15, n. 6; § 6-45, n. 7, 36.
Ross, Matter of—§ 8-2, n. 7.
Rosteck, Matter of—§ 7-5, n. 4; § 7-7, n. 2.
Roth, In re—§ 7-38, n. 1.
Rott, In re—§ 2-2, n. 15; § 9-24; § 9-24, n. 9.
Rotunda, Matter of—§ 8-22, n. 21.
Round Hill Travel, Inc., In re—§ 5-11, n. 2.
Rouse, In re—§ 6-72, n. 10.
Rouse, Matter of—§ 4-7, n. 12.
Roussin v. Johnson—§ 3-20, n. 11, 14.
Route 202 Corp., In re—§ 3-29, n. 14.
Rovine Corp., In re—§ 5-7; § 5-7, n. 18.
Rowan v. Morgan—§ 8-11, n. 3.
Rowe, In re—§ 9-14, n. 21.
Rowe, Matter of—§ 8-32, n. 5.
Rowland v. Strickland—§ 8-33, n. 16.
Row Steel, Inc., Matter of—§ 6-39, n. 3, 38; § 6-41, n. 38.
Roxse Homes, Inc., In re—§ 3-26, n. 9; § 6-73, n. 8.
Roxy Roller Rink Joint Venture, In re—§ 2-5; § 2-5, n. 37.
Roy v. Federal Nat. Mortg. Assn.—§ 6-54, n. 10; § 6-55, n. 13; § 6-56, n. 50.
Royal Coach Country, Inc., In re—§ 6-49, n. 40, 65, 66, 73; § 6-69, n. 11; § 6-87, n. 8.
Royal Crown Bottlers of North Alabama, Inc., In re—§ 6-49, n. 18, 49, 51, 58, 60; § 6-51; § 6-51, n. 25, 31, 36.
Royal Crown Bottling Co. of Boaz, Inc., In re—§ 6-44, n. 1.
Royal Food Markets, Inc., In re—§ 5-2, n. 2.
Royal Golf Products Corp., In re, 908 F.2d 91—§ 6-7, n. 11; § 6-9, n. 7.
Royal Golf Products Corp., In re, 79 B.R. 695—§ 6-9, n. 8.
Royal Palm Square Associates, In re—§ 3-25; § 3-25, n. 18, 61; § 3-27, n. 38; § 3-29, n. 15.
Rozel Industries, Inc., In re, 120 B.R. 944—§ 3-15, n. 6; § 3-27, n. 14; § 6-40, n. 6.
Rozel Industries, Inc., In re, 74 B.R. 643—§ 6-65, n. 12.

R. Purbeck & Associates, Ltd., In re—§ 6-49, n. 13, 28.
R & T Roofing Structures & Commercial Framing, Inc., In re—§ 6-7, n. 4.
R & T Roofing Structures & Commercial Framing, Inc., Matter of—§ 6-36, n. 15.
Rubin, In re, 875 F.2d 755—§ 7-26; § 7-26, n. 10, 13. 69.
Rubin, In re, 29 F.Supp. 416—§ 6-6, n. 2.
Rubin v. Manufacturers Hanover Trust Co.—§ 6-49; § 6-49, n. 39, 54; § 6-51; § 6-51, n. 5, 24, 28, 39, 44.
Rubin Bros. Footwear, Inc., In re, 119 B.R. 416—§ 6-48, n. 18; § 6-59, n. 2.
Rubin Bros. Footwear, Inc., In re, 73 B.R. 346—§ 6-4, n. 16; § 6-17; § 6-17, n. 16; § 6-20, n. 22; § 6-93, n. 28.
Rudd v. Laughlin—§ 2-2, n. 6.
Ruebeck, In re—§ 6-53, n. 6; § 6-55, n. 9, 13; § 6-56, n. 12, 17, 20, 25, 26, 27, 29, 34, 54; § 6-60, n. 17.
Ruespin Corp., In re—§ 9-17, n. 5.
Rumsey Sheet Metal, Inc., In re—§ 6-40, n. 5, 7; § 6-41, n. 52.
Rushton, In re—§ 9-14, n. 21.
Russell, In re, 927 F.2d 413—§ 6-47, n. 7; § 6-73, n. 21.
Russell, In re, 80 B.R. 662—§ 8-12, n. 4; § 8-13, n. 4.
Russell, In re, 44 B.R. 452—§ 10-17, n. 4.
Russell, Matter of—§ 6-72, n. 6, 7.
Rust, In re—§ 11-16, n. 4.
Rustia, In re—§ 6-25, n. 8, 11.
Rutherford, Matter of—§ 6-61, n. 79.
Ruti–Sweetwater, Inc., In re—§ 10-17, n. 4, 6.
Rutledge v. Johansen—§ 6-6, n. 2.
Rutty, Matter of—§ 6-15, n. 5.
Ryan, In re, 851 F.2d 502—§ 6-61, n. 18.
Ryan, In re, 100 B.R. 411—§ 3-23, n. 32; § 7-7, n. 3.
Ryan, In re, 78 B.R. 175—§ 9-4; § 9-4, n. 7, 13; § 9-20, n. 6.
Ryan, In re, 69 B.R. 598—§ 9-25; 9-25, n. 7.
Ryder, In re—§ 6-20, n. 18.

S

Saberman, In re—§ 6-62, n. 26.
Sacco, In re—§ 8-18, n. 16; § 8-23, n. 9; § 8-25, n. 8, 12.
Saco Local Development Corp., In re, 711 F.2d 441—§ 12-12, n. 5.
Saco Local Development Corp., In re, 30 B.R. 859—§ 6-19, n. 17, 19.
Sacramento Mansion, Ltd., In re—§ 6-77, n. 7, 11.
Sadler, Matter of—§ 2-11, n. 3; § 6-11, n. 6.
Safren, In re—§ 2-5, n. 7; § 11-32; § 11-32, n. 5, 6; § 11-33; § 11-37, n. 3.
Saint Peter's School, In re—§ 10-23, n. 4.
Sajkowski, In re—§ 8-13, n. 6.
Salamone, In re—§ 2-17, n. 15.
Salecki, In re—§ 3-20, n. 22, 33.
Salem Energy Supplies and Services, Inc., In re—§ 6-61, n. 53.
Saline State Bank v. Mahloch—§ 6-2, n. 24, 27; § 6-77, n. 11, 19.
Salisbury, In re—§ 3-30, n. 28.
Sam, Matter of—§ 7-27; § 7-27, n. 4.
Samar Fashions, Inc., In re—§ 6-87, n. 14.
Samar Fashions, Inc. v. Private Line, Inc.—§ 6-31, n. 17, 19.
Sambo's Restaurants, Inc., In re—§ 3-32, n. 2.
Sampsell v. Imperial Paper & Color Corporation—§ 2-4, n. 2.
Sampson, In re, 57 B.R. 304—§ 6-77, n. 19.
Sampson, In re, 51 B.R. 13—§ 7-37, n. 3.
Samuels, In re—§ 6-44, n. 1.
Sanchez, In re—§ 6-38, n. 21, 22; § 6-39, n. 2, 38.
Sanchez–Casis, In re—§ 6-71, n. 10, 20.
Sanderfoot, In re—§ 8-25, n. 17.
Sanders, In re, 110 B.R. 328—§ 7-26, n. 37, 44.
Sanders, In re, 61 B.R. 381—§ 8-25, n. 27.
Sandifer, In re—§ 3-10, n. 61, 63, 72.
Sandmar Corp., In re—§ 3-21, n. 34.
Sandra Cotton, Inc., In re—§ 6-82, n. 1; § 6-83, n. 16.
Sandy Ridge Development Corp., Matter of—§ 10-20; § 10-20, n. 13.
Sandy Ridge Oil Co., Inc., In re, 832 F.2d 75—§ 6-61, n. 53.

TABLE OF CASES

Sandy Ridge Oil Co., Inc., In re, 807 F.2d 1332—§ 6-61, n. 77.
San Felipe @ Voss, Ltd., In re—§ 10-20; § 10-20, n. 8.
Sanglier, In re—§ 8-28, n. 9, 23.
Sansone, In re—§ 3-33, n. 22.
Santa Clara Circuits West, Inc., In re—§ 3-9, n. 17, 23, 24, 28, 29, 34.
Santa Maria, In re—§ 3-12, n. 7; § 3-30, n. 10.
Santiago Vela, Matter of—§ 2-19, n. 5.
Santos & Nieves, Inc., In re—§ 6-61, n. 11, 16.
Sapp, In re—§ 6-73, n. 8.
Sarasota Plaza Associates Ltd. Partnership, In re—§ 6-88, n. 21.
Sarkis, In re—§ 6-38, n. 18; § 6-39, n. 2, 34.
Satterfield, In re—§ 4-9, n. 12.
Satterla, In re—§ 6-38, n. 18.
Sauber, In re—§ 9-18, n. 14.
Saugus General Hosp., Inc., In re—§ 6-38, n. 9; § 6-40, n. 2.
Saunders, Matter of—§ 9-13, n. 4.
Savage, In re—§ 8-22, n. 23; § 8-23, n. 6.
Savidge, In re—§ 6-61, n. 44, 55.
Savig, In re—§ 6-4, n. 14; § 6-35, n. 5, 54; § 6-38, n. 5, 9, 18; § 6-40, n. 14.
Sawmill Hydraulics, Inc., In re—§ 11-29, n. 1.
Sax, In re—§ 12-12, n. 10.
Saxon Associates v. Barton—§ 3-6, n. 18, 22.
Saxon Industries, In re—§ 10-7, n. 7.
Saylors, In re—§ 2-16; § 2-16, n. 28; § 9-30; § 9-30, n. 6, 8.
Sayman's, Inc., Matter of—§ 3-9, n. 12, 32; § 6-93, n. 40.
Scallywags, Inc., In re—§ 6-93, n. 41.
Scarboro, Matter of—§ 6-94, n. 5.
Scarborough v. Duke—§ 3-6, n. 45.
Scarlata, In re—§ 7-26, n. 19.
Scarlett v. Barnes—§ 8-33, n. 2.
Schaps v. Bally's Park Place, Inc.—§ 6-60, n. 20; § 6-88, n. 14, 49.
Scherbenske Excavating, Inc., In re—§ 6-36, n. 19.
Schewe, Matter of—§ 3-28, n. 13.
Schick Oil & Gas, Inc., In re—§ 6-17, n. 11.
Schiliro, In re—§ 6-40, n. 18; § 6-42, n. 3; § 6-44, n. 6.
Schipper, In re—§ 4-4, n. 1.
Schlee, In re—§ 8-17, n. 35, 36.
Schmidt, In re—§ 6-41, n. 44, 46, 49.
Schmit, In re—§ 8-32, n. 8, 9.
Schmitt, In re—§ 8-33, n. 22, 39.
Schneider, In re, 99 B.R. 974—§ 7-28; § 7-28, n. 6.
Schneider, In re, 9 B.R. 488—§ 8-9, n. 3; § 8-21, n. 10.
Schneider v. Beneficial Financial Co.—§ 8-29, n. 13.
Schnippel, In re—§ 3-14, n. 40.
Schoenthal v. Irving Trust Co.—§ 12-14, n. 15, 19.
Scholz, In re—§ 7-34, n. 13.
Schons, In re—§ 6-39, n. 15; § 6-40, n. 16.
Schroff, In re—§ 3-11; § 3-11, n. 3; § 8-29, n. 12, 14, 15.
Schuette, In re—§ 8-17, n. 24, 27.
Schultz, In re, 101 B.R. 68—§ 8-25, n. 25, 26, 27.
Schultz, In re, 69 B.R. 629—§ 10-8, n. 2.
Schultz Broadway Inn v. United States—§ 6-93, n. 66.
Schultz Broadway Inn, Ltd., In re—§ 6-93, n. 66.
Schulz, Matter of—§ 5-23, n. 10.
Schum, In re—§ 9-18, n. 14.
Schuman, In re—§ 6-12, n. 10; § 6-17, n. 10, 29.
Schutterle v. Schutterle—§ 8-7, n. 3.
Schwab v. Krauss—§ 8-10, n. 3.
Schwanz v. Teper—§ 8-13, n. 7.
Schwartz, In re, 954 F.2d 569—§ 3-32, n. 41, 42.
Schwartz, In re, 119 B.R. 207—§ 3-8, n. 17; § 3-32; § 3-32, n. 31, 35; § 6-73, n. 10.
Schwartz, In re, 58 B.R. 606—§ 8-17, n. 35, 36, 49.
Schwartz, Matter of—§ 6-88, n. 37; § 8-30, n. 3.
Schwartz v. Pierucci—§ 6-82, n. 2; § 6-84, n. 3.
Schweitzer v. Consolidated Rail Corp. (Conrail)—§ 4-10, n. 4; § 11-3, n. 8, 10; § 11-8; § 11-8, n. 15.
Schyma, In re—§ 8-24, n. 3; § 9-19, n. 5.
Scionti, In re—§ 6-39, n. 13, 34.
Scioto Valley Mortg. Co., In re—§ 11-17, n. 8.

Scott, In re, 121 B.R. 605—§ 3-25, n. 7, 8.
Scott, In re, 88 B.R. 196—§ 6-62, n. 27; § 8-23, n. 9.
Scott, In re, 77 B.R. 636—§ 9-22; § 9-22, n. 15.
Scott, United States v.—§ 8-9, n. 13; § 8-31, n. 4.
Scott Housing Systems, Inc., Matter of—§ 3-21, n. 57.
Scoviac, In re—§ 6-13, n. 4; § 6-24, n. 2.
Scoville v. Scoville—§ 8-7, n. 11.
Scrima v. John Devries Agency, Inc.—§ 3-14, n. 39; § 3-32, n. 1, 8, 10, 17, 18, 21.
Scruggs, In re—§ 6-72, n. 10.
S & D Foods, Inc., In re—§ 6-93, n. 11.
Seabloom, In re—§ 2-2, n. 15.
Sea Catch, Inc., In re—§ 6-61, n. 58.
Seacoast Products, Inc. v. Spring Valley Farms, Inc.—§ 5-20, n. 7.
Sea Island Motor Sales, Inc., In re—§ 3-31, n. 76.
Seattle-First Nat. Bank v. Westwood Lumber, Inc.—§ 3-6, n. 26.
Seaway Exp. Corp., In re, 912 F.2d 1125—§ 6-61, n. 11, 28, 38.
Seaway Exp. Corp., In re, 105 B.R. 28—§ 6-61, n. 18, 28, 38.
Seawinds Ltd., In re—§ 6-31, n. 17, 23.
Seawinds Ltd., Matter of—§ 6-31, n. 9.
S.E.C. v. First Financial Group of Texas—§ 3-21, n. 16, 44, 109, 116, 126.
S.E.C. v. Long—§ 3-21, n. 16.
Sechuan City, Inc., In re—§ 3-8; § 3-8, n. 5, 15; § 6-40, n. 4.
Secrist, In re—§ 6-73, n. 4.
Securities and Exchange Commission v. Canandaigua Enterprises Corp.—§ 10-1, n. 5.
Securities Group 1980, In re—§ 6-93, n. 33.
Security Savings & Loan Association v. Busch—§ 8-7, n. 15.
Sederstrom, In re—§ 8-17, n. 35, 36, 48.
Segal v. Rochelle—§ 2-8, n. 13.
Seguin, In re—§ 7-48; § 7-48, n. 3.
Seibert, Matter of—§ 7-29, n. 19, 23.
Seidel, In re, 752 F.2d 1382—§ 9-18; § 9-18, n. 17.
Seidel, In re, 27 B.R. 347—§ 6-6, n. 3, 7; § 8-22, n. 31.
Seidle v. GATX Leasing Corp.—§ 3-17, n. 16.
Seitles, United States v.—§ 3-5, n. 12, 19; § 3-21, n. 59; § 3-22, n. 5, 19, 21, 23, 25, 29.
Selby v. Ford Motor Co.—§ 6-62, n. 42.
Selden, Matter of—§ 6-77, n. 6, 19; § 6-78, n. 17.
Selgar Realty Corp., In re—§ 4-3; § 4-3, n. 9; § 4-4, n. 8.
Seligson v. New York Produce Exchange—§ 6-85; § 6-85, n. 17.
Sellers, In re—§ 9-13, n. 4; § 9-14, n. 13.
Selner, In re—§ 2-8, n. 23.
Seman, In re—§ 9-3, n. 8; § 9-14, n. 4.
Seneca Oil Co., In re, 906 F.2d 1445—§ 7-15, n. 3.
Seneca Oil Co., In re, 65 B.R. 902—§ 11-17, n. 8.
Sennhenn, In re—§ 9-18, n. 18.
Sensor Systems, Inc., In re—§ 6-82, n. 4; § 6-84, n. 2.
Sentry Park, Ltd., In re—§ 3-29, n. 15, 17.
Senyo, In re—§ 8-25, n. 7.
Sepco, Inc., In re, 750 F.2d 51—§ 6-92, n. 3, 5.
Sepco, Inc., In re, 36 B.R. 279—§ 6-92, n. 2; § 6-93, n. 4, 41, 63.
Sequoia Auto Brokers Ltd., Inc., In re—§ 12-1, n. 4.
Serafini, Matter of—§ 8-29, n. 15.
Serapiglia, In re—§ 8-29, n. 13.
Sergio, Inc., In re—§ 6-48, n. 8; § 6-87, n. 18.
Serra Builders, Inc., In re—§ 6-56, n. 8.
Service Bolt & Nut Co., Inc., In re, 98 B.R. 759—§ 6-3, n. 6.
Service Bolt & Nut Co., Inc., In re, 97 B.R. 892—§ 6-31, n. 17.
Service Decorating Co., In re—§ 6-44, n. 9; § 8-1, n. 20; § 11-3, n. 9.
S.E.T. Income Properties, III, In re—§ 11-17, n. 6.
7H Land & Cattle Co., Matter of—§ 2-5, n. 15.
Seven Stars Restaurant, Inc., In re—§ 3-28, n. 13; § 5-3, n. 2.
Severson, In re—§ 9-20, n. 11.
SFW, Inc., In re—§ 3-10, n. 38, 46, 47.
Shader, Matter of—§ 8-32, n. 5.
Shaffer, In re, 84 B.R. 63—§ 9-18, n. 10.
Shaffer, In re, 78 B.R. 783—§ 8-1, n. 15; § 8-6, n. 11.
Shamblin, In re—§ 3-16, n. 3, 11; § 3-32, n. 1, 15, 22; § 6-73, n. 11.
Shands, In re, 63 B.R. 121—§ 7-45, n. 13, 17.
Shands, In re, 57 B.R. 49—§ 8-25, n. 14.

TABLE OF CASES

Shank, In re—§ 7-25, n. 5.
Shanker, In re—§ 11-16, n. 4.
Shapiro, In re, 124 B.R. 974—§ 3-3, n. 2; § 6-4, n. 9; § 6-69, n. 8.
Shapiro, In re, 59 B.R. 844—§ 7-20, n. 2, 3.
Shapiro & Ornish, In re—§ 7-22, n. 4.
Shariyf, In re—§ 3-29, n. 13.
Sharon Steel Corp., In re, 111 B.R. 534—§ 6-16, n. 1.
Sharon Steel Corp., In re, 78 B.R. 762—§ 11-13, n. 3; § 11-14, n. 13; § 11-15; § 11-15, n. 12.
Sharon Steel Corp. v. National Fuel Gas Distribution Corp.—§ 3-9, n. 14.
Sharpe's Estate v. Metropolitan Nat. Bank—§ 6-38, n. 8.
Shaver v. Shaver—§ 7-29, n. 8.
Shaw, In re—§ 8-10; § 8-10, n. 15, 21.
Sheehan, In re—§ 3-27, n. 31.
Shehu, Matter of—§ 3-31; § 3-31, n. 61.
Shelby, In re—§ 3-23, n. 38; § 3-25, n. 8, 31.
Shelby Motel Group, Inc., Matter of—§ 6-2, n. 28.
Sheldon v. Munford, Inc.—§ 3-6, n. 30.
Shelter Enterprises, Inc., In re—§ 6-93, n. 21, 35, 37, 38, 43, 46.
Shelter Resources Corp., In re—§ 10-10; § 10-10, n. 1, 6.
Shelton, In re, 42 B.R. 547—§ 7-26, n. 35.
Shelton, In re, 33 B.R. 377—§ 6-48, n. 10; § 6-88, n. 19, 33.
Shepherd, In re, 75 B.R. 501—§ 2-2, n. 15; § 9-24, n. 22.
Shepherd, In re, 17 B.R. 278—§ 8-21, n. 4.
Shepherd, In re, 12 B.R. 151—§ 6-69, n. 9; § 6-74, n. 12; § 8-22, n. 35.
Shepler, In re—§ 8-25, n. 27.
Sheridan, In re—§ 8-17, n. 17, 33, 51.
Sherk, Matter of—§ 3-10, n. 22; § 3-14, n. 29; § 8-1, n. 13.
Sherman v. First City Bank of Dallas—§ 6-39, n. 24; § 6-40, n. 2, 6; § 6-41, n. 16, 23.
Sherwood, In re, 94 B.R. 679—§ 8-3, n. 21.
Sherwood, In re, 79 B.R. 399—§ 8-29, n. 3.
Sherwood Ford, Inc., In re—§ 6-77, n. 22.
Shestko–Montiel, In re—§ 8-25, n. 17.
Shirey, In re—§ 3-9, n. 16, 22.
Shirkey v. Leake—§ 8-1, n. 9.
Shore, In re—§ 7-33, n. 5.
Shoreham Paper Co., In re—§ 3-16, n. 6; § 3-18, n. 20; § 6-61, n. 59.
Short, In re—§ 7-28, n. 4, 5.
Shotwell v. Sioux Falls Sav. Bank—§ 6-38, n. 10.
Showinsky, In re—§ 8-25, n. 17.
Shropshire, In re—§ 3-35, n. 1.
Shrum, In re—§ 11-30, n. 11.
Shuman, In re—§ 3-6, n. 52.
Shumate v. Patterson—§ 8-33, n. 21.
S.I. Acquisition, Inc., Matter of—§ 3-10, n. 6, 23; § 3-14, n. 23, 25; § 3-22, n. 1; § 6-61, n. 8.
Sible, In re—§ 2-13, n. 1.
Sidebotham, In re—§ 8-18, n. 15, 17.
Sider Ventures & Services Corp., In re—§ 6-25, n. 20, 22.
Sidle v. Cheney—§ 8-31, n. 5.
Siegel, In re—§ 8-33, n. 17, 24.
Siegler, In re—§ 7-49, n. 9.
Sierer, In re—§ 6-62, n. 34.
Sierra, In re—§ 6-12, n. 18.
Sierra Steel, Inc., In re, 96 B.R. 275—§ 6-18, n. 3, 18, 30.
Sierra Steel, Inc., In re, 96 B.R. 271—§ 6-4, n. 2; § 6-7, n. 4, 7.
Sierra Switchboard Co. v. Westinghouse Elec. Corp.—§ 8-18, n. 2; § 8-33, n. 2.
Sikes v. Global Marine, Inc.—§ 3-32, n. 11, 30.
Silk Plants, Etc. Franchise Systems, Inc. v. Register—§ 5-7, n. 19.
Silldorff, In re—§ 8-17, n. 13; § 8-33, n. 39.
Silve, In re—§ 6-12, n. 7; § 6-27, n. 11, 13; § 6-29, n. 11.
Silverman, In re—§ 3-32, n. 6.
Silver Mill Frozen Foods, Inc., Matter of—§ 3-23, n. 6; § 6-83, n. 13, 16; § 6-84, n. 5.
Silver Wheel Freightlines, Inc., In re—§ 6-39, n. 13; § 6-48, n. 16; § 6-49, n. 43; § 6-50, n. 13; § 6-60, n. 18; § 6-84, n. 3.
Simasko Production Co., In re—§ 10-6; § 10-6, n. 2, 5.
Simmons, In re, 765 F.2d 547—§ 9-4; § 9-4, n. 16; § 9-20; § 9-20, n. 7.
Simmons, In re, 124 B.R. 606—§ 6-48, n. 2; § 6-49, n. 44.
Simmons, In re, 78 B.R. 300—§ 9-18, n. 13.
Simmons, Matter of—§ 8-25, n. 49.

Simon, In re—§ 8-17, n. 24, 25, 27; § 8-18, n. 3.
Simons, In re—§ 10-31, n. 1.
Simons v. Cogan—§ 6-52, n. 48.
Simonson, In re—§ 8-22, n. 12; § 8-27, n. 13; § 8-30, n. 9.
Simpkins, In re—§ 9-10, n. 10; § 9-18, n. 12, 14.
Simpson, In re—§ 6-17, n. 18; § 6-93, n. 44, 50.
Simpson Motor Co., In re—§ 3-31, n. 84.
Sims, In re—§ 8-23, n. 3, 5.
Sims, Matter of—§ 3-20, n. 5, 15.
Sims v. McFadden—§ 8-13, n. 7.
Sims Bros. Builders, Inc., In re—§ 6-83, n. 1.
Sims Office Supply, Inc., Matter of—§ 6-11, n. 6; § 6-16, n. 1; § 6-17, n. 6, 9; § 6-31, n. 4, 17.
Sinder, Matter of—§ 6-2, n. 3, 5, 9, 24, 30.
Singer Products Co., Inc., In re—§ 6-12, n. 7; § 6-20, n. 20; § 6-31, n. 14; § 6-86, n. 10.
Sin-Ko Inc., In re—§ 6-83, n. 5.
Siouxland Beef Processing Co., In re—§ 11-3, n. 21.
604 Columbus Ave. Realty Trust, In re—§ 6-93, n. 38, 41.
Skies Unlimited, Inc. of Colorado v. King—§ 10-29, n. 9.
Skinner, In re, 917 F.2d 444—§ 3-35, n. 2.
Skinner, In re, 90 B.R. 470—§ 3-16, n. 7; § 3-35, n. 5.
Skjonsby Truck Line, Inc., In re—§ 7-25, n. 2.
Sky Group Intern., Inc., In re—§ 7-43, n. 4.
Skyland, Inc., Matter of—§ 8-14, n. 12.
Skylark Travel, Inc., In re—§ 3-14, n. 59.
Sky Valley, Inc., In re—§ 4-13, n. 2.
Slater, In re—§ 6-35, n. 35.
Slaw Const. Corp., In re—§ 6-44, n. 9.
Sleepy Valley, Inc., In re—§ 6-18, n. 10, 23, 30; § 6-93; § 6-93, n. 20, 21, 34, 38, 39, 45, 46, 62.
Sluss, In re—§ 6-45, n. 22.
Small, In re—§ 9-17, n. 7.
Small v. Beverly Bank—§ 6-93, n. 49.
Small v. Hennepin County—§ 6-36, n. 3, 17; § 6-62, n. 5.
Small Business Admin. v. Rinehart—§ 3-14, n. 80; § 3-15, n. 6; § 3-34, n. 9; § 6-43, n. 15.
Smart, In re—§ 3-23, n. 5.
Smiley, Matter of—§ 7-19, n. 8, 9; § 8-32, n. 8, 14, 15.
Smith, In re, 876 F.2d 524—§ 3-32, n. 1, 8, 16, 17.
Smith, In re, 735 F.2d 459—§ 12-12, n. 27.
Smith, In re, 123 B.R. 423—§ 8-33, n. 34.
Smith, In re, 120 B.R. 588—§ 6-60, n. 20.
Smith, In re, 119 B.R. 757—§ 8-9, n. 13; § 8-27, n. 11; § 8-29, n. 7; § 8-31, n. 4.
Smith, In re, 119 B.R. 714—§ 8-1, n. 20.
Smith, In re, 119 B.R. 558—§ 6-76, n. 2.
Smith, In re, 117 B.R. 326—§ 8-28, n. 3.
Smith, In re, 113 B.R. 579—§ 8-32, n. 5, 14.
Smith, In re, 105 B.R. 217—§ 8-22, n. 8, 23, 38; § 8-25, n. 45.
Smith, In re, 103 B.R. 882—§ 8-33, n. 18, 24.
Smith, In re, 100 B.R. 330—§ 6-40, n. 4.
Smith, In re, 92 B.R. 127—§ 6-45, n. 7.
Smith, In re, 88 B.R. 297—§ 6-12, n. 8.
Smith, In re, 86 B.R. 92—§ 3-16, n. 7; § 6-74, n. 14.
Smith, In re, 84 B.R. 175—§ 12-16, n. 3.
Smith, In re, 81 B.R. 888—§ 7-7, n. 2.
Smith, In re, 75 B.R. 365—§ 8-9, n. 16.
Smith, In re, 72 B.R. 344—§ 6-76, n. 2.
Smith, In re, 51 B.R. 273—§ 9-3, n. 6.
Smith, In re, 50 B.R. 573—§ 7-26, n. 50.
Smith, In re, 45 B.R. 100—§ 6-6, n. 3, 7; § 8-23, n. 5.
Smith, In re, 42 B.R. 198—§ 9-10, n. 6.
Smith, In re, 27 B.R. 30—§ 8-21, n. 4.
Smith, In re, 24 B.R. 19—§ 6-49, n. 73; § 6-54, n. 10; § 6-55, n. 22; § 6-56, n. 17, 19, 22.
Smith, In re, 21 B.R. 345—§ 6-6, n. 3, 7; § 6-53, n. 8; § 6-56, n. 5.
Smith, Matter of, 640 F.2d 888—§ 8-20, n. 2.
Smith, Matter of, 123 B.R. 605—§ 6-7, n. 5.
Smith, Matter of, 123 B.R. 856—§ 6-61, n. 54.
Smith, Matter of, 78 B.R. 922—§ 8-9, n. 3; § 8-25, n. 52.
Smith, Matter of, 63 B.R. 15—§ 9-18, n. 14.
Smith v. Crocker First Nat. Bank of San Francisco—§ 6-15, n. 2.
Smith v. Dairymen, Inc.—§ 6-77, n. 1, 23; § 6-78, n. 13.

Smith v. Hoboken R.R. Warehouse & S.S. Connecting Co.—§ 5-12;. § 5-12, n. 2.
Smith v. Mark Twain Nat. Bank—§ 6-41, n. 47; § 6-73, n. 4.
Smith v. Mixon—§ 6-88, n. 21, 24, 26.
Smith v. Winter Park Software Inc.—§ 8-33, n. 16.
Smith Corset Shops, Inc., In re—§ 3-32; § 3-32, n. 12; § 6-74, n. 13.
Smith-Douglass, Inc., In re, 856 F.2d 12—§ 11-10, n. 5; § 11-11, n. 2.
Smith-Douglass, Inc., In re, 842 F.2d 729—§ 6-32, n. 8.
Smith, Richardson & Conroy, Inc., In re—§ 3-9, n. 26, 29.
Smurzynski, In re—§ 7-36; § 7-36, n. 1, 3.
Smythe, In re—§ 6-2, n. 24; § 6-36, n. 12; § 6-86, n. 4.
Snead, In re—§ 6-39, n. 1.
Snider Bros., Inc., In re—§ 11-41, n. 16.
Snipes, In re—§ 8-25, n. 32.
Snow, In re—§ 8-26, n. 5.
Snowshoe Co., Inc., In re—§ 4-13, n. 2; § 4-14; § 4-14, n. 2, 5; § 4-17, n. 2.
Snyder, In re, 108 B.R. 150—§ 8-22, n. 22.
Snyder, In re, 102 B.R. 874—§ 8-1, n. 12.
Snyder, In re, 61 B.R. 268—§ 6-2, n. 21.
Snyder, In re, 51 B.R. 432—§ 11-18, n. 8.
Snyder, Matter of—§ 11-17, n. 3.
Snyder v. State-Wide Properties, Inc.—§ 6-52, n. 48.
Snyder Elec. Co. v. Fleming—§ 6-59, n. 3.
Societe Nationale Algerienne v. Distrigas Corp.—§ 3-30, n. 23.
Solano, In re—§ 7-26, n. 21.
Solar Mfg. Corp., In re—§ 4-4; § 4-4, n. 9, 27.
Solberg, In re—§ 8-33, n. 36.
Solomon v. Davis—§ 8-7, n. 9, 14.
Solon Automated Services, Inc. v. Georgetown of Kettering, Ltd.—§ 10-32, n. 2.
Somero, In re—§ 6-77, n. 1, 11, 12.
Sonnax Industries, Inc., In re, 907 F.2d 1280—§ 3-30, n. 32; § 3-31, n. 67, 72.
Sonnax Industries, Inc., In re, 99 B.R. 591—§ 3-26, n. 3.
Sonora Convalescent Hosp., Inc., In re—§ 5-10, n. 3.
Sopkin, In re—§ 6-40, n. 19; § 8-17, n. 35, 36.
Sorlucco, In re—§ 6-56, n. 14.
Sorrels v. Texas Bank and Trust Co. of Jacksonville, Tex.—§ 6-63, n. 4.
Sound Emporium, Inc., In re, 70 B.R. 22—§ 6-39, n. 15, 17.
Sound Emporium, Inc., In re, 48 B.R. 1—§ 6-39, n. 17; § 6-44, n. 8.
Sounds Distributing, Inc., In re—§ 6-31, n. 16; § 6-34, n. 5, 17.
Sousa, In re—§ 9-4, n. 37.
Southard, In re—§ 6-82, n. 6; § 6-83, n. 5.
South Atlantic Packers Ass'n, Inc., In re—§ 6-33, n. 15.
South County Realty, Inc. II, Matter of—§ 3-25, n. 18.
Southeast Community Media, Inc., In re—§ 6-87, n. 8, 10; § 6-89, n. 12.
Southeast Forest Products Corp., In re—§ 6-31, n. 3, 19.
Southern Bank and Trust Co. v. Harley—§ 3-6, n. 30.
Southern Commodity Corp., In re—§ 6-2, n. 32; § 6-31, n. 15.
Southern Elec. Supply Co. v. Raleigh County Nat. Bank—§ 6-38, n. 11.
Southern Gardens, Inc., In re—§ 6-77, n. 19.
Southern Indus. Banking Corp., In re, 809 F.2d 329—§ 6-41; § 6-41, n. 23, 24, 27, 28; § 6-42, n. 2.
Southern Indus. Banking Corp., In re, 120 B.R. 921—§ 6-7, n. 7.
Southern Indus. Banking Corp., In re, 115 B.R. 930—§ 6-88, n. 24, 30, 38.
Southern Indus. Banking Corp., In re, 99 B.R. 827—§ 6-9, n. 5; § 6-88, n. 46.
Southern Indus. Banking Corp., In re, 92 B.R. 297—§ 6-3, n. 5; § 6-31, n. 6, 9, 16, 17, 19.
Southern Indus. Banking Corp., In re, 72 B.R. 512—§ 6-30; § 6-30, n. 5.
Southern Indus. Banking Corp., In re, 66 B.R. 349—§ 6-2, n. 32; § 6-84, n. 5.
Southern Indus. Banking Corp., In re, 63 B.R. 331—§ 6-40, n. 14.
Southern Indus. Banking Corp., In re, 48 B.R. 306—§ 6-41, n. 21, 25.
Southern Oregon Mortg., Inc., In re—§ 6-61, n. 16, 69.
Southern States Motor Inns, Inc., Matter of—§ 9-10, n. 12.
South Florida Title, Inc., In re—§ 6-87, n. 18; § 6-88, n. 32.
Southland Corp., In re—§ 11-23; § 11-23, n. 3.
Southmark Properties v. Charles House Corp.—§ 3-31, n. 54.
Southside Lawn & Garden/Suffolk Yard Guard, In re—§ 3-5, n. 15; § 3-10, n. 11; § 3-22, n. 24.
Southwest Aircraft Services, Inc., In re—§ 5-10; § 5-10, n. 7, 10; § 5-23, n. 6.
Southwest Oil Co. of Jourdanton, Inc., In re—§ 11-13, n. 3; § 11-15; § 11-15, n. 10, 17.
Southwest Products Co., Inc. v. United States Through I.R.S.—§ 3-23, n. 45.
Sovereign Estates, Ltd., In re—§ 4-4, n. 7.
Soviero v. Franklin Nat. Bank of Long Island—§ 11-40; § 11-40, n. 2; § 11-41; § 11-41, n. 1.

Sovran Bank, N.A. v. Anderson—§ 3-13, n. 5; § 3-25, n. 6; § 3-27, n. 22.
Spada, In re, 903 F.2d 971—§ 6-25, n. 33, 51.
Spada, In re, 91 B.R. 668—§ 6-25; § 6-25, n. 6, 43.
Spadel, In re—§ 9-18, n. 13.
Spader, In re—§ 9-18, n. 18.
Spain, In re—§ 8-1, n. 9, 13.
Spain, Matter of, 85 B.R. 874—§ 4-9; § 4-9, n. 5, 9, 13.
Spain, Matter of, 83 B.R. 61—§ 4-7, n. 6.
Sparmal Enterprises, Inc. v. Moffit Realty Corp.—§ 6-83, n. 12.
Spaude, In re—§ 3-23, n. 32.
Spearman, In re—§ 8-28, n. 14.
Spears, In re, 744 F.2d 1225—§ 8-26, n. 18.
Spears, In re, 39 B.R. 91—§ 6-65, n. 10.
Specialty Products, Inc., Matter of—§ 4-4, n. 2.
Spenard Ventures, Inc., In re—§ 2-15, n. 27.
Spencer, In re—§ 3-5, n. 17; § 3-6, n. 24; § 3-34, n. 8.
Spencer, Matter of—§ 3-6, n. 24; § 3-16, n. 10; § 3-26, n. 6.
Sperry, In re, 101 B.R. 767—§ 6-61, n. 18, 49, 70.
Sperry, In re, 101 B.R. 763—§ 6-60, n. 18.
Spicer Oaks Apartments, Ltd., In re—§ 12-6, n. 9; § 12-10, n. 7.
Spilotros, In re—§ 7-26, n. 37.
Spinelli, In re—§ 6-39, n. 13.
Spirtos, In re—§ 11-4, n. 31.
Spong, In re—§ 7-29, n. 10, 19, 22.
Sportfame of Ohio, Inc., In re—§ 3-8; § 3-8, n. 31.
Sports & Science, Ind., Inc., In re—§ 6-73, n. 8.
Sportswear Shoppe, Ltd., In re—§ 6-61, n. 67.
Sprecher, In re—§ 7-49, n. 3, 9.
Sprick, In re—§ 8-27, n. 3.
Spring Valley Farms, Inc., In re—§ 11-3, n. 21.
Spurlock, Matter of—§ 8-27, n. 11.
SPW Corp., In re, 96 B.R. 683—§ 6-31, n. 9.
SPW Corp., In re, 96 B.R. 676—§ 6-31, n. 19.
SSA Baltimore Federal Credit Union v. Bizon—§ 8-33, n. 20.
Stacy Farms, In re—§ 4-14, n. 6.
Stadium Management Corp., In re—§ 3-14, n. 21; § 3-22; § 3-22, n. 5, 26, 28.
Stafford, In re, 123 B.R. 415—§ 3-31, n. 97, 99, 100, 101.
Stafford, In re, 121 B.R. 109—§ 3-31, n. 65.
Stage, In re—§ 9-22; § 9-22, n. 6, 9.
Stahley, In re—§ 3-23, n. 23, 24, 28.
Staley, In re—§ 8-28, n. 3, 25.
Stall, In re—§ 6-39, n. 15, 16, 34.
Stalter & Co., Ltd., In re—§ 5-7, n. 3.
Stamford Municipal Employees' Credit Union v. Edwards—§ 9-22, n. 14.
Stamp v. Insurance Co. of North America—§ 6-40, n. 7.
Standard Food Services, Inc., In re—§ 6-27, n. 15.
Standard Furniture Co., In re—§ 6-39, n. 1; § 6-94, n. 6.
Standard Law Enforcement Supply Co. of Wisconsin, Matter of—§ 6-88, n. 33.
Standard Stores, Inc., In re—§ 6-17, n. 10, 23.
Standor Jewelers West, Inc., In re—§ 5-17, n. 3.
Staniforth, In re—§ 8-17, n. 35, 36.
Stanke, In re—§ 6-83, n. 18; § 6-84, n. 5.
Stanley Engineering Corporation, In re—§ 4-16, n. 2.
Stanley Hotel, Inc., In re—§ 11-17, n. 8.
Stanley Hotel, Inc., Matter of—§ 4-14, n. 5; § 4-17, n. 2.
Stanley–Southwest Investments, Inc., In re—§ 6-22, n. 2; § 6-88, n. 21.
Stann v. Mid–American Credit Union—§ 6-43, n. 29.
Stanton, In re—§ 3-31, n. 10.
Staples, In re—§ 6-50, n. 23; § 6-53, n. 3, 6; § 6-55, n. 9; § 6-56, n. 12, 46.
Starkey, In re, 116 B.R. 259—§ 8-33, n. 17, 24, 34.
Starkey, In re, 49 B.R. 984—§ 9-4, n. 14.
Starr, In re—§ 8-1, n. 10.
Star-Tel, Inc. v. Nacogdoches Telecommunications, Inc.—§ 3-5, n. 12, 19.
State v. ___ (see opposing party)
State Airlines, Inc., In re—§ 3-2, n. 9; § 3-6, n. 1.
State ex rel. v. ___ (see opposing party and relator)
State Farm Mutual Automobile Ins. Co. v. Continental Casualty Co.—§ 11-39, n. 1.
State of (see name of state)

Stearns v. Carlson—§ **6-56, n. 1.**
Stebbins By and Through Dahl, In re—§ **8-24, n. 5;** § **8-25, n. 18.**
Stebow Const. Co., Inc., In re—§ **6-61, n. 70.**
Steele, In re—§ **6-48, n. 17;** § **6-60, n. 20.**
Steele, Matter of—§ **6-86, n. 4, 10.**
Steeley v. Dunivant—§ **3-6, n. 49.**
Steel Imp. Co., In re—§ **6-31, n. 17, 19.**
Steel, Inc. v. Windstein—§ **6-83, n. 12, 13;** § **6-84, n. 5;** § **6-88, n. 18.**
SteelShip Corp., Matter of—§ **5-4, n. 16.**
Steelvest, Inc., In re—§ **6-2, n. 9;** § **6-7, n. 5.**
Stegall, Matter of—§ **11-27, n. 12;** § **11-29, n. 1.**
Stein, In re—§ **3-10, n. 49, 70;** § **7-45, n. 4.**
Stein and Day, Inc., In re—§ **10-8, n. 3.**
Stephens, In re—§ **7-28, n. 12.**
Stephens Industries, Inc. v. McClung—§ **3-25, n. 10;** § **3-31, n. 98;** § **4-4, n. 15.**
Stephen Smith Home For the Aged, Inc., In re—§ **12-5, n. 11.**
Stephenson, In re—§ **6-39, n. 15, 39;** § **6-40, n. 4;** § **6-44;** § **6-44, n. 10.**
Stereo Equipment Sales, Inc., In re—§ **6-16, n. 1.**
Stern, In re, 44 B.R. 15—§ **6-36, n. 3;** § **6-62, n. 3, 5, 22, 27;** § **7-7, n. 1.**
Stern, In re, 9 B.R. 747—§ **3-11, n. 14.**
Sternberg v. Rubenstein—§ **4-3, n. 2, 8.**
Stern–Slegman–Prins Co., In re—§ **6-93, n. 29, 33, 40.**
Stevens, In re, 112 B.R. 175—§ **6-47, n. 7;** § **6-48, n. 3.**
Stevens, In re, 68 B.R. 774—§ **3-21, n. 110;** § **11-10;** § **11-10, n. 3;** § **11-11, n. 2.**
Stevens v. Pike County Bank—§ **8-21, n. 10.**
Stevenson, In re—§ **6-48, n. 10, 11.**
Stewart, In re, 109 B.R. 998—§ **9-14, n. 21.**
Stewart, In re, 52 B.R. 281—§ **9-7, n. 3.**
Stewart, In re, 32 B.R. 132—§ **8-11, n. 16.**
Stewart, In re, 21 B.R. 329—§ **6-49, n. 34, 47.**
Stewart v. Gurley—§ **3-25;** § **3-25, n. 10, 17.**
Steyr-Daimler-Puch of America Corp. v. Pappas—§ **6-61, n. 8;** § **6-94, n. 7.**
St. George Island, Ltd. v. Pelham—§ **12-2, n. 10, 14, 19.**
Stiles, In re—§ **9-18, n. 8.**
Still, In re, 124 B.R. 24—§ **6-88, n. 24.**
Still, In re, 117 B.R. 251—§ **3-8, n. 4;** § **3-32, n. 30;** § **3-33, n. 27, 28.**
Still, In re, 113 B.R. 311—§ **6-88, n. 8.**
Stivers, In re—§ **3-32, n. 6.**
St. Louis Globe Democrat, Inc., In re, 99 B.R. 946—§ **6-16, n. 1;** § **6-25, n. 14;** § **6-31, n. 6.**
St. Louis Globe–Democrat, Inc., In re, 63 B.R. 131—§ **10-8, n. 3, 7, 11.**
St. Mary Hosp., In re, 89 B.R. 503—§ **6-43, n. 16.**
St. Mary Hosp., In re, 86 B.R. 393—§ **4-13, n. 5;** § **4-17;** § **4-17, n. 3.**
STN Enterprises, In re—§ **6-2, n. 28, 30.**
Stockhouse v. Hines Motor Supply (Wyoming), Inc.—§ **7-41;** § **7-41, n. 11.**
Stoffer, In re—§ **8-24, n. 4.**
Stoller's, Inc., In re—§ **6-56, n. 17, 20, 27, 28, 38.**
Stone, In re, 119 B.R. 222—§ **8-25, n. 14;** § **8-26, n. 7.**
Stone, In re, 94 B.R. 298— § **7-28, n. 17.**
Stone, In re, 91 B.R. 589— § **7-28, n. 4.**
Stone, In re, 90 B.R. 71— § **3-23, n. 32.**
Stone v. Stone—§ **8-33, n. 15.**
Stone's Pharmacy, Inc. v. Pharmacy Accounting Management, Inc.—§ **3-5, n. 10;** § **3-6, n. 20;** § **3-10, n. 22.**
Storage Technology Corp., In re, 48 B.R. 862—§ **6-66, n. 11.**
Storage Technology Corp., In re, 45 B.R. 363—§ **6-62, n. 18, 26.**
Storberg, In re—§ **10-22, n. 8.**
Stovall, Matter of—§ **7-29, n. 25.**
Stovall v. Stovall—§ **3-20, n. 11.**
St. Paul Fire & Marine Ins. Co. v. Vaughn—§ **7-30, n. 19;** § **12-13, n. 13.**
St. Petersburg Hotel Associates Ltd., Matter of, 44 B.R. 944—§ **4-13, n. 1;** § **4-14, n. 6.**
St. Petersburg Hotel Associates Ltd., Matter of, 37 B.R. 380—§ **11-36, n. 7.**
Straight, In re—§ **6-6, n. 3, 7;** § **8-30, n. 3.**
Stratbucker, Matter of—§ **4-14, n. 5.**
Stratford Hotel Co., In re—§ **3-25, n. 6, 15.**
Stratton, In re—§ **6-47, n. 7;** § **6-48, n. 15;** § **6-49, n. 44;** § **6-59, n. 2.**
Stratton, Matter of—§ **9-10, n. 10;** § **9-17, n. 8;** § **9-18, n. 12.**
Stratton v. Equitable Bank, N.A.—§ **6-44, n. 2;** § **6-48, n. 4;** § **6-49, n. 1, 2;** § **6-50, n. 5;** § **6-88, n. 35;** § **6-93, n. 46.**

Strause, In re—§ 9-30, n. 8.
Strauser, In re—§ 6-55, n. 3; § 6-56, n. 8.
Streets & Beard Farm Partnership, In re—§ 5-4, n. 14.
Strehlow, In re—§ 8-32, n. 8, 9.
Strelsky, In re—§ 7-7, n. 1.
Strickland, In re—§ 6-61, n. 74.
Stringer, In re—§ 3-1, n. 18; § 3-12, n. 20, 22, 23.
Strom, In re, 97 B.R. 532—§ 6-2, n. 3, 24; § 6-61, n. 30, 74, 77.
Strom, In re, 46 B.R. 144—§ 6-33, n. 20; § 6-89, n. 8, 23.
Strong, Matter of—§ 2-14, n. 4; § 7-45, n. 13; § 9-13, n. 4.
Stroop, In re—§ 2-5, n. 12.
Stroud Wholesale, Inc., Matter of—§ 4-7; § 4-7, n. 10, 14, 16.
Struggs, In re—§ 7-45, n. 13.
Stuckey, In re—§ 6-61, n. 11, 28.
Studio Five Designs (U.S.A.), Inc., In re—§ 6-15, n. 1, 5.
Sturgeon, In re—§ 9-2, n. 12.
Subscription Television of Greater Atlanta, In re—§ 5-23, n. 11.
Suburban Motor Freight, Inc., In re—§ 6-7, n. 4; § 6-49, n. 8, 46; § 6-52, n. 10.
Sugarek, In re—§ 8-25, n. 55.
Sulcer v. Northwestern Nat. Ins. Co. (of Milwaukee, Wis.)—§ 8-7, n. 3.
Sullivan, Matter of, 680 F.2d 1131—§ 8-3, n. 11, 13.
Sullivan, Matter of, 83 B.R. 623—§ 8-26, n. 5.
Sullivan Cent. Plaza I, Ltd., Matter of, 935 F.2d 723—§ 6-70, n. 3.
Sullivan Cent. Plaza I, Ltd., Matter of, 914 F.2d 731—§ 3-31, n. 1, 103.
Sullivan Cent. Plaza I Ltd. v. BancBoston Real Estate Capital Corp.—§ 3-31, n. 103.
Sullivan Ford Sales, Matter of—§ 4-16, n. 4.
Summers, In re, 108 B.R. 200—§ 8-3, n. 20.
Summers, In re, 85 B.R. 121—§ 6-58, n. 4; § 8-32, n. 8, 9, 13, 17, 19.
Summit Land Co., In re—§ 5-8, n. 8, 14.
Sumner, In re—§ 6-77, n. 1, 8, 21.
Sumy v. Schlossberg—§ 8-10, n. 25; § 12-12, n. 12.
Sunbelt Sav. Ass'n of Texas v. Truman—§ 3-22, n. 4, 29; § 3-31, n. 21, 39, 41, 43.
Sunbelt Vacation Travel, Inc., In re—§ 6-40, n. 2, 16, 36, 37; § 6-41, n. 46, 50; § 6-45, n. 3.
Sunberg, In re—§ 6-77, n. 1.
Sunberg, Matter of—§ 6-77, n. 1.
Suncrete Corp., In re—§ 6-44, n. 2.
Sundance Corp., In re—§ 12-10, n. 6.
Sun Island Foods, In re—§ 6-2, n. 6; § 6-77, n. 1.
Sunnyside Beverage, Inc., In re—§ 6-20, n. 20.
Sun Railings, Inc., In re—§ 6-7, n. 5.
Sun Runner Marine, Inc., In re—§ 5-14, n. 3.
Sunset Developers, In re—§ 2-5; § 2-5, n. 6; § 11-37, n. 3; § 11-38; § 11-38, n. 8.
Sunset Enterprises, Inc. v. B & B Coal Co., Inc.—§ 6-19, n. 16; § 6-70, n. 2.
Sun Spas by Schaeffer, Inc., In re—§ 6-47, n. 10.
Sun–Tel Communications, Inc., In re—§ 3-9, n. 22, 29, 33.
Sun Valley Ranches, Inc., In re—§ 3-27, n. 20.
Sun World Broadcasters, Inc., In re—§ 2-5, n. 46.
Sure–Snap Corp., In re—§ 6-47, n. 7.
Sutherland, In re—§ 9-7; § 9-7, n. 4, 7.
Sutliff, In re—§ 7-26, n. 21.
Suttles, In re—§ 7-22, n. 8.
Sutton, Matter of—§ 3-25, n. 10, 11, 12.
Sutton, United States v.—§ 3-12, n. 19.
Sutton Investments, Inc., In re—§ 6-39, n. 7, 38; § 6-40, n. 2; § 6-44, n. 2.
Swan v. Dervos—§ 3-21, n. 43.
Swansea Consol. Resources, Inc., In re—§ 3-25; § 3-25, n. 53, 57.
Swanson, In re, 873 F.2d 1121—§ 8-33, n. 7, 24, 26.
Swanson, In re, 12 B.R. 688—§ 7-26, n. 55.
Swanson, Matter of—§ 6-80, n. 12; § 8-29, n. 13.
Swartz, In re—§ 8-19, n. 10.
Swatara Coal Co., In re—§ 11-13, n. 3; § 11-18, n. 1.
Sweeney, In re—§ 7-42; § 7-42, n. 4.
Sweetapple Plastics, Inc., Matter of—§ 6-16, n. 1; § 6-20, n. 2, 11, 12, 17, 19; § 6-31, n. 15.
Sweetwater, In re, 884 F.2d 1323—§ 6-2, n. 32.
Sweetwater, In re, 57 B.R. 354—§ 11-17, n. 3.
Sweetwater, In re, 40 B.R. 733—§ 3-28; § 3-28, n. 6; § 5-24; § 5-24, n. 3.
S & W Enterprise, In re—§ 9-7, n. 1; § 10-22, n. 5; § 10-24, n. 9.
Swift, In re—§ 8-32, n. 5.

Swift Aire Lines, Inc., In re—§ 3-14; § 3-14, n. 57, 58.
Swift & Co., United States v.—§ 3-27, n. 44.
Swolsky, In re—§ 10-12, n. 12.
Sykes, In re—§ 3-22, n. 29.
Sylvester v. Dow Jones and Co., Inc.—§ 9-3, n. 12.
Sylvester v. Sylvester—§ 7-29; § 7-29, n. 8, 15, 18, 23.
Sylvester Bros. Development Co. v. Burlington Northern R.R.—§ 7-7, n. 15.
Synfax Mfg., Inc., Matter of—§ 3-21, n. 110.
Syrtveit, In re—§ 8-1, n. 12; § 8-3, n. 20.
Szabo, In re—§ 8-11, n. 1, 9.
Szabo v. Vinton Motors, Inc.—§ 6-63, n. 4.
S & Z Intern. Management, Inc., In re—§ 6-77, n. 1; § 6-78, n. 3.

T

Taber Farm Associates, In re—§ 5-10, n. 13.
Tabita, In re—§ 6-15, n. 1, 3; § 8-23, n. 5.
Tabor, Matter of—§ 3-9, n. 8.
Tabor Court Realty Corp., United States v.—§ 6-52, n. 11, 13, 21, 43.
Tabor Enterprises, Inc. v. People of State of Ill.—§ 6-54, n. 10; § 6-55, n. 22.
Taco Ed's, Inc., In re—§ 6-69, n. 9.
Taddeo, In re—§ 9-17, n. 2.
Taff, Matter of—§ 8-17, n. 45, 46, 48; § 9-13; § 9-13, n. 8, 9.
Tafoya, United States v.—§ 6-38, n. 16.
Taggatz, In re—§ 3-14, n. 57.
Takeuchi Manufacturing v. Fields (In re Fields)—§ 7-26, n. 59.
Talla, Inc., In re—§ 6-60, n. 20.
Talmadge, In re—§ 8-21, n. 9.
Tammey Jewels, Inc., In re—§ 5-23, n. 4.
Tampa Bay Associates, Ltd., Matter of—§ 10-26, n. 1.
Tampa Chain Co., Inc., In re—§ 3-6, n. 30, 38.
Tanner, In re—§ 11-30, n. 11.
Tape City, U.S.A., Inc., Matter of—§ 6-62, n. 3, 28.
Tarakjian v. Krone—§ 3-32, n. 38.
Tarnow, Matter of—§ 9-4; § 9-4, n. 17, 18.
Tarpley, In re—§ 8-9, n. 14.
Tart, In re—§ 9-24, n. 25.
Tash, In re—§ 6-2, n. 22; § 8-23, n. 7; § 8-25, n. 4.
Tashman, In re—§ 9-3, n. 9.
Tatsis, In re—§ 2-2, n. 7; § 2-13, n. 14; § 9-3, n. 33.
Taxman Clothing Co., Inc., Matter of—§ 6-18, n. 3, 11, 12, 30.
Taylor, In ro, 884 F.2d 478—§ 3-32, n. 27; § 3-33, n. 10, 13, 23.
Taylor, In re, 861 F.2d 550—§ 8-9, n. 2, 3; § 8-25, n. 57, 62.
Taylor, In re, 16 B.R. 323—§ 3-20, n. 24.
Taylor, In re, 15 B.R. 596—§ 9-3, n. 6.
Taylor, In re, 8 B.R. 578—§ 8-22, n. 30.
Taylor, Matter of, 913 F.2d 102—§ 5-15, n. 4.
Taylor, Matter of, 44 B.R. 548—§ 3-20, n. 33, 41.
Taylor v. First Federal Sav. & Loan Ass'n of Monessen—§ 3-6, n. 64; § 11-3, n. 1.
Taylor v. Freeland & Kronz—§ 8-1, n. 12; § 8-29, n. 7.
Taylor v. Standard Gas & Electric Co.—§ 6-93; § 6-93, n. 24.
Taylor Mfg., Inc., In re—§ 5-12; § 5-12, n. 6.
Taylor Motors, In re—§ 6-38, n. 21, 22; § 6-39, n. 2; § 6-40, n. 2, 5, 7, 14.
T & B General Contracting, Inc., Matter of—§ 6-40, n. 6, 7.
T.D.M.A., Inc., In re—§ 11-7, n. 8.
T & D Management Co., In re—§ 6-49, n. 40.
Teachers Ins. and Annuity Ass'n of America v. Butler—§ 3-5, n. 15; § 3-6, n. 30, 35; § 3-22, n. 34.
Teamsters Pension Trust Fund of Philadelphia and Vicinity v. Malone Realty Co.—§ 3-23, n. 44.
Technical Fabricators, Inc., In re—§ 2-5, n. 47.
Technology for Energy Corp., In re—§ 6-93, n. 46.
Teerlink Ranch Ltd., In re—§ 6-61, n. 8.
Teichman, In re—§ 7-6; § 7-6, n. 3.
Teigen, In re—§ 6-2, n. 13.
Telecash Industries, Inc., In re—§ 6-12, n. 7; § 6-27, n. 8, 13.
Telefest, Inc. v. VU–TV, Inc.—§ 6-51; § 6-51, n. 40, 41.
Tellier, In re—§ 3-27, n. 3, 32.

Teltronics Services, Inc., Matter of—§ 6-93, n. 38, 46.
T. E. Mercer Trucking Co., In re—§ 6-93, n. 18, 50.
Temple Retirement Community, Inc., In re—§ 11-18, n. 10.
Tenna Corp., In re—§ 6-20, n. 5, 6.
Tenneco Inc. v. First Virginia Bank of Tidewater—§ 8-33, n. 15.
Tennessee Wheel and Rubber Co., In re—§ 6-17, n. 6, 28.
Tennessee Wheel & Rubber Co., In re—§ 4-15; § 4-15, n. 9, 15; § 6-2, n. 32.
Tenney v. Terry—§ 9-3, n. 8.
Tenney Village Co., Inc., In re—§ 4-15, n. 12.
Terkeltaub, In re—§ 6-61, n. 18, 56.
Terrace Apartments, Ltd., Matter of—§ 5-15, n. 10.
Terrace Gardens Park Partnership, In re—§ 4-7, n. 12; § 6-92, n. 10.
Terra Villa Apartments, Ltd., In re—§ 6-61, n. 74.
Terrell, In re—§ 5-4, n. 14.
Territo, In re, 36 B.R. 667—§ 8-18; § 8-18, n. 12, 19.
Territo, In re, 35 B.R. 343—§ 6-62, n. 5.
Terry, In re, 780 F.2d 894—§ 9-17, n. 7.
Terry, In re, 78 B.R. 171—§ 9-7; § 9-7, n. 4, 14.
Terry, In re, 56 B.R. 538—§ 6-2, n. 21; § 6-6, n. 9; § 8-22, n. 33; § 8-23, n. 6.
Terry, In re, 12 B.R. 578—§ 3-30, n. 22.
Terry, In re, 9 B.R. 314—§ 9-14, n. 21.
Terry, In re, 7 B.R. 880—§ 8-31, n. 3.
Terry v. Chauffeurs, Teamsters and Helpers, Local 391—§ 3-5, n. 19; § 3-22, n. 33.
Terwilliger's Catering Plus, Inc., In re—§ 2-8, n. 42.
Tesmetges, In re—§ 6-48, n. 4; § 6-49, n. 39.
Texaco Inc., In re, 109 B.R. 609—§ 3-30, n. 27.
Texaco Inc., In re, 92 B.R. 38—§ 4-17, n. 2; § 10–14; § 10-14, n. 4.
Texaco Inc., In re, 89 B.R. 382—§ 12-9, n. 2.
Texaco Inc., In re, 81 B.R. 813—§ 11–19; § 11-19, n. 1.
Texaco Inc., In re, 79 B.R. 560—§ 10-12; § 10-12, n. 15.
Texaco Inc., In re, 76 B.R. 322—§ 11–13, n. 3; § 11–15; § 11-15, n. 5; § 11–18, n. 1.
Texaco, In re, Nos. 897 B. 20142, 20143 and 20144—§ 10-15, n. 4.
Texaco Inc. v. Louisiana Land and Exploration Co.—§ 5-15, n. 4.
Texas Corrugated Box Corp., In re—§ 6-43, n. 4.
Texas Extrusion Corp., Matter of—§ 11-17, n. 3.
Texas General Petroleum Corp., In re—§ 6-2, n. 32; § 6-19, n. 7.
Texas Research, Inc., Matter of—§ 4-15, n. 15; § 6-71, n. 22.
Texas Tri–Collar, Inc., In re—§ 6-76, n. 2; § 6-78, n. 6.
Texlon Corp., In re—§ 4-15; § 4-15, n. 7; § 10-34; § 10-34, n. 1.
Thames, In re—§ 6-48, n. 2; § 6-49, n. 13, 34.
THC Financial Corp., In re—§ 3-6, n. 62.
The Bible Speaks, In re—§ 11-6, n. 3, 13.
Theisen, In re—§ 6-60, n. 17, 28; § 8-32, n. 5.
The New 5510, Inc., In re—§ 6-61, n. 16.
Theo. Hamm Brewing Co. v. First Trust and Sav. Bank of Kankakee—§ 6-66, n. 3.
The Travel Shoppe, Inc., In re—§ 5-13, n. 3.
Thiel v. Thiel—§ 3-6, n. 33.
31–33 Corp., In re—§ 6-73; § 6-73, n. 4, 15.
Thomas, In re, 121 B.R. 94—§ 3-25, n. 8.
Thomas, In re, 91 B.R. 731—§ 6-39, n. 15; § 6-40, n. 4; § 6-44, n. 2.
Thomas, In re, 59 B.R. 758—§ 9-17, n. 5.
Thomas, In re, 47 B.R. 27—§ 7-6, n. 2.
Thomas, Matter of, 91 B.R. 117—§ 3-31, n. 5, 6.
Thomas, Matter of, 43 B.R. 201—§ 6-6, n. 6; § 8-22, n. 15.
Thomas v. Bennett—§ 6-38, n. 15.
Thomas v. Union Carbide Agr. Products Co.—§ 12-14, n. 12.
Thomas B. Hamilton Co., Inc., Matter of—§ 5-13; § 5-13, n. 5.
Thomas Farm Systems, Inc., In re—§ 6-18, n. 26, 30.
Thomas W. Garland, Inc., In re—§ 6-31, n. 7.
Thompson, In re, 884 F.2d 1100—§ 8-26, n. 19; § 8-31, n. 8.
Thompson, In re, 867 F.2d 416—§ 8-25, n. 55, 56, 60, 62.
Thompson, In re, 18 B.R. 67—§ 6-49, n. 73; § 6-56, n. 5.
Thompson, Matter of—§ 8-25, n. 48, 49.
Thomson McKinnon Securities Inc., In re—§ 6-9, n. 7; § 6-25, n. 13.
Thorne, In re—§ 9-10, n. 6.
Thornton, In re—§ 8-25, n. 38, 41.
Thorson, In re—§ 6-49, n. 66, 75, 76.
Three Star Telecast, Inc., Matter of—§ 3-28, n. 2, 5; § 5-24, n. 3.

Threet, In re—§ 9-17, n. 5.
3220 Erie Blvd. East, Inc., In re—§ 3-6, n. 11, 42; § 3-14, n. 67; § 3-30, n. 30.
Threewitt, In re—§ 8-33, n. 17.
Thrifty Dutchman, Inc., In re—§ 6-47, n. 7; § 6-49, n. 22, 78.
Thurmond, In re—§ 2-17, n. 16.
Thurston, In re—§ 9-18, n. 5.
Ticket Plus, Inc., In re—§ 3-20, n. 33.
Tidewater Memorial Hosp., Inc., In re—§ 6-45, n. 3.
TIE/Communications, Inc.—§ 11-23; § 11-23, n. 1.
Tignor, In re—§ 8-18, n. 2.
Tignor v. Parkinson—§ 8-1, n. 9, 11; § 8-18, n. 2; § 8-33, n. 2.
Tilco, Inc., Matter of—§ 5-8, n. 4.
Tillery, In re—§ 6-2, n. 16.
Tilley v. Jessee—§ 7-29; § 7-29, n. 2, 6, 8, 17, 23.
Tilston Roberts Corp., In re—§ 6-44, n. 1, 6.
Timberline Property Development, Inc., Matter of—§ 6-69, n. 6; § 6-76, n. 5.
Timbers of Inwood Forest Associates, Ltd., In re—§ 2-15, n. 4; § 3-27, n. 6; § 11-13, n. 9; § 11-15; § 11-15, n. 4, 15; § 11-36, n. 9.
Tim Wargo & Sons, Inc., In re—§ 9-24; § 9-24, n. 13.
Tinker, In re—§ 3-8, n. 35.
Tinsley and Groom, In re—§ 6-93, n. 46, 54.
Tisdale, Matter of—§ 8-33, n. 17, 20, 24, 26.
Titan Energy, Inc., In re, 837 F.2d 325—§ 12-5, n. 11.
Titan Energy Corp., In re, 82 B.R. 907—§ 6-4, n. 17.
Tleel, In re—§ 6-61, n. 28, 38.
TM Carlton House Partners, Ltd., In re, 97 B.R. 819—§ 5-7, n. 4.
TM Carlton House Partners, Ltd., In re, 93 B.R. 859—§ 6-39, n. 12, 38; § 6-40, n. 4; § 6-44, n. 1.
TM Carlton House Partners, Ltd., In re, 91 B.R. 349—§ 6-77, n. 20.
TMH Corp., In re—§ 6-61, n. 74.
T.M. Sweeney & Sons, LTL Services, Inc., In re—§ 6-12, n. 13; § 6-61, n. 30.
Todd, In re, 65 B.R. 249—§ 9-5, n. 5.
Todd, In re, 37 B.R. 836—§ 6-40, n. 14, 16, 19.
Todd Shipyards Corp., In re—§ 3-30, n. 35.
Toibb v. Radloff—§ 1-9, n. 1; § 2-2, n. 10; § 9-3; § 9-3, n. 34; § 10-2, n. 2.
Toledo Equipment Co., Inc., In re—§ 6-2, n. 28, 30; § 10-13, n. 13.
Tomasso, In re—§ 8-2, n. 4.
Tomer, In re—§ 6-61, n. 16, 28.
Tomko, In re—§ 8-13, n. 2, 3.
Tom McCormick Enterprises, Inc., In re—§ 4-15; § 4-15, n. 5; § 6-69, n. 13.
Tondreau, In re—§ 7-26, n. 21.
Toner, In re—§ 8-11, n. 18; § 8-33, n. 17, 24, 34.
Tony Downs Foods Co., In re—§ 11-13, n. 3; § 11-15, n. 9.
Top Sport Distributors, Inc., In re—§ 6-49, n. 34.
Torgerson Co., In re—§ 5-2, n. 2.
Torres, In re—§ 3-23, n. 40.
T.O.S. Industries, Inc. v. Ross Hill Controls Corp.—§ 12-12, n. 31.
Total Acquisition Corp., In re—§ 6-49, n. 36.
Total Transp., Inc., In re—§ 12-2, n. 10, 19.
Totten, In re—§ 6-36, n. 3, 7; § 6-62, n. 5.
Touchard, In re—§ 7-26, n. 21.
Towner Petroleum Co., In re—§ 11-5, n. 9; § 11-7, n. 11.
Townsend, In re, 84 B.R. 764—§ 12-11; § 12-11, n. 8.
Townsend, In re, 72 B.R. 960—§ 8-10, n. 25, 26.
Townsend v. Magic Graphics, Inc.—§ 3-6, n. 22.
T.P. Long Chemical, Inc., In re—§ 11-10; § 11-10, n. 8; § 11-11; § 11-11, n. 3.
Tractman, In re—§ 7-20, n. 3, 7.
Trainer's Inc., In re—§ 11-13, n. 3; § 11-14; § 11-14, n. 7; § 11-18, n. 1.
Trans Air, Inc., In re, 103 B.R. 322—§ 6-17, n. 8, 28; § 6-18, n. 21.
Trans Air, Inc., In re, 78 B.R. 351—§ 6-17, n. 8; § 6-25, n. 13; § 6-28, n. 2.
TransAmerican Natural Gas Corp., In re—§ 5-7; § 5-7, n. 15; § 11-5, n. 5; § 11-6, n. 11.
Trans Caribbean Lines, Inc. v. Tracor Marine, Inc.—§ 3-6, n. 46.
Transload & Transport, Inc. v. American Marine Underwriters, Inc.—§ 6-94, n. 8.
Transouth Financial Corp. v. Hill—§ 9-17, n. 5; § 9-18, n. 8.
Transouth Financial Corp. v. Paris—§ 8-2, n. 4; § 8-24, n. 3.
Transportation Design and Technology, Inc., In re—§ 6-76, n. 2; § 6-77, n. 7.
Transportation Systems Intern., Inc., In re—§ 3-6; § 3-6, n. 51, 63; § 3-14, n. 15.
Trans–Texas Petroleum Corp., In re—§ 6-77, n. 7; § 6-78, n. 6.
Trauger, In re, 109 B.R. 502—§ 6-88, n. 24.

Trauger, In re, 105 B.R. 120—§ **6-49**, n. 27, 43, 49, 52.
Traurig, In re—§ **8-10**, n. 25, 26.
Treadway, In re—§ **8-10**, n. 7.
Treadwell, Matter of—§ **6-49**, n. 41; § **8-11**, n. 3; § **8-17**, n. 10.
Treiber, In re—§ **6-6**, n. 3, 8.
Tremont Elec., Inc. v. Rampinelli Elec. Co., Inc.—§ **3-5**, n. 12; § **3-6**, n. 25.
Trending Cycles for Commodities, Inc., In re—§ **6-39**, n. 13; § **6-94**, n. 6.
Tressler, Matter of—§ **6-24**, n. 2.
Trevino, In re, 96 B.R. 608—§ **8–6**, n. 4, 5; § **8–22**, n. 21, 34.
Trevino, In re, 78 B.R. 29—§ **8-29**, n. 15.
Triangle Chemicals, Inc., Matter of—§ **1-4**, n. 6.
Trickett, In re—§ **8-10**, n. 25.
Trigwell, In re—§ **9-14**, n. 20; § **9-17**, n. 8.
Tri–L Corp., In re—§ **10-32**, n. 1.
Tringali v. Hathaway Machinery Co., Inc.—§ **3-10**, n. 27, 28; § **3-14**, n. 4, 36.
Trinity Baptist Church of Bradenton, Florida, Inc., Matter of—§ **6-48**, n. 17; § **6-60**, n. 4.
Trinsey, In re—§ **6-69**, n. 14.
Triple A Coal Co., Inc., Matter of—§ **6-38**, n. 10.
Triple R Holdings, L.P., In re—§ **11-27**, n. 17.
Tri–State Paving, Inc., Matter of—§ **6-59**, n. 3.
Trois Etoiles, Inc., In re—§ **6-69**, n. 7.
Tropicana Graphics, Inc., In re—§ **6-36**, n. 12; § **6-62**, n. 26, 27.
Trott, In re—§ **6-33**, n. 9.
Troxler Hosiery Co., Inc., United States v.—§ **3-20**, n. 5, 15.
Troyer, In re—§ **9-3**, n. 21.
Trustees of Amalgamated Ins. Fund v. McFarlin's, Inc.—§ **7-11**; § **7-11**, n. 2, 10.
Truxon, Matter of—§ **9-19**, n. 5.
Tryit Enterprises, In re—§ **6-51**, n. 27; § **6-60**, n. 20.
TS Industries, Inc., In re—§ **5-14**, n. 2.
Tsunis, Matter of—§ **4-9**; § **4-9**, n. 3, 4.
TSW Stores of Nanuet, Inc., In re—§ **5-20**, n. 9.
T & T Parts Warehouse, Inc., In re—§ **6-40**, n. 19; § **6-41**, n. 20, 26.
Tucker, In re—§ **9-3**, n. 6.
Tuckman v. Hayward—§ **8-8**, n. 6.
Tucson Estates, Inc., In re—§ **3-30**, n. 27.
Tudor Motor Lodge Associates, Ltd. Partnership, In re—§ **3-27**, n. 6.
Tull v. United States—§ **12-14**; § **12-14**, n. 7; § **12-15**.
Tunget, In re—§ **7-39**, n. 2.
Turbowind, Inc., In re—§ **3-14**, n. 5; § **12-2**, n. 6, 7.
Turchon, In re—§ **11-7**, n. 10.
Turner, In re, 724 F.2d 338—§ **8–1**, n. 13.
Turner, In re, 101 B.R. 751—§ **7-7**, n. 2, 3.
Turner, In re, 81 B.R. 387—§ **8-10**, n. 7, 25, 26.
Turner, In re, 78 B.R. 166—§ **6-60**, n. 20.
Turning Point Lounge, Ltd., In re—§ **3-23**, n. 34; § **10-31**, n. 1.
Tveten, In re—§ **12-12**, n. 24.
Twenty–Four Hour Nautilus Swim and Fitness Center, Inc., In re—§ **6-40**, n. 14.
TWI, Inc., In re—§ **12-2**, n. 8.
T.W. Koeger Trucking Co., In re—§ **2-2**, n. 8.
222 Liberty Associates, In re, 110 B.R. 196—§ **6-40**, n. 19; § **6-43**, n. 4; § **6-71**, n. 8.
222 Liberty Associates, In re, 94 B.R. 381—§ **4-15**, n. 5; § **6-71**, n. 9, 10, 11, 14, 20; § **6-74**, n. 14.
Tyler, In re, 18 B.R. 574—§ **10-8**, n. 3; § **10-10**, n. 1.
Tyler, In re, 15 B.R. 258—§ **3-11**, n. 13, 14.
Tynan, Matter of—§ **3-16**, n. 11, 15.
Tyndall, In re—§ **2-13**, n. 17.
Tyree, Matter of—§ **8-10**, n. 8.

U

Uhlmeyer, In re—§ **6-49**, n. 16, 28, 40.
Uiterwyk Corp., Matter of—§ **6-49**, n. 49, 52.
Ullman, Matter of—§ **6-31**, n. 15, 22; § **6-32**, n. 4.
U.L. Radio Corp., Matter of—§ **5-17**; § **5-17**, n. 5; § **5-20**, n. 9.
Underbakke, In re—§ **6-77**, n. 1, 23; § **6-78**, n. 18.
Underhill, In re—§ **7-20**; § **7-20**, n. 3, 5.
Underwood, In re, 103 B.R. 849—§ **8-24**, n. 3; § **8-25**, n. 4, 9, 23.

TABLE OF CASES

Underwood, In re, 7 B.R. 936—§ 2-13; § 2-13, n. 3.
Ungar, Matter of—§ 3-23, n. 37.
Unifirst Federal Sav. Bank v. American Ins. Co.—§ 3-14, n. 57.
Unimet Corp., Matter of—§ 6-31, n. 19.
Union Bank v. Wolas—§ 6-32; § 6-32, n. 6.
Union Cartage Co., In re—§ 6-41, n. 20, 21, 23, 24, 26, 46, 47, 51.
Union Cartage Co. v. Dollar Savings & Tr. Co.—§ 6-41, n. 25.
Union Scrap Iron & Metal, United States v.—§ 7-7; § 7-7, n. 13.
Unisys Corp. v. Dataware Products, Inc.—§ 3-14, n. 32, 33.
United Bank of Bismarck v. Selland—§ 8-31, n. 5.
United Church of the Ministers of God, In re—§ 12-5, n. 6.
United Companies Financial Corp. v. Brantley—§ 3-31, n. 68, 73.
United Energy Corp., In re—§ 6-49, n. 32.
United Kitchen Associates, Inc., In re—§ 2-5, n. 3.
United Missouri Bank of Kansas City, N.A., In re—§ 3-30, n. 29; § 12-16; § 12-16, n. 3, 6.
United Press Intern., Inc., In re, 60 B.R. 265—§ 11-13, n. 3; § 11-14; § 11-14, n. 8; § 11-15, n. 14; § 11-18, n. 1.
United Press Intern., Inc., In re, 55 B.R. 63—§ 5-13, n. 3.
United Sav. Ass'n of Texas v. Timbers of Inwood Forest Associates, Ltd.—§ 3-25; § 3-25, n. 33, 56; § 3-27; § 3-27, n. 7, 12; § 6-76, n. 1; § 9-23; § 9-23, n. 3; § 10-24, n. 1; § 10-25, n. 1.
United Sciences of America, Inc., In re—§ 6-43, n. 4.
United Sciences of America, Inc., Matter of—§ 6-39, n. 2; § 6-40, n. 6, 16; § 6-41, n. 10, 19, 26.
United States v. ___ (see opposing party)
United States Dept. of Energy v. West Texas Marketing Corp.—§ 7-15, n. 3.
United States Dept. of Health and Human Services v. Smith—§ 7-33; § 7-33, n. 4.
United States, Small Business Admin. v. Bridges—§ 7-27; § 7-27, n. 9.
U.S. Sprint Communications Co. v. Buscher—§ 3-20, n. 11.
United States Trust Co of New York v. Wabash W R Co—§ 5-5, n. 2.
United Virginia Bank v. Slab Fork Coal Co.—§ 6-77, n. 1; § 6-78, n. 5, 18.
United West, Inc., In re—§ 6-94, n. 5.
Unit Parts Co., In re—§ 11-5, n. 4.
Universal Clearing House Co., In re, 62 B.R. 118—§ 6-47, n. 7, 8; § 6-88, n. 18, 21, 23, 37, 45, 46, 47, 49.
Universal Clearing House Co., In re, 60 B.R. 985—§ 6-47, n. 8; § 6-49, n. 43; § 6-50, n. 14.
Universal Farming Industries, In re—§ 6-93, n. 16, 49.
Universal Life Church, United States v.—§ 3-8, n. 11; § 3-14, n. 80.
Universal Life Church, Inc., In re—§ 3-26, n. 2; § 3-30, n. 20.
Universal Profile, Inc., In re—§ 4-14, n. 5.
University Medical Center v. Sullivan, 125 B.R. 121—§ 3-33, n. 22; § 6-45, n. 16.
University Medical Center v. Sullivan, 122 B.R. 919—§ 3-15, n. 6; § 3-35, n. 2; § 5-25; § 5-25, n. 1, 4, 7; § 6-45, n. 22.
Unkefer, In re—§ 8-21, n. 10.
UNR Industries, Inc., In re, 72 B.R. 789—§ 11-13, n. 3; § 11-15, n. 17; § 11-18, n. 1.
UNR Industries, Inc., In re, 46 B.R. 671—§ 11-8, n. 10.
UNR Industries, Inc., In re, 46 B.R. 25—§ 6-93, n. 3, 32.
UNR Industries, Inc., In re, 30 B.R. 609—§ 10-13; § 10-13, n. 8.
UNR Industries, Inc., In re, 29 B.R. 741—§ 11-8; § 11-8, n. 9.
UNR Industries, Inc., In re, 23 B.R. 144—§ 3-31, n. 84.
UNR Industries, Inc., Matter of—§ 11-1, n. 6; § 11-8, n. 7, 11.
Upham, In re—§ 6-54, n. 10; § 6-55, n. 13; § 6-56, n. 8.
Upland/Euclid, Ltd., In re—§ 5-7, n. 4.
Urbanco, Inc., In re—§ 3-14; 3-14, n. 74, 78; § 3-23, n. 45; § 5-10, n. 15.
U.S. Aviex Co., Inc., In re—§ 12-11, n. 4, 7.
U.S. Bedding Co., Inc., In re—§ 6-41, n. 24, 27.
U.S. Elec., Inc., In re—§ 3-8, n. 10; § 3-14, n. 38; § 3-18, n. 17; § 6-62, n. 26.
Usery v. First Nat. Bank of Arizona—§ 8-11, n. 28.
U.S. Fax, Inc., In re—§ 5-10, n. 15.
U.S. Lines, Inc., In re—§ 6-20, n. 20.
U.S. Marketing Concepts, Inc., Matter of—§ 6-61, n. 11.
U.S.N. Co., Inc., In re—§ 6-39, n. 6.
U.S. Repeating Arms Co., In re—§ 10-33, n. 2.
U.S. Truck Co., Inc., In re—§ 10-21, n. 9; § 10-22; § 10-22, n. 6; § 11-27, n. 11; § 11-29, n. 1; § 11-30, n. 2.
Utica Floor Maintenance, Inc., In re, 41 B.R. 941—§ 6-39, n. 28; § 6-42, n. 2; § 6-43, n. 13.
Utica Floor Maintenance, Inc., In re, 31 B.R. 509—§ 3-9, n. 22.
Utica Floor Maintenance, Inc., In re, 25 B.R. 1010—§ 3-9, n. 22, 23.
UVAS Farming Corp., In re—§ 6-17, n. 10, 11, 13, 15.

V

Vadnais Lumber Supply, Inc., In re—§ 6-7, n. 5; § 6-18, n. 3; § 6-49, n. 8, 49; § 6-52, n. 7, 13, 49.
Vahlsing v. Commercial Union Ins. Co., Inc.—§ 3-33, n. 2.
Valairco, Inc., Matter of—§ 6-62, n. 26.
Val Decker Packing Co., Matter of—§ 6-35, n. 40.
Valdes, In re—§ 8-26, n. 5; § 8-28, n. 3.
Vale, In re—§ 8-25, n. 43.
Valentine, In re—§ 3-15, n. 6.
Valley Forge Plaza Associates v. Fireman's Fund Ins. Companies—§ 12-2, n. 20.
Valley Forge Plaza Associates v. Schwartz—§ 3-14, n. 40.
Valley Nat. Bank of Arizona, In re—§ 11-17, n. 3.
Valley Transit Mix of Ruidoso, Inc. v. Miller—§ 3-8, n. 2; § 3-10, n. 21.
Vanas, In re—§ 6-78, n. 15.
Vanasdale, Matter of—§ 6-77, n. 1; § 6-78, n. 14.
Vanasen, In re—§ 3-23, n. 35; § 9-20, n. 17.
Vance, In re—§ 9-14, n. 21.
Vance, Matter of—§ 6-24, n. 2.
Van De Kamp's Dutch Bakeries, In re—§ 6-86, n. 2.
Van Gordon, In re—§ 9-17, n. 8.
Vanguard Diversified, Inc., In re—§ 4-15; § 4-15, n. 12.
Vanguard Oil & Service Co., Inc., In re—§ 4-4, n. 8; § 4-17, n. 11.
Van Holt, In re—§ 7-49; § 7-49, n. 5, 6, 7, 9.
Van Horne, Matter of—§ 7-26; § 7-26, n. 58, 67.
Van Hove, In re—§ 8-3, n. 18.
Van Huffel Tube Corp., Matter of—§ 6-7, n. 6, 7, 12; § 6-20, n. 2, 17; § 6-25, n. 13; § 6-31, n. 15, 19; § 6-32, n. 3, 4.
Vaniman Intern., Inc., In re—§ 6-17, n. 6; § 6-48, n. 7, 8, 19; § 6-49, n. 18; § 6-52, n. 7, 9, 34, 35, 43, 47; § 6-60, n. 29.
Van Kylen, Matter of—§ 6-4, n. 4; § 6-61, n. 16.
Van Meter v. American State Bank—§ 7-36, n. 3.
Van Meter's Estate, In re—§ 8-7, n. 5.
Vann, In re, 113 B.R. 704—§ 8-1, n. 11; § 8-33, n. 24.
Vann, In re, 26 B.R. 148—§ 6-87, n. 6.
Van Ness Auto Plaza, Inc., In re—§ 5-16, n. 2.
Van Pelt, Matter of—§ 8-26; § 8-26, n. 3; § 8-29, n. 7.
Vanston Bondholders Protective Committee v. Green—§ 11-1, n. 7; § 11-3, n. 11.
Vantage Petroleum Corp., In re, 34 B.R. 650—§ 11-16, n. 6.
Vantage Petroleum Corp., In re, 25 B.R. 471—§ 3-21, n. 126, 128.
Vassilowitch, In re—§ 4-9, n. 11, 12.
Vasu Fabrics, Inc., In re—§ 6-19, n. 18.
Vaughan v. Central Bank of the South—§ 9-3; § 9-3, n. 12, 21, 22.
Vaughter, In re—§ 6-45, n. 6, 7, 22.
Vecco Const. Industries, Inc., In re—§ 2-4; § 2-4, n. 3; § 11-41, n. 12, 16.
Vedaa, In re—§ 6-87, n. 6, 8.
Velis, Matter of—§ 8-17, n. 17, 47, 49.
Velis v. Kardanis—§ 8-33, n. 17.
Venegas Munoz, Matter of—§ 3-10, n. 47, 51.
Venice Western Motel, Ltd., Matter of—§ 6-47, n. 7.
Vensel, In re—§ 9-12, n. 3; § 9-14, n. 21.
Venture Properties, Inc., In re—§ 11-35, n. 6.
Verco Industries, In re, 704 F.2d 1134—§ 6-39, n. 26; § 6-40, n. 27.
Verco Industries, In re, 10 B.R. 347—§ 6-60, n. 10.
Vermont Fiberglass, Inc., In re—§ 6-86, n. 4.
Vermont Real Estate Inv. Trust, In re, 25 B.R. 809—§ 3-28, n. 11.
Vermont Real Estate Inv. Trust, In re, 20 B.R. 33—§ 10-12, n. 12.
Vermont Toy Works, Inc., In re—§ 6-17, n. 6; § 6-61, n. 8.
Vern v. Roberts Supply, Inc.—§ 6-20, n. 20; § 6-61, n. 70.
Verna, In re—§ 6-54, n. 10; § 6-55, n. 9, 13; § 6-56, n. 8, 12.
Vescovo, In re—§ 6-49, n. 35; § 6-62, n. 13.
Veteran Plate Glass Co., Inc., Matter of—§ 6-62, n. 15.
Vetter, United States v.—§ 7-31, n. 14.
Via, In re—§ 6-37, n. 6, 7; § 8-22; § 8-22, n. 15, 27; § 8-23, n. 5.
Vibroflotation Foundation Co., In re—§ 6-40, n. 25.
Vickery, In re—§ 6-37; § 6-37, n. 5, 9; § 6-69, n. 3.
Victoria Grain Co. of Minneapolis, In re—§ 6-61, n. 60.

Victoria Station, Inc., In re—§ 5-10, n. 6.
Victory Const. Co., Inc., In re, 42 B.R. 145—§ 10-23, n. 5.
Victory Const. Co., Inc., In re, 9 B.R. 549—§ 3-26, n. 4
Victory Const. Co., Inc., In re—§ 3-26, n. 4; § 10-23, n. 5.
Vidana, In re—§ 6-57, n. 3.
Video King of Illinois, Inc., In re—§ 6-65, n. 1; § 6-67; § 6-67, n. 2, 4, 9, 10; § 6-86, n. 10.
Vienna Park Properties, In re—§ 6-61, n. 59; § 6-77, n. 20.
Vietri Homes, Inc., Matter of—§ 6-93, n. 47.
Vieweg, In re—§ 2-13, n. 14.
Village Properties, Ltd., Matter of—§ 6-77, n. 7, 11, 15, 19; § 6-78, n. 8.
Villarie, In re—§ 11-2, n. 6.
Villa Roel, Inc., In re, 57 B.R. 879—§ 6-49, n. 46; § 6-88, n. 18.
Villa Roel, Inc., In re, 57 B.R. 835—§ 6-60, n. 10.
Vilt, In re—§ 9-4, n. 25.
Vink v. SHV North America Holding Corp.—§ 8-33, n. 15.
Vinzant, In re—§ 6-12, n. 12; § 6-25, n. 15; § 6-49, n. 34, 64, 69.
Virginia Beach Federal Sav. and Loan Ass'n v. Wood—§ 6-77, n. 19.
Virginia Block Co., In re, 16 B.R. 771—§ 6-40, n. 25.
Virginia Block Co., In re, 16 B.R. 560—§ 6-40, n. 17, 22.
Virginia Block Co., In re, 8 B.R. 616—§ 6-40, n. 22.
Virginia Information Systems Corp., In re—§ 6-16, n. 1.
Virginia Packaging Supply Co., Inc., In re—§ 5-23, n. 3.
Virtual Network Services Corp., In re, 98 B.R. 343—§ 6-93, n. 66.
Virtual Network Services Corp., In re, 92 B.R. 784—§ 6-20, n. 6, 17.
Virtual Network Services Corp., Matter of—§ 6-93, n. 15.
Visiting Nurse Ass'n of Tampa Bay, Inc., Matter of—§ 3-15, n. 6; § 6-45, n. 5.
Vista VI, Inc., In re—§ 5-20, n. 9.
Vitreous Steel Products Co., Matter of—§ 6-2, n. 24; § 6-20, n. 22; § 6-93, n. 11.
Vitullo, In re—§ 8-27, n. 9.
Vlavianos, In re—§ 9-20, n. 6.
V.N. Deprizio Const. Co., In re, 86 B.R. 545—§ 6-9, n. 5.
V.N. DePrizio Const. Co., In re, 52 B.R. 283—§ 6-40, n. 16, 25.
Vogel, In re—§ 8-33, n. 20.
Vogel v. Russell Transfer, Inc.—§ 2-17, n. 19; § 6-4, n. 16; § 6-11, n. 6; § 6-70, n. 2, 3.
Voight, In re—§ 3-35, n. 1; § 6-38, n. 18; § 6-41, n. 27, 32; § 6-43, n. 4, 14, 15.
Vorek, In re—§ 7-34, n. 15.
Vreugdenhil v. Hoekstra—§ 6-2, n. 3, 21.
V. Savino Oil & Heating Co., Inc., In re—§ 6-2, n. 3, 5, 9, 24, 28, 29, 30.
VTN, Inc., In re—§ 10-12, n. 3.
Vunovich, In re—§ 6-25; § 6-25, n. 9; § 6-31, n. 22; § 6-34, n. 20.
Vurchio, In re—§ 6-18, n. 10, 21.
Vylene Enterprises, Inc., In re—§ 3-6, n. 36.

W

Wabash Valley Power Ass'n, Inc., In re—§ 6-77, n. 1.
Waddle, In re—§ 7-21, n. 11.
Wade, In re—§ 3-21, n. 113.
Wade v. Rathbun—§ 8-8, n. 4.
Wadsworth Bldg. Components, Inc., In re—§ 6-26; § 6-26, n. 2, 3; § 6-28, n. 2.
Wagner, In re, 87 B.R. 612—§ 3-23, n. 32; § 7-41, n. 2.
Wagner, In re, 74 B.R. 898—§ 3-33, n. 14.
Waites v. Braley—§ 7-45, n. 17.
Waites Co., Inc., In re—§ 6-59, n. 3.
Waits, In re—§ 12-10, n. 2.
Walat Farms, Inc., In re—§ 6-39, n. 15.
Waldman, In re, 81 B.R. 313—§ 8-3, n. 21; § 8-28, n. 7, 23, 24, 25.
Waldman, In re, 75 B.R. 1005—§ 9-4, n. 43.
Waldo, In re—§ 6-62, n. 23, 39.
Waldron, In re—§ 3-29, n. 9.
Waldron v. Farmers Home Admin.—§ 6-39, n. 15.
Waldschmidt v. CBS, Inc.—§ 6-45, n. 7, 10.
Waldvogel, In re—§ 6-2, n. 9; § 6-61, n. 76.
Walker, In re, 861 F.2d 597—§ 6-72, n. 8, 9, 10, 12, 13.
Walker, In re, 84 B.R. 888—§ 9-20; § 9-20, n. 9.
Walkers Mill Inn, Inc., In re—§ 3-25, n. 6.

Walkington, In re—§ 8-25, n. 54.
Wallace, In re, 102 B.R. 54—§ 7-36, n. 4; § 7-37, n. 2, 3.
Wallace, In re, 66 B.R. 834—§ 6-47, n. 7; § 6-49, n. 36, 44; § 6-56, n. 14.
Waller, Matter of—§ 6-40, n. 19; § 6-42, n. 2, 3.
Wallman, In re—§ 6-76, n. 2; § 6-77, n. 21.
Walls, In re, 125 B.R. 908—§ 8-27, n. 11.
Walls, In re, 45 B.R. 145—§ 8-10, n. 9.
Walls, In re, 17 B.R. 701—§ 6-2, n. 14, 16.
Wall Tube and Metal Products Co., In re—§ 11-10; § 11-10, n. 6.
Wally Findlay Galleries (New York), Inc., In re—§ 3-29, n. 12.
Walsey, In re—§ 9-2, n. 4.
Walter, In re, 108 B.R. 244—§ 3-29, n. 5.
Walter, In re, 47 B.R. 240—§ 12-10, n. 8.
Walters, In re, 868 F.2d 665—§ 12-1, n. 4.
Walters, In re, 61 B.R. 426—§ 6-15, n. 3, 8.
Walters, In re, 14 B.R. 92—§ 8-19, n. 7, 8, 17.
Walters, In re, 11 B.R. 567—§ 9-3, n. 17.
Walters, Matter of—§ 8-1, n. 17; § 8-24, n. 5.
Walters v. First Tennessee Bank, N.A. Memphis—§ 3-6, n. 13.
Walter's Disposal Service, Inc., Matter of—§ 8-22, n. 23.
Walton, In re—§ 2-14, n. 4, 5; § 7-45, n. 4, 8, 13, 17.
Wanderlich, In re—§ 2-17, n. 5.
Wandler, In re, 77 B.R. 735—§ 8-25, n. 32.
Wandler, In re, 77 B.R. 728—§ 10-28, n. 4.
Waner Corp., In re—§ 6-15, n. 5, 8.
Ward, In re, 857 F.2d 1082—§ 7-26, n. 21, 25, 29, 45.
Ward, In re, 837 F.2d 124—§ 3-25, n. 14; § 3-32, n. 1, 2; § 6-72, n. 5, 12, 13.
Ward, In re, 73 B.R. 119—§ 9-17, n. 7.
Ward, In re, 42 B.R. 946—§ 6-82, n. 1; § 6-86, n. 2, 4, 18.
Ward, In re, 36 B.R. 794—§ 6-6, n. 9; § 6-48, n. 15; § 6-49, n. 35; § 8-23, n. 6.
Ward v. Ward—§ 8-33, n. 15.
Ware, In re—§ 7-41, n. 18.
Ware, Matter of—§ 6-2, n. 20.
War Eagle Floats, Inc., In re—§ 6-49, n. 22, 27, 28.
Warner, In re—§ 2-13, n. 1.
Warner, Matter of—§ 6-48, n. 4; § 6-49, n. 15.
Warren, In re, 93 B.R. 710—§ 6-40, n. 16, 21.
Warren, In re, 91 B.R. 930—§ 8-25, n. 16.
Warren, In re, 89 B.R. 87—§ 9-13, n. 12; § 9-14; § 9-14, n. 7, 8, 22.
Wartels' Estate, In re—§ 8-7, n. 20.
Washburn & Roberts, Inc., In re—§ 6-61, n. 11, 21.
Washington, In re—§ 6-82, n. 4.
Washington Mfg. Co., In re—§ 3-6, n. 36.
Washington-St. Tammany Elec. Co-op., Inc., In re—§ 11-13, n. 3; § 11-14, n. 13; § 11-15, n. 17.
Washkowiak, Matter of—§ 6-20, n. 20; § 8-22, n. 35; § 8-23; § 8-23, n. 5, 10.
Washofsky, In re—§ 8-3, n. 21.
Wasserman, In re—§ 3-25, n. 37, 57; § 3-27, n. 23.
Waterfront Companies, Inc., In re v. Johnston—§ 4-3; § 4-3, n. 7; § 4-12, n. 2; § 10-6, n. 4.
Waterkist Corp., In re—§ 5-3, n. 4.
Waters, In re, 90 B.R. 946—§ 6-61, n. 29; § 6-77, n. 1, 6.
Waters, In re, 8 B.R. 163—§ 6-60, n. 20.
Waterside Const. Co., Inc., In re—§ 6-60, n. 4.
Waterville Timeshare Group, In re—§ 11-17, n. 3.
Waterways Barge Partnership, In re—§ 10-24, n. 6; § 10-28, n. 1.
Wathen's Elevators, Inc., In re, 37 B.R. 870—§ 6-19, n. 14, 17, 19.
Wathen's Elevators, Inc., In re, 32 B.R. 912—§ 6-66, n. 5; § 6-67, n. 10.
Watkins, Matter of—§ 8-33, n. 18, 20, 23.
Watkins v. Watkins—§ 6-61, n. 74.
Watkins Oil Service, Inc., In re—§ 11-4, n. 31.
Watson, In re, 116 B.R. 837—§ 8-28, n. 3.
Watson, In re, 78 B.R. 267—§ 6-40, n. 4.
Watson, In re, 78 B.R. 232—§ 3-6, n. 36; § 3-12, n. 2.
Watson, In re, 65 B.R. 9—§ 2-8, n. 18.
Watts, In re—§ 3-34, n. 6.
Watts v. Pennsylvania Housing Finance Co.—§ 3-14, n. 43; § 3-128BR1, n. 80.
Waugh, In re—§ 2-17, n. 6.
Weatherspoon, In re—§ 6-62, n. 16; § 8-25, n. 5, 6; § 8-27, n. 9.
Weaver, In re, 78 B.R. 135—§ 6-2, n. 21; § 8-22, n. 23, 32; § 8-23, n. 6; § 8-25, n. 44.

TABLE OF CASES

Weaver, In re, 69 B.R. 554—§ **6-2, n. 20.**
Weaver, In re, 8 B.R. 803—§ **3-10, n. 56, 70, 82.**
Weaver, Matter of—§ **8-17, n. 17, 49.**
Webb, In re, 121 B.R. 827—§ **8-3, n. 21.**
Webb, In re, 106 B.R. 517—§ **6-61, n. 16, 55.**
Webb, In re, 38 B.R. 541—§ **3-9, n. 6.**
Webb, In re, 29 B.R. 280—§ **8-21, n. 4, 11.**
Weber, Matter of—§ **7-28;** § **7-28, n. 16.**
Websco, Inc., In re—§ **6-22, n. 5;** § **6-31, n. 15, 19.**
Wedgewood Realty Group, Ltd., In re—§ **3-22, n. 4;** § **3-31;** § **3-31, n. 21, 33, 35, 40, 43.**
Wedgeworth v. Fibreboard Corp.—§ **3-5, n. 7;** § **3-22, n. 35.**
Wedtech Corp., In re, 121 B.R. 286—§ **6-60, n. 10, 20.**
Wedtech Corp., In re, 88 B.R. 619—§ **6-2, n. 9.**
Weeks, In re, 106 B.R. 257—§ **8-33, n. 17, 24.**
Weeks, In re, 28 B.R. 958—§ **6-93, n. 10, 11.**
Wegner, In re—§ **7-45, n. 8.**
Wegner v. Grunewaldt—§ **6-93, n. 45.**
Weidenhammer, In re—§ **3-12;** § **3-12, n. 14.**
Weis, Matter of—§ **6-6;** § **6-6, n. 3, 4, 8, 10;** § **6-57;** § **6-57, n. 2;** § **8-22, n. 21.**
Weiss, In re, 51 B.R. 224—§ **8-26, n. 19;** § **8-28, n. 4.**
Weiss, In re, 4 B.R. 327—§ **8-10, n. 21.**
Weiss-Wolf, Inc., In re—§ **11-17, n. 2, 8.**
Welco Industries, Inc., In re—§ **9-10, n. 12.**
Wellen, In re—§ **7-26, n. 21.**
Wellham, In re—§ **3-21, n. 50, 56, 59, 69.**
Wellington Const. Corp., Matter of—§ **6-18, n. 26;** § **6-22, n. 5;** § **6-25;** § **6-25, n. 39;** § **6-34, n. 10.**
Wellman v. Wellman—§ **6-87, n. 4.**
Weltman v. Independence Sav. Bank—§ **7-43, n. 6.**
Wenande, In re—§ **8-10, n. 26.**
Wenberg, In re—§ **2-2, n. 7.**
Wengert Transp., Inc., In re—§ **3-6, n. 49;** § **3-21, n. 13.**
Werner, In re, 79 B.R. 819—§ **8-3, n. 21;** § **8-13, n. 12;** § **8-25, n. 38, 63.**
Werner, In re, 31 B.R. 418—§ **8-17, n. 49, 50.**
Wernly, In re—§ **8-23, n. 6.**
Wesco Products Co., In re—§ **6-2, n. 9, 30.**
Wessels, In re—§ **7-21, n. 1, 9.**
West, In re, 101 B.R. 648—§ **7-39, n. 15.**
West, In re, 81 B.R. 22—§ **8-33, n. 20.**
West v. Costen—§ **9-22, n. 9.**
West, United States v.—§ **6-49, n. 18.**
Westchase I Associates, L.P., In re, 126 B.R. 692—§ **3-27;** § **3-27, n. 16, 18.**
Westchase I Associates, L.P., In re, 119 B.R. 521—§ **3-18, n. 21.**
Westchester Ave. Marina Realty, Inc., In re—§ **3-25, n. 2, 10;** § **3-27, n. 43.**
West Electronics Inc., Matter of—§ **3-14, n. 43;** § **3-26, n. 5;** § **3-31, n. 96;** § **5-15;** § **5-15, n. 3;** § **11-38, n. 5.**
Western Auto Supply Co. v. Bank of Imboden—§ **6-92, n. 3, 6.**
Western Pork Packers, Inc., Matter of—§ **11-16, n. 6.**
Western Real Estate Fund, Inc., In re, 922 F.2d 592—§ **3-10, n. 11;** § **3-22, n. 4, 5, 7, 20, 21, 24.**
Western Real Estate Fund, Inc., In re, 109 B.R. 455—§ **10-20, n. 14;** § **10-26, n. 1.**
Western Real Estate Fund, Inc., In re, 83 B.R. 52—§ **6-78, n. 2.**
Western Sur. Co. v. First Bank of South Dakota, N.A.—§ **6-38, n. 6.**
Western World Funding, Inc., In re, 54 B.R. 470—§ **6-19, n. 14, 16, 17, 18.**
Western World Funding, Inc., In re, 52 B.R. 743—§ **6-93, n. 16, 17, 32.**
Western World Funding, Inc., In re—§ **6-19, n. 14, 16, 17, 18;** § **6-93, n. 16, 17, 32.**
Westgate General Partnership, In re—§ **11-14;** § **11-14, n. 2;** § **11-18, n. 1.**
Westhem, In re—§ **8-6, n. 8, 9.**
Westinghouse Elec. Corp. v. Fidelity and Deposit Co. of Maryland—§ **6-39, n. 39;** § **6-40, n. 4;** § **6-45, n. 3, 6, 11, 17.**
Westlund v. State, Dept. of Licensing—§ **3-6, n. 40;** § **3-21, n. 9, 46, 109.**
Weston, In re—§ **3-23, n. 27.**
Westover Hills Ltd., In re—§ **2-2, n. 20.**
Westport-Sandpiper Associates Ltd. Partnership, In re—§ **3-18, n. 21;** § **6-77, n. 20.**
Westside Bank, United States v.—§ **6-67, n. 3.**
Westview 74th Street Drug Corp., In re—§ **5-20, n. 8;** § **5-23;** § **5-23, n. 6.**
Westwood Broadcasting, Inc., In re—§ **3-30, n. 35.**
W.E. Tucker Oil Co., Inc., In re, 55 B.R. 78—§ **6-47, n. 13;** § **6-49, n. 8, 39, 46.**
W.E. Tucker Oil, Inc., In re, 42 B.R. 897—§ **6-47, n. 7;** § **6-49, n. 46.**
Wey, In re—§ **6-19, n. 13, 14, 17.**

Wey, Matter of, 854 F.2d 196—§ 6-4; § 6-4, n. 10.
Wey, Matter of, 827 F.2d 140—§ 6-94, n. 7.
Wheeler, In re, 101 B.R. 39—§ 7-45, n. 17.
Wheeler, In re, 34 B.R. 818—§ 6-21, n. 4; § 6-53, n. 6; § 6-54, n. 10; § 6-55, n. 13; § 6-56, n. 51; § 8-23, n. 3.
Wheeling–Pittsburgh Steel Corp., In re, 108 B.R. 82—§ 12-15, n. 1.
Wheeling–Pittsburgh Steel Corp., In re, 74 B.R. 656—§ 6-65, n. 10; § 6-67, n. 3.
Wheeling–Pittsburgh Steel Corp., United States v.—§ 3-21, n. 7, 98.
WHET, Inc., In re—§ 4-4; § 4-4, n. 15, 16, 17.
Whilden, Matter of—§ 12-9, n. 2.
Whisenton, In re—§ 6-69, n. 3; § 8-22, n. 20, 35; § 8-23, n. 6.
Whispering Bay Campground, Inc., In re—§ 3-16, n. 11.
Whitaker, In re, 85 B.R. 788—§ 3-23, n. 46.
Whitaker, In re, 18 B.R. 314—§ 6-77, n. 1; § 6-78, n. 3.
Whitcomb & Keller Mortg. Co., Inc., Matter of—§ 5-22, n. 5.
White, In re, 851 F.2d 170—§ 3-6, n. 10; § 3-30, n. 10, 16, 17, 18.
White, In re, 727 F.2d 884—§ 12-12, n. 12.
White, In re, 61 B.R. 388—§ 8-17, n. 32.
White, In re, 64 B.R. 843—§ 6-36, n. 14.
White, In re, 49 B.R. 869—§ 7-45, n. 13.
White, In re, 47 B.R. 410—§ 8-33, n. 17.
White, In re, 47 B.R. 98—§ 6-50, n. 28; § 6-55, n. 13; § 6-56, n. 8.
White, In re, 28 B.R. 240—§ 6-58, n. 1; § 8-32, n. 8.
White v. Boston—§ 6-83, n. 17.
White v. Indiana Realty Associates, II—§ 3-14, n. 66.
White Beauty View, Inc., In re, 841 F.2d 524—§ 12-12, n. 17.
White Beauty View, Inc., In re, 81 B.R. 290—§ 6-61, n. 29.
White Beauty View, Inc., In re, 70 B.R. 90—§ 6-74, n. 14.
White Farm Equipment Co., In re—§ 10-2, n. 5.
Whitemont Associates Ltd. Partnership, Matter of—§ 3-25, n. 52.
White Motor Credit Corp., In re, 75 B.R. 944—§ 4-10; § 4-10, n. 2; § 11-3, n. 12; § 11-4, n. 7.
White Motor Credit Corp., In re, 37 B.R. 631—§ 10-2, n. 5.
White Motor Credit Corp., In re, 14 B.R. 584—§ 4-4; § 4-4, n. 14, 26.
White River Corp., In re—§ 6-25; § 6-25, n. 8, 13, 45.
Whitford, In re—§ 8-25, n. 8.
Whiting Pools, Inc., United States v.—§ 2-8, n. 2; § 3-14, n. 12.
Whitlow, In re—§ 6-61, n. 77.
Whitman, In re, 106 B.R. 654—§ 8-3, n. 21.
Whitman, In re, 38 B.R. 395—§ 6-39, n. 5, 38; § 6-40, n. 5; § 6-43, n. 3, 5; § 6-44, n. 16.
Whitney, In re—§ 8-9, n. 1; § 8-32, n. 6, 28.
Whitson v. Middleton—§ 7-34; § 7-34, n. 4, 14, 16.
Whittaker v. Philadelphia Elec. Co.—§ 3-9, n. 11; § 3-35, n. 7.
Whizco, Inc., United States v.—§ 7-8; § 7-8, n. 3.
Wicaco Mach. Co., Inc., In re—§ 4-3, n. 8.
Wickliffe, In re—§ 9-27, n. 15.
Wickstrom, Matter of—§ 6-6, n. 3; § 6-57, n. 1; § 8-2, n. 7; § 8-3, n. 21; § 8-22, n. 20, 21.
Wider v. Wootton—§ 6-85, n. 1, 7, 21.
Wieboldt Stores, Inc., In re—§ 4-17, n. 11.
Wieboldt Stores, Inc. v. Schottenstein—§ 6-52; § 6-52, n. 7, 9, 10, 12, 30, 36, 46.
Wiegand v. Wiegand—§ 8-7, n. 3.
Wiegmann, In re—§ 6-77, n. 1, 23; § 6-78, n. 5, 18.
Wiesel v. Ashcraft—§ 6-56, n. 1.
Wieseler, In re—§ 3-26, n. 12; § 3-27, n. 42, 43.
Wiford, In re—§ 8-3, n. 19, 21; § 8-26, n. 1.
Wiggins, In re—§ 8-17, n. 33.
Wiggles, Matter of—§ 9-3, n. 8.
Wiggs, In re—§ 6-2, n. 9; § 6-61, n. 78.
Wilcher, Matter of—§ 11-16, n. 6.
Wild, In re—§ 6-61, n. 27.
Wildcat Const. Co., Inc., In re—§ 3-31, n. 84, 85; § 6-43, n. 29.
Wilde, In re—§ 6-40, n. 2; § 6-42, n. 2, 3, 4; § 6-43, n. 29.
Wilder, In re—§ 6-61, n. 67.
Wilhelm, In re, 101 B.R. 120—§ 10-23, n. 3.
Wilhelm, In re, 6 B.R. 905—§ 9-3, n. 6.
Wilkes, In re—§ 7-45, n. 1, 13.
Wilkins, In re—§ 9-10, n. 8.
Wilkinson v. Carpenter—§ 8-7, n. 2.
Wilkins' Will, In re—§ 6-38, n. 13.

Wilks, In re—§ 3-25, n. 31; § 3-32, n. 11; § 7-47, n. 2.
Willardo, In re—§ 6-43, n. 13.
Willemain v. Kivitz—§ 4-17; § 4-17, n. 10.
William A. Smith Const. Co., Inc., In re—§ 10-8, n. 3.
William F. Gable Co., In re—§ 11-17, n. 5, 8.
William F. Wilke, Inc., United States v.—§ 3-5, n. 6; § 3-22, n. 5, 31.
William J. Brittingham, Inc., Matter of—§ 6-39, n. 13.
Williams, In re, 124 B.R. 864—§ 8-1, n. 12.
Williams, In re, 124 B.R. 311—§ 3-32; § 3-32, n. 1, 10, 14, 23, 27, 39; § 3-33, n. 5; § 6-61, n. 71.
Williams, In re, 109 B.R. 179—§ 8-1, n. 20; § 8-23, n. 7.
Williams, In re, 109 B.R. 36—§ 9-18, n. 6, 10.
Williams, In re, 106 B.R. 87—§ 7-26, n. 50.
Williams, In re, 104 B.R. 296—§ 6-69, n. 10; § 6-88, n. 18, 35, 36.
Williams, In re, 100 B.R. 726—§ 6-72, n. 4.
Williams, In re, 61 B.R. 567—§ 3-15, n. 5; § 6-38, n. 21, 22; § 6-39, n. 2; § 6-40, n. 2; § 6-43, n. 18, 29; § 6-74, n. 11.
Williams, In re, 51 B.R. 249—§ 9-3, n. 12, 17.
Williams, In re, 42 B.R. 474—§ 9-14, n. 13.
Williams, In re, 9 B.R. 83—§ 7-48, n. 5.
Williams, Matter of, 72 B.R. 508—§ 3-12, n. 15.
Williams, Matter of, 15 B.R. 655—§ 7-43, n. 2.
Williams v. California 1st Bank—§ 6-61, n. 8.
Williams v. First Nat. Bank & Trust Co. of Vinita—§ 6-92, n. 3, 6.
Williams v. Heller Financial, Inc.—§ 12-5, n. 2.
Williams v. Motley—§ 7-31, n. 4.
Williams v. Radivoj—§ 7-34, n. 12.
Williamson, Matter of, 844 F.2d 1166—§ 6-93, n. 62; § 8-2, n. 2.
Williamson, Matter of, 804 F.2d 1355—§ 2-17, n. 16; § 8-3, n. 22.
Williamson v. Fireman's Fund Ins. Co.—§ 7-21, n. 6, 8.
Williford v. Armstrong World Industries, Inc.—§ 3-3, n. 1; § 3-5, n. 19; § 3-6, n. 20; § 3-22, n. 35.
Willington Convalescent Home, Inc., In re—§ 3-34, n. 3.
Willis, In re, 48 B.R. 295—§ 6-53, n. 6; § 6-54, n. 10; § 6-55, n. 13; § 6-56, n. 5, 51, 52; § 8-23, n. 5, 16.
Willis, In re, 2 B.R. 643—§ 3-10, n. 44, 57.
Willoughby v. Jamison—§ 7-21, n. 11.
Will Rogers Jockey & Polo Club, Inc., In re—§ 7-41; § 7-41, n. 5, 10.
Willson Dairy Co., Matter of—§ 6-48, n. 4; § 6-49, n. 31.
Wilner Wood Products Co., In re—§ 3-34, n. 5.
Wilner Wood Products Co. v. State of Me., Dept. of Environmental Protection—§ 3-21, n. 120, 125; § 3-22, n. 3, 7.
Wilson, In re, 106 B.R. 125—§ 6-60, n. 11.
Wilson, In re, 94 B.R. 886—§ 2-8, n. 39.
Wilson, In re, 91 B.R. 74—§ 9-18, n. 8.
Wilson, In re, 85 B.R. 722—§ 3-30, n. 10, 16, 17, 18, 19; § 4-9, n. 11.
Wilson, In re, 77 B.R. 532—§ 6-2, n. 24.
Wilson, In re, 69 B.R. 960—§ 6-38, n. 18; § 6-49, n. 34.
Wilson, In re, 62 B.R. 43—§ 8-3, n. 21.
Wilson, In re, 56 B.R. 74—§ 6-69, n. 7.
Wilson, In re, 54 B.R. 796—§ 8-17, n. 33, 49.
Wilson, In re, 52 B.R. 637—§ 6-71, n. 7; § 6-72, n. 4, 15.
Wilson, In re, 49 B.R. 19—§ 6-44, n. 1.
Wilson, In re, 29 B.R. 54—§ 6-39, n. 19.
Wilson, Matter of, 694 F.2d 236—§ 8-1, n. 11; § 8-3, n. 30; § 8-19, n. 15; § 8-22, n. 5.
Wilson, Matter of, 11 B.R. 986—§ 9-17, n. 2.
Wilson v. Commonwealth Mortg. Corp.—§ 9-16, n. 5; § 9-18, n. 13.
Wilson Foods Corp., In re—§ 10-12; § 10-12, n. 14.
Wimbish, In re—§ 6-2, n. 3, 21; § 6-32, n. 2; § 8-22, n. 35; § 8-23, n. 6, 9, 15.
Windfelder, In re—§ 8-3, n. 21; § 8-28, n. 7; § 8-29, n. 2.
Windmill Farms, Inc., In re, 841 F.2d 1467—§ 5-4, n. 1.
Windmill Farms, Inc., In re, 70 B.R. 618—§ 12-12, n. 2.
Wind Power Systems, Inc., In re—§ 6-12; § 6-12, n. 23; § 6-61; § 6-61, n. 11, 43, 51, 53.
Windsor Communications Group, Inc., In re—§ 6-40, n. 16, 27; § 6-42, n. 2, 3, 4.
Windtech, Inc., Matter of—§ 12-10, n. 1, 3.
Wines, In re—§ 7-21, n. 3.
Wing, In re—§ 4-7, n. 18, 20.
Wingo, In re—§ 6-72, n. 2.
Wingspread Corp., In re, 120 B.R. 8—§ 6-34, n. 17.
Wingspread Corp., In re, 116 B.R. 915—§ 5-23, n. 3.

Winkle, In re—§ 6-7, n. 4; § 6-25, n. 3.
Winn, In re—§ 6-17, n. 8; § 6-19, n. 16; § 6-32, n. 5.
Winnett, In re, 102 B.R. 635—§ 6-24, n. 2; § 6-33, n. 9; § 6-61, n. 16.
Winnett, In re, 97 B.R. 7—§ 6-39, n. 7; § 6-42, n. 2.
Winshall Settlor's Trust, Matter of—§ 6-55, n. 3, 9; § 6-56, n. 8.
Winslow, Matter of—§ 3-31, n. 87, 88, 90, 92.
Winters, In re, 119 B.R. 283—§ 6-21, n. 4; § 6-53, n. 6; § 6-87, n. 8.
Winters, In re, 99 B.R. 658—§ 11-27; § 11-27, n. 3; § 11-29, n. 1.
Winters, In re, 69 B.R. 145—§ 7-39, n. 15.
Winzenburg, In re—§ 6-77, n. 8, 20; § 6-78, n. 6.
Wirick, In re—§ 7-43, n. 2.
Wissman, In re—§ 8-3, n. 21.
Wittenwyler, Matter of—§ 6-72, n. 17.
WJM, Inc., In re—§ 6-4, n. 14.
WJM, Inc. v. Massachusetts Dept. of Public Welfare—§ 6-2, n. 9; § 6-4, n. 2; § 6-18, n. 22; § 6-31, n. 3, 7; § 6-32, n. 3, 4; § 6-40, n. 16, 23, 38.
W. & L. Associates, Inc., In re—§ 5-8; § 5-8, n. 9.
W.L. Bradley Co., Inc., In re—§ 6-93, n. 62.
W.L. Jackson Mfg. Co., In re, 50 B.R. 506—§ 6-39, n. 19; § 6-40, n. 4.
W.L. Jackson Mfg. Co., In re, 50 B.R. 498—§ 6-40, n. 4.
Wlodarski, In re—§ 6-61, n. 53.
Wobig, Matter of—§ 6-77, n. 1.
Woker, In re—§ 6-31, n. 8; § 6-39, n. 36; § 6-40, n. 2.
Wolfe, In re, 68 B.R. 80—§ 12-13; § 12-13, n. 14.
Wolfe, In re, 12 B.R. 686—§ 7-43, n. 2.
Wolff, In re—§ 9-7, n. 4, 6.
Wolf & Vine, In re—§ 6-16, n. 1; § 6-31, n. 16.
Wolline, In re—§ 9-24; § 9-24, n. 11.
Woloschak Farms, In re—§ 3-34, n. 9.
Woloschak Farms, Matter of—§ 6-39, n. 15; § 6-43, n. 4, 15, 19, 32.
Wolverton Associates, In re—§ 6-69, n. 9.
Wommack, In re—§ 6-18, n. 6, 15, 22.
Wommack, Matter of—§ 8-17, n. 24, 25.
Wood, In re, 113 B.R. 253—§ 6-83, n. 16.
Wood, In re, 87 B.R. 170—§ 6-41; § 6-41, n. 12; § 6-42, n. 1.
Wood, In re, 23 B.R. 552—§ 9-3, n. 6.
Wood, Matter of, 825 F.2d 90—§ 11-1, n. 6; § 12-2, n. 14; § 12-3, n. 7.
Wood, Matter of, 47 B.R. 774—§ 10-29, n. 4.
Wood v. Wood (In re Wood)—§ 3-30, n. 27.
Wood Family Interests, Ltd., In re—§ 12-10, n. 6.
Woodford, In re—§ 8-17, n. 17, 49, 51.
Woodland Corp., In re—§ 3-9, n. 22, 31, 33.
Woods, In re—§ 7-26, n. 53.
Woods v. Alvarado State Bank—§ 8-7, n. 3.
Woodscape Ltd. Partnership, In re—§ 11-27, n. 17.
Woods Farmers Co-op. Elevator Co., In re—§ 6-62, n. 21, 26.
Woodson, In re—§ 8-1, n. 9, 12; § 8-19; § 8-19, n. 4, 6, 7, 18.
Woodstock Associates I, Inc., In re—§ 6-77, n. 15.
Woodworks Contemporary Furniture, Inc., Matter of—§ 6-86, n. 10.
Woolworth v. Micol Land Co.—§ 3-32, n. 6.
Wooten, In re—§ 8-26, n. 5.
Workmans Forest Products, Inc., In re—§ 6-11, n. 6.
World Financial Services, Inc., In re, 78 B.R. 239—§ 6-18, n. 23, 24, 26; § 6-20, n. 17, 22; § 6-26; § 6-26, n. 2, 5; § 6-27, n. 3; § 6-28, n. 2.
World Financial Services Center, Inc., In re, 64 B.R. 980—§ 6-73, n. 25; § 12-5, n. 2.
World Solar Corp., In re—§ 12-2, n. 9; § 12-5, n. 2, 5, 7.
Worrell, In re—§ 6-78, n. 14, 17.
Worth, In re—§ 8-26, n. 18.
Worthington, In re—§ 8-17, n. 35, 36.
Wrenn, In re—§ 7-30, n. 4.
Wright, In re, 128 B.R. 838—§ 3-25, n. 8.
Wright, In re, 99 B.R. 339—§ 8-3, n. 22.
Wright, In re, 82 B.R. 422—§ 9-4; § 9-4, n. 45.
Wright, In re, 66 B.R. 403—§ 7-34, n. 13.
Wright, Matter of—§ 6-48, n. 15; § 6-49, n. 49, 51; § 6-51, n. 25.
Writing Sales Ltd. Partnership, Matter of, 96 B.R. 179—§ 6-31, n. 15.
Writing Sales Ltd. Partnership, Matter of, 96 B.R. 175—§ 6-18, n. 3, 4, 10, 30; § 6-31, n. 4.
W.R.M.J. Johnson Fruit Farm, Inc., In re—§ 10-29, n. 4, 12.

W & T Enterprises, Inc., In re—§ 6-16, n. 1; § 6-69, n. 7, 13; § 6-74, n. 14.
W.T. Grant Co., In re—§ 6-51, n. 25; § 6-93, n. 4, 5, 48.
Wulf, Matter of—§ 2-2; § 2-2, n. 5; § 9-3, n. 33.
W.W. Gay Mechanical Contractor, Inc. v. Wharfside Two, Ltd.—§ 3-5, n. 8; § 3-6, n. 46.
WWG Industries, Inc., In re—§ 6-62, n. 25.
Wyles, In re—§ 8-33, n. 17.
Wynnewood House Associates, In re—§ 3-16, n. 8; § 3-18, n. 21; § 6-77, n. 20.
Wyoming County Bank & Trust Co. v. Kiley—§ 8-31, n. 5.

X

Xonics Imaging, Inc,, Matter of—§ 6-31, n. 15, 17.
Xonics, Inc., In re—§ 6-87, n. 4.
Xonics, Inc., Matter of—§ 10-29, n. 6; § 12-3, n. 7.
Xonics Photochemical, Inc., Matter of—§ 6-2, n. 9, 24, 28, 30; § 6-18, n. 18; § 6-51; § 6-51, n. 10.

Y

Yandell v. White City Amusement Park, Inc.—§ 6-15, n. 2.
Yanks, In re—§ 11-3, n. 11.
Yates, In re—§ 7-29; § 7-29, n. 4.
Yau, In re—§ 8-3, n. 21.
Yetter, Matter of—§ 6-15, n. 8; § 6-37, n. 4; § 8-25, n. 5, 6.
Yobe Elec., Inc., In re—§ 3-18, n. 17.
Yobe Elec., Inc., Matter of—§ 6-61, n. 58.
Yoder Co., In re—§ 10-31, n. 6.
Yohnke, In re—§ 8-18; § 8-18, n. 11.
Yonkers Hamilton Sanitarium Inc., In re, 34 B.R. 385—§ 6–45, n. 3, 5, 6, 7, 36.
Yonkers Hamilton Sanitarium Inc., In re, 22 B.R. 427—§ 6–17, n. 11.
Yost, In re—§ 6-48, n. 4; § 6-60, n. 4.
Youmans, In re—§ 3-30, n. 27.
Young, In re—§ 6-83, n. 5; § 6-84, n. 5.
Young, Matter of, 93 B.R. 590—§ 8–18, n. 7.
Young, Matter of, 76 B.R. 376—§ 3–29, n. 12.
Young, Matter of, 64 B.R. 611—§ 8–3, n. 10.
Young v. Schroeder—§ 6-56, n. 1.
Younger v. Harris—§ 3-20; § 3-20, n. 4, 29.
Youngs, In re—§ 3-28, n. 13.
Yu Chin T. Lim, Matter of—§ 6-93, n. 40.
Yukon Enterprises, Inc., In re—§ 2-15; § 2-15, n. 25.
Yurika Foods Corp., In re—§ 6-31, n. 17.

Z

Zachary v. Zachary—§ 8-25, n. 16.
Zagata Fabricators, Inc. v. Superior Air Products—§ 3-14, n. 64, 70.
Zaicek, In re—§ 7-48; § 7-48, n. 6; § 7-49, n. 2, 6.
Zaisan, Inc., In re—§ 6-62, n. 3, 20, 39.
Zarate v. Baldwin (In re Baldwin)—§ 7–26, n. 59.
Zarzynski, Matter of—§ 7-31, n. 13.
Zeman, In re—§ 6-47, n. 7; § 6-87, n. 8; § 6-89, n. 9.
Zenith Laboratories, Inc., In re—§ 3-5, n. 12; § 3-10, n. 35; § 3-22, n. 5, 19, 23, 29.
Zerodec Mega Corp., In re—§ 6-40, n. 4, 7, 11.
Zick, In re—§ 3-6, n. 25; § 3-12, n. 25; § 3-33, n. 10.
Ziegler, In re—§ 6-77, n. 19.
Zienel Furniture, Inc., Matter of—§ 6-39, n. 13.
Ziets, In re—§ 3-12, n. 24, 25.
Zilkha Energy Co. v. Leighton—§ 6-61, n. 8; § 6-83, n. 12.
Zimmerman, In re—§ 7-47, n. 4.
Zimmerman v. Morgan—§ 8-9, n. 16.
Zlogar, In re—§ 7-47, n. 2; § 11-30, n. 11.
Zook, Matter of—§ 11-10, n. 1.
Zouhar, In re—§ 8-32, n. 8, 22.
ZP Chandon, United States v.—§ 3-16, n. 2.

Zumbrun, In re—§ 3-33, n. 8.
Zuni, In re—§ 6-20, n. 20.
Zunich, In re—§ 3-32, n. 4.
Zwagerman, In re—§ 6-7, n. 4; § 6-31, n. 17.
Zyndorf, In re—§ 6-48, n. 8.
ZZZZ Best Co., Inc., In re—§ 6-32, n. 5.

Table of Statutes

EDITORIAL NOTE: A number of entries in this shared table relate to material appearing only in the three volume edition of this work. In those instances, see Epstein, Nickles and White, Bankruptcy, Practitioner Treatise Series.

UNITED STATES

UNITED STATES CONSTITUTION

Sec.	This Work Sec.	Note
I, § 8, cl. 4	1–1	
	8–3	11
III	12–16	
Amended		
7	12–14	
11	3–3	5
	3–34	
14, § 1	8–7	13

UNITED STATES CODE ANNOTATED

5 U.S.C.A.—Government Organization and Employees

Sec.	This Work Sec.	Note
8346	8–11	6

10 U.S.C.A.—Armed Forces

Sec.	This Work Sec.	Note
1408(d)(1)	7–6	

11 U.S.C.A.—Bankruptcy

Sec.	This Work Sec.	Note
24 (repealed)	6–6	5
35(a)(2)	11–37	6
35(a)(4)	7–28	9
57(d)	11–1	
70(a)	2–8	
101	1–10	
	2–1	
	2–2	11
	2–5	
	2–6	
	2–15	15

UNITED STATES CODE ANNOTATED
11 U.S.C.A.—Bankruptcy

Sec.	This Work Sec.	Note
101 (Cont'd)	2–16	
	7–5	3
	7–44	5
101(1)	6–8	2
101(2)	6–17	15
	12–7	
101(4)	7–5	
101(5)	3–6	56
	6–8	4
	6–18	17
	6–41	46
	7–4	
	7–5	
	7–7	
	9–30	
	11–2	
	11–2	2
101(5)(A)	6–3	9
	6–19	4
	6–37	15
	11–2	
	11–2	2
	11–3	
101(5)(B)	7–8	
	11–2	
	11–2	2
	11–9	
101(7)	2–8	8
101(8)	2–14	
	2–14	2
	3–10	45
	6–37	11
	6–37	15
	7–45	
101(9)(A)	11–3	22
101(10)(A)	6–3	9
	6–19	3
	11–2	4
101(11)	7–34	
101(12)	6–19	4
	6–37	15

1001

UNITED STATES CODE ANNOTATED
11 U.S.C.A.—Bankruptcy

Sec.	This Work Sec.	Note
101(12) (Cont'd)	7–5	
	7–31	10
101(13)	2–6	
	3–5	4
	6–3	8
101(15)	3–3	3
	6–88	3
	6–88	37
101(17)(A)	2–18	
101(17)(B)(ii)	9–24	24
101(18)	2–2	
	2–3	2
	8–9	3
	8–25	52
	9–24	
	9–24	1
101(18)(B)	9–24	
101(19)	9–24	
101(20)	8–25	52
	9–24	
101(21)	9–24	
	9–24	3
101(23)	2–6	
101(27)	3–3	3
	3–21	34
	7–31	
101(30)	9–3	2
101(31)	6–17	
	6–17	5
	6–17	10
	6–17	23
	6–17	26
	6–93	28
101(31)(E)	6–17	15
101(32)	6–18	2
	6–49	19
	6–66	11
101(32)(A)	6–3	10
	6–18	8
	6–49	8
	6–49	21
101(32)(A)(i)	6–18	5
101(32)(A)(ii)	6–18	6
101(32)(B)	6–18	8
	6–49	21
101(33)	10–12	3
101(36)	3–16	2
	6–36	10
	6–61	2
	6–62	9
	7–10	
	8–25	3
101(37)	3–16	2
	6–33	17
	6–61	2
	6–62	10
	7–10	
101(38–39)	6–85	10
101(41)	2–2	8
	2–2	16
	3–3	3
	3–33	4
101(43)	6–61	4

UNITED STATES CODE ANNOTATED
11 U.S.C.A.—Bankruptcy

Sec.	This Work Sec.	Note
101(43) (Cont'd)	6–62	25
101(45)	6–17	7
101(49)(A)(xiii)	6–93	33
101(50)	3–11	21
101(50) (former)	6–54	9
101(51)	3–11	22
	3–16	2
	6–33	3
	6–33	16
	6–35	29
	6–61	2
	6–62	8
	8–25	23
101(53)	3–16	2
	6–36	1
	6–36	8
	6–61	2
	6–62	7
	6–62	24
	6–62	41
	8–25	6
	8–25	10
	8–25	11
	8–25	23
101(54)	6–4	5
	6–5	6
	6–21	2
	6–24	5
	6–33	18
	6–47	7
	6–51	3
	6–54	
	6–54	1
	6–54	9
	6–69	6
	6–88	14
	7–19	8
102	2–9	1
	3–31	46
	3–31	49
102(1)	3–10	57
	3–31	
	3–31	44
	3–31	45
	4–16	
	4–16	1
	11–16	7
102(1)(A)	3–31	15
102(1)(B)	3–31	22
	4–16	
102(3)	6–17	10
103	1–3	3
103(a)	6–2	7
	6–2	19
	8–2	5
103(b)	6–93	66
	7–39	2
	11–32	
103(e)	6–2	7
103(g)	4–15	
105	2–4	
	2–11	8
	3–1	

TABLE OF STATUTES

UNITED STATES CODE ANNOTATED
11 U.S.C.A.—Bankruptcy

Sec.	This Work Sec.	Note
105 (Cont'd)	3–7	
	3–10	6
	3–20	
	3–21	125
	3–22	
	3–22	4
	3–22	19
	3–22	23
	3–22	29
	4–10	
	10–7	
	10–12	11
	11–36	
	11–36	1
	12–1	4
105(a)	2–9	1
	3–10	
	3–14	21
	3–16	11
	3–20	
	3–21	
	3–21	29
	3–21	120
	3–21	123
	3–22	
	3–22	1
	3–22	2
	3–22	3
	3–22	4
	3–22	5
	3–22	7
	3–22	21
	3–22	24
	3–22	26
	3–22	29
	3–31	
	3–31	38
	3–31	41
	3–31	95
	3–35	1
	4–10	
	6–93	64
	10–8	1
	11–34	
	11–34	1
	11–36	1
105(b)	10–8	1
106	3–34	
	3–34	1
	6–87	9
	6–88	4
106(a)	3–34	
	3–34	21
106(a–b)	3–34	
	3–34	10
106(b)	3–3	4
	3–34	
	3–34	21
	6–39	1
106(c)	3–3	5
	3–34	
106(c)(1)	3–34	
106(c)(2)	3–34	

UNITED STATES CODE ANNOTATED
11 U.S.C.A.—Bankruptcy

Sec.	This Work Sec.	Note
107(d)	6–56	3
107(d)(1)(E) (repealed)	6–49	39
107(d)(3)	6–59	8
107d(*l*)(e)(1) (repealed)	6–49	62
107d(*l*)(e)(2) (repealed)	6–49	62
108	3–14	46
	3–16	
	5–11	
108(a)	3–14	46
	6–60	26
	6–82	6
108(b)	3–14	46
	3–16	
	3–16	15
	5–11	
	5–11	2
108(b)(1)	3–16	17
108(b)(2)	3–16	16
108(c)	3–14	46
	3–16	
	3–16	19
	6–82	6
109	2–1	
	2–2	
	2–3	
	2–5	2
	2–6	
	9–25	
	10–15	6
109(a)	2–6	1
	12–7	2
109(b)	2–2	
109(b)(2)	2–5	2
109(b–f)	2–2	
109(c)	1–9	
109(d)	1–9	1
	2–2	
109(e)	1–8	
	2 2	
	2–3	2
	9–1	20
	9–3	
	9–3	1
	9–3	9
	9–3	10
109(f)	2–2	
	2–3	2
	2–11	4
	7–44	
	9–24	
109(g)	2–2	
	2–2	22
	2–16	
	2–16	1
	9–3	
	9–3	29
	9–25	
	9–25	13
	9–27	
	9–27	12
109(g)(1)	2–2	21
	9–2	17
	9–4	

1003

UNITED STATES CODE ANNOTATED
11 U.S.C.A.—Bankruptcy

Sec.	This Work Sec.	Note
109(g)(2)	2–2	
	9–2	17
	9–3	
	9–27	
110	4–7	3
110 (repealed)	6–6	1
130	2–17	14
141	2–15	1
157	11–5	
203	9–18	3
203(s)	9–18	3
249(b)	6–71	25
Ch. 3	5–12	
301	1–7	1
	2–1	
	2–2	
	2–3	
	2–10	
	3–9	2
302	2–1	
	2–3	
	2–3	1
	2–5	2
	2–10	
302(a)	8–21	1
302(b)	2–3	
	2–4	
303	Ch. 2, p. 51	
	2–1	
	2–4	2
	2–5	
	2–5	7
	2–10	
	6–71	
	7–2	1
	12–13	
	12–13	11
303(a)	2–5	
	9–3	1
303(b)	1–7	1
	2–5	
	6–71	2
303(b)(2)	2–5	
303(b)(3)	2–2	17
	2–2	19
	2–5	5
	2–5	14
303(b)(4)	2–5	14
	2–6	2
303(c)	2–5	13
	2–5	21
303(d)	2–5	23
303(e)	2–5	
303(f)	2–5	
	6–71	
	6–71	5
303(g)	2–5	28
	2–5	38
303(h)	2–5	
	2–5	2
	2–5	24
	3–9	3

UNITED STATES CODE ANNOTATED
11 U.S.C.A.—Bankruptcy

Sec.	This Work Sec.	Note
303(h)(1)	2–5	
303(h)(2)	2–5	
303(i)	2–5	
303(j)	2–5	40
	2–5	43
303(k)	2–5	2
	2–6	2
304	2–6	
	2–6	2
	2–10	
	2–10	1
304(b)	2–6	
304(c)	2–6	
	2–6	8
	2–10	1
304(c)(5)	2–6	
305	2–5	
	2–10	
	7–44	
305(2)(B)	2–10	1
321	10–9	1
321(b)	10–9	1
323(a)	6–94	2
326	1–7	4
	7–2	6
326(b)	9–4	39
327	7–2	6
	10–14	
	10–14	1
327(a)	6–73	
327(f)	10–9	1
328	10–14	
	10–14	2
329	6–69	14
330	7–2	6
	10–5	1
330(c)	9–4	38
341	7–2	
	9–4	
	11–16	4
	11–16	6
341(a)	7–2	3
	9–4	
	9–4	20
	11–16	
343	1–7	
	7–2	
	9–4	
	9–4	22
	11–16	
	11–16	4
346(i)	2–8	13
348	2–16	20
	2–17	
348(a)	2–11	2
	2–17	
	2–17	18
	2–18	
	3–2	8
	6–11	6
348(b)	2–17	
348(c)	2–17	
348(d)	2–16	20

TABLE OF STATUTES

UNITED STATES CODE ANNOTATED
11 U.S.C.A.—Bankruptcy

Sec.	This Work Sec.	Note
348(d) (Cont'd)	2–17	
349	2–11	
	3–23	24
349(a)	2–11	
	2–11	7
	3–23	29
349(b)	2–11	1
350	3–23	
350(a)	3–23	
	3–23	3
	3–23	10
352(a)(1)	3–14	82
352(a)(6)	3–1	13
356	3–10	21
361	3–1	
	3–27	
	3–27	27
	4–5	
	5–18	
	5–24	
	9–25	
	10–5	4
	12–14	16
361(3)	3–27	12
362	1–4	13
	2–5	
	2–5	29
	2–6	
	3–1	
	3–3	5
	3–5	
	3–5	6
	3–5	16
	3–5	19
	3–6	
	3–6	46
	3–6	61
	3–7	
	3–9	
	3–9	32
	3–10	
	3–10	11
	3–10	77
	3–11	26
	3–12	
	3–12	2
	3–13	
	3–13	5
	3–13	6
	3–14	
	3–14	39
	3–14	43
	3–15	
	3–15	4
	3–15	6
	3–16	
	3–18	
	3–21	
	3–21	29
	3–22	
	3–22	4
	3–27	15
	3–27	18

UNITED STATES CODE ANNOTATED
11 U.S.C.A.—Bankruptcy

Sec.	This Work Sec.	Note
362 (Cont'd)	3–32	
	3–32	28
	3–33	
	4–5	
	4–6	
	4–14	
	4–15	
	5–22	
	6–43	
	6–43	4
	6–45	
	6–73	
	6–73	10
	6–73	20
	6–76	5
	6–76	6
	6–90	
	7–5	
	7–13	
	7–40	
	9–4	
	9–20	
	10–7	
	10–7	1
	10–15	1
	10–20	6
	11–34	
	11–35	
	11–36	
	11–36	1
	12–14	
	12–14	16
362(a)	3–1	
	3–1	1
	3–1	2
	3–1	3
	3–1	4
	3–1	5
	3–2	1
	3–2	3
	3–3	
	3–3	2
	3–4	
	3–5	
	3–5	3
	3–5	12
	3–5	15
	3–5	19
	3–6	25
	3–6	40
	3–8	
	3–10	
	3–10	6
	3–12	
	3–12	2
	3–14	
	3–16	3
	3–18	
	3–19	
	3–20	
	3–21	
	3–21	113
	3–22	

TABLE OF STATUTES

UNITED STATES CODE ANNOTATED
11 U.S.C.A.—Bankruptcy

Sec.	This Work Sec.	Note
362(a) (Cont'd)	3–22	5
	3–22	7
	3–22	26
	3–23	
	3–23	46
	3–28	
	3–30	
	3–30	14
	3–30	33
	3–31	
	3–34	
	3–34	9
	6–43	10
	6–61	56
	6–66	6
	6–73	11
	6–74	3
	6–77	14
	8–1	21
	9–4	46
	9–20	
	11–2	4
	11–3	
	11–3	1
362(a)(1)	3–1	10
	3–6	
	3–6	7
	3–6	8
	3–6	24
	3–6	25
	3–6	35
	3–6	44
	3–6	46
	3–6	52
	3–6	53
	3–6	59
	3–6	64
	3–8	
	3–10	
	3–10	6
	3–10	11
	3–11	26
	3–12	
	3–12	21
	3–12	25
	3–14	
	3–14	68
	3–14	80
	3–16	
	3–16	3
	3–16	13
	3–16	21
	3–20	
	3–20	1
	3–21	
	3–21	1
	3–21	113
	3–22	2
	3–23	46
	3–30	
	3–30	1
362(a)(1–2)	3–5	1
	3–20	

UNITED STATES CODE ANNOTATED
11 U.S.C.A.—Bankruptcy

Sec.	This Work Sec.	Note
362(a)(1–2) (Cont'd)	3–21	
	3–21	69
362(a)(2)	3–8	
	3–10	21
	3–11	26
	3–13	
	3–13	3
	3–14	68
	3–21	
	3–21	28
362(a)(3)	2–8	
	3–3	2
	3–6	
	3–6	34
	3–8	
	3–8	2
	3–8	23
	3–9	
	3–10	
	3–10	20
	3–10	21
	3–10	27
	3–10	30
	3–10	32
	3–10	34
	3–13	
	3–14	
	3–14	1
	3–14	4
	3–14	9
	3–14	15
	3–14	20
	3–14	21
	3–14	34
	3–14	38
	3–14	39
	3–14	40
	3–14	42
	3–14	46
	3–14	65
	3–14	66
	3–14	80
	3–14	82
	3–15	
	3–15	6
	3–16	
	3–21	
	3–21	84
	3–21	109
	3–21	113
	3–21	114
	3–21	116
	3–21	120
	3–21	122
	3–22	
	3–22	16
	5–22	
	5–22	1
	6–43	26
	6–66	6
	9–20	
	13–1	1
362(a)(3–4)	3–6	

TABLE OF STATUTES

UNITED STATES CODE ANNOTATED
11 U.S.C.A.—Bankruptcy

Sec.	This Work Sec.	Note
362(a)(3–4) (Cont'd)	3–14	39
362(a)(4)	3–1	12
	3–8	
	3–11	14
	3–11	26
	3–13	
	3–13	2
	3–14	
	3–14	10
	3–14	18
	3–14	82
	3–16	
	3–16	1
	3–16	3
	3–16	4
	3–16	6
	3–16	8
	3–16	9
	3–16	20
	3–18	
	3–18	8
	3–18	21
	3–21	113
	6–61	56
	6–61	60
	6–66	6
	9–20	
362(a)(4–5)	3–18	
	3–21	69
	3–21	113
362(a)(4–6)	3–8	17
362(a)(5)	3–1	12
	3–5	2
	3–8	
	3–8	29
	3–11	
	3–11	2
	3–11	4
	3–11	12
	3–11	14
	3–11	17
	3–11	26
	3–12	
	3–14	18
	3–18	
	3–18	8
	3–23	46
	6–43	27
	6–66	6
362(a)(5–6)	3–11	14
	3–23	35
	3–23	46
362(a)(6)	3–1	11
	3–5	1
	3–8	
	3–8	1
	3–8	2
	3–8	11
	3–8	26
	3–9	
	3–9	8
	3–10	21
	3–14	

UNITED STATES CODE ANNOTATED
11 U.S.C.A.—Bankruptcy

Sec.	This Work Sec.	Note
362(a)(6) (Cont'd)	3–21	
	3–21	121
	3–21	122
	3–32	4
	6–43	28
	6–45	36
	6–66	6
	9–20	
362(a)(7)	3–13	
	3–13	4
	3–14	
	3–14	53
	3–15	
	3–15	1
	5–25	
	6–38	19
	6–39	37
	6–43	
	6–43	1
	6–43	20
362(a)(8)	3–5	1
	3–6	
362(a)(14)	3–15	
362(b)	3–1	
	3–1	14
	3–3	
	3–4	
	3–6	25
	3–18	21
	3–19	
	3–21	
	3–21	6
	3–21	45
	3–22	
	3–22	7
	6–66	6
362(b)(1)	3–1	15
	3–19	
	3–19	5
	3–20	
	3–20	2
	3–20	5
	3–20	6
	3–20	11
	3–20	12
	3–20	15
	3–20	19
	3–20	26
	3–22	3
362(b)(2)	3–1	17
	3–1	19
	3–12	
	3–12	3
	3–12	4
	3–12	5
	3–12	8
	3–12	10
	3–12	11
	3–12	15
	3–12	18
	3–12	25
	3–30	
	3–30	15

TABLE OF STATUTES

UNITED STATES CODE ANNOTATED
11 U.S.C.A.—Bankruptcy

Sec.	This Work Sec.	Note
362(b)(3)	3–18	
	3–18	9
	3–18	16
	3–18	17
	3–18	19
	3–18	20
	3–18	21
	3–18	24
	3–18	28
	3–18	29
	6–13	5
	6–61	61
	6–77	18
362(b)(4)	3–1	16
	3–7	4
	3–14	80
	3–16	2
	3–16	3
	3–19	6
	3–20	11
	3–21	
	3–21	2
	3–21	4
	3–21	5
	3–21	9
	3–21	14
	3–21	43
	3–21	44
	3–21	45
	3–21	46
	3–21	56
	3–21	60
	3–21	69
	3–21	73
	3–21	74
	3–21	82
	3–21	90
	3–21	112
	3–21	113
	3–21	116
	3–21	118
	3–22	3
	3–22	7
362(b)(4–5)	3–14	
	3–14	81
	3–16	3
	3–19	
	3–20	
	3–20	5
	3–20	11
	3–21	
	3–21	5
	3–21	44
	3–21	50
	3–21	73
	3–21	82
	3–21	109
	3–21	112
	3–21	116
	3–22	3
	3–22	7
	3–22	30
362(b)(5)	3–19	6

UNITED STATES CODE ANNOTATED
11 U.S.C.A.—Bankruptcy

Sec.	This Work Sec.	Note
362(b)(5) (Cont'd)	3–20	5
	3–20	11
	3–21	
	3–21	3
	3–21	4
	3–21	26
	3–21	44
	3–21	45
	3–21	69
	3–21	88
362(b)(6)	3–15	
	3–15	8
362(b)(7)	3–15	
	3–15	12
362(b)(8–9)	3–16	3
	3–19	4
362(b)(9)	3–8	
	3–8	18
	3–8	20
	3–8	21
362(b)(10)	3–14	
	3–14	75
	5–3	2
362(b)(11)	3–8	
	3–8	14
362(b)(12)	3–22	3
362(b)(12–13)	3–16	3
	3–19	4
362(b)(14)	3–15	13
	3–15	16
	6–85	22
362(c)	3–1	22
	3–23	
	3–23	1
362(c)(1)	3–23	
	3–23	45
	3–23	48
	10–29	6
362(c)(2)	3–1	23
	6–43	10
362(c)(2)(A)	3–23	2
362(c)(2)(B)	3–23	27
362(c)(2)(C)	3–11	14
	3–23	31
	3–23	44
	3–23	47
	10–29	7
362(d)	3–1	
	3–3	
	3–6	
	3–14	43
	3–23	
	3–28	
	3–31	
	3–31	1
	3–31	45
	3–31	89
	3–32	
	3–32	9
	5–24	
	6–43	7
	6–73	8
	7–13	

TABLE OF STATUTES

UNITED STATES CODE ANNOTATED
11 U.S.C.A.—Bankruptcy

Sec.	This Work Sec.	Note
362(d) (Cont'd)	10–5	4
362(d–f)	3–23	
362(d)(1)	2–15	20
	2–8	2
	3–1	
	3–1	24
	3–23	
	3–24	
	3–24	1
	3–25	64
	3–26	
	3–26	1
	3–27	
	3–27	1
	3–27	2
	3–27	10
	3–27	23
	3–27	38
	3–27	42
	3–28	
	3–28	12
	3–29	
	3–30	
	3–30	8
	3–31	
	5–24	
	6–43	10
362(d)(2)	2–15	20
	3–1	
	3–1	25
	3–24	
	3–24	3
	3–25	
	3–25	1
	3–25	2
	3–25	5
	3–25	6
	3–25	9
	3–25	10
	3–25	18
	3–25	45
	3–25	52
	3–26	
	3–27	20
	3–27	23
	3–27	38
	3–31	
	6–43	8
362(d)(2)(A)	3–25	
	3–25	6
362(d)(2)(B)	3–25	
	3–25	6
	3–25	23
362(d)(i)	2–16	
362(e)	3–1	22
	3–22	4
	3–23	
	3–31	
	3–31	16
	3–31	18
	3–31	20
	3–31	25
	3–31	31

UNITED STATES CODE ANNOTATED
11 U.S.C.A.—Bankruptcy

Sec.	This Work Sec.	Note
362(e) (Cont'd)	3–31	32
	3–31	41
	6–43	10
362(f)	3–23	
	3–31	
	3–31	49
	3–31	80
	3–31	84
	3–31	85
362(f)(2)(B)	5–6	
362(g)	3–27	6
	3–31	
	3–31	63
	3–31	64
362(g)(1)	3–25	3
362(g)(2)	3–25	4
362(h)	3–1	26
	3–33	
	3–33	1
	3–33	13
	3–33	18
	3–33	28
	3–33	31
	3–33	46
	3–34	
	3–34	8
	3–34	9
	3–35	
	3–35	2
	3–35	3
	6–43	15
	6–74	3
362(*l*)	6–73	5
363	1–5	2
	2–5	31
	2–8	2
	2–17	
	3–14	39
	3–15	
	3–15	4
	4–1	
	4–2	
	4–3	
	4–6	
	4–10	
	4–12	
	4–15	
	4–16	
	4–16	2
	4–17	
	5–6	4
	6–70	
	6–70	2
	6–71	
	6–71	4
	6–78	
	6–78	2
	8–10	
	8–10	7
	10–7	
	10–7	1
	10–15	3
	10–26	4

UNITED STATES CODE ANNOTATED
11 U.S.C.A.—Bankruptcy

Sec.	This Work Sec.	Note
363 (Cont'd)	12–2	
363(a)	3–15	5
	4–5	
	6–43	18
	6–43	23
	6–77	
	10–5	6
363(b)	4–2	
	4–4	
	4–4	14
	4–7	
	4–8	
	4–16	
	10–5	11
363(b)(1)	4–2	
	4–4	
	4–16	
363(b)(2)	4–16	
363(c)	4–7	
	4–16	
	6–43	18
363(c)(1)	3 28	2
	4–2	
	4–3	
	4–3	1
	6–70	2
	10–5	8
	10–6	
363(c)(2)	3–15	5
	3–21	110
	4–5	
	4–6	
	6–43	11
	6–43	24
	10–5	6
363(e)	3–21	110
	3–28	
	3–28	4
	3–31	84
	4–5	
	6–43	12
	6–43	18
	6–43	25
	10–5	4
	10–5	5
	10–5	6
	10–5	7
363(f)	2–8	12
	4–2	
	4–7	
	4–7	1
	4–8	
	4–9	1
	4–10	
	4–16	
	8–10	
	8–10	18
363(f)(1)	4–7	
	4–7	6
363(f)(2)	4–7	
	8–10	17
363(f)(3)	4–7	
	4–7	9

UNITED STATES CODE ANNOTATED
11 U.S.C.A.—Bankruptcy

Sec.	This Work Sec.	Note
363(f)(4)	4–7	
363(f)(5)	4–7	
	4–7	20
	4–10	
363(g)	4–16	
363(h)	2–8	12
	4–2	
	4–7	
	4–9	
	4–9	1
	4–9	2
	4–10	
	4–10	1
	4–10	8
	8–10	
	8–10	14
	8–10	26
363(h)(3)	8–10	20
363(i)	8–10	21
363(k)	4–2	
	4–7	
	4–8	
	10–20	16
	10–26	4
363(m)	3–31	103
	4–17	
363(n)	4–8	
364	2–5	
	4–1	
	4–6	
	4–11	
	4–12	
	4–12	3
	4–15	
	4–16	
	4–16	2
	4–17	
	5–14	3
	10–5	9
	10–7	1
	10–15	4
	12–2	
	12–14	
364(a)	2–5	
	2–5	38
	3–18	20
	4–3	
	4–11	
	4–12	
	6–61	60
364(b)	4–12	
	4–14	
	4–15	
	4–16	
	4–16	4
	10–5	12
364(c)	2–5	
	2–5	38
	4–11	
	4–13	
	4–14	
	4–15	
	4–16	

TABLE OF STATUTES

UNITED STATES CODE ANNOTATED
11 U.S.C.A.—Bankruptcy

Sec.	This Work Sec.	Note
364(c) (Cont'd)	4–16	4
	4–17	
	10–5	12
364(c)(1)	4–11	
364(d)	2–5	
	2–5	38
	4–11	
	4–13	
	4–14	
	4–14	5
	4–14	6
	4–15	
	4–16	
	4–16	4
	11–11	4
364(d)(1)(B)	4–14	
364(e)	4–17	
	4–17	8
365	3–6	
	3–8	22
	3–9	7
	3–14	
	3–14	43
	3–14	57
	3–17	
	3–28	
	3–28	12
	Ch. 5, p. 439	
	Ch. 5, p. 448	
	5–1	
	5–2	
	5–3	
	5–3	2
	5–4	
	5–4	1
	5–6	
	5–6	4
	5–7	
	5–7	12
	5–10	4
	5–11	
	5–16	
	5–18	
	5–21	2
	5–22	
	5–24	
	5–25	
	5–26	
	5–26	20
	7–7	
	7–40	
	7–41	
	11–37	6
	11–38	
365(a)	3–7	
	3–14	41
	3–14	69
	3–28	1
	5–8	
	5–10	4
	5–25	7

UNITED STATES CODE ANNOTATED
11 U.S.C.A.—Bankruptcy

Sec.	This Work Sec.	Note
365(b)	3–28	
	5–5	8
	5–12	5
	5–13	
	5–15	
	5–18	
	5–19	
	5–21	
	5–23	
	5–25	
	7–41	
365(b)(1)	3–9	7
	5–18	
365(b)(1)(C)	5–18	
365(b)(2)	5–12	5
	5–20	
365(b)(2)(C)	5–20	11
365(b)(2)(D)	5–20	11
365(b)(3)	5–17	
	5–18	1
	5–20	
	5–20	10
	5–21	
	5–26	2
365(b)(4)	5–20	10
	5–22	
365(c)	5–15	
	5–16	
	5–26	3
	11–38	
365(c)(1)	5–14	
	5–15	
	5–15	4
	5–15	5
	5–15	10
	5–16	
	11–38	
365(c)(1)(A)	5–15	
	5–15	7
	5–16	
	11–38	
365(c)(2)	3–14	43
	5–13	
	5–14	
	5–14	2
365(c)(2)(A)	11–38	
365(c)(2)(B)	5–13	
365(d)	3–14	71
	5–9	
	5–10	4
	5–11	
	5–26	4
365(d)(1)	5–8	
	5–9	1
	5–10	
	5–10	14
	5–23	
365(d)(2)	5–9	2
	5–10	4
	5–24	
	5–26	3
365(d)(3)	5–2	
	5–10	

TABLE OF STATUTES

UNITED STATES CODE ANNOTATED
11 U.S.C.A.—Bankruptcy

Sec.	This Work Sec.	Note
365(d)(3) (Cont'd)	5–22	3
	5–23	
	5–23	3
	5–23	6
	5–26	3
365(d)(4)	3–14	73
	3–14	74
	3–14	79
	5–2	
	5–8	
	5–10	
	5–10	2
	5–10	4
	5–10	14
	5–11	
	5–23	
	5–23	6
	5–26	3
365(e)	2–8	41
	5–12	
	11–38	
365(e)(1)	5–12	
365(e)(2)	3–14	43
	3–14	57
365(e)(2)(B)	3–14	43
365(f)	2–8	41
	5–16	
	5–17	
	5–21	
365(f)(1)	5–16	
	5–17	
	5–17	1
365(f)(2)	5–6	
	5–16	
	5–20	11
	5–21	
365(f)(2)(A)	5–16	
365(f)(2)(B)	5–17	
365(f)(3)	5–17	
	5–17	1
365(g)	3–14	72
	5–7	
	5–7	1
365(g)(1)	3–6	61
365(h)	5–7	
	5–7	3
	5–23	9
	5–26	5
	5–26	6
365(h)(1)	5–7	
365(h)(2)	5–7	
365(i)	5–4	
	5–26	6
365(j)	5–26	7
365(k)	5–6	
365(*l*)	5–21	
	5–21	2
365(m)	5–10	2
365(n)	5–7	
	5–23	9
	5–26	8
365(*o*)	5–26	9
366	3–9	

UNITED STATES CODE ANNOTATED
11 U.S.C.A.—Bankruptcy

Sec.	This Work Sec.	Note
366 (Cont'd)	3–9	7
	3–9	11
	3–9	16
	3–9	29
	3–9	35
	3–14	45
366(a)	3–9	
	3–9	1
	3–9	6
366(b)	3–9	
	3–9	13
	3–9	15
	3–9	31
	3–9	32
	3–9	34
	3–9	35
384(a)	6–71	13
407	8–11	3
421(i)	6–54	9
463(a)	6–54	6
	6–54	8
Ch. 5	6–2	
	6–2	7
	7–16	
	8–25	
501	7–3	
	11–4	
501—676	10–1	2
501(a)	11–4	3
	11–4	4
501(b)	12–14	17
	12–14	18
501(b)–(c)	11–4	7
501(c)	12–14	17
	12–14	18
501(d)	11–2	4
	11–4	
	11–4	9
502	5–1	
	6–82	
	6–93	32
	7–3	
	7–14	
	7–25	
	9–4	
	10–31	
	11–4	28
	12–14	
502(a)	7–3	
	7–15	
	11–4	18
502(b)	5–2	
	5–2	5
	6–20	9
	7–3	
	11–2	
	11–2	4
	11–4	19
502(b)(1)	10–25	
	10–25	5
	11–2	
	11–2	10
	11–4	20

TABLE OF STATUTES

UNITED STATES CODE ANNOTATED
11 U.S.C.A.—Bankruptcy

Sec.	This Work Sec.	Note
502(b)(2)	3–10	71
	7–3	
	7–25	
	11–4	21
	11–24	
502(b)(3)	6–41	1
	11–4	22
502(b)(4)	11–4	23
502(b)(5)	11–4	24
502(b)(6)	5–2	3
	5–7	17
	11–4	25
502(b)(7)	5–7	17
502(b)(7–8)	11–4	26
502(c)	11–4	
	11–5	
	11–6	
	11–7	
	11–7	8
502(c)(1)	2–15	15
502(c)(1)(B)	11–4	
502(c)(1)(C)	11–4	
502(d)	6–82	4
502(e)(2)	11–4	10
502(f)	2–5	34
	7–25	1
	10–15	7
	11–2	4
	11–4	14
502(g)	5–7	
	5–7	1
	11–4	11
502(h)	6–87	5
	6–88	19
	11–4	12
502(i)	9–4	
	11–4	13
502(j)	11–7	
	11–7	9
503	3–9	31
	5–1	
	5–13	
	7–3	
	7–9	
	10–14	
	11–10	
	11–10	1
	11–12	
503(b)	3–27	45
	4–12	
	6–69	14
	7–11	
	11–4	16
	11–10	
503(b)(1)	4–11	
	4–12	
	5–23	
	11–10	
503(b)(1)(A)	3–14	
	3–27	45
	4–12	
	4–13	
	7–11	1

UNITED STATES CODE ANNOTATED
11 U.S.C.A.—Bankruptcy

Sec.	This Work Sec.	Note
503(b)(1)(A) (Cont'd)	11–4	15
	11–10	
503(b)(1)(C)	6–93	66
503(b)(4)	7–11	
506	3–11	
	7–1	
	7–3	
	7–9	
	7–10	
	7–10	2
	7–47	
	7–47	2
	8–1	20
	8–28	
	9–3	10
	9–5	
	9–6	
	9–10	
	9–18	
	9–18	16
	12–14	
506(a)	3–11	28
	6–39	39
	6–43	9
	6–43	17
	6–43	23
	7–10	
	7–39	3
	7–47	
	7–47	2
	7–49	
	8–28	
	8–28	12
	10–20	3
	10–24	1
	10–25	
	10–25	1
	10–25	2
	10–27	
506(b)	1–3	
	3–27	
	3–27	14
	3–27	19
	6–78	3
506(c)	3–9	31
	3–21	110
	6–78	
	6–78	9
	6–78	14
	6–78	17
	11–11	
506(d)	3–11	28
	6–44	2
	7–39	4
	7–39	5
	7–47	
	7–47	2
	7–47	2
	8–27	13
	8–28	
	8–28	12
	9–4	
	9–20	

1013

TABLE OF STATUTES

UNITED STATES CODE ANNOTATED
11 U.S.C.A.—Bankruptcy

Sec.	This Work Sec.	Note
506(d) (Cont'd)	11–30	
507	1–7	
	2–8	43
	3–14	
	6–20	9
	6–20	12
	6–36	18
	7–3	
	7–9	
	7–10	
	7–11	
	7–12	
	7–14	
	7–15	
	7–25	
	9–6	
	11–10	
	11–12	
	11–33	
507(a)	7–12	
	7–12	1
	7–15	
	10–15	8
	11–4	16
507(a)(1)	3–21	112
	7–13	
	9–6	
	11–33	1
507(a)(2)	2–5	34
	7–12	
	7–25	
	7–25	1
507(a)(3)	4–15	
507(a)(5)	7–12	1
507(a)(6)(D)	7–25	2
507(a)(7)	7–12	
	7–12	1
	7–25	
	9–5	
507(a)(7)(A)	7–25	
507(a)(7)(A)(i)	7–25	
507(a)(7)(A)(ii)	7–25	
507(a)(7)(B)	7–12	1
	7–25	
507(a)(7)(C)	7–25	
	7–25	2
507(a)(7)(D)	7–25	2
507(a)(7)(E)	7–12	1
	7–25	
507(b)	3–27	
	3–27	45
	5–24	4
	7–13	
509	11–4	
	11–4	28
509(a)	11–4	
509(c)	11–4	
510	6–20	12
	6–91	
	7–9	
510(a)	6–91	2
	6–92	
	6–92	1

UNITED STATES CODE ANNOTATED
11 U.S.C.A.—Bankruptcy

Sec.	This Work Sec.	Note
510(b)	6–93	33
510(c)	3–30	
	6–2	25
	6–17	18
	6–91	2
	6–93	
	6–93	1
	6–93	5
	6–93	15
	6–93	32
	6–93	66
510(c)(2)	6–93	6
	8–22	9
521	1–7	
	7–39	
	7–39	14
	7–49	
521(1)	7–43	
	12–14	17
	12–14	18
521(2)	7–39	
	7–49	
522	1–4	12
	1–7	
	2–8	39
	2–17	
	6–1	10
	6–2	16
	6–2	21
	6–2	22
	6–58	
	6–78	
	7–47	
	7–48	
	7–48	5
	8–2	
	8–3	21
	8–11	
	8–21	
	8–21	4
	8–25	43
	8–28	
	8–30	8
	8–31	
	8–32	7
	8–33	
	9–9	
522(a)	6–76	6
522(a)(5)	8–24	5
522(a)(5)(C)	8–19	
522(b)	3–11	
	6–58	3
	6–77	7
	6–80	20
	8–1	10
	8–2	1
	8–3	
	8–3	1
	8–3	31
	8–21	5
	8–21	6
	8–21	7
	8–21	10

TABLE OF STATUTES

UNITED STATES CODE ANNOTATED
11 U.S.C.A.—Bankruptcy

Sec.	This Work Sec.	Note
522(b) (Cont'd)	8–22	1
	8–28	
522(b)(1)	8–1	6
	8–1	7
	8–1	8
	8–3	
	8–3	2
	8–3	9
	8–3	11
	8–33	31
522(b)(2)	8–1	5
	8–1	7
	8–3	
	8–33	
522(b)(2)(A)	2–17	
	8–3	3
	8–3	4
	8–3	9
	8–3	15
	8–3	18
	8–9	17
	8–11	
	8–11	1
	8–11	3
	8–11	12
	8–11	16
	8–11	18
	8–33	
	8–33	33
	8–33	34
522(b)(2)(B)	2–8	11
	6–57	3
	6–57	5
	8–3	5
	8–10	
	8–10	4
	8–10	7
	8–10	10
	8–10	12
	8–10	24
	8–21	
	8–33	2
522(b)(10)(E)	8–33	30
522(c)	8–1	16
	8–23	7
	8–31	
522(c)(1)	8–1	17
	8–24	5
	8–25	18
522(c)(2)	8–1	20
	8–31	6
522(c)(2)(A)	8–1	20
522(c)(2)(B)	8–1	20
	8–1	21
	8–23	7
522(d)	2–8	29
	6–57	3
	7–26	1
	7–47	
	8–1	
	8–1	6
	8–1	11
	8–3	

UNITED STATES CODE ANNOTATED
11 U.S.C.A.—Bankruptcy

Sec.	This Work Sec.	Note
522(d) (Cont'd)	8–3	10
	8–3	19
	8–3	31
	8–4	
	8–9	
	8–9	1
	8–10	
	8–10	7
	8–11	
	8–11	1
	8–11	3
	8–12	
	8–12	1
	8–12	3
	8–13	
	8–15	7
	8–18	
	8–19	
	8–19	14
	8–20	
	8–20	2
	8–21	
	8–21	4
	8–22	
	8–24	
	8–25	
	8–25	57
	8–25	62
	8–26	
	8–26	2
	8–33	
	8–33	29
	8–33	31
	8–33	34
	9–2	3
522(d)(1)	8–12	4
	8–13	
	8–13	1
	8–13	8
	8–13	11
	8–13	13
	8–20	
	8–21	4
522(d)(2)	7–47	
	8–15	1
	8–20	2
	8–25	61
522(d)(3)	8–15	2
	8–15	3
522(d)(4)	8–15	2
	8–15	4
522(d)(5)	7–47	
	8–3	21
	8–13	11
	8–13	14
	8–20	
	8–20	1
	8–20	2
	8–21	4
	8–25	62
	8–26	2
522(d)(6)	8–15	6
	8–21	4

UNITED STATES CODE ANNOTATED
11 U.S.C.A.—Bankruptcy

Sec.	This Work Sec.	Note
522(d)(6) (Cont'd)	8–25	
	8–25	59
	8–25	61
	8–25	62
522(d)(7)	8–19	
	8–19	1
	8–19	2
	8–19	3
	8–19	4
	8–19	8
	8–19	11
	8–19	20
522(d)(8)	8–19	
	8–19	9
	8–19	10
522(d)(9)	8–15	2
	8–15	5
522(d)(10)	2–8	29
	8–16	1
	8–17	
	8–17	1
	8–17	10
	8–17	33
	8–17	49
	8–18	
	8–18	3
522(d)(10)(A)	8–17	10
522(d)(10)(C)	8–16	
	8–17	7
522(d)(10)(D)	8–17	43
522(d)(10)(E)	8–17	13
	8–17	20
	8–17	21
	8–17	23
	8–17	24
	8–17	25
	8–17	27
	8–17	32
	8–17	33
	8–17	34
	8–17	35
	8–17	36
	8–17	42
	8–17	44
	8–17	47
	8–17	48
	8–17	49
	8–17	50
	8–17	51
	8–33	
522(d)(10)(E)(i)—(iii)	8–17	51
522(d)(10)(E)(iii)	8–17	39
	8–17	52
522(d)(11)	8–13	10
	8–16	
	8–16	2
	8–17	7
	8–18	
	8–18	1
	8–18	3
	8–18	19
522(d)(11)(B)–(C)	8–17	43
522(d)(11)(C)	8–19	

UNITED STATES CODE ANNOTATED
11 U.S.C.A.—Bankruptcy

Sec.	This Work Sec.	Note
522(d)(11)(C) (Cont'd)	8–19	13
522(d)(11)(D)	8–16	
	8–17	3
	8–18	
	8–18	6
	8–18	7
	8–18	8
	8–18	9
	8–18	10
	8–18	16
	8–18	19
	8–18	23
522(d)(11)(E)	8–16	
	8–17	3
	8–17	43
	8–18	
	8–18	5
	8–18	9
	8–18	16
	8–18	18
	8–18	19
	8–18	23
522(e)	8–9	
	8–9	11
	8–31	
	8–31	1
	8–31	3
	8–31	4
	8–31	10
	8–31	11
522(f)	3–11	16
	3–11	18
	3–30	
	6–1	10
	6–2	22
	6–6	7
	6–20	20
	6–80	
	6–80	9
	6–82	3
	7–29	26
	8–1	17
	8–1	24
	8–2	3
	8–2	4
	8–9	
	8–20	2
	8–24	
	8–24	1
	8–24	2
	8–24	3
	8–24	5
	8–25	
	8–25	4
	8–25	5
	8–25	8
	8–25	12
	8–25	15
	8–25	20
	8–25	24
	8–25	38
	8–25	55
	8–25	56

TABLE OF STATUTES

UNITED STATES CODE ANNOTATED
11 U.S.C.A.—Bankruptcy

Sec.	This Work Sec.	Note
522(f) (Cont'd)	8–25	57
	8–25	62
	8–25	64
	8–26	
	8–26	2
	8–26	5
	8–26	9
	8–26	12
	8–26	13
	8–26	18
	8–26	19
	8–26	20
	8–27	
	8–27	1
	8–27	2
	8–27	9
	8–27	10
	8–27	11
522(f)(2) (Cont'd)	8–27	13
	8–28	
	8–28	1
	8–28	3
	8–28	4
	8–28	6
	8–28	9
	8–28	12
	8–28	17
	8–28	20
	8–29	
	8–29	3
	8–29	7
	8–29	12
	8–29	13
	8–29	15
	8–30	4
	8–30	9
	8–31	9
	8–31	10
	11–30	
	11–30	10
522(f)(1)	7–29	26
	8–3	21
	8–9	8
	8–9	13
	8–23	
	8–25	1
	8–26	
	8–26	5
	8–26	14
	8–27	
	8–27	9
	8–28	
	8–30	9
522(f)(2)	6–6	6
	6–57	5
	8–15	
	8–15	7
	8–22	
	8–22	24
	8–24	
	8–25	
	8–25	2
	8–25	45

UNITED STATES CODE ANNOTATED
11 U.S.C.A.—Bankruptcy

Sec.	This Work Sec.	Note
522(f)(2) (Cont'd)	8–26	
	8–31	
	8–31	7
	11–30	
522(f)(2)(A)	8–25	
	8–25	40
	8–25	41
	8–25	43
	8–25	44
	8–25	46
	8–25	48
	8–25	49
	8–25	51
522(f)(2)(A)–(C)	8–25	
522(f)(2)(B)	8–25	
	8–25	38
	8–25	50
	8–25	51
	8–25	58
	8–25	62
	8–25	63
522(g)	6–6	
	6–6	6
	6–6	9
	6–57	4
	6–57	5
	8–1	22
	8–22	
	8–22	5
	8–22	6
	8–22	7
	8–22	8
	8–22	15
	8–22	17
	8–22	18
	8–22	19
	8–22	20
	8–22	23
	8–22	30
	8–22	35
	8–22	37
	8–23	
	8–23	5
	8–23	7
	8–31	7
522(g)(1)	8–22	
	8–22	23
	8–22	26
	8–23	
522(g)(1)(A)	8–22	13
	8–22	38
522(g)(1)(B)	8–22	36
522(g)(2)	8–22	
	8–22	24
522(h)	3–11	16
	6–1	10
	6–2	22
	6–6	7
	6–6	8
	8–1	23
	8–22	
	8–22	5
	8–22	17

TABLE OF STATUTES

UNITED STATES CODE ANNOTATED
11 U.S.C.A.—Bankruptcy

Sec.	This Work Sec.	Note
522(h) (Cont'd)	8–22	20
	8–23	
	8–23	2
	8–23	3
	8–23	4
	8–23	5
	8–23	6
	8–23	7
	8–23	8
	8–23	9
	8–23	15
	8–24	
	8–28	20
	8–28	22
	8–29	12
	8–30	
	8–31	7
522(h)(2)(A)	8–11	9
522(i)	8–22	
	8–22	5
	8–30	
	8–30	9
522(i)(1)	8–22	39
	8–30	2
	8–30	4
522(i)(2)	8–28	20
	8–30	7
	8–30	8
522(j)	8–30	5
522(*l*)	8–1	11
	8–1	12
	8–1	13
	8–2	7
	8–9	
	8–29	4
	8–29	5
522(m)	8–21	
	8–21	3
	8–21	4
	8–21	8
	8–21	9
	8–21	10
	8–21	11
523	1–7	
	2–16	
	3–12	
	6–48	4
	7–1	
	7–12	
	7–15	
	7–17	
	7–19	
	7–21	
	7–24	
	7–24	1
	7–25	
	7–26	
	7–27	
	7–29	
	7–30	
	7–31	
	7–32	
	7–33	

UNITED STATES CODE ANNOTATED
11 U.S.C.A.—Bankruptcy

Sec.	This Work Sec.	Note
523 (Cont'd)	7–35	
	7–42	
	9–2	13
	9–7	
	9–9	
	9–25	
	10–30	
	11–3	21
	11–9	
523(a)	3–12	1
	7–24	
	7–24	1
	7–33	
	8–9	6
	9–7	
	9–21	
523(a)(1)	7–24	
	7–25	
	7–32	
	7–33	
	8–1	17
	8–24	5
523(a)(1)(A)	7–15	
	7–25	
	7–32	
523(a)(1)(B)	7–25	
	7–32	
523(a)(1)(B)(i)	7–25	
523(a)(1)(B)(ii)	7–25	
523(a)(1)(C)	7–25	
523(a)(2)	4–6	
	7–24	
	7–25	
	7–26	
	7–27	
	7–31	
	7–33	
	7–38	
523(a)(2)(A)	7–26	
523(a)(2)(B)	7–26	
523(a)(2)(C)	7–26	
	7–26	1
	7–26	47
	7–26	48
523(a)(3)	7–24	
	7–27	
	7–27	1
523(a)(3)(A)	7–27	
523(a)(3)(B)	7–27	
523(a)(4)	4–6	
	7–24	
	7–25	
	7–27	
	7–28	
	7–28	1
	7–28	5
	7–28	18
	7–33	
523(a)(5)	3–12	
	7–24	1
	7–28	
	7–29	
	7–29	1

TABLE OF STATUTES

UNITED STATES CODE ANNOTATED
11 U.S.C.A.—Bankruptcy

Sec.	This Work Sec.	Note
523(a)(5) (Cont'd)	7–33	
	7–34	
	8–1	17
	8–25	18
	11–4	
523(a)(5)(A)	7–29	
523(a)(6)	7–24	
	7–25	
	7–27	
	7–30	
523(a)(7)	7–31	
	7–31	1
	7–32	
523(a)(7)(A)	7–32	
523(a)(7)(B)	7–32	
523(a)(8)	7–24	1
	7–29	16
	7–33	
	7–33	1
	9–7	
523(a)(8)(A)	7–24	
	7–33	
	7–33	1
523(a)(8)(B)	7–33	
523(a)(9)	7–24	1
	7–30	
	7–34	
	7–34	1
	7–34	2
	7–34	5
	7–34	6
	7–34	13
	7–34	14
523(c)	7–26	1
	7–27	
524	3–8	10
	3–11	14
	7–5	
	7–35	
	7–36	
	7–39	
	7–40	
	7–45	
	7–47	
524(a)	3–23	39
	7–1	
	7–16	
	7–40	
524(a)(1)	3–11	28
524(a)(2)	3–1	21
	3–11	6
	3–11	27
	7–16	
	7–36	
	10–29	8
524(a)(3)	2–8	8
524(c)	7–1	
	7–35	
	7–36	
	7–38	
	7–39	
	7–39	9
	7–47	

UNITED STATES CODE ANNOTATED
11 U.S.C.A.—Bankruptcy

Sec.	This Work Sec.	Note
524(c)(3)	7–35	
	7–37	
524(d)	7–2	
	7–35	
	7–36	
	7–38	
524(e)	3–10	19
524(f)	7–36	
525	3–8	35
	3–9	30
	7–1	
	7–36	
	7–40	
	7–41	
525(a)	3–8	35
	7–36	
	7–40	
	7–40	2
	7–41	
	7–42	
525(b)	3–8	35
	7–40	
	7–41	
	7–42	
533	6–45	2
533(a)	6–40	4
533(b)	8–23	5
541	2–5	
	2–5	30
	2–6	
	2–8	
	2–8	2
	2–8	3
	2–8	7
	2–8	29
	2–16	20
	3–10	20
	3–13	
	3–14	
	3–14	65
	5–1	
	5–15	
	6–3	2
	6–7	2
	6–61	
	6–61	8
	6–68	
	6–86	
	6–94	
	7–1	
	7–6	
	8–1	9
	12–8	
541(a)	2–8	
	3–11	1
	5–5	
	6–61	8
	6–68	1
	6–68	3
	6–69	4
	6–94	8
	7–11	8
541(a)(1)	2–8	

1019

UNITED STATES CODE ANNOTATED
11 U.S.C.A.—Bankruptcy

Sec.	This Work Sec.	Note
541(a)(1) (Cont'd)	2–8	21
	2–8	39
	3–10	20
	3–12	6
	5–5	
	5–7	14
	6–6	4
	6–71	3
	6–79	4
	6–94	8
	8–33	1
541(a)(2)	2–8	8
541(a)(3)	2–8	
	2–8	9
	2–8	20
	6–79	12
	6–80	
	6–80	15
	6–80	17
	6–80	18
	6–87	4
	8–22	4
541(a)(4)	2–8	
	6–80	17
	6–80	19
	6–80	20
	6–86	3
541(a)(5)	2–8	
	2–8	19
541(a)(5)—(a)(7)	8–1	11
541(a)(5)(A)	8–3	30
541(a)(5)(C)	8–19	20
541(a)(6)	2–8	
	2–8	14
	2–8	21
	3–12	6
	3–14	35
	6–74	13
	6–78	3
	7–45	13
541(a)(7)	2–8	
	3–14	34
541(b)	2–8	
	2–8	39
541(b)(1)	2–8	
	6–7	4
541(b)(2)	2–8	
	3–14	
	3–14	76
	5–3	2
	5–4	1
541(b)(3)	2–8	
541(c)	2–8	41
	5–15	
	7–39	
541(c)(1)	2–8	
	5–15	
	8–33	
541(c)(1)(A)	2–8	
	8–17	13
	8–33	2
	8–33	39
541(c)(1)(B)	3–14	44

UNITED STATES CODE ANNOTATED
11 U.S.C.A.—Bankruptcy

Sec.	This Work Sec.	Note
541(c)(2)	2–8	
	2–8	39
	6–61	38
	8–11	
	8–11	23
	8–17	13
	8–33	
	8–33	2
	8–33	3
	8–33	17
	8–33	18
	8–33	20
	8–33	24
	8–33	39
	9–2	3
541(d)	6–61	
	6–61	37
	6–61	38
541(e)	6–39	1
	6–94	1
542	2–8	2
	3–14	
	3–14	15
	3–32	
	3–33	
	3–34	
	6–43	
	6–45	
	6–73	
	6–73	20
	6–73	25
	6–82	1
	6–90	
	8–22	10
542(a)	2–8	2
	3–14	11
	6–73	13
	6–73	25
	6–74	1
	6–82	1
	6–90	4
542(a–b)	3–33	41
542(a)(3)	3–14	15
542(b)	3–14	15
	3–14	52
	3–15	
	3–15	2
	6–38	
	6–38	20
	6–43	22
	6–44	2
	6–45	38
	6–73	13
	6–74	
	6–74	2
	6–74	4
	12–2	10
542(c)	2–5	39
	3–32	
	6–69	9
	6–71	
	6–74	
	6–74	7

TABLE OF STATUTES

UNITED STATES CODE ANNOTATED
11 U.S.C.A.—Bankruptcy

Sec.	This Work Sec.	Note
542(c) (Cont'd)	6–74	10
	6–74	13
	6–74	14
542(c–d)	3–32	29
542(d)	8–19	10
543	2–8	2
	6–74	1
	6–82	1
	8–22	10
543(a)(6)	12–13	13
544	1–4	12
	2–17	
	3–17	20
	3–18	
	6–2	24
	6–50	5
	6–60	29
	6–61	8
	6–61	11
	6–61	51
	6–68	
	6–73	2
	6–78	
	6–78	3
	6–82	
	6–87	8
	6–88	
	8–22	2
544(a)	3–11	
	3–11	15
	3–18	
	3–18	1
	3–18	10
	6–2	2
	6–2	16
	6–2	24
	6–20	20
	6–38	
	6–60	
	6–61	
	6–61	1
	6–61	2
	6–61	8
	6–61	10
	6–61	11
	6–61	12
	6–61	13
	6–61	28
	6–61	34
	6–61	38
	6–61	42
	6–61	44
	6–61	49
	6–61	51
	6–61	52
	6–61	53
	6–61	54
	6–61	55
	6–61	58
	6–61	66
	6–61	67
	6–61	70
	6–61	74

UNITED STATES CODE ANNOTATED
11 U.S.C.A.—Bankruptcy

Sec.	This Work Sec.	Note
544(a) (Cont'd)	6–61	77
	6–61	78
	6–61	79
	6–61	80
	6–62	
	6–62	25
	6–62	28
	6–64	
	6–65	
	6–78	3
	6–80	1
	6–82	4
	6–82	6
	6–86	
	8–21	14
	8–22	23
	8–23	6
	8–32	8
	10–13	10
544(a)(1)	6–1	1
	6–61	
	6–61	3
	6–61	14
	6–61	34
	6–61	49
	6–61	53
	6–78	3
544(a)(2)	6–1	1
	6–61	7
	6–61	11
	6–61	49
	6–61	69
544(a)(3)	6–1	2
	6–61	
	6–61	5
	6–61	6
	6–61	11
	6–61	17
	6–61	38
	6–61	49
	6–61	53
	6–61	74
	6–86	4
	6–86	9
544(b)	2–8	7
	6–1	3
	6–2	2
	6–2	24
	6–46	
	6–46	8
	6–46	9
	6–48	4
	6–49	3
	6–50	5
	6–52	
	6–56	1
	6–59	
	6–59	3
	6–60	
	6–60	2
	6–60	4
	6–60	8
	6–60	10

TABLE OF STATUTES

UNITED STATES CODE ANNOTATED
11 U.S.C.A.—Bankruptcy

Sec.	This Work Sec.	Note
544(b) (Cont'd)	6–60	19
	6–60	20
	6–60	22
	6–60	24
	6–60	28
	6–60	29
	6–61	
	6–65	
	6–65	8
	6–80	1
	6–82	
	6–82	6
	6–82	7
	8–32	
	8–32	8
	10–13	12
	12–8	
545	2–8	43
	2–17	
	3–11	
	3–11	15
	3–18	
	3–18	13
	3–18	29
	6–1	4
	6–2	2
	6–2	24
	6–36	
	6–36	2
	6–36	12
	6–50	5
	6–62	
	6–62	1
	6–62	3
	6–62	5
	6–62	13
	6–62	20
	6–62	25
	6–62	28
	6–62	34
	6–62	39
	6–62	41
	6–64	
	6–68	
	6–73	2
	6–78	
	6–80	1
	6–82	
	6–88	
	8–22	2
	8–23	5
	8–23	7
	8–23	9
545(1)	6–62	
545(2)	3–18	
	3–18	1
	3–18	10
	6–36	12
	6–61	77
	6–62	
	6–62	25
	6–62	26
	6–62	28

UNITED STATES CODE ANNOTATED
11 U.S.C.A.—Bankruptcy

Sec.	This Work Sec.	Note
545(2) (Cont'd)	6–62	34
545(2)—522(h)	8–23	3
	6–62	37
545(3)	6–62	
	6–62	39
	6–86	6
545(4)	6–62	
	6–62	40
	6–62	42
546	3–18	21
	6–61	60
	6–66	7
	6–82	1
	6–82	4
	6–82	6
	8–23	9
546(a)	6–60	26
	6–60	27
	6–73	
	6–73	1
	6–73	2
	6–80	
	6–80	7
	6–80	8
	6–80	20
	6–80	21
	6–81	
	6–81	1
	6–81	2
	6–82	
	6–82	1
	6–82	3
	6–82	4
	6–82	6
	6–82	7
	6–83	
	6–83	8
	6–83	13
	6–83	15
	6–84	
	6–84	2
	6–90	
	6–90	1
	8–29	
	8–29	10
	8–29	12
546(a)(1)	6–11	6
	6–82	7
	6–83	
	6–83	3
	6–83	12
	6–83	16
	6–84	
546(a)(2)	6–83	
	6–83	13
	6–83	17
546(b)	3–18	
	3–18	15
	3–18	17
	3–18	19
	3–18	20
	3–18	21
	3–18	22

TABLE OF STATUTES

UNITED STATES CODE ANNOTATED
11 U.S.C.A.—Bankruptcy

Sec.	This Work Sec.	Note
546(b) (Cont'd)	3–18	29
	4–15	
	6–12	
	6–12	20
	6–61	
	6–61	58
	6–61	59
	6–61	60
	6–62	25
	6–77	
	6–77	16
	6–77	17
	6–77	19
546(c)	6–1	5
	6–63	6
	6–64	
	6–64	2
	6–65	
	6–65	2
	6–65	4
	6–65	9
	6–65	12
	6–65	17
	6–66	
	6–66	2
	6–66	11
	6–67	
	6–67	10
	6–67	11
	12–15	2
546(c)(1)	6–64	
	6–65	
	6–65	5
	6–66	1
	6–66	5
546(c)(2)	6–65	
	6–65	9
	6–67	
	6–67	10
	6–67	11
546(d)	6–64	2
546(e)	6–52	
	6–85	
	6–85	6
	6–85	16
	6–85	21
546(e–f)	6–85	5
546(f)	6–85	
	6–85	6
546(g)	6–85	
	6–85	22
547	1–2	
	1–4	14
	2–5	
	2–11	
	2–17	
	2–17	13
	3–11	
	3–18	
	3–34	
	4–7	
	4–15	
	6–3	

UNITED STATES CODE ANNOTATED
11 U.S.C.A.—Bankruptcy

Sec.	This Work Sec.	Note
547 (Cont'd)	6–4	
	6–5	
	6–6	
	6–6	3
	6–6	7
	6–6	8
	6–7	
	6–7	4
	6–10	
	6–10	13
	6–10	14
	6–10	18
	6–11	
	6–11	6
	6–12	
	6–12	8
	6–12	19
	6–13	
	6–14	
	6–16	
	6–18	
	6–19	
	6–20	20
	6–21	
	6–24	3
	6–25	
	6–27	
	6–32	
	6–34	
	6–35	
	6–35	5
	6–36	
	6–36	12
	6–38	
	6–38	18
	6–39	35
	6–39	39
	6–49	
	6–49	20
	6–50	5
	6–55	
	6–55	3
	6–59	
	6–59	11
	6–60	
	6–60	8
	6–61	
	6–61	38
	6–61	51
	6–62	
	6–62	5
	6–62	39
	6–64	
	6–65	
	6–68	
	6–69	13
	6–73	2
	6–78	
	6–82	
	6–88	
	8–22	2
	8–23	5
	8–23	9

UNITED STATES CODE ANNOTATED
11 U.S.C.A.—Bankruptcy

Sec.	This Work Sec.	Note
547 (Cont'd)	10–13	11
547(a)	6–25	4
	6–25	5
547(a)(1)	6–5	8
	6–9	
	6–35	21
	6–35	30
	6–35	32
547(a)(2)	6–25	2
	6–25	10
	6–25	16
	6–25	23
	6–25	31
	6–25	34
	6–25	38
	6–34	20
547(a)(3)	6–35	31
	6–35	33
547(b)	2–5	32
	3–11	15
	3–14	
	3–14	60
	3–18	
	3–18	1
	3–18	2
	3–18	25
	3–18	29
	6–1	6
	6–2	2
	6–3	
	6–4	
	6–4	1
	6–5	
	6–5	8
	6–6	
	6–6	7
	6–7	
	6–8	
	6–9	
	6–10	
	6–11	
	6–12	
	6–16	
	6–16	1
	6–18	30
	6–19	
	6–21	
	6–21	9
	6–22	
	6–23	
	6–24	
	6–25	
	6–27	
	6–27	17
	6–28	
	6–29	
	6–32	
	6–33	
	6–34	
	6–35	
	6–36	
	6–37	
	6–38	

UNITED STATES CODE ANNOTATED
11 U.S.C.A.—Bankruptcy

Sec.	This Work Sec.	Note
547(b) (Cont'd)	6–57	1
	6–59	
	6–61	
	6–62	
	6–65	15
	6–72	
	6–79	5
	6–79	10
	6–80	1
	6–86	
	6–87	14
	6–88	
	8–23	
	8–23	5
	8–23	9
547(b)(1)	3–14	61
	6–8	1
	6–9	
	6–10	7
	6–59	10
547(b)(2)	3–18	5
	6–19	
	6–19	1
	6–23	
	6–28	
547(b)(3)	6–18	1
547(b)(4)	6–11	
	6–11	6
	6–14	
	6–16	
	7–26	1
547(b)(4)(A)	6–11	3
	6–79	7
547(b)(4)(B)	6–10	7
	6–10	8
	6–11	4
	6–17	
	6–17	27
	6–79	6
547(b)(5)	6–9	
	6–10	7
	6–20	
	6–20	1
	6–20	3
	6–20	11
	6–20	12
	6–20	17
	6–20	21
	6–21	
	6–35	37
	6–36	16
	8–23	
	8–23	9
547(b)(5)(C)	6–20	12
547(c)	6–3	
	6–6	7
	6–10	
	6–16	
	6–19	
	6–20	21
	6–22	
	6–22	5
	6–25	52

TABLE OF STATUTES

UNITED STATES CODE ANNOTATED
11 U.S.C.A.—Bankruptcy

Sec.	This Work Sec.	Note
547(c) (Cont'd)	6–27	17
	6–28	
	6–31	16
	6–35	
	6–61	
	6–62	
	6–79	
	8–23	9
547(c)(1)	6–10	
	6–10	18
	6–10	19
	6–23	
	6–23	3
	6–24	
	6–24	2
	6–24	4
	6–24	6
	6–25	
	6–25	1
	6–25	2
	6–25	3
	6–25	13
	6–25	15
	6–25	20
	6–25	22
	6–25	40
	6–25	52
	6–26	
	6–26	7
	6–27	
	6–27	2
	6–27	15
	6–27	16
	6–28	
	6–28	2
	6–28	3
	6–29	
	6–33	
	6–34	
	6–35	
	6–35	6
	6–59	5
547(c)(1)(A)	6–25	20
	6–25	52
	6–26	1
	6–28	1
547(c)(1)(B)	6–27	1
547(c)(2)	6–19	17
	6–27	15
	6–29	
	6–29	6
	6–29	7
	6–29	9
	6–30	
	6–30	3
	6–30	7
	6–31	
	6–31	3
	6–31	7
	6–31	8
	6–31	15
	6–31	17
	6–31	19

UNITED STATES CODE ANNOTATED
11 U.S.C.A.—Bankruptcy

Sec.	This Work Sec.	Note
547(c)(2) (Cont'd)	6–31	21
	6–32	
	6–32	8
	6–32	9
	6–34	
	6–35	40
547(c)(2)(A)	6–29	14
	6–30	
	6–30	1
	6–30	9
547(c)(2)(B)	6–29	
	6–29	8
	6–29	9
	6–29	15
	6–30	9
	6–31	
	6–31	2
	6–31	19
	6–31	20
547(c)(2)(C)	6–29	16
	6–30	9
	6–31	
	6–31	19
	6–31	21
547(c)(3)	6–4	9
	6–13	4
	6–24	
	6–24	2
	6–24	7
	6–27	
	6–33	
	6–33	3
	6–33	6
	6–33	7
	6–33	9
	6–33	15
	6–33	20
	6–34	
	6–35	
	6–35	7
547(c)(3)(A)	6–33	
547(c)(3)(B)	6–24	7
	6–33	
	6–33	9
547(c)(4)	6–25	20
	6–34	
	6–34	1
	6–34	10
	6–34	18
	6–34	20
	6–34	27
	6–35	
	6–35	8
547(c)(4)(A)	6–34	21
547(c)(4)(B)	6–34	25
547(c)(5)	6–5	2
	6–5	3
	6–5	8
	6–35	
	6–35	8
	6–35	15
	6–35	16
	6–35	17

UNITED STATES CODE ANNOTATED
11 U.S.C.A.—Bankruptcy

Sec.	This Work Sec.	Note
547(c)(5) (Cont'd)	6–35	18
	6–35	22
	6–35	23
	6–35	24
	6–35	25
	6–35	27
	6–35	28
	6–35	29
	6–35	33
	6–35	36
	6–41	
547(c)(6)	3–18	29
	6–36	
	6–36	11
	6–36	12
	6–36	14
	6–36	15
	6–62	6
547(c)(7)	6–37	
	6–37	1
	6–37	2
	6–37	4
	6–37	10
547(d)	6–9	7
547(d)(5)	6–20	5
547(e)	6–5	4
	6–11	
	6–11	9
	6–12	
	6–13	4
	6–19	12
	6–24	
	6–27	
	6–27	11
	6–27	13
	6–33	
	6–34	
	6–34	13
547(e)(1)	6–14	
547(e)(1)(A)	6–11	15
	6–12	3
547(e)(1)(B)	6–11	16
	6–12	4
547(e)(2)	6–14	
	6–33	8
	6–34	14
	6–36	6
	6–36	13
547(e)(2)(A)	3–18	
	3–18	4
	3–18	12
	3–18	26
	6–11	12
	6–11	22
	6–12	2
	6–13	1
	6–16	
	6–24	9
	3–18	3
547(e)(2)(B)	6–11	13
	6–11	23
	6–12	1
	6–13	4

UNITED STATES CODE ANNOTATED
11 U.S.C.A.—Bankruptcy

Sec.	This Work Sec.	Note
547(e)(2)(B) (Cont'd)	6–27	10
	6–35	42
547(e)(2)(C)	3–18	6
	3–18	27
	6–11	14
	6–12	14
	6–34	16
	6–61	20
	3–18	7
547(e)(3)	6–11	17
	6–14	
	6–14	1
	6–14	2
	6–15	
	6–15	1
	6–35	4
547(f)	6–18	20
	6–49	20
	6–49	26
547(g)	6–3	12
	6–3	13
	6–18	19
	6–22	5
548	2–5	
	2–13	7
	2–17	
	6–2	21
	6–2	24
	6–2	32
	6–9	1
	6–19	5
	6–21	
	6–21	8
	6–21	11
	6–25	
	6–46	
	6–46	5
	6–47	
	6–47	1
	6–47	7
	6–47	9
	6–47	10
	6–47	13
	6–48	4
	6–49	
	6–49	20
	6–49	23
	6–49	40
	6–49	49
	6–50	
	6–50	5
	6–51	
	6–52	
	6–53	
	6–53	9
	6–54	
	6–54	1
	6–54	10
	6–55	
	6–56	
	6–56	14
	6–58	
	6–59	

TABLE OF STATUTES

UNITED STATES CODE ANNOTATED
11 U.S.C.A.—Bankruptcy

Sec.	This Work Sec.	Note
548 (Cont'd)	6–60	
	6–60	4
	6–60	6
	6–60	8
	6–61	38
	6–65	
	6–65	8
	6–68	
	6–71	
	6–71	25
	6–73	2
	6–78	
	6–82	
	6–88	
	6–93	5
	8–22	2
	8–23	3
	8–23	5
	8–32	
	8–32	8
	10–13	12
548(a)	6–1	7
	6–2	2
	6–25	37
	6–47	
	6–47	7
	6–47	8
	6–47	10
	6–49	3
	6–50	
	6–51	2
	6–51	3
	6–51	4
	6–52	
	6–52	39
	6–54	
	6–54	5
	6–54	8
	6–57	
	6–57	1
	6–59	
	6–59	3
	6–60	16
	6–80	1
548(a)(1)	6–46	6
	6–47	2
	6–47	9
	6–48	
	6–48	1
	6–48	5
	6–48	6
	6–48	18
	6–49	
	6–52	
	6–52	9
	6–57	
	6–57	3
	6–59	
	6–59	2
	6–59	3
	6–60	5
	8–32	9
548(a)(2)	6–9	1

UNITED STATES CODE ANNOTATED
11 U.S.C.A.—Bankruptcy

Sec.	This Work Sec.	Note
548(a)(2) (Cont'd)	6–46	7
	6–47	8
	6–48	
	6–49	
	6–49	1
	6–49	2
	6–49	43
	6–49	58
	6–50	
	6–51	
	6–52	
	6–52	39
	6–52	49
	6–53	
	6–55	
	6–56	
	6–56	14
	6–57	
	6–58	
	6–60	12
	6–71	16
	12–14	
548(a)(2)(A)	6–47	3
	6–47	4
	6–47	5
	6–48	23
	6–49	9
	6–49	29
	6–50	21
	6–71	23
548(a)(2)(B)(i)	6–47	3
	6–47	4
	6–47	5
	6–49	5
	6–49	6
	6–49	7
	6–49	8
	6–51	8
	6–51	18
548(b)	6–1	7
	6–2	2
	6–46	7
	6–47	
	6–47	6
	6–49	
	6–49	1
	6–49	2
	6–49	4
	6–49	10
	6–80	1
548(c)	6–49	62
	6–50	
	6–50	3
	6–50	5
	6–50	6
	6–50	10
	6–50	16
	6–50	18
	6–50	19
	6–50	21
	6–50	23
	6–50	24
	6–50	28

UNITED STATES CODE ANNOTATED
11 U.S.C.A.—Bankruptcy

Sec.	This Work Sec.	Note
548(c) (Cont'd)	6–50	35
	6–50	37
	6–52	
	6–52	39
	6–58	2
	6–60	29
	6–71	25
	6–87	3
	6–87	7
	6–88	23
	6–89	1
548(d)(1)	6–47	11
	6–47	12
	6–51	6
	6–55	
	6–55	1
548(d)(2)(A)	6–49	30
	6–49	32
	6–49	37
	6–49	42
	6–50	20
	6–56	49
	6–71	15
549	2–5	
	2–5	32
	2–8	20
	3–18	
	3–18	14
	3–18	15
	3–32	
	3–32	28
	3–32	35
	3–33	
	4–15	
	6–11	6
	6–16	
	6–65	
	6–68	
	6–69	2
	6–69	3
	6–69	7
	6–69	8
	6–69	9
	6–69	13
	6–70	3
	6–71	
	6–71	25
	6–72	10
	6–72	16
	6–72	17
	6–73	
	6–73	4
	6–73	10
	6–73	11
	6–73	20
	6–73	22
	6–76	
	6–77	7
	6–88	
	8–22	2
	8–28	
	12–15	
549(a)	3–18	

UNITED STATES CODE ANNOTATED
11 U.S.C.A.—Bankruptcy

Sec.	This Work Sec.	Note
549(a) (Cont'd)	3–18	11
	3–21	111
	3–32	36
	3–33	43
	6–1	8
	6–68	
	6–69	1
	6–69	2
	6–69	6
	6–69	10
	6–69	14
	6–70	
	6–70	2
	6–71	
	6–71	17
	6–72	
	6–72	10
	6–73	
	6–73	9
	6–73	14
	6–74	
	6–74	13
	6–76	5
	6–76	6
	6–80	1
	6–82	3
	8–28	21
549(a)(1)	3–32	24
	6–69	7
	6–69	8
549(a)(2)	2–17	
	2–17	20
549(a)(2)(A)	6–71	
	6–71	1
	6–71	6
549(a)(2)(B)	2–17	7
	4–15	
	6–70	1
549(b)	2–5	33
	3–32	27
	6–2	2
	6–71	
	6–71	8
	6–71	9
	6–71	10
	6–71	11
	6–71	16
	6–71	20
	6–71	21
	6–73	
	6–73	10
	6–74	
	6–87	3
	6–87	7
	6–89	1
549(c)	3–32	25
	3–32	26
	3–32	27
	6–71	
	6–71	12
	6–71	24
	6–71	25
	6–72	

TABLE OF STATUTES

UNITED STATES CODE ANNOTATED
11 U.S.C.A.—Bankruptcy

Sec.	This Work Sec.	Note
549(c) (Cont'd)	6–72	1
	6–72	3
	6–72	4
	6–72	5
	6–72	6
	6–72	7
	6–72	10
	6–72	12
	6–72	14
	6–72	16
	6–72	17
	6–73	
	6–73	10
	6–73	22
	6–74	
	6–87	3
	6–87	7
	6–89	1
549(d)	3–32	28
	3–33	47
	6–73	
	6–73	3
	6–73	4
	6–73	11
	6–73	20
	6–76	6
	6–82	3
550	2–8	17
	3–33	
	6–10	
	6–10	1
	6–10	14
	6–10	16
	6–52	
	6–60	29
	6–69	9
	6–71	21
	6–71	25
	6–72	16
	6–79	2
	6–80	
	6–80	8
	6–80	18
	6–80	20
	6–87	
	6–87	1
	6–87	3
	6–88	
	6–88	18
	6–88	30
	6–88	37
	6–89	
	6–90	
	8–22	
	8–22	8
	8–30	
550(a)	3–33	44
	3–34	
	6–10	
	6–10	11
	6–10	18
	6–50	
	6–50	1

UNITED STATES CODE ANNOTATED
11 U.S.C.A.—Bankruptcy

Sec.	This Work Sec.	Note
550(a) (Cont'd)	6–50	5
	6–52	30
	6–53	2
	6–53	4
	6–56	55
	6–60	29
	6–69	14
	6–71	25
	6–79	11
	6–80	2
	6–80	13
	6–80	18
	6–87	
	6–87	4
	6–88	
	6–88	1
	6–88	19
	6–88	35
	6–88	37
	6–88	46
	6–88	51
	6–89	
	6–89	2
	6–89	21
	8–22	3
	8–30	1
	12–14	
550(a)(1)	3–14	62
	3–14	63
	6–10	
	6–10	1
	6–10	14
	6–52	
	6–52	25
	6–52	26
	6–52	30
	6–52	39
	6–53	5
	6–72	16
	6–79	14
	6–87	3
	6–87	18
	6–88	
	6–88	6
	6–88	16
	6–88	18
	6–88	32
	6–88	36
	6–88	37
	6–88	44
	6–88	45
	6–88	47
	6–88	49
	6–89	10
550(a)(2)	6–10	1
	6–10	15
	6–52	30
	6–79	13
	6–88	
	6–88	7
	6–88	9
	6–88	12
	6–88	13

TABLE OF STATUTES

UNITED STATES CODE ANNOTATED
11 U.S.C.A.—Bankruptcy

Sec.	This Work Sec.	Note
550(a)(2) (Cont'd)	6–88	18
	6–88	21
	6–88	47
550(b)	6–10	15
	6–50	
	6–50	3
	6–50	34
	6–52	30
	6–52	40
	6–60	29
	6–79	15
	6–87	8
	6–88	
	6–88	5
	6–88	7
	6–88	18
	6–88	21
	6–88	37
	6–88	42
	6–88	47
550(b)(1)	6–50	34
	6–52	30
	6–88	
	6–88	10
	6–88	17
	6–88	21
	6–88	23
	6–88	24
	6–88	29
550(b)(2)	6–72	16
	6–88	
	6–88	11
550(c)	3–32	27
	6–10	1
	6–50	2
	6–88	33
	8–29	
550(d)	6–50	3
	6–50	23
	6–50	29
	6–50	31
	6–60	29
	6–87	3
	6–87	7
	6–87	13
	6–89	
	6–89	4
	6–89	16
	6–89	20
	6–89	31
550(d)(1)	6–89	
	6–89	5
	6–89	7
	6–89	11
	6–89	15
	6–89	22
550(d)(1)(A)	6–89	
	6–89	14
	6–89	16
	6–89	17
	6–89	20
550(d)(1)(B)	6–89	
	6–89	14

UNITED STATES CODE ANNOTATED
11 U.S.C.A.—Bankruptcy

Sec.	This Work Sec.	Note
550(d)(2)	6–89	
	6–89	6
550(d)(2)(A)	6–89	26
550(d)(2)(B)	6–89	27
550(d)(2)(C)	6–89	25
550(d)(2)(D)	6–89	4
	6–89	24
550(d)(2)(E)	6–89	28
550(e)	6–79	15
	6–80	7
	6–80	8
	6–80	10
	6–80	20
	6–90	
	6–90	3
	8–29	11
	8–29	12
551	2–8	17
	6–1	3
	6–61	12
	6–79	1
	6–79	8
	6–80	
	6–80	4
	6–80	16
	6–80	19
	6–80	20
	6–86	
	6–86	1
	6–86	2
	6–86	4
	6–86	5
	6–86	10
	6–86	16
	6–86	19
	8–22	
	8–28	
	8–28	18
	8–30	6
	8–30	8
	8–30	9
552	6–68	
	6–75	
	6–76	
	6–76	2
	6–76	3
	6–77	
	6–77	7
	6–77	8
	6–78	3
552(a)	3–11	
	3–11	19
	3–11	26
	6–67	16
	6–73	20
	6–76	
	6–76	2
	6–76	3
	6–76	5
	6–76	6
	6–77	
	6–77	1
	6–77	21

TABLE OF STATUTES

UNITED STATES CODE ANNOTATED
11 U.S.C.A.—Bankruptcy

Sec.	This Work Sec.	Note
552(b)	3–11	19
	3–11	26
	6–76	2
	6–76	3
	6–77	
	6–77	1
	6–77	6
	6–77	7
	6–77	8
	6–77	9
	6–77	10
	6–77	20
	6–77	21
	6–77	22
	6–78	
	6–78	3
	6–78	4
	6–78	14
	6–78	17
552(d)(10)(E)	8–17	17
553	3–15	
	5–25	
	6–4	
	6–31	8
	6–38	
	6–38	1
	6–38	3
	6–38	18
	6–39	
	6–39	1
	6–39	14
	6–39	39
	6–40	
	6–40	2
	6–40	3
	6–40	4
	6–40	5
	6–40	6
	6–40	9
	6–40	14
	6–40	16
	6–40	22
	6–40	38
	6–41	
	6–41	5
	6–41	7
	6–41	9
	6–41	36
	6–41	47
	6–42	
	6–43	
	6–44	2
	6–45	
	6–45	6
	6–73	2
	6–82	
	6–94	6
	8–22	2
	8–22	11
553(a)	3–14	54
	3–15	3
	6–1	9
	6–39	

UNITED STATES CODE ANNOTATED
11 U.S.C.A.—Bankruptcy

Sec.	This Work Sec.	Note
553(a) (Cont'd)	6–39	1
	6–40	
	6–41	9
	6–42	1
	6–43	2
	6–43	21
	6–45	6
	6–45	24
	6–45	33
553(a)(1)	6–41	1
553(a)(2)	6–41	
	6–41	2
	6–41	7
	6–41	9
	6–41	10
	6–41	11
553(a)(2)(A)	6–41	5
553(a)(2)(B)	6–41	6
553(a)(3)	6–41	
	6–41	3
	6–41	7
	6–41	9
	6–41	19
	6–41	23
	6–41	25
	6–41	26
553(b)	6–1	9
	6–41	
	6–41	4
	6–41	36
	6–41	46
	6–41	47
	6–80	1
	6–88	
	8–23	5
553(b)(1)	6–2	2
	6–41	34
	6–41	44
	6–41	49
	6–85	22
553(b)(1)(A)	6–41	49
553(b)(1)(B)	6–41	49
553(b)(2)	6–41	35
	6–41	43
	6–41	49
553(c)	6–41	8
553(h)	8–22	17
554	1–7	
	2–8	39
	7–47	
	7–48	
	8–33	
554(a)	11–9	
	6–86	2
	8–33	44
554(b)	6–60	20
	7–48	
555	5–26	10
	6–85	27
556	5–26	11
	6–85	26
557	5–26	12
558	6–39	1

TABLE OF STATUTES

UNITED STATES CODE ANNOTATED
11 U.S.C.A.—Bankruptcy

Sec.	This Work Sec.	Note
558 (Cont'd)	6–94	
	6–94	1
	6–94	2
	6–94	3
	6–94	4
559	5–1	
	5–26	13
	6–85	25
560	3–15	16
	5–1	
	5–26	14
	6–85	
	6–85	24
586	9–4	
586(e)(2)	9–4	44
647(b)(2)	6–8	5
Ch. 7	1–4	
	1–5	
	1–5	1
	1–6	
	1–7	
	1–7	3
	1–8	
	1–9	
	1–10	
	Ch. 2, p.68	
	2–1	
	2–1	1
	2–2	
	2–2	7
	2–2	9
	2–3	
	2–5	
	2–5	35
	2–8	
	2–8	2
	2–8	36
	2–12	
	2–13	
	2–13	7
	2–13	12
	2–13	13
	2–13	16
	2–14	
	2–14	2
	2–16	
	2–16	2
	2–16	7
	2–16	20
	2–17	
	2–18	
	2–18	2
	2–19	
	2–19	1
	2–19	5
	3–1	
	3–4	
	3–9	
	3–9	4
	3–10	
	3–10	81
	3–11	14

UNITED STATES CODE ANNOTATED
11 U.S.C.A.—Bankruptcy

Sec.	This Work Sec.	Note
Ch. 7 (Cont'd)	3–11	20
	3–12	
	3–12	5
	3–12	8
	3–20	47
	3–23	
	3–23	32
	3–23	42
	3–23	46
	3–25	5
	3–25	6
	3–27	22
	3–31	10
	3–32	4
	5–8	
	5–9	
	5–10	
	5–10	14
	5–12	
	5–17	
	6–2	
	6–2	7
	6–2	21
	6–2	24
	6–3	
	6–11	6
	6–20	
	6–20	3
	6–20	20
	6–20	23
	6–21	
	6–35	
	6–36	
	6–36	17
	6–39	15
	6–40	4
	6–44	
	6–44	6
	6–47	10
	6–58	
	6–61	51
	6–68	
	6–71	12
	6–73	4
	6–83	
	6–83	16
	6–88	14
	6–93	66
	7–1	
	7–2	
	7–2	6
	7–3	
	7–5	
	7–9	
	7–10	2
	7–11	
	7–13	
	7–14	
	7–15	
	7–16	
	7–17	
	7–18	
	7–19	

TABLE OF STATUTES

UNITED STATES CODE ANNOTATED
11 U.S.C.A.—Bankruptcy

Sec.	This Work Sec.	Note
Ch. 7 (Cont'd)	7–24	
	7–25	
	7–27	
	7–27	8
	7–29	
	7–30	
	7–31	
	7–33	
	7–35	
	7–36	
	7–39	
	7–39	2
	7–44	
	7–45	
	7–45	13
	7–45	17
	7–46	
	7–47	
	7–47	2
	7–47	5
	7–49	
	8–1	12
	8–2	
	8–2	5
	8–3	
	8–3	21
	8–3	22
	8–9	16
	8–22	19
	8–22	20
	8–24	
	8–28	3
	8–29	13
	8–32	8
	9–2	
	9–2	1
	9–2	3
	9–2	19
	9 2	23
	9–2	27
	9–3	
	9–6	
	9–7	
	9–8	
	9–9	
	9–10	
	9–11	
	9–12	
	9–14	
	9–14	21
	9–16	
	9–18	16
	9–19	
	9–21	
	9–23	
	9–25	
	9–27	
	9–30	
	9–30	8
	9–30	10
	10–2	
	10–15	
	10–18	

UNITED STATES CODE ANNOTATED
11 U.S.C.A.—Bankruptcy

Sec.	This Work Sec.	Note
Ch. 7 (Cont'd)	10–25	
	10–26	2
	10–30	
	10–31	
	10–31	2
	10–33	1
	10–34	
	11–2	2
	11–3	
	11–3	3
	11–4	
	11–8	
	11–9	
	11–10	
	11–11	
	11–12	
	11–17	
	11–32	
	11–33	
	12–1	
	12–10	
Ch. 7, § 350(b)	3–23	19
Ch. 7, Subch. III	1–5	
Ch. 7, Subch. IV	1–5	
701	6–83	
	7–2	
701—799	10–1	
701(a)(1)	6–68	4
	7–2	
702	1–7	
	6–83	
	7–2	
702(c)	1–4	2
702(d)	6–83	6
704	1–7	
	7–2	
	7–2	7
	9–2	3
704(1)	7–2	
704(2)	10–5	1
704(5)	10–5	1
704(7)	10–5	1
	11–18	2
704(8)	10–5	1
704(9)	10–5	1
705	7–2	
706	2–5	
	2–13	12
	2–16	29
	2–18	1
	7–1	
	7–2	
707	2–12	
	3–23	26
	7–1	
707(a)	2–13	
	2–13	2
	7–2	
	7–42	
	7–43	
	7–43	1
707(a)(1)	7–43	
707(a)(2)	2–2	24

TABLE OF STATUTES

UNITED STATES CODE ANNOTATED
11 U.S.C.A.—Bankruptcy

Sec.	This Work Sec.	Note
707(a)(2) (Cont'd)	7–43	
	7–43	5
707(a)(3)	7–43	
707(b)	2–14	
	2–14	1
	2–14	2
	7–2	
	7–42	
	7–44	
	7–45	
	7–45	13
	7–46	
721	1–5	1
	4–1	1
722	7–1	
	7–10	2
	7–37	
	7–39	
	7–39	1
	7–39	2
	7–39	3
	7–47	
	7–47	2
	7–48	
	7–48	5
	7–49	
	8–31	
	8–31	12
723	11–32	
	11–33	
	11–34	
	12–2	4
	12–15	
723(a)	11–32	
723(b)	11–32	
723(c)	11–33	
724	6–62	4
724(a)	6–1	10
	6–62	4
	6–88	
	8–22	2
724(b)	6–20	20
	6–36	18
	6–36	19
	6–62	4
726	1–7	
	6–3	1
	6–20	9
	6–20	12
	6–91	
	7–9	
	7–10	
	7–14	
	7–15	
	7–15	8
726(a)	6–91	1
	6–93	66
	7–14	
	7–15	
	11–33	
726(a)(1)	7–15	
	7–15	7
726(a)(2)	7–14	

UNITED STATES CODE ANNOTATED
11 U.S.C.A.—Bankruptcy

Sec.	This Work Sec.	Note
726(a)(2) (Cont'd)	7–15	
	7–15	19
726(a)(2)(C)	7–15	
	7–15	5
726(a)(3)	7–15	
	7–15	5
726(a)(4)	6–62	4
	6–93	66
	7–15	
726(a)(5)	7–14	
726(b)	10–31	
	2–5	35
726(c)	2–8	8
727	2–16	
	5–7	2
	6–58	
	7–1	
	7–5	
	7–17	
	7–18	
	7–21	
	7–36	
	9–7	
	10–30	
727(a)	1–7	
	6–58	5
	6–59	11
	7–17	
727(a)(1)	3–23	42
	7–16	
	7–17	
	7–18	
	10–30	
	10–30	3
	10–30	8
727(a)(1)—(a)(10)	9–2	14
727(a)(2)	6–58	6
	7–19	
	7–21	
727(a)(2)(A)	7–19	
	8–32	3
727(a)(3)	7–20	
	7–20	1
	7–20	4
	7–21	
	7–22	2
727(a)(3)(A)	7–19	
727(a)(4)	7–19	
	7–21	
	7–21	2
	7–26	
727(a)(4)(A)	7–21	
727(a)(5)	7–22	
	7–22	1
	7–22	2
727(a)(6)	7–23	
727(a)(8)	7–17	
	9–2	16
727(a)(9)	7–17	
	9–2	16
	9–12	
727(b)	3–11	5
	7–16	

UNITED STATES CODE ANNOTATED
11 U.S.C.A.—Bankruptcy

Sec.	This Work Sec.	Note
727(b) (Cont'd)	7–18	
727(c)	7–2	8
	11–33	1
741(5)	6–85	
	6–85	8
741(8)	6–85	
	6–85	9
761(15)	6–85	
	6–85	8
764(c)	6–85	
801—926	10–1	
Ch. 9	1–5	
	Ch. 2, p.68	
	2–15	
	2–15	2
	6–2	
	6–2	7
	7–24	
	7–30	
	11–4	
921	2–15	2
922	3–10	38
926(a)	6–2	7
1006(1)	9–1	16
1006(8)	9–1	10
1052	9–1	12
1061	9–1	11
	9–1	12
Ch. 11	1–4	
	1–4	6
	1–5	
	1–5	2
	1–6	
	1–9	
	1–9	1
	1–10	
	Ch. 2, p.68	
	2–1	
	2–1	1
	2–2	
	2–3	
	2–5	
	2–5	7
	2–5	27
	2–5	35
	2–8	
	2–8	2
	2–8	36
	2–8	37
	2–12	
	2–13	
	2–13	1
	2–13	7
	2–13	12
	2–15	
	2–15	10
	2–15	22
	2–15	24
	2–16	
	2–16	2
	2–16	20

UNITED STATES CODE ANNOTATED
11 U.S.C.A.—Bankruptcy

Sec.	This Work Sec.	Note
Ch. 11 (Cont'd)	2–17	
	2–18	
	2–18	2
	2–18	6
	2–19	
	2–19	5
	3–1	
	3–2	9
	3–5	6
	3–5	19
	3–9	
	3–10	
	3–11	
	3–11	12
	3–11	23
	3–14	65
	3–22	
	3–22	24
	3–22	29
	3–23	
	3–23	34
	3–23	44
	3–23	47
	3–23	48
	3–25	
	3–25	2
	3–25	6
	3–25	25
	3–25	31
	3–25	52
	3–27	15
	3–27	18
	3–27	35
	3–28	
	3–28	13
	3–29	
	3–29	5
	3–29	12
	3–29	13
	3–29	14
	3–31	84
	4–1	
	4–3	
	4–4	
	4–5	
	4–6	
	4–10	
	4–11	
	4–12	
	4–13	
	4–14	
	4–15	
	Ch. 5, p. 484	
	5–1	1
	5–2	
	5–2	7
	5–4	
	5–7	
	5–7	12
	5–9	
	5–10	
	5–10	4

TABLE OF STATUTES

UNITED STATES CODE ANNOTATED
11 U.S.C.A.—Bankruptcy

Sec.	Sec.	This Work Note
Ch. 11 (Cont'd)	5–11	
	5–12	
	5–14	2
	5–15	
	5–15	11
	5–22	
	5–23	
	5–24	
	6–2	
	6–2	7
	6–2	24
	6–2	28
	6–2	29
	6–2	30
	6–2	32
	6–11	6
	6–20	
	6–39	15
	6–40	4
	6–43	7
	6–44	5
	6–45	7
	6–47	10
	6–61	
	6–61	51
	6–67	
	6–70	
	6–71	13
	6–73	4
	6–75	
	6–77	1
	6–77	20
	6–83	
	6–83	12
	6–83	16
	6–93	66
	7–1	
	7–2	
	7–2	6
	7–3	
	7–5	
	7–7	
	7–7	15
	7–9	
	7–10	
	7–11	
	7–12	
	7–14	
	7–17	
	7–19	
	7–26	
	7–27	
	7–27	7
	7–29	
	7–31	
	7–41	
	7–42	
	8–1	12
	8–2	
	8–2	5
	8–3	
	8–3	21
	8–3	22

UNITED STATES CODE ANNOTATED
11 U.S.C.A.—Bankruptcy

Sec.	Sec.	This Work Note
Ch. 11 (Cont'd)	9–2	
	9–3	
	9–4	
	9–4	18
	9–5	
	9–6	
	9–7	
	9–11	
	9–12	13
	9–15	
	9–16	
	9–17	
	9–18	
	9–20	
	9–23	
	9–25	
	9–26	
	9–26	1
	9–27	
	9–30	
	10–1	
	10 1	1
	10–1	4
	10–2	
	10–2	2
	10–3	
	10–4	
	10–5	
	10–7	
	10–8	
	10–10	
	10–11	
	10–12	
	10–13	
	10–14	
	10–15	
	10–16	1
	10–17	
	10–18	
	10–21	
	10–22	8
	10–23	
	10–23	4
	10–24	12
	10–25	
	10–26	
	10–29	
	10–29	4
	10–30	
	10–31	
	10–31	2
	10–33	1
	10–33	2
	10–34	
	11–1	
	11–4	
	11–8	
	11–8	1
	11–9	
	11–10	
	11–11	
	11–12	
	11–13	

TABLE OF STATUTES

UNITED STATES CODE ANNOTATED
11 U.S.C.A.—Bankruptcy

Sec.	This Work Sec.	Note
Ch. 11 (Cont'd)	11–15	
	11–16	
	11–18	
	11–18	2
	11–21	
	11–22	
	11–24	
	11–30	
	11–30	22
	11–31	
	11–32	
	11–33	
	11–33	1
	11–35	
	11–36	
	11–36	7
	11–36	9
	11–37	
	11–38	
	11–40	
	11–41	
	12–1	
	12–4	
	12–5	
	12–6	9
	12–7	
	12–8	
	12–11	7
	12–13	
	12–15	
Ch. 11, Subch. 14	1–5	
1103(c)(3)	11–18	2
1103(c)(5)	6–2	29
	10–13	
1103(e)	10–13	1
1104	1–4	8
	6–2	10
	6–83	14
	10–7	5
	10–8	
1104(a)(1)	10–4	1
	10–8	
	10–8	4
1104(a)(2)	10–4	1
	10–8	11
1104(b)	10–10	
	11–24	5
1104(b)(1)	10–10	
1104(b)(2)	10–10	
	10–10	5
1105	10–8	4
1105(a)(2)	10–8	5
1106	6–2	10
1106(a)	10–9	1
1106(a)(1)	10–5	1
	11–18	2
1106(a)(2)	12–14	17
	12–14	18
1106(a)(3)	10–5	1
	11–18	2
1106(a)(4)	10–5	1
	11–18	2
1106(b)	1–4	6

UNITED STATES CODE ANNOTATED
11 U.S.C.A.—Bankruptcy

Sec.	This Work Sec.	Note
1106(b) (Cont'd)	10–10	
1107	1–4	6
	2–5	
	4–1	
	10–7	
	10–14	1
1107(a)	4–6	
	6–2	8
	6–61	75
	6–83	11
	10–5	1
1108	5–10	4
	10–9	1
	10–15	2
1109	10–13	2
1109(b)	1–4	6
	6–2	28
	6–2	29
	10–13	
	11–1	3
	11–8	
	11–8	10
1110	1–4	6
	3–17	
	3–17	1
	3–17	5
	3–17	18
	3–17	20
	5–1	
	5–26	15
1111(a)	9–20	
	10–29	12
	12–14	17
	12–14	18
1111(b)	9–6	
	10–25	
	10–27	4
1111(b)(1)	10–26	
1111(b)(1)(A)	10–26	1
1111(b)(1)(A)(ii)	10–26	3
1111(b)(1)(B)	10–28	
	10–28	2
1111(b)(1)(B)(i)	10–28	3
1111(b)(2)	9–23	
	10–20	3
	10–25	
	10–26	
	10–27	
	10–27	3
	10–27	5
	10–28	
	10–28	1
	10–28	6
1112	2–12	
	2–13	12
	2–15	
	2–15	4
	2–16	29
	2–18	
	2–18	2
	2–19	2
	3–23	26
	4–6	

UNITED STATES CODE ANNOTATED
11 U.S.C.A.—Bankruptcy

Sec.	This Work Sec.	Note
1112 (Cont'd)	12-6	9
1112(a)	1-4	6
1112(b)	2-13	
	2-16	
	2-18	
	2-19	4
	3-29	
	3-29	5
1112(f)	2-18	
1113	3-7	
	3-11	26
	5-1	
	5-26	16
	7-12	
1113(f)	3-22	7
1114	5-1	
	5-26	17
	7-12	
1121	10-3	
	10-11	3
	11-13	
	11-13	1
	11-14	
	11-14	2
	11-15	
	11-16	8
	11-18	
	11-27	
1121(b)	3-25	55
	5-10	
	9-25	
	10-16	1
	11-18	
	11-18	4
1121(c)	9-11	1
	10-16	1
1121(c)(2)	3-25	55
1121(d)	10-16	1
	11-13	2
	11-13	12
	11-14	
	11-14	1
	11-15	1
1122	9-5	
	9-7	
	10-22	
	10-22	8
	10-24	
	10-24	12
1122(a)	10-22	
	10-22	3
	10-24	
	10-24	5
	10-24	7
	10-24	9
1122(b)	10-24	8
	10-24	9
1123	4-15	
	6-2	
	6-2	32
	10-3	
1123(a)(3)	10-23	1
	4-15	

UNITED STATES CODE ANNOTATED
11 U.S.C.A.—Bankruptcy

Sec.	This Work Sec.	Note
1123(a)(3) (Cont'd)	10-16	5
1123(b)(3)(B)	6-2	
	6-2	31
1123(b)(4)	1-5	2
	10-15	5
1124	9-15	
	9-17	
	10-3	
	10-13	4
	10-17	1
	10-23	
	10-23	4
	10-23	5
	10-25	
1124(2)	9-15	
1124(2)(A)	9-17	9
1124(3)(B)	10-23	6
1125	4-4	
	10-3	
	10-16	2
	11-16	
	11-16	7
	11-18	
	11-18	8
	11-19	
	11-22	
1125(a)	11-16	
1125(a)(1)	11-18	
	11-18	3
1125(a)(2)(C)	11-18	2
1125(b)	11-16	
	11-16	7
	11-18	
	11-18	2
	11-18	10
	11-19	
1125(c)	11-16	
1125(e)	11-21	2
1126	4-4	
	10-3	
	10-17	6
	11-23	
	11-24	
1126(b)	10-20	
	11-22	
	11-23	
1126(b)(1)	11-22	
	11-23	
1126(b)(2)	11-22	
1126(c)	10-3	1
	10-17	6
	10-24	2
	11-27	
1126(d)	10-17	6
1126(f)	10-17	1
	10-23	2
1127	2-16	
	10-3	
1127(b)	2-16	13
	10-33	
1128	10-3	
1129	4-14	
	4-15	

TABLE OF STATUTES

UNITED STATES CODE ANNOTATED
11 U.S.C.A.—Bankruptcy

Sec.	This Work Sec.	Note
1129 (Cont'd)	4–4	
	4–7	
	9–6	3
	10–2	
	10–3	
	10–16	2
	10–20	
	10–22	
	10–27	
	10–33	
	11–16	
	11–17	
	11–27	
	11–27	8
	11–32	
	11–41	
1129(a)	3–25	
	3–25	38
	10–3	
	10–17	
	11–32	
1129(a)(1)	10–22	3
	11–17	
1129(a)(10)	10–17	4
	10–18	1
	10–24	9
	11–29	
1129(a)(11)	2–16	12
	10–3	
	10–16	6
1129(a)(3)	2–15	3
	4–15	
1129(a)(5)	11–17	
1129(a)(7)	4–4	
	7–14	
	10–3	
	10–17	6
	10–18	
	10–26	2
	11–17	
	11–30	
	11–32	
1129(a)(7)(A)(ii)	7–14	
	11–25	
	11–32	
1129(a)(8)	10–17	2
	10–17	6
	10–18	1
1129(a)(8)(A)	11–25	
1129(a)(9)	10–15	
	10–15	9
1129(a)(9)(A)	9–5	
1129(b)	3–25	
	3–25	39
	4–14	8
	4–7	
	10–3	
	10–13	
	10–16	
	10–17	
	10–17	6
	10–18	1
	10–19	

UNITED STATES CODE ANNOTATED
11 U.S.C.A.—Bankruptcy

Sec.	This Work Sec.	Note
1129(b) (Cont'd)	10–21	
	10–22	
	10–22	3
	10–24	
	10–24	12
	10–26	2
	10–27	
	10–28	
	11–25	
1129(b)(1)	9–7	
	10–19	1
	10–22	1
1129(b)(2)	3–11	8
	4–7	
	4–7	18
	9–11	
	9–6	
	10–25	
	11–25	
	11–27	
1129(b)(2)(A)	4–7	
	10–19	
	10–20	
	10–24	3
	10–26	4
1129(b)(2)(A)(i)(I)	10–20	2
1129(b)(2)(A)(i)(II)	10–27	
1129(b)(2)(A)(ii)	4–7	
	9–6	3
	10–20	4
	10–20	17
1129(b)(2)(A)(iii)	10–20	6
	10–20	14
1129(b)(2)(B)	4–4	
	10–19	
	10–21	2
	10–24	4
	11–17	
1129(b)(2)(B)(ii)	10–3	
	11–25	
	11–27	
1129(b)(2)(C)	10–19	
	10–21	4
1141	2–8	37
	4–10	
	5–7	2
	9–4	
	10–3	
	10–31	
	11–2	4
	11–3	
	11–3	21
	11–8	
1141(a)	10–31	
	10–31	1
	11–24	
1141(b)	2–16	20
	3–23	47
	10–29	3
1141(c)	3–11	7
	10–29	3
	10–29	10
1141(d)	3–23	33

TABLE OF STATUTES

UNITED STATES CODE ANNOTATED
11 U.S.C.A.—Bankruptcy

Sec.	This Work Sec.	Note
1141(d) (Cont'd)	3–23	47
	10–29	9
	10–29	14
	10–30	
	10–31	
1141(d)(1)	10–30	
	10–30	1
	10–30	4
	10–30	5
1141(d)(1)(A)	3–11	5
	11–3	21
1141(d)(2)	10–30	6
	10–31	1
1141(d)(3)	3–23	43
	10–30	7
	10–31	1
1142	6–70	2
	10–32	
1144	10–33	
1167	5–26	18
1168	3–17	
	3–17	2
1168	5–26	18
1171(b)	4–15	
Ch. 12	1–4	
	1–5	
	1–6	
	1–10	
	Ch. 2, p.68	
	2–1	1
	2–2	
	2–3	
	2–5	
	2–8	
	2–8	22
	2–12	
	2–13	
	2–13	16
	2–15	
	2–16	
	2–16	7
	2–17	
	2–18	
	2–19	
	3–1	
	3–10	
	3–10	65
	3–10	66
	3–10	73
	3–23	
	3–23	38
	4–11	
	6–2	
	6–2	7
	6–2	13
	6–39	15
	6–43	7
	6–44	
	6–83	
	6–87	8
	7–2	
	7–9	

UNITED STATES CODE ANNOTATED
11 U.S.C.A.—Bankruptcy

Sec.	This Work Sec.	Note
Ch. 12 (Cont'd)	7–10	
	7–14	
	7–17	
	7–29	
	7–31	
	8–2	
	8–2	3
	8–2	5
	8–24	
	8–24	2
	9–4	
	9–12	13
	9–15	
	9–16	
	9–18	
	9–23	
	9–23	1
	9–24	
	9–24	24
	9–25	
	9–26	
	9–27	
	9–28	
	9–29	
	9–30	
	9–30	9
	10–21	
	11–30	
1201	3–10	
	3–10	38
	3–10	82
	11–35	
1201—1231	10–1	7
1201(a)	3–10	
1201(a)(1)	3–10	52
1201(a)(2)	3–10	43
	3–10	82
1201(b)	3–10	54
1201(c)	3–10	55
1201(c)(1)	3–10	
1201(c)(2)	3–10	
	3–10	42
1201(c)(3)	3–10	
1201(d)	3–10	69
1202	6–2	11
	6–83	9
1203	4–1	1
	6–2	12
1204	9–25	2
1204(a)	6–2	13
1206	2–17	2
1207	2–8	22
1207(a)	2–8	
1208	2–12	
	2–16	
	2–16	29
	3–23	26
	9–27	
1208(a)	9–27	
1208(b)	2–13	
	2–13	16
1208(c)	9–27	
	9–27	7

TABLE OF STATUTES

UNITED STATES CODE ANNOTATED
11 U.S.C.A.—Bankruptcy

Sec.	This Work Sec.	Note
1208(c) (Cont'd)	9–27	11
1208(c)(5)	9–25	
1208(c)(9)	9–25	3
1208(d)	2–13	
	2–13	16
	2–19	1
1221	9–23	5
	9–25	
	9–25	5
1222	9–28	
1222(b)(3)	2–16	5
1224	9–25	
	9–25	1
1225	9–28	
1225(a)	9–27	
1225(a)(3)	2–15	3
	2–16	
1225(b)(1)	9–30	
1226	9–23	6
1227	6–44	47
1227(b)	3–23	47
1227(c)	6–44	12
1228	3–23	35
	3–23	36
	5–7	2
1228(c)	3–11	5
Ch. 13	1–4	
	1–5	
	1–6	
	1–8	
	1–9	
	1–10	
	Ch. 2, p.68	
	2–1	1
	2–2	
	2–2	7
	2–2	11
	2–3	
	2–3	3
	2–5	
	2–8	
	2–8	22
	2–12	
	2–13	
	2–13	12
	2–13	14
	2–13	16
	2–14	
	2–15	
	2–16	
	2–16	2
	2–16	7
	2–17	
	2–17	7
	2–18	
	2–19	
	2–19	5
	3–2	9
	3–5	18
	3–10	
	3–10	21
	3–10	81

UNITED STATES CODE ANNOTATED
11 U.S.C.A.—Bankruptcy

Sec.	This Work Sec.	Note
Ch. 13 (Cont'd)	3–11	
	3–11	10
	3–11	20
	3–11	26
	3–12	
	3–12	5
	3–12	10
	3–12	11
	3–12	15
	3–12	18
	3–15	6
	3–16	5
	3–16	9
	3–21	
	3–22	4
	3–22	5
	3–23	
	3–23	27
	3–23	37
	3–23	46
	3–23	47
	3–23	48
	3–25	
	3–25	8
	3–25	31
	3–28	12
	3–28	13
	3–29	9
	3–31	
	3–31	6
	3–31	84
	3–34	
	5–9	
	6–2	
	6–2	7
	6–2	16
	6–2	20
	6–2	22
	6–2	28
	6–11	6
	6–19	4
	6–40	4
	6–43	7
	6–44	2
	6–44	5
	6–61	12
	6–72	1
	6–83	
	6–83	16
	6–93	66
	7–2	
	7–9	
	7–10	
	7–14	
	7–17	
	7–24	
	7–24	1
	7–29	
	7–30	
	7–31	
	7–31	10
	7–33	
	7–37	

TABLE OF STATUTES

UNITED STATES CODE ANNOTATED
11 U.S.C.A.—Bankruptcy

Sec.	This Work Sec.	Note
Ch. 13 (Cont'd)	7–39	
	7–39	2
	7–45	
	7–45	17
	7–47	
	7–47	2
	7–47	5
	7–49	
	7–49	11
	8–2	
	8–2	4
	8–2	5
	8–3	22
	8–9	16
	8–11	3
	8–22	19
	8–22	20
	8–23	3
	8–23	5
	8–23	7
	8–24	
	8–24	3
	8–29	
	9–1	
	9–2	
	9–2	1
	9–2	3
	9–2	4
	9–2	10
	9–2	19
	9–2	23
	9–2	25
	9–2	27
	9–3	
	9–3	1
	9–3	33
	9–4	
	9–4	11
	9–4	14
	9–4	18
	9–4	19
	9–4	43
	9–5	
	9–6	
	9–7	
	9–7	14
	9–8	
	9–9	
	9–10	
	9–11	
	9–12	
	9–13	
	9–14	
	9–14	21
	9–14	27
	9–15	
	9–16	
	9–17	
	9–18	
	9–18	16
	9–19	
	9–20	
	9–22	

UNITED STATES CODE ANNOTATED
11 U.S.C.A.—Bankruptcy

Sec.	This Work Sec.	Note
Ch. 13 (Cont'd)	9–23	
	9–23	1
	9–23	6
	9–25	
	9–28	
	9–29	
	9–30	
	9–30	10
	10–22	
	10–22	8
	10–23	
	10–24	12
	11–4	
	12–5	5
1301	3–10	
	3–10	37
	3–10	38
	3–10	57
	3–10	82
	9–2	15
	9–4	
	9–4	47
	11–35	
1301 et seq.	9–1	17
1301(a)	3–10	
	3–10	36
	9–1	21
1301(a)(1)	3–10	52
1301(a)(2)	3–10	43
	3–10	82
1301(b)	3–10	54
1301(c)	3–10	55
1301(c)(1)	3–10	
1301(c)(2)	3–10	
	3–10	42
1301(c)(3)	3–10	
1301(d)	3–10	69
1302	6–2	14
	6–83	9
1302(a)	9–4	35
1302(c)	9–4	
1302(d)	9–4	35
1302(e)	9–4	35
1303	6–2	
	6–2	15
1305	9–4	
1305(a)	9–4	
1305(a)(1)	9–4	
1306	2–8	
	2–8	22
	3–23	47
	9–20	
1306(a)	3–10	21
1306(a)(1)	9–20	
1306(a)(2)	3–12	7
1306(b)	9–2	2
1307	2–12	
	2–16	
	2–16	29
	2–17	2
	2–19	2
	3–23	26
	4–1	1

TABLE OF STATUTES

UNITED STATES CODE ANNOTATED
11 U.S.C.A.—Bankruptcy

Sec.	This Work Sec.	Note
1307 (Cont'd)	9–20	
1307(b)	2–13	
	2–13	16
1307(c)	2–13	16
1307(c)(6)	9–20	
	9–20	19
1307(d)	2–13	16
1322	9–4	
	9–5	
	9–7	
	9–8	
	9–11	
	9–12	
	9–17	
	9–18	
	9–28	
	10–22	8
1322(a)(2)	9–4	12
	9–5	
	9–5	3
	9–6	
	9–6	4
1322(a)(3)	9–10	
1322(b)	9–7	
	9–16	1
	9–18	
1322(b)(1)	9–5	
	9–5	4
	9–5	6
	9–7	
	9–7	2
	9–7	6
	9–16	
	10–24	12
1322(b)(2)	9–12	
	9–15	
	9–15	1
	9–16	
	9–17	
	9–18	1
	9–18	2
	9–18	14
	9–23	
	9–30	
	9–30	11
1322(b)(3)	2–16	5
	9–15	
	9–15	2
	9–17	
	9–18	
1322(b)(5)	3–16	9
	9–16	
	9–16	1
	9–17	
	9–17	1
	9–18	
	9–18	4
	9–21	
1322(c)	9–1	24
	9–11	2
	9–12	
	9–12	1

UNITED STATES CODE ANNOTATED
11 U.S.C.A.—Bankruptcy

Sec.	This Work Sec.	Note
1322(c) (Cont'd)	9–12	2
	9–12	13
	9–12	14
	9–13	
	9–15	
	9–16	
	9–16	5
	9–18	
1324	9–4	
	9–4	27
	9–25	
1325	9–1	22
	9–4	
	9–5	
	9–6	3
	9–9	
	9–10	
	9–11	
	9–12	
	9–13	
	9–13	2
	9–14	
	9–14	21
	9–22	14
	9–28	
1325(a)(3)	2–15	3
	2–16	
	9–5	7
	9–7	
	9–7	9
	9–8	
	9–13	
	9–14	
	9–14	1
1325(a)(4)	9–10	
	9–4	10
	9–6	
	9–7	
	9–8	
	9–8	1
	9–9	
1325(a)(5)	3–11	9
	9–6	
	9–6	1
	9–10	
	9–15	
1325(a)(5)(A)	9–6	
1325(a)(5)(B)(ii)	9–6	3
	9–10	
1325(a)(6)	9–19	
	9–19	1
1325(b)	9–7	
	9–11	
	9–13	
	9–13	1
	9–13	12
	9–14	
1325(b)(1)	9–30	
1325(b)(1)(B)	9–8	
	9–11	
	9–11	4
	9–12	
	9–13	

1043

TABLE OF STATUTES

UNITED STATES CODE ANNOTATED
11 U.S.C.A.—Bankruptcy

Sec.	This Work Sec.	Note
1325(b)(1)(B) (Cont'd)	9–14	
	9–22	
1325(b)(2)	9–13	
1325(b)(5)	9–18	
1326	2–17	
	9–4	
1326(a)(1)	9–23	6
1326(b)	9–6	
	9–6	5
1326(b)(1)	9–5	
	9–5	2
1326(b)(2)	9–6	
1326(c)	9–4	
	9–4	40
1327	9–20	
1327(a)	9–1	23
	9–20	
1327(b)	3–12	9
	3–12	10
	3–23	47
	9–20	
1327(c)	3–11	9
	9–20	
1328	3–23	35
	3–23	36
	7–17	
	9–1	25
	9–4	
	9–7	
	9–16	2
	9–20	
	9–20	2
1328(a)	7–24	1
	7–31	
	7–31	10
	9–2	4
	9–2	10
	9–9	
	9–20	
	9–20	2
1328(a)(1)	9–16	
	9–18	
1328(a)(2)	9–20	
1328(a)(3)	7–31	
	7–34	10
	9–20	
1328(b)	7–31	9
	9–21	
	9–21	1
1328(b–c)	9–20	2
1328(b)(1)	9–21	
1328(b)(3)	9–21	
1328(c)	3–11	5
	9–21	
1329	9–21	
	9–22	
1329(a)	9–22	
	9–22	3
1329(b)(1)	9–22	
	9–22	5
1329(c)	9–22	9
1330(a)	9–22	10
1334	12–14	

UNITED STATES CODE ANNOTATED
11 U.S.C.A.—Bankruptcy

Sec.	This Work Sec.	Note
1334(c)(1)	12–5	
	12–5	9
1334(c)(2)	12–5	
	12–5	9
1338	5–7	2
1408	2–15	23
Ch. 19	2–16	
	9–30	
Ch. 20	2–16	
	9–30	
6323(a)	6–36	5

15 U.S.C.A.—Commerce and Trade

Sec.	This Work Sec.	Note
77a	11–21	2
77w	11–22	
303	8–11	26
1671—1677	8–11	25

18 U.S.C.A.—Crimes and Criminal Procedure

Sec.	This Work Sec.	Note
408	7–34	11

22 U.S.C.A.—Foreign Relations and Intercourse

Sec.	This Work Sec.	Note
4060(c)	8–11	2

25 U.S.C.A.—Indians

Sec.	This Work Sec.	Note
410	8–11	11
412(a)	8–11	11

26 U.S.C.A.—Internal Revenue Code

Sec.	This Work Sec.	Note
1 et seq.	8–11	8
382	11–24	
401(a)(13)(A)	8–33	14
6201 et seq.	7–25	9
6303	7–25	9
6321	6–36	4
	6–62	30
6322	6–62	30
	7–25	9
6323(a)	6–62	32
6323(b)	6–62	34
6323(b)(1)	6–62	33
	6–62	34
6323(b)(2)	6–62	33
6323(b)(3)	6–62	35
6323(f)	6–62	31
6331(a)	7–25	9
6402(a)	6–38	16

TABLE OF STATUTES

UNITED STATES CODE ANNOTATED
26 U.S.C.A.—Internal Revenue Code

Sec.	This Work Sec.	Note
6402(d)	6–38	15
7421(a)	3–22	5

28 U.S.C.A.—Judiciary and Judicial Procedure

Sec.	This Work Sec.	Note
151	12–16	
157	11–5	9
	12–1	
	12–2	
	12–2	8
157(b)	11–8	12
	12–2	
	12–16	
157(b)(1)	11–5	9
	12–2	
	12–3	
157(b)(2)	12–2	
157(b)(2)(A)	12–2	
157(b)(2)(B)	11–5	11
	12–4	
157(b)(2)(C)	12–2	
157(b)(2)(E)	12–2	
	12–2	10
157(b)(2)(O)	12–2	
157(b)(5)	12–4	
	12–4	2
	12–9	2
	12–13	
157(c)(1)	11–5	10
	12–3	
	12–5	7
	12–12	
157(c)(2)	12–3	
157(d)	12–1	2
158	12–12	
158(a)	12–12	
	12–12	20
158(b)	12–12	
158(b)(1)	12–12	1
158(b)(2)	12–12	1
158(b)(3)	12–12	1
554	11–9	
581	7–2	4
586	9–4	
586(b)	9–4	34
586(e)	9–4	
	9–4	36
586(e)(2)	9–4	
959	11–9	
	11–10	
959(a)	11–10	
959(b)	3–21	125
	11–10	
1141	12–14	
1292 (repealed)	12–12	21
1292(b)	11–14	
1293(b)	12–12	1
1334	3–30	27
	12–1	
	12–2	12

UNITED STATES CODE ANNOTATED
28 U.S.C.A.—Judiciary and Judicial Procedure

Sec.	This Work Sec.	Note
1334 (Cont'd)	12–5	
1334(a)	12–1	
1334(b)	12–1	
1334(c)	3–30	27
1334(c)(2)	3–30	27
	12–2	
1346	6–73	21
1404	12–11	5
1406	12–11	5
1408	12–6	
1408(1)	12–6	
	12–7	
	12–11	7
1408(2)	12–7	
	12–10	
1409	12–6	
	12–8	
1409(a)	12–8	
1409(b)	12–8	
1409(b)–(e)	12–8	
1409(c)	12–8	
1409(d)	12–8	
1411	3–30	28
	11–5	11
	12–13	
	12–16	
1411(a)	12–13	
1411(b)	12–13	11
1412	12–4	2
	12–9	1
	12–10	
	12–11	5
1473(b)	12–8	
1475	12–11	5
1477 (repealed)	12–11	
1477(a)	12–11	
1480	12–13	
	12–14	
	12–16	
1480(a)	12–13	
1480(b)	12–13	11
1481	3–22	5
1651(a)	3–22	1
1738	3–10	9
1930(a)(5)	9–25	15
1961(a)	6–87	14
2075	1–3	
	1–3	6
2283	3–22	5
2283(a)	3–22	5

29 U.S.C.A.—Labor

Sec.	This Work Sec.	Note
1001 et seq.	8–33	8
1002(1)	8–33	12
1002(2)(A)	8–33	13
1003(a)	8–33	10
1003(b)(1)	8–33	11
1051(1)	8–33	15
1056(d)(1)	8–11	17

UNITED STATES CODE ANNOTATED
29 U.S.C.A.—Labor

Sec.	This Work Sec.	Note
1056(d)(1) (Cont'd)	8–33	14
	8–33	15
1056(d)(3)	8–33	15
1144(b)(7)	8–33	15

33 U.S.C.A.—Navigation and Navigable Waters

Sec.	This Work Sec.	Note
916	8–11	7

38 U.S.C.A.—Veterans' Benefits

Sec.	This Work Sec.	Note
3101(a)	8–11	10
3101(b)	8–11	10

41 U.S.C.A.—Public Contracts

Sec.	This Work Sec.	Note
15	5–15	

42 U.S.C.A.—The Public Health and Welfare

Sec.	This Work Sec.	Note
294f(g)	9–2	10
407(a)	8–11	3
1717	8–11	4
1717(a)	8–11	5
1983	3–34	6
2000e et seq.	7–41	
9601 et seq.	3–31	110
9607(a)	11–11	6
9607(b)	11–11	6

43 U.S.C.A.—Public Lands

Sec.	This Work Sec.	Note
175 (repealed)	8–11	11
1181	8–11	11

45 U.S.C.A.—Railroads

Sec.	This Work Sec.	Note
231m(a)	8–11	8
352(e)	8–11	9

46 U.S.C.A.—Shipping

Sec.	This Work Sec.	Note
11109(a)	8–11	5

STATUTES AT LARGE

Year	This Work Sec.	Note
1898, July 1, Ch. 541, 30 Stat. 544	10–1	1
1898, July 1, Ch. 541, 30 Stat. 544–66	9–1	1
1898, July 1, Ch. 541, § 12, 30 Stat. 549	9–1	
	9–1	2
1898, July 1, Ch. 541, §606(8), 30 Stat. 565	9–1	10
1898, July 1, Ch. 541, § 652, 30 Stat. 565	9–1	12
1898, July 1, Ch. 541, § 661, 30 Stat. 565	9–1	12
	9–1	11
1933, March 3, P.L. 72–420, § 74, 47 Stat. 1467	9–1	
1933, March 3, P.L. 72–420, 47 Stat. 1467	9–1	4
1933, March 3, Ch. 204 § 75(a)–(r), 47 Stat. 1470	9–18	3
1935, July 28, Ch. 792, 49 Stat. 943	9–18	
1938, June 22, P.L. 74–696, 52 Stat. 840–940	9–1	7
1938, June 22, Ch. 575, § 1, 52 Stat. 930	9–1	10
1938, June 22, Ch. 575, § 1, 52 Stat. 934	9–1	
1938, June 22, Ch. 575, § 1, 52 Stat. 936	9–1	11
	9–1	12
1950, Dec. 29, Ch. 1193, 64 Stat. 1134	9–1	10
1952, July 7, Ch. 579, § 52, 66 Stat. 437	9–1	11
1959, May 13, P.L. 86–24, § 1, 73 Stat. 24	9–1	10
1960, July 20, P.L. 86–621, 74 Stat. 408	7–26	2
1965, Nov. 8, P.L. 89–239, § 439a, 79 Stat. 1247	7–33	3
1976, Oct. 12, P.L. 94–482 § 127(a), 90 Stat. 2141 (repealed)	7–33	3
1976, Oct. 21, P.L. 94–579, Tit. VII, § 702, 90 Stat. 2787	8–11	11
1978, Nov. 6, P.L. 95–598, 92 Stat. 2549	9–1	17
1978, Nov. 6, P.L. 95–598, § 317, 92 Stat. 2678	7–33	3
1978, Nov. 6, P.L. 95–598, § 402(a), 92 Stat. 2682	10–1	1

STATUTES AT LARGE

Year	This Work Sec.	Note
1978, Nov. 6, P.L. 95–598, Tit. IV,		
§ 405(d), 92 Stat. 2685	1–3	6
1981, Aug. 13, P.L. 97–35,		
95 Stat. 357	7–29	24
1981, Aug. 13, P.L. 97–35,		
§ 2344(b), 95 Stat. 863	7–29	24
1984, July 10, P.L. 98–353,		
98 Stat. 333	3–7	2
	4–7	9
	6–54	6
	7–29	24
	9–30	14
1984, July 10, P.L. 98–353,		
98 Stat. 390–91	3–7	2
1984, July 10, P.L. 98–353,		
98 Stat. 355	7–44	1
1984, July 10, P.L. 98–353,		
§ 317, 98 Stat. 356	9–30	14
1984, July 10, P.L. 98–353,		
§ 454(b), 98 Stat. 376	7–29	24
1986, Oct. 27, P.L. 99–554,		
100 Stat. 3088	9–30	14
1986, Oct. 27, P.L. 99–554,		
§ 219(b), 100 Stat. 3100	7–44	2
1986, Oct. 27, P.L. 99–554,		
§ 255, 100 Stat. 3111	9–30	14
1986, Oct. 27, P.L. 99–554,		
100 Stat. 3114	9–30	9
1986, Oct. 27, 99–554,		
§ 302(d)(3), 100 Stat. 3119	7–2	5
1990, Nov. 3, P.L. 101–508,		
§ 3007(b), 104 Stat. 1388–90	9–2	9
1990, Nov. 15, P.L. 101–581,		
104 Stat. 2865	9–2	9
1990, Nov. 15, P.L. 101–581,		
§ 3, 104 Stat. 2865	7–31	11
1990, Nov. 29, P.L. 101–647,		
104 Stat. 4789	7–5	
	7–24	2
1990, Nov. 29, P.L. 101–647,		
104 Stat. 4789	7–33	1
	7–5	

STATUTES AT LARGE

Year	This Work Sec.	Note
1990, Nov. 29, P.L. 101–647,		
§ 2522(a)(1), 104 Stat. 4865–66	7–24	2
1990, Nov. 29, P.L. 101–647,		
§ 2522(e), 104 Stat. 4867–68	7–5	3
1990, P.L. 101–647,		
§§ 3102(b)–3103, 104 Stat. 4916	9–2	9
1990, Nov. 29, P.L. 101–647,		
§ 3621, 104 Stat. 4964–65	7–33	1

STATE STATUTES

ALABAMA CONSTITUTION

Art.	This Work Sec.	Note
IX, § 210	8–9	10

ALABAMA CODE

Sec.	This Work Sec.	Note
6–10–120	8–9	10

ARIZONA REVISED STATUTES

Sec.	This Work Sec.	Note
33–1101	8–7	4

ARKANSAS CONSTITUTION

Art.	This Work Sec.	Note
IX, § 1	8–6	1
IX, § 2	8–6	1

ARKANSAS STATUTES

Sec.	This Work Sec.	Note
82–4709	11–11	5
82–4720	11–11	5

WEST'S ANNOTATED CALIFORNIA CONSTITUTION

Art.	This Work Sec.	Note
XX, § 1.5	8–7	4

WEST'S ANNOTATED CALIFORNIA CODE OF CIVIL PROCEDURE

Sec.	This Work Sec.	Note
680.190	8–8	6

WEST'S ANNOTATED CALIFORNIA CODE OF CIVIL PROCEDURE

Sec.	This Work Sec.	Note
704.01	8–8	6
704.710 et seq.	8–7	4
704.710(a)	8–7	21
704.710(b)	8–13	7
704.720(b)	8–13	7
704.960(a)	8–13	7

WEST'S ANNOTATED CALIFORNIA GOVERNMENT CODE

Sec.	This Work Sec.	Note
12419.5	6–38	17

CONNECTICUT GENERAL STATUTES ANNOTATED

Sec.	This Work Sec.	Note
22a–452a	11–11	5
52–352b(j)	8–8	6

DELAWARE CODE

Tit.	This Work Sec.	Note
8, § 160	6–52	49

WEST'S FLORIDA CONSTITUTION

Art.	This Work Sec.	Note
X, § 4	8–6	1

GEORGIA CODE

Sec.	This Work Sec.	Note
40–3–50(b)	6–13	3
44–13–1	8–6	1

ILLINOIS SMITH–HURD ANNOTATED

Ch.	This Work Sec.	Note
10, ¶ 12–906	8–13	7
110, ¶ 9–301	6–62	41
120, ¶ 441	7–25	4

IOWA CODE ANNOTATED

Sec.	This Work Sec.	Note
561.21	8–9	4
561.21	8–9	5
672.6(10)	8–6	2

MARYLAND ANNOTATED CODE

Sec.	This Work Sec.	Note
8–301—8–332	6–62	41

MASSACHUSETTS GENERAL LAWS ANNOTATED

Ch.	This Work Sec.	Note
21E	11–11	5

MICHIGAN CONSTITUTION

Art.	This Work Sec.	Note
X, § 3	8–7	4

MICHIGAN LOCAL BANKRUPTCY RULES

Rule	This Work Sec.	Note
33	12–16	11

MICHIGAN JUVENILE COURT RULES

Rule	This Work Sec.	Note
33(a)(3)(C)(i)	3–23	1

MINNESOTA STATUTES ANNOTATED

Sec.	This Work Sec.	Note
270.66	6–38	17
302A.551	6–52	49
302A.557	6–52	49
302A.559	6–52	49
302A.725(3)	6–52	48
550.37(12a)	8–6	
	8–8	1
550.37(19)	8–9	10

MISSISSIPPI CODE 1972

Sec.	This Work Sec.	Note
85–3–1	8–6	3
85–3–49	8–13	7

MONTANA CODE ANNOTATED

Sec.	This Work Sec.	Note
25–13–601	8–9	10

NEW HAMPSHIRE REVISED STATUTES ANNOTATED

Sec.	This Work Sec.	Note
147–B:10	11–11	5
480:1	8–7	4

NEW JERSEY STATUTES ANNOTATED

Sec.	This Work Sec.	Note
10–23.11(f)	11–11	5

NORTH DAKOTA CENTURY CODE

Sec.	This Work Sec.	Note
28–22–02(7)	8–13	7
28–22–02(9)	8–13	7

OHIO REVISED CODE

Sec.	This Work Sec.	Note
2329.66.1	8–9	10
4509.45	7–41	14

OREGON REVISED STATUTES

Sec.	This Work Sec.	Note
23.240(1)	8–7	4

PENNSYLVANIA STATUTES

Tit.	This Work Sec.	Note
39, § 151	6–59	2

TENNESSEE CODE ANNOTATED

Sec.	This Work Sec.	Note
26–2–301(a)	8–7	4
26–2–304	8–13	7
68–42–209	11–11	5

WISCONSIN STATUTES ANNOTATED

Sec.	This Work Sec.	Note
815.18(17)	8–13	7
815.20(L)	8–13	7

POPULAR NAME ACTS

BANKRUPTCY ACT

Sec.	This Work Sec.	Note
6	6–6	5
14(c)(2)	7–20	
	7–20	4
14(c)(7)	7–22	2
17	7–26	
17(a)(2)	7–26	
17(a)(4)	7–28	9
17(a)(7)	7–29	
	7–29	1
19	12–13	5
27(b)	5–15	8
59(g)	2–13	
63a(8)	11–1	11
63c	5–1	
67(d)(1)(E)	6–49	39
67(d)(3)	6–59	
67d	6–49	62
	6–54	

BANKRUPTCY ACT

Sec.	This Work Sec.	Note
67d (Cont'd)	6–56	3
67d(1)(e)(2)	6–49	62
67d(3)	6–59	8
70	5–5	
70(a)	2–8	3
70(f)	4–7	3
70(g)	4–7	3
70a	5–4	
	6–6	1
70b	5–1	
	5–3	1
	5–4	
	5–5	
	5–7	
	5–8	
	5–8	13
	5–12	
75	9–18	3
77	5–12	
	10–31	5
77A	11–1	
77B	11–1	
	11–26	
77B(f)	11–27	
	11–27	
116(1)	5–8	1
229c	2–16	13
313(1)	5–8	1
413(1)	5–8	1
442(d)	4–7	9
613(1)	5–8	1
606(1)	9–1	16
Ch. X	2–15	
	2–15	1
	2–16	13
	5–8	
	10–1	
	11–13	
	11–18	2
Ch. XI	5–8	
	5–12	
	10–1	
	10–1	2
	10–1	4
	11–13	
	11–21	
Ch. XII	5–8	
	10–1	
Ch. XII (repealed)	10–1	2
Ch. XIII	5–4	
	5–8	
	9–12	
	9–14	
	9–14	2

COMPREHENSIVE ENVIRONMENTAL RESPONSE, COMPENSATION AND LIABILITY ACT

Sec.	This Work Sec.	Note
107(a)	11–10	

CONSUMER CREDIT PROTECTION ACT

Sec.	This Work Sec.	Note
Tit. III	8–11	

EMPLOYEE RETIREMENT INCOME SECURITY ACT

Sec.	This Work Sec.	Note
Tit. IV	3–21	8
Tit. VII	3–21	8
	4–10	4
4062	3–14	

MODEL BUSINESS CORPORATION ACT

Sec.	This Work Sec.	Note
6.40	6–52	48
8.33	6–52	49

SECURITIES ACT OF 1933

Sec.	This Work Sec.	Note
17(a)	7–26	

SECURITIES ACT OF 1934

Sec.	This Work Sec.	Note
14	11–22	

SOCIAL SECURITY ACT

Sec.	This Work Sec.	Note
402(a)(26)	7–29	

UNIFORM COMMERCIAL CODE

Sec.	This Work Sec.	Note
1–201(22)	6–61	66
1–201(23)	2–5	
	6–66	10
1–201(25)	7–27	
1–201(26)	7–27	
1–201(27)	7–27	
	7–27	10
1–201(32)	6–67	7
1–201(33)	6–67	7
1–201(37)	3–17	
	5–2	
1–201(44)	6–11	20
1–209	6–92	8
Art. 2	6–36	12
	6–63	
	6–66	
	9–14	
2–105(1)	6–77	11
2–401(2)	6–11	18
2–403(1)	6–11	18
	6–63	5

UNIFORM COMMERCIAL CODE

Sec.	This Work Sec.	Note
2–403(1) (Cont'd)	6–67	5
	6–67	7
2–501	6–19	17
2–507	6–63	
2–507(1)	6–19	17
2–507(2)	6–63	2
2–507, Com. 3	6–63	3
2–511	6–63	
2–511(3)	6–63	2
2–607(1)	6–19	17
2–609	5–18	
2–702	6–65	
	6–67	3
2–702(2)	6–63	
	6–63	1
	6–63	3
	6–63	4
	6–63	5
	6–65	16
	6–66	
	6–66	3
	6–67	
2–702(3)	6–63	5
	6–63	6
	6–67	5
	6–67	7
2–705	6–65	16
Art. 3	6–16	
	6–69	15
3–118(e)	3–6	21
3–401(1)	6–16	4
3–409(1)	6–16	3
3–409(1)	6–16	5
3–415(5)	6–9	4
3–504(1)	3–8	14
3–603(1)	6–16	7
3–606	3–10	
3–802(1)(b)	6–16	7
3–802(1)(b)	6–16	7
Art. 4	6–16	
4–213(1)	6–16	6
4–303(1)	6–16	8
	6–16	9
4–402	6–74	5
4–403(1)	6–16	8
Art. 5	3–14	
5–111(1)	6–10	17
5–114(1)	3–14	57
5–114(3)	3–14	57
	6–9	9
	6–25	17
5–116(1–2)	3–14	57
5–116(2)	3–14	56
Art. 6	4–3	2
	6–60	
6–102(1)	4–3	2
6–104(1)	6–60	9
6–105	6–60	9
7–205	4–4	
7–209	6–62	3
	6–62	20
	6–62	39
Art. 9	3–11	
	3–11	14

TABLE OF STATUTES 1051

UNIFORM COMMERCIAL CODE		
		This Work
Sec.	Sec.	Note
Art. 9 (Cont'd)	3–11	26
	3–16	
	6–11	
	6–11	11
	6–12	
	6–12	8
	6–12	12
	6–14	
	6–15	
	6–20	20
	6–33	
	6–35	29
	6–53	
	6–56	1
	6–61	
	6–61	
	6–61	38
	6–61	66
	6–63	
	6–67	
	6–68	
	6–75	
	6–76	3
	6–77	
	6–77	7
	6–77	11
	6–79	
	6–86	
	6–92	
	6–92	3
	6–92	8
	7–10	
	7–47	
	7–49	
	8–22	
	8–22	26
	8–23	6
	8–31	5
9–102(1)	6–35	29
9–103(3)(d)	12–6	2
9–104	6–35	29
9–104(j)	6–77	11
9–105(1)(a)	3–14	56
9–105(1)(c)	6–76	3
9–105(1)(h)	6–77	11
9–105(1)(i)	6–35	33
9–105(1)(*l*)	6–76	3
9–106	6–35	33
	6–77	11
9–107	3–17	
	6–33	1
	8–25	29
9–107(a)	6–33	14
9–201	8–8	5
9–203(1)	6–11	10
	6–11	19
	6–68	5
9–204(1)	6–35	2
	6–68	5
	8–25	39
9–301	6–13	4
9–301(1)(b)	6–11	11
	6–11	21
	6–12	6

UNIFORM COMMERCIAL CODE		
		This Work
Sec.	Sec.	Note
9–301(1)(b) (Cont'd)	6–61	15
	6–61	57
	8–8	5
9–301(2)	6–33	9
	6–61	
9–302(1)	3–16	22
	6–11	11
	6–12	9
	6–61	63
9–302(2)	6–77	4
9–302(3)	6–13	3
9–302(3)(b)	6–12	8
9–303(1)	6–11	25
9–306	3–11	26
9–306(1)	6–35	34
	6–76	3
	6–77	3
	6–77	7
	6–77	22
9–306(2)	6–77	7
	6–77	22
9–306(3)	6–77	7
	6–78	3
9–306(4)	6–77	4
	6–77	7
	6–78	3
9–306(4)(d)	6–77	7
9–307(1)	4–7	
9–308(1)	6–77	8
9–312(3)	6–67	13
9–312(4)	6–33	9
	6–67	13
9–312(5)(a)	6–79	3
	6–79	9
	6–86	12
9–316	6–92	3
9–401	3–16	22
9–401(2)	6–61	77
9–402	3–16	22
9–402(1)	6–11	24
9–403(2)	3–16	23
	3–16	25
	3–16	26
	6–61	64
	6–61	65
	6–61	66
9–403(2–3)	3–16	24
9–503	2–8	2
	7–49	
9–504	2–8	2
	7–49	
9–506	2–8	2
	7–47	
	11–30	8
9–507(2)	6–56	1

UNIFORM EXEMPTION ACT		
		This Work
Sec.	Sec.	Note
6(b)	8–6	10
6(b), Com. 7	8–6	10

UNIFORM FRAUDULENT CONVEYANCE ACT

Sec.	This Work Sec.	Note
3	6–60	14
	6–60	15
4	6–46	4
	6–60	6
	6–60	12
	6–60	13
4(a)(1)	6–60	5
5	6–46	4
	6–60	6
	6–60	13
6	6–46	4
	6–60	6
	6–60	13
7	6–46	3
	6–60	5
8	6–46	4
	6–60	6
8(b)	6–60	13

UNIFORM FRAUDULENT TRANSFER ACT

Sec.	This Work Sec.	Note
1	6–51	16
3(a)	6–49	38
4(a)(1)	6–46	3
	6–60	5
4(a)(2)	6–46	4
	6–60	6
4(b)	6–48	6
5	6–46	4
	6–60	12
5(a)(2)	6–60	6
5(b)	6–59	2
7(a)(3)(iii)	6–52	

UNIFORM PARTNERSHIP ACT

Sec.	This Work Sec.	Note
31	2–5	
	2–5	7
31(1)(d)	11–37	1
31(4)	11–37	1
31(5)	11–32	
	11–37	
	11–37	1
33	2–5	
35	2–5	7
	11–37	

REVISED UNIFORM LIMITED PARTNERSHIP ACT

Sec.	This Work Sec.	Note
402	2–5	8

CODE OF FEDERAL REGULATIONS

Tit.	This Work Sec.	Note
16, § 444.1	8–25	43

CODE OF FEDERAL REGULATIONS

Tit.	This Work Sec.	Note
16, § 444.2(a)(2)	8–9	10
16, § 444.2(a)(4)	8–25	39
	11–30	9
17, § 229.501(c)(5)	11–22	
26, § 1.401(a)–13(b)(1)	8–33	14

TREASURY REGULATIONS

Sec.	This Work Sec.	Note
1.401(a)–13(b)(1)	8–33	14

FEDERAL RULES OF CIVIL PROCEDURE

Rule	This Work Sec.	Note
11	3–21	
15(c)	6–84	1
19(a)	3–6	19
19(b)	3–6	19
41(a)(2)	2–13	8
65	3–22	29

BANKRUPTCY RULES

Rule	This Work Sec.	Note
116(a)(2)	12–6	
205 (former)	11–16	6
205(a)(former)	11–16	6
606	4–7	3
805 (former)	3–31	103
1001	1–3	4
	1–3	5
1002	9–4	
1004(a)	2–2	17
1007	7–2	2
	7–3	
	7–27	
	11–16	
	11–16	3
1007(a)	9–4	
1007(b)(2)	9–4	
1007(h)	2–8	19
1011	2–5	23
1014	12–10	
	12–11	
1014(a)(1)	12–10	
1014(a)(2)	12–11	
	12–11	2
1015	2–5	7
1015(b)	8–21	1
2002	4–7	
	4–16	
	7–2	
	9–4	1
2002(a)	2–5	41
	4–16	
2002(b)(2)	11–23	2
2002(c)	4–16	
2003	7–2	
	9–4	3
2003(a)	9–4	21

TABLE OF STATUTES

BANKRUPTCY RULES

Rule	This Work Sec.	Note
2004	11–16	
	11–16	4
	11–16	5
	11–16	6
2004(b)	9–4	24
	11–16	4
2020	1–4	4
3001 et seq.	12–14	17
	12–14	18
3001(a)	11–4	3
3001(f)	11–4	17
3002	7–3	
	9–4	
	11–4	1
3002(a)	9–4	
	9–4	8
	9–4	9
	9–4	18
3002(c)	7–3	
	7–15	
	7–15	8
	9–4	
	11–4	6
3002(c)(1)–(5)	7–15	
3003(c)(2)	11–1	3
	11–4	2
3003(c)(3)	11–4	5
3003(c)(4)	12–14	17
	12–14	18
3002(c)(6)	7–15	
3004	7–15	
	9–4	
	9–4	4
	11–4	8
	12–14	17
	12–14	18
3014	10–27	3
3015	9–4	
	9–23	6
3016	11–16	
3016(a)	11–16	8
	11–18	
3017	11–16	
3017(a)	11–16	7
3018	11–24	
3018(b)	11–23	
3018(b)(2)	11–23	
3020	9–4	
3020(b)(2)	9–4	
	9–4	31
3022	3–23	9
4001	3–31	12
4001(a)(1)	3–31	9
	3–31	12
4001(a)(2)	3–31	
	3–31	28
	3–31	44
4001(a)(3)	3–31	81
	3–31	82

BANKRUPTCY RULES

Rule	This Work Sec.	Note
4001(a)(3) (Cont'd)	3–31	83
	3–31	86
4001(d)(1)	3–27	25
4003(a)	8–29	4
4003(b)	8–1	12
	8–29	7
4003(c)	8–1	14
	8–1	15
	8–18	16
	8–29	6
	8–29	8
4003(d)	8–29	2
4007(b)	7–33	
4007(c)	7–27	
5010	3–23	19
6001	6–71	14
6004	4–7	
	4–16	
6004(a)	5–21	1
6004(c)	4–16	
6004(d)	4–16	
6006	5–8	
6008	7–39	6
7001	8–29	1
8005	3–31	102
	3–31	103
9006	11–14	
9006(a)	6–11	8
	6–33	9
9006(b)	11–14	4
9006(b)(3)	7–3	
	7–3	2
9006(c)	4–16	
9009	1–7	2
	2–1	2
9011	4–6	
9013	4–16	
9014	3–31	9
	3–31	12
	3–31	20
	4–16	
	5–8	
	5–21	1
	9–4	

FEDERAL REGISTER

Vol.	This Work Sec.	Note
56, p. 28798	3–21	110
56, p. 28806	3–21	110

SECURITIES AND EXCHANGE COMMISSION RULE

Rule	This Work Sec.	Note
501(c)(5)	11–22	

Index

EDITORIAL NOTE: A number of entries in this shared index refer to text appearing only in the three volume edition of this work. In those instances, see Epstein, Nickles and White, Bankruptcy, Practitioner Treatise Series. References are to Sections.

ABSOLUTE PRIORITY RULE, 10–21, 11–25
New value exception, see New Value

ABSTENTION OF BANKRUPTCY COURTS, 12–5
Abstention under the Bankruptcy Code, 2–10

ACTS OF BANKRUPTCY
Under Bankruptcy Act of 1898, 2–5

ADEQUATE ASSURANCE
of Assignee performance, 5–21
for Assumption of executory contracts or leases on which debtor has defaulted, 5–18, 5–20
Utility service payments, 3–9

ADEQUATE PROTECTION
Adjustments of the protection, 3–27
Enhancing the value of the collateral, 3–27
Equity cushion, 3–27
Lifting the stay for lack of adequate protection, 3–27
Loans with priority over other administrative expenses, 4–14
of Nondebtor lessor during gap period, 5–24
Risks to, 3–27
Secured creditors, 4–14
Valuation of the secured interest, 3–27

ADEQUATE PROTECTION AGREEMENT
Lifting the stay, 3–27

ADEQUATE PROTECTION OF LESSORS
Lifting the stay, 3–28
Unexpired leases, 3–28

ADMINISTRATIVE EXPENSES
In general, 7–11
   See also Priority
Assumed lease or executory contract obligations, 5–5
GAP period rent, 5–22
Postpetition expenses, 7–11
Postpetition loans with priority over other administrative expenses, 4–13, 4–14

AIRCRAFT LIENS
Automatic stay, 3–17

ALIMONY
See Domestic Obligations

ALLOCATION OF EARNINGS & PROPERTY
See Property of the Estate

ANTECEDENT DEBT REQUIREMENT
Preferences, 6–19

APPEALS
Appealable orders, 12–12
Appeals jurisdiction, 12–12
Automatic stay, effects on appeals, 3–6
Court approval of non-ordinary course loans, 4–17
Court approval of sale/lease of property of the estate, 4–17
Orders granting or denying relief from the stay, 3–31

ASSETS
   See also Property of the Estate
Cash collateral, 4–5
   See, also, Cash Collateral
Distribution of assets, Chapter 7 liquidation, 7–14, 7–15
Loss of assets, failure to explain, denial of discharge, 7–22
Sale of assets, postpetition, 4–4
Subsidiary assets, sale of, 4–4

ASSIGNMENT OF CLAIM
Setoff, 6–41

ASSIGNMENT OF EXECUTORY CONTRACTS OR LEASES
See Executory Contracts; Leases

ASSIGNMENTS
Intangible personal property, 6–12

ASSUMPTION OF EXECUTORY CONTRACTS OR LEASES
See Executory Contracts; Leases

AUTHORIZED TRANSFERS
as Exceptions to avoidance, 6–70

AUTOMATIC STAY
   See also Exceptions to the Automatic Stay
Actions against debtor, 3–5, 3–6, 3–30

AUTOMATIC STAY—Cont'd
Actions covered, generally, 3–1, 3–5, 3–6, 3–8
Aircraft liens, 3–17
Aircraft security interests, 3–17
Annulment, 3–32
Appeals, effects on, 3–6
Applicability, 3–3
Breach of contract, 3–14
"Cause" for relief, 3–24
Causes of action, 3–14
Claims affected, 3–6
Claims assessment, 3–8
Codebtor,
    Consumer debt, 3–10
    Limitations, 3–10
    Protected, 3–10, 9–4
Collection activities, 3–1
Collection efforts, 3–8
Collective bargaining agreements, 3–7
Consequences, 3–1, 3–6
Consumer debt of codebtor, 3–10
Contract cancellation, 3–8
Contract rights, 3–14
Counterclaims by or against Debtor, effects on, 3–6
Creditors' rights, 3–1
Criminal actions excepted, 3–20
Criminal proceedings, 3–20
Damages for violation,
    Contempt, 3–35
Damages recoverable for willful violation, 3–33
Defined, 3–1
Discharge, effect on, 3–23
Dismissal, effects on, 3–6
Domestic obligations, 3–12, 3–30
Duration, 3–23
    See also, Lifting the Stay
Effect on creditors, 3–1
Effective date, 3–2
Effects of violation, 3–32
End of stay, 3–23
    See also, Lifting the Stay
Entities, defined, 3–3
Exceptions, 3–1
Exceptions to the stay, listed, 3–1
Foreclosure, 3–16
Foreign debtors (Section 304 petitions), 2–6
    Petitions for relief, 2–6
Fraudulent conveyances, 3–10
Freedom of contract, 3–8
Government action, 3–19, 3–21
Government actions excepted, 3–14, 3–19, 3–20, 3–21
Injunctive relief, 3–21
Insurers, effects on, 3–10
Involuntary petitions, 2–5
Judgment enforcement, 3–21
Judicial annulment of the stay, 3–32
Judicial relief, 3–24
Leasehold interest, 3–14
Leases, effects on, 3–14, 3–28
Legal and equitable annulment, 3–32
Letters of credit, effects on, 3–14
Liability insurers, 3–10
Licenses from government, 3–14, 3–21

AUTOMATIC STAY—Cont'd
Lien, effect on, 3–1
Liens,
    Affected, 3–11, 3–16, 3–18
    Perfection and enforcement, 3–16
Lift-stay motion, 3–1, 3–31
Lifting the stay, see Lifting the Stay
Limitation on litigation, 3–6
Nondebtors, protection of, 3–10, 11–34, 11–35
Overview, 3–1
Partnership cases, 11–34, 11–35
Party in interest, 3–31
Perfection of liens, 3–18
Post-petition, claims, 3–4
    Effects on, 3–6
Postpetition demand for reclamation, 6–66
Preexisting liens, 3–11
Pre-petition claims, 3–4
Procedural concerns, 3–31
Proceedings covered, 3–6
Property of the estate, 3–13, 3–14
Property without equity, 3–24
Protection of debtor, exceptions, 3–10
Protection of nondebtors, 3–10
Punitive damages recoverable, 3–33
Purchase-money security interest, 3–17
Purpose requirement, 3–6
Purposes, 3–1
Reimposing the stay, 3–31
Relation to debtor, 3–5
Relief, 3–23
    Creditor's interest, 3–10
Relief from the stay,
    See also, Lifting the Stay
    Dismissal, 2–2
Repurchase agreements, 3–15
Right of redemption, 3–16
Rights from government, 3–14
Scope, 3–4, 3–6
Scope and effect, 3–1
Setoff, 3–15, 6–38, 6–43
Supplemental injunctions, 3–22
Supplier of debtor, effects on, 3–8
Surety, effects on, 3–10
Swap agreements, 3–15
Tax lien, 3–8
Termination, 3–1, 3–23
Termination of the stay, see Lifting the Stay
Tort claims, effects on, 3–6
Unperfected liens, 3–11
Unsecured creditors, 3–1
Utility service, 3–9
Violation by creditor, 3–1
Violation of the stay, 3–32
    See also, Violation of the Stay
Violations, 3–31
    Contempt, 3–35
    Penalties, 6–43
"Voidable" violations, 3–32
When the stay arises, 3–2
Who is affected, 3–3, 3–5, 3–6, 3–10

AVOIDANCE POWERS
Chapter 9 exception, 6–2
Chapter 11, 6–2
Chapter 12, 6–2
Chapter 13, 6–2

AVOIDANCE POWERS—Cont'd
Consensual liens, 6–61
Consequences of avoidance, overview, 6–79
Constructive fraud, 6–49
Conversions, 2–17
Creditors' remedies, in pursuance of avoidance actions, 6–2
Debtors, 6–61, 8–24
Debtor's avoidance powers, 6–2, 8–24
    See also, Exemptions
Debtor's defenses asserted by trustee, 6–94
Debtor's representative, 6–2
Debtor's rights in Chapter 13, 6–2
Determination of insolvency, 6–18
Foreclosure sales, 6–21
Fraudulent transfers, 6–47
    See also, Fraudulent Transfers
    Forced sale of property, 6–50
Inequitable conduct, 6–93
Insufficiency of setoff, 6–41
Involuntary cases, 6–71
Involuntary transfers, 8–22
Margin payments, 6–85
Mortgages, 6–61
Nullification, 6–80
Overview, 6–1
Postpetition transactions, 6–68, 6–69
Postpetition transfers, see Postpetition Transactions
Preconversion, postpetition, 2–17
Preferences, see Preferences
Preservation of the avoided transfer, 6–86
Purposes, 6–1, 6–2
Reclamation of goods, see Reclamation of Goods
Recovery, 6–80, 6–87, 6–88, 6–89
    Damages, 6–87
    From initial transferee, 6–88
    Improvement liens as limitations on recovery, 6–89
    Prejudgment interest, 6–87
    Recovery of value, 6–87
    Time limitations, 6–90
    Who is liable, 6–88
Rejection of executory contracts as avoidance power, 5–7
Relation-back,
    Priority rules of state law, 6–61
    Rules of non-bankruptcy law, 6–12
Right of reclamation, 6–64
Secret conveyances, 6–27
Security interests, 6–61
Setoff, see Setoff
Settlement payments, 6–85
"Strong-arm" powers, 6–61
"Strong-arm" powers compare to statutory lien avoidance powers, 6–62
State fraudulent transfer laws, 6–60
Statute of limitations, 6–73
Statutory liens vulnerable to avoidance power, 6–62
Stockbroker defense, 6–85
Subordination, 6–91, 6–92, 6–93
Time limitations, 6–81, 6–82, 6–83, 6–84, 6–90
Trustee as bona fide purchaser, 6–61

AVOIDANCE POWERS—Cont'd
Trustee as hypothetical judicial lien creditor, 6–61
Trustee as judicial lienor, 6–61
Voidable preferences, see Preferences
Who may avoid transfers, 6–2

BAD FAITH
Criminal proceedings, 3–20

BAD FAITH FILING
Chapter 11, 3–29
Lifting the stay, 3–29
Reorganization, 3–29

BADGES OF FRAUD
of Fraudulent transfers, 6–48

BANK DEPOSITS
Setoff, 6–41

BANKRUPTCY
Compared to nonbankruptcy debt collection, 1–2
Crimes, denial of Chapter 7 discharge, 7–21
Origins of, 1–1
Purposes, goals of, 1–2

BANKRUPTCY CASE
Chapters 7, 11, 12, 13, commencement, 2–2
Closing, 3–23
Commencement, petition for relief, 2–1
Dismissal, 3–23
Grounds for dismissal, 2–12
Non-business debtors, 1–6
Termination,
Voluntary dismissal, 2–13
'Voluntary' distinguished from 'involuntary', 2–1

BANKRUPTCY CODE
Legislative history, 1–3
and State law, 1–3

BANKRUPTCY COURT
Discretionary injunction, 3–21
Dismissal sua sponte, 2–9
Supplemental injunctions, 3–22
Suspension of proceedings, 2–10

BANKRUPTCY CRIMES
Denial of discharge, 7–21

BANKRUPTCY JUDGE
Defined, 1–4

BANKRUPTCY LAW
As debt collection system, 1–2
Compared to English law, 1–1
Concept of 'Discharge', 1–3
Defined, 1–3
Distinguished from debt collection laws, 1–2
Distinguished from debtor-creditor laws, 1–3
Incorporation of state law, 1–3
Judicial construction, 1–3
Legislative history, 1–3
Origins, 1–1
Policy goals, 1–2
State common-law concepts, 1–3

BANKRUPTCY PROCEDURE
See also Venue
Chapter 13, petition for relief, 1–8
Collection, 1–7
Commencement of case, 1–7
Discharge, 1–7
Dismissal, frequent filings, 2–2
Distribution, 1–7
Joint administration, 2–4
Lift-stay motion, 3–31
Liquidation, 1–7
Meeting of debtors, 1–7
Pro rata distribution, exceptions, 1–7
Relief from the stay, 3–31
Trustee in bankruptcy, collection of property, 1–7

BANKRUPTCY REFORM ACT OF 1978
Substance of, 1–3

BANKRUPTCY RULES
Promulgation, 1–3

BANKS
Equitable setoff, 6–38
Freezing debtor's funds, 6–43
Postpetition payment of checks, 6–74
Violations of automatic stays, 6–43

BEST INTEREST TEST
in Chapter 11, 10–18
in Chapter 13, 9–9, 9–10
Court approval of non-ordinary course of business sale, 4–4
Court approval of reaffirmation of debts, 7–37

BIDDING IN, 4–8

BONA FIDE PURCHASER
Foreclosure sales, 6–55
Perfected federal tax liens, 6–62
Postpetition transactions, 6–72
Property of the estate, 4–17
Statutory liens, 6–62
Transfers, 6–12

BONA FIDE PURCHASER FOR VALUE
Real estate transfers, postpetition, 6–72
Trustee as, 6–61

BREACH OF CONTRACT
Automatic stay, 3–14
Rejection of executory contract as breach, 5–7

BROKERS
Setoff, 3–15

BUSINESS JUDGMENT TEST
Court approval of assumption or rejection of executory contracts or leases, 5–8

BUSINESS JUSTIFICATION
Test for court approval of non-ordinary course of business sale, 4–4

BUSINESS LICENSES
Property of the estate, 3–21

CASH COLLATERAL
Definition, 4–5
Restrictions on use, 4–5

CASH COLLATERAL—Cont'd
Sanctions for unauthorized use, 4–6
Setoff, 6–43

CASH COLLATERAL ORDER
Chapter 11, 4–5
Property of the estate, 4–5

CAUSES OF ACTION
as Property of the estate, 3–14

CERCLA LIABILITY
See Environmental Cleanup Obligations

CERTIFICATES OF DEPOSIT
Setoff, 6–41

CHANGE OF VENUE
See Venue

CHAPTER 7 (Bankruptcy Code)
See also Liquidation
Appointment of trustee, 7–2
Chapters 19 and 20, 9–30
Compared to Chapter 11, 1–9
Compared to Chapter 12, 1–10
Compared to Chapter 13, 1–8, 9–2
Debtors, conversion rights, 2–18
Discharge, 3–23
Dismissal of case,
  Substantial abuse, 2–14
Dismissal under, 7–43, 7–44, 7–45, 7–46
Distinguished from Chapter 13, 1–8
Distribution of assets, 7–14, 7–15
Election of creditors' committee, 7–2
Eligibility requirements, 2–2
Examination of debtor by trustee, 7–2
Filing a proof of claim, 7–3
Involuntary petitions, 2–5
Late claims, 7–3
Overview of a case, 1–7, 7–1, 7–2
Reaffirmation, see Reaffirmation
Superpriority claims, 7–13
Voluntary dismissal, 2–13
Who can file (filing by creditors), 1–8

CHAPTER 11 (Bankruptcy Code)
Absolute priority rule, 10–21
Avoidance powers, 6–2
Bad faith filing, 3–29
Best interest test, 10–18
Cash collateral order, 4–5
Claims, see Claims
Classification of claims, 10–22
Committee of creditors, 10–11, 10–12, 10–13, 10–14
Compared to Chapter 7, 1–9
Compared to Chapter 12, 1–10, 9–23
Compared to Chapter 13, 1–9
Corporate governance, effects on, 10–7
Cramdown, see Cramdown
Debtor in possession, see Debtor in Possession
Debtors, conversion rights, 2–18
Discharge upon confirmation, 10–30, 10–31
Discrimination between classes of creditors, 10–22, 10–24
Dismissal for bad faith, 2–15, 3–29
Dismissal of case, lack of good faith, 2–15
Distinguished from Chapters 7 and 13, 1–9

CHAPTER 11 (Bankruptcy Code)—Cont'd
Eligibility requirements, 2-2
Examiner, 10-10
Fair and equitable treatment, 10-20
History, 10-1
Impairment of claims, 10-23
Large vs. small reorganization, 10-2
Manipulation of classes of creditors, 10-24
Modification of the plan, 10-33
Nonbusiness debtors, 2-2
Overview, 10-2, 10-3, 10-34
Plan of reorganization, see Plan of Reorganization
Post-confirmation,
    Discharge of debtor, 10-30, 10-31
    Effect of the plan, 10-31
    Implementation of the plan, 10-32
    Modification of the plan, 10-33
    Return of property to the debtor, 10-29
    Revocation of the plan, 10-33
Recourse, 10-26, 10-27, 10-28
Reorganization plan, see Plan of Reorganization
Revocation of the plan, 10-33
Secured claims, 10-28
Tort claims, 11-8
Trustee, 10-8, 10-9
Voluntary dismissal, 2-13

CHAPTER 12 (Bankruptcy Code)
Avoidance powers, 6-2
Chapter 19, 9-30
Codebtors protected by the automatic stay, 3-10
Compared to Chapter 7, 1-10
Compared to Chapter 11, 1-10, 9-23
Compared to Chapter 13, 1-10, 9-23
Conversion, 9-27
Debtors, conversion rights, 2-18
Dismissal, 9-27
Eligibility requirements, 2-2, 9-24
Farming operation, defined, 9-24
Feasibility, 9-29
History, 9-23
Procedure, 9-25
Substantive rules, 9-28, 9-29
Time limitations, 9-25
Voluntary dismissal, 2-13

CHAPTER 13 (Bankruptcy Code)
Avoidance powers, 6-2
Best interest test, 9-9, 9-10
Chapter 20, 9-30
Codebtors protected by the automatic stay, 3-10, 9-4
Compared to Chapter 7, 1-8, 9-2
Compared to Chapter 11, 1-9
Compared to Chapter 12, 1-10, 9-23
Confirmation and post-confirmation, 9-20, 9-21
Confirmation meeting, 9-4
Creditors' meeting, 9-4
Debt limit, 2-2
Debtor as 'individual', 2-2
Debtors, conversion rights, 2-18
Discharge, 9-20, 9-21
Discrimination, 9-7

CHAPTER 13 (Bankruptcy Code)—Cont'd
Disposable income, 9-11, 9-13
Distinguished from Chapter 7, 1-8
Duration of the plan, 9-11, 9-12
Eligibility requirements, 2-2, 9-3
Frequency, increase in number, 9-2
Hardship discharge, 9-21
History, 9-1
Modification of confirmed plan, 9-22
Modification of creditors' rights, 9-15, 9-16, 9-17, 9-18, 9-22
Mortgage deacceleration, modification, 9-17, 9-18
Payment, minimum, 9-8
the Plan,
    Best interest test, 9-9, 9-10
    Confirmation, 9-20
    Cure of default, 9-17
    Deacceleration, 9-17
    Discrimination, 9-7
    Disposable income, 9-11, 9-13
    Duration, 9-12
    Feasibility, 9-19
    Good faith, 9-14
    Minimum payment, 9-8
    Modification of confirmed plan, 9-22
    Modification of creditors' rights, 9-15, 9-16, 9-17, 9-18, 9-22
    Mortgage modification, 9-17, 9-18
    Overview, 9-5
    Priority claims, 9-6
    Revocation of confirmed plan, 9-22
    Secured creditors, 9-6
Postpetition claims, 9-4
Procedure, 9-4
Revocation of confirmed plan, 9-22
Secured claims, 9-4
Trustee, 9-4
Voluntary dismissal, 2-13
Who can file, 1-8

CHAPTERS 19 AND 20, 9-30

CHECK PAYMENT
See Payment by Check

CHILD SUPPORT
See Domestic Obligations

CIVIL FORFEITURE
Automatic stay, effect on, 3-6

CLAIMHOLDER
    See also Claims; Secured Creditors; Unsecured Creditors
Definition, 1-4, 7-4

CLAIMS
Automatic stay, claims affected by, 3-6
Definition, in general, 3-6, 7-4, 11-2
Chapter 11 claims, impairment, 10-23
Contingent claims, 11-5
Criminal restitution, 3-20
Environmental claims, see Environmental Cleanup Obligations
Equitable remedy right as a claim, 7-8
Estimation of claims, 11-5, 11-6, 11-7
Hierarchy of claims, see Priority

CLAIMS—Cont'd
Impairment, Chapter 11 claims, 10–23
Origination, 3–6
Pension obligations, 7–6
Priority, see Priority
Proof of claim, see Proof of Claim
Secured claims, priority of, 7–10
Superpriority claims, 7–13
Tardy claims, 7–15
Tort claims, see Tort Claims
Valuation of claims, 11–5
    for Distribution purposes, 11–7
    for Voting purposes, 11–6
Wage and employee benefit claims, 7–12
What is a claim, 11–2
When arises, 7–5, 11–3
    Condominium fees, 7–7
    Environmental cleanup obligations, 7–7
    Pension obligations, 7–6

CLAIMS ASSESSMENT
Automatic stay, 3–8

CLASSES OF CREDITORS UNDER CHAPTER 11
    See also Chapter 11 (Bankruptcy Code)
Classification of claims, 10–22
Discrimination between, 10–22
Manipulation of, 10–24

CODEBTORS
    See also Joint Bankruptcies; Subsidiaries
Automatic stay, 3–10, 9–4
    Limitations, 3–10
Consumer debt, 3–10

COLLATERAL
    See also Cash Collateral; Security Interests
Avoidance of prepetition security interests, 6–75, 6–76, 6–77, 6–78
Decline in value, 3–27
Effect of automatic stay, 3–1
Equity cushion, calculation, 3–27
Floating liens, 6–35
Increase in value as voidable preference, 6–5
Inventory as collateral, floating lien, 6–35

COLLECTIVE BARGAINING AGREEMENTS
Automatic stay, effects of, 3–7

COMMENCEMENT
Consequences of, 2–7, 2–8
Involuntary cases, 2–5
Joint cases, 2–3
Overview, 2–1
Property of the estate, 2–8
Substantive consolidation, 2–4
Who may file, 2–2

COMMITTEE OF CREDITORS
Definition, 1–4
In general, 10–11, 10–12, 10–13, 10–14

CONDOMINIUM FEES, 7–7

CONFIRMATION
Chapter 13 confirmation, 9–20
Hearing, Chapter 13, 9–4

CONFIRMATION HEARING
Chapter 13 bankruptcy, 9–4

CONSENSUAL LIENS
Avoidance powers, 6–61
Postpetition property, 3–11

CONSOLIDATION OF CASES
Creditors, 2–4
Factors considered, 2–4
Statutory authority, 2–4

CONSOLIDATION OF ESTATES
See Substantive Consolidation

CONSTITUTIONAL ISSUES
Jurisdiction and the Marathon case, 12–1, 12–2
Jury trials, see Jury Trials in Bankruptcy Court
Takings clause, sale of estate property subject to co-owners' interest, 4–9

CONSTRUCTION LIENS
    See also, Liens, "Statutory liens"
Preferences, 6–36

CONSUMER BANKRUPTCY
    See also Chapter 13 (Bankruptcy Code)
Consumer debt, definition, 7–45
Dismissal for substantial abuse, 2–14, 7–45
Small transfers as exceptions to avoidance, 6–37

CONSUMER DEBT
Codebtor, 3–10

CONTEMPORANEOUS NEW VALUE
    See also, Preferences, "Exceptions to avoidance"
Intention of parties, 6–28

CONTEMPT
for Unauthorized use of cash collateral, 4–6
for Violating the stay, 3–35

CONTINGENT CLAIMS
Involuntary petitions,
    Petitioning creditors, 2–5

CONTINGENT LIABILITIES
Value in calculating insolvency, 6–51

CONTRACT CANCELLATION
Automatic stay, 3–8
Ipso facto clause, 3–14

CONTRACT CLAIMS
Lifting the stay, 3–30

CONTRACT RIGHTS
Property of the estate, 3–14

CONVERSION
Consequences, 2–17
Property of the estate, 2–17
Termination of trustee, 2–17

CONVERSION OF BANKRUPTCY CASE
Avoidance powers, 2–17, 6–82
of Chapter 13 case, 9–27
Consequences of, 2–17

CONVERSION OF BANKRUPTCY CASE
—Cont'd
as Creditor's right, 2-19
as Debtor's right, 2-18
Effect on automatic stay, 3-2
Exempt property, 2-17, 8-3
Exemptions, 8-3
of Involuntary cases, 2-5
Postpetition earnings, effects on, 2-17
Property of the estate, 2-17

CONVEYANCES
See Fraudulent Transfers; Transfer Restrictions

CO-OWNED PROPERTY
See also Entireties
Sale of estate property subject to co-owners' interests, 4-9

CORE PROCEEDINGS
See Jurisdiction of Bankruptcy Courts

CORPORATE GOVERNANCE
Effect of bankruptcy, 10-7

CORPORATIONS
Discharge, 7-18, 7-19

COUNTERCLAIMS
Automatic stay, effect on, 3-6

COUNTERCLAIMS IN BANKRUPTCY
Jurisdiction of bankruptcy courts, 12-2

COURSE OF BUSINESS
See Non-Ordinary Course of Business; Ordinary Course of Business

COVENANTS NOT TO COMPETE
Rejection of executory contracts, consequences of, 5-7

CRAMDOWN
Absolute priority rule, unsecured claims, 10-21
Discrimination between classes of creditors, 10-22
Fair and equitable treatment, secured claims, 10-20
In general, 10-19

CREDIT CARD DEBT
Exceptions to discharge, 7-26

CREDIT CARD FRAUD
Definition, 7-26

CREDITOR MEETING
Chapter 13, 9-4

CREDITORS
Collection efforts, 3-1
Definition, 1-4
Distribution, 1-7
 Dividends, 1-7
Foreign debtors, involuntary petitions, 2-6
Involuntary conversion rights, 2-19
Involuntary petitions, 2-5
Priority of postpetition creditors, 4-11, 4-13, 4-14

CREDITORS—Cont'd
Rights under debtor-creditor laws, 1-3
Secured claims, distribution, 1-7
Superpriority claims, 7-13
Unsecured claims,
 Distribution, 1-7
Violation of automatic stay, 3-1

CREDITORS' COMMITTEE
See also, Committee of Creditors
Chapter 11, 6-2, 10-12
Defined, 1-4
Liquidation, 7-2

CREDITOR'S RIGHT OF SETOFF
In general, 6-39
Limitations under bankruptcy law, 1-3

CRIMINAL PROCEEDINGS
Automatic stay, effects of, 3-19, 3-20
Bad faith, 3-20

CROSS-COLLATERALIZATION, 4-11, 4-15
Unsecured debt, 4-15

CURE OF DEFAULT
See Default

DAMAGES
Liquidated damages clauses in rejected executory contracts, 5-7
for Violation of the stay, 3-33, 3-34, 3-35

DEACCELERATION OF DEBT
Chapter 13, 9-17

DEBT COLLECTION
Long-term debt payments as exceptions to avoidance, 6-33
Mutual debt, see Setoff
Nonbankruptcy debt collection, compared to bankruptcy, 1-2
Prohibition under the stay, generally, 3-1, 3-8

DEBTOR
Definition, 1-4
Debtor's avoidance powers, 6-2

DEBTOR IN POSSESSION
See also Trustee
Avoidance powers, see Avoidance Powers
Chapters 11 and 12, 2-8
Definition, 1-4, 10-4
Limits on control of operations, 10-5, 10-6

DEBTORS
As indispensable party, effect on automatic stay, 3-6
Avoidance powers, 6-61, 8-23, 8-24
Conversion rights,
 Chapter 7, 2-18
 Chapter 11, 2-18
 Chapter 12, 2-18
 Chapter 13, 2-18
Defined, 1-4, 2-2
Discharge, 1-7
Discrimination,
 in General, 7-40
 by Employers, 7-40
 by Governmental units, 7-41

DEBTORS—Cont'd
Discrimination—Cont'd
  by Private employers, 7–42
Dismissal of case,
  Chapter 7, 2–13
  Chapters 12 and 13, 2–13
  Chapter 13, 2–13
  Grounds, 2–13
Exempt property, reclamation, 8–24
Extensions of credit, involuntary petitions, 2–5
Nonbankruptcy exemptions, 8–1

DEFALCATIONS
See Fraud

DEFAULT
Chapter 11 plan, refiling, 2–16
Cure of default, Chapter 13, 9–17
of Executory contracts by debtor, see Executory Contracts
of Leases by debtor, see Leases
of Plan obligations, refiling after, 2–16

DEFAULT CLAUSE
Redemption, 7–31

DEFINITIONS
of Participants in a bankruptcy, 1–4

DENIAL OF DISCHARGE
  See also, Discharge
Debts for luxury goods or services, 7–26
Fraudulent renewal of loan, 7–26

DEPOSIT
Utility service, 3–9

DISCHARGE
Chapter 11 discharge upon plan confirmation, 10–30, 10–31
Chapter 13 discharge, 9–20, 9–21
Corporations and partnerships, 7–17, 7–18
Defined, 1–7
Denial of discharge, Chapter 7,
  for Bankruptcy crimes, 7–21
    Distinguished from exception to discharge, 7–17
    for Failure to explain loss of assets, 7–22
    Financial disclosure condition, 7–20
    for Fraudulent conveyances, 7–19
    for "Loading up", 7–26
    for Refusal to obey court, 7–23
    Who is an individual, 7–18
Disclosure requirements, 7–20
Discriminatory treatment of discharged debtors, 7–40, 7–41, 7–42
Exceptions to discharge,
  Alimony, maintenance and support, 7–29
  Credit card debts, 7–26
  Driving while intoxicated, 7–34, 9–20
  Fines and penalties, 7–31, 7–32
  Fraud, false financial statement, 7–26
    Defalcation, embezzlement, 7–28
Fraudulent transfers, 7–19
  Legislative history, 7–24
  Loading up, 7–26
  Overview, 7–24
  Student loans, 7–33

DISCHARGE—Cont'd
Fraudulent transfers—Cont'd
  Taxes, tax penalties, 7–25, 7–32
  Unscheduled debts, 7–27
  Willful and malicious injury, 7–30
Overview, Chapter 7 discharge, 7–16
Reaffirmation, see Reaffirmation
Third party payments in marriage dissolution cases, 7–29
Under bankruptcy law, 1–3

DISCLOSURE BY DEBTOR
Adequate information, 11–17
Discharge condition, 7–20
Overview, 11–16
Pre-packaged plans, prepetition disclosure, 11–22
Purposes, 11–16

DISCLOSURE REQUIREMENTS
Discharge, 7–20

DISCRETIONARY INJUNCTION
Bankruptcy court, 3–21

DISCRIMINATORY TREATMENT OF CREDITORS
Chapter 11 plan, 10–22, 10–24
Chapter 13 plan, 9–7

DISCRIMINATORY TREATMENT OF DEBTORS
Discrimination by governmental units, 7–41
Discrimination by private employers/ees, 7–42
Overview, 7–40

DISMISSAL
Automatic stay, effects of, 3–6
for Bad faith, 2–15, 2–16, 3–29
of Chapter 7 case, 7–43, 7–44, 7–45, 7–46
of Chapter 12 case, 9–27
Consequences of, 2–11
Consumer cases, substantial abuse, 2–14, 7–45
Consumer debt requirement, 7–45
Debtors, Chapters 7 and 11, 2–13
Frequent filings, 2–2
Grounds for, 2–12, 7–43
of Involuntary petitions, 2–5
Motion by U.S. Trustee, 7–44
Single asset debtor, 2–15
Substantive requirements, 7–45
Successive Chapter 7 and Chapter 13 filings, 2–16
Voluntary dismissal, 2–13
Who can cause dismissal, 2–9

DISPOSABLE INCOME, 9–11, 9–13

DISTRIBUTION
Creditors, 1–7
Penalties, 7–15
Sales of assets, 1–7
Tardy claims, 7–15

DISTRIBUTION OF ASSETS
Estimating claims for distribution, 11–7
Liquidation, Chapter 7, 7–14, 7–15

DIVORCE
Automatic stay, effect on, 3–6

DIVORCE SETTLEMENTS
Debtor's avoidance powers, 8–25

DOMESTIC OBLIGATIONS
Automatic stay, effects of 3–12, 3–30
Effects on automatic stay, 3–30
Exceptions to discharge, 3–12, 7–29
Pension obligations, 7–6

DOMICILE
Definition, 8–3

DRUNK DRIVING
See Discharge, "Exceptions to discharge"

EARMARKING DOCTRINE, 6–7
See also Preferences

ELIGIBILITY FOR BANKRUPTCY, 2–2
Chapter 12, 9–24
Chapter 13, 9–2

EMBEZZLEMENT
See Fraud

EMERGENCY SALE OF ASSETS
Postpetition sale of all or substantially all assets, 4–4

EMPLOYEE BENEFITS
See also Retirement Benefits
Exemptions, 8–33
Priority of claims, 4–12

ENABLING SECURITY INTERESTS
See Purchase–Money Security Interests

ENCUMBRANCES
See Liens; Security Interests

ENTIRETIES
Exemption of, 8–10
Sale of estate property subject to co-owners' interests, 4–9

ENVIRONMENTAL CLEANUP OBLIGATIONS
Priority in relation to other claims, 11–9, 11–10, 11–12
as Secured claims, 11–11
When claim arises, 7–7

EQUITABLE SETOFF
In general, 6–38

EQUITY CUSHION
Adequate protection, 3–27

EQUITY IN PROPERTY
Debtor's equity, 3–25

ESCROW
as Preference transfer, 6–4

EVICTION
Automatic stay, effect on, 3–6

EVIDENCE
Fraudulent transfers, 6–48

EXAMINER
Appointment, 10–10
Definition, 1–4
Role, 10–10

EXCEPTIONS TO AVOIDANCE
See Preferences, "Exceptions to avoidance"

EXCEPTIONS TO DISCHARGE
See Discharge

EXCEPTIONS TO THE AUTOMATIC STAY
See also Automatic Stay
Aircraft security interests, 3–17
Collective bargaining agreements, 3–7
Criminal actions excepted, 3–19, 3–20
Domestic obligations, 3–12
Government actions, 3–14, 3–19, 3–20, 3–21
Leases, nonresidential, 3–14
Listed, 3–1
Perfection of liens within grace period, 3–18
Setoff exceptions, 3–15
Supplemental injunctions, 3–22

EXCLUSIVITY PERIOD
Cause for extension, 11–15
In general, 11–13
Procedure for extension, 11–14

EXECUTORY CONTRACTS
Adequate assurance of assignee performance, 5–21
Adequate assurance of future performance, 5–20
Assignee performance, adequate assurance of, 5–21
Assignment, consequences of, 5–6
Assumption, consequences of, 5–5
Court approval of assumption or rejection, 5–8
Default and adequate assurance, 5–20
Default cure and compensation, 5–19
Defaulted contracts, 5–18, 5–19, 5–20
Definition, 5–4
Gap period, see Gap Period
Intellectual property contracts, rejection by licensor, 5–7
Loans or Financial Accommodations, assumption of, 5–13, 5–14
Multiple executory contracts in one document, 5–4
Non–Assignable executory contracts, 5–15, 5–16, 5–17
Non–Assumable executory contracts, 5–12, 5–13, 5–14, 5–15
Obligations during gap period, see Gap Period
Partnership agreements, 11–38
Recoupment prior to debtor's assumption, 5–25
Rejection, consequences of, 5–7
"Special" executory contracts under the Code, 5–26
Termination clauses, 5–12
Time limits for assumption or rejection, 5–9, 5–11
Treatment in bankruptcy, 5–1

EXEMPT PROPERTY
Conversion to non-exempt property, 6–58
Fraudulent transfers, 6–57

EXEMPTIONS
Avoided transfers of exempt property,
    Debtor's avoidance powers, 8–24
    Determining if property is exempt, 8–26

EXEMPTIONS—Cont'd
Avoided transfers of exempt property—Cont'd
  Fixing of lien, 8–27
  Household goods, 8–25
  Impairment of exemption, 8–28
  Judicial lien, 8–25
  Procedural concerns, 8–29
  Security interest, 8–25
  Trade tools of debtor, 8–25
  Trustee's avoidance powers, 8–22
    Asserted by debtor, 8–23
Change in state exemption law after petition, 8–3
Chapter 7, consumer debtor, 1–7
Choice of laws by debtor, 8–3
Conversion of bankruptcy case, 8–3
Conversion of nonexempt property to exempt property as fraudulent transfer, 6–58, 8–32
Conversion (to a different chapter of bankruptcy), effects of, 2–17, 8–3
Employee benefits, 8–33
Entireties property, 8–10
ERISA, 8–33
Exemption value, definition, 8–28
Federal bankruptcy law exemptions, 8–12—8–20
  Benefits, 8–17
  Goods, 8–15
  Income, 8–16, 8–17, 8–18
  Life insurance, 8–19
  Recovery of losses, tort claims, 8–18
  Residence, 8–13
  Wild card exemption, 8–20
Hearings, 8–1
Homestead exemption, 8–7, 8–13
Impairment of exemption, for avoidance purposes, 8–28
Inalienable property, 8–33
Joint cases, 8–21
Lien avoidance, procedural requirements, 8–29
Natural persons, 8–2
Nonbankruptcy law exemptions, overview, 8–4
Nonbankruptcy law exemptions, federal, 8–11
"Opt out" clause, 8–2
Overview, 8–1, 8–4, 8–12
Pension benefits, 8–33
Personal property exemptions, 8–6, 8–14
Postpetition estate property, 8–3
Postpetition transactions, 8–3
Prepetition disposition of residence, 8–13
Property held by the entirety, 8–10
Real property exemptions, 8–7
Residence, 8–7, 8–13
Retirement benefits, 8–33
Secured debts, 8–1
State law exemptions, 8–6, 8–7, 8–8, 8–9, 8–25
Tenancy by the entirety, 8–10
Transfer of exempt property as fraudulent transfer, 6–57
Transfer of exempt property as voidable preference, 6–6
Trust funds, 8–33
Value limitations on state exemptions, 8–8
Voluntary transfers, 8–22

EXEMPTIONS—Cont'd
Waiver, 8–9, 8–31
Who is entitled to exemptions, 8–2

EXECUTORY CONTRACTS
Assignment, 5–1
Assumption, 5–1
Obligations of the estate, 5–5
Rejection, 5–1

FAILURE TO FILE
Grounds for dismissal, 7–43

FAIR AND EQUITABLE TREATMENT
of Secured creditors, Chapter 11, 10–20

FAMILY FARMER
Chapter 12,
  Eligibility requirements, 2–2

FARMER BANKRUPTCIES
See Chapter 12 (Bankruptcy Code)

FEASIBILITY OF THE REORGANIZATION PLAN
Chapter 12 plan, 9–29
Chapter 13 plan, 9–19
Lifting of the stay when Debtor lacks equity, 3–25

FEDERAL NONBANKRUPTCY LAW
Exemptions, 8–11

FEDERAL SETOFF
In general, 6–38

FEDERAL TAX LIENS
Bona fide purchasers, 6–62
Preferences, 6–36

FIDUCIARY RELATIONSHIP, 7–28

FILING FEES
Petition for relief, 2–2

FILING OF PETITION
  See also Commencement; Serial Filings
Bad faith filings, see Good Faith
Fees, 2–2
Foreclosure, filing on eve of, 2–15
Joint petition, 2–3
Who can file, 1–8, 2–2, 2–5

FINAL ORDERS
Distinguished from interlocutory orders, 12–12

FINANCIAL ACCOMMODATIONS
Assumption of, see Executory Contracts

FINANCIAL DISCLOSURE
False financial statement, exception to discharge, 7–26

FINANCIAL DISCLOSURE CONDITION
Denial of discharge, 7–20

FINES AND PENALTIES
Exceptions to discharge, 7–31, 7–32

FLOATING LIENS
  See also, Liens

INDEX

FLOATING LIENS—Cont'd
Collateral, valuation methods, 6–35
Setoff, 6–41

FLOATING SECURITY INTERESTS
Postpetition transactions, 6–76

FORECLOSURE
Automatic stay, 3–16
Filing on eve of, 2–15
Foreclosure sales as fraudulent transfers, 6–53, 6–54, 6–55, 6–56
Foreclosure sales as preferences, 6–21
"Lien-theory" state compared to "title-theory" state, 6–54

FORECLOSURE SALES
Avoidance powers, 6–21
Bona fide purchasers, 6–55
'Reasonably equivalent value', 6–56

FOREIGN DEBTORS, 2–6
Involuntary petitions, 2–6
Petitions for relief, 2–6

FRAUD
See also Good Faith
Credit card debt, exception to discharge, 7–26
Credit card fraud, elements, 7–26
Denial of discharge, scienter requirement, 7–26
False financial statements, 7–26
Fraud, false financial statements, exceptions to discharge, 7–26
Defalcation, embezzlement, exceptions to discharge, 7–28
Material misrepresentations, denial of discharge, 7–21
Standard of Proof, 7–26

FRAUDULENT CONVEYANCE
See Fraudulent Transfers

FRAUDULENT TRANSFERS
In general, 6–46, 6–47
'Actually' fraudulent and 'constructively' fraudulent, 6–46, 6–47
Automatic stay, 3–10
Avoidance powers, 6–47
Badges of fraud, 6–48, 7–19
Burden of proof, 6–48, 6–49
Conversion of nonexempt property to exempt property, 6–58
Defenses of transferee, 6–50
Denial of discharge, 7–19
Economic benefit to the debtor, 6–49
Evidence, 6–48
Exempt property, conversion from nonexempt property, 6–58
Exempt property, transfer of, 6–57
Foreclosure sales,
Overview, 6–53
"Reasonably equivalent value," 6–56
Timing of the transfer, 6–55
as Transfer of debtor's interest, 6–54
Fraud, actual, 6–48
Fraud, constructive, 6–49
Fraudulent transfers under state law, 6–60
'Good faith' defense of transferee, 6–50

FRAUDULENT TRANSFERS—Cont'd
Guaranties, 6–51
Insolvency, 6–49, 6–51
Intention of transferor, 6–48
Intracorporate guaranties, 6–51
Jury trials, 12–14
Leveraged buyouts, 6–52
Overview, 6–46, 6–47
Preferential transfers as fraudulent transfers, 6–59
"Reasonably equivalent value" received by debtor, 6–49, 6–56
Remedies of trustee, 6–50
State fraudulent transfer law, 6–60
to Subsequent transferees, 6–50
Trustee as successor to creditor, 6–60
Value received by debtor, determination of, 6–49

FREEDOM OF CONTRACT
Automatic stay, 3–8

GAP PERIOD
Adequate protection of nondebtor lessor during gap period, 5–24
Debtor's performance obligations, 5–23
Nondebtor's performance obligations, 5–22
Recoupment during gap period, 5–25

GARNISHMENT
During preference period, 6–15
Liens, see Liens, "Statutory liens"
Preference period, 6–15
Preferential and avoidable, 6–15

GENERAL PARTNERS
Partnerships,
Petition for relief, 2–2

GOOD FAITH
See also Fraud
Bad faith, determination of, 3–29
Chapter 13 plan, 9–14
Discharge of student loans, 7–33
Dismissal of Chapter 11 petition for bad faith, 2–15, 3–29
Dismissal of repetitive filing for bad faith, 2–16
Lifting the stay for bad faith filing, 3–29
Test for court approval of non-ordinary course of business sales, 4–4
Transferee of fraudulent transfer, 6–50, 6–52

GOVERNMENT ACTIONS
Discriminatory treatment towards discharged debtors, 7–41
Exceptions to the automatic stay, 3–14, 3–19, 3–20, 3–21
Fines and penalties, exceptions to discharge, 7–31
Governmental unit, definition, 7–41
Liens, see Liens, "Statutory liens"
Sovereign immunity, see Sovereign Immunity
Taxes, exception to discharge, 7–25

GOVERNMENTAL ENFORCEMENT POWERS
Exception from automatic stay, 3–21

GOVERNMENTAL REGULATORY ACTIONS
Exceptions from automatic stay, 3–21

GROUNDS FOR DISMISSAL
Failure to file, 7–43
Nonpayment of fees, 7–43
Substantial abuse by debtor, 7–43
Unreasonable delay, 7–43

GUARANTIES
Avoidable as fraudulent transfer, 6–51
Definition, 6–51

HARDSHIP DISCHARGE, 9–21

HEARINGS
See also, Bankruptcy Procedure
Exemptions, 8–1
Lift-stay motions, 3–31

HISTORY
of Bankruptcy, 1–1
Legislative history of Bankruptcy Code, 1–3

HOLDER OF A CLAIM
Defined, 1–4

HOLDER OF A SECURED CLAIM
Defined, 1–4

HOLDER OF AN UNSECURED CLAIM
Defined, 1–4

HOMESTEAD
Exemption, 8–7, 8–13
Sale of homestead subject to interest of co-owner, 4–9
State law exemptions, 8–7

IDENTITY OF INTEREST RULE
Guarantor and principal obligor, fraudulent transfers, 6–51
Nondebtors protected by the automatic stay, 3–10

IMPAIRMENT
of Claims, Chapter 11, 10–23
of Exemption on property, 8–28

IMPROVEMENT LIEN
See Liens

INDIRECT PREFERENCES
See Preferences

INDIRECT TRANSFER DOCTRINE, 6–9
See also Preferences

INDIVIDUAL
Definition, for purposes of discharge, 7–18

INDUBITABLE EQUIVALENT, 10–20

INEQUITABLE CONDUCT
Definition, 6–93
Justifying equitable subordination, 6–93

INJUNCTIONS
Actions against third-party nondebtors, 3–22
Creditor's actions against nondebtors, 3–22

INJUNCTIVE RELIEF
See also Automatic Stay

INJUNCTIVE RELIEF—Cont'd
Enforcement under the stay, 3–21
Equitable remedy right as a claim, 7–8
Partnership cases, staying creditors, 11–36
Reimposing the stay, 3–31
to Stay criminal proceedings, 3–20
Supplemental injunctions, 3–22
Third party nondebtors, 3–22

INSIDERS
See also Preferences
Definition of insider, 6–17
Inequitable conduct, 6–93
Loans from insiders as inequitable conduct subject to subordination, 6–93
Preference period for insiders, 6–17
Preferential transfers as fraudulent transfers, 6–59

INSOLVENCY
Calculation methods, for preference purposes, 6–18
Contingent liabilities, 6–51
Definition, 6–49
for Fraudulent transfer purposes, 6–49, 6–51
for Preference purposes, 6–18

INSOLVENT DEBTORS
Calculation methods, 6–18
Preferences, 6–18

INSURANCE POLICIES
Property of the estate, 3–14

INTELLECTUAL PROPERTY
Rejection of executory contract, consequences, 5–7

INTEREST
Tax debt, debtor's liability for interest, 7–25

INTERLOCUTORY ORDERS
Appeals of, 12–12
Distinguished from final orders, 12–12

INTRACORPORATE GUARANTIES
Fraudulent transfers, 6–51

INVENTORY SECURITY INTERESTS
See Liens, "Floating"

INVOLUNTARY CASES, 2–5
Involuntary conversion, 2–19
Involuntary gap, 2–5
Postpetition transfers as exceptions to avoidance, 6–71

INVOLUNTARY CONVERSION RIGHTS
Creditors, 2–19

INVOLUNTARY GAP
Involuntary petitions, 2–5

INVOLUNTARY PETITIONS
Answer by debtor, 2–5
Automatic stays, 2–5
Bad faith, dismissal, 2–5
Bankruptcy Act of 1898, 2–5
Chapter 7, 2–5
Commencement, 2–5
Creditors, 2–5

INVOLUNTARY PETITIONS—Cont'd
Debtors, extension of credit, 2–5
Dismissal, 2–5
Eligible debtors, 2–5
Foreign debtors, 2–6
Grounds, 2–5
Involuntary gap, 2–5
Orders for relief, 2–5
Partnerships, 2–5
Petitioning creditors, 2–5

INVOLUNTARY PROCEEDINGS
Distinguished from voluntary proceedings, 1–7

INVOLUNTARY TRANSFERS
Avoidance and exemption, 8–22, 8–23
Avoidance powers, 8–22
Debtor's avoidance powers, 8–23
Concealment, 8–22

JOINT ADMINISTRATION
Bankruptcy procedure, 2–4
Defined, 2–4
Distinguished from Substantive Consolidation, 2–4

JOINT BANKRUPTCIES
In general, 2–3
Exemptions, 8–21

JOINT CASES
Exemptions, 8–21
Husband and wife, consolidation, 2–3

JOINT PROPERTY
See also Entireties
Sale of estate property subject to co-owners' interests, 4–9

JUDGE (Bankruptcy Judge)
Approval of reaffirmation, 7–35
Definition, 1–4

JUDGMENTS
Enforcement under the stay, 3–21

JUDICIAL LIENS
Debtor's avoidance powers, 8–25
Distinguished from statutory liens, 6–36

JURISDICTION OF BANKRUPTCY COURTS
See also Jury Trials in Bankruptcy Court; Venue
Abstention, 12–5
Appeals, 12–12
Compared to other forums, 3–30
Core proceedings, 12–2
Related proceedings, 12–3
Overview, source, 12–1
Tort personal injury cases, 12–4

JURY TRIALS IN BANKRUPTCY COURT
Constitutionality, 3–30, 12–14
Right to jury trial, 12–13, 12–14, 12–15
Granfinanciera and after, 12–14, 12–15
History in bankruptcy, 12–13
Transfer of forum, 3–30
Which judge presides, 12–16

LAND SALES
Executory contracts, 5–4

LEASEHOLD INTEREST
Automatic stay, 3–14

LEASES
Adequate assurance of assignee performance, 5–21
Adequate assurance of future performance, 5–20
Adequate protection of nondebtor lessor during gap period, 5–24
Assignee performance, adequate assurance of, 5–21
Assignment, 5–1
Consequences of, 5–6
Assignment compared to subleasing, 5–6
Assumption, 5–1
Consequences of, 5–5
Automatic stay, effects of, 3–14, 3–28
Court approval of assumption or rejection, 5–8
Default and adequate assurance of future performance, 5–20
Default cure and compensation, 5–19
Defaulted leases, 5–18, 5–19, 5–20
Definition, 5–2
Gap period, see Gap Period
Non-Assignable leases, 5–15, 5–16, 5–17
Non-Assumable leases, 5–12, 5–15
Non-residential real property leases, 5–23
Obligations during gap period, see Gap Period
Obligations of the estate, 5–5
Property of the estate, 3–28
Rejection, 5–1
Consequences of, 5–7
Security lease, distinguished from true lease, 5–2
Shopping center leases, adequate assurance of future performance, 5–20
"Special" leases under the Code, 5–26
Termination clauses, 5–12
Time limits for assumption or rejection, 5–9, 5–10, 5–11
Treatment in bankruptcy, 5–1
Unexpired leases, definition, 5–3

LEGISLATIVE HISTORY
of Bankruptcy Code, 1–3
of Exceptions to discharge, 7–24
of Reaffirmation, 7–35

LETTERS OF CREDIT
Automatic stay, effects of, 3–14
Property of the estate, 3–14
as Voidable preferences, 6–9

LEVERAGED BUYOUTS
In general, 6–52
as Fraudulent transfers, 6–52
Policy considerations, 6–52

LIABILITY INSURERS
Automatic stay, 3–10

LICENSE REVOCATION
Automatic stay, effect on, 3–6

LIENS
See also Security Interests
Automatic stay, liens affected, 3–11, 3–16, 3–18
Avoidance of fixing of lien by debtor, 8–24, 8–25
Debtor's avoidance powers, 8–25
Debtor's right to exempt, 8–1
Fixing of lien, debtor's avoidance, 8–27
Floating liens, 6–35, 6–67, 6–75, 6–76, 6–77, 6–78
Improvement liens, 6–89
Judicial lien, avoidance by debtor, 8–25
Judicial lien, trustee as lien creditor, 6–61
Perfection, see Perfection, of liens, 3–18
Prepetition debts, 3–11
Prepetition transfers, exemptions, 8–1
Purchase-money liens as exceptions to avoidance, 6–24, 6–33
Reclamation of goods, see Reclamation of Goods
Statutory lien, definition, 6–36, 6–62
Statutory liens vulnerable to avoidance power, 6–62
Statutory liens as exceptions to avoidance, 6–36

LIFE INSURANCE
Exemptability under bankruptcy law, 8–19

LIFTING THE STAY
Actions in specialized forms, 3–30
Adequate protection agreement, 3–27
Adequate protection of lessors, 3–28
Annulment, 3–32
Appeal of orders granting or denying relief, 3–31
Bad faith filing, 3–29
Balancing test, 3–30
Burdens of proof, 3–31
for Cause, 3–26, 3–27, 3–28, 3–29, 3–30
Contract claims, 3–30
Debtor lacks equity in property, 3–25
Effects of lifting the stay, 3–31
for Estimation of claim in another court, 11–7
Ex parte relief, 3–31
Feasibility of reorganization, 3–25
"For cause", 3–26, 3–27
Forum more appropriate elsewhere, 3–30
Judicial annulment of the stay, 3–32
by Judicial default, 3–31
Lack of adequate protection, 3–27
Leases, 3–28
Lift-stay motion, 3–31, 3–25
Limited relief, 3–31
Overview, 3–24
"Party in interest", 3–31
Procedural concerns, 3–31
Reimposing the stay, 3–31
Tort claims, 3–30
Unsecured creditors, 3–26
Who can request relief, 3–31

LIFT-STAY HEARINGS
See Lift-Stay Motions

LIFT-STAY MOTIONS
Debtor's counterclaims, 3–31

LIFT-STAY MOTIONS—Cont'd
Hearings, 3–31
Issuance of orders, 3–31
Notice and hearing, 3–31
Time limits, 3–31

LIMITED PARTNERSHIPS
Involuntary cases, treatment in, 2–5
Petitioning creditors,
 Involuntary petitions, 2–5

LIQUIDATION
In general, 1–5, 7–1
 See also Chapter 7 (Bankruptcy Code)
Compared to rehabilitation, 1–5
Discharge, see Discharge
Distinguished from rehabilitation, 1–5
Distribution of assets, 7–14, 7–15
Filing proof of claim, 7–3
Hierarchy of claims, 7–10, 7–11, 7–12, 7–13
Meeting of creditors, 7–2
Order for relief, 7–2
Pension obligations, 7–6
Procedure, overview, 7–2
Property of the estate, 1–7
Reaffirmation, see Reaffirmation
Redemption, see Redemption
Schedule of assets and liabilities, 7–2
Superpriority claims, 7–13

LOADING UP
Denial of discharge, 7–26
Luxury goods and services, exceptions to discharge, 7–26

LOAN GUARANTOR
Consumer debt, automatic stay, 3–10

LOANS
Assumption of, see Executory Contracts
Fraudulently renewed loans, causation, exception to discharge, 7–26
Postpetition secured loans, 4–13, 4–14
Postpetition unsecured loans, 4–12
Student loans, exception to discharge, 7–33

LONG-TERM OBLIGATIONS
Ordinary course of business transfers, 6–32

LUXURY GOODS AND SERVICES
See Loading Up

MAINTENANCE AND SUPPORT
See Domestic Obligations

MATERIALMEN'S LIENS
Preferences, 6–36

MATURE DEBTS
Equitable setoff, 6–38

MECHANIC'S LIENS
Preferences, 6–36

MEETING OF CREDITORS
Liquidation, 7–2
Trustee, 7–2

MEETING OF DEBTORS
Location and evaluation of property, 1–7

MORTGAGES
Deacceleration, modification, 9–17, 9–18

MOTION FOR DISMISSAL
Who can move for dismissal, 2–9

MOTOR VEHICLES
Redemption, 7–49

MUTUAL DEBT
See Setoff

MUTUAL OBLIGATION
See Setoff

NEGOTIABLE INSTRUMENTS
Automatic stay, 3–8

NEW VALUE
Application of the New Value doctrine, 11–28, 11–29
Arguing for/against the new value exception to the absolute priority rule, 11–27, 11–30
Cases involving new value, 11–29
Contemporaneous new value as exception to avoidance, see Preferences, "Exceptions to avoidance"
Definition, 6–25
History, 11–26
Modification of pre-existing duty as new value, 6–25
Necessity requirement, 11–28
Purchase-money security interests as exceptions to avoidance, 6–33
Subsequent to preferential transfer, 6–34

N.L.R.B. PROCEEDINGS
Automatic stay, 3–21

NO–ASSET (CHAPTER 7)
Termination, 3–23

NON–BUSINESS DEBTORS
Bankruptcy cases, 1–6
Chapter 11, 2–2

NONCONSENSUAL LIEN CREDITOR
Postpetition interest, 1–3

NONDEBTORS
Automatic stay, 3–10

NON–ORDINARY COURSE OF BUSINESS
In general, 4–4
See also Ordinary Course of Business; Property of the Estate
Notice and hearing requirements, 4–16
Routine sales, court approval of, 4–4
Sale of all or substantially all assets, court approval of, 4–4
Unsecured loans, 4–12

NONPAYMENT OF FEES
Grounds for dismissal, 7–43

NONPOSSESSORY SECURITY INTERESTS
Debtor's avoidance powers, 8–25

NONRESIDENTIAL LEASES
Property of the estate, 3–14

NOTICE
of Bankruptcy case to creditors, 7–27
Bankruptcy court's powers, 4–16
Local rules, 4–16
Notice and hearing requirement, non-ordinary course transactions, 4–16

NOVATION
Pension obligations, 7–6

NULLIFICATION
See Avoidance Powers

OFFSET
See Setoff

OPT–OUT CLAUSES, 8–3

ORDER FOR RELIEF
Adjudication, 2–2
Foreign debtors, grounds, 2–6
Involuntary cases, 2–5
Involuntary petitions, 2–5
Liquidation, 7–2
Relief from the automatic stay, see Lifting the stay

ORDINARY COURSE OF BUSINESS
See also Non–Ordinary Course of Business; Property of the Estate
Distinguished from non-ordinary course, 4–3
Payments as exceptions to preferences, 6–29, 6–30, 6–31, 6–32
Postpetition transactions, 6–70
Unsecured creditors, 4–12
Unsecured loans, 4–12
Use/sale/lease of property of the estate, 4–3

ORDINARY COURSE OF BUSINESS TRANSFERS
Definition, 6–29
Payments on long-term debt, 6–32
Short-term obligations, 6–32
Subjective and objective tests, 6–31
Untimely payments, 6–31

ORDINARY DEBTS
See Ordinary Course of Business

ORIGINAL ISSUE DISCOUNT, 11–24

ORIGINS OF BANKRUPTCY, 1–1
Legislative history of Bankruptcy Code, 1–3

OVERSECURED CREDITORS
Lack of adequate protection, 3–27
Lifting the stay, 3–27
Postpetition interest, 3–27

PARTNERSHIP BANKRUPTCIES
See also Limited Partnerships
Automatic stay applied to partners, 11–34, 11–35
Differences from corporate bankruptcies, 11–31
Effects on partnership agreements, 11–37
Assumption, assignment, rejection, 11–38
Settlement and contribution by partner, 11–39
Eligibility for filing, commencement, 2–2

PARTNERSHIP BANKRUPTCIES—Cont'd
Injunctive relief to stay creditors, 11–36
Involuntary cases, 2–5
Jingle rule, 11–32
Liabilities to creditors, 11–32
Priority, 11–33
Venue, 12–6, 12–7

PARTNERSHIPS
Discharge, 7–18, 7–19
Involuntary petitions, Chapter 7, 2–5
Petition for relief, 2–2

PARTY IN INTEREST
Definition, 3–31
Lifting the stay, 3–31

PAYMENT BY CHECK
Perfection, 6–15
for Preference purposes, 6–16
Transfers, 6–15

PECUNIARY INTEREST TEST
Governmental action, effect on automatic stay, 3–21

PENALTIES
Definition, for purposes of Chapter 7 liquidation, 7–15
Exceptions to discharge, 7–31, 7–32

PENSION OBLIGATIONS
to Spouse, 7–6

PENSION PLANS
See also Retirement Benefits
Restoration after bankruptcy, 3–14

PERFECTION
of Liens, 3–18
Payment by check, 6–15
Postpetition perfection, 6–77
Postpetition rents and profits, 6–77
and the Preference period, 6–12, 6–13
Real property transfers, 6–12
Relation back of perfection, 6–13, 6–33
Third party interests, 6–61
Time limitation, 3–18, 6–11

PERSONAL SERVICE LIENS
See Liens, "Statutory liens"

PETITION FOR RELIEF
Automatic stay, initiation of bankruptcy case, 3–1
Chapter 13, 1–8
Creditors, 6–43
Foreign debtors, 2–6
Frequent filings, limitations, 2–2
Initiation of bankruptcy case, 3–1

PETITIONING CREDITORS
Involuntary petitions, contingent claims, 2–5

PETITIONS
Creditor filings, 2–5
Joint petitions, 2–3
Simultaneous petitions, 2–16

PIERCING THE CORPORATE VEIL
Distinguished from Substantive Consolidation, 2–4

PLAN OF REORGANIZATION
Chapter 13, see Chapter 13 (Bankruptcy Code), "Plan"
See also Chapter 11 (Bankruptcy Code)
Acceptance requirements, 10–17
Best interest test, 10–18
Classification of claims, 10–22
Competing plans, 11–18
Consummation, 3–23
Cramdown, 10–19
    Absolute priority rule, 10–21
    Discrimination between classes of creditors, 10–22
    Fair and equitable treatment, 10–20
Exclusivity period, 11–13
    Extension for cause, 11–15
    Extension procedure, 11–14
Feasibility, 3–25
Impairment of claims, 10–23
Implementation of the plan, 10–32
Manipulation of classes of creditors, 10–24
Modification of the plan, 10–33
New value, 11–27, 11–28, 11–29, 11–30
Overview, 10–15, 10–16
Post-confirmation, 10–31
Prepackaged plans, 11–21
    Advantages, disadvantages of pre-packaged plans, 11–24
    Prepetition disclosure, 11–22
    Prepetition solicitation, 11–23
Priority of claimants, 10–15
    See also Priority
Revocation of the plan, 10–33
Solicitation of rejection or acceptance of plans, 11–18
Voting, estimation of claims, 11–6
Voting agreements, 11–19
Voting in multiple plan cases, 11–20

POLICE AND REGULATORY POWERS
as Exceptions to the automatic stay, 3–21
Tests for, 3–21

POSSESSION OF PROPERTY
See also Reclamation of Goods
Automatic stay, effects of, 3–14
Effects on reclamation rights, 6–67

POSTPETITION CLAIMS
Allowance in Chapter 13 bankruptcy, 9–4
Automatic stay, 3–4
Chapter 13 bankruptcy, 9–4
Conversion and postpetition earnings, 2–17
Creditor priority, 4–11, 4–13, 4–14
Property or earnings, property of the estate, 2–8
Rents and profits of mortgaged property, 6–77

POSTPETITION EXPENSES
Administrative expenses, 7–11

POSTPETITION FUNDS
Payment of wages, 4–15

POSTPETITION INTEREST
Nonconsensual lien creditor, 1–3
Oversecured creditors, 3–27

POSTPETITION LOANS
Prepetition assets, secured by, 4–15

POSTPETITION PROPERTY
Consensual liens, 3–11

POSTPETITION TRANSACTIONS
See also Non–Ordinary Course of Business; Ordinary Course of Business; Property of the Estate
Agricultural set aside programs, 6–77
Authorized transfers, 6–70
Avoidance of postpetition transfers,
　Authorized transfers as exceptions to avoidance, 6–70
　Exceptions, 6–70, 6–71, 6–72, 6–77
　Floating liens, avoidance, 6–75, 6–76, 6–77, 6–78
　Innocent third-party transferors, 6–74
　Involuntary cases, exceptions to avoidance, 6–71
　Overview, 6–68
　Perfection postpetition, 6–77
　Real estate transfers as exceptions to avoidance, 6–72
　Scope, 6–68, 6–69
　Security interests, prepetition, 6–75, 6–76, 6–77, 6–78
　Third party transfers, 6–74
　Time limitations, 6–73
　Valuation of transfers, 6–71
Avoidance powers, 2–17, 6–69
Exemptions, 8–3
Floating security interests, 6–76
Involuntary cases, 6–71
Loans, creditors' priority, 4–11, 4–12, 4–13, 4–14
Notice and hearing requirements, 4–16
Ordinary course of business, 6–70
Personal property, 6–72
Prepetition security agreement, 6–68, 6–76
Property of the estate, 6–68, 6–69
Real estate, 6–72
Use/sale/lease of property of the estate, see Property of the Estate

PREEMPTION OF FEDERAL LAW
See State Law

PREEXISTING LIENS
Automatic stay, 3–11

PREFERENCES
Antecedent debt requirement, 6–19
Check payment, preference period, 6–16
Collateral appreciation, 6–5
Construction liens, 6–36
Consumer cases, small transfers as exceptions to avoidance, 6–37
Contemporaneous new value as exception to avoidance, 6–23, 6–27
Definition, 6–3
Earmarked funds or property, 6–7
Effect on third party transferees, 6–11

PREFERENCES—Cont'd
Escrow as preference transfer, 6–4
Exceptions to avoidance,
　Consumer cases, small transfers, 6–37
　Contemporaneous new value, generally, 6–23
　　Definition of contemporaneous, 6–27
　　Definition of exchange, 6–26
　　Definition of new value, 6–25
　　Intent requirement, 6–28
　　Scope of the exception, 6–24
　Floating liens on inventory or receivables, 6–35
　New value subsequent to preferential transfer, 6–34
　Ordinary course of business payments, generally, 6–29
　　Ordinary debt, 6–30
　　Ordinary payments, 6–31
　　Long-term debt, 6–32
　Overview, 6–22
　Purchase-money security interests, 6–33
　Statutory liens, 6–36
Exempt property transferred, 6–6
Exemption of small transfers in consumer bankruptcy cases, 6–37
Federal tax liens, 6–36
Floating liens, calculation method, 6–35
Floating liens on inventory or receivables, 6–35
Foreclosure sales as preferences, 6–21
Fraudulent transfers,
　See Fraudulent Transfers
　Preferential transfers as, 6–59
Friends as "insiders", 6–17
Garnishment during preference period, 6–15
Increase in value of collateral as a transfer, 6–5
Indirect preferences, 6–9
　Remedies, 6–10
Indirect preferences to insiders, 6–10
Insider preferences, preference period, 6–17
Insolvency requirement, 6–18
Jury trials, 12–14
Liens, statutory, 6–36
Long-term debt payment, 6–32
Materialmen's liens, 6–36
Mechanic's liens, 6–36
New value, contemporaneous new value as exception to avoidance, 6–23, 6–27
New value requirement, 6–25
New value subsequent to preferential transfer, 6–35
Ordinary course of business payments, 6–29, 6–30, 6–31, 6–32
Overview, 6–3
Payment by check, 6–15
Payment to creditor benefiting surety, 6–9
Perfection, 6–11, 6–12, 6–13
Preference period, generally, 6–11
　Caveat: no transfer until debtor acquires rights, 6–14
　Exception: perfection within ten days, 6–13
　Garnishment during preference period, 6–15

PREFERENCES—Cont'd
Preference period—Cont'd
  General rule, time of transfer is time of perfection, 6–12
  Insiders, 6–17
  Payment by check, 6–16
Preferential effect requirement, 6–20, 6–21
Preferential transfers as fraudulent transfers, 6–59
Purchase-money security interests, 6–33
Recoupment, see Recoupment
Relatives as "insiders", 6–17
Setoff, see Setoff
Small transfers, exemption of, 6–37
State fraudulent transfer laws, 6–60
State of mind irrelevant, 6–3
Statutory liens, 6–36, 6–62
Tangible value requirement, 6–25
Time of transfer, the preference period, 6–11, 6–12, 6–13, 6–14
"To or for the Benefit of a Creditor," defined, 6–8, 6–9
Transfer, definition, 6–4
Transfer of exempt property, 6–6
Transfer of third party property, 6–7
Transferees, direct and initial, 6–10
Transfers for the benefit of creditors, 6–8
Unsecured creditors, preferential effect of payments, 6–20
Undersecured creditors, preferential effect of payments, 6–20
Utility bills of debtor, 6–29

PRE-PACKAGED PLANS
See Plan of Reorganization

PREPETITION
Claims, definition, for purposes of setoff, 6–40
Debt, payment of and granting security for, 4–15
Disclosure, pre-packaged plans, 11–22
Solicitation, pre-packaged plans, 11–23

PREPETITION CLAIMS
Automatic stays, 3–4
  Effect on, 3–6
Liens, 3–11
Property of the estate, 3–6
Recoupment, 6–45

PREPETITION CREDITORS
Postpetition transfers, 4–15

PREPETITION DEBTS
Liens, 3–11
Setoff, 3–15
Utility service, 3–9

PREPETITION LOANS
Postpetition interest, 4–15

PREPETITION SECURITY AGREEMENTS
Postpetition transactions, 6–68

PREPETITION TRANSACTIONS
Automatic stay, effect on, 3–6
Exemptions, 8–1
Postpetition loans, 4–15

PRESENT VALUE
Computation, 9–10

PRESERVATION OF AVOIDED TRANSFERS, 6–86

PRIORITY
In general, 7–10, 7–11, 7–12, 7–13
Administrative expenses, 7–11
as Alternative remedy to reclamation of goods, 6–65
of Assumed lease or executory contract obligations, 5–5
Discrimination between classes of creditors, Chapter 11, 10–22
Environmental claims, see Environmental Cleanup Obligations
in Involuntary cases, 2–5
in Partnership cases, 11–33
of Postpetition creditors, 4–11
Postpetition loans with priority over other administrative expenses, 4–13, 4–14
Preservation of avoided transfer for the estate, 6–86
Secured claims, 7–10
State law effects, (trustee's section 544(a) claims), 6–61
Superpriority claims, 7–13
Tardy claims, 7–15
Trustee as judicial lienor, as bona fide purchaser, 6–61
Wage and employee benefits, 7–12

PROCEDURE
See Bankruptcy Procedure

PROOF OF CLAIM
Chapter 7 bankruptcy, 7–3
Chapter 13 bankruptcy, 9–4
Notice to creditor, 7–3
Time limits for filing, 7–3, 11–4

PROPERTY CASUALTY INSURANCE
Security interests, 3–27

PROPERTY OF THE ESTATE
In general, 2–8
  See also Executory Contracts; Leases
Assumed lease or executory contract, 5–5
Automatic stay, 3–13, 3–14
Bank accounts, 6–74
Bankruptcy procedure, 1–7
Bidding in by secured creditor, 4–8
Bona fide purchaser, 4–17
Business licenses, 3–21
Cash collateral, 4–5,
  See also, Cash Collateral
Cash collateral order, 4–5
of action, 3–14
Chapter 7, 2–8
Contract rights, 3–14
Conversion, 2–17
Contract rights, 3–14
Court-authorized sale or lease, appeals, 4–17
Debtor's equity in property, 3–25
Debtor's interest, state law, 2–8
Discharge, see Discharge
Dismissal of bankruptcy case, 3–23

PROPERTY OF THE ESTATE—Cont'd
Domestic obligations, 3–12
Executory contracts, 5–1
Exemptions, 8–1
    See also Exemptions
Exercise of control, 3–14
Governmental seizure, effect of automatic stay, 3–21
Insurance policies, 3–14
Involuntary petitions, disposal, 2–5
Joint tenancies, 2–8
Leasehold interest, 2–8
Leases, 3–28, 5–1
Letters of credit, 3–14
Liquidation, 1–7, 3–11
Mortgages, 2–8
Non-ordinary course of business, 4–4, 4–1, 4–2, 4–3
    Distinguished from ordinary course of business, 4–3
Nonresidential leases, 3–14
Notice and hearing requirements, 4–16
Ordinary course of business, 4–3, 4–1, 4–2
Pension plans, exemptions, 8–33
Postpetition earnings, property, 2–8
Postpetition interest, 2–8
Postpetition transactions, 6–68, 6–69
Prepetition claims, 3–6
Prepetition interest, statutory exceptions, 2–8
Real estate leases, 3–14
Return of property to the debtor, Chapter 11, 10–29
Sale of all or substantially all assets, 4–4
Sale of property subject to interests of others, Bidding in by creditor, 4–8
    Sale subject to co-owners' interests, 4–9
    Sale subject to partners' interests, 4–10
    Sale subject to security interests, 4–7
    Sale subject to tort claimants' interests, 4–10
Scope, 2–8
Statutory exclusions, 2–8
Subsidiary assets, sale of, 4–4
Successor liability, 4–10
Tenants in common, 2–8
Tenants in the entirety, 2–8
Tort claims, 4–10
Transfer restrictions, 2–8
Unperfected liens, 3–18
Use/sale/lease of property of the estate, overview, 4–1, 4–2

PURCHASE–MONEY SECURITY INTERESTS
Automatic stay, 3–17
as Exceptions to avoidance, 6–33

REAFFIRMATION
Admonition hearing requirement, 7–38
Approval by bankruptcy judge, 7–35
Best interest requirement, 7–37
Conditions required, 7–36
Legislative history, 7–35
Overview, 7–35
Procedural requirements, 7–36
Secured creditors and reaffirmation, redemption, negotiation, 7–39
Statement of intention, 7–39

REAFFIRMATION—Cont'd
Undue hardship, 7–37
Voluntary payment by debtor, 7–36

REAL ESTATE
Avoidance of postpetition transfers, 6–73
Exemptions, 8–7, 8–13

REAL ESTATE LEASES
Property of the estate, 3–14

REAL PROPERTY
State law exemptions, 8–3

REASONABLE RELIANCE
on False financial statement, 7–26

REASONABLY EQUIVALENT VALUE
In general, 6–49
Foreclosure sales, 6–56

RECLAMATION OF GOODS
Avoidance of reclamation, 6–65
Bankruptcy Code's effects on state reclamation rights, 6–64, 6–65
Possession by the debtor requirement, 6–67
Priority in the seller requirement, 6–67
Reclamation under state law, under the U.C.C., 6–63
Remedies alternative to reclamation, lien or priority claim, 6–65

RECOUPMENT
    In general, 6–45
        See also Setoff
Automatic stay, 6–45
Distinguished from setoff, 5–25, 6–45
During gap period, 5–25
Prepetition claim, 6–45
"Same transaction" requirement, 6–45

RECOURSE
Secured claims in Chapter 11, 10–26, 10–27, 10–28

RECOVERY
See Avoidance Powers

RECOVERY OF DAMAGES
Avoidance powers, 6–87

REDEMPTION
Consumer goods, 7–47
Enforcement of lien, 7–39
Exemption against unsecured creditors, 7–48
Installment payments, 7–39, 7–47
Installment redemption, 7–47
Lien stripping, 7–47
Lump sum payments, 7–47
Motor vehicles, 7–49
Overview, 7–47
of Secured debt, 7–39
Substantive requirements, 7–48
Valuation, 7–49
Wholesale vs. retail valuation, 7–49

REFEREE
See Judge (Bankruptcy Judge)

REHABILITATION
    In general, 1–5

REHABILITATION—Cont'd
Compared to liquidation, 1–5
Distinguished from liquidation, 1–5
Under Chapters 11, 12 & 13, 1–5

REJECTION OF EXECUTORY CONTRACTS OR LEASES
See Executory Contracts; Leases

RELATION BACK
of Perfection, 6–13, 6–33
of Pleadings to extend avoidance period, 6–84

REMEDIES
See
    also Damages
Avoidance remedies, 6–80
for Discriminatory treatment by a governmental unit, 7–41
for Discriminatory treatment by a private employer/ee, 7–42
Equitable remedy right as a claim, 7–8
for Fraudulent transfer, 6–50
for Indirect preference, 6–10
Remedies alternative to reclamation of goods, 6–65
Setoff, 6–38
for Violation of the stay, 3–33, 3–34, 3–35

REORGANIZATION
Bad faith filing, 3–28
Consummation of a plan, 3–23
Dismissal of case,
    Lack of good faith, 2–15
Lifting the stay, 3–25
Waiver of right of setoff, 6–43

REORGANIZATION PLAN
See Plan of Reorganization

REPURCHASE AGREEMENTS
Automatic stay, effects of, 3–15

RESIDENCE
Exemption, 8–7, 8–13

RESTITUTION
Dischargeability of criminal restitution, 7–31

RESTRICTIVE COVENANTS
Successor liability, 4–10

RETIREMENT BENEFITS
Exemption, exclusion, 8–17, 8–33

RIGHT OF RECLAMATION
Federal law requirements, 6–66
Seller of goods, 6–66
State law requirements, 6–66
Third-party priority in goods, 6–67

RIGHT OF REDEMPTION
Automatic stay, 3–16

SCHEDULES
Liquidation, 7–2

SECRET CONVEYANCES
Transfer restrictions, 6–27

SECURED CLAIMS
Chapter 11 bankruptcy, 10–28
Chapter 13 bankruptcy, 9–4
Creditors, distribution, 1–7
Setoff, 6–43

SECURED CREDITORS
See
    also Priority; Security Interests
Adequate protection, 4–14
Definition, 1–4
Fair and equitable treatment, Chapter 11, 10–20
Payment under Chapter 13 plan, 9–6
Perfected encumbrances, burden of proof, 3–31
Reaffirmation, redemption, negotiation, 7–39
Recourse, 10–26, 10–27, 10–28

SECURED DEBTS
Exemptions, 8–1

SECURITIES MARKET
Setoff, exceptions, 3–15

SECURITY INTERESTS
See also Liens; Priority
Aircraft security interests, excepted from the stay, 3–17
Avoidance by debtor, 8–25
Enabling security interests, see "Purchase-money security interests"
on Inventory, floating liens, 6–35, 6–67, 6–75, 6–76, 6–77, 6–78
Non-possessory, 6–11
Postpetition avoidance of prepetition floating liens, 6–75, 6–76, 6–77, 6–78
Postpetition transactions, 6–76
Property casualty insurance, 3–27
Purchase-money security interests, exceptions to avoidance, 6–33
Reaffirmation of secured debt, 7–39
Sale by trustee of estate property subject to security interest, 4–7
Valuation for purposes of adequate protection, 3–27

SERIAL FILINGS
Chapters 19 and 20, 9–30
Discharge limitations, 7–17
Dismissal, 2–16
Good faith problems, 2–16
Limitations, 2–2
Refiling after default, 2–16
Simultaneous petitions, 2–16

SETOFF
In general, 6–38, 6–39
    See also Recoupment
Amount of avoidance, 6–41
As secured claim, 6–43
Assignment of claim, 6–41
Automatic stay, 3–15, 6–43
Bank deposits, 6–41
Brokers, 3–15
Cash collateral, 6–43
Certificates of deposit, 6–41
Disallowed claims, 6–41

SETOFF—Cont'd
Distinguished from recoupment, 5–25, 6–45
Effect of bankruptcy law, 6–39
Equitable exceptions to setoff, 6–42
Equitable setoff, 6–38
Exceptions to setoff, substantive, 6–41, 6–42
Floating liens, 6–41
Freeze of debtor's assets by creditor, 6–43
Insufficiency of setoff, 6–41
Limitations on setoff, 6–41, 6–42
Maturity of debtor's obligation as prerequisite, 6–40
Modification of creditor's claim during 90–day prepetition period, 6–41
Mutual debt requirement, 6–40
Mutual obligation requirement, 6–40
Overview, 6–38
Petition for relief from the stay, 6–43
Prepetition debt requirement, 6–40
Prepetition debts, 3–15
Procedural effects of bankruptcy law on setoff, 6–43, 6–44
Recoupment, see Recoupment
Scope, 6–39
Statutory exceptions to setoff, 6–41
Substantive right under nonbankruptcy law, 6–40
Surety setoff, 6–41
Swap agreements, 3–15
Waiver, 6–43
Who may setoff, 6–39

SETOFF AND COUNTERCLAIM
Right of holder of secured claim, 1–4

SHAREHOLDERS AS CREDITORS
See New Value

SHORT-TERM OBLIGATIONS
Ordinary course of business transfers, 6–32

SIMULTANEOUS PETITIONS
Prohibitions, 2–16

SMALL TRANSFERS
Definition, 6–37

SOLICITATION, COMPETING PLANS, 11–18
Prepetition solicitation, pre-packaged plans, 11–23

SOVEREIGN IMMUNITY
Damages for violation of the stay, 3–34
Waiver, 3–34

SPENDTHRIFT TRUSTS
See Trust Funds

SPOUSE BANKRUPTCIES
See Domestic Obligations; Joint Bankruptcies

STATE FRAUDULENT TRANSFER LAWS
Statute of limitations, applicability, 6–60

STATE LAW
Abstention by bankruptcy courts, 12–5
and Bankruptcy Code, 1–3
Claims, determination of, 11–2, 11–3
Criminal proceedings enjoined, 3–20

STATE LAW—Cont'd
Domestic obligations, change in circumstances, 7–29
Exemption law, 8–6, 8–7, 8–8, 8–9
Fraudulent transfers under state law, 6–60
Reclamation of goods, see Reclamation of Goods
Retirement benefits, federal preemption, 8–33
State taxes excepted from discharge, 7–25

STATE PRIORITY LAW
Unperfected liens, 3–18

STATUTE OF LIMITATIONS
for Avoidance actions, 6–73

STATUTORY LIENS
See also Liens
Distinguished from judicial liens, 6–36

STAY
See Automatic Stay

STOCKBROKER DEFENSE
Avoidance powers, 6–85

"STRONG-ARM" AVOIDANCE POWERS, 6–61
Compared to statutory lien avoidance powers, 6–62

STUDENT LOANS
Exception to discharge, 7–33

SUBLEASE
Compared to assignment of a lease in bankruptcy, 5–6

SUBORDINATION
Claims, 6–91
Consensual subordination, 6–92
Equitable subordination, 6–93

SUBSIDIARIES
Sale of assets of subsidiary, approval of the court, 4–4

SUBSTANTIAL ABUSE STANDARD
Dismissal of Chapter 7 consumer cases, 7–45

SUBSTANTIVE CONSOLIDATION
In general, 2–4, 11–40
Cases and rules, 11–41
Distinguished from piercing the corporate veil, 2–4
Purposes, 11–40

SUCCESSIVE FILING
See Serial Filings

SUCCESSOR LIABILITY
Restrictive covenants, 4–10
Tort claims, 4–10

SUPERPRIORITY CLAIMS
Chapter 7, 7–13

SUPPLIER OF DEBTOR
Automatic stay, effects on, 3–8

SURETY
Automatic stay, effects of, 3–10

SURETY—Cont'd
Setoff, 6–41

SWAP AGREEMENTS
Automatic stay, effects of, 3–15
Setoff, 3–15

TAX LIENS
Automatic stay, 3–8
Postpetition property, 3–11

TAXES
Excepted from discharge, 7–25
    Penalties excepted from discharge, 7–32
Liens, see Liens, "Statutory liens"

TERMINATION CLAUSES
in Executory contracts and leases, 5–12

TIMING OF TRANSFERS
Foreclosure sales, 6–55

TORT CLAIMS
Automatic stay, claims affected, 3–6
Exemptability, 8–18
Jurisdiction of bankruptcy courts to hear tort claims, 12–4
Lifting the stay, 3–30
Mass tort claims and Chapter 11, 11–8
Negligent injury, dischargeability, 7–30
Partnerships, settlement and contribution, 11–39
Property of the estate, 3–14
Sale of estate property subject to tort claims, 4–10
Successor liability, 4–10
Willful and malicious injury, exception to discharge, 7–30
When arises, 7–5, 11–3

TRANSFER RESTRICTIONS
Effects on property of the estate, 2–8
Fraudulent transfers, see Fraudulent Transfers
Preferences, see Preferences
Property of the estate, 2–8
Postpetition transfers, see Postpetition Transactions
Secret conveyances, 6–27

TRANSFERS
Bona fide purchasers, 6–12
Contemporaneous new value, intention of parties, 6–28
Definition, 6–54
Insider time periods, 6–17
Payment by check, 6–16
Ten day grace period, 6–13

TRUST FUNDS
Exemptability, 8–33
for Mass tort claimants, 11–8

TRUST RELATIONSHIP, 7–28

TRUSTEE
    See also Debtor in Possession; U.S. Trustee
Avoidance powers, see Avoidance Powers
Chapter 11 trustee, appointment, 10–8
Chapter 11 trustee, powers, 10–9

TRUSTEE—Cont'd
Chapter 13 trustee, 9–4
Definition, 1–4
as Hypothetical lien creditor, 6–61
Interim, during involuntary gap, 2–5
Payment, Chapter 13, 9–4
as Purchaser, 6–61
as Successor to creditor, 6–60
U.S. trustee, definition, 1–4

TRUSTEE IN BANKRUPTCY
Appointment, 1–4, 1–7
Conversion, 2–17
Defined, 1–4
Meeting of creditors, 7–2
Postpetition transfers, avoidance, 2–17
Property of the estate, Chapter 7, 2–8
Recovery of prebankruptcy transfers, 1–2
Replacement by creditors, 1–4, 1–7
Transfer restrictions, property of the estate, 2–8
Unperfected liens, 3–18

UNDERSECURED CREDITORS
Floating liens, 6–35
Preferences, 6–20

UNDUE HARDSHIP
Dischargeability of student loans, 7–33
Reaffirmation of debts, 7–37

UNIFORM PARTNERSHIP ACT
Involuntary petitions,
    Partnerships, 2–5

UNPERFECTED LIENS
Avoidance, 3–11
Property of the estate, 3–18
State priority law, 3–18
Trustee in bankruptcy, 3–18

UNREASONABLE DELAY
Grounds for dismissal, 7–43

UNSATISFIED INDIVIDUAL CREDITOR
Powers in Chapter 11, 6–2

UNSECURED CLAIMS
Creditors,
    Distribution, 1–7

UNITED STATES TRUSTEE
    See also Trustee
Appointment of creditors' committee, Chapter 1 bankruptcy, 10–12
Appointment of interim trustee, 1–4
Appointment of private trustee, 1–4
Definition, 1–4, 7–2
Motion to dismiss, 7–44

UNSECURED CREDITORS
    See also Priority
Absolute priority rule, 10–21
As "party in interest", 3–31
Automatic stays, 3–1
Definition, 1–4
Lack of adequate protection, 3–27
Lifting the stay, 3–26
Ordinary course and nonordinary course loans, 4–12

UNSECURED CREDITORS—Cont'd
Postpetition unsecured loans, 4–12
Preference of payments, 6–20

UNSECURED DEBT
Cross-collateralization, 4–15

UTILITY BILLS
Preferences, 6–29

UTILITY SERVICE
Adequate assurance, 3–9
Automatic stay, 3–9
Bankruptcy, effect on, 3–9
Prepetition debts, 3–9

VALUATION OF PROPERTY
Collateral, valuation of floating lien for avoidance purposes, 6–35
Debtor's lack of equity, 3–25
for Exemption purposes, 8–8
New value, 11–30
Postpetition transfers, valuation of, 6–71
Present value, 9–10
"Reasonably equivalent value," fraudulent transfers, 6–49, 6–56
for Redemption purposes, 7–49
Valuation of secured interest for purposes of adequate protection, 3–27

VENUE
of Cases, 12–6, 12–7
Change of venue, 12–9
    Case filed in improper venue, 12–11
    Case filed in proper venue, 12–10
of Proceedings, 12–8

VIOLATION OF THE STAY
Contempt, 3–35
Damages, 3–33, 3–34, 3–35
Judicial annulment of the stay, 3–32
Setoff in violation of the stay, 6–43

VIOLATION OF THE STAY—Cont'd
Statutory exceptions, 3–32
"Voidable" actions compared with "Void" actions, 3–32
Voidance, 3–32

VOIDABLE PREFERENCES
See Preferences

VOIDANCE
See Violation of the Stay

VOLUNTARY PETITIONS
Commencement of bankruptcy case, 2–2
Eligibility requirements, 2–2
Ineligible debtors, conversion by court, 2–2
Motion to dismiss, 2–2

VOLUNTARY PROCEEDINGS
Distinguished from involuntary proceedings, 1–7

VOLUNTARY TRANSFERS
Definition, 8–22
Exemptions, 8–22

VOTING ON PLANS
Estimation of claims, 11–6
Multiple plan cases, 11–20
Voting agreements, 11–19

WAGE CLAIMS
Priority, 7–12

WAGES
Payment from postpetition funds, 4–15

WAIVER
of Exemptions, 8–9, 8–31

WILLFUL AND MALICIOUS INJURY
Exception to discharge, 7–30

†